THE BIBLE

Revised
King James Version
with New Testament Exegesis

Revise King James Version Bible with New Testament Exegesis ©2017 Donald Peart & Dameon Gibbs
All rights reserved. No part of this books translations may be used or reproduced in any manner whatsoever without written permission of the publisher, except for brief quotations in critical reviews, articles or for the inclusion in reviews and study. Printed in the United States of America.

Bible Translation Used:
The King James Version (Public Domain)
Dictionary references, includes, but not limited to, Strong's Concordance, BibleWorks Software, ISA2 Basic Software, Vines' Expository Dictionary, Thayer's Dictionary
Greek References:
Alexandrian Texts, Byzantine Majority Texts,
Textus Recptus (copies from the Majority Texts used for the King James translation)

Time Line of the Old Testament Prophets: Courtesy of *Theology of Work Project*: http://www.theologyofwork.org/old-testament/introduction-to-the-prophets/timeline-of-the-prophets/ISBN:

ISBN: 978-1-966856-01-6

This Revised King James Version Bible
Is Presented to
_____

_____

By

_____

_____

Date

_____

TABLE OF CONTENTS

- FORWARD 5
- ABOUT DAMEON GIBBS: 6
- 50 FACTS & 50 SCRIPTURES ABOUT JESUS CHRIST 7
- TIMELINES OF THE PROPHETS 0

OLD TESTAMENT 1

- GENESIS 1
- EXODUS 1
- LEVITICUS 1
- NUMBERS 1
- DEUTERONOMY 31
- JOSHUA 56
- JUDGES 73
- RUTH 90
- FIRST SAMUEL 93
- SECOND SAMUEL 115
- FIRST KINGS 133
- SECOND KINGS 154
- FIRST CHRONICLES 174
- SECOND CHRONICLES 193
- EZRA 215
- NEHEMIAH 222
- ESTHER 232
- JOB 237
- PSALMS 256
- THE PROVERBS 302
- ECCLESIASTES OR, THE PREACHER 318
- THE SONG OF SOLOMON 324
- ISAIAH 327
- JEREMIAH 359
- LAMENTATIONS OF JEREMIAH 396
- EZEKIEL 400
- DANIEL 435
- HOSEA 446
- JOEL 451
- AMOS 453
- OBADIAH 457
- JONAH 458
- MICAH 460
- NAHUM 463
- HABAKKUK 465
- ZEPHANIAH 467
- HAGGAI 469
- ZECHARIAH 470
- MALACHI 476

THE NEW TESTAMENT

- **HONOR** 1
- **COMMENTS** 2
- **TABLE OF CONTENTS** 4
- **THE GOSPEL OF MATTHEW** 1
- **THE GOSPEL OF MARK** 40
- **THE GOSPEL OF LUKE** 65
- **THE GOSPEL OF JOHN** 107
- **THE ACTS OF THE APOSTLES** 137
- **ROMANS** 180
- **1 CORINTHIANS** 196
- **2 CORINTHIANS** 212
- **GALATIANS** 222
- **EPHESIANS** 228

PHILIPPIANS	234
COLOSSIANS	238
1 THESSALONIANS	242
2 THESSALONIANS	246
1 TIMOTHY	248
2 TIMOTHY	253
TITUS	257
PHILEMON	259
HEBREWS	260
JAMES	273
1 PETER	277
2 PETER	282
1 JOHN	285
2 JOHN	289
3 JOHN	290
JUDE	291
THE REVELATION OF JESUS CHRIST	293
SYNOPTIC BIO OF DONALD PEART	312

FORWARD

The Revised King James Version study Bible contains the written notes and thoughts of Donald Peart, a pastor author and servant of the kingdom. Throughout the decades of ministering the gospel and diligently studying the scriptures, Donald Peart came to learn that the popular King James Version (public domain) of the Bible had deeper meaning when the scripture was translated back into its original Hebrew and Greek languages. Not stating that the King James Version is an inferior text by any means, for the King James Version has led many to the salvation in our Lord and Savior Jesus the Christ. However, for those that desire the deeper knowledge of the Father, they must read the scripture as it was originally written; which is the purpose of this Revised King James Version.

Readers must be made aware that the italicized words in the (Public Domain) King James Version and within some sections of King James Version are words that were added by the translators. Another major reason for using the Revised King James Version is that this version points out what has been added or removed by the public domain King James Version. Over the centuries there are places where proofreaders or publishers missed some of the italics, but for the most part all added words are italicized. Italicized words were added by the translators in order to convey the complete thought when moving from one language to another.

Many times, the added words do not change the meaning of the original text. However, in some instances the added words altered the overall meaning and context of the text. And in order to get the scriptures true meaning the added text must be deleted. In studying God's word from the King James Version readers should sometime read over or remove an italicized word to get the scripture true meaning. When doing so the reader will not be touching the original text as all italicized words were not part of the original manuscript but were added by translators. The Revised King James Version of the Bible does not take away from what God has already spoken in His word, however it does assist with clarifying the ancient text. It is one of the premire ways of coming to a deeper understanding of the Lord's word, by both using its easily understood resources and translations provided by Dr. Donald Peart.

Footnotes from Donald Peart personal study is italicized and underlined. Passages and words highlighted in gray are passages that interested him doing his thirty plus years of study.

Dameon Gibbs
Author and Historian

ABOUT DAMEON GIBBS:

Dameon Gibbs graduated from Salisbury University with his M.A in Classical History Studies and B.A in World History and Anthropology. He has been an avid writer since his days in high school during the late 1990s. He enjoys the creative process of all writing genres, whether it be biblical, poetic, science fiction, historical, biographies. Dameon has authored and co-authored over seven books, which include The Hole, The Seven Days of God, The World Around Them and He That Stands Upon the Mountain.

50 FACTS & 50 SCRIPTURES ABOUT JESUS CHRIST

Who Is Jesus?

1 - Jesus Was Never Created | **Micah 5:2**

2 - Jesus Essence Has Never Changed | **Hebrews 13:8**

3 - Jesus is God | **John 1:1**

4 - Jesus is The Creator of Everything | **Colossians 1:16**

5 - Jesus is All-Powerful | **Matthew 28:18**

6 - Jesus is All-Knowing | **Colossians 2:3**

7 - Jesus is Ever-Present | **Matthew 18:20**

8 - Jesus is Holy | **Luke 1:35**

9 - Jesus is Righteous | **Isaiah 53:11**

10 - Jesus is Just | **Zechariah 9:9**

11 - Jesus Had No Deceit | **1 Peter 2:22**

12 - Jesus is Sinless | **2 Corinthians 5:21**

13 - Jesus is Spotless | **1 Peter 1:19**

14 - Jesus is Innocent | **Matthew 27:4**

15 - Jesus is Gentle | **Matthew 11:29**

16 - Jesus is Merciful | **Hebrews 2:17**

17 - Jesus is Forgiving | **Luke 23:34**

18 - Jesus Receives Worship by Demons | **Mark 5:2,6**

19 - Jesus Receives Worship by Men | **John 9:38**

20 - Jesus Receives Worship by Angels | **Hebrews 1:6**

21 - Jesus Receives Worship by Disciples | **Luke 24:52**

22 - Jesus Receives Worship in Heaven | **Revelation 7:9-10**

23 - Jesus Will Receive Worship from Everyone | **Philippians 2:10-11**

24 - Jesus Was Human | **1 Timothy 2:5**

25 - Jesus Was Conceived by the Holy Spirit | **Luke 1:34-35**

26 - Jesus Took On Man's Nature | **Hebrews 2:9-18**

27 - Jesus Humbled Himself | **Philippians 2:8**

28 - Jesus Was Subject To Human Emotions | **Hebrews 5:7**

29 - Jesus Raised His Body From The Dead | **John 10:18**

30 - Jesus Blood Brings Reconciliation With God | **Ephesians 2:13-16**

31 - Jesus Blood Brings Redemption for Man | **Romans 3:24-25**

32 - Jesus Blood Allows Man To Be Justified before God | **Romans 5:9**

33 - Jesus Blood Sanctifies Man | **Hebrews 10:29**

34 - Jesus Blood Brings Spiritual Victory | **Revelations 12:11**

35 - Jesus Blood Brings Eternal Life | **John 6:53-56**

36 - Jesus Came to Save Sinners | **Luke 19:10**

37 - Jesus Will Bring in Everlasting Righteousness | **Daniel 9:24**

38 - Jesus Destroyed the Works of Satan | **1 John 3:8**

39 - Jesus Fulfilled the Old Testament | **Matthew 5:17**

40 - Jesus Gives Life Now | **John 10:10**

41 - Jesus Is Our Advocate | **1 John 2:1**

42 - Jesus Gives Eternal Life | **John 10:28**

43 - Jesus Is Eternal Life | **1 John 5:20**

44 - Jesus Sends The Holy Spirit To Us | **John 15:26**

45 - Jesus Will Take His People To Heaven | **John 14:3**

46 - Jesus Will Return To The Earth After The Tribulation | **Matthews 24:29**

47 - Jesus Will Return To The Earth In Power & Glory | **Matthew 24:30**

48 - Jesus Completes Revelation | **Hebrews 1:1**

49 - Jesus Will Never Send You Away If You Come To Him | **John 6:37**

50 - Jesus is the Way, the Truth, and the Life | **John 14:6**
Courtesy of: http://so4j.com/50-facts-about-jesus-christ

TIMELINES OF THE PROPHETS

The table below shows where in time the prophets fit within the northern kingdom of Israel and the southern kingdom of Judah.

Period	Northern Kings	Northern Prophets	Southern Kings	Southern Prophets
United kingdoms Under Saul, David, Solomon, c.1030-931 B.C.E				
David kingdom	Jeroboam (931-910) Nadab (910-909) Baasha (909-886) Elah (886) Zimri (885) Omri (885-874) Ahab (874-853) Jehoram (852-841) Jehu (841-814) Jehoahaz (814-798) Jehoash (798-782) Jeroboam II (793-753) Zechariah (753-752) Shallum (752) Menahem (752-742) Pekahiah (742-740) Pekah (752-732) Hoshea (732-722)	Elijah Elisha Amos Hosea	Rehoboam (931-913) Abijah (913) Asa (911-870) Jehoshaphat (873-848) Jehoram (853-841) Queen Athaliah (841-835) Joash (835-796) Amaziah (796-767) Uzziah (790-740) Jotham (750-731) Ahaz (735-715) Hezekiah (715-686) Manasseh (695-642) Amon (642-640) Josiah (640-609) Jehoahaz (609) Jehoiakim (609-597) Jehoiachin (597) Zedekia (597-586)	Obadiah Joel Jonah Isaiah Micah Jeremiah Zephaniah Nahum Habakkuk
Babylonian Exile				Ezekiel Daniel
Post-Exilic Prophets			Zerubbabel, governor Nehemiah, governor	Haggai Zechariah Malachi

Courtesy of *Theology of Work Project*: http://www.theologyofwork.org/old-testament/introduction-to-the-prophets/timeline-of-the-prophets/

OLD TESTAMENT

GENESIS
CHAPTER 1

1 In the beginning God created the **heavens** and the earth.
2 And the earth was without form, and **empty**; and darkness upon the face of the deep. And the Spirit of God **fluttered** upon the face of the waters.
3 And God said, Let there be light: and there was light.
4 And God saw the light, that *it was* good: and God divided the light from the darkness.
5 And God called the light Day, and the darkness he called Night. And the evening and the morning were the first day.
6 And God said, Let there be a firmament in the midst of the waters, and let it divide the waters from the waters.
7 And God made the firmament, and divided the waters which *were* under the firmament from the waters which *were* above the firmament: and it was so.
8 And God called the firmament Heaven. And the evening and the morning were the second day.
9 And God said, let the waters under the heaven be gathered together unto one place, and let the dry *land* appear: and it was so.
10 And God called the dry *land* Earth; and the gathering together of the waters called he Seas: and God saw that *it was* good.
11 And God said, let the earth bring forth grass, the herb yielding seed, *and* the fruit tree yielding fruit after his kind, whose seed *is* in itself, upon the earth: and it was so.
12 And the earth brought forth grass, *and* herb yielding seed after his kind, and the tree yielding fruit, whose seed *was* in itself, after his kind: and God saw that *it was* good.
13 And the evening and the morning were the third day.
14 And God said, let there be lights in the firmament of the heaven to divide the day from the night; and let them be for signs, and for seasons, and for days, and years:
15 And let them be for lights in the firmament of the heaven to give light upon the earth: and it was so.
16 And God made two great lights; the greater light to rule the day, and the lesser light to rule the night: *he made* the stars also.
17 And God set them in the firmament of the heaven to give light upon the earth,
18 And to rule over the day and over the night, and to divide the light from the darkness: and God saw that *it was* good.
19 And the evening and the morning were the fourth day.
20 And God said, let the waters bring forth abundantly the moving creature that hath life, and fowl *that* may fly above the earth in the open firmament of heaven.
21 And God created great whales, and every living **souls** that move, which the waters brought forth abundantly, after their kind, and every winged fowl after his kind: and God saw that *it was* good.
22 And God blessed them, saying, be fruitful, and multiply, and fill the waters in the seas, and let fowl multiply in the earth.
23 And the evening and the morning were the fifth day.
24 And God said, let the earth bring forth the living creature after his kind, cattle, and creeping thing, and beast of the earth after his kind: and it was so.
25 And God made the beast of the earth after his kind, and cattle after their kind, and everything that creep upon the earth after his kind: and God saw that *it was* good.
26 And God said, Let us make man in our image, after our likeness: and let them have dominion over the fish of the sea, and over the fowl of the air, and over the cattle, and over all the earth, and over every creeping thing that creep upon the earth.
27 So God created man in his *own* image, in the image of God created he him; male and female created he them.
28 And God blessed them, and God said unto them, be fruitful, and multiply, and replenish the earth, and subdue it: and have dominion over the fish of the sea, and over the fowl of the air, and over every living thing that move upon the earth.
29 And God said, Behold, I have given you every herb bearing seed, which *is* upon the face of all the earth, and every tree, in the which *is* the fruit of a tree yielding seed; to you it will be for meat.
30 And to every beast of the earth, and to every fowl of the air, and to everything that creep upon the earth, wherein *there is* life, *I have given* every green herb for meat: and it was so.
31 And God saw everything that he had made, and, behold, *it was* very good. And the evening and the morning were the sixth day.

CHAPTER 2

1 And the heavens and the earth were finished, and all the host of them.
2 And on the seventh day God ended his work which he had made; and he rested on the seventh day from all his work which he had made.
3 And God blessed the seventh day, and sanctified it: because that in it he had rested from all his work which God created and made.
4 These *are* the generations of the heavens and of the earth when they were created, in the day that the LORD God made the earth and the heavens,
5 And every plant[1] of the field before it was in the earth, and every herb of the field before it grew: for the LORD God had not caused it to rain upon the earth, and *there was* not a man to till the ground.
6 But there went up a mist from the earth, and watered[2] the whole face of the ground.
7 And the LORD God formed man *of* the dust[3] of the ground, and breathed into his nostrils the breath of life; and man became a living soul.
8 And the LORD God planted a garden eastward in Eden; and there he put the man whom he had formed.
9 And out of the ground made the LORD God to grow every tree that is pleasant to the sight, and good for food; the tree of life also in the midst of the garden, and the tree of knowledge of good and evil.
10 And a river went out of Eden to water the garden; and from thence it was parted, and became into four heads.
11 The name of the first *is* Pison[4]: that *is* it which compass the whole land of Havilah, where *there is* gold;
12 And the gold of that land *is* good: there *is* bdellium and the onyx stone.
13 And the name of the second river *is* Gihon[5]: the same *is* it that compasses the whole land of Ethiopia.

---

[1] <u>plant</u> – Hebrew word śîyach meaning a *shoot* (as if uttered or put forth), *shrubbery*, bush [Strgs#7880]. Root śîyach meaning to utter by speak, *ponder*, declare, converse (with oneself, and hence alond) [Strgs#7878]
[2] <u>watered</u> – to drink deeply [Strgs#8248]. Compare **Ps. 42:7**.
[3] <u>dust</u> - also mud, motar, ashes, earth and rubbish [Strgs#6083]
[4] Pison- the first river of Eden and a pool near Jerusalem. Its Hebrew word *pîyshôn*, meaningin increase and dispersive [Strgs#6376].
[5] Gihon- the second river of Eden. Its Hebrew word *gîychôn* meaning

14 And the name of the third river *is* Hiddekel[1]: that *is* it which goes toward the east of Assyria. And the fourth river *is* Euphrates[2].
15 And the LORD God took the man, and put him into the Garden of Eden to dress it and to keep it.
16 And the LORD God commanded the man, saying, of every tree of the garden you may freely eat:
17 But of the tree of the knowledge[3] of good and evil, you will not eat of it: for in the day that you eat of it [you will surely die][4].
18 And the LORD God said, *it is* not good that the man should be alone[5]; I will make him a help meet[6] for him.
19 And out of the ground the LORD God formed every beast of the field, and every fowl of the air; and brought *them* unto Adam[7] to see what he would call them: and whatsoever Adam called every living creature, that *was* the name thereof.
20 And Adam gave[8] names to all cattle, and to the fowl of the air, and to every beast of the field; but for Adam there was not found a help meet for him.
21 And the LORD God caused a deep sleep to fall upon Adam, and he slept: and he took one of his ribs, and closed up the flesh instead[9] thereof;
22 And the rib, which the LORD God had taken from man, made[10] him a woman, and brought her unto the man.
23 And Adam said, this *is* now[11] bone of my bones, and flesh[12] of my flesh: she will be called Woman, because she was taken out of Man.
24 Therefore will a man leave his father and his mother, and will cleave[13] unto his wife: and they will be one flesh.
25 And they were both naked, the man and his wife, and were not ashamed[14].

CHAPTER 3

1 Now the serpent was more subtle than any beast of the field which the LORD God had made. And he said unto the woman, yea[15], **have** God said, You will not eat of every tree of the garden?
2 And the woman said unto the serpent, We may eat of the fruit of the trees of the garden:
3 But of the fruit of the tree which *is* in the midst of the garden, God has said, you will not eat of it, neither will you touch it, [or you will die][16].
4 And the serpent said unto the woman, you will not surely die:
5 For God does know that in the day you eat of it, then your eyes will be opened[17], and you will be as gods, knowing good and evil.[18]
6 And when the woman saw that the tree *was* good for food, and that it *was* pleasant to the eyes, and a tree to be desired to make *one* wise, she took of the fruit of it, and did eat, and gave also unto her husband with her; and he did eat.
7 And the eyes of them both were opened, and they knew that they *were* naked[19]; and they sewed fig leaves together, and made themselves aprons[20].
8 And they heard the voice[21] of the LORD God walking in the garden in the cool of the day: and Adam and his wife hid themselves from the presence of the LORD God amongst the trees of the garden.
9 And the LORD God called unto Adam, and said unto him, where *are you*?
10 And he said, I heard your voice in the garden, and I was afraid, because I *was* naked; and I hid myself.
11 And he said, who told you that you were naked? Have you eaten of[22] the tree, that I commanded you that you should not eat?
12 And the man said, the woman who you gave *to be with* me, she gave me of the tree, and I did eat.
13 [And the LORD God said unto the woman, what *is* this *that* you have done? And the woman said, the serpent beguiled[23] me, and I did eat.][24]
14 And the LORD God said unto the serpent, Because you have done this, you are cursed above all cattle, and above every beast of the field; upon your belly you will go, and dust you will eat all the days of your life:
15 And I will put enmity between you and the woman, and between your seed and her seed; it will bruise your head, and you will bruise his heel.
16 Unto the woman he said, I will greatly multiply your sorrow[25] and your conception; in sorrow you will bring forth children; and your desire[26] *will be* to your husband, and he will rule over you.[27]
17 And unto Adam he said, Because you have hearkened unto the voice of your wife, and have eaten of the tree, of which I commanded you[28], saying, You will not eat of it: cursed *is* the

---

bursting, gush or break forth, labor to bring forth, come forth, draw, take out [Strgs#1521 & 1518].

[1] Hidekel- the third river of Eden. Its Hebrew word *chiddeqel* meaning rapid [Strgs# 2313].

[2] Euphrates- is the largest and longest river of western Asia. Its Hebrew word is *perâth*, meaning fruitfulness, it comes from an unused root word meaning to break forth. [Strgs# 6578].

[3] *knowledge* – comes from a Hebrew rootword meaning to know by seeing [Strgs#1847]

[4] lit. – dying you will die

[5] *alone* – as in separation from part of a body.

[6] Help meet- comes from the Hebrew word *'ezer*, ay'-zer; meaning *aid* and help. [Strgs#5828]. It come from the Hebrew root word *'âzar*, aw-zar'; meaning to *surround*, that is, *protect* or *aid*:- help, succor [Strgs#5826]. Also to expose predict and explain.

[7] Adam- the name of the first man. Ruddy, that is, a human being (an individual or the spiecies, mankind, etc.): -another, +hypocrite, common sort, low, man (mean, of low degree), person. [Strgs#120]. It also come from a root word meaning to show blood (in the face), that is, flush or turn rosy:-be (dyed, made) red (ruddy). [Strgs#119].

[8] *gave* – called (for, forth, self, upon), preach, proclaim, publish [Strgs#7121]

[9] *instead* - underneath

[10] *made* – to build a son, obtain children, repair, set (up) [Strgs#1129]

[11] *now* – trouble, stroke and agitate [Strgs#6471]

[12] *flesh* – Hebrew word bâsâr meaning internal flesh, nakedness, self [Strgs#1320]

[13] *cleave* – to catch by pursuit, impinge, cling, overtake, pursue hard [Strgs#1692]. Compare **1 Cor. 7:28** – Trouble of (in) my bones and my flesh.

[14] *ashamed* – to pale, be disappointed or delayed [Strgs#954]

[15] yea - *'aph* = anger, **nostril** [Strgs#637]

[16] Original King James Version reads - lest you die. Literally removal you die, lest [Strgs#6437]

[17] Their mind was not yet trained

[18] This tree was the 'meat' compare **Hebrews 5:14**.

[19] *naked* – comes from a Hebrew root word meaning cunning, crafty, naked by wisdom [Strgs#6191]

[20] *aprons* – belt, to narrow/curtail the waist, be afraid [Strgs#2296]

[21] *voice* – sound and to call aloud [Strgs#6963]

[22] Literally - a part of

[23] *beguiled* – or to owe for a debt

[24] Most problems in marriage is caused by the snake.

[25] *sorrow* – worry, labor pain [Strgs#6093]

[26] *desire* – longing or stretching out after [Strgs#8669]. Comes from root word meaning to run after the overflow [Strgs#7783].

[27] Compare **Genesis 4:7**, your desire to...husband...a desire to control.

[28] God gave the commandment to the man not the woman.

ground for your sake; in sorrow will you eat *of* it all the days of your life;
18 Thorns also and thistles will it bring forth to you; and you will eat the herb of the field;
19 In the sweat of your face[1] will you eat bread, until you return unto the ground; for out of it you were taken: for dust you *are*, and unto dust will you return.
20 And Adam called his wife's name Eve; because she was the mother of all living.
21 Unto Adam also and to his wife did the LORD God make coats of skins, and clothed them.
22 And the LORD God said, Behold, the man is become as one [of us][2], to know good and evil: and now, lest he put forth his hand, and take also of the tree of life, and eat, and live forever:
23 Therefore the LORD God sent him forth from the Garden of Eden, to till the ground from whence he was taken.
24 So he [drove out][3] the man; and he placed at the east of the garden of Eden Cherubims, and a flaming sword which turned every way, to keep the way of the tree of life.[4]

CHAPTER 4

1 And Adam knew Eve[5] his wife; and she conceived, and bare Cain, and said, I have gotten a man from the LORD.
2 And she again bares his brother Abel. And Abel was a keeper of sheep, but Cain was a tiller of the ground.
3 And [in process of time][6] it came to pass, that Cain brought of the fruit of the ground an offering unto the LORD.
4 And Abel, he also brought of the firstlings of his flock and of the fat thereof. And the LORD had respect unto Abel and to his offering:
5 But unto Cain and to his offering he had not respect. And Cain was very angry, and his countenance fell.
6 And the LORD said unto Cain, Why are you angry? And why is your countenance fallen?
7 If you do well, will you not be accepted[7]? And if you do not do well, sin lie at the door. And unto you *will be* his desire, and you will rule over him.
8 And Cain talked with Abel his brother: and it came to pass, when they were in the field, that Cain rose up against Abel his brother, and slew him.
9 And the LORD said unto Cain, Where *is* Abel your brother? And he said, I know not: *Am* I my brother's keeper?
10 And he said, what have you done? The voice of your brother's blood cries unto me from the ground.
11 And now *are* you cursed from the earth, which hath opened her mouth to receive your brother's blood from your hand;
12 When you till the ground, it will not bring forth yield unto you her strength; a fugitive and a vagabond you will be in the earth.
13 And Cain said unto the LORD, My punishment *is* greater than I can bear.
14 Behold, you have driven me out this day from the face of the earth; and from your face will I be hid; and I will be a fugitive and a vagabond in the earth; and it will come to pass, *that* every one that find me will slay me.
15 And the LORD said unto him, therefore whosoever slays Cain, vengeance will be taken on him sevenfold. And the LORD set a mark upon Cain, lest any finding him should kill him.
16 And Cain went out from the presence of the LORD, and dwelt in the land of Nod, on the east of Eden.
17 And Cain knew his wife; and she conceived, and bare Enoch[8]: and he built a city, and called the name of the city, after the name of his son, Enoch.
18 And unto Enoch was born Irad[9]: and Irad begat Mehujael[10]: and Mehujael begat Methusael[11]: and Methusael begat Lamech.
19 And Lamech took unto him two wives: the name of the one *was* Adah[12], and the name of the other Zillah[13].
20 And Adah bare Jabal: he was the father of such as dwell in tents, and *of such as have* cattle.
21 And his brother's name *was* Jubal: he was the father of all such as handle the harp and organ[14].
22 And Zillah, she also bare Tubal-cain, an instructer[15] of every artificer in brass and iron: and the sister of Tubal-cain *was* Naamah.
23 And Lamech said unto his wives, Adah and Zillah, Hear my voice; you wives of Lamech, hearken unto my speech: for I have slain a man to my wounding, and a young man to my hurt.
24 If Cain will be avenged sevenfold, truly Lamech seventy and sevenfold.
25 And Adam knew his wife again; and she bares a son, and called his name Seth[16]: For God, *said she*, hath appointed me another seed instead of Abel, whom Cain slew.
26 And to Seth, to him also there was born a son; and he called his name Enos[17]: then began men to call upon the name of the LORD.

CHAPTER 5

1 This *is* the book of the generations of Adam. In the day that God created man, in the likeness of God made he him;
2 Male and female created he them; and blessed them, and called their name Adam, in the day when they were created.
3 And Adam lived an hundred and thirty years, and begat *a son* in his own likeness, after his image; and called his name Seth:
4 And the days of Adam after he had begotten Seth were eight hundred years: and he begat sons and daughters
5 And all the days that Adam lived were nine hundred and thirty years: and he died.
6 And Seth lived an hundred and five years, and begat Enos:
7 And Seth lived after he begat Enos eight hundred and seven years, and begat sons and daughters:

---

[1] face - *'aph = anger*, **nostril** [Strgs#639]. Compare notes#3.
[2] Literall *a part of us*.
[3] *drove out* – divorce [Strgs#1644].
[4] The Devil is not driven out until **Rev. 12**.
[5] Eve- comes from the Hebrew word *chavvâh*, khav-vaw'; meaning *lifegiver*. [Strgs#2332]. It comes from the Hebrew root word *châvâh* meaning to *live*; implication (intensively) to *declare* or *show*:- show. [Strgs#2331]
[6] Literally at the end of days. In process = at the end of and an extremity [Strgs#7093]. Time = a day [Strgs#3117].
[7] *accepted* – to have the excelency, compare **Job 13:1 & Ps. 62:4**.
[8] Enoch – dedicated or initiated [Strgs#2585]
[9] Irad – literally means fleet or fugitive [Strgs#5897]
[10] Mehujael – smitten of God [Strgs#4232]
[11] Methusael – who is of God, with the relative interposed man who (is) of God [Strgs#4967]
[12] *Adah* – ornament, dubplicate, advance, continue [Strgs#5711 + 5710]
[13] Zillah – shade [Strgs#6741]
[14] Literally – instructment that uses breath.
[15] instructer- is the primitive Hebrew word *lâtash*, law-tash', meaning to hammer out (an edge), that is, to sharpen, whet [Strgs#3913].
[16] Seth – substituted or replacement [Strgs#8352]
[17] Enos – the mortal man [Strgs#583]

8 And all the days of Seth were nine hundred and twelve years: and he died.
9 And Enos lived ninety years, and begat Cainan:
10 And Enos lived after he begat Cainan eight hundred and fifteen years, and begat sons and daughters:
11 And all the days of Enos were nine hundred and five years: and he died.
12 And Cainan lived seventy years, and begat Mahalaleel:
13 And Cainan lived after he begat Mahalaleel eight hundred and forty years, and begat sons and daughters:
14 And all the days of Cainan were nine hundred and ten years: and he died.
15 And Mahalaleel lived sixty and five years, and begat Jared:
16 And Mahalaleel lived after he begat Jared eight hundred and thirty years, and begat sons and daughters:
17 And all the days of Mahalaleel were eight hundred ninety and five years: and he died.
18 And Jared lived an hundred sixty and two years, and he begat Enoch:
19 And Jared lived after he begat Enoch eight hundred years, and begat sons and daughters:
20 And all the days of Jared were nine hundred sixty and two years: and he died.
21 And Enoch lived sixty and five years, and begat Methuselah:
22 And Enoch walked with God after he begat Methuselah three hundred years, and begat sons and daughters:
23 And all the days of Enoch were three hundred sixty and five years:
24 And Enoch walked with God: and he *was* not; for God took him.
25 And Methuselah lived an hundred eighty and seven years, and begat Lamech:
26 And Methuselah lived after he begat Lamech seven hundred eighty and two years, and begat sons and daughters:
27 And all the days of Methuselah were nine hundred sixty and nine years: and he died.
28 And Lamech lived an hundred eighty and two years, and begat a son:
29 And he called his name Noah, saying, this *same* will comfort us concerning our work and toil of our hands, because of the ground which the LORD hath cursed.
30 And Lamech lived after he begat Noah five hundred ninety and five years, and begat sons and daughters:
31 And all the days of Lamech were seven hundred seventy and seven years: and he died.
32 And Noah was five hundred years old: and Noah begat Shem, Ham, and Japheth.

CHAPTER 6

1 And it came to pass, when men began to multiply on the face of the earth, and daughters were born unto them,
2 That the sons of God saw the daughters of men that they *were* fair; and they took[1] them wives of all which they chose.

3 And the LORD said, my spirit will not always strive with man, for that he also *is* flesh: yet his days will be an hundred and twenty years.
4 There were giants[2] in the earth in those days; and also after that, when the sons of God came in unto the daughters of men, and they bare[3] *children* to them, the same *became* mighty men which *were* of old[4], men of renown.
5 And GOD saw that the wickedness of man *was* great in the earth, and *that* every imagination of the thoughts of his heart *was* only evil continually.
6 And it repented the LORD that he had made man on the earth, and it grieved him at his heart.
7 And the LORD said, I will destroy man whom I have created from the face of the earth; both man, and beast, and the creeping thing, and the fowls of the air; for it repents me that I have made them.
8 But Noah[5] found grace in the eyes of the LORD.
9 These *are* the generations of Noah: Noah was a just man *and* perfect in his generations, *and* Noah walked with God.
10 And Noah begat three sons, Shem, Ham, and Japheth.
11 The earth also was corrupt before God, and the earth was filled with violence.
12 And God looked upon the earth, and, behold, it was corrupt; for all flesh had corrupted his way upon the earth.
13 And God said unto Noah, The end of all flesh is come before me; for the earth is filled with violence through them; and, behold, I will destroy them with the earth.
14 Make you an ark of gopher wood; rooms will you make in the ark, and will pitch it within and without with pitch.
15 And this *is the fashion* which you will make it *of*: The length of the ark *will be* three hundred cubits, the breadth of it fifty cubits, and the height of it thirty cubits.
16 A window will you make to the ark, and in a cubit will you finish it above; and the door of the ark will you set in the side thereof; *with* lower, second, and third *stories* will you make it.
17 And, behold, I, even I, do bring a flood of waters upon the earth, to destroy all flesh, wherein *is* the breath of life, from under heaven; *and* everything that *is* in the earth will die.
18 But with you will I establish my covenant; and you will come into the ark, you, and your sons, and your wife, and your sons' wives with you.
19 And of every living thing of all flesh, two of every *sort* will you bring into the ark, to keep *them* alive with you; they will be male and female.
20 Of fowls after their kind, and of cattle after their kind, of every creeping thing of the earth after his kind, two of every *sort* will come unto you, to keep *them* alive.
21 And take thou unto thee of all food that is eaten, and you will gather *it* to you; and it will be for food for you, and for them.
22 Thus did Noah; according to all that God commanded him, so did he.

---

[1] *took* – Hebrew word *lâqach* meaning to lay hold of, to take, mingle, win, take away, reserve, buy, carry away place [Strgs#3947]. The same Hebrew word used to describe when God took Enoch (see **Genesis 5:21-24**) and when God took Adam's rib (see **Genesis 2:21-22**).

[2] *giants* – Hebrew word *nephîyl* or *nephilim* meaning a feller, a bully or tyrant.

[3] bare – to act as a midwife, specifically to show lineage [Strgs#3205]

[4] old – the concealed, eternity, time out of mind, the banishing point [Strgs#5769]

[5] Noah- the patriarch of the flood. His name comes from the Hebrew word *nôach*, no'-akh; meaning *rest*. [Strgs#5146]

CHAPTER 7

1 And the LORD said unto Noah, Come you and your **entire** house into the ark; for you have I seen righteous before me in this generation.
2 Of every clean beast you will take to you by sevens, the male and his female: and of beasts that *are* not clean by two, the male and his female.
3 Of fowls also of the air by sevens, the male and the female; to keep seed alive upon the face of all the earth.[1]
4 For yet seven days, and I will cause it to rain upon the earth forty days and forty nights; and every living substance that I have made will I destroy from off the face of the earth.
5 And Noah did according unto all that the LORD commanded him.
6 And Noah *was* six hundred years old when the flood of waters was upon the earth.
7 And Noah went in, and his sons, and his wife, and his sons' wives with him, into the ark, because of the waters of the flood.
8 Of clean beasts, and of beasts that *are* not clean, and of fowls, and of everything that creep upon the earth,
9 There went in two and two unto Noah into the ark, the male and the female, as God had commanded Noah.
10 And it came to pass after seven days, that the waters of the flood were upon the earth.
11 In the six hundred year of Noah's life, in the second month, the seventeenth day of the month, the same day were all the fountains of the great deep broken up, and the windows of heaven were opened.
12 And the rain was upon the earth forty days and forty nights.
13 In the selfsame day entered Noah, and Shem, and Ham, and Japheth, the sons of Noah, and Noah's wife, and the three wives of his sons with them, into the ark;
14 They, and every beast after his kind, and all the cattle after their kind, and every creeping thing that creep upon the earth after his kind, and every fowl after his kind, every bird of every sort.
15 And they went in unto Noah into the ark, two and two of all flesh, wherein *is* the breath of life.
16 And they that went in, went in male and female of all flesh, as God had commanded him: and the LORD shut him in.
17 And the flood was forty days upon the earth; and the waters increased, and bare up the ark, and it was lift up above the earth.
18 And the waters prevailed, and were increased greatly upon the earth; and the ark went upon the face of the waters.
19 And the waters prevailed exceedingly upon the earth; and all the high hills, that *were* under the whole heaven, were covered.
20 Fifteen cubits upward did the waters prevail; and the mountains were covered.
21 And all flesh died that moved upon the earth, both of fowl, and of cattle, and of beast, and of every creeping thing that creep upon the earth, and every man:
22 All in whose nostrils *was* the breath of life, of all that *was* in the dry *land*, died.
23 And every living substance was destroyed which was upon the face of the ground, both man, and cattle, and the creeping things, and the fowl of the heaven; and they were destroyed from the earth: and Noah only remained *alive*, and they that *were* with him in the ark.
24 And the waters prevailed upon the earth an hundred and fifty days.

CHAPTER 8

1 And God remembered Noah, and every living thing, and all the cattle that *were* with him in the ark: and God made a wind to pass over the earth, and the waters **subsided**;
2 The fountains also of the deep and the windows of heaven were stopped, and the rain from heaven was restrained;
3 And the waters returned from off the earth continually: and after the end of the hundred and fifty days the waters were abated.
4 And the ark rested in the seventh month, on the seventeenth day of the month, upon the mountains of Ararat.
5 And the waters decreased continually until the tenth month: in the tenth *month*, on the first *day* of the month, were the tops of the mountains seen.
6 And it came to pass at the end of forty days, that Noah opened the window of the ark which he had made:
7 And he sent forth a raven, which went forth to and fro, until the waters were dried up from off the earth.
8 Also he sent forth a dove from him, to see if the waters were abated from off the face of the ground;
9 But the dove found no rest for the sole of her foot, and she returned unto him into the ark, for the waters *were* on the face of the whole earth: then he put forth his hand, and took her, and pulled her in unto him into the ark.
10 And he stayed yet other seven days; and again he sent forth the dove out of the ark;
11 And the dove came in to him in the evening; and, lo, in her mouth *was* an olive leaf plucked off: so Noah knew that the waters were abated from off the earth.
12 And he stayed yet other seven days; and sent forth the dove; which returned not again unto him anymore.
13 And it came to pass in the six hundred and first year, in the first *month*, the first *day* of the month, the waters were dried up from off the earth: and Noah removed the covering of the ark, and looked, and, behold, the face of the ground was dry.
14 And in the second month, on the seven and twentieth day of the month, was the earth dried.
15 And God spoke unto Noah, saying,
16 Go forth of the ark, you, and your wife, and your sons, and your sons' wives with you.
17 Bring forth with you every living thing that *is* with you, of all flesh, *both* of fowl, and of cattle, and of every creeping thing that creep upon the earth; that they may breed abundantly in the earth, and be fruitful, and multiply upon the earth.
18 And Noah went forth, and his sons, and his wife, and his sons' wives with him:
19 Every beast, every creeping thing, and every fowl, *and* whatsoever creep upon the earth, after their kinds went forth out of the ark.
20 And Noah built an altar unto the LORD; and took of every clean beast, and of every clean fowl, and offered burnt offerings on the altar.
21 And the LORD smelled a sweet savor; and the LORD said in his heart, I will not again curse the ground any more for man's sake; for the imagination of man's heart *is* evil from his youth; neither will I again smite any more everything living, as I have done.

---

[1] This eliminates the doctrine of same sex practices. God plan is to keep the seed alive through the male and female union.

22 While the earth remains, seedtime and harvest, and cold and heat, and summer and winter, and day and night will not cease.

CHAPTER 9

1 And God blessed Noah and his sons, and said unto them, be fruitful, and multiply, and replenish the earth.
2 And the fear of you and the dread of you will be upon every beast of the earth, and upon every fowl of the air, upon all that move *upon* the earth, and upon all the fishes of the sea; into your hand are they delivered.
3 Every moving thing that lives will be meat for you; even as the green herb have I given you all things.
4 But flesh with the life thereof, *which is* the blood thereof, will you not eat.
5 And surely your blood of your lives will I require; at the hand of every beast will I require it, and at the hand of man; at the hand of every man's brother will I require the life of man.
6 Who ever sheds man's blood, by man will his blood be shed: for in the image of God made he man.
7 And you, be you fruitful, and multiply; bring forth abundantly in the earth, and multiply therein.
8 And God spoke unto Noah, and to his sons with him, saying,
9 And I, behold, I establish my covenant with you, and with your seed after you;
10 And with every living creature that *is* with you, of the fowl, of the cattle, and of every beast of the earth with you; from all that go out of the ark, to every beast of the earth.
11 And I will establish my covenant with you; neither will all flesh be cut off any more by the waters of a flood; neither will there be any more floods to destroy the earth.
12 And God said, this *is* the token of the covenant which I make between me and you and every living creature that *is* with you, for perpetual generations:
13 I do set my bow in the cloud, and it will be for a token of a covenant between me and the earth.
14 And it will come to pass, when I bring a cloud over the earth, that the bow will be seen in the cloud:
15 And I will remember my covenant, which *is* between me and you and every living creature of all flesh; and the waters will no more become a flood to destroy all flesh.
16 And the bow will be in the cloud; and I will look upon it, that I may remember the everlasting covenant between God and every living creature of all flesh that *is* upon the earth.
17 And God said unto Noah, This *is* the token of the covenant, which I have established between me and all flesh that *is* upon the earth.
18 And the sons of Noah, that went forth of the ark, were Shem, and Ham, and Japheth: and Ham *is* the father of Canaan.
19 These *are* the three sons of Noah: and of them was the whole earth overspread.
20 And Noah began *to be* a husbandman, and he planted a vineyard:
21 And he drank of the wine, and was drunk; and he was uncovered within his tent.
22 [And Ham, the father of Canaan, saw the nakedness of his father, and told his two brethren without.]¹
23 And Shem and Japheth took a garment, and laid *it* upon both their shoulders, and went backward, and covered the nakedness of their father; and their faces *were* backward, and they saw not their father's nakedness.
24 And Noah awoke from his wine, and knew what his younger son had done unto him.
25 And he said, Cursed *be* Canaan; a servant of servants will he be unto his brethren.
26 And he said, blessed *is* the LORD God of Shem; and Canaan will be his servant.
27 God will enlarge Japheth, and he will dwell in the tents of Shem; and Canaan will be his servant.
28 And Noah lived after the flood three hundred and fifty years.
29 And all the days of Noah were nine hundred and fifty years: and he died.

CHAPTER 10

1 Now these *are* the generations of the sons of Noah, Shem, Ham, and Japheth: and unto them were sons born after the flood.
2 The sons of Japheth; Gomer, and Magog, and Madai, and Javan, and Tubal, and Meshech, and Tiras.
3 And the sons of Gomer; Ashkenaz, and Riphath, and Togarmah.
4 And the sons of Javan; Elishah, and Tarshish, Kittim, and Dodanim.
5 By these were the isles of the Gentiles divided in their lands; every one after his tongue, after their families, in their nations.
6 And the sons of Ham; Cush², and Mizraim, and Phut, and Canaan.
7 And the sons of Cush; Seba, and Havilah, and Sabtah, and Raamah³, and Sabtecha: and the sons of Raamah; Sheba, and Dedan.
8 And Cush begat Nimrod⁴: he began to be a mighty one in the earth.
9 He was a mighty hunter before the LORD: wherefore it is said, Even as Nimrod the mighty hunter before the LORD.
10 And the beginning of his kingdom was Babel, and Erech, and Accad, and Calneh, in the land of Shinar.
11 Out of that land went forth Asshur, and builded Nineveh, and the city Rehoboth, and Calah,
12 And Resen between Nineveh and Calah: the same *is* a great city.
13 And Mizraim begat Ludim, and Anamim, and Lehabim, and Naphtuhim,
14 And Pathrusim, and Casluhim, (out of whom came Philistim,) and Caphtorim.
15 And Canaan begat Sidon his firstborn, and Heth,
16 And the Jebusite, and the Amorite, and the Girgasite,
17 And the Hivite, and the Arkite, and the Sinite,
18 And the Arvadite, and the Zemarite, and the Hamathite and afterward were the families of the Canaanites spread abroad
19 And the border of the Canaanites was from Sidon, as you come to Gerar, unto Gaza; as you go, unto Sodom, and Gomorrah, and Admah, and Zeboim, even unto Lasha.
20 These *are* the sons of Ham, after their families, after their tongues, in their countries, *and* in their nations.
21 Unto Shem also, the father of all the children of Eber, the brother of Japheth the elder, even to him were *children* born.

---

¹ The start of Homosexuality, v.(25) serve his brethren, humble to men.
² Cush – black [Strgs#3568]
³ *Raamah* – horse's mane [Strgs#7484]. Root meaning thunder [Strgs#7483].
⁴ *Nimrod* – we will rebell, rebellion or the valiant [Strgs#5248]

22 The children of Shem; Elam, and Asshur, and Arphaxad, and Lud, and Aram.
23 And the children of Aram; Uz, and Hul, and Gether, and Mash.
24 And Arphaxad begat Salah; and Salah begat Eber.
25 And unto Eber were born two sons: the name of one *was* Peleg; for in his days was the earth divided; and his brother's name *was* Joktan.
26 And Joktan begat Almodad, and Sheleph, and Hazarmaveth, and Jerah,
27 And Hadoram, and Uzal, and Diklah,
28 And Obal, and Abimael, and Sheba,
29 And Ophir, and Havilah, and Jobab: all these *were* the sons of Joktan.
30 And their dwelling was from Mesha, as you go unto Sephar a mount of the east.
31 These *are* the sons of Shem, after their families, after their tongues, in their lands, after their nations.
32 These *are* the families of the sons of Noah, after their generations, in their nations: and by these were the nations divided in the earth after the flood.

CHAPTER 11

1 And the whole earth was of one language, and of one speech.
2 And it came to pass, as they journeyed from the east, that they found a plain[1] in the land of Shinar; and they dwelt there.
3 And they said one to another, Go to, let us make brick, and burn them thoroughly. And they had brick for stone, and slime had they for mortar.
4 And they said, Go to, let us build us a city and a tower, whose top *may reach* unto heaven; and let us make us a name, lest we be scattered abroad upon the face of the whole earth.
5 And the LORD came down to see the city and the tower, which the children of men built.
6 And the LORD said, Behold, the people *is* one, and they have all one language; and this they begin to do: and now nothing will be restrained from them, which they have imagined to do.
7 Go to, let us go down, and there confound their language, that they may not understand one another's speech.
8 So the LORD scattered them abroad from thence upon the face of all the earth: and they left off to build the city.
9 Therefore is the name of it called Babel; because the LORD did there confound the language of all the earth: and from thence did the LORD scatter them abroad upon the face of all the earth.
10 These *are* the generations of Shem: Shem *was* an hundred years old, and begat Arphaxad two years after the flood:
11 And Shem lived after he begat Arphaxad five hundred years, and begat sons and daughters.
12 And Arphaxad lived five and thirty years, and begat Salah:
13 And Arphaxad lived after he begat Salah four hundred and three years, and begat sons and daughters.
14 And Salah lived thirty years, and begat Eber:
15 And Salah lived after he begat Eber four hundred and three years, and begat sons and daughters.
16 And Eber lived four and thirty years, and begat Peleg:
17 And Eber lived after he begat Peleg four hundred and thirty years, and begat sons and daughters.
18 And Peleg lived thirty years, and begat Reu:
19 And Peleg lived after he begat Reu two hundred and nine years, and begat sons and daughters.
20 And Reu lived two and thirty years, and begat Serug:
21 And Reu lived after he begat Serug two hundred and seven years, and begat sons and daughters.
22 And Serug lived thirty years, and begat Nahor:
23 And Serug lived after he begat Nahor two hundred years, and begat sons and daughters.
24 And Nahor lived nine and twenty years, and begat Terah:
25 And Nahor lived after he begat Terah a hundred and nineteen years, and begat sons and daughters.
26 And Terah lived seventy years, and begat Abram, Nahor, and Haran.
27 Now these *are* the generations of Terah: Terah begat Abram[2], Nahor, and Haran; and Haran begat Lot[3].
28 And Haran died before his father Terah in the land of his nativity, in Ur of the Chaldees.
29 And Abram and Nahor took them wives: the name of Abram's wife *was* Sarai[4]; and the name of Nahor's wife, Milcah, the daughter of Haran, the father of Milcah, and the father of Iscah.
30 But Sarai was barren; she *had* no child.
31 And Terah took Abram his son, and Lot the son of Haran his son's son, and Sarai his daughter in law, his son Abram's wife; and they went forth with them from Ur of the Chaldees, to go into the land of Canaan; and they came unto Haran, and dwelt there.
32 And the days of Terah were two hundred and five years: and Terah died in Haran.

CHAPTER 12

1 Now the LORD had said unto Abram, Get you out of your country, and from your kindred, and from your father's house, unto a land that I will show you:
2 And I will make of you a great nation, and I will bless you, and make your name great; and you will be a blessing:
3 And I will bless them that bless you, and curse him that curses you: and in you will all families of the earth be blessed.
4 So Abram departed, as the LORD had spoken unto him; and Lot went with him: and Abram *was* seventy and five years old when he departed out of Haran.
5 And Abram took Sarai his wife, and Lot his brother's son, and all their substance that they had gathered, and the souls that they had gotten in Haran; and they went forth to go into the land of Canaan; and into the land of Canaan they came.
6 And Abram passed through the land unto the place of Sichem, unto the plain of Moreh. And the Canaanite *was* then in the land.
7 And the LORD appeared unto Abram, and said, unto your seed will I give this land: and there built he an altar unto the LORD, who appeared unto him.
8 And he removed from thence unto a mountain on the east of Beth-el, and pitched his tent, *having* Beth-el on the west, and Hai on the east: and there he built an altar unto the LORD, and called upon the name of the LORD.
9 And Abram journeyed, going on still toward the south.
10 And there was a famine in the land: and Abram went down into Egypt to sojourn there; for the famine *was* grievous in the land.
11 And it came to pass, when he was come near to enter into Egypt, that he said unto Sarai his wife, behold now, I know that you *are* a fair woman to look upon:

---

[1] *plain* – a *split*, a wide level *valley* between mountains [Strgs#1237]
[2] Abram- high father or exalted father [Strgs#87].
[3] Lot- covering, envelope [Strgs#3876].
[4] Sarai- princess [Strgs#8297].

12 Therefore it *will* come to pass, when the Egyptians will see you, that they will say, this *is* his wife: and they will kill me, but they will save you alive.
13 Say, I pray you, you *are* my sister: that it may be well with me for your sake; *and* my soul will live because of you.
14 And it came to pass, that, when Abram was come into Egypt, the Egyptians beheld the woman that she *was* very fair.
15 The princes also of Pharaoh saw her, and commended her before Pharaoh: and the woman was taken into Pharaoh's house.
16 And he entreated Abram well for her sake: and he had sheep, and oxen, and he asses, and menservants, and maidservants, and she asses, and camels.
17 And the LORD plagued Pharaoh and his house with great plagues because of Sarai Abram's wife.
18 And Pharaoh called Abram, and said, what *is* this *that* you have done unto me? Why did you not tell me that she *was* your wife?
19 Why said you, she *is* my sister? So I might have taken her to me to wife: now therefore behold your wife, take *her*, and go your way.
20 And Pharaoh commanded *his* men concerning him: and they sent him away, and his wife, and all that he had.

CHAPTER 13

1 And Abram went up out of Egypt, he, and his wife, and all that he had, and Lot with him, into the south.
2 And Abram *was* very rich in cattle, in silver, and in gold.
3 And he went on his journeys from the south even to Beth-el, unto the place where his tent had been at the beginning, between Beth-el and Hai;
4 Unto the place of the altar, which he had made there at the first: and there Abram called on the name of the LORD.
5 And Lot also, which went with Abram, had flocks, and herds, and tents.
6 And the land was not able to bear them, that they might dwell together: for their substance was great, so that they could not dwell together.
7 And there was strife between the herdmen of Abram's cattle and the herdmen of Lot's cattle: and the Canaanite and the Perizzite dwelled then in the land.
8 And Abram said unto Lot, Let there be no strife, I pray you, between me and you, and between my herdsmen and your herdsmen; for we *be* brethren.
9 *Is* not the whole land before you? Separate yourself, I pray you, from me: if *you will take* the left hand, then I will go to the right; or if *you depart* to the right hand, then I will go to the left.
10 And Lot lifted up his eyes, and beheld all the plain of Jordan, that it *was* well watered everywhere, before the LORD destroyed Sodom and Gomorrah, *even* as the garden of the LORD, like the land of Egypt, as you come unto Zoar.
11 Then Lot chose him all the plain of Jordan; and Lot journeyed east: and they separated themselves the one from the other.
12 Abram dwelt in the land of Canaan, and Lot dwelt in the cities of the plain, and pitched *his* tent toward Sodom.
13 But the men of Sodom *were* wicked and sinners before the LORD exceedingly.
14 And the LORD said unto Abram, after that Lot was separated from him, Lift up now your eyes, and look from the place where you are northward, and southward, and eastward, and westward:
15 For all the land which you see, to you will I give it, and to your seed for ever.
16 And I will make your seed as the dust of the earth: so that if a man can number the dust of the earth, *then* will your seed also be numbered.
17 Arise, walk through the land in the length of it and in the breadth of it; for I will give it unto you.
18 Then Abram removed *his* tent, and came and dwelt in the plain of Mamre, which *is* in Hebron, and built there an altar unto the LORD.

CHAPTER 14

1 And it came to pass in the days of Amraphel king of Shinar, Arioch king of Ellasar, Chedorlaomer king of Elam, and Tidal king of nations;
2 *That these* made war with Bera king of Sodom, and with Birsha king of Gomorrah, Shinab king of Admah, and Shemeber king of Zeboiim, and the king of Bela, which is Zoar.
3 All these were joined together in the vale of Siddim, which is the salt sea.
4 Twelve years they served Chedorlaomer, and in the thirteenth year they rebelled.
5 And in the fourteenth year came Chedorlaomer, and the kings that *were* with him, and smote the Rephaims in Ashteroth Karnaim, and the Zuzims in Ham, and the Emims in Shaveh Kiriathaim,
6 And the Horites in their mount Seir, unto El-paran, which *is* by the wilderness.
7 And they returned, and came to En-mishpat, which *is* Kadesh, and smote all the country of the Amalekites, and also the Amorites, that dwelt in Hazezon-tamar.
8 And there went out the king of Sodom, and the king of Gomorrah, and the king of Admah, and the king of Zeboiim, and the king of Bela (the same *is* Zoar;) and they joined battle with them in the vale of Siddim;
9 With Chedorlaomer the king of Elam, and with Tidal king of nations, and Amraphel king of Shinar, and Arioch king of Ellasar; four kings with five.
10 And the vale of Siddim *was full of* slime pits; and the kings of Sodom and Gomorrah fled, and fell there; and they that remained fled to the mountain.
11 And they took all the goods of Sodom and Gomorrah, and all their victuals, and went their way.
12 And they took Lot, Abram's brother's son, who dwelt in Sodom, and his goods, and departed.
13 And there came one that had escaped, and told Abram the Hebrew; for he dwelled in the plain of Mamre the Amorite, brother of Eshcol, and brother of Aner: and these *were* confederate with Abram.
14 And when Abram heard that his brother was taken captive, he armed his trained *servants*, born in his own house, three hundred and eighteen, and pursued *them* unto Dan.
15 And he divided himself against them, he and his servants, by night, and smote them, and pursued them unto Hobah, which *is* on the left hand of Damascus.
16 And he brought back all the goods, and also brought again his brother Lot, and his goods, and the women also, and the people.
17 And the king of Sodom went out to meet him after his return from the slaughter of Chedorlaomer, and of the kings that *were* with him, at the valley of Shaveh, which *is* the king's dale.

18 And Melchizedek[1] king of Salem brought forth bread and wine: and he *was* the priest of the most high God.
19 And he blessed him, and said, blessed *be* Abram of the most high God, possessor of heaven and earth:
20 And blessed be the most-high God, which hath delivered your enemies into your hand. And he gave him tithes of all.
21 And the king of Sodom said unto Abram, Give me the persons, and take the goods to yourself.
22 And Abram said to the king of Sodom, I have lift up mine hand unto the LORD, the most high God, the possessor of heaven and earth,
23 That I will not *take* from a thread even to a shoe latchet, and that I will not take any thing that *is* yours, lest you should say, I have made Abram rich:
24 Save only that which the young men have eaten, and the portion of the men which went with me, Aner, Eshcol, and Mamre; let them take their portion.

CHAPTER 15

1 After these things the word of the LORD came unto Abram in a vision, saying, fear not, Abram: I *am* your shield, *and* you're exceeding great reward.
2 And Abram said, Lord GOD, what will you give me, seeing I go childless, and the steward of my house *is* this Eliezer of Damascus?
3 And Abram said, Behold, to me you have given no seed: and, lo, one born in my house is mine heir.
4 And, behold, the word of the LORD *came* unto him, saying, this will not be your heir; but he that will come forth out of your own bowels will be your heir.
5 And he brought him forth abroad, and said, look now toward heaven, and tell the stars, if you be able to number them: and he said unto him, so will your seed be.[2]
6 And he believed in the LORD; and he counted it to him for righteousness.
7 And he said unto him, I *am* the LORD that brought you out of Ur of the Chaldees, to give you this land to inherit it.
8 And he said, Lord GOD, whereby will I know that I will inherit it?
9 And he said unto him, Take me a heifer of three years old, and a she goat of three years old, and a ram of three years old, and a turtledove, and a young pigeon.
10 And he took unto him all these, and divided them in the middle, and laid each piece one against another: but the birds divided he not.
11 And when the fowls came down upon the carcasses, Abram drove them away.
12 And when the sun was going down, a deep sleep fell upon Abram; and, lo, a horror of great darkness fell upon him.
13 And he said unto Abram, know of a sure that your seed will be a stranger in a land *that is* not theirs, and will serve them; and they will afflict them four hundred years;
14 And also that nation, whom they will serve, will I judge: and afterward will they come out with great substance.
15 And you will go to your fathers in peace; you will be buried in a good old age.
16 But in the fourth generation they will come here again: for the iniquity of the Amorites *is* not yet full.
17 And it came to pass, that, when the sun went down, and it was dark, behold a smoking furnace, and a burning lamp that passed between those pieces.
18 In the same day the LORD made a covenant with Abram, saying, unto your seed have I given this land, from the river of Egypt unto the great river, the river Euphrates:
19 The Kenites, and the Kenizzites, and the Kadmonites,
20 And the Hittites, and the Perizzites, and the Rephaims,
21 And the Amorites, and the Canaanites, and the Girgashites, and the Jebusites.

CHAPTER 16

1 Now Sarai Abram's wife bare him no children: and she had a handmaid, an Egyptian, whose name *was* Hagar.
2 And Sarai said unto Abram, Behold now, the LORD hath restrained me from bearing: I pray you, go in unto my maid; it may be that I may obtain children by her. And Abram hearkened to the voice of Sarai.
3 And Sarai Abram's wife took Hagar[3] her maid the Egyptian, after Abram had dwelled ten years in the land of Canaan, and gave her to her husband Abram to be his wife.
4 And he went in unto Hagar, and she conceived: and when she saw that she had conceived, her mistress was despised in her eyes.
5 And Sarai said unto Abram, My wrong *be* upon you: I have given my maid into your bosom; and when she saw that she had conceived, I was despised in her eyes: the LORD judge between me and you.
6 But Abram said unto Sarai, Behold, your maid *is* in your hand; do to her as it please you. And when Sarai dealt hardly with her, she fled from her face.
7 And the angel of the LORD found her by a fountain of water in the wilderness, by the fountain in the way to Shur.
8 And he said, Hagar, Sarai's maid, whence came you? And whither will you go? And she said, I flee from the face of my mistress Sarai.
9 And the angel of the LORD said unto her, return to your mistress, and submit yourself under her hands.
10 And the angel of the LORD said unto her, I will multiply your seed exceedingly, that it will not be numbered for multitude.
11 And the angel of the LORD said unto her, Behold, you *are* with child, and will bear a son, and will call his name Ishmael[4]; because the LORD hath heard your affliction.
12 And he will be a wild man; his hand *will be* against every man, and every man's hand against him; and he will dwell in the presence of all his brethren.
13 And she called the name of the LORD that spoke unto her, you God see me: for she said, have I also here looked after him that sees me?
14 Wherefore the well was called Beer-lahai-roi; behold, *it is* between Kadesh and Bered.
15 And Hagar bare Abram a son: and Abram called his son's name, which Hagar bare, Ishmael.

---

[1] Melchizedek- king of Salem and priest of the Most High God to who Abram paid tithe after the battle he fought to free Lot; the order of Melchizedek' the order of the priesthood to which Christ belongs (compare Hebrews 5:5-10). His name is defined as *king of right* or *my king is Sedek*.

[Strgs#4442= to 4428 & 6664]
[2] seeds = stars
[3] Hagar- flight, emigration [Strgs#1904].
[4] Ishmael- God will hear [Strgs#3458].

16 And Abram *was* fourscore and six years old, when Hagar bare Ishmael to Abram.

CHAPTER 17

1 And when Abram was ninety years old and nine, the LORD appeared to Abram, and said unto him, I *am* the Almighty God; walk before me, and be you perfect.
2 And I will make my covenant between me and you, and will multiply you exceedingly.
3 And Abram fell on his face: and God talked with him, saying,
4 As for me, behold, my covenant *is* with you, and you will be a father of many nations.
5 Neither will your name any more be called Abram, but your name will be Abraham[1]; for a father of many nations have I made you.
6 And I will make you exceeding fruitful, and I will make nations of you, and kings will come out of you.
7 And I will establish my covenant between me and you and your seed after you in their generations for an everlasting covenant, to be a God unto you, and to your seed after you.
8 And I will give unto you, and to your seed after you, the land wherein you are a stranger, all the land of Canaan, for an everlasting possession; and I will be their God.
9 And God said unto Abraham, You will keep my covenant therefore, you, and your seed after you in their generations.
10 This *is* my covenant[2], which you will keep, between me and you and your seed after you; every man child among you will be circumcised.
11 And you will circumcise the flesh of your foreskin; and it will be a token of the covenant between me and you.
12 And he that is eight days old will be circumcised among you, every man child in your generations, he that is born in the house, or bought with money of any stranger, which *is* not of your seed.
13 He that is born in your house, and he that is bought with your money, must need to be circumcised: and my covenant will be in your flesh for an everlasting covenant.
14 And the uncircumcised man child whose flesh of his foreskin is not circumcised, that soul will be cut off from his people; he has broken my covenant.
15 And God said unto Abraham, As for Sarai your wife, you will not call her name Sarai, but Sarah[3] *will* her name *be*.
16 And I will bless her, and give you a son also of her: yes, I will bless her, and she will be *a mother* of nations; kings of people will be of her.
17 Then Abraham fell upon his face, and laughed, and said in his heart, Will *a child* be born unto him that is an hundred years old? And will Sarah, that is ninety years old, bear?
18 And Abraham said unto God, O that Ishmael might live before you!
19 And God said, Sarah your wife will bear you a son indeed; and you will call his name Isaac: and I will establish my covenant with him for an everlasting covenant, *and* with his seed after him.
20 And as for Ishmael, I have heard you: Behold, I have blessed him, and will make him fruitful, and will multiply him exceedingly; twelve princes will he beget, and I will make him a great nation.
21 But my covenant will I establish with Isaac, which Sarah will bear unto you at this set time in the next year.
22 And he left off talking with him, and God went up from Abraham.

23 And Abraham took Ishmael his son, and all that were born in his house, and all that were bought with his money, every male among the men of Abraham's house; and circumcised the flesh of their foreskin in the selfsame day, as God had said unto him.
24 And Abraham *was* ninety years old and nine, when he was circumcised in the flesh of his foreskin.
25 And Ishmael his son *was* thirteen years old, when he was circumcised in the flesh of his foreskin.
26 In the selfsame day was Abraham circumcised, and Ishmael his son.
27 And all the men of his house, born in the house, and bought with money of the stranger, were circumcised with him.

CHAPTER 18

1 And the LORD appeared unto him in the plains of Mamre[4]: and he sat in the tent door in the heat of the day;
2 And he lifts up his eyes and looked, and, lo, three men stood by him: and when he saw *them*, he ran to meet them from the tent door, and bowed himself toward the ground,
3 And said, My Lord, if now I have found favor in your sight, pass not away, I pray you, from your servant:
4 Let a little water, I pray you, be fetched, and wash your feet, and rest yourselves under the tree:
5 And I will fetch a morsel of bread, and comfort you your hearts; after that you will pass on: for therefore are you come to your servant. And they said, so do, as you have said.
6 And Abraham hastened into the tent unto Sarah, and said, Make ready quickly three measures of fine meal, knead *it*, and make cakes upon the hearth.
7 And Abraham ran unto the herd, and fetched a calf tender and good, and gave *it* unto a young man; and he **speedily** to dress it.
8 And he took butter, and milk, and the calf which he had dressed, and set *it* before them; and he stood by them under the tree, and they did eat.
9 And they said unto him, where *is* Sarah your wife? And he said, Behold, in the tent.
10 And he said, I will certainly return unto you according to the time of life; and, lo, Sarah you wife will have a son. And Sarah heard *it* in the tent door, which *was* behind him.
11 Now Abraham and Sarah *were* old *and* well stricken in age; *and* it ceased to be with Sarah after the manner of women.
12 Therefore Sarah laughed within herself, saying, after I am waxed old will I have pleasure, my lord being old also?
13 And the LORD said unto Abraham, Wherefore did Sarah laugh, saying, Will I of a surety bear a child, which am old?
14 Is anything too hard for the LORD? At the time appointed I will return unto you, according to the time of life, and Sarah will have a son.
15 Then Sarah denied, saying, I laughed not; for she was afraid. And he said, No; but you didst laugh.
16 And the men rose up from there, and looked toward Sodom: and Abraham went with them to bring them on the way.
17 And the LORD said, Will I hide from Abraham that thing which I do;
18 Seeing that Abraham will surely become a great and mighty nation, and all the nations of the earth will be blessed in him?

---

[1] Abrahmham- father of a multitude or chief of multitude [Strgs#85].
[2] covenant- cutting flesh in two pieces and passing between them, an alliance, pledge [Strgs#1285].
[3] Sarah- noblewoman [Strgs#8283].
[4] mamre- firmness [Strgs#4471].

19 For I know him, that he will command his children and his household after him, and they will keep the way of the LORD, to do justice and judgment; that the LORD may bring upon Abraham that which he have spoken of him.
20 And the LORD said, because the cry of Sodom and Gomorrah is great, and because their sin is very grievous;
21 I will go down now, and see whether they have done altogether according to the cry of it, which is come unto me; and if not, I will know.
22 And the men turned their faces from thence, and went toward Sodom: but Abraham stood yet before the LORD.
23 And Abraham drew near, and said, Will you also destroy the righteous with the wicked?
24 Peradventure there are fifty righteous within the city: will you also destroy and not spare the place for the fifty righteous that *are* therein?
25 That be far from you to do after this manner, to slay the righteous with the wicked: and that the righteous should be as the wicked, that be far from you: Will not the Judge of all the earth do right?
26 And the LORD said, if I find in Sodom fifty righteous within the city, then I will spare the **entire** place for their sakes.
27 And Abraham answered and said, Behold now, I have taken upon me to speak unto the Lord, which *am but* dust and ashes:
28 Peradventure there will lack five of the fifty righteous: will you destroy the **entire** city for *lack of* five? And he said, if I find there forty and five, I will not destroy *it*.
29 And he spoke unto him yet again, and said, peradventure there will be forty found there. And he said, I will not do *it* for forty's sake.
30 And he said *unto him*, Oh let not the Lord be angry, and I will speak: Peradventure there will thirty be found there. And he said, I will not do *it*, if I find thirty there.
31 And he said, Behold now, I have taken upon me to speak unto the Lord: Peradventure there will be twenty found there. And he said, I will not destroy *it* for twenty's sake.
32 And he said, Oh let not the Lord be angry, and I will speak yet but this once: Peradventure ten will be found there. And he said, I will not destroy *it* for ten's sake.
33 And the LORD went his way, as soon as he had left communing with Abraham: and Abraham returned unto his place.

CHAPTER 19

1 And there came two angels to Sodom at even; and Lot sat in the gate of Sodom: and Lot seeing *them* rose up to meet them; and he bowed himself with his face toward the ground;
2 And he said, Behold now, my lords, turn in, I pray you, into your servant's house, and tarry all night, and wash your feet, and you will rise up early, and go on your ways. And they said, No; but we will abide in the street all night.
3 And he pressed upon them greatly; and they turned in unto him, and entered into his house; and he made them a feast, and did bake unleavened bread, and they did eat.
4 But before they lay down, the men[1] of the city, *even* the men of Sodom, compassed the house round, both old and young, all the people from every quarter:
5 And they called unto Lot, and said unto him, where *are* the men who came in to you this night? Bring them out unto us, that we may know them.[2]
6 And Lot went out at the door unto them, and shut the door after him,
7 And said, I pray you, brethren, do not so wickedly.
8 Behold now, I have two daughters which have not known man[3]; let me, I pray you, bring them out unto you, and do you to them as *is* good in your eyes: only unto these men do nothing; for therefore came they under the shadow of my roof.
9 And they said, Stand back. And they said *again*, this one *fellow* came in to sojourn, and he will needs be a judge: now will we deal worse with you, than with them. And they pressed sore upon the man, *even* Lot, and came near to break the door.
10 But the men put forth their hand, and pulled Lot into the house to them, and shut to the door.
11 And they smote the men that *were* at the door of the house with blindness, both small and great: so that they wearied themselves to find the door.[4]
12 And the men said unto Lot, have you here any besides? Son in law, and your sons, and your daughters, and whatsoever you have in the city, bring *them* out of this place:
13 For we will destroy this place, because the cry of them is waxen great before the face of the LORD; and the LORD hath sent us to destroy it.
14 And Lot went out, and spoke unto his sons in law, which married his daughters, and said, up, get you out of this place; for the LORD will destroy this city. But he seemed as one that mocked unto his sons in law.
15 And when the morning arose, then the angels hastened Lot, saying, Arise, take your wife, and your two daughters, which are here; lest you be consumed in the iniquity of the city.
16 And while he lingered, the men laid hold upon his hand, and upon the hand of his wife, and upon the hand of his two daughters; the LORD being merciful unto him: and they brought him forth, and set him without the city.
17 And it came to pass, when they had brought them forth abroad, that he said, Escape for your life; look not behind you, neither stay you in all the plain; escape to the mountain, lest you be consumed.
18 And Lot said unto them, Oh, not so, my Lord:
19 Behold now, your servant has found grace in your sight, and you have magnified your mercy, which you have showed unto me in saving my life; and I cannot escape to the mountain, lest some evil take me, and I die:
20 Behold now, this city *is* near to flee unto, and it *is* a little one: Oh, let me escape thither, (*is* it not a little one?) and my soul will live.
21 And he said unto him, See, I have accepted you concerning this thing also, that I will not overthrow this city, for which you have spoken.
22 **Hurry** you, escape here; for I cannot do anything until you come **here**. Therefore the name of the city was called Zoar.
23 The sun was raised upon the earth when Lot entered into Zoar.
24 Then the LORD rained upon Sodom and upon Gomorrah brimstone and fire from the LORD out of heaven;

---

[1] men – Hebrew *'ĕnôsh* meaning mortal man [Strgs#582]
[2] sex with angels – compare **Genesis 6** & **Jude**.
[3] *man* – Hebrew *'îysh* meaning man of high degree, husband, man, human being, servant, champion [Strgs#376]
[4] When sick men try to pervert men of God – blindness is their fate.

25 And he overthrew those cities, and all the plain, and all the inhabitants of the cities, and that which grew upon the ground.
26 But his wife looked back from behind him, and she became a pillar of salt.
27 And Abraham got up early in the morning to the place where he stood before the LORD:
28 And he looked toward Sodom and Gomorrah, and toward all the land of the plain, and beheld, and, lo, the smoke of the country went up as the smoke of a furnace.
29 And it came to pass, when God destroyed the cities of the plain, that God remembered Abraham, and sent Lot out of the midst of the overthrow, when he overthrew the cities in the which Lot dwelt.
30 And Lot went up out of Zoar, and dwelt in the mountain, and his two daughters with him; for he feared to dwell in Zoar: and he dwelt in a cave, he and his two daughters.
31 And the firstborn said unto the younger, our father *is* old, and *there is* not a man in the earth to come in unto us after the manner of all the earth:
32 Come, let us make our father drink wine, and we will lie with him, that we may preserve seed of our father.
33 And they made their father drink wine that night: and the firstborn went in, and lay with her father; and he perceived not when she lay down, or when she arose.
34 And it came to pass on the morrow, that the firstborn said unto the younger, Behold, I lay last night with my father: let us make him drink wine this night also; and go you in, *and* lie with him, that we may preserve seed of our father.
35 And they made their father drink wine that night also: and the younger arose, and lay with him; and he perceived not when she lay down, or when she arose.
36 They were both the daughters of Lot with child by their father.
37 And the firstborn bare a son, and called his name Moab: the same *is* the father of the Moabites unto this day.
38 And the younger, she also bares a son, and called his name Ben-ammi: the same *is* the father of the children of Ammon unto this day.

CHAPTER 20

1 And Abraham journeyed from thence toward the south country, and dwelled between Kadesh[1] and Shur[2], and sojourned in Gerar.
2 And Abraham said of Sarah his wife, she *is* my sister: and Abimelech king of Gerar sent, and took Sarah.
3 But God came to Abimelech in a dream by night, and said to him, Behold, you *are but* a dead man, for the woman which you have taken; for she *is* a man's wife.
4 But Abimelech had not come near her: and he said, Lord, will you slay also a righteous nation?
5 Said he not unto me, she *is* my sister? And she, even she herself said, He *is* my brother: in the integrity of my heart and innocence of my hands have I done this.
6 And God said unto him in a dream, Yes, I know that you didst this in the integrity of your heart; for I also withheld you from sinning against me: therefore suffered me you not to touch her.
7 Now therefore restore the man *his* wife; for he *is* a prophet, and he will pray for you, and you will live: and if you restore *her* not, know you that you will surely die, you, and all that *are* yours.

8 Therefore Abimelech rose early in the morning, and called all his servants, and told all these things in their ears: and the men were sore afraid.
9 Then Abimelech called Abraham, and said unto him, what have you done unto us? And what have I offended you, that you have brought on me and on my kingdom a great sin? You have done deeds unto me that ought not to be done.
10 And Abimelech said unto Abraham, what saw you that you have done this thing?
11 And Abraham said, because I thought, surely the fear of God *is* not in this place; and they will slay me for my wife's sake.
12 And yet indeed *she is* my sister; she *is* the daughter of my father, but not the daughter of my mother; and she became my wife.
13 And it came to pass, when God caused me to wander from my father's house, that I said unto her, This *is* your kindness which you will show unto me; at every place whither we will come, say of me, He *is* my brother.
14 And Abimelech took sheep, and oxen, and menservants, and women servants, and gave *them* unto Abraham, and restored him Sarah his wife.
15 And Abimelech said, Behold, my land *is* before you: dwell where it pleases you.
16 And unto Sarah he said, Behold, I have given your brother a thousand *pieces* of silver: behold, he *is* to you a covering of the eyes, unto all that *are* with you, and with all *other*: then she was reproved.
17 So Abraham prayed unto God: and God healed Abimelech, and his wife, and his maidservants; and they bare *children*.
18 For the LORD had fast closed up all the wombs of the house of Abimelech, because of Sarah Abraham's wife.

CHAPTER 21

1 And the LORD visited Sarah as he had said, and the LORD did unto Sarah as he had spoken.
2 For Sarah conceived, and bare Abraham a son in his old age, at the set time of which God had spoken to him.
3 And Abraham called the name of his son that was born unto him, whom Sarah bare to him, Isaac[3].
4 And Abraham circumcised his son Isaac being eight days old, as God had commanded him.
5 And Abraham was an hundred years old, when his son Isaac was born unto him.
6 And Sarah said, God hath made me to laugh, *so that* all that hear will laugh with me.
7 And she said, who would have said unto Abraham, that Sarah should have given children suck? For I have born *him* a son in his old age.
8 And the child grew, and was weaned: and Abraham made a great feast the *same* day that Isaac was weaned.
9 And Sarah saw the son of Hagar the Egyptian, which she had born unto Abraham, mocking.
10 Wherefore she said unto Abraham, cast out this bondwoman and her son: for the son of this bondwoman will not be heir with my son, *even* with Isaac.
11 And the thing was very grievous in Abraham's sight because of his son.

---

[1] Kadesh- holy, sanctuary [Strgs#6946].
[2] Shur- wall [Strgs#7793].

[3] Isaac- he laughs, laughter. [Strgs#3327]

12 And God said unto Abraham, Let it not be grievous in your sight because of the lad, and because of your bondwoman; in all that Sarah hath said unto you, hearken unto her voice; for in Isaac will your seed be called.
13 And also of the son of the bondwoman will I make a nation, because he *is* your seed.
14 And Abraham rose up early in the morning, and took bread, and a bottle of water, and gave *it* unto Hagar, putting *it* on her shoulder, and the child, and sent her away: and she departed, and wandered in the wilderness of Beer-sheba.
15 And the water was spent in the bottle, and she cast the child under one of the shrubs.
16 And she went, and sat her down over against *him* a good way off, as it were a bowshot: for she said, let me not see the death of the child. And she sat over against *him*, and lift up her voice, and wept.
17 And God heard the voice of the lad; and the angel of God called to Hagar out of heaven, and said unto her, what ails you, Hagar? Fear not; for God hath heard the voice of the lad where he *is*.
18 Arise, lift up the lad, and hold him in your hand; for I will make him a great nation.
19 And God opened her eyes, and she saw a well of water; and she went, and filled the bottle with water, and gave the lad drink.
20 And God was with the lad; and he grew, and dwelt in the wilderness, and became an archer.
21 And he dwelt in the wilderness of Paran: and his mother took him a wife out of the land of Egypt.
22 And it came to pass at that time, that Abimelech and Phichol the chief captain of his host spoke unto Abraham, saying, God *is* with you in all that you doest:
23 Now therefore swear unto me here by God that you will not deal falsely with me, or with my son, or with my son's son: *but* according to the kindness that I have done unto you, you will do unto me, and to the land wherein you have sojourned.
24 And Abraham said, I will swear.
25 And Abraham reproved Abimelech because of a well of water, which Abimelech's servants had violently taken away.
26 And Abimelech said, I will not who has done this thing: neither did you tell me, neither yet heard I *of it*, but to day.
27 And Abraham took sheep and oxen, and gave them unto Abimelech; and both of them made a covenant.
28 And Abraham set seven ewe lambs of the flock by themselves.
29 And Abimelech said unto Abraham, What *mean* these seven ewe lambs which you have set by themselves?
30 And he said, For *these* seven ewe lambs will you take of my hand, that they may be a witness unto me, that I have digged this well.
31 Wherefore he called that place Beer-sheba; because there they swore both of them.
32 Then they made a covenant at Beer-sheba: then Abimelech rose up, and Phichol the chief captain of his host, and they returned into the land of the Philistines.
33 And *Abraham* planted a grove in Beer-sheba, and called there on the name of the LORD, the everlasting God.
34 And Abraham sojourned in the Philistines' land many days.

---

[1] Beer-sheba – well of the sevenfold oath, well of oath or well of seven

CHAPTER 22

1 And it came to pass after these things, that God did tempt Abraham, and said unto him, Abraham: and he said, Behold, *here* I *am*.
2 And he said, Take now your son, your only *son* Isaac, who you love, and get you into the land of Moriah; and offer him there for a burnt offering upon one of the mountains which I will tell you of.
3 And Abraham rose up early in the morning, and saddled his ass, and took two of his young men with him, and Isaac his son, and clave the wood for the burnt offering, and rose up, and went unto the place of which God had told him.
4 Then on the third day Abraham lifted up his eyes, and saw the place afar off.
5 And Abraham said unto his young men, Abide you here with the ass; and I and the lad will go yonder and worship, and come again to you.
6 And Abraham took the wood of the burnt offering, and laid *it* upon Isaac his son; and he took the fire in his hand, and a knife; and they went both of them together.
7 And Isaac spoke unto Abraham his father, and said, my father: and he said, here *am* I, my son. And he said, behold the fire and the wood: but where *is* the lamb for a burnt offering?
8 And Abraham said, my son, God will provide himself a lamb for a burnt offering: so they went both of them together.
9 And they came to the place which God had told him of; and Abraham built an altar there, and laid the wood in order, and bound Isaac his son, and laid him on the altar upon the wood.
10 And Abraham stretched forth his hand, and took the knife to slay his son.
11 And the angel of the LORD called unto him out of heaven, and said, Abraham, Abraham: and he said, here *am* I.
12 And he said, lay not your hand upon the lad, neither do you anything unto him: for now I know that you fear God seeing you have not withheld your son, your only *son* from me.
13 And Abraham lifted up his eyes, and looked, and behold behind *him* a ram caught in a thicket by his horns: and Abraham went and took the ram, and offered him up for a burnt offering in the stead of his son.
14 And Abraham called the name of that place Jehovah-jireh: as it is said *to* this day, in the mount of the LORD it will be seen.
15 And the angel of the LORD called unto Abraham out of heaven the second time,
16 And said, by myself have I sworn, said the LORD, for because you have done this thing, and have not withheld your son, your only *son*:
17 That in blessing I will bless you, and in multiplying I will multiply your seed as the stars of the heaven, and as the sand which *is* upon the sea shore; and your seed will possess the gate of his enemies;
18 And in your seed will all the nations of the earth be blessed; because you have obeyed my voice.
19 So Abraham returned unto his young men, and they rose up and went together to Beer-sheba[1]; and Abraham dwelt at Beer-sheba.
20 And it came to pass after these things, that it was told Abraham, saying, Behold, Milcah, she have also born children unto your brother Nahor;

[Strgs#884]

21 Huz his firstborn, and Buz his brother, and Kemuel the father of Aram,
22 And Chesed, and Hazo, and Pildash, and Jidlaph, and Bethuel.
23 And Bethuel begat Rebekah: these eight Milcah did bear to Nahor, Abraham's brother.
24 And his concubine, whose name *was* Reumah, she bare also Tebah, and Gaham, and Thahash, and Maachah.

CHAPTER 23

1 And Sarah was an hundred and seven and twenty years old: *these were* the years of the life of Sarah.
2 And Sarah died in Kirjath-arba; the same *is* Hebron in the land of Canaan: and Abraham came to mourn for Sarah, and to weep for her.
3 And Abraham stood up from before his dead, and spoke unto the sons of Heth, saying,
4 I *am* a stranger and a sojourner with you: give me a possession of a burying place with you, that I may bury my dead out of my sight.
5 And the children of Heth answered Abraham, saying unto him,
6 Hear us, my lord: you *are* [a mighty prince]¹ among us: in the choice of our sepulchres bury your dead; none of us will withhold from you his sepulchre, but that you may bury your dead.
7 And Abraham stood up, and bowed himself to the people of the land, *even* to the children of Heth.
8 And he communed with them, saying, if it be your mind that I should bury my dead out of my sight; hear me, and entreat for me to Ephron the son of Zohar,
9 That he may give me the cave of Machpelah, which he hath, which *is* in the end of his field; for as much money as it is worth he will give it me for a possession of a burying place among you.
10 And Ephron dwelt among the children of Heth: and Ephron the Hittite answered Abraham in the audience of the children of Heth, *even* of all that went in at the gate of his city, saying,
11 Nay, my lord, hear me: the field give I **to** you, and the cave that *is* therein, I give it **to** you; in the presence of the sons of my people I give it **to** you: bury your dead.
12 And Abraham bowed down himself before the people of the land.
13 And he spoke unto Ephron in the audience of the people of the land, saying, But if you *will give it*, I pray you, hear me: I will give you money for the field; take *it* of me, and I will bury my dead there.
14 And Ephron answered Abraham, saying unto him,
15 My lord, hearken unto me: the land *is worth* four hundred shekels of silver; what *is* that between me and you? Bury therefore your dead.
16 And Abraham hearkened unto Ephron; and Abraham weighed to Ephron the silver, which he had named in the audience of the sons of Heth, four hundred shekels of silver, current *money* with the merchant.
17 And the field of Ephron, which *was* in Machpelah, which *was* before Mamre, the field, and the cave which *was* therein, and all the trees that *were* in the field, that *were* in all the borders round about, were made sure
18 Unto Abraham for a possession in the presence of the children of Heth, before all that went in at the gate of his city.
19 And after this, Abraham buried Sarah his wife in the cave of the field of Machpelah before Mamre: the same *is* Hebron in the land of Canaan.
20 And the field, and the cave that *is* therein, were made sure unto Abraham for a possession of a burying place by the sons of Heth.

CHAPTER 24

1 And Abraham was old, *and* well stricken in age: and the LORD had blessed Abraham in all things.
2 And Abraham said unto his eldest servant of his house, that ruled over all that he had, put, I pray you, your hand under my thigh:
3 And I will make you swear by the LORD, the God of heaven, and the God of the earth, that you will not take a wife unto my son of the daughters of the Canaanites, among whom I dwell:
4 But you will go unto my country, and to my kindred, and take a wife unto my son Isaac.
5 And the servant said unto him, Peradventure the woman will not be willing to follow me unto this land: must I needs bring your son again unto the land from where you came?
6 And Abraham said unto him, beware you that you bring not my son there again.
7 The LORD God of heaven, which took me from my father's house, and from the land of my kindred, and which spoke unto me, and that swore unto me, saying, Unto your seed will I give this land; he will send his angel before you, and you will take a wife unto my son from there.
8 And if the woman will not be willing to follow you, then you will be clear from this my oath: only bring not my son there again.
9 And the servant put his hand under the thigh of Abraham his master, and swore to him concerning that matter.
10 And the servant took ten camels of the camels of his master, and departed; for all the goods of his master *were* in his hand: and he arose, and went to Mesopotamia, unto the city of Nahor.
11 And he made his camels to kneel down without the city by a well of water at the time of the evening, *even* the time that women go out to draw *water*.
12 And he said, O LORD God of my master Abraham, I pray you, send me good speed this day, and show kindness unto my master Abraham.
13 Behold, I stand *here* by the well of water; and the daughters of the men of the city come out to draw water:
14 And let it come to pass, that the damsel to who I will say, Let down your pitcher, I pray you, that I may drink; and she will say, Drink, and I will give you camels drink also: *let the same be* she *that* you have appointed for your servant Isaac; and thereby will I know that you have showed kindness unto my master.
15 And it came to pass, before he had done speaking, that, behold, Rebekah came out, who was born to Bethuel, son of Milcah, the wife of Nahor, Abraham's brother, with her pitcher upon her shoulder.
16 And the damsel *was* very fair to look upon, a virgin, neither had any man known her: and she went down to the well, and filled her pitcher, and came up.
17 And the servant ran to meet her, and said, let me, I pray you, drink a little water of your pitcher.
18 And she said, Drink, my lord: and she hasted, and let down her pitcher upon her hand, and gave him drink.
19 And when she had done giving him drink, she said, I will draw w*ater* for your camels also, until they have done drinking.

---

¹ Literally – *a prince of God* [Strgs#430 = 5387]

20 And she hasted, and emptied her pitcher into the trough, and ran again unto the well to draw *water*, and drew for all his camels.
21 And the man wondering at her held his peace, to wit whether the LORD had made his journey prosperous or not.
22 And it came to pass, as the camels had done drinking, that the man took a golden earring of half a shekel weight, and two bracelets for her hands of ten *shekels* weight of gold;
23 And said, who daughter *are* you? Tell me, I pray you: is there room *in* your father's house for us to lodge in?
24 And she said unto him, I *am* the daughter of Bethuel the son of Milcah, which she bare unto Nahor.
25 She said moreover unto him, we have both straw and provender enough, and room to lodge in.
26 And the man bowed down his head, and worshipped the LORD.
27 And he said, blessed *be* the LORD God of my master Abraham, who has not left destitute my master of his mercy and his truth: I *being* in the way, the LORD led me to the house of my master's brethren.
28 And the damsel ran, and told *them of* her mother's house these things.
29 And Rebekah[1] had a brother, and his name *was* Laban: and Laban ran out unto the man, unto the well.
30 And it came to pass, when he saw the earring and bracelets upon his sister's hands, and when he heard the words of Rebekah his sister, saying, then spoke the man unto me; that he came unto the man; and, behold, he stood by the camels at the well.
31 And he said, Come in, you blessed of the LORD; wherefore stand you without? For I have prepared the house, and room for the camels.
32 And the man came into the house: and he ungirded his camels, and gave straw and provender for the camels, and water to wash his feet, and the men's feet that *were* with him.
33 And there was set *meat* before him to eat: but he said, I will not eat, until I have told mine errand. And he said, Speak on.
34 And he said, I *am* Abraham's servant.
35 And the LORD hath blessed my master greatly; and he is become great: and he hath given him flocks, and herds, and silver, and gold, and menservants, and maidservants, and camels, and asses.
36 And Sarah my master's wife bare a son to my master when she was old: and unto him hath he given all that he have.
37 And my master made me swear, saying, you will not take a wife to my son of the daughters of the Canaanites, in whose land I dwell:
38 But you will go unto my father's house, and to my kindred, and take a wife unto my son.
39 And I said unto my master, Peradventure the woman will not follow me.
40 And he said unto me, The LORD, before who I walk, will send his angel with you, and prosper your way; and you will take a wife for my son of my kindred, and of my father's house:
41 Then will you be clear from *this* my oath, when you come to my kindred; and if they give not you *one*, you will be clear from my oath.
42 And I came this day unto the well, and said, O LORD God of my master Abraham, if now you do prosper my way which I go:
43 Behold, I stand by the well of water; and it will come to pass, that when the virgin cometh forth to draw *water*, and I say to her, Give me, I pray you, a little water of your pitcher to drink;
44 And she say to me, both drink you, and I will also draw for your camels: *let* the same *be* the woman whom the LORD hath appointed out for my master's son.
45 And before I had done speaking in mine heart, behold, Rebekah came forth with her pitcher on her shoulder; and she went down unto the well, and drew *water*: and I said unto her, Let me drink, I pray you.
46 And she made haste, and let down her pitcher from her *shoulder*, and said, Drink, and I will give you camels drink also: so I drank, and she made the camels drink also.
47 And I asked her, and said, who daughter *are* you? And she said, the daughter of Bethuel, Nahor's son, whom Milcah bare unto him: and I put the earring upon her face, and the bracelets upon her hands.
48 And I bowed down my head, and worshipped the LORD, and blessed the LORD God of my master Abraham, which had led me in the right way to take my master's brother's daughter unto his son.
49 And now if you will deal kindly and truly with my master, tell me: and if not, tell me; that I may turn to the right hand, or to the left.
50 Then Laban and Bethuel answered and said, the thing proceed from the LORD: we cannot speak unto you bad or good.
51 Behold, Rebekah *is* before you, take *her*, and go, and let her be your master's son's wife, as the LORD has spoken.
52 And it came to pass, that, when Abraham's servant heard their words, he worshipped the LORD, *bowing himself* to the earth.
53 And the servant brought forth jewels of silver, and jewels of gold, and raiment, and gave *them* to Rebekah: he gave also to her brother and to her mother precious things.
54 And they did eat and drink, him and the men that *were* with him, and tarried all night; and they rose up in the morning, and he said, send me away unto my master.
55 And her brother and her mother said, let the damsel abide with us *a few* days, at the least ten; after that she will go.
56 And he said unto them, Hinder me not, seeing the LORD has prospered my way; send me away that I may go to my master.
57 And they said, we will call the damsel, and enquire at her mouth.
58 And they called Rebekah, and said unto her, Will you go with this man? And she said, I will go.
59 And they sent away Rebekah their sister, and her nurse, and Abraham's servant, and his men.
60 And they blessed Rebekah, and said unto her, you *are* our sister, be you *the mother* of thousands of millions, and let your seed possess the gate of those which hate them.
61 And Rebekah arose, and her damsels, and they rode upon the camels, and followed the man: and the servant took Rebekah, and went his way.
62 And Isaac came from the way of the well Laha-roi; for he dwelt in the south country.
63 And Isaac went out to meditate in the field at the eventide: and he lifted up his eyes, and saw, and, behold, the camels *were* coming.
64 And Rebekah lifted up her eyes, and when she saw Isaac, she lighted off the camel.

---

[1] Rebekah- ensnarer, fettering by beauty [Strgs#7259].

65 For she had said unto the servant, what man is this that walk in the field to meet us? And the servant had said, it is my master: therefore she took a veil, and covered herself.
66 And the servant told Isaac all things that he had done.
67 And Isaac brought her into his mother Sarah's tent, and took Rebekah, and she became his wife; and he loved her: and Isaac was comforted after his mother's death.

CHAPTER 25

1 Then again Abraham took a wife, and her name was Keturah.
2 And she bare him Zimran, and Jokshan, and Medan, and Midian, and Ishbak, and Shuah.
3 And Jokshan begat Sheba, and Dedan. And the sons of Dedan were Asshurim, and Letushim, and Leummim.
4 And the sons of Midian; Ephah, and Epher, and Hanoch, and Abida, and Eldaah. All these were the children of Keturah.
5 And Abraham gave all that he had unto Isaac.
6 But unto the sons of the concubines, which Abraham had, Abraham gave gifts, and sent them away from Isaac his son, while he yet lived, eastward, unto the east country.
7 And these are the days of the years of Abraham's life which he lived, an hundred threescore and fifteen years.
8 Then Abraham gave up the ghost, and died in a good old age, an old man, and full of years; and was gathered to his people.
9 And his sons Isaac and Ishmael buried him in the cave of Machpelah, in the field of Ephron the son of Zohar the Hittite, which is before Mamre;
10 The field which Abraham purchased of the sons of Heth: there was Abraham buried, and Sarah his wife.
11 And it came to pass after the death of Abraham, that God blessed his son Isaac; and Isaac dwelt by the well Lahai-roi.
12 Now these are the generations of Ishmael, Abraham's son, whom Hagar the Egyptian, Sarah's handmaid, bare unto Abraham:
13 And these are the names of the sons of Ishmael, by their names, according to their generations: the firstborn of Ishmael, Nebajoth; and Kedar, and Adbeel, and Mibsam,
14 And Mishma, and Dumah, and Massa,
15 Hadar, and Tema, Jetur, Naphish, and Kedemah:
16 These are the sons of Ishmael, and these are their names, by their towns, and by their castles; twelve princes according to their nations.
17 And these are the years of the life of Ishmael, an hundred and thirty and seven years: and he gave up the ghost and died; and was gathered unto his people.
18 And they dwelt from Havilah unto Shur, that is before Egypt, as you go toward Assyria: and he died in the presence of all his brethren.
19 And these are the generations of Isaac, Abraham's son: Abraham begat Isaac:
20 And Isaac was forty years old when he took Rebekah to wife, the daughter of Bethuel the Syrian of Padan-aram, the sister to Laban the Syrian.
21 And Isaac entreated the LORD for his wife, because she was barren: and the LORD was entreated of him, and Rebekah his wife conceived.
22 And the children struggled together within her; and she said, if it be so, why am I thus? And she went to enquire of the LORD.
23 And the LORD said unto her, two nations are in your womb, and two manners of people will be separated from your bowels; and the one people will be stronger than the other people; and the elder will serve the younger.
24 And when her days to be delivered were fulfilled, behold, there were twins in her womb.
25 And the first came out red, all over like a hairy garment; and they called his name Esau[1].
26 And after that came his brother out, and his hand took hold on Esau's heel; and his name was called Jacob[2]: and Isaac was threescore years old when she bare them.
27 And the boys grew: and Esau was a cunning hunter, a man of the field; and Jacob was a plain man, dwelling in tents.
28 And Isaac loved Esau, because he did eat of his venison: but Rebekah loved Jacob.
29 And Jacob sod pottage: and Esau came from the field, and he was faint:
30 And Esau said to Jacob, Feed me, I pray you, with that same red pottage; for I am faint: therefore was his name called Edom.
31 And Jacob said, Sell me this day your birthright.
32 And Esau said, Behold, I am at the point to die: and what profit will this birthright[3] do to me?
33 And Jacob said, Swear to me this day: and he swore unto him: and he sold his birthright unto Jacob.
34 Then Jacob gave Esau bread and pottage of lentiles; and he did eat and drink, and rose up, and went his way: thus Esau despised[4] his birthright.

CHAPTER 26

1 And there was a famine in the land, beside the first famine that was in the days of Abraham. And Isaac went unto Abimelech king of the Philistines unto Gerar.
2 And the LORD appeared unto him, and said, Go not down into Egypt; dwell in the land which I will tell you of:
3 Sojourn in this land, and I will be with you, and will bless you; for unto you, and unto your seed, I will give all these countries, and I will perform the oath which I swore unto Abraham your father;
4 And I will make your seed to multiply as the stars of heaven, and will give unto your seed all these countries; and in your seed will all the nations of the earth be blessed;
5 Because that Abraham obeyed my voice, and kept my charge, my commandments, my statutes, and my laws.
6 And Isaac dwelt in Gerar:
7 And the men of the place asked him of his wife; and he said, she is my sister: for he feared to say, she is my wife; lest, said he, the men of the place should kill me for Rebekah; because she was fair to look upon.
8 And it came to pass, when he had been there a long time, that Abimelech king of the Philistines looked out at a window, and saw, and, behold, Isaac was sporting with Rebekah his wife.
9 And Abimelech called Isaac, and said, Behold, of a surety she is your wife: and how said you, She is my sister? And Isaac said unto him, because I said, lest I die for her.
10 And Abimelech said, what is this you have done unto us? One of the people might lightly have lien with your wife, and you should have brought guiltiness upon us.

---

[1] Esau- hairy [Strgs#6215].
[2] Jacob- heel holder [Strgs#3290]
[3] *birthright* – (femine) first born of a mother, the right of the right woman to have a son.
[4] despised – to disesteem, disdain, contemn, think to scorn, vile person, held in contempt [Strgs#959]

11 And Abimelech charged all *his* people, saying, He that touch this man or his wife will surely be put to death.
12 Then Isaac sowed in that land, and received in the same year a hundredfold: and the LORD blessed him.
13 And the man waxed great, and went forward, and grew until he became very great:
14 For he had possession of flocks, and possession of herds, and great store of servants: and the Philistines envied him.
15 For all the wells which his father's servants had digged in the days of Abraham his father, the Philistines had stopped them, and filled them with earth.
16 And Abimelech said unto Isaac, Go from us; for you are much mightier than we.
17 And Isaac departed there, and pitched his tent in the valley of Gerar, and dwelt there.
18 And Isaac digged again the wells of water, which they had digged in the days of Abraham his father; for the Philistines had stopped them after the death of Abraham: and he called their names after the names by which his father had called them.
19 And Isaac's servants digged in the valley, and found there a well of springing water.
20 And the herdsmen of Gerar did strive with Isaac's herdsmen, saying, the water *is* ours: and he called the name of the well Esek; because they strove with him.
21 And they digged another well, and strove for that also: and he called the name of it Sitnah.
22 And he removed from thence, and digged another well; and for that they strove not: and he called the name of it Rehoboth; and he said, for now the LORD hath made room for us, and we will be fruitful in the land.
23 And he went up from there to Beer-sheba.
24 And the LORD appeared unto him the same night, and said, I *am* the God of Abraham your father: fear not, for I *am* with you, and will bless you, and multiply your seed for my servant Abraham's sake.
25 And he built an altar there, and called upon the name of the LORD, and pitched his tent there: and there Isaac's servants digged a well.
26 Then Abimelech went to him from Gerar, and Ahuzzath one of his friends, and Phichol the chief captain of his army.
27 And Isaac said unto them, wherefore come you to me, seeing you hate me, and have sent me away from you?
28 And they said, we saw certainly that the LORD was with you: and we said, Let there be now an oath between us, *even* between us and you, and let us make a covenant with you;
29 That you will do us no hurt, as we have not touched you, and as we have done unto you nothing but good, and have sent you away in peace: you *are* now the blessed of the LORD.
30 And he made them a feast, and they did eat and drink.
31 And they rose up betimes in the morning, and swore one to another: and Isaac sent them away, and they departed from him in peace.
32 And it came to pass the same day, that Isaac's servants came, and told him concerning the well which they had digged, and said unto him, we have found water.
33 And he called it Shebah: therefore the name of the city *is* Beer-sheba unto this day.
34 And Esau was forty years old when he took to wife Judith the daughter of Beeri the Hittite[1], and Bashemath[2] the daughter of Elon[3] the Hittite:
35 Which were a grief[4] of mind[5] unto Isaac and to Rebekah.

CHAPTER 27

1 And it came to pass, that when Isaac was old, and his eyes were dim, so that he could not see, he called Esau his eldest son, and said unto him, my son: and he said unto him, Behold, *here am* I.
2 And he said, Behold now, I am old, I know not the day of my death:
3 Now therefore take, I pray you, your weapons, your quiver and your bow, and go out to the field, and take me *some* venison;
4 And make me savory meat, such as I love, and bring *it* to me, that I may eat; that my soul may bless you before I die.
5 And Rebekah heard when Isaac spoke to Esau his son. And Esau went to the field to hunt *for* venison, *and* to bring *it*.
6 And Rebekah spoke unto Jacob her son, saying, Behold, I heard your father speak unto Esau your brother, saying,
7 Bring me venison, and make me savory meat, that I may eat, and bless you before the LORD before my death.
8 Now therefore, my son, obey my voice according to that which I command you.
9 Go now to the flock, and fetch me from there two good kids of the goats; and I will make them savory meat for your father, such as he loved:
10 And you will bring *it* to your father, that he may eat, and that he may bless you before his death.
11 And Jacob said to Rebekah his mother, Behold, Esau my brother *is* a hairy man, and I *am* a smooth man:
12 My father peradventure will feel me, and I will seem to him as a deceiver; and I will bring a curse upon me, and not a blessing.
13 And his mother said unto him, upon me *be* your curse, my son: only obey my voice, and go fetch me *them*.
14 And he went, and fetched, and brought *them* to his mother: and his mother made savory meat, such as his father loved.
15 And Rebekah took goodly raiment of her eldest son Esau, which *were* with her in the house, and put them upon Jacob her younger son:
16 And she put the skins of the kids of the goats upon his hands, and upon the smooth of his neck:
17 And she gave the savory meat and the bread, which she had prepared, into the hand of her son Jacob.
18 And he came unto his father, and said, my father: and he said, here *am* I; who *are* you, my son?
19 And Jacob said unto his father, I *am* Esau your firstborn; I have done according as you badest me: arise, I pray you, sit and eat of my venison, that your soul may bless me.
20 And Isaac said unto his son, how *is it* that you have found *it* so quickly, my son? And he said, because the LORD your God brought *it* to me.
21 And Isaac said unto Jacob, Come near, I pray you, that I may feel you, my son, whether you *be* my very son Esau or not.

---

[1] *Hittite* – descendant of Heth [Strgs#2850]. Derives from root word Heth meaning terror [Strgs#2845]
[2] *Bashemath* – spice or *fragrance* [Strgs#1315]
[3] *Elon* – mighty & oakgrove [Strgs#356]. Comes from a root word meaning ram (as food and sacrifice), strong & strength [Strgs#352]
[4] *grief* – bitterness [Strgs#4786]
[5] *mind* – spirit [Strgs#7307]

22 And Jacob went near unto Isaac his father; and he felt him, and said, the voice *is* Jacob's voice, but the hands *are* the hands of Esau.
23 And he discerned him not, because his hands were hairy, as his brother Esau's hands: so he blessed him.
24 And he said, *Are* you my very son Esau? And he said, I *am*.
25 And he said, Bring *it* near to me, and I will eat of my son's venison, that my soul may bless you. And he brought *it* near to him, and he did eat: and he brought him wine, and he drank.
26 And his father Isaac said unto him, Come near now, and kiss me, my son.
27 And he came near, and kissed him: and he smelled the smell of his raiment, and blessed him, and said, See, the smell of my son *is* as the smell of a field which the LORD has blessed:
28 Therefore God give you of the dew of heaven, and the fatness of the earth, and plenty of corn and wine:
29 Let people serve you, and nations bow down to you: be lord over your brethren, and let your mother's son's bow down to you: cursed *be* every one that curse you, and blessed *be* he that bless you.
30 And it came to pass, as soon as Isaac had made an end of blessing Jacob, and Jacob was yet scarce gone out from the presence of Isaac his father, that Esau his brother came in from his hunting.
31 And he also had made savory meat, and brought it unto his father, and said unto his father, Let my father arise, and eat of his son's venison, that your soul may bless me.
32 And Isaac his father said unto him, who *are* you? And he said, I *am* your son, your firstborn Esau.
33 And Isaac trembled very exceedingly, and said, who? Where *is* he that have taken venison, and brought *it* me, and I have eaten of all before you came, and have blessed him? Yes, *and* he will be blessed.
34 And when Esau heard the words of his father, he cried with a great and exceeding bitter cry, and said unto his father, bless me, *even* me also, O my father.
35 And he said, your brother came with subtlety, and have taken away your blessing.
36 And he said, is not he rightly named Jacob? For he have supplanted me these two times: he took away my birthright; and, behold, now he hath taken away my blessing. And he said, have you not reserved a blessing for me?
37 And Isaac answered and said unto Esau, Behold, I have made him your lord, and all his brethren have I given to him for servants; and with corn and wine have I sustained him: and what will I do now unto you, my son?
38 And Esau said unto his father, Have you but one blessing, my father? Bless me, *even* me also, O my father. And Esau lifted up his voice, and wept.
39 And Isaac his father answered and said unto him, Behold, your dwelling will be the fatness of the earth, and of the dew of heaven from above;
40 And by your sword will you live, and will serve your brother; and it will come to pass when you will have the dominion, that you will break his yoke from off your neck.
41 And Esau hated Jacob because of the blessing wherewith his father blessed him: and Esau said in his heart, the days of mourning for my father are at hand; then will I slay my brother Jacob.
42 And these words of Esau her elder son were told to Rebekah: and she sent and called Jacob her younger son, and said unto him, Behold, your brother Esau, as touching you, does comfort himself, *purposing* to kill you.
43 Now therefore, my son, obey my voice; and arise, flee you to Laban my brother to Haran;
44 And tarry with him a few days, until your brother's fury turn away;
45 Until your brother's anger turn away from you, and he forget *that* which you have done to him: then I will send, and fetch you from there: why should I be deprived also of you both in one day?
46 And Rebekah said to Isaac, I am weary of my life because of the daughters of Heth: if Jacob take a wife of the daughters of Heth, such as these *which are* of the daughters of the land, what good will my life do me?

CHAPTER 28

1 And Isaac called Jacob, and blessed him, and charged him, and said unto him, you will not take a wife of the daughters of Canaan.
2 Arise, go to Padan-aram, to the house of Bethuel your mother's father; and take you a wife from there of the daughters of Laban your mother's brother.
3 And God Almighty bless you, and make you fruitful, and multiply you, that you may be a multitude of people;
4 And give you the blessing of Abraham, to you, and to your seed with you; that you may inherit the land wherein you are a stranger, which God gave unto Abraham.
5 And Isaac sent away Jacob: and he went to Padan-aram unto Laban, son of Bethuel the Syrian, the brother of Rebekah, Jacob's and Esau's mother.
6 When Esau saw that Isaac had blessed Jacob, and sent him away to Padan-aram, to take him a wife from there; and that as he blessed him he gave him a charge, saying, You will not take a wife of the daughters of Canaan;
7 And that Jacob obeyed his father and his mother, and was gone to Padan-aram;
8 And Esau seeing that the daughters of Canaan pleased not Isaac his father;
9 Then went Esau unto Ishmael, and took unto the wives which he had Mahalath the daughter of Ishmael Abraham's son, the sister of Nebajoth, to be his wife.
10 And Jacob went out from Beer-sheba, and went toward Haran.
11 And he lighted upon a certain place, and tarried there all night, because the sun was set; and he took of the stones of that place, and put *them for* his pillows, and lay down in that place to sleep.
12 And he dreamed, and behold a ladder set up on the earth, and the top of it reached to heaven: and behold the angels of God ascending and descending on it.
13 And, behold, the LORD stood above it, and said, I *am* the LORD God of Abraham your father, and the God of Isaac: the land whereon you lie, to you will I give it, and to your seed;
14 And your seed will be as the dust of the earth, and you will spread abroad to the west, and to the east, and to the north, and to the south: and in you and in your seed will all the families of the earth be blessed.
15 And, behold, I *am* with you, and will keep you in all places whither you go, and will bring you again into this land; for I will not leave you, until I have done *that* which I have spoken to you of.
16 And Jacob awaked out of his sleep, and he said, surely the LORD is in this place; and I knew *it* not.

17 And he was afraid, and said, how dreadful *this place is*! This *is* none other but the house of God, and this *is* the gate of heaven.
18 And Jacob rose up early in the morning, and took the stone that he had put *for* his pillows, and set it up *for* a pillar, and poured oil upon the top of it.
19 And he called the name of that place Beth-el: but the name of that city *was called* Luz at the first.
20 And Jacob vowed a vow, saying, If God will be with me, and will keep me in this way that I go, and will give me bread to eat, and raiment to put on,
21 So that I come again to my father's house in peace; then will the LORD be my God:
22 And this stone, which I have set *for* a pillar, will be God's house: and of all that you will give me I will surely give the tenth unto you.

CHAPTER 29

1 Then Jacob went on his journey, and came into the land of the people of the east.
2 And he looked, and behold a well in the field, and, lo, there *were* three flocks of sheep lying by it; for out of that well they watered the flocks: and a great stone *was* upon the well's mouth.
3 And thither were all the flocks gathered: and they rolled the stone from the well's mouth, and watered the sheep, and put the stone again upon the well's mouth in his place.
4 And Jacob said unto them, my brethren, whence *be* you? And they said, Of Haran *are* we.
5 And he said unto them, know you Laban the son of Nahor? And they said, we know *him*.
6 And he said unto them, *is* he well? And they said, *he is* well: and, behold, Rachel his daughter come with the sheep.
7 And he said, lo, *it is* yet high day, neither *is it* time that the cattle should be gathered together: water you the sheep, and go *and* feed *them*.
8 And they said, we cannot, un*til* all the flocks be gathered together, and un*til* they roll the stone from the well's mouth; then we water the sheep.
9 And while he yet spoke with them, Rachel came with her father's sheep: for she kept them.
10 And it came to pass, when Jacob saw Rachel the daughter of Laban his mother's brother, and the sheep of Laban his mother's brother, that Jacob went near, and rolled the stone from the well's mouth, and watered the flock of Laban his mother's brother.
11 And Jacob kissed Rachel, and lifted up his voice, and wept.
12 And Jacob told Rachel that he *was* her father's brother, and that he *was* Rebekah's son: and she ran and told her father.
13 And it came to pass, when Laban heard the tidings of Jacob his sister's son, that he ran to meet him, and embraced him, and kissed him, and brought him to his house. And he told Laban all these things.
14 And Laban said to him, surely you *are* my bone and my flesh. And he abode with him the space of a month.
15 And Laban said unto Jacob, because you *are* my brother, should you therefore serve me for nought? Tell me, what *will* your wages *be*?
16 And Laban had two daughters: the name of the elder *was* Leah, and the name of the younger *was* Rachel.
17 Leah *was* tender eyed; but Rachel was beautiful and well favored.
18 And Jacob loved Rachel; and said, I will serve you seven years for Rachel you younger daughter.
19 And Laban said, *it is* better that I give her to you, than that I should give her to another man: abide with me.
20 And Jacob served seven years for Rachel; and they seemed unto him *but* a few days, for the love he had to her.
21 And Jacob said unto Laban, Give *me* my wife, for my days are fulfilled, that I may go in unto her.
22 And Laban gathered together all the men of the place, and made a feast.
23 And it came to pass in the evening, that he took Leah his daughter, and brought her to him; and he went in unto her.
24 And Laban gave unto his daughter Leah Zilpah his maid *for* a handmaid.
25 And it came to pass, that in the morning, behold, it *was* Leah: and he said to Laban, What *is* this you have done unto me? Did not I serve with you for Rachel? Wherefore then have you beguiled me?
26 And Laban said, it must not be so done in our country, to give the younger before the firstborn.
27 Fulfill her week, and we will give you this also for the service which you will serve with me yet seven other years.
28 And Jacob did so, and fulfilled her week: and he gave him Rachel his daughter to wife also.
29 And Laban gave to Rachel his daughter Bilhah his handmaid to be her maid.
30 And he went in also unto Rachel, and he loved also Rachel more than Leah, and served with him yet seven other years.
31 And when the LORD saw that Leah *was* hated, he opened her womb: but Rachel *was* barren.
32 And Leah conceived, and bare a son, and she called his name Reuben: for she said, surely the LORD hath looked upon my affliction; now therefore my husband will love me.
33 And she conceived again, and bare a son; and said, because the LORD hath heard that I *was* hated, he hath therefore given me this *son* also: and she called his name Simeon.
34 And she conceived again, and bare a son; and said, now this time will my husband be joined unto me, because I have born him three sons: therefore was his name called Levi.
35 And she conceived again, and bare a son: and she said, Now will I praise the LORD: therefore she called his name Judah; and left bearing.

CHAPTER 30

1 And when Rachel saw that she bare Jacob no children, Rachel envied her sister; and said unto Jacob, Give me children, or else I die.
2 And Jacob's anger was kindled against Rachel: and he said, *am* I in God's stead, who hath withheld from you the fruit of the womb?
3 And she said, Behold my maid Bilhah, go in unto her; and she will bear upon my knees, that I may also have children by her.
4 And she gave him Bilhah her handmaid to wife: and Jacob went in unto her.
5 And Bilhah conceived, and bare Jacob a son.
6 And Rachel said, God hath judged me, and hath also heard my voice, and hath given me a son: therefore called she his name Dan.
7 And Bilhah Rachel's maid conceived again, and bare Jacob a second son.
8 And Rachel said, with great wrestlings have I wrestled with my sister, and I have prevailed: and she called his name Naphtali.

9 When Leah saw that she had left bearing, she took Zilpah her maid, and gave her Jacob to wife.
10 And Zilpah Leah's maid bare Jacob a son.
11 And Leah said, a troop come: and she called his name Gad.
12 And Zilpah Leah's maid bare Jacob a second son.
13 And Leah said, Happy am I, for the daughters will call me blessed: and she called his name Asher.
14 And Reuben went in the days of wheat harvest, and found mandrakes in the field, and brought them unto his mother Leah. Then Rachel said to Leah, Give me, I pray you, of your son's mandrakes.
15 And she said unto her, *is it* a small matter that you have taken my husband? And would you take away my son's mandrakes also? And Rachel said, Therefore he will lie with you to night for your son's mandrakes.
16 And Jacob came out of the field in the evening, and Leah went out to meet him, and said, you must come in unto me; for surely I have hired you with my son's mandrakes. And he lay with her that night.
17 And God hearkened unto Leah, and she conceived, and bare Jacob the fifth son.
18 And Leah said, God hath given me my hire, because I have given my maiden to my husband: and she called his name Issachar.
19 And Leah conceived again, and bare Jacob the sixth son.
20 And Leah said, God hath endued me *with* a good dowry; now will my husband dwell with me, because I have born him six sons: and she called his name Zebulun.
21 And afterwards she bare a daughter, and called her name Dinah.
22 And God remembered Rachel, and God hearkened to her, and opened her womb.
23 And she conceived, and bare a son; and said, God hath taken away my reproach:
24 And she called his name Joseph; and said, The LORD will add to me another son.
25 And it came to pass, when Rachel had born Joseph, that Jacob said unto Laban, Send me away, that I may go unto mine own place, and to my country.
26 Give *me* my wives and my children, for whom I have served you, and let me go: for you know my service which I have done you.
27 And Laban said unto him, I pray you, if I have found favor in your eyes, *tarry: for* I have learned by experience that the LORD hath blessed me for your sake.
28 And he said, Appoint me your wages, and I will give *it*.
29 And he said unto him, you know how I have served you, and how your cattle was with me.
30 For *it was* little which you had before I *came*, and it is *now* increased unto a multitude; and the LORD has blessed you since my coming: and now when will I provide for mine own house also?
31 And he said, what will I give you? And Jacob said, you will not give me any thing: if you will do this thing for me, I will again feed *and* keep your flock:
32 I will pass through all your flock to day, removing from there all the speckled and spotted cattle, and all the brown cattle among the sheep, and the spotted and speckled among the goats: and *of such* will be my hire.
33 So will my righteousness answer for me in time to come, when it will come for my hire before your face: every one that *is* not speckled and spotted among the goats, and brown among the sheep, that will be counted stolen with me.
34 And Laban said, Behold, I would it might be according to your word.
35 And he removed that day the he goats that were ring streaked and spotted, and all the she goats that were speckled and spotted, *and* every one that had *some* white in it, and all the brown among the sheep, and gave *them* into the hand of his sons.
36 And he set three days' journey between himself and Jacob: and Jacob fed the rest of Laban's flocks.
37 And Jacob took him rods of green poplar, and of the hazel and chesnut tree; and pilled white strakes in them, and made the white appear which *was* in the rods.
38 And he set the rods which he had pilled before the flocks in the gutters in the watering troughs when the flocks came to drink, that they should conceive when they came to drink.
39 And the flocks conceived before the rods, and brought forth cattle ringstraked, speckled, and spotted.
40 And Jacob did separate the lambs, and set the faces of the flocks toward the ringstraked, and all the brown in the flock of Laban; and he put his own flocks by themselves, and put them not unto Laban's cattle.
41 And it came to pass, **whenever** the stronger cattle did conceive, that Jacob laid the rods before the eyes of the cattle in the gutters, that they might conceive among the rods.
42 But when the cattle were feeble, he put *them* not in: so the feebler were Laban's, and the stronger Jacob's.
43 And the man increased exceedingly, and had much cattle, and maidservants, and menservants, and camels, and asses.

CHAPTER 31

1 And he heard the words of Laban's sons, saying, Jacob **has** taken away all that *was* our father's; and of *that* which *was* our father's has he gotten all this glory.
2 And Jacob beheld the countenance of Laban, and, behold, it *was* not toward him as before.
3 And the LORD said unto Jacob, Return unto the land of your fathers, and to your kindred; and I will be with you.
4 And Jacob sent and called Rachel and Leah to the field unto his flock,
5 And said unto them, I see your father's countenance, that it *is* not toward me as before; but the God of my father has been with me.
6 And you know that with all my power I have served your father.
7 And your father hath deceived me, and changed my wages ten times; but God suffered him not to hurt me.
8 If he said thus, the speckled will be your wages; then all the cattle bare speckled: and if he said thus, the ring streaked will be your hire; then bare all the cattle ring streaked.
9 Thus God hath taken away the cattle of your father, and given *them* to me.
10 And it came to pass at the time that the cattle conceived that I lifted up mine eyes, and saw in a dream, and, behold, the rams which leaped upon the cattle *were* ring streaked, speckled, and spotted.
11 And the angel of God spoke unto me in a dream, *saying*, Jacob: And I said, here *am* I.
12 And he said, Lift up now your eyes, and see, all the rams which leap upon the cattle *are* ring streaked, speckled, and spotted: for I have seen all that Laban do unto you.

Genesis

13 I *am* the God of Beth-el, where you anointed the pillar, *and* where you vowed a vow unto me: now arise, get you out from this land, and return unto the land of your kindred.
14 And Rachel and Leah answered and said unto him, *is there* yet any portion or inheritance for us in our father's house?
15 Are we not counted of him strangers? For he has sold us, and hath quite devoured also our money.
16 For all the riches which God hath taken from our father, that *is* ours, and our children's: now then, whatsoever God has said unto you, do.
17 Then Jacob rose up, and set his sons and his wives upon camels;
18 And he carried away all his cattle, and all his goods which he had gotten, the cattle of his getting, which he had gotten in Padan-aram, for to go to Isaac his father in the land of Canaan.
19 And Laban went to shear his sheep: and Rachel had stolen the images that *were* her father's.
20 And Jacob stole away unawares to Laban the Syrian, in that he told him not that he fled.
21 So he fled with all that he had; and he rose up, and passed over the river, and set his face *toward* the mount Gilead.
22 And it was told Laban on the third day that Jacob was fled.
23 And he took his brethren with him, and pursued after him seven days' journey; and they overtook him in the mount Gilead.
24 And God came to Laban the Syrian in a dream by night, and said unto him, Take heed that you speak not to Jacob either good or bad.
25 Then Laban overtook Jacob. Now Jacob had pitched his tent in the mount: and Laban with his brethren pitched in the mount of Gilead.
26 And Laban said to Jacob, What have you done, that you have stolen away unawares to me, and carried away my daughters, as captives *taken* with the sword?
27 Wherefore did you flee away secretly, and steal away from me; and did not tell me, that I might have sent you away with mirth, and with songs, with tambourine, and with harp?
28 And has not suffered me to kiss my sons and my daughters? You have now done foolishly in *so* doing.
29 It is in the power of my hand to do you hurt: but the God of your father spoke unto me yester night, saying, take you heed that you speak not to Jacob either good or bad.
30 And now, *though* you would needs be gone, because you sore longed after your father's house, *yet* wherefore has you stolen my gods?
31 And Jacob answered and said to Laban, because I was afraid: for I said, peradventure you would take by force your daughters from me.
32 With whomsoever you find your gods, let him not live: before our brethren discern you what *is* yours with me, and take *it* to you. For Jacob knew not that Rachel had stolen them.
33 And Laban went into Jacob's tent, and into Leah's tent, and into the two maidservants' tents; but he found *them* not. Then went he out of Leah's tent, and entered into Rachel's tent.
34 Now Rachel had taken the images, and put them in the camel's furniture, and sat upon them. And Laban searched the **entire** tent, but found *them* not.
35 And she said to her father, Let it not displease my lord that I cannot rise up before you; for the custom of women *is* upon me. And he searched, but found not the images.
36 And Jacob was wroth, and chode with Laban: and Jacob answered and said to Laban, What *is* my trespass? What *is* my sin, that you have so hotly pursued after me?
37 Whereas you have searched all my stuff, what have you found of all your household stuff? Set *it* here before my brethren and your brethren, that they may judge between us both.
38 This twenty years *have* I *been* with you; your ewes and your she goats have not cast their young, and the rams of your flock have I not eaten.
39 That which was torn *of beasts* I brought not unto you, I bare the loss of it; of my hand did you require it, *whether* stolen by day, or stolen by night.
40 *Thus* I was; in the day the drought consumed me, and the frost by night; and my sleep departed from mine eyes.
41 You have I been twenty years in your house: I served you fourteen years for your two daughters, and six years for your cattle: and you have changed my wages ten times.
42 Except the God of my father, the God of Abraham, and the fear of Isaac, had been with me, surely you have sent me away now empty. God hath seen mine affliction and the labor of my hands, and rebuked *you* yester night.
43 And Laban answered and said unto Jacob, *These* daughters *are* my daughters, and *these* children *are* my children, and *these* cattle *are* my cattle, and all that you see *is* mine: and what can I do this day unto these my daughters, or unto their children which they have born?
44 Now therefore come you, let us make a covenant, I and you; and let it be for a witness between me and you.
45 And Jacob took a stone, and set it up *for* a pillar.
46 And Jacob said unto his brethren, Gather stones; and they took stones, and made a heap: and they did eat there upon the heap.
47 And Laban called it Jegarsahadutha: but Jacob called it Galeed.
48 And Laban said, this heap *is* a witness between me and you this day. Therefore was the name of it called Galeed;
49 And Mizpah; for he said, The LORD watch between me and you, when we are absent one from another.
50 If you will afflict my daughters, or if you will take *other* wives beside my daughters, no man *is* with us; see, God *is* witness between me and you.
51 And Laban said to Jacob, Behold this heap, and behold *this* pillar, which I have cast between me and you;
52 This heap *is* witness, and *this* pillar *is* witness, that I will not pass over this heap to you, and that you will not pass over this heap and this pillar unto me, for harm.
53 The God of Abraham, and the God of Nahor, the God of their father, judge between us. And Jacob swore by the fear of his father Isaac.
54 Then Jacob offered sacrifice upon the mount, and called his brethren to eat bread: and they did eat bread, and tarried all night in the mount.
55 And early in the morning Laban rose up, and kissed his sons and his daughters, and blessed them: and Laban departed, and returned unto his place.

CHAPTER 32

1 And Jacob went on his way, and the angels of God met him.
2 And when Jacob saw them, he said, this *is* God's host: and he called the name of that place Mahanaim.
3 And Jacob sent messengers before him to Esau his brother unto the land of Seir, the country of Edom.

4 And he commanded them, saying, then will you speak unto my lord Esau; your servant Jacob said this, I have sojourned with Laban, and stayed there until now:
5 And I have oxen, and asses, flocks, and menservants, and women servants: and I have sent to tell my lord, that I may find grace in your sight.
6 And the messengers returned to Jacob, saying, we came to your brother Esau, and also he cometh to meet you, and four hundred men with him.
7 Then Jacob was greatly afraid and distressed: and he divided the people that *were* with him, and the flocks, and herds, and the camels, into two bands;
8 And said, If Esau come to the one company, and smite it, and then the other company which is left will escape.
9 And Jacob said, O God of my father Abraham, and God of my father Isaac, the LORD which said unto me, Return unto your country, and to your kindred, and I will deal well with you:
10 I am not worthy of the least of all the mercies, and of all the truth, which you has showed unto your servant; for with my staff I passed over this Jordan; and now I am become two bands.
11 Deliver me, I pray you, from the hand of my brother, from the hand of Esau: for I fear him, lest he will come and smite me, *and* the mother with the children.
12 And you said, I will surely do you good, and make your seed as the sand of the sea, which cannot be numbered for multitude.
13 And he lodged there that same night; and took of that which came to his hand a present for Esau his brother;
14 Two hundred she goats, and twenty he goats, two hundred ewes, and twenty rams,
15 Thirty **nursing** camels with their colts, forty **heifers**, and ten bulls, twenty she asses, and ten foals.
16 And he delivered *them* into the hand of his servants, every drove by themselves; and said unto his servants, Pass over before me, and put a space between drove and drove.
17 And he commanded the foremost, saying, when Esau my brother meet you, and ask you, saying, whose *are* you? And whither go you? And whose *are* these before you?
18 Then you will say, *they* **are** your servant Jacob's; it *is* a present sent unto my lord Esau: and, behold, also he *is* behind us.
19 And so commanded he the second, and the third, and all that followed the droves, saying, on this manner will you speak unto Esau, when you find him.
20 And say you moreover, Behold, your servant Jacob *is* behind us. For he said, I will appease him with the present that go before me, and afterward I will see his face; peradventure he will accept of me.
21 So went the present over before him: and **he** lodged that night in the company.
22 And he rose up that night, and took his two wives, and his two women servants, and his eleven sons, and passed over the ford Jabbok.
23 And he took them, and sent them over the brook, and sent over that he had.
24 And Jacob was left alone; and there wrestled a man with him until the breaking of the day.
25 And when he saw that he prevailed not against him, he touched the hollow of his thigh; and the hollow of Jacob's thigh was out of joint, as he wrestled with him.

26 And he said, Let me go, for the day break. And he said, I will not let you go, except you bless me.
27 And he said unto him, what *is* your name? And he said, Jacob.
28 And he said, your name will be called no more Jacob, but Israel[1]: for as a prince has you power with God and with men, and **have** prevailed.
29 And Jacob asked *him*, and said, tell *me*, I pray you, your name. And he said, wherefore *is* it *that* you do ask after my name? And he blessed him there.
30 And Jacob called the name of the place Peniel[2]: for I have seen God face to face, and my life is preserved.
31 And as he passed over Penuel the sun rose upon him, and he halted upon his thigh.
32 Therefore the children of Israel eat not *of* the sinew which shrank, which *is* upon the hollow of the thigh, unto this day: because he touched the hollow of Jacob's thigh in the sinew that shrank.

CHAPTER 33

1 And Jacob lifted up his eyes, and looked, and, behold, Esau came, and with him four hundred men. And he divided the children unto Leah, and unto Rachel, and unto the two handmaids.
2 And he put the handmaids and their children foremost, and Leah and her children after, and Rachel and Joseph hindermost.
3 And he passed over before them, and bowed himself to the ground seven times, until he came near to his brother.
4 And Esau ran to meet him, and embraced him, and fell on his neck, and kissed him: and they wept.
5 And he lifted up his eyes, and saw the women and the children; and said, who *are* those with you? And he said, the children which God hath graciously given your servant.
6 Then the handmaidens came near, they and their children, and they bowed themselves.
7 And Leah also with her children came near, and bowed themselves: and after came Joseph near and Rachel, and they bowed themselves.
8 And he said, what *mean* you by this **entire** drove which I met? And he said, *these are* to find grace in the sight of my lord.
9 And Esau said, I have enough, my brother; keep that you has unto yourself.
10 And Jacob said, No, I pray you, if now I have found grace in your sight, then receive my present at my hand: for therefore I have seen your face, as though I had seen the face of God, and you was pleased with me.
11 Take, I pray you, my blessing that is brought to you; because God have dealt graciously with me, and because I have enough. And he urged him, and he took *it*.
12 And he said, Let us take our journey, and let us go, and I will go before you.
13 And he said unto him, my lord knows that the children *are* tender, and the flocks and herds with young *are* with me: and if men should overdrive them one day, all the flock will die.
14 Let my lord, I pray you, pass over before his servant: and I will lead on softly, according as the cattle that go before me and the children be able to endure, until I come unto my lord unto Seir.
15 And Esau said, Let me now leave with you *some* of the folk that *are* with me. And he said, what need it? Let me find grace in the sight of my lord.

---

[1] Israel- he will rule as God or God prevails [Strgs#3478].

[2] Peniel- face of God [Strgs#6439].

16 So Esau returned that day on his way unto Seir.

17 And Jacob journeyed to Succoth, and built him a house, and made booths for his cattle: therefore the name of the place is called Succoth.

18 And Jacob came to Shalem, a city of Shechem, which *is* in the land of Canaan, when he came from Padan-aram; and pitched his tent before the city.

19 And he bought a parcel of a field, where he had spread his tent, at the hand of the children of Hamor, Shechem's father, for an hundred pieces of money.

20 And he erected there an altar, and called it El-elohe-Israel.

CHAPTER 34

1 And Dinah the daughter of Leah, which she bare unto Jacob, went out to see the daughters of the land.

2 And when Shechem the son of Hamor the Hivite, prince of the country, saw her, he took her, and lay with her, and defiled her.

3 And his soul clave unto Dinah the daughter of Jacob, and he loved the damsel, and spoke kindly unto the damsel.

4 And Shechem spoke unto his father Hamor, saying, Get me this damsel to wife.

5 And Jacob heard that he had defiled Dinah his daughter: now his sons were with his cattle in the field: and Jacob held his peace until they were come.

6 And Hamor the father of Shechem went out unto Jacob to commune with him.

7 And the sons of Jacob came out of the field when they heard *it*: and the men were grieved, and they were very wroth, because he had wrought folly in Israel in lying with Jacob's daughter; which thing ought not to be done.

8 And Hamor communed with them, saying, the soul of my son Shechem longed for your daughter: I pray you give her him to wife.

9 And make you marriages with us, *and* give your daughters unto us, and take our daughters unto you.

10 And you will dwell with us: and the land will be before you; dwell and trade you therein, and get you possessions therein.

11 And Shechem said unto her father and unto her brethren, Let me find grace in your eyes, and what you will say unto me I will give.

12 Ask me never so much dowry and gift, and I will give according as you will say unto me: but give me the damsel to wife.

13 And the sons of Jacob answered Shechem and Hamor his father deceitfully, and said, because he had defiled Dinah their sister:

14 And they said unto them, we cannot do this thing, to give our sister to one that is uncircumcised; for that *were* a reproach unto us:

15 But in this will we consent unto you: If you will be as we *be*, that every male of you be circumcised;

16 Then will we give our daughters unto you, and we will take your daughters to us, and we will dwell with you, and we will become one people.

17 But if you will not hearken unto us, to be circumcised; then will we take our daughter, and we will be gone.

18 And their words pleased Hamor, and Shechem Hamor's son.

19 And the young man deferred not to do the thing, because he had delight in Jacob's daughter: and he *was* more honorable than all the house of his father.

20 And Hamor and Shechem his son came unto the gate of their city, and communed with the men of their city, saying,

21 These men *are* peaceable with us; therefore let them dwell in the land, and trade therein; for the land, behold, *it is* large enough for them; let us take their daughters to us for wives, and let us give them our daughters.

22 Only herein will the men consent unto us for to dwell with us, to be one people, if every male among us be circumcised, as they *are* circumcised.

23 *Will* not their cattle and their substance and every beast of theirs *be* ours? Only let us consent unto them, and they will dwell with us.

24 And unto Hamor and unto Shechem his son hearkened all that went out of the gate of his city; and every male was circumcised, all that went out of the gate of his city.

25 And it came to pass on the third day, when they were sore, that two of the sons of Jacob, Simeon and Levi, Dinah's brethren, took each man his sword, and came upon the city boldly, and slew all the males.

26 And they slew Hamor and Shechem his son with the edge of the sword, and took Dinah out of Shechem's house, and went out.

27 The sons of Jacob came upon the slain, and spoiled the city, because they had defiled their sister.

28 They took their sheep, and their oxen, and their asses, and that which *was* in the city, and that which *was* in the field,

29 And all their wealth, and all their little ones, and **take** their wives captive, and spoiled even all that *was* in the house.

30 And Jacob said to Simeon and Levi, You have troubled me to make me to stink among the inhabitants of the land, among the Canaanites and the Perizzites: and I *being* few in number, they will gather themselves together against me, and slay me; and I will be destroyed, I and my house.

31 And they said, should he deal with our sister as with a harlot?

CHAPTER 35

1 And God said unto Jacob, Arise, go up to Beth-el, and dwell there: and make there an altar unto God, that appeared unto you when you fled from the face of Esau your brother.

2 Then Jacob said unto his household, and to all that *were* with him, Put away the strange gods that *are* among you, and be clean, and change your garments:

3 And let us arise, and go up to Beth-el; and I will make there an altar unto God, who answered me in the day of my distress, and was with me in the way which I went.

4 And they gave unto Jacob all the strange gods which *were* in their hand, and *all their* earrings which *were* in their ears; and Jacob hid them under the oak which *was* by Shechem.

5 And they journeyed: and the terror of God was upon the cities that *were* round about them, and they did not pursue after the sons of Jacob.

6 So Jacob came to Luz, which *is* in the land of Canaan, that *is*, Beth-el, he and all the people that *were* with him.

7 And he built there an altar, and called the place El-beth-el: because there God appeared unto him, when he fled from the face of his brother.

8 But Deborah Rebekah's nurse died, and she was buried beneath Beth-el under an oak: and the name of it was called Allon-bachuth.

9 And God appeared unto Jacob again, when he came out of Padan-aram, and blessed him.

10 And God said unto him, your name *is* Jacob: your name will not be called any more Jacob, but Israel will be your name: and he called his name Israel.

11 And God said unto him, I *am* God Almighty: be fruitful and multiply; a nation and a company of nations will be of you, and kings will come out of your loins;

12 And the land which I gave Abraham and Isaac, to you I will give it, and to your seed after you will I give the land.

13 And God went up from him in the place where he talked with him.

14 And Jacob set up a pillar in the place where he talked with him, *even* a pillar of stone: and he poured a drink offering thereon, and he poured oil thereon.

15 And Jacob called the name of the place where God spoke with him, Beth-el.

16 And they journeyed from Beth-el; and there was but a little way to come to Ephrath: and Rachel travailed, and she had hard labor.

17 And it came to pass, when she was in hard labor, that the midwife said unto her, Fear not; you will have this son also.

18 And it came to pass, as her soul was in departing, (for she died) that she called his name Ben-oni: but his father called him Benjamin.

19 And Rachel died, and was buried in the way to Ephrath, which *is* Beth-lehem.

20 And Jacob set a pillar upon her grave: that *is* the pillar of Rachel's grave unto this day.

21 And Israel journeyed, and spread his tent beyond the tower of Edar.

22 And it came to pass, when Israel dwelt in that land, that Reuben went and **laid** with Bilhah his father's concubine: and Israel heard *it*. Now the sons of Jacob were twelve:

23 The sons of Leah; Reuben[1], Jacob's firstborn, and Simeon[2], and Levi[3], and Judah[4], and Issachar[5], and Zebulun[6]:

24 The sons of Rachel; Joseph[7], and Benjamin[8]:

25 And the sons of Bilhah, Rachel's handmaid; Dan[9], and Naphtali[10]:

26 And the sons of Zilpah, Leah's handmaid; Gad[11], and Asher[12]: these *are* the sons of Jacob, which were born to him in Padan-aram.

27 And Jacob came unto Isaac his father unto Mamre, unto the city of Arbah, which *is* Hebron, where Abraham and Isaac sojourned.

28 And the days of Isaac were an hundred and fourscore years.

29 And Isaac gave up the ghost, and died, and was gathered unto his people, *being* old and full of days: and his sons Esau and Jacob buried him.

CHAPTER 36

1 Now these *are* the generations of Esau, who *is* Edom.

2 Esau took his wives of the daughters of Canaan; Adah the daughter of Elon the Hittite, and Aholibamah the daughter of Anah the daughter of Zibeon the Hivite;

3 And Bashemath Ishmael's daughter, sister of Nebajoth.

4 And Adah bare to Esau Eliphaz; and Bashemath bare Reuel;

5 And Aholibamah bare Jeush, and Jaalam, and Korah: these *are* the sons of Esau, which were born unto him in the land of Canaan.

6 And Esau took his wives, and his sons, and his daughters, and all the persons of his house, and his cattle, and all his beasts, and all his substance, which he had got in the land of Canaan; and went into the country from the face of his brother Jacob.

7 For their riches were more than that they might dwell together; and the land wherein they were strangers could not bear them because of their cattle.

8 Thus dwelt Esau in mount Seir: Esau *is* Edom.

9 And these *are* the generations of Esau the father of the Edomites in mount Seir:

10 These *are* the names of Esau's sons; Eliphaz the son of Adah the wife of Esau, Reuel the son of Bashemath the wife of Esau.

11 And the sons of Eliphaz were Teman, Omar, Zepho, and Gatam, and Kenaz.

12 And Timna was concubine to Eliphaz Esau's son; and she bare to Eliphaz Amalek: these *were* the sons of Adah Esau's wife.

13 And these *are* the sons of Reuel; Nahath, and Zerah, Shammah, and Mizzah: these were the sons of Bashemath Esau's wife.

14 And these were the sons of Aholibamah, the daughter of Anah the daughter of Zibeon, Esau's wife: and she bare to Esau Jeush, and Jaalam, and Korah.

15 These *were* dukes of the sons of Esau: the sons of Eliphaz the firstborn *son* of Esau; duke Teman, duke Omar, duke Zepho, duke Kenaz,

16 Duke Korah, duke Gatam, *and* duke Amalek: these *are* the dukes *that* came of Eliphaz in the land of Edom; these *were* the sons of Adah.

17 And these *are* the sons of Reuel Esau's son; duke Nahath, duke Zerah, duke Shammah, duke Mizzah: these *are* the dukes *that* came of Reuel in the land of Edom; these *are* the sons of Bashemath Esau's wife.

18 And these *are* the sons of Aholibamah Esau's wife; duke Jeush, duke Jaalam, duke Korah: these *were* the dukes *that came* of Aholibamah the daughter of Anah, Esau's wife.

19 These *are* the sons of Esau, who *is* Edom, and these *are* their dukes.

20 These *are* the sons of Seir the Horite, who inhabited the land; Lotan, and Shobal, and Zibeon, and Anah,

21 And Dishon, and Ezer, and Dishan: these *are* the dukes of the Horites, the children of Seir in the land of Edom.

22 And the children of Lotan were Hori and Hemam; and Lotan's sister *was* Timna.

23 And the children of Shobal *were* these; Alvan, and Manahath, and Ebal, Shepho, and Onam.

24 And these *are* the children of Zibeon; both Ajah, and Anah: this *was that* Anah that found the mules in the wilderness, as he fed the asses of Zibeon his father.

25 And the children of Anah *were* these; Dishon, and Aholibamah the daughter of Anah.

26 And these *are* the children of Dishon; Hemdan, and Eshban, and Ithran, and Cheran.

27 The children of Ezer *are* these; Bilhan, and Zaavan, and Akan.

28 The children of Dishan *are* these; Uz, and Aran.

---

[1] Reuben- behold a son [Strgs#7205].
[2] Simeon- God hears [Strgs#8095].
[3] Levi- joined to [Strgs#3878].
[4] Judah- praised, celebrated [Strgs#3063].
[5] Issachar- he will bring a reward or there is recompense [Strgs#3485].
[6] Zebulun- dwelling, habitation [Strgs#2074].
[7] Joseph- may God add or Jehovah has added [Strgs#3130].
[8] Benjamin- son of the right hand [Strgs#1144].
[9] Dan- a judge [Strgs#1835].
[10] Naphtali- my wrestling [Strgs#5321].
[11] Gad- troop or good fortune [Strgs#1410].
[12] Asher- happy [Strgs#836].

29 These *are* the dukes *that came* of the Horites; duke Lotan, duke Shobal, duke Zibeon, duke Anah,
30 Duke Dishon, duke Ezer, duke Dishan: these *are* the dukes *that came* of Hori, among their dukes in the land of Seir.
31 And these *are* the kings that reigned in the land of Edom, before there reigned any king over the children of Israel.
32 And Bela the son of Beor reigned in Edom: and the name of his city *was* Dinhabah.
33 And Bela died, and Jobab the son of Zerah of Bozrah reigned in his stead.
34 And Jobab died, and Husham of the land of Temani reigned in his stead.
35 And Husham died, and Hadad the son of Bedad, who smote Midian in the field of Moab, reigned in his stead: and the name of his city *was* Avith.
36 And Hadad died, and Samlah of Masrekah reigned in his stead.
37 And Samlah died, and Saul of Rehoboth *by* the river reigned in his stead.
38 And Saul died, and Baal-hanan the son of Achbor reigned in his stead.
39 And Baal-hanan the son of Achbor died, and Hadar reigned in his stead: and the name of his city *was* Pau; and his wife's name *was* Mehetabel, the daughter of Matred, the daughter of Mezahab.
40 And these *are* the names of the dukes *that came* of Esau, according to their families, after their places, by their names; duke Timnah, duke Alvah, duke Jetheth,
41 Duke Aholibamah, duke Elah, duke Pinon,
42 Duke Kenaz, duke Teman, duke Mibzar,
43 Duke Magdiel, duke Iram: these *are* the dukes of Edom, according to their habitations in the land of their possession: he *is* Esau the father of the Edomites.

CHAPTER 37

1 And Jacob dwelt in the land wherein his father was a stranger, in the land of Canaan.
2 These *are* the generations of Jacob. Joseph, *being* seventeen years old, was feeding the flock with his brethren; and the lad *was* with the sons of Bilhah, and with the sons of Zilpah, his father's wives: and Joseph brought unto his father their evil report.
3 Now Israel loved Joseph more than all his children, because he *was* the son of his old age: and he made him a coat of *many* colors.
4 And when his brethren saw that their father loved him more than all his brethren, they hated him, and could not speak peaceably unto him.
5 And Joseph dreamed a dream, and he told *it* his brethren: and they hated him yet the more.
6 And he said unto them, Hear, I pray you, this dream which I have dreamed:
7 For, behold, we *were* binding sheaves in the field, and, lo, my sheaf arose, and also stood upright; and, behold, your sheaves stood round about, and made obeisance to my sheaf.
8 And his brethren said to him, Will you indeed reign over us? Or will you indeed have dominion over us? And they hated him yet the more for his dreams, and for his words.
9 And he dreamed yet another dream, and told it his brethren, and said, Behold, I have dreamed a dream more; and, behold, the sun and the moon and the eleven stars made obeisance to me.
10 And he told *it* to his father, and to his brethren: and his father rebuked him, and said unto him, what *is* this dream that you have dreamed? Will I and your mother and your brethren indeed come to bow down ourselves to you to the earth?
11 And his brethren envied him; but his father observed the saying.
12 And his brethren went to feed their father's flock in Shechem.
13 And Israel said unto Joseph, Do not your brethren feed *the flock* in Shechem? Come, and I will send you unto them. And he said to him, here *am I*.
14 And he said to him, Go, I pray you, see whether it be well with your brethren, and well with the flocks; and bring me word again. So he sent him out of the **valley** of Hebron, and he came to Shechem.
15 And a certain man found him, and, behold, *he was* wandering in the field: and the man asked him, saying, what seek you?
16 And he said, I seek my brethren: tell me, I pray you, where they feed *their flocks*.
17 And the man said, they are departed hence; for I heard them say, Let us go to Dothan. And Joseph went after his brethren, and found them in Dothan.
18 And when they saw him afar off, even before he came near unto them, they conspired against him to slay him.
19 And they said one to another, Behold, this dreamer cometh.
20 Come now therefore, and let us slay him, and cast him into some pit, and we will say, some evil beast hath devoured him: and we will see what will become of his dreams.
21 And Reuben heard *it*, and he delivered him out of their hands; and said, Let us not kill him.
22 And Reuben said unto them, Shed no blood, *but* cast him into this pit that *is* in the wilderness, and lay no hand upon him; that he might rid him out of their hands, to deliver him to his father again.
23 And it came to pass, when Joseph was come unto his brethren, that they strip Joseph out of his coat, *his* coat of *many* colors that *was* on him;
24 And they took him, and cast him into a pit: and the pit *was* empty, *there was* no water in it.
25 And they sat down to eat bread: and they lifted up their eyes and looked, and, behold, a company of Ishmeelites came from Gilead with their camels bearing spices and balm and myrrh, going to carry *it* down to Egypt.
26 And Judah said unto his brethren, what profit *is it* if we slay our brother, and conceal his blood?
27 Come, and let us sell him to the Ishmeelites, and let not our hand be upon him; for he *is* our brother *and* our flesh. And his brethren were content.
28 Then there passed by Midianites merchantmen; and they drew and lifted up Joseph out of the pit, and sold Joseph to the Ishmeelites for twenty *pieces* of silver: and they brought Joseph into Egypt.
29 And Reuben returned unto the pit; and, behold, Joseph *was* not in the pit; and he rent his clothes.
30 And he returned unto his brethren, and said, the child *is* not; and I, whither will I go?
31 And they took Joseph's coat, and killed a kid of the goats, and dipped the coat in the blood;
32 And they sent the coat of *many* colors, and they brought *it* to their father; and said, this have we found: know now whether it **is** your son's coat or no.
33 And he knew it, and said, *it is* my son's coat; an evil beast has devoured him; Joseph is without doubt rent in pieces.
34 And Jacob rent his clothes, and put sackcloth upon his loins, and mourned for his son many days.

35 And all his sons and all his daughters rose up to comfort him; but he refused to be comforted; and he said, for I will go down into the grave unto my son mourning. Thus his father wept for him.
36 And the Midianites sold him into Egypt unto Potiphar, an officer of Pharaoh's, *and* captain of the guard.

CHAPTER 38

1 And it came to pass at that time, that Judah went down from his brethren, and turned in to a certain Adullamite, whose name *was* Hirah.
2 And Judah saw there a daughter of a certain Canaanite, whose name *was* Shuah; and he took her, and went in unto her.
3 And she conceived, and bare a son; and he called his name Er.
4 And she conceived again, and bare a son; and she called his name Onan.
5 And she yet again conceived, and bares a son; and called his name Shelah: and he was at Chezib, when she bares him.
6 And Judah took a wife for Er his firstborn, whose name *was* Tamar.
7 And Er, Judah's firstborn, was wicked in the sight of the LORD; and the LORD slew him.
8 And Judah said unto Onan, Go in unto your brother's wife, and marry her, and raise up seed to your brother.
9 And Onan knew that the seed should not be his; and it came to pass, when he went in unto his brother's wife, that he spilled *it* on the ground, lest that he should give seed to his brother.
10 And the thing which he did displeased the LORD: wherefore he slew him also.
11 Then said Judah to Tamar his daughter in law, Remain a widow at your father's house, till Shelah my son be grown: for he said, lest peradventure he die also, as his brethren *did*. And Tamar went and dwelt in her father's house.
12 And in process of time the daughter of Shuah Judah's wife died; and Judah was comforted, and went up unto his sheepshearers to Timnath, he and his friend Hirah the Adullamite.
13 And it was told Tamar, saying, behold your father in law go up to Timnath to shear his sheep.
14 And she put her widow's garments off from her, and covered her with a veil, and wrapped herself, and sat in an open place, which *is* by the way to Timnath; for she saw that Shelah was grown, and she was not given unto him to wife.
15 When Judah saw her, he thought her *to be* a harlot; because she had covered her face.
16 And he turned unto her by the way, and said, go to, I pray you, let me come in unto you; (for he knew not that she *was* his daughter in law.) And she said, what will you give me, that you may come in unto me?
17 And he said, I will send *you* a kid from the flock. And she said, will you give *me* a pledge, until you send *it*?
18 And he said, what pledge will I give you? And she said, your signet, and your bracelets, and your staff that *is* in your hand. And he gave *it* her, and came in unto her, and she conceived by him.
19 And she arose, and went away, and laid by her veil from her, and put on the garments of her widowhood.
20 And Judah sent the kid by the hand of his friend the Adullamite, to receive *his* pledge from the woman's hand: but he found her not.
21 Then he asked the men of that place, saying, where *is* the harlot, that *was* openly by the way side? And they said, there was no harlot in this *place*.
22 And he returned to Judah, and said, I cannot find her; and also the men of the place said, *that* there was no harlot in this *place*.
23 And Judah said, Let her take *it* to her, lest we be shamed: behold, I sent this kid, and you has not found her.
24 And it came to pass about three months after, that it was told Judah, saying, Tamar your daughter in law has played the harlot; and also, behold, she *is* with child by whoredom. And Judah said, bring her forth, and let her be burnt.
25 When she *was* brought forth, she sent to her father in law, saying, By the man, whose these *are*, am I with child: and she said, Discern, I pray you, whose *are* these, the signet, and bracelets, and staff.
26 And Judah acknowledged *them*, and said, She hath been more righteous than I; because that I gave her not to Shelah my son. And he knew her again no more.
27 And it came to pass in the time of her travail, that, behold, twins *were* in her womb.
28 And it came to pass, when she travailed, that *the one* put out *his* hand: and the midwife took and bound upon his hand a scarlet thread, saying, this came out first.
29 And it came to pass, as he drew back his hand, that, behold, his brother came out: and she said, How has you broken forth? *This* breach *is* upon you: therefore his name was called Pharez.
30 And afterward came out his brother, that had the scarlet thread upon his hand: and his name was called Zarah

CHAPTER 39

1 And Joseph was brought down to Egypt; and Potiphar, an officer of Pharaoh, captain of the guard, an Egyptian, bought him of the hands of the Ishmeelites, which had brought him down thither.
2 And the LORD was with Joseph, and he was a prosperous man; and he was in the house of his master the Egyptian.
3 And his master saw that the LORD *was* with him, and that the LORD made all that he did to prosper in his hand.
4 And Joseph found grace in his sight, and he served him: and he made him overseer over his house, and all *that* he had he put into his hand.
5 And it came to pass from the time *that* he had made him overseer in his house, and over all that he had, that the LORD blessed the Egyptian's house for Joseph's sake; and the blessing of the LORD was upon all that he had in the house, and in the field.
6 And he left all that he had in Joseph's hand; and he knew not ought he had, save the bread which he did eat. And Joseph was *a* goodly *person*, and well favored.
7 And it came to pass after these things, that his master's wife cast her eyes upon Joseph; and she said, lie with me.
8 But he refused, and said unto his master's wife, Behold, my master wotteth not what *is* with me in the house, and he hath committed all that he hath to my hand;
9 *There is* none greater in this house than I; neither did he keep back anything from me but you, because you *are* his wife: how then can I do this great wickedness, and sin against God?
10 And it came to pass, as she spoke to Joseph day by day, that he hearkened not unto her, to lie by her, or to be with her.
11 And it came to pass about this time, that *Joseph* went into the house to do his business; and *there was* none of the men of the house there within.
12 And she caught him by his garment, saying, lie with me: and he left his garment in her hand, and fled, and got him out.

13 And it came to pass, when she saw that he had left his garment in her hand, and was fled forth,
14 That she called unto the men of her house, and spoke unto them, saying, See, he has brought in a Hebrew unto us to mock us; he came in unto me to lie with me, and I cried with a loud voice:
15 And it came to pass, when he heard that I lifted up my voice and cried, that he left his garment with me, and fled, and got him out.
16 And she laid up his garment by her, until his lord came home.
17 And she spoke unto him according to these words, saying, The Hebrew servant, which you have brought unto us, came in unto me to mock me:
18 And it came to pass, as I lifted up my voice and cried, that he left his garment with me, and fled out.
19 And it came to pass, when his master heard the words of his wife, which she spoke unto him, saying, after this manner did your servant to me; that his wrath was kindled.
20 And Joseph's master took him, and put him into the prison, a place where the king's prisoners *were* bound: and he was there in the prison.
21 But the LORD was with Joseph, and showed him mercy, and gave him favor in the sight of the keeper of the prison.
22 And the keeper of the prison committed to Joseph's hand all the prisoners that *were* in the prison; and whatsoever they did there, he was the doer *of it*.
23 The keeper of the prison looked not to anything *that was* under his hand; because the LORD was with him, and *that* which he did, the LORD made *it* to prosper.

CHAPTER 40

1 And it came to pass after these things, *that* the butler of the king of Egypt and *his* baker had offended their lord the king of Egypt.
2 And Pharaoh was wroth against two *of* his officers, against the chief of the butlers, and against the chief of the bakers.
3 And he put them in ward in the house of the captain of the guard, into the prison, the place where Joseph *was* bound.
4 And the captain of the guard charged Joseph with them, and he served them: and they continued a season in ward.
5 And they dreamed a dream both of them, each man his dream in one night, each man according to the interpretation of his dream, the butler and the baker of the king of Egypt, which *were* bound in the prison.
6 And Joseph came in unto them in the morning, and looked upon them, and, behold, they *were* sad.
7 And he asked Pharaoh's officers that *were* with him in the ward of his lord's house, saying, wherefore look you *so* sadly today?
8 And they said unto him, we have dreamed a dream, and *there is* no interpreter of it. And Joseph said unto them, *do* not interpretations *belong* to God? Tell me *them*, I pray you.
9 And the chief butler told his dream to Joseph, and said to him, in my dream, behold, a vine *was* before me;
10 And in the vine *were* three branches: and it *was* as though it budded, *and* her blossoms shot forth; and the clusters thereof brought forth ripe grapes:
11 And Pharaoh's cup *was* in my hand: and I took the grapes, and pressed them into Pharaoh's cup, and I gave the cup into Pharaoh's hand.
12 And Joseph said unto him, this *is* the interpretation of it: The three branches *are* three days:

13 Yet within three days will Pharaoh lift up your head, and restore you unto your place: and you will deliver Pharaoh's cup into his hand, after the former manner when you was his butler.
14 But think on me when it will be well with you, and show kindness, I pray you, unto me, and make mention of me unto Pharaoh, and bring me out of this house:
15 For indeed I was stolen away out of the land of the Hebrews: and here also have I done nothing that they should put me into the dungeon.
16 When the chief baker saw that the interpretation was good, he said unto Joseph, I also *was* in my dream, and, behold, *I had* three white baskets on my head:
17 And in the uppermost basket *there was* of all manner of bake meats for Pharaoh; and the birds did eat them out of the basket upon my head.
18 And Joseph answered and said, this *is* the interpretation thereof: The three baskets *are* three days:
19 Yet within three days will Pharaoh lift up your head from off you, and will hang you on a tree; and the birds will eat your flesh from off you.
20 And it came to pass the third day, *which was* Pharaoh's birthday, that he made a feast unto all his servants: and he lifted up the head of the chief butler and of the chief baker among his servants.
21 And he restored the chief butler unto his butlership again; and he gave the cup into Pharaoh's hand:
22 But he hanged the chief baker: as Joseph had interpreted to them.
23 Yet did not the chief butler remember Joseph, but forget him.

CHAPTER 41

1 And it came to pass at the end of two full years, that Pharaoh dreamed: and, behold, he stood by the river.
2 And, behold, there came up out of the river seven well favored heifer and fat fleshed; and they fed in a meadow.
3 And, behold, seven other heifer came up after them out of the river, ill favored and lean fleshed; and stood by the *other* heifer upon the brink of the river.
4 And the ill favored and lean fleshed heifer did eat up the seven well favored and fat **heifers**. So Pharaoh awoke.
5 And he slept and dreamed the second time: and, behold, seven ears of corn came up upon one stalk, rank and good.
6 And, behold, seven thin ears and blasted with the east wind sprung up after them.
7 And the seven thin ears devoured the seven rank and full ears. And Pharaoh awoke, and, behold, *it was* a dream.
8 And it came to pass in the morning that his spirit was troubled; and he sent and called for all the magicians of Egypt, and all the wise men thereof: and Pharaoh told them his dream; but *there was* none that could interpret them unto Pharaoh.
9 Then spoke the chief butler unto Pharaoh, saying, I do remember my faults this day:
10 Pharaoh was wroth with his servants, and put me in ward in the captain of the guard's house, *both* me and the chief baker:
11 And we dreamed a dream in one night, I and he; we dreamed each man according to the interpretation of his dream.
12 And *there was* there with us a young man, a Hebrew, servant to the captain of the guard; and we told him, and he interpreted to us our dreams; to each man according to his dream he did interpret.

13 And it came to pass, as he interpreted to us, so it was; me he restored unto mine office, and him he hanged.
14 Then Pharaoh sent and called Joseph, and they brought him hastily out of the dungeon: and he shaved *himself*, and changed his raiment, and came in unto Pharaoh.
15 And Pharaoh said unto Joseph, I have dreamed a dream, and *there is* none that can interpret it: and I have heard say of you, *that* you can understand a dream to interpret it.
16 And Joseph answered Pharaoh, saying, *it is* not in me: God will give Pharaoh an answer of peace.
17 And Pharaoh said unto Joseph, in my dream, behold, I stood upon the bank of the river:
18 And, behold, there came up out of the river seven **heifers**, fat fleshed and well favored; and they fed in a meadow:
19 And, behold, seven other **heifers** came up after them, poor and very ill favored and lean fleshed, such as I never saw in all the land of Egypt for badness:
20 And the lean and the ill favored **heifer** did eat up the first seven fat **heifers**:
21 And when they had eaten them up, it could not be known that they had eaten them; but they *were* still ill favored, as at the beginning. So I awoke.
22 And I saw in my dream, and, behold, seven ears came up in one stalk, full and good:
23 And, behold, seven ears, withered, thin, *and* blasted with the east wind, sprung up after them:
24 And the thin ears devoured the seven good ears: and I told *this* unto the magicians; but *there was* none that could declare *it* to me.
25 And Joseph said unto Pharaoh, The dream of Pharaoh *is* one: God hath showed Pharaoh what he *is* about to do.
26 The seven good **heifers** *are* seven years; and the seven good ears *are* seven years: the dream *is* one.
27 And the seven thin and ill favored heifer that came up after them *are* seven years; and the seven empty ears blasted with the east wind will be seven years of famine.
28 This *is* the thing which I have spoken unto Pharaoh: What God *is* about to do he showed unto Pharaoh.
29 Behold, there come seven years of great plenty throughout all the land of Egypt:
30 And there will arise after them seven years of famine; and all the plenty will be forgotten in the land of Egypt; and the famine will consume the land;
31 And the plenty will not be known in the land by reason of that famine following; for it *will be* very grievous.
32 And for that the dream was doubled unto Pharaoh twice; *it is* because the thing *is* established by God, and God will shortly bring it to pass.
33 Now therefore let Pharaoh look out a man discreet and wise, and set him over the land of Egypt.
34 Let Pharaoh do *this*, and let him appoint officers over the land, and take up the fifth part of the land of Egypt in the seven plenteous years.
35 And let them gather all the food of those good years that come, and lay up corn under the hand of Pharaoh, and let them keep food in the cities.
36 And that food will be for store to the land against the seven years of famine, which will be in the land of Egypt; that the land perish not through the famine.
37 And the thing was good in the eyes of Pharaoh, and in the eyes of all his servants.
38 And Pharaoh said unto his servants, Can we find *such a one* as this *is*, a man in whom the Spirit of God *is*?
39 And Pharaoh said unto Joseph, forasmuch as God hath showed you all this, *there is* none **as** discreet and wise as you *are*:
40 You will be over my house, and according unto your word will all my people be ruled: only in the throne will I be greater than you.
41 And Pharaoh said unto Joseph, See, I have set you over all the land of Egypt.
42 And Pharaoh took off his ring from his hand, and put it upon Joseph's hand, and arrayed him in vestures of fine linen, and put a gold chain about his neck;
43 And he made him to ride in the second chariot which he had; and they cried before him, Bow the knee: and he made him *ruler* over all the land of Egypt.
44 And Pharaoh said unto Joseph, I *am* Pharaoh, and without you will no man lift up his hand or foot in all the land of Egypt.
45 And Pharaoh called Joseph's name Zaphnath-paaneah; and he gave him to wife Asenath the daughter of Poti-pherah priest of On. And Joseph went out over *all* the land of Egypt.
46 And Joseph *was* thirty years old when he stood before Pharaoh King of Egypt. And Joseph went out from the presence of Pharaoh, and went throughout all the land of Egypt.
47 And in the seven plenteous years the earth brought forth by handfuls.
48 And he gathered up all the food of the seven years, which were in the land of Egypt, and laid up the food in the cities: the food of the field, which *was* round about every city, laid him up in the same.
49 And Joseph gathered corn as the sand of the sea, very much, until he left numbering; for *it was* without number.
50 And unto Joseph were born two sons before the years of famine came, which Asenath the daughter of Poti-pherah priest of On bare unto him.
51 And Joseph called the name of the firstborn Manasseh: For God, *said he*, hath made me forget all my toil, and my **entire** father's house.
52 And the name of the second called he Ephraim: For God hath caused me to be fruitful in the land of my affliction.
53 And the seven years of plenteousness, that was in the land of Egypt, were ended.
54 And the seven years of dearth began to come, according as Joseph had said: and the dearth was in all lands; but in all the land of Egypt there was bread.
55 And when all the land of Egypt was famished, the people cried to Pharaoh for bread: and Pharaoh said unto all the Egyptians, Go unto Joseph; what he said to you, do.
56 And the famine was over all the face of the earth: And Joseph opened all the storehouses, and sold unto the Egyptians and the famine waxed sore in the land of Egypt.
57 And all countries came into Egypt to Joseph for to buy *corn*; because that the famine was *so* sore in all lands.

CHAPTER 42

1 Now when Jacob saw that there was corn in Egypt, Jacob said unto his sons, why do you look one upon another?
2 And he said, Behold, I have heard that there is corn in Egypt: get you down there, and buy for us from there; that we may live, and not die.
3 And Joseph's ten brethren went down to buy corn in Egypt.
4 But Benjamin, Joseph's brother, Jacob sent not with his brethren; for he said, lest peradventure mischief befall him.

5 And the sons of Israel came to buy *corn* among those that came: for the famine was in the land of Canaan.
6 And Joseph *was* the governor over the land, *and he it was* that sold to all the people of the land: and Joseph's brethren came, and bowed down themselves before him *with* their faces to the earth.
7 And Joseph saw his brethren, and he knew them, but made himself strange unto them, and spoke roughly unto them; and he said unto them, where come you? And they said, from the land of Canaan to buy food.
8 And Joseph knew his brethren, but they knew not him.
9 And Joseph remembered the dreams which he dreamed of them, and said unto them, you *are* spies; to see the nakedness of the land you are come.
10 And they said unto him, No, my lord, but to buy food are your servants come.
11 We *are* all one man's sons; we *are* true *men*, your servants are no spies.
12 And he said unto them, No, but to see the nakedness of the land you are come.
13 And they said, your servants *are* twelve brethren, the sons of one man in the land of Canaan; and, behold, the youngest *is* this day with our father, and one *is* not.
14 And Joseph said unto them, that *is it* that I spoke unto you, saying, You *are* spies:
15 Hereby you will be proved: By the life of Pharaoh you will not go from here, except your youngest brother come here.
16 Send one of you, and let him fetch your brother, and you will be kept in prison, that your words may be proved, whether *there be* any truth in you: or else by the life of Pharaoh surely you *are* spies.
17 And he put them all together into ward three days.
18 And Joseph said unto them the third day, this do, and live; *for* I fear God:
19 If you *be* true *men*, let one of your brethren **is** bound in the house of your prison: go you, carry corn for the famine of your houses:
20 But bring your youngest brother unto me; so will your words be verified, and you will not die. And they did so.
21 And they said one to another, we *are* verily guilty concerning our brother, in that we saw the anguish of his soul, when he besought us, and we would not hear; therefore is this distress come upon us.
22 And Reuben answered them, saying, Spoke I not unto you, saying, Do not sin against the child; and you would not hear? Therefore, behold, also his blood is required.
23 And they knew not that Joseph understood *them*; for he spoke unto them by an interpreter.
24 And he turned himself about from them, and wept; and returned to them again, and communed with them, and took from them Simeon, and bound him before their eyes.
25 Then Joseph commanded to fill their sacks with corn, and to restore every man's money into his sack, and to give them provision for the way: and thus did he unto them.
26 And they laded their asses with the corn, and departed thence.
27 And as one of them opened his sack to give his ass provender in the inn, he espied his money; for, behold, it *was* in his sack's mouth.
28 And he said unto his brethren, my money is restored; and, lo, *it is* even in my sack: and their heart failed *them*, and they were afraid, saying one to another, what *is* this *that* God hath done unto us?
29 And they came unto Jacob their father unto the land of Canaan, and told him all that befell unto them; saying,
30 The man, *who is* the lord of the land, spoke roughly to us, and took us for spies of the country.
31 And we said unto him, we *are* true *men*; we are no spies:
32 We *are* twelve brethren, sons of our father; one *is* not, and the youngest *is* this day with our father in the land of Canaan.
33 And the man, the lord of the country, said unto us, hereby will I know that you *are* true *men*; leave one of your brethren *here* with me, and take *food for* the famine of your households, and be gone:
34 And bring your youngest brother unto me: then will I know that you *are* no spies, but *that* you *are* true *men*: so will I deliver you your brother, and you will traffic in the land.
35 And it came to pass as they emptied their sacks, that, behold, every man's bundle of money *was* in his sack: and when *both* they and their father saw the bundles of money, they were afraid.
36 And Jacob their father said unto them, me have you bereaved *of my children*: Joseph *is* not, and Simeon *is* not, and you will take Benjamin *away*: all these things are against me.
37 And Reuben spoke unto his father, saying, slay my two sons, if I bring him not to you: deliver him into my hand, and I will bring him to you again.
38 And he said, my son will not go down with you; for his brother is dead, and he is left alone: if mischief befall him by the way in the which you go, then will you bring down my gray hairs with sorrow to the grave.

CHAPTER 43

1 And the famine *was* sore in the land.
2 And it came to pass, when they had eaten up the corn which they had brought out of Egypt, their father said unto them, Go again, buy us a little food.
3 And Judah spoke unto him, saying, the man did solemnly protest unto us, saying, you will not see my face, except your brother *be* with you.
4 If you will send our brother with us, we will go down and buy you food:
5 But if you will not send *him*, we will not go down: for the man said unto us, you will not see my face, except your brother be with you.
6 And Israel said, wherefore dealt you *so* ill with me, *as* to tell the man whether you had yet a brother?
7 And they said, the man asked us straightly of our state, and of our kindred, saying, *is* your father yet alive? Have you *another* brother? And we told him according to the tenor of these words: could we certainly know that he would say, bring your brother down?
8 And Judah said unto Israel his father, Send the lad with me, and we will arise and go; that we may live, and not die, both we, and you, *and* also our little ones.
9 I will be surety for him; of my hand will you require him: if I bring him not unto you, and set him before you, then let me bear the blame for ever:
10 For except we had lingered, surely now we had returned this second time.
11 And their father Israel said unto them, if *it must be* so now, do this; take of the best fruits in the land in your vessels, and carry down the man a present, a little balm, and a little honey, spices, and myrrh, nuts, and almonds:

12 And take double money in your hand; and the money that was brought again in the mouth of your sacks, carry *it* again in your hand; peradventure it *was* an oversight:
13 Take also your brother, and arise, go again unto the man:
14 And God Almighty gives you mercy before the man, that he may send away your other brother, and Benjamin. If I be bereaved *of my children*, I am bereaved.
15 And the men took that present, and they took double money in their hand, and Benjamin; and rose up, and went down to Egypt, and stood before Joseph.
16 And when Joseph saw Benjamin with them, he said to the ruler of his house, Bring *these* men home, and slay, and make ready; for *these* men will dine with me at noon.
17 And the man did as Joseph bade; and the man brought the men into Joseph's house.
18 And the men were afraid, because they were brought into Joseph's house; and they said, Because of the money that was returned in our sacks at the first time are we brought in; that he may seek occasion against us, and fall upon us, and take us for bondmen, and our asses.
19 And they came near to the steward of Joseph's house, and they communed with him at the door of the house,
20 And said, O sir, we came indeed down at the first time to buy food:
21 And it came to pass, when we came to the inn, that we opened our sacks, and, behold, *every* man's money *was* in the mouth of his sack, our money in full weight: and we have brought it again in our hand.
22 And other money have we brought down in our hands to buy food: we cannot tell who put our money in our sacks.
23 And he said, Peace *be* to you, fear not: your God, and the God of your father, hath given you treasure in your sacks: I had your money. And he brought Simeon out unto them.
24 And the man brought the men into Joseph's house, and gave *them* water, and they washed their feet; and he gave their asses provender.
25 And they made ready the present against Joseph came at noon: for they heard that they should eat bread there.
26 And when Joseph came home, they brought him the present which *was* in their hand into the house, and bowed themselves to him to the earth.
27 And he asked them of *their* welfare, and said, *is* your father well, the old man of who you spoke? *Is* he yet alive?
28 And they answered, your servant our father *is* in good health, he *is* yet alive. And they bowed down their heads, and made obeisance.
29 And he lifted up his eyes, and saw his brother Benjamin, his mother's son, and said, *is* this your younger brother, of who you spoke unto me? And he said, God be gracious unto you, my son.
30 And Joseph made haste; for his bowels did yearn upon his brother: and he sought *where* to weep; and he entered into *his* chamber, and wept there.
31 And he washed his face, and went out, and refrained himself, and said, set on bread.
32 And they set on for him by himself, and for them by themselves, and for the Egyptians, which did eat with him, by themselves: because the Egyptians might not eat bread with the Hebrews; for that *is* an abomination unto the Egyptians.
33 And they sat before him, the firstborn according to his birthright, and the youngest according to his youth: and the men marveled one at another.
34 And he took *and sent* messes unto them from before him: but Benjamin's mess was five times so much as any of theirs. And they drank, and were merry with him.

CHAPTER 44

1 And he commanded the steward of his house, saying, Fill the men's sacks *with* food, as much as they can carry, and put every man's money in his sack's mouth.
2 And put my cup, the silver cup, in the sack's mouth of the youngest, and his corn money. And he did according to the word that Joseph had spoken.
3 As soon as the morning was light, the men were sent away, they and their asses.
4 *And* when they were gone out of the city, *and* not yet far off, Joseph said unto his steward, up, follow after the men; and when you do overtake them, say unto them, wherefore have you rewarded evil for good?
5 *Is* not this *it* in which my lord drink, and whereby indeed he divine? You have done evil in so doing.
6 And he overtook them, and he spoke unto them these same words.
7 And they said unto him, wherefore said my lord these words? God forbid that your servants should do according to this thing:
8 Behold, the money, which we found in our sacks' mouths, we brought again unto you out of the land of Canaan: how then should we steal out of your lord's house silver or gold?
9 With whomsoever of your servants it *is* found, both let him die, and we also will be my lord's bondmen.
10 And he said, now also *let* it *be* according unto your words: he with whom it is found will be my servant; and you will be blameless.
11 Then they speedily took down every man his sack to the ground, and opened every man his sack.
12 And he searched, *and* began at the eldest, and left at the youngest: and the cup was found in Benjamin's sack.
13 Then they rent their clothes, and laded every man his ass, and returned to the city.
14 And Judah and his brethren came to Joseph's house; for he *was* yet there: and they fell before him on the ground.
15 And Joseph said unto them, what deed *is* this that you have done? Wot you not that such a man as I can certainly divine?
16 And Judah said, what will we say unto my lord? What will we speak? Or how will we clear ourselves? God hath found out the iniquity of your servants: behold, we *are* my lord's servants, both we, and *he* also with whom the cup is found.
17 And he said, God forbid that I should do so: *but* the man in whose hand the cup is found, he will be my servant; and as for you, get you up in peace unto your father.
18 Then Judah came near unto him, and said, Oh my lord, let your servant, I pray you, speak a word in my lord's ears, and let not your anger burn against your servant: for you *are* even as Pharaoh.
19 My lord asked his servants, saying, Have you a father, or a brother?
20 And we said unto my lord, we have a father, an old man, and a child of his old age, a little one; and his brother is dead, and he alone is left of his mother, and his father love him.
21 And you said unto your servants, Bring him down unto me, that I may set mine eyes upon him.

22 And we said unto my lord, the lad cannot leave his father: for *if* he should leave his father, *his father* would die.
23 And you said unto your servants, except your youngest brother come down with you, you will see my face no more.
24 And it came to pass when we came up unto your servant my father, we told him the words of my lord.
25 And our father said, Go again, *and* buy us a little food.
26 And we said, we cannot go down: if our youngest brother be with us, then will we go down: for we may not see the man's face, except our youngest brother *be* with us.
27 And your servant my father said unto us, you know that my wife bare me two *sons*:
28 And the one went out from me, and I said, surely he is torn in pieces; and I saw him not since:
29 And if you take this also from me, and mischief befall him, you will bring down my gray hairs with sorrow to the grave.
30 Now therefore when I come to your servant my father, and the lad *is* not with us; seeing that his life is bound up in the lad's life;
31 It will come to pass, when he sees that the lad *is* not *with us*, that he will die: and your servants will bring down the gray hairs of your servant our father with sorrow to the grave.
32 For you servant became surety for the lad unto my father, saying, if I bring him not unto you, then I will bear the blame to my father forever.
33 Now therefore, I pray you, let your servant abide instead of the lad a bondman to my lord; and let the lad go up with his brethren.
34 For how will I go up to my father, and the lad is not with me? Lest peradventure I see the evil that will come on my father.

CHAPTER 45

1 Then Joseph could not refrain himself before all them that stood by him; and he cried, Cause every man to go out from me. And there stood no man with him, while Joseph made himself known unto his brethren.
2 And he wept aloud: and the Egyptians and the house of Pharaoh heard.
3 And Joseph said unto his brethren, I *am* Joseph; does my father yet live? And his brethren could not answer him; for they were troubled at his presence.
4 And Joseph said unto his brethren, Come near to me, I pray you. And they came near. And he said, I *am* Joseph your brother, whom you sold into Egypt.
5 Now therefore be not grieved, nor angry with yourselves, that you sold me hither: for God did send me before you to preserve life.
6 For these two years *hath* the famine *been* in the land: and yet *there are* five years, in the which *there will* neither *be* earing nor harvest.
7 And God sent me before you to preserve you a posterity in the earth, and to save your lives by a great deliverance.
8 So now *it was* not you *that* sent me here, but God: and he has made me a father to Pharaoh, and lord of his **entire** house, and a ruler throughout all the land of Egypt.
9 Haste you, and go up to my father, and say unto him, you said the son Joseph, God hath made me lord of all Egypt: come down unto me, tarry not:
10 And you will dwell in the land of Goshen, and you will be near unto me, you, and your children, and your children's children, and your flocks, and your herds, and all that you have:

11 And there will I nourish you; for yet *there are* five years of famine; lest you, and your household, and all that you have, come to poverty.
12 And, behold, your eyes see, and the eyes of my brother Benjamin, that *it is* my mouth that speak unto you.
13 And you will tell my father of all my glory in Egypt, and of all that you have seen; and you will haste and bring down my father hither.
14 And he fell upon his brother Benjamin's neck, and wept; and Benjamin wept upon his neck.
15 Moreover he kissed all his brethren, and wept upon them: and after that his brethren talked with him.
16 And the fame thereof was heard in Pharaoh's house, saying, Joseph's brethren are come: and it pleased Pharaoh well, and his servants.
17 And Pharaoh said unto Joseph, say unto your brethren, this do you; lade your beasts, and go, get you unto the land of Canaan;
18 And take your father and your households, and come unto me: and I will give you the good of the land of Egypt, and you will eat the fat of the land.
19 Now you are commanded, this do you; take you wagons out of the land of Egypt for your little ones, and for your wives, and bring your father, and come.
20 Also regard not your stuff; for the good of all the land of Egypt *is* yours.
21 And the children of Israel did so: and Joseph gave them wagons, according to the commandment of Pharaoh, and gave them provision for the way.
22 To all of them he gave each man changes of raiment; but to Benjamin he gave three hundred *pieces* of silver, and five changes of raiment.
23 And to his father he sent after this *manner;* ten asses laden with the good things of Egypt, and ten she asses laden with corn and bread and meat for his father by the way.
24 So he sent his brethren away, and they departed: and he said unto them, See that you fall not out by the way.
25 And they went up out of Egypt, and came into the land of Canaan unto Jacob their father,
26 And told him, saying, Joseph *is* yet alive, and he *is* governor over all the land of Egypt. And Jacob's heart fainted, for he believed them not.
27 And they told him all the words of Joseph, which he had said unto them: and when he saw the wagons which Joseph had sent to carry him, the spirit of Jacob their father revived:
28 And Israel said, *it is* enough; Joseph my son *is* yet alive: I will go and see him before I die.

CHAPTER 46

1 And Israel took his journey with all that he had, and came to Beer-sheba, and offered sacrifices unto the God of his father Isaac.
2 And God spoke unto Israel in the visions of the night, and said, Jacob, Jacob. And he said, here *am* I.
3 And he said, I *am* God, the God of your father: fear not to go down into Egypt; for I will there make of you a great nation:
4 I will go down with you into Egypt; and I will also surely bring you up *again*: and Joseph will put his hand upon your eyes.
5 And Jacob rose up from Beer-sheba: and the sons of Israel carried Jacob their father, and their little ones, and their wives, in the wagons which Pharaoh had sent to carry him.

6 And they took their cattle, and their goods, which they had gotten in the land of Canaan, and came into Egypt, Jacob, and all his seed with him:

7 His sons, and his sons' sons with him, his daughters, and his sons' daughters, and all his seed brought he with him into Egypt.

8 And these *are* the names of the children of Israel, which came into Egypt, Jacob and his sons: Reuben, Jacob's firstborn.

9 And the sons of Reuben; Hanoch, and Phallu, and Hezron, and Carmi.

10 And the sons of Simeon; Jemuel, and Jamin, and Ohad, and Jachin, and Zohar, and Shaul the son of a Canaanitish woman.

11 And the sons of Levi; Gershon, Kohath, and Merari.

12 And the sons of Judah; Er, and Onan, and Shelah, and Pharez, and Zerah: but Er and Onan died in the land of Canaan. And the sons of Pharez were Hezron and Hamul.

13 And the sons of Issachar; Tola, and Phuvah, and Job, and Shimron.

14 And the sons of Zebulun; Sered, and Elon, and Jahleel.

15 These are the sons of Leah, which she bare unto Jacob in Padan-aram, with his daughter Dinah: all the souls of his sons and his daughters *were* thirty and three.

16 And the sons of Gad; Ziphion, and Haggi, Shuni, and Ezbon, Eri, and Arodi, and Areli.

17 And the sons of Asher; Jimnah, and Ishuah, and Isui, and Beriah, and Serah their sister: and the sons of Beriah; Heber, and Malchiel.

18 These *are* the sons of Zilpah, whom Laban gave to Leah his daughter, and these she bare unto Jacob, *even* sixteen souls.

19 The sons of Rachel Jacob's wife; Joseph, and Benjamin.

20 And unto Joseph in the land of Egypt were born Manasseh and Ephraim, which Asenath the daughter of Poti-pherah priest of On bare unto him.

21 And the sons of Benjamin *were* Belah, and Becher, and Ashbel, Gera, and Naaman, Ehi, and Rosh, Muppim, and Huppim, and Ard.

22 These *are* the sons of Rachel, who were born to Jacob: all the souls *were* fourteen.

23 And the sons of Dan; Hushim.

24 And the sons of Naphtali; Jahzeel, and Guni, and Jezer, and Shillem.

25 These *are* the sons of Bilhah, which Laban gave unto Rachel his daughter, and she bares these unto Jacob: all the souls *were* seven.

26 All the souls that came with Jacob into Egypt, which came out of his loins, besides Jacob's sons' wives, all the souls *were* threescore and six;

27 And the sons of Joseph, which were born him in Egypt, *were* two souls: all the souls of the house of Jacob, which came into Egypt, *were* threescore and ten.

28 And he sent Judah before him unto Joseph, to direct his face unto Goshen; and they came into the land of Goshen.

29 And Joseph made ready his chariot, and went up to meet Israel his father, to Goshen, and presented himself unto him; and he fell on his neck, and wept on his neck a good while.

30 And Israel said unto Joseph, Now let me die, since I have seen your face, because you *are* yet alive.

31 And Joseph said unto his brethren, and unto his father's house, I will go up, and show Pharaoh, and say unto him, My brethren, and my father's house, which *were* in the land of Canaan, are come unto me;

32 And the men *are* shepherds, for their trade hath been to feed cattle; and they have brought their flocks, and their herds, and all that they have.

33 And it will come to pass, when Pharaoh will call you, and will say, what *is* your occupation?

34 That you will say, your servants' trade hath been about cattle from our youth even until now, both we, *and* also our fathers: that you may dwell in the land of Goshen; for every shepherd *is* an abomination unto the Egyptians.

CHAPTER 47

1 Then Joseph came and told Pharaoh, and said, my father and my brethren, and their flocks, and their herds, and all that they have, are come out of the land of Canaan; and, behold they *are* in the land of Goshen.

2 And he took some of his brethren, *even* five men, and presented them unto Pharaoh.

3 And Pharaoh said unto his brethren, what *is* your occupation? And they said unto Pharaoh, Your servants *are* shepherds, both we, *and* also our fathers.

4 They said moreover unto Pharaoh, For to sojourn in the land are we come; for your servants have no pasture for their flocks; for the famine *is* sore in the land of Canaan: now therefore, we pray you, let your servants dwell in the land of Goshen.

5 And Pharaoh spoke unto Joseph, saying, your father and your brethren are come unto you:

6 The land of Egypt *is* before you; in the best of the land make your father and brethren to dwell; in the land of Goshen let them dwell: and if you know *any* men of activity among them, then make them rulers over my cattle.

7 And Joseph brought in Jacob his father, and set him before Pharaoh: and Jacob blessed Pharaoh.

8 And Pharaoh said unto Jacob, How old *are* you?

9 And Jacob said unto Pharaoh, The days of the years of my pilgrimage *are* an hundred and thirty years: few and evil have the days of the years of my life been, and have not attained unto the days of the years of the life of my fathers in the days of their pilgrimage.

10 And Jacob blessed Pharaoh, and went out from before Pharaoh.

11 And Joseph placed his father and his brethren, and gave them a possession in the land of Egypt, in the best of the land, in the land of Rameses, as Pharaoh had commanded.

12 And Joseph nourished his father, and his brethren, and his **entire** father's household, with bread, according to *their* families.

13 And *there was* no bread in all the land; for the famine *was* very sore, so that the land of Egypt and *all* the land of Canaan fainted by reason of the famine.

14 And Joseph gathered up all the money that was found in the land of Egypt, and in the land of Canaan, for the corn which they bought: and Joseph brought the money into Pharaoh's house.

15 And when money failed in the land of Egypt, and in the land of Canaan, all the Egyptians came unto Joseph, and said, Give us bread: for why should we die in your presence? for the money failed.

16 And Joseph said, Give your cattle; and I will give you for your cattle, if money fail.

17 And they brought their cattle unto Joseph: and Joseph gave them bread *in exchange* for horses, and for the flocks, and for the

cattle of the herds, and for the asses: and he fed them with bread for all their cattle for that year.

18 When that year was ended, they came unto him the second year, and said unto him, we will not hide *it* from my lord, how that our money is spent; my lord also hath our herds of cattle; there is not ought left in the sight of my lord, but our bodies, and our lands:
19 Wherefore will we die before your eyes, both we and our land? Buy us and our land for bread, and we and our land will be servants unto Pharaoh: and give *us* seed, that we may live, and not die, that the land be not desolate.
20 And Joseph bought all the land of Egypt for Pharaoh; for the Egyptians sold every man his field, because the famine prevailed over them: so the land became Pharaoh's.
21 And as for the people, he removed them to cities from *one* end of the borders of Egypt even to the *other* end thereof.
22 Only the land of the priests bought him not; for the priests had a portion *assigned them* of Pharaoh, and did eat their portion which Pharaoh gave them: wherefore they sold not their lands.
23 Then Joseph said unto the people, Behold, I have bought you this day and your land for Pharaoh: lo, *here is* seed for you, and you will sow the land.
24 And it will come to pass in the increase, that you will give the fifth *part* unto Pharaoh, and four parts will be your own, for seed of the field, and for your food, and for them of your households, and for food for your little ones.
25 And they said, you have saved our lives: let us find grace in the sight of my lord, and we will be Pharaoh's servants.
26 And Joseph made it a law over the land of Egypt unto this day, *that* Pharaoh should have the fifth *part*; except the land of the priests only, *which* became not Pharaoh's.
27 And Israel dwelt in the land of Egypt, in the country of Goshen; and they had possessions therein, and grew, and multiplied exceedingly.
28 And Jacob lived in the land of Egypt seventeen years: so the whole age of Jacob was an hundred forty and seven years.
29 And the time drew nigh that Israel must die: and he called his son Joseph, and said unto him, If now I have found grace in your sight, put, I pray you, your hand under my thigh, and deal kindly and truly with me; bury me not, I pray you, in Egypt:
30 But I will lie with my fathers, and you will carry me out of Egypt, and bury me in their burying place. And he said, I will do as you have said.
31 And he said, Swear unto me. And he swore unto him. And Israel bowed himself upon the bed's head.

CHAPTER 48

1 And it came to pass after these things, that *one* told Joseph, Behold, your father *is* sick: and he took with him his two sons, Manasseh and Ephraim.
2 And *one* told Jacob, and said, Behold, your son Joseph comes unto you: and Israel strengthened himself, and sat upon the bed.
3 And Jacob said unto Joseph, God Almighty appeared unto me at Luz in the land of Canaan, and blessed me,
4 And said unto me, Behold, I will make you fruitful, and multiply you, and I will make of you a multitude of people; and will give this land to your seed after you *for* an everlasting possession.
5 And now your two sons, Ephraim and Manasseh, which were born unto you in the land of Egypt before I came unto you into Egypt, *are* mine; as Reuben and Simeon, they will be mine.

6 And your issue, which you begettest after them, will be yours, *and* will be called after the name of their brethren in their inheritance.
7 And as for me, when I came from Padan, Rachel died by me in the land of Canaan in the way, when yet *there was* but a little way to come unto Ephrath: and I buried her there in the way of Ephrath; the same *is* Beth-lehem.
8 And Israel beheld Joseph's sons, and said, who *are* these?
9 And Joseph said unto his father, they *are* my sons, whom God hath given me in this *place*. And he said, bring them, I pray you, unto me, and I will bless them.
10 Now the eyes of Israel were dim for age, *so that* he could not see. And he brought them near unto him; and he kissed them, and embraced them.
11 And Israel said unto Joseph, I had not thought to see your face: and, lo, God have showed me also your seed.
12 And Joseph brought them out from between his knees, and he bowed himself with his face to the earth.
13 And Joseph took them both, Ephraim in his right hand toward Israel's left hand, and Manasseh in his left hand toward Israel's right hand, and brought *them* near unto him.
14 And Israel stretched out his right hand, and laid *it* upon Ephraim's head, who *was* the younger, and his left hand upon Manasseh's head, guiding his hands wittingly; for Manasseh *was* the firstborn.
15 And he blessed Joseph, and said, God, before whom my fathers Abraham and Isaac did walk, the God which fed me all my life long unto this day,
16 The Angel which redeemed me from all evil, bless the lads; and let my name be named on them, and the name of my father's Abraham and Isaac; and let them grow into a multitude in the midst of the earth.
17 And when Joseph saw that his father laid his right hand upon the head of Ephraim, it displeased him: and he held up his father's hand, to remove it from Ephraim's head unto Manasseh's head.
18 And Joseph said unto his father, not so, my father: for this *is* the firstborn; put your right hand upon his head.
19 And his father refused, and said, I know *it*, my son, I know *it*: he also will become a people, and he also will be great: but truly his younger brother will be greater than he, and his seed will become a multitude of nations.
20 And he blessed them that day, saying, in you will Israel bless, saying, God make you as Ephraim and as Manasseh: and he set Ephraim before Manasseh.
21 And Israel said unto Joseph, Behold, I die: but God will be with you, and bring you again unto the land of your fathers.
22 Moreover I have given to you one portion above your brethren, which I took out of the hand of the Amorite with my sword and with my bow.

CHAPTER 49

1 And Jacob called unto his sons, and said, Gather yourselves together, that I may tell you *that* which will befall you in the last days.
2 Gather yourselves together, and hear, you sons of Jacob; and hearken unto Israel your father.
3 Reuben, you *are* my firstborn, my might, and the beginning of my strength, the excellency of dignity, and the excellency of power:
4 Unstable as water, you will not excel; because you went up to your father's bed; then defiled you *it*: he went up to my couch.

5 Simeon and Levi *are* brethren; instruments of cruelty *are in* their habitations.

6 O my soul, come not you into their secret; unto their assembly, mine honor, be not you united: for in their anger they slew a man, and in their self will they digged down a wall.

7 Cursed *be* their anger, for *it was* fierce; and their wrath, for it was cruel: I will divide them in Jacob, and scatter them in Israel.

8 Judah, you *are he* whom your brethren will praise: your hand *will be* in the neck of your enemies; your father's children will bow down before you.

9 Judah *is* a lion's whelp: from the prey, my son, you are gone up: he stooped down, he couched as a lion, and as an old lion; who will rouse him up?

10 The sceptre will not depart from Judah, or a lawgiver from between his feet, until Shiloh come; and unto him *will* the gathering of the people *be*.

11 Binding his foal unto the vine, and his ass's colt unto the choice vine; he washed his garments in wine, and his clothes in the blood of grapes:

12 His eyes *will be* red with wine, and his teeth white with milk.

13 Zebulun will dwell at the haven of the sea; and he *will be* for a haven of ships; and his border *will be* unto Zidon.

14 Issachar *is* a strong ass couching down between two burdens:

15 And he saw that rest *was* good, and the land that *it was* pleasant; and bowed his shoulder to bear, and became a servant unto tribute.

16 Dan will judge his people, as one of the tribes of Israel.

17 Dan will be a serpent by the way, an adder in the path, that bites the horse heels, so that his rider will fall backward.

18 I have waited for your salvation, O LORD.

19 Gad, a troop will overcome him: but he will overcome at the last.

20 Out of Asher his bread *will be* fat, and he will yield royal dainties.

21 Naphtali *is* a hind let loose: he give goodly words.

22 Joseph *is* a fruitful bough, *even* a fruitful bough by a well; *whose* branches run over the wall:

23 The archers have sorely grieved him, and shot *at him*, and hated him:

24 But his bow abode in strength, and the arms of his hands were made strong by the hands of the mighty *God* of Jacob; (from thence *is* the shepherd, the stone of Israel:)

25 *Even* by the God of your father, who will help you; and by the Almighty, who will bless you with blessings of heaven above, blessings of the deep that lie under, blessings of the breasts, and of the womb:

26 The blessings of your father have prevailed above the blessings of my progenitors unto the utmost bound of the everlasting hills: they will be on the head of Joseph, and on the crown of the head of him that was separate from his brethren.

27 Benjamin will ravin *as* a wolf: in the morning he will devour the prey, and at night he will divide the spoil.

28 All these *are* the twelve tribes of Israel: and this *is it* that their father spoke unto them, and blessed them; every one according to his blessing he blessed them.

29 And he charged them, and said unto them, I am to be gathered unto my people: bury me with my fathers in the cave that *is* in the field of Ephron the Hittite,

30 In the cave that *is* in the field of Machpelah, which *is* before Mamre, in the land of Canaan, which Abraham bought with the field of Ephron the Hittite for a possession of a burying place.

31 There they buried Abraham and Sarah his wife; there they buried Isaac and Rebekah his wife; and there I buried Leah.

32 The purchase of the field and of the cave that *is* therein *was* from the children of Heth.

33 And when Jacob had made an end of commanding his sons, he gathered up his feet into the bed, and yielded up the ghost, and was gathered unto his people.

CHAPTER 50

1 And Joseph fell upon his father's face, and wept upon him, and kissed him.

2 And Joseph commanded his servants the physicians to embalm his father: and the physicians embalmed Israel.

3 And forty days were fulfilled for him; for so are fulfilled the days of those which are embalmed: and the Egyptians mourned for him threescore and ten days.

4 And when the days of his mourning were past, Joseph spoke unto the house of Pharaoh, saying, If now I have found grace in your eyes, speak, I pray you, in the ears of Pharaoh, saying,

5 My father made me swear, saying, Lo, I die: in my grave which I have digged for me in the land of Canaan, there will you bury me. Now therefore let me go up, I pray you, and bury my father, and I will come again.

6 And Pharaoh said, Go up, and bury your father, according as he made you swear.

7 And Joseph went up to bury his father: and with him went up all the servants of Pharaoh, the elders of his house, and all the elders of the land of Egypt,

8 And all the house of Joseph, and his brethren, and his father's house: only their little ones, and their flocks, and their herds, they left in the land of Goshen.

9 And there went up with him both chariots and horsemen: and it was a very great company.

10 And they came to the threshing floor of Atad, which *is* beyond Jordan, and there they mourned with a great and very sore lamentation: and he made a mourning for his father seven days.

11 And when the inhabitants of the land, the Canaanites, saw the mourning in the floor of Atad, they said, this *is* a grievous mourning to the Egyptians: wherefore the name of it was called Abel-mizraim, which *is* beyond Jordan.

12 And his sons did unto him according as he commanded them:

13 For his sons carried him into the land of Canaan, and buried him in the cave of the field of Machpelah, which Abraham bought with the field for a possession of a burying place of Ephron the Hittite, before Mamre.

14 And Joseph returned into Egypt, he, and his brethren, and all that went up with him to bury his father, after he had buried his father.

15 And when Joseph's brethren saw that their father was dead, they said, Joseph will peradventure hate us, and will certainly requite us all the evil which we did unto him.

16 And they sent a messenger unto Joseph, saying, your father did command before he died, saying,

17 So will you say unto Joseph, Forgive, I pray you now, the trespass of your brethren, and their sin; for they did unto you evil: and now, we pray you, forgive the trespass of the servants of the God of your father. And Joseph wept when they spoke unto him.

18 And his brethren also went and fell down before his face; and they said, Behold, we *be* your servants.

19 And Joseph said unto them, Fear not: for *am* I in the place of God?
20 But as for you, you thought evil against me; *but* God meant it unto good, to bring to pass, as *it is* this day, to save much people alive.
21 Now therefore fear you not: I will nourish you, and your little ones. And he comforted them, and spoke kindly unto them.
22 And Joseph dwelt in Egypt, he, and his father's house: and Joseph lived an hundred and ten years.
23 And Joseph saw Ephraim's children of the third *generation*: the children also of Machir the son of Manasseh were brought up upon Joseph's knees.
24 And Joseph said unto his brethren, I die: and God will surely visit you, and bring you out of this land unto the land which he swore to Abraham, to Isaac, and to Jacob.
25 And Joseph took an oath of the children of Israel, saying, God will surely visit you, and you will carry up my bones from hence.
26 So Joseph died, *being* an hundred and ten years old: and they embalmed him, and he was put in a coffin in Egypt.

EXODUS

CHAPTER 1

1 Now these *are* the names of the children of Israel, which came into Egypt; every man and his household came with Jacob.
2 Reuben, Simeon, Levi, and Judah,
3 Issachar, Zebulun, and Benjamin,
4 Dan, and Naphtali, Gad, and Asher.
5 And all the souls that came out of the loins of Jacob were seventy souls: for Joseph was in Egypt *already*.
6 And Joseph died, and all his brethren, and all that generation.
7 And the children of Israel were fruitful, and increased abundantly, and multiplied, and waxed exceeding mighty; and the land was filled with them.
8 Now there arose up a new king over Egypt, which knew not Joseph.
9 And he said unto his people, Behold, the people of the children of Israel *are* more and mightier than we:
10 Come on, let us deal wisely with them; lest they multiply, and it come to pass, that, when there fall out any war, they join also unto our enemies, and fight against us, and *so* get them up out of the land.
11 Therefore they did set over them taskmasters to afflict them with their burdens. And they built for Pharaoh treasure cities, Pithom and Raamses.
12 But the more they afflicted them, the more they multiplied and grew. And they were grieved because of the children of Israel.
13 And the Egyptians made the children of Israel to serve with rigor:
14 And they made their lives bitter with hard bondage, in mortar, and in brick, and in all manner of service in the field: all their service, wherein they made them serve, *was* with rigor.
15 And the king of Egypt spoke to the Hebrew midwives, of which the name of the one *was* Shiphrah, and the name of the other Puah:
16 And he said, when you do the office of a midwife to the Hebrew women, and sees *them* upon the stools; if it *be* a son, then you will kill him: but if it *be* a daughter, then she will live.
17 But the midwives feared God, and did not as the king of Egypt commanded them, but saved the men children alive.
18 And the king of Egypt called for the midwives, and said unto them, Why have you done this thing, and have saved the men children alive?
19 And the midwives said unto Pharaoh, because the Hebrew women *are* not as the Egyptian women; for they *are* lively, and are delivered ere the midwives come in unto them.
20 Therefore God dealt well with the midwives: and the people multiplied, and waxed very mighty.
21 And it came to pass, because the midwives feared God, that he made them houses.
22 And Pharaoh charged all his people, saying, every son that is born you will cast into the river, and every daughter you will save alive.

CHAPTER 2

1 And there went a man of the house of Levi, and took *to wife* a daughter of Levi.
2 And the women conceived, and bare a son: and when she saw him that he *was a* goodly *child*, she hid him three months.
3 And when she could no longer hide him, she took for him an ark of bulrushes, and daubed it with slime and with pitch, and put the child therein; and she laid *it* in the flags by the river's brink.
4 And his sister stood afar off, to wit what would be done to him.
5 And the daughter of Pharaoh came down to wash *herself* at the river; and her maidens walked along by the river's side; and when she saw the ark among the flags, she sent her maid to fetch it.
6 And when she had opened *it*, she saw the child: and, behold, the babe wept. And she had compassion on him, and said, this *is one* of the Hebrews' children.
7 Then said his sister to Pharaoh's daughter, Will I go and call to you a nurse of the Hebrew women, that she may nurse the child for you?
8 And Pharaoh's daughter said to her, Go. And the maid went and called the child's mother.
9 And Pharaoh's daughter said unto her, Take this child away, and nurse it for me, and I will give *you* the wages. And the woman took the child, and nursed it.
10 And the child grew, and she brought him unto Pharaoh's daughter, and he became her son. And she called his name Moses[1]: and she said, because I drew him out of the water.
11 ¶ And it came to pass in those days, when Moses was grown, that he went out unto his brethren, and looked on their burdens: and he spied an Egyptian smiting an Hebrew, one of his brethren.
12 And he looked this way and that way, and when he saw that *there was* no man, he slew the Egyptian, and hid him in the sand.
13 And when he went out the second day, behold, two men of the Hebrews strove together: and he said to him that did the wrong, wherefore smite you your fellow?
14 And he said, who made you a prince and a judge over us? Intended you to kill me, as you killed the Egyptian? And Moses feared, and said, surely this thing is known.
15 Now when Pharaoh heard this thing, he sought to slay Moses. But Moses fled from the face of Pharaoh, and dwelt in the land of Midian: and he sat down by a well.
16 Now the priest of Midian had seven daughters: and they came and drew *water*, and filled the troughs to water their father's flock.
17 And the shepherds came and drove them away: but Moses stood up and helped them, and watered their flock.
18 And when they came to Reuel their father, he said, how *is it that* you are come so soon to day?
19 And they said, An Egyptian delivered us out of the hand of the shepherds, and also drew *water* enough for us, and watered the flock.
20 And he said unto his daughters, and where *is* he? Why *is it that* you have left the man? Call him, that he may eat bread.
21 And Moses was content to dwell with the man: and he gave Moses Zipporah his daughter.
22 And she bares *him* a son, and he called his name Gershom: for he said, I have been a stranger in a strange land.
23 And it came to pass in process of time, that the king of Egypt died: and the children of Israel sighed by reason of the bondage, and they cried, and their cry came up unto God by reason of the bondage.
24 And God heard their groaning, and God remembered his covenant with Abraham, with Isaac, and with Jacob.

---

[1] Moses- *môsheh*, mo-sheh'; *drawing out* (out of the water), that is, rescued [Strgs#4872].

25 And God looked upon the children of Israel, and God had respect unto *them*.

CHAPTER 3

1 Now Moses kept the flock of Jethro his father in law, the priest of Midian: and he led the flock to the backside of the desert, and came to the mountain of God, *even* to Horeb.
2 And the angel of the LORD appeared unto him in a flame of fire out of the midst of a bush: and he looked, and, beheld, the bush burned with fire, and the bush *was* not consumed.
3 And Moses said, I will now turn aside, and see this great sight[1], why the bush is not burnt.
4 And when the LORD saw that he turned aside to see, God called unto him out of the midst of the bush, and said, Moses, Moses. And he said, here *am* I.
5 And he said, Draw not near here: put off your shoes from off your feet, for the place whereon you stand *is* holy ground.
6 Moreover he said, I *am* the God of your father, the God of Abraham, the God of Isaac, and the God of Jacob. And Moses hid his face; for he was afraid to look upon God.
7 And the LORD said, I have surely seen the affliction of my people which *are* in Egypt, and have heard their cry by reason of their taskmasters; for I know their sorrows;
8 And I am come down to deliver them out of the hand of the Egyptians, and to bring them up out of that land unto a good land and a large, unto a land flowing with milk and honey; unto the place of the Canaanites, and the Hittites, and the Amorites, and the Perizzites, and the Hivites, and the Jebusites.
9 Now therefore, behold, the cry of the children of Israel is come unto me: and I have also seen the oppression wherewith the Egyptians oppress them.
10 Come now therefore, and I will send you unto Pharaoh, that you may bring forth my people the children of Israel out of Egypt.
11 And Moses said unto God, Who *am* I, that I should go unto Pharaoh, and that I should bring forth the children of Israel out of Egypt?
12 And he said, certainly I will be with you; and this will *be* a token unto you, that I have sent you: When you have brought forth the people out of Egypt, you will serve[2] God upon this mountain.
13 And Moses said unto God, Behold, *when* I come unto the children of Israel, and will say unto them, The God of your fathers have sent me unto you; and they will say to me, what *is* his name? What will I say unto them?
14 And God said unto Moses, I AM THAT I AM: and he said, This will you say unto the children of Israel, I AM have sent me unto you.
15 And God said moreover unto Moses, This will you say unto the children of Israel, The LORD God of your fathers, the God of Abraham, the God of Isaac, and the God of Jacob, hath sent me unto you: this *is* my name for ever, and this *is* my memorial unto all generations.
16 Go, and gather the elders of Israel together, and say unto them, The LORD God of your fathers, the God of Abraham, of Isaac, and of Jacob, appeared unto me, saying, I have surely visited you, and *seen* that which is done to you in Egypt:
17 And I have said, I will bring you up out of the affliction of Egypt unto the land of the Canaanites, and the Hittites, and the Amorites, and the Perizzites, and the Hivites, unto the Jebusites, unto a land flowing with milk and honey.
18 And they will hearken to your voice: and you will come, you and the elders of Israel, unto the king of Egypt, and you will say unto him, The LORD God of the Hebrews have met with us: and now let us go, we beseech you, three days' journey into the wilderness, that we may sacrifice to the LORD our God.
19 And I am sure that the king of Egypt will not let you go, no, not by a mighty hand.
20 And I will stretch out my hand, and smite Egypt with all my wonders which I will do in the midst thereof: and after that he will let you go.
21 And I will give this people favor in the sight of the Egyptians: and it will come to pass, that, when you go, you will not go empty:
22 But every woman will borrow of her neighbor, and of her that sojourn in her house, jewels of silver, and jewels of gold, and raiment: and you will put *them* upon your sons, and upon your daughters; and you will spoil the Egyptians.

CHAPTER 4

1 And Moses answered and said, but, behold, they will not believe me, or hearken unto my voice: for they will say, The LORD hath not appeared unto you.
2 And the LORD said unto him, what *is* that in your hand? And he said, a rod[3].
3 [And he said, Cast it on the ground. And he cast it on the ground, and it became a serpent; and Moses fled from before it.][4]
4 And the LORD said unto Moses, Put forth your hand, and take it by the tail[5]. And he put forth his hand, and caught[6] it, and it became a rod in his hand:
5 That they may believe that the LORD God of their fathers, the God of Abraham, the God of Isaac, and the God of Jacob, have appeared unto you.
6 And the LORD said furthermore unto him, Put now your hand into your bosom. And he put his hand into his bosom: and when he took it out, behold, his hand *was* leprous as snow.
7 And he said, put your hand into your bosom again. And he put his hand into your bosom again; and plucked it out of his bosom, and, behold, it was turned again as his *other* flesh.
8 And it will come to pass, if they will not believe you neither hearken to the voice of the first sign, that they will believe the voice of the latter sign.
9 And it will come to pass, if they will not believe also these two signs, neither hearken unto your voice, that you will take of the water of the river, and pour *it* upon the dry *land*: and the water which you take out of the river will become blood upon the dry *land*.
10 And Moses said unto the LORD, O my Lord, I *am* not eloquent, neither heretofore, nor since you have spoken unto your servant: but I *am* [slow of speech][7], and of a [slow tongue][8].

---

[1] *sight* – a *view*, *appearance*, a *shape*, *comeliness*, a *vision* [Strgs#4758]. Root word râ'âh meaning to *see* [Strgs#7200].
[2] *serve* – to work, to till, enslave [Strgs#5647]
[3] rod – a *branch* (as *extending*), a *tribe* [Strgs#4294]
[4] Compare **John 3:14**
[5] *tail* – the original sense of *flapping* [Strgs#2180]. Derives from *zânab* meaning *to cut off*, to wag, to curtail, cut off the rear, smite the hindmost [Strgs#2179]
[6] *caught* – to fasten upon; hence to seize, be strong (figuratively courageous, causatively strengthen, cure, help, repair, fortify), obstinate; to bind, restrain conquer [Strgs#2388]
[7] *slow of speech* – lit. heavy mouth [Strgs#3515 + 6310]
[8] *slow of tongue* – lit. heavy tongue [Strgs#3515+ 3956]

11 And the LORD said unto him, who has made man's mouth? Or who make the dumb, or deaf, or the seeing, or the blind? Have not I the LORD?
12 Now therefore go, and I will be with your mouth, and teach you what you will say.
13 And he said, O my Lord, send, I pray you, by the hand *of him whom* you will send.
14 And the anger of the LORD was kindled against Moses, and he said, *is* not Aaron the Levite your brother? I know that he can speak well. And also, behold, he comes forth to meet you: and when he sees you, he will be glad in his heart.
15 And you will speak unto him, and put words in his mouth: and I will be with your mouth, and with his mouth, and will teach you what you will do.
16 And he will be your spokesman unto the people: and he will be, *even* he will be to you instead of a mouth, and you will be to him instead of God.
17 And you will take this rod in your hand, wherewith you will do signs.
18 And Moses went and returned to Jethro his father in law, and said unto him, Let me go, I pray you, and return unto my brethren which *are* in Egypt, and see whether they be yet alive. And Jethro said to Moses, Go in peace.
19 [And the LORD said unto Moses in Midian, Go, return into Egypt: for all the men are dead which sought your life.]¹
20 And Moses took his wife and his sons, and set them upon an ass, and he returned to the land of Egypt: and Moses took the [rod of God]² in his hand.
21 And the LORD said unto Moses, When you go to return into Egypt, see that you do all those wonders before Pharaoh, which I have put in your hand: but I will harden his heart, that he will not let the people go.
22 [And you will say unto Pharaoh, This said the LORD, Israel *is* my son, *even* my firstborn:]³
23 And I say unto you, let my son go, that he may serve me: and if you refuse to let him go, behold, I will slay your son, *even* your firstborn.
24 And it came to pass by the way in the inn, that the LORD met him, and sought to kill him.
25 Then Zipporah took a sharp stone, and cut off the foreskin of her son, and cast *it* at his feet, and said, surely a bloody husband *are* you to me.
26 So he let him go: then she said, a bloody husband *you are*, because of the circumcision.
27 And the LORD said to Aaron, Go into the wilderness to meet Moses. And he went, and met him in the mount of God, and kissed him.
28 And Moses told Aaron all the words of the LORD who had sent him, and all the signs which he had commanded him.
29 And Moses and Aaron went and gathered together all the elders of the children of Israel:
30 And Aaron spoke all the words which the LORD had spoken unto Moses, and did the signs in the sight of the people.
31 And the people believed: and when they heard that the LORD had visited the children of Israel, and that he had looked upon their affliction, then they bowed their heads and worshipped.

---

¹ Compare **Matt. 2:20**
² Lit. – tribe of God . Rod = tribe [Stgrs#4294].
³ Compare **Rev. 12**

CHAPTER 5

1 And afterward Moses and Aaron went in, and told Pharaoh, This said the LORD God of Israel, Let my people go, that they may hold a feast unto me in the wilderness.
2 And Pharaoh said, who *is* the LORD, that I should obey his voice to let Israel go? I know not the LORD, neither will I let Israel go.
3 And they said, The God of the Hebrews hath met with us: let us go, we pray you, three days' journey into the desert, and sacrifice unto the LORD our God; lest he fall upon us with pestilence, or with the sword.
4 And the king of Egypt said unto them, wherefore do you, Moses and Aaron, let the people from their works? Get you unto your burdens.
5 And Pharaoh said, Behold, the people of the land now *are* many, and you make them rest from their burdens.
6 And Pharaoh commanded the same day the taskmasters of the people, and their officers, saying,
7 You will **no longer** give the people straw⁴ to make brick, as heretofore: let them go and gather straw for themselves.
8 And the tale of the bricks, which they did make heretofore, you will lay upon them; you will not diminish *ought* thereof: for they **are** idle; therefore they cry, saying, Let us go *and* sacrifice to our God.
9 Let there more work be laid upon the men, that they may labor therein; and let them not regard vain⁵ words.
10 And the taskmasters of the people went out, and their officers, and they spoke to the people, saying, this said Pharaoh, I will not give you straw.
11 Go you, get you straw where you can find it: yet not ought of your work will be diminished.
12 So the people were scattered abroad throughout all the land of Egypt to gather stubble instead of straw.
13 And the taskmasters hasted *them*, saying, Fulfill your works, *your* daily tasks, as when there was straw.
14 And the officers of the children of Israel, which Pharaoh's taskmasters had set over them, were beaten, *and* demanded, Wherefore have you not fulfilled your task in making brick both yesterday and today, as heretofore?
15 Then the officers of the children of Israel came and cried unto Pharaoh, saying, wherefore deal you this with your servants?
16 There is no straw given unto your servants, and they say to us, Make brick: and, behold, your servants *are* beaten; but the fault *is* in your own people.
17 But he said, you *are* idle, *you are* idle: therefore you say, Let us go *and* do sacrifice to the LORD.
18 Go therefore now, *and* work; for there will no straw be given you, yet will you deliver the tale of bricks.
19 And the officers of the children of Israel did see *that* they *were* in evil *case*, after it was said, you will not minish ought from your bricks of your daily task.
20 And they met Moses and Aaron, who stood in the way, as they came forth from Pharaoh:
21 And they said unto them, The LORD look upon you, and judge; because you have made our savor to be abhorred in the eyes of Pharaoh, and in the eyes of his servants, to put a sword in their hand to slay us.

---

⁴ *straw* – properly material [Strgs#1129]. Root meaning to build, to obtain children [Strgs#1129]
⁵ *vain* – an untruth, by implication a sham [Strgs#8267]

22 And Moses returned unto the LORD, and said, Lord, wherefore have you so evil entreated this people? Why is it that you have sent me?

23 For since I came to Pharaoh to speak in your name, he **has** done evil to this people; neither have you delivered your people at all.

CHAPTER 6

1 [Then the LORD said unto Moses, Now will you see what I will do to Pharaoh: for with a strong hand with he let them go, and with a strong hand will he drive them out of his land.][1]

2 And God spoke unto Moses, and said unto him, I am the LORD[2]:

3 And I appeared unto Abraham, unto Isaac, and unto Jacob, by the name of God Almighty, but by my name JEHOVAH[3] was I not known to them.

4 And I have also established[4] my covenant with them, to give them the land of Canaan, the land of their pilgrimage, wherein they were strangers.

5 And I have also heard the groaning of the children of Israel, whom the Egyptians keep in bondage; and I have remembered my covenant.

6 Wherefore say unto the children of Israel, I am the LORD, and I will bring you out from under the burdens of the Egyptians, and I will rid[5] you out of their bondage, and I will redeem you with a stretched out arm, and with great judgments:

7 And I will take you to me for a people, and I will be to you a God: and you will know that I am the LORD your God, which bring you out from under the burdens of the Egyptians.

8 [And I will bring you in unto the land, concerning **that** which I did swear[6] to give it to Abraham, to Isaac, and to Jacob; and I will give it you for an heritage: I am the LORD.][7]

9 And Moses spoke so unto the children of Israel: but they hearkened not unto Moses for anguish[8] of spirit, and for cruel bondage.

10 And the LORD spoke unto Moses, saying,

11 [Go in, speak unto Pharaoh King of Egypt, that he let the children of Israel go out of his land.][9]

12 And Moses spoke before the LORD, saying, Behold, the children of Israel have not hearkened unto me; how then will Pharaoh hear me, who am of uncircumcised[10] lips?

13 And the LORD spoke unto Moses and unto Aaron, and gave them a charge unto the children of Israel, and unto Pharaoh king of Egypt, to bring the children of Israel out of the land of Egypt.

14 These **are** the heads of their fathers' houses: The sons of Reuben the firstborn of Israel; Hanoch, and Pallu, Hezron, and Carmi: these be the families of Reuben.

15 And the sons of Simeon; Jemuel, and Jamin, and Ohad, and Jachin, and Zohar, and Shaul the son of a Canaanitish woman: these are the families of Simeon.

16 And these are the names of the sons of Levi according to their generations; Gershon, and Kohath, and Merari: and the years of the life of Levi were an hundred thirty and seven years.

17 The sons of Gershon; Libni, and Shimi, according to their families.

18 And the sons of Kohath; Amram, and Izhar, and Hebron, and Uzziel: and the years of the life of Kohath were an hundred thirty and three years.

19 And the sons of Merari; Mahali and Mushi: these are the families of Levi according to their generations.

20 And Amram took him Jochebed his father's sister to wife; and she bares him Aaron and Moses: and the years of the life of Amram were an hundred and thirty and seven years.

21 And the sons of Izhar; Korah, and Nepheg, and Zichri.

22 And the sons of Uzziel; Mishael, and Elzaphan, and Zithri.

23 And Aaron took him Elisheba, daughter of Amminadab[11], sister of Naashon[12], to wife; and she bares him Nadab, and Abihu, Eleazar, and Ithamar.

24 And the sons of Korah; Assir, and Elkanah, and Abiasaph: these are the families of the Korhites.

25 And Eleazar Aaron's son took him one of the daughters of Putiel to wife; and she bares him Phinehas: these are the heads of the fathers of the Levites according to their families.

26 These are that Aaron and Moses, to whom the LORD said, Bring out the children of Israel from the land of Egypt according to their armies.

27 These are they which spoke to Pharaoh king of Egypt to bring out the children of Israel from Egypt: these are that Moses and Aaron.

28 And it came to pass on the day when the LORD spoke unto Moses in the land of Egypt,

29 That the LORD spoke unto Moses, saying, I am the LORD: speak you unto Pharaoh king of Egypt all that I say unto you.

30 And Moses said before the LORD, Behold, I am of uncircumcised lips, and how will Pharaoh hearken unto me?

CHAPTER 7

1 And the LORD said unto Moses, See, I have made you a god to Pharaoh: and Aaron your brother will be your prophet.

2 You will speak all that I command you: and Aaron your brother will speak unto Pharaoh, that he sends the children of Israel out of his land.

3 And I will harden Pharaoh's heart, and multiply my signs and my wonders in the land of Egypt.

4 But Pharaoh will not hearken unto you, that I may lay[13] my hand upon Egypt, and bring forth mine armies, and my people the children of Israel, out of the land of Egypt by great judgments[14].

5 And the Egyptians will know that I am the LORD, when I stretch forth mine hand upon Egypt, and bring out the children of Israel from among them.

---

[1] see Exo. 8:8.
[2] Lit. – Jehovah meaning the self Existing one, self Existent or eternal. [Strgs#3068].
[3] [Strgs#3068]
[4] established – to rise, to rise again, resurrection.[Strgs#6965]
[5] rid – to snatch away [Strgs#5337].
[6] swear – comes from two Hebrew words nâsâ' and yâd; meaning to lift up the hand [Strgs#5375 + 3027].
[7] Compare **Rev. 10:5**.
[8] anguish – shortness (or spirit), impatience [Strgs#7115]

[9] People will not hear; God will send you to Pharaoh himself to demand that they be let go.
[10] uncircumcised – exposed, strip, go naked [Strgs#6189 + 6188].
[11] Amminadad – people of liberality [Strgs#5992]
[12] Naashon – enchanter [Strgs#5177]
[13] lay – to give, used with great latitude of application (put, make, etc.) [Strgs#5414]
[14] judgments – sentence, infliction [Strgs#8201]

6 And Moses and Aaron did as the LORD commanded them, so did they.
7 And Moses *was* fourscore years old, and Aaron fourscore and three years old, when they spoke unto Pharaoh.
8 And the LORD spoke unto Moses and unto Aaron, saying,
9 When Pharaoh will speak unto you, saying, Show[1] a miracle for you: then you will say unto Aaron, Take your rod, and cast *it* before Pharaoh, *and* it will become a serpent.
10 [And Moses and Aaron went in unto Pharaoh, and they did so as the LORD had commanded: and Aaron cast down his rod before Pharaoh, and before his servants, and it became a serpent.][2]
11 [Then Pharaoh also called the wise men and the sorcerers[3]: now the magicians of Egypt, they also did in like manner with their enchantments.
12 For they cast down every man his rod, and they became serpents: but Aaron's rod swallowed up their rods.][4]
13 And he hardened Pharaoh's heart, that he hearkened not unto them; as the LORD had said.
14 And the LORD said unto Moses, Pharaoh's heart *is* hardened, he refused to let the people go.
15 Get you unto Pharaoh in the morning; lo, he go out unto the water; and you will stand by the river's brink against he come; and the rod which was turned to a serpent will you take in your hand.
16 And you will say unto him, The LORD God of the Hebrews have sent me unto you, saying, Let my people go, that they may serve me in the wilderness: and, behold, hitherto you would not hear.
17 This said the LORD, in this you will know that I *am* the LORD: behold, I will smite with the rod that *is* in mine hand upon the waters which *are* in the river, and they will be turned to blood.
18 And the fish[5] that *is* in the river will die, and the river will stink; and the Egyptians will lothe to drink of the water of the river.
19 And the LORD spoke unto Moses, Say unto Aaron, Take your rod, and stretch out your hand upon the waters of Egypt, upon their streams, upon their rivers, and upon their ponds, and upon all their pools[6] of water, that they may become blood; and *that* there may be blood throughout all the land of Egypt, both in *vessels of* wood, and in *vessels of* stone.
20 And Moses and Aaron did so, as the LORD commanded; and he lifted up the rod, and smote the waters that *were* in the river, in the sight of Pharaoh, [and in the sight of his servants; and all the waters that *were* in the river were turned to blood.][7]
21 And the fish that *was* in the river died; and the river stank, and the Egyptians could not drink of the water of the river; and there was blood throughout all the land of Egypt.
22 And the magicians of Egypt did so with their enchantments: and Pharaoh's heart was hardened, neither did he hearken unto them; as the LORD had said.
23 And Pharaoh turned and went into his house, neither did he set his heart to this also.
24 And all the Egyptians dig round about the river for water to drink; for they could not drink of the water of the river.
25 And seven days were fulfilled, after that the LORD had smitten the river.

CHAPTER 8
1 And the LORD spoke unto Moses, Go unto Pharaoh, and say unto him, this said the LORD, Let my people go, that they may serve me.
2 And if you refuse to let *them* go, behold, I will smite all your borders[8] with frogs:
3 And the river you bring forth frogs abundantly, which you go up and come into your house, and into your bedchamber, and upon your bed, and into the house of your servants, and upon your people, and into your ovens, and into your kneading troughs:
4 And the frogs will come up both on you, and upon your people, and upon all your servants.
5 And the LORD spoke unto Moses, Say unto Aaron, Stretch forth your hand with your rod over the streams, over the rivers, and over the ponds, and cause frogs to come up upon the land of Egypt.
6 And Aaron stretched out his hand over the waters of Egypt; and the frogs came up, and covered the land of Egypt.
7 And the magicians did so with their enchantments, and brought up frogs upon the land of Egypt.
8 Then Pharaoh called for Moses and Aaron, and said, intreat the LORD, that he may take away the frogs from me, and from my people; and I will let the people go, that they may do sacrifice unto the LORD.
9 And Moses said unto Pharaoh, Glory over me: when will I *intreat* for you, and for your servants, and for your people, to destroy the frogs from you and your houses, *that* they may remain in the river only?
10 [And he said, tomorrow. And he said, *be it* according to you word: that you may know that *there is* none like unto the LORD our God.][9]
11 And the frogs will depart from you, and from your houses, and from your servants, and from your people; they will remain in the river only.
12 And Moses and Aaron went out from Pharaoh: and Moses cried unto the LORD because of the frogs which he had brought against Pharaoh.
13 And the LORD did according to the word of Moses; [and the frogs died out of the houses][10], out of the villages, and out of the fields.
14 And they gathered them together [upon heaps][11]: and the land stank.
15 But when Pharaoh saw that there was respite[12], he hardened his heart, and hearkened not unto them; as the LORD had said.

---

[1] *show* – to give [Strgs#5414]
[2] Jesus said, "Be wise as a serpent," – **Matt. 10:16**
[3] *sorcerers* – to *whisper* a spell, to *inchant* or practice magic [Strgs#3784]
[4] Compare **Matt. 10:16** = wisdom **John 3:14**
[5] Femine root for *dâg*, meaning a fis (as prolific); or as timid, sense of squirming, moving y the vibrator action of the tail [Strgs#1710 + 1709]
[6] *pools* – something waited for, confidence, a collection, a caravan or drove, abiding, linen yarn [Strgs#4723]. Comes from Hebrew root word *qâvâh*; meaning to bind together, collect, look, patiently, tarry [Strgs#6960]
[7] The place where the seeds of Israel were killed (compare **Rev. 16:3-7** & **Ex. 1:22**)

[8] *borders* – a *cord* (as *twisted*), a *boundary*; by extentsion the *territory* inclosed [Strgs#1366]
[9] They both (God and Satan) produced frogs, but only God can exterminate them.
[10] The frog spirit will die out of the houses (bodies) of people. God will kill the frog spirit in Revelations.
[11] *upon heaps* – a *bubbling* up, *mire* or clay (cement); homer or dry measure, motion, mortar [Strgs#2563]
[12] *respite* – relief, breathing [Strgs#7309]. From the root word revach meaning room, literally (an interval) or figuratively (delieverance): enlargement, space [Strgs#7305]

16 And the LORD said unto Moses, Say unto Aaron, stretch out your rod, and smite the dust of the land, that it may become lice throughout all the land of Egypt.

17 And they did so; for Aaron stretched out his hand with his rod, and smote the dust of the earth, and it became lice[1] in man, and in beast; all the dust of the land became lice throughout all the land of Egypt.

18 And the magicians did so with their enchantments to bring forth lice, but they could not: so there were lice upon man, and upon beast.

19 Then the magicians said unto Pharaoh, This *is* the finger of God: and Pharaoh's heart was hardened, and he hearkened not unto them; as the LORD had said.

20 And the LORD said unto Moses, Rise up early in the morning, and stand before Pharaoh; lo, he come forth to the water[2]; and say unto him, This said the LORD, Let my people go, that they may serve me.

21 Else, if you will not let my people go, behold, I will send swarms *of flies* upon you, and upon your servants, and upon your people, and into your houses: and the houses of the Egyptians will be full of swarms *of flies*, and also the ground whereon they *are*.

22 And I will sever in that day the land of Goshen, in which my people dwell, that no swarms *of flies* will be there; to the end you may know that I *am* the LORD in the midst of the earth.

23 And I will put a division[3] between my people and your people: tomorrow will this sign be.

24 And the LORD did so; and there came a grievous swarm *of flies* into the house of Pharaoh, and *into* his servants' houses, and into all the land of Egypt: the land was corrupted by reason of the swarm *of flies*.

25 And Pharaoh called for Moses and for Aaron, and said, Go you, sacrifice to your God in the land.

26 And Moses said, it is not meet so to do; for we will sacrifice the abomination of the Egyptians to the LORD our God: lo, will we sacrifice the abomination of the Egyptians before their eyes, and will they not stone us?

27 We will go three days' journey into the wilderness, and sacrifice to the LORD our God, as he will command us.

28 And Pharaoh said, I will let you go, that you may sacrifice to the LORD your God in the wilderness; only you will not go very far away: intreat for me.

29 And Moses said, Behold, I go out from you, and I will intreat the LORD that the swarms *of flies* may depart from Pharaoh, from his servants, and from his people, tomorrow: but let not Pharaoh deal deceitfully any more in not letting the people go to sacrifice to the LORD.

30 And Moses went out from Pharaoh, and intreated the LORD.

31 And the LORD did according to the word of Moses; and he removed the swarms *of flies* from Pharaoh, from his servants, and from his people; there remained not one.

32 And Pharaoh hardened his heart at this time also, neither would he let the people go.

CHAPTER 9

1 Then the LORD said unto Moses, Go in unto Pharaoh, and tell him, this said the LORD God of the Hebrews, Let my people go, that they may serve me.

2 For if you refuse to let *them* go, and will hold them still,

3 Behold, the hand of the LORD is upon your cattle which *are* in the field, upon the horses, upon the asses, upon the camels, upon the oxen, and upon the sheep: *there will be a very grievous murrain*[4].

4 And the LORD will sever between the cattle[5] of Israel and the cattle of Egypt: and there will nothing die of all *that is* the children's of Israel.

5 And the LORD appointed a set time, saying, Tomorrow the LORD will do this thing in the land.

6 And the LORD did that thing on the morrow, and all the cattle of Egypt died: but of the cattle of the children of Israel died not one.

7 And Pharaoh sent, and, behold, there was not one of the cattle of the Israelites dead. And the heart of Pharaoh was hardened, and he did not let the people go.

8 And the LORD said unto Moses and unto Aaron, Take to you handfuls[6] of ashes of the furnace, and let Moses sprinkle it toward the heaven in the sight of Pharaoh.

9 And it will become small dust in all the land of Egypt, and will be a boil breaking forth *with* blains[7] upon man, and upon beast, throughout all the land of Egypt.

10 And they took ashes of the furnace, and stood before Pharaoh; and Moses sprinkled it up toward heaven; and it became a boil breaking forth *with* blains upon man, and upon beast.

11 And the magicians could not stand before Moses because of the boils; for the boil was upon the magicians, and upon all the Egyptians.

12 And the LORD hardened the heart of Pharaoh, and he hearkened not unto them; as the LORD had spoken unto Moses.

13 And the LORD said unto Moses, Rise up early in the morning, and stand before Pharaoh, and say unto him, this said the LORD God of the Hebrews, Let my people go, that they may serve me.

14 For I will at this time send all my plagues upon your heart, and upon your servants, and upon your people; that you may know that *there is* none like me in all the earth.

15 For now I will stretch out my hand, that I may smite you and your people with pestilence; and you will be cut off from the earth.

16 And in very deed for this *cause* have I raised you up, for to show *in* you my power; and that my name may be declared throughout all the earth.

17 As yet exalt[8] you yourself against my people, that you will not let them go?

18 Behold, tomorrow about this time I will cause it to rain a very grievous hail, such as have not been in Egypt since the foundation thereof even until now.

19 Send therefore now, *and* gather your cattle, and all that you have in the field; *for upon* every man and beast which will be found in the field, and will not be brought home, the hail will come down upon them, and they will die.

---

[1] *lice* – I the sense of *fastening*; a *gnat* [Strgs#3654]. Root word set out, that is, *plant*; X vineyard [Strgs#3661]
[2] *water* = people (compare **Rev. 17:15**)
[3] *division* – distinction; also deliverance: - division, redeem, redemption [Strgs#6304]
[4] *murrain* – in the sense of destroying); a pestilence: plague [Strgs#1698]
[5] *cattle* – something *bought*, *property*, but only live stock; abstractly acquisition: possession [Strgs#4735]
[6] *handfuls* – comes from to Hebrew words meaning fistful [Strgs#4393]
[7] *blains* – blister, (meaning to *belch* forth); an inflammatory pustule (as eruption) [Strgs#76].
[8] *exalt* – to set self up as a dam, cast up, extol, make plain [Strgs#5549].

20 He that feared the word of the LORD among the servants of Pharaoh made his servants and his cattle flee into the houses:
21 And he that regarded not the word of the LORD left his servants and his cattle in the field.
22 And the LORD said unto Moses, Stretch forth your hand toward heaven, that there may be hail in all the land of Egypt, upon man, and upon beast, and upon every herb of the field, throughout the land of Egypt.
23 And Moses stretched forth his rod toward heaven: and the LORD sent thunder and hail, and the fire ran along upon the ground; and the LORD rained hail upon the land of Egypt.
24 So there was hail, and fire mingled with the hail, very grievous, such as there was none like it in all the land of Egypt since it became a nation.
25 And the hail smote throughout all the land of Egypt all that *was* in the field, both man and beast; and the hail smote every herb of the field, and break every tree of the field.
26 Only in the land of Goshen, where the children of Israel *were*, was there no hail.
27 And Pharaoh sent, and called for Moses and Aaron, and said unto them, I have sinned this time: the LORD *is* righteous, and I and my people *are* wicked.
28 Intreat the LORD (for *it is* enough) that there be no *more* [mighty thunderings]1 and hail; and I will let you go, and you will stay no longer.
29 And Moses said unto him, As soon as I am gone out of the city, I will spread abroad my hands unto the LORD; *and* the thunder will cease, neither will there be any more hail; that you may know how that the earth *is* the LORD'S.
30 But as for you and your servants, I know that you will not yet fear the LORD God.
31 And the flax and the barley was smitten: for the barley *was* in the ear, and the flax *was* bolled.
32 But the wheat and the rye were not smitten: for they *were* not grown up.
33 And Moses went out of the city from Pharaoh, and spread abroad his hands unto the LORD: and the thunders and hail ceased, and the rain was not poured upon the earth.
34 And when Pharaoh saw that the rain and the hail and the thunders were ceased, he sinned yet more, and hardened his heart, he and his servants.
35 And the heart of Pharaoh was hardened, neither would he let the children of Israel go; as the LORD had spoken by Moses.

CHAPTER 10

1 And the LORD said unto Moses, Go in unto Pharaoh: for I have hardened his heart, and the heart of his servants, that I might show these my signs before him:
2 And that you may tell in the ears of your son, and of your son's son, what things I have wrought in Egypt, and my signs which I have done among them; that you may know how that I *am* the LORD.
3 And Moses and Aaron came in unto Pharaoh, and said unto him, this said the LORD God of the Hebrews, How long will you refuse to humble yourself before me? Let my people go, that they may serve me.

4 Else, if you refuse to let my people go, behold, tomorrow will I bring the locusts into your coast:
5 And they will cover the face of the earth, that one cannot be able to see the earth: and they will eat the residue of that which is escaped, which remain unto you from the hail, and will eat every tree which grows for you out of the field:
6 And they will fill your houses, and the houses of all your servants, and the houses of all the Egyptians; which neither your fathers, or your fathers' fathers have seen, since the day that they were upon the earth unto this day. And he turned himself, and went out from Pharaoh.
7 And Pharaoh's servants said unto him, how long will this man be a snare unto us? Let the men go, that they may serve the LORD their God: know you not yet that Egypt is destroyed?
8 And Moses and Aaron were brought again unto Pharaoh: and he said unto them, Go, serve the LORD your God: *but* who *are* they that will go?
9 And Moses said, we will go with our young and with our old, with our sons and with our daughters, with our flocks and with our herds will we go; for we *must hold* a feast unto the LORD.
10 And he said unto them, Let the LORD be so with you, as I will let you go, and your little ones: look *to it*; for evil *is* before you.
11 Not so: go now you *that are* men, and serve the LORD; for that you did desire. And they were driven out from Pharaoh's presence.
12 And the LORD said unto Moses, Stretch out your hand over the land of Egypt for the locusts, that they may come up upon the land of Egypt, and eat every herb of the land, *even* all that the hail has left.
13 And Moses stretched forth his rod over the land of Egypt, and the LORD brought an east wind upon the land all that day and all *that* night; *and* when it was morning, the east wind brought the locusts.
14 And the locusts went up over all the land of Egypt, and rested in all the coasts of Egypt: very grievous *were they*; before them there were no such locusts as they, neither after them will be such.
15 For they covered the face of the whole earth, so that the land was darkened; and they did eat every herb of the land, and all the fruit of the trees which the hail had left: and there remained not any green thing in the trees, or in the herbs of the field, through all the land of Egypt.
16 Then Pharaoh called for Moses and Aaron in haste; and he said, I have sinned against the LORD your God, and against you.
17 Now therefore forgive, I pray you, my sin only this once, and intreat the LORD your God, that he may take away from me this death only.
18 And he went out from Pharaoh, and intreated the LORD.
19 And the LORD turned a mighty strong west2 wind3, which took away the locusts, and cast them into the Red sea; there remained not one locust in all the coasts of Egypt.
20 But the LORD hardened Pharaoh's heart, so that he would not let the children of Israel go.
21 And the LORD said unto Moses, Stretch out your hand toward heaven, that there may be darkness over the land of Egypt, even darkness *which* may be felt.
22 And Moses stretched forth his hand toward heaven; and there was a thick darkness in all the land of Egypt three days:

---

1 might thunderings – literally voices of God [Strgs#430 + 6963].
2 *west* – to roar; a sea (as breaking in noisy surf), the Mediterranean; sometimes a large river, or an artificial basin [Strgs#3220].

3 *wind* – by resemblance breath, a sensible (or even violent) exhalation; spirit, life, unsubstantiality; region of the sky, tempest, whirlwind [Strgs#7307]

Exodus

23 They saw not one another, neither **raised** any from his place for three days: but all the children of Israel had light in their dwellings.
24 And Pharaoh called unto Moses, and said, go you, serve the LORD; only let your flocks and your herds be stayed: let your little ones also go with you.
25 And Moses said, you must give us also sacrifices and burnt offerings, that we may sacrifice unto the LORD our God.
26 Our cattle also will go with us; there will not an hoof be left behind; for thereof must we take to serve the LORD our God; and we know not with what we must serve the LORD, until we come thither.
27 But the LORD hardened Pharaoh's heart, and he would not let them go.
28 And Pharaoh said unto him, Get you from me, take heed to yourself, see my face no more; for in *that* day you see my face you will die.
29 And Moses said, you have spoken well, I will see your face again no more.

CHAPTER 11

1 And the LORD said unto Moses, yet will I bring one plague *more* upon Pharaoh, and upon Egypt; afterwards he will let you go hence: when he will let *you* go, he will surely thrust you out hence altogether.
2 Speak now in the ears of the people, and let every man borrows of his neighbor, and every woman of her neighbor, jewels of silver, and jewels of gold.
3 And the LORD gave the people favor in the sight of the Egyptians. Moreover the man Moses *was* very great in the land of Egypt, in the sight of Pharaoh's servants, and in the sight of the people.
4 And Moses said, this said the LORD, About midnight will I go out into the midst of Egypt:
5 And all the firstborn in the land of Egypt will die, from the firstborn of Pharaoh that sit upon his throne, even unto the firstborn of the maidservant that *is* behind the mill; and all the firstborn of beasts.
6 And there will be [a great cry][1] throughout all the land of Egypt, such as there was none like it, or will be like it any more.
7 But against any of the children of Israel will not a dog move his tongue, against man or beast: that you may know how that the LORD does put a difference between the Egyptians and Israel.
8 And all your servants will come down unto me, and bow down themselves unto me, saying, Get you out, and all the people that follow you: and after that I will go out. And he went out from Pharaoh in a great anger.
9 And the LORD said unto Moses, Pharaoh will not hearken unto you; that my wonders may be multiplied in the land of Egypt.
10 And Moses and Aaron did all these wonders before Pharaoh: and the LORD hardened Pharaoh's heart, so that he would not let the children of Israel go out of his land.

CHAPTER 12

1 And the LORD spoke unto Moses and Aaron in the land of Egypt, saying,
2 This month *will be* unto you the beginning of months: it *will be* the first month of the year to you.
3 Speak you unto all the congregation of Israel, saying, in the tenth *day* of this month they will take to them every man a lamb, according to the house of *their* fathers, a lamb for a house:
4 And if the household be too little for the lamb, let him and his neighbor next unto his house take *it* according to the number of the souls; every man according to his eating will make your count for the lamb.
5 Your lamb will be without blemish, a male of the first year: you will take *it* out from the sheep, or from the goats:
6 And you will keep it up until the fourteenth day of the same month: and the whole assembly of the congregation of Israel will kill it in the evening.
7 And they will take of the blood, and strike *it* on the two side posts and on the upper door post of the houses, wherein they will eat it.
8 And they will eat the flesh in that night, roast with fire, and unleavened bread; *and* with bitter *herbs* they will eat it.
9 Eat not of it raw, nor sodden at all with water, but roast *with* fire; his head with his legs, and with the purtenance[2] thereof.
10 And you will let nothing of it remain until the morning; and that which remain of it until the morning you will burn with fire.
11 And then will you eat it; *with* your loins girded, your shoes on your feet, and your staff in your hand; and you will eat it in haste: it *is* the LORD'S Passover.
12 For I will pass through the land of Egypt this night, and will smite all the firstborn in the land of Egypt, both man and beast; and against all the gods of Egypt I will execute judgment[3]: I *am* the LORD.
13 And the blood will be to you for a token upon the houses where you *are*: and when I see the blood, I will pass over you, and the plague will not be upon you to destroy *you*, when I smite the land of Egypt.
14 And this day will be unto you for a memorial; and you will keep it a feast to the LORD throughout your generations; you will keep it a feast by an ordinance forever.
15 Seven days will you eat unleavened bread; even the first day you will put away leaven out of your houses: for whosoever eats leavened bread from the first day until the seventh day, that soul will be cut off from Israel.
16 And in the first day *there will be* a holy convocation, and in the seventh day there will be a holy convocation to you; no manner of work will be done in them, save *that* which every man must eat, that only may be done of you.
17 And you will observe *the feast of* unleavened bread; for in this selfsame day have I brought your armies out of the land of Egypt: therefore will you observe this day in your generations by an ordinance forever.
18 In the first *month*, on the fourteenth day of the month at even, you will eat unleavened bread, until the one and twentieth day of the month at even.
19 Seven days will there be no leaven found in your houses: for whosoever eats that which is leavened, even that soul will be cut off from the congregation of Israel, whether he be a stranger, or born in the land.
20 You will eat nothing leavened; in all your habitations will you eat unleavened bread.

---

[1] *a great cry* – demons leaving.
[2] *purtenance* – the *nearest* part [Strgs#7130]. Root word *qârab* meaning to *approach* (causatively *bring near*) [Strgs#7126].
[3] lit. *sentence* [Strgs#8201]

21 Then Moses called for all the elders of Israel, and said unto them, Draw out and takes you a lamb according to your families, and kills the Passover[1].
22 And you will take a bunch of hyssop, and dip *it* in the blood that *is* in the **bowl**, and strike the lintel and the two side posts with the blood that *is* in the **bowl**; and none of you will go out at the door of his house until the morning.
23 For the LORD will pass through to smite the Egyptians; and when he see the blood upon the lintel, and on the two side posts, the LORD will pass over the door, and will not suffer[2] the destroyer to come in unto your houses to smite *you*.
24 And you will observe this thing for an ordinance to you and to your sons forever.
25 And it will come to pass, when you be come to the land which the LORD will give you, according as he **has** promised, that you will keep this service.
26 And it will come to pass, when your children will say unto you, what mean you by this service?
27 That you will say, it *is* the sacrifice of the LORD'S Passover, who passed over the houses of the children of Israel in Egypt, when he smote the Egyptians, and delivered our houses. And the people bowed the head and worshipped.
28 And the children of Israel went away, and did as the LORD had commanded Moses and Aaron, so did they.
29 And it came to pass, that at midnight the LORD smote all the firstborn in the land of Egypt, from the firstborn of Pharaoh that sat on his throne unto the firstborn of the captive that *was* in the dungeon; and all the firstborn of cattle.
30 And Pharaoh rose up in the night, he, and all his servants, and all the Egyptians; and there was a great cry in Egypt; for *there was* not a house where *there was* not one dead.
31 And he called for Moses and Aaron by night, and said, Rise up, *and* get you forth from among my people, both you and the children of Israel; and go, serve the LORD, as you have said.
32 Also take your flocks and your herds, as you have said, and be gone; and bless me also.
33 And the Egyptians were urgent upon the people, that they might send them out of the land in haste; for they said, we *be* all dead *men*.
34 And the people took their dough before it was leavened, their kneading troughs being bound up in their clothes upon their shoulders.
35 And the children of Israel did according to the word of Moses; and they borrowed of the Egyptians jewels of silver, and jewels of gold, and raiment:
36 And the LORD gave the people favor in the sight of the Egyptians, so that they lent unto them *such things as they required*. And they spoiled the Egyptians.
37 And the children of Israel journeyed from Rameses to Succoth, about six hundred thousand on foot *that were* men, beside children.
38 And a mixed multitude went up also with them; and flocks, and herds, *even* very much cattle.
39 And they baked unleavened cakes of the dough which they brought forth out of Egypt, for it was not leavened; because they were thrust out of Egypt, and could not tarry, neither had they prepared for themselves any victual.
40 Now the sojourning of the children of Israel, who dwelt in Egypt, *was* four hundred and thirty years.
41 And it came to pass at the end of the four hundred and thirty years, even the selfsame day it came to pass, that all the hosts of the LORD went out from the land of Egypt.
42 It *is* a night to be much observed unto the LORD for bringing them out from the land of Egypt: this *is* that night of the LORD to be observed of all the children of Israel in their generations.
43 And the LORD said unto Moses and Aaron, This *is* the ordinance of the Passover: There will no stranger eat thereof:
44 But every man's servant that is bought for money, when you have circumcised him, then will he eat thereof.
45 A foreigner and a hired servant will not eat thereof.
46 In one house will it be eaten; you will not carry forth ought of the flesh abroad out of the house; neither will you break a bone thereof.
47 All the congregation of Israel will keep it.
48 And when a stranger will sojourn with you, and will keep the Passover to the LORD, let all his males be circumcised, and then let him come near and keep it; and he will be as one that is born in the land: for no uncircumcised person will eat thereof.
49 One law will be to him that is home born, and unto the stranger that sojourned among you.
50 This did all the children of Israel; as the LORD commanded Moses and Aaron, so did they.
51 And it came to pass the selfsame day, *that* the LORD did bring the children of Israel out of the land of Egypt by their armies.

CHAPTER 13

1 And the LORD spoke unto Moses, saying,
2 Sanctify unto me all the firstborn, whatsoever open the womb among the children of Israel, *both* of man and of beast: it *is* mine.
3 And Moses said unto the people, Remember this day, in which you came out from Egypt, out of the house of bondage; for by strength of hand the LORD brought you out from this *place*: there will no leavened bread be eaten.
4 This day came you out in the month Abib.
5 And it will be when the LORD will bring you into the land of the Canaanites, and the Hittites, and the Amorites, and the Hivites, and the Jebusites, which he swore unto your fathers to give you, a land flowing with milk and honey, that you will keep this service in this month.
6 Seven days you will eat unleavened bread, and in the seventh day will *be* a feast to the LORD.
7 Unleavened bread will be eaten seven days; and there will no leavened bread be seen with you, neither will there be leaven seen with you in all your quarters.
8 And you will shew your son in that day, saying, *this is done* because of that *which* the LORD did unto me when I came forth out of Egypt.
9 And it will be for a sign unto you upon your hand, and for a memorial between your eyes, that the LORD'S law may be in your mouth: for with a strong hand hath the LORD brought you out of Egypt.
10 You will therefore keep this ordinance in his season from year to year.

---

[1] *passover* – Hebrew word *pesach* meaning *pretermission, exemption* [Strgs#6453]. Root *pâsach* meaning *hop, skip over, spare, hesitate,* to *limp,* to *dance* [Strgs#6452]. "To let pass without mention or notice.
[2] lit. give [Strgs#5414]

11 And it will be when the LORD will bring you into the land of the Canaanites, as he swore unto you and to your fathers, and will give it you,
12 That you will set apart unto the LORD all that opened the matrix, and every firstling that cometh of a beast which you hast; the males will *be* the LORD'S.
13 And every firstling of an ass you will redeem with a lamb; and if you will not redeem it, then you will break his neck: and all the firstborn of man among your children will you redeem.
14 And it will be when your son asks you in time to come, saying, what *is* this? That you will say unto him, by strength of hand the LORD brought us out from Egypt, from the house of bondage:
15 And it came to pass, when Pharaoh would hardly let us go, that the LORD slew all the firstborn in the land of Egypt, both the firstborn of man, and the firstborn of beast: therefore I sacrifice to the LORD all that opened the matrix, being males; but all the firstborn of my children I redeem.
16 And it will be for a token upon your hand, and for frontlets between your eyes: for by strength of hand the LORD brought us forth out of Egypt.
17 And it came to pass, when Pharaoh had let the people go, that God led them not *through* the way of the land of the Philistines, although that *was* near; for God said, Lest peradventure the people repent when they see war, and they return to Egypt:
18 But God led the people about, *through* the way of the wilderness of the Red sea: and the children of Israel went up harnessed out of the land of Egypt.
19 And Moses took the bones of Joseph with him: for he had straightly sworn the children of Israel, saying, God will surely visit you; and you will carry up my bones away hence with you.
20 And they took their journey from Succoth, and encamped in Etham, in the edge of the wilderness.
21 And the LORD went before them by day in a pillar of a cloud, to lead them the way; and by night in a pillar of fire, to give them light; to go by day and night:
22 He took not away the pillar of the cloud by day, nor the pillar of fire by night, *from* before the people.

CHAPTER 14

1 And the LORD spoke unto Moses, saying,
2 Speak unto the children of Israel, that they turn and encamp before Pi-hahiroth, between Migdol and the sea, over against Baal-zephon: before it will you encamp by the sea.
3 For Pharaoh will say of the children of Israel, They *are* entangled in the land, the wilderness hath shut them in.
4 And I will harden Pharaoh's heart, that he will follow after them; and I will be honored upon Pharaoh, and upon his **entire** host; that the Egyptians may know that I *am* the LORD. And they did so.
5 And it was told the king of Egypt that the people fled: and the heart of Pharaoh and of his servants was turned against the people, and they said, why have we done this, that we have let Israel go from serving us?
6 And he made ready his chariot, and took his people with him:
7 And he took six hundred chosen chariots, and all the chariots of Egypt, and captains over every one of them.
8 And the LORD hardened the heart of Pharaoh king of Egypt, and he pursued after the children of Israel: and the children of Israel went out with a high hand.
9 But the Egyptians pursued after them, all the horses *and* chariots of Pharaoh, and his horsemen, and his army, and overtook them encamping by the sea, beside Pi-hahiroth, before Baal-zephon.
10 And when Pharaoh drew nigh, the children of Israel lifted up their eyes, and, behold, the Egyptians marched after them; and they were sore afraid: and the children of Israel cried out unto the LORD.
11 And they said unto Moses, because *there were* no graves in Egypt, have you taken us away to die in the wilderness? Wherefore have you dealt thus with us, to carry us forth out of Egypt?
12 *Is* not this the word that we did tell you in Egypt, saying, let us alone, that we may serve the Egyptians? For *it had been* better for us to serve the Egyptians, than that we should die in the wilderness.
13 And Moses said unto the people, Fear you not, stand still, and see the salvation of the LORD, which he will shew to you today: for the Egyptians whom you have seen today, you will see them again no more forever.
14 The LORD will fight for you, and you will hold your peace.
15 And the LORD said unto Moses, Wherefore cry you unto me? Speak unto the children of Israel, that they go forward:
16 But lift you up your rod, and stretch out your hand over the sea, and divide it: and the children of Israel will go on dry *ground* through the midst of the sea.
17 And I, behold, I will harden the hearts of the Egyptians, and they will follow them: and I will get me honor upon Pharaoh, and upon his **entire** host, upon his chariots, and upon his horsemen.
18 And the Egyptians will know that I *am* the LORD, when I have gotten me honor upon Pharaoh, upon his chariots, and upon his horsemen.
19 And the angel of God, which went before the camp of Israel, removed and went behind them; and the pillar of the cloud went from before their face, and stood behind them:
20 And it came between the camp of the Egyptians and the camp of Israel; and it was a cloud and darkness *to them*, but it gave light by night *to these*: so that the one came not near the other all the night.
21 And Moses stretched out his hand over the sea; and the LORD caused the sea to go *back* by a strong east wind all that night, and made the sea dry *land*, and the waters were divided.
22 And the children of Israel went into the midst of the sea upon the dry *ground*: and the waters *were* a wall unto them on their right hand, and on their left.
23 And the Egyptians pursued, and went in after them to the midst of the sea, *even* all Pharaoh's horses, his chariots, and his horsemen.
24 And it came to pass, that in the morning watch the LORD looked unto the host of the Egyptians through the pillar of fire and of the cloud, and troubled the host of the Egyptians,
25 And took off their chariot wheels, that they drive them heavily: so that the Egyptians said, Let us flee from the face of Israel; for the LORD fights for them against the Egyptians.
26 And the LORD said unto Moses, Stretch out your hand over the sea, that the waters may come again upon the Egyptians, upon their chariots, and upon their horsemen.
27 [And Moses stretched forth his hand over the sea, and the sea returned to his strength when the morning appeared; and the

Egyptians fled against it; and the LORD overthrew the Egyptians in the midst of the sea.]¹
28 And the waters returned, and covered the chariots, and the horsemen, *and* all the host of Pharaoh that came into the sea after them; there remained not so much as one of them.
29 But the children of Israel walked upon dry *land* in the midst of the sea; and the waters *were* a wall unto them on their right hand, and on their left.
30 Thus the LORD saved Israel that day out of the hand of the Egyptians; and Israel saw the Egyptians dead upon the sea shore.
31 And Israel saw that great work which the LORD did upon the Egyptians: and the people feared the LORD, and believed the LORD, and his servant Moses.

CHAPTER 15

1 Then sang Moses and the children of Israel this song unto the LORD, and spoke, saying, I will sing unto the LORD, for he hath triumphed gloriously: the horse and his rider hath he thrown into the sea.
2 The LORD *is* my strength and song, and he is become my salvation: he *is* my God, and I will prepare him a habitation; my father's God, and I will exalt him.
3 The LORD *is* a man of war: the LORD *is* his name.
4 Pharaoh's chariots and his host hath he cast into the sea: his chosen captains also are drowned in the Red sea.
5 The depths have covered them: they sank into the bottom as a stone.
6 Your right hand, O LORD, is become glorious in power: your right hand, O LORD, hath dashed in pieces the enemy.
7 And in the greatness of your Excellency you have overthrown them that rose up against you: you sent forth your wrath, *which* consumed them as stubble.
8 And with the blast of your nostrils the waters were gathered together, the floods stood upright as a heap, *and* the depths were congealed in the heart of the sea.
9 The enemy said, I will pursue, I will overtake, I will divide the spoil; my lust will be satisfied upon them; I will draw my sword, my hand will destroy them.
10 you didst blow with your wind, the sea covered them: they sank as lead in the mighty waters.
11 Who *is* like unto you, O LORD, among the gods? Who *is* like you, glorious in holiness, fearful *in* praises, doing wonders?
12 You stretched out your right hand, the earth swallowed them.
13 You in your mercy have led forth the people you have redeemed: you have guided *them* in your strength unto your holy habitation.
14 The people will hear, *and* be afraid: sorrow will take hold on the inhabitants of Palestina.
15 Then the dukes of Edom will be amazed; the mighty men of Moab, trembling will take hold upon them; all the inhabitants of Canaan will melt away.
16 Fear and dread will fall upon them; by the greatness of your arm they will be *as* still as a stone; till your people pass over, O LORD, till the people pass over, *which* you have purchased.
17 You will bring them in, and plant them in the mountain of your inheritance, *in* the place, O LORD, *which* you have made for you

to dwell in, *in* the Sanctuary, O Lord, *which* your hands have established.
18 The LORD will reign for ever and ever.
19 For the horse of Pharaoh went in with his chariots and with his horsemen into the sea, and the LORD brought again the waters of the sea upon them; but the children of Israel went on dry *and* in the midst of the sea.
20 And Miriam² the prophetess, the sister of Aaron, took a tambourine in her hand; and all the women went out after her with tambourine and with dances.
21 And Miriam answered them, Sing you to the LORD, for he hath triumphed gloriously; the horse and his rider hath he thrown into the sea.
22 So Moses brought Israel from the Red sea, and they went out into the wilderness of Shur; and they went three days in the wilderness, and found no water.
23 And when they came to Marah, they could not drink of the waters of Marah, for they *were* bitter: therefore the name of it was called Marah.
24 And the people murmured against Moses, saying, what will we drink?
25 And he cried unto the LORD; and the LORD showed³ him a tree, *which* when he had cast into the waters, the waters were made sweet: there he made for them a statute and an ordinance, and there he proved them,
26 And said, If you will diligently hearken to the voice of the LORD your God, and will do that which is right in his sight, and will give ear to his commandments, and keep all his statutes, I will put none of these diseases upon you, which I have brought upon the Egyptians: for I *am* the LORD that healed you.
27 And they came to Elim, where *were* twelve wells of water, and threescore and ten palm trees: and they encamped there by the waters.

CHAPTER 16

1 And they took their journey from Elim, and all the congregation of the children of Israel came **into** the wilderness of Sin, which *is* between Elim and Sinai, on the fifteenth day of the second month after their departing out of the land of Egypt.
2 And the whole congregation of the children of Israel murmured against Moses and Aaron in the wilderness:
3 And the children of Israel said unto them, Would to God we had died by the hand of the LORD in the land of Egypt, when we sat by the flesh pots, *and* when we did eat bread to the full; for you have brought us forth into this wilderness, to kill this whole assembly with hunger.
4 Then said the LORD unto Moses, Behold, I will rain bread from heaven for you; and the people will go out and gather a certain rate every day, that I may prove them, whether they will walk in my law, or no.
5 And it will come to pass, that on the sixth day they will prepare *that* which they bring in; and it will be twice as much as they gather daily.
6 And Moses and Aaron said unto all the children of Israel, at even, then you will know that the LORD hath brought you out from the land of Egypt:

---

¹ 12ᵗʰ Judgment
² Miriam- the sister of Aaron and Moses. Her name is defined as *rebelliously*. [Strgs#4813]

³ lit. *to flow as water*; transitively to *lay* or *throw* arrow, that is to shoot [Strgs#3384]

7 And in the morning, then you will see the glory of the LORD; for that he heard your murmurings against the LORD: and what *are* we, that you murmur against us?

8 And Moses said, *this will be*, when the LORD will give you in the evening flesh to eat, and in the morning bread to the full; for that the LORD heard your murmurings which you murmur against him: and what *are* we? Your murmurings *are* not against us, but against the LORD.

9 And Moses spoke unto Aaron, Say unto all the congregation of the children of Israel, Come near before the LORD: for he hath heard your murmurings.

10 And it came to pass, as Aaron spoke unto the whole congregation of the children of Israel, that they looked toward the wilderness, and, behold, the glory of the LORD appeared in the cloud.

11 And the LORD spoke unto Moses, saying,

12 I have heard the murmurings of the children of Israel: speak unto them, saying, at even you will eat flesh, and in the morning you will be filled with bread; and you will know that I *am* the LORD your God.

13 And it came to pass, that at even the quails came up, and covered the camp: and in the morning the dew lay round about the host.

14 And when the dew that lay was gone up, behold, upon the face of the wilderness *there lay* a small round thing, *as* small as the hoar frost on the ground.

15 And when the children of Israel saw *it*, they said one to another, It *is* manna: for they wist not what it *was*. And Moses said unto them, this *is* the bread which the LORD hath given you to eat.

16 This *is* the thing which the LORD hath commanded, Gather of it every man according to his eating, an omer for every man, *according to* the number of your persons; take you every man for *them* which *are* in his tents.

17 And the children of Israel did so, and gathered, some more, some less.

18 And when they did mete *it* with an omer, he that gathered much had nothing over, and he that gathered little had no lack; they gathered every man according to his eating.

19 And Moses said, Let no man leave of it till the morning.

20 Notwithstanding they hearkened not unto Moses; but some of them left of it until the morning, and it bred worms, and stank: and Moses was wroth with them.

21 And they gathered it every morning, every man according to his eating: and when the sun waxed hot, it melted.

22 And it came to pass, *that* on the sixth day they gathered twice as much bread, two omers[1] for one *man*: and all the rulers of the congregation came and told Moses.

23 And he said unto them, this *is that* which the LORD have said, tomorrow *is* the rest of the holy Sabbath unto the LORD: bake *that* which you will bake *today*, and seethe that you will seethe; and that which remain over lay up for you to be kept until the morning.

24 And they laid it up till the morning, as Moses bade: and it did not stink, neither was there any worm therein.

25 And Moses said, Eat that today; for today *is* a Sabbath unto the LORD: to day you will not find it in the field.

26 Six days you will gather it; but on the seventh day, *which is* the Sabbath, in it there will be none.

27 And it came to pass, *that* there went out *some* of the people on the seventh day for to gather, and they found none.

28 And the LORD said unto Moses, How long refuse you to keep my commandments and my laws?

29 See, for that the LORD hath given you the Sabbath, therefore he giveth you on the sixth day the bread of two days; abide you every man in his place, let no man go out of his place on the seventh day.

30 So the people rested on the seventh day.

31 And the house of Israel called the name thereof Manna: and it *was* like coriander seed, white; and the taste of it *was* like wafers *made* with honey.

32 And Moses said, this *is* the thing which the LORD commanded, fill an omer of it to be kept for your generations; that they may see the bread wherewith I have fed you in the wilderness, when I brought you forth from the land of Egypt.

33 And Moses said unto Aaron, Take a pot, and put an omer full of manna therein, and lay it up before the LORD, to be kept for your generations.

34 As the LORD commanded Moses, so Aaron laid it up before the Testimony, to be kept.

35 And the children of Israel did eat manna forty years, until they came to a land inhabited; they did eat manna, until they came unto the borders of the land of Canaan.

36 Now an omer *is* the tenth *part* of an ephah.

CHAPTER 17

1 And all the congregation of the children of Israel journeyed from the wilderness of Sin, after their journeys, according to the commandment of the LORD, and pitched in Rephidim: and *there was* no water for the people to drink.

2 Wherefore the people did chide with Moses, and said, give us water that we may drink. And Moses said unto them, why chide you with me? Wherefore do you tempt the LORD?

3 And the people thirsted there for water; and the people murmured against Moses, and said, wherefore *is* this *that* you have brought us up out of Egypt, to kill us and our children and our cattle with thirst?

4 And Moses cried unto the LORD, saying, what will I do unto this people? They are almost ready to stone me.

5 And the LORD said unto Moses, Go on before the people, and take with you of the elders of Israel; and your rod, wherewith you smite the river, take in your hand, and go.

6 Behold, I will stand before you there upon the rock in Horeb; and you will smite the rock, and there will come water out of it, that the people may drink. And Moses did so in the sight of the elders of Israel.

7 And he called the name of the place Massah, and Meribah, because of the chiding of the children of Israel, and because they tempted the LORD, saying, Is the LORD among us, or not?

8 Then came Amalek, and fought with Israel in Rephidim.

9 And Moses said unto Joshua, Choose us out men, and go out, fight with Amalek: tomorrow I will stand on the top of the hill with the rod of God in mine hand.

10 So Joshua did as Moses had said to him, and fought with Amalek: and Moses, Aaron, and Hur went up to the top of the hill.

11 And it came to pass, when Moses held up his hand, that Israel prevailed: and when he let down his hand, Amalek prevailed.

---

[1] omer – a measure of 1/10 ephah

12 But Moses' hands *were* heavy; and they took a stone, and put *it* under him, and he sat thereon; and Aaron and Hur stayed up his hands, the one on the one side, and the other on the other side; and his hands were steady until the going down of the sun.
13 And Joshua discomfited Amalek and his people with the edge of the sword.
14 And the LORD said unto Moses, Write this *for* a memorial in a book, and rehearse *it* in the ears of Joshua: for I will utterly put out the remembrance of Amalek from under heaven.
15 And Moses built an altar, and called the name of it Jehovah-nissi:
16 For he said, because the LORD hath sworn *that* the LORD *will have* war with Amalek from generation to generation.

CHAPTER 18

1 When Jethro, the priest of Midian, Moses' father in law, heard of all that God had done for Moses, and for Israel his people, *and* that the LORD had brought Israel out of Egypt;
2 Then Jethro, Moses' father in law, took Zipporah, Moses' wife, after he had sent her back,
3 And her two sons; of which the name of the one *was* Gershom; for he said, I have been an alien in a strange land:
4 And the name of the other *was* Eliezer; for the God of my father, *said he, was* mine help, and delivered me from the sword of Pharaoh:
5 And Jethro, Moses' father in law, came with his sons and his wife unto Moses into the wilderness, where he encamped at the mount of God:
6 And he said unto Moses, I your father in law Jethro am come unto you, and your wife, and her two sons with her.
7 And Moses went out to meet his father in law, and did obeisance, and kissed him; and they asked each other of *their* welfare; and they came into the tent.
8 And Moses told his father in law all that the LORD had done unto Pharaoh and to the Egyptians for Israel's sake, *and* all the travail that had come upon them by the way, and *how* the LORD delivered them.
9 And Jethro rejoiced for all the goodness which the LORD had done to Israel, whom he had delivered out of the hand of the Egyptians.
10 And Jethro said, blessed *be* the LORD, who hath delivered you out of the hand of the Egyptians, and out of the hand of Pharaoh, who hath delivered the people from under the hand of the Egyptians.
11 Now I know that the LORD *is* greater than all gods: for in the thing wherein they dealt proudly *he was* above them.
12 And Jethro, Moses' father in law, took a burnt offering and sacrifices for God: and Aaron came, and all the elders of Israel, to eat bread with Moses' father in law before God.
13 And it came to pass on **tomorrow**, that Moses sat to judge the people: and the people stood by Moses from the morning unto the evening.
14 And when Moses' father in law saw all that he did to the people, he said, what *is* this thing that you do to the people? Why sit alone, and all the people stand by you from morning unto even?
15 And Moses said unto his father in law, because the people come unto me to enquire of God:
16 When they have a matter, they come unto me; and I judge between one and another, and I do make *them* know the statutes of God, and his laws.
17 And Moses' father in law said unto him, the thing that you do *is* not good.
18 you will surely wear away, both thou, and this people that *is* with you: for this thing *is* too heavy for you; you are not able to perform it yourself alone.
19 Hearken now unto my voice, I will give you counsel, and God will be with you: Be you for the people to God-ward, that you may bring the causes unto God:
20 And you will teach them ordinances and laws, and will shew them the way wherein they must walk, and the work that they must do.
21 Moreover you will provide out of all the people able men, such as fear God, men of truth, hating covetousness; and place *such* over them, *to be* rulers of thousands, *and* rulers of hundreds, rulers of fifties, and rulers of tens:
22 And let them judge the people at all seasons: and it will be, *that* every great matter they will bring unto you, but every small matter they will judge: so will it be easier for yourself, and they will bear *the burden* with you.
23 If you will do this thing, and God command you *so*, then you will be able to endure, and this **entire** people will also go to their place in peace.
24 So Moses hearkened to the voice of his father in law, and did all that he have said.
25 And Moses chose able men out of all Israel, and made them heads over the people, rulers of thousands, rulers of hundreds, rulers of fifties, and rulers of tens.
26 And they judged the people at all seasons: the hard causes they brought unto Moses, but every small matter they judged themselves.
27 And Moses let his father in law depart; and he went his way into his own land.

CHAPTER 19

1 In the third month, when the children of Israel were gone forth out of the land of Egypt, the same day came they *into* the wilderness of Sinai.
2 For they were departed from Rephidim, and were come *to* the desert of Sinai, and had pitched in the wilderness; and there Israel camped before the mount.
3 And Moses went up unto God, and the LORD called unto him out of the mountain, saying, Thus will you say to the house of Jacob, and tell the children of Israel;
4 you have seen what I did unto the Egyptians, and *how* I bare you on eagles' wings, and brought you unto myself.
5 Now therefore, if you will obey my voice indeed, and keep my covenant, then you will be a peculiar treasure unto me above all people: for all the earth *is* mine:
6 And you will be unto me a kingdom of priests, and a holy nation. These *are* the words which you will speak unto the children of Israel.
7 And Moses came and called for the elders of the people, and laid before their faces all these words which the LORD commanded him.
8 And all the people answered together, and said, All that the LORD hath spoken we will do. And Moses returned the words of the people unto the LORD.
9 And the LORD said unto Moses, Lo, I come unto you in a thick cloud, that the people may hear when I speak with you, and believe

Exodus

you   forever. And Moses told the words of the people unto the LORD.
10 And the LORD said unto Moses, Go unto the people, and sanctify them today and tomorrow, and let them wash their clothes,
11 And be ready against the third day: for the third day the LORD will come down in the sight of all the people upon Mount Sinai.
12 And you will set bounds unto the people round about, saying, Take heed to yourselves, *that you* go *not* up into the mount, or touch the border of it: whosoever touched the mount will be surely put to death:
13 There will not an hand touch it, but he will surely be stoned, or shot through; whether *it be* beast or man, it will not live: when the trumpet sounded long, they will come up to the mount.
14 And Moses went down from the mount unto the people, and sanctified the people; and they washed their clothes.
15 And he said unto the people, be ready against the third day: come not at *your* wives.
16 And it came to pass on the third day in the morning, that there were thunders and lightning's, and a thick cloud upon the mount, and the voice of the trumpet exceeding loud; so that all the people that *was* in the camp trembled.
17 And Moses brought forth the people out of the camp to meet with God; and they stood at the nether part of the mount.
18 And Mount Sinai was altogether on a smoke, because the LORD descended upon it in fire: and the smoke thereof ascended as the smoke of a furnace, and the whole mount quaked greatly.
19 And when the voice of the trumpet sounded long, and waxed louder and louder, Moses spoke, and God answered him by a voice.
20 And the LORD came down upon Mount Sinai, on the top of the mount: and the LORD called Moses *up* to the top of the mount; and Moses went up.
21 And the LORD said unto Moses, Go down, charge the people, lest they break through unto the LORD to gaze, and many of them perish.
22 And let the priests also, which come near to the LORD, sanctify themselves, lest the LORD break forth upon them.
23 And Moses said unto the LORD, The people cannot come up to Mount Sinai: for you charged us, saying, Set bounds about the mount, and sanctify it.
24 And the LORD said unto him, Away, get you   down, and you will come up, thou, and Aaron with you: but let not the priests and the people break through to come up unto the LORD, lest he break forth upon them.
25 So Moses went down unto the people, and spoke unto them.

CHAPTER 20

1 And God spoke all these words, saying,
2 I *am* the LORD your God, which have brought you   out of the land of Egypt, out of the house of bondage.
3 You will have no other gods before me.
4 You will not make **for** you **cravings and** any representation **which** in **the** heaven**s** above, or **which** *is* in the earth beneath, or **which** *is* in the water **beneath** the earth:
5 you will not bow down yourself to them, nor serve them: for I the LORD your God *am* a jealous God, visiting the iniquity of the fathers upon the children unto the third and fourth *generation of* them that hate me;
6 And showing mercy unto thousands of them that love me, and keep my commandments.
7 you will not take the name of the LORD your God in vain; for the LORD will not hold him guiltless that taketh his name in vain.
8 Remember the Sabbath day, to keep it holy.
9 Six days will you labor, and do all your work:
10 But the seventh day *is* the Sabbath of the LORD your God: *in it* you will not do any work, thou, nor your son, nor your daughter, your manservant, nor your maidservant, nor your cattle, nor your stranger that *is* within your gates:
11 For *in* six days the LORD made heaven and earth, the sea, and all that in them *is*, and rested the seventh day: wherefore the LORD blessed the Sabbath day, and hallowed it.
12 Honor your father and your mother: that your days may be long upon the land which the LORD your God give you.
13 you will not kill.
14 you will not commit adultery.
15 you will not steal.
16 you will not bear false witness against your neighbor.
17 you will not covet your neighbor's house, you will not covet your neighbor's wife, or his manservant, or his maidservant, or his ox, or his ass, or any thing that *is* your neighbor's.
18 And all the people saw the thundering[1], and the lightnings, and the noise of the trumpet, and the mountain smoking: and when the people saw *it*, they removed, and stood afar off.
19 And they said unto Moses, Speak you with us, and we will hear: but let not God speak with us, lest we die.
20 And Moses said unto the people, Fear not: for God is come to prove you, and that his fear may be before your faces, that you sin not.
21 And the people stood afar off, and Moses drew near unto the thick darkness where God *was*.
22 And the LORD said unto Moses, Thus you will say unto the children of Israel, you have seen that I have talked with you from heaven.
23 you will not make with me gods of silver, neither will you make unto you gods of gold.
24 An altar of earth you will make unto me, and will sacrifice thereon your burnt offerings, and your peace offerings, your sheep, and your oxen: in all places where I record my name I will come unto you, and I will bless you.
25 And if you will make me an altar of stone, you will not build it of hewn stone: for if you lift up your tool upon it, you have polluted it.
26 Neither will you go up by steps unto mine altar, that your nakedness be not discovered thereon.

CHAPTER 21

1 Now these *are* the judgments which you will set before them.
2 If you buy a Hebrew servant, six years he will serve: and in the seventh he will go out free for nothing.
3 If he came in by himself, he will go out by himself: if he were married, then his wife will go out with him.
4 If his master has given him a wife, and she have born him sons or daughters; the wife and her children will be her master's, and he will go out by himself.
5 And if the servant will plainly say, I love my master, my wife, and my children; I will not go out free:

---
[1] lit. voices or sounds [Strgs#6963]

6 Then his master will bring him unto the judges; he will also bring him to the door, or unto the door post; and his master will bore his ear through with an aul; and he will serve him forever.
7 And if a man sells his daughter to be a maidservant, she will not go out as the menservants do.
8 If she pleases not her master, who hath betrothed her to himself, then will he let her be redeemed: to sell her unto a strange nation he will have no power, seeing he hath dealt deceitfully with her.
9 And if he has betrothed her unto his son, he will deal with her after the manner of daughters.
10 If he takes him another *wife*; her food, her raiment, and her duty of marriage, will he not diminished.
11 And if he does not these three unto her, then will she go out free without money.
12 He that smites a man, so that he dies, will be surely put to death.
13 And if a man lie not in wait, but God deliver *him* into his hand; then I will appoint you a place whither he will flee.
14 But if a man come presumptuously upon his neighbor, to slay him with guile; you will take him from mine altar, that he may die.
15 And he that smites his father, or his mother, will be surely put to death.
16 And he that steal a man, and sells him, or if he be found in his hand, he will surely be put to death.
17 And he that curses his father, or his mother, will surely be put to death.
18 And if men strive together, and one smite another with a stone, or with *his* fist, and he die not, but keeps *his* bed:
19 If he rise again, and walk abroad upon his staff, then will he that smote *him* be quit: only he will pay *for* the loss of his time, and will cause *him* to be thoroughly healed.
20 And if a man smite his servant, or his maid, with a rod, and he die under his hand; he will be surely punished.
21 Notwithstanding, if he continues a day or two, he will not be punished: for he *is* his money.
22 If men strive, and hurt a woman with child, so that her fruit depart *from her*, and yet no mischief follows: he will be surely punished, according as the woman's husband will lay upon him; and he will pay as the judges *determine*.
23 And if *any* mischief follows, then you will give life for life,
24 Eye for eye, tooth for tooth, hand for hand, foot for foot,
25 Burning for burning, wound for wound, stripe for stripe.
26 And if a man smite the eye of his servant, or the eye of his maid, that it perish; he will let him go free for his eye's sake.
27 And if he smite out his manservant's tooth, or his maidservant's tooth; he will let him go free for his tooth's sake.
28 If an ox gore a man or a woman, that they die: then the ox will be surely stoned, and his flesh will not be eaten; but the owner of the ox will *be* quit.
29 But if the ox were wont to push with his horn in time past, and it hath been testified to his owner, and he hath not kept him in, but that he hath killed a man or a woman; the ox will be stoned, and his owner also will be put to death.
30 If there be laid on him a sum of money, then he will give for the ransom of his life whatsoever is laid upon him.
31 Whether he have gored a son, or have gored a daughter, according to this judgment will it be done unto him.
32 If the ox will push a manservant or a maidservant; he will give unto their master thirty shekels of silver, and the ox will be stoned.
33 And *if a man will* open *a* pit, or if a man will dig a pit, and not cover it, and an ox or an ass fall therein;
34 The owner of the pit will make *it* good, *and* give money unto the owner of them; and the dead *beast* will be his.
35 And if one man's ox hurt another's, that he die; then they will sell the live ox, and divide the money of it; and the dead ox also they will divide.
36 Or if it be known that the ox hath used to push in time past, and his owner hath not kept him in; he will surely pay ox for ox; and the dead will be his own.

CHAPTER 22

1 If a man will steal an ox, or a sheep, and kill it, or sell it; he will restore five oxen for an ox, and four sheep for a sheep.
2 If a thief be found breaking up, and be smitten that he die, *there will* no blood *be shed* for him.
3 If the sun be **raised** upon him, *there will be* blood *shed* for him; *for* he should make full restitution; if he has nothing, then he will be sold for his theft.
4 If the theft be certainly found in his hand alive, whether it be ox, or ass, or sheep; he will restore double.
5 If a man will cause a field or vineyard to be eaten, and will put in his beast, and will feed in another man's field; of the best of his own field, and of the best of his own vineyard, will he make restitution.
6 If fire break out, and catch in thorns, so that the stacks of corn, or the standing corn, or the field, be consumed *therewith*; he that kindled the fire will surely make restitution.
7 If a man will deliver unto his neighbor money or stuff to keep, and it be stolen out of the man's house; if the thief be found, let him pay double.
8 If the thief be not found, then the master of the house will be brought unto the judges, *to see* whether he have put his hand unto his neighbor's goods.
9 For all manner of trespass, *whether it be* for ox, for ass, for sheep, for raiment, *or* for any manner of lost thing, which *another* challenged to be his, the cause of both parties will come before the judges; *and* whom the judges will condemn, he will pay double unto his neighbor.
10 If a man deliver unto his neighbor an ass, or an ox, or a sheep, or any beast, to keep; and it die, or be hurt, or driven away, no man seeing *it*:
11 *Then* will an oath of the LORD be between them both, that he hath not put his hand unto his neighbor's goods; and the owner of it will accept *thereof*, and he will not make *it* good.
12 And if it be stolen from him, he will make restitution unto the owner thereof.
13 If it be torn in pieces, *then* let him bring it *for* witness, *and* he will not make good that which was torn.
14 And if a man borrow *ought* of his neighbor, and it be hurt, or die, the owner thereof *being* not with it, he will surely make *it* good.
15 *But* if the owner thereof *be* with it, he will not make *it* good: if it *be* a hired *thing*, it came for his hire.
16 And if a man entices a maid that is not betrothed, and lie with her, he will surely endow her to be his wife.
17 If her father utterly refuses to give her unto him, he will pay money according to the dowry of virgins.
18 You will not suffer a witch to live.
19 Whosoever lies with a beast will surely be put to death.
20 He that sacrifice unto *any* god, save unto the LORD only, he will be utterly destroyed.

21 You will neither vex a stranger, nor oppress him: for you were strangers in the land of Egypt.
22 You will not afflict any widow, or fatherless child.
23 If you afflict them in any wise, and they cry at all unto me, I will surely hear their cry;
24 And my wrath will wax hot, and I will kill you with the sword; and your wives will be widows, and your children fatherless.
25 If you lend money to *any of* my people *that is* poor by you, you will not be to him as a usurer, neither will you lay upon him usury.
26 If you at all take your neighbor's raiment to pledge, you will deliver it unto him by that the sun goes down:
27 For that *is* his covering only, it *is* his raiment for his skin: wherein will he sleep? And it will come to pass, when he cries unto me, that I will hear; for I *am* gracious.
28 You will not revile the gods, nor curse the ruler of your people.
29 You will not delay *to offer* the first of your ripe fruits, and of your liquors: the firstborn of your sons will you give unto me.
30 Likewise will you do with your oxen, *and* with your sheep: seven days it will be with his dam; on the eighth day you will give it me.
31 And you will be holy men unto me: neither will you eat *any* flesh *that is* torn of beasts in the field; you will cast it to the dogs.

CHAPTER 23

1 You will not raise a false report: put not your hand with the wicked to be an unrighteous witness.
2 You will not follow a multitude to *do* evil; neither will you speak in a cause to decline after many to wrest *judgment*:
3 Neither will you countenance a poor man in his cause.
4 If you meet your enemy's ox or his ass going astray, you will surely bring it back to him again.
5 If you see the ass of him that hated you lying under his burden, and would forbear to help him, you will surely help with him.
6 you will not wrest the judgment of your poor in his cause.
7 Keep you far from a false matter; and the innocent and righteous slay you not: for I will not justify the wicked.
8 And you will take no gift: for the gift blinded the wise, and perverted the words of the righteous.
9 Also you will not oppress a stranger: for you know the heart of a stranger, seeing you were strangers in the land of Egypt.
10 And six years you will sow your land, and will gather in the fruits thereof:
11 But the seventh *year* you will let it rest and lie still; that the poor of your people may eat: and what they leave the beasts of the field will eat. In like manner you will deal with your vineyard, *and* with your olive yard.
12 Six days you will do your work, and on the seventh day you will rest: that your ox and your ass may rest, and the son of your handmaid, and the stranger, may be refreshed.
13 And in all *things* that I have said unto you be circumspect: and make no mention of the name of other gods, neither let it be heard out of your mouth.
14 Three times you will keep a feast unto me in the year.
15 you will keep the feast of unleavened bread: (thou will eat unleavened bread seven days, as I commanded you, in the time appointed of the month Abib; for in it you **come** out from Egypt: and none will appear before me empty:)
16 And the feast of harvest, the first fruits of your labors, which you have sown *in* the field: *and* the feast of ingathering, *which is* in the end of the year, when you have gathered in your labors out of the field.
17 Three times in the year all your males will appear before the Lord GOD.
18 you will not offer the blood of my sacrifice with leavened bread; neither will the fat of my sacrifice remain until the morning.
19 The first of the first fruits of your land you will bring into the house of the LORD your God. You will not seethe a kid in his mother's milk.
20 Behold, I send an Angel before you, to keep you in the way, and to bring you into the place which I have prepared.
21 Beware of him, and obey his voice, provoke him not; for he will not pardon your transgressions: for my name *is* in him.
22 But if you will indeed obey his voice, and do all that I speak; then I will be an enemy unto your enemies, and an adversary unto your adversaries.
23 For mine Angel will go before you, and bring you in unto the Amorites, and the Hittites, and the Perizzites, and the Canaanites, the Hivites, and the Jebusites: and I will cut them off.
24 You will not bow down to their gods, nor serve them, nor do after their works: but you will utterly overthrow them, and quite break down their images.
25 And you will serve the LORD your God, and he will bless your bread, and your water; and I will take sickness away from the midst of you.
26 There will nothing cast their young, nor be barren, in your land: the number of your days I will fulfil.
27 I will send my fear before you, and will destroy all the people to whom you will come, and I will make all your enemies turn their backs unto you.
28 And I will send hornets before you, which will drive out the Hivite, the Canaanite, and the Hittite, from before you.
29 I will not drive them out from before you in one year; lest the land become desolate, and the beast of the field multiply against you.
30 By little and little I will drive them out from before you, until you be increased, and inherit the land.
31 And I will set your bounds from the Red sea even unto the sea of the Philistines, and from the desert unto the river: for I will deliver the inhabitants of the land into your hand; and you will drive them out before you.
32 You will make no covenant with them, or with their gods.
33 They will not dwell in your land, lest they make you sin against me: for if you serve their gods, it will surely be a snare unto you.

CHAPTER 24

1 And he said unto Moses, Come up unto the LORD, thou, and Aaron, Nadab, and Abihu, and seventy of the elders of Israel; and worship you afar off.
2 And Moses alone will come near the LORD: but they will not come nigh; neither will the people go up with him.
3 And Moses came and told the people all the words of the LORD, and all the judgments: and all the people answered with one voice, and said, all the words which the LORD hath said will we do.
4 And Moses wrote all the words of the LORD, and rose up early in the morning, and builds an altar under the hill, and twelve pillars, according to the twelve tribes of Israel.
5 And he sent young men of the children of Israel, which offered burnt offerings, and sacrificed peace offerings of oxen unto the LORD.

6 And Moses took half of the blood, and put *it* in basons; and half of the blood he sprinkled on the altar.
7 And he took the book of the covenant, and read in the audience of the people: and they said, all that the LORD hath said will we do, and be obedient.
8 And Moses took the blood, and sprinkled *it* on the people, and said, Behold the blood of the covenant, which the LORD hath made with you concerning all these words.
9 Then went up Moses, and Aaron, Nadab, and Abihu, and seventy of the elders of Israel:
10 And they saw the God of Israel: and *there was* under his feet as it were a paved work of a sapphire stone, and as it were the body of heaven in *his* clearness.
11 And upon the nobles of the children of Israel he laid not his hand: also they saw God, and did eat and drink.
12 [And the LORD said unto Moses, Come up to me into the mount, and be there: and I will give you tables of stone, and a law, and commandments which I have written; that you may teach them.]¹
13 And Moses rose up, and his minister Joshua: and Moses went up into the mount of God.
14 And he said unto the elders, Tarry you here for us, until we come again unto you: and, behold, Aaron and Hur *are* with you: if any man have any matters to do, let him come unto them.
15 And Moses went up into the mount, and a cloud covered the mount.
16 [And the glory of the LORD abode upon Mount Sinai, and the cloud covered it six days: and the seventh day he called unto Moses out of the midst of the cloud.]²
17 And the sight of the glory of the LORD *was* like devouring fire on the top of the mount in the eyes of the children of Israel.
18 And Moses went into the midst of the cloud, and gat him up into the mount: and Moses was in the mount forty days and forty nights.

CHAPTER 25

1 And the LORD spoke unto Moses, saying,
2 Speak unto the children of Israel, that they bring me an offering: of every man that giveth it willingly with his heart you will take my offering.
3 And this *is* the offering which you will take of them; gold, and silver, and brass,
4 And blue, and purple, and scarlet, and fine linen, and goats' *hair*,
5 And rams' skins dyed red, and badgers' skins, and shittim wood,
6 Oil for the light, spices for anointing oil, and for sweet incense,
7 Onyx stones, and stones to be set in the ephod, and in the breastplate.
8 And let them make me a sanctuary; that I may dwell among them.
9 According to all that I shew you, *after* the pattern of the tabernacle, and the pattern of all the instruments thereof, even so will you make *it*.
10 And they will make an ark *of* shittim wood: two cubits and a half will *be* the length thereof, and a cubit and a half the breadth thereof, and a cubit and a half the height thereof.
11 And you will overlay it with pure gold, within and without will you overlay it, and will make upon it a crown of gold round about.
12 And you will cast four rings of gold for it, and put *them* in the four corners thereof; and two rings will *be* in the one side of it, and two rings in the other side of it.

13 And you will make staves *of* shittim wood, and overlay them with gold.
14 And you will put the staves into the rings by the sides³ of the ark, that the ark may be borne with them.
15 The staves will be in the rings of the ark: they will not be taken from it.
16 And you will put into the ark the testimony which I will give you.
17 And you will make a mercy seat *of* pure gold: two cubits and a half will *be* the length thereof, and a cubit and a half the breadth thereof.
18 And you will make two cherubim's *of* gold, *of* beaten work will you make them, in the two ends of the mercy seat.
19 And make one cherub on the one end, and the other cherub on the other end: *even of* the mercy seat will you make the cherubim's on the two ends thereof.
20 And the cherubim's will stretch forth *their* wings on high, covering the mercy seat with their wings, and their faces will look one to another; toward the mercy seat will the faces of the cherubim's be.
21 And you will put the mercy seat above upon the ark; and in the ark you will put the testimony that I will give you.
22 And there I will meet with you, and I will commune with you from above the mercy seat, from between the two cherubim's which *are* upon the ark of the testimony, of all *things* which I will give you in commandment unto the children of Israel.
23 You will also make a table *of* shittim wood: two cubits will *be* the length thereof, and a cubit the breadth thereof, and a cubit and a half the height thereof.
24 And you will overlay it with pure gold, and make thereto a crown of gold round about.
25 And you will make unto it a border of a hand breadth round about, and you will make a golden crown to the border thereof round about.
26 And you will make for it four rings of gold, and put the rings in the four corners that *are* on the four feet thereof.
27 Over against the border will the rings be for places of the staves to bear the table.
28 And you will make the staves *of* shittim wood, and overlay them with gold, that the table may be borne with them.
29 And you will make the dishes thereof, and spoons thereof, and covers thereof, and bowls thereof, to cover withal: *of* pure gold will you make them.
30 And you will set upon the table shewbread before me always.
31 And you will make a candlestick *of* pure gold: *of* beaten work will the candlestick be made: his shaft, and his branches, his bowls, his knops, and his flowers, will be of the same.
32 And six branches will come out of the sides of it; three branches of the candlestick out of the one side, and three branches of the candlestick out of the other side:
33 Three bowls made like unto almonds, *with* a knop and a flower in one branch; and three bowls made like almonds in the other branch, *with* a knop and a flower: so in the six branches that come out of the candlestick.
34 And in the candlestick will *be* four bowls made like unto almonds, *with* their knops and their flowers.
35 And *there will be* a knop under two branches of the same, and a knop under two branches of the same, and a knop under two

---

¹ The revelation of your house-law will come through fasting.
² It took seven days for God to speak.

³ sides – a rib (a curved) of the body, figuratively of a door that is leaf [Strgs#6763]

branches of the same, according to the six branches that proceed out of the candlestick.

36 Their knops and their branches will be of the same: all it will *be* one beaten work *of* pure gold.

37 And you will make the seven lamps thereof: and they will light the lamps thereof, that they may give light over against it.

38 And the tongs thereof, and the snuff dishes thereof, will *be of* pure gold.

39 *Of* a talent of pure gold will he make it, with all these vessels.

40 And look that you make *them* after their pattern, which was shewed you in the mount.

CHAPTER 26

1 Moreover you will make the tabernacle *with* ten curtains *of* fine twined linen, and blue, and purple, and scarlet: *with* cherubim's of cunning work will you make them.

2 The length of one curtain will *be* eight and twenty cubits, and the breadth of one curtain four cubits: and every one of the curtains will have one measure.

3 The five curtains will be coupled together one to another; and *other* five curtains will *be* coupled one to another.

4 And you will make loops of blue upon the edge of the one curtain from the selvedge in the coupling; and likewise will you make in the uttermost edge of *another* curtain, in the coupling of the second.

5 Fifty loops will you make in the one curtain, and fifty loops will you make in the edge of the curtain that *is* in the coupling of the second; that the loops may take hold one of another.

6 And you will make fifty **belaying pins** of gold, and couple the curtains together with the **belaying pins**: and it will be one tabernacle.

7 And you will make curtains *of* goats' *hair* to be a covering upon the tabernacle: eleven curtains will you make.

8 The length of one curtain will *be* thirty cubits, and the breadth of one curtain four cubits: and the eleven curtains will *be all* of one measure.

9 And you will couple five curtains by themselves, and six curtains by themselves, and will double the sixth curtain in the forefront of the tabernacle.

10 And you will make fifty loops on the edge of the one curtain *that is* outmost in the coupling, and fifty loops in the edge of the curtain which couples the second.

11 And you will make fifty **belaying pins** of brass, and put the **belaying pins** into the loops, and couple the tent together, that it may be one.

12 And the remnant that remained of the curtains of the tent, the half curtain that remained, will hang over the backside of the tabernacle.

13 And a cubit on the one side, and a cubit on the other side of that which remained in the length of the curtains of the tent, it will hang over the sides of the tabernacle on this side and on that side, to cover it.

14 And you will make a covering for the tent *of* rams' skins dyed red, and a covering above *of* badgers' skins.

15 And you will make boards for the tabernacle *of* shittim wood standing up.

16 Ten cubits will *be* the length of a board, and a cubit and a half will *be* the breadth of one board.

17 Two tenons will *there be* in one board, set in order one against another: thus will you make for all the boards of the tabernacle.

18 And you will make the boards for the tabernacle, twenty boards on the south side southward.

19 And you will make forty sockets of silver under the twenty boards; two sockets under one board for his two tenons, and two sockets under another board for his two tenons.

20 And for the second side of the tabernacle on the north side *there will be* twenty boards:

21 And their forty sockets *of* silver; two sockets under one board, and two sockets under another board.

22 And for the sides of the tabernacle westward you will make six boards.

23 And two boards will you make for the corners of the tabernacle in the two sides.

24 And they will be coupled together beneath, and they will be coupled together above the head of it unto one ring: thus will it be for them both; they will be for the two corners.

25 And they will be eight boards, and their sockets *of* silver, sixteen sockets; two sockets under one board, and two sockets under another board.

26 And you will make bars *of* shittim wood; five for the boards of the one side of the tabernacle,

27 And five bars for the boards of the other side of the tabernacle, and five bars for the boards of the side of the tabernacle, for the two sides westward.

28 And the middle bar in the midst of the boards will reach from end to end.

29 And you will overlay the boards with gold, and make their rings *of* gold *for* places for the bars: and you will overlay the bars with gold.

30 And you will rear up the tabernacle according to the fashion thereof which was shewed you in the mount.

31 And you will make a vail *of* blue, and purple, and scarlet, and fine twined linen of cunning work: with cherubims will it be made:

32 And you will hang it upon four pillars of shittim *wood* overlaid with gold: their hooks will *be of* gold, upon the four sockets of silver.

33 And you will hang up the vail under the **belaying pins**, that you may bring in thither within the vail the ark of the testimony: and the vail will divide unto you between the holy *place* and the most holy.

34 And you will put the mercy seat upon the ark of the testimony in the most holy *place*.

35 And you will set the table without the vail, and the candlestick over against the table on the side of the tabernacle toward the south: and you will put the table on the north side.

36 And you will make a hanging for the door of the tent, *of* blue, and purple, and scarlet, and fine twined linen, wrought with needlework.

37 And you will make for the hanging five pillars *of* shittim wood, and overlay them with gold, *and* their hooks will *be of* gold: and you will cast five sockets of brass for them.

CHAPTER 27

1 And you will make an altar *of* shittim wood, five cubits long, and five cubits broad; the altar will be foursquare: and the height thereof will *be* three cubits.

2 And you will make the horns of it upon the four corners thereof: his horns will be of the same: and you will overlay it with brass.

3 And you will make his pans to receive his ashes, and his shovels, and his bowls, and his flesh hooks, and his firepans: all the vessels thereof you will make *of* brass.

4 And you will make for it a grate of network *of* brass; and upon the net will you make four brasen rings in the four corners thereof.
5 And you will put it under the compass of the altar beneath, that the net may be even to the midst of the altar.
6 And you will make staves for the altar, staves *of* shittim wood, and overlay them with brass.
7 And the staves will be put into the rings, and the staves will be upon the two sides of the altar, to bear it.
8 Hollow[1] with boards will you make it: as it was shewed you in the mount, so will they make *it*.
9 And you will make the court of the tabernacle: for the south side southward *there will be* hangings for the court *of* fine twined linen of an hundred cubits long for one side:
10 And the twenty pillars thereof and their twenty sockets will *be of* brass; the hooks of the pillars and their fillets will *be of* silver.
11 And likewise for the north side in length *there will be* hangings of an hundred *cubits* long, and his twenty pillars and their twenty sockets *of* brass; the hooks of the pillars and their fillets *of* silver.
12 And *for* the breadth of the court on the west side will *be* hangings of fifty cubits: their pillars ten, and their sockets ten.
13 And the breadth of the court on the east side eastward will *be* fifty cubits.
14 The hangings of one side *of the gate will be* fifteen cubits: their pillars three, and their sockets three.
15 And on the other side will *be* hangings fifteen *cubits*: their pillars three, and their sockets three.
16 And for the gate of the court will *be* a hanging of twenty cubits, *of* blue, and purple, and scarlet, and fine twined linen, wrought with needlework: *and* their pillars will *be* four, and their sockets four.
17 All the pillars round about the court will *be* filleted with silver; their hooks will *be of* silver, and their sockets *of* brass.
18 The length of the court will *be* an hundred cubits, and the breadth fifty everywhere, and the height five cubits *of* fine twined linen, and their sockets *of* brass.
19 All the vessels of the tabernacle in all the service thereof, and all the pins thereof, and all the pins of the court, will *be of* brass.
20 And you will command the children of Israel, that they bring you pure oil olive beaten for the light, to cause the lamp to burn always.
21 In the tabernacle of the congregation without the vail, which *is* before the testimony, Aaron and his sons will order it from evening to morning before the LORD: *it will be* a statute forever unto their generations on the behalf of the children of Israel.

CHAPTER 28

1 And take you unto you Aaron your brother, and his sons with him, from among the children of Israel, that he may minister unto me in the priest's office, *even* Aaron, Nadab and Abihu, Eleazar and Ithamar, Aaron's sons.
2 And you will make holy garments for Aaron your brother for glory and for beauty.
3 And you will speak unto all *that are* wise hearted, whom I have filled with the spirit of wisdom, that they may make Aaron's garments to consecrate him, that he may minister unto me in the priest's office.
4 And these *are* the garments which they will make; a breastplate, and an ephod, and a robe, and a broidered coat, a turban, and a girdle: and they will make holy garments for Aaron your brother, and his sons, that he may minister unto me in the priest's office.

5 And they will take gold, and blue, and purple, and scarlet, and fine linen.
6 And they will make the ephod *of* gold, *of* blue, and *of* purple, *of* scarlet, and fine twined linen, with cunning work.
7 It will have the two shoulder pieces thereof joined at the two edges thereof; and *so* it will be joined together.
8 And the curious girdle of the ephod, which *is* upon it, will be of the same, according to the work thereof; *even of* gold, *of* blue, and purple, and scarlet, and fine twined linen.
9 And you will take two onyx stones, and grave on them the names of the children of Israel:
10 Six of their names on one stone, and *the other* six names of the rest on the other stone, according to their birth.
11 With the work of an engraver in stone, *like* the engravings of a signet, will you engrave the two stones with the names of the children of Israel: you will make them to be set in ouches of gold.
12 And you will put the two stones upon the shoulders of the ephod *for* stones of memorial unto the children of Israel: and Aaron will bear their names before the LORD upon his two shoulders for a memorial.
13 And you will make ouches *of* gold;
14 And two chains *of* pure gold at the ends; *of* wreathen work will you make them, and fasten the wreathen chains to the ouches.
15 And you will make the breastplate of judgment with cunning work; after the work of the ephod you will make it; *of* gold, *of* blue, and *of* purple, and *of* scarlet, and *of* fine twined linen, will you make it.
16 Foursquare it will be *being* doubled; a span will *be* the length thereof, and a span will *be* the breadth thereof.
17 And you will set in it settings of stones, *even* four rows of stones: *the first* row will *be* a sardius, a topaz, and a carbuncle: *this will be* the first row.
18 And the second row will *be* an emerald, a sapphire, and a diamond.
19 And the third row a ligure[2], an agate, and an amethyst.
20 And the fourth row a beryl, and an onyx, and a jasper: they will be set in gold in their enclosings.
21 And the stones will be with the names of the children of Israel, twelve, according to their names, *like* the engravings of a signet; every one with his name will they be according to the twelve tribes.
22 And you will make upon the breastplate chains at the ends *of* wreathen work *of* pure gold.
23 And you will make upon the breastplate two rings of gold, and will put the two rings on the two ends of the breastplate.
24 And you will put the two wreathen *chains* of gold in the two rings *which are* on the ends of the breastplate.
25 And *the other* two ends of the two wreathen *chains* you will fasten in the two ouches, and put *them* on the shoulder pieces of the ephod before it.
26 And you will make two rings of gold, and you will put them upon the two ends of the breastplate in the border thereof which *is* in the side of the ephod inward.
27 And two *other* rings of gold you will make, and will put them on the two sides of the ephod underneath, toward the forepart thereof, over against the *other* coupling thereof, above the curious girdle of the ephod.

---

[1] lit. to pierce, or figuratively foolish [Strgs#5014]. Compare **1 Cor. 1:18-25**.

[2] ligure- a gem, perhaps the *jacinth*. A precious stone in the high priest's breast-plate. [Strgs#3958]

Exodus

28 And they will bind the breastplate by the rings thereof unto the rings of the ephod with a lace of blue, that *it* may be above the curious girdle of the ephod, and that the breastplate be not loosed from the ephod.
29 And Aaron will bear the names of the children of Israel in the breastplate of judgment upon his heart, when he goes in unto the holy *place*, for a memorial before the LORD continually.
30 And you will put in the breastplate of judgment the Urim and the Thummim; and they will be upon Aaron's heart, when he goes in before the LORD: and Aaron will bear the judgment of the children of Israel upon his heart before the LORD continually.
31 And you will make the robe of the ephod all *of* blue.
32 And there will be an hole in the top of it, in the midst thereof: it will have a binding of woven work round about the hole of it, as it were the hole of an habergeon, that it be not rent.
33 And *beneath* upon the hem of it you will make pomegranates *of* blue, and *of* purple, and *of* scarlet, round about the hem thereof; and bells of gold between them round about:
34 A golden bell and a pomegranate, a golden bell and a pomegranate, upon the hem of the robe round about.
35 And it will be upon Aaron to minister: and his sound will be heard when he goes in unto the holy *place* before the LORD, and when he cometh out, that he die not.
36 And you will make a plate *of* pure gold, and grave upon it, *like* the engravings of a signet, HOLINESS TO THE LORD.
37 And you will put it on a blue lace, that it may be upon the turban; upon the forefront of the turban it will be.
38 And it will be upon Aaron's forehead, that Aaron may bear the iniquity of the holy things, which the children of Israel will hallow in all their holy gifts; and it will be always upon his forehead, that they may be accepted before the LORD.
39 And you will embroider the coat of fine linen, and you will make the turban *of* fine linen, and you will make the girdle *of* needlework.
40 And for Aaron's sons you will make coats, and you will make for them girdles, and bonnets will you make for them, for glory and for beauty.
41 And you will put them upon Aaron your brother, and his sons with him; and will anoint them, and consecrate them, and sanctify them, that they may minister unto me in the priest's office.
42 And you will make them linen breeches to cover their nakedness; from the loins even unto the thighs they will reach:
43 And they will be upon Aaron, and upon his sons, when they come in unto the tabernacle of the congregation, or when they come near unto the altar to minister in the holy *place*; that they bear not iniquity, and die: *it will be* a statute forever unto him and his seed after him.

CHAPTER 29

1 And this *is* the thing that you will do unto them to hallow them, to minister unto me in the priest's office: Take one young bullock, and two rams without blemish,
2 And unleavened bread, and cakes unleavened tempered with oil, and wafers unleavened anointed with oil: *of* wheaten flour will you make them.
3 And you will put them into one basket, and bring them in the basket, with the bullock and the two rams.
4 And Aaron and his sons you will bring unto the door of the tabernacle of the congregation, and will wash them with water.
5 And you will take the garments, and put upon Aaron the coat, and the robe of the ephod, and the ephod, and the breastplate, and gird him with the curious girdle of the ephod:
6 And you will put the turban upon his head, and put the holy crown upon the turban.
7 Then will you take the anointing oil, and pour *it* upon his head, and anoint him.
8 And you will bring his sons, and put coats upon them.
9 And you will gird them with girdles, Aaron and his sons, and put the bonnets on them: and the priest's office will be theirs for a perpetual statute: and you will consecrate Aaron and his sons.
10 And you will cause a bullock to be brought before the tabernacle of the congregation: and Aaron and his sons will put their hands upon the head of the bullock.
11 And you will kill the bullock before the LORD, *by* the door of the tabernacle of the congregation.
12 And you will take of the blood of the bullock, and put *it* upon the horns of the altar with your finger, and pour all the blood beside the bottom of the altar.
13 And you will take all the fat that covered the inwards, and the caul *that is* above the liver, and the two kidneys, and the fat that *is* upon them, and burn *them* upon the altar.
14 But the flesh of the bullock, and his skin, and his dung, will you burn with fire without the camp: it *is* a sin offering.
15 you will also take one ram; and Aaron and his sons will put their hands upon the head of the ram.
16 And you will slay the ram, and you will take his blood, and sprinkle *it* round about upon the altar.
17 And you will cut the ram in pieces, and wash the inwards of him, and his legs, and put *them* unto his pieces, and unto his head.
18 And you will burn the whole ram upon the altar: it *is* a burnt offering unto the LORD: it *is* a sweet savor, an offering made by fire unto the LORD.
19 And you will take the other ram; and Aaron and his sons will put their hands upon the head of the ram.
20 Then will you kill the ram, and take of his blood, and put *it* upon the tip of the right ear of Aaron, and upon the tip of the right ear of his sons, and upon the thumb of their right hand, and upon the great toe of their right foot, and sprinkle the blood upon the altar round about.
21 And you will take of the blood that *is* upon the altar, and of the anointing oil, and sprinkle *it* upon Aaron, and upon his garments, and upon his sons, and upon the garments of his sons with him: and he will be hallowed, and his garments, and his sons and his sons' garments with him.
22 Also you will take of the ram the fat and the rump, and the fat that covered the inwards, and the caul *above* the liver, and the two kidneys, and the fat that *is* upon them, and the right shoulder; for it *is* a ram of consecration:
23 And one loaf of bread, and one cake of oiled bread, and one wafer out of the basket of the unleavened bread that *is* before the LORD:
24 And you will put all in the hands of Aaron, and in the hands of his sons; and will wave them *for* a wave offering before the LORD.
25 And you will receive them of their hands, and burn *them* upon the altar for a burnt offering, for a sweet savor before the LORD: it *is* an offering made by fire unto the LORD.
26 And you will take the breast of the ram of Aaron's consecration, and wave it *for* a wave offering before the LORD: and it will be your part.

27 And you will sanctify the breast of the wave offering, and the shoulder of the heave offering, which is waved, and which is heaved up, of the ram of the consecration, *even* of *that* which *is* for Aaron, and of *that* which is for his sons:

28 And it will be Aaron's and his sons' by a statute forever from the children of Israel: for it *is* an heave offering: and it will be an heave offering from the children of Israel of the sacrifice of their peace offerings, *even* their heave offering unto the LORD.

29 And the holy garments of Aaron will be his sons' after him, to be anointed therein, and to be consecrated in them.

30 *And* that son that is priest in his stead will put them on seven days, when he cometh into the tabernacle of the congregation to minister in the holy *place*.

31 And you will take the ram of the consecration, and seethe his flesh in the holy place.

32 And Aaron and his sons will eat the flesh of the ram, and the bread that *is* in the basket, *by* the door of the tabernacle of the congregation.

33 And they will eat those things wherewith the atonement was made, to consecrate *and* to sanctify them: but a stranger will not eat *thereof*, because they *are* holy.

34 And if ought of the flesh of the consecrations, or of the bread, remain unto the morning, then you will burn the remainder with fire: it will not be eaten, because it *is* holy.

35 And thus will you do unto Aaron, and to his sons, according to all *things* which I have commanded you: seven days will you consecrate them.

36 And you will offer every day a bullock *for* a sin offering for atonement: and you will cleanse the altar, when you have made atonement for it, and you will anoint it, to sanctify it.

37 Seven days you will make atonement for the altar, and sanctify it; and it will be an altar most holy: whatsoever touch the altar will be holy.

38 Now this *is that* which you will offer upon the altar; two lambs of the first year day by day continually.

39 The one lamb you will offer in the morning; and the other lamb you will offer at even:

40 And with the one lamb a tenth deal of flour mingled with the fourth part of a hin of beaten oil; and the fourth part of an hin of wine *for* a drink offering.

41 And the other lamb you will offer at even, and will do thereto according to the meat offering of the morning, and according to the drink offering thereof, for a sweet savor, an offering made by fire unto the LORD.

42 *This will be* a continual burnt offering throughout your generations *at* the door of the tabernacle of the congregation before the LORD: where I will meet you, to speak there unto you.

43 And there I will meet with the children of Israel, and *the tabernacle* will be sanctified by my glory.

44 And I will sanctify the tabernacle of the congregation, and the altar: I will sanctify also both Aaron and his sons, to minister to me in the priest's office.

45 And I will dwell among the children of Israel, and will be their God.

46 And they will know that I *am* the LORD their God, that brought them forth out of the land of Egypt, that I may dwell among them: I *am* the LORD their God.

CHAPTER 30

1 And you will make an altar to [burn incense]¹ upon: of shittim wood will you make it.

2 A cubit will *be* the length thereof, and a cubit the breadth thereof; foursquare will it be: and two cubits will *be* the height thereof: the horns thereof will *be* of the same.

3 And you will overlay it with pure gold, the **roof** thereof, and the **walls** thereof round about, and the horns thereof; and you will make unto it a crown² of gold round about.

4 And two golden rings³ will you make to it under the crown of it, by the two corners⁴ thereof, upon the two sides of it will you make *it*; and they will be for places for the staves⁵ to bear it withal.

5 And you will make the staves *of* shittim wood, and overlay them with gold.

6 And you will put it before the vail that *is* by the ark of the testimony, before the mercy seat that *is* over the testimony, where I will meet with you.

7 And Aaron will burn thereon sweet incense [every morning]⁶: when [he dressed]⁷ the lamps, he will burn incense upon it.

8 And when Aaron lighted⁸ the lamps at even, he will burn incense upon it, a perpetual incense before the LORD throughout your generations.

9 you will offer no strange⁹ incense thereon, nor burnt sacrifice, nor meat offering; neither will you pour drink offering thereon.

10 And Aaron will make atonement upon the horns of it once in a year with the blood of the sin offering of atonements: once in the year will he make atonement upon it throughout your generations: it *is* most holy unto the LORD.

11 And the LORD spoke unto Moses, saying,

12 When you takes the sum of the children of Israel after their number, then will they give every man a ransom for his soul unto the LORD, when you number them; that there be no plague among them, when you number them.

13 This they will give, every one that passes among them that are numbered, half a shekel after the shekel of the sanctuary: (a shekel *is* twenty gerahs:) an half shekel will *be* the offering of the LORD.

14 Every one that passes among them that are numbered, from twenty years old and above, will give an offering unto the LORD.

15 The rich will not give more, and the poor will not give less than half a shekel, when *they* give an offering unto the LORD, to make atonement for your souls.

16 And you will take the atonement money of the children of Israel, and will appoint it for the service of the tabernacle of the congregation; that it may be a memorial unto the children of Israel before the LORD, to make atonement for your souls.

17 And the LORD spoke unto Moses, saying,

---

¹ lit. incense of incese [Strgs#4729, 6999 + 7004].

² <u>crown</u> - in the sense of *scattering*, a *chaplet* (as spread around the top), (specifically) a border *molding* [Strgs#2213].

³ <u>rings</u> – properly as *seal* (as sunk into the wax), that *signet* (for sealing); hence a *ring* of any kind [Strgs#2885].

⁴ <u>corners</u> – a *rib* (as curved) [Strgs#6763]. Jesus was pierced in his side (rib).

⁵ <u>staves</u> – properly *separation*, by implication a *part* of the body, *branch* of a tree, bar for carrying; figuratively *chief* of a city [Strgs#905].

⁶ lit. dawn as the break of day [Strgs#1242].

⁷ <u>he dresses</u> - to be, make well, sound, beautiful, happy, successful, right [Strgs#3190].

⁸ <u>lights</u> – Hebrew word 'âlâh meaning to *ascend* or actively *mounting* [Strgs#5927]

⁹ <u>strange</u> – to *turn* aside (especially for lodging); hence to be a *foreigner*, *profane*; specifically active to *commit adultery* [Strgs#2114].

18 you will also make a laver *of* brass, and his foot *also of* brass, to wash *withal*: and you will put it between the tabernacle of the congregation and the altar, and you will put water therein.
19 For Aaron and his sons will wash their hands and their feet thereat:
20 When they go into the tabernacle of the congregation, they will wash with water, that they die not; or when they come near to the altar to minister, to burn offering made by fire unto the LORD:
21 So they will wash their hands and their feet, that they die not: and it will be a statute for ever to them, *even* to him and to his seed throughout their generations.
22 Moreover the LORD spoke unto Moses, saying,
23 Take you also unto you principal spices, of pure myrrh five hundred *shekels*, and of sweet cinnamon half so much, *even* two hundred and fifty *shekels*, and of sweet calamus two hundred and fifty *shekels*,
24 And of cassia five hundred *shekels*, after the shekel of the sanctuary, and of oil olive a hin:
25 And you will make it an oil of holy ointment[1], an ointment[2] compound after the are of the apothecary[3]: it will be an holy anointing oil.
26 And you will anoint the tabernacle of the congregation therewith, and the ark of the testimony,
27 And the table and all his vessels, and the candlestick and his vessels, and the altar of incense,
28 And the altar of burnt offering with all his vessels, and the laver and his foot.
29 And you will sanctify them, that they may be most holy: whatsoever touches them will be holy.
30 And you will anoint Aaron and his sons, and consecrate them, that *they* may minister unto me in the priest's office.
31 And you will speak unto the children of Israel, saying, This will be an holy anointing oil unto me throughout your generations.
32 Upon man's flesh will it not be poured, neither will you make *any other* like it, after the composition of it: it *is* holy, *and* it will be holy unto you.
33 Whosoever compound *any* like it, or whosoever puts *any* of it upon a stranger, will even be cut off from his people.
34 And the LORD said unto Moses, Take unto you sweet spices, stacte, and onycha, and galbanum; *these* sweet spices with pure frankincense: of each will there be a like *weight*:
35 And you will make it a perfume, a confection after the are of the apothecary, tempered together, pure *and* holy:
36 And you will beat *some* of it very small, and put of it before the testimony in the tabernacle of the congregation, where I will meet with you: it will be unto you most holy.
37 And *as for* the perfume which you will make, you will not make to yourselves according to the composition thereof: it will be unto you holy for the LORD.
38 Whosoever will make like unto that, to smell thereto, will even be cut off from his people.

CHAPTER 31

1 And the LORD spoke unto Moses, saying,
2 See, I have called by name Bezaleel the son of Uri, the son of Hur, of the tribe of Judah:
3 And I have filled him with the spirit of God, in wisdom, and in understanding, and in knowledge, and in all manner of workmanship,
4 To devise cunning works, to work in gold, and in silver, and in brass,
5 [And in cutting of stones, to set *them*, and in carving of timber, to work in all manner of workmanship.][4]
6 And I, behold, I have given with him Aholiab, the son of Ahisamach, of the tribe of Dan: and in the hearts of all that are wise hearted I have put wisdom, that they may make all that I have commanded you;
7 The tabernacle of the congregation, and the ark of the testimony, and the mercy seat that *is* thereupon, and all the furniture of the tabernacle,
8 And the table and his furniture, and the pure candlestick with all his furniture, and the altar of incense,
9 And the altar of burnt offering with all his furniture, and the laver and his foot,
10 And the cloths of service, and the holy garments for Aaron the priest, and the garments of his sons, to minister in the priest's office,
11 And the anointing oil, and sweet incense for the holy *place*: according to all that I have commanded you will they do.
12 And the LORD spoke unto Moses, saying,
13 Speak you also unto the children of Israel, saying, verily my Sabbaths you will keep: for it *is* a sign between me and you throughout your generations; that you may know that I *am* the LORD that does sanctify you.
14 you will keep the Sabbath therefore; for it *is* holy unto you: every one that defiles it will surely be put to death: for whosoever doeth *any* work therein, that soul will be cut off from among his people.
15 Six days may work be done; but in the seventh *is* the Sabbath of rest, holy to the LORD: whosoever doeth *any* work in the Sabbath day, he will surely be put to death.
16 Wherefore the children of Israel will keep the Sabbath, to observe the Sabbath throughout their generations, *for a* perpetual covenant.
17 It *is* a sign between me and the children of Israel for ever: for *in* six days the LORD made heaven and earth, and on the seventh day he rested, and was refreshed.
18 And he gave unto Moses, when he had made an end of communing with him upon mount Sinai, two tables of testimony, tables of stone, written with the finger of God.

CHAPTER 32

1 And when the people saw that Moses delayed to come down out of the mount, the people gathered themselves together unto Aaron, and said unto him, Up, make us gods, which will go before us; for *as for* this Moses, the man that brought us up out of the land of Egypt, we wot not what is become of him.
2 And Aaron said unto them, Break off the golden earrings, which *are* in the ears of your wives, of your sons, and of your daughters, and bring *them* unto me.
3 And all the people brake off the golden earrings which *were* in their ears, and brought *them* unto Aaron.
4 And he received *them* at their hand, and fashioned it with a graving tool, after he had made it a molten calf: and they said,

---

[1] ointment – unction (the act) by implication a consecratory gift [Strgs#4888].
[2] ointment – aromatic [Strgs#7545]
[3] lit. perfume, prepare spice [Strgs#7543].
[4] God places in men that which He calls us to build.

these *be* your gods, O Israel, which brought you up out of the land of Egypt.

5 And when Aaron saw *it*, he built an altar before it; and Aaron made proclamation, and said, tomorrow *is* a feast to the LORD.

6 And they rose up early on the morrow, and offered burnt offerings, and brought peace offerings; and the people sat down to eat and to drink, and rose up to play.

7 And the LORD said unto Moses, Go, get you down; for your people, which you brought out of the land of Egypt, have corrupted *themselves*:

8 They have turned aside quickly out of the way which I commanded them: they have made them a molten calf, and have worshipped it, and have sacrificed thereunto, and said, these *be* your gods, O Israel, which has brought you up out of the land of Egypt.

9 And the LORD said unto Moses, I have seen this people, and, behold, it *is* a stiff-necked people:

10 Now therefore let me alone, that my wrath may wax hot against them, and that I may consume them: and I will make of you a great nation.

11 And Moses besought the LORD his God, and said, LORD, why does your wrath wax hot against your people, which you have brought forth out of the land of Egypt with great power, and with a mighty hand?

12 Wherefore should the Egyptians speak, and say, for mischief did he bring them out, to slay them in the mountains, and to consume them from the face of the earth? Turn from your fierce wrath, and repent of this evil against your people.

13 Remember Abraham, Isaac, and Israel, your servants, to whom you swore by your own self, and said unto them, I will multiply your seed as the stars of heaven, and all this land that I have spoken of will I give unto your seed, and they will inherit *it* forever.

14 And the LORD repented of the evil which he thought to do unto his people.

15 And Moses turned, and went down from the mount, and the two tables of the testimony *were* in his hand: the tables *were* written on both their sides; on the one side and on the other *were* they written.

16 And the tables *were* the work of God, and the writing *was* the writing of God, graven upon the tables.

17 And when Joshua heard the noise of the people as they shouted, he said unto Moses, *There is* a noise of war in the camp.

18 And he said, *it is* not the voice of *them that* shout for mastery, neither *is it* the voice of *them that* cry for being overcome: *but* the noise of *them that* sing do I hear.

19 And it came to pass, as soon as he came nigh unto the camp, that he saw the calf, and the dancing: and Moses' anger waxed hot, and he cast the tables out of his hands, and break them beneath the mount.

20 And he took the calf which they had made, and burnt *it* in the fire, and ground *it* to powder, and strawed *it* upon the water, and made the children of Israel drink *of it*.

21 And Moses said unto Aaron, What did this people unto you, that you have brought so great a sin upon them?

22 And Aaron said, let not the anger of my lord wax hot: you know the people, that they *are set* on mischief.

23 For they said unto me, make us gods, which will go before us: for *as for* this Moses, the man that brought us up out of the land of Egypt, we wot not what is become of him.

24 And I said unto them, whosoever hath any gold, let them break *it* off. So they gave *it* me: then I cast it into the fire, and there came out this calf.

25 And when Moses saw that the people *were* naked; (for Aaron had made them naked unto *their* shame among their enemies:)

26 Then Moses stood in the gate of the camp, and said, who *is* on the LORD'S side? *Let him come* unto me. And all the sons of Levi gathered themselves together unto him.

27 And he said unto them, Thus said the LORD God of Israel, Put every man his sword by his side, *and* go in and out from gate to gate throughout the camp, and slay every man his brother, and every man his companion, and every man his neighbor.

28 And the children of Levi did according to the word of Moses: and there fell of the people that day about three thousand men.

29 For Moses had said, consecrate yourselves to day to the LORD, even every man upon his son, and upon his brother; that he may bestow upon you a blessing this day.

30 And it came to pass on the morrow, that Moses said unto the people, you have sinned a great sin: and now I will go up unto the LORD; peradventure I will make atonement for your sin.

31 And Moses returned unto the LORD, and said, oh, this people have sinned a great sin, and have made them gods of gold.

32 Yet now, if you will forgive their sin--; and if not, blot me, I pray you, out of your book which you have written.

33 And the LORD said unto Moses, Whosoever hath sinned against me, him will I blot out of my book.

34 Therefore now go, lead the people unto *the place* of which I have spoken unto you: behold, mine Angel will go before you: nevertheless in the day when I visit I will visit their sin upon them.

35 And the LORD plagued the people, because they made the calf, which Aaron made.

CHAPTER 33

1 And the LORD said unto Moses, Depart, *and* go up hence, you and the people which you have brought up out of the land of Egypt, unto the land which I swore unto Abraham, to Isaac, and to Jacob, saying, Unto your seed will I give it:

2 And I will send an angel before you; and I will drive out the Canaanite, the Amorite, and the Hittite, and the Perizzite, the Hivite, and the Jebusite:

3 Unto a land flowing with milk and honey: for I will not go up in the midst of you; for you are a stiff-necked people: lest I consume you in the way.

4 And when the people heard these evil tidings, they mourned: and no man did put on him his ornaments.

5 For the LORD had said unto Moses, Say unto the children of Israel, you *are* a stiff-necked people: I will come up into the midst of you in a moment, and consume you: therefore now put off your ornaments from you, that I may know what to do unto you.

6 And the children of Israel stripped themselves of their ornaments by the mount Horeb.

7 And Moses took the tabernacle, and pitched it without the camp, afar off from the camp, and called it the Tabernacle of the congregation. And it came to pass, *that* everyone who sought the LORD went out unto the tabernacle of the congregation, which *was* without the camp.

8 And it came to pass, when Moses went out unto the tabernacle, *that* all the people rose up, and stood every man *at* his tent door, and looked after Moses, until he was gone into the tabernacle.

9 And it came to pass, as Moses entered into the tabernacle, the cloudy pillar descended, and stood *at* the door of the tabernacle, and *the* LORD talked with Moses.
10 And all the people saw the cloudy pillar stand *at* the tabernacle door: and all the people rose up and worshipped, every man *in* his tent door.
11 And the LORD spoke unto Moses face to face, as a man speak unto his friend. And he turned again into the camp: but his servant Joshua, the son of Nun, a young man, departed not out of the tabernacle.
12 And Moses said unto the LORD, See, you say unto me, Bring up this people: and you have not let me know whom you will send with me. Yet you have said, I know you by name[1], and you have also found grace in my sight.
13 Now therefore, I pray you, if I have found grace in your sight, shew me now your way, that I may know you, that I may find grace in your sight: and consider that this nation *is* your people.
14 And he said, my presence[2] will go *with you*, and I will give you rest.
15 And he said unto him, if your presence goes not *with me*, carry us not up hence.
16 For wherein will it be known here that I and your people have found grace in your sight? *Is it* not in that you go with us? So will we be separated, I and your people, from all the people that *are* upon the face of the earth.
17 And the LORD said unto Moses, I will do this thing also that you have spoken: for you have found grace in my sight, and I know you by name.
18 And he said, I beseech you, show me your glory.
19 And he said, I will make all my goodness pass before you, and I will proclaim the name of the LORD before you; and will be gracious to whom I will be gracious, and will shew mercy on whom I will shew mercy.
20 And he said, you canst not see my face: for there will no man see me, and live.
21 And the LORD said, Behold, *there is* a place by[3] me, and you will stand upon a rock:
22 And it will come to pass, while my glory passes by, that I will put you in a cliff[4] of the rock, and will cover you with my hand while I pass by:
23 And I will take away mine hand, and you will [see my back][5] parts: but my face will not be seen.

CHAPTER 34

1 And the LORD said unto Moses, Hew you two tables of stone like unto the first: and I will write upon *these* tables the words that were in the first tables, which you broke.
2 And be ready in the morning, and come up in the morning unto Mount Sinai, and present yourself there to me in the top of the mount.
3 And no man will come up with you, neither let any man be seen throughout the **entire** mount; neither let the flocks or herds feed before that mount.
4 And he hewed two tables of stone like unto the first; and Moses rose up early in the morning, and went up unto Mount Sinai, as the LORD had commanded him, and took in his hand the two tables of stone.
5 And the LORD descended in the cloud, and stood with him there, and proclaimed the name of the LORD.
6 And the LORD passed by before him, and proclaimed, The LORD, The LORD God, merciful and gracious, longsuffering, and abundant in goodness and truth,
7 Keeping mercy for thousands, forgiving iniquity and transgression and sin, and that will by no means clear *the guilty*; visiting the iniquity of the fathers upon the children, and upon the children's children, unto the third and to the fourth *generation*.
8 And Moses made haste, and bowed his head toward the earth, and worshipped.
9 And he said, if now I have found grace in your sight, O Lord, let my Lord, I pray you, go among[6] us; for it *is* a stiff-necked people; and pardon our iniquity and our sin, and take us for your inheritance.
10 And he said, Behold, I make a covenant: before all your people I will do marvels, such as have not been done[7] in all the earth, nor in any nation: and all the people among which you are will see the work of the LORD: for it *is* a terrible thing that I will do with you.
11 Observe you that which I command you this day behold, I drive out before you the Amorite, and the Canaanite, and the Hittite, and the Perizzite, and the Hivite, and the Jebusite.
12 Take heed to yourself, lest you make a covenant with the inhabitants of the land whither you go, lest it be for a snare in the midst of you:
13 But you will destroy their altars, break their images, and cut down their groves:
14 For you will worship no other god: for the LORD, whose name *is* Jealous, *is* a jealous God:
15 Lest you make a covenant with the inhabitants of the land, and they go a whoring after their gods, and do sacrifice unto their gods, and *one* call you, and you eat of his sacrifice;
16 And you take of their daughters unto your sons, and their daughters go a whoring after their gods, and make your sons go a whoring after their gods.
17 you will make you no molten gods.
18 The feast of unleavened bread will you keep. Seven days you will eat unleavened bread, as I commanded you, in the time of the month Abib: for in the month Abib you came out from Egypt.
19 All that opened the matrix *is* mine; and every firstling among your cattle, *whether* ox or sheep, *that is male*.
20 But the firstling of an ass you will redeem with a lamb: and if you redeem *him* not, then will you break his neck. All the firstborn of your sons you will redeem. And none will appear before me empty.
21 Six days you will work, but on the seventh day you will rest: in earing time and in harvest you will rest.
22 And you will observe the feast of weeks, of the first fruits of wheat harvest, and the feast of ingathering at the [year's end].[8]
23 Thrice in the year will all your men children appear before the Lord GOD, the God of Israel.

---

[1] compare Exodus 31:2
[2] presence = face [Strgs#6440]
[3] lit. with
[4] cliff = fissure, hole [Strgs#5366]. Derives from a root word meaning to bore, dig, pick out, pierce, thrust [Strgs#5365].
[5] compare Hebrews 11:27
[6] among = the nearest part [Strgs#7130]
[7] done = to create [Strgs#1254]
[8] year's end = revolution of year [Strgs'8141 + 8622]. End comes from Hebrew root word meaning to strike violently, to surround [Strgs#5362]

24 For I will cast out the nations before you, and enlarge your borders: neither will any man desire your land, when you will go up to appear before the LORD your God thrice in the year.
25 you will not offer the blood of my sacrifice with leaven; neither will the sacrifice of the feast of the Passover be left unto the morning.
26 The first of the first fruits of your land you will bring unto the house of the LORD your God. You will not seethe a kid in his mother's milk.
27 And the LORD said unto Moses, write you these words: for after the tenor of these words I have made a covenant with you and with Israel.
28 And he was there with the LORD forty days and forty nights; he did neither eat bread, nor drink water. And he wrote upon the tables the words of the covenant, the Ten Commandments.
29 [And it came to pass, when Moses came down from mount Sinai with the two tables of testimony in Moses' hand, when he came down from the mount, that Moses wist not that the skin of his face shone while he talked with him.][1]
30 And when Aaron and all the children of Israel saw Moses, behold, the skin of his face shone; and they were afraid to come nigh him.
31 And Moses called unto them; and Aaron and all the rulers of the congregation returned unto him: and Moses talked with them.
32 And afterward all the children of Israel came nigh: and he gave them in commandment all that the LORD had spoken with him in Mount Sinai.
33 And *till* Moses had done speaking with them, he put a vail on his face.
34 But when Moses went in before the LORD to speak with him, he took the vail off, until he came out. And he came out, and spoke unto the children of Israel *that* which he was commanded.
35 And the children of Israel saw the face of Moses, that the skin of Moses' face shone: and Moses put the vail upon his face again, until he went in to speak with him.

CHAPTER 35

1 And Moses gathered all the congregation of the children of Israel together, and said unto them, these *are* the words which the LORD hath commanded, that you should do them.
2 Six days will work be done, but on the seventh day there will be to you an holy day, a Sabbath of rest to the LORD: whosoever doeth work therein will be put to death.
3 you will kindle no fire throughout your habitations upon the Sabbath day.
4 And Moses spoke unto all the congregation of the children of Israel, saying, this *is* the thing which the LORD commanded, saying,
5 Take you from among you an offering unto the LORD: whosoever *is* of a willing heart, let him bring it, an offering of the LORD; gold, and silver, and brass,
6 And blue, and purple, and scarlet, and fine linen, and goats' *hair*,
7 And rams' skins dyed red, and badgers' skins, and shittim wood,
8 And oil for the light, and spices for anointing oil, and for the sweet incense,
9 And onyx stones, and stones to be set for the ephod, and for the breastplate.
10 And every wise hearted among you will come, and make all that the LORD hath commanded;
11 The tabernacle, his tent, and his covering, his **belaying pins**, and his boards, his bars, his pillars, and his sockets,
12 The ark, and the staves thereof, *with* the mercy seat, and the vail of the covering,
13 The table, and his staves, and all his vessels, and the shewbread,
14 The candlestick also for the light, and his furniture, and his lamps, with the oil for the light,
15 And the incense altar, and his staves, and the anointing oil, and the sweet incense, and the hanging for the door at the entering in of the tabernacle,
16 The altar of burnt offering, with his brasen grate, his staves, and all his vessels, the laver and his foot,
17 The hangings of the court, his pillars, and their sockets, and the hanging for the door of the court,
18 The pins of the tabernacle, and the pins of the court, and their cords,
19 The cloths of service, to do service in the holy *place*, the holy garments for Aaron the priest, and the garments of his sons, to minister in the priest's office.
20 And all the congregation of the children of Israel departed from the presence of Moses.
21 And they came, every one whose heart stirred him up, and every one whom his spirit made willing, *and* they brought the LORD'S offering to the work of the tabernacle of the congregation, and for all his service, and for the holy garments.
22 And they came, both men and women, as many as were willing hearted, *and* brought bracelets, and earrings, and rings, and tablets, all jewels of gold: and every man that offered an offering of gold unto the LORD.
23 And every man, with whom was found blue, and purple, and scarlet, and fine linen, and goats' *hair*, and red skins of rams, and badgers' skins, brought *them*.
24 Every one that did offer an offering of silver and brass brought the LORD'S offering: and every man, with whom was found shittim wood for any work of the service, brought *it*.
25 And all the women that were wise hearted did spin with their hands, and brought that which they had spun, *both* of blue, and of purple, *and* of scarlet, and of fine linen.
26 And all the women whose heart stirred them up in wisdom spun goats' *hair*.
27 And the rulers brought onyx stones, and stones to be set, for the ephod, and for the breastplate;
28 And spice, and oil for the light, and for the anointing oil, and for the sweet incense.
29 The children of Israel brought a willing offering unto the LORD, every man and woman, whose heart made them willing to bring for all manner of work, which the LORD had commanded to be made by the hand of Moses.
30 And Moses said unto the children of Israel, See, the LORD hath called by name Bezaleel the son of Uri, the son of Hur, of the tribe of Judah;
31 And he hath filled him with the spirit of God, in wisdom, in understanding, and in knowledge, and in all manner of workmanship;
32 And to devise curious works, to work in gold, and in silver, and in brass,

---
[1] Why? Compare Ex. 33:12-14 & Deut. 34:10

33 And in the cutting of stones, to set *them*, and in carving of wood, to make any manner of cunning work.
34 And he hath put in his heart that he may teach, *both* he, and Aholiab, the son of Ahisamach, of the tribe of Dan.
35 Them hath he filled with wisdom of heart, to work all manner of work, of the engraver, and of the cunning workman, and of the embroiderer, in blue, and in purple, in scarlet, and in fine linen, and of the weaver, *even* of them that do any work, and of those that devise cunning work.

CHAPTER 36

1 Then wrought Bezaleel and Aholiab, and every wise hearted man, in whom the LORD put wisdom and understanding to know how to work all manner of work for the service of the sanctuary, according to all that the LORD had commanded.
2 And Moses called Bezaleel and Aholiab, and every wise hearted man, in whose heart the LORD had put wisdom, *even* every one whose heart stirred him up to come unto the work to do it:
3 And they received of Moses all the offering, which the children of Israel had brought for the work of the service of the sanctuary, to make it *withal*. And they brought yet unto him free offerings every morning.
4 And all the wise men, that wrought all the work of the sanctuary, came every man from his work which they made;
5 And they spoke unto Moses, saying, The people bring much more than enough for the service of the work, which the LORD commanded to make.
6 And Moses gave commandment, and they caused it to be proclaimed throughout the camp, saying, Let neither man nor woman make any more work for the offering of the sanctuary. So the people were restrained from bringing.
7 For the stuff they had was sufficient for all the work to make it, and too much.
8 And every wise hearted man among them that wrought the work of the tabernacle made ten curtains *of* fine twined linen, and blue, and purple, and scarlet: *with* cherubims of cunning work made he them.
9 The length of one curtain *was* twenty and eight cubits, and the breadth of one curtain four cubits: the curtains *were* all of one size.
10 And he coupled the five curtains one unto another: and *the other* five curtains he coupled one unto another.
11 And he made loops of blue on the edge of one curtain from the selvedge in the coupling: likewise he made in the uttermost side of *another* curtain, in the coupling of the second.
12 Fifty loops made he in one curtain, and fifty loops made he in the edge of the curtain which *was* in the coupling of the second: the loops held one *curtain* to another.
13 And he made fifty **belaying pins** of gold, and coupled the curtains one unto another with the **belaying pins**: so it became one tabernacle.
14 And he made curtains *of* goats' *hair* for the tent over the tabernacle: eleven curtains he made them.
15 The length of one curtain *was* thirty cubits, and four cubits *was* the breadth of one curtain: the eleven curtains *were* of one size.
16 And he coupled five curtains by themselves, and six curtains by themselves.
17 And he made fifty loops upon the uttermost edge of the curtain in the coupling, and fifty loops made he upon the edge of the curtain which coupled the second.
18 And he made fifty **belaying pins** of brass to couple the tent together, that it might be one.
19 And he made a covering for the tent *of* rams' skins dyed red, and a covering *of* badgers' skins above *that*.
20 And he made boards for the tabernacle *of* shittim wood, standing up.
21 The length of a board *was* ten cubits, and the breadth of a board one cubit and a half.
22 One board had two tenons, equally distant one from another: thus did he make for all the boards of the tabernacle.
23 And he made boards for the tabernacle; twenty boards for the south side southward:
24 And forty sockets of silver he made under the twenty boards; two sockets under one board for his two tenons, and two sockets under another board for his two tenons.
25 And for the other side of the tabernacle, *which is* toward the north corner, he made twenty boards,
26 And their forty sockets of silver; two sockets under one board, and two sockets under another board.
27 And for the sides of the tabernacle westward he made six boards.
28 And two boards made he for the corners of the tabernacle in the two sides.
29 And they were coupled beneath, and coupled together at the head thereof, to one ring: thus he did to both of them in both the corners.
30 And there were eight boards; and their sockets *were* sixteen sockets of silver, under every board two sockets.
31 And he made bars of shittim wood; five for the boards of the one side of the tabernacle,
32 And five bars for the boards of the other side of the tabernacle, and five bars for the boards of the tabernacle for the sides westward.
33 And he made the middle bar to shoot through the boards from the one end to the other.
34 And he overlaid the boards with gold, and made their rings *of* gold *to be* places for the bars, and overlaid the bars with gold.
35 And he made a vail *of* blue, and purple, and scarlet, and fine twined linen: *with* cherubim's made he it of cunning work.
36 And he made thereunto four pillars *of* shittim wood, and overlaid them with gold: their hooks *were* of gold; and he cast for them four sockets of silver.
37 And he made a hanging for the tabernacle door *of* blue, and purple, and scarlet, and fine twined linen, of needlework;
38 And the five pillars of it with their hooks: and he overlaid their chapiters and their fillets with gold: but their five sockets *were* of brass.

CHAPTER 37

1 And Bezaleel made the ark *of* shittim wood: two cubits and a half *was* the length of it, and a cubit and a half the breadth of it, and a cubit and a half the height of it:
2 And he overlaid it with pure gold within and without, and made a crown of gold to it round about.
3 And he cast for it four rings of gold, *to be set* by the four corners of it; even two rings upon the one side of it, and two rings upon the other side of it.
4 And he made staves *of* shittim wood, and overlaid them with gold.

5 And he put the staves into the rings by the sides of the ark, to bear the ark.
6 And he made the mercy seat *of* pure gold: two cubits and a half *were* the length thereof, and one cubit and a half the breadth thereof.
7 And he made two cherubims *of* gold, beaten out of one piece made he them, on the two ends of the mercy seat;
8 One cherub on the end on this side, and another cherub on the *other* end on that side: out of the mercy seat made he the cherubims on the two ends thereof.
9 And the cherubims spread out *their* wings on high, *and* covered with their wings over the mercy seat, with their faces one to another; *even* to the mercy seatward were the faces of the cherubims.
10 And he made the table *of* shittim wood: two cubits *were* the length thereof, and a cubit the breadth thereof, and a cubit and a half the height thereof:
11 And he overlaid it with pure gold, and made thereunto a crown of gold round about.
12 Also he made thereunto a border of a handbreadth round about; and made a crown of gold for the border thereof round about.
13 And he cast for it four rings of gold, and put the rings upon the four corners that *were* in the four feet thereof.
14 Over against the border were the rings, the places for the staves to bear the table.
15 And he made the staves *of* shittim wood, and overlaid them with gold, to bear the table.
16 And he made the vessels which *were* upon the table, his dishes, and his spoons, and his bowls, and his covers to cover withal, *of* pure gold.
17 And he made the candlestick *of* pure gold: *of* beaten work made he the candlestick; his shaft, and his branch, his bowls, his knops, and his flowers, were of the same:
18 And six branches going out of the sides thereof; three branches of the candlestick out of the one side thereof, and three branches of the candlestick out of the other side thereof:
19 Three bowls made after the fashion of almonds in one branch, a knop and a flower; and three bowls made like almonds in another branch, a knop and a flower: so throughout the six branches going out of the candlestick.
20 And in the candlestick *were* four bowls made like almonds, his knops, and his flowers:
21 And a knop under two branches of the same, and a knop under two branches of the same, and a knop under two branches of the same, according to the six branches going out of it.
22 Their knops and their branches were of the same: all of it *was* one beaten work *of* pure gold.
23 And he made his seven lamps, and his snuffers, and his snuff dishes, *of* pure gold.
24 *Of* a talent of pure gold made he it, and all the vessels thereof.
25 And he made the incense altar *of* shittim wood: the length of it *was* a cubit, and the breadth of it a cubit; *it was* foursquare; and two cubits *was* the height of it; the horns thereof were of the same.
26 And he overlaid it with pure gold, *both* the top of it, and the sides thereof round about, and the horns of it: also he made unto it a crown of gold round about.
27 And he made two rings of gold for it under the crown thereof, by the two corners of it, upon the two sides thereof, to be places for the staves to bear it withal.
28 And he made the staves *of* shittim wood, and overlaid them with gold.
29 And he made the holy anointing oil, and the pure incense of sweet spices, according to the work of the apothecary.

CHAPTER 38

1 And he made the altar of burnt offering *of* shittim wood: five cubits *was* the length thereof, and five cubits the breadth thereof; *it was* foursquare; and three cubits the height thereof.
2 And he made the horns thereof on the four corners of it; the horns thereof were of the same: and he overlaid it with brass.
3 And he made all the vessels of the altar, the pots, and the shovels, and the basons, *and* the fleshhooks, and the firepans: all the vessels thereof made he *of* brass.
4 And he made for the altar a brasen grate of network under the compass thereof beneath unto the midst of it.
5 And he cast four rings for the four ends of the grate of brass, *to be* places for the staves.
6 And he made the staves *of* shittim wood, and overlaid them with brass.
7 And he put the staves into the rings on the sides of the altar, to bear it withal; he made the altar hollow with boards.
8 And he made the laver *of* brass, and the foot of it *of* brass, of the looking glasses of *the women* assembling, which assembled *at* the door of the tabernacle of the congregation.
9 And he made the court: on the south side southward the hangings of the court *were of* fine twined linen, an hundred cubits:
10 Their pillars *were* twenty, and their brasen sockets twenty; the hooks of the pillars and their fillets *were of* silver.
11 And for the north side *the hangings were* an hundred cubits, their pillars *were* twenty, and their sockets of brass twenty; the hooks of the pillars and their fillets *of* silver.
12 And for the west side *were* hangings of fifty cubits, their pillars ten, and their sockets ten; the hooks of the pillars and their fillets *of* silver.
13 And for the east side eastward fifty cubits.
14 The hangings of the one side *of the gate were* fifteen cubits; their pillars three, and their sockets three.
15 And for the other side of the court gate, on this hand and that hand, *were* hangings of fifteen cubits; their pillars three, and their sockets three.
16 All the hangings of the court roundabout *were of* fine twined linen.
17 And the sockets for the pillars *were of* brass; the hooks of the pillars and their fillets *of* silver; and the overlaying of their chapiters *of* silver; and all the pillars of the court *were* filleted with silver.
18 And the hanging for the gate of the court *was* needlework, *of* blue, and purple, and scarlet, and fine twined linen: and twenty cubits *was* the length, and the height in the breadth *was* five cubits, answerable to the hangings of the court.
19 And their pillars *were* four, and their sockets *of* brass four; their hooks *of* silver, and the overlaying of their chapiters and their fillets *of* silver.
20 And all the pins of the tabernacle, and of the court round about, *were of* brass.
21 This is the sum of the tabernacle, *even of* the tabernacle of testimony, as it was counted, according to the commandment of Moses, *for* the service of the Levites, by the hand of Ithamar, son to Aaron the priest.

22 And Bezaleel the son of Uri, the son of Hur, of the tribe of Judah, made all that the LORD commanded Moses.
23 And with him *was* Aholiab, son of Ahisamach, of the tribe of Dan, an engraver, and a cunning workman, and an embroiderer in blue, and in purple, and in scarlet, and fine linen.
24 All the gold that was occupied for the work in all the work of the holy *place*, even the gold of the offering, was twenty and nine talents, and seven hundred and thirty shekels, after the shekel of the sanctuary.
25 And the silver of them that were numbered of the congregation *was* an hundred talents, and a thousand seven hundred and threescore and fifteen shekels, after the shekel of the sanctuary:
26 A bekah for every man, *that is*, half a shekel, after the shekel of the sanctuary, for every one that went to be numbered, from twenty years old and upward, for six hundred thousand and three thousand and five hundred and fifty *men*.
27 And of the hundred talents of silver were cast the sockets of the sanctuary, and the sockets of the vail; an hundred sockets of the hundred talents, a talent for a socket.
28 And of the thousand seven hundred seventy and five shekels he made hooks for the pillars, and overlaid their chapiters, and filleted them.
29 And the brass of the offering *was* seventy talents, and two thousand and four hundred shekels.
30 And therewith he made the sockets to the door of the tabernacle of the congregation, and the brasen altar, and the brasen grate for it, and all the vessels of the altar,
31 And the sockets of the court round about, and the sockets of the court gate, and all the pins of the tabernacle, and all the pins of the court round about.

CHAPTER 39

1 And of the blue, and purple, and scarlet, they made cloths of service, to do service in the holy *place*, and made the holy garments for Aaron; as the LORD commanded Moses.
2 And he made the ephod *of* gold, blue, and purple, and scarlet, and fine twined linen.
3 And they did beat the gold into thin plates, and cut *it into* wires, to work *it* in the blue, and in the purple, and in the scarlet, and in the fine linen, *with* cunning work.
4 They made shoulder pieces for it, to couple *it* together: by the two edges was it coupled together.
5 And the curious girdle of his ephod, that *was* upon it, *was* of the same, according to the work thereof; *of* gold, blue, and purple, and scarlet, and fine twined linen; as the LORD commanded Moses.
6 And they wrought onyx stones enclosed in ouches of gold, graven, as signets are graven, with the names of the children of Israel.
7 And he put them on the shoulders of the ephod, *that they should be* stones for a memorial to the children of Israel; as the LORD commanded Moses.
8 And he made the breastplate *of* cunning work, like the work of the ephod; *of* gold, blue, and purple, and scarlet, and fine twined linen.
9 It was foursquare; they made the breastplate double: a span *was* the length thereof, and a span the breadth thereof, *being* doubled.
10 And they set in it four rows of stones: *the first* row *was* a sardius, a topaz, and a carbuncle: this *was* the first row.
11 And the second row, an emerald, a sapphire, and a diamond.
12 And the third row, a ligure, an agate, and an amethyst.
13 And the fourth row, a beryl, an onyx, and a jasper: *they were* enclosed in ouches of gold in their inclosing's.
14 And the stones *were* according to the names of the children of Israel, twelve, according to their names, *like* the engravings of a signet, everyone with his name, according to the twelve tribes.
15 And they made upon the breastplate chains at the ends, *of* wreathen work *of* pure gold.
16 And they made two ouches *of* gold, and two gold rings; and put the two rings in the two ends of the breastplate.
17 And they put the two wreathen chains of gold in the two rings on the ends of the breastplate.
18 And the two ends of the two wreathen chains they fastened in the two ouches, and put them on the shoulder pieces of the ephod, before it.
19 And they made two rings of gold, and put *them* on the two ends of the breastplate, upon the border of it, which *was* on the side of the ephod inward.
20 And they made two *other* golden rings, and put them on the two sides of the ephod underneath, toward the forepart of it, over against the *other* coupling thereof, above the curious girdle of the ephod.
21 And they did bind the breastplate by his rings unto the rings of the ephod with a lace of blue, that it might be above the curious girdle of the ephod, and that the breastplate might not be loosed from the ephod; as the LORD commanded Moses.
22 And he made the robe of the ephod *of* woven work, all *of* blue.
23 And *there was* a hole in the midst of the robe, as the hole of a habergeon, *with* a band round about the hole, that it should not rend.
24 And they made upon the hems of the robe pomegranates *of* blue, and purple, and scarlet, *and* twined *linen*.
25 And they made bells *of* pure gold, and put the bells between the pomegranates upon the hem of the robe, round about between the pomegranates;
26 A bell and a pomegranate, a bell and a pomegranate, round about the hem of the robe to minister *in*; as the LORD commanded Moses.
27 And they made coats *of* fine linen *of* woven work for Aaron, and for his sons,
28 And a of fine linen, and goodly bonnets *of* fine linen, and linen breeches *of* fine twined linen,
29 And a girdle *of* fine twined linen, and blue, and purple, and scarlet, *of* needlework; as the LORD commanded Moses.
30 And they made the plate of the holy crown *of* pure gold, and wrote upon it a writing, *like to* the engravings of a signet, HOLINESS TO THE LORD.
31 And they tied unto it a lace of blue, to fasten *it* on high upon the turban; as the LORD commanded Moses.
32 Thus was all the work of the tabernacle of the tent of the congregation finished: and the children of Israel did according to all that the LORD commanded Moses, so did they.
33 And they brought the tabernacle unto Moses, the tent and all his furniture, his **belaying pins**, his boards, his bars, and his pillars, and his sockets,
34 And the covering of rams' skins dyed red, and the covering of badgers' skins, and the vail of the covering,
35 The ark of the testimony, and the staves thereof, and the mercy seat,
36 The table, *and* all the vessels thereof, and the shewbread,

37 The pure candlestick, *with* the lamps thereof, *even with* the lamps to be set in order, and all the vessels thereof, and the oil for light,

38 And the golden altar, and the anointing oil, and the sweet incense, and the hanging for the tabernacle door,

39 The brasen altar, and his grate of brass, his staves, and all his vessels, the laver and his foot,

40 The hangings of the court, his pillars, and his sockets, and the hanging for the court gate, his cords, and his pins, and all the vessels of the service of the tabernacle, for the tent of the congregation,

41 The cloths of service to do service in the holy *place*, and the holy garments for Aaron the priest, and his sons' garments, to minister in the priest's office.

42 According to all that the LORD commanded Moses, so the children of Israel made all the work.

43 And Moses did look upon all the work, and, behold, they had done it as the LORD had commanded, even so had they done it: and Moses blessed them.

CHAPTER 40

1 And the LORD spoke unto Moses, saying,

2 On the first day of the first month will you set up the tabernacle of the tent of the congregation.

3 And you will put therein the ark of the testimony, and cover the ark with the vail.

4 And you will bring in the table, and set in order the things that are to be set in order upon it; and you will bring in the candlestick, and light the lamps thereof.

5 And you will set the altar of gold for the incense before the ark of the testimony, and put the hanging of the door to the tabernacle.

6 And you will set the altar of the burnt offering before the door of the tabernacle of the tent of the congregation.

7 And you will set the laver between the tent of the congregation and the altar, and will put water therein.

8 And you will set up the court round about, and hang up the hanging at the court gate.

9 And you will take the anointing oil, and anoint the tabernacle, and all that *is* therein, and will hallow it, and all the vessels thereof: and it will be holy.

10 And you will anoint the altar of the burnt offering, and all his vessels, and sanctify the altar: and it will be an altar most holy.

11 And you will anoint the laver and his foot, and sanctify it.

12 And you will bring Aaron and his sons unto the door of the tabernacle of the congregation, and wash them with water.

13 And you will put upon Aaron the holy garments, and anoint him, and sanctify him; that he may minister unto me in the priest's office.

14 And you will bring his sons, and clothe them with coats:

15 And you will anoint them, as you didst anoint their father, that they may minister unto me in the priest's office: for their anointing will surely be an everlasting priesthood throughout their generations.

16 Thus did Moses: according to all that the LORD commanded him, so did he.

17 And it came to pass in the first month in the second year, on the first *day* of the month, *that* the tabernacle was reared up.

18 And Moses reared up the tabernacle, and fastened his sockets, and set up the boards thereof, and put in the bars thereof, and reared up his pillars.

19 And he spread abroad the tent over the tabernacle, and put the covering of the tent above upon it; as the LORD commanded Moses.

20 And he took and put the testimony into the ark, and set the staves on the ark, and put the mercy seat above upon the ark:

21 And he brought the ark into the tabernacle, and set up the vail of the covering, and covered the ark of the testimony; as the LORD commanded Moses.

22 And he put the table in the tent of the congregation, upon the side of the tabernacle northward, without the vail.

23 And he set the bread in order upon it before the LORD; as the LORD had commanded Moses.

24 And he put the candlestick in the tent of the congregation, over against the table, on the side of the tabernacle southward.

25 And he lighted the lamps before the LORD; as the LORD commanded Moses.

26 And he put the golden altar in the tent of the congregation before the vail:

27 And he burnt sweet incense thereon; as the LORD commanded Moses.

28 And he set up the hanging *at* the door of the tabernacle.

29 And he put the altar of burnt offering *by* the door of the tabernacle of the tent of the congregation, and offered upon it the burnt offering and the meat offering; as the LORD commanded Moses.

30 And he set the laver between the tent of the congregation and the altar, and put water there, to wash *withal*.

31 And Moses and Aaron and his sons washed their hands and their feet thereat:

32 When they went into the tent of the congregation, and when they came near unto the altar, they washed; as the LORD commanded Moses.

33 And he reared up the court round about the tabernacle and the altar, and set up the hanging of the court gate. So Moses finished the work.

34 Then a cloud covered the tent of the congregation, and the glory of the LORD filled the tabernacle.

35 And Moses was not able to enter into the tent of the congregation, because the cloud abode thereon, and the glory of the LORD filled the tabernacle.

36 And when the cloud was taken up from over the tabernacle, the children of Israel went onward in all their journeys:

37 But if the cloud were not taken up, then they journeyed not till the day that it was taken up.

38 For the cloud of the LORD *was* upon the tabernacle by day, and fire was on it by night, in the sight of all the house of Israel, throughout all their journeys.

LEVITICUS
CHAPTER 1

1 And the LORD called unto Moses, and spoke unto him out of the tabernacle of the congregation, saying,
2 Speak unto the children of Israel, and say unto them, if any man of you brings an offering unto the LORD, you will bring your offering of the cattle, *even* of the herd, and of the flock.
3 If his offering *be* a burnt sacrifice of the herd, let him offer a male without blemish: he will offer it of his own voluntary will at the door of the tabernacle of the congregation before the LORD.
4 And he will put his hand upon the head of the burnt offering; and it will be accepted for him to make atonement for him.
5 And he will kill the bullock before the LORD: and the priests, Aaron's sons, will bring the blood, and sprinkle the blood round about upon the altar that *is by* the door of the tabernacle of the congregation.
6 And he will flay the burnt offering, and cut it into his pieces.
7 And the sons of Aaron the priest will put fire upon the altar, and lay the wood in order upon the fire:
8 And the priests, Aaron's sons, will lay the parts, the head, and the fat, in order upon the wood that *is* on the fire which *is* upon the altar:
9 But his inwards and his legs will he wash in water: and the priest will burn all on the altar, *to be* a burnt sacrifice, an offering made by fire, of a sweet savor unto the LORD.
10 And if his offering *be* of the flocks, *namely*, of the sheep, or of the goats, for a burnt sacrifice; he will bring it a male without blemish.
11 And he will kill it on the side of the altar northward before the LORD: and the priests, Aaron's sons, will sprinkle his blood round about upon the altar.
12 And he will cut it into his pieces, with his head and his fat: and the priest will lay them in order on the wood that *is* on the fire which *is* upon the altar:
13 But he will wash the inwards and the legs with water: and the priest will bring *it* all, and burn *it* upon the altar: it *is* a burnt sacrifice, an offering made by fire, of a sweet savor unto the LORD.
14 And if the burnt sacrifice for his offering to the LORD *be* of fowls, then he will bring his offering of turtledoves, or of young pigeons.
15 And the priest will bring it unto the altar, and wring off his head, and burn *it* on the altar; and the blood thereof will be wrung out at the side of the altar:
16 And he will pluck away his crop with his feathers, and cast it beside the altar on the east part, by the place of the ashes:
17 And he will cleave it with the wings thereof, *but* will not divide *it* asunder: and the priest will burn it upon the altar, upon the wood that *is* upon the fire: it *is* a burnt sacrifice, an offering made by fire, of a sweet savor unto the LORD.

CHAPTER 2

1 And when any will offer a meat offering unto the LORD, his offering will be *of* fine flour; and he will pour oil upon it, and put frankincense thereon:
2 And he will bring it to Aaron's sons the priests: and he will take there out his handful of the flour thereof, and of the oil thereof, with all the frankincense thereof; and the priest will burn the memorial of it upon the altar, *to be* an offering made by fire, of a sweet savor unto the LORD:
3 And the remnant of the meat offering will *be* Aaron's and his sons': *it is* a thing most holy of the offerings of the LORD made by fire.
4 And if you bring an oblation of a meat offering baked in the oven, *it will be* unleavened cakes of fine flour mingled with oil, or unleavened wafers anointed with oil.
5 And if your oblation *be* a meat offering *baked* in a pan, it will be *of* fine flour unleavened, mingled with oil.
6 you will part it in pieces, and pour oil thereon: it *is* a meat offering.
7 And if your oblation *be* a meat offering *baked* in the frying pan, it will be made *of* fine flour with oil.
8 And you will bring the meat offering that is made of these things unto the LORD: and when it is presented unto the priest, he will bring it unto the altar.
9 And the priest will take from the meat offering a memorial thereof, and will burn *it* upon the altar: it *is* an offering made by fire, of a sweet savor unto the LORD.
10 And that which is left of the meat offering will *be* Aaron's and his sons': *it is* a thing most holy of the offerings of the LORD made by fire.
11 No meat offering, which you will bring unto the LORD, will be made with leaven: for you will burn no leaven, nor any honey, in any offering of the LORD made by fire.
12 As for the oblation of the first fruits, you will offer them unto the LORD: but they will not be burnt on the altar for a sweet savor.
13 And every oblation of your meat offering will you season with salt; neither will you suffer the salt of the covenant of your God to be lacking from your meat offering: with all your offerings you will offer salt.
14 And if you offer a meat offering of your first fruits unto the LORD, you will offer for the meat offering of your first fruits green ears of corn dried by the fire, *even* corn beaten out of full ears.
15 And you will put oil upon it, and lay frankincense thereon: it *is* a meat offering.
16 And the priest will burn the memorial of it, *part* of the beaten corn thereof, and *part* of the oil thereof, with all the frankincense thereof: it *is* an offering made by fire unto the LORD.

CHAPTER 3

1 And if his oblation *be* a sacrifice of peace offering, if he offers *it* of the herd; whether *it is* a male or female, he will offer it without blemish before the LORD.
2 And he will lay his hand upon the head of his offering, and kill it *at* the door of the tabernacle of the congregation: and Aaron's sons the priests will sprinkle the blood upon the altar round about.
3 And he will offer of the sacrifice of the peace offering an offering made by fire unto the LORD; the fat that covers the inwards, and all the fat that *is* upon the inwards,
4 And the two kidneys, and the fat that *is* on them, which *is* by the flanks, and the fat above the liver, with the kidneys, it will he take away.
5 And Aaron's sons will burn it on the altar upon the burnt sacrifice, which *is* upon the wood that *is* on the fire: it *is* an offering made by fire, of a sweet savor unto the LORD.
6 And if his offering for a sacrifice of peace offering unto the LORD *be* of the flock; male or female, he will offer it without blemish.
7 If he offers a lamb for his offering, then will he offer it before the LORD.
8 And he will lay his hand upon the head of his offering, and kill it before the tabernacle of the congregation: and Aaron's sons will sprinkle the blood thereof round about upon the altar.

9 And he will offer of the sacrifice of the peace offering an offering made by fire unto the LORD; the fat thereof, *and* the whole rump, it will he take off hard by the backbone; and the fat that covers the inwards, and all the fat that *is* upon the inwards,

10 And the two kidneys, and the fat that *is* upon them, which *is* by the flanks, and the fat above the liver, with the kidneys, it will he take away.

11 And the priest will burn it upon the altar: *it is* the food of the offering made by fire unto the LORD.

12 And if his offering *be* a goat, then he will offer it before the LORD.

13 And he will lay his hand upon the head of it, and kill it before the tabernacle of the congregation: and the sons of Aaron will sprinkle the blood thereof upon the altar round about.

14 And he will offer thereof his offering, *even* an offering made by fire unto the LORD; the fat that covers the inwards, and all the fat that *is* upon the inwards,

15 And the two kidneys, and the fat that *is* upon them, which *is* by the flanks, and the fat above the liver, with the kidneys, it will he take away.

16 And the priest will burn them upon the altar: *it is* the food of the offering made by fire for a sweet savor: all the fat *is* the LORD'S.

17 *It will be* a perpetual statute for your generations throughout all your dwellings, that you eat neither fat nor blood.

CHAPTER 4

1 And the LORD spoke unto Moses, saying,

2 Speak unto the children of Israel, saying, if a soul will sin through ignorance against any of the commandments of the LORD *concerning things* which ought not to be done, and will do against any of them:

3 If the priest that is anointed does sin according to the sin of the people; then let him bring for his sin, which he hath sinned, a young bullock without blemish unto the LORD for a sin offering.

4 And he will bring the bullock unto the door of the tabernacle of the congregation before the LORD; and will lay his hand upon the bullock's head, and kill the bullock before the LORD.

5 And the priest that is anointed will take of the bullock's blood, and bring it to the tabernacle of the congregation:

6 And the priest will dip his finger in the blood, and sprinkle of the blood seven times before the LORD, before the veil of the sanctuary.

7 And the priest will put *some* of the blood upon the horns of the altar of sweet incense before the LORD, which *is* in the tabernacle of the congregation; and will pour all the blood of the bullock at the bottom of the altar of the burnt offering, which *is at* the door of the tabernacle of the congregation.

8 And he will take off from it all the fat of the bullock for the sin offering; the fat that covers the inwards, and all the fat that *is* upon the inwards,

9 And the two kidneys, and the fat that *is* upon them, which *is* by the flanks, and the fat above the liver, with the kidneys, it will he take away,

10 As it was taken off from the bullock of the sacrifice of peace offerings: and the priest will burn them upon the altar of the burnt offering.

11 And the skin of the bullock, and all his flesh, with his head, and with his legs, and his inwards, and his dung,

12 Even the whole bullock will he carry forth without the camp unto a clean place, where the ashes are poured out, and burn him on the wood with fire: where the ashes are poured out will he be burnt.

13 And if the whole congregation of Israel sin through ignorance, and the thing be hid from the eyes of the assembly, and they have done *somewhat against* any of the commandments of the LORD *concerning things* which should not be done, and are guilty;

14 When the sin, which they have sinned against it, is known, then the congregation will offer a young bullock for the sin, and bring him before the tabernacle of the congregation.

15 And the elders of the congregation will lay their hands upon the head of the bullock before the LORD: and the bullock will be killed before the LORD.

16 And the priest that is anointed will bring of the bullock's blood to the tabernacle of the congregation:

17 And the priest will dip his finger *in some* of the blood, and sprinkle *it* seven times before the LORD, *even* before the veil.

18 And he will put *some* of the blood upon the horns of the altar which *is* before the LORD, that *is* in the tabernacle of the congregation, and will pour out all the blood at the bottom of the altar of the burnt offering, which *is at* the door of the tabernacle of the congregation.

19 And he will take all his fat from him, and burn *it* upon the altar.

20 And he will do with the bullock as he did with the bullock for a sin offering, so will he do with this: and the priest will make atonement for them, and it will be forgiven them.

21 And he will carry forth the bullock without the camp, and burn him as he burned the first bullock: it *is* a sin offering for the congregation.

22 When a ruler hath sinned, and done *somewhat* through ignorance *against* any of the commandments of the LORD his God *concerning things* which should not be done, and is guilty;

23 Or if his sin, wherein he hath sinned, come to his knowledge; he will bring his offering, a kid of the goats, a male without blemish:

24 And he will lay his hand upon the head of the goat, and kill it in the place where they kill the burnt offering before the LORD: it *is* a sin offering.

25 And the priest will take of the blood of the sin offering with his finger, and put *it* upon the horns of the altar of burnt offering, and will pour out his blood at the bottom of the altar of burnt offering.

26 And he will burn all his fat upon the altar, as the fat of the sacrifice of peace offerings: and the priest will make atonement for him as concerning his sin, and it will be forgiven him.

27 And if any one of the common people sin through ignorance, while he doeth *somewhat against* any of the commandments of the LORD *concerning things* which ought not to be done, and be guilty;

28 Or if his sin, which he hath sinned, comes to his knowledge: then he will bring his offering, a kid of the goats, a female without blemish, for his sin which he hath sinned.

29 And he will lay his hand upon the head of the sin offering, and slay the sin offering in the place of the burnt offering.

30 And the priest will take of the blood thereof with his finger, and put *it* upon the horns of the altar of burnt offering, and will pour out all the blood thereof at the bottom of the altar.

31 And he will take away all the fat thereof, as the fat is taken away from off the sacrifice of peace offerings; and the priest will burn *it* upon the altar for a sweet savor unto the LORD; and the priest will make an atonement for him, and it will be forgiven him.

32 And if he brings a lamb for a sin offering, he will bring it a female without blemish.

33 And he will lay his hand upon the head of the sin offering, and slay it for a sin offering in the place where they kill the burnt offering.

34 And the priest will take of the blood of the sin offering with his finger, and put *it* upon the horns of the altar of burnt offering, and will pour out all the blood thereof at the bottom of the altar:
35 And he will take away all the fat thereof, as the fat of the lamb is taken away from the sacrifice of the peace offerings; and the priest will burn them upon the altar, according to the offerings made by fire unto the LORD: and the priest will make an atonement for his sin that he hath committed, and it will be forgiven him.

CHAPTER 5

1 And if a soul sin, and hear the voice of swearing, and *is* a witness, whether he hath seen or known *of it*; if he do not utter *it*, then he will bear his iniquity.
2 Or if a soul touch any unclean thing, whether *it be* a carcass of an unclean beast, or a carcass of unclean cattle, or the carcass of unclean creeping things, and *if* it be hidden from him; he also will be unclean, and guilty.
3 Or if he touch the uncleanness of man, whatsoever uncleanness *it be* that a man will be defiled withal, and it be hid from him; when he knows *of it*, then he will be guilty.
4 Or if a soul swear, pronouncing with *his* lips to do evil, or to do good, whatsoever *it be* that a man will pronounce with an oath, and it be hid from him; when he knows *of it*, then he will be guilty in one of these.
5 And it will be, when he will be guilty in one of these *things*, that he will confess that he hath sinned in that *thing*:
6 And he will bring his trespass offering unto the LORD for his sin which he hath sinned, a female from the flock, a lamb or a kid of the goats, for a sin offering; and the priest will make atonement for him concerning his sin.
7 And if he be not able to bring a lamb, then he will bring for his trespass, which he hath committed, two turtledoves, or two young pigeons, unto the LORD; one for a sin offering, and the other for a burnt offering.
8 And he will bring them unto the priest, who will offer *that* which *is* for the sin offering first, and wring off his head from his neck, but will not divide *it* asunder:
9 And he will sprinkle of the blood of the sin offering upon the side of the altar; and the rest of the blood will be wrung out at the bottom of the altar: it *is* a sin offering.
10 And he will offer the second *for* a burnt offering, according to the manner: and the priest will make atonement for him for his sin which he hath sinned, and it will be forgiven him.
11 But if he be not able to bring two turtledoves, or two young pigeons, then he that sinned will bring for his offering the tenth part of an ephah of fine flour for a sin offering; he will put no oil upon it, neither will he put *any* frankincense thereon: for it *is* a sin offering.
12 Then will he bring it to the priest, and the priest will take his handful of it, *even* a memorial thereof, and burn *it* on the altar, according to the offerings made by fire unto the LORD: it *is* a sin offering.
13 And the priest will make an atonement for him as touching his sin that he hath sinned in one of these, and it will be forgiven him: and *the remnant* will be the priest's, as a meat offering.
14 And the LORD spoke unto Moses, saying,
15 If a soul commit a trespass, and sin through ignorance, in the holy things of the LORD; then he will bring for his trespass unto the LORD a ram without blemish out of the flocks, with your estimation by shekels of silver, after the shekel of the sanctuary, for a trespass offering:
16 And he will make amends for the harm that he hath done in the holy thing, and will add the fifth part thereto, and give it unto the priest: and the priest will make atonement for him with the ram of the trespass offering, and it will be forgiven him.
17 And if a soul sin, and commit any of these things which are forbidden to be done by the commandments of the LORD; though he wist *it* not, yet is he guilty, and will bear his iniquity.
18 And he will bring a ram without blemish out of the flock, with your estimation, for a trespass offering, unto the priest: and the priest will make atonement for him concerning his ignorance wherein he erred and wist *it* not, and it will be forgiven him.
19 It *is* a trespass offering: he hath certainly trespassed against the LORD.

CHAPTER 6

1 And the LORD spoke unto Moses, saying,
2 If a soul sin, and commit a trespass against the LORD, and lie unto his neighbor in that which was delivered him to keep, or in fellowship, or in a thing taken away by violence, or hath deceived his neighbor;
3 Or have found that which was lost, and lie concerning it, and swear falsely; in any of all these that a man doeth, sinning therein:
4 Then it will be, because he hath sinned, and is guilty, that he will restore that which he took violently away, or the thing which he hath deceitfully gotten, or that which was delivered him to keep, or the lost thing which he found,
5 Or all that about which he hath sworn falsely; he will even restore it in the principal, and will add the fifth part more thereto, *and* give it unto him to whom it appertain, in the day of his trespass offering.
6 And he will bring his trespass offering unto the LORD, a ram without blemish out of the flock, with your estimation, for a trespass offering, unto the priest:
7 And the priest will make atonement for him before the LORD: and it will be forgiven him for any thing of all that he hath done in trespassing therein.
8 And the LORD spoke unto Moses, saying,
9 Command Aaron and his sons, saying, this *is* the law of the burnt offering: It *is* the burnt offering, because of the burning upon the altar all night unto the morning, and the fire of the altar will be burning in it.
10 And the priest will put on his linen garment, and his linen breeches will he put upon his flesh, and take up the ashes which the fire hath consumed with the burnt offering on the altar, and he will put them beside the altar.
11 And he will put off his garments, and put on other garments, and carry forth the ashes without the camp unto a clean place.
12 And the fire upon the altar will be burning in it; it will not be put out: and the priest will burn wood on it every morning, and lays the burnt offering in order upon it; and he will burn thereon the fat of the peace offerings.
13 The fire will ever be burning upon the altar; it will never go out.
14 And this *is* the law of the meat offering: the sons of Aaron will offer it before the LORD, before the altar.
15 And he will take of it his handful, of the flour of the meat offering, and of the oil thereof, and all the frankincense which *is* upon the meat offering, and will burn *it* upon the altar *for* a sweet savor, *even* the memorial of it, unto the LORD.
16 And the remainder thereof will Aaron and his sons eat: with unleavened bread will it be eaten in the holy place; in the court of the tabernacle of the congregation they will eat it.

17 It will not be baked with leaven. I have given it *unto them for* their portion of my offerings made by fire; it *is* most holy, as *is* the sin offering, and as the trespass offering.
18 All the males among the children of Aaron will eat of it. *It will be* a statute forever in your generations concerning the offerings of the LORD made by fire: every one that touch them will be holy.
19 And the LORD spoke unto Moses, saying,
20 This *is* the offering of Aaron and of his sons, which they will offer unto the LORD in the day when he is anointed; the tenth part of an ephah of fine flour for a meat offering perpetual, half of it in the morning, and half thereof at night.
21 In a pan it will be made with oil; *and when it is* baked, you will bring it in: *and* the baked pieces of the meat offering will you offer *for* a sweet savor unto the LORD.
22 And the priest of his sons that is anointed in his stead will offer it: *it is* a statute for ever unto the LORD; it will be wholly burnt.
23 For every meat offering for the priest will be wholly burnt: it will not be eaten.
24 And the LORD spoke unto Moses, saying,
25 Speak unto Aaron and to his sons, saying, this *is* the law of the sin offering: In the place where the burnt offering is killed will the sin offering be killed before the LORD: it *is* most holy.
26 The priest that offered it for sin will eat it: in the holy place will it be eaten, in the court of the tabernacle of the congregation.
27 Whatsoever will touch the flesh thereof will be holy: and when there is sprinkled of the blood thereof upon any garment, you will wash that whereon it was sprinkled in the holy place.
28 But the earthen vessel wherein it is sodden will be broken: and if it be sodden in a brazen pot, it will be both scoured, and rinsed in water.
29 All the males among the priests will eat thereof: it *is* most holy.
30 And no sin offering, whereof *any* of the blood is brought into the tabernacle of the congregation to reconcile *withal* in the holy *place,* will be eaten: it will be burnt in the fire.

CHAPTER 7

1 Likewise this *is* the law of the trespass offering: it *is* most holy.
2 In the place where they kill the burnt offering will they kill the trespass offering: and the blood thereof will he sprinkle round about upon the altar.
3 And he will offer of it all the fat thereof; the rump, and the fat that covers the inwards,
4 And the two kidneys, and the fat that *is* on them, which *is* by the flanks, and the fat *that is* above the liver, with the kidneys, it will he take away:
5 And the priest will burn them upon the altar *for* an offering made by fire unto the LORD: it *is* a trespass offering.
6 Every male among the priests will eat thereof: it will be eaten in the holy place: it *is* most holy.
7 As the sin offering *is,* so *is* the trespass offering: *there is* one law for them: the priest that make atonement therewith will have *it.*
8 And the priest that offer any man's burnt offering, *even* the priest will have to himself the skin of the burnt offering which he hath offered.
9 And all the meat offering that is baked in the oven, and all that is dressed in the frying pan, and in the pan, will be the priest's that offer it.
10 And every meat offering, mingled with oil, and dry, will all the sons of Aaron have, one *as much* as another.
11 And this *is* the law of the sacrifice of peace offerings, which he will offer unto the LORD.
12 If he offer it for a thanksgiving, then he will offer with the sacrifice of thanksgiving unleavened cakes mingled with oil, and unleavened wafers anointed with oil, and cakes mingled with oil, of fine flour, fried.
13 Besides the cakes, he will offer *for* his offering leavened bread with the sacrifice of thanksgiving of his peace offerings.
14 And of it he will offer one out of the whole oblation *for* an heave offering unto the LORD, *and* it will be the priest's that sprinkles the blood of the peace offerings.
15 And the flesh of the sacrifice of his peace offerings for thanksgiving will be eaten the same day that it is offered; he will not leave any of it until the morning.
16 But if the sacrifice of his offering *be* a vow, or a voluntary offering, it will be eaten the same day that he offer his sacrifice: and on the morrow also the remainder of it will be eaten:
17 But the remainder of the flesh of the sacrifice on the third day will be burnt with fire.
18 And if *any* of the flesh of the sacrifice of his peace offerings be eaten at all on the third day, it will not be accepted, neither will it be imputed unto him that offer it: it will be an abomination, and the soul that eat of it will bear his iniquity.
19 And the flesh that touches any unclean *thing* will not be eaten; it will be burnt with fire: and as for the flesh, all that is clean will eat thereof.
20 But the soul that eat *of* the flesh of the sacrifice of peace offerings, that *pertain* unto the LORD, having his uncleanness upon him, even that soul will be cut off from his people.
21 Moreover the soul that will touch any unclean *thing, as* the uncleanness of man, or *any* unclean beast, or any abominable unclean *thing,* and eat of the flesh of the sacrifice of peace offerings, which *pertain* unto the LORD, even that soul will be cut off from his people.
22 ¶ And the LORD spoke unto Moses, saying,
23 Speak unto the children of Israel, saying, you will eat no manner of fat, of ox, or of sheep, or of goat.
24 And the fat of the beast that dies of itself, and the fat of that which is torn with beasts, may be used in any other use: but you will in no wise eat of it.
25 For whosoever eat the fat of the beast, of which men offer an offering made by fire unto the LORD, even the soul that eat *it* will be cut off from his people.
26 Moreover you will eat no manner of blood, *whether it be* of fowl or of beast, in any of your dwellings.
27 Whatsoever soul *it be* that eats any manner of blood even that soul will be cut off from his people.
28 And the LORD spoke unto Moses, saying,
29 Speak unto the children of Israel, saying, He that offeres the sacrifice of his peace offerings unto the LORD will bring his oblation unto the LORD of the sacrifice of his peace offerings.
30 His own hands will bring the offerings of the LORD made by fire, the fat with the breast, it will he bring, that the breast may be waved *for* a wave offering before the LORD.
31 And the priest will burn the fat upon the altar: but the breast will be Aaron's and his sons'.
32 And the right shoulder will you give unto the priest *for* an heave offering of the sacrifices of your peace offerings.
33 He among the sons of Aaron, that offer the blood of the peace offerings, and the fat, will have the right shoulder for *his* part.
34 For the wave breast and the heave shoulder have I taken of the children of Israel from off the sacrifices of their peace offerings,

and have given them unto Aaron the priest and unto his sons by a statute for ever from among the children of Israel.
35 This *is the portion* of the anointing of Aaron, and of the anointing of his sons, out of the offerings of the LORD made by fire, in the day *when* he presented them to minister unto the LORD in the priest's office;
36 Which the LORD commanded to be given them of the children of Israel, in the day that he anointed them, *by* a statute for ever throughout their generations.
37 This *is* the law of the burnt offering, of the meat offering, and of the sin offering, and of the trespass offering, and of the consecrations, and of the sacrifice of the peace offerings;
38 Which the LORD commanded Moses in Mount Sinai, in the day that he commanded the children of Israel to offer their oblations unto the LORD, in the wilderness of Sinai.

CHAPTER 8

1 And the LORD spoke unto Moses, saying,
2 Take Aaron and his sons with him, and the garments, and the anointing oil, and a bullock for the sin offering, and two rams, and a basket of unleavened bread;
3 And gather you the **entire** congregation together unto the door of the tabernacle of the congregation.
4 And Moses did as the LORD commanded him; and the assembly was gathered together unto the door of the tabernacle of the congregation.
5 And Moses said unto the congregation, This *is* the thing which the LORD commanded to be done.
6 And Moses brought Aaron and his sons, and washed them with water.
7 And he put upon him the coat, and girded him with the girdle, and clothed him with the robe, and put the ephod upon him, and he girded him with the curious girdle of the ephod, and bound *it* unto him therewith.
8 And he put the breastplate upon him: also he put in the breastplate the Urim and the Thummim.
9 And he put the turban upon his head; also upon the turban, *even* upon his forefront, did he put the golden plate, the holy crown; as the LORD commanded Moses.
10 And Moses took the anointing oil, and anointed the tabernacle and all that *was* therein, and sanctified them.
11 And he sprinkled thereof upon the altar seven times, and anointed the altar and all his vessels, both the laver and his foot, to sanctify them.
12 And he poured of the anointing oil upon Aaron's head, and anointed him, to sanctify him.
13 And Moses brought Aaron's sons, and put coats upon them, and girded them with girdles, and put bonnets upon them; as the LORD commanded Moses.
14 And he brought the bullock for the sin offering: and Aaron and his sons laid their hands upon the head of the bullock for the sin offering.
15 And he slew *it*; and Moses took the blood, and put *it* upon the horns of the altar roundabout with his finger, and purified the altar, and poured the blood at the bottom of the altar, and sanctified it, to make reconciliation upon it.
16 And he took all the fat that *was* upon the inwards, and the fat *above* the liver, and the two kidneys, and their fat, and Moses burned *it* upon the altar.
17 But the bullock, and his hide, his flesh, and his dung, he burnt with fire without the camp; as the LORD commanded Moses.

18 And he brought the ram for the burnt offering: and Aaron and his sons laid their hands upon the head of the ram.
19 And he killed *it*; and Moses sprinkled the blood upon the altar round about.
20 And he cut the ram into pieces; and Moses burnt the head, and the pieces, and the fat.
21 And he washed the inwards and the legs in water; and Moses burnt the whole ram upon the altar: it *was* a burnt sacrifice for a sweet savor, *and* an offering made by fire unto the LORD; as the LORD commanded Moses.
22 And he brought the other ram, the ram of consecration: and Aaron and his sons laid their hands upon the head of the ram.
23 And he slew *it*; and Moses took of the blood of it, and put *it* upon the tip of Aaron's right ear, and upon the thumb of his right hand, and upon the great toe of his right foot.
24 And he brought Aaron's sons, and Moses put of the blood upon the tip of their right ear, and upon the thumbs of their right hands, and upon the great toes of their right feet: and Moses sprinkled the blood upon the altar round about.
25 And he took the fat, and the rump, and all the fat that *was* upon the inwards, and the fat *above* the liver, and the two kidneys, and their fat, and the right shoulder:
26 And out of the basket of unleavened bread, that *was* before the LORD, he took one unleavened cake, and a cake of oiled bread, and one wafer, and put *them* on the fat, and upon the right shoulder:
27 And he put all upon Aaron's hands, and upon his sons' hands, and waved them *for* a wave offering before the LORD.
28 And Moses took them from off their hands, and burnt *them* on the altar upon the burnt offering: they *were* consecrations for a sweet savor: it *is* an offering made by fire unto the LORD.
29 And Moses took the breast, and waved it *for* a wave offering before the LORD: *for* of the ram of consecration it was Moses' part; as the LORD commanded Moses.
30 And Moses took of the anointing oil, and of the blood which *was* upon the altar, and sprinkled *it* upon Aaron, *and* upon his garments, and upon his sons, and upon his sons' garments with him; and sanctified Aaron, *and* his garments, and his sons, and his sons' garments with him.
31 And Moses said unto Aaron and to his sons, boil the flesh *at* the door of the tabernacle of the congregation: and there eat it with the bread that *is* in the basket of consecrations, as I commanded, saying, Aaron and his sons will eat it.
32 And that which remain of the flesh and of the bread will you burn with fire.
33 And you will not go out of the door of the tabernacle of the congregation *in* seven days, until the days of your consecration be at an end: for seven days will he consecrate you.
34 As he hath done this day, *so* the LORD hath commanded to do, to make atonement for you.
35 Therefore will you abide *at* the door of the tabernacle of the congregation day and night seven days, and keep the charge of the LORD, that you die not: for so I am commanded.
36 So Aaron and his sons did all things which the LORD commanded by the hand of Moses.

CHAPTER 9

1 And it came to pass on the eighth day, *that* Moses called Aaron and his sons, and the elders of Israel;

2 And he said unto Aaron, Take thee a young calf for a sin offering, and a ram for a burnt offering, without blemish, and offer *them* before the LORD.
3 And unto the children of Israel you will speak, saying, take you a kid of the goats for a sin offering; and a calf and a lamb, *both* of the first years, without blemish, for a burnt offering;
4 Also a bullock and a ram for peace offerings, to sacrifice before the LORD; and a meat offering mingled with oil: for today the LORD will appear unto you.
5 And they brought *that* which Moses commanded before the tabernacle of the congregation: and the **entire** congregation drew near and stood before the LORD.
6 And Moses said, this *is* the thing which the LORD commanded that you should do: and the glory of the LORD will appear unto you.
7 And Moses said unto Aaron, Go unto the altar, and offer your sin offering, and your burnt offering, and make atonement for thyself, and for the people: and offer the offering of the people, and make atonement for them; as the LORD commanded.
8 Aaron therefore went unto the altar, and slew the calf of the sin offering, which *was* for himself.
9 And the sons of Aaron brought the blood unto him: and he dipped his finger in the blood, and put *it* upon the horns of the altar, and poured out the blood at the bottom of the altar:
10 But the fat, and the kidneys, and the fat above the liver of the sin offering, he burnt upon the altar; as the LORD commanded Moses.
11 And the flesh and the hide he burnt with fire without the camp.
12 And he slew the burnt offering; and Aaron's sons presented unto him the blood, which he sprinkled round about upon the altar.
13 And they presented the burnt offering unto him, with the pieces thereof, and the head: and he burnt *them* upon the altar.
14 And he did wash the inwards and the legs, and burnt *them* upon the burnt offering on the altar.
15 And he brought the people's offering, and took the goat, which *was* the sin offering for the people, and slew it, and offered it for sin, as the first.
16 And he brought the burnt offering, and offered it according to the manner.
17 And he brought the meat offering, and took a handful thereof, and burnt *it* upon the altar, beside the burnt sacrifice of the morning.
18 He slew also the bullock and the ram *for* a sacrifice of peace offerings, which *was* for the people: and Aaron's sons presented unto him the blood, which he sprinkled upon the altar round about,
19 And the fat of the bullock and of the ram, the rump, and that which covered *the inwards*, and the kidneys, and the fat *above* the liver:
20 And they put the fat upon the breasts, and he burnt the fat upon the altar:
21 And the breasts and the right shoulder Aaron waved *for* a wave offering before the LORD; as Moses commanded.
22 And Aaron lifted up his hand toward the people, and blessed them, and came down from offering of the sin offering, and the burnt offering, and peace offerings.
23 And Moses and Aaron went into the tabernacle of the congregation, and came out, and blessed the people: and the glory of the LORD appeared unto all the people.
24 And there came a fire out from before the LORD, and consumed upon the altar the burnt offering and the fat: *which* when all the people saw, they shouted, and fell on their faces.

CHAPTER 10

1 And Nadab and Abihu, the sons of Aaron, took either of them his censer, and put fire therein, and put incense thereon, and offered strange fire before the LORD, which he commanded them not.
2 And there went out fire from the LORD, and devoured them, and they died before the LORD.
3 Then Moses said unto Aaron, This *is it* that the LORD spoke, saying, I will be sanctified in them that come nigh me, and before all the people I will be glorified. And Aaron held his peace.
4 And Moses called Mishael and Elzaphan, the sons of Uzziel the uncle of Aaron, and said unto them, Come near, carry your brethren from before the sanctuary out of the camp.
5 So they went near, and carried them in their coats out of the camp; as Moses had said.
6 And Moses said unto Aaron, and unto Eleazar and unto Ithamar, his sons, Uncover not your heads, neither rend your clothes; lest you die, and lest wrath come upon all the people: but let your brethren, the whole house of Israel, bewail the burning which the LORD hath kindled.
7 And you will not go out from the door of the tabernacle of the congregation, lest you die: for the anointing oil of the LORD *is* upon you. And they did according to the word of Moses.
8 And the LORD spoke unto Aaron, saying,
9 Do not drink wine nor strong drink, thou, nor your sons with thee, when you go into the tabernacle of the congregation, lest you die: *it will be* a statute for ever throughout your generations:
10 And that you may put difference between holy and unholy, and between unclean and clean;
11 And that you may teach the children of Israel all the statutes which the LORD hath spoken unto them by the hand of Moses.
12 And Moses spoke unto Aaron, and unto Eleazar and unto Ithamar, his sons that were left, Take the meat offering that remain of the offerings of the LORD made by fire, and eat it without leaven beside the altar: for it *is* most holy:
13 And you will eat it in the holy place, because it *is* your due, and your sons' due, of the sacrifices of the LORD made by fire: for so I am commanded.
14 And the wave breast and heave shoulder will you eat in a clean place; thou, and your sons, and your daughters with thee: for *they be* your due, and your sons' due, *which* are given out of the sacrifices of peace offerings of the children of Israel.
15 The heave shoulder and the wave breast will they bring with the offerings made by fire of the fat, to wave *it for* a wave offering before the LORD; and it will be your, and your sons' with thee, by a statute for ever; as the LORD hath commanded.
16 And Moses diligently sought the goat of the sin offering, and, behold, it was burnt: and he was angry with Eleazar and Ithamar, the sons of Aaron *which were* left *alive*, saying,
17 Wherefore have you not eaten the sin offering in the holy place, seeing it *is* most holy, and *God* hath given it you to bear the iniquity of the congregation, to make atonement for them before the LORD?
18 Behold, the blood of it was not brought in within the holy *place*: you should indeed have eaten it in the holy *place*, as I commanded.
19 And Aaron said unto Moses, Behold, this day have they offered their sin offering and their burnt offering before the LORD; and such things have befallen me: and *if* I had eaten the sin offering today, should it have been accepted in the sight of the LORD?
20 And when Moses heard *that*, he was content.

CHAPTER 11

1 And the LORD spoke unto Moses and to Aaron, saying unto them,

2 Speak unto the children of Israel, saying, these *are* the beasts which you will eat among all the beasts that *are* on the earth.

3 Whatsoever part the hoof, and is cloven footed, *and* chew the cud, among the beasts, that will you eat.

4 Nevertheless these will you not eat of them that chew the cud, or of them that divide the hoof: *as* the camel, because he chewed the cud, but divided not the hoof; he *is* unclean unto you.

5 And the coney[1], because he chewed the cud, but divided not the hoof; he *is* unclean unto you.

6 And the hare, because he chewed the cud, but divided not the hoof; he *is* unclean unto you.

7 And the swine, though he divide the hoof, and be cloven-footed, yet he chewed not the cud; he *is* unclean to you.

8 Of their flesh will you not eat, and their carcass will you not touch; they *are* unclean to you.

9 These will you eat of all that *are* in the waters: whatsoever hath fins and scales in the waters, in the seas, and in the rivers, them will you eat.

10 And all that have not fins and scales in the seas, and in the rivers, of all that move in the waters, and of any living thing which *is* in the waters, they will *be* an abomination unto you:

11 They will be even an abomination unto you; you will not eat of their flesh, but you will have their carcasses in abomination.

12 Whatsoever hath no fins or scales in the waters, that will *be* an abomination unto you.

13 And these *are they which* you will have in abomination among the fowls; they will not be eaten, they *are* an abomination: the eagle, and the ossifrage, and the ospray,

14 And the vulture, and the kite after his kind;

15 Every raven after his kind;

16 And the owl, and the night hawk, and the cuckow, and the hawk after his kind,

17 And the little owl, and the cormorant, and the great owl,

18 And the swan, and the pelican, and the gier eagle[2],

19 And the stork, the heron after her kind, and the lapwing, and the bat.

20 All fowls that creep, going upon *all* four, will *be* an abomination unto you.

21 Yet these may you eat of every flying creeping thing that goes upon *all* four, which have legs above their feet, to leap withal upon the earth;

22 *Even* these of them you may eat; the locust after his kind, and the bald locust after his kind, and the beetle after his kind, and the grasshopper after his kind.

23 But all *other* flying creeping things, which have four feet, will *be* an abomination unto you.

24 And for these you will be unclean: whosoever touched the carcass of them will be unclean until the evening.

25 And whosoever bears *ought* of the carcass of them will wash his clothes, and be unclean until the evening.

26 *The carcasses* of every beast which divided the hoof, and *is* not cloven footed, or chew the cud, *are* unclean unto you: every one that touches them will be unclean.

27 And whatsoever goes upon his paws, among all manner of beasts that go on *all* four, those *are* unclean unto you: whoso touches their carcass will be unclean until the evening.

28 And he that bears the carcass of them will wash his clothes, and be unclean until the evening: they *are* unclean unto you.

29 These also will *be* unclean unto you among the creeping things that creep upon the earth; the weasel, and the mouse, and the tortoise after his kind,

30 And the ferret, and the chameleon, and the lizard, and the snail, and the mole.

31 These *are* unclean to you among all that creep: whosoever does touch them, when they be dead, will be unclean until the evening.

32 And upon whatsoever *any* of them, when they are dead, does fall, it will be unclean; whether *it be* any vessel of wood, or raiment, or skin, or sack, whatsoever vessel *it be*, wherein *any* work is done, it must be put into water, and it will be unclean until the evening; so it will be cleansed.

33 And every earthen vessel, where into *any* of them fall, whatsoever *is* in it will be unclean; and you will break it.

34 Of all meat which may be eaten, *that* on which *such* water cometh will be unclean: and all drink that may be drunk in every *such* vessel will be unclean.

35 And every*thing* whereupon *any part* of their carcass fall will be unclean; *whether it be* oven, or ranges for pots, they will be broken down: *for* they *are* unclean, and will be unclean unto you.

36 Nevertheless a fountain or pit, *wherein there is* plenty of water, will be clean: but that which touches their carcass will be unclean.

37 And if *any part* of their carcass falls upon any sowing seed which is to be sown, it will *be* clean.

38 But if *any* water be put upon the seed, and *any part* of their carcass fall thereon, it will *be* unclean unto you.

39 And if any beast, of which you may eat, die; he that touches the carcass thereof will be unclean until the evening.

40 And he that eats of the carcass of it will wash his clothes, and be unclean until the evening: he also that bears the carcass of it will wash his clothes, and be unclean until the evening.

41 And every creeping thing that creeps upon the earth will *be* an abomination; it will not be eaten.

42 Whatsoever go upon the belly, and whatsoever go upon *all* four, or whatsoever hath more feet among all creeping things that creep upon the earth, them you will not eat; for they *are* an abomination.

43 you will not make yourselves abominable with any creeping thing that creeps, neither will you make yourselves unclean with them, that you should be defiled thereby.

44 For I *am* the LORD your God: you will therefore sanctify yourselves, and you will be holy; for I *am* holy: neither will you defile yourselves with any manner of creeping thing that creeps upon the earth.

45 For I *am* the LORD that brought you up out of the land of Egypt, to be your God: you will therefore be holy, for I *am* holy.

46 This *is* the law of the beasts, and of the fowl, and of every living creature that moves in the waters, and of every creature that creeps upon the earth:

47 To make a difference between the unclean and the clean, and between the beast that may be eaten and the beast that may not be eaten.

---

[1] Coney – a species of rock rabbit. [Strgs#8227]

[2] Gier Eagle – a kind of vulture (suppose to be tender towards its young).

[Strgs#7360]

CHAPTER 12

1 And the LORD spoke unto Moses, saying,
2 Speak unto the children of Israel, saying, if a woman have conceived seed, and born a man child: then she will be unclean seven days; according to the days of the separation for her infirmity will she be unclean.
3 And in the eighth day the flesh of his foreskin will be circumcised.
4 And she will then continue in the blood of her purifying three and thirty days; she will touch no hallowed thing, nor come into the sanctuary, until the days of her purifying be fulfilled.
5 But if she bears a maid child, then she will be unclean two weeks, as in her separation: and she will continue in the blood of her purifying threescore and six days.
6 And when the days of her purifying are fulfilled, for a son, or for a daughter, she will bring a lamb of the first year for a burnt offering, and a young pigeon, or a turtledove, for a sin offering, unto the door of the tabernacle of the congregation, unto the priest:
7 Who will offer it before the LORD, and make atonement for her; and she will be cleansed from the issue of her blood. This *is* the law for her that hath born a male or a female.
8 And if she be not able to bring a lamb, then she will bring two turtles, or two young pigeons; the one for the burnt offering, and the other for a sin offering: and the priest will make atonement for her, and she will be clean.

CHAPTER 13

1 And the LORD spoke unto Moses and Aaron, saying,
2 When a man will have in the skin of his flesh a rising, a scab, or bright spot, and it be in the skin of his flesh *like* the plague of leprosy; then he will be brought unto Aaron the priest, or unto one of his sons the priests:
3 And the priest will look on the plague in the skin of the flesh: and *when* the hair in the plague is turned white, and the plague in sight *is* deeper than the skin of his flesh, it *is* a plague of leprosy: and the priest will look on him, and pronounce him unclean.
4 If the bright spot *be* white in the skin of his flesh, and in sight *be* not deeper than the skin, and the hair thereof be not turned white; then the priest will shut up *him that hath* the plague seven days:
5 And the priest will look on him the seventh day: and, behold, *if* the plague in his sight be at a stay, *and* the plague spread not in the skin; then the priest will shut him up seven days more:
6 And the priest will look on him again the seventh day: and, behold, *if* the plague be somewhat dark, *and* the plague spread not in the skin, the priest will pronounce him clean: it *is but* a scab: and he will wash his clothes, and be clean.
7 But if the scab spread much abroad in the skin, after that he hath been seen of the priest for his cleansing, he will be seen of the priest again:
8 And *if* the priest sees that, behold, the scab spread in the skin, then the priest will pronounce him unclean: it *is* a leprosy.
9 When the plague of leprosy is in a man, then he will be brought unto the priest;
10 And the priest will see *him*: and, behold, *if* the rising *be* white in the skin, and it have turned the hair white, and *there be* quick raw flesh in the rising;
11 It *is* an old leprosy in the skin of his flesh, and the priest will pronounce him unclean, and will not shut him up: for he *is* unclean.
12 And if a leprosy break out abroad in the skin, and the leprosy cover all the skin of *him that hath* the plague from his head even to his foot, wherever the priest look;
13 Then the priest will consider: and, behold, *if* the leprosy have covered all his flesh, he will pronounce *him* clean *that hath* the plague: it is all turned white: he *is* clean.
14 But when raw flesh appears in him, he will be unclean.
15 And the priest will see the raw flesh, and pronounce him to be unclean: *for* the raw flesh *is* unclean: it *is* leprosy.
16 Or if the raw flesh turn again, and be changed unto white, he will come unto the priest;
17 And the priest will see him: and, behold, *if* the plague be turned into white; then the priest will pronounce *him* clean *that hath* the plague: he *is* clean.
18 The flesh also, in which, *even* in the skin thereof was a boil, and is healed,
19 And in the place of the boil there be a white rising, or a bright spot, white, and somewhat reddish, and it be showed to the priest;
20 And if, when the priest sees it, behold, it *be* in sight lower than the skin, and the hair thereof be turned white; the priest will pronounce him unclean: it *is* a plague of leprosy broken out of the boil.
21 But if the priest looks on it, and, behold, *there be* no white hairs therein, and *if it be* not lower than the skin, but *be* somewhat dark; then the priest will shut him up seven days:
22 And if it spread much abroad in the skin, then the priest will pronounce him unclean: it *is* a plague.
23 But if the bright spot stay in his place, *and* spread not, it *is* a burning boil; and the priest will pronounce him clean.
24 Or if there be *any* flesh, in the skin whereof *there is* a hot burning, and the quick *flesh* that burns have a white bright spot, somewhat reddish, or white;
25 Then the priest will look upon it: and, behold, *if* the hair in the bright spot be turned white, and it *be in* sight deeper than the skin; it *is* a leprosy broken out of the burning: wherefore the priest will pronounce him unclean: it *is* the plague of leprosy.
26 But if the priest look on it, and, behold, *there be* no white hair in the bright spot, and it *be* no lower than the *other* skin, but *be* somewhat dark; then the priest will shut him up seven days:
27 And the priest will look upon him the seventh day: *and* if it be spread much abroad in the skin, then the priest will pronounce him unclean: it *is* the plague of leprosy.
28 And if the bright spot stay in his place, *and* spread not in the skin, but it *be* somewhat dark; it *is* a rising of the burning, and the priest will pronounce him clean: for it *is* an inflammation of the burning.
29 If a man or woman have a plague upon the head or the beard;
30 Then the priest will see the plague: and, behold, if it *be* in sight deeper than the skin; *and there be* in it a yellow thin hair; then the priest will pronounce him unclean: it *is* a dry **scab**, *even* a leprosy upon the head or beard.
31 And if the priest looks on the plague of the **scab**, and, behold, it *be* not in sight deeper than the skin, and *that there is* no black hair in it; then the priest will shut up *him that hath* the plague of the **scab** seven days:
32 And in the seventh day the priest will look on the plague: and, behold, *if* the **scab** spread not, and there be in it no yellow hair, and the **scab** *be* not in sight deeper than the skin;
33 He will be shaven, but the **scab** wills he not shave; and the priest will shut up *him that hath* the **scab** seven days more:
34 And in the seventh day the priest will look on the **scab**: and, behold, *if* the **scab** be not spread in the skin, nor *be* in sight deeper

than the skin; then the priest will pronounce him clean: and he will wash his clothes, and be clean.
35 But if the **scab** spread much in the skin after his cleansing;
36 Then the priest will look on him: and, behold, if the **scab** be spread in the skin, the priest will not seek for yellow hair; he *is* unclean.
37 But if the **scab** be in his sight at a stay, and *that* there is black hair grown up therein; the **scab** is healed, he *is* clean: and the priest will pronounce him clean.
38 If a man also or a woman have in the skin of their flesh bright spots, *even* white bright spots;
39 Then the priest will look: and, behold, *if* the bright spots in the skin of their flesh *be* darkish white; it *is* a freckled spot *that* grows in the skin; he *is* clean.
40 And the man whose hair is fallen off his head, he *is* bald; *yet is* he clean.
41 And he that hath his hair fallen off from the part of his head toward his face, he *is* forehead bald: *yet is* he clean.
42 And if there be in the bald head, or bald forehead, a white reddish sore; it *is* a leprosy sprung up in his bald head, or his bald forehead.
43 Then the priest will look upon it: and, behold, *if* the rising of the sore *be* white reddish in his bald head, or in his bald forehead, as the leprosy appears in the skin of the flesh;
44 He is a leprous man, he *is* unclean: the priest will pronounce him utterly unclean; his plague *is* in his head.
45 And the leper in whom the plague *is*, his clothes will be rent, and his head bare, and he will put a covering upon his upper lip, and will cry, Unclean, unclean.
46 All the days wherein the plague will *be* in him he will be defiled; he *is* unclean: he will dwell alone; without the camp will his habitation *be*.
47 The garment also that the plague of leprosy is in, *whether it be* a woolen garment, or a linen garment;
48 Whether *it is* in the warp, or woof; of linen, or of woolen; whether in a skin, or in any thing made of skin;
49 And if the plague be greenish or reddish in the garment, or in the skin, either in the warp, or in the woof, or in any thing of skin; it *is* a plague of leprosy, and will be showed unto the priest:
50 And the priest will look upon the plague, and shut up *it that hath* the plague seven days:
51 And he will look on the plague on the seventh day: if the plague be spread in the garment, either in the warp, or in the woof, or in a skin, *or* in any work that is made of skin; the plague *is* a fretting leprosy; it *is* unclean.
52 He will therefore burn that garment, whether warp or woof, in woolen or in linen, or anything of skin, wherein the plague is: for it *is* a fretting leprosy; it will be burnt in the fire.
53 And if the priest will look, and, behold, the plague be not spread in the garment, either in the warp, or in the woof, or in any thing of skin;
54 Then the priest will command that they wash *the thing* wherein the plague *is*, and he will shut it up seven days more:
55 And the priest will look on the plague, after that it is washed: and, behold, *if* the plague have not changed his color, and the plague be not spread; it *is* unclean; you will burn it in the fire; it *is* fret inward, *whether* it *be* bare within or without.
56 And if the priest looks, and, behold, the plague *be* somewhat dark after the washing of it; then he will rend it out of the garment, or out of the skin, or out of the warp, or out of the woof:
57 And if it appear still in the garment, either in the warp, or in the woof, or in any thing of skin; it *is* a spreading *plague*: you will burn that wherein the plague *is* with fire.
58 And the garment, either warp, or woof, or whatsoever thing of skin *it be*, which you will wash, if the plague be departed from them, then it will be washed the second time, and will be clean.
59 This *is* the law of the plague of leprosy in a garment of woolen or linen, either in the warp, or woof, or anything of skins, to pronounce it clean, or to pronounce it unclean.

CHAPTER 14

1 And the LORD spoke unto Moses, saying,
2 This will be the law of the leper in the day of his cleansing: He will be brought unto the priest:
3 And the priest will go forth out of the camp; and the priest will look, and, behold, *if* the plague of leprosy be healed in the leper;
4 Then will the priest command to take for him that is to be cleansed two birds alive *and* clean, and cedar wood, and scarlet, and hyssop:
5 And the priest will command that one of the birds be killed in an earthen vessel over running water:
6 As for the living bird, he will take it, and the cedar wood, and the scarlet, and the hyssop, and will dip them and the living bird in the blood of the bird *that was* killed over the running water:
7 And he will sprinkle upon him that is to be cleansed from the leprosy seven times, and will pronounce him clean, and will let the living bird loose into the open field.
8 And he that is to be cleansed will wash his clothes, and shave off all his hair, and wash himself in water, that he may be clean: and after that he will come into the camp, and will tarry abroad out of his tent seven days.
9 But it will be on the seventh day, that he will shave all his hair off his head and his beard and his eyebrows, even all his hair he will shave off: and he will wash his clothes, also he will wash his flesh in water, and he will be clean.
10 And on the eighth day he will take two he lambs without blemish, and one ewe lamb of the first year without blemish, and three tenth deals of fine flour *for* a meat offering, mingled with oil, and one log of oil.
11 And the priest that makes *him* clean will present the man that is to be made clean, and those things, before the LORD, *at* the door of the tabernacle of the congregation:
12 And the priest will take one he lamb, and offer him for a trespass offering, and the log of oil, and wave them *for* a wave offering before the LORD:
13 And he will slay the lamb in the place where he will kill the sin offering and the burnt offering, in the holy place: for as the sin offering *is* the priest's, *so is* the trespass offering: it *is* most holy:
14 And the priest will take *some* of the blood of the trespass offering, and the priest will put *it* upon the tip of the right ear of him that is to be cleansed, and upon the thumb of his right hand, and upon the great toe of his right foot:
15 And the priest will take *some* of the log of oil, and pour *it* into the palm of his own left hand:
16 And the priest will dip his right finger in the oil that *is* in his left hand, and will sprinkle of the oil with his finger seven times before the LORD:
17 And of the rest of the oil that *is* in his hand will the priest put upon the tip of the right ear of him that is to be cleansed, and upon the thumb of his right hand, and upon the great toe of his right foot, upon the blood of the trespass offering:

18 And the remnant of the oil that *is* in the priest's hand he will pour upon the head of him that is to be cleansed: and the priest will make atonement for him before the LORD.
19 And the priest will offer the sin offering, and make atonement for him that is to be cleansed from his uncleanness; and afterward he will kill the burnt offering:
20 And the priest will offer the burnt offering and the meat offering upon the altar: and the priest will make atonement for him, and he will be clean.
21 And if he *be* poor, and cannot get so much; then he will take one lamb *for* a trespass offering to be waved, to make an atonement for him, and one tenth deal of fine flour mingled with oil for a meat offering, and a log of oil;
22 And two turtledoves, or two young pigeons, such as he is able to get; and the one will be a sin offering, and the other a burnt offering.
23 And he will bring them on the eighth day for his cleansing unto the priest, unto the door of the tabernacle of the congregation, before the LORD.
24 And the priest will take the lamb of the trespass offering, and the log of oil, and the priest will wave them *for* a wave offering before the LORD:
25 And he will kill the lamb of the trespass offering, and the priest will take *some* of the blood of the trespass offering, and put *it* upon the tip of the right ear of him that is to be cleansed, and upon the thumb of his right hand, and upon the great toe of his right foot:
26 And the priest will pour of the oil into the palm of his own left hand:
27 And the priest will sprinkle with his right finger *some* of the oil that *is* in his left hand seven times before the LORD:
28 And the priest will put of the oil that *is* in his hand upon the tip of the right ear of him that is to be cleansed, and upon the thumb of his right hand, and upon the great toe of his right foot, upon the place of the blood of the trespass offering:
29 And the rest of the oil that *is* in the priest's hand he will put upon the head of him that is to be cleansed, to make atonement for him before the LORD.
30 And he will offer the one of the turtledoves, or of the young pigeons, such as he can get;
31 *Even* such as he is able to get, the one *for* a sin offering, and the other *for* a burnt offering, with the meat offering: and the priest will make atonement for him that is to be cleansed before the LORD.
32 This *is* the law *of him* in who *is* the plague of leprosy, whose hand is not able to get *that which pertains* to his cleansing.
33 And the LORD spoke unto Moses and unto Aaron, saying,
34 When you be come into the land of Canaan, which I give to you for a possession, and I put the plague of leprosy in a house of the land of your possession;
35 And he that owns the house will come and tell the priest, saying, it seems to me *there is* as it were a plague in the house:
36 Then the priest will command that they empty the house, before the priest go *into it* to see the plague, that all that *is* in the house be not made unclean: and afterward the priest will go in to see the house:
37 And he will look on the plague, and, behold, *if* the plague *be* in the walls of the house with hollow strakes, greenish or reddish, which in sight *are* lower than the wall;
38 Then the priest will go out of the house to the door of the house, and shut up the house seven days:
39 And the priest will come again the seventh day, and will look: and, behold, *if* the plague be spread in the walls of the house;
40 Then the priest will command that they take away the stones in which the plague *is*, and they will cast them into an unclean place without the city:
41 And he will cause the house to be scraped within round about, and they will pour out the dust that they scrape off without the city into an unclean place:
42 And they will take other stones, and put *them* in the place of those stones; and he will take other mortar, and will plaster the house.
43 And if the plague come again, and break out in the house, after that he hath taken away the stones, and after he hath scraped the house, and after it is plastered;
44 Then the priest will come and look, and, behold, *if* the plague be spread in the house, it *is* a fretting leprosy in the house: it *is* unclean.
45 And he will break down the house, the stones of it, and the timber thereof, and all the mortar of the house; and he will carry *them* forth out of the city into an unclean place.
46 Moreover he that goes into the house all the while that it is shut up will be unclean until the evening.
47 And he that lies in the house will wash his clothes; and he that eats in the house will wash his clothes.
48 And if the priest will come in, and look *upon it*, and, behold, the plague hath not spread in the house, after the house was plastered: then the priest will pronounce the house clean, because the plague is healed.
49 And he will take to cleanse the house two birds, and cedar wood, and scarlet, and hyssop:
50 And he will kill the one of the birds in an earthen vessel over running water:
51 And he will take the cedar wood, and the hyssop, and the scarlet, and the living bird, and dip them in the blood of the slain bird, and in the running water, and sprinkle the house seven times:
52 And he will cleanse the house with the blood of the bird, and with the running water, and with the living bird, and with the cedar wood, and with the hyssop, and with the scarlet:
53 But he will let go the living bird out of the city into the open fields, and make atonement for the house: and it will be clean.
54 This *is* the law for all manner of plague of leprosy, and scab,
55 And for the leprosy of a garment, and of a house,
56 And for a rising, and for a scab, and for a bright spot:
57 To teach when *it is* unclean, and when *it is* clean: this *is* the law of leprosy.

CHAPTER 15

1 And the LORD spoke unto Moses and to Aaron, saying,
2 Speak unto the children of Israel, and say unto them, when any man hath a running issue out of his flesh, *because of* his issue he *is* unclean.
3 And this will be his uncleanness in his issue: whether his flesh run with his issue, or his flesh is stopped from his issue, it *is* his uncleanness.
4 Every bed, whereon he lies that has the issue, is unclean: and everything, whereon he sits, will be unclean.
5 And whosoever touches his bed will wash his clothes, and bathe *himself* in water, and be unclean until the evening.
6 And he that sits on *anything* whereon he sat that hath the issue will wash his clothes, and bathe *himself* in water, and be unclean until the evening.

Leviticus

7 And he that touches the flesh of him that hath the issue will wash his clothes, and bathe *himself* in water, and be unclean until the even.

8 And if he that hath the issue spit upon him that is clean; then he will wash his clothes, and bathe *himself* in water, and be unclean until the evening.

9 And **whatever** saddle he rides upon that has the issue will be unclean.

10 And whosoever touches anything that was under him will be unclean until the evening: and he that bears *any of* those things will wash his clothes, and bathe *himself* in water, and be unclean until the evening.

11 And whomsoever he touches that hath the issue, and hath not rinsed his hands in water, he will wash his clothes, and bathe *himself* in water, and be unclean until the evening.

12 And the vessel of earth, that he touches which hath the issue, will be broken: and every vessel of wood will be rinsed in water.

13 And when he that hath an issue is cleansed of his issue; then he will number to himself seven days for his cleansing, and wash his clothes, and bathe his flesh in running water, and will be clean.

14 And on the eighth day he will take to him two turtledoves, or two young pigeons, and come before the LORD unto the door of the tabernacle of the congregation, and give them unto the priest:

15 And the priest will offer them, the one *for* a sin offering, and the other *for* a burnt offering; and the priest will make atonement for him before the LORD for his issue.

16 And if any man's seed of copulation go out from him, then he will wash all his flesh in water, and be unclean until the evening.

17 And every garment, and every skin, whereon is the seed of copulation, will be washed with water, and be unclean until the evening.

18 The woman also with **who** the man will lie *with* seed of copulation, they will *both* bathe *themselves* in water, and be unclean until the evening.

19 And if a woman has an issue, *and* her issue in her flesh is blood, she will be put apart seven days: and whosoever touches her will be unclean until the evening.

20 And everything that she lay upon in her separation will be unclean: everything also that she sits upon will be unclean.

21 And whosoever touches her bed will wash his clothes, and bathe *himself* in water, and be unclean until the evening.

22 And whosoever touches any thing that she sat upon will wash his clothes, and bathe *himself* in water, and be unclean until the evening.

23 And if it *be* on *her* bed, or on anything whereon she sits, when he touches it, he will be unclean until the evening.

24 And if any man lie with her at all, and her flowers be upon him, he will be unclean seven days; and all the bed whereon he lay will be unclean.

25 And if a woman have an issue of her blood many days out of the time of her separation, or if it run beyond the time of her separation; all the days of the issue of her uncleanness will be as the days of her separation: she will *be* unclean.

26 Every bed whereon she lay all the days of her issue will be unto her as the bed of her separation: and whatsoever she sits upon will be unclean, as the uncleanness of her separation.

27 And whosoever touches those things will be unclean, and will wash his clothes, and bathe *himself* in water, and be unclean until the evening.

28 But if she be cleansed of her issue, then she will number to herself seven days, and after that she will be clean.

29 And on the eighth day she will take unto her two turtles, or two young pigeons, and bring them unto the priest, to the door of the tabernacle of the congregation.

30 And the priest will offer the one *for* a sin offering, and the other *for* a burnt offering; and the priest will make atonement for her before the LORD for the issue of her uncleanness.

31 Thus will you separate the children of Israel from their uncleanness; that they die not in their uncleanness, when they defile my tabernacle that *is* among them.

32 This *is* the law of him that hath an issue, and *of him* whose seed goes from him, and is defiled therewith;

33 And of her that is sick of her flowers, and of him that hath an issue, of the man, and of the woman, and of him that lay with her that is unclean.

CHAPTER 16

1 And the LORD spoke unto Moses after the death of the two sons of Aaron, when they offered before the LORD, and died;

2 [And the LORD said unto Moses, Speak unto Aaron your brother, that he come not at all times into the holy *place* within[1] the veil before the mercy seat, which *is* upon the ark; that he die not: for I will appear[2] in the cloud[3] upon the mercy seat.][4]

3 Thus will Aaron come into the holy *place*: with a young bullock for a sin offering, and a ram for a burnt offering.

4 He will put on the holy linen coat, and he will have the linen breeches[5] upon his flesh, and will be girded with a linen girdle, and with the linen **turban**[6] will he be attired: these *are* holy garments; therefore will he wash his flesh in water, and *so* put them on.

5 And he will take of the congregation of the children of Israel two kids of the goats for a sin offering, and one ram for a burnt offering.

6 And Aaron will offer his bullock of the sin offering, which *is* for himself, and make atonement for himself, and for his house.

7 And he will take the two goats, and present them before the LORD *at* the door of the tabernacle of the congregation.

8 And Aaron will cast lots upon the two goats; one lot for the LORD, and the other lot for the scapegoat.

9 And Aaron will bring the goat upon which the LORD'S lot fell, and offer him *for* a sin offering.

10 But the goat, on which the lot fell to be the scapegoat[7], will be presented alive before the LORD, to make atonement with him, *and* to let him go for a scapegoat into the wilderness.

11 And Aaron will bring the **young bull** of the sin offering, which *is* for himself, and will make atonement for himself, and for his house, and will kill the bullock of the sin offering which *is* for himself:

12 And he will take a censer full of burning coals of fire from off the altar before the LORD, and his hands full of sweet incense beaten small, and bring *it* within the veil:

---

[1] lit. within = house [Strgs#1004]
[2] lit. appear = see [Strgs#7200]
[3] lit. cloud = thunder cloud [Strgs#6061]
[4] v2 = produced by prayer
[5] breeches = sense of *hiding*; drawers (from concealing the provate parts)

[Strgs#4370]. Root word kâmas meaning to *store away* [Strgs#3647].
[6] also translate as diadem or mitre [Strgs#4701]
[7] scapegoat = goat of departure [Strgs#5799]. Root femine = she goat + departure or a complete removal.

13 And he will put the incense upon the fire before the LORD, that the cloud[1] of the incense may cover the mercy seat that *is* upon the testimony, that he die not:
14 And he will take of the blood of the bullock, and sprinkle *it* with his finger upon the mercy seat eastward; and before the mercy seat will he sprinkle of the blood with his finger seven times.
15 Then will he kill the goat of the sin offering that is for the people and bring his blood within the veil, and do with that blood as he did with the blood of the bullock, and sprinkle it upon the mercy seat, and before the mercy seat:
16 And he will make atonement for the holy *place*, because of the uncleanness[2] of the children of Israel, and because of their transgressions in all their sins: and so will he do for the tabernacle of the congregation, that remained among them in the midst of their uncleanness.
17 And there will be no man in the tabernacle of the congregation when he goes in to make an atonement in the holy *place*, until he come out, and have made an atonement for himself, and for his household, and for all the congregation of Israel.
18 And he will go out unto the altar that *is* before the LORD, and make atonement for it; and will take of the blood of the bullock, and of the blood of the goat, and put *it* upon the horns of the altar round about.
19 And he will sprinkle of the blood upon it with his finger seven times, and cleanse it, and hallow it from the uncleanness of the children of Israel.
20 And when he hath made an end of reconciling the holy *place*, and the tabernacle of the congregation, and the altar, he will bring the live goat:
21 And Aaron will lay both his hands upon the head of the live goat, and confess[3] over him all the iniquities[4] of the children of Israel, and all their transgressions[5] in all their sins, putting them upon the head of the goat[6], and will send *him* away by the hand of a fit man into the wilderness:
22 And the goat will bear upon him all their iniquities unto a land not inhabited[7]: and he will let go the goat in the wilderness.
23 And Aaron will come into the tabernacle of the congregation, and will put off the linen garments, which he put on when he went into the holy *place*, and will leave them there:
24 And he will wash his flesh with water in the holy place, and put on his garments, and come forth, and offer his burnt offering, and the burnt offering of the people, and make atonement for himself, and for the people.
25 And the fat of the sin offering will he burn upon the altar.
26 And he that let go the goat for the scapegoat will wash his clothes, and bathe his flesh in water, and afterward come into the camp.
27 And the bullock *for* the sin offering, and the goat *for* the sin offering, whose blood was brought in to make atonement in the holy *place*, will *one* carry forth without the camp; and they will burn in the fire their skins, and their flesh, and their dung.
28 And he that burns them will wash his clothes, and bathe his flesh in water, and afterward he will come into the camp.
29 And *this* will be a statute for ever unto you: *that* in the seventh month, on the tenth *day* of the month, you will afflict your souls, and do no work at all, *whether it be* one of your own country, or a stranger that sojourneth among you:
30 For on that day will *the priest* make an atonement for you, to cleanse you, *that* you may be clean from all your sins before the LORD.
31 It will *be* a Sabbath of rest unto you, and you will afflict your souls, by a statute forever.
32 And the priest, whom he will anoint, and whom he will consecrate to minister in the priest's office in his father's stead, will make the atonement, and will put on the linen clothes, *even* the holy garments:
33 And he will make atonement for the holy sanctuary, and he will make atonement for the tabernacle of the congregation, and for the altar, and he will make atonement for the priests, and for all the people of the congregation.
34 And this will be an everlasting statute unto you, to make atonement for the children of Israel for all their sins once a year. And he did as the LORD commanded Moses.

CHAPTER 17

1 And the LORD spoke unto Moses, saying,
2 Speak unto Aaron, and unto his sons, and unto all the children of Israel, and say unto them; this *is* the thing which the LORD hath commanded, saying,
3 What man soever *there be* of the house of Israel, that kills an ox, or lamb, or goat, in the camp, or that kills *it* out of the camp,
4 And brings it not unto the door of the tabernacle of the congregation, to offer an offering unto the LORD before the tabernacle of the LORD; blood will be imputed unto that man; he hath shed blood; and that man will be cut off from among his people:
5 To the end that the children of Israel may bring their sacrifices, which they offer in the open field, even that they may bring them unto the LORD, unto the door of the tabernacle of the congregation, unto the priest, and offer them *for* peace offerings unto the LORD.
6 And the priest will sprinkle the blood upon the altar of the LORD *at* the door of the tabernacle of the congregation, and burn the fat for a sweet savor unto the LORD.
7 And they will no more offer their sacrifices unto devils, after **which** they have gone a whoring. This will be a statute for ever unto them throughout their generations.
8 And you will say unto them, whatever man *there be* of the house of Israel, or of the strangers which sojourn among you, that offers a burnt offering or sacrifice,
9 And brings it not unto the door of the tabernacle of the congregation, to offer it unto the LORD; even that man will be cut off from among his people.
10 And whatever man *there be* of the house of Israel, or of the strangers that sojourn among you, that eats any manner of blood; I will even set my face against that soul that eats blood, and will cut him off from among his people.
11 For the life of the flesh *is* in the blood: and I have given it to you upon the altar to make atonement for your souls: for it *is* the blood *that* makes atonement for the soul.

---

[1] lit. thunder cloud compare **Rev. 8:5**.
[2] uncleanness = pollution, religious impurity [Strgs#2932]. Root *tâmê* meaning to be foul, contaminated [Strgs#2930].
[3] confess = to worship with the hand or use the hand [Strgs#3034]
[4] lit. *evil* or *perversity* [Strgs#5771].
[5] lit. revolt [Strgs#6588].
[6] lit. satyr, devil, he goat, faun [Strgs#8163].
[7] inhabited = Hebrew word *gezêrâh* meaning desert (as separated) [Strgs#1509]. Derives from the root word *gâzar* meaning to cut down or off, to destroy, divide, exlude or decide, snatch [Strgs1504].

12 Therefore I said unto the children of Israel, No soul of you will eat blood, neither will any stranger that sojourned among you eat blood.
13 And whatever man *there is* of the children of Israel, or of the strangers that sojourn among you, which hunted and **caught** any beast or fowl that may be eaten; he will even pour out the blood thereof, and cover it with dust.
14 For *it is* the life of all flesh; the blood of it *is* for the life thereof: therefore I said unto the children of Israel, you will eat the blood of no manner of flesh: for the life of all flesh *is* the blood thereof: whosoever eats it will be cut off.
15 And every soul that eats that which died *of itself*, or that which was torn *with beasts, whether it be* one of your own country, or a stranger, he will both wash his clothes, and bathe *himself* in water, and be unclean until the evening: then will he be clean.
16 But if he wash *them* not, nor bathe his flesh; then he will bear his iniquity.

CHAPTER 18

1 And the LORD spoke unto Moses, saying,
2 Speak unto the children of Israel, and say unto them, I am the LORD your God.
3 After the doings of the land of Egypt, wherein you dwelt, will you not do: and after the doings of the land of Canaan, whither I bring you, will you not do: neither will you walk in their ordinances.
4 you will do my judgments, and keep mine ordinances, to walk therein: I *am* the LORD your God.
5 you will therefore keep my statutes, and my judgments: which if a man do, he will live in them: I *am* the LORD.
6 None of you will approach to any that is near of kin to him, to uncover *their* nakedness: I *am* the LORD.
7 The nakedness of your father, or the nakedness of your mother, will you not uncover: she *is* your mother; you will not uncover her nakedness.
8 The nakedness of your father's wife will you not uncover: it *is* your father's nakedness.
9 The nakedness of your sister, the daughter of your father, or daughter of your mother, *whether she be* born at home, or born abroad, *even* their nakedness you will not uncover.
10 The nakedness of your son's daughter, or of your daughter's daughter, *even* their nakedness you will not uncover: for theirs *is* your own nakedness.
11 The nakedness of your father's wife's daughter, begotten of your father, she *is* your sister, you will not uncover her nakedness.
12 you will not uncover the nakedness of your father's sister: she *is* your father's near kinswoman.
13 you will not uncover the nakedness of your mother's sister: for she *is* your mother's near kinswoman.
14 you will not uncover the nakedness of your father's brother, you will not approach to his wife: she *is* your aunt.
15 you will not uncover the nakedness of your daughter in law: she *is* your son's wife; you will not uncover her nakedness.
16 you will not uncover the nakedness of your brother's wife: it *is* your brother's nakedness.
17 you will not uncover the nakedness of a woman and her daughter, neither will you take her son's daughter, or her daughter's daughter, to uncover her nakedness; *for* they *are* her near kinswomen: it *is* wickedness.
18 Neither will you take a wife to her sister, to vex *her*, to uncover her nakedness, beside the other in her life *time*.
19 Also you will not approach unto a woman to uncover her nakedness, as long as she is put apart for her uncleanness.
20 Moreover you will not lie carnally with your neighbor's wife, to defile thyself with her.
21 And you will not let any of your seed pass through *the fire* to Molech[1], neither will you profane the name of your God: I *am* the LORD.
22 you will not lie with mankind, as with womankind: it *is* abomination.
23 Neither will you lie with any beast to defile thyself therewith: neither will any woman stand before a beast to lie down thereto: it *is* confusion.
24 Defile not you yourselves in any of these things: for in all these the nations are defiled which I cast out before you:
25 And the land is defiled: therefore I do visit the iniquity thereof upon it, and the land itself vomited out her inhabitants.
26 You will therefore keep my statutes and my judgments, and will not commit *any* of these abominations; *neither* any of your own nation, nor any stranger that sojourned among you:
27 (For all these abominations have the men of the land done, which *were* before you, and the land is defiled;)
28 That the land **vomits** not you out also, when you defile it, as it **vomited** out the nations that *were* before you.
29 For whosoever will commit any of these abominations, even the souls that commit *them* will be cut off from among their people.
30 Therefore will you keep mine ordinance, that you commit not *any one* of these abominable customs, which were committed before you, and that you defile not yourselves therein: I *am* the LORD your God.

CHAPTER 19

1 And the LORD spoke unto Moses, saying,
2 Speak unto all the congregation of the children of Israel, and say unto them, you will be holy: for I the LORD your God *am* holy.
3 you will fear every man his mother, and his father, and keep my Sabbaths: I *am* the LORD your God.
4 Turn you not unto idols, nor make to yourselves molten gods: I *am* the LORD your God.
5 And if you offer a sacrifice of peace offerings unto the LORD, you will offer it at your own will.
6 It will be eaten the same day you offer it, and on the morrow: and if ought remain until the third day, it will be burnt in the fire.
7 And if it be eaten at all on the third day, it *is* abominable; it will not be accepted.
8 Therefore *everyone* that eats it will bear his iniquity, because he hath profaned the hallowed thing of the LORD: and that soul will be cut off from among his people.
9 And when you reap the harvest of your land, you will not wholly reap the corners of your field, neither will you gather the gleanings of your harvest.
10 And you will not glean your vineyard, neither will you gather *every* grape of your vineyard; you will leave them for the poor and stranger: I *am* the LORD your God.
11 you will not steal, neither deal falsely, neither lay one to another.
12 And you will not swear by my name falsely, neither will you profane the name of your God: I *am* the LORD.

---

[1] Molek (that is, king)- the chief deity of the Ammonites. [Strgs#4432]

Leviticus

13 you will not defraud your neighbor, neither rob *him*: the wages of him that is hired will not abide with thee all night until the morning.
14 you will not curse the deaf, nor put a stumbling block before the blind, but will fear your God: I *am* the LORD.
15 you will do no unrighteousness in judgment: you will not respect the person of the poor, nor honor the person of the mighty: *but* in righteousness will you judge your neighbor.
16 you will not go up and down *as* a talebearer among your people: neither will you stand against the blood of your neighbor: I *am* the LORD.
17 you will not hate your brother in your heart: you will in any wise rebuke your neighbor, and not suffer sin upon him.
18 you will not avenge, nor bear any grudge against the children of your people, but you will love your neighbor as thyself: I *am* the LORD.
19 You will keep my statutes. You will not let your cattle gender with a diverse kind: you will not sow your field with mingled seed: neither will a garment mingled **with** linen and woolen come upon thee.
20 And whosoever lay carnally with a woman, that *is* a bondmaid, betrothed to a husband, and not at all redeemed, or freedom given her; she will be scourged; they will not be put to death, because she was not free.
21 And he will bring his trespass offering unto the LORD, unto the door of the tabernacle of the congregation, *even* a ram for a trespass offering.
22 And the priest will make atonement for him with the ram of the trespass offering before the LORD for his sin which he hath done: and the sin which he hath done will be forgiven him.
23 And when you will come into the land, and will have planted all manner of trees for food, then you will count the fruit thereof as uncircumcised: three years will it be as uncircumcised unto you: it will not be eaten of.
24 But in the fourth year all the fruit thereof will be holy to praise the LORD *withal*.
25 And in the fifth year will you eat of the fruit thereof, that it may yield unto you the increase thereof: I *am* the LORD your God.
26 you will not eat *anything* with the blood: neither will you use enchantment, nor observe times.
27 you will not round the corners of your heads, neither will you mar the corners of your beard.
28 you will not make any cuttings in your flesh for the dead, nor print any marks upon you: I *am* the LORD.
29 Do not prostitute¹ your daughter, to cause her to be a whore; lest the land fall to whoredom, and the land become full of wickedness.
30 You will keep my Sabbaths, and reverence my sanctuary: I *am* the LORD.
31 Regard not them that have familiar spirits, neither seek after wizards, to be defiled² by them: I *am* the LORD your God.
32 you will rise up before the hoary head, and honor the face of the old man, and fear your God: I *am* the LORD.
33 And if a stranger sojourn with thee in your land, you will not vex him.
34 *But* the stranger that dwell with you will be unto you as one born among you, and you will love him as thyself; for you were strangers in the land of Egypt: I *am* the LORD your God.
35 You will do no unrighteousness in judgment, in meteyard, in weight, or in measure.
36 Just balances, just weights, a just ephah, and a just hin, will you have: I *am* the LORD your God, which brought you out of the land of Egypt.
37 Therefore will you observe all my statutes, and all my judgments, and do them: I *am* the LORD.

CHAPTER 20

1 And the LORD spoke unto Moses, saying,
2 Again, you will say to the children of Israel, Whosoever, **whether** *he be* of the children of Israel, or of the strangers that sojourn in Israel, that give *any* of his seed unto Molech; he will surely be put to death: the people of the land will stone him with stones.
3 And I will set my face against that man, and will cut him off from among his people; because he hath given of his seed unto Molech, to defile my sanctuary, and to profane my holy name.
4 And if the people of the land do any ways hide their eyes from the man, when he give of his seed unto Molech, and kill him not:
5 Then I will set my face against that man, and against his family, and will cut him off, and all that go a whoring after him, to commit whoredom with Molech, from among their people.
6 And the soul that turn after such as have familiar spirits, and after wizards, to go a whoring after them, I will even set my face against that soul, and will cut him off from among his people.
7 Sanctify yourselves therefore, and be holy: for I *am* the LORD your God.
8 And you will keep my statutes, and do them: I *am* the LORD which sanctify you.
9 For every one that curses his father or his mother will surely **be** put to death: he has cursed his father or his mother; his blood will *be* upon him.
10 And the man that commit adultery with *another* man's wife, *even* he that commit adultery with his neighbor's wife, the adulterer and the adulteress will surely be put to death.
11 And the man that lay with his father's wife has uncovered his father's nakedness: both of them will surely be put to death; their blood will *be* upon them.
12 And if a man lie with his daughter in law, both of them will surely be put to death: they have wrought confusion; their blood will *be* upon them.
13 If a man also lie with mankind, as he lie with a woman, both of them have committed an abomination: they will surely be put to death; their blood will *be* upon them.
14 And if a man take a wife and her mother, it *is* wickedness: they will be burnt with fire, both he and they; that there be no wickedness among you.
15 And if a man lay with a beast, he will surely be put to death: and you will slay the beast.
16 And if a woman approach unto any beast, and lie down thereto, you will kill the woman, and the beast: they will surely be put to death; their blood will *be* upon them.
17 And if a man will take his sister, his father's daughter, or his mother's daughter, *and* see her nakedness, *and* she see his nakedness; it is a wicked thing; and they will be cut off in the sight

---

¹ prostitute = to *bore*, to *wound*, to *dissolve*, to *profane*, to *break* (one's word), to *begin* (as if by an openingwedge) [Strgs2490]. Compare to *be rubbed* or *worn*, to *be weak, sick afflicted*; or to *grieve, make sick* [Strgs#2470].

² lit. to be foul, contaminated. Compare **2 Cor. 5:10**.

of their people: he hath uncovered his sister's nakedness; he will bear his iniquity.

18 And if a man will lie with a woman having her sickness, and will uncover her nakedness; he hath discovered her fountain, and she hath uncovered the fountain of her blood: and both of them will be cut off from among their people.

19 And you will not uncover the nakedness of your mother's sister, or of your father's sister: for he uncovered his near kin: they will bear their iniquity.

20 And if a man will lie with his uncle's wife, he hath uncovered his uncle's nakedness: they will bear their sin; they will die childless.

21 And if a man will take his brother's wife, it *is* an unclean thing: he hath uncovered his brother's nakedness; they will be childless.

22 You will therefore keep all my statutes, and all my judgments, and do them: that the land, whither I bring you to dwell therein, and **vomit** you not out.

23 And you will not walk in the manners of the nation, which I cast out before you: for they committed all these things, and therefore I abhorred them.

24 But I have said unto you, you will inherit their land, and I will give it unto you to possess it, a land that flow with milk and honey: I *am* the LORD your God, which has separated you from *other* people.

25 you will therefore put difference between clean beasts and unclean, and between unclean fowls and clean: and you will not make your souls abominable by beast, or by fowl, or by any manner of living thing that creeps on the ground, which I have separated from you as unclean.

26 And you will be holy unto me: for I the LORD *am* holy, and have severed you from *other* people, that you should be mine.

27 A man also or woman that hath a familiar spirit, or that is a wizard, will surely be put to death: they will stone them with stones: their blood will *be* upon them.

CHAPTER 21

1 And the LORD said unto Moses, Speak unto the priests the sons of Aaron, and say unto them, there will none be defiled for the dead among his people:

2 But for his kin, that is near unto him, *that is*, for his mother, and for his father, and for his son, and for his daughter, and for his brother,

3 And for his sister a virgin, that is nigh unto him, which hath had no husband; for her may he be defiled.

4 *But* he will not defile himself, *being* a chief man among his people, to profane himself.

5 They will not make baldness upon their head, neither will they shave off the corner of their beard, nor make any cuttings in their flesh.

6 They will be holy unto their God, and not profane the name of their God: for the offerings of the LORD made by fire, *and* the bread of their God, they do offer: therefore they will be holy.

7 They will not take a wife *that is* a whore, or profane; neither will they take a woman put away from her husband: for he *is* holy unto his God.

8 you will sanctify him therefore; for he offered the bread of your God: he will be holy unto thee: for I the LORD, which sanctify you, *am* holy.

9 And the daughter of any priest, if she profane herself by playing the whore, she profane her father: she will be burnt with fire.

10 And *he that is* the high priest among his brethren, upon whose head the anointing oil was poured, and that is consecrated to put on the garments, will not uncover his head, nor rend his clothes;

11 Neither will he go in to any dead body, nor defile himself for his father, or for his mother;

12 Neither will he go out of the sanctuary, nor profane the sanctuary of his God; for the crown of the anointing oil of his God *is* upon him: I *am* the LORD.

13 And he will take a wife in her virginity.

14 A widow, or a divorced woman, or profane, *or* a harlot, these will he not take: but he will take a virgin of his own people to wife.

15 Neither will he profane his seed among his people: for I the LORD do sanctify him.

16 And the LORD spoke unto Moses, saying,

17 Speak unto Aaron, saying, Whoever *he be* of your seed in their generations that hath *any* blemish, let him not approach to offer the bread of his God.

18 For whatsoever man *he be* that hath a blemish, he will not approach: a blind man, or a lame, or he that hath a flat nose, or any thing superfluous,

19 Or a man that is broken footed, or broken handed,

20 Or crookback, or a dwarf, or that hath a blemish in his eye, or be scurvy, or scabbed, or hath his stones broken;

21 No man that hath a blemish of the seed of Aaron the priest will come nigh to offer the offerings of the LORD made by fire: he hath a blemish; he will not come nigh to offer the bread of his God.

22 He will eat the bread of his God, *both* of the most holy, and of the holy.

23 Only he will not go in unto the veil, or come nigh unto the altar, because he hath a blemish; that he profane not my sanctuaries: for I the LORD do sanctify them.

24 And Moses told *it* unto Aaron, and to his sons, and unto all the children of Israel.

CHAPTER 22

1 And the LORD spoke unto Moses, saying,

2 Speak unto Aaron and to his sons, that they separate themselves from the holy things of the children of Israel, and that they profane not my holy name *in those things* which they hallow unto me: I *am* the LORD.

3 Say unto them, whoever *he is* of all your seed among your generations, that goes unto the holy things, which the children of Israel hallow unto the LORD, having his uncleanness upon him, that soul will be cut off from my presence: I *am* the LORD.

4 What man soever of the seed of Aaron *is* a leper, or hath a running issue; he will not eat of the holy things, until he be clean. And **whoever** touches anything *that is* unclean *by* the dead, or a man whose seed goes from him;

5 Or whosoever touches any creeping thing, whereby he may be made unclean, or a man of whom he may take uncleanness, whatsoever uncleanness he hath;

6 The soul which hath touched any such will be unclean until even, and will not eat of the holy things, unless he washes his flesh with water.

7 And when the sun is down, he will be clean, and will afterward eat of the holy things; because it *is* his food.

8 That which dies of itself, or is torn *with beasts*, he will not eat to defile himself therewith: I *am* the LORD.

9 They will therefore keep mine ordinance, lest they bear sin for it, and die therefore, if they profane it: I the LORD do sanctify them.

10 There will no stranger eat *of* the holy thing: a sojourner of the priest, or a hired servant, will not eat *of* the holy thing.
11 But if the priest buys *any* soul with his money, he will eat of it, and he that is born in his house: they will eat of his meat.
12 If the priest's daughter also be *married* unto a stranger, she may not eat of an offering of the holy things.
13 But if the priest's daughter be a widow, or divorced, and have no child, and is returned unto her father's house, as in her youth, she will eat of her father's meat: but there will no stranger eat thereof.
14 And if a man eats *of* the holy thing unwittingly, then he will put the fifth *part* thereof unto it, and will give *it* unto the priest with the holy thing.
15 And they will not profane the holy things of the children of Israel, which they offer unto the LORD;
16 Or suffer them to bear the iniquity of trespass, when they eat their holy things: for I the LORD do sanctify them.
17 And the LORD spoke unto Moses, saying,
18 Speak unto Aaron, and to his sons, and unto all the children of Israel, and say unto them, Whatsoever *he be* of the house of Israel, or of the strangers in Israel, that will offer his oblation for all his vows, and for all his freewill offerings, which they will offer unto the LORD for a burnt offering;
19 you will *offer* at your own will a male without blemish, of the beeves, of the sheep, or of the goats.
20 *But* whatsoever hath a blemish, *that* will you not offer: for it will not be acceptable for you.
21 And whosoever offered a sacrifice of peace offerings unto the LORD to accomplish *his* vow, or a freewill offering in beeves or sheep, it will be perfect to be accepted; there will be no blemish therein.
22 Blind, or broken, or maimed, or having **running sores**, or scurvy, or scabbed, you will not offer these unto the LORD, nor make an offering by fire of them upon the altar unto the LORD.
23 Either a bullock or a lamb that hath anything superfluous or lacking in his parts, that may you offer *for* a freewill offering; but for a vow it will not be accepted.
24 you will not offer unto the LORD that which is bruised, or crushed, or broken, or cut; neither will you make *any offering thereof* in your land.
25 Neither from a stranger's hand will you offer the bread of your God of any of these; because their corruption *is* in them, *and* blemishes are in them: they will not be accepted for you.
26 And the LORD spoke unto Moses, saying,
27 When a bullock, or a sheep, or a goat, is brought forth, then it will be seven days under the dam; and from the eighth day and thenceforth it will be accepted for an offering made by fire unto the LORD.
28 And *whether it* **is** cow or ewe, you will not kill it and her young both in one day.
29 And when you will offer a sacrifice of thanksgiving unto the LORD, offer *it* at your own will.
30 On the same day it will be eaten up; you will leave none of it until the morrow: I *am* the LORD.
31 Therefore will you keep my commandments, and do them: I *am* the LORD.
32 Neither will you profane my holy name; but I will be hallowed among the children of Israel: I *am* the LORD which hallow you,
33 That brought you out of the land of Egypt, to be your God: I *am* the LORD.

CHAPTER 23

1 And the LORD spoke unto Moses, saying,
2 Speak unto the children of Israel, and say unto them, *concerning* the feasts of the LORD, which you will proclaim *to be* holy convocations, *even* these *are* my feasts.
3 Six days will work be done: but the seventh day *is* the Sabbath of rest, a holy convocation; you will do no work *therein*: it *is* the Sabbath of the LORD in all your dwellings.
4 These *are* the feasts of the LORD, *even* holy convocations, which you will proclaim in their seasons.
5 In the fourteenth *day* of the first month at even *is* the LORD'S Passover.
6 And on the fifteenth day of the same month *is* the feast of unleavened bread unto the LORD: seven days you must eat unleavened bread.
7 In the first day you will have a holy convocation: you will do no servile work therein.
8 But you will offer an offering made by fire unto the LORD seven days: in the seventh day *is* a holy convocation: you will do no servile work *therein*.
9 And the LORD spoke unto Moses, saying,
10 Speak unto the children of Israel, and say unto them, when you come into the land which I give unto you, and will reap the harvest thereof, then you will bring a sheaf of the first fruits of your harvest unto the priest:
11 And he will wave the sheaf before the LORD, to be accepted for you: on the morrow after the Sabbath the priest will wave it.
12 And you will offer that day when you wave the sheaf a **male** lamb without blemish of the first year for a burnt offering unto the LORD.
13 And the meat offering thereof will *be* two tenth deals of fine flour mingled with oil, an offering made by fire unto the LORD *for* a sweet savor: and the drink offering thereof will *be* of wine, the fourth *part* of a hin.
14 And you will eat neither bread, nor parched corn, nor green ears, until the selfsame day that you have brought an offering unto your God: *it will be* a statute for ever throughout your generations in all your dwellings.
15 And you will count unto you from the morrow after the Sabbath, from the day that you brought the sheaf of the wave offering; seven Sabbaths will be complete:
16 Even unto the morrow after the seventh Sabbath will you number fifty days; and you will offer a new meat offering unto the LORD.
17 you will bring out of your habitations two wave loaves of two tenth deals: they will be of fine flour; they will be baked with leaven; *they are* the first fruits unto the LORD.
18 And you will offer with the bread seven lambs without blemish of the first year, and one young bullock, and two rams: they will be *for* a burnt offering unto the LORD, with their meat offering, and their drink offerings, *even* an offering made by fire, of sweet savor unto the LORD.
19 Then you will sacrifice one kid of the goats for a sin offering, and two lambs of the first year for a sacrifice of peace offerings.
20 And the priest will wave them with the bread of the first fruits *for* a wave offering before the LORD, with the two lambs: they will be holy to the LORD for the priest.
21 And you will proclaim on the selfsame day, *that* it may be a holy convocation unto you: you will do no servile work *therein: it will be* a statute forever in all your dwellings throughout your generations.

22 And when you reap the harvest of your land, you will not make clean riddance of the corners of your field when you reap, neither will you gather any gleaning of your harvest: you will leave them unto the poor, and to the stranger: I *am* the LORD your God.
23 And the LORD spoke unto Moses, saying,
24 Speak unto the children of Israel, saying, in the seventh month, in the first *day* of the month, will you have a Sabbath, a memorial of blowing of trumpets, a holy convocation.
25 you will do no servile work *therein*: but you will offer an offering made by fire unto the LORD.
26 And the LORD spoke unto Moses, saying,
27 Also on the tenth *day* of this seventh month *there will be* a day of atonement: it will be a holy convocation unto you; and you will afflict your souls, and offer an offering made by fire unto the LORD.
28 And you will do no work in that same day: for it *is* a day of atonement, to make atonement for you before the LORD your God.
29 For whatever soul *it be* that will not be afflicted in that same day, he will be cut off from among his people.
30 And whatsoever soul *it be* that doeth any work in that same day, the same soul will I destroy from among his people.
31 you will do no manner of work: *it will be* a statute for ever throughout your generations in all your dwellings.
32 It will *be* unto you a Sabbath of rest, and you will afflict your souls: in the ninth *day* of the month at even, from even unto even, will you celebrate your Sabbath.
33 And the LORD spoke unto Moses, saying,
34 Speak unto the children of Israel, saying, the fifteenth day of this seventh month will *be* the feast of tabernacles *for* seven days unto the LORD.
35 On the first day will *be* a holy convocation: you will do no servile work *therein*.
36 Seven days you will offer an offering made by fire unto the LORD: on the eighth day will be a holy convocation unto you; and you will offer an offering made by fire unto the LORD: it *is* a solemn assembly; *and* you will do no servile work *therein*.
37 These *are* the feasts of the LORD, which you will proclaim *to be* holy convocations, to offer an offering made by fire unto the LORD, a burnt offering, and a meat offering, a sacrifice, and drink offerings, everything upon his day:
38 Beside the Sabbaths of the LORD, and beside your gifts, and beside all your vows, and beside all your freewill offerings, which you give unto the LORD.
39 Also in the fifteenth day of the seventh month, when you have gathered in the fruit of the land, you will keep a feast unto the LORD seven days: on the first day will *be* a Sabbath, and on the eighth day will *be* a Sabbath.
40 And you will take you on the first day the boughs of goodly trees, branches of palm trees, and the boughs of thick trees, and willows of the brook; and you will rejoice before the LORD your God seven days.
41 And you will keep it a feast unto the LORD seven days in the year. *It will be* a statute forever in your generations: you will celebrate it in the seventh month.
42 you will dwell in booths seven days; all that are Israelites born will dwell in booths:
43 That your generations may know that I made the children of Israel to dwell in booths, when I brought them out of the land of Egypt: I *am* the LORD your God.
44 And Moses declared unto the children of Israel the feasts of the LORD.

CHAPTER 24

1 And the LORD spoke unto Moses, saying,
2 Command the children of Israel, that they bring unto tree pure oil olive beaten for the light, to cause the lamps to burn continually.
3 Without the veil of the testimony, in the tabernacle of the congregation, will Aaron order it from the evening unto the morning before the LORD continually: *it will be* a statute forever in your generations.
4 He will order the lamps upon the pure candlestick before the LORD continually.
5 And you will take fine flour, and bake twelve cakes thereof: two tenth deals will be in one cake.
6 And you will set them in two rows, six on a row, upon the pure table before the LORD.
7 And you will put pure frankincense upon *each* row, that it may be on the bread for a memorial, *even* an offering made by fire unto the LORD.
8 Every Sabbath he will set it in order before the LORD continually, *being taken* from the children of Israel by an everlasting covenant.
9 And it will be Aaron's and his sons'; and they will eat it in the holy place: for it *is* most holy unto him of the offerings of the LORD made by fire by a perpetual statute.
10 And the son of an Israelitish woman, whose father *was* an Egyptian, went out among the children of Israel: and this son of the Israelitish *woman* and a man of Israel strove together in the camp;
11 And the Israelitish woman's son blasphemed the name *of the LORD*, and cursed. And they brought him unto Moses: (and his mother's name *was* Shelomith, the daughter of Dibri, of the tribe of Dan:)
12 And they put him in ward, that the mind of the LORD might be showed them.
13 And the LORD spoke unto Moses, saying,
14 Bring forth him that hath cursed without the camp; and let all that heard *him* lay their hands upon his head, and let the entire congregation stone him.
15 And you will speak unto the children of Israel, saying, Whoever curses his God will bear his sin.
16 And he that blaspheme the name of the LORD, he will surely be put to death, *and* all the congregation will certainly stone him: as well the stranger, as he that is born in the land, when he blaspheme the name *of the LORD*, will be put to death.
17 And he that kills any man will surely be put to death.
18 And he that kills a beast will make it good; beast for beast.
19 And if a man causes a blemish in his neighbor; as he hath done, so will it be done to him;
20 Breach for breach, eye for eye, and tooth for tooth: as he hath caused a blemish in a man, so will it be done to him *again*.
21 And he that kills a beast, he will restore it: and he that kills a man, he will be put to death.
22 you will have one manner of law, as well for the stranger, as for one of your own country: for I *am* the LORD your God.
23 And Moses spoke to the children of Israel, that they should bring forth him that had cursed out of the camp, and stone him with stones. And the children of Israel did as the LORD commanded Moses.

CHAPTER 25

1 And the LORD spoke unto Moses in Mount Sinai, saying,
2 Speak unto the children of Israel, and say unto them, when you come into the land which I give you, then will the land keep a Sabbath unto the LORD.

3 Six years you will sow your field, and six years you will prune your vineyard, and gather in the fruit thereof;
4 But in the seventh year will be a Sabbath of rest unto the land, a Sabbath for the LORD: you will neither sow your field, nor prune your vineyard.
5 That which grows of its own accord of your harvest you will not reap, neither gather the grapes of your vine undressed: *for* it is a year of rest unto the land.
6 And the Sabbath of the land will be meat for you; for thee, and for your servant, and for your maid, and for your hired servant, and for your stranger that sojourned with thee,
7 And for your cattle, and for the beast that *are* in your land, will all the increase thereof be meat.
8 And you will number seven Sabbaths of years unto thee, seven times seven years; and the space of the seven Sabbaths of years will be unto thee forty and nine years.
9 Then will you cause the trumpet of the jubilee to sound on the tenth *day* of the seventh month, in the Day of Atonement will you make the trumpet sound throughout all your land.
10 And you will hallow the fiftieth year, and proclaim liberty throughout *all* the land unto all the inhabitants thereof: it will be a jubilee unto you; and you will return every man unto his possession, and you will return every man unto his family.
11 A jubilee will that fiftieth year be unto you: you will not sow, neither reaps that which grows of itself in it, or gather *the grapes* in it of your vine undressed.
12 For it *is* the jubilee; it will be holy unto you: you will eat the increase thereof out of the field.
13 In the year of this jubilee you will return every man unto his possession.
14 And if you sell ought unto your neighbor, or buy *ought* of your neighbor's hand, you will not oppress one another:
15 According to the number of years after the jubilee you will buy of your neighbor, *and* according unto the number of years of the fruits he will sell unto thee:
16 According to the multitude of years you will increase the price thereof, and according to the fewness of years you will diminish the price of it: for *according* to the number *of the years* of the fruits does he sell unto thee.
17 you will not therefore oppress one another; but you will fear your God: for I *am* the LORD your God.
18 Wherefore you will do my statutes, and keep my judgments, and do them; and you will dwell in the land in safety.
19 And the land will yield her fruit, and you will eat your fill, and dwell therein in safety.
20 And if you will say, what will we eat the seventh year? Behold, we will not sow, nor gather in our increase:
21 Then I will command my blessing upon you in the sixth year, and it will bring forth fruit for three years.
22 And you will sow the eighth year, and eat *yet* of old fruit until the ninth year; until her fruits come in you will eat *of the old store*.
23 The land will not be sold for ever: for the land *is* mine; for you *are* strangers and sojourners with me.
24 And in all the land of your possession you will grant redemption for the land.
25 If your brother be waxen poor, and hath sold away *some* of his possession, and if any of his kin come to redeem it, then will he redeem that which his brother sold.
26 And if the man has none to redeem it, and himself be able to redeem it;
27 Then let him count the years of the sale thereof, and restore the over plus unto the man to whom he sold it; that he may return unto his possession.
28 But if he be not able to restore *it* to him, then that which is sold will remain in the hand of him that hath bought it until the year of jubilee: and in the jubilee it will go out, and he will return unto his possession.
29 And if a man sell a dwelling house in a walled city, then he may redeem it within a whole year after it is sold; *within* a full year may he redeem it.
30 And if it be not redeemed within the space of a full year, then the house that *is* in the walled city will be established for ever to him that bought it throughout his generations: it will not go out in the jubilee.
31 But the houses of the villages which have no wall round about them will be counted as the fields of the country: they may be redeemed, and they will go out in the jubilee.
32 Notwithstanding the cities of the Levites, *and* the houses of the cities of their possession, may the Levites redeem at any time.
33 And if a man purchase of the Levites, then the house that was sold, and the city of his possession, will go out in *the year of* jubilee: for the houses of the cities of the Levites *are* their possession among the children of Israel.
34 But the field of the suburbs of their cities may not be sold; for it *is* their perpetual possession.
35 And if your brother be waxen poor, and fallen in decay with thee; then you will relieve him: *yea, though he be* a stranger, or a sojourner; that he may live with thee.
36 Take you no usury of him, or increase: but fear your God; that your brother may live with thee.
37 you will not give him your money upon usury, nor lend him your victuals for increase.
38 I *am* the LORD your God, which brought you forth out of the land of Egypt, to give you the land of Canaan, *and* to be your God.
39 And if your brother *that dwell* by you be waxen poor, and be sold unto thee; you will not compel him to serve as a bondservant:
40 *But* as a hired servant, *and* as a sojourner, he will be with thee, *and* will serve thee unto the year of jubilee:
41 And *then* will he depart from thee, *both* he and his children with him, and will return unto his own family, and unto the possession of his father's will he return.
42 For they *are* my servants, which I brought forth out of the land of Egypt: they will not be sold as bondmen.
43 You will not rule over him with rigor; but will fear your God.
44 Both your bondmen, and your bondmaids, which you will have, will *be* of the heathen that are round about you; of them will you buy bondmen and bondmaids.
45 Moreover of the children of the strangers that do sojourn among you, of them will you buy, and of their families that *are* with you, which they begat in your land: and they will be your possession.
46 And you will take them as an inheritance for your children after you, to inherit *them for* a possession; they will be your bondmen for ever: but over your brethren the children of Israel, you will not rule one over another with rigor.
47 And if a sojourner or stranger wax rich by you, and your brother *that dwell* by him wax poor, and sell himself unto the stranger *or* sojourner by thee, or to the stock of the stranger's family:
48 After that he is sold he may be redeemed again; one of his brethren may redeem him:

49 Either his uncle, or his uncle's son, may redeem him, or *any* that is nigh of kin unto him of his family may redeem him; or if he be able, he may redeem himself.
50 And he will reckon with him that bought him from the year that he was sold to him unto the year of jubilee: and the price of his sale will be according unto the number of years, according to the time of a hired servant will it be with him.
51 If *there be* yet many years *behind*, according unto them he will give again the price of his redemption out of the money that he was bought for.
52 And if there remain but few years unto the year of jubilee, then he will count with him, *and* according unto his years will he give him again the price of his redemption.
53 *And* as a yearly hired servant will he be with him: *and the other* will not rule with rigor over him in your sight.
54 And if he be not redeemed in these *years*, then he will go out in the year of jubilee, *both* he, and his children with him.
55 For unto me the children of Israel *are* servants; they *are* my servants whom I brought forth out of the land of Egypt: I *am* the LORD your God.

CHAPTER 26

1 you will make you no idols nor graven image, neither rear you up a standing image, neither will you set up *any* image of stone in your land, to bow down unto it: for I *am* the LORD your God.
2 you will keep my Sabbaths, and reverence my sanctuary: I *am* the LORD.
3 If you walk in my statutes, and keep my commandments, and do them;
4 Then I will give you rain in due season, and the land will yield her increase, and the trees of the field will yield their fruit.
5 And your threshing will reach unto the vintage, and the vintage will reach unto the sowing time: and you will eat your bread to the full, and dwell in your land safely.
6 And I will give peace in the land, and you will lie down, and none will make *you* afraid: and I will rid evil beasts out of the land, neither will the sword go through your land.
7 And you will chase your enemies, and they will fall before you by the sword.
8 And five of you will chase an hundred, and an hundred of you will put ten thousand to flight: and your enemies will fall before you by the sword.
9 For I will have respect unto you, and make you fruitful, and multiply you, and establish my covenant with you.
10 And you will eat old store, and bring forth the old because of the new.
11 And I will set my tabernacle among you: and my soul will not abhor you.
12 And I will walk among you, and will be your God, and you will be my people.
13 I *am* the LORD your God, which brought you forth out of the land of Egypt, that you should not be their bondmen; and I have broken the bands of your yoke, and made you go upright.
14 But if you will not hearken unto me, and will not do all these commandments;
15 And if you will despise my statutes, or if your soul abhor my judgments, so that you will not do all my commandments, *but that* you break my covenant:
16 I also will do this unto you; I will even appoint over you terror, consumption, and the burning ague, that will consume the eyes, and cause sorrow of heart: and you will sow your seed in vain, for your enemies will eat it.
17 And I will set my face against you, and you will be slain before your enemies: they that hate you will reign over you; and you will flee when none pursue you.
18 And if you will not yet for all this hearken unto me, then I will punish you seven times more for your sins.
19 And I will break the pride of your power; and I will make your heaven as iron, and your earth as brass:
20 And your strength will be spent in vain: for your land will not yield her increase, neither will the trees of the land yield their fruits.
21 And if you walk contrary unto me, and will not hearken unto me; I will bring seven times more plagues upon you according to your sins.
22 I will also send wild beasts among you, which will rob you of your children, and destroy your cattle, and make you few in number; and your *high* ways will be desolate.
23 And if you will not be reformed by me by these things, but will walk contrary unto me;
24 Then will I also walk contrary unto you, and will punish you yet seven times for your sins.
25 And I will bring a sword upon you, that will avenge the quarrel of *my* covenant: and when you are gathered together within your cities, I will send the pestilence among you; and you will be delivered into the hand of the enemy.
26 *And* when I have broken the staff of your bread, ten women will bake your bread in one oven, and they will deliver *you* your bread again by weight: and you will eat, and not be satisfied.
27 And if you will not for all this hearken unto me, but walk contrary unto me;
28 Then I will walk contrary unto you also in fury; and I, even I, will chastise you seven times for your sins.
29 And you will eat the flesh of your sons, and the flesh of your daughters will you eat.
30 And I will destroy your high places, and cut down your images, and cast your carcass upon the carcasses of your idols, and my soul will abhor you.
31 And I will make your cities waste, and bring your sanctuaries unto desolation, and I will not smell the savor of your sweet odors.
32 And I will bring the land into desolation: and your enemies which dwell therein will be astonished at it.
33 And I will scatter you among the heathen, and will draw out a sword after you: and your land will be desolate, and your cities waste.
34 Then will the land enjoy her Sabbaths, as long as it **lay** desolate, and you *be* in your enemies' land; *even* then will the land rest, and enjoy her Sabbaths.
35 As long as it **lay** desolate it will rest; because it did not rest in your Sabbaths, when you dwelt upon it.
36 And upon them that are left *alive* of you I will send a faintness into their hearts in the lands of their enemies; and the sound of a shaken leaf will chase them; and they will flee, as fleeing from a sword; and they will fall when none pursue.
37 And they will fall one upon another, as it were before a sword, when none pursue: and you will have no power to stand before your enemies.
38 And you will perish among the heathen, and the land of your enemies will eat you up.

39 And they that are left of you will pine away in their iniquity in your enemies' lands; and also in the iniquities of their fathers will they pine away with them.
40 If they will confess their iniquity, and the iniquity of their fathers, with their trespass which they trespassed against me, and that also they have walked contrary unto me;
41 And *that* I also have walked contrary unto them, and have brought them into the land of their enemies; if then their uncircumcised hearts be humbled, and they then accept of the punishment of their iniquity:
42 Then will I remember my covenant with Jacob, and also my covenant with Isaac, and also my covenant with Abraham will I remember; and I will remember the land.
43 The land also will be left of them, and will enjoy her Sabbaths, while she **lay** desolate without them: and they will accept of the punishment of their iniquity: because, even because they despised my judgments, and because their soul abhorred my statutes.
44 And yet for all that, when they be in the land of their enemies, I will not cast them away, neither will I abhor them, to destroy them utterly, and to break my covenant with them: for I *am* the LORD their God.
45 But I will for their sakes remember the covenant of their ancestors, whom I brought forth out of the land of Egypt in the sight of the heathen, that I might be their God: I *am* the LORD.
46 These *are* the statutes and judgments and laws, which the LORD made between him and the children of Israel in Mount Sinai by the hand of Moses.

CHAPTER 27

1 And the LORD spoke unto Moses, saying,
2 Speak unto the children of Israel, and say unto them, when a man will make a singular vow, the persons will *be* for the LORD by your estimation.
3 And your estimation will be of the male from twenty years old even unto sixty years old, even your estimation will be fifty shekels of silver, after the shekel of the sanctuary.
4 And if it *be* a female, then your estimation will be thirty shekels.
5 And if *it be* from five years old even unto twenty years old, then your estimation will be of the male twenty shekels, and for the female ten shekels.
6 And if *it be* from a month old even unto five years old, then your estimation will be of the male five shekels of silver, and for the female your estimation will *be* three shekels of silver.
7 And if *it be* from sixty years old and above; if *it be* a male, then your estimation will be fifteen shekels, and for the female ten shekels.
8 But if he be poorer than your estimation, then he will present himself before the priest, and the priest will value him; according to his ability that vowed will the priest value him.
9 And if *it be* a beast, whereof men bring an offering unto the LORD, all that *any man* gives of such unto the LORD will be holy.
10 He will not alter it, nor change it, a good for a bad, or a bad for a good: and if he will at all change beast for beast, then it and the exchange thereof will be holy.
11 And if *it be* any unclean beast, of which they do not offer a sacrifice unto the LORD, then he will present the beast before the priest:
12 And the priest will value it, whether it is good or bad: as you value it, *who are* the priest, so will it be.
13 But if he will at all redeem it, then he will add a fifth *part* thereof unto your estimation.
14 And when a man will sanctify his house *to be* holy unto the LORD, then the priest will estimate it, whether it is good or bad: as the priest will estimate it, so will it stand.
15 And if he that sanctified it will redeem his house, then he will add the fifth *part* of the money of your estimation unto it, and it will be his.
16 And if a man will sanctify unto the LORD *some part* of a field of his possession, then your estimation will be according to the seed thereof: a homer of barley seed will *be valued* at fifty shekels of silver.
17 If he sanctifies his field from the year of jubilee, according to your estimation it will stand.
18 But if he sanctify his field after the jubilee, then the priest will reckon unto him the money according to the years that remain, even unto the year of the jubilee, and it will be abated from your estimation.
19 And if he that sanctified the field will in any wise redeem it, then he will add the fifth *part* of the money of your estimation unto it, and it will be assured to him.
20 And if he will not redeem the field, or if he has sold the field to another man, it will not be redeemed any more.
21 But the field, when it goes out in the jubilee, will be holy unto the LORD, as a field devoted; the possession thereof will be the priest's.
22 And if *a man* sanctify unto the LORD a field which he hath bought, which *is* not of the fields of his possession;
23 Then the priest will reckon unto him the worth of your estimation, *even* unto the year of the jubilee: and he will give your estimation in that day, *as* a holy thing unto the LORD.
24 In the year of the jubilee the field will return unto him of whom it was bought, *even* to him to whom the possession of the land *did belong*.
25 And all your estimations will be according to the shekel of the sanctuary: twenty gerahs will be the shekel.
26 Only the firstling of the beasts, which should be the LORD'S firstling, no man will sanctify it; whether *it is* ox, or sheep: it *is* the LORD'S.
27 And if *it be* of an unclean beast, then he will redeem *it* according to your estimation, and will add a fifth *part* of it thereto: or if it be not redeemed, then it will be sold according to your estimation.
28 Notwithstanding no devoted thing, that a man will devote unto the LORD of all that he have, *both* of man and beast, and of the field of his possession, will be sold or redeemed: every devoted thing *is* most holy unto the LORD.
29 None devoted, which will be devoted of men, will be redeemed; *but* will surely be put to death.
30 And all the tithe of the land, *whether* of the seed of the land, *or* of the fruit of the tree, *is* the LORD'S: *it is* holy unto the LORD.
31 And if a man will at all redeem *ought* of his tithes, he will add thereto the fifth *part* thereof.
32 And concerning the tithe of the herd, or of the flock, *even* of whatsoever passes under the rod, the tenth will be holy unto the LORD.
33 He will not search whether it is good or bad, neither will he change it: and if he changes it at all, then both it and the change thereof will be holy; it will not be redeemed.
34 These *are* the commandments, which the LORD commanded Moses for the children of Israel in Mount Sinai.

NUMBERS
CHAPTER 1

1 And the LORD spoke unto Moses in the wilderness of Sinai, in the tabernacle of the congregation, on the first *day* of the second month, in the second year after they were come out of the land of Egypt, saying,
2 Take you the sum of all the congregation of the children of Israel, after their families, by the house of their fathers, with the number of *their* names, every male by their polls;
3 From twenty years old and upward, all that are able to go forth to war in Israel: you and Aaron will number them by their armies.
4 And with you there will be a man of every tribe; every one head of the house of his fathers.
5 And these *are* the names of the men that will stand with you: of *the tribe of* Reuben; Elizur the son of Shedeur.
6 Of Simeon; Shelumiel the son of Zurishaddai.
7 Of Judah; Nahshon the son of Amminadab.
8 Of Issachar; Nethaneel the son of Zuar.
9 Of Zebulun; Eliab the son of Helon.
10 Of the children of Joseph: of Ephraim; Elishama the son of Ammihud: of Manasseh; Gamaliel the son of Pedahzur.
11 Of Benjamin; Abidan the son of Gideoni.
12 Of Dan; Ahiezer the son of Ammishaddai.
13 Of Asher; Pagiel the son of Ocran.
14 Of Gad; Eliasaph the son of Deuel.
15 Of Naphtali; Ahira the son of Enan.
16 These *were* the renowned of the congregation, princes of the tribes of their fathers, heads of thousands in Israel.
17 And Moses and Aaron took these men which are expressed by *their* names:
18 And they assembled the entire congregation together on the first *day* of the second month, and they declared their pedigrees threescore and fourteen thousand and six hundred.
28 Of the children of Issachar, by their generations, after their families, by the house of their fathers, according to the number of the names, from twenty years old and upward, all that were able to go forth to war;
29 Those that were numbered of them, *even* of the tribe of Issachar, *were* fifty and four thousand and four hundred.
30 Of the children of Zebulun, by their generations, after their families, by the house of their fathers, according to the number of the names, from twenty years old and upward, all that were able to go forth to war;
31 Those that were numbered of them, *even* of the tribe of Zebulun, *were* fifty and seven thousand and four hundred.
32 Of the children of Joseph, *namely*, of the children of Ephraim, by their generations, after their families, by the house of their fathers, according to the number of the names, from twenty years old and upward, all that were able to go forth to war;
33 Those that were numbered of them, *even* of the tribe of Ephraim, *were* forty thousand and five hundred.
34 Of the children of Manasseh, by their generations, after their families, by the house of their fathers, according to the number of the names, from twenty years old and upward, all that were able to go forth to war;
35 Those that were numbered of them, *even* of the tribe of Manasseh, *were* thirty and two thousand and two hundred.
36 Of the children of Benjamin, by their generations, after their families, by the house of their fathers, according to the number of the names, after their families, by the house of their fathers, according to the number of the names, from twenty years old and upward, by their polls.
19 As the LORD commanded Moses, so he numbered them in the wilderness of Sinai.
20 And the children of Reuben, Israel's eldest son, by their generations, after their families, by the house of their fathers, according to the number of the names, by their polls, every male from twenty years old and upward, all that were able to go forth to war;
21 Those that were numbered of them, *even* of the tribe of Reuben, *were* forty and six thousand and five hundred.
22 Of the children of Simeon, by their generations, after their families, by the house of their fathers, those that were numbered of them, according to the number of the names, by their polls, every male from twenty years old and upward, all that were able to go forth to war;
23 Those that were numbered of them, *even* of the tribe of Simeon, *were* fifty and nine thousand and three hundred.
24 Of the children of Gad, by their generations, after their families, by the house of their fathers, according to the number of the names, from twenty years old and upward, all that were able to go forth to war;
25 Those that were numbered of them, *even* of the tribe of Gad, *were* forty and five thousand six hundred and fifty.
26 Of the children of Judah, by their generations, after their families, by the house of their fathers, according to the number of the names, from twenty years old and upward, all that were able to go forth to war;
27 Those that were numbered of them, *even* of the tribe of Judah, *were*

the names, from twenty years old and upward, all that were able to go forth to war;
37 Those that were numbered of them, *even* of the tribe of Benjamin, *were* thirty and five thousand and four hundred.
38 Of the children of Dan, by their generations, after their families, by the house of their fathers, according to the number of the names, from twenty years old and upward, all that were able to go forth to war;
39 Those that were numbered of them, *even* of the tribe of Dan, *were* threescore and two thousand and seven hundred.
40 Of the children of Asher, by their generations, after their families, by the house of their fathers, according to the number of the names, from twenty years old and upward, all that were able to go forth to war;
41 Those that were numbered of them, *even* of the tribe of Asher, *were* forty and one thousand and five hundred.
42 Of the children of Naphtali, throughout their generations, after their families, by the house of their fathers, according to the number of the names, from twenty years old and upward, all that were able to go forth to war;
43 Those that were numbered of them, *even* of the tribe of Naphtali, *were* fifty and three thousand and four hundred.
44 These *are* those that were numbered, which Moses and Aaron numbered, and the princes of Israel, *being* twelve men each one was for the house of his fathers.

45 So were all those that were numbered of the children of Israel, by the house of their fathers, from twenty years old and upward, all that were able to go forth to war in Israel;
46 Even all they that were numbered were six hundred thousand and three thousand and five hundred and fifty.
47 But the Levites after the tribe of their fathers were not numbered among them.
48 For the LORD had spoken unto Moses, saying,
49 Only you will not number the tribe of Levi, neither take the sum of them among the children of Israel:
50 But you will appoint the Levites over the tabernacle of testimony, and over all the vessels thereof, and over all things that *belong* to it: they will bear the tabernacle, and all the vessels thereof; and they will minister unto it, and will encamp round about the tabernacle.
51 And when the tabernacle **is to go** forward, the Levites will take it down: and when the tabernacle is to be pitched, the Levites will set it up: and the stranger that cometh nigh will be put to death.
52 And the children of Israel will pitch their tents, every man by his own camp, and every man by his own standard, throughout their hosts.
53 But the Levites will pitch round about the tabernacle of testimony, that there is no wrath upon the congregation of the children of Israel: and the Levites will keep the charge of the tabernacle of testimony.
54 And the children of Israel did according to all that the LORD commanded Moses, so did they.

CHAPTER 2

1 And the LORD spoke unto Moses and unto Aaron, saying,
2 Every man of the children of Israel will pitch by his own standard, with the ensign of their father's house: far off about the tabernacle of the congregation will they pitch.
3 And on the east side toward the rising of the sun will they of the standard of the camp of Judah pitch throughout their armies: and Nahshon the son of Amminadab will *be* captain of the children of Judah.
4 And his host, and those that were numbered of them, *were* threescore and fourteen thousand and six hundred.
5 And those that do pitch next unto him will *be* the tribe of Issachar: and Nethaneel the son of Zuar will *be* captain of the children of Issachar.
6 And his host, and those that were numbered thereof, *were* fifty and four thousand and four hundred.
7 *Then* the tribe of Zebulun: and Eliab the son of Helon will *be* captain of the children of Zebulun.
8 And his host, and those that were numbered thereof, *were* fifty and seven thousand and four hundred.
9 All that were numbered in the camp of Judah *were* an hundred thousand and fourscore thousand and six thousand and four hundred, throughout their armies. These will first set forth.
10 On the south side will *be* the standard of the camp of Reuben according to their armies: and the captain of the children of Reuben will *be* Elizur the son of Shedeur.
11 And his host, and those that were numbered thereof, *were* forty and six thousand and five hundred.
12 And those which pitch by him will *be* the tribe of Simeon: and the captain of the children of Simeon will *be* Shelumiel the son of Zurishaddai.
13 And his host, and those that were numbered of them, *were* fifty and nine thousand and three hundred.
14 Then the tribe of Gad: and the captain of the sons of Gad will *be* Eliasaph the son of Reuel.
15 And his host, and those that were numbered of them, *were* forty and five thousand and six hundred and fifty.
16 All that were numbered in the camp of Reuben *were* an hundred thousand and fifty and one thousand and four hundred and fifty, throughout their armies. And they will set forth in the second rank.
17 Then the tabernacle of the congregation will set forward with the camp of the Levites in the midst of the camp: as they encamp, so will they set forward, every man in his place by their standards.
18 On the west side will *be* the standard of the camp of Ephraim according to their armies: and the captain of the sons of Ephraim will *be* Elishama the son of Ammihud.
19 And his host, and those that were numbered of them, *were* forty thousand and five hundred.
20 And by him will *be* the tribe of Manasseh: and the captain of the children of Manasseh will *be* Gamaliel the son of Pedahzur.
21 And his host, and those that were numbered of them, *were* thirty and two thousand and two hundred.
22 Then the tribe of Benjamin: and the captain of the sons of Benjamin will *be* Abidan the son of Gideoni.
23 And his host, and those that were numbered of them, *were* thirty and five thousand and four hundred.
24 All that were numbered of the camp of Ephraim *were* an hundred thousand and eight thousand and an hundred throughout their armies. And they will go forward in the third rank.
25 The standard of the camp of Dan will *be* on the north side by their armies: and the captain of the children of Dan will *be* Ahiezer the son of Ammishaddai.
26 And his host, and those that were numbered of them, *were* threescore and two thousand and seven hundred.
27 And those that encamp by him will *be* the tribe of Asher: and the captain of the children of Asher will *be* Pagiel the son of Ocran.
28 And his host, and those that were numbered of them *were* forty and one thousand and five hundred.
29 Then the tribe of Naphtali: and the captain of the children of Naphtali will *be* Ahira the son of Enan.
30 And his host, and those that were numbered of them, *were* fifty and three thousand and four hundred.
31 All they that were numbered in the camp of Dan *were* an hundred thousand and fifty and seven thousand and six hundred. They will go hindmost with their standards.
32 These *are* those which were numbered of the children of Israel by the house of their fathers: all those that were numbered of the camps throughout their hosts *were* six hundred thousand and three thousand and five hundred and fifty.
33 But the Levites were not numbered among the children of Israel; as the LORD commanded Moses.
34 And the children of Israel did according to all that the LORD commanded Moses: so they pitched by their standards, and so they set forward, every one after their families, according to the house of their fathers.

CHAPTER 3

1 These also *are* the generations of Aaron and Moses in the day *that* the LORD spoke with Moses in Mount Sinai.
2 And these *are* the names of the sons of Aaron; Nadab the firstborn, and Abihu, Eleazar, and Ithamar.

3 These *are* the names of the sons of Aaron, the priests which were anointed, whom he consecrated to minister in the priest's office.
4 And Nadab and Abihu died before the LORD, when they offered strange fire before the LORD, in the wilderness of Sinai, and they had no children: and Eleazar and Ithamar ministered in the priest's office in the sight of Aaron their father.
5 And the LORD spoke unto Moses, saying,
6 Bring the tribe of Levi near, and present them before Aaron the priest, that they may minister unto him.
7 And they will keep his charge, and the charge of the whole congregation before the tabernacle of the congregation, to do the service of the tabernacle.
8 And they will keep all the instruments of the tabernacle of the congregation, and the charge of the children of Israel, to do the service of the tabernacle.
9 And you will give the Levites unto Aaron and to his sons: they *are* wholly given unto him out of the children of Israel.
10 And you will appoint Aaron and his sons, and they will wait on their priest's office: and the stranger that cometh nigh will be put to death.
11 And the LORD spoke unto Moses, saying,
12 And I, behold, I have taken the Levites from among the children of Israel instead of all the firstborn that opened the matrix among the children of Israel: therefore the Levites will be mine;
13 Because all the firstborn *are* mine; *for* on the day that I smote all the firstborn in the land of Egypt I hallowed unto me all the firstborn in Israel, both man and beast: mine will they be: I *am* the LORD.
14 And the LORD spoke unto Moses in the wilderness of Sinai, saying,
15 Number the children of Levi after the house of their fathers, by their families: every male from a month old and upward will you number them.
16 And Moses numbered them according to the word of the LORD, as he was commanded.
17 And these were the sons of Levi by their names; Gershon, and Kohath, and Merari.
18 And these *are* the names of the sons of Gershon by their families; Libni, and Shimei.
19 And the sons of Kohath by their families; Amram, and Izehar, Hebron, and Uzziel.
20 And the sons of Merari by their families; Mahli, and Mushi. These *are* the families of the Levites according to the house of their fathers.
21 Of Gershon *was* the family of the Libnites, and the family of the Shimites: these *are* the families of the Gershonites.
22 Those that were numbered of them, according to the number of all the males, from a month old and upward, *even* those that were numbered of them *were* seven thousand and five hundred.
23 The families of the Gershonites will pitch behind the tabernacle westward.
24 And the chief of the house of the father of the Gershonites will *be* Eliasaph the son of Lael.
25 And the charge of the sons of Gershon in the tabernacle of the congregation will *be* the tabernacle, and the tent, the covering thereof, and the hanging for the door of the tabernacle of the congregation,
26 And the hangings of the court, and the curtain for the door of the court, which *is* by the tabernacle, and by the altar round about, and the cords of it for all the service thereof.
27 And of Kohath *were* the family of the Amramites, and the family of the Izeharites, and the family of the Hebronites, and the family of the Uzzielites: these *are* the families of the Kohathites.
28 In the number of all the males, from a month old and upward, *were* eight thousand and six hundred, keeping the charge of the sanctuary.
29 The families of the sons of Kohath will pitch on the side of the tabernacle southward.
30 And the chief of the house of the father of the families of the Kohathites will *be* Elizaphan the son of Uzziel.
31 And their charge will *be* the ark, and the table, and the candlestick, and the altars, and the vessels of the sanctuary wherewith they minister, and the hanging, and all the service thereof.
32 And Eleazar the son of Aaron the priest will *be* chief over the chief of the Levites, *and have* the oversight of them that keep the charge of the sanctuary.
33 Of Merari *was* the family of the Mahlites, and the family of the Mushites: these *are* the families of Merari.
34 And those that were numbered of them, according to the number of all the males, from a month old and upward, *were* six thousand and two hundred.
35 And the chief of the house of the father of the families of Merari *was* Zuriel the son of Abihail: *these* will pitch on the side of the tabernacle northward.
36 And *under* the custody and charge of the sons of Merari will *be* the boards of the tabernacle, and the bars thereof, and the pillars thereof, and the sockets thereof, and all the vessels thereof, and all that serveth thereto,
37 And the pillars of the court round about, and their sockets, and their pins, and their cords.
38 But those that encamp before the tabernacle toward the east, *even* before the tabernacle of the congregation eastward, will *be* Moses, and Aaron and his sons, keeping the charge of the sanctuary for the charge of the children of Israel; and the stranger that cometh nigh will be put to death.
39 All that were numbered of the Levites, which Moses and Aaron numbered at the commandment of the LORD, throughout their families, all the males from a month old and upward, *were* twenty and two thousand.
40 And the LORD said unto Moses, Number all the firstborn of the males of the children of Israel from a month old and upward, and take the number of their names.
41 And you will take the Levites for me (I *am* the LORD) instead of all the firstborn among the children of Israel; and the cattle of the Levites instead of all the firstlings among the cattle of the children of Israel.
42 And Moses numbered, as the LORD commanded him, all the firstborn among the children of Israel.
43 And all the firstborn males by the number of names, from a month old and upward, of those that were numbered of them, were twenty and two thousand two hundred and threescore and thirteen.
44 And the LORD spoke unto Moses, saying,
45 Take the Levites instead of all the firstborn among the children of Israel, and the cattle of the Levites instead of their cattle; and the Levites will be mine: I *am* the LORD.

46 And for those that are to be redeemed of the two hundred and threescore and thirteen of the firstborn of the children of Israel, which are more than the Levites;
47 you will even take five shekels apiece by the poll, after the shekel of the sanctuary will you take *them*: (the shekel *is* twenty gerahs:)
48 And you will give the money, wherewith the odd number of them is to be redeemed, unto Aaron and to his sons.
49 And Moses took the redemption money of them that were over and above them that were redeemed by the Levites:
50 Of the firstborn of the children of Israel he took the money; a thousand three hundred and threescore and five *shekels*, after the shekel of the sanctuary:
51 And Moses gave the money of them that were redeemed unto Aaron and to his sons, according to the word of the LORD, as the LORD commanded Moses.

CHAPTER 4

1 And the LORD spoke unto Moses and unto Aaron, saying,
2 Take the sum of the sons of Kohath from among the sons of Levi, after their families, by the house of their fathers,
3 From thirty years old and upward even until fifty years old, all that enters into the host, to do the work in the tabernacle of the congregation.
4 This will *be* the service of the sons of Kohath in the tabernacle of the congregation, *about* the most holy things:
5 And when the camp **is to go** forward, Aaron will come, and his sons, and they will take down the covering veil, and cover the ark of testimony with it:
6 And will put thereon the covering of badgers' skins, and will spread over *it* a cloth wholly of blue, and will put in the staves thereof.
7 And upon the table of showbread they will spread a cloth of blue, and put thereon the dishes, and the spoons, and the bowls, and covers to cover withal: and the continual bread will be thereon:
8 And they will spread upon them a cloth of scarlet, and cover the same with a covering of badgers' skins, and will put in the staves thereof.
9 And they will take a cloth of blue, and cover the candlestick of the light, and his lamps, and his tongs, and his snuffdishes, and all the oil vessels thereof, wherewith they minister unto it:
10 And they will put it and all the vessels thereof within a covering of badgers' skins, and will put *it* upon a bar.
11 And upon the golden altar they will spread a cloth of blue, and cover it with a covering of badgers' skins, and will put to the staves thereof:
12 And they will take all the instruments of ministry, wherewith they minister in the sanctuary, and put *them* in a cloth of blue, and cover them with a covering of badgers' skins, and will put *them* on a bar:
13 And they will take away the ashes from the altar, and spread a purple cloth thereon:
14 And they will put upon it all the vessels thereof, wherewith they minister about it, *even* the censers, the flesh hooks, and the shovels, and the bowls, all the vessels of the altar; and they will spread upon it a covering of badgers' skins, and put to the staves of it.
15 And when Aaron and his sons have made an end of covering the sanctuary, and all the vessels of the sanctuary, as the camp is to set forward; after that, the sons of Kohath will come to bear *it*: but they will not touch *any* holy thing, lest they die. These *things are* the burden of the sons of Kohath in the tabernacle of the congregation.
16 And to the office of Eleazar the son of Aaron the priest *pertained* the oil for the light, and the sweet incense, and the daily meat offering, and the anointing oil, *and* the oversight of all the tabernacle, and of all that therein *is*, in the sanctuary and in the vessels thereof.
17 And the LORD spoke unto Moses and unto Aaron, saying,
18 Cut you not off the tribe of the families of the Kohathites from among the Levites:
19 But thus do unto them, that they may live, and not die, when they approach unto the most holy things: Aaron and his sons will go in, and appoint them every one to his service and to his burden:
20 But they will not go in to see when the holy things are covered, lest they die.
21 And the LORD spoke unto Moses, saying,
22 Take also the sum of the sons of Gershon, throughout the houses of their fathers, by their families;
23 From thirty years old and upward until fifty years old will you number them; all that enter in to perform the service, to do the work in the tabernacle of the congregation.
24 This *is* the service of the families of the Gershonites, to serve, and for burdens:
25 And they will bear the curtains of the tabernacle, and the tabernacle of the congregation, his covering, and the covering of the badgers' skins that *is* above upon it, and the hanging for the door of the tabernacle of the congregation,
26 And the hangings of the court, and the hanging for the door of the gate of the court, which *is* by the tabernacle and by the altar round about, and their cords, and all the instruments of their service, and all that is made for them: so will they serve.
27 At the appointment of Aaron and his sons will be all the service of the sons of the Gershonites, in all their burdens, and in all their service: and you will appoint unto them in charge all their burdens.
28 This *is* the service of the families of the sons of Gershon in the tabernacle of the congregation: and their charge will *be* under the hand of Ithamar the son of Aaron the priest.
29 As for the sons of Merari, you will number them after their families, by the house of their fathers;
30 From thirty years old and upward even unto fifty years old will you number them, every one that entered into the service, to do the work of the tabernacle of the congregation.
31 And this *is* the charge of their burden, according to all their service in the tabernacle of the congregation; the boards of the tabernacle, and the bars thereof, and the pillars thereof, and sockets thereof,
32 And the pillars of the court round about, and their sockets, and their pins, and their cords, with all their instruments, and with all their service: and by name you will reckon the instruments of the charge of their burden.
33 This *is* the service of the families of the sons of Merari, according to all their service, in the tabernacle of the congregation, under the hand of Ithamar the son of Aaron the priest.
34 And Moses and Aaron and the chief of the congregation numbered the sons of the Kohathites after their families, and after the house of their fathers,
35 From thirty years old and upward even unto fifty years old, every one that entered into the service, for the work in the tabernacle of the congregation:

36 And those that were numbered of them by their families were two thousand seven hundred and fifty.
37 These *were* they that were numbered of the families of the Kohathites, all that might do service in the tabernacle of the congregation, which Moses and Aaron did number according to the commandment of the LORD by the hand of Moses.
38 And those that were numbered of the sons of Gershon, throughout their families, and by the house of their fathers,
39 From thirty years old and upward even unto fifty years old, every one that entered into the service, for the work in the tabernacle of the congregation,
40 Even those that were numbered of them, throughout their families, by the house of their fathers, were two thousand and six hundred and thirty.
41 These *are* they that were numbered of the families of the sons of Gershon, of all that might do service in the tabernacle of the congregation, whom Moses and Aaron did number according to the commandment of the LORD.
42 And those that were numbered of the families of the sons of Merari, throughout their families, by the house of their fathers,
43 From thirty years old and upward even unto fifty years old, every one that entered into the service, for the work in the tabernacle of the congregation,
44 Even those that were numbered of them after their families, were three thousand and two hundred.
45 These *are* those that were numbered of the families of the sons of Merari, whom Moses and Aaron numbered according to the word of the LORD by the hand of Moses.
46 All those that were numbered of the Levites, whom Moses and Aaron and the chief of Israel numbered, after their families, and after the house of their fathers,
47 From thirty years old and upward even unto fifty years old, every one that came to do the service of the ministry, and the service of the burden in the tabernacle of the congregation,
48 Even those that were numbered of them, were eight thousand and five hundred and fourscore.
49 According to the commandment of the LORD they were numbered by the hand of Moses, every one according to his service, and according to his burden: thus were they numbered of him, as the LORD commanded Moses.

CHAPTER 5

1 And the LORD spoke unto Moses, saying,
2 Command the children of Israel, that they put out of the camp every leper, and every one that has an issue, and whosoever is defiled by the dead:
3 Both male and female will you put out, without the camp will you put them; that they defile not their camps, in the midst whereof I dwell.
4 And the children of Israel did so, and put them out without the camp: as the LORD spoke unto Moses, so did the children of Israel.
5 And the LORD spoke unto Moses, saying,
6 Speak unto the children of Israel, when a man or woman will commit any sin that men commit, to do a trespass against the LORD, and that person be guilty;
7 Then they will confess their sin which they have done: and he will recompense his trespass with the principal thereof, and add unto it the fifth *part* thereof, and give *it* unto *him* against whom he has trespassed.
8 But if the man has no kinsman to recompense the trespass unto, let the trespass be recompensed unto the LORD, *even* to the priest; beside the ram of the atonement, whereby atonement will be made for him.
9 And every offering of all the holy things of the children of Israel, which they bring unto the priest, will be his.
10 And every man's hallowed things will be his: whatsoever any man gives the priest, it will be his.
11 And the LORD spoke unto Moses, saying,
12 Speak unto the children of Israel, and say unto them, if any man's wife go aside, and commit a trespass against him,
13 And a man lie with her carnally, and it be hid from the eyes of her husband, and be kept close, and she be defiled, and *there be* no witness against her, neither she be taken *with the manner*;
14 And the spirit of jealousy comes upon him, and he is jealous of his wife, and she is defiled: or if the spirit of jealousy comes upon him, and he is jealous of his wife, and she is not defiled:
15 Then will the man bring his wife unto the priest, and he will bring her offering for her, the tenth *part* of an ephah of barley meal; he will pour no oil upon it, or put frankincense thereon; for it *is* an offering of jealousy, an offering of memorial, bringing iniquity to remembrance.
16 And the priest will bring her near, and set her before the LORD:
17 And the priest will take holy water in an earthen vessel; and of the dust that is in the floor of the tabernacle the priest will take, and put *it* into the water:
18 And the priest will set the woman before the LORD, and uncover the woman's head, and put the offering of memorial in her hands, which *is* the jealousy offering: and the priest will have in his hand the bitter water that causes the curse:
19 And the priest will charge her by an oath, and say unto the woman, if no man has lain with you, and if you hast not gone aside to uncleanness *with another* instead of your husband, be you free from this bitter water that causes the curse:
20 But if you have gone aside *to another* instead of your husband, and if you **are** defiled, and some man has **lain** with you besides your husband:
21 Then the priest will charge the woman with an oath of cursing, and the priest will say unto the woman, The LORD make you a curse and an oath among your people, when the LORD does make your thigh to rot, and your belly to swell;
22 And this water that causes the curse will go into your bowels, to make your belly to swell, and your thigh to rot: And the woman will say, Amen, amen.
23 And the priest will write these curses in a book, and he will blot *them* out with the bitter water:
24 And he will cause the woman to drink the bitter water that causes the curse: and the water that causes the curse will enter into her, *and become* bitter.
25 Then the priest will take the jealousy offering out of the woman's hand, and will wave the offering before the LORD, and offer it upon the altar:
26 And the priest will take a handful of the offering, *even* the memorial thereof, and burn *it* upon the altar, and afterward will cause the woman to drink the water.
27 And when he has made her to drink the water, then it will come to pass, *that*, if she be defiled, and have done trespass against her husband, that the water that causes the curse will enter into her, *and become* bitter, and her belly will swell, and her thigh will rot: and the woman will be a curse among her people.

28 And if the woman be not defiled, but be clean; then she will be free, and will conceive seed.
29 This *is* the law of jealousies, when a wife goes aside *to another* instead of her husband, and is defiled;
30 Or when the spirit of jealousy cometh upon him, and he be jealous over his wife, and will set the woman before the LORD, and the priest will execute upon her all this law.
31 Then will the man be guiltless from iniquity, and this woman will bear her iniquity.

CHAPTER 6

1 And the LORD spoke unto Moses, saying,
2 Speak unto the children of Israel, and say unto them, when either man or woman will separate *themselves* to vow a vow of a Nazarite, to separate *themselves* unto the LORD:
3 He will separate *himself* from wine and strong drink, and will drink no vinegar of wine, or vinegar of strong drink, neither will he drink any liquor of grapes, nor eat moist grapes, or dried.
4 All the days of his separation will he eat nothing that is made of the vine tree, from the kernels even to the husk.
5 All the days of the vow of his separation there will no razor come upon his head: until the days **are** fulfilled, in which he **will** separate *himself* unto the LORD, he will be holy, *and* will let the locks of the hair of his head grow.
6 All the days that he separates *himself* unto the LORD he will come at no dead body.
7 He will not make himself unclean for his father, or for his mother, for his brother, or for his sister, when they die: because the consecration of his God *is* upon his head.
8 All the days of his separation he *is* holy unto the LORD.
9 And if any man die very suddenly by him, and he has defiled the head of his consecration; then he will shave his head in the day of his cleansing, on the seventh day will he shave it.
10 And on the eighth day he will bring two turtles, or two young pigeons, to the priest, to the door of the tabernacle of the congregation:
11 And the priest will offer the one for a sin offering, and the other for a burnt offering, and make atonement for him, for that he sinned by the dead, and will hallow[1] his head that same day.
12 And he will consecrate unto the LORD the days of his separation, and will bring a lamb of the first year for a trespass offering: but the days that were before will be lost, because his separation was defiled.
13 And this *is* the law of the Nazarite, when the days of his separation are fulfilled: he will be brought unto the door of the tabernacle of the congregation:
14 And he will offer his offering unto the LORD, one he lamb of the first year without blemish for a burnt offering, and one ewe lamb of the first year without blemish for a sin offering, and one ram without blemish for peace offerings,
15 And a basket of unleavened bread, cakes of fine flour mingled with oil, and wafers of unleavened bread anointed with oil, and their meat offering, and their drink offerings.
16 And the priest will bring *them* before the LORD, and will offer his sin offering, and his burnt offering:
17 And he will offer the ram *for* a sacrifice of peace offerings unto the LORD, with the basket of unleavened bread: the priest will offer also his meat offering, and his drink offering.
18 And the Nazarite will shave the head of his separation *at* the door of the tabernacle of the congregation, and will take the hair of the head of his separation, and put *it* in the fire which *is* under the sacrifice of the peace offerings.
19 And the priest will take the sodden shoulder of the ram, and one unleavened cake out of the basket, and one unleavened wafer, and will put *them* upon the hands of the Nazarite, after *the hair of* his separation is shaven:
20 And the priest will wave them *for* a wave offering before the LORD: this *is* holy for the priest, with the wave breast and heave shoulder: and after that the Nazarite may drink wine.
21 This *is* the law of the Nazarite who has vowed, *and of* his offering unto the LORD for his separation, beside *that* that his hand will get: according to the vow which he vowed, so he must do after the law of his separation.
22 And the LORD spoke unto Moses, saying,
23 Speak unto Aaron and unto his sons, saying, on this wise you will bless the children of Israel, saying unto them,
24 The LORD blesses you, and keeps you:
25 The LORD make his face shines upon you, and is gracious unto you:
26 The LORD lifts up his countenance upon you, and gives you peace.
27 And they will put my name upon the children of Israel; and I will bless them.

CHAPTER 7

1 And it came to pass on the day that Moses had fully set up the tabernacle, and had anointed it, and sanctified it, and all the instruments thereof, both the altar and all the vessels thereof, and had anointed them, and sanctified them;
2 That the princes of Israel, heads of the house of their fathers, who *were* the princes of the tribes, and were over them that were numbered, offered:
3 And they brought their offering before the LORD, six covered wagons, and twelve oxen; a wagon for two of the princes, and for each one an ox: and they brought them before the tabernacle.
4 And the LORD spoke unto Moses, saying,
5 Take *it* of them, that they may be to do the service of the tabernacle of the congregation; and you will give them unto the Levites, to every man according to his service.
6 And Moses took the wagons and the oxen, and gave them unto the Levites.
7 Two wagons and four oxen he gave unto the sons of Gershon, according to their service:
8 And four wagons and eight oxen he gave unto the sons of Merari, according unto their service, under the hand of Ithamar the son of Aaron the priest.
9 But unto the sons of Kohath he gave none: because the service of the sanctuary belonging unto them *was that* they should bear upon their shoulders.
10 And the princes offered for dedicating of the altar in the day that it was anointed, even the princes offered their offering before the altar.
11 And the LORD said unto Moses, They will offer their offering, each prince on his day, for the dedicating of the altar.
12 And he that offered his offering the first day was Nahshon the son of Amminadab, of the tribe of Judah:

---

[1] hallow- is the Hebrew word *qâdash*- to (*make, pronounce, observe* as) *clean, kept holy, purify* or *sanctify*. [Strgs#6942]

13 And his offering *was* one silver charger, the weight thereof *was* an hundred and thirty *shekels*, one silver bowl of seventy shekels, after the shekel of the sanctuary; both of them *were* full of fine flour mingled with oil for a meat offering:
14 One spoon of ten *shekels* of gold, full of incense:
15 One young bullock, one ram, one lamb of the first year, for a burnt offering:
16 One kid of the goats for a sin offering:
17 And for a sacrifice of peace offerings, two oxen, five rams, five he goats, five lambs of the first year: this *was* the offering of Nahshon the son of Amminadab.
18 On the second day Nethaneel the son of Zuar, prince of Issachar, did offer:
19 He offered *for* his offering one silver charger, the weight whereof *was* an hundred and thirty *shekels*, one silver bowl of seventy shekels, after the shekel of the sanctuary; both of them full of fine flour mingled with oil for a meat offering:
20 One spoon of gold of ten *shekels*, full of incense:
21 One young bullock, one ram, one lamb of the first year, for a burnt offering:
22 One kid of the goats for a sin offering:
23 And for a sacrifice of peace offerings, two oxen, five rams, five he goats, five lambs of the first year: this *was* the offering of Nethaneel the son of Zuar.
24 On the third day Eliab the son of Helon, prince of the children of Zebulun, *did offer*:
25 His offering *was* one silver charger, the weight whereof *was* an hundred and thirty *shekels*, one silver bowl of seventy shekels, after the shekel of the sanctuary; both of them full of fine flour mingled with oil for a meat offering:
26 One golden spoon of ten *shekels*, full of incense:
27 One young bullock, one ram, one lamb of the first year, for a burnt offering:
28 One kid of the goats for a sin offering:
29 And for a sacrifice of peace offerings, two oxen, five rams, five he goats, five lambs of the first year: this *was* the offering of Eliab the son of Helon.
30 On the fourth day Elizur the son of Shedeur, prince of the children of Reuben, *did offer*:
31 His offering *was* one silver charger of the weight of an hundred and thirty *shekels*, one silver bowl of seventy shekels, after the shekel of the sanctuary; both of them full of fine flour mingled with oil for a meat offering:
32 One golden spoon of ten *shekels*, full of incense:
33 One young bullock, one ram, one lamb of the first year, for a burnt offering:
34 One kid of the goats for a sin offering:
35 And for a sacrifice of peace offerings, two oxen, five rams, five he goats, five lambs of the first year: this *was* the offering of Elizur the son of Shedeur.
36 On the fifth day Shelumiel the son of Zurishaddai, prince of the children of Simeon, *did offer*:
37 His offering *was* one silver charger, the weight whereof *was* an hundred and thirty *shekels*, one silver bowl of seventy shekels, after the shekel of the sanctuary; both of them full of fine flour mingled with oil for a meat offering:
38 One golden spoon of ten *shekels*, full of incense:
39 One young bullock, one ram, one lamb of the first year, for a burnt offering:
40 One kid of the goats for a sin offering:
41 And for a sacrifice of peace offerings, two oxen, five rams, five he goats, five lambs of the first year: this *was* the offering of Shelumiel the son of Zurishaddai.
42 On the sixth day Eliasaph the son of Deuel, prince of the children of Gad, *offered*:
43 His offering *was* one silver charger of the weight of an hundred and thirty *shekels*, a silver bowl of seventy shekels, after the shekel of the sanctuary; both of them full of fine flour mingled with oil for a meat offering:
44 One golden spoon of ten *shekels*, full of incense:
45 One young bullock, one ram, one lamb of the first year, for a burnt offering:
46 One kid of the goats for a sin offering:
47 And for a sacrifice of peace offerings, two oxen, five rams, five he goats, five lambs of the first year: this *was* the offering of Eliasaph the son of Deuel.
48 On the seventh day Elishama the son of Ammihud, prince of the children of Ephraim, *offered*:
49 His offering *was* one silver charger, the weight whereof *was* an hundred and thirty *shekels*, one silver bowl of seventy shekels, after the shekel of the sanctuary; both of them full of fine flour mingled with oil for a meat offering:
50 One golden spoon of ten *shekels*, full of incense:
51 One young bullock, one ram, one lamb of the first year, for a burnt offering:
52 One kid of the goats for a sin offering:
53 And for a sacrifice of peace offerings, two oxen, five rams, five he goats, five lambs of the first year: this *was* the offering of Elishama the son of Ammihud.
54 On the eighth day *offered* Gamaliel the son of Pedahzur, prince of the children of Manasseh:
55 His offering *was* one silver charger of the weight of an hundred and thirty *shekels*, one silver bowl of seventy shekels, after the shekel of the sanctuary; both of them full of fine flour mingled with oil for a meat offering:
56 One golden spoon of ten *shekels*, full of incense:
57 One young bullock, one ram, one lamb of the first year, for a burnt offering:
58 One kid of the goats for a sin offering:
59 And for a sacrifice of peace offerings, two oxen, five rams, five he goats, five lambs of the first year: this *was* the offering of Gamaliel the son of Pedahzur.
60 On the ninth day Abidan the son of Gideoni, prince of the children of Benjamin, *offered*:
61 His offering *was* one silver charger, the weight whereof *was* an hundred and thirty *shekels*, one silver bowl of seventy shekels, after the shekel of the sanctuary; both of them full of fine flour mingled with oil for a meat offering:
62 One golden spoon of ten *shekels*, full of incense:
63 One young bullock, one ram, one lamb of the first year, for a burnt offering:
64 One kid of the goats for a sin offering:
65 And for a sacrifice of peace offerings, two oxen, five rams, five he goats, five lambs of the first year: this *was* the offering of Abidan the son of Gideoni.
66 On the tenth day Ahiezer the son of Ammishaddai, prince of the children of Dan, *offered*:
67 His offering *was* one silver charger, the weight whereof *was* an hundred and thirty *shekels*, one silver bowl of seventy shekels,

after the shekel of the sanctuary; both of them full of fine flour mingled with oil for a meat offering:

68 One golden spoon of ten *shekels*, full of incense:

69 One young bullock, one ram, one lamb of the first year, for a burnt offering:

70 One kid of the goats for a sin offering:

71 And for a sacrifice of peace offerings, two oxen, five rams, five he goats, five lambs of the first year: this *was* the offering of Ahiezer the son of Ammishaddai.

72 On the eleventh day Pagiel the son of Ocran, prince of the children of Asher, *offered*:

73 His offering *was* one silver charger, the weight whereof *was* an hundred and thirty *shekels*, one silver bowl of seventy shekels, after the shekel of the sanctuary; both of them full of fine flour mingled with oil for a meat offering:

74 One golden spoon of ten *shekels*, full of incense:

75 One young bullock, one ram, one lamb of the first year, for a burnt offering:

76 One kid of the goats for a sin offering:

77 And for a sacrifice of peace offerings, two oxen, five rams, five he goats, five lambs of the first year: this *was* the offering of Pagiel the son of Ocran.

78 On the twelfth day Ahira the son of Enan, prince of the children of Naphtali, *offered*:

79 His offering *was* one silver charger, the weight whereof *was* an hundred and thirty *shekels*, one silver bowl of seventy shekels, after the shekel of the sanctuary; both of them full of fine flour mingled with oil for a meat offering:

80 One golden spoon of ten *shekels*, full of incense:

81 One young bullock, one ram, one lamb of the first year, for a burnt offering:

82 One kid of the goats for a sin offering:

83 And for a sacrifice of peace offerings, two oxen, five rams, five he goats, five lambs of the first year: this *was* the offering of Ahira the son of Enan.

84 This *was* the dedication of the altar, in the day when it was anointed, by the princes of Israel: twelve chargers of silver, twelve silver bowls, twelve spoons of gold:

85 Each charger of silver *weighing* an hundred and thirty *shekels*, each bowl seventy: all the silver vessels *weighed* two thousand and four hundred *shekels*, after the shekel of the sanctuary:

86 The golden spoons *were* twelve, full of incense, *weighing* ten *shekels* apiece, after the shekel of the sanctuary: all the gold of the spoons *was* an hundred and twenty *shekels*.

87 All the oxen for the burnt offering *were* twelve bullocks, the rams twelve, the lambs of the first year twelve, with their meat offering: and the kids of the goats for sin offering twelve.

88 And all the oxen for the sacrifice of the peace offerings *were* twenty and four bullocks, the rams sixty, the he goats sixty, the lambs of the first year sixty. This *was* the dedication of the altar, after that it was anointed.

89 And when Moses was gone into the tabernacle of the congregation to speak with him, then he heard the voice of one speaking unto him from off the mercy seat that *was* upon the ark of testimony, from between the two cherubims: and he spoke unto him.

CHAPTER 8

1 And the LORD spoke unto Moses, saying,

2 Speak unto Aaron, and say unto him, When you lightest the lamps, the seven lamps will give light over against the candlestick.

3 And Aaron did so; he lighted the lamps thereof over against the candlestick, as the LORD commanded Moses.

4 And this work of the candlestick *was of* beaten gold, unto the shaft thereof, unto the flowers thereof, *was* beaten work: according unto the pattern which the LORD had shewed Moses, so he made the candlestick.

5 And the LORD spoke unto Moses, saying,

6 Take the Levites from among the children of Israel, and cleanse them.

7 And thus will you do unto them, to cleanse them: Sprinkle water of purifying upon them, and let them shave all their flesh, and let them wash their clothes, and so make themselves clean.

8 Then let them take a young bullock with his meat offering, *even* fine flour mingled with oil, and another young bullock will you take for a sin offering.

9 And you will bring the Levites before the tabernacle of the congregation: and you will gather the whole assembly of the children of Israel together:

10 And you will bring the Levites before the LORD: and the children of Israel will put their hands upon the Levites:

11 And Aaron will offer the Levites before the LORD for an offering of the children of Israel, that they may execute the service of the LORD.

12 And the Levites will lay their hands upon the heads of the bullocks: and you will offer the one *for* a sin offering, and the other *for* a burnt offering, unto the LORD, to make an atonement for the Levites.

13 And you will set the Levites before Aaron, and before his sons, and offer them *for* an offering unto the LORD.

14 Thus will you separate the Levites from among the children of Israel: and the Levites will be mine.

15 And after that will the Levites go in to do the service of the tabernacle of the congregation: and you will cleanse them, and offer them *for* an offering.

16 For they *are* wholly given unto me from among the children of Israel; instead of such as open every womb, *even instead of* the firstborn of all the children of Israel, have I taken them unto me.

17 For all the firstborn of the children of Israel *are* mine, *both* man and beast: on the day that I smote every firstborn in the land of Egypt I sanctified them for myself.

18 And I have taken the Levites for all the firstborn of the children of Israel.

19 And I have given the Levites *as* a gift to Aaron and to his sons from among the children of Israel, to do the service of the children of Israel in the tabernacle of the congregation, and to make an atonement for the children of Israel: that there be no plague among the children of Israel, when the children of Israel come nigh unto the sanctuary.

20 And Moses, and Aaron, and all the congregation of the children of Israel, did to the Levites according unto all that the LORD commanded Moses concerning the Levites, so did the children of Israel unto them.

21 And the Levites were purified, and they washed their clothes; and Aaron offered them *as* an offering before the LORD; and Aaron made an atonement for them to cleanse them.

22 And after that went the Levites in to do their service in the tabernacle of the congregation before Aaron, and before his sons:

as the LORD had commanded Moses concerning the Levites, so did they unto them.
23 And the LORD spoke unto Moses, saying,
24 This *is it* that *belongs* unto the Levites: from twenty and five years old and upward they will go in to wait upon the service of the tabernacle of the congregation:
25 And from the age of fifty years they will cease waiting upon the service *thereof*, and will serve no more:
26 But will minister with their brethren in the tabernacle of the congregation, to keep the charge, and will do no service. Thus will you do unto the Levites touching their charge.

CHAPTER 9

1 And the LORD spoke unto Moses in the wilderness of Sinai, in the first month of the second year after they were come out of the land of Egypt, saying,
2 Let the children of Israel also keep the Passover at his appointed season.
3 In the fourteenth day of this month, at even, you will keep it in his appointed season: according to all the rites of it, and according to all the ceremonies thereof, will you keep it.
4 And Moses spoke unto the children of Israel, that they should keep the Passover.
5 And they kept the Passover on the fourteenth day of the first month at even in the wilderness of Sinai: according to all that the LORD commanded Moses, so did the children of Israel.
6 And there were certain men, who were defiled by the dead body of a man, that they could not keep the Passover on that day: and they came before Moses and before Aaron on that day:
7 And those men said unto him, we *are* defiled by the dead body of a man: wherefore are we kept back, that we may not offer an offering of the LORD in his appointed season among the children of Israel?
8 And Moses said unto them, standstill, and I will hear what the LORD will command concerning you.
9 And the LORD spoke unto Moses, saying,
10 Speak unto the children of Israel, saying, if any man of you or of your posterity will be unclean by reason of a dead body, or *be* in a journey afar off, yet he will keep the Passover unto the LORD.
11 The fourteenth day of the second month at even they will keep it, *and* eat it with unleavened bread and bitter *herbs*.
12 They will leave none of it unto the morning, nor break any bone of it: according to all the ordinances of the Passover they will keep it.
13 But the man that *is* clean, and is not in a journey, and forbear to keep the Passover, even the same soul will be cut off from among his people: because he brought not the offering of the LORD in his appointed season, that man will bear his sin.
14 And if a stranger will sojourn among you, and will keep the Passover unto the LORD; according to the ordinance of the Passover, and according to the manner thereof, so will he do: you will have one ordinance, both for the stranger, and for him that was born in the land.
15 And on the day that the tabernacle was reared up the cloud covered the tabernacle, *namely*, the tent of the testimony: and at even there was upon the tabernacle as it were the appearance of fire, until the morning.
16 So it was always: the cloud covered it *by day*, and the appearance of fire by night.
17 And when the cloud was taken up from the tabernacle, then after that the children of Israel journeyed: and in the place where the cloud abode, there the children of Israel pitched their tents.
18 At the commandment of the LORD the children of Israel journeyed, and at the commandment of the LORD they pitched: as long as the cloud abode upon the tabernacle they rested in their tents.
19 And when the cloud tarried long upon the tabernacle many days, then the children of Israel kept the charge of the LORD, and journeyed not.
20 And *so* it was, when the cloud was a few days upon the tabernacle; according to the commandment of the LORD they abode in their tents, and according to the commandment of the LORD they journeyed.
21 And *so* it was, when the cloud abode from even unto the morning, and *that* the cloud was taken up in the morning, then they journeyed: whether *it was* by day or by night that the cloud was taken up, they journeyed.
22 Or *whether it were* two days, or a month, or a year, that the cloud tarried upon the tabernacle, remaining thereon, the children of Israel abode in their tents, and journeyed not: but when it was taken up, they journeyed.
23 At the commandment of the LORD they rested in the tents, and at the commandment of the LORD they journeyed: they kept the charge of the LORD, at the commandment of the LORD by the hand of Moses.

CHAPTER 10

1 And the LORD spoke unto Moses, saying,
2 Make you two trumpets of silver; of a whole piece will you make them: that you may use them for the calling of the assembly, and for the journeying of the camps.
3 And when they will blow with them, all the assembly will assemble themselves to you at the door of the tabernacle of the congregation.
4 And if they blow *but* with one *trumpet*, then the princes, *which are* heads of the thousands of Israel, will gather themselves unto you.
5 When you blow an alarm, then the camps that lie on the east parts will go forward.
6 When you blow an alarm the second time, then the camps that lie on the south side will take their journey: they will blow an alarm for their journeys.
7 But when the congregation is to be gathered together, you will blow, but you will not sound an alarm.
8 And the sons of Aaron, the priests, will blow with the trumpets; and they will be to you for an ordinance for ever throughout your generations.
9 And if you go to war in your land against the enemy that oppresses you, then you will blow an alarm with the trumpets; and you will be remembered before the LORD your God, and you will be saved from your enemies.
10 Also in the day of your gladness, and in your solemn days, and in the beginnings of your months, you will blow with the trumpets over your burnt offerings, and over the sacrifices of your peace offerings; that they may be to you for a memorial before your God: I *am* the LORD your God.
11 And it came to pass on the twentieth *day* of the second month, in the second year, that the cloud was taken up from off the tabernacle of the testimony.

12 And the children of Israel took their journeys out of the wilderness of Sinai; and the cloud rested in the wilderness of Paran.
13 And they first took their journey according to the commandment of the LORD by the hand of Moses.
14 In the first *place* went the standard of the camp of the children of Judah according to their armies: and over his host *was* Nahshon the son of Amminadab.
15 And over the host of the tribe of the children of Issachar *was* Nethaneel the son of Zuar.
16 And over the host of the tribe of the children of Zebulun *was* Eliab the son of Helon.
17 And the tabernacle was taken down; and the sons of Gershon and the sons of Merari set forward, bearing the tabernacle.
18 And the standard of the camp of Reuben set forward according to their armies: and over his host *was* Elizur the son of Shedeur.
19 And over the host of the tribe of the children of Simeon *was* Shelumiel the son of Zurishaddai.
20 And over the host of the tribe of the children of Gad *was* Eliasaph the son of Deuel.
21 And the Kohathites set forward, bearing the sanctuary: and *the other* did set up the tabernacle **for their arrival**.
22 And the standard of the camp of the children of Ephraim set forward according to their armies: and over his host *was* Elishama the son of Ammihud.
23 And over the host of the tribe of the children of Manasseh *was* Gamaliel the son of Pedahzur.
24 And over the host of the tribe of the children of Benjamin *was* Abidan the son of Gideoni.
25 And the standard of the camp of the children of Dan set forward, *which was* the reward of all the camps throughout their hosts: and over his host *was* Ahiezer the son of Ammishaddai.
26 And over the host of the tribe of the children of Asher *was* Pagiel the son of Ocran.
27 And over the host of the tribe of the children of Naphtali *was* Ahira the son of Enan.
28 Thus *were* the journeying of the children of Israel according to their armies, when they set forward.
29 And Moses said unto Hobab, the son of Raguel the Midianite, Moses' father in law, We are journeying unto the place of which the LORD said, I will give it you: come you with us, and we will do you good: for the LORD has spoken good concerning Israel.
30 And he said unto him, I will not go; but I will depart to mine own land, and to my kindred.
31 And he said, Leave us not, I pray you; forasmuch as you know how we are to encamp in the wilderness, and you may be to us instead of eyes.
32 And it will be, if you go with us, yea, it will be, that what goodness the LORD will do unto us, the same will we do unto you.
33 And they departed from the mount of the LORD three days' journey: and the ark of the covenant of the LORD went before them in the three days' journey, to search out a resting place for them.
34 And the cloud of the LORD *was* upon them by day, when they went out of the camp.
35 And it came to pass, when the ark set forward, that Moses said, Rise up, LORD, and let your enemies be scattered; and let them that hate you flee before you.
36 And when it rested, he said, Return, O LORD, unto the many thousands of Israel.

CHAPTER 11

1 And *when* the people complained, it displeased the LORD: and the LORD heard *it*; and his anger was kindled; and the fire of the LORD burnt among them, and consumed *them that were* in the uttermost parts of the camp.
2 And the people cried unto Moses; and when Moses prayed unto the LORD, the fire was quenched.
3 And he called the name of the place Taberah: because the fire of the LORD burnt among them.
4 And the mixed multitude that *was* among them fell a lusting: and the children of Israel also wept again, and said, who will give us flesh to eat?
5 We remember the fish, which we did eat in Egypt freely; the cucumbers, and the melons, and the leeks, and the onions, and the garlic:
6 But now our soul *is* dried away: *there is* nothing at all, beside this manna, *before* our eyes.
7 And the manna *was* as coriander seed, and the color thereof as the color of bdellium.
8 *And* the people went about, and gathered *it*, and ground *it* in mills, or beat *it* in a mortar, and baked *it* in pans, and made cakes of it: and the taste of it was as the taste of fresh oil.
9 And when the dew fell upon the camp in the night, the manna fell upon it.
10 Then Moses heard the people weep throughout their families, every man in the door of his tent: and the anger of the LORD was kindled greatly; Moses also was displeased.
11 And Moses said unto the LORD, Wherefore hast you afflicted your servant? And wherefore have I not found favor in your sight, that you lay the burden of all this people upon me?
12 Have I conceived this **entire** people? Have I begotten them, that you should say unto me, Carry them in your bosom, as a nursing father bears the sucking child, unto the land which you swore unto their fathers?
13 Where should I have flesh to give unto this **entire** people? For they weep unto me, saying, give us flesh, that we may eat.
14 I am not able to bear all this people alone, because *it is* too heavy for me.
15 And if you deal thus with me, kill me, I pray you, out of hand, if I have found favor in your sight; and let me not see my wretchedness.
16 And the LORD said unto Moses, Gather unto me seventy men of the elders of Israel, who you know to be the elders of the people, and officers over them; and bring them unto the tabernacle of the congregation, that they may stand there with you.
17 And I will come down and talk with you there: and I will take of the spirit which *is* upon you, and will put *it* upon them; and they will bear the burden of the people with you, that you bear *it* not yourself alone.
18 And say you unto the people, Sanctify yourselves against tomorrow, and you will eat flesh: for you have wept in the ears of the LORD, saying, who will give us flesh to eat? For *it was* well with us in Egypt: therefore the LORD will give you flesh and you will eat.
19 You will not eat one day, nor two days, nor five days, neither ten days or twenty days;
20 *But* even a whole month, until it come out at your nostrils, and it be loathsome unto you: because that you have despised the

LORD which *is* among you, and have wept before him, saying, Why came we forth out of Egypt?

21 And Moses said, the people, among whom I *am*, *are* six hundred thousand footmen; and you hast said, I will give them flesh, that they may eat a whole month.

22 will the flocks and the herds be slain for them, to suffice them? Or will all the fish of the sea be gathered together for them, to suffice them?

23 And the LORD said unto Moses, Is the LORD'S hand waxed short? You will see now whether my word will come to pass unto you or not.

24 And Moses went out, and told the people the words of the LORD, and gathered the seventy men of the elders of the people, and set them round about the tabernacle.

25 And the LORD came down in a cloud, and spoke unto him, and took of the spirit that *was* upon him, and gave *it* unto the seventy elders: and it came to pass, *that*, when the spirit rested upon them, they prophesied, and did not cease.

26 But there remained two *of the* men in the camp, the name of the one *was* Eldad, and the name of the other Medad: and the spirit rested upon them; and they *were* of them that were written, but went not out unto the tabernacle: and they prophesied in the camp.

27 And there ran a young man, and told Moses, and said, Eldad and Medad do prophesy in the camp.

28 And Joshua the son of Nun, the servant of Moses, *one* of his young men, answered and said, my lord Moses, forbid them.

29 And Moses said unto him, envy you for my sake? Would God that all the LORD'S people were prophets, *and* that the LORD would put his spirit upon them!

30 And Moses gat him into the camp, he and the elders of Israel.

31 And there went forth a wind from the LORD, and brought quails from the sea, and let *them* fall by the camp, as it were a day's journey on this side, and as it were a day's journey on the other side, round about the camp, and as it were two cubits *high* upon the face of the earth.

32 And the people stood up all that day, and all *that* night, and all the next day, and they gathered the quails: he that gathered least gathered ten homers: and they spread *them* all abroad for themselves round about the camp.

33 And while the flesh *was* yet between their teeth, ere it was chewed, the wrath of the LORD was kindled against the people, and the LORD smote the people with a very great plague.

34 And he called the name of that place Kibroth-hattaavah[1]: because there they buried the people that lusted.

35 *And* the people journeyed from Kibroth-hattaavah unto Hazeroth; and abode at Hazeroth.

CHAPTER 12

1 And Miriam and Aaron spoke against Moses because of the Ethiopian woman whom he had married: for he had married an Ethiopian woman.

2 And they said, has the LORD indeed spoken only by Moses? Has he not spoken also by us? And the LORD heard *it*.

3 (Now the man Moses *was* very meek, above all the men **that** *were* upon the face of the earth.)

4 And the LORD spoke suddenly unto Moses, and unto Aaron, and unto Miriam, Come out you three unto the tabernacle of the congregation. And they three came out.

5 And the LORD came down in the pillar of the cloud, and stood *in* the door of the tabernacle, and called Aaron and Miriam: and they both came forth.

6 And he said, hear now my words: If there be a prophet among you, *I* the LORD will make myself known unto him in a vision, *and* will speak unto him in a dream.

7 My servant Moses *is* not so, who *is* faithful in all mine house.

8 With him will I speak mouth to mouth, even apparently, and not in dark speeches; and the similitude of the LORD will he behold: wherefore then were you not afraid to speak against my servant Moses?

9 And the anger of the LORD was kindled against them; and he departed.

10 And the cloud departed from off the tabernacle; and behold, Miriam *became* leprous, *white* as snow: and Aaron looked upon Miriam, and, behold, *she was* leprous.

11 And Aaron said unto Moses, Alas, my lord, I beseech you, lay not the sin upon us, wherein we have done foolishly, and wherein we have sinned.

12 Let her not be as one dead, of whom the flesh is half consumed when he cometh out of his mother's womb.

13 And Moses cried unto the LORD, saying, Heal her now, O God, I beseech you.

14 And the LORD said unto Moses, if her father had but spit in her face, should she not be ashamed seven days? Let her be shut out from the camp seven days, and after that let her be received in *again*.

15 And Miriam was shut out from the camp seven days: and the people journeyed not till Miriam was brought in *again*.

16 And afterward the people removed from Hazeroth, and pitched in the wilderness of Paran.

CHAPTER 13

1 And the LORD spoke unto Moses, saying,

2 Send you men, that they may search the land of Canaan, which I give unto the children of Israel: of every tribe of their fathers will you send a man, everyone a ruler among them.

3 And Moses by the commandment of the LORD sent them from the wilderness of Paran: all those men *were* heads of the children of Israel.

4 And these *were* their names: of the tribe of Reuben, Shammua the son of Zaccur.

5 Of the tribe of Simeon, Shaphat the son of Hori.

6 Of the tribe of Judah, Caleb the son of Jephunneh.

7 Of the tribe of Issachar, Igal the son of Joseph.

8 Of the tribe of Ephraim, Oshea the son of Nun.

9 Of the tribe of Benjamin, Palti the son of Raphu.

10 Of the tribe of Zebulun, Gaddiel the son of Sodi.

11 Of the tribe of Joseph, *namely*, of the tribe of Manasseh, Gaddi the son of Susi.

12 Of the tribe of Dan, Ammiel the son of Gemalli.

13 Of the tribe of Asher, Sethur the son of Michael.

14 Of the tribe of Naphtali, Nahbi the son of Vophsi.

15 Of the tribe of Gad, Geuel the son of Machi.

16 These *are* the names of the men which Moses sent to spy out the land. And Moses called Oshea the son of Nun Jehoshua.

---

[1] Kibroth-hattaavah = graves of lust or *graves of the longing* [Strgs#6914].

17 And Moses sent them to spy out the land of Canaan, and said unto them, Get you up this *way* southward, and go up into the mountain:
18 And see the land, what it *is*; and the people that dwelled therein, whether they *are* strong or weak, few or many;
19 And what the land *is* that they dwell in, whether it *is* good or bad; and what cities *they be* that they dwell in, whether in tents, or in strong holds;
20 And what the land *is*, whether it *be* fat or lean, whether there be wood therein, or not. And be you of good courage, and bring of the fruit of the land. Now the time *was* the time of the first ripe grapes.
21 So they went up, and searched the land from the wilderness of Zin unto Rehob, as men come to Hamath.
22 And they ascended by the south, and came unto Hebron; where Ahiman, Sheshai, and Talmai, the children of Anak, *were*. (Now Hebron was built seven years before Zoan in Egypt.)
23 And they came unto the brook of Eshcol, and cut down from thence a branch with one cluster of grapes, and they bare it between two upon a staff; and *they brought* of the pomegranates, and of the figs.
24 The place was called the brook Eshcol, because of the cluster of grapes which the children of Israel cut down from thence.
25 And they returned from searching of the land after forty days.
26 And they went and came to Moses, and to Aaron, and to the entire congregation of the children of Israel, unto the wilderness of Paran, to Kadesh; and brought back word unto them, and unto the entire congregation, and showed them the fruit of the land.
27 And they told him, and said, we came unto the land where you sent us, and surely it flowed with milk and honey; and this *is* the fruit of it.
28 Nevertheless the people *are* strong that dwell in the land, and the cities *are* walled, *and* very great: and moreover we saw the children of Anak there.
29 The Amalekites dwell in the land of the south: and the Hittites, and the Jebusites, and the Amorites, dwell in the mountains: and the Canaanites dwell by the sea, and by the coast of Jordan.
30 And Caleb stilled the people before Moses, and said, Let us go up at once, and possess it; for we are well able to overcome it.
31 But the men that went up with him said, we are not able to go up against the people; for they *are* stronger than we.
32 And they brought up an evil report of the land which they had searched unto the children of Israel, saying, the land, through which we have gone to search it, is a land that eats up the inhabitants thereof; and all the people that we saw in it are men of a great stature.
33 And there we saw the giants, the sons of Anak, *which come* of the giants: and we were in our own sight as grasshoppers, and so we were in their sight.

CHAPTER 14

1 And the **entire** congregation lifted up their voice, and cried; and the people wept that night.
2 And all the children of Israel murmured against Moses and against Aaron: and the whole congregation said unto them, Would God that we had died in the land of Egypt! Or would God we had died in this wilderness!
3 And wherefore has the LORD brought us unto this land, to fall by the sword, that our wives and our children should be a prey? Was it not better for us to return into Egypt?
4 And they said one to another, Let us make a captain, and let us return into Egypt.
5 Then Moses and Aaron fell on their faces before all the assembly of the congregation of the children of Israel.
6 And Joshua the son of Nun, and Caleb the son of Jephunneh, *which were* of them that searched the land, rent their clothes:
7 And they spoke unto all the company of the children of Israel, saying, the land, which we passed through to search it, *is* an exceeding good land.
8 If the LORD delight in us, then he will bring us into this land, and give it us; a land which flowed with milk and honey.
9 Only rebel not you against the LORD, neither fear you the people of the land; for they *are* bread for us: their defense is departed from them, and the LORD *is* with us: fear them not.
10 But all the congregation bade stone them with stones. And the glory of the LORD appeared in the tabernacle of the congregation before all the children of Israel.
11 And the LORD said unto Moses, How long will this people provoke me? And how long will it be ere they believe me, for all the signs which I have showed among them?
12 I will smite them with the pestilence, and disinherit them, and will make of you a greater nation and mightier than they.
13 And Moses said unto the LORD, then the Egyptians will hear *it*, (for you brought up this people in your might from among them;)
14 And they will tell *it* to the inhabitants of this land: for they have heard that you LORD are among this people, that you LORD are seen face to face, and *that* your cloud stand over them, and *that* you goes before them, by day time in a pillar of a cloud, and in a pillar of fire by night.
15 Now *if* you will kill *all* this people as one man, then the nations which have heard the fame of you will speak, saying,
16 Because the LORD was not able to bring this people into the land which he swore unto them, therefore he has slain them in the wilderness.
17 And now, I beseech you, let the power of my Lord be great, according as you hast spoken, saying,
18 The LORD *is* longsuffering, and of great mercy, forgiving iniquity and transgression, and by no means clearing *the guilty*, visiting the iniquity of the fathers upon the children unto the third and fourth *generation*.
19 Pardon, I beseech you, the iniquity of this people according unto the greatness of your mercy, and as you hast forgiven this people, from Egypt even until now.
20 And the LORD said, I have pardoned according to your word:
21 But *as* truly *as* I live, all the earth will be filled with the glory of the LORD.
22 Because all those men which have seen my glory, and my miracles, which I did in Egypt and in the wilderness, and have tempted me now these ten times, and have not hearkened to my voice;
23 Surely they will not see the land which I swore unto their fathers, neither will any of them that provoked me see it:
24 But my servant Caleb, because he had another spirit with him, and has followed me fully, him will I bring into the land where into he went; and his seed will possess it.
25 (Now the Amalekites and the Canaanites dwelt in the valley.) Tomorrow turn you, and get you into the wilderness by the way of the Red sea.
26 And the LORD spoke unto Moses and unto Aaron, saying,

27 How long will *I bear with* this evil congregation, which murmur against me? I have heard the murmurings of the children of Israel, which they murmur against me.
28 Say unto them, *as truly as* I live, said the LORD, as you have spoken in mine ears, so will I do to you:
29 Your carcasses will fall in this wilderness; and all that were numbered of you, according to your whole number, from twenty years old and upward, which have murmured against me,
30 Doubtless you will not come into the land, *concerning* which I swore to make you dwell therein, save Caleb the son of Jephunneh, and Joshua the son of Nun.
31 But your little ones, which you said should be a prey, them will I bring in, and they will know the land which you have despised.
32 But *as for* you, your carcasses, they will fall in this wilderness.
33 And your children will wander in the wilderness forty years, and bear your whoredoms, until your carcasses be wasted in the wilderness.
34 After the number of the days in which you searched the land, *even* forty days, each day for a year, will you bear your iniquities, *even* forty years, and you will know my breach of promise.
35 I the LORD have said, I will surely do it unto this **entire** evil congregation that are gathered together against me: in this wilderness they will be consumed, and there they will die.
36 And the men, which Moses sent to search the land, who returned, and made the **entire** congregation to murmur against him, by bringing up a slander upon the land,
37 Even those men that did bring up the evil report upon the land, died by the plague before the LORD.
38 But Joshua the son of Nun, and Caleb the son of Jephunneh, *which were* of the men that went to search the land, lived *still*.
39 And Moses told these sayings unto all the children of Israel: and the people mourned greatly.
40 And they rose up early in the morning, and gat them up into the top of the mountain, saying, lo, we *are here*, and will go up unto the place which the LORD has promised: for we have sinned.
41 And Moses said, wherefore now do you transgress the commandment of the LORD? But it will not prosper.
42 Go not up, for the LORD *is* not among you; that you are not slayed before your enemies.
43 For the Amalekites and the Canaanites *are* there before you, and you will fall by the sword: because you are turned away from the LORD, therefore the LORD will not be with you.
44 But they presumed to go up unto the hill top: nevertheless the ark of the covenant of the LORD, and Moses, departed not out of the camp.
45 Then the Amalekites came down, and the Canaanites which dwelt in that hill, and smote them, and discomfited them, *even* unto Hormah.

CHAPTER 15

1 And the LORD spoke unto Moses, saying,
2 Speak unto the children of Israel, and say unto them, when you are come into the land of your habitations, which I give unto you,
3 And will make an offering by fire unto the LORD, a burnt offering, or a sacrifice in performing a vow, or in a freewill offering, or in your solemn feasts, to make a sweet savor unto the LORD, of the herd, or of the flock:
4 Then will he that offered his offering unto the LORD bring a meat offering of a tenth deal of flour mingled with the fourth *part* of a hin of oil.
5 And the fourth *part* of a hin of wine for a drink offering will you prepare with the burnt offering or sacrifice, for one lamb.
6 Or for a ram, you will prepare *for* a meat offering two tenth deals of flour mingled with the third *part* of a hin of oil.
7 And for a drink offering you will offer the third *part* of a hin of wine, *for* a sweet savor unto the LORD.
8 And when you prepare a bullock *for* a burnt offering, or *for* a sacrifice in performing a vow, or peace offerings unto the LORD:
9 Then will he bring with a bullock a meat offering of three tenth deals of flour mingled with half a hin of oil.
10 And you will bring for a drink offering half a hin of wine, *for* an offering made by fire, of a sweet savor unto the LORD.
11 Thus will it be done for one bullock, or for one ram, or for a lamb, or a kid.
12 According to the number that you will prepare, so will you do to everyone according to their number.
13 All that are born of the country will do these things after this manner, in offering an offering made by fire, of a sweet savor unto the LORD.
14 And if a stranger sojourn with you, or whosoever *be* among you in your generations, and will offer an offering made by fire, of a sweet savor unto the LORD; as you do, so he will do.
15 One ordinance will *be both* for you of the congregation, and also for the stranger that sojourned *with you*, an ordinance forever in your generations: as you *are*, so will the stranger be before the LORD.
16 One law and one manner will be for you, and for the stranger that sojourned with you.
17 And the LORD spoke unto Moses, saying,
18 Speak unto the children of Israel, and say unto them, when you come into the land where I bring you,
19 Then it will be, that, when you eat of the bread of the land, you will offer up an heave offering unto the LORD.
20 you will offer up a cake of the first of your dough *for* a heave offering: as you *do* the heave offering of the threshing floor, so will you have it.
21 Of the first of your dough you will give unto the LORD a heave offering in your generations.
22 And if you have erred, and not observed all these commandments, which the LORD has spoken unto Moses,
23 *Even* all that the LORD has commanded you by the hand of Moses, from the day that the LORD commanded *Moses*, and henceforward among your generations;
24 Then it will be, if *ought* be committed by ignorance without the knowledge of the congregation, that all the congregation will offer one young bullock for a burnt offering, for a sweet savor unto the LORD, with his meat offering, and his drink offering, according to the manner, and one kid of the goats for a sin offering.
25 And the priest will make atonement for all the congregation of the children of Israel, and it will be forgiven them; for it *is* ignorance: and they will bring their offering, a sacrifice made by fire unto the LORD, and their sin offering before the LORD, for their ignorance:
26 And it will be forgiven all the congregation of the children of Israel, and the stranger that sojourned among them; seeing all the people *were* in ignorance.
27 And if any soul sin through ignorance, then he will bring a she goat of the first year for a sin offering.
28 And the priest will make atonement for the soul that sin ignorantly, when he sins by ignorance before the LORD, to make atonement for him; and it will be forgiven him.

29 You will have one law for him that sins through ignorance, *both for* him that is born among the children of Israel, and for the stranger that sojourned among them.
30 But the soul that doeth *ought* presumptuously, *whether he be* born in the land, or a stranger, the same reproach the LORD; and that soul will be cut off from among his people.
31 Because he has despised the word of the LORD, and has broken his commandment, that soul will utterly be cut off; his iniquity will *be* upon him.
32 And while the children of Israel were in the wilderness, they found a man that gathered sticks upon the Sabbath day.
33 And they that found him gathering sticks brought him unto Moses and Aaron, and unto the **entire** congregation.
34 And they put him in ward, because it was not declared what should be done to him.
35 And the LORD said unto Moses, The man will be surely put to death: the **entire** congregation will stone him with stones without the camp.
36 And the **entire** congregation brought him without the camp, and stoned him with stones, and he died; as the LORD commanded Moses.
37 And the LORD spoke unto Moses, saying,
38 Speak unto the children of Israel, and bid them that they make them fringes in the borders of their garments throughout their generations, and that they put upon the fringe of the borders a ribband of blue:
39 And it will be unto you for a fringe, that you may look upon it, and remember all the commandments of the LORD, and do them; and that you seek not after your own heart and your own eyes, after which you use to go a whoring:
40 That you may remember, and do all my commandments, and be holy unto your God.
41 I *am* the LORD your God, which brought you out of the land of Egypt, to be your God: I *am* the LORD your God.

CHAPTER 16

1 Now Korah, the son of Izhar, the son of Kohath, the son of Levi, and Dathan and Abiram, the sons of Eliab, and On, the son of Peleth, sons of Reuben, took *men*:
2 And they rose up before Moses, with certain of the children of Israel, two hundred and fifty princes of the assembly, famous in the congregation, men of renown:
3 And they gathered themselves together against Moses and against Aaron, and said unto them, you *take* too much upon you, seeing all the congregation *are* holy, every one of them, and the LORD *is* among them: wherefore then lift you up yourselves above the congregation of the LORD?
4 And when Moses heard *it*, he fell upon his face:
5 And he spoke unto Korah and unto all his company, saying, even tomorrow the LORD will show who *are* his, and *who is* holy; and will cause *him* to come near unto him: even *him* whom he has chosen will he cause to come near unto him.
6 This *does*; Take you censers, Korah, and all his company;
7 And put fire therein, and put incense in them before the LORD tomorrow: and it will be *that* the man whom the LORD does choose, he will *be* holy: you *take* too much upon you, you sons of Levi.
8 And Moses said unto Korah, Hear, I pray you, you sons of Levi:
9 *It* **seems** *but* a small thing unto you, that the God of Israel has separated you from the congregation of Israel, to bring you near to himself to do the service of the tabernacle of the LORD, and to stand before the congregation to minister unto them?
10 And he has brought you near *to him*, and all your brethren the sons of Levi with you: and seek you the priesthood also?
11 For which cause *both* you and all your company are gathered together against the LORD: and what *is* Aaron, that you murmur against him?
12 And Moses sent to call Dathan and Abiram, the sons of Eliab: which said, we will not come up:
13 *Is it* a small thing that you hast brought us up out of a land that flows with milk and honey, to kill us in the wilderness, except you make yourself altogether a prince over us?
14 Moreover you hast not brought us into a land that flows with milk and honey, or given us inheritance of fields and vineyards: wilt you put out the eyes of these men? We will not come up.
15 And Moses was very wroth, and said unto the LORD, Respect not you their offering: I have not taken one ass from them, neither have I hurt one of them.
16 And Moses said unto Korah, Be you and all your company before the LORD, thou, and they, and Aaron, tomorrow:
17 And take every man his censer, and put incense in them, and bring you before the LORD every man his censer, two hundred and fifty censers; you also, and Aaron, each *of you* his censer.
18 And they took every man his censer, and put fire in them, and laid incense thereon, and stood in the door of the tabernacle of the congregation with Moses and Aaron.
19 And Korah gathered the **entire** congregation against them unto the door of the tabernacle of the congregation: and the glory of the LORD appeared unto the **entire** congregation.
20 And the LORD spoke unto Moses and unto Aaron, saying,
21 Separate **you** from among this congregation, that I may consume them in a moment.
22 And they fell upon their faces, and said, O God, the God of the spirits of all flesh, will one man sin, and will you be angry with the **entire** congregation?
23 And the LORD spoke unto Moses, saying,
24 Speak unto the congregation, saying, Get you up from about the tabernacle of Korah, Dathan, and Abiram.
25 And Moses rose up and went unto Dathan and Abiram; and the elders of Israel followed him.
26 And he spoke unto the congregation, saying, Depart, I pray you, from the tents of these wicked men, and touch nothing of theirs, lest you be consumed in all their sins.
27 So they **got** up from the tabernacle of Korah, Dathan, and Abiram, on every side: and Dathan and Abiram came out, and stood in the door of their tents, and their wives, and their sons, and their little children.
28 And Moses said, hereby you will know that the LORD has sent me to do all these works; for *I have* not *done them* of mine own mind.
29 If these men die the common death of all men, or if they be visited after the visitation of all men; *then* the LORD has not sent me.
30 But if the LORD make a new thing, and the earth open her mouth, and swallow them up, with all that *appertain* unto them, and they go down quick into the pit; then you will understand that these men have provoked the LORD.
31 And it came to pass, as he had made an end of speaking all these words, that the ground clave asunder that *was* under them:

32 And the earth opened her mouth, and swallowed them up, and their houses, and all the men that *appertained* unto Korah, and all *their* goods.
33 They, and all that *appertained* to them, went down alive into the pit, and the earth closed upon them: and they perished from among the congregation.
34 And all Israel that *were* round about them fled at the cry of them: for they said, lest the earth swallow us up *also*.
35 And there came out a fire from the LORD, and consumed the two hundred and fifty men that offered incense.
36 And the LORD spoke unto Moses, saying,
37 Speak unto Eleazar the son of Aaron the priest, that he take up the censers out of the burning, and scatter you the fire yonder; for they are hallowed.
38 The censers of these sinners against their own souls, let them make them broad plates *for* a covering of the altar: for they offered them before the LORD, therefore they are hallowed: and they will be a sign unto the children of Israel.
39 And Eleazar the priest took the brasen censers, wherewith they that were burnt had offered; and they were made broad *plates for* a covering of the altar:
40 *To be* a memorial unto the children of Israel, that no stranger, which *is* not of the seed of Aaron, come near to offer incense before the LORD; that he be not as Korah, and as his company: as the LORD said to him by the hand of Moses.
41 But on the morrow all the congregation of the children of Israel murmured against Moses and against Aaron, saying, you have killed the people of the LORD.
42 And it came to pass, when the congregation was gathered against Moses and against Aaron, that they looked toward the tabernacle of the congregation: and, behold, the cloud covered it, and the glory of the LORD appeared.
43 And Moses and Aaron came before the tabernacle of the congregation.
44 And the LORD spoke unto Moses, saying,
45 Get you up from among this congregation, that I may consume them as in a moment. And they fell upon their faces.
46 And Moses said unto Aaron, Take a censer, and put fire therein from off the altar, and put on incense, and go quickly unto the congregation, and make an atonement for them: for there is wrath gone out from the LORD; the plague is begun.
47 And Aaron took as Moses commanded, and ran into the midst of the congregation; and, behold, the plague was begun among the people: and he put on incense, and made an atonement for the people.
48 And he stood between the dead and the living; and the plague was stayed.
49 Now they that died in the plague were fourteen thousand and seven hundred, beside them that died about the matter of Korah.
50 And Aaron returned unto Moses unto the door of the tabernacle of the congregation: and the plague was stayed.

CHAPTER 17

1 And the LORD spoke unto Moses, saying,
2 Speak unto the children of Israel, and take of every one of them a rod[1] according to the house of *their* fathers, of all their princes according to the house of their fathers twelve rods: write you every man's name upon his rod.
3 And you will write Aaron's name upon the rod of Levi: for one rod will *be* for the head of the house of their fathers.
4 And you will lay them up in the tabernacle of the congregation before the testimony, where I will meet with you.
5 And it will come to pass, *that* the man's rod, whom I will choose, will blossom: and I will make to cease from me the murmurings of the children of Israel, whereby they murmur against you.
6 And Moses spoke unto the children of Israel, and every one of their princes gave him a rod apiece, for each prince one, according to their fathers' houses, *even* twelve rods: and the rod of Aaron *was* among their rods.
7 And Moses laid up the rods before the LORD in the tabernacle of witness.
8 And it came to pass, that on the morrow Moses went into the tabernacle of witness; and, behold, the rod of Aaron for the house of Levi was budded, and brought forth buds, and bloomed blossoms, and yielded almonds.
9 And Moses brought out all the rods from before the LORD unto all the children of Israel: and they looked, and took every man his rod.
10 And the LORD said unto Moses, Bring Aaron's rod again before the testimony, to be kept for a token against the rebels and you will quite take away their murmurings from me, that they die not.
11 And Moses did *so*: as the LORD commanded him, so did he.
12 And the children of Israel spoke unto Moses, saying, Behold, we die, we perish, we all perish.
13 Whosoever cometh any thing near unto the tabernacle of the LORD will die: will we be consumed with dying?

CHAPTER 18

1 And the LORD said unto Aaron, you and your sons and your father's house with you will bear the iniquity of the sanctuary: and you and your sons with you will bear the iniquity of your priesthood.
2 And your brethren also of the tribe of Levi, the tribe of your father, bring you with you, that they may be joined unto you, and minister unto you: but you and your sons with you will *minister* before the tabernacle of witness.
3 And they will keep your charge, and the charge of the entire tabernacle: only they will not come nigh the vessels of the sanctuary and the altar, that neither they, nor you also, die.
4 And they will be joined unto you, and keep the charge of the tabernacle of the congregation, for all the service of the tabernacle: and a stranger will not come nigh unto you.
5 And you will keep the charge of the sanctuary, and the charge of the altar: that there is no wrath any more upon the children of Israel.
6 And I, behold, I have taken your brethren the Levites from among the children of Israel: to you *they are* given *as* a gift for the LORD, to do the service of the tabernacle of the congregation
7 Therefore you and your sons with you will keep your priest's office for everything of the altar, and within the veil; and you will serve: I have given your priest's office *unto you* as a service of gift: and the stranger that cometh nigh will be put to death.
8 And the LORD spoke unto Aaron, Behold, I also have given you the charge of mine heave offerings of all the hallowed things of the children of Israel; unto you have I given them by reason of the anointing, and to your sons, by an ordinance forever.

---

[1] rod = derives from the Hebrew word *maṭṭeh* which is defined as *a branch* (as extending); a *tribe*; also a rod whether for chastising (figuratively correction) [Strgs#4294].

9 This will be your of the most holy things, *reserved* from the fire: every oblation of theirs, every meat offering of theirs, and every sin offering of theirs, and every trespass offering of theirs, which they will render unto me, will *be* most holy for you and for your sons.

10 In the most holy *place* will you eat it; every male will eat it: it will be holy unto you.

11 And this *is* yours; the heave offering of their gift, with all the wave offerings of the children of Israel: I have given them unto you, and to your sons and to your daughters with you, by a statute for ever: every one that is clean in your house will eat of it.

12 All the best of the oil, and all the best of the wine, and of the wheat, the first fruits of them which they will offer unto the LORD, them have I given you.

13 *And* whatsoever is first ripe in the land, which they will bring unto the LORD, will be yours; every one that is clean in your house will eat *of* it.

14 Everything devoted in Israel will be yours.

15 Everything that opens the matrix in all flesh, which they bring unto the LORD, *whether it be* of men or beasts, will be yours: nevertheless the firstborn of man will you surely redeem, and the firstling of unclean beasts will you redeem.

16 And those that are to be redeemed from a month old will you redeem, according to your estimation, for the money of five shekels, after the shekel of the sanctuary, which *is* twenty gerahs.

17 But the firstling of a cow, or the firstling of a sheep, or the firstling of a goat, you will not redeem; they *are* holy: you will sprinkle their blood upon the altar, and will burn their fat *for* an offering made by fire, for a sweet savor unto the LORD.

18 And the flesh of them will be yours, as the wave breast and as the right shoulder are yours.

19 All the heave offerings of the holy things, which the children of Israel offer unto the LORD, have I given you, and your sons and your daughters with you, by a statute for ever: it *is* a covenant of salt for ever before the LORD unto you and to your seed with you.

20 And the LORD spoke unto Aaron, you will have no inheritance in their land, neither will you have any part among them: I *am* your part and your inheritance among the children of Israel.

21 And, behold, I have given the children of Levi all the tenth in Israel for an inheritance, for their service which they serve, *even* the service of the tabernacle of the congregation.

22 Neither must the children of Israel henceforth come nigh the tabernacle of the congregation, lest they bear sin, and die.

23 But the Levites will do the service of the tabernacle of the congregation, and they will bear their iniquity: *it will be* a statute for ever throughout your generations, that among the children of Israel they have no inheritance.

24 But the tithes of the children of Israel, which they offer *as* an heave offering unto the LORD, I have given to the Levites to inherit: therefore I have said unto them, Among the children of Israel they will have no inheritance.

25 And the LORD spoke unto Moses, saying,

26 Thus speak unto the Levites, and say unto them, When you take of the children of Israel the tithes which I have given you from them for your inheritance, then you will offer up an heave offering of it for the LORD, *even* a tenth *part* of the tithe.

27 And *this* your heave offering will be reckoned unto you, as though *it were* the corn of the threshing floor, and as the fullness of the winepress.

28 Thus you also will offer an heave offering unto the LORD of all your tithes, which you receive of the children of Israel; and you will give thereof the LORD'S heave offering to Aaron the priest.

29 Out of all your gifts you will offer every heave offering of the LORD, of all the best thereof, *even* the hallowed part thereof out of it.

30 Therefore you will say unto them, When you have heaved the best thereof from it, then it will be counted unto the Levites as the increase of the threshing floor, and as the increase of the winepress.

31 And you will eat it in every place, you and your households: for it *is* your reward for your service in the tabernacle of the congregation.

32 And you will bear no sin by reason of it, when you have heaved from it the best of it: neither will you pollute the holy things of the children of Israel, lest you die.

CHAPTER 19

1 And the LORD spoke unto Moses and unto Aaron, saying,

2 This *is* the ordinance of the law which the LORD has commanded, saying, Speak unto the children of Israel, that they bring you a red heifer without spot, wherein *is* no blemish, *and* upon which never came yoke:

3 And you will give her unto Eleazar the priest, that he may bring her forth without the camp, and *one* will slay her before his face:

4 And Eleazar the priest will take of her blood with his finger, and sprinkle of her blood directly before the tabernacle of the congregation seven times:

5 And *one* will burn the heifer in his sight; her skin, and her flesh, and her blood, with her dung, will he burn:

6 And the priest will take cedar wood, and hyssop, and scarlet, and cast *it* into the midst of the burning of the heifer.

7 Then the priest will wash his clothes, and he will bathe his flesh in water, and afterward he will come into the camp, and the priest will be unclean until the even.

8 And he that burneth her will wash his clothes in water, and bathe his flesh in water, and will be unclean until the even.

9 And a man *that is* clean will gather up the ashes of the heifer, and lay *them* up without the camp in a clean place, and it will be kept for the congregation of the children of Israel for a water of separation: it *is* a purification for sin.

10 And he that gathers the ashes of the heifer will wash his clothes, and be unclean until the even: and it will be unto the children of Israel, and unto the stranger that sojourns among them, for a statute forever.

11 He that touches the dead body of any man will be unclean seven days.

12 He will purify himself with it on the third day, and on the seventh day he will be clean: but if he purify not himself the third day, then the seventh day he will not be clean.

13 Whosoever touches the dead body of any man that is dead, and purifies not himself, defiles the tabernacle of the LORD; and that soul will be cut off from Israel: because the water of separation was not sprinkled upon him, he will be unclean; his uncleanness *is* yet upon him.

14 This *is* the law, when a man dies in a tent: all that come into the tent, and all that *is* in the tent, will be unclean seven days.

15 And every open vessel, which has no covering bound upon it, *is* unclean.

16 And whosoever touches one that is slain with a sword in the open fields, or a dead body, or a bone of a man, or a grave, will be unclean seven days.
17 And for an unclean *person* they will take of the ashes of the burnt heifer of purification for sin, and running water will be put thereto in a vessel:
18 And a clean person will take hyssop, and dip *it* in the water, and sprinkle *it* upon the tent, and upon all the vessels, and upon the persons that were there, and upon him that touched a bone, or one slain, or one dead, or a grave:
19 And the clean *person* will sprinkle upon the unclean on the third day, and on the seventh day: and on the seventh day he will purify himself, and wash his clothes, and bathe himself in water, and will be clean at even.
20 But the man that will be unclean, and will not purify himself, that soul will be cut off from among the congregation, because he has defiled the sanctuary of the LORD: the water of separation has not been sprinkled upon him; he *is* unclean.
21 And it will be a perpetual statute unto them, that he that sprinkles the water of separation will wash his clothes; and he that touches the water of separation will be unclean until even.
22 And whatsoever the unclean *person* touches will be unclean; and the soul that touches *it* will be unclean until even.

CHAPTER 20

1 Then came the children of Israel, *even* the whole congregation, into the desert of Zin in the first month: and the people abode in Kadesh; and Miriam died there, and was buried there.
2 And there was no water for the congregation: and they gathered themselves together against Moses and against Aaron.
3 And the people chode with Moses, and spoke, saying, Would God that we had died when our brethren died before the LORD!
4 And why have you brought up the congregation of the LORD into this wilderness, that we and our cattle should die there?
5 And wherefore have you made us to come up out of Egypt, to bring us in unto this evil place? it *is* no place of seed, or of figs, or of vines, or of pomegranates; neither *is* there any water to drink.
6 And Moses and Aaron went from the presence of the assembly unto the door of the tabernacle of the congregation, and they fell upon their faces: and the glory of the LORD appeared unto them.
7 And the LORD spoke unto Moses, saying,
8 Take the rod, and gather you the assembly together, thou, and Aaron your brother, and speak you unto the rock before their eyes; and it will give forth his water, and you will bring forth to them water out of the rock: so you will give the congregation and their beasts drink.
9 And Moses took the rod from before the LORD, as he commanded him.
10 And Moses and Aaron gathered the congregation together before the rock, and he said unto them, Hear now, you rebels; must we fetch you water out of this rock?
11 And Moses lifted up his hand, and with his rod he smote the rock twice: and the water came out abundantly, and the congregation drank, and their beasts *also*.
12 And the LORD spoke unto Moses and Aaron, Because you believed me not, to sanctify me in the eyes of the children of Israel, therefore you will not bring this congregation into the land which I have given them.
13 This *is* the water of Meribah; because the children of Israel strove with the LORD, and he was sanctified in them.
14 And Moses sent messengers from Kadesh unto the king of Edom, Thus said your brother Israel, you know all the travail that has befallen us:
15 How our fathers went down into Egypt, and we have dwelt in Egypt a long time; and the Egyptians vexed us, and our fathers:
16 And when we cried unto the LORD, he heard our voice, and sent an angel, and has brought us forth out of Egypt: and, behold, we *are* in Kadesh, a city in the uttermost of your border:
17 Let us pass, I pray you, through your country: we will not pass through the fields, or through the vineyards, neither will we drink *of* the water of the wells: we will go by the king's *high* way, we will not turn to the right hand nor to the left, until we have passed your borders.
18 And Edom said unto him, you will not pass by me, lest I come out against you with the sword.
19 And the children of Israel said unto him, we will go by the high way: and if I and my cattle drink of your water, then I will pay for it: I will only, without *doing* anything *else*, go through on my feet.
20 And he said, you will not go through. And Edom came out against him with much people, and with a strong hand.
21 Thus Edom refused to give Israel passage through his border: wherefore Israel turned away from him.
22 And the children of Israel, *even* the whole congregation, journeyed from Kadesh, and came unto mount Hor.
23 And the LORD spoke unto Moses and Aaron in mount Hor, by the coast of the land of Edom, saying,
24 Aaron will be gathered unto his people: for he will not enter into the land which I have given unto the children of Israel, because you rebelled against my word at the water of Meribah.
25 Take Aaron and Eleazar his son, and bring them up unto mount Hor:
26 And strip Aaron of his garments, and put them upon Eleazar his son: and Aaron will be gathered *unto his people*, and will die there.
27 And Moses did as the LORD commanded: and they went up into mount Hor in the sight of all the congregation.
28 And Moses stripped Aaron of his garments, and put them upon Eleazar his son; and Aaron died there in the top of the mount: and Moses and Eleazar came down from the mount.
29 And when all the congregation saw that Aaron was dead, they mourned for Aaron thirty days, *even* all the house of Israel.

CHAPTER 21

1 And *when* king Arad the Canaanite, which dwelt in the south, heard tell that Israel came by the way of the spies; then he fought against Israel, and took *some* of them prisoners.
2 And Israel vowed a vow unto the LORD, and said, f you wilt indeed deliver this people into my hand, then I will utterly destroy their cities.
3 And the LORD hearkened to the voice of Israel, and delivered up the Canaanites; and they utterly destroyed them and their cities: and he called the name of the place Hormah.
4 And they journeyed from mount Hor by the way of the Red sea, to compass the land of Edom: and the soul of the people was much discouraged because of the way.
5 And the people spoke against God, and against Moses, Wherefore have you brought us up out of Egypt to die in the wilderness? for *there is* no bread, neither *is there* any water; and our soul loathes this light bread.

6 And the LORD sent [fiery serpents]¹ among the people, and they bit the people; and much people of Israel died.
7 Therefore the people came to Moses, and said, We have sinned, for we have spoken against the LORD, and against you; pray unto the LORD, that he take away the serpents from us. And Moses prayed for the people.
8 And the LORD said unto Moses, Make you a fiery serpent, and set it upon a pole: and it will come to pass, that every one that is bitten², when he looks upon it, will live.
9 [And Moses made a serpent of brass, and put it upon a pole, and it came to pass, that if a serpent had bitten any man, when he beheld the serpent of brass, he lived.]³
10 And the children of Israel set forward, and pitched in Oboth.
11 And they journeyed from Oboth, and pitched at Ije-abarim, in the wilderness which *is* before Moab, toward the sun rising.
12 From thence they removed, and pitched in the valley of Zared.
13 From thence they removed, and pitched on the other side of Arnon, which *is* in the wilderness that cometh out of the coasts of the Amorites: for Arnon *is* the border of Moab, between Moab and the Amorites.
14 Wherefore it is said in the book of the wars of the LORD, What he did in the Red sea, and in the brooks of Arnon,
15 And at the stream of the brooks that goes down to the dwelling of Ar, and lies upon the border of Moab.
16 And from thence *they went* to Beer: that *is* the well whereof the LORD spoke unto Moses, Gather the people together, and I will give them water.
17 Then Israel sang this song, Spring up, O well; sing you unto it:
18 The princes digged the well, the nobles of the people digged it, by *the direction of* the lawgiver, with their staves. And from the wilderness *they went* to Mattanah:
19 And from Mattanah to Nahaliel: and from Nahaliel to Bamoth:
20 And from Bamoth *in* the valley, that *is* in the country of Moab, to the top of Pisgah, which looketh toward Jeshimon.
21 And Israel sent messengers unto Sihon king of the Amorites, saying,
22 Let me pass through your land: we will not turn into the fields, or into the vineyards; we will not drink *of* the waters of the well: *but* we will go along by the king's *high* way, until we be past your borders.
23 And Sihon would not suffer Israel to pass through his border: but Sihon gathered all his people together, and went out against Israel into the wilderness: and he came to Jahaz, and fought against Israel.
24 And Israel smote him with the edge of the sword, and possessed his land from Arnon unto Jabbok, even unto the children of Ammon: for the border of the children of Ammon *was* strong.
25 And Israel took all these cities: and Israel dwelt in all the cities of the Amorites, in Heshbon, and in all the villages thereof.
26 For Heshbon *was* the city of Sihon the king of the Amorites, who had fought against the former king of Moab, and taken all his land out of his hand, even unto Arnon.
27 Wherefore they that speak in proverbs say, Come into Heshbon, let the city of Sihon be built and prepared:
28 For there is a fire gone out of Heshbon, a flame from the city of Sihon: it has consumed Ar of Moab, *and* the lords of the high places of Arnon.
29 Woe to you, Moab! you are undone, O people of Chemosh: he has given his sons that escaped, and his daughters, into captivity unto Sihon king of the Amorites.
30 We have shot at them; Heshbon is perished even unto Dibon, and we have laid them waste even unto Nophah, which *reacheth* unto Medeba.
31 Thus Israel dwelt in the land of the Amorites.
32 And Moses sent to spy out Jaazer, and they took the villages thereof, and drove out the Amorites that *were* there.
33 And they turned and went up by the way of Bashan: and Og the king of Bashan went out against them, he, and all his people, to the battle at Edrei.
34 And the LORD said unto Moses, Fear him not: for I have delivered him into your hand, and all his people, and his land; and you will do to him as you didst unto Sihon king of the Amorites, which dwelt at Heshbon.
35 So they smote him, and his sons, and all his people, until there was none left him alive: and they possessed his land.

CHAPTER 22

1 And the children of Israel set forward, and pitched in the plains of Moab on this side Jordan *by* Jericho.
2 And Balak the son of Zippor saw all that Israel had done to the Amorites.
3 And Moab was sore afraid of the people, because they *were* many: and Moab was distressed because of the children of Israel.
4 And Moab said unto the elders of Midian, Now will this company lick up all *that are* round about us, as the ox licketh up the grass of the field. And Balak the son of Zippor *was* king of the Moabites at that time.
5 He sent messengers therefore unto Balaam the son of Beor to Pethor, which *is* by the river of the land of the children of his people, to call him, saying, Behold, there is a people come out from Egypt: behold, they cover the face of the earth, and they abide over against me:
6 Come now therefore, I pray you, curse me this people; for they *are* too mighty for me: peradventure I will prevail, *that* we may smite them, and *that* I may drive them out of the land: for I wot that he whom you blesses *is* blessed, and he whom you curses is cursed.
7 And the elders of Moab and the elders of Midian departed with the rewards of divination in their hand; and they came unto Balaam, and spoke unto him the words of Balak.
8 And he said unto them, Lodge here this night, and I will bring you word again, as the LORD will speak unto me: and the princes of Moab abode with Balaam.
9 And God came unto Balaam, and said, what men *are* these with you?
10 And Balaam said unto God, Balak the son of Zippor, king of Moab, has sent unto me, *saying,*
11 Behold, *there is* a people come out of Egypt, which covers the face of the earth: come now, curse me them; peradventure I will be able to overcome them, and drive them out.

---
¹ fiery serpent = Hebrew *śârâph* meaning *burning, poisonous* (serpent) [Strgs#8314].
² bitten = Hebrew word *nâshak* which is defined as to *strike* with a sting (as a serpent); figuratively, to *oppress* with interest on a loan [Strgs#5391].
³ compare **John 3:14**

12 And God said unto Balaam, you will not go with them; you will not curse the people: for they *are* blessed.
13 And Balaam rose up in the morning, and said unto the princes of Balak, Get you into your land: for the LORD refuses to give me leave to go with you.
14 And the princes of Moab rose up, and they went unto Balak, and said, Balaam refuses to come with us.
15 And Balak sent yet again princes, more, and more honorable than they.
16 And they came to Balaam, and said to him, thus said Balak the son of Zippor, Let nothing, I pray you, hinder you from coming unto me:
17 For I will promote you unto very great honor, and I will do whatsoever you say unto me: come therefore, I pray you, curse me this people.
18 And Balaam answered and said unto the servants of Balak, If Balak would give me his house full of silver and gold, I cannot go beyond the word of the LORD my God, to do less or more.
19 Now therefore, I pray you, tarry you also here this night, that I may know what the LORD will say unto me more.
20 And God came unto Balaam at night, and said unto him, If the men come to call you, rise up, *and* go with them; but yet the word which I will say unto you, that will you do.
21 And Balaam rose up in the morning, and saddled his ass, and went with the princes of Moab.
22 And God's anger was kindled because he went: and the angel of the LORD stood in the way for an adversary against him. Now he was riding upon his ass, and his two servants *were* with him.
23 And the ass saw the angel of the LORD standing in the way, and his sword drawn in his hand: and the ass turned aside out of the way, and went into the field: and Balaam smote the ass, to turn her into the way.
24 But the angel of the LORD stood in a path of the vineyards, a wall *being* on this side, and a wall on that side.
25 And when the ass saw the angel of the LORD, she thrust herself unto the wall, and crushed Balaam's foot against the wall: and he smote her again.
26 And the angel of the LORD went further, and stood in a narrow place, where *was* no way to turn either to the right hand or to the left.
27 And when the ass saw the angel of the LORD, she fell down under Balaam: and Balaam's anger was kindled, and he smote the ass with a staff.
28 And the LORD opened the mouth of the ass, and she said unto Balaam, What have I done unto you, that you hast smitten me these three times?
29 And Balaam said unto the ass, Because you hast mocked me: I would there were a sword in mine hand, for now would I kill you.
30 And the ass said unto Balaam, *Am* not I your ass, upon which you hast ridden ever since *I was* your unto this day? was I ever wont to do so unto you? And he said, Nay.
31 Then the LORD opened the eyes of Balaam, and he saw the angel of the LORD standing in the way, and his sword drawn in his hand: and he bowed down his head, and fell flat on his face.
32 And the angel of the LORD said unto him, Wherefore hast you smitten your ass these three times? behold, I went out to withstand you, because your way is perverse before me:
33 And the ass saw me, and turned from me these three times: unless she had turned from me, surely now also I had slain you, and saved her alive.
34 And Balaam said unto the angel of the LORD, I have sinned; for I knew not that you stood in the way against me: now therefore, if it displease you, I will get me back again.
35 And the angel of the LORD said unto Balaam, Go with the men: but only the word that I will speak unto you, that you will speak. So Balaam went with the princes of Balak.
36 And when Balak heard that Balaam was come, he went out to meet him unto a city of Moab, which *is* in the border of Arnon, which *is* in the utmost coast.
37 And Balak said unto Balaam, Did I not earnestly send unto you to call you? Wherefore come you not unto me? Am I not able indeed to promote you to honor?
38 And Balaam said unto Balak, Lo, I am come unto you: have I now any power at all to say anything? the word that God puts in my mouth, that will I speak.
39 And Balaam went with Balak, and they came unto Kirjath-huzoth.
40 And Balak offered oxen and sheep, and sent to Balaam, and to the princes that *were* with him.
41 And it came to pass on the morrow, that Balak took Balaam, and brought him up into the high places of Baal, that thence he might see the utmost *part* of the people.

CHAPTER 23

1 And Balaam said unto Balak, Build me here seven altars, and prepare me here seven oxen and seven rams.
2 And Balak did as Balaam had spoken; and Balak and Balaam offered on *every* altar a bullock and a ram.
3 And Balaam said unto Balak, Stand by your burnt offering, and I will go: peradventure the LORD will come to meet me: and whatsoever he shows me I will tell you. And he went to an high place.
4 And God met Balaam: and he said unto him, I have prepared seven altars, and I have offered upon *every* altar a bullock and a ram.
5 And the LORD put a word in Balaam's mouth, and said, Return unto Balak, and thus you will speak.
6 And he returned unto him, and, lo, he stood by his burnt sacrifice, he, and all the princes of Moab.
7 And he took up his parable, and said, Balak the king of Moab has brought me from Aram, out of the mountains of the east, *saying*, Come, curse me Jacob, and come, defy Israel.
8 How will I curse, whom God has not cursed? or how will I defy, *whom* the LORD has not defied?
9 For from the top of the rocks I see him, and from the hills I behold him: lo, the people will dwell alone, and will not be reckoned among the nations.
10 Who can count the dust of Jacob, and the number of the fourth *part* of Israel? Let me die the death of the righteous, and let my last end be like his!
11 And Balak said unto Balaam, What hast you done unto me? I took you to curse mine enemies, and, behold, you hast blessed *them* altogether.
12 And he answered and said, Must I not take heed to speak that which the LORD has put in my mouth?
13 And Balak said unto him, Come, I pray you, with me unto another place, from whence you may see them: you will see but the utmost part of them, and will not see them all: and curse me them from thence.

14 And he brought him into the field of Zophim, to the top of Pisgah, and built seven altars, and offered a bullock and a ram on *every* altar.
15 And he said unto Balak, Stand here by your burnt offering, while I meet *the* LORD yonder.
16 And the LORD met Balaam, and put a word in his mouth, and said, Go again unto Balak, and say thus.
17 And when he came to him, behold, he stood by his burnt offering, and the princes of Moab with him. And Balak said unto him, what has the LORD spoken?
18 And he took up his parable, and said, Rise up, Balak, and hear; hearken unto me, you son of Zippor:
19 God *is* not a man, that he should lie; neither the son of man, that he should repent: has he said, and will he not do *it*? or has he spoken, and will he not make it good?
20 Behold, I have received *commandment* to bless: and he has blessed; and I cannot reverse it.
21 He has not beheld iniquity in Jacob, neither has he seen perverseness in Israel: the LORD his God *is* with him, and the shout of a king *is* among them.
22 God brought them out of Egypt; he has as it were the strength of an unicorn.
23 Surely *there is* no enchantment against Jacob, neither *is there* any divination against Israel: according to this time it will be said of Jacob and of Israel, What has God wrought!
24 Behold, the people will rise up as a great lion, and lift up himself as a young lion: he will not lie down until he eat *of* the prey, and drink the blood of the slain.
25 And Balak said unto Balaam, Neither curse them at all, nor bless them at all.
26 But Balaam answered and said unto Balak, Told not I you, saying, All that the LORD speaks, that I must do?
27 And Balak said unto Balaam, Come, I pray you, I will bring you unto another place; peradventure it will please God that you may curse me them from thence.
28 And Balak brought Balaam unto the top of Peor, that looks toward Jeshimon.
29 And Balaam said unto Balak, Build me here seven altars, and prepare me here seven bullocks and seven rams.
30 And Balak did as Balaam had said, and offered a bullock and a ram on *every* altar.

CHAPTER 24

1 And when Balaam saw that it pleased the LORD to bless Israel, he went not, as at other times, to seek for enchantments, but he set his face toward the wilderness.
2 And Balaam lifted up his eyes, and he saw Israel abiding *in his tents* according to their tribes; and the spirit of God came upon him.
3 And he took up his parable, and said, Balaam the son of Beor has said, and the man whose eyes are open has said:
4 He has said, which heard the words of God, which saw the vision of the Almighty, falling *into a trance*, but having his eyes open:
5 How goodly are your tents, O Jacob, *and* your tabernacles, O Israel!
6 As the valleys are they spread forth, as gardens by the river's side, as the trees of lign aloes which the LORD has planted, *and* as cedar trees beside the waters.
7 He will pour the water out of his buckets, and his seed will *be* in many waters, and his king will be higher than Agag, and his kingdom will be exalted.
8 God brought him forth out of Egypt; he has as it were the strength of an unicorn: he will eat up the nations his enemies, and will break their bones, and pierce *them* through with his arrows.
9 He couched, he lay down as a lion, and as a great lion: who will stir him up? Blessed *is* he that blesses you, and cursed *is* he that curses you.
10 And Balak's anger was kindled against Balaam, and he smote his hands together: and Balak said unto Balaam, I called you to curse mine enemies, and, behold, you hast altogether blessed *them* these three times.
11 Therefore now flee you to your place: I thought to promote you unto great honor; but, lo, the LORD has kept you back from honor.
12 And Balaam said unto Balak, spoke I not also to your messengers which you sent unto me, saying,
13 If Balak would give me his house full of silver and gold, I cannot go beyond the commandment of the LORD, to do *either* good or bad of mine own mind; *but* what the LORD said, that will I speak?
14 And now, behold, I go unto my people: come *therefore, and* I will advertise you what this people will do to your people in the latter days.
15 And he took up his parable, and said, Balaam the son of Beor has said, and the man whose eyes are open has said:
16 He has said, which heard the words of God, and knew the knowledge of the most High, *which* saw the vision of the Almighty, falling *into a trance*, but having his eyes open:
17 I will see him, but not now: I will behold him, but not nigh: there will come a Star out of Jacob, and a Scepter will rise out of Israel, and will smite the corners of Moab, and destroy all the children of Sheth.
18 And Edom will be a possession, Seir also will be a possession for his enemies; and Israel will do valiantly.
19 Out of Jacob will come he that will have dominion, and will destroy him that remains of the city.
20 And when he looked on Amalek, he took up his parable, and said, Amalek *was* the first of the nations; but his latter end will *be* that he perish forever.
21 And he looked on the Kenites, and took up his parable, and said, Strong is your dwelling place, and you put your nest in a rock.
22 Nevertheless the Kenite will be wasted, until Asshur will carry you away captive.
23 And he took up his parable, and said, Alas, who will live when God doeth this!
24 And ships will *come* from the coast of Chittim, and will afflict Asshur, and will afflict Eber, and he also will perish for ever.
25 And Balaam rose up, and went and returned to his place: and Balak also went his way.

CHAPTER 25

1 And Israel abode in Shittim, and the people began to commit whoredom with the daughters of Moab.
2 And they called the people unto the sacrifices of their gods: and the people did eat, and bowed down to their gods.
3 And Israel joined himself unto Baal-peor: and the anger of the LORD was kindled against Israel.
4 And the LORD said unto Moses, Take all the heads of the people, and hang them up before the LORD against the sun, that the fierce anger of the LORD may be turned away from Israel.
5 And Moses said unto the judges of Israel, Slay you every one his men that were joined unto Baal-peor.

6 And, behold, one of the children of Israel came and brought unto his brethren a Midianitish woman in the sight of Moses, and in the sight of all the congregation of the children of Israel, who were weeping before the door of the tabernacle of the congregation.
7 And when Phinehas, the son of Eleazar, the son of Aaron the priest, saw it, he rose up from among the congregation, and took a javelin in his hand;
8 And he went after the man of Israel into the tent, and thrust both of them through, the man of Israel, and the woman through her belly. So the plague was stayed from the children of Israel.
9 And those that died in the plague were twenty and four thousand.
10 And the LORD spoke unto Moses, saying,
11 Phinehas, the son of Eleazar, the son of Aaron the priest, has turned my wrath away from the children of Israel, while he was zealous for my sake among them, that I consumed not the children of Israel in my jealousy.
12 Wherefore say, Behold, I give unto him my covenant of peace:
13 And he will have it, and his seed after him, even the covenant of an everlasting priesthood; because he was zealous for his God, and made an atonement for the children of Israel.
14 Now the name of the Israelite that was slain, even that was slain with the Midianitish woman, was Zimri, the son of Salu, a prince of a chief house among the Simeonites.
15 And the name of the Midianitish woman that was slain was Cozbi, the daughter of Zur; he was head over a people, and of a chief house in Midian.
16 And the LORD spoke unto Moses, saying,
17 Vex the Midianites, and smite them:
18 For they vex you with their wiles, wherewith they have beguiled you in the matter of Peor, and in the matter of Cozbi, the daughter of a prince of Midian, their sister, which was slain in the day of the plague for Peor's sake.

CHAPTER 26

1 And it came to pass after the plague, that the LORD spoke unto Moses and unto Eleazar the son of Aaron the priest, saying,
2 Take the sum of all the congregation of the children of Israel, from twenty years old and upward, throughout their fathers' house, all that are able to go to war in Israel.
3 And Moses and Eleazar the priest spoke with them in the plains of Moab by Jordan near Jericho, saying,
4 Take the sum of the people, from twenty years old and upward; as the LORD commanded Moses and the children of Israel, which went forth out of the land of Egypt.
5 Reuben, the eldest son of Israel: the children of Reuben; Hanoch, of whom cometh the family of the Hanochites: of Pallu, the family of the Palluites:
6 Of Hezron, the family of the Hezronites: of Carmi, the family of the Carmites.
7 These are the families of the Reubenites: and they that were numbered of them were forty and three thousand and seven hundred and thirty.
8 And the sons of Pallu; Eliab.
9 And the sons of Eliab; Nemuel, and Dathan, and Abiram. This is that Dathan and Abiram, which were famous in the congregation, who strove against Moses and against Aaron in the company of Korah, when they strove against the LORD:
10 And the earth opened her mouth, and swallowed them up together with Korah, when that company died, what time the fire devoured two hundred and fifty men: and they became a sign.
11 Notwithstanding the children of Korah died not.
12 The sons of Simeon after their families: of Nemuel, the family of the Nemuelites: of Jamin, the family of the Jaminites: of Jachin, the family of the Jachinites:
13 Of Zerah, the family of the Zarhites: of Shaul, the family of the Shaulites.
14 These are the families of the Simeonites, twenty and two thousand and two hundred.
15 The children of Gad after their families: of Zephon, the family of the Zephonites: of Haggi, the family of the Haggites: of Shuni, the family of the Shunites:
16 Of Ozni, the family of the Oznites: of Eri, the family of the Erites:
17 Of Arod, the family of the Arodites: of Areli, the family of the Arelites.
18 These are the families of the children of Gad according to those that were numbered of them, forty thousand and five hundred.
19 The sons of Judah were Er and Onan: and Er and Onan died in the land of Canaan.
20 And the sons of Judah after their families were; of Shelah, the family of the Shelanites: of Pharez, the family of the Pharzites: of Zerah, the family of the Zarhites.
21 And the sons of Pharez were; of Hezron, the family of the Hezronites: of Hamul, the family of the Hamulites.
22 These are the families of Judah according to those that were numbered of them, threescore and sixteen thousand and five hundred.
23 Of the sons of Issachar after their families: of Tola, the family of the Tolaites: of Pua, the family of the Punites:
24 Of Jashub, the family of the Jashubites: of Shimron, the family of the Shimronites.
25 These are the families of Issachar according to those that were numbered of them, threescore and four thousand and three hundred.
26 Of the sons of Zebulun after their families: of Sered, the family of the Sardites: of Elon, the family of the Elonites: of Jahleel, the family of the Jahleelites.
27 These are the families of the Zebulunites according to those that were numbered of them, threescore thousand and five hundred.
28 The sons of Joseph after their families were Manasseh and Ephraim.
29 Of the sons of Manasseh: of Machir, the family of the Machirites: and Machir begat Gilead: of Gilead come the family of the Gileadites.
30 These are the sons of Gilead: of Jeezer, the family of the Jeezerites: of Helek, the family of the Helekites:
31 And of Asriel, the family of the Asrielites: and of Shechem, the family of the Shechemites:
32 And of Shemida, the family of the Shemidaites: and of Hepher, the family of the Hepherites.
33 And Zelophehad the son of Hepher had no sons, but daughters: and the names of the daughters of Zelophehad were Mahlah, and Noah, Hoglah, Milcah, and Tirzah.
34 These are the families of Manasseh, and those that were numbered of them, fifty and two thousand and seven hundred.
35 These are the sons of Ephraim after their families: of Shuthelah, the family of the Shuthalhites: of Becher, the family of the Bachrites: of Tahan, the family of the Tahanites.
36 And these are the sons of Shuthelah: of Eran, the family of the Eranites.

37 These *are* the families of the sons of Ephraim according to those that were numbered of them, thirty and two thousand and five hundred. These *are* the sons of Joseph after their families.
38 The sons of Benjamin after their families: of Bela, the family of the Belaites: of Ashbel, the family of the Ashbelites: of Ahiram, the family of the Ahiramites:
39 Of Shupham, the family of the Shuphamites: of Hupham, the family of the Huphamites.
40 And the sons of Bela were Ard and Naaman: *of Ard*, the family of the Ardites: *and* of Naaman, the family of the Naamites.
41 These *are* the sons of Benjamin after their families: and they that were numbered of them *were* forty and five thousand and six hundred.
42 These *are* the sons of Dan after their families: of Shuham, the family of the Shuhamites. These *are* the families of Dan after their families.
43 All the families of the Shuhamites, according to those that were numbered of them, *were* threescore and four thousand and four hundred.
44 *Of* the children of Asher after their families: of Jimna, the family of the Jimnites: of Jesui, the family of the Jesuites: of Beriah, the family of the Beriites.
45 Of the sons of Beriah: of Heber, the family of the Heberites: of Malchiel, the family of the Malchielites.
46 And the name of the daughter of Asher *was* Sarah.
47 These *are* the families of the sons of Asher according to those that were numbered of them; *who were* fifty and three thousand and four hundred.
48 *Of* the sons of Naphtali after their families: of Jahzeel, the family of the Jahzeelites: of Guni, the family of the Gunites:
49 Of Jezer, the family of the Jezerites: of Shillem, the family of the Shillemites.
50 These *are* the families of Naphtali according to their families: and they that were numbered of them *were* forty and five thousand and four hundred.
51 These *were* the numbered of the children of Israel, six hundred thousand and a thousand seven hundred and thirty.
52 And the LORD spoke unto Moses, saying,
53 Unto these the land will be divided for an inheritance according to the number of names.
54 To many you will give the more inheritance, and to few you will give the less inheritance: to everyone will his inheritance be given according to those that were numbered of him.
55 Notwithstanding the land will be divided by lot: according to the names of the tribes of their fathers they will inherit.
56 According to the lot will the possession thereof be divided between many and few.
57 And these *are* they that were numbered of the Levites after their families: of Gershon, the family of the Gershonites: of Kohath, the family of the Kohathites: of Merari, the family of the Merarites.
58 These *are* the families of the Levites: the family of the Libnites, the family of the Hebronites, the family of the Mahlites, the family of the Mushites, the family of the Korathites. And Kohath begat Amram.
59 And the name of Amram's wife *was* Jochebed, the daughter of Levi, whom *her mother* bare to Levi in Egypt: and she bare unto Amram Aaron and Moses, and Miriam their sister.
60 And unto Aaron was born Nadab, and Abihu, Eleazar, and Ithamar.
61 And Nadab and Abihu died, when they offered strange fire before the LORD.
62 And those that were numbered of them were twenty and three thousand, all males from a month old and upward: for they were not numbered among the children of Israel, because there was no inheritance given them among the children of Israel.
63 These *are* they that were numbered by Moses and Eleazar the priest, who numbered the children of Israel in the plains of Moab by Jordan *near* Jericho.
64 But among these there was not a man of them whom Moses and Aaron the priest numbered, when they numbered the children of Israel in the wilderness of Sinai.
65 For the LORD had said of them, they will surely die in the wilderness. And there was not left a man of them, save Caleb the son of Jephunneh, and Joshua the son of Nun.

CHAPTER 27

1 Then came the daughters of Zelophehad, the son of Hepher, the son of Gilead, the son of Machir, the son of Manasseh, of the families of Manasseh the son of Joseph: and these *are* the names of his daughters; Mahlah, Noah, and Hoglah, and Milcah, and Tirzah.
2 And they stood before Moses, and before Eleazar the priest, and before the princes and the **entire** congregation, *by the* door of the tabernacle of the congregation, saying,
3 Our father died in the wilderness, and he was not in the company of them that gathered themselves together against the LORD in the company of Korah; but died in his own sin, and had no sons.
4 Why should the name of our father be done away from among his family, because he has no son? Give unto us therefore a possession among the brethren of our father.
5 And Moses brought their cause before the LORD.
6 And the LORD spoke unto Moses, saying,
7 The daughters of Zelophehad speak right: you will surely give them a possession of an inheritance among their fathers brethren; and you will cause the inheritance of their father to pass unto them.
8 And you will speak unto the children of Israel, saying, If a man die, and have no son, then you will cause his inheritance to pass unto his daughter.
9 And if he has no daughter, then you will give his inheritance unto his brethren.
10 And if he has no brethren, then you will give his inheritance unto his father's brethren.
11 And if his father have no brethren, then you will give his inheritance unto his kinsman that is next to him of his family, and he will possess it: and it will be unto the children of Israel a statute of judgment, as the LORD commanded Moses.
12 And the LORD said unto Moses, Get you up into this mount Abarim, and see the land which I have given unto the children of Israel.
13 And when you hast seen it, you also will be gathered unto your people, as Aaron your brother was gathered.
14 For you rebelled against my commandment in the desert of Zin, in the strife of the congregation, to sanctify me at the water before their eyes: that *is* the water of Meribah in Kadesh in the wilderness of Zin.
15 And Moses spoke unto the LORD, saying,
16 Let the LORD, the God of the spirits of all flesh, set a man over the congregation,

17 Which may go out before them, and which may go in before them, and which may lead them out, and which may bring them in; that the congregation of the LORD be not as sheep which have no shepherd.
18 And the LORD said unto Moses, Take you Joshua the son of Nun, a man in whom *is* the spirit, and lay your hand upon him;
19 And set him before Eleazar the priest, and before the entire congregation; and give him a charge in their sight.
20 And you will put *some* of your honor upon him, that all the congregation of the children of Israel may be obedient.
21 And he will stand before Eleazar the priest, who will ask *counsel* for him after the judgment of Urim before the LORD: at his word will they go out, and at his word they will come in, *both* he, and all the children of Israel with him, even all the congregation.
22 And Moses did as the LORD commanded him: and he took Joshua, and set him before Eleazar the priest, and before the entire congregation:
23 And he laid his hands upon him, and gave him a charge, as the LORD commanded by the hand of Moses.

CHAPTER 28

1 And the LORD spoke unto Moses, saying,
2 Command the children of Israel, and say unto them, my offering, *and* my bread for my sacrifices made by fire, *for* a sweet savor unto me, will you observe to offer unto me in their due season.
3 And you will say unto them, This *is* the offering made by fire which you will offer unto the LORD; two lambs of the first year without spot day by day, *for* a continual burnt offering.
4 The one lamb will you offer in the morning, and the other lamb will you offer at even;
5 And a tenth *part* of an ephah of flour for a meat offering, mingled with the fourth *part* of a hin of beaten oil.
6 *It is* a continual burnt offering, which was ordained in Mount Sinai for a sweet savor, a sacrifice made by fire unto the LORD.
7 And the drink offering thereof will *be* the fourth *part* of a hin for the one lamb: in the holy *place* will you cause the strong wine to be poured unto the LORD *for* a drink offering.
8 And the other lamb will you offer at even: as the meat offering of the morning, and as the drink offering thereof, you will offer *it*, a sacrifice made by fire, of a sweet savor unto the LORD.
9 And on the Sabbath day two lambs of the first year without spot, and two tenth deals of flour *for* a meat offering, mingled with oil, and the drink offering thereof:
10 *This is* the burnt offering of every Sabbath, beside the continual burnt offering, and his drink offering.
11 ¶ And in the beginnings of your months you will offer a burnt offering unto the LORD; two young bullocks, and one ram, seven lambs of the first year without spot;
12 And three tenth deals of flour *for* a meat offering, mingled with oil, for one bullock; and two tenth deals of flour *for* a meat offering, mingled with oil, for one ram;
13 And a several tenth deal of flour mingled with oil *for* a meat offering unto one lamb; *for* a burnt offering of a sweet savor, a sacrifice made by fire unto the LORD.
14 And their drink offerings will be half a hin of wine unto a bullock, and the third *part* of a hin unto a ram, and a fourth *part* of a hin unto a lamb: this *is* the burnt offering of every month throughout the months of the year.

15 And one kid of the goats for a sin offering unto the LORD will be offered, beside the continual burnt offering, and his drink offering.
16 And in the fourteenth day of the first month *is* the Passover of the LORD.
17 And in the fifteenth day of this month *is* the feast: seven days will unleavened bread be eaten.
18 In the first day will *be* a holy convocation; you will do no manner of servile work *therein*:
19 But you will offer a sacrifice made by fire *for* a burnt offering unto the LORD; two young bullocks, and one ram, and seven lambs of the first year: they will be unto you without blemish:
20 And their meat offering will *be of* flour mingled with oil: three tenth deals will you offer for a bullock, and two tenth deals for a ram;
21 A several tenth deal will you offer for every lamb, throughout the seven lambs:
22 And one goat *for* a sin offering, to make atonement for you.
23 you will offer these beside the burnt offering in the morning, which *is* for a continual burnt offering.
24 After this manner you will offer daily, throughout the seven days, the meat of the sacrifice made by fire, of a sweet savor unto the LORD: it will be offered beside the continual burnt offering, and his drink offering.
25 And on the seventh day you will have a holy convocation; you will do no servile work.
26 Also in the day of the first fruits, when you bring a new meat offering unto the LORD, after your weeks *are out*, you will have a holy convocation; you will do no servile work:
27 But you will offer the burnt offering for a sweet savor unto the LORD; two young bullocks, one ram, seven lambs of the first year;
28 And their meat offering of flour mingled with oil, three tenth deals unto one bullock, two tenth deals unto one ram,
29 A several tenth deal unto one lamb, throughout the seven lambs;
30 *And* one kid of the goats, to make atonement for you.
31 you will offer *them* beside the continual burnt offering, and his meat offering, (they will be unto you without blemish) and their drink offerings.

CHAPTER 29

1 And in the seventh month, on the first *day* of the month, you will have a holy convocation; you will do no servile work: it is a day of blowing the trumpets unto you.
2 And you will offer a burnt offering for a sweet savor unto the LORD; one young bullock, one ram, *and* seven lambs of the first year without blemish:
3 And their meat offering will *be of* flour mingled with oil, three tenth deals for a bullock, *and* two tenth deals for a ram,
4 And one tenth deal for one lamb, throughout the seven lambs:
5 And one kid of the goats *for* a sin offering, to make atonement for you:
6 Beside the burnt offering of the month, and his meat offering, and the daily burnt offering, and his meat offering, and their drink offerings, according unto their manner, for a sweet savor, a sacrifice made by fire unto the LORD.
7 And you will have on the tenth *day* of this seventh month a holy convocation; and you will afflict your souls: you will not do any work *therein*:

8 But you will offer a burnt offering unto the LORD *for* a sweet savor; one young bullock, one ram, *and* seven lambs of the first year; they will be unto you without blemish:
9 And their meat offering will *be of* flour mingled with oil, three tenth deals to a bullock, *and* two tenth deals to one ram,
10 A several tenth deal for one lamb, throughout the seven lambs:
11 One kid of the goats *for* a sin offering; beside the sin offering of atonement, and the continual burnt offering, and the meat offering of it, and their drink offerings.
12 And on the fifteenth day of the seventh month you will have a holy convocation; you will do no servile work, and you will keep a feast unto the LORD seven days:
13 And you will offer a burnt offering, a sacrifice made by fire, of a sweet savor unto the LORD; thirteen young bullocks, two rams, *and* fourteen lambs of the first year; they will be without blemish:
14 And their meat offering will *be of* flour mingled with oil, three tenth deals unto every bullock of the thirteen bullocks, two tenth deals to each ram of the two rams,
15 And a several tenth deal to each lamb of the fourteen lambs:
16 And one kid of the goats *for* a sin offering; beside the continual burnt offering, his meat offering, and his drink offering.
17 And on the second day you *will offer* twelve young bullocks, two rams, fourteen lambs of the first year without spot:
18 And their meat offering and their drink offerings for the bullocks, for the rams, and for the lambs, will *be* according to their number, after the manner:
19 And one kid of the goats *for* a sin offering; beside the continual burnt offering, and the meat offering thereof, and their drink offerings.
20 And on the third day eleven bullocks, two rams, fourteen lambs of the first year without blemish;
21 And their meat offering and their drink offerings for the bullocks, for the rams, and for the lambs, will *be* according to their number, after the manner:
22 And one goat *for* a sin offering; beside the continual burnt offering, and his meat offering, and his drink offering.
23 And on the fourth day ten bullocks, two rams, *and* fourteen lambs of the first year without blemish:
24 Their meat offering and their drink offerings for the bullocks, for the rams, and for the lambs, will *be* according to their number, after the manner:
25 And one kid of the goats *for* a sin offering; beside the continual burnt offering, his meat offering, and his drink offering.
26 And on the fifth day nine bullocks, two rams, *and* fourteen lambs of the first year without spot:
27 And their meat offering and their drink offerings for the bullocks, for the rams, and for the lambs, will *be* according to their number, after the manner:
28 And one goat *for* a sin offering; beside the continual burnt offering, and his meat offering, and his drink offering.
29 And on the sixth day eight bullocks, two rams, *and* fourteen lambs of the first year without blemish:
30 And their meat offering and their drink offerings for the bullocks, for the rams, and for the lambs, will *be* according to their number, after the manner:
31 And one goat *for* a sin offering; beside the continual burnt offering, his meat offering, and his drink offering.
32 And on the seventh day seven bullocks, two rams, *and* fourteen lambs of the first year without blemish:
33 And their meat offering and their drink offerings for the bullocks, for the rams, and for the lambs, will *be* according to their number, after the manner:
34 And one goat *for* a sin offering; beside the continual burnt offering, his meat offering, and his drink offering.
35 On the eighth day you will have a solemn assembly you will do no servile work *therein*:
36 But you will offer a burnt offering, a sacrifice made by fire, of a sweet savor unto the LORD: one bullock, one ram, seven lambs of the first year without blemish:
37 Their meat offering and their drink offerings for the bullock, for the ram, and for the lambs, will *be* according to their number, after the manner:
38 And one goat *for* a sin offering; beside the continual burnt offering, and his meat offering, and his drink offering.
39 These *things* you will do unto the LORD in your set feasts, beside your vows, and your freewill offerings, for your burnt offerings, and for your meat offerings, and for your drink offerings, and for your peace offerings.
40 And Moses told the children of Israel according to all that the LORD commanded Moses.

CHAPTER 30

1 And Moses spoke unto the heads of the tribes concerning the children of Israel, saying, this *is* the thing which the LORD has commanded.
2 If a man vow a vow unto the LORD, or swear an oath to bind his soul with a bond; he will not break his word, he will do according to all that proceeded out of his mouth.
3 If a woman also vow a vow unto the LORD, and bind herself by a bond, *being* in her father's house in her youth;
4 And her father hears her vow, and her bond wherewith she has bound her soul, and her father will hold his peace at her: then all her vows will stand, and every bond wherewith she has bound her soul will stand.
5 But if her father disallows her in the day that he hears; not any of her vows, or of her bonds wherewith she has bound her soul, will stand: and the LORD will forgive her, because her father disallowed her.
6 And if she had at all a husband, when she vowed, or uttered ought out of her lips, wherewith she bound her soul;
7 And her husband heard *it,* and held his peace at her in the day that he heard *it*: then her vows will stand, and her bonds wherewith she bound her soul will stand.
8 But if her husband disallowed her on the day that he heard *it*; then he will make her vow which she vowed, and that which she uttered with her lips, wherewith she bound her soul, of none effect: and the LORD will forgive her.
9 But every vow of a widow, and of her that is divorced, wherewith they have bound their souls, will stand against her.
10 And if she vowed in her husband's house, or bound her soul by a bond with an oath;
11 And her husband heard *it*, and held his peace at her, *and* disallowed her not: then all her vows will stand, and every bond wherewith she bound her soul will stand.
12 But if her husband has utterly made them void on the day he heard *them; then* whatsoever proceeded out of her lips concerning her vows, or concerning the bond of her soul, will not stand: her husband has made them void; and the LORD will forgive her.

13 Every vow, and every binding oath to afflict the soul, her husband may establish it, or her husband may make it void.
14 But if her husband altogether hold his peace at her from day to day; then he established all her vows, or all her bonds, which *are* upon her: he confirmed them, because he held his peace at her in the day that he heard *them*.
15 But if he will any ways make them void after that he has heard *them*; then he will bear her iniquity.
16 These *are* the statutes, which the LORD commanded Moses, between a man and his wife, between the father and his daughter, *being yet* in her youth in her father's house.

CHAPTER 31

1 And the LORD spoke unto Moses, saying,
2 Avenge the children of Israel of the Midianites: afterward will you be gathered unto your people.
3 And Moses spoke unto the people, saying, Arm some of yourselves unto the war, and let them go against the Midianites, and avenge the LORD of Midian.
4 Of every tribe a thousand, throughout all the tribes of Israel, will you send to the war.
5 So there were delivered out of the thousands of Israel, a thousand of *every* tribe, twelve thousand armed for war.
6 And Moses sent them to the war, a thousand of *every* tribe, them and Phinehas the son of Eleazar the priest, to the war, with the holy instruments, and the trumpets to blow in his hand.
7 And they warred against the Midianites, as the LORD commanded Moses; and they slew all the males.
8 And they slew the kings of Midian, beside the rest of them that were slain; *namely*, Evi, and Rekem, and Zur, and Hur, and Reba, five kings of Midian: Balaam also the son of Beor they slew with the sword.
9 And the children of Israel took *all* the women of Midian captives, and their little ones, and took the spoil of all their cattle, and all their flocks, and all their goods.
10 And they burnt all their cities wherein they dwelt, and all their goodly castles, with fire.
11 And they took all the spoil, and all the prey, *both* of men and of beasts.
12 And they brought the captives, and the prey, and the spoil, unto Moses, and Eleazar the priest, and unto the congregation of the children of Israel, unto the camp at the plains of Moab, which *are* by Jordan *near* Jericho.
13 And Moses, and Eleazar the priest, and all the princes of the congregation, went forth to meet them without the camp.
14 And Moses was wroth with the officers of the host, *with* the captains over thousands, and captains over hundreds, which came from the battle.
15 And Moses said unto them, have you saved all the women alive?
16 Behold, these caused the children of Israel, through the counsel of Balaam, to commit trespass against the LORD in the matter of Peor, and there was a plague among the congregation of the LORD.
17 Now therefore kill every male among the little ones, and kill every woman that has known man by lying with him.
18 But all the women children, that have not known a man by lying with him, keep alive for yourselves.
19 And do you abide without the camp seven days: whosoever has killed any person, and whosoever has touched any slain, purify *both* yourselves and your captives on the third day, and on the seventh day.
20 And purify all *your* raiment, and all that is made of skins, and all work of goats' *hair*, and all things made of wood.
21 And Eleazar the priest said unto the men of war which went to the battle, this *is* the ordinance of the law which the LORD commanded Moses;
22 Only the gold, and the silver, the brass, the iron, the tin, and the lead,
23 Everything that may abide the fire, you will make *it* go through the fire, and it will be clean: nevertheless it will be purified with the water of separation: and all that **enter** not the fire you will make go through the water.
24 And you will wash your clothes on the seventh day, and you will be clean, and afterward you will come into the camp.
25 And the LORD spoke unto Moses, saying,
26 Take the sum of the prey that was taken, *both* of man and of beast, thou, and Eleazar the priest, and the chief fathers of the congregation:
27 And divide the prey into two parts; between them that took the war upon them, who went out to battle, and between all the congregations:
28 And levy a tribute unto the LORD of the men of war which went out to battle: one soul of five hundred, *both* of the persons, and of the beeves, and of the asses, and of the sheep:
29 Take *it* of their half, and give it unto Eleazar the priest, *for* a heave offering of the LORD.
30 And of the children of Israel's half, you will take one portion of fifty, of the persons, of the beeves, of the asses, and of the flocks, of all manner of beasts, and give them unto the Levites, which keep the charge of the tabernacle of the LORD.
31 And Moses and Eleazar the priest did as the LORD commanded Moses.
32 And the booty, *being* the rest of the prey which the men of war had caught, was six hundred thousand and seventy thousand and five thousand sheep,
33 And threescore and twelve thousand beeves,
34 And threescore and one thousand asses,
35 And thirty and two thousand persons in all, of women that had not known man by lying with him.
36 And the half, *which was* the portion of them that went out to war, was in number three hundred thousand and seven and thirty thousand and five hundred sheep:
37 And the LORD'S tribute of the sheep was six hundred and threescore and fifteen.
38 And the beeves *were* thirty and six thousand; of which the LORD'S tribute *was* threescore and twelve.
39 And the asses *were* thirty thousand and five hundred: of which the LORD'S tribute *was* threescore and one.
40 And the persons *were* sixteen thousand; of which the LORD'S tribute *was* thirty and two persons.
41 And Moses gave the tribute, *which was* the LORD'S heave offering, unto Eleazar the priest, as the LORD commanded Moses.
42 And of the children of Israel's half, which Moses divided from the men that warred,
43 (Now the half *that pertained unto* the congregation was three hundred thousand and thirty thousand *and* seven thousand and five hundred sheep,
44 And thirty and six thousand beeves,
45 And thirty thousand asses and five hundred,

46 And sixteen thousand persons;)
47 Even of the children of Israel's half, Moses took one portion of fifty, *both* of man and of beast, and gave them unto the Levites, which kept the charge of the tabernacle of the LORD; as the LORD commanded Moses.
48 And the officers **who** *were* over thousands of the host, the captains of thousands, and captains of hundreds, came near unto Moses:
49 And they said unto Moses, your servants have taken the sum of the men of war which *are* under our charge, and there lack not one man of us.
50 We have therefore brought an oblation for the LORD, what every man has gotten, of jewels of gold, chains, and bracelets, rings, earrings, and tablets, to make an atonement for our souls before the LORD.
51 And Moses and Eleazar the priest took the gold of them, *even* all wrought jewels.
52 And all the gold of the offering that they offered up to the LORD, of the captains of thousands, and of the captains of hundreds, was sixteen thousand seven hundred and fifty shekels.
53 (*For* the men of war had taken spoil, every man for himself.)
54 And Moses and Eleazar the priest took the gold of the captains of thousands and of hundreds, and brought it into the tabernacle of the congregation, *for* a memorial for the children of Israel before the LORD.

CHAPTER 32

1 Now the children of Reuben and the children of Gad had a very great multitude of cattle: and when they saw the land of Jazer, and the land of Gilead, that, behold, the place *was* a place for cattle;
2 The children of Gad and the children of Reuben came and spoke unto Moses, and to Eleazar the priest, and unto the princes of the congregation, saying,
3 Ataroth, and Dibon, and Jazer, and Nimrah, and Heshbon, and Elealeh, and Shebam, and Nebo, and Beon,
4 *Even* the country which the LORD smote before the congregation of Israel, *is* a land for cattle, and your servants have cattle:
5 Wherefore, said they, if we have found grace in your sight, let this land be given unto your servants for a possession, *and* bring us not over Jordan.
6 And Moses said unto the children of Gad and to the children of Reuben, will your brethren go to war, and will you sit here?
7 And wherefore discourage you the heart of the children of Israel from going over into the land which the LORD has given them?
8 Thus did your fathers, when I sent them from Kadesh-barnea to see the land.
9 For when they went up unto the valley of Eshcol, and saw the land, they discouraged the heart of the children of Israel, that they should not go into the land which the LORD had given them.
10 And the LORD'S anger was kindled the same time, and he swore, saying,
11 Surely none of the men that came up out of Egypt, from twenty years old and upward, will see the land which I swore unto Abraham, unto Isaac, and unto Jacob; because they have not wholly followed me:
12 Save Caleb the son of Jephunneh the Kenezite, and Joshua the son of Nun: for they have wholly followed the LORD.
13 And the LORD'S anger was kindled against Israel, and he made them wander in the wilderness forty years, until all the generation, that had done evil in the sight of the LORD, was consumed.
14 And, behold, you are risen up in your fathers' stead, an increase of sinful men, to augment yet the fierce anger of the LORD toward Israel.
15 For if you turn away from after him, he will yet again leave them in the wilderness; and you will destroy this **entire** people.
16 And they came near unto him, and said, we will build sheepfolds here for our cattle, and cities for our little ones:
17 But we ourselves will go ready armed before the children of Israel, until we have brought them unto their place: and our little ones will dwell in the fenced cities because of the inhabitants of the land.
18 We will not return unto our houses, until the children of Israel have inherited every man his inheritance.
19 For we will not inherit with them on yonder side Jordan, or forward; because our inheritance is fallen to us on this side Jordan eastward.
20 And Moses said unto them, If you will do this thing, if you will go armed before the LORD to war,
21 And will go all of you armed over Jordan before the LORD, until he has driven out his enemies from before him,
22 And the land is subdued before the LORD: then afterward you will return, and be guiltless before the LORD, and before Israel; and this land will be your possession before the LORD.
23 But if you will not do so, behold, you have sinned against the LORD: and be sure your sin will find you out.
24 Build you cities for your little ones, and folds for your sheep; and do that which has proceeded out of your mouth.
25 And the children of Gad and the children of Reuben spoke unto Moses, saying, your servants will do as my lord commanded.
26 Our little ones, our wives, our flocks, and all our cattle, will be there in the cities of Gilead:
27 But your servants will pass over, every man armed for war, before the LORD to battle, as my lord said.
28 So concerning them Moses commanded Eleazar the priest, and Joshua the son of Nun, and the chief fathers of the tribes of the children of Israel:
29 And Moses said unto them, if the children of Gad and the children of Reuben will pass with you over Jordan, every man armed to battle, before the LORD, and the land will be subdued before you; then you will give them the land of Gilead for a possession:
30 But if they will not pass over with you armed, they will have possessions among you in the land of Canaan.
31 And the children of Gad and the children of Reuben answered, saying, As the LORD has said unto your servants, so will we do.
32 We will pass over armed before the LORD into the land of Canaan, that the possession of our inheritance on this side Jordan *may be* ours.
33 And Moses gave unto them, *even* to the children of Gad, and to the children of Reuben, and unto half the tribe of Manasseh the son of Joseph, the kingdom of Sihon king of the Amorites, and the kingdom of Og king of Bashan, the land, with the cities thereof in the coasts, *even* the cities of the country round about.
34 And the children of Gad built Dibon, and Ataroth, and Aroer,
35 And Atroth, Shophan, and Jaazer, and Jogbehah,
36 And Beth-nimrah, and Beth-haran, fenced cities: and folds for sheep.
37 And the children of Reuben built Heshbon, and Elealeh, and Kirjathaim,

38 And Nebo, and Baal-meon, (their names being changed,) and Shibmah: and gave other names unto the cities which they built.
39 And the children of Machir the son of Manasseh went to Gilead, and took it, and dispossessed the Amorite which *was* in it.
40 And Moses gave Gilead unto Machir the son of Manasseh; and he dwelt therein.
41 And Jair the son of Manasseh went and took the small towns thereof, and called them Havoth-jair.
42 And Nobah went and took Kenath, and the villages thereof, and called it Nobah, after his own name.

CHAPTER 33

1 These *are* the journeys of the children of Israel, which went forth out of the land of Egypt with their armies under the hand of Moses and Aaron.
2 And Moses wrote their goings out according to their journeys by the commandment of the LORD: and these *are* their journeys according to their goings out.
3 And they departed from Rameses in the first month, on the fifteenth day of the first month; on the morrow after the Passover the children of Israel went out with a high hand in the sight of all the Egyptians.
4 For the Egyptians buried all *their* firstborn, **whom** the LORD had smitten among them: upon their gods also the LORD executed judgments.
5 And the children of Israel removed from Rameses, and pitched in Succoth.
6 And they departed from Succoth, and pitched in Etham, which *is* in the edge of the wilderness.
7 And they removed from Etham, and turned again unto Pi-hahiroth, which *is* before Baal-zephon: and they pitched before Migdol.
8 And they departed from before Pi-hahiroth, and passed through the midst of the sea into the wilderness, and went three days' journey in the wilderness of Etham, and pitched in Marah.
9 And they removed from Marah, and came unto Elim: and in Elim *were* twelve fountains of water, and threescore and ten palm trees; and they pitched there.
10 And they removed from Elim, and encamped by the Red sea.
11 And they removed from the Red sea, and encamped in the wilderness of Sin.
12 And they took their journey out of the wilderness of Sin, and encamped in Dophkah.
13 And they departed from Dophkah, and encamped in Alush.
14 And they removed from Alush, and encamped at Rephidim, where was no water for the people to drink.
15 And they departed from Rephidim, and pitched in the wilderness of Sinai.
16 And they removed from the desert of Sinai, and pitched at Kibroth-hattaavah.
17 And they departed from Kibroth-hattaavah, and encamped at Hazeroth.
18 And they departed from Hazeroth, and pitched in Rithmah.
19 And they departed from Rithmah, and pitched at Rimmon-parez.
20 And they departed from Rimmon-parez, and pitched in Libnah.
21 And they removed from Libnah, and pitched at Rissah.
22 And they journeyed from Rissah, and pitched in Kehelathah.
23 And they went from Kehelathah, and pitched in mount Shapher.
24 And they removed from mount Shapher, and encamped in Haradah.
25 And they removed from Haradah, and pitched in Makheloth.
26 And they removed from Makheloth, and encamped at Tahath.
27 And they departed from Tahath, and pitched at Tarah.
28 And they removed from Tarah, and pitched in Mithcah.
29 And they went from Mithcah, and pitched in Hashmonah.
30 And they departed from Hashmonah, and encamped at Moseroth.
31 And they departed from Moseroth, and pitched in Bene-jaakan.
32 And they removed from Bene-jaakan, and encamped at Hor-hagidgad.
33 And they went from Hor-hagidgad, and pitched in Jotbathah.
34 And they removed from Jotbathah, and encamped at Ebronah.
35 And they departed from Ebronah, and encamped at Ezion-gaber.
36 And they removed from Ezion-gaber, and pitched in the wilderness of Zin, which *is* Kadesh.
37 And they removed from Kadesh, and pitched in mount Hor, in the edge of the land of Edom.
38 And Aaron the priest went up into mount Hor at the commandment of the LORD, and died there, in the fortieth year after the children of Israel **had** come out of the land of Egypt, in the first *day* of the fifth month.
39 And Aaron *was* an hundred and twenty and three years old when he died in mount Hor.
40 And king Arad the Canaanite, which dwelt in the south in the land of Canaan, heard of the coming of the children of Israel.
41 And they departed from mount Hor, and pitched in Zalmonah.
42 And they departed from Zalmonah, and pitched in Punon.
43 And they departed from Punon, and pitched in Oboth.
44 And they departed from Oboth, and pitched in Ije-abarim, in the border of Moab.
45 And they departed from Iim, and pitched in Dibon-gad.
46 And they removed from Dibon-gad, and encamped in Almon-diblathaim.
47 And they removed from Almon-diblathaim, and pitched in the mountains of Abarim, before Nebo.
48 And they departed from the mountains of Abarim, and pitched in the plains of Moab by Jordan *near* Jericho.
49 And they pitched by Jordan, from Beth-jesimoth *even* unto Abel-shittim in the plains of Moab.
50 And the LORD spoke unto Moses in the plains of Moab by Jordan *near* Jericho, saying,
51 Speak unto the children of Israel, and say unto them, when you are passed over Jordan into the land of Canaan;
52 Then you will drive out all the inhabitants of the land from before you, and destroy all their pictures, and destroy all their molten images, and quite pluck down all their high places:
53 And you will dispossess *the inhabitants* of the land, and dwell therein: for I have given you the land to possess it.
54 And you will divide the land by lot for an inheritance among your families: *and* to the more you will give the more inheritance, and to the fewer you will give the less inheritance: every man's *inheritance* will be in the place where his lot fell; according to the tribes of your fathers you will inherit.
55 But if you will not drive out the inhabitants of the land from before you; then it will come to pass, that those which you let remain of them will *be* pricks in your eyes, and thorns in your sides, and will vex you in the land wherein you dwell.

56 Moreover it will come to pass, *that* I will do unto you, as I thought to do unto them.

CHAPTER 34

1 And the LORD spoke unto Moses, saying,
2 Command the children of Israel, and say unto them, when you come into the land of Canaan; (this *is* the land that will fall unto you for an inheritance, *even* the land of Canaan with the coasts thereof:)
3 Then your south quarter will be from the wilderness of Zin along by the coast of Edom, and your south border will be the outmost coast of the salt sea eastward:
4 And your border will turn from the south to the ascent of Akrabbim, and pass on to Zin: and the going forth thereof will be from the south to Kadesh-barnea, and will go on to Hazar-addar, and pass on to Azmon:
5 And the border will fetch a compass from Azmon unto the river of Egypt, and the goings out of it will be at the sea.
6 And *as for* the western border, you will even have the great sea for a border: this will be your west border.
7 And this will be your north border: from the great sea you will point out for you mount Hor:
8 From mount Hor you will point out *your border* unto the entrance of Hamath; and the goings forth of the border will be to Zedad:
9 And the border will go on to Ziphron, and the goings out of it will be at Hazar-enan: this will be your north border.
10 And you will point out your east border from Hazar-enan to Shepham:
11 And the coast will go down from Shepham to Riblah, on the east side of Ain; and the border will descend, and will reach unto the side of the sea of Chinnereth eastward:
12 And the border will go down to Jordan, and the goings out of it will be at the salt sea: this will be your land with the coasts thereof round about.
13 And Moses commanded the children of Israel, saying, this *is* the land which you will inherit by lot, which the LORD commanded to give unto the nine tribes, and to the half tribe:
14 For the tribe of the children of Reuben according to the house of their fathers, and the tribe of the children of Gad according to the house of their fathers, have received *their inheritance*; and half the tribe of Manasseh has received their inheritance:
15 The two tribes and the half tribe have received their inheritance on this side Jordan *near* Jericho eastward, toward the sun rising.
16 And the LORD spoke unto Moses, saying,
17 These *are* the names of the men which will divide the land unto you: Eleazar the priest, and Joshua the son of Nun.
18 And you will take one prince of every tribe, to divide the land by inheritance.
19 And the names of the men *are* these: Of the tribe of Judah, Caleb the son of Jephunneh.
20 And of the tribe of the children of Simeon, Shemuel the son of Ammihud.
21 Of the tribe of Benjamin, Elidad the son of Chislon.
22 And the prince of the tribe of the children of Dan, Bukki the son of Jogli.
23 The prince of the children of Joseph, for the tribe of the children of Manasseh, Hanniel the son of Ephod.
24 And the prince of the tribe of the children of Ephraim, Kemuel the son of Shiphtan.
25 And the prince of the tribe of the children of Zebulun, Elizaphan the son of Parnach.
26 And the prince of the tribe of the children of Issachar, Paltiel the son of Azzan.
27 And the prince of the tribe of the children of Asher, Ahihud the son of Shelomi.
28 And the prince of the tribe of the children of Naphtali, Pedahel the son of Ammihud.
29 These *are they* whom the LORD commanded to divide the inheritance unto the children of Israel in the land of Canaan.

CHAPTER 35

1 And the LORD spoke unto Moses in the plains of Moab by Jordan *near* Jericho, saying,
2 Command the children of Israel, that they give unto the Levites of the inheritance of their possession cities to dwell in; and you will give *also* unto the Levites suburbs for the cities round about them.
3 And the cities will they have to dwell in; and the suburbs of them will be for their cattle, and for their goods, and for all their beasts.
4 And the suburbs of the cities, which you will give unto the Levites, will *reach* from the wall of the city and outward a thousand cubits round about.
5 And you will measure from without the city on the east side two thousand cubits, and on the south side two thousand cubits, and on the west side two thousand cubits, and on the north side two thousand cubits; and the city will *be* in the midst: this will be to them the suburbs of the cities.
6 And among the cities which you will give unto the Levites *there will be* six cities for refuge, which you will appoint for the manslayer, that he may flee thither: and to them you will add forty and two cities.
7 *So* all the cities which you will give to the Levites will *be* forty and eight cities: them will you *give* with their suburbs.
8 And the cities which you will give will *be* of the possession of the children of Israel: from *them that have* many you will give many; but from *them that have* few you will give few: everyone will give of his cities unto the Levites according to his inheritance which he inherited.
9 And the LORD spoke unto Moses, saying,
10 Speak unto the children of Israel, and say unto them, when you **go** over Jordan into the land of Canaan;
11 Then you will appoint you cities to be cities of refuge for you; that the slayer may flee thither, which kills any person at unawares.
12 And they will be unto you cities for refuge from the avenger; that the manslayer die not, until he stand before the congregation in judgment.
13 And of these cities which you will give six cities will you have for refuge.
14 you will give three cities on this side Jordan, and three cities will you give in the land of Canaan, *which* will be cities of refuge.
15 These six cities will be a refuge, *both* for the children of Israel, and for the stranger, and for the sojourner among them: that every one that kills any person unawares may flee thither.
16 And if he **strikes** him with an instrument of iron, so that he dies, he *is* a murderer: the murderer will surely be put to death.
17 And if he **strikes** him with throwing a stone, wherewith he may die, and he dies, he *is* a murderer: the murderer will surely be put to death.

18 Or *if* he **strikes** him with a hand weapon of wood, wherewith he may die, and he dies, he *is* a murderer: the murderer will surely be put to death.

19 The revenger of blood himself will slay the murderer: when he meets him, he will slay him.

20 But if he thrust him of hatred, or hurl at him by laying of wait, that he die;

21 Or in enmity smite him with his hand, that he dies: he that smote *him* will surely be put to death; *for* he *is* a murderer: the revenger of blood will slay the murderer, when he meets him.

22 But if he thrust him suddenly without enmity, or have cast upon him anything without laying of wait,

23 Or with any stone, wherewith a man may die, seeing *him* not, and cast *it* upon him, that he die, and *was* not his enemy, neither sought his harm:

24 Then the congregation will judge between the slayer and the revenger of blood according to these judgments:

25 And the congregation will deliver the slayer out of the hand of the revenger of blood, and the congregation will restore him to the city of his refuge, where he was fled: and he will abide in it unto the death of the high priest, which was anointed with the holy oil.

26 But if the slayer will at any time come without the border of the city of his refuge, where he was fled;

27 And the revenger of blood finds him without the borders of the city of his refuge, and the revenger of blood kill the slayer; he will not be guilty of blood:

28 Because he should have remained in the city of his refuge until the death of the high priest: but after the death of the high priest the slayer will return into the land of his possession.

29 So these *things* will be for a statute of judgment unto you throughout your generations in all your dwellings.

30 Whoso kills any person, the murderer will be put to death by the mouth of witnesses: but one witness will not testify against any person *to cause him* to die.

31 Moreover you will take no satisfaction for the life of a murderer, which *is* guilty of death: but he will be surely put to death.

32 And you will take no satisfaction for him that is fled to the city of his refuge, that he should come again to dwell in the land, until the death of the priest.

33 So you will not pollute the land wherein you *are*: for blood it defiles the land: and the land cannot be cleansed of the blood that is shed therein, but by the blood of him that shed it.

34 Defile not therefore the land which you will inhabit, wherein I dwell: for I the LORD dwell among the children of Israel.

CHAPTER 36

1 And the chief fathers of the families of the children of Gilead, the son of Machir, the son of Manasseh, of the families of the sons of Joseph, came near, and spoke before Moses, and before the princes, the chief fathers of the children of Israel:

2 And they said, The LORD commanded my lord to give the land for an inheritance by lot to the children of Israel: and my lord was commanded by the LORD to give the inheritance of Zelophehad our brother unto his daughters.

3 And if they be married to any of the sons of the *other* tribes of the children of Israel, then will their inheritance be taken from the inheritance of our fathers, and will be put to the inheritance of the tribe whereunto they are received: so will it be taken from the lot of our inheritance.

4 And when the jubilee of the children of Israel will be, then will their inheritance be put unto the inheritance of the tribe whereunto they are received: so will their inheritance be taken away from the inheritance of the tribe of our fathers.

5 And Moses commanded the children of Israel according to the word of the LORD, saying, the tribe of the sons of Joseph has said well.

6 This *is* the thing which the LORD does command concerning the daughters of Zelophehad, saying, Let them marry to whom they think best; only to the family of the tribe of their father will they marry.

7 So will not the inheritance of the children of Israel remove from tribe to tribe: for every one of the children of Israel will keep himself to the inheritance of the tribe of his fathers.

8 And every daughter, that possesses an inheritance in any tribe of the children of Israel, will be wife unto one of the family of the tribe of her father, that the children of Israel may enjoy every man the inheritance of his fathers.

9 Neither will the inheritance remove from *one* tribe to another tribe; but every one of the tribes of the children of Israel will keep himself to his own inheritance.

10 Even as the LORD commanded Moses, so did the daughters of Zelophehad:

11 For Mahlah, Tirzah, and Hoglah, and Milcah, and Noah, the daughters of Zelophehad, were married unto their father's brothers' sons:

12 *And* they were married into the families of the sons of Manasseh the son of Joseph, and their inheritance remained in the tribe of the family of their father.

13 These *are* the commandments and the judgments, which the LORD commanded by the hand of Moses unto the children of Israel in the plains of Moab by Jordan *near* Jericho.

DEUTERONOMY

CHAPTER 1

1 These *are* the words which Moses spoke unto all Israel on this side Jordan in the wilderness, in the plain over against the Red *sea*, between Paran, and Tophel, and Laban, and Hazeroth, and Dizahab.

2 (*There are* eleven days' *journey* from Horeb by the way of mount Seir unto Kadesh-barnea.)

3 And it came to pass in the fortieth year, in the eleventh month, on the first *day* of the month, *that* Moses spoke unto the children of Israel, according unto all that the LORD had given him in commandment unto them;

4 After he had slain Sihon the king of the Amorites, which dwelt in Heshbon, and Og the king of Bashan, which dwelt at Astaroth in Edrei:

5 On this side Jordan, in the land of Moab, began Moses to declare this law, saying,

6 The LORD our God spoke unto us in Horeb, saying, you have dwelt long enough in this mount:

7 Turn you, and take your journey, and go to the mount of the Amorites, and unto all *the places* nigh thereunto, in the plain, in the hills, and in the vale, and in the south, and by the sea side, to the land of the Canaanites, and unto Lebanon, unto the great river, the river Euphrates.

8 Behold, I have set the land before you: go in and possess the land which the LORD swore unto your fathers, Abraham, Isaac, and Jacob, to give unto them and to their seed after them.

9 And I spoke unto you at that time, saying, I am not able to bear you myself alone:

10 The LORD your God has multiplied you, and, behold, you *are* this day as the stars of heaven for multitude.

11 (The LORD God of your fathers make you a thousand times so many more as you *are*, and bless you, as he has promised you!)

12 How can I myself alone bear your cumbrance, and your burden, and your strife?

13 Take you wise men, and understanding, and known among your tribes, and I will make them rulers over you.

14 And you answered me, and said, the thing which you have spoken *is* good *for us* to do.

15 So I took the chief of your tribes, wise men, and known, and made them heads over you, captains over thousands, and captains over hundreds, and captains over fifties, and captains over tens, and officers among your tribes.

16 And I charged your judges at that time, saying, hear *the causes* between your brethren, and judge righteously between *every* man and his brother, and the stranger *that is* with him.

17 you will not respect persons in judgment; *but* you will hear the small as well as the great; you will not be afraid of the face of man; for the judgment *is* God's: and the cause that is too hard for you, bring *it* unto me, and I will hear it.

18 And I commanded you at that time all the things which you should do.

19 And when we departed from Horeb, we went through all that great and terrible wilderness, which you saw by the way of the mountain of the Amorites, as the LORD our God commanded us; and we came to Kadesh-barnea.

20 And I said unto you, you are come unto the mountain of the Amorites, which the LORD our God does give unto us.

21 Behold, the LORD your God has set the land before you: go up *and* possess *it*, as the LORD God of your fathers has said unto you; fear not, neither be discouraged.

22 And you came near unto me every one of you, and said, We will send men before us, and they will search us out the land, and bring us word again by what way we must go up, and into what cities we will come.

23 And the saying pleased me well: and I took twelve men of you, one of a tribe:

24 And they turned and went up into the mountain, and came unto the valley of Eshcol, and searched it out.

25 And they took of the fruit of the land in their hands, and brought *it* down unto us, and brought us word again, and said, *it is* a good land which the LORD our God does give us.

26 Notwithstanding you would not go up, but rebelled against the commandment of the LORD your God:

27 And you murmured in your tents, and said, because the LORD hated us, he has brought us forth out of the land of Egypt, to deliver us into the hand of the Amorites, to destroy us.

28 Whither will we go up? Our brethren have discouraged our heart, saying, the people *is* greater and taller than we; the cities *are* great and walled up to heaven; and moreover we have seen the sons of the Anakims there.

29 Then I said unto you, Dread not, neither be afraid of them.

30 The LORD your God which goes before you, he will fight for you, according to all that he did for you in Egypt before your eyes;

31 And in the wilderness, where you have seen how that the LORD your God bare you, as a man does bear his son, in all the way that you went, until you came into this place.

32 Yet in this thing you did not believe the LORD your God,

33 Who went in the way before you, to search you out a place to pitch your tents *in*, in fire by night, to show you by what way you should go, and in a cloud by day.

34 And the LORD heard the voice of your words, and was angered, and swore, saying,

35 Surely there will not one of these men of this evil generation see that good land, which I swore to give unto your fathers,

36 Save Caleb the son of Jephunneh; he will see it, and to him will I give the land that he has trodden upon, and to his children, because he has wholly followed the LORD.

37 Also the LORD was angry with me for your sakes, saying, you also will not go in thither.

38 *But* Joshua the son of Nun, which stands before you, he will go in thither: encourage him: for he will cause Israel to inherit it.

39 Moreover your little ones, which you said should be a prey, and your children, which in that day had no knowledge between good and evil, they will go in thither, and unto them will I give it, and they will possess it.

40 But *as for* you, turn you, and take your journey into the wilderness by the way of the Red sea.

41 Then you answered and said unto me, we have sinned against the LORD, we will go up and fight, according to all that the LORD our God commanded us. And when you had girded on every man his weapons of war, you were ready to go up into the hill.

42 And the LORD said unto me, Say unto them, Go not up, neither fight; for I *am* not among you; lest you be smitten before your enemies.

43 So I spoke unto you; and you would not hear, but rebelled against the commandment of the LORD, and went presumptuously up into the hill.

44 And the Amorites, which dwelt in that mountain, came out against you, and chased you, as bees do, and destroyed you in Seir, *even* unto Hormah.
45 And you returned and wept before the LORD; but the LORD would not hearken to your voice, nor give ear unto you.
46 So you abide in Kadesh many days, according unto the days that you abide *there*.

CHAPTER 2

1 Then we turned, and took our journey into the wilderness by the way of the Red sea, as the LORD spoke unto me: and we compassed mount Seir many days.
2 And the LORD spoke unto me, saying,
3 you have compassed this mountain long enough: turn you northward.
4 And command you the people, saying, you *are* to pass through the coast of your brethren the children of Esau, which dwell in Seir; and they will be afraid of you: take you good heed unto yourselves therefore:
5 Meddle not with them; for I will not give you of their land, no, not as much as a foot breadth; because I have given mount Seir unto Esau *for* a possession.
6 you will buy meat of them for money, that you may eat; and you will also buy water of them for money, that you may drink.
7 For the LORD your God has blessed you in all the works of your hand: he knows you're walking through this great wilderness: these forty years the LORD your God has *been* with you; you have lacked nothing.
8 And when we passed by from our brethren the children of Esau, which dwelt in Seir, through the way of the plain from Elath, and from Ezion-gaber, we turned and passed by the way of the wilderness of Moab.
9 And the LORD said unto me, Distress not the Moabites, neither contends with them in battle: for I will not give you of their land *for* a possession; because I have given Ar unto the children of Lot *for* a possession.
10 The Emims dwelt therein in times past, a people great, and many, and tall, as the Anakims;
11 Which also were accounted giants, as the Anakims; but the Moabites call them Emims.
12 The Horims also dwelt in Seir beforetime; but the children of Esau succeeded them, when they had destroyed them from before them, and dwelt in their stead; as Israel did unto the land of his possession, which the LORD gave unto them.
13 Now rise up, *said I*, and get you over the brook Zered. And we went over the brook Zered.
14 And the space in which we came from Kadesh-barnea, until we were come over the brook Zered, *was* thirty and eight years; until all the generation of the men of war were wasted out from among the host, as the LORD swore unto them.
15 For indeed the hand of the LORD were against them, to destroy them from among the host, until they were consumed.
16 So it came to pass, when all the men of war were consumed and dead from among the people,
17 That the LORD spoke unto me, saying,
18 you are to pass over through Ar, the coast of Moab, this day:
19 And *when* you comest nigh over against the children of Ammon, distress them not, nor meddle with them: for I will not give you of the land of the children of Ammon *any* possession; because I have given it unto the children of Lot *for* a possession.
20 (That also was accounted a land of giants: giants dwelt therein in old time; and the Ammonites call them Zamzummims;
21 A people great, and many, and tall, as the Anakims; but the LORD destroyed them before them; and they succeeded them, and dwelt in their stead:
22 As he did to the children of Esau, which dwelt in Seir, when he destroyed the Horims from before them; and they succeeded them, and dwelt in their stead even unto this day:
23 And the Avims which dwelt in Hazerim, *even* unto Azzah, the Caphtorims, which came forth out of Caphtor, destroyed them, and dwelt in their stead.)
24 Rise you up, take your journey, and pass over the river Arnon: behold, I have given into your hand Sihon the Amorite, king of Heshbon, and his land: begin to possess *it*, and contend with him in battle.
25 This day will I begin to put the dread of you and the fear of you upon the nations *that are* under the whole heaven, who will hear report of you, and will tremble, and be in anguish because of you.
26 And I sent messengers out of the wilderness of Kedemoth unto Sihon king of Heshbon with words of peace, saying,
27 Let me pass through your land: I will go along by the high way, I will neither turn unto the right hand nor to the left.
28 you will sell me meat for money, that I may eat; and give me water for money, that I may drink: only I will pass through on my feet;
29 (As the children of Esau which dwell in Seir, and the Moabites which dwell in Ar, did unto me;) until I will pass over Jordan into the land which the LORD our God giveth us.
30 But Sihon king of Heshbon would not let us pass by him: for the LORD your God hardened his spirit, and made his heart obstinate, that he might deliver him into your hand, as *appeared* this day.
31 And the LORD said unto me, Behold, I have begun to give Sihon and his land before you: begin to possess, that you may inherit his land.
32 Then Sihon came out against us, him and all his people, to fight at Jahaz.
33 And the LORD our God delivered him before us; and we smote him, and his sons, and all his people.
34 And we took all his cities at that time, and utterly destroyed the men, and the women, and the little ones, of every city, we left none to remain:
35 Only the cattle we took for a prey unto ourselves, and the spoil of the cities which we took.
36 From Aroer, which *is* by the brink of the river of Arnon, and *from* the city that *is* by the river, even unto Gilead, there was not one city too strong for us: the LORD our God delivered all unto us:
37 Only unto the land of the children of Ammon you came not, *nor* unto any place of the river Jabbok, nor unto the cities in the mountains, nor unto whatsoever the LORD our God forbids us.

CHAPTER 3

1 Then we turned, and went up the way to Bashan: and Og the king of Bashan came out against us, him and all his people, to battle at Edrei.
2 And the LORD said unto me, Fear him not: for I will deliver him, and all his people, and his land, into your hand; and you will do unto him as you didst unto Sihon king of the Amorites, which dwelt at Heshbon.

Deuteronomy

3 So the LORD our God delivered into our hands Og also, the king of Bashan, and all his people: and we smote him until none was left to him remaining.
4 And we took all his cities at that time, there was not a city which we took not from them, threescore cities, all the region of Argob, the kingdom of Og in Bashan.
5 All these cities *were* fenced with high walls, gates, and bars; beside unwalled towns a great many.
6 And we utterly destroyed them, as we did unto Sihon king of Heshbon, utterly destroying the men, women, and children, of every city.
7 But all the cattle, and the spoil of the cities, we took for a prey to ourselves.
8 And we took at that time out of the hand of the two kings of the Amorites the land that *was* on this side Jordan, from the river of Arnon unto Mount Hermon;
9 (*Which* Hermon the Sidonians call Sirion; and the Amorites call it Shenir;)
10 All the cities of the plain, and all Gilead, and all Bashan, unto Salchah and Edrei, cities of the kingdom of Og in Bashan.
11 For only Og king of Bashan remained of the remnant of giants; behold, his bedstead *was* a bedstead of iron; *is* it not in Rabbath of the children of Ammon? Nine cubits *was* the length thereof, and four cubits the breadth of it, after the cubit of a man.
12 And this land, *which* we possessed at that time, from Aroer, which *is* by the river Arnon, and half mount Gilead, and the cities thereof, gave I unto the Reubenites and to the Gadites.
13 And the rest of Gilead, and all Bashan, *being* the kingdom of Og, gave I unto the half tribe of Manasseh; all the region of Argob, with all Bashan, which was called the land of giants.
14 Jair the son of Manasseh took all the country of Argob unto the coasts of Geshuri and Maachathi; and called them after his own name, Bashan-havoth-jair, unto this day.
15 And I gave Gilead unto Machir.
16 And unto the Reubenites and unto the Gadites I gave from Gilead even unto the river Arnon half the valley, and the border even unto the river Jabbok, *which is* the border of the children of Ammon;
17 The plain also, and Jordan, and the coast *thereof*, from Chinnereth even unto the sea of the plain, *even* the salt sea, under Ashdoth-pisgah eastward.
18 And I commanded you at that time, saying, The LORD your God has given you this land to possess it: you will pass over armed before your brethren the children of Israel, all *that are* meet for the war.
19 But your wives, and your little ones, and your cattle, (*for* I know that you have many cattle,) will abide in your cities which I have given you;
20 Until the LORD has given rest unto your brethren, as well as unto you, and *until* they also possess the land which the LORD your God has given them beyond Jordan: and *then* will you return every man unto his possession, which I have given you.
21 And I commanded Joshua at that time, saying, your eyes have seen all that the LORD your God has done unto these two kings: so will the LORD do unto all the kingdoms whither you pass.
22 you will not fear them: for the LORD your God he will fight for you.
23 And I besought the LORD at that time, saying,
24 O Lord GOD, you have begun to show your servant your greatness, and your mighty hand: for what God *is there* in heaven or in earth, that can do according to your works, and according to your might?
25 I pray you, let me go over, and see the good land that *is* beyond Jordan, that goodly mountain, and Lebanon.
26 But the LORD was wroth with me for your sakes, and would not hear me: and the LORD said unto me, Let it suffice you; speak no more unto me of this matter.
27 Get you up into the top of Pisgah, and lift up your eyes westward, and northward, and southward, and eastward, and behold *it* with your eyes: for you will not go over this Jordan.
28 But charge Joshua, and encourage him, and strengthen him: for he will go over before this people, and he will cause them to inherit the land which you will see.
29 So we abode in the valley over against Beth-peor.

CHAPTER 4

1 Now therefore hearken, O Israel, unto the statutes and unto the judgments, which I teach you, for to do *them*, that you may live, and go in and possess the land which the LORD God of your fathers gives you.
2 you will not add unto the word which I command you, neither will you diminish *ought* from it, that you may keep the commandments of the LORD your God which I command you.
3 Your eyes have seen what the LORD did because of Baal-peor: for all the men that followed Baal-peor, the LORD your God has destroyed them from among you.
4 But you that did cleave unto the LORD your God *are* alive every one of you this day.
5 Behold, I have taught you statutes and judgments, even as the LORD my God commanded me, that you should do so in the land whither you go to possess it.
6 Keep therefore and do *them*; for this *is* your wisdom and your understanding in the sight of the nations, which will hear all these statutes, and say, surely this great nation *is* a wise and understanding people.
7 For what nation *is there so* great, who has God *so* nigh unto them, as the LORD our God *is* in all *things that* we call upon him *for*?
8 And what nation *is there so* great, that have statutes and judgments *as* righteous as all this law, which I set before you this day?
9 Only take heed to thyself, and keep your soul diligently lest you forget the things which your eyes have seen, and lest they depart from your heart all the days of your life: but teach them your sons, and your sons' sons;
10 *Specially* the day that you stood before the LORD your God in Horeb, when the LORD said unto me, gather me the people together, and I will make them hear my words, that they may learn to fear me all the days that they will live upon the earth, and *that* they may teach their children.
11 And you came near and stood under the mountain, and the mountain burned with fire unto the midst of heaven, with darkness, clouds, and thick darkness.
12 And the LORD spoke unto you out of the midst of the fire: you heard the voice of the words, but saw no similitude; only you *heard* a voice.
13 And he declared unto you his covenant, which he commanded you to perform, *even* Ten Commandments; and he wrote them upon two tables of stone.

14 And the LORD commanded me at that time to teach you statutes and judgments, that you might do them in the land whither you go over to possess it.
15 Take you therefore good heed unto yourselves; for you saw no manner of similitude on the day *that* the LORD spoke unto you in Horeb out of the midst of the fire:
16 Lest you corrupt *yourselves*, and make you a graven image, the similitude of any figure, the likeness of male or female,
17 The likeness of any beast that *is* on the earth, the likeness of any winged fowl that flies in the air,
18 The likeness of anything that creeps on the ground, the likeness of any fish that *is* in the waters beneath the earth:
19 And lest you lift up your eyes unto heaven, and when you see the sun, and the moon, and the stars, *even* all the host of heaven, should be driven to worship them, and serve them, which the LORD your God has divided unto all nations under the whole heaven.
20 But the LORD has taken you, and brought you forth out of the iron furnace, *even* out of Egypt, to be unto him a people of inheritance, as you *are* this day.
21 Furthermore the LORD was angry with me for your sakes, and swore that I should not go over Jordan, and that I should not go in unto that good land, which the LORD your God gives you *for* an inheritance:
22 But I must die in this land, I must not go over Jordan: but you will go over, and possess that good land.
23 Take heed unto yourselves, lest you forget the covenant of the LORD your God, which he made with you, and make you a graven image, *or* the likeness of any*thing*, which the LORD your God has forbidden you.
24 For the LORD your God *is* a consuming fire, *even* a jealous God.
25 When you will beget children, and children's children, and you will have remained long in the land, and will corrupt *yourselves*, and make a graven image, *or* the likeness of any*thing*, and will do evil in the sight of the LORD your God, to provoke him to anger:
26 I call heaven and earth to witness against you this day, that you will soon utterly perish from off the land whereunto you go over Jordan to possess it; you will not prolong *your* days upon it, but will utterly be destroyed.
27 And the LORD will scatter you among the nations, and you will be left few in number among the heathen, whither the LORD will lead you.
28 And there you will serve gods, the work of men's hands, wood and stone, which neither see, nor hear, nor eat, nor smell.
29 But if from thence you will seek the LORD your God, you will find *him*, if you seek him with all your heart and with all your soul.
30 When you are in tribulation, and all these things are come upon you, *even* in the latter days, if you turn to the LORD your God, and will be obedient unto his voice;
31 (For the LORD your God *is* a merciful God;) he will not forsake you, neither destroy you, or forget the covenant of your fathers which he swore unto them.
32 For ask now of the days that are past, which were before you, since the day that God created man upon the earth, and *ask* from the one side of heaven unto the other, whether there has been *any such thing* as this great thing *is*, or has been heard like it?
33 Did *ever* people hear the voice of God speaking out of the midst of the fire, as you have heard, and live?
34 Or has God assayed to go *and* take him a nation from the midst of *another* nation, by temptations, by signs, and by wonders, and by war, and by a mighty hand, and by a stretched out arm, and by great terrors, according to all that the LORD your God did for you in Egypt before your eyes?
35 Unto you it was showed, that you might know that the LORD he *is* God; *there is* none else beside him.
36 Out of heaven he made you to hear his voice, that he might instruct you: and upon earth he showed you his great fire; and you heard his words out of the midst of the fire.
37 And because he loved your fathers, therefore he chose their seed after them, and brought you out in his sight with his mighty power out of Egypt;
38 To drive out nations from before you greater and mightier than you *art*, to bring you in, to give you their land *for* an inheritance, as *it is* this day.
39 Know therefore this day, and consider *it* in your heart, that the LORD he *is* God in heaven above, and upon the earth beneath: *there is* none else.
40 you will keep therefore his statutes, and his commandments, which I command you this day, that it may go well with you, and with your children after you, and that you may prolong your days upon the earth, which the LORD your God gives you, forever.
41 Then Moses severed three cities on this side Jordan toward the sun rising;
42 That the slayer might flee thither, which should kill his neighbor unawares, and hated him not in times past; and that fleeing unto one of these cities he might live:
43 *Namely*, Bezer in the wilderness, in the plain country, of the Reubenites; and Ramoth in Gilead, of the Gadites; and Golan in Bashan, of the Manassites.
44 And this *is* the law which Moses set before the children of Israel:
45 These *are* the testimonies, and the statutes, and the judgments, which Moses spoke unto the children of Israel, after they came forth out of Egypt,
46 On this side Jordan, in the valley over against Beth-peor, in the land of Sihon king of the Amorites, who dwelt at Heshbon, whom Moses and the children of Israel smote, after they were come forth out of Egypt:
47 And they possessed his land, and the land of Og king of Bashan, two kings of the Amorites, which *were* on this side Jordan toward the sun rising;
48 From Aroer, which *is* by the bank of the river Arnon, even unto mount Sion, which *is* Hermon,
49 And all the plain on this side Jordan eastward, even unto the sea of the plain, under the springs of Pisgah.

CHAPTER 5

1 And Moses called all Israel, and said unto them, Hear, O Israel, the statutes and judgments which I speak in your ears this day, that you may learn them, and keeps, and does them.
2 The LORD our God made a covenant with us in Horeb.
3 The LORD made not this covenant with our fathers, but with us, *even* us, who *are* all of us here alive this day.
4 The LORD talked with you face to face in the mount out of the midst of the fire,
5 (I stood between the LORD and you at that time, to show you the word of the LORD: for you were afraid by reason of the fire, and went not up into the mount;) saying,

6 I *am* the LORD your God, which brought you out of the land of Egypt, from the house of bondage.
7 you will have none other gods before me.
8 you will not make you *any* graven image, *or* any likeness *of anything* that *is* in heaven above, or that *is* in the earth beneath, or that *is* in the waters beneath the earth:
9 you will not bow down thyself unto them, nor serve them: for I the LORD your God *am* a jealous God, visiting the iniquity of the fathers upon the children unto the third and fourth *generation* of them that hate me,
10 And showing mercy unto thousands of them that love me and keep my commandments.
11 you will not take the name of the LORD your God in vain: for the LORD will not hold *him* guiltless that takes his name in vain.
12 Keep the Sabbath day to sanctify it, as the LORD your God has commanded you.
13 Six days you will labor, and do all your work:
14 But the seventh day *is* the Sabbath of the LORD your God: *in it* you will not do any work, you, nor your son, nor your daughter, nor your manservant, nor your maidservant, nor your ox, nor your ass, nor any of your cattle, nor your stranger that *is* within your gates; that your manservant and your maidservant may rest as well as you.
15 And remember that you were a servant in the land of Egypt, and *that* the LORD your God brought you out thence through a mighty hand and by a stretched out arm: therefore the LORD your God commanded you to keep the Sabbath day.
16 Honor your father and your mother, as the LORD your God has commanded you; that your days may be prolonged, and that it may go well with you, in the land which the LORD your God gives you.
17 you will not kill.
18 Neither will you commit adultery.
19 Neither will you steal.
20 Neither will you bear false witness against your neighbor.
21 Neither will you desire your neighbor's wife, neither will you covet your neighbor's house, his field, or his manservant, or his maidservant, his ox, or his ass, or any*thing* that *is* your neighbor's.
22 These words the LORD spoke unto all your assembly in the mount out of the midst of the fire, of the cloud, and of the thick darkness, with a great voice: and he added no more. And he wrote them in two tables of stone, and delivered them unto me.
23 And it came to pass, when you heard the voice out of the midst of the darkness, (for the mountain did burn with fire,) that you came near unto me, *even* all the heads of your tribes, and your elders;
24 And you said, Behold, the LORD our God has showed us his glory and his greatness, and we have heard his voice out of the midst of the fire: we have seen this day that God does talk with man, and he lives.
25 Now therefore why should we die? For this great fire will consume us: if we hear the voice of the LORD our God any more, then we will die.
26 For who *is there of* all flesh, that has heard the voice of the living God speaking out of the midst of the fire, as we *have*, and lived?
27 Go you near, and hear all that the LORD our God will say: and speak you unto us all that the LORD our God will speak unto you; and we will hear *it*, and do *it*.
28 And the LORD heard the voice of your words, when you spoke unto me; and the LORD said unto me, I have heard the voice of the words of this people, which they have spoken unto you: they have well said all that they have spoken.
29 O that there were such an heart in them, that they would fear me, and keep all my commandments always, that it might be well with them, and with their children forever!
30 Go say to them, Get you into your tents again.
31 But as for you, stand you here by me, and I will speak unto you all the commandments, and the statutes, and the judgments, which you will teach them, that they may do *them* in the land which I give them to possess it.
32 you will observe to do therefore as the LORD your God has commanded you: you will not turn aside to the right hand or to the left.
33 you will walk in all the ways which the LORD your God has commanded you, that you may live, and *that it may be* well with you, and *that* you may prolong *your* days in the land which you will possess.

CHAPTER 6

1 Now these *are* the commandments, the statutes, and the judgments, which the LORD your God commanded to teach you, that you might do *them* in the land whither you go to possess it:
2 That you might fear the LORD your God, to keep all his statutes and his commandments, which I command you, you, and your son, and your son's son, all the days of your life; and that your days may be prolonged.
3 Hear therefore, O Israel, and observe to do *it*; that it may be well with you, and that you may increase mightily, as the LORD God of your fathers has promised you, in the land that flows with milk and honey.
4 Hear, O Israel: The LORD our God *is* one LORD:
5 And you will love the LORD your God with all your heart, and with all your soul, and with all your might.
6 And these words, which I command you this day, will be in your heart:
7 And you will teach them diligently unto your children, and will talk of them when you sit in your house, and when you walk by the way, and when you lay down, and when you rise up.
8 And you will bind them for a sign upon your hand, and they will be as frontlets between your eyes.
9 And you will write them upon the posts of your house, and on your gates.
10 And it will be, when the LORD your God will have brought you into the land which he swore unto your fathers, to Abraham, to Isaac, and to Jacob, to give you great and goodly cities, which you built not,
11 And houses full of all good *things*, which you filled not, and wells digged, which you digged not, vineyards and olive trees which you planted not; when you will have eaten and be full;
12 *Then* beware lest you forget the LORD, which brought you forth out of the land of Egypt, from the house of bondage.
13 you will fear the LORD your God, and serve him, and will swear by his name.
14 you will not go after other gods, of the gods of the people which *are* round about you;
15 (For the LORD your God *is* a jealous God among you) lest the anger of the LORD your God be kindled against you, and destroy you from off the face of the earth.
16 you will not tempt the LORD your God, as you tempted *him* in Massah.

17 you will diligently keep the commandments of the LORD your God, and his testimonies, and his statutes, which he has commanded you.
18 And you will do *that which is* right and good in the sight of the LORD: that it may be well with you, and that you may go in and possess the good land which the LORD swore unto your fathers,
19 To cast out all your enemies from before you, as the LORD has spoken.
20 *And* when your son ask you in time to come, saying, what *mean* the testimonies, and the statutes, and the judgments, which the LORD our God has commanded you?
21 Then you will say unto your son, we were Pharaoh's bondmen in Egypt; and the LORD brought us out of Egypt with a mighty hand:
22 And the LORD showed signs and wonders, great and sore, upon Egypt, upon Pharaoh, and upon his **entire** household, before our eyes:
23 And he brought us out from there, that he might bring us in, to give us the land which he swore unto our fathers.
24 And the LORD commanded us to do all these statutes, to fear the LORD our God, for our good always, that he might preserve us alive, as *it is* at this day.
25 And it will be our righteousness, if we observe to do all these commandments before the LORD our God, as he has commanded us.

CHAPTER 7

1 When the LORD your God will bring you into the land whither you go to possess it, and has cast out many nations before you, the Hittites, and the Girgashites, and the Amorites, and the Canaanites, and the Perizzites, and the Hivites, and the Jebusites, seven nations greater and mightier than you;
2 And when the LORD your God will deliver them before you; you will smite them, *and* utterly destroy them; you will make no covenant with them, or show mercy unto them:
3 Neither will you make marriages with them; your daughter you will not give unto his son, or his daughter will you take unto your son.
4 For they will turn away your son from following me, that they may serve other gods: so will the anger of the LORD be kindled against you, and destroy you suddenly.
5 But thus will you deal with them; you will destroy their altars, and break down their images, and cut down their groves, and burn their graven images with fire.
6 For you *are* a holy people unto the LORD your God: the LORD your God has chosen you to be a special people unto himself, above all people that *are* upon the face of the earth.
7 The LORD did not set his love upon you, nor choose you, because you were more in number than any people; for you *were* the fewest of all people:
8 But because the LORD loved you, and because he would keep the oath which he had sworn unto your fathers, has the LORD brought you out with a mighty hand, and redeemed you out of the house of bondmen, from the hand of Pharaoh King of Egypt.
9 Know therefore that the LORD your God, he *is* God, the faithful God, which keeps covenant and mercy with them that love him and keep his commandments to a thousand generations;
10 And repay them that hate him to their face, to destroy them: he will not be slack to him that hates him, he will repay him to his face.

11 you will therefore keep the commandments, and the statutes, and the judgments, which I command you this day, to do them.
12 Wherefore it will come to pass, if you hearken to these judgments, and keep, and do them, that the LORD your God will keep unto you the covenant and the mercy which he swore unto your fathers:
13 And he will love you, and bless you, and multiply you: he will also bless the fruit of your womb, and the fruit of your land, your corn, and your wine, and your oil, the increase of your ox, and the flocks of your sheep, in the land which he swore unto your fathers to give you.
14 you will be blessed above all people: there will not be male or female barren among you, or among your cattle.
15 And the LORD will take away from you all sickness, and will put none of the evil diseases of Egypt, which you know, upon you; but will lay them upon all *them* that hate you.
16 And you will consume all the people which the LORD your God will deliver you; your eye will have no pity upon them: neither will you serve their gods; for that *will be* a snare unto you.
17 If you will say in your heart, these nations *are* more than I; how can I dispossess them?
18 you will not be afraid of them: *but* will well remember what the LORD your God did unto Pharaoh, and unto all Egypt;
19 The great temptations which your eyes saw, and the signs, and the wonders, and the mighty hand, and the stretched out arm, whereby the LORD your God brought you out: so will the LORD your God do unto all the people of whom you are afraid
20 Moreover the LORD your God will send the hornet among them, until they that are left, and hide themselves from you, be destroyed.
21 you will not be affrighted at them: for the LORD your God *is* among you, a mighty God and terrible.
22 And the LORD your God will put out those nations before you by little and little: you may not consume them at once, lest the beasts of the field increase upon you.
23 But the LORD your God will deliver them unto you, and will destroy them with a mighty destruction, until they be destroyed.
24 And he will deliver their kings into your hand, and you will destroy their name from under heaven: there will no man be able to stand before you, until you have destroyed them.
25 The graven images of their gods will you burn with fire: you will not desire the silver or gold *that is* on them, nor take *it* unto you, lest you be snared therein: for it *is* an abomination to the LORD your God.
26 Neither will you bring an abomination into your house, lest you be a cursed thing like it: *but* you will utterly detest it, and you will utterly abhor it; for it *is* a cursed thing.

CHAPTER 8

1 All the commandments which I command you this day will you observe to do, that you may live, and multiply, and go in and possess the land which the LORD swore unto your fathers.
2 And you will remember all the way which the LORD your God led you these forty years in the wilderness, to humble you, *and* to prove you, to know what *was* in your heart, whether you would keep his commandments, or no.
3 And he humbled you, and suffered you to hunger, and fed you with manna, which you knew not, neither did your fathers know; that he might make you know that man does not live by bread only, but by every *word* that proceeds out of the mouth of the LORD does man live.

4 your raiment waxed not old upon you, neither did your foot swell, these forty years.

5 you will also consider in your heart, that, as a man chasten his son, *so* the LORD your God chasten you.

6 Therefore you will keep the commandments of the LORD your God, to walk in his ways, and to fear him.

7 For the LORD your God brings you into a good land, a land of brooks of water, of fountains and depths that spring out of valleys and hills;

8 A land of wheat, and barley, and vines, and fig trees, and pomegranates; a land of oil olive, and honey;

9 A land wherein you will eat bread without scarceness, you will not lack any *thing* in it; a land whose stones *are* iron, and out of whose hills you may dig brass.

10 When you have eaten and are full, then you will bless the LORD your God for the good land which he has given you.

11 Beware that you forget not the LORD your God, in not keeping his commandments, and his judgments, and his statutes, which I command you this day:

12 Lest *when* you have eaten and are full, and have built goodly houses, and dwelt *therein*;

13 And *when* your herds and your flocks multiply, and your silver and your gold are multiplied, and all that you have is multiplied;

14 Then your heart be lifted up, and you forget the LORD your God, which brought you forth out of the land of Egypt, from the house of bondage;

15 [Who led you through that great and terrible wilderness, *wherein were* [fiery serpents]¹, and scorpions, and drought, where *there was* no water; who brought you forth water out of the rock of flint;]²

16 Who fed you in the wilderness with manna, which your fathers knew not, that he might humble you, and that he might prove you, to do you good at your latter end;

17 And you say in your heart, my power and the might of *mine* hand has gotten me this wealth.

18 But you will remember the LORD your God: for *it is* he that gives you power to get wealth, that he may establish his covenant which he swore unto your fathers, as *it is* this day.

19 And it will be, if you do at all forget the LORD your God, and walk after other gods, and serve them, and worship them, I testify against you this day that you will surely perish.

20 As the nations which the LORD destroyed before your face, so will you perish; because you would not be obedient unto the voice of the LORD your God.

CHAPTER 9

1 Hear, O Israel: you are to pass over Jordan this day, to go in to possess nations greater and mightier than thyself, cities great and fenced up to heaven,

2 A people great and tall, the children of the Anakims, whom you know, and *of whom* you have heard *say*, who can stand before the children of Anak!

3 Understand therefore this day, that the LORD your God *is* he which goes over before you; *as* a consuming fire he will destroy them, and he will bring them down before your face: so will you drive them out, and destroy them quickly, as the LORD has said unto you.

4 Speak not you in your heart, after that the LORD your God has cast them out from before you, saying, For my righteousness the LORD has brought me in to possess this land: but for the wickedness of these nations the LORD does drive them out from before you.

5 Not for your righteousness, or for the uprightness of your heart, dost you go to possess their land: but for the wickedness of these nations the LORD your God does drive them out from before you, and that he may perform the word which the LORD swore unto your fathers, Abraham, Isaac, and Jacob.

6 Understand therefore, that the LORD your God gives you not this good land to possess it for your righteousness; for you *are* a stiff-necked people.

7 Remember, *and* forget not, how you provoked the LORD your God to wrath in the wilderness: from the day that you didst depart out of the land of Egypt, until you came unto this place, you have been rebellious against the LORD.

8 Also in Horeb you provoked the LORD to wrath, so that the LORD was angry with you to have destroyed you.

9 When I was gone up into the mount to receive the tables of stone, *even* the tables of the covenant which the LORD made with you, then I abode in the mount forty days and forty nights, I neither did eat bread nor drink water:

10 And the LORD delivered unto me two tables of stone written with the finger of God; and on them *was written* according to all the words, which the LORD spoke with you in the mount out of the midst of the fire in the day of the assembly.

11 [And it came to pass at the end of forty days and forty nights, *that* the LORD gave me the two tables of stone, *even* the tables of the covenant.]³

12 And the LORD said unto me, Arise, get you down quickly from hence; for your people which you have brought forth out of Egypt have corrupted *themselves*; they are quickly turned aside out of the way which I commanded them; they have made them a molten image.

13 Furthermore the LORD spoke unto me, saying, I have seen this people, and, behold, it *is* a stiff-necked people:

14 Let me alone, that I may destroy them, and blot out their name from under heaven: and I will make of you a nation mightier and greater than they.

15 So I turned and came down from the mount, and the mount burned with fire: and the two tables of the covenant *were* in my two hands.

16 And I looked, and, behold, you had sinned against the LORD your God, *and* had made you a molten calf: you had turned aside quickly out of the way which the LORD had commanded you.

17 And I took the two tables, and cast them out of my two hands, and break them before your eyes.

18 [And I fell down before the LORD, as at the first, forty days and forty nights: I did neither eat bread, nor drink water, because of all your sins which you sinned, in doing wickedly in the sight of the LORD, to provoke him to anger.]⁴

19 For I was afraid of the anger and hot displeasure, wherewith the LORD was wroth against you to destroy you. But the LORD hearkened unto me at that time also.

---

¹ fiery serpent = śârâph meaning burning or poisonous (serpent) [Strgs#8314].
² compare Ez. 2:6 & Luke 10:19
³ compare Ex. 24:12-18
⁴ compare **Ex. 32:31**

20 And the LORD was very angry with Aaron to have destroyed him: and I prayed for Aaron also the same time.
21 And I took your sin, the calf which you had made, and burnt it with fire, and stamped it, *and* ground *it* very small, *even* until it was as small as dust: and I cast the dust thereof into the brook that descended out of the mount.
22 And at Taberah, and at Massah, and at Kibroth-hattaavah, you provoked the LORD to wrath.
23 Likewise when the LORD sent you from Kadesh-barnea, saying, Go up and possess the land which I have given you; then you rebelled against the commandment of the LORD your God, and you believed him not, nor hearkened to his voice.
24 you have been rebellious against the LORD from the day that I knew you.
25 Thus I fell down before the LORD forty days and forty nights, as I fell down *at the first*; because the LORD had said he would destroy you.
26 I prayed therefore unto the LORD, and said, O Lord GOD, destroy not your people and your inheritance, which you have redeemed through your greatness, which you have brought forth out of Egypt with a mighty hand.
27 Remember your servants, Abraham, Isaac, and Jacob; look not unto the stubbornness of this people, nor to their wickedness, nor to their sin:
28 Lest the land where you brought us out say, because the LORD was not able to bring them into the land which he promised them, and because he hated them, he has brought them out to slay them in the wilderness.
29 Yet they *are* your people and your inheritance, which you brought out by your mighty power and by your stretched out arm.

CHAPTER 10

1 At that time the LORD said unto me, hew you two tables of stone like unto the first, and come up unto me into the mount, and make you an ark of wood.
2 And I will write on the tables the words that were in the first tables which you break, and you will put them in the ark.
3 And I made an ark *of* **sticks of** wood, and hewed two tables of stone like unto the first, and went up into the mount, having the two tables in mine hand.
4 And he wrote on the tables, according to the first writing, the Ten Commandments, which the LORD spoke unto you in the mount out of the midst of the fire in the day of the assembly: and the LORD gave them unto me.
5 And I turned myself and came down from the mount, and put the tables in the ark which I had made; and there they are, as the LORD commanded me.
6 And the children of Israel took their journey from Beeroth of the children of Jaakan to Mosera: there Aaron died, and there he was buried; and Eleazar his son ministered in the priest's office in his stead.
7 From thence they journeyed unto Gudgodah; and from Gudgodah to Jotbath, a land of rivers of waters.
8 At that time the LORD separated the tribe of Levi, to bear the ark of the covenant of the LORD, to stand before the LORD to minister unto him, and to bless in his name, unto this day.
9 Wherefore Levi has no part or inheritance with his brethren; the LORD *is* his inheritance, according as the LORD your God promised him.
10 And I stayed in the mount, according to the first time, forty days and forty nights; and the LORD hearkened unto me at that time also, *and* the LORD would not destroy you.
11 And the LORD said unto me, Arise, take your journey before the people, that they may go in and possess the land, which I swore unto their fathers to give unto them.
12 And now, Israel, what does the LORD your God require of you, but to fear the LORD your God, to walk in all his ways, and to love him, and to serve the LORD your God with all your heart and with all your soul,
13 To keep the commandments of the LORD, and his statutes, which I command you this day for your good?
14 Behold, the heaven and the heaven of heavens *is* the LORD'S your God, the earth *also*, with all that therein *is*.
15 Only the LORD had a delight in your fathers to love them, and he chose their seed after them, *even* you above all people, as *it is* this day.
16 Circumcise therefore the foreskin of your heart, and be no more stiff-necked.
17 For the LORD your God *is* God of gods, and Lord of lords, a great God, a mighty, and a terrible, which regards not persons, or takes reward:
18 He does execute the judgment of the fatherless and widow, and loves the stranger, in giving him food and raiment.
19 Love you therefore the stranger: for you were strangers in the land of Egypt.
20 you will fear the LORD your God; him will you serve and to him will you cleave, and swear by his name.
21 He *is* your praise, and he *is* your God, that has done for you these great and terrible things, which your eyes have seen.
22 your fathers went down into Egypt with threescore and ten persons; and now the LORD your God has made you as the stars of heaven for multitude.

CHAPTER 11

1 Therefore you will love the LORD your God, and keep his charge, and his statutes, and his judgments, and his commandments, always.
2 And know you this day: for *I speak* not with your children which have not known, and which have not seen the chastisement of the LORD your God, his greatness, his mighty hand, and his stretched out arm,
3 And his miracles, and his acts, which he did in the midst of Egypt unto Pharaoh the king of Egypt, and unto all his land;
4 And what he did unto the army of Egypt, unto their horses, and to their chariots; how he made the water of the Red sea to overflow them as they pursued after you, and *how* the LORD has destroyed them unto this day;
5 And what he did unto you in the wilderness, until you came into this place;
6 And what he did unto Dathan and Abiram, the sons of Eliab, the son of Reuben: how the earth opened her mouth, and swallowed them up, and their households, and their tents, and all the substance that *was* in their possession, in the midst of all Israel:
7 But your eyes have seen all the great acts of the LORD which he did.
8 Therefore will you keep all the commandments which I command you this day, that you may be strong, and go in and possess the land, whither you go to possess it;

9 And that you may prolong *your* days in the land, which the LORD swore unto your fathers to give unto them and to their seed, a land that flows with milk and honey.

10 For the land, whither you go in to possess it, *is* not as the land of Egypt, from where you came out, where you sowe your seed, and watered *it* with your foot, as a garden of herbs:

11 But the land, whither you go to possess it, *is* a land of hills and valleys, *and* drink water of the rain of heaven:

12 A land which the LORD your God cares for: the eyes of the LORD your God *is* always upon it, from the beginning of the year even unto the end of the year.

13 And it will come to pass, if you will hearken diligently unto my commandments which I command you this day, to love the LORD your God, and to serve him with all your heart and with all your soul,

14 That I will give *you* the rain of your land in his due season, the first rain and the latter rain, that you may gather in your corn, and your wine, and your oil.

15 And I will send grass in your fields for your cattle, that you may eat and be full.

16 Take heed to yourselves, that your heart be not deceived, and you turn aside, and serve other gods, and worship them;

17 And *then* the LORD'S wrath be kindled against you, and he shut up the heaven, that there be no rain, and that the land yield not her fruit; and *lest* you perish quickly from off the good land which the LORD gives you.

18 Therefore will you lay up these my words in your heart and in your soul, and bind them for a sign upon your hand, that they may be as frontlets between your eyes.

19 And you will teach them your children, speaking of them when you sit in your house, and when you walk by the way, when you lie down, and when you rise up.

20 And you will write them upon the door posts of your house, and upon your gates:

21 That your days may be multiplied, and the days of your children, in the land which the LORD swore unto your fathers to give them, as the days of heaven upon the earth.

22 For if you will diligently keep all these commandments which I command you, to do them, to love the LORD your God, to walk in all his ways, and to cleave unto him;

23 Then will the LORD drive out all these nations from before you, and you will possess greater nations and mightier than yourselves.

24 Every place whereon the soles of your feet will tread will be yours: from the wilderness and Lebanon, from the river, the river Euphrates, even unto the uttermost sea will your coast be.

25 There will no man be able to stand before you: *for* the LORD your God will lay the fear of you and the dread of you upon all the land that you will tread upon, as he has said unto you.

26 Behold, I set before you this day a blessing and a curse;

27 A blessing, if you obey the commandments of the LORD your God, which I command you this day:

28 And a curse, if you will not obey the commandments of the LORD your God, but turn aside out of the way which I command you this day, to go after other gods, which you have not known.

29 And it will come to pass, when the LORD your God has brought you in unto the land whither you go to possess it, that you will put the blessing upon mount Gerizim, and the curse upon mount Ebal.

30 *Are* they not on the other side Jordan, by the way where the sun goes down, in the land of the Canaanites, which dwell in the champaign[1] over against Gilgal, beside the plains of Moreh?

31 For you will pass over Jordan to go in to possess the land which the LORD your God gives you, and you will possess it, and dwell therein.

32 And you will observe to do all the statutes and judgments which I set before you this day.

CHAPTER 12

1 These *are* the statutes and judgments, which you will observe to do in the land, which the LORD God of your fathers gives you to possess it, all the days that you live upon the earth.

2 you will utterly destroy all the places, wherein the nations which you will possess served their gods, upon the high mountains, and upon the hills, and under every green tree:

3 And you will overthrow their altars, and break their pillars, and burn their groves with fire; and you will hew down the graven images of their gods, and destroy the names of them out of that place.

4 you will not do so unto the LORD your God.

5 But unto the place which the LORD your God will choose out of all your tribes to put his name there, *even* unto his habitation will you seek, and thither you will come:

6 And thither you will bring your burnt offerings, and your sacrifices, and your tithes, and heave offerings of your hand, and your vows, and your freewill offerings, and the firstlings of your herds and of your flocks:

7 And there you will eat before the LORD your God, and you will rejoice in all that you put your hand unto, you and your households, wherein the LORD your God has blessed you.

8 you will not do after all *the things* that we do here this day, every man whatsoever *is* right in his own eyes.

9 For you are not as yet come to the rest and to the inheritance, which the LORD your God gives you.

10 But *when* you go over Jordan, and dwell in the land which the LORD your God gives you to inherit, and *when* he gives you rest from all your enemies round about, so that you dwell in safety;

11 Then there will be a place which the LORD your God will choose to cause his name to dwell there; thither will you bring all that I command you; your burnt offerings, and your sacrifices, your tithes, and the heave offering of your hand, and all your choice vows which you vow unto the LORD:

12 And you will rejoice before the LORD your God, you, and your sons, and your daughters, and your menservants and your maidservants, and the Levite that *is* within your gates; forasmuch as he has no part or inheritance with you.

13 Take heed to thyself that you offer not your burnt offerings in every place that you see:

14 But in the place which the LORD will choose in one of your tribes, there you will offer your burnt offerings, and there you will do all that I command you.

15 Notwithstanding you may kill and eat flesh in all your gates, whatsoever your soul lusts after, according to the blessing of the LORD your God which he has given you: the unclean and the clean may eat thereof, as of the roebuck, and as of the hart

16 Only you will not eat the blood; you will pour it upon the earth as water.

---

[1] Champaign- in the sense of sterility, a desert, sterile valley of the Jordan and its continuation to the Red Sea. [Strgs#6160]

17 you may not eat within your gates the tithe of your corn, or of your wine, or of your oil, or the firstlings of your herds or of your flock, nor any of your vows which you vow, nor your freewill offerings, or heave offering of your hand:
18 But you must eat them before the LORD your God in the place which the LORD your God will choose, you, and your son, and your daughter, and your manservant, and your maidservant, and the Levite that *is* within your gates: and you will rejoice before the LORD your God in all that you put your hands unto.
19 Take heed to thyself that you forsake not the Levite as long as you live upon the earth.
20 When the LORD your God will enlarge your border, as he has promised you, and you will say, I will eat flesh, because your soul longs to eat flesh; you may eat flesh, whatsoever your soul lusteth after.
21 If the place which the LORD your God has chosen to put his name there be too far from you, then you will kill of your herd and of your flock, which the LORD has given you, as I have commanded you, and you will eat in your gates whatsoever your soul lusteth after.
22 Even as the roebuck and the hart is eaten, so you will eat them: the unclean and the clean will eat *of* them alike.
23 Only be sure that you eat not the blood: for the blood *is* the life; and you may not eat the life with the flesh.
24 you will not eat it; you will pour it upon the earth as water.
25 you will not eat it; that it may go well with you, and with your children after you, when you will do *that which is* right in the sight of the LORD.
26 Only your holy things which you hast, and your vows, you will take, and go unto the place which the LORD will choose:
27 And you will offer your burnt offerings, the flesh and the blood, upon the altar of the LORD your God: and the blood of your sacrifices will be poured out upon the altar of the LORD your God, and you will eat the flesh.
28 Observe and hear all these words which I command you, that it may go well with you, and with your children after you forever, when you doest *that which is* good and right in the sight of the LORD your God.
29 When the LORD your God will cut off the nations from before you, whither you goes to possess them, and you succeed them, and dwell in their land;
30 Take heed to yourself that you be not snared by following them, after that they be destroyed from before you; and that you enquire not after their gods, saying, How did these nations serve their gods? Even so will I do likewise.
31 you will not do so unto the LORD your God: for every abomination to the LORD, which he hates, have they done unto their gods; for even their sons and their daughters they have burnt in the fire to their gods.
32 What thing so ever I command you, observe to do it: you will not add thereto, nor diminish from it.

CHAPTER 13

1 If there arise among you a prophet, or a dreamer of dreams, and give you a sign or a wonder[1],
2 And the sign or the wonder come to pass, whereof he spoke unto you, saying, Let us go after other gods, which you have not known, and let us serve them;
3 you will not hearken unto the words of that prophet, or that dreamer of dreams: [for the LORD your God proves you][2], to know whether you love the LORD your God with all your heart and with all your soul.
4 you will walk after the LORD your God, and fear him, and keep his commandments, and obey his voice, and you will serve him, and cleave unto him.
5 And that prophet, or that dreamer of dreams, will be put to death; because he has spoken to turn *you* away from the LORD your God, which brought you out of the land of Egypt, and redeemed you out of the house of bondage, to thrust you out of the way, which the LORD your God commanded you to walk in. So will you put the evil away from the midst of you.
6 If your brother, the son of your mother, or your son, or your daughter, or the wife of your bosom, or your friend, which *is* as your own soul, entice you secretly, saying, Let us go and serve other gods, which you have not known, you, nor your fathers;
7 *Namely*, of the gods of the people which *are* round about you, nigh unto you, or far off from you, from the *one* end of the earth even unto the *other* end of the earth;
8 you will not consent unto him, nor hearken unto him; neither will your eye pity him, neither will you spare, neither will you conceal him:
9 But you will surely kill him; your hand will be first upon him to put him to death, and afterwards the hand of all the people.
10 And you will stone him with stones, that he die; because he has sought to thrust you away from the LORD your God, which brought you out of the land of Egypt, from the house of bondage
11 And all Israel will hear, and fear, and will do no more any such wickedness as this is among you.
12 If you will hear *say* in one of your cities, which the LORD your God has given you to dwell there, saying,
13 *Certain* men, the children of Belial, are gone out from among you, and have withdrawn the inhabitants of their city, saying, Let us go and serve other gods, which you have not known;
14 Then will you enquire, and make search, and ask diligently; and, behold, *if it be* truth, *and* the thing certain, *that* such abomination is wrought among you;
15 you will surely smite the inhabitants of that city with the edge of the sword, destroying it utterly, and all that *is* therein, and the cattle thereof, with the edge of the sword.
16 And you will gather all the spoil of it into the midst of the street thereof, and will burn with fire the city, and all the spoil thereof every whit, for the LORD your God: and it will be a heap forever; it will not be built again.
17 And there will cleave nought of the cursed thing to your hand: that the LORD may turn from the fierceness of his anger, and show you mercy, and have compassion upon you, and multiply you, as he has sworn unto your fathers;
18 When you will hearken to the voice of the LORD your God, to keep all his commandments which I command you this day, to do *that which is* right in the eyes of the LORD your God.

---

[1] wonder = conspicuousness; a miracle; by implication a token or omen [Strgs#4159]. Derives from the root word yâphâh meaning to be bright, beautiful [Strgs#3302].

[2] God allow the false signs and wonders. It was given unto him...compare **Rev. 13:11-17**.

CHAPTER 14

1 you *are* the children of the LORD your God: you will not cut yourselves, nor make any baldness between your eyes for the dead.
2 For you *are* a holy people unto the LORD your God, and the LORD has chosen you to be a peculiar people unto himself, above all the nations that *are* upon the earth.
3 you will not eat any abominable thing.
4 These *are* the beasts which you will eat: the ox, the sheep, and the goat,
5 The hart, and the roebuck, and the fallow deer, and the wild goat, and the pygarg[1], and the wild ox, and the chamois[2].
6 And every beast that parts the hoof, and cleaves the cleft into two claws, *and* chews the cud among the beasts, that you will eat.
7 Nevertheless these you will not eat of them that chew the cud, or of them that divide the cloven hoof; *as* the camel, and the hare, and the coney[3]: for they chew the cud, but divide not the hoof; *therefore* they *are* unclean unto you.
8 And the swine, because it divides the hoof, yet chews not the cud, it *is* unclean unto you: you will not eat of their flesh, nor touch their dead carcass.
9 These you will eat of all that *are* in the waters: all that have fins and scales will you eat:
10 And whatsoever has not fins and scales you may not eat; it *is* unclean unto you.
11 *Of* all clean birds you will eat.
12 But these *are they* of which you will not eat: the eagle, and the ossifrage[4], and the ospray,
13 And the glede[5], and the kite, and the vulture after his kind,
14 And every raven after his kind,
15 And the owl, and the night hawk, and the cuckow[6], and the hawk after his kind,
16 The little owl, and the great owl, and the swan,
17 And the pelican, and the gier eagle, and the cormorant,
18 And the stork, and the heron after her kind, and the lapwing, and the bat.
19 And every creeping thing that flies *is* unclean unto you: they will not be eaten.
20 *But of* all clean fowls you may eat.
21 You will not eat *of* anything that dies of itself: you will give it unto the stranger that *is* in your gates, that he may eat it; or you may sell it unto an alien: for you *are* a holy people unto the LORD your God. You will not seethe a kid in his mother's milk.
22 you will truly tithe all the increase of your seed, that the field brings forth year by year.
23 And you will eat before the LORD your God, in the place which he will choose to place his name there, the tithe of your corn, of your wine, and of your oil, and the firstlings of your herds and of your flocks; that you may learn to fear the LORD your God always.
24 And if the way be too long for you, so that you are not able to carry it; *or* if the place be too far from you, which the LORD your God will choose to set his name there, when the LORD your God has blessed you:
25 Then will you turn *it* into money, and bind up the money in your hand, and will go unto the place which the LORD your God will choose:
26 And you will bestow that money for whatsoever your soul lusts after, for oxen, or for sheep, or for wine, or for strong drink, or for whatsoever your soul desires: and you will eat there before the LORD your God, and you will rejoice, you, and your household,
27 And the Levite that *is* within your gates; you will not forsake him; for he has no part or inheritance with you.
28 At the end of three years you will bring forth all the tithe of your increase the same year, and will lay *it* up within your gates
29 And the Levite, (because he has no part or inheritance with you,) and the stranger, and the fatherless, and the widow, which *are* within your gates, will come, and will eat and be satisfied; that the LORD your God may bless you in all the work of your hand which you doest.

CHAPTER 15

1 At the end of *every* seven years you will make a release
2 And this *is* the manner of the release: Every creditor that lends *ought* unto his neighbor will release *it*; he will not exact *it* of his neighbor, or of his brother; because it is called the LORD'S release.
3 Of a foreigner you may exact *it again*: but *that* which is your with your brother your hand will release;
4 Save when there will be no poor among you; for the LORD will greatly bless you in the land which the LORD your God gives you *for* an inheritance to possess it:
5 Only if you carefully hearken unto the voice of the LORD your God, to observe to do all these commandments which I command you this day.
6 For the LORD your God blessed you, as he promised you: and you will lend unto many nations, but you will not borrow; and you will reign over many nations, but they will not reign over you.
7 If there be among you a poor man of one of your brethren within any of your gates in your land which the LORD your God give you, you will not harden your heart, nor shut your hand from your poor brother:
8 But you will open your hand wide unto him, and will surely lend him sufficient for his need, *in that* which he wantd.
9 Beware that there be not a thought in your wicked heart, saying, The seventh year, the year of release, is at hand; and your eye be evil against your poor brother, and you gives him nought; and he cry unto the LORD against you, and it be sin unto you.
10 you will surely give him, and your heart will not be grieved when you gives unto him: because that for this thing the LORD your God will bless you in all your works, and in all that you puts your hand unto.
11 For the poor will never cease out of the land: therefore I command you, saying, you will open your hand wide unto your brother, to your poor, and to your needy, in your land.
12 *And* if your brother, an Hebrew man, or an Hebrew woman, be sold unto you, and serve you six years; then in the seventh year you will let him go free from you.
13 And when you sends him out free from you, you will not let him go away empty:

---

[1] Pygarg- literally antelope. [Strgs#1788]
[2] Chamois- literally a gazelle due to its feet lightly touching the ground. [Strgs#2169]
[3] coney- a species of rock rabbit, probably the hyrax. [Strgs#8227]
[4] ossifrage- a kind of eagle [Strgs#6538]
[5] glede- believed to be the vulture due to it sharp eye sight. [Strgs#7201]
[6] cuckow- believed to be an extinct species of a seagull. [Strgs#7828]

14 You will furnish him liberally out of your flock, and out of your floor, and out of your winepress: *of that* wherewith the LORD your God has blessed you, you will give unto him.
15 And you will remember that you were a bondman in the land of Egypt, and the LORD your God redeemed you: therefore I command you this thing to day.
16 And it will be, if he says unto you, I will not go away from you; because he loves you and your house, because he is well with you;
17 Then you will take an aul[1], and thrust *it* through his ear unto the door, and he will be your servant forever. And also unto your maidservant you will do likewise.
18 It will not seem hard unto you, when you sends him away free from you; for he has been worth a double hired servant *to you*, in serving you six years: and the LORD your God will bless you in all that you doest.
19 All the firstling males that come of your herd and of your flock you will sanctify unto the LORD your God: you will do no work with the firstling of your bullock, nor shear the firstling of your sheep.
20 you will eat *it* before the LORD your God year by year in the place which the LORD will choose, you and your household.
21 And if there be *any* blemish therein, *as if it be* lame, or blind, *or have* any ill blemish, you will not sacrifice it unto the LORD your God.
22 you will eat it within your gates: the unclean and the clean *person will eat it* alike, as the roebuck, and as the hart.
23 Only you will not eat the blood thereof; you will pour it upon the ground as water.

CHAPTER 16
1 Observe the month of Abib, and keep the Passover unto the LORD your God: for in the month of Abib the LORD your God brought you forth out of Egypt by night.
2 you will therefore sacrifice the Passover unto the LORD your God, of the flock and the herd, in the place which the LORD will choose to place his name there.
3 you will eat no leavened bread with it; seven days will you eat unleavened bread therewith, *even* the bread of affliction; for you came forth out of the land of Egypt in haste: that you may remember the day when you came forth out of the land of Egypt all the days of your life.
4 And there will be no leavened bread seen with you in your **entire** coast seven days; neither will there *anything* of the flesh, which you sacrifices the first day at even, remain all night until the morning.
5 you may not sacrifice the Passover within any of your gates, which the LORD your God give you:
6 But at the place which the LORD your God will choose to place his name in, there you will sacrifice the Passover at even, at the going down of the sun, at the season that you come forth out of Egypt.
7 And you will roast and eat *it* in the place which the LORD your God will choose: and you will turn in the morning, and go unto your tents.
8 Six days you will eat unleavened bread: and on the seventh day will *be* a solemn assembly to the LORD your God: you will do no work *therein*.

9 Seven weeks will you number unto you: begin to number the seven weeks from *such time as* you begin *to put* the sickle to the corn.
10 And you will keep the feast of weeks unto the LORD your God with a tribute of a freewill offering of your hand, which you will give *unto the LORD your God*, according as the LORD your God has blessed you:
11 And you will rejoice before the LORD your God, you, and your son, and your daughter, and your manservant, and your maidservant, and the Levite that *is* within your gates, and the stranger, and the fatherless, and the widow, that *are* among you, in the place which the LORD your God has chosen to place his name there.
12 And you will remember that you were a bondman in Egypt: and you will observe and do these statutes.
13 you will observe the feast of tabernacles seven days, after that you have gathered in your corn and your wine:
14 And you will rejoice in your feast, you, and your son, and your daughter, and your manservant, and your maidservant, and the Levite, the stranger, and the fatherless, and the widow, that *are* within your gates.
15 Seven days will you keep a solemn feast unto the LORD your God in the place which the LORD will choose: because the LORD your God will bless you in all your increase, and in all the works of your hands, therefore you will surely rejoice.
16 Three times in a year will all your males appear before the LORD your God in the place which he will choose; in the feast of unleavened bread, and in the feast of weeks, and in the feast of tabernacles: and they will not appear before the LORD empty:
17 Every man will *give* as he is able, according to the blessing of the LORD your God which he has given you.
18 Judges and officers will you make you in all your gates, which the LORD your God give you, throughout your tribes: and they will judge the people with just judgment.
19 you will not wrest judgment; you will not respect persons, neither take a gift: for a gift does blind the eyes of the wise, and pervert the words of the righteous.
20 That which is altogether just will you follow, that you may live, and inherit the land which the LORD your God gives you.
21 you will not plant you a grove of any trees near unto the altar of the LORD your God, which you will make you.
22 Neither will you set you up *any* image; which the LORD your God hates.

CHAPTER 17
1 you will not sacrifice unto the LORD your God *any* bullock, or sheep, wherein is blemish, *or* any evil-favouredness[2]: for that *is* an abomination unto the LORD your God.
2 If there be found among you, within any of your gates which the LORD your God gives you, man or woman, that has wrought wickedness in the sight of the LORD your God, in transgressing his covenant,
3 And has gone and served other gods, and worshipped them, either the sun, or moon, or any of the host of heaven, which I have not commanded;
4 And it be told you, and you have heard *of it*, and enquired diligently, and, behold, *it be* true, *and* the thing certain, *that* such abomination is wrought in Israel:

---

[1] aul- a boring instrument. [Strgs#4836]
[2] Is the Hebrew word *ra'rä'âh*, <u>rah</u>, defined as bad or evil naturally or morally. Also adversity, affliction and calamity.

Deuteronomy

5 Then will you bring forth that man or that woman, which have committed that wicked thing, unto your gates, even that man or that woman, and will stone them with stones, till they die.

6 At the mouth of two witnesses, or three witnesses, will he that is worthy of death be put to death; but at the mouth of one witness he will not be put to death.

7 The hands of the witnesses will be first upon him to put him to death, and afterward the hands of all the people. So you will put the evil away from among you.

8 If there arise a matter too hard for you in judgment, between blood and blood, between plea and plea, and between stroke and stroke, being matters of controversy within your gates: then will you arise, and get you up into the place which the LORD your God will choose;

9 And you will come unto the priests the Levites, and unto the judge that will be in those days, and enquire; and they will show you the sentence of judgment:

10 And you will do according to the sentence, which they of that place which the LORD will choose will show you; and you will observe to do according to all that they inform you:

11 According to the sentence of the law which they will teach you, and according to the judgment which they will tell you, you will do: you will not decline from the sentence which they will show you, to the right hand, nor to the left.

12 And the man that will do presumptuously, and will not hearken unto the priest that stands to minister there before the LORD your God, or unto the judge, even that man will die: and you will put away the evil from Israel.

13 And all the people will hear, and fear, and do no more presumptuously.

14 When you are come unto the land which the LORD your God gives you, and will possess it, and will dwell therein, and will say, I will set a king over me, like as all the nations that are about me;

15 you will in any wise set him king over you, whom the LORD your God will choose: one from among your brethren will you set king over you: you may not set a stranger over you, which is not your brother.

16 But he will not multiply horses to himself, nor cause the people to return to Egypt, to the end that he should multiply horses: forasmuch as the LORD has said unto you, you will henceforth return no more that way.

17 Neither will he multiply wives to himself, that his heart turns not away: neither will he greatly multiply to himself silver and gold.

18 And it will be, when he sits upon the throne of his kingdom, that he will write him a copy of this law in a book out of that which is before the priests the Levites:

19 And it will be with him, and he will read therein all the days of his life: that he may learn to fear the LORD his God, to keep all the words of this law and these statutes, to do them:

20 That his heart be not lifted up above his brethren, and that he turn not aside from the commandment, to the right hand, or to the left: to the end that he may prolong his days in his kingdom, he, and his children, in the midst of Israel.

CHAPTER 18

1 The priests the Levites, and all the tribe of Levi, will have no part nor inheritance with Israel: they will eat the offerings of the LORD made by fire, and his inheritance.

2 Therefore will they have no inheritance among their brethren: the LORD is their inheritance, as he has said unto them.

3 And this will be the priest's due from the people, from them that offer a sacrifice, whether it be ox or sheep; and they will give unto the priest the shoulder, and the two cheeks, and the maw.

4 The first fruit also of your corn, of your wine, and of your oil, and the first of the fleece of your sheep, will you give him.

5 For the LORD your God has chosen him out of all your tribes, to stand to minister in the name of the LORD, him and his sons forever.

6 And if a Levite comes from any of your gates out of all Israel, where he sojourned, and come with all the desire of his mind unto the place which the LORD will choose;

7 Then he will minister in the name of the LORD his God, as all his brethren the Levites do, which stand there before the LORD.

8 They will have like portions to eat, beside that which cometh of the sale of his patrimony.

9 When you are come into the land which the LORD your God giveth you, you will not learn to do after the abominations of those nations.

10 There will not be found among you anyone that makes his son or his daughter to pass through the fire, or that use divination, or an [observer of times][1], or an enchanter[2], or a witch,

11 Or a charmer[3], or a consulter with familiar spirits, or a wizard, or a necromancer[4].

12 For all that do these things are an abomination unto the LORD: and because of these abominations the LORD your God does drive them out from before you.

13 you will be perfect with the LORD your God.

14 For these nations, which you will possess, hearkened unto observers of times, and unto diviners: but as for you, the LORD your God has not suffered you so to do.

15 The LORD your God will raise up unto you a Prophet from the midst of you, of your brethren, like unto me; unto him you will hearken;

16 According to all that you desired of the LORD your God in Horeb in the day of the assembly, saying, Let me not hear again the voice of the LORD my God, neither let me see this great fire any more, that I die not.

17 And the LORD said unto me, they have well spoken that which they have spoken.

18 I will raise them up a Prophet from among their brethren, like unto you, and will put my words in his mouth; and he will speak unto them all that I will command him.

19 And it will come to pass, that whosoever will not hearken unto my words which he will speak in my name[5], I will require it of him.

20 But the prophet, which will presume[6] to speak a word in my name, which I have not commanded him to speak, or that will speak in the name of other gods, even that prophet will die.

---

[1] lit. to cloud over [Strgs#6049]. Root word 'ānân meaning nimbus or thunder cloud [Strgs#6051].

[2] enchanter = to hiss, whisper a (magic) spell, to whisper as a serpent [Strgs#5172].

[3] charmer = to join a society or to join by means of spells or to fascinate [Strgs#2266 + 2267].

[4] necromancer = to seek and worship the dead [Strgs#1875 – 4191].

[5] name = position, appellation, as a mark or memorial of individuality; by implication honor, authority, character [Strgs8034].

[6] presume = to seeth, a state of rapid agitated movement; boil; to curn or foam as if boiling [Strgs2102].

21 And if you say in your heart, how will we know the word which the LORD has not spoken?
22 When a prophet speaks in the name of the LORD, if the thing follows[1] not, or [come to pass][2], that is the thing which the LORD has not spoken, but the prophet has spoken it presumptuously: you will not be afraid of him.

CHAPTER 19

1 When the LORD your God has cut off the nations, whose land the LORD your God gives you, and you succeed them, and dwell in their cities, and in their houses;
2 you will separate three cities for you in the midst of your land, which the LORD your God gives you to possess it.
3 you will prepare you a way, and divide the coasts of your land, which the LORD your God gives you to inherit, into three parts, that every slayer may flee thither.
4 And this is the case of the slayer, which will flee thither, that he may live: Whoso kills his neighbor ignorantly, whom he hated not in time past;
5 As when a man goes into the wood with his neighbor to hew wood, and his hand fetches a stroke with the axe to cut down the tree, and the head slips from the helve[3], and lights[4] upon his neighbor, that he die; he will flee unto one of those cities, and live:
6 Lest the avenger of the blood pursue the slayer, while his heart is hot, and overtake him, because the way is long, and slay him; whereas he was not worthy of death, inasmuch as he hated him not in time past.
7 Wherefore I command you, saying, you will separate three cities for you.
8 And if the LORD your God enlarge your coast, as he has sworn unto your fathers, and give you all the land which he promised to give unto your fathers;
9 If you will keep all these commandments to do them, which I command you this day, to love the LORD your God, and to walk ever in his ways; then will you add three cities more for you, beside these three:
10 That innocent blood is not shed in your land, which the LORD your God gives you for an inheritance, and so blood is upon you.
11 But if any man hate his neighbor, and lie in wait for him, and rise up against him, and smite him mortally that he die, and flees into one of these cities:
12 Then the elders of his city will send and fetch him thence, and deliver him into the hand of the avenger of blood, that he may die.
13 your eye will not pity him, but you will put away the guilt of innocent blood from Israel, that it may go well with you.
14 you will not remove your neighbor's landmark, which they of old time have set in your inheritance, which you will inherit in the land that the LORD your God gives you to possess it.
15 One witness will not rise up against a man for any iniquity, or for any sin, in any sin that he sins: at the mouth of two witnesses, or at the mouth of three witnesses, will the matter be established.
16 If a false witness rise up against any man to testify against him that which is wrong;
17 Then both the men, between whom the controversy is, will stand before the LORD, before the priests and the judges, which will be in those days;
18 And the judges will make diligent inquisition: and, behold, if the witness be a false witness, and has testified falsely against his brother;
19 Then will you do unto him, as he had thought to have done unto his brother: so will you put the evil away from among you.
20 And those which remain will hear, and fear, and will henceforth commit no more any such evil among you.
21 And your eye will not pity; but life will go for life, eye for eye, tooth for tooth, hand for hand, foot for foot.

CHAPTER 20

1 When you go out to battle against your enemies, and sees horses, and chariots, and a people more than you, be not afraid of them: for the LORD your God is with you, which brought you up out of the land of Egypt.
2 And it will be, when you are come nigh unto the battle, that the priest will approach and speak unto the people,
3 And will say unto them, Hear, O Israel, you approach this day unto battle against your enemies: let not your hearts faint, fear not, and do not tremble, neither be you terrified because of them;
4 For the LORD your God is he that goes with you, to fight for you against your enemies, to save you.
5 And the officers will speak unto the people, saying, what man is there that has built a new house, and has not dedicated it? Let him go and return to his house, lest he dies in the battle, and another man dedicates it.
6 And what man is he that has planted a vineyard, and has not yet eaten of it? Let him also go and return unto his house, lest he dies in the battle, and another man eats of it.
7 And what man is there that has betrothed a wife, and has not taken her? Let him go and return unto his house, lest he dies in the battle, and another man takes her.
8 And the officers will speak further unto the people, and they will say, what man is there that is fearful and fainthearted? Let him go and return unto his house, lest his brethren's heart faint as well as his heart.
9 And it will be, when the officers have made an end of speaking unto the people, that they will make captains of the armies to lead the people.
10 When you come near unto a city to fight against it, then proclaim peace unto it.
11 And it will be, if it make you answer of peace, and open unto you, then it will be, that all the people that is found therein will be tributaries unto you, and they will serve you.
12 And if it will make no peace with you, but will make war against you, then you will besiege it:
13 And when the LORD your God has delivered it into your hands, you will smite every male thereof with the edge of the sword:
14 But the women, and the little ones, and the cattle, and all that is in the city, even all the spoil thereof, will you take unto thyself; and you will eat the spoil of your enemies, which the LORD your God has given you.
15 Thus will you do unto all the cities which are very far off from you, which are not of the cities of these nations.
16 But of the cities of these people, which the LORD your God does give you for an inheritance, you will save alive nothing that breathes:

---

[1] follow = to exist.
[2] lit. to come or go [Strgs#935].

[3] literally the handle.
[4] literally to cause to come on or upon.

17 But you will utterly destroy them; *namely*, the Hittites, and the Amorites, the Canaanites, and the Perizzites, the Hivites, and the Jebusites; as the LORD your God has commanded you:
18 That they teach you not to do after all their abominations, which they have done unto their gods; so should you sin against the LORD your God.
19 When you will besiege a city a long time, in making war against it to take it, you will not destroy the trees thereof by forcing an axe against them: for you may eat of them, and you will not cut them down (for the tree of the field *is* man's *life*) to employ *them* in the siege:
20 Only the trees which you knows that they *be* not trees for meat, you will destroy and cut them down; and you will build bulwarks against the city that makes war with you, until it be subdued.

CHAPTER 21
1 If *one* be found slain in the land which the LORD your God gives you to possess it, lying in the field, *and* it be not known who has slain him:
2 Then your elders and your judges will come forth, and they will measure unto the cities which *are* round about him that is slain:
3 And it will be, *that* the city which *is* next unto the slain man, even the elders of that city will take an heifer, which has not been wrought with, *and* which has not drawn in the yoke;
4 And the elders of that city will bring down the heifer unto a rough valley, which is neither eared nor sown, and will strike off the heifer's neck there in the valley:
5 And the priests the sons of Levi will come near; for them the LORD your God has chosen to minister unto him, and to bless in the name of the LORD; and by their word will every controversy and every stroke be *tried*:
6 And all the elders of that city, *that are* next unto the slain *man*, will wash their hands over the heifer that is beheaded in the valley:
7 And they will answer and say, our hands have not shed this blood, neither have our eyes seen *it*.
8 Be merciful, O LORD, unto your people Israel, whom you have redeemed, and lay not innocent blood unto your people of Israel's charge. And the blood will be forgiven them.
9 So will you put away the *guilt of* innocent blood from among you, when you will do *that which is* right in the sight of the LORD.
10 When you go forth to war against your enemies, and the LORD your God has delivered them into your hands, and you have taken them captive,
11 And see among the captives a beautiful woman, and have a desire unto her, that you would have her to your wife;
12 Then you will bring her home to your house; and she will shave her head, and pare her nails;
13 And she will put the raiment of her captivity from off her, and will remain in your house, and bewail her father and her mother a full month: and after that you will go in unto her, and be her husband, and she will be your wife.
14 And it will be, if you have no delight in her, then you will let her go whither she will; but you will not sell her at all for money, you will not make merchandise of her, because you have humbled her.
15 If a man have two wives, one beloved, and another hated, and they have born him children, *both* the beloved and the hated; and *if* the firstborn son be hers that was hated:
16 Then it will be, when he makes his sons to inherit *that* which he hath, *that* he may not make the son of the beloved firstborn before the son of the hated, *which is indeed* the firstborn:
17 But he will acknowledge the son of the hated *for* the firstborn, by giving him a double portion of all that he hath: for he *is* the beginning of his strength; the right of the firstborn *is* his.
18 If a man have a stubborn and rebellious son, which will not obey the voice of his father, or the voice of his mother, and *that*, when they have chastened him, will not hearken unto them:
19 Then will his father and his mother lay hold on him, and bring him out unto the elders of his city, and unto the gate of his place;
20 And they will say unto the elders of his city, this our son *is* stubborn and rebellious, he will not obey our voice; *he is* a glutton, and a drunkard.
21 And all the men of his city will stone him with stones, that he dies: so will you put evil away from among you; and all Israel will hear, and fear.
22 And if a man have committed a sin worthy of death, and he be to be put to death, and you hang him on a tree:
23 His body will not remain all night upon the tree, but you will in any wise bury him that day; (for he that is hanged *is* cursed of God;) that your land be not defiled, which the LORD your God gives you *for* an inheritance.

CHAPTER 22
1 you will not see your brother's ox or his sheep go astray, and hide thyself from them: you will in any case bring them again unto your brother.
2 And if your brother *be* not nigh unto you, or if you know him not, then you will bring it unto your own house, and it will be with you until your brother seek after it, and you will restore it to him again.
3 In like manner will you do with his ass; and so will you do with his raiment; and with all lost thing of your brother's, which he has lost, and you have found, will you do likewise: you may not hide thyself.
4 you will not see your brother's ass or his ox fall down by the way, and hide thyself from them: you will surely help him to lift *them* up again.
5 The woman will not wear that which pertained unto a man, neither will a man put on a woman's garment: for all that do so *are* abomination unto the LORD your God.
6 If a bird's nest chance to be before you in the way in any tree, or on the ground, *whether they be* young ones, or eggs, and the dam sitting upon the young, or upon the eggs, you will not take the dam with the young:
7 *But* you will in any wise let the dam go, and take the young to you; that it may be well with you, and *that* you may prolong your days.
8 When you build a new house, then you will make a battlement for your roof, that you bring not blood upon your house, if any man falls from there.
9 you will not sow your vineyard with divers seeds: lest the fruit of your seed which you have sown, and the fruit of your vineyard, be defiled.
10 you will not plow with an ox and an ass together.
11 you will not wear a garment of **diverse** sorts, *as* of woolen and linen together.
12 you will make you fringes upon the four quarters of your vesture, wherewith you cover *yourself*.
13 If any man take a wife, and go in unto her, and hate her,
14 And give occasions of speech against her, and bring up an evil name upon her, and say, I took this woman, and when I came to her, I found her not a maid:

15 Then will the father of the damsel, and her mother, take and bring forth *the tokens of* the damsel's virginity unto the elders of the city in the gate:
16 And the damsel's father will say unto the elders, I gave my daughter unto this man to wife, and he hates her;
17 And, lo, he has given occasions of speech *against her*, saying, I found not your daughter a maid; and yet these *are the tokens of* my daughter's virginity. And they will spread the cloth before the elders of the city.
18 And the elders of that city will take that man and chastise him;
19 And they will amerce him in an hundred *shekels* of silver, and give *them* unto the father of the damsel, because he has brought up an evil name upon a virgin of Israel: and she will be his wife; he may not put her away all his days.
20 But if this thing be true, *and the tokens of* virginity be not found for the damsel:
21 Then they will bring out the damsel to the door of her father's house, and the men of her city will stone her with stones that she dies: because she has wrought folly in Israel, to play the whore in her father's house: so will you put evil away from among you.
22 If a man be found lying with a woman married to an husband, then they will both of them die, *both* the man that lay with the woman, and the woman: so will you put away evil from Israel.
23 If a damsel *that is* a virgin be betrothed unto a husband, and a man find her in the city, and lie with her;
24 Then you will bring them both out unto the gate of that city, and you will stone them with stones that they die; the damsel, because she cried not, *being* in the city; and the man, because he has humbled his neighbor's wife: so you will put away evil from among you.
25 But if a man find a betrothed damsel in the field, and the man force her, and lie with her: then the man only that lay with her will die:
26 But unto the damsel you will do nothing; *there is* in the damsel no sin *worthy* of death: for as when a man rises against his neighbor, and slays him, even so *is* this matter:
27 For he found her in the field, *and* the betrothed damsel cried, and *there was* none to save her.
28 If a man find a damsel *that is* a virgin, which is not betrothed, and lay hold on her, and lie with her, and they be found;
29 Then the man that lay with her will give unto the damsel's father fifty *shekels* of silver, and she will be his wife; because he has humbled her, he may not put her away all his days.
30 A man will not take his father's wife, nor discover his father's skirt.

CHAPTER 23

1 He that is wounded in the stones, or has his privy member cut off, will not enter into the congregation of the LORD.
2 A bastard will not enter into the congregation of the LORD; even to his tenth generation will he not enter into the congregation of the LORD.
3 An Ammonite or Moabite will not enter into the congregation of the LORD; even to their tenth generation will they not enter into the congregation of the LORD for ever:
4 Because they met you not with bread and with water in the way, when you came forth out of Egypt; and because they hired against you Balaam the son of Beor of Pethor of Mesopotamia, to curse you.
5 Nevertheless the LORD your God would not hearken unto Balaam; but the LORD your God turned the curse into a blessing unto you, because the LORD your God loved you.
6 You will not seek their peace nor their prosperity all your days for ever.
7 you will not abhor an Edomite; for he *is* your brother: you will not abhor an Egyptian; because you **were** a stranger in his land.
8 The children that are begotten of them will enter into the congregation of the LORD in their third generation.
9 When the host goes forth against your enemies, then keep you from every wicked thing.
10 If there be among you any man, that is not clean by reason of uncleanness that chances him by night, then will he go abroad out of the camp, he will not come within the camp:
11 But it will be, when evening cometh on, he will wash *himself* with water: and when the sun is down, he will come into the camp *again.*
12 you will have a place also without the camp, whither you will go forth abroad:
13 And you will have a paddle upon your weapon; and it will be, when you wilt ease thyself abroad, you will dig therewith, and will turn back and cover that which cometh from you:
14 For the LORD your God walks in the midst of your camp, to deliver you, and to give up your enemies before you; therefore will your camp be holy: that he see no unclean thing in you, and turn away from you.
15 you will not deliver unto his master the servant which is escaped from his master unto you:
16 He will dwell with you, *even* among you, in that place which he will choose in one of your gates, where it likes him best: you will not oppress him.
17 There will be no whore of the daughters of Israel, or a sodomite of the sons of Israel.
18 you will not bring the hire of a whore, or the price of a dog, into the house of the LORD your God for any vow: for even both these *are* abomination unto the LORD your God.
19 you will not lend upon usury to your brother; usury of money, usury of victuals, usury of anything that is lent upon usury:
20 Unto a stranger you may lend upon usury; but unto your brother you will not lend upon usury: that the LORD your God may bless you in all that you sets your hand to in the land whither you go to possess it.
21 When you will vow a vow unto the LORD your God, you will not slack to pay it: for the LORD your God will surely require it of you; and it would be sin in you.
22 But if you will forbear to vow, it will be no sin in you.
23 That which is gone out of your lips you will keep and perform; *even* a freewill offering, according as you have vowed unto the LORD your God, which you have promised with your mouth.
24 When you come into your neighbor's vineyard, then you may eat grapes your fill at your own pleasure; but you will not put *any* in your vessel.
25 When you come into the standing corn of your neighbor, then you may pluck the ears with your hand; but you will not move a sickle unto your neighbor's standing corn.

CHAPTER 24

1 When a man has taken a wife, and married her, and it come to pass that she find no favor in his eyes, because he has found some uncleanness in her: then let him write her a bill of divorcement, and give it in her hand, and send her out of his house.

2 And when she is departed out of his house, she may go and be another man's *wife*.

3 And *if* the latter husband hate her, and write her a bill of divorcement, and gives *it* in her hand, and sends her out of his house; or if the latter husband die, which took her *to be* his wife;

4 Her former husband, which sent her away, may not take her again to be his wife, after that she is defiled; for that *is* abomination before the LORD: and you will not cause the land to sin, which the LORD your God gives you *for* an inheritance.

5 When a man has taken a new wife, he will not go out to war, neither will he be charged with any business: *but* he will be free at home one year, and will cheer up his wife which he has taken.

6 No man will take the nether or the upper millstone to pledge: for he takes *a man's* life to pledge.

7 If a man be found stealing any of his brethren of the children of Israel, and makes merchandise of him, or sells him; then that thief will die; and you will put evil away from among you.

8 Take heed in the plague of leprosy, that you observe diligently, and do according to all that the priests the Levites will teach you: as I commanded them, *so* you will observe to do.

9 Remember what the LORD your God did unto Miriam by the way, after that you were come forth out of Egypt.

10 When you dost lend your brother anything, you will not go into his house to fetch his pledge.

11 you will stand abroad, and the man to whom you dost lend will bring out the pledge abroad unto you.

12 And if the man *be* poor, you will not sleep with his pledge:

13 In any case you will deliver him the pledge again when the sun goes down, that he may sleep in his own raiment, and bless you: and it will be righteousness unto you before the LORD your God.

14 you will not oppress an hired servant *that is* poor and needy, *whether he be* of your brethren, or of your strangers that *are* in your land within your gates:

15 At his day you will give *him* his hire, neither will the sun go down upon it; for he *is* poor, and sets his heart upon it: lest he cry against you unto the LORD, and it be sin unto you.

16 The fathers will not be put to death for the children, neither will the children be put to death for the fathers: every man will be put to death for his own sin.

17 you will not pervert the judgment of the stranger, *nor* of the fatherless; nor take a widow's raiment to pledge:

18 But you will remember that you **were** a bondman in Egypt, and the LORD your God redeemed you thence: therefore I command you to do this thing.

19 When you cuts down your harvest in your field, and have forgot a sheaf in the field, you will not go again to fetch it: it will be for the stranger, for the fatherless, and for the widow: that the LORD your God may bless you in all the work of your hands.

20 When you beat your olive tree, you will not go over the boughs again: it will be for the stranger, for the fatherless, and for the widow.

21 When you gather the grapes of your vineyard, you will not glean *it* afterward: it will be for the stranger, for the fatherless, and for the widow.

22 And you will remember that you **were** a bondman in the land of Egypt: therefore I command you to do this thing.

CHAPTER 25

1 If there be a controversy between men, and they come unto judgment, that *the judges* may judge them; then they will justify the righteous, and condemn the wicked.

2 And it will be, if the wicked man *be* worthy to be beaten, that the judge will cause him to lie down, and to be beaten before his face, according to his fault, by a certain number.

3 Forty stripes he may give him, *and* not exceed: lest, *if* he should exceed, and beat him above these with many stripes, then your brother should seem vile unto you.

4 you will not muzzle the ox when he treads out *the corn*.

5 If brethren dwell together, and one of them die, and have no child, the wife of the dead will not marry without unto a stranger: her husband's brother will go in unto her, and take her to him to wife, and perform the duty of a husband's brother unto her.

6 And it will be, *that* the firstborn which she bears will succeed in the name of his brother *which is* dead, that his name be not put out of Israel.

7 And if the man like not to take his brother's wife, then let his brother's wife go up to the gate unto the elders, and say, My husband's brother refuses to raise up unto his brother a name in Israel, he will not perform the duty of my husband's brother.

8 Then the elders of his city will call him, and speak unto him: and *if* he stand *to it*, and say, I like not to take her;

9 Then will his brother's wife come unto him in the presence of the elders, and loose his shoe from off his foot, and spit in his face, and will answer and say, so will it be done unto that man that will not build up his brother's house.

10 And his name will be called in Israel, The house of him that has his shoe loosed.

11 When men strive together one with another, and the wife of the one draws near for to deliver her husband out of the hand of him that smites him, and puts forth her hand, and takes him by the secrets:

12 Then you will cut off her hand, your eye will not pity *her*.

13 You will not have in your bag diverse weights, a great and a small.

14 You will not have in your house diverse measures, a great and a small.

15 *But* you will have a perfect and just weight, a perfect and just measure will you have: that your days may be lengthened in the land which the LORD your God gives you.

16 For all that do such things, *and* all that do unrighteously, *are* an abomination unto the LORD your God.

17 Remember what Amalek did unto you by the way, when you were come forth out of Egypt;

18 How he met you by the way, and smote the hindmost of you, *even* all *that were* feeble behind you, when you were faint and weary; and he feared not God.

19 Therefore it will be, when the LORD your God has given you rest from all your enemies round about, in the land which the LORD your God gives you *for* an inheritance to possess it, *that* you will blot out the remembrance of Amalek from under heaven; you will not forget *it*.

CHAPTER 26

1 And it will be, when you *are* come in unto the land which the LORD your God gives you *for* an inheritance, and possesses it, and dwell therein;

2 That you will take of the first of all the fruit of the earth, which you will bring of your land that the LORD your God gives you, and will put *it* in a basket, and will go unto the place which the LORD your God will choose to place his name there.
3 And you will go unto the priest that will be in those days, and say unto him, I profess this day unto the LORD your God, that I am come unto the country which the LORD swore unto our fathers for to give us.
4 And the priest will take the basket out of your hand, and set it down before the altar of the LORD your God.
5 And you will speak and say before the LORD your God, A Syrian ready to perish *was* my father, and he went down into Egypt, and sojourned there with a few, and became there a nation, great, mighty, and populous:
6 And the Egyptians evil entreated us, and afflicted us, and laid upon us hard bondage:
7 And when we cried unto the LORD God of our fathers, the LORD heard our voice, and looked on our affliction, and our labor, and our oppression:
8 And the LORD brought us forth out of Egypt with a mighty hand, and with an outstretched arm, and with great terribleness, and with signs, and with wonders:
9 And he has brought us into this place, and has given us this land, *even* a land that flows with milk and honey.
10 And now, behold, I have brought the first fruits of the land, which you, O LORD, have given me. And you will set it before the LORD your God, and worship before the LORD your God:
11 And you will rejoice in every good *thing* which the LORD your God has given unto you, and unto your house, you, and the Levite, and the stranger that *is* among you.
12 When you have made an end of tithing all the tithes of your increase the third year, *which is* the year of tithing, and have given *it* unto the Levite, the stranger, the fatherless, and the widow, that they may eat within your gates, and be filled;
13 Then you will say before the LORD your God, I have brought away the hallowed things out of *mine* house, and also have given them unto the Levite, and unto the stranger, to the fatherless, and to the widow, according to all your commandments which you have commanded me: I have not transgressed your commandments, neither have I forgotten *them*:
14 I have not eaten thereof in my mourning, neither have I taken away *ought* thereof for *any* unclean *use*, nor given *ought* thereof for the dead: *but* I have hearkened to the voice of the LORD my God, *and* have done according to all that you have commanded me.
15 Look down from your holy habitation, from heaven, and bless your people Israel, and the land which you have given us, as you swore unto our fathers, a land that flows with milk and honey.
16 This day the LORD your God has commanded you to do these statutes and judgments: you will therefore keep and do them with all your heart, and with all your soul.
17 you have avouched the LORD this day to be your God, and to walk in his ways, and to keep his statutes, and his commandments, and his judgments, and to hearken unto his voice:
18 And the LORD has avouched you this day to be his peculiar people, as he has promised you, and that you should keep all his commandments;
19 And to make you high above all nations which he has made, in praise, and in name, and in honor; and that you may be a holy people unto the LORD your God, as he has spoken.

CHAPTER 27

1 And Moses with the elders of Israel commanded the people, saying, keep all the commandments which I command you this day.
2 And it will be on the day when you will pass over Jordan unto the land which the LORD your God gives you, that you will set you up great stones, and plaster them with plaster:
3 And you will write upon them all the words of this law, when you are passed over, that you may go in unto the land which the LORD your God gives you, a land that flows with milk and honey; as the LORD God of your fathers has promised you.
4 Therefore it will be when you be gone over Jordan, *that* you will set up these stones, which I command you this day, in mount Ebal, and you will plaster them with plaster.
5 And there will you build an altar unto the LORD your God, an altar of stones: you will not lift up *any* iron *tool* upon them.
6 you will build the altar of the LORD your God of whole stones: and you will offer burnt offerings thereon unto the LORD your God:
7 And you will offer peace offerings, and will eat there, and rejoice before the LORD your God.
8 And you will write upon the stones all the words of this law very plainly.
9 And Moses and the priests the Levites spoke unto all Israel, saying, Take heed, and hearken, O Israel; this day you are become the people of the LORD your God.
10 you will therefore obey the voice of the LORD your God, and do his commandments and his statutes, which I command you this day.
11 And Moses charged the people the same day, saying,
12 These will stand upon mount Gerizim to bless the people, when you are come over Jordan; Simeon, and Levi, and Judah, and Issachar, and Joseph, and Benjamin:
13 And these will stand upon mount Ebal to curse; Reuben, Gad, and Asher, and Zebulun, Dan, and Naphtali.
14 And the Levites will speak, and say unto all the men of Israel with a loud voice,
15 Cursed *be* the man that makes *any* graven or molten image, an abomination unto the LORD, the work of the hands of the craftsman, and puts *it* in *a* secret *place*. And all the people will answer and say, Amen.
16 Cursed *be* he that set light by his father or his mother. And all the people will say, Amen.
17 Cursed *be* he that remove his neighbor's landmark. And all the people will say, Amen.
18 Cursed *be* he that make the blind to wander out of the way. And all the people will say, Amen.
19 Cursed *be* he that perverts the judgment of the stranger, fatherless, and widow. And all the people will say, Amen.
20 Cursed *be* he that lies with his father's wife; because he uncovers his father's skirt. And all the people will say, Amen.
21 Cursed *be* he that lies with any manner of beast. And all the people will say, Amen.
22 Cursed *be* he that lies with his sister, the daughter of his father, or the daughter of his mother. And all the people will say, Amen.
23 Cursed *be* he that lies with his mother in law. And all the people will say, Amen.
24 Cursed *be* he that smites his neighbor secretly. And all the people will say, Amen.

25 Cursed *be* he that takes reward to slay an innocent person. And all the people will say, Amen.
26 Cursed *be* he that confirms not *all* the words of this law to do them. And all the people will say, Amen.

CHAPTER 28

1 And it will come to pass, if you will hearken diligently unto the voice of the LORD your God, to observe *and* to do all his commandments which I command you this day, that the LORD your God will set you on high above all nations of the earth:
2 And all these blessings will come on you, and overtake you, if you will hearken unto the voice of the LORD your God.
3 Blessed will you *be* in the city, and blessed will you *be* in the field.
4 Blessed will *be* the fruit of your body, and the fruit of your ground, and the fruit of your cattle, the increase of heifer, and the flocks of your sheep.
5 Blessed will *be* your basket and your store.
6 Blessed will you *be* when you come in, and blessed will you *be* when you go out.
7 The LORD will cause your enemies that rise up against you to be smitten before your face: they will come out against you one way, and flee before you seven ways.
8 The LORD will command the blessing upon you in your storehouses, and in all that you set your hand unto; and he will bless you in the land which the LORD your God gives you.
9 The LORD will establish you a holy people unto himself, as he has sworn unto you, if you will keep the commandments of the LORD your God, and walk in his ways.
10 And all people of the earth will see that you are called by the name of the LORD; and they will be afraid of you.
11 And the LORD will make you plenteous in goods, in the fruit of your body, and in the fruit of your cattle, and in the fruit of your ground, in the land which the LORD swore unto your fathers to give you.
12 The LORD will open unto you his good treasure, the heaven to give the rain unto your land in his season, and to bless all the work of your hand: and you will lend unto many nations, and you will not borrow.
13 And the LORD will make you the head, and not the tail; and you will be above only, and you will not be beneath; if that you hearken unto the commandments of the LORD your God, which I command you this day, to observe and to do *them*:
14 And you will not go aside from any of the words which I command you this day, *to* the right hand, or *to* the left, to go after other gods to serve them.
15 But it will come to pass, if you will not hearken unto the voice of the LORD your God, to observe to do all his commandments and his statutes which I command you this day; that all these curses will come upon you, and overtake you:
16 Cursed will you *be* in the city, and cursed will you *be* in the field.
17 Cursed will *be* your basket and your store.
18 Cursed will *be* the fruit of your body, and the fruit of your land, the increase of your heifer, and the flocks of your sheep.
19 Cursed will you *be* when you come in, and cursed will you *be* when you go out.
20 The LORD will send upon you cursing, vexation, and rebuke, in all that you set your hand unto for to do, until you are destroyed, and until you perish quickly; because of the wickedness of your doings, whereby you have forsaken me.

21 The LORD will make the pestilence cleave unto you, until he have consumed you from off the land, whither you go to possess it.
22 The LORD will smite you with consumption, and with a fever, and with an inflammation, and with an extreme burning, and with the sword, and with blasting, and with mildew; and they will pursue you until you perish.
23 And your heaven that *is* over your head will be brass, and the earth that is under you will *be* iron.
24 The LORD will make the rain of your land powder and dust: from heaven will it come down upon you, until you are destroyed.
25 The LORD will cause you to be smitten before your enemies: you will go out one way against them, and flee seven ways before them: and will be removed into all the kingdoms of the earth.
26 And your carcass will be meat unto all fowls of the air, and unto the beasts of the earth, and no man will fray *them* away.
27 The LORD will smite you with the botch of Egypt, and with the emerods[1], and with the scab, and with the itch, whereof you canst not be healed.
28 The LORD will smite you with madness, and blindness, and astonishment of heart:
29 And you will grope at noonday, as the blind gropes in darkness, and you will not prosper in your ways: and you will be only oppressed and spoiled evermore, and no man will save *you*.
30 you will betroth a wife, and another man will lie with her: you will build a house, and you will not dwell therein: you will plant a vineyard, and will not gather the grapes thereof.
31 your ox will *be* slain before your eyes, and you will not eat thereof: your ass will *be* violently taken away from before your face, and will not be restored to you: your sheep will *be* given unto your enemies, and you will have none to rescue *them*.
32 your sons and your daughters will *be* given unto another people, and your eyes will look, and fail *with longing* for them all day long: and *there will be* no might in your hand.
33 The fruit of your land, and all your labors, will a nation which you knowest not eat up; and you will be only oppressed and crushed alway:
34 So that you will be mad for the sight of your eyes which you will see.
35 The LORD will smite you in the knees, and in the legs, with a sore botch that cannot be healed, from the sole of your foot unto the top of your head.
36 The LORD will bring you, and your king which you will set over you, unto a nation which neither you nor your fathers have known; and there will you serve other gods, wood and stone.
37 And you will become an astonishment, a proverb, and a byword, among all nations whither the LORD will lead you.
38 you will carry much seed out into the field, and will gather *but* little in; for the locust will consume it.
39 you will plant vineyards, and dress *them*, but will neither drink *of* the wine, nor gather *the grapes*; for the worms will eat them.
40 you will have olive trees throughout all your coasts, but you will not anoint *thyself* with the oil; for your olive will cast *his fruit*.
41 you will beget sons and daughters, but you will not enjoy them; for they will go into captivity.
42 All your trees and fruit of your land will the locust consume.
43 The stranger that *is* within you will get up above you very high; and you will come down very low.

---

[1] emerod- meaning to burn, a boil or ulcer (from the inflammation), especially a tumor in the anus or pudenda. [Strgs#2914 & 6076]

44 He will lend to you, and you will not lend to him: he will be the head, and you will be the tail.

45 Moreover all these curses will come upon you, and will pursue you, and overtake you, until you are destroyed; because you hearkened not unto the voice of the LORD your God, to keep his commandments and his statutes which he commanded you:

46 And they will be upon you for a sign and for a wonder, and upon your seed for ever.

47 Because you served not the LORD your God with joyfulness, and with gladness of heart, for the abundance of all *things*;

48 Therefore will you serve your enemies which the LORD will send against you, in hunger, and in thirst, and in nakedness, and in want of all *things*: and he will put a yoke of iron upon your neck, until he has destroyed you.

49 The LORD will bring a nation against you from far, from the end of the earth, *as swift* as the eagle flies; a nation whose tongue you will not understand;

50 A nation of fierce countenance, which will not regard the person of the old, nor show favor to the young:

51 And he will eat the fruit of your cattle, and the fruit of your land, until you are destroyed: which *also* will not leave you *either* corn, wine, or oil, *or* the increase of your heifer, or flocks of your sheep, until he have destroyed you.

52 And he will besiege you in all your gates, until your high and fenced walls come down, wherein you trusted, throughout all your land: and he will besiege you in all your gates throughout all your land, which the LORD your God has given you.

53 And you will eat the fruit of your own body, the flesh of your sons and of your daughters, which the LORD your God has given you, in the siege, and in the straitness[1], wherewith your enemies will distress you:

54 *So that* the man *that is* tender among you, and very delicate, his eye will be evil toward his brother, and toward the wife of his bosom, and toward the remnant of his children which he will leave:

55 So that he will not give to any of them of the flesh of his children whom he will eat: because he has nothing left him in the siege, and in the straitness, wherewith your enemies will distress you in all your gates.

56 The tender and delicate woman among you, which would not adventure to set the sole of her foot upon the ground for delicateness and tenderness, her eye will be evil toward the husband of her bosom, and toward her son, and toward her daughter,

57 And toward her young one that cometh out from between her feet, and toward her children which she will bear: for she will eat them for want of all *things* secretly in the siege and straitness, wherewith your enemy will distress you in your gates.

58 If you wilt not observe to do all the words of this law that are written in this book, that you may fear this glorious and fearful name, THE LORD your GOD;

59 Then the LORD will make your plagues wonderful, and the plagues of your seed, *even* great plagues, and of long continuance, and sore sicknesses, and of long continuance.

60 Moreover he will bring upon you all the diseases of Egypt, which you wast afraid of; and they will cleave unto you.

61 Also every sickness, and every plague, which *is* not written in the book of this law, them will the LORD bring upon you, until you be destroyed.

62 And you will be left few in number, whereas you were as the stars of heaven for multitude; because you wouldest not obey the voice of the LORD your God.

63 And it will come to pass, *that* as the LORD rejoiced over you to do you good, and to multiply you; so the LORD will rejoice over you to destroy you, and to bring you to nought; and you will be plucked from off the land whither you goest to possess it.

64 And the LORD will scatter you among all people, from the one end of the earth even unto the other; and there you will serve other gods, which neither you nor your fathers have known, *even* wood and stone.

65 And among these nations will you find no ease, neither will the sole of your foot have rest: but the LORD will give you there a trembling heart, and failing of eyes, and sorrow of mind:

66 And your life will hang in doubt before you; and you will fear day and night, and will have none assurance of your life:

67 In the morning you will say, Would God it were even! And at even you will say, Would God it were morning! For the fear of your heart wherewith you will fear, and for the sight of your eyes which you will see.

68 And the LORD will bring you into Egypt again with ships, by the way whereof I spoke unto you, you will see it no more again: and there you will be sold unto your enemies for bondmen and bondwomen, and no man will buy *you*.

CHAPTER 29

1 These *are* the words of the covenant, which the LORD commanded Moses to make with the children of Israel in the land of Moab, beside the covenant which he made with them in Horeb.

2 And Moses called unto all Israel, and said unto them, you have seen all that the LORD did before your eyes in the land of Egypt unto Pharaoh, and unto all his servants, and unto all his land;

3 The great temptations which your eyes have seen, the signs, and those great miracles:

4 Yet the LORD has not given you a heart to perceive, and eyes to see, and ears to hear, unto this day.

5 And I have led you forty years in the wilderness: your clothes are not waxen old upon you, and your shoe is not waxen old upon your foot.

6 You have not eaten bread, neither have you drink wine or strong drink: that you might know that I *am* the LORD your God.

7 And when you came unto this place, Sihon the king of Heshbon, and Og the king of Bashan, came out against us unto battle, and we smote them:

8 And we took their land, and gave it for an inheritance unto the Reubenites, and to the Gadites, and to the half tribe of Manasseh.

9 Keep therefore the words of this covenant, and do them, that you may prosper in all that you do.

10 You stand this day all of you before the LORD your God; your captains of your tribes, your elders, and your officers, *with* all the men of Israel,

11 Your little ones, your wives, and your stranger that *is* in your camp, from the hewer of your wood unto the drawer of your water:

12 That you should enter into covenant with the LORD your God, and into his oath, which the LORD your God makes with you this day:

13 That he may establish you today for a people unto himself, and *that* he may be unto you a God, as he has said unto you, and as

---

[1] straitness- a narrow place, that is (either abstract or figuratively) confinement or disability: anguish or distress. [Strgs#4689]

he has sworn unto your fathers, to Abraham, to Isaac, and to Jacob.
14 Neither with you only do I make this covenant and this oath;
15 But with *him* that stands here with us this day before the LORD our God, and also with *him* that *is* not here with us this day:
16 (For you know how we have dwelt in the land of Egypt; and how we came through the nations which you passed by;
17 And you have seen their abominations, and their idols, wood and stone, silver and gold, which *were* among them:)
18 Lest there should be among you man, or woman, or family, or tribe, whose heart turns away this day from the LORD our God, to go *and* serve the gods of these nations; lest there should be among you a root that bares gall[1] and wormwood[2];
19 And it come to pass, when he hears the words of this curse, that he bless himself in his heart, saying, I will have peace, though I walk in the imagination of mine heart, to add drunkenness to thirst:
20 The LORD will not spare him, but then the anger of the LORD and his jealousy will smoke against that man, and all the curses that are written in this book will lie upon him, and the LORD will blot out his name from under heaven.
21 And the LORD will separate him unto evil out of all the tribes of Israel, according to all the curses of the covenant that are written in this book of the law:
22 So that the generation to come of your children that will rise up after you, and the stranger that will come from afar land, will say, when they see the plagues of that land, and the sicknesses which the LORD has laid upon it;
23 And that the whole land thereof *is* brimstone, and salt, *and* burning, *that* it is not sown, or bear, or any grass grows therein, like the overthrow of Sodom, and Gomorrah, Admah, and Zeboim, which the LORD overthrew in his anger, and in his wrath:
24 Even all nations will say, wherefore has the LORD done thus unto this land? What *means* the heat of this great anger?
25 Then men will say, because they have forsaken the covenant of the LORD God of their fathers, which he made with them when he brought them forth out of the land of Egypt:
26 For they went and served other gods, and worshipped them, gods whom they knew not, and *whom* he had not given unto them:
27 And the anger of the LORD was kindled against this land, to bring upon it all the curses that are written in this book:
28 And the LORD rooted them out of their land in anger, and in wrath, and in great indignation, and cast them into another land, as *it is* this day.
29 The secret *things belong* unto the LORD our God: but those *things which are* revealed *belong* unto us and to our children for ever, that *we* may do all the words of this law.

CHAPTER 30

1 And it will come to pass, when all these things are come upon you, the blessing and the curse, which I have set before you, and you will call *them* to mind among all the nations, whither the LORD your God has driven you,
2 And will return unto the LORD your God, and will obey his voice according to all that I command you this day, you and your children, with all your heart, and with all your soul;
3 That then the LORD your God will turn your captivity, and have compassion upon you, and will return and gather you from all the nations, whither the LORD your God has scattered you.
4 If *any* of your be driven out unto the outmost *parts* of heaven, from thence will the LORD your God gather you, and from thence will he fetch you:
5 And the LORD your God will bring you into the land which your fathers possessed, and you will possess it; and he will do you good, and multiply you above your fathers.
6 And the LORD your God will circumcise your heart, and the heart of your seed, to love the LORD your God with all your heart, and with all your soul, that you may live.
7 And the LORD your God will put all these curses upon your enemies, and on them that hate you, which persecuted you.
8 And you will return and obey the voice of the LORD, and do all his commandments which I command you this day.
9 And the LORD your God will make you plenteous in every work of your hand, in the fruit of your body, and in the fruit of your cattle, and in the fruit of your land, for good: for the LORD will again rejoice over you for good, as he rejoiced over your fathers:
10 If you will hearken unto the voice of the LORD your God, to keep his commandments and his statutes which are written in this book of the law, *and* if you turn unto the LORD your God with all your heart, and with all your soul.
11 For this commandment which I command you this day, it *is* not hidden from you, neither *is* it far off.
12 It *is* not in heaven, that you should say, who will go up for us to heaven, and bring it unto us, that we may hear it, and do it?
13 Neither *is* it beyond the sea, that you should say, who will go over the sea for us, and bring it unto us, that we may hear it, and do it?
14 But the word *is* very nigh unto you, in your mouth, and in your heart, that you may do it.
15 See, I have set before you this day life and good, and death and evil;
16 In that I command you this day to love the LORD your God, to walk in his ways, and to keep his commandments and his statutes and his judgments, that you may live and multiply: and the LORD your God will bless you in the land whither you go to possess it.
17 But if your heart turn away, so that you will not hear, but will be drawn away, and worship other gods, and serve them;
18 I denounce unto you this day, that you will surely perish, *and that* you will not prolong *your* days upon the land, whither you pass over Jordan to go to possess it.
19 I call heaven and earth to record this day against you, *that* I have set before you life and death, blessing and cursing: therefore choose life, that both you and your seed may live:
20 That you may love the LORD your God, *and* that you may obey his voice, and that you may cleave unto him: for he *is* your life, and the length of your days: that you may dwell in the land which the LORD swore unto your fathers, to Abraham, to Isaac, and to Jacob, to give them.

CHAPTER 31

1 And Moses went and spoke these words unto all Israel.
2 And he said unto them, I *am* an hundred and twenty years old this day; I can no more go out and come in: also the LORD has said unto me, you will not go over this Jordan.

---

[1] gall- a poisonous plant, probably the poppy; generally poison (even as serpents): hemlock, poison and venom. [Strgs#7219]

[2] wormwood- also regarded as poisonous and therefore cursed: hemlock. [Strgs#3939]

3 The LORD your God, he will go over before you, *and* he will destroy these nations from before you, and you will possess them: *and* Joshua, he will go over before you, as the LORD has said.
4 And the LORD will do unto them as he did to Sihon and to Og, kings of the Amorites, and unto the land of them, whom he destroyed.
5 And the LORD will give them up before your face, that you may do unto them according unto all the commandments which I have commanded you.
6 Be strong and of a good courage, fear not, or be afraid of them: for the LORD your God, he that does go with you; he will not fail you, or forsake you.
7 And Moses called unto Joshua, and said unto him in the sight of all Israel, Be strong and of a good courage: for you must go with this people unto the land which the LORD has sworn unto their fathers to give them; and you will cause them to inherit it.
8 And the LORD, he that does go before you; he will be with you, he will not fail you, neither forsakes you: fear not, neither is dismayed.
9 And Moses wrote this law, and delivered it unto the priests the sons of Levi, which bare the Ark of the Covenant of the LORD, and unto all the elders of Israel.
10 And Moses commanded them, saying, at the end of *every* seven years, in the solemnity of the year of release, in the feast of tabernacles,
11 When all Israel is come to appear before the LORD your God in the place which he will choose, you will read this law before all Israel in their hearing.
12 Gather the people together, men, and women, and children, and your stranger that *is* within your gates, that they may hear, and that they may learn, and fear the LORD your God, and observe to do all the words of this law:
13 And *that* their children, which have not known *anything*, may hear, and learn to fear the LORD your God, as long as you live in the land whither you go over Jordan to possess it.
14 And the LORD said unto Moses, Behold, your days approach that you must die: call Joshua, and present yourselves in the tabernacle of the congregation, that I may give him a charge. And Moses and Joshua went, and presented themselves in the tabernacle of the congregation.
15 And the LORD appeared in the tabernacle in a pillar of a cloud: and the pillar of the cloud stood over the door of the tabernacle.
16 And the LORD said unto Moses, Behold, you will sleep with your fathers; and this people will rise up, and go a whoring after the gods of the strangers of the land, whither they go *to be* among them, and will forsake me, and break my covenant which I have made with them.
17 Then my anger will be kindled against them in that day, and I will forsake them, and I will hide my face from them, and they will be devoured, and many evils and troubles will befall them; so that they will say in that day, are not these evils come upon us, because our God *is* not among us?
18 And I will surely hide my face in that day for all the evils which they will have wrought, in that they are turned unto other gods.
19 Now therefore write you this song for you, and teach it the children of Israel: put it in their mouths, that this song may be a witness for me against the children of Israel.
20 For when I will have brought them into the land which I swore unto their fathers, that flows with milk and honey; and they will have eaten and filled themselves, and waxen fat; then will they turn unto other gods, and serve them, and provoke me, and break my covenant.
21 And it will come to pass, when many evils and troubles are befallen them, that this song will testify against them as a witness; for it will not be forgotten out of the mouths of their seed: for I know their imagination which they go about, even now, before I have brought them into the land which I swore.
22 Moses therefore wrote this song the same day, and taught it the children of Israel.
23 And he gave Joshua the son of Nun a charge, and said, be strong and of a good courage: for you will bring the children of Israel into the land which I swore unto them: and I will be with you.
24 And it came to pass, when Moses had made an end of writing the words of this law in a book, until they were finished,
25 That Moses commanded the Levites, which bare the ark of the covenant of the LORD, saying,
26 Take this book of the law, and put it in the side of the ark of the covenant of the LORD your God, that it may be there for a witness against you.
27 For I know your rebellion, and your stiff neck: behold, while I am yet alive with you this day, you have been rebellious against the LORD; and how much more after my death?
28 Gather unto me all the elders of your tribes, and your officers, that I may speak these words in their ears, and call heaven and earth to record against them.
29 For I know that after my death you will utterly corrupt *yourselves*, and turn aside from the way which I have commanded you; and evil will befall you in the latter days; because you will do evil in the sight of the LORD, to provoke him to anger through the work of your hands.
30 And Moses spoke in the ears of all the congregation of Israel the words of this song, until they were ended.

CHAPTER 32

1 Give ear, O you heavens, and I will speak; and hear, O earth, the words of my mouth.
2 My doctrine will drop as the rain, my speech will distil as the dew, as the small rain upon the tender herb, and as the showers upon the grass:
3 Because I will publish the name of the LORD: ascribe you greatness unto our God.
4 *He is* the Rock, his work *is* perfect: for all his ways *is* judgment: a God of truth and without iniquity, just and right *is* he.
5 They have corrupted themselves, their spot *is* not *the spot* of his children: *they are* a perverse and crooked generation.
6 Do you thus requite the LORD, O foolish people and unwise? *Is* not he your father *that* has bought you? Has he not made you, and established you?
7 Remember the days of old, consider the years of many generations: ask your father, and he will show you; your elders, and they will tell you.
8 When the most High divided to the nations their inheritance, when he separated the sons of Adam, he set the bounds of the people according to the number of the children of Israel.
9 For the LORD'S portion *are* his people; Jacob *is* the lot of his inheritance.
10 He found him in a desert land, and in the waste howling wilderness; he led him about, he instructed him, he kept him as the apple of his eye.

11 As an eagle stirs up her nest, flutters over her young, spreads abroad her wings, takes them, and bears them on her wings:
12 So the LORD alone did lead him, and *there was* no strange god with him.
13 He made him ride on the high places of the earth, that he might eat the increase of the fields; and he made him to suck honey out of the rock, and oil out of the flinty rock;
14 Butter of heifer, and milk of sheep, with fat of lambs, and rams of the breed of Bashan, and goats, with the fat of kidneys of wheat; and you didst drink the pure blood of the grape.
15 But Jeshurun waxed fat, and kicked: you are waxen fat, you are grown thick, you are covered *with fatness*; then he forsook God *which* made him, and lightly esteemed the Rock of his salvation.
16 They provoked him to jealousy with strange *gods*, with abominations provoked they him to anger.
17 They sacrificed unto devils, not to God; to gods whom they knew not, to new *gods that* came newly up, whom your fathers feared not.
18 Of the Rock *that* begat you, you are unmindful, and have forgotten God that formed you.
19 And when the LORD saw *it*, he abhorred *them*, because of the provoking of his sons, and of his daughters.
20 And he said, I will hide my face from them, I will see what their end will *be*: for they *are* a very forward generation, children in whom *is* no faith.
21 They have moved me to jealousy with *that which is* not God; they have provoked me to anger with their vanities: and I will move them to jealousy with *those which are* not a people; I will provoke them to anger with a foolish nation.
22 For a fire is kindled in mine anger, and will burn unto the lowest hell, and will consume the earth with her increase, and set on fire the foundations of the mountains.
23 I will heap mischiefs upon them; I will spend mine arrows upon them.
24 *They will be* burnt with hunger, and devoured with burning heat, and with bitter destruction: I will also send the teeth of beasts upon them, with the poison of serpents of the dust.
25 The sword without, and terror within, will destroy both the young man and the virgin, the suckling *also* with the man of gray hairs.
26 I said, I would scatter them into corners, I would make the remembrance of them to cease from among men:
27 Were it not that I feared the wrath of the enemy, lest their adversaries should behave themselves strangely, *and* lest they should say, our hand *is* high, and the LORD has not done all this.
28 For they *are* a nation void of counsel, neither *is there any* understanding in them.
29 O that they were wise, *that* they understood this, *that* they would consider their latter end!
30 How should one chase a thousand, and two put ten thousand to flight, except their Rock had sold them, and the LORD had shut them up?
31 For their rock *is* not as our Rock, even our enemies themselves *being* judges.
32 For their vine *is* of the vine of Sodom, and of the fields of Gomorrah: their grapes *are* grapes of gall, their clusters *are* bitter:
33 Their wine *is* the poison of dragons, and the cruel venom of asps.
34 *Is* not this laid up in store with me, *and* sealed up among my treasures?
35 To me *belonged* vengeance, and recompense; their foot will slide in *due* time: for the day of their calamity *is* at hand, and the things that will come upon them make haste.
36 For the LORD will judge his people, and repent himself for his servants, when he sees that *their* power is gone, and *there is* none shut up, or left.
37 And he will say, where *are* their gods, *their* rock in whom they trusted,
38 Which did eat the fat of their sacrifices, *and* drank the wine of their drink offerings? Let them rise up and help you, *and* be your protection.
39 See now that I, *even* I, *am* he, and *there is* no god with me: I kill, and I make alive; I wound, and I heal: neither *is there any* that can deliver out of my hand.
40 For I lift up my hand to heaven, and say, I live forever.
41 If I whet my glittering sword, and mine hand take hold on judgment; I will render vengeance to mine enemies, and will reward them that hate me.
42 I will make mine arrows drunk with blood, and my sword will devour flesh; *and that* with the blood of the slain and of the captives, from the beginning of revenges upon the enemy.
43 Rejoice, O you nations, *with* his people: for he will avenge the blood of his servants, and will render vengeance to his adversaries, and will be merciful unto his land, *and* to his people.
44 And Moses came and spoke all the words of this song in the ears of the people, he, and Hoshea the son of Nun.
45 And Moses made an end of speaking all these words to all Israel:
46 And he said unto them, set your hearts unto all the words which I testify among you this day, which you will command your children to observe to do, all the words of this law.
47 For it *is* not a vain thing for you; because it *is* your life: and through this thing you will prolong *your* days in the land, whither you go over Jordan to possess it.
48 And the LORD spoke unto Moses that selfsame day, saying,
49 Get you up into this mountain Abarim, *unto* mount Nebo, which *is* in the land of Moab, that *is* over against Jericho; and behold the land of Canaan, which I give unto the children of Israel for a possession:
50 And die in the mount whither you go up, and be gathered unto your people; as Aaron your brother died in mount Hor, and was gathered unto his people:
51 Because you trespassed against me among the children of Israel at the waters of Meribah-Kadesh, in the wilderness of Zin; because you sanctified me not in the midst of the children of Israel.
52 Yet you will see the land before *you*; but you will not go thither unto the land which I give the children of Israel.

CHAPTER 33

1 And this *is* the blessing, wherewith Moses the man of God blessed the children of Israel before his death.
2 And he said, The LORD came from Sinai, and rose up from Seir unto them; he shined forth from mount Paran, and he came with ten thousands of saints: from his right hand *went* a fiery law for them.
3 Yea, he loved the people; all his saints *are* in your hand: and they sat down at your feet; *everyone* will receive of your words.
4 Moses commanded us a law, *even* the inheritance of the congregation of Jacob.

5 And he was king in Jeshurun, when the heads of the people *and* the tribes of Israel were gathered together.
6 Let Reuben live, and not die; and let *not* his men be few.
7 And this *is the blessing* of Judah: and he said, Hear, LORD, the voice of Judah, and bring him unto his people: let his hands be sufficient for him; and be you a help *to him* from his enemies.
8 And of Levi he said, *let* your Thummim and your Urim *be* with your holy one, whom you didst prove at Massah[1], *and with* whom you didst strive at the waters of Meribah;
9 Who said unto his father and to his mother, I have not seen him; neither did he acknowledge his brethren, nor knew his own children: for they have observed your word, and kept your covenant.
10 They will teach Jacob your judgments, and Israel your law: they will put incense before you, and [whole burnt sacrifice][2] upon your altar.
11 Bless, LORD, his substance, and accept the work of his hands: smite through the loins of them that rise against him, and of them that hate him, that they rise not again.
12 *And* of Benjamin he said, the beloved of the LORD will dwell in safety by him; *and the LORD* will cover him all the day long, and he will dwell between his shoulders.
13 And of Joseph he said, blessed of the LORD *be* his land, for the precious things of heaven, for the dew, and for the deep that coucheth beneath,
14 And for the precious fruits *brought forth* by the sun, and for the precious things put forth by the moon,
15 And for the chief things of the ancient mountains, and for the precious things of the lasting hills,
16 And for the precious things of the earth and fullness thereof, and *for* the good will of him that dwelt in the bush: let *the blessing* come upon the head of Joseph, and upon the top of the head of him *that was* separated from his brethren.
17 His glory *is like* the firstling of his bullock, and his horns *are like* the horns of unicorns: with them he will push the people together to the ends of the earth: and they *are* the ten thousands of Ephraim, and they *are* the thousands of Manasseh.
18 And of Zebulun he said, Rejoice, Zebulun, in your going out; and, Issachar, in your tents.
19 They will call the people unto the mountain; there they will offer sacrifices of righteousness: for they will suck *of* the abundance of the seas, and *of* treasures hid in the sand.
20 And of Gad he said, blessed *be* he that enlarges Gad: he dwelled as a lion, and tears the arm with the crown of the head.
21 And he provided the first part for himself, because there, *in* a portion of the lawgiver, *was he* seated; and he came with the heads of the people, he executed the justice of the LORD, and his judgments with Israel.
22 And of Dan he said, Dan *is* a lion's whelp: he will leap from Bashan.
23 And of Naphtali he said, O Naphtali, satisfied with favor, and full with the blessing of the LORD: possess you the west and the south.
24 And of Asher he said, *Let* Asher *be* blessed with children; let him be acceptable to his brethren, and let him dip his foot in oil.
25 Your shoes will *be* iron and brass; and as your days, *so will your* strength *be*.
26 *There is* none like unto the God of Jeshurun, *who* rides upon the heaven in your help, and in his excellency on the sky.
27 The eternal God *is your* refuge, and underneath *are* the everlasting arms: and he will thrust out the enemy from before you; and will say, Destroy *them*.
28 Israel then will dwell in safety alone: the fountain of Jacob will *be* upon a land of corn and wine; also his heavens will drop down dew.
29 Happy are you, O Israel: who *is* like unto you, O people saved by the LORD, the shield of your help, and who *is* the sword of your excellency! And your enemies will be found liars unto you; and you will tread upon their high places.

CHAPTER 34

1 And Moses went up from the plains of Moab unto the mountain of Nebo, to the top of Pisgah, that *is* over against Jericho. And the LORD showed him all the land of Gilead, unto Dan,
2 And all Naphtali, and the land of Ephraim, and Manasseh, and all the land of Judah, unto the utmost sea,
3 And the south, and the plain of the valley of Jericho, the city of palm trees, unto Zoar.
4 And the LORD said unto him, this *is* the land which I swore unto Abraham, unto Isaac, and unto Jacob, saying, I will give it unto your seed: I have caused you to see *it* with your eyes, but you will not go over thither.
5 [So Moses the servant of the LORD died there in the land of Moab, according to the word of the LORD.][3]
6 And he buried him in a valley in the land of Moab, over against Beth-peor: but no man knows of his sepulcher unto this day.
7 And Moses *was* an hundred and twenty years old when he died: his eye was not dim, nor his [natural force][4] abated.
8 And the children of Israel wept for Moses in the plains of Moab thirty days: so the days of weeping *and* mourning for Moses were ended.
9 And Joshua the son of Nun was full of the spirit of wisdom; for Moses had laid his hands upon him: and the children of Israel hearkened unto him, and did as the LORD commanded Moses.
10 And there arose not a prophet since in Israel like unto Moses, whom the LORD knew face to face,
11 In all the signs and the wonders, which the LORD sent him to do in the land of Egypt to Pharaoh, and to all his servants, and to all his land,
12 And in all that mighty hand, and in all the great terror which Moses showed in the sight of all Israel.

---

[1] Massah – lit. testing. The place in the wilderness where the Iserlites tested Jehovah. [Strgs#4532]
[2] lit. complete, the *whole* (specifically a sacrifice entirely consumed); fully [Strgs#3632].
[3] that is God commanded him to die, see **Deut. 32:49-55**
[4] natural force – *freshness*, green, to be new, moisture [Strgs#3893].

JOSHUA
CHAPTER 1

1 Now after the death of Moses the servant of the LORD it came to pass, that the LORD spoke unto Joshua[1] the son of Nun, Moses' minister, saying,
2 Moses my servant is dead; now therefore arise, go over this Jordan[2], you, and this **entire** people, unto the land which I do give to them, *even* to the children of Israel.
3 Every place that the sole of your foot will tread upon, that have I given unto you, as I said unto Moses.
4 From the wilderness and this Lebanon even unto the great river, the river Euphrates, all the land of the Hittites, and unto the great sea toward the going down of the sun, will be your coast.
5 There will not any man be able to stand before you all the days of your life: as I was with Moses, *so* I will be with you: I will not fail you, nor forsake you.
6 Be strong and of a good courage: for unto this people will you divide for an inheritance the land, which I swore unto their fathers to give them.
7 Only be you strong and very courageous, that you may observe to do according to all the law, which Moses my servant commanded you: turn not from it *to* the right hand or *to* the left, that you may prosper whithersoever you go.
8 This book of the law will not depart out of your mouth; but you will meditate therein day and night, that you may observe to do according to all that is written therein: for then you will make your way prosperous, and then you will have good success.
9 Have not I commanded you? Be strong and of a good courage; be not afraid, neither be you dismayed: for the LORD your God *is* with you whithersoever you go.
10 Then Joshua commanded the officers of the people, saying,
11 Pass through the host, and command the people, saying, Prepare you victuals; for within three days you will pass over this Jordan, to go in to possess the land, which the LORD your God gives you to possess it.
12 And to the Reubenites, and to the Gadites, and to half the tribe of Manasseh, spoke Joshua, saying,
13 Remember the word which Moses the servant of the LORD commanded you, saying, The LORD your God hath given you rest, and have given you this land.
14 Your wives, your little ones, and your cattle, will remain in the land which Moses gave you on this side Jordan; but you will pass before your brethren armed, all the mighty men of valor, and help them;
15 Until the LORD have given your brethren rest, as *he hath given* you, and they also have possessed the land which the LORD your God gives them: then you will return unto the land of your possession, and enjoy it, which Moses the LORD'S servant gave you on this side Jordan toward the sun rising.
16 And they answered Joshua, saying, all that you commanded us we will do, and whithersoever you send us, we will go.
17 According as we hearkened unto Moses in all things, so will we hearken unto you: only the LORD your God be with you, as he was with Moses.
18 Whosoever *he be* that does rebel against your commandment, and will not hearken unto your words in all that you commanded him, he will be put to death: only be strong and of a good courage.

CHAPTER 2

1 And Joshua the son of Nun sent out of Shittim two men to spy secretly, saying, Go view the land, even Jericho. And they went, and came into a harlot's house, named Rahab, and lodged there.
2 And it was told the king of Jericho, saying, Behold, there came men in here to night of the children of Israel to search out the country.
3 And the king of Jericho sent unto Rahab, saying, Bring forth the men that are come to you, which are entered into your house: for they be come to search out all the country.
4 And the woman took the two men, and hid them, and said thus, there came men unto me, but I wist[3] not where they *were*:
5 And it came to pass *about the time* of shutting of the gate, when it was dark, that the men went out: whither the men went I wot[4] not: pursue after them quickly; for you will overtake them.
6 But she had brought them up to the roof of the house, and hid them with the stalks of flax, which she had laid in order upon the roof.
7 And the men pursued after them the way to Jordan unto the fords: and as soon as they which pursued after them were gone out, they shut the gate.
8 And before they were laid down, she came up unto them upon the roof;
9 And she said unto the men, I know that the LORD hath given you the land, and that your terror is fallen upon us, and that all the inhabitants of the land faint because of you.
10 For we have heard how the LORD dried up the water of the Red sea for you, when you came out of Egypt; and what you did unto the two kings of the Amorites, that *were* on the other side Jordan, Sihon and Og, whom you utterly destroyed.
11 And as soon as we had heard *these things*, our hearts did melt, neither did there remain any more courage in any man, because of you: for the LORD your God, he *is* God in heaven above, and in earth beneath.
12 Now therefore, I pray you, swear unto me by the LORD, since I have showed you kindness, that you will also show kindness unto my father's house, and give me a true token:
13 And *that* you will save alive my father, and my mother, and my brethren, and my sisters, and all that they have, and deliver our lives from death.
14 And the men answered her, our life for yours, if you utter not this our business. And it will be, when the LORD hath given us the land, that we will deal kindly and truly with you.
15 Then she let them down by a cord through the window: for her house *was* upon the town wall, and she dwelt upon the wall.
16 And she said unto them, Get you to the mountain lest the pursuers meet you; and hide yourselves there three days, until the pursuers are returned: and afterward may you go your way.
17 And the men said unto her, we *will be* blameless of this your oath which you have made us swear.
18 Behold, *when* we come into the land, you will bind this line of scarlet thread in the window which you didst let us down by: and you will bring your father, and your mother, and your brethren, and your father's **entire** household, home unto you.

---

[1] Joshua- Jehovah saved or Jehovah is salvation. [Strgs#3091]
[2] Jordan- is the principle river of Palestine. It comes from the Hebrew word *yardên*, meaning descender. [Strgs#3383]
[3] wist- Old English word meaning to know by seeing: acknowledge, acquaintance, advise and to appoint. [Strgs#3045]
[4] wot- equal to wist.

19 And it will be, *that* whosoever will go out of the doors of your house into the street, his blood will *be* upon his head, and we *will be* guiltless: and whosoever will be with you in the house, his blood will *be* on our head, if *any* hand be upon him.
20 And if you utter this our business, then we will be quit of your oath which you have made us to swear.
21 And she said, according unto your words, so *be* it. And she sent them away, and they departed: and she bound the scarlet line in the window.
22 And they went, and came unto the mountain, and abode there three days, until the pursuers were returned: and the pursuers sought *them* throughout all the way, but found *them* not.
23 So the two men returned, and descended from the mountain, and passed over, and came to Joshua the son of Nun, and told him all *things* that befell them:
24 And they said unto Joshua, truly the LORD hath delivered into our hands all the land; for even all the inhabitants of the country do faint because of us.

CHAPTER 3

1 And Joshua rose early in the morning; and they removed from Shittim, and came to Jordan, he and all the children of Israel, and lodged there before they passed over.
2 And it came to pass after three days, that the officers went through the host;
3 And they commanded the people, saying, when you see the ark of the covenant of the LORD your God, and the priests the Levites bearing it, then you will remove from your place, and go after it.
4 Yet there will be a space between you and it, about two thousand cubits by measure: come not near unto it, that you may know the way by which you must go: for you have not passed *this* way heretofore[1].
5 And Joshua said unto the people, sanctify yourselves: for tomorrow the LORD will do wonders among you.
6 And Joshua spoke unto the priests, saying, take up the Ark of the Covenant, and pass over before the people. And they took up the Ark of the Covenant, and went before the people.
7 And the LORD said unto Joshua, this day will I begin to magnify you in the sight of all Israel, that they may know that, as I was with Moses, *so* I will be with you.
8 And you will command the priests that bear the Ark of the Covenant, saying, when you are come to the brink of the water of Jordan, you will stand still in Jordan.
9 And Joshua said unto the children of Israel, come hither, and hear the words of the LORD your God.
10 And Joshua said, Hereby you will know that the living God *is* among you, and *that* he will without fail drive out from before you the Canaanites, and the Hittites, and the Hivites, and the Perizzites, and the Girgashites, and the Amorites, and the Jebusites.
11 Behold, the Ark of the Covenant of the Lord of all the earth passes over before you into Jordan.
12 Now therefore take you twelve men out of the tribes of Israel, out of every tribe a man.
13 And it will come to pass, as soon as the soles of the feet of the priests that bear the ark of the LORD, the Lord of all the earth, will rest in the waters of Jordan, *that* the waters of Jordan will be [cut off][2] *from* the waters that come down from above; and they will stand upon an heap.
14 And it came to pass, when the people removed from their tents, to pass over Jordan, and the priests bearing the Ark of the Covenant before the people;
15 And as they that bare the ark were come unto Jordan, and the feet of the priests that bare the ark were dipped in the brim of the water, (for Jordan overflows all his banks all the time of harvest,)
16 That the waters which came down from above stood *and* rose up upon an heap very far from the city Adam[3], that *is* beside Zaretan[4]: and those that came down toward the sea of the plain, *even* the salt sea, failed, *and* were cut off: and the people passed over right against Jericho.
17 And the priests that bare the ark of the covenant of the LORD stood firm on dry ground in the midst of Jordan, and all the Israelites passed over on dry ground, until all the people were passed clean over Jordan.

CHAPTER 4

1 And it came to pass, when all the people were clean passed over Jordan, that the LORD spoke unto Joshua, saying,
2 Take you twelve men out of the people, out of every tribe a man,
3 And command you them, saying, Take you hence out of the midst of Jordan, out of the place where the priests' feet stood firm, twelve stones, and you will carry them over with you, and leave them in the lodging place, where you will lodge this night.
4 Then Joshua called the twelve men, whom he had prepared of the children of Israel, out of every tribe a man:
5 And Joshua said unto them, Pass over before the ark of the LORD your God into the midst of Jordan, and take you up every man of you a stone upon his shoulder, according unto the number of the tribes of the children of Israel:
6 That this may be a sign among you, *that* when your children ask *their fathers* in time to come, saying, what *mean* you by these stones?
7 Then you will answer them, that the waters of Jordan were cut off before the ark of the covenant of the LORD; when it passed over Jordan, the waters of Jordan were cut off: and these stones will be for a memorial unto the children of Israel for ever.
8 And the children of Israel did so as Joshua commanded, and took up twelve stones out of the midst of Jordan, as the LORD spoke unto Joshua, according to the number of the tribes of the children of Israel, and carried them over with them unto the place where they lodged, and laid them down there.
9 And Joshua set up twelve stones in the midst of Jordan, in the place where the feet of the priests which bare the Ark of the Covenant stood: and they are there unto this day.
10 For the priests which bare the ark stood in the midst of Jordan, until everything was finished that the LORD commanded Joshua to speak unto the people, according to all that Moses commanded Joshua: and the people hasted and passed over.
11 And it came to pass, when all the people were clean passed over, that the ark of the LORD passed over, and the priests, in the presence of the people.
12 And the children of Reuben, and the children of Gad and half the tribe of Manasseh, passed over armed before the children of Israel, as Moses spoke unto them:

---

[1] heretofore – since yesterday and the third day [Strgs#8543 + 8032]
[2] cut off – to *covenant*, to *cut*, *destroy* or consume [Strgs#3772].
[3] Adam- the name of the first man. The word Adam also mean red, to show blood (in the face) to be flush or turn rosy. Also a place in Palestine.
[Strgs#121]
[4] Zarethan- perhaps for *tsarethan*, a place in Palestine. Zarethan comes from the Hebrew root word meaning to pierce and puncture. [Strgs#6819]

13 About forty thousand prepared for war passed over before the LORD unto battle, to the plains of Jericho.
14 On that day the LORD magnified Joshua in the sight of all Israel; and they feared him, as they feared Moses, all the days of his life.
15 And the LORD spoke unto Joshua, saying,
16 Command the priests that bear the ark of the testimony, that they come up out of Jordan.
17 Joshua therefore commanded the priests, saying, come you up out of Jordan.
18 And it came to pass, when the priests that bare the ark of the covenant of the LORD were come up out of the midst of Jordan, *and* the soles of the priests' feet were lifted up unto the dry land, that the waters of Jordan returned unto their place, and flowed over all his banks, as *they did* before.
19 And the people came up out of Jordan on the tenth *day* of the first month, and encamped in Gilgal[1], in the east border of Jericho.
20 And those twelve stones, which they took out of Jordan, did Joshua pitch in Gilgal.
21 And he spoke unto the children of Israel, saying, when your children will ask their fathers in time to come, saying, what *mean* these stones?
22 Then you will let your children know, saying, Israel came over this Jordan on dry land.
23 For the LORD your God dried up the waters of Jordan from before you, until you were passed over, as the LORD your God did to the Red sea, which he dried up from before us, until we were gone over:
24 That all the people of the earth might know the hand of the LORD, that it *is* mighty: that you might fear the LORD your God for ever.

CHAPTER 5

1 And it came to pass, when all the kings of the Amorites, which *were* on the side of Jordan westward, and all the kings of the Canaanites, which *were* by the sea, heard that the LORD had dried up the waters of Jordan from before the children of Israel, until we were passed over, that their heart melted, neither was there spirit in them anymore, because of the children of Israel.
2 At that time the LORD said unto Joshua, Make you sharp knives, and circumcise again the children of Israel the second time.
3 And Joshua made him sharp knives, and circumcised the children of Israel at the hill of the foreskins.
4 And this *is* the cause why Joshua did circumcise: All the people that came out of Egypt, *that were* males, *even* all the men of war, died in the wilderness by the way, after they came out of Egypt.
5 Now all the people that came out were circumcised: but all the people *that were* born in the wilderness by the way as they came forth out of Egypt, *them* they had not circumcised.
6 For the children of Israel walked forty years[2] in the wilderness, till all the people *that were* men of war, which came out of Egypt, were consumed, because they obeyed not the voice of the LORD: unto whom the LORD swore that he would not show them the land, which the LORD swore unto their fathers that he would give us, a land that flows with milk and honey.
7 And their children, *whom* he raised up in their stead, them Joshua circumcised: for they were uncircumcised, because they had not circumcised them by the way.

8 And it came to pass, when they had done circumcising all the people, that they abode in their places in the camp, till they were whole.
9 And the LORD said unto Joshua, This day have I rolled away the reproach of Egypt from off you. Wherefore the name of the place is called Gilgal unto this day.
10 And the children of Israel encamped in Gilgal, and kept the Passover on the fourteenth day of the month at even in the plains of Jericho.
11 And they did eat of the old corn of the land on the morrow after the Passover, unleavened cakes, and parched *corn* in the selfsame day.
12 And the manna ceased on the morrow after they had eaten of the old corn of the land; neither had the children of Israel manna anymore; but they did eat of the fruit of the land of Canaan that year.
13 And it came to pass, when Joshua was by Jericho, that he lifted up his eyes and looked, and, behold, there stood a man over against him with his sword drawn in his hand: and Joshua went unto him, and said unto him, are you for us, or for our adversaries?
14 And he said, Nay; but *as* captain of the host of the LORD am I now come. And Joshua fell on his face to the earth, and did worship, and said unto him, what said my lord unto his servant?
15 And the captain of the LORD'S host said unto Joshua, Loose your shoe from off your foot; for the place where you stand on *is* holy. And Joshua did so.

CHAPTER 6

1 Now Jericho was straightly shut up because of the children of Israel: none went out, and none came in.
2 And the LORD said unto Joshua, See, I have given into your hand Jericho, and the king thereof, *and* the mighty men of valor.
3 And you will compass the city, all you men of war, *and* go round about the city once. Thus will you do six days.
4 And seven priests will bear before the ark seven trumpets of rams' horns: and the seventh day you will compass the city seven times, and the priests will blow with the trumpets.
5 And it will come to pass, that when they make a long *blast* with the ram's horn, *and* when you hear the sound of the trumpet, all the people will shout with a great shout; and the wall of the city will fall down flat, and the people will ascend up every man straight before him.
6 And Joshua the son of Nun called the priests, and said unto them, Take up the Ark of the Covenant, and let seven priests bear seven trumpets of rams' horns before the ark of the LORD.
7 And he said unto the people, Pass on, and compass the city, and let him that is armed pass on before the ark of the LORD.
8 And it came to pass, when Joshua had spoken unto the people, that the seven priests bearing the seven trumpets of rams' horns passed on before the LORD, and blew with the trumpets: and the ark of the covenant of the LORD followed them.
9 And the armed men went before the priests that blew with the trumpets, and the rereward came after the ark, *the priests* going on, and blowing with the trumpets.
10 And Joshua had commanded the people, saying, you will not shout, nor make any noise with your voice, neither will *any* word

---

[1] Gilgal- defined as a wheel or rolling. The first site of an Israelite camp west of the Jordan, east of Jericho. Here Samuel was judge and Saul was made king (**1 Samuel 11:15**; **13:4-12**; **15:12-33**), it would later be used for illicit worship (**Hosea 4:15**; **Amos 5:5**). [Strgs#1537]

[2] years – Hebrew word *shâneh*; defined as a revolution of time [Strgs#8141]. Derives from the Hebrew root word *shânâh* meaning to fold, duplicate; by implication oto transmute [Strgs#8138].

proceed out of your mouth, until the day I bid you shout; then will you shout.

11 So the ark of the LORD compassed the city, going about *it* once: and they came into the camp, and lodged in the camp.

12 And Joshua rose early in the morning, and the priests took up the ark of the LORD.

13 And seven priests bearing seven trumpets of rams' horns before the ark of the LORD went on continually, and blew with the trumpets: and the armed men went before them; but the rereward came after the ark of the LORD, *the priests* going on, and blowing with the trumpets.

14 And the second day they compassed the city once, and returned into the camp: so they did six days.

15 And it came to pass on the seventh day, that they rose early about the dawning of the day, and compassed the city after the same manner seven times: only on that day they compassed the city seven times.

16 And it came to pass at the seventh time, when the priests blew with the trumpets, Joshua said unto the people, Shout; for the LORD hath given you the city.

17 [And the city will be accursed, *even* it, and all that *are* therein, to the LORD: only Rahab the harlot will live, she and all that *are* with her in the house, because she hid[1] the messengers that we sent.][2]

18 And you, in any wise keep *yourselves* from the accursed thing, lest you make *yourselves* accursed[3], when you take of the accursed thing, and make the camp of Israel a curse, and trouble it.

19 But all the silver, and gold, and vessels of brass and iron, *are* consecrated unto the LORD: they will come into the treasury of the LORD.

20 So the people shouted when *the priests* blew with the trumpets: and it came to pass, when the people heard[4] the sound of the trumpet, and the people shouted with a great shout, that the wall fell down flat, so that the people went up into the city, every man straight before him, and they took the city.

21 And they utterly destroyed all that *was* in the city, both man and woman, young and old, and ox, and sheep, and ass, with the edge of the sword.

22 But Joshua had said unto the two men that had spied out the country, Go into the harlot's house, and bring out thence the woman, and all that she hath, as you swore unto her.

23 And the young men that were spies went in, and brought out Rahab, and her father, and her mother, and her brethren, and all that she had; and they brought out all her kindred, and left them without the camp of Israel.

24 And they burnt the city with fire[5], and all that *was* therein: only the silver, and the gold, and the vessels of brass and of iron, they put into the treasury of the house of the LORD.

25 And Joshua saved Rahab the harlot alive, and her father's household, and all that she had; and she dwelled in Israel *even* unto this day; because she hid the messengers, which Joshua sent to spy out Jericho.

26 And Joshua adjured *them* at that time, saying, cursed *be* the man before the LORD, that rises up and builds this city Jericho: he will lay the foundation thereof in his firstborn, and in his youngest *son* will he set up the gates of it.

27 So the LORD was with Joshua; and his fame was *noised* throughout all the country.

CHAPTER 7

1 But the children of Israel committed a trespass in the accursed thing: for Achan, the son of Carmi, the son of Zabdi, the son of Zerah, of the tribe of Judah, took of the accursed thing: and the anger of the LORD was kindled against the children of Israel.

2 And Joshua sent men from Jericho to Ai, which *is* beside Beth-aven, on the east side of Beth-el, and spoke unto them, saying, Go up and view the country. And the men went up and viewed Ai.

3 And they returned to Joshua, and said unto him, Let not all the people go up; but let about two or three thousand men go up and smite Ai; *and* make not all the people to labor thither; for they *are but* few.

4 So there went up thither of the people about three thousand men: and they fled before the men of Ai.

5 And the men of Ai smote of them about thirty and six men: for they chased them *from* before the gate *even* unto Shebarim[6], and smote them in the going down: wherefore the hearts of the people melted, and became as water.

6 And Joshua rent his clothes, and fell to the earth upon his face before the ark of the LORD until the eventide, he and the elders of Israel, and put dust upon their heads.

7 And Joshua said, Alas, O Lord GOD, wherefore have you at all brought this people over Jordan, to deliver us into the hand of the Amorites, to destroy us? would to God we had been content, and dwelt on the other side Jordan!

8 O Lord, what will I say, when Israel turneth their backs before their enemies!

9 For the Canaanites and all the inhabitants of the land will hear *of it*, and will environ us round, and cut off our name from the earth: and what will you do unto your great name?

10 And the LORD said unto Joshua, Get you up; wherefore lies you thus upon your face?

11 Israel hath sinned, and they have also transgressed my covenant which I commanded them: for they have even taken of the accursed thing, and have also stolen, and dissembled also, and they have put *it* even among their own stuff[7].

12 Therefore the children of Israel could not stand before their enemies, *but* turned *their* backs before their enemies, because they were accursed: neither will I be with you any more, except you destroy the accursed from among you.

13 Up, sanctify the people, and say, sanctify yourselves against tomorrow: for thus said the LORD God of Israel, *There is* an accursed thing in the midst of you, O Israel: you canst not stand before your enemies, until you take away the accursed thing from among you.

---

[1] hid – to secrete, do secretly [Strgs#2244]. Comes from the Hebrew root word *châbab* meaning to *hide*, to *cherish* (with affection), love [Strgs#2245].
[2] compare – Matt. 21:28-31
[3] accursed – Hebrew word *chêrem*, *things that should have been destroyed*, shut in a net, *doomed*, *extermination*, utter destruction [Strgs#2764]
[4] heard – to *hear intelligently*, certain sound [Strgs#8085]. Compare **1 Cor.** 14:8.
[5] fire – lit. judgment
[6] Shebarim- literally the breaches, it's from a root word meaning ruins, affliction, crashing destruction, hurt interpretation and vexation. [Strgs#7671]
[7] Note: personal things, church.

14 [In the morning therefore you will be brought according to your tribes: and it will be, *that* the tribe which the LORD takes will come according to the families *thereof*; and the family which the LORD will take will come by households; and the household which the LORD will take will come man by man.]¹
15 And it will be, *that* he that is taken with the accursed thing will be burnt with fire, he and all that he hath: because he hath transgressed the covenant of the LORD, and because he hath wrought folly in Israel.
16 So Joshua rose up early in the morning, and brought Israel by their tribes; and the tribe of Judah was taken:
17 And he brought the family of Judah; and he took the family of the Zarhites: and he brought the family of the Zarhites man by man; and Zabdi was taken:
18 And he brought his household man by man; and Achan, the son of Carmi, the son of Zabdi, the son of Zerah, of the tribe of Judah, was taken.
19 And Joshua said unto Achan, My son, give, I pray you, glory to the LORD God of Israel, and make confession unto him; and tell me now what you have done; hide *it* not from me.
20 And Achan answered Joshua, and said, indeed I have sinned against the LORD God of Israel, and thus and thus have I done:
21 When I saw among the spoils a goodly Babylonian garment, and two hundred shekels of silver, and a wedge of gold of fifty shekels weight, then I coveted them, and took them; and, behold, they *are* hid in the earth in the midst of my tent², and the silver under it.
22 So Joshua sent messengers, and they ran unto the tent; and, behold, *it was* hid in his tent, and the silver under it.
23 And they took them out of the midst of the tent, and brought them unto Joshua, and unto all the children of Israel, and laid them out before the LORD.
24 And Joshua, and all Israel with him, took Achan the son of Zerah, and the silver, and the garment, and the wedge of gold, and his sons, and his daughters, and his oxen, and his asses, and his sheep, and his tent, and all that he had: and they brought them unto the valley of Achor.
25 And Joshua said, why have you troubled³ us? The LORD will trouble you this day. And all Israel stoned him with stones, and burned them with fire, after they had stoned them with stones.⁴
26 And they raised over him a great heap of stones unto this day. So the LORD turned from the fierceness of his anger.⁵ Wherefore the name of that place was called, the valley of Achor, unto this day.

CHAPTER 8

1 And the LORD said unto Joshua, Fear not, neither **are** you dismayed: take all the people of war with you, and arise, go up to Ai: see, I have given into your hand the king of Ai, and his people, and his city, and his land:
2 And you will do to Ai and her king as you didst unto Jericho and her king: only the spoil thereof, and the cattle thereof, will you take for a prey unto yourselves: lay you an ambush for the city behind it.
3 So Joshua arose, and all the people of war, to go up against Ai: and Joshua chose out thirty thousand mighty men of valor, and sent them away by night.
4 And he commanded them, saying, Behold, you will lie in wait against the city, *even* behind the city: go not very far from the city, but be you all ready:
5 And I, and all the people that *are* with me, will approach unto the city: and it will come to pass, when they come out against us, as at the first, that we will flee before them,
6 (For they will come out after us) till we have drawn them from the city; for they will say, they flee before us, as at the first: therefore we will flee before them.
7 Then you will rise up from the ambush, and seize upon the city: for the LORD your God will deliver it into your hand.
8 And it will be, when you have taken the city, *that* you will set the city on fire: according to the commandment of the LORD will you do. See, I have commanded you.
9 Joshua therefore sent them forth: and they went to lie in ambush, and abode between Beth-el and Ai, on the west side of Ai: but Joshua lodged that night among the people.
10 And Joshua rose up early in the morning, and numbered the people, and went up, he and the elders of Israel, before the people to Ai.
11 And all the people, *even the people* of war that *were* with him, went up, and drew nigh, and came before the city, and pitched on the north side of Ai: now *there was* a valley between them and Ai.
12 And he took about five thousand men, and set them to lie in ambush between Beth-el and Ai, on the west side of the city.
13 And when they had set the people, *even* all the host that *was* on the north of the city, and their liers in wait on the west of the city, Joshua went that night into the midst of the valley.
14 And it came to pass, when the king of Ai saw *it*, that they hasted and rose up early, and the men of the city went out against Israel to battle, he and all his people, at a time appointed, before the plain; but he **knew** not that *there were* liers in ambush against him behind the city.
15 And Joshua and all Israel made as if they were beaten before them, and fled by the way of the wilderness.
16 And all the people that *were* in Ai were called together to pursue after them: and they pursued after Joshua, and were drawn away from the city.
17 And there was not a man left in Ai or Beth-el, that went not out after Israel: and they left the city open, and pursued after Israel.
18 And the LORD said unto Joshua, Stretch out the spear that *is* in your hand toward Ai; for I will give it into your hand. And Joshua stretched out the spear that *he had* in his hand toward the city.
19 And the ambush arose quickly out of their place, and they ran as soon as he had stretched out his hand: and they entered into the city, and took it, and hasted and set the city on fire.
20 And when the men of Ai looked behind them, they saw, and, behold, the smoke of the city ascended up to heaven, and they had no power to flee this way or that way: and the people that fled to the wilderness turned back upon the pursuers.
21 And when Joshua and all Israel saw that the ambush had taken the city, and that the smoke of the city ascended, then they turned again, and slew the men of Ai.
22 And the other issued out of the city against them; so they were in the midst of Israel, some on this side, and some on that side: and they smote them, so that they let none of them remain or escape.

---

¹ God is searching households.
² ie. home, church
³ trouble – to roil water, disturb or afflict [Strgs#5916]
⁴ compare 1 Cor. 12:26, 1 Peter 4:17
⁵ Trouble stops when Go judges

23 And the king of Ai they took alive, and brought him to Joshua.
24 And it came to pass, when Israel had made an end of slaying all the inhabitants of Ai in the field, in the wilderness wherein they chased them, and when they were all fallen on the edge of the sword, until they were consumed, that all the Israelites returned unto Ai, and smote it with the edge of the sword.
25 And *so it was, that* all that fell that day, both of men and women, *were* twelve thousand, *even* all the men of Ai.
26 For Joshua drew not his hand back, wherewith he stretched out the spear, until he had utterly destroyed all the inhabitants of Ai.
27 Only the cattle and the spoil of that city Israel took for a prey unto themselves, according unto the word of the LORD which he commanded Joshua.
28 And Joshua burnt Ai, and made it a heap forever, *even* desolation unto this day.
29 And the king of Ai he hanged on a tree until eventide: and as soon as the sun was down, Joshua commanded that they should take his carcass down from the tree, and cast it at the entering of the gate of the city, and raise thereon a great heap of stones, *that remained* unto this day.
30 Then Joshua built an altar unto the LORD God of Israel in mount Ebal,
31 As Moses the servant of the LORD commanded the children of Israel, as it is written in the book of the Law of Moses, an altar of whole stones, over which no man hath lift up *any* iron: and they offered thereon burnt offerings unto the LORD, and sacrificed peace offerings.
32 And he wrote there upon the stones a copy of the Law of Moses, which he wrote in the presence of the children of Israel.
33 And all Israel, and their elders, and officers, and their judges, stood on this side the ark and on that side before the priests the Levites, which bare the ark of the covenant of the LORD, as well the stranger, as he that was born among them; half of them over against mount Gerizim, and half of them over against mount Ebal; as Moses the servant of the LORD had commanded before, that they should bless the people of Israel.
34 And afterward he read all the words of the law, the blessings and cursing, according to all that is written in the book of the law.
35 There was not a word of all that Moses commanded, which Joshua read not before all the congregation of Israel, with the women, and the little ones, and the strangers that were conversant among them.

CHAPTER 9

1 And it came to pass, when all the kings which *were* on this side Jordan, in the hills, and in the valleys, and in all the coasts of the great sea over against Lebanon, the Hittite, and the Amorite, the Canaanite, the Perizzite, the Hivite, and the Jebusite, heard *thereof*;
2 That they gathered themselves together, to fight with Joshua and with Israel, with one accord.
3 And when the inhabitants of Gibeon heard what Joshua had done unto Jericho and to Ai,
4 They did work wilily, and went and made as if they had been ambassadors, and took old sacks upon their asses, and wine bottles, old, and rent, and bound up;
5 And old shoes and clouted upon their feet, and old garments upon them; and all the bread of their provision was dry *and* moldy.
6 And they went to Joshua unto the camp at Gilgal, and said unto him, and to the men of Israel, We are come from a far country: now therefore make you a league with us.
7 And the men of Israel said unto the Hivites, Peradventure you dwell among us; and how will we make a league with you?
8 And they said unto Joshua, We *are* your servants. And Joshua said unto them, who *are* ye? And from whence come ye?
9 And they said unto him, from a very far country your servants are come because of the name of the LORD your God: for we have heard the fame of him, and all that he did in Egypt,
10 And all that he did to the two kings of the Amorites, that *were* beyond Jordan, to Sihon king of Heshbon, and to Og king of Bashan, which *was* at Ashtaroth.
11 Wherefore our elders and all the inhabitants of our country spoke to us, saying, Take victuals with you for the journey, and go to meet them, and say unto them, we *are* your servants: therefore now make you a league with us.
12 This our bread we took hot *for* our provision out of our houses on the day we came forth to go unto you; but now, behold, t is dry, and it is moldy:
13 And these bottles of wine, which we filled, *were* new; and, behold, they are rent: and these our garments and our shoes are become old by reason of the very long journey.
14 And the men took of their victuals, and asked not *counsel* at the mouth of the LORD.
15 And Joshua made peace with them, and made a league with them, to let them live: and the princes of the congregation swore unto them.
16 And it came to pass at the end of three days after they had made a league with them, that they heard that they were their neighbors, and *that* they dwelt among them.
17 And the children of Israel journeyed, and came unto their cities on the third day. Now their cities *were* Gibeon, and Chephirah, and Beeroth, and Kirjath-jearim.
18 And the children of Israel smote them not, because the princes of the congregation had sworn unto them by the LORD God of Israel. And the **entire** congregation murmured against the princes.
19 But all the princes said unto the entire congregation, we have sworn unto them by the LORD God of Israel: now therefore we may not touch them.
20 This we will do to them; we will even let them live, lest wrath be upon us, because of the oath which we swore unto them
21 And the princes said unto them, Let them live; but let them be hewers of wood and drawers of water unto the entire congregation; as the princes had promised them.
22 And Joshua called for them, and he spoke unto them, saying, wherefore have you beguiled us, saying, we *are* very far from you; when you dwell among us?
23 Now therefore you *are* cursed, and there will none of you be freed from being bondmen, and hewers of wood and drawers of water for the house of my God.
24 And they answered Joshua, and said, Because it was certainly told your servants, how that the LORD your God commanded his servant Moses to give you all the land, and to destroy all the inhabitants of the land from before you, therefore we were sore afraid of
our lives because of you, and have done this thing.
25 And now, behold, we *are* in your hand: as it seems good and right unto you to do unto us, do.
26 And so did he unto them, and delivered them out of the hand of the children of Israel, that they slaughter them not.

27 And Joshua made them that day hewers[1] of wood and drawers of water for the congregation, and for the altar of the LORD, even unto this day, in the place which he should choose.

CHAPTER 10

1 Now it came to pass, when Adoni-zedek king of Jerusalem had heard how Joshua had taken Ai, and had utterly destroyed it; as he had done to Jericho and her king, so he had done to Ai and her king; and how the inhabitants of Gibeon had made peace with Israel, and were among them;

2 That they feared greatly, because Gibeon *was* a great city, as one of the royal cities, and because it *was* greater than Ai, and all the men thereof *were* mighty.

3 Wherefore Adoni-zedek king of Jerusalem sent unto Hoham king of Hebron, and unto Piram king of Jarmuth, and unto Japhia king of Lachish, and unto Debir king of Eglon, saying,

4 Come up unto me, and help me, that we may smite Gibeon: for it hath made peace with Joshua and with the children of Israel.

5 Therefore the five kings of the Amorites, the king of Jerusalem, the king of Hebron, the king of Jarmuth, the king of Lachish, the king of Eglon, gathered themselves together, and went up, they and all their hosts, and encamped before Gibeon, and made war against it.

6 And the men of Gibeon sent unto Joshua to the camp to Gilgal, saying, Slack not your hand from your servants; come up to us quickly, and save us, and help us: for all the kings of the Amorites that dwell in the mountains are gathered together against us.

7 So Joshua ascended from Gilgal, he, and all the people of war with him, and all the mighty men of valor.

8 And the LORD said unto Joshua, Fear them not: for I have delivered them into your hand; there will not **be** a man of them **that can** stand before you.

9 Joshua therefore came unto them suddenly, *and* went up from Gilgal all night.

10 And the LORD discomfited them before Israel, and slew them with a great slaughter at Gibeon, and chased them along the way that goes up to Beth-horon, and smote them to Azekah, and unto Makkedah[2].

11 And it came to pass, as they fled from before Israel, *and* were in the going down to Beth-horon, that the LORD cast down great stones from heaven upon them unto Azekah, and they died: *they were* more which died with hailstones than *they* whom the children of Israel slaughtered with the sword.

12 Then spoke Joshua to the LORD in the day when the LORD delivered up the Amorites before the children of Israel, and he said in the sight of Israel, Sun, stand you still upon Gibeon; and you, Moon, in the valley of Ajalon.

13 And the sun stood still, and the moon stayed, until the people had avenged themselves upon their enemies. *Is* not this written in the book of Jasher[3]? So the sun stood still in the midst of heaven, and hasted not to go down about a whole day.

14 And there was no day like that before it or after it, that the LORD hearkened unto the voice of a man: for the LORD fought for Israel.

15 And Joshua returned, and all Israel with him, unto the camp to Gilgal.

16 But these five kings fled, and hid themselves in a cave at Makkedah.

17 And it was told Joshua, saying, the five kings are found hid in a cave at Makkedah.

18 And Joshua said, Roll great stones upon the mouth of the cave, and set men by it for to keep them:

19 And stay you not, *but* pursue after your enemies, and smite the hindmost of them[4]; suffer them not to enter into their cities: for the LORD your God hath delivered them into your hand.

20 And it came to pass, when Joshua and the children of Israel had made an end of slaying them with a very great slaughter, till they were consumed, that the rest *which* remained of them entered into fenced cities.

21 And all the people returned to the camp to Joshua at Makkedah in peace: none moved his tongue against any of the children of Israel.

22 Then said Joshua, Open the mouth of the cave, and bring out those five kings unto me out of the cave.

23 And they did so, and brought forth those five kings unto him out of the cave, the king of Jerusalem, the king of Hebron, the king of Jarmuth, the king of Lachish, *and* the king of Eglon.

24 And it came to pass, when they brought out those kings unto Joshua, that Joshua called for all the men of Israel, and said unto the captains of the men of war which went with him, come near, put your feet upon the necks of these kings. And they came near, and put their feet upon the necks of them.

25 And Joshua said unto them, Fear not, nor be dismayed, be strong and of good courage: for thus will the LORD do to all your enemies against whom you fight.

26 And afterward Joshua smote them, and slew them, and hanged them on five trees: and they were hanging upon the trees until the evening.

27 And it came to pass at the time of the going down of the sun, *that* Joshua commanded, and they took them down off the trees, and cast them into the cave wherein they had been hid, and laid great stones in the cave's mouth, *which remain* until this very day.

28 And that day Joshua took Makkedah, and smote it with the edge of the sword, and the king thereof he utterly destroyed them, and all the souls that *were* therein; he let none remain: and he did to the king of Makkedah as he did unto the king of Jericho.

29 Then Joshua passed from Makkedah, and all Israel with him, unto Libnah, and fought against Libnah:

30 And the LORD delivered it also, and the king thereof, into the hand of Israel; and he smote it with the edge of the sword, and all the souls that *were* therein; he let none remain in it; but did unto the king thereof as he did unto the king of Jericho.

31 And Joshua passed from Libnah, and all Israel with him, unto Lachish, and encamped against it, and fought against it.

32 And the LORD delivered Lachish into the hand of Israel, which took it on the second day, and smote it with the edge of the sword, and all the souls that *were* therein, according to all that he had done to Libnah.

33 Then Horam king of Gezer came up to help Lachish; and Joshua smote him and his people, until he had left him none remaining.

---

[1] hewers- those that cut and gathered. A primitive root; to chop or carve wood:- cut down, polish. [Strgs#2404]

[2] Mekkedah- defined as place of shepherds. It's the location of a cave in Judah where Joshua captured and executed five Canaanite kings during his conquest. [Strgs#4719]

[3] Jasher- defined as straight or pleased well righteous. The Book of Jasher was an ancient collection of verses, now lost, which described great events in the history of Israel. The book contained Joshua's poetic address to the sun and the moon at the battle of Gibeon (Joshua 10:12 13) and the "Song of the Bow," which is David's lament over the death of Saul and Jonathan (**II Sam. 1:17-27**). [Strgs#4719]

[4] lit. you shall cut off their tail

34 And from Lachish Joshua passed unto Eglon, and all Israel with him; and they encamped against it, and fought against it:

35 And they took it on that day, and smote it with the edge of the sword, and all the souls that *were* therein he utterly destroyed that day, according to all that he had done to Lachish.

36 And Joshua went up from Eglon, and all Israel with him, unto Hebron; and they fought against it:

37 And they took it, and smote it with the edge of the sword, and the king thereof, and all the cities thereof, and all the souls that *were* therein; he left none remaining, according to all that he had done to Eglon; but destroyed it utterly, and all the souls that *were* therein.

38 And Joshua returned, and all Israel with him, to Debir; and fought against it:

39 And he took it, and the king thereof, and all the cities thereof; and they smote them with the edge of the sword, and utterly destroyed all the souls that *were* therein; he left none remaining: as he had done to Hebron, so he did to Debir, and to the king thereof; as he had done also to Libnah, and to her king.

40 So Joshua smote all the country of the hills, and of the south, and of the vale, and of the springs, and all their kings: he left none remaining, but utterly destroyed all that breathed, as the LORD God of Israel commanded.

41 And Joshua smote them from Kadesh-barnea even unto Gaza, and all the country of Goshen, even unto Gibeon.

42 And all these kings and their land did Joshua take at one time, because the LORD God of Israel fought for Israel.

43 And Joshua returned, and all Israel with him, unto the camp to Gilgal.

CHAPTER 11

1 And it came to pass, when Jabin king of Hazor had heard *those things*, that he sent to Jobab king of Madon, and to the king of Shimron, and to the king of Achshaph,

2 And to the kings that *were* on the north of the mountains, and of the plains south of Chinneroth, and in the valley, and in the borders of Dor on the west,

3 *And to* the Canaanite on the east and on the west, and *to* the Amorite, and the Hittite, and the Perizzite, and the Jebusite in the mountains, and *to* the Hivite under Hermon in the land of Mizpeh.

4 And they went out, they and all their hosts with them, much people, even as the sand that *is* upon the sea shore in multitude, with horses and chariots very many.

5 And when all these kings were met together, they came and pitched together at the waters of Merom, to fight against Israel.

6 And the LORD said unto Joshua, be not afraid because of them: for tomorrow about this time will I deliver them up all slain before Israel: you will **exterminate** their horses, and burn their chariots with fire.

7 So Joshua came, and all the people of war with him, against them by the waters of Merom suddenly; and they fell upon them.

8 And the LORD delivered them into the hand of Israel, who smote them, and chased them unto great Zidon, and unto Misrephoth-maim, and unto the valley of Mizpeh eastward; and they smote them, until they left them none remaining.

9 And Joshua did unto them as the LORD bade him: he **exterminated** their horses, and burnt their chariots with fire.

10 And Joshua at that time turned back, and took Hazor, and smote the king thereof with the sword: for Hazor beforetime was the head of all those kingdoms.

11 And they smote all the souls that *were* therein with the edge of the sword, utterly destroying *them*: there was not any left to breathe: and he burnt Hazor with fire.

12 And all the cities of those kings, and all the kings of them, did Joshua take, and smote them with the edge of the sword, *and* he utterly destroyed them, as Moses the servant of the LORD commanded.

13 But *as for* the cities that stood still in their strength, Israel burned none of them, save Hazor only; *that* did Joshua burn.

14 And all the spoil of these cities, and the cattle, the children of Israel took for a prey unto themselves; but every man they smote with the edge of the sword, until they had destroyed them, neither left **them** any to breathe.

15 As the LORD commanded Moses his servant, so did Moses command Joshua, and so did Joshua; he left nothing undone of all that the LORD commanded Moses.

16 So Joshua took all that land, the hills, and all the south country, and all the land of Goshen, and the valley, and the plain, and the mountain of Israel, and the valley of the same;

17 *Even* from the mount Halak, that goes up to Seir[1], even unto Baal-gad in the valley of Lebanon under Mount Hermon: and all their kings he took, and smote them, and slew them.

18 Joshua made war a long time with all those kings.

19 There was not a city that made peace with the children of Israel, save the Hivites the inhabitants of Gibeon: all *other* they took in battle.

20 For it was of the LORD to harden their hearts, that they should come against Israel in battle, that he might destroy them utterly, *and* that they might have no favor, but that he might destroy them, as the LORD commanded Moses.

21 And at that time came Joshua, and cut off the Anakims from the mountains, from Hebron, from Debir, from Anab, and from all the mountains of Judah, and from all the mountains of Israel: Joshua destroyed them utterly with their cities.

22 There was none of the Anakims left in the land of the children of Israel: only in Gaza, in Gath, and in Ashdod, there remained.

23 So Joshua took the whole land, according to all that the LORD said unto Moses; and Joshua gave it for an inheritance unto Israel according to their divisions by their tribes. And the land rested from war.

CHAPTER 12

1 Now these *are* the kings of the land, which the children of Israel smote, and possessed their land on the other side Jordan toward the rising of the sun, from the river Arnon unto mount Hermon, and all the plain on the east:

2 Sihon king of the Amorites, who dwelt in Heshbon, *and* ruled from Aroer, which *is* upon the bank of the river Arnon, and from the middle of the river, and from half Gilead, even unto the river Jabbok, *which is* the border of the children of Ammon;

3 And from the plain to the sea of Chinneroth on the east, and unto the sea of the plain, *even* the salt sea on the east, the way to Beth-jeshimoth; and from the south, under Ashdoth-pisgah:

4 And the coast of Og king of Bashan, *which was* of the remnant of the giants, that dwelt at Ashtaroth and at Edrei,

---

[1] Seir- comes from the Hebrew root word *śâiyr* meaning hairy, rough, goat, faun, devil, kid and satyr. [Strgs#8165]

5 And reigned in Mount Hermon, and in Salcah, and in all Bashan, unto the border of the Geshurites and the Maachathites, and half Gilead, the border of Sihon king of Heshbon.
6 Them did Moses the servant of the LORD and the children of Israel smite: and Moses the servant of the LORD gave it *for a* possession unto the Reubenites, and the Gadites, and the half tribe of Manasseh.
7 And these *are* the kings of the country which Joshua and the children of Israel smote on this side Jordan on the west, from Baal-gad in the valley of Lebanon even unto the mount Halak, that goes up to Seir; which Joshua gave unto the tribes of Israel *for a* possession according to their divisions;
8 In the mountains, and in the valleys, and in the plains, and in the springs, and in the wilderness, and in the south country; the Hittites, the Amorites, and the Canaanites, the Perizzites, the Hivites, and the Jebusites:
9 The king of Jericho, one; the king of Ai, which *is* beside Beth-el, one;
10 The king of Jerusalem, one; the king of Hebron, one;
11 The king of Jarmuth, one; the king of Lachish, one;
12 The king of Eglon, one; the king of Gezer, one;
13 The king of Debir, one; the king of Geder, one;
14 The king of Hormah, one; the king of Arad, one;
15 The king of Libnah, one; the king of Adullam, one;
16 The king of Makkedah, one; the king of Beth-el, one;
17 The king of Tappuah, one; the king of Hepher, one;
18 The king of Aphek, one; the king of Lasharon, one;
19 The king of Madon, one; the king of Hazor, one;
20 The king of Shimron-meron, one; the king of Achshaph, one;
21 The king of Taanach, one; the king of Megiddo, one;
22 The king of Kedesh, one; the king of Jokneam of Carmel, one;
23 The king of Dor in the coast of Dor, one; the king of the nations of Gilgal, one;
24 The king of Tirzah, one: all the kings thirty and one.

CHAPTER 13

1 Now Joshua was old *and* stricken in years; and the LORD said unto him, you are old *and* stricken in years, and there remains yet very much land to be possessed.
2 This *is* the land that yet remains: all the borders of the Philistines, and all Geshuri,
3 From Sihor, which *is* before Egypt, even unto the borders of Ekron northward, *which* is counted to the Canaanite: five lords of the Philistines; the Gazathites, and the Ashdothites, the Eshkalonites, the Gittites, and the Ekronites; also the Avites:
4 From the south, all the land of the Canaanites, and Mearah that *is* beside the Sidonians, unto Aphek, to the borders of the Amorites:
5 And the land of the Giblites, and all Lebanon, toward the sun rising, from Baal-gad under Mount Hermon unto the entering into Hamath.
6 All the inhabitants of the hill country from Lebanon unto Misrephoth-maim, *and* all the Sidonians, them will I drive out from before the children of Israel: only divide you it by lot unto the Israelites for an inheritance, as I have commanded you.
7 Now therefore divide this land for an inheritance unto the nine tribes, and the half tribe of Manasseh,
8 With whom the Reubenites and the Gadites have received their inheritance, which Moses gave them, beyond Jordan eastward, *even* as Moses the servant of the LORD gave them;
9 From Aroer, that *is* upon the bank of the river Arnon, and the city that *is* in the midst of the river, and all the plain of Medeba unto Dibon;
10 And all the cities of Sihon king of the Amorites, which reigned in Heshbon, unto the border of the children of Ammon
11 And Gilead, and the border of the Geshurites and Maachathites, and all mount Hermon, and all Bashan unto Salcah;
12 All the kingdom of Og in Bashan, which reigned in Ashtaroth and in Edrei, who remained of the remnant of the giants: for these did Moses smite, and cast them out.
13 Nevertheless the children of Israel expelled not the Geshurites, nor the Maachathites: but the Geshurites and the Maachathites dwell among the Israelites until this day.
14 Only unto the tribe of Levi he gave none inheritance; the sacrifices of the LORD God of Israel made by fire *are* their inheritance, as he said unto them.
15 And Moses gave unto the tribe of the children of Reuben *inheritance* according to their families.
16 And their coast was from Aroer, that *is* on the bank of the river Arnon, and the city that *is* in the midst of the river, and all the plain by Medeba;
17 Heshbon, and all her cities that *are* in the plain; Dibon, and Bamoth-baal, and Beth-baal-meon,
18 And Jahazah, and Kedemoth, and Mephaath,
19 And Kirjathaim, and Sibmah, and Zareth-shahar in the mount of the valley,
20 And Beth-peor, and Ashdoth-pisgah, and Beth-jeshimoth,
21 And all the cities of the plain, and all the kingdom of Sihon king of the Amorites, which reigned in Heshbon, whom Moses smote with the princes of Midian, Evi, and Rekem, and Zur, and Hur, and Reba, *which were* dukes of Sihon, dwelling in the country.
22 Balaam also the son of Beor, the soothsayer, did the children of Israel slay with the sword among them that were slain by them.
23 And the border of the children of Reuben was Jordan, and the border *thereof*. This *was* the inheritance of the children of Reuben after their families, the cities and the villages thereof.
24 And Moses gave *inheritance* unto the tribe of Gad, *even* unto the children of Gad according to their families.
25 And their coast was Jazer, and all the cities of Gilead, and half the land of the children of Ammon, unto Aroer that *is* before Rabbah;
26 And from Heshbon unto Ramath-mizpeh, and Betonim; and from Mahanaim unto the border of Debir;
27 And in the valley, Beth-aram, and Beth-nimrah, and Succoth, and Zaphon, the rest of the kingdom of Sihon king of Heshbon, Jordan and *his* border, *even* unto the edge of the sea of Chinnereth on the other side Jordan eastward.
28 This *is* the inheritance of the children of Gad after their families, the cities, and their villages.
29 And Moses gave *inheritance* unto the half tribe of Manasseh: and *this* was the *possession* of the half tribe of the children of Manasseh by their families.
30 And their coast was from Mahanaim, all Bashan, all the kingdom of Og king of Bashan, and all the towns of Jair, which *are* in Bashan, threescore cities:
31 And half Gilead, and Ashtaroth, and Edrei, cities of the kingdom of Og in Bashan, *were pertaining* unto the children of Machir the son of Manasseh, *even* to the one half of the children of Machir by their families.

32 These *are* the *countries* which Moses did distribute for inheritance in the plains of Moab, on the other side Jordan, by Jericho, eastward.
33 But unto the tribe of Levi Moses gave not *any* inheritance: the LORD God of Israel *was* their inheritance, as he said unto them.

CHAPTER 14

1 And these *are* the *countries* which the children of Israel inherited in the land of Canaan, which Eleazar the priest, and Joshua the son of Nun, and the heads of the fathers of the tribes of the children of Israel, distributed for inheritance to them.
2 By lot *was* their inheritance, as the LORD commanded by the hand of Moses, for the nine tribes, and *for* the half tribe.
3 For Moses had given the inheritance of two tribes and a half tribe on the other side Jordan: but unto the Levites he gave none inheritance among them.
4 For the children of Joseph were two tribes, Manasseh and Ephraim: therefore they gave no part unto the Levites in the land, save cities to dwell *in*, with their suburbs for their cattle and for their substance.
5 As the LORD commanded Moses, so the children of Israel did, and they divided the land.
6 Then the children of Judah came unto Joshua in Gilgal: and Caleb the son of Jephunneh the Kenezite said unto him, you know the thing that the LORD said unto Moses the man of God concerning me and you in Kadesh-barnea.
7 Forty years old *was* I when Moses the servant of the LORD sent me from Kadesh-barnea to espy out the land; and I brought him word again as *it was* in mine heart.
8 Nevertheless my brethren that went up with me made the heart of the people melt: but I wholly followed the LORD my God.
9 And Moses swore on that day, saying, surely the land whereon your feet have trodden will be your inheritance, and your children's forever, because you hast wholly followed the LORD my God.
10 And now, behold, the LORD hath kept me alive, as he said, these forty and five years, even since the LORD spoke this word unto Moses, while *the children of* Israel wandered in the wilderness: and now, lo, I *am* this day fourscore and five years old.
11 As yet I *am as* strong this day as *I was* in the day that Moses sent me: as my strength *was* then, even so *is* my strength now, for war, both to go out, and to come in.
12 Now therefore give me this mountain, whereof the LORD spoke in that day; for you heard in that day how the Anakims *were* there, and *that* the cities *were* great *and* fenced: if so be the LORD *will be* with me, then I will be able to drive them out, as the LORD said.
13 And Joshua blessed him, and gave unto Caleb the son of Jephunneh Hebron for an inheritance.
14 Hebron therefore became the inheritance of Caleb the son of Jephunneh the Kenezite unto this day, because that he wholly followed the LORD God of Israel.
15 And the name of Hebron before *was* Kirjath-arba; *which Arba was* a great man among the Anakims. And the land had rest from war.

CHAPTER 15

1 *This* then was the lot of the tribe of the children of Judah by their families; *even* to the border of Edom the wilderness of Zin southward *was* the uttermost part of the south coast.
2 And their south border was from the shore of the salt sea, from the bay that looks southward:
3 And it went out to the south side to Maaleh-acrabbim, and passed along to Zin, and ascended up on the south side unto Kadesh-barnea, and passed along to Hezron, and went up to Adar, and fetched a compass to Karkaa:
4 *From thence* it passed toward Azmon, and went out unto the river of Egypt; and the goings out of that coast were at the sea: this will be your south coast.
5 And the east border *was* the salt sea, *even* unto the end of Jordan. And *their* border in the north quarter *was* from the bay of the sea at the uttermost part of Jordan:
6 And the border went up to Beth-hogla, and passed along by the north of Beth-arabah; and the border went up to the stone of Bohan the son of Reuben:
7 And the border went up toward Debir from the valley of Achor, and so northward, looking toward Gilgal, that *is* before the going up to Adummim, which *is* on the south side of the river: and the border passed toward the waters of En-shemesh, and the goings out thereof were at En-rogel:
8 And the border went up by the valley of the son of Hinnom unto the south side of the Jebusite; the same *is* Jerusalem: and the border went up to the top of the mountain that *lies* before the valley of Hinnom westward, which *is* at the end of the valley of the giants northward:
9 And the border was drawn from the top of the hill unto the fountain of the water of Nephtoah, and went out to the cities of mount Ephron; and the border was drawn to Baalah, which *is* Kirjath-jearim:
10 And the border compassed from Baalah westward unto mount Seir, and passed along unto the side of mount Jearim, which *is* Chesalon, on the north side, and went down to Beth-shemesh, and passed on to Timnah:
11 And the border went out unto the side of Ekron northward: and the border was drawn to Shicron, and passed along to mount Baalah, and went out unto Jabneel; and the goings out of the border were at the sea.
12 And the west border *was* to the great sea, and the coast *thereof*. This *is* the coast of the children of Judah round about according to their families.
13 And unto Caleb the son of Jephunneh he gave a part among the children of Judah, according to the commandment of the LORD to Joshua, *even* the city of Arba the father of Anak, which *city is* Hebron.
14 And Caleb drove thence the three sons of Anak, Sheshai, and Ahiman, and Talmai, the children of Anak.
15 And he went up thence to the inhabitants of Debir: and the name of Debir before *was* Kirjath-sepher.
16 And Caleb said, He that smiteth Kirjath-sepher, and taketh it, to him will I give Achsah my daughter to wife.
17 And Othniel the son of Kenaz, the brother of Caleb, took it: and he gave him Achsah his daughter to wife.
18 And it came to pass, as she came *unto him*, that she moved him to ask of her father a field: and she lighted off *her* ass; and Caleb said unto her, what would you?
19 Who answered, Give me a blessing; for you have given me a south land; give me also springs of water. And he gave her the upper springs, and the nether springs.
20 This *is* the inheritance of the tribe of the children of Judah according to their families.
21 And the uttermost cities of the tribe of the children of Judah toward the coast of Edom southward were Kabzeel, and Eder, and Jagur,
22 And Kinah, and Dimonah, and Adadah,
23 And Kedesh, and Hazor, and Ithnan,

24 Ziph, and Telem, and Bealoth,
25 And Hazor, Hadattah, and Kerioth, *and* Hezron, which *is* Hazor,
26 Amam, and Shema, and Moladah,
27 And Hazar-gaddah, and Heshmon, and Beth-palet,
28 And Hazar-shual, and Beer-sheba, and Bizjothjah,
29 Baalah, and Iim, and Azem,
30 And Eltolad, and Chesil, and Hormah,
31 And Ziklag, and Madmannah, and Sansannah,
32 And Lebaoth, and Shilhim, and Ain, and Rimmon: all the cities *are* twenty and nine, with their villages:
33 *And* in the valley, Eshtaol, and Zoreah, and Ashnah,
34 And Zanoah, and En-gannim, Tappuah, and Enam,
35 Jarmuth, and Adullam, Socoh, and Azekah,
36 And Sharaim, and Adithaim, and Gederah, and Gederothaim; fourteen cities with their villages:
37 Zenan, and Hadashah, and Migdal-gad,
38 And Dilean, and Mizpeh, and Joktheel,
39 Lachish, and Bozkath, and Eglon,
40 And Cabbon, and Lahmam, and Kithlish,
41 And Gederoth, Beth-dagon, and Naamah, and Makkedah; sixteen cities with their villages:
42 Libnah, and Ether, and Ashan,
43 And Jiphtah, and Ashnah, and Nezib,
44 And Keilah, and Achzib, and Mareshah; nine cities with their villages:
45 Ekron, with her towns and her villages:
46 From Ekron even unto the sea, all that *lay* near Ashdod, with their villages:
47 Ashdod with her towns and her villages, Gaza with her towns and her villages, unto the river of Egypt, and the great sea, and the border *thereof*:
48 And in the mountains, Shamir, and Jattir, and Socoh,
49 And Dannah, and Kirjath-sannah, which *is* Debir,
50 And Anab, and Eshtemoh, and Anim,
51 And Goshen, and Holon, and Giloh; eleven cities with their villages:
52 Arab, and Dumah, and Eshean,
53 And Janum, and Beth-tappuah, and Aphekah,
54 And Humtah, and Kirjath-arba, which *is* Hebron, and Zior; nine cities with their villages:
55 Maon, Carmel, and Ziph, and Juttah,
56 And Jezreel, and Jokdeam, and Zanoah,
57 Cain, Gibeah, and Timnah; ten cities with their villages:
58 Halhul, Beth-zur, and Gedor,
59 And Maarath, and Beth-anoth, and Eltekon; six cities with their villages:
60 Kirjath-baal, which *is* Kirjath-jearim, and Rabbah; two cities with their villages:
61 In the wilderness, Beth-arabah, Middin, and Secacah,
62 And Nibshan, and the city of Salt, and En-gedi; six cities with their villages.
63 As for the Jebusites the inhabitants of Jerusalem, the children of Judah could not drive them out: but the Jebusites dwell with the children of Judah at Jerusalem unto this day.

CHAPTER 16

1 And the lot of the children of Joseph fell from Jordan by Jericho, unto the water of Jericho on the east, to the wilderness that goes up from Jericho throughout mount Beth-el,
2 And goes out from Beth-el to Luz, and passes along unto the borders of Archi to Ataroth,
3 And goes down westward to the coast of Japhleti, unto the coast of Beth-horon the nether, and to Gezer: and the goings out thereof are at the sea.
4 So the children of Joseph, Manasseh and Ephraim, took their inheritance.
5 And the border of the children of Ephraim according to their families was *thus*: even the border of their inheritance on the east side was Ataroth-addar, unto Beth-horon the upper;
6 And the border went out toward the sea to Michmethah on the north side; and the border went about eastward unto Taanath-shiloh, and passed by it on the east to Janohah;
7 And it went down from Janohah to Ataroth, and to Naarath, and came to Jericho, and went out at Jordan.
8 The border went out from Tappuah westward unto the river Kanah; and the goings out thereof were at the sea. This *is* the inheritance of the tribe of the children of Ephraim by their families.
9 And the separate cities for the children of Ephraim *were* among the inheritance of the children of Manasseh, all the cities with their villages.
10 And they drove not out the Canaanites that dwelt in Gezer: but the Canaanites dwell among the Ephraimites unto this day, and serve under tribute.

CHAPTER 17

1 There was also a lot for the tribe of Manasseh; for he *was* the firstborn of Joseph; *to wit*, for Machir the firstborn of Manasseh, the father of Gilead: because he was a man of war, therefore he had Gilead and Bashan.
2 There was also *a* lot for the rest of the children of Manasseh by their families; for the children of Abiezer, and for the children of Helek, and for the children of Asriel, and for the children of Shechem, and for the children of Hepher, and for the children of Shemida: these *were* the male children of Manasseh the son of Joseph by their families.
3 But Zelophehad, the son of Hepher, the son of Gilead, the son of Machir, the son of Manasseh, had no sons, but daughters: and these *are* the names of his daughters, Mahlah, and Noah, Hoglah, Milcah, and Tirzah.
4 And they came near before Eleazar the priest, and before Joshua the son of Nun, and before the princes, saying, The LORD commanded Moses to give us an inheritance among our brethren. Therefore according to the commandment of the LORD he gave them an inheritance among the brethren of their father.
5 And there fell ten portions to Manasseh, beside the land of Gilead and Bashan, which *were* on the other side Jordan;
6 Because the daughters of Manasseh had an inheritance among his sons: and the rest of Manasseh's sons had the land of Gilead.
7 And the coast of Manasseh was from Asher to Michmethah, that *lies* before Shechem; and the border went along on the right hand unto the inhabitants of En-tappuah.
8 *Now* Manasseh had the land of Tappuah: but Tappuah on the border of Manasseh *belonged* to the children of Ephraim;
9 And the coast descended unto the river Kanah, southward of the river: these cities of Ephraim *are* among the cities of Manasseh: the coast of Manasseh also *was* on the north side of the river, and the outgoings of it were at the sea:
10 Southward *it was* Ephraim's, and northward *it was* Manasseh's, and the sea is his border; and they met together in Asher on the north, and in Issachar on the east.
11 And Manasseh had in Issachar and in Asher Beth-shean and her towns, and Ibleam and her towns, and the inhabitants of Dor

and her towns, and the inhabitants of En-dor and her towns, and the inhabitants of Taanach and her towns, and the inhabitants of Megiddo and her towns, *even* three countries.

12 Yet the children of Manasseh could not drive out *the inhabitants of* those cities; but the Canaanites would dwell in that land.

13 Yet it came to pass, when the children of Israel were waxen strong, that they put the Canaanites to tribute; but did not utterly drive them out.

14 And the children of Joseph spoke unto Joshua, saying, why have you given me *but* one lot and one portion to inherit, seeing I *am* a great people, forasmuch as the LORD hath blessed me hitherto?

15 And Joshua answered them, if you *be* a great people, *then* get you up to the wood *country*, and cut down for yourself there in the land of the Perizzites and of the giants, if mount Ephraim be too narrow for you.

16 And the children of Joseph said, the hill is not enough for us: and all the Canaanites that dwell in the land of the valley have chariots of iron, *both they* who *are* of Beth-shean and her towns, and *they* who *are* of the valley of Jezreel.

17 And Joshua spoke unto the house of Joseph, *even* to Ephraim and to Manasseh, saying, you are a great people, and have great power: you will not have one lot *only*:

18 But the mountain will be thine; for it *is* a wood, and you will cut it down: and the outgoings of it will be thine: for you will drive out the Canaanites, though they have iron chariots, *and* though they *are* strong.

CHAPTER 18

1 And the whole congregation of the children of Israel assembled together at Shiloh, and set up the tabernacle of the congregation there. And the land was subdued before them.

2 And there remained among the children of Israel seven tribes, which had not yet received their inheritance.

3 And Joshua said unto the children of Israel, How long *are* you slack to go to possess the land, which the LORD God of your fathers hath given you?

4 Give out from among you three men for *each* tribe: and I will send them, and they will rise, and go through the land, and describe it according to the inheritance of them; and they will come *again* to me.

5 And they will divide it into seven parts: Judah will abide in their coast on the south, and the house of Joseph will abide in their coasts on the north.

6 you will therefore describe the land *into* seven parts, and bring *the description* here to me, that I may cast lots for you here before the LORD our God.

7 But the Levites have no part among you; for the priesthood of the LORD *is* their inheritance: and Gad, and Reuben, and half the tribe of Manasseh, have received their inheritance beyond Jordan on the east, which Moses the servant of the LORD gave them.

8 And the men arose, and went away: and Joshua charged them that went to describe the land, saying, Go and walk through the land, and describe it, and come again to me, that I may here cast lots for you before the LORD in Shiloh.

9 And the men went and passed through the land, and described it by cities into seven parts in a book, and came again to Joshua to the host at Shiloh.

10 And Joshua cast lots for them in Shiloh before the LORD: and there Joshua divided the land unto the children of Israel according to their divisions.

11 And the lot of the tribe of the children of Benjamin came up according to their families: and the coast of their lot came forth between the children of Judah and the children of Joseph

12 And their border on the north side was from Jordan; and the border went up to the side of Jericho on the north side, and went up through the mountains westward; and the goings out thereof were at the wilderness of Beth-aven.

13 And the border went over from thence toward Luz, to the side of Luz, which *is* Beth-el, southward; and the border descended to Ataroth-adar, near the hill that *lies* on the south side of the nether Beth-horon.

14 And the border was drawn *thence*, and compassed the corner of the sea southward, from the hill that *lies* before Beth-horon southward; and the goings out thereof were at Kirjath-baal, which *is* Kirjath-jearim, a city of the children of Judah: this *was* the west quarter.

15 And the south quarter *was* from the end of Kirjath-jearim, and the border went out on the west, and went out to the well of waters of Nephtoah:

16 And the border came down to the end of the mountain that *lies* before the valley of the son of Hinnom, *and* which *is* in the valley of the giants on the north, and descended to the valley of Hinnom, to the side of Jebusi on the south, and descended to En-rogel,

17 And was drawn from the north, and went forth to En-shemesh, and went forth toward Geliloth, which *is* over against the going up of Adummim, and descended to the stone of Bohan the son of Reuben,

18 And passed along toward the side over against Arabah northward, and went down unto Arabah:

19 And the border passed along to the side of Beth-hoglah northward: and the outgoings of the border were at the north bay of the salt sea at the south end of Jordan: this *was* the south coast.

20 And Jordan was the border of it on the east side. This *was* the inheritance of the children of Benjamin, by the coasts thereof round about, according to their families.

21 Now the cities of the tribe of the children of Benjamin according to their families were Jericho, and Beth-hoglah, and the valley of Keziz,

22 And Beth-arabah, and Zemaraim, and Beth-el,

23 And Avim, and Parah, and Ophrah,

24 And Chephar-haammonai, and Ophni, and Gaba; twelve cities with their villages:

25 Gibeon, and Ramah, and Beeroth,

26 And Mizpeh, and Chephirah, and Mozah,

27 And Rekem, and Irpeel, and Taralah,

28 And Zelah, Eleph, and Jebusi, which *is* Jerusalem, Gibeath, *and* Kirjath; fourteen cities with their villages. This *is* the inheritance of the children of Benjamin according to their families.

CHAPTER 19

1 And the second lot came forth to Simeon, *even* for the tribe of the children of Simeon according to their families: and their inheritance was within the inheritance of the children of Judah.

2 And they had in their inheritance Beer-sheba, or Sheba, and Moladah,

3 And Hazar-shual, and Balah, and Azem,

4 And Eltolad, and Bethul, and Hormah,

5 And Ziklag, and Beth-marcaboth, and Hazar-susah,

6 And Beth-lebaoth, and Sharuhen; thirteen cities and their villages:

7 Ain, Remmon, and Ether, and Ashan; four cities and their villages:
8 And all the villages that *were* round about these cities to Baalath-beer, Ramath of the south. This *is* the inheritance of the tribe of the children of Simeon according to their families.
9 Out of the portion of the children of Judah *was* the inheritance of the children of Simeon: for the part of the children of Judah was too much for them: therefore the children of Simeon had their inheritance within the inheritance of them.
10 And the third lot came up for the children of Zebulun according to their families: and the border of their inheritance was unto Sarid:
11 And their border went up toward the sea, and Maralah, and reached to Dabbasheth, and reached to the river that *is* before Jokneam;
12 And turned from Sarid eastward toward the sun rising unto the border of Chisloth-tabor, and then go out to Daberath, and go up to Japhia,
13 And from there pass on along on the east to Gittah-hepher, to Ittah-kazin, and goes out to Remmon-methoar to Neah;
14 And the border compassed it on the north side to Hannathon: and the outgoings thereof are in the valley of Jiphthah-el:
15 And Kattath, and Nahallal, and Shimron, and Idalah, and Beth-lehem: twelve cities with their villages.
16 This *is* the inheritance of the children of Zebulun according to their families, these cities with their villages.
17 *And* the fourth lot came out to Issachar, for the children of Issachar according to their families.
18 And their border was toward Jezreel, and Chesulloth, and Shunem,
19 And Haphraim, and Shion, and Anaharath,
20 And Rabbith, and Kishion, and Abez,
21 And Remeth, and En-gannim, and En-haddah, and Beth-pazzez;
22 And the coast reached to Tabor, and Shahazimah, and Beth-shemesh; and the outgoings of their border were at Jordan: sixteen cities with their villages.
23 This *is* the inheritance of the tribe of the children of Issachar according to their families, the cities and their villages.
24 And the fifth lot came out for the tribe of the children of Asher according to their families.
25 And their border was Helkath, and Hali, and Beten, and Achshaph,
26 And Alammelech, and Amad, and Misheal; and reached to Carmel westward, and to Shihor-libnath;
27 And turned toward the sun rising to Beth-dagon, and reached to Zebulun, and to the valley of Jiphthah-el toward the north side of Beth-emek, and Neiel, and go out to Cabul on the left hand,
28 And Hebron, and Rehob, and Hammon, and Kanah, *even* unto great Zidon;
29 And *then* the coast turned to Ramah, and to the strong city Tyre; and the coast turned to Hosah; and the outgoings thereof are at the sea from the coast to Achzib:
30 Ummah also, and Aphek, and Rehob: twenty and two cities with their villages.
31 This *is* the inheritance of the tribe of the children of Asher according to their families, these cities with their villages.

32 The sixth lot came out to the children of Naphtali, *even* for the children of Naphtali according to their families.
33 And their coast was from Heleph, from Allon to Zaanannim, and Adami, Nekeb, and Jabneel, unto Lakum; and the outgoings thereof were at Jordan:
34 And *then* the coast turned westward to Aznoth-tabor, and goes out from there to Hukkok, and reached to Zebulun on the south side, and reached to Asher on the west side, and to Judah upon Jordan toward the sun rising.
35 And the fenced cities *are* Ziddim, Zer, and Hammath, Rakkath, and Chinnereth,
36 And Adamah, and Ramah, and Hazor,
37 And Kedesh, and Edrei, and En-hazor,
38 And Iron, and Migdal-el, Horem, and Beth-anath, and Beth-shemesh; nineteen cities with their villages.
39 This *is* the inheritance of the tribe of the children of Naphtali according to their families, the cities and their villages.
40 *And* the seventh lot came out for the tribe of the children of Dan according to their families.
41 And the coast of their inheritance was Zorah, and Eshtaol, and Ir-shemesh,
42 And Shaalabbin, and Ajalon, and Jethlah,
43 And Elon, and Thimnathah, and Ekron,
44 And Eltekeh, and Gibbethon, and Baalath,
45 And Jehud, and Bene-berak, and Gath-rimmon,
46 And Me-jarkon, and Rakkon, with the border before Japho.
47 And the coast of the children of Dan went out *too little* for them: therefore the children of Dan went up to fight against Leshem, and took it, and smote it with the edge of the sword, and possessed it, and dwelt therein, and called Leshem, Dan, after the name of Dan their father.
48 This *is* the inheritance of the tribe of the children of Dan according to their families, these cities with their villages.
49 When they had made an end of dividing the land for inheritance by their coasts, the children of Israel gave an inheritance to Joshua the son of Nun among them:
50 According to the word of the LORD they gave him the city which he asked, *even* Timnath-serah[1] in mount Ephraim: and he built the city, and dwelt therein.
51 These *are* the inheritances, which Eleazar the priest, and Joshua the son of Nun, and the heads of the fathers of the tribes of the children of Israel, divided for an inheritance by lot in Shiloh before the LORD, at the door of the tabernacle of the congregation. So they made an end of dividing the country.

CHAPTER 20

1 The LORD also spoke unto Joshua, saying,
2 Speak to the children of Israel, saying, Appoint out for you cities of refuge, whereof I spoke unto you by the hand of Moses:
3 That the slayer that kills *any* person unawares *and* unwittingly may flee thither: and they will be your refuge from the avenger of blood.
4 And when he that does flee unto one of those cities will stand at the entering of the gate of the city, and will declare his cause in the ears of the elders of that city, they will take him into the city unto them, and give him a place, that he may dwell among them.

---

[1] lit. a portion of the sun. Derives from two root words: the first being the Hebrew word *timnâh* meaning a portion assigned [Strgs#8553]. The second *cheres* meaning to scrape; the itch; also (perhaps from the mediating idea of the sun) [Strgs#2775].

5 And if the avenger of blood pursue after him, then they will not deliver the slayer up into his hand; because he smote his neighbor unwittingly, and hated him not beforetime.

6 And he will dwell in that city, until he stand before the congregation for judgment, *and* until the death of the high priest that will be in those days: then will the slayer return, and come unto his own city, and unto his own house, unto the city from whence he fled.

7 And they appointed Kedesh in Galilee in mount Naphtali, and Shechem in mount Ephraim, and Kirjath-arba, which *is* Hebron, in the mountain of Judah.

8 And on the other side Jordan by Jericho eastward, they assigned Bezer in the wilderness upon the plain out of the tribe of Reuben, and Ramoth in Gilead out of the tribe of Gad, and Golan in Bashan out of the tribe of Manasseh.

9 These were the cities appointed for all the children of Israel, and for the stranger that sojourns among them, that whosoever kills *any* person at unawares might flee thither, and not die by the hand of the avenger of blood, until he stood before the congregation.

CHAPTER 21

1 Then came near the heads of the fathers of the Levites unto Eleazar the priest, and unto Joshua the son of Nun, and unto the heads of the fathers of the tribes of the children of Israel;

2 And they spoke unto them at Shiloh in the land of Canaan, saying, The LORD commanded by the hand of Moses to give us cities to dwell in, with the suburbs thereof for our cattle.

3 And the children of Israel gave unto the Levites out of their inheritance, at the commandment of the LORD, these cities and their suburbs.

4 And the lot came out for the families of the Kohathites: and the children of Aaron the priest, *which were* of the Levites, had by lot out of the tribe of Judah, and out of the tribe of Simeon, and out of the tribe of Benjamin, thirteen cities.

5 And the rest of the children of Kohath *had* by lot out of the families of the tribe of Ephraim, and out of the tribe of Dan, and out of the half tribe of Manasseh, ten cities.

6 And the children of Gershon *had* by lot out of the families of the tribe of Issachar, and out of the tribe of Asher, and out of the tribe of Naphtali, and out of the half tribe of Manasseh in Bashan, thirteen cities.

7 The children of Merari by their families *had* out of the tribe of Reuben, and out of the tribe of Gad, and out of the tribe of Zebulun, twelve cities.

8 And the children of Israel gave by lot unto the Levites these cities with their suburbs, as the LORD commanded by the hand of Moses.

9 And they gave out of the tribe of the children of Judah, and out of the tribe of the children of Simeon, these cities which are *here* mentioned by name,

10 Which the children of Aaron, *being* of the families of the Kohathites, *who were* of the children of Levi, had: for theirs was the first lot.

11 And they gave them the city of Arba the father of Anak, which *city is* Hebron, in the hill *country* of Judah, with the suburbs thereof round about it.

12 But the fields of the city, and the villages thereof, gave they to Caleb the son of Jephunneh for his possession.

13 Thus they gave to the children of Aaron the priest Hebron with her suburbs, *to be* a city of refuge for the slayer; and Libnah with her suburbs,

14 And Jattir with her suburbs, and Eshtemoa with her suburbs,

15 And Holon with her suburbs, and Debir with her suburbs,

16 And Ain with her suburbs, and Juttah with her suburbs, *and* Beth-shemesh with her suburbs; nine cities out of those two tribes.

17 And out of the tribe of Benjamin, Gibeon with her suburbs, Geba with her suburbs,

18 Anathoth with her suburbs, and Almon with her suburbs; four cities.

19 All the cities of the children of Aaron, the priests, *were* thirteen cities with their suburbs.

20 And the families of the children of Kohath, the Levites which remained of the children of Kohath, even they had the cities of their lot out of the tribe of Ephraim.

21 For they gave them Shechem with her suburbs in mount Ephraim, *to be* a city of refuge for the slayer; and Gezer with her suburbs,

22 And Kibzaim with her suburbs, and Beth-horon with her suburbs; four cities.

23 And out of the tribe of Dan, Eltekeh with her suburbs, Gibbethon with her suburbs,

24 Aijalon with her suburbs, Gath-rimmon with her suburbs; four cities.

25 And out of the half tribe of Manasseh, Tanach with her suburbs, and Gath-rimmon with her suburbs; two cities.

26 All the cities *were* ten with their suburbs for the families of the children of Kohath that remained.

27 And unto the children of Gershon, of the families of the Levites, out of the *other* half tribe of Manasseh *they gave* Golan in Bashan with her suburbs, *to be* a city of refuge for the slayer; and Beesh-terah with her suburbs; two cities.

28 And out of the tribe of Issachar, Kishon with her suburbs, Dabareh with her suburbs,

29 Jarmuth with her suburbs, En-gannim with her suburbs; four cities.

30 And out of the tribe of Asher, Mishal with her suburbs, Abdon with her suburbs,

31 Helkath with her suburbs, and Rehob with her suburbs; four cities.

32 And out of the tribe of Naphtali, Kedesh in Galilee with her suburbs, *to be* a city of refuge for the slayer; and Hammoth-dor with her suburbs, and Kartan with her suburbs; three cities.

33 All the cities of the Gershonites according to their families *were* thirteen cities with their suburbs.

34 And unto the families of the children of Merari, the rest of the Levites, out of the tribe of Zebulun, Jokneam with her suburbs, and Kartah with her suburbs,

35 Dimnah with her suburbs, Nahalal with her suburbs; four cities.

36 And out of the tribe of Reuben, Bezer with her suburbs, and Jahazah with her suburbs,

37 Kedemoth with her suburbs, and Mephaath with her suburbs; four cities.

38 And out of the tribe of Gad, Ramoth in Gilead with her suburbs, *to be* a city of refuge for the slayer; and Mahanaim with her suburbs,

39 Heshbon with her suburbs, Jazer with her suburbs four cities in all.

40 So all the cities for the children of Merari by their families, which were remaining of the families of the Levites, were *by* their lot twelve cities.

41 All the cities of the Levites within the possession of the children of Israel *were* forty and eight cities with their suburbs.
42 These cities were everyone with their suburbs round about them: thus *were* all these cities.
43 And the LORD gave unto Israel all the land which he swore to give unto their fathers; and they possessed it, and dwelt therein.
44 And the LORD gave them rest round about, according to all that he swore unto their fathers: and there stood not a man of all their enemies before them; the LORD delivered all their enemies into their hand.
45 There failed not ought of any good thing which the LORD had spoken unto the house of Israel; all came to pass.

CHAPTER 22

1 Then Joshua called the Reubenites, and the Gadites, and the half tribe of Manasseh,
2 And said unto them, you have kept all that Moses the servant of the LORD commanded you, and have obeyed my voice in all that I commanded you:
3 you have not left your brethren these many days unto this day, but have kept the charge of the commandment of the LORD your God.
4 And now the LORD your God hath given rest unto your brethren, as he promised them: therefore now return you, and get you unto your tents, *and* unto the land of your possession, which Moses the servant of the LORD gave you on the other side Jordan.
5 But take diligent heed to do the commandment and the law, which Moses the servant of the LORD charged you, to love the LORD your God, and to walk in all his ways, and to keep his commandments, and to cleave unto him, and to serve him with all your heart and with all your soul.
6 So Joshua blessed them, and sent them away: and they went unto their tents.
7 Now to the *one* half of the tribe of Manasseh Moses had given *possession* in Bashan: but unto the *other* half thereof gave Joshua among their brethren on this side Jordan westward. And when Joshua sent them away also unto their tents, then he blessed them,
8 And he spoke unto them, saying, Return with much riches unto your tents, and with very much cattle, with silver, and with gold, and with brass, and with iron, and with very much raiment: divide the spoil of your enemies with your brethren.
9 And the children of Reuben and the children of Gad and the half tribe of Manasseh returned, and departed from the children of Israel out of Shiloh, which *is* in the land of Canaan, to go unto the country of Gilead, to the land of their possession, whereof they were possessed, according to the word of the LORD by the hand of Moses.
10 And when they came unto the borders of Jordan, that *are* in the land of Canaan, the children of Reuben and the children of Gad and the half tribe of Manasseh built there an altar by Jordan, a great altar to see to.
11 And the children of Israel heard say, Behold, the children of Reuben and the children of Gad and the half tribe of Manasseh have built an altar over against the land of Canaan, in the borders of Jordan, at the passage of the children of Israel.
12 And when the children of Israel heard *of it*, the whole congregation of the children of Israel gathered themselves together at Shiloh, to go up to war against them.
13 And the children of Israel sent unto the children of Reuben, and to the children of Gad, and to the half tribe of Manasseh, into the land of Gilead, Phinehas the son of Eleazar the priest,
14 And with him ten princes, of each chief house a prince throughout all the tribes of Israel; and each one *was* a head of the house of their fathers among the thousands of Israel.
15 And they came unto the children of Reuben, and to the children of Gad, and to the half tribe of Manasseh, unto the land of Gilead, and they spoke with them, saying,
16 Thus said the whole congregation of the LORD, What trespass *is* this that you have committed against the God of Israel, to turn away this day from following the LORD, in that you have built you an altar, that you might rebel this day against the LORD?
17 *Is* the iniquity of Peor too little for us, from which we are not cleansed until this day, although there was a plague in the congregation of the LORD,
18 But that you must turn away this day from following the LORD? And it will be, *seeing* you rebel today against the LORD, that tomorrow he will be angry with the whole congregation of Israel.
19 Notwithstanding, if the land of your possession *be* unclean, *then* pass you over unto the land of the possession of the LORD, wherein the LORD'S tabernacle dwelled, and take possession among us: but rebel not against the LORD, or rebel against us, in building you an altar beside the altar of the LORD our God.
20 Did not Achan the son of Zerah commit a trespass in the accursed thing, and wrath fell on all the congregation of Israel? And that man perished not alone in his iniquity.
21 Then the children of Reuben and the children of Gad and the half tribe of Manasseh answered, and said unto the heads of the thousands of Israel,
22 The LORD God of gods, the LORD God of gods, he know, and Israel he will know; if *it be* in rebellion, or if in transgression against the LORD, (save us not this day,)
23 That we have built us an altar to turn from following the LORD, or if to offer thereon burnt offering or meat offering, or if to offer peace offerings thereon, let the LORD himself require *it*.
24 And if we have not *rather* done it for fear of *this* thing, saying, In time to come your children might speak unto our children, saying, What have you to do with the LORD God of Israel?
25 For the LORD have made Jordan a border between us and you, you children of Reuben and children of Gad; you have no part in the LORD: so will your children make our children cease from fearing the LORD.
26 Therefore we said, Let us now prepare to build us an altar, not for burnt offering, nor for sacrifice:
27 But *that* it *may be* a witness between us, and you, and our generations after us, that we might do the service of the LORD before him with our burnt offerings, and with our sacrifices, and with our peace offerings; that your children may not say to our children in time to come, you have no part in the LORD.
28 Therefore said we, that it will be, when they should *so* say to us or to our generations in time to come, that we may say *again*, Behold the pattern of the altar of the LORD, which our fathers made, not for burnt offerings, nor for sacrifices; but it *is* a witness between us and you.
29 God forbid that we should rebel against the LORD, and turn this day from following the LORD, to build an altar for burnt offerings, for meat offerings, or for sacrifices, beside the altar of the LORD our God that *is* before his tabernacle.
30 And when Phinehas the priest, and the princes of the congregation and heads of the thousands of Israel which *were* with

him, heard the words that the children of Reuben and the children of Gad and the children of Manasseh spoke, it pleased them.
31 And Phinehas the son of Eleazar the priest said unto the children of Reuben, and to the children of Gad, and to the children of Manasseh, This day we perceive that the LORD *is* among us, because you have not committed this trespass against the LORD: now you have delivered the children of Israel out of the hand of the LORD.
32 And Phinehas the son of Eleazar the priest, and the princes, returned from the children of Reuben, and from the children of Gad, out of the land of Gilead, unto the land of Canaan, to the children of Israel, and brought them word again.
33 And the thing pleased the children of Israel; and the children of Israel blessed God, and did not intend to go up against them in battle, to destroy the land wherein the children of Reuben and Gad dwelt.
34 And the children of Reuben and the children of Gad called the altar *Ed*: for it will *be* a witness between us that the LORD *is* God.

CHAPTER 23

1 And it came to pass a long time after that the LORD had given rest unto Israel from all their enemies round about, that Joshua waxed old *and* stricken in age.
2 And Joshua called for all Israel, *and* for their elders, and for their heads, and for their judges, and for their officers, and said unto them, I am old *and* stricken in age:
3 And you have seen all that the LORD your God hath done unto all these nations because of you; for the LORD your God *is* he that hath fought for you.
4 Behold, I have divided unto you by lot these nations that remain, to be an inheritance for your tribes, from Jordan, with all the nations that I have cut off, even unto the great sea westward.
5 And the LORD your God, he will expel them from before you, and drive them from out of your sight; and you will possess their land, as the LORD your God hath promised unto you.
6 Be you therefore very courageous to keep and to do all that is written in the book of the law of Moses, that you turn not aside therefrom *to* the right hand or *to* the left;
7 That you come not among these nations, these that remain among you; neither make mention of the name of their gods, nor cause to swear *by them*, neither serve them, nor bow yourselves unto them:
8 But cleave unto the LORD your God, as you have done unto this day.
9 For the LORD hath driven out from before you great nations and strong: but *as for* you, no man hath been able to stand before you unto this day.
10 One man of you will chase a thousand: for the LORD your God, he *it is* that fights for you, as he hath promised you.
11 Take good heed therefore unto yourselves, that you love the LORD your God.
12 Else if you do in any wise go back, and cleave unto the remnant of these nations, *even* these that remain among you, and will make marriages with them, and go in unto them, and they to you:
13 Know for a certainty that the LORD your God will no more drive out *any of* these nations from before you; but they will be snares and traps unto you, and scourges in your sides, and thorns in your eyes, until you perish from off this good land which the LORD your God hath given you.
14 And, behold, this day I *am* going the way of all the earth: and you know in all your hearts and in all your souls, that not one thing hath failed of all the good things which the LORD your God spoke concerning you; all are come to pass unto you, *and* not one thing hath failed thereof.
15 Therefore it will come to pass, *that* as all good things are come upon you, which the LORD your God promised you; so will the LORD bring upon you all evil things, until he have destroyed you from off this good land which the LORD your God hath given you.
16 When you have transgressed the covenant of the LORD your God, which he commanded you, and have gone and served other gods, and bowed yourselves to them; then will the anger of the LORD be kindled against you, and you will perish quickly from off the good land which he hath given unto you.

CHAPTER 24

1 And Joshua gathered all the tribes of Israel to Shechem, and called for the elders of Israel, and for their heads, and for their judges, and for their officers; and they presented themselves before God.
2 And Joshua said unto all the people, Thus said the LORD God of Israel, Your fathers dwelt on the other side of the flood in old time, *even* Terah, the father of Abraham, and the father of Nachor: and they served other gods.
3 And I took your father Abraham from the other side of the flood, and led him throughout all the land of Canaan, and multiplied his seed, and gave him Isaac.
4 And I gave unto Isaac Jacob and Esau: and I gave unto Esau mount Seir, to possess it; but Jacob and his children went down into Egypt.
5 I sent Moses also and Aaron, and I plagued Egypt, according to that which I did among them: and afterward I brought you out.
6 And I brought your fathers out of Egypt: and you came unto the sea; and the Egyptians pursued after your fathers with chariots and horsemen unto the Red sea.
7 And when they cried unto the LORD, he put darkness between you and the Egyptians, and brought the sea upon them, and covered them; and your eyes have seen what I have done in Egypt: and you dwelt in the wilderness a long season.
8 And I brought you into the land of the Amorites, which dwelt on the other side Jordan; and they fought with you: and I gave them into your hand, that you might possess their land; and I destroyed them from before you.
9 Then Balak the son of Zippor, king of Moab, arose and warred against Israel, and sent and called Balaam the son of Beor to curse you:
10 But I would not hearken unto Balaam; therefore he blessed you still: so I delivered you out of his hand.
11 And you went over Jordan, and came unto Jericho: and the men of Jericho fought against you, the Amorites, and the Perizzites, and the Canaanites, and the Hittites, and the Girgashites, the Hivites, and the Jebusites; and I delivered them into your hand
12 And I sent the hornet before you, which drive them out from before you, *even* the two kings of the Amorites; *but* not with your sword, nor with your bow.
13 And I have given you a land for which you did not labor, and cities which you built not, and you dwell in them; of the vineyards and olive yards which you planted not do you eat.
14 Now therefore fear the LORD, and serve him in sincerity and in truth: and put away the gods which your fathers served on the other side of the flood, and in Egypt; and serve you the LORD.
15 And if it seems evil unto you to serve the LORD, choose you this day who you will serve; whether the gods which your fathers

served that *were* on the other side of the flood, or the gods of the Amorites, in whose land you dwell: but as for me and my house, we will serve the LORD.

16 And the people answered and said, God forbid that we should forsake the LORD, to serve other gods;

17 For the LORD our God, he *it is* that brought us up and our fathers out of the land of Egypt, from the house of bondage, and which did those great signs in our sight, and preserved us in all the way wherein we went, and among all the people through whom we passed:

18 And the LORD drive out from before us all the people, even the Amorites which dwelt in the land: *therefore* will we also serve the LORD; for he *is* our God.

19 And Joshua said unto the people, you cannot serve the LORD: for he *is* a holy God; he *is* a jealous God; he will not forgive your transgressions or your sins.

20 If you forsake the LORD, and serve strange gods, then he will turn and do you hurt, and consume you, after that he hath done you good.

21 And the people said unto Joshua, Nay; but we will serve the LORD.

22 And Joshua said unto the people, you *are* witnesses against yourselves that you have chosen you the LORD, to serve him. And they said, *we are* witnesses.

23 Now therefore put away, *said he*, the strange gods which *are* among you, and incline your heart unto the LORD God of Israel.

24 And the people said unto Joshua, The LORD our God will we serve, and his voice will we obey.

25 So Joshua made a covenant with the people that day, and set them a statute and an ordinance in Shechem.

26 And Joshua wrote these words in the book of the law of God, and took a great stone, and set it up there under an oak, that *was* by the sanctuary of the LORD.

27 And Joshua said unto all the people, Behold, this stone will be a witness unto us; for it hath heard all the words of the LORD which he spoke unto us: it will be therefore a witness unto you, lest you deny your God.

28 So Joshua let the people depart, every man unto his inheritance.

29 And it came to pass after these things, that Joshua the son of Nun, the servant of the LORD, died, *being* an hundred and ten years old.

30 And they buried him in the border of his inheritance in Timnath-serah, which *is* in mount Ephraim, on the north side of the hill of Gaash.

31 And Israel served the LORD all the days of Joshua, and all the days of the elders that over lived Joshua, and which had known all the works of the LORD, that he had done for Israel.

32 And the bones of Joseph, which the children of Israel brought up out of Egypt, buried they in Shechem, in a parcel of ground which Jacob bought of the sons of Hamor the father of Shechem for an hundred pieces of silver: and it became the inheritance of the children of Joseph.

33 And Eleazar the son of Aaron died; and they buried him in a hill *that pertained to* Phinehas his son, which was given him in mount Ephraim.

JUDGES
CHAPTER 1

1 Now after the death of Joshua it came to pass, that the children of Israel asked the LORD, saying, who will go up for us against the Canaanites first, to fight against them?
2 And the LORD said, Judah will go up: behold, I have delivered the land into his hand.
3 And Judah said unto Simeon his brother, come up with me into my lot, that we may fight against the Canaanites; and I likewise will go with you into your lot. So Simeon went with him.
4 And Judah went up; and the LORD delivered the Canaanites and the Perizzites into their hand: and they slew of them in Bezek ten thousand men.
5 And they found Adoni-bezek in Bezek: and they fought against him, and they slew the Canaanites and the Perizzites.
6 But Adoni-bezek fled; and they pursued after him, and caught him, and cut off his thumbs and his great toes.
7 And Adoni-bezek said, Threescore and ten kings, having their thumbs and their great toes cut off, gathered *their meat* under my table: as I have done, so God hath requited me. And they brought him to Jerusalem, and there he died.
8 Now the children of Judah had fought against Jerusalem, and had taken it, and smitten it with the edge of the sword, and set the city on fire.
9 And afterward the children of Judah went down to fight against the Canaanites, that dwelt in the mountain, and in the south, and in the valley.
10 And Judah went against the Canaanites that dwelt in Hebron: (now the name of Hebron before *was* Kirjath-arba:) and they slew Sheshai, and Ahiman, and Talmai.
11 And from thence he went against the inhabitants of Debir: and the name of Debir before *was* Kirjath-sepher:
12 And Caleb said, He that slaughtered Kirjath-sepher, and taketh it, to him will I give Achsah my daughter to wife.
13 And Othniel the son of Kenaz, Caleb's younger brother, took it: and he gave him Achsah his daughter to wife.
14 And it came to pass, when she came *to him*, that she moved him to ask of her father a field: and she lighted from off *her* ass; and Caleb said unto her, what will you?
15 And she said unto him, Give me a blessing: for you have given me a south land; give me also springs of water. And Caleb gave her the upper springs and the nether springs.
16 And the children of the Kenite, Moses' father in law, went up out of the city of palm trees with the children of Judah into the wilderness of Judah, which lie in the south of Arad; and they went and dwelt among the people.
17 And Judah went with Simeon his brother, and they slew the Canaanites that inhabited Zephath, and utterly destroyed it. And the name of the city was called Hormah.
18 Also Judah took Gaza with the coast thereof, and Askelon with the coast thereof, and Ekron with the coast thereof.
19 And the LORD was with Judah; and he drive out *the inhabitants of* the mountain; but could not drive out the inhabitants of the valley, because they had chariots of iron.
20 And they gave Hebron unto Caleb, as Moses said: and he expelled thence the three sons of Anak.
21 And the children of Benjamin did not drive out the Jebusites that inhabited Jerusalem; but the Jebusites dwell with the children of Benjamin in Jerusalem unto this day.
22 And the house of Joseph, they also went up against Beth-el: and the LORD *was* with them.
23 And the house of Joseph sent to descry Beth-el. (Now the name of the city before *was* Luz.)
24 And the spies saw a man come forth out of the city, and they said unto him, show us, we pray you, the entrance into the city, and we will show you mercy.
25 And when he showed them the entrance into the city, they smote the city with the edge of the sword; but they let go the man and all his family.
26 And the man went into the land of the Hittites, and built a city, and called the name thereof Luz: which *is* the name thereof unto this day.
27 Neither did Manasseh drive out *the inhabitants of* Beth-shean and her towns, or Taanach and her towns, or the inhabitants of Dor and her towns, or the inhabitants of Ibleam and her towns, or the inhabitants of Megiddo[1] and her towns: but the Canaanites would dwell in that land.
28 And it came to pass, when Israel was strong, that they put the Canaanites to tribute, and did not utterly drive them out.
29 Neither did Ephraim drive out the Canaanites that dwelt in Gezer; but the Canaanites dwelt in Gezer among them.
30 Neither did Zebulun drive out the inhabitants of Kitron, or the inhabitants of Nahalol; but the Canaanites dwelt among them, and became tributaries.
31 Neither did Asher drive out the inhabitants of Accho, or the inhabitants of Zidon, or of Ahlab, or of Achzib, or of Helbah, or of Aphik, or of Rehob:
32 But the Asherites dwelt among the Canaanites, the inhabitants of the land: for they did not drive them out.
33 Neither did Naphtali drive out the inhabitants of Beth-shemesh, or the inhabitants of Beth-anath; but he dwelt among the Canaanites, the inhabitants of the land: nevertheless the inhabitants of Beth-shemesh and of Beth-anath became tributaries unto them.
34 And the Amorites forced the children of Dan into the mountain: for they would not suffer them to come down to the valley:
35 But the Amorites would dwell in mount Heres in Aijalon, and in Shaalbim: yet the hand of the house of Joseph prevailed, so that they became tributaries.
36 And the coast of the Amorites *was* from the going up to Akrabbim, from the rock, and upward.

CHAPTER 2
1 And an angel of the LORD came up from Gilgal to Bochim, and said, I made you to go up out of Egypt, and have brought you unto the land which I swore unto your fathers; and I said, I will never break my covenant with you.
2 And you will make no league with the inhabitants of this land; you will throw down their altars: but you have not obeyed my voice: why have you done this?
3 Wherefore I also said, I will not drive them out from before you; but they will be *as thorns* in your sides, and their gods will be a snare unto you.

---

[1] Megiddo –an ancient city of Canaan assigned to Manasseh and located on the southern rim of the plains of Esdraelon 6 miles from Nazareth. Defined as place of crowds, derives from the Hebrew root word *gâdad*, gaw-dad, meaning to crowd, to gash (as if by pressing into), to assemble selves by troops, to cut selves. [Strgs#4023]

4 And it came to pass, when the angel of the LORD spoke these words unto all the children of Israel, that the people lifted up their voice, and wept.
5 And they called the name of that place Bochim: and they sacrificed there unto the LORD.
6 And when Joshua had let the people go, the children of Israel went every man unto his inheritance to possess the land.
7 And the people served the LORD all the days of Joshua, and all the days of the elders that outlived Joshua, who had seen all the great works of the LORD, that he did for Israel.
8 And Joshua the son of Nun, the servant of the LORD, died, *being* an hundred and ten years old.
9 And they buried him in the border of his inheritance in Timnath-heres, in the mount of Ephraim, on the north side of the hill Gaash.
10 [And also all that generations were gathered unto their fathers: and there arose another generation after them, which knew not the LORD, or yet the works which he had done for Israel.]1
11 And the children of Israel did evil in the sight of the LORD, and served Baalim:
12 And they forsook the LORD God of their fathers, which brought them out of the land of Egypt, and followed other gods, of the gods of the people that *were* round about them, and bowed themselves unto them, and provoked the LORD to anger.
13 And they forsook the LORD, and served Baal and Ashtaroth.
14 And the anger of the LORD was hot against Israel, and he delivered them into the hands of spoilers that spoiled them, and he sold them into the hands of their enemies round about, so that they could not any longer stand before their enemies.
15 Whithersoever they went out, the hand of the LORD was against them for evil, as the LORD had said, and as the LORD had sworn unto them: and they were greatly distressed.
16 Nevertheless the LORD raised up judges, which delivered them out of the hand of those that spoiled them.
17 And yet they would not hearken unto their judges, but they went a whoring after other gods, and bowed themselves unto them: they turned quickly out of the way which their fathers walked in, obeying the commandments of the LORD; *but* they did not so.
18 And when the LORD raised them up judges, then the LORD was with the judge, and delivered them out of the hand of their enemies all the days of the judge: for it repented the LORD because of their groanings by reason of them that oppressed them and vexed them.
19 And it came to pass, when the judge was dead, *that* they returned, and corrupted *themselves* more than their fathers, in following other gods to serve them, and to bow down unto them; they ceased not from their own doings, or from their stubborn way.
20 And the anger of the LORD was hot against Israel; and he said, because that this people hath transgressed my covenant which I commanded their fathers, and have not hearkened unto my voice;
21 I also will not henceforth drive out any from before them of the nations which Joshua left when he died:
22 That through them I may prove Israel, whether they will keep the way of the LORD to walk therein, as their fathers did keep *it*, or not.
23 Therefore the LORD left those nations, without driving them out hastily; neither delivered he them into the hand of Joshua.

CHAPTER 3

1 Now these *are* the nations which the LORD left, to prove Israel by them, *even* as many *of Israel* as had not known all the wars of Canaan;
2 Only that the generations of the children of Israel might know, to teach them war, at the least such as before knew nothing thereof;
3 *Namely*, five lords of the Philistines, and all the Canaanites, and the Sidonians, and the Hivites that dwelt in Mount Lebanon, from Mount Baal-hermon unto the entering in of Hamath.
4 And they were to prove Israel by them, to know whether they would hearken unto the commandments of the LORD, which he commanded their fathers by the hand of Moses.
5 And the children of Israel dwelt among the Canaanites, Hittites, and Amorites, and Perizzites, and Hivites, and Jebusites:
6 And they took their daughters to be their wives, and gave their daughters to their sons, and served their gods.
7 And the children of Israel did evil in the sight of the LORD, and forgot the LORD their God, and served Baalim and the groves.
8 Therefore the anger of the LORD was hot against Israel, and he sold them into the hand of Chushan-rishathaim2 king of Mesopotamia: and the children of Israel served Chushan-rishathaim eight years.
9 And when the children of Israel cried unto the LORD, the LORD raised up a deliverer to the children of Israel, who delivered them, *even* Othniel3 the son of Kenaz, Caleb's younger brother.
10 And the Spirit of the LORD came upon him, and he judged Israel, and went out to war: and the LORD delivered Chushan-rishathaim king of Mesopotamia into his hand; and his hand prevailed against Chushan-rishathaim.
11 And the land had rest forty years. And Othniel the son of Kenaz died.
12 And the children of Israel did evil again in the sight of the LORD: and the LORD strengthened Eglon the king of Moab against Israel, because they had done evil in the sight of the LORD.
13 And he gathered unto him the children of Ammon and Amalek, and went and smote Israel, and possessed the city of palm trees.
14 So the children of Israel served Eglon the king of Moab eighteen years.
15 But when the children of Israel cried unto the LORD, the LORD raised them up a deliverer, Ehud the son of Gera, a Benjamite, a man left-handed: and by him the children of Israel sent a present unto Eglon the king of Moab.
16 But Ehud made him a dagger which had two edges, of a cubit length; and he did gird it under his raiment upon his right thigh.
17 And he brought the present unto Eglon king of Moab: and Eglon *was* a very fat man.
18 And when he had made an end to offer the present, he sent away the people that bare the present.
19 But he himself turned again from the quarries that *were* by Gilgal, and said, I have a secret errand unto you, O king: who said, Keep silence. And all that stood by him went out from him.
20 And Ehud came unto him; and he was sitting in a summer parlor, which he had for himself alone. And Ehud said, I have a message from God unto you. And he arose out of *his* seat.
21 And Ehud put forth his left hand, and took the dagger from his right thigh, and thrust it into his belly:

---

1 The other generations did not evangelize the next generation: compare **Ps. 78:6-8**.
2 Chushan-rishathaim- defined as Cushan of double wickedness. It derives from two other words. The first being *kûsh* meaning black, probably of foreign origin (Ethiopia), the name of a son of Ham and of his territory. The second being *râsha* meaning wrong, to disturb, violate, condemn, make trouble, vex, be wickedly. [Strgs#3573]
3 Othniel- defined lion of God or force of God. [Strgs#6274]

22 And the haft also went in after the blade; and the fat closed upon the blade, so that he could not draw the dagger out of his belly; and the dirt came out.
23 Then Ehud went forth through the porch, and shut the doors of the parlor upon him, and locked them.
24 When he was gone out, his servants came; and when they saw that, behold, the doors of the parlor *were* locked, they said, Surely he covered his feet in his summer chamber.
25 And they tarried till they were ashamed: and, behold, he opened not the doors of the parlor; therefore they took a key, and opened *them*: and, behold, their lord *was* fallen down dead on the earth.
26 And Ehud escaped while they tarried, and passed beyond the quarries, and escaped unto Seirath.
27 And it came to pass, when he was come, that he blew a trumpet in the mountain of Ephraim, and the children of Israel went down with him from the mount, and he before them.
28 And he said unto them, Follow after me: for the LORD hath delivered your enemies the Moabites into your hand. And they went down after him, and took the fords of Jordan toward Moab, and suffered not a man to pass over.
29 And they slew of Moab at that time about ten thousand men, all lusty, and all men of valor; and there escaped not a man.
30 So Moab was subdued that day under the hand of Israel. And the land had rest fourscore years.
31 And after him was Shamgar the son of Anath, which slew of the Philistines six hundred men with an ox goad: and he also delivered Israel.

CHAPTER 4

1 And the children of Israel again did evil in the sight of the LORD, when Ehud was dead.
2 And the LORD sold them into the hand of Jabin king of Canaan, that reigned in Hazor; the captain of whose host *was* Sisera, which dwelt in Harosheth of the Gentiles.
3 And the children of Israel cried unto the LORD: for he had nine hundred chariots of iron; and twenty years he mightily oppressed the children of Israel.
4 And Deborah, a prophetess, the wife of Lapidoth, she judged Israel at that time.
5 And she dwelt under the palm tree of Deborah between Ramah and Beth-el in mount Ephraim: and the children of Israel came up to her for judgment.
6 And she sent and called Barak the son of Abinoam out of Kedesh-naphtali, and said unto him, Hath not the LORD God of Israel commanded, *saying*, Go and draw toward mount Tabor, and take with you ten thousand men of the children of Naphtali and of the children of Zebulun?
7 And I will draw unto you to the river Kishon Sisera, the captain of Jabin's army, with his chariots and his multitude; and I will deliver him into thine hand.
8 And Barak said unto her, if you will go with me, then I will go: but if you will not go with me, *then* I will not go.
9 And she said, I will surely go with you: notwithstanding the journey that you take will not be for your honor; for the LORD will sell Sisera into the hand of a woman. And Deborah arose, and went with Barak to Kedesh.
10 And Barak called Zebulun and Naphtali to Kedesh; and he went up with ten thousand men at his feet: and Deborah went up with him.
11 Now Heber the Kenite, *which was* of the children of Hobab the father in law of Moses, had severed himself from the Kenites, and pitched his tent unto the plain of Zaanaim, which *is* by Kedesh.
12 And they showed Sisera that Barak the son of Abinoam was gone up to mount Tabor.
13 And Sisera gathered together all his chariots, *even* nine hundred chariots of iron, and all the people that *were* with him, from Harosheth of the Gentiles unto the river of Kishon.
14 And Deborah said unto Barak, up; for this *is* the day in which the LORD hath delivered Sisera into thine hand: is not the LORD gone out before you? So Barak went down from mount Tabor, and ten thousand men after him.
15 And the LORD discomfited Sisera, and all *his* chariots, and all *his* host, with the edge of the sword before Barak; so that Sisera lighted down off *his* chariot, and fled away on his feet.
16 But Barak pursued after the chariots, and after the host, unto Harosheth of the Gentiles: and all the host of Sisera fell upon the edge of the sword; *and* there was not a man left.
17 Howbeit Sisera fled away on his feet to the tent of Jael the wife of Heber the Kenite: for *there was* peace between Jabin the king of Hazor and the house of Heber the Kenite.
18 And Jael went out to meet Sisera, and said unto him, Turn in, my lord, turn in to me; fear not. And when he had turned in unto her into the tent, she covered him with a mantle.
19 And he said unto her, Give me, I pray you, a little water to drink; for I am thirsty. And she opened a bottle of milk, and gave him drink, and covered him.
20 Again he said unto her, Stand in the door of the tent, and it will be, when any man doth come and enquire of you, and say, is there any man here? That you will say, no.
21 Then Jael Heber's wife took a nail of the tent, and took a hammer in her hand, and went softly unto him, and **struck** the nail into his temples, and fastened it into the ground: for he was fast asleep and weary. So he died.
22 And, behold, as Barak pursued Sisera, Jael came out to meet him, and said unto him, come, and I will show you the man who you seek. And when he came into her *tent*, behold, Sisera lay dead, and the nail *was* in his temples.
23 So God subdued on that day Jabin the king of Canaan before the children of Israel.
24 And the hand of the children of Israel prospered, and prevailed against Jabin the king of Canaan, until they had destroyed Jabin king of Canaan.

CHAPTER 5

1 Then sang Deborah and Barak the son of Abinoam on that day, saying,
2 Praise you the LORD for the avenging of Israel, when the people willingly offered themselves.
3 Hear, O you kings; give ear, O you princes; I, *even* I, will sing unto the LORD; I will sing *praise* to the LORD God of Israel.
4 LORD, when you went out of Seir, when you marched out of the field of Edom, the earth trembled, and the heavens dropped, the clouds also dropped water.
5 The mountains melted from before the LORD, *even* that Sinai from before the LORD God of Israel.
6 In the days of Shamgar the son of Anath, in the days of Jael, the highways were unoccupied, and the travelers walked through byways.
7 *The inhabitants of* the villages ceased, they ceased in Israel, until that I Deborah arose, that I arose a mother in Israel.

8 They chose new gods; then **there** *was* war in the gates: was there a shield or spear seen among forty thousand in Israel?
9 My heart *is* toward the governors of Israel, that offered themselves willingly among the people. Bless you the LORD.
10 Speak, you that ride on white asses, you that sit in judgment, and walk by the way.
11 *They that are delivered* from the noise of archers in the places of drawing water, there will they rehearse the righteous acts of the LORD, *even* the righteous acts *toward the inhabitants* of his villages in Israel: then will the people of the LORD go down to the gates.
12 Awake, awake, Deborah: awake, awake, utter a song: arise, Barak, and lead your captivity captive, you son of Abinoam.
13 Then he made him that remained have dominion over the nobles among the people: the LORD made me have dominion over the mighty.
14 Out of Ephraim *was there* a root of them against Amalek; after you, Benjamin, among your people; out of Machir came down governors, and out of Zebulun they that handle the pen of the writer.
15 And the princes of Issachar *were* with Deborah; even Issachar, and also Barak: he was sent on foot into the valley. For the divisions of Reuben *there were* great thoughts of heart.
16 Why **dwell** you among the sheepfolds, to hear the bleatings of the flocks? For the divisions of Reuben *there were* great searching of heart.
17 Gilead abode beyond Jordan: and why did Dan remain in ships? Asher continued on the sea shore, and abode in his breaches.
18 Zebulun and Naphtali *were* a people *that* jeopardize their lives unto the death in the high places of the field.
19 The kings came *and* fought, then fought the kings of Canaan in Taanach by the waters of Megiddo; they took no gain of money.
20 They fought from heaven; the stars in their courses fought against Sisera.
21 The river of Kishon swept them away, that ancient river, the river Kishon. O my soul, you have trodden down strength.
22 Then were the horsehoofs broken by the means of the pransings, the pransings of their mighty ones.
23 Curse you Meroz, said the angel of the LORD, curse you bitterly the inhabitants thereof; because they came not to the help of the LORD, to the help of the LORD against the mighty.
24 Blessed above women will Jael the wife of Heber the Kenite be, blessed will she be above women in the tent.
25 He asked water, *and* she gave *him* milk; she brought forth butter in a lordly dish.
26 She put her hand to the nail, and her right hand to the workmen's hammer; and with the hammer she smote Sisera, she smote off his head, when she had pierced and stricken through his temples.
27 At her feet he bowed, he fell, he lay down: at her feet he bowed, he fell: where he bowed, there he fell down dead.
28 The mother of Sisera looked out at a window, and cried through the lattice, why is his chariot *so* long in coming? Why tarry the wheels of his chariots?
29 Her wise ladies answered her, yea, she returned answer to herself,
30 Have they not sped? have they *not* divided the prey; to every man a damsel *or* two; to Sisera a prey of divers colors, a prey of divers colors of needlework, of divers colors of needlework on both sides, *meet* for the necks of *them that take* the spoil?
31 So let all thine enemies perish, O LORD: but *let* them that love him *be* as the sun when he go forth in his might. And the land had rest forty years.

CHAPTER 6

1 And the children of Israel did evil in the sight of the LORD: and the LORD delivered them into the hand of Midian seven years.
2 And the hand of Midian prevailed against Israel: *and* because of the Midianites the children of Israel made them the dens which *are* in the mountains, and caves, and strong holds.
3 And *so* it was, when Israel had sown, that the Midianites came up, and the Amalekites, and the children of the east, even they came up against them;
4 And they encamped against them, and destroyed the increase of the earth, till you come unto Gaza, and left no sustenance for Israel, neither sheep, or ox, or ass.
5 For they came up with their cattle and their tents, and they came as grasshoppers for multitude; *for* both they and their camels were without number: and they entered into the land to destroy it.
6 And Israel was greatly impoverished because of the Midianites; and the children of Israel cried unto the LORD.
7 And it came to pass, when the children of Israel cried unto the LORD because of the Midianites,
8 That the LORD sent a prophet unto the children of Israel, which said unto them, thus said the LORD God of Israel, I brought you up from Egypt, and brought you forth out of the house of bondage;
9 And I delivered you out of the hand of the Egyptians, and out of the hand of all that oppressed you, and drive them out from before you, and gave you their land;
10 And I said unto you, I *am* the LORD your God; fear not the gods of the Amorites, in whose land you dwell: but you have not obeyed my voice.
11 And there came an angel of the LORD, and sat under an oak which *was* in Ophrah, that *pertained* unto Joash the Abiezrite: and his son Gideon threshed wheat by the winepress, to hide *it* from the Midianites.
12 And the angel of the LORD appeared unto him, and said unto him, The LORD *is* with you, you mighty man of valor.
13 And Gideon said unto him, Oh my Lord, if the LORD be with us, why then is all this befallen us? And where *be* all his miracles which our fathers told us of, saying, did not the LORD bring us up from Egypt? But now the LORD hath forsaken us, and delivered us into the hands of the Midianites.
14 And the LORD looked upon him, and said, go in this your might, and you will save Israel from the hand of the Midianites: have not I sent you?
15 And he said unto him, Oh my Lord, wherewith will I save Israel? Behold, my family *is* poor in Manasseh, and I *am* the least in my father's house.
16 And the LORD said unto him, surely I will be with you, and you will smite the Midianites as one man.
17 And he said unto him, if now I have found grace in your sight, then show me a sign that you talk with me.
18 Depart not hence, I pray you, until I come unto you, and bring forth my present, and set *it* before you. And he said, I will tarry until you come again.
19 And Gideon went in, and made ready a kid, and unleavened cakes of an ephah of flour: the flesh he put in a basket, and he put the broth in a pot, and brought *it* out unto him under the oak, and presented *it*.

20 And the angel of God said unto him, Take the flesh and the unleavened cakes, and lay *them* upon this rock, and pour out the broth. And he did so.
21 Then the angel of the LORD put forth the end of the staff that *was* in his hand, and touched the flesh and the unleavened cakes; and there rose up fire out of the rock, and consumed the flesh and the unleavened cakes. Then the angel of the LORD departed out of his sight.
22 And when Gideon perceived that he *was* an angel of the LORD, Gideon said, Alas, O Lord GOD! For because I have seen an angel of the LORD face to face.
23 And the LORD said unto him, Peace *be* unto you; fear not: you will not die.
24 Then Gideon built an altar there unto the LORD, and called it Jehovah-shalom: unto this day it *is* yet in Ophrah of the Abiezrites.
25 And it came to pass the same night, that the LORD said unto him, Take your father's young bullock, even the second bullock of seven years old, and throw down the altar of Baal that your father hath, and cut down the grove that *is* by it:
26 And build an altar unto the LORD your God upon the top of this rock, in the ordered place, and take the second bullock, and offer a burnt sacrifice with the wood of the grove which you will cut down.
27 Then Gideon took ten men of his servants, and did as the LORD had said unto him: and *so* it was, because he feared his father's household, and the men of the city, that he could not do *it* by day, that he did *it* by night.
28 And when the men of the city arose early in the morning, behold, the altar of Baal was cast down, and the grove was cut down that *was* by it, and the second bullock was offered upon the altar *that was* built.
29 And they said one to another, who hath done this thing? And when they enquired and asked, they said, Gideon the son of Joash hath done this thing.
30 Then the men of the city said unto Joash, Bring out your son, that he may die: because he hath cast down the altar of Baal, and because he hath cut down the grove that *was* by it.
31 And Joash said unto all that stood against him, Will you plead for Baal? Will you save him? He that will plead for him, let him be put to death while *it is yet* morning: if he *be* a god, let him plead for himself, because *one* hath cast down his altar.
32 Therefore on that day he called him Jerubbaal, saying, let Baal plead against him, because he hath thrown down his altar.
33 Then all the Midianites and the Amalekites and the children of the east were gathered together, and went over, and pitched in the valley of Jezreel.
34 But the Spirit of the LORD came upon Gideon, and he blew a trumpet; and Abiezer was gathered after him.
35 And he sent messengers throughout all Manasseh; who also was gathered after him: and he sent messengers unto Asher, and unto Zebulun, and unto Naphtali; and they came up to meet them.
36 And Gideon said unto God, if you will save Israel by mine hand, as you have said,
37 Behold, I will put a fleece of wool in the floor; *and* if the dew be on the fleece only, and *it be* dry upon all the earth *beside*, then will I know that you will save Israel by mine hand, as you have said.
38 And it was so: for he rose up early on the morrow, and thrust the fleece together, and wringed the dew out of the fleece, a bowl full of water.
39 And Gideon said unto God, Let not thine anger be hot against me, and I will speak but this once: let me prove, I pray you, but this once with the fleece; let it now be dry only upon the fleece, and upon all the ground let there be dew.
40 And God did so that night: for it was dry upon the fleece only, and there was dew on all the ground.

CHAPTER 7

1 Then Jerubbaal, who *is* Gideon, and all the people that *were* with him, rose up early, and pitched beside the well of Harod: so that the host of the Midianites were on the north side of them, by the hill of Moreh, in the valley.
2 And the LORD said unto Gideon, The people that *are* with you *are* too many for me to give the Midianites into their hands, lest Israel vaunt themselves against me, saying, Mine own hand hath saved me.
3 Now therefore go to, proclaim in the ears of the people, saying, whosoever *is* fearful and afraid, let him return and depart early from mount Gilead. And there returned of the people twenty and two thousand; and there remained ten thousand.
4 And the LORD said unto Gideon, The people *are* yet too many; bring them down unto the water, and I will try them for you there: and it will be, *that* of who I say unto you, This will go with you, the same will go with you; and of whomsoever I say unto you, This will not go with you, the same will not go.
5 So he brought down the people unto the water: and the LORD said unto Gideon, Everyone that **licks** of the water with his tongue, as a dog **licks**, him will you set by himself; likewise everyone that bows down upon his knees to drink.
6 And the number of them that licks, *putting* their hand to their mouth, were three hundred men: but all the rest of the people bowed down upon their knees to drink water.
7 And the LORD said unto Gideon, by the three hundred men that lapped will I save you, and deliver the Midianites into thine hand: and let all the *other* people go every man unto his place.
8 So the people took victuals in their hand, and their trumpets: and he sent all *the rest of* Israel every man unto his tent, and retained those three hundred men: and the host of Midian was beneath him in the valley.
9 And it came to pass the same night, that the LORD said unto him, Arise, get you down unto the host; for I have delivered it into thine hand.
10 But if you fear to go down, go you with Phurah your servant down to the host:
11 And you will hear what they say; and afterward will thine hands be strengthened to go down unto the host. Then he went down with Phurah his servant unto the outside of the armed men that *were* in the host.
12 And the Midianites and the Amalekites and all the children of the east lay along in the valley like grasshoppers for multitude; and their camels *were* without number, as the sand by the sea side for multitude.
13 And when Gideon was come, behold, *there was* a man that told a dream unto his fellow, and said, Behold, I dreamed a dream, and, lo, a cake of barley bread tumbled into the host of Midian, and came unto a tent, and smote it that it fell, and overturned it, that the tent lay along.
14 And his fellow answered and said, this *is* nothing else save the sword of Gideon the son of Joash, a man of Israel: *for* into his hand hath God delivered Midian, and the **entire** host.
15 And it was *so*, when Gideon heard the telling of the dream, and the interpretation thereof, that he worshipped, and returned into

the host of Israel, and said, Arise; for the LORD hath delivered into your hand the host of Midian.

16 And he divided the three hundred men *into* three companies, and he put a trumpet in every man's hand, with empty pitchers, and lamps within the pitchers.

17 And he said unto them, Look on me, and do likewise: and, behold, when I come to the outside of the camp, it will be *that*, as I do, so will you do.

18 When I blow with a trumpet, I and all that *are* with me, then blow you the trumpets also on every side of all the camp, and say, *the sword* of the LORD, and of Gideon.

19 So Gideon, and the hundred men that *were* with him, came unto the outside of the camp in the beginning of the middle watch; and they had but newly set the watch: and they blew the trumpets, and broke the pitchers that *were* in their hands.

20 And the three companies blew the trumpets, and broke the pitchers, and held the lamps in their left hands, and the trumpets in their right hands to blow *withal*: and they cried, the sword of the LORD, and of Gideon.

21 And they stood every man in his place round about the camp: and all the host ran, and cried, and fled.

22 And the three hundred blew the trumpets, and the LORD set every man's sword against his fellow, even throughout the **entire** host: and the host fled to Beth-shittah in Zererath, *and* to the border of Abel-meholah, unto Tabbath.

23 And the men of Israel gathered themselves together out of Naphtali, and out of Asher, and out of all Manasseh, and pursued after the Midianites.

24 And Gideon sent messengers throughout all mount Ephraim, saying, Come down against the Midianites, and take before them the waters unto Beth-barah and Jordan. Then all the men of Ephraim gathered themselves together, and took the waters unto Beth-barah and Jordan.

25 And they took two princes of the Midianites, Oreb and Zeeb; and they slew Oreb upon the rock Oreb, and Zeeb they slew at the winepress of Zeeb, and pursued Midian, and brought the heads of Oreb and Zeeb to Gideon on the other side Jordan.

CHAPTER 8

1 And the men of Ephraim said unto him, why have you served us thus, that you called us not, when you went to fight with the Midianites? And they did chide with him sharply.

2 And he said unto them, what have I done now in comparison of you? *Is* not the gleaning of the grapes of Ephraim better than the vintage of Abiezer?

3 God hath delivered into your hands the princes of Midian, Oreb and Zeeb: and what was I able to do in comparison of you? Then their anger was abated toward him, when he had said that.

4 And Gideon came to Jordan, *and* passed over, he, and the three hundred men that *were* with him, faint, yet pursuing *them*.

5 And he said unto the men of Succoth, Give, I pray you, loaves of bread unto the people that follow me; for they *are* faint, and I am pursuing after Zebah and Zalmunna, kings of Midian.

6 And the princes of Succoth said, *Are* the hands of Zebah and Zalmunna now in thine hand, that we should give bread unto thine army?

7 And Gideon said, therefore when the LORD hath delivered Zebah and Zalmunna into mine hand, then I will tear your flesh with the thorns of the wilderness and with briers.

8 And he went up thence to Penuel, and spoke unto them likewise: and the men of Penuel answered him as the men of Succoth had answered *him*.

9 And he spoke also unto the men of Penuel, saying, When I come again in peace, I will break down this tower.

10 Now Zebah and Zalmunna *were* in Karkor, and their hosts with them, about fifteen thousand *men*, all that were left of all the hosts of the children of the east: for there fell an hundred and twenty thousand men that drew sword.

11 And Gideon went up by the way of them that dwelt in tents on the east of Nobah and Jogbehah, and smote the host for the host was secure.

12 And when Zebah and Zalmunna fled, he pursued after them, and took the two kings of Midian, Zebah and Zalmunna, and discomfited[1] the **enitire** host.

13 And Gideon the son of Joash returned from battle before the sun *was* up,

14 And caught a young man of the men of Succoth, and enquired of him: and he described unto him the princes of Succoth, and the elders thereof, *even* threescore and seventeen men.

15 And he came unto the men of Succoth, and said, Behold Zebah and Zalmunna, with who you did upbraid me, saying, *Are* the hands of Zebah and Zalmunna now in thine hand, that we should give bread unto your men *that are* weary?

16 And he took the elders of the city, and thorns of the wilderness and briers, and with them he taught the men of Succoth.

17 And he beat down the tower of Penuel[2], and slew the men of the city.

18 Then said he unto Zebah and Zalmunna, What manner of men *were they* who you slew at Tabor? And they answered, as you are, so *were* they; each one resembled the children of a king.

19 And he said, they *were* my brethren, *even* the sons of my mother: *as* the LORD lives, if you had saved them alive, I would not slay you.

20 And he said unto Jether his firstborn, up, *and* slay them. But the youth drew not his sword: for he feared, because he *was* yet a youth.

21 Then Zebah and Zalmunna said, rise you, and fall upon us: for as the man *is, so is* his strength. And Gideon arose, and slew Zebah and Zalmunna, and took away the ornaments that *were* on their camels' necks.

22 Then the men of Israel said unto Gideon, Rule you over us, both thou, and your son, and your son's son also: for you have delivered us from the hand of Midian.

23 And Gideon said unto them, I will not rule over you, neither will my son rule over you: the LORD will rule over you.

24 And Gideon said unto them, I would desire a request of you, that you would give me every man the earrings of his prey. (For they had golden earrings, because they *were* Ishmaelites.)

25 And they answered, we will willingly give *them*. And they spread a garment, and did cast therein every man the earrings of his prey.

26 And the weight of the golden earrings that he requested was a thousand and seven hundred *shekels* of gold; beside ornaments, and collars, and purple raiment that *was* on the kings of Midian, and beside the chains that *were* about their camels' necks.

---

[1] discomfited- is the Hebrew word *chârad*, khaw-rad, meaning to shudder with terror, hence to fear, to hasten with anxiety, to be afraid and tremble. [Strgs#2729]

[2] Penuel- literally means face of God or facing God. [Strgs#6439]

27 And Gideon made an ephod thereof, and put it in his city, *even* in Ophrah: and all Israel went there a whoring after it: which thing became a snare unto Gideon, and to his house.
28 Thus was Midian subdued before the children of Israel, so that they lifted up their heads no more. And the country was in quietness forty years in the days of Gideon.
29 And Jerubbaal the son of Joash went and dwelt in his own house.
30 And Gideon had threescore and ten sons of his body begotten: for he had many wives.
31 And his concubine that *was* in Shechem, she also bares him a son, whose name he called Abimelech.
32 And Gideon the son of Joash died in a good old age, and was buried in the sepulcher of Joash his father, in Ophrah of the Abiezrites.
33 And it came to pass, as soon as Gideon was dead, that the children of Israel turned again, and went a whoring after Baalim, and made Baal-berith their god.
34 And the children of Israel remembered not the LORD their God, who had delivered them out of the hands of all their enemies on every side:
35 Neither showed they kindness to the house of Jerubbaal, *namely*, Gideon, according to all the goodness which he had showed unto Israel.

CHAPTER 9

1 And Abimelech the son of Jerubbaal went to Shechem unto his mother's brethren, and communed with them, and with all the family of the house of his mother's father, saying,
2 Speak, I pray you, in the ears of all the men of Shechem, whether *is* better for you, either all the sons of Jerubbaal, *which are* threescore and ten persons, reign over you, or that one reign over you? Remember also that I *am* your bone and your flesh.
3 And his mother's brethren spoke of him in the ears of all the men of Shechem all these words: and their hearts inclined to follow Abimelech; for they said, He *is* our brother.
4 And they gave him threescore and ten *pieces* of silver out of the house of Baal-berith, wherewith Abimelech hired vain and light persons, which followed him.
5 And he went unto his father's house at Ophrah, and slew his brethren the sons of Jerubbaal, *being* threescore and ten persons, upon one stone: notwithstanding yet Jotham the youngest son of Jerubbaal was left; for he hid himself.
6 And all the men of Shechem gathered together, and all the house of Millo, and went, and made Abimelech king, by the plain of the pillar that *was* in Shechem.
7 And when they told *it* to Jotham, he went and stood in the top of mount Gerizim, and lifted up his voice, and cried, and said unto them, Hearken unto me, you men of Shechem, that God may hearken unto you.
8 The trees went forth *on a time* to anoint a king over them; and they said unto the olive tree, reign you over us.
9 But the olive tree said unto them, Should I leave my fatness, wherewith by me they honor God and man, and go to be promoted over the trees?
10 And the trees said to the fig tree, Come thou, *and* reign over us.
11 But the fig tree said unto them, Should I forsake my sweetness, and my good fruit, and go to be promoted over the trees?
12 Then said the trees unto the vine, Come thou, *and* reign over us.
13 And the vine said unto them, should I leave my wine, which cheered God and man, and go to be promoted over the trees?
14 Then said all the trees unto the bramble, Come thou, *and* reign over us.
15 And the bramble said unto the trees, If in truth you anoint me king over you, *then* come *and* put your trust in my shadow: and if not, let fire come out of the bramble, and devour the cedars of Lebanon.
16 Now therefore, if you have done truly and sincerely, in that you have made Abimelech king, and if you have dealt well with Jerubbaal and his house, and have done unto him according to the deserving of his hands;
17 (For my father fought for you, and adventured his life far, and delivered you out of the hand of Midian:
18 And you are risen up against my father's house this day, and have slain his sons, threescore and ten persons, upon one stone, and have made Abimelech, the son of his maidservant, king over the men of Shechem, because he *is* your brother;)
19 If you then have dealt truly and sincerely with Jerubbaal and with his house this day, *then* rejoice you in Abimelech, and let him also rejoice in you:
20 But if not, let fire come out from Abimelech, and devour the men of Shechem, and the house of Millo; and let fire come out from the men of Shechem, and from the house of Millo, and devour Abimelech.
21 And Jotham ran away, and fled, and went to Beer, and dwelt there, for fear of Abimelech his brother.
22 When Abimelech had reigned three years over Israel,
23 Then God sent an evil spirit between Abimelech and the men of Shechem; and the men of Shechem dealt treacherously with Abimelech:
24 That the cruelty *done* to the threescore and ten sons of Jerubbaal might come, and their blood be laid upon Abimelech their brother, which slew them; and upon the men of Shechem, which aided him in the killing of his brethren.
25 And the men of Shechem set **ambushers** in wait for him in the top of the mountains, and they robbed all that came along that way by them: and it was told Abimelech.
26 And Gaal the son of Ebed came with his brethren, and went over to Shechem: and the men of Shechem put their confidence in him.
27 And they went out into the fields, and gathered their vineyards, and trode *the grapes*, and made merry, and went into the house of their god, and did eat and drink, and cursed Abimelech.
28 And Gaal the son of Ebed said, who *is* Abimelech, and who *is* Shechem, that we should serve him? *Is* not *he* the son of Jerubbaal? And Zebul his officer? Serve the men of Hamor the father of Shechem: for why should we serve him?
29 And would to God this people were under my hand! Then would I remove Abimelech. And he said to Abimelech, Increase thine army, and come out.
30 And when Zebul the ruler of the city heard the words of Gaal the son of Ebed, his anger was kindled.
31 And he sent messengers unto Abimelech privily, saying, Behold, Gaal the son of Ebed and his brethren be come to Shechem; and, behold, they fortify the city against you.
32 Now therefore up by night, you and the people that *are* with you, and lie in wait in the field:
33 And it will be, *that* in the morning, as soon as the sun is up, you will rise early, and set upon the city: and, behold, *when* he and the

people that *is* with him come out against you, then may you do to them as you will find occasion.

34 And Abimelech rose up, and all the people that *were* with him, by night, and they laid wait against Shechem in four companies.

35 And Gaal the son of Ebed went out, and stood in the entering of the gate of the city: and Abimelech rose up, and the people that *were* with him, from lying in wait.

36 And when Gaal saw the people, he said to Zebul, Behold, there come people down from the top of the mountains. And Zebul said unto him, you see the shadow of the mountains as *if they were* men.

37 And Gaal spoke again and said, see there come people down by the middle of the land, and another company come along by the plain of Meonenim[1].

38 Then said Zebul unto him, where *is* now your mouth, wherewith you said, who *is* Abimelech, that we should serve him? *Is* not this the people that you have despised? Go out, I pray now, and fight with them.

39 And Gaal went out before the men of Shechem, and fought with Abimelech.

40 And Abimelech chased him, and he fled before him, and many were overthrown *and* wounded, *even* unto the entering of the gate.

41 And Abimelech dwelt at Arumah: and Zebul thrust out Gaal and his brethren, that they should not dwell in Shechem.

42 And it came to pass on the morrow, that the people went out into the field; and they told Abimelech.

43 And he took the people, and divided them into three companies, and laid wait in the field, and looked, and, behold, the people *were* come forth out of the city; and he rose up against them, and smote them.

44 And Abimelech, and the company that *was* with him, rushed forward, and stood in the entering of the gate of the city: and the two *other* companies ran upon all *the people* that *were* in the fields, and slew them.

45 And Abimelech fought against the city all that day; and he took the city, and slew the people that *was* therein, and beat down the city, and sowed it with salt.

46 And when all the men of the tower of Shechem heard *that*, they entered into a hold of the house of the god Berith[2].

47 And it was told Abimelech, that all the men of the tower of Shechem were gathered together.

48 And Abimelech gat him up to mount Zalmon, he and all the people that *were* with him; and Abimelech took an axe in his hand, and cut down a bough from the trees, and took it, and laid *it* on his shoulder, and said unto the people that *were* with him, What you have seen me do, make haste, *and* do as I *have done*.

49 And all the people likewise cut down every man his bough, and followed Abimelech, and put *them* to the hold, and set the hold on fire upon them; so that all the men of the tower of Shechem died also, about a thousand men and women.

50 Then went Abimelech to Thebez, and encamped against Thebez, and took it.

51 But there was a strong tower within the city, and there fled all the men and women, and all they of the city, and shut *it* to them, and gat them up to the top of the tower.

52 And Abimelech came unto the tower, and fought against it, and went hard unto the door of the tower to burn it with fire.

53 And a certain woman cast a piece of a millstone upon Abimelech's head, and all to break his skull.

54 Then he called hastily unto the young man his armorbearer, and said unto him, Draw your sword, and slay me, that men say not of me, a woman slew him. And his young man thrust him through, and he died.

55 And when the men of Israel saw that Abimelech was dead, they departed every man unto his place.

56 Thus God rendered the wickedness of Abimelech, which he did unto his father, in slaying his seventy brethren:

57 And all the evil of the men of Shechem did God render upon their heads: and upon them came the curse of Jotham the son of Jerubbaal.

CHAPTER 10

1 And after Abimelech there arose to defend Israel Tola the son of Puah, the son of Dodo, a man of Issachar; and he dwelt in Shamir in mount Ephraim.

2 And he judged Israel twenty and three years, and died, and was buried in Shamir.

3 And after him arose Jair, a Gileadite, and judged Israel twenty and two years.

4 And he had thirty sons that rode on thirty ass colts, and they had thirty cities, which are called Havoth-jair unto this day, which *are* in the land of Gilead.

5 And Jair died, and was buried in Camon.

6 And the children of Israel did evil again in the sight of the LORD, and served Baalim, and Ashtaroth, and the gods of Syria, and the gods of Zidon, and the gods of Moab, and the gods of the children of Ammon, and the gods of the Philistines, and forsook the LORD, and served not him.

7 And the anger of the LORD was hot against Israel, and he sold them into the hands of the Philistines, and into the hands of the children of Ammon.

8 And that year they vexed and oppressed the children of Israel: eighteen years, all the children of Israel that *were* on the other side Jordan in the land of the Amorites, which *is* in Gilead.

9 Moreover the children of Ammon passed over Jordan to fight also against Judah, and against Benjamin, and against the house of Ephraim; so that Israel was sore distressed.

10 And the children of Israel cried unto the LORD, saying we have sinned against you, both because we have forsaken our God, and also served Baalim.

11 And the LORD said unto the children of Israel, *Did not I deliver you* from the Egyptians, and from the Amorites, from the children of Ammon, and from the Philistines?

12 The Zidonians also, and the Amalekites, and the Maonites, did oppress you; and you cried to me, and I delivered you out of their hand.

13 Yet you have forsaken me, and served other gods: wherefore I will deliver you no more.

14 Go and cry unto the gods which you have chosen; let them deliver you in the time of your tribulation.

15 And the children of Israel said unto the LORD, We have sinned: do you unto us whatsoever seems good unto you; deliver us only, we pray you, this day.

16 And they put away the strange gods from among them, and served the LORD: and his soul was grieved for the misery of Israel.

---

[1] Meonenim- to cloud over, to act covertly, to practice magic, to be an enchanter, soothsayer, sorcerer. [Strgs#6049]

[2] Berith- an earlier name which Baal was worshipped. [Strgs#1286]

17 Then the children of Ammon were gathered together, and encamped in Gilead. And the children of Israel assembled themselves together, and encamped in Mizpeh.
18 And the people *and* princes of Gilead said one to another, what man *is he* that will begin to fight against the children of Ammon? He will be head over all the inhabitants of Gilead.

CHAPTER 11

1 Now Jephthah the Gileadite was a mighty man of valor, and he *was* the son of a harlot: and Gilead begat Jephthah.
2 And Gilead's wife bare him sons; and his wife's sons grew up, and they thrust out Jephthah, and said unto him, you will not inherit in our father's house; for you *are* the son of a strange woman.
3 Then Jephthah fled from his brethren, and dwelt in the land of Tob: and there were gathered vain men to Jephthah, and went out with him.
4 And it came to pass in process of time, that the children of Ammon made war against Israel.
5 And it was so, that when the children of Ammon made war against Israel, the elders of Gilead went to fetch Jephthah out of the land of Tob:
6 And they said unto Jephthah, Come, and be our captain, that we may fight with the children of Ammon.
7 And Jephthah said unto the elders of Gilead, Did not you hate me, and expel me out of my father's house? And why are you come unto me now when you are in distress?
8 And the elders of Gilead said unto Jephthah, Therefore we turn again to you now, that you may go with us, and fight against the children of Ammon, and be our head over all the inhabitants of Gilead.
9 And Jephthah said unto the elders of Gilead, if you bring me home again to fight against the children of Ammon, and the LORD deliver them before me, will I be your head?
10 And the elders of Gilead said unto Jephthah, The LORD is witness between us, if we do not so according to your words.
11 Then Jephthah went with the elders of Gilead, and the people made him head and captain over them: and Jephthah uttered all his words before the LORD in Mizpeh.
12 And Jephthah sent messengers unto the king of the children of Ammon, saying, what have you to do with me, that you are come against me to fight in my land?
13 And the king of the children of Ammon answered unto the messengers of Jephthah, Because Israel took away my land, when they came up out of Egypt, from Arnon even unto Jabbok, and unto Jordan: now therefore restore those *lands* again peaceably.
14 And Jephthah sent messengers again unto the king of the children of Ammon:
15 And said unto him, thus said Jephthah, Israel took not away the land of Moab, or the land of the children of Ammon:
16 But when Israel came up from Egypt, and walked through the wilderness unto the Red sea, and came to Kadesh;
17 Then Israel sent messengers unto the king of Edom, saying, let me, I pray you, pass through your land: but the king of Edom would not hearken *thereto*. And in like manner they sent unto the king of Moab: but he would not *consent*: and Israel abode in Kadesh.
18 Then they went along through the wilderness, and compassed the land of Edom, and the land of Moab, and came by the east side of the land of Moab, and pitched on the other side of Arnon, but came not within the border of Moab: for Arnon *was* the border of Moab.
19 And Israel sent messengers unto Sihon king of the Amorites, the king of Heshbon; and Israel said unto him, Let us pass, we pray you, through your land into my place.
20 But Sihon trusted not Israel to pass through his coast: but Sihon gathered all his people together, and pitched in Jahaz, and fought against Israel.
21 And the LORD God of Israel delivered Sihon and all his people into the hand of Israel, and they smote them: so Israel possessed all the land of the Amorites, the inhabitants of that country.
22 And they possessed all the coasts of the Amorites, from Arnon even unto Jabbok, and from the wilderness even unto Jordan.
23 So now the LORD God of Israel hath dispossessed the Amorites from before his people Israel, and should you possess it?
24 will not you possess that which Chemosh your god giveth you to possess? So whomsoever the LORD our God will drive out from before us, them will we possess.
25 And now are you anything better than Balak the son of Zippor, king of Moab? Did he ever strive against Israel, or did he ever fight against them,
26 While Israel dwelt in Heshbon and her towns, and in Aroer and her towns, and in all the cities that *be* along by the coasts of Arnon, three hundred years? Why therefore did you not recover *them* within that time?
27 Wherefore I have not sinned against you, but you do me wrong to war against me: the LORD the Judge be judge this day between the children of Israel and the children of Ammon.
28 Howbeit the king of the children of Ammon hearkened not unto the words of Jephthah which he sent him.
29 Then the Spirit of the LORD came upon Jephthah, and he passed over Gilead, and Manasseh, and passed over Mizpeh of Gilead, and from Mizpeh of Gilead he passed over unto the children of Ammon.
30 And Jephthah vowed a vow unto the LORD, and said, f you will without fail deliver the children of Ammon into mine hands,
31 Then it will be, that whatsoever cometh forth of the doors of my house to meet me, when I return in peace from the children of Ammon, will surely be the LORD'S, and I will offer it up for a burnt offering.
32 So Jephthah passed over unto the children of Ammon to fight against them; and the LORD delivered them into his hands.
33 And he smote them from Aroer, even till you come to Minnith, *even* twenty cities, and unto the plain of the vineyards, with a very great slaughter. Thus the children of Ammon were subdued before the children of Israel.
34 And Jephthah came to Mizpeh unto his house, and, behold, his daughter came out to meet him with **tambourines** and with dances: and she *was his* only child; beside her he had neither son or daughter.
35 And it came to pass, when he saw her, that he rent his clothes, and said, alas, my daughter! You have brought me very low, and you are one of them that trouble me: for I have opened my mouth unto the LORD, and I cannot go back.
36 And she said unto him, my father, *if* you have opened your mouth unto the LORD, do to me according to that which hath proceeded out of your mouth; forasmuch as the LORD hath taken vengeance for you of thine enemies, *even* of the children of Ammon.
37 And she said unto her father, Let this thing be done for me: let me alone two months, that I may go up and down upon the mountains, and bewail my virginity, I and my fellows.

38 And he said, go. And he sent her away *for* two months: and she went with her companions, and bewailed her virginity upon the mountains.
39 And it came to pass at the end of two months, that she returned unto her father, who did with her *according* to his vow which he had vowed: and she knew no man. And it was a custom in Israel,
40 *That* the daughters of Israel went yearly to lament the daughter of Jephthah the Gileadite four days in a year.

CHAPTER 12

1 And the men of Ephraim gathered themselves together, and went northward, and said unto Jephthah, Wherefore passes you over to fight against the children of Ammon, and didst not call us to go with you? We will burn thine house upon you with fire.
2 And Jephthah said unto them, I and my people were at great strife with the children of Ammon; and when I called you, you delivered me not out of their hands.
3 And when I saw that you delivered *me* not, I put my life in my hands, and passed over against the children of Ammon, and the LORD delivered them into my hand: wherefore then are you come up unto me this day, to fight against me?
4 Then Jephthah gathered together all the men of Gilead, and fought with Ephraim: and the men of Gilead smote Ephraim, because they said, you Gileadites *are* fugitives of Ephraim among the Ephraimites, *and* among the Manassites.
5 And the Gileadites took the passages of Jordan before the Ephraimites: and it was *so*, that when those Ephraimites which were escaped said, Let me go over; that the men of Gilead said unto him, are you an Ephraimite? If he said, No;
6 Then said they unto him, Say now Shibboleth: and he said Sibboleth: for he could not frame to pronounce *it* right. Then they took him, and slew him at the passages of Jordan: and there fell at that time of the Ephraimites forty and two thousand.
7 And Jephthah judged Israel six years. Then died Jephthah the Gileadite, and was buried in *one of* the cities of Gilead.
8 And after him Ibzan of Beth-lehem judged Israel.
9 And he had thirty sons, and thirty daughters, who he sent abroad, and took in thirty daughters from abroad for his sons. And he judged Israel seven years.
10 Then died Ibzan, and was buried at Beth-lehem.
11 And after him Elon, a Zebulonite, judged Israel; and he judged Israel ten years.
12 And Elon the Zebulonite died, and was buried in Aijalon in the country of Zebulun.
13 And after him Abdon the son of Hillel, a Pirathonite, judged Israel.
14 And he had forty sons and thirty nephews, that rode on threescore and ten ass colts: and he judged Israel eight years.
15 And Abdon the son of Hillel the Pirathonite died, and was buried in Pirathon in the land of Ephraim, in the mount of the Amalekites.

CHAPTER 13

1 And the children of Israel did evil again in the sight of the LORD; and the LORD delivered them into the hand of the Philistines forty years.
2 And there was a certain man of Zorah, of the family of the Danites, whose name *was* Manoah; and his wife *was* barren, and bare not.
3 And the angel of the LORD appeared unto the woman, and said unto her, Behold now, you are barren, and bear not: but you will conceive, and bear a son.
4 Now therefore beware, I pray you, and drink not vine or strong drink, and eat not any unclean *thing*:
5 For, lo, you will conceive, and bear a son; and no razor will come on his head: for the child will be a Nazarite unto God from the womb: and he will begin to deliver Israel out of the hand of the Philistines.
6 Then the woman came and told her husband, saying, a man of God came unto me, and his countenance *was* like the countenance of an angel of God, very terrible: but I asked him not whence he *was*, neither told he me his name:
7 But he said unto me, Behold, you will conceive, and bear a son; and now drink no wine or strong drink, neither eat any unclean *thing*: for the child will be a Nazarite to God from the womb to the day of his death.
8 Then Manoah **prayed to** the LORD, and said, O my Lord, let the man of God which you did send come again unto us, and teach us what we will do unto the child that will be born.
9 And God hearkened to the voice of Manoah; and the angel of God came again unto the woman as she sat in the field: but Manoah her husband *was* not with her.
10 And the woman made haste, and ran, and showed her husband, and said unto him, Behold, the man has appeared unto me, that came unto me the *other* day.
11 And Manoah arose, and went after his wife, and came to the man, and said unto him, *are* you the man that spoke unto the woman? And he said, I *am*.
12 And Manoah said, Now let your words come to pass. How will we **have** order the child, and *how* will we do unto him?
13 And the angel of the LORD said unto Manoah, of all that I said unto the woman let her beware.
14 She may not eat of any*thing* that cometh of the vine, neither let her drink wine or strong drink, or eat any unclean *thing*: all that I commanded her let her observe.
15 And Manoah said unto the angel of the LORD, I pray you, let us detain you, until we will have made ready a kid for you.
16 And the angel of the LORD said unto Manoah, though you detain me, I will not eat of your bread: and if you will offer a burnt offering, you must offer it unto the LORD. For Manoah knew not that he *was* an angel of the LORD.
17 And Manoah said unto the angel of the LORD, What *is* your name, that when your sayings come to pass we may do you honors?
18 And the angel of the LORD said unto him, Why ask you thus after my name, seeing it *is* secret?
19 So Manoah took a kid with a meat offering, and offered *it* upon a rock unto the LORD: and *the angel* did wondrously; and Manoah and his wife looked on.
20 For it came to pass, when the flame went up toward heaven from off the altar, that the angel of the LORD ascended in the flame of the altar. And Manoah and his wife looked on *it*, and fell on their faces to the ground.
21 But the angel of the LORD did no more appear to Manoah and to his wife. Then Manoah knew that he *was* an angel of the LORD.
22 And Manoah said unto his wife, we will surely die, because we have seen God.
23 But his wife said unto him, If the LORD were pleased to kill us, he would not have received a burnt offering and a meat offering at our hands, neither would he have showed us all these *things*, or would as at this time have told us *such things* as these.

24 And the woman bares a son, and called his name Samson[1]: and the child grew, and the LORD blessed him.
25 And the Spirit of the LORD began to move him at times in the camp of Dan between Zorah and Eshtaol.

CHAPTER 14

1 And Samson went down to Timnath, and saw a woman in Timnath of the daughters of the Philistines.
2 And he came up, and told his father and his mother, and said, I have seen a woman in Timnath of the daughters of the Philistines: now therefore get her for me to wife.
3 Then his father and his mother said unto him, *Is there* never a woman among the daughters of your brethren, or among all my people, that you go to take a wife of the uncircumcised Philistines? And Samson said unto his father, get her for me; for she pleases me well.
4 But his father and his mother knew not that it *was* of the LORD, that he sought an occasion against the Philistines: for at that time the Philistines had dominion over Israel.
5 Then went Samson down, and his father and his mother, to Timnath, and came to the vineyards of Timnath: and, behold, a young lion roared against him.
6 And the Spirit of the LORD came mightily upon him, and he rent him as he would have rent a kid, and *he had* nothing in his hand: but he told not his father or his mother what he had done.
7 And he went down, and talked with the woman; and she pleased Samson well.
8 And after a time he returned to take her, and he turned aside to see the carcass of the lion: and, behold, *there was* a swarm of bees and honey in the carcass of the lion.
9 And he took thereof in his hands, and went on eating, and came to his father and mother, and he gave them, and they did eat: but he told not them that he had taken the honey out of the carcass of the lion.
10 So his father went down unto the woman: and Samson made there a feast; for so used the young men to do.
11 And it came to pass, when they saw him, that they brought thirty companions to be with him.
12 And Samson said unto them, I will now put forth a riddle unto you: if you can certainly declare it me within the seven days of the feast, and find *it* out, then I will give you thirty sheets and thirty change of garments:
13 But if you cannot declare *it* me, then will you give me thirty sheets and thirty change of garments. And they said unto him, put forth your riddle, that we may hear it.
14 And he said unto them, Out of the eater came forth meat, and out of the strong came forth sweetness. And they could not in three days expound the riddle.
15 And it came to pass on the seventh day, that they said unto Samson's wife, Entice your husband, that he may declare unto us the riddle, lest we burn you and your father's house with fire: have you called us to take that we have? *Is it* not *so*?
16 And Samson's wife wept before him, and said, you dost but hate me, and loves me not: you have put forth a riddle unto the children of my people, and have not told *it* me. And he said unto her, Behold, I have not told *it* my father or my mother, and will I tell *it* you?
17 And she wept before him the seven days, while their feast lasted: and it came to pass on the seventh day, that he told her, because she lay sore upon him: and she told the riddle to the children of her people.
18 And the men of the city said unto him on the seventh day before the sun went down, what *is* sweeter than honey? And what *is* stronger than a lion? And he said unto them, if you had not plowed with my heifer, you had not found out my riddle.
19 And the Spirit of the LORD came upon him, and he went down to Ashkelon, and slew thirty men of them, and took their spoil, and gave change of garments unto them which expounded the riddle. And his anger was kindled, and he went up to his father's house.
20 But Samson's wife was *given* to his companion, who he had used as his friend.

CHAPTER 15

1 But it came to pass within a while after, in the time of wheat harvest, that Samson visited his wife with a kid; and he said, I will go in to my wife into the chamber. But her father would not suffer him to go in.
2 And her father said, I verily thought that you had utterly hated her; therefore I gave her to your companion: *is* not her younger sister fairer than she? Take her, I pray you, instead of her.
3 And Samson said concerning them, now will I be more blameless than the Philistines, though I do them displeasure.
4 And Samson went and caught three hundred foxes, and took firebrands, and turned tail to tail, and put a firebrand in the midst between two tails.
5 And when he had set the brands on fire, he let *them* go into the standing corn of the Philistines, and burnt up both the shocks, and also the standing corn, with the vineyards *and* olives.
6 Then the Philistines said, who hath done this? And they answered, Samson, the son in law of the Timnite, because he had taken his wife, and given her to his companion. And the Philistines came up, and burnt her and her father with fire.
7 And Samson said unto them, though you have done this, yet will I be avenged of you, and after that I will cease.
8 And he smote them hip and thigh with a great slaughter: and he went down and dwelt in the top of the rock Etam.
9 Then the Philistines went up, and pitched in Judah, and spread themselves in Lehi.
10 And the men of Judah said, why are you come up against us? And they answered, to bind Samson are we come up, to do to him as he hath done to us.
11 Then three thousand men of Judah went to the top of the rock Etam, and said to Samson, know you not that the Philistines *are* rulers over us? What *is* this *that* you have done unto us? And he said unto them, as they did unto me, so have I done unto them.
12 And they said unto him, we are come down to bind you, that we may deliver you into the hand of the Philistines. And Samson said unto them, Swear unto me, that you will not fall upon me yourselves.
13 And they spoke unto him, saying, No; but we will bind you fast, and deliver you into their hand: but surely we will not kill you. And they bound him with two new cords, and brought him up from the rock.
14 *And* when he came unto Lehi, the Philistines shouted against him: and the Spirit of the LORD came mightily upon him, and the cords that *were* upon his arms became as flax that was burnt with fire, and his bands loosed from off his hands.

---

[1] Samson- is defined as *like the sun* or *sunlight*. [8123]

15 And he found a new jawbone of an ass, and put forth his hand, and took it, and slew a thousand men therewith.
16 And Samson said, with the jawbone of an ass, heaps upon heaps, with the jaw of an ass have I slain a thousand men.
17 And it came to pass, when he had made an end of speaking, that he cast away the jawbone out of his hand, and called that place Ramath-lehi.
18 And he was sore athirst, and called on the LORD, and said, you have given this great deliverance into the hand of your servant: and now will I die for thirst, and fall into the hand of the uncircumcised?
19 But God clave a hollow place that *was* in the jaw, and there came water thereout; and when he had drunk, his spirit came again, and he revived: wherefore he called the name thereof En-hakkore, which *is* in Lehi unto this day.
20 And he judged Israel in the days of the Philistines twenty years.

CHAPTER 16

1 Then went Samson to Gaza, and saw there a harlot, and went in unto her.
2 *And it was told* the Gazites, saying, Samson is come hither. And they compassed *him* in, and laid wait for him all night in the gate of the city, and were quiet all the night, saying, in the morning, when it is day, we will kill him.
3 And Samson lay till midnight, and arose at midnight, and took the doors of the gate of the city, and the two posts, and went away with them, bar and all, and put *them* upon his shoulders, and carried them up to the top of a hill that *is* before Hebron.
4 And it came to pass afterward, that he loved a woman in the valley of Sorek[1], whose name *was* Delilah[2].
5 And the lords of the Philistines came up unto her, and said unto her, entice him, and see wherein his great strength *lies*, and by what *means* we may prevail against him, that we may bind him to afflict him: and we will give you every one of us eleven hundred *pieces* of silver.
6 And Delilah said to Samson, tell me, I pray you, wherein your great strength *lies*, and wherewith you might be bound to afflict you.
7 And Samson said unto her, if they bind me with seven green **cords** that were never dried, then will I be weak, and be as another man.
8 Then the lords of the Philistines brought up to her seven green **cords** which had not been dried, and she bound him with them.
9 Now *there were* men lying in wait, abiding with her in the chamber. And she said unto him, The Philistines *be* upon you, Samson. And he broke the **cords**, as a thread of tow is broken when it touches the fire. So his strength was not known.
10 And Delilah said unto Samson, behold, you have mocked me, and told me lies: now tell me, I pray you, wherewith you might be bound.
11 And he said unto her, if they bind me fast with new ropes that never were occupied, then will I be weak, and be as another man.
12 Delilah therefore took new ropes, and bound him therewith, and said unto him, The Philistines *be* upon you, Samson. And *there were* **ambushers** in wait abiding in the chamber. And he broke them from off his arms like a thread.
13 And Delilah said unto Samson, hitherto you have mocked me, and told me lies: tell me wherewith you might be bound. And he said unto her, if you weave the seven locks of my head with the web.
14 And she fastened *it* with the pin, and said unto him, The Philistines *be* upon you, Samson. And he awaked out of his sleep, and went away with the pin of the beam, and with the web.
15 And she said unto him, how can you say, I love you when your heart *is* not with me? You have mocked me these three times, and have not told me wherein your great strength *lies*.
16 [And it came to pass, when she pressed him daily with her words, and urged him, so that his soul was vexed[3] unto death;][4]
17 That he told her all his heart, and said unto her, There has not come a razor upon mine head; for I *have been* a Nazarite unto God from my mother's womb: if I be shaven, then my strength will go from me, and I will become weak, and be like any *other* man.
18 And when Delilah saw that he had told her all his heart, she sent and called for the lords of the Philistines, saying, come up this once, for he has showed me all his heart. Then the lords of the Philistines came up unto her, and brought money in their hand.
19 And she made him sleep upon her knees; and she called for a man, and she caused him to shave off the seven locks of his head; and she began to afflict him, and his strength went from him.
20 And she said, The Philistines *be* upon you, Samson. And he awoke out of his sleep, and said, I will go out as at other times before, and shake myself. And he was not that the LORD was departed from him.
21 [But the Philistines took him, and put out his eyes, and brought him down to Gaza, and bound him with fetters of brass; and he did grind in the prison house.][5]
22 Howbeit the hair of his head began to grow again after he was shaven.
23 [Then the lords of the Philistines gathered them together for to offer a great sacrifice unto Dagon their god, and to rejoice: for they said, our god has delivered Samson our enemy into our hand.][6]
24 And when the people saw him, they praised their god: for they said, our god has delivered into our hands our enemy, and the destroyer of our country, which slaughtered many of us
25 And it came to pass, when their hearts were merry, that they said, call for Samson, that he may make us sport. And they called for Samson out of the prison house; and he made them sport: and they set him between the pillars.
26 And Samson said unto the lad that held him by the hand, suffer me that I may feel the pillars whereupon the house stands, that I may lean upon them.
27 Now the house was full of men and women; and all the lords of the Philistines *were* there; and *there were* upon the roof about three thousand men and women, that beheld while Samson made sport.
28 And Samson called unto the LORD, and said, O Lord GOD, remember me, I pray you, and strengthen me, I pray you, only this once, O God, that I may be at once avenged of the Philistines for my two eyes.

---

[1] Sorek- a vine, a vine stock that yields grapes and wine. It comes from two root words, the first being *shâraq*, meaning to be shrill, to whistle or hiss. The second is *śârûq*, meaning bright red (as piercing to the sight), and speckled. [Strgs#7796]
[2] Delilah- literally means lanquishing, comes from a root word that means to slacken, be feeble, to be oppressed, bring low, dry up, to be emptied, not equal, fail, to be impoverished and to be made thin. [Strgs#1809]
[3] vexed – to dock off, curtail, to harvest, cut down, discourage [Strgs#7114]
[4] Samson died soul wise
[5] you will loose your eyes when you tell the secret of your strength.
[6] false witness victories of Islam does not make it true.

29 And Samson took hold of the two middle pillars upon which the house stood, and on which it was borne up, of the one with his right hand, and of the other with his left.
30 And Samson said, let me die with the Philistines. And he **stretched** himself with *all his* might; and the house fell upon the lords, and upon all the people that *were* therein. So the dead which he slaughtered at his death were more than *they* which he slaughtered in his life.
31 Then his brethren and all the house of his father came down, and took him, and brought *him* up, and buried him between Zorah and Eshtaol in the burying place of Manoah his father. And he judged Israel twenty years.

CHAPTER 17

1 And there was a man of mount Ephraim, whose name *was* Micah.
2 And he said unto his mother, the eleven hundred *shekels* of silver that were taken from you, about which you cursed, and spoke of also in mine ears, behold, the silver *is* with me; I took it. And his mother said, blessed *be you* of the LORD, my son.
3 And when he had restored the eleven hundred *shekels* of silver to his mother, his mother said, I had wholly dedicated the silver unto the LORD from my hand for my son, to make a graven image and a molten image: now therefore I will restore it unto you.
4 Yet he restored the money unto his mother; and his mother took two hundred *shekels* of silver, and gave them to the founder, who made thereof a graven image and a molten image: and they were in the house of Micah.
5 And the man Micah had a house of gods, and made an ephod[1], and teraphim[2], and consecrated one of his sons, who became his priest.
6 In those days *there was* no king in Israel, *but* every man did *that* which *was* right in his own eyes.
7 And there was a young man out of Beth-lehem-judah of the family of Judah, who *was* a Levite, and he sojourned there.
8 And the man departed out of the city from Beth-lehem-judah to sojourn where he could find *a place*: and he came to mount Ephraim to the house of Micah, as he journeyed.
9 And Micah said unto him, where come you? And he said unto him, I *am* a Levite of Beth-lehem-judah, and I go to sojourn where I may find *a place*.
10 And Micah said unto him, Dwell with me, and be unto me a father and a priest, and I will give you ten *shekels* of silver by the year, and a suit of apparel, and your victuals. So the Levite went in.
11 And the Levite was content to dwell with the man; and the young man was unto him as one of his sons.
12 And Micah consecrated the Levite; and the young man became his priest, and was in the house of Micah.
13 Then said Micah, Now know I that the LORD will do me good, seeing I have a Levite to *my* priest.

CHAPTER 18

1 In those days *there was* no king in Israel: and in those days the tribe of the Danites sought them an inheritance to dwell in; for unto that day *all their* inheritance had not fallen unto them among the tribes of Israel.
2 And the children of Dan sent of their family five men from their coasts, men of valor, from Zorah, and from Eshtaol, to spy out the land, and to search it; and they said unto them, Go, search the land: who when they came to mount Ephraim, to the house of Micah, they lodged there.
3 When they *were* by the house of Micah, they knew the voice of the young man the Levite: and they turned in thither, and said unto him, who brought you hither? And what makes you in this *place*? And what have you here?
4 And he said unto them, thus and thus deals Micah with me, and has hired me, and I am his priest.
5 And they said unto him, ask counsel, we pray you, of God, that we may know whether our way which we go will be prosperous.
6 And the priest said unto them, go in peace: before the LORD *is* your way wherein you go.
7 Then the five men departed, and came to Laish, and saw the people that *were* therein, how they dwelt careless, after the manner of the Zidonians, quiet and secure; and *there was* no magistrate in the land, that might put *them* to shame in *any*thing; and they *were* far from the Zidonians, and had no business with *any* man.
8 And they came unto their brethren to Zorah and Eshtaol: and their brethren said unto them, what *say* you?
9 And they said, Arise, that we may go up against them: for we have seen the land, and, behold, it *is* very good: and *are* you still? Be not slothful to go, *and* to enter to possess the land.
10 When you go, you will come unto a people secure, and to a large land: for God hath given it into your hands; a place where *there is* no want of anything that *is* in the earth.
11 And there went from thence of the family of the Danites, out of Zorah and out of Eshtaol, six hundred men appointed with weapons of war.
12 And they went up, and pitched in Kirjath-jearim, in Judah: wherefore they called that place Mahaneh-dan unto this day: behold, *it is* behind Kirjath-jearim.
13 And they passed thence unto mount Ephraim, and came unto the house of Micah.
14 Then answered the five men that went to spy out the country of Laish, and said unto their brethren, Do you know that there is in these houses an ephod, and teraphim, and a graven image, and a molten image? Now therefore consider what you have to do.
15 And they turned thitherward, and came to the house of the young man the Levite, *even* unto the house of Micah, and saluted him.
16 And the six hundred men appointed with their weapons of war, which *were* of the children of Dan, stood by the entering of the gate.
17 And the five men that went to spy out the land went up, *and* came in thither, *and* took the graven image, and the ephod, and the teraphim, and the molten image: and the priest stood in the entering of the gate with the six hundred men *that were* appointed with weapons of war.
18 And these went into Micah's house, and fetched the carved image, the ephod, and the teraphim, and the molten image. Then said the priest unto them, what do you?
19 And they said unto him, Hold your peace, lay thine hand upon your mouth, and go with us, and be to us a father and a priest: *is it* better for you to be a priest unto the house of one man, or that you be a priest unto a tribe and a family in Israel?

---

[1] ephod- a priestly garment, shoulder-cape or mantle, outer garment, a girdle; also generally an image. [Strgs#646]

[2] teraphim- a family idol. [Strgs#8655]

20 And the priest's heart was glad, and he took the ephod, and the teraphim, and the graven image, and went in the midst of the people.

21 So they turned and departed, and put the little ones and the cattle and the carriage before them.

22 *And* when they were a good way from the house of Micah, the men that *were* in the houses near to Micah's house were gathered together, and overtook the children of Dan.

23 And they cried unto the children of Dan. And they turned their faces, and said unto Micah, What ails you, that you come with such a company?

24 And he said, you have taken away my gods which I made, and the priest, and you are gone away: and what have I more? and what *is* this *that* you say unto me, What ails you?

25 And the children of Dan said unto him, Let not your voice be heard among us, lest angry fellows run upon you, and you lose your life, with the lives of your household.

26 And the children of Dan went their way: and when Micah saw that they *were* too strong for him, he turned and went back unto his house.

27 And they took *the things* which Micah had made, and the priest which he had, and came unto Laish, unto a people *that were* at quiet and secure: and they smote them with the edge of the sword, and burnt the city with fire.

28 And *there was* no deliverer, because it *was* far from Zidon, and they had no business with *any* man; and it was in the valley that lie by Beth-rehob. And they built a city, and dwelt therein.

29 And they called the name of the city Dan, after the name of Dan their father, who was born unto Israel: howbeit the name of the city *was* Laish at the first.

30 And the children of Dan set up the graven image: and Jonathan, the son of Gershom, the son of Manasseh, he and his sons were priests to the tribe of Dan until the day of the captivity of the land.

31 And they set them up Micah's graven image, which he made, all the time that the house of God was in Shiloh.

CHAPTER 19

1 And it came to pass in those days, when *there was* no king in Israel, that there was a certain Levite sojourning on the side of mount Ephraim, who took to him a concubine out of Beth-lehem-judah.

2 And his concubine played the whore against him, and went away from him unto her father's house to Beth-lehem-judah, and was there four whole months.

3 And her husband arose, and went after her, to speak friendly unto her, *and* to bring her again, having his servant with him, and a couple of asses: and she brought him into her father's house: and when the father of the damsel saw him, he rejoiced to meet him.

4 And his father in law, the damsel's father, retained him; and he abode with him three days: so they did eat and drink, and lodged there.

5 And it came to pass on the fourth day, when they arose early in the morning, that he rose up to depart: and the damsel's father said unto his son in law, Comfort thine heart with a morsel of bread, and afterward go your way.

6 And they sat down, and did eat and drink both of them together: for the damsel's father had said unto the man, be content, I pray you, and tarry all night, and let thine heart be merry.

7 And when the man rose up to depart, his father in law urged him: therefore he lodged there again.

8 And he arose early in the morning on the fifth day to depart: and the damsel's father said, Comfort thine heart, I pray you. And they tarried until afternoon, and they did eat both of them.

9 And when the man rose up to depart, he, and his concubine, and his servant, his father in law, the damsel's father, said unto him, Behold, now the day draws toward evening, I pray you tarry all night: behold, the day grows to an end, lodge here, that thine heart may be merry; and tomorrow get you early on your way, that you may go home.

10 But the man would not tarry that night, but he rose up and departed, and came over against Jebus, which *is* Jerusalem; and *there were* with him two asses saddled, his concubine also *was* with him.

11 *And* when they *were* by Jebus, the day was far spent; and the servant said unto his master, Come, I pray you, and let us turn in into this city of the Jebusites, and lodge in it.

12 And his master said unto him, we will not turn aside hither into the city of a stranger, that *is* not of the children of Israel; we will pass over to Gibeah.

13 And he said unto his servant, Come, and let us draw near to one of these places to lodge all night, in Gibeah, or in Ramah.

14 And they passed on and went their way; and the sun went down upon them *when they were* by Gibeah, which *belongs* to Benjamin.

15 And they turned aside thither, to go in *and* to lodge in Gibeah: and when he went in, he sat him down in a street of the city: for *there was* no man that took them into his house to lodging.

16 And, behold, there came an old man from his work out of the field at even, which *was* also of mount Ephraim; and he sojourned in Gibeah: but the men of the place *were* Benjamites.

17 And when he had lifted up his eyes, he saw a wayfaring man in the street of the city: and the old man said, whither go you? And where come you?

18 And he said unto him, we *are* passing from Beth-lehem-judah toward the side of mount Ephraim; from thence *am* I: and I went to Beth-lehem-judah, but I *am now* going to the house of the LORD; and there *is* no man that receives me to house.

19 Yet there is both straw and provender for our asses; and there is bread and wine also for me, and for your handmaid and for the young man *which is* with your servants: *there is* no want of anything.

20 And the old man said, Ppace *be* with you; howsoever *let* all your wants *lie* upon me; only lodge not in the street.

21 So he brought him into his house, and gave provender unto the asses: and they washed their feet, and did eat and drink.

22 *Now* as they were making their hearts merry, behold, the men of the city, certain sons of Belial, beset the house round about, *and* beat at the door, and spoke to the master of the house, the old man, saying, Bring forth the man that came into thine house, that we may know him.

23 And the man, the master of the house, went out unto them, and said unto them, No, my brethren, *no*, I pray you, do not so wickedly; seeing that this man is come into mine house, do not this folly.

24 Behold, *here is* my daughter a maiden, and his concubine; them I will bring out now, and humble you them, and do with them what seems good unto you: but unto this man do not so vile a thing.

25 But the men would not hearken to him: so the man took his concubine, and brought her forth unto them; and they knew her, and abused her all the night until the morning: and when the day began to spring, they let her go.

26 Then came the woman in the dawning of the day, and fell down at the door of the man's house where her lord *was*, till it was light.

27 And her lord rose up in the morning, and opened the doors of the house, and went out to go his way: and, behold, the woman his concubine was fallen down *at* the door of the house, and her hands *were* upon the threshold.

28 And he said unto her, Up, and let us be going. But none answered. Then the man took her *up* upon an ass, and the man rose up, and gat him unto his place.

29 And when he was come into his house, he took a knife, and laid hold on his concubine, and divided her, *together* with her bones, into twelve pieces, and sent her into all the coasts of Israel.

30 And it was so, that all that saw it said, there was no such deed done or seen from the day that the children of Israel came up out of the land of Egypt unto this day: consider of it, take advice, and speak *your minds*.

CHAPTER 20

1 Then all the children of Israel went out, and the congregation was gathered together as one man, from Dan even to Beer-sheba, with the land of Gilead, unto the LORD in Mizpeh.

2 And the chief of all the people, *even* of all the tribes of Israel, presented themselves in the assembly of the people of God, four hundred thousand footmen that drew sword.

3 (Now the children of Benjamin heard that the children of Israel were gone up to Mizpeh.) Then said the children of Israel, Tell *us*, how was this wickedness?

4 And the Levite, the husband of the woman that was slain, answered and said, I came into Gibeah that *belongs* to Benjamin, I and my concubine, to lodge.

5 And the men of Gibeah rose against me, and beset the house round about upon me by night, *and* thought to have slain me: and my concubine have they forced, that she is dead.

6 And I took my concubine, and cut her in pieces, and sent her throughout all the country of the inheritance of Israel: for they have committed lewdness and folly in Israel.

7 Behold, you *are* all children of Israel; give here your advice and counsel.

8 And all the people arose as one man, saying, we will not any *of us* go to his tent, neither will we any *of us* turn into his house.

9 But now this will *be* the thing which we will do to Gibeah; *we will go up* by lot against it;

10 And we will take ten men of an hundred throughout all the tribes of Israel, and an hundred of a thousand, and a thousand out of ten thousand, to fetch victual for the people, that they may do, when they come to Gibeah of Benjamin, according to all the folly that they have wrought in Israel.

11 So all the men of Israel were gathered against the city, knit together as one man.

12 And the tribes of Israel sent men through all the tribe of Benjamin, saying, what wickedness *is* this that is done among you?

13 Now therefore deliver *us* the men, the children of Belial, which *are* in Gibeah, that we may put them to death, and put away evil from Israel. But the children of Benjamin would not hearken to the voice of their brethren the children of Israel:

14 But the children of Benjamin gathered themselves together out of the cities unto Gibeah, to go out to battle against the children of Israel.

15 And the children of Benjamin were numbered at that time out of the cities twenty and six thousand men that drew sword, beside the inhabitants of Gibeah, which were numbered seven hundred chosen men.

16 Among all this people *there were* seven hundred chosen men left-handed; every one could sling stones at a hair *breadth*, and not miss.

17 And the men of Israel, beside Benjamin, were numbered four hundred thousand men that drew sword: all these *were* men of war.

18 And the children of Israel arose, and went up to the house of God, and asked counsel of God, and said, which of us will go up first to the battle against the children of Benjamin? And the LORD said, Judah will *go up* first.

19 And the children of Israel rose up in the morning, and encamped against Gibeah.

20 And the men of Israel went out to battle against Benjamin; and the men of Israel put themselves in array to fight against them at Gibeah.

21 And the children of Benjamin came forth out of Gibeah, and destroyed down to the ground of the Israelites that day twenty and two thousand men.

22 And the people the men of Israel encouraged themselves, and set their battle again in array in the place where they put themselves in array the first day.

23 (And the children of Israel went up and wept before the LORD until even, and asked counsel of the LORD, saying, will I go up again to battle against the children of Benjamin my brother? And the LORD said, Go up against him.)

24 And the children of Israel came near against the children of Benjamin the second day.

25 And Benjamin went forth against them out of Gibeah the second day, and destroyed down to the ground of the children of Israel again eighteen thousand men; all these drew the sword.

26 Then all the children of Israel, and all the people, went up, and came unto the house of God, and wept, and sat there before the LORD, and fasted that day until even, and offered burnt offerings and peace offerings before the LORD.

27 And the children of Israel enquired of the LORD, (for the ark of the covenant of God *was* there in those days,

28 And Phinehas, the son of Eleazar, the son of Aaron, stood before it in those days,) saying, will I yet again go out to battle against the children of Benjamin my brother, or will I cease? And the LORD said, Go up; for tomorrow I will deliver them into thine hand.

29 And Israel set **ambushers** in wait round about Gibeah.

30 And the children of Israel went up against the children of Benjamin on the third day, and put themselves in array against Gibeah, as at other times.

31 And the children of Benjamin went out against the people, *and* were drawn away from the city; and they began to smite of the people, *and* kill, as at other times, in the highways, of which one go up to the house of God, and the other to Gibeah n the field, about thirty men of Israel.

32 And the children of Benjamin said, they *are* smitten down before us, as at the first. But the children of Israel said, Let us flee, and draw them from the city unto the highways.

33 And all the men of Israel rose up out of their place, and put themselves in array at Baal-tamar: and the **ambushers** in wait of Israel came forth out of their places, *even* out of the meadows of Gibeah.

34 And there came against Gibeah ten thousand chosen men out of all Israel, and the battle was sore: but they knew not that evil *was* near them.

35 And the LORD smote Benjamin before Israel: and the children of Israel destroyed of the Benjamites that day twenty and five thousand and an hundred men: all these drew the sword.
36 So the children of Benjamin saw that they were smitten: for the men of Israel gave place to the Benjamites, because they trusted unto the **ambushers** in wait which they had set beside Gibeah.
37 And the liers in wait hasted, and rushed upon Gibeah; and the liers in wait drew *themselves* along, and smote the **entire** city with the edge of the sword.
38 Now there was an appointed sign between the men of Israel and the **ambushers** in wait, that they should make a great flame with smoke rise up out of the city.
39 And when the men of Israel retired in the battle, Benjamin began to smite *and* kill of the men of Israel about thirty persons: for they said, surely they are smitten down before us, as *in* the first battle.
40 But when the flame began to arise up out of the city with a pillar of smoke, the Benjamites looked behind them, and, behold, the flame of the city ascended up to heaven.
41 And when the men of Israel turned again, the men of Benjamin were amazed: for they saw that evil was come upon them.
42 Therefore they turned *their backs* before the men of Israel unto the way of the wilderness; but the battle overtook them; and them which *came* out of the cities they destroyed in the midst of them.
43 *Thus* they **surrounded** the Benjamites round about, *and* chased them, *and* **overran** them down with ease over against Gibeah toward the rising sun.
44 And there fell of Benjamin eighteen thousand men; all these *were* men of valor.
45 And they turned and fled toward the wilderness unto the rock of Rimmon: and they gleaned of them in the highways five thousand men; and pursued hard after them unto Gidom, and slew two thousand men of them.
46 So that all which fell that day of Benjamin were twenty and five thousand men that drew the sword; all these *were* men of valor.
47 But six hundred men turned and fled to the wilderness unto the rock Rimmon, and abode in the rock Rimmon four months.
48 And the men of Israel turned again upon the children of Benjamin, and smote them with the edge of the sword, as well the men of *every* city, as the beast, and all that came to hand: also they set on fire all the cities that they came to.

CHAPTER 21

1 Now the men of Israel had sworn in Mizpeh, saying, There will not any of us give his daughter unto Benjamin to wife.
2 And the people came to the house of God, and abode there till even before God, and lifted up their voices, and wept sore;
3 And said, O LORD God of Israel, why is this come to pass in Israel, that there should be to day one tribe lacking in Israel?
4 And it came to pass on the morrow, that the people rose early, and built there an altar, and offered burnt offerings and peace offerings.
5 And the children of Israel said, who *is there* among all the tribes of Israel that came not up with the congregation unto the LORD? For they had made a great oath concerning him that came not up to the LORD to Mizpeh, saying, He will surely be put to death.
6 And the children of Israel repented them for Benjamin their brother, and said, there is one tribe cut off from Israel this day.
7 How will we do for wives for them that remain, seeing we have sworn by the LORD that we will not give them of our daughters to wives?
8 And they said, what one *is there* of the tribes of Israel that came not up to Mizpeh to the LORD? And, behold, there came none to the camp from Jabesh-gilead to the assembly.
9 For the people were numbered, and, behold, *there were* none of the inhabitants of Jabesh-gilead there.
10 And the congregation sent there twelve thousand men of the valiantest, and commanded them, saying, Go and kill the inhabitants of Jabesh-gilead with the edge of the sword, with the women and the children.
11 And this *is* the thing that you will do, you will utterly destroy every male, and every woman that hath lain by man.
12 And they found among the inhabitants of Jabesh-gilead four hundred young virgins, that had known no man by lying with any male: and they brought them unto the camp to Shiloh, which *is* in the land of Canaan.
13 And the whole congregation sent *some* to speak to the children of Benjamin that *were* in the rock Rimmon, and to call peaceably unto them.
14 And Benjamin came again at that time; and they gave them wives which they had saved alive of the women of Jabesh-gilead: and yet so they sufficed them not.
15 And the people repented them for Benjamin, because that the LORD had made a breach in the tribes of Israel.
16 Then the elders of the congregation said, how will we do for wives for them that remain, seeing the women are destroyed out of Benjamin?
17 And they said, There must *be* an inheritance for them that be escaped of Benjamin, that a tribe be not destroyed out of Israel.
18 Howbeit we may not give them wives of our daughters: for the children of Israel have sworn, saying, cursed *be* he that gives a wife to Benjamin.
19 Then they said, Behold, *there is* a feast of the LORD in Shiloh yearly *in a place* which *is* on the north side of Beth-el, on the east side of the highway that go up from Beth-el to Shechem, and on the south of Lebonah.
20 Therefore they commanded the children of Benjamin, saying, Go and lie in wait in the vineyards;
21 And see, and, behold, if the daughters of Shiloh come out to dance in dances, then come you out of the vineyards, and catch you every man his wife of the daughters of Shiloh, and go to the land of Benjamin.
22 And it will be, when their fathers or their brethren come unto us to complain, that we will say unto them, Be favorable unto them for our sakes: because we reserved not to each man his wife in the war: for you did not give unto them at this time, *that* you should be guilty.
23 And the children of Benjamin did so, and took *them* wives, according to their number, of them that danced, who they caught: and they went and returned unto their inheritance, and repaired the cities, and dwelt in them.
24 And the children of Israel departed there at that time, every man to his tribe and to his family, and they went out from there every man to his inheritance.
25 In those days *there was* no king in Israel: every man did *that which was* right in his own eyes.

RUTH

CHAPTER 1

1 Now it came to pass in the days when the judges ruled, that there was a famine in the land. And a certain man of Beth-lehem-judah went to sojourn in the country of Moab, he, and his wife, and his two sons.
2 And the name of the man *was* Elimelech[1], and the name of his wife Naomi[2], and the name of his two sons Mahlon[3] and Chilion[4], Ephrathites of Beth-lehem-judah. And they came into the country of Moab, and continued there.
3 And Elimelech Naomi's husband died; and she was left, and her two sons.
4 And they took them wives of the women of Moab; the name of the one *was* Orpah[5], and the name of the other Ruth[6]: and they dwelled there about ten years.
5 And Mahlon and Chilion died also both of them; and the woman was left of her two sons and her husband.
6 Then she arose with her daughters in law, that she might return from the country of Moab: for she had heard in the country of Moab how that the LORD had visited his people in giving them bread.
7 Wherefore she went forth out of the place where she was, and her two daughters in law with her; and they went on the way to return unto the land of Judah.
8 And Naomi said unto her two daughters in law, Go, return each to her mother's house: the LORD deal kindly with you, as you have dealt with the dead, and with me.
9 The LORD grants you that you may find rest, each *of you* in the house of her husband. Then she kissed them; and they lifted up their voice, and wept.
10 And they said unto her, surely we will return with you unto your people.
11 And Naomi said, Turn again, my daughters: why will you go with me? *Are* there yet *any more* sons in my womb, that they may be your husband's?
12 Turn again, my daughters, go *your way*; for I am too old to have a husband. If I should say, I have hope, *if* I should have a husband also to night, and should also bear sons;
13 Would you tarry for them till they were grown? Would you stay for them from having husbands? Nay, my daughters; for it grieves me much for your sakes that the hand of the LORD is gone out against me.
14 And they lifted up their voice, and wept again: and Orpah kissed her mother in law; but Ruth clave unto her.
15 And she said, Behold, your sister in law is gone back unto her people, and unto her gods: return you after your sister in law.
16 And Ruth said, cause me not to leave you, *or* to return from following after you: for wherever you go, I will go; and where you lodge, I will lodge: your people will *be* my people, and your God my God:
17 Where you die, will I die, and there will I be buried: the LORD do so to me, and more also, *if ought* but death part you and me.
18 When she saw that she was steadfastly minded to go with her, then she left speaking unto her.
19 So they two went until they came to Beth-lehem. And it came to pass, when they were come to Beth-lehem, that all the city was moved about them, and they said, is this Naomi?
20 And she said unto them, Call me not Naomi, call me Mara: for the Almighty has dealt very bitterly with me.
21 I went out full, and the LORD has brought me home again empty: why *then* call you me Naomi, seeing the LORD has testified against me, and the Almighty has afflicted me?
22 So Naomi returned, and Ruth the Moabitess, her daughter in law, with her, which returned out of the country of Moab: and they came to Beth-lehem in the beginning of barley harvest.

CHAPTER 2

1 And Naomi had a kinsman of her husband's, a mighty man of wealth, of the family of Elimelech; and his name *was* Boaz[7].
2 And Ruth the Moabitess said unto Naomi, Let me now go to the field, and glean ears of corn after *him* in whose sight I will find grace. And she said unto her, Go, my daughter.
3 And she went, and came, and gleaned in the field after the reapers: and her hap was to light on a part of the field *belonging* unto Boaz, who *was* of the kindred of Elimelech.
4 And, behold, Boaz came from Beth-lehem, and said unto the reapers, The LORD *be* with you. And they answered him, The LORD bless you.
5 Then said Boaz unto his servant that was set over the reapers, whose damsel *is* this?
6 And the servant that was set over the reapers answered and said, it *is* the Moabitish damsel that came back with Naomi out of the country of Moab:
7 And she said, I pray you, let me glean and gather after the reapers among the sheaves: so she came, and has continued even from the morning until now, that she tarried a little in the house.
8 Then said Boaz unto Ruth, hear you not, my daughter? Go not to glean in another field, neither go from hence, but abide here fast by my maidens:
9 *Let* your eyes *be* on the field that they do reap, and go you after them: have I not charged the young men that they will not touch you? And when you are **thirsty**, go unto the vessels, and drink of *that* which the young men have drawn.
10 Then she fell on her face, and bowed herself to the ground, and said unto him, why have I found grace in your eyes, that you should take knowledge of me, seeing I *am* a stranger?
11 And Boaz answered and said unto her, it has fully been showed me, all that you hast done unto your mother in law since the death of your husband: and how you hast left your father and your mother, and the land of your nativity, and are come unto a people which you knew not heretofore.
12 The LORD recompense your work, and a full reward be given you of the LORD God of Israel, under whose wings you are come to trust.
13 Then she said, let me find favor in your sight, my lord; for that you hast comforted me, and for that you hast spoken friendly unto your handmaid, though I **am** not like unto one of your handmaidens.

---

[1] Elimelech- God of king or my God is king. [Strgs#458]
[2] Naomi- my delight. [Strgs#5281]
[3] Mahlon- sick, worn, put to pain, to be weak. [Strgs#4248]
[4] Chilion- pining, destruction, consumption, failing. [Strgs#3630]
[5] Orpah- literally stiff-neck. [Strgs#6204]
[6] Ruth- friend, neighbor. [Strgs#7327]
[7] Boaz- in him is strength. Also the name of one of two bronze pillars in front of King Solomon's temple (**II Chr. 3:17**), the name of the second was Jachin. [Strgs#1162]

Ruth

14 And Boaz said unto her, at mealtime come you here, and eat of the bread, and dip your morsel in the vinegar. And she sat beside the reapers: and he reached her parched *corn*, and she did eat, and was sufficed, and left.
15 And when she was risen up to glean, Boaz commanded his young men, saying, let her glean even among the sheaves, and reproach her not:
16 And let fall also *some* of the handfuls of purpose for her, and leave *them*, that she may glean *them*, and rebuke her not.
17 So she gleaned in the field until even, and beat out that she had gleaned: and it was about an ephah of barley.
18 And she took *it* up, and went into the city: and her mother in law saw what she had gleaned: and she brought forth, and gave to her that she had reserved after she was sufficed.
19 And her mother in law said unto her, where have you gleaned today? And where wroughtest you? Blessed be he that did take knowledge of you. And she showed her mother in law with whom she had wrought, and said, the man's name with who I wrought today *is* Boaz.
20 And Naomi said unto her daughter in law, blessed *be* he of the LORD, who has not left off his kindness to the living and to the dead. And Naomi said unto her, the man *is* near of kin unto us, one of our next kinsmen.
21 And Ruth the Moabitess said, He said unto me also, you will keep fast by my young men, until they have ended all my harvest.
22 And Naomi said unto Ruth her daughter in law, *It is* good, my daughter, that you go out with his maidens, that they meet you not in any other field.
23 So she kept fast by the maidens of Boaz to glean unto the end of barley harvest and of wheat harvest; and dwelt with her mother in law.

CHAPTER 3

1 Then Naomi her mother in law said unto her, my daughter, will I not seek rest for you, that it may be well with you?
2 And now *is* not Boaz of our kindred, with whose maidens you were? Behold, he **fans** barley tonight in the threshing floor.
3 Wash yourself therefore, and anoint you, and put your raiment upon you, and get you down to the floor: *but* make not yourself known unto the man, until he will have done eating and drinking.
4 And it will be, when he lay down, that you will mark the place where he will lie, and you will go in, and uncover his feet, and lay you down; and he will tell you what you will do.
5 And she said unto her, all that you say unto me I will do.
6 And she went down unto the floor, and did according to all that her mother in law bade her.
7 And when Boaz had eaten and drunk, and his heart was merry, he went to lie down at the end of the heap of corn: and she came softly, and uncovered his feet, and laid her down.
8 And it came to pass at midnight, that the man was afraid, and turned himself: and, behold, a woman lay at his feet.
9 And he said, who are you? And she answered, I *am* Ruth your handmaid: spread therefore your skirt over your handmaid; for you are a near kinsman.
10 And he said, blessed *be* you of the LORD, my daughter: *for* you hast showed more kindness in the latter end than at the beginning, inasmuch as you followed not young men, whether poor or rich.
11 And now, my daughter, fear not; I will do to you all that you require: for all the city of my people doth know that you are a virtuous woman.
12 And now it is true that I *am your* near kinsman: howbeit there is a kinsman nearer than I.
13 Tarry this night, and it will be in the morning, *that* if he will perform unto you the part of a kinsman, well; let him do the kinsman's part: but if he will not do the part of a kinsman to you, then will I do the part of a kinsman to you, *as* the LORD lives: lie down until the morning.
14 And she lay at his feet until the morning: and she rose up before one could know another. And he said, let it not be known that a woman came into the floor.
15 Also he said, bring the veil that you *have* upon you, and hold it. And when she held it, he measured six *measures* of barley, and laid *it* on her: and she went into the city.
16 And when she came to her mother in law, she said, who are you, my daughter? And she told her all that the man had done to her.
17 And she said, these six *measures* of barley gave he me; for he said to me, go not empty unto your mother in law.
18 Then said she, Sit still, my daughter, until you know how the matter will fall: for the man will not be in rest, until he have finished the thing this day.

CHAPTER 4

1 Then went Boaz up to the gate, and sat him down there: and, behold, the kinsman of whom Boaz spoke came by; unto whom he said, Ho, such a one! Turn aside, sit down here. And he turned aside, and sat down.
2 And he took ten men of the elders of the city, and said, sit you down here. And they sat down.
3 And he said unto the kinsman, Naomi, that is come again out of the country of Moab, sell a parcel of land, which *was* our brother Elimelech's:
4 And I thought to advertise you, saying, buy *it* before the inhabitants, and before the elders of my people. If you will redeem *it*, redeem *it*: but if you will not redeem *it*, then tell me, that I may know: for *there is* none to redeem *it* beside you; and I *am* after you. And he said, I will redeem *it*.
5 Then said Boaz, what day you buy the field of the hand of Naomi, you must buy *it* also of Ruth the Moabitess, the wife of the dead, to raise up the name of the dead upon his inheritance.
6 And the kinsman said, I cannot redeem *it* for myself, lest I mar mine own inheritance: redeem you my right to thyself; for I cannot redeem *it*.
7 Now this *was the manner* in former time in Israel concerning redeeming and concerning changing, for to confirm all things; a man plucked off his shoe, and gave *it* to his neighbor: and this *was* a testimony in Israel.
8 Therefore the kinsman said unto Boaz, Buy *it* for you. So he drew off his shoe.
9 And Boaz said unto the elders, and *unto* all the people, you *are* witnesses this day, that I have bought all that *was* Elimelech's, and all that *was* Chilion's and Mahlon's, of the hand of Naomi.
10 Moreover Ruth the Moabitess, the wife of Mahlon, have I purchased to be my wife, to raise up the name of the dead upon his inheritance, that the name of the dead be not cut off from among his brethren, and from the gate of his place: you *are* witnesses this day.
11 [And all the people that *were* in the gate, and the elders, said, *we are* witnesses. The LORD make the woman that is come into your house like Rachel and like Leah, which two did build the

house of Israel:]¹ and do you worthily in Ephratah, [and be famous in Beth-lehem:]²

12 And let your house be like the house of Pharez, whom Tamar bare unto Judah, of the seed which the LORD will give you of this young woman.

13 So Boaz took Ruth, and she was his wife: and when he went in unto her, the LORD gave her conception³, and she bares a son.

14 And the women said unto Naomi, Blessed *be* the LORD, which has not left you this day without a kinsman, that his name may be famous in Israel.

15 And he will be unto you a restorer of your life, and a nourisher of your old age: for your daughter in law, which loves you, which is better to you than seven sons, has born him.

16 And Naomi took the child, and laid it in her bosom, and became nurse unto it.

17 And the women her neighbors gave it a name, saying, there is a son born to Naomi; and they called his name Obed: he *is* the father of Jesse, the father of David.

18 Now these *are* the generations of Pharez: Pharez begat Hezron,

19 And Hezron begat Ram, and Ram begat Amminadab,

20 And Amminadab begat Nahshon, and Nahshon begat Salmon,

21 And Salmon begat Boaz, and Boaz begat Obed,

22 And Obed begat Jesse, and Jesse begat David.

---

¹ women build the house of Israel by having children.
² this was fulfilled when Jesus was born.

³ conception – is something the Lord gives. The husband should make God's name famous in Israel.

FIRST SAMUEL
CHAPTER 1

1 Now there was a certain man of Ramathaim-zophim, of mount Ephraim, and his name *was* Elkanah, the son of Jeroham, the son of Elihu, the son of Tohu, the son of Zuph, an Ephrathite:
2 And he had two wives; the name of the one *was* Hannah, and the name of the other Peninnah: and Peninnah had children, but Hannah had no children.
3 And this man went up out of his city yearly to worship and to sacrifice unto the LORD of hosts in Shiloh. And the two sons of Eli, Hophni and Phinehas, the priests of the LORD, *were* there.
4 And when the time was that Elkanah offered, he gave to Peninnah his wife, and to all her sons and her daughters, portions:
5 But unto Hannah he gave a worthy portion; for he loved Hannah: but the LORD had shut up her womb.
6 And her adversary also provoked her sore, for to make her fret, because the LORD had shut up her womb.
7 And *as* he did so year by year, when she went up to the house of the LORD, so she provoked her; therefore she wept, and did not eat.
8 Then said Elkanah her husband to her, Hannah, why weep you? And why eat you not? And why is your heart grieved? *Am* not I better to you than ten sons?
9 So Hannah rose up after they had eaten in Shiloh, and after they had drunk. Now Eli the priest sat upon a seat by a post of the temple of the LORD.
10 And she *was* in bitterness of soul, and prayed unto the LORD, and wept sore.
11 And she vowed a vow, and said, O LORD of hosts, if you will indeed look on the affliction of your handmaid, and remember me, and not forget your handmaid, but will give unto your handmaid a man child, then I will give him unto the LORD all the days of his life, and there will no razor come upon his head.
12 And it came to pass, as she continued praying before the LORD, that Eli marked her mouth.
13 Now Hannah, she spoke in her heart; only her lips moved, but her voice was not heard: therefore Eli thought she had been drunken.
14 And Eli said unto her, how long will you be drunken? Put away your wine from you.
15 And Hannah answered and said, No, my lord, I *am* a woman of a sorrowful spirit: I have drunk neither wine or strong drink, but have poured out my soul before the LORD.
16 Count not your handmaid for a daughter of Belial: for out of the abundance of my complaint and grief have I spoken here.
17 Then Eli answered and said, go in peace: and the God of Israel grants you your petition that you have asked of him.
18 And she said, let your handmaid find grace in your sight. So the woman went her way, and did eat, and her countenance was no more *sad*.
19 And they rose up in the morning early, and worshipped before the LORD, and returned, and came to their house to Ramah: and Elkanah knew Hannah his wife; and the LORD remembered her.
20 Wherefore it came to pass, when the time was come about after Hannah had conceived, that she bare a son, and called his name Samuel[1], *saying*, because I have asked him of the LORD.
21 And the man Elkanah, and his **entire** house, went up to offer unto the LORD the yearly sacrifice, and his vow.
22 But Hannah went not up; for she said unto her husband, *I will not go up* until the child be weaned, and *then* I will bring him, that he may appear before the LORD, and there abide forever.
23 And Elkanah her husband said unto her, Do what seems you good; tarry until you have weaned him; only the LORD establish his word. So the woman abode, and gave her son suck until she weaned him.
24 And when she had weaned him, she took him up with her, with three bullocks, and one ephah of flour, and a bottle of wine, and brought him unto the house of the LORD in Shiloh: and the child *was* young.
25 And they slew a bullock, and brought the child to Eli.
26 And she said, oh my lord, *as* your soul lives, my lord, *I am* the woman that stood by you here, praying unto the LORD.
27 For this child I prayed; and the LORD has given me my petition which I asked of him:
28 Therefore also I have lent him to the LORD; as long as he lives he will be lent to the LORD. And he worshipped the LORD there.

CHAPTER 2

1 And Hannah prayed, and said, My heart rejoices in the LORD, mine horn is exalted in the LORD: my mouth is enlarged over mine enemies; because I rejoice in your salvation.
2 *There is* none holy as the LORD: for *there is* none beside you: neither *is there* any rock like our God.
3 Talk no more so exceeding proudly; let *not* arrogancy come out of your mouth: for the LORD *is* a God of knowledge, and by him actions are weighed.
4 The bows of the mighty men *are* broken, and they that stumbled are girded with strength.
5 *They that were* full have hired out themselves for bread; and *they that were* hungry ceased: so that the barren has born seven; and she that has many children is waxed feeble.
6 The LORD kills, and makes alive: he brings down to the grave, and brings up.
7 The LORD makes poor, and makes rich: he brings low, and lifts up.
8 He raises up the poor out of the dust, *and* lifts up the beggar from the dunghill, to set *them* among princes, and to make them inherit the throne of glory: for the pillars of the earth *are* the LORD'S, and he has set the world upon them.
9 He will keep the feet of his saints, and the wicked will be silent in darkness; for by strength will no man prevail.
10 The adversaries of the LORD will be broken to pieces; out of heaven will he thunder upon them: the LORD will judge the ends of the earth; and he will give strength unto his king, and exalt the horn of his anointed.
11 And Elkanah went to Ramah to his house. And the child did minister unto the LORD before Eli the priest.
12 Now the sons of Eli *were* sons of Belial; they knew not the LORD.
13 And the priests' custom with the people *was, that,* when any man offered sacrifice, the priest's servant came, while the flesh was in seething, with a flesh hook of three teeth in his hand;
14 And he struck *it* into the pan, or kettle, or caldron, or pot; all that the flesh hook brought up the priest took for himself. So they did in Shiloh unto all the Israelites that came there.

---

[1] Samuel- name of God or his name is El. [Strgs#8050]

15 Also before they burnt the fat, the priest's servant came, and said to the man that sacrificed, Give flesh to roast for the priest; for he will not have sodden flesh of you, but raw.
16 And *if* any man said unto him, Let them not fail to burn the fat presently, and *then* take *as* much as your soul desires; then he would answer him, *Nay*; but you will give *it me* now: and if not, I will take *it* by force.
17 Wherefore the sin of the young men was very great before the LORD: for men abhorred the offering of the LORD.
18 But Samuel ministered before the LORD, *being* a child, girded with a linen ephod.
19 Moreover his mother made him a little coat, and brought *it* to him from year to year, when she came up with her husband to offer the yearly sacrifice.
20 And Eli blessed Elkanah and his wife, and said, The LORD give you seed of this woman for the loan which is lent to the LORD. And they went unto their own home.
21 And the LORD visited Hannah, so that she conceived, and bare three sons and two daughters. And the child Samuel grew before the LORD.
22 Now Eli was very old, and heard all that his sons did unto all Israel; and how they lay with the women that assembled *at* the door of the tabernacle of the congregation.
23 And he said unto them, why do you such things? For I hear of your evil dealings by this **entire** people.
24 Nay, my sons; for *it is* no good report that I hear: you make the LORD'S people to transgress.
25 If one man sin against another, the judge will judge him: but if a man sin against the LORD, who will intreat for him? Not with standing they hearkened not unto the voice of their father, because the LORD would slay them.
26 And the child Samuel grew on, and was in favor both with the LORD, and also with men.
27 And there came a man of God unto Eli, and said unto him, Thus said the LORD, Did I plainly appear unto the house of your father, when they were in Egypt in Pharaoh's house?
28 And did I choose him out of all the tribes of Israel *to be* my priest, to offer upon mine altar, to burn incense, to wear an ephod before me? And did I give unto the house of your father all the offerings made by fire of the children of Israel?
29 Wherefore kick you at my sacrifice and at mine offering, which I have commanded *in my* habitation; and honor your sons above me, to make yourselves fat with the chief of all the offerings of Israel my people?
30 Wherefore the LORD God of Israel said, I said indeed *that* your house, and the house of your father, should walk before me forever: but now the LORD said, Be it far from me; for them that honor me I will honor, and they that despise me will be lightly esteemed.
31 Behold, the days come, that I will cut off your arm, and the arm of your father's house, that there will not be an old man in your house.
32 And you will see an enemy *in my* habitation, in all *the wealth* which *God* will give Israel: and there will not be an old man in your house for ever.
33 And the man of your, *whom* I will not cut off from mine altar, will *be* to consume your eyes, and to grieve your heart: and all the increase of your house will die in the flower of their age.
34 And this will *be* a sign unto you, that will come upon your two sons, on Hophni[1] and Phinehas[2]; in one day they will die both of them.
35 And I will raise me up a faithful priest, *that* will do according to *that* which *is* in mine heart and in my mind: and I will build him a sure house; and he will walk before mine anointed forever.
36 And it will come to pass, *that* every one that is left in your house will come *and* crouch to him for a piece of silver and a morsel of bread, and will say, Put me, I pray you, into one of the priests' offices, that I may eat a piece of bread.

CHAPTER 3

1 And the child Samuel ministered unto the LORD before Eli. And the word of the LORD was precious in those days; *there was* no open vision.
2 And it came to pass at that time, when Eli *was* laid down in his place, and his eyes began to wax dim, *that* he could not see;
3 And ere the lamp of God went out in the temple of the LORD, where the ark of God *was*, and Samuel was laid down *to sleep*;
4 That the LORD called Samuel: and he answered, here *am* I.
5 And he ran unto Eli, and said, here *am* I; for you called me. And he said, I called not; lie down again. And he went and lay down.
6 And the LORD called yet again, Samuel. And Samuel arose and went to Eli, and said, here *am* I; for you didst call me. And he answered, I called not, my son; lie down again.
7 Now Samuel did not yet know the LORD, neither was the word of the LORD yet revealed unto him.
8 And the LORD called Samuel again the third time. And he arose and went to Eli, and said, here *am* I; for you didst call me. And Eli perceived that the LORD had called the child.
9 Therefore Eli said unto Samuel, Go, lay down: and it will be, if he call you, that you will say, Speak, LORD; for your servant hears. So Samuel went and lay down in his place.
10 And the LORD came, and stood, and called as at other times, Samuel, Samuel. Then Samuel answered, Speak; for your servant hears.
11 And the LORD said to Samuel, Behold, I will do a thing in Israel, at which both the ears of every one that hears it will tingle.
12 In that day I will perform against Eli all *things* which I have spoken concerning his house: when I begin, I will also make an end.
13 For I have told him that I will judge his house for ever for the iniquity which he knows; because his sons made themselves vile, and he restrained them not.
14 And therefore I have sworn unto the house of Eli, that the iniquity of Eli's house will not be purged with sacrifice or offering forever.
15 And Samuel lay until the morning, and opened the doors of the house of the LORD. And Samuel feared to show Eli the vision.
16 Then Eli called Samuel, and said, Samuel, my son. And he answered, Here *am* I.
17 And he said, what *is* the thing that *the LORD* has said unto you? I pray you hide *it* not from me: God do so to you, and more also, if you hide *any*thing from me of all the things that he said unto you.
18 And Samuel told him every whit, and hid nothing from him. And he said, It *is* the LORD: let him do what seems him good.
19 And Samuel grew, and the LORD was with him, and did let none of his words fall to the ground.

---

[1] Hophni- tadpoll, pugilist. [Strgs#2652].

[2] Phinehas- mouth of a serpent or mouth of brass. [Strgs#6372]

20 And all Israel from Dan even to Beer-sheba[1] knew that Samuel *was* established *to be* a prophet of the LORD.

21 And the LORD appeared again in Shiloh: for the LORD revealed himself to Samuel in Shiloh by the word of the LORD.

CHAPTER 4

1 And the word of Samuel came to all Israel. Now Israel went out against the Philistines to battle, and pitched beside Eben-ezer[2]: and the Philistines pitched in Aphek.

2 And the Philistines put themselves in array against Israel: and when they joined battle, Israel was smitten before the Philistines: and they slew of the army in the field about four thousand men.

3 And when the people were come into the camp, the elders of Israel said, Wherefore has the LORD smitten us to day before the Philistines? Let us fetch the ark of the covenant of the LORD out of Shiloh unto us, that, when it cometh among us, it may save us out of the hand of our enemies.

4 So the people sent to Shiloh, that they might bring from there the ark of the covenant of the LORD of hosts, which dwells *between* the cherubims: and the two sons of Eli, Hophni and Phinehas, *were* there with the ark of the covenant of God.

5 And when the ark of the covenant of the LORD came into the camp, all Israel shouted with a great shout, so that the earth rang again.

6 And when the Philistines heard the noise of the shout, they said, what *means* the noise of this great shout in the camp of the Hebrews? And they understood that the ark of the LORD was come into the camp.

7 And the Philistines were afraid, for they said, God is come into the camp. And they said, Woe unto us! For there has not been such a thing heretofore.

8 Woe unto us! Who will deliver us out of the hand of these mighty Gods? These *are* the Gods that smote the Egyptians with all the plagues in the wilderness.

9 Be strong, and quit yourselves like men, O you Philistines, that you are not servants unto the Hebrews, as they have been to you: quit yourselves like men, and fight.

10 And the Philistines fought, and Israel was smitten, and they fled every man into his tent: and there was a very great slaughter; for there fell of Israel thirty thousand footmen.

11 And the ark of God was taken; and the two sons of Eli, Hophni and Phinehas, were slain.

12 And there ran a man of Benjamin out of the army, and came to Shiloh the same day with his clothes rent, and with earth upon his head.

13 And when he came, lo, Eli sat upon a seat by the wayside watching: for his heart trembled for the ark of God. And when the man came into the city, and told *it*, the **entire** city cried out.

14 And when Eli heard the noise of the crying, he said, what *means* the noise of this tumult? And the man came in hastily, and told Eli.

15 Now Eli was ninety and eight years old; and his eyes were dim, that he could not see.

16 And the man said unto Eli, I *am* he that came out of the army, and I fled to day out of the army. And he said, what is there done, my son?

17 And the messenger answered and said, Israel is fled before the Philistines, and there has been also a great slaughter among the people, and your two sons also, Hophni and Phinehas, are dead, and the ark of God is taken.

18 And it came to pass, when he made mention of the ark of God, that he fell from off the seat backward by the side of the gate, and his neck brake, and he died: for he was an old man, and heavy. And he had judged Israel forty years.

19 And his daughter in law, Phinehas' wife, was with child, *near* to be delivered: and when she heard the tidings that the ark of God was taken, and that her father in law and her husband were dead, she bowed herself and travailed; for her pains came upon her.

20 And about the time of her death the women that stood by her said unto her, Fear not; for you have born a son. But she answered not, neither did she regard *it*.

21 And she named the child I-chabod, saying, the glory is departed from Israel: because the ark of God was taken, and because of her father in law and her husband.

22 And she said, the glory is departed from Israel: for the ark of God is taken.

CHAPTER 5

1 And the Philistines took the ark of God, and brought it from Eben-ezer unto Ashdod.

2 When the Philistines took the ark of God, they brought it into the house of Dagon, and set it by Dagon.

3 And when they of Ashdod arose early on the morrow, behold, Dagon *was* fallen upon his face to the earth before the ark of the LORD. And they took Dagon, and set him in his place again.

4 And when they arose early on the morrow morning, behold, Dagon *was* fallen upon his face to the ground before the ark of the LORD; and the head of Dagon and both the palms of his hands *were* cut off upon the threshold; only *the stump of* Dagon was left to him.

5 Therefore neither the priests of Dagon, or any that come into Dagon's house, tread on the threshold of Dagon in Ashdod unto this day.

6 But the hand of the LORD was heavy upon them of Ashdod, and he destroyed them, and smote them with emerods, *even* Ashdod and the coasts thereof.

7 And when the men of Ashdod saw that *it was* so, they said, the ark of the God of Israel will not abide with us: for his hand is sore upon us, and upon Dagon our god.

8 They sent therefore and gathered all the lords of the Philistines unto them, and said, what will we do with the ark of the God of Israel? And they answered, Let the ark of the God of Israel be carried about unto Gath. And they carried the ark of the God of Israel about *there*.

9 And it was *so*, that, after they had carried it about, the hand of the LORD was against the city with a very great destruction: and he smote the men of the city, both small and great, and they had emerods in their secret parts.

10 Therefore they sent the ark of God to Ekron. And it came to pass, as the ark of God came to Ekron, that the Ekronites cried out, saying, They have brought about the ark of the God of Israel to us, to slay us and our people.

11 So they sent and gathered together all the lords of the Philistines, and said, Send away the ark of the God of Israel, and let it go again to his own place, that it slays us not, and our people: for there was a deadly destruction throughout the **entire** city; the hand of God was very heavy there.

12 And the men that died not were smitten with the emerods: and the cry of the city went up to heaven.

---

[1] Beersheba – well of the sevenfold oath. [Strgs#884]

[2] Ebenezer- stone of the help or stone of help. [Strgs#72]

CHAPTER 6

1 And the ark of the LORD was in the country of the Philistines seven months.
2 And the Philistines called for the priests and the diviners, saying, what will we do to the ark of the LORD? Tell us wherewith we will send it to his place.
3 And they said, if you send away the ark of the God of Israel, send it not empty; but in any wise return him a trespass offering: then you will be healed, and it will be known to you why his hand is not removed from you.
4 Then said they, what will *be* the trespass offering which we will return to him? They answered, five golden emerods, and five golden mice, *according to* the number of the lords of the Philistines: for one plague *was* on you all, and on your lords.
5 Wherefore you will make images of your emerods, and images of your mice that mar the land; and you will give glory unto the God of Israel: peradventure he will lighten his hand from off you, and from off your gods, and from off your land.
6 Wherefore then do you harden your hearts, as the Egyptians and Pharaoh hardened their hearts? When he had wrought wonderfully among them, did they not let the people go, and they departed?
7 Now therefore make a new cart, and take two **nursing heifers**, on which there has come no yoke, and tie the **heifer** to the cart, and bring their calves' home from them:
8 And take the ark of the LORD, and lay it upon the cart; and put the jewels of gold, which you return him *for* a trespass offering, in a coffer by the side thereof; and send it away, that it may go.
9 And see, if it goes up by the way of his own coast to Beth-shemesh, *then* he has done us this great evil: but if not, then we will know that *it is* not his hand *that* smote us: it *was* a chance *that* happened to us.
10 And the men did so; and took two **nursing heifers**, and tied them to the cart, and shut up their calves at home:
11 And they laid the ark of the LORD upon the cart, and the coffer with the mice of gold and the images of their emerods.
12 And the **heifer** took the straight way to the way of Beth-shemesh, *and* went along the highway, lowing as they went, and turned not aside *to* the right hand or *to* the left; and the lords of the Philistines went after them unto the border of Beth-shemesh.
13 And *they of* Beth-shemesh *were* reaping their wheat harvest in the valley: and they lifted up their eyes, and saw the ark, and rejoiced to see *it*.
14 And the cart came into the field of Joshua, a Beth-shemite, and stood there, where *there was* a great stone: and they clave the wood of the cart, and offered the **heifer as** a burnt offering unto the LORD.
15 And the Levites took down the ark of the LORD, and the coffer that *was* with it, wherein the jewels of gold *were*, and put *them* on the great stone: and the men of Beth-shemesh offered burnt offerings and sacrificed sacrifices the same day unto the LORD.
16 And when the five lords of the Philistines had seen *it*, they returned to Ekron the same day.
17 And these *are* the golden emerods which the Philistines returned *for* a trespass offering unto the LORD; for Ashdod one, for Gaza one, for Askelon one, for Gath one, for Ekron one;
18 And the golden mice, *according to* the number of all the cities of the Philistines *belonging* to the five lords, *both* of fenced cities, and of country villages, *even* unto the great *stone of* Abel, whereon they set down the ark of the LORD: *which stone* remains unto this day in the field of Joshua, the Beth-shemite.
19 And he smote the men of Beth-shemesh, because they had looked into the ark of the LORD, even he smote of the people fifty thousand and threescore and ten men: and the people lamented, because the LORD had smitten *many* of the people with a great slaughter.
20 And the men of Beth-shemesh said, who is able to stand before this holy LORD God? And to whom will he go up from us?
21 And they sent messengers to the inhabitants of Kirjath-jearim, saying, The Philistines have brought again the ark of the LORD; come you down, *and* fetch it up to you.

CHAPTER 7

1 And the men of Kirjath-jearim came, and fetched up the ark of the LORD, and brought it into the house of Abinadab in the hill, and sanctified Eleazar his son to keep the ark of the LORD.
2 And it came to pass, while the ark abode in Kirjath-jearim, that the time was long; for it was twenty years: and all the house of Israel lamented after the LORD.
3 And Samuel spoke unto all the house of Israel, saying, if you do return unto the LORD with all your hearts, *then* put away the strange gods and Ashtaroth from among you, and prepare your hearts unto the LORD, and serve him only: and he will deliver you out of the hand of the Philistines.
4 Then the children of Israel did put away Baalim and Ashtaroth, and served the LORD only.
5 And Samuel said, Gather all Israel to Mizpeh, and I will pray for you unto the LORD.
6 And they gathered together to Mizpeh, and drew water, and poured *it* out before the LORD, and fasted on that day, and said there, we have sinned against the LORD. And Samuel judged the children of Israel in Mizpeh.
7 And when the Philistines heard that the children of Israel were gathered together to Mizpeh, the lords of the Philistines went up against Israel. And when the children of Israel heard *it*, they were afraid of the Philistines.
8 And the children of Israel said to Samuel, Cease not to cry unto the LORD our God for us, that he will save us out of the hand of the Philistines.
9 And Samuel took a sucking lamb, and offered *it for* a burnt offering wholly unto the LORD: and Samuel cried unto the LORD for Israel; and the LORD heard him.
10 And as Samuel was offering up the burnt offering, the Philistines drew near to battle against Israel: but the LORD thundered with a great thunder on that day upon the Philistines, and discomfited them; and they were smitten before Israel.
11 And the men of Israel went out of Mizpeh, and pursued the Philistines, and smote them, until *they came* under Beth-car.
12 Then Samuel took a stone, and set *it* between Mizpeh and Shen, and called the name of it Eben-ezer, saying, here has the LORD helped us.
13 So the Philistines were subdued, and they came no more into the coast of Israel: and the hand of the LORD was against the Philistines all the days of Samuel.
14 And the cities which the Philistines had taken from Israel were restored to Israel, from Ekron even unto Gath; and the coasts thereof did Israel deliver out of the hands of the Philistines. And there was peace between Israel and the Amorites.
15 And Samuel judged Israel all the days of his life.
16 And he went from year to year in circuit to Beth-el, and Gilgal, and Mizpeh, and judged Israel in all those places.

17 And his return *was* to Ramah; for there *was* his house; and there he judged Israel; and there he built an altar unto the LORD.

CHAPTER 8

1 And it came to pass, when Samuel was old, that he made his sons judges over Israel.
2 Now the name of his firstborn was Joel; and the name of his second, Abiah: *they were* judges in Beer-sheba.
3 And his sons walked not in his ways, but turned aside after lucre, and took bribes, and perverted judgment.
4 Then all the elders of Israel gathered themselves together, and came to Samuel unto Ramah,
5 And said unto him, Behold, you are old, and your sons walk not in your ways: now make us a king to judge us like all the nations.
6 But the thing displeased Samuel, when they said, Give us a king to judge us. And Samuel prayed unto the LORD.
7 And the LORD said unto Samuel, Hearken unto the voice of the people in all that they say unto you: for they have not rejected you, but they have rejected me, that I should not reign over them.
8 According to all the works which they have done since the day that I brought them up out of Egypt even unto this day, wherewith they have forsaken me, and served other gods, so do they also unto you.
9 Now therefore hearken unto their voice: howbeit yet protest solemnly unto them, and show them the manner of the king that will reign over them.
10 And Samuel told all the words of the LORD unto the people that asked of him a king.
11 And he said, this will be the manner of the king that will reign over you: He will take your sons, and appoint *them* for himself, for his chariots, and *to be* his horsemen; and *some* will run before his chariots.
12 And he will appoint him captains over thousands, and captains over fifties; and *will set them* to **plow** his ground, and to reap his harvest, and to make his instruments of war, and instruments of his chariots.
13 And he will take your daughters *to be* confectionaries, and *to be* cooks, and *to be* bakers.
14 And he will take your fields, and your vineyards, and your olive yards, *even* the best *of them*, and give *them* to his servants.
15 And he will take the tenth of your seed, and of your vineyards, and give to his officers, and to his servants.
16 And he will take your menservants, and your maidservants, and your goodliest young men, and your asses, and put *them* to his work.
17 He will take the tenth of your sheep: and you will be his servants.
18 And you will cry out in that day because of your king which you will have chosen you; and the LORD will not hear you in that day.
19 Nevertheless the people refused to obey the voice of Samuel; and they said, nay; but we will have a king over us;
20 That we also may be like all the nations; and that our king may judge us, and go out before us, and fight our battles.
21 And Samuel heard all the words of the people, and he rehearsed them in the ears of the LORD.
22 And the LORD said to Samuel, Hearken unto their voice, and make them a king. And Samuel said unto the men of Israel, Go you every man unto his city.

CHAPTER 9

1 Now there was a man of Benjamin, whose name *was* Kish, the son of Abiel, the son of Zeror, the son of Bechorath, the son of Aphiah, a Benjamite, a mighty man of power.
2 And he had a son, whose name *was* Saul[1], a choice young man, and a goodly: and *there was* not among the children of Israel a goodlier person than he: from his shoulders and upward *he was* higher than any of the people.
3 And the asses of Kish Saul's father were lost. And Kish said to Saul his son, Take now one of the servants with you, and arise, go seek the asses.
4 And he passed through mount Ephraim, and passed through the land of Shalisha, but they found *them* not: then they passed through the land of Shalim, and *there they were* not: and he passed through the land of the Benjamites, but they found *them* not.
5 *And* when they were come to the land of Zuph, Saul said to his servant that *was* with him, Come, and let us return; lest my father leave *caring* for the asses, and take thought for us.
6 And he said unto him, Behold now, *there is* in this city a man of God, and *he is* an honorable man; all that he said cometh surely to pass: now let us go there; peradventure he can show us our way that we should go.
7 Then said Saul to his servant, But, behold, *if* we go, what will we bring the man? For the bread is spent in our vessels, and *there is* not a present to bring to the man of God: what have we?
8 And the servant answered Saul again, and said, Behold, I have here at hand the fourth part of a shekel of silver: *that* will I give to the man of God, to tell us our way.
9 (Beforetime in Israel, when a man went to enquire of God, thus he spoke, Come, and let us go to the seer: for *he that is* now *called* a Prophet was beforetime called a Seer.)
10 Then said Saul to his servant, well said; come, let us go. So they went unto the city where the man of God *was*.
11 *And* as they went up the hill to the city, they found young maidens going out to draw water, and said unto them, is the seer here?
12 And they answered them, and said, He is; behold, *he is* before you: make haste now, for he came to day to the city; for *there is* a sacrifice of the people today in the high place:
13 As soon as you come into the city, you will straightway find him, before he goes up to the high place to eat: for the people will not eat until he come, because he does bless the sacrifice; *and* afterwards they eat that be bidden. Now therefore get you up; for about this time you will find him.
14 And they went up into the city: *and* when they were come into the city, behold, Samuel came out against them, for to go up to the high place.
15 Now the LORD had told Samuel in his ear a day before Saul came, saying,
16 To morrow about this time I will send you a man out of the land of Benjamin, and you will anoint him *to be* captain over my people Israel, that he may save my people out of the hand of the Philistines: for I have looked upon my people, because their cry is come unto me.
17 And when Samuel saw Saul, the LORD said unto him, Behold the man whom I spoke to you **about**! This same will reign over my people.

---

[1] Saul- literally desired or asked. [Strgs#7586]

18 Then Saul drew near to Samuel in the gate, and said, tell me, I pray you, where the seer's house *is*.
19 And Samuel answered Saul, and said, I *am* the seer: go up before me unto the high place; for you will eat with me today, and tomorrow I will let you go, and will tell you all that *is* in your heart.
20 And as for your asses that were lost three days ago, set not your mind on them; for they are found. And on whom *is* all the desire of Israel? *Is it* not on you, and on all your father's house?
21 And Saul answered and said, *Am* not I a Benjamite, of the smallest of the tribes of Israel? And my family the least of all the families of the tribe of Benjamin? Wherefore then speak you so to me?
22 And Samuel took Saul and his servant, and brought them into the parlor, and made them sit in the chief's place among them that were bidden, which *were* about thirty persons.
23 And Samuel said unto the cook, bring the portion which I gave you, of which I said unto you, set it by you.
24 And the cook took up the shoulder, and *that* which *was* upon it, and set *it* before Saul. And *Samuel* said, behold that which is left! Set *it* before you, *and* eat: for unto this time has it been kept for you since I said, I have invited the people. So Saul did eat with Samuel that day.
25 And when they were come down from the high place into the city, *Samuel* communed with Saul upon the top of the house.
26 And they arose early: and it came to pass about the spring of the day, that Samuel called Saul to the top of the house, saying, up, that I may send you away. And Saul arose, and they went out both of them, he and Samuel, abroad.
27 *And* as they were going down to the end of the city, Samuel said to Saul, Bid the servant pass on before us, (and he passed on,) but stand you still a while, that I may show you the word of God.

CHAPTER 10

1 Then Samuel took a vial of oil, and poured *it* upon his head, and kissed him, and said, *is it* not because the LORD has anointed you *to be* captain over his inheritance?
2 When you are departed from me today, then you will find two men by Rachel's sepulcher in the border of Benjamin at Zelzah; and they will say unto you, The asses which you went to seek are found: and, lo, your father has left the care of the asses, and sorrows for you, saying, What will I do for my son?
3 Then will you go on forward from there, and you will come to the plain of Tabor, and there will meet you three men going up to God to Beth-el, one carrying three kids, and another carrying three loaves of bread, and another carrying a bottle of wine:
4 And they will salute you, and give you two *loaves* of bread; which you will receive of their hands.
5 After that you will come to the hill of God, where *is* the garrison of the Philistines: and it will come to pass, when you are come here to the city, that you will meet a company of prophets coming down from the high place with a psaltery, and a **tambourine**, and a pipe, and a harp, before them; and they will prophesy:
6 And the Spirit of the LORD will come upon you, and you will prophesy with them, and will be turned into another man.
7 And let it be, when these signs are come unto you, *that* you do as occasion serve you; for God *is* with you.
8 And you will go down before me to Gilgal; and, behold, I will come down unto you, to offer burnt offerings, *and* to sacrifice sacrifices of peace offerings: seven days will you tarry, till I come to you, and show you what you will do.
9 And it was *so*, that when he had turned his back to go from Samuel, God gave him another heart: and all those signs came to pass that day.
10 And when they came there to the hill, behold, a company of prophets met him; and the Spirit of God came upon him, and he prophesied among them.
11 And it came to pass, when all that knew him beforetime saw that, behold, he prophesied among the prophets, then the people said one to another, What *is* this *that* is come unto the son of Kish? *Is* Saul also among the prophets?
12 And one of the same place answered and said, but who *is* their father? Therefore it became a proverb, *is* Saul also among the prophets?
13 And when he had made an end of prophesying, he came to the high place.
14 And Saul's uncle said unto him and to his servant, whither went you? And he said, to seek the asses: and when we saw that *they were* nowhere, we came to Samuel.
15 And Saul's uncle said, Tell me, I pray you, what Samuel said unto you.
16 And Saul said unto his uncle, He told us plainly that the asses were found. But of the matter of the kingdom, whereof Samuel spoke, he told him not.
17 And Samuel called the people together unto the LORD to Mizpeh;
18 And said unto the children of Israel, Thus said the LORD God of Israel, I brought up Israel out of Egypt, and delivered you out of the hand of the Egyptians, and out of the hand of all kingdoms, *and* of them that oppressed you:
19 And you have this day rejected your God, who himself saved you out of all your adversities and your tribulations; and you have said unto him, *Nay*, but set a king over us. Now therefore present yourselves before the LORD by your tribes, and by your thousands.
20 And when Samuel had caused all the tribes of Israel to come near, the tribe of Benjamin was taken.
21 When he had caused the tribe of Benjamin to come near by their families, the family of Matri was taken, and Saul the son of Kish was taken: and when they sought him, he could not be found.
22 Therefore they enquired of the LORD further, if the man should yet come there. And the LORD answered, Behold, he has hid himself among the stuff.
23 And they ran and fetched him there: and when he stood among the people, he was higher than any of the people from his shoulders and upward.
24 And Samuel said to all the people, see you him whom the LORD has chosen, that *there is* none like him among all the people? And all the people shouted, and said, God save the king.
25 Then Samuel told the people the manner of the kingdom, and wrote *it* in a book, and laid *it* up before the LORD. And Samuel sent all the people away, every man to his house.
26 And Saul also went home to Gibeah; and there went with him a band of men, whose hearts God had touched.
27 But the children of Belial said, how will this man save us? And they despised him, and brought him no presents. But he held his peace.

CHAPTER 11

1 Then Nahash the Ammonite came up, and encamped against Jabesh-gilead[1]: and all the men of Jabesh said unto Nahash, Make a covenant with us, and we will serve you.
2 And Nahash the Ammonite answered them, on this *condition* will I make *a covenant* with you, that I may thrust out all your right eyes, and lay it *for* a reproach upon all Israel.
3 And the elders of Jabesh said unto him, Give us seven days' respite, that we may send messengers unto all the coasts of Israel: and then, if *there be* no man to save us, we will come out to you.
4 Then came the messengers to Gibeah of Saul, and told the tidings in the ears of the people: and all the people lifted up their voices, and wept.
5 And, behold, Saul came after the herd out of the field; and Saul said, what *ailes* the people that they weep? And they told him the tidings of the men of Jabesh.
6 And the Spirit of God came upon Saul when he heard those tidings, and his anger was kindled greatly.
7 And he took a yoke of oxen, and hewed them in pieces, and sent *them* throughout all the coasts of Israel by the hands of messengers, saying, whosoever cometh not forth after Saul and after Samuel, so will it be done unto his oxen. And the fear of the LORD fell on the people, and they came out with one consent.
8 And when he numbered them in Bezek, the children of Israel were three hundred thousand, and the men of Judah thirty thousand.
9 And they said unto the messengers that came, thus will you say unto the men of Jabesh-gilead, tomorrow, by *that time* the sun be hot, you will have help. And the messengers came and showed *it* to the men of Jabesh; and they were glad.
10 Therefore the men of Jabesh said, tomorrow we will come out unto you, and you will do with us all that seems good unto you.
11 And it was *so* on the morrow, that Saul put the people in three companies; and they came into the midst of the host in the morning watch, and slew the Ammonites until the heat of the day: and it came to pass, that they which remained were scattered, so that two of them were not left together.
12 And the people said unto Samuel, Who *is* he that said, will Saul reign over us? Bring the men, that we may put them to death.
13 And Saul said, there will not a man be put to death this day: for today the LORD has wrought salvation in Israel.
14 Then said Samuel to the people, Come, and let us go to Gilgal, and renew the kingdom there.
15 And all the people went to Gilgal; and there they made Saul king before the LORD in Gilgal; and there they sacrificed sacrifices of peace offerings before the LORD; and there Saul and all the men of Israel rejoiced greatly.

CHAPTER 12

1 And Samuel said unto all Israel, Behold, I have hearkened unto your voice in all that you said unto me, and have made a king over you.
2 And now, behold, the king walks before you: and I am old and gray-headed; and, behold, my sons *are* with you: and I have walked before you from my childhood unto this day.
3 Behold, here I *am*: witness against me before the LORD, and before his anointed: whose ox have I taken? Or whose ass have I taken? Or whom have I defrauded? Whom have I oppressed? Or of whose hand have I received *any* bribe to blind mine eyes therewith? And I will restore it you.
4 And they said, you have not defrauded us, or oppressed us, neither have you taken ought of any man's hand.
5 And he said unto them, The LORD *is* witness against you, and his anointed *is* witness this day, that you have not found ought in my hand. And they answered, *He is* witness.
6 And Samuel said unto the people, *it is* the LORD that advanced Moses and Aaron, and that brought your fathers up out of the land of Egypt.
7 Now therefore stand still, that I may reason with you before the LORD of all the righteous acts of the LORD, which he did to you and to your fathers.
8 When Jacob was come into Egypt, and your fathers cried unto the LORD, then the LORD sent Moses and Aaron, which brought forth your fathers out of Egypt, and made them dwell in this place.
9 And when they forget the LORD their God, he sold them into the hand of Sisera, captain of the host of Hazor, and into the hand of the Philistines, and into the hand of the king of Moab, and they fought against them.
10 And they cried unto the LORD, and said, we have sinned, because we have forsaken the LORD, and have served Baalim and Ashtaroth: but now deliver us out of the hand of our enemies, and we will serve you.
11 And the LORD sent Jerubbaal, and Bedan, and Jephthah, and Samuel, and delivered you out of the hand of your enemies on every side, and you dwelled safe.
12 And when you saw that Nahash the king of the children of Ammon came against you, you said unto me, Nay; but a king will reign over us: when the LORD your God *was* your king.
13 Now therefore behold the king whom you have chosen, *and* whom you have desired! And, behold, the LORD has set a king over you.
14 If you will fear the LORD, and serve him, and obey his voice, and not rebel against the commandment of the LORD, then will both you and also the king that reigns over you continue following the LORD your God:
15 But if you will not obey the voice of the LORD, but rebel against the commandment of the LORD, then will the hand of the LORD be against you, as *it was* against your fathers.
16 Now therefore stand and see this great thing, which the LORD will do before your eyes.
17 *Is it* not wheat harvest today? I will call unto the LORD, and he will send thunder and rain; that you may perceive and see that your wickedness *is* great, which you have done in the sight of the LORD, in asking you a king.
18 So Samuel called unto the LORD; and the LORD sent thunder and rain that day: and all the people greatly feared the LORD and Samuel.
19 And all the people said unto Samuel, Pray for your servants unto the LORD your God, that we die not: for we have added unto all our sins *this* evil, to ask us a king.
20 And Samuel said unto the people, Fear not: you have done all this wickedness: yet turn not aside from following the LORD, but serve the LORD with all your heart;

---

[1] Jabeshgilead- is a combination of Jabesh (literally dry) and gilead (rocky). Jabesh is a town in the territory of Gilead, and according to Eusebius, it is beyond the Jordan, 6 miles from Pella on the mountain road of Gerasea. Gilead is a mountainous region bounded on the west by the Jordan, on the north by Bashan, on the east by the Arabian plateau, and on the south by Moab and Ammon.[Strgs#3003]

21 And turn you not aside: for *then should you go* after vain *things*, which cannot profit or deliver; for they *are* vain.
22 For the LORD will not forsake his people for his great name's sake: because it has pleased the LORD to make you his people.
23 Moreover as for me, God forbid that I should sin against the LORD in ceasing to pray for you: but I will teach you the good and the right way:
24 Only fear the LORD, and serve him in truth with all your heart: for consider how great *things* he has done for you.
25 But if you will still do wickedly, you will be consumed, both you and your king.

CHAPTER 13

1 Saul reigned one year; and when he had reigned two years over Israel,
2 Saul chose him three thousand *men* of Israel; *whereof* two thousand were with Saul in Michmash and in mount Beth-el, and a thousand were with Jonathan in Gibeah of Benjamin: and the rest of the people he sent every man to his tent.
3 And Jonathan smote the garrison of the Philistines that *was* in Geba, and the Philistines heard *of it*. And Saul blew the trumpet throughout all the land, saying, Let the Hebrews hear.
4 And all Israel heard say *that* Saul had smitten a garrison of the Philistines, and *that* Israel also was had in abomination with the Philistines. And the people were called together after Saul to Gilgal.
5 And the Philistines gathered themselves together to fight with Israel, thirty thousand chariots, and six thousand horsemen, and people as the sand which *is* on the sea shore in multitude: and they came up, and pitched in Michmash, eastward from Beth-aven.
6 When the men of Israel saw that they were in a strait, (for the people were distressed,) then the people did hide themselves in caves, and in thickets, and in rocks, and in high places, and in pits.
7 And *some of* the Hebrews went over Jordan to the land of Gad and Gilead. As for Saul, he *was* yet in Gilgal, and all the people followed him trembling.
8 And he tarried seven days, according to the set time that Samuel *had appointed*: but Samuel came not to Gilgal; and the people were scattered from him.
9 And Saul said, Bring here a burnt offering to me, and peace offerings. And he offered the burnt offering.
10 And it came to pass, that as soon as he had made an end of offering the burnt offering, behold, Samuel came; and Saul went out to meet him, that he might salute him.
11 And Samuel said, what have you done? And Saul said, because I saw that the people were scattered from me, and *that* you came not within the days appointed, and *that* the Philistines gathered themselves together at Michmash;
12 Therefore said I, The Philistines will come down now upon me to Gilgal, and I have not made supplication unto the LORD: I forced myself therefore, and offered a burnt offering.
13 And Samuel said to Saul, you have done foolishly: you have not kept the commandment of the LORD your God, which he commanded you: for now would the LORD have established your kingdom upon Israel for ever.
14 But now your kingdom will not continue: the LORD has sought him a man after his own heart, and the LORD has commanded him *to be* captain over his people, because you have not kept *that* which the LORD commanded you.

15 And Samuel arose, and gat him up from Gilgal unto Gibeah of Benjamin. And Saul numbered the people *that were* present with him, about six hundred men.
16 And Saul, and Jonathan his son, and the people *that were* present with them, abode in Gibeah of Benjamin: but the Philistines encamped in Michmash.
17 And the spoilers came out of the camp of the Philistines in three companies: one company turned unto the way *that leads to* Ophrah, unto the land of Shual:
18 And another company turned the way *to* Beth-horon: and another company turned *to* the way of the border that looks to the valley of Zeboim toward the wilderness.
19 Now there was no smith found throughout all the land of Israel: for the Philistines said, lest the Hebrews make *them* swords or spears:
20 But all the Israelites went down to the Philistines, to sharpen every man his share, and his coulter, and his axe, and his mattock.
21 Yet they had a file for the mattocks, and for the coulters, and for the forks, and for the axes, and to sharpen the goads.
22 So it came to pass in the day of battle, that there was neither sword or spear found in the hand of any of the people that *were* with Saul and Jonathan: but with Saul and with Jonathan his son was there found.
23 And the garrison of the Philistines went out to the passage of Michmash.

CHAPTER 14

1 Now it came to pass upon a day, that Jonathan the son of Saul said unto the young man that bare his armor, come, and let us go over to the Philistines' garrison, that *is* on the other side. But he told not his father.
2 And Saul tarried in the uttermost part of Gibeah under a pomegranate tree which *is* in Migron: and the people that *were* with him *were* about six hundred men;
3 And Ahiah, the son of Ahitub, I-chabod's brother, the son of Phinehas, the son of Eli, the LORD'S priest in Shiloh, wearing an ephod. And the people knew not that Jonathan was gone.
4 And between the passages, by which Jonathan sought to go over unto the Philistines' garrison, *there was* a sharp rock on the one side, and a sharp rock on the other side: and the name of the one *was* Bozez, and the name of the other Seneh.
5 The forefront of the one *was* situate northward over against Michmash, and the other southward over against Gibeah.
6 And Jonathan said to the young man that bare his armor, Come, and let us go over unto the garrison of these uncircumcised: it may be that the LORD will work for us: for *there is* no restraint to the LORD to save by many or by few.
7 And his armor-bearer said unto him, Do all that *is* in your heart: turn you; behold, I *am* with you according to your heart.
8 Then said Jonathan, Behold, we will pass over unto these men, and we will discover ourselves unto them.
9 If they say thus unto us, Tarry until we come to you; then we will stand still in our place, and will not go up unto them.
10 But if they say thus, Come up unto us; then we will go up: for the LORD has delivered them into our hand: and this will be a sign unto us.
11 And both of them discovered themselves unto the garrison of the Philistines: and the Philistines said, Behold, the Hebrews come forth out of the holes where they had hid themselves.
12 And the men of the garrison answered Jonathan and his armor-bearer, and said, Come up to us, and we will show you a thing.

And Jonathan said unto his armorbearer, come up after me: for the LORD has delivered them into the hand of Israel.

13 And Jonathan climbed up upon his hands and upon his feet, and his armorbearer after him: and they fell before Jonathan; and his armorbearer slew after him.

14 And that first slaughter, which Jonathan and his armor-bearer made, was about twenty men, within as it were an half acre of land, *which* a yoke *of oxen might plow.*

15 And there was trembling in the host, in the field, and among all the people: the garrison, and the spoilers, they also trembled, and the earth quaked: so it was a very great trembling.

16 And the watchmen of Saul in Gibeah of Benjamin looked; and, behold, the multitude melted away, and they went on beating down *one another.*

17 Then said Saul unto the people that *were* with him, Number now, and see who is gone from us. And when they had numbered, behold, Jonathan and his armor-bearer *were* not *there.*

18 And Saul said unto Ahiah, Bring here the ark of God. For the ark of God was at that time with the children of Israel.

19 And it came to pass, while Saul talked unto the priest, that the noise that *was* in the host of the Philistines went on and increased: and Saul said unto the priest, Withdraw your hand.

20 And Saul and all the people that *were* with him assembled themselves, and they came to the battle: and, behold, every man's sword was against his fellow, *and there was* a very great discomfiture.

21 Moreover the Hebrews *that* were with the Philistines before that time, which went up with them into the camp *from the country* round about, even they also *turned* to be with the Israelites that *were* with Saul and Jonathan.

22 Likewise all the men of Israel which had hid themselves in mount Ephraim, *when* they heard that the Philistines fled, even they also followed hard after them in the battle.

23 So the LORD saved Israel that day: and the battle passed over unto Beth-aven.

24 And the men of Israel were distressed that day: for Saul had adjured the people, saying, Cursed *be* the man that eats *any* food until evening, that I may be avenged on mine enemies. So none of the people tasted *any* food.

25 And all *they of* the land came to a wood; and there was honey upon the ground.

26 And when the people were come into the wood, behold, the honey dropped; but no man put his hand to his mouth: for the people feared the oath.

27 But Jonathan heard not when his father charged the people with the oath: wherefore he put forth the end of the rod that *was* in his hand, and dipped it in a honeycomb, and put his hand to his mouth; and his eyes were enlightened.

28 Then answered one of the people, and said, your father straightly charged the people with an oath, saying, cursed *be* the man that eats *any* food this day. And the people were faint.

29 Then said Jonathan, My father has troubled the land: see, I pray you, how mine eyes have been enlightened, because I tasted a little of this honey.

30 How much more, if haply the people had eaten freely to day of the spoil of their enemies which they found? For had there not been now a much greater slaughter among the Philistines?

31 And they smote the Philistines that day from Michmash to Aijalon: and the people were very faint.

32 And the people flew upon the spoil, and took sheep, and oxen, and calves, and slew *them* on the ground: and the people did eat *them* with the blood.

33 Then they told Saul, saying, Behold, the people sin against the LORD, in that they eat with the blood. And he said, you have transgressed: roll a great stone unto me this day.

34 And Saul said, Disperse yourselves among the people, and say unto them, Bring me here every man his ox, and every man his sheep, and slay *them* here, and eat; and sin not against the LORD in eating with the blood. And all the people brought every man his ox with him that night, and slew *them* there.

35 And Saul built an altar unto the LORD: the same was the first altar that he built unto the LORD.

36 And Saul said, Let us go down after the Philistines by night, and spoil them until the morning light, and let us not leave a man of them. And they said, do whatsoever seems good unto you. Then said the priest, Let us draw near here unto God.

37 And Saul asked counsel of God, will I go down after the Philistines? Will you deliver them into the hand of Israel? But he answered him not that day.

38 And Saul said, draw you near hither, all the chief of the people: and know and see wherein this sin has been this day.

39 For, *as* the LORD lives, which saves Israel, though it be in Jonathan my son, he will surely die. But *there was* not a man among all the people *that* answered him.

40 Then said he unto all Israel, Be you on one side, and I and Jonathan my son will be on the other side. And the people said unto Saul, Do what seems good unto you.

41 Therefore Saul said unto the LORD God of Israel, Give a perfect *lot.* And Saul and Jonathan were taken: but the people escaped.

42 And Saul said, cast *lots* between me and Jonathan my son. And Jonathan was taken.

43 Then Saul said to Jonathan, tell me what you have done. And Jonathan told him, and said, I did but taste a little honey with the end of the rod that *was* in mine hand, *and,* lo, I must die.

44 And Saul answered, God do so and more also: for you will surely die, Jonathan.

45 And the people said unto Saul, will Jonathan die, who has wrought this great salvation in Israel? God forbid: *as* the LORD lives, there will not one hair of his head fall to the ground; for he has wrought with God this day. So the people rescued Jonathan, that he died not.

46 Then Saul went up from following the Philistines: and the Philistines went to their own place.

47 So Saul took the kingdom over Israel, and fought against all his enemies on every side, against Moab, and against the children of Ammon, and against Edom, and against the kings of Zobah, and against the Philistines: and whithersoever he turned himself, he vexed *them.*

48 And he gathered a host, and smote the Amalekites, and delivered Israel out of the hands of them that spoiled them.

49 Now the sons of Saul were Jonathan, and Ishui, and Melchi-shua: and the names of his two daughters *were these;* the name of the firstborn Merab, and the name of the younger Michal:

50 And the name of Saul's wife *was* Ahinoam, the daughter of Ahimaaz: and the name of the captain of his host *was* Abner, the son of Ner, Saul's uncle.

51 And Kish *was* the father of Saul; and Ner the father of Abner *was* the son of Abiel.

52 And there was sore war against the Philistines all the days of Saul: and when Saul saw any strong man, or any valiant man, he took him unto him.

CHAPTER 15

1 Samuel also said unto Saul, The LORD sent me to anoint you *to be* king over his people, over Israel: now therefore hearken you unto the voice of the words of the LORD.
2 Thus said the LORD of hosts, I remember *that* which Amalek did to Israel, how he laid *wait* for him in the way, when he came up from Egypt.
3 Now go and smite Amalek, and utterly destroy all that they have, and spare them not; but slay both man and woman, infant and suckling, ox and sheep, camel and ass.
4 And Saul gathered the people together, and numbered them in Telaim, two hundred thousand footmen, and ten thousand men of Judah.
5 And Saul came to a city of Amalek, and laid wait in the valley.
6 And Saul said unto the Kenites, Go, depart, get you down from among the Amalekites, lest I destroy you with them: for you showed kindness to all the children of Israel, when they came up out of Egypt. So the Kenites departed from among the Amalekites.
7 And Saul smote the Amalekites from Havilah *until* you come to Shur, that *is* over against Egypt.
8 And he took Agag the king of the Amalekites alive, and utterly destroyed all the people with the edge of the sword.
9 But Saul and the people spared Agag, and the best of the sheep, and of the oxen, and of the fatlings, and the lambs, and all *that was* good, and would not utterly destroy them: but everything *that was* vile and refuse, that they destroyed utterly.
10 Then came the word of the LORD unto Samuel, saying,
11 It repents me that I have set up Saul *to be* king: for he is turned back from following me, and has not performed my commandments. And it grieved Samuel; and he cried unto the LORD all night.
12 And when Samuel rose early to meet Saul in the morning, it was told Samuel, saying, Saul came to Carmel, and, behold, he set him up a place, and is gone about, and passed on, and gone down to Gilgal.
13 And Samuel came to Saul: and Saul said unto him, blessed *be* you of the LORD: I have performed the commandment of the LORD.
14 And Samuel said, what *means* then this bleating of the sheep in mine ears, and the lowing of the oxen which I hear?
15 And Saul said, they have brought them from the Amalekites: for the people spared the best of the sheep and of the oxen, to sacrifice unto the LORD your God; and the rest we have utterly destroyed.
16 Then Samuel said unto Saul, Stay, and I will tell you what the LORD has said to me this night. And he said unto him, Say on.
17 And Samuel said, When you were little in your own sight, were you not *made* the head of the tribes of Israel, and the LORD anointed you king over Israel?
18 And the LORD sent you on a journey, and said, Go and utterly destroy the sinners the Amalekites, and fight against them until they be consumed.
19 Wherefore then didst you not obey the voice of the LORD, but didst fly upon the spoil, and did evil in the sight of the LORD?
20 And Saul said unto Samuel, Yea, I have obeyed the voice of the LORD, and have gone the way which the LORD sent me, and have brought Agag the king of Amalek, and have utterly destroyed the Amalekites.
21 But the people took of the spoil, sheep and oxen, the chief of the things which should have been utterly destroyed, to sacrifice unto the LORD your God in Gilgal.
22 And Samuel said, has the LORD *as great* delight in burnt offerings and sacrifices, as in obeying the voice of the LORD? Behold, to obey *is* better than sacrifice, *and* to hearken than the fat of rams.
23 For rebellion *is as* the sin of witchcraft, and stubbornness *is as* iniquity and idolatry. Because you have rejected the word of the LORD, he has also rejected you from *being* king.
24 And Saul said unto Samuel, I have sinned: for I have transgressed the commandment of the LORD, and your words: because I feared the people, and obeyed their voice.
25 Now therefore, I pray you, pardon my sin, and turn again with me, that I may worship the LORD.
26 And Samuel said unto Saul, I will not return with you: for you have rejected the word of the LORD, and the LORD has rejected you from being king over Israel.
27 And as Samuel turned about to go away, he laid hold upon the skirt of his mantle, and it rent.
28 And Samuel said unto him, The LORD has rent the kingdom of Israel from you this day, and has given it to a neighbor of yours, *that is* better than you.
29 And also the Strength of Israel will not lie or repent: for he *is* not a man, that he should repent.
30 Then he said, I have sinned: *yet* honor me now, I pray you, before the elders of my people, and before Israel, and turn again with me, that I may worship the LORD your God.
31 So Samuel turned again after Saul; and Saul worshipped the LORD.
32 Then said Samuel, Bring you here to me Agag the king of the Amalekites. And Agag came unto him delicately. And Agag said, surely the bitterness of death is past.
33 And Samuel said, as your sword has made women childless, so will your mother be childless among women. And Samuel hewed Agag in pieces before the LORD in Gilgal.
34 Then Samuel went to Ramah; and Saul went up to his house to Gibeah of Saul.
35 And Samuel came no more to see Saul until the day of his death: nevertheless Samuel mourned for Saul: and the LORD repented that he had made Saul king over Israel.

CHAPTER 16

1 And the LORD said unto Samuel, How long will you mourn for Saul, seeing I have rejected him from reigning over Israel? Fill your horn with oil, and go, I will send you to Jesse the Bethlehemite: for I have provided me a king among his sons.
2 And Samuel said, how can I go? If Saul hears *it*, he will kill me. And the LORD said, take a heifer with you, and say, I am come to sacrifice to the LORD.
3 And call Jesse to the sacrifice, and I will show you what you will do: and you will anoint unto me *him* whom I name unto you.
4 And Samuel did that which the LORD spoke, and came to Bethlehem. And the elders of the town trembled at his coming, and said, come you **peaceably**?
5 And he said, **peacefully**: I am come to sacrifice unto the LORD: sanctify yourselves, and come with me to the sacrifice. And he sanctified Jesse and his sons, and called them to the sacrifice.

6 And it came to pass, when they were come, that he looked on Eliab, and said, surely the LORD'S anointed *is* before him.
7 But the LORD said unto Samuel, Look not on his countenance, or on the height of his stature; because I have refused him: for *the LORD sees* not as man sees; for man looks on the outward appearance, but the LORD looks on the heart.
8 Then Jesse called Abinadab, and made him pass before Samuel. And he said, neither has the LORD chosen this.
9 Then Jesse made Shammah to pass by. And he said, neither has the LORD chosen this.
10 Again, Jesse made seven of his sons to pass before Samuel. And Samuel said unto Jesse, The LORD has not chosen these.
11 And Samuel said unto Jesse, are here all your children? And he said, there remains yet the youngest, and, behold, he keeps the sheep. And Samuel said unto Jesse, send and fetch him: for we will not sit down until he come here.
12 And he sent, and brought him in. Now he *was* ruddy, *and* withal of a beautiful countenance, and goodly to look to. And the LORD said, arise, anoint him: for this *is* he.
13 Then Samuel took the horn of oil, and anointed him in the midst of his brethren: and the Spirit of the LORD came upon David[1] from that day forward. So Samuel rose up, and went to Ramah.
14 But the Spirit of the LORD departed from Saul, and an evil spirit from the LORD troubled him.
15 And Saul's servants said unto him, Behold now, an evil spirit from God troubles you.
16 Let our lord now command your servants, *which are* before you, to seek out a man, *who is* a cunning player on a harp: and it will come to pass, when the evil spirit from God is upon you, that he will play with his hand, and you will be well.
17 And Saul said unto his servants, provide me now a man that can play well, and bring *him* to me.
18 Then answered one of the servants, and said, Behold, I have seen a son of Jesse the Beth-lehemite, *that is* cunning in playing, and a mighty valiant man, and a man of war, and prudent in matters, and a comely person, and the LORD *is* with him.
19 Wherefore Saul sent messengers unto Jesse, and said, send me David your son, which *is* with the sheep.
20 And Jesse took an ass laden with bread, and a bottle of wine, and a kid, and sent *them* by David his son unto Saul.
21 And David came to Saul, and stood before him: and he loved him greatly; and he became his armor-bearer.
22 And Saul sent to Jesse, saying, Let David, I pray you, stand before me; for he has found favor in my sight.
23 And it came to pass, when the *evil* spirit from God was upon Saul, that David took a harp, and played with his hand: so Saul was refreshed, and was well, and the evil spirit departed from him.

CHAPTER 17

1 Now the Philistines gathered together their armies to battle, and were gathered together at Shochoh, which *belongs* to Judah, and pitched between Shochoh and Azekah, in Ephes-dammim.
2 And Saul and the men of Israel were gathered together, and pitched by the valley of Elah, and set the battle in array against the Philistines.
3 And the Philistines stood on a mountain on the one side, and Israel stood on a mountain on the other side: and *there was* a valley between them.

4 And there went out a champion out of the camp of the Philistines, named Goliath, of Gath, whose height *was* six cubits and a span.
5 And *he had* a helmet of brass upon his head, and he *was* armed with a coat of mail; and the weight of the coat *was* five thousand shekels of brass.
6 And *he had* greaves of brass upon his legs, and a target[2] of brass between his shoulders.
7 And the staff of his spear *was* like a weaver's beam; and his spear's head *weighed* six hundred shekels of iron: and one bearing a shield[3] went before him.
8 And he stood and cried unto the armies of Israel, and said unto them, why are you come out to set *your* battle in array? *Am* not I a Philistine, and you servants to Saul? Choose you a man for you, and let him come down to me.
9 If he be able to fight with me, and to kill me, then will we be your servants: but if I prevail against him, and kill him, then will you be our servants, and serve us.
10 And the Philistine said, I defy the armies of Israel this day; give me a man, that we may fight together.
11 When Saul and all Israel heard those words of the Philistine, they were dismayed, and greatly afraid.
12 Now David *was* the son of that Ephrathite of Beth-lehem-judah, whose name *was* Jesse; and he had eight sons: and the man went among men *for* an old man in the days of Saul.
13 And the three eldest sons of Jesse went *and* followed Saul to the battle: and the names of his three sons that went to the battle *were* Eliab the firstborn, and next unto him Abinadab, and the third Shammah.
14 And David *was* the youngest: and the three eldest followed Saul.
15 But David went and returned from Saul to feed his father's sheep at Beth-lehem.
16 And the Philistine drew near morning and evening, and presented himself forty days.
17 And Jesse said unto David his son, Take now for your brethren an ephah of this parched *corn*, and these ten loaves, and run to the camp to your brethren;
18 And carry these ten cheeses unto the captain of *their* thousand, and look how your brethren fare, and take their pledge.
19 Now Saul, and they, and all the men of Israel, *were* in the valley of Elah, fighting with the Philistines.
20 And David rose up early in the morning, and left the sheep with a keeper, and took, and went, as Jesse had commanded him; and he came to the trench, as the host was going forth to the fight, and shouted for the battle.
21 For Israel and the Philistines had put the battle in array, army against army.
22 And David left his carriage in the hand of the keeper of the carriage, and ran into the army, and came and saluted his brethren.
23 And as he talked with them, behold, there came up the champion, the Philistine of Gath, Goliath by name, out of the armies of the Philistines, and spoke according to the same words: and David heard *them*.
24 And all the men of Israel, when they saw the man, fled from him, and were sore afraid.
25 And the men of Israel said, have you seen this man that is come up? Surely to defy Israel is he come up: and it will be, *that* the man

---

[1] David- is defined as beloved. [Strgs#1732]
[2] target – spear, to strike with, that is, a dart. [Strgs#3591]
[3] shield – a *hook* (as pointed); also a large *shield* (as if guarding by prickliness), also cold (as piercing) hook, buckler. [Strgs#6793]

who kills him, the king will enrich him with great riches, and will give him his daughter, and make his father's house free in Israel.

26 And David spoke to the men that stood by him, saying, what will be done to the man that kills this Philistine, and takes away the reproach from Israel? For who *is* this uncircumcised Philistine, that he should defy the armies of the living God?

27 And the people answered him after this manner, saying, so will it be done to the man that kills him.

28 And Eliab his eldest brother heard when he spoke unto the men; and Eliab's anger was kindled against David, and he said, why **do you** come down here? And with whom have you left those few sheep in the wilderness? I know your pride, and the naughtiness of your heart; for you are come down that you might see the battle.

29 And David said, what have I done now? *Is there* not a cause?

30 [And he turned from him toward another, and spoke after the same manner: and the people answered him again after the former manner.]¹

31 And when the words were heard which David spoke, they rehearsed *them* before Saul: and he sent for him.

32 And David said to Saul, Let no man's heart fail because of him; your servant will go and fight with this Philistine.

33 And Saul said to David, you are not able to go against this Philistine to fight with him: for you are *but* a youth, and he's a man of war from his youth.

34 And David said unto Saul, your servant kept his father's sheep, and there came a lion, and a bear, and took a lamb out of the flock:

35 And I went out after him, and smote him, and delivered *it* out of his mouth: and when he arose against me, I caught *him* by his beard, and smote him, and slew him.

36 your servant slew both the lion and the bear: and this uncircumcised Philistine will be as one of them, seeing he has defied the armies of the living God.

37 David said moreover, The LORD that delivered me out of the paw of the lion, and out of the paw of the bear, he will deliver me out of the hand of this Philistine. And Saul said unto David, Go, and the LORD be with you.

38 And Saul armed David with his armor, and he put a helmet of brass upon his head; also he armed him with a coat of mail.

39 And David girded his sword upon his armor, and he assayed to go; for he had not proved *it*. And David said unto Saul, I cannot go with these; for I have not proved *them*. And David put them off him.

40 And he took his staff in his hand, and chose² him five smooth stones³ out of the brook, and put them in a shepherd's bag⁴ which he had, even in a scrip⁵; and his sling *was* in his hand: and he drew near to the Philistine.

41 And the Philistine came on and drew near unto David; and the man that bare the shield *went* before him.

42 And when the Philistine looked about, and saw David, he disdained him: for he was *but* a youth, and ruddy, and of a fair countenance.

43 And the Philistine said unto David, *Am* I a dog, that you come to me with staves? And the Philistine cursed David by his gods.

44 And the Philistine said to David, Come to me, and I will give your flesh unto the fowls of the air, and to the beasts of the field.

45 Then said David to the Philistine, you come to me with a sword, and with a spear, and with a shield: but I come to you in the name of the LORD of hosts, the God of the armies of Israel, whom you have defied.

46 This day will the LORD deliver you into mine hand; and I will smite you, and take your head from you; and I will give the carcasses of the host of the Philistines this day unto the fowls of the air, and to the wild beasts of the earth; that all the earth may know that there is a God in Israel.

47 And all this assembly will know that the LORD saves not with sword and spear: for the battle *is* the LORD'S, and he will give you into our hands.

48 And it came to pass, when the Philistine arose, and came and drew nigh to meet David, that David hasted, and ran toward the army to meet the Philistine.

49 And David put his hand in his bag, and took there a stone, and slangs *it*, and smote the Philistine in his forehead, that the stone sunk into his forehead; and he fell upon his face to the earth.

50 So David prevailed over the Philistine with a sling and with a stone, and smote the Philistine, and slew him; but *there was* no sword in the hand of David.

51 Therefore David ran, and stood upon the Philistine and took his sword, and drew it out of the sheath thereof, and slew him, and cut off his head therewith. And when the Philistines saw their champion was dead, they fled.

52 And the men of Israel and of Judah arose, and shouted, and pursued the Philistines, until you come to the valley, and to the gates of Ekron. And the wounded of the Philistines fell down by the way to Shaaraim⁶, even unto Gath⁷, and unto Ekron⁸.

53 And the children of Israel returned from chasing after the Philistines, and they spoiled their tents.

54 And David took the head of the Philistine, and brought it to Jerusalem; but he put his armor in his tent.

55 And when Saul saw David go forth against the Philistine, he said unto Abner, the captain of the host, Abner, whose son *is* this youth? And Abner said, *as* your soul lives, O king, I cannot tell.

56 And the king said, Enquire you whose son the stripling⁹ *is*.

57 And as David returned from the slaughter of the Philistine, Abner took him, and brought him before Saul with the head of the Philistine in his hand.

58 And Saul said to him, whose son are you, you young man? And David answered, I *am* the son of your servant Jesse the Bethlehemite.

CHAPTER 18

1 And it came to pass, when he had made an end of speaking unto Saul, that the soul of Jonathan was knit with the soul of David, and Jonathan loved him as his own soul.

2 And Saul took him that day, and would let him go no more home to his father's house.

3 Then Jonathan and David made a covenant, because he loved him as his own soul.

4 And Jonathan stripped himself of the robe that *was* upon him, and gave it to David, and his garments, even to his sword and to his bow, and to his girdle.

---

¹ sometimes we must turn from our brothers to 'another' or a leader will turn from his practices to do God's will.
² chose – to *try*, that is (by implication) select. [Strgs#977]
³ stones – to build [Strgs#68]
⁴ bag – something prepared, vessel, weapon, dress, armor [Strgs#3627]
⁵ Scrip- a traveling pouch. [Strgs#3219]
⁶ Shaaraim – *double gate* [Strgs#8189]
⁷ Gath – *wine press* [Strgs#1661]
⁸ Ekron – emigration or *torn up by the roots, eradication.* [Strgs#6138]
⁹ stripling – keep out of sight [Strgs#5958]

5 And David went out whithersoever Saul sent him, *and* behaved himself wisely: and Saul set him over the men of war, and he was accepted in the sight of all the people, and also in the sight of Saul's servants.
6 And it came to pass as they came, when David was returned from the slaughter of the Philistine, that the women came out of all cities of Israel, singing and dancing, to meet King Saul, with tambourines, with joy, and with instruments of music.
7 And the women answered *one another* as they played, and said, Saul has slain his thousands, and David his ten thousands.
8 And Saul was very wroth, and the saying displeased him; and he said, they have ascribed unto David ten thousands, and to me they have ascribed *but* thousands: and *what* can he have more but the kingdom?
9 And Saul eyed David from that day and forward.
10 And it came to pass on the morrow, that the evil spirit from God came upon Saul, and he prophesied in the midst of the house: and David played with his hand, as at other times: and *there was* a javelin in Saul's hand.
11 And Saul cast the javelin; for he said, I will smite David even to the wall *with it*. And David avoided out of his presence twice.
12 And Saul was afraid of David, because the LORD was with him, and was departed from Saul.
13 Therefore Saul removed him from him, and made him his captain over a thousand; and he went out and came in before the people.
14 And David behaved himself wisely in all his ways; and the LORD *was* with him.
15 Wherefore when Saul saw that he behaved himself very wisely, he was afraid of him.
16 But all Israel and Judah loved David, because he went out and came in before them.
17 And Saul said to David, Behold my elder daughter Merab, her will I give you to wife: only be you valiant for me, and fight the LORD'S battles. For Saul said, Let not mine hand be upon him, but let the hand of the Philistines be upon him.
18 And David said unto Saul, Who *am* I? And what *is* my life, *or* my father's family in Israel, that I should be son in law to the king?
19 But it came to pass at the time when Merab Saul's daughter should have been given to David, that she was given unto Adriel the Meholathite to wife.
20 And Michal Saul's daughter loved David: and they told Saul, and the thing pleased him.
21 And Saul said, I will give him her, that she may be a snare to him, and that the hand of the Philistines may be against him. Wherefore Saul said to David, you will this day be my son in law in *the one of* the twain.
22 And Saul commanded his servants, *saying*, Commune with David secretly, and say, Behold, the king has delight in you, and all his servants love you: now therefore be the king's son in law.
23 And Saul's servants spoke those words in the ears of David. And David said, seems it to you *a* light *thing* to be a king's son in law, seeing that I *am* a poor man, and lightly esteemed?
24 And the servants of Saul told him, saying, on this manner spoke David.
25 And Saul said, Thus will you say to David, The king desires not any dowry, but an hundred foreskins of the Philistines, to be avenged of the king's enemies. But Saul thought to make David fall by the hand of the Philistines.
26 And when his servants told David these words, it pleased David well to be the king's son in law: and the days were not expired.
27 Wherefore David arose and went, he and his men, and slew of the Philistines two hundred men; and David brought their foreskins, and they gave them in full tale to the king, that he might be the king's son in law. And Saul gave him Michal his daughter to wife.
28 And Saul saw and knew that the LORD *was* with David, and *that* Michal Saul's daughter loved him.
29 And Saul was yet the more afraid of David; and Saul became David's enemy continually.
30 Then the princes of the Philistines went forth: and it came to pass, after they went forth, *that* David behaved himself more wisely than all the servants of Saul; so that his name was much set by.

CHAPTER 19

1 And Saul spoke to Jonathan his son, and to all his servants, that they should kill David.
2 But Jonathan Saul's son delighted much in David: and Jonathan told David, saying, Saul my father seeks to kill you: now therefore, I pray you, take heed to yourself until the morning, and abide in a secret *place*, and hide yourself:
3 And I will go out and stand beside my father in the field where you *art*, and I will commune with my father of you; and what I see, that I will tell you.
4 And Jonathan spoke good of David unto Saul his father, and said unto him, Let not the king sin against his servant, against David; because he has not sinned against you, and because his works *have been* to you-ward very good:
5 For he did put his life in his hand, and slew the Philistine, and the LORD wrought a great salvation for all Israel: you saw *it*, and didst rejoice: wherefore then will you sin against innocent blood, to slay David without a cause?
6 And Saul hearkened unto the voice of Jonathan: and Saul swore, *As* the LORD lives, he will not be slain.
7 And Jonathan called David, and Jonathan showed him all those things. And Jonathan brought David to Saul, and he was in his presence, as in times past.
8 And there was war again: and David went out, and fought with the Philistines, and slew them with a great slaughter; and they fled from him.
9 And the evil spirit from the LORD was upon Saul, as he sat in his house with his javelin in his hand: and David played with *his* hand.
10 And Saul sought to smite David even to the wall with the javelin; but he slipped away out of Saul's presence, and he smote the javelin into the wall: and David fled, and escaped that night.
11 Saul also sent messengers unto David's house, to watch him, and to slay him in the morning: and Michal David's wife told him, saying, If you save not your life tonight, tomorrow you will be slain.
12 So Michal let David down through a window: and he went, and fled, and escaped.
13 And Michal took an image, and laid *it* in the bed, and put a pillow of goats' *hair* for his bolster, and covered *it* with a cloth.
14 And when Saul sent messengers to take David, she said, He *is* sick.
15 And Saul sent the messengers *again* to see David, saying, Bring him up to me in the bed, that I may slay him.
16 And when the messengers were come in, behold, *there was* an image in the bed, with a pillow of goats' *hair* for his bolster.

17 And Saul said unto Michal, Why have you deceived me so, and sent away mine enemy, that he is escaped? And Michal answered Saul, He said unto me, Let me go; why should I kill you?
18 So David fled, and escaped, and came to Samuel to Ramah, and told him all that Saul had done to him. And he and Samuel went and dwelt in Naioth.
19 And it was told Saul, saying, Behold, David *is* at Naioth in Ramah.
20 And Saul sent messengers to take David: and when they saw the company of the prophets prophesying, and Samuel standing *as* appointed over them, the Spirit of God was upon the messengers of Saul, and they also prophesied.
21 And when it was told Saul, he sent other messengers, and they prophesied likewise. And Saul sent messengers again the third time, and they prophesied also.
22 Then went he also to Ramah, and came to a great well that *is* in Sechu: and he asked and said, where *are* Samuel and David? And *one* said, Behold, *they be* at Naioth in Ramah.
23 And he went there to Naioth in Ramah: and the Spirit of God was upon him also, and he went on, and prophesied, until he came to Naioth in Ramah.
24 And he stripped off his clothes also, and prophesied before Samuel in like manner, and lay down naked all that day and all that night. Wherefore they say, *Is* Saul also among the prophets?

CHAPTER 20

1 And David fled from Naioth in Ramah, and came and said before Jonathan, What have I done? What *is* mine iniquity? And what *is* my sin before your father, that he seeks my life?
2 And he said unto him, God forbid; you will not die: behold, my father will do nothing either great or small, but that he will show it me: and why should my father hide this thing from me? it *is* not *so*.
3 And David swore moreover, and said, your father certainly knows that I have found grace in your eyes; and he said, Let not Jonathan know this, lest he be grieved: but truly *as* the LORD lives, and *as* your soul lives, *there is* but a step between me and death.
4 Then said Jonathan unto David, Whatsoever your soul desires, I will even do *it* for you.
5 And David said unto Jonathan, Behold, tomorrow *is* the new moon, and I should not fail to sit with the king at meat: but let me go, that I may hide myself in the field unto the third *day* at even.
6 If your father at all miss me, then say, David earnestly asked *leave* of me that he might run to Beth-lehem his city: for *there is* a yearly sacrifice there for all the family.
7 If he say thus, *It is* well; your servant will have peace: but if he be very wroth, *then* be sure that evil is determined by him.
8 Therefore you will deal kindly with your servant; for you have brought your servant into a covenant of the LORD with you: notwithstanding, if there be in me iniquity, slay me yourself; for why should you bring me to your father?
9 And Jonathan said, far be it from you: for if I knew certainly that evil were determined by my father to come upon you, then would not I tell it you?
10 Then said David to Jonathan, Who will tell me? Or what *if* your father answer you roughly?
11 And Jonathan said unto David, Come, and let us go out into the field. And they went out both of them into the field.
12 And Jonathan said unto David, O LORD God of Israel, when I have sounded my father about tomorrow any time, *or* the third *day*, and, behold, *if there be* good toward David, and I then send not unto you, and show it you;
13 The LORD do so and much more to Jonathan: but if it please my father *to do* you evil, then I will show it you, and send you away, that you may go in peace: and the LORD be with you as he has been with my father.
14 And you will not only while yet I live show me the kindness of the LORD, that I die not:
15 But *also* you will not cut off your kindness from my house for ever: no, not when the LORD has cut off the enemies of David everyone from the face of the earth.
16 So Jonathan made *a* covenant with the house of David, *saying*, Let the LORD even require *it* at the hand of David's enemies.
17 And Jonathan caused David to swear again, because he loved him: for he loved him as he loved his own soul.
18 Then Jonathan said to David, tomorrow *is* the new moon: and you will be missed, because your seat will be empty.
19 And *when* you have stayed three days, *then* you will go down quickly, and come to the place where you didst hide yourself when the business was *in* hand, and will remain by the stone Ezel.
20 And I will shoot three arrows on the side *thereof*, as though I shot at a mark.
21 And, behold, I will send a lad, *saying*, Go, find out the arrows. If I expressly say unto the lad, Behold, the arrows *are* on this side of you, take them; then come you: for *there is* peace to you, and no hurt; *as* the LORD lives.
22 But if I say thus unto the young man, Behold, the arrows *are* beyond you; go your way: for the LORD has sent you away.
23 And *as touching* the matter which you and I have spoken of, behold, the LORD *be* between you and me forever.
24 So David hid himself in the field: and when the new moon was come, the king sat him down to eat meat.
25 And the king sat upon his seat, as at other times, *even* upon a seat by the wall: and Jonathan arose, and Abner sat by Saul's side, and David's place was empty.
26 Nevertheless Saul spoke not anything that day: for he thought, something has befallen him, he *is* not clean; surely he *is* not clean.
27 And it came to pass on the morrow, *which was* the second *day* of the month, that David's place was empty: and Saul said unto Jonathan his son, wherefore cometh not the son of Jesse to meat, neither yesterday, or to day?
28 And Jonathan answered Saul, David earnestly asked *leave* of me to go to Beth-lehem:
29 And he said, Let me go, I pray you; for our family has a sacrifice in the city; and my brother, he has commanded me *to be there*: and now, if I have found favor in your eyes, let me get away, I pray you, and see my brethren. Therefore he cometh not unto the king's table.
30 Then Saul's anger was kindled against Jonathan, and he said unto him, you son of the perverse rebellious *woman*, do not I know that you have chosen the son of Jesse to your own confusion, and unto the confusion of your mother's nakedness?
31 For as long as the son of Jesse lives upon the ground, you will not be established, or your kingdom. Wherefore now send and fetch him unto me, for he will surely die.
32 And Jonathan answered Saul his father, and said unto him, wherefore will he be slain? What has he done?
33 And Saul cast a javelin at him to smite him: whereby Jonathan knew that it was determined of his father to slay David.
34 So Jonathan arose from the table in fierce anger, and did eat no meat the second day of the month: for he was grieved for David, because his father had done him shame.

35 And it came to pass in the morning, that Jonathan went out into the field at the time appointed with David, and a little lad with him.
36 And he said unto his lad, run, find out now the arrows which I shoot. *And* as the lad ran, he shot an arrow beyond him.
37 And when the lad was come to the place of the arrow which Jonathan had shot, Jonathan cried after the lad, and said, *Is not* the arrow beyond you?
38 And Jonathan cried after the lad, make speed, haste, stay not. And Jonathan's lad gathered up the arrows, and came to his master.
39 But the lad knew not anything: only Jonathan and David knew the matter.
40 And Jonathan gave his artillery unto his lad, and said unto him, Go, carry *them* to the city.
41 *And* as soon as the lad was gone, David arose out of *a place* toward the south, and fell on his face to the ground, and bowed himself three times: and they kissed one another, and wept one with another, until David exceeded.
42 And Jonathan said to David, go in peace, forasmuch as we have sworn both of us in the name of the LORD, saying, The LORD be between me and you, and between my seed and your seed forever. And he arose and departed: and Jonathan went into the city.

CHAPTER 21

1 Then came David to Nob to Ahimelech the priest: and Ahimelech was afraid at the meeting of David, and said unto him, why are you alone, and no man with you?
2 And David said unto Ahimelech the priest, The king has commanded me a business, and has said unto me, Let no man know anything of the business where about I send you, and what I have commanded you: and I have appointed *my* servants to such and such a place.
3 Now therefore what is under your hand? Give *me* five *loaves of* bread in mine hand, or what there is present.
4 And the priest answered David, and said, *there is* no common bread under **my** hand, but there is hallowed bread; if the young men have kept themselves at least from women.
5 And David answered the priest, and said unto him, Of a truth women *have been* kept from us about these three days, since I came out, and the vessels of the young men are holy, and *the bread is* in a manner common, yea, though it were sanctified this day in the vessel.
6 So the priest gave him hallowed *bread*: for there was no bread there but the showbread, that was taken from before the LORD, to put hot bread in the day when it was taken away.
7 Now a certain man of the servants of Saul *was* there that day, detained before the LORD; and his name *was* Doeg[1], an Edomite, the chief of the herdsmen that *belonged* to Saul.
8 And David said unto Ahimelech, And is there not here under your hand spear or sword? For I have neither brought my sword or my weapons with me, because the king's business required haste.
9 And the priest said, the sword[2] of Goliath the Philistine, whom you slaughter in the valley of Elah, behold, it *is here* wrapped in a cloth behind the ephod: if you will take that, take *it*: for *there is* no other save that here. And David said, *there is* none like that; give it me.
10 And David arose, and fled that day for fear of Saul, and went to Achish the king of Gath.
11 And the servants of Achish said unto him, *Is* not this David the king of the land? Did they not sing one to another of him in dances, saying, Saul has slain his thousands, and David his ten thousands?
12 And David laid up these words in his heart, and was sore afraid of Achish the king of Gath.
13 And he changed his behavior before them, and feigned himself mad in their hands, and scrabbled on the doors of the gate, and let his spittle fall down upon his beard.
14 Then said Achish unto his servants, Lo, you see the man is mad: wherefore *then* have you brought him to me?
15 Have I need of mad men, that you have brought this *fellow* to play the mad man in my presence? Will this *fellow* come into my house?

CHAPTER 22

1 David therefore departed there, and escaped to the cave Adullam: and when his brethren and his **entire** father's house heard *it*, they went down there to him.
2 And every one *that was* in distress, and every one that *was* in debt, and every one *that was* discontented, gathered themselves unto him; and he became a captain over them: and there were with him about four hundred men.
3 And David went there to Mizpeh of Moab: and he said unto the king of Moab, Let my father and my mother, I pray you, come forth, *and be* with you, till I know what God will do for me.
4 And he brought them before the king of Moab: and they dwelt with him all the while that David was in the hold.
5 And the prophet Gad said unto David, Abide not in the hold; depart, and get you into the land of Judah. Then David departed, and came into the forest of Hareth.
6 When Saul heard that David was discovered, and the men that *were* with him, (now Saul abode in Gibeah under a tree in Ramah, having his spear in his hand, and all his servants *were* standing about him;)
7 Then Saul said unto his servants that stood about him, Hear now, you Benjamites; will the son of Jesse give every one of you fields and vineyards, *and* make you all captains of thousands, and captains of hundreds;
8 That all of you have conspired against me, and *there is* none that shows me that my son has made a league with the son of Jesse, and *there is* none of you that is sorry for me, or shows unto me that my son has stirred up my servant against me, to lie in wait, as at this day?
9 Then answered Doeg the Edomite, which was set over the servants of Saul, and said, I saw the son of Jesse coming to Nob, to Ahimelech the son of Ahitub.
10 And he enquired of the LORD for him, and gave him victuals, and gave him the sword of Goliath the Philistine.
11 Then the king sent to call Ahimelech the priest, the son of Ahitub, and his **entire** father's house, the priests that *were* in Nob: and they came all of them to the king.
12 And Saul said, Hear now, you son of Ahitub. And he answered, Here I *am*, my lord.
13 And Saul said unto him, Why have you conspired against me, you and the son of Jesse, in that you have given him bread, and a

---

[1] Doeg – fearing, anxious [Strgs#1673]
[2] the same word the Devil used against Jesus is the same word's Jesus use to over His enemies, compare **Matthew 4**.

sword, and have enquired of God for him, that he should rise against me, to lie in wait, as at this day?

14 Then Ahimelech answered the king, and said, and who *is so* faithful among all your servants as David, which is the king's son in law, and goes at your bidding, and is honorable in your house?

15 Did I then begin to enquire of God for him? Be it far from me: let not the king impute *any*thing unto his servant, or to all the house of my father: for your servant knew nothing of all this, less or more.

16 And the king said, you will surely die, Ahimelech, you, and your **entire** father's house.

17 And the king said unto the footmen that stood about him, Turn, and slay the priests of the LORD; because their hand also *is* with David, and because they knew when he fled, and did not show it to me. But the servants of the king would not put forth their hand to fall upon the priests of the LORD.

18 And the king said to Doeg, Turn you, and fall upon the priests. And Doeg the Edomite turned, and he fell upon the priests, and slew on that day fourscore and five persons that did wear a linen ephod.

19 And Nob, the city of the priests, smote he with the edge of the sword, both men and women, children and sucklings, and oxen, and asses, and sheep, with the edge of the sword.

20 And one of the sons of Ahimelech the son of Ahitub, named Abiathar, escaped, and fled after David.

21 And Abiathar showed David that Saul had slain the LORD'S priests.

22 And David said unto Abiathar, I knew *it* that day, when Doeg the Edomite *was* there, that he would surely tell Saul: I have occasioned *the death* of all the persons of your father's house.

23 Abide you with me, fear not: for he that seeks my life seeks your life: but with me you will *be* in safeguard.

CHAPTER 23

1 Then they told David, saying, Behold, the Philistines fight against Keilah, and they rob the threshing floors.

2 Therefore David enquired of the LORD, saying, will I go and smite these Philistines? And the LORD said unto David, Go, and smite the Philistines, and save Keilah.

3 And David's men said unto him, Behold, we be afraid here in Judah: how much more then if we come to Keilah against the armies of the Philistines?

4 Then David enquired of the LORD yet again. And the LORD answered him and said, Arise, go down to Keilah; for I will deliver the Philistines into your hand.

5 So David and his men went to Keilah, and fought with the Philistines, and brought away their cattle, and smote them with a great slaughter. So David saved the inhabitants of Keilah.

6 And it came to pass, when Abiathar the son of Ahimelech fled to David to Keilah, *that* he came down *with* an ephod in his hand.

7 And it was told Saul that David was come to Keilah. And Saul said, God has delivered him into mine hand; for he is shut in, by entering into a town that has gates and bars.

8 And Saul called all the people together to war, to go down to Keilah, to besiege David and his men.

9 And David knew that Saul secretly practised mischief against him; and he said to Abiathar the priest, bring here the ephod.

10 Then said David, O LORD God of Israel, your servant has certainly heard that Saul seeks to come to Keilah, to destroy the city for my sake.

11 Will the men of Keilah deliver me up into his hand? Will Saul come down, as your servant has heard? O LORD God of Israel, I beseech you, tell your servant. And the LORD said, He will come down.

12 Then said David, Will the men of Keilah deliver me and my men into the hand of Saul? And the LORD said, they will deliver you up.

13 Then David and his men, *which were* about six hundred, arose and departed out of Keilah, and went whithersoever they could go. And it was told to Saul that David was escaped from Keilah; and he **left** to go forth.

14 And David abode in the wilderness in strong holds, and remained in a mountain in the wilderness of Ziph. And Saul sought him every day, but God delivered him not into his hand.

15 And David saw that Saul was come out to seek his life: and David *was* in the wilderness of Ziph in a wood.

16 And Jonathan Saul's son arose, and went to David into the wood, and strengthened his hand in God.

17 And he said unto him, Fear not: for the hand of Saul my father will not find you; and you will be king over Israel, and I will be next unto you; and that also Saul my father knows.

18 And they two made a covenant before the LORD: and David abode in the wood, and Jonathan went to his house.

19 Then came up the Ziphites to Saul to Gibeah, saying, does not David hide himself with us in strong holds in the wood, in the hill of Hachilah, which *is* on the south of Jeshimon?

20 Now therefore, O king, come down according to all the desire of your soul to come down; and our part will *be* to deliver him into the king's hand.

21 And Saul said, blessed *be* you of the LORD; for you have compassion on me.

22 Go, I pray you, prepare yet, and know and see his place where his haunt is, *and* who has seen him there: for it is told me *that* he deals very **cunningly**.

23 See therefore, and take knowledge of all the lurking places where he hides himself, and come you again to me with the certainty, and I will go with you: and it will come to pass, if he be in the land, that I will search him out throughout all the thousands of Judah.

24 And they arose, and went to Ziph before Saul: but David and his men *were* in the wilderness of Maon, in the plain on the south of Jeshimon.

25 Saul also and his men went to seek *him*. And they told David: wherefore he came down into a rock, and abode in the wilderness of Maon. And when Saul heard *that*, he pursued after David in the wilderness of Maon.

26 And Saul went on this side of the mountain, and David and his men on that side of the mountain: and David made haste to get away for fear of Saul; for Saul and his men compassed David and his men round about to take them.

27 But there came a messenger unto Saul, saying, Haste you, and come; for the Philistines have invaded the land.

28 Wherefore Saul returned from pursuing after David, and went against the Philistines: therefore they called that place Selahammahlekoth[1].

29 And David went up from there, and dwelt in strong holds at En-gedi.

---

[1] Selahammahlekoth- rock of division or the cliff of escapes. [Strgs#5555]

CHAPTER 24

1 And it came to pass, when Saul was returned from following the Philistines, that it was told him, saying, Behold, David *is* in the wilderness of En-gedi.
2 Then Saul took three thousand chosen men out of all Israel, and went to seek David and his men upon the rocks of the wild goats.
3 And he came to the sheepcotes by the way, where *was* a cave; and Saul went in to cover his feet: and David and his men remained in the sides of the cave.
4 And the men of David said unto him, Behold the day of which the LORD said unto you, Behold, I will deliver your enemy into your hand, that you may do to him as it will seem good unto you. Then David arose, and cut off the skirt of Saul's robe privily[1].
5 And it came to pass afterward, that David's heart smote him, because he had cut off Saul's skirt.
6 And he said unto his men, The LORD forbid that I should do this thing unto my master, the LORD'S anointed, to stretch forth mine hand against him, seeing he *is* the anointed of the LORD.
7 So David stayed his servants with these words, and suffered them not to rise against Saul. But Saul rose up out of the cave, and went on *his* way.
8 David also arose afterward, and went out of the cave, and cried after Saul, saying, my lord the king. And when Saul looked behind him, David stooped with his face to the earth, and bowed himself.
9 And David said to Saul, Wherefore hear you men's words, saying, Behold, David seeks your hurt?
10 Behold, this day your eyes have seen how that the LORD had delivered you today into mine hand in the cave: and *some* bade *me* kill you: but *mine eye* spared you; and I said, I will not put forth mine hand against my lord; for he *is* the LORD'S anointed.
11 Moreover, my father, see, yea, see the skirt of your robe in my hand: for in that I cut off the skirt of your robe, and killed you not, know you and see that *there is* neither evil or transgression in mine hand, and I have not sinned against you; yet you hunt my soul to take it.
12 The LORD judge between me and you, and the LORD avenge me of you: but mine hand will not be upon you.
13 As said the proverb of the ancients, Wickedness proceeds from the wicked: but mine hand will not be upon you.
14 After whom is the king of Israel come out? After whom dost you pursue? After a dead dog, after a flea.
15 The LORD therefore is judge, and judge between me and you, and sees, and pleads my cause, and delivers me out of your hand.
16 And it came to pass, when David had made an end of speaking these words unto Saul, that Saul said, *is* this your voice, my son David? And Saul lifted up his voice, and wept.
17 And he said to David, you are more righteous than I: for you have rewarded me good, whereas I have rewarded you evil.
18 And you have showed this day how that you have dealt well with me: forasmuch as when the LORD had delivered me into your hand, you killed me not.
19 For if a man finds his enemy, will he let him go well away? Wherefore the LORD rewards you good for that you have done unto me this day.
20 And now, behold, I know well that you will surely be king, and that the kingdom of Israel will be established in your hand.
21 Swear now therefore unto me by the LORD, that you will not cut off my seed after me, and that you will not destroy my name out of my father's house.
22 And David swore unto Saul. And Saul went home; but David and his men gat them up unto the hold.

CHAPTER 25

1 And Samuel died; and all the Israelites were gathered together, and lamented him, and buried him in his house at Ramah And David arose, and went down to the wilderness of Paran.
2 And *there was* a man in Maon, whose possessions *were* in Carmel; and the man *was* very great, and he had three thousand sheep, and a thousand goats: and he was shearing his sheep in Carmel.
3 Now the name of the man *was* Nabal; and the name of his wife Abigail: and *she was* a woman of good understanding, and of a beautiful countenance: but the man *was* churlish and evil in his doings; and he *was* of the house of Caleb.
4 And David heard in the wilderness that Nabal did shear his sheep.
5 And David sent out ten young men, and David said unto the young men, Get you up to Carmel, and go to Nabal, and greet him in my name:
6 And thus will you say to him that lives *in prosperity*, Peace *be* both to you, and peace *be* to your house, and peace *be* unto all that you hast.
7 And now I have heard that you have shearers: now your shepherds which were with us, we hurt them not, neither was there ought missing unto them, all the while they were in Carmel.
8 Ask your young men, and they will show you. Wherefore let the young men find favor in your eyes: for we come in a good day: give, I pray you, whatsoever cometh to your hand unto your servants, and to your son David.
9 And when David's young men came, they spoke to Nabal according to all those words in the name of David, and ceased.
10 And Nabal answered David's servants, and said, who *is* David? And who *is* the son of Jesse? There are many servants now days that break away every man from his master.
11 will I then take my bread, and my water, and my flesh that I have killed for my shearers, and give *it* unto men, whom I know not where they *be*?
12 So David's young men turned their way, and went again, and came and told him all those sayings.
13 And David said unto his men, Gird you on every man his sword. And they girded on every man his sword; and David also girded on his sword: and there went up after David about four hundred men; and two hundred abode by the stuff.
14 But one of the young men told Abigail, Nabal's wife, saying, Behold, David sent messengers out of the wilderness to salute our master; and he railed on them.
15 But the men *were* very good unto us, and we were not hurt, neither missed we anything, as long as we were conversant with them, when we were in the fields:
16 They were a wall unto us both by night and day, all the while we were with them keeping the sheep.
17 Now therefore know and consider what you will do; for evil is determined against our master, and against his **entire** household: for he *is* such a son of Belial, that *a man* cannot speak to him.

---

[1] privily- is defined as covered, that which is secret or covertly, enchantment and softly. It derives from to root words one meaning muffled, silently and softly. And the second meaning to wrap up and cast. [Strgs#3909]

18 Then Abigail made haste, and took two hundred loaves, and two bottles of wine, and five sheep ready dressed, and five measures of parched *corn*, and an hundred clusters of raisins, and two hundred cakes of figs, and laid *them* on asses.
19 And she said unto her servants, Go on before me; behold, I come after you. But she told not her husband Nabal.
20 And it was *so, as* she rode on the ass, that she came down by the covert of the hill, and, behold, David and his men came down against her; and she met them.
21 Now David had said, surely in vain have I kept all that this *fellow* has in the wilderness, so that nothing was missed of all that *pertained* unto him: and he has requited me evil for good.
22 So and more also do God unto the enemies of David, if I leave of all that *pertain* to him by the morning light any that urinates against the wall.
23 And when Abigail saw David, she hasted, and lighted off the ass, and fell before David on her face, and bowed herself to the ground,
24 And fell at his feet, and said, upon me, my lord, *upon* me *let this* iniquity *be*: and let your handmaid, I pray you, speak in your audience, and hear the words of your handmaid.
25 Let not my lord, I pray you, regard this man of Belial, *even* Nabal: for as his name *is*, so *is* he; Nabal *is* his name, and folly *is* with him: but I your handmaid saw not the young men of my lord, whom you didst send.
26 Now therefore, my lord, *as* the LORD lives, and *as* your soul lives, seeing the LORD has withheld you from coming to *shed* blood, and from avenging yourself with your own hand, now let your enemies, and they that seek evil to my lord, be as Nabal.
27 And now this blessing which your handmaid has brought unto my lord, let it even be given unto the young men that follow my lord.
28 I pray you, forgive the trespass of your handmaid: for the LORD will certainly make my lord a sure house; because my lord fights the battles of the LORD, and evil has not been found in you *all* your days.
29 Yet a man is raised to pursue you, and to seek your soul: but the soul of my lord will be bound in the bundle of life with the LORD your God; and the souls of your enemies, them will he sling out, *as out* of the middle of a sling.
30 And it will come to pass, when the LORD will have done to my lord according to all the good that he has spoken concerning you, and will have appointed you ruler over Israel;
31 That this will be no grief unto you, or offence of heart unto my lord, either that you have shed blood causeless, or that my lord has avenged himself: but when the LORD will have dealt well with my lord, then remember your handmaid.
32 And David said to Abigail, Blessed *be* the LORD God of Israel, which sent you this day to meet me:
33 And blessed *be* your advice, and blessed *be* you, which have kept me this day from coming to *shed* blood, and from avenging myself with mine own hand.
34 For in very deed, *as* the LORD God of Israel lives, which has kept me back from hurting you, except you **have** hasted and come to meet me, surely there had not been left unto Nabal by the morning light any that urinates against the wall.
35 So David received of her hand *that* which she had brought him, and said unto her, Go up in peace to your house; see, I have hearkened to your voice, and have accepted your person.
36 And Abigail came to Nabal; and, behold, he held a feast in his house, like the feast of a king; and Nabal's heart *was* merry within him, for he *was* very drunken: wherefore she told him nothing, less or more, until the morning light.
37 But it came to pass in the morning, when the wine was gone out of Nabal, and his wife had told him these things that his heart died within him, and he became *as* a stone.
38 And it came to pass about ten days *after*, that the LORD smote Nabal, that he died.
39 And when David heard that Nabal was dead, he said, blessed *be* the LORD, that has pleaded the cause of my reproach from the hand of Nabal, and has kept his servant from evil for the LORD has returned the wickedness of Nabal upon his own head. And David sent and communed with Abigail, to take her to him to wife.
40 And when the servants of David were come to Abigail to Carmel, they spoke unto her, saying, David sent us unto you, to take you to him to wife.
41 And she arose, and bowed herself on *her* face to the earth, and said, Behold, *let* your handmaid *be* a servant to wash the feet of the servants of my lord.
42 And Abigail hasted, and arose, and rode upon an ass, with five damsels of hers that went after her; and she went after the messengers of David, and became his wife.
43 David also took Ahinoam of Jezreel; and they were also both of them his wives.
44 But Saul had given Michal his daughter, David's wife, to Phalti the son of Laish, which *was* of Gallim.

CHAPTER 26

1 And the Ziphites came unto Saul to Gibeah, saying, does not David hide himself in the hill of Hachilah, *which is* before Jeshimon?
2 Then Saul arose, and went down to the wilderness of Ziph, having three thousand chosen men of Israel with him, to seek David in the wilderness of Ziph.
3 And Saul pitched in the hill of Hachilah, which *is* before Jeshimon, by the way. But David abode in the wilderness, and he saw that Saul came after him into the wilderness.
4 David therefore sent out spies, and understood that Saul was come in very deed.
5 And David arose, and came to the place where Saul had pitched: and David beheld the place where Saul lay, and Abner the son of Ner, the captain of his host: and Saul lay in the trench, and the people pitched round about him.
6 Then answered David and said to Ahimelech the Hittite, and to Abishai the son of Zeruiah, brother to Joab, saying, who will go down with me to Saul to the camp? And Abishai said, I will go down with you.
7 So David and Abishai came to the people by night: and, behold, Saul lay sleeping within the trench, and his spear stuck in the ground at his bolster: but Abner and the people lay round about him.
8 Then said Abishai to David, God has delivered your enemy into your hand this day: now therefore let me smite him, I pray you, with the spear even to the earth at once, and I will not *smite* him the second time.
9 And David said to Abishai, Destroy him not: for who can stretch forth his hand against the LORD'S anointed, and be guiltless?
10 David said furthermore, *As* the LORD lives, the LORD will smite him; or his day will come to die; or he will descend into battle, and perish.

11 The LORD forbid that I should stretch forth mine hand against the LORD'S anointed: but, I pray you, take you now the spear that *is* at his bolster, and the cruse of water, and let us go.
12 So David took the spear and the cruse of water from Saul's bolster; and they gat them away, and no man saw *it*, or knew *it*, neither awaked: for they *were* all asleep; because a deep sleep from the LORD was fallen upon them.
13 Then David went over to the other side, and stood on the top of an hill afar off; a great space *being* between them:
14 And David cried to the people, and to Abner the son of Ner, saying, answered you not, Abner? Then Abner answered and said, who are you *that* cried to the king?
15 And David said to Abner, are not you a *valiant* man? and who *is* like to you in Israel? Wherefore then have you not kept your lord the king? for there came one of the people in to destroy the king your lord.
16 This thing *is* not good that you have done. As the LORD lives, you *are* worthy to die, because you have not kept your master, the LORD'S anointed. And now see where the king's spear *is*, and the cruse of water that *was* at his bolster.
17 And Saul knew David's voice, and said, *Is* this your voice, my son David? And David said, *it is* my voice, my lord, O king.
18 And he said, wherefore does my lord thus pursue after his servant? For what have I done? Or what evil *is* in mine hand?
19 Now therefore, I pray you, let my lord the king hear the words of his servant. If the LORD have stirred you up against me, let him accept an offering: but if *they be* the children of men, cursed *be* they before the LORD; for they have driven me out this day from abiding in the inheritance of the LORD, saying, Go, serve other gods.
20 Now therefore, let not my blood fall to the earth before the face of the LORD: for the king of Israel is come out to seek a flea, as when one does hunt a partridge in the mountains.
21 Then said Saul, I have sinned: return, my son David: for I will no more do you harm, because my soul was precious in your eyes this day: behold, I have played the fool, and have erred exceedingly.
22 And David answered and said, behold the king's spear! And let one of the young men come over and fetch it.
23 The LORD render to every man his righteousness and his faithfulness: for the LORD delivered you into *my* hand to day, but I would not stretch forth mine hand against the LORD'S anointed.
24 And, behold, as your life was much set by this day in mine eyes, so let my life be much set by in the eyes of the LORD, and let him deliver me out of all tribulation.
25 Then Saul said to David, Blessed *be* you, my son David: you will both do great *things*, and also will still prevail. So David went on his way, and Saul returned to his place.

CHAPTER 27

1 And David said in his heart, I will now perish one day by the hand of Saul: *there is* nothing better for me than that I should speedily escape into the land of the Philistines; and Saul will despair of me, to seek me any more in any coast of Israel: so will I escape out of his hand.
2 And David arose, and he passed over with the six hundred men that *were* with him unto Achish, the son of Maoch, king of Gath.
3 And David dwelt with Achish at Gath, he and his men, every man with his household, *even* David with his two wives, Ahinoam the Jezreelitess, and Abigail the Carmelitess, Nabal's wife.
4 And it was told Saul that David was fled to Gath: and he sought no more again for him.
5 And David said unto Achish, If I have now found grace in your eyes, let them give me a place in some town in the country, that I may dwell there: for why should your servant dwell in the royal city with you?
6 Then Achish gave him Ziklag that day: wherefore Ziklag pertains unto the kings of Judah unto this day.
7 [And the time that David dwelt in the country of the Philistines was a full year and four months.]¹
8 And David and his men went up, and invaded the Geshurites, and the Gezrites, and the Amalekites: for those *nations were* of old the inhabitants of the land, as you go to Shur, even unto the land of Egypt.
9 And David smote the land, and left neither man or woman alive, and took away the sheep, and the oxen, and the asses, and the camels, and the apparel, and returned, and came to Achish.
10 And Achish said, whither have you made a road to day? And David said, against the south of Judah, and against the south of the Jerahmeelites, and against the south of the Kenites.
11 And David saved neither man or woman alive, to bring *tidings* to Gath, saying, Lest they should tell on us, saying, So did David, and so *will be* his manner all the while he dwells in the country of the Philistines.
12 And Achish believed David, saying, He has made his people Israel utterly to abhor him; therefore he will be my servant forever.

CHAPTER 28

1 And it came to pass in those days, that the Philistines gathered their armies together for warfare, to fight with Israel. And Achish said unto David, Know you assuredly, that you will go out with me to battle, you and your men.
2 And David said to Achish, Surely you will know what your servant can do. And Achish said to David, Therefore will I make you keeper of mine head for ever.
3 Now Samuel was dead, and all Israel had lamented him, and buried him in Ramah, even in his own city. And Saul had put away those that had familiar spirits, and the wizards, out of the land.
4 And the Philistines gathered themselves together, and came and pitched in Shunem: and Saul gathered all Israel together, and they pitched in Gilboa.
5 And when Saul saw the host of the Philistines, he was afraid, and his heart greatly trembled.
6 And when Saul enquired of the LORD, the LORD answered him not, neither by dreams, or by Urim, or by prophets.
7 Then said Saul unto his servants, seek me a woman that has a familiar spirit, that I may go to her, and enquire of her. And his servants said to him, Behold, *there is* a woman that has a familiar spirit at En-dor².
8 And Saul disguised himself, and put on other raiment, and he went, and two men with him, and they came to the woman by night: and he said, I pray you, divine unto me by the familiar spirit, and bring me *him* up, whom I will name unto you.
9 And the woman said unto him, Behold, you know what Saul has done, how he has cut off those that have familiar spirits, and the

---
¹ lit. 480 day
² Endor- fountain of dwelling or fountain of Dor. Endor is the combination of two Hebrew root words, the first being *'ayin*, which means an eye (being mental and spiritual). The second root word being *dôr*, which means a revolution of time, an age or generation, also a dwelling, evermore posterity. [Strgs#5874=5869+1755]

wizards, out of the land: wherefore then lay you a snare for my life, to cause me to die?

10 And Saul swore to her by the LORD, saying, *As* the LORD lives, there will no punishment happen to you for this thing.

11 Then said the woman, whom will I bring up unto you? And he said, bring me up Samuel.

12 And when the woman saw Samuel, she cried with a loud voice: and the woman spoke to Saul, saying, why have you deceived me? For you are Saul.

13 And the king said unto her, Be not afraid: for what saw you? And the woman said unto Saul, I saw gods ascending out of the earth.

14 And he said unto her, what form *is* he of? And she said, an old man cometh up; and he *is* covered with a mantle. And Saul perceived that it *was* Samuel, and he stooped with *his* face to the ground, and bowed himself.

15 And Samuel said to Saul, why have you disquieted me, to bring me up? And Saul answered, I am sore distressed; for the Philistines make war against me, and God is departed from me, and answer me no more, neither by prophets, or by dreams: therefore I have called you, that you may make known unto me what I will do.

16 Then said Samuel, Wherefore then dost you ask of me, seeing the LORD is departed from you, and is become your enemy?

17 And the LORD has done to him, as he spoke by me: for the LORD has rent the kingdom out of your hand, and given it to your neighbor, *even* to David:

18 Because you obeyed not the voice of the LORD, or executed his fierce wrath upon Amalek, therefore has the LORD done this thing unto you this day.

19 Moreover the LORD will also deliver Israel with you into the hand of the Philistines: and tomorrow will you and your sons *be* with me: the LORD also will deliver the host of Israel into the hand of the Philistines.

20 Then Saul fell straightway all along on the earth, and was sore afraid, because of the words of Samuel: and there was no strength in him; for he had eaten no bread all the day, or all the night.

21 And the woman came unto Saul, and saw that he was sore troubled, and said unto him, Behold, your handmaid has obeyed your voice, and I have put my life in my hand, and have hearkened unto your words which you spoke unto me.

22 Now therefore, I pray you, hearken you also unto the voice of your handmaid, and let me set a morsel of bread before you; and eat, that you may have strength, when you go on your way.

23 But he refused, and said, I will not eat. But his servants, together with the woman, compelled him; and he hearkened unto their voice. So he arose from the earth, and sat upon the bed.

24 And the woman had a fat calf in the house; and she hasted, and killed it, and took flour, and kneaded *it*, and did bake unleavened bread thereof:

25 And she brought *it* before Saul, and before his servants; and they did eat. Then they rose up, and went away that night.

CHAPTER 29

1 Now the Philistines gathered together all their armies to Aphek: and the Israelites pitched by a fountain which *is* in Jezreel.

2 And the lords of the Philistines passed on by hundreds, and by thousands: but David and his men passed on in the rereward[1] with Achish.

3 Then said the princes of the Philistines, What *do* these Hebrews *here*? And Achish said unto the princes of the Philistines, *Is* not this David, the servant of Saul the king of Israel, which has been with me these days, or these years, and I have found no fault in him since he fell *unto me* unto this day?

4 And the princes of the Philistines were wroth with him; and the princes of the Philistines said unto him, Make this fellow return, that he may go again to his place which you have appointed him, and let him not go down with us to battle, lest in the battle he be an adversary to us: for wherewith should he reconcile himself unto his master? Should it not be with the heads of these men?

5 *Is* not this David, of whom they sang one to another in dances, saying, Saul slew his thousands, and David his ten thousands?

6 Then Achish called David, and said unto him, Surely, *as* the LORD lives, you have been upright, and your going out and your coming in with me in the host *is* good in my sight: for I have not found evil in you since the day of your coming unto me unto this day: nevertheless the lords favor you not.

7 Wherefore now return, and go in peace, that you displease not the lords of the Philistines.

8 And David said unto Achish, but what have I done? And what have you found in your servant so long as I have been with you unto this day, that I may not go fight against the enemies of my lord the king?

9 And Achish answered and said to David, I know that you are good in my sight, as an angel of God: notwithstanding the princes of the Philistines have said, He will not go up with us to the battle.

10 Wherefore now rise up early in the morning with your master's servants that are come with you: and as soon as you be up early in the morning, and have light, depart.

11 So David and his men rose up early to depart in the morning, to return into the land of the Philistines. And the Philistines went up to Jezreel.

CHAPTER 30

1 And it came to pass, when David and his men were come to Ziklag on the third day, that the Amalekites had invaded the south, and Ziklag, and smitten Ziklag, and burned it with fire;

2 And had taken the women captives, that *were* therein: they slew not any, either great or small, but carried *them* away, and went on their way.

3 So David and his men came to the city, and, behold, *it was* burned with fire; and their wives, and their sons, and their daughters, were taken captives.

4 Then David and the people that *were* with him lifted up their voice and wept, until they had no more power to weep.

5 And David's two wives were taken captives, Ahinoam the Jezreelitess, and Abigail the wife of Nabal the Carmelite.

6 And David was greatly distressed; for the people spoke of stoning him, because the soul of all the people was grieved, every man for his sons and for his daughters: but David encouraged himself in the LORD his God.

7 And David said to Abiathar the priest, Ahimelech's son, I pray you, bring me here the ephod. And Abiathar brought there the ephod to David.

8 And David enquired at the LORD, saying, will I pursue after this troop? Will I overtake them? And he answered him, Pursue: for you will surely overtake *them*, and without fail recover *all*.

---

[1] rereward- hinder; generally late or last; specifically (as facing the east) western: after, to come, following, hind, last, latter, uttermost. [Strgs#314]

9 So David went, he and the six hundred men that *were* with him, and came to the brook Besor, where those that were left behind stayed.
10 But David pursued, he and four hundred men: for two hundred abode behind, which were so faint that they could not go over the brook Besor.
11 And they found an Egyptian in the field, and brought him to David, and gave him bread, and he did eat; and they made him drink water;
12 And they gave him a piece of a cake of figs, and two clusters of raisins: and when he had eaten, his spirit came again to him: for he had eaten no bread, or drunk *any* water, three days and three nights.
13 And David said unto him, to whom *belongs* you? And where are you? And he said, I *am* a young man of Egypt, servant to an Amalekite; and my master left me, because three days ago I fell sick.
14 We made an invasion *upon* the south of the Cherethites, and upon *the coast* which *belongs* to Judah, and upon the south of Caleb; and we burned Ziklag with fire.
15 And David said to him, Canst you bring me down to this company? And he said, Swear unto me by God, that you will neither kill me, or deliver me into the hands of my master, and I will bring you down to this company.
16 And when he had brought him down, behold, *they were* spread abroad upon all the earth, eating and drinking, and dancing, because of all the great spoil that they had taken out of the land of the Philistines, and out of the land of Judah.
17 And David smote them from the twilight even unto the evening of the next day: and there escaped not a man of them, save four hundred young men, which rode upon camels, and fled.
18 And David recovered all that the Amalekites had carried away: and David rescued his two wives.
19 And there was nothing lacking to them, neither small or great, neither sons or daughters, neither spoil, or any*thing* that they had taken to them: David recovered all.
20 And David took all the flocks and the herds, *which* they drove before those *other* cattle, and said, this *is* David's spoil.
21 And David came to the two hundred men, which were so faint that they could not follow David, whom they had made also to abide at the brook Besor: and they went forth to meet David, and to meet the people that *were* with him: and when David came near to the people, he saluted them.
22 Then answered all the wicked men and *men* of Belial, of those that went with David, and said, because they went not with us, we will not give them *ought* of the spoil that we have recovered, save to every man his wife and his children, that they may lead *them* away, and depart.
23 Then said David, you will not do so, my brethren, with that which the LORD has given us, who has preserved us, and delivered the company that came against us into our hand.
24 For who will hearken unto you in this matter? But as his part *is* that goes down to the battle, so will his part *be* that tarries by the stuff: they will part alike.
25 And it was *so* from that day forward, that he made it a statute and an ordinance for Israel unto this day.
26 And when David came to Ziklag, he sent of the spoil unto the elders of Judah, *even* to his friends, saying, Behold a present for you of the spoil of the enemies of the LORD;
27 To *them* which *were* in Beth-el, and to *them* which *were* in south Ramoth, and to *them* which *were* in Jattir,
28 And to *them* which *were* in Aroer, and to *them* which *were* in Siphmoth, and to *them* which *were* in Eshtemoa,
29 And to *them* which *were* in Rachal, and to *them* which *were* in the cities of the Jerahmeelites, and to *them* which *were* in the cities of the Kenites,
30 And to *them* which *were* in Hormah, and to *them* which *were* in Chorashan, and to *them* which *were* in Athach,
31 And to *them* which *were* in Hebron, and to all the places where David himself and his men were wont to haunt.

CHAPTER 31

1 Now the Philistines fought against Israel: and the men of Israel fled from before the Philistines, and fell down slain in mount Gilboa.
2 And the Philistines followed hard upon Saul and upon his sons; and the Philistines slew Jonathan, and Abinadab, and Malchi-shua, Saul's sons.
3 And the battle went sore against Saul, and the archers hit him; and he was sore wounded of the archers.
4 Then said Saul unto his armor-bearer, Draw your sword, and thrust me through therewith; lest these uncircumcised come and thrust me through, and abuse me. But his armor-bearer would not; for he was sore afraid. Therefore Saul took a sword, and fell upon it.
5 And when his armor-bearer saw that Saul was dead, he fell likewise upon his sword, and died with him.
6 So Saul died, and his three sons, and his armor-bearer, and all his men, that same day together.
7 And when the men of Israel that *were* on the other side of the valley, and *they* that *were* on the other side Jordan, saw that the men of Israel fled, and that Saul and his sons were dead, they forsook the cities, and fled; and the Philistines came and dwelt in them.
8 And it came to pass on the morrow, when the Philistines came to strip the slain, that they found Saul and his three sons fallen in mount Gilboa.
9 And they cut off his head, and stripped off his armor, and sent into the land of the Philistines round about, to publish *it in* the house of their idols, and among the people.
10 And they put his armor in the house of Ashtaroth: and they fastened his body to the wall of Beth-shan.
11 And when the inhabitants of Jabesh-gilead heard of that which the Philistines had done to Saul;
12 All the valiant men arose, and went all night, and took the body of Saul and the bodies of his sons from the wall of Beth-shan, and came to Jabesh, and burnt them there.
13 And they took their bones, and buried *them* under a tree at Jabesh, and fasted seven days.

SECOND SAMUEL
CHAPTER 1

1 Now it came to pass after the death of Saul, when David was returned from the slaughter of the Amalekites, and David had abode two days in Ziklag;

2 It came even to pass on the third day, that, behold, a man came out of the camp from Saul with his clothes rent, and earth upon his head: and so it was, when he came to David, that he fell to the earth, and did obeisance.

3 And David said unto him, from where come you? And he said unto him, Out of the camp of Israel am I escaped.

4 And David said unto him, how went the matter? I pray you, tell me. And he answered, that the people are fled from the battle, and many of the people also are fallen and dead; and Saul and Jonathan his son are dead also.

5 And David said unto the young man that told him, how **do you** know that Saul and Jonathan his son **are** dead?

6 And the young man that told him said, as I happened by chance upon mount Gilboa, behold Saul leaned upon his spear; and, lo, the chariots and horsemen followed hard after him.

7 And when he looked behind him, he saw me, and called unto me. And I answered, here am I.

8 And he said unto me, who are you? And I answered him, I am an Amalekite.

9 He said unto me again, Stand, I pray you, upon me, and slay me: for anguish is come upon me, because my life is yet whole in me.

10 So I stood upon him, and slew him, because I was sure that he could not live after that he was fallen: and I took the crown that was upon his head, and the bracelet that was on his arm, and have brought them here unto my lord.

11 Then David took hold on his clothes, and rent them; and likewise all the men that were with him:

12 And they mourned, and wept, and fasted until even, for Saul, and for Jonathan his son, and for the people of the LORD, and for the house of Israel; because they were fallen by the sword.

13 And David said unto the young man that told him, where are you? And he answered, I am the son of a stranger, an Amalekite.

14 And David said unto him, how were you not afraid to stretch forth your hand to destroy the LORD'S anointed?

15 And David called one of the young men, and said, go near, and fall upon him. And he smote him that he died.

16 And David said unto him, your blood be upon your head; for your mouth has testified against you, saying, I have slain the LORD'S anointed.

17 And David lamented with this lamentation over Saul and over Jonathan his son:

18 (Also he bade them teach the children of Judah the use of the bow: behold, it is written in the book of Jasher.)

19 The beauty of Israel is slain upon your high places: how are the mighty fallen!

20 Tell it not in Gath, publish it not in the streets of Askelon; lest the daughters of the Philistines rejoice, lest the daughters of the uncircumcised triumph.

21 you mountains of Gilboa, let there be no dew, neither let there be rain, upon you, or fields of offerings: for there the shield of the mighty is vilely cast away, the shield of Saul, as though he had not been anointed with oil.

22 From the blood of the slain, from the fat of the mighty, the bow of Jonathan turned not back, and the sword of Saul returned not empty.

23 Saul and Jonathan were lovely and pleasant in their lives, and in their death they were not divided: they were swifter than eagles, they were stronger than lions.

24 you daughters of Israel, weep over Saul, who clothed you in scarlet, with other delights, who put on ornaments of gold upon your apparel.

25 How are the mighty fallen in the midst of the battle! O Jonathan, you were slain in your high places.

26 I am distressed for you, my brother Jonathan: very pleasant have you been unto me: your love to me was wonderful, passing the love of women.

27 How are the mighty fallen, and the weapons of war perished!

CHAPTER 2

1 And it came to pass after this, that David enquired of the LORD, saying, will I go up into any of the cities of Judah? And the LORD said unto him, Go up. And David said, whither will I go up? And he said, Unto Hebron.

2 So David went up thither, and his two wives also, Ahinoam the Jezreelitess, and Abigail Nabal's wife the Carmelite.

3 And his men that were with him did David bring up, every man with his household: and they dwelt in the cities of Hebron.

4 And the men of Judah came, and there they anointed David king over the house of Judah. And they told David, saying, that the men of Jabesh-gilead were they that buried Saul.

5 And David sent messengers unto the men of Jabesh-gilead, and said unto them, blessed be you of the LORD, that you have showed this kindness unto your lord, even unto Saul, and have buried him.

6 And now the LORD show kindness and truth unto you: and I also will requite you this kindness, because you have done this thing.

7 Therefore now let your hands be strengthened, and be you valiant: for your master Saul is dead, and also the house of Judah has anointed me king over them.

8 But Abner the son of Ner, captain of Saul's host, took Ish-bosheth the son of Saul, and brought him over to Mahanaim;

9 And made him king over Gilead, and over the Ashurites, and over Jezreel, and over Ephraim, and over Benjamin, and over all Israel.

10 Ish-bosheth Saul's son was forty years old when he began to reign over Israel, and reigned two years. But the house of Judah followed David.

11 And the time that David was king in Hebron over the house of Judah was seven years and six months.

12 And Abner the son of Ner, and the servants of Ish-bosheth the son of Saul, went out from Mahanaim to Gibeon.

13 And Joab the son of Zeruiah, and the servants of David, went out, and met together by the pool of Gibeon: and they sat down, the one on the one side of the pool, and the other on the other side of the pool.

14 And Abner said to Joab, Let the young men now arise, and play before us. And Joab said, Let them arise.

15 Then there arose and went over by number twelve of Benjamin, which pertained to Ish-bosheth the son of Saul, and twelve of the servants of David.

16 And they caught everyone his fellow by the head, and thrust his sword in his fellow's side; so they fell down together: wherefore that place was called Helkath-hazzurim, which is in Gibeon.

17 And there was a very sore battle that day; and Abner was beaten, and the men of Israel, before the servants of David.
18 And there were three sons of Zeruiah there, Joab, and Abishai, and Asahel: and Asahel was as light of foot as a wild roe.
19 And Asahel pursued after Abner; and in going he turned not to the right hand or to the left from following Abner.
20 Then Abner looked behind him, and said, are you Asahel? And he answered, I am.
21 And Abner said to him, Turn you aside to your right hand or to your left, and lay you hold on one of the young men, and take you his armour. But Asahel would not turn aside from following of him.
22 And Abner said again to Asahel, Turn you aside from following me: wherefore should I smite you to the ground? How then should I hold up my face to Joab your brother?
23 Howbeit he refused to turn aside: wherefore Abner with the hinder end of the spear smote him under the fifth rib, that the spear came out behind him; and he fell down there, and died in the same place: and it came to pass, that as many as came to the place where Asahel fell down and died stood still.
24 Joab also and Abishai pursued after Abner: and the sun went down when they were come to the hill of Ammah that lay before Giah by the way of the wilderness of Gibeon.
25 And the children of Benjamin gathered themselves together after Abner, and became one troop, and stood on the top of a hill.
26 Then Abner called to Joab, and said, will the sword devour forever? knowest you not that it will be bitterness in the latter end? How long will it be then, ere you bid the people return from following their brethren?
27 And Joab said, as God lives, unless you have spoken, surely then in the morning the people had gone up every one from following his brother.
28 So Joab blew a trumpet, and all the people stood still, and pursued after Israel no more, neither fought they any more.
29 And Abner and his men walked all that night through the plain, and passed over Jordan, and went through all Bithron, and they came to Mahanaim.
30 And Joab returned from following Abner: and when he had gathered all the people together, there lacked of David's servants nineteen men and Asahel.
31 But the servants of David had smitten of Benjamin, and of Abner's men, so that three hundred and threescore men died.
32 And they took up Asahel, and buried him in the sepulcher of his father, which was in Beth-lehem. And Joab and his men went all night, and they came to Hebron at break of day.

CHAPTER 3

1 Now there was long war between the house of Saul and the house of David: but David waxed stronger and stronger, and the house of Saul waxed weaker and weaker.
2 And unto David were sons born in Hebron: and his firstborn was Amnon, of Ahinoam the Jezreelitess;
3 And his second, Chileab, of Abigail the wife of Nabal the Carmelite; and the third, Absalom the son of Maacah the daughter of Talmai king of Geshur;
4 And the fourth, Adonijah the son of Haggith; and the fifth, Shephatiah the son of Abital;
5 And the sixth, Ithream, by Eglah David's wife. These were born to David in Hebron.
6 And it came to pass, while there was war between the house of Saul and the house of David, that Abner made himself strong for the house of Saul.

7 And Saul had a concubine, whose name was Rizpah, the daughter of Aiah: and Ish-bosheth said to Abner, Wherefore have you gone in unto my father's concubine?
8 Then was Abner very wroth for the words of Ish-bosheth, and said, Am I a dog's head, which against Judah do show kindness this day unto the house of Saul your father, to his brethren, and to his friends, and have not delivered you into the hand of David, that you charges me today with a fault concerning this woman?
9 So do God to Abner, and more also, except, as the LORD has sworn to David, even so I do to him;
10 To translate the kingdom from the house of Saul, and to set up the throne of David over Israel and over Judah, from Dan even to Beer-sheba.
11 And he could not answer Abner a word again, because he feared him.
12 And Abner sent messengers to David on his behalf, saying, whose is the land? Saying also, Make your league with me, and, behold, my hand will be with you, to bring about all Israel unto you.
13 And he said, well; I will make a league with you: but one thing I require of you, that is, you will not see my face, except you first bring Michal Saul's daughter, when you come to see my face.
14 And David sent messengers to Ish-bosheth Saul's son, saying, deliver me my wife Michal, which I espoused to me for an hundred foreskins of the Philistines.
15 And Ish-bosheth sent, and took her from her husband, even from Phaltiel the son of Laish.
16 And her husband went with her along weeping behind her to Bahurim. Then said Abner unto him, Go, return. And he returned.
17 And Abner had communication with the elders of Israel, saying, you sought for David in times past to be king over you:
18 Now then do it: for the LORD has spoken of David, saying, by the hand of my servant David I will save my people Israel out of the hand of the Philistines, and out of the hand of all their enemies.
19 And Abner also spoke in the ears of Benjamin: and Abner went also to speak in the ears of David in Hebron all that seemed good to Israel, and that seemed good to the whole house of Benjamin.
20 So Abner came to David to Hebron, and twenty men with him. And David made Abner and the men that were with him a feast.
21 And Abner said unto David, I will arise and go, and will gather all Israel unto my lord the king, that they may make a league with you, and that you may reign over all that your heart desires. And David sent Abner away; and he went in peace.
22 And, behold, the servants of David and Joab came from pursuing a troop, and brought in a great spoil with them: but Abner was not with David in Hebron; for he had sent him away, and he was gone in peace.
23 When Joab and all the host that was with him were come, they told Joab, saying, Abner the son of Ner came to the king, and he has sent him away, and he is gone in peace.
24 Then Joab came to the king, and said, what have you done? Behold, Abner came unto you; why is it that you have sent him away, and he is quite gone?
25 you knowest Abner the son of Ner, that he came to deceive you, and to know **you are** going out and **you're** coming in, and to know all that you do.
26 And when Joab was come out from David, he sent messengers after Abner, which brought him again from the well of Sirah: but David knew it not.

27 And when Abner was returned to Hebron, Joab took him aside in the gate to speak with him quietly, and smote him there under the fifth *rib*, that he died, for the blood of Asahel his brother.
28 And afterward when David heard *it*, he said, I and my kingdom *are* guiltless before the LORD for ever from the blood of Abner the son of Ner:
29 Let it rest on the head of Joab, and on his **entire** father's house; and let there not fail from the house of Joab one that has an issue, or that is a leper, or that leaneth on a staff, or that falls on the sword, or that lacks bread.
30 So Joab and Abishai his brother slew Abner, because he had slain their brother Asahel at Gibeon in the battle.
31 And David said to Joab, and to all the people that *were* with him, **tear** your clothes, and gird you with sackcloth, and mourn before Abner. And King David *himself* followed the bier.
32 And they buried Abner in Hebron: and the king lifted up his voice, and wept at the grave of Abner; and all the people wept.
33 And the king lamented over Abner, and said, Died Abner as a fool dies?
34 Your hands *were* not bound, or your feet put into **chains**: as a man falls before wicked men, *so* you fell. And all the people wept again over him.
35 And when all the people came to cause David to eat meat while it was yet day, David swore, saying, So do God to me, and more also, if I taste bread, or ought else, till the sun be down.
36 And all the people took notice *of it*, and it pleased them: as whatsoever the king did pleased all the people.
37 For all the people and all Israel understood that day that it was not of the king to slay Abner the son of Ner.
38 And the king said unto his servants, Know you not that there is a prince and a great man fallen this day in Israel?
39 And I *am* this day weak, though anointed king; and these men the sons of Zeruiah *be* too hard for me: the LORD will reward the doer of evil according to his wickedness.

CHAPTER 4

1 And when Saul's son heard that Abner was dead in Hebron, his hands were feeble, and all the Israelites were troubled.
2 And Saul's son had two men *that were* captains of bands: the name of the one *was* Baanah, and the name of the other Rechab, the sons of Rimmon a Beerothite, of the children of Benjamin: (for Beeroth also was reckoned to Benjamin:
3 And the Beerothites fled to Gittaim, and were sojourners there until this day.)
4 And Jonathan, Saul's son, had a son *that was* lame of *his* feet. He was five years old when the tidings came of Saul and Jonathan out of Jezreel, and his nurse took him up, and fled: and it came to pass, as she made haste to flee, that he fell, and became lame. And his name *was* Mephibosheth.
5 And the sons of Rimmon the Beerothite, Rechab and Baanah, went, and came about the heat of the day to the house of Ish-bosheth, who lay on a bed at noon.
6 And they came there into the midst of the house, *as though* they would have fetched wheat; and they smote him under the fifth *rib*: and Rechab and Baanah his brother escaped.
7 For when they came into the house, he lay on his bed in his bedchamber, and they **killed** him, and **slaughtered** him, and beheaded him, and took his head, and **departed** away through the plain all night.
8 And they brought the head of Ish-bosheth unto David to Hebron, and said to the king, Behold the head of Ish-bosheth the son of Saul your enemy, which sought your life; and the LORD has avenged my lord the king this day of Saul, and of his seed.
9 And David answered Rechab and Baanah his brother, the sons of Rimmon the Beerothite, and said unto them, As the LORD lives, who has redeemed my soul out of all adversity,
10 When one told me, saying, Behold, Saul is dead, thinking to have brought good tidings, I took hold of him, and slew him in Ziklag, who *thought* that I would have given him a reward for his tidings:
11 How much more, when wicked men have slain a righteous person in his own house upon his bed? Will I not therefore now require his blood of your hand, and take you away from the earth?
12 And David commanded his young men, and they slew them, and cut off their hands and their feet, and hanged *them* up over the pool in Hebron. But they took the head of Ish-bosheth, and buried *it* in the sepulcher of Abner in Hebron.

CHAPTER 5

1 Then came all the tribes of Israel to David unto Hebron, and spoke, saying, behold, we *are* your bone and your flesh.
2 Also in time past, when Saul was king over us, you were he that led out and brought in Israel: and the LORD said to you, you will feed my people Israel, and you will be a captain over Israel.
3 So all the elders of Israel came to the king to Hebron; and King David made a league with them in Hebron before the LORD: and they anointed David king over Israel.
4 David *was* thirty years old when he began to reign, *and* he reigned forty years.
5 In Hebron he reigned over Judah seven years and six months: and in Jerusalem he reigned thirty and three years over all Israel and Judah.
6 And the king and his men went to Jerusalem unto the Jebusites, the inhabitants of the land: which spoke unto David, saying, except you take away the blind and the lame, you will not come in hither: thinking, David cannot come in hither.
7 Nevertheless David took the strong hold of Zion: the same *is* the city of David.
8 And David said on that day, whosoever gets up to the gutter, and **slaughter** the Jebusites, and the lame and the blind, *that are* hated of David's soul, *he will be chief and captain*. Wherefore they said, the blind and the lame will not come into the house.
9 So David dwelt in the fort, and called it the city of David. And David built round about from Millo and inward.
10 And David went on, and grew great, and the LORD God of hosts *was* with him.
11 And Hiram king of Tyre sent messengers to David, and cedar trees, and carpenters, and masons: and they built David a house.
12 And David perceived that the LORD had established him king over Israel, and that he had exalted his kingdom for his people Israel's sake.
13 And David took *him* more concubines and wives out of Jerusalem, after he was come from Hebron: and there were yet sons and daughters born to David.
14 And these *be* the names of those that were born unto him in Jerusalem; Shammua, and Shobab, and Nathan, and Solomon,
15 Ibhar also, and Elishua, and Nepheg, and Japhia,
16 And Elishama, and Eliada, and Eliphalet.
17 But when the Philistines heard that they had anointed David king over Israel, all the Philistines came up to seek David; and David heard *of it*, and went down to the hold.

18 The Philistines also came and spread themselves in the valley of Rephaim.
19 And David enquired of the LORD, saying, will I go up to the Philistines? Will you deliver them into mine hand? And the LORD said unto David, Go up: for I will doubtless deliver the Philistines into your hand.
20 And David came to Baal-perazim, and David smote them there, and said, The LORD has broken forth upon mine enemies before me, as the breach of waters. Therefore he called the name of that place Baal-perazim.
21 And there they left their images, and David and his men burned them.
22 And the Philistines came up yet again, and spread themselves in the valley of Rephaim.
23 And when David enquired of the LORD, he said, you will not go up; *but* fetch a compass behind them, and come upon them over against the mulberry trees.
24 And let it be, when you hear the sound of a going in the tops of the mulberry trees, that then you will bestir thyself: for then will the LORD go out before you, to smite the host of the Philistines.
25 And David did so, as the LORD had commanded him; and smote the Philistines from Geba until you come to Gazer.

CHAPTER 6

1 Again, David gathered together all *the* chosen *men* of Israel, thirty thousand.
2 And David arose, and went with all the people that *were* with him from Baale of Judah, to bring up from there the ark of God, whose name is called by the name of the LORD of hosts that dwells *between* the cherubims.
3 And they set the ark of God upon a new cart, and brought it out of the house of Abinadab that *was* in Gibeah: and Uzzah and Ahio, the sons of Abinadab, drove the new cart.
4 And they brought it out of the house of Abinadab which *was* at Gibeah, accompanying the ark of God: and Ahio went before the ark.
5 And David and all the house of Israel played before the LORD on all manner of *instruments made of* fir wood, even on harps, and on psalteries, and on **tambourines**, and on cornets, and on cymbals.
6 And when they came to Nachon's threshing-floor, Uzzah put forth *his* hand to the ark of God, and took hold of it; for the oxen shook *it*.
7 And the anger of the LORD was kindled against Uzzah; and God smote him there for *his* error; and there he died by the ark of God.
8 And David was displeased, because the LORD had made a breach upon Uzzah: and he called the name of the place Perez-uzzah to this day.
9 And David was afraid of the LORD that day, and said, how will the ark of the LORD come to me?
10 So David would not remove the ark of the LORD unto him into the city of David: but David carried it aside into the house of Obed-edom the Gittite.
11 And the ark of the LORD continued in the house of Obed-edom the Gittite three months: and the LORD blessed Obed-edom, and his **entire** household.
12 And it was told King David, saying, The LORD has blessed the house of Obed-edom, and all that *pertains* unto him, because of the ark of God. So David went and brought up the ark of God from the house of Obed-edom into the city of David with gladness.
13 And it was *so*, that when they that bare the ark of the LORD had gone six paces, he sacrificed oxen and fatlings.
14 And David danced before the LORD with all *his* might; and David *was* girded with a linen ephod.
15 So David and all the house of Israel brought up the ark of the LORD with shouting, and with the sound of the trumpet.
16 And as the ark of the LORD came into the city of David, Michal Saul's daughter looked through a window, and saw King David leaping and dancing before the LORD; and she despised him in her heart.
17 And they brought in the ark of the LORD, and set it in his place, in the midst of the tabernacle that David had pitched for it: and David offered burnt offerings and peace offerings before the LORD.
18 And as soon as David had made an end of offering burnt offerings and peace offerings, he blessed the people in the name of the LORD of hosts.
19 And he dealt among all the people, *even* among the whole multitude of Israel, as well to the women as men, to everyone a cake of bread, and a good piece *of flesh*, and a flagon *of wine*. So the **entire** people departed everyone to his house.
20 Then David returned to bless his household. And Michal the daughter of Saul came out to meet David, and said, how glorious was the king of Israel to day, who uncovered himself to day in the eyes of the handmaids of his servants, as one of the vain fellows shamelessly uncovers himself!
21 And David said unto Michal, *It was* before the LORD, which chose me before your father, and before his **entire** house, to appoint me ruler over the people of the LORD, over Israel: therefore will I play before the LORD.
22 And I will yet be more vile than you, and will be base in mine own sight: and of the maidservants which you have spoken of, of them will I be had in honor.
23 Therefore Michal the daughter of Saul had no child unto the day of her death.

CHAPTER 7

1 And it came to pass, when the king sat in his house, and the LORD had given him rest round about from all his enemies;
2 That the king said unto Nathan the prophet, See now, I dwell in an house of cedar, but the ark of God dwells within curtains.
3 And Nathan said to the king, Go, do all that *is* in your heart; for the LORD *is* with you.
4 And it came to pass that night, that the word of the LORD came unto Nathan, saying,
5 Go and tell my servant David, you said the LORD, will you build me an house for me to dwell in?
6 Whereas I have not dwelt in *any* house since the time that I brought up the children of Israel out of Egypt, even to this day, but have walked in a tent and in a tabernacle.
7 In all *the places* wherein I have walked with all the children of Israel spoke I a word with any of the tribes of Israel, whom I commanded to feed my people Israel, saying, Why build you not me an house of cedar?
8 Now therefore so will you say unto my servant David, Thus said the LORD of hosts, I took you from the sheepcote, from following the sheep, to be ruler over my people, over Israel:
9 And I was with you whithersoever you went, and have cut off all your enemies out of your sight, and have made you a great name, like unto the name of the great *men* that *are* in the earth.

10 Moreover I will appoint a place for my people Israel, and will plant them, that they may dwell in a place of their own, and move no more; neither will the children of wickedness afflict them anymore, as beforetime,
11 And as since the time that I commanded judges to be over my people Israel, and have caused you to rest from all your enemies. Also the LORD tells you that he will make you a house.
12 And when your days be fulfilled, and you will sleep with your fathers, I will set up your seed after you, which will proceed out of your bowels, and I will establish his kingdom.
13 He will build a house for my name, and I will establish the throne of his kingdom forever.
14 I will be his father, and he will be my son. If he commits iniquity, I will chasten him with the rod of men, and with the stripes of the children of men:
15 But my mercy will not depart away from him, as I took it from Saul, whom I put away before you.
16 And your house and your kingdom will be established for ever before you: your throne will be established for ever.
17 According to all these words, and according to all this vision, so did Nathan speak unto David.
18 Then went King David in, and sat before the LORD, and he said, who am I, O Lord GOD? And what is my house, that you have brought me hitherto?
19 And this was yet a small thing in your sight, O Lord GOD; but you have spoken also of your servant's house for a great while to come. And is this the manner of man, O Lord GOD?
20 And what can David say more unto you? For you, Lord GOD, knows your servant.
21 For your word's sake, and according to your own heart, have you done all these great things, to make your servant know them.
22 Wherefore you are great, O LORD God: for there is none like you, neither is there any God beside you, according to all that we have heard with our ears.
23 And what one nation in the earth is like your people, even like Israel, whom God went to redeem for a people to himself, and to make him a name, and to do for you great things and terrible, for your land, before your people, which you redeemed to you from Egypt, from the nations and their gods?
24 For you have confirmed to yourself your people Israel to be a people unto you forever: and you, LORD, are become their God.
25 And now, O LORD God, the word that you have spoken concerning your servant, and concerning his house, establish it forever, and do as you have said.
26 And let your name be magnified forever, saying, The LORD of hosts is the God over Israel: and let the house of your servant David be established before you.
27 For you, O LORD of hosts, God of Israel, have revealed to your servant, saying, I will build you a house: therefore has your servant found in his heart to pray this prayer unto you.
28 And now, O Lord GOD, you are that God, and your words are true, and you have promised this goodness unto your servant:
29 Therefore now let it please you to bless the house of your servant, that it may continue forever before you: for you, O Lord GOD, have spoken it: and with your blessing let the house of your servant be blessed forever.

---

[1] hough- to pluck up by the roots, to hamstring, to exterminate, dig down.

CHAPTER 8

1 And after this it came to pass, that David smote the Philistines, and subdued them: and David took Metheg-ammah out of the hand of the Philistines.
2 And he smote Moab, and measured them with a line, casting them down to the ground; even with two lines measured he to put to death, and with one full line to keep alive. And so the Moabites became David's servants, and brought gifts.
3 David smote also Hadadezer, the son of Rehob, king of Zobah, as he went to recover his border at the river Euphrates.
4 And David took from him a thousand chariots, and seven hundred horsemen, and twenty thousand footmen: and David houghed[1] all the chariot horses, but reserved of them for an hundred chariots.
5 And when the Syrians of Damascus came to succour Hadadezer king of Zobah, David slew of the Syrians two and twenty thousand men.
6 Then David put garrisons in Syria of Damascus: and the Syrians became servants to David, and brought gifts. And the LORD preserved David whithersoever he went.
7 And David took the shields of gold that were on the servants of Hadadezer, and brought them to Jerusalem.
8 And from Betah, and from Berothai, cities of Hadadezer, king David took exceeding much brass.
9 When Toi king of Hamath heard that David had smitten all the host of Hadadezer,
10 Then Toi sent Joram his son unto King David, to salute him, and to bless him, because he had fought against Hadadezer, and smitten him: for Hadadezer had wars with Toi. And Joram brought with him vessels of silver, and vessels of gold, and vessels of brass:
11 Which also king David did dedicate unto the LORD, with the silver and gold that he had dedicated of all nations which he subdued;
12 Of Syria, and of Moab, and of the children of Ammon, and of the Philistines, and of Amalek, and of the spoil of Hadadezer, son of Rehob, king of Zobah.
13 And David gat him a name when he returned from smiting of the Syrians in the valley of salt, being eighteen thousand men.
14 And he put garrisons in Edom; throughout all Edom put he garrisons, and all they of Edom became David's servants. And the LORD preserved David whithersoever he went.
15 And David reigned over all Israel; and David executed judgment and justice unto all his people.
16 And Joab the son of Zeruiah was over the host; and Jehoshaphat the son of Ahilud was recorder;
17 And Zadok the son of Ahitub, and Ahimelech the son of Abiathar, were the priests; and Seraiah was the scribe
18 And Benaiah the son of Jehoiada was over both the Cherethites and the Pelethites; and David's sons were chief rulers.

CHAPTER 9

1 And David said, Is there yet any that is left of the house of Saul, that I may show him kindness for Jonathan's sake?
2 And there was of the house of Saul a servant whose name was Ziba. And when they had called him unto David, the king said unto him, are you Ziba? And he said, your servant is he.

[Strgs#6131]

3 And the king said, *Is* there not yet any of the house of Saul, that I may show the kindness of God unto him? And Ziba said unto the king, Jonathan has yet a son, *which is* lame on *his* feet.
4 And the king said unto him, Where *is* he? And Ziba said unto the king, Behold, he *is* in the house of Machir, the son of Ammiel, in Lo-debar.
5 Then king David sent, and fetched him out of the house of Machir, the son of Ammiel, from Lo-debar.
6 Now when Mephibosheth, the son of Jonathan, the son of Saul, was come unto David, he fell on his face, and did reverence. And David said, Mephibosheth. And he answered, Behold your servant!
7 And David said unto him, Fear not: for I will surely show you kindness for Jonathan your father's sake, and will restore you all the land of Saul your father; and you will eat bread at my table continually.
8 And he bowed himself, and said, what *is* your servant, that you should look upon such a dead dog as I *am*?
9 Then the king called to Ziba, Saul's servant, and said unto him, I have given unto your master's son all that pertained to Saul and to his **entire** house.
10 you therefore, and your sons, and your servants, will till the land for him, and you will bring in *the fruits*, that your master's son may have food to eat: but Mephibosheth¹ your master's son will eat bread always at my table. Now Ziba had fifteen sons and twenty servants.
11 Then said Ziba unto the king, According to all that my lord the king has commanded his servant, so will your servant do. As for Mephibosheth, *said the king*, he will eat at my table, as one of the king's sons.
12 And Mephibosheth had a young son, whose name *was* Micha. And all that dwelt in the house of Ziba *were* servants unto Mephibosheth.
13 So Mephibosheth dwelt in Jerusalem: for he did eat continually at the king's table; and was lame on both his feet.

CHAPTER 10
1 And it came to pass after this, that the king of the children of Ammon died, and Hanun his son reigned in his stead.
2 Then said David, I will show kindness unto Hanun the son of Nahash, as his father showed kindness unto me. And David sent to comfort him by the hand of his servants for his father. And David's servants came into the land of the children of Ammon.
3 And the princes of the children of Ammon said unto Hanun their lord, thank you that David does honor your father, that he has sent comforters unto you? Has not David *rather* sent his servants unto you, to search the city, and to spy it out, and to overthrow it?
4 Wherefore Hanun took David's servants, and shaved off the one half of their beards, and cut off their garments in the middle, *even* to their buttocks, and sent them away.
5 When they told *it* unto David, he sent to meet them, because the men were greatly ashamed: and the king said, tarry at Jericho until your beards are grown, and *then* return.
6 And when the children of Ammon saw that they stank before David, the children of Ammon sent and hired the Syrians of Beth-rehob, and the Syrians of Zoba, twenty thousand footmen, and of king Maacah a thousand men, and of Ish-tob twelve thousand men.

7 And when David heard of *it*, he sent Joab, and all the host of the mighty men.
8 And the children of Ammon came out, and put the battle in array at the entering in of the gate: and the Syrians of Zoba, and of Rehob, and Ish-tob, and Maacah, *were* by themselves in the field.
9 When Joab saw that the front of the battle was against him before and behind, he chose of all the choice *men* of Israel, and put *them* in array against the Syrians:
10 And the rest of the people he delivered into the hand of Abishai his brother, that he might put *them* in array against the children of Ammon.
11 And he said, if the Syrians be too strong for me, then you will help me: but if the children of Ammon be too strong for you, then I will come and help you.
12 Be of good courage, and let us play the men for our people, and for the cities of our God: and the LORD does that which seems him good.
13 And Joab drew nigh, and the people that *were* with him, unto the battle against the Syrians: and they fled before him
14 And when the children of Ammon saw that the Syrians were fled, then fled they also before Abishai, and entered into the city. So Joab returned from the children of Ammon, and came to Jerusalem.
15 And when the Syrians saw that they were smitten before Israel, they gathered themselves together.
16 And Hadarezer sent, and brought out the Syrians that *were* beyond the river: and they came to Helam; and Shobach the captain of the host of Hadarezer *went* before them.
17 And when it was told David, he gathered all Israel together, and passed over Jordan, and came to Helam. And the Syrians set themselves in array against David, and fought with him.
18 And the Syrians fled before Israel; and David **slaughtered** *the men of* seven hundred chariots of the Syrians, and forty thousand horsemen, and smote Shobach the captain of their host, who died there.
19 And when all the kings *that were* servants to Hadarezer saw that they were smitten before Israel, they made peace with Israel, and served them. So the Syrians feared to help the children of Ammon anymore.

CHAPTER 11
1 And it came to pass, after the year was expired, at the time when kings go forth *to battle*, that David sent Joab, and his servants with him, and all Israel; and they destroyed the children of Ammon, and besieged Rabbah. But David tarried still at Jerusalem.
2 And it came to pass in an evening tide, that David arose from off his bed, and walked upon the roof of the king's house: and from the roof he saw a woman washing herself; and the woman *was* very beautiful to look upon.
3 And David sent and enquired after the woman. And *one* said, *Is* not this Bath-sheba, the daughter of Eliam, the wife of Uriah the Hittite?
4 And David sent messengers, and took her; and she came in unto him, and he lay with her; for she was purified from her uncleanness: and she returned unto her house.
5 And the woman conceived, and sent and told David, and said, I *am* with child.

---
¹ Mephibosheth- a son of Jonathan and grandson of Saul. Mephiboshet was also called Merib-Baal (**I Chr. 8:34; 9:40**), but his name was later changed because the word Baal was associated with idol worship. Mephiboshet is defined as dispeller of shame (that is, of Baal) or exterminating the idol. [Strgs#4648]

6 And David sent to Joab, *saying*, Send me Uriah the Hittite. And Joab sent Uriah to David.
7 And when Uriah was come unto him, David demanded *of him* how Joab did, and how the people did, and how the war prospered.
8 And David said to Uriah, Go down to your house, and wash your feet. And Uriah departed out of the king's house, and there followed him a mess *of meat* from the king.
9 But Uriah slept at the door of the king's house with all the servants of his lord, and went not down to his house.
10 And when they had told David, saying, Uriah went not down unto his house, David said unto Uriah, **did** you not come from your journey? Why *then* **do** you not go down to your house?
11 And Uriah said unto David, The ark, and Israel, and Judah, abide in tents; and my lord Joab, and the servants of my lord, are encamped in the open fields; will I then go into mine house, to eat and to drink, and to lie with my wife? *As* you live, and *as* your soul lives, I will not do this thing.
12 And David said to Uriah, Tarry here today also, and tomorrow I will let you depart. So Uriah abode in Jerusalem that day, and the morrow.
13 And when David had called him, he did eat and drink before him; and he made him drunk: and at even he went out to lie on his bed with the servants of his lord, but went not down to his house.
14 And it came to pass in the morning, that David wrote a letter to Joab, and sent *it* by the hand of Uriah.
15 And he wrote in the letter, saying, Set you Uriah in the forefront of the hottest battle, and retire you from him, that he may be smitten, and die.
16 And it came to pass, when Joab observed the city, that he assigned Uriah unto a place where he knew that valiant men *were*.
17 And the men of the city went out, and fought with Joab: and there fell *some* of the people of the servants of David; and Uriah the Hittite died also.
18 Then Joab sent and told David all the things concerning the war;
19 And charged the messenger, saying, when you have made an end of telling the matters of the war unto the king,
20 And if so be that the king's wrath arise, and he say unto you, Wherefore approached you so nigh unto the city when you did fight? Knew you not that they would shoot from the wall?
21 Who smote Abimelech the son of Jerubbesheth? Did not a woman cast a piece of a millstone upon him from the wall, that he died in Thebez? Why went you nigh the wall? Then say you, your servant Uriah the Hittite is dead also.
22 So the messenger went, and came and showed David all that Joab had sent him for.
23 And the messenger said unto David, Surely the men prevailed against us, and came out unto us into the field, and we were upon them even unto the entering of the gate.
24 And the shooters shot from off the wall upon your servants; and *some* of the king's servants be dead, and your servant Uriah the Hittite is dead also.
25 Then David said unto the messenger, Thus will you say unto Joab, Let not this thing displease you, for the sword devours one as well as another: make your battle more strong against the city, and overthrow it: and encourage you him.
26 And when the wife of Uriah heard that Uriah her husband was dead, she mourned for her husband.
27 And when the mourning was past, David sent and fetched her to his house, and she became his wife, and bare him a son. But the thing that David had done displeased the LORD.

CHAPTER 12

1 And the LORD sent Nathan unto David. And he came unto him, and said unto him, there were two men in one city; the one rich, and the other poor.
2 The rich *man* had exceeding many flocks and herds:
3 But the poor *man* had nothing, save one little ewe lamb which he had bought and nourished up: and it grew up together with him, and with his children; it did eat of his own meat, and drank of his own cup, and lay in his bosom, and was unto him as a daughter.
4 And there came a traveler unto the rich man, and he spared to take of his own flock and of his own herd, to dress for the wayfaring man that was come unto him; but took the poor man's lamb, and dressed it for the man that was come to him.
5 And David's anger was greatly kindled against the man; and he said to Nathan, *As* the LORD lives, the man that has done this *thing* will surely die:
6 And he will restore the lamb fourfold, because he did this thing, and because he had no pity.
7 And Nathan said to David, you are the man. Thus said the LORD God of Israel, I anointed you king over Israel, and I delivered you out of the hand of Saul;
8 And I gave you your master's house, and your master's wives into your bosom, and gave you the house of Israel and of Judah; and if *that had been* too little, I would moreover have given unto you such and such things.
9 Wherefore have you despised the commandment of the LORD, to do evil in his sight? You have killed Uriah the Hittite with the sword, and have taken his wife *to be* your wife, and have slain him with the sword of the children of Ammon.
10 Now therefore the sword will never depart from your house; because you have despised me, and have taken the wife of Uriah the Hittite to be your wife.
11 Thus said the LORD, Behold, I will rise up evil against you out of your own house, and I will take your wives before your eyes, and give *them* unto your neighbor, and he will lie with your wives in the sight of this sun.
12 For you did *it* secretly: but I will do this thing before all Israel, and before the sun.
13 And David said unto Nathan, I have sinned against the LORD. And Nathan said unto David, The LORD also has put away your sin; you will not die.
14 Howbeit, because by this deed you have given great occasion to the enemies of the LORD to blaspheme, the child also *that is* born unto you will surely die.
15 And Nathan departed unto his house. And the LORD struck the child that Uriah's wife bare unto David, and it was very sick.
16 David therefore sought God for the child; and David fasted, and went in, and lay all night upon the earth.
17 And the elders of his house arose, *and went* to him, to raise him up from the earth: but he would not, neither did he eat bread with them.
18 And it came to pass on the seventh day, that the child died. And the servants of David feared to tell him that the child was dead: for they said, Behold, while the child was yet alive, we spoke unto him, and he would not hearken unto our voice: how will he then vex himself, if we tell him that the child is dead?

19 But when David saw that his servants whispered, David perceived that the child was dead: therefore David said unto his servants, is the child dead? And they said, he is dead.
20 Then David arose from the earth, and washed, and anointed *himself*, and changed his apparel, and came into the house of the LORD, and worshipped: then he came to his own house; and when he required, they set bread before him, and he did eat.
21 Then said his servants unto him, what thing *is* this that you have done? You did fast and weep for the child, *while it was* alive; but when the child was dead, you did rise and eat bread.
22 And he said, while the child was yet alive, I fasted and wept: for I said, who can tell *whether* GOD will be gracious to me, that the child may live?
23 But now he is dead, wherefore should I fast? Can I bring him back again? I will go to him, but he will not return to me.
24 And David comforted Bath-sheba his wife, and went in unto her, and lay with her: and she bares a son, and he called his name Solomon: and the LORD loved him.
25 And he sent by the hand of Nathan the prophet; and he called his name Jedidiah, because of the LORD.
26 And Joab fought against Rabbah of the children of Ammon, and took the royal city.
27 And Joab sent messengers to David, and said, I have fought against Rabbah, and have taken the city of waters.
28 Now therefore gather the rest of the people together, and encamp against the city, and take it: lest I take the city, and called *it* after my name.
29 And David gathered all the people together, and went to Rabbah, and fought against it, and took it.
30 And he took their king's crown from off his head, the weight whereof *was* a talent of gold with the precious stones: and it was *set* on David's head. And he brought forth the spoil of the city in great abundance.
31 And he brought forth the people that *were* therein, and put *them* under saws, and under harrows of iron, and under axes of iron, and made them pass through the **brick-making**: and thus did he unto all the cities of the children of Ammon. So David and all the people returned unto Jerusalem.

CHAPTER 13

1 And it came to pass after this, that Absalom the son of David had a fair sister, whose name *was* Tamar; and Amnon the son of David loved her.
2 And Amnon was so vexed, that he fell sick for his sister Tamar; for she *was* a virgin; and Amnon thought it hard for him to do anything to her.
3 But Amnon had a friend, whose name *was* Jonadab, the son of Shimeah David's brother: and Jonadab *was* a very subtle man.
4 And he said unto him, Why are you, *being* the king's son, lean from day to day? Will you not tell me? And Amnon said unto him, I love Tamar, my brother Absalom's sister.
5 And Jonadab said unto him, Lay you down on your bed, and make yourself sick: and when your father cometh to see you, say unto him, I pray you, let my sister Tamar come, and give me meat, and dress the meat in my sight, that I may see *it*, and eat *it* at her hand.
6 So Amnon lay down, and made himself sick: and when the king was come to see him, Amnon said unto the king, I pray you, let Tamar my sister come, and make me a couple of cakes in my sight, that I may eat at her hand.
7 Then David sent home to Tamar, saying, Go now to your brother Amnon's house, and dress him meat.
8 So Tamar went to her brother Amnon's house; and he was laid down. And she took flour, and kneaded *it*, and made cakes in his sight, and did bake the cakes.
9 And she took a pan, and poured *them* out before him; but he refused to eat. And Amnon said, Have out all men from me. And they went out every man from him.
10 And Amnon said unto Tamar, bring the meat into the chamber, that I may eat of your hand. And Tamar took the cakes which she had made, and brought *them* into the chamber to Amnon her brother.
11 And when she had brought *them* unto him to eat, he took hold of her, and said unto her, come lie with me, my sister
12 And she answered him, Nay, my brother, do not force me; for no such thing ought to be done in Israel: do not you this folly.
13 And I, whither will I cause my shame to go? and as for you, you will be as one of the fools in Israel. Now therefore, I pray you, speak unto the king; for he will not withhold me from you.
14 Howbeit he would not hearken unto her voice but, being stronger than she, forced her, and lay with her.
15 Then Amnon hated her exceedingly; so that the hatred wherewith he hated her *was* greater than the love wherewith he had loved her. And Amnon said unto her, Arise, be gone.
16 And she said unto him, *there is* no cause: this evil in sending me away *is* greater than the other that you did unto me. But he would not hearken unto her.
17 Then he called his servant that ministered unto him, and said, Put now this *woman* out from me, and bolt the door after her.
18 And *she had* a garment of **multiple** colors upon her: for with such robes were the king's daughters *that were* virgins appareled. Then his servant brought her out, and bolted the door after her.
19 And Tamar put ashes on her head, and rent her garment of **multiple** colors that *was* on her, and laid her hand on her head, and went on crying.
20 And Absalom her brother said unto her, has Amnon your brother been with you? But hold now your peace, my sister: he *is* your brother; regard not this thing. So Tamar remained desolate in her brother Absalom's house.
21 But when king David heard of all these things, he was very wroth.
22 And Absalom spoke unto his brother Amnon neither good or bad: for Absalom hated Amnon, because he had forced his sister Tamar.
23 And it came to pass after two full years, that Absalom had sheepshearers in Baal-hazor, which *is* beside Ephraim: and Absalom invited all the king's sons.
24 And Absalom came to the king, and said, Behold now, your servant has sheepshearers; let the king, I beseech you, and his servants go with your servant.
25 And the king said to Absalom, Nay, my son, let us not all now go, lest we be chargeable unto you. And he pressed him: howbeit he would not go, but blessed him.
26 Then said Absalom, if not, I pray you, let my brother Amnon go with us. And the king said unto him, why should he go with you?
27 But Absalom pressed him, that he let Amnon and all the king's sons go with him.
28 Now Absalom had commanded his servants, saying, Mark you now when Amnon's heart is merry with wine, and when I say unto

you, Smite Amnon; then kill him, fear not: have not I commanded you? Be courageous, and be valiant.

29 And the servants of Absalom did unto Amnon as Absalom had commanded. Then all the king's sons arose, and every man gat him up upon his mule, and fled.

30 And it came to pass, while they were in the way, that tidings came to David, saying, Absalom has slain all the king's sons, and there is not one of them left.

31 Then the king arose, and tare his garments, and lay on the earth; and all his servants stood by with their clothes rent.

32 And Jonadab, the son of Shimeah David's brother, answered and said, Let not my lord suppose *that* they have slain all the young men the king's sons; for Amnon only is dead: for by the appointment of Absalom this has been determined from the day that he forced his sister Tamar.

33 Now therefore let not my lord the king take the thing to his heart, to think that all the king's sons are dead: for Amnon only is dead.

34 But Absalom fled. And the young man that kept the watch lifted up his eyes, and looked, and, behold, there came much people by the way of the hill side behind him.

35 And Jonadab said unto the king, Behold, the king's sons come: as your servant said, so it is.

36 And it came to pass, as soon as he had made an end of speaking, that, behold, the king's sons came, and lifted up their voice and wept: and the king also and all his servants wept very sore.

37 But Absalom fled, and went to Talmai, the son of Ammihud, king of Geshur. And *David* mourned for his son every day.

38 So Absalom fled, and went to Geshur, and was there three years.

39 And *the soul of* King David longed to go forth unto Absalom: for he was comforted concerning Amnon, seeing he was dead.

CHAPTER 14

1 Now Joab the son of Zeruiah perceived that the king's heart *was* toward Absalom.

2 And Joab sent to Tekoah, and fetched there a wise woman, and said unto her, I pray you, feign yourself to be a mourner, and put on now mourning apparel, and anoint not yourself with oil, but be as a woman that had a long time mourned for the dead:

3 And come to the king, and speak on this manner unto him. So Joab put the words in her mouth.

4 And when the woman of Tekoah spoke to the king, she fell on her face to the ground, and did obeisance, and said, Help, O king.

5 And the king said unto her, what ails you? And she answered, I *am* indeed a widow woman, and mine husband is dead.

6 And your handmaid had two sons, and they two strove together in the field, and *there was* none to part them, but the one smote the other, and slew him.

7 And, behold, the whole family is risen against your handmaid, and they said, Deliver him that smote his brother, that we may kill him, for the life of his brother whom he slew; and we will destroy the heir also: and so they will quench my coal which is left, and will not leave to my husband *neither* name or remainder upon the earth.

8 And the king said unto the woman, Go to your house, and I will give charge concerning you.

9 And the woman of Tekoah said unto the king, my lord, O king, the iniquity *be* on me, and on my father's house: and the king and his throne *be* guiltless.

10 And the king said, whosoever said *ought* unto you, bring him to me, and he will not touch you anymore.

11 Then said she, I pray you, let the king remember the LORD your God, that you would not suffer the revengers of blood to destroy any more, lest they destroy my son. And he said, *As* the LORD lives, there will not one hair of your son fall to the earth.

12 Then the woman said, let your handmaid, I pray you, speak *one* word unto my lord the king. And he said, Say on.

13 And the woman said, wherefore then have you thought such a thing against the people of God? For the king does speak this thing as one which is faulty, in that the king does not fetch home again his banished.

14 For we must needs die, and *are* as water spilt on the ground, which cannot be gathered up again; neither does God respect *any* person: yet does he devise means, that his banished be not expelled from him.

15 Now therefore that I am come to speak of this thing unto my lord the king, *it is* because the people have made me afraid: and your handmaid said, I will now speak unto the king; it may be that the king will perform the request of his handmaid.

16 For the king will hear, to deliver his handmaid out of the hand of the man *that would* destroy me and my son together out of the inheritance of God.

17 Then your handmaid said, the word of my lord the king will now be comfortable: for as an angel of God, so *is* my lord the king to discern good and bad: therefore the LORD your God will be with you.

18 Then the king answered and said unto the woman Hide not from me, I pray you, the thing that I will ask you. And the woman said, Let my lord the king now speak.

19 And the king said, *Is not* the hand of Joab with you in all this? And the woman answered and said, *as* your soul lives, my lord the king, none can turn to the right hand or to the left from ought that my lord the king has spoken: for your servant Joab, he bade me, and he put all these words in the mouth of your handmaid:

20 To fetch about this form of speech has your servant Joab done this thing: and my lord *is* wise, according to the wisdom of an angel of God, to know all *things* that *are* in the earth.

21 And the king said unto Joab, Behold now, I have done this thing: go therefore, bring the young man Absalom again.

22 And Joab fell to the ground on his face, and bowed himself, and thanked the king: and Joab said, today your servant knows that I have found grace in your sight, my lord, O king, in that the king has fulfilled the request of his servant.

23 So Joab arose and went to Geshur, and brought Absalom to Jerusalem.

24 And the king said, Let him turn to his own house, and let him not see my face. So Absalom returned to his own house, and saw not the king's face.

25 But in all Israel there was none to be so much praised as Absalom for his beauty: from the sole of his foot even to the crown of his head there was no blemish in him.

26 And when he polled his head, (for it was at every year's end that he polled *it*: because *the hair* was heavy on him, therefore he polled it:) he weighed the hair of his head at two hundred shekels after the king's weight.

27 And unto Absalom there were born three sons, and one daughter, whose name *was* Tamar: she was a woman of a fair countenance.

28 So Absalom dwelt two full years in Jerusalem, and saw not the king's face.

29 Therefore Absalom sent for Joab, to have sent him to the king; but he would not come to him: and when he sent again the second time, he would not come.
30 Therefore he said unto his servants, See, Joab's field is near mine, and he has barley there; go and set it on fire. And Absalom's servants set the field on fire.
31 Then Joab arose, and came to Absalom unto *his* house, and said unto him, wherefore have your servants set my field on fire?
32 And Absalom answered Joab, Behold, I sent unto you, saying, come hither, that I may send you to the king, to say, wherefore am I come from Geshur? *It had been* good for me *to have been* there still: now therefore let me see the king's face; and if there be *any* iniquity in me, let him kill me.
33 So Joab came to the king, and told him: and when he had called for Absalom, he came to the king, and bowed himself on his face to the ground before the king: and the king kissed Absalom.

CHAPTER 15

1 And it came to pass after this, that Absalom prepared him chariots and horses, and fifty men to run before him.
2 And Absalom rose up early, and stood beside the way of the gate: and it was *so*, that when any man that had a controversy came to the king for judgment, then Absalom called unto him, and said, Of what city are you? And he said, your servant *is* of one of the tribes of Israel.
3 And Absalom said unto him, See, your matters *are* good and right; but *there is* no man *deputed* of the king to hear you.
4 Absalom said moreover, Oh that I *was* made judge in the land, that every man which has any suit or cause might come unto me, and I would do him justice!
5 And it was *so*, that when any man came nigh *to him* to do him obeisance, he put forth his hand, and took him, and kissed him.
6 And on this manner did Absalom to all Israel that came to the king for judgment: so Absalom stole the hearts of the men of Israel.
7 And it came to pass after forty years, that Absalom said unto the king, I pray you, let me go and pay my vow, which I have vowed unto the LORD, in Hebron.
8 For your servant vowed a vow while I abode at Geshur in Syria, saying, If the LORD will bring me again indeed to Jerusalem, then I will serve the LORD.
9 And the king said unto him, Go in peace. So he arose, and went to Hebron.
10 But Absalom sent spies throughout all the tribes of Israel, saying, As soon as you hear the sound of the trumpet, then you will say, Absalom reigns in Hebron.
11 And with Absalom went two hundred men out of Jerusalem, *that were* called; and they went in their simplicity, and they knew not any thing.
12 And Absalom sent for Ahithophel the Gilonite, David's counselor, from his city, *even* from Giloh, while he offered sacrifices. And the conspiracy was strong; for the people increased continually with Absalom.
13 And there came a messenger to David, saying, the hearts of the men of Israel are after Absalom.
14 And David said unto all his servants that *were* with him at Jerusalem, Arise, and let us flee; for we will not *else* escape from Absalom: make speed to depart, lest he overtake us suddenly, and bring evil upon us, and smite the city with the edge of the sword.
15 And the king's servants said unto the king, Behold, your servants *are ready to do* whatsoever my lord the king will appoint.

16 And the king went forth, and his **entire** household after him. And the king left ten women, *which were* concubines, to keep the house.
17 And the king went forth, and all the people after him, and tarried in a place that was far off.
18 And all his servants passed on beside him; and all the Cherethites, and all the Pelethites, and all the Gittites, six hundred men which came after him from Gath, passed on before the king.
19 Then said the king to Ittai the Gittite, Wherefore go you also with us? Return to your place, and abide with the king: for you are a stranger, and also an exile.
20 Whereas you came *but* yesterday, should I this day make you go up and down with us? Seeing I go whither I may, return you, and take back your brethren: mercy and truth *be* with you.
21 And Ittai answered the king, and said, *As* the LORD lives, and *as* my lord the king lives, surely in what place my lord the king will be, whether in death or life, even there also will your servant be.
22 And David said to Ittai, Go and pass over. And Ittai the Gittite passed over, and all his men, and all the little ones that *were* with him.
23 And all the country wept with a loud voice, and all the people passed over: the king also himself passed over the brook Kidron, and all the people passed over, toward the way of the wilderness.
24 And lo Zadok also, and all the Levites *were* with him, bearing the ark of the covenant of God: and they set down the ark of God; and Abiathar went up, until all the people had done passing out of the city.
25 And the king said unto Zadok, Carry back the ark of God into the city: if I will find favor in the eyes of the LORD, he will bring me again, and show me *both* it, and his habitation:
26 But if he thus say, I have no delight in you; behold, *here am* I, let him do to me as seems good unto him.
27 The king said also unto Zadok the priest, are *not* you a seer? Return into the city in peace, and your two sons with you, Ahimaaz your son, and Jonathan the son of Abiathar.
28 See, I will tarry in the plain of the wilderness, until there come word from you to certify me.
29 Zadok therefore and Abiathar carried the ark of God again to Jerusalem: and they tarried there.
30 And David went up by the ascent of *mount* Olivet, and wept as he went up, and had his head covered, and he went barefoot: and all the people that *was* with him covered every man his head, and they went up, weeping as they went up.
31 And *one* told David, saying, Ahithophel *is* among the conspirators with Absalom. And David said, O LORD, I pray you, turn the counsel of Ahithophel into foolishness.
32 And it came to pass, that *when* David was come to the top *of the mount*, where he worshipped God, behold, Hushai the Archite came to meet him with his coat rent, and earth upon his head:
33 Unto whom David said, if you pass on with me, then you will be a burden unto me:
34 But if you return to the city, and say unto Absalom, I will be your servant, O king; *as I have been* your father's servant hitherto, so *will* I now also *be* your servant: then may you for me defeat the counsel of Ahithophel.
35 And have *you* not there with you Zadok and Abiathar the priests? Therefore it will be, *that* what thing soever you will hear out of the king's house, you will tell *it* to Zadok and Abiathar the priests.

36 Behold, *they have* there with them their two sons, Ahimaaz Zadok's *son*, and Jonathan Abiathar's *son*; and by them you will send unto me everything that you can hear.
37 So Hushai David's friend came into the city, and Absalom came into Jerusalem.

CHAPTER 16

1 And when David was a little past the top *of the hill*, behold, Ziba the servant of Mephibosheth met him, with a couple of asses saddled, and upon them two hundred *loaves* of bread, and an hundred bunches of raisins, and an hundred of summer fruits, and a bottle of wine.
2 And the king said unto Ziba, What meanest you by these? And Ziba said, the asses *are* for the king's household to ride on; and the bread and summer fruit for the young men to eat; and the wine, that such as be faint in the wilderness may drink.
3 And the king said, and where *is* your master's son? And Ziba said unto the king, Behold, he abides at Jerusalem: for he said, today will the house of Israel restore me the kingdom of my father.
4 Then said the king to Ziba, Behold, your *are* all that *pertained* unto Mephibosheth. And Ziba said, I humbly beseech you *that* I may find grace in your sight, my lord, O king.
5 And when king David came to Bahurim, behold, there came out a man of the family of the house of Saul, whose name *was* Shimei, the son of Gera: he came forth, and cursed still as he came.
6 And he cast stones at David, and at all the servants of King David: and all the people and all the mighty men *were* on his right hand and on his left.
7 And thus said Shimei when he cursed, Come out, come out, you bloody man, and you man of Belial:
8 The LORD has returned upon you all the blood of the house of Saul, in whose stead you have reigned; and the LORD has delivered the kingdom into the hand of Absalom your son: and, behold, you are *taken* in your mischief, because you are a bloody man.
9 Then said Abishai the son of Zeruiah unto the king, why should this dead dog curse my lord the king? Let me go over, I pray you, and take off his head.
10 And the king said, what have I to do with you, you sons of Zeruiah? So let him curse, because the LORD has said unto him, Curse David. Who will then say, wherefore have you done so?
11 And David said to Abishai, and to all his servants, Behold, my son, which came forth of my bowels, seeks my life: how much more now *may this* Benjamite *do it*? Let him alone, and let him curse; for the LORD has bidden him.
12 It may be that the LORD will look on mine affliction, and that the LORD will requite[1] me good for his cursing this day.
13 And as David and his men went by the way, Shimei went along on the hill's side over against him, and cursed as he went, and threw stones at him, and cast dust.
14 And the king, and all the people that *were* with him, came weary, and refreshed themselves there.
15 And Absalom, and all the people the men of Israel, came to Jerusalem, and Ahithophel with him.
16 And it came to pass, when Hushai the Archite, David's friend, was come unto Absalom, that Hushai said unto Absalom, God save the king, God save the king.
17 And Absalom said to Hushai, *Is* this your kindness to your friend? Why **did** you not **go** with your friend?

---

[1] requite- to turn back, build, circumcise, deliver again, refresh, reverse, reward, fetch home again. [Strgs#7725]

18 And Hushai said unto Absalom, Nay; but whom the LORD, and this people, and all the men of Israel, choose, his will I be, and with him will I abide.
19 And again, whom should I serve? *Should I* not *serve* in the presence of his son? As I have served in your father's presence, so will I be in your presence.
20 Then said Absalom to Ahithophel, Give counsel among you what we will do.
21 And Ahithophel said unto Absalom, Go in unto your father's concubines, which he has left to keep the house; and all Israel will hear that you are abhorred of your father: then will the hands of all that *are* with you be strong.
22 So they spread Absalom a tent upon the top of the house; and Absalom went in unto his father's concubines in the sight of all Israel.
23 And the counsel of Ahithophel, which he counseled in those days, *was* as if a man had enquired at the oracle of God: so *was* all the counsel of Ahithophel both with David and with Absalom.

CHAPTER 17

1 Moreover Ahithophel said unto Absalom, Let me now choose out twelve thousand men, and I will arise and pursue after David this night:
2 And I will come upon him while he *is* weary and weak handed, and will make him afraid: and all the people that *are* with him will flee; and I will smite the king only:
3 And I will bring back all the people unto you: the man whom you seek *is* as if all returned: *so* all the people will be in peace.
4 And the saying pleased Absalom well, and all the elders of Israel.
5 Then said Absalom, call now Hushai the Archite also, and let us hear likewise what he said.
6 And when Hushai was come to Absalom, Absalom spoke unto him, saying, Ahithophel has spoken after this manner: will we do *after* his saying? If not; speak you.
7 And Hushai said unto Absalom, the counsel that Ahithophel has given *is* not good at this time.
8 For, said Hushai, you know your father and his men, that they *be* mighty men, and they *be* chafed in their minds, as a bear robbed of her whelps in the field: and your father *is* a man of war, and will not lodge with the people.
9 Behold, he is hid now in some pit, or in some *other* place: and it will come to pass, when some of them be overthrown at the first, that whosoever hears it will say, there is a slaughter among the people that follow Absalom.
10 And he also *that is* valiant, whose heart *is* as the heart of a lion, will utterly melt: for all Israel knows that your father *is* a mighty man, and *they* which *be* with him *are* valiant men.
11 Therefore I counsel that all Israel be generally gathered unto you, from Dan even to Beer-sheba, as the sand that *is* by the sea for multitude; and that you go to battle in your own person.
12 So will we come upon him in some place where he will be found, and we will light upon him as the dew falls on the ground: and of him and of all the men that *are* with him there will not be left so much as one.
13 Moreover, if he be gotten into a city, then will all Israel bring ropes to that city, and we will draw it into the river, until there be not one small stone found there.
14 And Absalom and all the men of Israel said, the counsel of Hushai the Archite *is* better than the counsel of Ahithophel. For the

LORD had appointed to defeat the good counsel of Ahithophel, to the intent that the LORD might bring evil upon Absalom.

15 Then said Hushai unto Zadok and to Abiathar the priests, thus and thus did Ahithophel counsel Absalom and the elders of Israel; and thus and thus have I counseled.

16 Now therefore send quickly, and tell David, saying, Lodge not this night in the plains of the wilderness, but speedily pass over; lest the king be swallowed up, and all the people that *are* with him.

17 Now Jonathan and Ahimaaz stayed by En-rogel; for they might not be seen to come into the city: and a wench went and told them; and they went and told King David.

18 Nevertheless a lad saw them, and told Absalom: but they went both of them away quickly, and came to a man's house in Bahurim, which had a well in his court; whither they went down.

19 And the woman took and spread a covering over the well's mouth, and spread ground corn thereon; and the thing was not known.

20 And when Absalom's servants came to the woman to the house, they said, where *is* Ahimaaz and Jonathan? And the woman said unto them, they *are* gone over the brook of water. And when they had sought and could not find *them*, they returned to Jerusalem.

21 And it came to pass, after they were departed, that they came up out of the well, and went and told king David, and said unto David, Arise, and pass quickly over the water: for thus has Ahithophel counseled against you.

22 Then David arose, and all the people that *were* with him, and they passed over Jordan: by the morning light there lacked not one of them that was not gone over Jordan.

23 And when Ahithophel saw that his counsel was not followed, he saddled *his* ass, and arose, and gat him home to his house, to his city, and put his household in order, and hanged himself, and died, and was buried in the sepulcher of his father.

24 Then David came to Mahanaim. And Absalom passed over Jordan, he and all the men of Israel with him.

25 And Absalom made Amasa captain of the host instead of Joab: which Amasa *was* a man's son, whose name *was* Ithra an Israelite, that went in to Abigail the daughter of Nahash, sister to Zeruiah Joab's mother.

26 So Israel and Absalom pitched in the land of Gilead.

27 And it came to pass, when David was come to Mahanaim, that Shobi the son of Nahash of Rabbah of the children of Ammon, and Machir the son of Ammiel of Lo-debar, and Barzillai the Gileadite of Rogelim,

28 Brought beds, and **bowls**, and earthen vessels, and wheat, and barley, and flour, and parched *corn*, and beans, and lentils, and parched *pulse*,

29 And honey, and butter, and sheep, and cheese of **heifer**, for David, and for the people that *were* with him, to eat: for they said, the people *are* hungry, and weary, and thirsty, in the wilderness.

CHAPTER 18

1 And David numbered the people that *were* with him, and set captains of thousands and captains of hundreds over them.

2 And David sent forth a third part of the people under the hand of Joab, and a third part under the hand of Abishai the son of Zeruiah, Joab's brother, and a third part under the hand of Ittai the Gittite. And the king said unto the people, I will surely go forth with you myself also.

3 But the people answered, you will not go forth: for if we flee away, they will not care for us; neither if half of us die, will they care for us: but now you *are* worth ten thousand of us: therefore now *it is* better that you **help** us out of the city.

4 And the king said unto them, what seems best **to you** I will do. And the king stood by the gate side, and all the people came out by hundreds and by thousands.

5 And the king commanded Joab and Abishai and Ittai, saying, *deal* gently for my sake with the young man, *even* with Absalom. And all the people heard when the king gave all the captains charge concerning Absalom.

6 So the people went out into the field against Israel: and the battle was in the wood of Ephraim;

7 Where the people of Israel were slain before the servants of David, and there was there a great slaughter that day of twenty thousand *men*.

8 For the battle was there scattered over the face of all the country: and the wood devoured more people that day than the sword devoured.

9 And Absalom met the servants of David. And Absalom rode upon a mule, and the mule went under the thick boughs of a great oak, and his head caught hold of the oak, and he was taken up between the heaven and the earth; and the mule that *was* under him went away.

10 And a certain man saw *it*, and told Joab, and said, Behold, I saw Absalom hanged in an oak.

11 And Joab said unto the man that told him, and, behold, you saw *him*, and why did you not smite him there to the ground? And I would have given you ten *shekels* of silver, and a girdle.

12 And the man said unto Joab, Though I should receive a thousand *shekels* of silver in mine hand, *yet* would I not put forth mine hand against the king's son: for in our hearing the king charged you and Abishai and Ittai, saying, Beware that none *touch* the young man Absalom.

13 Otherwise I should have wrought falsehood against mine own life: for there is no matter hid from the king, and you yourself would have set yourself against *me*.

14 Then said Joab, I may not tarry thus with you. And he took three darts in his hand, and thrust them through the heart of Absalom, while he *was* yet alive in the midst of the oak.

15 And ten young men that bare Joab's armor compassed about and smote Absalom, and slew him.

16 And Joab blew the trumpet, and the people returned from pursuing after Israel: for Joab held back the people.

17 And they took Absalom, and cast him into a great pit in the wood, and laid a very great heap of stones upon him: and all Israel fled everyone to his tent.

18 Now Absalom in his lifetime had taken and reared up for himself a pillar, which *is* in the king's dale: for he said, I have no son to keep my name in remembrance: and he called the pillar after his own name: and it is called unto this day, Absalom's place.

19 Then said Ahimaaz the son of Zadok, Let me now run, and bear the king tidings, how that the LORD has avenged him of his enemies.

20 And Joab said unto him, you will not bear tidings this day, but you will bear tidings another day: but this day you will bear no tidings, because the king's son is dead.

21 Then said Joab to Cushi, Go tell the king what you have seen. And Cushi bowed himself unto Joab, and ran.

22 Then said Ahimaaz the son of Zadok yet again to Joab, But howsoever, let me, I pray you, also run after Cushi. And Joab said, wherefore will you run, my son, seeing that you have no tidings ready?

23 But howsoever, *said he*, let me run. And he said unto him, run. Then Ahimaaz ran by the way of the plain, and overran Cushi.
24 And David sat between the two gates: and the watchman went up to the roof over the gate unto the wall, and lifted up his eyes, and looked, and behold a man running alone.
25 And the watchman cried, and told the king. And the king said, If he *be* alone, *there is* tidings in his mouth. And he came apace, and drew near.
26 And the watchman saw another man running: and the watchman called unto the porter, and said, Behold *another* man running alone. And the king said, He also brings tidings.
27 And the watchman said, I think the running of the foremost is like the running of Ahimaaz the son of Zadok. And the king said, He *is* a good man, and cometh with good tidings.
28 And Ahimaaz called, and said unto the king, All is well. And he fell down to the earth upon his face before the king, and said, Blessed *be* the LORD your God, which has delivered[1] up the men that lifted up their hand against my lord the king.
29 And the king said, Is the young man Absalom safe? And Ahimaaz answered, when Joab sent the king's servant, and *me* your servant, I saw a great tumult, but I knew not what *it was*.
30 And the king said *unto him*, turn aside, *and* stand here. And he turned aside, and stood still.
31 And, behold, Cushi came; and Cushi said, Tidings, my lord the king: for the LORD has avenged you this day of all them that rose up against you.
32 And the king said unto Cushi, Is the young man Absalom safe? And Cushi answered, the enemies of my lord the king, and all that rise against you to do you hurt, be as *that* young man *is*.
33 And the king was much moved, and went up to the chamber over the gate, and wept: and as he went, thus he said, O my son Absalom, my son, my son Absalom! Would God I had died for you, O Absalom, my son, my son!

CHAPTER 19

1 And it was told Joab, behold, the king weeps and mourns for Absalom.
2 And the victory that day was *turned* into mourning unto all the people: for the people heard say that day how the king was grieved for his son.
3 And the people **came upon** them by stealth that day into the city, as people being ashamed steal away when they flee in battle.
4 But the king covered his face, and the king cried with a loud voice, O my son Absalom, O Absalom, my son, my son!
5 And Joab came into the house to the king, and said, you have shamed this day the faces of all your servants, which this day have saved your life, and the lives of your sons and of your daughters, and the lives of your wives, and the lives of your concubines;
6 In that you love your enemies, and hate your friends. For you have declared this day, that you regard neither princes or servants: for this day I perceive, that if Absalom had lived, and all we had died this day, then it had pleased you well.
7 Now therefore arise, go forth, and speak comfortably unto your servants: for I swear by the LORD, if you go not forth, there will not tarry one with you this night: and that will be worse unto you than all the evil that befell you from your youth until now.
8 Then the king arose, and sat in the gate. And they told unto all the people, saying, Behold, the king does sit in the gate. And all the people came before the king: for Israel had fled every man to his tent.
9 And all the people were at strife throughout all the tribes of Israel, saying, the king saved us out of the hand of our enemies and he delivered us out of the hand of the Philistines; and now he is fled out of the land for Absalom.
10 And Absalom, whom we anointed over us, is dead in battle. Now therefore why speak you not a word of bringing the king back?
11 And King David sent to Zadok and to Abiathar the priests, saying, Speak unto the elders of Judah, saying, Why are you the last to bring the king back to his house? Seeing the speech of all Israel is come to the king, *even* to his house.
12 you *are* my brethren, you *are* my bones and my flesh: wherefore then are you the last to bring back the king?
13 And say you to Amasa, are you not of my bone, and of my flesh? God do so to me, and more also, if you be not captain of the host before me continually in the room of Joab.
14 And he bowed the heart of all the men of Judah, even as *the heart of* one man; so that they sent *this word* unto the king, Return you, and all your servants.
15 So the king returned, and came to Jordan. And Judah came to Gilgal, to go to meet the king, to conduct the king over Jordan.
16 And Shimei the son of Gera, a Benjamite, which *was* of Bahurim, hasted and came down with the men of Judah to meet King David.
17 And *there were* a thousand men of Benjamin with him, and Ziba the servant of the house of Saul, and his fifteen sons and his twenty servants with him; and they went over Jordan before the king.
18 And there went over a ferry boat to carry over the king's household, and to do what he thought **was** good. And Shimei the son of Gera fell down before the king, as he was come over Jordan;
19 And said unto the king, Let not my lord impute iniquity unto me, neither do you remember that which your servant did perversely the day that my lord the king went out of Jerusalem, that the king should take it to his heart.
20 For your servant does know that I have sinned: therefore, behold, I am come the first this day of all the house of Joseph to go down to meet my lord the king.
21 But Abishai the son of Zeruiah answered and said, will not Shimei be put to death for this, because he cursed the LORD'S anointed?
22 And David said, what have I to do with you, you sons of Zeruiah, that you should this day be adversaries unto me? Will there any man be put to death this day in Israel? For do not I know that I *am* this day king over Israel?
23 Therefore the king said unto Shimei, you will not die. And the king swore unto him.
24 And Mephibosheth the son of Saul came down to meet the king, and had neither dressed his feet, or trimmed his beard, or washed his clothes, from the day the king departed until the day he came *again* in peace.
25 And it came to pass, when he was come to Jerusalem to meet the king, that the king said unto him, wherefore wentest not you with me, Mephibosheth?
26 And he answered, my lord, O king, my servant deceived me: for your servant said, I will saddle me an ass, that I may ride thereon, and go to the king; because your servant *is* lame.

---

[1] lit. to shut up, to surrender, repair [Strgs#5462]

27 And he has slandered your servant unto my lord the king; but my lord the king *is* as an angel of God: do therefore *what is* good in your eyes.

28 For all *of* my father's house were but dead men before my lord the king: yet did you set your servant among them that did eat at your own table. What right therefore have I yet to cry any more unto the king?

29 And the king said unto him, why speak you any more of your matters? I have said, you and Ziba divide the land.

30 And Mephibosheth said unto the king, yea, let him take all, forasmuch as my lord the king is come again in peace unto his own house.

31 And Barzillai the Gileadite came down from Rogelim, and went over Jordan with the king, to conduct him over Jordan.

32 Now Barzillai was a very aged man, *even* fourscore years old: and he had provided the king of sustenance while he lay at Mahanaim; for he *was* a very great man.

33 And the king said unto Barzillai, Come you over with me, and I will feed you with me in Jerusalem.

34 And Barzillai said unto the king, how long have I to live, that I should go up with the king unto Jerusalem?

35 I *am* this day fourscore years old: *and* can I discern between good and evil? Can your servant taste what I eat or what I drink? Can I hear any more the voice of singing men and singing women? Wherefore then should your servant be yet a burden unto my lord the king?

36 Your servant will go a little way over Jordan with the king: and why should the king recompense it me with such a reward?

37 Let your servant, I pray you, turn back again, that I may die in mine own city, *and be buried* by the grave of my father and of my mother. But behold your servant Chimham; let him go over with my lord the king; and do to him what will seem good unto you.

38 And the king answered, Chimham will go over with me, and I will do to him that which will seem good unto you: and whatsoever you will require of me, *that* will I do for you.

39 And all the people went over Jordan. And when the king was come over, the king kissed Barzillai, and blessed him; and he returned unto his own place.

40 Then the king went on to Gilgal, and Chimham went on with him: and all the people of Judah conducted the king, and also half the people of Israel.

41 And, behold, all the men of Israel came to the king, and said unto the king, Why have our brethren the men of Judah stolen you away, and have brought the king, and his household, and all David's men with him, over Jordan?

42 And all the men of Judah answered the men of Israel, because the king *is* near of kin to us: wherefore then be you angry for this matter? Have we eaten at all of the king's *cost*? Or has he given us any gift?

43 And the men of Israel answered the men of Judah, and said, we have ten parts in the king, and we have also more *right* in David than ye: why then did you despise us, that our advice should not be first had in bringing back our king? And the words of the men of Judah were fiercer than the words of the men of Israel.

CHAPTER 20

1 And there happened to be there a man of Belial, whose name *was* Sheba, the son of Bichri, a Benjamite: and he blew a trumpet, and said, we have no part in David, neither have we inheritance in the son of Jesse: every man to his tents, O Israel.

2 So every man of Israel went up from after David, *and* followed Sheba the son of Bichri: but the men of Judah clave unto their king, from Jordan even to Jerusalem.

3 And David came to his house at Jerusalem; and the king took the ten women *his* concubines, whom he had left to keep the house, and put them in ward, and fed them, but went not in unto them. So they were shut up unto the day of their death, living in widowhood.

4 Then said the king to Amasa, Assemble me the men of Judah within three days, and be you here present.

5 So Amasa went to assemble *the men of* Judah: but he tarried longer than the set time which he had appointed him.

6 And David said to Abishai, Now will Sheba the son of Bichri do us more harm than *did* Absalom: take you your lord's servants, and pursue after him, lest he get him fenced cities, and escape us.

7 And there went out after him Joab's men, and the Cherethites, and the Pelethites, and all the mighty men: and they went out of Jerusalem, to pursue after Sheba the son of Bichri.

8 When they *were* at the great stone which *is* in Gibeon, Amasa went before them. And Joab's garment that he had put on was girded unto him, and upon it a girdle *with* a sword fastened upon his loins in the sheath thereof; and as he went forth it fell out.

9 And Joab said to Amasa, are you in health, my brother? And Joab took Amasa by the beard with the right hand to kiss him.

10 But Amasa took no heed to the sword that *was* in Joab's hand: so he **struck** him therewith in the fifth *rib*, and shed out his bowels to the ground, and struck him not again; and he died. So Joab and Abishai his brother pursued after Sheba the son of Bichri.

11 And one of Joab's men stood by him, and said, He that favor Joab, and he that *is* for David, *let him go* after Joab.

12 And Amasa wallowed in blood in the midst of the highway. And when the man saw that all the people stood still, he removed Amasa out of the highway into the field, and cast a cloth upon him, when he saw that every one that came by him stood still.

13 When he was removed out of the highway, all the people went on after Joab, to pursue after Sheba the son of Bichri.

14 And he went through all the tribes of Israel unto Abel, and to Beth-maachah, and all the Berites: and they were gathered together, and went also after him.

15 And they came and besieged him in Abel of Beth-maachah, and they cast up a bank against the city, and it stood in the trench: and all the people that *were* with Joab battered the wall, to throw it down.

16 Then cried a wise woman out of the city, hear, hear; say, I pray you, unto Joab, Come near hither, that I may speak with you.

17 And when he was come near unto her, the woman said, are you Joab? And he answered, I *am he*. Then she said unto him, hear the words of your handmaid. And he answered, I do hear.

18 Then she spoke, saying, they were wont to speak in old time, saying, they will surely ask *counsel* at Abel: and so they ended *the matter*.

19 I *am one of them that are* peaceable *and* faithful in Israel: you seek to destroy a city and a mother in Israel: why will you swallow up the inheritance of the LORD?

20 And Joab answered and said, far be it, far be it from me, that I should swallow up or destroy.

21 The matter *is* not so: but a man of mount Ephraim, Sheba the son of Bichri by name, has lifted up his hand against the king, *even* against David: deliver him only, and I will depart from the city. And the woman said unto Joab, Behold, his head will be thrown to you over the wall.

22 Then the woman went unto all the people in her wisdom. And they cut off the head of Sheba the son of Bichri, and cast *it* out to Joab. And he blew a trumpet, and they retired from the city, every man to his tent. And Joab returned to Jerusalem unto the king.
23 Now Joab *was* over all the host of Israel: and Benaiah the son of Jehoiada *was* over the Cherethites and over the Pelethites:
24 And Adoram *was* over the tribute: and Jehoshaphat the son of Ahilud *was* recorder:
25 And Sheva *was* scribe: and Zadok and Abiathar *were* the priests:
26 And Ira also the Jairite was a chief ruler about David.

CHAPTER 21

1 Then there was a famine in the days of David three years, year after year; and David enquired of the LORD. And the LORD answered, *it is* for Saul, and for *his* bloody house, because he slew the Gibeonites.
2 And the king called the Gibeonites, and said unto them; (now the Gibeonites *were* not of the children of Israel, but of the remnant of the Amorites; and the children of Israel had sworn unto them: and Saul sought to slay them in his zeal to the children of Israel and Judah.)
3 Wherefore David said unto the Gibeonites, What will I do for you? And wherewith will I make the atonement, that you may bless the inheritance of the LORD?
4 And the Gibeonites said unto him, we will have no silver or gold of Saul, or of his house; neither for us will you kill any man in Israel. And he said, what you will say, *that* will I do for you.
5 And they answered the king, the man that consumed us, and that devised against us *that* we should be destroyed from remaining in any of the coasts of Israel,
6 Let seven men of his sons be delivered unto us, and we will hang them up unto the LORD in Gibeah of Saul, *whom* the LORD did choose. And the king said, I will give *them*.
7 But the king spared Mephibosheth, the son of Jonathan the son of Saul, because of the LORD'S oath that *was* between them, between David and Jonathan the son of Saul.
8 But the king took the two sons of Rizpah the daughter of Aiah, whom she bare unto Saul, Armoni and Mephibosheth; and the five sons of Michal the daughter of Saul, whom she brought up for Adriel the son of Barzillai the Meholathite:
9 And he delivered them into the hands of the Gibeonites, and they hanged them in the hill before the LORD: and they fell *all* seven together, and were put to death in the days of harvest, in the first *days,* in the beginning of barley harvest.
10 And Rizpah the daughter of Aiah took sackcloth, and spread it for her upon the rock, from the beginning of harvest until water dropped upon them out of heaven, and suffered neither the birds of the air to rest on them by day, or the beasts of the field by night.
11 And it was told David what Rizpah the daughter of Aiah, the concubine of Saul, had done.
12 And David went and took the bones of Saul and the bones of Jonathan his son from the men of Jabesh-gilead, which had stolen them from the street of Beth-shan, where the Philistines had hanged them, when the Philistines had slain Saul in Gilboa:
13 And he brought up from there the bones of Saul and the bones of Jonathan his son; and they gathered the bones of them that were hanged.
14 And the bones of Saul and Jonathan his son buried they in the country of Benjamin in Zelah, in the sepulchre of Kish his father: and they performed all that the king commanded. And after that God was intreated for the land.
15 Moreover the Philistines had yet war again with Israel; and David went down, and his servants with him, and fought against the Philistines: and David waxed faint.
16 And Ishbi-benob, which *was* of the sons of the giant, the weight of whose spear *weighed* three hundred *shekels* of brass in weight, he being girded with a new *sword*, thought to have slain David.
17 But Abishai the son of Zeruiah succoured him, and smote the Philistine, and killed him. Then the men of David swore unto him, saying, you will go no more out with us to battle, that you quench not the light of Israel.
18 And it came to pass after this, that there was again a battle with the Philistines at Gob: then Sibbechai the Hushathite slew Saph, which *was* of the sons of the giant.
19 And there was again a battle in Gob with the Philistines, where Elhanan the son of Jaare-oregim, a Beth-lehemite, slew *the brother of* Goliath the Gittite, the staff of whose spear *was* like a weaver's beam.
20 And there was yet a battle in Gath, where was a man of *great* stature, that had on every hand six fingers, and on every foot six toes, four and twenty in number; and he also was born to the giant.
21 And when he defied Israel, Jonathan the son of Shimea the brother of David slew him.
22 These four were born to the giant in Gath, and fell by the hand of David, and by the hand of his servants.

CHAPTER 22

1 And David spoke unto the LORD the words of this song in the day *that* the LORD had delivered him out of the hand of all his enemies, and out of the hand of Saul:
2 And he said, The LORD *is* my rock, and my fortress, and my deliverer;
3 The God of my rock; in him will I trust: *he is* my shield, and the horn of my salvation, my high tower, and my refuge, my savior; you saved me from violence.
4 I will call on the LORD, *who is* worthy to be praised: so will I be saved from mine enemies.
5 When the waves of death compassed me, the floods of ungodly men made me afraid;
6 The sorrows of hell compassed me about; the snares of death prevented me;
7 In my distress I called upon the LORD, and cried to my God: and he did hear my voice out of his temple, and my cry *did enter* into his ears.
8 Then the earth shook and trembled; the foundations of heaven moved and shook, because he was **angry**.
9 There went up a smoke out of his nostrils, and fire out of his mouth devoured: coals were kindled by it.
10 He bowed the heavens also, and came down; and darkness *was* under his feet.
11 And he rode upon a cherub, and did fly: and he was seen upon the wings of the wind.
12 And he made darkness pavilions round about him, dark waters, *and* thick clouds of the skies.
13 Through the brightness before him were coals of fire kindled.
14 The LORD thundered from heaven, and the most High uttered his voice.
15 And he sent out arrows, and scattered them; lightning, and discomfited them.

16 And the channels of the sea appeared, the foundations of the world were discovered, at the rebuking of the LORD, at the blast of the breath of his nostrils.
17 He sent from above, he took me; he drew me out of many waters;
18 He delivered me from my strong enemy, *and* from them that hated me: for they were too strong for me.
19 They prevented me in the day of my calamity: but the LORD was my stay.
20 He brought me forth also into a large place: he delivered me, because he delighted in me.
21 The LORD rewarded me according to my righteousness: according to the cleanness of my hands has he recompensed me.
22 For I have kept the ways of the LORD, and have not wickedly departed from my God.
23 For all his judgments *were* before me: and *as for* his statutes, I did not depart from them.
24 I was also upright before him, and have kept myself from mine iniquity.
25 Therefore the LORD has recompensed me according to my righteousness; according to my cleanness in his eye sight.
26 With the merciful you will show yourself merciful, *and* with the upright man you will show yourself upright.
27 With the pure you will show yourself pure; and with the **distorted** you will show yourself unsavory.
28 And the afflicted people you will save: but your eyes *are* upon the haughty, *that* you may bring *them* down.
29 For you are my lamp, O LORD: and the LORD will lighten my darkness.
30 For by you I have run through a troop: by my God have I leaped over a wall.
31 *As for* God, his way *is* perfect; the word of the LORD *is* tried: he *is* a buckler to all them that trust in him.
32 For who *is* God, save the LORD? And who *is* a rock, save our God?
33 God *is* my strength *and* power: and he makes my way perfect.
34 He makes my feet like hinds' *feet*: and sets me upon my high places.
35 He teaches my hands to war; so that a bow of steel is broken by mine arms.
36 you have also given me the shield of your salvation: and your gentleness has [made me great]¹.
37 you have enlarged my steps under me; so that my feet did not slip.
38 I have pursued mine enemies, and destroyed them; and turned not again until I had consumed them.
39 And I have consumed them, and wounded them, that they could not arise: yea, they are fallen under my feet.
40 For you have girded me with strength to battle: them that rose up against me have you subdued under me.
41 you have also given me the necks of mine enemies, that I might destroy them that hate me.
42 They looked, but *there was* none to save; *even* unto the LORD, but he answered them not.
43 Then did I beat them as small as the dust of the earth, I did stamp them as the mire of the street, *and* did spread them abroad.
44 you also have delivered me from the strivings of my people, you have kept me *to be* head of the heathen: a people *which* I knew not will serve me.

45 Strangers will submit themselves unto me: as soon as they hear, they will be obedient unto me.
46 Strangers will fade away, and they will be afraid out of their close places.
47 The LORD lives; and blessed *be* my rock; and exalted be the God of the rock of my salvation.
48 *It is* God that avenges me, and that brings down the people under me,
49 And that brings me forth from mine enemies: you also have lifted me up on high above them that rose up against me: you have delivered me from the violent man.
50 Therefore I will give thanks unto you, O LORD among the heathen, and I will sing praises unto your name.
51 *He is* the tower of salvation for his king: and showed mercy to his anointed, unto David, and to his seed for evermore.

CHAPTER 23

1 Now these *be* the last words of David. David the son of Jesse said, and the man *who was* raised up on high, the anointed of the God of Jacob, and the sweet psalmist of Israel, said,
2 The Spirit of the LORD spoke by me, and his word *was* in my tongue.
3 The God of Israel said, the Rock of Israel spoke to me, He that rules over men *must be* just, ruling in the fear of God.
4 And *he will be* as the light of the morning, *when* the sun rises, *even* a morning without clouds; *as* the tender grass springing out of the earth by clear shining after rain.
5 Although my house *be* not so with God; yet he has made with me an everlasting covenant, ordered in all *things*, and sure: for *this is* all my salvation, and all *my* desire, although he make *it* not to grow.
6 But *the sons* of Belial will *be* all of them as thorns thrust away, because they cannot be taken with hands:
7 But the man *that* will touch them must be fenced with iron and the staff of a spear; and they will be utterly burned with fire in the *same* place.
8 These *be* the names of the mighty men whom David had: The Tachmonite that sat in the seat, chief among the captains; the same *was* Adino the Eznite: *he lift up his spear* against eight hundred, whom he slew at one time.
9 And after him *was* Eleazar the son of Dodo the Ahohite, *one of* the three mighty men with David, when they defied the Philistines *that* were there gathered together to battle, and the men of Israel were gone away:
10 He arose, and smote the Philistines until his hand was weary, and his hand clave unto the sword: and the LORD wrought a great victory that day; and the people returned after him only to spoil.
11 And after him *was* Shammah the son of Agee the Hararite. And the Philistines were gathered together into a troop, where was a piece of ground full of lentiles: and the people fled from the Philistines.
12 But he stood in the midst of the ground, and defended it, and slew the Philistines: and the LORD wrought a great victory.
13 And three of the thirty chief went down, and came to David in the harvest time unto the cave of Adullam: and the troop of the Philistines pitched in the valley of Rephaim.
14 And David *was* then in a hold, and the garrison of the Philistines *was* then *in* Beth-lehem.

---

¹ lit. multiplied me or to increase [Strgs#7235]

15 And David longed, and said, Oh that one would give me drink of the water of the well of Beth-lehem, which is by the gate!
16 And the three mighty men brake through the host of the Philistines, and drew water out of the well of Beth-lehem, that was by the gate, and took it, and brought it to David: nevertheless he would not drink thereof, but poured it out unto the LORD.
17 And he said, be it far from me, O LORD, that I should do this: is not this the blood of the men that went in jeopardy of their lives? Therefore he would not drink it. These things did these three mighty men.
18 And Abishai, the brother of Joab, the son of Zeruiah, was chief among three. And he lifted up his spear against three hundred, and slew them, and had the name among three.
19 Was he not most honorable of three? Therefore he was their captain: howbeit he attained not unto the first three.
20 And Benaiah the son of Jehoiada, the son of a valiant man, of Kabzeel, who had done many acts, he slew two lion-like men of Moab: he went down also and slew a lion in the midst of a pit in time of snow:
21 And he slew an Egyptian, a goodly man: and the Egyptian had a spear in his hand; but he went down to him with a staff, and plucked the spear out of the Egyptian's hand, and slew him with his own spear.
22 These things did Benaiah the son of Jehoiada, and had the name among three mighty men.
23 He was more honorable than the thirty, but he attained not to the first three. And David set him over his guard.
24 Asahel the brother of Joab was one of the thirty; Elhanan the son of Dodo of Beth-lehem,
25 Shammah the Harodite, Elika the Harodite,
26 Helez the Paltite, Ira the son of Ikkesh the Tekoite,
27 Abiezer the Anethothite, Mebunnai the Hushathite,
28 Zalmon the Ahohite, Maharai the Netophathite,
29 Heleb the son of Baanah, a Netophathite, Ittai the son of Ribai out of Gibeah of the children of Benjamin,
30 Benaiah the Pirathonite, Hiddai of the brooks of Gaash,
31 Abi-albon the Arbathite, Azmaveth the Barhumite,
32 Eliahba the Shaalbonite, of the sons of Jashen, Jonathan,
33 Shammah the Hararite, Ahiam the son of Sharar the Hararite,
34 Eliphelet the son of Ahasbai, the son of the Maachathite, Eliam the son of Ahithophel the Gilonite,
35 Hezrai the Carmelite, Paarai the Arbite,
36 Igal the son of Nathan of Zobah, Bani the Gadite,
37 Zelek the Ammonite, Naharai the Beerothite, armourbearer to Joab the son of Zeruiah,
38 Ira an Ithrite, Gareb an Ithrite,
39 Uriah the Hittite: thirty and seven in all.

CHAPTER 24

1 And again the anger of the LORD was kindled against Israel, and he moved David against them to say, go, number Israel and Judah.
2 For the king said to Joab the captain of the host, which was with him, Go now through all the tribes of Israel, from Dan even to Beer-sheba, and number you the people, that I may know the number of the people.
3 And Joab said unto the king, now the LORD your God add unto the people, how many so ever they be, an hundredfold, and that the eyes of my lord the king may see it: but why does my lord the king delight in this thing?
4 Notwithstanding the king's word prevailed against Joab, and against the captains of the host. And Joab and the captains of the host went out from the presence of the king, to number the people of Israel.
5 And they passed over Jordan, and pitched in Aroer, on the right side of the city that lies in the midst of the river of Gad, and toward Jazer:
6 Then they came to Gilead, and to the land of Tahtim-hocshi; and they came to Dan-jaan, and about to Zidon,
7 And came to the strong hold of Tyre, and to all the cities of the Hivites, and of the Canaanites: and they went out to the south of Judah, even to Beer-sheba.
8 So when they had gone through all the land, they came to Jerusalem at the end of nine months and twenty days.
9 And Joab gave up the sum of the number of the people unto the king: and there were in Israel eight hundred thousand valiant men that drew the sword; and the men of Judah were five hundred thousand men.
10 And David's heart smote him after that he had numbered the people. And David said unto the LORD, I have sinned greatly in that I have done: and now, I beseech you, O LORD, take away the iniquity of your servant; for I have done very foolishly.
11 For when David was up in the morning, the word of the LORD came unto the prophet Gad, David's seer, saying,
12 Go and say unto David, Thus said the LORD, I offer you three things; choose you one of them, that I may do it unto you.
13 So Gad came to David, and told him, and said unto him, will seven years of famine come unto you in your land? Or will you flee three months before your enemies, while they pursue you? Or that there be three days' pestilence in your land? Now advise, and see what answer I will return to him that sent me.
14 And David said unto Gad, I am in a great strait: let us fall now into the hand of the LORD; for his mercies are great: and let me not fall into the hand of man.
15 So the LORD sent a pestilence upon Israel from the morning even to the time appointed: and there died of the people from Dan even to Beer-sheba seventy thousand men.
16 And when the angel stretched out his hand upon Jerusalem to destroy it, the LORD repented him of the evil, and said to the angel that destroyed the people, it is enough: stay now your hand. And the angel of the LORD was by the threshing place of Araunah the Jebusite.
17 And David spoke unto the LORD when he saw the angel that smote the people, and said, Lo, I have sinned, and I have done wickedly: but these sheep, what have they done? Let your hand, I pray you, be against me, and against my father's house.
18 And Gad came that day to David, and said unto him, Go up, rear an altar unto the LORD in the threshing floor of Araunah the Jebusite.
19 And David, according to the saying of Gad, went up as the LORD commanded.
20 And Araunah looked, and saw the king and his servants coming on toward him: and Araunah went out, and bowed himself before the king on his face upon the ground.
21 And Araunah said, wherefore is my lord the king come to his servant? And David said, to buy the threshing floor of you, to build an altar unto the LORD, that the plague may be stayed from the people.
22 And Araunah said unto David, Let my lord the king take and offer up what seems good unto him: behold, here be oxen for burnt sacrifice, and threshing instruments and other instruments of the oxen for wood.

23 All these *things* did Araunah, *as* a king, give unto the king. And Araunah said unto the king, The LORD your God accept you.
24 And the king said unto Araunah, Nay; but I will surely buy *it* of you at a price: neither will I offer burnt offerings unto the LORD my God of that which does cost me nothing. So David bought the threshing floor and the oxen for fifty shekels of silver.
25 And David built there an altar unto the LORD, and offered burnt offerings and peace offerings. So the LORD was intreated for the land, and the plague was stayed from Israel.

FIRST KINGS

CHAPTER 1

1 Now King David was old *and* stricken in years; and they covered him with clothes, but he gat no heat.
2 Wherefore his servants said unto him, Let there be sought for my lord the king a young virgin: and let her stand before the king, and let her cherish him, and let her lie in your bosom, that my lord the king may get heat.
3 So they sought for a fair damsel throughout all the coasts of Israel, and found Abishag a Shunammite, and brought her to the king.
4 And the damsel *was* very fair, and cherished the king, and ministered to him: but the king knew her not.
5 Then Adonijah the son of Haggith exalted himself, saying, I will be king: and he prepared him chariots and horsemen, and fifty men to run before him.
6 And his father had not displeased him at any time in saying, why have you done so? And he also *was a* very goodly *man*; and *his* mother bare him after Absalom.
7 And he conferred with Joab the son of Zeruiah, and with Abiathar the priest: and they following Adonijah helped *him*.
8 But Zadok the priest, and Benaiah the son of Jehoiada, and Nathan the prophet, and Shimei, and Rei, and the mighty men which *belonged* to David, were not with Adonijah.
9 And Adonijah slaughtered sheep and oxen and fat cattle by the stone of Zoheleth[1], which *is* by En-rogel, and called all his brethren the king's sons, and all the men of Judah the king's servants:
10 But Nathan the prophet, and Benaiah, and the mighty men, and Solomon his brother, he called not.
11 Wherefore Nathan spoke unto Bath-sheba the mother of Solomon, saying, have you not heard that Adonijah the son of Haggith does reign, and David our lord knows *it* not?
12 Now therefore come, let me, I pray you, give you counsel, that you may save your own life, and the life of your son Solomon.
13 Go and get you in unto King David, and say unto him, did not thou, my lord, O king, swear unto your handmaid, saying, Assuredly Solomon your son will reign after me, and he will sit upon my throne? Why then does Adonijah reign?
14 Behold, while you yet talk there with the king, I also will come in after you, and confirm your words.
15 And Bath-sheba went in unto the king into the chamber: and the king was very old; and Abishag the Shunammite ministered unto the king.
16 And Bath-sheba bowed, and did obeisance unto the king. And the king said, what would you?
17 And she said unto him, my lord, you swore by the LORD your God unto your handmaid, *saying*, Assuredly Solomon your son will reign after me, and he will sit upon my throne.
18 And now, behold, Adonijah reigneth; and now, my lord the king, you know *it* not:
19 And he has slain oxen and fat cattle and sheep in abundance, and has called all the sons of the king, and Abiathar the priest, and Joab the captain of the host: but Solomon your servant has he not called.
20 And you, my lord, O king, the eyes of all Israel *are* upon you, that you should tell them who will sit on the throne of my lord the king after him.
21 Otherwise it will come to pass, when my lord the king will sleep with his fathers, that I and my son Solomon will be counted offenders.
22 And, lo, while she yet talked with the king, Nathan the prophet also came in.
23 And they told the king, saying, Behold Nathan the prophet. And when he was come in before the king, he bowed himself before the king with his face to the ground.
24 And Nathan said, my lord, O king, have you said, Adonijah will reign after me, and he will sit upon my throne?
25 For he is gone down this day, and has slain oxen and fat cattle and sheep in abundance, and has called all the king's sons, and the captains of the host, and Abiathar the priest; and, behold, they eat and drink before him, and say, God save king Adonijah.
26 But me, *even* me your servant, and Zadok the priest, and Benaiah the son of Jehoiada, and your servant Solomon, has he not called.
27 Is this thing done by my lord the king, and you have not showed *it* unto your servant, who should sit on the throne of my lord the king after him?
28 Then King David answered and said, call me Bath-sheba. And she came into the king's presence, and stood before the king.
29 And the king swore, and said, *As* the LORD lives, that has redeemed my soul out of all distress,
30 Even as I swore unto you by the LORD God of Israel, saying, Assuredly Solomon your son will reign after me, and he will sit upon my throne in my stead; even so will I certainly do this day.
31 Then Bath-sheba bowed with *her* face to the earth, and did reverence to the king, and said, let my lord king David live forever.
32 And king David said, Call me Zadok the priest, and Nathan the prophet, and Benaiah the son of Jehoiada. And they came before the king.
33 The king also said unto them, take with you the servants of your lord, and cause Solomon my son to ride upon mine own mule, and bring him down to Gihon:
34 And let Zadok the priest and Nathan the prophet anoint him there king over Israel: and blow you with the trumpet, and say, God save king Solomon.
35 Then you will come up after him, that he may come and sit upon my throne; for he will be king in my stead: and I have appointed him to be ruler over Israel and over Judah.
36 And Benaiah the son of Jehoiada answered the king, and said, Amen: the LORD God of my lord the king say so *too*.
37 As the LORD has been with my lord the king, even so be he with Solomon, and make his throne greater than the throne of my lord king David.
38 So Zadok the priest, and Nathan the prophet, and Benaiah the son of Jehoiada, and the Cherethites, and the Pelethites, went down, and caused Solomon to ride upon King David's mule, and brought him to Gihon.
39 And Zadok the priest took a horn of oil out of the tabernacle, and anointed Solomon. And they blew the trumpet; and all the people said, God save King Solomon.
40 And all the people came up after him, and the people piped with pipes, and rejoiced with great joy, so that the earth rent with the sound of them.
41 And Adonijah and all the guests that *were* with him heard *it* as they had made an end of eating. And when Joab heard the sound

---

[1] Zoheleth- crawling (that is serpent), a boundary stone in Palestine.

[Strgs#2120]

of the trumpet, he said, wherefore *is this* noise of the city being in an uproar?

42 And while he yet spoke, behold, Jonathan the son of Abiathar the priest came: and Adonijah said unto him, Come in; for you are a valiant man, and brings good tidings.

43 And Jonathan answered and said to Adonijah, Verily our lord king David has made Solomon king.

44 And the king has sent with him Zadok the priest, and Nathan the prophet, and Benaiah the son of Jehoiada, and the Cherethites, and the Pelethites, and they have caused him to ride upon the king's mule:

45 And Zadok the priest and Nathan the prophet have anointed him king in Gihon: and they are come up from there rejoicing, so that the city rang again. This *is* the noise that you have heard.

46 And also Solomon sits on the throne of the kingdom.

47 And moreover the king's servants came to bless our lord king David, saying, God make the name of Solomon better than your name, and make his throne greater than your throne. And the king bowed himself upon the bed.

48 And also thus said the king, blessed *be* the LORD God of Israel, which has given *one* to sit on my throne this day, mine eyes even seeing *it*.

49 And all the guests that *were* with Adonijah were afraid, and rose up, and went every man his way.

50 And Adonijah feared because of Solomon, and arose, and went, and caught hold on the horns of the altar.

51 And it was told Solomon, saying, Behold, Adonijah fears King Solomon: for, lo, he has caught hold on the horns of the altar, saying, Let king Solomon swear unto me to day that he will not slay his servant with the sword.

52 And Solomon said, if he will show himself a worthy man, there will not a hair of him fall to the earth: but if wickedness will be found in him, he will die.

53 So King Solomon sent, and they brought him down from the altar. And he came and bowed himself to King Solomon: and Solomon said unto him, Go to your house.

CHAPTER 2

1 Now the days of David drew nigh that he should die; and he charged Solomon his son, saying,

2 I go the way of all the earth: be you strong therefore, and show yourself a man;

3 And keep the charge of the LORD your God, to walk in his ways, to keep his statutes, and his commandments, and his judgments, and his testimonies, as it is written in the Law of Moses, that you may prosper in all that you doest, and whithersoever you turn yourself:

4 That the LORD may continue his word which he spoke concerning me, saying, If your children take heed to their way, to walk before me in truth with all their heart and with all their soul, there will not fail you (said he) a man on the throne of Israel.

5 Moreover you know also what Joab the son of Zeruiah did to me, *and* what he did to the two captains of the hosts of Israel, unto Abner the son of Ner, and unto Amasa the son of Jether, whom he slew, and shed the blood of war in peace, and put the blood of war upon his girdle that *was* about his loins, and in his shoes that *were* on his feet.

6 Do therefore according to your wisdom, and let not his hoar head go down to the grave in peace.

7 But show kindness unto the sons of Barzillai the Gileadite, and let them be of those that eat at your table: for so they came to me when I fled because of Absalom your brother.

8 And, behold, you have with you Shimei the son of Gera, a Benjamite of Bahurim, which cursed me with a grievous curse in the day when I went to Mahanaim: but he came down to meet me at Jordan, and I swore to him by the LORD, saying, I will not put you to death with the sword.

9 Now therefore hold him not guiltless: for you are a wise man, and know what you ought to do unto him; but his hoar head bring you down to the grave with blood.

10 So David slept with his fathers, and was buried in the city of David.

11 And the days that David reigned over Israel *were* forty years: seven years reigned he in Hebron, and thirty and three years reigned he in Jerusalem.

12 Then sat Solomon upon the throne of David his father; and his kingdom was established greatly.

13 And Adonijah the son of Haggith came to Bath-sheba the mother of Solomon. And she said, come you peaceably? And he said, peaceably.

14 He said moreover, I have somewhat to say unto you. And she said, Say on.

15 And he said, you know that the kingdom was mine and *that* all Israel set their faces on me, that I should reign: howbeit the kingdom is turned about, and is become my brother's: for it was his from the LORD.

16 And now I ask one petition of you, deny me not. And she said unto him, Say on.

17 And he said, Speak, I pray you, unto Solomon the king, (for he will not say you nay,) that he give me Abishag the Shunammite to wife.

18 And Bath-sheba said, well; I will speak for you unto the king.

19 Bath-sheba therefore went unto King Solomon, to speak unto him for Adonijah. And the king rose up to meet her, and bowed himself unto her, and sat down on his throne, and caused a seat to be set for the king's mother; and she sat on his right hand.

20 Then she said, I desire one small petition of you; *I pray you*, say me not nay. And the king said unto her, Ask on, my mother: for I will not say you nay.

21 And she said, Let Abishag the Shunammite be given to Adonijah your brother to wife.

22 And King Solomon answered and said unto his mother, and why dost you ask Abishag the Shunammite for Adonijah? ask for him the kingdom also; for he *is* mine elder brother; even for him, and for Abiathar the priest, and for Joab the son of Zeruiah.

23 Then King Solomon swore by the LORD, saying, God do so to me, and more also, if Adonijah have not spoken this word against his own life.

24 Now therefore, *as* the LORD lives, which has established me, and set me on the throne of David my father, and who has made me an house, as he promised, Adonijah will be put to death this day.

25 And King Solomon sent by the hand of Benaiah the son of Jehoiada; and he fell upon him that he died.

26 And unto Abiathar the priest said the king, Get you to Anathoth, unto your own fields; for you are worthy of death: but I will not at this time put you to death, because you barest the ark of the Lord GOD before David my father, and because you have been afflicted in all wherein my father was afflicted.

27 So Solomon thrust out Abiathar from being priest unto the LORD; that he might fulfill the word of the LORD, which he spoke concerning the house of Eli in Shiloh.
28 Then tidings came to Joab: for Joab had turned after Adonijah, though he turned not after Absalom. And Joab fled unto the tabernacle of the LORD, and caught hold on the horns of the altar.
29 And it was told King Solomon that Joab was fled unto the tabernacle of the LORD; and, behold, *he is* by the altar. Then Solomon sent Benaiah the son of Jehoiada, saying, go, fall upon him.
30 And Benaiah came to the tabernacle of the LORD, and said unto him, thus said the king, come forth. And he said, nay; but I will die here. And Benaiah brought the king word again, saying, Thus said Joab, and thus he answered me.
31 And the king said unto him, Do as he has said, and fall upon him, and bury him; that you may take away the innocent blood, which Joab shed, from me, and from the house of my father.
32 And the LORD will return his blood upon his own head, who fell upon two men more righteous and better than he, and slew them with the sword, my father David not knowing *thereof, to wit*, Abner the son of Ner, captain of the host of Israel, and Amasa the son of Jether, captain of the host of Judah.
33 Their blood will therefore return upon the head of Joab, and upon the head of his seed for ever: but upon David, and upon his seed, and upon his house, and upon his throne, will there be peace for ever from the LORD.
34 So Benaiah the son of Jehoiada went up, and fell upon him, and slew him: and he was buried in his own house in the wilderness.
35 And the king put Benaiah the son of Jehoiada in his room over the host: and Zadok the priest did the king put in the room of Abiathar.
36 And the king sent and called for Shimei, and said unto him, Build you a house in Jerusalem, and dwell there, and go not forth there any whither.
37 For it will be, *that* on the day you go out, and pass over the brook Kidron, you will know for certain that you will surely die: your blood will be upon your own head.
38 And Shimei said unto the king, the saying *is* good: as my lord the king has said, so will your servant do. And Shimei dwelt in Jerusalem many days.
39 And it came to pass at the end of three years, that two of the servants of Shimei ran away unto Achish son of Maachah king of Gath. And they told Shimei, saying, Behold, your servants *be* in Gath.
40 And Shimei arose, and saddled his ass, and went to Gath to Achish to seek his servants: and Shimei went, and brought his servants from Gath.
41 And it was told Solomon that Shimei had gone from Jerusalem to Gath, and was come again.
42 And the king sent and called for Shimei, and said unto him, did I not make you to swear by the LORD, and protested unto you, saying, Know for a certain, on the day you go out, and walk abroad any whither, that you will surely die? And you said unto me, the word *that* I have heard *is* good.
43 Why then have you not kept the oath of the LORD, and the commandment that I have charged you with?
44 The king said moreover to Shimei, you know all the wickedness which your heart is privy to, that you did to David my father: therefore the LORD will return your wickedness upon your own head;
45 And King Solomon will *be* blessed, and the throne of David will be established before the LORD forever.
46 So the king commanded Benaiah the son of Jehoiada; which went out, and fell upon him, that he died. And the kingdom was established in the hand of Solomon.

CHAPTER 3

1 And Solomon made affinity with Pharaoh King of Egypt, and took Pharaoh's daughter, and brought her into the city of David, until he had made an end of building his own house, and the house of the LORD, and the wall of Jerusalem round about.
2 Only the people sacrificed in high places, because there was no house built unto the name of the LORD, until those days.
3 And Solomon loved the LORD, walking in the statutes of David his father: only he sacrificed and burnt incense in high places.
4 And the king went to Gibeon to sacrifice there; for that *was* the great high place: a thousand burnt offerings did Solomon offer upon that altar.
5 In Gibeon the LORD appeared to Solomon in a dream by night: and God said, Ask what I will give you.
6 And Solomon said, you have showed unto your servant David my father great mercy, according as he walked before you in truth, and in righteousness, and in uprightness of heart with you; and you have kept for him this great kindness, that you have given him a son to sit on his throne, as *it is* this day.
7 And now, O LORD my God, you have made your servant king instead of David my father: and I *am but* a little child: I know not *how* to go out or come in.
8 And your servant *is* in the midst of your people which you have chosen, a great people, that cannot be numbered or counted for multitude.
9 [Give therefore your servant an understanding heart to judge your people, that I may discern between good and bad[1] for who is able to judge this your so great[2] a people?][3]
10 And the speech pleased the Lord, that Solomon had asked this thing.
11 And God said unto him, Because you have asked this thing, and have not asked for yourself long life; neither have asked riches for thyself, or have asked the life of your enemies; but have asked for yourself understanding to discern[4] judgment;
12 Behold, I have done according to your words: lo, I have given you a wise and an understanding[5] heart[6]; so that there was none like you before you, neither after you will any arise like unto you.
13 And I have also given you that which you have not asked, both riches, and honor: so that there will not be any among the kings like unto you all your days.
14 And if you will walk in my ways, to keep my statutes and my commandments, as your father David did walk, then I will lengthen your days.
15 And Solomon awoke; and, behold, *it was* a dream. And he came to Jerusalem, and stood before the ark of the covenant of the

---

[1] bad – evil [Strgs#7451]
[2] great – heavy; figuratively in a good sense (numerous) or in a bad sense (severe, difficult, stupid) [Strgs#3515]
[3] compare – Hebrews 11:4, Job 12:11 & John 5:30
[4] discern – to *hear intelligently* [Strgs#8085]
[5] understand – to *separate mentally* (or distinguish) [Strgs#995]
[6] heart – the heart, the will and event the intellect [Strgs#3820]

LORD, and offered up burnt offerings, and offered peace offerings, and made a feast to all his servants.

16 Then came there two women, *that were* harlots, unto the king, and stood before him.

17 And the one woman said, O my lord, I and this woman dwell in one house; and I was delivered of a child with her in the house.

18 And it came to pass the third day after that I was delivered, that this woman was delivered also: and we *were* together; *there was* no stranger with us in the house, save we two in the house.

19 And this woman's child died in the night; because she overlaid it.

20 And she arose at midnight, and took my son from beside me, while your handmaid slept, and laid it in her bosom, and laid her dead child in my bosom.

21 And when I rose in the morning to give my child suck, behold, it was dead: but when I had considered it in the morning, behold, it was not my son, which I did bear.

22 And the other woman said, nay; but the living *is* my son, and the dead *is* your son. And this said, No; but the dead *is* your son, and the living *is* my son. Thus they spoke before the king.

23 Then said the king, the one said, this *is* my son that lives, and your son *is* the dead: and the other said, nay; but your son *is* the dead, and my son *is* the living.

24 And the king said, Bring me a sword. And they brought a sword before the king.

25 And the king said, Divide the living child in two, and give half to the one, and half to the other.

26 Then spoke the woman whose the living child *was* unto the king, for her bowels[1] yearned upon her son, and she said, O my lord, give her the living child, and in no wise slay it. But the other said, Let it be neither mine or yours, *but* divide *it*.

27 Then the king answered and said, Give her the living child, and in no wise slay it: she *is* the mother thereof.

28 And all Israel heard of the judgment which the king had judged; and they feared the king: for they saw that the wisdom of God *was* in him, to do judgment.

CHAPTER 4

1 So King Solomon was king over all Israel.

2 And these *were* the princes which he had; Azariah the son of Zadok the priest,

3 Elihoreph and Ahiah, the sons of Shisha, scribes; Jehoshaphat[2] the son of Ahilud, the recorder.

4 And Benaiah the son of Jehoiada *was* over the host: and Zadok and Abiathar *were* the priests:

5 And Azariah the son of Nathan *was* over the officers: and Zabud the son of Nathan *was* principal officer, *and* the king's friend:

6 And Ahishar *was* over the household: and Adoniram the son of Abda *was* over the tribute.

7 And Solomon had twelve officers over all Israel, which provided victuals for the king and his household: each man his month in a year made provision.

8 And these *are* their names: The son of Hur, in mount Ephraim:

9 The son of Dekar, in Makaz, and in Shaalbim, and Beth-shemesh, and Elon-beth-hanan:

10 The son of Hesed, in Aruboth; to him *pertained* Sochoh, and all the land of Hepher:

11 The son of Abinadab, in all the region of Dor; which had Taphath the daughter of Solomon to wife:

12 Baana the son of Ahilud; *to him pertained* Taanach and Megiddo, and all Beth-shean, which *is* by Zartanah beneath Jezreel, from Beth-shean to Abel-meholah, *even unto* the place that is beyond Jokneam:

13 The son of Geber, in Ramoth-gilead; to him *pertained* the towns of Jair the son of Manasseh, which *are* in Gilead; to him *also pertained* the region of Argob, which *is* in Bashan, threescore great cities with walls and brasen bars:

14 Ahinadab the son of Iddo *had* Mahanaim:

15 Ahimaaz *was* in Naphtali; he also took Basmath the daughter of Solomon to wife:

16 Baanah the son of Hushai *was* in Asher and in Aloth:

17 Jehoshaphat the son of Paruah, in Issachar:

18 Shimei the son of Elah, in Benjamin:

19 Geber the son of Uri *was* in the country of Gilead, *in* the country of Sihon king of the Amorites, and of Og king of Bashan; and *he was* the only officer which *was* in the land.

20 Judah and Israel *were* many, as the sand which *is* by the sea in multitude, eating and drinking, and making merry.

21 And Solomon reigned over all kingdoms from the river unto the land of the Philistines, and unto the border of Egypt: they brought presents, and served Solomon all the days of his life.

22 And Solomon's provision for one day was thirty measures of fine flour, and threescore measures of meal,

23 Ten fat oxen, and twenty oxen out of the pastures, and an hundred sheep, beside harts, and roebucks, and fallowdeer, and fatted fowl.

24 For he had dominion over **the entire** region on this side the river, from Tiphsah even to Azzah, over all the kings on this side the river: and he had peace on all sides round about him.

25 And Judah and Israel dwelt safely, every man under his vine and under his fig tree, from Dan even to Beer-sheba, all the days of Solomon.

26 And Solomon had forty thousand stalls of horses for his chariots, and twelve thousand horsemen.

27 And those officers provided victual for King Solomon, and for all that came unto King Solomon's table, every man in his month: they lacked nothing.

28 Barley also and straw for the horses and dromedaries brought they unto the place where *the officers* were, every man according to his charge.

29 And God gave Solomon wisdom and understanding exceeding much, and largeness of heart, even as the sand that *is* on the sea shore.

30 And Solomon's wisdom excelled the wisdom of all the children of the east country, and all the wisdom of Egypt.

31 For he was wiser than all men; than Ethan the Ezrahite, and Heman, and Chalcol, and Darda, the sons of Mahol: and his fame was in all nations round about.

32 And he spoke three thousand proverbs: and his songs were a thousand and five.

33 And he spoke of trees, from the cedar tree that *is* in Lebanon even unto the hyssop that springs out of the wall: he spoke also of beasts, and of fowl, and of creeping things, and of fishes.

34 And there came of all people to hear the wisdom of Solomon, from all kings of the earth, which had heard of his wisdom

---

[1] bowels – *compassion,* by extension the *womb* (as *cherishing* the fetus); by implication a *maiden* [Strgs#7356]

[2] Jehoshaphat- Jehovah has judged. [Strgs#3092]

CHAPTER 5

1 And Hiram king of Tyre sent his servants unto Solomon; for he had heard that they had anointed him king in the room of his father: for Hiram was ever a lover of David.
2 And Solomon sent to Hiram, saying,
3 You know how that David my father could not build an house unto the name of the LORD his God for the wars which were about him on every side, until the LORD put them under the soles of his feet.
4 But now the LORD my God has given me rest on every side, *so that there is* neither adversary or evil occurrent[1].
5 And, behold, I purpose to build a house unto the name of the LORD my God, as the LORD spoke unto David my father, saying, your son, whom I will set upon your throne in your room, he will build a house unto my name.
6 Now therefore command you that they hew me cedar trees out of Lebanon; and my servants will be with your servants: and unto you will I give hire for your servants according to all that you will appoint: for you know that *there is* not among us any that can skill to hew timber like unto the Sidonians.
7 And it came to pass, when Hiram heard the words of Solomon, that he rejoiced greatly, and said, blessed *be* the LORD this day, which has given unto David a wise son over this great people.
8 And Hiram sent to Solomon, saying, I have considered the things which you sent to me for: *and* I will do all your desire concerning timber of cedar, and concerning timber of fir.
9 My servants will bring *them* down from Lebanon unto the sea: and I will convey them by sea in floats unto the place that you will appoint me, and will cause them to be discharged there, and you will receive *them*: and you will accomplish my desire, in giving food for my household.
10 So Hiram gave Solomon cedar trees and fir trees *according to* all his desire.
11 And Solomon gave Hiram twenty thousand measures of wheat *for* food to his household, and twenty measures of pure oil: thus gave Solomon to Hiram year by year.
12 And the LORD gave Solomon wisdom, as he promised him: and there was peace between Hiram and Solomon; and they two made a league together.
13 And King Solomon raised a levy out of all Israel; and the levy was thirty thousand men.
14 And he sent them to Lebanon, ten thousand a month by courses: a month they were in Lebanon, *and* two months at home: and Adoniram *was* over the levy.
15 And Solomon had threescore and ten thousand that bare burdens, and fourscore thousand hewers in the mountains;
16 Beside the chief of Solomon's officers which *were* over the work, three thousand and three hundred, which ruled over the people that wrought in the work.
17 And the king commanded, and they brought great stones, costly stones, *and* hewed stones, to lay the foundation of the house.
18 And Solomon's builders and Hiram's builders did hew *them*, and the stones-quarers: so they prepared timber and stones to build the house.

CHAPTER 6

1 And it came to pass in the four hundred and eightieth year after the children of Israel were come out of the land of Egypt, in the fourth year of Solomon's reign over Israel, in the month Zif, which *is* the second month, that he began to build the house of the LORD.
2 And the house which King Solomon built for the LORD, the length thereof *was* threescore cubits, and the breadth thereof twenty *cubits*, and the height thereof thirty cubits.
3 And the porch before the temple of the house, twenty cubits *was* the length thereof, according to the breadth of the house; *and* ten cubits *was* the breadth thereof before the house.
4 And for the house he made windows of narrow lights.
5 And against the wall of the house he built chambers round about, *against* the walls of the house round about, *both* of the temple and of the oracle: and he made chambers round about:
6 The nethermost chamber *was* five cubits broad, and the middle *was* six cubits broad, and the third *was* seven cubits broad: for without *in the wall* of the house he made narrowed rests round about, that *the beams* should not be fastened in the walls of the house.
7 And the house, when it was in building, was built of stone made ready before it was brought thither: so that there was neither hammer or axe or any tool of iron heard in the house, while it was in building.
8 The door for the middle chamber *was* in the right side of the house: and they went up with winding stairs into the middle *chamber*, and out of the middle into the third.
9 So he built the house, and finished it; and covered the house with beams and boards of cedar.
10 And *then* he built chambers against the **entire** house, five cubits high: and they rested on the house *with* timber of cedar.
11 And the word of the LORD came to Solomon, saying,
12 *Concerning* this house which you are in building, if you will walk in my statutes, and execute my judgments, and keep all my commandments to walk in them; then will I perform my word with you, which I spoke unto David your father:
13 And I will dwell among the children of Israel, and will not forsake my people Israel.
14 So Solomon built the house, and finished it.
15 And he built the walls of the house within with boards of cedar, both the floor of the house, and the walls of the ceiling: *and* he covered *them* on the inside with wood, and covered the floor of the house with planks of fir.
16 And he built twenty cubits on the sides of the house, both the floor and the walls with boards of cedar: he even built *them* for it within, *even* for the oracle, *even* for the most holy *place*.
17 And the house, that *is*, the temple before it, was forty cubits *long*.
18 And the cedar of the house within *was* carved with knops and open flowers: all *was* cedar; there was no stone seen.
19 And the [oracle he prepared in the house within][2], to set there the ark of the covenant of the LORD.
20 And the oracle in the forepart[3] *was* twenty cubits in length, and twenty cubits in breadth, and twenty cubits in the height thereof: and he overlaid it with pure gold; and *so* covered the altar which *was of* cedar.
21 So Solomon overlaid the house within with pure gold: and he made a partition by the chains of gold before the oracle; and he overlaid it with gold.

---

[1] occurrent- literally impact, chance. [Strgs#6294]
[2] the Most Holy, see v16
[3] lit. face [Strgs#6440]

22 And the whole house he overlaid with gold, until he had finished the entire house: also the whole altar that *was* by the oracle he overlaid with gold.
23 And within the oracle he made two cherubims *of* olive tree, *each* ten[1] cubits high.
24 And five cubits *was* the one wing of the cherub, and five cubits the other wing of the cherub: from the uttermost part of the one wing unto the uttermost part of the other *were* ten cubits.
25 And the other cherub *was* ten cubits: both the cherubims *were* of one measure and one size.
26 The height of the one cherub *was* ten cubits, and so *was it* of the other cherub.
27 And he set the cherubims within the inner house: and they stretched forth the wings of the cherubims, so that the wing of the one touched the *one* wall, and the wing of the other cherub touched the other wall; and their wings touched one another in the midst of the house.
28 And he overlaid the cherubims with gold.
29 And he carved all the walls of the house round about with carved figures of cherubims and palm trees and open flowers, within and without.
30 And the floor of the house he overlaid with gold, within and without.
31 And for the entering of the oracle he made doors *of* olive tree: the lintel *and* side posts *were* a fifth part *of the wall*.
32 The two doors also *were of* olive tree; and he carved upon them carvings of cherubims and palm trees and open flowers, and overlaid *them* with gold, and spread gold upon the cherubims, and upon the palm trees.
33 So also made he for the door of the temple posts *of* olive tree, a fourth part *of the wall*.
34 And the two doors *were of* fir tree: the two leaves of the one door *were* folding, and the two leaves of the other door *were* folding.
35 And he carved *thereon* cherubims and palm trees and open flowers: and covered *them* with gold fitted upon the carved work.
36 And he built the inner court with three rows of hewed stone, and a row of cedar beams.
37 In the fourth year was the foundation of the house of the LORD laid, in the month Zif[2]:
38 And in the eleventh year, in the month Bul, which *is* the eighth month, was the house finished throughout all the parts thereof, and according to all the fashion of it. So was he seven years in building it.

CHAPTER 7

1 But Solomon was building his own house thirteen years, and he finished his **entire** house.
2 He built also the house of the forest of Lebanon; the length thereof *was* an hundred cubits, and the breadth thereof fifty cubits, and the height thereof thirty cubits, upon four rows of cedar pillars, with cedar beams upon the pillars.
3 And *it was* covered with cedar above upon the beams, that *lay* on forty five pillars, fifteen *in* a row.
4 And *there were* windows *in* three rows, and light *was* against light *in* three ranks.
5 And all the doors and posts *were* square, with the windows: and light *was* against light *in* three ranks.
6 And he made a porch of pillars; the length thereof *was* fifty cubits, and the breadth thereof thirty cubits: and the porch *was* before them: and the *other* pillars and the thick beam *were* before them.
7 Then he made a porch for the throne where he might judge, *even* the porch of judgment: and *it was* covered with cedar[3] from one side of the floor[4] to the other.
8 And his house where he dwelt *had* another court within the porch, which was of the like work. Solomon made also a house for Pharaoh's daughter, whom he had taken *to wife*, like unto this porch.
9 All these *were of* costly stones, according to the measures of hewed stones, sawed with saws, within and without, even from the foundation unto the coping, and *so* on the outside toward the great court.
10 And the foundation *was of* costly stones, even great stones, stones of ten cubits, and stones of eight cubits.
11 And above *were* costly stones, after the measures of hewed stones, and cedars.
12 And the great court round about *was* with three rows of hewed stones, and a row of cedar beams, both for the inner court of the house of the LORD, and for the porch of the house.
13 And King Solomon sent and fetched Hiram out of Tyre.
14 He *was* a widow's son of the tribe of Naphtali, and his father *was* a man of Tyre, a worker in brass: and he was filled with wisdom, and understanding, and cunning to work all works in brass. And he came to King Solomon, and wrought all his work.
15 For he cast two pillars of brass, of eighteen cubits high apiece: and a line of twelve cubits did compass either of them about.
16 And he made two chapiters *of* molten brass, to set upon the tops of the pillars: the height of the one chapiter *was* five cubits, and the height of the other chapiter *was* five cubits:
17 *And* nets of checker work, and wreaths of chain work, for the chapiters[5] which *were* upon the top of the pillars; seven for the one chapiter, and seven for the other chapiter.
18 And he made the pillars, and two rows round about upon the one network, to cover the chapiters that *were* upon the top, with pomegranates: and so did he for the other chapiter.
19 And the chapiters that *were* upon the top of the pillars *were* of lily work in the porch, four cubits.
20 And the chapiters upon the two pillars *had pomegranates* also above, over against the belly which *was* by the network: and the pomegranates *were* two hundred in rows round about upon the other chapiter.
21 And he set up the pillars in the porch of the temple: and he set up the right pillar, and called the name thereof Jachin: and he set up the left pillar, and called the name thereof Boaz.
22 And upon the top of the pillars *was* lily work: so was the work of the pillars finished.
23 And he made a molten sea, ten cubits from the one brim to the other: *it was* round all about, and his height *was* five cubits: and a line of thirty cubits did compass it round about.

---

[1] ten – Hebrew word *'aśârâh* meaning an accumulation to the extent of the digits [Strgs#6235]. Derives from the root word *'âśar* meaning *tithe* [Strgs#6237].

[2] Zif – to *be prominent, brightness*, the month of *flowers* (corresponding to Ijar or May) [Strgs#2099]

[3] cedar – comes from a Hebrew root word meaing *to be firm* [Strgs#729]

[4] floor – as if a pavement of pieces or *tesserae* [Strgs#7172]. Derives from a root word meaning to *rend*, literally or figuratively (*revile, paint the eyes*, as if enlarging them [Strgs#7167].

[5] chapiters- the capital of a column. [Strgs#3805]

24 And under the brim of it round about *there were* knops compassing it, ten in a cubit, compassing the sea round about: the knops *were* cast in two rows, when it was cast.

25 It stood upon twelve oxen, three looking toward the north, and three looking toward the west, and three looking toward the south, and three looking toward the east: and the sea *was set* above upon them, and all their hinder parts *were* inward[1].

26 And it *was* a hand breadth thick, and the brim thereof was wrought like the brim of a cup, with flowers of lilies: it contained two thousand baths.

27 And he made ten bases of brass; four cubits *was* the length of one base, and four cubits the breadth thereof, and three cubits the height of it.

28 And the work of the bases *was* on this *manner*: they had borders, and the borders *were* between the ledges:

29 And on the borders that *were* between the ledges *were* lions[2], oxen[3], and cherubims[4]: and upon the ledges *there was* a base above: and beneath the lions and oxen *were* certain additions made of thin work.

30 And every base had four brasen wheels, and plates of brass: and the four corners thereof had undersetters: under the laver *were* undersetters[5] molten, at the side of every addition.

31 And the mouth of it within the chapter and above *was* a cubit: but the mouth thereof *was* round *after* the work of the base, a cubit and an half: and also upon the mouth of it *were* gravings with their borders, foursquare, not round.

32 And under the borders *were* four wheels; and the axletrees of the wheels *were joined* to the base: and the height of a wheel *was* a cubit and half a cubit.

33 And the work of the wheels *was* like the work of a chariot wheel: their axletrees[6], and their naves, and their felloes[7], and their spokes, *were* all molten.

34 And *there were* four undersetters to the four corners of one base: *and* the undersetters *were* of the very base itself.

35 And in the top of the base *was there* a round compass of half a cubit high: and on the top of the base the ledges thereof and the borders thereof *were* of the same.

36 For on the plates of the ledges thereof, and on the borders thereof, he graved cherubims, lions, and palm trees, according to the proportion of every one, and additions round about.

37 After this *manner* he made the ten bases: all of them had one casting, one measure, *and* one size.

38 Then made he ten lavers of brass: one laver contained forty baths: *and* every laver was four cubits: *and* upon every one of the ten bases one laver.

39 And he put five bases on the right side of the house, and five on the left side of the house: and he set the sea on the right side of the house eastward over against the south.

40 And Hiram made the lavers, and the shovels, and the basons. So Hiram made an end of doing all the work that he made king Solomon for the house of the LORD:

41 The two pillars, and the *two* bowls of the chapiters that *were* on the top of the two pillars; and the two networks, to cover the two bowls of the chapiters which *were* upon the top of the pillars;

42 And four hundred pomegranates for the two networks, *even* two rows of pomegranates for one network, to cover the two bowls of the chapiters that *were* upon the pillars;

43 And the ten bases, and ten lavers on the bases;

44 And one sea, and twelve oxen under the sea;

45 And the pots, and the shovels, and the basons: and all these vessels, which Hiram made to King Solomon for the house of the LORD, *were of* bright brass.

46 In the plain of Jordan did the king cast them, in the clay ground between Succoth and Zarthan.

47 And Solomon left all the vessels *unweighed*, because they were exceeding many: neither was the weight of the brass found out.

48 And Solomon made all the vessels that *pertained* unto the house of the LORD: the altar of gold, and the table of gold, whereupon the showbread *was*,

49 And the candlesticks of pure gold, five on the right *side*, and five on the left, before the oracle, with the flowers, and the lamps, and the tongs *of* gold,

50 And the bowls, and the snuffers, and the basons and the spoons, and the censers *of* pure gold; and the hinges *of* gold, *both* for the doors of the inner house, the most holy *place, and* for the doors of the house, *to wit*, of the temple.

51 So was ended all the work that king Solomon made for the house of the LORD. And Solomon brought in the things which David his father had dedicated; *even* the silver, and the gold, and the vessels, did he put among the treasures of the house of the LORD.

CHAPTER 8

1 Then Solomon assembled the elders of Israel, and all the heads of the tribes, the chief of the fathers of the children of Israel, unto King Solomon in Jerusalem, that they might bring up the ark of the covenant of the LORD out of the city of David, which *is* Zion.

2 And all the men of Israel assembled themselves unto King Solomon at the feast in the month Ethanim, which *is* the seventh month.

3 And all the elders of Israel came, and the priests took up the ark.

4 And they brought up the ark of the LORD, and the tabernacle of the congregation, and all the holy vessels that *were* in the tabernacle, even those did the priests and the Levites bring up.

5 And King Solomon, and all the congregation of Israel, that were assembled unto him, *were* with him before the ark, sacrificing sheep and oxen, that could not be told or numbered for multitude.

6 And the priests brought in the ark of the covenant of the LORD unto his place, into the oracle of the house, to the most holy *place, even* under the wings of the cherubims.

7 For the cherubims spread forth *their* two wings over the place of the ark, and the cherubims covered the ark and the staves thereof above.

8 And they drew out the staves, that the ends of the staves were seen out in the holy *place* before the oracle, and they were not seen without: and there they are unto this day.

---

[1] compare Luke 9:62 & Phil. 3:12-14
[2] authority
[3] servant & intercession
[4] glory
[5] undersetter- from an unused root meaning to clothe, the shoulder (proper, that is upper end of the arm; as being the spot where the garments hand); figuratively side piece or lateral projection or anything; arm, corner, shoulder (-piece), side. [Strgs#3802]
[6] axletrees – is the Hebrew word *yâd* meaning *hand* (the open one, indicating *power, means, direction*) [Strgs#3027]
[7] felloes – *conjoined*, a *wheel* spoke or rod connecting the hub with the rim [Strgs#2839]. Its root word is translated as to *cling, join to love, delight* in [Strgs#2836].

9 *There was* nothing in the ark save the two tables of stone, which Moses put there at Horeb, when the LORD made *a covenant* with the children of Israel, when they came out of the land of Egypt.
10 And it came to pass, when the priests were come out of the holy *place*, that the cloud filled the house of the LORD,
11 So that the priests could not stand to minister because of the cloud: for the glory of the LORD had filled the house of the LORD.
12 Then spoke Solomon, The LORD said that he would dwell in the thick darkness.
13 I have surely built you a house to dwell in, a settled place for you to abide in forever.
14 And the king turned his face about, and blessed all the congregation of Israel: (and all the congregation of Israel stood;)
15 And he said, Blessed *be* the LORD God of Israel, which spoke with his mouth unto David my father, and has with his hand fulfilled *it*, saying,
16 Since the day that I brought forth my people Israel out of Egypt, I chose no city out of all the tribes of Israel to build a house, that my name might be therein; but I chose David to be over my people Israel.
17 And it was in the heart of David my father to build a house for the name of the LORD God of Israel.
18 And the LORD said unto David my father, whereas it was in your heart to build a house unto my name, you did well that it was in your heart.
19 Nevertheless you will not build the house; but your son that will come forth out of your loins; he will build the house unto my name.
20 And the LORD has performed his word that he spoke, and I am risen up in the room of David my father, and sit on the throne of Israel, as the LORD promised, and have built a house for the name of the LORD God of Israel.
21 And I have set there a place for the ark, wherein *is* the covenant of the LORD, which he made with our fathers, when he brought them out of the land of Egypt.
22 And Solomon stood before the altar of the LORD in the presence of all the congregation of Israel, and spread forth his hands toward heaven:
23 And he said, LORD God of Israel, *there is* no God like you, in heaven above, or on earth beneath, who keep covenant and mercy with your servants that walk before you with all their heart:
24 Who have kept with your servant David my father that you promised him: you spoke also with your mouth, and have fulfilled *it* with your hand, as *it is* this day.
25 Therefore now, LORD God of Israel, keep with your servant David my father that you promised him, saying, There will not fail you a man in my sight to sit on the throne of Israel; so that your children take heed to their way, that they walk before me as you have walked before me.
26 And now, O God of Israel, let your word, I pray you, be verified, which you spoke unto your servant David my father.
27 But will God indeed dwell on the earth? Behold, the heaven and heaven of heavens cannot contain you; how much less this house that I have built?
28 Yet have you respect unto the prayer of your servant, and to his supplication, O LORD my God, to hearken unto the cry and to the prayer, which your servant prayed before you today:
29 That your eyes may be open toward this house night and day, *even* toward the place of which you have said, My name will be there: that you may hearken unto the prayer which your servant will make toward this place.
30 And hearken you to the supplication of your servant, and of your people Israel, when they will pray toward this place: and hear you in heaven your dwelling place: and when you heard, forgive.
31 If any man trespass against his neighbor, and an oath be laid upon him to cause him to swear, and the oath come before your altar in this house:
32 Then hear you in heaven, and do, and judge your servants, condemning the wicked, to bring his way upon his head; and justifying the righteous, to give him according to his righteousness.
33 When your people Israel be smitten down before the enemy, because they have sinned against you, and will turn again to you, and confess your name, and pray, and make supplication unto you in this house:
34 Then hear you in heaven, and forgive the sin of your people Israel, and bring them again unto the land which you gave unto their fathers.
35 When heaven is shut up, and there is no rain, because they have sinned against you; if they pray toward this place, and confess your name, and turn from their sin, when you afflicted them:
36 Then hear you in heaven, and forgive the sin of your servants, and of your people Israel, that you teach them the good way wherein they should walk, and give rain upon your land, which you have given to your people for an inheritance.
37 If there be in the land famine, if there be pestilence, blasting, mildew, locust, *or* if there be caterpillar; if their enemy besiege them in the land of their cities; whatsoever plague, whatsoever sickness *there be*;
38 What prayer and supplication so ever be *made* by any man, *or* by all your people Israel, which will know every man the plague of his own heart, and spread forth his hands toward this house:
39 Then hear you in heaven your dwelling place, and forgive, and do, and give to every man according to his ways, whose heart you know; (for thou, *even* you only, know the hearts of all the children of men;)
40 That they may fear you all the days that they live in the land which you gave unto our fathers.
41 Moreover concerning a stranger, that *is* not of your people Israel, but cometh out of a far country for your name's sake;
42 (For they will hear of your great name, and of your strong hand, and of your stretched out arm;) when he will come and pray toward this house;
43 Hear you in heaven your dwelling place, and do according to all that the stranger called to you for: that all people of the earth may know your name, to fear you, as *do* your people Israel; and that they may know that this house, which I have built, is called by your name.
44 If your people go out to battle against their enemy, whithersoever you will send them, and will pray unto the LORD toward[1] the city[2] which you have chosen, and *toward* the house that I have built for your name:
45 Then hear you in heaven their prayer and their supplication, and maintain[3] their cause[4].

---

[1] towards – a *road* (as *trodden*), figurateively a *course* of life or mode of action [Strgs#1870]. The way of the city.
[2] city – a *city*, excitement, anguish, of terror, a place guarded by *waking* or a watch, *encampment* or *post* [Strgs#5892].
[3] maintain – to do, fashion, accomplish to do or make [Stgs#6213]
[4] right – a *verdict*, *right* [Strgs#4941]

46 If they sin against you, (for *there is* no man that sins not,) and you be angry with them, and deliver them to the enemy, so that they carry them away captives unto the land of the enemy, far or near;

47 *Yet* if they will bethink themselves in the land whither they were carried captives, and repent, and make supplication unto you in the land of them that carried them captives, saying, We have sinned, and have done perversely, we have committed wickedness;

48 And *so* return unto you with all their heart, and with all their soul, in the land of their enemies, which led them away captive, and pray unto you toward their land, which you gave unto their fathers, the city which you have chosen, and the house which I have built for your name:

49 Then hear you their prayer and their supplication in heaven your dwelling place, and maintain their cause,

50 And forgive your people that have sinned against you, and all their transgressions wherein they have transgressed against you, and give them compassion before them who carried them captive, that they may have compassion on them:

51 For they *be* your people, and your inheritance, which you brought forth out of Egypt, from the midst of the furnace of iron:

52 That your eyes may be open unto the supplication of your servant, and unto the supplication of your people Israel, to hearken unto them in all that they call for unto you.

53 For you did separate them from among all the people of the earth, *to be* your inheritance, as you spoke by the hand of Moses your servant, when you brought our fathers out of Egypt, O Lord GOD.

54 And it was *so*, that when Solomon had made an end of praying all this prayer and supplication unto the LORD, he arose from before the altar of the LORD, from kneeling on his knees with his hands spread up to heaven.

55 And he stood, and blessed all the congregation of Israel with a loud voice, saying,

56 Blessed *be* the LORD, that has given rest unto his people Israel, according to all that he promised: there has not failed one word of all his good promise, which he promised by the hand of Moses his servant.

57 The LORD our God be with us, as he was with our fathers: let him not leave us, or forsake us:

58 That he may incline our hearts unto him, to walk in all his ways, and to keep his commandments, and his statutes, and his judgments, which he commanded our fathers.

59 And let these my words, wherewith I have made supplication before the LORD, be nigh unto the LORD our God day and night, that he maintain the cause of his servant, and the cause of his people Israel at all times, as the matter will require:

60 That all the people of the earth may know that the LORD *is* God, *and that there is* none else.

61 Let your heart therefore be perfect with the LORD our God, to walk in his statutes, and to keep his commandments, as at this day.

62 And the king, and all Israel with him, offered sacrifice before the LORD.

63 And Solomon offered a sacrifice of peace offerings, which he offered unto the LORD, two and twenty thousand oxen, and an hundred and twenty thousand sheep. So the king and all the children of Israel dedicated the house of the LORD.

64 The same day did the king hallow the middle of the court that *was* before the house of the LORD: for there he offered burnt offerings, and meat offerings, and the fat of the peace offerings: because the brasen altar that *was* before the LORD *was* too little to receive the burnt offerings, and meat offerings, and the fat of the peace offerings.

65 And at that time Solomon held a feast, and all Israel with him, a great congregation, from the entering in of Hamath unto the river of Egypt, before the LORD our God, seven days and seven days, *even* fourteen days.

66 On the eighth day he sent the people away: and they blessed the king, and went unto their tents joyful and glad of heart for all the goodness that the LORD had done for David his servant, and for Israel his people.

CHAPTER 9

1 And it came to pass, when Solomon had finished the building of the house of the LORD, and the king's house, and all Solomon's desire which he was pleased to do,

2 That the LORD appeared to Solomon the second time, as he had appeared unto him at Gibeon.

3 And the LORD said unto him, I have heard your prayer and your supplication, that you have made before me: I have hallowed this house, which you have built, to put my name there forever; and mine eyes and mine heart will be there perpetually.

4 And if you will walk before me, as David your father walked, in integrity of heart, and in uprightness, to do according to all that I have commanded you, *and* will keep my statutes and my judgments:

5 Then I will establish the throne of your kingdom upon Israel for ever, as I promised to David your father, saying, there will not fail you a man upon the throne of Israel.

6 *But* if you will at all turn from following me, you or your children, and will not keep my commandments *and* my statutes which I have set before you, but go and serve other gods, and worship them:

7 Then will I cut off Israel out of the land which I have given them; and this house, which I have hallowed for my name, will cast out of my sight; and Israel will be a proverb and a byword among all people:

8 And at this house, *which* is high, every one that passes by it will be astonished, and will hiss; and they will say, Why has the LORD done thus unto this land, and to this house?

9 And they will answer, because they forsook the LORD their God, who brought forth their fathers out of the land of Egypt, and have taken hold upon other gods, and have worshipped them, and served them: therefore has the LORD brought upon them all this evil.

10 And it came to pass at the end of twenty years, when Solomon had built the two houses, the house of the LORD, and the king's house,

11 (*Now* Hiram the king of Tyre had furnished Solomon with cedar trees and fir trees, and with gold, according to all his desire,) that then king Solomon gave Hiram twenty cities in the land of Galilee.

12 And Hiram came out from Tyre to see the cities which Solomon had given him; and they pleased him not.

13 And he said, what cities *are* these which you have given me, my brother? And he called them the land of Cabul unto this day.

14 And Hiram sent to the king sixscore talents of gold.

15 And this *is* the reason of the levy which king Solomon raised; for to build the house of the LORD, and his own house, and Millo, and the wall of Jerusalem, and Hazor, and Megiddo, and Gezer.

16 *For* Pharaoh King of Egypt had gone up, and taken Gezer, and burnt it with fire, and slain the Canaanites that dwelt in the city, and given it *for* a present unto his daughter, Solomon's wife.
17 And Solomon built Gezer, and Beth-horon the nether,
18 And Baalath, and Tadmor in the wilderness, in the land,
19 And all the cities of store that Solomon had, and cities for his chariots and cities for his horsemen, and that which Solomon desired to build in Jerusalem, and in Lebanon, and in all the land of his dominion.
20 *And* all the people *that were* left of the Amorites, Hittites, Perizzites, Hivites, and Jebusites, which *were* not of the children of Israel,
21 Their children that were left after them in the land, whom the children of Israel also were not able utterly to destroy, upon those did Solomon levy a tribute of bond-service unto this day.
22 But of the children of Israel did Solomon make no bondmen: but they *were* men of war, and his servants, and his princes, and his captains, and rulers of his chariots, and his horsemen.
23 These *were* the chief of the officers that *were* over Solomon's work, five hundred and fifty, which bare rule over the people that wrought in the work.
24 But Pharaoh's daughter came up out of the city of David unto her house which *Solomon* had built for her: then did he build Millo.
25 And three times in a year did Solomon offer burnt offerings and peace offerings upon the altar which he built unto the LORD, and he burnt incense upon the altar that *was* before the LORD. So he finished the house.
26 And King Solomon made a navy of ships in Ezion-geber, which *is* beside Eloth, on the shore of the Red sea, in the land of Edom.
27 And Hiram sent in the navy his servants, shipmen that had knowledge of the sea, with the servants of Solomon.
28 And they came to Ophir, and fetched from there gold, four hundred and twenty talents, and brought *it* to King Solomon.

CHAPTER 10

1 And when the queen of Sheba heard of the fame of Solomon concerning the name of the LORD, she came to prove him with hard questions.
2 And she came to Jerusalem with a very great train, with camels that bare spices, and very much gold, and precious stones: and when she was come to Solomon, she communed with him of all that was in her heart.
3 And Solomon told her all her questions: there was not *any*thing hid from the king, which he told her not.
4 And when the queen of Sheba had seen all Solomon's wisdom, and the house that he had built,
5 And the meat of his table, and the sitting of his servants, and the attendance of his ministers, and their apparel, and his cupbearers, and his ascent by which he went up unto the house of the LORD; there was no more spirit in her.
6 And she said to the king, It was a true report that I heard in mine own land of your acts and of your wisdom.
7 Howbeit I believed not the words, until I came, and mine eyes had seen *it*: and, behold, the half was not told me: your wisdom and prosperity exceeded the fame which I heard.

8 Happy *are* your men, happy *are* these your servants, which stand continually before you, *and* that hear your wisdom.
9 Blessed be the LORD your God, which delighted in you, to set you on the throne of Israel: because the LORD loved Israel for ever, therefore made he you king, to do judgment and justice.
10 And she gave the king a hundred and twenty talents of gold, and of spices very great store, and precious stones: there came no more such abundance of spices as these which the queen of Sheba gave to king Solomon.
11 And the navy also of Hiram, that brought gold from Ophir, brought in from Ophir great plenty of almug trees, and precious stones.
12 And the king made of the almug trees pillars for the house of the LORD, and for the king's house, harps also and psalteries for singers: there came no such almug trees, or were seen unto this day.
13 And King Solomon gave unto the queen of Sheba all her desire, whatsoever she asked, beside *that* which Solomon gave her of his royal bounty. So she turned and went to her own country, she and her servants.
14 Now the weight of gold that came to Solomon in one year was six hundred threescore and six talents of gold,
15 Beside *that he had* of the merchantmen, and of the traffic of the spice merchants, and of all the kings of Arabia, and of the governors of the country.
16 And King Solomon made two hundred targets *of* beaten gold: six hundred *shekels* of gold went to one target.
17 And *he made* three hundred shields *of* beaten gold; three pound of gold went to one shield: and the king put them in the house of the forest of Lebanon.
18 Moreover the king made a great throne of ivory, and overlaid [1]it with the best[2] gold.
19 The throne had six steps, and the top[3] of the throne *was* round behind: and *there were* stays[4] on either side on the place of the seat[5], and two lions stood beside[6] the stays.
20 And twelve lions stood there on the one side and on the other upon the six steps[7]: there was not the like made in any kingdom.
21 And all king Solomon's drinking vessels *were of* gold, and all the vessels of the house of the forest of Lebanon *were of* pure gold; none *were of* silver: it was nothing accounted of in the days of Solomon.
22 For the king had at sea a navy of Tharshish with the navy of Hiram: once in three years came the navy of Tharshish, bringing gold, and silver, ivory, and apes, and peacocks.
23 So king Solomon exceeded all the kings of the earth for riches and for wisdom.
24 And all the earth sought to Solomon, to hear his wisdom, which God had put in his heart.
25 And they brought every man his present, vessels of silver, and vessels of gold, and garments, and armor, and spices, horses, and mules, a rate year by year.
26 And Solomon gathered together chariots and horsemen: and he had a thousand and four hundred chariots, and twelve thousand horsemen, whom he bestowed in the cities for chariots, and with the king at Jerusalem.

---

[1] overlaid – is the Hebrew word *tsâphâh* meaning *expansion*, to *sheet over*, cover [Strgs#6823]. Its root word means to *lean* forward that is to peer into the distance, to *observe*, *await* [Strgs#6822].
[2] best – refined [Strgs#6338]
[3] top – the *head*, to shake the head [Strgs#7218].
[4] stays – hand, the open one indicating power, means, direction

[Strgs#3027]
[5] seat – *session*, an *abode* or *locality* [Strgs#7675]. Its root word means to sit [Strgs#3427].
[6] besides – in the sense of *joining*, *near* [Strgs#681].
[7] steps – *elevation* (literally a *journey* to a higher place, a *thought* arising), *superiority* of station, climatic *progression* [Strgs#4609].

27 And the king made silver *to be* in Jerusalem as stones, and cedars made he *to be* as the sycomore trees that *are* in the vale, for abundance.
28 And Solomon had horses brought out of Egypt, and linen yarn: the king's merchants received the linen yarn at a price.
29 And a chariot came up and went out of Egypt for six hundred *shekels* of silver, and an horse for an hundred and fifty: and so for all the kings of the Hittites, and for the kings of Syria, did they bring *them* out by their means.

CHAPTER 11

1 But King Solomon loved many strange women, together with the daughter of Pharaoh, women of the Moabites, Ammonites, Edomites, Zidonians, *and* Hittites;
2 Of the nations *concerning* which the LORD said unto the children of Israel, you will not go in to them, neither will they come in unto you: *for* surely they will turn away your heart after their gods: Solomon clave unto these in love.
3 And he had seven hundred wives, princesses, and three hundred concubines: and his wives turned away his heart.
4 For it came to pass, when Solomon was old, *that* his wives turned away his heart after other gods: and his heart was not perfect with the LORD his God, as *was* the heart of David his father.
5 For Solomon went after Ashtoreth the goddess of the Zidonians, and after Milcom the abomination of the Ammonites.
6 And Solomon did evil in the sight of the LORD, and went not fully after the LORD, as *did* David his father.
7 Then did Solomon build a high place for Chemosh, the abomination of Moab, in the hill that *is* before Jerusalem, and for Molech, the abomination of the children of Ammon.
8 And likewise did he for all his strange wives, which burnt incense and sacrificed unto their gods.
9 And the LORD was angry with Solomon, because his heart was turned from the LORD God of Israel, which had appeared unto him twice,
10 And had commanded him concerning this thing, that he should not go after other gods: but he kept not that which the LORD commanded.
11 Wherefore the LORD said unto Solomon, Forasmuch as this is done of you, and you have not kept my covenant and my statutes, which I have commanded you, I will surely rend the kingdom from you, and will give it to your servant.
12 Notwithstanding in your days I will not do it for David your father's sake: *but* I will rend it out of the hand of your son.
13 Howbeit I will not rend away the **entire** kingdom; *but* will give one tribe to your son for David my servant's sake, and for Jerusalem's sake which I have chosen.
14 And the LORD stirred up an adversary unto Solomon, Hadad the Edomite: he *was* of the king's seed in Edom.
15 For it came to pass, when David was in Edom, and Joab the captain of the host was gone up to bury the slain, after he had smitten every male in Edom;
16 (For six months did Joab remain there with all Israel, until he had cut off every male in Edom:)
17 That Hadad fled, he and certain Edomites of his father's servants with him, to go into Egypt; Hadad *being* yet a little child.
18 And they arose out of Midian, and came to Paran: and they took men with them out of Paran, and they came to Egypt, unto Pharaoh King of Egypt; which gave him a house, and appointed him victuals, and gave him land.
19 And Hadad found great favor in the sight of Pharaoh, so that he gave him to wife the sister of his own wife, the sister of Tahpenes the queen.
20 And the sister of Tahpenes bare him Genubath his son, whom Tahpenes weaned in Pharaoh's house: and Genubath was in Pharaoh's household among the sons of Pharaoh.
21 And when Hadad heard in Egypt that David slept with his fathers, and that Joab the captain of the host was dead, Hadad said to Pharaoh, Let me depart, that I may go to mine own country.
22 Then Pharaoh said unto him, but what have you lacked with me, that, behold, you seek to go to your own country? And he answered, nothing: howbeit let me go in any wise.
23 And God stirred him up *another* adversary, Rezon the son of Eliadah, which fled from his lord Hadadezer king of Zobah:
24 And he gathered men unto him, and became captain over a band, when David slew them *of Zobah*: and they went to Damascus, and dwelt therein, and reigned in Damascus.
25 And he was an adversary to Israel all the days of Solomon, beside the mischief that Hadad *did*: and he abhorred Israel, and reigned over Syria.
26 And Jeroboam the son of Nebat, an Ephrathite of Zereda, Solomon's servant, whose mother's name *was* Zeruah, a widow woman, even he lifted up *his* hand against the king.
27 And this *was* the cause that he lifted up *his* hand against the king: Solomon built Millo, *and* repaired the breaches of the city of David his father.
28 And the man Jeroboam *was* a mighty man of valor: and Solomon seeing the young man that he was industrious, he made him ruler over all the charge of the house of Joseph.
29 And it came to pass at that time when Jeroboam went out of Jerusalem, that the prophet Ahijah the Shilonite found him in the way; and he had clad himself with a new garment; and they two *were* alone in the field:
30 And Ahijah caught the new garment that *was* on him, and rent it *in* twelve pieces:
31 And he said to Jeroboam, take you ten pieces: for thus said the LORD, the God of Israel, Behold, I will rend the kingdom out of the hand of Solomon, and will give ten tribes to you:
32 (But he will have one tribe for my servant David's sake, and for Jerusalem's sake, the city which I have chosen out of all the tribes of Israel:)
33 Because that they have forsaken me, and have worshipped Ashtoreth the goddess of the Zidonians, Chemosh the god of the Moabites, and Milcom the god of the children of Ammon, and have not walked in my ways, to do *that which is* right in mine eyes, and *to keep* my statutes and my judgments, as *did* David his father.
34 Howbeit I will not take the whole kingdom out of his hand: but I will make him prince all the days of his life for David my servant's sake, whom I chose, because he kept my commandments and my statutes:
35 But I will take the kingdom out of his son's hand, and will give it unto you, *even* ten tribes.
36 And unto his son will I give one tribe, that David my servant may have a light always before me in Jerusalem, the city which I have chosen me to put my name there.
37 And I will take you, and you will reign according to all that your soul desires, and will be king over Israel.
38 And it will be, if you will hearken unto all that I command you, and will walk in my ways, and do *that is* right in my sight, to keep my statutes and my commandments, as David my servant did; that

I will be with you, and build you a sure house, as I built for David, and will give Israel unto you.

39 And I will for this afflict the seed of David, but not for ever.

40 Solomon sought therefore to kill Jeroboam. And Jeroboam arose, and fled into Egypt, unto Shishak King of Egypt, and was in Egypt until the death of Solomon.

41 And the rest of the acts of Solomon, and all that he did, and his wisdom, *are* they not written in the book of the acts of Solomon?

42 And the time that Solomon reigned in Jerusalem over all Israel *was* forty years.

43 And Solomon slept with his fathers, and was buried in the city of David his father: and Rehoboam his son reigned in his stead.

CHAPTER 12

1 And Rehoboam went to Shechem: for all Israel were come to Shechem to make him king.

2 And it came to pass, when Jeroboam the son of Nebat, who was yet in Egypt, heard *of it*, (for he was fled from the presence of king Solomon, and Jeroboam dwelt in Egypt;)

3 That they sent and called him. And Jeroboam and all the congregation of Israel came, and spoke unto Rehoboam, saying,

4 your father made our yoke grievous: now therefore make you the grievous service of your father, and his heavy yoke which he put upon us, lighter, and we will serve you.

5 And he said unto them, depart yet *for* three days, then come again to me. And the people departed.

6 And king Rehoboam consulted with the old men, that stood before Solomon his father while he yet lived, and said, how do you advise that I may answer this people?

7 And they spoke unto him, saying, If you will be a servant unto this people this day, and will serve them, and answer them, and speak good words to them, then they will be your servants forever.

8 But he forsook the counsel of the old men, which they had given him, and consulted with the young men that were grown up with him, *and* which stood before him:

9 And he said unto them, what counsel give you that we may answer this people, who have spoken to me, saying, make the yoke which your father did put upon us lighter?

10 And the young men that were grown up with him spoke unto him, saying, Thus will you speak unto this people that spoke unto you, saying, your father made our yoke heavy, but make you *it* lighter unto us; thus will you say unto them, My little *finger* will be thicker than my father's loins.

11 And now whereas my father did lade you with a heavy yoke, I will add to your yoke: my father has chastised you with whips, but I will chastise you with scorpions.

12 So Jeroboam and all the people came to Rehoboam the third day, as the king had appointed, saying, Come to me again the third day.

13 And the king answered the people roughly, and forsook the old men's counsel that they gave him;

14 And spoke to them after the counsel of the young men, saying, My father made your yoke heavy, and I will add to your yoke: my father *also* chastised you with whips, but I will chastise you with scorpions.

15 Wherefore the king hearkened not unto the people; for the cause was from the LORD, that he might perform his saying, which the LORD spoke by Ahijah the Shilonite unto Jeroboam the son of Nebat.

16 So when all Israel saw that the king hearkened not unto them, the people answered the king, saying, what portion have we in David? Neither *have we* inheritance in the son of Jesse: to your tents, O Israel: now see to your own house, David. So Israel departed unto their tents.

17 But *as for* the children of Israel which dwelt in the cities of Judah, Rehoboam reigned over them.

18 Then king Rehoboam sent Adoram, who *was* over the tribute; and all Israel stoned him with stones, that he died. Therefore king Rehoboam made speed to get him up to his chariot, to flee to Jerusalem.

19 So Israel rebelled against the house of David unto this day.

20 And it came to pass, when all Israel heard that Jeroboam was come again, that they sent and called him unto the congregation, and made him king over all Israel: there was none that followed the house of David, but the tribe of Judah only.

21 And when Rehoboam was come to Jerusalem, he assembled all the house of Judah, with the tribe of Benjamin, an hundred and fourscore thousand chosen men, which were warriors, to fight against the house of Israel, to bring the kingdom again to Rehoboam the son of Solomon.

22 But the word of God came unto Shemaiah the man of God, saying,

23 Speak unto Rehoboam, the son of Solomon, king of Judah, and unto all the house of Judah and Benjamin, and to the remnant of the people, saying,

24 Thus said the LORD, you will not go up, or fight against your brethren the children of Israel: return every man to his house; for this thing is from me. They hearkened therefore to the word of the LORD, and returned to depart, according to the word of the LORD.

25 Then Jeroboam built Shechem in mount Ephraim, and dwelt therein; and went out from there, and built Penuel.

26 And Jeroboam said in his heart, now will the kingdom return to the house of David:

27 If this people go up to do sacrifice in the house of the LORD at Jerusalem, then will the heart of this people turn again unto their lord, *even* unto Rehoboam king of Judah, and they will kill me, and go again to Rehoboam king of Judah.

28 [Whereupon the king took counsel, and made two calves *of* gold, and said unto them, It is too much for you to go up to Jerusalem: behold your gods, O Israel, which brought you up out of the land of Egypt.][1]

29 And he set the one in Beth-el, and the other put he in Dan.

30 And this thing became a sin: for the people went to *worship* before the one, *even* unto Dan.

31 And he made a house of high places, and made priests of the lowest of the people, which were not of the sons of Levi.

32 And Jeroboam ordained a feast in the eighth month, on the fifteenth day of the month, like unto the feast that *is* in Judah, and he offered upon the altar. So did he in Beth-el, sacrificing unto the calves that he had made: and he placed in Beth-el the priests of the high places which he had made.

33 So he offered upon the altar which he had made in Beth-el the fifteenth day of the eighth month, *even* in the month which he had devised of his own heart; and ordained a feast unto the children of Israel: and he offered upon the altar, and burnt incense.

---

[1] compare Exodus 32:4, Ps. 106:19-20 & Romans 1:24 (Homosexuality).

CHAPTER 13

1 And, behold, there came a man of God out of Judah by the word of the LORD unto Beth-el: and Jeroboam stood by the altar to burn incense.
2 And he cried against the altar in the word of the LORD, and said, O altar, altar, thus said the LORD; Behold, a child will be born unto the house of David, Josiah[1] by name; and upon you will he offer the priests of the high places that burn incense upon you, and men's bones will be burnt upon you.
3 And he gave a sign the same day, saying, this *is* the sign which the LORD has spoken; Behold, the altar will be rent, and the ashes that *are* upon it will be poured out.
4 And it came to pass, when king Jeroboam[2] heard the saying of the man of God, which had cried against the altar in Beth-el, that he put forth his hand from the altar, saying, lay hold on him. And his hand, which he put forth against him, dried up, so that he could not pull it in again to him.
5 The altar also was rent, and the ashes poured out from the altar, according to the sign which the man of God had given by the word of the LORD.
6 And the king answered and said unto the man of God, Intreat now the face of the LORD your God, and pray for me, that my hand may be restored me again. And the man of God besought the LORD, and the king's hand was restored him again, and became as *it was* before.
7 And the king said unto the man of God, Come home with me, and refresh thyself, and I will give you a reward.
8 And the man of God said unto the king, If you will give me half your house, I will not go in with you, neither will I eat bread or drink water in this place:
9 For so was it charged me by the word of the LORD, saying, Eat no bread, or drink water, or turn again by the same way that you came.
10 So he went another way, and returned not by the way that he came to Beth-el.
11 Now there dwelt an old prophet in Beth-el; and his sons came and told him all the works[3] that the man of God had done that day in Beth-el: the words which he had spoken unto the king, them they told also to their father.
12 And their father said unto them, what way went he? For his sons had seen what way the man of God went, which came from Judah.
13 And he said unto his sons, Saddle me the ass. So they saddled him the ass: and he rode thereon,
14 And went after the man of God, and found him sitting under an oak: and he said unto him, are you the man of God that came from Judah? And he said, I *am*.
15 Then he said unto him, Come home with me, and eat bread.
16 And he said, I may not return with you, or go in with you: neither will I eat bread or drink water with you in this place:
17 For it was said to me by the word of the LORD, you will eat no bread or drink water there, or turn again to go by the way that you came.
18 He said unto him, I *am* a prophet also as you *are*; and an angel spoke unto me by the word of the LORD, saying, Bring him back with you into your house, that he may eat bread and drink water. *But* he lied[4] unto him.
19 So he went back with him, and did eat bread in his house, and drank water.
20 And it came to pass, as they sat at the table, that the word of the LORD came unto the prophet that brought him back:
21 And he cried unto the man of God that came from Judah, saying, Thus said the LORD, Forasmuch as you have disobeyed the mouth of the LORD, and have not kept the commandment which the LORD your God commanded you,
22 But came back, and have eaten bread and drunk water in the place, of the which *the LORD* did say to you, Eat no bread, and drink no water; your carcass will not come unto the sepulcher of your fathers.
23 And it came to pass, after he had eaten bread, and after he had drunk, that he saddled for him the ass, *to wit*, for the prophet whom he had brought back.
24 And when he was gone, a lion met him by the way, and slew him: and his carcass was cast in the way, and the ass stood by it, the lion also stood by the carcass.
25 And, behold, men passed by, and saw the carcass cast in the way, and the lion standing by the carcass: and they came and told *it* in the city where the old prophet dwelt.
26 And when the prophet that brought him back from the way heard *thereof*, he said, It *is* the man of God, who was disobedient unto the word of the LORD: therefore the LORD has delivered him unto the lion, which has torn him, and slain him, according to the word of the LORD, which he spoke unto him.
27 And he spoke to his sons, saying, Saddle me the ass. And they saddled *him*.
28 And he went and found his carcass cast in the way, and the ass and the lion standing by the carcass: the lion had not eaten the carcass, or torn the ass.
29 And the prophet took up the carcass of the man of God, and laid it upon the ass, and brought it back: and the old prophet came to the city, to mourn and to bury him.
30 And he laid his carcass in his own grave; and they mourned over him, *saying*, Alas, my brother!
31 And it came to pass, after he had buried him, that he spoke to his sons, saying, when I am dead, then bury me in the sepulcher wherein the man of God *is* buried; lay my bones beside his bones:
32 For the saying which he cried by the word of the LORD against the altar in Beth-el, and against all the houses of the high places which *are* in the cities of Samaria, will surely come to pass.
33 After this thing Jeroboam returned not from his evil way, but made again of the lowest of the people priests of the high places: whosoever would, he consecrated him, and he became one of the priests of the high places.
34 And this thing became sin unto the house of Jeroboam, even to cut *it* off, and to destroy *it* from off the face of the earth.

CHAPTER 14

1 At that time Abijah[5] the son of Jeroboam fell sick.
2 And Jeroboam said to his wife, Arise, I pray you, and disguise thyself, that you be not known to be the wife of Jeroboam; and get

---

[1] Josiah – *whom Jehovah heals* [Strgs#2977]. It comes from two root words, the first is defined as *foundation* and the second *Jehovah* [Strgs#803+3050]. Literally the foundation of Jehovah.
[2] Jeroboam – the *people will contend* [Strgs#3379].
[3] Jesus 'worked' the 'works' of God.
[4] lied – to *be untrue*, in word (to *feign*, *disown*) or deed (to *disappoint*, *fail*, *cringe*), deal falsely, submit selves [Strgs#3584]. False submission, compare **2 Samuel 22:45**.
[5] Abijah- Jehovah is my father. [Strgs#29]

you to Shiloh: behold, there *is* Ahijah the prophet, which told me that *I should be* king over this people.

3 And take with you ten loaves, and cracknels, and a cruse¹ of honey, and go to him: he will tell you what will become of the child.

4 And Jeroboam's wife did so, and arose, and went to Shiloh, and came to the house of Ahijah. But Ahijah could not see; for his eyes were set by reason of his age.

5 And the LORD said unto Ahijah, Behold, the wife of Jeroboam cometh to ask a thing of you for her son; for he *is* sick: thus and thus will you say unto her: for it will be, when she cometh in, that she will feign herself *to be* another *woman*.

6 And it was *so*, when Ahijah heard the sound of her feet, as she came in at the door, that he said, Come in, you wife of Jeroboam; why feigns you yourself *to be* another? For I *am* sent to you *with* heavy *tidings*.

7 Go, tell Jeroboam, Thus said the LORD God of Israel, Forasmuch as I exalted you from among the people, and made you prince over my people Israel,

8 And rent the kingdom away from the house of David, and gave it you: and *yet* you have not been as my servant David, who kept my commandments, and who followed me with all his heart, to do *that* only *which was* right in mine eyes;

9 But have done evil above all that were before you: for you have gone and made you other gods, and molten images, to provoke me to anger, and have cast me behind your back:

10 Therefore, behold, I will bring evil upon the house of Jeroboam, and will cut off from Jeroboam him that pisses against the wall, *and* him that is shut up and left in Israel, and will take away the remnant of the house of Jeroboam, as a man takes away dung, till it be all gone.

11 Him that dies of Jeroboam in the city will the dogs eat; and him that dies in the field will the fowls of the air eat: for the LORD has spoken *it*.

12 Arise you therefore, get you to your own house: *and* when your feet enter into the city, the child will die.

13 And all Israel will mourn for him, and bury him: for he only of Jeroboam will come to the grave, because in him there is found *some* good thing toward the LORD God of Israel in the house of Jeroboam.

14 Moreover the LORD will raise him up a king over Israel, who will cut off the house of Jeroboam that day: but what? Even now.

15 For the LORD will smite Israel, as a reed is shaken in the water, and he will root up Israel out of this good land, which he gave to their fathers, and will scatter them beyond the river, because they have made their groves, provoking the LORD to anger.

16 And he will give Israel up because of the sins of Jeroboam, who did sin, and who made Israel to sin.

17 And Jeroboam's wife arose, and departed, and came to Tirzah: *and* when she came to the threshold of the door, the child died;

18 And they buried him; and all Israel mourned for him, according to the word of the LORD, which he spoke by the hand of his servant Ahijah the prophet.

19 And the rest of the acts of Jeroboam, how he warred, and how he reigned, behold, they *are* written in the book of the chronicles of the kings of Israel.

20 And the days which Jeroboam reigned *were* two and twenty years: and he slept with his fathers, and Nadab his son reigned in his stead.

21 And Rehoboam the son of Solomon reigned in Judah. Rehoboam *was* forty and one years old when he began to reign, and he reigned seventeen years in Jerusalem, the city which the LORD did choose out of all the tribes of Israel, to put his name there. And his mother's name *was* Naamah an Ammonitess.

22 And Judah did evil in the sight of the LORD, and they provoked him to jealousy with their sins which they had committed, above all that their fathers had done.

23 For they also built them high places, and images and groves, on every high hill, and under every green tree.

24 And there were also sodomites in the land: *and* they did according to all the abominations of the nations which the LORD cast out before the children of Israel.

25 And it came to pass in the fifth year of king Rehoboam, *that* Shishak king of Egypt came up against Jerusalem:

26 And he took away the treasures of the house of the LORD, and the treasures of the king's house; he even took away all: and he took away all the shields of gold which Solomon had made.

27 And king Rehoboam made in their stead brasen shields, and committed *them* unto the hands of the chief of the guard, which kept the door of the king's house.

28 And it was *so*, when the king went into the house of the LORD, that the guard bare them, and brought them back into the guard chamber.

29 Now the rest of the acts of Rehoboam, and all that he did, *are* they not written in the book of the chronicles of the kings of Judah?

30 And there was war between Rehoboam and Jeroboam all *their* days.

31 And Rehoboam slept with his fathers, and was buried with his fathers in the city of David. And his mother's name *was* Naamah an Ammonitess. And Abijam his son reigned in his stead.

CHAPTER 15

1 Now in the eighteenth year of king Jeroboam the son of Nebat reigned Abijam over Judah.

2 Three years reigned he in Jerusalem. And his mother's name *was* Maachah, the daughter of Abishalom.

3 And he walked in all the sins of his father, which he had done before him: and his heart was not perfect with the LORD his God, as the heart of David his father.

4 Nevertheless for David's sake did the LORD his God give him a lamp in Jerusalem, to set up his son after him, and to establish Jerusalem:

5 Because David did *that which was* right in the eyes of the LORD, and turned not aside from any*thing* that he commanded him all the days of his life, save only in the matter of Uriah the Hittite.

6 And there was war between Rehoboam and Jeroboam all the days of his life.

7 Now the rest of the acts of Abijam, and all that he did, *are* they not written in the book of the chronicles of the kings of Judah? And there was war between Abijam and Jeroboam.

8 And Abijam slept with his fathers; and they buried him in the city of David: and Asa his son reigned in his stead.

9 And in the twentieth year of Jeroboam king of Israel reigned Asa over Judah.

10 And forty and one years reigned he in Jerusalem. And his mother's name *was* Maachah, the daughter of Abishalom.

11 And Asa did *that which was* right in the eyes of the LORD, as *did* David his father.

---

¹ cruse- bottle(from the gurgling in empting). [Strgs#1228]

12 And he took away the sodomites out of the land, and removed all the idols that his fathers had made.

13 And also Maachah his mother, even her he removed from *being* queen, because she had made an idol in a grove; and Asa destroyed her idol, and burnt *it* by the brook Kidron.

14 But the high places were not removed: nevertheless Asa's heart was perfect with the LORD all his days.

15 And he brought in the things which his father had dedicated, and the things which himself had dedicated, into the house of the LORD, silver, and gold, and vessels.

16 And there was war between Asa and Baasha king of Israel all their days.

17 And Baasha king of Israel went up against Judah, and built Ramah, that he might not suffer any to go out or come in to Asa king of Judah.

18 Then Asa took all the silver and the gold *that were* left in the treasures of the house of the LORD, and the treasures of the king's house, and delivered them into the hand of his servants: and king Asa sent them to Ben-hadad, the son of Tabrimon, the son of Hezion, king of Syria, that dwelt at Damascus, saying,

19 *There is* a league between me and you, *and* between my father and your father: behold, I have sent unto you a present of silver and gold; come and break your league with Baasha king of Israel, that he may depart from me.

20 So Ben-hadad hearkened unto king Asa, and sent the captains of the hosts which he had against the cities of Israel, and smote Ijon, and Dan, and Abel-beth-maachah, and all Cinneroth, with all the land of Naphtali.

21 And it came to pass, when Baasha heard *thereof*, that he left off building of Ramah, and dwelt in Tirzah.

22 Then king Asa made a proclamation throughout all Judah; none *was* exempted: and they took away the stones of Ramah, and the timber thereof, wherewith Baasha had **built**; and king Asa built with them Geba of Benjamin, and Mizpah.

23 The rest of all the acts of Asa, and all his might, and all that he did, and the cities which he built, *are* they not written in the book of the chronicles of the kings of Judah? Nevertheless in the time of his old age he was diseased in his feet.

24 And Asa slept with his fathers, and was buried with his father's in the city of David his father: and Jehoshaphat his son reigned in his stead.

25 And Nadab the son of Jeroboam began to reign over Israel in the second year of Asa king of Judah, and reigned over Israel two years.

26 And he did evil in the sight of the LORD, and walked in the way of his father, and in his sin wherewith he made Israel to sin.

27 And Baasha the son of Ahijah, of the house of Issachar, conspired against him; and Baasha smote him at Gibbethon, which *belonged* to the Philistines; for Nadab and all Israel laid siege to Gibbethon.

28 Even in the third year of Asa king of Judah did Baasha slay him, and reigned in his stead.

29 And it came to pass, when he reigned, *that* he smote all the house of Jeroboam; he left not to Jeroboam any that breathed, until he had destroyed him, according unto the saying of the LORD, which he spoke by his servant Ahijah the Shilonite:

30 Because of the sins of Jeroboam which he sinned, and which he made Israel sin, by his provocation wherewith he provoked the LORD God of Israel to anger.

31 Now the rest of the acts of Nadab, and all that he did, *are* they not written in the book of the chronicles of the kings of Israel?

32 And there was war between Asa and Baasha king of Israel all their days.

33 In the third year of Asa king of Judah began Baasha the son of Ahijah to reign over all Israel in Tirzah, twenty and four years.

34 And he did evil in the sight of the LORD, and walked in the way of Jeroboam, and in his sin wherewith he made Israel to sin.

CHAPTER 16

1 Then the word of the LORD came to Jehu the son of Hanani against Baasha, saying,

2 Forasmuch as I exalted you out of the dust, and made you prince over my people Israel; and you have walked in the way of Jeroboam, and have made my people Israel to sin, to provoke me to anger with their sins;

3 Behold, I will take away the posterity of Baasha, and the posterity of his house; and will make your house like the house of Jeroboam the son of Nebat.

4 Him that dies of Baasha in the city will the dogs eat; and him that dies of his in the fields will the fowls of the air eat.

5 Now the rest of the acts of Baasha, and what he did, and his might, *are* they not written in the book of the chronicles of the kings of Israel?

6 So Baasha slept with his fathers, and was buried in Tirzah: and Elah his son reigned in his stead.

7 And also by the hand of the prophet Jehu the son of Hanani came the word of the LORD against Baasha, and against his house, even for all the evil that he did in the sight of the LORD, in provoking him to anger with the work of his hands, in being like the house of Jeroboam; and because he killed him.

8 In the twenty and sixth year of Asa king of Judah began Elah the son of Baasha to reign over Israel in Tirzah, two years.

9 And his servant Zimri, captain of half *his* chariots, conspired against him, as he was in Tirzah, drinking himself drunk in the house of Arza steward of *his* house in Tirzah.

10 And Zimri went in and smote him, and killed him, in the twenty and seventh year of Asa king of Judah, and reigned in his stead.

11 And it came to pass, when he began to reign, as soon as he sat on his throne, *that* he slew all the house of Baasha: he left him not one that pisses against a wall, neither of his kinsfolks, or of his friends.

12 Thus did Zimri destroy all the house of Baasha, according to the word of the LORD, which he spoke against Baasha by Jehu the prophet,

13 For all the sins of Baasha, and the sins of Elah his son, by which they sinned, and by which they made Israel to sin, in provoking the LORD God of Israel to anger with their vanities.

14 Now the rest of the acts of Elah, and all that he did, *are* they not written in the book of the chronicles of the kings of Israel?

15 In the twenty and seventh year of Asa king of Judah did Zimri reign seven days in Tirzah. And the people *were* encamped against Gibbethon, which *belonged* to the Philistines.

16 And the people *that were* encamped heard say, Zimri has conspired, and has also slain the king: wherefore all Israel made Omri, the captain of the host, king over Israel that day in the camp.

17 And Omri went up from Gibbethon, and all Israel with him, and they besieged Tirzah.

18 And it came to pass, when Zimri saw that the city was taken, that he went into the palace of the king's house, and burnt the king's house over him with fire, and died,

19 For his sins which he sinned in doing evil in the sight of the LORD, in walking in the way of Jeroboam, and in his sin which he did, to make Israel to sin.
20 Now the rest of the acts of Zimri, and his treason that he wrought, *are* they not written in the book of the chronicles of the kings of Israel?
21 Then were the people of Israel divided into two parts: half of the people followed Tibni the son of Ginath, to make him king; and half followed Omri.
22 But the people that followed Omri prevailed against the people that followed Tibni the son of Ginath: so Tibni died, and Omri reigned.
23 In the thirty and first year of Asa king of Judah began Omri to reign over Israel, twelve years: six years reigned he in Tirzah.
24 And he bought the hill Samaria of Shemer for two talents of silver, and built on the hill, and called the name of the city which he built, after the name of Shemer, owner of the hill, Samaria.
25 But Omri wrought evil in the eyes of the LORD, and did worse than all that *were* before him.
26 For he walked in all the way of Jeroboam the son of Nebat, and in his sin wherewith he made Israel to sin, to provoke the LORD God of Israel to anger with their vanities.
27 Now the rest of the acts of Omri which he did, and his might that he showed, *are* they not written in the book of the chronicles of the kings of Israel?
28 So Omri slept with his fathers, and was buried in Samaria: and Ahab his son reigned in his stead.
29 And in the thirty and eighth year of Asa king of Judah began Ahab the son of Omri to reign over Israel: and Ahab the son of Omri reigned over Israel in Samaria twenty and two years.
30 And Ahab the son of Omri did evil in the sight of the LORD above all that *were* before him.
31 And it came to pass, as if it had been a light thing for him to walk in the sins of Jeroboam the son of Nebat, that he took to wife Jezebel the daughter of Ethbaal king of the Zidonians, and went and served Baal, and worshipped him.
32 And he reared up an altar for Baal in the house of Baal, which he had built in Samaria.
33 And Ahab made a grove; and Ahab did more to provoke the LORD God of Israel to anger than all the kings of Israel that were before him.
34 In his days did Hiel the Beth-elite build Jericho: he laid the foundation thereof in Abiram his firstborn, and set up the gates thereof in his youngest *son* Segub, according to the word of the LORD, which he spoke by Joshua the son of Nun.

CHAPTER 17

1 And Elijah[1] the Tishbite, *who was* of the inhabitants of Gilead, said unto Ahab, As the LORD God of Israel lives, before whom I stand, there will not be dew or rain these years, but according to my word.
2 And the word of the LORD came unto him, saying,
3 Get you hence, and turn you eastward, and hide yourself by the brook Cherith, that *is* before Jordan.
4 And it will be, *that* you will drink of the brook; and I have commanded the ravens to feed you there.
5 So he went and did according unto the word of the LORD: for he went and dwelt by the brook Cherith, that *is* before Jordan.
6 And the ravens brought him bread and flesh in the morning, and bread and flesh in the evening; and he drank of the brook.
7 And it came to pass after a while, that the brook dried up, because there had been no rain in the land.
8 And the word of the LORD came unto him, saying,
9 Arise, get you to Zarephath[2], which *belongs* to Zidon[3], and dwell there: behold, I have commanded a widow woman there to sustain you.
10 So he arose and went to Zarephath. And when he came to the gate of the city, behold, the widow woman *was* there gathering of sticks: and he called to her, and said, fetch me, I pray you, a little water in a vessel, that I may drink.
11 And as she was going to fetch *it*, he called to her, and said, bring me, I pray you, a morsel of bread in your hand.
12 And she said, *As* the LORD your God lives, I have not a cake, but an handful of meal in a barrel, and a little oil in a cruse: and, behold, I *am* gathering two sticks, that I may go in and dress it for me and my son, that we may eat it, and die.
13 And Elijah said unto her, Fear not; go *and* do as you have said: but make me thereof a little cake first, and bring *it* unto me, and after make for you and for your son.
14 For thus said the LORD God of Israel, The barrel of meal will not waste, neither will the cruse of oil fail, until the day *that* the LORD sends rain upon the earth.
15 And she went and did according to the sayings of Elijah: and she, and he, and her house, did eat *many* days.
16 *And* the barrel of meal wasted not, neither did the cruse of oil fail, according to the word of the LORD, which he spoke by Elijah.
17 And it came to pass after these things, *that* the son of the woman, the mistress of the house, fell sick; and his sickness was so sore, that there was no breath left in him.
18 And she said unto Elijah, What have I to do with you, O you man of God? are you come unto me to call my sin to remembrance, and to slay my son?
19 And he said unto her, Give me your son. And he took him out of her bosom, and carried him up into a loft, where he abode, and laid him upon his own bed.
20 And he cried unto the LORD, and said, O LORD my God, have you also brought evil upon the widow with whom I sojourn, by slaying her son?
21 And he stretched himself upon the child three times, and cried unto the LORD, and said, O LORD my God, I pray you, let this child's soul come into him again.
22 And the LORD heard the voice of Elijah; and the soul of the child came into him again, and he revived.
23 And Elijah took the child, and brought him down out of the chamber into the house, and delivered him unto his mother: and Elijah said, See, your son lives.
24 And the woman said to Elijah, now by this I know that you are a man of God, *and* that the word of the LORD in your mouth *is* truth.

CHAPTER 18

1 And it came to pass *after* many days, that the word of the LORD came to Elijah in the third year, saying, go, show yourself unto Ahab; and I will send rain upon the earth.
2 And Elijah went to show himself unto Ahab. And *there was* a sore famine in Samaria.

---

[1] Elijah- God is Jehovah. [Strgs#452]
[2] Zarephath – refinery or refinement [Strgs#6886]. Comes from a root word meaning to fuse metal [Strgs#6884].
[3] lit. to *catch fish, fishery* [Strgs#6721]. Has a root word meaning to *lie* alongside in wait, to catch an animal, to *victual* for a journey, take provision [Strgs#6679].

3 And Ahab called Obadiah, which *was* the governor of *his* house. (Now Obadiah feared the LORD greatly:
4 For it was *so*, when Jezebel cut off the prophets of the LORD, that Obadiah took an hundred prophets, and hid them by fifty in a cave, and fed them with bread and water.)
5 And Ahab said unto Obadiah, Go into the land, unto all fountains of water, and unto all brooks: peradventure we may find grass to save the horses and mules alive, that we lose not all the beasts.
6 So they divided the land between them to pass throughout it: Ahab went one way by himself, and Obadiah went another way by himself.
7 And as Obadiah was in the way, behold, Elijah met him: and he knew him, and fell on his face, and said, are you that my lord Elijah?
8 And he answered him, I *am*: go, tell your lord, Behold, Elijah *is here*.
9 And he said, what have I sinned, that you would deliver your servant into the hand of Ahab, to slay me?
10 *As* the LORD your God lives, there is no nation or kingdom, where my lord has not sent to seek you: and when they said, *He is* not *there*; he took an oath of the kingdom and nation, that they found you not.
11 And now you say, go, tell your lord, Behold, Elijah *is here*.
12 And it will come to pass, *as soon as* I am gone from you, that the Spirit of the LORD will carry you where I know not; and *so* when I come and tell Ahab, and he cannot find you, he will slay me: but I your servant fear the LORD from my youth.
13 Was it not told my lord what I did when Jezebel slew the prophets of the LORD, how I hid an hundred men of the LORD'S prophets by fifty in a cave, and fed them with bread and water?
14 And now you say, Go, tell your lord, Behold, Elijah *is here*: and he will slay me.
15 And Elijah said, *As* the LORD of hosts lives, before whom I stand, I will surely show myself unto him to day.
16 So Obadiah went to meet Ahab, and told him: and Ahab went to meet Elijah.
17 And it came to pass, when Ahab saw Elijah, that Ahab said unto him, are you he that troubles Israel?
18 And he answered, I have not troubled Israel; but thou, and your father's house, in that you have forsaken the commandments of the LORD, and you have followed Baalim[1].
19 Now therefore send, *and* gather to me all Israel unto Mount Carmel, and the prophets of Baal four hundred and fifty, and the prophets of the groves four hundred, which eat at Jezebel's table.[2]
20 So Ahab sent unto all the children of Israel, and gathered the prophets together unto Mount Carmel.
21 And Elijah came unto all the people, and said, how long halt you between two opinions? if the LORD *be* God, follow him: but if Baal, *then* follow him. And the people answered him not a word.
22 Then said Elijah unto the people, I, *even* I only, remain a prophet of the LORD; but Baal's prophets *are* four hundred and fifty men.
23 Let them therefore give us two bullocks; and let them choose one bullock for themselves, and cut it in pieces, and lay *it* on wood, and put no fire *under*: and I will dress the other bullock, and lay *it* on wood, and put no fire *under*.
24 And call you on the name of your gods, and I will call on the name of the LORD: and the God that answers by fire, let him be God. And all the people answered and said, It is well spoken.
25 And Elijah said unto the prophets of Baal, Choose you one bullock for yourselves, and dress *it* first; for you *are* many; and call on the name of your gods, but put no fire *under*.
26 And they took the bullock which was given them, and they dressed *it*, and called on the name of Baal from morning even until noon, saying, O Baal, hear us. But *there was* no voice, or any that answered. And they leaped upon the altar which was made.
27 And it came to pass at noon, that Elijah mocked them, and said, cry aloud: for he *is* a god; either he is talking, or he is pursuing, or he is in a journey, *or* peradventure he sleeps, and must be awaked.
28 And they cried aloud, and cut themselves after their manner with knives and lancets, till the blood gushed out upon them.
29 And it came to pass, when midday was past, and they prophesied until the *time* of the offering of the *evening* sacrifice, that *there was* neither voice, or any to answer, or any that regarded.
30 And Elijah said unto all the people, come near unto me. And all the people came near unto him. And he repaired the altar of the LORD *that was* broken down.
31 And Elijah took twelve stones, according to the number of the tribes of the sons of Jacob, unto whom the word of the LORD came, saying, Israel will be your name:
32 [And with the stones he built an altar in the name of the LORD: and he made a trench about the altar, [as great as would contain][3] two measures of seed.][4]
33 And he put the wood in order, and cut the bullock in pieces, and laid *him* on the wood, and said, Fill four barrels with water, and pour *it* on the burnt sacrifice, and on the wood.
34 And he said, Do *it* the second time. And they did *it* the second time. And he said, Do *it* the third time. And they did *it* the third time.
35 And the water ran round about the altar; and he filled the trench also with water.
36 And it came to pass at *the time of* the offering of the *evening* sacrifice, that Elijah the prophet came near, and said, LORD God of Abraham, Isaac, and of Israel, let it be known this day that you are God in Israel, and *that* I *am* your servant, and *that* I have done all these things at your word.
37 Hear me, O LORD, hear me, that this people may know that you are the LORD God, and *that* you have turned their heart back again.
38 Then the fire of the LORD fell, and consumed the burnt sacrifice, and the wood, and the stones, and the dust, and licked up the water that *was* in the trench.
39 And when all the people saw *it*, they fell on their faces: and they said, the LORD, he *is* the God; the LORD, he *is* the God.
40 And Elijah said unto them, Take the prophets of Baal; let not one of them escape. And they took them: and Elijah brought them down to the brook Kishon, and slew them there.[5]
41 And Elijah said unto Ahab, Get you up, eat and drink; for *there is* a sound of abundance of rain.

---

[1] Baalim – lord, the same as Baal the Phoenician deity [Strgs#1168]. Plural includes Beelzebub.
[2] Prophets of Satan/Prophets of sex – Baal was the leader see v21 & Mark 3:22.
[3] lit. a house or family [Strgs#1004].
[4] we are at two measures = 2,000 years of seed being baptized.
[5] it appears that he did not kill the other 400, see v19, v22, v26, v40 with **1 Kings 22:6**. Although Elijah heard, he still had to pray, see v3€ & v42.

42 So Ahab went up to eat and to drink. And Elijah went up to the top of Carmel; and he cast himself down upon the earth[1], and put his face between his knees,

43 And said to his servant, Go up now, look toward the sea. And he went up, and looked, and said, *there is* nothing. And he said, Go again seven times.

44 And it came to pass at the seventh time, that he said, Behold, there arises a little cloud out of the sea, like a man's hand. And he said, Go up, say unto Ahab, Prepare your *chariot*, and get you down, that the rain stop you not.

45 And it came to pass in the mean while, that the heaven was black with clouds and wind, and there was a great rain. And Ahab rode, and went to Jezreel.

46 And the hand of the LORD was on Elijah; and he girded up his loins, and ran before Ahab to the entrance of Jezreel.

CHAPTER 19

1 And Ahab told Jezebel all that Elijah had done, and withal how he had slain all the prophets with the sword.

2 Then Jezebel sent a messenger unto Elijah, saying, so let the gods do *to me*, and more also, if I make not your life as the life of one of them by tomorrow about this time.

3 And when he saw *that*, he arose, and went for his life, and came to Beer-sheba, which *belongs* to Judah, and left his servant there.

4 But he himself went a day's journey into the wilderness, and came and sat down under a juniper tree: and he requested for himself that he might die; and said, it is enough; now, O LORD, take away my life; for I *am* not better than my fathers.

5 And as he lay and slept under a juniper tree, behold, then an angel touched him, and said unto him, arise *and* eat.

6 And he looked, and, behold, *there was* a cake baking on the coals, and a cruse of water at his head[2]. And he did eat and drink, and laid him down again.

7 And the angel of the LORD came again the second time, and touched him, and said, Arise *and* eat; because the journey *is* too great for you.

8 And he arose, and did eat and drink, and went in the strength of that meat forty days and forty nights unto Horeb[3] the mount of God.

9 And he came there unto a cave, and lodged there; and, behold, the word of the LORD *came* to him, and he said unto him, what **do** you here, Elijah?

10 And he said, I have been very jealous for the LORD God of hosts: for the children of Israel have forsaken your covenant, thrown down your altars, and slain your prophets with the sword; and I, *even* I only, am left; and they seek my life, to take it away.

11 And he said, Go forth, and stand upon the mount before the LORD. And, behold, the LORD passed by, and a great and strong wind rent the mountains, and brake in pieces the rocks before the LORD; *but* the LORD *was* not in the wind: and after the wind an earthquake; *but* the LORD *was* not in the earthquake:

12 And after the earthquake a fire; *but* the LORD *was* not in the fire: and after the fire a still small voice.

13 And it was *so*, when Elijah heard *it*, that he wrapped his face in his mantle, and went out, and stood in the entering in of the cave. And, behold, *there came* a voice unto him, and said, what **do** you here, Elijah?

14 And he said, I have been very jealous for the LORD God of hosts: because the children of Israel have forsaken your covenant, thrown down your altars, and slain your prophets with the sword; and I, *even* I only, am left; and they seek my life, to take it away.

15 And the LORD said unto him, Go, return on your way to the wilderness of Damascus: and when you come, anoint Hazael[4] *to be* king over Syria:

16 And Jehu[5] the son of Nimshi will you anoint *to be* king over Israel: and Elisha[6] the son of Shaphat of Abelmeholah will you anoint *to be* prophet in your room.

17 And it will come to pass, *that* him that escapes the sword of Hazael will Jehu slay: and him that escapes from the sword of Jehu will Elisha slay.

18 Yet I have left *me* seven thousand in Israel, all the knees which have not bowed unto Baal, and every mouth which has not kissed him.

19 So he departed there, and found Elisha the son of Shaphat, who *was* plowing *with* twelve yoke *of oxen* before him, and he with the twelfth: and Elijah passed by him, and cast his mantle upon him.

20 And he left the oxen, and ran after Elijah, and said, let me, I pray you, kiss my father and my mother, and *then* I will follow you. And he said unto him, Go back again: for what have I done to you?

21 And he returned back from him, and took a yoke of oxen, and slew them, and boiled their flesh with the instruments of the oxen, and gave unto the people, and they did eat. Then he arose, and went after Elijah, and ministered unto him.

CHAPTER 20

1 And Ben-hadad the king of Syria gathered his **entire** host together: and *there were* thirty and two kings with him, and horses, and chariots: and he went up and besieged Samaria, and warred against it.

2 And he sent messengers to Ahab king of Israel into the city, and said unto him, thus said Ben-hadad,

3 your silver and your gold *is* mine; your wives also and your children, *even* the goodliest, *are* mine.

4 And the king of Israel answered and said, My lord, O king, according to your saying, I *am* yours, and all that I have.

5 And the messengers came again, and said, thus speaks Ben-hadad, saying, Although I have sent unto you, saying, you will deliver me your silver, and your gold, and your wives, and your children;

6 Yet I will send my servants unto you tomorrow about this time, and they will search your house, and the houses of your servants; and it will be, *that* whatsoever is pleasant in your eyes, they will put *it* in their hand, and take *it* away.

7 Then the king of Israel called all the elders of the land, and said, Mark, I pray you, and see how this *man* seeks mischief: for he sent unto me for my wives, and for my children, and for my silver, and for my gold; and I denied him not.

8 And all the elders and all the people said unto him, Hearken not *unto him*, or consent.

9 Wherefore he said unto the messengers of Ben-hadad, tell my lord the king, All that you did send for to your servant at the first I will do: but this thing I may not do. And the messengers departed, and brought him word again.

---

[1] lit. to *be firm*, the *earth* (as large or partitively a *land*) [Strgs#776].
[2] head – headpiece, head rest or headship [Strgs#4763].
[3] Horeb – *desert & desolate* [Strgs#2717]. It's root word is defined as *to parch*, to *desolate*, *destroy*, *kill* & *decay* [Strgs#2717].

[4] Hazael- one who sees God or God has seen. [Strgs#2317]
[5] Jehu- Jehovah is He. [Strgs#3058]
[6] Elisha- God is salvation. [Strgs#477]

10 And Ben-hadad sent unto him, and said, the gods do so unto me, and more also, if the dust of Samaria will suffice for handfuls for all the people that follow me.
11 And the king of Israel answered and said, tell *him*, Let not him that girdes on *his harness* boast himself as he that puts it off.
12 And it came to pass, when *Ben-hadad* heard this message, as he *was* drinking, he and the kings in the pavilions, that he said unto his servants, set *yourselves in array*. And they set *themselves in array* against the city.
13 And, behold, there came a prophet unto Ahab king of Israel, saying, Thus said the LORD, have you seen all this great multitude? Behold, I will deliver it into your hand this day; and you will know that I *am* the LORD.
14 And Ahab said, by whom? And he said, thus said the LORD, *Even* by the young men of the princes of the provinces. Then he said, who will order the battle? And he answered, you.
15 Then he numbered the young men of the princes of the provinces, and they were two hundred and thirty two: and after them he numbered all the people, *even* all the children of Israel, *being* seven thousand.
16 And they went out at noon. But Ben-hadad *was* drinking himself drunk in the pavilions, he and the kings, the thirty and two kings that helped him.
17 And the young men of the princes of the provinces went out first; and Ben-hadad sent out, and they told him, saying, there are men come out of Samaria.
18 And he said, whether they be come out for peace, take them alive; or whether they be come out for war, take them alive.
19 So these young men of the princes of the provinces came out of the city, and the army which followed them.
20 And they slew everyone his man: and the Syrians fled; and Israel pursued them: and Ben-hadad the king of Syria escaped on a horse with the horsemen.
21 And the king of Israel went out, and smote the horses and chariots, and slew the Syrians with a great slaughter.
22 And the prophet came to the king of Israel, and said unto him, Go, strengthen thyself, and mark, and see what you doest: for at the return of the year the king of Syria will come up against you.
23 And the servants of the king of Syria said unto him, their gods *are* gods of the hills; therefore they were stronger than we; but let us fight against them in the plain, and surely we will be stronger than they.
24 And do this thing, Take the kings away, every man out of his place, and put captains in their rooms:
25 And number you an army, like the army that you have lost, horse for horse, and chariot for chariot: and we will fight against them in the plain, *and* surely we will be stronger than they. And he hearkened unto their voice, and did so.
26 And it came to pass at the return of the year, that Ben-hadad numbered the Syrians, and went up to Aphek, to fight against Israel.
27 And the children of Israel were numbered, and were all present, and went against them: and the children of Israel pitched before them like two little flocks of kids; but the Syrians filled the country.
28 And there came a man of God, and spoke unto the king of Israel, and said, Thus said the LORD, Because the Syrians have said, The LORD *is* God of the hills, but he *is* not God of the valleys, therefore will I deliver all this great multitude into your hand, and you will know that I *am* the LORD.
29 And they pitched one over against the other seven days. And *so* it was, that in the seventh day the battle was joined: and the children of Israel slew of the Syrians an hundred thousand footmen in one day.
30 But the rest fled to Aphek, into the city; and *there* a wall fell upon twenty and seven thousand of the men *that were* left. And Ben-hadad fled, and came into the city, into an inner chamber.
31 And his servants said unto him, Behold now, we have heard that the kings of the house of Israel *are* merciful kings: let us, I pray you, put sackcloth on our loins, and ropes upon our heads, and go out to the king of Israel: peradventure he will save your life.
32 So they girded sackcloth on their loins, and *put* ropes on their heads, and came to the king of Israel, and said, your servant Ben-hadad said, I pray you, let me live. And he said, *is* he yet alive? he *is* my brother.
33 Now the men did diligently observe whether *any thing would come* from him, and did hastily catch *it*: and they said, your brother Ben-hadad. Then he said, Go ye, bring him. Then Ben-hadad came forth to him; and he caused him to come up into the chariot.
34 And *Ben-hadad* said unto him, the cities, which my father took from your father, I will restore; and you will make streets for you in Damascus, as my father made in Samaria. Then *said* Ahab, I will send you away with this covenant. So he made a covenant with him, and sent him away.
35 And a certain man of the sons of the prophets said unto his neighbor in the word of the LORD, Smite me, I pray you. And the man refused to smite him.
36 Then said he unto him, because you have not obeyed the voice of the LORD, behold, as soon as you are departed from me, a lion will slay you. And as soon as he was departed from him, a lion found him, and slew him.
37 Then he found another man, and said, smite me, pray you. And the man smote him, so that in smiting he wounded *him*.
38 So the prophet departed, and waited for the king by the way, and disguised himself with ashes upon his face.
39 And as the king passed by, he cried unto the king: and he said, your servant went out into the midst of the battle; and, behold, a man turned aside, and brought a man unto me, and said, Keep this man: if by any means he be missing, then will your life be for his life, or else you will pay a talent of silver.
40 And as your servant was busy here and there, he was gone. And the king of Israel said unto him, so will your judgment *be*; yourself have decided *it*.
41 And he hasted, and took the ashes away from his face; and the king of Israel discerned him that he *was* of the prophets.
42 And he said unto him, thus said the LORD, because you have let go out of your hand a man whom I appointed to utter destruction, therefore your life will go for his life, and your people for his people.
43 And the king of Israel went to his house heavy and displeased, and came to Samaria.

CHAPTER 21

1 And it came to pass after these things, *that* Naboth the Jezreelite had a vineyard, which *was* in Jezreel, hard by the palace of Ahab king of Samaria.
2 And Ahab spoke unto Naboth, saying, Give me your vineyard, that I may have it for a garden of herbs, because it *is* near unto my house: and I will give you for it a better vineyard than it; *or*, if it seem good to you, I will give you the worth of it in money.
3 And Naboth said to Ahab, The LORD forbid it me, that I should give the inheritance of my father's unto you.

4 And Ahab came into his house heavy and displeased because of the word which Naboth the Jezreelite had spoken to him: for he had said, I will not give you the inheritance of my fathers. And he laid him down upon his bed, and turned away his face, and would eat no bread.

5 But Jezebel his wife came to him, and said unto him, why is your spirit so sad, that you eat no bread?

6 And he said unto her, because I spoke unto Naboth the Jezreelite, and said unto him, give me your vineyard for money; or else, if it pleases you, I will give you *another* vineyard for it: and he answered, I will not give you my vineyard.

7 And Jezebel his wife said unto him, **do** you now govern the kingdom of Israel? Arise, *and* eat bread, and let your heart be merry: I will give you the vineyard of Naboth the Jezreelite.

8 So she wrote letters in Ahab's name, and sealed *them* with his seal, and sent the letters unto the elders and to the nobles that *were* in his city, dwelling with Naboth.

9 And she wrote in the letters, saying, proclaim a fast, and set Naboth on high among the people:

10 And set two men, sons of Belial, before him, to bear witness against him, saying, you did blaspheme God and the king. And *then* carry him out, and stone him, that he may die.

11 And the men of his city, *even* the elders and the nobles who were the inhabitants in his city, did as Jezebel had sent unto them, *and* as it *was* written in the letters which she had sent unto them.

12 They proclaimed a fast, and set Naboth on high among the people.

13 And there came in two men, children of Belial, and sat before him: and the men of Belial witnessed against him, *even* against Naboth, in the presence of the people, saying, Naboth did blaspheme God and the king. Then they carried him forth out of the city, and stoned him with stones, that he died.

14 Then they sent to Jezebel, saying, Naboth is stoned, and is dead.

15 And it came to pass, when Jezebel heard that Naboth was stoned, and was dead, that Jezebel said to Ahab, Arise, take possession of the vineyard of Naboth the Jezreelite, which he refused to give you for money: for Naboth is not alive, but dead.

16 And it came to pass, when Ahab heard that Naboth was dead, that Ahab rose up to go down to the vineyard of Naboth the Jezreelite, to take possession of it.

17 And the word of the LORD came to Elijah the Tishbite, saying,

18 Arise, go down to meet Ahab king of Israel, which *is* in Samaria: behold, *he is* in the vineyard of Naboth, where he is gone down to possess it.

19 And you will speak unto him, saying, thus said the LORD, have you killed, and also taken possession? And you will speak unto him, saying, thus said the LORD, In the place where dogs licked the blood of Naboth will dogs lick your blood, even yours.

20 And Ahab said to Elijah, have you found me, O mine enemy? And he answered, I have found *you*: because you have sold yourself to work evil in the sight of the LORD.

21 Behold, I will bring evil upon you, and will take away your posterity, and will cut off from Ahab him that pisses against the wall, and him that is shut up and left in Israel,

22 And will make your house like the house of Jeroboam the son of Nebat, and like the house of Baasha the son of Ahijah, for the provocation wherewith you have provoked *me* to anger, and made Israel to sin.

23 And of Jezebel also spoke the LORD, saying, the dogs will eat Jezebel by the wall of Jezreel.

24 Him that dies of Ahab in the city the dogs will eat; and him that dies in the field will the fowls of the air eat.

25 But there was none like unto Ahab, which did sell himself to work wickedness in the sight of the LORD, whom Jezebel his wife stirred up.

26 And he did very abominably in following idols, according to all *things* as did the Amorites, whom the LORD cast out before the children of Israel.

27 And it came to pass, when Ahab heard those words, that he rent his clothes, and put sackcloth upon his flesh, and fasted, and lay in sackcloth, and went softly.

28 And the word of the LORD came to Elijah the Tishbite, saying,

29 See you how Ahab humbles himself before me? Because he humbles himself before me, I will not bring the evil in his days: *but* in his son's days will I bring the evil upon his house.

CHAPTER 22

1 And they continued three years without war between Syria and Israel.

2 And it came to pass in the third year, that Jehoshaphat the king of Judah came down to the king of Israel.

3 And the king of Israel said unto his servants, Know you that Ramoth in Gilead *is* our's, and we *be* still, *and* take it not out of the hand of the king of Syria?

4 And he said unto Jehoshaphat, will you go with me to battle to Ramoth-gilead? And Jehoshaphat said to the king of Israel, I *am* as you *art*, my people as your people, my horses as your horses.

5 And Jehoshaphat said unto the king of Israel, Enquire, I pray you, at the word of the LORD today.

6 Then the king of Israel gathered the prophets together, about four hundred men, and said unto them, will I go against Ramoth-gilead to battle, or will I forbear? And they said, Go up; for the Lord will deliver *it* into the hand of the king.

7 And Jehoshaphat said, *is there* not here a prophet of the LORD besides, that we might enquire of him?

8 And the king of Israel said unto Jehoshaphat, *there is* yet one man, Micaiah the son of Imlah, by whom we may enquire of the LORD: but I hate him; for he does not prophesy good concerning me, but evil. And Jehoshaphat said, Let not the king say so.

9 Then the king of Israel called an officer, and said, hasten here Micaiah the son of Imlah.

10 And the king of Israel and Jehoshaphat the king of Judah sat each on his throne, having put on their robes, in a void place in the entrance of the gate of Samaria; and all the prophets prophesied before them.

11 And Zedekiah the son of Chenaanah made him horns of iron: and he said, thus said the LORD, with these will you push the Syrians, until you have consumed them.

12 And all the prophets prophesied so, saying, Go up to Ramoth-gilead, and prosper: for the LORD will deliver *it* into the king's hand.

13 And the messenger that was gone to call Micaiah spoke unto him, saying, Behold now, the words of the prophets *declare* good unto the king with one mouth: let your word, I pray you, be like the word of one of them, and speak *that which is* good.

14 And Micaiah said, *As* the LORD lives, what the LORD said unto me, that will I speak.

15 So he came to the king. And the king said unto him, Micaiah, will we go against Ramoth-gilead to battle, or will we forbear? And he answered him, Go, and prosper: for the LORD will deliver *it* into the hand of the king.

16 And the king said unto him, how many times will I adjure you that you tell me nothing but *that which is* true in the name of the LORD?

17 And he said, I saw all Israel scattered upon the hills, as sheep that have not a shepherd: and the LORD said, these have no master: let them return every man to his house in peace.

18 And the king of Israel said unto Jehoshaphat, Did I not tell you that he would prophesy no good concerning me, but evil?

19 And he said, hear you therefore the word of the LORD: I saw the LORD sitting on his throne, and all the host of heaven standing by him on his right hand and on his left.

20 And the LORD said, who will persuade Ahab, that he may go up and fall at Ramoth-gilead? And one said on this manner, and another said on that manner.

21 And there came forth a spirit, and stood before the LORD, and said, I will persuade him.

22 And the LORD said unto him, wherewith? And he said, I will go forth, and I will be a lying spirit in the mouth of all his prophets. And he said, you will persuade *him*, and prevail also: go forth, and do so.

23 Now therefore, behold, the LORD has put a lying spirit in the mouth of all these, your prophets, and the LORD has spoken evil concerning you.

24 But Zedekiah the son of Chenaanah went near, and smote Micaiah on the cheek, and said, which way went the Spirit of the LORD from me to speak unto you?

25 And Micaiah said, Behold, you will see in that day, when you will go into an inner chamber to hide thyself.

26 And the king of Israel said, take Micaiah, and carry him back unto Amon the governor of the city, and to Joash the king's son;

27 And say, thus said the king, put this *fellow* in the prison, and feed him with bread of affliction and with water of affliction, until I come in peace.

28 And Micaiah said, if you return at all in peace, the LORD has not spoken by me. And he said, Hearken, O people, every one of you.

29 So the king of Israel and Jehoshaphat the king of Judah went up to Ramoth-gilead.

30 And the king of Israel said unto Jehoshaphat, I will disguise myself, and enter into the battle; but put you on your robes. And the king of Israel disguised himself, and went into the battle.

31 But the king of Syria commanded his thirty and two captains that had rule over his chariots, saying, fight neither with small or great, save only with the king of Israel.

32 And it came to pass, when the captains of the chariots saw Jehoshaphat, that they said, surely it *is* the king of Israel. And they turned aside to fight against him: and Jehoshaphat cried out.

33 And it came to pass, when the captains of the chariots perceived that it *was* not the king of Israel, that they turned back from pursuing him.

34 And a *certain* man drew a bow at a venture, and smote the king of Israel between the joints of the harness: wherefore he said unto the driver of his chariot, turn your hand, and carry me out of the host; for I am wounded.

35 And the battle increased that day: and the king was stayed up in his chariot against the Syrians, and died at even: and the blood ran out of the wound into the midst of the chariot.

36 And there went a proclamation throughout the host about the going down of the sun, saying, every man to his city, and every man to his own country.

37 So the king died, and was brought to Samaria; and they buried the king in Samaria.

38 And *one* washed the chariot in the pool of Samaria; and the dogs licked up his blood; and they washed his armor; according unto the word of the LORD which he spoke.

39 Now the rest of the acts of Ahab, and all that he did, and the ivory house which he made, and all the cities that he built, *are* they not written in the book of the chronicles of the kings of Israel?

40 So Ahab slept with his father's; and Ahaziah his son reigned in his stead.

41 And Jehoshaphat the son of Asa began to reign over Judah in the fourth year of Ahab king of Israel.

42 Jehoshaphat *was* thirty and five years old when he began to reign; and he reigned twenty and five years in Jerusalem. And his mother's name *was* Azubah the daughter of Shilhi.

43 And he walked in all the ways of Asa his father; he turned not aside from it, doing *that which was* right in the eyes of the LORD: nevertheless the high places were not taken away; *for* the people offered and burnt incense yet in the high places.

44 And Jehoshaphat made peace with the king of Israel.

45 Now the rest of the acts of Jehoshaphat, and his might that he showed, and how he warred, *are* they not written in the book of the chronicles of the kings of Judah?

46 And the remnant of the sodomites, which remained in the days of his father Asa, he took out of the land.

47 *There was* then no king in Edom: a deputy *was* king.

48 Jehoshaphat made ships of Tharshish to go to Ophir for gold: but they went not; for the ships were broken at Ezion-geber.

49 Then said Ahaziah the son of Ahab unto Jehoshaphat, let my servants go with your servants in the ships. But Jehoshaphat would not.

50 And Jehoshaphat slept with his fathers, and was buried with his father's in the city of David his father: and Jehoram his son reigned in his stead.

51 Ahaziah the son of Ahab began to reign over Israel in Samaria the seventeenth year of Jehoshaphat king of Judah, and reigned two years over Israel.

52 And he did evil in the sight of the LORD, and walked in the way of his father, and in the way of his mother, and in the way of Jeroboam the son of Nebat, who made Israel to sin:

53 For he served Baal, and worshipped him, and provoked to anger the LORD God of Israel, according to all that his father had done.

SECOND KINGS
CHAPTER 1

1 Then Moab rebelled against Israel after the death of Ahab.

2 And Ahaziah fell down through a lattice in his upper chamber that *was* in Samaria, and was sick: and he sent messengers, and said unto them, Go, enquire of Baal-zebub the god of Ekron whether I will recover of this disease.

3 But the angel of the LORD said to Elijah the Tishbite, Arise, go up to meet the messengers of the king of Samaria, and say unto them, *Is it* not because *there is* not a God in Israel, *that* you go to enquire of Baal-zebub the god of Ekron?

4 Now therefore thus said the LORD, you will not come down from that bed on which you are gone up, but will surely die. And Elijah departed.

5 And when the messengers turned back unto him, he said unto them, why are you now turned back?

6 And they said unto him, There came a man up to meet us, and said unto us, Go, turn again unto the king that sent you, and say unto him, Thus said the LORD, *Is it* not because *there is* not a God in Israel, *that* you send to enquire of Baal-zebub the god of Ekron? Therefore you will not come down from that bed on which you are gone up, but will surely die.

7 And he said unto them, what manner of man *was he* which came up to meet you, and told you these words?

8 And they answered him, *He was* a hairy man, and girt with a girdle of leather about his loins. And he said, it *is* Elijah the Tishbite.

9 Then the king sent unto him a captain of fifty with his fifty. And he went up to him: and, behold, he sat on the top of a hill. And he spoke unto him, you man of God, the king has said, come down.

10 And Elijah answered and said to the captain of fifty, if I *be* a man of God, then let fire come down from heaven, and consume you and your fifty. And there came down fire from heaven, and consumed him and his fifty.

11 Again also he sent unto him another captain of fifty with his fifty. And he answered and said unto him, O man of God, thus has the king said, come down quickly.

12 And Elijah answered and said unto them, if I *be* a man of God, let fire come down from heaven, and consumes you and your fifty. And the fire of God came down from heaven, and consumed him and his fifty.

13 And he sent again a captain of the third fifty with his fifty. And the third captain of fifty went up, and came and fell on his knees before Elijah, and besought him, and said unto him, O man of God, I pray you , let my life, and the life of these fifty your servants, be precious in your sight.

14 Behold, there came fire down from heaven, and burnt up the two captains of the former fifties with their fifties: therefore let my life now be precious in your sight.

15 And the angel of the LORD said unto Elijah, Go down with him: be not afraid of him. And he arose, and went down with him unto the king.

16 And he said unto him, thus said the LORD, Forasmuch as you have sent messengers to enquire of Baal-zebub the god of Ekron, *is it* not because *there is* no God in Israel to enquire of his word? Therefore you will not come down off that bed on which you are gone up, but will surely die.

17 So he died according to the word of the LORD which Elijah had spoken. And Jehoram reigned in his stead in the second year of Jehoram the son of Jehoshaphat king of Judah; because he had no son.

18 Now the rest of the acts of Ahaziah which he did, *are* they not written in the book of the chronicles of the kings of Israel?

CHAPTER 2

1 And it came to pass, when the LORD would take up Elijah into heaven by a whirlwind, that Elijah went with Elisha from Gilgal.

2 And Elijah said unto Elisha, Tarry here, I pray you; for the LORD has sent me to Beth-el. And Elisha said *unto him*, As the LORD lives, and *as* your soul lives, I will not leave you. So they went down to Beth-el.

3 And the sons of the prophets that *were* at Beth-el came forth to Elisha, and said unto him, know you that the LORD will take away your master from your head today? And he said, Yea, I know *it*; hold you your peace.

4 And Elijah said unto him, Elisha, tarry here, I pray you; for the LORD has sent me to Jericho. And he said, As the LORD lives, and *as* your soul lives, I will not leave you. So they came to Jericho.

5 And the sons of the prophets that *were* at Jericho came to Elisha, and said unto him, knows you that the LORD will take away your master from your head today? And he answered, yea; I know *it*; hold you your peace.

6 And Elijah said unto him, Tarry, I pray you, here; for the LORD has sent me to Jordan. And he said, As the LORD lives, and *as* your soul lives, I will not leave you. And they two went on.

7 And fifty men of the sons of the prophets went, and stood to view afar off: and they two stood by Jordan.

8 And Elijah took his mantle, and wrapped *it* together, and smote the waters, and they were divided here and thither, so that they two went over on dry ground.

9 And it came to pass, when they were gone over, that Elijah said unto Elisha, Ask what I will do for you, before I be taken away from you. And Elisha said, I pray you, let a double portion of your spirit be upon me.

10 And he said, you have asked a hard thing: *nevertheless*, if you see me *when I am* taken from you, it will be so unto you; but if not, it will not be *so*.

11 And it came to pass, as they still went on, and talked, that, behold, *there appeared* a chariot of fire, and horses of fire, and parted them both asunder; and Elijah went up by a whirlwind into heaven.

12 And Elisha saw *it*, and he cried my father, my father, the chariot of Israel, and the horsemen thereof. And he saw him no more: and he took hold of his own clothes, and rent them in two pieces.

13 He took up also the mantle of Elijah that fell from him, and went back, and stood by the bank of Jordan;

14 And he took the mantle of Elijah that fell from him, and smote the waters, and said, where *is* the LORD God of Elijah? And when he also had smitten the waters, they parted here and thither: and Elisha went over.

15 And when the sons of the prophets which *were* to view at Jericho saw him, they said, The spirit of Elijah does rest on Elisha. And they came to meet him, and bowed themselves to the ground before him.

16 And they said unto him, Behold now, there be with your servants fifty strong men; let them go, we pray you, and seek your master: lest peradventure the Spirit of the LORD has taken him up, and cast him upon some mountain, or into some valley. And he said, you will not send.

17 And when they urged him till he was ashamed, he said, Send. They sent therefore fifty men; and they sought three days, but found him not.
18 And when they came again to him, (for he tarried at Jericho,) he said unto them, did I not say unto you, Go not?
19 And the men of the city said unto Elisha, Behold, I pray you, the situation of this city *is* pleasant, as my lord see: but the water *is* naught, and the ground barren.
20 And he said, bring me a new cruse, and put salt therein. And they brought *it* to him.
21 And he went forth unto the spring of the waters, and cast the salt in there, and said, Thus said the LORD, I have healed these waters; there will not be from here anymore death or barren *land*.
22 So the waters were healed unto this day, according to the saying of Elisha which he spoke.
23 And he went up from here unto Beth-el: and as he was going up by the way, there came forth little children out of the city, and mocked him, and said unto him, Go up, you bald head; go up, you bald head.
24 And he turned back, and looked on them, and cursed them in the name of the LORD. And there came forth two she bears out of the wood, and tare forty and two children of them.
25 And he went from here to Mount Carmel, and from here he returned to Samaria.

CHAPTER 3

1 Now Jehoram the son of Ahab began to reign over Israel in Samaria the eighteenth year of Jehoshaphat king of Judah, and reigned twelve years.
2 And he wrought evil in the sight of the LORD; but not like his father, and like his mother: for he put away the image of Baal that his father had made.
3 Nevertheless he cleaved unto the sins of Jeroboam the son of Nebat, which made Israel to sin; he departed not there from.
4 And Mesha king of Moab was a sheep master, and rendered unto the king of Israel an hundred thousand lambs, and an hundred thousand rams, with the wool.
5 But it came to pass, when Ahab was dead, that the king of Moab rebelled against the king of Israel.
6 And king Jehoram went out of Samaria the same time, and numbered all Israel.
7 And he went and sent to Jehoshaphat the king of Judah, saying, the king of Moab has rebelled against me: will you go with me against Moab to battle? And he said, I will go up: I *am* as you *are*, my people as your people, *and* my horses as your horses.
8 And he said, which way will we go up? And he answered, the way through the wilderness of Edom.
9 So the king of Israel went, and the king of Judah, and the king of Edom: and they fetched a compass of seven days' journey: and there was no water for the host, and for the cattle that followed them.
10 And the king of Israel said, Alas! That the LORD has called these three kings together, to deliver them into the hand of Moab!
11 But Jehoshaphat said, *is there* not here a prophet of the LORD, that we may enquire of the LORD by him? And one of the kings of Israel's servants answered and said, here *is* Elisha the son of Shaphat, which poured water on the hands of Elijah.
12 And Jehoshaphat said, the word of the LORD is with him. So the king of Israel and Jehoshaphat and the king of Edom went down to him.
13 And Elisha said unto the king of Israel, What have I to do with you? Get you to the prophets of your father, and to the prophets of your mother. And the king of Israel said unto him, nay: for the LORD has called these three kings together, to deliver them into the hand of Moab.
14 And Elisha said, *As* the LORD of hosts lives, before whom I stand, surely, were it not that I regard the presence of Jehoshaphat the king of Judah, I would not look toward you, or see you.
15 But now bring me a minstrel. And it came to pass, when the minstrel played, that the hand of the LORD came upon him.
16 And he said, thus said the LORD, Make this valley full of ditches.
17 For thus said the LORD, you will not see wind, neither will you see rain; yet that valley will be filled with water, that you may drink, both ye, and your cattle, and your beasts.
18 And this is *but* a light thing in the sight of the LORD: he will deliver the Moabites also into your hand.
19 And you will smite every fenced city, and every choice city, and will fell every good tree, and stop all wells of water, and mar every good piece of land with stones.
20 And it came to pass in the morning, when the meat offering was offered, that, behold, there came water by the way of Edom, and the country was filled with water.
21 And when all the Moabites heard that the kings were come up to fight against them, they gathered all that were able to put on armor, and upward, and stood in the border.
22 And they rose up early in the morning, and the sun shone upon the water, and the Moabites saw the water on the other side *as* red as blood:
23 And they said, this *is* blood: the kings are surely slain, and they have smitten one another: now therefore, Moab, to the spoil.
24 And when they came to the camp of Israel, the Israelites rose up and smote the Moabites, so that they fled before them: but they went forward smiting the Moabites, even in *their* country.
25 And they beat down the cities, and on every good piece of land cast every man his stone, and filled it; and they stopped all the wells of water, and felled all the good trees: only in Kir-haraseth left they the stones thereof; howbeit the slingers went about *it*, and smote it.
26 And when the king of Moab saw that the battle was too sore for him, he took with him seven hundred men that drew swords, to break through *even* unto the king of Edom: but they could not.
27 Then he took his eldest son that should have reigned in his stead, and offered him *for* a burnt offering upon the wall. And there was great indignation against Israel: and they departed from him, and returned to *their own* land.

CHAPTER 4

1 Now there cried a certain woman of the wives of the sons of the prophets unto Elisha, saying, your servant my husband is dead; and you know that your servant did fear the LORD: and the creditor is come to take unto him my two sons to be bondmen
2 And Elisha said unto her, what will I do for you? Tell me, what have you in the house? And she said, your handmaid has not anything in the house, save a pot of oil.
3 Then he said, Go, borrow you vessels abroad of all your neighbors, *even* empty vessels; borrow not a few.

4 And when you are come in, you will shut the door upon you and upon your sons, and will pour out into all those vessels, and you will set aside that which is full.
5 So she went from him, and shut the door upon her and upon her sons, who brought *the vessels* to her; and she poured out.
6 And it came to pass, when the vessels were full, that she said unto her son, Bring me yet a vessel. And he said unto her, *there is* not a vessel more. And the oil stayed.
7 Then she came and told the man of God. And he said, Go, sell the oil, and pay your debt, and live you and your children of the rest.
8 And it fell on a day, that Elisha passed to Shunem, where *was a* great woman; and she constrained him to eat bread. And *so* it was, *that* as oft¹ as he passed by, he turned in there to eat bread.
9 And she said unto her husband, Behold now, I perceive that this *is* a holy man of God, which passes by us continually.
10 Let us make a little chamber, I pray you, on the wall; and let us set for him there a bed, and a table, and a stool, and a candlestick: and it will be, when he cometh to us, that he will turn in thither.
11 And it fell on a day, that he came thither, and he turned into the chamber, and lay there.
12 And he said to Gehazi his servant, Call this Shunammite. And when he had called her, she stood before him.
13 And he said unto him, Say now unto her, Behold, you have been careful for us with all this care; what *is* to be done for you? Would you be spoken for to the king, or to the captain of the host? And she answered, I dwell among mine own people.
14 And he said, what then *is* to be done for her? And Gehazi answered, verily she has no child, and her husband is old.
15 And he said, call her. And when he had called her, she stood in the door.
16 And he said, About this season, according to the time of life, you will embrace a son. And she said, Nay, my lord, you man of God, do not lie unto your handmaid.
17 And the woman conceived, and bare a son at that season that Elisha had said unto her, according to the time of life.
18 And when the child was grown, it fell on a day, that he went out to his father to the reapers.
19 And he said unto his father, my head, my head. And he said to a lad, Carry him to his mother.
20 And when he had taken him, and brought him to his mother, he sat on her knees till noon, and *then* died.
21 And she went up, and laid him on the bed of the man of God, and shut *the door* upon him, and went out.
22 And she called unto her husband, and said, send me, I pray you, one of the young men, and one of the asses, that I may run to the man of God, and come again.
23 And he said, wherefore will you go to him today? *It is* neither new moon, or Sabbath. And she said, *it will be* well.
24 Then she saddled an ass, and said to her servant, Drive, and go forward; slack not your riding for me, except I bid you.
25 So she went and came unto the man of God to Mount Carmel. And it came to pass, when the man of God saw her afar off, that he said to Gehazi his servant, Behold, *yonder is* that Shunammite:
26 Run now, I pray you, to meet her, and say unto her, *Is it* well with you? *Is it* well with your husband? *Is it* well with the child? And she answered, *it is* well.
27 And when she came to the man of God to the hill, she caught him by the feet: but Gehazi came near to thrust her away. And the man of God said, let her alone; for her soul *is* vexed within her: and the LORD has hid *it* from me, and has not told me.
28 Then she said, did I desire a son of my lord? Did I not say, Do not deceive me?
29 Then he said to Gehazi, Gird up your loins, and take my staff in your hand, and go your way: if you meet any man, salute him not; and if any salute you, answer him not again: and lay my staff upon the face of the child.
30 And the mother of the child said, *As* the LORD lives, and *as* your soul lives, I will not leave you. And he arose, and followed her.
31 And Gehazi passed on before them, and laid the staff upon the face of the child; but *there was* neither voice, or hearing. Wherefore he went again to meet him, and told him, saying, the child is not awaked.
32 And when Elisha was come into the house, behold the child was dead, *and* laid upon his bed.
33 He went in therefore, and shut the door upon them twain, and prayed unto the LORD.
34 And he went up, and lay upon the child, and put his mouth upon his mouth, and his eyes upon his eyes, and his hands upon his hands: and he stretched himself upon the child; and the flesh of the child waxed warm.
35 Then he returned, and walked in the house to and fro; and went up, and stretched himself upon him: and the child sneezed seven times, and the child opened his eyes.
36 And he called Gehazi, and said, call this Shunammite. So he called her. And when she was come in unto him, he said, take up your son.
37 Then she went in, and fell at his feet, and bowed herself to the ground, and took up her son, and went out.
38 And Elisha came again to Gilgal: and *there was* a dearth in the land; and the sons of the prophets *were* sitting before him: and he said unto his servant, Set on the great pot, and seethe pottage for the sons of the prophets.
39 And one went out into the field to gather herbs, and found a wild vine, and gathered thereof wild gourds his lap full, and came and shred *them* into the pot of pottage: for they knew *them* not.
40 So they poured out for the men to eat. And it came to pass, as they were eating of the pottage, that they cried out, and said, O you man of God, *there is* death in the pot. And they could not eat *thereof*.
41 But he said, then bring meal. And he cast *it* into the pot; and he said, Pour out for the people, that they may eat. And there was no harm in the pot.
42 And there came a man from Baal-shalisha, and brought the man of God bread of the first-fruits, twenty loaves of barley, and full ears of corn in the husk thereof. And he said, Give unto the people, that they may eat.
43 And his servitor said, what, should I set this before an hundred men? He said again, Give the people, that they may eat: for thus said the LORD, They will eat, and will leave *thereof*.
44 So he set *it* before them, and they did eat, and left *thereof*, according to the word of the LORD.

---

¹ oft- of uncertain derivation, *enough*, used chiefly with preposition in phrases: able, according to, after (ability), among, (more than) enough, sufficient (-ly), too much, very, when. [Strgs#1767]

CHAPTER 5

1 Now Naaman, captain of the host of the king of Syria, was a great man with his master, and honorable, because by him the LORD had given deliverance unto Syria: he was also a mighty man in valor, *but he was* a leper.
2 And the Syrians had gone out by companies, and had brought away captive out of the land of Israel a little maid; and she waited on Naaman's wife.
3 And she said unto her mistress, Would God my lord *were* with the prophet that *is* in Samaria! For he would recover him of his leprosy.
4 And *one* went in, and told his lord, saying, thus and thus said the maid that *is* of the land of Israel.
5 And the king of Syria said, Go to, go, and I will send a letter unto the king of Israel. And he departed, and took with him ten talents of silver, and six thousand *pieces* of gold, and ten changes of raiment.
6 And he brought the letter to the king of Israel, saying, Now when this letter is come unto you, behold; I have *therewith* sent Naaman my servant to you, that you may recover him of his leprosy.
7 And it came to pass, when the king of Israel had read the letter, that he rent his clothes, and said, *Am* I God, to kill and to make alive, that this man does send unto me to recover a man of his leprosy? Wherefore consider, I pray you, and see how he seeks a quarrel against me.
8 And it was *so*, when Elisha the man of God had heard that the king of Israel had rent his clothes, that he sent to the king, saying, wherefore have you rent your clothes? Let him come now to me, and he will know that there is a prophet in Israel.
9 So Naaman came with his horses and with his chariot, and stood at the door of the house of Elisha.
10 And Elisha sent a messenger unto him, saying, Go and wash in Jordan seven times, and your flesh will come again to you, and you will be clean.
11 But Naaman was **angry**, and went away, and said, Behold, I thought, He will surely come out to me, and stand, and call on the name of the LORD his God, and strike his hand over the place, and recover the leper.
12 *Are* not Abana and Pharpar, rivers of Damascus, better than all the waters of Israel? May I not wash in them, and be clean? So he turned and went away in a rage.
13 And his servants came near, and spoke unto him, and said, my father, *if* the prophet had bid you *do some* great thing, would you not have done *it*? How much rather then, when he said to you, wash, and be clean?
14 Then went he down, and dipped himself seven times in Jordan, according to the saying of the man of God: and his flesh came again like unto the flesh of a little child, and he was clean.
15 And he returned to the man of God, he and all his company, and came, and stood before him: and he said, Behold, now I know that *there is* no God in all the earth, but in Israel: now therefore, I pray you , take a blessing of your servant.
16 But he said, *As* the LORD lives, before whom I stand, I will receive none. And he urged him to take *it*; but he refused.
17 And Naaman said, will there not then, I pray you, be given to your servant two mules' burden of earth? For your servant will henceforth offer neither burnt offering or sacrifice unto other gods, but unto the LORD.
18 In this thing the LORD pardon your servant, *that* when my master goes into the house of Rimmon to worship there, and he leans on my hand, and I bow myself in the house of Rimmon when I bow down myself in the house of Rimmon, the LORD pardon your servant in this thing.
19 And he said unto him, Go in peace. So he departed from him a little way.
20 But Gehazi[1], the servant of Elisha the man of God, said, Behold, my master has spared Naaman this Syrian, in not receiving at his hands that which he brought: but, *as* the LORD lives, I will run after him, and take somewhat of him.
21 So Gehazi followed after Naaman. And when Naaman saw *him* running after him, he lighted down from the chariot to meet him, and said, *is* all well?
22 And he said, all *is* well. My master has sent me, saying, Behold, even now there be come to me from mount Ephraim two young men of the sons of the prophets: give them, I pray you , a talent of silver, and two changes of garments.
23 And Naaman said, Be content, take two talents. And he urged him, and bound two talents of silver in two bags, with two changes of garments, and laid *them* upon two of his servants; and they bare *them* before him.
24 And when he came to the tower, he took *them* from their hand, and bestowed *them* in the house: and he let the men go, and they departed.
25 But he went[2] in, and stood before his master. And Elisha said unto him, where *come you*, Gehazi? And he said, your servant went no whither.
26 [And he said unto him, Went not mine heart *with you,* when the man turned again from his chariot to meet you? *Is it* a time to receive money, and to receive garments, and olive yards, and vineyards, and sheep, and oxen, and menservants, and maidservants?][3]
27 The leprosy therefore of Naaman will cleave unto you, and unto your seed for ever. And he went out from his presence a leper *as white* as snow.

CHAPTER 6

1 And the sons of the prophets said unto Elisha, Behold now, the place where we dwell with you is too strait for us.
2 Let us go, we pray you, unto Jordan, and take here every man a beam, and let us make us a place there, where we may dwell. And he answered, Go ye.
3 And one said, Be content, I pray you, and go with your servants. And he answered, I will go.
4 So he went with them. And when they came to Jordan, they cut down wood.
5 But as one was felling a beam, the axe head fell into the water: and he cried, and said, Alas, master! For it was borrowed.
6 And the man of God said, where fell it? And he showed him the place. And he cut down a stick, and cast *it* in thither; and the iron did swim.
7 Therefore said he, take *it* up to you. And he put out his hand, and took it.
8 Then the king of Syria warred against Israel, and took counsel with his servants, saying, in such and such a place will *be* my camp.

---

[1] Gehazi – *valley of a visionary* [Strgs#1522].
[2] went – to *walk* [Strgs#1980].

[3] compare **Col. 2:5** & **1 Cor. 5:4**, the heart can be a sense (sight), walk, organ.

9 And the man of God sent unto the king of Israel, saying, Beware that you pass not such a place; for there the Syrians are come down.

10 And the king of Israel sent to the place which the man of God told him and warned him of, and saved himself there, not once or twice.

11 Therefore the heart of the king of Syria was sore troubled for this thing; and he called his servants, and said unto them, Will you not show me which of us *is* for the king of Israel?

12 And one of his servants said, none, my lord, O king: but Elisha, the prophet that *is* in Israel, tells the king of Israel the words that you speak in your bedchamber.

13 And he said, Go and spy where he *is*, that I may send and fetch him. And it was told him, saying, Behold, *he is* in Dothan.

14 Therefore sent he there horses, and chariots, and a great host: and they came by night, and compassed the city about.

15 And when the servant of the man of God was risen early, and gone forth, behold, a host compassed the city both with horses and chariots. And his servant said unto him, alas, my master! How will we do?

16 And he answered, Fear not: for they that *be* with us *are* more than they that *be* with them.

17 And Elisha prayed, and said, LORD, I pray you, open his eyes, that he may see. And the LORD opened the eyes of the young man; and he saw: and, behold, the mountain *was* full of horses and chariots of fire round about Elisha.

18 And when they came down to him, Elisha prayed unto the LORD, and said, Smite this people, I pray you, with blindness. And he smote them with blindness according to the word of Elisha.

19 And Elisha said unto them, this *is* not the way, neither *is* this the city: follow me, and I will bring you to the man whom you seek. But he led them to Samaria.

20 And it came to pass, when they were come into Samaria, that Elisha said, LORD, open the eyes of these *men*, that they may see. And the LORD opened their eyes, and they saw; and, behold, *they were* in the midst of Samaria.

21 And the king of Israel said unto Elisha, when he saw them, my father, will I smite *them*? Will I smite *them*?

22 And he answered, you will not smite *them*: would you smite those whom you have taken captive with your sword and with your bow? Set bread and water before them, that they may eat and drink, and go to their master.

23 And he prepared great provision for them: and when they had eaten and drunk, he sent them away, and they went to their master. So the bands of Syria came no more into the land of Israel.

24 And it came to pass after this, that Ben-hadad king of Syria gathered his **entire** host, and went up, and besieged Samaria.

25 And there was a great famine in Samaria: and, behold, they besieged it, until an ass's head was *sold* for fourscore *pieces* of silver, and the fourth part of a cab of dove's dung for five *pieces* of silver.

26 And as the king of Israel was passing by upon the wall, there cried a woman unto him, saying, Help, my lord, O king.

27 And he said, if the LORD do not help you, where will I help you? Out of the barn floor, or out of the winepress?

28 And the king said unto her, what ails you? And she answered, this woman said unto me, give your son, that we may eat him to day, and we will eat my son tomorrow.

29 So we boiled my son, and did eat him: and I said unto her on the next day, Give your son, that we may eat him: and she has hid her son.

30 And it came to pass, when the king heard the words of the woman, that he rent his clothes; and he passed by upon the wall, and the people looked, and, behold, *he had* sackcloth within upon his flesh.

31 Then he said, God do so and more also to me, if the head of Elisha the son of Shaphat will stand on him this day.

32 But Elisha sat in his house, and the elders sat with him; and *the king* sent a man from before him: but ere the messenger came to him, he said to the elders, See you how this son of a murderer has sent to take away mine head? Look, when the messenger comes, shut the door, and hold him fast at the door: *is* not the sound of his master's feet behind him?

33 And while he yet talked with them, behold, the messenger came down unto him: and he said, Behold, this evil *is* of the LORD; what should I wait for the LORD any longer?

CHAPTER 7

1 Then Elisha said, Hear you the word of the LORD; thus said the LORD, tomorrow about this time will a measure of fine flour *be sold* for a shekel, and two measures of barley for a shekel in the gate of Samaria.

2 Then a lord on whose hand the king leaned answered the man of God, and said, Behold, *if* the LORD would make windows in heaven, might this thing be? And he said, Behold, you will see *it* with your eyes, but will not eat thereof.

3 And there were four leprous men at the entering in of the gate: and they said one to another, why sit we here until we die?

4 If we say, we will enter into the city, then the famine *is* in the city, and we will die there: and if we sit still here, we die also. Now therefore come, and let us fall unto the host of the Syrians: if they save us alive, we will live; and if they kill us, we will but die.

5 And they rose up in the twilight, to go unto the camp of the Syrians: and when they were come to the uttermost part of the camp of Syria, behold, *there was* no man there.

6 For the Lord had made the host of the Syrians to hear a noise of chariots, and a noise of horses, *even* the noise of a great host: and they said one to another, Lo, the king of Israel has hired against us the kings of the Hittites, and the kings of the Egyptians, to come upon us.

7 Wherefore they arose and fled in the twilight, and left their tents, and their horses, and their asses, even the camp as it *was*, and fled for their life.

8 And when these lepers came to the uttermost part of the camp, they went into one tent, and did eat and drink, and carried here silver, and gold, and raiment, and went and hid *it*; and came again, and entered into another tent, and carried here *also*, and went and hid *it*.

9 Then they said one to another, we do not well: this day *is* a day of good tidings, and we hold our peace: if we tarry till the morning light, some mischief will come upon us: now therefore come, that we may go and tell the king's household.

10 So they came and called unto the porter of the city: and they told them, saying, We came to the camp of the Syrians, and, behold, *there was* no man there, neither voice of man, but horses tied, and asses tied, and the tents as they *were*.

11 And he called the porters; and they told *it* to the king's house within.

12 And the king arose in the night, and said unto his servants, I will now show you what the Syrians have done to us. They know that we *be* hungry; therefore are they gone out of the camp to hide themselves in the field, saying, When they come out of the city, we will catch them alive, and get into the city.
13 And one of his servants answered and said, Let *some* take, I pray you, five of the horses that remain, which are left in the city, (behold, they *are* as all the multitude of Israel that are left in it: behold, *I say*, they *are* even as all the multitude of the Israelites that are consumed:) and let us send and see.
14 They took therefore two chariot horses; and the king sent after the host of the Syrians, saying, Go and see.
15 And they went after them unto Jordan: and, lo, all the way *was* full of garments and vessels, which the Syrians had cast away in their haste. And the messengers returned, and told the king.
16 And the people went out, and spoiled the tents of the Syrians. So a measure of fine flour was *sold* for a shekel, and two measures of barley for a shekel, according to the word of the LORD.
17 And the king appointed the lord on whose hand he leaned to have the charge of the gate: and the people **trample** upon him in the gate, and he died, as the man of God had said, who spoke when the king came down to him.
18 And it came to pass as the man of God had spoken to the king, saying, two measures of barley for a shekel, and a measure of fine flour for a shekel, will be tomorrow about this time in the gate of Samaria:
19 And that lord answered the man of God, and said, now, behold, *if* the LORD should make windows in heaven, might such a thing be? And he said, Behold, you will see it with your eyes, but will not eat thereof.
20 And so it fell out unto him: for the people **trample** upon him in the gate, and he died.

CHAPTER 8

1 Then spoke Elisha unto the woman, whose son he had restored to life, saying, arise, and go you and your household, and sojourn wheresoever you can sojourn: for the LORD has called for a famine; and it will also come upon the land seven years.
2 And the woman arose, and did after the saying of the man of God: and she went with her household, and sojourned in the land of the Philistines seven years.
3 And it came to pass at the seven years' end, that the woman returned out of the land of the Philistines: and she went forth to cry unto the king for her house and for her land.
4 And the king talked with Gehazi the servant of the man of God, saying, Tell me, I pray you, all the great things that Elisha has done.
5 And it came to pass, as he was telling the king how he had restored a dead body to life, that, behold, the woman, whose son he had restored to life, cried to the king for her house and for her land. And Gehazi said, My lord, O king, this *is* the woman, and this *is* her son, whom Elisha restored to life.
6 And when the king asked the woman, she told him. So the king appointed unto her a certain officer, saying, Restore all that *was* hers, and all the fruits of the field since the day that she left the land, even until now.
7 And Elisha came to Damascus; and Ben-hadad the king of Syria was sick; and it was told him, saying, the man of God is come hither.

8 And the king said unto Hazael, Take a present in your hand, and go, meet the man of God, and enquire of the LORD by him, saying, will I recover of this disease?
9 So Hazael went to meet him, and took a present with him, even of every good thing of Damascus, forty camels' burden, and came and stood before him, and said, your son Ben-hadad king of Syria has sent me to you , saying, will I recover of this disease?
10 And Elisha said unto him, Go, say unto him, you may certainly recover: howbeit the LORD has showed me that he will surely die.
11 And he settled his countenance stedfastly, until he was ashamed: and the man of God wept.
12 And Hazael said, why weeps my lord? And he answered, because I know the evil that you will do unto the children of Israel: their strong holds will you set on fire, and their young men will you slay with the sword, and will dash their children, and rip up their women with child.
13 And Hazael said, but what, *is* your servant a dog, that he should do this great thing? And Elisha answered; The LORD has showed me that you will *be* king over Syria.
14 So he departed from Elisha, and came to his master; who said to him, what said Elisha to you? And he answered, He told me *that* you should surely recover.
15 And it came to pass on the morrow, that he took a thick cloth, and dipped *it* in water, and spread *it* on his face, so that he died: and Hazael reigned in his stead.
16 And in the fifth year of Joram the son of Ahab king of Israel, Jehoshaphat *being* then king of Judah, Jehoram the son of Jehoshaphat king of Judah began to reign.
17 Thirty and two years old was he when he began to reign; and he reigned eight years in Jerusalem.
18 And he walked in the way of the kings of Israel, as did the house of Ahab: for the daughter of Ahab was his wife: and he did evil in the sight of the LORD.
19 Yet the LORD would not destroy Judah for David his servant's sake, as he promised him to give him alway a light, *and* to his children.
20 In his days Edom revolted from under the hand of Judah, and made a king over themselves.
21 So Joram went over to Zair, and all the chariots with him: and he rose by night, and smote the Edomites which compassed him about, and the captains of the chariots: and the people fled into their tents.
22 Yet Edom revolted from under the hand of Judah unto this day. Then Libnah revolted at the same time.
23 And the rest of the acts of Joram, and all that he did, *are* they not written in the book of the chronicles of the kings of Judah?
24 And Joram slept with his fathers, and was buried with his fathers in the city of David: and Ahaziah his son reigned in his stead
25 In the twelfth year of Joram the son of Ahab king of Israel did Ahaziah the son of Jehoram king of Judah begin to reign.
26 Two and twenty years old *was* Ahaziah when he began to reign; and he reigned one year in Jerusalem. And his mother's name *was* Athaliah, the daughter of Omri king of Israel.
27 And he walked in the way of the house of Ahab, and did evil in the sight of the LORD, as *did* the house of Ahab: for he *was* the son in law of the house of Ahab.
28 And he went with Joram the son of Ahab to the war against Hazael king of Syria in Ramoth-gilead; and the Syrians wounded Joram.

29 And king Joram went back to be healed in Jezreel[1] of the wounds which the Syrians had given him at Ramah, when he fought against Hazael king of Syria. And Ahaziah the son of Jehoram king of Judah went down to see Joram the son of Ahab in Jezreel, because he was sick.

CHAPTER 9

1 And Elisha the prophet called one of the children of the prophets, and said unto him, Gird up your loins, and take this box of oil in your hand, and go to Ramoth-gilead:
2 And when you comest thither, look out there Jehu the son of Jehoshaphat the son of Nimshi, and go in, and make him arise up from among his brethren, and carry him to an inner chamber;
3 Then take the box of oil, and pour *it* on his head, and say, thus said the LORD, I have anointed you king over Israel. Then open the door, and flee, and tarry not.
4 So the young man, *even* the young man the prophet, went to Ramoth-gilead.
5 And when he came, behold, the captains of the host *were* sitting; and he said, I have an errand to you, O captain. And Jehu said, unto which of all us? And he said, to you, O captain.
6 And he arose, and went into the house; and he poured the oil on his head, and said unto him, Thus said the LORD God of Israel, I have anointed you king over the people of the LORD, *even* over Israel.
7 And you will smite the house of Ahab your master, that I may avenge the blood of my servants the prophets, and the blood of all the servants of the LORD, at the hand of Jezebel[2].
8 For the whole house of Ahab will perish: and I will cut off from Ahab him that pisses against the wall, and him that is shut up and left in Israel:
9 And I will make the house of Ahab like the house of Jeroboam the son of Nebat, and like the house of Baasha the son of Ahijah:
10 And the dogs will eat Jezebel in the portion of Jezreel, and *there will be* none to bury *her*. And he opened the door, and fled.
11 Then Jehu came forth to the servants of his lord: and *one* said unto him, *Is* all well? Wherefore came this mad *fellow* to you? And he said unto them, you know the man, and his communication.
12 And they said, *it is* false; tell us now. And he said, Thus and thus spoke he to me, saying, thus said the LORD, I have anointed you king over Israel.
13 Then they hasted, and took every man his garment, and put *it* under him on the top of the stairs, and blew with trumpets, saying, Jehu is king.
14 So Jehu the son of Jehoshaphat the son of Nimshi conspired against Joram. (Now Joram had kept Ramoth-gilead, he and all Israel, because of Hazael king of Syria.
15 But king Joram was returned to be healed in Jezreel of the wounds which the Syrians had given him, when he fought with Hazael king of Syria.) And Jehu said, if it be your minds, *then* let none go forth or escape out of the city to go to tell *it* in Jezreel.
16 So Jehu rode in a chariot, and went to Jezreel; for Joram lay there. And Ahaziah king of Judah was come down to see Joram.
17 And there stood a watchman on the tower in Jezreel, and he spied the company of Jehu as he came, and said, I see a company. And Joram said, Take a horseman, and send to meet them, and let him say, *is it* peace?
18 So there went one on horseback to meet him, and said, thus said the king, *is it* peace? And Jehu said, what have you to do with peace? Turn you behind me. And the watchman told, saying, the messenger came to them, but he cometh not again.
19 Then he sent out a second on horseback, which came to them, and said, thus said the king, *Is it* peace? And Jehu answered, what have you to do with peace? Turn you behind me.
20 And the watchman told, saying, He came even unto them, and cometh not again: and the driving *is* like the driving of Jehu the son of Nimshi; for he drives furiously.
21 And Joram said, Make ready. And his chariot was made ready. And Joram king of Israel and Ahaziah king of Judah went out, each in his chariot, and they went out against Jehu, and met him in the portion of Naboth the Jezreelite.
22 And it came to pass, when Joram saw Jehu, that he said, *is it* peace, Jehu? And he answered, what peace, so long as the whoredoms of your mother Jezebel and her witchcrafts *are so* many?
23 And Joram turned his hands, and fled, and said to Ahaziah, *There is* treachery, O Ahaziah.
24 And Jehu drew a bow with his full strength, and smote Jehoram between his arms, and the arrow went out at his heart, and he sunk down in his chariot.
25 Then said *Jehu* to Bidkar his captain, Take up, *and* cast him in the portion of the field of Naboth the Jezreelite: for remember how that, when I and you rode together after Ahab his father, the LORD laid this burden upon him;
26 Surely I have seen yesterday the blood of Naboth, and the blood of his sons, said the LORD; and I will requite you in this plat, said the LORD. Now therefore take *and* cast him into the plat *of ground*, according to the word of the LORD.
27 But when Ahaziah the king of Judah saw *this*, he fled by the way of the garden house. And Jehu followed after him, and said, smite him also in the chariot. *And they did so* at the going up to Gur, which *is* by Ibleam. And he fled to Megiddo, and died there.
28 And his servants carried him in a chariot to Jerusalem, and buried him in his sepulcher with his fathers in the city of David.
29 And in the eleventh year of Joram the son of Ahab began Ahaziah to reign over Judah.
30 And when Jehu was come to Jezreel, Jezebel heard *of it*; and she painted her face, and tired her head, and looked out at a window.
31 And as Jehu entered in at the gate, she said, *had* Zimri peace, who slew his master?
32 And he lifted up his face to the window, and said, who *is* on my side? Who? And there looked out to him two *or* three eunuchs.
33 And he said, Throw her down. So they threw her down: and *some* of her blood was sprinkled on the wall, and on the horses: and he **trample** her under foot.
34 And when he was come in, he did eat and drink, and said, Go, see now this cursed *woman*, and bury her: for *she is* a king's daughter.
35 And they went to bury her: but they found no more of her than the skull, and the feet, and the palms of *her* hands
36 Wherefore they came again, and told him. And he said, this *is* the word of the LORD, which he spoke by his servant Elijah the Tishbite, saying, In the portion of Jezreel will dogs eat the flesh of Jezebel:

---

[1] Jezreel- God sows or God will sow. [Strgs#3157]
[2] Jezebel- the wife of King Ahab. Her name is defined as *Baal exalts or Baal is husband/unchaste.* [Strgs#348]

37 And the carcase of Jezebel will be as dung upon the face of the field in the portion of Jezreel; *so* that they will not say, this *is* Jezebel.

CHAPTER 10

1 And Ahab had seventy sons in Samaria. And Jehu wrote letters, and sent to Samaria, unto the rulers of Jezreel, to the elders, and to them that brought up Ahab's *children*, saying,
2 Now as soon as this letter cometh to you, seeing your master's sons *are* with you, and *there are* with you chariots and horses, a fenced city also, and armor;
3 Look even out the best and meet of your master's sons, and set *him* on his father's throne, and fight for your master's house.
4 But they were exceedingly afraid, and said, Behold, two kings stood not before him: how then will we stand?
5 And he that *was* over the house, and he that *was* over the city, the elders also, and the bringers up *of the children*, sent to Jehu, saying, We *are* your servants, and will do all that you will bid us; we will not make any king: do you *that which is* good in your eyes.
6 Then he wrote a letter the second time to them, saying, if you *be* mine, and *if* you will hearken unto my voice, take you the heads of the men your master's sons, and come to me to Jezreel by tomorrow this time. Now the king's sons, *being* seventy persons, *were* with the great men of the city, which brought them up.
7 And it came to pass, when the letter came to them, that they took the king's sons, and slew seventy persons, and put their heads in baskets, and sent him *them* to Jezreel.
8 And there came a messenger, and told him, saying, they have brought the heads of the king's sons. And he said, Lay you them in two heaps at the entering in of the gate until the morning.
9 And it came to pass in the morning, that he went out, and stood, and said to all the people, you *be* righteous: behold, I conspired against my master, and slew him: but who slew all these?
10 Know now that there will fall unto the earth nothing of the word of the LORD, which the LORD spoke concerning the house of Ahab: for the LORD has done *that* which he spoke by his servant Elijah.
11 So Jehu slew all that remained of the house of Ahab in Jezreel, and all his great men, and his kinsfolks, and his priests, until he left him none remaining.
12 And he arose and departed, and came to Samaria. *And* as he *was* at the shearing house in the way,
13 Jehu met with the brethren of Ahaziah king of Judah, and said, who *are* ye? And they answered, we *are* the brethren of Ahaziah; and we go down to salute the children of the king and the children of the queen.
14 And he said, Take them alive. And they took them alive, and slew them at the pit of the shearing house, *even* two and forty men; neither left he any of them.
15 And when he was departed thence, he lighted on Jehonadab the son of Rechab *coming* to meet him: and he saluted him, and said to him, is your heart right, as my heart *is* with your heart? And Jehonadab answered, it is. If it be, give *me* your hand. And he gave *him* his hand; and he took him up to him into the chariot.
16 And he said, Come with me, and see my zeal for the LORD. So they made him ride in his chariot.

17 And when he came to Samaria, he slew all that remained unto Ahab in Samaria, till he had destroyed him, according to the saying of the LORD, which he spoke to Elijah.
18 And Jehu gathered all the people together, and said unto them, Ahab served Baal a little; *but* Jehu will serve him much.
19 Now therefore call unto me all the prophets of Baal, all his servants, and all his priests; let none be wanting: for I have a great sacrifice *to do* to Baal; whosoever will be wanting, he will not live. But Jehu did *it* in subtlety, to the intent that he might destroy the worshippers of Baal.
20 And Jehu said, Proclaim a solemn assembly for Baal. And they proclaimed *it*.
21 And Jehu sent through all Israel: and all the worshippers of Baal came, so that there was not a man left that came not. And they came into the house of Baal; and the house of Baal was full from one end to another.
22 And he said unto him that *was* over the vestry[1], Bring forth vestments[2] for all the worshippers of Baal. And he brought them forth vestments.
23 And Jehu went, and Jehonadab the son of Rechab, into the house of Baal, and said unto the worshippers of Baal, Search, and look that there be here with you none of the servants of the LORD, but the worshippers of Baal only.
24 And when they went in to offer sacrifices and burnt offerings, Jehu appointed fourscore men without, and said, *if* any of the men whom I have brought into your hands escape, *he that lets him go*, his life will *be* for the life of him.
25 And it came to pass, as soon as he had made an end of offering the burnt offering, that Jehu said to the guard and to the captains, go in, *and* slay them; let none come forth. And they smote them with the edge of the sword; and the guard and the captains cast *them* out, and went to the city of the house of Baal.
26 And they brought forth the images out of the house of Baal, and burned them.
27 And they broke down the image of Baal, and brake down the house of Baal, and made it a draught house unto this day.
28 Thus Jehu destroyed Baal out of Israel.
29 Howbeit *from* the sins of Jeroboam the son of Nebat, who made Israel to sin, Jehu departed not from after them, *to wit*, the golden calves that *were* in Beth-el, and that *were* in Dan.
30 And the LORD said unto Jehu, Because you have done well in executing *that which is* right in mine eyes, *and* have done unto the house of Ahab according to all that *was* in mine heart, your children of the fourth *generation* will sit on the throne of Israel.
31 But Jehu took no heed to walk in the law of the LORD God of Israel with all his heart: for he departed not from the sins of Jeroboam, which made Israel to sin.
32 In those days the LORD began to cut Israel short: and Hazael smote them in all the coasts of Israel;
33 From Jordan eastward, all the land of Gilead, the Gadites, and the Reubenites, and the Manassites, from Aroer, which *is* by the river Arnon, even Gilead and Bashan.
34 Now the rest of the acts of Jehu, and all that he did, and all his might, *are* they not written in the book of the chronicles of the kings of Israel?
35 And Jehu slept with his fathers: and they buried him in Samaria. And Jehoahaz his son reigned in his stead.

---

[1] vestry- from an unused root meaning to *spread out*; a *wardrobe* (that is, room where clothing is spread) [Strgs# 4458].

[2] vestments- a *garment* (literally or figuratively); by implication (euphemistically) a *wife*:- apparel, clothed with, clothing, garment, raiment, vesture. [Strgs# 3830].

36 And the time that Jehu reigned over Israel in Samaria *was* twenty and eight years.

CHAPTER 11

1 And when Athaliah the mother of Ahaziah saw that her son was dead, she arose and destroyed all the seed royal.
2 But Jehosheba, the daughter of king Joram, sister of Ahaziah, took Joash the son of Ahaziah, and stole him from among the king's sons *which were* slain; and they hid him, *even* him and his nurse, in the bedchamber from Athaliah, so that he was not slain.
3 And he was with her hid in the house of the LORD six years. And Athaliah did reign over the land.
4 And the seventh year Jehoiada sent and fetched the rulers over hundreds, with the captains and the guard, and brought them to him into the house of the LORD, and made a covenant with them, and took an oath of them in the house of the LORD, and showed them the king's son.
5 And he commanded them, saying, This *is* the thing that you will do; A third part of you that enter in on the Sabbath will even be keepers of the watch of the king's house;
6 And a third part will *be* at the gate of Sur; and a third part at the gate behind the guard: so will you keep the watch of the house, that it be not broken down.
7 And two parts of all you that go forth on the Sabbath, even they will keep the watch of the house of the LORD about the king.
8 And you will compass the king round about, every man with his weapons in his hand: and he that cometh within the ranges, let him be slain: and be you with the king as he goes out and as he cometh in.
9 And the captains over the hundreds did according to all *things* that Jehoiada the priest commanded: and they took every man his men that were to come in on the Sabbath, with them that should go out on the Sabbath, and came to Jehoiada the priest.
10 And to the captains over hundreds did the priest give king David's spears and shields, that *were* in the temple of the LORD.
11 And the guard stood, every man with his weapons in his hand, round about the king, from the right corner of the temple to the left corner of the temple, *along* by the altar and the temple.
12 And he brought forth the king's son, and put the crown upon him, and *gave him* the testimony; and they made him king, and anointed him; and they clapped their hands, and said, God save the king.
13 And when Athaliah heard the noise of the guard *and* of the people, she came to the people into the temple of the LORD.
14 And when she looked, behold, the king stood by a pillar, as the manner *was*, and the princes and the trumpeters by the king, and all the people of the land rejoiced, and blew with trumpets: and Athaliah rent her clothes, and cried, Treason, Treason.
15 But Jehoiada the priest commanded the captains of the hundreds, the officers of the host, and said unto them, Have her forth without the ranges: and him that follows her kill with the sword. For the priest had said, let her not be slain in the house of the LORD.
16 And they laid hands on her; and she went by the way by the which the horses came into the king's house: and there was she slain.
17 And Jehoiada made a covenant between the LORD and the king and the people, that they should be the LORD'S people; between the king also and the people.
18 And all the people of the land went into the house of Baal, and **broke** it down; his altars and his images **they broke** in pieces thoroughly, and slew Mattan the priest of Baal before the altars. And the priest appointed officers over the house of the LORD.
19 And he took the rulers over hundreds, and the captains, and the guard, and all the people of the land; and they brought down the king from the house of the LORD, and came by the way of the gate of the guard to the king's house. And he sat on the throne of the kings.
20 And all the people of the land rejoiced, and the city was in quiet: and they slew Athaliah with the sword *beside* the king's house.
21 Seven years old *was* Jehoash when he began to reign.

CHAPTER 12

1 In the seventh year of Jehu Jehoash began to reign; and forty years reigned he in Jerusalem. And his mother's name *was* Zibiah of Beer-sheba.
2 And Jehoash did *that which was* right in the sight of the LORD all his days wherein Jehoiada the priest instructed him.
3 But the high places were not taken away: the people still sacrificed and burnt incense in the high places.
4 And Jehoash said to the priests, All the money of the dedicated things that is brought into the house of the LORD, *even* the money of every one that passes *the account*, the money that every man is set at, *and* all the money that cometh into any man's heart to bring into the house of the LORD,
5 Let the priests take *it* to them, every man of his acquaintance: and let them repair the breaches of the house, wheresoever any breach will be found.
6 But it was *so, that* in the three and twentieth year of king Jehoash the priests had not repaired the breaches of the house.
7 Then king Jehoash called for Jehoiada the priest, and the *other* priests, and said unto them, why repair you not the breaches of the house? Now therefore receive no *more* money of your acquaintance, but deliver it for the breaches of the house.
8 And the priests consented to receive no *more* money of the people, neither to repair the breaches of the house.
9 But Jehoiada the priest took a chest, and bored a hole in the lid of it, and set it beside the altar, on the right side as one cometh into the house of the LORD: and the priests that kept the door put therein all the money *that was* brought into the house of the LORD.
10 And it was *so*, when they saw that *there was* much money in the chest, that the king's scribe and the high priest came up, and they put up in bags, and told the money that was found in the house of the LORD.
11 And they gave the money, being told, into the hands of them that did the work, that had the oversight of the house of the LORD: and they laid it out to the carpenters and builders, that wrought upon the house of the LORD,
12 And to masons, and hewers of stone, and to buy timber and hewed stone to repair the breaches of the house of the LORD, and for all that was laid out for the house to repair *it*.
13 Howbeit there were not made for the house of the LORD bowls of silver, snuffers, basons, trumpets, any vessels of gold, or vessels of silver, of the money *that was* brought into the house of the LORD:
14 But they gave that to the workmen, and repaired therewith the house of the LORD.
15 Moreover they reckoned not with the men, into whose hand they delivered the money to be bestowed on workmen: for they dealt faithfully.
16 The trespass money and sin money was not brought into the house of the LORD: it was the priests'.

17 Then Hazael king of Syria went up, and fought against Gath, and took it: and Hazael set his face to go up to Jerusalem.
18 And Jehoash king of Judah took all the hallowed things that Jehoshaphat, and Jehoram, and Ahaziah, his fathers, kings of Judah, had dedicated, and his own hallowed things, and all the gold *that was* found in the treasures of the house of the LORD, and in the king's house, and sent *it* to Hazael king of Syria: and he went away from Jerusalem.
19 And the rest of the acts of Joash, and all that he did, *are* they not written in the book of the chronicles of the kings of Judah?
20 And his servants arose, and made a conspiracy, and slew Joash in the house of Millo, which goeth down to Silla.
21 For Jozachar the son of Shimeath, and Jehozabad the son of Shomer, his servants, smote him, and he died; and they buried him with his fathers in the city of David: and Amaziah his son reigned in his stead.

CHAPTER 13

1 In the three and twentieth year of Joash the son of Ahaziah king of Judah Jehoahaz the son of Jehu began to reign over Israel in Samaria, *and reigned* seventeen years.
2 And he did *that which was* evil in the sight of the LORD, and followed the sins of Jeroboam the son of Nebat, which made Israel to sin; he departed not there from.
3 And the anger of the LORD was kindled against Israel, and he delivered them into the hand of Hazael king of Syria, and into the hand of Ben-hadad the son of Hazael, all *their* days.
4 And Jehoahaz besought the LORD, and the LORD hearkened unto him: for he saw the oppression of Israel, because the king of Syria oppressed them.
5 (And the LORD gave Israel a savior, so that they went out from under the hand of the Syrians: and the children of Israel dwelt in their tents, as beforetime.
6 Nevertheless they departed not from the sins of the house of Jeroboam, who made Israel sin, *but* walked therein: and there remained the grove also in Samaria.)
7 Neither did he leave of the people to Jehoahaz but fifty horsemen, and ten chariots, and ten thousand footmen; for the king of Syria had destroyed them, and had made them like the dust by threshing.
8 Now the rest of the acts of Jehoahaz, and all that he did, and his might, *are* they not written in the book of the chronicles of the kings of Israel?
9 And Jehoahaz slept with his fathers; and they buried him in Samaria: and Joash his son reigned in his stead.
10 In the thirty and seventh year of Joash king of Judah began Jehoash the son of Jehoahaz to reign over Israel in Samaria, *and reigned* sixteen years.
11 And he did *that which was* evil in the sight of the LORD; he departed not from all the sins of Jeroboam the son of Nebat, who made Israel sin: *but* he walked therein.
12 And the rest of the acts of Joash, and all that he did, and his might wherewith he fought against Amaziah king of Judah, *are* they not written in the book of the chronicles of the kings of Israel?
13 And Joash slept with his fathers; and Jeroboam sat upon his throne: and Joash was buried in Samaria with the kings of Israel.
14 Now Elisha was fallen sick of his sickness whereof he died. And Joash the king of Israel came down unto him, and wept over his face, and said, O my father, my father, the chariot of Israel, and the horsemen thereof.
15 And Elisha said unto him, Take bow and arrows. And he took unto him bow and arrows.
16 And he said to the king of Israel, Put your hand upon the bow. And he put his hand *upon it*: and Elisha put his hands upon the king's hands.
17 And he said, Open the window eastward. And he opened *it*. Then Elisha said, Shoot. And he shot. And he said, The arrow of the LORD'S deliverance, and the arrow of deliverance from Syria: for you will smite the Syrians in Aphek, till you have consumed *them*.
18 And he said, take the arrows. And he took *them*. And he said unto the king of Israel, Smite upon the ground. And he smote thrice, and stayed.
19 And the man of God was wroth with him, and said, you should have smitten five or six times; then had you smitten Syria till you had consumed *it*: whereas now you will smite Syria but thrice.
20 And Elisha died, and they buried him. And the bands of the Moabites invaded the land at the coming in of the year.
21 And it came to pass, as they were burying a man, that, behold, they spied a band *of men*; and they cast the man into the sepulcher of Elisha: and when the man was let down, and touched the bones of Elisha, he revived, and stood up on his feet.
22 But Hazael king of Syria oppressed Israel all the days of Jehoahaz.
23 And the LORD was gracious unto them, and had compassion on them, and had respect unto them, because of his covenant with Abraham, Isaac, and Jacob, and would not destroy them, neither cast he them from his presence as yet.
24 So Hazael king of Syria died; and Ben-hadad his son reigned in his stead.
25 And Jehoash the son of Jehoahaz took again out of the hand of Ben-hadad the son of Hazael the cities, which he had taken out of the hand of Jehoahaz his father by war. Three times did Joash beat him, and recovered the cities of Israel.

CHAPTER 14

1 In the second year of Joash son of Jehoahaz king of Israel reigned Amaziah the son of Joash king of Judah.
2 He was twenty and five years old when he began to reign, and reigned twenty and nine years in Jerusalem. And his mother's name *was* Jehoaddan of Jerusalem.
3 And he did *that which was* right in the sight of the LORD, yet not like David his father: he did according to all things as Joash his father did.
4 Howbeit the high places were not taken away: as yet the people did sacrifice and burnt incense on the high places.
5 And it came to pass, as soon as the kingdom was confirmed in his hand, that he slew his servants which had slain the king his father.
6 But the children of the murderers he slew not: according unto that which is written in the book of the law of Moses, wherein the LORD commanded, saying, the fathers will not be put to death for the children, or the children be put to death for the fathers; but every man will be put to death for his own sin.
7 He slew of Edom in the valley of salt ten thousand, and took Selah[1] by war, and called the name of it Joktheel[2] unto this day.

---

[1] Selah- literally means *the rock*. A place in Edom, perhaps an early name for Petra, the rock city of Idumaea. [Strgs#5554].

[2] Joktheel- literally means the blessedness of God or veneration of God. [Strgs#3371]

8 Then Amaziah sent messengers to Jehoash, the son of Jehoahaz son of Jehu, king of Israel, saying, Come, let us look one another in the face.
9 And Jehoash the king of Israel sent to Amaziah king of Judah, saying, The thistle that *was* in Lebanon sent to the cedar that *was* in Lebanon, saying, Give your daughter to my son to wife: and there passed by a wild beast that *was* in Lebanon, and **trample** down the thistle.
10 you have indeed smitten Edom, and your heart has lifted you up: glory *of this*, and tarry at home: for why should you meddle to your hurt, that you should fall, *even* you, and Judah with you ?
11 But Amaziah would not hear. Therefore Jehoash king of Israel went up; and he and Amaziah king of Judah looked one another in the face at Beth-shemesh, which *belongs* to Judah.
12 And Judah was put to the worse before Israel; and they fled every man to their tents.
13 And Jehoash king of Israel took Amaziah king of Judah, the son of Jehoash the son of Ahaziah, at Beth-shemesh, and came to Jerusalem, and brake down the wall of Jerusalem from the gate of Ephraim unto the corner gate, four hundred cubits.
14 And he took all the gold and silver, and all the vessels that were found in the house of the LORD, and in the treasures of the king's house, and hostages, and returned to Samaria.
15 Now the rest of the acts of Jehoash which he did, and his might, and how he fought with Amaziah king of Judah, *are* they not written in the book of the chronicles of the kings of Israel?
16 And Jehoash slept with his fathers, and was buried in Samaria with the kings of Israel; and Jeroboam his son reigned in his stead.
17 And Amaziah the son of Joash king of Judah lived after the death of Jehoash son of Jehoahaz king of Israel fifteen years.
18 And the rest of the acts of Amaziah, *are* they not written in the book of the chronicles of the kings of Judah?
19 Now they made a conspiracy against him in Jerusalem: and he fled to Lachish; but they sent after him to Lachish, and slew him there.
20 And they brought him on horses: and he was buried at Jerusalem with his fathers in the city of David.
21 And all the people of Judah took Azariah, which *was* sixteen years old, and made him king instead of his father Amaziah.
22 He built Elath, and restored it to Judah, after that the king slept with his fathers.
23 In the fifteenth year of Amaziah the son of Joash king of Judah Jeroboam the son of Joash king of Israel began to reign in Samaria, *and reigned* forty and one years.
24 And he did *that which was* evil in the sight of the LORD: he departed not from all the sins of Jeroboam the son of Nebat, who made Israel to sin.
25 He restored the coast of Israel from the entering of Hamath unto the sea of the plain, according to the word of the LORD God of Israel, which he spoke by the hand of his servant Jonah[1], the son of Amittai, the prophet, which *was* of Gath-hepher[2].
26 For the LORD saw the affliction of Israel, *that it was* very bitter: for *there was* not any shut up, or any left, or any helper for Israel.
27 And the LORD said not that he would blot out the name of Israel from under heaven: but he saved them by the hand of Jeroboam the son of Joash.
28 Now the rest of the acts of Jeroboam, and all that he did, and his might, how he warred, and how he recovered Damascus, and Hamath, *which belonged* to Judah, for Israel, are they not written in the book of the chronicles of the kings of Israel?
29 And Jeroboam slept with his fathers, *even* with the kings of Israel; and Zachariah his son reigned in his stead.

CHAPTER 15

1 In the twenty and seventh year of Jeroboam king of Israel began Azariah son of Amaziah king of Judah to reign.
2 Sixteen years old was he when he began to reign, and he reigned two and fifty years in Jerusalem. And his mother's name *was* Jecholiah of Jerusalem.
3 And he did *that which was* right in the sight of the LORD, according to all that his father Amaziah had done;
4 Save that the high places were not removed: he people sacrificed and burnt incense still on the high places.
5 And the LORD smote the king, so that he was a leper unto the day of his death, and dwelt in a several house. And Jotham the king's son *was* over the house, judging the people of the land.
6 And the rest of the acts of Azariah, and all that he did, *are* they not written in the book of the chronicles of the kings of Judah?
7 So Azariah slept with his fathers; and they buried him with his fathers in the city of David: and Jotham his son reigned in his stead.
8 In the thirty and eighth year of Azariah king of Judah did Zachariah the son of Jeroboam reign over Israel in Samaria six months.
9 And he did *that which was* evil in the sight of the LORD, as his fathers had done: he departed not from the sins of Jeroboam the son of Nebat, who made Israel to sin.
10 And Shallum the son of Jabesh conspired against him, and smote him before the people, and slew him, and reigned in his stead.
11 And the rest of the acts of Zachariah, behold, they *are* written in the book of the chronicles of the kings of Israel.
12 This *was* the word of the LORD which he spoke unto Jehu, saying, your sons will sit on the throne of Israel unto the fourth *generation*. And so it came to pass.
13 Shallum the son of Jabesh began to reign in the nine and thirtieth year of Uzziah king of Judah; and he reigned a full month in Samaria.
14 For Menahem the son of Gadi went up from Tirzah, and came to Samaria, and smote Shallum the son of Jabesh in Samaria, and slew him, and reigned in his stead.
15 And the rest of the acts of Shallum, and his conspiracy which he made, behold, they *are* written in the book of the chronicles of the kings of Israel.
16 Then Menahem smote Tiphsah, and all that *were* therein, and the coasts thereof from Tirzah: because they opened not *to him*, therefore he smote *it; and* all the women therein that were with child he ripped up.
17 In the nine and thirtieth year of Azariah king of Judah began Menahem the son of Gadi to reign over Israel, *and reigned* ten years in Samaria.
18 And he did *that which was* evil in the sight of the LORD: he departed not all his days from the sins of Jeroboam the son of Nebat, who made Israel to sin.

---

[1] Jonah- literally *dove*. [Strgs#3124]
[2] Gathhelper- (*literally the winepress of digging or wine press of the well*) a border town in the territory of Zebulun, about five kilometers (*three miles*) northeast of Nazareth. Gathhelper was the hometown of the prophet Jonah (**II Kings 14:25**). [Strgs#1662]

19 *And* Pul the king of Assyria came against the land: and Menahem gave Pul a thousand talents of silver, that his hand might be with him to confirm the kingdom in his hand.
20 And Menahem exacted the money of Israel, *even* of all the mighty men of wealth, of each man fifty shekels of silver, to give to the king of Assyria. So the king of Assyria turned back, and stayed not there in the land.
21 And the rest of the acts of Menahem, and all that he did, *are* they not written in the book of the chronicles of the kings of Israel?
22 And Menahem slept with his fathers; and Pekahiah his son reigned in his stead.
23 In the fiftieth year of Azariah king of Judah Pekahiah the son of Menahem began to reign over Israel in Samaria, *and reigned* two years.
24 And he did *that which was* evil in the sight of the LORD: he departed not from the sins of Jeroboam the son of Nebat, who made Israel to sin.
25 But Pekah the son of Remaliah, a captain of his, conspired against him, and smote him in Samaria, in the palace of the king's house, with Argob and Arieh, and with him fifty men of the Gileadites: and he killed him, and reigned in his room.
26 And the rest of the acts of Pekahiah, and all that he did, behold, they *are* written in the book of the chronicles of the kings of Israel.
27 In the two and fiftieth year of Azariah king of Judah Pekah the son of Remaliah began to reign over Israel in Samaria, *and reigned* twenty years.
28 And he did *that which was* evil in the sight of the LORD: he departed not from the sins of Jeroboam the son of Nebat, who made Israel to sin.
29 In the days of Pekah king of Israel came Tiglath-pileser king of Assyria, and took Ijon, and Abel-beth-maachah, and Janoah, and Kedesh, and Hazor, and Gilead, and Galilee, all the land of Naphtali, and carried them captive to Assyria.
30 And Hoshea the son of Elah made a conspiracy against Pekah the son of Remaliah, and smote him, and slew him, and reigned in his stead, in the twentieth year of Jotham the son of Uzziah.
31 And the rest of the acts of Pekah, and all that he did, behold, they *are* written in the book of the chronicles of the kings of Israel.
32 In the second year of Pekah the son of Remaliah king of Israel began Jotham the son of Uzziah king of Judah to reign.
33 Five and twenty years old was he when he began to reign, and he reigned sixteen years in Jerusalem. And his mother's name *was* Jerusha, the daughter of Zadok.
34 And he did *that which was* right in the sight of the LORD: he did according to all that his father Uzziah had done.
35 Howbeit the high places were not removed: the people sacrificed and burned incense still in the high places. He built the higher gate of the house of the LORD.
36 Now the rest of the acts of Jotham, and all that he did, *are* they not written in the book of the chronicles of the kings of Judah?
37 In those days the LORD began to send against Judah Rezin the king of Syria, and Pekah the son of Remaliah.
38 And Jotham slept with his fathers, and was buried with his fathers in the city of David his father: and Ahaz his son reigned in his stead.

CHAPTER 16

1 In the seventeenth year of Pekah the son of Remaliah Ahaz the son of Jotham king of Judah began to reign.
2 Twenty years old *was* Ahaz when he began to reign, and reigned sixteen years in Jerusalem, and did not *that which was* right in the sight of the LORD his God, like David his father.
3 But he walked in the way of the kings of Israel, yea, and made his son to pass through the fire, according to the abominations of the heathen, whom the LORD cast out from before the children of Israel.
4 And he sacrificed and burnt incense in the high places, and on the hills, and under every green tree.
5 Then Rezin king of Syria and Pekah son of Remaliah king of Israel came up to Jerusalem to war: and they besieged Ahaz, but could not overcome *him*.
6 At that time Rezin king of Syria recovered Elath to Syria, and drave the Jews from Elath: and the Syrians came to Elath, and dwelt there unto this day.
7 So Ahaz sent messengers to Tiglath-pileser king of Assyria, saying, I *am* your servant and your son: come up, and save me out of the hand of the king of Syria, and out of the hand of the king of Israel, which rise up against me.
8 And Ahaz took the silver and gold that was found in the house of the LORD, and in the treasures of the king's house, and sent *it for* a present to the king of Assyria.
9 And the king of Assyria hearkened unto him: for the king of Assyria went up against Damascus, and took it, and carried *the people of* it captive to Kir, and slew Rezin.
10 And king Ahaz went to Damascus to meet Tiglath-pileser king of Assyria, and saw an altar that *was* at Damascus: and king Ahaz sent to Urijah the priest the fashion of the altar, and the pattern of it, according to all the workmanship thereof.
11 And Urijah the priest built an altar according to all that king Ahaz had sent from Damascus: so Urijah the priest made *it* against king Ahaz came from Damascus.
12 And when the king was come from Damascus, the king saw the altar: and the king approached to the altar, and offered thereon.
13 And he burnt his burnt offering and his meat offering, and poured his drink offering, and sprinkled the blood of his peace offerings, upon the altar.
14 And he brought also the brasen altar, which *was* before the LORD, from the forefront of the house, from between the altar and the house of the LORD, and put it on the north side of the altar.
15 And king Ahaz commanded Urijah the priest, saying, Upon the great altar burn the morning burnt offering, and the evening meat offering, and the king's burnt sacrifice, and his meat offering, with the burnt offering of all the people of the land, and their meat offering, and their drink offerings; and sprinkle upon it all the blood of the burnt offering, and all the blood of the sacrifice: and the brasen altar will be for me to enquire *by*.
16 Thus did Urijah the priest, according to all that king Ahaz commanded.
17 And king Ahaz cut off the borders of the bases, and removed the laver from off them; and took down the sea from off the brasen oxen that *were* under it, and put it upon a pavement of stones.
18 And the covert for the Sabbath that they had built in the house, and the king's entry without, turned he from the house of the LORD for the king of Assyria.
19 Now the rest of the acts of Ahaz which he did, *are* they not written in the book of the chronicles of the kings of Judah?
20 And Ahaz slept with his fathers, and was buried with his fathers in the city of David: and Hezekiah his son reigned in his stead.

CHAPTER 17

1 In the twelfth year of Ahaz king of Judah began Hoshea the son of Elah to reign in Samaria over Israel nine years.
2 And he did *that which was* evil in the sight of the LORD, but not as the kings of Israel that were before him.
3 Against him came up Shalmaneser king of Assyria; and Hoshea became his servant, and gave him presents.
4 And the king of Assyria found conspiracy in Hoshea: for he had sent messengers to so king of Egypt, and brought no present to the king of Assyria, as *he had done* year by year: therefore the king of Assyria shut him up, and bound him in prison.
5 Then the king of Assyria came up throughout all the land, and went up to Samaria, and besieged it three years.
6 In the ninth year of Hoshea the king of Assyria took Samaria, and carried Israel away into Assyria, and placed them in Halah and in Habor *by* the river of Gozan, and in the cities of the Medes.
7 For *so* it was, that the children of Israel had sinned against the LORD their God, which had brought them up out of the land of Egypt, from under the hand of Pharaoh king of Egypt, and had feared other gods,
8 And walked in the statutes of the heathen, whom the LORD cast out from before the children of Israel, and of the kings of Israel, which they had made.
9 And the children of Israel did secretly *those* things that *were* not right against the LORD their God, and they built them high places in all their cities, from the tower of the watchmen to the fenced city.
10 And they set them up images and groves in every high hill, and under every green tree:
11 And there they burnt incense in all the high places, as *did* the heathen whom the LORD carried away before them; and wrought wicked things to provoke the LORD to anger:
12 For they served idols, whereof the LORD had said unto them, you will not do this thing.
13 Yet the LORD testified against Israel, and against Judah, by all the prophets, *and by* all the seers, saying, Turn you from your evil ways, and keep my commandments *and* my statutes, according to all the law which I commanded your fathers, and which I sent to you by my servants the prophets.
14 Notwithstanding they would not hear, but hardened their necks, like to the neck of their fathers, that did not believe in the LORD their God.
15 And they rejected his statutes, and his covenant that he made with their fathers, and his testimonies which he testified against them; and they followed vanity, and became vain, and went after the heathen that *were* round about them, *concerning* whom the LORD had charged them, that they should not do like them.
16 And they left all the commandments of the LORD their God, and made them molten images, *even* two calves, and made a grove, and worshipped all the host of heaven, and served Baal.
17 And they caused their sons and their daughters to pass through the fire, and used divination and enchantments, and sold themselves to do evil in the sight of the LORD, to provoke him to anger.
18 Therefore the LORD was very angry with Israel, and removed them out of his sight: there was none left but the tribe of Judah only.
19 Also Judah kept not the commandments of the LORD their God, but walked in the statutes of Israel which they made.
20 And the LORD rejected all the seed of Israel, and afflicted them, and delivered them into the hand of spoilers, until he had cast them out of his sight.
21 For he rent Israel from the house of David; and they made Jeroboam the son of Nebat king: and Jeroboam drove Israel from following the LORD, and made them sin a great sin.
22 For the children of Israel walked in all the sins of Jeroboam which he did; they departed not from them;
23 Until the LORD removed Israel out of his sight, as he had said by all his servants the prophets. So was Israel carried away out of their own land to Assyria unto this day.
24 And the king of Assyria brought *men* from Babylon, and from Cuthah, and from Ava, and from Hamath, and from Sepharvaim, and placed *them* in the cities of Samaria instead of the children of Israel: and they possessed Samaria, and dwelt in the cities thereof.
25 And *so* it was at the beginning of their dwelling there, *that* they feared not the LORD: therefore the LORD sent lions among them, which slew *some* of them.
26 Wherefore they spoke to the king of Assyria, saying, The nations which you have removed, and placed in the cities of Samaria, know not the manner of the God of the land: therefore he has sent lions among them, and, behold, they slay them, because they know not the manner of the God of the land.
27 Then the king of Assyria commanded, saying, Carry there one of the priests whom you brought from thence; and let them go and dwell there, and let him teach them the manner of the God of the land.
28 Then one of the priests whom they had carried away from Samaria came and dwelt in Beth-el, and taught them how they should fear the LORD.
29 Howbeit every nation made gods of their own, and put *them* in the houses of the high places which the Samaritans had made, every nation in their cities wherein they dwelt.
30 And the men of Babylon made Succoth-benoth, and the men of Cuth made Nergal, and the men of Hamath made Ashima,
31 And the Avites made Nibhaz and Tartak, and the Sepharvites burnt their children in fire to Adrammelech and Anammelech, the gods of Sepharvaim.
32 So they feared the LORD, and made unto themselves of the lowest of them priests of the high places, which sacrificed for them in the houses of the high places.
33 They feared the LORD, and served their own gods, after the manner of the nations whom they carried away from thence.
34 Unto this day they do after the former manners: they fear not the LORD, neither do they after their statutes, or after their ordinances, or after the law and commandment which the LORD commanded the children of Jacob, whom he named Israel;
35 With whom the LORD had made a covenant, and charged them, saying, you will not fear other gods, or bow yourselves to them, or serve them, or sacrifice to them:
36 But the LORD, who brought you up out of the land of Egypt with great power and a stretched out arm, him will you fear, and him will you worship, and to him will you do sacrifice.
37 And the statutes, and the ordinances, and the law, and the commandment, which he wrote for you, you will observe to do for evermore; and you will not fear other gods.
38 And the covenant that I have made with you, you will not forget; neither will you fear other gods.
39 But the LORD your God you will fear; and he will deliver you out of the hand of all your enemies.

40 Howbeit they did not hearken, but they did after their former manner.

41 So these nations feared the LORD, and served their graven images, both their children, and their children's children: as did their fathers, so do they unto this day.

CHAPTER 18

1 Now it came to pass in the third year of Hoshea son of Elah king of Israel, *that* Hezekiah the son of Ahaz king of Judah began to reign.

2 Twenty and five years old was he when he began to reign; and he reigned twenty and nine years in Jerusalem. His mother's name also *was* Abi, the daughter of Zachariah.

3 And he did *that which was* right in the sight of the LORD, according to all that David his father did.

4 He removed the high places, and brake the images, and cut down the groves, and brake in pieces the brasen serpent that Moses had made: for unto those days the children of Israel did burn incense to it: and he called it Nehushtan.

5 He trusted in the LORD God of Israel; so that after him was none like him among all the kings of Judah, or *any* that were before him.

6 For he clave to the LORD, *and* departed not from following him, but kept his commandments, which the LORD commanded Moses.

7 And the LORD was with him; *and* he prospered whithersoever he went forth: and he rebelled against the king of Assyria, and served him not.

8 He smote the Philistines, *even* unto Gaza, and the borders thereof, from the tower of the watchmen to the fenced city.

9 And it came to pass in the fourth year of King Hezekiah, which *was* the seventh year of Hoshea son of Elah king of Israel, *that* Shalmaneser king of Assyria came up against Samaria, and besieged it.

10 And at the end of three years they took it: *even* in the sixth year of Hezekiah, that *is* the ninth year of Hoshea king of Israel, Samaria was taken.

11 And the king of Assyria did carry away Israel unto Assyria, and put them in Halah and in Habor *by* the river of Gozan, and in the cities of the Medes:

12 Because they obeyed not the voice of the LORD their God, but transgressed his covenant, *and* all that Moses the servant of the LORD commanded, and would not hear *them*, or do *them*.

13 Now in the fourteenth year of king Hezekiah did Sennacherib king of Assyria come up against all the fenced cities of Judah, and took them.

14 And Hezekiah king of Judah sent to the king of Assyria to Lachish, saying, I have offended; return from me: that which you puttest on me will I bear. And the king of Assyria appointed unto Hezekiah king of Judah three hundred talents of silver and thirty talents of gold.

15 And Hezekiah gave *him* all the silver that was found in the house of the LORD, and in the treasures of the king's house.

16 At that time did Hezekiah cut off *the gold from* the doors of the temple of the LORD, and *from* the pillars which Hezekiah king of Judah had overlaid, and gave it to the king of Assyria.

17 And the king of Assyria sent Tartan and Rabsaris and Rabshakeh from Lachish to King Hezekiah with a great host against Jerusalem. And they went up and came to Jerusalem. And when they were come up, they came and stood by the conduit of the upper pool, which *is* in the highway of the fuller's field.

18 And when they had called to the king, there came out to them Eliakim the son of Hilkiah, which *was* over the household, and Shebna the scribe, and Joah the son of Asaph the recorder.

19 And Rabshakeh said unto them, Speak you now to Hezekiah, Thus said the great king, the king of Assyria, What confidence *is* this wherein you trust?

20 you say, (but *they are but* vain words,) *I have* counsel and strength for the war. Now on whom dost you trust, that you rebell against me?

21 Now, behold, you trusts upon the staff of this bruised reed, *even* upon Egypt, on which if a man lean, it will go into his hand, and pierce it: so *is* Pharaoh king of Egypt unto all that trust on him.

22 But if you say unto me, we trust in the LORD our God: *is* not that he, whose high places and whose altars Hezekiah has taken away, and has said to Judah and Jerusalem, you will worship before this altar in Jerusalem?

23 Now therefore, I pray you, give pledges to my lord the king of Assyria, and I will deliver you two thousand horses, if you be able on your part to set riders upon them.

24 How then will you turn away the face of one captain of the least of my master's servants, and put your trust on Egypt for chariots and for horsemen?

25 Am I now come up without the LORD against this place to destroy it? The LORD said to me, Go up against this and, and destroy it.

26 Then said Eliakim the son of Hilkiah, and Shebna, and Joah, unto Rabshakeh, speak, I pray you, to your servants in the Syrian language; for we understand *it*: and talk not with us in the Jews' language in the ears of the people that *are* on the wall.

27 But Rabshakeh said unto them, has my master sent me to your master, and to you, to speak these words? Has *he* not sent *me* to the men who sit on the wall, that they may eat their own dung, and drink their own piss with you?

28 Then Rabshakeh stood and cried with a loud voice in the Jews' language, and spoke, saying, hear the word of the great king, the king of Assyria:

29 Thus said the king, Let not Hezekiah deceive you: for he will not be able to deliver you out of his hand:

30 Neither let Hezekiah make you trust in the LORD, saying, The LORD will surely deliver us, and this city will not be delivered into the hand of the king of Assyria.

31 Hearken not to Hezekiah: for thus said the king of Assyria, Make *an agreement* with me by a present, and come out to me, and *then* eat you every man of his own vine, and every one of his fig tree, and drink you every one the waters of his cistern:

32 Until I come and take you away to a land like your own land, a land of corn and wine, a land of bread and vineyards, a land of oil olive and of honey, that you may live, and not die: and hearken not unto Hezekiah, when he persuades you, saying, The LORD will deliver us.

33 Has any of the gods of the nations delivered at all his land out of the hand of the king of Assyria?

34 Where *are* the gods of Hamath, and of Arpad? Where *are* the gods of Sepharvaim, Hena, and Ivah? Have they delivered Samaria out of mine hand?

35 Who *are* they among all the gods of the countries, that have delivered their country out of mine hand, that the LORD should deliver Jerusalem out of mine hand?

36 But the people held their peace, and answered him not a word: for the king's commandment was, saying, Answer him not.

37 Then came Eliakim the son of Hilkiah, which *was* over the household, and Shebna the scribe, and Joah the son of Asaph the recorder, to Hezekiah with *their* clothes rent, and told him the words of Rabshakeh.

CHAPTER 19

1 And it came to pass, when King Hezekiah heard *it*, that he rent his clothes, and covered himself with sackcloth, and went into the house of the LORD.
2 And he sent Eliakim, which *was* over the household, and Shebna the scribe, and the elders of the priests, covered with sackcloth, to Isaiah the prophet the son of Amoz.
3 And they said unto him, Thus said Hezekiah, This day *is* a day of trouble, and of rebuke, and blasphemy: for the children are come to the birth, and *there is* not strength to bring forth.
4 It may be the LORD your God will hear all the words of Rabshakeh, whom the king of Assyria his master has sent to reproach the living God; and will reprove the words which the LORD your God has heard: wherefore lift up your prayer for the remnant that are left.
5 So the servants of King Hezekiah came to Isaiah.
6 And Isaiah said unto them, Thus will you say to your master, Thus said the LORD, Be not afraid of the words which you have heard, with which the servants of the king of Assyria have blasphemed me.
7 Behold, I will send a blast upon him, and he will hear a rumor, and will return to his own land; and I will cause him to fall by the sword in his own land.
8 So Rabshakeh returned, and found the king of Assyria warring against Libnah: for he had heard that he was departed from Lachish.
9 And when he heard say of Tirhakah king of Ethiopia, Behold, he is come out to fight against you: he sent messengers again unto Hezekiah, saying,
10 Thus will you speak to Hezekiah king of Judah, saying, Let not your God in whom you trust deceive you, saying, Jerusalem will not be delivered into the hand of the king of Assyria.
11 Behold, you have heard what the kings of Assyria have done to all lands, by destroying them utterly: and will you be delivered?
12 Have the gods of the nations delivered them which my fathers have destroyed; *as* Gozan, and Haran, and Rezeph, and the children of Eden which *were* in Thelasar?
13 Where *is* the king of Hamath, and the king of Arpad, and the king of the city of Sepharvaim, of Hena, and Ivah?
14 And Hezekiah received the letter of the hand of the messengers, and read it: and Hezekiah went up into the house of the LORD, and spread it before the LORD.
15 And Hezekiah prayed before the LORD, and said, O LORD God of Israel, which dwells *between* the cherubims, you are the God, *even* you alone, of all the kingdoms of the earth; you have made heaven and earth.
16 LORD, bow down your ear, and hear: open, LORD, your eyes, and see: and hear the words of Sennacherib, which has sent him to reproach the living God.
17 Of a truth, LORD, the kings of Assyria have destroyed the nations and their lands,
18 And have cast their gods into the fire: for they *were* no gods, but the work of men's hands, wood and stone: therefore they have destroyed them.
19 Now therefore, O LORD our God, I beseech you, save you us out of his hand, that all the kingdoms of the earth may know that you are the LORD God, *even* you only.
20 Then Isaiah the son of Amoz sent to Hezekiah, saying, Thus said the LORD God of Israel, *That* which you have prayed to me against Sennacherib king of Assyria I have heard.
21 This *is* the word that the LORD has spoken concerning him; The virgin the daughter of Zion has despised you, *and* laughed you to scorn; the daughter of Jerusalem has shaken her head at you.
22 Whom have you reproached and blasphemed? And against whom have you exalted your voice, and lifted up your eyes on high? *Even* against the Holy *One* of Israel.
23 By your messengers you have reproached the Lord, and have said, With the multitude of my chariots I am come up to the height of the mountains, to the sides of Lebanon, and will cut down the tall cedar trees thereof, *and* the choice fir trees thereof: and I will enter into the lodgings of his borders, *and into* the forest of his Carmel.
24 I have digged and drunk strange waters, and with the sole of my feet have I dried up all the rivers of besieged places.
25 have you not heard long ago *how* I have done it, *and* of ancient times that I have formed it? Now have I brought it to pass, that you should be to lay waste fenced cities *into* ruinous heaps.
26 Therefore their inhabitants were of small power, they were dismayed and confounded; they were *as* the grass of the field, and *as* the green herb, *as* the grass on the housetops, and *as corn* blasted before it be grown up.
27 But I know your abode, and your going out, and your coming in, and your rage against me.
28 Because your rage against me and your tumult is come up into mine ears, therefore I will put my hook in your nose, and my bridle in your lips, and I will turn you back by the way by which you came.
29 And this will *be* a sign unto you, you will eat this year such things as grow of themselves, and in the second year that which springs of the same; and in the third year sow ye, and reap, and plant vineyards, and eat the fruits thereof.
30 And the remnant that is escaped of the house of Judah will yet again take root downward, and bear fruit upward.
31 For out of Jerusalem will go forth a remnant, and they that escape out of mount Zion: the zeal of the LORD *of hosts* will do this.
32 Therefore thus said the LORD concerning the king of Assyria, He will not come into this city, or shoot an arrow there, or come before it with shield, or cast a bank against it.
33 By the way that he came, by the same will he return, and will not come into this city, said the LORD.
34 For I will defend this city, to save it, for mine own sake, and for my servant David's sake.
35 And it came to pass that night, that the angel of the LORD went out, and smote in the camp of the Assyrians an hundred fourscore and five thousand: and when they arose early in the morning, behold, they *were* all dead corpses.
36 So Sennacherib king of Assyria departed, and went and returned, and dwelt at Nineveh.
37 And it came to pass, as he was worshipping in the house of Nisroch his god, that Adrammelech and Sharezer his sons smote him with the sword: and they escaped into the land of Armenia. And Esar-haddon his son reigned in his stead.

CHAPTER 20

1 In those days was Hezekiah sick unto death. And the prophet Isaiah the son of Amoz came to him, and said unto him, thus said the LORD, Set your house in order; for you will die, and not live.
2 Then he turned his face to the wall, and prayed unto the LORD, saying,
3 I beseech you, O LORD, remember now how I have walked before you in truth and with a perfect heart, and have done *that which is* good in your sight. And Hezekiah wept sore.
4 And it came to pass, afore Isaiah was gone out into the middle court, that the word of the LORD came to him, saying,
5 Turn again, and tell Hezekiah the captain of my people, Thus said the LORD, the God of David your father, I have heard your prayer, I have seen your tears: behold, I will heal you: on the third day you will go up unto the house of the LORD.
6 And I will add unto your days fifteen years; and I will deliver you and this city out of the hand of the king of Assyria; and I will defend this city for mine own sake, and for my servant David's sake.
7 And Isaiah said, Take a lump of figs. And they took and laid *it* on the boil, and he recovered.
8 And Hezekiah said unto Isaiah, What will *be* the sign that the LORD will heal me, and that I will go up into the house of the LORD the third day?
9 And Isaiah said, this sign will you have of the LORD, that the LORD will do the thing that he has spoken: will the shadow go forward ten degrees, or go back ten degrees?
10 And Hezekiah answered, It is a light thing for the shadow to go down ten degrees: nay, but let the shadow return backward ten degrees.
11 And Isaiah the prophet cried unto the LORD: and he brought the shadow ten degrees backward, by which it had gone down in the dial of Ahaz.
12 At that time Berodach-baladan, the son of Baladan, king of Babylon, sent letters and a present unto Hezekiah: for he had heard that Hezekiah had been sick.
13 And Hezekiah hearkened unto them, and showed them all the house of his precious things, the silver, and the gold, and the spices, and the precious ointment, and *all* the house of his armor, and all that was found in his treasures: there was nothing in his house, or in all his dominion, that Hezekiah showed them not.
14 Then came Isaiah the prophet unto king Hezekiah, and said unto him, What said these men? And from where came they unto you? And Hezekiah said, they are come from a far country, *even* from Babylon.
15 And he said, what have they seen in your house? And Hezekiah answered, all *the things* that *are* in mine house have they seen: there is nothing among my treasures that I have not showed them.
16 And Isaiah said unto Hezekiah, Hear the word of the LORD.
17 Behold, the days come, that all that *is* in your house, and that which your fathers have laid up in store unto this day, will be carried into Babylon: nothing will be left, said the LORD.
18 And of your sons that will issue from you, which will beget, will they take away; and they will be eunuchs in the palace of the king of Babylon.
19 Then said Hezekiah unto Isaiah, Good *is* the word of the LORD which you have spoken. And he said, *Is it* not *good*, if peace and truth be in my days?
20 And the rest of the acts of Hezekiah, and all his might, and how he made a pool, and a conduit, and brought water into the city, *are* they not written in the book of the chronicles of the kings of Judah?
21 And Hezekiah slept with his fathers: and Manasseh his son reigned in his stead.

CHAPTER 21

1 Manasseh *was* twelve years old when he began to reign, and reigned fifty and five years in Jerusalem. And his mother's name *was* Hephzi-bah.
2 And he did *that which was* evil in the sight of the LORD, after the abominations of the heathen, whom the LORD cast out before the children of Israel.
3 For he built up again the high places which Hezekiah his father had destroyed; and he reared up altars for Baal, and made a grove, as did Ahab king of Israel; and worshipped all the host of heaven, and served them.
4 And he built altars in the house of the LORD, of which the LORD said, In Jerusalem will I put my name.
5 And he built altars for all the host of heaven in the two courts of the house of the LORD.
6 And he made his son pass through the fire, and [observed times][1], and used enchantments, and dealt with familiar spirits and wizards: he wrought much wickedness in the sight of the LORD, to provoke *him* to anger.
7 And he set a graven image of the grove that he had made in the house, of which the LORD said to David, and to Solomon his son, In this house, and in Jerusalem, which I have chosen out of all tribes of Israel, will I put my name for ever:
8 Neither will I make the feet of Israel move any more out of the land which I gave their fathers; only if they will observe to do according to all that I have commanded them, and according to all the law that my servant Moses commanded them.
9 But they hearkened not: and Manasseh seduced them to do more evil than did the nations whom the LORD destroyed before the children of Israel.
10 And the LORD spoke by his servants the prophets, saying,
11 Because Manasseh king of Judah has done these abominations, *and* has done wickedly above all that the Amorites did, which *were* before him, and has made Judah also to sin with his idols:
12 Therefore thus said the LORD God of Israel, Behold, I *am* bringing *such* evil upon Jerusalem and Judah, that whosoever hears of it, both his ears will tingle.
13 And I will stretch over Jerusalem the line of Samaria, and the plummet of the house of Ahab: and I will wipe Jerusalem as *a man* wipes a dish, wiping *it*, and turning *it* upside down.
14 And I will forsake the remnant of mine inheritance, and deliver them into the hand of their enemies; and they will become a prey and a spoil to all their enemies;
15 Because they have done *that which was* evil in my sight, and have provoked me to anger, since the day their fathers came forth out of Egypt, even unto this day.
16 Moreover Manasseh shed innocent blood very much, till he had filled Jerusalem from one end to another; beside his sin wherewith he made Judah to sin, in doing *that which was* evil in the sight of the LORD.

---

[1] lit. to cloud over, to act covertly, that is, practice magic, enchanter, observe times, soothsayer & sorcerer [Strgs#6049].

17 Now the rest of the acts of Manasseh, and all that he did, and his sin that he sinned, *are* they not written in the book of the chronicles of the kings of Judah?
18 And Manasseh slept with his fathers, and was buried in the garden of his own house, in the garden of Uzza: and Amon his son reigned in his stead.
19 Amon *was* twenty and two years old when he began to reign, and he reigned two years in Jerusalem. And his mother's name *was* Meshullemeth, the daughter of Haruz of Jotbah.
20 And he did *that which was* evil in the sight of the LORD, as his father Manasseh did.
21 And he walked in all the way that his father walked in, and served the idols that his father served, and worshipped them:
22 And he forsook the LORD God of his fathers, and walked not in the way of the LORD.
23 And the servants of Amon conspired against him, and slew the king in his own house.
24 And the people of the land slew all them that had conspired against king Amon; and the people of the land made Josiah his son king in his stead.
25 Now the rest of the acts of Amon which he did, *are* they not written in the book of the chronicles of the kings of Judah?
26 And he was buried in his sepulcher in the garden of Uzza: and Josiah his son reigned in his stead.

CHAPTER 22

1 Josiah *was* eight years old when he began to reign, and he reigned thirty and one years in Jerusalem. And his mother's name *was* Jedidah, the daughter of Adaiah of Boscath.
2 And he did *that which was* right in the sight of the LORD, and walked in all the way of David his father, and turned not aside to the right hand or to the left.
3 And it came to pass in the eighteenth year of king Josiah, *that* the king sent Shaphan the son of Azaliah, the son of Meshullam, the scribe, to the house of the LORD, saying,
4 Go up to Hilkiah the high priest, that he may sum the silver which is brought into the house of the LORD, which the keepers of the door have gathered of the people:
5 And let them deliver it into the hand of the doers of the work, that have the oversight of the house of the LORD: and let them give it to the doers of the work which *is* in the house of the LORD, to repair the breaches of the house,
6 Unto carpenters, and builders, and masons, and to buy timber and hewn stone to repair the house.
7 Howbeit there was no reckoning made with them of the money that was delivered into their hand, because they dealt faithfully.
8 And Hilkiah the high priest said unto Shaphan the scribe, I have found the book of the law in the house of the LORD. And Hilkiah gave the book to Shaphan, and he read it.
9 And Shaphan the scribe came to the king, and brought the king word again, and said, your servants have gathered the money that was found in the house, and have delivered it into the hand of them that do the work, that have the oversight of the house of the LORD.
10 And Shaphan the scribe showed the king, saying, Hilkiah the priest has delivered me a book. And Shaphan read it before the king.
11 And it came to pass, when the king had heard the words of the book of the law, that he rent his clothes.
12 And the king commanded Hilkiah the priest, and Ahikam the son of Shaphan, and Achbor the son of Michaiah, and Shaphan the scribe, and Asahiah a servant of the king's, saying,
13 Go ye, enquire of the LORD for me, and for the people, and for all Judah, concerning the words of this book that is found: for great *is* the wrath of the LORD that is kindled against us, because our fathers have not hearkened unto the words of this book, to do according unto all that which is written concerning us.
14 So Hilkiah the priest, and Ahikam, and Achbor, and Shaphan, and Asahiah, went unto Huldah the prophetess, the wife of Shallum the son of Tikvah, the son of Harhas, keeper of the wardrobe; (now she dwelt in Jerusalem in the college;) and they communed with her.
15 And she said unto them, Thus said the LORD God of Israel, Tell the man that sent you to me,
16 Thus said the LORD, Behold; I will bring evil upon this place, and upon the inhabitants thereof, *even* all the words of the book which the king of Judah has read:
17 Because they have forsaken me, and have burned incense unto other gods, that they might provoke me to anger with all the works of their hands; therefore my wrath will be kindled against this place, and will not be quenched.
18 But to the king of Judah which sent you to enquire of the LORD, thus will you say to him, Thus said the LORD God of Israel, *as touching* the words which you have heard;
19 Because your heart was tender, and you have humbled yourself before the LORD, when you heardest what I spoke against this place, and against the inhabitants thereof, that they should become a desolation and a curse, and have rent your clothes, and wept before me; I also have heard you, said the LORD.
20 Behold therefore, I will gather you unto your fathers, and you will be gathered into your grave in peace; and your eyes will not see all the evil which I will bring upon this place. And they brought the king word again.

CHAPTER 23

1 And the king sent, and they gathered unto him all the elders of Judah and of Jerusalem.
2 And the king went up into the house of the LORD, and all the men of Judah and all the inhabitants of Jerusalem with him, and the priests, and the prophets, and all the people, both small and great: and he read in their ears all the words of the book of the covenant which was found in the house of the LORD.
3 And the king stood by a pillar, and made a covenant before the LORD, to walk after the LORD, and to keep his commandments and his testimonies and his statutes with all *their* heart and all *their* soul, to perform the words of this covenant that were written in this book. And all the people stood to the covenant.
4 And the king commanded Hilkiah the high priest, and the priests of the second order, and the keepers of the door, to bring forth out of the temple of the LORD all the vessels that were made for Baal, and for the grove, and for all the host of heaven: and he burned them without Jerusalem in the fields of Kidron, and carried the ashes of them unto Beth-el.
5 And he put down the idolatrous priests, whom the kings of Judah had ordained to burn incense in the high places in the cities of Judah, and in the places round about Jerusalem; them also that burned incense unto Baal, to the sun, and to the moon, and to the planets, and to all the host of heaven.
6 And he brought out the grove from the house of the LORD, without Jerusalem, unto the brook Kidron, and burned it at the brook Kidron, and stamped *it* small to powder, and cast the powder thereof upon the graves of the children of the people.

7 And he broke down the houses of the sodomites, that *were* by the house of the LORD, where the women wove hangings for the grove.
8 And he brought all the priests out of the cities of Judah, and defiled the high places where the priests had burned incense, from Geba to Beer-sheba, and brake down the high places of the gates that *were* in the entering in of the gate of Joshua the governor of the city, which *were* on a man's left hand at the gate of the city.
9 Nevertheless the priests of the high places came not up to the altar of the LORD in Jerusalem, but they did eat of the unleavened bread among their brethren.
10 And he defiled Topheth, which *is* in the valley of the children of Hinnom, that no man might make his son or his daughter to pass through the fire to Molech.
11 And he took away the horses that the kings of Judah had given to the sun, at the entering in of the house of the LORD, by the chamber of Nathan-melech the chamberlain, which *was* in the suburbs, and burned the chariots of the sun with fire.
12 And the altars that *were* on the top of the upper chamber of Ahaz, which the kings of Judah had made, and the altars which Manasseh had made in the two courts of the house of the LORD, did the king beat down, and brake *them* down from thence, and cast the dust of them into the brook Kidron.
13 And the high places that *were* before Jerusalem, which *were* on the right hand of the mount of corruption, which Solomon the king of Israel had builded for Ashtoreth the abomination of the Zidonians, and for Chemosh the abomination of the Moabites, and for Milcom the abomination of the children of Ammon, did the king defile.
14 And he broke in pieces the images, and cut down the groves, and filled their places with the bones of men.
15 Moreover the altar that *was* at Beth-el, *and* the high place which Jeroboam the son of Nebat, who made Israel to sin, had made, both that altar and the high place he broke down, and burned the high place, *and* stamped *it* small to powder, and burned the grove.
16 And as Josiah turned himself, he spied the sepulchers that *were* there in the mount, and sent, and took the bones out of the sepulchers, and burned *them* upon the altar, and polluted it, according to the word of the LORD which the man of God proclaimed, who proclaimed these words.
17 Then he said, what title *is* that that I see? And the men of the city told him, *it is* the sepulcher of the man of God, which came from Judah, and proclaimed these things that you have done against the altar of Beth-el.
18 And he said, let him alone; let no man move his bones. So they let his bones alone, with the bones of the prophet that came out of Samaria.
19 And all the houses also of the high places that *were* in the cities of Samaria, which the kings of Israel had made to provoke *the LORD* to anger, Josiah took away, and did to them according to all the acts that he had done in Beth-el.
20 And he slew all the priests of the high places that *were* there upon the altars, and burned men's bones upon them, and returned to Jerusalem.
21 And the king commanded all the people, saying, keep the Passover unto the LORD your God, as *it is* written in the book of this covenant.
22 Surely there was not holden such a passover from the days of the judges that judged Israel, or in all the days of the kings of Israel, or of the kings of Judah;
23 But in the eighteenth year of king Josiah, *wherein* this passover was holden to the LORD in Jerusalem.
24 Moreover the *workers with* familiar spirits, and the wizards, and the images, and the idols, and all the abominations that were spied in the land of Judah and in Jerusalem, did Josiah put away, that he might perform the words of the law which were written in the book that Hilkiah the priest found in the house of the LORD.
25 And like unto him was there no king before him, that turned to the LORD with all his heart, and with all his soul, and with all his might, according to all the law of Moses; neither after him arose there *any* like him.
26 Notwithstanding the LORD turned not from the fierceness of his great wrath, wherewith his anger was kindled against Judah, because of all the provocations that Manasseh had provoked him withal.
27 And the LORD said, I will remove Judah also out of my sight, as I have removed Israel, and will cast off this city Jerusalem which I have chosen, and the house of which I said, My name will be there.
28 Now the rest of the acts of Josiah, and all that he did *are* they not written in the book of the chronicles of the kings of Judah?
29 In his days Pharaoh-nechoh king of Egypt went up against the king of Assyria to the river Euphrates: and king Josiah went against him; and he slew him at Megiddo, when he had seen him.
30 And his servants carried him in a chariot dead from Megiddo, and brought him to Jerusalem, and buried him in his own sepulchre. And the people of the land took Jehoahaz the son of Josiah, and anointed him, and made him king in his father's stead.
31 Jehoahaz *was* twenty and three years old when he began to reign; and he reigned three months in Jerusalem. And his mother's name *was* Hamutal, the daughter of Jeremiah of Libnah.
32 And he did *that which was* evil in the sight of the LORD, according to all that his fathers had done.
33 And Pharaoh-nechoh put him in bands at Riblah in the land of Hamath, that he might not reign in Jerusalem; and put the land to a tribute of an hundred talents of silver, and a talent of gold.
34 And Pharaoh-nechoh made Eliakim the son of Josiah king in the room of Josiah his father, and turned his name to Jehoiakim, and took Jehoahaz away: and he came to Egypt, and died there.
35 And Jehoiakim gave the silver and the gold to Pharaoh; but he taxed the land to give the money according to the commandment of Pharaoh: he exacted the silver and the gold of the people of the land, of every one according to his taxation, to give *it* unto Pharaoh-nechoh.
36 Jehoiakim *was* twenty and five years old when he began to reign; and he reigned eleven years in Jerusalem. And his mother's name *was* Zebudah, the daughter of Pedaiah of Rumah.
37 And he did *that which was* evil in the sight of the LORD, according to all that his fathers had done.

CHAPTER 24

1 In his days Nebuchadnezzar king of Babylon came up, and Jehoiakim became his servant three years: then he turned and rebelled against him.
2 And the LORD sent against him bands of the Chaldees, and bands of the Syrians, and bands of the Moabites, and bands of the children of Ammon, and sent them against Judah to destroy it, according to the word of the LORD, which he spoke by his servants the prophets.

3 Surely at the commandment of the LORD came *this* upon Judah, to remove *them* out of his sight, for the sins of Manasseh, according to all that he did;

4 And also for the innocent blood that he shed: for he filled Jerusalem with innocent blood; which the LORD would not pardon.

5 Now the rest of the acts of Jehoiakim, and all that he did, *are* they not written in the book of the chronicles of the kings of Judah?

6 So Jehoiakim slept with his fathers: and Jehoiachin his son reigned in his stead.

7 And the king of Egypt came not again any more out of his land: for the king of Babylon had taken from the river of Egypt unto the river Euphrates all that pertained to the king of Egypt.

8 Jehoiachin *was* eighteen years old when he began to reign, and he reigned in Jerusalem three months. And his mother's name *was* Nehushta, the daughter of Elnathan of Jerusalem.

9 And he did *that which was* evil in the sight of the LORD, according to all that his father had done.

10 At that time the servants of Nebuchadnezzar king of Babylon came up against Jerusalem, and the city was besieged.

11 And Nebuchadnezzar king of Babylon came against the city, and his servants did besiege it.

12 And Jehoiachin the king of Judah went out to the king of Babylon, he, and his mother, and his servants, and his princes, and his officers: and the king of Babylon took him in the eighth year of his reign.

13 And he carried out here all the treasures of the house of the LORD, and the treasures of the king's house, and cut in pieces all the vessels of gold which Solomon king of Israel had made in the temple of the LORD, as the LORD had said.

14 And he carried away all Jerusalem, and all the princes, and all the mighty men of valour, *even* ten thousand captives, and all the craftsmen and smiths: none remained, save the poorest sort of the people of the land.

15 And he carried away Jehoiachin to Babylon, and the king's mother, and the king's wives, and his officers, and the mighty of the land, *those* carried he into captivity from Jerusalem to Babylon.

16 And all the men of might, *even* seven thousand, and craftsmen and smiths a thousand, all *that were* strong *and* apt for war, even them the king of Babylon brought captive to Babylon.

17 And the king of Babylon made Mattaniah his father's brother king in his stead, and changed his name to Zedekiah.

18 Zedekiah *was* twenty and one years old when he began to reign, and he reigned eleven years in Jerusalem. And his mother's name *was* Hamutal, the daughter of Jeremiah of Libnah.

19 And he did *that which was* evil in the sight of the LORD, according to all that Jehoiakim had done.

20 For through the anger of the LORD it came to pass in Jerusalem and Judah, until he had cast them out from his presence, that Zedekiah rebelled against the king of Babylon.

CHAPTER 25

1 And it came to pass in the ninth year of his reign, in the tenth month, in the tenth *day* of the month, *that* Nebuchadnezzar king of Babylon came, he, and his **entire** host, against Jerusalem, and pitched against it; and they built forts against it round about.

2 And the city was besieged unto the eleventh year of King Zedekiah.

3 And on the ninth *day* of the *fourth* month the famine prevailed in the city, and there was no bread for the people of the land.

4 And the city was broken up, and all the men of war *fled* by night by the way of the gate between two walls, which *is* by the king's garden: (now the Chaldees *were* against the city round about:) and the king went the way toward the plain.

5 And the army of the Chaldees pursued after the king, and overtook him in the plains of Jericho: and all his army were scattered from him.

6 So they took the king, and brought him up to the king of Babylon to Riblah; and they gave judgment upon him.

7 And they slew the sons of Zedekiah before his eyes, and put out the eyes of Zedekiah, and bound him with fetters of brass, and carried him to Babylon.

8 And in the fifth month, on the seventh *day* of the month, which *is* the nineteenth year of king Nebuchadnezzar king of Babylon, came Nebuzar-adan, captain of the guard, a servant of the king of Babylon, unto Jerusalem:

9 And he burnt the house of the LORD, and the king's house, and all the houses of Jerusalem, and every great *man's* house burnt he with fire.

10 And all the army of the Chaldees, that *were with* the captain of the guard, brake down the walls of Jerusalem round about.

11 Now the rest of the people *that were* left in the city, and the fugitives that fell away to the king of Babylon, with the remnant of the multitude, did Nebuzar-adan the captain of the guard carry away.

12 But the captain of the guard left of the poor of the land *to be* vinedressers and husbandmen.

13 And the pillars of brass that *were* in the house of the LORD, and the bases, and the brasen sea that *was* in the house of the LORD, did the Chaldees break in pieces, and carried the brass of them to Babylon.

14 And the pots, and the shovels, and the snuffers, and the spoons, and all the vessels of brass wherewith they ministered, took they away.

15 And the firepans, and the bowls, *and* such things as *were* of gold, *in* gold, and of silver, *in* silver, the captain of the guard took away.

16 The two pillars, one sea, and the bases which Solomon had made for the house of the LORD; the brass of all these vessels was without weight.

17 The height of the one pillar *was* eighteen cubits, and the chapiter upon it *was* brass: and the height of the chapiter three cubits; and the wreathen work, and pomegranates upon the chapiter round about, all of brass: and like unto these had the second pillar with wreathen work.

18 And the captain of the guard took Seraiah the chief priest, and Zephaniah the second priest, and the three keepers of the door:

19 And out of the city he took an officer that was set over the men of war, and five men of them that were in the king's presence, which were found in the city, and the principal scribe of the host, which mustered the people of the land, and threescore men of the people of the land *that were* found in the city:

20 And Nebuzar-adan captain of the guard took these, and brought them to the king of Babylon to Riblah:

21 And the king of Babylon smote them, and slew them at Riblah in the land of Hamath. So Judah was carried away out of their land.

22 And *as for* the people that remained in the land of Judah, whom Nebuchadnezzar king of Babylon had left, even over them he made Gedaliah the son of Ahikam, the son of Shaphan, ruler.

23 And when all the captains of the armies, they and their men, heard that the king of Babylon had made Gedaliah governor, there came to Gedaliah to Mizpah, even Ishmael the son of Nethaniah, and Johanan the son of Careah, and Seraiah the son of

Tanhumeth the Netophathite, and Jaazaniah the son of a Maachathite, they and their men.

24 And Gedaliah swore to them, and to their men, and said unto them, Fear not to be the servants of the Chaldees: dwell in the land, and serve the king of Babylon; and it will be well with you.

25 But it came to pass in the seventh month, that Ishmael the son of Nethaniah, the son of Elishama, of the seed royal, came, and ten men with him, and smote Gedaliah, that he died, and the Jews and the Chaldees that were with him at Mizpah.

26 And all the people, both small and great, and the captains of the armies, arose, and came to Egypt: for they were afraid of the Chaldees.

27 And it came to pass in the seven and thirtieth year of the captivity of Jehoiachin king of Judah, in the twelfth month, on the seven and twentieth *day* of the month, *that* Evil-merodach king of Babylon in the year that he began to reign did lift up the head of Jehoiachin king of Judah out of prison;

28 And he spoke kindly to him, and set his throne above the throne of the kings that *were* with him in Babylon;

29 And changed his prison garments: and he did eat bread continually before him all the days of his life.

30 And his allowance *was* a continual allowance given him of the king, a daily rate for every day, all the days of his life.

FIRST CHRONICLES

CHAPTER 1

1 Adam, Sheth, Enosh,
2 Kenan, Mahalaleel, Jered,
3 Henoch, Methuselah, Lamech,
4 Noah, Shem, Ham, and Japheth.
5 The sons of Japheth; Gomer, and Magog, and Madai, and Javan, and Tubal, and Meshech, and Tiras.
6 And the sons of Gomer; Ashchenaz, and Riphath, and Togarmah.
7 And the sons of Javan; Elishah, and Tarshish, Kittim, and Dodanim.
8 The sons of Ham; Cush, and Mizraim, Put, and Canaan.
9 And the sons of Cush; Seba, and Havilah, and Sabta, and Raamah, and Sabtecha. And the sons of Raamah; Sheba, and Dedan.
10 And Cush begat Nimrod: he began to be mighty upon the earth.
11 And Mizraim begat Ludim, and Anamim, and Lehabim, and Naphtuhim,
12 And Pathrusim, and Casluhim, (of whom came the Philistines,) and Caphthorim.
13 And Canaan begat Zidon his firstborn, and Heth,
14 The Jebusite also, and the Amorite, and the Girgashite,
15 And the Hivite, and the Arkite, and the Sinite,
16 And the Arvadite, and the Zemarite, and the Hamathite.
17 The sons of Shem; Elam, and Asshur, and Arphaxad, and Lud, and Aram, and Uz, and Hul, and Gether, and Meshech.
18 And Arphaxad begat Shelah, and Shelah begat Eber.
19 And unto Eber were born two sons: the name of the one was Peleg; because in his days the earth was divided: and his brother's name was Joktan.
20 And Joktan begat Almodad, and Sheleph, and Hazarmaveth, and Jerah,
21 Hadoram also, and Uzal, and Diklah,
22 And Ebal, and Abimael, and Sheba,
23 And Ophir, and Havilah, and Jobab. All these were the sons of Joktan.
24 Shem, Arphaxad, Shelah,
25 Eber, Peleg, Reu,
26 Serug, Nahor, Terah,
27 Abram; the same is Abraham.
28 The sons of Abraham; Isaac, and Ishmael.
29 These are their generations: The firstborn of Ishmael, Nebaioth; then Kedar, and Adbeel, and Mibsam,
30 Mishma, and Dumah, Massa, Hadad, and Tema,
31 Jetur, Naphish, and Kedemah. These are the sons of Ishmael.
32 Now the sons of Keturah, Abraham's concubine: she bare Zimran, and Jokshan, and Medan, and Midian, and Ishbak, and Shuah. And the sons of Jokshan; Sheba, and Dedan.
33 And the sons of Midian; Ephah, and Epher, and Henoch, and Abida, and Eldaah. All these are the sons of Keturah.
34 And Abraham begat Isaac. The sons of Isaac; Esau and Israel.
35 The sons of Esau; Eliphaz, Reuel, and Jeush, and Jaalam, and Korah.
36 The sons of Eliphaz; Teman, and Omar, Zephi, and Gatam, Kenaz, and Timna, and Amalek.
37 The sons of Reuel; Nahath, Zerah, Shammah, and Mizzah.
38 And the sons of Seir; Lotan, and Shobal, and Zibeon, and Anah, and Dishon, and Ezer, and Dishan.
39 And the sons of Lotan; Hori, and Homam: and Timna was Lotan's sister.
40 The sons of Shobal; Alian, and Manahath, and Ebal, Shephi, and Onam. And the sons of Zibeon; Aiah, and Anah.
41 The sons of Anah; Dishon. And the sons of Dishon; Amram, and Eshban, and Ithran, and Cheran.
42 The sons of Ezer; Bilhan, and Zavan, and Jakan The sons of Dishan; Uz, and Aran.
43 Now these are the kings that reigned in the land of Edom before any king reigned over the children of Israel; Bela the son of Beor: and the name of his city was Dinhabah.
44 And when Bela was dead, Jobab the son of Zerah of Bozrah reigned in his stead.
45 And when Jobab was dead, Husham of the land of the Temanites reigned in his stead.
46 And when Husham was dead, Hadad the son of Bedad, which smote Midian in the field of Moab, reigned in his stead: and the name of his city was Avith.
47 And when Hadad was dead, Samlah of Masrekah reigned in his stead.
48 And when Samlah was dead, Shaul of Rehoboth by the river reigned in his stead.
49 And when Shaul was dead, Baal-hanan the son of Achbor reigned in his stead.
50 And when Baal-hanan was dead, Hadad reigned in his stead: and the name of his city was Pai; and his wife's name was Mehetabel, the daughter of Matred, the daughter of Mezahab.
51 Hadad died also. And the dukes of Edom were; duke Timnah, duke Aliah, duke Jetheth,
52 Duke Aholibamah, duke Elah, duke Pinon,
53 Duke Kenaz, duke Teman, duke Mibzar,
54 Duke Magdiel, duke Iram. These are the dukes of Edom.

CHAPTER 2

1 These are the sons of Israel; Reuben, Simeon, Levi, and Judah, Issachar, and Zebulun,
2 Dan, Joseph, and Benjamin, Naphtali, Gad, and Asher.
3 The sons of Judah; Er, and Onan, and Shelah: which three were born unto him of the daughter of Shua the Canaanitess. And Er, the firstborn of Judah, was evil in the sight of the LORD; and he slew him.
4 And Tamar his daughter in law bare him Pharez and Zerah. All the sons of Judah were five.
5 The sons of Pharez; Hezron, and Hamul.
6 And the sons of Zerah; Zimri, and Ethan, and Heman, and Calcol, and Dara: five of them in all.
7 And the sons of Carmi; Achar, the troubler of Israel, who transgressed in the thing accursed.
8 And the sons of Ethan; Azariah.
9 The sons also of Hezron, that were born unto him; Jerahmeel, and Ram, and Chelubai.
10 And Ram begat Amminadab; and Amminadab begat Nahshon, prince of the children of Judah;
11 And Nahshon begat Salma, and Salma begat Boaz,
12 And Boaz begat Obed, and Obed begat Jesse,
13 And Jesse begat his firstborn Eliab, and Abinadab the second, and Shimma the third,
14 Nethaneel the fourth, Raddai the fifth,
15 Ozem the sixth, David the seventh:
16 Whose sisters were Zeruiah, and Abigail. And the sons of Zeruiah; Abishai, and Joab, and Asahel, three.

17 And Abigail bare Amasa: and the father of Amasa was Jether the Ishmeelite.

18 And Caleb the son of Hezron begat children of Azubah his wife, and of Jerioth: her sons are these; Jesher, and Shobab, and Ardon.

19 And when Azubah was dead, Caleb took unto him Ephrath, which bare him Hur.

20 And Hur begat Uri, and Uri begat Bezaleel.

21 And afterward Hezron went in to the daughter of Machir the father of Gilead, whom he married when he was threescore years old; and she bare him Segub.

22 And Segub begat Jair, who had three and twenty cities in the land of Gilead.

23 And he took Geshur, and Aram, with the towns of Jair, from them, with Kenath, and the towns thereof, even threescore cities. All these belonged to the sons of Machir the father of Gilead.

24 And after that Hezron was dead in Caleb-ephratah, then Abiah Hezron's wife bare him Ashur the father of Tekoa.

25 And the sons of Jerahmeel the firstborn of Hezron were, Ram the firstborn, and Bunah, and Oren, and Ozem, and Ahijah.

26 Jerahmeel had also another wife, whose name was Atarah; she was the mother of Onam.

27 And the sons of Ram the firstborn of Jerahmeel were, Maaz, and Jamin, and Eker.

28 And the sons of Onam were, Shammai, and Jada. And the sons of Shammai; Nadab, and Abishur.

29 And the name of the wife of Abishur was Abihail, and she bare him Ahban, and Molid.

30 And the sons of Nadab; Seled, and Appaim: but Seled died without children.

31 And the sons of Appaim; Ishi. And the sons of Ishi; Sheshan. And the children of Sheshan; Ahlai.

32 And the sons of Jada the brother of Shammai; Jether, and Jonathan: and Jether died without children.

33 And the sons of Jonathan; Peleth, and Zaza. These were the sons of Jerahmeel.

34 Now Sheshan had no sons, but daughters. And Sheshan had a servant, an Egyptian, whose name was Jarha.

35 And Sheshan gave his daughter to Jarha his servant to wife; and she bare him Attai.

36 And Attai begat Nathan, and Nathan begat Zabad,

37 And Zabad begat Ephlal, and Ephlal begat Obed,

38 And Obed begat Jehu, and Jehu begat Azariah,

39 And Azariah begat Helez, and Helez begat Eleasah,

40 And Eleasah begat Sisamai, and Sisamai begat Shallum,

41 And Shallum begat Jekamiah, and Jekamiah begat Elishama.

42 Now the sons of Caleb the brother of Jerahmeel were, Mesha his firstborn, which was the father of Ziph; and the sons of Mareshah the father of Hebron.

43 And the sons of Hebron; Korah, and Tappuah, and Rekem, and Shema.

44 And Shema begat Raham, the father of Jorkoam: and Rekem begat Shammai.

45 And the son of Shammai was Maon: and Maon was the father of Beth-zur.

46 And Ephah, Caleb's concubine, bare Haran, and Moza, and Gazez: and Haran begat Gazez.

47 And the sons of Jahdai; Regem, and Jotham, and Gesham, and Pelet, and Ephah, and Shaaph.

48 Maachah, Caleb's concubine, bare Sheber, and Tirhanah.

49 She bare also Shaaph the father of Madmannah, Sheva the father of Machbenah, and the father of Gibea: and the daughter of Caleb was Achsa.

50 These were the sons of Caleb the son of Hur, the firstborn of Ephratah; Shobal the father of Kirjath-jearim,

51 Salma the father of Beth-lehem, Hareph the father of Beth-gader.

52 And Shobal the father of Kirjath-jearim had sons; Haroeh, and half of the Manahethites.

53 And the families of Kirjath-jearim; the Ithrites, and the Puhites, and the Shumathites, and the Mishraites; of them came the Zareathites, and the Eshtaulites.

54 The sons of Salma; Beth-lehem, and the Netophathites, Ataroth, the house of Joab, and half of the Manahethites, the Zorites.

55 And the families of the scribes which dwelt at Jabez; the Tirathites, the Shimeathites, and Suchathites. These are the Kenites that came of Hemath, the father of the house of Rechab.

CHAPTER 3

1 Now these were the sons of David, which were born unto him in Hebron; the firstborn Amnon, of Ahinoam the Jezreelitess; the second Daniel, of Abigail the Carmelitess:

2 The third, Absalom the son of Maachah the daughter of Talmai king of Geshur: the fourth, Adonijah the son of Haggith:

3 The fifth, Shephatiah of Abital: the sixth, Ithream by Eglah his wife.

4 These six were born unto him in Hebron; and there he reigned seven years and six months: and in Jerusalem he reigned thirty and three years.

5 And these were born unto him in Jerusalem; Shimea, and Shobab, and Nathan, and Solomon, four, of Bath-shua the daughter of Ammiel:

6 Ibhar also, and Elishama, and Eliphelet,

7 And Nogah, and Nepheg, and Japhia,

8 And Elishama, and Eliada, and Eliphelet, nine.

9 These were all the sons of David, beside the sons of the concubines, and Tamar their sister.

10 And Solomon's son was Rehoboam, Abia his son, Asa his son, Jehoshaphat his son,

11 Joram his son, Ahaziah his son, Joash his son,

12 Amaziah his son, Azariah his son, Jotham his son,

13 Ahaz his son, Hezekiah his son, Manasseh his son,

14 Amon his son, Josiah his son.

15 And the sons of Josiah were, the firstborn Johanan, the second Jehoiakim, the third Zedekiah, the fourth Shallum.

16 And the sons of Jehoiakim: Jeconiah his son, Zedekiah his son.

17 And the sons of Jeconiah; Assir, Salathiel his son,

18 Malchiram also, and Pedaiah, and Shenazar, Jecamiah, Hoshama, and Nedabiah.

19 And the sons of Pedaiah were, Zerubbabel, and Shimei: and the sons of Zerubbabel; Meshullam, and Hananiah, and Shelomith their sister:

20 And Hashubah, and Ohel, and Berechiah, and Hasadiah, Jushab-hesed, five.

21 And the sons of Hananiah; Pelatiah, and Jesaiah: the sons of Rephaiah, the sons of Arnan, the sons of Obadiah, the sons of Shechaniah.

22 And the sons of Shechaniah; Shemaiah: and the sons of Shemaiah; Hattush, and Igeal, and Bariah, and Neariah, and Shaphat, six.

23 And the sons of Neariah; Elioenai, and Hezekiah, and Azrikam, three.
24 And the sons of Elioenai were, Hodaiah, and Eliashib, and Pelaiah, and Akkub, and Johanan, and Dalaiah, and Anani, seven.

CHAPTER 4

1 The sons of Judah; Pharez, Hezron, and Carmi, and Hur, and Shobal.
2 And Reaiah the son of Shobal begat Jahath; and Jahath begat Ahumai, and Lahad. These are the families of the Zorathites.
3 And these were of the father of Etam; Jezreel, and Ishma, and Idbash: and the name of their sister was Hazelelponi:
4 And Penuel the father of Gedor, and Ezer the father of Hushah. These are the sons of Hur, the firstborn of Ephratah, the father of Beth-lehem.
5 And Ashur the father of Tekoa had two wives, Helah and Naarah.
6 And Naarah bare him Ahuzam, and Hepher, and Temeni, and Haahashtari. These were the sons of Naarah.
7 And the sons of Helah were, Zereth, and Jezoar, and Ethnan.
8 And Coz begat Anub, and Zobebah, and the families of Aharhel the son of Harum.
9 And Jabez was more honourable than his brethren: and his mother called his name Jabez, saying, Because I bare him with sorrow.
10 And Jabez called on the God of Israel, saying, Oh that you wouldest bless me indeed, and enlarge my coast, and that your hand might be with me, and that you wouldest keep me from evil, that it may not grieve me! And God granted him that which he requested.
11 And Chelub the brother of Shuah begat Mehir, which was the father of Eshton.
12 And Eshton begat Beth-rapha, and Paseah, and Tehinnah the father of Ir-nahash. These are the men of Rechah.
13 And the sons of Kenaz; Othniel, and Seraiah: and the sons of Othniel; Hathath.
14 And Meonothai begat Ophrah: and Seraiah begat Joab, the father of the valley of Charashim; for they were craftsmen.
15 And the sons of Caleb the son of Jephunneh; Iru, Elah, and Naam: and the sons of Elah, even Kenaz.
16 And the sons of Jehaleleel; Ziph, and Ziphah, Tiria, and Asareel.
17 And the sons of Ezra were, Jether, and Mered, and Epher, and Jalon: and she bare Miriam, and Shammai, and Ishbah the father of Eshtemoa.
18 And his wife Jehudijah bare Jered the father of Gedor, and Heber the father of Socho, and Jekuthiel the father of Zanoah. And these are the sons of Bithiah the daughter of Pharaoh, which Mered took.
19 And the sons of his wife Hodiah the sister of Naham, the father of Keilah the Garmite, and Eshtemoa the Maachathite.
20 And the sons of Shimon were, Amnon, and Rinnah, Ben-hanan, and Tilon. And the sons of Ishi were, Zoheth, and Ben-zoheth.
21 The sons of Shelah the son of Judah were, Er the father of Lecah, and Laadah the father of Mareshah, and the families of the house of them that wrought fine linen, of the house of Ashbea,
22 And Jokim, and the men of Chozeba, and Joash, and Saraph, who had the dominion in Moab, and Jashubi-lehem. And these are ancient things.
23 These were the potters, and those that dwelt among plants and hedges: there they dwelt with the king for his work.

24 The sons of Simeon were, Nemuel, and Jamin, Jarib, Zerah, and Shaul:
25 Shallum his son, Mibsam his son, Mishma his son.
26 And the sons of Mishma; Hamuel his son, Zacchur his son, Shimei his son.
27 And Shimei had sixteen sons and six daughters; but his brethren had not many children, neither did all their family multiply, like to the children of Judah.
28 And they dwelt at Beer-sheba, and Moladah, and Hazar-shual,
29 And at Bilhah, and at Ezem, and at Tolad,
30 And at Bethuel, and at Hormah, and at Ziklag,
31 And at Beth-marcaboth, and Hazar-susim, and at Beth-birei, and at Shaaraim. These were their cities unto the reign of David.
32 And their villages were, Etam, and Ain, Rimmon, and Tochen, and Ashan, five cities:
33 And all their villages that were round about the same cities, unto Baal. These were their habitations, and their genealogy.
34 And Meshobab, and Jamlech, and Joshah the son of Amaziah,
35 And Joel, and Jehu the son of Josibiah, the son of Seraiah, the son of Asiel,
36 And Elioenai, and Jaakobah, and Jeshohaiah, and Asaiah, and Adiel, and Jesimiel, and Benaiah,
37 And Ziza the son of Shiphi, the son of Allon, the son of Jedaiah, the son of Shimri, the son of Shemaiah;
38 These mentioned by their names were princes in their families: and the house of their fathers increased greatly.
39 And they went to the entrance of Gedor, even unto the east side of the valley, to seek pasture for their flocks.
40 And they found fat pasture and good, and the land was wide, and quiet, and peaceable; for they of Ham had dwelt there of old.
41 And these written by name came in the days of Hezekiah king of Judah, and smote their tents, and the habitations that were found there, and destroyed them utterly unto this day, and dwelt in their rooms: because there was pasture there for their flocks.
42 And some of them, even of the sons of Simeon, five hundred men, went to mount Seir, having for their captains Pelatiah, and Neariah, and Rephaiah, and Uzziel, the sons of Ishi.
43 And they smote the rest of the Amalekites that were escaped, and dwelt there unto this day.

CHAPTER 5

1 Now the sons of Reuben the firstborn of Israel, (for he was the firstborn; but, forasmuch as he defiled his father's bed, his birthright was given unto the sons of Joseph the son of Israel: and the genealogy is not to be reckoned after the birthright.
2 For Judah prevailed above his brethren, and of him came the chief ruler; but the birthright was Joseph's:)
3 The sons, I say, of Reuben the firstborn of Israel were, Hanoch, and Pallu, Hezron, and Carmi.
4 The sons of Joel; Shemaiah his son, Gog his son, Shimei his son,
5 Micah his son, Reaia his son, Baal his son,
6 Beerah his son, whom Tilgath-pilneser king of Assyria carried away captive: he was prince of the Reubenites.
7 And his brethren by their families, when the genealogy of their generations was reckoned, were the chief, Jeiel, and Zechariah,
8 And Bela the son of Azaz, the son of Shema, the son of Joel, who dwelt in Aroer, even unto Nebo and Baal-meon:
9 And eastward he inhabited unto the entering in of the wilderness from the river Euphrates: because their cattle were multiplied in the land of Gilead.

10 And in the days of Saul they made war with the Hagarites, who fell by their hand: and they dwelt in their tents throughout all the east *land* of Gilead.
11 And the children of Gad dwelt over against them, in the land of Bashan unto Salchah:
12 Joel the chief, and Shapham the next, and Jaanai, and Shaphat in Bashan.
13 And their brethren of the house of their fathers *were*, Michael, and Meshullam, and Sheba, and Jorai, and Jachan, and Zia, and Heber, seven.
14 These *are* the children of Abihail the son of Huri, the son of Jaroah, the son of Gilead, the son of Michael, the son of Jeshishai, the son of Jahdo, the son of Buz;
15 Ahi the son of Abdiel, the son of Guni, chief of the house of their fathers.
16 And they dwelt in Gilead in Bashan, and in her towns, and in all the suburbs of Sharon, upon their borders.
17 All these were reckoned by genealogies in the days of Jotham king of Judah, and in the days of Jeroboam king of Israel.
18 The sons of Reuben, and the Gadites, and half the tribe of Manasseh, of valiant men, men able to bear buckler and sword, and to shoot with bow, and skilful in war, *were* four and forty thousand seven hundred and threescore, that went out to the war.
19 And they made war with the Hagarites, with Jetur, and Nephish, and Nodab.
20 And they were helped against them, and the Hagarites were delivered into their hand, and all that *were* with them: for they cried to God in the battle, and he was intreated of them; because they put their trust in him.
21 And they took away their cattle; of their camels fifty thousand, and of sheep two hundred and fifty thousand, and of asses two thousand, and of men an hundred thousand.
22 For there fell down many slain, because the war *was* of God. And they dwelt in their steads until the captivity.
23 And the children of the half tribe of Manasseh dwelt in the land: they increased from Bashan unto Baal-hermon and Senir, and unto Mount Hermon.
24 And these *were* the heads of the house of their fathers, even Epher, and Ishi, and Eliel, and Azriel, and Jeremiah, and Hodaviah, and Jahdiel, mighty men of valour, famous men, *and* heads of the house of their fathers.
25 And they transgressed against the God of their fathers, and went a whoring after the gods of the people of the land, whom God destroyed before them.
26 And the God of Israel stirred up the spirit of Pul king of Assyria, and the spirit of Tilgath-pilneser king of Assyria, and he carried them away, even the Reubenites, and the Gadites, and the half tribe of Manasseh, and brought them unto Halah, and Habor, and Hara, and to the river Gozan, unto this day.

CHAPTER 6

1 The sons of Levi; Gershon, Kohath, and Merari.
2 And the sons of Kohath; Amram, Izhar, and Hebron, and Uzziel.
3 And the children of Amram; Aaron, and Moses, and Miriam. The sons also of Aaron; Nadab, and Abihu, Eleazar, and Ithamar.
4 Eleazar begat Phinehas, Phinehas begat Abishua,
5 And Abishua begat Bukki, and Bukki begat Uzzi,
6 And Uzzi begat Zerahiah, and Zerahiah begat Meraioth,
7 Meraioth begat Amariah, and Amariah begat Ahitub,
8 And Ahitub begat Zadok, and Zadok begat Ahimaaz,
9 And Ahimaaz begat Azariah, and Azariah begat Johanan,
10 And Johanan begat Azariah, (he *it is* that executed the priest's office in the temple that Solomon built in Jerusalem:)
11 And Azariah begat Amariah, and Amariah begat Ahitub,
12 And Ahitub begat Zadok, and Zadok begat Shallum,
13 And Shallum begat Hilkiah, and Hilkiah begat Azariah,
14 And Azariah begat Seraiah, and Seraiah begat Jehozadak,
15 And Jehozadak went *into captivity*, when the LORD carried away Judah and Jerusalem by the hand of Nebuchadnezzar.
16 The sons of Levi; Gershom, Kohath, and Merari.
17 And these *are* the names of the sons of Gershom; Libni, and Shimei.
18 And the sons of Kohath *were*, Amram, and Izhar, and Hebron, and Uzziel.
19 The sons of Merari; Mahli, and Mushi. And these *are* the families of the Levites according to their fathers.
20 Of Gershom; Libni his son, Jahath his son, Zimmah his son,
21 Joah his son, Iddo his son, Zerah his son, Jeaterai his son.
22 The sons of Kohath; Amminadab his son, Korah his son, Assir his son,
23 Elkanah his son, and Ebiasaph his son, and Assir his son,
24 Tahath his son, Uriel his son, Uzziah his son, and Shaul his son.
25 And the sons of Elkanah; Amasai, and Ahimoth.
26 *As for* Elkanah: the sons of Elkanah; Zophai his son, and Nahath his son,
27 Eliab his son, Jeroham his son, Elkanah his son.
28 And the sons of Samuel; the firstborn Vashni, and Abiah.
29 The sons of Merari; Mahli, Libni his son, Shimei his son, Uzza his son,
30 Shimea his son, Haggiah his son, Asaiah his son.
31 And these *are they* whom David set over the service of song in the house of the LORD, after that the ark had rest.
32 And they ministered before the dwelling place of the tabernacle of the congregation with singing, until Solomon had built the house of the LORD in Jerusalem: and *then* they waited on their office according to their order.
33 And these *are* they that waited with their children. Of the sons of the Kohathites: Heman a singer, the son of Joel, the son of Shemuel,
34 The son of Elkanah, the son of Jeroham, the son of Eliel, the son of Toah,
35 The son of Zuph, the son of Elkanah, the son of Mahath, the son of Amasai,
36 The son of Elkanah, the son of Joel, the son of Azariah, the son of Zephaniah,
37 The son of Tahath, the son of Assir, the son of Ebiasaph, the son of Korah,
38 The son of Izhar, the son of Kohath, the son of Levi, the son of Israel.
39 And his brother Asaph, who stood on his right hand, *even* Asaph the son of Berachiah, the son of Shimea,
40 The son of Michael, the son of Baaseiah, the son of Malchiah,
41 The son of Ethni, the son of Zerah, the son of Adaiah,
42 The son of Ethan, the son of Zimmah, the son of Shimei,
43 The son of Jahath, the son of Gershom, the son of Levi.
44 And their brethren the sons of Merari *stood* on the left hand: Ethan the son of Kishi, the son of Abdi, the son of Malluch,
45 The son of Hashabiah, the son of Amaziah, the son of Hilkiah,
46 The son of Amzi, the son of Bani, the son of Shamer,

47 The son of Mahli, the son of Mushi, the son of Merari, the son of Levi.
48 Their brethren also the Levites *were* appointed unto all manner of service of the tabernacle of the house of God.
49 But Aaron and his sons offered upon the altar of the burnt offering, and on the altar of incense, *and were appointed* for all the work of the *place* most holy, and to make atonement for Israel, according to all that Moses the servant of God had commanded.
50 And these *are* the sons of Aaron; Eleazar his son, Phinehas his son, Abishua his son,
51 Bukki his son, Uzzi his son, Zerahiah his son,
52 Meraioth his son, Amariah his son, Ahitub his son,
53 Zadok his son, Ahimaaz his son.
54 Now these *are* their dwelling places throughout their castles in their coasts, of the sons of Aaron, of the families of the Kohathites: for their's was the lot.
55 And they gave them Hebron in the land of Judah, and the suburbs thereof round about it.
56 But the fields of the city, and the villages thereof, they gave to Caleb the son of Jephunneh.
57 And to the sons of Aaron they gave the cities of Judah, *namely*, Hebron, *the city* of refuge, and Libnah with her suburbs, and Jattir, and Eshtemoa, with their suburbs,
58 And Hilen with her suburbs, Debir with her suburbs,
59 And Ashan with her suburbs, and Beth-shemesh with her suburbs:
60 And out of the tribe of Benjamin; Geba with her suburbs, and Alemeth with her suburbs, and Anathoth with her suburbs. All their cities throughout their families *were* thirteen cities.
61 And unto the sons of Kohath, *which were* left of the family of that tribe, *were cities given* out of the half tribe, *namely, out of* the half *tribe* of Manasseh, by lot, ten cities.
62 And to the sons of Gershom throughout their families out of the tribe of Issachar, and out of the tribe of Asher, and out of the tribe of Naphtali, and out of the tribe of Manasseh in Bashan, thirteen cities.
63 Unto the sons of Merari *were given* by lot, throughout their families, out of the tribe of Reuben, and out of the tribe of Gad, and out of the tribe of Zebulun, twelve cities.
64 And the children of Israel gave to the Levites *these* cities with their suburbs.
65 And they gave by lot out of the tribe of the children of Judah, and out of the tribe of the children of Simeon, and out of the tribe of the children of Benjamin, these cities, which are called by *their* names.
66 And *the residue* of the families of the sons of Kohath had cities of their coasts out of the tribe of Ephraim.
67 And they gave unto them, *of* the cities of refuge, Shechem in mount Ephraim with her suburbs; *they gave* also Gezer with her suburbs,
68 And Jokmeam with her suburbs, and Beth-horon with her suburbs,
69 And Aijalon with her suburbs, and Gath-rimmon with her suburbs:
70 And out of the half tribe of Manasseh; Aner with her suburbs, and Bileam with her suburbs, for the family of the remnant of the sons of Kohath.
71 Unto the sons of Gershom *were given* out of the family of the half tribe of Manasseh, Golan in Bashan with her suburbs, and Ashtaroth with her suburbs:
72 And out of the tribe of Issachar; Kedesh with her suburbs, Daberath with her suburbs,
73 And Ramoth with her suburbs, and Anem with her suburbs:
74 And out of the tribe of Asher; Mashal with her suburbs, and Abdon with her suburbs,
75 And Hukok with her suburbs, and Rehob with her suburbs:
76 And out of the tribe of Naphtali; Kedesh in Galilee with her suburbs, and Hammon with her suburbs, and Kirjathaim with her suburbs.
77 Unto the rest of the children of Merari *were given* out of the tribe of Zebulun, Rimmon with her suburbs, Tabor with her suburbs:
78 And on the other side Jordan by Jericho, on the east side of Jordan, *were given them* out of the tribe of Reuben, Bezer in the wilderness with her suburbs, and Jahzah with her suburbs,
79 Kedemoth also with her suburbs, and Mephaath with her suburbs:
80 And out of the tribe of Gad; Ramoth in Gilead with her suburbs, and Mahanaim with her suburbs,
81 And Heshbon with her suburbs, and Jazer with her suburbs.

CHAPTER 7

1 Now the sons of Issachar *were*, Tola, and Puah, Jashub, and Shimron, four.
2 And the sons of Tola; Uzzi, and Rephaiah, and Jeriel, and Jahmai, and Jibsam, and Shemuel, heads of their father's house, *to wit*, of Tola: they were valiant men of might in their generations; whose number *was* in the days of David two and twenty thousand and six hundred.
3 And the sons of Uzzi; Izrahiah: and the sons of Izrahiah; Michael, and Obadiah, and Joel, Ishiah, five: all of them chief men.
4 And with them, by their generations, after the house of their fathers, *were* bands of soldiers for war, six and thirty thousand *men*: for they had many wives and sons.
5 And their brethren among all the families of Issachar *were* valiant men of might, reckoned in all by their genealogies fourscore and seven thousand.
6 *The sons* of Benjamin; Bela, and Becher, and Jediael, three.
7 And the sons of Bela; Ezbon, and Uzzi, and Uzziel, and Jerimoth, and Iri, five; heads of the house of *their* fathers, mighty men of valour; and were reckoned by their genealogies twenty and two thousand and thirty and four.
8 And the sons of Becher; Zemira, and Joash, and Eliezer, and Elioenai, and Omri, and Jerimoth, and Abiah, and Anathoth, and Alameth. All these *are* the sons of Becher.
9 And the number of them, after their genealogy by their generations, heads of the house of their fathers, mighty men of valour, *was* twenty thousand and two hundred.
10 The sons also of Jediael; Bilhan: and the sons of Bilhan; Jeush, and Benjamin, and Ehud, and Chenaanah, and Zethan, and Tharshish, and Ahishahar.
11 All these the sons of Jediael, by the heads of their fathers, mighty men of valour, *were* seventeen thousand and two hundred *soldiers*, fit to go out for war *and* battle.
12 Shuppim also, and Huppim, the children of Ir, *and* Hushim, the sons of Aher.
13 The sons of Naphtali; Jahziel, and Guni, and Jezer, and Shallum, the sons of Bilhah.
14 The sons of Manasseh; Ashriel, whom she bare *(but his* concubine the Aramitess bare Machir the father of Gilead:

15 And Machir took to wife *the sister* of Huppim and Shuppim, whose sister's name *was* Maachah;) and the name of the second *was* Zelophehad: and Zelophehad had daughters.
16 And Maachah the wife of Machir bare a son, and she called his name Peresh; and the name of his brother *was* Sheresh; and his sons *were* Ulam and Rakem.
17 And the sons of Ulam; Bedan. These *were* the sons of Gilead, the son of Machir, the son of Manasseh.
18 And his sister Hammoleketh bare Ishod, and Abiezer, and Mahalah.
19 And the sons of Shemidah were, Ahian, and Shechem, and Likhi, and Aniam.
20 And the sons of Ephraim; Shuthelah, and Bered his son, and Tahath his son, and Eladah his son, and Tahath his son,
21 And Zabad his son, and Shuthelah his son, and Ezer, and Elead, whom the men of Gath *that were* born in *that* land slew, because they came down to take away their cattle.
22 And Ephraim their father mourned many days, and his brethren came to comfort him.
23 And when he went in to his wife, she conceived, and bare a son, and he called his name Beriah, because it went evil with his house.
24 (And his daughter *was* Sherah, who built Beth-horon the nether, and the upper, and Uzzen-sherah.)
25 And Rephah *was* his son, also Resheph, and Telah his son, and Tahan his son,
26 Laadan his son, Ammihud his son, Elishama his son,
27 Non his son, Jehoshua his son.
28 And their possessions and habitations *were*, Beth-el and the towns thereof, and eastward Naaran, and westward Gezer, with the towns thereof; Shechem also and the towns thereof, unto Gaza and the towns thereof:
29 And by the borders of the children of Manasseh, Beth-shean and her towns, Taanach and her towns, Megiddo and her towns, Dor and her towns. In these dwelt the children of Joseph the son of Israel.
30 The sons of Asher; Imnah, and Isuah, and Ishuai, and Beriah, and Serah their sister.
31 And the sons of Beriah; Heber, and Malchiel, who *is* the father of Birzavith.
32 And Heber begat Japhlet, and Shomer, and Hotham, and Shua their sister.
33 And the sons of Japhlet; Pasach, and Bimhal, and Ashvath. These *are* the children of Japhlet.
34 And the sons of Shamer; Ahi, and Rohgah, Jehubbah, and Aram.
35 And the sons of his brother Helem; Zophah, and Imna, and Shelesh, and Amal.
36 The sons of Zophah; Suah, and Harnepher, and Shual, and Beri, and Imrah,
37 Bezer, and Hod, and Shamma, and Shilshah, and Ithran, and Beera.
38 And the sons of Jether; Jephunneh, and Pispah, and Ara.
39 And the sons of Ulla; Arah, and Haniel, and Rezia.
40 All these *were* the children of Asher, heads of *their* father's house, choice *and* mighty men of valour, chief of the princes. And the number throughout the genealogy of them that were apt to the war *and* to battle *was* twenty and six thousand men.

CHAPTER 8

1 Now Benjamin begat Bela his firstborn, Ashbel the second, and Aharah the third,
2 Nohah the fourth, and Rapha the fifth.
3 And the sons of Bela were, Addar, and Gera, and Abihud,
4 And Abishua, and Naaman, and Ahoah,
5 And Gera, and Shephuphan, and Huram.
6 And these *are* the sons of Ehud: these are the heads of the fathers of the inhabitants of Geba, and they removed them to Manahath:
7 And Naaman, and Ahiah, and Gera, he removed them, and begat Uzza, and Ahihud.
8 And Shaharaim begat *children* in the country of Moab, after he had sent them away; Hushim and Baara *were* his wives.
9 And he begat of Hodesh his wife, Jobab, and Zibia, and Mesha, and Malcham,
10 And Jeuz, and Shachia, and Mirma. These *were* his sons, heads of the fathers.
11 And of Hushim he begat Abitub, and Elpaal.
12 The sons of Elpaal; Eber, and Misham, and Shamed, who built Ono, and Lod, with the towns thereof:
13 Beriah also, and Shema, who *were* heads of the fathers of the inhabitants of Aijalon, who drove away the inhabitants of Gath:
14 And Ahio, Shashak, and Jeremoth,
15 And Zebadiah, and Arad, and Ader,
16 And Michael, and Ispah, and Joha, the sons of Beriah;
17 And Zebadiah, and Meshullam, and Hezeki, and Heber,
18 Ishmerai also, and Jezliah, and Jobab, the sons of Elpaal;
19 And Jakim, and Zichri, and Zabdi,
20 And Elienai, and Zilthai, and Eliel,
21 And Adaiah, and Beraiah, and Shimrath, the sons of Shimhi;
22 And Ishpan, and Heber, and Eliel,
23 And Abdon, and Zichri, and Hanan,
24 And Hananiah, and Elam, and Antothijah,
25 And Iphedeiah, and Penuel, the sons of Shashak;
26 And Shamsherai, and Shehariah, and Athaliah,
27 And Jaresiah, and Eliah, and Zichri, the sons of Jeroham.
28 These *were* heads of the fathers, by their generations, chief *men*. These dwelt in Jerusalem.
29 And at Gibeon dwelt the father of Gibeon; whose wife's name *was* Maachah:
30 And his firstborn son Abdon, and Zur, and Kish, and Baal, and Nadab,
31 And Gedor, and Ahio, and Zacher.
32 And Mikloth begat Shimeah. And these also dwelt with their brethren in Jerusalem, over against them.
33 And Ner begat Kish, and Kish begat Saul, and Saul begat Jonathan, and Malchi-shua, and Abinadab, and Esh-baal.
34 And the son of Jonathan *was* Merib-baal; and Merib-baal begat Micah.
35 And the sons of Micah *were*, Pithon, and Melech, and Tarea, and Ahaz.
36 And Ahaz begat Jehoadah; and Jehoadah begat Alemeth, and Azmaveth, and Zimri; and Zimri begat Moza,
37 And Moza begat Binea: Rapha *was* his son, Eleasah his son, Azel his son:
38 And Azel had six sons, whose names *are* these, Azrikam, Bocheru, and Ishmael, and Sheariah, and Obadiah, and Hanan. All these *were* the sons of Azel.

39 And the sons of Eshek his brother were, Ulam his firstborn, Jehush the second, and Eliphelet the third.
40 And the sons of Ulam were mighty men of valour, archers, and had many sons, and sons' sons, an hundred and fifty. All these are of the sons of Benjamin.

CHAPTER 9

1 So all Israel were reckoned by genealogies; and, behold, they were written in the book of the kings of Israel and Judah, who were carried away to Babylon for their transgression.
2 Now the first inhabitants that dwelt in their possessions in their cities were, the Israelites, the priests, Levites, and the Nethinims.
3 And in Jerusalem dwelt of the children of Judah, and of the children of Benjamin, and of the children of Ephraim, and Manasseh;
4 Uthai the son of Ammihud, the son of Omri, the son of Imri, the son of Bani, of the children of Pharez the son of Judah.
5 And of the Shilonites; Asaiah the firstborn, and his sons.
6 And of the sons of Zerah; Jeuel, and their brethren, six hundred and ninety.
7 And of the sons of Benjamin; Sallu the son of Meshullam, the son of Hodaviah, the son of Hasenuah,
8 And Ibneiah the son of Jeroham, and Elah the son of Uzzi, the son of Michri, and Meshullam the son of Shephathiah, the son of Reuel, the son of Ibnijah;
9 And their brethren, according to their generations, nine hundred and fifty and six. All these men were chief of the fathers in the house of their fathers.
10 And of the priests; Jedaiah, and Jehoiarib, and Jachin,
11 And Azariah the son of Hilkiah, the son of Meshullam, the son of Zadok, the son of Meraioth, the son of Ahitub, the ruler of the house of God;
12 And Adaiah the son of Jeroham, the son of Pashur, the son of Malchijah, and Maasiai the son of Adiel, the son of Jahzerah, the son of Meshullam, the son of Meshillemith, the son of Immer;
13 And their brethren, heads of the house of their fathers, a thousand and seven hundred and threescore; very able men for the work of the service of the house of God.
14 And of the Levites; Shemaiah the son of Hasshub, the son of Azrikam, the son of Hashabiah, of the sons of Merari;
15 And Bakbakkar, Heresh, and Galal, and Mattaniah the son of Micah, the son of Zichri, the son of Asaph;
16 And Obadiah the son of Shemaiah, the son of Galal, the son of Jeduthun, and Berechiah the son of Asa, the son of Elkanah, that dwelt in the villages of the Netophathites.
17 And the porters were, Shallum, and Akkub, and Talmon, and Ahiman, and their brethren: Shallum was the chief;
18 Who hitherto waited in the king's gate eastward: they were porters in the companies of the children of Levi.
19 And Shallum the son of Kore, the son of Ebiasaph, the son of Korah, and his brethren, of the house of his father, the Korahites, were over the work of the service, keepers of the gates of the tabernacle: and their fathers, being over the host of the LORD, were keepers of the entry.
20 And Phinehas the son of Eleazar was the ruler over them in time past, and the LORD was with him.
21 And Zechariah the son of Meshelemiah was porter of the door of the tabernacle of the congregation.
22 All these which were chosen to be porters in the gates were two hundred and twelve. These were reckoned by their genealogy in their villages, whom David and Samuel the seer did ordain in their set office.
23 So they and their children had the oversight of the gates of the house of the LORD, namely, the house of the tabernacle, by wards.
24 In four quarters were the porters, toward the east, west, north, and south.
25 And their brethren, who were in their villages, were to come after seven days from time to time with them.
26 For these Levites, the four chief porters, were in their set office, and were over the chambers and treasuries of the house of God.
27 And they lodged round about the house of God, because the charge was upon them, and the opening thereof every morning pertained to them.
28 And certain of them had the charge of the ministering vessels, that they should bring them in and out by tale.
29 Some of them also were appointed to oversee the vessels, and all the instruments of the sanctuary, and the fine flour, and the wine, and the oil, and the frankincense, and the spices.
30 And some of the sons of the priests made the ointment of the spices.
31 And Mattithiah, one of the Levites, who was the firstborn of Shallum the Korahite, had the set office over the things that were made in the pans.
32 And other of their brethren, of the sons of the Kohathites, were over the shewbread, to prepare it every sabbath.
33 And these are the singers, chief of the fathers of the Levites, who remaining in the chambers were free: for they were employed in that work day and night.
34 These chief fathers of the Levites were chief throughout their generations; these dwelt at Jerusalem.
35 And in Gibeon dwelt the father of Gibeon, Jehiel, whose wife's name was Maachah:
36 And his firstborn son Abdon, then Zur, and Kish, and Baal, and Ner, and Nadab,
37 And Gedor, and Ahio, and Zechariah, and Mikloth.
38 And Mikloth begat Shimeam. And they also dwelt with their brethren at Jerusalem, over against their brethren.
39 And Ner begat Kish; and Kish begat Saul; and Saul begat Jonathan, and Malchi-shua, and Abinadab, and Esh-baal.
40 And the son of Jonathan was Merib-baal: and Merib-baal begat Micah.
41 And the sons of Micah were, Pithon, and Melech, and Tahrea, and Ahaz.
42 And Ahaz begat Jarah; and Jarah begat Alemeth, and Azmaveth, and Zimri; and Zimri begat Moza;
43 And Moza begat Binea; and Rephaiah his son, Eleasah his son, Azel his son.
44 And Azel had six sons, whose names are these, Azrikam, Bocheru, and Ishmael, and Sheariah, and Obadiah, and Hanan: these were the sons of Azel.

CHAPTER 10

1 Now the Philistines fought against Israel; and the men of Israel fled from before the Philistines, and fell down slain in mount Gilboa.
2 And the Philistines followed hard after Saul, and after his sons; and the Philistines slew Jonathan, and Abinadab, and Malchi-shua, the sons of Saul.
3 And the battle went sore against Saul, and the archers hit him, and he was wounded of the archers.

4 Then said Saul to his armourbearer, Draw your sword, and thrust me through therewith; lest these uncircumcised come and abuse me. But his armourbearer would not; for he was sore afraid. So Saul took a sword, and fell upon it.
5 And when his armourbearer saw that Saul was dead, he fell likewise on the sword, and died.
6 So Saul died, and his three sons and his **entire** house died together.
7 And when all the men of Israel that *were* in the valley saw that they fled, and that Saul and his sons were dead, then they forsook their cities, and fled: and the Philistines came and dwelt in them.
8 And it came to pass on the morrow, when the Philistines came to strip the slain, that they found Saul and his sons fallen in mount Gilboa.
9 And when they had stripped him, they took his head, and his armour, and sent into the land of the Philistines round about, to carry tidings unto their idols, and to the people.
10 And they put his armour in the house of their gods, and fastened his head in the temple of Dagon.
11 And when all Jabesh-gilead heard all that the Philistines had done to Saul,
12 They arose, all the valiant men, and took away the body of Saul, and the bodies of his sons, and brought them to Jabesh, and buried their bones under the oak in Jabesh, and fasted seven days.
13 ¶ So Saul died for his transgression which he committed against the LORD, *even* against the word of the LORD, which he kept not, and also for asking *counsel* of *one that had* a familiar spirit, to enquire *of it*;
14 And enquired not of the LORD: therefore he slew him, and turned the kingdom unto David the son of Jesse.

CHAPTER 11

1 Then all Israel gathered themselves to David unto Hebron, saying, Behold, we *are* your bone and your flesh.
2 And moreover in time past, even when Saul was king, you were he that leddest out and broughtest in Israel: and the LORD your God said unto you, you will feed my people Israel, and you will be ruler over my people Israel.
3 Therefore came all the elders of Israel to the king to Hebron; and David made a covenant with them in Hebron before the LORD; and they anointed David king over Israel, according to the word of the LORD by Samuel.
4 And David and all Israel went to Jerusalem, which *is* Jebus; where the Jebusites *were*, the inhabitants of the land.
5 And the inhabitants of Jebus said to David, you will not come hither. Nevertheless David took the castle of Zion, which *is* the city of David.
6 And David said, whosoever smiteth the Jebusites first will be chief and captain. So Joab the son of Zeruiah went first up, and was chief.
7 And David dwelt in the castle; therefore they called it the city of David.
8 And he built the city round about, even from Millo round about: and Joab repaired the rest of the city.
9 So David waxed greater and greater: for the LORD of hosts *was* with him.
10 These also *are* the chief of the mighty men whom David had, who strengthened themselves with him in his kingdom, *and* with all Israel, to make him king, according to the word of the LORD concerning Israel.
11 And this *is* the number of the mighty men whom David had; Jashobeam, an Hachmonite, the chief of the captains: he lifted up his spear against three hundred slain *by him* at one time.
12 And after him *was* Eleazar the son of Dodo, the Ahohite, who *was one* of the three mighties.
13 He was with David at Pas-dammim, and there the Philistines were gathered together to battle, where was a parcel of ground full of barley; and the people fled from before the Philistines.
14 And they set themselves in the midst of *that* parcel, and delivered it, and slew the Philistines; and the LORD saved them by a great deliverance.
15 Now three of the thirty captains went down to the rock to David, into the cave of Adullam; and the host of the Philistines encamped in the valley of Rephaim.
16 And David *was* then in the hold, and the Philistines' garrison *was* then at Beth-lehem.
17 And David longed, and said, Oh that one would give me drink of the water of the well of Beth-lehem, that *is* at the gate!
18 And the three brake through the host of the Philistines, and drew water out of the well of Beth-lehem, that *was* by the gate, and took *it*, and brought *it* to David: but David would not drink *of* it, but poured it out to the LORD,
19 And said, My God forbid it me, that I should do this thing: will I drink the blood of these men that have put their lives in jeopardy? for with *the jeopardy of* their lives they brought it. Therefore he would not drink it. These things did these three mightiest.
20 And Abishai the brother of Joab, he was chief of the three: for lifting up his spear against three hundred, he slew *them*, and had a name among the three.
21 Of the three, he was more honorable than the two; for he was their captain: howbeit he attained not to the *first* three.
22 Benaiah the son of Jehoiada, the son of a valiant man of Kabzeel, who had done many acts; he slew two lionlike men of Moab: also he went down and slew a lion in a pit in a snowy day.
23 And he slew an Egyptian, a man of *great* stature, five cubits high; and in the Egyptian's hand *was* a spear like a weaver's beam; and he went down to him with a staff, and plucked the spear out of the Egyptian's hand, and slew him with his own spear.
24 These *things* did Benaiah the son of Jehoiada, and had the name among the three mighties.
25 Behold, he was honourable among the thirty, but attained not to the *first* three: and David set him over his guard.
26 Also the valiant men of the armies *were*, Asahel the brother of Joab, Elhanan the son of Dodo of Beth-lehem,
27 Shammoth the Harorite, Helez the Pelonite,
28 Ira the son of Ikkesh the Tekoite, Abiezer the Antothite,
29 Sibbecai the Hushathite, Ilai the Ahohite,
30 Maharai the Netophathite, Heled the son of Baanah the Netophathite,
31 Ithai the son of Ribai of Gibeah, *that pertained* to the children of Benjamin, Benaiah the Pirathonite,
32 Hurai of the brooks of Gaash, Abiel the Arbathite,
33 Azmaveth the Baharumite, Eliahba the Shaalbonite,
34 The sons of Hashem the Gizonite, Jonathan the son of Shage the Hararite,
35 Ahiam the son of Sacar the Hararite, Eliphal the son of Ur,
36 Hepher the Mecherathite, Ahijah the Pelonite,
37 Hezro the Carmelite, Naarai the son of Ezbai,
38 Joel the brother of Nathan, Mibhar the son of Haggeri,

39 Zelek the Ammonite, Naharai the Berothite, the armourbearer of Joab the son of Zeruiah,
40 Ira the Ithrite, Gareb the Ithrite,
41 Uriah the Hittite, Zabad the son of Ahlai,
42 Adina the son of Shiza the Reubenite, a captain of the Reubenites, and thirty with him,
43 Hanan the son of Maachah, and Joshaphat the Mithnite,
44 Uzzia the Ashterathite, Shama and Jehiel the sons of Hothan the Aroerite,
45 Jediael the son of Shimri, and Joha his brother, the Tizite,
46 Eliel the Mahavite, and Jeribai, and Joshaviah, the sons of Elnaam, and Ithmah the Moabite,
47 Eliel, and Obed, and Jasiel the Mesobaite.

CHAPTER 12

1 Now these *are* they that came to David to Ziklag, while he yet kept himself close because of Saul the son of Kish: and they *were* among the mighty men, helpers of the war.
2 *They were* armed with bows, and could use both the right hand and the left in *hurling* stones and *shooting* arrows out of a bow, *even* of Saul's brethren of Benjamin.
3 The chief *was* Ahiezer, then Joash, the sons of Shemaah the Gibeathite; and Jeziel, and Pelet, the sons of Azmaveth; and Berachah, and Jehu the Antothite,
4 And Ismaiah the Gibeonite, a mighty man among the thirty, and over the thirty; and Jeremiah, and Jahaziel, and Johanan, and Josabad the Gederathite,
5 Eluzai, and Jerimoth, and Bealiah, and Shemariah, and Shephatiah the Haruphite,
6 Elkanah, and Jesiah, and Azareel, and Joezer, and Jashobeam, the Korhites,
7 And Joelah, and Zebadiah, the sons of Jeroham of Gedor.
8 And of the Gadites there separated themselves unto David into the hold to the wilderness men of might, *and* men of war *fit* for the battle, that could handle shield and buckler, whose faces *were like* the faces of lions, and *were* as swift as the roes upon the mountains;
9 Ezer the first, Obadiah the second, Eliab the third,
10 Mishmannah the fourth, Jeremiah the fifth,
11 Attai the sixth, Eliel the seventh,
12 Johanan the eighth, Elzabad the ninth,
13 Jeremiah the tenth, Machbanai the eleventh.
14 These *were* of the sons of Gad, captains of the host: one of the least *was* over an hundred and the greatest over a thousand.
15 These *are* they that went over Jordan in the first month, when it had overflown all his banks; and they put to flight all *them* of the valleys, *both* toward the east, and toward the west.
16 And there came of the children of Benjamin and Judah to the hold unto David.
17 And David went out to meet them, and answered and said unto them, If you be come peaceably unto me to help me, mine heart will be knit unto you: but if you *be come* to betray me to mine enemies, seeing *there is* no wrong in mine hands, the God of our fathers look *thereon*, and rebuke *it*.
18 Then the spirit came upon Amasai, *who was* chief of the captains, *and he said*, your *are we*, David, and on your side, you son of Jesse: peace, peace *be* unto you, and peace *be* to your helpers; for your God helpeth you. Then David received them, and made them captains of the band.
19 And there fell *some* of Manasseh to David, when he came with the Philistines against Saul to battle: but they helped them not: for the lords of the Philistines upon advisement sent him away, saying, He will fall to his master Saul to *the jeopardy of* our heads.
20 As he went to Ziklag, there fell to him of Manasseh, Adnah, and Jozabad, and Jediael, and Michael, and Jozabad, and Elihu, and Zilthai, captains of the thousands that *were* of Manasseh.
21 And they helped David against the band *of the rovers*: for they *were* all mighty men of valour, and were captains in the host.
22 For at *that* time day by day there came to David to help him, until *it was* a great host, like the host of God.
23 And these *are* the numbers of the bands *that were* ready armed to the war, *and* came to David to Hebron, to turn the kingdom of Saul to him, according to the word of the LORD.
24 The children of Judah that bare shield and spear *were* six thousand and eight hundred, ready armed to the war.
25 Of the children of Simeon, mighty men of valour for the war, seven thousand and one hundred.
26 Of the children of Levi four thousand and six hundred.
27 And Jehoiada *was* the leader of the Aaronites, and with him *were* three thousand and seven hundred;
28 And Zadok, a young man mighty of valour, and of his father's house twenty and two captains.
29 And of the children of Benjamin, the kindred of Saul, three thousand: for hitherto the greatest part of them had kept the ward of the house of Saul.
30 And of the children of Ephraim twenty thousand and eight hundred, mighty men of valour, famous throughout the house of their fathers.
31 And of the half tribe of Manasseh eighteen thousand, which were expressed by name, to come and make David king.
32 And of the children of Issachar, *which were men* that had understanding of the times, to know what Israel ought to do; the heads of them *were* two hundred; and all their brethren *were* at their commandment.
33 Of Zebulun, such as went forth to battle, expert in war, with all instruments of war, fifty thousand, which could keep rank: *they were* not of double heart.
34 And of Naphtali a thousand captains, and with them with shield and spear thirty and seven thousand.
35 And of the Danites expert in war twenty and eight thousand and six hundred.
36 And of Asher, such as went forth to battle, expert in war, and forty thousand.
37 And on the other side of Jordan, of the Reubenites, and the Gadites, and of the half tribe of Manasseh, with all manner of instruments of war for the battle, an hundred and twenty thousand.
38 All these men of war, that could keep rank, came with a perfect heart to Hebron, to make David king over all Israel: and all the rest also of Israel *were* of one heart to make David king.
39 And there they were with David three days, eating and drinking: for their brethren had prepared for them.
40 Moreover they that were nigh them, *even* unto Issachar and Zebulun and Naphtali, brought bread on asses, and on camels, and on mules, and on oxen, *and* meat, meal, cakes of figs, and bunches of raisins, and wine, and oil, and oxen, and sheep abundantly: for *there was* joy in Israel.

CHAPTER 13

1 And David consulted with the captains of thousands and hundreds, *and* with every leader.
2 And David said unto all the congregation of Israel, If *it seem* good unto you, and *that it be* of the LORD our God, let us send abroad

unto our brethren every where, *that are* left in all the land of Israel, and with them *also* to the priests and Levites *which are* in their cities *and* suburbs, that they may gather themselves unto us:

3 And let us bring again the ark of our God to us: for we enquired not at it in the days of Saul.

4 And all the congregation said that they would do so: for the thing was right in the eyes of all the people.

5 So David gathered all Israel together, from Shihor of Egypt even unto the entering of Hemath, to bring the ark of God from Kirjath-jearim.

6 And David went up, and all Israel, to Baalah, *that is*, to Kirjath-jearim, which *belonged* to Judah, to bring up **from there** the ark of God the LORD, that dwelleth *between* the cherubims, whose name is called *on it*.

7 And they carried the ark of God in a new cart out of the house of Abinadab: and Uzza and Ahio **drove** the cart.

8 And David and all Israel played before God with all *their* might, and with singing, and with harps, and with psalteries, and with timbrels, and with cymbals, and with trumpets.

9 And when they came unto the threshingfloor of Chidon, Uzza put forth his hand to hold the ark; for the oxen stumbled.

10 And the anger of the LORD was kindled against Uzza, and he smote him, because he put his hand to the ark: and there he died before God.

11 And David was displeased, because the LORD had made a breach upon Uzza: wherefore that place is called Perez-uzza to this day.

12 And David was afraid of God that day, saying, how will I bring the ark of God *home* to me?

13 So David brought not the ark *home* to himself to the city of David, but carried it aside into the house of Obed-edom the Gittite.

14 And the ark of God remained with the family of Obed-edom in his house three months. And the LORD blessed the house of Obed-edom, and all that he had.

CHAPTER 14

1 Now Hiram king of Tyre sent messengers to David, and timber of cedars, with masons and carpenters, to build him a house.

2 And David perceived that the LORD had confirmed him king over Israel, for his kingdom was lifted up on high, because of his people Israel.

3 And David took more wives at Jerusalem: and David begat more sons and daughters.

4 Now these *are* the names of *his* children which he had in Jerusalem; Shammua, and Shobab, Nathan, and Solomon,

5 And Ibhar, and Elishua, and Elpalet,

6 And Nogah, and Nepheg, and Japhia,

7 And Elishama, and Beeliada, and Eliphalet.

8 And when the Philistines heard that David was anointed king over all Israel, all the Philistines went up to seek David. And David heard *of it*, and went out against them.

9 And the Philistines came and spread themselves in the valley of Rephaim.

10 And David enquired of God, saying, will I go up against the Philistines? and will you deliver them into mine hand? And the LORD said unto him, Go up; for I will deliver them into your hand.

11 So they came up to Baal-perazim; and David smote them there. Then David said, God has broken in upon mine enemies by mine hand like the breaking forth of waters: therefore they called the name of that place Baal-perazim.

12 And when they had left their gods there, David gave a commandment, and they were burned with fire.

13 And the Philistines yet again spread themselves abroad in the valley.

14 Therefore David enquired again of God; and God said unto him, Go not up after them; turn away from them, and come upon them over against the mulberry trees.

15 And it will be, when you will hear a sound of going in the tops of the mulberry trees, *that* then you will go out to battle: for God is gone forth before you to smite the host of the Philistines.

16 David therefore did as God commanded him: and they smote the host of the Philistines from Gibeon even to Gazer.

17 And the fame of David went out into all lands; and the LORD brought the fear of him upon all nations.

CHAPTER 15

1 And *David* made him houses in the city of David, and prepared a place for the ark of God, and pitched for it a tent.

2 Then David said none ought to carry the ark of God but the Levites: for them has the LORD chosen to carry the ark of God, and to minister unto him for ever.

3 And David gathered all Israel together to Jerusalem, to bring up the ark of the LORD unto his place, which he had prepared for it.

4 And David assembled the children of Aaron, and the Levites:

5 Of the sons of Kohath; Uriel the chief, and his brethren an hundred and twenty:

6 Of the sons of Merari; Asaiah the chief, and his brethren two hundred and twenty:

7 Of the sons of Gershom; Joel the chief, and his brethren an hundred and thirty:

8 Of the sons of Elizaphan; Shemaiah the chief, and his brethren two hundred:

9 Of the sons of Hebron; Eliel the chief, and his brethren fourscore:

10 Of the sons of Uzziel; Amminadab the chief, and his brethren an hundred and twelve.

11 And David called for Zadok and Abiathar the priests and for the Levites, for Uriel, Asaiah, and Joel, Shemaiah, and Eliel, and Amminadab,

12 And said unto them, you *are* the chief of the fathers of the Levites: sanctify yourselves, *both* you and your brethren, that you may bring up the ark of the LORD God of Israel unto t*he place that* I have prepared for it.

13 For because you *did it* not at the first, the LORD our God made a breach upon us, for that we sought him not after the due order.

14 So the priests and the Levites sanctified themselves to bring up the ark of the LORD God of Israel.

15 And the children of the Levites bare the ark of God upon their shoulders with the staves thereon, as Moses commanded according to the word of the LORD.

16 And David spoke to the chief of the Levites to appoint their brethren *to be* the singers with instruments of musick, psalteries and harps and cymbals, sounding, by lifting up the voice with joy.

17 So the Levites appointed Heman the son of Joel; and of his brethren, Asaph the son of Berechiah; and of the sons of Merari their brethren, Ethan the son of Kushaiah;

18 And with them their brethren of the second *degree*, Zechariah, Ben, and Jaaziel, and Shemiramoth, and Jehiel, and Unni, Eliab, and Benaiah, and Maaseiah, and Mattithiah, and Elipheleh, and Mikneiah, and Obed-edom, and Jeiel, the porters.

19 So the singers, Heman, Asaph, and Ethan, *were appointed* to sound with cymbals of brass;

20 And Zechariah, and Aziel, and Shemiramoth, and Jehiel, and Unni, and Eliab, and Maaseiah, and Benaiah, with psalteries on Alamoth;
21 And Mattithiah, and Elipheleh, and Mikneiah, and Obed-edom, and Jeiel, and Azaziah, with harps on the Sheminith to excel.
22 And Chenaniah, chief of the Levites, *was* for song: he instructed about the song, because he *was* skilful.
23 And Berechiah and Elkanah *were* doorkeepers for the ark.
24 And Shebaniah, and Jehoshaphat, and Nethaneel, and Amasai, and Zechariah, and Benaiah, and Eliezer, the priests, did blow with the trumpets before the ark of God: and Obed-edom and Jehiah *were* doorkeepers for the ark.
25 So David, and the elders of Israel, and the captains over thousands, went to bring up the ark of the covenant of the LORD out of the house of Obed-edom with joy.
26 And it came to pass, when God helped the Levites that bare the ark of the covenant of the LORD, that they offered seven bullocks and seven rams.
27 And David *was* clothed with a robe of fine linen, and all the Levites that bare the ark, and the singers, and Chenaniah the master of the song with the singers: David also *had* upon him an ephod of linen.
28 Thus all Israel brought up the ark of the covenant of the LORD with shouting, and with sound of the cornet, and with trumpets, and with cymbals, making a noise with psalteries and harps.
29 And it came to pass, *as* the ark of the covenant of the LORD came to the city of David, that Michal the daughter of Saul looking out at a window saw King David dancing and playing: and she despised him in her heart.

CHAPTER 16

1 So they brought the ark of God, and set it in the midst of the tent that David had pitched for it: and they offered burnt sacrifices and peace offerings before God.
2 And when David had made an end of offering the burnt offerings and the peace offerings, he blessed the people in the name of the LORD.
3 And he dealt to every one of Israel, both man and woman, to every one a loaf of bread, and a good piece of flesh, and a flagon *of wine*.
4 And he appointed *certain* of the Levites to minister before the ark of the LORD, and to record, and to thank and praise the LORD God of Israel:
5 Asaph the chief, and next to him Zechariah, Jeiel, and Shemiramoth, and Jehiel, and Mattithiah, and Eliab, and Benaiah, and Obed-edom: and Jeiel with psalteries and with harps; but Asaph made a sound with cymbals;
6 Benaiah also and Jahaziel the priests with trumpets continually before the ark of the covenant of God.
7 Then on that day David delivered first *this psalm* to thank the LORD into the hand of Asaph and his brethren.
8 Give thanks unto the LORD, call upon his name, make known his deeds among the people.
9 Sing unto him, sing psalms unto him, talk you of all his wondrous works.
10 Glory you in his holy name: let the heart of them rejoice that seek the LORD.
11 Seek the LORD and his strength, seek his face continually.
12 Remember his marvellous works that he has done, his wonders, and the judgments of his mouth;
13 O you seed of Israel his servant, you children of Jacob, his chosen ones.
14 He *is* the LORD our God; his judgments *are* in all the earth.
15 Be you mindful always of his covenant; the word *which* he commanded to a thousand generations;
16 *Even of the covenant* which he made with Abraham, and of his oath unto Isaac;
17 And has confirmed the same to Jacob for a law, *and* to Israel *for* an everlasting covenant,
18 Saying, unto you will I give the land of Canaan, the lot of your inheritance;
19 When you were but few, even a few, and strangers in it.
20 And *when* they went from nation to nation and from *one* kingdom to another people;
21 He suffered no man to do them wrong: yea, he reproved kings for their sakes,
22 *Saying*, Touch not mine anointed, and do my prophets no harm.
23 Sing unto the LORD, all the earth; show forth from day to day his salvation.
24 Declare his glory among the heathen; his marvellous works among all nations.
25 For great *is* the LORD, and greatly to be praised: he also *is* to be feared above all gods.
26 For all the gods of the people *are* idols: but the LORD made the heavens.
27 Glory and honour *are* in his presence; strength and gladness *are* in his place.
28 Give unto the LORD, you kindreds of the people, give unto the LORD glory and strength.
29 Give unto the LORD the glory *due* unto his name: bring an offering, and come before him: worship the LORD in the beauty of holiness.
30 Fear before him, all the earth: the world also will be stable, that it be not moved.
31 Let the heavens be glad, and let the earth rejoice: and let *men* say among the nations, The LORD reigneth.
32 Let the sea roar, and the fulness thereof: let the fields rejoice, and all that *is* therein.
33 Then will the trees of the wood sing out at the presence of the LORD, because he cometh to judge the earth.
34 O give thanks unto the LORD; for *he is* good; for his mercy *endureth* for ever.
35 And say you, save us, O God of our salvation, and gather us together, and deliver us from the heathen, that we may give thanks to your holy name, *and* glory in your praise.
36 Blessed *be* the LORD God of Israel for ever and ever. And all the people said, Amen, and praised the LORD.
37 So he left there before the ark of the covenant of the LORD Asaph and his brethren, to minister before the ark continually, as every day's work required:
38 And Obed-edom with their brethren, threescore and eight; Obed-edom also the son of Jeduthun and Hosah *to be* porters:
39 And Zadok the priest, and his brethren the priests, before the tabernacle of the LORD in the high place that *was* at Gibeon,
40 To offer burnt offerings unto the LORD upon the altar of the burnt offering continually morning and evening, and *to do* according to all that is written in the law of the LORD, which he commanded Israel;

41 And with them Heman and Jeduthun, and the rest that were chosen, who were expressed by name, to give thanks to the LORD, because his mercy *endureth* for ever;
42 And with them Heman and Jeduthun with trumpets and cymbals for those that should make a sound, and with musical instruments of God. And the sons of Jeduthun *were* porters.
43 And all the people departed every man to his house: and David returned to bless his house.

CHAPTER 17

1 Now it came to pass, as David sat in his house, that David said to Nathan the prophet, Lo, I dwell in an house of cedars, but the ark of the covenant of the LORD *remaineth* under curtains.
2 Then Nathan said unto David, Do all that *is* in your heart; for God *is* with you.
3 And it came to pass the same night, that the word of God came to Nathan, saying,
4 Go and tell David my servant, Thus said the LORD, you will not build me a house to dwell in:
5 For I have not dwelt in an house since the day that I brought up Israel unto this day; but have gone from tent to tent, and from *one* tabernacle *to another*.
6 Wheresoever I have walked with all Israel, spoke I a word to any of the judges of Israel, whom I commanded to feed my people, saying, why have you not built me an house of cedars?
7 Now therefore thus will you say unto my servant David, Thus said the LORD of hosts, I took you from the sheepcote, *even* from following the sheep, that you shouldest be ruler over my people Israel:
8 And I have been with you whithersoever you have walked, and have cut off all your enemies from before you, and have made you a name like the name of the great men that *are* in the earth.
9 Also I will ordain a place for my people Israel, and will plant them, and they will dwell in their place, and will be moved no more; neither will the children of wickedness waste them any more, as at the beginning,
10 And since the time that I commanded judges *to be* over my people Israel. Moreover I will subdue all your enemies. Furthermore I tell you that the LORD will build you an house.
11 And it will come to pass, when your days be expired that you must go *to be* with your fathers, that I will raise up your seed after you, which will be of your sons; and I will establish his kingdom.
12 He will build me an house, and I will stablish his throne for ever.
13 I will be his father, and he will be my son: and I will not take my mercy away from him, as I took *it* from *him* that was before you:
14 But I will settle him in mine house and in my kingdom for ever: and his throne will be established for evermore.
15 According to all these words, and according to all this vision, so did Nathan speak unto David.
16 And David the king came and sat before the LORD, and said, who *am* I, O LORD God, and what *is* mine house, that you have brought me hitherto?
17 And *yet* this was a small thing in your eyes, O God; for you have *also* spoken of your servant's house for a great while to come, and have regarded me according to the estate of a man of high degree, O LORD God.
18 What can David *speak* more to you for the honour of your servant? for you knowest your servant.
19 O LORD, for your servant's sake, and according to your own heart, have you done all this greatness, in making known all *these* great things.
20 O LORD, *there is* none like you, neither *is there any* God beside you, according to all that we have heard with our ears.
21 And what one nation in the earth *is* like your people Israel, whom God went to redeem *to be* his own people, to make you a name of greatness and terribleness, by driving out nations from before your people, whom you have redeemed out of Egypt?
22 For your people Israel did you make your own people for ever; and you, LORD, becamest their God.
23 Therefore now, LORD, let the thing that you have spoken concerning your servant and concerning his house be established for ever, and do as you have said.
24 Let it even be established, that your name may be magnified for ever, saying, The LORD of hosts *is* the God of Israel, *even a* God to Israel: and *let* the house of David your servant *be* established before you.
25 For you, O my God, have told your servant that you will build him an house: therefore your servant has found *in his heart* to pray before you.
26 And now, LORD, you are God, and have promised this goodness unto your servant:
27 Now therefore let it please you to bless the house of your servant, that it may be before you for ever: for you blessest, O LORD, and *it will be* blessed for ever.

CHAPTER 18

1 Now after this it came to pass, that David smote the Philistines, and subdued them, and took Gath and her towns out of the hand of the Philistines.
2 And he **slaughtered** Moab; and the Moabites became David's servants, *and* brought gifts.
3 And David smote Hadarezer king of Zobah unto Hamath, as he went to stablish his dominion by the river Euphrates.
4 And David took from him a thousand chariots, and seven thousand horsemen, and twenty thousand footmen: David also houghed all the chariot *horses*, but reserved of them an hundred chariots.
5 And when the Syrians of Damascus came to help Hadarezer king of Zobah, David slew of the Syrians two and twenty thousand men.
6 Then David put *garrisons* in Syria-damascus; and the Syrians became David's servants, *and* brought gifts. Thus the LORD preserved David whithersoever he went.
7 And David took the shields of gold that were on the servants of Hadarezer, and brought them to Jerusalem.
8 Likewise from Tibhath, and from Chun, cities of Hadarezer, brought David very much brass, wherewith Solomon made the brasen sea, and the pillars, and the vessels of brass.
9 Now when Tou king of Hamath heard how David had smitten all the host of Hadarezer king of Zobah;
10 He sent Hadoram his son to king David, to enquire of his welfare, and to congratulate him, because he had fought against Hadarezer, and smitten him; (for Hadarezer had war with Tou;) and *with him* all manner of vessels of gold and silver and brass.
11 Them also king David dedicated unto the LORD, with the silver and the gold that he brought from all *these* nations; from Edom, and from Moab, and from the children of Ammon, and from the Philistines, and from Amalek.
12 Moreover Abishai the son of Zeruiah slew of the Edomites in the valley of salt eighteen thousand.
13 And he put garrisons in Edom; and all the Edomites became David's servants. Thus the LORD preserved David whithersoever he went.

14 So David reigned over all Israel, and executed judgment and justice among all his people.
15 And Joab the son of Zeruiah *was* over the host; and Jehoshaphat the son of Ahilud, recorder.
16 And Zadok the son of Ahitub, and Abimelech the son of Abiathar, *were* the priests; and Shavsha was scribe;
17 And Benaiah the son of Jehoiada *was* over the Cherethites and the Pelethites; and the sons of David *were* chief about the king.

CHAPTER 19

1 Now it came to pass after this, that Nahash the king of the children of Ammon died, and his son reigned in his stead.
2 And David said, I will show kindness unto Hanun the son of Nahash, because his father shewed kindness to me. And David sent messengers to comfort him concerning his father. So the servants of David came into the land of the children of Ammon to Hanun, to comfort him.
3 But the princes of the children of Ammon said to Hanun, Thinkest you that David does honour your father, that he has sent comforters unto you? Are not his servants come unto you for to search, and to overthrow, and to spy out the land?
4 Wherefore Hanun took David's servants, and shaved them, and cut off their garments in the midst hard by their buttocks, and sent them away.
5 Then there went *certain*, and told David how the men were served. And he sent to meet them: for the men were greatly ashamed. And the king said, Tarry at Jericho until your beards be grown, and *then* return.
6 And when the children of Ammon saw that they had made themselves odious to David, Hanun and the children of Ammon sent a thousand talents of silver to hire them chariots and horsemen out of Mesopotamia, and out of Syria-maachah, and out of Zobah.
7 So they hired thirty and two thousand chariots, and the king of Maachah and his people; who came and pitched before Medeba. And the children of Ammon gathered themselves together from their cities, and came to battle.
8 And when David heard *of it*, he sent Joab, and all the host of the mighty men.
9 And the children of Ammon came out, and put the battle in array before the gate of the city: and the kings that were come *were* by themselves in the field.
10 Now when Joab saw that the battle was set against him before and behind, he chose out of all the choice of Israel, and put *them* in array against the Syrians.
11 And the rest of the people he delivered unto the hand of Abishai his brother, and they set *themselves* in array against the children of Ammon.
12 And he said, If the Syrians be too strong for me, then you will help me: but if the children of Ammon be too strong for you, then I will help you.
13 Be of good courage, and let us behave ourselves valiantly for our people, and for the cities of our God: and let the LORD do *that which is* good in his sight.
14 So Joab and the people that *were* with him drew nigh before the Syrians unto the battle; and they fled before him.
15 And when the children of Ammon saw that the Syrians were fled, they likewise fled before Abishai his brother, and entered into the city. Then Joab came to Jerusalem.
16 And when the Syrians saw that they were put to the worse before Israel, they sent messengers, and drew forth the Syrians that *were* beyond the river: and Shophach the captain of the host of Hadarezer *went* before them.
17 And it was told David; and he gathered all Israel, and passed over Jordan, and came upon them, and set *the battle* in array against them. So when David had put the battle in array against the Syrians, they fought with him.
18 But the Syrians fled before Israel; and David slew of the Syrians seven thousand *men which fought in* chariots, and forty thousand footmen, and killed Shophach the captain of the host.
19 And when the servants of Hadarezer saw that they were put to the worse before Israel, they made peace with David, and became his servants: neither would the Syrians help the children of Ammon any more.

CHAPTER 20

1 And it came to pass, that after the year was expired, at the time that kings go out *to battle*, Joab led forth the power of the army, and wasted the country of the children of Ammon, and came and besieged Rabbah. But David tarried at Jerusalem. And Joab smote Rabbah, and destroyed it.
2 And David took the crown of their king from off his head, and found it to weigh a talent of gold, and *there were* precious stones in it; and it was set upon David's head: and he brought also exceeding much spoil out of the city.
3 And he brought out the people that *were* in it, and cut *them* with saws, and with harrows of iron, and with axes. Even so dealt David with all the cities of the children of Ammon. And David and all the people returned to Jerusalem.
4 And it came to pass after this, that there arose war at Gezer with the Philistines; at which time Sibbechai the Hushathite slew Sippai, *that was* of the children of the giant: and they were subdued.
5 And there was war again with the Philistines; and Elhanan the son of Jair slew Lahmi the brother of Goliath the Gittite, whose spear staff *was* like a weaver's beam.
6 And yet again there was war at Gath, where was a man of *great* stature, whose fingers and toes *were* four and twenty, six *on each hand*, and six *on each foot*: and he also was the son of the giant.
7 But when he defied Israel, Jonathan the son of Shimea David's brother slew him.
8 These were born unto the giant in Gath; and they fell by the hand of David, and by the hand of his servants.

CHAPTER 21

1 And Satan stood up against Israel, and provoked David to number Israel.
2 And David said to Joab and to the rulers of the people, go, number Israel from Beer-sheba even to Dan; and bring the number of them to me, that I may know *it*.
3 And Joab answered, The LORD makes his people an hundred times so many more as they *be*: but, my lord the king, *are* they not all my lord's servants? Why then does my lord require this thing? Why will he be a cause of trespass to Israel?
4 Nevertheless the king's word prevailed against Joab. Wherefore Joab departed, and went throughout all Israel, and came to Jerusalem.
5 And Joab gave the sum of the number of the people unto David. And all *they of* Israel were a thousand thousand and an hundred thousand men that drew sword: and Judah *was* four hundred threescore and ten thousand men that drew sword.
6 But Levi and Benjamin counted he not among them: for the king's word was abominable to Joab.

# First Chronicles

7 And God was displeased with this thing; therefore he smote Israel.
8 And David said unto God, I have sinned greatly, because I have done this thing: but now, I beseech you; do away the iniquity of your servant; for I have done very foolishly.
9 And the LORD spoke unto Gad, David's seer, saying,
10 Go and tell David, saying, thus said the LORD, I offer you three *things*: choose you one of them, that I may do *it* unto you.
11 So Gad came to David, and said unto him, thus said the LORD, Choose you.
12 Either three years' famine; or three months to be destroyed before your foes, while that the sword of your enemies overtaketh you; or else three days the sword of the LORD, even the pestilence, in the land, and the angel of the LORD destroying throughout all the coasts of Israel. Now therefore advise yourself what word I will bring again to him that sent me.
13 And David said unto Gad, I am in a great strait: let me fall now into the hand of the LORD; for very great *are* his mercies: but let me not fall into the hand of man.
14 So the LORD sent pestilence upon Israel: and there fell of Israel seventy thousand men.
15 And God sent an angel unto Jerusalem to destroy it: and as he was destroying, the LORD beheld, and he repented him of the evil, and said to the angel that destroyed, It is enough, stay now your hand. And the angel of the LORD stood by the threshingfloor of Ornan the Jebusite.
16 And David lifted up his eyes, and saw the angel of the LORD stand between the earth and the heaven, having a drawn sword in his hand stretched out over Jerusalem. Then David and the elders *of Israel, who were* clothed in sackcloth, fell upon their faces.
17 And David said unto God, *Is it* not I *that* commanded the people to be numbered? Even I it is that have sinned and done evil indeed; but *as for* these sheep, what have they done? let your hand, I pray you, O LORD my God, be on me, and on my father's house; but not on your people, that they should be plagued.
18 Then the angel of the LORD commanded Gad to say to David, that David should go up, and set up an altar unto the LORD in the threshingfloor of Ornan the Jebusite.
19 And David went up at the saying of Gad, which he spoke in the name of the LORD.
20 And Ornan turned back, and saw the angel; and his four sons with him hid themselves. Now Ornan was threshing wheat.
21 And as David came to Ornan, Ornan looked and saw David, and went out of the threshingfloor, and bowed himself to David with *his* face to the ground.
22 Then David said to Ornan, Grant me the place of *this* threshingfloor, that I may build an altar therein unto the LORD: you will grant it me for the full price: that the plague may be stayed from the people.
23 And Ornan said unto David, Take *it* to you, and let my lord the king do *that which is* good in his eyes: lo, I give you the oxen *also* for burnt offerings, and the threshing instruments for wood, and the wheat for the meat offering; I give it all.
24 And King David said to Ornan, Nay; but I will verily buy it for the full price: for I will not take *that* which *is* yours for the LORD, or offer burnt offerings without cost.
25 So David gave to Ornan for the place six hundred shekels of gold by weight.
26 And David built there an altar unto the LORD, and offered burnt offerings and peace offerings, and called upon the LORD; and he answered him from heaven by fire upon the altar of burnt offering.
27 And the LORD commanded the angel; and he put up his sword again into the sheath thereof.
28 At that time when David saw that the LORD had answered him in the threshingfloor of Ornan the Jebusite, then he sacrificed there.
29 For the tabernacle of the LORD, which Moses made in the wilderness, and the altar of the burnt offering, *were* at that season in the high place at Gibeon.
30 But David could not go before it to enquire of God: for he was afraid because of the sword of the angel of the LORD.

CHAPTER 22

1 Then David said, this *is* the house of the LORD God, and this *is* the altar of the burnt offering for Israel.
2 And David commanded to gather together the strangers that *were* in the land of Israel; and he set masons to hew wrought stones to build the house of God.
3 And David prepared iron in abundance for the nails for the doors of the gates, and for the joinings; and brass in abundance without weight;
4 Also cedar trees in abundance: for the Zidonians and they of Tyre brought much cedar wood to David.
5 And David said, Solomon my son *is* young and tender, and the house *that is* to be builded for the LORD *must be* exceeding magnifical, of fame and of glory throughout all countries: I will *therefore* now make preparation for it. So David prepared abundantly before his death.
6 Then he called for Solomon his son, and charged him to build an house for the LORD God of Israel.
7 And David said to Solomon, My son, as for me, it was in my mind to build a house unto the name of the LORD my God:
8 But the word of the LORD came to me, saying, you have shed blood abundantly, and have made great wars: you will not build a house unto my name, because you have shed much blood upon the earth in my sight.
9 Behold, a son will be born to you, who will be a man of rest; and I will give him rest from all his enemies round about: for his name will be Solomon and I will give peace and quietness unto Israel in his days.
10 He will build a house for my name; and he will be my son, and I *will be* his father; and I will establish the throne of his kingdom over Israel for ever.
11 Now, my son, **may** the LORD be with you; and prosper you, and build the house of the LORD your God, as he has said of you.
12 Only the LORD give you wisdom and understanding, and give you charge concerning Israel, that you may keep the law of the LORD your God.
13 Then will you prosper, if you takest heed to fulfil the statutes and judgments which the LORD charged Moses with concerning Israel: be strong, and of good courage; dread not, or be dismayed.
14 Now, behold, in my trouble I have prepared for the house of the LORD an hundred thousand talents of gold, and a thousand thousand talents of silver; and of brass and iron without weight; for it is in abundance: timber also and stone have I prepared; and you mayest add thereto.
15 Moreover *there are* workmen with you in abundance, hewers and workers of stone and timber, and all manner of cunning men for every manner of work.
16 Of the gold, the silver, and the brass, and the iron, *there is* no number. Arise *therefore*, and be doing, and the LORD be with you.

17 David also commanded all the princes of Israel to help Solomon his son, *saying*,
18 *Is* not the LORD your God with you? And has he *not* given you rest on every side? For he has given the inhabitants of the land into mine hand; and the land is subdued before the LORD, and before his people.
19 Now set your heart and your soul to seek the LORD your God; arise therefore, and build you the sanctuary of the LORD God, to bring the ark of the covenant of the LORD, and the holy vessels of God, into the house that is to be built to the name of the LORD.

CHAPTER 23

1 So when David was old and full of days, he made Solomon his son king over Israel.
2 And he gathered together all the princes of Israel, with the priests and the Levites.
3 Now the Levites were numbered from the age of thirty years and upward: and their number by their polls, man by man, was thirty and eight thousand.
4 Of which, twenty and four thousand *were* to set forward the work of the house of the LORD; and six thousand *were* officers and judges:
5 Moreover four thousand *were* porters; and four thousand praised the LORD with the instruments which I made, *said David*, to praise *therewith*.
6 And David divided them into courses among the sons of Levi, *namely*, Gershon, Kohath, and Merari.
7 Of the Gershonites *were*, Laadan, and Shimei.
8 The sons of Laadan; the chief *was* Jehiel, and Zetham, and Joel, three.
9 The sons of Shimei; Shelomith, and Haziel, and Haran, three. These *were* the chief of the fathers of Laadan.
10 And the sons of Shimei *were*, Jahath, Zina, and Jeush, and Beriah. These four *were* the sons of Shimei.
11 And Jahath was the chief and Zizah the second: but Jeush and Beriah had not many sons; therefore they were in one reckoning, according to *their* father's house.
12 The sons of Kohath; Amram, Izhar, Hebron, and Uzziel, four.
13 The sons of Amram; Aaron and Moses: and Aaron was separated, that he should sanctify the most holy things, he and his sons for ever, to burn incense before the LORD, to minister unto him, and to bless in his name for ever.
14 Now *concerning* Moses the man of God, his sons were named of the tribe of Levi.
15 The sons of Moses *were*, Gershom, and Eliezer.
16 Of the sons of Gershom, Shebuel *was* the chief.
17 And the sons of Eliezer *were*, Rehabiah the chief. And Eliezer had none other sons; but the sons of Rehabiah were very many.
18 Of the sons of Izhar; Shelomith the chief.
19 Of the sons of Hebron; Jeriah the first, Amariah the second, Jahaziel the third, and Jekameam the fourth.
20 Of the sons of Uzziel; Michah the first, and Jesiah the second.
21 The sons of Merari; Mahli, and Mushi. The sons of Mahli; Eleazar, and Kish.
22 And Eleazar died, and had no sons, but daughters: and their brethren the sons of Kish took them.
23 The sons of Mushi; Mahli, and Eder, and Jeremoth, three.
24 These *were* the sons of Levi after the house of their fathers; *even* the chief of the fathers, as they were counted by number of names by their polls, that did the work for the service of the house of the LORD, from the age of twenty years and upward.
25 For David said, The LORD God of Israel has given rest unto his people, that they may dwell in Jerusalem for ever:
26 And also unto the Levites; they will no *more* carry the tabernacle, or any vessels of it for the service thereof.
27 For by the last words of David the Levites *were* numbered from twenty years old and above:
28 Because their office *was* to wait on the sons of Aaron for the service of the house of the LORD, in the courts, and in the chambers, and in the purifying of all holy things, and the work of the service of the house of God;
29 Both for the shewbread, and for the fine flour for meat offering, and for the unleavened cakes, and for *that which is baked in* the pan, and for that which is fried, and for all manner of measure and size;
30 And to stand every morning to thank and praise the LORD, and likewise at even;
31 And to offer all burnt sacrifices unto the LORD in the sabbaths, in the new moons, and on the set feasts, by number, according to the order commanded unto them, continually before the LORD:
32 And that they should keep the charge of the tabernacle of the congregation, and the charge of the holy *place*, and the charge of the sons of Aaron their brethren, in the service of the house of the LORD.

CHAPTER 24

1 Now *these are* the divisions of the sons of Aaron. The sons of Aaron; Nadab, and Abihu, Eleazar, and Ithamar.
2 But Nadab and Abihu died before their father, and had no children: therefore Eleazar and Ithamar executed the priest's office.
3 And David distributed them, both Zadok of the sons of Eleazar, and Ahimelech of the sons of Ithamar, according to their offices in their service.
4 And there were more chief men found of the sons of Eleazar than of the sons of Ithamar; and *thus* were they divided. Among the sons of Eleazar *there were* sixteen chief men of the house of *their* fathers, and eight among the sons of Ithamar according to the house of their fathers.
5 Thus were they divided by lot, one sort with another; for the governors of the sanctuary, and governors *of the house* of God, were of the sons of Eleazar, and of the sons of Ithamar.
6 And Shemaiah the son of Nethaneel the scribe, *one* of the Levites, wrote them before the king, and the princes, and Zadok the priest, and Ahimelech the son of Abiathar, and *before* the chief of the fathers of the priests and Levites: one principal household being taken for Eleazar, and *one* taken for Ithamar.
7 Now the first lot came forth to Jehoiarib, the second to Jedaiah,
8 The third to Harim, the fourth to Seorim,
9 The fifth to Malchijah, the sixth to Mijamin,
10 The seventh to Hakkoz, the eighth to Abijah,
11 The ninth to Jeshua, the tenth to Shecaniah,
12 The eleventh to Eliashib, the twelfth to Jakim,
13 The thirteenth to Huppah, the fourteenth to Jeshebeab,
14 The fifteenth to Bilgah, the sixteenth to Immer,
15 The seventeenth to Hezir, the eighteenth to Aphses,
16 The nineteenth to Pethahiah, the twentieth to Jehezekel,
17 The one and twentieth to Jachin, the two and twentieth to Gamul,
18 The three and twentieth to Delaiah, the four and twentieth to Maaziah.

19 These *were* the orderings of them in their service to come into the house of the LORD, according to their manner, under Aaron their father, as the LORD God of Israel had commanded him.

20 And the rest of the sons of Levi *were* these: Of the sons of Amram; Shubael: of the sons of Shubael; Jehdeiah.

21 Concerning Rehabiah: of the sons of Rehabiah, the first *was* Isshiah.

22 Of the Izharites; Shelomoth: of the sons of Shelomoth; Jahath.

23 And the sons *of Hebron*; Jeriah *the first*, Amariah the second, Jahaziel the third, Jekameam the fourth.

24 *Of* the sons of Uzziel; Michah: of the sons of Michah; Shamir.

25 The brother of Michah *was* Isshiah: of the sons of Isshiah; Zechariah.

26 The sons of Merari *were* Mahli and Mushi: the sons of Jaaziah; Beno.

27 The sons of Merari by Jaaziah; Beno, and Shoham, and Zaccur, and Ibri.

28 Of Mahli *came* Eleazar, who had no sons.

29 Concerning Kish: the son of Kish *was* Jerahmeel.

30 The sons also of Mushi; Mahli, and Eder, and Jerimoth. These *were* the sons of the Levites after the house of their fathers.

31 These likewise cast lots over against their brethren the sons of Aaron in the presence of David the king, and Zadok, and Ahimelech, and the chief of the fathers of the priests and Levites, even the principal fathers over against their younger brethren.

CHAPTER 25

1 Moreover David and the captains of the host separated to the service of the sons of Asaph[1], and of Heman[2], and of Jeduthun[3], who should prophesy with harps, with psalteries, and with cymbals: and the number of the workmen according to their service was:

2 Of the sons of Asaph; Zaccur, and Joseph, and Nethaniah, and Asarelah, the sons of Asaph under the hands of Asaph, which prophesied according to the order of the king[4].

3 Of Jeduthun: the sons of Jeduthun; Gedaliah, and Zeri, and Jeshaiah, Hashabiah, and Mattithiah, six, under the hands of their father Jeduthun, [who prophesied with a harp, to give thanks and to praise the LORD][5].

4 Of Heman: the sons of Heman; Bukkiah, Mattaniah, Uzziel, Shebuel, and Jerimoth, Hananiah, Hanani, Eliathah, Giddalti, and Romamti-ezer, Joshbekashah, Mallothi, Hothir, *and* Mahazioth:

5 All these *were* the sons of Heman the king's seer in the words of God, to lift up the horn. And God gave to Heman fourteen sons and three daughters.

6 All these *were* under the hands of their father for song *in* the house of the LORD, with cymbals, psalteries, and harps, for the service of the house of God, according to the king's order to Asaph, Jeduthun, and Heman.

7 So the number of them, with their brethren that were instructed in the [songs of the LORD][6], *even* all that were cunning, was two hundred fourscore and eight.

8 [And they cast lots, ward[7] against *ward*, as well the small as the great, the teacher as the scholar.][8]

9 Now the first lot came forth for Asaph to Joseph: the second to Gedaliah, who with his brethren and sons *were* twelve:

10 The third to Zaccur, *he*, his sons, and his brethren, *were* twelve:

11 The fourth to Izri, *he*, his sons, and his brethren, *were* twelve:

12 The fifth to Nethaniah, *he*, his sons, and his brethren, *were* twelve:

13 The sixth to Bukkiah, *he*, his sons, and his brethren, *were* twelve:

14 The seventh to Jesharelah, *he*, his sons, and his brethren, *were* twelve:

15 The eighth to Jeshaiah, *he*, his sons, and his brethren, *were* twelve:

16 The ninth to Mattaniah, *he*, his sons, and his brethren, *were* twelve:

17 The tenth to Shimei, *he*, his sons, and his brethren, *were* twelve:

18 The eleventh to Azareel, *he*, his sons, and his brethren, *were* twelve:

19 The twelfth to Hashabiah, *he*, his sons, and his brethren, *were* twelve:

20 The thirteenth to Shubael, *he*, his sons, and his brethren, *were* twelve:

21 The fourteenth to Mattithiah, *he*, his sons, and his brethren, *were* twelve:

22 The fifteenth to Jeremoth, *he*, his sons, and his brethren, *were* twelve:

23 The sixteenth to Hananiah, *he*, his sons, and his brethren, *were* twelve:

24 The seventeenth to Joshbekashah, *he*, his sons, and his brethren, *were* twelve:

25 The eighteenth to Hanani, *he*, his sons, and his brethren, *were* twelve:

26 The nineteenth to Mallothi[9], *he*, his sons, and his brethren, *were* twelve:

27 The twentieth to Eliathah[10], *he*, his sons, and his brethren, *were* twelve:

28 The one and twentieth to Hothir[11], *he*, his sons, and his brethren, *were* twelve:

29 The two and twentieth to Giddalti[12], *he*, his sons, and his brethren, *were* twelve:

30 The three and twentieth to Mahazioth[13], *he*, his sons, and his brethren, *were* twelve:

31 The four and twentieth to Romamti-ezer[14], *he*, his sons, and his brethren, *were* twelve.

CHAPTER 26

1 Concerning the divisions of the porters: Of the Korhites *was* Meshelemiah the son of Kore, of the sons of Asaph.

2 And the sons of Meshelemiah *were*, Zechariah the firstborn, Jediael the second, Zebadiah the third, Jathniel the fourth,

3 Elam the fifth, Jehohanan the sixth, Elioenai the seventh.

4 Moreover the sons of Obed-edom *were*, Shemaiah the firstborn, Jehozabad the second, Joah the third, and Sacar the fourth, and Nethaneel the fifth,

---

[1] Asaph – gatherer or *collector* [Strgs#623]
[2] Heman – *faithful* [Strgs#1968]
[3] Jeduthun – *praising*, to *revere*, *worship* (with extended hands), to *throw* (a stone or an arrow) [Strgs#3038+3034]
[4] lit. by the hands of the king.
[5] giving thanks & prasing to God is prophesying.
[6] which is prophetic, see v1 & v3.
[7] ward – *watch*, the act (custody), the *sentry*, *preservation*, *observance*, *duty* [Strgs#4931].
[8] no respect of person, different class yet peers.
[9] Mallothi – I have uttered, *I have talked* [Strgs#4413]
[10] Eliathah – God has come, *God of* (his) *consent* [Strgs#448].
[11] Hothir – abundance, *he has caused to remain* [Strgs#1956].
[12] Giddalti – I make great, *I have made great* [Strgs#1437].
[13] Mahazioth – visions [Strgs#4238].
[14] Romamtiezer – I have exalted the Helper, *I have raised up a help* [Strgs#7320].

5 Ammiel the sixth, Issachar the seventh, Peulthai the eighth: for God blessed him.
6 Also unto Shemaiah his son were sons born, that ruled throughout the house of their father: for they *were* mighty men of valour.
7 The sons of Shemaiah; Othni, and Rephael, and Obed, Elzabad, whose brethren *were* strong men, Elihu, and Semachiah.
8 All these of the sons of Obed-edom: they and their sons and their brethren, able men for strength for the service, *were* threescore and two of Obed-edom.
9 And Meshelemiah had sons and brethren, strong men, eighteen.
10 Also Hosah, of the children of Merari, had sons; Simri the chief, (for *though* he was not the firstborn, yet his father made him the chief;)
11 Hilkiah the second, Tebaliah the third, Zechariah the fourth: all the sons and brethren of Hosah *were* thirteen.
12 Among these *were* the divisions of the porters, *even* among the chief men, *having* wards one against another, to minister in the house of the LORD.
13 And they cast lots, as well the small as the great, according to the house of their fathers, for every gate.
14 And the lot eastward fell to Shelemiah. Then for Zechariah his son, a wise counsellor, they cast lots; and his lot came out northward.
15 To Obed-edom southward; and to his sons the house of Asuppim.
16 To Shuppim and Hosah *the lot came forth* westward, with the gate Shallecheth, by the causeway of the going up, ward against ward.
17 Eastward *were* six Levites, northward four a day, southward four a day, and toward Asuppim two *and* two.
18 At Parbar westward, four at the causeway, *and* two at Parbar.
19 These *are* the divisions of the porters among the sons of Kore, and among the sons of Merari.
20 And of the Levites, Ahijah *was* over the treasures of the house of God, and over the treasures of the dedicated things.
21 *As concerning* the sons of Laadan; the sons of the Gershonite Laadan, chief fathers, *even* of Laadan the Gershonite, *were* Jehieli.
22 The sons of Jehieli; Zetham, and Joel his brother, *which were* over the treasures of the house of the LORD.
23 Of the Amramites, *and* the Izharites, the Hebronites, *and* the Uzzielites:
24 And Shebuel the son of Gershom, the son of Moses, *was* ruler of the treasures.
25 And his brethren by Eliezer; Rehabiah his son, and Jeshaiah his son, and Joram his son, and Zichri his son, and Shelomith his son.
26 Which Shelomith and his brethren *were* over all the treasures of the dedicated things, which David the king, and the chief fathers, the captains over thousands and hundreds, and the captains of the host, had dedicated.
27 Out of the spoils won in battles did they dedicate to maintain the house of the LORD.
28 And all that Samuel the seer, and Saul the son of Kish, and Abner the son of Ner, and Joab the son of Zeruiah, had dedicated; *and* whosoever had dedicated *any thing, it was* under the hand of Shelomith, and of his brethren.
29 Of the Izharites, Chenaniah and his sons *were* for the outward business over Israel, for officers and judges.
30 And of the Hebronites, Hashabiah and his brethren, men of valour, a thousand and seven hundred, *were* officers among them of Israel on this side Jordan westward in all the business of the LORD, and in the service of the king.
31 Among the Hebronites *was* Jerijah the chief, *even* among the Hebronites, according to the generations of his fathers. In the fortieth year of the reign of David they were sought for, and there were found among them mighty men of valour at Jazer of Gilead.
32 And his brethren, men of valour, *were* two thousand and seven hundred chief fathers, whom King David made rulers over the Reubenites, the Gadites, and the half tribe of Manasseh, for every matter pertaining to God, and affairs of the king.

CHAPTER 27

1 Now the children of Israel after their number, *to wit*, the chief fathers and captains of thousands and hundreds, and their officers that served the king in any matter of the courses, which came in and went out month by month throughout all the months of the year, of every course *were* twenty and four thousand.
2 Over the first course for the first month *was* Jashobeam the son of Zabdiel: and in his course *were* twenty and four thousand.
3 Of the children of Perez *was* the chief of all the captains of the host for the first month.
4 And over the course of the second month *was* Dodai an Ahohite, and of his course *was* Mikloth also the ruler: in his course likewise *were* twenty and four thousand.
5 The third captain of the host for the third month *was* Benaiah the son of Jehoiada, a chief priest: and in his course *were* twenty and four thousand.
6 This *is that* Benaiah, *who was* mighty *among* the thirty, and above the thirty: and in his course *was* Ammizabad his son.
7 The fourth *captain* for the fourth month *was* Asahel the brother of Joab, and Zebadiah his son after him: and in his course *were* twenty and four thousand.
8 The fifth captain for the fifth month *was* Shamhuth the Izrahite: and in his course *were* twenty and four thousand.
9 The sixth *captain* for the sixth month *was* Ira the son of Ikkesh the Tekoite: and in his course *were* twenty and four thousand.
10 The seventh *captain* for the seventh month *was* Helez the Pelonite, of the children of Ephraim: and in his course *were* twenty and four thousand.
11 The eighth *captain* for the eighth month *was* Sibbecai the Hushathite, of the Zarhites: and in his course *were* twenty and four thousand.
12 The ninth *captain* for the ninth month *was* Abiezer the Anetothite, of the Benjamites: and in his course *were* twenty and four thousand.
13 The tenth *captain* for the tenth month *was* Maharai the Netophathite, of the Zarhites: and in his course *were* twenty and four thousand.
14 The eleventh *captain* for the eleventh month *was* Benaiah the Pirathonite, of the children of Ephraim: and in his course *were* twenty and four thousand.
15 The twelfth *captain* for the twelfth month *was* Heldai the Netophathite, of Othniel: and in his course *were* twenty and four thousand.
16 Furthermore over the tribes of Israel: the ruler of the Reubenites *was* Eliezer the son of Zichri: of the Simeonites, Shephatiah the son of Maachah:
17 Of the Levites, Hashabiah the son of Kemuel: of the Aaronites, Zadok:

18 Of Judah, Elihu, *one* of the brethren of David: of Issachar, Omri the son of Michael:
19 Of Zebulun, Ishmaiah the son of Obadiah: of Naphtali, Jerimoth the son of Azriel:
20 Of the children of Ephraim, Hoshea the son of Azaziah: of the half tribe of Manasseh, Joel the son of Pedaiah:
21 Of the half *tribe* of Manasseh in Gilead, Iddo the son of Zechariah: of Benjamin, Jaasiel the son of Abner:
22 Of Dan, Azareel the son of Jeroham. These *were* the princes of the tribes of Israel.
23 But David took not the number of them from twenty years old and under: because the LORD had said he would increase Israel like to the stars of the heavens.
24 Joab the son of Zeruiah began to number, but he finished not, because there fell wrath for it against Israel; neither was the number put in the account of the chronicles of King David.
25 And over the king's treasures *was* Azmaveth the son of Adiel: and over the storehouses in the fields, in the cities, and in the villages, and in the castles, *was* Jehonathan the son of Uzziah:
26 And over them that did the work of the field for tillage of the ground *was* Ezri the son of Chelub:
27 And over the vineyards *was* Shimei the Ramathite: over the increase of the vineyards for the wine cellars *was* Zabdi the Shiphmite:
28 And over the olive trees and the sycomore trees that *were* in the low plains *was* Baal-hanan the Gederite: and over the cellars of oil *was* Joash:
29 And over the herds that fed in Sharon *was* Shitrai the Sharonite: and over the herds *that were* in the valleys *was* Shaphat the son of Adlai:
30 Over the camels also *was* Obil the Ishmaelite: and over the asses *was* Jehdeiah the Meronothite:
31 And over the flocks *was* Jaziz the Hagerite. All these *were* the rulers of the substance which *was* King David's.
32 Also Jonathan David's uncle was a counsellor, a wise man, and a scribe: and Jehiel the son of Hachmoni *was* with the king's sons:
33 And Ahithophel *was* the king's counsellor: and Hushai the Archite *was* the king's companion:
34 And after Ahithophel *was* Jehoiada the son of Benaiah, and Abiathar: and the general of the king's army *was* Joab.

CHAPTER 28

1 And David assembled all the princes of Israel, the princes of the tribes, and the captains of the companies that ministered to the king by course, and the captains over the thousands, and captains over the hundreds, and the stewards over all the substance and possession of the king, and of his sons, with the officers, and with the mighty men, and with all the valiant men, unto Jerusalem.
2 Then David the king stood up upon his feet, and said, Hear me, my brethren, and my people: As for me, I *had* in mine heart to build an house of rest for the ark of the covenant of the LORD, and for the footstool of our God, and had made ready for the building:
3 But God said unto me, you will not build an house for my name, because you have *been* a man of war, and have shed blood.
4 Howbeit the LORD God of Israel chose me before all the house of my father to be king over Israel for ever: for he has chosen Judah *to be* the ruler; and of the house of Judah, the house of my father; and among the sons of my father he liked me to make *me* king over all Israel:
5 And of all my sons, (for the LORD has given me many sons,) he has chosen Solomon my son to sit upon the throne of the kingdom of the LORD over Israel.
6 And he said unto me, Solomon your son, he will build my house and my courts: for I have chosen him *to be* my son, and I will be his father.
7 Moreover I will establish his kingdom for ever, if he be constant to do my commandments and my judgments, as at this day.
8 Now therefore in the sight of all Israel the congregation of the LORD, and in the audience of our God, keep and seek for all the commandments of the LORD your God: that you may possess this good land, and leave *it* for an inheritance for your children after you for ever.
9 And you, Solomon my son, know you the God of your father, and serve him with a perfect heart and with a willing mind: for the LORD searcheth all hearts, and understandeth all the imaginations of the thoughts: if you seek him, he will be found of you; but if you forsake him, he will cast you off for ever.
10 Take heed now; for the LORD has chosen you to build an house for the sanctuary: be strong, and do *it*.
11 Then David gave to Solomon his son the pattern of the porch, and of the houses thereof, and of the treasuries thereof, and of the upper chambers thereof, and of the inner parlours thereof, and of the place of the mercy seat,
12 And the pattern of all that he had by the spirit, of the courts of the house of the LORD, and of all the chambers round about, of the treasuries of the house of God, and of the treasuries of the dedicated things:
13 Also for the courses of the priests and the Levites, and for all the work of the service of the house of the LORD, and for all the vessels of service in the house of the LORD.
14 *He gave* of gold by weight for *things* of gold, for all instruments of all manner of service; *silver also* for all instruments of silver by weight, for all instruments of every kind of service:
15 Even the weight for the candlesticks of gold, and for their lamps of gold, by weight for every candlestick, and for the lamps thereof: and for the candlesticks of silver by weight, *both* for the candlestick, and *also* for the lamps thereof, according to the use of every candlestick.
16 And by weight *he gave* gold for the tables of shewbread, for every table; and *likewise* silver for the tables of silver:
17 Also pure gold for the fleshhooks, and the bowls, and the cups: and for the golden basons *he gave gold* by weight for every bason; and *likewise silver* by weight for every bason of silver:
18 And for the altar of incense refined gold by weight; and gold for the pattern of the chariot of the cherubims, that spread out *their wings*, and covered the ark of the covenant of the LORD.
19 All *this, said David*, the LORD made me understand in writing by *his* hand upon me, *even* all the works of this pattern.
20 And David said to Solomon his son, be strong and of good courage, and do *it*: fear not, or be dismayed: for the LORD God, *even* my God, *will be* with you; he will not fail you, or forsake you, until you have finished all the work for the service of the house of the LORD.
21 And, behold, the courses of the priests and the Levites, *even they will be with you* for all the service of the house of God: and *there will be* with you for all manner of workmanship every willing skilful man, for any manner of service: also the princes and all the people *will be* wholly at your commandment.

CHAPTER 29

1 Furthermore David the king said unto the **entire** congregation, Solomon my son, whom alone God has chosen, *is yet* young and tender, and the work *is* great: for the palace *is* not for man, but for the LORD God.
2 Now I have prepared with all my might for the house of my God the gold for *things to be made* of gold, and the silver for *things* of silver, and the brass for *things* of brass, the iron for *things* of iron, and wood for *things* of wood; onyx stones, and *stones* to be set, glistering stones, and of divers colours, and all manner of precious stones, and marble stones in abundance.
3 Moreover, because I have set my affection to the house of my God, I have of mine own proper good, of gold and silver, *which* I have given to the house of my God, over and above all that I have prepared for the holy house,
4 *Even* three thousand talents of gold, of the gold of Ophir, and seven thousand talents of refined silver, to overlay the walls of the houses *withal*:
5 The gold for *things* of gold, and the silver for *things* of silver, and for all manner of work *to be made* by the hands of artificers. And who *then* is willing to consecrate his service this day unto the LORD?
6 Then the chief of the fathers and princes of the tribes of Israel, and the captains of thousands and of hundreds, with the rulers of the king's work, offered willingly,
7 And gave for the service of the house of God of gold five thousand talents and ten thousand drams, and of silver ten thousand talents, and of brass eighteen thousand talents, and one hundred thousand talents of iron.
8 And they with whom *precious* stones were found gave *them* to the treasure of the house of the LORD, by the hand of Jehiel the Gershonite.
9 Then the people rejoiced, for that they offered willingly, because with perfect heart they offered willingly to the LORD: and David the king also rejoiced with great joy.
10 Wherefore David blessed the LORD before the **entire** congregation: and David said, blessed *be* you, LORD God of Israel our father, for ever and ever.
11 Thine, O LORD, *is* the greatness, and the power, and the glory, and the victory, and the majesty: for all *that is* in the heaven and in the earth *is thine*; your *is* the kingdom, O LORD, and you are exalted as head above all.
12 Both riches and honour *come* of you, and you reignest over all; and in your hand *is* power and might; and in your hand *it is* to make great, and to give strength unto all.
13 Now therefore, our God, we thank you, and praise your glorious name.
14 But who *am* I, and what *is* my people, that we should be able to offer so willingly after this sort? For all things *come* of you, and of your own have we given you.
15 For we *are* strangers before you, and sojourners, as *were* all our fathers: our days on the earth *are* as a shadow, and *there is* none abiding.
16 O LORD our God, all this store that we have prepared to build you an house for your holy name *cometh* of your hand, and *is* all your own.
17 I know also, my God, that you triest the heart, and have pleasure in uprightness. As for me, in the uprightness of mine heart I have willingly offered all these things: and now have I seen with joy your people, which are present here, to offer willingly unto you.
18 O LORD God of Abraham, Isaac, and of Israel, our fathers, keep this for ever in the imagination of the thoughts of the heart of your people, and prepare their heart unto you:
19 And give unto Solomon my son a perfect heart, to keep your commandments, your testimonies, and your statutes, and to do all *these things*, and to build the palace, *for* which I have made provision.
20 And David said to the **entire** congregation, now bless the LORD your God. And the **entire** congregation blessed the LORD God of their fathers, and bowed down their heads, and worshipped the LORD, and the king.
21 And they sacrificed sacrifices unto the LORD, and offered burnt offerings unto the LORD, on the morrow after that day, *even* a thousand bullocks, a thousand rams, *and* a thousand lambs, with their drink offerings, and sacrifices in abundance for all Israel:
22 And did eat and drink before the LORD on that day with great gladness. And they made Solomon the son of David king the second time, and anointed *him* unto the LORD *to be* the chief governor, and Zadok *to be* priest.
23 Then Solomon sat on the throne of the LORD as king instead of David his father, and prospered; and all Israel obeyed him.
24 And all the princes, and the mighty men, and all the sons likewise of king David, submitted themselves unto Solomon the king.
25 And the LORD magnified Solomon exceedingly in the sight of all Israel, and bestowed upon him *such* royal majesty as had not been on any king before him in Israel.
26 Thus David the son of Jesse reigned over all Israel.
27 And the time that he reigned over Israel *was* forty years; seven years reigned he in Hebron, and thirty and three *years* reigned he in Jerusalem.
28 And he died in a good old age, full of days, riches, and honour: and Solomon his son reigned in his stead.
29 Now the acts of David the king, first and last, behold they *are* written in the book of Samuel the seer, and in the book of Nathan the prophet, and in the book of Gad the seer,
30 With all his reign and his might, and the times that went over him, and over Israel, and over all the kingdoms of the countries.

SECOND CHRONICLES

CHAPTER 1

1 And Solomon the son of David was strengthened in his kingdom, and the LORD his God *was* with him, and magnified him exceedingly.
2 Then Solomon spoke unto all Israel, to the captains of thousands and of hundreds, and to the judges, and to every governor in all Israel, the chief of the fathers.
3 So Solomon, and the **entire** congregation with him, went to the high place that *was* at Gibeon; for there was the tabernacle of the congregation of God, which Moses the servant of the LORD had made in the wilderness.
4 But the ark of God had David brought up from Kirjath-jearim[1] to *the place which* David had prepared for it: for he had pitched a tent for it at Jerusalem.
5 Moreover the brasen altar, that Bezaleel the son of Uri, the son of Hur, had made, he put before the tabernacle of the LORD: and Solomon and the congregation sought unto it.
6 And Solomon went up there to the brasen altar before the LORD, which *was* at the tabernacle of the congregation, and offered a thousand burnt offerings upon it.
7 In that night did God appear unto Solomon, and said unto him, Ask what I will give you.
8 And Solomon said unto God, you have showed great mercy unto David my father, and hast made me to reign in his stead.
9 Now, O LORD God, let your promise unto David my father be established: for you hast made me king over a people like the dust of the earth in multitude.
10 Give me now wisdom and knowledge, that I may go out and come in before this people: for who can judge this your people, *that is so* great?
11 And God said to Solomon, Because this was in your heart, and you hast not asked riches, wealth, or honor, nor the life of your enemies, neither yet hast asked long life; but hast asked wisdom and knowledge for thyself, that you may judge my people, over whom I have made you king:
12 Wisdom and knowledge *is* granted unto you; and I will give you riches, and wealth, and honor, such as none of the kings have had that *have been* before you, neither will there any after you have the like.
13 Then Solomon came *from his journey* to the high place that *was* at Gibeon to Jerusalem, from before the tabernacle of the congregation, and reigned over Israel.
14 And Solomon gathered chariots and horsemen: and he had a thousand and four hundred chariots, and twelve thousand horsemen, which he placed in the chariot cities, and with the king at Jerusalem.
15 And the king made silver and gold at Jerusalem *as plenteous* as stones, and cedar trees made he as the sycomore trees that *are* in the vale for abundance.
16 And Solomon had horses brought out of Egypt, and linen yarn: the king's merchants received the linen yarn at a price.
17 And they fetched up, and brought forth out of Egypt a chariot for six hundred *shekels* of silver, and an horse for an hundred and fifty: and so brought they out *horses* for all the kings of the Hittites, and for the kings of Syria, by their means.

CHAPTER 2

1 And Solomon determined to build a house for the name of the LORD, and an house for his kingdom.
2 And Solomon told out threescore and ten thousand men to bear burdens, and fourscore thousand to hew in the mountain, and three thousand and six hundred to oversee them.
3 And Solomon sent to Huram the king of Tyre, saying, as you did deal with David my father, and did send him cedars to build him a house to dwell therein, *even so deal with me*.
4 Behold, I build a house to the name of the LORD my God, to dedicate *it* to him, *and* to burn before him sweet incense, and for the continual shewbread, and for the burnt offerings morning and evening, on the Sabbaths, and on the new moons, and on the solemn feasts of the LORD our God. This *is an ordinance* for ever to Israel.
5 And the house which I build *is* great: for great *is* our God above all gods.
6 But who is able to build him a house, seeing the heaven and heaven of heavens cannot contain him? Who *am* I then, that I should build him an house, save only to burn sacrifice before him?
7 Send me now therefore a man cunning to work in gold, and in silver, and in brass, and in iron, and in purple, and crimson, and blue, and that can skill to grave with the cunning men that *are* with me in Judah and in Jerusalem, whom David my father did provide.
8 Send me also cedar trees, fir trees, and algum trees, out of Lebanon: for I know that your servants can skill to cut timber in Lebanon; and, behold, my servants will *be* with your servants,
9 Even to prepare me timber in abundance: for the house which I am about to build will *be* wonderful great.
10 And, behold, I will give to your servants, the hewers that cut timber, twenty thousand measures of beaten wheat, and twenty thousand measures of barley, and twenty thousand baths of wine, and twenty thousand baths of oil.
11 Then Huram the king of Tyre answered in writing, which he sent to Solomon, because the LORD has loved his people, he has made you king over them.
12 Huram said moreover, blessed *be* the LORD God of Israel, that made heaven and earth, who has given to David the king a wise son, endued with prudence and understanding, that might build an house for the LORD, and an house for his kingdom.
13 And now I have sent a cunning man, endued with understanding, of Huram my father's,
14 The son of a woman of the daughters of Dan, and his father *was* a man of Tyre, skilful to work in gold, and in silver, in brass, in iron, in stone, and in timber, in purple, in blue, and in fine linen, and in crimson; also to grave any manner of graving, and to find out every device which will be put to him, with your cunning men, and with the cunning men of my lord David your father.
15 Now therefore the wheat, and the barley, the oil, and the wine, which my lord has spoken of, let him send unto his servants:
16 And we will cut wood out of Lebanon, as much as you will need: and we will bring it to you in **rafts** by sea to Joppa; and you will carry it up to Jerusalem.
17 And Solomon numbered all the strangers that *were* in the land of Israel, after the numbering wherewith David his father had numbered them; and they were found an hundred and fifty thousand and three thousand and six hundred.

---

[1] Kirjathjearim- defined as city of forest. [Strgs#7157]

18 And he set threescore and ten thousand of them *to be* bearers of burdens, and fourscore thousand *to be* hewers in the mountain, and three thousand and six hundred overseers to set the people a work.

CHAPTER 3

1 Then Solomon began to build the house of the LORD at Jerusalem in mount Moriah, where *the LORD* appeared unto David his father, in the place that David had prepared in the threshing floor of Ornan the Jebusite.
2 And he began to build in the second *day* of the second month, in the fourth year of his reign.
3 Now these *are the things wherein* Solomon was instructed for the building of the house of God. The length by cubits after the first measure *was* threescore cubits, and the breadth twenty cubits.
4 And the porch that *was* in the front *of the house*, the length *of it was* according to the breadth of the house, twenty cubits, and the height *was* an hundred and twenty: and he overlaid it within with pure gold.
5 And the greater house he **covered** with fir tree, which he overlaid with fine gold, and set thereon palm trees and chains.
6 And he garnished the house with precious stones for beauty: and the gold *was* gold of Parvaim.
7 He overlaid also the house, the beams, the posts, and the walls thereof, and the doors thereof, with gold; and graved cherubims on the walls.
8 And he made the most holy house, the length whereof *was* according to the breadth of the house, twenty cubits, and the breadth thereof twenty cubits: and he overlaid it with fine gold, *amounting* to six hundred talents.
9 And the weight of the nails *was* fifty shekels of gold. And he overlaid the upper chambers with gold.
10 And in the most holy house he made two cherubims of image work, and overlaid them with gold.
11 And the wings of the cherubims *were* twenty cubits long: one wing *of the one cherub was* five cubits, reaching to the wall of the house: and the other wing *was likewise* five cubits, reaching to the wing of the other cherub.
12 And *one* wing of the other cherub *was* five cubits, reaching to the wall of the house: and the other wing *was* five cubits *also*, joining to the wing of the other cherub.
13 The wings of these cherubims spread themselves forth twenty cubits: and they stood on their feet, and their faces *were* inward.
14 And he made the veil *of* blue, and purple, and crimson, and fine linen, and wrought cherubims thereon.
15 Also he made before the house two pillars of thirty and five cubits high, and the chapiter that *was* on the top of each of them *was* five cubits.
16 And he made chains, *as* in the oracle, and put *them* on the heads of the pillars; and made an hundred pomegranates, and put *them* on the chains.
17 And he reared up the pillars before the temple, one on the right hand, and the other on the left; and called the name of that on the right hand Jachin, and the name of that on the left Boaz.

CHAPTER 4

1 Moreover he made an altar of brass, twenty cubits the length thereof, and twenty cubits the breadth thereof, and ten cubits the height thereof.
2 Also he made a molten sea of ten cubits from brim to brim, round in compass, and five cubits the height thereof; and a line of thirty cubits did compass it round about.
3 And under it *was* the similitude of oxen, which did compass it round about: ten in a cubit, compassing the sea round about. Two rows of oxen *were* cast, when it was cast.
4 It stood upon twelve oxen, three looking toward the north, and three looking toward the west, and three looking toward the south, and three looking toward the east: and the sea *was set* above upon them, and all their hinder parts *were* inward.
5 And the thickness of it *was* a handbreadth, and the brim of it like the work of the brim of a cup, with flowers of lilies; *and* it received and held three thousand baths.
6 He made also ten lavers, and put five on the right hand, and five on the left, to wash in them: such things as they offered for the burnt offering they washed in them; but the sea *was* for the priests to wash in.
7 And he made ten candlesticks of gold according to their form, and set *them* in the temple, five on the right hand, and five on the left.
8 He made also ten tables, and placed *them* in the temple, five on the right side, and five on the left. And he made an hundred basons of gold.
9 Furthermore he made the court of the priests, and the great court, and doors for the court, and overlaid the doors of them with brass.
10 And he set the sea on the right side of the east end, over against the south.
11 And Huram made the pots, and the shovels, and the basons. And Huram finished the work that he was to make for King Solomon for the house of God;
12 *To wit*, the two pillars, and the pommels, and the chapiters *which were* on the top of the two pillars, and the two wreaths to cover the two pommels of the chapiters which *were* on the top of the pillars;
13 And four hundred pomegranates on the two wreaths; two rows of pomegranates on each wreath, to cover the two pommels of the chapiters which *were* upon the pillars.
14 He made also bases, and lavers made he upon the bases;
15 One sea, and twelve oxen under it.
16 The pots also, and the shovels, and the flesh-hooks, and all their instruments, did Huram his father make to King Solomon for the house of the LORD of bright brass.
17 In the plain of Jordan did the king cast them, in the clay ground between Succoth and Zeredathah.
18 Thus Solomon made all these vessels in great abundance: for the weight of the brass could not be found out.
19 And Solomon made all the vessels that *were for* the house of God, the golden altar also, and the tables whereon the shewbread *was set*;
20 Moreover the candlesticks with their lamps, that they should burn after the manner before the oracle, of pure gold;
21 And the flowers, and the lamps, and the tongs, *made he of* gold, *and* that perfect gold;
22 And the snuffers, and the basons, and the spoons, and the censers, *of* pure gold: and the entry of the house, the inner doors thereof for the most holy *place*, and the doors of the house of the temple, *were of* gold.

CHAPTER 5

1 Thus all the work that Solomon made for the house of the LORD was finished: and Solomon brought in *all* the things that David his father had dedicated; and the silver, and the gold, and all the instruments, put he among the treasures of the house of God.

2 Then Solomon assembled the elders of Israel, and all the heads of the tribes, the chief of the fathers of the children of Israel, unto Jerusalem, to bring up the ark of the covenant of the LORD out of the city of David, which *is* Zion.
3 Wherefore all the men of Israel assembled themselves unto the king in the feast which *was* in the seventh month.
4 And all the elders of Israel came; and the Levites took up the ark.
5 And they brought up the ark, and the tabernacle of the congregation, and all the holy vessels that *were* in the tabernacle, these did the priests *and* the Levites bring up.
6 Also King Solomon, and all the congregation of Israel that were assembled unto him before the ark, sacrificed sheep and oxen, which could not be told nor numbered for multitude.
7 And the priests brought in the ark of the covenant of the LORD unto his place, to the oracle of the house, into the most holy *place, even* under the wings of the cherubims:
8 For the cherubims spread forth *their* wings over the place of the ark, and the cherubims covered the ark and the staves thereof above.
9 And they drew out the staves *of the ark* that the ends of the staves were seen from the ark before the oracle; but they were not seen without. And there it is unto this day.
10 *There was* nothing in the ark save the two tables which Moses put *therein* at Horeb, when the LORD made *a* covenant with the children of Israel, when they came out of Egypt.
11 And it came to pass, when the priests were come out of the holy *place*: (for all the priests *that were* present were sanctified, *and* did not *then* wait by course:
12 Also the Levites *which were* the singers, all of them of Asaph, of Heman, of Jeduthun, with their sons and their brethren, *being* arrayed in white linen, having cymbals and psalteries and harps, stood at the east end of the altar, and with them an hundred and twenty priests sounding with trumpets:)
13 It came even to pass, as the trumpeters and singers *were* as one, to make one sound to be heard in praising and thanking the LORD; and when they lifted up *their* voice with the trumpets and cymbals and instruments of music, and praised the LORD, *saying*, For *he is* good; for his mercy *endures* for ever: that *then* the house was filled with a cloud, *even* the house of the LORD;
14 So that the priests could not stand to minister by reason of the cloud: for the glory of the LORD had filled the house of God.

CHAPTER 6

1 Then said Solomon, The LORD has said that he would dwell in the thick darkness.
2 But I have built a house of habitation for you, and a place for your dwelling forever.
3 And the king turned his face, and blessed the whole congregation of Israel: and all the congregation of Israel stood.
4 And he said, Blessed *be* the LORD God of Israel, who has with his hands fulfilled *that* which he spoke with his mouth to my father David, saying,
5 Since the day that I brought forth my people out of the land of Egypt I chose no city among all the tribes of Israel to build a house in, that my name might be there; neither chose I any man to be a ruler over my people Israel:
6 But I have chosen Jerusalem, that my name might be there; and have chosen David to be over my people Israel.
7 Now it was in the heart of David my father to build a house for the name of the LORD God of Israel.
8 But the LORD said to David my father, Forasmuch as it was in your heart to build a house for my name, you did well in that it was in your heart:
9 Notwithstanding you will not build the house; but your son which will come forth out of your loins; he will build the house for my name.
10 The LORD therefore has performed his word that he has spoken: for I am risen up in the room of David my father and am set on the throne of Israel, as the LORD promised, and have built the house for the name of the LORD God of Israel.
11 And in it have I put the ark, wherein *is* the covenant of the LORD, that he made with the children of Israel.
12 And he stood before the altar of the LORD in the presence of all the congregation of Israel, and spread forth his hands:
13 For Solomon had made a brazen scaffold, of five cubits long, and five cubits broad, and three cubits high, and had set it in the midst of the court: and upon it he stood, and kneeled down upon his knees before all the congregation of Israel, and spread forth his hands toward heaven,
14 And said, O LORD God of Israel, *there is* no God like you in the heaven, nor in the earth; which keeps covenant, and *shows* mercy unto your servants, that walk before you with all their hearts:
15 You which have kept with your servant David my father that which you hast promised him; and spoke with your mouth and hast fulfilled *it* with your hand, as *it is* this day.
16 Now therefore, O LORD God of Israel, keep with your servant David my father that which you hast promised him, saying, There will not fail you a man in my sight to sit upon the throne of Israel; yet so that your children take heed to their way to walk in my law, as you hast walked before me.
17 Now then, O LORD God of Israel, let your word be verified, which you hast spoken unto your servant David.
18 But will God in very deed dwell with men on the earth? Behold, heaven and the heaven of heavens cannot contain you; how much less this house which I have built!
19 Have respect therefore to the prayer of your servant, and to his supplication, O LORD my God, to hearken unto the cry and the prayer which your servant prays before you:
20 That your eyes may be open upon this house day and night, upon the place whereof you hast said that you would put your name there; to hearken unto the prayer which your servant prays toward this place.
21 Hearken therefore unto the supplications of your servant, and of your people Israel, which they will make toward this place: hear you from your dwelling place, *even* from heaven; and when you hear, forgive.
22 If a man sin against his neighbor, and an oath be laid upon him to make him swear, and the oath come before your altar in this house;
23 Then hear you from heaven, and do, and judge your servants, by requiting the wicked, by recompensing his way upon his own head; and by justifying the righteous, by giving him according to his righteousness.
24 And if your people Israel be put to the worse before the enemy, because they have sinned against you; and will return and confess your name, and pray and make supplication before you in this house;
25 Then hear you from the heavens, and forgive the sin of your people Israel, and bring them again unto the land which you gave to them and to their fathers.

26 When the heaven is shut up, and there is no rain, because they have sinned against you; *yet* if they pray toward this place, and confess your name, and turn from their sin, when you dost afflict them;

27 Then hear you from heaven, and forgive the sin of your servants, and of your people Israel, when you hast taught them the good way, wherein they should walk; and send rain upon your land, which you hast given unto your people for an inheritance.

28 If there be dearth in the land, if there be pestilence, if there be blasting, or mildew, locusts, or caterpillars; if their enemies besiege them in the cities of their land; whatsoever sore or whatsoever sickness *there be*:

29 *Then* what prayer *or* what supplication soever will be made of any man, or of all your people Israel, when everyone will know his own sore and his own grief, and will spread forth his hands in this house:

30 Then hear you from heaven your dwelling place, and forgive, and render unto every man according unto all his ways, whose heart you know; (for you only know the hearts of the children of men:)

31 That they may fear you, to walk in your ways, so long as they live in the land which you gave unto our fathers.

32 Moreover concerning the stranger, which is not of your people Israel, but is come from a far country for your great name's sake, and your mighty hand, and your stretched out arm; if they come and pray in this house;

33 Then hear you from the heavens, *even* from your dwelling place, and do according to all that the stranger called to you for; that all people of the earth may know your name, and fear you, as does your people Israel, and may know that this house which I have built is called by your name.

34 If your people go out to war against their enemies by the way that you will send them, and they pray unto you toward this city which you hast chosen, and the house which I have built for your name;

35 Then hear you from the heavens their prayer and their supplication, and maintain their cause.

36 If they sin against you, (for *there is* no man which sins not,) and you be angry with them, and deliver them over before *their* enemies, and they carry them away captives unto a land far off or near;

37 Yet *if* they bethink themselves in the land where they are carried captive, and turn and pray unto you in the land of their captivity, saying, We have sinned, we have done amiss, and have dealt wickedly;

38 If they return to you with all their heart and with all their soul in the land of their captivity, where they have carried them captives, and pray toward their land, which you gave unto their fathers, and *toward* the city which you hast chosen, and toward the house which I have built for your name:

39 Then hear you from the heavens, *even* from your dwelling place, their prayer and their supplications, and maintain their cause, and forgive your people which have sinned against you.

40 Now, my God, let, I beseech you, your eyes be open, and *let* your ears *be* **attentive** unto the prayer *that is made* in this place.

41 Now therefore arise, O LORD God, into your resting place, thou, and the ark of your strength: let your priests, O LORD God, be clothed with salvation, and let your saints rejoice in goodness.

42 O LORD God, turn not away the face of your anointed: remember the mercies of David your servant.

CHAPTER 7

1 Now when Solomon had made an end of praying, the fire came down from heaven, and consumed the burnt offering and the sacrifices; and the glory of the LORD filled the house.

2 And the priests could not enter into the house of the LORD, because the glory of the LORD had filled the LORD'S house.

3 And when all the children of Israel saw how the fire came down, and the glory of the LORD upon the house, they bowed themselves with their faces to the ground upon the pavement, and worshipped, and praised the LORD, *saying*, For *he is* good; for his mercy *endures* forever.

4 Then the king and all the people offered sacrifices before the LORD.

5 And king Solomon offered a sacrifice of twenty and two thousand oxen, and an hundred and twenty thousand sheep: so the king and all the people dedicated the house of God.

6 And the priests waited on their offices: the Levites also with instruments of music of the LORD, which David the king had made to praise the LORD, because his mercy *endures* forever, when David praised by their ministry; and the priests sounded trumpets before them, and all Israel stood.

7 Moreover Solomon hallowed the middle of the court that *was* before the house of the LORD: for there he offered burnt offerings, and the fat of the peace offerings, because the brazen altar which Solomon had made was not able to receive the burnt offerings, and the meat offerings, and the fat.

8 Also at the same time Solomon kept the feast seven days, and all Israel with him, a very great congregation, from the entering in of Hamath unto the river of Egypt.

9 And in the eighth day they made a solemn assembly: for they kept the dedication of the altar seven days, and the feast seven days.

10 And on the three and twentieth day of the seventh month he sent the people away into their tents, glad and merry in heart for the goodness that the LORD had showed unto David, and to Solomon, and to Israel his people.

11 Thus Solomon finished the house of the LORD, and the king's house: and all that came into Solomon's heart to make in the house of the LORD, and in his own house, he prosperously effected.

12 And the LORD appeared to Solomon by night, and said unto him, I have heard your prayer, and have chosen this place to myself for a house of sacrifice.

13 If I shut up heaven that there be no rain, or if I command the locusts to devour the land, or if I send pestilence among my people;

14 If my people, which are called by my name, will humble themselves, and pray, and seek my face, and turn from their wicked ways; then will I hear from heaven, and will forgive their sin, and will heal their land.

15 Now mine eyes will be open, and mine ears **attentive** unto the prayer *that is made* in this place.

16 For now have I chosen and sanctified this house, that my name may be there forever: and mine eyes and mine heart will be there perpetually.

17 And as for you, if you will walk before me, as David your father walked, and do according to all that I have commanded you, and will observe my statutes and my judgments;

18 [Then will I establish the throne of your kingdom, according as I have covenanted with David your father, saying, There will not fail you a man *to be* ruler in Israel.][1]
19 But if ye turn away, and forsake my statutes and my commandments, which I have set before you, and will go and serve other gods, and worship them;
20 Then will I pluck them up by the roots out of my land which I have given them; and this house, which I have sanctified for my name, will I cast out of my sight, and will make it *to be* a proverb and a byword among all nations.
21 And this house, which is high, will be an astonishment to everyone that passes by it; so that he will say, Why has the LORD done thus unto this land, and unto this house?
22 And it will be answered, because they forsook the LORD God of their fathers, which brought them forth out of the land of Egypt, and laid hold on other gods, and worshipped them, and served them: therefore has he brought all this evil upon them.

CHAPTER 8

1 And it came to pass at the end of twenty years, wherein Solomon had built the house of the LORD, and his own house,
2 That the cities which Huram had restored to Solomon, Solomon built them, and caused the children of Israel to dwell there.
3 And Solomon went to Hamath-zobah, and prevailed against it.
4 And he built Tadmor in the wilderness, and all the store cities, which he built in Hamath.
5 Also he built Beth-horon the upper, and Beth-horon the nether, fenced cities, with walls, gates, and bars;
6 And Baalath, and all the store cities that Solomon had, and all the chariot cities, and the cities of the horsemen, and all that Solomon desired to build in Jerusalem, and in Lebanon, and throughout all the land of his dominion.
7 *As for* all the people *that were* left of the Hittites, and the Amorites, and the Perizzites, and the Hivites, and the Jebusites, which *were* not of Israel,
8 *But* of their children, who were left after them in the land, whom the children of Israel consumed not, them did Solomon make to pay tribute until this day.
9 But of the children of Israel did Solomon make no servants for his work; but they *were* men of war, and chief of his captains, and captains of his chariots and horsemen.
10 And these *were* the chief of King Solomon's officers, *even* two hundred and fifty, that bare rule over the people.
11 And Solomon brought up the daughter of Pharaoh out of the city of David unto the house that he had built for her: for he said, my wife will not dwell in the house of David king of Israel, because *the places are* holy, whereunto the ark of the LORD has come.
12 Then Solomon offered burnt offerings unto the LORD on the altar of the LORD, which he had built before the porch,
13 Even after a certain rate every day, offering according to the commandment of Moses, on the Sabbaths, and on the new moons, and on the solemn feasts, three times in the year, *even* in the feast of unleavened bread, and in the feast of weeks, and in the feast of tabernacles.
14 And he appointed, according to the order of David his father, the courses of the priests to their service, and the Levites to their charges, to praise and minister before the priests, as the duty of every day required: the porters also by their courses at every gate: for so had David the man of God commanded.
15 And they departed not from the commandment of the king unto the priests and Levites concerning any matter, or concerning the treasures.
16 Now all the work of Solomon was prepared unto the day of the foundation of the house of the LORD, and until it was finished. So the house of the LORD was perfected.
17 Then went Solomon to Ezion-geber, and to Eloth, at the sea side in the land of Edom.
18 And Huram sent him by the hands of his servants ships, and servants that had knowledge of the sea; and they went with the servants of Solomon to Ophir, and took **from there** four hundred and fifty talents of gold, and brought *them* to King Solomon.

CHAPTER 9

1 And when the queen of Sheba heard of the fame of Solomon, she came to prove Solomon with hard questions at Jerusalem, with a very great company, and camels that bare spices, and gold in abundance, and precious stones: and when she was come to Solomon, she communed with him of all that was in her heart.
2 And Solomon told her all her questions: and there was nothing hid from Solomon which he told her not.
3 And when the queen of Sheba had seen the Wisdom of Solomon, and the house that he had built,
4 And the meat of his table, and the sitting of his servants, and the attendance of his ministers, and their apparel; his cupbearers also, and their apparel; and his ascent by which he went up into the house of the LORD; there was no more spirit in her.
5 And she said to the king, *it was* a true report which I heard in mine own land of your acts, and of your wisdom:
6 Howbeit I believed not their words, until I came, and mine eyes had seen *it*: and, behold, the one half of the greatness of your wisdom was not told me: *for* you exceeds the fame that I heard.
7 Happy *are* your men, and happy *are* these your servants, which stand continually before you, and hear your wisdom.
8 Blessed be the LORD your God, which delighted in you to set you on his throne, *to be* king for the LORD your God: because your God loved Israel, to establish them forever, therefore made he you king over them, to do judgment and justice.
9 And she gave the king a hundred and twenty talents of gold, and of spices great abundance, and precious stones: neither was there any such spice as the queen of Sheba gave King Solomon.
10 And the servants also of Huram, and the servants of Solomon, which brought gold from Ophir, brought algum trees and precious stones.
11 And the king made *of* the algum trees terraces to the house of the LORD, and to the king's palace, and harps and psalteries for singers: and there were none such seen before in the land of Judah.
12 And King Solomon gave to the queen of Sheba all her desire, whatsoever she asked, beside *that* which she had brought unto the king. So she turned, and went away to her own land, she and her servants.
13 Now the weight of gold that came to Solomon in one year was six hundred and threescore and six talents of gold;
14 Beside *that which* chapmen and merchants brought. And all the kings of Arabia and governors of the country brought gold and silver to Solomon.
15 And King Solomon made two hundred targets *of* beaten gold: six hundred *shekels* of beaten gold went to one target.

---

[1] compare – Daniel 9:26 & Hagai 2:5

16 And three hundred shields *made he of* beaten gold: three hundred *shekels* of gold went to one shield. And the king put them in the house of the forest of Lebanon.
17 Moreover the king made a great throne of ivory, and overlaid it with pure gold.
18 And *there were* six steps to the throne, with a footstool of gold, *which were* fastened to the throne, and stays on each side of the sitting place, and two lions standing by the stays:
19 And twelve lions stood there on the one side and on the other upon the six steps. There was not the like made in any kingdom.
20 And all the drinking vessels of King Solomon *were of* gold, and all the vessels of the house of the forest of Lebanon *were of* pure gold: none *were of* silver; it was *not* anything accounted of in the days of Solomon.
21 For the king's ships went to Tarshish with the servants of Huram: every three years once came the ships of Tarshish bringing gold, and silver, ivory, and apes, and peacocks.
22 And king Solomon passed all the kings of the earth in riches and wisdom.
23 And all the kings of the earth sought the presence of Solomon, to hear his wisdom, that God had put in his heart.
24 And they brought every man his present, vessels of silver, and vessels of gold, and raiment, harness, and spices, horses, and mules, a rate year by year.
25 And Solomon had four thousand stalls for horses and chariots, and twelve thousand horsemen; whom he bestowed in the chariot cities, and with the king at Jerusalem.
26 And he reigned over all the kings from the river even unto the land of the Philistines, and to the border of Egypt.
27 And the king made silver in Jerusalem as stones, and cedar trees made he as the sycamore trees that *are* in the low plains in abundance.
28 And they brought unto Solomon horses out of Egypt, and out of all lands.
29 Now the rest of the acts of Solomon, first and last, *are* they not written in the book of Nathan the prophet, and in the prophecy of Ahijah the Shilonite, and in the visions of Iddo the seer against Jeroboam the son of Nebat?
30 And Solomon reigned in Jerusalem over all Israel forty years.
31 And Solomon slept with his fathers, and he was buried in the city of David his father: and Rehoboam his son reigned in his stead.

CHAPTER 10

1 And Rehoboam went to Shechem: for to Shechem were all Israel come to make him king.
2 And it came to pass, when Jeroboam the son of Nebat, who *was* in Egypt, where he had fled from the presence of Solomon the king, heard *it*, that Jeroboam returned out of Egypt.
3 And they sent and called him. So Jeroboam and all Israel came and spoke to Rehoboam, saying,
4 your father made our yoke grievous: now therefore ease you somewhat the grievous servitude of your father, and his heavy yoke that he put upon us, and we will serve you.
5 And he said unto them, come again unto me after three days. And the people departed.
6 And king Rehoboam took counsel with the old men that had stood before Solomon his father while he yet lived, saying, What counsel give you *me* to return answer to this people?
7 And they spoke unto him, saying, if you be kind to this people, and please them, and speak good words to them, they will be your servants forever.
8 But he forsook the counsel which the old men gave him, and took counsel with the young men that were brought up with him, that stood before him.
9 And he said unto them, what advice give ye that we may return answer to this people, which have spoken to me, saying, ease somewhat the yoke that your father did put upon us?
10 And the young men that were brought up with him spoke unto him, saying, Thus will you answer the people that spoke unto you, saying, your father made our yoke heavy, but make you *it* somewhat lighter for us; thus will you say unto them, My little *finger* will be thicker than my father's loins.
11 For whereas my father put a heavy yoke upon you, I will put more to your yoke: my father chastised you with whips, but I *will chastise you* with scorpions.
12 So Jeroboam and all the people came to Rehoboam on the third day, as the king bade, saying, come again to me on the third day.
13 And the king answered them roughly; and king Rehoboam forsook the counsel of the old men,
14 And answered them after the advice of the young men, saying, My father made your yoke heavy, but I will add thereto: my father chastised you with whips, but I *will chastise you* with scorpions.
15 So the king hearkened not unto the people: for the cause was of God, that the LORD might perform his word, which he spoke by the hand of Ahijah the Shilonite to Jeroboam the son of Nebat.
16 And when all Israel *saw* that the king would not hearken unto them, the people answered the king, saying, what portion have we in David? And *we have* none inheritance in the son of Jesse: every man to your tents, O Israel: *and* now, David, see to your own house. So all Israel went to their tents.
17 But *as for* the children of Israel that dwelt in the cities of Judah, Rehoboam reigned over them.
18 Then king Rehoboam sent Hadoram that *was* over the tribute; and the children of Israel stoned him with stones, that he died. But king Rehoboam made speed to get him up to *his* chariot, to flee to Jerusalem.
19 And Israel rebelled against the house of David unto this day.

CHAPTER 11

1 And when Rehoboam was come to Jerusalem, he gathered of the house of Judah and Benjamin an hundred and fourscore thousand chosen *men*, which were warriors, to fight against Israel, that he might bring the kingdom again to Rehoboam.
2 But the word of the LORD came to Shemaiah the man of God, saying,
3 Speak unto Rehoboam the son of Solomon, king of Judah, and to all Israel in Judah and Benjamin, saying,
4 Thus said the LORD, you will not go up, nor fight against your brethren: return every man to his house: for this thing is done of me. And they obeyed the words of the LORD, and returned from going against Jeroboam.
5 And Rehoboam dwelt in Jerusalem, and built cities for defence in Judah.
6 He built even Beth-lehem, and Etam, and Tekoa,
7 And Beth-zur, and Shoco, and Adullam,
8 And Gath, and Mareshah, and Ziph,
9 And Adoraim, and Lachish, and Azekah,
10 And Zorah, and Aijalon, and Hebron, which *are* in Judah and in Benjamin fenced cities.

11 And he fortified the strong holds, and put captains in them, and store of victual, and of oil and wine.
12 And in every several city *he put* shields and spears, and made them exceeding strong, having Judah and Benjamin on his side.
13 And the priests and the Levites that *were* in all Israel resorted to him out of all their coasts.
14 For the Levites left their suburbs and their possession, and came to Judah and Jerusalem: for Jeroboam and his sons had cast them off from executing the priest's office unto the LORD:
15 And he ordained him priests for the high places, and for the devils, and for the calves which he had made.
16 And after them out of all the tribes of Israel such as set their hearts to seek the LORD God of Israel came to Jerusalem, to sacrifice unto the LORD God of their fathers.
17 So they strengthened the kingdom of Judah, and made Rehoboam the son of Solomon strong, three years: for three years they walked in the way of David and Solomon.
18 And Rehoboam took him Mahalath the daughter of Jerimoth the son of David to wife, *and* Abihail the daughter of Eliab the son of Jesse;
19 Which bare him children; Jeush, and Shamariah, and Zaham.
20 And after her he took Maachah the daughter of Absalom; which bare him Abijah, and Attai, and Ziza, and Shelomith.
21 And Rehoboam loved Maachah the daughter of Absalom above all his wives and his concubines: (for he took eighteen wives, and threescore concubines; and begat twenty and eight sons, and threescore daughters.)
22 And Rehoboam made Abijah the son of Maachah the chief, *to be* ruler among his brethren: for *he thought* to make him king.
23 And he dealt wisely, and dispersed of all his children throughout all the countries of Judah and Benjamin, unto every fenced city: and he gave them victual in abundance. And he desired many wives.

CHAPTER 12

1 And it came to pass, when Rehoboam had established the kingdom, and had strengthened himself, he forsook the law of the LORD, and all Israel with him.
2 And it came to pass, *that* in the fifth year of king Rehoboam Shishak king of Egypt came up against Jerusalem, because they had transgressed against the LORD,
3 With twelve hundred chariots, and threescore thousand horsemen: and the people *were* without number that came with him out of Egypt; the Lubims, the Sukkiims, and the Ethiopians.
4 And he took the fenced cities which *pertained* to Judah, and came to Jerusalem.
5 Then came Shemaiah the prophet to Rehoboam, and *to* the princes of Judah, that were gathered together to Jerusalem because of Shishak, and said unto them, Thus said the LORD, you have forsaken me, and therefore have I also left you in the hand of Shishak.
6 Whereupon the princes of Israel and the king humbled themselves; and they said, The LORD *is* righteous.
7 And when the LORD saw that they humbled themselves, the word of the LORD came to Shemaiah, saying, they have humbled themselves; *therefore* I will not destroy them, but I will grant them some deliverance; and my wrath will not be poured out upon Jerusalem by the hand of Shishak.
8 Nevertheless they will be his servants; that they may know my service, and the service of the kingdoms of the countries.
9 So Shishak king of Egypt came up against Jerusalem, and took away the treasures of the house of the LORD, and the treasures of the king's house; he took all: he carried away also the shields of gold which Solomon had made.
10 Instead of which king Rehoboam made shields of brass, and committed *them* to the hands of the chief of the guard, that kept the entrance of the king's house.
11 And when the king entered into the house of the LORD, the guard came and fetched them, and brought them again into the guard chamber.
12 And when he humbled himself, the wrath of the LORD turned from him, that he would not destroy *him* altogether: and also in Judah things went well.
13 So king Rehoboam strengthened himself in Jerusalem, and reigned: for Rehoboam *was* one and forty years old when he began to reign, and he reigned seventeen years in Jerusalem, the city which the LORD had chosen out of all the tribes of Israel, to put his name there. And his mother's name *was* Naamah an Ammonitess.
14 And he did evil, because he prepared not his heart to seek the LORD.
15 Now the acts of Rehoboam, first and last, *are* they not written in the book of Shemaiah the prophet, and of Iddo the seer concerning genealogies? And *there were* wars between Rehoboam and Jeroboam continually.
16 And Rehoboam slept with his fathers, and was buried in the city of David: and Abijah his son reigned in his stead.

CHAPTER 13

1 Now in the eighteenth year of king Jeroboam began Abijah to reign over Judah.
2 He reigned three years in Jerusalem. His mother's name also *was* Michaiah the daughter of Uriel of Gibeah. And there was war between Abijah and Jeroboam.
3 And Abijah set the battle in array with an army of valiant men of war, *even* four hundred thousand chosen men: Jeroboam also set the battle in array against him with eight hundred thousand chosen men, *being* mighty men of valor.
4 And Abijah stood up upon mount Zemaraim, which *is* in mount Ephraim, and said, Hear me, you Jeroboam, and all Israel;
5 Ought you not to know that the LORD God of Israel gave the kingdom over Israel to David forever, *even* to him and to his sons by a covenant of salt?
6 Yet Jeroboam the son of Nebat, the servant of Solomon the son of David, is risen up, and has rebelled against his lord.
7 And there are gathered unto him vain men, the children of Belial, and have strengthened themselves against Rehoboam the son of Solomon, when Rehoboam was young and tenderhearted, and could not withstand them.
8 And now you think to withstand the kingdom of the LORD in the hand of the sons of David; and you *be* a great multitude, and *there are* with you golden calves, which Jeroboam made you for gods.
9 Have you not cast out the priests of the LORD, the sons of Aaron, and the Levites, and have made you priests after the manner of the nations of *other* lands? So that whosoever cometh to consecrate himself with a young bullock and seven rams, *the same* may be a priest of *them that are* no gods.
10 But as for us, the LORD *is* our God, and we have not forsaken him; and the priests, which minister unto the LORD, *are* the sons of Aaron, and the Levites *wait* upon *their* business:

11 And they burn unto the LORD every morning and every evening burnt sacrifices and sweet incense: the shewbread also *set* **them** *in order* upon the pure table; and the candlestick of gold with the lamps thereof, to burn every evening: for we keep the charge of the LORD our God; but you have forsaken him.
12 And, behold, God himself *is* with us for *our* captain, and his priests with sounding trumpets to cry alarm against you. O children of Israel, fight you not against the LORD God of your fathers; for you will not prosper.
13 But Jeroboam caused an **ambush** to come about behind them: so they were before Judah, and the **ambush** *was* behind them.
14 And when Judah looked back, behold, the battle *was* before and behind: and they cried unto the LORD, and the priests sounded with the trumpets.
15 Then the men of Judah gave a shout: and as the men of Judah shouted, it came to pass, that God smote Jeroboam and all Israel before Abijah and Judah.
16 And the children of Israel fled before Judah: and God delivered them into their hand.
17 And Abijah and his people slew them with a great slaughter: so there fell down slain of Israel five hundred thousand chosen men.
18 Thus the children of Israel were brought under at that time, and the children of Judah prevailed, because they relied upon the LORD God of their fathers.
19 And Abijah pursued after Jeroboam, and took cities from him, Beth-el with the towns thereof, and Jeshanah with the towns thereof, and Ephrain with the towns thereof.
20 Neither did Jeroboam recover strength again in the days of Abijah: and the LORD struck him, and he died.
21 But Abijah waxed mighty, and married fourteen wives, and begat twenty and two sons, and sixteen daughters.
22 And the rest of the acts of Abijah, and his ways, and his sayings, *are* written in the story of the prophet Iddo.

CHAPTER 14

1 So Abijah slept with his fathers, and they buried him in the city of David: and Asa his son reigned in his stead. In his days the land was quiet ten years.
2 And Asa did *that which was* good and right in the eyes of the LORD his God:
3 For he took away the altars of the strange *gods*, and the high places, and broke down the images, and cut down the groves:
4 And commanded Judah to seek the LORD God of their fathers, and to do the law and the commandment.
5 Also he took away out of all the cities of Judah the high places and the images: and the kingdom was quiet before him.
6 And he built fenced cities in Judah: for the land had rest, and he had no war in those years; because the LORD had given him rest.
7 Therefore he said unto Judah, Let us build these cities, and make about *them* walls, and towers, gates, and bars, *while* the land *is* yet before us; because we have sought the LORD our God, we have sought *him*, and he has given us rest on every side. So they built and prospered.
8 And Asa had an army *of men* that bare targets and spears, out of Judah three hundred thousand; and out of Benjamin, that bare shields and drew bows, two hundred and fourscore thousand: all these *were* mighty men of valor.
9 And there came out against them Zerah the Ethiopian with a host of a thousand thousand, and three hundred chariots; and came unto Mareshah.
10 Then Asa went out against him, and they set the battle in array in the valley of Zephathah at Mareshah.
11 And Asa cried unto the LORD his God, and said, LORD, *it is* nothing with you to help, whether with many, or with them that have no power: help us, O LORD our God; for we rest on you, and in your name we go against this multitude. O LORD, you are our God; let not man prevail against you.
12 So the LORD smote the Ethiopians before Asa, and before Judah; and the Ethiopians fled.
13 And Asa and the people that *were* with him pursued them unto Gerar: and the Ethiopians were overthrown, that they could not recover themselves; for they were destroyed before the LORD, and before his host; and they carried away very much spoil.
14 And they smote all the cities round about Gerar; for the fear of the LORD came upon them: and they spoiled all the cities; for there was exceeding much spoil in them.
15 They smote also the tents of cattle, and carried away sheep and camels in abundance, and returned to Jerusalem.

CHAPTER 15

1 And the Spirit of God came upon Azariah the son of Oded:
2 And he went out to meet Asa, and said unto him, hear you me, Asa, and all Judah and Benjamin; The LORD *is* with you, while you be with him; and if you seek him, he will be found of you; but if you forsake him, he will forsake you.
3 Now for a long season Israel has *been* without the true God, and without a teaching priest, and without law.
4 But when they in their trouble did turn unto the LORD God of Israel, and sought him, he was found of them.
5 And in those times *there was* no peace to him that went out, nor to him that came in, but great vexations *were* upon all the inhabitants of the countries.
6 And nation was destroyed of nation, and city of city: for God did vex them with all adversity.
7 Be you strong therefore, and let not your hands be weak: for your work will be rewarded.
8 And when Asa heard these words, and the prophecy of Oded the prophet, he took courage, and put away the abominable idols out of all the land of Judah and Benjamin, and out of the cities which he had taken from mount Ephraim, and renewed the altar of the LORD, that *was* before the porch of the LORD.
9 And he gathered all Judah and Benjamin, and the strangers with them out of Ephraim and Manasseh, and out of Simeon: for they fell to him out of Israel in abundance, when they saw that the LORD his God *was* with him.
10 So they gathered themselves together at Jerusalem in the third month, in the fifteenth year of the reign of Asa.
11 And they offered unto the LORD the same time, of the spoil which they had brought, seven hundred oxen and seven thousand sheep.
12 And they entered into a covenant to seek the LORD God of their fathers with all their heart and with all their soul;
13 That whosoever would not seek the LORD God of Israel should be put to death, whether small or great, whether man or woman.
14 And they swore unto the LORD with a loud voice, and with shouting, and with trumpets, and with cornets.
15 And all Judah rejoiced at the oath: for they had sworn with all their heart, and sought him with their whole desire; and he was found of them: and the LORD gave them rest round about.
16 And also *concerning* Maachah the mother of Asa the king, he removed her from *being* queen, because she had made an idol in

a grove: and Asa cut down her idol, and stamped *it*, and burnt *it* at the brook Kidron.

17 But the high places were not taken away out of Israel: nevertheless the heart of Asa was perfect all his days.

18 And he brought into the house of God the things that his father had dedicated, and that he himself had dedicated, silver, and gold, and vessels.

19 And there was no *more* war unto the five and thirtieth year of the reign of Asa.

CHAPTER 16

1 In the six and thirtieth year of the reign of Asa Baasha king of Israel came up against Judah, and built Ramah, to the intent that he might let none go out or come in to Asa king of Judah.

2 Then Asa brought out silver and gold out of the treasures of the house of the LORD and of the king's house, and sent to Ben-hadad king of Syria, that dwelt at Damascus, saying,

3 *There is* a league between me and you, as *there was* between my father and your father: behold, I have sent you silver and gold; go, break your league with Baasha king of Israel, that he may depart from me.

4 And Ben-hadad hearkened unto king Asa, and sent the captains of his armies against the cities of Israel; and they smote Ijon, and Dan, and Abel-maim, and all the store cities of Naphtali.

5 And it came to pass, when Baasha heard *it*, that he left off building of Ramah, and let his work cease.

6 Then Asa the king took all Judah; and they carried away the stones of Ramah, and the timber thereof, wherewith Baasha was building; and he built therewith Geba and Mizpah.

7 And at that time Hanani the seer came to Asa king of Judah, and said unto him, because you have relied on the king of Syria, and not relied on the LORD your God, therefore is the host of the king of Syria escaped out of your hand.

8 Were not the Ethiopians and the Lubims a huge host, with very many chariots and horsemen? Yet, because you did rely on the LORD, he delivered them into your hand.

9 For the eyes of the LORD run to and fro throughout the whole earth, to show himself strong in the behalf of *them* whose heart *is* perfect toward him. Herein you have done foolishly: therefore from henceforth you will have wars.

10 Then Asa was wroth with the seer, and put him in a prison house; for *he was* in a rage with him because of this *thing*. And Asa oppressed *some* of the people the same time.

11 And, behold, the acts of Asa, first and last, lo, they *are* written in the book of the kings of Judah and Israel.

12 And Asa in the thirty and ninth year of his reign was diseased in his feet, until his disease *was* exceeding *great*: yet in his disease he sought not to the LORD, but to the physicians.

13 And Asa slept with his fathers, and died in the one and fortieth year of his reign.

14 And they buried him in his own sepulchers, which he had made for himself in the city of David, and laid him in the bed which was filled with sweet odors and divers kinds *of spices* prepared by the apothecaries' art: and they made a very great burning for him.

CHAPTER 17

1 And Jehoshaphat his son reigned in his stead, and strengthened himself against Israel.

2 And he placed forces in all the fenced cities of Judah, and set garrisons in the land of Judah, and in the cities of Ephraim, which Asa his father had taken.

3 And the LORD was with Jehoshaphat, because he walked in the first ways of his father David, and sought not unto Baalim;

4 But sought to the LORD God of his father, and walked in his commandments, and not after the doings of Israel.

5 Therefore the LORD established the kingdom in his hand; and all Judah brought to Jehoshaphat presents; and he had riches and honor in abundance.

6 And his heart was lifted up in the ways of the LORD: moreover he took away the high places and groves out of Judah.

7 Also in the third year of his reign he sent to his princes, *even* to Benhail, and to Obadiah, and to Zechariah, and to Nethaneel, and to Michaiah, to teach in the cities of Judah.

8 And with them *he sent* Levites, *even* Shemaiah, and Nethaniah, and Zebadiah, and Asahel, and Shemiramoth, and Jehonathan, and Adonijah, and Tobijah, and Tobadonijah, Levites; and with them Elishama and Jehoram, priests.

9 And they taught in Judah, and *had* the book of the law of the LORD with them, and went about throughout all the cities of Judah, and taught the people.

10 And the fear of the LORD fell upon all the kingdoms of the lands that *were* round about Judah, so that they made no war against Jehoshaphat.

11 Also *some* of the Philistines brought Jehoshaphat presents, and tribute silver; and the Arabians brought him flocks, seven thousand and seven hundred rams, and seven thousand and seven hundred he goats.

12 And Jehoshaphat waxed great exceedingly; and he built in Judah castles, and cities of store.

13 And he had much business in the cities of Judah: and the men of war, mighty men of valor, *were* in Jerusalem.

14 And these *are* the numbers of them according to the house of their fathers: Of Judah, the captains of thousands; Adnah the chief, and with him mighty men of valor three hundred thousand.

15 And next to him *was* Jehohanan the captain, and with him two hundred and fourscore thousand.

16 And next *to* him *was* Amasiah the son of Zichri, who willingly offered himself unto the LORD; and with him two hundred thousand mighty men of valor.

17 And of Benjamin; Eliada a mighty man of valor, and with him armed men with bow and shield two hundred thousand.

18 And next *to* him *was* Jehozabad, and with him a hundred and fourscore thousand ready prepared for the war.

19 These waited on the king, beside *those* whom the king put in the fenced cities throughout all Judah.

CHAPTER 18

1 Now Jehoshaphat had riches and honor in abundance, and joined affinity with Ahab.

2 And after *certain* years he went down to Ahab to Samaria. And Ahab killed sheep and oxen for him in abundance, and for the people that *he had* with him, and persuaded him to go up *with him* to Ramoth-gilead.

3 And Ahab king of Israel said unto Jehoshaphat king of Judah, will you go with me to Ramoth-gilead? And he answered him, I *am* as you *art*, and my people as your people; and *we will be* with you in the war.

4 And Jehoshaphat said unto the king of Israel, Enquire, I pray you, at the word of the LORD today.

5 Therefore the king of Israel gathered together of prophets four hundred men, and said unto them, will we go to Ramoth-gilead to battle, or will I forbear? And they said, Go up; for God will deliver it into the king's hand.

6 But Jehoshaphat said, is there not here a prophet of the LORD besides, that we might enquire of him?

7 And the king of Israel said unto Jehoshaphat, There is yet one man, by whom we may enquire of the LORD: but I hate him; for he never prophesied good unto me, but always evil[1]: the same is Micaiah the son of Imla. And Jehoshaphat said, let not the king say so.

8 And the king of Israel called for one of his officers, and said, fetch quickly Micaiah the son of Imla.

9 And the king of Israel and Jehoshaphat king of Judah sat either of them on his throne, clothed in their robes, and they sat in a void place at the entering in of the gate of Samaria; and [all the prophets prophesied before them][2].

10 And Zedekiah the son of Chenaanah had made him horns of iron, and said, Thus said the LORD, With these you will push Syria until they be consumed.

11 And all the prophets prophesied so, saying, Go up to Ramoth-gilead, and prosper: for the LORD will deliver it into the hand of the king.

12 And the messenger that went to call Micaiah spoke to him, saying, Behold, the words of the prophets declare good to the king with one assent; let your word therefore, I pray you, be like one of their's, and speak you good.

13 And Micaiah said, As the LORD lives, even what my God saith, that will I speak.

14 And when he was come to the king, the king said unto him, Micaiah, will we go to Ramoth-gilead to battle, or will I forbear? And he said, Go you up, and prosper, and they will be delivered into your hand.

15 And the king said to him, how many times will I adjure you that you say nothing but the truth to me in the name of the LORD?

16 Then he said, I did see all Israel scattered upon the mountains, as sheep that have no shepherd: and the LORD said, these have no master; let them return therefore every man to his house in peace.

17 And the king of Israel said to Jehoshaphat, Did I not tell you that he would not prophesy good unto me, but evil?

18 Again he said, therefore hear the word of the LORD; I saw the LORD sitting upon his throne, and all the host of heaven standing on his right hand and on his left.

19 And the LORD said, who will entice Ahab king of Israel, that he may go up and fall at Ramoth-gilead? And one spoke saying after this manner, and another saying after that manner.

20 Then there came out a spirit, and stood before the LORD, and said, I will entice him. And the LORD said unto him, wherewith?

21 And he said, I will go out, and be a lying spirit in the mouth[3] of all his prophets. And the LORD said, you will entice him, and you will also prevail: go out, and do even so.

22 Now therefore, behold, the LORD has put a lying spirit in the mouth of these your prophets, and the LORD has spoken evil against you.

23 Then Zedekiah the son of Chenaanah came near, and smote Micaiah upon the cheek, and said, which way went the Spirit of the LORD from me to speak unto you?

24 And Micaiah said, Behold, you will see on that day when you will go into an inner chamber to hide thyself.

25 Then the king of Israel said, Take you Micaiah, and carry him back to Amon the governor of the city, and to Joash the king's son;

26 And say, Thus said the king, Put this fellow in the prison, and feed him with bread of affliction and with water of affliction, until I return in peace.

27 And Micaiah said, if you certainly return in peace, then has not the LORD spoken by me. And he said, Hearken, all you people.

28 So the king of Israel and Jehoshaphat the king of Judah went up to Ramoth-gilead.

29 And the king of Israel said unto Jehoshaphat, I will disguise myself, and will go to the battle; but put you on your robes. So the king of Israel disguised himself; and they went to the battle.

30 Now the king of Syria had commanded the captains of the chariots that were with him, saying, Fight you not with small or great, save only with the king of Israel.

31 And it came to pass, when the captains of the chariots saw Jehoshaphat, that they said, It is the king of Israel. Therefore they compassed about him to fight: but Jehoshaphat cried out, and the LORD helped him; and God moved them to depart from him.

32 For it came to pass, that, when the captains of the chariots perceived that it was not the king of Israel, they turned back again from pursuing him.

33 And a certain man drew a bow at a venture, and smote the king of Israel between the joints of the harness: therefore he said to his chariot man, Turn your hand, that you may carry me out of the host; for I am wounded.

34 And the battle increased that day: howbeit the king of Israel stayed himself up in his chariot against the Syrians until the even: and about the time of the sun going down he died.

CHAPTER 19

1 And Jehoshaphat the king of Judah returned to his house in peace to Jerusalem.

2 And Jehu the son of Hanani the seer went out to meet him, and said to King Jehoshaphat, Shouldest you help the ungodly, and love them that hate the LORD? Therefore is wrath upon you from before the LORD.

3 Nevertheless there are good things found in you, in that you have taken away the groves out of the land, and have prepared your heart to seek God.

4 And Jehoshaphat dwelt at Jerusalem: and he went out again through the people from Beer-sheba to mount Ephraim, and brought them back unto the LORD God of their fathers.

5 And he set judges in the land throughout all the fenced cities of Judah, city by city,

6 And said to the judges, take heed what you do: for you judge not for man, but for the LORD, who is with you in the judgment.

7 Wherefore now let the fear of the LORD be upon you; take heed and do it: for there is no iniquity with the LORD our God, or respect of persons, or taking of gifts.

8 Moreover in Jerusalem did Jehoshaphat set of the Levites, and of the priests, and of the chief of the fathers of Israel, for the judgment of the LORD, and for controversies, when they returned to Jerusalem.

9 And he charged them, saying, Thus will you do in the fear of the LORD, faithfully, and with a perfect heart.

10 And what cause so ever will come to you of your brethren that dwell in their cities, between blood and blood, between law and

---

[1] lit. evil all his days [Strgs#7451]
[2] compare **Rev. 13:12-14**

[3] compare **Rev. 16:13**

commandment, statutes and judgments, you will even warn them that they trespass not against the LORD, and so wrath come upon you, and upon your brethren: this do, and you will not trespass.

11 And, behold, Amariah the chief priest *is* over you in all matters of the LORD; and Zebadiah the son of Ishmael, the ruler of the house of Judah, for all the king's matters: also the Levites will *be* officers before you. Deal courageously, and the LORD will be with the good.

CHAPTER 20

1 It came to pass after this also, *that* the children of Moab, and the children of Ammon, and with them *other* beside the Ammonites, came against Jehoshaphat to battle.
2 Then there came some that told Jehoshaphat, saying, There cometh a great multitude against you from beyond the sea on this side Syria; and, behold, they *be* in Hazazon-tamar, which *is* En-gedi.
3 And Jehoshaphat feared, and set himself to seek the LORD, and proclaimed a fast throughout all Judah.
4 And Judah gathered themselves together, to ask *help* of the LORD: even out of all the cities of Judah they came to seek the LORD.
5 And Jehoshaphat stood in the congregation of Judah and Jerusalem, in the house of the LORD, before the new court,
6 And said, O LORD God of our fathers, are not you God in heaven? And rules *not* you over all the kingdoms of the heathen? And in your hand *is there not* power and might, so that none is able to withstand you?
7 *Are* not you our God, *who* did drive out the inhabitants of this land before your people Israel, and gave it to the seed of Abraham your friend forever?
8 And they dwelt therein, and have built you a sanctuary therein for your name, saying,
9 If, *when* evil cometh upon us, *as* the sword, judgment, or pestilence, or famine, we stand before this house, and in your presence, (for your name *is* in this house,) and cry unto you in our affliction, then you will hear and help.
10 And now, behold, the children of Ammon and Moab and mount Seir, whom you would not let Israel invade, when they came out of the land of Egypt, but they turned from them, and destroyed them not;
11 Behold, *I say, how* they reward us, to come to cast us out of your possession, which you have given us to inherit.
12 O our God, will you not judge them? For we have no might against this great company that cometh against us; neither know we what to do: but our eyes *are* upon you.
13 And all Judah stood before the LORD, with their little ones, their wives, and their children.
14 Then upon Jahaziel the son of Zechariah, the son of Benaiah, the son of Jeiel, the son of Mattaniah, a Levite of the sons of Asaph, came the Spirit of the LORD in the midst of the congregation;
15 And he said, Hearken ye, all Judah, and you inhabitants of Jerusalem, and you king Jehoshaphat, Thus said the LORD unto you, Be not afraid or dismayed by reason of this great multitude; for the battle *is* not yours, but God's.
16 To morrow go you down against them: behold, they come up by the cliff of Ziz; and you will find them at the end of the brook, before the wilderness of Jeruel.
17 you will not *need* to fight in this *battle*: set yourselves, stand you *still*, and see the salvation of the LORD with you, O Judah and Jerusalem: fear not, or be dismayed; tomorrow go out against them: for the LORD *will be* with you.
18 And Jehoshaphat bowed his head with *his* face to the ground: and all Judah and the inhabitants of Jerusalem fell before the LORD, worshipping the LORD.
19 And the Levites, of the children of the Kohathites, and of the children of the Korhites, stood up to praise the LORD God of Israel with a loud voice on high.
20 And they rose early in the morning, and went forth into the wilderness of Tekoa: and as they went forth, Jehoshaphat stood and said, hear me, O Judah, and you inhabitants of Jerusalem; Believe in the LORD your God, so will you be established; believe his prophets, so will you prosper.
21 And when he had consulted with the people, he appointed singers unto the LORD, and that should praise the beauty of holiness, as they went out before the army, and to say, Praise the LORD; for his mercy *endures* forever.
22 And when they began to sing and to praise, the LORD set ambushments against the children of Ammon, Moab, and mount Seir, which were come against Judah; and they were smitten.
23 For the children of Ammon and Moab stood up against the inhabitants of mount Seir, utterly to slay and destroy *them*: and when they had made an end of the inhabitants of Seir, every one helped to destroy another.
24 And when Judah came toward the watch tower in the wilderness, they looked unto the multitude, and, behold, they *were* dead bodies fallen to the earth, and none escaped.
25 And when Jehoshaphat and his people came to take away the spoil of them, they found among them in abundance both riches with the dead bodies, and precious jewels, which they stripped off for themselves, more than they could carry away: and they were three days in gathering of the spoil, it was so much.
26 And on the fourth day they assembled themselves in the valley of Berachah; for there they blessed the LORD: therefore the name of the same place was called, the valley of Berachah, unto this day.
27 Then they returned, every man of Judah and Jerusalem, and Jehoshaphat in the forefront of them, to go again to Jerusalem with joy; for the LORD had made them to rejoice over their enemies.
28 And they came to Jerusalem with psalteries and harps and trumpets unto the house of the LORD.
29 And the fear of God was on all the kingdoms of *those* countries, when they had heard that the LORD fought against the enemies of Israel.
30 So the realm of Jehoshaphat was quiet: for his God gave him rest round about.
31 And Jehoshaphat reigned over Judah: *he was* thirty and five years old when he began to reign, and he reigned twenty and five years in Jerusalem. And his mother's name *was* Azubah the daughter of Shilhi.
32 And he walked in the way of Asa his father, and departed not from it, doing *that which was* right in the sight of the LORD.
33 Howbeit the high places were not taken away: for as yet the people had not prepared their hearts unto the God of their fathers.
34 Now the rest of the acts of Jehoshaphat, first and last, behold, they *are* written in the book of Jehu the son of Hanani, who *is* mentioned in the book of the kings of Israel.
35 And after this did Jehoshaphat king of Judah join himself with Ahaziah King of Israel, who did very wickedly:
36 And he joined himself with him to make ships to go to Tarshish: and they made the ships in Ezion-geber.

37 Then Eliezer the son of Dodavah of Mareshah prophesied against Jehoshaphat, saying, because you have joined yourself with Ahaziah, the LORD has broken your works. And the ships were broken, that they were not able to go to Tarshish.

CHAPTER 21

1 Now Jehoshaphat slept with his fathers, and was buried with his fathers in the city of David. And Jehoram his son reigned in his stead.

2 And he had brethren the sons of Jehoshaphat, Azariah, and Jehiel, and Zechariah, and Azariah, and Michael, and Shephatiah: all these *were* the sons of Jehoshaphat king of Israel.

3 And their father gave them great gifts of silver, and of gold, and of precious things, with fenced cities in Judah: but the kingdom **he** gave to Jehoram; because he *was* the firstborn.

4 Now when Jehoram was risen up to the kingdom of his father, he strengthened himself, and slew all his brethren with the sword, and *divers* also of the princes of Israel.

5 Jehoram *was* thirty and two years old when he began to reign, and he reigned eight years in Jerusalem.

6 And he walked in the way of the kings of Israel, like as did the house of Ahab: for he had the daughter of Ahab to wife: and he wrought *that which was* evil in the eyes of the LORD.

7 Howbeit the LORD would not destroy the house of David, because of the covenant that he had made with David, and as he promised to give a light to him and to his sons forever.

8 In his days the Edomites revolted from under the dominion of Judah, and made themselves a king.

9 Then Jehoram went forth with his princes, and all his chariots with him: and he rose up by night, and smote the Edomites which compassed him in, and the captains of the chariots.

10 So the Edomites revolted from under the hand of Judah unto this day. The same time *also* did Libnah revolt from under his hand; because he had forsaken the LORD God of his fathers.

11 Moreover he made high places in the mountains of Judah, and caused the inhabitants of Jerusalem to commit fornication, and compelled Judah *thereto*.

12 And there came a writing to him from Elijah the prophet, saying, Thus said the LORD God of David your father, Because you have not walked in the ways of Jehoshaphat your father, or in the ways of Asa king of Judah,

13 But have walked in the way of the kings of Israel, and have made Judah and the inhabitants of Jerusalem to go a whoring, like to the whoredoms of the house of Ahab, and also have slain your brethren of your father's house, *which were* better than thyself:

14 Behold, with a great plague will the LORD smite your people, and your children, and your wives, and all your goods:

15 And you will *have* great sickness by disease of your bowels, until your bowels fall out by reason of the sickness day by day.

16 Moreover the LORD stirred up against Jehoram the spirit of the Philistines, and of the Arabians, that *were* near the Ethiopians:

17 And they came up into Judah, and brake into it, and carried away all the substance that was found in the king's house, and his sons also, and his wives; so that there was never a son left him, save Jehoahaz, the youngest of his sons.

18 And after all this the LORD smote him in his bowels with an incurable disease.

19 And it came to pass, that in process of time, after the end of two years, his bowels fell out by reason of his sickness: so he died of sore diseases. And his people made no burning for him, like the burning of his fathers.

20 Thirty and two years old was he when he began to reign, and he reigned in Jerusalem eight years, and departed without being desired. Howbeit they buried him in the city of David, but not in the sepulchres of the kings.

CHAPTER 22

1 And the inhabitants of Jerusalem made Ahaziah his youngest son king in his stead: for the band of men that came with the Arabians to the camp had slain all the eldest. So Ahaziah the son of Jehoram king of Judah reigned.

2 Forty and two years old *was* Ahaziah when he began to reign, and he reigned one year in Jerusalem. His mother's name also *was* Athaliah the daughter of Omri.

3 He also walked in the ways of the house of Ahab: for his mother was his counselor to do wickedly.

4 Wherefore he did evil in the sight of the LORD like the house of Ahab: for they were his counselors after the death of his father to his destruction.

5 He walked also after their counsel, and went with Jehoram the son of Ahab king of Israel to war against Hazael king of Syria at Ramoth-gilead: and the Syrians smote Joram.

6 And he returned to be healed in Jezreel because of the wounds which were given him at Ramah, when he fought with Hazael king of Syria. And Azariah the son of Jehoram king of Judah went down to see Jehoram the son of Ahab at Jezreel, because he was sick.

7 And the destruction of Ahaziah was of God by coming to Joram: for when he was come, he went out with Jehoram against Jehu the son of Nimshi, whom the LORD had anointed to cut off the house of Ahab.

8 And it came to pass, that, when Jehu was executing judgment upon the house of Ahab, and found the princes of Judah, and the sons of the brethren of Ahaziah, that ministered to Ahaziah, he slew them.

9 And he sought Ahaziah: and they caught him, (for he was hid in Samaria,) and brought him to Jehu: and when they had slain him, they buried him: Because, said they, he *is* the son of Jehoshaphat, who sought the LORD with all his heart. So the house of Ahaziah had no power to keep still the kingdom.

10 But when Athaliah the mother of Ahaziah saw that her son was dead, she arose and destroyed all the seed royal of the house of Judah.

11 But Jehoshabeath, the daughter of the king, took Joash the son of Ahaziah, and stole him from among the king's sons that were slain, and put him and his nurse in a bedchamber. So Jehoshabeath, the daughter of king Jehoram, the wife of Jehoiada the priest, (for she was the sister of Ahaziah,) hid him from Athaliah, so that she slew him not.

12 And he was with them hid in the house of God six years: and Athaliah reigned over the land.

CHAPTER 23

1 And in the seventh year Jehoiada strengthened himself, and took the captains of hundreds, Azariah the son of Jeroham, and Ishmael the son of Jehohanan, and Azariah the son of Obed, and Maaseiah the son of Adaiah, and Elishaphat the son of Zichri, into covenant with him.

2 And they went about in Judah, and gathered the Levites out of all the cities of Judah, and the chief of the fathers of Israel, and they came to Jerusalem.

3 And the **entire** congregation made a covenant with the king in the house of God. And he said unto them, Behold, the king's son will reign, as the LORD has said of the sons of David.

4 This *is* the thing that you will do; A third part of you entering on the Sabbath, of the priests and of the Levites, will *be* porters of the doors;

5 And a third part will *be* at the king's house; and a third part at the gate of the foundation: and all the people will *be* in the courts of the house of the LORD.

6 But let none come into the house of the LORD, save the priests, and they that minister of the Levites; they will go in, for they *are* holy: but all the people will keep the watch of the LORD.

7 And the Levites will compass the king round about, every man with his weapons in his hand; and whosoever *else* cometh into the house, he will be put to death: but be you with the king when he cometh in, and when he goes out.

8 So the Levites and all Judah did according to all things that Jehoiada the priest had commanded, and took every man his men that were to come in on the Sabbath, with them that were to go *out* on the Sabbath: for Jehoiada the priest dismissed not the courses.

9 Moreover Jehoiada the priest delivered to the captains of hundreds spears, and bucklers, and shields, that *had been* King David's, which *were* in the house of God.

10 And he set all the people, every man having his weapon in his hand, from the right side of the temple to the left side of the temple, along by the altar and the temple, by the king round about.

11 Then they brought out the king's son, and put upon him the crown, and *gave him* the testimony, and made him king. And Jehoiada and his sons anointed him, and said, God save the king.

12 Now when Athaliah heard the noise of the people running and praising the king, she came to the people into the house of the LORD:

13 And she looked, and, behold, the king stood at his pillar at the entering in, and the princes and the trumpets by the king: and all the people of the land rejoiced, and sounded with trumpets, also the singers with instruments of music, and such as taught to sing praise. Then Athaliah rent her clothes, and said, Treason, Treason.

14 Then Jehoiada the priest brought out the captains of hundreds that were set over the host, and said unto them, have her forth of the ranges: and **whosoever** follows her, let him be slain with the sword. For the priest said, slay her not in the house of the LORD.

15 So they laid hands on her; and when she was come to the entering of the horse gate by the king's house, they slew her there.

16 And Jehoiada made a covenant between him, and between all the people, and between the king, that they should be the LORD'S people.

17 Then all the people went to the house of Baal, and broke it down, and **broke** his altars and his images in pieces, and **slaughtered** Mattan the priest of Baal before the altars.

18 Also Jehoiada appointed the offices of the house of the LORD by the hand of the priests the Levites, whom David had distributed in the house of the LORD, to offer the burnt offerings of the LORD, as *it is* written in the Law of Moses, with rejoicing and with singing, *as it was ordained* by David.

19 And he set the porters at the gates of the house of the LORD, that none *which was* unclean in anything should enter in.

20 And he took the captains of hundreds, and the nobles, and the governors of the people, and all the people of the land, and brought down the king from the house of the LORD: and they came through the high gate into the king's house, and set the king upon the throne of the kingdom.

21 And all the people of the land rejoiced: and the city was quiet, after that they had slain Athaliah with the sword.

CHAPTER 24

1 Joash *was* seven years old when he began to reign, and he reigned forty years in Jerusalem. His mother's name also *was* Zibiah of Beer-sheba.

2 And Joash did *that which was* right in the sight of the LORD all the days of Jehoiada the priest.

3 And Jehoiada took for him two wives; and he begat sons and daughters.

4 And it came to pass after this, *that* Joash was minded to repair the house of the LORD.

5 And he gathered together the priests and the Levites, and said to them, Go out unto the cities of Judah, and gather of all Israel money to repair the house of your God from year to year, and see that you hasten the matter. Howbeit the Levites hastened *it* not.

6 And the king called for Jehoiada the chief, and said unto him, why have you not required of the Levites to bring in out of Judah and out of Jerusalem the collection, *according to the commandment* of Moses the servant of the LORD, and of the congregation of Israel, for the tabernacle of witness?

7 For the sons of Athaliah, that wicked woman, had broken up the house of God; and also all the dedicated things of the house of the LORD did they bestow upon Baalim.

8 And at the king's commandment they made a chest, and set it without at the gate of the house of the LORD.

9 And they made a proclamation through Judah and Jerusalem, to bring in to the LORD the collection *that* Moses the servant of God *laid* upon Israel in the wilderness.

10 And all the princes and all the people rejoiced, and brought in, and cast into the chest, until they had made an end.

11 Now it came to pass, that at what time the chest was brought unto the king's office by the hand of the Levites, and when they saw that *there was* much money, the king's scribe and the high priest's officer came and emptied the chest, and took it, and carried it to his place again. Thus they did day by day, and gathered money in abundance.

12 And the king and Jehoiada gave it to such as did the work of the service of the house of the LORD, and hired masons and carpenters to repair the house of the LORD, and also such as wrought iron and brass to mend the house of the LORD.

13 So the workmen wrought, and the work was perfected by them, and they set the house of God in his state, and strengthened it.

14 And when they had finished *it*, they brought the rest of the money before the king and Jehoiada, whereof were made vessels for the house of the LORD, *even* vessels to minister, and to offer withal, and spoons, and vessels of gold and silver. And they offered burnt offerings in the house of the LORD continually all the days of Jehoiada.

15 But Jehoiada waxed old, and was full of days when he died; an hundred and thirty years old *was he* when he died.

16 And they buried him in the city of David among the kings, because he had done good in Israel, both toward God, and toward his house.

17 Now after the death of Jehoiada came the princes of Judah, and made obeisance to the king. Then the king hearkened unto them.

18 And they left the house of the LORD God of their fathers, and served groves and idols: and wrath came upon Judah and Jerusalem for this their trespass.

19 Yet he sent prophets to them, to bring them again unto the LORD; and they testified against them: but they would not give ear.

20 And the Spirit of God came upon Zechariah the son of Jehoiada the priest, which stood above the people, and said unto them, thus said God, why transgress you the commandments of the LORD, that you cannot prosper? Because you have forsaken the LORD, he has also forsaken you.
21 And they conspired against him, and stoned him with stones at the commandment of the king in the court of the house of the LORD.
22 Thus Joash the king remembered not the kindness which Jehoiada his father had done to him, but slew his son. And when he died, he said, The LORD look upon *it*, and require *it*.
23 And it came to pass at the end of the year, *that* the host of Syria came up against him: and they came to Judah and Jerusalem, and destroyed all the princes of the people from among the people, and sent all the spoil of them unto the king of Damascus.
24 For the army of the Syrians came with a small company of men, and the LORD delivered a very great host into their hand, because they had forsaken the LORD God of their fathers. So they executed judgment against Joash.
25 And when they were departed from him, (for they left him in great diseases,) his own servants conspired against him for the blood of the sons of Jehoiada the priest, and slew him on his bed, and he died: and they buried him in the city of David, but they buried him not in the sepulchers of the kings.
26 And these are they that conspired against him; Zabad the son of Shimeath an Ammonitess, and Jehozabad the son of Shimrith a Moabitess.
27 Now *concerning* his sons, and the greatness of the burdens *laid* upon him, and the repairing of the house of God, behold, they *are* written in the story of the book of the kings. And Amaziah his son reigned in his stead.

CHAPTER 25

1 Amaziah *was* twenty and five years old *when* he began to reign, and he reigned twenty and nine years in Jerusalem. And his mother's name *was* Jehoaddan of Jerusalem.
2 And he did *that which was* right in the sight of the LORD, but not with a perfect heart.
3 Now it came to pass, when the kingdom was established to him, that he slew his servants that had killed the king his father.
4 But he slew not their children, but *did* as *it is* written in the law in the book of Moses, where the LORD commanded, saying, The fathers will not die for the children, neither will the children die for the fathers, but every man will die for his own sin.
5 Moreover Amaziah gathered Judah together, and made them captains over thousands, and captains over hundreds, according to the houses of *their* fathers, throughout all Judah and Benjamin: and he numbered them from twenty years old and above, and found them three hundred thousand choice *men, able* to go forth to war, that could handle spear and shield.
6 He hired also an hundred thousand mighty men of valor out of Israel for an hundred talents of silver.
7 But there came a man of God to him, saying, O king, let not the army of Israel go with you; for the LORD *is* not with Israel, *to wit, with* all the children of Ephraim.
8 But if you will go, do *it*, be strong for the battle: God will make you fall before the enemy: for God has power to help, and to cast down.
9 And Amaziah said to the man of God, but what will we do for the hundred talents which I have given to the army of Israel? And the man of God answered, The LORD is able to give you much more than this.
10 Then Amaziah separated them, *to wit*, the army that was come to him out of Ephraim, to go home again: wherefore their anger was greatly kindled against Judah, and they returned home in great anger.
11 And Amaziah strengthened himself, and led forth his people, and went to the valley of salt, and smote of the children of Seir ten thousand.
12 And *other* ten thousand *left* alive did the children of Judah carry away captive, and brought them unto the top of the rock, and cast them down from the top of the rock, that they all were broken in pieces.
13 But the soldiers of the army which Amaziah sent back, that they should not go with him to battle, fell upon the cities of Judah, from Samaria even unto Beth-horon, and smote three thousand of them, and took much spoil.
14 Now it came to pass, after that Amaziah was come from the slaughter of the Edomites, that he brought the gods of the children of Seir, and set them up *to be* his gods, and bowed down himself before them, and burned incense unto them.
15 Wherefore the anger of the LORD was kindled against Amaziah, and he sent unto him a prophet, which said unto him, why have you sought after the gods of the people, which could not deliver their own people out of your hand?
16 And it came to pass, as he talked with him, that *the king* said unto him, are you made of the King's Counsel? Forbear; why should you be smitten? Then the prophet forbare, and said, I know that God has determined to destroy you, because you have done this, and have not hearkened unto my counsel.
17 Then Amaziah king of Judah took advice, and sent to Joash, the son of Jehoahaz, the son of Jehu, king of Israel, saying, Come, let us see one another in the face.
18 And Joash king of Israel sent to Amaziah king of Judah, saying, The thistle that *was* in Lebanon sent to the cedar that *was* in Lebanon, saying, Give your daughter to my son to wife: and there passed by a wild beast that *was* in Lebanon and **trample** down the thistle.
19 You say, Lo, you have smitten the Edomites; and your heart lifts you up to boast: abide now at home; why should you meddle to your hurt, that you should fall, *even* thou, and Judah with you?
20 But Amaziah would not hear; for it came of God, that he might deliver them into the hand *of their enemies*, because they sought after the gods of Edom.
21 So Joash the king of Israel went up; and they saw one another in the face, *both* he and Amaziah king of Judah, at Beth-shemesh, which *belongs* to Judah.
22 And Judah was put to the worse before Israel, and they fled every man to his tent.
23 And Joash the king of Israel took Amaziah king of Judah, the son of Joash, the son of Jehoahaz, at Beth-shemesh, and brought him to Jerusalem, and brake down the wall of Jerusalem from the gate of Ephraim to the corner gate, four hundred cubits.
24 And *he took* all the gold and the silver, and all the vessels that were found in the house of God with Obed-edom, and the treasures of the king's house, the hostages also, and returned to Samaria.
25 And Amaziah the son of Joash king of Judah lived after the death of Joash son of Jehoahaz king of Israel fifteen years.
26 Now the rest of the acts of Amaziah, first and last, behold, *are* they not written in the book of the kings of Judah and Israel?

27 Now after the time that Amaziah did turn away from following the LORD they made a conspiracy against him in Jerusalem; and he fled to Lachish: but they sent to Lachish after him, and slew him there.
28 And they brought him upon horses, and buried him with his fathers in the city of Judah.

CHAPTER 26

1 Then all the people of Judah took Uzziah, who *was* sixteen years old, and made him king in the room of his father Amaziah.
2 He built Eloth, and restored it to Judah, after that the king slept with his fathers.
3 Sixteen years old *was* Uzziah when he began to reign, and he reigned fifty and two years in Jerusalem. His mother's name also *was* Jecoliah of Jerusalem.
4 And he did *that which was* right in the sight of the LORD, according to all that his father Amaziah did.
5 And he sought God in the days of Zechariah, who had understanding in the visions of God: and as long as he sought the LORD, God made him to prosper.
6 And he went forth and warred against the Philistines, and brake down the wall of Gath, and the wall of Jabneh, and the wall of Ashdod, and built cities about Ashdod, and among the Philistines.
7 And God helped him against the Philistines, and against the Arabians that dwelt in Gurbaal, and the Mehunims.
8 And the Ammonites gave gifts to Uzziah: and his name spread abroad *even* to the entering in of Egypt; for he strengthened *himself* exceedingly.
9 Moreover Uzziah built towers in Jerusalem at the corner gate, and at the valley gate, and at the turning *of the wall*, and fortified them.
10 Also he built towers in the desert, and digged many wells: for he had much cattle, both in the low country, and in the plains: husbandmen *also*, and vine dressers in the mountains, and in Carmel: for he loved husbandry.
11 Moreover Uzziah had an host of fighting men, that went out to war by bands, according to the number of their account by the hand of Jeiel the scribe and Maaseiah the ruler, under the hand of Hananiah, *one* of the king's captains.
12 The whole number of the chief of the fathers of the mighty men of valor *were* two thousand and six hundred.
13 And under their hand *was* an army, three hundred thousand and seven thousand and five hundred, that made war with mighty power, to help the king against the enemy.
14 And Uzziah prepared for them throughout all the host shields, and spears, and helmets, and habergeons, and bows, and slings *to cast* stones.
15 And he made in Jerusalem engines, invented by cunning men, to be on the towers and upon the bulwarks, to shoot arrows and great stones withal. And his name spread far abroad; for he was marvelously helped, till he was strong.
16 But when he was strong, his heart was lifted up to *his* destruction: for he transgressed against the LORD his God, and went into the temple of the LORD to burn incense upon the altar of incense.
17 And Azariah the priest went in after him, and with him fourscore priests of the LORD, *that were* valiant men:
18 And they withstood Uzziah the king, and said unto him, *It appertains* not unto you, Uzziah, to burn incense unto the LORD, but to the priests the sons of Aaron, that are consecrated to burn incense: go out of the sanctuary; for you have trespassed; neither will *it be* for your honour from the LORD God.
19 Then Uzziah was **angry**, and *had* a censer in his hand to burn incense: and while he was wroth with the priests, the leprosy even rose up in his forehead before the priests in the house of the LORD, from beside the incense altar.
20 And Azariah the chief priest, and all the priests, looked upon him, and, behold, he *was* leprous in his forehead, and they thrust him out from thence; yea, himself hasted also to go out, because the LORD had smitten him.
21 And Uzziah the king was a leper unto the day of his death, and dwelt in a several house, *being* a leper; for he was cut off from the house of the LORD: and Jotham his son *was* over the king's house, judging the people of the land.
22 Now the rest of the acts of Uzziah, first and last, did Isaiah the prophet, the son of Amoz, write.
23 So Uzziah slept with his fathers, and they buried him with his fathers in the field of the burial which *belonged* to the kings; for they said, He *is* a leper: and Jotham his son reigned in his stead.

CHAPTER 27

1 Jotham *was* twenty and five years old when he began to reign, and he reigned sixteen years in Jerusalem. His mother's name also *was* Jerushah, the daughter of Zadok.
2 And he did *that which was* right in the sight of the LORD, according to all that his father Uzziah did: howbeit he entered not into the temple of the LORD. And the people did yet corruptly.
3 He built the high gate of the house of the LORD, and on the wall of Ophel he built much.
4 Moreover he built cities in the mountains of Judah, and in the forests he built castles and towers.
5 He fought also with the king of the Ammonites, and prevailed against them. And the children of Ammon gave him the same year an hundred talents of silver, and ten thousand measures of wheat, and ten thousand of barley. So much did the children of Ammon pay unto him, both the second year, and the third.
6 So Jotham became mighty, because he prepared his ways before the LORD his God.
7 Now the rest of the acts of Jotham, and all his wars, and his ways, lo, they *are* written in the book of the kings of Israel and Judah.
8 He was five and twenty years old when he began to reign, and reigned sixteen years in Jerusalem.
9 And Jotham slept with his fathers, and they buried him in the city of David: and Ahaz his son reigned in his stead.

CHAPTER 28

1 Ahaz *was* twenty years old when he began to reign, and he reigned sixteen years in Jerusalem: but he did not **do** *that which was* right in the sight of the LORD, like David his father:
2 For he walked in the ways of the kings of Israel, and made also molten images for Baalim.
3 Moreover he burnt incense in the valley of the son of Hinnom, and burnt his children in the fire, after the abominations of the heathen whom the LORD had cast out before the children of Israel.
4 He sacrificed also and burnt incense in the high places, and on the hills, and under every green tree.
5 Wherefore the LORD his God delivered him into the hand of the king of Syria; and they **slaughtered** him, and carried away a great multitude of them captives, and brought *them* to Damascus. And he was also delivered into the hand of the king of Israel, who smote him with a great slaughter.

6 For Pekah the son of Remaliah slew in Judah an hundred and twenty thousand in one day, *which were* all valiant men; because they had forsaken the LORD God of their fathers.

7 And Zichri, a mighty man of Ephraim, slew Maaseiah the king's son, and Azrikam the governor of the house, and Elkanah *that was* next to the king.

8 And the children of Israel carried away captive of their brethren two hundred thousand, women, sons, and daughters, and took also away much spoil from them, and brought the spoil to Samaria.

9 But a prophet of the LORD was there, whose name *was* Oded: and he went out before the host that came to Samaria, and said unto them, Behold, because the LORD God of your fathers was wroth with Judah, he has delivered them into your hand, and you have slain them in a rage *that* reaches up unto heaven.

10 And now you purpose to keep under the children of Judah and Jerusalem for bondmen and bondwomen unto you: *but are there* not with you, even with you, sins against the LORD your God?

11 Now hear me therefore, and deliver the captives again, which you have taken captive of your brethren: for the fierce wrath of the LORD *is* upon you.

12 Then certain of the heads of the children of Ephraim, Azariah the son of Johanan, Berechiah the son of Meshillemoth, and Jehizkiah the son of Shallum, and Amasa the son of Hadlai, stood up against them that came from the war,

13 And said unto them, you will not bring in the captives hither: for whereas we have offended against the LORD *already*, you intend to add *more* to our sins and to our trespass: for our trespass is great, and *there is* fierce wrath against Israel.

14 So the armed men left the captives and the spoil before the princes and the **entire** congregation.

15 And the men which were expressed by name rose up, and took the captives, and with the spoil clothed all that were naked among them, and arrayed them, and shod them, and gave them to eat and to drink, and anointed them, and carried all the feeble of them upon asses, and brought them to Jericho, the city of palm trees, to their brethren: then they returned to Samaria.

16 At that time did king Ahaz send unto the kings of Assyria to help him.

17 For again the Edomites had come and smitten Judah, and carried away captives.

18 The Philistines also had invaded the cities of the low country, and of the south of Judah, and had taken Beth-shemesh, and Ajalon, and Gederoth, and Shocho with the villages thereof, and Timnah with the villages thereof, Gimzo also and the villages thereof: and they dwelt there.

19 For the LORD brought Judah low because of Ahaz king of Israel; for he made Judah naked, and transgressed sore against the LORD.

20 And Tilgath-pilneser king of Assyria came unto him, and distressed him, but strengthened him not.

21 For Ahaz took away a portion *out* of the house of the LORD, and *out* of the house of the king, and of the princes, and gave *it* unto the king of Assyria: but he helped him not.

22 And in the time of his distress did he trespass yet more against the LORD: this *is that* king Ahaz.

23 For he sacrificed unto the gods of Damascus, which smote him: and he said, because the gods of the kings of Syria help them, *therefore* will I sacrifice to them, that they may help me. But they were the ruin of him, and of all Israel.

24 And Ahaz gathered together the vessels of the house of God, and cut in pieces the vessels of the house of God, and shut up the doors of the house of the LORD, and he made him altars in every corner of Jerusalem.

25 And in every several city of Judah he made high places to burn incense unto other gods, and provoked to anger the LORD God of his fathers.

26 Now the rest of his acts and of all his ways, first and last, behold, they *are* written in the book of the kings of Judah and Israel.

27 And Ahaz slept with his fathers, and they buried him in the city, *even* in Jerusalem: but they brought him not into the sepulchers of the kings of Israel: and Hezekiah his son reigned in his stead.

CHAPTER 29

1 Hezekiah began to reign *when he was* five and twenty years old, and he reigned nine and twenty years in Jerusalem. And his mother's name *was* Abijah, the daughter of Zechariah.

2 And he did *that which was* right in the sight of the LORD, according to all that David his father had done.

3 He in the first year of his reign, in the first month, opened the doors of the house of the LORD, and repaired them.

4 And he brought in the priests and the Levites, and gathered them together into the east street,

5 And said unto them, Hear me, you Levites, sanctify now yourselves, and sanctify the house of the LORD God of your fathers, and carry forth the filthiness out of the holy *place*.

6 For our fathers have trespassed, and done *that which was* evil in the eyes of the LORD our God, and have forsaken him, and have turned away their faces from the habitation of the LORD, and turned *their* backs.

7 Also they have shut up the doors of the porch, and put out the lamps, and have not burned incense or offered burnt offerings in the holy *place* unto the God of Israel.

8 Wherefore the wrath of the LORD was upon Judah and Jerusalem, and he has delivered them to trouble, to astonishment, and to hissing, as you see with your eyes.

9 For, lo, our fathers have fallen by the sword, and our sons and our daughters and our wives *are* in captivity for this.

10 Now *it is* in mine heart to make a covenant with the LORD God of Israel, that his fierce wrath may turn away from us.

11 My sons, be not now negligent: for the LORD has chosen you to stand before him, to serve him, and that you should minister unto him, and burn incense.

12 Then the Levites arose, Mahath the son of Amasai, and Joel the son of Azariah, of the sons of the Kohathites: and of the sons of Merari, Kish the son of Abdi, and Azariah the son of Jehalelel: and of the Gershonites; Joah the son of Zimmah, and Eden the son of Joah:

13 And of the sons of Elizaphan; Shimri, and Jeiel: and of the sons of Asaph; Zechariah, and Mattaniah:

14 And of the sons of Heman; Jehiel, and Shimei: and of the sons of Jeduthun; Shemaiah, and Uzziel.

15 And they gathered their brethren, and sanctified themselves, and came, according to the commandment of the king, by the words of the LORD, to cleanse the house of the LORD.

16 And the priests went into the inner part of the house of the LORD, to cleanse *it*, and brought out all the uncleanness that they found in the temple of the LORD into the court of the house of the LORD. And the Levites took *it*, to carry *it* out abroad into the brook Kidron.

17 Now they began on the first *day* of the first month to sanctify, and on the eighth day of the month came they to the porch of the

LORD: so they sanctified the house of the LORD in eight days; and in the sixteenth day of the first month they made an end.

18 Then they went in to Hezekiah the king, and said, we have cleansed all the house of the LORD, and the altar of burnt offering, with all the vessels thereof, and the shewbread table, with all the vessels thereof.

19 Moreover all the vessels, which king Ahaz in his reign did cast away in his transgression, have we prepared and sanctified, and, behold, they *are* before the altar of the LORD.

20 Then Hezekiah the king rose early, and gathered the rulers of the city, and went up to the house of the LORD.

21 And they brought seven bullocks, and seven rams, and seven lambs, and seven he goats, for a sin offering for the kingdom, and for the sanctuary, and for Judah. And he commanded the priests the sons of Aaron to offer *them* on the altar of the LORD.

22 So they killed the bullocks, and the priests received the blood, and sprinkled *it* on the altar: likewise, when they had killed the rams, they sprinkled the blood upon the altar: they killed also the lambs, and they sprinkled the blood upon the altar.

23 And they brought forth the he goats *for* the sin offering before the king and the congregation; and they laid their hands upon them:

24 And the priests killed them, and they made reconciliation with their blood upon the altar, to make atonement for all Israel: for the king commanded *that* the burnt offering and the sin offering *should be made* for all Israel.

25 And he set the Levites in the house of the LORD with cymbals, with psalteries, and with harps, according to the commandment of David, and of Gad the king's seer, and Nathan the prophet: for *so was* the commandment of the LORD by his prophets.

26 And the Levites stood with the instruments of David, and the priests with the trumpets.

27 And Hezekiah commanded to offer the burnt offering upon the altar. And when the burnt offering began, the song of the LORD began *also* with the trumpets, and with the instruments *ordained* by David king of Israel.

28 And the **entire** congregation worshipped, and the singers sang, and the trumpeters sounded: *and* all this continued until the burnt offering was finished.

29 And when they had made an end of offering, the king and all that were present with him bowed themselves, and worshipped.

30 Moreover Hezekiah the king and the princes commanded the Levites to sing praise unto the LORD with the words of David, and of Asaph the seer. And they sang praises with gladness, and they bowed their heads and worshipped.

31 Then Hezekiah answered and said, now you have consecrated yourselves unto the LORD, come near and bring sacrifices and thank offerings into the house of the LORD. And the congregation brought in sacrifices and thank offerings; and as many as were of a free heart burnt offerings.

32 And the number of the burnt offerings, which the congregation brought, was threescore and ten bullocks, an hundred rams, *and* two hundred lambs: all these *were* for a burnt offering to the LORD.

33 And the consecrated things *were* six hundred oxen and three thousand sheep.

34 But the priests were too few, so that they could not flay all the burnt offerings: wherefore their brethren the Levites did help them, till the work was ended, and until the *other* priests had sanctified themselves: for the Levites *were* more upright in heart to sanctify themselves than the priests.

35 And also the burnt offerings *were* in abundance, with the fat of the peace offerings, and the drink offerings for *every* burnt offering. So the service of the house of the LORD was set in order.

36 And Hezekiah rejoiced, and all the people, that God had prepared the people: for the thing was *done* suddenly.

CHAPTER 30

1 And Hezekiah sent to all Israel and Judah, and wrote letters also to Ephraim and Manasseh, that they should come to the house of the LORD at Jerusalem, to keep the Passover unto the LORD God of Israel.

2 For the king had taken counsel, and his princes, and the **entire** congregation in Jerusalem, to keep the Passover in the second month.

3 For they could not keep it at that time, because the priests had not sanctified themselves sufficiently, neither had the people gathered themselves together to Jerusalem.

4 And the thing pleased the king and the **entire** congregation.

5 So they established a decree to make proclamation throughout all Israel, from Beer-sheba even to Dan, that they should come to keep the Passover unto the LORD God of Israel at Jerusalem: for they had not done *it* of a long *time in such sort* as it was written.

6 So the posts went with the letters from the king and his princes throughout all Israel and Judah, and according to the commandment of the king, saying, you children of Israel, turn again unto the LORD God of Abraham, Isaac, and Israel, and he will return to the remnant of you, that are escaped out of the hand of the kings of Assyria.

7 And be not you like your fathers, and like your brethren, which trespassed against the LORD God of their fathers, *who* therefore gave them up to desolation, as you see.

8 Now be you not stiff-neck, as your fathers *were*, but yield yourselves unto the LORD, and enter into his sanctuary, which he has sanctified for ever: and serve the LORD your God, that the fierceness of his wrath may turn away from you.

9 For if you turn again unto the LORD, your brethren and your children will *find* compassion before them that lead them captive, so that they will come again into this land: for the LORD your God *is* gracious and merciful, and will not turn away *his* face from you, if you return unto him.

10 So the posts passed from city to city through the country of Ephraim and Manasseh even unto Zebulun: but they laughed them to scorn, and mocked them.

11 Nevertheless divers of Asher and Manasseh and of Zebulun humbled themselves, and came to Jerusalem.

12 Also in Judah the hand of God was to give them one heart to do the commandment of the king and of the princes, by the word of the LORD.

13 And there assembled at Jerusalem much people to keep the feast of unleavened bread in the second month, a very great congregation.

14 And they arose and took away the altars that *were* in Jerusalem, and all the altars for incense took they away, and cast *them* into the brook Kidron.

15 Then they killed the Passover on the fourteenth *day* of the second month: and the priests and the Levites were ashamed, and sanctified themselves, and brought in the burnt offerings into the house of the LORD.

16 And they stood in their place after their manner, according to the Law of Moses the man of God: the priests sprinkled the blood, *which they received* of the hand of the Levites.

17 For *there were* many in the congregation that were not sanctified: therefore the Levites had the charge of the killing of the Passovers for everyone *that was* not clean, to sanctify *them* unto the LORD.

18 For a multitude of the people, *even* many of Ephraim, and Manasseh, Issachar, and Zebulun, had not cleansed themselves, yet did they eat the Passover otherwise than it was written. But Hezekiah prayed[1] for them, saying, the good LORD pardon every one

19 [*That* prepares his heart to seek God, the LORD God of his fathers, though *he be* not *cleansed* according to the purification of the sanctuary.][2]

20 And the LORD hearkened to Hezekiah, and healed the people.

21 And the children of Israel that were present at Jerusalem kept the feast of unleavened bread seven days with great gladness: and the Levites and the priests praised the LORD day by day, *singing* with loud instruments unto the LORD.

22 And Hezekiah spoke comfortably unto all the Levites that taught the good knowledge of the LORD: and they did eat throughout the feast seven days, offering peace offerings, and making confession to the LORD God of their fathers.

23 And the whole assembly took counsel to keep other seven days: and they kept *other* seven days with gladness.

24 For Hezekiah king of Judah did give to the congregation a thousand bullocks and seven thousand sheep; and the princes gave to the congregation a thousand bullocks and ten thousand sheep: and a great number of priests sanctified themselves.

25 And all the congregation of Judah, with the priests and the Levites, and the **entire** congregation that came out of Israel, and the strangers that came out of the land of Israel, and that dwelt in Judah, rejoiced.

26 So there was great joy in Jerusalem: for since the time of Solomon the son of David king of Israel *there was* not the like in Jerusalem.

27 Then the priests the Levites arose and blessed the people: and their voice was heard, and their prayer came *up* to his holy dwelling place, *even* unto heaven.

CHAPTER 31

1 Now when all this was finished, all Israel that were present went out to the cities of Judah, and brake the images in pieces, and cut down the groves, and threw down the high places and the altars out of all Judah and Benjamin, in Ephraim also and Manasseh, until they had utterly destroyed them all. Then all the children of Israel returned, every man to his possession, into their own cities.

2 And Hezekiah appointed the courses of the priests and the Levites after their courses, every man according to his service, the priests and Levites for burnt offerings and for peace offerings, to minister, and to give thanks, and to praise in the gates of the tents of the LORD.

3 *He appointed* also the king's portion of his substance for the burnt offerings, *to wit*, for the morning and evening burnt offerings, and the burnt offerings for the Sabbaths, and for the new moons, and for the set feasts, as *it is* written in the law of the LORD.

4 Moreover he commanded the people that dwelt in Jerusalem to give the portion of the priests and the Levites, that they might be encouraged in the law of the LORD.

5 And as soon as the commandment came abroad, the children of Israel brought in abundance the first fruits of corn, wine, and oil, and honey, and of all the increase of the field; and the tithe of all *things* brought they in abundantly.

6 And *concerning* the children of Israel and Judah, that dwelt in the cities of Judah, they also brought in the tithe of oxen and sheep, and the tithe of holy things which were consecrated unto the LORD their God, and laid *them* by heaps.

7 In the third month they began to lay the foundation of the heaps, and finished *them* in the seventh month.

8 And when Hezekiah and the princes came and saw the heaps, they blessed the LORD, and his people Israel.

9 Then Hezekiah questioned with the priests and the Levites concerning the heaps.

10 And Azariah the chief priest of the house of Zadok answered him, and said, since *the people* began to bring the offerings into the house of the LORD, we have had enough to eat, and have left plenty: for the LORD has blessed his people; and that which is left *is* this great store.

11 Then Hezekiah commanded to prepare chambers in the house of the LORD; and they prepared *them*,

12 And brought in the offerings and the tithes and the dedicated *things* faithfully: over which Cononiah the Levite *was* ruler, and Shimei his brother *was* the next.

13 And Jehiel, and Azaziah, and Nahath, and Asahel, and Jerimoth, and Jozabad, and Eliel, and Ismachiah, and Mahath, and Benaiah, *were* overseers under the hand of Cononiah and Shimei his brother, at the commandment of Hezekiah the king, and Azariah the ruler of the house of God.

14 And Kore the son of Imnah the Levite, the porter toward the east, *was* over the freewill offerings of God, to distribute the oblations of the LORD, and the most holy things.

15 And next him *were* Eden, and Miniamin, and Jeshua, and Shemaiah, Amariah, and Shecaniah, in the cities of the priests, in *their* set office, to give to their brethren by courses, as well to the great as to the small:

16 Beside their genealogy of males, from three years old and upward, *even* unto everyone that enters into the house of the LORD, his daily portion for their service in their charges according to their courses;

17 Both to the genealogy of the priests by the house of their fathers, and the Levites from twenty years old and upward, in their charges by their courses;

18 And to the genealogy of all their little ones, their wives, and their sons, and their daughters, through the **entire** congregation: for in their set office they sanctified themselves in holiness:

19 Also of the sons of Aaron the priests, *which were* in the fields of the suburbs of their cities, in every several city, the men that were expressed by name, to give portions to all the males among the priests, and to all that were reckoned by genealogies among the Levites.

20 And thus did Hezekiah throughout all Judah, and wrought *that which was* good and right and truth before the LORD his God.

21 And in every work that he began in the service of the house of God, and in the law, and in the commandments, to seek his God, he did *it* with all his heart, and prospered.

---

[1] prayed – to judge (officially or mentally); by extension to interceded [Strgs#6419].

[2] sometimes this happens and Jesus has to intercede for us or to judge for us.

CHAPTER 32

1 After these things, and the establishment thereof, Sennacherib king of Assyria came, and entered into Judah, and encamped against the fenced cities, and thought to win them for himself.
2 And when Hezekiah saw that Sennacherib was come, and that he was purposed to fight against Jerusalem,
3 He took counsel with his princes and his mighty men to stop the waters of the fountains which were without the city: and they did help him.
4 So there was gathered much people together, who stopped all the fountains, and the brook that ran through the midst of the land, saying, why should the kings of Assyria come, and find much water?
5 He also strengthened himself, and built up the **entire** wall that was broken, and raised it up to the towers, and another wall without, and repaired Millo in the city of David, and made darts and shields in abundance.
6 And he set captains of war over the people, and gathered them together to him in the street of the gate of the city, and spoke comfortably to them, saying,
7 Be strong and courageous, be not afraid or dismayed for the king of Assyria, or for the **entire** multitude that is with him: for there be more with us than with him:
8 With him is an arm of flesh; but with us is the LORD our God to help us, and to fight our battles. And the people rested themselves upon the words of Hezekiah king of Judah.
9 After this did Sennacherib king of Assyria send his servants to Jerusalem, (but he himself laid siege against Lachish, and all his power with him,) unto Hezekiah king of Judah, and unto all Judah that were at Jerusalem, saying,
10 Thus said Sennacherib king of Assyria, Whereon do you trust, that you abide in the siege in Jerusalem?
11 Does not Hezekiah persuade you to give over yourselves to die by famine and by thirst, saying, The LORD our God will deliver us out of the hand of the king of Assyria?
12 has not the same Hezekiah taken away his high places and his altars, and commanded Judah and Jerusalem, saying, you will worship before one altar, and burn incense upon it?
13 Know you not what I and my fathers have done unto all the people of other lands? Were the gods of the nations of those lands any ways able to deliver their lands out of mine hand?
14 Who was there among all the gods of those nations that my fathers utterly destroyed, that could deliver his people out of mine hand, that your God should be able to deliver you out of mine hand?
15 Now therefore let not Hezekiah deceive you, or persuade you on this manner, neither yet believe him: for no god of any nation or kingdom was able to deliver his people out of mine hand, and out of the hand of my fathers: how much less will your God deliver you out of mine hand?
16 And his servants spoke yet more against the LORD God, and against his servant Hezekiah.
17 He wrote also letters to rail on the LORD God of Israel, and to speak against him, saying, As the gods of the nations of other lands have not delivered their people out of mine hand, so will not the God of Hezekiah deliver his people out of mine hand.
18 Then they cried with a loud voice in the Jews' speech unto the people of Jerusalem that were on the wall, to affright them, and to trouble them; that they might take the city.
19 And they spoke against the God of Jerusalem, as against the gods of the people of the earth, which were the work of the hands of man.
20 And for this cause Hezekiah the king, and the prophet Isaiah the son of Amoz, prayed and cried to heaven.
21 And the LORD sent an angel, which cut off all the mighty men of valor, and the leaders and captains in the camp of the king of Assyria. So he returned with shame of face to his own land. And when he was come into the house of his god, they that came forth of his own bowels slew him there with the sword.
22 Thus the LORD saved Hezekiah and the inhabitants of Jerusalem from the hand of Sennacherib the king of Assyria, and from the hand of all other, and guided them on every side.
23 And many brought gifts unto the LORD to Jerusalem, and presents to Hezekiah king of Judah: so that he was magnified in the sight of all nations from thenceforth.
24 In those days Hezekiah was sick to the death, and prayed unto the LORD: and he spoke unto him, and he gave him a sign.
25 But Hezekiah rendered not again according to the benefit done unto him; for his heart was lifted up: therefore there was wrath upon him, and upon Judah and Jerusalem.
26 Notwithstanding Hezekiah humbled himself for the pride of his heart, both he and the inhabitants of Jerusalem, so that the wrath of the LORD came not upon them in the days of Hezekiah.
27 And Hezekiah had exceeding much riches and honor: and he made himself treasuries for silver, and for gold, and for precious stones, and for spices, and for shields, and for all manner of pleasant jewels;
28 Storehouses also for the increase of corn, and wine, and oil; and stalls for all manner of beasts, and cotes for flocks.
29 Moreover he provided him cities, and possessions of flocks and herds in abundance: for God had given him substance very much.
30 This same Hezekiah also stopped the upper watercourse of Gihon, and brought it straight down to the west side of the city of David. And Hezekiah prospered in all his works.
31 Howbeit in the business of the ambassadors of the princes of Babylon, who sent unto him to enquire of the wonder that was done in the land, God left him, to try him, that he might know all that was in his heart.
32 Now the rest of the acts of Hezekiah, and his goodness, behold, they are written in the vision of Isaiah the prophet, the son of Amoz, and in the book of the kings of Judah and Israel.
33 And Hezekiah slept with his fathers, and they buried him in the chiefs of the sepulchers of the sons of David: and all Judah and the inhabitants of Jerusalem did him honor at his death. And Manasseh his son reigned in his stead.

CHAPTER 33

1 Manasseh was twelve years old when he began to reign, and he reigned fifty and five years in Jerusalem:
2 But did that which was evil in the sight of the LORD, like unto the abominations of the heathen, whom the LORD had cast out before the children of Israel.
3 For he built again the high places which Hezekiah his father had broken down, and he reared up altars for Baalim, and made groves, and worshipped all the host of heaven, and served them.
4 Also he built altars in the house of the LORD, whereof the LORD had said, In Jerusalem will my name be forever.
5 And he built altars for all the host of heaven in the two courts of the house of the LORD.

6 And he caused his children to pass through the fire in the valley of the son of Hinnom: also he observed times, and used enchantments, and used witchcraft, and dealt with a familiar spirit, and with wizards: he wrought much evil in the sight of the LORD, to provoke him to anger.
7 And he set a carved image, the idol which he had made, in the house of God, of which God had said to David and to Solomon his son, In this house, and in Jerusalem, which I have chosen before all the tribes of Israel, will I put my name for ever:
8 Neither will I any more remove the foot of Israel from out of the land which I have appointed for your fathers; so that they will take heed to do all that I have commanded them, according to the whole law and the statutes and the ordinances by the hand of Moses.
9 So Manasseh made Judah and the inhabitants of Jerusalem to err, *and* to do worse than the heathen, whom the LORD had destroyed before the children of Israel.
10 And the LORD spoke to Manasseh, and to his people: but they would not hearken.
11 Wherefore the LORD brought upon them the captains of the host of the king of Assyria, which took Manasseh among the thorns, and bound him with fetters, and carried him to Babylon.
12 And when he was in affliction, he besought the LORD his God, and humbled himself greatly before the God of his fathers,
13 And prayed unto him: and he was intreated of him, and heard his supplication, and brought him again to Jerusalem into his kingdom. Then Manasseh knew that the LORD he *was* God.
14 Now after this he built a wall without the city of David, on the west side of Gihon, in the valley, even to the entering in at the fish gate, and compassed about Ophel, and raised it up a very great height, and put captains of war in all the fenced cities of Judah.
15 And he took away the strange gods, and the idol out of the house of the LORD, and all the altars that he had built in the mount of the house of the LORD, and in Jerusalem, and cast *them* out of the city.
16 And he repaired the altar of the LORD, and sacrificed thereon peace offerings and thanks offerings, and commanded Judah to serve the LORD God of Israel.
17 Nevertheless the people did sacrifice still in the high places, *yet* unto the LORD their God only.
18 Now the rest of the acts of Manasseh, and his prayer unto his God, and the words of the seers that spoke to him in the name of the LORD God of Israel, behold, they *are written* in the book of the kings of Israel.
19 His prayer also, and *how God* was intreated of him, and all his sin, and his trespass, and the places wherein he built high places, and set up groves and graven images, before he was humbled: behold, they *are* written among the sayings of the seers.
20 So Manasseh slept with his fathers, and they buried him in his own house: and Amon his son reigned in his stead.
21 Amon *was* two and twenty years old when he began to reign, and reigned two years in Jerusalem.
22 But he did *that which was* evil in the sight of the LORD, as did Manasseh his father: for Amon sacrificed unto all the carved images which Manasseh his father had made, and served them;
23 And humbled not himself before the LORD, as Manasseh his father had humbled himself; but Amon trespassed more and more.
24 And his servants conspired against him, and slew him in his own house.
25 But the people of the land slew all them that had conspired against king Amon; and the people of the land made Josiah his son king in his stead.

CHAPTER 34

1 Josiah *was* eight years old when he began to reign, and he reigned in Jerusalem one and thirty years.
2 And he did *that which was* right in the sight of the LORD, and walked in the ways of David his father, and declined neither to the right hand, or to the left.
3 For in the eighth year of his reign, while he was yet young, he began to seek after the God of David his father: and in the twelfth year he began to purge Judah and Jerusalem from the high places, and the groves, and the carved images, and the molten images.
4 And they broke down the altars of Baalim in his presence; and the images, that *were* on high above them, he cut down; and the groves, and the carved images, and the molten images, he brake in pieces, and made dust *of them*, and **scattered** *it* upon the graves of them that had sacrificed unto them.
5 And he burnt the bones of the priests upon their altars, and cleansed Judah and Jerusalem.
6 And *so did he* in the cities of Manasseh, and Ephraim, and Simeon, even unto Naphtali, with their mattocks round about.
7 And when he had broken down the altars and the groves, and had beaten the graven images into powder, and cut down all the idols throughout all the land of Israel, he returned to Jerusalem.
8 Now in the eighteenth year of his reign, when he had purged the land, and the house, he sent Shaphan the son of Azaliah, and Maaseiah the governor of the city, and Joah the son of Joahaz the recorder, to repair the house of the LORD his God.
9 And when they came to Hilkiah the high priest, they delivered the money that was brought into the house of God, which the Levites that kept the doors had gathered of the hand of Manasseh and Ephraim, and of the **entire** remnant of Israel, and of all Judah and Benjamin; and they returned to Jerusalem.
10 And they put *it* in the hand of the workmen that had the oversight of the house of the LORD, and they gave it to the workmen that wrought in the house of the LORD, to repair and amend the house:
11 Even to the artificers and builders gave they *it*, to buy hewn stone, and timber for couplings, and to floor the houses which the kings of Judah had destroyed.
12 And the men did the work faithfully: and the overseers of them *were* Jahath and Obadiah, the Levites, of the sons of Merari; and Zechariah and Meshullam, of the sons of the Kohathites, to set *it* forward; and *other of* the Levites, all that could skill of instruments of musick.
13 Also *they were* over the bearers of burdens, and *were* overseers of all that wrought the work in any manner of service: and of the Levites *there were* scribes, and officers, and porters.
14 And when they brought out the money that was brought into the house of the LORD, Hilkiah the priest found a book of the law of the LORD *given* by Moses.
15 And Hilkiah answered and said to Shaphan the scribe, I have found the book of the law in the house of the LORD. And Hilkiah delivered the book to Shaphan.
16 And Shaphan carried the book to the king, and brought the king word back again, saying, all that was committed to your servants, they do *it*.
17 And they have gathered together the money that was found in the house of the LORD, and have delivered it into the hand of the overseers, and to the hand of the workmen.
18 Then Shaphan the scribe told the king, saying, Hilkiah the priest has given me a book. And Shaphan read it before the king.

19 And it came to pass, when the king had heard the words of the law, that he rent his clothes.
20 And the king commanded Hilkiah, and Ahikam the son of Shaphan, and Abdon the son of Micah, and Shaphan the scribe, and Asaiah a servant of the king's, saying,
21 Go, enquire of the LORD for me, and for them that are left in Israel and in Judah, concerning the words of the book that is found: for great *is* the wrath of the LORD that is poured out upon us, because our fathers have not kept the word of the LORD, to do after all that is written in this book.
22 And Hilkiah, and *they* that the king *had appointed,* went to Huldah the prophetess, the wife of Shallum the son of Tikvath, the son of Hasrah, keeper of the wardrobe; (now she dwelt in Jerusalem in the college:) and they spoke to her to that *effect.*
23 And she answered them, thus said the LORD God of Israel, Tell you the man that sent you to me,
24 Thus said the LORD, Behold; I will bring evil upon this place, and upon the inhabitants thereof, *even* all the curses that are written in the book which they have read before the king of Judah:
25 Because they have forsaken me, and have burned incense unto other gods, that they might provoke me to anger with all the works of their hands; therefore my wrath will be poured out upon this place, and will not be quenched.
26 And as for the king of Judah, who sent you to enquire of the LORD, so will you say unto him, thus said the LORD God of Israel *concerning* the words which you have heard;
27 Because your heart was tender, and you did humble yourself before God, when you heard his words against this place, and against the inhabitants thereof, and humbled yourself before me, and did rend your clothes, and weep before me; I have even heard you also, said the LORD.
28 Behold, I will gather you to your fathers, and you will be gathered to your grave in peace, neither will your eyes see all the evil that I will bring upon this place, and upon the inhabitants of the same. So they brought the king word again.
29 Then the king sent and gathered together all the elders of Judah and Jerusalem.
30 And the king went up into the house of the LORD, and all the men of Judah, and the inhabitants of Jerusalem, and the priests, and the Levites, and all the people, great and small: and he read in their ears all the words of the book of the covenant that was found in the house of the LORD.
31 And the king stood in his place, and made a covenant before the LORD, to walk after the LORD, and to keep his commandments, and his testimonies, and his statutes, with all his heart, and with all his soul, to perform the words of the covenant which are written in this book.
32 And he caused all that were present in Jerusalem and Benjamin to stand *to it.* And the inhabitants of Jerusalem did according to the covenant of God, the God of their fathers.
33 And Josiah took away all the abominations out of all the countries that *pertained* to the children of Israel, and made all that were present in Israel to serve, *even* to serve the LORD their God. *And* all his days they departed not from following the LORD, the God of their fathers.

CHAPTER 35

1 Moreover Josiah kept a Passover unto the LORD in Jerusalem: and they killed the Passover on the fourteenth *day* of the first month.
2 And he set the priests in their charges, and encouraged them to the service of the house of the LORD,
3 And said unto the Levites that taught all Israel, which were holy unto the LORD, Put the holy ark in the house which Solomon the son of David king of Israel did build; *it will* not *be* a burden upon *your* shoulders: serve now the LORD your God, and his people Israel,
4 And prepare *yourselves* by the houses of your fathers, after your courses, according to the writing of David king of Israel, and according to the writing of Solomon his son.
5 And stand in the holy *place* according to the divisions of the families of the fathers of your brethren the people, and *after* the division of the families of the Levites.
6 So kill the Passover, and sanctify yourselves, and prepare your brethren, that *they* may do according to the word of the LORD by the hand of Moses.
7 And Josiah gave to the people, of the flock, lambs and kids, all for the Passover offerings, for all that were present, to the number of thirty thousand, and three thousand bullocks: these *were* of the king's substance.
8 And his princes gave willingly unto the people, to the priests, and to the Levites: Hilkiah and Zechariah and Jehiel, rulers of the house of God, gave unto the priests for the Passover offerings two thousand and six hundred *small cattle,* and three hundred oxen.
9 Conaniah also, and Shemaiah and Nethaneel, his brethren, and Hashabiah and Jeiel and Jozabad, chief of the Levites, gave unto the Levites for Passover offerings five thousand *small cattle,* and five hundred oxen.
10 So the service was prepared, and the priests stood in their place, and the Levites in their courses, according to the king's commandment.
11 And they killed the Passover, and the priests sprinkled *the blood* from their hands, and the Levites flayed *them.*
12 And they removed the burnt offerings, that they might give according to the divisions of the families of the people, to offer unto the LORD, as *it is* written in the book of Moses. And so *did they* with the oxen.
13 And they roasted the Passover with fire according to the ordinance: but the *other* holy *offerings* sod they in pots, and in caldrons, and in pans, and divided *them* speedily among all the people.
14 And afterward they made ready for themselves, and for the priests: because the priests the sons of Aaron *were busied* in offering of burnt offerings and the fat until night; therefore the Levites prepared for themselves, and for the priests the sons of Aaron.
15 And the singers the sons of Asaph *were* in their place, according to the commandment of David, and Asaph, and Heman, and Jeduthun the king's seer; and the porters *waited* at every gate; they might not depart from their service; for their brethren the Levites prepared for them.
16 So all the service of the LORD was prepared the same day, to keep the Passover, and to offer burnt offerings upon the altar of the LORD, according to the commandment of King Josiah.
17 And the children of Israel that were present kept the Passover at that time, and the feast of unleavened bread seven days.
18 And there was no Passover like to that kept in Israel from the days of Samuel the prophet; neither did all the kings of Israel keep such a Passover as Josiah kept, and the priests, and the Levites, and all Judah and Israel that were present, and the inhabitants of Jerusalem.

19 In the eighteenth year of the reign of Josiah was this Passover kept.
20 After all this, when Josiah had prepared the temple, Necho king of Egypt came up to fight against Carchemish by Euphrates: and Josiah went out against him.
21 But he sent ambassadors to him, saying, what have I to do with you, you king of Judah? *I come* not against you this day, but against the house wherewith I have war: for God commanded me to make haste: forbear you from *meddling with* God, who *is* with me, that he destroys you not.
22 Nevertheless Josiah would not turn his face from him, but disguised himself, that he might fight with him, and hearkened not unto the words of Necho from the mouth of God, and came to fight in the valley of Megiddo.
23 And the archers shot at king Josiah; and the king said to his servants, Have me away; for I am sore wounded.
24 His servants therefore took him out of that chariot, and put him in the second chariot that he had; and they brought him to Jerusalem, and he died, and was buried in *one of* the sepulchers of his fathers. And all Judah and Jerusalem mourned for Josiah.
25 And Jeremiah lamented for Josiah: and all the singing men and the singing women spoke of Josiah in their lamentations to this day, and made them an ordinance in Israel: and, behold, they *are* written in the lamentations.
26 Now the rest of the acts of Josiah, and his goodness, according to *that which was* written in the law of the LORD,
27 And his deeds, first and last, behold, they *are* written in the book of the kings of Israel and Judah.

CHAPTER 36

1 Then the people of the land took Jehoahaz the son of Josiah, and made him king in his father's stead in Jerusalem.
2 Jehoahaz *was* twenty and three years old when he began to reign, and he reigned three months in Jerusalem.
3 And the king of Egypt put him down at Jerusalem, and condemned the land in an hundred talents of silver and a talent of gold.
4 And the king of Egypt made Eliakim his brother king over Judah and Jerusalem, and turned his name to Jehoiakim. And Necho took Jehoahaz his brother, and carried him to Egypt.
5 Jehoiakim *was* twenty and five years old when he began to reign, and he reigned eleven years in Jerusalem: and he did *that which was* evil in the sight of the LORD his God.
6 Against him came up Nebuchadnezzar king of Babylon, and bound him in fetters, to carry him to Babylon.
7 Nebuchadnezzar also carried of the vessels of the house of the LORD to Babylon, and put them in his temple at Babylon.
8 Now the rest of the acts of Jehoiakim, and his abominations which he did, and that which was found in him, behold, they *are* written in the book of the kings of Israel and Judah: and Jehoiachin his son reigned in his stead.
9 Jehoiachin *was* eight years old when he began to reign, and he reigned three months and ten days in Jerusalem: and he did *that which was* evil in the sight of the LORD.
10 And when the year was expired, king Nebuchadnezzar sent, and brought him to Babylon, with the goodly vessels of the house of the LORD, and made Zedekiah his brother king over Judah and Jerusalem.
11 Zedekiah *was* one and twenty years old when he began to reign, and reigned eleven years in Jerusalem.
12 And he did *that which was* evil in the sight of the LORD his God, *and* humbled not himself before Jeremiah the prophet *speaking* from the mouth of the LORD.
13 And he also rebelled against king Nebuchadnezzar, who had made him swear by God: but he stiffened his neck, and hardened his heart from turning unto the LORD God of Israel.
14 Moreover all the chief of the priests, and the people, transgressed very much after all the abominations of the heathen; and polluted the house of the LORD which he had hallowed in Jerusalem.
15 And the LORD God of their fathers sent to them by his messengers, rising up betimes, and sending; because he had compassion on his people, and on his dwelling place:
16 But they mocked the messengers of God, and despised his words, and misused his prophets, until the wrath of the LORD arose against his people, till *there was* no remedy.
17 Therefore he brought upon them the king of the Chaldees, who slew their young men with the sword in the house of their sanctuary, and had no compassion upon young man or maiden, old man, or him that stooped for age: he gave *them* all into his hand.
18 And all the vessels of the house of God, great and small, and the treasures of the house of the LORD, and the treasures of the king, and of his princes; all *these* he brought to Babylon.
19 And they burnt the house of God, and brake down the wall of Jerusalem, and burnt all the palaces thereof with fire, and destroyed all the goodly vessels thereof.
20 And them that had escaped from the sword carried he away to Babylon; where they were servants to him and his sons until the reign of the kingdom of Persia:
21 To fulfill the word of the LORD by the mouth of Jeremiah, until the land had enjoyed her Sabbaths: *for* as long as she lay desolate she kept Sabbath, to fulfill threescore and ten years.
22 Now in the first year of Cyrus king of Persia, that the word of the LORD *spoken* by the mouth of Jeremiah might be accomplished, the LORD stirred up the spirit of Cyrus king of Persia, that he made a proclamation throughout all his kingdom, and *put it* also in writing, saying,
23 Thus said Cyrus king of Persia, All the kingdoms of the earth has the LORD God of heaven given me; and he has charged me to build him a house in Jerusalem, which *is* in Judah. Who *is there* among you of all his people? The LORD his God be with him, and let him go up.

EZRA

CHAPTER 1

1 Now in the first year of Cyrus[1] King of Persia, that the word of the LORD by the mouth of Jeremiah might be fulfilled, the LORD stirred up the spirit of Cyrus king of Persia, that he made a proclamation throughout all his kingdom, and *put it* also in writing, saying,

2 Thus said Cyrus king of Persia, the LORD God of heaven has given me all the kingdoms of the earth; and he has charged me to build him an house at Jerusalem, which *is* in Judah.

3 Who *is there* among you of all his people? his God be with him, and let him go up to Jerusalem, which *is* in Judah, and build the house of the LORD God of Israel, (he *is* the God,) which *is* in Jerusalem.

4 And whosoever remains in any place where he sojourns, let the men of his place help him with silver, and with gold, and with goods, and with beasts, beside the freewill offering for the house of God that *is* in Jerusalem.

5 Then **raised** up the chief of the fathers of Judah and Benjamin, and the priests, and the Levites, with all *them* whose spirit God had raised, to go up to build the house of the LORD which *is* in Jerusalem.

6 And all they that *were* about them strengthened their hands with vessels of silver, with gold, with goods, and with beasts, and with precious things, beside all *that* was willingly offered.

7 Also Cyrus the king brought forth the vessels of the house of the LORD, which Nebuchadnezzar had brought forth out of Jerusalem, and had put them in the house of his gods;

8 Even those did Cyrus king of Persia bring forth by the hand of Mithredath the treasurer, and numbered them unto Sheshbazzar, the prince of Judah.

9 And this *is* the number of them: thirty chargers of gold, a thousand chargers of silver, nine and twenty knives,

10 Thirty **bowls** of gold, silver **bowls** of a second *sort* four hundred and ten, *and* other vessels a thousand.

11 All the vessels of gold and of silver *were* five thousand and four hundred. All *these* did Sheshbazzar bring up with *them of* the captivity that were brought up from Babylon unto Jerusalem.

CHAPTER 2

1 Now these *are* the children of the province that went up out of the captivity, of those which had been carried away, whom Nebuchadnezzar the king of Babylon had carried away unto Babylon, and came again unto Jerusalem and Judah, every one unto his city;

2 Which came with Zerubbabel: Jeshua, Nehemiah, Seraiah, Reelaiah, Mordecai, Bilshan, Mispar, Bigvai, Rehum, Baanah. The number of the men of the people of Israel:

3 The children of Parosh, two thousand an hundred seventy and two.

4 The children of Shephatiah, three hundred seventy and two.

5 The children of Arah, seven hundred seventy and five.

6 The children of Pahath-moab, of the children of Jeshua *and* Joab, two thousand eight hundred and twelve.

7 The children of Elam, a thousand two hundred fifty and four.

8 The children of Zattu, nine hundred forty and five.

9 The children of Zaccai, seven hundred and threescore.

10 The children of Bani, six hundred forty and two.

11 The children of Bebai, six hundred twenty and three.

12 The children of Azgad, a thousand two hundred twenty and two.

13 The children of Adonikam, six hundred sixty and six.

14 The children of Bigvai, two thousand fifty and six.

15 The children of Adin, four hundred fifty and four.

16 The children of Ater of Hezekiah, ninety and eight.

17 The children of Bezai, three hundred twenty and three.

18 The children of Jorah, an hundred and twelve.

19 The children of Hashum, two hundred twenty and three.

20 The children of Gibbar, ninety and five.

21 The children of Beth-lehem, an hundred twenty and three.

22 The men of Netophah, fifty and six.

23 The men of Anathoth, an hundred twenty and eight.

24 The children of Azmaveth, forty and two.

25 The children of Kirjath-arim, Chephirah, and Beeroth, seven hundred and forty and three.

26 The children of Ramah and Gaba, six hundred twenty and one.

27 The men of Michmas, an hundred twenty and two.

28 The men of Beth-el and Ai, two hundred twenty and three.

29 The children of Nebo, fifty and two.

30 The children of Magbish, an hundred fifty and six.

31 The children of the other Elam, a thousand two hundred fifty and four.

32 The children of Harim, three hundred and twenty.

33 The children of Lod, Hadid, and Ono, seven hundred twenty and five.

34 The children of Jericho, three hundred forty and five.

35 The children of Senaah, three thousand and six hundred and thirty.

36 The priests: the children of Jedaiah, of the house of Jeshua, nine hundred seventy and three.

37 The children of Immer, a thousand fifty and two.

38 The children of Pashur, a thousand two hundred forty and seven.

39 The children of Harim, a thousand and seventeen.

40 The Levites: the children of Jeshua and Kadmiel, of the children of Hodaviah, seventy and four.

41 The singers: the children of Asaph, an hundred twenty and eight.

42 The children of the porters: the children of Shallum, the children of Ater, the children of Talmon, the children of Akkub, the children of Hatita, the children of Shobai, *in* all an hundred thirty and nine.

43 The Nethinims: the children of Ziha, the children of Hasupha, the children of Tabbaoth,

44 The children of Keros, the children of Siaha, the children of Padon,

45 The children of Lebanah, the children of Hagabah, the children of Akkub,

---

[1] Cyrus- His name means *posses you the furnace* [Strgs#3566]. He was the powerful king of Persia (c.559-530), sometimes called "Cyrus the Great," who allowed the Jewish captives to return to their homeland in Jerusalem after he led Persians to become the dominant nation in the ancient world. Within 20 years after become king of Persia, Cyrus had conquered the Medes, Lydians, and Babylonians (549-, 547, and 539 B.C). Cyrus was known in Persia as a wise and tolerant ruler. He was able to gain the goodwill of the varied ethnic and religious groups within his large empire, which extended from India to the western edge of Asia Minor (modern Turkey). The Old Testament describes him as chosen by the Lord God of Israel as the deliverer of His people. It was not that Cyrus became a follower of Israel's God; rather, he described himself as the one who received "all the kingdoms of the earth," he declared that God "commanded me to build Him a house at Jerusalem" (II Chr.36:23).

46 The children of Hagab, the children of Shalmai, the children of Hanan,
47 The children of Giddel, the children of Gahar, the children of Reaiah,
48 The children of Rezin, the children of Nekoda, the children of Gazzam,
49 The children of Uzza, the children of Paseah, the children of Besai,
50 The children of Asnah, the children of Mehunim, the children of Nephusim,
51 The children of Bakbuk, the children of Hakupha, the children of Harhur,
52 The children of Bazluth, the children of Mehida, the children of Harsha,
53 The children of Barkos, the children of Sisera, the children of Thamah,
54 The children of Neziah, the children of Hatipha.
55 The children of Solomon's servants: the children of Sotai, the children of Sophereth, the children of Peruda,
56 The children of Jaalah, the children of Darkon, the children of Giddel,
57 The children of Shephatiah, the children of Hattil, the children of Pochereth of Zebaim, the children of Ami.
58 All the Nethinims, and the children of Solomon's servants, *were* three hundred ninety and two.
59 And these *were* they which went up from Tel-melah, Tel-harsa, Cherub, Addan, *and* Immer: but they could not shew their father's house, and their seed, whether they *were* of Israel:
60 The children of Delaiah, the children of Tobiah, the children of Nekoda, six hundred fifty and two.
61 And of the children of the priests: the children of Habaiah, the children of Koz, the children of Barzillai; which took a wife of the daughters of Barzillai the Gileadite, and was called after_their name:
62 These sought their register *among* those that were reckoned by genealogy, but they were not found: therefore were they, as polluted, put from the priesthood.
63 And the Tirshatha said unto them, that they should not eat of the most holy things, till there stood up a priest with Urim and with Thummim.
64 The whole congregation together *was* forty and two thousand three hundred *and* threescore,
65 Beside their servants and their maids, of whom *there were* seven thousand three hundred thirty and seven: and *there were* among them two hundred singing men and singing women.
66 Their horses *were* seven hundred thirty and six; their mules, two hundred forty and five;
67 Their camels, four hundred thirty and five; *their* asses, six thousand seven hundred and twenty.
68 And *some* of the chief of the fathers, when they came to the house of the LORD which *is* at Jerusalem, offered freely for the house of God to set it up in his place:
69 They gave after their ability unto the treasure of the work threescore and one thousand drams of gold, and five thousand pound of silver, and one hundred priests' garments.
70 So the priests, and the Levites, and *some* of the people, and the singers, and the porters, and the Nethinims, dwelt in their cities, and all Israel in their cities.

CHAPTER 3

1 And when the seventh month was come, and the children of Israel *were* in the cities, the people gathered themselves together as one man to Jerusalem.
2 Then stood up Jeshua the son of Jozadak, and his brethren the priests, and Zerubbabel the son of Shealtiel, and his brethren, and **built** the altar of the God of Israel, to offer burnt offerings thereon, as *it is* written in the Law of Moses the man of God.
3 And they set the altar upon his bases; for fear *was* upon them because of the people of those countries: and they offered burnt offerings thereon unto the LORD, *even* burnt offerings morning and evening.
4 They kept also the feast of tabernacles, as *it is* written, and *offered* the daily burnt offerings by number, according to the custom, as the duty of every day required;
5 And afterward *offered* the continual burnt offering, both of the new moons, and of all the set feasts of the LORD that were consecrated, and of every one that willingly offered a freewill offering unto the LORD.
6 From the first day of the seventh month began they to offer burnt offerings unto the LORD. But the foundation of the temple of the LORD was not *yet* laid.
7 They gave money also unto the masons, and to the carpenters; and meat, and drink, and oil, unto them of Zidon, and to them of Tyre, to bring cedar trees from Lebanon to the sea of Joppa, according to the grant that they had of Cyrus king of Persia.
8 Now in the second year of their coming unto the house of God at Jerusalem, in the second month, began Zerubbabel the son of Shealtiel, and Jeshua the son of Jozadak, and the remnant of their brethren the priests and the Levites, and all they that were come out of the captivity unto Jerusalem; and appointed the Levites, from twenty years old and upward, to set forward the work of the house of the LORD.
9 Then stood Jeshua *with* his sons and his brethren, Kadmiel and his sons, the sons of Judah, together, to set forward the workmen in the house of God: the sons of Henadad, *with* their sons and their brethren the Levites.
10 And when the builders laid the foundation of the temple of the LORD, they set the priests in their apparel with trumpets, and the Levites the sons of Asaph with cymbals, to praise the LORD, after the ordinance of David king of Israel.
11 And they sang together by course in praising and giving thanks unto the LORD; because *he is* good, for his mercy *endures* forever toward Israel. And all the people shouted with a great shout, when they praised the LORD, because the foundation of the house of the LORD was laid.
12 But many of the priests and Levites and chief of the fathers, *who were* ancient men, that had seen the first house, when the foundation of this house was laid before their eyes wept with a loud voice; and many shouted aloud for joy:
13 So that the people could not discern the noise of the shout of joy from the noise of the weeping of the people: for the people shouted with a loud shout, and the noise was heard afar off.

CHAPTER 4

1 Now when the adversaries of Judah and Benjamin heard that the children of the captivity **built** the temple unto the LORD God of Israel;
2 Then they came to Zerubbabel, and to the chief of the fathers, and said unto them, Let us build with you: for we seek your God,

as you *do*; and we do sacrifice unto him since the days of Esarhaddon king of Assur, which brought us up hither.

3 But Zerubbabel, and Jeshua, and the rest of the chief of the fathers of Israel, said unto them, you have nothing to do with us to build a house unto our God; but we ourselves together will build unto the LORD God of Israel, as King Cyrus the king of Persia has commanded us.

4 Then the people of the land weakened the hands of the people of Judah, and troubled them in building,

5 And hired counselors against them, to frustrate their purpose, all the days of Cyrus king of Persia, even until the reign of Darius king of Persia.

6 And in the reign of Ahasuerus, in the beginning of his reign, wrote they *unto him* an accusation against the inhabitants of Judah and Jerusalem.

7 And in the days of Artaxerxes wrote Bishlam, Mithredath, Tabeel, and the rest of their companions, unto Artaxerxes king of Persia; and the writing of the letter *was* written in the Syrian tongue, and interpreted in the Syrian tongue.

8 Rehum the chancellor and Shimshai the scribe wrote a letter against Jerusalem to Artaxerxes the king in this sort:

9 Then *wrote* Rehum the chancellor, and Shimshai the scribe, and the rest of their companions; the Dinaites, the Apharsathchites, the Tarpelites, the Apharsites, the Archevites, the Babylonians, the Susanchites, the Dehavites, *and* the Elamites,

10 And the rest of the nations whom the great and noble Asnappar brought over, and set in the cities of Samaria, and the rest *that are* on this side the river, and at such a time.

11 This *is* the copy of the letter that they sent unto him, *even unto* Artaxerxes the king; your servants the men on this side the river, and at such a time.

12 Be it known unto the king, that the Jews which came up from you to us are come unto Jerusalem, building the rebellious and the bad city, and have set up the walls *thereof*, and joined the foundations.

13 Be it known now unto the king, that, if this city be **built**, and the walls set up *again, then* will they not pay toll, tribute, and custom, and *so* you will endamage[1] the revenue of the kings.

14 Now because we have maintenance from *the king's* palace, and it was not meet for us to see the king's dishonor, therefore have we sent and certified the king;

15 That search may be made in the book of the records of your fathers: so will you find in the book of the records, and know that this city *is* a rebellious city, and hurtful unto kings and provinces, and that they have moved sedition within the same of old time: for which cause was this city destroyed.

16 We certify the king that, if this city be **built** *again*, and the walls thereof set up, by this means you will have no portion on this side the river.

17 *Then* sent the king an answer unto Rehum the chancellor, and *to* Shimshai the scribe, and *to* the rest of their companions that dwell in Samaria, and *unto* the rest beyond the river, Peace, and at such a time.

18 The letter which you sent unto us has been plainly read before me.

19 And I commanded, and search has been made, and it is found that this city of old time has made insurrection against kings, and *that* rebellion and sedition have been made therein.

20 There have been mighty kings also over Jerusalem, which have ruled over all *countries* beyond the river; and toll, tribute, and custom, was paid unto them.

21 Give you now commandment to cause these men to cease, and that this city be not **built**, until *another* commandment will be given from me.

22 Take heed now that you fail not to do this: why should damage grow to the hurt of the kings?

23 Now when the copy of King Artaxerxes' letter *was* read before Rehum, and Shimshai the scribe, and their companions, they went up in haste to Jerusalem unto the Jews, and made them to cease by force and power.

24 Then ceased the work of the house of God which *is* at Jerusalem. So it ceased unto the second year of the reign of Darius king of Persia.

CHAPTER 5

1 Then the prophets, Haggai the prophet, and Zechariah the son of Iddo, prophesied unto the Jews that *were* in Judah and Jerusalem in the name of the God of Israel, *even* unto them.

2 Then raised up Zerubbabel the son of Shealtiel, and Jeshua the son of Jozadak, and began to build the house of God which *is* at Jerusalem: and with them *were* the prophets of God helping them.

3 At the same time came to them Tatnai, governor on this side the river, and Shethar-boznai, and their companions, and said thus unto them, who has commanded you to build this house, and to make up this wall?

4 Then said we unto them after this manner, what are the names of the men that make this building?

5 But the eye of their God was upon the elders of the Jews, that they could not cause them to cease, till the matter came to Darius: and then they returned answer by letter concerning this *matter*.

6 The copy of the letter that Tatnai, governor on this side the river, and Shethar-boznai, and his companions the Apharsachites, which *were* on this side the river, sent unto Darius the king:

7 They sent a letter unto him, wherein was written thus; Unto Darius the king, all peace.

8 Be it known unto the king, that we went into the province of Judea, to the house of the great God, which is built with great stones, and timber is laid in the walls, and this work goes fast on, and prospers in their hands.

9 Then asked we those elders, *and* said unto them thus, Who commanded you to build this house, and to make up these walls?

10 We asked their names also, to certify you, that we might write the names of the men that *were* the chief of them.

11 And thus they returned us answer, saying, we are the servants of the God of heaven and earth, and build the house that was built these many years ago, which a great king of Israel built and set up.

12 But after that our fathers had provoked the God of heaven unto wrath, he gave them into the hand of Nebuchadnezzar the king of Babylon, the Chaldean, who destroyed this house, and carried the people away into Babylon.

13 But in the first year of Cyrus the king of Babylon *the same* king Cyrus made a decree to build this house of God.

14 And the vessels also of gold and silver of the house of God, which Nebuchadnezzar took out of the temple that *was* in Jerusalem, and brought them into the temple of Babylon, those did Cyrus the king take out of the temple of Babylon, and they were

---

[1] endamage- to suffer (causatively inflict) loss, have damage, hurtful. It comes from the Hebrew root word *nêzeq*, nay´zek; which is defined as to injure, loss and damage.

delivered unto *one*, whose name *was* Sheshbazzar, whom he had made governor;

15 And said unto him, Take these vessels, go, carry them into the temple that *is* in Jerusalem, and let the house of God be **built** in his place.

16 Then came the same Sheshbazzar, *and* laid the foundation of the house of God which *is* in Jerusalem: and since that time even until now has it been in building, and *yet* it is not finished.

17 Now therefore, if *it seem* good to the king, let there be search made in the king's treasure house, which *is* there at Babylon, whether it be *so*, that a decree was made of Cyrus the king to build this house of God at Jerusalem, and let the king send his pleasure to us concerning this matter.

CHAPTER 6

1 Then Darius the king made a decree, and search was made in the house of the rolls, where the treasures were laid up in Babylon.

2 And there was found at Achmetha, in the palace that *is* in the province of the Medes, a roll, and therein *was* a record thus written:

3 In the first year of Cyrus the king *the same* Cyrus the king made a decree *concerning* the house of God at Jerusalem, Let the house be built, the place where they offered sacrifices, and let the foundations thereof be strongly laid; the height thereof threescore cubits, *and* the breadth thereof threescore cubits;

4 *With* three rows of great stones, and a row of new timber: and let the expenses be given out of the king's house:

5 And also let the golden and silver vessels of the house of God, which Nebuchadnezzar took forth out of the temple which *is* at Jerusalem, and brought unto Babylon, be restored, and brought again unto the temple which *is* at Jerusalem, *every one* to his place, and place *them* in the house of God.

6 Now *therefore*, Tatnai, governor beyond the river, Shethar-boznai, and your companions the Apharsachites, which *are* beyond the river, be you far from thence:

7 Let the work of this house of God alone; let the governor of the Jews and the elders of the Jews build this house of God in his place.

8 Moreover I make a decree what you will do to the elders of these Jews for the building of this house of God: that of the king's goods, *even* of the tribute beyond the river, forthwith expenses be given unto these men, that they be not hindered.

9 And that which they have need of, both young bullocks, and rams, and lambs, for the burnt offerings of the God of heaven, wheat, salt, wine, and oil, according to the appointment of the priests which *are* at Jerusalem, let it be given them day by day without fail:

10 That they may offer sacrifices of sweet savors unto the God of heaven, and pray for the life of the king, and of his sons.

11 Also I have made a decree, that whosoever will alter this word, let timber be pulled down from his house, and being set up, let him be hanged thereon; and let his house be made a dunghill for this.

12 And the God that has caused his name to dwell there destroy all kings and people, that will put to their hand to alter *and* to destroy this house of God which *is* at Jerusalem. I Darius have made a decree; let it be done with speed.

13 Then Tatnai, governor on this side the river, Shethar-boznai, and their companions, according to that which Darius the king had sent, so they did speedily.

14 And the elders of the Jews **built**, and they prospered through the prophesying of Haggai the prophet and Zechariah the son of Iddo. And they **built**, and finished *it*, according to the commandment of the God of Israel, and according to the commandment of Cyrus, and Darius, and Artaxerxes king of Persia.

15 And this house was finished on the third day of the month Adar, which was in the sixth year of the reign of Darius the king.

16 And the children of Israel, the priests, and the Levites, and the rest of the children of the captivity, kept the dedication of this house of God with joy,

17 And offered at the dedication of this house of God an hundred bullocks, two hundred rams, four hundred lambs; and for a sin offering for all Israel, twelve he goats, according to the number of the tribes of Israel.

18 And they set the priests in their divisions, and the Levites in their courses, for the service of God, which *is* at Jerusalem; as it is written in the book of Moses.

19 And the children of the captivity kept the Passover upon the fourteenth *day* of the first month.

20 For the priests and the Levites were purified together, all of them *were* pure, and killed the Passover for all the children of the captivity, and for their brethren the priests, and for themselves.

21 And the children of Israel, which were come again out of captivity, and all such as had separated themselves unto them from the filthiness of the heathen of the land, to seek the LORD God of Israel, did eat,

22 And kept the feast of unleavened bread seven days with joy: for the LORD had made them joyful, and turned the heart of the king of Assyria unto them, to strengthen their hands in the work of the house of God, the God of Israel.

CHAPTER 7

1 Now after these things, in the reign of Artaxerxes[1] king of Persia, Ezra the son of Seraiah, the son of Azariah, the son of Hilkiah,

2 The son of Shallum, the son of Zadok, the son of Ahitub,

3 The son of Amariah, the son of Azariah, the son of Meraioth,

4 The son of Zerahiah, the son of Uzzi, the son of Bukki,

5 The son of Abishua, the son of Phinehas, the son of Eleazar, the son of Aaron the chief priest:

6 This Ezra went up from Babylon; and he *was* a ready scribe in the Law of Moses, which the LORD God of Israel had given: and the king granted him all his request, according to the hand of the LORD his God upon him.

7 And there went up *some* of the children of Israel, and of the priests, and the Levites, and the singers, and the porters, and the Nethinims, unto Jerusalem, in the seventh year of Artaxerxes the king.

8 And he came to Jerusalem in the fifth month, which *was* in the seventh year of the king.

9 For upon the first *day* of the first month began he to go up from Babylon, and on the first *day* of the fifth month came he to Jerusalem, according to the good hand of his God upon him.

---

[1] Artaxerxes – (*possessor of an exalted kingdom*) a king of Persia in whose court Ezra and Nehemiah were officials (**Ezra 7:1, 7**). Known as Artaxerxes I Longimanus (long-handed), he temporarily halted the rebuilding program at Jerusalem that Cyrus, his predecessor, had encouraged (**Ezra 4:7-23**), but later allowed it to continue (**Ezra 6:14**). In the seventh year of his reign (c.458 B.C), he authorized the mission of Ezra to lead a large number of Israelites back from the Captivity to Jerusalem (**Ezra 7:1-28**). In the 20th year of his reign, he allowed Nehemiah to return to Jerusalem and to begin rebuilding the walls of that city (**Nehemiah 2:1-10; 13 6**).

10 For Ezra had prepared his heart to seek the law of the LORD, and to do *it*, and to teach in Israel statutes and judgments.

11 Now this *is* the copy of the letter that the king Artaxerxes gave unto Ezra the priest, the scribe, *even* a scribe of the words of the commandments of the LORD, and of his statutes to Israel.

12 Artaxerxes, king of kings, unto Ezra the priest, a scribe of the law of the God of heaven, perfect *peace*, and at such a time.

13 I make a decree, that all they of the people of Israel, and *of* his priests and Levites, in my realm, which are minded of their own freewill to go up to Jerusalem, go with you.

14 Forasmuch as you are sent of[1] the king, and of his seven counselors, to enquire concerning Judah and Jerusalem, according to the law of your God which *is* in your hand;

15 And to carry the silver and gold, which the king and his counselors have freely offered unto the God of Israel, whose habitation *is* in Jerusalem,

16 And all the silver and gold that you canst find in all the province of Babylon, with the freewill offering of the people, and of the priests, offering willingly for the house of their God which *is* in Jerusalem:

17 That you may buy speedily with this money **bulls**, rams, lambs, with their meat offerings and their drink offerings, and offer them upon the altar of the house of your God which *is* in Jerusalem.

18 And whatsoever will seems good to you, and to your brethren, to do with the rest of the silver and the gold, that do after the will of your God.

19 The vessels also that are given you for the service of the house of your God, *those* deliver you before the God of Jerusalem.

20 And whatsoever more will be needful for the house of your God, which you will have occasion to bestow, bestow *it* out of the king's treasure house.

21 And I, *even* I Artaxerxes the king, do make a decree to all the treasurers which *are* beyond the river, that whatsoever Ezra the priest, the scribe of the law of the God of heaven, will require of you, it be done speedily,

22 Unto an hundred talents of silver, and to an hundred measures of wheat, and to an hundred baths of wine, and to an hundred baths of oil, and salt without prescribing *how much*.

23 Whatsoever is commanded by the God of Heaven, let it be diligently done for the house of the God of heaven: for why should there be wrath against the realm of the king and his sons?

24 Also we certify you, that touching any of the priests and Levites, singers, porters, Nethinims, or ministers of this house of God, it will not be lawful to impose toll, tribute, or custom, upon them.

25 And thou, Ezra, after the wisdom of your God, that *is* in your hand, set magistrates and judges, which may judge all the people that *are* beyond the river, all such as know the laws of your God; and teach you them that know *them* not.

26 [And whosoever will not do the law of your God, and the law of the king, let judgment be executed speedily upon him, whether *it be* unto death, or to banishment, or to confiscation of goods, or to imprisonment.][2]

27 Blessed *be* the LORD God of our fathers, which has put *such a thing* as this in the king's heart, to beautify the house of the LORD which *is* in Jerusalem:

28 And has extended mercy unto me before the king, and his counselors, and before all the king's mighty princes. And I was strengthened as the hand of the LORD my God *was* upon me, and I gathered together out of Israel chief men to go up with me.

CHAPTER 8

1 These *are* now the chief of their fathers, and *this is* the genealogy of them that went up with me from Babylon, in the reign of Artaxerxes the king.

2 Of the sons of Phinehas; Gershom: of the sons of Ithamar; Daniel: of the sons of David; Hattush.

3 Of the sons of Shechaniah, of the sons of Pharosh; Zechariah: and with him were reckoned by genealogy of the males an hundred and fifty.

4 Of the sons of Pahath-moab; Elihoenai the son of Zerahiah, and with him two hundred males.

5 Of the sons of Shechaniah; the son of Jahaziel, and with him three hundred males.

6 Of the sons also of Adin; Ebed the son of Jonathan, and with him fifty males.

7 And of the sons of Elam; Jeshaiah the son of Athaliah, and with him seventy males.

8 And of the sons of Shephatiah; Zebadiah the son of Michael, and with him fourscore males.

9 Of the sons of Joab; Obadiah the son of Jehiel, and with him two hundred and eighteen males.

10 And of the sons of Shelomith; the son of Josiphiah, and with him an hundred and threescore males.

11 And of the sons of Bebai; Zechariah the son of Bebai, and with him twenty and eight males.

12 And of the sons of Azgad; Johanan the son of Hakkatan, and with him an hundred and ten males.

13 And of the last sons of Adonikam, whose names *are* these, Eliphelet, Jeiel, and Shemaiah, and with them threescore males.

14 Of the sons also of Bigvai; Uthai, and Zabbud, and with them seventy males.

15 And I gathered them together to the river that runneth to Ahava; and there abode we in tents three days: and I viewed the people, and the priests, and found there none of the sons of Levi.

16 Then sent I for Eliezer, for Ariel, for Shemaiah, and for Elnathan, and for Jarib, and for Elnathan, and for Nathan, and for Zechariah, and for Meshullam, chief men; also for Joiarib, and for Elnathan, men of understanding.

17 And I sent them with commandment unto Iddo the chief at the place Casiphia, and I told them what they should say unto Iddo, *and* to his brethren the Nethinims, at the place Casiphia, that they should bring unto us ministers for the house of our God.

18 And by the good hand of our God upon us they brought us a man of understanding, of the sons of Mahli, the son of Levi, the son of Israel; and Sherebiah, with his sons and his brethren, eighteen;

19 And Hashabiah, and with him Jeshaiah of the sons of Merari, his brethren and their sons, twenty;

20 Also of the Nethinims, whom David and the princes had appointed for the service of the Levites, two hundred and twenty Nethinims: all of them were expressed by name.

21 Then I proclaimed a fast there, at the river of Ahava, that we might afflict ourselves before our God, to seek of him a right way for us, and for our little ones, and for all our substance.

22 For I was ashamed to require of the king a band of soldiers and horsemen to help us against the enemy in the way: because we had spoken unto the king, saying, The hand of our God *is* upon all

---

[1] lit. from before [Strgs#4481]

[2] compare **Ecc. 8:11**

them for good that seek him; but his power and his wrath *is* against all them that forsake him.

23 So we fasted and besought our God for this: and he was intreated of us.

24 Then I separated twelve of the chief of the priests, Sherebiah, Hashabiah, and ten of their brethren with them,

25 And weighed unto them the silver, and the gold, and the vessels, *even* the offering of the house of our God, which the king, and his counselors, and his lords, and all Israel *their* present, had offered:

26 I even weighed unto their hand six hundred and fifty talents of silver, and silver vessels an hundred talents, *and* of gold an hundred talents;

27 Also twenty **bowls** of gold, of a thousand drams; and two vessels of fine copper, precious as gold.

28 And I said unto them, you *are* holy unto the LORD; the vessels *are* holy also; and the silver and the gold *are* a freewill offering unto the LORD God of your fathers.

29 Watch you, and keep *them*, until you weigh *them* before the chief of the priests and the Levites, and chief of the fathers of Israel, at Jerusalem, in the chambers of the house of the LORD.

30 So took the priests and the Levites the weight of the silver, and the gold, and the vessels, to bring *them* to Jerusalem unto the house of our God.

31 Then we departed from the river of Ahava on the twelfth *day* of the first month, to go unto Jerusalem: and the hand of our God was upon us, and he delivered us from the hand of the enemy, and of such as lay in wait by the way.

32 And we came to Jerusalem, and **remained** there three days.

33 Now on the fourth day was the silver and the gold and the vessels weighed in the house of our God by the hand of Meremoth the son of Uriah the priest; and with him *was* Eleazar the son of Phinehas; and with them *was* Jozabad the son of Jeshua, and Noadiah the son of Binnui, Levites;

34 By number *and* by weight of everyone: and all the weight was written at that time.

35 *Also* the children of those that had been carried away, which were come out of the captivity, offered burnt offerings unto the God of Israel, twelve **bulls** for all Israel, ninety and six rams, seventy and seven lambs, twelve he goats *for* a sin offering: all *this was* a burnt offering unto the LORD.

36 And they delivered the king's commissions unto the king's lieutenants and to the governors on this side the river: and they furthered the people, and the house of God.

CHAPTER 9

1 Now when these things were done, the princes came to me, saying, The people of Israel, and the priests, and the Levites, have not separated themselves from the people of the lands, *doing* according to their abominations, *even* of the Canaanites, the Hittites, the Perizzites, the Jebusites, the Ammonites, the Moabites, the Egyptians, and the Amorites.

2 For they have taken of their daughters for themselves, and for their sons: so that the holy seed have mingled themselves with the people of *those* lands: **yes**, the hand of the princes and rulers has been chief in this trespass.

3 And when I heard this thing, I rent my garment and my mantle, and plucked off the hair of my head and of my beard, and sat down **astonished**.

4 Then were assembled unto me every one that trembled at the words of the God of Israel, because of the transgression of those that had been carried away; and I sat **astonished** until the evening sacrifice.

5 And at the evening sacrifice I arose up from my heaviness; and having rent my garment and my mantle, I fell upon my knees, and spread out my hands unto the LORD my God,

6 And said, O my God, I am ashamed and blush to lift up my face to you, my God: for our iniquities are increased over *our* head, and our trespass is grown up unto the heavens.

7 Since the days of our fathers *have* we *been* in a great trespass unto this day; and for our iniquities have we, our kings, *and* our priests, been delivered into the hand of the kings of the lands, to the sword, to captivity, and to a spoil, and to confusion of face, as *it is* this day.

8 And now for a little space grace has been *showed* from the LORD our God, to leave us a remnant to escape, and to give us a nail in his holy place, that our God may lighten our eyes, and give us a little reviving in our bondage.

9 For we *were* bondmen; yet our God has not forsaken us in our bondage, but has extended mercy unto us in the sight of the kings of Persia, to give us a reviving, to set up the house of our God, and to repair the desolations thereof, and to give us a wall in Judah and in Jerusalem.

10 And now, O our God, what will we say after this? For we have forsaken your commandments,

11 Which you hast commanded by your servants the prophets, saying, the land, unto which you go to possess it, is an unclean land with the filthiness of the people of the lands, with their abominations, which have filled it from one end to another with their uncleanness.

12 Now therefore give not your daughters unto their sons, neither take their daughters unto your sons, nor seek their peace or their wealth for ever: that you may be strong, and eat the good of the land, and leave *it* for an inheritance to your children for ever.

13 And after all that is come upon us for our evil deeds, and for our great trespass, seeing that you our God hast punished us less than our iniquities *deserve*, and hast given us *such* deliverance as this;

14 Should we again break your commandments, and join in affinity with the people of these abominations? Would not you be angry with us till you had consumed *us*, so that *there* should be no remnant or escaping?

15 O LORD God of Israel, you are righteous: for we remain yet escaped, as *it is* this day: behold, we *are* before you in our trespasses: for we cannot stand before you because of this.

CHAPTER 10

1 Now when Ezra had prayed, and when he had confessed, weeping and casting himself down before the house of God, there assembled unto him out of Israel a very great congregation of men and women and children: for the people wept very sore.

2 And Shechaniah the son of Jehiel, *one* of the sons of Elam, answered and said unto Ezra, We have trespassed against our God, and have taken strange wives of the people of the land: yet now there is hope in Israel concerning this thing.

3 Now therefore let us make a covenant with our God to put away all the wives, and such as are born of them, according to the counsel of my lord, and of those that tremble at the commandment of our God; and let it be done according to the law.

4 Arise; for *this* matter *belongs* unto you: we also *will be* with you: be of good courage, and do *it*.

5 Then arose Ezra, and made the chief priests, the Levites, and all Israel, to swear that they should do according to this word. And they swore.

6 Then Ezra rose up from before the house of God, and went into the chamber of Johanan the son of Eliashib: and *when* he came thither, he did eat no bread, nor drink water: for he mourned because of the transgression of them that had been carried away.

7 And they made proclamation throughout Judah and Jerusalem unto all the children of the captivity, that they should gather themselves together unto Jerusalem;

8 And that whosoever would not come within three days, according to the counsel of the princes and the elders, all his substance should be forfeited, and himself separated from the congregation of those that had been carried away.

9 Then all the men of Judah and Benjamin gathered themselves together unto Jerusalem within three days. It *was* the ninth month, on the twentieth *day* of the month; and all the people sat in the street of the house of God, trembling because of *this* matter, and for the great rain.

10 And Ezra the priest stood up, and said unto them, you have transgressed, and have taken strange wives, to increase the trespass of Israel.

11 Now therefore make confession unto the LORD God of your fathers, and do his pleasure: and separate yourselves from the people of the land, and from the strange wives.

12 Then the **entire** congregation answered and said with a loud voice, As you hast said, so must we do.

13 But the people *are* many, and *it is* a time of much rain, and we are not able to stand without, neither *is* this a work of one day or two: for we are many that have transgressed in this thing.

14 Let now our rulers of all the congregation stand, and let all them which have taken strange wives in our cities come at appointed times, and with them the elders of every city, and the judges thereof, until the fierce wrath of our God for this matter be turned from us.

15 Only Jonathan the son of Asahel and Jahaziah the son of Tikvah were employed about this *matter*: and Meshullam and Shabbethai the Levite helped them.

16 And the children of the captivity did so. And Ezra the priest, *with* certain chief of the fathers, after the house of their fathers, and all of them by *their* names, were separated, and sat down in the first day of the tenth month to examine the matter.

17 And they made an end with all the men that had taken strange wives by the first day of the first month.

18 And among the sons of the priests there were found that had taken strange wives: *namely*, of the sons of Jeshua the son of Jozadak, and his brethren; Maaseiah, and Eliezer, and Jarib, and Gedaliah.

19 And they gave their hands that they would put away their wives; and *being* guilty, *they offered* a ram of the flock for their trespass.

20 And of the sons of Immer; Hanani, and Zebadiah.

21 And of the sons of Harim; Maaseiah, and Elijah, and Shemaiah, and Jehiel, and Uzziah.

22 And of the sons of Pashur; Elioenai, Maaseiah, Ishmael, Nethaneel, Jozabad, and Elasah.

23 Also of the Levites; Jozabad, and Shimei, and Kelaiah, (the same *is* Kelita,) Pethahiah, Judah, and Eliezer.

24 Of the singers also; Eliashib: and of the porters; Shallum, and Telem, and Uri.

25 Moreover of Israel: of the sons of Parosh; Ramiah, and Jeziah, and Malchiah, and Miamin, and Eleazar, and Malchijah, and Benaiah.

26 And of the sons of Elam; Mattaniah, Zechariah, and Jehiel, and Abdi, and Jeremoth, and Eliah.

27 And of the sons of Zattu; Elioenai, Eliashib, Mattaniah, and Jeremoth, and Zabad, and Aziza.

28 Of the sons also of Bebai; Jehohanan, Hananiah, Zabbai, *and* Athlai.

29 And of the sons of Bani; Meshullam, Malluch, and Adaiah, Jashub, and Sheal, and Ramoth.

30 And of the sons of Pahath-moab; Adna, and Chelal, Benaiah, Maaseiah, Mattaniah, Bezaleel, and Binnui, and Manasseh.

31 And *of* the sons of Harim; Eliezer, Ishijah, Malchiah, Shemaiah, Shimeon,

32 Benjamin, Malluch, *and* Shemariah.

33 Of the sons of Hashum; Mattenai, Mattathah, Zabad, Eliphelet, Jeremai, Manasseh, *and* Shimei.

34 Of the sons of Bani; Maadai, Amram, and Uel,

35 Benaiah, Bedeiah, Chelluh,

36 Vaniah, Meremoth, Eliashib,

37 Mattaniah, Mattenai, and Jaasau,

38 And Bani, and Binnui, Shimei,

39 And Shelemiah, and Nathan, and Adaiah,

40 Machnadebai, Shashai, Sharai,

41 Azareel, and Shelemiah, Shemariah,

42 Shallum, Amariah, *and* Joseph.

43 Of the sons of Nebo; Jeiel, Mattithiah, Zabad, Zebina, Jadau, and Joel, Benaiah.

44 All these had taken strange wives: and *some* of them had wives by whom they had children.

NEHEMIAH

CHAPTER 1

1 The words of Nehemiah[1] the son of Hachaliah. And it came to pass in the month Chisleu, in the twentieth year, as I was in Shushan the palace,
2 That Hanani, one of my brethren, came, he and *certain* men of Judah; and I asked them concerning the Jews that had escaped, which were left of the captivity, and concerning Jerusalem.
3 And they said unto me, the remnants that are left of the captivity there in the province *are* in great affliction and reproach: the wall of Jerusalem also *is* broken down, and the gates thereof are burned with fire.
4 And it came to pass, when I heard these words, that I sat down and wept, and mourned *certain* days, and fasted, and prayed before the God of heaven,
5 And said, I beseech you, O LORD God of heaven, the great and terrible God, that keep covenant and mercy for them that love him and observe his commandments:
6 Let your ear now be attentive, and your eyes open, that you may hear the prayer of your servant, which I pray before you now, day and night, for the children of Israel your servants, and confess the sins of the children of Israel, which we have sinned against you: both I and my father's house have sinned.
7 We have dealt very corruptly against you, and have not kept the commandments, or the statutes, or the judgments, which you commanded your servant Moses.
8 Remember, I beseech you, the word that you commanded your servant Moses, saying, *if* you transgress, I will scatter you abroad among the nations:
9 But *if* you turn unto me, and keep my commandments, and do them; though there were of you cast out unto the uttermost part of the heaven, *yet* will I gather them from thence, and will bring them unto the place that I have chosen to set my name there.
10 Now these *are* your servants and your people, whom you have redeemed by your great power, and by your strong hand.
11 O Lord, I beseech you, let now your ear be attentive to the prayer of your servant, and to the prayer of your servants, who desire to fear your name: and prosper, I pray you, your servant this day, and grant him mercy in the sight of this man. For I was the king's cupbearer.

CHAPTER 2

1 And it came to pass in the month Nisan, in the twentieth year of Artaxerxes the king, *that* wine *was* before him: and I took up the wine, and gave *it* unto the king. Now I had not been *beforetime* sad in his presence.
2 Wherefore the king said unto me, why *is* your countenance sad, seeing you are not sick? This *is* nothing *else* but sorrow of heart. Then I was very sore afraid,
3 And said unto the king, Let the king live forever: why should not my countenance be sad, when the city, the place of my fathers' sepulchers, *lies* waste, and the gates thereof are consumed with fire?
4 Then the king said unto me, for what dost you make request? So I prayed to the God of heaven.
5 And I said unto the king, if it pleases the king, and if your servant **has** found favor in your sight, that you would send me unto Judah, unto the city of my fathers' sepulchers, that I may build it.
6 And the king said unto me, (the queen also sitting by him,) for how long will your journey be? And when will you return? So it pleased the king to send me; and I set him a time.
7 Moreover I said unto the king, If it please the king, let letters be given me to the governors beyond the river, that they may convey me over till I come into Judah;
8 And a letter unto Asaph the keeper of the king's forest, that he may give me timber to make beams for the gates of the palace which *appertained* to the house, and for the wall of the city, and for the house that I will enter into. And the king granted me, according to the good hand of my God upon me.
9 Then I came to the governors beyond the river, and gave them the king's letters. Now the king had sent captains of the army and horsemen with me.
10 When Sanballat the Horonite[2], and Tobiah the servant, the Ammonite, heard *of it*, it grieved them exceedingly that there **has** come a man to seek the welfare of the children of Israel.
11 So I came to Jerusalem, and was there three days.
12 [And I arose in the night, I and some few men with me; neither told I *any* man what my God had put in my heart to do at Jerusalem: neither *was there any* beast with me, save the beast that I rode upon.][3]
13 And I went out by night by the gate of the valley, even before the dragon well[4], and to the dung port, and viewed the walls of Jerusalem, which were broken down, and the gates thereof were consumed with fire.
14 Then I went on to the gate of the fountain, and to the king's pool: but *there was* no place for the beast *that was* under me to pass.
15 Then went I up in the night by the brook, and viewed the wall, and turned back, and entered by the gate of the valley, and *so* returned.
16 And the rulers knew not where I went, or what I did; neither had I as yet told *it* to the Jews, or to the priests, or to the nobles, or to the rulers, or to the rest that did the work.
17 Then said I unto them, you see the distress that *we are* in, how Jerusalem *lie* waste, and the gates thereof are burned with fire: come, and let us build up the wall of Jerusalem, that we be no more a reproach.
18 Then I told them of the hand of my God which was good upon me; as also the king's words that he had spoken unto me. And they said, Let us rise up and build. So they strengthened their hands for *this* good *work*.
19 But when Sanballat[5] the Horonite[6], and Tobiah[7] the servant, the Ammonite, and Geshem[8] the Arabian, heard *it*, they laughed us to scorn, and despised us, and said, what *is* this thing that you do? Will you rebel against the king?
20 Then answered I them, and said unto them, The God of heaven, he will prosper us; therefore we his servants will arise and build: but you have no portion, or right, or memorial, in Jerusalem.

---

[1] Nehemiah- Jehovah comforts or consolation of Jah.[Strgs#5166]
[2] <u>Sanballat the Horonite</u> – double cave town. Comes from root word meaning crevice of a serpent or cell of a prison.
[3] compare Gal. 1:12-16, John 5:34 & 2:24-25
[4] well – comes from to Hebrew words, the first being *'ayin* meaning an *eye* and *fountain* [Strgs#5869]. The second is *'êyn tannîym* meaning fountain of the jackal or fountain of jackals [Strgs#5886].
[5] Sanballat- is a Babylonian name meaning Sin has given life. Sin was a Babylonian moon god.[Strgs#5571]
[6] <u>Horonite</u> – derives from a Hebrew root word meaning two caves or *double cave town* [Strgs#2773].
[7] Tobiah- goodness of Jehovah or Jehovah is good. [Strgs#2900]
[8] Geshem- violent rain. [Strgs31654]

CHAPTER 3

1 Then Eliashib the high priest rose up with his brethren the priests, and they built the sheep gate; they sanctified it, and set up the doors of it; even unto the tower of Meah they sanctified it, unto the tower of Hananeel.

2 And next unto him built the men of Jericho. And next to them built Zaccur the son of Imri.

3 But the fish gate did the sons of Hassenaah build, who *also* laid the beams thereof, and set up the doors thereof, the locks thereof, and the bars thereof.

4 And next unto them repaired Meremoth the son of Urijah, the son of Koz. And next unto them repaired Meshullam the son of Berechiah, the son of Meshezabeel. And next unto them repaired Zadok the son of Baana.

5 And next unto them the Tekoites repaired; but their nobles put not their necks to the work of their Lord.

6 Moreover the old gate repaired Jehoiada the son of Paseah, and Meshullam the son of Besodeiah; they laid the beams thereof, and set up the doors thereof, and the locks thereof, and the bars thereof.

7 And next unto them repaired Melatiah the Gibeonite, and Jadon the Meronothite, the men of Gibeon, and of Mizpah, unto the throne of the governor on this side the river.

8 Next unto him repaired Uzziel the son of Harhaiah, of the goldsmiths. Next unto him also repaired Hananiah the son of *one of* the apothecaries, and they fortified Jerusalem unto the broad wall.

9 And next unto them repaired Rephaiah the son of Hur, the ruler of the half part of Jerusalem.

10 And next unto them repaired Jedaiah the son of Harumaph, even over against his house. And next unto him repaired Hattush the son of Hashabniah.

11 Malchijah the son of Harim, and Hashub the son of Pahath-moab, repaired the other piece, and the tower of the furnaces.

12 And next unto him repaired Shallum the son of Halohesh, the ruler of the half part of Jerusalem, he and his daughters.

13 The valley gate repaired Hanun, and the inhabitants of Zanoah; they built it, and set up the doors thereof, the locks thereof, and the bars thereof, and a thousand cubits on the wall unto the dung gate.

14 But the dung gate repaired Malchiah the son of Rechab, the ruler of part of Beth-haccerem; he built it, and set up the doors thereof, the locks thereof, and the bars thereof.

15 But the gate of the fountain repaired Shallun the son of Col-hozeh, the ruler of part of Mizpah; he built it, and covered it, and set up the doors thereof, the locks thereof, and the bars thereof, and the wall of the pool of Siloah by the king's garden, and unto the stairs that go down from the city of David.

16 After him repaired Nehemiah the son of Azbuk, the ruler of the half part of Beth-zur, unto *the place* over against the sepulchers of David, and to the pool that was made, and unto the house of the mighty.

17 After him repaired the Levites, Rehum the son of Bani. Next unto him repaired Hashabiah, the ruler of the half part of Keilah, in his part.

18 After him repaired their brethren, Bavai the son of Henadad, the ruler of the half part of Keilah.

19 And next to him repaired Ezer the son of Jeshua, the ruler of Mizpah, another piece over against the going up to the armory at the turning *of the wall*.

20 After him Baruch the son of Zabbai earnestly repaired the other piece, from the turning *of the wall* unto the door of the house of Eliashib the high priest.

21 After him repaired Meremoth the son of Urijah the son of Koz another piece, from the door of the house of Eliashib even to the end of the house of Eliashib.

22 And after him repaired the priests, the men of the plain.

23 After him repaired Benjamin and Hashub over against their house. After him repaired Azariah the son of Maaseiah the son of Ananiah by his house.

24 After him repaired Binnui the son of Henadad another piece, from the house of Azariah unto the turning *of the wall*, even unto the corner.

25 Palal the son of Uzai, over against the turning *of the wall*, and the tower which lieth out from the king's high house, that *was* by the court of the prison. After him Pedaiah the son of Parosh.

26 Moreover the Nethinims dwelt in Ophel, unto *the place* over against the water gate toward the east, and the tower that lies out.

27 After them the Tekoites repaired another piece, over against the great tower that lies out, even unto the wall of Ophel.

28 From above the horse gate repaired the priests, every one over against his house.

29 After them repaired Zadok the son of Immer over against his house. After him repaired also Shemaiah the son of Shechaniah, the keeper of the east gate.

30 After him repaired Hananiah the son of Shelemiah, and Hanun the sixth son of Zalaph, another piece. After him repaired Meshullam the son of Berechiah over against his chamber.

31 After him repaired Malchiah the goldsmith's son unto the place of the Nethinims, and of the merchants, over against the gate Miphkad, and to the going up of the corner.

32 And between the going up of the corner unto the sheep gate repaired the goldsmiths and the merchants.

CHAPTER 4

1 But it came to pass, that when Sanballat[1] heard that we built the wall, he was **angry**, and took great indignation, and mocked the Jews.

2 And he spoke before his brethren and the army of Samaria[2], and said, what do these feeble Jews? Will they fortify themselves? Will they sacrifice? Will they make an end in a day? Will they revive the stones out of the heaps of the rubbish which are burned?

3 Now Tobiah the Ammonite[3] *was* by him, and he said, even that which they build, if a fox go up, he will even break down their stone wall.

4 Hear, O our God; for we are despised: and turn their reproach upon their own head, and give them for a prey in the land of captivity:

5 And cover not their iniquity, and let not their sin be blotted out from before you: for they have provoked you to anger before the builders.

6 So built we the wall; and all the wall was joined together unto the half thereof: for the people had a mind to work.

7 But it came to pass, *that* when Sanballat, and Tobiah, and the Arabians, and the Ammonites, and the Ashdodites, heard that the

---

[1] Sanballat – sin (the moon god has given life).
[2] Samaria – watch station (in this context of the enemy) [Strgs#8111].

[3] Ammonite – inbred, son of my relative [Strgs#5984+5983]

walls of Jerusalem [were made up]¹, *and* that the breaches began to be stopped, then they were very angry,

8 And conspired all of them together to come *and* to fight against Jerusalem, and [to hinder it]².

9 Nevertheless we made our prayer unto our God, and set a watch³ against them day and night, because of them.

10 And Judah said, the strength of the bearers of burdens is decayed, and *there is* much rubbish; so that we are not able to build the wall.

11 And our adversaries said, They will not know, neither see, till we come in the midst among them, and slay them, and cause the work to cease.

12 And it came to pass, that when the Jews which dwelt by them came, they said unto us ten times, from all places where you will return unto us *they will be upon you*.

13 Therefore set I in the lower places behind the wall, *and* on the higher places, I even set the people after their families with their swords, their spears, and their bows.

14 And I looked, and rose up, and said unto the nobles, and to the rulers, and to the rest of the people, be not you afraid of them: remember the Lord, *which is* great and terrible, and fight for your brethren, your sons, and your daughters, your wives, and your houses.

15 And it came to pass, when our enemies heard that it was known unto us, and God had brought their counsel to nought⁴, that we returned all of us to the wall, every one unto his work.

16 And it came to pass from that time forth, *that* the half of my servants wrought in the work, and the other half of them held both the spears, the shields, and the bows, and the habergeons⁵; and the rulers *were* behind all the house of Judah.

17 They which built on the wall, and they that bare burdens, with those that **load**, *everyone* with one of his hands wrought in the work, and with the other *hand* held a weapon.

18 For the builders, everyone had his sword girded [by his side]⁶, and *so* built. And he that sounded the trumpet *was* by me.

19 And I said unto the nobles, and to the rulers, and to the rest of the people, the work *is* great and large, and we are separated upon the wall, one far from another.

20 In what place *therefore* you hear the sound of the trumpet, resort you there unto us: our God will fight for us.

21 So we labored in the work: and half of them held the spears from the rising of the morning till the stars appeared.

22 Likewise at the same time said I unto the people, let everyone with his servant lodge within Jerusalem, that in the night they may be a guard to us, and labor on the day.

23 So neither I, or my brethren, or my servants, or the men of the guard which followed me, none of us put off our clothes, *saving that* every one put them off for washing.

CHAPTER 5

1 And there was a great cry of the people and of their wives against their brethren the Jews.

2 For there were that said, we, our sons, and our daughters, *are* many: therefore we take up corn *for them*, that we may eat, and live.

3 *Some* also there were that said, we have mortgaged our lands, vineyards, and houses, that we might buy corn, because of the dearth.

4 There were also that said, we have borrowed money for the king's tribute, *and that upon* our lands and vineyards.

5 Yet now our flesh *is* as the flesh of our brethren, our children as their children: and, lo, we bring into bondage our sons and our daughters to be servants, and *some* of our daughters are brought unto bondage *already*: neither *is it* in our power *to redeem them*; for other men have our lands and vineyards.

6 And I was very angry when I heard their cry and these words.

7 Then I consulted with myself, and I rebuked the nobles, and the rulers, and said unto them, you exact usury, every one of his brother. And I set a great assembly against them.

8 And I said unto them, we after our ability have redeemed our brethren the Jews, which were sold unto the heathen; and will you even sell your brethren? Or shall they be sold unto us? Then held **them** their peace, and found nothing *to answer*.

9 Also I said, It *is* not good that you do: ought you not to walk in the fear of our God because of the reproach of the heathen our enemies?

10 I likewise, *and* my brethren, and my servants, might exact of them money and corn: I pray you, let us leave off this usury.

11 Restore, I pray you, to them, even this day, their lands, their vineyards, their oliveyards, and their houses, also the hundredth *part* of the money, and of the corn, the wine, and the oil, that you exact of them.

12 Then said they, we will restore *them*, and will require nothing of them; so will we do as you say. Then I called the priests, and took an oath of them, that they should do according to this promise.

13 Also I shook my lap, and said, So God shake out every man from his house, and from his labor, that performs not this promise, even thus be he shaken out, and emptied. And the **entire** congregation said, Amen, and praised the LORD. And the people did according to this promise.

14 Moreover from the time that I was appointed to be their governor in the land of Judah, from the twentieth year even unto the two and thirtieth year of Artaxerxes the king, *that is*, twelve years, I and my brethren have not eaten the bread of the governor.

15 But the former governors that *had been* before me were chargeable unto the people, and had taken of them bread and wine, beside forty shekels of silver; yea, even their servants bare rule over the people: but so did not I, because of the fear of God.

16 Yea, also I continued in the work of this wall, neither bought we any land: and all my servants *were* gathered there unto the work.

17 Moreover *there were* at my table an hundred and fifty of the Jews and rulers, beside those that came unto us from among the heathen that *are* about us.

18 Now *that* which was prepared *for me* daily *was* one ox *and* six choice sheep; also fowls were prepared for me, and once in ten days store of all sorts of wine: yet for all this required not I the bread of the governor, because the bondage was heavy upon this people.

19 Think upon me, my God, for good, *according* to all that I have done for this people.

---

¹ lit. restoring to soundness by ascending [Strgs#724+5927].
² lit. make an error to it or make a mistake of it [Strgs#6213+8442].
³ watch – when trouble comes post a guard [Strgs#4929+8104].
⁴ nought- is the Hebrew word *pàrar*, paw-rar'; it's defined as to break up, to violate, frustrate, cast off, cause to cease, defeat, dissolve, divide, fail, to make void, to make of none effect. [Strgs#6565]
⁵ habergeons – a corslet, *coat of mail, armor* [Strgs#8302]
⁶ lit. on his loins as slender, to be slender, the waist or small of the back [Strgs#4975].

CHAPTER 6

1 Now it came to pass, when Sanballat, and Tobiah, and Geshem the Arabian, and the rest of our enemies, heard that I had built the wall, and *that* there was no breach left therein; (though at that time I had not set up the doors upon the gates;)
2 That Sanballat and Geshem sent unto me, saying, come, let us meet together in *some one of* the villages in the plain of Ono. But they thought to do me mischief.
3 And I sent messengers unto them, saying, I *am* doing a great work, so that I cannot come down: why should the work cease, whilst I leave it, and come down to you?
4 Yet they sent unto me four times after this sort; and I answered them after the same manner.
5 Then sent Sanballat his servant unto me in like manner the fifth time with an open letter in his hand;
6 Wherein *was* written, it is reported among the heathen, and Gashmu said *it, that* you and the Jews think to rebel: for which cause you built the wall, that you may be their king, according to these words.
7 And you have also appointed prophets to preach of you at Jerusalem, saying, *there is* a king in Judah: and now will it be reported to the king according to these words. Come now therefore, and let us take counsel together.
8 Then I sent unto him, saying, there are no such things done as you say, but you feigns them out of your own heart.
9 For they all made us afraid, saying, their hands will be weakened from the work, that it be not done. Now therefore, O God, strengthen my hands.
10 Afterward I came unto the house of Shemaiah the son of Delaiah the son of Mehetabeel, who *was* shut up; and he said, Let us meet together in the house of God, within the temple, and let us shut the doors of the temple: for they will come to slay you; yea, in the night will they come to slay you.
11 And I said, should such a man as I flee? And who *is there*, that, *being* as I *am*, would go into the temple to save his life? I will not go in.
12 And, lo, I perceived that God had not sent him; but that he pronounced this prophecy against me: for Tobiah and Sanballat had hired him.
13 Therefore *was* he hired, that I should be afraid, and do so, and sin, and *that* they might have *matter* for an evil report, that they might reproach me.
14 My God, think you upon Tobiah and Sanballat according to these their works, and on the prophetess Noadiah, and the rest of the prophets, that would have put me in fear.
15 So the wall was finished in the twenty and fifth *day of the month* Elul, in fifty and two days.
16 And it came to pass, that when all our enemies heard *thereof*, and all the heathen that *were* about us saw *these things*, they were much cast down in their own eyes: for they perceived that this work was wrought of our God.
17 Moreover in those days the nobles of Judah sent many letters unto Tobiah, and *the letters* of Tobiah came unto them.
18 For *there were* many in Judah sworn unto him, because he *was* the son in law of Shechaniah the son of Arah; and his son Johanan had taken the daughter of Meshullam the son of Berechiah.
19 Also they reported his good deeds before me, and uttered my words to him. *And* Tobiah sent letters to put me in fear.

---
[1] Raamiah – thunder of Jehovah or *Jah has shaken* [Strgs#7485].

CHAPTER 7

1 Now it came to pass, when the wall was built, and I had set up the doors, and the porters and the singers and the Levites were appointed,
2 That I gave my brother Hanani, and Hananiah the ruler of the palace, charge over Jerusalem: for he *was* a faithful man, and feared God above many.
3 And I said unto them, Let not the gates of Jerusalem be opened until the sun be hot; and while they stand by, let them shut the doors, and bar *them*: and appoint watches of the inhabitants of Jerusalem, everyone in his watch, and every one *to be* over against his house.
4 Now the city *was* large and great: but the people *were* few therein, and the houses *were* not built.
5 And my God put into mine heart to gather together the nobles, and the rulers, and the people, that they might be reckoned by genealogy. And I found a register of the genealogy of them which came up at the first, and found written therein,
6 These *are* the children of the province, that went up out of the captivity, of those that had been carried away, whom Nebuchadnezzar the king of Babylon had carried away, and came again to Jerusalem and to Judah, every one unto his city;
7 Who came with Zerubbabel, Jeshua, Nehemiah, Azariah, Raamiah[1], Nahamani, Mordecai, Bilshan, Mispereth, Bigvai, Nehum, Baanah. The number, *I say*, of the men of the people of Israel *was this*;
8 The children of Parosh, two thousand an hundred seventy and two.
9 The children of Shephatiah, three hundred seventy and two.
10 The children of Arah, six hundred fifty and two.
11 The children of Pahath-moab, of the children of Jeshua and Joab, two thousand and eight hundred *and* eighteen.
12 The children of Elam, a thousand two hundred fifty and four.
13 The children of Zattu, eight hundred forty and five.
14 The children of Zaccai, seven hundred and threescore.
15 The children of Binnui, six hundred forty and eight.
16 The children of Bebai, six hundred twenty and eight.
17 The children of Azgad, two thousand three hundred twenty and two.
18 The children of Adonikam, six hundred threescore and seven.
19 The children of Bigvai, two thousand threescore and seven.
20 The children of Adin, six hundred fifty and five.
21 The children of Ater of Hezekiah, ninety and eight.
22 The children of Hashum, three hundred twenty and eight.
23 The children of Bezai, three hundred twenty and four.
24 The children of Hariph, an hundred and twelve.
25 The children of Gibeon, ninety and five.
26 The men of Beth-lehem and Netophah, an hundred fourscore and eight.
27 The men of Anathoth, an hundred twenty and eight.
28 The men of Beth-azmaveth, forty and two.
29 The men of Kirjath-jearim, Chephirah, and Beeroth, seven hundred forty and three.
30 The men of Ramah and Geba, six hundred twenty and one.
31 The men of Michmas, an hundred and twenty and two.
32 The men of Beth-el and Ai, an hundred twenty and three.
33 The men of the other Nebo, fifty and two.

34 The children of the other Elam, a thousand two hundred fifty and four.
35 The children of Harim, three hundred and twenty.
36 The children of Jericho, three hundred forty and five.
37 The children of Lod, Hadid, and Ono, seven hundred twenty and one.
38 The children of Senaah, three thousand nine hundred and thirty.
39 The priests: the children of Jedaiah, of the house of Jeshua, nine hundred seventy and three.
40 The children of Immer, a thousand fifty and two.
41 The children of Pashur, a thousand two hundred forty and seven.
42 The children of Harim, a thousand and seventeen.
43 The Levites: the children of Jeshua, of Kadmiel, *and* of the children of Hodevah, seventy and four.
44 The singers: the children of Asaph, an hundred forty and eight.
45 The porters: the children of Shallum, the children of Ater, the children of Talmon, the children of Akkub, the children of Hatita, the children of Shobai, an hundred thirty and eight.
46 The Nethinims: the children of Ziha, the children of Hashupha, the children of Tabbaoth,
47 The children of Keros, the children of Sia, the children of Padon,
48 The children of Lebana, the children of Hagaba, the children of Shalmai,
49 The children of Hanan, the children of Giddel, the children of Gahar,
50 The children of Reaiah, the children of Rezin, the children of Nekoda,
51 The children of Gazzam, the children of Uzza, the children of Phaseah,
52 The children of Besai, the children of Meunim, the children of Nephishesim,
53 The children of Bakbuk, the children of Hakupha, the children of Harhur,
54 The children of Bazlith, the children of Mehida, the children of Harsha,
55 The children of Barkos, the children of Sisera, the children of Tamah,
56 The children of Neziah, the children of Hatipha.
57 The children of Solomon's servants: the children of Sotai, the children of Sophereth, the children of Perida,
58 The children of Jaala, the children of Darkon, the children of Giddel,
59 The children of Shephatiah, the children of Hattil, the children of Pochereth of Zebaim, the children of Amon.
60 All the Nethinims, and the children of Solomon's servants, *were* three hundred ninety and two.
61 And these *were* they which went up *also* from Tel-melah, Tel-haresha, Cherub, Addon, and Immer: but they could not show their father's house, or their seed, whether they *were* of Israel.
62 The children of Delaiah, the children of Tobiah, the children of Nekoda, six hundred forty and two.
63 And of the priests: the children of Habaiah, the children of Koz, the children of Barzillai, which took *one* of the daughters of Barzillai the Gileadite to wife, and was called after their name.
64 These sought their register among those that were reckoned by genealogy, but it was not found: therefore were they, as polluted, put from the priesthood.

65 And the Tirshatha said unto them, that they should not eat of the most holy things, till there stood *up* a priest with Urim and Thummim.
66 The whole congregation together *was* forty and two thousand three hundred and threescore,
67 Beside their man-servants and their maidservants, of whom *there were* seven thousand three hundred thirty and seven: and they had two hundred forty and five singing men and singing women.
68 Their horses, seven hundred thirty and six: their mules, two hundred forty and five:
69 *Their* camels, four hundred thirty and five: six thousand seven hundred and twenty asses.
70 And some of the chief of the fathers gave unto the work. The Tirshatha gave to the treasure a thousand drams of gold, fifty bowls, and five hundred and thirty priests' garments.
71 And *some* of the chief of the fathers gave to the treasure of the work twenty thousand drams of gold, and two thousand and two hundred pound of silver.
72 And *that* which the rest of the people gave *was* twenty thousand drams of gold, and two thousand pound of silver, and threescore and seven priests' garments.
73 So the priests, and the Levites, and the porters, and the singers, and *some* of the people, and the Nethinims, and all Israel, dwelt in their cities; and when the seventh month came, the children of Israel *were* in their cities.

CHAPTER 8

1 And all the people gathered themselves together as one man into the street that *was* before the water gate; and they spoke unto Ezra the scribe to bring the book of the Law of Moses, which the LORD had commanded to Israel.
2 And Ezra the priest brought the law before the congregation both of men and women, and all [that could hear with understanding]¹, upon the first day of the seventh month.
3 And he read therein before the street that *was* before the water gate from the morning until midday, before the men and the women, and those that could understand; and the ears of all the people *were attentive* unto the book of the law.
4 And Ezra the scribe stood upon a pulpit of wood, which they had made for the purpose; and beside him stood Mattithiah, and Shema, and Anaiah, and Urijah, and Hilkiah, and Maaseiah, on his right hand; and on his left hand, Pedaiah, and Mishael, and Malchiah, and Hashum, and Hashbadana, Zechariah, *and* Meshullam.
5 And Ezra opened the book in the sight of all the people; (for he was above all the people;) and when he opened it, all the people stood up:
6 And Ezra blessed the LORD, the great God. And all the people answered, Amen, Amen, with lifting up their hands: and they bowed their heads, and worshipped the LORD with *their* faces to the ground.
7 Also Jeshua, and Bani, and Sherebiah, Jamin, Akkub, Shabbethai, Hodijah, Maaseiah, Kelita, Azariah, Jozabad, Hanan, Pelaiah, and the Levites, caused the people to understand the law: and the people *stood* in their place.
8 So they read in the book in the law of God distinctly, and gave the sense, and caused *them* to understand the reading.

---

¹ lit. – that which is understood in hearing [Strgs#8085+995].

9 And Nehemiah, which *is* the Tirshatha, and Ezra the priest the scribe, and the Levites that taught the people, said unto all the people, This day *is* holy unto the LORD your God; mourn not, or weep. For all the people wept, when they heard the words of the law.
10 Then he said unto them, Go your way, eat the fat, and drink the sweet, and send portions unto them for whom nothing is prepared: for *this* day *is* holy unto our Lord: neither be you sorry; for the joy of the LORD is your strength.
11 So the Levites stilled all the people, saying, hold your peace, for the day *is* holy; neither be you grieved.
12 And all the people went their way to eat, and to drink, and to send portions, and to make great mirth, because they had understood the words that were declared unto them.
13 And on the second day were gathered together the chief of the fathers of all the people, the priests, and the Levites, unto Ezra the scribe, even to understand the words of the law.
14 And they found written in the law which the LORD had commanded by Moses, that the children of Israel should dwell in booths in the feast of the seventh month:
15 And that they should publish and proclaim in all their cities, and in Jerusalem, saying, Go forth unto the mount, and fetch olive branches, and pine branches, and myrtle branches, and palm branches, and branches of thick trees, to make booths, as *it is* written.
16 So the people went forth, and brought *them*, and made themselves booths, every one upon the roof of his house, and in their courts, and in the courts of the house of God, and in the street of the water gate, and in the street of the gate of Ephraim.
17 And all the congregation of them that were come again out of the captivity made booths, and sat under the booths: for since the days of Jeshua the son of Nun unto that day had not the children of Israel done so. And there was very great gladness.
18 Also day by day, from the first day unto the last day, he read in the book of the law of God. And they kept the feast seven days; and on the eighth day *was* a solemn assembly, according unto the manner.

CHAPTER 9

1 Now in the twenty and fourth day of this month the children of Israel were assembled with fasting, and with sackclothes, and earth upon them.
2 And the seed of Israel separated themselves from all strangers, and stood and confessed their sins, and the iniquities of their fathers.
3 And they stood up in their place, and read in the book of the law of the LORD their God *one* fourth part of the day; and *another* fourth part they confessed, and worshipped the LORD their God.
4 Then stood up upon the stairs, of the Levites, Jeshua, and Bani, Kadmiel, Shebaniah, Bunni, Sherebiah, Bani, *and* Chenani, and cried with a loud voice unto the LORD their God.
5 Then the Levites, Jeshua, and Kadmiel, Bani, Hashabniah, Sherebiah, Hodijah, Shebaniah, *and* Pethahiah, said, Stand up *and* bless the LORD your God forever and ever: and blessed be your glorious name, which is exalted above all blessing and praise.
6 Thou, *even* thou, are LORD alone; you have made heaven, the heaven of heavens, with all their host, the earth, and all *things* that *are* therein, the seas, and all that *is* therein, and you preserves them all; and the host of heaven worships you.
7 you are the LORD the God, who did choose Abram, and brought him forth out of Ur of the Chaldees, and gave him the name of Abraham;
8 And found his heart faithful before you, and made a covenant with him to give the land of the Canaanites, the Hittites, the Amorites, and the Perizzites, and the Jebusites, and the Girgashites, to give *it, I say*, to his seed, and have performed your words; for you are righteous:
9 And did see the affliction of our fathers in Egypt, and heard their cry by the Red sea;
10 And showed signs and wonders upon Pharaoh, and on all his servants, and on all the people of his land: for you knew that they dealt proudly against them. So did you **make** you a name[1], as *it is* this day.
11 And you did divide the sea before them, so that they went through the midst of the sea on the dry land; and their persecutors you threw into the deeps, as a stone into the mighty waters.
12 Moreover you led them in the day by a cloudy pillar; and in the night by a pillar of fire, to give them light in the way wherein they should go.
13 you came down also upon mount Sinai, and spoke with them from heaven, and gave them right judgments, and true laws, good statutes and commandments:
14 And made known unto them your holy Sabbath, and commanded them precepts, statutes, and laws, by the hand of Moses your servant:
15 And gave them bread from heaven for their hunger, and brought forth water for them out of the rock for their thirst, and promised them that they should go in to possess the land which you had sworn to give them.
16 But they and our fathers dealt proudly, and hardened their necks, and hearkened not to your commandments,
17 And refused to obey, neither were mindful of your wonders that you did among them; but hardened their necks, and in their rebellion appointed a captain to return to their bondage: but you are a God ready to pardon, gracious and merciful, slow to anger, and of great kindness, and forsook them not.
18 Yea, when they had made them a molten calf, and said, this *is* your God that brought you up out of Egypt, and had wrought great provocations;
19 Yet you in your manifold mercies forsook them not in the wilderness: the pillar of the cloud departed not from them by day, to lead them in the way; neither the pillar of fire by night, to show them light, and the way wherein they should go.
20 you gave also your good spirit to instruct them, and withheld not your manna from their mouth, and gave them water for their thirst.
21 Yes, forty years did you sustain them in the wilderness, *so that* they lacked nothing; their clothes waxed not old, and their feet swelled not.
22 Moreover you gave them kingdoms and nations, and did divide them into corners: so they possessed the land of Sihon, and the land of the king of Heshbon, and the land of Og king of Bashan.
23 Their children also multiplied you as the stars of heaven, and brought them into the land, concerning which you had promised to their fathers, that they should go in to possess *it*.
24 So the children went in and possessed the land, and you subdued before them the inhabitants of the land, the Canaanites,

---

[1] name- the word name here does not only refer to an actual name. Name here also translate as position, a mark, memorial of individuality, honor, authority, character, famous, renown and report. [Strgs#8034]

and gave them into their hands, with their kings, and the people of the land, that they might do with them as they would.

25 And they took strong cities, and a fat land, and possessed houses full of all goods, wells **dug**, vineyards, and oliveyards, and fruit trees in abundance: so they did eat, and were filled, and became fat, and delighted themselves in your great goodness.

26 Nevertheless they were disobedient, and rebelled against you, and cast your law behind their backs, and **slaughtered** your prophets **who** testified against them to turn them to you, and they wrought great provocations.

27 Therefore you delivered them into the hand of their enemies, who vexed them: and in the time of their trouble, when they cried unto you, you heard *them* from heaven; and according to your manifold mercies you gave them saviors, who saved them out of the hand of their enemies.

28 But after they had rest, they did evil again before you: therefore left you them in the hand of their enemies, so that they had the dominion over them: yet when they returned, and cried unto you, you heard *them* from heaven; and many times did you deliver them according to your mercies;

29 And testified against them, that you might bring them again unto your law: yet they dealt proudly, and hearkened not unto your commandments, but sinned against your judgments, (which if a man do, he will live in them;) and withdrew the shoulder, and hardened their neck, and would not hear.

30 Yet many years did you forbear them, and testify against them by your spirit in your prophets: yet would they not give ear: therefore gave you them into the hand of the people of the lands.

31 Nevertheless for your great mercies' sake you did not utterly consume them, or forsake them; for you are a gracious and merciful God.

32 Now therefore, our God, the great, the mighty, and the terrible God, who keeps[1] covenant and mercy, let not all the trouble seem little before you, that has come upon us, on our kings, on our princes, and on our priests, and on our prophets, and on our fathers, and on all your people, since the time of the kings of Assyria unto this day.

33 Howbeit you are just in all that is brought upon us; for you have done right, but we have done wickedly:

34 Neither **has** our kings, our princes, our priests, or our fathers, kept your law, or hearkened unto your commandments and your testimonies, wherewith you did testify against them.

35 For they have not served you in their kingdom, and in your great goodness that you gave them, and in the large and fat land which you gave before them, neither turned they from their wicked works.

36 Behold, we *are* servants this day, and *for* the land that you gave unto our fathers to eat the fruit thereof and the good thereof, behold, we *are* servants in it:

37 And it yields much increase unto the kings whom you have set over us because of our sins: also they have dominion over our bodies, and over our cattle, at their pleasure, and we *are* in great distress.

38 And because of all this we make a sure *covenant*, and write *it*; and our princes, Levites, *and* priests, seal *unto it*.

CHAPTER 10

1 Now those that sealed *were*, Nehemiah, the Tirshatha, the son of Hachaliah, and Zidkijah,

2 Seraiah, Azariah, Jeremiah,

3 Pashur, Amariah, Malchijah,

4 Hattush, Shebaniah, Malluch,

5 Harim, Meremoth, Obadiah,

6 Daniel, Ginnethon, Baruch,

7 Meshullam, Abijah, Mijamin,

8 Maaziah, Bilgai, Shemaiah: these *were* the priests.

9 And the Levites: both Jeshua the son of Azaniah, Binnui of the sons of Henadad, Kadmiel;

10 And their brethren, Shebaniah, Hodijah, Kelita, Pelaiah, Hanan,

11 Micha, Rehob, Hashabiah,

12 Zaccur, Sherebiah, Shebaniah,

13 Hodijah, Bani, Beninu.

14 The chief of the people; Parosh, Pahath-moab, Elam, Zatthu, Bani,

15 Bunni, Azgad, Bebai,

16 Adonijah, Bigvai, Adin,

17 Ater, Hizkijah, Azzur,

18 Hodijah, Hashum, Bezai,

19 Hariph, Anathoth, Nebai,

20 Magpiash, Meshullam, Hezir,

21 Meshezabeel, Zadok, Jaddua,

22 Pelatiah, Hanan, Anaiah,

23 Hoshea, Hananiah, Hashub,

24 Hallohesh, Pileha, Shobek,

25 Rehum, Hashabnah, Maaseiah,

26 And Ahijah, Hanan, Anan,

27 Malluch, Harim, Baanah.

28 And the rest of the people, the priests, the Levites, the porters, the singers, the Nethinims, and all they that had separated themselves from the people of the lands unto the law of God, their wives, their sons, and their daughters, every one having knowledge, and having understanding;

29 They clave to their brethren, their nobles, and entered into a curse, and into an oath, to walk in God's law, which was given by Moses the servant of God, and to observe and do all the commandments of the LORD our Lord, and his judgments and his statutes;

30 And that we would not give our daughters unto the people of the land, or take their daughters for our sons:

31 And *if* the people of the land bring ware or any victuals on the Sabbath day to sell, *that* we would not buy it of them on the Sabbath, or on the holy day: and *that* we would leave the seventh year, and the exaction of every debt.

32 Also we made ordinances for us, to charge ourselves yearly with the third part of a shekel for the service of the house of our God;

33 For the shewbread, and for the continual meat offering, and for the continual burnt offering, of the Sabbaths, of the new moons, for the set feasts, and for the holy *things*, and for the sin offerings to make an atonement for Israel, and *for* all the work of the house of our God.

34 And we cast the lots among the priests, the Levites, and the people, for the wood offering, to bring *it* into the house of our God, after the houses of our fathers, at times appointed year by year, to burn upon the altar of the LORD our God, as *it is* written in the law:

---

[1] keep- is the Hebrew word *shâmar*, <u>shaw-mar'</u>, which is translated as to hedge about (as with thorns), guard, to protect, attend to, to be circumspect, take heed (to self), observe, preserve, regard, reserve, save (self), wait for, watch.

So God not only keeps His covenant with believers, but He protects and circumvents it, that it may remain preserved. [Strgs#8104]

35 And to bring the first-fruits of our ground, and the first-fruits of all fruit of all trees, year by year, unto the house of the LORD:

36 Also the firstborn of our sons, and of our cattle, as *it is* written in the law, and the firstlings of our herds and of our flocks, to bring to the house of our God, unto the priests that minister in the house of our God:

37 And *that* we should bring the first-fruits of our dough, and our offerings, and the fruit of all manner of trees, of wine and of oil, unto the priests, to the chambers of the house of our God; and the tithes of our ground unto the Levites, that the same Levites might have the tithes in all the cities of our tillage.

38 And the priest the son of Aaron will be with the Levites, when the Levites take tithes: and the Levites will bring up the tithe of the tithes unto the house of our God, to the chambers, into the treasure house.

39 For the children of Israel and the children of Levi will bring the offering of the corn, of the new wine, and the oil, unto the chambers, where *are* the vessels of the sanctuary, and the priests that minister, and the porters, and the singers: and we will not forsake the house of our God.

CHAPTER 11

1 And the rulers of the people dwelt at Jerusalem: the rest of the people also cast lots, to bring one of ten to dwell in Jerusalem the holy city, and nine parts *to dwell* in *other* cities.

2 And the people blessed all the men, that willingly offered themselves to dwell at Jerusalem.

3 Now these *are* the chief of the province that dwelt in Jerusalem: but in the cities of Judah dwelt everyone in his possession in their cities, *to wit*, Israel, the priests, and the Levites, and the Nethinims, and the children of Solomon's servants.

4 And at Jerusalem dwelt *certain* of the children of Judah, and of the children of Benjamin. Of the children of Judah; Athaiah the son of Uzziah, the son of Zechariah, the son of Amariah, the son of Shephatiah, the son of Mahalaleel, of the children of Perez;

5 And Maaseiah the son of Baruch, the son of Col-hozeh, the son of Hazaiah, the son of Adaiah, the son of Joiarib, the son of Zechariah, the son of Shiloni.

6 All the sons of Perez that dwelt at Jerusalem *were* four hundred threescore and eight valiant men.

7 And these *are* the sons of Benjamin; Sallu the son of Meshullam, the son of Joed, the son of Pedaiah, the son of Kolaiah, the son of Maaseiah, the son of Ithiel, the son of Jesaiah.

8 And after him Gabbai, Sallai, nine hundred twenty and eight.

9 And Joel the son of Zichri *was* their overseer: and Judah the son of Senuah *was* second over the city.

10 Of the priests: Jedaiah the son of Joiarib, Jachin.

11 Seraiah the son of Hilkiah, the son of Meshullam, the son of Zadok, the son of Meraioth, the son of Ahitub, *was* the ruler of the house of God.

12 And their brethren that did the work of the house *were* eight hundred twenty and two: and Adaiah the son of Jeroham, the son of Pelaliah, the son of Amzi, the son of Zechariah, the son of Pashur, the son of Malchiah,

13 And his brethren, chief of the fathers, two hundred forty and two: and Amashai the son of Azareel, the son of Ahasai, the son of Meshillemoth, the son of Immer,

14 And their brethren, mighty men of valor, an hundred twenty and eight: and their overseer *was* Zabdiel, the son of *one of* the great men.

15 Also of the Levites: Shemaiah the son of Hashub, the son of Azrikam, the son of Hashabiah, the son of Bunni;

16 And Shabbethai and Jozabad, of the chief of the Levites, *had* the oversight of the outward business of the house of God

17 And Mattaniah the son of Micha, the son of Zabdi, the son of Asaph, *was* the principal to begin the thanksgiving in prayer: and Bakbukiah the second among his brethren, and Abda the son of Shammua, the son of Galal, the son of Jeduthun.

18 All the Levites in the holy city *were* two hundred fourscore and four.

19 Moreover the porters, Akkub, Talmon, and their brethren that kept the gates, *were* an hundred seventy and two.

20 And the residue of Israel, of the priests, *and* the Levites, *were* in all the cities of Judah, everyone in his inheritance.

21 But the Nethinims dwelt in Ophel: and Ziha and Gispa *were* over the Nethinims.

22 The overseer also of the Levites at Jerusalem *was* Uzzi the son of Bani, the son of Hashabiah, the son of Mattaniah, the son of Micha. Of the sons of Asaph, the singers *were* over the business of the house of God.

23 For *it was* the king's commandment concerning them, that a certain portion should be for the singers, due for every day.

24 And Pethahiah the son of Meshezabeel, of the children of Zerah the son of Judah, *was* at the king's hand in all matters concerning the people.

25 And for the villages, with their fields, *some* of the children of Judah dwelt at Kirjath-arba, and *in* the villages thereof, and at Dibon, and *in* the villages thereof, and at Jekabzeel, and *in* the villages thereof,

26 And at Jeshua, and at Moladah, and at Beth-phelet,

27 And at Hazar-shual, and at Beer-sheba, and *in* the villages thereof,

28 And at Ziklag, and at Mekonah, and in the villages thereof,

29 And at En-rimmon, and at Zareah, and at Jarmuth,

30 Zanoah, Adullam, and *in* their villages, at Lachish, and the fields thereof, at Azekah, and *in* the villages thereof. And they dwelt from Beer-sheba unto the valley of Hinnom.

31 The children also of Benjamin from Geba *dwelt* at Michmash, and Aija, and Beth-el, and *in* their villages,

32 *And* at Anathoth, Nob, Ananiah,

33 Hazor, Ramah, Gittaim,

34 Hadid, Zeboim, Neballat,

35 Lod, and Ono, the valley of craftsmen.

36 And of the Levites *were* divisions *in* Judah, *and* in Benjamin.

CHAPTER 12

1 Now these *are* the priests and the Levites that went up with Zerubbabel the son of Shealtiel, and Jeshua: Seraiah, Jeremiah, Ezra,

2 Amariah, Malluch, Hattush,

3 Shechaniah, Rehum, Meremoth,

4 Iddo, Ginnetho, Abijah,

5 Miamin, Maadiah, Bilgah,

6 Shemaiah, and Joiarib, Jedaiah,

7 Sallu, Amok, Hilkiah, Jedaiah. These *were* the chief of the priests and of their brethren in the days of Jeshua.

8 Moreover the Levites: Jeshua, Binnui, Kadmiel, Sherebiah, Judah, *and* Mattaniah, *which was* over the thanksgiving, he and his brethren.

9 Also Bakbukiah and Unni, their brethren, *were* over against them in the watches.

10 And Jeshua begat Joiakim, Joiakim also begat Eliashib, and Eliashib begat Joiada,
11 And Joiada begat Jonathan, and Jonathan begat Jaddua.
12 And in the days of Joiakim were priests, the chief of the fathers: of Seraiah, Meraiah; of Jeremiah, Hananiah;
13 Of Ezra, Meshullam; of Amariah, Jehohanan;
14 Of Melicu, Jonathan; of Shebaniah, Joseph;
15 Of Harim, Adna; of Meraioth, Helkai;
16 Of Iddo, Zechariah; of Ginnethon, Meshullam;
17 Of Abijah, Zichri; of Miniamin, of Moadiah, Piltai;
18 Of Bilgah, Shammua; of Shemaiah, Jehonathan;
19 And of Joiarib, Mattenai; of Jedaiah, Uzzi;
20 Of Sallai, Kallai; of Amok, Eber;
21 Of Hilkiah, Hashabiah; of Jedaiah, Nethaneel.
22 The Levites in the days of Eliashib, Joiada, and Johanan, and Jaddua, were recorded chief of the fathers: also the priests, to the reign of Darius the Persian.
23 The sons of Levi, the chief of the fathers, were written in the book of the chronicles, even until the days of Johanan the son of Eliashib.
24 And the chief of the Levites: Hashabiah, Sherebiah, and Jeshua the son of Kadmiel, with their brethren over against them, to praise and to give thanks, according to the commandment of David the man of God, ward over against ward.
25 Mattaniah, and Bakbukiah, Obadiah, Meshullam, Talmon, Akkub, were porters keeping the ward at the thresholds of the gates.
26 These were in the days of Joiakim the son of Jeshua, the son of Jozadak, and in the days of Nehemiah the governor, and of Ezra the priest, the scribe.
27 And at the dedication of the wall of Jerusalem they sought the Levites out of all their places, to bring them to Jerusalem, to keep the dedication with gladness, both with thanksgivings, and with singing, with cymbals, psalteries, and with harps.
28 And the sons of the singers gathered themselves together, both out of the plain country round about Jerusalem, and from the villages of Netophathi;
29 Also from the house of Gilgal, and out of the fields of Geba and Azmaveth: for the singers had **built** them villages round about Jerusalem.
30 And the priests and the Levites purified themselves, and purified the people, and the gates, and the wall.
31 Then I brought up the princes of Judah upon the wall, and appointed two great *companies of them that gave* thanks, *whereof one* went on the right hand upon the wall toward the dung gate:
32 And after them went Hoshaiah, and half of the princes of Judah,
33 And Azariah, Ezra, and Meshullam,
34 Judah, and Benjamin, and Shemaiah, and Jeremiah,
35 And *certain* of the priests' sons with trumpets; *namely*, Zechariah the son of Jonathan, the son of Shemaiah, the son of Mattaniah, the son of Michaiah, the son of Zaccur, the son of Asaph:
36 And his brethren, Shemaiah, and Azarael, Milalai, Gilalai, Maai, Nethaneel, and Judah, Hanani, with the musical instruments of David the man of God, and Ezra the scribe before them.
37 And at the fountain gate, which was over against them, they went up by the stairs of the city of David, at the going up of the wall, above the house of David, even unto the water gate eastward.

38 And the other *company of them that gave* thanks went over against *them*, and I after them, and the half of the people upon the wall, from beyond the tower of the furnaces even unto the broad wall;
39 And from above the gate of Ephraim, and above the old gate, and above the fish gate, and the tower of Hananeel, and the tower of Meah, even unto the sheep gate: and they stood still in the prison gate.
40 So stood the two *companies of them that gave* thanks in the house of God, and I, and the half of the rulers with me:
41 And the priests; Eliakim, Maaseiah, Miniamin, Michaiah, Elioenai, Zechariah, *and* Hananiah, with trumpets;
42 And Maaseiah, and Shemaiah, and Eleazar, and Uzzi, and Jehohanan, and Malchijah, and Elam, and Ezer. And the singers sang loud, with Jezrahiah *their* overseer.
43 Also that day they offered great sacrifices, and rejoiced: for God had made them rejoice with great joy: the wives also and the children rejoiced: so that the joy of Jerusalem was heard even afar off.
44 And at that time were some appointed over the chambers for the treasures, for the offerings, for the first-fruits, and for the tithes, to gather into them out of the fields of the cities the portions of the law for the priests and Levites: for Judah rejoiced for the priests and for the Levites that waited.
45 And both the singers and the porters kept the ward of their God, and the ward of the purification, according to the commandment of David, *and* of Solomon his son.
46 For in the days of David and Asaph of old *there* were chief of the singers, and songs of praise and thanksgiving unto God.
47 And all Israel in the days of Zerubbabel, and in the days of Nehemiah, gave the portions of the singers and the porters, every day his portion: and they sanctified *holy things* unto the Levites; and the Levites sanctified *them* unto the children of Aaron.

CHAPTER 13

1 On that day they read in the book of Moses in the audience of the people; and therein was found written, that the Ammonite and the Moabite should not come into the congregation of God for ever;
2 Because they met not the children of Israel with bread and with water, but hired Balaam against them, that he should curse them: howbeit our God turned the curse into a blessing.
3 Now it came to pass, when they had heard the law, that they separated from Israel the **entire** mixed multitude.
4 And before this, Eliashib the priest, having the oversight of the chamber of the house of our God, *was* allied unto Tobiah:
5 And he had prepared for him a great chamber, where aforetime they laid the [meat offerings][1], the frankincense, and the vessels, and the tithes of the [corn][2], the new wine, and the oil, which was commanded *to be given* to the Levites, and the singers, and the porters; and the offerings of the priests.
6 But in all this *time* was not I at Jerusalem: for in the two and thirtieth year of Artaxerxes king of Babylon came I unto the king, and after certain days obtained I leave of the king:
7 And I came to Jerusalem, and understood of the evil that Eliashib[3] did for Tobiah, in preparing him a chamber in the courts of the house of God.
8 And it grieved me sore: therefore I cast forth all the household stuff of Tobiah out of the chamber.

---

[1] lit. something prepared, to *apportion*, *bestow*, a *donation*, *tribute*, *offering* [Strgs#4503].

[2] corn – *increase*, grain, wheat [Strgs#1715].
[3] Eliashib – God will restore [Strgs#475].

9 Then I commanded, and they cleansed the chambers: and there brought I again the vessels of the house of God, with the meat offering and the frankincense.
10 And I perceived that the portions of the Levites had not been given *them*: for the Levites and the singers, that did the work, were fled everyone to his field.
11 Then contended I with the rulers, and said, why is the house of God forsaken? And I gathered them together, and set them in their place¹.
12 Then brought all Judah the tithe of the corn and the new wine and the oil unto the treasuries.
13 And I made treasurers over the treasuries, Shelemiah the priest, and Zadok the scribe, and of the Levites, Pedaiah: and next to them *was* Hanan the son of Zaccur, the son of Mattaniah: for they were counted faithful, and their office *was* to distribute unto their brethren.
14 Remember me, O my God, concerning this, and wipe not out my good deeds that I have done for the house of my God, and for the offices thereof.
15 In those days saw I in Judah *some* treading wine presses on the Sabbath, and bringing in sheaves, and lading asses; as also wine, grapes, and figs, and all *manner of* burdens, which they brought into Jerusalem on the Sabbath day: and I testified *against them* in the day wherein they sold victuals.
16 There dwelt men of Tyre also therein, which brought fish, and all manner of ware, and sold on the Sabbath unto the children of Judah, and in Jerusalem.
17 Then I contended with the nobles of Judah, and said unto them, what evil thing *is* this that you do, and profane the Sabbath day?
18 Did not your fathers thus, and did not our God bring all this evil upon us, and upon this city? Yet you bring more wrath upon Israel by profaning the Sabbath.
19 And it came to pass, that when the gates of Jerusalem began to be dark before the Sabbath, I commanded that the gates should be shut, and charged that they should not be opened till after the Sabbath: and *some* of my servants set I at the gates, *that* there should no burden be brought in on the Sabbath day.
20 So the merchants and sellers of all kind of ware lodged without Jerusalem once or twice.
21 Then I testified against them, and said unto them, why lodge you about the wall? If you do *so* again, I will lay hands on you. From that time forth came they no *more* on the Sabbath.
22 And I commanded the Levites that they should cleanse themselves, and *that* they should come *and* keep the gates, to sanctify the Sabbath day. Remember me, O my God, *concerning* this also, and spare me according to the greatness of your mercy.
23 In those days also saw I Jews *that* had married wives of Ashdod, of Ammon, *and* of Moab:
24 And their children spoke half in the speech of Ashdod², and could not speak in the Jews' language, but according to the language of each people.
25 And I contended with them, and cursed them, and smote certain of them, and plucked off their hair, and made them swear by God, *saying*, you will not give your daughters unto their sons, or take their daughters unto your sons, or for yourselves.
26 Did not Solomon king of Israel sin by these things? Yet among many nations was there no king like him, who was beloved of his God, and God made him king over all Israel: nevertheless even him did outlandish women cause to sin.
27 will we then hearken unto you to do all this great evil, to transgress against our God in marrying strange wives?
28 And *one* of the sons of Joiada³, the son of Eliashib the high priest, *was* son in law to Sanballat the Horonite: therefore I chased him from me.
29 Remember them, O my God, because they have defiled the priesthood, and the covenant of the priesthood, and of the Levites.
30 Thus cleansed I them from all strangers, and appointed the wards of the priests and the Levites, everyone in his business;
31 And for the wood offering, at times appointed, and for the firstfruits. Remember me, O my God, for good.

---

¹ place – standing place, a *spot* (as being *fixed*), stood, upright [Strgs#5977]. Apostolic order.
² Ashdod – derives from Hebrew words meaning *ravager*, *burly*, impregnable, and robber [Strgs#797+796+795+7703].
³ Joiada – *Jehovah knows* [Strgs#3111].

ESTHER
CHAPTER 1

1 Now it came to pass in the days of Ahasuerus[1], (this *is* Ahasuerus which reigned, from India even unto Ethiopia, *over* an hundred and seven and twenty provinces:)

2 *That* in those days, when the King Ahasuerus sat on the throne of his kingdom, which *was* in Shushan the palace,

3 In the third year of his reign, he made a feast unto all his princes and his servants; the power of Persia and Media, the nobles and princes of the provinces, *being* before him:

4 When he showed the riches of his glorious kingdom and the honor of his excellent majesty many days, *even* an hundred and fourscore days.

5 And when these days were expired, the king made a feast unto all the people that were present in Shushan the palace, both unto great and small, seven days, in the court of the garden of the king's palace;

6 *Where were* white, green, and blue, *hangings*, fastened with cords of fine linen and purple to silver rings and pillars of marble: the beds *were of* gold and silver, upon a pavement of red, and blue, and white, and black, marble.

7 And they gave *them* drink in vessels of gold, (the vessels being diverse one from another,) and royal wine in abundance, according to the state of the king.

8 And the drinking *was* according to the law; none did compel: for so the king had appointed to all the officers of his house, that they should do according to every man's pleasure.

9 Also Vashti[2] the queen made a feast for the women *in* the royal house which *belonged* to king Ahasuerus.

10 On the seventh day, when the heart of the king was merry with wine, he commanded Mehuman, Biztha, Harbona, Bigtha, and Abagtha, Zethar, and Carcas, the seven chamberlains that served in the presence of Ahasuerus the king,

11 To bring Vashti the queen before the king with the crown royal[3], to show the people and the princes her beauty: for she *was* fair to look on.

12 But the queen Vashti refused to come at the king's commandment by *his* chamberlains: therefore was the king very **angry**[4], and his anger burned in him.

13 Then the king said to the wise men, which knew the times, (for so *was* the king's manner toward all that knew law and judgment:

14 And the next unto him *was* Carshena, Shethar, Admatha, Tarshish, Meres, Marsena, *and* Memucan, the seven princes of Persia and Media, which saw the king's face, *and* which sat the first in the kingdom;)

15 What will we do unto the queen Vashti according to law, because she has not performed the commandment of the king Ahasuerus by the chamberlains?

16 And Memucan answered before the king and the princes, Vashti the queen has not done wrong to the king only, but also to all the princes, and to all the people that *are* in all the provinces of the king Ahasuerus.

17 For *this* deed of the queen will come abroad unto all women, so that they will despise their husbands in their eyes, when it will be reported, The king Ahasuerus commanded Vashti the queen to be brought in before him, but she came not.

18 *Likewise* will the ladies of Persia and Media say this day unto all the king's princes, which have heard of the deed of the queen. Thus will *there arise* too much contempt and wrath[5].

19 If it please the king, let there go a royal commandment from him, and let it be written among the laws of the Persians and the Medes, that it be not altered, that Vashti come no more before king Ahasuerus; and let the king give her royal estate unto another that is better than she.

20 And when the king's decree which he will make will be published throughout all his empire, (for it is great,) all the wives will give to their husbands honor[6], both to great and small.

21 And the saying pleased the king and the princes; and the king did according to the word of Memucan:

22 For he sent letters into all the king's provinces, into every province according to the writing thereof, and to every people after their language, that every man should [bear rule][7] in his own house, and that *it* should be published according to the language of every people.

CHAPTER 2

1 After these things, when the wrath of king Ahasuerus was appeased, he remembered Vashti, and what she had done, and what was decreed against her.

2 Then said the king's servants that ministered unto him, Let there be fair young virgins sought for the king:

3 And let the king appoint officers in all the provinces of his kingdom, that they may gather together all the fair young virgins unto Shushan the palace, to the house of the women, unto the custody of Hege the king's chamberlain, keeper of the women; and let their things for purification be given *them*:

4 And let the maiden which pleases the king be queen instead of Vashti. And the thing pleased the king; and he did so.

5 *Now* in Shushan the palace there was a certain Jew, whose name *was* Mordecai, the son of Jair, the son of Shimei, the son of Kish, a Benjamite;

6 Who had been carried away from Jerusalem with the captivity which had been carried away with Jeconiah king of Judah, whom Nebuchadnezzar the king of Babylon had carried away.

7 And he brought up Hadassah[8], that *is*, Esther[9], his uncle's daughter: for she had neither father or mother, and the maid *was* fair and beautiful; whom Mordecai[10], when her father and mother were dead, took for his own daughter.

8 So it came to pass, when the king's commandment and his decree was heard, and when many maidens were gathered together unto Shushan the palace, to the custody of Hegai, that Esther was brought also unto the king's house, to the custody of Hegai, keeper of the women.

9 And the maiden pleased him, and she obtained kindness of him; and he speedily gave her, her things for purification, with such things as belonged to her, and seven maidens, *which were* meet

---

[1] Ahasuerus- literally *I will be silent and poor*. See index for more details.[Strgs#325]

[2] Vashti- *beautiful*. [Strgs#2060]

[3] royalty – concretely a dominion [Strgs#4438]. Crown of Royalty, Crown of Rule or Crown of Dominion.

[4] Originally KJV uses the word wroth instead of angry, wroth is defined as to *crack* off, *burst*, out in rage [Strgs#7107].

[5] wrath – *splinter* (as *chipped* off); figuratively *rage* or *strife*: - foam, indignation, sore [Strgs#7110].

[6] honor – *value*, wealth, costliness, dignity [Strgs#3366].

[7] bear rule – have dominion, exercise dominion or get dominion [Strgs#8323].

[8] Haddassah- *myrtle*. [Strgs#1919]

[9] Esther- *star*. [Strgs#635]

[10] Mordecai- the name is of foreign derivation meaning little man or worshipper of Mars. [Strgs#4782]

to be given her, out of the king's house: and he preferred[1] her and her maids unto the best *place* of the house of the women.

10 Esther had not showed her people or her kindred: for Mordecai had charged her that she should not show *it*.

11 And Mordecai walked every day before the court of the women's house, to know how Esther did, and what should become of her.

12 Now when every maid's turn was come to go in to king Ahasuerus, after that she had been twelve months, according to the manner of the women, (for so were the days of their purifications accomplished, *to wit*, six months with oil of myrrh, and six months with sweet odors, and with *other* things for the purifying of the women;)

13 Then thus came *every* maiden unto the king; whatsoever she desired was given her to go with her out of the house of the women unto the king's house.

14 [In the evening she went, and on the morrow she returned into the second house of the women, to the custody of Shaashgaz, the king's chamberlain, which kept the concubines: she came in unto the king no more, except the king delighted in her, and that she were called by name.][2]

15 Now when the turn of Esther, the daughter of Abihail the uncle of Mordecai, who had taken her for his daughter, was come to go in unto the king, she required nothing but what Hegai the king's chamberlain, the keeper of the women, appointed. And Esther obtained favor in the sight of all them that looked upon her.

16 So Esther was taken unto king Ahasuerus into his house royal in the tenth month, which *is* the month Tebeth, in the seventh year of his reign.

17 And the king loved Esther above all the women, and she obtained grace and favor in his sight more than all the virgins; so that he set the royal crown upon her head, and made her queen instead of Vashti.

18 Then the king made a great feast unto all his princes and his servants, *even* Esther's feast; and he made a release to the provinces, and gave gifts, according to the state of the king.

19 And when the virgins were gathered together the second time, then Mordecai sat in the king's gate.

20 Esther had not *yet* showed her kindred or her people; as Mordecai had charged her: for Esther did the commandment of Mordecai, like as when she was brought up with him.

21 In those days, while Mordecai sat in the king's gate, two of the king's chamberlains, Bigthan and Teresh, of those which kept the door[3], were angry, and sought to lay hand on the king Ahasuerus.

22 And the thing was known to Mordecai, who told *it* unto Esther the queen; and Esther certified the king *thereof* in Mordecai's name.

23 And when inquisition was made of the matter, it was found out; therefore they were both hanged on a tree: and it was written in the book of the chronicles before the king.

CHAPTER 3

1 After these things did king Ahasuerus promote Haman the son of Hammedatha the Agagite, and advanced him, and set his seat above all the princes that *were* with him.

2 And all the king's servants, that *were* in the king's gate, bowed, and reverenced Haman: for the king had so commanded concerning him. But Mordecai bowed not, or did *him* reverence.

3 Then the king's servants, which *were* in the king's gate, said unto Mordecai, why transgresses you the king's commandment?

4 Now it came to pass, when they spoke daily unto him, and he hearkened not unto them, that they told Haman, to see whether Mordecai's matters would stand: for he had told them that he *was* a Jew.

5 And when Haman saw that Mordecai bowed not, or did him reverence, then was Haman full of wrath.

6 And he thought scorn to lay hands on Mordecai alone; for they had showed him the people of Mordecai: wherefore Haman sought to destroy all the Jews that *were* throughout the whole kingdom of Ahasuerus, *even* the people of Mordecai.

7 In the first month, that *is*, the month Nisan, in the twelfth year of king Ahasuerus, they cast Pur, that *is*, the lot, before Haman from day to day, and from month to month, *to* the twelfth *month*, that *is*, the month Adar.

8 And Haman said unto king Ahasuerus, there is a certain people scattered abroad and dispersed among the people in all the provinces of your kingdom; and their laws *are* diverse from all people; neither keep they the king's laws: therefore it *is* not for the king's profit to suffer them.

9 If it pleases the king, let it be written that they may be destroyed: and I will pay ten thousand talents of silver to the hands of those that have the charge of the business, to bring *it* into the king's treasuries.

10 And the king took his ring from his hand, and gave it unto Haman the son of Hammedatha the Agagite, the Jews' enemy.

11 And the king said unto Haman, The silver *is* given to you, the people also, to do with them as it seems good to you.

12 Then were the king's scribes called on the thirteenth day of the first month, and there was written according to all that Haman had commanded unto the king's lieutenants, and to the governors that *were* over every province, and to the rulers of every people of every province according to the writing thereof, and *to* every people after their language; in the name of king Ahasuerus was it written, and sealed with the king's ring.

13 And the letters were sent by posts into all the king's provinces, to destroy, to kill, and to cause to perish, all Jews, both young and old, little children and women, in one day, *even* upon the thirteenth *day* of the twelfth month, which is the month Adar, and *to take* the spoil of them for a prey.

14 The copy of the writing for a commandment to be given in every province was published unto all people, that they should be ready against that day.

15 The posts went out, being hastened by the king's commandment, and the decree was given in Shushan the palace. And the king and Haman sat down to drink; but the city Shushan was perplexed.

CHAPTER 4

1 When Mordecai perceived all that was done, Mordecai rent his clothes, and put on sackcloth with ashes, and went out into the midst of the city, and cried with a loud and a bitter cry;

2 And came even before the king's gate: for none *might* enter into the king's gate clothed with sackcloth.

3 And in every province, whithersoever the king's commandment and his decree came, *there was* great mourning among the Jews,

---

[1] preferred – to *fold, duplicate, transmute*, change, disguise, (be) diverse, pervert, repeat [Strgs#8138].
[2] sexual involvement
[3] door – in the original sense of containing; a *vestibule* (as a *limit*), threshold; also a *dish* [Strgs#5592].

and fasting, and weeping, and wailing; and many lay in sackcloth and ashes.

4 So Esther's maids and her chamberlains came and told *it* her. Then was the queen exceedingly grieved; and she sent raiment to clothe Mordecai, and to take away his sackcloth from him: but he received *it* not.

5 Then called Esther for Hatach, *one* of the king's chamberlains, whom he had appointed to attend upon her, and gave him a commandment to Mordecai, to know what it *was*, and why it *was*.

6 So Hatach went forth to Mordecai unto the street of the city, which *was* before the king's gate.

7 And Mordecai told him of all that had happened unto him, and of the sum of the money that Haman had promised to pay to the king's treasuries for the Jews, to destroy them.

8 Also he gave him the copy of the writing of the decree that was given at Shushan to destroy them, to show *it* unto Esther, and to declare *it* unto her, and to charge her that she should go in unto the king, to make supplication unto him, and to make request before him for her people.

9 And Hatach came and told Esther the words of Mordecai.

10 Again Esther spoke unto Hatach, and gave him commandment unto Mordecai;

11 All the king's servants, and the people of the king's provinces, do know, that whosoever, whether man or woman, will come unto the king into the inner court, who is not called, *there is* one law of his to put *him* to death, except such to whom the king will hold out the golden sceptre, that he may live: but I have not been called to come in unto the king these thirty days.

12 And they told to Mordecai Esther's words.

13 Then Mordecai commanded to answer Esther, Think not with yourself that you will escape in the king's house, more than all the Jews.

14 For if you altogether hold your peace at this time, *then* will there enlargement and deliverance arises to the Jews from another place; but you and your father's house will be destroyed: and who knows whether you are come to the kingdom for *such* a time as this?

15 Then Esther bade *them* return Mordecai *this answer*,

16 Go, gather together all the Jews that are present in Shushan, and fast you for me, and neither eat or drink three days, night or day: I also and my maidens will fast likewise; and so will I go in unto the king, which *is* not according to the law: and if I perish, I perish.

17 So Mordecai went his way, and did according to all that Esther had commanded him.

CHAPTER 5

1 Now it came to pass on the third day, that Esther put on *her royal apparel*, and stood in the inner court of the king's house, over against the king's house: and the king sat upon his royal throne in the royal house, over against the gate of the house.

2 And it was so, when the king saw Esther the queen standing in the court, *that* she obtained favor in his sight: and the king held out to Esther the golden scepter that *was* in his hand. So Esther drew near, and touched the top of the scepter.

3 Then said the king unto her, what will thou, Queen Esther? And what *is* your request? It will be even given you to the half of the kingdom.

4 And Esther answered, if *it seems* good unto the king, let the king and Haman come this day unto the banquet that I have prepared for him.

5 Then the king said, Cause Haman to make haste, that he may do as Esther has said. So the king and Haman came to the banquet that Esther had prepared.

6 And the king said unto Esther at the banquet of wine, what *is* your petition? And it will be granted you: and what *is* your request? even to the half of the kingdom it will be performed.

7 Then answered Esther, and said, my petition and my request *is*;

8 If I have found favor in the sight of the king, and if it please the king to grant my petition, and to perform my request, let the king and Haman come to the banquet that I will prepare for them, and I will do tomorrow as the king has said.

9 Then went Haman forth that day joyful and with a glad heart: but when Haman saw Mordecai in the king's gate, that he stood not up, or moved for him, he was full of indignation against Mordecai.

10 Nevertheless Haman refrained himself: and when he came home, he sent and called for his friends, and Zeresh his wife.

11 And Haman told them of the glory of his riches, and the multitude of his children, and all *the things* wherein the king had promoted him, and how he had advanced him above the princes and servants of the king.

12 Haman said moreover, Yea, Esther the queen did let no man come in with the king unto the banquet that she had prepared but myself; and tomorrow am I invited unto her also with the king.

13 Yet all this avails me nothing, so long as I see Mordecai the Jew sitting at the king's gate.

14 Then said Zeresh his wife and all his friends unto him, Let a gallows be made of fifty cubits high, and tomorrow speak you unto the king that Mordecai may be hanged thereon: then go you in merrily with the king unto the banquet. And the thing pleased Haman; and he caused the gallows to be made.

CHAPTER 6

1 On that night could not the king sleep, and he commanded to bring the book of records of the chronicles; and they were read before the king.

2 And it was found written, that Mordecai had told of Bigthana and Teresh, two of the king's chamberlains, the keepers of the door, who sought to lay hand on the king Ahasuerus.

3 And the king said, what honor and dignity has been done to Mordecai for this? Then said the king's servants that ministered unto him, There is nothing done for him.

4 And the king said, who *is* in the court? Now Haman was come into the outward court of the king's house, to speak unto the king to hang Mordecai on the gallows that he had prepared for him.

5 And the king's servants said unto him, Behold, Haman stands in the court. And the king said, Let him come in.

6 So Haman came in. And the king said unto him, what will be done unto the man whom the king delights to honor? Now Haman thought in his heart, to whom would the king delight to do honor more than to myself?

7 And Haman answered the king, for the man whom the king delights to honor,

8 Let the royal apparel be brought which the king *uses* to wear, and the horse that the king rides upon, and the crown royal which is set upon his head:

9 And let this apparel and horse be delivered to the hand of one of the king's most noble princes, that they may array the man *withal* whom the king delights to honor, and bring him on horseback through the street of the city, and proclaim before him, Thus will it be done to the man whom the king delights to honor.

10 Then the king said to Haman, Make haste, *and* take the apparel and the horse, as you have said, and do even so to Mordecai the Jew, that sits at the king's gate: let nothing fail of all that you have spoken.

11 Then took Haman the apparel and the horse, and arrayed Mordecai, and brought him on horseback through the street of the city, and proclaimed before him, thus will it be done unto the man whom the king delights to honor.

12 And Mordecai came again to the king's gate. But Haman hasted to his house mourning, and having his head covered.

13 And Haman told Zeresh his wife and all his friends every*thing* that had befallen him. Then said his wise men and Zeresh his wife unto him, If Mordecai *be* of the seed of the Jews, before whom you have begun to fall, you will not prevail against him, but will surely fall before him.

14 And while they *were* yet talking with him, came the king's chamberlains, and hasted to bring Haman unto the banquet that Esther had prepared.

CHAPTER 7

1 So the king and Haman came to banquet[1] with Esther the queen.

2 And the king said again unto Esther on the second day at the banquet of wine, what *is* your petition, Queen Esther? And it will be granted you: and what *is* your request? And it will be performed, *even* to the half of the kingdom.

3 Then Esther the queen answered and said, If I have found favor in your sight, O king, and if it please the king, let my life be given me at my petition, and my people at my request:

4 For we are sold, I and my people, to be destroyed, to be slain, and to perish. But if we had been sold for bondmen and bondwomen, I had held my tongue, although the enemy could not countervail the king's damage.

5 Then the king Ahasuerus answered and said unto Esther the queen, who is he, and where is he, that durst presume in his heart to do so?

6 And Esther said, the adversary[2] and enemy *is* this wicked Haman. Then Haman was afraid before the king and the queen.

7 And the king arising from the banquet of wine in his wrath *went* into the palace garden: and Haman stood up to make request for his life to Esther the queen; for he saw that there was evil determined against him by the king.

8 Then the king returned out of the palace garden into the place of the banquet of wine; and Haman was fallen upon the bed whereon Esther *was*. Then said the king, Will he force the queen also before me in the house? As the word went out of the king's mouth, they covered Haman's face.

9 And Harbonah, one of the chamberlains, said before the king, Behold also, the gallows fifty cubits high, which Haman had made for Mordecai, who had spoken good for the king, stands in the house of Haman. Then the king said, Hang him thereon.

10 So they hanged Haman on the gallows that he had prepared for Mordecai. Then was the king's wrath pacified.

CHAPTER 8

1 On that day did the king Ahasuerus give the house of Haman the Jews' enemy unto Esther the queen. And Mordecai came before the king; for Esther had told what he *was* unto her.

2 And the king took off his ring, which he had taken from Haman, and gave it unto Mordecai. And Esther set Mordecai over the house of Haman.

3 And Esther spoke yet again before the king, and fell down at his feet, and besought him with tears to put away the mischief of Haman the Agagite, and his device that he had devised against the Jews.

4 Then the king held out the golden scepter toward Esther. So Esther arose, and stood before the king,

5 And said, If it please the king, and if I have found favor in his sight, and the thing *seem* right before the king, and I *be* pleasing in his eyes, let it be written to reverse the letters devised by Haman the son of Hammedatha the Agagite, which he wrote to destroy the Jews which *are* in all the king's provinces:

6 For how can I endure to see the evil that will come unto my people? or how can I endure to see the destruction of my kindred?

7 Then the king Ahasuerus said unto Esther the queen and to Mordecai the Jew, Behold, I have given Esther the house of Haman, and him they have hanged upon the gallows, because he laid his hand upon the Jews.

8 Write you also for the Jews, as it likes you, in the king's name, and seal *it* with the king's ring: for the writing which is written in the king's name, and sealed with the king's ring, may no man reverse.

9 Then were the king's scribes called at that time in the third month, that *is*, the month Sivan, on the three and twentieth *day* thereof; and it was written according to all that Mordecai commanded unto the Jews, and to the lieutenants, and the deputies and rulers of the provinces which *are* from India unto Ethiopia, an hundred twenty and seven provinces, unto every province according to the writing thereof, and unto every people after their language, and to the Jews according to their writing, and according to their language.

10 And he wrote in the king Ahasuerus' name, and sealed *it* with the king's ring, and sent letters by posts on horseback, *and* riders on mules, camels, *and* young dromedaries:

11 Wherein the king granted the Jews which *were* in every city to gather themselves together, and to stand for their life, to destroy, to slay, and to cause to perish, all the power of the people and province that would assault them, *both* little ones and women, and *to take* the spoil of them for a prey,

12 Upon one day in all the provinces of king Ahasuerus, *namely*, upon the thirteenth *day* of the twelfth month, which *is* the month Adar.

13 The copy of the writing for a commandment to be given in every province *was* published[3] unto all people, and that the Jews should be ready against that day to avenge themselves on their enemies.

14 So the posts that rode upon mules *and* camels went out, being hastened and pressed on by the king's commandment. And the decree was given at Shushan the palace.

15 And Mordecai went out from the presence of the king in royal apparel of blue and white, and with a great crown of gold, and with a garment of fine linen and purple: and the city of Shushan rejoiced and was glad.

16 The Jews had light, and gladness, and joy, and honor.

17 And in every province, and in every city, whithersoever the king's commandment and his decree came, the Jews had joy and gladness, a feast and a good day. And many of the people of the land became Jews; for the fear of the Jews fell upon them.

---

[1] banquet – to imbibe, drink [Strgs#8354].
[2] lit. the man adversary [Strgs#376+6862]. Compare **Matthew 13:28**.

[3] published – to *denude*, to *exile*, discover to reveal [Strgs#1540].

CHAPTER 9

1 Now in the twelfth month, that *is*, the month Adar, on the thirteenth day of the same, when the king's commandment and his decree drew near to be put in execution, in the day that the enemies of the Jews hoped to have power over them, (though it was turned to the contrary, that the Jews had rule over them that hated them;)
2 The Jews gathered themselves together in their cities throughout all the provinces of the king Ahasuerus, to lay hand on such as sought their hurt: and no man could withstand them; for the fear of them fell upon all people.
3 And all the rulers of the provinces, and the lieutenants, and the deputies, and officers of the king, helped the Jews; because the fear of Mordecai fell upon them.
4 For Mordecai *was* great in the king's house, and his fame went out throughout all the provinces: for this man Mordecai waxed greater and greater.
5 Thus the Jews smote all their enemies with the stroke of the sword, and slaughter, and destruction, and did what they would unto those that hated them.
6 And in Shushan the palace the Jews slew and destroyed five hundred men.
7 And Parshandatha, and Dalphon, and Aspatha,
8 And Poratha, and Adalia, and Aridatha,
9 And Parmashta, and Arisai, and Aridai, and Vajezatha,
10 The ten sons of Haman the son of Hammedatha, the enemy of the Jews, slew they; but on the spoil laid they not their hand.
11 On that day the number of those that were slain in Shushan the palace was brought before the king.
12 And the king said unto Esther the queen, The Jews have slain and destroyed five hundred men in Shushan the palace, and the ten sons of Haman; what have they done in the rest of the king's provinces? Now what *is* your petition? And it will be granted you: or what *is* your request further? And it will be done.
13 Then said Esther, If it please the king, let it be granted to the Jews which *are* in Shushan to do to morrow also according unto this day's decree, and let Haman's ten sons be hanged upon the gallows.
14 And the king commanded it so to be done: and the decree was given at Shushan; and they hanged Haman's ten sons.
15 For the Jews that *were* in Shushan gathered themselves together on the fourteenth day also of the month Adar, and slew three hundred men at Shushan; but on the prey they laid not their hand.
16 But the other Jews that *were* in the king's provinces gathered themselves together, and stood for their lives, and had rest from their enemies, and slew of their foes seventy and five thousand, but they laid not their hands on the prey,
17 On the thirteenth day of the month Adar; and on the fourteenth day of the same rested they, and made it a day of feasting and gladness.
18 But the Jews that *were* at Shushan assembled together on the thirteenth *day* thereof, and on the fourteenth thereof; and on the fifteenth *day* of the same they rested, and made it a day of feasting and gladness.
19 Therefore the Jews of the villages, that dwelt in the unwalled towns, made the fourteenth day of the month Adar *a day of* gladness and feasting, and a good day, and of sending portions one to another.
20 And Mordecai wrote these things, and sent letters unto all the Jews that *were* in all the provinces of the king Ahasuerus, *both* nigh and far,
21 To establish *this* among them, that they should keep the fourteenth day of the month Adar, and the fifteenth day of the same, yearly,
22 As the days wherein the Jews rested from their enemies, and the month which was turned unto them from sorrow to joy, and from mourning into a good day: that they should make them days of feasting and joy, and of sending portions one to another, and gifts to the poor.
23 And the Jews undertook to do as they had begun, and as Mordecai had written unto them;
24 Because Haman the son of Hammedatha, the Agagite, the enemy of all the Jews, had devised against the Jews to destroy them, and had cast Pur, that *is*, the lot, to consume them, and to destroy them;
25 But when *Esther* came before the king, he commanded by letters that his wicked device, which he devised against the Jews, should return upon his own head, and that he and his sons should be hanged on the gallows.
26 Wherefore they called these days Purim after the name of Pur. Therefore for all the words of this letter, and *of that* which they had seen concerning this matter, and which had come unto them,
27 The Jews ordained, and took upon them, and upon their seed, and upon all such as joined themselves unto them, so as it should not fail, that they would keep these two days according to their writing, and according to their *appointed* time every year;
28 And *that* these days *should be* remembered and kept throughout every generation, every family, every province, and every city; and *that* these days of Purim should not fail from among the Jews, or the memorial of them perish from their seed.
29 Then Esther the queen, the daughter of Abihail, and Mordecai the Jew, wrote with all authority, to confirm this second letter of Purim.
30 And he sent the letters unto all the Jews, to the hundred twenty and seven provinces of the kingdom of Ahasuerus *with* words of peace and truth,
31 To confirm these days of Purim in their times *appointed*, according as Mordecai the Jew and Esther the queen had enjoined them, and as they had decreed for themselves and for their seed, the matters of the fasting and their cry.
32 And the decree of Esther confirmed these matters of Purim; and it was written in the book.

CHAPTER 10

1 And the king Ahasuerus laid a tribute upon the land, and *upon* the isles of the sea.
2 And all the acts of his power and of his might, and the declaration of the greatness of Mordecai, whereunto the king advanced him, *are* they not written in the book of the chronicles of the kings of Media and Persia?
3 For Mordecai the Jew *was* next unto king Ahasuerus, and great among the Jews, and accepted of the multitude of his brethren, seeking the wealth of his people, and speaking peace to all his seed.

JOB
CHAPTER 1

1 There was a man in the land of Uz, whose name *was* Job; and that man was perfect and upright, and one that feared God, and eschewed evil.
2 And there were born unto him seven sons and three daughters.
3 His substance also was seven thousand sheep, and three thousand camels, and five hundred yoke of oxen, and five hundred she asses, and a very great household; so that this man was the greatest of all the men of the east.
4 And his sons went and feasted *in their* houses, everyone his day; and sent and called for their three sisters to eat and to drink with them.
5 And it was so, when the days of *their* feasting were gone about, that Job sent and sanctified them, and rose up early in the morning, and offered burnt offerings *according* to the number of them all: for Job said, It may be that my sons have sinned, and cursed God in their hearts. Thus did Job continually.
6 Now there was a day when the sons of God came to present themselves before the LORD, and Satan came also among them.
7 And the LORD said unto Satan, where **did you** come **from**? Then Satan answered the LORD, and said, from going to and fro in the earth, and from walking up and down in it.
8 And the LORD said unto Satan, have you considered my servant Job, that *there is* none like him in the earth, a perfect and an upright man, one that fears God, and eschewsh[1] evil?
9 Then Satan answered the LORD, and said, does Job fear God for nought?
10 Have not you made a hedge about him, and about his house, and about all that he has on every side? You have blessed the work of his hands, and his substance is increased in the land.
11 But put forth your hand now, and touch all that he hath, and he will curse you to your face.
12 And the LORD said unto Satan, Behold, all that he has *is* in your power; only upon himself put not forth your hand. So Satan went forth from the presence of the LORD.
13 And there was a day when his sons and his daughters *were* eating and drinking wine in their eldest brother's house:
14 And there came a messenger unto Job, and said, the oxen were plowing, and the asses feeding beside them:
15 And the Sabeans fell *upon them*, and took them away; yea, they have slain the servants with the edge of the sword; and I only am escaped alone to tell you.
16 While he *was* yet speaking, there came also another, and said, the fire of God is fallen from heaven, and has burned up the sheep, and the servants, and consumed them; and I only am escaped alone to tell you.
17 While he *was* yet speaking, there came also another, and said, The Chaldeans made out three bands, and fell upon the camels, and have carried them away, yea, and slain the servants with the edge of the sword; and I only am escaped alone to tell you.
18 While he *was* yet speaking, there came also another, and said, your sons and your daughters *were* eating and drinking wine in their eldest brother's house:
19 And, behold, there came a great wind from the wilderness, and smote the four corners of the house, and it fell upon the young men, and they are dead; and I only am escaped alone to tell you.
20 Then Job arose, and rent his mantle, and shaved his head, and fell down upon the ground, and worshipped,
21 And said, Naked came I out of my mother's womb, and naked will I return thither: the LORD gave, and the LORD has taken away; blessed be the name of the LORD.
22 In all this Job sinned not, or charged God foolishly.

CHAPTER 2

1 Again there was a day when the sons of God came to present themselves before the LORD, and Satan came also among them to present himself before the LORD.
2 And the LORD said unto Satan, from **where did you** come? And Satan answered the LORD, and said, from going to and fro in the earth, and from walking up and down in it.
3 And the LORD said unto Satan, have you considered my servant Job, that *there is* none like him in the earth, a perfect and an upright man, one that fears God, and eschews evil? And still he holds fast his integrity, although you moved me against him, to destroy him without cause.
4 And Satan answered the LORD, and said, Skin for skin, yea, all that a man has will he give for his life.
5 But put forth your hand now, and touch his bone and his flesh, and he will curse you to your face.
6 And the LORD said unto Satan, Behold, he *is* in your hand; but save his life.
7 So went Satan forth from the presence of the LORD, and smote Job with sore boils from the sole of his foot unto his crown.
8 And he took him a potsherd to scrape himself withal; and he sat down among the ashes.
9 Then said his wife unto him, do you still retain your integrity? Curse God, and die.
10 But he said unto her, you speak as one of the foolish women speaks. What? Will we receive good at the hand of God, and will we not receive evil? In all this did not Job sin with his lips.
11 Now when Job's three friends heard of all this evil that was come upon him, they everyone came from his own place; Eliphaz the Temanite, and Bildad the Shuhite, and Zophar the Naamathite: for they had made an appointment together to come to mourn with him and to comfort him.
12 And when they lifted up their eyes afar off, and knew him not, they lifted up their voice, and wept; and they rent everyone his mantle, and sprinkled dust upon their heads toward heaven.
13 So they sat down with him upon the ground seven days and seven nights, and none spoke a word unto him: for they saw that *his* grief was very great.

CHAPTER 3

1 After this opened Job his mouth, and cursed his day.
2 And Job spoke, and said,
3 Let the day perish wherein I was born, and the night *in which* it was said, there is a man child conceived.
4 Let that day be darkness; let not God regard it from above, neither let the light shine upon it.
5 Let darkness and the shadow of death stain it; let a cloud dwell upon it; let the blackness of the day terrify it.
6 As *for* that night, let darkness seize upon it; let it not be joined unto the days of the year, let it not come into the number of the months.
7 Lo, let that night be solitary, let no joyful voice come therein.

---

[1] eschew- withdraws from. [Strgs#5493]

8 Let them curse it that curse the day, who are ready to raise up their mourning.
9 Let the stars of the twilight thereof be dark; let it look for light, but *have* none; neither let it see the dawning of the day:
10 Because it shut not up the doors of my *mother's* womb, nor hid sorrow from mine eyes.
11 Why died I not from the womb? *Why* did I *not* give up the ghost when I came out of the belly?
12 Why did the knees prevent me? Or why the breasts that I should suck?
13 For now should I have lain still and been quiet, I should have slept: then had I been at rest,
14 With kings and counselors of the earth, which built desolate places for themselves;
15 Or with princes that had gold, who filled their houses with silver:
16 Or as a hidden untimely birth I had not been; as infants *which* never saw light.
17 There the wicked cease *from* troubling; and there the weary be at rest.
18 *There* the prisoners rest together; they hear not the voice of the oppressor.
19 The small and great are there; and the servant *is* free from his master.
20 Wherefore is light given to him that is in misery, and life unto the bitter *in* soul;
21 Which long for death, but it *cometh* not; and dig for it more than for hid treasures;
22 Which rejoice exceedingly, *and* are glad, when they can find the grave?
23 *Why is light given* to a man whose way is hid, and whom God has hedged in?
24 For my sighing cometh before I eat, and my roarings are poured out like the waters.
25 For the thing which I greatly feared is come upon me, and that which I was afraid of is come unto me.
26 I was not in safety, neither had I rest, neither was I quiet; yet trouble came.

CHAPTER 4

1 Then Eliphaz[1] the Temanite answered and said,
2 *If* we assay to commune with you, will you be grieved? But who can withhold himself from speaking?
3 Behold, you have instructed many, and you have strengthened the weak hands.
4 Your words have **upheld** him that was falling, and you have strengthened the feeble knees.
5 But now it is come upon you, and you faintest; it touches you, and you are troubled.
6 *Is* not *this* your fear, your confidence, your hope, and the uprightness of your ways?
7 Remember, I pray you, who *ever* perished, being innocent? Or where were the righteous cut off?
8 Even as I have seen, they that plow iniquity, and sow wickedness, reap the same.
9 By the blast of God they perish, and by the breath of his nostrils are they consumed.
10 The roaring of the lion, and the voice of the fierce lion, and the teeth of the young lions, are broken.

11 The old lion perishes for lack of prey, and the stout lion's whelps are scattered abroad.
12 Now a thing was secretly brought to me, and mine ear received a little thereof.
13 In thoughts from the visions of the night, when deep sleep falls on men,
14 Fear came upon me, and trembling, which made all my bones to shake.
15 Then a spirit passed before my face; the hair of my flesh stood up:
16 It stood still, but I could not discern the form thereof: an image *was* before mine eyes, *there was* silence, and I heard a voice, *saying*,
17 Will mortal man be more just than God? Will a man be more pure than his maker?
18 Behold, he put no trust in his servants; and his angels he charged with folly:
19 How much less *in* them that dwell in houses of clay, whose foundation *is* in the dust, *which* are crushed before the moth?
20 They are destroyed from morning to evening: they perish for ever without any regarding *it*.
21 Does not their excellency *which is* in them go away? They die, even without wisdom.

CHAPTER 5

1 Call now, if there be any that will answer you; and to which of the saints will you turn?
2 For wrath kills the foolish man, and envy slays the silly one.
3 I have seen the foolish taking root: but suddenly I cursed his habitation.
4 His children are far from safety, and they are crushed in the gate, neither *is there* any to deliver *them*.
5 Whose harvest the hungry eats up, and takes it even out of the thorns and the robber swallows up their substance.
6 Although affliction cometh not forth of the dust, neither does trouble spring out of the ground;
7 Yet man is born unto trouble, as the sparks fly upward.
8 I would seek unto God, and unto God would I commit my cause:
9 Which doeth great things and unsearchable; marvelous things without number:
10 Who gives rain upon the earth, and sends waters upon the fields:
11 To set up on high those that be low; that those which mourn may be exalted to safety.
12 He disappoints the devices of the crafty, so that their hands cannot perform *their* enterprise.
13 He takes the wise in their own craftiness: and the counsel of the forward is carried headlong.
14 They meet with darkness in the daytime, and grope in the noonday as in the night.
15 But he saves the poor from the sword, from their mouth, and from the hand of the mighty.
16 So the poor has hope, and iniquity stops her mouth.
17 Behold, happy *is* the man whom God corrects: therefore despise not you the chastening of the Almighty:
18 For he makes sore, and binds up: he wounds, and his hands make whole.
19 He will deliver you in six troubles: yea, in seven there will no evil touch you.

---

[1] Eliphaz- *God is victorious* or *my God is fine gold* the name of one of Job's friends, and of a son of Esau. [Strgs#464]

20 In famine he will redeem you from death: and in war from the power of the sword.
21 you will be hid from the scourge of the tongue: neither will you be afraid of destruction when it cometh.
22 At destruction and famine you will laugh: neither will you be afraid of the beasts of the earth.
23 For you will be in league with the stones of the field: and the beasts of the field will be at peace with you.
24 And you will know that your tabernacle will *be* in peace; and you will visit your habitation, and will not sin.
25 You will know also that your seed will *be* great, and your offspring as the grass of the earth.
26 You will come to your grave in a full age, like as a shock of corn comes in his season.
27 Lo this, we have searched it, so it *is*; hear it, and know you *it* for your good.

CHAPTER 6

1 But Job answered and said,
2 Oh that my grief **was** thoroughly weighed, and my calamity laid in the balances together!
3 For now it would be heavier than the sand of the sea: therefore my words are swallowed up.
4 For the arrows of the Almighty *are* within me, the poison whereof drinks up my spirit: the terrors of God do set themselves in array against me.
5 Does the wild ass bray when he has grass? Or lowers the ox over his fodder?
6 Can that which is unsavory be eaten without salt? Or is there *any* taste in the white of an egg?
7 The things *that* my soul refused to touch *are* as my sorrowful meat.
8 Oh that I might have my request; and that God would grant *me* the thing that I long for!
9 Even that it would please God to destroy me; that he would let loose his hand, and cut me off!
10 Then should I yet have comfort; yea, I would harden myself in sorrow: let him not spare; for I have not concealed the words of the Holy One.
11 What *is* my strength, that I should hope? And what *is* mine end, that I should prolong my life?
12 *Is* my strength the strength of stones? Or *is* my flesh of brass?
13 *Is* not my help in me? And is wisdom driven quite from me?
14 To him that is afflicted pity *should be showed* from his friend; but he forsakes the fear of the Almighty.
15 My brethren have dealt deceitfully as a brook, *and* as the stream of brooks they pass away;
16 Which are blackish by reason of the ice, *and* wherein the snow is hid:
17 What time they wax warm, they vanish: when it is hot, they are consumed out of their place.
18 The paths of their way are turned aside; they go to nothing, and perish.
19 The troops of Tema looked, the companies of Sheba waited for them.
20 They were confounded because they had hoped; they came thither, and were ashamed.
21 For now ye are nothing; ye see *my* casting down, and are afraid.

22 Did I say, Bring unto me? Or, Give a reward for me of your substance?
23 Or, Deliver me from the enemy's hand? or, Redeem me from the hand of the mighty?
24 Teach me, and I will hold my tongue: and cause me to understand wherein I have erred.
25 How forcible[1] are right words! But what does your arguing reprove?
26 Do you imagine to reprove words, and the speeches of one that is desperate, *which are* as wind?
27 Yea, ye overwhelm the fatherless, and ye dig *a pit* for your friend.
28 Now therefore be content, look upon me; for *it is* evident unto you if I lie.
29 Return, I pray you, let it not be iniquity; yea, return again, my righteousness *is* in it.
30 Is there iniquity in my tongue? Cannot my taste discern perverse things?

CHAPTER 7

1 *Is there* not an appointed time to man upon earth? *Are not* his days also like the days of a hireling?
2 As a servant earnestly desires the shadow, and as a hireling looks for *the reward of* his work:
3 So am I made to possess months of vanity, and wearisome nights are appointed to me.
4 When I lie down, I say, when will I arise, and the night be gone? And I am full of tossings to and fro unto the dawning of the day.
5 My flesh is clothed with worms and clods of dust; my skin is broken, and become loathsome.
6 My days are swifter than a weaver's shuttle, and are spent without hope.
7 O remember that my life *is* wind: mine eye will no more see good.
8 The eye of him that has seen me will see me no *more*: your eyes *are* upon me, and I *am* not.
9 *As* the cloud is consumed and vanishes away: so he that goes down to the grave will come up no *more*.
10 He will return no more to his house, neither will his place know him anymore.
11 Therefore I will not refrain my mouth; I will speak in the anguish of my spirit; I will complain in the bitterness of my soul.
12 *Am* I a sea, or a whale, that you set a watch over me?
13 When I say, my bed will comfort me, my couch will ease my complaint;
14 Then you scare me with dreams, and terrifies me through visions:
15 So that my soul chooses strangling, *and* death rather than my life.
16 I loathe *it*; I would not live always: let me alone; for my days *are* vanity.
17 What *is* man, that you should magnify him? And that you should set your heart upon him?
18 And *that* you should visit him every morning, *and* try him every moment?
19 How long will you not depart from me, nor let me alone till I swallow down my spittle?
20 I have sinned; what will I do unto you, O you preserver of men? Why have you set me as a mark against you, so that I am a burden to myself?

---

[1] forcible – to *press*, to be *pungent* or vehement; to *irritate*, embolden

[Strgs#4834].

21 And why dost you not pardon my transgression, and take away mine iniquity? For now will I sleep in the dust; and you will seek me in the morning, but I will not *be*.

CHAPTER 8

1 Then answered Bildad[1] the Shuhite, and said,
2 How long will you speak these *things*? And *how long will* the words of your mouth *be like* a strong wind?
3 does God pervert judgment? Or does the Almighty pervert justice?
4 If your children have sinned against him, and he have cast them away for their transgression;
5 If you would seek unto God betimes, and make your supplication to the Almighty;
6 If you *wert* pure and upright; surely now he would awake for you, and make the habitation of your righteousness prosperous.
7 Though your beginning was small[2], yet your latter end should greatly[3] increase[4].
8 For enquire, I pray you, of the former age, and prepare yourself to the search of their fathers:
9 (For we *are but of* yesterday, and know nothing, because our days upon earth *are* a shadow:)
10 will not they teach you, *and* tell you, and utter words out of their heart?
11 Can the rush grow up without mire? Can the flag grow without water?
12 While it *is* yet in his greenness, *and* not cut down, it withers before any *other* herb.
13 So *are* the paths of all that forget God; and the hypocrite's hope will perish:
14 Whose hope will be cut off, and whose trust will *be* a spider's web.
15 He will lean upon his house, but it will not stand: he will hold it fast, but it will not endure.
16 He *is* green before the sun, and his branch shoots forth in his garden.
17 His roots are wrapped about the heap, *and* sees the place of stones.
18 If he destroys him from his place, then *it* will deny him, *saying*, I have not seen you.
19 Behold, this *is* the joy of his way, and out of the earth will others grow.
20 Behold, God will not cast away a perfect *man*, neither will he help the evil doers:
21 Till he fill your mouth with laughing, and your lips with rejoicing.
22 They that hate you will be clothed with shame; and the dwelling place of the wicked will come to **nothing**.

CHAPTER 9

1 Then Job answered and said,
2 I know *it is* so of a truth: but how should man be just with God?
3 If he will contend with him, he cannot answer him one of a thousand.
4 *He is* wise in heart, and mighty in strength: who has hardened *himself* against him, and has prospered?
5 Which removes the mountains, and they know not: which overturns them in his anger.
6 Which shakes the earth out of her place, and the pillars thereof tremble.
7 Which commands the sun, and it rises not; and seals up the stars.
8 Which alone spreads out the heavens, and treads upon the waves of the sea.
9 Which makes Arcturus, Orion, and Pleiades, and the chambers of the south.
10 Which doeth great things past finding out; yea, and wonders without number.
11 Lo, he goes by me, and I see *him* not: he passes on also, but I perceive him not.
12 Behold, he takes away, who can hinder him? Who will say unto him, what does you?
13 *If* God will not withdraw his anger, the proud helpers do stoop under him.
14 How much less will I answer him, *and* choose out my words *to reason* with him?
15 Whom, though I were righteous, *yet* would I not answer, *but* I would make supplication to my judge.
16 If I had called, and he had answered me; *yet* would I not believe that he had hearkened unto my voice.
17 For he breaks me with a tempest, and multiplies my wounds without cause.
18 He will not suffer me to take my breath, but fills me with bitterness.
19 If *I* speak of strength, lo, *he is* strong: and if of judgment, who will set me a time *to plead*?
20 If I justify myself, mine own mouth will condemn me: *if I say*, I *am* perfect, it will also prove me perverse.
21 *Though* I *were* perfect, *yet* would I not know my soul: I would despise my life.
22 This *is* one *thing*, therefore I said *it*, and He destroys the perfect and the wicked.
23 If the scourge slay suddenly, he will laugh at the trial of the innocent.
24 The earth is given into the hand of the wicked he covers the faces of the judges thereof; if not, where, *and* who *is* he?
25 Now my days are swifter than a post: they flee away, they see no good.
26 They are passed away as the swift ships: as the eagle *that* haste to the prey.
27 If I say, I will forget my complaint, I will leave off my heaviness, and comfort *myself*:
28 I am afraid of all my sorrows, I know that you will not hold me innocent.
29 *If* I be wicked, why then labor I in vain?
30 If I wash myself with snow water, and make my hands never so clean;
31 Yet will you plunge me in the ditch, and mine own clothes will abhor me.
32 For *he is* not a man, as I *am, that* I should answer him, *and* we should come together in judgment.
33 Neither is there any days man betwixt us, *that* might lay his hand upon us both.

---

[1] Bildad- (defined by BDB biblical dictionary as *confusing love* by mingling) Bildad expressed the belief that all suffering is the direct result of one's sin. He had little patience with the questionings and searchings of Job. He is called "Bildad the Shuhite" (**Job 2:11**), which means he belonged to an Aramean nomadic tribe that live in the Transjordan area southeast of Palestine. [Strgs#1085]
[2] lit. petty (in size or number); a short (time): - little one [Strgs#4705].
[3] lit. forceful energy, *vehemently, wholly, speedily* [Strgs#3966].
[4] lit. enlarge, increase upward [Strgs#7685].

34 Let him take his rod away from me, and let not his fear terrify me:
35 Then would I speak, and not fear him; but *it is* not so with me.

CHAPTER 10
1 My soul is weary of my life; I will leave my complaint upon myself; I will speak in the bitterness of my soul.
2 I will say unto God, Do not condemn me; show me wherefore you contends with me.
3 *Is it* good unto you that you should oppress, that you should despise the work of your hands, and shine upon the counsel of the wicked?
4 have you eyes of flesh? Or sees you as man sees
5 *Are* your days as the days of man? *Are* your years as man's days,
6 That you enquires after mine iniquity, and searches after my sin?
7 you knows that I am not wicked; and *there is* none that can deliver out of your hand.
8 your hands have made me and fashioned me together round about; yet you dost destroy me.
9 Remember, I beseech you, that you have made me as the clay; and will you bring me into dust again?
10 have you not poured me out as milk, and curdled me like cheese?
11 you have clothed me with skin and flesh, and have fenced me with bones and sinews.
12 you have granted me life and favor, and your visitation has preserved my spirit.
13 And these *things* have you hid in your heart: I know that this *is* with you.
14 If I sin, then you mark me, and you will not acquit me from mine iniquity.
15 If I be wicked, woe unto me; and *if* I be righteous, *yet* will I not lift up my head. *I am* full of confusion; therefore see you mine affliction;
16 For it increases. You hunt me as a fierce lion: and again you show yourself marvelous upon me.
17 you renews your witnesses against me, and increases your indignation upon me; changes and war *are* against me.
18 Wherefore then have you brought me forth out of the womb? Oh that I had given up the ghost, and no eye had seen me!
19 I should have been as though I had not been; I should have been carried from the womb to the grave.
20 *Are* not my days few? Cease *then, and* let me alone, that I may take comfort a little,
21 Before I go *whence* I will not return, *even* to the land of darkness and the shadow of death;
22 A land of darkness, as darkness *itself; and* of the shadow of death, without any order, and *where* the light *is* as darkness.

CHAPTER 11
1 Then answered Zophar[1] the Naamathite, and said,
2 Should not the multitude of words be answered? And should a man full of talk be justified?
3 Should your lies make men hold their peace? And when you mockes, will no man make you ashamed?
4 For you have said, my doctrine *is* pure, and I am clean in your eyes.
5 But oh that God would speak, and open his lips against you;
6 And that he would show you the secrets of wisdom, that *they are* double to that which is! Know therefore that God exacts of you *less* than your iniquity *deserves*.
7 Canst you by searching find out God? Canst you find out the Almighty unto perfection?
8 *It is* as high as heaven; what canst you do? Deeper than hell; what canst you know?
9 The measure thereof *is* longer than the earth, and broader than the sea.
10 If he cut off, and shut up, or gather together, then who can hinder him?
11 For he knows vain men: he sees wickedness also; will he not then consider *it*?
12 For vain man would be wise, though man be born *like* a wild ass's colt.
13 If you prepare your heart, and stretch out your hands toward him;
14 If iniquity *be* in your hand, put it far away, and let not wickedness dwell in your tabernacles.
15 For then will you lift up your face without spot; yea, you will be steadfast, and will not fear:
16 Because you will forget your misery, *and* remember *it* as waters *that* pass away:
17 And your age will be clearer than the noonday; you will shine forth, you will be as the morning.
18 And you will be secure, because there is hope; yea, you will dig *about you, and* you will take your rest in safety.
19 Also you will lie down, and none will make you afraid; yea, many will make suit unto you.
20 But the eyes of the wicked will fail, and they will not escape, and their hope will *be as* the giving up of the ghost.

CHAPTER 12
1 And Job answered and said,
2 No doubt but ye *are* the people, and wisdom will die with you.
3 But I have understanding as well as you; I *am* not inferior to you: yea, who knows not such things as these?
4 I am *as* one mocked of his neighbor, who calls upon God, and he answers him: the just upright *man is* laughed to scorn.
5 He that is ready to slip with *his* feet *is as* a lamp despised in the thought of him that is at ease.
6 The tabernacles of robbers prosper, and they that provoke God are secure; into whose hand God brings *abundantly*.
7 But ask now the beasts, and they will teach you; and the fowls of the air, and they will tell you:
8 Or speak to the earth, and it will teach you: and the fishes of the sea will declare unto you.
9 Who knows not in all these that the hand of the LORD has wrought this?
10 In whose hand *is* the soul of every living thing, and the breath of all mankind.
11 <u>Does not the ear try words? And the mouth tastes his meat</u>?
12 With the ancient *is* wisdom; and in length of days understanding.
13 With him *is* wisdom and strength, he has counsel and understanding.
14 Behold, he breaks down, and it cannot be built again: he shuts up a man, and there can be no opening.

---

[1] Zophar- (*sparrow* or *twittering bird*) He is called a Naamathite (**Job 2:11, 11:1, 20:1**; **42:9**), indicating he was from Naamah, in northern Arabia. Zophar's two discourses are found in **Job 11:1-20** and **20:1-29**. He accused Job of wickedness and hypocrisy, urged Job to turn from his rebellion, and charged that God was punishing Job far less than his sins deserved (**Job 11:6**). [Stgrs#6691]

15 Behold, he withheld the waters, and they dry up: also he sends them out, and they overturn the earth.
16 [With him *is* strength and wisdom: the deceived and the deceiver *are* his.]¹
17 He leads counselors away spoiled, and makes the judges fools.
18 He looses the bond of kings, and girds their loins with a girdle.
19 He leads princes away spoiled, and overthrows the mighty.
20 He removes away the speech of the trusty, and takes away the understanding of the aged.
21 He pours contempt upon princes, and weakens the strength of the mighty.
22 He discovers deep things out of darkness, and brings out to light the shadow of death.
23 He increases the nations, and destroys them: he enlarges the nations, and straitens them *again*.
24 He takes away the heart of the chief of the people of the earth, and causes them to wander in a wilderness *where there is* no way.
25 They grope in the dark without light, and he makes them to stagger like *a* drunken *man*.

CHAPTER 13

1 Lo, mine eye has seen all *this*, mine ear has heard and understood it.
2 What ye know, *the same* do I know also: I *am* not inferior unto you.
3 Surely I would speak to the Almighty, and I desire to reason with God.
4 But ye *are* forgers of lies, ye *are* all physicians of no value.
5 O that ye would altogether hold your peace! And it should be your wisdom.
6 Hear now my reasoning, and hearken to the pleadings of my lips.
7 Will ye speak wickedly for God? And talk deceitfully for him?
8 Will ye accept his person? Will ye contend for God?
9 Is it good that he should search you out? Or as one man mocks another, do ye *so* mock him?
10 He will surely reprove you, if ye do secretly accept persons.
11 Will not his excellency make you afraid? And his dread fall upon you?
12 Your remembrances *are* like unto ashes, your bodies to bodies of clay.
13 Hold your peace, let me alone, that I may speak, and let come on me what *will*.
14 Wherefore do I take my flesh in my teeth, and put my life in mine hand?
15 Though he slay me, yet will I trust in him: but I will maintain mine own ways before him.
16 He also will *be* my salvation: for a hypocrite will not come before him.
17 Hear diligently my speech, and my declaration with your ears.
18 Behold now, I have ordered *my* cause; I know that I will be justified.
19 Who *is* he *that* will plead with me? For now, if I hold my tongue, I will give up the ghost.
20 Only do not two *things* unto me: then will I not hide myself from you.
21 Withdraw your hand far from me: and let not your dread make me afraid.
22 Then call you, and I will answer: or let me speak, and answer you me.

23 How many *are* mine iniquities and sins? Make me to know my transgression and my sin.
24 Wherefore hides you your face, and holds me for your enemy?
25 will you break a leaf driven to and fro? And will you pursue the dry stubble?
26 For you write bitter things against me, and make me to possess the iniquities of my youth.
27 you put my feet also in the stocks, and looks narrowly unto all my paths; you sets a print upon the heels of my feet.
28 And he, as a rotten thing, consumes, as a garment that is moth eaten.

CHAPTER 14

1 Man *that is* born of a woman *is* of few days, and full of trouble.
2 He cometh forth like a flower, and is cut down: he flees also as a shadow, and continues not.
3 And dost you open your eyes upon such a one, and brings me into judgment with you?
4 Who can bring a clean *thing* out of an unclean? Not one.
5 Seeing his days *are* determined, the number of his months *are* with you, you have appointed his bounds that he cannot pass;
6 Turn from him, that he may rest, till he will accomplish, as a hireling, his day.
7 For there is hope of a tree, if it be cut down, that it will sprout again, and that the tender branch thereof will not cease.
8 Though the root thereof wax old in the earth, and the stock thereof die in the ground;
9 *Yet* through the scent of water it will bud, and bring forth boughs like a plant.
10 But man dies, and wastes away: yea, man gives up the ghost, and where *is* he?
11 *As* the waters fail from the sea, and the flood decays and dries up:
12 So man lies down, and rises not: till the heavens *be* no more, they will not awake, nor be raised out of their sleep
13 O that you would hide me in the grave, that you would keep me secret, until your wrath be past, that you would appoint me a set time, and remember me!
14 If a man die, will he live *again*? All the days of my appointed time will I wait, till my change come.
15 you will call, and I will answer you: you will have a desire to the work of your hands.
16 For now you number my steps: dost you not watch over my sin?
17 My transgression *is* sealed up in a bag, and you sew up mine iniquity.
18 And surely the mountain falling comes to nothing, and the rock is removed out of his place.
19 The waters wear the stones: you washes away the things which grow *out* of the dust of the earth; and you destroys the hope of man.
20 you prevails for ever against him, and he passes: you changes his countenance, and sends him away.
21 His sons come to honor, and he knows *it* not; and they are brought low, but he perceives *it* not of them.
22 But his flesh upon him will have pain, and his soul within him will mourn.

CHAPTER 15

1 Then answered Eliphaz the Temanite, and said,

---

¹ compare 2 Chron. 18:20

2 Should a wise man utter vain knowledge, and fill his belly with the east wind?
3 Should he reason with unprofitable talk? Or with speeches wherewith he can do no good?
4 Yea, you cast off fear, and restrains prayer before God.
5 For your mouth utters your iniquity, and you chooses the tongue of the crafty.
6 your own mouth condemns you, and not I: yea, your own lips testify against you.
7 are you the first man *that* was born? Or **were** you made before the hills?
8 have you heard the secret of God? And dost you restrain wisdom to thyself?
9 What knows you, that we know not? *What* understands you, which *is* not in us?
10 With us *are* both the gray-headed and very aged men, much elder than your father.
11 *Are* the consolations of God small with you? Is there any secret thing with you?
12 Why does your heart carry you away? And what do your eyes wink at,
13 That you turns your spirit against God, and lets *such* words go out of your mouth?
14 What *is* man, that he should be clean? And *he which is* born of a woman, that he should be righteous?
15 Behold, he puts no trust in his saints; yea, the heavens are not clean in his sight.
16 How much more abominable and filthy *is* man, which drinks iniquity like water?
17 I will show you, hear me; and that *which* I have seen I will declare;
18 Which wise men have told from their fathers, and have not hid *it*:
19 Unto whom alone the earth was given, and no stranger passed among them.
20 The wicked man travails with pain all *his* days, and the number of years is hidden to the oppressor.
21 A dreadful sound *is* in his ears: in prosperity the destroyer will come upon him.
22 He believeth not that he will return out of darkness, and he is waited for of the sword.
23 He wanders abroad for bread, *saying*, Where *is it*? He knows that the day of darkness is ready at his hand.
24 Trouble and anguish will make him afraid; they will prevail against him, as a king ready to the battle.
25 For he stretches out his hand against God, and strengthens himself against the Almighty.
26 He runs upon him, *even* on *his* neck, upon the thick bosses of his bucklers:
27 Because he covers his face with his fatness, and makes collops of fat on *his* flanks.
28 And he dwells in desolate cities, *and* in houses which no man inhabits, which are ready to become heaps.
29 He will not be rich, neither will his substance continue, neither will he prolong the perfection thereof upon the earth.
30 He will not depart out of darkness; the flame will dry up his branches, and by the breath of his mouth will he go away.
31 Let not him that is deceived trust in vanity: for vanity will be his recompence[1].
32 It will be accomplished before his time, and his branch will not be green.
33 He will shake off his unripe grape as the vine, and will cast off his flower as the olive.
34 For the congregation of hypocrites will *be* desolate, and fire will consume the tabernacles of bribery.
35 They conceive mischief, and bring forth vanity, and their belly prepares deceit.

CHAPTER 16

1 Then Job answered and said,
2 I have heard many such things: miserable comforters *are* ye all.
3 will vain words have an end? or what emboldens you that you answers?
4 I also could speak as ye *do*: if your soul were in my soul's stead, I could heap up words against you, and shake mine head at you.
5 *But* I would strengthen you with my mouth, and the moving of my lips should asswage[2] *your* grief.
6 Though I speak, my grief is not asswaged: and *though* I forbear, what am I eased?
7 But now he has made me weary: you have made desolate all my company.
8 And you have filled me with wrinkles[3], *which* is a witness against me: and [my leanness][4] rising up in me [bears witness][5] to my face.
9 He tears *me* in his wrath, who hates me: he gnashs[6] upon me with his teeth; mine enemy sharpens his eyes upon me.
10 They have gaped upon me with their mouth; they have smitten me upon the cheek reproachfully; they have gathered themselves together against me.
11 God has delivered me to the ungodly, and turned me over into the hands of the wicked.
12 I was at ease, but he has broken me asunder: he has also taken *me* by my neck, and shaken me to pieces, and set me up for his mark.
13 His archers compass me round about, he cleaves my reins asunder, and does not spare; he pours out my gall upon the ground.
14 He breaks me with breach upon breach, he runs upon me like a giant.
15 I have sewed sackcloth upon my skin, and defiled my horn in the dust.
16 My face is foul with weeping, and on my eyelids *is* the shadow of death;
17 Not for *any* injustice in mine hands: also my prayer *is* pure.
18 O earth, cover not you my blood, and let my cry have no place.
19 Also now, behold, my witness *is* in heaven, and my record *is* on high.
20 My friends scorn me: *but* mine eye pours out *tears* unto God.
21 O that one might plead for a man with God, as a man pleads for his neighbor!
22 When a few years are come, then I will go the way whence I will not return.

---

[1] recompense- is the Hebrew word *temûrâh* and translates as barter, compensation, (ex) change (ing), restitution.[Strgs#8545]
[2] asswage- a prim root; to *restrain* or *refrain*; by implication to assuage, spare, preserve; also (by interchange with to observe, assuage, forbear, hinder, hold back, keep (back), punish, reserve and withhold. [Strgs#2820]

[3] wrinkles – to *pluck*, destroy, cut down [Strgs#7059].
[4] lit. lying, a *failure* of flesh, *emaciation; hypocrisy* [Strgs#3585].
[5] lit. to *eye* or to *heed, pay attention, sing, shout*, scholar, *respond, testify, announce* [Strgs#6030].
[6] Gnash- to grate the teeth. [Strgs#2786]

CHAPTER 17

1 My breath is corrupt, my days are extinct, the graves *are ready* for me.
2 *Are there* not mockers with me? And does not mine eye continue in their provocation?
3 Lay down now, put me in a surety with you; who *is* he *that* will strike hands with me?
4 For you have hid their heart from understanding: therefore will you not exalt *them*.
5 He that speaks flattery to *his* friends, even the eyes of his children will fail.
6 He has made me also a byword of the people; and aforetime I was as a tabret¹.
7 Mine eye also is dim by reason of sorrow, and all my members *are* as a shadow.
8 Upright *men* will be **astonished** at this, and the innocent will stir up himself against the hypocrite.
9 The righteous also will hold on his way, and he that has clean hands will be stronger and stronger.
10 But as for you all, do ye return, and come now: for I cannot find *one* wise *man* among you.
11 My days are past, my purposes are broken off, *even* the thoughts of my heart.
12 They change the night into day: the light *is* short because of darkness.
13 If I wait, the grave *is* mine house: I have made my bed in the darkness.
14 I have said to corruption, you *are* my father: to the worm, you *are* my mother, and my sister.
15 And where *is* now my hope? As for my hope, who will see it?
16 They will go down to the bars of the pit, when *our* rest together *is* in the dust.

CHAPTER 18

1 Then answered Bildad the Shuhite, and said,
2 How long *will it be ere* ye make an end of words? Mark, and afterwards we will speak.
3 Wherefore are we counted as beasts, *and* reputed vile in your sight?
4 He tears himself in his anger: will the earth be forsaken for you? And will the rock be removed out of his place?
5 Yea, the light of the wicked will be put out, and the spark of his fire will not shine.
6 The light will be dark in his tabernacle, and his candle will be put out with him.
7 The steps of his strength will be straitened, and his own counsel will cast him down.
8 For he is cast into a net by his own feet, and he walks upon a snare.
9 [The gin will take *him* by the heel, *and* the robber will prevail against him.]²
10 The snare *is* laid for him in the ground, and a trap for him in the way.
11 Terrors will make him afraid on every side, and will drive him to his feet.
12 His strength will be hunger bitten, and destruction³ will *be* ready at his side.
13 It will devour the strength of his skin: *even* the firstborn of death will devour his strength.
14 His confidence will be rooted out of his tabernacle, and it will bring him to the king of terrors.
15 It will dwell in his tabernacle, because *it is* none of his: brimstone will be scattered upon his habitation.
16 His roots will be dried up beneath, and above will his branch be cut off.
17 His remembrance will perish from the earth, and he will have no name in the street.
18 He will be driven from light into darkness, and chased out of the world.
19 He will neither have son nor nephew among his people, or any remaining in his dwellings.
20 They that come after *him* will be **astonished** at his day, as they that went before were affrighted.
21 Surely such *are* the dwellings of the wicked, and this *is* the place *of him that* knows not God.

CHAPTER 19

1 Then Job answered and said,
2 How long will ye vex my soul, and break me in pieces with words?
3 These ten times have ye reproached me: ye are not ashamed *that* ye make yourselves strange to me.
4 And be it indeed *that* I have erred, mine error remains with myself.
5 If indeed ye will magnify *yourselves* against me, and plead against me my reproach:
6 Know now that God has overthrown me, and has compassed me with his net.
7 Behold, I cry out of wrong, but I am not heard: I cry aloud, but *there is* no judgment.
8 He has fenced up my way that I cannot pass, and he has set darkness in my paths.
9 He has stripped me of my glory, and taken the crown *from* my head.
10 He has destroyed me on every side, and I am gone: and mine hope has he removed like a tree.
11 He has also kindled his wrath against me, and he counts me unto him as *one of* his enemies.
12 His troops come together, and raise up their way against me, and encamp round about my tabernacle.
13 He has put my brethren far from me, and mine acquaintance are verily estranged from me.
14 My kinsfolk have failed, and my familiar friends have forgotten me.
15 They that dwell in mine house, and my maids count me for a stranger: I am an alien in their sight.
16 I called my servant, and he gave *me* no answer; I intreated⁴ him with my mouth.
17 My breath⁵ is strange to my wife, though I intreated⁶ for the children's *sake* of mine own body.

---

¹ tabret- is the Hebrew root word *tôpheth* and it is defined as an act of *spitting*, a *smiting*, that is contempt. [Strgs#8611]
² Satan contrast **Rev. 12**.
³ lit. a burden, load; heavy misfortune, calamity, ruin, destruction [Strgs#343]. Compare **Job 21:17, 21:30, 30:12**.
⁴ intreated- to bend or stoop in kindness to an inferior, to favor, bestow, causatively to implore, to move to favor by petition, beseech, favorable, be gracious, merciful, pray and to have pity upon. [Strgs#2603]
⁵ lit. *spirit*, resemblance *breath*, by extension a *region of* the sky, *life*, *anger*, *unsubstantiality* [Strgs#7307].
⁶ intreated – in the sense of prayer; supplication, be gracious [Strgs#2589]. Root word meaning to *bend* or stoop in kindness to an inferior, to *favor*,

18 Yea, young children despised me; I arose, and they spoke against me.
19 All my [inward friends]¹ abhorred me: and they whom I loved are turned against me.
20 My bone cleaves to my skin and to my flesh, and I am escaped with the skin of my teeth.
21 Have pity upon me, have pity upon me, O ye my friends; for the hand of God has touched me.
22 Why do ye persecute me as God, and are not satisfied with my flesh?
23 Oh that my words were now written! Oh that they were printed in a book!
24 That they were graven with an iron pen and lead in the rock forever!
25 For I know *that* my redeemer lives, and *that* he will stand at the latter *day* upon the earth:
26 And *though* after my skin *worms* destroy this *body*, yet in my flesh will I see God:
27 Whom I will see for myself, and mine eyes will behold, and not another; *though* my reins be consumed within me.
28 But ye should say, why persecute we him, seeing the root of the matter is found in me?
29 Be ye afraid of the sword: for wrath *brings* the punishments of the sword, that ye may know *there is* a judgment.

CHAPTER 20

1 Then answered Zophar the Naamathite, and said,
2 Therefore do my thoughts cause me to answer, and for *this* I make haste.
3 I have heard the check of my reproach, and the spirit of my understanding causes me to answer.
4 Knows you *not* this of old, since man was placed upon earth,
5 That the triumphing of the wicked *is* short, and the joy of the hypocrite *but* for a moment?
6 Though his excellency mount up to the heavens, and his head reach unto the clouds;
7 *Yet* he will perish for ever like his own dung: they which have seen him will say, where *is* he?
8 He will fly away as a dream, and will not be found: yea, he will be chased away as a vision of the night.
9 The eye also *which* saw him will *see him* no more; neither will his place any more behold him.
10 His children will seek to please the poor, and his hands will restore their goods.
11 His bones are full *of the sin* of his youth, which will lie down with him in the dust.
12 Though wickedness be sweet in his mouth, *though* he hide it under his tongue;
13 *Though* he spares it, and forsakes it not; but keep it still within his mouth:
14 *Yet* his meat in his bowels is turned, *it is* the gall of asps within him.
15 He has swallowed down riches, and he will vomit them up again: God will cast them out of his belly.
16 He will suck the poison of asps: the viper's tongue will slay him.
17 He will not see the rivers, the floods, the brooks of honey and butter.

18 That which he labored for will he restore, and will not swallow *it* down: according to *his* substance will the restitution *be*, and he will not rejoice *therein*.
19 Because he has oppressed *and* has forsaken the poor; *because* he has violently taken away a house which he built not;
20 Surely he will not feel quietness in his belly, he will not save of that which he desired.
21 There will none of his meat be left; therefore will no man look for his goods.
22 In the fullness of his sufficiency he will be in straits: every hand of the wicked will come upon him.
23 *When* he is about to fill his belly, *God* will cast the fury of his wrath upon him, and will rain *it* upon him while he is eating.
24 He will flee from the iron weapon, *and* the bow of steel will strike him through.
25 It is drawn, and cometh out of the body; yea, the glittering sword cometh out of his gall: terrors *are* upon him.
26 All darkness will *be* hid in his secret places: a fire not blown will consume him; it will go ill with him that is left in his tabernacle.
27 The heaven will reveal his iniquity; and the earth will rise up against him.
28 The increase of his house will depart, *and his goods* will flow away in the day of his wrath.
29 This *is* the portion of a wicked man from God, and the heritage appointed unto him by God.

CHAPTER 21

1 But Job answered and said,
2 Hear diligently my speech, and let this be your consolations.
3 Suffer me that I may speak; and after that I have spoken, mock on.
4 As for me, *is* my complaint to man? And if *it were so*, why should not my spirit be troubled?
5 Mark me, and be astonished, and lay *your* hand upon *your* mouth.
6 Even when I remember I am afraid, and trembling takes hold on my flesh.
7 Wherefore do the wicked live, become old, yea, are mighty in power?
8 Their seed is established in their sight with them, and their offspring before their eyes.
9 Their houses *are* safe from fear, neither *is* the rod of God upon them.
10 Their bull genders, and fails not; their cow calves, and casts not her calf.
11 They send forth their little ones like a flock, and their children dance.
12 They take the **tambourine** and harp, and rejoice at the sound of the organ.
13 They spend their days in wealth, and in a moment go down to the grave.
14 Therefore they say unto God, Depart from us; for we desire not the knowledge of your ways.
15 What *is* the Almighty, that we should serve him? And what profit should we have, if we pray unto him?
16 Lo, their good *is* not in their hand: the counsel of the wicked is far from me.

---

bestow; implore [Strgs#2603].
¹ inward – a session, company of persons (in close deliberation); by implication intimacy, consultation, a secret [Strgs#5475]. Friends – an adult, a man [Strgs#4962]. When the two words are put together it literally men of my secrets.

17 How oft is the candle of the wicked put out! And *how oft* cometh their destruction upon them! *God* distributes sorrows in his anger.
18 They are as stubble before the wind, and as chaff that the storm carries away.
19 God lays up his iniquity for his children: he rewards him, and he will know *it*.
20 His eyes will see his destruction, and he will drink of the wrath of the Almighty.
21 For what pleasure has he in his house after him, when the number of his months is cut off in the midst?
22 will *any* teach God knowledge? Seeing he judges those that are high.
23 One dies in his full strength, being wholly at ease and quiet.
24 His breasts are full of milk, and his bones are moistened with marrow.
25 And another dies in the bitterness of his soul, and never eats with pleasure.
26 They will lie down alike in the dust, and the worms will cover them.
27 Behold, I know your thoughts, and the devices *which* ye wrongfully imagine against me.
28 For ye say, where *is* the house of the prince? And where *are* the dwelling places of the wicked?
29 Have ye not asked them that go by the way? And do ye not know their tokens,
30 That the wicked is reserved to the day of destruction? They will be brought forth to the day of wrath.
31 Who will declare his way to his face? And who will repay him *what* he has done?
32 Yet will he be brought to the grave, and will remain in the tomb.
33 The clods of the valley will be sweet unto him, and every man will draw after him, as *there are* innumerable before him.
34 How then comfort ye me in vain, seeing in your answers there remains falsehood?

CHAPTER 22

1 Then Eliphaz the Temanite answered and said,
2 Can a man be profitable unto God, as he that is wise may be profitable unto himself?
3 *Is it* any pleasure to the Almighty, that you are righteous? Or *is it* gain *to him*, that you makes your ways perfect?
4 Will he reprove you for fear of you? Will he enter with you into judgment?
5 *Is* not your wickedness great? And your iniquities infinite?
6 For you have taken a pledge from your brother for **nothing**, and stripped the naked of their clothing.
7 you have not given water to the weary to drink, and you have **withheld** bread from the hungry.
8 But *as for* the mighty man, he had the earth; and the honorable man dwelt in it.
9 you have sent widows away empty, and the arms of the fatherless have been broken.
10 Therefore snares *are* round about you, and sudden fear troubles you;
11 Or darkness, *that* you canst not see; and abundance of waters cover you.
12 *Is* not God in the height of heaven? And behold the height of the stars, how high they are!
13 And you says, how does God know? Can he judge through the dark cloud?
14 Thick clouds *are* a covering to him, that he sees not; and he walks in the circuit of heaven.
15 have you marked the old way which wicked men have trodden?
16 Which were cut down out of time, whose foundation was **overflows** with a flood:
17 Which said unto God, Depart from us: and what can the Almighty do for them?
18 Yet he filled their houses with good *things*: but the counsel of the wicked is far from me.
19 The righteous see *it*, and are glad: and the innocent laugh them to scorn.
20 Whereas our substance is not cut down, but the remnant of them the fire consumes.
21 Acquaint now yourself with him, and be at peace: thereby good will come unto you.
22 Receive, I pray you, the law from his mouth, and lay up his words in your heart.
23 If you return to the Almighty, you will be built up, you will put away iniquity far from your tabernacles.
24 Then will you lay up gold as dust, and the *gold* of Ophir as the stones of the brooks.
25 Yes, the Almighty will be your defense, and you will have plenty of silver.
26 For then will you have your delight in the Almighty, and will lift up your face unto God.
27 you will make your prayer unto him, and he will hear you, and you will pay your vows.
28 you will also decree a thing, and it will be established unto you: and the light will shine upon your ways.
29 When *men* are cast down, then you will say, *there is* lifting up; and he will save the humble person.
30 He will deliver the island of the innocent: and it is delivered by the pureness of your hands.

CHAPTER 23

1 Then Job answered and said,
2 Even today *is* my complaint bitter: my stroke is heavier than my groaning.
3 Oh that I knew where I might find him! *That* I might come *even* to his seat!
4 I would order *my* cause before him, and fill my mouth with arguments.
5 I would know the words *which* he would answer me, and understand what he would say unto me.
6 Will he plead against me with *his* great power? No; but he would put *strength* in me.
7 There the righteous might dispute with him; so should I be delivered for ever from my judge.
8 Behold, I go forward, but he *is* not *there*; and backward, but I cannot perceive him:
9 On the left hand, where he does work, but I cannot behold *him*: he hides himself on the right hand, that I cannot see *him*:
10 But he knows the way that I take: *when* he has tried me, I will come forth as gold.
11 My foot has held his steps, his way have I kept, and not declined.
12 Neither have I gone back from the commandment of his lips; I have esteemed the words of his mouth more than my necessary *food*.
13 But he *is* in one *mind*, and who can turn him? and *what* his soul desires, even *that* he doeth.

14 For he performs *the thing that is* appointed for me: and many such *things are* with him.
15 Therefore am I troubled at his presence: when I consider, I am afraid of him.
16 For God makes my heart soft, and the Almighty troubles me:
17 Because I was not cut off before the darkness, *neither* has he covered the darkness from my face.

CHAPTER 24

1 Why, seeing times are not hidden from the Almighty, do they that know him not see his days?
2 *Some* remove the landmarks; they violently take away flocks, and feed *thereof*.
3 They drive away the ass of the fatherless, they take the widow's ox for a pledge.
4 They turn the needy out of the way: the poor of the earth hide themselves together.
5 Behold, *as* wild asses in the desert, go they forth to their work; rising betimes for a prey: the wilderness *yields* food for them *and* for *their* children.
6 They reap everyone his corn in the field: and they gather the vintage of the wicked.
7 They cause the naked to lodge without clothing, that *they have* no covering in the cold.
8 They are wet with the showers of the mountains, and embrace the rock for want of a shelter.
9 They pluck the fatherless from the breast, and take a pledge of the poor.
10 They cause *him* to go naked without clothing, and they take away the sheaf *from* the hungry;
11 *Which* make oil within their walls, *and* tread *their* winepresses, and suffer thirst.
12 Men groan from out of the city, and the soul of the wounded cries out: yet God lays not folly *to them*.
13 They are of those that rebel against the light; they know not the ways thereof, nor abide in the paths thereof.
14 The murderer rising with the light kills the poor and needy, and in the night is as a thief.
15 The eye also of the adulterer waits for the twilight, saying, No eye will see me: and disguises *his* face.
16 In the dark they dig through houses, *which* they had marked for themselves in the daytime: they know not the light.
17 For the morning *is* to them even as the shadow of death: if *one* know *them, they are in* the terrors of the shadow of death.
18 He *is* swift as the waters; their portion is cursed in the earth: he beholds not the way of the vineyards.
19 Drought and heat consume the snow waters: *so does* the grave *those which* have sinned.
20 The womb will forget him; the worm will feed sweetly on him; he will be no more remembered; and wickedness will be broken as a tree.
21 He evil entreats the barren *that* bears not: and doeth not good to the widow.
22 He draws also the mighty with his power: he rises up, and no *man* is sure of life.
23 *Though* it be given him *to be* in safety, whereon he rests; yet his eyes *are* upon their ways.

24 They are exalted for a little while, but are gone and brought low; they are taken out of the way as all *other*, and cut off as the tops of the ears of corn.
25 And if *it be* not *so* now, who will make me a liar, and make my speech nothing worth?

CHAPTER 25

1 Then answered Bildad the Shuhite, and said,
2 Dominion and fear *are* with him, he makes peace in his high places.
3 Is there any number of his armies? And upon whom does not his light arise?
4 How then can man be justified with God? Or how can he be clean *that is* born of a woman?
5 Behold even to the moon, and it shines not; yea, the stars are not pure in his sight.
6 How much less man, *that is* a worm? And the son of man, *which is* a worm?

CHAPTER 26

1 But Job answered and said,
2 How have you helped *him that is* without power? *How* saves you the arm *that has* no strength?
3 How have you counseled *him that has* no wisdom? and *how* have you plentifully declared the thing as it is?
4 To **who** have you uttered words? And whose spirit came from you?
5 Dead *things* are formed from under the waters, and the inhabitants thereof.
6 Hell *is* naked before him, and destruction has no covering.
7 He stretches out the north over the empty place, *and* hangs the earth upon nothing.
8 He binds up the waters in his thick clouds; and the cloud is not rent under them.
9 He holds back the face of his throne, *and* spreads his cloud upon it.
10 He has compassed the waters with bounds, until the day and night come to an end.
11 The pillars of heaven tremble and are astonished at his reproof.
12 He divides the sea with his power, and by his understanding he smites through the proud.
13 By his spirit he has garnished the heavens; his hand has formed the crooked serpent.
14 Lo, these *are* parts of his ways: but how little a portion is heard of him? But the thunder of his power[1] who can understand?

CHAPTER 27

1 Moreover Job continued his parable, and said,
2 *As* God lives, *who* has taken away my judgment; and the Almighty, *who* has vexed my soul;
3 All the while my breath *is* in me, and the spirit of God *is* in my nostrils;
4 My lips will not speak wickedness, nor my tongue utter deceit.
5 God forbid that I should justify you: till I die I will not remove mine integrity from me.
6 My righteousness I hold fast, and will not let it go: my heart will not reproach *me* so long as I live.
7 Let mine enemy be as the wicked, and he that rises up against me as the unrighteous.

---

[1] lit. force

8 For what *is* the hope of the hypocrite, though he has gained, when God takes away his soul?
9 Will God hear his cry when trouble cometh upon him?
10 Will he delight himself in the Almighty? Will he always call upon God?
11 I will teach you by the hand of God: *that* which *is* with the Almighty will I not conceal.
12 Behold, all ye yourselves have seen *it*; why then are ye thus altogether vain?
13 This *is* the portion of a wicked man with God, and the heritage of oppressors, *which* they will receive of the Almighty.
14 If his children be multiplied, *it is* for the sword: and his offspring will not be satisfied with bread.
15 Those that remain of him will be buried in death: and his widows will not weep.
16 Though he heap up silver as the dust, and prepare raiment as the clay;
17 He may prepare *it*, but the just will put *it* on, and the innocent will divide the silver.
18 He builds his house as a moth, and as a booth *that* the keeper makes.
19 The rich man will lie down, but he will not be gathered: he opens his eyes, and he *is* not.
20 Terrors take hold on him as waters, a tempest steals him away in the night.
21 The east wind carries him away, and he departs: and as a storm hurls him out of his place.
22 For *God* will cast upon him, and not spare: he would fain flee out of his hand.
23 *Men* will clap their hands at him, and will hiss him out of his place.

CHAPTER 28

1 Surely there is a vein for the silver, and a place for gold *where* they fine *it*.
2 Iron is taken out of the earth, and brass *is* molten *out of* the stone.
3 He sits an end to darkness, and searches out all perfection: the stones of darkness, and the shadow of death.
4 The flood breaks out from the inhabitant; *even the waters* forgotten of the foot: they are dried up, they are gone away from men.
5 *As for* the earth, out of it cometh bread: and under it is turned up as it were fire.
6 The stones of it *are* the place of sapphires: and it has dust of gold.
7 *There is* a path which no fowl knows, and which the vulture's eye has not seen:
8 The lion's whelps have not trodden it, nor the fierce lion passed by it.
9 He puts forth his hand upon the rock; he overturns the mountains by the roots.
10 He cuts out rivers among the rocks; and his eye sees every precious thing.
11 He binds the floods from overflowing; and *the thing that is* hid brings he forth to light.
12 But where will wisdom be found? And where *is* the place of understanding?
13 Man knows not the price thereof; neither is it found in the land of the living.
14 The depth said, it *is* not in me: and the sea said, *It is* not with me.
15 It cannot be gotten for gold, neither will silver be weighed *for* the price thereof.
16 It cannot be valued with the gold of Ophir, with the precious onyx, or the sapphire.
17 The gold and the crystal cannot equal it: and the exchange of it will *not be for* jewels of fine gold.
18 No mention will be made of coral, or of pearls: for the price of wisdom *is* above rubies.
19 The topaz of Ethiopia will not equal it, neither will it be valued with pure gold.
20 Whence then cometh wisdom? And where *is* the place of understanding?
21 Seeing it is hid from the eyes of all living, and kept close from the fowls of the air.
22 Destruction and death say, we have heard the fame thereof with our ears.
23 God understands the way thereof, and he knows the place thereof.
24 For he looks to the ends of the earth, *and* sees under the whole heaven;
25 To make the weight for the winds; and he weighs the waters by measure.
26 When he made a decree for the rain, and a way for the lightning of the thunder:
27 Then did he see it, and declare it; he prepared it, yea, and searched it out.
28 And unto man he said, Behold, the fear of the Lord, that *is* wisdom; and to depart from evil *is* understanding.

CHAPTER 29

1 Moreover Job continued his parable, and said,
2 Oh that I were as *in* months past, as *in* the days *when* God preserved me;
3 When his candle shined upon my head, *and when* by his light I walked *through* darkness;
4 As I was in the days of my youth, when the secret of God *was* upon my tabernacle;
5 When the Almighty *was* yet with me, *when* my children *were* about me;
6 When I washed my steps with butter, and the rock poured me out rivers of oil;
7 When I went out to the gate through the city, *when* I prepared my seat in the street!
8 The young men saw me, and hid themselves: and the aged arose, *and* stood up.
9 The princes refrained talking, and laid *their* hand on their mouth.
10 The nobles held their peace, and their tongue cleaved to the roof of their mouth.
11 When the ear heard *me*, then it blessed me; and when the eye saw *me*, it gave witness to me:
12 Because I delivered the poor that cried, and the fatherless, and *him that had* none to help him.
13 The blessing of him that was ready to perish came upon me: and I caused the widow's heart to sing for joy.
14 I put on righteousness, and it clothed me: my judgment *was* as a robe and a diadem.
15 I was eyes to the blind, and feet *was* I to the lame.
16 I *was* a father to the poor: and the cause *which* I knew not I searched out.
17 And I broke the jaws of the wicked, and plucked the spoil out of his teeth.

18 Then I said, I will die in my nest, and I will multiply *my* days as the sand.
19 My root *was* spread out by the waters, and the dew lay all night upon my branch.
20 My glory *was* fresh in me, and my bow was renewed in my hand.
21 Unto me *men* gave ear, and waited, and kept silence at my counsel.
22 After my words they spoke not again; and my speech dropped upon them.
23 And they waited for me as for the rain; and they opened their mouth wide *as* for the latter rain.
24 *If* I laughed on them, they believed *it* not; and the light of my countenance they cast not down.
25 I chose out their way, and sat chief, and dwelt as a king in the army, as one *that* comforts the mourners.

CHAPTER 30

1 But now *they that are* younger than I have me in derision, whose fathers I would have disdained to have set with the dogs of my flock.
2 Yea, whereto *might* the strength of their hands *profit* me, in whom old age was perished?
3 For want and famine *they were* solitary; fleeing into the wilderness in former time desolate and waste.
4 Who cut up mallows by the bushes, and juniper roots *for* their meat.
5 They were driven forth from among *men*, (they cried after them as *after* a thief;)
6 To dwell in the cliffs of the valleys, *in* caves of the earth, and *in* the rocks.
7 Among the bushes they brayed; under the nettles they were gathered together.
8 *They were* children of fools, yes, children of base men: they were viler than the earth.
9 And now am I their song, yea, I am their byword.
10 They abhor me, they flee far from me, and spare not to spit in my face.
11 Because he has loosed my cord, and afflicted me, they have also let loose the bridle before me.
12 Upon *my* right *hand* rise the youth; they push away my feet, and they raise up against me the ways of their destruction.
13 They mar my path, they set forward my calamity, they have no helper.
14 They came *upon me* as a wide breaking in *of waters*: in the desolation they rolled themselves *upon me*.
15 Terrors are turned upon me: they pursue my soul as the wind: and my welfare pass away as a cloud.
16 And now my soul is poured out upon me; the days of affliction have taken hold upon me.
17 My bones are pierced in me in the night season: and my sinews take no rest.
18 By the great force *of my disease* is my garment changed: it binds me about as the collar of my coat.
19 He has cast me into the mire, and I am become like dust and ashes.
20 I cry unto you, and you dost not hear me: I stand up, and you regards me *not*.
21 you are become cruel to me: with your strong hand you opposes yourself against me.
22 you lift me up to the wind; you causes me to ride *upon it*, and dissolves my substance.
23 For I know *that* you will bring me *to* death, and *to* the house appointed for all living.
24 Howbeit he will not stretch out *his* hand to the grave, though they cry in his destruction.
25 Did not I weep for him that was in trouble? Was *not* my soul grieved for the poor?
26 When I looked for good, then evil came *unto me*: and when I waited for light, there came darkness.
27 My bowels boiled, and rested not: the days of affliction prevented me.
28 I went mourning without the sun: I stood up, *and* I cried in the congregation.
29 I am a brother to dragons, and a companion to owls.
30 My skin is black upon me, and my bones are burned with heat.
31 My harp also is *turned* to mourning, and my organ into the voice of them that weep.

CHAPTER 31

1 I made¹ a covenant with mine eyes; why then should I think upon a maid?
2 For what portion of God *is there* from above? And *what* inheritance of the Almighty from on high?
3 *Is* not destruction to the wicked? And a strange *punishment* to the workers of iniquity?
4 does not he see my ways, and count all my steps?
5 If I have walked with vanity, or if my foot has hasted to deceit;
6 Let me be weighed in an even balance, that God may know mine integrity.
7 If my step has turned out of the way, and mine heart walked after mine eyes, and if any blot has cleaved to mine hands;
8 *Then* let me sow, and let another eat; yes, let my offspring be rooted out.
9 If mine heart have been deceived² by a woman, or *if* I have laid wait at my neighbor's door;
10 *Then* let my wife grind unto another³, and let others⁴ bow down upon her.
11 [For this *is* an heinous crime; yea, it *is* an iniquity *to be punished by* the judges.]⁵
12 For it *is* a fire *that* consumes to destruction, and would root out all mine increase⁶.
13 If I did despise the cause of my manservant or of my maidservant, when they contended with me;
14 What then will I do when God rises up? And when he visits, what will I answer him?
15 Did not he that made me in the womb make him? And did not one fashion us in the womb?
16 If I have withheld the poor from *their* desire, or have caused the eyes of the widow to fail;
17 Or have eaten my morsel myself alone, and the fatherless has not eaten thereof;

---

¹ lit. to *cut*, *destroy*, covenant, or *consume* [Strgs#3772].
² deceived – is the Greek word *pâthâh* meaning to open, seduce, flatter, *simple* [Strgs#6601].
³ another – comes from the Hebrew word *'achêr* meaning *hinder* [Strgs#312]. It derives from the Hebrew root word *'âchar* meaning *be behind*, *loiter*; by implication to *procrastinate* [Strgs#309].
⁴ Ibid
⁵ compare **1 Cor. 5:4**
⁶ lit. income [Strgs#8393]. Compare **Proverbs 6:26**.

18 (For from my youth he was brought up with me, as *with* a father, and I have guided her from my mother's womb;)
19 If I have seen any perish for want of clothing, or any poor without covering;
20 If his loins have not blessed me, and *if* he were *not* warmed with the fleece of my sheep;
21 If I have lifted up my hand against the fatherless, when I saw my help in the gate:
22 *Then* let mine arm fall from my shoulder blade, and mine arm be broken from the bone.
23 For destruction *from* God *was* a terror to me, and by reason of his highness I could not endure.
24 If I have made gold my hope, or have said to the fine gold, you are my confidence;
25 If I rejoiced because my wealth *was* great, and because mine hand had gotten much;
26 If I beheld the sun when it shined, or the moon walking *in* brightness;
27 And my heart has been secretly enticed, or my mouth has kissed my hand:
28 This also *were* an iniquity *to be punished by* the judge: for I should have denied the God *that is* above.
29 If I rejoiced at the destruction of him that hated me, or lifted up myself when evil found him:
30 Neither have I suffered my mouth to sin by wishing a curse to his soul.
31 If the men of my tabernacle said not, oh that we had of his flesh! we cannot be satisfied.
32 The stranger did not lodge in the street: *but* I opened my doors to the traveler.
33 If I covered my transgressions as Adam, by hiding mine iniquity in my bosom:
34 Did I fear a great multitude, or did the contempt of families terrify me, that I kept silence, *and* went not out of the door?
35 Oh that one would hear me! Behold, my desire *is, that* the Almighty would answer me, and *that* mine adversary had written a book.
36 Surely I would take it upon my shoulder, *and* bind it *as* a crown to me.
37 I would declare unto him the number of my steps; as a prince would I go near unto him.
38 If my land cry against me, or that the furrows likewise thereof complain;
39 If I have eaten the fruits thereof without money, or have caused the owners thereof to lose their life:
40 Let thistles grow instead of wheat, and cockle instead of barley. The words of Job are ended.

CHAPTER 32

1 So these three men ceased to answer Job, because he *was* righteous in his own eyes.
2 Then was kindled the wrath of Elihu[1] the son of Barachel the Buzite, of the kindred of Ram: against Job was his wrath kindled, because he justified himself rather than God.
3 Also against his three friends was his wrath kindled, because they had found no answer, and *yet* had condemned Job.
4 Now Elihu had waited till Job had spoken, because they *were* elder than he.
5 When Elihu saw that *there was* no answer in the mouth of *these* three men, then his wrath was kindled.
6 And Elihu the son of Barachel the Buzite answered and said, I *am* young, and ye *are* very old; wherefore I was afraid, and durst not shew you mine opinion.
7 I said, Days should speak, and multitude of years should teach wisdom.
8 But *there is* a spirit in man: and the inspiration of the Almighty gives them understanding.
9 Great men are not *always* wise: neither do the aged understand judgment.
10 Therefore I said, Hearken to me; I also will show mine opinion.
11 Behold, I waited for your words; I gave ear to your reasons, whilst ye searched out what to say.
12 Yea, I attended unto you, and, behold, *there was* none of you that convinced Job, *or* that answered his words:
13 Lest ye should say, we have found out wisdom: God thrusts him down, not man.
14 Now he has not directed *his* words against me: neither will I answer him with your speeches.
15 They were amazed, they answered no more: they left off speaking.
16 When I had waited, (for they spoke not, but stood still, *and* answered no more;)
17 *I said*, I will answer also my part, I also will show mine opinion.
18 For I am full of matter, the spirit within me constrains me.
19 Behold, my belly *is* as wine *which* has no vent; it is ready to burst like new bottles.
20 I will speak, that I may be refreshed: I will open my lips and answer.
21 Let me not, I pray you, accept any man's person, neither let me give flattering titles unto man.
22 For I know not to give flattering titles; *in so doing* my maker would soon take me away.

CHAPTER 33

1 Wherefore, Job, I pray you, hear my speeches, and hearken to all my words.
2 Behold, now I have opened my mouth, my tongue has spoken in my mouth.
3 My words will *be of* the uprightness of my heart: and my lips will utter knowledge clearly. 4 The Spirit of God has made me, and the breath of the Almighty has given me life.
5 If you canst answer me, set your *words* in order before me, stand up.
6 Behold, I *am* according to your wish in God's stead: I also am formed out of the clay.
7 Behold, my terror will not make you afraid, neither will my hand be heavy upon you.
8 Surely you have spoken in mine hearing, and I have heard the voice of your words, *saying*,
9 I am clean without transgression, I *am* innocent; neither *is there* iniquity in me.
10 Behold, he finds occasions against me, he counts me for his enemy,
11 He puts my feet in the stocks, he marks all my paths.
12 Behold, *in* this you are not just: I will answer you, that God is greater than man.

---

[1] Elihu- (*He is my God* or *God of him*) the youngest of Job's comforters. Elihu spoke to Job after the three friends—Eliphaz, Bildad and Zophar—failed to give convincing answers to Job's questions. Elihu is called "the son of Barachel the Buzite: of the family of Ram" (**Job 32:2**). Like Job's other friends, Elihu was probably from the Transjordan area southeast of Palestine.

13 Why dost you strive against him? For he gives not account of any of his matters.
14 For God speaks once, yea twice, *yet man* perceives it not.
15 In a dream, in a vision of the night, when deep sleep falls upon men, in slumberings upon the bed;
16 Then he opens the ears of men, and seals their instruction,
17 That he may withdraw man *from his* purpose, and hide pride from man.
18 He keeps back his soul from the pit, and his life from perishing by the sword.
19 He is chastened also with pain upon his bed, and the multitude of his bones with strong *pain*:
20 So that his life abhors bread, and his soul dainty meat.
21 His flesh is consumed away, that it cannot be seen; and his bones *that* were not seen stick out.
22 Yea, his soul draws near unto the grave, and his life to the destroyers.
23 If there be a messenger with him, an interpreter, one among a thousand, to show unto man his uprightness:
24 Then he is gracious unto him, and said, Deliver him from going down to the pit: I have found a ransom.
25 His flesh will be fresher than a child's: he will return to the days of his youth:
26 He will pray unto God, and he will be favorable unto him: and he will see his face with joy: for he will render unto man his righteousness.
27 He looks upon men, and *if any* say, I have sinned, and perverted *that which was* right, and it profited me not;
28 He will deliver his soul from going into the pit, and his life will see the light.
29 Lo, all these *things* works God oftentimes with man,
30 To bring back his soul from the pit, to be enlightened with the light of the living.
31 Mark well, O Job, hearken unto me: hold your peace, and I will speak.
32 If you have anything to say, answer me: speak, for I desire to justify you.
33 If not, hearken unto me: hold your peace, and I will teach you wisdom.

CHAPTER 34

1 Furthermore Elihu answered and said,
2 Hear my words, O ye wise *men*; and give ear unto me, ye that have knowledge.
3 For the ear tries words, as the mouth tastes meat.
4 Let us choose to us judgment: let us know among ourselves what *is* good.
5 For Job has said, I am righteous: and God has taken away my judgment.
6 Should I lie against my right? My wound *is* incurable without transgression.
7 What man *is* like Job, *who* drinks up scorning like water?
8 Which goes in company with the workers of iniquity, and walks with wicked men.
9 For he has said, it profits a man nothing that he should delight himself with God.
10 Therefore hearken unto me, ye men of understanding: far be it from God, *that he should do* wickedness; and *from* the Almighty, *that he should commit* iniquity.
11 For the work of a man will he render unto him, and cause every man to find according to *his* ways.

12 Yea, surely God will not do wickedly, neither will the Almighty pervert judgment.
13 Who has given him a charge over the earth? Or who has disposed the whole world?
14 If he set his heart upon man, *if* he gather unto himself his spirit and his breath;
15 All flesh will perish together, and man will turn again unto dust.
16 If now you have understanding, hear this: hearken to the voice of my words.
17 will even he that hates right govern? And will you condemn him that is most just?
18 *Is it fit* to say to a king, you are wicked? *And* to princes, *you are* ungodly?
19 *How much less to him* that accepts not the persons of princes, or regards the rich more than the poor? For they all *are* the work of his hands.
20 In a moment will they die, and the people will be troubled at midnight, and pass away: and the mighty will be taken away without hand.
21 For his eyes *are* upon the ways of man, and he sees his **entire** goings.
22 *There is* no darkness, nor shadow of death, where the workers of iniquity may hide themselves.
23 For he will not lay upon man more *than right*; that he should enter into judgment with God.
24 He will break in pieces mighty men without number, and set others in their stead.
25 Therefore he knows their works, and he overturns *them* in the night, so that they are destroyed.
26 He strikes them as wicked men in the open sight of others;
27 Because they turned back from him, and would not consider any of his ways:
28 So that they cause the cry of the poor to come unto him, and he hears the cry of the afflicted.
29 When he gives quietness, who then can make trouble? And when he hides *his* face, who then can behold him? Whether it be done against a nation, or against a man only:
30 That the hypocrite reign not, lest the people be ensnared
31 Surely it is meet to be said unto God, I have borne *chastisement*, I will not offend *any more*:
32 *That which* I see not **teaches** you me: if I have done iniquity, I will do no more.
33 *Should it be* according to your mind? He will recompense it, whether you refuse, or whether you choose; and not I: therefore speak what you knows.
34 Let men of understanding tell me, and let a wise man hearken unto me.
35 Job has spoken without knowledge, and his words *were* without wisdom.
36 My desire *is that* Job may be tried unto the end because of *his* answers for wicked men.
37 For he adds rebellion unto his sin, he claps *his hands* among us, and multiplies his words against God.

CHAPTER 35

1 Elihu spoke moreover, and said,
2 **Do you think** this to be right, *that* you said, my righteousness *is* more than God's?
3 For you said, what advantage will it be unto you? *And*, what profit will I have, *if I be cleansed* from my sin?
4 I will answer you, and your companions with you.

5 Look unto the heavens, and see; and behold the clouds *which* are higher than you.
6 If you sins, what does you against him? or *if* your transgressions be multiplied, what does you unto him?
7 If you be righteous, what gives you him? Or what receives he of your hand?
8 your wickedness *may hurt* a man as you *art*; and your righteousness *may profit* the son of man.
9 By reason of the multitude of oppressions they make *the oppressed* to cry: they cry out by reason of the arm of the mighty.
10 But none said, where *is* God my maker, who gives songs in the night;
11 Who teaches us more than the beasts of the earth, and makes us wiser than the fowls of heaven?
12 There they cry, but none gives answer, because of the pride of evil men.
13 Surely God will not hear vanity, neither will the Almighty regard it.
14 Although you say you will not see him, *yet* judgment *is* before him; therefore trust you in him.
15 But now, because *it is* not *so*, he has visited in his anger; yet he knows *it* not in great extremity:
16 Therefore does Job open his mouth in vain; he multiplies words without knowledge.

CHAPTER 36

1 Elihu also proceeded, and said,
2 Suffer me a little, and I will show you that *I have* yet to speak on God's behalf.
3 I will fetch my knowledge from afar, and will ascribe righteousness to my Maker.
4 For truly my words will not *be* false: he that is perfect in knowledge *is* with you.
5 Behold, God *is* mighty, and despises not *any*: he *is* mighty in strength *and* wisdom.
6 He preserves not the life of the wicked: but gives right to the poor.
7 He withdraws not his eyes from the righteous: but with kings *are* they on the throne; yea, he does establish them forever, and they are exalted.
8 And if *they be* bound in fetters, *and* be held in cords of affliction;
9 Then he shows them their work, and their transgressions that they have exceeded.
10 He opens also their ear to discipline, and commands that they return from iniquity.
11 If they obey and serve *him*, they will spend their days in prosperity, and their years in pleasures.
12 But if they obey not, they will perish by the sword, and they will die without knowledge.
13 But the hypocrites in heart heap up wrath: they cry not when he binds them.
14 They die in youth, and their life *is* among the unclean.
15 He delivers the poor in his affliction, and opens their ears in oppression.

16 Even so would he have removed you out of the strait *into* a broad place, where *there is* no straitness[1]; and that which should be set on your table *should be* full of fatness.
17 But you have fulfilled the judgment of the wicked: judgment and justice take hold *on you*.
18 Because *there is* wrath, *beware* lest he take you away with *his* stroke: then a great ransom cannot deliver you.
19 Will he esteem your riches? *No*, not gold, nor all the forces of strength.
20 Desire not the night, when people are cut off in their place.
21 Take heed, regard not iniquity: for this have you chosen rather than affliction.
22 Behold, God exalts by his power: who teaches like him?
23 Who has enjoined him his way? Or who can say, you have wrought iniquity?
24 Remember that you magnify his work, which men behold.
25 Every man may see it; man may behold *it* afar off.
26 Behold, God *is* great, and we know *him* not, neither can the number of his years be searched out.
27 For he makes small the drops of water: they pour down rain according to the vapor thereof:
28 Which the clouds do drop *and* distil upon man abundantly.
29 Also can *any* understand the **expansion** of the clouds, *or* the noise of his tabernacle?
30 Behold, he spreads his light upon it, and covers the bottom of the sea.
31 For by them judges he the people; he gives meat in abundance.
32 [With clouds he covers the light; and commands it *not to shine* by *the cloud* that cometh betwixt.][2]
33 The noise thereof shows[3] concerning it, the cattle[4] also concerning [the vapor][5].

CHAPTER 37

1 At this also my heart trembles, and is moved out of his place.
2 Hear attentively the noise of his voice, and the sound *that* goes out of his mouth.
3 He directs[6] it under the whole heaven, and his lightning unto the ends of the earth.
4 After it a voice roars: he thunders with the voice of his excellency; and he will not stay them when his voice is heard.
5 God thunders marvelously[7] with his voice; **and does great things**, which we cannot comprehend[8].
6 For he said to the snow, Be you *on* the earth; likewise to the small rain, and to the great rain of his strength.
7 He seals up the hand of every man; that all men may know his work.
8 Then the beasts go into dens, and remain in their places.
9 Out of the south cometh the whirlwind: and cold out of the north.
10 By the breath of God frost is given: and the breadth of the waters is straitened.
11 Also by watering he wearies the thick cloud: he scatters his bright cloud:

---

[1] straitness- here is defined as narrowness, figuratively distress, anguish, is straitened. [Strgs#4164]
[2] lit. He covers (His) hands with lightining and commands it to strike the mark.
[3] shows – properly to *front*, stand bodly out oppositie; by implication to *manifest*; figuratively to announce (always by word of mouth to one present; specifically to *expose*, *predict*, *explain*, *praise* [Strgs#5046].
[4] lit. something bought, *property*, but only live *stock*; abstractly *acquisition* [Strgs#4735].
[5] vapors – to *ascend*, intransitively (be *high*) or active (*mount*), that which goes up [Strgs#5927].
[6] lit. to be straight or even; figuratively to be (causatively to *make*) right, *pleasant* and *prosperous* [Strgs#3474].
[7] marvelously – to separate, *distinguish*, to *be great*, *difficult*, *wonderful*, accomplish [Strgs#6381].
[8] comprehend – to know by seeing [Strgs#3045].

12 And it is turned round about by his counsels: that they may do whatsoever he commands them upon the face of the world in the earth.
13 He causes it to come, whether for correction, or for his land, or for mercy.
14 Hearken unto this, O Job: standstill, and consider the wondrous works of God.
15 Dost you know when God disposed them, and caused the light of his cloud to shine?
16 Do you know the balancing of the clouds, the wondrous works of him which is perfect in knowledge?
17 How your garments *are* warm, when he quiets the earth by the south *wind*?
18 have you with him spread out the sky, *which is* strong, *and* as a molten looking glass?
19 Teach us what we will say unto him; *for* we cannot order *our speech* by reason of darkness.
20 will it be told him that I speak? If a man speak, surely he will be swallowed up.
21 And now *men* see not the bright light which *is* in the clouds: but the wind passes, and cleans them.
22 Fair weather cometh out of the north: with God *is* terrible majesty.
23 *Touching* the Almighty, we cannot find him out: *he is* excellent in power, and in judgment, and in plenty of justice: he will not afflict.
24 Men do therefore fear him: he respects not any *that are* wise of heart.

CHAPTER 38

1 Then the LORD answered Job out of the whirlwind, and said,
2 Who *is* this that darkens counsel by words without knowledge?
3 Gird up now your loins like a man; for I will demand of you, and answer you me.
4 Where were you when I laid the foundations of the earth? Declare, if you have understanding.
5 Who has laid the measures thereof, if you knows? Or who has stretched the line upon it?
6 Whereupon are the foundations thereof fastened? Or who laid the corner stone thereof;
7 When the morning stars sang together, and all the sons of God shouted for joy?
8 Or *who* shut up the sea with doors, when it brakes forth, *as if* it had issued out of the womb?
9 When I made the cloud the garment thereof, and thick darkness a swaddling-band for it,
10 And brakes up for it my decreed *place*, and set bars and doors,
11 And said, Hitherto will you come, but no further: and here will your proud waves be stayed?
12 have you commanded the morning since your days; *and* caused the dayspring to know his place;
13 That it might take hold of the ends of the earth, that the wicked might be shaken out of it?
14 It is turned as clay *to* the seal; and they stand as a garment.
15 And from the wicked their light is **withheld**, and the high arm will be broken.
16 have you entered into the springs of the sea? Or have you walked in the search of the depth?
17 Have the gates of death been opened unto you? Or have you seen the doors of the shadow of death?
18 have you perceived the breadth of the earth? Declare if you knows it all.
19 Where *is* the way *where* light dwells? And *as for* darkness, where *is* the place thereof,
20 That you should take it to the bound thereof, and that you should know the paths *to* the house thereof?
21 Knows you *it*, because you **were** then born? Or *because* the number of your days *is* great?
22 have you entered into the treasures of the snow? Or have you seen the treasures of the hail,
23 Which I have reserved against the time of trouble, against the day of battle and war?
24 By what way is the light parted, *which* scatters the east wind upon the earth?
25 Who has divided a watercourse for the overflowing of waters, or a way for the lightning of thunder;
26 To cause it to rain on the earth, *where* no man *is; on* the wilderness, wherein *there is* no man;
27 To satisfy the desolate and waste *ground*; and to cause the bud of the tender herb to spring forth?
28 Has the rain a father? Or who has begotten the drops of dew?
29 Out of whose womb came the ice? And the hoary frost of heaven, who has gendered it?
30 The waters are hid as *with* a stone, and the face of the deep is frozen.
31 Canst you bind the sweet influences of Pleiades, or loose the bands of Orion?
32 Can you bring forth Mazzaroth[1] in his season? Or can you guide Arcturus[2] with his sons?
33 Know you the ordinances of heaven? Can you set the dominion thereof in the earth?
34 Can you lift up your voice to the clouds, that abundance of waters may cover you?
35 Can you send lightnings, that they may go, and say unto you, Here we *are*?
36 Who has put wisdom in the inward parts? Or who has given understanding to the heart?
37 Who can number the clouds in wisdom? Or who can stay the bottles of heaven,
38 When the dust grows into hardness, and the clods cleave fast together?
39 will you hunt the prey for the lion? Or fill the appetite of the young lions,
40 When they couch in *their* dens, *and* abide in the covert to lie in wait?
41 Who provides for the raven his food? When his young ones cry unto God, they wander for lack of meat.

CHAPTER 39

1 Know you the time when the wild goats of the rock bring forth? *Or* canst you mark when the hinds do calve?
2 Canst you number the months *that* they fulfill? Or knows you the time when they bring forth?
3 They bow themselves, they bring forth their young ones they cast out their sorrows.

---

[1] Mazzaroth- (*the scattered ones*) a feature either of the starry heavens or the changing seasons. It is often translated as constellations. [Strgs#4216]
[2] Arcturus- (*the bear keeper*) King James Version of a Hebrew word meaning "crowd," and referring to a constellation of stars. The NKJV translates the word as "the Bear" (**Job 9:9**) and "the Great Bear with its cubs" (**Job 38:32**)—the "cubs" being a reference to the seven main stars of this constellation. [Strgs#5906]

4 Their young ones are in good liking, they grow up with corn; they go forth, and return not unto them.
5 Who has sent out the wild ass free? Or who has loosed the bands of the wild ass?
6 Whose house I have made the wilderness, and the barren land his dwellings.
7 He scorns the multitude of the city, neither regards he the crying of the driver.
8 The range of the mountains *is* his pasture, and he searches after every green thing.
9 Will the unicorn be willing to serve you, or abide by your crib?
10 Canst you bind the unicorn with his band in the furrow? Or will he harrow the valleys after you?
11 will you trust him, because his strength *is* great? Or will you leave your labor to him?
12 will you believe him, that he will bring home your seed, and gather *it into* your barn?
13 *Gave you* the goodly wings unto the peacocks? Or wings and feathers unto the ostrich?
14 Which leaves her eggs in the earth, and warms them in dust,
15 And forgets that the foot may crush them, or that the wild beast may break them.
16 She is hardened against her young ones, as though *they were* not hers: her labor is in vain without fear;
17 Because God has deprived her of wisdom, neither has he imparted to her understanding.
18 What time [she lifts up][1] herself on high, she scorns the horse and his rider.
19 have you given the horse strength? Have you clothed his neck with thunder?
20 Canst you make him afraid as a grasshopper? The glory of his nostrils[2] *is* terrible.
21 He paws in the valley, and rejoices in *his* strength: he goes on to meet the armed men.
22 He mocks at fear, and is not affrighted; neither turns he back from the sword.
23 The quiver rattles against him, the glittering spear and the shield.
24 He swallows the ground with fierceness and rage: neither believeth he that *it is* the sound of the trumpet.
25 He said among the trumpets, Ha, ha; and he smells the battle afar off, the thunder of the captains, and the shouting.
26 Does the hawk fly by your wisdom, *and* stretch her wings toward the south?
27 Does the eagle mount up at your command, and make her nest on high?
28 She dwells and abides on the rock, upon the crag of the rock, and the strong place.
29 From thence she seeks the prey, *and* her eyes behold afar off.
30 Her young ones also suck up blood: and where the slain *are*, there *is* she.

CHAPTER 40

1 Moreover the LORD answered Job, and said,
2 will he that contends with the Almighty instruct him? He that reproves God, let him answer it.
3 Then Job answered the LORD, and said,
4 Behold, I am vile; what will I answer you? I will lay mine hand upon my mouth.
5 Once have I spoken; but I will not answer: yea, twice; but I will proceed no further.
6 Then answered the LORD unto Job out of the whirlwind, and said,
7 Gird up your loins now like a man: I will demand of you, and declare you unto me.
8 will you also disannul my judgment? Will you condemn me, that you may be righteous?
9 have you an arm like God? Or canst you thunder with a voice like him?
10 Deck yourself now *with* majesty and excellency; and array yourself with glory and beauty.
11 Cast abroad the rage of your wrath: and behold every one *that is* proud, and abase him.
12 Look on every one *that is* proud, *and* bring him low; and tread down the wicked in their place.
13 Hide them in the dust together; *and* bind their faces in secret.
14 Then will I also confess unto you that your own right hand can save you.
15 Behold now behemoth, which I made with you; he eats grass as an ox.
16 Lo now, his strength *is* in his loins, and his force *is* in the navel of his belly.
17 He moves his tail like a cedar: the sinews of his stones are wrapped together.
18 His bones *are as* strong pieces of brass; his bones *are* like bars of iron.
19 He *is* the chief of the ways of God: he that made him can make his sword to approach *unto him*.
20 Surely the mountains bring him forth food, where all the beasts of the field play.
21 He lies under the shady trees, in the covert of the reed, and fens.
22 The shady trees cover him *with* their shadow; the willows of the brook compass him about.
23 Behold, he drinks up a river, *and* haste not: he trusted that he can draw up Jordan into his mouth.
24 He takes it with his eyes: *his* nose pierces through snares.

CHAPTER 41

1 Can you draw out Leviathan[3] with a hook? Or his tongue[4] with a cord *which* you lets down?
2 Can you put a hook into his nose? Or bore[5] his jaw through with a thorn?
3 Will he make many supplications unto you? Will he speak soft *words* unto you?
4 Will he make a covenant with you? Will you take him for a servant forever?

---

[1] lit. to *rebel*; hence (through the idea of *maltreating*) to *whip, lash* [Strgs#4754].
[2] nostrils – to *snort*. Compare **John 11:33**.
[3] Leviathan- a wreathed animal, that is a serpent; figuratively the constellation of the dragon; also as a symbol of Babylon:- mourning. [Strgs#3882]
[4] tongue- the tongue (of man or animals), used literally (as the instrument of licking, eating, or speech), and figuratively (speech, an ingot, a fork of flame, a cove of water): -+ babbler, bay, + evil speaker, language and wedge. [Strgs#3956]
[5] bore- to puncture, literally (to perforate, with more or less violence) or figuratively (to specify, designate, libel): -appoint, blaspheme, curse, express, with holes, name, pierce, strike through. [Strgs#5344]

5 Will you play with him as *with* a bird? Or will you bind him for your maidens?
6 Will the companions make a banquet of him? Will they part him among the merchants?
7 Can you fill his skin with barbed irons? Or his head with fish spears?
8 Lay your hand upon him, remember the battle, do no more.
9 Behold, the hope of him is in vain: will not *one* be cast down even at the sight of him?
10 None *is* so fierce that dare stir him up: who then is able to stand before me?
11 Who has prevented me, that I should repay *him*? Whatsoever *is* under the whole heaven is mine.
12 I will not conceal his parts, nor his power, nor his comely proportion.
13 Who can discover the face of his garment? *Or* who can come *to him* with his double bridle?
14 Who can open the doors of his face? His teeth *are* terrible round about.
15 *His* scales *are his* pride, shut up together *as with* a close seal.
16 One is so near to another, that no air can come between them.
17 They are joined one to another, they stick together, that they cannot be sundered.
18 By his **sneezing**[1] a light does shine, and his eyes *are* like the eyelids of the morning.
19 Out of his mouth go burning lamps, *and* sparks of fire leap out.
20 Out of his nostrils goes smoke, as *out* of a seething pot or caldron.
21 His breath kindles coals, and a flame goes out of his mouth.
22 In his neck remains strength, and sorrow is turned into joy before him.
23 The flakes of his flesh are joined together: they are firm in themselves; they cannot be moved.
24 His heart is as firm as a stone; yea, as hard as a piece of the nether *millstone*.
25 When he raises up himself, the mighty are afraid: by reason of breakings they purify themselves.
26 The sword of him that lays at him cannot hold: the spear, the dart, or the habergeon.
27 He esteems iron as straw, *and* brass as rotten wood.
28 The arrow cannot make him flee: sling-stones are turned with him into stubble.
29 Darts are counted as stubble: he laughs at the shaking of a spear.
30 Sharp stones *are* under him: he spreads sharp pointed things upon the mire.
31 He makes the deep to boil like a pot: he makes the sea like a pot of ointment.
32 He makes a path to shine after him; *one* would think the deep *to be* hoary.
33 Upon earth there is not his like, who is made without fear.
34 He beheld all high *things*: he *is* a king over all the children of pride.

CHAPTER 42

1 Then Job answered the LORD, and said,
2 I know that you canst do everyt*hing*, and *that* no thought can be withheld from you.
3 Who *is* he that hides counsel without knowledge? Therefore have I uttered that I understood not; things too wonderful for me, which I knew not.
4 Hear, I beseech you, and I will speak: I will demand of you, and declare you unto me.
5 I have heard of you by the hearing of the ear: but now mine eye sees you.
6 Wherefore I abhor *myself*, and repent in dust and ashes.
7 And it was *so*, that after the LORD had spoken these words unto Job, the LORD said to Eliphaz the Temanite, My wrath is kindled against you, and against your two friends: for ye have not spoken of me *the thing that is* right, as my servant Job *hath*.
8 Therefore take unto you now seven bullocks and seven rams, and go to my servant Job, and offer up for yourselves a burnt offering; and my servant Job will pray for you: for him will I accept: lest I deal with you *after your* folly, in that ye have not spoken of me *the thing which is* right, like my servant Job.
9 So Eliphaz the Temanite and Bildad the Shuhite *and* Zophar the Naamathite went, and did according as the LORD commanded them: the LORD also accepted Job.
10 And the LORD turned the captivity of Job, when he prayed for his friends: also the LORD gave Job twice as much as he had before.
11 Then came there unto him all his brethren, and all his sisters, and all they that had been of his acquaintance before, and did eat bread with him in his house: and they bemoaned him, and comforted him over all the evil that the LORD had brought upon him: every man also gave him a piece of money, and everyone an earring of gold.
12 So the LORD blessed the latter end of Job more than his beginning: for he had fourteen thousand sheep, and six thousand camels, and a thousand yoke of oxen, and a thousand she asses.
13 He had also seven sons and three daughters.
14 And he called the name of the first, Jemima[2]; and the name of the second, Kezia[3]; and the name of the third, Keren-happuch[4].
15 And in all the land were no women found *so* fair as the daughters of Job: and their father gave them inheritance among their brethren.
16 After this lived Job an hundred and forty years, and saw his sons, and his sons' sons, *even* four generations.
17 So Job died, *being* old and full of days.

---

[1] The KJV uses the word neesings.
[2] Jemima- is the Hebrew word *yemîymâh*, <u>yem-ee-maw'</u> meaning warm, that is affectionate, hence dove. [Strgs#3224]
[3] Kezia- is the Hebrew word *qetsîy'âh*, <u>kets-ee-aw'</u>, the same as cassia meaning a spice, a powdered blark like cinnamon. [Strgs#7103]
[4] Kerenhappuch- from the Hebrew word qeren happûk, keh'-ren hap-pook', which translate as the horn of antimony or horn of cosmetic. [Strgs#7163]

PSALMS

PSALM 1

1 Blessed *is* the man that walks not in the counsel of the ungodly, or stands in the way of sinners, or sits in the seat of the scornful.
2 But his delight *is* in the law of the LORD; and in his law does he meditate day and night.
3 And he will be like a tree planted by the rivers of water, that brings forth his fruit in his season; his leaf also will not wither; and whatsoever he doeth will prosper.
4 The ungodly *are* not so: but *are* like the chaff which the wind drives away.
5 Therefore the ungodly will not stand in the judgment, or sinners in the congregation of the righteous.
6 For the LORD knows the way of the righteous: but the way of the ungodly will perish.

PSALM 2

1 Why do the heathen rage, and the people imagine a vain thing?
2 The kings of the earth set themselves, and the rulers take counsel together, against the LORD, and against his anointed, *saying*,
3 Let us break their bands asunder, and cast away their cords from us.
4 He that sits in the heavens will laugh: the Lord will have them in derision.
5 Then will he speak unto them in his wrath, and vex them in his sore displeasure.
6 Yet have I set my king upon my holy hill of Zion.
7 I will declare the decree: the LORD has said unto me, you are my Son; this day have I begotten you.
8 Ask of me, and I will give you the heathen *for* your inheritance, and the uttermost parts of the earth *for* your possession.
9 you will break them with a rod of iron; you will dash them in pieces like a potter's vessel.
10 Be wise now therefore, O you kings: be instructed, you judges of the earth.
11 Serve the LORD with fear, and rejoice with trembling.
12 Kiss the Son, lest he be angry, and you perish *from* the way, when his wrath is kindled but a little. Blessed *are* all they that put their trust in him.

PSALM 3

A Psalm of David, when he fled from Absalom his son.

1 LORD, how are they increased that trouble me! Many *are* they that rise up against me.
2 Many *there be* which say of my soul, There *is* no help for him in God. Selah.
3 But you, O LORD, are a shield for me; my glory, and the lifter up of mine head.
4 I cried unto the LORD with my voice, and he heard me out of his holy hill. Selah.
5 I laid me down and slept; I awaked; for the LORD sustained me.
6 I will not be afraid of ten thousands of people, that have set *themselves* against me round about.
7 Arise, O LORD; save me, O my God: for you have smitten all mine enemies *upon* the cheek bone; you have broken the teeth of the ungodly.
8 Salvation *belongs* unto the LORD: your blessing *is* upon your people. Selah.

PSALM 4

To the chief Musician on Neginoth, A Psalm of David.

1 Hear me when I call, O God of my righteousness you have enlarged me *when I was* in distress; have mercy upon me, and hear my prayer.
2 O you sons of men, how long *will you turn* my glory into shame? *How long* will you love vanity, *and* seek after leasing? Selah.
3 But know that the LORD has set apart him that *is* godly for himself: the LORD will hear when I call unto him.
4 Stand in awe, and sin not: commune with your own heart upon your bed, and be still. Selah.
5 Offer the sacrifices of righteousness, and put your trust in the LORD.
6 *There be* many that say, who will show us *any* good? LORD, lift you up the light of your countenance upon us.
7 you have put gladness in my heart, more than in the time *that* their corn and their wine increased.
8 I will both lay me down in peace, and sleep: for you, LORD, only makes me dwell in safety.

PSALM 5

To the chief Musician upon Nehiloth, A Psalm of David.

1 Give ear to my words, O LORD, consider my meditation.
2 Hearken unto the voice of my cry, my King, and my God: for unto you will I pray.
3 My voice will you hear in the morning, O LORD; in the morning will I direct *my prayer* unto you, and will look up.
4 For you are not a God that has pleasure in wickedness: neither will evil dwell with you.
5 The foolish will not stand in your sight: you hate all workers of iniquity.
6 you will destroy them that speak leasing: the LORD will abhor the bloody and deceitful man.
7 But as for me, I will come *into* your house in the multitude of your mercy: *and* in your fear will I worship toward your holy temple.
8 Lead me, O LORD, in your righteousness because of mine enemies; make your way straight before my face.
9 For *there is* no faithfulness in their mouth; their inward part *is* very wickedness; their throat *is* an open sepulcher; they flatter with their tongue.
10 Destroy you them, O God; let them fall by their own counsels; cast them out in the multitude of their transgressions; for they have rebelled against you.
11 But let all those that put their trust in you rejoice: let them ever shout for joy, because you defend them: let them also that love your name be joyful in you.
12 For you, LORD, will bless the righteous; with favor will you compass him as *with* a shield.

PSALM 6

To the chief Musician on Neginoth upon Sheminith, A Psalm of David.

1 O LORD, rebuke me not in your anger, neither chasten me in your hot displeasure.
2 Have mercy upon me, O LORD; for I *am* weak O LORD, heal me; for my bones are vexed.
3 My soul is also sore vexed: but you, O LORD, how long?

4 Return, O LORD, deliver my soul: oh save me for your mercies' sake.
5 For in death *there is* no remembrance of you: in the grave who will give you thanks?
6 I am weary with my groaning; all the night make I my bed to swim; I water my couch with my tears.
7 Mine eye is consumed because of grief; it waxes old because of all mine enemies.
8 Depart from me, all you workers of iniquity; for the LORD has heard the voice of my weeping.
9 The LORD has heard my supplication; the LORD will receive my prayer.
10 Let all mine enemies be ashamed and sore vexed: let them return *and* be ashamed suddenly.

PSALM 7

Shiggaion of David, which he sang unto the LORD, concerning the words of Cush the Benjamite.

1 O LORD my God, in you do I put my trust: save me from all them that persecute me, and deliver me:
2 Lest he tear my soul like a lion, rending *it* in pieces, while *there is* none to deliver.
3 O LORD my God, if I have done this; if there be iniquity in my hands;
4 If I have rewarded evil unto him that was at peace with me; (yea, I have delivered him that without cause is mine enemy:)
5 Let the enemy persecute my soul, and take *it*; yea, let him tread down my life upon the earth, and lay mine honor in the dust. Selah.
6 Arise, O LORD, in your anger, lift up yourself because of the rage of mine enemies: and awake for me *to* the judgment *that* you have commanded.
7 So will the congregation of the people compass you about: for their sakes therefore return you on high.
8 The LORD will judge the people: judge me, O LORD, according to my righteousness, and according to mine integrity *that is* in me.
9 Oh let the wickedness of the wicked come to an end; but establish the just: for the righteous God tries the hearts and reins.
10 My defense *is* of God, which saves the upright in heart.
11 God judges the righteous, and God is angry *with the wicked* every day.
12 If he turn not, he will whet his sword; he has bent his bow, and made it ready.
13 He has also prepared for him the instruments of death; he ordains his arrows against the persecutors.
14 Behold, he travails with iniquity, and has conceived mischief, and brought forth falsehood.
15 He made a pit, and **dug** it, and is fallen into the ditch *which* he made.
16 His mischief will return upon his own head, and his violent dealing will come down upon his own pate.
17 I will praise the LORD according to his righteousness: and will sing praise to the name of the LORD most high.

PSALM 8

To the chief Musician upon Gittith, A Psalm of David.

1 O LORD our Lord, how excellent *is* your name in all the earth! who have set your glory above the heavens.
2 Out of the mouth of babes and sucklings have you ordained strength because of your enemies, that you might still the enemy and the avenger.
3 When I consider your heavens, the work of your fingers, the moon and the stars, which you have ordained;
4 What is man, that you are mindful of him? And the son of man, that you visits him?
5 For you have made him a little lower than the angels, and have crowned him with glory and honor.
6 you made him to have dominion over the works of your hands; you have put all *things* under his feet:
7 All sheep and oxen, yea, and the beasts of the field;
8 The fowl of the air, and the fish of the sea, *and whatsoever* passes through the paths of the seas.
9 O LORD our Lord, how excellent *is* your name in all the earth!

PSALM 9

To the chief Musician upon Muth-labben, A Psalm of David

1 I will praise you, O LORD, with my whole heart; I will show forth all your marvelous works.
2 I will be glad and rejoice in you: I will sing praise to your name, O you most High.
3 When mine enemies are turned back, they will fall and perish at your presence.
4 For you have maintained my right and my cause; you sat in the throne judging right.
5 you have rebuked the heathen, you have destroyed the wicked, you have put out their name forever and ever.
6 O you enemy, destructions are come to a perpetual end: and you have destroyed cities; their memorial is perished with them.
7 But the LORD will endure for ever: he has prepared his throne for judgment.
8 And he will judge the world in righteousness, he will minister judgment to the people in uprightness.
9 The LORD also will be a refuge for the oppressed, a refuge in times of trouble.
10 And they that know your name will put their trust in you: for you, LORD, have not forsaken them that seek you.
11 Sing praises to the LORD, which dwells in Zion: declare among the people his doings.
12 When he makes inquisition for blood, he remembers them: he forgets not the cry of the humble.
13 Have mercy upon me, O LORD; consider my trouble *which I suffer* of them that hate me, you that lifts me up from the gates of death:
14 That I may show forth all your praise in the gates of the daughter of Zion: I will rejoice in your salvation.
15 The heathen are sunk down in the pit *that* they made: in the net which they hid is their own foot taken.
16 The LORD is known *by* the judgment *which* he executes: the wicked is snared in the work of his own hands. Higgaion[1]. Selah.
17 The wicked will be turned into hell, *and* all the nations that forget God.
18 For the needy will not always be forgotten: the expectation of the poor will *not* perish forever.
19 Arise, O LORD; let not man prevail: let the heathen be judged in your sight.

---

[1] Higgaion- muttering (sounds spoken to no one in particular), meditation, melody, device, solemn sound. [Strgs#1902]

20 Put them in fear, O LORD: *that* the nations may know themselves *to be but* men. Selah.

PSALM 10

1 Why stands you afar off, O LORD? *Why* hide you yourself in times of trouble?
2 The wicked in *his* pride does persecute the poor: let them be taken in the devices that they have imagined.
3 For the wicked boasts of his heart's desire, and blesses the covetous, *whom* the LORD abhorreth[1].
4 The wicked, through the pride of his countenance, will not seek *after God*: God *is* not in all his thoughts.
5 His ways are always grievous; your judgments *are* far above out of his sight: *as for* all his enemies, he puffs at them.
6 He has said in his heart, I will not be moved: for *I will* never *be* in adversity.
7 His mouth is full of cursing and deceit and fraud: under his tongue *is* mischief and vanity.
8 He sits in the lurking places of the villages: in the secret places does he murder the innocent: his eyes are privily set against the poor.
9 He lies in wait secretly as a lion in his den: he lies in wait to catch the poor: he does catch the poor, when he draws him into his net.
10 He crouches, *and* humbles himself, that the poor may fall by his strong ones.
11 He has said in his heart, God has forgotten: he hides his face; he will never see *it*.
12 Arise, O LORD; O God, lift up your hand: forget not the humble.
13 Wherefore do the wicked contemn God? He has said in his heart, you will not require *it*.
14 you have seen *it*; for you behold mischief and spite, to requite *it* with your hand: the poor commits himself unto you; you are the helper of the fatherless.
15 Break you the arm of the wicked and the evil *man*: seek out his wickedness *till* you find none.
16 The LORD *is* King forever and ever: the heathen are perished out of his land.
17 LORD, you have heard the desire of the humble: you will prepare their heart, you will cause your ear to hear:
18 To judge the fatherless and the oppressed, that the man of the earth may no more oppress.

PSALM 11

To the chief Musician, *A Psalm* of David.

1 In the LORD put I my trust: how say you to my soul, Flee *as* a bird to your mountain?
2 For, lo, the wicked bend *their* bow, they make ready their arrow upon the string, that they may privily shoot at the upright in heart.
3 If the foundations be destroyed, what can the righteous do?
4 The LORD *is* in his holy temple, the LORD'S throne *is* in heaven: his eyes behold, his eyelids try, the children of men.
5 The LORD tries the righteous: but the wicked and him that loves violence his soul hates.
6 Upon the wicked he will rain snares, fire and brimstone, and a horrible tempest: *this will be* the portion of their cup.
7 For the righteous LORD loves righteousness; his countenance does behold the upright.

PSALM 12

To the chief Musician upon Sheminith, A Psalm of David.

1 Help, LORD; for the godly man ceases; for the faithful fail from among the children of men.
2 They speak vanity every one with his neighbor: *with* flattering lips *and* with a double heart do they speak.
3 The LORD will cut off all flattering lips, *and* the tongue that speaks proud things:
4 Who have said, with our tongue will we prevail; our lips *are* our own: who *is* lord over us?
5 For the oppression of the poor, for the sighing of the needy, now will I arise, said the LORD; I will set *him* in safety from him that puffs at him.
6 The words of the LORD *are* pure words: *as* silver tried in a furnace of earth, purified seven times.
7 you will keep them, O LORD, you will preserve them from this generation forever.
8 The wicked walk on every side, when the vilest men are exalted.

PSALM 13

To the chief Musician, A Psalm of David.

1 How long will you forget me, O LORD? Forever? How long will you hide your face from me?
2 How long will I take counsel in my soul, *having* sorrow in my heart daily? How long will mine enemy be exalted over me?
3 Consider *and* hear me, O LORD my God: lighten mine eyes, lest I sleep the *sleep of* death;
4 Lest mine enemy say, I have prevailed against him; *and* those that trouble me rejoice when I am moved.
5 But I have trusted in your mercy; my heart will rejoice in your salvation.
6 I will sing unto the LORD, because he has dealt bountifully with me.

PSALM 14

To the chief Musician, *A Psalm* of David.

1 The fool has said in his heart, *there is* no God. They are corrupt, they have done abominable works, *there is* none that doeth good.
2 The LORD looked down from heaven upon the children of men, to see if there were any that did understand, *and* seek God.
3 They are all gone aside, they are *all* together become filthy: *there is* none that doeth good, no, not one.
4 Have all the workers of iniquity no knowledge? Who eat up my people *as* they eat bread, and call not upon the LORD.
5 There were they in great fear: for God *is* in the generation of the righteous.
6 you have shamed the counsel of the poor, because the LORD *is* his refuge.
7 Oh that the salvation of Israel *were come* out of Zion! When the LORD brings back the captivity of his people, Jacob will rejoice, *and* Israel will be glad.

PSALM 15

A Psalm of David.

1 LORD, who will abide in your tabernacle? Who will dwell in your holy hill?

---

[1] abhorreth- to bloom, (give occasion to) blaspheme, contemn, despise, flourish, provoke. [Strgs#5006]

2 He that walks uprightly, and works righteousness, and speaks the truth in his heart.
3 *He that* backbites not with his tongue, or doeth evil to his neighbor, or takes up a reproach against his neighbor.
4 In whose eyes a vile person is contemned; but he honors them that fear the LORD. *He that* swears to *his own* hurt, and changes not.
5 *He that* puts not out his money to usury, or takes reward against the innocent. He that doeth these *things* will never be moved.

PSALM 16
Michtam of David.

1 Preserve me, O God: for in you do I put my trust.
2 *O my soul*, you have said unto the LORD, you are my Lord: my goodness *extends* not to you;
3 *But* to the saints that *are* in the earth, and *to* the excellent, in whom *is* all my delight.
4 Their sorrows will be multiplied *that* hasten *after* another *god*: their drink offerings of blood will I not offer, or take up their names into my lips.
5 The LORD *is* the portion of mine inheritance and of my cup: you maintain my lot.
6 The lines are fallen unto me in pleasant *places*; yea, I have a goodly heritage.
7 I will bless the LORD, who has given me counsel: my reins also instruct me in the night seasons.
8 I have set the LORD always before me: because *he is* at my right hand, I will not be moved.
9 Therefore my heart is glad, and my glory rejoices: my flesh also will rest in hope.
10 For you will not leave my soul in hell; neither will you suffer your Holy One to see corruption.
11 you will show me the path of life: in your presence *is* fullness of joy; at your right hand *there are* pleasures for evermore.

PSALM 17
A Prayer of David.

1 Hear the right, O LORD, attend unto my cry, give ear unto my prayer, *that goes* not out of feigned lips.
2 Let my sentence come forth from your presence; let your eyes behold the things that are equal.
3 you have proved mine heart; you have visited *me* in the night; you have tried me, *and* will find nothing; I am purposed *that* my mouth will not transgress.
4 Concerning the works of men, by the word of your lips I have kept *me from* the paths of the destroyer.
5 Hold up my goings in your paths, *that* my footsteps slip not.
6 I have called upon you, for you will hear me, O God: incline your ear unto me, *and hear* my speech.
7 Show your marvelous loving-kindness, O you that saves by your right hand them which put their trust *in you* from those that rise up *against them*.
8 Keep me as the apple of the eye, hide me under the shadow of your wings,
9 From the wicked that oppresses me, *from* my deadly enemies, *who* compass me about.
10 They are **enclosed** in their own fat: with their mouth they speak proudly.
11 They have now compassed us in our steps: they have set their eyes bowing down to the earth;
12 Like as a lion *that* is greedy of his prey, and as it were a young lion lurking in secret places.
13 Arise, O LORD, disappoint him, cast him down: deliver my soul from the wicked, *which is* your sword:
14 From men *which are* your hand, O LORD, from men of the world, *which have* their portion in *this* life, and whose belly you fill with your hid *treasure*: they are full of children, and leave the rest of their *substance* to their babes.
15 As for me, I will behold your face in righteousness: I will be satisfied, when I awake, with your likeness.

PSALM 18
To the chief Musician, *A Psalm* of David, the servant of the LORD, who spoke unto the LORD the words of this song in the day *that* the LORD delivered him from the hand of all his enemies, and from the hand of Saul: And he said,

1 I will love you, O LORD, my strength.
2 The LORD *is* my rock, and my fortress, and my deliverer; my God, my strength, in whom I will trust; my buckler, and the horn of my salvation, *and* my high tower.
3 I will call upon the LORD, *who is worthy* to be praised: so will I be saved from mine enemies.
4 The sorrows of death compassed me, and the floods of ungodly men made me afraid.
5 The sorrows of hell compassed me about: the snares of death prevented me.
6 In my distress I called upon the LORD, and cried unto my God: he heard my voice out of his temple, and my cry came before him, *even* into his ears.
7 Then the earth shook and trembled; the foundations also of the hills moved and were shaken, because he was **angry**.
8 There went up a smoke out of his nostrils, and fire out of his mouth devoured: coals were kindled by it.
9 He bowed the heavens also, and came down: and darkness *was* under his feet.
10 And he rode upon a cherub, and did fly: yes, he did fly upon the wings of the wind.
11 He made darkness his secret place; his pavilion round about him *were* dark waters *and* thick clouds of the skies.
12 At the brightness *that was* before him his thick clouds passed, hail *stones* and coals of fire.
13 The LORD also thundered in the heavens, and the Highest gave his voice; hail *stones* and coals of fire.
14 Yea, he sent out his arrows, and scattered them; and he shot out lightnings, and discomfited them.
15 Then the channels of waters were seen, and the foundations of the world were discovered at your rebuke, O LORD, at the blast of the breath of your nostrils.
16 He sent from above, he took me, he drew me out of many waters.
17 He delivered me from my strong enemy, and from them which hated me: for they were too strong for me.
18 They prevented me in the day of my calamity: but the LORD was my stay.
19 He brought me forth also into a large place; he delivered me, because he delighted in me.
20 The LORD rewarded me according to my righteousness; according to the cleanness of my hands has he recompensed me.
21 For I have kept the ways of the LORD, and have not wickedly departed from my God.

22 For all his judgments *were* before me, and I did not put away his statutes from me.
23 I was also upright before him, and I kept myself from mine iniquity.
24 Therefore has the LORD recompensed me according to my righteousness, according to the cleanness of my hands in his eyesight.
25 With the merciful you will show yourself merciful; with an upright man you will show yourself upright;
26 With the pure you will show yourself pure; and with the **distorted** you will show yourself **distorted**.
27 For you will save the afflicted people; but will bring down high looks.
28 For you will light my candle: the LORD my God will enlighten my darkness.
29 For by you I have run through a troop; and by my God have I leaped over a wall.
30 *As for* God, his way *is* perfect: the word of the LORD is tried: he *is* a buckler to all those that trust in him.
31 For who *is* God save the LORD? or who *is* a rock save our God?
32 *It is* God that **binds** me with strength, and makes my way perfect.
33 He makes my feet like hinds' *feet*, and sets me upon my high places.
34 He teaches my hands to war, so that a bow of steel is broken by mine arms.
35 you have also given me the shield of your salvation: and your right hand has **held** me up, and your gentleness has made me great.
36 you have enlarged my steps under me, that my feet did not slip.
37 I have pursued mine enemies, and overtaken them: neither did I turn again till they were consumed.
38 I have wounded them that they were not able to rise: they are fallen under my feet.
39 For you have girded me with strength unto the battle: you have subdued under me those that rose up against me.
40 you have also given me the necks of mine enemies; that I might destroy them that hate me.
41 They cried, but *there was* none to save *them*: *even* unto the LORD, but he answered them not.
42 Then did I beat them small as the dust before the wind: I did cast them out as the dirt in the streets.
43 you have delivered me from the strivings of the people; *and* you have made me the head of the heathen: a people *whom* I have not known will serve me.
44 As soon as they hear of me, they will obey me: the strangers will submit themselves unto me.
45 The strangers will fade away, and be afraid out of their close places.
46 The LORD lives; and blessed *be* my rock; and let the God of my salvation be exalted.
47 *It is* God that avenges me, and subdues the people under me.
48 He delivers me from mine enemies: yea, you lifts me up above those that rise up against me: you have delivered me from the violent man.
49 Therefore will I give thanks unto you, O LORD, among the heathen, and sing praises unto your name.
50 Great deliverance gives he to his king; and shows mercy to his anointed, to David, and to his seed for evermore.

PSALM 19
To the chief Musician, A Psalm of David.

1 The heavens declare the glory of God; and the firmament show his handiwork.
2 Day unto day utters speech, and night unto night show knowledge.
3 *There is* no speech or language, *where* their voice is not heard.
4 Their line is gone out through all the earth, and their words to the end of the world. In them has he set a tabernacle for the sun,
5 Which *is* as a bridegroom coming out of his chamber, *and* rejoices as a strong man to run a race.
6 His going forth *is* from the end of the heaven, and his circuit unto the ends of it: and there is nothing hid from the heat thereof.
7 The law of the LORD *is* perfect, converting the soul: the testimony of the LORD *is* sure, making wise the simple.
8 The statutes of the LORD *are* right, rejoicing the heart: the commandment of the LORD *is* pure, enlightening the eyes.
9 The fear of the LORD *is* clean, enduring for ever: the judgments of the LORD *are* true *and* righteous altogether.
10 More to be desired *are they* **then** gold, yea, than much fine gold: sweeter also than honey and the honeycomb.
11 Moreover by them is your servant warned: *and* in keeping of them *there is* great reward.
12 Who can understand *his* errors? Cleanse you me from secret *faults*.
13 Keep back your servant also from presumptuous *sins*; let them not have dominion over me: then will I be upright, and I will be innocent from the great transgression.
14 Let the words of my mouth, and the meditation of my heart, be acceptable in your sight, O LORD, my strength, and my redeemer.

PSALM 20
To the chief Musician, A Psalm of David.

1 The LORD hear you in the day of trouble; the name of the God of Jacob defend you;
2 Send you help from the sanctuary, and strengthen you out of Zion;
3 Remember all your offerings, and accept your burnt sacrifice; Selah.
4 Grant you according to your own heart, and fulfill all your counsel.
5 We will rejoice in your salvation, and in the name of our God we will set up *our* banners: the LORD fulfils all your petitions.
6 Now know I that the LORD saves his anointed; he will hear him from his holy heaven with the saving strength of his right hand.
7 Some *trust* in chariots, and some in horses: but we will remember the name of the LORD our God.
8 They are brought down and fallen: but we are risen, and stand upright.
9 Save, LORD: let the king hear us when we call.

PSALM 21
To the chief Musician, A Psalm of David.

1 The king will joy in your strength, O LORD; and in your salvation how greatly will he rejoice!
2 you have given him his heart's desire, and have not withheld the request of his lips. Selah.
3 For you prevents him with the blessings of goodness: you set a crown of pure gold on his head.

4 He asked life of you, *and* you gave *it* him, *even* length of days forever and ever.
5 His glory *is* great in your salvation: honor and majesty have you laid upon him.
6 For you have made him most blessed for ever: you have made him exceeding glad with your countenance.
7 For the king trusts in the LORD, and through the mercy of the most High he will not be moved.
8 your hand will find out all your enemies: your right hand will find out those that hate you.
9 you will make them as a fiery oven in the time of your anger: the LORD will swallow them up in his wrath, and the fire will devour them.
10 Their fruit will you destroy from the earth, and their seed from among the children of men.
11 For they intended evil against you: they imagined a mischievous device, *which* they are not able *to perform*.
12 Therefore will you make them turn their back, *when* you will make ready your *arrows* upon your strings against the face of them.
13 Be you exalted, LORD, in your own strength: *so* will we sing and praise your power.

PSALM 22
To the chief Musician upon Aijeleth Shahar, A Psalm of David.

1 My God, my God, why have you forsaken me? *Why are you so* far from helping me, *and from* the words of my roaring?
2 O my God, I cry in the daytime, but you hears not; and in the night season, and am not silent.
3 But you are holy, *O you* that inhabits the praises of Israel.
4 Our fathers trusted in you: they trusted, and you did deliver them.
5 They cried unto you, and were delivered: they trusted in you, and were not confounded.
6 But I *am* a worm, and no man; a reproach of men, and despised of the people.
7 All they that see me laugh me to scorn: they shoot out the lip, they shake the head, *saying*,
8 He trusted on the LORD *that* he would deliver him: let him deliver him, seeing he delighted in him.
9 But you are he that took me out of the womb: you did make me hope *when I was* upon my mother's breasts.
10 I was cast upon you from the womb: you are my God from my mother's belly.
11 Be not far from me; for trouble *is* near; for *there is* none to help.
12 Many bulls have compassed me: strong *bulls* of Bashan have beset me round.
13 They gaped upon me *with* their mouths, *as* a ravening and a roaring lion.
14 I am poured out like water, and all my bones are out of joint: my heart is like wax; it is melted in the midst of my bowels.
15 My strength is dried up like a potsherd; and my tongue cleaves to my jaws; and you have brought me into the dust of death.
16 For dogs have compassed me: the assembly of the wicked have **enclosed** me: they pierced my hands and my feet.
17 I may tell all my bones: they look *and* stare upon me.
18 They part my garments among them, and cast lots upon my vesture.
19 But be not you far from me, O LORD: O my strength, haste you to help me.
20 Deliver my soul from the sword; my darling from the power of the dog.
21 Save me from the lion's mouth: for you have heard me from the horns of the unicorns.
22 I will declare your name unto my brethren: in the midst of the congregation will I praise you.
23 you that fear the LORD, praise him; all you the seed of Jacob, glorify him; and fear him, all you the seed of Israel.
24 For he has not despised or abhorred the affliction of the afflicted; neither has he hid his face from him; but when he cried unto him, he heard.
25 My praise will *be* of you in the great congregation: I will pay my vows before them that fear him.
26 The meek will eat and be satisfied: they will praise the LORD that seek him: your heart will live forever.
27 All the ends of the world will remember and turn unto the LORD: and all the kindreds of the nations will worship before you.
28 For the kingdom *is* the LORD'S: and he *is* the governor among the nations.
29 All *they that be* fat upon earth will eat and worship: all they that go down to the dust will bow before him: and none can keep alive his own soul.
30 A seed will serve him; it will be accounted to the Lord for a generation.
31 They will come, and will declare his righteousness unto a people that will be born, that he has done *this*.

PSALM 23
A Psalm of David.

1 The LORD *is* my shepherd; I will not want.
2 He makes me to lie down in [green pastures][1]: he leads me beside the still waters.
3 He restores my soul: he leads me in the paths of righteousness for his name's sake.
4 Yea, though I walk through the valley of the shadow of death, I will fear no evil: for you are with me; your rod and your staff they comfort me.
5 you prepares a table before me in the presence of mine enemies: you anoints my head with oil; my cup runs over.
6 Surely goodness and mercy will follow me all the days of my life: and I will dwell in the house of the LORD forever.

PSALM 24
A Psalm of David.

1 The earth *is* the LORD'S, and the fullness thereof; the world, and they that dwell therein.
2 For he has founded it upon the seas, and established it upon the floods.
3 Who will ascend into the hill of the LORD? Or who will stand in his holy place?
4 He that has clean hands, and a pure heart; who has not lifted up his soul unto vanity, or sworn deceitfully.
5 He will receive the blessing from the LORD, and righteousness from the God of his salvation.
6 This *is* the generation of them that seek him, that seek your face, O Jacob. Selah.

---
[1] lit. home of tender green grass. Compare **Zec. 10:1**, **Rev. 8:7** & **9:4**.

7 Lift up your heads, O you gates; and be you lift up, you everlasting doors; and the King of glory will come in.
8 Who *is* this King of glory? The LORD strong and mighty, the LORD mighty in battle.
9 Lift up your heads, O you gates; even lift *them* up, you everlasting doors; and the King of glory will come in.
10 Who is this King of glory? The LORD of hosts, he *is* the King of glory. Selah.

PSALM 25
A Psalm of David.

1 Unto you, O LORD, do I lift up my soul.
2 O my God, I trust in you: let me not be ashamed, let not mine enemies triumph over me.
3 Yea, let none that wait on you be ashamed: let them be ashamed which transgress without cause.
4 show me your ways, O LORD; teach me your paths.
5 Lead me in your truth, and teach me: for you are the God of my salvation; on you do I wait all the day.
6 Remember, O LORD, your tender mercies and your loving kindnesses; for they *have been* ever of old.
7 Remember not the sins of my youth, or my transgressions: according to your mercy remember you me for your goodness' sake, O LORD.
8 Good and upright *is* the LORD: therefore will he teach sinners in the way.
9 The meek will he guide in judgment: and the meek will he teach his way.
10 All the paths of the LORD *are* mercy and truth unto such as keep his covenant and his testimonies.
11 For your name's sake, O LORD, pardon mine iniquity; for it *is* great.
12 What man *is* he that fears the LORD? Him will he teach in the way *that* he will choose.
13 His soul will dwell at ease; and his seed will inherit the earth.
14 The secret of the LORD *is* with them that fear him; and he will show them his covenant.
15 Mine eyes *are* ever toward the LORD; for he will pluck my feet out of the net.
16 Turn you unto me, and have mercy upon me; for I *am* desolate and afflicted.
17 The troubles of my heart are enlarged: *O* bring you me out of my distresses.
18 Look upon mine affliction and my pain; and forgive all my sins.
19 Consider mine enemies; for they are many; and they hate me with cruel hatred.
20 O keep my soul, and deliver me: let me not be ashamed; for I put my trust in you.
21 Let integrity and uprightness preserve me; for I wait on you.
22 Redeem Israel, O God, out of all his troubles.

PSALM 26
A Psalm of David.

1 Judge me, O LORD; for I have walked in mine integrity: I have trusted also in the LORD; *therefore* I will not slide.
2 Examine me, O LORD, and prove me; try my reins and my heart.
3 For your loving-kindness *is* before mine eyes: and I have walked in your truth.
4 I have not sat with vain persons, neither will go in with dissemblers.
5 I have hated the congregation of evil doers; and will not sit with the wicked.
6 I will wash mine hands in innocency[1]: so will I compass your altar, O LORD:
7 That I may publish with the voice of thanksgiving, and tell of all your wondrous works.
8 LORD, I have loved the habitation of your house, and the place where your honor dwells.
9 Gather not my soul with sinners, or my life with bloody men:
10 In whose hands *is* mischief, and their right hand is full of bribes.
11 But as for me, I will walk in mine integrity: redeem me, and be merciful unto me.
12 My foot stands in an even place: in the congregations will I bless the LORD.

PSALM 27
A Psalm of David.

1 The LORD *is* my light and my salvation; whom will I fear? The LORD *is* the strength of my life; of whom will I be afraid?
2 When the wicked, *even* mine enemies and my foes, came upon me to eat up my flesh, they stumbled and fell.
3 Though a host should encamp against me, my heart will not fear: though war should rise against me, in this *will* I *be* confident.
4 One *thing* have I desired of the LORD, that will I seek after; that I may dwell in the house of the LORD all the days of my life, to behold the beauty of the LORD, and to enquire in his temple.
5 For in the time of trouble he will hide me in his pavilion: in the secret of his tabernacle will he hide me; he will set me up upon a rock.
6 And now will mine head be lifted up above mine enemies round about me: therefore will I offer in his tabernacle sacrifices of joy; I will sing, yea, I will sing praises unto the LORD.
7 Hear, O LORD, *when* I cry with my voice: have mercy also upon me, and answer me.
8 *When you said*, Seek you my face; my heart said unto you, your face, LORD, will I seek.
9 Hide not your face *far* from me; put not your servant away in anger: you have been my help; leave me not, neither forsake me, O God of my salvation.
10 When my father and my mother forsake me, then the LORD will take me up.
11 Teach me your way, O LORD, and lead me in a plain path, because of mine enemies.
12 Deliver me not over unto the will of mine enemies: for false witnesses are risen up against me, and such as breathe out cruelty.
13 *I had fainted*, unless I had believed to see the goodness of the LORD in the land of the living.
14 Wait on the LORD: be of good courage, and he will strengthen your heart: wait, I say, on the LORD.

PSALM 28
A Psalm of David.

1 Unto you will I cry, O LORD my rock; be not silent to me: lest, *if* you be silent to me, I become like them that go down into the pit.

---

[1] innocency- literally defined as clearness or cleanness. [Strgs#5356]

2 Hear the voice of my supplications, when I cry unto you, when I lift up my hands toward your holy oracle.
3 Draw me not away with the wicked, and with the workers of iniquity, which speak peace to their neighbors, but mischief *is* in their hearts.
4 Give them according to their deeds, and according to the wickedness of their endeavors: give them after the work of their hands; render to them their desert.
5 Because they regard not the works of the LORD, or the operation of his hands, he will destroy them, and not build them up.
6 Blessed *be* the LORD, because he has heard the voice of my supplications.
7 The LORD *is* my strength and my shield; my heart trusted in him, and I am helped: therefore my heart greatly rejoices; and with my song will I praise him.
8 The LORD *is* their strength, and he *is* the saving strength of his anointed.
9 Save your people, and bless your inheritance: feed them also, and lift them up forever.

PSALM 29
A Psalm of David.

1 Give unto the LORD, O you mighty, give unto the LORD glory and strength.
2 Give unto the LORD the glory due unto his name; worship the LORD in the beauty of holiness.
3 The voice of the LORD *is* upon the waters: the God of glory thunders: the LORD *is* upon many waters.
4 The voice of the LORD *is* powerful; the voice of the LORD *is* full of majesty.
5 The voice of the LORD breaks the cedars; yea, the LORD breaks the cedars of Lebanon.
6 He makes them also to skip like a calf; Lebanon and Sirion like a young unicorn.
7 The voice of the LORD divides the flames of fire.
8 The voice of the LORD shakes the wilderness; the LORD shakes the wilderness of Kadesh.
9 The voice of the LORD makes the hinds to calve, and discovers the forests: and in his temple does every one speak of *his* glory.
10 The LORD sits upon the flood; yea, the LORD sits King forever.
11 The LORD will give strength unto his people; the LORD will bless his people with peace.

PSALM 30
A Psalm *and* Song *at* the dedication of the house of David.

1 I will extol you, O LORD; for you have lifted me up, and have not made my foes to rejoice over me.
2 O LORD my God, I cried unto you, and you have healed me.
3 O LORD, you have brought up my soul from the grave: you have kept me alive, that I should not go down to the pit.
4 Sing unto the LORD, O you saints of his, and give thanks at the remembrance of his holiness.
5 For his anger *endures but* a moment; in his favor *is* life: weeping may endure for a night, but joy *cometh* in the morning.
6 And in my prosperity I said, I will never be moved.
7 LORD, by your favor you have made my mountain to stand strong: you did hide your face, *and* I was troubled.
8 I cried to you, O LORD; and unto the LORD I made supplication.
9 What profit *is there* in my blood, when I go down to the pit? will the dust praise you? will it declare your truth?
10 Hear, O LORD, and have mercy upon me: LORD, be you my helper.
11 you have turned for me my mourning into dancing: you have put off my sackcloth, and girded me with gladness;
12 To the end that *my* glory may sing praise to you, and not be silent. O LORD my God, I will give thanks unto you forever.

PSALM 31
To the chief Musician, A Psalm of David.

1 In you, O LORD, do I put my trust; let me never be ashamed: deliver me in your righteousness.
2 Bow down your ear to me; deliver me speedily: be you my strong rock, for a house of defense to save me.
3 For you are my rock and my fortress; therefore for your name's sake lead me, and guide me.
4 Pull me out of the net that they have laid privily for me: for you are my strength.
5 Into your hand I commit my spirit: you have redeemed me, O LORD God of truth.
6 I have hated them that regard lying vanities: but I trust in the LORD.
7 I will be glad and rejoice in your mercy: for you have considered my trouble; you have known my soul in adversities;
8 And have not shut me up into the hand of the enemy: you have set my feet in a large room.
9 Have mercy upon me, O LORD, for I am in trouble: mine eye is consumed with grief, *yea*, my soul and my belly.
10 For my life is spent with grief, and my years with sighing: my strength fails because of mine iniquity, and my bones are consumed.
11 I was a reproach among all mine enemies, but especially among my neighbors, and a fear to mine acquaintance: they that did see me without fled from me.
12 I am forgotten as a dead man out of mind: I am like a broken vessel.
13 For I have heard the slander of many: fear *was* on every side: while they took counsel together against me, they devised to take away my life.
14 But I trusted in you, O LORD: I said, you are my God.
15 My times *are* in your hand: deliver me from the hand of mine enemies, and from them that persecute me.
16 Make your face to shine upon your servant: save me for your mercies' sake.
17 Let me not be ashamed, O LORD; for I have called upon you: let the wicked be ashamed, *and* let them be silent in the grave.
18 Let the lying lips be put to silence; which speak grievous things proudly and contemptuously against the righteous.
19 *Oh* how great *is* your goodness, which you have laid up for them that fear you; *which* you have wrought for them that trust in you before the sons of men!
20 you will hide them in the secret of your presence from the pride of man: you will keep them secretly in a pavilion from the strife of tongues.
21 Blessed *be* the LORD: for he has showed me his marvelous kindness in a strong city.
22 For I said in my haste, I am cut off from before your eyes: nevertheless you heard the voice of my supplications when I cried unto you.
23 O love the LORD, all you his saints: *for* the LORD preserves the faithful, and plentifully rewards the proud doer.

24 Be of good courage, and he will strengthen your heart, all you that hope in the LORD.

PSALM 32
A Psalm of David, Maschil.

1 Blessed *is he whose* transgression *is* forgiven, *whose* sin *is* covered.
2 Blessed *is* the man unto whom the LORD imputes not iniquity, and in whose spirit *there is* no guile.
3 When I kept silence, my bones waxed old through my roaring all the day long.
4 For day and night your hand was heavy upon me: my moisture is turned into the drought of summer. Selah.
5 I acknowledged my sin unto you, and mine iniquity have I not hid. I said, I will confess my transgressions unto the LORD; and you forgave the iniquity of my sin. Selah.
6 For this will every one that is godly pray unto you in a time when you may be found: surely in the floods of great waters they will not come nigh unto him.
7 you are my hiding place; you will preserve me from trouble; you will compass me about with songs of deliverance. Selah.
8 I will instruct you and teach you in the way which you will go: I will guide you with mine eye.
9 Be you not as the horse, *or* as the mule, *which* have no understanding: whose mouth must be held in with bit and bridle, lest they come near unto you.
10 Many sorrows will *be* to the wicked: but he that trusts in the LORD, mercy will compass him about.
11 Be glad in the LORD, and rejoice, you righteous: and shout for joy, all you *that are* upright in heart.

PSALM 33

1 Rejoice in the LORD, O you righteous: *for* praise is comely for the upright.
2 Praise the LORD with harp: sing unto him with the psaltery *and* an instrument of ten strings.
3 Sing unto him a new song; play skillfully with a loud noise.
4 For the word of the LORD *is* right; and all his works *are done* in truth.
5 He loves righteousness and judgment: the earth is full of the goodness of the LORD.
6 By the word of the LORD were the heavens made; and all the host of them by the breath of his mouth.
7 He gathers the waters of the sea together as an heap: he lays up the depth in storehouses.
8 Let all the earth fear the LORD: let all the inhabitants of the world stand in awe of him.
9 For he spoke, and it was *done*; he commanded, and it stood fast.
10 The LORD brings the counsel of the heathen to **break**: he makes the devices of the people of none effect.
11 The counsel of the LORD stands for ever, the thoughts of his heart to all generations.
12 Blessed *is* the nation whose God *is* the LORD; *and* the people *whom* he has chosen for his own inheritance.
13 The LORD looks from heaven; he **beheld** all the sons of men.
14 From the place of his habitation he looks upon all the inhabitants of the earth.
15 He fashions their hearts alike; he considers all their works.
16 There is no king saved by the multitude of a host: a mighty man is not delivered by much strength.
17 An horse *is* a vain thing for safety: neither will he deliver *any* by his great strength.
18 Behold, the eye of the LORD *is* upon them that fear him, upon them that hope in his mercy;
19 To deliver their soul from death, and to keep them alive in famine.
20 Our soul waits for the LORD: he *is* our help and our shield.
21 For our heart will rejoice in him, because we have trusted in his holy name.
22 Let your mercy, O LORD, be upon us, according as we hope in you.

PSALM 34
A Psalm of David, when he changed his behavior before Abimelech; who drove him away, and he departed.

1 I will bless the LORD at all times: his praise will continually *be* in my mouth.
2 My soul will make her boast in the LORD: the humble will hear *thereof*, and be glad.
3 O magnify the LORD with me, and let us exalt his name together.
4 I sought the LORD, and he heard me, and delivered me from all my fears.
5 They looked unto him, and were lightened: and their faces were not ashamed.
6 This poor man cried, and the LORD heard *him*, and saved him out of all his troubles.
7 The angel of the LORD encamps round about them that fear him, and delivers them.
8 O taste and see that the LORD *is* good: blessed *is* the man *that* trusts in him.
9 O fear the LORD, you his saints: for *there is* no want to them that fear him.
10 The young lions do lack, and suffer hunger: but they that seek the LORD will not want any good *thing*.
11 Come, you children, hearken unto me: I will teach you the fear of the LORD.
12 What man *is he that* desires life, *and* loves *many* days, that he may see good?
13 Keep your tongue from evil, and your lips from speaking guile.
14 Depart from evil, and do good; seek peace, and pursue it.
15 The eyes of the LORD *are* upon the righteous, and his ears *are open* unto their cry.
16 The face of the LORD *is* against them that do evil, to cut off the remembrance of them from the earth.
17 *The righteous* cry, and the LORD hears, and delivers them out of all their troubles.
18 The LORD *is* nigh unto them that are of a broken heart; and saves such as be of a contrite spirit.
19 Many *are* the afflictions of the righteous: but the LORD delivered him out of them all.
20 He keeps all his bones: not one of them is broken.
21 Evil will slay the wicked: and they that hate the righteous will be desolate.
22 The LORD redeems the soul of his servants: and none of them that trust in him will be desolate.

PSALM 35
A Psalm of David.

1 Plead *my cause*, O LORD, with them that strive with me: fight against them that fight against me.

2 Take hold of shield and buckler, and stand up for mine help.
3 Draw out also the spear, and stop *the way* against them that persecute me: say unto my soul, I *am* your salvation.
4 Let them be confounded and put to shame that seek after my soul: let them be turned back and brought to confusion that devise my hurt.
5 Let them be as chaff before the wind: and let the angel of the LORD chase *them*.
6 Let their way be dark and slippery: and let the angel of the LORD persecute them.
7 For without cause have they hid for me their net *in* a pit, *which* without cause they have **dug** for my soul.
8 Let destruction come upon him at unawares; and let his net that he has hid catch himself: into that very destruction let him fall.
9 And my soul will be joyful in the LORD: it will rejoice in his salvation.
10 All my bones will say, LORD, who *is* like unto you, which delivers the poor from him that is too strong for him, yea, the poor and the needy from him that spoils him?
11 False witnesses did rise up; they laid to my charge *things* that I knew not.
12 They rewarded me evil for good *to* the spoiling of my soul.
13 [But as for me, when they were sick, my clothing *was* sackcloth: I humbled my soul with fasting; and my prayer returned into mine own bosom.]¹
14 I behaved myself as though *he had been* my friend *or* brother: I bowed down heavily, as one that mourns *for his* mother.
15 But in mine adversity they rejoiced, and gathered themselves together: *yes*, the **smiters** gathered themselves together against me, and I knew *it* not; they did tear *me*, and ceased not:
16 With hypocritical mockers in feasts, they gnashed upon me with their teeth.
17 Lord, how long will you look on? Rescue my soul from their destructions, my darling from the lions.
18 I will give you thanks in the great congregation: I will praise you among much people.
19 Let not them that are mine enemies wrongfully rejoice over me: *neither* let them wink with the eye that hate me without a cause.
20 For they speak not peace: but they devise deceitful matters against *them that are* quiet in the land.
21 Yea, they opened their mouth wide against me, *and* said, Aha, aha, our eye has seen *it*.
22 *This* you have seen, O LORD: keep not silence: O Lord, be not far from me.
23 Stir up yourself, and awake to my judgment, *even* unto my cause, my God and my Lord.
24 Judge me, O LORD my God, according to your righteousness; and let them not rejoice over me.
25 Let them not say in their hearts, Ah, so would we have it: let them not say, we have swallowed him up.
26 Let them be ashamed and brought to confusion together that rejoice at mine hurt: let them be clothed with shame and dishonor that magnify *themselves* against me.
27 Let them shout for joy, and be glad, that favor my righteous cause: yea, let them say continually, let the LORD be magnified, which has pleasure in the prosperity of his servant.
28 And my tongue will speak of your righteousness *and* of your praise all the day long.

PSALM 36
To the chief Musician, *A Psalm* of David the servant of the LORD.

1 The transgression of the wicked said within my heart, *that there is* no fear of God before his eyes.
2 For he flatters himself in his own eyes, until his iniquity be found to be hateful.
3 The words of his mouth *are* iniquity and deceit: he has left off to be wise, *and* to do good.
4 He devises mischief upon his bed; he set himself in a way *that is* not good; he abhorred not evil.
5 your mercy, O LORD, *is* in the heavens; *and* your faithfulness *reaches* unto the clouds.
6 your righteousness *is* like the great mountains; your judgments *are* a great deep: O LORD, you preserves man and beast.
7 How excellent *is* your loving-kindness, O God! Therefore the children of men put their trust under the shadow of your wings.
8 They will be abundantly satisfied with the fatness of your house; and you will make them drink of the river of your pleasures
9 For with you *is* the fountain of life: in your light will we see light.
10 O continue your loving-kindness unto them that know you; and your righteousness to the upright in heart.
11 Let not the foot of pride come against me, and let not the hand of the wicked remove me.
12 There are the workers of iniquity fallen: they are cast down, and will not be able to rise.

PSALM 37
A Psalm of David.

1 Fret not yourself because of evildoers, neither be you envious against the workers of iniquity.
2 For they will soon be cut down like the grass², and wither as the green herb.
3 Trust in the LORD, and do good; *so* will you dwell in the land, and verily you will be fed.
4 Delight yourself also in the LORD; and he will give you the desires of your heart.
5 Commit your way unto the LORD; trust also in him; and he will bring *it* to pass.
6 And he will bring forth your righteousness as the light, and your judgment as the noonday.
7 Rest in the LORD, and wait patiently for him: fret not yourself because of him who prospers in his way, because of the man who brings wicked devices to pass.
8 Cease from anger, and forsake wrath: fret not yourself in any wise to do evil.
9 For evildoers will be cut off: but those that wait upon the LORD, they will inherit the earth.
10 For yet a little while, and the wicked will not *be*: yea, you will diligently consider his place, and it will not *be*.
11 But the meek will inherit the earth; and will delight themselves in the abundance of peace.
12 The wicked plots against the just, and **grinds** upon him with his teeth.
13 The Lord will laugh at him: for he sees that his day is coming.
14 The wicked have drawn out the sword, and have bent their bow, to cast down the poor and needy, *and* to slay such as be of upright conversation.

---

¹ compare Daniel 10:12

² compare 1Peter 1:24, Rev. 8:7, Is. 51:12 & Micah 5:7.

15 Their sword will enter into their own heart, and their bows will be broken.
16 A little that a righteous man has *is* better than the riches of many wicked.
17 For the arms of the wicked will be broken: but the LORD uphold the righteous.
18 The LORD knows the days of the upright: and their inheritance will be forever.
19 They will not be ashamed in the evil time: and in the days of famine they will be satisfied.
20 But the wicked will perish, and the enemies of the LORD will *be* as the fat of lambs: they will consume; into smoke will they consume away.
21 The wicked borrows, and pays not again: but the righteous shows mercy, and gives.
22 For *such as be* blessed of him will inherit the earth; and *they that be* cursed of him will be cut off.
23 The steps of a *good* man are ordered by the LORD: and he delights in his way.
24 Though he fall, he will not be utterly cast down: for the LORD uphold *him with* his hand.
25 I have been young, and *now* am old; yet have I not seen the righteous forsaken, or his seed begging bread.
26 *He is* ever merciful, and lends; and his seed *is* blessed.
27 Depart from evil, and do good; and dwell for evermore.
28 For the LORD loves judgment, and forsakes not his saints; they are preserved for ever: but the seed of the wicked will be cut off.
29 The righteous will inherit the land, and dwell therein forever.
30 The mouth of the righteous speaks wisdom, and his tongue talks of judgment.
31 The law of his God *is* in his heart; none of his steps will slide.
32 The wicked watches the righteous, and seeks to slay him.
33 The LORD will not leave him in his hand, or condemn him when he is judged.
34 Wait on the LORD, and keep his way, and he will exalt you to inherit the land: when the wicked are cut off, you will see *it*.
35 I have seen the wicked in great power, and spreading himself like a green bay tree.
36 Yet he passed away, and, lo, he *was* not: yea, I sought him, but he could not be found.
37 Mark the perfect *man*, and behold the upright: for the end of *that* man *is* peace.
38 But the transgressors will be destroyed together: the end of the wicked will be cut off.
39 But the salvation of the righteous *is* of the LORD: *he is* their strength in the time of trouble.
40 And the LORD will help them, and deliver them: he will deliver them from the wicked, and save them, because they trust in him.

PSALM 38

A Psalm of David, to bring to remembrance.

1 O LORD, rebuke me not in your wrath: neither chasten me in your hot displeasure.
2 For your arrows stick fast in me, and your hand presses me sore.
3 *There is* no soundness in my flesh because of your anger; neither *is there any* rest in my bones because of my sin.
4 For mine iniquities are gone over mine head: as a heavy burden they are too heavy for me.
5 My wounds stink *and* are corrupt because of my foolishness.
6 I am troubled; I am bowed down greatly; I go mourning all the day long.
7 For my loins are filled with a loathsome *disease*: and *there is* no soundness in my flesh.
8 I am feeble and sore broken: I have roared by reason of the disquietness[1] of my heart.
9 Lord, all my desire *is* before you; and my groaning is not hid from you.
10 My heart pants, my strength fails me: as for the light of mine eyes, it also is gone from me.
11 My lovers and my friends stand aloof from my sore; and my kinsmen stand afar off.
12 They also that seek after my life lay snares *for me*: and they that seek my hurt speak mischievous things, and imagine deceits all the day long.
13 But I, as a deaf *man*, heard not; and *I was* as a dumb man *that* opens not his mouth.
14 Thus I was as a man that hears not, and in whose mouth *are* no reproofs.
15 For in you, O LORD, do I hope: you will hear, O Lord my God.
16 For I said, *hear me*, lest *otherwise* they should rejoice over me: when my foot slips, they magnify *themselves* against me.
17 For I *am* ready to halt, and my sorrow *is* continually before me.
18 For I will declare mine iniquity; I will be sorry for my sin.
19 But mine enemies *are* lively, *and* they are strong: and they that hate me wrongfully are multiplied.
20 They also that render evil for good are mine adversaries; because I follow *the thing that* good *is*.
21 Forsake me not, O LORD: O my God, be not far from me.
22 Make haste to help me, O Lord my salvation.

PSALM 39

To the chief Musician, *even* to Jeduthun, A Psalm of David.

1 I said, I will take heed to my ways, that I sin not with my tongue: I will keep my mouth with a bridle, while the wicked is before me.
2 I was dumb with silence, I held my peace, *even* from good; and my sorrow was stirred.
3 My heart was hot within me, while I was musing the fire burned: *then* spoke I with my tongue,
4 LORD, make me to know mine end, and the measure of my days, what it *is; that* I may know how frail I *am*.
5 Behold, you have made my days *as* an handbreadth; and mine age *is* as nothing before you: verily every man at his best state *is* altogether vanity. Selah.
6 Surely every man walks in a vain show: surely they are disquieted in vain: he heaps up *riches*, and knows not who will gather them.
7 And now, Lord, what wait I for? My hope *is* in you.
8 Deliver me from all my transgressions: make me not the reproach of the foolish.
9 I was dumb, I opened not my mouth; because you did *it*.
10 Remove your stroke away from me: I am consumed by the blow of your hand.
11 When you with rebukes dost correct man for iniquity, you makes his beauty to consume away like a moth: surely every man *is* vanity. Selah.

---

[1] disquietness- to growl, groaning, snarling. [Strgs#5100]

12 Hear my prayer, O LORD, and give ear unto my cry; hold not your peace at my tears: for I *am* a stranger with you, *and* a sojourner, as all my fathers *were*.
13 O spare me, that I may recover strength, before I go hence, and be no more.

PSALM 40

To the chief Musician, A Psalm of David.

1 I waited patiently for the LORD; and he inclined unto me, and heard my cry.
2 He brought me up also out of a horrible pit, out of the miry clay, and set my feet upon a rock, *and* established my goings.
3 And he has put a new song in my mouth, *even* praise unto our God: many will see *it*, and fear, and will trust in the LORD.
4 Blessed *is* that man that makes the LORD his trust, and respects not the proud, or such as turn aside to lies.
5 Many, O LORD my God, *are* your wonderful works *which* you have done, and your thoughts *which are* to us-ward: they cannot be reckoned up in order unto you: *if* I would declare and speak *of them*, they are more than can be numbered.
6 Sacrifice and offering you did not desire; mine ears have you opened: burnt offering and sin offering have you not required.
7 Then said I, Lo, I come: in the volume of the book *it is* written of me,
8 I delight to do your will, O my God: yea, your law *is* within my heart.
9 I have preached righteousness in the great congregation: lo, I have not refrained my lips, O LORD, you knows.
10 I have not hid your righteousness within my heart; I have declared your faithfulness and your salvation: I have not concealed your loving-kindness and your truth from the great congregation.
11 Withhold not you your tender mercies from me, O LORD: let your loving-kindness and your truth continually preserve me.
12 For innumerable evils have compassed me about: mine iniquities have taken hold upon me, so that I am not able to look up; they are more than the hairs of mine head: therefore my heart fails me.
13 Be pleased, O LORD, to deliver me: O LORD, make haste to help me.
14 Let them be ashamed and confounded together that seek after my soul to destroy it; let them be driven backward and put to shame that wish me evil.
15 Let them be desolate for a reward of their shame that say unto me, Aha, aha.
16 Let all those that seek you rejoice and be glad in you: let such as love your salvation say continually, The LORD be magnified.
17 But I *am* poor and needy; *yet* the Lord thinks upon me: you are my help and my deliverer; make no tarrying, O my God.

PSALM 41

To the chief Musician, A Psalm of David.

1 Blessed *is* he that considers the poor: the LORD will deliver him in time of trouble.
2 The LORD will preserve him, and keep him alive; *and* he will be blessed upon the earth: and you will not deliver him unto the will of his enemies.
3 The LORD will strengthen him upon the bed of languishing: you will make all his bed in his sickness.
4 I said, LORD, be merciful unto me: heal my soul; for I have sinned against you.
5 Mine enemies speak evil of me, when will he die, and his name perish?
6 And if he come to see *me*, he speaks vanity: his heart gathers iniquity to itself; *when* he goes abroad, he tells *it*.
7 All that hate me whisper together against me: against me do they devise my hurt.
8 An evil disease, *say they*, cleaves fast unto him: and *now* that he lies he will rise up no more.
9 Yea, mine own familiar friend, in whom I trusted, which did eat of my bread, has lifted up *his* heel against me.
10 But you, O LORD, be merciful unto me, and raise me up, that I may requite[1] them.
11 By this I know that you favors me, because mine enemy does not triumph over me.
12 And as for me, you uphold me in mine integrity, and set me before your face forever.
13 Blessed *be* the LORD God of Israel from everlasting, and to everlasting. Amen, and Amen.

PSALM 42

To the chief Musician, Maschil, for the sons of Korah.

1 As the **ram longs** after the water brooks, so **longs** my soul after you, O God.
2 My soul thirsts for God, for the living God: when will I come and appear before God?
3 My tears have been my meat day and night, while they continually say unto me, where *is* your God?
4 When I remember these *things*, I pour out my soul in me: for I had gone with the multitude, I went with them to the house of God, with the voice of joy and praise, with a multitude that kept holyday.
5 Why are you cast down, O my soul? And *why* are you disquieted in me? Hope you in God: for I will yet praise him *for* the help of his countenance.
6 O my God, my soul is cast down within me: therefore will I remember you from the land of Jordan, and of the Hermonites, from the hill Mizar.
7 Deep calls unto deep at the noise of your waterspouts: all your waves and your billows are gone over me.
8 *Yet* the LORD will command his loving-kindness in the daytime, and in the night his song will *be* with me, *and* my prayer unto the God of my life.
9 I will say unto God my rock, why have you forgotten me? why go I mourning because of the oppression of the enemy?
10 *As* with a sword in my bones, mine enemies reproach me; while they say daily unto me, where *is* your God?
11 Why are you cast down, O my soul? And why are you disquieted within me? Hope you in God: for I will yet praise him, *who is* the health of my countenance, and my God.

PSALM 43

1 Judge me, O God, and plead my cause against an ungodly nation: O deliver me from the deceitful and unjust man.
2 For you are the God of my strength: why dost you cast me off? why go I mourning because of the oppression of the enemy?

---

[1] requite- a primitive root to be safe (in mind, body or estate); figuratively to be completed; by implication to be friendly, make amends, peaceable, that is perfect, render, restore. [Strgs#7999]

3 O send out your light and your truth: let them lead me; let them bring me unto your holy hill, and to your tabernacles.
4 Then will I go unto the altar of God, unto God my exceeding joy: yea, upon the harp will I praise you, O God my God.
5 Why are you cast down, O my soul? And why are you disquieted within me? hope in God: for I will yet praise him, *who is* the health of my countenance, and my God.

PSALM 44

To the chief Musician for the sons of Korah, Maschil.

1 We have heard with our ears, O God, our fathers have told us, *what* work you did in their days, in the times of old.
2 *How* you did drive out the heathen with your hand, and planted them; *how* you did afflict the people, and cast them out.
3 For they got not the land in possession by their own sword, neither did their own arm save them: but your right hand, and your arm, and the light of your countenance, because you had a favor unto them.
4 you are my King, O God: command deliverances for Jacob.
5 Through you will we push down our enemies: through your name will we tread them under that rise up against us.
6 For I will not trust in my bow, neither will my sword save me.
7 But you have saved us from our enemies, and have put them to shame that hated us.
8 In God we boast all the day long, and praise your name for ever. Selah.
9 But you have cast off, and put us to shame; and go not forth with our armies.
10 You makes us to turn back from the enemy: and they which hate us spoil for themselves.
11 You have given us like sheep *appointed* for meat; and have scattered us among the heathen.
12 You sells your people for **riches**, and do not increase your *wealth* by their price.
13 You make us a reproach to our neighbors, a scorn and a derision to them that are round about us.
14 You make us a byword among the heathen, a shaking of the head among the people.
15 My confusion *is* continually before me, and the shame of my face has covered me,
16 For the voice of him that reproaches and blasphemes; by reason of the enemy and avenger.
17 All this is come upon us; yet have we not forgotten you, neither have we dealt falsely in your covenant.
18 Our heart is not turned back, neither have our steps declined from your way;
19 Though you have sore broken us in the place of dragons, and covered us with the shadow of death.
20 If we have forgotten the name of our God, or stretched out our hands to a strange god;
21 will not God search this out? For he knows the secrets of the heart.
22 Yea, for your sake are we killed all day long; we are counted as sheep for the slaughter.
23 Awake, why sleeps you, O Lord? Arise, cast *us* not off for ever.
24 Wherefore hide you your face, *and* forgets our affliction and our oppression?
25 For our soul is bowed down to the dust: our belly cleaves unto the earth.
26 Arise for our help, and redeem us for your mercies' sake.

PSALM 45

To the chief Musician upon Shoshannim, for the sons of Korah, Maschil, A Song of loves.

1 My heart is **gushing** a good matter: I speak of the things which I have made touching the king: my tongue *is* the pen of a ready writer.
2 You are fairer than the children of men: grace is poured into your lips: therefore God has blessed you forever.
3 Gird your sword upon your thigh, O *most* mighty, with your glory and your majesty.
4 And in your majesty ride prosperously because of truth and meekness *and* righteousness; and your right hand will teach you terrible things.
5 your arrows *are* sharp in the heart of the king's enemies; *whereby* the people fall under you.
6 your throne, O God, *is* forever and ever: the scepter of your kingdom *is* a right scepter.
7 you love righteousness, and hate wickedness: therefore God, your God, has anointed you with the oil of gladness above your fellows.
8 All your garments *smell* of myrrh, and aloes, *and* cassia, out of the ivory palaces, whereby they have made you glad.
9 Kings' daughters *were* among your honorable women: upon your right hand did stand the queen in gold of Ophir.
10 Hearken, O daughter, and consider, and incline your ear; forget also your own people, and your father's house;
11 So will the king greatly desire your beauty: for he is your Lord; and worship you him.
12 And the daughter of Tyre¹ will *be there* with a gift; *even* the rich among the people will intreat² your favor.
13 The king's daughter *is* all glorious within: her clothing *is* of wrought gold.
14 She will be brought unto the king in raiment of needlework: the virgins her companions that follow her will be brought unto you.
15 With gladness and rejoicing will they be brought: they will enter into the king's palace.
16 Instead of your fathers will be your children, whom you may make princes in all the earth.
17 I will make your name to be remembered in all generations: therefore will the people praise you forever and ever.

PSALM 46

To the chief Musician for the sons of Korah, A Song upon Alamoth.

1 God *is* our refuge and strength, a very present help in trouble.
2 Therefore will not we fear, though the earth be removed, and though the mountains be carried into the midst of the sea;
3 *Though* the waters thereof roar *and* be troubled, though the mountains shake with the swelling thereof. Selah.
4 *There is* a river, the streams whereof will make glad the city of God, the holy *place* of the tabernacles of the most High.
5 God *is* in the midst of her; she will not be moved: God will help her, *and that* right early.

---

¹ Tyre or Tyrus- the Phoenician city on the Mediterranean coast. Its name means a rock. [Strgs#6865]
² intreat- to be rubbed or worn; hence to figuratively speak of weakness, sickness, afflicted or to grievous, to stroke, woman in travail to be wounded. [Strgs#2470]

6 The heathen raged, the kingdoms were moved: he uttered his voice, the earth melted.
7 The LORD of hosts *is* with us; the God of Jacob *is* our refuge. Selah.
8 Come, behold the works of the LORD, what desolations he has made in the earth.
9 He makes wars to cease unto the end of the earth; he breaks the bow, and cut the spear in sunder; he burn the chariot in the fire.
10 Be still, and know that I *am* God: I will be exalted among the heathen, I will be exalted in the earth.
11 The LORD of hosts *is* with us; the God of Jacob *is* our refuge. Selah.

PSALM 47
To the chief Musician, A Psalm for the sons of Korah.

1 O clap your hands, all you people; shout unto God with the voice of triumph.
2 For the LORD most high *is* terrible; *he is* a great King over all the earth.
3 He will subdue the people under us, and the nations under our feet.
4 He will choose our inheritance for us, the excellency of Jacob whom he loved. Selah.
5 God is gone up with a shout, the LORD with the sound of a trumpet.
6 Sing praises to God, sing praises: sing praises unto our King, sing praises.
7 For God *is* the King of all the earth: sing you praises with understanding.
8 God reigns over the heathen: God sits upon the throne of his holiness.
9 The princes of the people are gathered together, *even* the people of the God of Abraham: for the shields of the earth *belong* unto God: he is greatly exalted.

PSALM 48
A Song *and* Psalm for the sons of Korah.

1 Great *is* the LORD, and greatly to be praised in the city of our God, *in* the mountain of his holiness.
2 Beautiful for situation, the joy of the whole earth, *is* mount Zion, *on* the sides of the north, the city of the great King.
3 God is known in her palaces for a refuge.
4 For, lo, the kings were assembled, they passed by together.
5 They saw *it, and* so they marveled; they were troubled, *and* hasted away.
6 Fear took hold upon them there, *and* pain, as of a woman in travail.
7 You break the ships of Tarshish[1] with an east wind.
8 As we have heard, so have we seen in the city of the LORD of hosts, in the city of our God: God will establish it forever. Selah.
9 We have thought of your loving-kindness, O God, in the midst of your temple.
10 According to your name, O God, so *is* your praise unto the ends of the earth: your right hand is full of righteousness.
11 Let mount Zion rejoice, let the daughters of Judah be glad, because of your judgments.
12 Walk about Zion, and go round about her: tell the towers thereof.
13 Mark you well her bulwarks, consider her palaces; that you may tell *it* to the generation following.
14 For this God *is* our God forever and ever: he will be our guide *even* unto death.

PSALM 49
To the chief Musician, A Psalm for the sons of Korah.

1 Hear this, all you people; give ear, all you inhabitants of the world:
2 Both low and high, rich and poor, together.
3 My mouth will speak of wisdom; and the meditation of my heart will *be* of understanding.
4 I will incline mine ear to a parable: I will open my dark saying upon the harp.
5 Wherefore should I fear in the days of evil, *when* the iniquity of my heels will compass me about?
6 They that trust in their wealth, and boast themselves in the multitude of their riches;
7 None *of them* can by any means redeem his brother, or give to God a ransom for him:
8 (For the redemption of their soul *is* precious, and it ceases forever:)
9 That he should still live forever, *and* not see corruption.
10 For he sees *that* wise men die, likewise the fool and the brutish person perish, and leave their wealth to others.
11 Their inward thought *is, that* their houses will continue forever, *and* their dwelling places to all generations; they call their lands after their own names.
12 Nevertheless man *being* in honor abides not: he is like the beasts *that* perish.
13 This their way *is* their folly: yet their posterity approve their sayings. Selah.
14 Like sheep they are laid in the grave; death will feed on them; and the upright will have dominion over them in the morning; and their beauty will consume in the grave from their dwelling.
15 But God will redeem my soul from the power of the grave: for he will receive me. Selah.
16 Be not you afraid when one is made rich, when the glory of his house is increased;
17 For when he dies he will carry nothing away: his glory will not descend after him.
18 Though while he lived he blessed his soul: and *men* will praise you, when you doest well to yourself.
19 He will go to the generation of his fathers; they will never see light.
20 Man *that is* in honor, and understands not, is like the beasts *that* perish.

PSALM 50
A Psalm of Asaph.

1 The mighty God, *even* the LORD, has spoken, and called the earth from the rising of the sun unto the going down thereof.
2 Out of Zion, the perfection of beauty, God has shined.
3 Our God will come, and will not keep silence: a fire will devour before him, and it will be very tempestuous round about him.

---

[1] Tarshish- the name of a type of ship that carried great wealth (**II Chr. 20:35**; **Is. 2:16-17**), a city or territory (**II Chr. 9:21**; **Ps. 72:10**), a man (**Esth. 1:14**) and a precious stone in the Old Testament (**Ex. 28:20**, **Ezek. 1:16**; **28:13**, **Dan. 10:6**). [Strgs#8659]

4 He will call to the heavens from above, and to the earth, that he may judge his people.
5 Gather my saints together unto me; those that have made a covenant with me by sacrifice.
6 And the heavens will declare his righteousness: for God *is* judge himself. Selah.
7 Hear, O my people, and I will speak; O Israel, and I will testify against you: I *am* God, *even* your God.
8 I will not reprove you for your sacrifices or your burnt offerings, *to have been* continually before me.
9 I will take no bullock out of your house, or he goats out of your folds.
10 For every beast of the forest *is* mine, *and* the cattle upon a thousand hills.
11 I know all the fowls of the mountains: and the wild beasts of the field *are* mine.
12 If I were hungry, I would not tell you: for the world *is* mine, and the fullness thereof.
13 Will I eat the flesh of bulls, or drink the blood of goats?
14 Offer unto God thanksgiving; and pay your vows unto the most High:
15 And call upon me in the day of trouble: I will deliver you, and you will glorify me.
16 But unto the wicked God said, what have you to do to declare my statutes, or *that* you should take my covenant in your mouth?
17 Seeing you hate instruction, and cast my words behind you.
18 When you saw a thief, then you consented with him, and have been partaker with adulterers.
19 You give your mouth to evil, and your tongue frames deceit.
20 You sit *and* speak against your brother; you slander your own mother's son.
21 These *things* have you done, and I kept silence; you thought that I was altogether *such a one* as yourself: *but* I will reprove you, and set *them* in order before your eyes.
22 Now consider this, you that forget God, lest I tear *you* in pieces, and *there be* none to deliver.
23 Whoso offers praise glorifies me: and to him that orders *his* conversation *aright* will I show the salvation of God.

PSALM 51

To the chief Musician, A Psalm of David, when Nathan the prophet came unto him, after he had gone in to Bath-sheba.

1 Have mercy upon me, O God, according to your loving-kindness: according unto the multitude of your tender mercies blot out my transgressions.
2 Wash me thoroughly from mine iniquity, and cleanse me from my sin.
3 For I acknowledge my transgressions: and my sin *is* ever before me.
4 Against you, you only, have I sinned, and done *this* evil in your sight: that you might be justified when you speaks, *and* be clear when you judges.
5 Behold, I was shapen[1] in iniquity; and in sin did my mother conceive me.
6 Behold, you desire truth in the inward parts: and in the hidden *part* you will make me to know wisdom.

7 Purge me with hyssop, and I will be clean: wash me, and I will be whiter than snow.
8 Make me to hear joy and gladness; *that* the bones *which* you have broken may rejoice.
9 Hide your face from my sins, and blot out all mine iniquities.
10 Create in me a clean heart, O God; and renew a right spirit within me.
11 Cast me not away from your presence; and take not your holy spirit from me.
12 Restore unto me the joy of your salvation; and uphold me *with your* free spirit.
13 *Then* will I teach transgressors your ways; and sinners will be converted unto you.
14 Deliver me from blood guiltiness, O God, you God of my salvation: *and* my tongue will sing aloud of your righteousness.
15 O Lord, open you my lips; and my mouth will show forth your praise.
16 For you desires not sacrifice; else would I give *it*: you delight not in burnt offering.
17 The sacrifices of God *are* a broken spirit: a broken and a contrite heart, O God, you will not despise.
18 Do good in your good pleasure unto Zion: build you the walls of Jerusalem.
19 Then will you be pleased with the sacrifices of righteousness, with burnt offering and whole burnt offering: then will they offer bullocks upon your altar.

PSALM 52

To the chief Musician, Maschil, *A Psalm* of David, when Doeg the Edomite came and told Saul, and said unto him, David is come to the house of Ahimelech.

1 Why boast you yourself in mischief, O mighty man? the goodness of God *endures* continually.
2 Your tongue devises mischiefs; like a sharp razor, working deceitfully.
3 You love evil more than good; *and* lying rather than to speak righteousness. Selah.
4 You love all devouring words, O you deceitful tongue.
5 God will likewise destroy you forever, he will take you away, and pluck you out of your dwelling place, and root you out of the land of the living. Selah.
6 The righteous also will see, and fear, and will laugh at him:
7 Lo, *this is* the man *that* made not God his strength; but trusted in the abundance of his riches, *and* strengthened himself in his wickedness.
8 But I *am* like a green olive tree in the house of God: I trust in the mercy of God forever and ever.
9 I will praise you forever, because you have done *it*: and I will wait on your name; for *it is* good before your saints.

PSALM 53

To the chief Musician upon Mahalath, Maschil, *A Psalm* of David.

1 The fool has said in his heart, *there is* no God. Corrupt are they, and have done abominable iniquity: *there is* none that doeth good.
2 God looked down from heaven upon the children of men, to see if there were *any* that did understand, that did seek God.

---

[1] shapen- comes from the Hebrew word *chûl*, <u>khool</u>; it translates as to twist, whirl (in a circular or spiral manner), to dance, to writhe in pain or fear, to figuratively wait, to pervert, bear, bring forth, dance, drive away, form, to be grievous, hope, travail, tremble, trust, wait carefully, to be wounded. [Strgs#2342]

3 Every one of them is gone back: they are altogether become filthy; *there is* none that doeth good, no, not one.
4 Have the workers of iniquity no knowledge? Who eat up my people *as* they eat bread: they have not called upon God.
5 There were they in great fear, *where* no fear was: for God has scattered the bones of him that encamps *against* you: you have put *them* to shame, because God has despised them.
6 Oh that the salvation of Israel *were* come out of Zion! When God brings back the captivity of his people, Jacob will rejoice, *and* Israel will be glad.

PSALM 54
To the chief Musician on Neginoth, Maschil, *A Psalm* of David, when the Ziphims came and said to Saul, does not David hide himself with us?

1 Save me, O God, by your name, and judge me by your strength.
2 Hear my prayer, O God; give ear to the words of my mouth.
3 For strangers are risen up against me, and oppressors seek after my soul: they have not set God before them. Selah.
4 Behold, God *is* mine helper: the Lord *is* with them that uphold my soul.
5 He will reward evil unto mine enemies: cut them off in your truth.
6 I will freely sacrifice unto you: I will praise your name, O LORD; for *it is* good.
7 For he has delivered me out of all trouble: and mine eye has seen *his desire* upon mine enemies.

PSALM 55
To the chief Musician on Neginoth, Maschil, *A Psalm* of David.

1 Give ear to my prayer, O God; and hide not yourself from my supplication.
2 Attend unto me, and hear me: I mourn in my complaint, and make a noise;
3 Because of the voice of the enemy, because of the oppression of the wicked: for they cast iniquity upon me, and in wrath they hate me.
4 My heart is sore pained within me: and the terrors of death are fallen upon me.
5 Fearfulness and trembling are come upon me, and horror has overwhelmed me.
6 And I said, Oh that I had wings like a dove! *For then* would I fly away, and be at rest.
7 Lo, *then* would I wander far off, *and* remain in the wilderness. Selah.
8 I would hasten my escape from the windy storm *and* tempest.
9 Destroy, O Lord, *and* divide their tongues: for I have seen violence and strife in the city.
10 Day and night they go about it upon the walls thereof: mischief also and sorrow *are* in the midst of it.
11 Wickedness *is* in the midst thereof: deceit and guile depart not from her streets.
12 For *it was* not an enemy *that* reproached me; then I could have borne *it*: neither *was it* he that hated me *that* did magnify *himself* against me; then I would have hid myself from him:
13 But *it was* you, a man mine equal, my guide, and mine acquaintance.
14 We took sweet counsel together, *and* walked unto the house of God in company.
15 Let death seize upon them, *and* let them go down quick into hell: for wickedness *is* in their dwellings, *and* among them.
16 As for me, I will call upon God; and the LORD will save me.
17 Evening, and morning, and at noon, will I pray, and cry aloud: and he will hear my voice.
18 He has delivered my soul in peace from the battle *that was* against me: for there were many with me.
19 God will hear, and afflict them, even he that abides of old. Selah. Because they have no changes, therefore they fear not God.
20 He has put forth his hands against such as be at peace with him: he has broken his covenant.
21 *The words* of his mouth were smoother than butter, but war *was* in his heart: his words were softer than oil, yet *were* they drawn swords.
22 Cast your burden upon the LORD, and he will sustain you: he will never suffer the righteous to be moved.
23 But you, O God, will bring them down into the pit of destruction: bloody and deceitful men will not live out half their days; but I will trust in you.

PSALM 56
To the chief Musician upon Jonath-elem-rechokim, Michtam of David, when the Philistines took him in Gath.

1 Be merciful unto me, O God: for man would swallow me up; he fighting daily oppresses me.
2 Mine enemies would daily swallow *me* up: for *they be* many that fight against me, O you most High.
3 What time I am afraid, I will trust in you.
4 In God I will praise his word, in God I have put my trust; I will not fear what flesh can do unto me.
5 Every day they wrest my words: all their thoughts *are* against me for evil.
6 They gather themselves together, they hide themselves, they mark my steps, when they wait for my soul.
7 will they escape by iniquity? In your anger cast down the people, O God.
8 You tell my wanderings: put you my tears into your bottle: *are they* not in your book?
9 When I cry *unto you*, then will mine enemies turn back: this I know; for God *is* for me.
10 In God will I praise *his* word: in the LORD will I praise *his* word.
11 In God have I put my trust: I will not be afraid what man can do unto me.
12 your vows *are* upon me, O God: I will render praises unto you.
13 For you have delivered my soul from death: will not you *deliver* my feet from falling, that I may walk before God in the light of the living?

PSALM 57
To the chief Musician, Al-taschith, Michtam of David, when he fled from Saul in the cave.

1 Be merciful unto me, O God, be merciful unto me: for my soul trusts in you: yea, in the shadow of your wings will I make my refuge, until *these* calamities be over past.
2 I will cry unto God most high; unto God that performs *all things* for me.
3 He will send from heaven, and save me *from* the reproach of him that would swallow me up. Selah. God will send forth his mercy and his truth.

4 My soul *is* among lions: and I lie *even* among them that are set on fire, *even* the sons of men, whose teeth *are* spears and arrows, and their tongue a sharp sword.
5 Be you exalted, O God, above the heavens; *let* your glory *be* above all the earth.
6 They have prepared a net for my steps; my soul is bowed down: they have **dug** a pit before me, into the midst whereof they are fallen *themselves*. Selah.
7 My heart is fixed, O God, my heart is fixed: I will sing and give praise.
8 Awake up, my glory; awake, psaltery and harp: I *myself* will awake early.
9 I will praise you, O Lord, among the people: I will sing unto you among the nations.
10 For your mercy *is* great unto the heavens, and your truth unto the clouds.
11 Be you exalted, O God, above the heavens: *let* your glory *be* above all the earth.

PSALM 58
To the chief Musician, Al-taschith, Michtam of David.

1 Do you indeed speak righteousness, O congregation? Do you judge uprightly, O you sons of men?
2 Yea, in heart you work wickedness; you weigh the violence of your hands in the earth.
3 The wicked are estranged from the womb: they go astray as soon as they be born, speaking lies.
4 Their poison *is* like the poison of a serpent: *they are* like the deaf adder *that* stops her ear;
5 Which will not hearken to the voice of charmers, charming never so wisely.
6 Break their teeth, O God, in their mouth: break out the great teeth of the young lions, O LORD.
7 Let them melt away as waters *which* run continually: *when* he bends *his bow to shoot* his arrows, let them be as cut in pieces.
8 As a snail *which* melts, let *every one of them* pass away: *like* the untimely birth of a woman, *that* they may not see the sun.
9 Before your pots can feel the thorns, he will take them away as with a whirlwind, both living, and in *his* wrath.
10 The righteous will rejoice when he sees the vengeance: he will wash his feet in the blood of the wicked.
11 So that a man will say, Verily *there is* a reward for the righteous: verily he is a God that judges in the earth.

PSALM 59
To the chief Musician, Al-taschith, Michtam of David; when Saul sent, and they watched the house to kill him.

1 Deliver me from mine enemies, O my God: defend me from them that rise up against me.
2 Deliver me from the workers of iniquity, and save me from bloody men.
3 For, lo, they lie in wait for my soul: the mighty are gathered against me; not *for* my transgression, or *for* my sin, O LORD.
4 They run and prepare themselves without *my* fault: awake to help me, and behold.
5 you therefore, O LORD God of hosts, the God of Israel, awake to visit all the heathen: be not merciful to any wicked transgressors. Selah.
6 They return at evening: they make a noise like a dog, and go round about the city.
7 Behold, they belch out with their mouth: swords *are* in their lips: for who, *say they*, does hear?
8 But you, O LORD, will laugh at them; you will have all the heathen in derision.
9 *Because of* his strength will I wait upon you: for God *is* my defence.
10 The God of my mercy will prevent me: God will let me see *my desire* upon mine enemies.
11 Slay them not, lest my people forget: scatter them by your power; and bring them down, O Lord our shield.
12 *For* the sin of their mouth *and* the words of their lips let them even be taken in their pride: and for cursing and lying *which* they speak.
13 Consume *them* in wrath, consume *them*, that they *may* not *be*: and let them know that God rules in Jacob unto the ends of the earth. Selah.
14 And at evening let them return; *and* let them make a noise like a dog, and go round about the city.
15 Let them wander up and down for meat, and grudge if they be not satisfied.
16 But I will sing of your power; yea, I will sing aloud of your mercy in the morning: for you have been my defence and refuge in the day of my trouble.
17 Unto you, O my strength, will I sing: for God *is* my defence, *and* the God of my mercy.

PSALM 60
To the chief Musician upon Shushan-eduth, Michtam of David, to teach; when he strove with Aram-naharaim and with Aram-zobah, when Joab returned, and smote of Edom in the valley of salt twelve thousand.

1 O God, you have cast us off, you have scattered us, you have been displeased; O turn yourself to us again.
2 you have made the earth to tremble; you have broken it: heal the breaches thereof; for it shakes.
3 you have showed your people hard things: you have made us to drink the wine of astonishment.
4 you have given a banner to them that fear you, that it may be displayed because of the truth. Selah.
5 That your beloved may be delivered; save *with* your right hand, and hear me.
6 God has spoken in his holiness; I will rejoice, I will divide Shechem, and mete out the valley of Succoth.
7 Gilead *is* mine, and Manasseh *is* mine; Ephraim also *is* the strength of mine head; Judah *is* my lawgiver;
8 Moab *is* my wash pot; over Edom will I cast out my shoe: Philistia, triumph you because of me.
9 Who will bring me *into* the strong city? Who will lead me into Edom?
10 will not you, O God, *which* have cast us off? And you, O God, *which* did not go out with our armies?
11 Give us help from trouble: for vain *is* the help of man.
12 Through God we will do valiantly: for he *it is that* will tread down our enemies.

PSALM 61
To the chief Musician upon Neginah, *A Psalm* of David.

1 Hear my cry, O God; attend unto my prayer.
2 From the end of the earth will I cry unto you, when my heart is overwhelmed: lead me to the rock *that* is higher than I.

3 For you have been a shelter for me, *and* a strong tower from the enemy.
4 I will abide in your tabernacle for ever: I will trust in the covert of your wings. Selah.
5 For you, O God, have heard my vows: you have given *me* the heritage of those that fear your name.
6 you will prolong the king's life: *and* his years as many generations.
7 He will abide before God for ever: O prepare mercy and truth, *which* may preserve him.
8 So will I sing praise unto your name for ever, that I may daily perform my vows.

PSALM 62

To the chief Musician, to Jeduthun, A Psalm of David.

1 Truly my soul waits upon God: from him *cometh* my salvation.
2 He only *is* my rock and my salvation; *he is* my defence; I will not be greatly moved.
3 How long will you imagine mischief against a man? you will be slain all of you: as a bowing wall will you *be, and as* a tottering fence.
4 They only consult to cast *him* down from his excellency: they delight in lies: they bless with their mouth, but they curse inwardly. Selah.
5 My soul, wait you only upon God; for my expectation *is* from him.
6 He only *is* my rock and my salvation: *he is* my defence; I will not be moved.
7 In God *is* my salvation and my glory: the rock of my strength, *and* my refuge, *is* in God.
8 Trust in him at all times; you people, pour out your heart before him: God *is* a refuge for us. Selah.
9 Surely men of low degree *are* vanity, *and* men of high degree *are* a lie: to be laid in the balance, they *are* altogether *lighter* than vanity.
10 Trust not in oppression, and become not vain in robbery: if riches increase, set not your heart *upon them*.
11 God has spoken once; twice have I heard this; that power *belongs* unto God.
12 Also unto you, O Lord, *belongs* mercy: for you renders to every man according to his work.

PSALM 63

A Psalm of David, when he was in the wilderness of Judah.

1 O God, you are my God; early will I seek you: my soul thirsts for you, my flesh longs for you in a dry and thirsty land, where no water is;
2 To see your power and your glory, so *as* I have seen you in the sanctuary.
3 Because your loving-kindness *is* better than life, my lips will praise you.
4 Thus will I bless you while I live: I will lift up my hands in your name.
5 My soul will be satisfied as *with* marrow and fatness; and my mouth will praise you with joyful lips:
6 When I remember you upon my bed, *and* meditate on you in the *night* watches.
7 Because you have been my help, therefore in the shadow of your wings will I rejoice.
8 My soul follows hard after you: your right hand upholds me.

9 But those *that* seek my soul, to destroy *it*, will go into the lower parts of the earth.
10 They will fall by the sword: they will be a portion for foxes.
11 But the king will rejoice in God; every one that swears by him will glory: but the mouth of them that speak lies will be stopped.

PSALM 64

To the chief Musician, A Psalm of David.

1 Hear my voice, O God, in my prayer: preserve my life from fear of the enemy.
2 Hide me from the secret counsel of the wicked; from the insurrection of the workers of iniquity:
3 Who whet their tongue like a sword, *and* bend *their* bows *to* shoot their arrows, *even* bitter words:
4 That they may shoot in secret at the perfect: suddenly do they shoot at him, and fear not.
5 They encourage themselves *in* an evil matter: they commune of laying snares privily; they say, who will see them?
6 They search out iniquities; they accomplish a diligent search: both the inward *thought* of every one *of them*, and the heart, *is* deep.
7 But God will shoot at them *with* an arrow; suddenly will they be wounded.
8 So they will make their own tongue to fall upon themselves: all that see them will flee away.
9 And all men will fear, and will declare the work of God; for they will wisely consider of his doing.
10 The righteous will be glad in the LORD, and will trust in him; and all the upright in heart will glory.

PSALM 65

To the chief Musician, A Psalm *and* Song of David.

1 Praise waits for you, O God, in Sion: and unto you will the vow be performed.
2 O you that hears prayer, unto you will all flesh come.
3 Iniquities prevail against me: *as for* our transgressions, you will purge them away.
4 Blessed *is the man whom* you choose, and causes to approach *unto you, that* he may dwell in your courts: we will be satisfied with the goodness of your house, *even* of your holy temple.
5 *By* terrible things in righteousness will you answer us, O God of our salvation; *who are* the confidence of all the ends of the earth, and of them that are afar off *upon* the sea:
6 Which by his strength set fast the mountains; *being* girded with power:
7 Which stills the noise of the seas, the noise of their waves, and the tumult of the people.
8 They also that dwell in the uttermost parts are afraid at your tokens: you make the outgoings of the morning and evening to rejoice.
9 You visit the earth, and waters it: you greatly enriches it with the river of God, *which* is full of water: you prepares them corn, when you have so provided for it.
10 You water the ridges thereof abundantly: you settles the furrows thereof: you makest it soft with showers: you bless the springing thereof.
11 You crown the year with your goodness; and your paths drop fatness.
12 They drop *upon* the pastures of the wilderness: and the little hills rejoice on every side.

13 The pastures are clothed with flocks; the valleys also are covered over with corn; they shout for joy, they also sing.

PSALM 66

To the chief Musician, A Song *or* Psalm.

1 Make a joyful noise unto God, all you lands:
2 Sing forth the honor of his name: make his praise glorious.
3 Say unto God, How terrible are you *in* your works! Through the greatness of your power will your enemies submit themselves unto you.
4 All the earth will worship you, and will sing unto you; they will sing *to* your name. Selah.
5 Come and see the works of God: *he is* terrible *in his* doing toward the children of men.
6 He turned the sea into dry *land*: they went through the flood on foot: there did we rejoice in him.
7 He rules by his power for ever; his eyes behold the nations: let not the rebellious exalt themselves. Selah.
8 O bless our God, you people, and make the voice of his praise to be heard:
9 Which holds our soul in life, and suffers not our feet to be moved.
10 For you, O God, have proved us: you have tried us, as silver is tried.
11 you brought us into the net; you laid affliction upon our loins.
12 you have caused men to ride over our heads; we went through fire and through water: but you brought us out into a wealthy *place*.
13 I will go into your house with burnt offerings: I will pay you my vows,
14 Which my lips have uttered, and my mouth has spoken, when I was in trouble.
15 I will offer unto you burnt sacrifices of fatlings, with the incense of rams; I will offer bullocks with goats. Selah.
16 Come *and* hear, all you that fear God, and I will declare what he has done for my soul.
17 I cried unto him with my mouth, and he was extolled with my tongue.
18 If I regard iniquity in my heart, the Lord will not hear *me*:
19 *But* verily God has heard *me*; he has attended to the voice of my prayer.
20 Blessed *be* God, which has not turned away my prayer, or his mercy from me.

PSALM 67

To the chief Musician on Neginoth, A Psalm *or* Song.

1 God be merciful unto us, and bless us; *and* cause his face to shine upon us; Selah.
2 That your way may be known upon earth, your saving health among all nations.
3 Let the people praise you, O God; let all the people praise you.
4 O let the nations be glad and sing for joy: for you will judge the people righteously, and govern the nations upon earth. Selah.
5 Let the people praise you, O God; let all the people praise you.
6 *Then* will the earth yield her increase; *and* God, *even* our own God, will bless us.
7 God will bless us; and all the ends of the earth will fear him.

PSALM 68

To the chief Musician, A Psalm *or* Song of David.

1 Let God arise, let his enemies be scattered: let them also that hate him flee before him.
2 As smoke is driven away, *so* drive *them* away: as wax melts before the fire, *so* let the wicked perish at the presence of God.
3 But let the righteous be glad; let them rejoice before God: yea, let them exceedingly rejoice.
4 Sing unto God, sing praises to his name: extol him that rides upon the heavens by his name JAH, and rejoice before him.
5 A father of the fatherless, and a judge of the widows, *is* God in his holy habitation.
6 God sets the solitary in families: he brings out those which are bound with chains: but the rebellious dwell in a dry land.
7 O God, when you went forth before your people, when you did march through the wilderness; Selah:
8 The earth shook, the heavens also dropped at the presence of God: *even* Sinai itself *was* moved at the presence of God, the God of Israel.
9 You, O God, did send a plentiful rain, whereby you did confirm your inheritance, when it was weary.
10 your congregation has dwelt therein: you, O God, have prepared of your goodness for the poor.
11 The Lord gave the word: great *was* the company of those that published *it*.
12 Kings of armies did flee apace: and she that tarried at home divided the spoil.
13 Though you have lien among the pots, *yet will you be as* the wings of a dove covered with silver, and her feathers with yellow gold.
14 When the Almighty scattered kings in it, it was *white* as snow in Salmon.
15 The hill of God *is as* the hill of Bashan; an high hill *as* the hill of Bashan.
16 Why leap you, you high hills? *this is* the hill *which* God desires to dwell in; yea, the LORD will dwell *in it* for ever.
17 The chariots of God *are* twenty thousand, *even* thousands of angels[1]: the Lord *is* among them, *as in* Sinai, in the holy *place*.
18 you have ascended on high, you have led captivity captive: you have received gifts for men; yea, *for* the rebellious also, that the LORD God might dwell *among them*.
19 Blessed *be* the Lord, *who* daily loads us *with* benefits, *even* the God of our salvation. Selah.
20 *He that is* our God *is* the God of salvation; and unto GOD the Lord *belong* the issues from death.
21 But God will wound the head of his enemies, *and the* hairy scalp of such a one as goes on still in his trespasses.
22 The Lord said, I will bring again from Bashan, I will bring *my people* again from the depths of the sea:
23 That your foot may be dipped in the blood of your enemies, *and* the tongue of your dogs in the same.
24 They have seen your goings, O God; *even* the goings of my God, my King, in the sanctuary.
25 The singers went before, the players on instruments *followed* after; among *them were* the damsels playing with tambourines.
26 Bless you God in the congregations, *even* the Lord, from the fountain of Israel.
27 There *is* little Benjamin *with* their ruler, the princes of Judah *and* their council, the princes of Zebulun, *and* the princes of Naphtali.

---

[1] angels – is the Hebrew word *shin'ân* meaning *change, repetition* [Strgs#8136]. It comes from the root word *shânâ'* which translate as *alter*

[Strgs#8132]. Literally alters changes.

28 your God has commanded your strength: strengthen, O God, that which you have wrought for us.
29 Because of your temple at Jerusalem will kings bring presents unto you.
30 Rebuke the company of spearmen, the multitude of the bulls, with the calves of the people, *till every one* submit himself with pieces of silver: scatter you the people *that* delight in war.
31 Princes will come out of Egypt; Ethiopia will soon stretch out her hands unto God.
32 Sing unto God, you kingdoms of the earth; O sing praises unto the Lord; Selah:
33 To him that rides upon the heavens of heavens, *which were* of old; lo, he does send out his voice, *and that* a mighty voice.
34 Ascribe you strength unto God: his excellency *is* over Israel, and his strength *is* in the clouds.
35 O God, you *are* terrible out of your holy places: the God of Israel *is* he that gives strength and power unto *his* people. Blessed *be* God.

PSALM 69
To the chief Musician upon Shoshannim, *A Psalm* of David.

1 Save me, O God; for the waters are come in unto *my* soul.
2 I sink in deep mire, where *there is* no standing: I am come into deep waters, where the floods overflow me.
3 I am weary of my crying: my throat is dried: mine eyes fail while I wait for my God.
4 They that hate me without a cause are more than the hairs of mine head: they that would destroy me, *being* mine enemies wrongfully, are mighty: then I restored *that* which I took not away.
5 O God, you know my foolishness; and my sins are not hid from you.
6 Let not them that wait on you, O Lord GOD of hosts, be ashamed for my sake: let not those that seek you be confounded for my sake, O God of Israel.
7 Because for your sake I have borne reproach; shame has covered my face.
8 I am become a stranger unto my brethren, and an alien unto my mother's children.
9 For the zeal of your house has eaten me up; and the reproaches of them that reproached you are fallen upon me.
10 When I wept, *and chastened* my soul with fasting, that was to my reproach.
11 I made sackcloth also my garment; and I became a proverb to them.
12 They that sit in the gate speak against me; and I *was* the song of the drunkards.
13 But as for me, my prayer *is* unto you, O LORD, *in* an acceptable time: O God, in the multitude of your mercy hear me, in the truth of your salvation.
14 Deliver me out of the mire, and let me not sink: let me be delivered from them that hate me, and out of the deep waters.
15 Let not the water flood overflow me, neither let the deep swallow me up, and let not the pit shut her mouth upon me.
16 Hear me, O LORD; for your loving-kindness *is* good: turn unto me according to the multitude of your tender mercies.
17 And hide not your face from your servant; for I am in trouble: hear me speedily.
18 Draw nigh unto my soul, *and* redeem it: deliver me because of mine enemies.
19 you have known my reproach, and my shame, and my dishonor: mine adversaries *are* all before you.
20 Reproach has broken my heart; and I am full of heaviness: and I looked *for some* to take pity, but *there was* none; and for comforters, but I found none.
21 They gave me also gall for my meat; and in my thirst they gave me vinegar to drink.
22 Let their table become a snare before them: and *that which should have been* for *their* welfare, *let it become* a trap.
23 Let their eyes be darkened, that they see not; and make their loins continually to shake.
24 Pour out your indignation upon them, and let your wrathful anger take hold of them.
25 Let their habitation be desolate; *and* let none dwell in their tents.
26 For they persecute *him* whom you have smitten; and they talk to the grief of those whom you have wounded.
27 Add iniquity unto their iniquity: and let them not come into your righteousness.
28 Let them be blotted out of the book of the living, and not be written with the righteous.
29 But I *am* poor and sorrowful: let your salvation, O God, set me up on high.
30 I will praise the name of God with a song, and will magnify him with thanksgiving.
31 *This* also will please the LORD better than an ox *or* bullock that has horns and hoofs.
32 The humble will see *this, and* be glad: and your heart will live that seek God.
33 For the LORD hears the poor, and despises not his prisoners.
34 Let the heaven and earth praise him, the seas, and everything that moves therein.
35 For God will save Zion, and will build the cities of Judah: that they may dwell there, and have it in possession.
36 The seed also of his servants will inherit it: and they that love his name will dwell therein.

PSALM 70
To the chief Musician, *A Psalm* of David, to bring to remembrance.

1 *Make haste*, O God, to deliver me; make haste to help me, O LORD.
2 Let them be ashamed and confounded that seek after my soul: let them be turned backward, and put to confusion, that desire my hurt.
3 Let them be turned back for a reward of their shame that say, Aha, aha.
4 Let all those that seek you rejoice and be glad in you: and let such as love your salvation say continually, Let God be magnified.
5 But I *am* poor and needy: make haste unto me, O God: you are my help and my deliverer; O LORD, make no tarrying.

PSALM 71
1 In you, O LORD, do I put my trust: let me never be put to confusion.
2 Deliver me in your righteousness, and cause me to escape: incline your ear unto me, and save me.
3 Be you my strong habitation, whereunto I may continually resort: you have given commandment to save me; for you are my rock and my fortress.
4 Deliver me, O my God, out of the hand of the wicked, out of the hand of the unrighteous and cruel man.

5 For you are my hope, O Lord GOD: you *are* my trust from my youth.
6 By you have I been **held** up from the womb: you are he that took me out of my mother's bowels: my praise will *be* continually of you.
7 I am as a wonder unto many; but you are my strong refuge.
8 Let my mouth be filled *with* your praise *and with* your honor all the day.
9 Cast me not off in the time of old age; forsake me not when my strength fails.
10 For mine enemies speak against me; and they that lay wait for my soul take counsel together,
11 Saying, God has forsaken him: persecute and take him; for *there is* none to deliver *him*.
12 O God, be not far from me: O my God, make haste for my help.
13 Let them be confounded *and* consumed that are adversaries to my soul; let them be covered *with* reproach and dishonor that seek my hurt.
14 But I will hope continually, and will yet praise you more and more.
15 My mouth will show forth your righteousness *and* your salvation all the day; for I know not the numbers *thereof*.
16 I will go in the strength of the Lord GOD: I will make mention of your righteousness, *even* of your only.
17 O God, you have taught me from my youth: and hitherto have I declared your wondrous works.
18 Now also when I am old and gray headed, O God, forsake me not; until I have showed your strength unto *this* generation, *and* your power to everyone *that* is to come.
19 your righteousness also, O God, *is* very high, who have done great things: O God, who *is* like unto you!
20 Y*ou*, which have showed me great and sore troubles, will quicken me again, and will bring me up again from the depths of the earth.
21 you will increase my greatness, and comfort me on every side.
22 I will also praise you with the psaltery, *even* your truth, O my God: unto you will I sing with the harp, O you Holy One of Israel.
23 My lips will greatly rejoice when I sing unto you; and my soul, which you have redeemed.
24 My tongue also will talk of your righteousness all day long: for they are confounded, for they are brought unto shame, that seek my hurt.

PSALM 72

A *Psalm* for Solomon.

1 Give the king your judgments, O God, and your righteousness unto the king's son.
2 He will judge your people with righteousness, and your poor with judgment.
3 The mountains will bring peace to the people, and the little hills, by righteousness.
4 He will judge the poor of the people, he will save the children of the needy, and will break in pieces the oppressor.
5 They will fear you as long as the sun and moon endure, throughout all generations.
6 He will come down like rain upon the mown grass: as showers *that* water the earth.
7 In his days will the righteous flourish; and abundance of peace so long as the moon endures.
8 He will have dominion also from sea to sea, and from the river unto the ends of the earth.
9 They that dwell in the wilderness will bow before him; and his enemies will lick the dust.
10 The kings of Tarshish and of the isles will bring presents: the kings of Sheba and Seba will offer gifts.
11 Yea, all kings will fall down before him: all nations will serve him.
12 For he will deliver the needy when he cries; the poor also, and *him* that has no helper.
13 He will spare the poor and needy, and will save the souls of the needy.
14 He will redeem their soul from deceit and violence: and precious will their blood be in his sight.
15 And he will live, and to him will be given of the gold of Sheba: prayer also will be made for him continually; *and* daily will he be praised.
16 There will be an handful of corn in the earth upon the top of the mountains; the fruit thereof will shake like Lebanon: and *they* of the city will flourish like grass of the earth.
17 His name will endure for ever: his name will be continued as long as the sun: and *men* will be blessed in him: all nations will call him blessed.
18 Blessed *be* the LORD God, the God of Israel, who only doeth wondrous things.
19 And blessed *be* his glorious name for ever: and let the whole earth be filled *with* his glory; Amen, and Amen.
20 The prayers of David the son of Jesse are ended.

PSALM 73

A Psalm of Asaph.

1 Truly God *is* good to Israel, *even* to such as are of a clean heart.
2 But as for me, my feet were almost gone; my steps had well nigh slipped.
3 For I was envious at the foolish, *when* I saw the prosperity of the wicked.
4 For *there are* no bands in their death: but their strength *is* firm.
5 They *are* not in trouble *as other* men; neither are they plagued like *other* men.
6 Therefore pride compasses them about as a chair; violence covers them *as* a garment.
7 Their eyes stand out with fatness: they have more than heart could wish.
8 They are corrupt, and speak wickedly *concerning* oppression: they speak loftily.
9 They set their mouth against the heavens, and their tongue walks through the earth.
10 Therefore his people return here: and waters of a full *cup* are wrung out to them.
11 And they say, how does God know? And is there knowledge in the most High?
12 Behold, these *are* the ungodly, which prosper in the world; they increase *in* riches.
13 Verily I have cleansed my heart *in* vain, and washed my hands in innocency.
14 For all day long have I been plagued, and chastened every morning.
15 If I say, I will speak thus; behold, I should offend *against* the generation of your children.
16 When I thought to know this, it *was* too painful for me;
17 Until I went into the sanctuary of God; *then* understood I their end.

18 Surely you did set them in slippery places: you casted them down into destruction.
19 How are they *brought* into desolation, as in a moment! they are utterly consumed with terrors.
20 As a dream when *one* awakes; *so*, O Lord, when you awake, you will despise their image.
21 Thus my heart was grieved, and I was pricked in my reins.
22 So foolish *was* I, and ignorant: I was *as* a beast before you.
23 Nevertheless I *am* continually with you: you have **held** *me* by my right hand.
24 you will guide me with your counsel, and afterward receive me *to* glory.
25 Who have I in heaven *but* you? And *there is* none upon earth *that* I desire beside you.
26 My flesh and my heart fails: *but* God *is* the strength of my heart, and my portion forever.
27 For, lo, they that are far from you will perish: you have destroyed all them that go a whoring from you.
28 But *it is* good for me to draw near to God: I have put my trust in the Lord GOD, that I may declare all your works.

PSALM 74
Maschil of Asaph.

1 O God, why have you cast *us* off forever? *Why* does your anger smoke against the sheep of your pasture?
2 Remember your congregation, *which* you have purchased of old; the rod of your inheritance, *which* you have redeemed; this mount Zion, wherein you have dwelt.
3 Lift up your feet unto the perpetual desolations; *even* all *that* the enemy has done wickedly in the sanctuary.
4 Your enemies roar in the midst of your congregations; they set up their ensigns *for* signs.
5 *A man* was famous according as he had lifted up axes upon the thick trees.
6 But now they break down the carved work thereof at once with axes and hammers.
7 They have cast fire into your sanctuary, they have defiled *by casting down* the dwelling place of your name to the ground.
8 They said in their hearts, Let us destroy them together: they have burned up all the synagogues of God in the land.
9 We see not our signs: *there is* no more any prophet: neither *is there* among us any that knows how long.
10 O God, how long will the adversary reproach? will the enemy blaspheme your name forever?
11 Why withdraw you your hand, even your right hand? pluck *it* out of your bosom.
12 For God *is* my King of old, working salvation in the midst of the earth.
13 you did divide the sea by your strength: you brake the heads of the dragons in the waters.
14 You break the heads of leviathan in pieces, *and* gave him *to be* meat to the people inhabiting the wilderness.
15 You did cleave the fountain and the flood: you dried up mighty rivers.
16 The day *is* your, the night also *is* your: you have prepared the light and the sun.
17 you have set all the borders of the earth: you have made summer and winter.
18 Remember this, *that* the enemy has reproached, O LORD, and *that* the foolish people have blasphemed your name.
19 O deliver not the soul of your turtledove unto the multitude *of the wicked*: forget not the congregation of your poor forever.
20 Have respect unto the covenant: for the dark places of the earth are full of the habitations of cruelty.
21 O let not the oppressed return ashamed: let the poor and needy praise your name.
22 Arise, O God, plead your own cause: remember how the foolish man reproaches you daily.
23 Forget not the voice of your enemies: the tumult of those that rise up against you increases continually.

PSALM 75
To the chief Musician, Al-taschith, A Psalm *or* Song of Asaph.

1 Unto you, O God, do we give thanks, *unto you* do we give thanks: for *that* your name is near your wondrous works declare.
2 When I will receive the congregation I will judge uprightly.
3 The earth and all the inhabitants thereof are dissolved: I bear up the pillars of it. Selah.
4 I said unto the fools, Deal not foolishly: and to the wicked, lift not up the horn:
5 Lift not up your horn on high: speak *not with* a stiff neck.
6 For promotion *cometh* neither from the east, or from the west, or from the south.
7 But God *is* the judge: he puts down one and sets up another.
8 For in the hand of the LORD *there is* a cup, and the wine is red; it is full of mixture; and he pours out of the same: but the dregs thereof, all the wicked of the earth will wring *them* out, *and* drink *them*.
9 But I will declare for ever; I will sing praises to the God of Jacob.
10 All the horns of the wicked also will I cut off; *but* the horns of the righteous will be exalted.

PSALM 76
To the chief Musician on Neginoth, A Psalm *or* Song of Asaph.

1 In Judah *is* God known: his name *is* great in Israel.
2 In Salem also is his tabernacle, and his dwelling place in Zion.
3 There **broke** he the arrows of the bow, the shield, and the sword, and the battle. Selah.
4 you are more glorious *and* excellent than the mountains of prey.
5 The stouthearted are spoiled, they have slept their sleep: and none of the men of might have found their hands.
6 At your rebuke, O God of Jacob, both the chariot and horse are cast into a dead sleep.
7 You, *even* you, are to be feared: and who may stand in your sight when once you are angry?
8 you did cause judgment to be heard from heaven; the earth feared, and was still,
9 When God arose to judgment, to save all the meek of the earth. Selah.
10 Surely the wrath of man will praise you: the remainder of wrath will you restrain
11 Vow, and pay unto the LORD your God: let all that be round about him bring presents unto him that ought to be feared.
12 He will cut off the spirit of princes: *he is* terrible to the kings of the earth.

PSALM 77
To the chief Musician, to Jeduthun, A Psalm of Asaph.

1 I cried unto God with my voice, *even* unto God with my voice; and he gave ear unto me.
2 In the day of my trouble I sought the Lord: my sore ran in the night, and ceased not: my soul refused to be comforted.
3 I remembered God, and was troubled: I complained, and my spirit was overwhelmed. Selah.
4 You **held** mine eyes waking: I am so troubled that I cannot speak.
5 I have considered the days of old, the years of ancient times.
6 I call to remembrance my song in the night: I commune with mine own heart: and my spirit made diligent search.
7 Will the Lord cast off forever? And will he be favorable no more?
8 Is his mercy clean gone forever? Does *his* promise fail for evermore?
9 Have God forgotten to be gracious? Has he in anger shut up his tender mercies? Selah.
10 And I said, this *is* my infirmity: *but I will remember* the years of the right hand of the most High.
11 I will remember the works of the LORD: surely I will remember your wonders of old.
12 I will meditate also of all your work, and talk of your doings.
13 Your way, O God, *is* [in the sanctuary]¹: who *is* so great a God as *our* God?
14 You are the God that does wonders: you have declared your strength among the people.
15 you have with your arm redeemed your people, the sons of Jacob and Joseph. Selah.
16 The waters saw you, O God, the waters saw you; they were afraid: the depths also were troubled.
17 The clouds poured out water: the skies² sent out a sound³: your arrows also went abroad.
18 The voice of your thunder *was* in the heaven⁴: the lightnings lightened the world: the earth trembled and shook.
19 your way *is* in the sea, and your path in the great waters, and your footsteps are not known.
20 You led your people like a flock by the hand of Moses and Aaron.

PSALM 78

Maschil of Asaph.

1 Give ear, O my people, *to* my law: incline your ears to the words of my mouth.
2 I will open my mouth in a parable: I will utter dark sayings of old:
3 Which we have heard and known, and our fathers have told us.
4 We will not hide *them* from their children, showing to the generation to come the praises of the LORD, and his strength, and his wonderful works that he has done.
5 For he established a testimony in Jacob, and appointed a law in Israel, which he commanded our fathers, that they should make them known to their children:
6 That the generation to come [might know]⁵ *them, even* the children *which* should be born; *who* should arise and declare *them* to their children:
7 That they might set their hope in God, and not forget the works of God, but keep his commandments:
8 And might not be as their fathers, a stubborn and rebellious generation; a generation *that* set not their heart aright, and whose spirit was not steadfast with God.

9 The children of Ephraim, *being* armed, *and* carrying bows, turned back in the day of battle.
10 They kept not the covenant of God, and refused to walk in his law;
11 And forgot his works, and his wonders that he had showed them.
12 Marvelous things did he in the sight of their fathers, in the land of Egypt, *in* the field of Zoan.
13 He divided the sea, and caused them to pass through; and he made the waters to stand as an heap.
14 In the daytime also he led them with a cloud, and all the night with a light of fire.
15 He clave the rocks in the wilderness, and gave *them* drink as *out of* the great depths.
16 He brought streams also out of the rock, and caused waters to run down like rivers.
17 And they sinned yet more against him by provoking the most High in the wilderness.
18 And they tempted God in their heart by asking meat for their lust.
19 Yea, they spoke against God; they said, Can God furnish a table in the wilderness?
20 Behold, he smote the rock, that the waters gushed out, and the streams overflowed; can he give bread also? Can he provide flesh for his people?
21 Therefore the LORD heard *this*, and was wroth: so a fire was kindled against Jacob, and anger also came up against Israel;
22 Because they believed not in God, and trusted not in his salvation:
23 Though he had commanded the clouds from above, and opened the doors of heaven,
24 And had rained down manna upon them to eat, and had given them of the corn of heaven.
25 Man did eat angels' food: he sent them meat to the full.
26 He caused an east wind to blow in the heaven: and by his power he brought in the south wind.
27 He rained flesh also upon them as dust, and feathered fowls like as the sand of the sea:
28 And he let *it* fall in the midst of their camp, round about their habitations.
29 So they did eat, and were well filled: for he gave them their own desire;
30 They were not estranged from their lust. But while their meat *was* yet in their mouths,
31 The wrath of God came upon them, and slew the fattest of them, and smote down the chosen *men* of Israel.
32 For all this they sinned still, and believed not for his wondrous works.
33 Therefore their days did he consume in vanity, and their years in trouble.
34 When he slew them, then they sought him: and they returned and enquired early after God.
35 And they remembered that God *was* their rock, and the high God their redeemer.
36 Nevertheless they did flatter him with their mouth, and they lied unto him with their tongues.

---

¹ lit. a clean/sacred place or thing, *sanctity* [Strgs#6944].
² skies – a *powder* (as *beaten* small); by analogy a thin *vapor*; by extension the *firmament* [Strgs#7834].
³ sound – to *call* aloud; a *voice* [Strgs#6963].
⁴ heaven – a *wheel*, *whirlwind*; also dust (as whirled) [Strgs#1534].
⁵ see Judges 2:10

37 For their heart was not right with him, neither were they steadfast in his covenant.
38 But he, *being* full of compassion, forgave *their* iniquity, and destroyed *them* not: yea, many a time turned he his anger away, and did not stir up all his wrath.
39 For he remembered that they *were but* flesh; a wind that passes away, and cometh not again.
40 How oft did they provoke him in the wilderness, *and* grieve him in the desert!
41 Yea, they turned back and tempted God, and limited[1] the Holy One of Israel.
42 They remembered not his hand, *or* the day when he delivered them from the enemy.
43 How he had wrought his signs in Egypt, and his wonders in the field of Zoan[2]:
44 And had turned their rivers into blood; and their floods, that they could not drink.
45 [He sent divers sorts of flies among them, which devoured them; and frogs, which destroyed[3] them.][4]
46 He gave also their increase unto the caterpillar, and their labor unto the locust.
47 He destroyed their vines with hail, and their sycamore trees with frost.
48 He gave up their cattle also to the hail, and their flocks to hot thunderbolts.
49 He cast upon them the fierceness of his anger, wrath, and indignation, and trouble, by sending evil angels *among them*.
50 He made a way to his anger; he spared not their soul from death, but gave their life over to the pestilence;
51 And smote all the firstborn in Egypt; the chief of *their* strength in the tabernacles of Ham:
52 But made his own people to go forth like sheep, and guided them in the wilderness like a flock.
53 And he led them on safely, so that they feared not: but the sea overwhelmed their enemies.
54 And he brought them to the border of his sanctuary, *even to* this mountain, *which* his right hand had purchased.
55 He cast out the heathen also before them, and divided them an inheritance by line, and made the tribes of Israel to dwell in their tents.
56 Yet they tempted and provoked the most high God, and kept not his testimonies:
57 But turned back, and dealt unfaithfully like their fathers: they were turned aside like a deceitful bow.
58 For they provoked him to anger with their high places, and moved him to jealousy with their graven images.
59 When God heard *this*, he was **angered**, and greatly abhorred Israel:
60 So that he forsook the tabernacle of Shiloh, the tent *which* he placed among men;
61 And delivered his strength into captivity, and his glory into the enemy's hand.
62 He gave his people over also unto the sword; and was wroth with his inheritance.
63 The fire consumed their young men; and their maidens were not given to marriage.
64 Their priests fell by the sword; and their widows made no lamentation.
65 Then the Lord awaked as one out of sleep, *and* like a mighty man that shouts by reason of wine.
66 And he smote his enemies in the hinder parts: he put them to a perpetual reproach.
67 Moreover he refused the tabernacle of Joseph, and chose not the tribe of Ephraim:
68 But chose the tribe of Judah, the mount Zion which he loved.
69 And he built his sanctuary like high *palaces*, like the earth which he has established for ever.
70 He chose David also his servant, and took him from the sheepfolds:
71 From following the ewes great with young he brought him to feed Jacob his people, and Israel his inheritance.
72 So he fed them according to the integrity of his heart; and guided them by the skillfulness of his hands.

PSALM 79
A Psalm of Asaph.

1 O God, the heathen are come into your inheritance; your holy temple have they defiled; they have laid Jerusalem on heaps.
2 The dead bodies of your servants have they given *to be* meat unto the fowls of the heaven, the flesh of your saints unto the beasts of the earth.
3 Their blood have they shed like water round about Jerusalem; and *there was* none to bury *them*.
4 We are become a reproach to our neighbors, a scorn and derision to them that are round about us.
5 How long, LORD? Will you be angry forever? Will your jealousy burn like fire?
6 Pour out your wrath upon the heathen that have not known you, and upon the kingdoms that have not called upon your name.
7 For they have devoured Jacob, and laid waste his dwelling place.
8 O remember not against us former iniquities: let your tender mercies speedily prevent us: for we are brought very low.
9 Help us, O God of our salvation, for the glory of your name: and deliver us, and purge away our sins, for your name's sake.
10 Wherefore should the heathen say, where *is* their God? let him be known among the heathen in our sight *by* the revenging of the blood of your servants *which is* shed.
11 Let the sighing of the prisoner come before you; according to the greatness of your power preserve you those that are appointed to die;
12 And render unto our neighbors sevenfold into their bosom their reproach, wherewith they have reproached you, O Lord.
13 So we your people and sheep of your pasture will give you thanks for ever: we will show forth your praise to all generations.

PSALM 80
To the chief Musician upon Shoshannim-Eduth, A Psalm of Asaph.

1 Give ear, O Shepherd of Israel, you that lead Joseph like a flock; you that dwells *between* the cherubims, shine forth.
2 Before Ephraim and Benjamin and Manasseh stir up your strength, and come *and* save us.

---

[1] limited – is the Hebrew word *tāvâh* meaning scraping to pieces; to grieve [Strgs#8428].
[2] Zoan- an ancient city in Egypt dating back to Abraham, often called Tanis by the Greeks. It was built seven after Hebron (**Num. 13:22**), Zoan has often been identified with one of the royal cities in northern Egypt. [Strgs#6814]
[3] lit. to *decay* and *ruin*.
[4] see Psalm 105:30

3 Turn us again, O God, and cause your face to shine; and we will be saved.
4 O LORD God of hosts, how long will you be angry against the prayer of your people?
5 You feed them with the bread of tears; and give them tears to drink in great measure.
6 You make us a strife unto our neighbors: and our enemies laugh among themselves.
7 Turn us again, O God of hosts, and cause your face to shine; and we will be saved.
8 You have brought a vine out of Egypt: you have cast out the heathen, and planted it.
9 You prepared *room* before it, and did cause it to take deep root, and it filled the land.
10 The hills were covered with the shadow of it, and the boughs thereof *were like* the goodly cedars.
11 She sent out her boughs unto the sea, and her branches unto the river.
12 Why have you *then* broken down her hedges, so that all they which pass by the way do pluck her?
13 The boar out of the wood does waste it, and the wild beast of the field does devour it.
14 Return, we beseech you, O God of hosts: look down from heaven, and behold, and visit this vine;
15 And the vineyard which your right hand has planted, and the branch *that* you made strong for yourself.
16 *It is* burned with fire, *it is* cut down: they perish at the rebuke of your countenance.
17 Let your hand be upon the man of your right hand, upon the son of man *whom* you made strong for yourself.
18 So will not we go back from you: quicken us, and we will call upon your name.
19 Turn us again, O LORD God of hosts, cause your face to shine; and we will be saved.

PSALM 81

To the chief Musician upon Gittith, *A Psalm* of Asaph.

1 Sing aloud unto God our strength: make a joyful noise unto the God of Jacob.
2 Take a psalm, and bring here the **tambourine**, the pleasant harp with the psaltery.
3 Blow up the trumpet in the new moon, in the time appointed, on our solemn feast day.
4 For this *was* a statute for Israel, *and* a law of the God of Jacob.
5 This he ordained in Joseph *for* a testimony, when he went out through the land of Egypt: *where* I heard a language *that* I understood not.
6 I removed his shoulder from the burden: his hands were delivered from the pots.
7 You called in trouble, and I delivered you; I answered you in the [secret place of thunder][1]: I proved you at the waters of Meribah. Selah.
8 Hear, O my people, and I will testify unto you: O Israel, if you will hearken unto me;
9 There will no strange god be in you; neither will you worship any strange god.
10 I *am* the LORD your God, which brought you out of the land of Egypt: open your mouth wide, and I will fill it.

---

[1] lit. the secret of thunder.

11 But my people would not hearken to my voice; and Israel would none of me.
12 So I gave them up unto their own hearts' lust: *and* they walked in their own counsels.
13 Oh that my people had hearkened unto me, *and* Israel had walked in my ways!
14 I should soon have subdued their enemies, and turned my hand against their adversaries.
15 The haters of the LORD should have submitted themselves unto him: but their time should have endured forever.
16 He should have fed them also with the finest of the wheat: and with honey out of the rock should I have satisfied you.

PSALM 82

A Psalm of Asaph.

1 God stands in the congregation of the mighty; he judges among the gods.
2 How long will you judge unjustly, and accept the persons of the wicked? Selah.
3 Defend the poor and fatherless: do justice to the afflicted and needy.
4 Deliver the poor and needy: rid *them* out of the hand of the wicked.
5 They know not, neither will they understand; they walk on in darkness: all the foundations of the earth are out of course.
6 I have said, you *are* gods; and all of you *are* children of the most High.
7 But you will die like men, and fall like one of the princes.
8 Arise, O God, judge the earth: for you will inherit all nations.

PSALM 83

A Song *or* Psalm of Asaph.

1 Keep not you silence, O God: hold not your peace, and be not still, O God.
2 For, lo, your enemies make a tumult: and they that hate you have lifted up the head.
3 They have taken crafty counsel against your people, and consulted against your hidden ones.
4 They have said, Come, and let us cut them off from *being* a nation; that the name of Israel may be no more in remembrance.
5 For they have consulted together with one consent: they are confederate against you:
6 The tabernacles of Edom, and the Ishmaelites; of Moab, and the Hagarenes;
7 Gebal, and Ammon, and Amalek; the Philistines with the inhabitants of Tyre;
8 Assur also is joined with them: they have holpen the children of Lot. Selah.
9 Do unto them as *unto* the Midianites; as *to* Sisera, as *to* Jabin, at the brook of Kison:
10 *Which* perished at En-dor: they became *as* dung for the earth.
11 Make their nobles like Oreb, and like Zeeb: yea, all their princes as Zebah, and as Zalmunna:
12 Who said, Let us take to ourselves the houses of God in possession.
13 O my God, make them like a wheel; as the stubble before the wind.

14 As the fire burns a wood, and as the flame sets the mountains on fire;
15 So persecute them with your tempest, and make them afraid with your storm.
16 Fill their faces with shame; that they may seek your name, O LORD.
17 Let them be confounded and troubled for ever; yea, let them be put to shame, and perish:
18 That *men* may know that you, whose name alone *is* JEHOVAH, are the most high over all the earth.

PSALM 84
To the chief Musician upon Gittith, A Psalm for the sons of Korah.

1 How amiable *are* your tabernacles, O LORD of hosts!
2 My soul longs, yea, even faints for the courts of the LORD: my heart and my flesh cries out for the living God.
3 Yea, the sparrow has found an house, and the swallow a nest for herself, where she may lay her young, *even* your altars, O LORD of hosts, my King, and my God.
4 Blessed *are* they that dwell in your house: they will be still praising you. Selah.
5 Blessed *is* the man whose strength *is* in you; in whose heart *are* the ways *of them*.
6 *Who* passing through the valley of Baca make it a well; the rain also fills the pools.
7 They go from strength to strength, *every one of them* in Zion appears before God.
8 O LORD God of hosts, hear my prayer: give ear, O God of Jacob. Selah.
9 Behold, O God our shield, and look upon the face of your anointed.
10 For a day in your courts *is* better than a thousand. I had rather be a doorkeeper in the house of my God, than to dwell in the tents of wickedness.
11 For the LORD God *is* a sun and shield: the LORD will give grace and glory: no good *thing* will he withhold from them that walk uprightly.
12 O LORD of hosts, blessed *is* the man that trusts in you.

PSALM 85
To the chief Musician, A Psalm for the sons of Korah.

1 LORD, you have been favorable unto your land: you have brought back the captivity of Jacob.
2 you have forgiven the iniquity of your people, you have covered all their sin. Selah.
3 You have taken away all your wrath: you have turned yourself from the fierceness of your anger.
4 Turn us, O God of our salvation, and cause your anger toward us to cease.
5 will you be angry with us forever? Will you draw out your anger to all generations?
6 will you not revive us again: that your people may rejoice in you?
7 show us your mercy, O LORD, and grant us your salvation.
8 I will hear what God the LORD will speak: for he will speak peace unto his people, and to his saints: but let them not turn again to folly.
9 Surely his salvation *is* nigh them that fear him; that glory may dwell in our land.
10 Mercy and truth are met together; righteousness and peace have kissed *each other*.
11 Truth will spring out of the earth; and righteousness will look down from heaven.
12 Yea, the LORD will give *that which is* good; and our land will yield her increase.
13 Righteousness will go before him; and will set *us* in the way of his steps.

PSALM 86
A Prayer of David.

1 Bow down your ear, O LORD, hear me: for I *am* poor and needy.
2 Preserve my soul; for I *am* holy: O you my God, save your servant that trusts in you.
3 Be merciful unto me, O Lord: for I cry unto you daily.
4 Rejoice the soul of your servant: for unto you, O Lord, do I lift up my soul.
5 For you, Lord, are good, and ready to forgive; and plenteous in mercy unto all them that call upon you.
6 Give ear, O LORD, unto my prayer; and attend to the voice of my supplications.
7 In the day of my trouble I will call upon you: for you will answer me.
8 Among the gods *there is* none like unto you, O Lord; neither *are there any works* like unto your works.
9 All nations whom you have made will come and worship before you, O Lord; and will glorify your name.
10 For you are great, and doest wondrous things: you are God alone.
11 Teach me your way, O LORD; I will walk in your truth: unite my heart to fear your name.
12 I will praise you, O Lord my God, with all my heart: and I will glorify your name for evermore.
13 For great *is* your mercy toward me: and you have delivered my soul from the lowest hell.
14 O God, the proud are risen against me, and the assemblies of violent *men* have sought after my soul; and have not set you before them.
15 But you, O Lord, are a God full of compassion, and gracious, longsuffering, and plenteous in mercy and truth.
16 O turn unto me, and have mercy upon me; give your strength unto your servant, and save the son of your handmaid.
17 Show me a token for good; that they which hate me may see *it*, and be ashamed: because you, LORD, have **help**[1] me, and comforted me.

PSALM 87
A Psalm *or* Song for the sons of Korah.

1 His foundation *is* in the holy mountains.
2 The LORD loves the gates of Zion more than all the dwellings of Jacob.
3 Glorious things are spoken of you, O city of God. Selah.
4 I will make mention of Rahab and Babylon to them that know me: behold Philistia, and Tyre, with Ethiopia; this *man* was born there.
5 And of Zion it will be said, This and that man was born in her: and the highest himself will establish her.
6 The LORD will count, when he writes up the people, *that* this *man* was born there. Selah.

---

[1] The KJV uses the word <u>holpen</u> instead of help. Holpen is an old English word meaning to surround, to protect, aid and help. [Strgs#5826]

7 As well the singers as the players on instruments will *be there*: all my springs *are* in you.

PSALM 88

A Song *or* Psalm for the sons of Korah, to the chief Musician upon Mahalath Leannoth, Maschil of Heman the Ezrahite.

1 O LORD God of my salvation, I have cried day *and* night before you:
2 Let my prayer come before you: incline your ear unto my cry;
3 For my soul is full of troubles: and my life draws nigh unto the grave.
4 I am counted with them that go down into the pit: I am as a man *that has* no strength:
5 Free among the dead, like the slain that lie in the grave, whom you remembers no more: and they are cut off from your hand.
6 you have laid me in the lowest pit, in darkness, in the deeps.
7 your wrath lies hard upon me, and you have afflicted *me* with all your waves. Selah.
8 you have put away mine acquaintance far from me; you have made me an abomination unto them: *I am* shut up, and I cannot come forth.
9 Mine eye mourns by reason of affliction: LORD, I have called daily upon you, I have stretched out my hands unto you.
10 will you show wonders to the dead? Will the dead arise *and* praise you? Selah.
11 will your loving-kindness be declared in the grave? *Or* your faithfulness in destruction?
12 will your wonders be known in the dark? And your righteousness in the land of forgetfulness?
13 But unto you have I cried, O LORD; and in the morning will my prayer prevent you.
14 LORD, why casts you off my soul? *Why* hide you your face from me?
15 I *am* afflicted and ready to die from *my* youth up: *while* I suffer your terrors I am distracted.
16 Your fierce wrath goes over me; your terrors have cut me off.
17 They came round about me daily like water; they compassed me about together.
18 Lover and friend have you put far from me, *and* mine acquaintance into darkness.

PSALM 89

Maschil of Ethan the Ezrahite.

1 I will sing of the mercies of the LORD for ever: with my mouth will I make known your faithfulness to all generations.
2 For I have said, Mercy will be built up forever: your faithfulness will you establish in the very heavens.
3 I have made a covenant with my chosen, I have sworn unto David my servant,
4 your seed will I establish forever, and build up your throne to all generations. Selah.
5 And the heavens will praise your wonders, O LORD: your faithfulness also in the congregation of the saints.
6 For who in the heaven can be compared unto the LORD? *Who* among the sons of the mighty can be likened unto the LORD?
7 God is greatly to be feared in the assembly of the saints, and to be had in reverence of all *them that are* about him.
8 O LORD God of hosts, who *is* a strong LORD like unto you? or to your faithfulness round about you?
9 You rule the raging of the sea: when the waves thereof arise, you stillest them.
10 you have broken Rahab in pieces, as one that is slain; you have scattered your enemies with your strong arm.
11 The heavens *are* your, the earth also *is* your: *as for* the world and the fullness thereof, you have founded them.
12 The north and the south you have created them: Tabor and Hermon will rejoice in your name.
13 you have a mighty arm: strong is your hand, *and* high is your right hand.
14 Justice and judgment *are* the habitation of your throne: mercy and truth will go before your face.
15 Blessed *is* the people that know the joyful sound they will walk, O LORD, in the light of your countenance.
16 In your name will they rejoice all the day and in your righteousness will they be exalted.
17 For you are the glory of their strength: and in your favor our horn will be exalted.
18 For the LORD *is* our defence; and the Holy One of Israel *is* our king.
19 Then you **spoke** in vision to your holy one, and said, I have laid help upon *one that is* mighty; I have exalted *one* chosen out of the people.
20 I have found David my servant; with my holy oil have I anointed him:
21 With whom my hand will be established: mine arm also will strengthen him.
22 The enemy will not exact upon him; or the son of wickedness afflict him.
23 And I will beat down his foes before his face, and plague them that hate him.
24 But my faithfulness and my mercy will *be with* him: and in my name will his horn be exalted.
25 I will set his hand also in the sea, and his right hand in the rivers.
26 He will cry unto me, you are my father, my God, and the rock of my salvation.
27 Also I will make him *my* firstborn, higher than the kings of the earth.
28 My mercy will I keep for him for evermore, and my covenant will stand fast with him.
29 His seed also will I make *to endure* forever, and his throne as the days of heaven.
30 If his children forsake my law, and walk not in my judgments;
31 If they break my statutes, and keep not my commandments;
32 Then will I visit their transgression with the rod, and their iniquity with stripes.
33 Nevertheless my loving-kindness will I not utterly take from him, or suffer my faithfulness to fail.
34 My covenant will I not break, or alter the thing that is gone out of my lips.
35 Once have I sworn by my holiness that I will not lie unto David.
36 His seed will endure forever, and his throne as the sun before me.
37 It will be established for ever as the moon, and *as* a faithful witness in heaven. Selah.
38 But you have cast off and abhorred, you have been wroth with your anointed.
39 you have made void the covenant of your servant: you have profaned his crown *by casting it* to the ground.

40 you have broken down all his hedges; you have brought his strong holds to ruin.
41 All that pass by the way spoil him: he is a reproach to his neighbors.
42 you have set up the right hand of his adversaries; you have made all his enemies to rejoice.
43 you have also turned the edge of his sword, and have not made him to stand in the battle.
44 you have made his glory to cease, and cast his throne down to the ground.
45 The days of his youth have you shortened: you have covered him with shame. Selah.
46 How long, LORD? Will you hide yourself forever? Will your wrath burn like fire?
47 Remember how short my time is: wherefore have you made all men in vain?
48 What man *is he that* lives, and will not see death? Will he deliver his soul from the hand of the grave? Selah.
49 Lord, where *are* your former loving kindnesses, *which* you **swore** unto David in your truth?
50 Remember, Lord, the reproach of your servants; *how* I do bear in my bosom *the reproach of* all the mighty people;
51 Wherewith your enemies have reproached, O LORD; wherewith they have reproached the footsteps of your anointed.
52 Blessed *be* the LORD for evermore. Amen, and Amen.

PSALM 90

A Prayer of Moses the man of God.

1 Lord, you have been our dwelling place in all generations.
2 Before the mountains were brought forth, **or even before you** formed the earth and the world, even from everlasting to everlasting, you are God.
3 You turn man to destruction; and say, Return, you children of men.
4 For a thousand years in your sight *are but* as yesterday when it is past, and *as* a watch in the night.
5 You **carry** them away as with a flood; they are *as* a sleep: in the morning *they are* like grass *which* grows up.
6 In the morning it flourishes, and grows up; in the evening it is cut down, and withers.
7 For we are consumed by your anger, and by your wrath are we troubled.
8 you have set our iniquities before you, our secret *sins* in the light of your countenance.
9 For all our days are passed away in your wrath: we spend our years as a tale *that is told*.
10 The days of our years *are* threescore years and ten; and if by reason of strength *they be* fourscore years, yet *is* their strength labor and sorrow; for it is soon cut off, and we fly away.
11 Who knows the power of your anger? Even according to your fear, *so is* your wrath.
12 So teach *us* to number our days, that we may apply *our* hearts unto wisdom.
13 Return, O LORD, how long? And let it repent you concerning your servants.
14 O satisfy us early with your mercy; that we may rejoice and be glad all our days.
15 Make us glad according to the days *wherein* you have afflicted us, *and* the years *wherein* we have seen evil.
16 Let your work appear unto your servants, and your glory unto their children.
17 And let the beauty of the LORD our God be upon us: and establish you the work of our hands upon us; yea, the work of our hands establish you it.

PSALM 91

1 He that dwells in the secret place of the most High will abide under the shadow of the Almighty.
2 I will say of the LORD, *He is* my refuge and my fortress: my God; in him will I trust.
3 Surely he will deliver you from the snare of the fowler, and from the noisome pestilence.
4 He will cover you with his feathers, and under his wings will you trust: his truth will *be your* shield and buckler.
5 you will not be afraid for the terror by night; or for the arrow *that* flies by day;
6 or for the pestilence *that* walks in darkness; or for the destruction *that* wastes at noonday.
7 A thousand will fall at your side, and ten thousand at your right hand; *but* it will not come nigh you.
8 Only with your eyes will you behold and see the reward of the wicked.
9 Because you have made the LORD, *which is* my refuge, *even* the most High, your habitation;
10 There will no evil befall you, neither will any plague come nigh your dwelling.
11 For he will give his angels charge over you, to keep you in all your ways.
12 They will bear you up in *their* hands, lest you dash your foot against a stone.
13 you will tread upon the lion and adder: the young lion and the dragon will you trample under feet.
14 Because he has set his love upon me, therefore will I deliver him: I will set him on high, because he has known my name.
15 He will call upon me, and I will answer him: I *will be with* him in trouble; I will deliver him, and honor him.
16 With long life will I satisfy him, and show him my salvation.

PSALM 92

A Psalm *or* Song for the Sabbath day.

1 *It is a* good *thing* to give thanks unto the LORD, and to sing praises unto your name, O most High:
2 To show forth your loving-kindness in the morning, and your faithfulness every night,
3 Upon an instrument of ten strings, and upon the psaltery; upon the harp with a solemn sound.
4 For you, LORD, have made me glad through your work: I will triumph in the works of your hands.
5 O LORD, how great are your works! *And* your thoughts are very deep.
6 A brutish man knows not; neither does a fool understand this.
7 When the wicked spring as the grass, and when all the workers of iniquity do flourish; *it is* that they will be destroyed for ever:
8 But you, LORD, are *most* high for evermore.
9 For, lo, your enemies, O LORD, for, lo, your enemies will perish; all the workers of iniquity will be scattered.
10 But my horn will you exalt like *the horn of* an unicorn: I will be anointed with fresh oil.
11 Mine eye also will see *my desire* on mine enemies, *and* mine ears will hear *my desire* of the wicked that rise up against me.

12 The righteous will flourish like the palm tree: he will grow like a cedar in Lebanon.
13 Those that be planted in the house of the LORD will flourish in the courts of our God.
14 They will still bring forth fruit in old age; they will be fat and flourishing;
15 To show that the LORD *is* upright: *he is* my rock, and *there is* no unrighteousness in him.

PSALM 93

1 The LORD reigns, he is clothed with majesty; the LORD is clothed with strength, *wherewith* he has girded himself: the world also is **established**, that it cannot be moved.
2 Your throne *is* established of old: you are from everlasting.
3 The floods have lifted up, O LORD, the floods have lifted up their voice; the floods lift up their waves.
4 The LORD on high *is* mightier than the noise of many waters, *yea, than* the mighty waves of the sea.
5 Your testimonies are very sure: holiness becomes your house, O LORD, forever.

PSALM 94

1 O LORD God, to who vengeance belongs; O God, to who vengeance belongs, show yourself.
2 Lift up yourself, you judge of the earth: render a reward to the proud.
3 LORD, how long will the wicked, how long will the wicked triumph?
4 *How long* will they utter *and* speak hard things? *And* all the workers of iniquity boast themselves?
5 They break in pieces your people, O LORD, and afflict your heritage.
6 They slay the widow and the stranger, and murder the fatherless.
7 Yet they say, The LORD will not see, neither will the God of Jacob regard *it*.
8 Understand, you brutish among the people: and you fools, when will you be wise?
9 He that planted the ear, will he not hear? he that formed the eye, will he not see?
10 He that chastises the heathen, will not he correct? He that teaches man knowledge, will *not he know*?
11 The LORD knows the thoughts of man, that they *are* vanity.
12 Blessed *is* the man whom you chasten, O LORD, and teaches him out of your law;
13 That you may give him rest from the days of adversity, until the pit be **dug** for the wicked.
14 For the LORD will not cast off his people, neither will he forsake his inheritance.
15 But judgment will return unto righteousness: and all the upright in heart will follow it.
16 Who will rise up for me against the evildoers? *Or* who will stand up for me against the workers of iniquity?
17 Unless the LORD *had been* my help, my soul had almost dwelt in silence.
18 When I said, my foot slips your mercy, O LORD, held me up.
19 In the multitude of my thoughts within me your comforts delight my soul.
20 will the throne of iniquity have fellowship with you, which frames mischief by a law?
21 They gather themselves together against the soul of the righteous, and condemn the innocent blood.
22 But the LORD is my defence; and my God *is* the rock of my refuge.
23 And he will bring upon them their own iniquity, and will cut them off in their own wickedness; *yea*, the LORD our God will cut them off.

PSALM 95

1 O come, let us sing unto the LORD: let us make a joyful noise to the rock of our salvation.
2 Let us come before his presence with thanksgiving, and make a joyful noise unto him with psalms.
3 For the LORD *is* a great God, and a great King above all gods.
4 In his hand *are* the deep places of the earth: the strength of the hills *is* his also.
5 The sea *is* his, and he made it: and his hands formed the dry *land*.
6 O come, let us worship and bow down: let us kneel before the LORD our maker.
7 For he *is* our God; and we *are* the people of his pasture, and the sheep of his hand. Today if you will hear his voice,
8 Harden not your heart, as in the provocation, *and as in* the day of temptation in the wilderness:
9 When your fathers tempted me, proved me, and saw my work.
10 Forty years long was I grieved with *this* generation, and said, It *is* a people that do err in their heart, and they have not known my ways:
11 Unto whom I swore in my wrath that they should not enter into my rest.

PSALM 96

1 O sing unto the LORD a new song: sing unto the LORD, all the earth.
2 Sing unto the LORD, bless his name; show forth his salvation from day to day.
3 Declare his glory among the heathen, his wonders among all people.
4 For the LORD *is* great, and greatly to be praised: he *is* to be feared above all gods.
5 For all the gods of the nations *are* idols: but the LORD made the heavens.
6 Honor and majesty *are* before him: strength and beauty *are* in his sanctuary.
7 Give unto the LORD, O you kindred's of the people, give unto the LORD glory and strength.
8 Give unto the LORD the glory *due unto* his name: bring an offering, and come into his courts.
9 O worship the LORD in the beauty of holiness: fear before him, all the earth.
10 Say among the heathen *that* the LORD reigns: the world also will be established that it will not be moved: he will judge the people righteously.
11 Let the heavens rejoice, and let the earth be glad; let the sea roar, and the fullness thereof.
12 Let the field be joyful, and all that *is* therein: then will all the trees of the wood rejoice
13 Before the LORD: for he cometh, for he cometh to judge the earth: he will judge the world with righteousness, and the people with his truth.

PSALM 97

1 The LORD reigns; let the earth rejoice; let the multitude of isles be glad *thereof*.

2 Clouds and darkness *are* round about him: righteousness and judgment *are* the habitation of his throne.
3 A fire goes before him, and burns up his enemies round about.
4 His lightnings enlightened the world: the earth saw, and trembled.
5 The hills melted like wax at the presence of the LORD, at the presence of the Lord of the whole earth.
6 The heavens declare his righteousness, and all the people see his glory.
7 Confounded be all they that serve graven images, that boast themselves of idols: worship him, all you gods.
8 Zion heard, and was glad; and the daughters of Judah rejoiced because of your judgments, O LORD.
9 For you, LORD, are high above all the earth: you are exalted far above all gods.
10 You that love the LORD, hate evil: he preserves the souls of his saints; he delivers them out of the hand of the wicked.
11 Light is sown for the righteous, and gladness for the upright in heart.
12 Rejoice in the LORD, you righteous; and give thanks at the remembrance of his holiness.

PSALM 98
A Psalm.

1 O sing unto the LORD a new song; for he has done marvelous things: his right hand, and his holy arm, has gotten him the victory.
2 The LORD has made known his salvation: his righteousness has he openly showed in the sight of the heathen.
3 He has remembered his mercy and his truth toward the house of Israel: all the ends of the earth have seen the salvation of our God.
4 Make a joyful noise unto the LORD, all the earth: make a loud noise, and rejoice, and sing praise.
5 Sing unto the LORD with the harp; with the harp, and the voice of a psalm.
6 With trumpets and sound of cornet make a joyful noise before the LORD, the King.
7 Let the sea roar, and the fullness thereof; the world, and they that dwell therein.
8 Let the floods clap *their* hands: let the hills be joyful together
9 Before the LORD; for he cometh to judge the earth: with righteousness will he judge the world, and the people with equity.

PSALM 99

1 The LORD reigns; let the people tremble: he sits *between* the cherubims; let the earth be moved.
2 The LORD *is* great in Zion; and he *is* high above all the people.
3 Let them praise your great and terrible name; *for* it *is* holy.
4 The king's strength also loves judgment; you dost establish equity, you executes judgment and righteousness in Jacob.
5 Exalt you the LORD our God, and worship at his footstool; *for* he *is* holy.
6 Moses and Aaron among his priests, and Samuel among them that call upon his name; they called upon the LORD, and he answered them.
7 He spoke unto them in the cloudy pillar: they kept his testimonies, and the ordinance *that* he gave them.
8 You answered them, O LORD our God: you were a God that forgave them, though you took vengeance of their inventions.
9 Exalt the LORD our God, and worship at his holy hill; for the LORD our God *is* holy.

PSALM 100
A Psalm of praise.

1 Make a joyful noise unto the LORD, all you lands.
2 Serve the LORD with gladness: come before his presence with singing.
3 Know you that the LORD he *is* God: *it is* he *that* has made us, and not we ourselves; *we are* his people, and the sheep of his pasture.
4 Enter into his gates with thanksgiving, *and* into his courts with praise: be thankful unto him, *and* bless his name.
5 For the LORD *is* good; his mercy *is* everlasting; and his truth *endures* to all generations.

PSALM 101
A Psalm of David.

1 I will sing of mercy and judgment: unto you, O LORD, will I sing.
2 I will behave myself wisely in a perfect way. O when will you come unto me? I will walk within my house with a perfect heart.
3 I will set no wicked thing before mine eyes: I hate the work of them that turn aside; *it* will not cleave to me.
4 A forward heart will depart from me: I will not know a wicked *person*.
5 Whoso privily slanders his neighbor, him will I cut off: him that has an high look and a proud heart will not I suffer.
6 Mine eyes will *be* upon the faithful of the land, that they may dwell with me: he that walks in a perfect way, he will serve me.
7 He that works deceit will not dwell within my house: he that tells lies will not tarry in my sight.
8 I will early destroy all the wicked of the land; that I may cut off all wicked doers from the city of the LORD.

PSALM 102
A Prayer of the afflicted, when he is overwhelmed, and pours out his complaint before the LORD.

1 Hear my prayer, O LORD, and let my cry come unto you.
2 Hide not your face from me in the day *when* I am in trouble; incline your ear unto me: in the day *when* I call answer me speedily.
3 For my days are consumed like smoke, and my bones are burned as an hearth.
4 My heart is smitten, and withered like grass; so that I forget to eat my bread.
5 By reason of the voice of my groaning my bones cleave to my skin.
6 I am like a pelican of the wilderness: I am like an owl of the desert.
7 I watch, and am as a sparrow alone upon the house top.
8 Mine enemies reproach me all the day; *and* they that are mad against me are sworn against me.
9 For I have eaten ashes like bread, and mingled my drink with weeping,
10 Because of your indignation and your wrath: for you have lifted me up, and cast me down.
11 My days *are* like a shadow that declines; and I am withered like grass.
12 But you, O LORD, will endure for ever; and your remembrance unto all generations.
13 you will arise, *and* have mercy upon Zion: for the time to favor her, yea, the set time, is come.

14 For your servants take pleasure in her stones, and favor the dust thereof.
15 So the heathen will fear the name of the LORD, and all the kings of the earth your glory.
16 When the LORD will build up Zion, he will appear in his glory.
17 He will regard the prayer of the destitute, and not despise their prayer.
18 [This will be written for the generation to come: and the people which will be created will praise the LORD.]¹
19 For he has looked down from the height of his sanctuary; from heaven did the LORD behold the earth;
20 To hear the groaning of the prisoner; to loose those that are appointed to death;
21 To declare the name of the LORD in Zion, and his praise in Jerusalem;
22 When the people are gathered together, and the kingdoms, to serve the LORD.
23 He weakened my strength in the way; he shortened my days.
24 I said, O my God, take me not away in the midst of my days: your years *are* throughout all generations.
25 Of old have you laid the foundation of the earth: and the heavens *are* the work of your hands.
26 They will perish, but you will endure: yea, all of them will wax old like a garment; as a vesture will you change them, and they will be changed:
27 But you are the same, and your years will have no end.
28 The children of your servants will continue, and their seed will be established before you.

PSALM 103

A Psalm of David.

1 Bless the LORD, O my soul: and all that is within me, *bless* his holy name.
2 Bless the LORD, O my soul, and forget not all his benefits:
3 Who forgives all your iniquities; who heals all your diseases;
4 Who redeems your life from destruction; who crowns you with loving-kindness and tender mercies;
5 Who satisfies your mouth with good *things; so that* your youth is renewed like the eagle's.
6 The LORD execute righteousness and judgment for all that are oppressed.
7 He made known his ways unto Moses, his acts unto the children of Israel.
8 The LORD *is* merciful and gracious, slow to anger, and plenteous in mercy.
9 He will not always chide: neither will he keep *his anger* for ever.
10 He has not dealt with us after our sins; or rewarded us according to our iniquities.
11 For as the heaven is high above the earth, *so* great is his mercy toward them that fear him.
12 As far as the east is from the west, *so* far has he removed our transgressions from us.
13 Like as a father pities *his* children, *so* the LORD pities them that fear him.
14 For he knows our frame; he remembers that we *are* dust.
15 *As for* man, his days *are* as grass: as a flower of the field, so he flourishes.
16 For the wind passes over it, and it is gone; and the place thereof will know it no more.
17 But the mercy of the LORD *is* from everlasting to everlasting upon them that fear him, and his righteousness unto children's children;
18 To such as keep his covenant, and to those that remember his commandments to do them.
19 The LORD has prepared his throne in the heavens; and his kingdom rules over all.
20 Bless the LORD, you his angels, that excel in strength, that do his commandments, hearkening unto the voice of his word.
21 Bless you the LORD, all you his hosts; you ministers of his, that do his pleasure.
22 Bless the LORD, all his works in all places of his dominion: bless the LORD, O my soul.

PSALM 104

1 Bless the LORD, O my soul. O LORD my God, you are very great; you are clothed with honor and majesty.
2 Who covers yourself with light as *with* a garment: who stretches out the heavens like a curtain:
3 Who lays the beams of his chambers in the waters: who makes the clouds his chariot: who walks upon the wings of the wind:
4 Who makes his angels spirits; his ministers a flaming fire:
5 *Who* laid the foundations of the earth, *that* it should not be removed for ever.
6 You covered it with the deep as *with* a garment: the waters stood above the mountains.
7 [At your rebuke they fled; at the voice of your thunder they hasted away.]²
8 They go up by the mountains; they go down by the valleys unto the place which you have founded for them.
9 you have set a bound that they may not pass over; that they turn not again to cover the earth.
10 He sends the springs into the valleys, *which* run among the hills.
11 They give drink to every beast of the field: the wild asses quench their thirst.
12 By them will the fowls of the heaven have their habitation, *which* sing among the branches.
13 He waters the hills from his chambers: the earth is satisfied with the fruit of your works.
14 He causes the grass to grow for the cattle, and herb for the service of man: that he may bring forth food out of the earth;
15 And wine *that* makes glad the heart of man, *and* oil to make *his* face to shine, and bread *which* strengthens man's heart.
16 The trees of the LORD are full *of sap*; the cedars of Lebanon, which he has planted;
17 Where the birds make their nests: *as for* the stork, the fir trees *are* her house.
18 The high hills *are* a refuge for the wild goats; *and* the rocks for the conies.
19 He appointed the moon for seasons: the sun knows his going down.
20 you makes darkness, and it is night: wherein all the beasts of the forest do creep *forth*.
21 The young lions roar after their prey, and seek their meat from God.
22 The sun arises, they gather themselves together, and lay them down in their dens.

---

¹ see Rev. 3:14

² voice of thunder cause water to 'haste away'.

23 Man goes forth unto his work and to his labor until the evening.
24 O LORD, how manifold are your works! in wisdom have you made them all: the earth is full of your riches.
25 *So is* this great and wide sea, wherein *are* things creeping innumerable, both small and great beasts.
26 There go the ships: *there is* that leviathan, *who* you have made to play therein.
27 These wait all upon you; that you may give *them* their meat in due season.
28 *That* you give them they gather: you opens your hand, they are filled with good.
29 You hide your face, they are troubled: you take away their breath, they die, and return to their dust.
30 [You send forth your spirit, they are created: and you renew the face of the earth.]¹
31 The glory of the LORD will endure for ever: the LORD will rejoice in his works.
32 He looks on the earth, and it trembles: he touches the hills, and they smoke.
33 I will sing unto the LORD as long as I live: I will sing praise to my God while I have my being.
34 My meditation of him will be sweet: I will be glad in the LORD.
35 Let the sinners be consumed out of the earth, and let the wicked be no more. Bless you the LORD, O my soul. Praise you the LORD.

PSALM 105

1 O give thanks unto the LORD; call upon his name: make known his deeds among the people.
2 Sing unto him, sing psalms unto him: talk you of all his wondrous works.
3 Glory you in his holy name: let the heart of them rejoice that seek the LORD.
4 Seek the LORD, and his strength: seek his face evermore.
5 Remember his marvelous works that he has done; his wonders, and the judgments of his mouth;
6 O you seed of Abraham his servant, you children of Jacob his chosen.
7 He *is* the LORD our God: his judgments *are* in all the earth.
8 He has remembered his covenant forever, the word which he commanded to a thousand generations.
9 Which *covenant* he made with Abraham, and his oath unto Isaac;
10 And confirmed the same unto Jacob for a law, *and* to Israel *for* an everlasting covenant:
11 Saying, unto you will I give the land of Canaan, the lot of your inheritance:
12 When they were *but* a few men in number; yea, very few, and strangers in it.
13 When they went from one nation to another, from *one* kingdom to another people;
14 He suffered no man to do them wrong: yea, he reproved kings for their sakes;
15 *Saying*, Touch not mine anointed, and do my prophets no harm.
16 Moreover he called for a famine upon the land: he brake the whole staff of bread.
17 He sent² a man before them, *even* Joseph, *who* was sold for a servant:

18 Whose feet they hurt with fetters: he was laid in iron:
19 Until the time that his word came: the word of the LORD tried him.
20 The king sent and loosed him; *even* the ruler of the people, and let him go free.
21 He made him lord of his house, and ruler of all his substance:
22 To bind his princes at his pleasure; and teach his senators wisdom.
23 Israel also came into Egypt; and Jacob sojourned in the land of Ham.
24 And he increased his people greatly; and made them stronger than their enemies.
25 He turned their heart to hate his people, to deal subtly with his servants.
26 He sent Moses his servant; *and* Aaron whom he had chosen.
27 They showed his signs³ among them, and wonders in the land of Ham.
28 He sent darkness, and made it dark; and they rebelled not against his word.
29 He turned their waters into blood, and slew their fish.
30 [Their land brought forth frogs⁴ in abundance, in the chambers of their kings.]⁵
31 He spoke, and there came divers sorts of flies, *and* lice in all their coasts.
32 He gave them hail for rain, *and* flaming fire in their land.
33 He smote their vines also and their fig trees; and brake the trees of their coasts.
34 He spoke, and the locusts came, and caterpillars, and that without number,
35 And did eat up all the herbs in their land, and devoured the fruit of their ground.
36 He smote also all the firstborn in their land, the chief of all their strength.
37 He brought them forth also with silver and gold: and *there was* not one feeble *person* among their tribes.
38 Egypt was glad when they departed: for the fear of them fell upon them.
39 He spread a cloud for a covering; and fire to give light in the night.
40 *The people* asked, and he brought quails, and satisfied them with the bread of heaven.
41 He opened the rock, and the waters gushed out; they ran in the dry places *like* a river.
42 For he remembered his holy promise, *and* Abraham his servant.
43 And he brought forth his people with joy, *and* his chosen with gladness:
44 And gave them the lands of the heathen: and they inherited the labor of the people;
45 That they might observe his statutes, and keep his laws. Praise you the LORD.

PSALM 106

1 Praise you the LORD. O give thanks unto the LORD; for *he is* good: for his mercy *endures* forever.
2 Who can utter the mighty acts of the LORD? who can show forth all his praise?

---

¹ compare Genesis 1:1
² sent – is the Greek word *apostello*. Note: the apostle was sold for a slave.
³ signs – comes from two Hebrew words. The first being *'ôth* meaning a *signal*, as *flag, beacon, monument, omen, prodigy, evidence* [Strgs#226].

The second word *dâbâr* meaning a *word*; by implication a matter (as *spoken of*) of *thing* [Strgs#1697]. Literally words of His signs.
⁴ lit. *swamp; a marsh leaper* [Strgs#6854]
⁵ compare Psalm 78:45

3 Blessed *are* they that keep judgment, *and* he that doeth righteousness at all times.
4 Remember me, O LORD, with the favor *that you bears unto* your people: O visit me with your salvation;
5 That I may see the good of your chosen, that I may rejoice in the gladness of your nation, that I may glory with your inheritance.
6 We have sinned with our fathers, we have committed iniquity, we have done wickedly.
7 Our fathers understood not your wonders in Egypt; they remembered not the multitude of your mercies; but provoked *him* at the sea, *even* at the Red sea.
8 Nevertheless he saved them for his name's sake, that he might make his mighty power to be known.
9 He rebuked the Red sea also, and it was dried up: so he led them through the depths, as through the wilderness.
10 And he saved them from the hand of him that hated *them*, and redeemed them from the hand of the enemy.
11 And the waters covered their enemies: there was not one of them left.
12 Then believed they his words; they sang his praise.
13 They soon forgot his works; they waited not for his counsel:
14 But lusted exceedingly in the wilderness, and tempted God in the desert.
15 And he gave them their request; but sent leanness into their soul.
16 They envied Moses also in the camp, *and* Aaron the saint of the LORD.
17 The earth opened and swallowed up Dathan, and covered the company of Abiram.
18 And a fire was kindled in their company; the flame burned up the wicked.
19 They made a calf in Horeb, and worshipped the molten image.
20 [Thus they changed their glory into the similitude of an ox that eats grass.]¹
21 They forgot God their savior, which had done great things in Egypt;
22 Wondrous works in the land of Ham, *and* terrible things by the Red sea.
23 Therefore he said that he would destroy them, had not Moses his chosen stood before him in the breach, to turn away his wrath, lest he should destroy *them*.
24 Yea, they despised the pleasant land, they believed not his word:
25 But murmured in their tents, *and* hearkened not unto the voice of the LORD.
26 Therefore he lifted up his hand against them, to overthrow them in the wilderness:
27 To overthrow their seed also among the nations, and to scatter them in the lands.
28 They joined themselves also unto Baal-peor, and ate the sacrifices of the dead.
29 Thus they provoked *him* to anger with their inventions: and the plague brake in upon them.
30 Then stood up Phinehas, and executed judgment: and *so* the plague was stayed.
31 And that was counted unto him for righteousness unto all generations for evermore.
32 They angered *him* also at the waters of strife, so that it went ill with Moses for their sakes:
33 Because they provoked his spirit, so that he spoke unadvisedly with his lips.
34 They did not destroy the nations, concerning whom the LORD commanded them:
35 But were mingled among the heathen, and learned their works.
36 And they served their idols: which were a snare unto them.
37 Yea, they sacrificed their sons and their daughters unto devils,
38 And shed innocent blood, *even* the blood of their sons and of their daughters, whom they sacrificed unto the idols of Canaan: and the land was polluted with blood.
39 Thus were they defiled with their own works, and went a whoring with their own inventions.
40 Therefore was the wrath of the LORD kindled against his people, insomuch that he abhorred his own inheritance.
41 And he gave them into the hand of the heathen; and they that hated them ruled over them.
42 Their enemies also oppressed them, and they were brought into subjection under their hand.
43 Many times did he deliver them; but they provoked *him* with their counsel, and were brought low for their iniquity.
44 Nevertheless he regarded their affliction, when he heard their cry:
45 And he remembered for them his covenant, and repented according to the multitude of his mercies.
46 He made them also to be pitied of all those that carried them captives.
47 Save us, O LORD our God, and gather us from among the heathen, to give thanks unto your holy name, *and* to triumph in your praise.
48 Blessed *be* the LORD God of Israel from everlasting to everlasting: and let all the people say, Amen. Praise you the LORD.

PSALM 107

1 O give thanks unto the LORD, for *he is* good: for his mercy *endures* forever.
2 Let the redeemed of the LORD say *so*, whom he has redeemed from the hand of the enemy;
3 And gathered them out of the lands, from the east, and from the west, from the north, and from the south.
4 They wandered in the wilderness in a solitary way; they found no city to dwell in.
5 Hungry and thirsty, their soul fainted in them.
6 Then they cried unto the LORD in their trouble, *and* he delivered them out of their distresses.
7 And he led them forth by the right way, that they might go to a city of habitation.
8 Oh that *men* would praise the LORD *for* his goodness, and *for* his wonderful works to the children of men!
9 For he satisfies the longing soul, and fills the hungry soul with goodness.
10 Such as sit in darkness and in the shadow of death, *being* bound in affliction and iron;
11 Because they rebelled against the words of God, and contemned the counsel of the most High:
12 Therefore he brought down their heart with labor; they fell down, and *there was* none to help.
13 Then they cried unto the LORD in their trouble, *and* he saved them out of their distresses.

---

¹ compare Romans 1:24, 1 Kings 12:25-28 & Exodus 32:4 – homosexuality.

14 He brought them out of darkness and the shadow of death, and brake their bands in sunder.
15 Oh that *men* would praise the LORD *for* his goodness, and *for* his wonderful works to the children of men!
16 For he has broken the gates of brass, and cut the bars of iron in sunder.
17 Fools because of their transgression, and because of their iniquities, are afflicted.
18 Their soul abhorrers all manner of meat; and they draw near unto the gates of death.
19 Then they cry unto the LORD in their trouble, *and* he saves them out of their distresses.
20 He sent his word, and healed them, and delivered *them* from their destructions.
21 Oh that *men* would praise the LORD *for* his goodness, and *for* his wonderful works to the children of men!
22 And let them sacrifice the sacrifices of thanksgiving, and declare his works with rejoicing.
23 They that go down to the sea in ships, that do business in great waters;
24 These see the works of the LORD, and his wonders in the deep.
25 For he commands, and raises the stormy wind, which lifts up the waves thereof.
26 They mount up to the heaven, they go down again to the depths: their soul is melted because of trouble.
27 They reel to and fro, and stagger like a drunken man, and are at their wits' end.
28 Then they cry unto the LORD in their trouble, and he brings them out of their distresses.
29 He makes the storm a calm, so that the waves thereof are still.
30 Then are they glad because they be quiet; <u>so he brings them unto their desired haven</u>.
31 Oh that *men* would praise the LORD *for* his goodness, and *for* his wonderful works to the children of men!
32 Let them exalt him also in the congregation of the people, and praise him in the assembly of the elders.
33 He turns rivers into a wilderness, and the water-springs into dry ground;
34 A fruitful land into barrenness, for the wickedness of them that dwell therein.
35 He turns the wilderness into a standing water, and dry ground into water-springs.
36 And there he makes the hungry to dwell, that they may prepare a city for habitation;
37 And sow the fields, and plant vineyards, which may yield fruits of increase.
38 He blesses them also, so that they are multiplied greatly; and suffers not their cattle to decrease.
39 Again, they are minished and brought low through oppression, affliction, and sorrow.
40 He pours contempt upon princes, and causes them to wander in the wilderness, *where there is* no way.
41 Yet sets he the poor on high from affliction, and makes *him* families like a flock.
42 The righteous will see *it*, and rejoice: and all iniquity will stop her mouth.
43 Whoso *is* wise, and will observe these *things*, even they will understand the loving-kindness of the LORD.

PSALM 108
A Song *or* Psalm of David.

1 O God, my heart is fixed; I will sing and give praise, even with my glory.
2 Awake, psaltery and harp: I *myself* will awake early.
3 I will praise you, O LORD, among the people: and I will sing praises unto you among the nations.
4 For your mercy *is* great above the heavens: and your truth *reaches* unto the clouds.
5 Be you exalted, O God, above the heavens: and your glory above all the earth;
6 That your beloved may be delivered: save *with* your right hand, and answer me.
7 God has spoken in his holiness; I will rejoice, I will divide Shechem, and mete out the valley of Succoth.
8 Gilead *is* mine; Manasseh *is* mine; Ephraim also *is* the strength of mine head; Judah *is* my lawgiver;
9 Moab *is* my wash-pot; over Edom will I cast out my shoe; over Philistia will I triumph.
10 Who will bring me into the strong city? Who will lead me into Edom?
11 Will not you, O God, *who* have cast us off? And will not you, O God, go forth with our hosts?
12 Give us help from trouble: for vain *is* the help of man.
13 Through God we will do valiantly: for he *it is that* will tread down our enemies.

PSALM 109
To the chief Musician, A Psalm of David.

1 Hold not your peace, O God of my praise;
2 For the mouth of the wicked and the mouth of the deceitful are opened against me: they have spoken against me with a lying tongue.
3 They compassed me about also with words of hatred; and fought against me without a cause.
4 For my love they are my adversaries: but I *give myself unto* prayer.
5 And they have rewarded me evil for good, and hatred for my love.
6 Set you a wicked man over him: and let Satan stand at his right hand.
7 When he will be judged, let him be condemned: and let his prayer become sin.
8 Let his days be few; *and* let another take his office.
9 Let his children be fatherless, and his wife a widow.
10 Let his children be continually vagabonds, and beg let them seek *their bread* also out of their desolate places.
11 Let the extortioner catch all that he hath; and let the strangers spoil his labor.
12 Let there be none to extend mercy unto him: neither let there be any to favor his fatherless children.
13 Let his posterity be cut off; *and* in the generation following let their name be blotted out.
14 Let the iniquity of his fathers be remembered with the LORD; and let not the sin of his mother be blotted out.
15 Let them be before the LORD continually, that he may cut off the memory of them from the earth.
16 Because that he remembered not to show mercy, but persecuted the poor and needy man, that he might even slay the broken in heart.
17 As he loved cursing, so let it come unto him: as he delighted not in blessing, so let it be far from him.

18 As he clothed himself with cursing like as with his garment, so let it come into his bowels like water, and like oil into his bones.
19 Let it be unto him as the garment *which* covers him, and for a girdle wherewith he is girded continually.
20 *Let* this *be* the reward of mine adversaries from the LORD, and of them that speak evil against my soul.
21 But do you for me, O GOD the Lord, for your name's sake: because your mercy *is* good, deliver you me.
22 For I *am* poor and needy, and my heart is wounded within me.
23 I am gone like the shadow when it declines: I am tossed up and down as the locust.
24 My knees are weak through fasting; and my flesh fails of fatness.
25 I became also a reproach unto them: *when* they looked upon me they shake their heads.
26 Help me, O LORD my God: O save me according to your mercy:
27 That they may know that this *is* your hand; *that* you, LORD, have done it.
28 Let them curse, but bless you: when they arise, let them be ashamed; but let your servant rejoice.
29 Let mine adversaries be clothed with shame, and let them cover themselves with their own confusion, as with a mantle.
30 I will greatly praise the LORD with my mouth; yea, I will praise him among the multitude.
31 For he will stand at the right hand of the poor, to save *him* from those that condemn his soul.

PSALM 110
A Psalm of David.

1 The LORD said unto my Lord, Sit you at my right hand, until I make your enemies your footstool.
2 The LORD will send the rod of your strength out of Zion: rule you in the midst of your enemies.
3 your people will *be* willing in the day of your power, in the beauties of holiness from the womb of the morning: you have the dew of your youth.
4 The LORD has sworn, and will not repent, you are a priest for ever after the order of Melchizedek.
5 The Lord at your right hand will strike through kings in the day of his wrath.
6 He will judge among the heathen, he will fill *the places* with the dead bodies; he will wound the heads over many countries.
7 He will drink of the brook in the way: therefore will he lift up the head.

PSALM 111
1 Praise you the LORD. I will praise the LORD with *my* whole heart, in the assembly of the upright, and *in* the congregation.
2 The works of the LORD *are* great, sought out of all them that have pleasure therein.
3 His work *is* honorable and glorious: and his righteousness endures forever.
4 He has made his wonderful works to be remembered: the LORD *is* gracious and full of compassion.
5 He has given meat unto them that fear him: he will ever be mindful of his covenant.
6 He has showed his people the power of his works, that he may give them the heritage of the heathen.
7 The works of his hands *are* verity and judgment; all his commandments *are* sure.
8 They stand fast forever and ever, *and are* done in truth and uprightness.
9 He sent redemption unto his people: he has commanded his covenant for ever: holy and reverend *is* his name.
10 The fear of the LORD *is* the beginning of wisdom: a good understanding have all they that do *his commandments*: his praise endures forever.

PSALM 112
1 Praise you the LORD. Blessed *is* the man *that* fears the LORD, *that* delights greatly in his commandments.
2 His seed will be mighty upon earth: the generation of the upright will be blessed.
3 Wealth and riches will *be* in his house: and his righteousness endures forever.
4 Unto the upright there arises light in the darkness: *he is* gracious, and full of compassion, and righteous.
5 A good man shows favor, and lends: he will guide his affairs with discretion.
6 Surely he will not be moved for ever: the righteous will be in everlasting remembrance.
7 He will not be afraid of evil tidings: his heart is fixed, trusting in the LORD.
8 His heart *is* established, he will not be afraid, until he see *his desire* upon his enemies.
9 He has dispersed, he has given to the poor; his righteousness endures for ever; his horn will be exalted with honor.
10 The wicked will see *it*, and be grieved; he will gnash with his teeth, and melt away: the desire of the wicked will perish.

PSALM 113
1 Praise you the LORD. Praise, O you servants of the LORD, praise the name of the LORD.
2 Blessed be the name of the LORD from this time forth and for evermore.
3 From the rising of the sun unto the going down of the same the LORD'S name *is* to be praised.
4 The LORD *is* high above all nations, *and* his glory above the heavens.
5 Who *is* like unto the LORD our God, who dwells on high,
6 Who humbles *himself* to behold *the things that are* in heaven, and in the earth!
7 He raises up the poor out of the dust, *and* lifts the needy out of the dunghill;
8 That he may set *him* with princes, *even* with the princes of his people.
9 He make the barren woman to keep house, *and to be* a joyful mother of children. Praise you the LORD.

PSALM 114
1 When Israel went out of Egypt, the house of Jacob from a people of strange language;
2 Judah was his sanctuary, *and* Israel his dominion.
3 The sea saw *it*, and fled: Jordan was driven back.
4 The mountains skipped like rams, *and* the little hills like lambs.
5 What *ailed* you, O you sea, that you fleddest? You Jordan, *that* you were driven back?
6 you mountains, *that* you skipped like rams; *and* you little hills, like lambs?
7 Tremble, you earth, at the presence of the Lord, at the presence of the God of Jacob;

8 Which turned the rock *into* a standing water, the flint into a fountain of waters.

PSALM 115

1 Not unto us, O LORD, not unto us, but unto your name give glory, for your mercy, *and* for your truth's sake.
2 Wherefore should the heathen say, where *is* now their God?
3 But our God *is* in the heavens: he has done whatsoever he has pleased.
4 Their idols *are* silver and gold, the work of men's hands.
5 They have mouths, but they speak not: eyes have they, but they see not:
6 They have ears, but they hear not: noses have they, but they smell not:
7 They have hands, but they handle not: feet have they, but they walk not: neither speak they through their throat.
8 They that make them are like unto them; *so is* every one that trusts in them.
9 O Israel, trust you in the LORD: he *is* their help and their shield.
10 O house of Aaron, trust in the LORD: he *is* their help and their shield.
11 you that fear the LORD, trust in the LORD: he *is* their help and their shield.
12 The LORD has been mindful of us: he will bless *us*; he will bless the house of Israel; he will bless the house of Aaron.
13 He will bless them that fear the LORD, *both* small and great.
14 The LORD will increase you more and more, you and your children.
15 you *are* blessed of the LORD which made heaven and earth.
16 The heaven, *even* the heavens, *are* the LORD'S: but the earth has he given to the children of men.
17 The dead praise not the LORD, neither any that go down into silence.
18 But we will bless the LORD from this time forth and for evermore. Praise the LORD.

PSALM 116

1 I love the LORD, because he has heard my voice *and* my supplications.
2 Because he has inclined his ear unto me, therefore will I call upon *him* as long as I live.
3 The sorrows of death compassed me, and the pains of hell gat hold upon me: I found trouble and sorrow.
4 Then called I upon the name of the LORD; O LORD, I beseech you, deliver my soul.
5 Gracious *is* the LORD, and righteous; yea, our God *is* merciful.
6 The LORD preserves the simple: I was brought low, and he helped me.
7 Return unto your rest, O my soul; for the LORD has dealt bountifully with you.
8 For you have delivered my soul from death, mine eyes from tears, *and* my feet from falling.
9 I will walk before the LORD in the land of the living.
10 I believed, therefore have I spoken: I was greatly afflicted:
11 I said in my haste, All men *are* liars.
12 What will I render unto the LORD *for* all his benefits toward me?
13 I will take the cup of salvation, and call upon the name of the LORD.
14 I will pay my vows unto the LORD now in the presence of all his people.
15 Precious in the sight of the LORD *is* the death of his saints.
16 O LORD, truly I *am* your servant; I *am* your servant, *and* the son of your handmaid: you have loosed my bonds.
17 I will offer to you the sacrifice of thanksgiving, and will call upon the name of the LORD.
18 I will pay my vows unto the LORD now in the presence of all his people,
19 In the courts of the LORD'S house, in the midst of you, O Jerusalem. Praise you the LORD.

PSALM 117

1 O praise the LORD, all you nations: praise him, all you people.
2 For his merciful kindness is great toward us: and the truth of the LORD *endures* forever. Praise you the LORD.

PSALM 118

1 O give thanks unto the LORD; for *he is* good: because his mercy *endures* forever.
2 Let Israel now say, that his mercy *endures* forever.
3 Let the house of Aaron now say, that his mercy *endures* forever.
4 Let them now that fear the LORD say, that his mercy *endures* forever.
5 I called upon the LORD in distress: the LORD answered me, *and set me* in a large place.
6 The LORD *is* on my side; I will not fear: what can man do unto me?
7 The LORD takes my part with them that help me: therefore will I see *my desire* upon them that hate me.
8 *It is* better to trust in the LORD than to put confidence in man.
9 *It is* better to trust in the LORD than to put confidence in princes.
10 All nations compassed me about: but in the name of the LORD will I destroy them.
11 They compassed me about; yea, they compassed me about: but in the name of the LORD I will destroy them.
12 They compassed me about like bees; they are quenched as the fire of thorns: for in the name of the LORD I will destroy them.
13 you have thrust sore at me that I might fall: but the LORD helped me.
14 The LORD *is* my strength and song, and is become my salvation.
15 The voice of rejoicing and salvation *is* in the tabernacles of the righteous: the right hand of the LORD does valiantly.
16 The right hand of the LORD is exalted: the right hand of the LORD does valiantly.
17 I will not die, but live, and declare the works of the LORD.
18 The LORD has chastened me sore: but he has not given me over unto death.
19 Open to me the gates of righteousness: I will go into them, *and* I will praise the LORD:
20 This gate of the LORD, into which the righteous will enter.
21 I will praise you: for you have heard me, and are become my salvation.
22 The stone *which* the builders refused is become the head *stone* of the corner.
23 This is the LORD'S doing; it *is* marvelous in our eyes.
24 This *is* the day *which* the LORD has made; we will rejoice and be glad in it.
25 Save now, I beseech you, O LORD: O LORD, I beseech you, send now prosperity.
26 Blessed *be* he that cometh in the name of the LORD: we have blessed you out of the house of the LORD.
27 God *is* the LORD, which has showed us light: bind the sacrifice with cords, *even* unto the horns of the altar.

28 you are my God, and I will praise you: you *are* my God, I will exalt you.
29 O give thanks unto the LORD; for *he is* good: for his mercy *endures* forever.

PSALM 119
ALEPH.

1 Blessed *are* the undefiled in the way, who walk in the law of the LORD.
2 Blessed *are* they that keep his testimonies, *and that* seek him with the whole heart.
3 They also do no iniquity: they walk in his ways.
4 you have commanded *us* to keep your precepts diligently.
5 O that my ways were directed to keep your statutes!
6 Then will I not be ashamed, when I have respect unto all your commandments.
7 I will praise you with uprightness of heart, when I will have learned your righteous judgments.
8 I will keep your statutes: O forsake me not utterly.

BETH.

9 Wherewithal will a young man cleanse his way? By taking heed *thereto* according to your word.
10 With my whole heart have I sought you: O let me not wander from your commandments.
11 your word have I hid in mine heart, that I might not sin against you.
12 Blessed are you, O LORD: teach me your statutes.
13 With my lips have I declared all the judgments of your mouth.
14 I have rejoiced in the way of your testimonies, as *much as* in all riches.
15 I will meditate in your precepts, and have respect unto your ways.
16 I will delight myself in your statutes: I will not forget your word.

GIMEL.

17 Deal bountifully with your servant, *that* I may live, and keep your word.
18 Open you mine eyes, that I may behold wondrous things out of your law.
19 I *am* a stranger in the earth: hide not your commandments from me.
20 My soul breaks for the longing *that it has* unto your judgments at all times.
21 you have rebuked the proud *that are* cursed, which do err from your commandments.
22 Remove from me reproach and contempt; for I have kept your testimonies.
23 Princes also did sit *and* speak against me: *but* your servant did meditate in your statutes.
24 Your testimonies also *are* my delight *and* my counselors¹.

DALETH.

25 My soul cleaves unto the dust: quicken you me according to your word.
26 I have declared my ways, and you heard me: teach me your statutes.

27 Make me to understand the way of your precepts: so will I talk of your wondrous works.
28 My soul melts for heaviness: strengthen you me according unto your word.
29 Remove from me the way of lying: and grant me your law graciously.
30 I have chosen the way of truth: your judgments have I laid *before me*.
31 I have stuck unto your testimonies: O LORD, put me not to shame.
32 I will run the way of your commandments, when you will enlarge my heart.

HE.

33 Teach me, O LORD, the way of your statutes; and I will keep it *unto* the end.
34 Give me understanding, and I will keep your law; yea, I will observe it with *my* whole heart.
35 Make me to go in the path of your commandments; for therein do I delight.
36 Incline my heart unto your testimonies, *and* not to covetousness.
37 Turn away mine eyes from beholding vanity; *and* quicken you me in your way.
38 **Establish** your word unto your servant, who *is devoted* to your fear.
39 Turn away my reproach which I fear: for your judgments *are* good.
40 Behold, I have longed after your precepts: quicken me in your righteousness.

VAU.

41 Let your mercies come also unto me, O LORD, *even* your salvation, according to your word.
42 So will I have wherewith to answer him that reproaches me: for I trust in your word.
43 And take not the word of truth utterly out of my mouth; for I have hoped in your judgments.
44 So will I keep your law continually forever and ever.
45 And I will walk at liberty: for I seek your precepts.
46 I will speak of your testimonies also before kings, and will not be ashamed.
47 And I will delight myself in your commandments, which I have loved.
48 My hands also will I lift up unto your commandments, which I have loved; and I will meditate in your statutes.

ZAIN.

49 Remember the word unto your servant, upon which you have caused me to hope.
50 This *is* my comfort in my affliction: for your word has quickened me.
51 The proud have had me greatly in derision: *yet* have I not declined from your law.
52 I remembered your judgments of old, O LORD; and have comforted myself.
53 Horror has taken hold upon me because of the wicked that forsake your law.

---

¹ counsel – comes from two Hebrew words meaning men of counsel or men of advice [Strgs#582+6098].

54 your statutes have been my songs in the house of my pilgrimage.
55 I have remembered your name, O LORD, in the night, and have kept your law.
56 This I had, because I kept your precepts.

CHETH.

57 you *are* my portion, O LORD: I have said that I would keep your words.
58 I intreated your favor with *my* whole heart: be merciful unto me according to your word.
59 I thought on my ways, and turned my feet unto your testimonies.
60 I made haste, and delayed not to keep your commandments.
61 The bands of the wicked have robbed me: *but* I have not forgotten your law.
62 At midnight I will rise to give thanks unto you because of your righteous judgments.
63 I *am* a companion of all *them* that fear you, and of them that keep your precepts.
64 The earth, O LORD, is full of your mercy: teach me your statutes.

TETH.

65 you have dealt well with your servant, O LORD, according unto your word.
66 Teach me good judgment and knowledge: for I have believed your commandments.
67 Before I was afflicted I went astray: but now have I kept your word.
68 you are good, and doest good; teach me your statutes.
69 The proud have forged a lie against me: *but* I will keep your precepts with *my* whole heart.
70 Their heart is as fat as grease; *but* I delight in your law.
71 *It is* good for me that I have been afflicted; that I might learn your statutes.
72 The law of your mouth *is* better unto me than thousands of gold and silver.

JOD.

73 your hands have made me and fashioned me: give me understanding, that I may learn your commandments.
74 They that fear you will be glad when they see me; because I have hoped in your word.
75 I know, O LORD, that your judgments *are* right, and *that* you in faithfulness have afflicted me.
76 Let, I pray you, your merciful kindness be for my comfort, according to your word unto your servant.
77 Let your tender mercies come unto me, that I may live: for your law *is* my delight.
78 Let the proud be ashamed; for they dealt perversely with me without a cause: *but* I will meditate in your precepts.
79 Let those that fear you turn unto me, and those that have known your testimonies.
80 Let my heart be sound in your statutes; that I be not ashamed.

CAPH.

81 My soul faints for your salvation: *but* I hope in your word.
82 Mine eyes fail for your word, saying, when will you comfort me?
83 For I am become like a bottle in the smoke; *yet* do I not forget your statutes.
84 How many *are* the days of your servant? when will you execute judgment on them that persecute me?
85 The proud have digged pits for me, which *are* not after your law.
86 All your commandments *are* faithful: they persecute me wrongfully; help you me.
87 They had almost consumed me upon earth; but I forsook not your precepts.
88 Quicken me after your loving-kindness; so will I keep the testimony of your mouth.

LAMED.

89 Forever, O LORD, your word is settled in heaven.
90 your faithfulness *is* unto all generations: you have established the earth, and it abides.
91 They continue this day according to your ordinances: for all *are* your servants.
92 Unless your law *had been* my delights, I should then have perished in mine affliction.
93 I will never forget your precepts: for with them you have quickened me.
94 I *am* yours, save me; for I have sought your precepts.
95 The wicked have waited for me to destroy me: *but* I will consider your testimonies.
96 I have seen an end of all perfection: *but* your commandment *is* exceeding broad.

MEM.

97 O how love I your law! it *is* my meditation all the day.
98 you through your commandments have made me wiser than mine enemies: for they *are* ever with me.
99 I have more understanding than all my teachers: for your testimonies *are* my meditation.
100 I understand more than the ancients, because I keep your precepts.
101 I have refrained my feet from every evil way, that I might keep your word.
102 I have not departed from your judgments: for you have taught me.
103 How sweet are your words unto my taste! *yea, sweeter* than honey to my mouth!
104 Through your precepts I get understanding: therefore I hate every false way.

NUN.

105 your word *is* a lamp unto my feet, and a light unto my path.
106 I have sworn, and I will perform *it*, that I will keep your righteous judgments.
107 I am afflicted very much: quicken me, O LORD, according unto your word.
108 Accept, I beseech you, the freewill offerings of my mouth, O LORD, and teach me your judgments.
109 My soul *is* continually in my hand: yet do I not forget your law.
110 The wicked have laid a snare for me: yet I erred not from your precepts.
111 your testimonies have I taken as an heritage for ever: for they *are* the rejoicing of my heart.
112 I have inclined mine heart to perform your statutes always, *even unto* the end.

SAMECH.

113 I hate *vain* thoughts: but your law do I love.
114 you are my hiding place and my shield: I hope in your word.
115 Depart from me, you evildoers: for I will keep the commandments of my God.
116 Uphold me according unto your word, that I may live: and let me not be ashamed of my hope.
117 Hold you me up, and I will be safe: and I will have respect unto your statutes continually.
118 you have trodden down all them that err from your statutes: for their deceit *is* falsehood.
119 You put away all the wicked of the earth *like* dross: therefore I love your testimonies.
120 My flesh trembles for fear of you; and I am afraid of your judgments.

AIN.

121 I have done judgment and justice: leave me not to mine oppressors.
122 Be surety for your servant for good: let not the proud oppress me.
123 Mine eyes fail for your salvation, and for the word of your righteousness.
124 Deal with your servant according unto your mercy, and teach me your statutes.
125 I *am* your servant; give me understanding, that I may know your testimonies.
126 *It is* time for you, LORD, to work: *for* they have made void your law.
127 Therefore I love your commandments above gold; yea, above fine gold.
128 Therefore I esteem all your precepts *concerning* all *things to be* right; *and* I hate every false way.

PE.

129 your testimonies *are* wonderful: therefore does my soul keep them.
130 The entrance of your words gives light; it gives understanding unto the simple.
131 I opened my mouth, and panted: for I longed for your commandments.
132 Look you upon me, and be merciful unto me, as you use to do unto those that love your name.
133 Order my steps in your word: and let not any iniquity have dominion over me.
134 Deliver me from the oppression of man: so will I keep your precepts.
135 Make your face to shine upon your servant; and teach me your statutes.
136 Rivers of waters run down mine eyes, because they keep not your law.

TZADDI.

137 Righteous are you, O LORD, and upright *are* your judgments.
138 your testimonies *that* you have commanded *are* righteous and very faithful.
139 My zeal has consumed me, because mine enemies have forgotten your words.
140 your word *is* very pure: therefore your servant loveth it.
141 I *am* small and despised: *yet* do not I forget your precepts.
142 your righteousness *is* an everlasting righteousness, and your law *is* the truth.
143 Trouble and anguish have taken hold on me: *yet* your commandments *are* my delights.
144 The righteousness of your testimonies *is* everlasting: give me understanding, and I will live.

KOPH.

145 I cried with *my* whole heart; hear me, O LORD: I will keep your statutes.
146 I cried unto you; save me, and I will keep your testimonies.
147 I prevented the dawning of the morning, and cried: I hoped in your word.
148 Mine eyes prevent the *night* watches, that I might meditate in your word.
149 Hear my voice according unto your loving-kindness: O LORD, quicken me according to your judgment.
150 They draw nigh that follow after mischief: they are far from your law.
151 you are near, O LORD; and all your commandments *are* truth.
152 Concerning your testimonies, I have known of old that you have founded them forever.

RESH.

153 Consider mine affliction, and deliver me: for I do not forget your law.
154 Plead my cause, and deliver me: quicken me according to your word.
155 Salvation *is* far from the wicked: for they seek not your statutes.
156 Great *are* your tender mercies, O LORD: quicken me according to your judgments.
157 Many *are* my persecutors and mine enemies; *yet* do I not decline from your testimonies.
158 I beheld the transgressors, and was grieved; because they kept not your word.
159 Consider how I love your precepts: quicken me, O LORD, according to your loving-kindness.
160 your word *is* true *from* the beginning: and every one of your righteous judgments *endures* forever.

SCHIN.

161 Princes have persecuted me without a cause: but my heart stands in awe of your word.
162 I rejoice at your word, as one that finds great spoil.
163 I hate and abhor lying: *but* your law do I love.
164 Seven times a day do I praise you because of your righteous judgments.
165 Great peace have they which love your law: and nothing will offend them.
166 LORD, I have hoped for your salvation, and done your commandments.
167 My soul has kept your testimonies; and I love them exceedingly.
168 I have kept your precepts and your testimonies: for all my ways *are* before you.

TAU.

169 Let my cry come near before you, O LORD give me understanding according to your word.

170 Let my supplication come before you: deliver me according to your word.
171 My lips will utter praise, when you have taught me your statutes.
172 My tongue will speak of your word: for all your commandments *are* righteousness.
173 Let your hand help me; for I have chosen your precepts.
174 I have longed for your salvation, O LORD; and your law *is* my delight.
175 Let my soul live, and it will praise you; and let your judgments help me.
176 I have gone astray like a lost sheep; seek your servant; for I do not forget your commandments.

PSALM 120
A Song of degrees.

1 In my distress I cried unto the LORD, and he heard me.
2 Deliver my soul, O LORD, from lying lips, *and* from a deceitful tongue.
3 What will be given unto you? or what will be done unto you, you false tongue?
4 Sharp arrows of the mighty, with coals of juniper.
5 Woe is me, that I sojourn in Mesech, *that* I dwell in the tents of Kedar!
6 My soul has long dwelt with him that hates peace.
7 I *am for* peace: but when I speak, they *are* for war.

PSALM 121
A Song of degrees.

1 I will lift up mine eyes unto the hills, from where comes my help.
2 My help *cometh* from the LORD, which made heaven and earth.
3 He will not suffer your foot to be moved: he that keeps you will not slumber.
4 Behold, he that keeps Israel will neither slumber or sleep.
5 The LORD *is* your keeper: the LORD *is* your shade upon your right hand.
6 The sun will not smite you by day, or the moon by night.
7 The LORD will preserve you from all evil: he will preserve your soul.
8 The LORD will preserve your going out and your coming in from this time forth, and even for evermore.

PSALM 122
A Song of degrees of David.

1 I was glad when they said unto me, Let us go into the house of the LORD.
2 Our feet will stand within your gates, O Jerusalem.
3 Jerusalem is built as a city that is **joined**[1] together:
4 Where the tribes go up, the tribes of the LORD, unto the testimony of Israel, to give thanks unto the name of the LORD.
5 For there are set thrones of judgment, the thrones of the house of David.
6 Pray for the peace of Jerusalem: they will prosper that love you.
7 Peace be within your walls, *and* prosperity within your palaces.
8 For my brethren and companions' sakes, I will now say, Peace *be* within you.
9 Because of the house of the LORD our God I will seek your good.

PSALM 123
A Song of degrees.

1 Unto you lift I up mine eyes, O you that dwell in the heavens.
2 Behold, as the eyes of servants *look* unto the hand of their masters, *and* as the eyes of a maiden unto the hand of her mistress; so our eyes *wait* upon the LORD our God, until that he have mercy upon us.
3 Have mercy upon us, O LORD, have mercy upon us: for we are exceedingly filled with contempt.
4 Our soul is exceedingly filled with the scorning of those that are at ease, *and* with the contempt of the proud.

PSALM 124
A Song of degrees of David.

1 If *it had not been* the LORD who was on our side, now may Israel say;
2 If *it had not been* the LORD who was on our side, when men rose up against us:
3 Then they had swallowed us up quick, when their wrath was kindled against us:
4 Then the waters had overwhelmed us, the stream had gone over our soul:
5 Then the proud waters had gone over our soul.
6 Blessed *be* the LORD, who has not given us *as* a prey to their teeth.
7 Our soul is escaped as a bird out of the snare of the fowlers: the snare is broken, and we are escaped.
8 Our help *is* in the name of the LORD, who made heaven and earth.

PSALM 125
A Song of degrees.

1 They that trust in the LORD will *be* as mount Zion, *which* cannot be removed, *but* abides forever.
2 As the mountains *are* round about Jerusalem, so the LORD *is* round about his people from henceforth even forever.
3 For the rod of the wicked will not rest upon the lot of the righteous; lest the righteous put forth their hands unto iniquity.
4 Do good, O LORD, unto *those that be* good, and *to them that are* upright in their hearts.
5 As for such as turn aside unto their crooked ways, the LORD will lead them forth with the workers of iniquity: *but* peace will *be* upon Israel.

PSALM 126

A Song of degrees.

1 When the LORD turned again the captivity of Zion, we were like them that dream.
2 Then was our mouth filled with laughter, and our tongue with singing: then said they among the heathen, The LORD has done great things for them.
3 The LORD has done great things for us; *whereof* we are glad.

---

[1] The King James Version uses the word <u>compact</u>. It is the Hebrew word *châbar*, khaw-bar'; which is defined as to *join* (literally or figuratively; specifically (by means of spells) to *fascinate*:- charm (-er), be compact, couple (together), have fellowship with, heap up, join (self, together), league. [Strgs#2266]

4 Turn again our captivity, O LORD, as the streams in the south.
5 They that sow in tears will reap in joy.
6 He that goes forth and weeps, bearing precious seed, will doubtless come again with rejoicing, bringing his sheaves *with him*.

PSALM 127

A Song of degrees for Solomon.

1 Except the LORD build the house, they labor in vain that build it: except the LORD keep the city, the watchman wakes *but* in vain.
2 *It is* vain for you to rise up early, to sit up late, to eat the bread of sorrows: *for* so he gives his beloved sleep.
3 Lo, children *are* an heritage of the LORD: *and* the fruit of the womb *is his* reward.
4 As arrows *are* in the hand of a mighty man; so *are* children of the youth.
5 Happy *is* the man that has his quiver full of them: they will not be ashamed, but they will speak with the enemies in the gate.

PSALM 128

A Song of degrees.

1 Blessed *is* every one that fears the LORD; that walks in his ways.
2 For you will eat the labor of your hands: happy will you *be*, and *it will be* well with you.
3 Your wife will *be* as a fruitful vine by the sides of your house: your children like olive plants round about your table.
4 Behold, that thus will the man be blessed that fears the LORD.
5 The LORD will bless you out of Zion: and you will see the good of Jerusalem all the days of your life.
6 Yea, you will see your children's children, *and* peace upon Israel.

PSALM 129

A Song of degrees.

1 Many a time have they afflicted me from my youth, may Israel now say:
2 Many a time have they afflicted me from my youth: yet they have not prevailed against me.
3 The plowers[1] plowed upon my back: they made long their furrows.
4 The LORD *is* righteous: he has cut asunder the cords of the wicked.
5 Let them all be confounded and turned back that hate Zion.
6 Let them be as the grass *upon* the housetops, which withers afore it grows up:
7 Wherewith the mower fills not his hand; or he that binds sheaves his bosom.
8 Neither do they which go by say, The blessing of the LORD *be* upon you: we bless you in the name of the LORD.

PSALM 130

A Song of degrees.

1 Out of the depths have I cried unto you, O LORD.
2 Lord, hear my voice: let your ears be attentive to the voice of my supplications.
3 If you, LORD, should mark iniquities, O Lord, who will stand?
4 But *there is* forgiveness with you, that you may be feared.

---

[1] Plowers- is the Hebrew word chârash, khaw-rash'. A primitive root; to *scratch*, that is, (by implication) to *engrave*, *plough*; hence (from theuse of

5 I wait for the LORD, my soul does wait, and in his word do I hope.
6 My soul *waits* for the Lord more than they that watch for the morning: *I say, more than* they that watch for the morning.
7 Let Israel hope in the LORD: for with the LORD *there is* mercy, and with him *is* plenteous redemption.
8 And he will redeem Israel from all his iniquities.

PSALM 131

A Song of degrees of David.

1 LORD, my heart is not haughty, or mine eyes lofty: neither do I exercise myself in great matters, or in things too high for me.
2 Surely I have behaved and quieted myself, as a child that is weaned of his mother: my soul *is* even as a weaned child.
3 Let Israel hope in the LORD from henceforth and forever.

PSALM 132

A Song of degrees.

1 LORD, remember David, *and* all his afflictions:
2 How he swore unto the LORD, *and* vowed unto the mighty God of Jacob;
3 Surely I will not come into the tabernacle of my house, or go up into my bed;
4 I will not give sleep to mine eyes, *or* slumber to mine eyelids,
5 Until I find out a place for the LORD, a habitation for the mighty God of Jacob.
6 Lo, we heard of it at Ephratah: we found it in the fields of the wood.
7 We will go into his tabernacles: we will worship at his footstool.
8 Arise, O LORD, into your rest; you, and the ark of your strength.
9 Let your priests be clothed with righteousness; and let your saints shout for joy.
10 For your servant David's sake turn not away the face of your anointed.
11 The LORD has sworn *in* truth unto David; he will not turn from it; Of the fruit of your body will I set upon your throne.
12 If your children will keep my covenant and my testimony that I will teach them, their children will also sit upon your throne for evermore.
13 For the LORD has chosen Zion; he has desired *i.* for his habitation.
14 This *is* my rest for ever: here will I dwell; for I have desired it.
15 I will abundantly bless her provision: I will satisfy her poor with bread.
16 I will also clothe her priests with salvation: and her saints will shout aloud for joy.
17 There will I make the horn of David to bud: I have ordained a lamp for mine anointed.
18 His enemies will I clothe with shame: but upon himself will his crown flourish.

PSALM 133

A Song of degrees of David.

1 Behold, how good and how pleasant *it is* for brethren to dwell together in unity!
2 *It is* like the precious ointment upon the head, that ran down upon the beard, *even* Aaron's beard: that went down to the skirts of his garments;

---

tools) to *fabricate* (of any material); figuratively to devise (in a bad sense); hence (from the idea of secrecy) to be *silent*, to *let alone*. [Strgs#2790]

3 As the dew of Hermon, *and as the dew* that descended upon the mountains of Zion: for there the LORD commanded the blessing, *even* life for evermore.

PSALM 134
A Song of degrees.

1 Behold, bless you the LORD, all you servants of the LORD, which by night stand in the house of the LORD.
2 Lift up your hands *in* the sanctuary, and bless the LORD.
3 The LORD that made heaven and earth bless you out of Zion.

PSALM 135

1 Praise you the LORD. Praise you the name of the LORD; praise *him*, O you servants of the LORD.
2 you that stand in the house of the LORD, in the courts of the house of our God,
3 Praise the LORD; for the LORD *is* good: sing praises unto his name; for *it is* pleasant.
4 For the LORD has chosen Jacob unto himself, *and* Israel for his peculiar treasure.
5 For I know that the LORD *is* great, and *that* our Lord *is* above all gods.
6 Whatsoever the LORD pleased, *that* did he in heaven, and in earth, in the seas, and all deep places.
7 He causes the vapors[1] to ascend from the ends of the earth; he makes lightnings for the rain; he brings the wind out of his treasuries.
8 Who smote the firstborn of Egypt, both of man and beast.
9 *Who* sent tokens and wonders into the midst of you, O Egypt, upon Pharaoh, and upon all his servants.
10 Who smote great nations, and slew mighty kings;
11 Sihon king of the Amorites, and Og king of Bashan, and all the kingdoms of Canaan:
12 And gave their land *for* an heritage, an heritage unto Israel his people.
13 your name, O LORD, *endures* forever; *and* your memorial, O LORD, throughout all generations.
14 For the LORD will judge his people, and he will repent himself concerning his servants.
15 The idols of the heathen *are* silver and gold, the work of men's hands.
16 They have mouths, but they speak not; eyes have they, but they see not;
17 They have ears, but they hear not; neither is there *any* breath in their mouths.
18 They that make them are like unto them: *so is* every one that trusts in them.
19 Bless the LORD, O house of Israel: bless the LORD, O house of Aaron:
20 Bless the LORD, O house of Levi: you that fear the LORD, bless the LORD.
21 Blessed be the LORD out of Zion, which dwells at Jerusalem. Praise you the LORD.

PSALM 136

1 O give thanks unto the LORD; for *he is* good: for his mercy *endures* forever.
2 O give thanks unto the God of gods: for his mercy *endures* forever.
3 O give thanks to the Lord of lords: for his mercy *endures* forever.
4 To him who alone doeth great wonders: for his mercy *endures* forever.
5 To him that by wisdom made the heavens: for his mercy *endures* forever.
6 To him that stretched out the earth above the waters: for his mercy *endures* forever.
7 To him that made great lights: for his mercy *endures* forever:
8 The sun to rule by day: for his mercy *endures* forever:
9 The moon and stars to rule by night: for his mercy *endures* forever.
10 To him that smote Egypt in their firstborn: for his mercy *endures* forever.
11 And brought out Israel from among them: for his mercy *endures* forever.
12 With a strong hand, and with a stretched out arm: for his mercy *endures* forever.
13 To him which divided the Red sea into parts: for his mercy *endures* for ever:
14 And made Israel to pass through the midst of it: for his mercy *endures* forever:
15 But overthrew Pharaoh and his host in the Red sea: for his mercy *endures* forever.
16 To him which led his people through the wilderness: for his mercy *endures* forever.
17 To him which smote great kings: for his mercy *endures* forever:
18 And slew famous kings: for his mercy *endures* for ever:
19 Sihon king of the Amorites: for his mercy *endures* forever:
20 And Og the king of Bashan: for his mercy *endures* forever:
21 And gave their land for an heritage: for his mercy *endures* forever:
22 *Even* a heritage unto Israel his servant: for his mercy *endures* forever.
23 Who remembered us in our low estate: for his mercy *endures* forever:
24 And has redeemed us from our enemies: for his mercy *endures* forever.
25 Who gives food to all flesh: for his mercy *endures* forever.
26 O give thanks unto the God of heaven: for his mercy *endures* forever.

PSALM 137

1 By the rivers of Babylon, there we sat down, yea, we wept, when we remembered Zion.
2 We hanged our harps upon the willows in the midst thereof.
3 For there they that carried us away captive required of us a song; and they that wasted us *required of us* mirth, *saying*, Sing us *one* of the songs of Zion.
4 How will we sing the LORD'S song in a strange land?
5 If I forget you, O Jerusalem, let my right hand forget *her cunning*.
6 If I do not remember you, let my tongue cleave to the roof of my mouth; if I prefer not Jerusalem above my chief joy.
7 Remember, O LORD, the children of Edom in the day of Jerusalem; who said, Rase *it*, rase *it*, *even* to the foundation thereof.
8 O daughter of Babylon, who are to be destroyed; happy *will he be*, that rewards you as you have served us.
9 Happy *will he be*, that takes and dashes your little ones against the stones.

---

[1] vapors – an *exalted one*, a *king* or *sheik*; also a rising *mist* [Strgs#5387].

PSALM 138
A Psalm of David.

1 I will praise you with my whole heart: before the gods will I sing praise unto you.
2 I will worship toward your holy temple, and praise your name for your loving-kindness and for your truth: for you have magnified your word above all your name.
3 In the day when I cried you answered me, *and* strengthened me *with* strength in my soul.
4 All the kings of the earth will praise you, O LORD, when they hear the words of your mouth.
5 Yea, they will sing in the ways of the LORD: for great *is* the glory of the LORD.
6 Though the LORD *be* high, yet has he respect unto the lowly: but the proud he knows afar off.
7 Though I walk in the midst of trouble, you will revive me: you will stretch forth your hand against the wrath of mine enemies, and your right hand will save me.
8 The LORD will perfect *that which* concerns me: your mercy, O LORD, *endures* forever: forsake not the works of your own hands.

PSALM 139
To the chief Musician, A Psalm of David.

1 O LORD, you have searched me, and known *me*.
2 you knows my down sitting and mine uprising, you understands my thought afar off.
3 You compasses my path and my lying down, and are acquainted *with* all my ways.
4 For *there is* not a word in my tongue, *but,* lo, O LORD, you knows it altogether.
5 you have beset me behind and before, and laid your hand upon me.
6 *Such* knowledge *is* too wonderful for me; it is high, I cannot *attain* unto it.
7 Where will I go from your spirit? Or where will I flee from your presence?
8 If I ascend up into heaven, you are there: if I make my bed in hell, behold, you *are there*.
9 *If* I take the wings of the morning, *and* dwell in the uttermost parts of the sea;
10 Even there will your hand lead me, and your right hand will hold me.
11 If I say, surely the darkness will cover me; even the night will be light about me.
12 Yea, the darkness hides not from you; but the night shines as the day: the darkness and the light *are* both alike *to you*.
13 For you have possessed my reins: you have covered me in my mother's womb.
14 I will praise you; for I am fearfully *and* wonderfully made: marvelous *are* your works; and *that* my soul knows right well.
15 My substance was not hid from you, when I was made in secret, *and* curiously wrought in the lowest parts of the earth.
16 Your eyes did see my substance, yet being unperfect[1]; and in your book all *my members* were written, *which* in continuance were fashioned, when *as yet there was* none of them.

17 How precious also are your thoughts unto me, O God! how great is the sum of them!
18 *If* I should count them, they are more in number than the sand: when I awake, I am still with you.
19 Surely you will slay the wicked, O God: depart from me therefore, you bloody men.
20 For they speak against you wickedly, *and* your enemies take your *name* in vain.
21 Do not I hate them, O LORD, that hate you? And am not I grieved with those that rise up against you?
22 I hate them with perfect hatred: I count them mine enemies.
23 Search me, O God, and know my heart: try me, and know my thoughts:
24 And see if *there be any* wicked way in me, and lead me in the way everlasting.

PSALM 140
To the chief Musician, A Psalm of David.

1 Deliver me, O LORD, from the evil man: preserve me from the violent man;
2 Which imagine mischiefs in *their* heart; continually are they gathered together *for* war.
3 They have sharpened their tongues like a serpent; adders' poison *is* under their lips. Selah.
4 Keep me, O LORD, from the hands of the wicked; preserve me from the violent man; who have purposed to overthrow my goings.
5 The proud have hid a snare for me, and cords; they have spread a net by the wayside; they have set gins for me. Selah.
6 I said unto the LORD, you are my God: hear the voice of my supplications, O LORD.
7 O GOD the Lord, the strength of my salvation, you have covered my head in the day of battle.
8 Grant not, O LORD, the desires of the wicked: further not his wicked device; *lest* they exalt themselves. Selah.
9 *As for* the head of those that compass me about, let the mischief of their own lips cover them.
10 Let burning coals fall upon them: let them be cast into the fire; into deep pits, that they rise not up again.
11 Let not an evil speaker be established in the earth: evil will hunt the violent man to overthrow *him*.
12 I know that the LORD will maintain the cause of the afflicted, *and* the right of the poor.
13 Surely the righteous will give thanks unto your name: the upright will dwell in your presence.

PSALM 141
A Psalm of David.

1 LORD, I cry unto you: make haste unto me; give ear unto my voice, when I cry unto you.
2 Let my prayer be set forth before you *as* incense; *and* the lifting up of my hands *as* the evening sacrifice.
3 Set a watch, O LORD, before my mouth; keep the door of my lips.
4 Incline not my heart to *any* evil thing, to practice wicked works with men that work iniquity: and let me not eat of their dainties.

---

[1] unperfect- comes from the Hebrew word *golem*, go'-lem; which translate as a wrapped (and unformed mass, that is, the embryo):- substance yet being unperfect. [Strgs#1564]

5 Let the righteous smite me; *it will be* a kindness: and let him reprove me; *it will be* an excellent oil, *which* will not break my head: for yet my prayer also will *be* in their calamities.
6 When their judges are overthrown in stony places, they will hear my words; for they are sweet.
7 Our bones are scattered at the grave's mouth, as when one cuts and cleaves *wood* upon the earth.
8 But mine eyes *are* unto you, O GOD the Lord: in you is my trust; leave not my soul destitute.
9 Keep me from the snares *which* they have laid for me, and the gins of the workers of iniquity.
10 Let the wicked fall into their own nets, whilst that I withal escape.

PSALM 142
Maschil of David; A Prayer when he was in the cave.

1 I cried unto the LORD with my voice; with my voice unto the LORD did I make my supplication.
2 I poured out my complaint before him; I showed before him my trouble.
3 When my spirit was overwhelmed within me, then you knew my path. In the way wherein I walked have they privily laid a snare for me.
4 I looked on *my* right hand, and beheld, but *there was* no man that would know me: refuge failed me; no man cared for my soul.
5 I cried unto you, O LORD: I said, you are my refuge *and* my portion in the land of the living.
6 Attend unto my cry; for I am brought very low: deliver me from my persecutors; for they are stronger than I.
7 Bring my soul out of prison, that I may praise your name: the righteous will compass me about; for you will deal bountifully with me.

PSALM 143
A Psalm of David.

1 Hear my prayer, O LORD, give ear to my supplications: in your faithfulness answer me, *and* in your righteousness.
2 And enter not into judgment with your servant: for in your sight will no man living be justified.
3 For the enemy has persecuted my soul; he has smitten my life down to the ground; he has made me to dwell in darkness, as those that have been long dead.
4 Therefore is my spirit overwhelmed within me; my heart within me is desolate.
5 I remember the days of old; I meditate on all your works; I muse on the work of your hands.
6 I stretch forth my hands unto you: my soul *thirsts* after you, as a thirsty land. Selah.
7 Hear me speedily, O LORD: my spirit fails: hide not your face from me, lest I be like unto them that go down into the pit.
8 Cause me to hear your loving-kindness in the morning; for in you do I trust: cause me to know the way wherein I should walk; for I lift up my soul unto you.
9 Deliver me, O LORD, from mine enemies: I flee unto you to hide me.
10 Teach me to do your will; for you are my God: your spirit *is* good; lead me into the land of uprightness.
11 Quicken me, O LORD, for your name's sake: for your righteousness' sake bring my soul out of trouble.
12 And of your mercy cut off mine enemies, and destroy all them that afflict my soul: for I *am* your servant.

PSALM 144
A Psalm of David.

1 Blessed *be* the LORD my strength, which teaches my hands to war, *and* my fingers to fight:
2 My goodness, and my fortress; my high tower, and my deliverer; my shield, and *he* in whom I trust; who subdues my people under me.
3 LORD, what *is* man, that you takes knowledge of him! *Or* the son of man, that you makes account of him!
4 Man is like to vanity: his days *are* as a shadow that passes away.
5 Bow your heavens, O LORD, and come down: touch the mountains, and they will smoke.
6 Cast forth lightning, and scatter them: shoot out your arrows, and destroy them.
7 Send your hand from above; rid me, and deliver me out of great waters, from the hand of strange children;
8 Whose mouth speaks vanity, and their right hand *is* a right hand of falsehood.
9 I will sing a new song unto you, O God: upon a psaltery *and* an instrument of ten strings will I sing praises unto you.
10 *It is he* that gives salvation unto kings: who delivers David his servant from the hurtful sword.
11 Rid me, and deliver me from the hand of strange children, whose mouth speaks vanity, and their right hand *is* a right hand of falsehood:
12 That our sons *may be* as plants grown up in their youth; *that* our daughters *may be* as corner stones, polished *after* the similitude of a palace:
13 *That* our garners *may be* full, affording all manner of store: *that* our sheep may bring forth thousands and ten thousands in our streets:
14 *That* our oxen *may be* strong to labor; *that there be* no breaking in, or going out; that *there be* no complaining in our streets.
15 Happy *is that* people, that is in such a case: *yea, happy is that* people, whose God *is* the LORD.

PSALM 145
David's *Psalm* of praise.

1 I will extol you, my God, O king; and I will bless your name forever and ever.
2 Every day will I bless you; and I will praise your name forever and ever.
3 Great *is* the LORD, and greatly to be praised; and his greatness *is* unsearchable.
4 One generation will praise your works to another, and will declare your mighty acts.
5 I will speak of the glorious honor of your majesty, and of your wondrous works.
6 And *men* will speak of the might of your terrible acts: and I will declare your greatness.
7 They will abundantly utter the memory of your great goodness, and will sing of your righteousness.
8 The LORD *is* gracious, and full of compassion; slow to anger, and of great mercy.
9 The LORD *is* good to all: and his tender mercies *are* over all his works.
10 All your works will praise you, O LORD; and your saints will bless you.

11 They will speak of the glory of your kingdom, and talk of your power;
12 To make known to the sons of men his mighty acts, and the glorious majesty of his kingdom.
13 your kingdom *is* an everlasting kingdom, and your dominion *endures* throughout all generations.
14 The LORD upholds all that fall, and raises up all *those that be* bowed down.
15 The eyes of all wait upon you; and you gives them their meat in due season.
16 you opens your hand, and satisfies the desire of every living thing.
17 The LORD *is* righteous in all his ways, and holy in all his works.
18 The LORD *is* nigh unto all them that call upon him, to all that call upon him in truth.
19 He will fulfill the desire of them that fear him: he also will hear their cry, and will save them.
20 The LORD preserves all them that love him: but all the wicked will he destroy.
21 My mouth will speak the praise of the LORD: and let all flesh bless his holy name forever and ever.

PSALM 146

1 Praise you the LORD. Praise the LORD, O my soul.
2 While I live will I praise the LORD: I will sing praises unto my God while I have any being.
3 Put not your trust in princes, or in the son of man, in whom *there is* no help.
4 His breath goes forth, he returns to his earth; in that very day his thoughts perish.
5 Happy *is he* that has the God of Jacob for his help, whose hope *is* in the LORD his God:
6 Which made heaven, and earth, the sea, and all that therein *is*: which keeps truth forever:
7 Which executes judgment for the oppressed: which gives food to the hungry. The LORD looses the prisoners:
8 The LORD opens *the eyes of* the blind: the LORD raises them that are bowed down: the LORD loves the righteous:
9 The LORD preserves the strangers; he relieves the fatherless and widow: but the way of the wicked he turns upside down.
10 The LORD will reign forever, *even* your God, O Zion, unto all generations. Praise you the LORD.

PSALM 147

1 Praise you the LORD: for *it is* good to sing praises unto our God; for *it is* pleasant; *and* praise is comely.
2 The LORD does build up Jerusalem: he gathers together the outcasts of Israel.
3 He heals the broken in heart, and binds up their wounds.
4 He tells the number of the stars; he calls them all by *their* names.
5 Great *is* our Lord, and of great power: his understanding *is* infinite.
6 The LORD lifts up the meek: he casts the wicked down to the ground.
7 Sing unto the LORD with thanksgiving; sing praise upon the harp unto our God:
8 Who covers the heaven with clouds, who prepares rain for the earth, who makes grass to grow upon the mountains.
9 He gives to the beast his food, *and* to the young ravens which cry.
10 He delights not in the strength of the horse: he takes not pleasure in the legs of a man.
11 The LORD takes pleasure in them that fear him, in those that hope in his mercy.
12 Praise the LORD, O Jerusalem; praise your God, O Zion.
13 For he has strengthened the bars of your gates; he has blessed your children within you.
14 He makes peace *in* your borders, *and* fills you with the finest of the wheat.
15 He sends forth his commandment *upon* earth: his word runs very swiftly.
16 He gives snow like wool: he scatters the hoarfrost like ashes.
17 He casts forth his ice like morsels: who can stand before his cold?
18 He sends out his word, and melts them: he causes his wind to blow, *and* the waters flow.
19 He shows his word unto Jacob, his statutes and his judgments unto Israel.
20 He has not dealt so with any nation: and *as for his* judgments, they have not known them. Praise you the LORD.

PSALM 148

1 Praise you the LORD. Praise you the LORD from the heavens: praise him in the heights.
2 Praise you him, all his angels: praise you him, all his hosts.
3 Praise you him, sun and moon: praise him, all you stars of light.
4 Praise him, you heavens of heavens, and you waters that *be* above the heavens.
5 Let them praise the name of the LORD: for he commanded, and they were created.
6 He has also established them forever and ever: he has made a decree which will not pass.
7 Praise the LORD from the earth, you dragons, and all deeps:
8 Fire, and hail; snow, and vapor; stormy wind fulfilling his word:
9 Mountains, and all hills; fruitful trees, and all cedars:
10 Beasts, and all cattle; creeping things, and flying fowl:
11 Kings of the earth, and all people; princes, and all judges of the earth:
12 Both young men, and maidens; old men, and children
13 Let them praise the name of the LORD: for his name alone is excellent; his glory *is* above the earth and heaven.
14 He also exalts the horn of his people, the praise of all his saints; *even* of the children of Israel, a people near unto him. Praise you the LORD.

PSALM 149

1 Praise you the LORD. Sing unto the LORD a new song, *and* his praise in the congregation of saints.
2 Let Israel rejoice in him that made him: let the children of Zion be joyful in their King.
3 Let them praise his name in the dance: let them sing praises unto him with the tambourine and harp.
4 For the LORD takes pleasure in his people: he will beautify the meek with salvation.
5 Let the saints be joyful in glory: let them sing aloud upon their beds.
6 *Let* the high *praises* of God *be* in their mouth, and a two-edged sword in their hand;
7 To execute vengeance upon the heathen, *and* punishments upon the people;
8 To bind their kings with chains, and their nobles with fetters of iron;
9 To execute upon them the judgment written: this honor have all his saints. Praise you the LORD.

PSALM 150

1 Praise you the LORD. Praise God in his sanctuary: praise him in the firmament of his power.
2 Praise him for his mighty acts: praise him according to his excellent greatness.
3 Praise him with the sound of the trumpet: praise him with the psaltery and harp.
4 Praise him with the tambourine and dance: praise him with stringed instruments and organs.
5 Praise him upon the loud cymbals: praise him upon the high sounding cymbals.
6 Let everything that has breath praise the LORD. Praise you the LORD.

THE PROVERBS

CHAPTER 1

1 The proverbs of Solomon the son of David, king of Israel;
2 To know wisdom and instruction; to perceive the words of understanding;
3 To receive the instruction of wisdom, justice, and judgment, and equity;
4 To give subtlety to the simple, to the young man knowledge and discretion.
5 A wise *man* will hear, and will increase learning; and a man of understanding will attain unto wise counsels:
6 To understand a proverb, and the interpretation; the words of the wise, and their dark sayings.
7 The fear of the LORD *is* the beginning of knowledge: *but* fools despise wisdom and instruction.
8 My son, hear the instruction of your father, and forsake not the law of your mother:
9 For they will *be* an ornament of grace unto your head, and chains about your neck.
10 My son, if sinners entice you, consent you not.
11 If they say, Come with us, let us lay wait for blood, let us lurk privily[1] for the innocent without cause.
12 Let us swallow them up alive as the grave; and whole, as those that go down into the pit:
13 We will find all precious substance, we will fill our houses with spoil:
14 Cast in your lot among us; let us all have one purse:
15 My son, walk not you in the way with them; refrain your foot from their path:
16 For their feet run to evil, and make haste to shed blood.
17 Surely in vain the net is spread in the sight of any bird.
18 And they lay wait for their *own* blood; they lurk privily for their *own* lives.
19 So *are* the ways of every one that is greedy of gain; *which* takes away the life of the owners thereof.
20 Wisdom cries without; she utters her voice in the streets:
21 She cries in the chief place of concourse, in the openings of the gates: in the city she utters her words, *saying*,
22 How long, you simple ones, will you love simplicity? And the scorners delight in their scorning, and fools hate knowledge?
23 Turn you at my reproof: behold, I will pour out my spirit unto you, I will make known my words unto you.
24 Because I have called, and you refused; I have stretched out my hand, and no man regarded;
25 But you have set at nought[2] all my counsel, and would none of my reproof:
26 I also will laugh at your calamity; I will mock when your fear cometh;
27 When your fear cometh as desolation, and your destruction cometh as a whirlwind; when distress and anguish cometh upon you.
28 Then will they call upon me, but I will not answer; they will seek me early, but they will not find me:
29 For that they hated knowledge, and did not choose the fear of the LORD:
30 They would none of my counsel: they despised all my reproof.
31 Therefore will they eat of the fruit of their own way, and be filled with their own devices.
32 For the turning away of the simple will slay them, and the prosperity of fools will destroy them.
33 But whoso hearkens unto me will dwell safely, and will be quiet from fear of evil.

CHAPTER 2

1 My son, if you will receive my words, and hide my commandments with you;
2 So that you incline your ear unto wisdom, *and* apply your heart to understanding;
3 Yea, if you cry after knowledge, *and* lifts up your voice for understanding;
4 If you seeks her as silver, and searches for her *as for* hid treasures;
5 [Then will you understand the fear of the LORD, and find the knowledge of God.][3]
6 For the LORD gives wisdom: out of his mouth *comes* knowledge and understanding.
7 He lays up sound wisdom for the righteous: *he is* a buckler to them that walk uprightly.
8 He keeps the paths of judgment, and preserves the way of his saints.
9 Then will you understand righteousness, and judgment, and equity; *yea*, every good path.
10 [When wisdom enters into your heart, and knowledge is pleasant unto your soul;][4]
11 Discretion will preserve you, understanding will keep you:
12 To deliver you from the way of the evil *man*, from the man that speaks forward things;
13 Who leave the paths of uprightness, to walk in the ways of darkness;
14 Who rejoice to do evil, *and* delight in the forwardness of the wicked;
15 Whose ways *are* crooked, and *they* forward in their paths:
16 To deliver you from the strange woman, *even* from the stranger *which* flatters with her words;
17 Which forsakes the guide of her youth, and forgotten the covenant of her God.
18 For her house inclines unto death, and her paths unto the dead.
19 None that go unto her return again, neither take they hold of the paths of life.
20 That you may walk in the way of good *men*, and keep the paths of the righteous.
21 For the upright will dwell in the land, and the perfect[5] will remain in it.
22 But the wicked will be cut off from the earth, and the transgressors will be rooted out of it.

CHAPTER 3

1 My son, forget not my law; but let your heart keep my commandments:

---

[1] privily- is defined as to hide (by covering over), by implication to *hoard* or *reserve*, figuratively to deny; specifically (favorable) to *protect*, (unfavorably) to *lurk*: esteem, hide or hidden oneself, layup, lurk (be set), (keep) secret, treasure, store up. [Strgs#6845]
[2] nought- a primitive root; to loosen; by implication to *expose, dismiss*; figuratively *absolve, begin*; -avenge, avoid, bare, go back, let, (make) naked, set at nought, perish, refuse, uncover. [Strgs#6544]
[3] In wisdom you understand the fear of the Lord and find knowledge of God.
[4] When you take pleasure in knowledge, discretion will preserve you.
[5] spirit of just men made perfect.

The Proverbs

2 For length of days, and long life, and peace, will they add to you.
3 Let not mercy and truth forsake you: bind them about your neck; write them upon the table of your heart:
4 So will you find favor and good understanding in the sight of God and man.
5 Trust in the LORD with all your heart; and lean not unto your own understanding.
6 In all your ways acknowledge him, and he will direct your paths.[1]
7 Be not wise in your own eyes: fear the LORD, and depart from evil.
8 It will be health to your navel, and marrow to your bones.
9 Honor the LORD with your substance, and with the first-fruits of all your increase:
10 So will your barns be filled with plenty, and your presses will burst out with new wine.
11 My son, despise not the chastening of the LORD; neither be weary of his correction[2]:
12 For whom the LORD loves he corrects; even as a father the son *in whom* he delights.
13 Happy *is* the man *that* finds[3] wisdom, and the man *that* gets understanding.
14 For the merchandise of it *is* better than the merchandise of silver, and the gain thereof than fine gold.
15 She *is* more precious than rubies: and all the things you canst desire are not to be compared unto her.
16 Length of days *is* in her right hand; *and* in her left hand riches and honor.
17 Her ways *are* ways of pleasantness, and all her paths *are* peace.
18 She *is* a tree of life to them that lay hold upon her: and happy *is every one* that retains her.
19 The LORD by wisdom has founded the earth; by understanding has he established the heavens.
20 By his knowledge the depths are broken up, and the clouds drop down the dew.
21 My son, let not them depart from your eyes: keep [sound wisdom][4] and discretion[5]:
22 So will they be life unto your soul, and grace to your neck.
23 Then will you walk in your way safely, and your foot will not stumble.
24 When you lie down, you will not be afraid: yea, you will lie down, and your sleep will be sweet.
25 Be not afraid of sudden fear, neither of the desolation[6] of the wicked, when it cometh.
26 For the LORD will be your confidence, and will keep your foot from being taken.
27 Withhold not good from them to whom it is due, when it is in the power of your hand to do *it*.
28 Say not unto your neighbor, Go, and come again, and tomorrow I will give; when you have it by you.
29 Devise not evil against your neighbor, seeing he dwells securely by you.
30 Strive not with a man without cause, if he **has** done you no harm.
31 Envy you not the oppressor[7], and choose none of his ways.
32 For the forward *is* abomination to the LORD: but his secret *is* with the righteous.
33 The curse of the LORD *is* in the house of the wicked: but he blesses the habitation of the just.
34 Surely he scorns the scorners: but he gives grace unto the lowly.
35 The wise will inherit glory: but shame will be the promotion of fools.

CHAPTER 4

1 Hear, you children, the instruction of a father, and attend to know understanding.
2 For I give you good doctrine, forsake you not my law.
3 For I was my father's son, tender and only *beloved* in the sight of my mother.
4 He taught me also, and said unto me, Let your heart retain my words: keep my commandments, and live.
5 Get wisdom, get understanding: forget[8] *it* not; neither decline[9] from the words of my mouth.
6 Forsake her not, and she will preserve you: love her, and she will keep you.
7 Wisdom *is* the principal thing; *therefore* get[10] wisdom: and with all your getting[11] get understanding.
8 Exalt her, and she will promote you: she will bring you to honor, when you dost embrace her.
9 She will give to your head an ornament of grace: a crown of glory will she delivers[12] to you.
10 Hear, O my son, and receive my sayings; and the years of your life will be many.
11 I have taught you in the way of wisdom; I have led you in right paths.
12 When you go, your steps will not be straitened; and when you run, you will not stumble.
13 Take fast hold of instruction; let *her* not go: keep her; for she *is* your life.
14 Enter not into the path of the wicked, and go not in the way of evil *men*.
15 Avoid it, pass not by it, turn from it, and pass away.
16 For they sleep not, except they have done mischief; and their sleep is taken away, unless they cause *some* to fall.
17 For they eat the bread of wickedness, and drink the wine of violence.
18 But the path of the just *is* as the shining light, that shines more and more unto the perfect day.
19 The way of the wicked *is* as darkness: they know not at what they stumble.
20 My son, attend to my words; incline your ear unto my sayings.
21 Let them not depart from your eyes; keep them in the midst of your heart.
22 For they *are* life unto those that find them, and health to all their flesh.

---

[1] compare Proverbs 11:5
[2] lit. chastisement, refutation, proof [Strgs#8433]. Comes from a Hebrew root word meaning to be right, argue, justify or convict [Strgs#3198].
[3] lit. to come forth [Strgs#4672].
[4] sound wisdom – *substantiate*, support, ability, help, undertaking, understanding [Strgs#8454].
[5] discretion – a plan [Strgs#4209].
[6] lit. storm tempest [Strgs#7722].

[7] oppressor – derives from two Hebrew words to mean a man of violence [Strgs#376+2555].
[8] forget – to mislay [Strgs#7911].
[9] lit. to stretch away [Strgs#5186].
[10] lit. to erect, create, to procure, own, buy, sell [Strgs#7069].
[11] lit. creation [Strgs#7075].
[12] deliver – to shield, encompass, to rescue, to hand safely over, surrender [Strgs#4042].

23 Keep your heart with all diligence; for out of it *are* the issues of life.
24 Put away from you a forward mouth, and perverse lips put far from you.
25 Let your eyes look right on, and let your eyelids look straight before you.
26 Ponder the path of your feet, and let all your ways be established.
27 Turn not to the right hand or to the left: remove your foot from evil.

CHAPTER 5

1 My son, attend unto my wisdom, *and* bow your ear to my understanding:
2 That you may regard discretion, and *that* your lips may keep knowledge.
3 [For the lips of a strange woman drop *as* a honeycomb, and her mouth *is* smoother than oil:
4 But her end is bitter as wormwood, sharp as a two-edged sword.
5 Her feet go down to death; her steps take hold on hell.]¹
6 Lest you should ponder the path of life, her ways are moveable, *that* you canst not know *them*.
7 Hear me now therefore, O you children, and depart not from the words of my mouth.
8 Remove your way far from her, and come not nigh the door of her house:
9 Lest you give your honor unto others, and your years unto the cruel:
10 Lest strangers be filled with your wealth; and your labors *be* in the house of a stranger;
11 And you mourn at the last, when your flesh and your body are consumed,
12 And say, how have I hated instruction, and my heart despised reproof;
13 And have not obeyed the voice of my teachers, or inclined mine ear to them that instructed me!
14 I was almost in all evil in the midst of the congregation and assembly.
15 Drink waters out of your own cistern, and running waters out of your own well.
16 Let your fountains be dispersed abroad, *and* rivers of waters in the streets.
17 Let them be only your own, and not strangers' with you.
18 Let your fountain be blessed: and rejoice with the wife of your youth.
19 *Let her be as* the loving hind and pleasant roe; let her breasts satisfy you at all times; and be you ravished always with her love.
20 And why will you, my son, be ravished with a strange woman, and embrace the bosom of a stranger?
21 For the ways of man *are* before the eyes of the LORD, and he ponders all his goings.
22 His own iniquities will take the wicked himself, and he will be **held** with the cords of his sins.
23 He will die without instruction; and in the greatness of his folly he will go astray.

CHAPTER 6

1 My son, if you be surety for your friend, *if* you have stricken your hand with a stranger,
2 you are snared with the words of your mouth, you are taken with the words of your mouth.
3 Do this now, my son, and deliver yourself, when you are come into the hand of your friend; go, humble yourself, and make sure your friend.
4 Give not sleep to your eyes, or slumber to your eyelids.
5 Deliver yourself as a roe from the hand *of the hunter*, and as a bird from the hand of the fowler.
6 Go to the ant, you sluggard; consider her ways, and be wise:
7 Which having no guide, overseer, or ruler,
8 Provides her meat in the summer, *and* gathers her food in the harvest.
9 How long will you sleep, O sluggard? When will you arise out of your sleep?
10 *Yet* a little sleep, a little slumber, a little folding of the hands to sleep:
11 So will your poverty come as one that travels, and your want as an armed man.
12 A naughty person, a wicked man, walks with a forward mouth.
13 He winks with his eyes, he speaks with his feet, he teaches with his fingers;
14 Forwardness *is* in his heart, he devises mischief continually; he sows discord.
15 Therefore will his calamity come suddenly; suddenly will he be broken without remedy.
16 These six *things* does the LORD hate: yea, seven *are* an abomination unto him:
17 A proud look, a lying tongue, and hands that shed innocent blood,
18 An heart that devises wicked imaginations, feet that be swift in running to mischief,
19 A false witness *that* speaks lies, and he that sows discord among brethren.
20 My son, keep your father's commandment, and forsake not the law of your mother:
21 Bind them continually upon your heart, *and* tie them about your neck.
22 When you go, it will lead you; when you sleep, it will keep you; and *when* you awake, it will talk with you.
23 For the commandment *is* a lamp; and the law *is* light; and reproofs of instruction *are* the way of life:
24 To keep you from the evil woman, from the flattery of the tongue of a strange woman.
25 Lust not after her beauty in your heart; neither let her take you with her eyelids.
26 [For by means of a whorish woman *a man is brought* to a piece of bread: and the adulteress will hunt for the precious life.]²
27 Can a man take fire in his bosom, and his clothes not be burned?
28 Can one go upon hot coals, and his feet not be burned?
29 So he that goes in to his neighbor's wife; whosoever touches her will not be innocent.
30 *Men* do not despise a thief, if he steals to satisfy his soul when he is hungry;
31 But *if* he be found, he will restore sevenfold; he will give all the substance of his house.
32 *But* whoso commits adultery with a woman lacks understanding³: he *that* doeth it destroys his own soul.

---

¹ see Ecc. 7:26
² compare **Job 31:12**

³ understanding – the heart [Strgs#3820]. Out of the heart, compare **Mark:7:20-23**.

33 A wound and dishonor will he get; and his reproach will not be wiped away.
34 For jealousy *is* the rage of a man: therefore he will not spare in the day of vengeance.
35 He will not regard any ransom; neither will he rest content, though you give many gifts.

CHAPTER 7

1 My son, keep my words, and lay up my commandments with you.
2 Keep my commandments, and live; and my law as the apple of your eye.
3 Bind them upon your fingers, write them upon the table of your heart.
4 Say unto wisdom, you are my sister; and call understanding your kinswoman:
5 That they may keep you from the strange woman, from the stranger *which* flatters with her words.
6 For at the window of my house I looked through my casement,
7 And beheld among the simple ones, I discerned among the youths¹, a young man void of understanding,
8 Passing through the street near her corner; and he went the way to her house,
9 In the twilight, in the evening, in the black and dark night:
10 And, behold, there met him a woman *with* the attire of an harlot, and subtle of heart.
11 (She *is* loud and stubborn; her feet abide not in her house:
12 Now *is she* without, now in the streets, and lies in wait at every² corner.)
13 So she caught him, and kissed him, *and* with an impudent face said unto him,
14 *I have* peace offerings with me; this day have I **paid** my vows.
15 Therefore **I came** forth to meet you, diligently to seek your face, and I have found you.
16 I have decked my bed with coverings of tapestry, with carved *works*, with fine linen of Egypt.
17 I have perfumed my bed with myrrh, aloes, and cinnamon.
18 Come, let us take our fill of love until the morning: let us solace ourselves with loves.
19 For the goodman *is* not at home, he is gone a long journey:
20 He has taken a bag of money with him, *and* will come home at the day appointed³.
21 With her much fair speech she caused him to yield, with the flattering of her lips she forced him.
22 He goes after her straightway, as an ox goes to the slaughter, or as a fool to the correction of the stocks;
23 Till a dart strike through his liver; as a bird haste to the snare, and knows not that it *is* for his life.
24 Hearken unto me now therefore, O you children, and attend to the words of my mouth.
25 Let not your heart decline to her ways, go not astray in her paths.
26 For she has cast down many wounded: yea, many strong *men* have been slain by her.
27 Her house *is* the way to hell, going down to the chambers of death.

CHAPTER 8

1 does not wisdom cry? And understanding put forth her voice?
2 She stands in the top of high places, by the way in the places of the paths.
3 She cries at the gates, at the entry of the city, at the coming in at the doors.
4 Unto you, O men, I call; and my voice *is* to the sons of man.
5 O you simple, understand wisdom: and, you fools, be you of an understanding heart.
6 Hear; for I will speak of excellent things; and the opening of my lips will *be* right things.
7 For my mouth will speak truth; and wickedness *is* an abomination to my lips.
8 All the words of my mouth *are* in righteousness; *there is* nothing forward or perverse in them.
9 They *are* all plain to him that understands, and right to them that find knowledge.
10 Receive my instruction, and not silver; and knowledge rather than choice gold.
11 For wisdom *is* better than rubies; and all the things that may be desired are not to be compared to it.
12 I wisdom dwell with prudence, and find out knowledge of witty inventions.
13 The fear of the LORD *is* to hate evil: pride, and arrogancy, and the evil way, and the forward mouth, do I hate.
14 Counsel *is* mine, and sound wisdom: I *am* understanding; I have strength.
15 By me kings reign, and princes decree justice.
16 By me princes rule, and nobles, *even* all the judges of the earth.
17 I love them that love me; and those that seek me early will find me.
18 Riches and honor *are* with me; *yea*, durable riches and righteousness.
19 My fruit *is* better than gold, yea, than fine gold; and my revenue than choice silver.
20 I lead in the way of righteousness, in the midst of the paths of judgment:
21 That I may cause those that love me to inherit substance; and I will fill their treasures.
22 The LORD possessed me in the beginning of his way, before his works of old.
23 I was set up from everlasting, from the beginning, or ever the earth was.
24 When *there were* no depths, I was brought forth; when *there were* no fountains abounding with water.
25 Before the mountains were settled, before the hills was I brought forth:
26 While as yet he had not made the earth, or the fields, or the highest part of the dust of the world.
27 When he prepared the heavens, I *was* there: when he set a compass upon the face of the depth:
28 When he established the clouds above: when he strengthened the fountains of the deep:
29 When he gave to the sea his decree, that the waters should not pass his commandment: when he appointed the foundations of the earth:
30 Then I was by him, *as* one brought up *with him*: and I was daily *his* delight, rejoicing always before him;
31 Rejoicing in the habitable part of his earth; and my delights *were* with the sons of men

---

¹ lit. sons [Strgs#1121].
² she is also spiritual

³ lit. fullness or full moon [Strgs#3677].

32 Now therefore hearken unto me, O you children: for blessed *are they that* keep my ways.
33 Hear instruction, and be wise, and refuse it not.
34 Blessed *is* the man that hears me, watching daily at my gates, waiting at the posts of my doors.
35 For whoso finds me finds life, and will obtain favor of the LORD.
36 But he that sins against me wrongs his own soul: all they that hate me love death.

CHAPTER 9

1 Wisdom has **built** her house, she has hewn out her seven pillars:
2 She has killed her beasts; she has mingled her wine; she has also furnished her table.
3 She has sent forth her maidens: she cries upon the highest places of the city,
4 Whoso *is* simple, let him turn in hither: *as for* him that wants understanding, she said to him,
5 Come, eat of my bread, and drink of the wine *which* I have mingled.
6 Forsake the foolish, and live; and go in the way of understanding.
7 He that reproves a scorner gets to himself shame: and he that rebukes a wicked *man gets* himself a blot.
8 Reprove not a scorner, lest he hate you: rebuke a wise man, and he will love you.
9 Give *instruction* to a wise *man*, and he will be yet wiser: teach a just *man*, and he will increase in learning.
10 The fear of the LORD *is* the beginning of wisdom: and the knowledge of the holy *is* understanding.
11 For by me your days will be multiplied, and the years of your life will be increased.
12 If you be wise, you will be wise for yourself: but *if* you scorns, you alone will bear *it*.
13 A foolish woman *is* clamorous: *she is* simple, and knows nothing.
14 For she sits at the door of her house, on a seat in the high places of the city,
15 To call passengers who go right on their ways:
16 Whoso *is* simple, let him turn in here: and *as for* him that wants understanding, she said to him,
17 Stolen waters are sweet, and bread [*eaten* in secret is pleasant]¹.
18 But he knows not that the dead *are* there; *and that* her guests *are* in the depths of hell.

CHAPTER 10

1 The proverbs of Solomon. A wise son makes a glad father: but a foolish son *is* the heaviness of his mother.
2 Treasures of wickedness profit nothing: but righteousness delivers from death.
3 The LORD will not suffer the soul of the righteous to famish: but he casts away the substance of the wicked.
4 He becomes poor that deals *with* a slack hand: but the hand of the diligent makes rich.
5 He that gathers in summer *is* a wise son: *but* he that sleeps in harvest *is* a son that causes shame.

6 Blessings *are* upon the head of the just: but violence covers the mouth of the wicked.
7 The memory of the just *is* blessed: but the name of the wicked will rot.
8 The wise in heart will receive commandments: but a prating fool will fall.
9 He that walks uprightly walks surely: but he that perverts his ways will be known.
10 He that winks with the eye causes sorrow: but a prating² fool will fall.
11 The mouth of a righteous *man is* a well of life: but violence covers the mouth of the wicked.
12 Hatred stirs up strife: but love covers all sins.
13 In the lips of him that has understanding wisdom is found: but a rod *is* for the back of him that is void of understanding.
14 Wise *men* layup knowledge: but the mouth of the foolish *is* near destruction.
15 The rich man's wealth *is* his strong city: the destruction of the poor *is* their poverty.
16 The labor of the righteous *tends* to life: the fruit of the wicked to sin.
17 He *is in* the way of life that keeps instruction: but he that refuses reproof errs.
18 He that hides hatred *with* lying lips, and he that utters a slander, *is* a fool.
19 In the multitude of words there wants not sin: but he that refrains his lips *is* wise.
20 The tongue of the just *is as* choice silver: the heart of the wicked *is* little worth.
21 The lips of the righteous feed many: but fools die for want of wisdom.
22 The blessing of the LORD, it makes rich, and he adds no sorrow with it.
23 *It is* as sport to a fool to do mischief: but a man of understanding has wisdom.
24 The fear of the wicked, it will come upon him: but the desire of the righteous will be granted.
25 As the whirlwind passes, so *is* the wicked no *more*: but the righteous *is* an everlasting foundation.
26 As vinegar to the teeth, and as smoke to the eyes, so *is* the sluggard to them that send him.
27 The fear of the LORD prolongs days: but the years of the wicked will be shortened.
28 The hope of the righteous will *be* gladness: but the expectation of the wicked will perish.
29 The way of the LORD *is* strength to the upright: but destruction will *be* to the workers of iniquity.
30 The righteous will never be removed: but the wicked will not inhabit the earth.
31 The mouth of the just brings forth wisdom: but the forward tongue will be cut out.
32 The lips of the righteous know what is acceptable: but the mouth of the wicked *speaks* forwardness.

---

¹ lit. bread of secrecies is pleasant
² prating- is the Hebrew word *śâphâh*, saw-faw'; it is the idea of *termination*; the *lip* (as a natural boundary); by implication *language*; by analogy a *margin*; band, bank, binding, border, brim, brink, edge, shore, side, speech, talk, [vain] words. *Śâphâh* comes from two Hebrew root words, the first being *sâphâh*, meaning to *scrape* (literally to *shave*; but usually figuratively) together (that is, to *accumulate* or *increase*) or away (that is, to *scatter*, *remove* or *ruin*; intransitively to *perish*):- add, augment, consume, destroy, heap, join. The second root word being shâphâh, meaning to *abrade*, that is *bare*: -high, stick out. [Strgs#8193]

CHAPTER 11

1 A false balance *is* abomination to the LORD: but a just weight *is* his delight.
2 *When* pride cometh, then cometh shame: but with the lowly *is* wisdom.
3 The integrity[1] of the upright will guide them: but the perverseness of transgressors will destroy them.
4 Riches profit not in the day of wrath: but righteousness delivers from death.
5 The righteousness of the perfect will direct[2] his way: but the wicked will fall by his own wickedness.
6 The righteousness of the upright will deliver them: but transgressors will be taken in *their own* naughtiness.
7 When a wicked man dies, *his* expectation will perish: and the hope of unjust *men* perishes.
8 The righteous is delivered out of trouble, and the wicked cometh in his stead.
9 An hypocrite with *his* mouth destroys his neighbor: but through knowledge will the just be delivered.
10 When it goes well with the righteous, the city rejoices: and when the wicked perish, *there is* shouting.
11 By the blessing of the upright the city is exalted: but it is overthrown by the mouth of the wicked.
12 He that is void of wisdom despises his neighbor: but a man of understanding holds his peace.
13 A talebearer reveals secrets: but he that is of a faithful spirit conceals the matter.
14 Where no counsel *is*, the people fall: but in the multitude of counselors *there is* safety.
15 He that is surety[3] for a stranger will smart *for it*: and he that hates suretiship[4] is sure.
16 A gracious woman retains honor: and strong *men* retain riches.
17 The merciful man doeth good to his own soul: but *he that is* cruel troubles his own flesh.
18 The wicked works a deceitful work: but to *him that* sows righteousness will *be* a sure reward.
19 As righteousness tends to life: so he that pursues evil *pursues it* to his own death.
20 They that are of a forward heart *are* abomination to the LORD: but *such as are* upright in *their* way *are* his delight.
21 *Though* hand *join* in hand, the wicked will not be unpunished: but the seed of the righteous will be delivered.
22 *As* a jewel of gold in a swine's snout, *so is* a fair woman which is without discretion.
23 The desire of the righteous *is* only good: *but* the expectation of the wicked *is* wrath.
24 There is that scatters, and yet increases; and *there is* that withholds more than is meet, *but it tends* to poverty.
25 The *liberal* soul will be made fat: and he that waters will be watered also himself.
26 He that withholds corn, the people will curse him: but blessing will *be* upon the head of him that sells *it*.
27 He that diligently seeks good procures favor: but he that seeks mischief, *it will* come unto him.
28 He that trusts in his riches will fall: but the righteous will flourish as a branch.
29 He that troubles his own house will inherit the wind: and the fool will *be* servant to the wise of heart.
30 The fruit of the righteous *is* a tree of life; and he that wins souls *is* wise.
31 Behold, the righteous will be recompensed in the earth: much more the wicked and the sinner.

CHAPTER 12

1 Whoso loves instruction loves knowledge: but he that hates reproof *is* brutish.
2 A good *man* obtains favor of the LORD: but a man of wicked devices will he condemn.
3 A man will not be established by wickedness: but the root of the righteous will not be moved.
4 A virtuous woman *is* a crown to her husband: but she that makes ashamed *is* as rottenness in his bones.
5 The thoughts of the righteous *are* right: *but* the counsels of the wicked *are* deceit.
6 The words of the wicked *are* to lie in wait for blood: but the mouth of the upright will deliver them.
7 The wicked are overthrown, and *are* not: but the house of the righteous will stand.
8 A man will be commended according to his wisdom: but he that is of a perverse heart will be despised.
9 *He that is* despised, and has a servant, *is* better than he that honors himself, and lacks bread.
10 A righteous *man* regards the life of his beast: but the tender mercies of the wicked *are* cruel.
11 He that tills his land will be satisfied with bread: but he that follows vain *persons is* void of understanding.
12 The wicked desires the net of evil *men*: but the root of the righteous yields *fruit*.
13 The wicked is snared by the transgression of *his* lips: but the *just will* come out of trouble.
14 A man will be satisfied with good by the fruit of *his* mouth: and the recompence[5] of a man's hands will be rendered unto him.
15 The way of a fool *is* right in his own eyes: but he that hearkens unto counsel *is* wise.
16 A fool's wrath is presently known: but a prudent *man* covers shame.
17 *He that* speaks truth shows forth righteousness: but a false witness deceit.
18 There is that speaks like the piercings of a sword: but the tongue of the wise *is* health.
19 The lip of truth will be established for ever: but a lying tongue *is* but for a moment.
20 Deceit *is* in the heart of them that imagine evil: but to the counselors of peace *is* joy.
21 There will no evil happen to the just: but the wicked will be filled with mischief.
22 Lying lips *are* abomination to the LORD: but they that deal truly *are* his delight.

---

[1] integrity – <u>innocence, complete</u> [Strgs#8538+8537].
[2] lit. to be straight, even, right, pleasant, prosperous [Strgs#3474].
[3] surety- is the Hebrew word 'ârab, aw-rab', a primitive root; to *braid*, that is, *intermix*; technically to *traffic* (as if by barter); also to *give* or *be security* (as a kind of exchange):- engage, (inter-) meddle (with), mingle (self), mortgage, occupy, give pledges, be (-come, put in) surety, undertake. [Strgs#6148]
[4] suretiship- a primitive root; to *clatter*, that is, *slap* (the hands together), *clang* (an instrument); by analogy to *drive* (a nail or tent pin, a dart, etc.); by implication to *become bondsman* (by hand-clasping); -blow [a trumpet], cast, clap, fasten, pitch [tent], smite, sound, strike, thrust. [Strgs#8628]
[5] recompence- literally *acts* (of good or ill). [Strgs#1576]

23 A prudent man conceals knowledge: but the heart of fools proclaims foolishness.
24 The hand of the diligent will bear rule: but the slothful will be under tribute.
25 Heaviness in the heart of man makes it stoop: but a good word makes it glad.
26 The righteous *is* more excellent than his neighbor: but the way of the wicked seduces them.
27 The slothful *man* roasts not that which he took in hunting: but the substance of a diligent man *is* precious.
28 In the way of righteousness *is* life; and *in* the pathway thereof *there is* no death.

CHAPTER 13

1 A wise son *hears* his father's instruction: but a scorner hears not rebuke.
2 A man will eat good by the fruit of *his* mouth: but the soul of the transgressors will *eat* violence.
3 He that keeps his mouth keeps his life: *but* he that opens wide his lips will have destruction.
4 The soul of the sluggard desires, and has nothing: but the soul of the diligent will be made fat.
5 A righteous *man* hates lying: but a wicked *man* is loathsome, and cometh to shame.
6 Righteousness keeps *him that is* upright in the way: but wickedness overthrows the sinner.
7 There is that makes himself rich, yet has nothing: *there is* that makes himself poor, yet has great riches.
8 The ransom of a man's life *are* his riches: but the poor hears not rebuke.
9 The light of the righteous rejoices: but the lamp of the wicked will be put out.
10 Only by pride cometh contention: but with the well advised *is* wisdom.
11 Wealth *gotten* by vanity will be diminished: but he that gathers by labor will increase.
12 Hope deferred makes the heart sick: but *when* the desire cometh, *it is* a tree of life.
13 Whoso despises the word will be destroyed: but he that fears the commandment will be rewarded.
14 The law of the wise *is* a fountain of life, to depart from the snares of death.
15 Good understanding gives favor: but the way of transgressors *is* hard.
16 Every prudent *man* deals with knowledge: but a fool lays open *his* folly.
17 A wicked messenger falls into mischief: but a faithful ambassador *is* health.
18 Poverty and shame will *be to* him that refuses instruction: but he that regards reproof will be honored.
19 The desire accomplished is sweet to the soul: but *it is* abomination to fools to depart from evil.
20 He that walks with wise *men* will be wise: but a companion of fools will be destroyed.
21 Evil pursues sinners: but to the righteous good will be repayed.
22 A good *man* leaves an inheritance to his children's children: and the wealth of the sinner *is* laid up for the just.

23 Much food *is in* the tillage of the poor: but there is *that is* destroyed for want of judgment.
24 He that spares his rod hates his son: but he that loves him chastens him betimes.
25 The righteous eats to the satisfying of his soul: but the belly of the wicked will want.

CHAPTER 14

1 Every wise woman builds her house: but the foolish plucks it down with her hands.
2 He that walks in his uprightness fears the LORD: but *he that is* perverse in his ways despises him.
3 In the mouth of the foolish *is* a rod of pride: but the lips of the wise will preserve them.
4 Where no oxen *are*, the crib *is* clean: but much increase *is* by the strength of the ox.
5 A faithful witness will not lie: but a false witness will utter lies.
6 A scorner seeks wisdom, and *finds it* not: but knowledge *is* easy unto him that understands.
7 Go from the presence of a foolish man, when you perceive not *in him* the lips of knowledge.
8 The wisdom of the prudent *is* to understand his way: but the folly of fools *is* deceit.
9 Fools make a mock at sin: but among the righteous *there is* favor[1].
10 The heart knows his own bitterness; and a stranger does not intermeddle with his joy.
11 The house of the wicked will be overthrown: but the tabernacle of the upright will flourish.
12 There is a way which seems right unto a man, but the end thereof *are* the ways of death.
13 Even in laughter the heart is sorrowful; and the end of that mirth *is* heaviness.
14 The backslider in heart will be filled with *his* own ways: and a good man *will be satisfied* from himself.
15 The simple believeth every word: but *the* prudent *man* looks well to his going.
16 A wise *man* fears, and departs from evil: but the fool rages, and is confident.
17 *He that is* soon angry deals foolishly: and a man of wicked devices is hated.
18 The simple inherit folly: but the prudent are crowned with knowledge.
19 The evil bow before the good; and the wicked at the gates of the righteous.
20 The poor is hated even of his own neighbor: but the rich has many friends.
21 He that despises his neighbor sins: but he that has mercy on the poor, happy *is* he.
22 Do they not err that devise evil? but mercy and truth will *be* to them that devise good.
23 [In all labor there is profit: but the talk of the lips *tends* only to penury[2].][3]
24 The crown of the wise *is* their riches: but the foolishness of fools *is* folly.
25 A true witness delivers souls: but a deceitful *witness* speaks lies.

---

[1] favor – <u>delight, be pleased with</u> [Strgs#7522+7521].
[2] lit. *deficiency*; hence *impoverishment* [Strgs#4270].

[3] Some are poor in spiritual things because they talk only and labor not in the spirit. They have no prophet.

26 In the fear of the LORD *is* strong confidence: and his children will have a place of refuge.
27 The fear of the LORD *is* a fountain of life, to depart from the snares of death.
28 In the multitude of people *is* the king's honor: but in the want of people *is* the destruction of the prince.
29 *He that is* slow to wrath *is* of great understanding: but *he that is* hasty of spirit exalts folly.
30 A sound heart *is* the life of the flesh: but envy the rottenness of the bones.
31 He that oppresses the poor reproaches his Maker: but he that honors him has mercy on the poor.
32 The wicked is driven away in his wickedness: but the righteous has hope in his death.
33 Wisdom rests in the heart of him that has understanding: but *that which is* in the midst of fools is made known.
34 Righteousness exalts a nation: but sin *is* a reproach to any people.
35 The king's favor *is* toward a wise servant: but his wrath is *against* him that causes shame.

CHAPTER 15

1 A soft[1] answer turns away wrath: but grievous[2] words stir up anger.
2 The tongue of the wise uses knowledge aright: but the mouth of fools pours out foolishness.
3 The eyes of the LORD *are* in every place, beholding the evil and the good.
4 A wholesome tongue *is* a tree of life: but perverseness therein *is* a breach in the spirit.
5 A fool despises his father's instruction: but he that regards reproof is prudent.
6 In the house of the righteous *is* much treasure: but in the revenues of the wicked is trouble.
7 The lips of the wise disperse knowledge: but the heart of the foolish *doeth* not so.
8 The sacrifice of the wicked *is* an abomination to the LORD: but the prayer of the upright *is* his delight.
9 The way of the wicked *is* an abomination unto the LORD: but he loves him that follows after righteousness.
10 Correction *is* grievous unto him that forsakes the way: *and* he that hates reproof will die.
11 Hell and destruction *are* before the LORD: how much more then the hearts of the children of men?
12 A scorner loves not one that reproves him: neither will he go unto the wise.
13 A merry heart makes a cheerful countenance: but by sorrow of the heart the spirit is broken.
14 The heart of him that has understanding seeks knowledge: but the mouth of fools feeds on foolishness.
15 All the days of the afflicted *are* evil: but he that is of a merry heart has a continual feast.
16 Better *is* little with the fear of the LORD than great treasure and trouble therewith.
17 Better *is* a dinner of herbs where love is, than a stalled ox and hatred therewith.
18 A wrathful man stirs up strife: but *he that is* slow to anger appeases strife.

19 The way of the slothful *man is* as a hedge of thorns: but the way of the righteous *is* made plain.
20 A wise son makes a glad father: but a foolish man despises his mother.
21 Folly *is* joy to *him that is* destitute of wisdom: but a man of understanding walks uprightly.
22 Without counsel purposes are disappointed: but in the multitude of counselors they are established.
23 A man has joy by the answer of his mouth: and a word *spoken* in due season, how good *is it*!
24 The way of life *is* above to the wise, that he may depart from hell beneath.
25 The LORD will destroy the house of the proud: but he will establish the border of the widow.
26 The thoughts of the wicked *are* an abomination to the LORD: but *the words* of the pure *are* pleasant words.
27 He that is greedy of gain troubles his own house; but he that hates gifts will live.
28 The heart of the righteous studies to answer: but the mouth of the wicked pours out evil things.
29 The LORD *is* far from the wicked: but he hears the prayer of the righteous.
30 The light of the eyes rejoices the heart: *and* a good report makes the bones fat.
31 The ear that hears the reproof of life abides among the wise.
32 He that refuses instruction despises his own soul: but he that hears reproof gets understanding.
33 The fear of the LORD *is* the instruction of wisdom; and before honor *is* humility.

CHAPTER 16

1 The preparations of the heart in man, and the answer of the tongue, *is* from the LORD.
2 All the ways of a man *are* clean in his own eyes; but the LORD weights the spirits.
3 Commit your works unto the LORD, and your thoughts will be established.
4 The LORD has made all *things* for himself: yea, even the wicked for the day of evil.
5 Every one *that is* proud in heart *is* an abomination to the LORD: *though* hand *join* in hand, he will not be unpunished.
6 By mercy and truth iniquity is purged: and by the fear of the LORD men depart from evil.
7 When a man's ways please the LORD, he makes even his enemies to be at peace with him.
8 Better *is* a little with righteousness than great revenues without right.
9 A man's heart devises his way: but the LORD directs his steps.
10 A divine sentence *is* in the lips of the king: his mouth transgresses not in judgment.
11 A just weight and balance *are* the LORD'S: all the weights of the bag *are* his work.
12 *It is* an abomination to kings to commit wickedness: for the throne is established by righteousness.
13 Righteous lips *are* the delight of kings; and they love him that speaks right.
14 The wrath of a king *is* as messengers of death: but a wise man will pacify it.

---

[1] lit. tender[Strgs#7390]
[2] grievous – painful, an earthen vessel, toil; also a pang [Strgs#6089]. Root word to carve, fabricate or fashion, worry, pain or anger [Strgs#6087].

15 In the light of the king's countenance *is* life; and his favor *is* as a cloud of the latter rain.
16 How much better *is it* to get wisdom than gold! And to get understanding rather to be chosen than silver!
17 The highway of the upright *is* to depart from evil: he that keeps his way preserves his soul.
18 Pride *goes* before destruction, and **a** haughty spirit before a fall.
19 Better *it is to be* of **a** humble spirit with the lowly, than to divide the spoil with the proud.
20 He that handles a matter wisely will find good: and whoso trusts in the LORD, happy *is* he.
21 The wise in heart will be called prudent: and the sweetness of the lips increases learning.
22 Understanding *is* a wellspring of life unto him that has it: but the instruction of fools *is* folly.
23 The heart of the wise teaches his mouth, and adds learning to his lips.
24 Pleasant words *are as* **a** honeycomb, sweet to the soul, and health to the bones.
25 There is a way that seems right unto a man, but the end thereof *are* the ways of death.
26 He that labors, labors for himself; for his mouth craves it of him.
27 An ungodly man digs up evil: and in his lips *there is* as a burning fire.
28 A forward man sows strife: and a whisperer separates chief friends.
29 A violent man entices his neighbor, and leads him into the way *that is* not good.
30 He shuts his eyes to devise forward things: moving his lips he brings evil to pass.
31 The hoary head *is* a crown of glory, *if* it be found in the way of righteousness.
32 *He that is* slow to anger *is* better than the mighty; and he that rules his spirit than he that takes a city.
33 The lot is cast into the lap; but the whole disposing thereof *is* of the LORD.

CHAPTER 17

1 Better *is* a dry morsel, and quietness therewith, than an house full of sacrifices *with* strife.
2 A wise servant will have rule over a son that causes shame, and will have part of the inheritance among the brethren.
3 The fining pot *is* for silver, and the furnace for gold: but the LORD tries the hearts.
4 A wicked doer gives heed to false lips; *and* a liar gives ear to a naughty tongue.
5 Whoso mocks the poor reproaches his Maker: *and* he that is glad at calamities will not be unpunished.
6 Children's children *are* the crown of old men; and the glory of children *are* their fathers.
7 Excellent speech becomes not a fool: much less do lying lips a prince.
8 A gift *is as* a precious stone in the eyes of him that has it: whithersoever it turns, it prospers.
9 He that covers a transgression seeks love; but he that repeats a matter separates *very* friends.
10 A reproof enters more into a wise man than an hundred stripes into a fool.

11 An evil *man* seeks only rebellion: therefore a cruel messenger will be sent against him.
12 Let a bear robbed of her whelps meet a man, rather than a fool in his folly.
13 Whoso rewards evil for good, evil will not depart from his house.
14 The beginning of strife *is as* when one lets out water: therefore leave off contention, before it be meddled with.
15 He that justifies the wicked, and he that condemns the just, even they both *are* abomination to the LORD.
16 Wherefore *is there* a price in the hand of a fool to get wisdom, seeing *he has* no heart *to it*?
17 A friend loves at all times, and a brother is born for adversity.
18 A man void of understanding strikes hands, *and* becomes surety in the presence of his friend.
19 He loves transgression that loves strife: *and* he that exalts his gate seeks destruction.
20 He that has a forward heart finds no good: and he that has a perverse tongue falls into mischief.
21 He that **begotten** a fool *does it* to his sorrow: and the father of a fool has no joy.
22 A merry heart doeth good *like* a medicine: but a broken spirit dries the bones.
23 A wicked *man* takes a gift out of the bosom to pervert the ways of judgment.
24 Wisdom *is* before him that has understanding; but the eyes of a fool *are* in the ends of the earth.
25 A foolish son *is* a grief to his father, and bitterness to her that bare him.
26 Also to punish the just *is* not good, or to strike princes for equity.
27 He that has knowledge spares his words: *and* a man of understanding is of an excellent spirit.
28 Even a fool, when he holds his peace, is counted wise: *and* he that shuts his lips *is esteemed* a man of understanding.

CHAPTER 18

1 Through desire a man, having separated himself, seeks *and* intermeddles[1] with all wisdom.
2 A fool has no delight in understanding, but that his heart may discover itself.
3 When the wicked cometh, *then* cometh also contempt, and with ignominy reproach.
4 The words of a man's mouth *are as* deep waters, *and* the wellspring of wisdom *as* a flowing brook.
5 *It is* not good to accept the person of the wicked, to overthrow the righteous in judgment.
6 A fool's lips enter into contention, and his mouth calls for strokes.
7 A fool's mouth *is* his destruction, and his lips *are* the snare of his soul.
8 The words of a talebearer *are* as wounds, and they go down into the innermost parts of the belly.
9 He also that is slothful in his work is brother to him that is a great waster.
10 The name of the LORD *is* a strong tower the righteous runs into it, and is safe.
11 The rich man's wealth *is* his strong city, and as a high wall in his own conceit.
12 Before destruction the heart of man is haughty, and before honor *is* humility.

---

[1] intermeddle- a primitive root; to be obstinate:- (inter-) meddle (with). [Strgs#1566]. BDB defines it as to expose, lay bare, to disclose oneself, break out.

The Proverbs

13 He that answers a matter before he hears *it*, *it is* folly and shame unto him.
14 The spirit of a man will sustain his infirmity; but a wounded spirit who can bear?
15 The heart of the prudent gets knowledge; and the ear of the wise seeks knowledge.
16 A man's gift makes room for him, and brings him before great men.
17 *He that is* first in his own cause *seems* just; but his neighbor cometh and searches him.
18 The lot causes contentions to cease, and parts between the mighty.
19 A brother offended *is harder to be won* than a strong city: and *their* contentions *are* like the bars of a castle.
20 A man's belly will be satisfied with the fruit of his mouth; *and* with the increase of his lips will he be filled.
21 Death and life *are* in the power of the tongue: and they that love it will eat the fruit thereof.
22 *Whoso* finds a wife finds a good *thing*, and obtains favor of the LORD.
23 The poor uses intreaties[1]; but the rich answers roughly.
24 A man *that has* friends must show himself friendly: and there is a friend *that* sticks closer than a brother.

CHAPTER 19

1 Better *is* the poor that walks in his integrity, than *he that is* perverse in his lips, and is a fool.
2 Also, *that* the soul *be* without knowledge, *it is* not good; and he that hastes with *his* feet sins.
3 The foolishness of man perverts his way: and his heart frets against the LORD.
4 Wealth makes many friends; but the poor is separated from his neighbor.
5 A false witness will not be unpunished, and *he that* speaks lies will not escape.
6 Many will intreat the favor of the prince: and every man *is* a friend to him that gives gifts.
7 All the brethren of the poor do hate him: how much more do his friends go far from him? He pursues *them* with words, *yet they are* wanting *to him*.
8 He that gets wisdom loves his own soul: he that keeps understanding will find good.
9 A false witness will not be unpunished, and *he that* speaks lies will perish.
10 Delight is not seemly for a fool; much less for a servant to have rule over princes.
11 The discretion of a man defers his anger; and *it is* his glory to pass over a transgression.
12 The king's wrath *is* as the roaring of a lion; but his favor *is* as dew upon the grass.
13 A foolish son *is* the calamity of his father: and the contentions of a wife *are* a continual dropping.
14 House and riches *are* the inheritance of fathers: and a prudent wife *is* from the LORD.
15 Slothfulness casts into a deep sleep; and an idle soul will suffer hunger.
16 He that keeps the commandment keeps his own soul; *but* he that despises his ways will die.
17 He that has pity upon the poor lends unto the LORD; and that which he has given will he pay him again.
18 Chasten your son while there is hope, and let not your soul spare for his crying.
19 A man of great wrath will suffer punishment: for if you deliver *him*, yet you must do it again.
20 Hear counsel, and receive instruction, that you may be wise in your latter end.
21 *There are* many devices in a man's heart; nevertheless the counsel of the LORD, that will stand.
22 The desire of a man *is* his kindness: and a poor man *is* better than a liar.
23 The fear of the LORD *tends* to life: and *he that has it* will abide satisfied; he will not be visited with evil.
24 A slothful *man* hides his hand in *his* bosom, and will not so much as bring it to his mouth again.
25 Smite a scorner, and the simple will beware: and reprove one that has understanding, *and* he will understand knowledge.
26 He that wastes *his* father, *and* chases away *his* mother, *is* a son that causes shame, and brings reproach.
27 Cease, my son, to hear the instruction *that causes* to err from the words of knowledge.
28 An ungodly witness scorns judgment: and the mouth of the wicked devours iniquity.
29 Judgments are prepared for scorners[2], and stripes for the back of fools.

CHAPTER 20

1 Wine *is* a mocker, strong drink *is* raging: and whosoever is deceived thereby is not wise.
2 The fear of a king *is* as the roaring of a lion: whoso provokes him to anger sins *against* his own soul.
3 *It is* an honor for a man to cease from strife: but every fool will be meddling.
4 The sluggard will not plow by reason of the cold; *therefore* will he beg in harvest, and *have* nothing.
5 Counsel in the heart of man *is like* deep water; but a man of understanding will draw it out.
6 Most men will proclaim everyone his own goodness: but a faithful man who can find?
7 The just *man* walks in his integrity: his children *are* blessed after him.
8 A king that sits in the throne of judgment scatters away all evil with his eyes.
9 Who can say, I have made my heart clean, I am pure from my sin?
10 Divers weights, *and* divers measures, both of them *are* alike abomination to the LORD.
11 Even a child is known by his doings, whether his work *be* pure, and whether *it be* right.
12 The hearing ear, and the seeing eye, the LORD has made even both of them.
13 Love not sleep, lest you come to poverty; open your eyes, *and* you will be satisfied with bread.
14 *It is* naught, *it is* naught, said the buyer: but when he is gone his way, then he boasts.

---

[1] intreaties- literally earnest prayer: -intreat or supplication. [Strgs#8469]
[2] scorners- the Hebrew word *lûts*, <u>loots</u>; to <u>make mouths</u> at, that is, to scoff; hence (from the effort to pronounce a foreign language) to *interpret*, or (generally) *intercede*: -ambassador, have in derision, interpreter, make a mock, mocker, teacher. [Strgs#3887]

15 There is gold, and a multitude of rubies: but the lips of knowledge *are* a precious jewel.
16 Take his garment that is surety *for* a stranger: and take a pledge of him for a strange woman.
17 Bread of deceit *is* sweet to a man; but afterwards his mouth will be filled with gravel.
18 *Every* purpose is established by counsel: and with good advice make war.
19 He that goes about *as* a talebearer reveals secrets: therefore meddle not with him that flatters with his lips.
20 Whoso curses his father or his mother, his lamp will be put out in obscure darkness.
21 An inheritance *may be* gotten hastily at the beginning; but the end thereof will not be blessed.
22 Say not you, I will recompense evil; *but* wait on the LORD, and he will save you.
23 Divers weights *are* an abomination unto the LORD; and a false balance *is* not good.
24 Man's goings *are* of the LORD; how can a man then understand his own way?
25 *It is* a snare to the man *who* devours *that which is* holy, and after vows to make enquiry.
26 A wise king scatters the wicked, and brings the wheel over them.
27 The spirit of man *is* the candle of the LORD, searching all the inward parts of the belly.
28 Mercy and truth preserve the king: and his throne is upheld by mercy.
29 The glory of young men *is* their strength: and the beauty of old men *is* the gray head.
30 The blueness of a wound cleans away evil: so *do* stripes the inward parts of the belly.

CHAPTER 21

1 The king's heart *is* in the hand of the LORD, *as* the rivers of water: he turns it whithersoever he will.
2 Every way of a man *is* right in his own eyes: but the LORD ponders the hearts.
3 To do justice and judgment *is* more acceptable to the LORD than sacrifice.
4 An high look, and a proud heart, *and* the plowing of the wicked, *is* sin.
5 The thoughts of the diligent *tend* only to plenteousness; but of every one *that is* hasty only to want.
6 The getting of treasures by a lying tongue *is* a vanity tossed to and fro of them that seek death.
7 The robbery of the wicked will destroy them; because they refuse to do judgment.
8 The way of man *is* forward and strange: but *as for* the pure, his work *is* right.
9 *It is* better to dwell in a corner of the housetop, than with a brawling woman in a wide house.
10 The soul of the wicked desires evil: his neighbor finds no favor in his eyes.
11 When the scorner is punished, the simple is made wise: and when the wise is instructed, he receives knowledge.
12 The righteous *man* wisely considers the house of the wicked: *but God* overthrows the wicked for *their* wickedness.
13 Whoso stops his ears at the cry of the poor, he also will cry himself, but will not be heard.
14 A gift in secret pacifies anger: and a reward in the bosom strong wrath.
15 *It is* joy to the just to do judgment: but destruction will *be* to the workers of iniquity.
16 The man that wanders out of the way of understanding will remain in the congregation of the dead.
17 He that loves pleasure will *be* a poor man: he that loves wine and oil will not be rich.
18 The wicked will *be* a ransom for the righteous, and the transgressor for the upright.
19 *It is* better to dwell in the wilderness, than with a contentious and an angry woman.
20 *There is* treasure to be desired and oil in the dwelling of the wise; but a foolish man spends it up.
21 He that follows after righteousness and mercy finds life, righteousness, and honor.
22 A wise *man* scales the city of the mighty, and casts down the strength of the confidence thereof.
23 Whoso keeps his mouth and his tongue keeps his soul from troubles.
24 Proud *and* haughty scorner *is* his name, who deals in proud wrath.
25 The desire of the slothful kills him; for his hands refuse to labor.
26 He covets greedily all the daylong: but the righteous gives and spares not.
27 The sacrifice of the wicked *is* abomination: how much more, *when* he brings it with a wicked mind?
28 A false witness will perish: but the man that hears speaks constantly.
29 A wicked man hardens his face: but *as for* the upright, he directs his way.
30 *There is* no wisdom or understanding or counsel against the LORD.
31 The horse *is* prepared against the day of battle: but safety *is* of the LORD.

CHAPTER 22

1 A *good* name *is* rather to be chosen than great riches, *and* loving favor rather than silver and gold.
2 The rich and poor meet together: the LORD *is* the maker of them all.
3 A prudent *man* foresees the evil, and hides himself: but the simple pass on, and are punished.
4 By humility *and* the fear of the LORD *are* riches, and honor, and life.
5 Thorns *and* snares *are* in the way of the forward: he that does keep his soul will be far from them.
6 Train up a child in the way he should go: and when he is old, he will not depart from it.
7 The rich rules over the poor, and the borrower *is* servant to the lender.
8 He that sows iniquity will reap vanity: and the rod of his anger will fail.
9 He that has a bountiful eye will be blessed; for he gives of his bread to the poor.
10 Cast out the scorner, and contention will go out; yea, strife and reproach will cease.
11 He that loves pureness of heart, *for* the grace of his lips the king will *be* his friend.
12 The eyes of the LORD preserve knowledge, and he overthrows the words of the transgressor.

13 The slothful *man* said, *there is* a lion without, I will be slain in the streets.
14 The mouth of strange women *is* a deep pit: he that is abhorred of the LORD will fall therein.
15 Foolishness *is* bound in the heart of a child; *but* the rod of correction will drive it far from him.
16 He that oppresses the poor to increase his *riches, and* he that gives to the rich, will surely *come* to want.
17 Bow down your ear, and hear the words of the wise, and apply your heart unto my knowledge.
18 For *it is* a pleasant thing if you keep them [within you]¹; they will withal be fitted in your lips.
19 That your trust may be in the LORD, I have made known to you this day, even to you.
20 Have not I written to you excellent things in counsels and knowledge,
21 That I might make you know the certainty of the words of truth; that you might answer the words of truth to them that send unto you?
22 Rob not the poor, because he *is* poor: neither oppresses the afflicted in the gate:
23 For the LORD will plead their cause, and spoil the soul of those that spoiled them.
24 Make no friendship with an angry man; and with a furious man you will not go:
25 Lest you learn his ways, and get a snare to your soul.
26 Be not you *one* of them that strike hands, *or* of them that are sureties for debts.
27 If you have nothing to pay, why should he take away your bed from under you?
28 Remove not the ancient landmark, which your fathers have set.
29 See you a man diligent in his business? He will stand before kings; he will not stand before mean *men*.

CHAPTER 23

1 When you sits to eat with a ruler, consider diligently what *is* before you:
2 And put a knife to your throat, if you *be* a man given to appetite.
3 Be not desirous of his dainties: for they *are* deceitful meat.
4 Labor not to be rich: cease from your own wisdom.
5 will you set your eyes upon that which is not? For *riches* certainly make themselves wings; they fly away as an eagle toward heaven.
6 Eat you not the bread of *him that has* an evil eye, neither desire you his dainty meats:
7 For as he thinks in his heart, so *is* he: Eat and drink, said he to you; but his heart *is* not with you.
8 The morsel *which* you have eaten will you vomit up, and lose your sweet words.
9 Speak not in the ears of a fool: for he will despise the wisdom of your words.
10 Remove not the old landmark; and enter not into the fields of the fatherless:
11 For their redeemer *is* mighty; he will plead their cause with you.
12 Apply your heart unto instruction, and your ears to the words of knowledge.
13 Withhold not correction from the child: for *if* you beat him with the rod, he will not die.
14 you will beat him with the rod, and will deliver his soul from hell.
15 My son, if your heart be wise, my heart will rejoice, even mine.
16 Yea, my reins will rejoice, when your lips speak right things.
17 Let not your heart envy sinners: but *be you* in the fear of the LORD all the day long.
18 For surely there is an end; and your expectation will not be cut off.
19 Hear you, my son, and be wise, and guide your heart in the way.
20 Be not among winebibbers; among riotous eaters of flesh:
21 For the drunkard and the glutton will come to poverty: and drowsiness will clothe *a man* with rags.
22 Hearken unto your father that begat you, and despise not your mother when she is old.
23 Buy the truth, and sell *it* not; *also* wisdom, and instruction, and understanding.
24 The father of the righteous will greatly rejoice: and he that begets a wise *child* will have joy of him.
25 your father and your mother will be glad, and she that bare you will rejoice.
26 My son, give me your heart, and let your eyes observe my ways.
27 For a whore *is* a deep ditch; and a strange woman *is* a narrow pit.
28 She also lies in wait as *for* a prey, and increases the transgressors among men.
29 Who has woe? Who has sorrow? Who has contentions? Who has babbling? Who has wounds without cause? Who has redness of eyes?
30 They that tarry long at the wine; they that go to seek mixed wine.
31 Look not you upon the wine when it is red, when it gives his color in the cup, *when* it moves itself aright.
32 At the last it bites like a serpent, and stings like an adder².
33 your eyes will behold strange women, and your heart will utter perverse things.
34 Yea, you will be as he that lies down in the midst of the sea, or as he that lies upon the top of a mast.
35 They have stricken me, will you *say, and* I was not sick; they have beaten me, *and* I felt *it* not: when will I awake? I will seek it yet again.

CHAPTER 24

1 Be not you envious against evil men, neither desire to be with them.
2 For their heart studies destruction, and their lips talk of mischief.
3 Through wisdom is a house built; and by understanding it is established:
4 And by knowledge will the chambers be filled with all precious and pleasant riches.
5 A wise man *is* strong; yea, a man of knowledge increases strength.
6 For by wise counsel you will make your war: and in multitude of counselors *there is* safety.
7 Wisdom *is* too high for a fool: he opens not his mouth in the gate.
8 He that devises to do evil will be called a mischievous person.
9 The thought of foolishness *is* sin: and the scorner *is* an abomination to men.
10 *If* you faint in the day of adversity, your strength *is* small.
11 If you forbear to deliver *them that are* drawn unto death, and *those that are* ready to be slain;

---

¹ lit. in your belly [Strgs#990].
² adder- is a horned viper snake that is native to Israel. Adder is defined as to extrude; a viper (as thrusting out the tongue, that is, hissing). [Strgs##6848]

12 If you say, Behold, we knew it not; does not he that ponders the heart consider *it*? And he that keeps your soul, does *not* he know *it*? And will *not* he render to *every* man according to his works?
13 My son, eat you honey, because *it is* good; and the honeycomb, *which is* sweet to your taste:
14 So will the knowledge of wisdom *be* unto your soul: when you have found *it*, then there will be a reward, and your expectation will not be cut off.
15 Lay not wait, O wicked *man*, against the dwelling of the righteous; spoil not his resting place:
16 For a just *man* falls seven times, and rises up again: but the wicked will fall into mischief.
17 Rejoice not when your enemy fall, and let not your heart be glad when he stumbles:
18 Lest the LORD see *it*, and it displease him, and he turn away his wrath from him.
19 Fret not yourself because of evil *men*, neither be you envious at the wicked;
20 For there will be no reward to the evil *man*; the candle of the wicked will be put out.
21 My son, fear you the LORD and the king: *and* meddle not with them that are given to change:
22 For their calamity will rise suddenly; and who knows the ruin of them both?
23 These *things* also *belong* to the wise. *It is* not good to have respect of persons in judgment.
24 He that said unto the wicked, you are righteous; him will the people curse, nations will abhor him:
25 But to them that rebuke *him* will be delight, and a good blessing will come upon them.
26 *Every man* will kiss *his* lips that gives a right answer.
27 Prepare your work without, and make it fit for yourself in the field; and afterwards build your house.
28 Be not a witness against your neighbor without cause; and deceive *not* with your lips.
29 Say not, I will do so to him as he has done to me: I will render to the man according to his work.
30 I went by the field of the slothful, and by the vineyard of the man void of understanding;
31 And, lo, it was all grown over with thorns, *and* nettles had covered the face thereof, and the stone wall thereof was broken down.
32 Then I saw, *and* considered *it* well: I looked upon *it, and* received instruction.
33 *Yet* a little sleep, a little slumber, a little folding of the hands to sleep:
34 So will your poverty come *as* one that travels; and your want as an armed man.

CHAPTER 25

1 These *are* also proverbs of Solomon, which the men of Hezekiah king of Judah copied out.
2 *It is* the glory of God to conceal a thing: but the honor of kings *is* to search out a matter.
3 The heaven for height, and the earth for depth, and the heart of kings *is* unsearchable.
4 Take away the dross from the silver, and there will come forth a vessel for the finer.
5 Take away the wicked *from* before the king, and his throne will be established in righteousness.
6 Put not forth yourself in the presence of the king, and stand not in the place of great *men*:
7 For better *it is* that it be said unto you, Come up hither; than that you should be put lower in the presence of the prince whom your eyes have seen.
8 Go not forth hastily to strive, lest you *know not* what to do in the end thereof, when your neighbor has put you to shame.
9 Debate your cause with your neighbor *himself*; and discover not a secret to another:
10 Lest he that hears *it* put you to shame, and your infamy turn not away.
11 A word fitly spoken *is like* apples of gold in pictures of silver.
12 *As* an earring of gold, and an ornament of fine gold, *so is* a wise reprover[1] upon an obedient ear.
13 As the cold of snow in the time of harvest, *so is* a faithful messenger to them that send him: for he refreshes the soul of his masters.
14 Whoso boasts himself of a false gift *is like* clouds[2] and wind without rain.
15 By long forbearing is a prince persuaded, and a soft tongue breaks the bone.
16 have you found honey? Eat so much as is sufficient for you, lest you be filled therewith, and vomit it.
17 Withdraw your foot from your neighbor's house; lest he be weary of you, and *so* hate you.
18 A man that bears false witness against his neighbor *is* a maul, and a sword, and a sharp arrow.
19 Confidence in an unfaithful man in time of trouble *is like* a broken tooth, and a foot out of joint.
20 *As* he that takes away a garment in cold weather, *and as* vinegar upon nitre[3], so *is* he that sings songs to a heavy heart.
21 If your enemy be hungry, give him bread to eat; and if he be thirsty, give him water to drink:
22 For you will heap coals of fire upon his head, and the LORD will reward you.
23 The north wind drives away rain: so does an angry countenance a backbiting tongue.
24 *It is* better to dwell in the corner of the housetop, than with a brawling woman and in a wide house.
25 *As* cold waters to a thirsty soul, so *is* good news from a far country.
26 A righteous man falling down before the wicked *is as* a troubled fountain, and a corrupt spring.
27 *It is* not good to eat much honey: so *for men* to search their own glory *is not* glory.
28 He that has no rule over his own spirit *is like* a city *that is* broken down, *and* without walls.

CHAPTER 26

1 As snow in summer, and as rain in harvest, so honor is not seemly for a fool.
2 As the bird by wandering, as the swallow by flying, so the curse causeless will not come.

---

[1] reprove- is the Hebrew word *yâkach*, <u>yaw-wahh'</u>; which is defined as to *be right* (that is, correct); reciprocally to *argue*; causatively to *decide*, *justify* or *convict*: -appoint, argue, chasten, convince, correct(ion), daysman, plead, reason, dispute, judge. [Strgs#3198]

[2] lit. *an exalted one* [Strgs#5387].
[3] nitre- comes from the Hebrew root word *nâthar*, <u>naw-thar'</u>, meaning to *jump*, that is, be violently *agitated*; causatively, to *terrify*, *shake off*, *untie*: -make, move, undo. [Strgs#5427]

3 A whip for the horse, a bridle for the ass, and a rod for the fool's back.
4 Answer not a fool according to his folly, lest you also be like unto him.
5 Answer a fool according to his folly, lest he be wise in his own conceit.
6 He that sends a message by the hand of a fool cuts off the feet, *and* drinks damage.
7 The legs of the lame are not equal: so *is* a parable in the mouth of fools.
8 As he that binds a stone in a sling, so *is* he that gives honor to a fool.
9 *As* a thorn goes up into the hand of a drunkard, so *is* a parable in the mouth of fools.
10 The great *God* that formed all *things* both rewards the fool, and rewards transgressors.
11 As a dog returns to his vomit, *so* a fool returns to his folly.
12 See you a man wise in his own conceit? There is more hope of a fool than of him.
13 The slothful *man* said, *there is* a lion in the way; a lion *is* in the streets.
14 *As* the door turns upon his hinges, so does the slothful upon his bed.
15 The slothful hides his hand in *his* bosom; it grieves him to bring it again to his mouth.
16 The sluggard *is* wiser in his own conceit than seven men that can render a reason.
17 He that passes by, *and* meddles with strife *belonging* not to him, *is like* one that takes a dog by the ears.
18 As a mad *man* who casts firebrands, arrows, and death,
19 So *is* the man *that* deceives his neighbor, and said, Am not I in sport?
20 Where no wood is, *there* the fire goes out: so where *there is* no talebearer, the strife ceases.
21 *As* coals *are* to burning coals, and wood to fire; so *is* a contentious man to kindle strife.
22 The words of a talebearer *are* as wounds, and they go down into the innermost parts of the belly.
23 Burning lips and a wicked heart *are like* a potsherd covered with silver dross.
24 He that hates dissembles with his lips, and lays up deceit within him;
25 When he speaks fair, believe him not: for *there are* seven abominations in his heart.
26 *Whose* hatred is covered by deceit, his wickedness will be showed before the *whole* congregation.
27 Whoso digs a pit will fall therein: and he that rolls a stone, it will return upon him.
28 A lying tongue hates *those that are* afflicted by it; and a flattering mouth works ruin.

CHAPTER 27

1 Boast not yourself of tomorrow; for you knows not what a day may bring forth.
2 Let another man praise you, and not your own mouth; a stranger, and not your own lips.
3 A stone *is* heavy, and the sand weighty; but a fool's wrath *is* heavier than them both.
4 Wrath *is* cruel, and anger *is* outrageous; but who *is* able to stand before envy?
5 Open rebuke *is* better than secret love.
6 Faithful *are* the wounds of a friend; but the kisses of an enemy *are* deceitful.
7 The full soul loathes a honeycomb; but to the hungry soul every bitter thing is sweet.
8 As a bird that wanders from her nest, so *is* a man that wanders from his place.
9 Ointment and perfume rejoice the heart: so does the sweetness of a man's friend by hearty counsel.
10 your own friend, and your father's friend, forsake not; neither go into your brother's house in the day of your calamity: *for* better *is* a neighbor *that is* near than a brother far off.
11 My son, be wise, and make my heart glad, that I may answer him that reproaches me.
12 A prudent *man* foresees the evil, *and* hides himself but the simple pass on, *and* are punished.
13 Take his garment that is surety for a stranger, and take a pledge of him for a strange woman.
14 He that blesses his friend with a loud voice, rising early in the morning, it will be counted a curse to him.
15 A continual dropping in a very rainy day and a contentious woman are alike.
16 Whosoever hides her hides the wind, and the ointment of his right hand, *which* bewrays[1] *itself*.
17 Iron sharpens iron; so a man sharpens the countenance of his friend.
18 Whoso keeps the fig tree will eat the fruit thereof: so he that waits on his master will be honored.
19 As in water face *answers* to face, so the heart of man to man.
20 Hell and destruction are never full; so the eyes of man are never satisfied.
21 *As* the fining pot for silver, and the furnace for gold; so *is* a man to his praise.
22 Though you should bray a fool in a mortar among wheat with a pestle, *yet* will not his foolishness depart from him.
23 Be you diligent to know the state of your flocks, *and* look well to your herds.
24 For riches *are* not for ever: and does the crown endure to every generation?
25 The hay appears, and the tender grass shows itself, and herbs of the mountains are gathered.
26 The lambs *are* for your clothing, and the goats *are* the price of the field.
27 And you will have goats' milk enough for your food, for the food of your household, and *for* the maintenance for your maidens.

CHAPTER 28

1 The wicked flee when no man pursues: but the righteous are bold as a lion.
2 For the transgression of a land many *are* the princes thereof: but by a man of understanding *and* knowledge the state *thereof* will be prolonged.
3 A poor man that oppresses the poor *is like* a sweeping rain which leaves no food.
4 They that forsake the law praise the wicked: but such as keep the law contend with them.

---

[1] bewrays- to call out (that is, properly address by name, but used in a wide variety of applications). [Strgs#7121]

5 Evil men understand not judgment: but they that seek the LORD understand all *things*.
6 Better *is* the poor that walks in his uprightness, than *he that is* perverse *in his* ways, though he *be* rich.
7 Whoso keeps the law *is* a wise son: but he that is a companion of riotous *men* shames his father.
8 He that by usury and unjust gain increases his substance, he will gather it for him that will pity the poor.
9 He that turns away his ear from hearing the law, even his prayer will *be* abomination.
10 Whoso causes the righteous to go astray in an evil way, he will fall himself into his own pit: but the upright will have good *things* in possession.
11 The rich man *is* wise in his own conceit; but the poor that has understanding searches him out.
12 When righteous *men* do rejoice, *there is* great glory: but when the wicked rise, a man is hidden.
13 He that covers his sins will not prosper: but whoso confesses and forsakes *them* will have mercy.
14 Happy *is* the man that fears always: but he that hardens his heart will fall into mischief.
15 *As* a roaring lion, and a ranging bear; *so is* a wicked ruler over the poor people.
16 The prince that wants understanding *is* also a great oppressor: *but* he that hates covetousness will prolong *his* days.
17 A man that doeth violence to the blood of *any* person will flee to the pit; let no man stay him.
18 Whoso walks uprightly will be saved: but *he that is* perverse *in* his ways will fall at once.
19 He that tills his land will have plenty of bread: but he that follows after vain *persons* will have poverty enough.
20 A faithful man will abound with blessings: but he that makes haste to be rich will not be innocent.
21 To have respect of persons *is* not good: for a piece of bread *that* man will transgress.
22 He that **haste's** to be rich has an evil eye, and considers not that poverty will come upon him.
23 He that rebukes a man afterwards will find more favor than he that flatters with the tongue.
24 Whoso robs his father or his mother, and said, *It is* no transgression; the same *is* the companion of a destroyer.
25 He that is of a proud heart stirs up strife: but he that puts his trust in the LORD will be made fat.
26 He that trusts in his own heart is a fool: but whoso walks wisely, he will be delivered.
27 He that gives unto the poor will not lack: but he that hides his eyes will have many a curse.
28 When the wicked rise, men hide themselves: but when they perish, the righteous increase.

CHAPTER 29

1 He, that being often reproved hardens *his* neck, will suddenly be destroyed, and that without remedy.
2 When the righteous are in authority, the people rejoice: but when the wicked bears rule, the people mourn.
3 Whoso loves wisdom rejoices his father: but he that keeps company with harlots spends *his* substance.

4 The king by judgment establishes the land: but he that receives gifts overthrows it.
5 A man that flatters his neighbor spreads a net for his feet.
6 In the transgression of an evil man *there is* a snare: but the righteous does sing and rejoice.
7 The righteous considers the cause of the poor: *but* the wicked regards not to know *it*.
8 Scornful men bring a city into a snare: but wise *men* turn away wrath.
9 *If* a wise man contends with a foolish man, whether he rage or laugh, *there is* no rest.
10 The bloodthirsty hate the upright: but the just seek his soul.
11 A fool utters all his mind: but a wise *man* keeps it in till afterwards.
12 If a ruler hearkens to lies, all his servants *are* wicked.
13 The poor and the deceitful man meet together: the LORD lightens both their eyes.
14 The king that faithfully judges the poor, his throne will be established for ever.
15 The rod and reproof give wisdom: but a child left *to himself* brings his mother to shame.
16 When the wicked are multiplied, transgression increases: but the righteous will see their fall.
17 Correct your son, and he will give you rest; yea, he will give delight unto your soul.
18 Where *there is* no vision[1], the people perish[2]: but he that keeps the law, happy *is* he.
19 A servant will not be corrected by words: for though he understand he will not answer.
20 Sees you a man *that is* hasty in his words? *There is* more hope of a fool than of him.
21 He that delicately brings up his servant from a child will have him become *his* son at the length.
22 An angry man stirs up strife, and a furious man abounds in transgression.
23 A man's pride will bring him low: but honor will uphold the humble in spirit.
24 Whoso is partner with a thief hates his own soul: he hears cursing, and bewrays *it* not.
25 The fear of man brings a snare: but whoso puts his trust in the LORD will be safe.
26 Many seek the ruler's favor; but *every* man's judgment *cometh* from the LORD.
27 An unjust man *is* an abomination to the just: and *he that is* upright in the way *is* abomination to the wicked.

CHAPTER 30

1 The words of Agur the son of Jakeh, *even* the prophecy: the man spoke unto Ithiel, even unto Ithiel and Ucal,
2 Surely I *am* more brutish than *any* man, and have not the understanding of a man.
3 I neither learned wisdom, or have the knowledge of the holy.
4 Who has ascended up into heaven, or descended? Who has gathered the wind in his fists? Who has bound the waters in a garment? Who has established all the ends of the earth? What *is* his name, and what *is* his son's name, if you canst tell?
5 Every word of God *is* pure: he *is* a shield unto them that put their trust in him.

---

[1] lit. mental sight, mental revelation, dream oracle [Strgs#2377].
[2] perish – to *loosen*, to *expose*, *dismiss*, *absolve*, to make naked [Strgs#6544].

6 Add you not unto his words, lest he reprove you, and you be found a liar.
7 Two *things* have I required of you; deny me *them* not before I die:
8 Remove far from me vanity and lies: give me neither poverty or riches; feed me with food convenient for me:
9 Lest I be full, and deny you, and say, Who *is* the LORD? Or lest I be poor, and steal, and take the name of my God *in vain*.
10 Accuse not a servant unto his master, lest he curse you, and you be found guilty.
11 *There is* a generation *that* curses their father, and does not bless their mother.
12 *There is* a generation *that are* pure in their own eyes, and *yet* is not washed from their filthiness.
13 *There is* a generation, O how lofty are their eyes! And their eyelids are lifted up.
14 *There is* a generation, whose teeth *are as* swords, and their jaw teeth *as* knives, to devour the poor from off the earth, and the needy from *among* men.
15 The horse-leach has two daughters, *crying*, Give, give. There are three *things that* are never satisfied, *yea*, four *things* say not, *It is* enough:
16 The grave; and the barren womb; the earth *that* is not filled with water; and the fire *that* said not, *It is* enough.
17 The eye *that* mocks at *his* father, and despises to obey *his* mother, the ravens of the valley will pick it out, and the young eagles will eat it.
18 There be three *things which* are too wonderful for me, yea, four which I know not:
19 The way of an eagle in the air; the way of a serpent upon a rock; the way of a ship in the midst of the sea; and the way of a man with a maid.
20 Such *is* the way of an adulterous woman; she eats, and wipes her mouth, and said, I have done no wickedness.
21 For three *things* the earth is disquieted, and for four *which* it cannot bear:
22 For a servant when he reigns; and a fool when he is filled with meat;
23 For an odious *woman* when she is married; and a handmaid that is heir to her mistress.
24 There be four *things which* are little upon the earth, but they *are* exceeding wise:
25 The ants *are* a people not strong, yet they prepare their meat in the summer;
26 The conies *are but* a feeble folk, yet make they their houses in the rocks;
27 The locusts have no king, yet go they forth all of them by bands;
28 The spider takes hold with her hands, and is in kings' palaces.
29 There be three *things* which go well, yea, four are comely in going:
30 A lion *which is* strongest among beasts, and turns not away for any;
31 A greyhound; a he goat also; and a king, against whom *there is* no rising up.
32 If you have done foolishly in lifting up yourself, or if you have thought evil, *lay* your hand upon your mouth.
33 Surely the churning of milk brings forth butter, and the wringing of the nose brings forth blood: so the forcing of wrath brings forth strife.

CHAPTER 31

1 The words of king Lemuel, the prophecy that his mother taught him.
2 What, my son? And what, the son of my womb? and what, the son of my vows?
3 Give not your strength unto women, or your ways to that which destroys kings.
4 *It is* not for kings, O Lemuel, *it is* not for kings to drink wine; or for princes strong drink:
5 Lest they drink, and forget the law, and pervert the judgment of any of the afflicted.
6 Give strong drink unto him that is ready to perish, and wine unto those that be of heavy hearts.
7 Let him drink, and forget his poverty, and remember his misery no more.
8 Open your mouth for the dumb in the cause of all such as are appointed to destruction.
9 Open your mouth, judge righteously, and plead the cause of the poor and needy.
10 Who can find a virtuous woman? For her price *is* far above rubies.
11 The heart of her husband does safely trust in her, so that he will have no need of spoil.
12 She will do him good and not evil all the days of her life.
13 She seeks wool, and flax, and works willingly with her hands.
14 She is like the merchants' ships; she brings her food from afar.
15 She rises also while it is yet night, and gives meat to her household, and a portion to her maidens.
16 She considers a field, and buys it: with the fruit of her hands she plants a vineyard.
17 She girds her loins with strength, and strengthens her arms.
18 She perceives that her merchandise *is* good: her candle goes not out by night.
19 She lays her hands to the spindle, and her hands hold the distaff.
20 She stretches out her hand to the poor; yea, she reaches forth her hands to the needy.
21 She is not afraid of the snow for her household: for all her household *are* clothed with scarlet.
22 She makes herself coverings of tapestry; her clothing *is* silk and purple.
23 Her husband is known in the gates, when he sits among the elders of the land.
24 She makes fine linen, and sells *it*; and delivers girdles unto the merchant.
25 Strength and honor *are* her clothing; and she will rejoice in time to come.
26 She opens her mouth with wisdom; and in her tongue *is* the law of kindness.
27 She looks well to the ways of her household, and eats not the bread of idleness.
28 Her children arise up, and call her blessed; her husband *also*, and he praises her.
29 Many daughters have done virtuously, but you excel them all.
30 Favor *is* deceitful, and beauty *is* vain: *but* a woman *that* fears the LORD, she will be praised.
31 Give her of the fruit of her hands; and let her own works praise her in the gates.

ECCLESIASTES OR, THE PREACHER

CHAPTER 1

1 The words of the Preacher, the son of David, king in Jerusalem.
2 Vanity of vanities, said the Preacher, vanity of vanities; all *is* vanity.
3 What profit has a man of all his labor which he takes under the sun?
4 *One* generation passes away, and *another* generation cometh: but the earth abides forever.
5 The sun also arises, and the sun goes down, and haste to his place where he arose.
6 The wind goes toward the south, and turns about unto the north; it whirls about continually, and the wind returns again according to his circuits.
7 All the rivers run into the sea; yet the sea *is* not full; unto the place from whence the rivers come, thither they return again.
8 All things [*are* full of labor][1]; man cannot utter *it*: the eye is not satisfied with seeing, or the ear filled with hearing.
9 The thing that has been, it *is that* which will be; and that which is done *is* that which will be done: and *there is* no new *thing* under the sun.
10 Is there *any*thing whereof it may be said, See, this *is* new? It has been already [of old time][2], which was before us.
11 *There is* no remembrance of former *things*; neither will there be *any* remembrance of *things* that are to come with *those* that will come after.
12 I the Preacher was king over Israel in Jerusalem.
13 And I gave my heart to seek and search out by wisdom concerning all *things* that are done under heaven: this sore travail has God given to the sons of man to be exercised therewith.
14 I have seen all the works that are done under the sun; and, behold, all *is* vanity and vexation of spirit.
15 That which *is* crooked cannot be made straight: and that which is wanting cannot be numbered.
16 I communed with mine own heart, saying, Lo, I am come to great estate, and have gotten more wisdom than all *they* that have been before me in Jerusalem: yea, my heart had great experience of wisdom and knowledge.
17 And I gave my heart to know wisdom, and to know madness and folly: I perceived that this also is vexation of spirit.
18 For in much wisdom *is* much grief: and he that increases knowledge increases sorrow.

CHAPTER 2

1 I said in mine heart, Go to now, I will prove you with mirth, therefore enjoy pleasure: and, behold, this also *is* vanity.
2 I said of laughter, *it is* mad: and of mirth[3], what does it?
3 I sought in mine heart to give myself unto wine, yet acquainting mine heart with wisdom; and to lay hold on folly, till I might see what *was* that good for the sons of men, which they should do under the heaven all the days of their life.
4 I made me great works; I built me houses; I planted me vineyards:
5 I made me gardens and orchards, and I planted trees in them of all *kind of* fruits:
6 I made me pools of water, to water therewith the wood that brings forth trees:
7 I got *me* servants and maidens, and had servants born in my house; also I had great possessions of great and small cattle above all that were in Jerusalem before me:
8 I gathered me also silver and gold, and the peculiar treasure of kings and of the provinces: I get me men singers and women singers, and the delights of the sons of men, *as* musical instruments, and that of all sorts.
9 So I was great, and increased more than all that were before me in Jerusalem: also my wisdom remained with me.
10 And whatsoever mine eyes desired I kept not from them, I withheld not my heart from any joy; for my heart rejoiced in all my labor: and this was my portion of all my labor.
11 Then I looked on all the works that my hands had wrought, and on the labor that I had labored to do: and, behold, all *was* vanity and vexation of spirit, and *there was* no profit under the sun.
12 And I turned myself to behold wisdom, and madness, and **foolishness**: for what *can* the man *do* that comes after the king? *Even* that which has been already done.
13 Then I saw that wisdom excels folly, as far as light excels darkness.
14 The wise man's eyes *are* in his head; but the fool walks in darkness: and I myself perceived also that one event happens to them all.
15 Then said I in my heart, as it happens to the fool, so it happens even to me; and why was I then more wise? Then said in my heart, that this also *is* vanity.
16 For *there is* no remembrance of the wise more than of the fool for ever; seeing that which now *is* in the days to come will all be forgotten. And how dies the wise *man*? As the fool.
17 Therefore I hated life; because the work that is wrought under the sun *is* grievous unto me: for all *is* vanity and vexation of spirit.
18 Yea, I hated all my labor which I had taken under the sun: because I should leave it unto the man that will be after me.
19 And who knows whether he will be a wise *man* or a fool? Yet will he have rule over all my labor wherein I have labored, and wherein I have showed myself wise under the sun. This *is* also vanity.
20 Therefore I went about to cause my heart to despair of all the labor which I took under the sun.
21 For there is a man whose labor *is* in wisdom, and in knowledge, and in **success**; yet to a man that have not labored therein will he leave it *for* his portion. This also *is* vanity and a great evil.
22 For what has man of all his labor, and of the **desires** of his heart, wherein he has labored under the sun?
23 For all his days *are* sorrows, and his travail grief; yes, his heart takes not rest in the night. This is also vanity.
24 *There is* nothing better for a man, *than* that he should eat and drink, and *that* he should make his soul enjoy good in his labor. This also I saw, that it *was* from the hand of God.
25 For who can eat, or who else can hasten *hereunto*, more than I?
26 For *God* gives to a man that *is* good in his sight wisdom, and knowledge, and joy: but to the sinner he gives travail, to gather and

---

[1] lit. *tired, tiresome* [Strgs#3023]. It comes from the root word *yâga'*, meaning to gasp; hence to be exhausted, toil [Strgs#3021].
[2] lit. *concealed*, banishing point, *time out of mind* (past or future) [Strgs#5769].
[3] mirth- blithesomeness or glee, (religious or festival): - exceeding (-ly), gladness, joy (-fulness), pleasure, rejoice. [Strgs#8057]

to heap up, that he may give to *him that is* good before God. This also *is* vanity[1] and vexation[2] of spirit.

CHAPTER 3

1 To every*thing there is* a season[3], and a time to every purpose under the heaven:

2 A time to be born, and a time to die; a time to plant, and a time to pluck up *that which is* planted;

3 A time to kill, and a time to heal; a time to break down, and a time to build up;

4 A time to weep, and a time to laugh; a time to mourn, and a time to dance;

5 A time to cast away stones, and a time to gather stones together; a time to embrace, and a time to refrain from embracing;

6 A time to get, and a time to lose; a time to keep, and a time to cast away;

7 A time to rend, and a time to sew; a time to keep silence, and a time to speak;

8 A time to love, and a time to hate; a time of war, and a time of peace.

9 What profit has he that works in that wherein he labors?

10 I have seen the travail, which God has given to the sons of men to be exercised in it.

11 He has made every*thing* beautiful in his time: also he has set the world in their heart, [so that][4] no man can find out the work that God makes from the beginning to the end.

12 I know that *there is* no good in them, but for *a man* to rejoice, and to do good in his life.

13 And also that every man should eat and drink, and enjoy the good of all his labor, it *is* the gift of God.

14 I know that, whatsoever God doeth, it will be forever: nothing can be put to it, or anything taken from it: and God doeth *it*, that *men* should fear before him.

15 That which has been is now; and that which is to be has already been; and God requires that which is past.

16 And moreover I saw under the sun the place of judgment, *that* wickedness *was* there; and the place of righteousness, *that* iniquity *was* there.

17 I said in mine heart, God will judge the righteous and the wicked: for *there is* a time there for every purpose and for every work.

18 I said in mine heart concerning the estate of the sons of men, that God might manifest them, and that they might see that they themselves are beasts.

19 For that which befalls the sons of men befalls beasts; even one thing befalls them: as the one dies, so dies the other; yea, they have all one breath; so that a man has no preeminence above a beast: for all *is* vanity.

20 All go unto one place; all are of the dust, and all turn to dust again.

21 Who knows the spirit of man that goes upward, and the spirit of the beast that goes downward to the earth?

22 Wherefore I perceive that *there is* nothing better, than that a man should rejoice in his own works; for that *is* his portion: for who will bring him to see what will be after him?

CHAPTER 4

1 So I returned, and considered all the oppressions that are done under the sun: and behold the tears of *such as were* oppressed, and they had no comforter; and on the side of their oppressors *there was* power; but they had no comforter.

2 Wherefore I praised the dead which are already dead more than the living which are yet alive.

3 Yes, better *is he* then both they, which has not yet been, who has not seen the evil work that is done under the sun.

4 Again, I considered all travail, and every right work, that for this a man is envied of his neighbor. This *is* also vanity and vexation of spirit.

5 The fool folds his hands together, and eats his own flesh.

6 Better *is* a handful *with* quietness, than both the hands full *with* travail and vexation of spirit.

7 Then I returned, and I saw vanity under the sun.

8 There is one *alone*, and *there is* not a second; yea, he has neither child or brother: yet *is there* no end of all his labor; neither is his eye satisfied with riches; neither said *he*, For whom do I labor, and bereave my soul of good? This *is* also vanity, yes, it *is* an **evil business**.

9 Two *are* better than one; because they have a good reward for their labor.

10 For if they fall, the one will lift up his fellow: but woe to him *that is* alone when he falls; for *he has* not another to help him up.

11 Again, if two lie together, then they have heat: but how can one be warm *alone*?

12 And if one prevail against him, two will withstand him; and a threefold cord is not quickly broken.

13 Better *is* a poor and a wise child than an old and foolish king, who will no more be admonished.

14 For out of prison he comes to reign; whereas also *he that is* born in his kingdom becomes poor.

15 I considered all the living which walk under the sun, with the second child that will stand up in his stead.

16 *There is* no end of all the people, *even* of all that have been before them: they also that come after will not rejoice in him. Surely this also *is* vanity and vexation of spirit.

CHAPTER 5

1 Keep your foot when you go to the house of God, and be more ready to hear, than to give the sacrifice of fools: for they consider not that they do evil.

2 Be not rash with your mouth, and let not your heart be hasty to utter any*thing* before God: for God *is* in heaven, and you upon earth: therefore let your words be few.

3 For a dream comes through the multitude of business; and a fool's voice *is known* by multitude of words.

4 When you vow a vow unto God, defer not to pay it; for *he has* no pleasure in fools: pay that which you hast vowed.

---

[1] vanity- *emptiness* or *vanity*; figuratively something transitory and unsatisfactory; often used as an adverb: - altogether, vain. [Strgs#1892]

[2] Vexation- is the Hebrew word re'ûth, <u>reh-ooth'</u>, which is defined as *feeding* upon, that is, grasping after. [Strgs#7469]. Vanity comes from the Hebrew root word râ'âh, <u>raw-aw'</u>, a primitive root; to tend a flock, that is, *pasture* it; intransitively to *graze* (literally or figuratively); generally to *rule*; by extension to *associate* with (as a friend): - break, companion, keep company with, devour, eat up evil entreat, use as a friend, make friendship with, herdman, keep [sheep], shearing house, shepherd, wander, waste. [Strgs#7462]

[3] season- literally an appointed occasion: time. [Strgs#2165]

[4] lit. *failure, nothing, destruction,* <u>without</u>, *not yet, because not, as long as* [Strgs#1097]. God wanted man to 'find' out His work.

5 Better *is it* that you should not vow, than that you should vow and not pay.
6 Suffer not your mouth to cause your flesh to sin; neither say you before the angel, that it *was* an error: wherefore should God be angry at your voice, and destroy the work of your hands?
7 For in the multitude of dreams and many words *there are* also *divers* vanities: but fear you God.
8 If you see the oppression of the poor, and violent perverting of judgment and justice in a province, marvel not at the matter: for *he that is* higher than the highest regards; and *there be* higher than they.
9 Moreover the profit of the earth is for all: the king *himself* is served by the field.
10 He that loves silver will not be satisfied with silver; or he that loves abundance with increase: this *is* also vanity.
11 When goods increase, they are increased that eat them: and what good *is there* to the owners thereof, saving the beholding *of them* with their eyes?
12 The sleep of a laboring man *is* sweet, whether he eat little or much: but the abundance of the rich will not suffer him to sleep.
13 There is a [sore evil]¹ *which* I have seen under the sun, *namely*, riches kept² for the owners thereof to their hurt.
14 But those riches perish by evil travail: and he begets a son, and *there is* nothing in his hand.
15 As he came forth of his mother's womb, naked will he return to go as he came, and will take nothing of his labor, which he may carry away in his hand.
16 And this also *is* a sore evil, *that* in all points as he came, so will he go: and what profit has he that have labored for the wind?
17 All his days also he eats in darkness, and *he has* much sorrow and wrath with his sickness.
18 Behold *that* which I have seen: *it is* good and comely *for one* to eat and to drink, and to enjoy the good of all his labor that he takes under the sun all the days of his life, which God gives him: for it *is* his portion.
19 Every man also to whom God has given riches and wealth, and has given him power to eat thereof, and to take his portion, and to rejoice in his labor; this *is* the gift of God.
20 For he will not much remember the days of his life; because God answers *him* in the joy of his heart.

CHAPTER 6

1 There is an evil which I have seen under the sun, and it *is* common among men:
2 A man to whom God has given riches, wealth³, and honor, so that he wants nothing for his soul of all that he desires, yet God gives him not power to eat thereof, but a stranger⁴ eats it: this *is* vanity, and it *is* an evil disease.
3 If a man beget an hundred *children*, and live many years, so that the days of his years be many, and his soul be not filled with good, and also *that* he have no burial; I say, *that* an untimely birth *is* better than he.
4 For he comes in with vanity, and departs in darkness, and his name will be covered with darkness.
5 Moreover he has not seen the sun, or known *anything*: this has more rest than the other.
6 Yea, though he lives a thousand years twice *told*, yet have he seen no good: do not all go to one place?
7 All the labor of man *is* for his mouth, and yet the appetite is not filled.
8 For what have the wise more than the fool? What have the poor, that knows to walk before the living?
9 Better *is* the sight of the eyes than the wandering of the desire: this *is* also vanity and vexation of spirit.
10 That which have been is named already, and it is known that it *is* man: neither may he contend with him that is mightier than he.
11 Seeing there be many things that increase vanity, what *is* man the better?
12 For who knows what *is* good for man in *this* life, all the days of his vain life which he spends as a shadow? For who can tell a man what will be after him under the sun?

CHAPTER 7

1 A good name *is* better than precious ointment; and the day of death than the day of one's birth.
2 *It is* better to go to the house of mourning, than to go to the house of feasting: for that *is* the end of all men; and the living will lay *it* to his heart.
3 Sorrow *is* better than laughter: for by the sadness of the countenance the heart is made better.
4 The heart of the wise *is* in the house of mourning; but the heart of fools *is* in the house of mirth.
5 *It is* better to hear the rebuke of the wise, than for a man to hear the song of fools.
6 For as the crackling of thorns under a pot, so *is* the laughter of the fool: this also *is* vanity.
7 Surely oppression makes a wise man mad; and a gift destroys the heart.
8 Better *is* the end of a thing than the beginning thereof: *and* the patient in spirit *is* better than the proud in spirit.
9 Be not hasty in your spirit to be angry: for anger rests in the bosom of fools.
10 Say not you, What is *the cause* that the former days were better than these? for you dost not enquire wisely concerning this.
11 Wisdom *is* good with an inheritance: and *by it there is* profit to them that see the sun.
12 For wisdom *is* a defense, *and* money *is* a defense: but the **profit** of knowledge *is, that* wisdom gives life to them [that have it]⁵.
13 Consider the work of God: for who can make *that* straight, which he have made crooked?
14 In the day of prosperity be joyful, but in the day of adversity consider: God also have set the one over against the other, to the end that man should find nothing after him.
15 All *things* have I seen in the days of my vanity: there is a just *man* that perishes in his righteousness, and there is a wicked *man* that prolongs *his life* in his wickedness.
16 Be not righteous over much; neither make thyself over wise: why should you destroy thyself?
17 Be not over much wicked, neither be you foolish: why should you die before your time?
18 *It is* good that you should take hold of this; yea, also from this withdraw not your hand: for he that fears God will come forth of them all.
19 Wisdom strengthens the wise more than ten mighty *men* which are in the city.

---

¹ lit. evil deseased [Strgs#2470+7451].
² kept – <u>no giving</u>, to *hedge* about, *guard, protect, attend to* [Strgs#8104].
³ lit. <u>*treasure*</u>, to *accumulate* [Strgs#5233].
⁴ lit. a strange man.
⁵ lit. <u>*master*</u>, hence *husband* or *owner* [Strgs#1167].

20 For *there is* not a just man upon earth, that doeth good, and sins not.
21 Also take no heed unto all words that are spoken; lest you hear your servant curse you:
22 For oftentimes also your own heart knows that you thyself likewise hast cursed others.
23 All this have I proved by wisdom: I said, I will be wise; but it *was* far from me.
24 That which is far off, and exceeding deep, who can find it out?
25 I applied mine heart to know, and to search, and to seek out wisdom, and the reason *of things*, and to know the wickedness of folly, even of foolishness *and* madness:
26 And I find more bitter than death the woman, whose heart *is* snares and nets, *and* her hands *as* bands: whoso pleases God will escape from her; but the sinner will be taken by her.
27 Behold, this have I found, said the preacher, *counting* one by one, to find out the account[1]:
28 Which yet my soul seeks, but I find not: one man among a thousand have I found; but a woman among all those have I not found.
29 Lo, this only have I found, that God have made man upright; but they have sought out many inventions.

CHAPTER 8

1 Who *is* as the wise *man*? And who knows the interpretation of a thing? A man's wisdom makes his face to shine, and the boldness of his face will be changed.
2 I *counsel you* to keep the king's commandment, and *that* in regard of the oath of God.
3 Be not hasty to go out of his sight: stand not in an evil thing; for he doeth whatsoever pleases him.
4 Where the word of a king *is, there is* power: and who may say unto him, what **are you doing**?
5 [Whoso keeps the commandment will feel no evil thing: and a wise man's heart discerns both time and judgment.][2]
6 Because to every purpose there is time and judgment[3], therefore the misery[4] of man *is* great upon him.
7 [For he knows not that which will be: for who can tell him when it will be?][5]
8 *There is* no man that has power over the spirit to retain the spirit; neither has *he* power in the day of death: and *there is* no discharge[6] in *that* war; neither will wickedness deliver[7] those that are given to it.
9 All this have I seen, and applied my heart unto every work that is done under the sun: *there is* a time wherein one man rules over another to his own hurt.
10 And so I saw the wicked buried, who had come and gone from the place of the holy, and they were forgotten in the city where they had so done: this *is* also vanity.
11 [Because sentence against an evil work is not executed speedily, therefore the heart of the sons of men is fully set in them to do evil.][8]

12 Though a sinner do evil an hundred times, and his *days* be prolonged, yet surely I know that it will be well with them that fear God, which fear before him:
13 But it will not be well with the wicked, neither will he prolong *his* days, *which are* as a shadow; because he fears not before God.
14 There is a vanity which is done upon the earth; that there be just *men*, unto whom it happens according to the work of the wicked; again, there be wicked *men*, to whom it happens according to the work of the righteous: I said that this also *is* vanity.
15 Then I commended mirth, because a man has no better thing under the sun, than to eat, and to drink, and to be merry: for that will abide with him of his labor the days of his life, which God gives him under the sun.
16 When I applied mine heart to know wisdom, and to see the business that is done upon the earth: (for also *there is that* neither day or night sees sleep with his eyes:)
17 Then I beheld all the work of God, that a man cannot find out the work that is done under the sun: because though a man labor to seek *it* out, yet he will not find *it*; yes further; though a wise *man* think to know *it*, yet will he not be able to find *it*.

CHAPTER 9

1 For all this I considered in my heart even to declare all this, that the righteous, and the wise, and their works, *are* in the hand of God: no man knows either love or hatred *by* all *that is* before them.
2 All *things come* alike to all: *there is* one event to the righteous, and to the wicked; to the good and to the clean, and to the unclean; to him that sacrifices, and to him that sacrifices not: as *is* the good, so *is* the sinner; *and* he that swears, as *he* that fears an oath.
3 This *is* an evil among all *things* that are done under the sun, that *there is* one event unto all: yea, also the heart of the sons of men is full of evil, and madness *is* in their heart while they live, and after that *they go* to the dead.
4 For to him that is joined to all the living there is hope[9]: for a living dog is better than a dead lion.
5 For the living know that they will die: but the dead know not anything, neither have they any more a reward; for the memory of them is forgotten.
6 Also their love, and their hatred, and their envy, is now perished; neither have they any more a portion forever in any*thing* that is done under the sun.
7 Go your way, eat your bread with joy, and drink your wine with a merry heart; for God now accepts your works.
8 Let your garments be always white; and let your head lack no ointment.
9 Live joyfully with the wife whom you loves all the days of the life of your vanity, which he has given you under the sun, all the days of your vanity: for that *is* your portion in *this* life, and in your labor which you takes under the sun.
10 Whatsoever your hand finds to do, do *it* with your might; for *there is* no work, or device, or knowledge, or wisdom, in the grave, whither you go.
11 I returned, and saw under the sun, that the race *is* not to the swift, or the battle to the strong, neither yet bread to the wise, or

---

[1] account – *contrivance*; by implication *intelligence*, reason [Strgs#2808].
[2] compare Matthew 16:3
[3] judgment – *a verdict*, *divine law*, *justice*, *right*, *privilege* or even *a style* [Strgs4941].
[4] lit. bad, evil [Strgs#7451].
[5] i.e. the sentence, verdict that is attached to every purpose.
[6] discharge – is the Hebrew word *mishlachath* meaing a *mission*, casting off a weapon, *release*, an *army* [Strgs#4917]. Derives from a root word meaning *sending out*, *presentation*, *seizure*, *dismissal* or a *business* to be discharged [Strgs#4916].
[7] lit. to be *smooth*, *escape* (as if by *slipperiness*), to release or *rescue*, to *bring forth*, emit, birth [Strgs#4422]. Compare **Acts 2:24.**
[8] see Ezra 7:26 & Isaiah 26:9
[9] hope – *trust & confidence* [Strgs#986]. Similar to the Hebrew root word *châsâh* meaning to flee for protection, to *confide* in [Strgs#2620].

yet riches to men of understanding, or yet favor to men of skill; but time and chance happens to them all.

12 For man also knows not his time: as the fishes that are taken in an evil net, and as the birds that are caught in the snare; so *are* the sons of men snared in an evil time, when it falls suddenly[1] upon them.

13 This wisdom have I seen also under the sun, and it *seemed* great unto me:

14 *There was* a little city, and few men within it; and there came a great king against it, and besieged it, and built great bulwarks against it:

15 Now there was found in it a poor wise man, and he by his wisdom delivered the city; yet no man remembered that same poor man.

16 Then said I, Wisdom *is* better than strength: nevertheless the poor man's wisdom *is* despised, and his words are not heard.

17 The words of wise *men are* heard in quiet more than the cry of him that rules among fools.

18 Wisdom *is* better than weapons of war: but one sinner destroys much good.

CHAPTER 10

1 Dead flies cause the ointment of the apothecary to send forth a stinking savor: *so doth* a little folly him that is in reputation for wisdom *and* honor.

2 A wise man's heart *is* at his right hand; but a fool's heart at his left.

3 Yes also, when he that is a fool walks by the way, his wisdom fails *him*, and he said to everyone *that* he *is* a fool.

4 If the spirit of the ruler rise up against thee, leave not your place; for yielding pacifies great offences.

5 There is an evil *which* I have seen under the sun, as an error *which* proceeds from the ruler:

6 Folly is set in great dignity, and the rich sit in low place.

7 I have seen servants upon horses, and princes walking as servants upon the earth.

8 He that digs a pit will fall into it; and whoso breaks a hedge, a serpent will bite him.

9 Whoso removes stones[2] will be hurt therewith; *and* he that cleaves wood will be endangered thereby.

10 If the iron be blunt, and he do not whet[3] the edge[4], then must he put to more strength: but wisdom *is* profitable to direct.

11 Surely the serpent will bite without enchantment; and a babbler[5] is no better.

12 [The words of a wise man's mouth *are* gracious; but the lips of a fool will swallow up himself.][6]

13 The beginning of the words of his mouth *is* foolishness: and the end of his talk *is* mischievous madness.

14 A fool also is full of words: a man cannot tell what will be; and what will be after him, who can tell him?

15 The labor of the foolish **worries** every one of them, because he knows not how to go to the city.

16 Woe to thee, O land, when your king *is* a child, and your princes eat in the morning!

17 Blessed *art* you, O land, when your king *is* the son of nobles, and your princes eat in due season, for strength, and not for drunkenness!

18 By much slothfulness the building decays; and through idleness of the hands the house drops through.

19 A feast is made for laughter, and wine makes merry: but money answers all *things*.

20 Curse not the king, no not in your thought and curse not the rich in your bedchamber: for a bird of the air will carry the voice, and that which has wings will tell the matter.

CHAPTER 11

1 Cast your bread upon the waters: for you will find it after many days.

2 Give a portion to seven, and also to eight; for you knows not what evil will be upon the earth.

3 If the clouds be full of rain, they empty *themselves* upon the earth: and if the tree falls toward the south, or toward the north, in the place where the tree falls, there it will be.

4 He that observes the wind will not sow; and he that regards the clouds will not reap.

5 As you knows not what *is* the way of the spirit, or how the bones *do grow* in the womb of her that is with child: even so you knows not the works of God who makes all.

6 In the morning sow your seed, and in the evening withhold not your hand: for you know not whether will prosper, either this or that, or whether they both will *be* alike good.

7 Truly the light *is* sweet, and a pleasant *thing it is* for the eyes to behold the sun:

8 But if a man live many years, *and* rejoice in them all; yet let him remember the days of darkness; for they will be many. All that comes *is* vanity.

9 Rejoice, O young man, in your youth; and let your heart cheer you in the days of your youth, and walk in the ways of your heart, and in the sight of your eyes: but know you, that for all these *things* God will bring you into judgment.

10 Therefore remove sorrow from your heart, and put away evil from your flesh: for childhood and youth *are* vanity.

CHAPTER 12

1 Remember now your Creator in the days of your youth, while the evil days come not, or the years draw nigh, when you will say, I have no pleasure in them;

2 While the sun, or the light, or the moon, or the stars, be not darkened, or the clouds return after the rain:

3 In the day when the keepers of the house will tremble, and the strong men will bow themselves, and the grinders cease because they are few, and those that look out of the windows be darkened,

4 And the doors will be shut in the streets, when the sound of the grinding is low, and he will rise up at the voice of the bird, and all the daughters of will be brought low;

5 Also *when* they will be afraid of *that which is* high, and fears will *be* in the way, and the almond tree will flourish, and the grasshopper will be a burden, and desire will fail: because man goes to his long home, and the mourners go about the streets:

---

[1] lit. *instantly* [Strgs#6597]. Its root word means <u>to open</u>, *wink, moment, quickly* or *unexpectedly* [Strgs#6621].
[2] stones – to *build*; a *stone* [Strgs#68]. <u>Living Stones</u>,compare **1Peter 2:5**.
[3] lit. to <u>make light</u>, *swift, small, sharp, easy, trifling, vile* [Strgs#7043].
[4] edge – is the Hebrew word *pânîym* meaning <u>face</u>, employ, endure, countenance, before, was purposed [Strgs#6440].
[5] babbler - comes from two Hebrew words meaning master of the tongue [Strgs#3956+1167].
[6] balance, compare **Ps. 45:2** & **Luke 4:22-11**

6 Or ever the silver cord be loosed, or the golden bowl be broken, or the pitcher be broken at the fountain, or the wheel broken at the cistern.
7 Then will the dust return to the earth as it was: and the spirit will return unto God who gave it.
8 Vanity of vanities, said the preacher; all *is* vanity.
9 And moreover, because the preacher was wise, he still taught the people knowledge; yea, he gave good heed, and sought out, *and* set in order many proverbs.
10 The preacher sought to find out acceptable words: and *that which was* written *was* upright, *even* words of truth.
11 The words of the wise *are* as goads, and as nails fastened *by* the masters of assemblies, *which* are given from one shepherd.
12 And further, by these, my son, be admonished: of making many books *there is* no end; and much study *is* a weariness of the flesh.
13 Let us hear the conclusion of the whole matter: Fear God, and keep his commandments: for this *is* the whole *duty* of man.
14 For God will bring every work into judgment, with every secret thing, whether *it be* good, or whether *it be* evil.

THE SONG OF SOLOMON

CHAPTER 1

1 The song of songs, which *is* Solomon's.
2 Let him kiss me with the kisses of his mouth: for your love *is* better than wine.
3 Because of the savor of your good ointments your name *is as* ointment poured forth, therefore do the virgins love you.
4 Draw me, we will run after you: the king has brought me into his chambers: we will be glad and rejoice in you, we will remember your love more than wine: the upright love you.
5 I *am* black, but comely, O you daughters of Jerusalem, as the tents of Kedar, as the curtains of Solomon.
6 Look not upon me, because I *am* black, because the sun has looked upon me: my mother's children were angry with me; they made me the keeper of the vineyards; *but* mine own vineyard have I not kept.
7 Tell me, O you whom my soul loves, where you feeds where you makes your *flock* to rest at noon: for why should I be as one that [turns aside][1] by the flocks of your companions?
8 If you know not, O you fairest among women, go your way forth by the footsteps of the flock, and feed your kids beside the shepherds' tents.
9 I have compared you, O my love, to a company of horses in Pharaoh's chariots.
10 your cheeks are comely with rows *of jewels*, your neck with chains *of gold*.
11 We will make you borders of gold with studs of silver.
12 While the king *sits* at his table, my spikenard sends forth the smell thereof.
13 A bundle of myrrh *is* my well beloved unto me; he shall lie all night betwixt my breasts.
14 My beloved *is* unto me *as* a cluster of camphire[2] in the vineyards of En-gedi[3].
15 Behold, you are fair, my love; behold, you are fair; you *have* doves' eyes.
16 Behold, you are fair, my beloved, yes, pleasant: also our bed *is* green.
17 The beams of our house *are* cedar, *and* our rafters of fir.

CHAPTER 2

1 I *am* the rose of Sharon, *and* the lily of the valleys.
2 As the lily among thorns, so *is* my love among the daughters.
3 As the apple tree among the trees of the wood, so *is* my beloved among the sons. I sat down under his shadow with great delight, and his fruit *was* sweet to my taste.
4 He brought me to the banqueting[4] house, and his banner over me *was* love.
5 Stay me with flagons, comfort[5] me with apples: for I *am* sick of love.
6 His left hand *is* under my head, and his right hand doth embrace me.
7 I charge you, O you daughters of Jerusalem, by the roes, and by the hinds of the field, that you stir not up, or awake *my* love, til he please.
8 The voice of my beloved! Behold, he cometh leaping upon the mountains, skipping upon the hills.
9 My beloved is like a roe or a young hart: behold, he stands behind our wall, he looks forth at the windows, showing[6] himself through the lattice.
10 My beloved spoke, and said unto me, Rise up, my love, my fair one, and come away.
11 For, lo, the winter is past, the rain is over *and* gone;
12 The flowers appear on the earth; the time of the singing *of* birds is come, and the voice of the turtle is heard in our land;
13 The fig tree puts forth her green figs, and the vines *with* the tender grape give a *good* smell. Arise, my love, my fair one, and come away.
14 O my dove, *that are* in the clefts of the rock, in the secret *places* of the stairs, let me see your countenance, let me hear your voice; for sweet *is* your voice, and your countenance *is* comely.
15 Take us the foxes, the little foxes, that spoil the vines: for our vines *have* tender grapes.
16 My beloved *is* mine, and I *am* his: he feeds among the lilies.
17 Until the day break, and the shadows flee away, turn, my beloved, and be you like a roe or a young hart upon the mountains of Bether[7].

CHAPTER 3

1 By night on my bed I sought him whom my soul loves: I sought him, but I found him not.
2 I will rise now, and go about the city in the streets, and in the broad ways I will seek him whom my soul loves: I sought him, but I found him not.
3 The watchmen that go about the city found me: *to whom I said*, saw you him whom my soul loves?
4 *It was* but a little that I passed from them, but I found him whom my soul loves: I held him, and would not let him go, until I had brought him into my mother's house, and into the chamber of her that conceived me.
5 I charge you, O you daughters of Jerusalem, by the roes, and by the hinds of the field, that you stir not up, nor awake *my* love, till he please.
6 Who *is* this that cometh out of the wilderness like pillars of smoke, perfumed with myrrh and frankincense, with all powders of the merchant?
7 Behold his bed, which *is* Solomon's; threescore valiant men *are* about it, of the valiant of Israel.
8 They all hold swords, *being* expert in war: every man has his sword upon his thigh because of fear in the night.
9 King Solomon made himself a chariot of the wood of Lebanon.
10 He made the pillars thereof *of* silver, the bottom thereof *of* gold, the covering of it *of* purple, the midst thereof being paved *with* love, for the daughters of Jerusalem.

---

[1] lit. to wrap, cover, <u>veil</u>, clothe or roll [Strgs#5844].
[2] camphire- properly a cover, that is, (literally) a village (as covered in): (specifically) bitumen (as used for coating), and the henna plant (as used for dyeing); figuratively a redemption price: - bribe, pitch, ransom, satisfaction, sum of money, village. [Strgs#3724]
[3] Engedi- a town in the wilderness of Judah on the western shore of the Dead Sea. Its name meaning *fountain of a kid*. [Strgs#5872]
[4] lit. to *effervesce*, *intoxication*, bibber, <u>House of wine</u> [Strgs#3196].
[5] comfort – to <u>spread</u>, to *refresh* [Strgs#7502].
[6] showing – to *twinkle*, *glance*, to <u>blossom</u> (figuratively *flourish* [Strgs#6692].
[7] Bether- a mountainous region in Palestine. It's name meaning a craggy place. [Strgs#1336]

11 Go forth, O you daughters of Zion, and behold King Solomon with the crown wherewith his mother crowned him in the day of his espousals¹, and in the day of the gladness of his heart.

CHAPTER 4

1 Behold, you *are* fair, my love; behold, you *are* fair; you have doves' eyes within your locks²: your hair *is* as a flock of goats, that appear from mount Gilead.
2 Your teeth *are* like a flock *of sheep that are even* shorn, which came up from the washing; whereof every one bear twins, and none *is* barren among them.
3 Your lips *are* like a thread of scarlet, and your speech³ *is* comely: your temples⁴ *are* like a piece⁵ of a pomegranate⁶ within your locks⁷.
4 Your neck *is* like the tower of David built for an armory, whereon there hang a thousand bucklers, all shields of mighty men.
5 Your two breasts *are* like two young roes that are twins, which feed among the lilies.
6 Until the day break, and the shadows flee away, I will get me to the mountain of myrrh, and to the hill of frankincense.
7 You are all fair, my love; *there is* no spot in you.
8 Come with me from Lebanon, *my* spouse, with me from Lebanon: look from the top of Amana, from the top of Shenir and Hermon, from the lions' dens, from the mountains of the leopards.
9 You have ravished my heart, my sister, *my* spouse; you have ravished my heart with one of your eyes, with one chain of your neck.
10 How fair is your love, my sister, *my* spouse! How much better is your love than wine! And the smell of your ointments than all spices!
11 Your lips, O *my* spouse, drop *as* the honeycomb: honey and milk *are* under your tongue; and the smell of your garments *is* like the smell of Lebanon.
12 A garden enclosed *is* my sister, *my* spouse; a spring shut up, a fountain sealed.
13 Your plants *are* an orchard of pomegranates, with pleasant fruits; camphire, with spikenard,
14 Spikenard and saffron; calamus and cinnamon, with all trees of frankincense; myrrh and aloes, with all the chief spices:
15 A fountain of gardens, a well of living waters, and streams from Lebanon.
16 Awake, O north wind; and come, you south; blow upon my garden, *that* the spices thereof may flow out. Let my beloved come into his garden, and eat his pleasant fruits.

CHAPTER 5

1 I am come into my garden, my sister, *my* spouse: I have gathered my myrrh with my spice; I have eaten my honeycomb with my honey; I have drunk my wine with my milk: eat, O friends; drink, yes, drink abundantly, O beloved.
2 I sleep, but my heart wakes: *it is* the voice of my beloved that knocks, *saying*, Open to me, my sister, my love, my dove, my undefiled: for my head is filled with dew, *and* my locks with the drops of the night.
3 I have put off my coat; how shall I put it on? I have washed my feet; how shall I defile them?
4 My beloved put in his hand by the hole *of the door*, and my bowels were moved for him.
5 I rose up to open to my beloved; and my hands dropped *with* myrrh, and my fingers *with* sweet smelling myrrh, upon the handles of the lock.
6 I opened to my beloved; but my beloved had withdrawn himself, *and* was gone: my soul failed when he spoke: I sought him, but I could not find him; I called him, but he gave me no answer.
7 The watchmen that went about the city found me, they smote me, they wounded me; the keepers of the walls took away my veil from me.
8 I charge you, O daughters of Jerusalem, if you find my beloved, that you tell him, that I *am* sick of love.
9 What *is* your beloved more than *another* beloved, O you fairest among women? What *is* your beloved more than *another* beloved, that you dost so charge us?
10 My beloved *is* white and ruddy, the chief among ten thousand.
11 His head *is as* the most fine gold, his locks *are* bushy, *and* black as a raven.
12 His eyes *are as the eyes* of doves by the rivers of waters, washed with milk, *and* fitly set.
13 His cheeks *are* as a bed of spices, *as* sweet flowers: his lips *like* lilies, dropping sweet smelling myrrh.
14 His hands *are as* gold rings set with the beryl: his belly *is as* bright ivory overlaid *with* sapphires.
15 His legs *are as* pillars of marble, set upon sockets of fine gold: his countenance *is* as Lebanon, excellent as the cedars.
16 His mouth *is* most sweet: yes, he *is* altogether lovely. This *is* my beloved, and this *is* my friend, O daughters of Jerusalem.

CHAPTER 6

1 Whither is your beloved gone, O you fairest among women? Whither is your beloved turned aside? That we may seek him with you.
2 My beloved is gone down into his garden, to the beds of spices, to feed in the gardens, and to gather lilies.
3 I *am* my beloved's, and my beloved *is* mine: he feeds among the lilies.
4 You are beautiful, O my love, as Tirzah⁸, comely as Jerusalem, terrible as *an army* with banners.
5 Turn away your eyes from me, for they have overcome me: your hair *is* as a flock of goats that appear from Gilead.
6 Your teeth *are* as a flock of sheep which go up from the washing, whereof every one bears twins, and *there is* not one barren among them.
7 As a piece of a pomegranate *are* your temples within your locks.
8 There are threescore queens, and fourscore concubines, and virgins without number.
9 My dove, my undefiled is *but* one; she *is* the *only one* of her mother, she *is* the choice *one* of her that bare her. The daughters saw her, and blessed her; *yea*, the queens and the concubines, and they praised her.

---

¹ espousal- wedding [Strgs#2861]
² lit. to *fasten* on; a *veil* [Strgs#6777].
³ speech – *driving*; a *pasture* (that is, open field, whither cattle are driven); a *desert*, *wilderness* [Strgs#4057].
⁴ lit. *thinness*, the *side* of the head [Strgs#7541].
⁵ lit. *slice*, piece [Strgs#6400].
⁶ pomegranate – is the Hebrew word *rimmôn* meaning the tree (from its *upright* growth) or the fruit (also an artificial ornament) [Strgs#7416]. Derives from the root word *râmam* meaning to *rise*, exalt, get (oneself) up, lift up, mount up [Strgs#7426].
⁷ See note two above.
⁸ Tirzah- (*favourable* or *delightsomeness*) a Canaanite city, later capital of the northern kingdom of Israel. One of the kingdoms on the west of the Jordan conquered by Joshua and the Israelites. [Strgs#8656]

10 Who *is* she *that* looks forth as the morning, fair as the moon, clear as the sun, *and* terrible as *an army* with banners?
11 I went down into the garden of nuts to see the fruits of the valley, *and* to see whether the vine flourished, *and* the pomegranates budded.
12 Or ever I was aware, my soul made me *like* the chariots of Amminadib.
13 Return, return, O Shulamite[1]; return, return, that we may look upon you. What will you see in the Shulamite? As it were the company of two armies.

CHAPTER 7

1 How beautiful are your feet with shoes, O prince's daughter! The joints of your thighs *are* like jewels, the work of the hands of a cunning workman.
2 Your navel *is like* a round goblet, *which* wants not liquor: your belly *is like* a heap of wheat set about with lilies.
3 Your two breasts *are* like two young roes *that are* twins.
4 Your neck *is* as a tower of ivory; your eyes *like* the fish-pools in Heshbon, by the gate of Bath-rabbim: your nose *is* as the tower of Lebanon which looks toward Damascus.
5 Your head upon you *is* like Carmel, and the hair of your head like purple; the king *is* held in the galleries.
6 How fair and how pleasant are thou, O love, for delights!
7 This your stature is like to a palm tree, and your breasts to clusters *of grapes*.
8 I said, I will go up to the palm tree, I will take hold of the boughs thereof: now also your breasts shall be as clusters of the vine, and the smell of your nose like apples;
9 And the roof of your mouth like the best wine for my beloved, that goes *down* sweetly, causing the lips of those that are asleep to speak.
10 I *am* my beloved's, and his desire *is* toward me.
11 Come, my beloved, let us go forth into the field; let us lodge in the villages.
12 Let us get up early to the vineyards; let us see if the vine flourish, *whether* the tender grape appear, *and* the pomegranates bud forth: there will I give you my loves.
13 The mandrakes give a smell, and at our gates *are* all manner of pleasant *fruits*, new and old, *which* I have laid up for you, O my beloved.

CHAPTER 8

1 O that you *were* as my brother, that sucked the breasts of my mother! *When* I should find you without, I would kiss you; yea, I should not be despised.
2 I would lead you, *and* bring you into my mother's house, *who* would instruct me: I would cause you to drink of spiced wine of the juice of my pomegranate.
3 His left hand *should be* under my head, and his right hand should embrace me.
4 I charge you, O daughters of Jerusalem, that you stir not up, nor awake *my* love, until he please.
5 Who *is* this that cometh up from the wilderness, leaning upon her beloved? I raised you up under the apple tree: there your mother brought you forth: there she brought you forth *that* bare you.
6 Set me as a seal upon your heart, as a seal upon your arm: for love *is* strong as death; jealousy *is* cruel as the grave: the coals thereof *are* coals of fire, *which has a* most vehement flame.
7 Many waters cannot quench love, neither can the floods drown it: if *a* man would give all the substance of his house for love, it would utterly be contemned.
8 We have a little sister, and she has no breasts: what shall we do for our sister in the day when she shall be spoken for?
9 If she *be* a wall, we will build upon her a palace of silver: and if she *be* a door, we will enclose her with boards of cedar.
10 I *am* a wall, and my breasts like towers: then was I in his eyes as one that found favor.
11 Solomon had a vineyard at Baal-hamon[2]; he let out the vineyard unto keepers; every one for the fruit thereof was to bring a thousand *pieces* of silver.
12 My vineyard, which *is* mine, *is* before me: you, O Solomon, *must have* a thousand, and those that keep the fruit thereof two hundred.
13 You that dwell in the gardens, the companions hearken to your voice: cause me to hear *it*.
14 Make haste, my beloved, and be you like to a roe or to a young hart upon the mountains of spices.

---

[1] Shulamite- literally the *perfect*, the *peaceful*. [Strgs#7759]
[2] Baalhamon- lord (possessor) of abundance or *possessor of a multitude*.

[Strgs#1174]

ISAIAH

CHAPTER 1

1 The vision of Isaiah[1] the son of Amoz, which he saw concerning Judah and Jerusalem in the days of Uzziah, Jotham, Ahaz, *and* Hezekiah, kings of Judah.

2 Hear, O heavens, and give ear, O earth: for the LORD has spoken, I have nourished and brought up children, and they have rebelled against me.

3 The ox knows his owner, and the ass his master's crib: *but* Israel does not know, my people does not consider.

4 Ah sinful nation, a people laden with iniquity, a seed of evildoers, children that are corrupters: they have forsaken the LORD, they have provoked the Holy One of Israel unto anger, they are gone away backward.

5 Why should you be stricken anymore? You will revolt more and more: the whole head is sick, and the whole heart faint.

6 From the sole of the foot even unto the head *there is* no soundness in it; *but* wounds, and bruises, and putrefying sores: they have not been closed, neither bound up, neither mollified with ointment.

7 Your country *is* desolate, your cities *are* burned with fire: your land, strangers devour it in your presence, and *it is* desolate, as overthrown by strangers.

8 And the daughter of Zion is left as a cottage in a vineyard, as a lodge in a garden of cucumbers, as a besieged city.

9 Except the LORD of hosts had left unto us a very small remnant, we should have been as Sodom, *and* we should have been like unto Gomorrah.

10 Hear the word of the LORD, you rulers of Sodom; give ear unto the law of our God, you people of Gomorrah.

11 To what purpose *is* the multitude of your sacrifices unto me? Said the LORD: I am full of the burnt offerings of rams, and the fat of fed beasts; and I delight not in the blood of bullocks, or of lambs, or of he goats.

12 When you come to appear before me, who has required this at your hand, to tread my courts?

13 Bring no more vain oblations; incense is an abomination unto me; the new moons and Sabbaths, the calling of assemblies, I cannot away with; *it is* iniquity, even the solemn meeting.

14 Your new moons and your appointed feasts my soul hates: they are a trouble unto me; I am weary to bear *them*.

15 And when you spread forth your hands, I will hide mine eyes from you: yea, when you make many prayers, I will not hear: your hands are full of blood.

16 Wash you, make you clean; put away the evil of your doings from before mine eyes; cease to do evil;

17 Learn to do well; seek judgment, relieve[2] the oppressed[3] judge the fatherless[4], plead for the widow.

18 Come now, and let us reason together, said the LORD: though your sins be as scarlet, they will be as white as snow; though they be red like crimson, they will be as wool.

19 If you be willing[5] and obedient, you will eat the good of the land:

20 But if you refuse and rebel, you will be devoured with the sword: for the mouth of the LORD has spoken *it*.

21 How is the faithful city become an harlot! It was full of judgment; righteousness lodged in it; but now murderers[6].

22 your silver is become dross, your wine mixed with water.

23 Your princes *are* rebellious, and companions of thieves: everyone loves gifts, and follows after rewards: they judge not the fatherless, neither does the cause[7] of the widow come unto them.

24 Therefore said the Lord, the LORD of hosts, the mighty One of Israel, Ah, I will ease me of mine adversaries, and avenge me of mine enemies:

25 And I will turn my hand upon you, and purely purge away your dross, and take away all your tin:

26 And I will restore your judges[8] as at the first[9], and your counselors[10] as at the beginning: afterward you will be called, the city of righteousness, the faithful city.

27 Zion will be redeemed with judgment, and her converts with righteousness.

28 And the destruction[11] of the transgressors and of the sinners will *be* together, and they that forsake the LORD will be consumed.

29 For they will be ashamed of [the oaks][12] which you have desired, and you will be confounded for the gardens[13] that you have chosen.

30 For you will be as an oak whose leaf fades, and as a garden that has no water.

31 And the strong[14] will be as tow[15], and the maker of it as a spark, and they will both burn together, and none will quench *them*.

CHAPTER 2

1 The word that Isaiah the son of Amoz[16] saw concerning Judah and Jerusalem.

2 And it will come to pass in the last days, *that* the mountain of the LORD'S house will [be established][17] in the top of the mountains, and will be exalted above the hills; and all nations will flow unto it.

3 And many people will go and say, Come you, and let us go up to the mountain of the LORD, to the house of the God of Jacob; and he will teach us of his ways, and we will walk in his paths: for out of Zion will go forth the law, and the word of the LORD from Jerusalem.

4 And he will judge among the nations, and will rebuke[18] many people: and they will beat their swords into plowshares, and their

---

[1] Isaiah- *Jehovah has saved* or *Jah has saved*. Other variations would include Jesaiah, Jeshaiah. [Strgs#3470]

[2] relieve – is the Hebrew word *'âshar* meaning to *be straight* (used I the widest sense, especially to be *level*, *right*, *happy*); figuratively to *go forward, be honest, prosper* [Strgs#833].

[3] lit. *violent*, by implication a *robber* [Strgs#2541].

[4] lit. to *be lonely*; a *bereaved* person, orphan [Strgs#3490].

[5] willing – Hebrew word *'âbâh*; which is defined as *to breathe after*, to be *acquiescent*, rest content, consent [Strgs#14].

[6] murderers – to *dash in pieces*, kill (a human being), *to murder*, man slayer [Strgs#7523].

[7] lit. a *contest* (personal or legal) *adversary*, contend, controversy, pleading strife, suit [Strgs#7379].

[8] Judges are symbolic of the New Testament Apostles.

[9] symbolic of the beginning of the church era.

[10] Seven Spirits of God, compare Ezra 7:14

[11] destruction – a *fracture*, ruin; specifically a *solution* (of a dream): affliction breach, crashing, interpretation [Strgs#7667].

[12] oaks – *strength*; anything *strong*, a *chief* (politically) also a *ram*, pilaster (as a strong support) [Strgs#352].

[13] gardens – from Hebrew root word meaning *fenced* [Strgs#1588]. Symbolic of protection.

[14] strong – from Hebrew word meaning powerful [Strgs2634]. Derives from a root word meaning to be *compact*, to *hoard*, lay up [Strgs#2630].

[15] lit. *something shaken out*, tow (as the refuse of flaw) [Strgs#5296].

[16] Amoz- is the Hebrew word *'âmôts, aw-mohts'*; meaning *strong*. [Strgs#531].

[17] compare Ezekiel 43:12

[18] rebuke – *to be right*, reciprocally to *argue*; causatively to *decide, justify* or convict [Strgs#3198].

spears into pruning-hooks: nation will not lift up sword against nation, neither will they learn war any more.

5 O house of Jacob, come you, and let us walk in the light of the LORD.

6 Therefore you have forsaken your people the house of Jacob, because they be replenished from the east, and *are* soothsayers like the Philistines, and they please themselves in the children of strangers.

7 Their land also is full of silver and gold, neither *is there any* end of their treasures; their land is also full of horses, neither *is there any* end of their chariots:

8 Their land also is full of idols; they worship the work of their own hands, that which their own fingers have made:

9 And the mean man bows down, and the great man humbles himself: therefore forgive them not.

10 Enter into the rock, and hide you in the dust, for fear of the LORD, and for the glory of his majesty.

11 The lofty looks of man will be humbled, and the haughtiness of men will be bowed down, and the LORD alone will be exalted in that day.

12 For the day of the LORD of hosts will *be* upon every *one that is* proud and lofty, and upon every *one that is* lifted up; and he will be brought low:

13 And upon all the cedars of Lebanon, *that are* high and lifted up, and upon all the oaks of Bashan,

14 And upon all the high mountains, and upon all the hills *that are* lifted up,

15 And upon every high tower, and upon every fenced wall,

16 And upon all the ships of Tarshish, and upon all pleasant pictures.

17 And the loftiness of man will be bowed down, and the haughtiness of men will be made low: and the LORD alone will be exalted in that day.

18 And the idols he will utterly abolish.

19 And they will go into the holes of the rocks, and into the caves of the earth, for fear of the LORD, and for the glory of his majesty, when he arises to shake terribly the earth.

20 In that day a man will cast his idols of silver, and his idols of gold, which they made *each one* for himself to worship, to the moles and to the bats;

21 To go into the clefts of the rocks, and into the tops of the ragged rocks, for fear of the LORD, and for the glory of his majesty, when he arises to shake terribly the earth.

22 Cease you from man, whose breath *is* in his nostrils: for wherein is he to be accounted of?

CHAPTER 3

1 For, behold, the Lord, the LORD of hosts, does take away from Jerusalem and from Judah the stay and the staff, the whole stay of bread, and the whole stay of water,

2 The mighty man, and the man of war, the judge, and the prophet, and the prudent, and the ancient,

3 The captain of fifty, and the honorable man, and the counselor, and the cunning artificer, and the eloquent orator.

4 And I will give children *to be* their princes, and babes will rule over them.

5 And the people will be oppressed, everyone by another, and every one by his neighbor: the child will behave himself proudly against the ancient, and the base against the honorable.

6 When a man will take hold of his brother of the house of his father, *saying*, you have clothing, be you our ruler, and *let* this ruin *be* under your hand:

7 In that day will he swear, saying, I will not be a healer; for in my house *is* neither bread or clothing: make me not a ruler of the people.

8 For Jerusalem is ruined, and Judah is fallen: because their tongue and their doings *are* against the LORD, to provoke the eyes of his glory.

9 The show of their countenance does witness against them; and they declare their sin as Sodom, they hide *it* not. Woe unto their soul! for they have rewarded evil unto themselves.

10 Say you to the righteous, that *it will be* well *with him*: for they will eat the fruit of their doings.

11 Woe unto the wicked! *It will be* ill *with him*: for the reward of his hands will be given him.

12 *As for* my people, children *are* their oppressors, and women rule over them. O my people, they which lead you cause you to err, and destroy the way of your paths.

13 The LORD stands up to plead, and stands to judge the people.

14 The LORD will enter into judgment with the ancients of his people, and the princes thereof: for you have eaten up the vineyard; the spoil of the poor *is* in your houses.

15 What mean you *that* you beat my people to pieces, and grind the faces of the poor? Said the Lord GOD of hosts.

16 Moreover the LORD said, because the daughters of Zion are haughty, and walk with stretched forth necks and wanton eyes, walking and mincing *as* they go, and making a tinkling with their feet:

17 Therefore the Lord will smite with a scab the crown of the head of the daughters of Zion, and the LORD will discover their secret parts.

18 In that day the Lord will take away the bravery of *their* tinkling ornaments *about their feet*, and *their* cauls, and *their* round tires like the moon,

19 The chains, and the bracelets, and the mufflers,

20 The bonnets, and the ornaments of the legs, and the headbands, and the tablets, and the earrings,

21 The rings, and nose jewels,

22 The changeable suits of apparel, and the mantles, and the wimples, and the crisping pins,

23 The glasses, and the fine linen, and the hoods, and the veils.

24 And it will come to pass, *that* instead of sweet smell there will be stink; and instead of a girdle a rent; and instead of well set hair baldness; and instead of a stomacher a girding of sackcloth; *and* burning instead of beauty.

25 your men will fall by the sword, and your mighty in the war.

26 And her gates will lament and mourn; and she *being* desolate will sit upon the ground.

CHAPTER 4

1 And in that day seven women will take hold of one man, saying, we will eat our own bread, and wear our own apparel only let us be called by your name, to take away our reproach.

2 In that day will the branch of the LORD be beautiful and glorious, and the fruit of the earth will *be* excellent and comely for them that are escaped of Israel.

3 And it will come to pass, *that he that is* left in Zion, and *he that* remains in Jerusalem, will be called holy, *even* every one that is written among the living in Jerusalem:

4 When the Lord will have washed away the filth of the daughters of Zion, and will have purged the blood of Jerusalem from the midst thereof by the spirit of judgment, and by the spirit of burning.
5 And the LORD will create upon every dwelling place of mount Zion, and upon her assemblies, a cloud and smoke by day, and the shining of a flaming fire by night: for upon all the glory will *be* a defence.
6 And there will be a tabernacle for a shadow in the daytime from the heat, and for a place of refuge, and for a covert from storm and from rain.

CHAPTER 5

1 Now will I sing to my well beloved a song of my beloved touching his vineyard. My well beloved has a vineyard in a very [fruitful hill][1]:
2 And he fenced it, and gathered out the stones thereof, and planted it with the choicest vine, and built a tower in the midst of it, and also made a winepress therein: and he looked that it should bring forth grapes, and it brought forth wild grapes[2].
3 And now, O inhabitants of Jerusalem, and men of Judah, judge, I pray you, betwixt me and my vineyard.
4 What could have been done more to my vineyard, that I have not done in it? Wherefore, when I looked that it should bring forth grapes, brought it forth wild grapes?
5 And now go to; I will tell you what I will do to my vineyard: I will take away the hedge thereof, and it will be eaten up; *and* break down the wall thereof, and it will be trodden down:
6 And I will lay it waste: it will not be pruned, or digged; but there will come up briers and thorns: I will also command the clouds that they rain no rain upon it.
7 For the vineyard of the LORD of hosts *is* the house of Israel, and the men of Judah his pleasant plant: and he looked for judgment, but behold oppression; for righteousness, but behold a cry.
8 Woe unto them that join house to house, *that* lay field to field, till *there be* no place, that they may be placed alone in the midst of the earth!
9 In mine ears *said* the LORD of hosts, Of a truth many houses will be desolate, *even* great and fair, without inhabitant.
10 Yea, ten acres of vineyard will yield one bath, and the seed of an homer will yield an ephah.
11 Woe unto them that rise up early in the morning, *that* they may follow strong drink; that continue until night, *till* wine inflame them!
12 And the harp, and the viol, the **tambourine**, and pipe, and wine, are in their feasts: but they regard not the work of the LORD, neither consider the operation of his hands.
13 Therefore my people are gone into captivity, because *they have* no knowledge: and their honorable men *are* famished, and their multitude dried up with thirst.
14 Therefore hell has enlarged herself, and opened her mouth without measure: and their glory, and their multitude, and their pomp, and he that rejoices, will descend into it.
15 And the mean man will be brought down, and the mighty man will be humbled, and the eyes of the lofty will be humbled:
16 But the LORD of hosts will be exalted in judgment, and God that is holy will be sanctified in righteousness.
17 Then will the lambs feed after their manner, and the waste places of the fat ones will strangers eat.
18 Woe unto them that draw iniquity with cords of vanity, and sin as it were with a cart rope:
19 That say, Let him make speed, *and* hasten his work, that we may see *it*: and let the counsel of the Holy One of Israel draw nigh and come, that we may know *it*!
20 Woe unto them that call evil good, and good evil; that put darkness for light, and light for darkness; that put bitter for sweet, and sweet for bitter!
21 Woe unto *them that are* wise in their own eyes, and prudent in their own sight!
22 Woe unto *them that are* mighty to drink wine, and men of strength to mingle strong drink:
23 Which justify the wicked for reward, and take away the righteousness of the righteous from him!
24 Therefore as the fire devours the stubble, and the flame consumes the chaff, *so* their root will be as rottenness, and their blossom will go up as dust: because they have cast away the law of the LORD of hosts, and despised the word of the Holy One of Israel.
25 Therefore is the anger of the LORD kindled against his people, and he has stretched forth his hand against them, and has smitten them: and the hills did tremble, and their carcasses *were* torn in the midst of the streets. For all this his anger is not turned away, but his hand *is* stretched out still.
26 And he will lift up an ensign to the nations from far, and will hiss unto them from the end of the earth: and, behold, they will come with speed swiftly:
27 None will be weary or stumble among them; none will slumber or sleep; neither will the girdle of their loins be loosed, or the latchet of their shoes be broken:
28 Whose arrows *are* sharp, and all their bows bent, their horses' hoofs will be counted like flint, and their wheels like a whirlwind:
29 Their roaring will *be* like a lion, they will roar like young lions: yea, they will roar, and lay hold of the prey, and will carry *it* away safe, and none will deliver *it*.
30 And in that day they will roar against them like the roaring of the sea: and if *one* look unto the land, behold darkness *and* sorrow, and the light is darkened in the heavens thereof.

CHAPTER 6

1 In the year that king Uzziah died I saw also the Lord sitting upon a throne, high and lifted up, and his train filled the temple.
2 Above it stood the seraphims: each one had six wings; with twain he covered his face, and with twain he covered his feet, and with twain he did fly.
3 And one cried unto another, and said, Holy, holy, holy, *is* the LORD of hosts: the whole earth *is* full of his glory.
4 And the posts[3] of the door[4] moved at the voice of him that cried, and the house was filled with smoke.
5 Then said I, Woe *is* me! For I am undone[5]; because I *am* a man of unclean lips, and I dwell in the midst of a people of unclean lips: for mine eyes have seen the King, the LORD of hosts.

---

[1] lit. – 'A horn of the son of oil (olive)'. Fruitful comes from two Hebrew words, the first being *bên* meaning <u>a son</u> (as a builder of the family name) [Strgs#1121]. The second word is *shemen* meaning *grease*, especially liquid (as from the *olive*, often perfumed) figuratively *richness*, anointing, ointment [Strgs#8081]. Hill derives from the Hebrew word *qeren* meaning a *horn* (as projecting); by implication a *flask*, <u>cornet</u>; by resemblance an elephant's tooth (that is *ivory*), a *corner* (of the altar), a *peak* (of a <u>mountain</u>), a *ray* (of light); figuratively *power* [Strgs#7161].

[2] grapes – is defined as *poison berries* [Strgs#891]. Derives from a Hebrew root word meaning *stench*, <u>stink</u> [Strgs#889].
[3] posts – a <u>mother</u> (that is, *unit*) of measure, or the forearm (below the elbow), a <u>cubit</u>; also a door *base* (as a *bond* of the entrance) [Strgs#520].
[4] door – in its original sense of *containing*; a *vestibule* (as a *limit*); also a *dish* (for holding blood or wine): cup, bason, door post, <u>bowl</u> (compare **Exodus 12:22**), gate, <u>threshold</u> (compare **Ezekiel 40:6**) [Strgs#5592].
[5] lit. to *be dumb* or *silent*; hence to *fail* or *perish*; to *destroy*: be cut down

6 Then flew one of the seraphims[1] unto me, having a live coal in his hand, *which* he had taken with the tongs from off the altar:
7 And he laid *it* upon my mouth, and said, lo, this has touched your lips; and your iniquity is taken away, and your sin purged.
8 Also I heard the voice of the Lord, saying, whom will I send, and who will go for us? Then said I, Here *am* I; send me.
9 And he said, Go, and tell this people, hear you indeed, but understand not; and see you indeed, but perceive[2] not.
10 Make the heart of this people fat, and make their ears heavy, and shut their eyes; lest they see with their eyes, and hear with their ears, and understand with their heart, and convert, and be healed.
11 Then said I, Lord, how long? And he answered, until the cities be wasted without inhabitant, and the houses without man, and the land be utterly desolate,
12 And the LORD has removed men far away, and *there be* a great forsaking in the midst of the land.
13 But yet in it will *be* a tenth, and *it* will return, and will be eaten: as a teil tree, and as an oak, whose substance *is* in them, when they cast *their* leaves: *so* the holy seed will *be* the substance thereof.

CHAPTER 7

1 And it came to pass in the days of Ahaz[3] the son of Jotham, the son of Uzziah, king of Judah, *that* Rezin the king of Syria, and Pekah the son of Remaliah, king of Israel, went up toward Jerusalem to war against it, but could not prevail against it.
2 And it was told the house of David, saying, Syria is confederate with Ephraim. And his heart was moved, and the heart of his people, as the trees of the wood are moved with the wind.
3 Then said the LORD unto Isaiah, Go forth now to meet Ahaz, you, and Shear-jashub your son, at the end of the conduit of the upper pool in the highway of the fuller's field;
4 And say unto him, take heed, and be quiet; fear not, neither be fainthearted for the two tails of these smoking firebrands, for the fierce anger of Rezin with Syria, and of the son of Remaliah.
5 Because Syria, Ephraim, and the son of Remaliah, have taken evil counsel against you, saying,
6 Let us go up against Judah, and vex it, and let us make a breach therein for us, and set a king in the midst of it, *even* the son of Tabeal:
7 Thus said the Lord GOD, It will not stand, neither will it come to pass.
8 For the head of Syria *is* Damascus, and the head of Damascus *is* Rezin; and within threescore and five years will Ephraim be broken, that it be not a people.
9 And the head of Ephraim *is* Samaria, and the head of Samaria *is* Remaliah's son. If you will not believe, surely you will not be established.
10 Moreover the LORD spoke again unto Ahaz, saying,
11 Ask you a sign of the LORD your God; ask it either in the depth, or in the height above.
12 But Ahaz said, I will not ask, neither will I tempt the LORD.
13 And he said, Hear you now, O house of David; *Is it* a small thing for you to weary men, but will you weary my God also?

14 Therefore the Lord himself will give you a sign; Behold, a virgin will conceive, and bear a son, and will call his name Immanuel.
15 Butter and honey will he eat, that he may know to refuse the evil, and choose the good.
16 For before the child will know to refuse the evil, and choose the good, the land that you abhor will be forsaken of both her kings.
17 The LORD will bring upon you, and upon your people, and upon your father's house, days that have not come, from the day that Ephraim departed from Judah; *even* the king of Assyria.
18 And it will come to pass in that day, *that* the LORD will hiss for the fly that *is* in the uttermost part of the rivers of Egypt, and for the bee that *is* in the land of Assyria.
19 And they will come, and will rest all of them in the desolate valleys, and in the holes of the rocks, and upon all thorns, and upon all bushes.
20 In the same day will the Lord shave with a razor that is hired, *namely*, by them beyond the river, by the king of Assyria, the head, and the hair of the feet: and it will also consume the beard.
21 And it will come to pass in that day, *that* a man will nourish a young cow, and two sheep;
22 And it will come to pass, for the abundance of milk *that* they will give he will eat butter: for butter and honey will every one eat that is left in the land.
23 And it will come to pass in that day, *that* every place will be, where there were a thousand vines at a thousand silverlings, it will *even* be for briers and thorns.
24 With arrows and with bows will *men* come thither; because all the land will become briers and thorns.
25 And *on* all hills that will be digged with the mattock, there will not come there the fear of briers and thorns: but it will be for the sending forth of oxen, and for the treading of lesser cattle.

CHAPTER 8

1 Moreover the LORD said unto me, take you a great roll, and write in it with a man's pen concerning Maher-shalal-hash-baz.
2 And I took unto me faithful witnesses to record, Uriah the priest, and Zechariah the son of Jeberechiah.
3 And I went unto the prophetess; and she conceived, and bare a son. Then said the LORD to me, Call his name Maher-shalal-hash-baz.
4 For before the child will have knowledge to cry, my father, and my mother, the riches of Damascus and the spoil of Samaria will be taken away before the king of Assyria.
5 The LORD spoke also unto me again, saying,
6 Forasmuch as this people refuses the waters of Shiloah that go softly, and rejoice in Rezin and Remaliah's son;
7 Now therefore, behold, the Lord brings up upon them the waters of the river, strong and many, *even* the king of Assyria, and all his glory: and he will come up over all his channels, and go over all his banks:
8 And he will pass through Judah; he will overflow and go over, he will reach *even* to the neck; and the stretching out of his wings will fill the breadth of your land, O Immanuel.
9 Associate yourselves, O you people, and you will be broken in pieces; and give ear, all you of far countries: gird yourselves, and

---

(off), be brought to silence [Strgs#1820].
[1] seraphims- *burning*, that is, (figuratively) *poisonous* (serpent); specifically a seraph or symbolical creature (from their copper color):- fiery (serpent), seraph. [Strgs#8314] Majestic beings with six wings, human hands or voices in attendance upon God.

[2] perceive – is the Hebrew word *yâda'* meaning to *know* (properly to ascertain by seeing), *observation, care, recognition, instruction, designation, punishment* [Strgs#3045].
[3] Ahaz- he has grasped or possessor. [Strgs#271]

you will be broken in pieces; gird yourselves, and you will be broken in pieces.
10 Take counsel together, and it will come to nought[1]; speak the word, and it will not stand: for God *is* with us.
11 For the LORD spoke this to me with a strong hand, and instructed me that I should not walk in the way of this people, saying,
12 Say you not, A confederacy, to all *them to* whom this people will say, A confederacy; neither fear you their fear, or be afraid.
13 Sanctify the LORD of hosts himself; and *let* him *be* your fear, and *let* him *be* your dread.
14 And he will be for a sanctuary; but for a stone of stumbling and for a rock of offence to both the houses of Israel, for a gin and for a snare to the inhabitants of Jerusalem.
15 And many among them will stumble, and fall, and be broken, and be snared, and be taken.
16 Bind up the testimony, seal the law among my disciples.
17 And I will wait upon the LORD, that hides his face from the house of Jacob, and I will look for him.
18 Behold, I and the children whom the LORD has given me *are* for signs and for wonders in Israel from the LORD of hosts, which dwells in mount Zion.
19 And when they will say unto you, Seek unto them that have familiar spirits, and unto wizards that peep, and that mutter: should not a people seek unto their God? For the living to the dead?
20 To the law and to the testimony: if they speak not according to this word, *it is* because *there is* no light in them.
21 And they will pass through it, hardly bestead and hungry: and it will come to pass, that when they will be hungry, they will fret themselves, and curse their king and their God, and look upward.
22 And they will look unto the earth; and behold trouble and darkness, dimness of anguish; and *they will be* driven to darkness.

CHAPTER 9

1 Nevertheless the dimness will not *be* such as *was* in her vexation, when at the first he lightly afflicted the land of Zebulun and the land of Naphtali, and afterward did more grievously afflict her *by* the way of the sea, beyond Jordan, in Galilee of the nations.
2 The people that walked in darkness have seen a great light: they that dwell in the land[2] of the shadow of death, upon them has the light shined.
3 You have multiplied the nation, *and* not increased the joy: they joy before you according to the joy in harvest, *and* as *men* rejoice when they divide the spoil.
4 For you have broken the yoke of his burden, and the staff of his shoulder, the rod of his oppressor, as in the day of Midian.
5 For every battle of the warrior *is* with confused noise, and garments rolled in blood; but *this* will be with burning *and* fuel of fire.
6 For unto us a child is born, unto us a son is given: and the government will be upon his shoulder: and his name will be called Wonderful, Counselor, The mighty God, The everlasting Father, The Prince of Peace.
7 Of the increase of *his* government and peace *there will be* no end, upon the throne of David, and upon his kingdom, to order it, and to establish it with judgment and with justice from henceforth even forever. The zeal of the LORD of hosts will perform this.

8 The Lord sent a word into Jacob, and it has lighted upon Israel.
9 And all the people will know, *even* Ephraim and the inhabitant of Samaria, that say in the pride and stoutness of heart,
10 The bricks are fallen down, but we will build with hewn stones: the sycamores are cut down, but we will change *them into* cedars.
11 Therefore the LORD will set up the adversaries of Rezin against him, and join his enemies together;
12 The Syrians before, and the Philistines behind; and they will devour Israel with open mouth. For all this his anger is not turned away, but his hand *is* stretched out still.
13 For the people turns not unto him that smites them, neither do they seek the LORD of hosts.
14 Therefore the LORD will cut off from Israel head and tail branch and rush, in one day.
15 The ancient and honorable, he *is* the head; and the prophet that teaches lies, he *is* the tail.
16 For the leaders of this people cause *them* to err; and *they that are* led of them *are* destroyed[3].
17 Therefore the Lord will have no joy in their young men, neither will have mercy on their fatherless and widows: for everyone *is* an hypocrite and an evildoer, and every mouth speaks folly. For all this his anger is not turned away, but his hand *is* stretched out still.
18 For wickedness burns as the fire: it will devour the briers and thorns, and will kindle in the thickets of the forest, and they will mount up *like* the lifting up of smoke.
19 Through the wrath of the LORD of hosts is the land darkened, and the people will be as the fuel of the fire: no man will spare his brother.
20 And he will snatch on the right hand, and be hungry; and he will eat on the left hand, and they will not be satisfied: they will eat every man the flesh of his own arm:
21 Manasseh, Ephraim; and Ephraim, Manasseh: *and* they together will *be* against Judah. For all this his anger is not turned away, but his hand *is* stretched out still.

CHAPTER 10

1 Woe unto them that decree unrighteous decrees, and that write grievousness *which* they have prescribed;
2 To turn aside the needy from judgment, and to take away the right from the poor of my people, that widows may be their prey, and *that* they may rob the fatherless!
3 And what will you do in the day of visitation, and in the desolation *which* will come from far? To whom will you flee for help? And where will you leave your glory?
4 Without me they will bow down under the prisoners, and they will fall under the slain. For all this his anger is not turned away, but his hand *is* stretched out still.
5 O Assyrian, the rod of mine anger, and the staff in their hand is mine indignation.
6 I will send him against a hypocritical nation, and against the people of my wrath will I give him a charge, to take the spoil, and to take the prey, and to tread them down like the mire of the streets.
7 Howbeit he means not so, neither does his heart think so; but *it is* in his heart to destroy and cut off nations not a few.
8 For he said, *are* not my princes altogether kings?
9 *Is* not Calno as Carchemish? *Is* not Hamath as Arpad? *Is* not Samaria as Damascus?

---

[1] nought- *to break up* (usually figuratively, that is, *to violate*, frustrate):- any ways, break (asunder), cast off, cause to cease, X clean, defeat, disannul, disappoint, dissolve, divide, make of none effect, fail, frustrate, bring (come) to nought, X utterly, make void. [Strgs#6565]

[2] lit. from an unused root probably meaning to *be firm*, the *earth*, region [Strgs#7760. Compare **Matthew 4:16**.

[3] destroyed – to *make away with* (specifically by swallowing; generally to *destroy*: cover, devour, eat up, spend up [Strgs#1104].

10 As my hand has found the kingdoms of the idols, and whose graven images did excel them of Jerusalem and of Samaria;
11 will I not, as I have done unto Samaria and her idols, so do to Jerusalem and her idols?
12 Wherefore it will come to pass, *that* when the Lord has performed his whole work upon mount Zion and on Jerusalem, I will punish the fruit of the stout heart of the king of Assyria, and the glory of his high looks.
13 For he said, by the strength of my hand I have done *it*, and by my wisdom; for I am prudent: and I have removed the bounds of the people, and have robbed their treasures, and I have put down the inhabitants like a valiant *man*:
14 And my hand has found as a nest the riches of the people: and as one gathers eggs *that are* left, have I gathered all the earth; and there was none that moved the wing, or opened the mouth, or peeped.
15 will the axe boast itself against him that hews therewith? *or* will the saw magnify itself against him that shakes it? As if the rod should shake *itself* against them that lift it up, *or* as if the staff should lift up *itself, as if it were* no wood.
16 Therefore will the Lord, the Lord of hosts, send among his fat ones leanness; and under his glory he will kindle a burning like the burning of a fire.
17 And the light of Israel will be for a fire, and his Holy One for a flame: and it will burn and devour his thorns and his briers in one day;
18 And will consume the glory of his forest, and of his fruitful field, both soul and body: and they will be as when a standard bearer faints.
19 And the rest of the trees of his forest will be few, that a child may write them.
20 And it will come to pass in that day, *that* the remnant of Israel, and such as are escaped of the house of Jacob, will no more again stay upon him that smote them; but will stay upon the LORD, the Holy One of Israel, in truth.
21 The remnant will return, *even* the remnant of Jacob, unto the mighty God.
22 For though your people Israel be as the sand of the sea, *yet* a remnant of them will return: the consumption decreed will overflow with righteousness.
23 For the Lord GOD of hosts will make a consumption, even determined, in the midst of all the land.
24 Therefore thus said the Lord GOD of hosts, O my people that dwells in Zion, be not afraid of the Assyrian: he will smite you with a rod, and will lift up his staff against you, after the manner of Egypt.
25 For yet a very little while, and the indignation will cease, and mine anger in their destruction.
26 And the LORD of hosts will stir up a scourge for him according to the slaughter of Midian at the rock of Oreb: and *as* his rod *was* upon the sea, so will he lift it up after the manner of Egypt.
27 And it will come to pass in that day, *that* his burden will be taken away from off your shoulder, and his yoke from off your neck, and the yoke will be destroyed because of the anointing.
28 He is come to Aiath, he is passed to Migron; at Michmash he has laid up his carriages:
29 They are gone over the passage: they have taken up their lodging at Geba; Ramah is afraid; Gibeah of Saul is fled.
30 Lift up your voice, O daughter of Gallim: cause it to be heard unto Laish, O poor Anathoth.
31 Madmenah is removed; the inhabitants of Gebim gather themselves to flee.
32 As yet will he remain at Nob that day: he will shake his hand *against* the mount of the daughter of Zion, the hill of Jerusalem.
33 Behold, the Lord, the LORD of hosts, will lop the bough with terror: and the high ones of stature will *be* hewn down, and the haughty will be humbled.
34 And he will cut down the thickets of the forest with iron, and Lebanon will fall by a mighty one.

CHAPTER 11

1 And there will come forth a rod out of the stem of Jesse, and a Branch will grow out of his roots:
2 And the spirit of the LORD will rest upon him, the spirit of wisdom and understanding, the spirit of counsel and might, the spirit of knowledge and of the fear of the LORD;
3 And will make him of [quick understanding][1] in the fear of the LORD: and he will not judge after the sight of his eyes, neither reprove after the hearing of his ears:
4 But with righteousness will he judge the poor, and reprove with equity for the meek of the earth: and he will smite the earth with the rod of his mouth, and with the breath[2] of his lips will he slay the wicked.
5 And righteousness will be the girdle of his loins, and faithfulness the girdle of his reins.
6 The wolf also will dwell with the lamb, and the leopard will lie down with the kid; and the calf and the young lion and the fatling together; and a little child will lead them.
7 And the cow and the bear will feed; their young ones will lie down together: and the lion will eat straw like the ox.
8 And the sucking child will play on the hole of the asp, and the weaned child will put his hand on the cockatrice' den.
9 They will not hurt or destroy in my **entire** holy mountain: for the earth will be full of the knowledge of the LORD, as the waters cover the sea.
10 And in that day there will be a root of Jesse, which will stand for an ensign of the people; to it will the Gentiles seek: and his rest will be glorious.
11 And it will come to pass in that day, *that* the Lord will set his hand again the second time to recover the remnant of his people, which will be left, from Assyria, and from Egypt, and from Pathros, and from Cush, and from Elam, and from Shinar, and from Hamath, and from the islands of the sea.
12 And he will set up an ensign for the nations, and will assemble the outcasts of Israel, and gather together the dispersed of Judah from the four corners of the earth.
13 The envy also of Ephraim will depart, and the adversaries of Judah will be cut off: Ephraim will not envy Judah, and Judah will not vex Ephraim.
14 But they will fly upon the shoulders of the Philistines toward the west; they will spoil them of the east together: they will lay their hand upon Edom and Moab; and the children of Ammon will obey them.
15 And the LORD will utterly destroy the tongue of the Egyptian sea; and with his mighty wind will he shake his hand over the river,

---

[1] lit. to *blow, breathe*, to *smell, perceive*, to *anticipate, enjoy* [Strgs#7306].
[2] lit. *wind, life, anger, unsubstantiality, region of the sky, spirit* [Strgs#7307].

and will smite it in the seven streams, and make *men* go over dryshod[1].

16 And there will be a highway for the remnant of his people, which will be left, from Assyria; like as it was to Israel in the day that he came up out of the land of Egypt.

CHAPTER 12

1 And in that day you will say, O LORD, I will praise you: though you were angry with me, your anger is turned away, and you comforted me.

2 Behold, God *is* my salvation; I will trust, and not be afraid: for the LORD JEHOVAH *is* my strength and *my* song; he also is become my salvation.

3 Therefore with joy will you draw water out of the wells of salvation.

4 And in that day will you say, Praise the LORD, call upon his name, declare his doings among the people, make mention that his name is exalted.

5 Sing unto the LORD; for he has done excellent things: this *is* known in all the earth.

6 Cry out and shout, you inhabitant of Zion: for great *is* the Holy One of Israel in the midst of you.

CHAPTER 13

1 The burden of Babylon, which Isaiah the son of Amoz did see.

2 Lift you up a banner upon the high mountain, exalt the voice unto them, shake the hand, that they may go into the gates of the nobles.

3 I have commanded my sanctified ones, I have also called my mighty ones for mine anger, *even* them that rejoice in my highness.

4 The noise of a multitude in the mountains, like as of a great people; a tumultuous noise of the kingdoms of nations gathered together: the LORD of hosts musters the host of the battle.

5 They come from a far country, from the end of heaven, *even* the LORD, and the weapons of his indignation, to destroy the whole land.

6 Howl you; for the day of the LORD *is* at hand; it will come as a destruction from the Almighty.

7 Therefore will all hands be faint, and every man's heart will melt:

8 And they will be afraid: pangs and sorrows will take hold of them; they will be in pain as a woman that travails: they will be amazed one at another; their faces will *be as* flames.

9 Behold, the day of the LORD cometh, cruel both with wrath and fierce anger, to lay the land desolate: and he will destroy the sinners thereof out of it.

10 For the stars of heaven and the constellations thereof will not give their light: the sun will be darkened in his going forth, and the moon will not cause her light to shine.

11 And I will punish the world for *their* evil, and the wicked for their iniquity; and I will cause the arrogance of the proud to cease, and will lay low the haughtiness of the terrible.

12 I will make a man more precious than fine gold; even a man than the golden wedge of Ophir.

13 Therefore I will shake the heavens, and the earth will remove out of her place, in the wrath of the LORD of hosts, and in the day of his fierce anger.

14 And it will be as the chased roe, and as a sheep that no man takes up: they will every man turn to his own people, and flee every one into his own land.

---

[1] dryshod- properly a sandal tongue; by extension a sandal or slipper (sometimes as a symbol of occupancy, a refusal to marry, or of something

15 Every one that is found will be thrust through; and every one that is joined *unto them* will fall by the sword.

16 Their children also will be dashed to pieces before their eyes; their houses will be spoiled, and their wives ravished.

17 Behold, I will stir up the Medes against them, which will not regard silver; and *as for* gold, they will not delight in it.

18 *Their* bows also will dash the young men to pieces; and they will have no pity on the fruit of the womb; their eye will not spare children.

19 And Babylon, the glory of kingdoms, the beauty of the Chaldees' excellency, will be as when God overthrew Sodom and Gomorrah.

20 It will never be inhabited, neither will it be dwelt in from generation to generation: neither will the Arabian pitch tent there; neither will the shepherds make their fold there.

21 But wild beasts of the desert will lie there; and their houses will be full of doleful creatures; and owls will dwell there, and satyrs will dance there.

22 And the wild beasts of the islands will cry in their desolate houses, and dragons in *their* pleasant palaces: and her time *is* near to come, and her days will not be prolonged.

CHAPTER 14

1 For the LORD will have mercy on Jacob, and will yet choose Israel, and set them in their own land: and the strangers will be joined with them, and they will cleave to the house of Jacob.

2 And the people will take them, and bring them to their place: and the house of Israel will possess them in the land of the LORD for servants and handmaids: and they will take them captives, whose captives they were; and they will rule over their oppressors.

3 And it will come to pass in the day that the LORD will give you rest from your sorrow, and from your fear, and from the hard bondage wherein you were made to serve,

4 That you will take up this proverb against the king of Babylon, and say, how has the oppressor ceased! The golden city ceased!

5 The LORD has broken the staff of the wicked, *and* the scepter of the rulers.

6 He who smote the people in wrath with a continual stroke, he that ruled the nations in anger, is persecuted, *and* none hinders.

7 The whole earth is at rest, *and* is quiet: they break forth into singing.

8 Yea, the fir trees rejoice at you, *and* the cedars of Lebanon, *saying*, since you are laid down, no feller is come up against us.

9 Hell from beneath is moved for you to meet you at your coming: it stirs up the dead for you, *even* all the chief ones of the earth; it has raised up from their thrones all the kings of the nations.

10 All they will speak and say unto you, are you also become weak as we? Are you become like unto us?

11 your pomp is brought down to the grave, *and* the noise of your viols: the worm is spread under you, and the worms cover you.

12 How are you fallen from heaven, O Lucifer, son of the morning! *How* are you cut down to the ground, which did weaken the nations!

13 For you have said in your heart, I will ascend into heaven, I will exalt my throne above the stars of God: I will sit also upon the mount of the congregation, in the sides of the north:

14 I will ascend above the heights of the clouds; I will be like the most High.

---

valueless. [Strgs#5275]

15 Yet you will be brought down to hell, to the sides of the pit.
16 They that see you will narrowly look upon you, *and* consider you, *saying, is* this the man that made the earth to tremble, that did shake kingdoms;
17 *That* made the world as a wilderness, and destroyed the cities thereof; *that* opened not the house of his prisoners?
18 All the kings of the nations, *even* all of them, lie in glory, everyone in his own house.
19 But you are cast out of your grave like an abominable branch, *and as* the raiment of those that are slain, thrust through with a sword, that go down to the stones of the pit; as a carcass trodden under feet.
20 you will not be joined with them in burial, because you have destroyed your land, *and* slain your people: the seed of evildoers will never be renowned.
21 Prepare slaughter for his children for the iniquity of their fathers; that they do not rise, or possess the land, or fill the face of the world with cities.
22 For I will rise up against them, said the LORD of hosts, and cut off from Babylon the name, and remnant, and son, and nephew, said the LORD.
23 I will also make it a possession for the bittern, and pools of water: and I will sweep it with the besom of destruction, said the LORD of hosts.
24 The LORD of hosts has sworn, saying, Surely as I have thought, so will it come to pass; and as I have purposed, *so* will it stand:
25 That I will break the Assyrian in my land, and upon my mountains tread him under foot: then will his yoke depart from off them, and his burden depart from off their shoulders.
26 This *is* the purpose that is purposed upon the whole earth: and this *is* the hand that is stretched out upon all the nations.
27 For the LORD of hosts has purposed, and who will disannul *it*? And his hand *is* stretched out, and who will turn it back?
28 In the year that king Ahaz died was this burden.
29 Rejoice not thou, whole Palestina, because the rod of him that smote you is broken: for out of the serpent's root will come forth a cockatrice, and his fruit will *be* a fiery flying serpent.
30 And the firstborn of the poor will feed, and the needy will lie down in safety: and I will kill your root with famine, and he will slay your remnant.
31 Howl, O gate; cry, O city; thou, whole Palestina, are dissolved: for there will come from the north a smoke, and none will *be* alone in his appointed times.
32 What will *one* then answer the messengers of the nation? That the LORD has founded Zion, and the poor of his people will trust in it.

CHAPTER 15

1 The burden of Moab. Because in the night Ar of Moab is laid waste, *and* brought to silence; because in the night Kir of Moab is laid waste, *and* brought to silence;
2 He is gone up to Bajith, and to Dibon, the high places, to weep: Moab will howl over Nebo, and over Medeba: on all their heads will *be* baldness, *and* every beard cut off.
3 In their streets they will gird themselves with sackcloth: on the tops of their houses, and in their streets, everyone will howl, weeping abundantly.
4 And Heshbon will cry, and Elealeh: their voice will be heard *even* unto Jahaz: therefore the armed soldiers of Moab will cry out; his life will be grievous unto him.
5 My heart will cry out for Moab; his fugitives will *flee* unto Zoar, a heifer of three years old: for by the mounting up of Luhith with weeping will they go it up; for in the way of Horonaim they will raise up a cry of destruction.
6 For the waters of Nimrim will be desolate: for the hay is withered away, the grass fails, there is no green thing.
7 Therefore the abundance they have gotten, and that which they have laid up, will they carry away to the brook of the willows.
8 For the cry is gone round about the borders of Moab; the howling thereof unto Eglaim, and the howling thereof unto Beer-elim.
9 For the waters of Dimon will be full of blood: for I will bring more upon Dimon, lions upon him that escapes of Moab, and upon the remnant of the land.

CHAPTER 16

1 Send you the lamb to the ruler of the land from Sela to the wilderness, unto the mount of the daughter of Zion.
2 For it will be, *that*, as a wandering bird cast out of the nest, *so* the daughters of Moab will be at the fords of Arnon.
3 Take counsel, execute judgment; make your shadow as the night in the midst of the noonday; hide the outcasts; bewray[1] not him that wanders.
4 Let mine outcasts dwell with you, Moab; be you a covert to them from the face of the spoiler: for the extortioner is a an end, the spoiler ceases, the oppressors are consumed out of the land.
5 And in mercy will the throne be established: and he will sit upon it in truth in the tabernacle of David, judging, and seeking judgment, and hasting righteousness.
6 We have heard of the pride of Moab; *he is* very proud: *even* of his haughtiness, and his pride, and his wrath: *but his* lies will not *be* so.
7 Therefore will Moab howl for Moab, everyone will howl: for the foundations of Kir-haraseth[2] will you mourn; surely *they are* stricken.
8 For the fields of Heshbon languish, *and* the vine of Sibmah: the lords of the heathen have broken down the principal plants thereof, they are come *even* unto Jazer, they wandered through the wilderness: her branches are stretched out, they are gone over the sea.
9 Therefore I will bewail with the weeping of Jazer the vine of Sibmah: I will water you with my tears, O Heshbon, and Elealeh: for the shouting for your summer fruits and for your harvest is fallen.
10 And gladness is taken away, and joy out of the plentiful field; and in the vineyards there will be no singing, neither will there be shouting: the treaders will tread out no wine in *their* presses; I have made *their vintage* shouting to cease.
11 Wherefore my bowels will sound like a harp for Moab, and mine inward parts for Kir-haresh.
12 And it will come to pass, when it is seen that Moab is weary on the high place, that he will come to his sanctuary to pray; but he will not prevail.
13 This *is* the word that the LORD has spoken concerning Moab since that time.

---

[1] bewray- a primitive root; to denude (especially in a disgraceful sense); by implication to exile (captives being usually stripped); figuratively to reveal:-+ advertise, appear, bring, (carry, lead, go) captive (into captivity), depart, disclose, discover, publish, remove, uncover. [Strgs#1540]
[2] Kirhareseth- a place in Moab. It is translated as *wall of potsherds* or fortress of earthenware. [Strgs#7025]

14 But now the LORD has spoken, saying, within three years, as the years of a hireling, and the glory of Moab will be contemned, with all that great multitude; and the remnant will *be* very small *and* feeble.

CHAPTER 17

1 The burden of Damascus. Behold, Damascus is taken away from *being* a city, and it will be a ruinous heap.
2 The cities of Aroer[1] *are* forsaken: they will be for flocks, which will lie down, and none will make *them* afraid.
3 The fortress also will cease from Ephraim, and the kingdom from Damascus, and the remnant of Syria: they will be as the glory of the children of Israel, said the LORD of hosts.
4 And in that day it will come to pass, *that* the glory of Jacob will be made thin, and the fatness of his flesh will wax lean.
5 And it will be as when the harvestman gathers the corn, and reaps the ears with his arm; and it will be as he that gathers ears in the valley of Rephaim.
6 Yet gleaning grapes will be left in it, as the shaking of an olive tree, two *or* three berries in the top of the uppermost bough, four *or* five in the outmost fruitful branches thereof, said the LORD God of Israel.
7 At that day will a man look to his Maker, and his eyes will have respect to the Holy One of Israel.
8 And he will not look to the altars, the work of his hands, neither will respect *that* which his fingers have made, either the groves, or the images.
9 In that day will his strong cities be as a forsaken bough, and an uppermost branch, which they left because of the children of Israel: and there will be desolation.
10 Because you have forgotten the God of your salvation, and have not been mindful of the rock of your strength, therefore will you plant pleasant plants, and will set it with strange slips:
11 In the day will you make your plant to grow, and in the morning will you make your seed to flourish: *but* the harvest will *be* a heap in the day of grief and of desperate sorrow.
12 Woe to the multitude of many people, *which* make a noise like the noise of the seas; and to the rushing of nations, *that* make a rushing like the rushing of mighty waters!
13 The nations will rush like the rushing of many waters: but *God* will rebuke them, and they will flee far off, and will be chased as the chaff of the mountains before the wind, and like a rolling thing before the whirlwind.
14 And behold at evening tide trouble; *and* before the morning he *is* not. This *is* the portion of them that spoil us, and the lot of them that rob us.

CHAPTER 18

1 Woe to the land shadowing with wings, which *is* beyond the rivers of Ethiopia:
2 That sends ambassadors by the sea, even in vessels of bulrushes upon the waters, *saying*, Go, you swift messengers, to a nation scattered and peeled, to a people terrible from their beginning hitherto; a nation meted out and trodden down, whose land the rivers have spoiled!
3 All you inhabitants of the world, and dwellers on the earth, see you, when he lifts up an ensign on the mountains; and when he blows a trumpet, hear ye.

4 For so the LORD said unto me, I will take my rest, and I will consider in my dwelling place like a clear heat upon herbs, *and* like a cloud of dew in the heat of harvest.
5 For afore the harvest, when the bud is perfect, and the sour grape is ripening in the flower, he will both cut off the sprigs with pruning hooks, and take away *and* cut down the branches.
6 They will be left together unto the fowls of the mountains and to the beasts of the earth: and the fowls will summer upon them, and all the beasts of the earth will winter upon them.
7 In that time will the present be brought unto the LORD of hosts of a people scattered and peeled, and from a people terrible from their beginning hitherto; a nation meted out and trodden under foot, whose land the rivers have spoiled, to the place of the name of the LORD of hosts, the mount Zion.

CHAPTER 19

1 The burden of Egypt. Behold, the LORD rides upon a swift cloud, and will come into Egypt: and the idols of Egypt will be moved at his presence, and the heart of Egypt will melt in the midst of it.
2 And I will set the Egyptians against the Egyptians: and they will fight every one against his brother, and every one against his neighbor; city against city, *and* kingdom against kingdom.
3 And the spirit of Egypt will fail in the midst thereof; and I will destroy the counsel thereof: and they will seek to the idols, and to the charmers, and to them that have familiar spirits, and to the wizards.
4 And the Egyptians will I give over into the hand of a cruel lord; and a fierce king will rule over them, said the Lord, the LORD of hosts.
5 And the waters will fail from the sea, and the river will be wasted and dried up.
6 And they will turn the rivers far away; *and* the brooks of defense will be emptied and dried up: the reeds and flags will wither.
7 The paper reeds by the brooks, by the mouth of the brooks, and everything sown by the brooks, will wither, be driven away, and be no *more*.
8 The fishers also will mourn, and all they that cast angle into the brooks will lament, and they that spread nets upon the waters will languish.
9 Moreover they that work in fine flax, and they that weave networks, will be confounded.
10 And they will be broken in the purposes thereof, all that make sluices *and* ponds for fish.
11 Surely the princes of Zoan *are* fools, the counsel of the wise counselors of Pharaoh is become brutish: how say you unto Pharaoh, I *am* the son of the wise, the son of ancient kings?
12 Where *are* they? Where *are* your wise *men*? And let them tell you now, and let them know what the LORD of hosts has purposed upon Egypt.
13 The princes of Zoan are become fools, the princes of Noph are deceived; they have also seduced Egypt, *even they that are* the stay of the tribes thereof.
14 The LORD has mingled a perverse spirit in the midst thereof: and they have caused Egypt to err in every work thereof, as a drunken *man* staggers in his vomit.
15 Neither will there be *any* work for Egypt, which the head or tail, branch or rush, may do.

---

[1] Aroer- *nudity of situation.* The name of three places in or near Palestine.

[Strgs#6177]

16 In that day will Egypt be like unto women: and it will be afraid and fear because of the shaking of the hand of the LORD of hosts, which he shakes over it.

17 And the land of Judah will be a terror unto Egypt, every one that makes mention thereof will be afraid in himself, because of the counsel of the LORD of hosts, which he has determined against it.

18 In that day will five cities in the land of Egypt speak the language of Canaan, and swear to the LORD of hosts; one will be called, The city of destruction.

19 In that day will there be an altar to the LORD in the midst of the land of Egypt, and a pillar at the border thereof to the LORD.

20 And it will be for a sign and for a witness unto the LORD of hosts in the land of Egypt: for they will cry unto the LORD because of the oppressors, and he will send them a savior, and a great one, and he will deliver them.

21 And the LORD will be known to Egypt, and the Egyptians will know the LORD in that day, and will do sacrifice and oblation; yea, they will vow a vow unto the LORD, and perform *it*.

22 And the LORD will smite Egypt: he will smite and heal *it*: and they will return *even* to the LORD, and he will be intreated of them, and will heal them.

23 In that day will there be a highway out of Egypt to Assyria, and the Assyrian will come into Egypt, and the Egyptian into Assyria, and the Egyptians will serve with the Assyrians.

24 In that day will Israel be the third with Egypt and with Assyria, *even* a blessing in the midst of the land:

25 Whom the LORD of hosts will bless, saying, Blessed *be* Egypt my people, and Assyria the work of my hands, and Israel mine inheritance.

CHAPTER 20

1 In the year that Tartan came unto Ashdod, (when Sargon the king of Assyria sent him,) and fought against Ashdod, and took it;

2 At the same time spoke the LORD by Isaiah the son of Amoz, saying, Go and loose the sackcloth from off your loins, and put off your shoe from your foot. And he did so, walking naked and barefoot.

3 And the LORD said, Like as my servant Isaiah has walked naked and barefoot three years *for* a sign and wonder upon Egypt and upon Ethiopia;

4 So will the king of Assyria lead away the Egyptians prisoners, and the Ethiopians captives, young and old, naked and barefoot, even with *their* buttocks uncovered, to the shame of Egypt.

5 And they will be afraid and ashamed of Ethiopia their expectation, and of Egypt their glory.

6 And the inhabitant of this isle will say in that day, Behold, such *is* our expectation, where we flee for help to be delivered from the king of Assyria: and how will we escape?

CHAPTER 21

1 The burden of the desert of the sea. As whirlwinds in the south pass through; *so* it cometh from the desert, from a terrible land.

2 A grievous vision is declared unto me; the treacherous dealer deals treacherously, and the spoiler spoils. Go up, O Elam: besiege, O Media; all the sighing thereof have I made to cease.

3 Therefore are my loins filled with pain: pangs have taken hold upon me, as the pangs of a woman that travails: I was bowed down at the hearing *of it*; I was dismayed at the seeing *of it*.

4 My heart panted, fearfulness affrighted me: the night of my pleasure has he turned into fear unto me.

5 Prepare the table, watch in the watchtower, eat, drink: arise, you princes, *and* anoint the shield.

6 For thus has the Lord said unto me, Go, set a watchman, let him declare what he sees.

7 And he saw a chariot *with* a couple of horsemen a chariot of asses, *and* a chariot of camels; and he hearkened diligently with much heed:

8 And he cried, A lion: My lord, I stand continually upon the watchtower in the daytime, and I am set in my ward whole nights:

9 And, behold, here cometh a chariot of men, *with* a couple of horsemen. And he answered and said, Babylon is fallen, is fallen; and all the graven images of her gods he has broken unto the ground.

10 O my threshing, and the corn of my floor: that which I have heard of the LORD of hosts, the God of Israel, have I declared unto you.

11 The burden of Dumah. He calls to me out of Seir, Watchman, what of the night? Watchman, what of the night?

12 The watchman said, the morning comes, and also the night: if you will enquire, enquire ye: return, come.

13 The burden upon Arabia. In the forest in Arabia will you lodge, O you travelling companies of Dedanim.

14 The inhabitants of the land of Tema brought water to him that was thirsty, they prevented with their bread him that fled.

15 For they fled from the swords, from the drawn sword, and from the bent bow, and from the grievousness of war.

16 For thus has the Lord said unto me, within a year, according to the years of a hireling, and all the glory of Kedar will fail:

17 And the residue of the number of archers, the mighty men of the children of Kedar, will be diminished: for the LORD God of Israel has spoken *it*.

CHAPTER 22

1 The burden of the valley of vision. What ails you now, that you are wholly gone up to the housetops?

2 You that are full of stirs, a tumultuous city, a joyous city: your slain *men are* not slain with the sword, or dead in battle.

3 All your rulers are fled together, they are bound by the archers: all that are found in you are bound together, *which* have fled from far.

4 Therefore said I, Look away from me; I will weep bitterly, labor not to comfort me, because of the spoiling of the daughter of my people.

5 For *it is* a day of trouble, and of treading down, and of perplexity by the Lord GOD of hosts in the valley of vision, breaking down the walls, and of crying to the mountains.

6 And Elam bare the quiver with chariots of men *and* horsemen, and Kir uncovered the shield.

7 And it will come to pass, *that* your choicest valleys will be full of chariots, and the horsemen will set themselves in array at the gate.

8 And he discovered the covering of Judah, and you did look in that day to the armor of the house of the forest.

9 you have seen also the breaches of the city of David, that they are many: and you gathered together the waters of the lower pool.

10 And you have numbered the houses of Jerusalem, and the houses have you broken down to fortify the wall.

11 you made also a ditch between the two walls for the water of the old pool: but you have not looked unto the maker thereof, neither had respect unto him that fashioned it long ago.

12 And in that day did the Lord GOD of hosts call to weeping, and to mourning, and to baldness, and to girding with sackcloth:

13 And behold joy and gladness, slaying oxen, and killing sheep, eating flesh, and drinking wine: let us eat and drink; for tomorrow we will die.
14 And it was revealed in mine ears by the LORD of hosts, surely this iniquity will not be purged from you till you die, said the Lord GOD of hosts.
15 Thus said the Lord GOD of hosts, Go, get you unto this treasurer, *even* unto Shebna, which *is* over the house, *and say*,
16 What have you here? And who have you here, that you have hewed you out a sepulcher here, *as* he that hews him out a sepulcher on high, *and* that graves an habitation for himself in a rock?
17 Behold, the LORD will carry you away with a mighty captivity, and will surely cover you.
18 He will surely violently turn and toss you *like* a ball into a large country: there will you die, and there the chariots of your glory will *be* the shame of your lord's house.
19 And I will drive you from your station, and from your state will he pull you down.
20 And it will come to pass in that day, that I will call my servant Eliakim the son of Hilkiah:
21 And I will clothe him with your robe, and strengthen him with your girdle, and I will commit your government into his hand: and he will be a father to the inhabitants of Jerusalem, and to the house of Judah.
22 And the key of the house of David will I lay upon his shoulder; so he will open, and none will shut; and he will shut, and none will open.
23 And I will fasten him *as* a nail in a sure place; and he will be for a glorious throne to his father's house.
24 And they will hang upon him all the glory of his father's house, the offspring and the issue, all vessels of small quantity, from the vessels of cups, even to all the vessels of flagons.
25 In that day, said the LORD of hosts, will the nail that is fastened in the sure place be removed, and be cut down, and fall; and the burden that *was* upon it will be cut off: for the LORD has spoken *it*.

CHAPTER 23

1 The burden of Tyre. Howl, you ships of Tarshish; for it is laid waste, so that there is no house, no entering in: from the land of Chittim it is revealed to them.
2 Be still, you inhabitants of the isle; you whom the merchants of Zidon, that pass over the sea, have replenished.
3 And by great waters the seed of Sihor, the harvest of the river, *is* her revenue; and she is a mart of nations.
4 Be you ashamed, O Zidon: for the sea has spoken, *even* the strength of the sea, saying, I travail not, or bring forth children, neither do I nourish up young men, or bring up virgins.
5 As at the report concerning Egypt, *so* will they be sorely pained at the report of Tyre.
6 Pass you over to Tarshish; howl, you inhabitants of the isle.
7 *Is* this your joyous *city*, whose antiquity *is* of ancient days? Her own feet will carry her afar off to sojourn.
8 Who has taken this counsel against Tyre, the crowning *city*, whose merchants *are* princes, whose traffickers *are* the honorable of the earth?
9 The LORD of hosts has purposed it, to stain the pride of all glory, *and* to bring into contempt all the honorable of the earth.
10 Pass through your land as a river, O daughter of Tarshish: *there is* no more strength.
11 He stretched out his hand over the sea, he shook the kingdoms: the LORD has given a commandment against the merchant *city*, to destroy the strong holds thereof.
12 And he said, you will no more rejoice, O you oppressed virgin, daughter of Zidon: arise, pass over to Chittim; there also will you have no rest.
13 Behold the land of the Chaldeans; this people was not, *till* the Assyrian founded it for them that dwell in the wilderness: they set up the towers thereof, they raised up the palaces thereof; *and* he brought it to ruin.
14 Howl, you ships of Tarshish: for your strength is laid waste.
15 And it will come to pass in that day, that Tyre will be forgotten seventy years, according to the days of one king: after the end of seventy years will Tyre sing as a harlot.
16 Take a harp, go about the city, you harlot that have been forgotten; make sweet melody, sing many songs, that you may be remembered.
17 And it will come to pass after the end of seventy years, that the LORD will visit Tyre, and she will turn to her hire, and will commit fornication with all the kingdoms of the world upon the face of the earth.
18 And her merchandise and her hire will be holiness to the LORD: it will not be treasured or laid up; for her merchandise will be for them that dwell before the LORD, to eat sufficiently, and for durable clothing.

CHAPTER 24

1 Behold, the LORD makes the earth empty, and makes it waste, and turns it upside down, and scatters abroad the inhabitants thereof.
2 And it will be, as with the people, so with the priest; as with the servant, so with his master; as with the maid, so with her mistress; as with the buyer, so with the seller; as with the lender, so with the borrower; as with the taker of usury, so with the giver of usury to him.
3 The land will be utterly emptied, and utterly spoiled: for the LORD has spoken this word.
4 The earth mourns *and* fades away, the world languishes *and* fades away, the haughty people of the earth do languish.
5 The earth also is defiled under the inhabitants thereof; because they have transgressed the laws, changed the ordinance, broken the everlasting covenant.
6 Therefore has the curse devoured the earth, and they that dwell therein are desolate: therefore the inhabitants of the earth are burned, and few men left.
7 The new wine mourns, the vine languishes, all the merry-hearted do sigh.
8 The mirth of tambourines ceases, the noise of them that rejoice ends, the joy of the harp ceases.
9 They will not drink wine with a song; strong drink will be bitter to them that drink it.
10 The city of confusion is broken down: every house is shut up, that no man may come in.
11 *There is* a crying for wine in the streets; all joy is darkened, the mirth of the land is gone.
12 In the city is left desolation, and the gate is smitten with destruction.
13 When thus it will be in the midst of the land among the people, *there will be* as the shaking of an olive tree, *and* as the gleaning grapes when the vintage is done.

14 They will lift up their voice, they will sing for the majesty of the LORD, they will cry aloud from the sea.
15 Wherefore glorify you the LORD in the fires, *even* the name of the LORD God of Israel in the isles of the sea.
16 From the uttermost part of the earth have we heard songs, *even* glory to the righteous. But I said, my leanness, my leanness, woe unto me! The treacherous dealers have dealt treacherously; yea, the treacherous dealers have dealt very treacherously.
17 Fear, and the pit, and the snare, *are* upon you, O inhabitant of the earth.
18 And it will come to pass, *that* he who flees from the noise of the fear will fall into the pit; and he that cometh up out of the midst of the pit will be taken in the snare: for the windows from on high are open, and the foundations of the earth do shake.
19 The earth is utterly broken down, the earth is clean dissolved, the earth is moved exceedingly.
20 The earth will reel to and fro like a drunkard, and will be removed like a cottage; and the transgression thereof will be heavy upon it; and it will fall, and not rise again.
21 And it will come to pass in that day, *that* the LORD will punish the host of the high ones *that are* on high, and the kings of the earth upon the earth.
22 And they will be gathered together, *as* prisoners are gathered in the pit, and will be shut up in the prison, and after many days will they be visited.
23 Then the moon will be confounded, and the sun ashamed, when the LORD of hosts will reign in mount Zion, and in Jerusalem, and before his ancients gloriously.

CHAPTER 25

1 O LORD, you are my God; I will exalt you, I will praise your name; for you have done wonderful *things; your* counsels of old *are* faithfulness *and* truth.
2 For you have made of a city a heap; *of* a defended city a ruin: a palace of strangers to be no city; it will never be built.
3 Therefore will the strong people glorify you, the city of the terrible nations will fear you.
4 For you have been a strength to the poor, a strength to the needy in his distress, a refuge from the storm, a shadow from the heat, when the blast of the terrible ones *is* as a storm *against* the wall.
5 you will bring down the noise of strangers, as the heat in a dry place; *even* the heat with the shadow of a cloud: the branch of the terrible ones will be brought low.
6 And in this mountain will the LORD of hosts make unto all people a feast of fat things, a feast of wines on the lees, of fat things full of marrow, of wines on the lees well refined.
7 And he will destroy in this mountain the face of the covering cast over all people, and the veil that is spread over all nations.
8 He will swallow up death in victory; and the Lord GOD will wipe away tears from off all faces; and the rebuke of his people will he take away from off all the earth: for the LORD has spoken *it*.
9 And it will be said in that day, Lo, this *is* our God; we have waited for him, and he will save us: this *is* the LORD; we have waited for him, we will be glad and rejoice in his salvation.
10 For in this mountain will the hand of the LORD rest, and Moab will be trodden down under him, even as straw is trodden down for the dunghill.
11 And he will spread forth his hands in the midst of them, as he that swims spreads forth *his hands* to swim: and he will bring down their pride together with the spoils of their hands.
12 And the fortress of the high fort of your walls will he bring down, lay low, *and* bring to the ground, *even* to the dust.

CHAPTER 26

1 In that day will this song be sung in the land of Judah; we have a strong city; salvation will *God* appoint *for* walls and bulwarks.
2 Open you the gates, that the righteous nation which keeps the truth may enter in.
3 you will keep *him* in perfect peace, *whose* mind *is* stayed *on you*: because he trusts in you.
4 Trust you in the LORD for ever: for in the LORD JEHOVAH *is* everlasting strength:
5 For he brings down them that dwell on high; the lofty city, he lays it low; he lays it low, *even* to the ground; he brings it *even* to the dust.
6 The foot will tread it down, *even* the feet of the poor, *and* the steps of the needy.
7 The way of the just *is* uprightness: thou, most upright, dost weigh the path of the just.
8 Yea, in the way of your judgments, O LORD, have we waited for you; the desire of *our* soul *is* to your name, and to the remembrance of you.
9 With my soul have I desired you in the night; yes, with my spirit within me will I seek you early: for when your judgments *are* in the earth, the inhabitants of the world will learn righteousness.
10 Let favor be showed to the wicked, *yet* will he not learn righteousness: in the land of uprightness will he deal unjustly, and will not behold the majesty of the LORD.
11 LORD, *when* your hand is lifted up, they will not see: *but* they will see, and be ashamed for *their* envy at the people: yea, the fire of your enemies will devour them.
12 LORD, you will ordain peace for us: for you also have wrought all our works in us.
13 O LORD our God, *other* lords beside you have had dominion over us: *but* by you only will we make mention of your name.
14 *They are* dead, they will not live; *they are* deceased, they will not rise: therefore have you visited and destroyed them, and made all their memory to perish.
15 You have increased the nation, O LORD, you have increased the nation: you are glorified: you had removed *it* far *unto* all the ends of the earth.
16 LORD, in trouble have they visited you, they poured out a prayer *when* your chastening *was* upon them.
17 Like as a woman with child, *that* draws near the time of her delivery, is in pain, *and* cries out in her pangs; so have we been in your sight, O LORD.
18 [We have been with child, we have been in pain, we have as it were brought forth wind[1]; we have not wrought any deliverance in the earth; neither have the inhabitants[2] of the world fallen.][3]
19 your dead *men* will live, *together with* my dead body will they arise. Awake and sing, you that dwell in dust: for your dew *is as* the dew of herbs, and the earth will cast out the dead.
20 Come, my people, enter you into your chambers, and shut your doors about you: hide yourself as it were for a little moment, until the indignation be over-past.

---

[1] Wind of Doctrine, compare **Eph. 4:14**.
[2] inhabitants – *to sit down as judge, in ambush,* to *dwell,* to *remain,* to *settle,* to *marry* [Strgs#3427]. Seat = throne, powers of darkness.
[3] Our wind of doctrine have not delivered people from the seat of demons.

21 For, behold, the LORD cometh out of his place to punish the inhabitants of the earth for their iniquity: the earth also will disclose her blood, and will no more cover her slain.

CHAPTER 27

1 In that day the LORD with his sore and great and strong sword will punish leviathan the piercing serpent, even leviathan that crooked serpent; and he will slay the dragon that *is* in the sea.
2 In that day sing you unto her, a vineyard of red wine.
3 I the LORD do keep it; I will water it every moment: lest *any* hurt it, I will keep it night and day.
4 Fury *is* not in me: who would set the briers *and* thorns against me in battle? I would go through them, I would burn them together.
5 Or let him take hold of my strength, *that* he may make peace with me; *and* he will make peace with me.
6 He will cause them that come of Jacob to take root: Israel will blossom and bud, and fill the face of the world with fruit.
7 Has he smitten him, as he smote those that smote him? *Or* is he slain according to the slaughter of them that are slain by him?
8 In measure, when it shoots forth, you will debate with it: he stays his rough wind in the day of the east wind.
9 By this therefore will the iniquity of Jacob be purged; and this *is* all the fruit to take away his sin; when he makes all the stones of the altar as chalkstones that are beaten in sunder, the groves and images will not stand up.
10 Yet the defended city will *be* desolate, *and* the habitation forsaken, and left like a wilderness: there will the calf feed, and there will he lie down, and consume the branches thereof.
11 When the boughs thereof are withered, they will be broken off: the women come, *and* set them on fire: for it *is* a people of no understanding: therefore he that made them will not have mercy on them, and he that formed them will show them no favor.
12 And it will come to pass in that day, *that* the LORD will beat off from the channel of the river unto the stream of Egypt, and you will be gathered one by one, O you children of Israel.
13 And it will come to pass in that day, *that* the great trumpet will be blown, and they will come which were ready to perish in the land of Assyria, and the outcasts in the land of Egypt, and will worship the LORD in the holy mount at Jerusalem.

CHAPTER 28

1 Woe to the crown of pride, to the drunkards of Ephraim, whose glorious beauty *is* a fading flower, which *are* on the head of the fat valleys of them that are overcome with wine!
2 Behold, the Lord has a mighty and strong one, *which* as a tempest of hail *and* a destroying storm, as a flood of mighty waters overflowing, will cast down to the earth with the hand.
3 The crown of pride, the drunkards of Ephraim, will be trodden under feet:
4 And the glorious beauty, which *is* on the head of the fat valley, will be a fading flower, *and* as the hasty fruit before the summer; which *when* he that looks upon it sees, while it is yet in his hand he eats it up.
5 In that day will the LORD of hosts be for a crown of glory, and for a diadem of beauty, unto the residue of his people,
6 And for a spirit of judgment to him that sits in judgment, and for strength to them that turn the battle to the gate.
7 But they also have erred through wine, and through strong drink are out of the way; the priest and the prophet have erred through strong drink, they are swallowed up of wine, they are out of the way through strong drink; they err in vision, they stumble *in* judgment.
8 For all tables are full of vomit *and* filthiness, *so that there is* no place clean.
9 Whom will he teach knowledge? And whom will he make to understand doctrine? *Them that are* weaned from the milk, *and* drawn from the breasts.
10 For precept *must be* upon precept, precept upon precept; line upon line, line upon line; here a little, *and* there a little:
11 For with stammering lips and another tongue will he speak to this people.
12 To whom he said, this *is* the rest wherewith you may cause the weary to rest; and this *is* the refreshing: yet they would not hear.
13 But the word of the LORD was unto them precept upon precept, precept upon precept; line upon line, line upon line; here a little, *and* there a little; that they might go, and fall backward, and be broken, and snared, and taken.
14 Wherefore hear the word of the LORD, you scornful men, that rule this people which *is* in Jerusalem.
15 Because you have said, We have made a covenant with death, and with hell are we at agreement; when the overflowing scourge will pass through, it will not come unto us: for we have made lies our refuge, and under falsehood have we hid ourselves:
16 Therefore thus said the Lord GOD, Behold, I lay in Zion for a foundation a stone, a tried stone, a precious corner *stone*, a sure foundation: he that believeth will not make haste.
17 Judgment also will I lay to the line, and righteousness to the plummet: and the hail will sweep away the refuge of lies, and the waters will overflow the hiding place.
18 And your covenant with death will be disannulled, and your agreement with hell will not stand; when the overflowing scourge will pass through, then you will be trodden down by it.
19 From the time that it goes forth it will take you: for morning by morning will it pass over, by day and by night: and it will be a vexation only *to* understand the report.
20 For the bed is shorter than that *a man* can stretch himself *on it*: and the covering narrower than that he can wrap himself *in it*.
21 For the LORD will rise up as *in* mount Perazim, he will be **angry** as *in* the valley of Gibeon, that he may do his work, his strange work; and bring to pass his act, his strange act.
22 Now therefore be you not mockers, lest your bands be made strong: for I have heard from the Lord GOD of hosts a consumption, even determined upon the whole earth.
23 Give you ear, and hear my voice; hearken, and hear my speech.
24 Does the plowman plow all day to sow? Does he open and break the clods of his ground?
25 When he has made plain the face thereof, does he not cast abroad the fitches, and scatter the cummin[1], and cast in the principal wheat and the appointed barley and the **rye** in their place?
26 For his God does instruct him to discretion, *and* does teach him.
27 For the fitches are not threshed with a threshing instrument, neither is a cart wheel turned about upon the cummin; but the fitches are beaten out with a staff, and the cummin with a rod.
28 Bread *corn* is bruised; because he will not ever be threshing it, or break *it with* the wheel of his cart, or bruise it *with* his horsemen.
29 This also cometh forth from the LORD of hosts, *which* is wonderful in counsel, *and* excellent in working.

---

[1] cummin- is the Hebrew word *kammôn*, kam-mone'; meaning to store up or preserve. [Strgs#3646]

CHAPTER 29

1 Woe to Ariel, to Ariel, the city *where* David dwelt! Add you year to year; let them kill sacrifices.
2 Yet I will distress Ariel, and there will be heaviness and sorrow: and it will be unto me as Ariel.
3 And I will camp against you round about, and will lay siege against you with a mount, and I will raise forts against you.
4 And you will be brought down, *and* will speak out of the ground, and your speech will be low out of the dust, and your voice will be, as of one that has a familiar spirit, out of the ground, and your speech will whisper out of the dust.
5 Moreover the multitude of your strangers will be like small dust, and the multitude of the terrible ones will *be* as chaff that passes away: yea, it will be at an instant suddenly.
6 you will be visited of the LORD of hosts with thunder, and with earthquake, and great noise, with storm and tempest, and the flame of devouring fire.
7 And the multitude of all the nations that fight against Ariel, even all that fight against her and her munitions, and that distress her, will be as a dream of a night vision.
8 It will even be as when an hungry *man* dreams, and, behold, he eats; but he awakes, and his soul is empty: or as when a thirsty man dreams, and, behold, he drinks; but he awakes, and, behold, *he is* faint, and his soul has appetite: so will the multitude of all the nations be, that fight against mount Zion.
9 Stay yourselves, and wonder; cry you out, and cry: they are drunken, but not with wine; they stagger, but not with strong drink.
10 For the LORD has poured out upon you the spirit of deep sleep, and has closed your eyes: the prophets and your rulers, the seers has he covered.
11 And the vision of all is become unto you as the words of a book that is sealed, which *men* deliver to one that is learned, saying, Read this, I pray you: and he said, I cannot; for it *is* sealed:
12 And the book is delivered to him that is not learned, saying, Read this, I pray you: and he said, I am not learned.
13 ¶ Wherefore the Lord said, Forasmuch as this people draw near *me* with their mouth, and with their lips do honor me, but have removed their heart far from me, and their fear toward me is taught by the precept of men:
14 Therefore, behold, I will proceed to do a marvelous work among this people, *even* a marvelous work and a wonder: for the wisdom of their wise *men* will perish, and the understanding of their prudent *men* will be hid.
15 Woe unto them that seek deep to hide their counsel from the LORD, and their works are in the dark, and they say, who sees us? And who knows us?
16 Surely your turning of things upside down will be esteemed as the potter's clay: for will the work say of him that made it, He made me not? Or will the thing framed say of him that framed it, He had no understanding?
17 *Is* it not yet a very little while, and Lebanon will be turned into a fruitful field, and the fruitful field will be esteemed as a forest?
18 And in that day will the deaf hear the words of the book, and the eyes of the blind will see out of obscurity, and out of darkness.
19 The meek also will increase *their* joy in the LORD, and the poor among men will rejoice in the Holy One of Israel.
20 For the terrible one is brought to nought, and the scorner is consumed, and all that watch for iniquity are cut off:
21 That make a man an offender for a word, and lay a snare for him that reproves in the gate, and turn aside the just for a thing of nought.
22 Therefore thus said the LORD, who redeemed Abraham, concerning the house of Jacob, Jacob will not now be ashamed, neither will his face now wax pale.
23 But when he sees his children, the work of mine hands, in the midst of him, they will sanctify my name, and sanctify the Holy One of Jacob, and will fear the God of Israel.
24 They also that erred in spirit will come to understanding, and they that murmured will learn doctrine.

CHAPTER 30

1 Woe to the rebellious children, said the LORD, that take counsel, but not of me; and that cover with a covering, but not of my spirit, that they may add sin to sin:
2 That walk to go down into Egypt, and have not asked at my mouth; to strengthen themselves in the strength of Pharaoh, and to trust in the shadow of Egypt!
3 Therefore will the strength of Pharaoh be your shame, and the trust in the shadow of Egypt *your* confusion.
4 For his princes were at Zoan, and his ambassadors came to Hanes.
5 They were all ashamed of a people *that* could not profit them, or be an help or profit, but a shame, and also a reproach.
6 The burden of the beasts of the south: into the land of trouble and anguish, from where *come* the young and old lion, the viper and fiery flying serpent, they will carry their riches upon the shoulders of young asses, and their treasures upon the bunches of camels, to a people *that* will not profit *them*.
7 For the Egyptians will help in vain, and to no purpose: therefore have I cried concerning this, their strength *is* to sit still.
8 Now go, write it before them in a table, and note it in a book, that it may be for the time to come forever and ever:
9 That this *is* a rebellious people, lying children, children *that* will not hear the law of the LORD:
10 Which say to the seers, See not; and to the prophets, prophesy not unto us right things, speak unto us smooth things, prophesy deceits:
11 Get you out of the way, turn aside out of the path, cause the Holy One of Israel to cease from before us.
12 Wherefore thus said the Holy One of Israel, Because you despise this word, and trust in oppression and perverseness, and stay thereon:
13 Therefore this iniquity will be to you as a breach ready to fall, swelling out in a high wall, whose breaking cometh suddenly at an instant.
14 And he will break it as the breaking of the potters' vessel that is broken in pieces; he will not spare: so that there will not be found in the bursting of it a sherd to take fire from the hearth, or to take water *withal* out of the pit.
15 For thus said the Lord GOD, the Holy One of Israel; in returning and rest will you be saved; in quietness and in confidence will be your strength: and you would not.
16 But you said, No; for we will flee upon horses; therefore will you flee: and, we will ride upon the swift; therefore will they that pursue you be swift.
17 One thousand will *flee* at the rebuke of one; at the rebuke of five will you flee: till you be left as a beacon upon the top of a mountain, and as an ensign on an hill.

18 And therefore will the LORD wait, that he may be gracious unto you, and therefore will he be exalted, that he may have mercy upon you: for the LORD *is* a God of judgment: blessed *are* all they that wait for him.
19 For the people will dwell in Zion at Jerusalem: you will weep no more: he will be very gracious unto you at the voice of your cry; when he will hear it, he will answer you.
20 And *though* the Lord give you the bread of adversity, and the water of affliction, yet will not your teachers be removed into a corner any more, but your eyes will see your teachers:
21 And your ears will hear a word behind you, saying, this *is* the way, walk you in it, when you turn to the right hand, and when you turn to the left.
22 You will defile also the covering of your graven images of silver, and the ornament of your molten images of gold: you will cast them away as a menstruous[1] cloth; you will say unto it, get you hence.
23 Then will he give the rain of your seed, that you will sow the ground withal; and bread of the increase of the earth, and it will be fat and plenteous: in that day will your cattle feed in large pastures.
24 The oxen likewise and the young asses that ear the ground will eat clean provender, which has been winnowed with the shovel and with the fan.
25 And there will be upon every high mountain, and upon every high hill, rivers *and* streams of waters in the day of the great slaughter, when the towers fall.
26 Moreover the light of the moon will be as the light of the sun, and the light of the sun will be sevenfold, as the light of seven days, in the day that the LORD binds up the breach of his people, and heals the stroke of their wound.
27 Behold, the name of the LORD cometh from far, burning *with* his anger, and the burden *thereof is* heavy: his lips are full of indignation, and his tongue as a devouring fire:
28 And his breath, as an overflowing stream, will reach to the midst of the neck, to sift the nations with the sieve of vanity: and *there will be* a bridle in the jaws of the people, causing *them* to err.
29 you will have a song, as in the night *when* a holy solemnity is kept; and gladness of heart, as when one goes with a pipe to come into the mountain of the LORD, to the mighty One of Israel.
30 And the LORD will cause his glorious voice to be heard, and will show the lighting down of his arm, with the indignation of *his* anger, and *with* the flame of a devouring fire, *with* scattering, and tempest, and hailstones.
31 For through the voice of the LORD will the Assyrian be beaten down, *which* smote with a rod.
32 And *in* every place where the grounded staff will pass, which the LORD will lay upon him, *it* will be with tambourines and harps: and in battles of shaking will he fight with it.
33 For Tophet[2] *is* ordained of old; yea, for the king it is prepared; he has made *it* deep *and* large: the pile thereof *is* fire and much wood; the breath of the LORD, like a stream of brimstone, does kindle it.

CHAPTER 31

1 Woe to them that go down to Egypt for help; and stay on horses, and trust in chariots, because *they are* many; and in horsemen, because they are very strong; but they look not unto the Holy One of Israel, neither seek the LORD!
2 Yet he also *is* wise, and will bring evil, and will not call back his words: but will arise against the house of the evildoers, and against the help of them that work iniquity.
3 Now the Egyptians *are* men, and not God; and their horses flesh, and not spirit. When the LORD will stretch out his hand, both he that helps will fall, and he that is holpen[3] will fall down, and they all will fail together.
4 For thus has the LORD spoken unto me, Like as the lion and the young lion roaring on his prey, when a multitude of shepherds is called forth against him, *he* will not be afraid of their voice, or abase himself for the noise of them: so will the LORD of hosts come down to fight for mount Zion, and for the hill thereof.
5 As birds flying, so will the LORD of hosts defend Jerusalem; defending also he will deliver *it; and* passing over he will preserve it.
6 Turn you unto *him from* whom the children of Israel have deeply revolted.
7 For in that day every man will cast away his idols of silver, and his idols of gold, which your own hands have made unto you *for* a sin.
8 Then will the Assyrian fall with the sword, not of a mighty man; and the sword, not of a mean man, will devour him: but he will flee from the sword, and his young men will be discomfited.
9 And he will pass over to his strong hold for fear, and his princes will be afraid of the ensign, said the LORD, whose fire *is* in Zion, and his furnace in Jerusalem.

CHAPTER 32

1 Behold, a king will reign in righteousness, and princes will rule in judgment.
2 And a man will be as a hiding place from the wind, and a covert from the tempest; as rivers of water in a dry place, as the shadow of a great rock in a weary land.
3 And the eyes of them that see will not be dim, and the ears of them that hear will hearken.
4 The heart also of the rash will understand knowledge and the tongue of the stammerers will be ready to speak plainly.
5 The vile person will be no more called liberal, or the churl said *to be* bountiful.
6 For the vile person will speak villainy, and his heart will work iniquity, to practice hypocrisy, and to utter error against the LORD, to make empty the soul of the hungry, and he will cause the drink of the thirsty to fail.
7 The instruments also of the churl *are* evil: he devises wicked devices to destroy the poor with lying words, even when the needy speaks right.
8 But the liberal devises liberal things; and by liberal things will he stand.
9 Rise up, you women that are at ease; hear my voice, you careless daughters; give ear unto my speech.
10 Many days and years will you be troubled, you careless women: for the vintage will fail, the gathering will not come.
11 Tremble, you women that are at ease; be troubled, you careless ones: strip you, and make you bare, and gird *sackcloth* upon *your* loins.
12 They will lament for the teats, for the pleasant fields, for the fruitful vine.

---

[1] menstruous- *sick*, (especially in Menstruation):- faint, menstruous cloth, she that is sick, having sickness. [Strgs#1739]
[2] Tophet- *place of fire*. Probably a form of *Topheh*, a place of cremation. A place in the southeast end of the valley of the son of Hinnom, south of Jerusalem. [Strgs#8613]
[3] holpen- is the Hebrew word *'âzar*, <u>awzar'</u>; which is a primitive root, to *surround*, that is *protect* or *aid*:- help, succor. [Strgs#5826]

13 Upon the land of my people will come up thorns *and* briers; yea, upon all the houses of joy *in* the joyous city:
14 Because the palaces will be forsaken; the multitude of the city will be left; the forts and towers will be for dens forever, a joy of wild asses, a pasture of flocks;
15 Until the spirit be poured upon us from on high, and the wilderness be a fruitful field, and the fruitful field be counted for a forest.
16 Then judgment will dwell in the wilderness, and righteousness remain in the fruitful field.
17 And the work of righteousness will be peace; and the effect of righteousness quietness and assurance forever.
18 And my people will dwell in a peaceable habitation, and in sure dwellings, and in quiet resting places;
19 When it will hail, coming down on the forest; and the city will be low in a low place.
20 Blessed *are* you that sow beside all waters, that send forth there the feet of the ox and the ass.

CHAPTER 33

1 Woe to you that spoils and you were not spoiled; and deals treacherously, and they dealt not treacherously with you! When you will cease to spoil, you will be spoiled; *and* when you will make an end to deal treacherously, they will deal treacherously with you.
2 O LORD, be gracious unto us; we have waited for you: be you their arm every morning, our salvation also in the time of trouble.
3 At the noise of the tumult the people fled; at the lifting up of yourself the nations were scattered.
4 And your spoil will be gathered *like* the gathering of the caterpiller: as the running to and fro of locusts will he run upon them.
5 The LORD is exalted; for he dwells on high: he has filled Zion with judgment and righteousness.
6 And wisdom and knowledge will be the stability of your times, *and* strength of salvation: the fear of the LORD *is* his treasure.
7 Behold, their valiant ones will cry without: the ambassadors of peace will weep bitterly.
8 The highways lie waste, the wayfaring man ceases: he has broken the covenant, he has despised the cities, he regards no man.
9 The earth mourns *and* languishes: Lebanon is ashamed *and* hewn down: Sharon is like a wilderness; and Bashan and Carmel shake off *their fruits*.
10 Now will I rise, said the LORD; now will I be exalted; now will I lift up myself.
11 you will conceive chaff, you will bring forth stubble: your breath, *as* fire, will devour you.
12 And the people will be *as* the burnings of lime: *as* thorns cut up will they be burned in the fire.
13 Hear, you *that are* far off, what I have done; and, you *that are* near, acknowledge my might.
14 The sinners in Zion are afraid; fearfulness has surprised the hypocrites. Who among us will dwell with the devouring fire? Who among us will dwell with everlasting burnings?
15 He that walks righteously, and speaks uprightly; he that despises the gain of oppressions, that shakes his hands from holding of bribes, that stops his ears from hearing of blood, and shuts his eyes from seeing evil;
16 He will dwell on high: his place of defense will *be* the munitions of rocks: bread will be given him; his waters will *be* sure.
17 your eyes will see the king in his beauty: they will behold the land that is very far off.
18 your heart will meditate terror. Where *is* the scribe? Where *is* the receiver? Where *is* he that counted the towers?
19 you will not see a fierce people, a people of a deeper speech than you canst perceive; of a stammering tongue, *that you canst* not understand.
20 Look upon Zion, the city of our solemnities: your eyes will see Jerusalem a quiet habitation, a tabernacle *that* will not be taken down; not one of the stakes thereof will ever be removed, neither will any of the cords thereof be broken.
21 But there the glorious LORD *will be* unto us a place of broad rivers *and* streams; wherein will go no galley with oars, neither will gallant ship pass thereby.
22 For the LORD *is* our judge, the LORD *is* our lawgiver, the LORD *is* our king; he will save us.
23 Your tacklings are loosed; they could not well strengthen their mast, they could not spread the sail: then is the prey of a great spoil divided; the lame take the prey.
24 And the inhabitant will not say, I am sick: the people that dwell therein will *be* forgiven *their* iniquity.

CHAPTER 34

1 Come near, you nations, to hear; and hearken, you people: let the earth hear, and all that is therein; the world, and all things that come forth of it.
2 For the indignation of the LORD *is* upon all nations, and *his* fury upon all their armies: he has utterly destroyed them, he has delivered them to the slaughter.
3 Their slain also will be cast out, and their stink will come up out of their carcasses, and the mountains will be melted with their blood.
4 And all the host of heaven will be dissolved, and the heavens will be rolled together as a scroll: and all their host will fall down, as the leaf falls off from the vine, and as a falling *fig* from the fig tree.
5 For my sword will be bathed in heaven: behold, it will come down upon Idumea, and upon the people of my curse, to judgment.
6 The sword of the LORD is filled with blood, it is made fat with fatness, *and* with the blood of lambs and goats, with the fat of the kidneys of rams: for the LORD has a sacrifice in Bozrah, and a great slaughter in the land of Idumea.
7 And the unicorns will come down with them, and the bullocks with the bulls; and their land will be soaked with blood, and their dust made fat with fatness.
8 For *it is* the day of the LORD'S vengeance, *and* the year of recompences for the controversy of Zion.
9 And the streams thereof will be turned into pitch, and the dust thereof into brimstone, and the land thereof will become burning pitch.
10 It will not be quenched night or day; the smoke thereof will go up forever: from generation to generation it will lie waste; none will pass through it forever and ever.
11 But the cormorant and the bittern will possess it; the owl also and the raven will dwell in it: and he will stretch out upon it the line of confusion, and the stones of emptiness.
12 They will call the nobles thereof to the kingdom, but none will *be* there, and all her princes will be nothing.
13 And thorns will come up in her palaces, nettles and brambles in the fortresses thereof: and it will be a habitation of dragons, *and* a court for owls.

14 The wild beasts of the desert will also meet with the wild beasts of the island, and the satyr will cry to his fellow; the screech owl also will rest there, and find for herself a place of rest.
15 There will the great owl make her nest, and lay, and hatch, and gather under her shadow: there will the vultures also be gathered, everyone with her mate.
16 Seek you out of the book of the LORD, and read: no one of these will fail, none will want her mate: for my mouth it has commanded, and his spirit it has gathered them.
17 And he has cast the lot for them, and his hand has divided it unto them by line: they will possess it forever, from generation to generation will they dwell therein.

CHAPTER 35

1 The wilderness and the solitary place will be glad for them; and the desert will rejoice, and blossom as the rose.
2 It will blossom abundantly, and rejoice even with joy and singing: the glory of Lebanon will be given unto it, the excellency of Carmel and Sharon, they will see the glory of the LORD, *and* the excellency of our God.
3 Strengthen you the weak hands, and confirm the feeble knees.
4 Say to them *that are* of a fearful heart, Be strong, fear not: behold, your God will come *with* vengeance, *even* God *with* a recompence; he will come and save you.
5 Then the eyes of the blind will be opened, and the ears of the deaf will be unstopped.
6 Then will the lame *man* leap as an hart, and the tongue of the dumb sing: for in the wilderness will waters break out, and streams in the desert.
7 And the parched ground will become a pool, and the thirsty land springs of water: in the habitation of dragons, where each lay, will *be* grass with reeds and rushes.
8 And an highway will be there, and a way, and it will be called The way of holiness; the unclean will not pass over it; but it will *be* for those: the wayfaring men, though fools, will not err *therein*.
9 No lion will be there, or *any* ravenous beast will go up thereon, it will not be found there; but the redeemed will walk *there*:
10 And the ransomed of the LORD will return, and come to Zion with songs and everlasting joy upon their heads: they will obtain joy and gladness, and sorrow and sighing will flee away.

CHAPTER 36

1 Now it came to pass in the fourteenth year of King Hezekiah[1], *that* Sennacherib king of Assyria came up against all the defenced cities of Judah, and took them.
2 And the king of Assyria sent Rabshakeh from Lachish to Jerusalem unto king Hezekiah with a great army. And he stood by the conduit of the upper pool in the highway of the fuller's field.
3 Then came forth unto him Eliakim, Hilkiah's son, which was over the house, and Shebna the scribe, and Joah, Asaph's son, the recorder.
4 And Rabshakeh said unto them, Say you now to Hezekiah, Thus said the great king, the king of Assyria, What confidence *is* this wherein you trustest?
5 I say, *sayest you*, (but *they are but* vain words) *I have* counsel and strength for war: now on whom dost you trust, that you rebells against me?
6 Lo, you trust in the staff of this broken reed, on Egypt; whereon if a man lean, it will go into his hand, and pierce it: so *is* Pharaoh king of Egypt to all that trust in him.

---

[1] Hezekiah- Jehovah is my strength or *strengthened of Jah*. [Strgs#2396]

7 But if you say to me, we trust in the LORD our God: *is it* not he, whose high places and whose altars Hezekiah has taken away, and said to Judah and to Jerusalem, you will worship before this altar?
8 Now therefore give pledges, I pray you, to my master the king of Assyria, and I will give you two thousand horses, if you be able on your part to set riders upon them.
9 How then will you turn away the face of one captain of the least of my master's servants, and put your trust on Egypt for chariots and for horsemen?
10 And am I now come up without the LORD against this land to destroy it? The LORD said unto me, Go up against this land, and destroy it.
11 Then said Eliakim and Shebna and Joah unto Rabshakeh, Speak, I pray you, unto your servants in the Syrian language; for we understand *it*: and speak not to us in the Jews' language, in the ears of the people that *are* on the wall.
12 But Rabshakeh said, has my master sent me to your master and to you to speak these words? Has *he* not *sent me* to the men that sit upon the wall, that they may eat their own dung, and drink their own piss with you?
13 Then Rabshakeh stood, and cried with a loud voice in the Jews' language, and said, hear you the words of the great king, the king of Assyria.
14 Thus said the king, Let not Hezekiah deceive you: for he will not be able to deliver you.
15 Neither let Hezekiah make you trust in the LORD, saying, The LORD will surely deliver us: this city will not be delivered into the hand of the king of Assyria.
16 Hearken not to Hezekiah: for thus said the king of Assyria, Make *an agreement* with me *by* a present, and come out to me: and eat you every one of his vine, and every one of his fig tree, and drink you every one the waters of his own cistern;
17 Until I come and take you away to a land like your own land, a land of corn and wine, a land of bread and vineyards.
18 *Beware* lest Hezekiah persuade you, saying, The LORD will deliver us. Has any of the gods of the nations delivered his land out of the hand of the king of Assyria?
19 Where *are* the gods of Hamath and Arphad? Where *are* the gods of Sepharvaim? And have they delivered Samaria out of my hand?
20 Who *are they* among all the gods of these lands, that have delivered their land out of my hand, that the LORD should deliver Jerusalem out of my hand?
21 But they held their peace, and answered him not a word: for the king's commandment was, saying, answer him not.
22 Then came Eliakim, the son of Hilkiah, that *was* over the household, and Shebna the scribe, and Joah, the son of Asaph, the recorder, to Hezekiah with *their* clothes rent, and told him the words of Rabshakeh.

CHAPTER 37

1 And it came to pass, when King Hezekiah heard *it*, that he rent his clothes, and covered himself with sackcloth, and went into the house of the LORD.
2 And he sent Eliakim, who *was* over the household, and Shebna the scribe, and the elders of the priests covered with sackcloth, unto Isaiah the prophet the son of Amoz.

3 And they said unto him, Thus said Hezekiah, This day *is* a day of trouble, and of rebuke, and of blasphemy: for the children are come to the birth, and *there is* not strength to bring forth.
4 It may be the LORD your God will hear the words of Rabshakeh, whom the king of Assyria his master has sent to reproach the living God, and will reprove the words which the LORD your God has heard: wherefore lift up your prayer for the remnant that is left.
5 So the servants of king Hezekiah came to Isaiah.
6 And Isaiah said unto them, Thus will you say unto your master, thus said the LORD, Be not afraid of the words that you have heard, wherewith the servants of the king of Assyria have blasphemed me.
7 Behold, I will send a blast upon him, and he will hear a rumor, and return to his own land; and I will cause him to fall by the sword in his own land.
8 So Rabshakeh returned, and found the king of Assyria warring against Libnah: for he had heard that he was departed from Lachish.
9 And he heard say concerning Tirhakah king of Ethiopia, He is come forth to make war with you. And when he heard *it*, he sent messengers to Hezekiah, saying,
10 Thus will you speak to Hezekiah king of Judah, saying, let not your God, in whom you trustest, deceive you, saying, Jerusalem will not be given into the hand of the king of Assyria.
11 Behold, you have heard what the kings of Assyria have done to all lands by destroying them utterly; and will you be delivered?
12 Have the gods of the nations delivered them which my fathers have destroyed, *as* Gozan, and Haran, and Rezeph, and the children of Eden which *were* in Telassar?
13 Where *is* the king of Hamath, and the king of Arphad, and the king of the city of Sepharvaim, Hena, and Ivah?
14 And Hezekiah received the letter from the hand of the messengers, and read it: and Hezekiah went up unto the house of the LORD, and spread it before the LORD.
15 And Hezekiah prayed unto the LORD, saying,
16 O LORD of hosts, God of Israel, that dwells *between* the cherubims, you are the God, *even* you alone, of all the kingdoms of the earth: you have made heaven and earth.
17 Incline your ear, O LORD, and hear; open your eyes, O LORD, and see: and hear all the words of Sennacherib, which has sent to reproach the living God.
18 Of a truth, LORD, the kings of Assyria have laid waste all the nations, and their countries,
19 And have cast their gods into the fire: for they *were* no gods, but the work of men's hands, wood and stone: therefore they have destroyed them.
20 Now therefore, O LORD our God, save us from his hand, that all the kingdoms of the earth may know that you are the LORD, *even* you only.
21 Then Isaiah the son of Amoz sent unto Hezekiah, saying, Thus said the LORD God of Israel, Whereas you have prayed to me against Sennacherib king of Assyria:
22 This *is* the word which the LORD has spoken concerning him; The virgin, the daughter of Zion, has despised you, *and* laughed you to scorn; the daughter of Jerusalem has shaken her head at you.
23 Whom have you reproached and blasphemed? And against whom have you exalted your voice, and lifted up your eyes on high? *Even* against the Holy One of Israel.
24 By your servants have you reproached the Lord, and have said, By the multitude of my chariots am I come up to the height of the mountains, to the sides of Lebanon; and I will cut down the tall cedars thereof, *and* the choice fir trees thereof: and I will enter into the height of his border, *and* the forest of his Carmel
25 I have digged, and drunk water; and with the sole of my feet have I dried up all the rivers of the besieged places.
26 have you not heard long ago, *how* I have done it; *and* of ancient times, that I have formed it? Now have I brought it to pass, that you should be to lay waste defenced cities *into* ruinous heaps.
27 Therefore their inhabitants *were* of small power, they were dismayed and confounded: they were *as* the grass of the field, and *as* the green herb, *as* the grass on the housetops, *and as* corn blasted before it be grown up.
28 But I know your abode, and your going out, and your coming in, and your rage against me.
29 Because your rage against me, and your tumult, is come up into mine ears, therefore will I put my hook in your nose, and my bridle in your lips, and I will turn you back by the way by which you came.
30 And this will *be* a sign unto you, you will eat *this* year such as grows of itself; and the second year that which springs of the same: and in the third year sow you, and reap, and plant vineyards, and eat the fruit thereof.
31 And the remnant that is escaped of the house of Judah will again take root downward, and bear fruit upward:
32 For out of Jerusalem will go forth a remnant, and they that escape out of mount Zion: the zeal of the LORD of hosts will do this.
33 Therefore thus said the LORD concerning the king of Assyria, He will not come into this city, or shoot an arrow there, or come before it with shields, or cast a bank against it.
34 By the way that he came, by the same will he return, and will not come into this city, said the LORD.
35 For I will defend this city to save it for mine own sake, and for my servant David's sake.
36 Then the angel of the LORD went forth, and smote in the camp of the Assyrians a hundred and fourscore and five thousand: and when they arose early in the morning, behold, they *were* all dead corpses.
37 So Sennacherib king of Assyria departed, and went and returned, and dwelt at Nineveh.
38 And it came to pass, as he was worshipping in the house of Nisroch his god, that Adrammelech and Sharezer his sons smote him with the sword; and they escaped into the land of Armenia: and Esar-haddon his son reigned in his stead.

CHAPTER 38

1 In those days was Hezekiah sick unto death. And Isaiah the prophet the son of Amoz came unto him, and said unto him, thus said the LORD, Set your house in order: for you will die, and not live.
2 Then Hezekiah turned his face toward the wall, and prayed unto the LORD,
3 And said, Remember now, O LORD, I beseech you, how I have walked before you in truth and with a perfect heart, and have done *that which is* good in your sight. And Hezekiah wept sore
4 Then came the word of the LORD to Isaiah, saying,
5 Go, and say to Hezekiah, Thus said the LORD, the God of David your father, I have heard your prayer, I have seen your tears: behold, I will add unto your days fifteen years.

6 And I will deliver you and this city out of the hand of the king of Assyria: and I will defend this city.
7 And this will be a sign unto you from the LORD, that the LORD will do this thing that he has spoken;
8 Behold, I will bring again the shadow of the degrees, which is gone down in the sun dial of Ahaz, ten degrees backward. So the sun returned ten degrees, by which degrees it was gone down.
9 The writing of Hezekiah king of Judah, when he had been sick, and was recovered of his sickness:
10 I said in the cutting off of my days, I will go to the gates of the grave: I am deprived of the residue of my years.
11 I said, I will not see the LORD, even the LORD, in the land of the living: I will behold man no more with the inhabitants of the world.
12 Mine age is departed, and is removed from me as a shepherd's tent: I have cut off like a weaver my life: he will cut me off with pining sickness: from day even tonight will you make an end of me.
13 I reckoned till morning, that, as a lion, so will he break all my bones: from day even tonight will you make an end of me.
14 Like a crane or a swallow, so did I chatter: I did mourn as a dove: mine eyes fail with looking upward: O LORD, I am oppressed; undertake for me.
15 What will I say? He has both spoken unto me, and himself has done it: I will go softly all my years in the bitterness of my soul.
16 O Lord, by these things men live, and in all these things is the life of my spirit: so will you recover me, and make me to live.
17 Behold, for peace I had great bitterness: but you have in love to my soul delivered it from the pit of corruption: for you have cast all my sins behind your back.
18 For the grave cannot praise you, death cannot celebrate you: they that go down into the pit cannot hope for your truth.
19 The living, the living, he will praise you, as I do this day: the father to the children will make known your truth.
20 The LORD was ready to save me: therefore we will sing my songs to the stringed instruments all the days of our life in the house of the LORD.
21 For Isaiah had said, let them take a lump of figs, and lay it for a plaister[1] upon the boil, and he will recover.
22 Hezekiah also had said, what is the sign that I will go up to the house of the LORD?

CHAPTER 39

1 At that time Merodach-baladan, the son of Baladan, king of Babylon, sent letters and a present to Hezekiah: for he had heard that he had been sick, and was recovered.
2 And Hezekiah was glad of them, and showed them the house of his precious things, the silver, and the gold, and the spices, and the precious ointment, and all the house of his armor, and all that was found in his treasures: there was nothing in his house, or in all his dominion, that Hezekiah showed them not.
3 Then came Isaiah the prophet unto king Hezekiah, and said unto him, What said these men? And from where came they unto you? And Hezekiah said, they are come from a far country unto me, even from Babylon.
4 Then said he, what have they seen in your house? And Hezekiah answered, All that is in mine house have they seen: there is nothing among my treasures that I have not showed them.
5 Then said Isaiah to Hezekiah, Hear the word of the LORD of hosts:
6 Behold, the days come, that all that is in your house, and that which your fathers have laid up in store until this day, will be carried to Babylon: nothing will be left, said the LORD.
7 And of your sons that will issue from you, which you will beget, will they take away; and they will be eunuchs in the palace of the king of Babylon.
8 Then said Hezekiah to Isaiah, Good is the word of the LORD which you have spoken. He said moreover, for there will be peace and truth in my days.

CHAPTER 40

1 Comfort you, comfort you my people, said your God.
2 Speak you comfortably to Jerusalem, and cry unto her, that her warfare is accomplished, that her iniquity is pardoned: for she has received of the LORD'S hand double for all her sins.
3 The voice of him that cries in the wilderness, prepare you the way of the LORD, make straight in the desert a highway for our God.
4 Every valley will be exalted, and every mountain and hill will be made low: and the crooked will be made straight and the rough places plain:
5 And the glory of the LORD will be revealed, and all flesh will see it together: for the mouth of the LORD has spoken it.
6 The voice said, Cry. And he said, what will I cry? All flesh is grass, and all the goodliness thereof is as the flower of the field:
7 The grass withers, the flower fades: because the spirit of the LORD blows upon it: surely the people is grass.
8 The grass withers, the flower fades: but the word of our God will stand for ever.
9 O Zion, that brings good tidings, get you up into the high mountain; O Jerusalem, that brings good tidings, lift up your voice with strength; lift it up, be not afraid; say unto the cities of Judah, Behold your God!
10 Behold, the Lord GOD will come with strong hand, and his arm will rule for him: behold, his reward is with him, and his work before him.
11 He will feed his flock like a shepherd: he will gather the lambs with his arm, and carry them in his bosom, and will gently lead those that are with young.
12 Who has measured the waters in the hollow of his hand, and meted out heaven with the span, and comprehended the dust of the earth in a measure, and weighed the mountains in scales, and the hills in a balance?
13 Who has directed the Spirit of the LORD, or being his counselor has taught him?
14 With whom took he counsel, and who instructed him, and taught him in the path of judgment, and taught him knowledge, and showed to him the way of understanding?
15 Behold, the nations are as a drop of a bucket, and are counted as the small dust of the balance: behold, he takes up the isles as a very little thing.
16 And Lebanon is not sufficient to burn, or the beasts thereof sufficient for a burnt offering.
17 All nations before him are as nothing; and they are counted to him less than nothing, and vanity.
18 To whom then will you liken God? or what likeness will you compare unto him?
19 The workman melts a graven image, and the goldsmith spreads it over with gold, and casts silver chains.

---

[1] plaister- a primitive root; properly to soften by rubbing or pressure; heance (medicinally) to apply as an emollient:- lay for a plaister. [Strgs#4799]

20 He that *is* so impoverished that he has no oblation chooses a tree *that* will not rot; he seeks unto him a cunning workman to prepare a graven image, *that* will not be moved.

21 Have you not known? Have you not heard? Has it not been told you from the beginning? Have you not understood from the foundations of the earth?

22 *It is* he that sits upon the circle of the earth, and the inhabitants thereof *are* as grasshoppers; that stretches out the heavens as a curtain, and spreads them out as a tent to dwell in:

23 That brings the princes to nothing; he makes the judges of the earth as vanity.

24 Yea, they will not be planted; yea, they will not be sown: yea, their stock will not take root in the earth: and he will also blow upon them, and they will wither, and the whirlwind will take them away as stubble.

25 To whom then will you liken me, or will I be equal? Said the Holy One.

26 Lift up your eyes on high, and behold who has created these *things*, that brings out their host by number: he calls them all by names by the greatness of his might, for that *he is* strong in power; not one fails.

27 Why say thou, O Jacob, and speaks, O Israel, My way is hid from the LORD, and my judgment is passed over from my God?

28 have you not known? Have you not heard, *that* the everlasting God, the LORD, the Creator of the ends of the earth, faint not, neither is weary? *There is* no searching of his understanding.

29 He gives power to the faint; and to *them that have* no might he increases strength.

30 Even the youths will faint and be weary, and the young men will utterly fall:

31 But they that wait upon the LORD will renew *their* strength; they will mount up with wings as eagles; they will run, and not be weary; *and* they will walk, and not faint.

CHAPTER 41

1 Keep silence before me, O islands; and let the people renew *their* strength: let them come near; then let them speak: let us come near together to judgment.

2 Who raised up the righteous *man* from the east, called him to his foot, gave the nations before him, and made *him* rule over kings? he gave *them* as the dust to his sword, *and* as driven stubble to his bow.

3 He pursued them, *and* passed safely; *even* by the way *that* he had not gone with his feet.

4 Who has wrought and done *it*, calling the generations from the beginning? I the LORD, the first, and with the last; I *am* he.

5 The isles saw *it*, and feared; the ends of the earth were afraid, drew near, and came.

6 They helped everyone his neighbor; and *every one* said to his brother, Be of good courage.

7 So the carpenter encouraged the goldsmith, *and* he that smoothes *with* the hammer him that smote the anvil, saying, it *is* ready for the sodering: and he fastened it with nails, *that* it should not be moved.

8 But thou, Israel, *are* my servant, Jacob whom I have chosen, the seed of Abraham my friend.

9 you whom I have taken from the ends of the earth, and called you from the chief men thereof, and said unto you, you are my servant; I have chosen you, and not cast you away.

10 Fear you not; for I *am* with you: be not dismayed; for I *am* your God: I will strengthen you; yea, I will help you; yea, I will uphold you with the right hand of my righteousness.

11 Behold, all they that were incensed against you will be ashamed and confounded: they will be as nothing; and they that strive with you will perish.

12 you will seek them, and will not find them, *even* them that contended with you: they that war against you will be as nothing, and as a thing of nought.

13 For I the LORD your God will hold your right hand, saying unto you, Fear not; I will help you.

14 Fear not, you worm Jacob, *and* you men of Israel; I will help you, said the LORD, and your redeemer, the Holy One of Israel.

15 Behold, I will make you a new sharp threshing instrument having teeth: you will thresh the mountains, and beat *them* small, and will make the hills as chaff.

16 you will fan them, and the wind will carry them away, and the whirlwind will scatter them: and you will rejoice in the LORD, *and* will glory in the Holy One of Israel.

17 *When* the poor and needy seek water, and *there is* none, *and* their tongue fails for thirst, I the LORD will hear them, I the God of Israel will not forsake them.

18 I will open rivers in high places, and fountains in the midst of the valleys: I will make the wilderness a pool of water, and the dry land springs of water.

19 I will plant in the wilderness the cedar, the shittah tree, and the myrtle, and the oil tree; I will set in the desert the fir tree, *and* the pine, and the box tree together:

20 That they may see, and know, and consider, and understand together, that the hand of the LORD has done this, and the Holy One of Israel has created it.

21 Produce your cause, said the LORD; bring forth your strong *reasons*, said the King of Jacob.

22 Let them bring *them* forth, and show us what will happen: let them show the former things, what they *be*, that we may consider them, and know the latter end of them; or declare us things for to come.

23 show the things that are to come hereafter, that we may know that you *are* gods: yea, do good, or do evil, that we may be dismayed, and behold *it* together.

24 Behold, you *are* of nothing, and your work of nought: an abomination *is he that* chooses you.

25 I have raised up *one* from the north, and he will come: from the rising of the sun will he call upon my name: and he will come upon princes as *upon* morter, and as the potter treads clay.

26 Who has declared from the beginning, that we may know? And beforetime, that we may say, He *is* righteous? Yea, *there is* none that shows, yea, *there is* none that declares, yea, *there is* none that hears your words.

27 The first will *say* to Zion, Behold, behold them: and I will give to Jerusalem one that brings good tidings.

28 For I beheld, and *there was* no man; even among them, and *there was* no counselor, that, when I asked of them, could answer a word.

29 Behold, they *are* all vanity; their works *are* nothing: their molten images *are* wind and confusion.

CHAPTER 42

1 Behold my servant, whom I uphold; mine elect, *in whom* my soul delights; I have put my spirit upon him: he will bring forth judgment to the Gentiles.

2 He will not cry, or lift up, or cause his voice to be heard in the street.
3 A bruised reed will he not break, and the smoking flax will he not quench: he will bring forth judgment unto truth.
4 He will not fail or be discouraged, till he have set judgment in the earth: and the isles will wait for his law.
5 Thus said God the LORD, he that created the heavens, and stretched them out; he that spread forth the earth, and that which cometh out of it; he that gives breath unto the people upon it, and spirit to them that walk therein:
6 I the LORD have called you in righteousness, and will hold your hand, and will keep you, and give you for a covenant of the people, for a light of the Gentiles;
7 To open the blind eyes, to bring out the prisoners from the prison, *and* them that sit in darkness out of the prison house.
8 I *am* the LORD: that *is* my name: and my glory will I not give to another, neither my praise to graven images.
9 Behold, the former things are come to pass, and new things do I declare: before they spring forth I tell you of them.
10 Sing unto the LORD a new song, *and* his praise from the end of the earth, you that go down to the sea, and all that is therein; the isles, and the inhabitants thereof.
11 Let the wilderness and the cities thereof lift up *their voice*, the villages *that* Kedar does inhabit: let the inhabitants of the rock sing, let them shout from the top of the mountains.
12 Let them give glory unto the LORD, and declare his praise in the islands.
13 The LORD will go forth as a mighty man, he will stir up jealousy like a man of war: he will cry, yea, roar; he will prevail against his enemies.
14 I have long time **held** my peace; I have been still, *and* refrained myself: *now* will I cry like a travailing woman; I will destroy and devour at once.
15 I will make waste mountains and hills, and dry up all their herbs; and I will make the rivers islands, and I will dry up the pools.
16 And I will bring the blind by a way *that* they knew not; I will lead them in paths *that* they have not known: I will make darkness light before them, and crooked things straight. These things will I do unto them, and not forsake them.
17 They will be turned back, they will be greatly ashamed, that trust in graven images, that say to the molten images, you *are* our gods.
18 Hear, you deaf; and look, you blind, that you may see.
19 Who *is* blind, but my servant? or deaf, as my messenger *that* I sent? Who *is* blind as *he that is* perfect, and blind as the LORD'S servant?
20 Seeing many things, but you observe not; opening the ears, but he hears not.
21 The LORD is well pleased for his righteousness' sake; he will magnify the law, and make *it* honorable.
22 But this *is* a people robbed and spoiled; *they are* all of them snared in holes, and they are hid in prison houses: they are for a prey, and none delivers; for a spoil, and none said, Restore.
23 Who among you will give ear to this? *Who* will hearken and hear for the time to come?
24 Who gave Jacob for a spoil, and Israel to the robbers? Did not the LORD, he against whom we have sinned? For they would not walk in his ways, neither were they obedient unto his law.
25 Therefore he has poured upon him the fury of his anger, and the strength of battle: and it has set him on fire round about, yet he knew not; and it burned him, yet he laid *it* not to heart.

CHAPTER 43

1 But now thus said the LORD that created you, O Jacob, and he that formed you, O Israel, Fear not: for I have redeemed you, I have called you by your name; you are mine.
2 When you passes through the waters, I *will be* with you; and through the rivers, they will not overflow you: when you walk through the fire, you will not be burned; neither will the flame kindle upon you.
3 For I *am* the LORD your God, the Holy One of Israel, your Savior: I gave Egypt *for* your ransom, Ethiopia and Seba for you.
4 Since you were precious in my sight, you have been honorable, and I have loved you: therefore will I give men for you, and people for your life.
5 Fear not: for I *am* with you: I will bring your seed from the east, and gather you from the west;
6 I will say to the north, Give up; and to the south, keep not back: bring my sons from far, and my daughters from the ends of the earth;
7 *Even* every one that is called by my name: for I have created him for my glory, I have formed him; yea, I have made him.
8 Bring forth the blind people that have eyes, and the deaf that have ears.
9 Let all the nations be gathered together, and let the people be assembled: who among them can declare this, and show us former things? let them bring forth their witnesses, that they may be justified: or let them hear, and say, *It is* truth.
10 you *are* my witnesses, said the LORD, and my servant whom I have chosen: that you may know and believe me, and understand that I *am* he: before me there was no God formed, neither will there be after me.
11 I, *even* I, *am* the LORD; and beside me *there is* no savior.
12 I have declared, and have saved, and I have showed, when *there was* no strange *god* among you: therefore you *are* my witnesses, said the LORD, that I *am* God.
13 Yea, before the day *was* I *am* he; and *there is* none that can deliver out of my hand: I will work, and who will let it?
14 Thus said the LORD, your redeemer, the Holy One of Israel; for your sake I have sent to Babylon, and have brought down all their nobles, and the Chaldeans, whose cry *is* in the ships.
15 I *am* the LORD, your Holy One, the creator of Israel, your King.
16 Thus said the LORD, which makes a way in the sea, and a path in the mighty waters;
17 Which brings forth the chariot and horse, the army and the power; they will lie down together, they will not rise: they are extinct, they are quenched as tow.
18 Remember you not the former things, neither consider the things of old.
19 Behold, I will do a new thing; now it will spring forth; will you not know it? I will even make a way in the wilderness, *and* rivers in the desert.
20 The beast of the field will honor me, the dragons and the owls: because I give waters in the wilderness, *and* rivers in the desert, to give drink to my people, my chosen.
21 This people have I formed for myself; they will show forth my praise.
22 But you have not called upon me, O Jacob; but you have been weary of me, O Israel.
23 you have not brought me the small cattle of your burnt offerings; neither have you honored me with your sacrifices. I have not caused you to serve with an offering, or wearied you with incense.

24 you have bought me no sweet cane with money, neither have you filled me with the fat of your sacrifices: but you have made me to serve with your sins, you have wearied me with your iniquities.
25 I, *even* I, *am* he that blots out your transgressions for mine own sake, and will not remember your sins.
26 Put me in remembrance: let us plead together: declare thou, that you may be justified.
27 your first father has sinned, and your teachers have transgressed against me.
28 Therefore I have profaned the princes of the sanctuary, and have given Jacob to the curse, and Israel to reproaches.

CHAPTER 44

1 Yet now hear, O Jacob my servant; and Israel, whom I have chosen:
2 Thus said the LORD that made you, and formed you from the womb, *which* will help you; Fear not, O Jacob, my servant; and you, Jesurun[1], whom I have chosen.
3 For I will pour water upon him that is thirsty, and floods upon the dry ground: I will pour my spirit upon your seed, and my blessing upon your offspring:
4 And they will spring up *as* among the grass, as willows by the water courses.
5 One will say, I *am* the LORD'S; and another will call *himself* by the name of Jacob; and another will subscribe *with* his hand unto the LORD, and surname *himself* by the name of Israel.
6 Thus said the LORD the King of Israel, and his redeemer the LORD of hosts; I *am* the first, and I *am* the last; and beside me *there is* no God.
7 And who, as I, will call, and will declare it, and set it in order for me, since I appointed the ancient people? And the things that are coming, and will come, let them show unto them.
8 Fear you not, neither be afraid: have not I told you from that time, and have declared *it*? You *are* even my witnesses. Is there a God beside me? Yes, *there is* no God; I know not *any*.
9 They that make a graven image *are* all of them vanity; and their delectable things will not profit; and they *are* their own witnesses; they see not, or know; that they may be ashamed.
10 Who has formed a god, or molten a graven image *that* is profitable for nothing?
11 Behold, all his fellows will be ashamed: and the workmen, they *are* of men: let them all be gathered together, let them stand up; *yet* they will fear, *and* they will be ashamed together.
12 The smith with the tongs both works in the coals, and fashions it with hammers, and works it with the strength of his arms: yea, he is hungry, and his strength fails: he drinks no water, and is faint.
13 The carpenter stretches out *his* rule; he marks it out with a line; he fits it with planes, and he marks it out with the compass, and makes it after the figure of a man, according to the beauty of a man; that it may remain in the house.
14 He hews him down cedars, and takes the cypress and the oak, which he strengthens for himself among the trees of the forest: he plants an ash, and the rain does nourish *it*.
15 Then will it be for a man to burn: for he will take thereof, and warm himself; yea, he kindles *it*, and bakes bread; yea, he makes a god, and worships *it*; he makes it a graven image, and falls down thereto.
16 He burns part thereof in the fire; with part thereof he eats flesh; he roasts roast, and is satisfied: yea, he warms *himself*, and said, Aha, I am warm, I have seen the fire:
17 And the residue thereof he makes a god, *even* his graven image: he falls down unto it, and worships *it*, and prays unto it, and said, deliver me; for you are my god.
18 They have not known or understood: for he has shut their eyes, that they cannot see; *and* their hearts, that they cannot understand.
19 And none considers in his heart, neither *is there* knowledge or understanding to say, I have burned part of it in the fire; yea, also I have baked bread upon the coals thereof; I have roasted flesh, and eaten *it*: and will I make the residue thereof an abomination? Will I fall down to the stock of a tree?
20 He feeds on ashes: a deceived heart has turned him aside, that he cannot deliver his soul, or say, *is there* not a lie in my right hand?
21 Remember these, O Jacob and Israel; for you are my servant: I have formed you; you are my servant: O Israel, you will not be forgotten of me.
22 I have blotted out, as a thick cloud, your transgressions, and, as a cloud, your sins: return unto me; for I have redeemed you.
23 Sing, O you heavens; for the LORD has done *it*: shout, you lower parts of the earth: break forth into singing, you mountains, O forest, and every tree therein: for the LORD has redeemed Jacob, and glorified himself in Israel.
24 Thus said the LORD, your redeemer, and he that formed you from the womb, I *am* the LORD that makes all *things*; that stretches forth the heavens alone; that spreads abroad the earth by myself;
25 That frustrates the tokens of the liars, and makes diviners mad; that turns wise *men* backward, and makes their knowledge foolish;
26 That confirms the word of his servant, and performs the counsel of his messengers; that said to Jerusalem, you will be inhabited; and to the cities of Judah, you will be built, and I will raise up the decayed places thereof:
27 That said to the deep, be dry, and I will dry up your rivers:
28 That said of Cyrus, He *is* my shepherd, and will perform all my pleasure: even saying to Jerusalem, you will be built and to the temple, your foundation will be laid.

CHAPTER 45

1 Thus said the LORD to his anointed, to Cyrus, whose right hand I have **held**, to subdue nations before him; and I will loose the loins of kings, to open before him the two leaved gates; and the gates will not be shut;
2 I will go before you, and make the crooked places straight: I will break in pieces the gates of brass, and cut in sunder the bars of iron:
3 And I will give you the treasures of darkness, and hidden riches of secret places, that you may know that I, the LORD, which call you by your name, *am* the God of Israel.
4 For Jacob my servant's sake, and Israel mine elect, I have even called you by your name: I have surnamed you, though you have not known me.
5 I *am* the LORD, and *there is* none else, *there is* no God beside me: I girded you, though you have not known me:
6 That they may know from the rising of the sun, and from the west, that *there is* none beside me. I *am* the LORD, and *there is* none else.

---

[1] Jeshurun- defined as *upright one*, a symbolic name for Israel describing her ideal character. [Strgs#3484]

7 I form the light, and create darkness: I make peace, and create evil: I the LORD do all these *things*.
8 Drop down, you heavens, from above, and let the skies pour down righteousness: let the earth open, and let them bring forth salvation, and let righteousness spring up together; I the LORD have created it.
9 Woe unto him that strives with his Maker! *Let* the potsherd *strive* with the potsherds of the earth. Will the clay say to him that fashions it, what makes you? Or your work, He has no hands?
10 Woe unto him that said unto *his* father, what beget you? Or to the woman, what have you brought forth?
11 Thus said the LORD, the Holy One of Israel, and his Maker, Ask me of things to come concerning my sons, and concerning the work of my hands command you me.
12 I have made the earth, and created man upon it: I, *even* my hands, have stretched out the heavens, and all their host have I commanded.
13 I have raised him up in righteousness, and I will direct all his ways: he will build my city, and he will let go my captives, not for price or reward, said the LORD of hosts.
14 Thus said the LORD, The labor of Egypt, and merchandise of Ethiopia and of the Sabeans, men of stature, will come over unto you, and they will be yours: they will come after you; in chains they will come over, and they will fall down unto you, they will make supplication unto you, *saying*, Surely God *is* in you; and *there is* none else, *there is* no God.
15 Verily you are a God that hide yourself, O God of Israel, the Savior.
16 They will be ashamed, and also confounded, all of them: they will go to confusion together *that are* makers of idols.
17 *But* Israel will be saved in the LORD with an everlasting salvation: you will not be ashamed or confounded world without end.
18 For thus said the LORD that created the heavens; God himself that formed the earth and made it; he has established it, he created it not in vain, he formed it to be inhabited: I *am* the LORD; and *there is* none else.
19 I have not spoken in secret, in a dark place of the earth: I said not unto the seed of Jacob, Seek you me in vain: I the LORD speak righteousness, I declare things that are right.
20 Assemble yourselves and come; draw near together, you *that are* escaped of the nations: they have no knowledge that set up the wood of their graven image, and pray unto a god *that* cannot save.
21 Tell you, and bring *them* near; yea, let them take counsel together: who has declared this from ancient time? *Who* has told it from that time? *Have* not I the LORD? And *there is* no God else beside me; a just God and a Savior; *there is* none beside me.
22 Look unto me, and be you saved, all the ends of the earth: for I *am* God, and *there is* none else.
23 I have sworn by myself, the word is gone out of my mouth *in* righteousness, and will not return, That unto me every knee will bow, every tongue will swear.
24 Surely, will *one* say, in the LORD have I righteousness and strength: *even* to him will *men* come; and all that are incensed against him will be ashamed.
25 In the LORD will all the seed of Israel be justified, and will glory.

CHAPTER 46

1 Bel bows down, Nebo stoops, their idols were upon the beasts, and upon the cattle: your carriages *were* heavy loaden; *they are* a burden to the weary *beast*.
2 They stoop, they bow down together; they could not deliver the burden, but themselves are gone into captivity.
3 Hearken unto me, O house of Jacob, and all the remnant of the house of Israel, which are borne *by me* from the belly, which are carried from the womb:
4 And *even* to *your* old age I *am* he; and *even* to hoar hairs will I carry *you*: I have made, and I will **bear**; even I will carry, and will deliver *you*.
5 To whom will you liken me, and make *me* equal, and compare me, that we may be like?
6 They lavish gold out of the bag, and weigh silver in the balance, *and* hire a goldsmith; and he makes it a god: they fall down yea, they worship.
7 They bear him upon the shoulder, they carry him, and set him in his place, and he stands; from his place will he not remove: yea, *one* will cry unto him, yet can he not answer, or save him out of his trouble.
8 Remember this, and show yourselves men: bring *it* again to mind, O you transgressors.
9 Remember the former things of old: for I *am* God, and *there is* none else; *I am* God, and *there is* none like me,
10 Declaring the end from the beginning, and from ancient times *the things* that are not *yet* done, saying, My counsel will stand, and I will do all my pleasure:
11 Calling a ravenous bird from the east, the man that executes my counsel from a far country: yes, I have spoken *it*, I will also bring it to pass; I have purposed *it*, I will also do it.
12 Hearken unto me, you stouthearted, that *are* far from righteousness:
13 I bring near my righteousness; it will not be far off, and my salvation will not tarry: and I will place salvation in Zion for Israel my glory.

CHAPTER 47

1 Come down, and sit in the dust, O virgin daughter of Babylon, sit on the ground: *there is* no throne, O daughter of the Chaldeans: for you will no more be called tender and delicate.
2 Take the millstones, and grind meal: uncover your locks, make bare the leg, uncover the thigh, passes over the rivers.
3 your nakedness will be uncovered, yea, your shame will be seen: I will take vengeance, and I will not meet you *as* a man.
4 *As for* our redeemer, the LORD of hosts *is* his name, the Holy One of Israel.
5 Sit you silent, and get you into darkness, O daughter of the Chaldeans: for you will no more be called, the lady of kingdoms.
6 I was wroth with my people, I have polluted mine inheritance, and given them into your hand: you did show them no mercy; upon the ancient have you very heavily laid your yoke.
7 And you said, I will be a lady for ever: *so* that you did not lay these *things* to your heart, neither did remember the latter end of it.
8 Therefore hear now this, you *that are* given to pleasures, that dwells carelessly, that says in your heart, I *am*, and none else beside me; I will not sit *as* a widow, neither will I know the loss of children:
9 But these two *things* will come to you in a moment in one day, the loss of children, and widowhood: they will come upon you in

their perfection for the multitude of your sorceries, *and* for the great abundance[1] of your enchantments[2].

10 For you have trusted in your wickedness: you have said, none sees me. your wisdom and your knowledge, it has perverted you; and you have said in your heart, I *am*, and none else beside me.

11 Therefore will evil come upon you; you will not know from where it rises: and mischief will fall upon you; you will not be able to put it off: and desolation will come upon you suddenly, *which* you will not know.

12 Stand now with your enchantments, and with the multitude of your sorceries, wherein you have labored from your youth; if so be you will be able to profit[3], if so be you may prevail.

13 You are wearied in the multitude of your counsels. Let now the astrologers[4], the stargazers[5], the monthly prognosticators, stand up, and save you from *these things* that will come upon you.

14 Behold, they will be as stubble; the fire will burn them; they will not deliver themselves from the power of the flame: *there will* not *be* a coal to warm at, or fire to sit before it.

15 Thus will they be unto you with whom you have labored, *even* your merchants, from your youth: they will wander everyone to his quarter; none will save you.

CHAPTER 48

1 Hear you this, O house of Jacob, which are called by the name of Israel, and are come forth out of the waters of Judah, which swear by the name of the LORD, and make mention of the God of Israel, *but* not in truth, or in righteousness.

2 For they call themselves of the holy city, and stay themselves upon the God of Israel; The LORD of hosts *is* his name.

3 I have declared the former things from the beginning; and they went forth out of my mouth, and I showed them; I did *them* suddenly, and they came to pass.

4 Because I knew that you are obstinate, and your neck *is* an iron sinew, and your brow brass;

5 I have even from the beginning declared *it* to you; before it came to pass I showed[6] *it* you: lest you should say, Mine idol has done them, and my graven image, and my molten image, has commanded them.

6 you have heard, see all this; and will not you declare *it*? I have showed you new things from this time, even hidden things, and you did not know them.

7 They are created now, and not from the beginning; even before the day when you heard them not; lest you should say, Behold, I knew them.

8 Yea, you heard not; yes, you knew not; yea, from that time *that* your ear was not opened: for I knew that you would deal very treacherously, and were called a transgressor from the womb.

9 For my name's sake will I defer mine anger, and for my praise will I refrain for you, that I cut you not off.

10 Behold, I have refined you, but not with silver; I have chosen you in the furnace of affliction.

11 For mine own sake, *even* for mine own sake, will I do *it*: for how should *my name* be polluted? And I will not give my glory unto another.

12 Hearken unto me, O Jacob and Israel, my called; I *am* he; I *am* the first, I also *am* the last.

13 Mine hand also has laid the foundation of the earth, and my right hand has spanned the heavens: *when* I call unto them, they stand up together.

14 All you, assemble yourselves, and hear; which among them has declared these *things*? The LORD has loved him he will do his pleasure on Babylon, and his arm will *be on* the Chaldeans.

15 I, *even* I, have spoken; yea, I have called him: I have brought him, and he will make his way prosperous.

16 Come you near unto me, hear you this; I have not spoken in secret from the beginning; from the time that it was, there *am* I: and now the Lord GOD, and his Spirit, has sent me.

17 Thus said the LORD, your Redeemer, the Holy One of Israel; I *am* the LORD your God which teaches you to profit, which leads you by the way *that* you should go.

18 O that you had hearkened to my commandments! Then had your peace been as a river, and your righteousness as the waves of the sea:

19 your seed also had been as the sand, and the offspring of your bowels like the gravel thereof; his name should not have been cut off or destroyed from before me.

20 Go you forth of Babylon, flee you from the Chaldeans, with a voice of singing declare you, tell this, utter it *even* to the end of the earth; say you, The LORD has redeemed his servant Jacob.

21 And they thirsted not *when* he led them through the deserts: he caused the waters to flow out of the rock for them he clave the rock also, and the waters gushed out.

22 *There is* no peace, said the LORD, unto the wicked.

CHAPTER 49

1 Listen, O isles, unto me; and hearken, you people from far; The LORD has called me from the womb; from the bowels of my mother has he made mention of my name.

2 And he has made my mouth like a sharp sword; in the shadow of his hand has he hid me, and made me a polished shaft; in his quiver has he hid me;

3 And said unto me, you are my servant, O Israel, in whom I will be glorified.

4 Then I said, I have labored in vain, I have spent my strength for nought, and in vain: *yet* surely my judgment *is* with the LORD, and my work with my God.

5 And now, said the LORD that formed me from the womb *to be* his servant, to bring Jacob again to him, though Israel be not gathered, yet will I be glorious in the eyes of the LORD, and my God will be my strength.

6 And he said, it is a light thing that you should be my servant to raise up the tribes of Jacob, and to restore the preserved of Israel: I will also give you for a light to the Gentiles, that you may be my salvation unto the end of the earth.

7 Thus said the LORD, the Redeemer of Israel, *and* his Holy One, to him whom man despises, to him whom the nation abhors, to a servant of rulers, Kings will see and arise, princes also will worship, because of the LORD that is faithful, *and* the Holy One of Israel, and he will choose you.

---

[1] abundance – powerfulness [Strgs#6109].
[2] enchantments – a *society*; also a *spell* [Strgs#2267]. Root word *to join*; means of spells to *fascinate*, charm [Strgs#2266].
[3] lit. to *ascend*, to *be valuable* [Strgs#3276]. Compare Isaiah 14:13-14.
[4] astrologers – to be a horoscopist or viewer of Heaven [Strgs#1895].
[5] stargazer – derives from two Hebrew words, the first being *chôzeh* meaning beholder in vision, compact (as looked upon with approval) agreement, prophet, see, seer [Strgs#2374]. Second being *kôkâb* meaning rolling or (in the sense of blazing) a star (as round or as shining) [Strgs#3556].
[6] showed – to *hear* intelligently, causatively to *tell* [Strgs#8085].

8 Thus said the LORD, in an acceptable time have I heard you, and in a day of salvation have I helped you: and I will preserve you, and give you for a covenant of the people, to establish the earth, to cause to inherit the desolate heritages;
9 That you may say to the prisoners, Go forth; to them that *are* in darkness, show yourselves. They will feed in the ways, and their pastures will *be* in all high places.
10 They will not hunger or thirst; neither will the heat or sun smite them: for he that has mercy on them will lead them, even by the springs of water will he guide them.
11 And I will make all my mountains a way, and my highways will be exalted.
12 Behold, these will come from far: and, lo, these from the north and from the west; and these from the land of Sinim.
13 Sing, O heavens; and be joyful, O earth; and break forth into singing, O mountains: for the LORD has comforted his people, and will have mercy upon his afflicted.
14 But Zion said, The LORD has forsaken me, and my Lord has forgotten me.
15 Can a woman forget her sucking child, that she should not have compassion on the son of her womb? Yes, they may forget, yet will I not forget you.
16 Behold, I have graven you upon the palms of *my* hands; your walls *are* continually before me.
17 your children will make haste; your destroyers and they that made you waste will go forth of you.
18 Lift up your eyes round about, and behold: all these gather themselves together, *and* come to you. *As* I live, said the LORD, you will surely clothe you with them all, as with an ornament, and bind them *on you*, as a bride *does*.
19 For your waste and your desolate places, and the land of your destruction, will even now be too narrow by reason of the inhabitants, and they that swallowed you up will be far away.
20 The children which you will have, after you have lost the other, will say again in your ears, The place *is* too strait for me: give place to me that I may dwell.
21 Then will you say in your heart, who has begotten me these, seeing I have lost my children, and am desolate, a captive, and removing to and fro? And who has brought up these? Behold, I was left alone; these, where *had* they *been*?
22 Thus said the Lord GOD, Behold; I will lift up mine hand to the Gentiles, and set up my standard to the people: and they will bring your sons in *their* arms, and your daughters will be carried upon *their* shoulders.
23 And kings will be your nursing fathers, and their queens your nursing mothers: they will bow down to you with *their* face toward the earth, and lick up the dust of your feet; and you will know that I *am* the LORD: for they will not be ashamed that wait for me.
24 will the prey be taken from the mighty, or the lawful captive delivered?
25 But thus said the LORD, Even the captives of the mighty will be taken away, and the prey of the terrible will be delivered: for I will contend with him that contends with you, and I will save your children.
26 And I will feed them that oppress you with their own flesh; and they will be drunken with their own blood, as with sweet wine: and all flesh will know that I the LORD *am* your Savior and your Redeemer, the mighty One of Jacob.

CHAPTER 50

1 Thus said the LORD, Where *is* the bill of your mother's divorcement, whom I have put away? Or which of my creditors *is it* to whom I have sold you? Behold, for your iniquities have you sold yourselves, and for your transgressions is your mother put away.
2 Wherefore, when I came, *was there* no man? When I called, *was there* none to answer? Is my hand shortened at all, that it cannot redeem? Or have I no power to deliver? Behold, at my rebuke I dry up the sea, I make the rivers a wilderness: their fish stinks, because *there is* no water, and dies for thirst.
3 I clothe the heavens with blackness, and I make sackcloth their covering.
4 The Lord GOD has given me the tongue of the learned, that I should know how to speak a word in season to *him that is* weary: he wakens morning by morning, he wakens mine ear to hear as the learned.
5 The Lord GOD has opened mine ear, and I was not rebellious, neither turned away back.
6 I gave my back to the smiters, and my cheeks to them that plucked off the hair: I hid not my face from shame and spitting.
7 For the Lord GOD will help me; therefore will I not be confounded: therefore have I set my face like a flint, and I know that I will not be ashamed.
8 *He is* near that justifies me; who will contend with me? let us stand together: who *is* mine adversary? Let him come near to me.
9 Behold, the Lord GOD will help me; who *is* he *that* will condemn me? Lo, they all will wax old as a garment; the moth will eat them up.
10 Who *is* among you that fears the LORD, that obeys the voice of his servant, that walks *in* darkness, and has no light? Let him trust in the name of the LORD, and stay upon his God.
11 Behold, all you that kindle a fire, that compass *yourselves* about with sparks: walk in the light of your fire, and in the sparks *that* you have kindled. This will you have of mine hand; you will lie down in sorrow.

CHAPTER 51

1 Hearken to me, you that follow after righteousness, you that seek the LORD: look unto the rock where you are hewn, and to the hole of the pit where you are digged.
2 Look unto Abraham your father, and unto Sarah *that* bare you: for I called him alone, and blessed him, and increased him.
3 For the LORD will comfort Zion: he will comfort all her waste places; and he will make her wilderness like Eden, and her desert like the garden of the LORD; joy and gladness will be found therein, thanksgiving, and the voice of melody.
4 Hearken unto me, my people; and give ear unto me, O my nation: for a law will proceed from me, and I will make my judgment to rest for a light of the people.
5 My righteousness *is* near; my salvation is gone forth, and mine arms will judge the people; the isles will wait upon me, and on mine arm will they trust.
6 Lift up your eyes to the heavens, and look upon the earth beneath: for the heavens will vanish away like smoke, and the earth will wax old like a garment, and they that dwell therein will die in like manner: but my salvation will be forever, and my righteousness will not be abolished.
7 Hearken unto me, you that know righteousness, the people in whose heart *is* my law; fear you not the reproach of men, neither be you afraid of their revilings.

8 For the moth will eat them up like a garment, and the worm will eat them like wool: but my righteousness will be forever and my salvation from generation to generation.
9 Awake, awake, put on strength, O arm of the LORD; awake, as in the ancient days, in the generations of old. Are you not it that has cut Rahab[1], *and* wounded the dragon?
10 Are you not it which has dried the sea, the waters of the great deep; that has made the depths of the sea a way for the ransomed to pass over?
11 Therefore the redeemed of the LORD will return, and come with singing unto Zion; and everlasting joy will *be* upon their head: they will obtain gladness and joy; *and* sorrow and mourning will flee away.
12 I, *even* I, *am* he that comforts you: who are thou, that you should be afraid of a man *that* will die, and of the son of man *which* will be made *as* grass;
13 And forgets the LORD your maker, that has stretched forth the heavens, and laid the foundations of the earth; and have feared continually every day because of the fury of the oppressor, as if he were ready to destroy? And where *is* the fury of the oppressor?
14 The captive exile hastens that he may be loosed, and that he should not die in the pit, or that his bread should fail.
15 But I *am* the LORD your God, that divided the sea, whose waves roared: The LORD of hosts *is* his name.
16 And I have put my words in your mouth, and I have covered you in the shadow of mine hand, that I may plant the heavens, and lay the foundations of the earth, and say unto Zion, you are my people.
17 Awake, awake, stand up, O Jerusalem, which have drunk at the hand of the LORD the cup of his fury; you have drunken the dregs of the cup of trembling, *and* wrung *them* out.
18 *There is* none to guide her among all the sons *whom* she has brought forth; neither *is there any* that takes her by the hand of all the sons *that* she has brought up.
19 These two *things* are come unto you; who will be sorry for you? Desolation, and destruction, and the famine, and the sword: by whom will I comfort you?
20 your sons have fainted, they lie at the head of all the streets, as a wild bull in a net: they are full of the fury of the LORD, the rebuke of your God.
21 Therefore hear now this, you afflicted, and drunken, but not with wine:
22 Thus said your Lord the LORD, and your God *that* pleads the cause of his people, Behold, I have taken out of your hand the cup of trembling, *even* the dregs of the cup of my fury; you will no more drink it again:
23 But I will put it into the hand of them that afflict you; which have said to your soul, Bow down, that we may go over: and you have laid your body as the ground, and as the street, to them that went over.

CHAPTER 52

1 Awake, awake; put on your strength, O Zion; put on your beautiful garments, O Jerusalem, the holy city: for henceforth there will no more come into you the uncircumcised and the unclean.
2 Shake yourself from the dust; arise, *and* sit down, O Jerusalem: loose yourself from the bands of your neck, O captive daughter of Zion.

3 For thus said the LORD, you have sold yourselves for nought; and you will be redeemed without money.
4 For thus said the Lord GOD, My people went down aforetime into Egypt to sojourn there; and the Assyrian oppressed them without cause.
5 Now therefore, what have I here, said the LORD, that my people is taken away for nought? They that rule over them make them to howl, said the LORD; and my name continually every day *is* blasphemed.
6 Therefore my people will know my name: therefore *they will know* in that day that I *am* he that does speak: behold, *it is* I.
7 How beautiful upon the mountains are the feet of him that brings good tidings, that publishes peace; that brings good tidings of good, that publishes salvation; that said unto Zion, your God reigns!
8 Your watchmen will lift up the voice; with the voice together will they sing: for they will see eye to eye, when the LORD will bring again Zion.
9 Break forth into joy, sing together, you waste places of Jerusalem: for the LORD has comforted his people, he has redeemed Jerusalem.
10 The LORD has made bare his holy arm in the eyes of all the nations; and all the ends of the earth will see the salvation of our God.
11 Depart you, depart you, go you out from there, touch no unclean *thing*; go you out of the midst of her; be you clean, that bear the vessels of the LORD.
12 For you will not go out with haste, or go by flight: for the LORD will go before you; and the God of Israel *will be* your reward.
13 Behold, my servant will deal prudently, he will be exalted and extolled, and be very high.
14 As many were **astonished** at you; his [visage was so marred][2] more than any man, and his form[3] more than the sons of men:
15 So will he sprinkle many nations; the kings will shut their mouths at him: for *that* which had not been told them will they see; and *that* which they had not heard will they consider.

CHAPTER 53

1 Who has believed our report? And to whom is the arm of the LORD revealed?
2 [For he will grow up before him as a tender plant, and as a root out of a dry ground: he has no form[4] or comeliness; and when we will see him, *there is* no beauty that we should desire him.][5]
3 He is despised and rejected of men; a man of sorrows, and acquainted with grief: and we hid as it were *our* faces from him; he was despised, and we esteemed him not.
4 Surely he has borne our griefs, and carried our sorrows: yet we did esteem him stricken, smitten of God, and afflicted.
5 But he *was* wounded for our transgressions, *he was* bruised for our iniquities: the chastisement of our peace *was* upon him; and with his stripes we are healed.
6 All we like sheep have gone astray; we have turned everyone to his own way; and the LORD has laid on him the iniquity of us all.
7 He was oppressed, and he was afflicted, yet he opened not his mouth: he is brought as a lamb to the slaughter, and as a sheep before her shearers is dumb, so he opens not his mouth.

---

[1] Rahab- BDB Definition: breadth; storm, arrogance, mythical sea monster. That is to boaster, an epithet of Egypt. [Strgs#7294]
[2] lit. disfigured
[3] form – <u>outline</u>, figure or appearance, beautiful [Strgs#8389].
[4] Ibid.
[5] This is in contrast to **Genesis 2:6**.

8 He was taken from prison and from judgment: and who will declare his generation? For he was cut off out of the land of the living: for the transgression of my people was he stricken.
9 And he made his grave with the wicked, and with the rich in his death; because he had done no violence, neither *was any* deceit in his mouth.
10 Yet it pleased the LORD to bruise him; he has put *him* to grief: when you will make his soul an offering for sin, he will see *his* seed, he will prolong *his* days, and the pleasure of the LORD will prosper in his hand.
11 He will see of the travail of his soul, *and* will be satisfied: by his knowledge will my righteous servant justify many; for he will bear their iniquities.
12 Therefore will I divide him *a portion* with the great, and he will divide the spoil with the strong; because he has poured out his soul unto death: and he was numbered with the transgressors; and he bare the sin of many, and made intercession for the transgressors.

CHAPTER 54

1 Sing, O barren, you *that* did not bear; break forth into singing, and cry aloud, you *that* did not travail with child: for more *are* the children of the desolate than the children of the married wife, said the LORD.
2 Enlarge the place of your tent, and let them stretch forth the curtains of your habitations: spare not, lengthen your cords, and strengthen your stakes;
3 For you will break forth on the right hand and on the left; and your seed will inherit the Gentiles, and make the desolate cities to be inhabited.
4 Fear not; for you will not be ashamed: neither be you confounded; for you will not be put to shame: for you will forget the shame of your youth, and will not remember the reproach of your widowhood any more.
5 For your Maker *is* your husband; the LORD of hosts *is* his name; and your Redeemer the Holy One of Israel; the God of the whole earth will he be called.
6 For the LORD has called you as a woman forsaken and grieved in spirit, and a wife of youth, when you were refused, said your God.
7 For a small moment have I forsaken you; but with great mercies will I gather you.
8 In a little wrath I hid my face from you for a moment; but with everlasting kindness will I have mercy on you, said the LORD your Redeemer.
9 For this *is as* the waters of Noah unto me: for *as* I have sworn that the waters of Noah should no more go over the earth; so have I sworn that I would not be **angry** with you, or rebuke you.
10 For the mountains will depart, and the hills be removed; but my kindness will not depart from you, neither will the covenant of my peace be removed, said the LORD that has mercy on you.
11 O you afflicted, tossed with tempest, *and* not comforted, behold, I will lay your stones with fair colors, and lay your foundations with sapphires.
12 And I will make your windows of agates[1], and your gates of carbuncles[2], and all your borders of pleasant stones.
13 And all your children will *be* taught of the LORD; and great will *be* the peace of your children.

---

[1] agates – *striking fire, a sparkling gem* [Strgs#3539]. Comes from the Hebrew root word *kad* meaning *to deepen*, a *pail*, a *jar* [Strgs#3537].
[2] carbuncles – derives from two Hebrew words the first being *'eben*

14 In righteousness will you be established: you will be far from oppression; for you will not fear: and from terror; for it will not come near you.
15 Behold, they will surely gather together, *but* not by me: whosoever will gather together against you will fall for your sake.
16 Behold, I have created the smith that blows the coals in the fire, and that brings forth an instrument for his work; and I have created the waster to destroy.
17 No weapon that is formed against you will prosper; and every tongue *that* will rise against you in judgment you will condemn This *is* the heritage of the servants of the LORD, and their righteousness *is* of me, said the LORD.

CHAPTER 55

1 Ho, every one that thirsts, come you to the waters, and he that has no money; come you, buy, and eat; yea, come, buy wine and milk without money and without price.
2 Wherefore do you spend money for *that which is* not bread? And your labor for *that which* satisfies not? Hearken diligently unto me, and eat you *that which is* good, and let your soul delight itself in fatness.
3 Incline your ear, and come unto me: hear, and your soul will live; and I will make an everlasting covenant with you, *even* the sure mercies of David.
4 Behold, I have given him *for* a witness to the people, a leader and commander to the people.
5 Behold, you will call a nation *that* you knows not, and nations *that* knew not you will run unto you because of the LORD your God, and for the Holy One of Israel; for he has glorified you.
6 Seek you the LORD while he may be found, call you upon him while he is near:
7 Let the wicked forsake his way, and the unrighteous man his thoughts: and let him return unto the LORD, and he will have mercy upon him; and to our God, for he will abundantly pardon.
8 For my thoughts *are* not your thoughts, neither *are* your ways my ways, said the LORD.
9 For *as* the heavens are higher than the earth, so are my ways higher than your ways, and my thoughts than your thoughts.
10 For as the rain cometh down, and the snow from heaven, and returns not thither, but waters the earth, and makes it bring forth and bud, that it may give seed to the sower, and bread to the eater:
11 So will my word be that goes forth out of my mouth: it will not return unto me void, but it will accomplish that which I please, and it will prosper *in the thing* whereto I sent it.
12 For you will go out with joy, and be led forth with peace: the mountains and the hills will break forth before you into singing, and all the trees of the field will clap *their* hands.
13 Instead of the thorn will come up the fir tree, and instead of the brier will come up the myrtle tree: and it will be to the LORD for a name, for an everlasting sign *that* will not be cut off.

CHAPTER 56

1 Thus said the LORD, Keep you judgment, and do justice: for my salvation *is* near to come, and my righteousness to be revealed.
2 Blessed *is* the man *that* doeth this, and the son of man *that* lay hold on it; that keeps the Sabbath from polluting it, and keeps his hand from doing any evil.

---

meaning *to build, a stone* [Strgs#68]. The second word being *'eqdâch* meaning *burning*, or *fiery gem* [Strgs#688]. Literally Stones of Fire.

3 Neither let the son of the stranger, that has joined himself to the LORD, speak, saying, The LORD has utterly separated me from his people: neither let the eunuch say, Behold, I *am* a dry tree.
4 For thus said the LORD unto the eunuchs that keep my Sabbaths, and choose *the things* that please me, and take hold of my covenant;
5 Even unto them will I give in mine house and within my walls a place and a name better than of sons and of daughters: I will give them an everlasting name, that will not be cut off.
6 Also the sons of the stranger, that join themselves to the LORD, to serve him, and to love the name of the LORD, to be his servants, every one that keeps the Sabbath from polluting it, and takes hold of my covenant;
7 Even them will I bring to my holy mountain, and make them joyful in my house of prayer: their burnt offerings and their sacrifices will *be* accepted upon mine altar; for mine house will be called a house of prayer for all people.
8 The Lord GOD which gathers the outcasts of Israel says, yet will I gather *others* to him, beside those that are gathered unto him.
9 All you beasts of the field, come to devour, *yea*, all you beasts in the forest.
10 His watchmen *are* blind: they are all ignorant, they *are* all dumb dogs, they cannot bark; sleeping, lying down, loving to slumber.
11 Yea, *they are* greedy dogs *which* can never have enough, and they *are* shepherds *that* cannot understand: they all look to their own way, every one for his gain, from his quarter.
12 Come you, *say they*, I will fetch wine, and we will fill ourselves with strong drink; and tomorrow will be as this day, *and* much more abundant.

CHAPTER 57

1 The righteous perishes, and no man lay *it* to heart: and merciful men *are* taken away, none considering that the righteous is taken away from the evil *to come*.
2 He will enter into peace: they will rest in their beds, *each one* walking *in* his uprightness.
3 But draw near hither, you sons of the sorceress, the seed of the adulterer and the whore.
4 Against whom do you sport yourselves? Against whom make you a wide mouth, *and* draw out the tongue? *Are* you not children of transgression, a seed of falsehood,
5 Enflaming yourselves with idols under every green tree, slaying the children in the valleys under the cliffs of the rocks?
6 Among the smooth *stones* of the stream *is* your portion; they, they *are* your lot: even to them have you poured a drink offering, you have offered a meat offering. Should I receive comfort in these?
7 Upon a lofty and high mountain have you set your bed: even there went you up to offer sacrifice.
8 Behind the doors also and the posts have you set up your remembrance: for you have discovered yourself *to another* than me, and are gone up; you have enlarged your bed, and made you *a covenant* with them; you loved their bed where you saw *it*.
9 And you went to the king with ointment, and did increase your perfumes, and did send your messengers far off, and did debase yourself *even* unto hell.
10 You are wearied in the greatness of your way; *yet* said you not, there is no hope: you have found the life of your hand; therefore you were not grieved.
11 And of whom have you been afraid or feared, that you have lied, and have not remembered me, or laid *it* to your heart? Have not I held my peace even of old, and you fear me not?
12 I will declare your righteousness, and your works; for they will not profit you.
13 When you cries, let your companies deliver you; but the wind will carry them all away; vanity will take *them*: but he that puts his trust in me will possess the land, and will inherit my holy mountain;
14 And will say, cast you up, cast you up, prepare the way, take up the stumbling block out of the way of my people.
15 For thus said the high and lofty One that inhabits eternity, whose name *is* Holy; I dwell in the high and holy place, with him also *that is* of a contrite and humble spirit, to revive the spirit of the humble, and to revive the heart of the contrite ones.
16 For I will not contend for ever, neither will I be always wroth: for the spirit should fail before me, and the souls which I have made.
17 For the iniquity of his covetousness was I wroth, and smote him: I hid me, and was **angry**, and he went on forwardly in the way of his heart.
18 I have seen his ways, and will heal him: I will lead him also, and restore comforts unto him and to his mourners.
19 I create the fruit of the lips; Peace, peace to *him that is* far off, and to *him that is* near, said the LORD; and I will heal him.
20 But the wicked *are* like the troubled sea, when it cannot rest, whose waters cast up mire and dirt.
21 *There is* no peace, said my God, to the wicked.

CHAPTER 58

1 Cry aloud, spare not, lift up your voice like a trumpet, and show my people their transgression, and the house of Jacob their sins.
2 Yet they seek me daily, and delight to know my ways, as a nation that did righteousness, and forsook not the ordinance of their God: they ask of me the ordinances of justice; they take delight in approaching to God.
3 Wherefore have we fasted, *say they*, and you see not? *Wherefore* have we afflicted our soul, and you take no knowledge? Behold, in the day of your fast you find pleasure, and exact all your labors.
4 Behold, you fast for strife and debate, and to smite with the fist of wickedness: you will not fast as you *do this* day, to make your voice to be heard on high.
5 Is it such a fast that I have chosen? a day for a man to afflict his soul? *Is it* to bow down his head as a bulrush, and to spread sackcloth and ashes *under him*? Will you call this a fast, and an acceptable day to the LORD?
6 *Is* not this the fast that I have chosen? To lose the bands of wickedness, to undo the heavy burdens, and to let the oppressed go free, and that you break every yoke?
7 *Is it* not to deal your bread to the hungry, and that you bring the poor that are cast out to your house? When you see the naked, that you cover him; and that you hide not yourself from your own flesh?
8 Then will your light break forth as the morning, and your health will spring forth speedily: and your righteousness will go before you; the glory of the LORD will be your reward.
9 Then will you call, and the LORD will answer; you will cry, and he will say, here I *am*. If you take away from the midst of you the yoke, the putting forth of the finger, and speaking vanity;
10 And *if* you draw out your soul to the hungry, and satisfy the afflicted soul; then will your light rise in obscurity, and your darkness *be* as the noonday:

11 And the LORD will guide you continually, and satisfy your soul in drought, and make fat your bones: and you will be like a watered garden, and like a spring of water, whose waters fail not.
12 And *they that will be* of you will build the old waste places: you will raise up the foundations of many generations; and you will be called, The repairer of the breach, The restorer of paths to dwell in.
13 If you turn away your foot from the Sabbath, *from* doing your pleasure on my holy day; and call the Sabbath a delight, the holy of the LORD, honorable; and will honor him, not doing your own ways, or finding your own pleasure, or speaking your *own* words:
14 Then will you delight yourself in the LORD; and I will cause you to ride upon the high places of the earth, and feed you with the heritage of Jacob your father: for the mouth of the LORD has spoken *it*.

CHAPTER 59

1 Behold, the LORD'S hand is not shortened, that it cannot save; neither his ear heavy, that it cannot hear:
2 But your iniquities have separated between you and your God, and your sins have hid *his* face from you, that he will not hear.
3 For your hands are defiled with blood, and your fingers with iniquity; your lips have spoken lies, your tongue has muttered perverseness.
4 None calls for justice, or *any* pleads for truth: they trust in vanity, and speak lies; they conceive mischief, and bring forth iniquity.
5 They hatch cockatrice' eggs, and weave the spider's web: he that eats of their eggs dies, and that which is crushed breaks out into a viper.
6 Their webs will not become garments, neither will they cover themselves with their works: their works *are* works of iniquity, and the act of violence *is* in their hands.
7 Their feet run to evil, and they make haste to shed innocent blood: their thoughts *are* thoughts of iniquity; wasting and destruction *are* in their paths.
8 The way of peace they know not; and *there is* no judgment in their goings: they have made them crooked paths: whosoever goes therein will not know peace.
9 Therefore is judgment far from us, neither does justice overtake us: we wait for light, but behold obscurity; for brightness, *but* we walk in darkness.
10 We grope for the wall like the blind, and we grope as if *we had* no eyes: we stumble at noonday as in the night; *we are* in desolate places as dead *men*.
11 We roar all like bears, and mourn sore like doves: we look for judgment, but *there is* none; for salvation, *but* it is far off from us.
12 For our transgressions are multiplied before you, and our sins testify against us: for our transgressions *are* with us; and *as for* our iniquities, we know them;
13 In transgressing and lying against the LORD, and departing away from our God, speaking oppression and revolt, conceiving and uttering from the heart words of falsehood.
14 And judgment is turned away backward, and justice stands afar off: for truth is fallen in the street, and equity cannot enter.
15 Yea, truth fails; and he *that* departs from evil makes himself a prey: and the LORD saw *it*, and it displeased him that *there was* no judgment.
16 And he saw that *there was* no man, and wondered that *there was* no intercessor: therefore his arm brought salvation unto him; and his righteousness, it sustained him.
17 For he put on righteousness as a breastplate, and a helmet of salvation upon his head; and he put on the garments of vengeance *for* clothing, and was clad with zeal as a cloak.
18 According to *their* deeds, accordingly he will repay, fury to his adversaries, recompense to his enemies; to the islands he will repay recompense.
19 So will they fear the name of the LORD from the west, and his glory from the rising of the sun. When the enemy will come in like a flood, the Spirit of the LORD will lift up a standard against him.
20 And the Redeemer will come to Zion, and unto them that turn from transgression in Jacob, said the LORD.
21 As for me, this *is* my covenant with them, said the LORD; My spirit that *is* upon you, and my words which I have put in your mouth, will not depart out of your mouth, or out of the mouth of your seed, or out of the mouth of your seed's seed, said the LORD, from henceforth and forever.

CHAPTER 60

1 Arise, shine; for your light is come, and the glory of the LORD is risen upon you.
2 For, behold, the darkness will cover the earth, and gross darkness the people: but the LORD will arise upon you, and his glory will be seen upon you.
3 And the Gentiles will come to your light, and kings to the brightness of your rising.
4 Lift up your eyes round about, and see: all they gather themselves together, they come to you: your sons will come from far, and your daughters will be nursed at your side.
5 Then you will see, and flow together, and your heart will fear, and be enlarged; because the abundance of the sea will be converted unto you, the forces of the Gentiles will come unto you.
6 The multitude of camels will cover you, the dromedaries of Midian and Ephah; all they from Sheba will come: they will bring gold and incense; and they will show forth the praises of the LORD.
7 All the flocks of Kedar will be gathered together unto you, the rams of Nebaioth will minister unto you: they will come up with acceptance on mine altar, and I will glorify the house of my glory.
8 Who *are* these *that* fly as a cloud, and as the doves to their windows?
9 Surely the isles will wait for me, and the ships of Tarshish first, to bring your sons from far, their silver and their gold with them, unto the name of the LORD your God, and to the Holy One of Israel, because he has glorified you.
10 And the sons of strangers will build up your walls, and their kings will minister unto you: for in my wrath I smote you, but in my favor have I had mercy on you.
11 Therefore your gates will be open continually; they will not be shut day or night; that *men* may bring unto you the forces of the Gentiles, and *that* their kings *may be* brought.
12 For the nation and kingdom that will not serve you will perish; yea, *those* nations will be utterly wasted.
13 The glory of Lebanon will come unto you, the fir tree, the pine tree, and the box together, to beautify the place of my sanctuary; and I will make the place of my feet glorious.
14 The sons also of them that afflicted you will come bending unto you; and all they that despised you will bow themselves down at the soles of your feet; and they will call you, the city of the LORD, The Zion of the Holy One of Israel.
15 Whereas you have been forsaken and hated, so that no man went through you, I will make you an eternal excellency, a joy of many generations.

16 you will also suck the milk of the Gentiles, and will suck the breast of kings: and you will know that I the LORD am your Savior and your Redeemer, the mighty One of Jacob.

17 For brass I will bring gold, and for iron I will bring silver, and for wood brass, and for stones iron: I will also make your officers peace, and your exactors righteousness.

18 Violence will no more be heard in your land, wasting or destruction within your borders; but you will call your walls Salvation, and your gates Praise.

19 The sun will be no more your light by day; neither for brightness will the moon give light unto you: but the LORD will be unto you an everlasting light, and your God your glory.

20 your sun will no more go down; neither will your moon withdraw itself: for the LORD will be your everlasting light, and the days of your mourning will be ended.

21 your people also will be all righteous: they will inherit the land for ever, the branch of my planting, the work of my hands, that I may be glorified.

22 A little one will become a thousand, and a small one a strong nation: I the LORD will hasten it in his time.

CHAPTER 61

1 The Spirit of the Lord GOD is upon me; because the LORD has anointed me to preach good tidings unto the meek; he has sent me to bind up the brokenhearted, to proclaim liberty to the captives, and the opening of the prison to them that are bound;

2 To proclaim the acceptable[1] year of the LORD, and the day of vengeance of our God; to comfort all that mourn;

3 To appoint unto them that mourn in Zion, to give unto them beauty for ashes, the oil of joy for mourning, the garment of praise for the spirit of heaviness; that they might be called trees of righteousness, the planting of the LORD, that he might be glorified.

4 And they will build the old wastes, they will raise up the former desolations, and they will repair the waste cities, the desolations of many generations.

5 And strangers will stand and feed your flocks, and the sons of the alien will be your plowmen and your vinedressers.

6 But you will be named the Priests of the LORD: men will call you the Ministers of our God: you will eat the riches of the Gentiles, and in their glory will you boast yourselves.

7 For your shame you will have double; and for confusion they will rejoice in their portion: therefore in their land they will possess the double: everlasting joy will be unto them.

8 For I the LORD love judgment, I hate robbery for burnt offering; and I will direct their work in truth, and I will make an everlasting covenant with them.

9 And their seed will be known among the Gentiles, and their offspring among the people: all that see them will acknowledge them, that they are the seed which the LORD has blessed.

10 I will greatly rejoice in the LORD, my soul will be joyful in my God; for he has clothed me with the garments of salvation, he has covered me with the robe of righteousness, as a bridegroom decks himself with ornaments, and as a bride adorns herself with her jewels.

11 For as the earth brings forth her bud, and as the garden causes the things that are sown in it to spring forth; so the Lord GOD will cause righteousness and praise to spring forth before all the nations.

CHAPTER 62

1 For Zion's sake will I not hold my peace, and for Jerusalem's sake I will not rest, until the righteousness thereof go forth as brightness, and the salvation thereof as a lamp that burns.

2 And the Gentiles will see your righteousness, and all kings your glory: and you will be called by a new name, which the mouth of the LORD will name.

3 You will also be a crown of glory in the hand of the LORD, and a royal diadem in the hand of your God.

4 You will no more be termed Forsaken; neither will your land any more be termed Desolate: but you will be called Hephzi-bah, and your land Beulah: for the LORD delights in you, and your land will be married.

5 For as a young man marries a virgin, so will your sons marry you: and as the bridegroom rejoices over the bride, so will your God rejoice over you.

6 I have set watchmen upon your walls, O Jerusalem, which will never hold their peace day or night: you that make mention of the LORD, keep not silence,

7 And give him no rest, till he establishes, and till he makes Jerusalem a praise in the earth.

8 The LORD has sworn by his right hand, and by the arm of his strength, surely I will no more give your corn to be meat for your enemies; and the sons of the stranger will not drink your wine, for the which you have labored:

9 But they that have gathered it will eat it, and praise the LORD; and they that have brought it together will drink it in the courts of my holiness.

10 Go through, go through the gates; prepare you the way of the people; cast up, cast up the highway; gather out the stones; lift up a standard for the people.

11 Behold, the LORD has proclaimed unto the end of the world, Say you to the daughter of Zion, Behold, your salvation cometh; behold, his reward is with him, and his work before him.

12 And they will call them, the holy people, The redeemed of the LORD: and you will be called, Sought out, A city not forsaken.

CHAPTER 63

1 Who is this that cometh from Edom, with dyed garments from Bozrah? This that is glorious in his apparel, travelling in the greatness of his strength? I that speak in righteousness, mighty to save.

2 Wherefore are you red in your apparel, and your garments like him that treads in the wine-fat?

3 I have trodden the winepress alone; and of the people there was none with me: for I will tread them in mine anger, and trample them in my fury; and their blood will be sprinkled upon my garments, and I will stain all my raiment.

4 For the day of vengeance is in mine heart, and the year of my redeemed is come.

5 And I looked, and there was none to help; and I wondered that there was none to uphold: therefore mine own arm brought salvation unto me; and my fury, it upheld me.

6 And I will tread down the people in mine anger, and make them drunk in my fury, and I will bring down their strength to the earth.

7 I will mention the loving-kindnesses of the LORD, and the praises of the LORD, according to all that the LORD has bestowed on us, and the great goodness toward the house of Israel, which he has

---

[1] lit. delight, desire, favor [Strgs#7522]. Comes from root word meaning to be pleased with, to satisfy, a debt [Strgs#7521].

bestowed on them according to his mercies, and according to the multitude of his loving-kindnesses.

8 For he said, surely they *are* my people, children *that* will not lie: so he was their Savior.

9 In their **entire** affliction he was afflicted, and the angel of his presence saved them: in his love and in his pity he redeemed them; and he bare them, and carried them all the days of old.

10 But they rebelled, and vexed his Holy Spirit: therefore he was turned to be their enemy, *and* he fought against them.

11 Then he remembered the days of old, Moses, *and* his people, *saying*, where *is* he that brought them up out of the sea with the shepherd of his flock? Where *is* he that put his Holy Spirit within him?

12 That led *them* by the right hand of Moses with his glorious arm, dividing the water before them, to make himself an everlasting name?

13 That led them through the deep, as a horse in the wilderness, *that* they should not stumble?

14 As a beast goes down into the valley, the Spirit of the LORD caused him to rest: so did you lead your people, to make yourself a glorious name.

15 Look down from heaven, and behold from the habitation of your holiness and of your glory: where *is* your zeal and your strength, the sounding of your bowels and of your mercies toward me? Are they restrained?

16 Doubtless you are our father, though Abraham be ignorant of us, and Israel acknowledge us not: thou, O LORD, are our father, our redeemer; your name *is* from everlasting.

17 O LORD, why have you made us to err from your ways, *and* hardened our heart from your fear? Return for your servants' sake, the tribes of your inheritance.

18 The people of your holiness have possessed *it* but a little while: our adversaries have trodden down your sanctuary.

19 We are *yours*: you never bare rule over them; they were not called by your name.

CHAPTER 64

1 Oh that you would rend the heavens, that you would come down, that the mountains might flow down at your presence,

2 As *when* the melting fire burns, the fire causes the waters to boil, to make your name known to your adversaries, *that* the nations may tremble at your presence!

3 When you did terrible things *which* we looked not for, you came down, the mountains flowed down at your presence.

4 [For since the beginning of the world]¹ *men* have not heard, or perceived by the ear, neither has the eye seen, O God, beside you, *what* he has prepared for him that waits for him.

5 You meet him that rejoices and works righteousness, *those that* remember you in your ways: behold, you are **angry**; for we have sinned: in those is continuance, and we will be saved.

6 But we are all as an unclean *thing*, and all our righteousness *are* as filthy rags; and we all do fade as a leaf; and our iniquities, like the wind, have taken us away.

7 And *there is* none that calls upon your name, that stirs up himself to take hold of you: for you have hid your face from us, and have consumed us, [because of our iniquities.]²

8 But now, O LORD, you are our father; we *are* the clay, and you our potter; and we all *are* the work of your hand.

9 Be not wroth very sore, O LORD, neither remember iniquity for ever: behold, see, we beseech you, we *are* all your people.

10 Your holy cities are a wilderness, Zion is a wilderness, Jerusalem a desolation.

11 Our holy and our beautiful house, where our fathers praised you, is burned up with fire: and all our pleasant things are laid waste.

12 Will you refrain yourself for these *things*, O LORD? Will you hold your peace, and afflict us very sore?

CHAPTER 65

1 I am sought of *them that* asked not *for me*; I am found of *them that* sought me not: I said, Behold me, behold me, unto a nation *that* was not called by my name.

2 I have spread out my hands all the day unto a rebellious people, which walks in a way *that was* not good, after their own thoughts;

3 A people that provokes me to anger continually to my face; that sacrifices in gardens, and burns incense upon altars of brick;

4 Which remain among the graves, and lodge in the monuments, which eat swine's flesh, and broth of abominable *things is in* their vessels;

5 Which say, Stand by thyself, come not near to me; for I am holier than you. These *are* a smoke in my nose, a fire that burns all the day.

6 Behold, *it is* written before me: I will not keep silence, but will recompense, even recompense into their bosom,

7 Your iniquities, and the iniquities of your fathers together, said the LORD, which have burned incense upon the mountains, and blasphemed me upon the hills: therefore will I measure their former work into their bosom.

8 Thus said the LORD, as the new wine is found in the cluster, and *one* said, Destroy it not; for a blessing *is* in it: so will I do for my servants' sakes, that I may not destroy them all.

9 And I will bring forth a seed out of Jacob, and out of Judah an inheritor of my mountains: and mine elect will inherit it, and my servants will dwell there.

10 And Sharon will be a fold of flocks, and the valley of Achor a place for the herds to lie down in, for my people that have sought me.

11 But you *are* they that forsake the LORD, that forget my holy mountain, that prepare³ a table for that troop⁴, and that furnish⁵ the drink offering unto [that number]⁶.

12 Therefore will I number you to the sword, and you will all bow down to the slaughter: because when I called, you did not answer; when I spoke, you did not hear; but did evil before mine eyes, and did choose *that* wherein I delighted not.

13 Therefore thus said the Lord GOD, Behold, my servants will eat, but you will be hungry: behold, my servants will drink, but you will be thirsty: behold, my servants will rejoice, but you will be ashamed:

14 Behold, my servants will sing for joy of heart, but you will cry for sorrow of heart, and will howl for vexation of spirit.

15 And you will leave your name for a curse unto my chosen: for the Lord GOD will slay you, and call his servants by another name:

---

¹ lit. concealed, time out of mind.
² By the hand of our iniquity.
³ lit. set in a row [Strgs#6186].
⁴ troop – comes from a root word meaning *to crowd upon* [Strgs#1409 + 1464].
⁵ lit. *to fill* or *be full of* [Strgs#4390].
⁶ lit. Apportioner [Strgs#4507], compare **Rev. 13:7**.

16 That he who blesses himself in the earth will bless himself in the God of truth; and he that swears in the earth will swear by the God of truth; because the former troubles are forgotten, and because they are hid from mine eyes.
17 For, behold, I create new heavens and a new earth: and the former will not be remembered, or come into mind.
18 But be you glad and rejoice forever *in that* which I create: for, behold, I create Jerusalem a rejoicing, and her people a joy.
19 And I will rejoice in Jerusalem, and joy in my people: and the voice of weeping will be no more heard in her, or the voice of crying.
20 There will be no more thence an infant of days, or an old man that has not filled his days: for the child will die an hundred years old; but the sinner *being* an hundred years old will be accursed.
21 And they will build houses, and inhabit *them*; and they will plant vineyards, and eat the fruit of them.
22 They will not build, and another inhabit; they will not plant, and another eat: for as the days of a tree *are* the days of my people, and mine elect will long enjoy the work of their hands.
23 They will not labor in vain, or bring forth for trouble; for they *are* the seed of the blessed of the LORD, and their offspring with them.
24 And it will come to pass, that before they call, I will answer; and while they are yet speaking, I will hear.
25 The wolf and the lamb will feed together, and the lion will eat straw like the bullock: and dust will *be* the serpent's meat. They will not hurt or destroy in all my holy mountain, said the LORD.

CHAPTER 66

1 Thus said the LORD, The heaven *is* my throne, and the earth *is* my footstool: where *is* the house that you build unto me? And where *is* the place of my rest?
2 For all those *things* has mine handmade, and all those *things* have been, said the LORD: but to this *man* will I look, *even to him that is* poor and of a contrite spirit, and trembles at my word.
3 He that kills an ox *is as if* he slew a man; he that sacrifices a lamb, *as if* he cut off a dog's neck; he that offers an oblation, *as if he offered* swine's blood; he that burns incense, *as if* he blessed an idol. Yea, they have chosen their own ways, and their soul delights in their abominations.
4 I also will choose their delusions, and will bring their fears upon them; because when I called, none did answer; when I spoke, they did not hear: but they did evil before mine eyes, and chose *that* in which I delighted not.
5 Hear the word of the LORD, you that tremble at his word; your brethren that hated you, that cast you out for my name's sake, said, let the LORD be glorified: but he will appear to your joy, and they will be ashamed.
6 A voice of noise from the city, a voice from the temple, a voice of the LORD that renders recompense to his enemies.
7 Before she travailed, she brought forth; before her pain came, she was delivered of a man child.
8 Who has heard such a thing? Who has seen such things? Will the earth be made to bring forth in one day? *Or* will a nation be born at once? For as soon as Zion travailed, she brought forth her children.
9 will I bring to the birth, and not cause to bring forth? Said the LORD: will I cause to bring forth, and shut *the womb*? Said your God.
10 Rejoice you with Jerusalem, and be glad with her, all you that love her: rejoice for joy with her, all you that mourn for her:
11 That you may suck, and be satisfied with the breasts of her consolations; that you may milk out, and be delighted with the abundance of her glory.
12 For thus said the LORD, Behold, I will extend peace to her like a river, and the glory of the Gentiles like a flowing stream: then will you suck, you will be borne upon *her* sides, and be dandled upon *her* knees.
13 As one whom his mother comforts, so will I comfort you; and you will be comforted in Jerusalem.
14 And when you see *this*, your heart will rejoice, and your bones will flourish like an herb: and the hand of the LORD will be known toward his servants, and *his* indignation toward his enemies.
15 For, behold, the LORD will come with fire, and with his chariots like a whirlwind, to render his anger with fury, and his rebuke with flames of fire.
16 For by fire and by his sword will the LORD plead with all flesh: and the slain of the LORD will be many.
17 They that sanctify themselves, and purify themselves in the gardens behind one *tree* in the midst, eating swine's flesh, and the abomination, and the mouse, will be consumed together, said the LORD.
18 For I *know* their works and their thoughts: it will come, that I will gather all nations and tongues; and they will come, and see my glory.
19 And I will set a sign among them, and I will send those that escape of them unto the nations, *to* Tarshish, Pul, and Lud, that draw the bow, *to* Tubal, and Javan, *to* the isles afar off, that have not heard my fame, neither have seen my glory; and they will declare my glory among the Gentiles.[1]
20 And they will bring all your brethren *for* an offering unto the LORD out of all nations upon horses, and in chariots, and in litters, and upon mules, and upon swift beasts, to my holy mountain Jerusalem, said the LORD, as the children of Israel bring an offering in a clean vessel into the house of the LORD.
21 And I will also take of them for priests *and* for Levites, said the LORD.
22 For as the new heavens and the new earth, which I will make, will remain before me, said the LORD, so will your seed and your name remain.
23 And it will come to pass, *that* from one new moon to another, and from one Sabbath to another, will all flesh come to worship before me, said the LORD.
24 And they will go forth, and look upon the carcasses of the men that have transgressed against me: for their worm will not die, neither will their fire be quenched; and they will be an abhorring unto all flesh.

---

[1] The Septuagint (Greek translation of the Old Testament) reads, "And I will leave a sign upon them, and I will send forth them that have escaped of them to the nations, to Tharsis, and Phud, and Lud, and Mosoch, and to Thobel, and to Greece, and to the isles afar off, to those who have not heard my name, or seen my glory; and they shall declare my glory among the Gentiles."

JEREMIAH

CHAPTER 1

1 The words of Jeremiah[1] the son of Hilkiah, of the priests that *were* in Anathoth in the land of Benjamin:
2 To whom [the word of the LORD came in][2] the days of Josiah the son of Amon king of Judah, in the thirteenth year of his reign.[3]
3 It came also in the days of Jehoiakim the son of Josiah king of Judah, unto the end of the eleventh year of Zedekiah the son of Josiah king of Judah, unto the carrying away of Jerusalem captive in the fifth month.
4 Then the word of the LORD came unto me, saying,
5 Before I formed you in the belly I knew you; and before you came forth out of the womb I sanctified you, *and* I ordained you a prophet unto the nations.
6 Then said I, Ah, Lord GOD! Behold, I cannot speak: for I *am* a child.
7 But the LORD said unto me, Say not, I *am* a child: for you will go to all that I will send you, and whatsoever I command you, you will speak.
8 Be not afraid of their faces: for I *am* with you to deliver you, said the LORD.
9 Then the LORD put forth his hand, and touched my mouth. And the LORD said unto me, Behold, I have put my words in your mouth.
10 See, I have this day set you over the nations and over the kingdoms, to root out, and to pull down, and to destroy, and to throw down, to build, and to plant.
11 Moreover the word of the LORD came unto me, saying, Jeremiah, what **do you** see? And I said, I see a rod of an almond tree.
12 Then said the LORD unto me, you have well seen: for I will hasten my word to perform it.
13 And the word of the LORD came unto me the second time, saying, what **do you** see? And I said, I see a seething pot; and the face thereof *is* toward the north.
14 Then the LORD said unto me, Out of the north[4] an evil will break forth upon all the inhabitants of the land.
15 For, lo, I will call all the families of the kingdoms of the north, said the LORD; and they will come, and they will set everyone his throne at the entering of the gates of Jerusalem, and against all the walls thereof round about, and against all the cities of Judah.
16 And I will utter my judgments against them touching all their wickedness, who have forsaken me, and have burned incense unto other gods, and worshipped the works of their own hands.
17 You therefore gird up your loins, and arise, and speak unto them all that I command you: be not dismayed at their faces, lest I confound you before them.
18 [For, behold, I have made you this day a defenced city, and an iron pillar, and brasen walls against the whole land, against the kings of Judah, against the princes thereof, against the priests thereof, and against the people of the land.][5]
19 And they will fight against you; but they will not prevail against you; for I *am* with you, said the LORD, to deliver you.

CHAPTER 2

1 Moreover the word of the LORD came to me, saying,
2 Go and cry in the ears of Jerusalem, saying, Thus said the LORD; I remember you, the kindness of your youth, the love of your espousals, when you went after me in the wilderness, in a land *that was* not sown.
3 Israel *was* holiness unto the LORD, *and* the first-fruits of his increase: all that devour him will offend; evil will come upon them, said the LORD.
4 Hear you the word of the LORD, O house of Jacob, and all the families of the house of Israel:
5 Thus said the LORD, what iniquity have your fathers found in me, that they are gone far from me, and have walked after vanity, and are become vain?
6 Neither said they, Where *is* the LORD that brought us up out of the land of Egypt, that led us through the wilderness, through a land of deserts and of pits, through a land of drought, and of the shadow of death, through a land that no man passed through, and where no man dwelt?
7 And I brought you into a plentiful country, to eat the fruit thereof and the goodness thereof; but when you entered, you defiled my land, and made mine heritage an abomination.
8 The priests said not, where *is* the LORD? And they that handle the law knew me not: the pastors also transgressed against me, and the prophets prophesied by Baal, and walked after *things that* do not profit.
9 Wherefore I will yet plead with you, said the LORD, and with your children's children will I plead.
10 For pass over the isles of Chittim, and see; and send unto Kedar, and consider diligently, and see if there be such a thing.
11 have a nation changed *their* gods, which *are* yet no gods? But my people have changed their glory for *that which* does not profit.
12 Be astonished[6], O you heavens, at this, and [be horribly afraid][7], be you very desolate[8], said the LORD.
13 For my people have committed two evils; they have forsaken me the fountain of living waters, *and* hewed them out cisterns, broken cisterns, that can hold no water.
14 *Is* Israel a servant? *Is* he a home born *slave*? Why is he spoiled?
15 The young lions roared upon him, *and* yelled, and they made his land waste: his cities are burned without inhabitant.
16 Also the children of Noph[9] and Tahapanes[10] have broken the crown of your head.
17 have you not procured this unto yourself, in that you have forsaken the LORD your God, when he led you by the way?
18 And now what have you to do in the way of Egypt, to drink the waters of Sihor[11]? Or what have you to do in the way of Assyria, to drink the waters of the river?
19 your own wickedness will correct you, and your backslidings will reprove you: know therefore and see that *it is* an evil *thing* and

---

[1] Jeremiah- *whom Jehovah has appointed*. [Strgs#3414]
[2] Principle: no prophet should prophesy unless the word of the Lord comes to him. He must hold his peace until god's word come to Him. Anything else is false.
[3] compare Ez. 1:3, Ez. 3:26-27, 1Samuel 3:7, 1 Samuel 3:20-21, Luke 3:2.
[4] north – hidden, dark [Strgs#6828].
[5] compare Ezkiel 13:2 & 17
[6] lit. to stun [Strgs#8074].
[7] lit. storm, to shiver, fear [Strgs#8175].
[8] lit. to parch [2717].
[9] Noph – is the Hebrew name for Memphis an ancient city and the capital of Egypt. Located on the western bank of the Nile and south of what is now Cairo. (see **Isaiah 19:13**). [Strgs#5297].
[10] Tahapanes – translate as *thou will fill hands with pity*. A city in Egypt; modern Tel Defenneh or Tel Defneh located approximately 18 miles east southeast from Tanis (compare **Ezekiel 30:18**). [Strgs#8471]
[11] Sihor- dark, that is, turbid, a stream of Egypt. [Strgs#7883].

bitter, that you have forsaken the LORD your God, and that my fear *is* not in you, said the Lord GOD of hosts.

20 For of old time I have broken your yoke, *and* burst your bands; and you said, I will not transgress; when upon every high hill and under every green tree you wandered, playing the harlot.

21 Yet I had planted you a noble vine, wholly a right seed: how then are you turned into the degenerate plant of a strange vine unto me?

22 For though you wash you with nitre[1], and take you much soap, *yet* your iniquity is marked before me, said the Lord GOD.

23 How canst you say, I am not polluted, I have not gone after Baalim? See your way in the valley, know what you have done: you *are* a swift dromedary traversing her ways;

24 A wild ass used to the wilderness, *that* snuffs[2] up the wind at her pleasure; in her occasion who can turn her away? All they that seek her will not weary themselves; in her month they will find her.

25 Withhold your foot from being unshod, and your throat from thirst: but you said, there is no hope: no; for I have loved strangers, and after them will I go.

26 As the thief is ashamed when he is found, so is the house of Israel ashamed; they, their kings, their princes, and their priests, and their prophets,

27 Saying to a stock, you are my father; and to a stone, you have brought me forth: for they have turned *their* back unto me, and not *their* face: but in the time of their trouble they will say, Arise, and save us.

28 But where *are* your gods that you have made you? Let them arise, if they can save you in the time of your trouble: for *according to* the number of your cities are your gods, O Judah.

29 Wherefore will you plead with me? You all have transgressed against me, said the LORD.

30 In vain have I smitten your children; they received no correction: your own sword **has** devoured your prophets, like a destroying lion.

31 O generation, see you the word of the LORD. Have I been a wilderness unto Israel? a land of darkness? Wherefore say my people, we are lords; we will come no more unto you?

32 Can a maid forget her ornaments, *or* a bride her attire? Yet my people have forgotten me days without number.

33 **Why trim your way to seek love?** Therefore have you also taught the wicked ones your ways.

34 Also in your skirts is found the blood of the souls of the poor innocents: I have not found it by secret search, but upon all these.

35 Yet you say, because I am innocent, surely his anger will turn from me. Behold, I will plead with you, because you say, I have not sinned.

36 Why gad you about so much to change your way? You also will be ashamed of Egypt, as you were ashamed of Assyria.

37 Yea, you will go forth from him, and your hands upon your head: for the LORD have rejected your confidences, and you will not prosper in them.

CHAPTER 3

1 They say, if a man put away his wife, and she go from him, and become another man's, will he return unto her again? Will not that land be greatly polluted? But you have played the harlot with many lovers; yet return again to me, said the LORD.

2 Lift up your eyes unto the high places, and see where you have not been lien with. In the ways have you sat for them, as the Arabian in the wilderness; and you have polluted the land with your whoredoms and with your wickedness.

3 Therefore the showers have been withheld, and there have been no latter rain; and you had a whore's forehead, you refused to be ashamed.

4 will you not from this time cry unto me, my father, you are the guide of my youth?

5 Will he reserve *his anger* forever? Will he keep *it* to the end? Behold, you have spoken and done evil things as you could.

6 The LORD said also unto me in the days of Josiah the king, have you seen *that* which backsliding Israel **has** done? She is gone up upon every high mountain and under every green tree, and there have played the harlot.

7 And I said after she had done all these *things*, Turn you unto me. But she returned not. And her treacherous sister Judah saw *it*.

8 And I saw, when for all the causes whereby backsliding Israel committed adultery I had put her away, and given her a bill of divorce; yet her treacherous sister Judah feared not, but went and played the harlot also.

9 And it came to pass through the lightness of her whoredom, that she defiled the land, and committed adultery with stones and with stocks.

10 And yet for all this her treacherous sister Judah have not turned unto me with her whole heart, but feignedly, said the LORD.

11 And the LORD said unto me, the backsliding Israel have justified herself more than treacherous Judah.

12 Go and proclaim these words toward the north, and say, Return, you backsliding Israel, said the LORD; *and* I will no cause mine anger to fall upon you: for I *am* merciful, said the LORD, *and* I will not keep *anger* forever.

13 Only acknowledge your iniquity, that you have transgressed against the LORD your God, and have scattered your ways to the strangers under every green tree, and you have not obeyed my voice, said the LORD.

14 Turn, O backsliding children, said the LORD; for I am married unto you: and I will take you one of a city, and two of a family, and I will bring you to Zion:

15 And I will give you pastors according to mine heart, which will feed you with knowledge and understanding.

16 And it will come to pass, when you be multiplied and increased in the land, in those days, said the LORD, they will say no more, The ark of the covenant of the LORD: neither will it come to mind: neither will they remember it; neither will they visit *it*; neither will *that* be done any more.

17 At that time they will call Jerusalem the throne of the LORD; and all the nations will be gathered unto it, to the name of the LORD, to Jerusalem: neither will they walk any more after the imagination of their evil heart.

18 In those days the house of Judah will walk with the house of Israel, and they will come together out of the land of the north to the land that I have given for an inheritance unto your fathers.

19 But I said, how will I put you among the children, and give you a pleasant land, a goodly heritage of the hosts of nations? And I said, you will call me, my father; and will not turn away from me.

---

[1] nitre – is the Hebrew word *nether*, neh'-ther; meaning mineral potash (so called from effervescing with acid. [Strgs#5427]. It comes from the Hebrew root word *nâthar*, naw-thar' meaning to jump, that is, be violently agitated; causatively, to terrify, shake off, untie: drive asunder, leap, loose, make, move, undo. [Strgs#5425].

[2] snuffs- to inhale eagerly, figuratively to covet; by implication to be angry; also to hasten; - desire (earnestly), devour, pant, swallow up. [Strgs#7602]

Jeremiah

20 Surely *as* a wife treacherously departs from her husband, so have you dealt treacherously with me, O house of Israel, said the LORD.
21 A voice was heard upon the high places, weeping *and* supplications of the children of Israel: for they have perverted their way, *and* they have forgotten the LORD their God.
22 Return, you backsliding children, *and* I will heal your backslidings. Behold, we come unto you; for you are the LORD our God.
23 Truly in vain *is salvation hoped for* from the hills, *and from* the multitude of mountains: truly in the LORD our God *is* the salvation of Israel.
24 For shame have devoured the labor of our fathers from our youth; their flocks and their herds, their sons and their daughters.
25 We lie down in our shame, and our confusion covers us: for we have sinned against the LORD our God, we and our fathers, from our youth even unto this day, and have not obeyed the voice of the LORD our God.

CHAPTER 4

1 If you will return, O Israel, said the LORD, return unto me: and if you will put away your abominations out of my sight, then will you not remove.
2 And you will swear, The LORD lives, in truth, in judgment, and in righteousness; and the nations will bless themselves in him, and in him will they glory.
3 For thus said the LORD to the men of Judah and Jerusalem, Break up your fallow ground, and sow not among thorns.
4 Circumcise yourselves to the LORD, and take away the foreskins of your heart, you men of Judah and inhabitants of Jerusalem: lest my fury come forth like fire, and burn that none can quench *it*, because of the evil of your doings.
5 Declare you in Judah, and publish in Jerusalem; and say, Blow you the trumpet in the land: cry, gather together, and say, Assemble yourselves, and let us go into the defenced cities.
6 Set up the standard toward Zion: retire, stay not: for I will bring evil from the north, and a great destruction[1].
7 The lion is come up from his thicket, and the destroyer of the Gentiles is on his way; he is gone forth from his place to make your land desolate; *and* your cities will be laid waste, without an inhabitant.
8 For this gird you with sackcloth, lament and howl: for the fierce anger of the LORD is not turned back from us.
9 And it will come to pass at that day, said the LORD, *that* the heart of the king will perish, and the heart of the princes; and the priests will be astonished, and the prophets will wonder.
10 Then said I, Ah, Lord GOD! Surely you have greatly deceived this people and Jerusalem, saying, you will have peace; whereas the sword reaches unto the soul.
11 At that time will it be said to this people and to Jerusalem, A dry wind of the high places in the wilderness toward the daughter of my people, not to fan, or to cleanse,
12 *Even* a full wind from those *places* will come unto me: now also will I give sentence against them.
13 Behold, he will come up as clouds, and his chariots will *be* as a whirlwind: his horses are swifter than eagles. Woe unto us! For we are spoiled.
14 O Jerusalem, wash your heart from wickedness, that you may be saved. How long will your vain thoughts lodge within you?
15 For a voice declares from Dan, and publishes affliction from mount Ephraim.
16 Make you mention to the nations; behold, publish against Jerusalem, *that* watchers come from a far country, and give out their voice against the cities of Judah.
17 As keepers of a field, are they against her round about; because she have been rebellious against me, said the LORD.
18 your way and your doings have procured these *things* unto you; this *is* your wickedness, because it is bitter, because it reaches unto your heart.
19 My bowels, my bowels! I am pained at my very heart; my heart makes a noise in me; I cannot hold my peace, because you have heard, O my soul, the sound of the trumpet, the alarm of war
20 Destruction upon destruction is cried; for the whole land is spoiled: suddenly are my tents spoiled, *and* my curtains in a moment.
21 How long will I see the standard, *and* hear the sound of the trumpet?
22 For my people *is* foolish, they have not known me; they *are* sottish[2] children, and they have none understanding: they *are* wise to do evil, but to do good they have no knowledge.
23 I beheld the earth, and, lo, *it was* without form, and void; and the heavens, and they *had* no light.
24 I beheld the mountains, and, lo, they trembled, and all the hills moved lightly.
25 I beheld, and, lo, *there was* no man, and all the birds of the heavens were fled.
26 I beheld, and, lo, the fruitful place *was* a wilderness, and all the cities thereof were broken down at the presence of the LORD, *and* by his fierce anger.
27 For thus have the LORD said, the whole land will be desolate; yet will I not make a full end.
28 For this will the earth mourn, and the heavens above be black: because I have spoken *it*, I have purposed *it*, and will not repent, neither will I turn back from it.
29 The whole city will flee for the noise of the horsemen and bowmen; they will go into thickets, and climb up upon the rocks: every city will *be* forsaken, and not a man dwell therein.
30 And *when* you are spoiled, what will you do? Though you clothe yourself with crimson, though you deck **yourself** with ornaments of gold, though you rent your face with painting, in vain will you make yourself fair; your lovers will despise you, they will seek your life.
31 For I have heard a voice as of a woman in travail, *and* the anguish as of her that brings forth her first child, the voice of the daughter of Zion, *that* bewails herself, *that* spreads her hands, *saying*, Woe *is* me now! For my soul is wearied because of murderers.

CHAPTER 5

1 Run you to and fro through the streets of Jerusalem, and see now, and know, and seek in the broad places thereof, if you can find a man, if there be *any* that executes judgment, that seeks the truth; and I will pardon it.
2 And though they say, The LORD lives; surely they swear falsely.

---

[1] destruction – a fracture, ruin, a solution (of a dream) breaking [Strgs#7667].

[2] sottish- literally silly or foolish. [Strgs#5530]

3 O LORD, *are* not your eyes upon the truth? You have stricken them, but they have not grieved; you have consumed them, *but* they have refused to receive correction: they have made their faces harder than a rock; they have refused to return.

4 Therefore I said, surely these *are* poor; they are foolish: for they know not the way of the LORD, or the judgment of their God.

5 I will get me unto the great men, and will speak unto them; for they have known the way of the LORD, *and* the judgment of their God: but these have altogether broken the yoke, *and* burst the bonds.

6 Wherefore a lion out of the forest will slay them, *and* a wolf of the evenings will spoil them, a leopard will watch over their cities: every one that goes out there will be torn in pieces: because their transgressions are many, *and* their backslidings are increased.

7 How will I pardon you for this? Your children have forsaken me, and sworn by *them that are* no gods: when I had fed them to the full, they then committed adultery, and assembled themselves by troops in the harlots' houses.

8 They were *as* fed horses in the morning: every one neighed after his neighbor's wife.

9 Will I not visit for these *things*? Said the LORD: and will not my soul be avenged on such a nation as this?

10 Go you up upon her walls, and destroy; but make not a full end: take away her battlements; for they *are* not the LORD'S.

11 For the house of Israel and the house of Judah have dealt very treacherously against me, said the LORD.

12 They have belied the LORD, and said, *it is* not he; neither will evil come upon us; neither will we see sword or famine:

13 And the prophets will become wind, and the word *is* not in them: thus will it be done unto them.

14 Wherefore thus said the LORD God of hosts, because you speak this word, behold, I will make my words in your mouth fire, and this people wood, and it will devour them.

15 Lo, I will bring a nation upon you from far, O house of Israel, said the LORD: it *is* a mighty nation, it *is* an ancient nation, a nation whose language you knows not, neither understands what they say.

16 Their quiver *is* as an open sepulcher, they *are* all mighty men.

17 And they will eat up your harvest, and your bread, *which* your sons and your daughters should eat: they will eat up your flocks and your herds: they will eat up your vines and your fig trees: they will impoverish your fenced cities, wherein you trust, with the sword.

18 Nevertheless in those days, said the LORD, I will not make a full end with you.

19 And it will come to pass, when you will say, wherefore doeth the LORD our God all these *things* unto us? then will you answer them, Like as you have forsaken me, and served strange gods in your land, so will you serve strangers in a land *that is* not your's.

20 Declare this in the house of Jacob, and publish it in Judah, saying,

21 Hear now this, O foolish people, and without understanding; which have eyes, and see not; which have ears, and hear not:

22 Fear you not me? said the LORD: will you not tremble at my presence, which have placed the sand *for* the bound of the sea by a perpetual decree, that it cannot pass it: and though the waves thereof toss themselves, yet can they not prevail; though they roar, yet can they not pass over it?

23 But this people have a revolting and a rebellious heart; they are revolted and gone.

24 Neither say they in their heart, Let us now fear the LORD our God, that gives rain, both the former and the latter in his season: he reserves unto us the appointed weeks of the harvest.

25 Your iniquities have turned away these *things* and your sins have withheld good *things* from you.

26 For among my people are found wicked *men*: they lay wait, as he that sets snares; they set a trap, they catch men.

27 As a cage is full of birds, so *are* their houses full of deceit: therefore they are become great, and waxen rich.

28 They are waxen fat, they shine: yea, they overpass the deeds of the wicked: they judge not the cause, the cause of the fatherless, yet they prosper; and the right of the needy do they not judge.

29 Will I not visit for these *things*? Said the LORD: will not my soul be avenged on such a nation as this?

30 A wonderful and horrible thing is committed in the land;

31 The prophets prophesy falsely, and the priests bear rule by their means; and my people love *to have it* so: and what will you do in the end thereof?

CHAPTER 6

1 O you children of Benjamin, gather yourselves to flee out of the midst of Jerusalem, and blow the trumpet in Tekoa, and set up a sign of fire in Beth-haccerem[1]: for evil appears out of the north, and great destruction.

2 I have likened the daughter of Zion to a comely and delicate *woman*.

3 The shepherds with their flocks will come unto her; they will pitch *their* tents against her round about; they will feed everyone in his place.

4 Prepare you war against her; arise, and let us go up at noon. Woe unto us! For the day goes away, for the shadows of the evening are stretched out.

5 Arise, and let us go by night, and let us destroy her palaces.

6 For thus have the LORD of hosts said, hew you down trees, and cast a mount against Jerusalem: this *is* the city to be visited; she *is* wholly oppression in the midst of her.

7 As a fountain casts out her waters, so she casts out her wickedness: violence and spoil is heard in her; before me continually *is* grief and wounds.

8 Be you instructed, O Jerusalem, lest my soul depart from you; lest I make you desolate, a land not inhabited.

9 Thus said the LORD of hosts, They will thoroughly glean the remnant of Israel as a vine: turn back your hand as a grape-gatherer into the baskets.

10 To whom will I speak, and give warning, that they may hear? behold, their ear *is* uncircumcised, and they cannot hearken: behold, the word of the LORD is unto them a reproach; they have no delight in it.

11 Therefore I am full of the fury of the LORD; I am weary with holding in: I will pour it out upon the children abroad and upon the assembly of young men together: for even the husband with the wife will be taken, the aged with *him that is* full of days.

12 And their houses will be turned unto others, *with their* fields and wives together: for I will stretch out my hand upon the inhabitants of the land, said the LORD.

---

[1] Beth-haccerem – is defined as *house of the vineyard*. [Strgs#1021]. It was a place in Palestine where signal fires were set to warn of an invasion (See Neh. 3:14)

13 For from the least of them even unto the greatest of them every one *is* given to covetousness; and from the prophet even unto the priest every one deals falsely.
14 They have healed also the hurt *of the daughter* of my people slightly, saying, Peace, peace; when *there is* no peace.
15 Were they ashamed when they had committed abomination? No, they were not at all ashamed, neither could they blush: therefore they will fall among them that fall: at the time *that* I visit them they will be cast down, said the LORD.
16 Thus said the LORD, Stand you in the ways, and see, and ask for the old paths, where *is* the good way, and walk therein, and you will find rest for your souls. But they said, we will not walk *therein*.
17 Also I set watchmen over you, *saying*, Hearken to the sound of the trumpet. But they said, we will not hearken.
18 Therefore hear, you nations, and know, O congregation, what *is* among them.
19 Hear, O earth: behold, I will bring evil upon this people, *even* the fruit of their thoughts, because they have not hearkened unto my words, or to my law, but rejected it.
20 To what purpose comes there to me incense from Sheba, and the sweet cane from a far country? Your burnt offerings *are* not acceptable, or your sacrifices sweet unto me.
21 Therefore thus said the LORD, Behold, I will lay stumbling blocks before this people, and the fathers and the sons together will fall upon them; the neighbor and his friend will perish.
22 Thus said the LORD, Behold, a people comes from the north country, and a great nation will be raised from the sides of the earth.
23 They will lay hold on bow and spear; they *are* cruel, and have no mercy; their voice roars like the sea; and they ride upon horses, set in array as men for war against you, O daughter of Zion.
24 We have heard the fame thereof: our hands wax feeble: anguish have taken hold of us, *and* pain, as of a woman in travail.
25 Go not forth into the field, or walk by the way; for the sword of the enemy *and* fear *is* on every side.
26 O daughter of my people, gird you with sackcloth, and wallow yourself in ashes: make you mourning, *as for* an only son, most bitter lamentation: for the spoiler will suddenly come upon us.
27 I have set you *for* a tower[1] *and* a fortress[2] among my people, that you may know and try their way.[3]
28 They *are* all grievous revolters, walking with slanders: *they are* brass and iron; they *are* all corrupters.
29 The bellows are burned, the lead is consumed of the fire; the founder melts in vain: for the wicked are not plucked away.
30 Reprobate silver will *men* call them, because the LORD have rejected them.

CHAPTER 7

1 The word that came to Jeremiah from the LORD, saying,
2 Stand in the gate of the LORD'S house, and proclaim there this word, and say, Hear the word of the LORD, all you *of* Judah, that enter in at these gates to worship the LORD.
3 Thus said the LORD of hosts, the God of Israel, Amend your ways and your doings, and I will cause you to dwell in this place.
4 Trust you not in lying words, saying, The temple of the LORD, The temple of the LORD, The temple of the LORD, *are* these.
5 For if you thoroughly amend your ways and your doings; if you thoroughly execute judgment between a man and his neighbor;
6 *If* you oppress not the stranger, the fatherless, and the widow, and shed not innocent blood in this place, neither walks after other gods to your hurt:
7 Then will I cause you to dwell in this place, in the land that I gave to your fathers, forever and ever.
8 Behold, you trust in lying words, that cannot profit.
9 Will you steal, murder, and commit adultery, and swear falsely, and burn incense unto Baal, and walk after other gods whom you know not;
10 And come and stand before me in this house, which is called by my name, and say, we are delivered to do all these abominations?
11 Is this house, which is called by my name, become a den of robbers in your eyes? Behold, even I have seen *it*, said the LORD.
12 But go you now unto my place which *was* in Shiloh, where I set my name at the first, and see what I did to it for the wickedness of my people Israel.
13 And now, because you have done all these works, said the LORD, and I spoke unto you, rising up early and speaking, but you heard not; and I called you, but you answered not;
14 Therefore will I do unto *this* house, which is called by my name, wherein you trust, and unto the place which I gave to you and to your fathers, as I have done to Shiloh.
15 And I will cast you out of my sight, as I have cast out all your brethren, *even* the whole seed of Ephraim.
16 Therefore pray not you for this people, neither lift up cry or prayer[4] for them, neither make intercession to me: for I will not hear you.[5]
17 See you not what they do in the cities of Judah and in the streets of Jerusalem?
18 The children gather wood, and the fathers kindle the fire, and the women knead *their* dough, to make cakes to the queen of heaven, and to pour out drink offerings unto other gods, that they may provoke me to anger.
19 Do they provoke me to anger? Said the LORD: *do they* not *provoke* themselves to the confusion of their own faces?
20 Therefore thus said the Lord GOD; Behold, mine anger and my fury will be poured out upon this place, upon man, and upon beast, and upon the trees of the field, and upon the fruit of the ground; and it will burn, and will not be quenched.[6]
21 Thus said the LORD of hosts, the God of Israel; Put your burnt offerings unto your sacrifices, and eat flesh.
22 For I spoke not unto your fathers, or commanded them in the day that I brought them out of the land of Egypt, concerning burnt offerings or sacrifices:
23 But this thing commanded I them, saying, Obey my voice, and I will be your God, and you will be my people: and walk you in all the ways that I have commanded you, that it may be well unto you.
24 But they hearkened not, or inclined their ear, but walked in the counsels *and* in the imagination of their evil heart, and went backward, and not forward.
25 Since the day that your fathers came forth out of the land of Egypt unto this day I have even sent unto you all my servants the prophets, daily rising up early and sending *them*:
26 Yet they hearkened not unto me, or inclined their ear, but hardened their neck: they did worse than their fathers.

---

[1] tower – assayer of metals [Strgs#969].
[2] fortress – fortification, castle, fortified city, defender [Strgs#4013].
[3] compare Ez. 14:22-23.

[4] compare Amos 5:13 & Ex. 39:10
[5] compare Jer. 15:1 & Ez. 14:14-22
[6] compare Rev. 8:7, Rev. 16

27 Therefore you will speak all these words unto them; but they will not hearken to you: you will also call unto them; but they will not answer you.
28 But you will say unto them, this *is* a nation that obeys not the voice of the LORD their God, or receives correction: truth is perished, and is cut off from their mouth.
29 Cut off your hair, *O Jerusalem*, and cast *it* away, and take up a lamentation on high places; for the LORD have rejected and forsaken the generation of his wrath.
30 For the children of Judah have done evil in my sight, said the LORD: they have set their abominations in the house which is called by my name, to pollute it.
31 And they have built the high places of Tophet[1], which *is* in the valley of the son of Hinnom, to burn their sons and their daughters in the fire; which I commanded *them* not, neither came it into my heart.
32 Therefore, behold, the days come, said the LORD, that it will no more be called Tophet, or the valley of the son of Hinnom, but the valley of slaughter: for they will bury in Tophet, till there be no place.
33 And the carcasses of this people will be meat for the fowls of the heaven, and for the beasts of the earth; and none will fray *them* away.
34 Then will I cause to cease from the cities of Judah, and from the streets of Jerusalem, the voice of mirth, and the voice of gladness, the voice of the bridegroom, and the voice of the bride: for the land will be desolate.

CHAPTER 8

1 At that time, said the LORD, they will bring out the bones of the kings of Judah, and the bones of his princes, and the bones of the priests, and the bones of the prophets, and the bones of the inhabitants of Jerusalem, out of their graves:
2 And they will spread them before the sun, and the moon, and all the host of heaven, whom they have loved, and whom they have served, and after whom they have walked, and whom they have sought, and whom they have worshipped: they will not be gathered, or be buried; they will be for dung upon the face of the earth.
3 And death will be chosen rather than life by all the residue of them that remain of this evil family, which remain in all the places where I have driven them, said the LORD of hosts.
4 Moreover you will say unto them, thus said the LORD; will they fall, and not arise? Will he turn away, and not return?
5 Why *then* is this people of Jerusalem slidden back by a perpetual backsliding? They hold fast deceit, they refuse to return.
6 I hearkened and heard, *but* they spoke not aright: no man repented him of his wickedness, saying, what have I done? Everyone turned to his course, as the horse rushes into the battle.
7 Yea, the stork in the heaven knows her appointed times; and the turtle and the crane and the swallow observe the time of their coming; but my people know not the judgment of the LORD.
8 How do you say, we *are* wise, and the law of the LORD *is* with us? Lo, certainly in vain made he *it*; the pen of the scribes *is* in vain.
9 The wise *men* are ashamed, they are dismayed and taken: lo, they have rejected the word of the LORD; and what wisdom *is* in them?

10 Therefore will I give their wives unto others, *and* their fields to them that will inherit *them*: for everyone from the least even unto the greatest is given to covetousness, from the prophet even unto the priest every one deals falsely.
11 For they have healed the hurt of the daughter of my people slightly, saying, Peace, peace; when *there is* no peace.
12 Were they ashamed when they had committed abomination? No, they were not at all ashamed, neither could they blush: therefore will they fall among them that fall: in the time of their visitation they will be cast down, said the LORD.
13 I will surely consume them, said the LORD: *there will be* no grapes on the vine, or figs on the fig tree, and the leaf will fade; and *the things that* I have given them will pass away from them.
14 Why do we sit still? Assemble yourselves, and let us enter into the defenced cities, and let us be silent there: for the LORD our God have put us to silence, and given us water of gall to drink, because we have sinned against the LORD.
15 We looked for peace, but no good *came; and* for a time of health, and behold trouble!
16 The snorting of his horses was heard from Dan: the whole land trembled at the sound of the neighing of his strong ones; for they are come, and have devoured the land, and all that is in it; the city, and those that dwell therein.
17 For, behold, I will send serpents, cockatrices, among you, which *will* not *be* charmed, and they will bite you, said the LORD.
18 *When* I would comfort myself against sorrow, my heart *is* faint in me.
19 Behold the voice of the cry of the daughter of my people because of them that dwell in a far country: *Is* not the LORD in Zion? *Is* not her king in her? Why have they provoked me to anger with their graven images, *and* with strange vanities?
20 The harvest is past, the summer is ended, and we are not saved.
21 For the hurt of the daughter of my people am I hurt; I am black; astonishment **has** taken hold on me.
22 *Is there* no balm in Gilead; *is there* no physician there? Why then is not the health of the daughter of my people recovered?

CHAPTER 9

1 Oh that my head were waters, and mine eyes a fountain of tears, that I might weep day and night for the slain of the daughter of my people!
2 Oh that I had in the wilderness a lodging place of wayfaring men; that I might leave my people, and go from them! For they *be* all adulterers, an assembly of treacherous men.
3 And they bend their tongues *like* their bow *for* lies: but they are not valiant for the truth upon the earth; for they proceed from evil to evil, and they know not me, said the LORD.
4 Take you heed every one of his neighbor, and trust you not in any brother: for every brother will utterly supplant, and every neighbor will walk with slanders.
5 And they will deceive everyone his neighbor, and will not speak the truth: they have taught their tongue to speak lies, *and* weary themselves to commit iniquity.
6 your habitation *is* in the midst of deceit; through deceit they refuse to know me, said the LORD.
7 Therefore thus said the LORD of hosts, Behold; I will melt them, and try them; for how will I do for the daughter of my people?

---

[1] see Reference Index

8 Their tongue *is as* an arrow shot out; it speaks deceit: *one* speaks peaceably to his neighbor with his mouth, but in heart he lays his wait.
9 will I not visit them for these *things*? Said the LORD: will not my soul be avenged on such a nation as this?
10 For the mountains will I take up a weeping and wailing, and for the habitations of the wilderness a lamentation, because they are burned up, so that none can pass through *them*; neither can *men* hear the voice of the cattle; both the fowl of the heavens and the beast are fled; they are gone.
11 And I will make Jerusalem heaps, *and* a den of dragons; and I will make the cities of Judah desolate, without an inhabitant.
12 Who *is* the wise man, that may understand this? and *who is he* to whom the mouth of the LORD have spoken, that he may declare it, for what the land perishes *and* is burned up like a wilderness, that none passes through?
13 And the LORD said, Because they have forsaken my law which I set before them, and have not obeyed my voice, neither walked therein;
14 But have walked after the imagination of their own heart, and after Baalim, which their fathers taught them:
15 Therefore thus said the LORD of hosts, the God of Israel; Behold, I will feed them, *even* this people, with wormwood, and give them water of gall to drink.
16 I will scatter them also among the heathen, whom neither they or their fathers have known: and I will send a sword after them, till I have consumed them.
17 Thus said the LORD of hosts, Consider ye, and call for the mourning women, that they may come; and send for cunning *women*, that they may come:
18 And let them make haste, and take up a wailing for us, that our eyes may run down with tears, and our eyelids gush out with waters.
19 For a voice of wailing is heard out of Zion, How are we spoiled! We are greatly confounded, because we have forsaken the land, because our dwellings have cast *us* out.
20 Yet hear the word of the LORD, O you women, and let your ear receive the word of his mouth, and teach your daughters wailing, and everyone her neighbor lamentation.
21 For death is come up into our windows, *and* is entered into our palaces, to cut off the children from without, *and* the young men from the streets.
22 Speak, Thus said the LORD, Even the carcasses of men will fall as dung upon the open field, and as the handful after the harvestman, and none will gather *them*.
23 Thus said the LORD, Let not the wise *man* glory in his wisdom, neither let the mighty *man* glory in his might, let not the rich *man* glory in his riches:
24 But let him that glories, glory in this, that he understands and knows me, that I *am* the LORD which exercise loving-kindness, judgment, and righteousness, in the earth: for in these *things* I delight, said the LORD.
25 Behold, the days come, said the LORD, that I will punish all *them which are* circumcised with the uncircumcised;
26 Egypt, and Judah, and Edom, and the children of Ammon[1], and Moab, and all *that are* in the utmost corners, that dwell in the wilderness: for all *these* nations *are* uncircumcised, and all the house of Israel *are* uncircumcised in the heart.

---

[1] see Reference Index

CHAPTER 10
1 Hear you the word which the LORD speaks unto you, O house of Israel:
2 Thus said the LORD, Learn not the way of the heathen, and be not dismayed at the signs of heaven; for the heathen are dismayed at them.
3 For the customs of the people *are* vain: for *one* cuts a tree out of the forest, the work of the hands of the workman, with the axe.
4 They deck it with silver and with gold; they fasten it with nails and with hammers, that it move not.
5 They *are* upright as the palm tree, but speak not: they must needs be borne, because they cannot go. Be not afraid of them; for they cannot do evil, neither also *is it* in them to do good.
6 Forasmuch as *there is* none like unto you, O LORD; you are great, and your name *is* great in might.
7 Who would not fear you, O King of nations? For to you does it appertain: forasmuch as among all the wise *men* of the nations, and in all their kingdoms, *there is* none like unto you.
8 But they are altogether brutish and foolish: the stock *is* a doctrine of vanities.
9 Silver spread into plates is brought from Tarshish, and gold from Uphaz, the work of the workman, and of the hands of the founder: blue and purple *is* their clothing: they *are* all the work of cunning *men*.
10 But the LORD *is* the true God, he *is* the living God, and an everlasting king: at his wrath the earth will tremble, and the nations will not be able to abide his indignation.
11 Thus will you say unto them, the gods that have not made the heavens and the earth, *even* they will perish from the earth and from under these heavens.
12 He have made the earth by his power, he have established the world by his wisdom, and have stretched out the heavens by his discretion.
13 When he utters his voice, *there is* a multitude of waters in the heavens, and he causes the vapors to ascend from the ends of the earth; he makes lightning's with rain, and brings forth the wind out of his treasures.
14 Every man is brutish in *his* knowledge: every founder is confounded by the graven image: for his molten image *is* falsehood, and *there is* no breath in them.
15 They *are* vanity, *and* the work of errors: in the time of their visitation they will perish.
16 The portion of Jacob *is* not like them: for he *is* the former of all *things*; and Israel *is* the rod of his inheritance: The LORD of hosts *is* his name.
17 Gather up your wares out of the land, O inhabitant of the fortress.
18 For thus said the LORD, Behold, I will sling out the inhabitants of the land at this once, and will distress them, that they may find *it so*.
19 Woe is me for my hurt! My wound is grievous: but I said, truly this *is* a grief, and I must bear it.
20 My tabernacle is spoiled, and all my cords are broken: my children are gone forth of me, and they *are* not: *there is* none to stretch forth my tent any more, and to set up my curtains.
21 For the pastors are become brutish, and have not sought the LORD: therefore they will not prosper, and all their flocks will be scattered.

22 Behold, the noise of the bruit is come, and a great commotion out of the north country, to make the cities of Judah desolate, *and* a den of dragons.

23 O LORD, I know that the way of man *is* not in himself: *it is* not in man that walks to direct his steps.

24 O LORD, correct me, but with judgment; not in your anger, lest you bring me to nothing.

25 Pour out your fury upon the heathen that know you not, and upon the families that call not on your name: for they have eaten up Jacob, and devoured him, and consumed him, and have made his habitation desolate.

CHAPTER 11

1 The word that came to Jeremiah from the LORD, saying,

2 Hear you the words of this covenant, and speak unto the men of Judah, and to the inhabitants of Jerusalem;

3 And say you unto them, thus said the LORD God of Israel; cursed *be* the man that obeys not the words of this covenant,

4 Which I commanded your fathers in the day *that* I brought them forth out of the land of Egypt, from the iron furnace, saying, Obey my voice, and do them, according to all which I command you: so will you be my people, and I will be your God:

5 That I may perform the oath which I have sworn unto your fathers, to give them a land flowing with milk and honey, as *it is* this day. Then answered I, and said, so be it, O LORD.

6 Then the LORD said unto me, proclaim all these words in the cities of Judah, and in the streets of Jerusalem, saying, hear you the words of this covenant, and do them.

7 For I earnestly protested unto your fathers in the day *that* I brought them up out of the land of Egypt, *even* unto this day, rising early and protesting, saying, Obey my voice.

8 Yet they obeyed not, or inclined their ear, but walked everyone in the imagination of their evil heart: therefore I will bring upon them all the words of this covenant, which I commanded *them* to do; but they did *them* not.

9 And the LORD said unto me, a conspiracy is found among the men of Judah, and among the inhabitants of Jerusalem.

10 They are turned back to the iniquities of their forefathers, which refused to hear my words; and they went after other gods to serve them: the house of Israel and the house of Judah have broken my covenant which I made with their fathers.

11 Therefore thus said the LORD, Behold, I will bring evil upon them, which they will not be able to escape; and though they will cry unto me, I will not hearken unto them.

12 Then will the cities of Judah and inhabitants of Jerusalem go, and cry unto the gods unto whom they offer incense: but they will not save them at all in the time of their trouble.

13 For *according to* the number of your cities were your gods, O Judah; and *according to* the number of the streets of Jerusalem have you set up altars to *that* shameful thing, *even* altars to burn incense unto Baal.

14 Therefore pray not you for this people, neither lift up a cry or prayer for them: for I will not hear *them* in the time that they cry unto me for their trouble.

15 What have my beloved to do in mine house, *seeing* she have wrought lewdness with many, and the holy flesh is passed from you? When you doest evil, then you rejoices.

16 The LORD called your name, a green olive tree, fair, *and* of goodly fruit: with the noise of a great tumult he have kindled fire upon it, and the branches of it are broken.

17 For the LORD of hosts, that planted you, have pronounced evil against you, for the evil of the house of Israel and of the house of Judah, which they have done against themselves to provoke me to anger in offering incense unto Baal.

18 And the LORD have given me knowledge *of it*, and I know *it*: then you showed me their doings.

19 But I *was* like a lamb *or* an ox *that* is brought to the slaughter; and I knew not that they had devised devices against me, *saying*, Let us destroy the tree with the fruit thereof, and let us cut him off from the land of the living, that his name may be no more remembered.

20 But, O LORD of hosts, that judges righteously, that tries the reins and the heart, let me see your vengeance on them: for unto you have I revealed my cause.

21 Therefore thus said the LORD of the men of Anathoth[1], that seek your life, saying, Prophesy not in the name of the LORD, that you die not by our hand:

22 Therefore thus said the LORD of hosts, Behold, I will punish them: the young men will die by the sword; their sons and their daughters will die by famine:

23 And there will be no remnant of them: for I will bring evil upon the men of Anathoth, *even* the year of their visitation.

CHAPTER 12

1 Righteous are you, O LORD, when I plead with you: yet let me talk with you of your judgments: Wherefore does the way of the wicked prosper? *Wherefore* are all they happy that deal very treacherously?

2 you have planted them, yea, they have taken root: they grow, yes, they bring forth fruit: you are near in their mouth, and far from their reins.

3 But you, O LORD, know me: you have seen me, and tried mine heart toward you: pull them out like sheep for the slaughter, and prepare them for the day of slaughter.

4 How long will the land mourn, and the herbs of every field wither, for the wickedness of them that dwell therein? The beasts are consumed, and the birds; because they said, He will not see our last end.

5 If you have run with the footmen, and they have wearied you, then how canst you contend with horses? And *if* in the land of peace, *wherein* you trusted, *they wearied you*, then how will you do in the swelling of Jordan?

6 For even your brethren, and the house of your father, even they have dealt treacherously with you; yes, they have called a multitude after you: believe them not, though they speak fair words unto you.

7 I have forsaken mine house, I have left mine heritage; I have given the dearly beloved of my soul into the hand of her enemies.

8 Mine heritage is unto me as a lion in the forest; it cries out against me: therefore have I hated it.

9 Mine heritage *is* unto me *as* a speckled bird, the birds round about *are* against her; come you, assemble all the beasts of the field, come to devour.

---

[1] Anathoth- is defined as *answered prayers*. It's the birth place of the prophet Jeremiah (see **Jeremiah 1:1**; **29:27**), the name of two men and one city. Son of Becher and grandson of Benjamin (see **1 Chronicles 7:8**). One of the heads of the people who signed the covenant with Nehemiah (see **Nehemiah 10:19**). A city of Benjamin allotted to the priest; located approximately three miles from Jerusalem (see **1Kings 2:26**). [Strgs#6068]

Jeremiah

10 Many pastors have destroyed my vineyard, they have trodden my portion under foot, they have made my pleasant portion a desolate wilderness.
11 They have made it desolate, *and being* desolate it mourns unto me; the whole land is made desolate, because no man lays *it* to heart.
12 The spoilers are come upon all high places through the wilderness: for the sword of the LORD will devour from the *one* end of the land even to the *other* end of the land: no flesh will have peace.
13 They have sown wheat, but will reap thorns: they have put themselves to pain, *but* will not profit: and they will be ashamed of your revenues because of the fierce anger of the LORD.
14 Thus said the LORD against all mine evil neighbors, that touch the inheritance which I have caused my people Israel to inherit; Behold, I will pluck them out of their land, and pluck out the house of Judah from among them.
15 And it will come to pass, after that I have plucked them out I will return, and have compassion on them, and will bring them again, every man to his heritage, and every man to his land.
16 And it will come to pass, if they will diligently learn the ways of my people, to swear by my name, The LORD lives; as they taught my people to swear by Baal; then will they be built in the midst of my people.
17 But if they will not obey, I will utterly pluck up and destroy that nation, said the LORD.

CHAPTER 13

1 Thus said the LORD unto me, Go and get you a linen girdle, and put it upon your loins, and put it not in water.
2 So I got a girdle according to the word of the LORD, and put *it* on my loins.
3 And the word of the LORD came unto me the second time, saying,
4 Take the girdle that you have got, which *is* upon your loins, and arise, go to Euphrates, and hide it there in a hole of the rock.
5 So I went, and hid it by Euphrates, as the LORD commanded me.
6 And it came to pass after many days, that the LORD said unto me, Arise, go to Euphrates, and take the girdle from thence, which I commanded you to hide there.
7 Then I went to Euphrates, and digged, and took the girdle from the place where I had hid it: and, behold, the girdle was marred, it was profitable for nothing.
8 Then the word of the LORD came unto me, saying,
9 Thus said the LORD, after this manner will I mar the pride of Judah, and the great pride of Jerusalem.
10 This evil people, which refuse to hear my words, which walk in the imagination of their heart, and walk after other gods, to serve them, and to worship them, will even be as this girdle, which is good for nothing.
11 For as the girdle cleaves to the loins of a man, so have I caused to cleave unto me the whole house of Israel and the whole house of Judah, said the LORD; that they might be unto me for a people, and for a name, and for a praise, and for a glory: but they would not hear.
12 Therefore you will speak unto them this word; thus said the LORD God of Israel, Every bottle will be filled with wine: and they will say unto you, do we not certainly know that every bottle will be filled with wine?
13 Then will you say unto them, Thus said the LORD, Behold, I will fill all the inhabitants of this land, even the kings that sit upon David's throne, and the priests, and the prophets, and all the inhabitants of Jerusalem, with drunkenness.
14 And I will dash them one against another, even the fathers and the sons together, said the LORD: I will not pity, or spare, or have mercy, but destroy them.
15 Hear you, and give ear; be not proud: for the LORD have spoken.
16 Give glory to the LORD your God, before he cause darkness, and before your feet stumble upon the dark mountains, and, while you look for light, he turn it into the shadow of death, *and* make *it* gross darkness.
17 But if you will not hear it, my soul will weep in secret places for *your* pride; and mine eye will weep sore, and run down with tears, because the LORD'S flock is carried away captive.
18 Say unto the king and to the queen, humble yourselves, sit down: for your principalities will come down, *even* the crown of your glory.
19 The cities of the south will be shut up, and none will open *them*: Judah will be carried away captive all of it, it will be wholly carried away captive.
20 Lift up your eyes, and behold them that come from the north: where *is* the flock *that* was given you, your beautiful flock?
21 What will you say when he will punish you? For you have taught them *to be* captains, *and* as chief over you: will not sorrows take you, as a woman in travail?
22 And if you say in your heart, wherefore come these things upon me? For the greatness of your iniquity are your skirts discovered, *and* your heels made bare.
23 Can the Ethiopian change his skin, or the leopard his spots? *Then* may you also do good, that are accustomed to do evil.
24 Therefore will I scatter them as the stubble that passes away by the wind of the wilderness.
25 This *is* your lot, the portion of your measures from me, said the LORD; because you have forgotten me, and trusted in falsehood.
26 Therefore will I discover your skirts upon your face, that your shame may appear.
27 I have seen your adulteries, and your neighings[1], the lewdness of your whoredom, *and* your abominations on the hills in the fields. Woe unto you, O Jerusalem! Will you not be made clean? When will *it* once *be*?

CHAPTER 14

1 The word of the LORD that came to Jeremiah concerning the dearth.
2 Judah mourns, and the gates thereof languish; they are black unto the ground; and the cry of Jerusalem is gone up.
3 And their nobles have sent their little ones to the waters: they came to the pits, *and* found no water; they returned with their vessels empty; they were ashamed and confounded, and covered their heads.
4 Because the ground is chapt[2], for there was no rain in the earth, the plowmen were ashamed, they covered their heads.
5 Yea, the hind also calved in the field, and forsook *it*, because there was no grass.

---

[1] neighing- literally a whinnying (through impatience for battle or lust. [Strgs#468]
[2] chapt- is the Hebrew word *châthath*, <u>khaw-thath</u>; meaning properly to prostrate; hence to *break* down, either (literally) by violence, or (figuratively) by confusion and fear:- abolish, affright, be (make) afraid, amase, beaddown, discourage, (cause to) dismay, go down, scare, terrify.

6 And the wild asses did stand in the high places, they snuffed up the wind like dragons; their eyes did fail, because *there was* no grass.

7 O LORD, though our iniquities testify against us, do you *it* for your name's sake: for our backslidings are many; we have sinned against you.

8 O the hope of Israel, the savior thereof in time of trouble, why should you be as a stranger in the land, and as a wayfaring man *that* turns aside to tarry for a night?

9 Why should you be as a man **astonished**, as a mighty man *that* cannot save? Yet you, O LORD, are in the midst of us, and we are called by your name; leave us not.

10 Thus said the LORD unto this people, Thus have they loved to wander, they have not refrained their feet, therefore the LORD does not accept them; he will now remember their iniquity, and visit their sins.

11 Then said the LORD unto me, Pray not for this people for *their* good.

12 When they fast, I will not hear their cry; and when they offer burnt offering and an oblation, I will not accept them: but I will consume them by the sword, and by the famine, and by the pestilence.

13 Then said I, Ah, Lord GOD! behold, the prophets say unto them, you will not see the sword, neither will you have famine; but I will give you assured peace in this place.

14 Then the LORD said unto me, the prophets prophesy lies in my name: I sent them not, neither have I commanded them, neither spoke unto them: they prophesy unto you a false vision and divination, and a thing of **vanity**, and the deceit of their heart.

15 Therefore thus said the LORD concerning the prophets that prophesy in my name, and I sent them not, yet they say, Sword and famine will not be in this land; by sword and famine will those prophets be consumed.

16 And the people to whom they prophesy will be cast out in the streets of Jerusalem because of the famine and the sword; and they will have none to bury them, them, their wives, or their sons, or their daughters: for I will pour their wickedness upon them.

17 Therefore you will say this word unto them; let mine eyes run down with tears night and day, and let them not cease: for the virgin daughter of my people is broken with a great breach, with a very grievous blow.

18 If I go forth into the field, then behold the slain with the sword! and if I enter into the city, then behold them that are sick with famine! yea, both the prophet and the priest go about into a land that they know not.

19 have you utterly rejected Judah? Have your soul lothed Zion? Why have you smitten us, and *there is* no healing for us? We looked for peace, and *there is* no good; and for the time of healing, and behold trouble!

20 We acknowledge, O LORD, our wickedness, *and* the iniquity of our fathers: for we have sinned against you.

21 Do not abhor *us*, for your name's sake, do not disgrace the throne of your glory: remember, break not your covenant with us.

22 Are there *any* among the vanities of the Gentiles that can cause rain? Or can the heavens give showers? Are not you he, O LORD our God? Therefore we will wait upon you: for you have made all these *things*.

[Strgs#2865]
[1] lanquish- to droop, by implication to be sick, to mourn; - languish, be weak, wax feeble. [Strgs#535]

Jeremiah

CHAPTER 15

1 Then said the LORD unto me, Though Moses and Samuel stood before me, *yet* my mind *could* not *be* toward this people: cast *them* out of my sight, and let them go forth.

2 And it will come to pass, if they say unto you, where will we go forth? Then you will tell them, thus said the LORD; such as *are* for death, to death; and such as *are* for the sword, to the sword; and such as *are* for the famine, to the famine; and such as *are* for the captivity, to the captivity.

3 And I will appoint over them four kinds, said the LORD: the sword to slay, and the dogs to tear, and the fowls of the heaven, and the beasts of the earth, to devour and destroy.

4 And I will cause them to be removed into all kingdoms of the earth, because of Manasseh the son of Hezekiah king of Judah, for *that* which he did in Jerusalem.

5 For who will have pity upon you, O Jerusalem? Or who will bemoan you? Or who will go aside to ask how you doest?

6 you have forsaken me, said the LORD, you are gone backward: therefore will I stretch out my hand against you, and destroy you; I am weary with repenting.

7 And I will fan them with a fan in the gates of the land; I will bereave *them* of children, I will destroy my people, *since* they return not from their ways.

8 Their widows are increased to me above the sand of the seas: I have brought upon them against the mother of the young men a spoiler at noonday: I have caused *him* to fall upon it suddenly, and terrors upon the city.

9 She that have borne seven languishes[1]: she have given up the ghost; her sun is gone down while *it was* yet day: she have been ashamed and confounded: and the residue of them will I deliver to the sword before their enemies, said the LORD.

10 Woe is me, my mother, that you have borne me a man of strife and a man of contention to the whole earth! I have neither lent on usury, or men have lent to me on usury; *yet* every one of them does curse me.

11 The LORD said, Verily it will be well with your remnant; verily I will cause the enemy to entreat you *well* in the time of evil and in the time of affliction.

12 will iron break the northern iron and the steel?

13 your substance and your treasures will I give to the spoil without price, and *that* for all your sins, even in all your borders.

14 And I will make you to pass with your enemies into a land *which* you knows not: for a fire is kindled in mine anger, *which* will burn upon you.

15 O LORD, you knows: remember me, and visit me, and revenge me of my persecutors; take me not away in your longsuffering: know that for your sake I have suffered rebuke.

16 your words were found, and I did eat them; and your word was unto me the joy and rejoicing of mine heart: for I am called by your name, O LORD God of hosts.

17 I sat not in the assembly of the mockers, or rejoiced; I sat alone because of your hand: for you have filled me with indignation.

18 Why is my pain[2] perpetual, and my wound incurable, *which* refuses to be healed? Will you be altogether unto me as a liar, *and* as waters *that* fail[3]?

19 Therefore thus said the LORD, If you return, then will I bring you again, *and* you will stand before me: and if you take forth the

---

[2] pain – *suffering* (physical or mental), *adversity*: -grief pain, sorrow [Strgs#3511].
[3] lit. no build up, no support, no trust, no go to the right hand [Strgs#539].

precious from the vile, you will be as my mouth: let them return unto you; but return not you unto them.
20 And I will make you unto this people a fenced brasen wall: and they will fight against you, but they will not prevail against you: for I *am* with you to save you and to deliver you, said the LORD.
21 And I will deliver you out of the hand of the wicked, and I will redeem you out of the hand of the terrible.

CHAPTER 16

1 The word of the LORD came also unto me, saying,
2 you will not take you a wife, neither will you have sons or daughters in this place.
3 For thus said the LORD concerning the sons and concerning the daughters that are born in this place, and concerning their mothers that bare them, and concerning their fathers that begat them in this land;
4 They will die of grievous deaths; they will not be lamented; neither will they be buried; *but* they will be as dung upon the face of the earth: and they will be consumed by the sword, and by famine; and their carcasses will be meat for the fowls of heaven, and for the beasts of the earth.
5 For thus said the LORD, Enter not into the house of mourning, neither go to lament or bemoan them: for I have taken away my peace from this people, said the LORD, *even* loving-kindness and mercies.
6 Both the great and the small will die in this land: they will not be buried, neither will *men* lament for them, or cut themselves, or make themselves bald for them:
7 Neither will *men* tear *themselves* for them in mourning, to comfort them for the dead; neither will *men* give them the cup of consolation to drink for their father or for their mother.
8 You will not also go into the house of feasting, to sit with them to eat and to drink.
9 For thus said the LORD of hosts, the God of Israel; Behold, I will cause to cease out of this place in your eyes, and in your days, the voice of mirth, and the voice of gladness, the voice of the bridegroom, and the voice of the bride.
10 And it will come to pass, when you will show this people all these words, and they will say unto you, wherefore have the LORD pronounced all this great evil against us? Or what *is* our iniquity? Or what *is* our sin that we have committed against the LORD our God?
11 Then will you say unto them, Because your fathers have forsaken me, said the LORD, and have walked after other gods, and have served them, and have worshipped them, and have forsaken me, and have not kept my law;
12 And you have done worse than your fathers; for, behold, you walk every one after the imagination of his evil heart, that they may not hearken unto me:
13 Therefore will I cast you out of this land into a land that you know not, *neither* you or your fathers; and there will you serve other gods day and night; where I will not show you favor.
14 Therefore, behold, the days come, said the LORD, that it will no more be said, The LORD lives, that brought up the children of Israel out of the land of Egypt;
15 But, the LORD lives, that brought up the children of Israel from the land of the north, and from all the lands where he had driven them: and I will bring them again into their land that I gave unto their fathers.
16 Behold, I will send for many fishers, said the LORD, and they will fish them; and after will I send for many hunters, and they will hunt them from every mountain, and from every hill, and out of the holes of the rocks.
17 For mine eyes *are* upon all their ways: they are not hid from my face, neither is their iniquity hid from mine eyes.
18 And first I will recompense their iniquity and their sin double; because they have defiled my land, they have filled mine inheritance with the carcasses of their detestable and abominable things.
19 O LORD, my strength, and my fortress, and my refuge in the day of affliction, the Gentiles will come unto you from the ends of the earth, and will say, surely our fathers have inherited lies, vanity, and *things* wherein *there is* no profit.
20 will a man make gods unto himself, and they *are* no gods?
21 Therefore, behold, I will this once cause them to know, I will cause them to know mine hand and my might; and they will know that my name *is* The LORD.

CHAPTER 17

1 The sin of Judah *is* written with a pen of iron, *and* with the point of a diamond: *it is* graven upon the table of their heart, and upon the horns of your altars;
2 Whilst their children remember their altars and their groves by the green trees upon the high hills.
3 O my mountain in the field, I will give your substance *and* all your treasures to the spoil, *and* your high places for sin, throughout all your borders.
4 And you, even thyself, will discontinue from your heritage that I gave you; and I will cause you to serve your enemies in the land which you knows not: for you have kindled a fire in mine anger, *which* will burn forever.
5 Thus said the LORD; cursed *be* the man that trusts in man, and makes flesh his arm, and whose heart departs from the LORD.
6 For he will be like the heath in the desert, and will not see when good cometh; but will inhabit the parched places in the wilderness, *in* a salt land and not inhabited.
7 Blessed *is* the man that trusts in the LORD, and whose hope the LORD is.
8 For he will be as a tree planted by the waters, and *that* spreads out her roots by the river, and will not see when heat cometh, but her leaf will be green; and will not be careful in the year of drought, neither will cease from yielding fruit.
9 The heart *is* deceitful above all *things*, and desperately wicked: who can know it?
10 I the LORD search the heart, *I* try the reins, even to give every man according to his ways, *and* according to the fruit of his doings.
11 *As* the partridge sits *on eggs*, and hatches *them* not; *so* he that gets riches, and not by right, will leave them in the midst of his days, and at his end will be a fool.
12 A glorious high throne from the beginning *is* the place of our sanctuary.
13 O LORD, the hope of Israel, all that forsake you will be ashamed, *and* they that depart from me will be written in the earth, because they have forsaken the LORD, the fountain of living waters.
14 Heal me, O LORD, and I will be healed; save me, and I will be saved: for you are my praise.
15 Behold, they say unto me, where *is* the word of the LORD? Let it come now.
16 As for me, I have not hastened from *being* a pastor to follow you: neither have I desired the woeful day; you know: that which came out of my lips was *right* before you.

17 Be not a terror unto me: you are my hope in the day of evil.
18 Let them be confounded that persecute me, but let not me be confounded: let them be dismayed, but let not me be dismayed: bring upon them the day of evil, and destroy them with double destruction.
19 Thus said the LORD unto me; Go and stand in the gate of the children of the people, whereby the kings of Judah come in, and by which they go out, and in all the gates of Jerusalem;
20 And say unto them, Hear you the word of the LORD, you kings of Judah, and all Judah, and all the inhabitants of Jerusalem, that enter in by these gates:
21 Thus said the LORD; Take heed to yourselves, and bear no burden on the Sabbath day, or bring *it* in by the gates of Jerusalem;
22 Neither carry forth a burden out of your houses on the Sabbath day, neither do you any work, but hallow you the Sabbath day, as I commanded your fathers.
23 But they obeyed not, neither inclined their ear, but made their neck stiff, that they might not hear, or receive instruction.
24 And it will come to pass, if you diligently hearken unto me, said the LORD, to bring in no burden through the gates of this city on the Sabbath day, but hallow the Sabbath day, to do no work therein;
25 Then will there enter into the gates of this city kings and princes sitting upon the throne of David, riding in chariots and on horses, they, and their princes, the men of Judah, and the inhabitants of Jerusalem: and this city will remain forever.
26 And they will come from the cities of Judah, and from the places about Jerusalem, and from the land of Benjamin, and from the plain, and from the mountains, and from the south, bringing burnt offerings, and sacrifices, and meat offerings, and incense, and bringing sacrifices of praise, unto the house of the LORD.
27 But if you will not hearken unto me to hallow the Sabbath day, and not to bear a burden, even entering in at the gates of Jerusalem on the Sabbath day; then will I kindle a fire in the gates thereof, and it will devour the palaces of Jerusalem, and it will not be quenched.

CHAPTER 18

1 The word which came to Jeremiah from the LORD, saying,
2 Arise, and go down to the potter's house, and there I will cause you to hear my words.
3 Then I went down to the potter's house, and, behold, he wrought a work on the wheels.
4 And the vessel that he made of clay was marred in the hand of the potter: so he made it again another vessel, as seemed good to the potter to make *it*.
5 Then the word of the LORD came to me, saying,
6 O house of Israel, cannot I do with you as this potter? Said the LORD. Behold, as the clay *is* in the potter's hand, so *are* you in mine hand, O house of Israel.
7 *At what* instant I will speak concerning a nation, and concerning a kingdom, to pluck up, and to pull down, and to destroy *it*;
8 If that nation, against whom I have pronounced, turn from their evil, I will repent of the evil that I thought to do unto them.
9 And *at what* instant I will speak concerning a nation, and concerning a kingdom, to build and to plant *it*;
10 If it do evil in my sight, that it obey not my voice, then I will repent of the good, wherewith I said I would benefit them.
11 Now therefore go to, speak to the men of Judah, and to the inhabitants of Jerusalem, saying, Thus said the LORD; Behold, I frame evil against you, and devise a device against you: return you now everyone from his evil way, and make your ways and your doings good.
12 And they said, there is no hope: but we will walk after our own devices, and we will every one do the imagination of his evil heart.
13 Therefore thus said the LORD; ask you now among the heathen, who have heard such things: the virgin of Israel have done a very horrible thing.
14 Will *a man* leave the snow of Lebanon *which cometh* from the rock of the field? *Or* will the cold flowing waters that come from another place be forsaken?
15 Because my people have forgotten me, they have burned incense to vanity, and they have caused them to stumble in their ways *from* the ancient paths, to walk in paths, *in* a way not cast up;
16 To make their land desolate, *and* a perpetual hissing; every one that passes thereby will be astonished, and wag his head.
17 I will scatter them as with an east wind before the enemy; I will show them the back, and not the face, in the day of their calamity.
18 Then said they, Come, and let us devise devices against Jeremiah; for the law will not perish from the priest, or counsel from the wise, or the word from the prophet. Come, and let us smite him with the tongue, and let us not give heed to any of his words.
19 Give heed to me, O LORD, and hearken to the voice of them that contend with me.
20 will evil be recompensed for good? For they have dig a pit for my soul. Remember that I stood before you to speak good for them, *and* to turn away your wrath from them.
21 Therefore deliver up their children to the famine, and pour out their *blood* by the force of the sword; and let their wives be bereaved of their children, and *be* widows; and let their men be put to death; *let* their young men *be* slain by the sword in battle.
22 Let a cry be heard from their houses, when you will bring a troop suddenly upon them: for they have dig a pit to take me, and hid snares for my feet.
23 Yet, LORD, you know all their counsel against me to slay *me*: forgive not their iniquity, neither blot out their sin from your sight, but let them be overthrown before you; deal *thus* with them in the time of your anger.

CHAPTER 19

1 Thus said the LORD, Go and get a potter's earthen bottle, and *take* of the ancients of the people, and of the ancients of the priests;
2 And go forth unto the valley of the son of Hinnom, which *is* by the entry of the east gate, and proclaim there the words that I will tell you,
3 And say, hear you the word of the LORD, O kings of Judah, and inhabitants of Jerusalem; Thus said the LORD of hosts, the God of Israel; Behold, I will bring evil upon this place, the which whosoever hears, his ears will tingle.
4 Because they have forsaken me, and have estranged this place, and have burned incense in it unto other gods, whom neither they or their fathers have known, or the kings of Judah, and have filled this place with the blood of innocents;
5 They have built also the high places of Baal, to burn their sons with fire *for* burnt offerings unto Baal, which I commanded not, or spoke *it*, neither came *it* into my mind:
6 Therefore, behold, the days come, said the LORD, that this place will no more be called Tophet, or The valley of the son of Hinnom, but The valley of slaughter.
7 And I will make void the counsel of Judah and Jerusalem in this place; and I will cause them to fall by the sword before their

enemies, and by the hands of them that seek their lives: and their carcasses will I give to be meat for the fowls of the heaven, and for the beasts of the earth.

8 And I will make this city desolate, and a hissing; every one that passes thereby will be astonished and hiss because of all the plagues thereof.

9 And I will cause them to eat the flesh of their sons and the flesh of their daughters, and they will eat every one the flesh of his friend in the siege and straitness[1], wherewith their enemies, and they that seek their lives, will straighten[2] them.[3]

10 Then will you break the bottle in the sight of the men that go with you,

11 And will say unto them, Thus said the LORD of hosts; Even so will I break this people and this city, as *one* breaks a potter's vessel, that cannot be made whole again: and they will bury *them* in Tophet, till *there be* no place to bury.

12 Thus will I do unto this place, said the LORD, and to the inhabitants thereof, and *even* make this city as Tophet:

13 And the houses of Jerusalem, and the houses of the kings of Judah, will be defiled as the place of Tophet, because of all the houses upon whose roofs they have burned incense unto all the host of heaven, and have poured out drink offerings unto other gods.

14 Then came Jeremiah from Tophet, where the LORD had sent him to prophesy; and he stood in the court of the LORD'S house; and said to all the people,

15 Thus said the LORD of hosts, the God of Israel; Behold, I will bring upon this city and upon all her towns all the evil that I have pronounced against it, because they have hardened their necks, that they might not hear my words.

CHAPTER 20

1 Now Pashur[4] the son of Immer the priest, who *was* also chief governor in the house of the LORD, heard that Jeremiah prophesied these things.

2 Then Pashur smote Jeremiah the prophet, and put him in the stocks that *were* in the high gate of Benjamin, which *was* by the house of the LORD.

3 And it came to pass on the morrow, that Pashur brought forth Jeremiah out of the stocks. Then said Jeremiah unto him, The LORD **has** not called your name Pashur, but Magor-missabib[5].

4 For thus said the LORD, Behold, I will make you a terror to thyself, and to all your friends: and they will fall by the sword of their enemies, and your eyes will behold *it*: and I will give all Judah into the hand of the king of Babylon, and he will carry them captive into Babylon, and will slay them with the sword.

5 Moreover I will deliver all the strength of this city, and all the labors thereof, and all the precious things thereof, and all the treasures of the kings of Judah will I give into the hand of their enemies, which will spoil them, and take them, and carry them to Babylon.

6 And you, Pashur, and all that dwell in your house will go into captivity: and you will come to Babylon, and there you will die, and will be buried there, you, and all your friends, to whom you have prophesied lies.

7 O LORD, you have deceived me, and I was deceived: you are stronger than I, and have prevailed: I am in derision daily, every one mocks me.

8 For since I spoke, I cried out, I cried violence and spoil; because the word of the LORD was made a reproach unto me, and a derision, daily.

9 Then I said, I will not make mention of him, or speak any more in his name. But *his word* was in mine heart as a burning fire shut up in my bones, and I was weary with forbearing, and I could not *stay*.

10 For I heard the defaming of many, fear on every side. Report, *say they*, and we will report it. All my familiars watched for my halting, *saying*, Peradventure he will be enticed, and we will prevail against him, and we will take our revenge on him.

11 But the LORD *is* with me as a mighty terrible one: therefore my persecutors will stumble, and they will not prevail: they will be greatly ashamed; for they will not prosper: *their* everlasting confusion will never be forgotten.

12 But, O LORD of hosts, that tries the righteous, *and* sees the reins and the heart, let me see your vengeance on them: for unto you have I opened my cause.

13 Sing unto the LORD, praise you the LORD: for he **has** delivered the soul of the poor from the hand of evildoers.

14 Cursed *be* the day wherein I was born: let not the day wherein my mother bare me be blessed.

15 Cursed *be* the man who brought tidings to my father, *saying*, a man child is born unto you; making him very glad.

16 And let that man be as the cities which the LORD overthrew, and repented not: and let him hear the cry in the morning, and the shouting at noontide;

17 Because he slew me not from the womb; or that my mother might have been my grave, and her womb *to be* always great *with me*.

18 Wherefore came I forth out of the womb to see labor and sorrow, that my days should be consumed with shame?

CHAPTER 21

1 The word which came unto Jeremiah from the LORD, when king Zedekiah sent unto him Pashur the son of Melchiah, and Zephaniah the son of Maaseiah the priest, saying,

2 Enquire, I pray you, of the LORD for us; for Nebuchadrezzar[6] king of Babylon makes war against us; if so be that the LORD will deal with us according to all his wondrous works, that he may go up from us.

3 Then said Jeremiah unto them, Thus will you say to Zedekiah:

4 Thus said the LORD God of Israel; Behold, I will turn back the weapons of war that *are* in your hands, wherewith you fight against the king of Babylon, and *against* the Chaldeans, which besiege

---

[1] straitness- literally means a *narrow* place, that is (abstractly and figuratively) *confinement* or *disability*:- anguish and distress. [Strgs#4689]
[2] straighten- is a Hebrew word meaning to *compress*, that is (figuratively) *oppress, distress*: -constrain, lie sore. [Strgs#6693]
[3] In the Tanak **Jeremiah 19:9** reads, "And I will cause them to eat the flesh of their sons and the flesh of their daughters, and they shall devor one another's flesh—because of the desperate straits to which they will be reduced by their enemies, who seek their life" The Septuagint reads, "And they shall eat the flesh of their sons, and the flesh of their daughters; and they shall eat everyone the flesh of his neighbor in the blockade, and in the siege wherewith their enemies shall besiege them."
[4] Pashur- his name means *freedom*. [Strgs#6583]
[5] Magormissabib- the symbolic name given to Pashur the priest by Jeremiah after being put in the stocks. Pashur means terror on every side or *affright from around*. [Strgs#4036]
[6] Nebuchadrezzar- the great king of Babylon who captured Jerusalem and carried Judah captive. He ruled as king in Babylon from 605-562 B C.). His name means may Nebo protect the crown (see **Jeremiah 21-52**; **Daniel 1:1-5:18**, **2 Kings 24:1-25:22**; **Ezra 1:7-6:5**; and **Ezekiel 26:7-30:10**). [Strgs#5019]

you without the walls, and I will assemble them into the midst of this city.

5 And I myself will fight against you with an outstretched hand and with a strong arm, even in anger, and in fury, and in great wrath.

6 And I will smite the inhabitants of this city, both man and beast: they will die of a great pestilence.

7 And afterward, said the LORD, I will deliver Zedekiah king of Judah, and his servants, and the people, and such as are left in this city from the pestilence, from the sword, and from the famine, into the hand of Nebuchadrezzar king of Babylon, and into the hand of their enemies, and into the hand of those that seek their life: and he will smite them with the edge of the sword; he will not spare them, neither have pity, or have mercy.

8 And unto this people you will say, thus said the LORD; Behold, I set before you the way of life, and the way of death.

9 He that abides in this city will die by the sword, and by the famine, and by the pestilence: but he that goes out, and falls to the Chaldeans that besiege you, he will live, and his life will be unto him for a prey.

10 For I have set my face against this city for evil, and not for good, said the LORD: it will be given into the hand of the king of Babylon, and he will burn it with fire.

11 And touching the house of the king of Judah, *say*, hear you the word of the LORD;

12 O house of David, thus said the LORD; Execute judgment in the morning, and deliver *him that is* spoiled out of the hand of the oppressor, lest my fury go out like fire, and burn that none can quench *it*, because of the evil of your doings.

13 Behold, I *am* against you, O inhabitant of the valley, *and* rock of the plain, said the LORD; which say, who will come down against us? Or who will enter into our habitations?

14 But I will punish you according to the fruit of your doings, said the LORD: and I will kindle a fire in the forest thereof, and it will devour all things round about it.

CHAPTER 22

1 Thus said the LORD; Go down to the house of the king of Judah, and speak there this word,

2 And say, hear the word of the LORD, O king of Judah, that sits upon the throne of David, you, and your servants, and your people that enter in by these gates:

3 Thus said the LORD; execute you judgment and righteousness, and deliver the spoiled out of the hand of the oppressor: and do no wrong, do no violence to the stranger, the fatherless, or the widow, neither shed innocent blood in this place.

4 For if you do this thing indeed, then will there enter in by the gates of this house kings sitting upon the throne of David, riding in chariots and on horses, he, and his servants, and his people.

5 But if you will not hear these words, I swear by myself, said the LORD, that this house will become a desolation.

6 For thus said the LORD unto the king's house of Judah; you are Gilead unto me, *and* the head of Lebanon: yet surely I will make you a wilderness, *and* cities which are not inhabited.

7 And I will prepare destroyers against you, everyone with his weapons: and they will cut down your choice cedars, and cast them into the fire.

8 And many nations will pass by this city, and they will say every man to his neighbor, wherefore have the LORD done thus unto this great city?

9 Then they will answer, because they have forsaken the covenant of the LORD their God, and worshipped other gods, and served them.

10 Weep you not for the dead, neither bemoan[1] him: but weep sore for him that goes away: for he will return no more, or see his native country.

11 For thus said the LORD touching Shallum the son of Josiah king of Judah, which reigned instead of Josiah his father, which went forth out of this place; He will not return there any more:

12 But he will die in the place where they have led him captive, and will see this land no more.

13 Woe unto him that builds his house by unrighteousness, and his chambers by wrong; *that* uses his neighbor's service without wages, and gives him not for his work;

14 That said, I will build me a wide house and large chambers, and cuts him out windows; and *it is* cieled[2] with cedar, and painted with vermilion.

15 will you reign, because you closest yourself in cedar? Did not your father eat and drink, and do judgment and justice, *and* then *it was* well with him?

16 He judged the cause of the poor and needy; then *it was* well *with him: was* not this to know me? Said the LORD.

17 But your eyes and your heart *are* not but for your covetousness, and for to shed innocent blood, and for oppression, and for violence, to do *it*.

18 Therefore thus said the LORD concerning Jehoiakim the son of Josiah king of Judah; they will not lament for him, *saying*, Ah my brother! Or, Ah sister! They will not lament for him, *saying*, Ah lord! Or, Ah his glory!

19 He will be buried with the burial of an ass, drawn and cast forth beyond the gates of Jerusalem.

20 Go up to Lebanon, and cry; and lift up your voice in Bashan, and cry from the passages: for all your lovers are destroyed.

21 I spoke unto you in your prosperity; *but* you said, I will not hear. This **has** *been* your manner from your youth, that you obeyed not my voice.

22 The wind will eat up all your pastors, and your lovers will go into captivity: surely then will you be ashamed and confounded for all your wickedness.

23 O inhabitant of Lebanon, that makes your nest in the cedars, how gracious will you be when pangs come upon you, the pain as of a woman in travail!

24 *As* I live, said the LORD, though Coniah[3] the son of Jehoiakim king of Judah were the signet upon my right hand, yet would I pluck you thence;

25 And I will give you into the hand of them that seek your life, and into the hand *of them* whose face you fear, even into the hand of Nebuchadrezzar king of Babylon, and into the hand of the Chaldeans.

26 And I will cast you out, and your mother that bare you, into another country, where you were not born; and there will you die.

---

[1] Bemoan- to **nod**, that is, waver, figuratively to *wander*, *flee*, *disappear*; also (from *shaking* the head in sympathy), to *console*, *deplore*, or (from *tossing* the head in scorn) *taunt*: mourn, make to move, take pity, shake, skip for joy, be sorry, vagabond. [Strgs#5110]

[2] ceiled- to hide by covering; specifically to roof (passive participle as noun, a roof) or wainscot; figuratively to reserve: seated. [Strgs#5503]

[3] Coniah – another name for king Jehoiachin of Judah, the next to last king on the throne before the captivity. His name means Jehovah will establish. [Strgs#3659]

27 But to the land whereunto they desire to return, there will they not return.
28 *Is* this man Coniah a despised broken idol? *is he* a vessel wherein *is* no pleasure? Wherefore are they cast out, he and his seed, and are cast into a land which they know not?
29 O earth, earth, earth, hear the word of the LORD.
30 Thus said the LORD, Write you this man childless, a man *that* will not prosper in his days: for no man of his seed will prosper, sitting upon the throne of David, and ruling any more in Judah.

CHAPTER 23

1 Woe be unto the pastors that destroy and scatter the sheep of my pasture! Said the LORD.
2 Therefore thus said the LORD God of Israel against the pastors that feed my people; you have scattered my flock, and driven them away, and have not visited them: behold, I will visit upon you the evil of your doings, said the LORD.
3 And I will gather the remnant of my flock out of all countries where I have driven them, and will bring them again to their folds; and they will be fruitful and increase.
4 And I will set up shepherds over them which will feed them: and they will fear no more, or be dismayed, neither will they be lacking, said the LORD.
5 Behold, the days come, said the LORD, that I will raise unto David a righteous Branch, and a King will reign and prosper, and will execute judgment and justice in the earth.
6 In his days Judah will be saved, and Israel will dwell safely: and this *is* his name whereby he will be called, THE LORD OUR RIGHTEOUSNESS.
7 Therefore, behold, the days come, said the LORD, that they will no more say, The LORD lives, which brought up the children of Israel out of the land of Egypt;
8 But, the LORD lives, which brought up and which led the seed of the house of Israel out of the north country, and from all countries where I had driven them; and they will dwell in their own land.
9 Mine heart within me is broken because of the prophets; all my bones shake; I am like a drunken man, and like a man whom wine have overcome, because of the LORD, and because of the words of his holiness.
10 For the land is full of adulterers; for because of swearing the land mourns; the pleasant places of the wilderness are dried up, and their course[1] is evil, and their force *is* not right.
11 For both prophet and priest are profane[2]; yea, in my house have I found their wickedness, said the LORD.
12 Wherefore their way will be unto them as slippery *ways* in the darkness: they will be driven on, and fall therein: for I will bring evil upon them, *even* the year of their visitation, said the LORD.
13 And I have seen folly in the prophets of Samaria; they prophesied in Baal, and caused my people Israel to err.
14 I have seen also in the prophets of Jerusalem a horrible thing: they commit adultery, and walk in lies: they strengthen also the hands of evildoers[3], that none does return from his wickedness: they are all of them unto me as Sodom, and the inhabitants thereof as Gomorrah[4].
15 Therefore thus said the LORD of hosts concerning the prophets; Behold, [I will feed them with wormwood, and make them drink the water of gall][5]: for from the prophets of Jerusalem is profaneness gone forth into all the land.
16 Thus said the LORD of hosts, Hearken not unto the words of the prophets that prophesy unto you: they make you vain: they speak a vision of their own heart, *and* not out of the mouth of the LORD.
17 They say still unto them that despise me, The LORD have said, you will have peace; and they say unto every one that walks after the imagination of his own heart, No evil will come upon you.
18 For who have stood in the counsel[6] of the LORD, and have perceived and heard his word? Who have marked[7] his word, and heard *it*?
19 Behold, a whirlwind of the LORD is gone forth in fury, even a grievous whirlwind: it will fall grievously upon the head of the wicked.
20 The anger of the LORD will not return, until he **has** executed, and till he **has** performed the thoughts of his heart: in the latter days you will consider it perfectly.
21 I have not sent these prophets, yet they ran: I have not spoken to them, yet they prophesied.
22 [But if they had stood in my counsel, and had caused my people to hear my words, then they should have turned them from their evil way, and from the evil of their doings.][8]
23 *Am* I a God at hand, said the LORD, and not a God afar off?
24 Can any hide himself in secret places that I will not see him? Said the LORD. Do not I fill heaven and earth? Said the LORD.
25 I have heard what the prophets said, that prophesy lies in my name, saying, I have dreamed, I have dreamed.
26 How long will *this* be in the heart of the prophets that prophesy lies? Yea, *they are* prophets of the deceit of their own heart;
27 Which think to cause my people to forget my name by their dreams which they tell every man to his neighbor, as their fathers have forgotten my name for Baal[9].
28 The prophet that have a dream, let him tell a dream; and he that have my word, let him speak my word faithfully. What *is* the chaff to the wheat? Said the LORD.
29 *Is* not my word like as a fire? Said the LORD; and like a hammer *that* breaks the rock in pieces?
30 Therefore, behold, I *am* against the prophets, said the LORD, that steal my words everyone from his neighbor.
31 Behold, I *am* against the prophets, said the LORD, that use their tongues, and say, He said.
32 Behold, I *am* against them that prophesy false dreams, said the LORD, and do tell them, and cause my people to err by their lies, and by their lightness; yet I sent them not, or commanded them: therefore they will not profit this people at all, said the LORD.
33 And when this people, or the prophet, or a priest, will ask you, saying, what *is* the burden of the LORD? You will then say unto them, what burden? I will even forsake you, said the LORD.
34 And *as for* the prophet, and the priest, and the people, that will say, The burden of the LORD, I will even punish that man and his house.
35 Thus will you say everyone to his neighbor, and every one to his brother, what have the LORD answered? And, what have the LORD spoken?

---

[1] course – *a race*, running [Strgs#4794].
[2] lit. *to soil*, corrupt, defile, pollute [Strgs#2610].
[3] True prophets weaken the hands of evil doers.
[4] False Prophets often practice homosexuality.
[5] compare Rev. 8:10-11
[6] counsel – a *session*, company of persons (in close deliberation) *intimacy, consultation*, a *secret*, assembly [Strgs#5475].
[7] lit. *to prick up the ears*, hearken, attend [Strgs#7181].
[8] As true prophets wait/hear God, people will stop being evil.
[9] Dreams has to do with Baal.

36 And the burden of the LORD will you mention no more: for every man's word will be his burden; for you have perverted the words of the living God, of the LORD of hosts our God.
37 Thus will you say to the prophet, what have the LORD answered you? And, What have the LORD spoken?
38 But since you say, the burden of the LORD; therefore thus said the LORD; Because you say this word, The burden of the LORD, and I have sent unto you, saying, you will not say, The burden of the LORD;
39 Therefore, behold, I, even I, will utterly forget you, and I will forsake you, and the city that I gave you and your fathers, *and cast you* out of my presence:
40 And I will bring an everlasting reproach upon you, and a perpetual shame, which will not be forgotten.

CHAPTER 24

1 The LORD showed me, and, behold, two baskets of figs *were* set before the temple of the LORD, after that Nebuchadrezzar king of Babylon had carried away captive Jeconiah the son of Jehoiakim king of Judah, and the princes of Judah, with the carpenters and smiths, from Jerusalem, and had brought them to Babylon.
2 One basket *had* very good figs, *even* like the figs *that are* first ripe: and the other basket *had* very naughty figs, which could not be eaten, they were so bad.
3 Then said the LORD unto me, what see you, Jeremiah? And I said, Figs; the good figs, very good; and the evil, very evil, that cannot be eaten, they are so evil.
4 Again the word of the LORD came unto me, saying,
5 Thus said the LORD, the God of Israel; like these good figs, so will I acknowledge them that are carried away captive of Judah, whom I have sent out of this place into the land of the Chaldeans for *their* good.
6 For I will set mine eyes upon them for good, and I will bring them again to this land: and I will build them, and not pull *them* down; and I will plant them, and not pluck *them* up.
7 And I will give them and heart to know me, that I *am* the LORD: and they will be my people, and I will be their God: for they will return unto me with their whole heart.
8 And as the evil figs, which cannot be eaten, they are so evil; surely thus said the LORD, So will I give Zedekiah the king of Judah, and his princes, and the residue of Jerusalem, that remain in this land, and them that dwell in the land of Egypt:
9 And I will deliver them to be removed into all the kingdoms of the earth for *their* hurt, *to be* a reproach and a proverb, a taunt and a curse, in all places where I will drive them.
10 And I will send the sword, the famine, and the pestilence, among them, till they be consumed from off the land that I gave unto them and to their fathers.

CHAPTER 25

1 The word that came to Jeremiah concerning all the people of Judah in the fourth year of Jehoiakim the son of Josiah king of Judah, that *was* the first year of Nebuchadrezzar king of Babylon;
2 The which Jeremiah the prophet spoke unto all the people of Judah, and to all the inhabitants of Jerusalem, saying,
3 From the thirteenth year of Josiah the son of Amon king of Judah, even unto this day, that *is* the three and twentieth year, the word of the LORD have come unto me, and I have spoken unto you, rising early and speaking; but you have not hearkened.
4 And the LORD have sent unto you all his servants the prophets, rising early and sending *them*; but you have not hearkened, or inclined your ear to hear.
5 They said, Turn you again now everyone from his evil way, and from the evil of your doings, and dwell in the land that the LORD have given unto you and to your fathers forever and ever:
6 And go not after other gods to serve them, and to worship them, and provoke me not to anger with the works of your hands; and I will do you no hurt.
7 Yet you have not hearkened unto me, said the LORD; that you might provoke me to anger with the works of your hands to your own hurt.
8 Therefore thus said the LORD of hosts; because you have not heard my words,
9 Behold, I will send and take all the families of the north, said the LORD, and Nebuchadrezzar the king of Babylon, my servant, and will bring them against this land, and against the inhabitants thereof, and against all these nations round about, and will utterly destroy them, and make them an astonishment, and an hissing, and perpetual desolations.
10 Moreover I will take from them the voice of mirth, and the voice of gladness, the voice of the bridegroom, and the voice of the bride, the sound of the millstones, and the light of the candle.
11 And this whole land will be a desolation, *and an* astonishment; and these nations will serve the king of Babylon seventy years.
12 And it will come to pass, when seventy years are accomplished, *that* I will punish the king of Babylon, and that nation, said the LORD, for their iniquity, and the land of the Chaldeans, and will make it perpetual desolations.
13 And I will bring upon that land all my words which I have pronounced against it, *even* all that is written in this book, which Jeremiah have prophesied against all the nations.
14 For many nations and great kings will serve themselves of them also: and I will recompense them according to their deeds, and according to the works of their own hands.
15 For thus said the LORD God of Israel unto me; take the wine cup of this fury at my hand, and cause all the nations, to whom I send you, to drink it.
16 And they will drink, and be moved, and be mad, because of the sword that I will send among them.
17 Then took I the cup at the LORD'S hand, and made all the nations to drink, unto whom the LORD had sent me:
18 *To wit*, Jerusalem, and the cities of Judah, and the kings thereof, and the princes thereof, to make them a desolation, an astonishment, an hissing, and a curse; as *it is* this day;
19 Pharaoh king of Egypt, and his servants, and his princes, and all his people;
20 And all the mingled people, and all the kings of the land of Uz, and all the kings of the land of the Philistines, and Ashkelon, and Azzah, and Ekron, and the remnant of Ashdod,
21 Edom, and Moab, and the children of Ammon,
22 And all the kings of Tyrus, and all the kings of Zidon, and the kings of the isles which *are* beyond the sea,
23 Dedan, and Tema, and Buz, and all *that are* in the utmost corners,
24 And all the kings of Arabia, and all the kings of the mingled people that dwell in the desert,
25 And all the kings of Zimri, and all the kings of Elam, and all the kings of the Medes,

26 And all the kings of the north, far and near, one with another, and all the kingdoms of the world, which are upon the face of the earth: and the king of Sheshach will drink after them.

27 Therefore you will say unto them, thus said the LORD of hosts, the God of Israel; Drink you, and be drunken, and **vomit**, and fall, and rise no more, because of the sword which I will send among you.

28 And it will be, if they refuse to take the cup at your hand to drink, then will you say unto them, Thus said the LORD of hosts; you will certainly drink.

29 For, lo, I begin to bring evil on the city which is called by my name, and should you be utterly unpunished? You will not be unpunished: for I will call for a sword upon all the inhabitants of the earth, said the LORD of hosts.

30 Therefore prophesy you against them all these words, and say unto them, The LORD will roar from on high, and utter his voice from his holy habitation; he will mightily roar upon his habitation; he will give a shout, as they that tread the grapes, against all the inhabitants of the earth.

31 A noise will come even to the ends of the earth; for the LORD have a controversy with the nations, he will plead with all flesh; he will give them that are wicked to the sword, said the LORD.

32 Thus said the LORD of hosts, Behold, evil will go forth from nation to nation, and a great whirlwind will be raised up from the coasts of the earth.

33 And the slain of the LORD will be at that day from one end of the earth even unto the other end of the earth: they will not be lamented, neither gathered, or buried; they will be dung upon the ground.

34 Howl, you shepherds, and cry; and wallow yourselves in the ashes, you principal of the flock: for the days of your slaughter and of your dispersions are accomplished; and you will fall like a pleasant vessel.

35 And the shepherds will have no way to flee, or the principal of the flock to escape.

36 A voice of the cry of the shepherds, and a howling of the principal of the flock, will be heard: for the LORD have spoiled their pasture.

37 And the peaceable habitations are cut down because of the fierce anger of the LORD.

38 He have forsaken his covert, as the lion: for their land is desolate because of the fierceness of the oppressor, and because of his fierce anger.

CHAPTER 26

1 In the beginning of the reign of Jehoiakim the son of Josiah king of Judah came this word from the LORD, saying,

2 Thus said the LORD; Stand in the court of the LORD'S house, and speak unto all the cities of Judah, which come to worship in the LORD'S house, all the words that I command you to speak unto them; diminish not a word:

3 If so be they will hearken, and turn every man from his evil way, that I may repent me of the evil, which I purpose to do unto them because of the evil of their doings.

4 And you will say unto them, thus said the LORD; If you will not hearken to me, to walk in my law, which I have set before you,

5 To hearken to the words of my servants the prophets, whom I sent unto you, both rising up early, and sending them, but you have not hearkened;

6 Then will I make this house like Shiloh, and will make this city a curse to all the nations of the earth.

7 So the priests and the prophets and all the people heard Jeremiah speaking these words in the house of the LORD.

8 Now it came to pass, when Jeremiah had made an end of speaking all that the LORD had commanded him to speak unto all the people, that the priests and the prophets and all the people took him, saying, you will surely die.

9 Why have you prophesied in the name of the LORD, saying, this house will be like Shiloh, and this city will be desolate without an inhabitant? And all the people were gathered against Jeremiah in the house of the LORD.

10 When the princes of Judah heard these things, then they came up from the king's house unto the house of the LORD, and sat down in the entry of the new gate of the LORD'S house.

11 Then spoke the priests and the prophets unto the princes and to all the people, saying, This man is worthy to die; for he have prophesied against this city, as you have heard with your ears.

12 Then spoke Jeremiah unto all the princes and to all the people, saying, The LORD sent me to prophesy against this house and against this city all the words that you have heard.

13 Therefore now amend your ways and your doings, and obey the voice of the LORD your God; and the LORD will repent him of the evil that he have pronounced against you.

14 As for me, behold, I am in your hand: do with me as seems good and meet unto you.

15 But know you for certain, that if you put me to death, you will surely bring innocent blood upon yourselves, and upon this city, and upon the inhabitants thereof: for of a truth the LORD have sent me unto you to speak all these words in your ears.

16 Then said the princes and all the people unto the priests and to the prophets; this man is not worthy to die: for he **has** spoken to us in the name of the LORD our God.

17 Then rose up certain of the elders of the land, and spoke to all the assembly of the people, saying,

18 Micah the Morasthite prophesied in the days of Hezekiah king of Judah, and spoke to all the people of Judah, saying, thus said the LORD of hosts; Zion will be plowed like a field, and Jerusalem will become heaps, and the mountain of the house as the high places of a forest.

19 Did Hezekiah king of Judah and all Judah put him at all to death? did he not fear the LORD, and besought the LORD, and the LORD repented him of the evil which he had pronounced against them? Thus might we procure great evil against our souls.

20 And there was also a man that prophesied in the name of the LORD, Urijah the son of Shemaiah of Kirjath-jearim, who prophesied against this city and against this land according to all the words of Jeremiah:

21 And when Jehoiakim the king, with all his mighty men, and all the princes, heard his words, the king sought to put him to death: but when Urijah heard it, he was afraid, and fled, and went into Egypt;

22 And Jehoiakim the king sent men into Egypt, namely, Elnathan the son of Achbor, and certain men with him into Egypt.

23 And they fetched forth Urijah out of Egypt, and brought him unto Jehoiakim the king; who slew him with the sword, and cast his dead body into the graves of the common people.

24 Nevertheless the hand of Ahikam the son of Shaphan was with Jeremiah, that they should not give him into the hand of the people to put him to death.

CHAPTER 27

1 In the beginning of the reign of Jehoiakim the son of Josiah king of Judah came this word unto Jeremiah from the LORD, saying,
2 Thus said the LORD to me; Make you bonds and yokes, and put them upon your neck,
3 And send them to the king of Edom, and to the king of Moab, and to the king of the Ammonites, and to the king of Tyrus, and to the king of Zidon, by the hand of the messengers which come to Jerusalem unto Zedekiah king of Judah;
4 And command them to say unto their masters, Thus said the LORD of hosts, the God of Israel; Thus will you say unto your masters;
5 I have made the earth, the man and the beast that *are* upon the ground, by my great power and by my outstretched arm, and have given it unto whom it seemed meet unto me.
6 And now have I given all these lands into the hand of Nebuchadnezzar the king of Babylon, my servant; and the beasts of the field have I given him also to serve him.
7 And all nations will serve him, and his son, and his son's son, until the very time of his land come: and then many nations and great kings will serve themselves of him.
8 And it will come to pass, *that* the nation and kingdom which will not serve the same Nebuchadnezzar the king of Babylon, and that will not put their neck under the yoke of the king of Babylon, that nation will I punish, said the LORD, with the sword, and with the famine, and with the pestilence, until I have consumed them by his hand.
9 Therefore hearken not you to your prophets, or to your diviners, or to your dreamers, or to your enchanters, or to your sorcerers, which speak unto you, saying, you will not serve the king of Babylon:
10 For they prophesy a lie unto you, to remove you far from your land; and that I should drive you out, and you should perish.
11 But the nations that bring their neck under the yoke of the king of Babylon, and serve him, those will I let remain still in their own land, said the LORD; and they will till it, and dwell therein.
12 I spoke also to Zedekiah king of Judah according to all these words, saying, Bring your necks under the yoke of the king of Babylon, and serve him and his people, and live.
13 Why will you die, you and your people, by the sword, by the famine, and by the pestilence, as the LORD have spoken against the nation that will not serve the king of Babylon?
14 Therefore hearken not unto the words of the prophets that speak unto you, saying, you will not serve the king of Babylon: for they prophesy a lie unto you.
15 For I have not sent them, said the LORD, yet they prophesy a lie in my name; that I might drive you out, and that you might perish, ye, and the prophets that prophesy unto you.
16 Also I spoke to the priests and to all this people, saying, Thus said the LORD; Hearken not to the words of your prophets that prophesy unto you, saying, Behold, the vessels of the LORD'S house will now shortly be brought again from Babylon: for they prophesy a lie unto you.
17 Hearken not unto them; serve the king of Babylon, and live: wherefore should this city be laid waste?
18 [But if they *be* prophets, and if the word of the LORD be with them, let them now make intercession to the LORD of hosts, that the vessels which are left in the house of the LORD, and *in the* house of the king of Judah, and at Jerusalem, go not to Babylon.][1]
19 For thus said the LORD of hosts concerning the pillars, and concerning the sea, and concerning the bases, and concerning the residue of the vessels that remain in this city,
20 Which Nebuchadnezzar king of Babylon took not, when he carried away captive Jeconiah the son of Jehoiakim king of Judah from Jerusalem to Babylon, and all the nobles of Judah and Jerusalem;
21 Yea, thus said the LORD of hosts, the God of Israel, concerning the vessels that remain *in* the house of the LORD, and *in* the house of the king of Judah and of Jerusalem;
22 They will be carried to Babylon, and there will they be until the day that I visit them, said the LORD; then will I bring them up, and restore them to this place.

CHAPTER 28

1 And it came to pass the same year, in the beginning of the reign of Zedekiah king of Judah, in the fourth year, *and* in the fifth month, *that* Hananiah the son of Azur the prophet, which *was* of Gibeon, spoke unto me in the house of the LORD, in the presence of the priests and of all the people, saying,
2 Thus speaks the LORD of hosts, the God of Israel, saying, I have broken the yoke of the king of Babylon.
3 Within two full years will I bring again into this place all the vessels of the LORD'S house, that Nebuchadnezzar king of Babylon took away from this place, and carried them to Babylon:
4 And I will bring again to this place Jeconiah the son of Jehoiakim king of Judah, with all the captives of Judah, that went into Babylon, said the LORD: for I will break the yoke of the king of Babylon.
5 Then the prophet Jeremiah said unto the prophet Hananiah in the presence of the priests, and in the presence of all the people that stood in the house of the LORD,
6 Even the prophet Jeremiah said, Amen: the LORD do so: the LORD perform your words which you have prophesied, to bring again the vessels of the LORD'S house, and all that is carried away captive, from Babylon into this place.
7 Nevertheless hear you now this word that I speak in your ears, and in the ears of all the people;
8 The prophets that have been before me and before you of old prophesied both against many countries, and against great kingdoms, of war, and of evil, and of pestilence.
9 The prophet which prophesies of peace, when the word of the prophet will come to pass, *then* will the prophet be known, that the LORD have truly sent him.
10 Then Hananiah the prophet took the yoke from off the prophet Jeremiah's neck, and **broke**[2] it.
11 And Hananiah spoke in the presence of all the people, saying, thus said the LORD; Even so will I break the yoke of Nebuchadnezzar king of Babylon from the neck of all nations within the space of two full years. And the prophet Jeremiah went his way.
12 Then the word of the LORD came unto Jeremiah *the prophet*, after that Hananiah the prophet had broken the yoke from off the neck of the prophet Jeremiah, saying,
13 Go and tell Hananiah, saying, thus said the LORD; you have broken the yokes of wood; but you will make for them yokes of iron.

---

[1] The privaledge of true prophets only after God speaks.
[2] broke- a primitive root; to *burst* (literally or figuratively): -break (down, off, in pieces, up), bring to the birth, crush, destroy, hurt, quench, tear. [Strgs#7665]

14 For thus said the LORD of hosts, the God of Israel; I have put a yoke of iron upon the neck of all these nations, that they may serve Nebuchadnezzar king of Babylon; and they will serve him: and I have given him the beasts of the field also.
15 Then said the prophet Jeremiah unto Hananiah the prophet, Hear now, Hananiah; The LORD have not sent you; but you makes this people to trust in a lie.
16 Therefore thus said the LORD; Behold, I will cast you from off the face of the earth: this year you will die, because you have taught rebellion against the LORD.
17 So Hananiah the prophet died the same year in the seventh month.

CHAPTER 29

1 Now these *are* the words of the letter that Jeremiah the prophet sent from Jerusalem unto the residue of the elders which were carried away captives, and to the priests, and to the prophets, and to all the people whom Nebuchadnezzar had carried away captive from Jerusalem to Babylon;
2 (After that Jeconiah the king, and the queen, and the eunuchs, the princes of Judah and Jerusalem, and the carpenters, and the smiths, were departed from Jerusalem;)
3 By the hand of Elasah the son of Shaphan, and Gemariah the son of Hilkiah, (whom Zedekiah king of Judah sent unto Babylon to Nebuchadnezzar king of Babylon) saying,
4 Thus said the LORD of hosts, the God of Israel, unto all that are carried away captives, whom I have caused to be carried away from Jerusalem unto Babylon;
5 Build you houses, and dwell *in them*; and plant gardens, and eat the fruit of them;
6 Take you wives, and beget sons and daughters; and take wives for your sons, and give your daughters to husbands, that they may bear sons and daughters; that you may be increased there, and not diminished.
7 And seek the peace of the city where I have caused you to be carried away captives, and pray unto the LORD for it: for in the peace thereof will you have peace.
8 For thus said the LORD of hosts, the God of Israel; Let not your prophets and your diviners, that *be* in the midst of you, deceive you, neither hearken to your dreams which you cause to be dreamed.
9 For they prophesy falsely unto you in my name: I have not sent them, said the LORD.
10 For thus said the LORD, that after seventy years be accomplished at Babylon I will visit you, and perform my good word toward you, in causing you to return to this place.
11 For I know the thoughts that I think toward you, said the LORD, thoughts of peace, and not of evil, to give you an expected end.
12 Then will you call upon me, and you will go and pray unto me, and I will hearken unto you.
13 And you will seek me, and find *me*, when you will search for me with all your heart.
14 And I will be found of you, said the LORD: and I will turn away your captivity, and I will gather you from all the nations, and from all the places where I have driven you, said the LORD; and I will bring you again into the place where I caused you to be carried away captive.
15 Because you have said, The LORD has raised us up prophets in Babylon;
16 *Know* that thus said the LORD of the king that sits upon the throne of David, and of all the people that dwells in this city, and of your brethren that are not gone forth with you into captivity;
17 Thus said the LORD of hosts; Behold, I will send upon them the sword, the famine, and the pestilence, and will make them like vile figs, that cannot be eaten, they are so evil.
18 And I will persecute them with the sword, with the famine, and with the pestilence, and will deliver them to be removed to all the kingdoms of the earth, to be a curse, and an astonishment, and an hissing, and a reproach, among all the nations where I have driven them:
19 Because they have not hearkened to my words, said the LORD, which I sent unto them by my servants the prophets, rising up early and sending *them*; but you would not hear, said the LORD.
20 Hear you therefore the word of the LORD, all you of the captivity, whom I have sent from Jerusalem to Babylon:
21 Thus said the LORD of hosts, the God of Israel, of Ahab the son of Kolaiah, and of Zedekiah the son of Maaseiah, which prophesy a lie unto you in my name; Behold, I will deliver them into the hand of Nebuchadrezzar king of Babylon; and he will slay them before your eyes;
22 And of them will be taken up a curse by all the captivity of Judah which *are* in Babylon, saying, The LORD make you like Zedekiah and like Ahab, whom the king of Babylon roasted in the fire;
23 Because they have committed villany in Israel, and have committed adultery with their neighbors' wives, and have spoken lying words in my name, which I have not commanded them; even I know, and *am* a witness, said the LORD.
24 *Thus* will you also speak to Shemaiah the Nehelamite, saying,
25 Thus speaks the LORD of hosts, the God of Israel, saying, Because you have sent letters in your name unto all the people that *are* at Jerusalem, and to Zephaniah the son of Maaseiah the priest, and to all the priests, saying,
26 The LORD have made you priest in the stead of Jehoiada the priest, that you should be officers in the house of the LORD, for every man *that is* mad, and makes himself a prophet, that you should put him in prison, and in the stocks.
27 Now therefore why have you not reproved Jeremiah of Anathoth, which makes himself a prophet to you?
28 For therefore he sent unto us *in* Babylon, saying, this *captivity is* long: build you houses, and dwell *in them*; and plant gardens, and eat the fruit of them.
29 And Zephaniah the priest read this letter in the ears of Jeremiah the prophet.
30 Then came the word of the LORD unto Jeremiah, saying,
31 Send to all them of the captivity, saying, Thus said the LORD concerning Shemaiah the Nehelamite; Because that Shemaiah have prophesied unto you, and I sent him not, and he caused you to trust in a lie:
32 Therefore thus said the LORD; Behold, I will punish Shemaiah the Nehelamite, and his seed: he will not have a man to dwell among this people; neither will he behold the good that I will do for my people, said the LORD; because he have taught rebellion against the LORD.

CHAPTER 30

1 The word that came to Jeremiah from the LORD, saying,
2 Thus speaks the LORD God of Israel, saying, write[1] you all the words that I have spoken unto you in a book.

---

[1] write- to grave; by implication to write (describe, inscribe, prescribe, subscribe): - record. [Strgs#3789]

3 For, lo, the days come, said the LORD, that I will bring again the captivity of my people Israel and Judah, said the LORD: and I will cause them to return to the land that I gave to their fathers, and they will possess it.
4 And these *are* the words that the LORD spoke concerning Israel and concerning Judah.
5 For thus said the LORD; we have heard a voice of trembling, of fear, and not of peace.
6 Ask you now, and see whether a man does travail with child? Wherefore do I see every man with his hands on his loins, as a woman in travail, and all faces are turned into paleness?
7 Alas! For that day *is* great, so that none *is* like it: it *is* even the time of Jacob's trouble; but he will be saved out of it.
8 For it will come to pass in that day, said the LORD of hosts, *that* I will break his yoke from off your neck, and will burst your bonds, and strangers will no more serve themselves of him:
9 But they will serve the LORD their God, and David their king, whom I will raise up unto them.
10 Therefore fear you not, O my servant Jacob, said the LORD; neither be dismayed, O Israel: for, lo, I will save you from afar, and your seed from the land of their captivity; and Jacob will return, and will be in rest, and be quiet, and none will make *him* afraid.
11 For I *am* with you, said the LORD, to save you: though I make a full end of all nations where I have scattered you, yet will I not make a full end of you: but I will correct you in measure, and will not leave you altogether unpunished.
12 For thus said the LORD, your bruise *is* incurable, *and* your wound *is* grievous.
13 *There is* none to plead your cause, that you may be bound up: you have no healing medicines.
14 All your lovers have forgotten you; they seek you not; for I have wounded you with the wound of an enemy, with the chastisement of a cruel one, for the multitude of your iniquity; *because* your sins were increased.
15 Why cries you for your affliction? Your sorrow *is* incurable for the multitude of your iniquity: *because* your sins were increased, I have done these things unto you.
16 Therefore all they that devour you will be devoured; and all your adversaries, every one of them, will go into captivity; and they that spoil you will be a spoil, and all that prey upon you will I give for a prey.
17 For I will restore health unto you, and I will heal you of your wounds, said the LORD; because they called you an Outcast, *saying,* this *is* Zion, whom no man seeks after.
18 Thus said the LORD; Behold, I will bring again the captivity of Jacob's tents, and have mercy on his dwelling places; and the city will be **built** upon her own heap, and the palace will remain after the manner thereof.
19 And out of them will proceed thanksgiving and the voice of them that make merry: and I will multiply them, and they will not be few; I will also glorify them, and they will not be small.
20 Their children also will be as aforetime, and their congregation will be established before me, and I will punish all that oppress them.
21 And their nobles will be of themselves, and their governor will proceed from the midst of them; and I will cause him to draw near, and he will approach unto me: for who *is* this that engaged his heart to approach unto me? Said the LORD.
22 And you will be my people, and I will be your God.
23 Behold, the whirlwind of the LORD goes forth with fury, a continuing whirlwind: it will fall with pain upon the head of the wicked.
24 The fierce anger of the LORD will not return, until he **has** done *it,* and until he **has** performed the intents of his heart: in the latter days you will consider it.

CHAPTER 31

1 At the same time, said the LORD, will I be the God of all the families of Israel, and they will be my people.
2 Thus said the LORD, The people *which were* left of the sword found grace in the wilderness; *even* Israel, when I went to cause him to rest.
3 The LORD **has** appeared of old unto me, *saying,* Yea, I have loved you with an everlasting love: therefore with loving-kindness have I drawn you.
4 Again I will build you, and you will be built, O virgin of Israel: you will again be adorned with your **tambourines**, and will go forth in the dances of them that make merry.
5 you will yet plant vines upon the mountains of Samaria: the planters will plant, and will eat *them* as common things.
6 For there will be a day, *that* the watchmen upon the mount Ephraim will cry, Arise ye, and let us go up to Zion unto the LORD our God.
7 For thus said the LORD; Sing with gladness for Jacob, and shout among the chief of the nations: publish ye, praise ye, and say, O LORD, save your people, the remnant of Israel.
8 Behold, I will bring them from the north country, and gather them from the coasts of the earth, *and* with them the blind and the lame, the woman with child and her that travails with child together: a great company will return thither.
9 They will come with weeping, and with supplications will I lead them: I will cause them to walk by the rivers of waters in a straight way, wherein they will not stumble: for I am a father to Israel, and Ephraim *is* my firstborn.
10 Hear the word of the LORD, O you nations, and declare *it* in the isles afar off, and say, He that scattered Israel will gather him, and keep him, as a shepherd does his flock.
11 For the LORD have redeemed Jacob, and ransomed him from the hand of *him that was* stronger than he.
12 Therefore they will come and sing in the height of Zion, and will flow together to the goodness of the LORD, for wheat, and for wine, and for oil, and for the young of the flock and of the herd: and their soul will be as a watered garden; and they will not sorrow any more at all.
13 Then will the virgin rejoice in the dance, both young men and old together: for I will turn their mourning into joy, and will comfort them, and make them rejoice from their sorrow.
14 And I will satiate the soul of the priests with fatness, and my people will be satisfied with my goodness, said the LORD.
15 Thus said the LORD; a voice was heard in Ramah, lamentation, *and* bitter weeping; Rahel weeping for her children refused to be comforted for her children, because they *were* not.
16 Thus said the LORD; Refrain your voice from weeping, and your eyes from tears: for your work will be rewarded, said the LORD; and they will come again from the land of the enemy.
17 And there is hope in your end, said the LORD, that your children will come again to their own border.
18 I have surely heard Ephraim bemoaning himself *thus;* you have chastised me, and I was chastised, as a bullock un accustomed *to*

the yoke: turn you me, and I will be turned; for you are the LORD my God.

19 Surely after that I was turned, I repented; and after that I was instructed, I smote upon *my* thigh: I was ashamed, yea, even confounded, because I did bear the reproach of my youth.

20 *Is* Ephraim my dear son? *Is he* a pleasant child? For since I spoke against him, I do earnestly remember him still: therefore my bowels are troubled for him; I will surely have mercy upon him, said the LORD.

21 Set you up way marks, make you high heaps: set your heart toward the highway, *even* the way *which* you went: turn again, O virgin of Israel, turn again to these your cities.

22 How long will you go about, O you backsliding daughter? For the LORD have created a new thing in the earth, a woman will compass a man.

23 Thus said the LORD of hosts, the God of Israel; As yet they will use this speech in the land of Judah and in the cities thereof, when I will bring again their captivity; The LORD bless you, O habitation of justice, *and* mountain of holiness.

24 And there will dwell in Judah itself, and in all the cities thereof together, husbandmen, and they *that* go forth with flocks.

25 For I have satiated the weary soul, and I have replenished every sorrowful soul.

26 Upon this I awaked, and beheld; and my sleep was sweet unto me.

27 Behold, the days come, said the LORD, that I will sow the house of Israel and the house of Judah with the seed of man, and with the seed of beast.

28 And it will come to pass, *that* like as I have watched over them, to pluck up, and to break down, and to throw down, and to destroy, and to afflict; so will I watch over them, to build, and to plant, said the LORD.

29 In those days they will say no more, the fathers have eaten a sour grape, and the children's teeth are set on edge.

30 But everyone will die for his own iniquity: every man that eats the sour grape, his teeth will be set on edge.

31 Behold, the days come, said the LORD, that I will make a new covenant with the house of Israel, and with the house of Judah:

32 Not according to the covenant that I made with their fathers in the day *that* I took them by the hand to bring them out of the land of Egypt; which my covenant they brake, although I was an husband unto them, said the LORD:

33 But this will *be* the covenant that I will make with the house of Israel; After those days, said the LORD, I will put my law in their inward parts, and write it in their hearts; and will be their God, and they will be my people.

34 And they will teach no more every man his neighbor, and every man his brother, saying, Know the LORD: for they will all know me, from the least of them unto the greatest of them, said the LORD: for I will forgive their iniquity, and I will remember their sin no more.

35 Thus said the LORD, which gives the sun for a light by day, *and* the ordinances of the moon and of the stars for a light by night, which divides the sea when the waves thereof roar; The LORD of hosts *is* his name:

36 If those ordinances depart from before me, said the LORD, *then* the seed of Israel also will cease from being a nation before me forever.

37 Thus said the LORD; If heaven above can be measured, and the foundations of the earth searched out beneath, I will also cast off all the seed of Israel for all that they have done, said the LORD.

38 Behold, the days come, said the LORD, that the city will be built to the LORD from the tower of Hananeel unto the gate of the corner.

39 And the measuring line will yet go forth over against it upon the hill Gareb, and will compass about to Goath.

40 And the whole valley of the dead bodies, and of the ashes, and all the fields unto the brook of Kidron, unto the corner of the horse gate toward the east, will *be* holy unto the LORD; it will not be plucked up, or thrown down any more forever.

CHAPTER 32

1 The word that came to Jeremiah from the LORD in the tenth year of Zedekiah king of Judah, which *was* the eighteenth year of Nebuchadrezzar.

2 For then the king of Babylon's army besieged Jerusalem: and Jeremiah the prophet was shut up in the court of the prison, which *was* in the king of Judah's house.

3 For Zedekiah king of Judah had shut him up, saying, Wherefore dost you prophesy, and say, Thus said the LORD, Behold, I will give this city into the hand of the king of Babylon, and he will take it;

4 And Zedekiah king of Judah will not escape out of the hand of the Chaldeans, but will surely be delivered into the hand of the king of Babylon, and will speak with him mouth to mouth, and his eyes will behold his eyes;

5 And he will lead Zedekiah to Babylon, and there will he be until I visit him, said the LORD: though you fight with the Chaldeans, you will not prosper.

6 And Jeremiah said, the word of the LORD came unto me, saying,

7 Behold, Hanameel the son of Shallum your uncle will come unto you, saying, Buy you my field that *is* in Anathoth: for the right of redemption *is* your to buy *it*.

8 So Hanameel mine uncle's son came to me in the court of the prison according to the word of the LORD, and said unto me, Buy my field, I pray you, that *is* in Anathoth, which *is* in the country of Benjamin: for the right of inheritance *is* yours, and the redemption *is* yours; buy *it* for thyself. Then I knew that this *was* the word of the LORD.

9 And I bought the field of Hanameel my uncle's son, that *was* in Anathoth, and weighed him the money, *even* seventeen shekels of silver.

10 And I subscribed the evidence, and sealed *it*, and took witnesses, and weighed *him* the money in the balances.

11 So I took the evidence of the purchase, *both* that which was sealed *according* to the law and custom, and that which was open:

12 And I gave the evidence of the purchase unto Baruch the son of Neriah, the son of Maaseiah, in the sight of Hanameel mine uncle's *son*, and in the presence of the witnesses that subscribed the book of the purchase, before all the Jews that sat in the court of the prison.

13 And I charged Baruch before them, saying,

14 Thus said the LORD of hosts, the God of Israel; Take these evidences, this evidence of the purchase, both which is sealed, and this evidence which is open; and put them in an earthen vessel, that they may continue many days.

15 For thus said the LORD of hosts, the God of Israel; Houses and fields and vineyards will be possessed again in this land.

16 Now when I had delivered the evidence of the purchase unto Baruch the son of Neriah, I prayed unto the LORD, saying,

17 Ah Lord GOD! Behold, you have made the heaven and the earth by your great power and stretched out arm, *and* there is nothing too hard for you:
18 you show loving-kindness unto thousands, and recompenses the iniquity of the fathers into the bosom of their children after them: the Great, the Mighty God, the LORD of hosts, *is* his name,
19 Great in counsel, and mighty in work: for your eyes *are* open upon all the ways of the sons of men: to give everyone according to his ways, and according to the fruit of his doings:
20 Which have set signs and wonders in the land of Egypt, *even* unto this day, and in Israel, and among *other* men; and have made you a name, as at this day;
21 And have brought forth your people Israel out of the land of Egypt with signs, and with wonders, and with a strong hand, and with a stretched out arm, and with great terror;
22 And have given them this land, which you did swear to their fathers to give them, a land flowing with milk and honey;
23 And they came in, and possessed it; but they obeyed not your voice, neither walked in your law; they have done nothing of all that you commanded them to do: therefore you have caused all this evil to come upon them:
24 Behold the mounts, they are come unto the city to take it; and the city is given into the hand of the Chaldeans, that fight against it, because of the sword, and of the famine, and of the pestilence: and what you have spoken is come to pass; and, behold, you see *it*.
25 And you have said unto me, O Lord GOD, Buy you the field for money, and take witnesses; for the city is given into the hand of the Chaldeans.
26 Then came the word of the LORD unto Jeremiah, saying,
27 Behold, I *am* the LORD, the God of all flesh: is there anything too hard for me?
28 Therefore thus said the LORD; Behold, I will give this city into the hand of the Chaldeans, and into the hand of Nebuchadrezzar king of Babylon, and he will take it:
29 And the Chaldeans, that fight against this city, will come and set fire on this city, and burn it with the houses, upon whose roofs they have offered incense unto Baal, and poured out drink offerings unto other gods, to provoke me to anger.
30 For the children of Israel and the children of Judah have only done evil before me from their youth: for the children of Israel have only provoked me to anger with the work of their hands, said the LORD.
31 For this city have been to me *as* a provocation of mine anger and of my fury from the day that they built it even unto this day; that I should remove it from before my face,
32 Because of all the evil of the children of Israel and of the children of Judah, which they have done to provoke me to anger, they, their kings, their princes, their priests, and their prophets, and the men of Judah, and the inhabitants of Jerusalem.
33 And they have turned unto me the back, and not the face: though I taught them, rising up early and teaching *them*, yet they have not hearkened to receive instruction.
34 But they set their abominations in the house, which is called by my name, to defile it.
35 And they built the high places of Baal, which *are* in the valley of the son of Hinnom, to cause their sons and their daughters to pass through *the fire* unto Molech; which I commanded them not, neither came it into my mind, that they should do this abomination, to cause Judah to sin.
36 And now therefore thus said the LORD, the God of Israel, concerning this city, whereof you say, It will be delivered into the hand of the king of Babylon by the sword, and by the famine, and by the pestilence;
37 Behold, I will gather them out of all countries, where I have driven them in mine anger, and in my fury, and in great wrath; and I will bring them again unto this place, and I will cause them to dwell safely:
38 And they will be my people, and I will be their God:
39 And I will give them one heart, and one way, that they may fear me forever, for the good of them, and of their children after them:
40 And I will make an everlasting covenant with them that I will not turn away from them, to do them good; but I will put my fear in their hearts, that they will not depart from me.
41 Yea, I will rejoice over them to do them good, and I will plant them in this land assuredly with my whole heart and with my whole soul.
42 For thus said the LORD; Like as I have brought all this great evil upon this people, so will I bring upon them all the good that I have promised them.
43 And fields will be bought in this land, whereof you say, *it is* desolate without man or beast; it is given into the hand of the Chaldeans.
44 Men will buy fields for money, and subscribe evidences, and seal *them*, and take witnesses in the land of Benjamin, and in the places about Jerusalem, and in the cities of Judah, and in the cities of the mountains, and in the cities of the valley, and in the cities of the south: for I will cause their captivity to return, said the LORD.

CHAPTER 33

1 Moreover the word of the LORD came unto Jeremiah the second time, while he was yet shut up in the court of the prison, saying,
2 Thus said the LORD the maker thereof, the LORD that formed it, to establish it; the LORD *is* his name;
3 Call unto me, and I will answer you, and show you great and mighty things, which you know not.
4 For thus said the LORD, the God of Israel, concerning the houses of this city, and concerning the houses of the kings of Judah, which are thrown down by the mounts, and by the sword;
5 They come to fight with the Chaldeans, but *it is* to fill them with the dead bodies of men, whom I have slain in mine anger and in my fury, and for all whose wickedness I have hid my face from this city.
6 Behold, I will bring it health and cure, and I will cure them, and will reveal unto them the abundance of peace and truth.
7 And I will cause the captivity of Judah and the captivity of Israel to return, and will build them, as at the first.
8 And I will cleanse them from all their iniquity, whereby they have sinned against me; and I will pardon all their iniquities, whereby they have sinned, and whereby they have transgressed against me.
9 And it will be to me a name of joy, a praise and an honor before all the nations of the earth, which will hear all the good that I do unto them: and they will fear and tremble for all the goodness and for all the prosperity that I procure unto it.
10 Thus said the LORD; Again there will be heard in this place, which you say will *be* desolate without man and without beast, *even* in the cities of Judah, and in the streets of Jerusalem, that are desolate, without man, and without inhabitant, and without beast,

11 The voice of joy, and the voice of gladness, the voice of the bridegroom, and the voice of the bride, the voice of them that will say, Praise the LORD of hosts: for the LORD *is* good; for his mercy *endures* for ever: *and* of them that will bring the sacrifice of praise into the house of the LORD. For I will cause to return the captivity of the land, as at the first, said the LORD.
12 Thus said the LORD of hosts; Again in this place, which is desolate without man and without beast, and in all the cities thereof, will be an habitation of shepherds causing *their* flocks to lie down.
13 In the cities of the mountains, in the cities of the vale, and in the cities of the south, and in the land of Benjamin, and in the places about Jerusalem, and in the cities of Judah, will the flocks pass again under the hands of him that tells *them*, said the LORD.
14 Behold, the days come, said the LORD, that I will perform that good thing which I have promised unto the house of Israel and to the house of Judah.
15 In those days, and at that time, will I cause the Branch of righteousness to grow up unto David; and he will execute judgment and righteousness in the land.
16 In those days will Judah be saved, and Jerusalem will dwell safely: and this *is the name* wherewith she will be called, The LORD our righteousness.
17 For thus said the LORD; David will never want a man to sit upon the throne of the house of Israel;
18 Neither will the priests the Levites want a man before me to offer burnt offerings, and to kindle meat offerings, and to do sacrifice continually.
19 And the word of the LORD came unto Jeremiah, saying,
20 Thus said the LORD; if you can break my covenant of the day, and my covenant of the night, and that there should not be day and night in their season;
21 *Then* may also my covenant be broken with David my servant, that he should not have a son to reign upon his throne; and with the Levites the priests, my ministers.
22 As the host of heaven cannot be numbered, neither the sand of the sea measured: so will I multiply the seed of David my servant, and the Levites that minister unto me.
23 Moreover the word of the LORD came to Jeremiah, saying,
24 Considers you not what this people have spoken, saying, the two families which the LORD have chosen, he have even cast them off? thus they have despised my people, that they should be no more a nation before them.
25 Thus said the LORD; if my covenant *be* not with day and night, *and if* I have not appointed the ordinances of heaven and earth;
26 Then will I cast away the seed of Jacob, and David my servant, *so that* I will not take *any* of his seed *to be* rulers over the seed of Abraham, Isaac, and Jacob: for I will cause their captivity to return, and have mercy on them.

CHAPTER 34

1 The word which came unto Jeremiah from the LORD, when Nebuchadnezzar king of Babylon, and all his army, and all the kingdoms of the earth of his dominion, and all the people, fought against Jerusalem, and against all the cities thereof, saying,
2 Thus said the LORD, the God of Israel; Go and speak to Zedekiah king of Judah, and tell him, Thus said the LORD; Behold, I will give this city into the hand of the king of Babylon, and he will burn it with fire:
3 And you will not escape out of his hand, but will surely be taken, and delivered into his hand; and your eyes will behold the eyes of the king of Babylon, and he will speak with you mouth to mouth, and you will go to Babylon.
4 Yet hear the word of the LORD, O Zedekiah king of Judah; Thus said the LORD of you, you will not die by the sword:
5 *But* you will die in peace: and with the burnings of your fathers, the former kings which were before you, so will they burn *odors* for you; and they will lament you, *saying*, Ah lord! For I have pronounced the word, said the LORD.
6 Then Jeremiah the prophet spoke all these words unto Zedekiah king of Judah in Jerusalem,
7 When the king of Babylon's army fought against Jerusalem, and against all the cities of Judah that were left, against Lachish, and against Azekah: for these **defensive** cities remained of the cities of Judah.
8 *This is* the word that came unto Jeremiah from the LORD, after that the king Zedekiah had made a covenant with all the people which *were* at Jerusalem, to proclaim liberty unto them;
9 That every man should let his manservant, and every man his maidservant, *being* a Hebrew or an Hebrewess, go free; that none should serve himself of them, *to wit*, of a Jew his brother.
10 Now when all the princes, and all the people, which had entered into the covenant, heard that everyone should let his manservant, and everyone his maidservant, go free, that none should serve themselves of them anymore, then they obeyed, and let *them* go.
11 But afterward they turned, and caused the servants and the handmaids, whom they had let go free, to return, and brought them into subjection for servants and for handmaids.
12 Therefore the word of the LORD came to Jeremiah from the LORD, saying,
13 Thus said the LORD, the God of Israel; I made a covenant with your fathers in the day that I brought them forth out of the land of Egypt, out of the house of bondmen, saying,
14 At the end of seven years let you go every man his brother an Hebrew, which have been sold unto you; and when he have served you six years, you will let him go free from you: but your fathers hearkened not unto me, neither inclined their ear.
15 And you were now turned, and had done right in my sight, in proclaiming liberty every man to his neighbor; and you had made a covenant before me in the house which is called by my name:
16 But you turned and polluted my name, and caused every man his servant, and every man his handmaid, whom you had set at liberty at their pleasure, to return, and brought into subjection, to be unto you for servants and for handmaids.
17 Therefore thus said the LORD; you have not hearkened unto me, in proclaiming liberty, every one to his brother, and every man to his neighbor: behold, I proclaim a liberty for you, said the LORD, to the sword, to the pestilence, and to the famine; and I will make you to be removed into all the kingdoms of the earth.
18 And I will give the men that have transgressed my covenant, which have not performed the words of the covenant which they had made before me, when they cut the calf in twain, and passed between the parts thereof,
19 The princes of Judah, and the princes of Jerusalem, the eunuchs, and the priests, and all the people of the land, which passed between the parts of the calf;
20 I will even give them into the hand of their enemies, and into the hand of them that seek their life: and their dead bodies will be for meat unto the fowls of the heaven, and to the beasts of the earth.
21 And Zedekiah king of Judah and his princes will I give into the hand of their enemies, and into the hand of them that seek their

life, and into the hand of the king of Babylon's army, which are gone up from you.

22 Behold, I will command, said the LORD, and cause them to return to this city; and they will fight against it, and take it, and burn it with fire: and I will make the cities of Judah a desolation without an inhabitant.

CHAPTER 35

1 The word which came unto Jeremiah from the LORD in the days of Jehoiakim the son of Josiah king of Judah, saying,

2 Go unto the house of the Rechabites, and speak unto them, and bring them into the house of the LORD, into one of the chambers, and give them wine to drink.

3 Then I took Jaazaniah the son of Jeremiah, the son of Habaziniah, and his brethren, and all his sons, and the whole house of the Rechabites;

4 And I brought them into the house of the LORD, into the chamber of the sons of Hanan, the son of Igdaliah, a man of God, which *was* by the chamber of the princes, which *was* above the chamber of Maaseiah the son of Shallum, the keeper of the door:

5 And I set before the sons of the house of the Rechabites pots full of wine, and cups, and I said unto them, Drink you wine.

6 But they said, we will drink no wine: for Jonadab the son of Rechab our father commanded us, saying, you will drink no wine, *neither ye*, or your sons for ever:

7 Neither will you build house, or sow seed, or plant vineyard, or have *any*: but all your days you will dwell in tents; that you may live many days in the land where you *be* strangers.

8 Thus have we obeyed the voice of Jonadab the son of Rechab our father in all that he have charged us, to drink no wine all our days, we, our wives, our sons, or our daughters;

9 or to build houses for us to dwell in: neither have we vineyard, or field, or seed:

10 But we have dwelt in tents, and have obeyed, and done according to all that Jonadab our father commanded us.

11 But it came to pass, when Nebuchadrezzar king of Babylon came up into the land, that we said, Come, and let us go to Jerusalem for fear of the army of the Chaldeans, and for fear of the army of the Syrians: so we dwell at Jerusalem.

12 Then came the word of the LORD unto Jeremiah, saying,

13 Thus said the LORD of hosts, the God of Israel; Go and tell the men of Judah and the inhabitants of Jerusalem, Will you not receive instruction to hearken to my words? Said the LORD.

14 The words of Jonadab the son of Rechab, that he commanded his sons not to drink wine, are performed; for unto this day they drink none, but obey their father's commandment: notwithstanding I have spoken unto you, rising early and speaking; but you hearkened not unto me.

15 I have sent also unto you all my servants the prophets, rising up early and sending *them*, saying, Return you now every man from his evil way, and amend your doings, and go not after other gods to serve them, and you will dwell in the land which I have given to you and to your fathers: but you have not inclined your ear, or hearkened unto me.

16 Because the sons of Jonadab the son of Rechab have performed the commandment of their father, which he commanded them; but this people have not hearkened unto me:

17 Therefore thus said the LORD God of hosts, the God of Israel; Behold, I will bring upon Judah and upon all the inhabitants of Jerusalem all the evil that I have pronounced against them: because I have spoken unto them, but they have not heard; and I have called unto them, but they have not answered.

18 And Jeremiah said unto the house of the Rechabites, Thus said the LORD of hosts, the God of Israel; because you have obeyed the commandment of Jonadab your father, and kept all his precepts, and done according unto all that he have commanded you:

19 Therefore thus said the LORD of hosts, the God of Israel; Jonadab the son of Rechab will not want a man to stand before me forever.

CHAPTER 36

1 And it came to pass in the fourth year of Jehoiakim the son of Josiah king of Judah, *that* this word came unto Jeremiah from the LORD, saying,

2 Take you a roll of a book, and write therein all the words that I have spoken unto you against Israel, and against Judah, and against all the nations, from the day I spoke unto you, from the days of Josiah, even unto this day.

3 It may be that the house of Judah will hear all the evil which I purpose to do unto them; that they may return every man from his evil way; that I may forgive their iniquity and their sin.

4 Then Jeremiah called Baruch the son of Neriah: and Baruch wrote from the mouth of Jeremiah all the words of the LORD, which he had spoken unto him, upon a roll of a book.

5 And Jeremiah commanded Baruch, saying, I *am* shut up; I cannot go into the house of the LORD:

6 Therefore go you, and read in the roll, which you have written from my mouth, the words of the LORD in the ears of the people in the LORD'S house upon the fasting day: and also you will read them in the ears of all Judah that come out of their cities.

7 It may be they will present their supplication before the LORD, and will return everyone from his evil way: for great *is* the anger and the fury that the LORD **has** pronounced against this people.

8 And Baruch the son of Neriah did according to all that Jeremiah the prophet commanded him, reading in the book the words of the LORD in the LORD'S house.

9 And it came to pass in the fifth year of Jehoiakim the son of Josiah king of Judah, in the ninth month, *that* they proclaimed a fast before the LORD to all the people in Jerusalem, and to all the people that came from the cities of Judah unto Jerusalem.

10 Then read Baruch in the book the words of Jeremiah in the house of the LORD, in the chamber of Gemariah the son of Shaphan the scribe, in the higher court, at the entry of the new gate of the LORD'S house, in the ears of all the people.

11 When Michaiah the son of Gemariah, the son of Shaphan, had heard out of the book all the words of the LORD,

12 Then he went down into the king's house, into the scribe's chamber: and, lo, all the princes sat there, *even* Elishama the scribe, and Delaiah the son of Shemaiah, and Elnathan the son of Achbor, and Gemariah the son of Shaphan, and Zedekiah the son of Hananiah, and all the princes.

13 Then Michaiah declared unto them all the words that he had heard, when Baruch read the book in the ears of the people.

14 Therefore all the princes sent Jehudi the son of Nethaniah, the son of Shelemiah, the son of Cushi, unto Baruch, saying, Take in your hand the roll wherein you have read in the ears of the people, and come. So Baruch the son of Neriah took the roll in his hand, and came unto them.

15 And they said unto him, Sit down now, and read it in our ears. So Baruch read *it* in their ears.

16 Now it came to pass, when they had heard all the words, they were afraid both one and other, and said unto Baruch, We will surely tell the king of all these words.
17 And they asked Baruch, saying, Tell us now, How did you write all these words at his mouth?
18 Then Baruch answered them, He pronounced all these words unto me with his mouth, and I wrote *them* with ink in the book.
19 Then said the princes unto Baruch, Go, hide you, you and Jeremiah; and let no man know where you be.
20 And they went in to the king into the court, but they laid up the roll in the chamber of Elishama the scribe, and told all the words in the ears of the king.
21 So the king sent Jehudi to fetch the roll: and he took it out of Elishama the scribe's chamber. And Jehudi read it in the ears of the king, and in the ears of all the princes which stood beside the king.
22 Now the king sat in the winterhouse in the ninth month: and *there was a fire* on the hearth burning before him.
23 And it came to pass, *that* when Jehudi had read three or four leaves, he cut it with the penknife, and cast *it* into the fire that *was* on the hearth, until all the roll was consumed in the fire that *was* on the hearth.
24 Yet they were not afraid, or rent their garments, *neither* the king, or any of his servants that heard all these words.
25 Nevertheless Elnathan and Delaiah and Gemariah had made intercession to the king that he would not burn the roll: but he would not hear them.
26 But the king commanded Jerahmeel the son of Hammelech, and Seraiah the son of Azriel, and Shelemiah the son of Abdeel, to take Baruch the scribe and Jeremiah the prophet: but the LORD hid them.
27 Then the word of the LORD came to Jeremiah, after that the king had burned the roll, and the words which Baruch wrote at the mouth of Jeremiah, saying,
28 Take you again another roll, and write in it all the former words that were in the first roll, which Jehoiakim the king of Judah have burned.
29 And you will say to Jehoiakim king of Judah, Thus said the LORD; you have burned this roll, saying, Why have you written therein, saying, The king of Babylon will certainly come and destroy this land, and will cause to cease from thence man and beast?
30 Therefore thus said the LORD of Jehoiakim king of Judah; He will have none to sit upon the throne of David: and his dead body will be cast out in the day to the heat, and in the night to the frost.
31 And I will punish him and his seed and his servants for their iniquity; and I will bring upon them, and upon the inhabitants of Jerusalem, and upon the men of Judah, all the evil that I have pronounced against them; but they hearkened not.
32 Then took Jeremiah another roll, and gave it to Baruch the scribe, the son of Neriah; who wrote therein from the mouth of Jeremiah all the words of the book which Jehoiakim king of Judah had burned in the fire: and there were added besides unto them many like words.

CHAPTER 37

1 And king Zedekiah the son of Josiah reigned instead of Coniah the son of Jehoiakim, whom Nebuchadrezzar king of Babylon made king in the land of Judah.
2 But neither he, or his servants, or the people of the land, did hearken unto the words of the LORD, which he spoke by the prophet Jeremiah.
3 And Zedekiah the king sent Jehucal the son of Shelemiah and Zephaniah the son of Maaseiah the priest to the prophet Jeremiah, saying, Pray now unto the LORD our God for us.
4 Now Jeremiah came in and went out among the people: for they had not put him into prison.
5 Then Pharaoh's army was come forth out of Egypt: and when the Chaldeans that besieged Jerusalem heard tidings of them, they departed from Jerusalem.
6 Then came the word of the LORD unto the prophet Jeremiah, saying,
7 Thus said the LORD, the God of Israel; Thus will you say to the king of Judah, that sent you unto me to enquire of me; Behold, Pharaoh's army, which is come forth to help you, will return to Egypt into their own land.
8 And the Chaldeans will come again, and fight against this city, and take it, and burn it with fire.
9 Thus said the LORD; Deceive not yourselves, saying, The Chaldeans will surely depart from us: for they will not depart.
10 For though you had smitten the whole army of the Chaldeans that fight against you, and there remained *but* wounded men among them, *yet* should they rise up every man in his tent, and burn this city with fire.
11 And it came to pass, that when the army of the Chaldeans was broken up from Jerusalem for fear of Pharaoh's army,
12 Then Jeremiah went forth out of Jerusalem to go into the land of Benjamin, to separate himself thence in the midst of the people.
13 And when he was in the gate of Benjamin, a captain of the ward *was* there, whose name *was* Irijah, the son of Shelemiah, the son of Hananiah; and he took Jeremiah the prophet, saying, you fallest away to the Chaldeans.
14 Then said Jeremiah, *It is* false; I fall not away to the Chaldeans. But he hearkened not to him: so Irijah took Jeremiah, and brought him to the princes.
15 Wherefore the princes were wroth with Jeremiah, and smote him, and put him in prison in the house of Jonathan the scribe: for they had made that the prison.
16 When Jeremiah was entered into the dungeon, and into the cabins, and Jeremiah had remained there many days;
17 Then Zedekiah the king sent, and took him out: and the king asked him secretly in his house, and said, Is there *any* word from the LORD? And Jeremiah said, there is: for, said he, you will be delivered into the hand of the king of Babylon.
18 Moreover Jeremiah said unto King Zedekiah, What have I offended against you, or against your servants, or against this people, that you have put me in prison?
19 Where *are* now your prophets which prophesied unto you, saying, The king of Babylon will not come against you, or against this land?
20 Therefore hear now, I pray you, O my lord the king: let my supplication, I pray you, be accepted before you; that you cause me not to return to the house of Jonathan the scribe, lest I die there.
21 Then Zedekiah the king commanded that they should commit Jeremiah into the court of the prison, and that they should give him daily a piece of bread out of the bakers' street, until all the bread in the city were spent. Thus Jeremiah remained in the court of the prison.

CHAPTER 38

1 Then Shephatiah the son of Mattan, and Gedaliah the son of Pashur, and Jucal the son of Shelemiah, and Pashur the son of Malchiah, heard the words that Jeremiah had spoken unto all the people, saying,

2 Thus said the LORD, He that remaineth in this city will die by the sword, by the famine, and by the pestilence: but he that goeth forth to the Chaldeans will live; for he will have his life for a prey, and will live.

3 Thus said the LORD, This city will surely be given into the hand of the king of Babylon's army, which will take it.

4 Therefore the princes said unto the king, We beseech you, let this man be put to death: for thus he weakeneth the hands of the men of war that remain in this city, and the hands of all the people, in speaking such words unto them: for this man seeketh not the welfare of this people, but the hurt.

5 Then Zedekiah the king said, Behold, he *is* in your hand: for the king *is* not *he that* can do *any*thing against you.

6 Then **they took** Jeremiah, and cast him into the dungeon of Malchiah the son of Hammelech, that *was* in the court of the prison: and they let down Jeremiah with cords. And in the dungeon *there was* no water, but mire: so Jeremiah sunk in the mire.

7 Now when Ebed-melech the Ethiopian, one of the eunuchs which was in the king's house, heard that they had put Jeremiah in the dungeon; the king then sitting in the gate of Benjamin;

8 Ebed-melech went forth out of the king's house, and spoke to the king, saying,

9 My lord the king, these men have done evil in all that they have done to Jeremiah the prophet, whom they have cast into the dungeon; and he is like to die for hunger in the place where he is: for *there is* no more bread in the city.

10 Then the king commanded Ebed-melech the Ethiopian, saying, Take from hence thirty men with you, and take up Jeremiah the prophet out of the dungeon, before he die.

11 So Ebed-melech took the men with him, and went into the house of the king under the treasury, and took thence old cast clouts and old rotten rags, and let them down by cords into the dungeon to Jeremiah.

12 And Ebed-melech the Ethiopian said unto Jeremiah, Put now *these* old cast clouts and rotten rags under your armholes under the cords. And Jeremiah did so.

13 So they drew up Jeremiah with cords, and took him up out of the dungeon: and Jeremiah remained in the court of the prison.

14 Then Zedekiah the king sent, and took Jeremiah the prophet unto him into the third entry that *is* in the house of the LORD: and the king said unto Jeremiah, I will ask you a thing; hide nothing from me.

15 Then Jeremiah said unto Zedekiah, If I declare *it* unto you, will you not surely put me to death? And if I give you counsel, will you not hearken unto me?

16 So Zedekiah the king swore secretly unto Jeremiah, saying, *As* the LORD lives, that made us this soul, I will not put you to death, neither will I give you into the hand of these men that seek your life.

17 Then said Jeremiah unto Zedekiah, Thus said the LORD, the God of hosts, the God of Israel; If you will assuredly go forth unto the king of Babylon's princes, then your soul will live, and this city will not be burned with fire; and you will live, and your house:

18 But if you will not go forth to the king of Babylon's princes, then will this city be given into the hand of the Chaldeans, and they will burn it with fire, and you will not escape out of their hand.

19 And Zedekiah the king said unto Jeremiah, I am afraid of the Jews that are fallen to the Chaldeans, lest they deliver me into their hand, and they mock me.

20 But Jeremiah said, they will not deliver you. Obey, I beseech you, the voice of the LORD, which I speak unto you: so it will be well unto you, and your soul will live.

21 But if you refuse to go forth, this *is* the word that the LORD have showed me:

22 And, behold, all the women that are left in the king of Judah's house will *be* brought forth to the king of Babylon's princes, and those *women* will say, your friends have set you on, and have prevailed against you: your feet are sunk in the mire *and* they are turned away back.

23 So they will bring out all your wives and your children to the Chaldeans: and you will not escape out of their hand, but will be taken by the hand of the king of Babylon: and you will cause this city to be burned with fire.

24 Then said Zedekiah unto Jeremiah, Let no man know of these words, and you will not die.

25 But if the princes hear that I have talked with you, and they come unto you, and say unto you, Declare unto us now what you have said unto the king, hide it not from us, and we will not put you to death; also what the king said unto you:

26 Then you will say unto them, I presented my supplication before the king, that he would not cause me to return to Jonathan's house, to die there.

27 Then came all the princes unto Jeremiah, and asked him: and he told them according to all these words that the king had commanded. So they left off speaking with him; for the matter was not perceived.

28 So Jeremiah abode in the court of the prison until the day that Jerusalem was taken: and he was *there* when Jerusalem was taken.

CHAPTER 39

1 In the ninth year of Zedekiah king of Judah, in the tenth month, came Nebuchadrezzar king of Babylon and all his army against Jerusalem, and they besieged it.

2 *And* in the eleventh year of Zedekiah, in the fourth month, the ninth *day* of the month, the city was broken up.

3 And all the princes of the king of Babylon came in and sat in the middle gate, *even* Nergal-sharezer, Samgar-nebo, Sarsechim, Rab-saris, Nergal-sharezer, Rab-mag, with all the residue of the princes of the king of Babylon.

4 And it came to pass, *that* when Zedekiah the king of Judah saw them, and all the men of war, then they fled, and went forth out of the city by night, by the way of the king's garden, by the gate betwixt the two walls: and he went out the way of the plain.

5 But the Chaldeans' army pursued after them, and overtook Zedekiah in the plains of Jericho: and when they had taken him, they brought him up to Nebuchadnezzar king of Babylon to Riblah in the land of Hamath, where he gave judgment upon him.

6 Then the king of Babylon slew the sons of Zedekiah in Riblah before his eyes: also the king of Babylon slew all the nobles of Judah.

7 Moreover he put out Zedekiah's eyes, and bound him with chains, to carry him to Babylon.

8 And the Chaldeans burned the king's house, and the houses of the people, with fire, and brake down the walls of Jerusalem.
9 Then Nebuzar-adan the captain of the guard carried away captive into Babylon the remnant of the people that remained in the city, and those that fell away, that fell to him, with the rest of the people that remained.
10 But Nebuzar-adan the captain of the guard left of the poor of the people, which had nothing, in the land of Judah, and gave them vineyards and fields at the same time.
11 Now Nebuchadrezzar king of Babylon gave charge concerning Jeremiah to Nebuzar-adan the captain of the guard, saying,
12 Take him, and look well to him, and do him no harm; but do unto him even as he will say unto you.
13 So Nebuzar-adan the captain of the guard sent, and Nebushasban, Rab-saris, and Nergal-sharezer, Rab-mag, and all the king of Babylon's princes;
14 Even they sent, and took Jeremiah out of the court of the prison, and committed him unto Gedaliah the son of Ahikam the son of Shaphan, that he should carry him home: so he dwelt among the people.
15 Now the word of the LORD came unto Jeremiah, while he was shut up in the court of the prison, saying,
16 Go and speak to Ebed-melech the Ethiopian, saying, Thus said the LORD of hosts, the God of Israel; Behold, I will bring my words upon this city for evil, and not for good; and they will be *accomplished* in that day before you.
17 But I will deliver you in that day, said the LORD: and you will not be given into the hand of the men of whom you are afraid.
18 For I will surely deliver you, and you will not fall by the sword, but your life will be for a prey unto you: because you have put your trust in me, said the LORD.

CHAPTER 40

1 The word that came to Jeremiah from the LORD, after that Nebuzar-adan the captain of the guard had let him go from Ramah, when he had taken him being bound in chains among all that were carried away captive of Jerusalem and Judah, which were carried away captive unto Babylon.
2 And the captain of the guard took Jeremiah, and said unto him, The LORD your God have pronounced this evil upon this place.
3 Now the LORD have brought *it*, and done according as he have said: because you have sinned against the LORD, and have not obeyed his voice, therefore this thing is come upon you.
4 And now, behold, I loose you this day from the chains which *were* upon your hand. If it seem good unto you to come with me into Babylon, come; and I will look well unto you: but if it seem ill unto you to come with me into Babylon, forbear: behold, all the land *is* before you: where it seems good and convenient for you to go, there go.
5 Now while he was not yet gone back, *he said*, Go back also to Gedaliah the son of Ahikam the son of Shaphan, whom the king of Babylon have made governor over the cities of Judah, and dwell with him among the people: or go wheresoever it seemeth convenient unto you to go. So the captain of the guard gave him victuals and a reward, and let him go.
6 Then went Jeremiah unto Gedaliah the son of Ahikam to Mizpah; and dwelt with him among the people that were left in the land.
7 Now when all the captains of the forces which *were* in the fields, *even* they and their men, heard that the king of Babylon had made Gedaliah the son of Ahikam governor in the land, and had committed unto him men, and women, and children, and of the poor of the land, of them that were not carried away captive to Babylon;
8 Then they came to Gedaliah to Mizpah, even Ishmael the son of Nethaniah, and Johanan and Jonathan the sons of Kareah and Seraiah the son of Tanhumeth, and the sons of Epha the Netophathite, and Jezaniah the son of a Maachathite, they and their men.
9 And Gedaliah the son of Ahikam the son of Shaphan swore unto them and to their men, saying, Fear not to serve the Chaldeans: dwell in the land, and serve the king of Babylon, and it will be well with you.
10 As for me, behold, I will dwell at Mizpah to serve the Chaldeans, which will come unto us: but ye, gather you wine, and summer fruits, and oil, and put *them* in your vessels, and dwell in your cities that you have taken.
11 Likewise when all the Jews that *were* in Moab, and among the Ammonites, and in Edom, and that *were* in all the countries, heard that the king of Babylon had left a remnant of Judah, and that he had set over them Gedaliah the son of Ahikam the son of Shaphan;
12 Even all the Jews returned out of all places where they were driven, and came to the land of Judah, to Gedaliah, unto Mizpah, and gathered wine and summer fruits very much.
13 Moreover Johanan the son of Kareah, and all the captains of the forces that *were* in the fields, came to Gedaliah to Mizpah,
14 And said unto him, Do you certainly know that Baalis the king of the Ammonites have sent Ishmael the son of Nethaniah to slay you? But Gedaliah the son of Ahikam believed them not.
15 Then Johanan the son of Kareah spoke to Gedaliah in Mizpah secretly, saying, Let me go, I pray you, and I will slay Ishmael the son of Nethaniah, and no man will know *it*: wherefore should he slay you, that all the Jews which are gathered unto you should be scattered, and the remnant in Judah perish?
16 But Gedaliah the son of Ahikam said unto Johanan the son of Kareah, you will not do this thing: for you speak falsely of Ishmael.

CHAPTER 41

1 Now it came to pass in the seventh month, *that* Ishmael the son of Nethaniah the son of Elishama, of the seed royal, and the princes of the king, even ten men with him, came unto Gedaliah the son of Ahikam to Mizpah; and there they did eat bread together in Mizpah.
2 Then arose Ishmael the son of Nethaniah, and the ten men that were with him, and smote Gedaliah the son of Ahikam the son of Shaphan with the sword, and slew him, whom the king of Babylon had made governor over the land.
3 Ishmael also slew all the Jews that were with him, *even* with Gedaliah, at Mizpah, and the Chaldeans that were found there, *and* the men of war.
4 And it came to pass the second day after he had slain Gedaliah, and no man knew *it*,
5 That there came certain from Shechem, from Shiloh, and from Samaria, *even* fourscore men, having their beards shaven, and their clothes rent, and having cut themselves, with offerings and incense in their hand, to bring *them* to the house of the LORD.
6 And Ishmael the son of Nethaniah went forth from Mizpah to meet them, weeping all along as he went: and it came to pass, as he met them, he said unto them, come to Gedaliah the son of Ahikam.
7 And it was *so*, when they came into the midst of the city, that Ishmael the son of Nethaniah slew them, *and cast them* into the midst of the pit, he, and the men that *were* with him.

8 But ten men were found among them that said unto Ishmael, Slay us not: for we have treasures in the field, of wheat, and of barley, and of oil, and of honey. So he forbare, and slew them not among their brethren.
9 Now the pit wherein Ishmael had cast all the dead bodies of the men, whom he had slain because of Gedaliah, *was* it which Asa the king had made for fear of Baasha king of Israel: *and* Ishmael the son of Nethaniah filled it with *them that were* slain.
10 Then Ishmael carried away captive all the residue of the people that *were* in Mizpah, *even* the king's daughters, and all the people that remained in Mizpah, whom Nebuzar-adan the captain of the guard had committed to Gedaliah the son of Ahikam: and Ishmael the son of Nethaniah carried them away captive, and departed to go over to the Ammonites.
11 But when Johanan the son of Kareah, and all the captains of the forces that *were* with him, heard of all the evil that Ishmael the son of Nethaniah had done,
12 Then they took all the men, and went to fight with Ishmael the son of Nethaniah, and found him by the great waters that *are* in Gibeon.
13 Now it came to pass, *that* when all the people which *were* with Ishmael saw Johanan the son of Kareah, and all the captains of the forces that *were* with him, then they were glad.
14 So all the people that Ishmael had carried away captive from Mizpah cast about and returned, and went unto Johanan the son of Kareah.
15 But Ishmael the son of Nethaniah escaped from Johanan with eight men, and went to the Ammonites.
16 Then took Johanan the son of Kareah, and all the captains of the forces that *were* with him, all the remnant of the people whom he had recovered from Ishmael the son of Nethaniah, from Mizpah, after *that* he had slain Gedaliah the son of Ahikam, *even* mighty men of war, and the women, and the children, and the eunuchs, whom he had brought again from Gibeon:
17 And they departed, and dwelt in the habitation of Chimham, which is by Beth-lehem, to go to enter into Egypt,
18 Because of the Chaldeans: for they were afraid of them, because Ishmael the son of Nethaniah had slain Gedaliah the son of Ahikam, whom the king of Babylon made governor in the land.

CHAPTER 42

1 Then all the captains of the forces, and Johanan the son of Kareah, and Jezaniah the son of Hoshaiah, and all the people from the least even unto the greatest, came near,
2 And said unto Jeremiah the prophet, Let, we beseech you, our supplication be accepted before you, and pray for us unto the LORD your God, *even* for all this remnant; (for we are left *but* a few of many, as your eyes do behold us:)
3 That the LORD your God may show us the way wherein we may walk, and the thing that we may do.
4 Then Jeremiah the prophet said unto them, I have heard *you*; behold, I will pray unto the LORD your God according to your words; and it will come to pass, *that* whatsoever thing the LORD will answer you, I will declare *it* unto you; I will keep nothing back from you.
5 Then they said to Jeremiah, The LORD be a true and faithful witness between us, if we do not even according to all things for the which the LORD your God will send you to us.
6 Whether *it be* good, or whether *it be* evil, we will obey the voice of the LORD our God, to whom we send you; that it may be well with us, when we obey the voice of the LORD our God.

7 And it came to pass after ten days, that the word of the LORD came unto Jeremiah.
8 Then called he Johanan the son of Kareah, and all the captains of the forces which *were* with him, and all the people from the least even to the greatest,
9 And said unto them, thus said the LORD, the God of Israel, unto whom you sent me to present your supplication before him;
10 If you will still abide in this land, then will I build you, and not pull *you* down, and I will plant you, and not pluck *you* up: for I repent me of the evil that I have done unto you.
11 Be not afraid of the king of Babylon, of whom you are afraid; be not afraid of him, said the LORD: for I *am* with you to save you, and to deliver you from his hand.
12 And I will show mercies unto you, that he may have mercy upon you, and cause you to return to your own land.
13 But if you say, we will not dwell in this land, neither obey the voice of the LORD your God,
14 Saying, No; but we will go into the land of Egypt, where we will see no war, or hear the sound of the trumpet, or have hunger of bread; and there will we dwell:
15 And now therefore hear the word of the LORD, you remnant of Judah; Thus said the LORD of hosts, the God of Israel; If you wholly set your faces to enter into Egypt, and go to sojourn there;
16 Then it will come to pass, *that* the sword, which you feared, will overtake you there in the land of Egypt, and the famine, whereof you were afraid, will follow close after you there in Egypt; and there you will die.
17 So will it be with all the men that set their faces to go into Egypt to sojourn there; they will die by the sword, by the famine, and by the pestilence: and none of them will remain or escape from the evil that I will bring upon them.
18 For thus said the LORD of hosts, the God of Israel; As mine anger and my fury have been poured forth upon the inhabitants of Jerusalem; so will my fury be poured forth upon you, when you will enter into Egypt: and you will be an execration, and an astonishment, and a curse, and a reproach; and you will see this place no more.
19 The LORD have said concerning you, O you remnant of Judah; Go you not into Egypt: know certainly that I have admonished you this day.
20 For you dissembled in your hearts, when you sent me unto the LORD your God, saying, Pray for us unto the LORD our God; and according unto all that the LORD our God will say, so declare unto us, and we will do *it*.
21 And *now* I have this day declared *it* to you; but you have not obeyed the voice of the LORD your God, or anything for the which he have sent me unto you.
22 Now therefore know certainly that you will die by the sword, by the famine, and by the pestilence, in the place where you desire to go *and* to sojourn.

CHAPTER 43

1 And it came to pass, *that* when Jeremiah had made an end of speaking unto all the people all the words of the LORD their God, for which the LORD their God had sent him to them, *even* all these words,
2 Then spoke Azariah the son of Hoshaiah, and Johanan the son of Kareah, and all the proud men, saying unto Jeremiah, you speak falsely: the LORD our God have not sent you to say, Go not into Egypt to sojourn there:

3 But Baruch the son of Neriah sets you on against us, for to deliver us into the hand of the Chaldeans, that they might put us to death, and carry us away captives into Babylon.
4 So Johanan the son of Kareah, and all the captains of the forces, and all the people, obeyed not the voice of the LORD, to dwell in the land of Judah.
5 But Johanan the son of Kareah, and all the captains of the forces, took all the remnant of Judah, that were returned from all nations, where they had been driven, to dwell in the land of Judah;
6 *Even* men, and women, and children, and the king's daughters, and every person that Nebuzar-adan the captain of the guard had left with Gedaliah the son of Ahikam the son of Shaphan, and Jeremiah the prophet, and Baruch the son of Neriah.
7 So they came into the land of Egypt: for they obeyed not the voice of the LORD: thus came they *even* to Tahpanhes.
8 Then came the word of the LORD unto Jeremiah in Tahpanhes, saying,
9 Take great stones in your hand, and hide them in the clay in the **brickwork**, which *is* at the entry of Pharaoh's house in Tahpanhes, in the sight of the men of Judah;
10 And say unto them, Thus said the LORD of hosts, the God of Israel; Behold, I will send and take Nebuchadrezzar the king of Babylon, my servant, and will set his throne upon these stones that I have hid; and he will spread his royal pavilion over them.
11 And when he cometh, he will smite the land of Egypt, *and* deliver such *as are* for death to death; and such *as are* for captivity to captivity; and such *as are* for the sword to the sword.
12 And I will kindle a fire in the houses of the gods of Egypt; and he will burn them, and carry them away captives: and he will array himself with the land of Egypt, as a shepherd puts on his garment; and he will go forth from thence in peace.
13 He will break also the images of Beth-shemesh, that *is* in the land of Egypt; and the houses of the gods of the Egyptians will he burn with fire.

CHAPTER 44

1 The word that came to Jeremiah concerning all the Jews which dwell in the land of Egypt, which dwell at Migdol, and at Tahpanhes, and at Noph, and in the country of Pathros, saying,
2 Thus said the LORD of hosts, the God of Israel; you have seen all the evil that I have brought upon Jerusalem, and upon all the cities of Judah; and, behold, this day they *are* a desolation, and no man dwells therein,
3 Because of their wickedness which they have committed to provoke me to anger, in that they went to burn incense, *and* to serve other gods, whom they knew not, *neither* they, you, or your fathers.
4 Howbeit I sent unto you all my servants the prophets, rising early and sending *them*, saying, Oh, do not this abominable thing that I hate.
5 But they hearkened not, or inclined their ear to turn from their wickedness, to burn no incense unto other gods.
6 Wherefore my fury and mine anger was poured forth, and was kindled in the cities of Judah and in the streets of Jerusalem; and they are wasted *and* desolate, as at this day.
7 Therefore now thus said the LORD, the God of hosts, the God of Israel; Wherefore commit you *this* great evil against your souls, to cut off from you man and woman, child and suckling, out of Judah, to leave you none to remain;
8 In that you provoke me unto wrath with the works of your hands, burning incense unto other gods in the land of Egypt, where you be gone to dwell, that you might cut yourselves off, and that you might be a curse and a reproach among all the nations of the earth?
9 Have you forgotten the wickedness of your fathers, and the wickedness of the kings of Judah, and the wickedness of their wives, and your own wickedness, and the wickedness of your wives, which they have committed in the land of Judah, and in the streets of Jerusalem?
10 They are not humbled *even* unto this day, neither have they feared, or walked in my law, or in my statutes, that I set before you and before your fathers.
11 Therefore thus said the LORD of hosts, the God of Israel; Behold, I will set my face against you for evil, and to cut off all Judah.
12 And I will take the remnant of Judah, that have set their faces to go into the land of Egypt to sojourn there, and they will all be consumed, *and* fall in the land of Egypt; they will *even* be consumed by the sword *and* by the famine: they will die, from the least even unto the greatest, by the sword and by the famine: and they will be an execration, *and* an astonishment, and a curse, and a reproach.
13 For I will punish them that dwell in the land of Egypt, as I have punished Jerusalem, by the sword, by the famine, and by the pestilence:
14 So that none of the remnant of Judah, which are gone into the land of Egypt to sojourn there, will escape or remain, that they should return into the land of Judah, to the which they have a desire to return to dwell there: for none will return but such as will escape.
15 Then all the men which knew that their wives had burned incense unto other gods, and all the women that stood by, a great multitude, even all the people that dwelt in the land of Egypt, in Pathros, answered Jeremiah, saying,
16 *As for* the word that you have spoken unto us in the name of the LORD, we will not hearken unto you.
17 But we will certainly do whatsoever thing goes forth out of our own mouth, to burn incense unto the queen of heaven, and to pour out drink offerings unto her, as we have done, we, and our fathers, our kings, and our princes, in the cities of Judah, and in the streets of Jerusalem: for *then* had we plenty of victuals, and were well, and saw no evil.
18 But since we left off to burn incense to the queen of heaven, and to pour out drink offerings unto her, we have wanted all *things*, and have been consumed by the sword and by the famine.
19 And when we burned incense to the queen of heaven, and poured out drink offerings unto her, did we make her cakes to worship her, and pour out drink offerings unto her, without our men?
20 Then Jeremiah said unto all the people, to the men, and to the women, and to all the people which had given him *that* answer, saying,
21 The incense that you burned in the cities of Judah, and in the streets of Jerusalem, ye, and your fathers, your kings, and your princes, and the people of the land, did not the LORD remember them, and came it *not* into his mind?
22 So that the LORD could no longer bear, because of the evil of your doings, *and* because of the abominations which you have committed; therefore is your land a desolation, and an astonishment, and a curse, without an inhabitant, as at this day.
23 Because you have burned incense, and because you have sinned against the LORD, and have not obeyed the voice of the

LORD, or walked in his law, or in his statutes, or in his testimonies; therefore this evil is happened unto you, as at this day.

24 Moreover Jeremiah said unto all the people, and to all the women, Hear the word of the LORD, all Judah that *are* in the land of Egypt:

25 Thus said the LORD of hosts, the God of Israel, saying; you and your wives have both spoken with your mouths, and fulfilled with your hand, saying, We will surely perform our vows that we have vowed, to burn incense to the queen of heaven, and to pour out drink offerings unto her: you will surely accomplish your vows, and surely perform your vows.

26 Therefore hear you the word of the LORD, all Judah that dwell in the land of Egypt; Behold, I have sworn by my great name, said the LORD, that my name will no more be named in the mouth of any man of Judah in all the land of Egypt, saying, The Lord GOD lives.

27 Behold, I will watch over them for evil, and not for good: and all the men of Judah that *are* in the land of Egypt will be consumed by the sword and by the famine, until there be an end of them.

28 Yet a small number that escape the sword will return out of the land of Egypt into the land of Judah, and all the remnant of Judah, that are gone into the land of Egypt to sojourn there, will know whose words will stand, mine, or theirs.

29 And this will *be* a sign unto you, said the LORD, that I will punish you in this place, that you may know that my words will surely stand against you for evil:

30 Thus said the LORD; Behold, I will give Pharaoh-hophra king of Egypt into the hand of his enemies, and into the hand of them that seek his life; as I gave Zedekiah king of Judah into the hand of Nebuchadrezzar king of Babylon, his enemy, and that sought his life.

CHAPTER 45

1 The word that Jeremiah the prophet spoke unto Baruch the son of Neriah, when he had written these words in a book at the mouth of Jeremiah, in the fourth year of Jehoiakim the son of Josiah king of Judah, saying,

2 Thus said the LORD, the God of Israel, unto you, O Baruch;

3 You did say, Woe is me now! for the LORD have added grief to my sorrow; I fainted in my sighing, and I find no rest.

4 Thus will you say unto him, The LORD said thus; Behold, *that* which I have built will I break down, and that which I have planted I will pluck up, even this whole land.

5 And seek you great things for thyself? seek *them* not: for, behold, I will bring evil upon all flesh, said the LORD: but your life will I give unto you for a prey in all places where you go.

CHAPTER 46

1 The word of the LORD which came to Jeremiah the prophet against the Gentiles;

2 Against Egypt, against the army of Pharaoh-necho king of Egypt, which was by the river Euphrates in Carchemish, which Nebuchadrezzar king of Babylon smote in the fourth year of Jehoiakim the son of Josiah king of Judah.

3 Order you the buckler and shield, and draw near to battle.

4 Harness the horses; and get up, you horsemen, and stand forth with *your* helmets; furbish the spears, *and* put on the brigandines.

5 Wherefore have I seen them dismayed *and* turned away back? and their mighty ones are beaten down, and are fled apace, and look not back: *for* fear *was* round about, said the LORD.

6 Let not the swift flee away, or the mighty man escape; they will stumble, and fall toward the north by the river Euphrates.

7 Who *is* this *that* cometh up as a flood, whose waters are moved as the rivers?

8 Egypt rises up like a flood, and *his* waters are moved like the rivers; and he said, I will go up, *and* will cover the earth; I will destroy the city and the inhabitants thereof.

9 Come up, you horses; and rage, you chariots; and let the mighty men come forth; the Ethiopians and the Libyans, that handle the shield; and the Lydians, that handle *and* bend the bow.

10 For this *is* the day of the Lord GOD of hosts, a day of vengeance, that he may avenge him of his adversaries: and the sword will devour, and it will be satiate and made drunk with their blood: for the Lord GOD of hosts have a sacrifice in the north country by the river Euphrates.

11 Go up into Gilead, and take balm, O virgin, the daughter of Egypt: in vain will you use many medicines; *for* you will not be cured.

12 The nations have heard of your shame, and your cry have filled the land: for the mighty man have stumbled against the mighty, *and* they are fallen both together.

13 The word that the LORD spoke to Jeremiah the prophet, how Nebuchadrezzar king of Babylon should come *and* smite the land of Egypt.

14 Declare you in Egypt, and publish in Migdol, and publish in Noph and in Tahpanhes: say you, Stand fast, and prepare you; for the sword will devour round about you.

15 Why are your valiant *men* swept away? They stood not, because the LORD did drive them.

16 He made many to fall, yea, one fell upon another: and they said, Arise, and let us go again to our own people, and to the land of our nativity, from the oppressing sword.

17 They did cry there, Pharaoh King of Egypt *is but* a noise; he have passed the time appointed.

18 *As* I live, said the King, whose name *is* the LORD of hosts, Surely as Tabor *is* among the mountains, and as Carmel by the sea, *so* will he come.

19 O you daughter dwelling in Egypt, furnish yourself to go into captivity: for Noph will be waste and desolate without an inhabitant.

20 Egypt *is like* a very fair heifer, *but* destruction cometh; it cometh out of the north.

21 Also her hired men *are* in the midst of her like fatted bullocks; for they also are turned back, *and* are fled away together: they did not stand, because the day of their calamity was come upon them, *and* the time of their visitation.

22 The voice thereof will go like a serpent; for they will march with an army, and come against her with axes, as hewers of wood.

23 They will cut down her forest, said the LORD, though it cannot be searched; because they are more than the grasshoppers, and *are* innumerable.

24 The daughter of Egypt will be confounded; she will be delivered into the hand of the people of the north.

25 The LORD of hosts, the God of Israel, said; Behold, I will punish the multitude of No, and Pharaoh, and Egypt, with their gods, and their kings; even Pharaoh, and *all* them that trust in him:

26 And I will deliver them into the hand of those that seek their lives, and into the hand of Nebuchadrezzar king of Babylon, and into the hand of his servants: and afterward it will be inhabited, as in the days of old, said the LORD.

27 But fear not you, O my servant Jacob, and be not dismayed, O Israel: for, behold, I will save you from afar off, and your seed from the land of their captivity; and Jacob will return, and be in rest and at ease, and none will make *him* afraid.

28 Fear you not, O Jacob my servant, said the LORD: for I am with you; for I will make a full end of all the nations where I have driven you: but I will not make a full end of you, but correct you in measure; yet will I not leave you wholly unpunished.[1]

CHAPTER 47

1 The word of the LORD that came to Jeremiah the prophet against the Philistines, before that Pharaoh smote Gaza.
2 Thus said the LORD; Behold, waters rise up out of the north, and will be an overflowing flood, and will overflow the land, and all that is therein; the city, and them that dwell therein: then the men will cry, and all the inhabitants of the land will howl.
3 At the noise of the stamping of the hoofs of his strong *horses*, at the rushing of his chariots, *and at* the rumbling of his wheels, the fathers will not look back to *their* children for feebleness of hands;
4 Because of the day that cometh to spoil all the Philistines, *and* to cut off from Tyrus and Zidon every helper that remaineth: for the LORD will spoil the Philistines, the remnant of the country of Caphtor.
5 Baldness is come upon Gaza; Ashkelon is cut off *with* the remnant of their valley: how long will you cut yourself?
6 O you sword of the LORD, how long *will it be* ere you be quiet? Put up yourself into your scabbard, rest, and be still.
7 How can it be quiet, seeing the LORD have given it a charge against Ashkelon, and against the sea shore? There have he appointed it.

CHAPTER 48

1 Against Moab thus said the LORD of hosts, the God of Israel; Woe unto Nebo! For it is spoiled: Kiriathaim is confounded *and* taken: Misgab is confounded and dismayed.
2 *There will be* no more praise of Moab: in Heshbon they have devised evil against it; come, and let us cut it off from *being* a nation. Also you will be cut down, O Madmen; the sword will pursue you.
3 A voice of crying will *be* from Horonaim, spoiling and great destruction.
4 Moab is destroyed; her little ones have caused a cry to be heard.
5 For in the going up of Luhith continual weeping will go up; for in the going down of Horonaim the enemies have heard a cry of destruction.
6 Flee, save your lives, and be like the heath in the wilderness.
7 For because you have trusted in your works and in your treasures, you will also be taken: and Chemosh will go forth into captivity *with* his priests and his princes together.
8 And the spoiler will come upon every city, and no city will escape: the valley also will perish, and the plain will be destroyed, as the LORD have spoken.
9 Give wings unto Moab, that it may flee and get away: for the cities thereof will be desolate, without any to dwell therein.
10 Cursed *be* he that doeth the work of the LORD deceitfully, and cursed *be* he that keeps back his sword from blood.
11 Moab **has** been at ease from his youth, and he have settled on his lees[2], and have not been emptied from vessel to vessel, neither have he gone into captivity: therefore his taste remained in him, and his scent[3] is not changed.
12 Therefore, behold, the days come, said the LORD, that I will send unto him wanderers[4], that will cause him to wander[5], and will empty his vessels, and break their bottles.
13 And Moab will be ashamed of Chemosh[6], as the house of Israel was ashamed of Beth-el their confidence.
14 How say you, we *are* mighty and strong men for the war?
15 Moab is spoiled, and gone up *out of* her cities, and his chosen young men are gone down to the slaughter, said the King, whose name *is* the LORD of hosts.
16 The calamity of Moab *is* near to come, and his affliction hastens fast.
17 All you that are about him, bemoan him; and all you that know his name, say, How is the strong staff broken, *and* the beautiful rod!
18 you daughter that dost inhabit Dibon, come down from your glory, and sit in thirst; for the spoiler of Moab will come upon you, *and* he will destroy your strong holds.
19 O inhabitant of Aroer, stand by the way, and espy; ask him that flees, and her that escapes, *and* say, what is done?
20 Moab is confounded; for it is broken down: howl and cry; tell you it in Arnon, that Moab is spoiled,
21 And judgment is come upon the plain country; upon Holon, and upon Jahazah, and upon Mephaath,
22 And upon Dibon, and upon Nebo, and upon Beth-diblathaim,
23 And upon Kiriathaim, and upon Beth-gamul, and upon Beth-meon,
24 And upon Kerioth, and upon Bozrah, and upon all the cities of the land of Moab, far or near.
25 The horn of Moab is cut off, and his arm is broken, said the LORD.
26 Make you him drunken: for he magnified *himself* against the LORD: Moab also will wallow in his vomit, and he also will be in derision.
27 For was not Israel a derision unto you? Was he found among thieves? For since you spoke of him, you skipped for joy.
28 O you that dwell in Moab, leave the cities, and dwell in the rock, and be like the dove *that* makes her nest in the sides of the hole's mouth.
29 We have heard the pride of Moab, (he is exceeding proud) his loftiness, and his arrogancy, and his pride, and the haughtiness of his heart.
30 I know his wrath, said the LORD; but *it will* not *be* so; his lies will not so effect *it*.
31 Therefore will I howl for Moab, and I will cry out for all Moab; *mine heart* will mourn for the men of Kir-heres.
32 O vine of Sibmah, I will weep for you with the weeping of Jazer: your plants are gone over the sea, they reach *even* to the sea of Jazer: the spoiler is fallen upon your summer fruits and upon your vintage.
33 And joy and gladness is taken from the plentiful field, and from the land of Moab; and I have caused wine to fail from the winepresses: none will tread with shouting; *their* shouting will *be* no shouting.
34 From the cry of Heshbon *even* unto Elealeh, *and even* unto Jahaz, have they uttered their voice, from Zoar *even* unto

---

[1] compare Eph. 4:13 & Rev. 11:1
[2] lees – <u>something *preserved*</u>, the *settlings* (plural only) of wine [Strgs#8105].
[3] scent – odor (as if blown) [Strgs#7381]. <u>Scent of incest of Sodom</u>.
[4] wanderers – *to tip over* (for the purpose of *spilling* or *pouring* out), *depopulate*; by implication to *imprison* or *conquer*; (reflexively) to *lie down* (for coition) [Strgs#6808].
[5] Ibid.
[6] Chemosh – to *subdue*; the *powerful*; *Kemosh*, the god of the Moabites [Strgs#3645].

Horonaim, *as* a heifer of three years old: for the waters also of Nimrim will be desolate.

35 Moreover I will cause to cease in Moab, said the LORD, him that offers in the high places, and him that burns incense to his gods.

36 Therefore mine heart will sound for Moab like pipes, and mine heart will sound like pipes for the men of Kir-heres: because the riches *that* he have gotten are perished.

37 For every head will *be* bald, and every beard clipped: upon all the hands will *be* cuttings, and upon the loins sackcloth.

38 *There will be* lamentation generally upon all the housetops of Moab, and in the streets thereof: for I have broken Moab like a vessel wherein *is* no pleasure, said the LORD.

39 They will howl, *saying*, how is it broken down! How have Moab turned the back with shame! So will Moab be a derision[1] and a dismaying to all them about him.

40 For thus said the LORD; behold, he will fly as an eagle, and will spread his wings over Moab.

41 Kerioth is taken[2], and the strong holds are surprised, and the mighty men's hearts in Moab at that day will be as the heart of a woman in her pangs.

42 And Moab will be destroyed from *being* a people, because he have magnified *himself* against the LORD.

43 Fear, and the pit, and the snare, will *be* upon you, O inhabitant of Moab, said the LORD.

44 He that flees from the fear will fall into the pit; and he that gets up out of the pit will be taken in the snare: for I will bring upon it, *even* upon Moab, the year of their visitation, said the LORD.

45 They that fled stood under the shadow of Heshbon because of the force: but a fire will come forth out of Heshbon, and a flame from the midst of Sihon, and will devour the corner of Moab, and the crown of the head of the tumultuous ones.

46 Woe be unto you, O Moab! The people of Chemosh perishes: for your sons are taken captives, and your daughters captives.

47 Yet will I bring again the captivity of Moab in the latter days, said the LORD. Thus far *is* the judgment of Moab.

CHAPTER 49

1 Concerning the Ammonites, thus said the LORD; have Israel no sons? Have he no heir? Why *then* does their king inherit Gad, and his people dwell in his cities?

2 Therefore, behold, the days come, said the LORD, that I will cause an alarm of war to be heard in Rabbah of the Ammonites; and it will be a desolate heap, and her daughters will be burned with fire: then will Israel be heir unto them that were his heirs, said the LORD.

3 Howl, O Heshbon, for Ai is spoiled: cry, you daughters of Rabbah, gird you with sackcloth; lament, and run to and fro by the hedges; for their king will go into captivity, *and* his priests and his princes together.

4 Wherefore glory you in the valleys, your flowing valley, O backsliding daughter? That trusted in her treasures, *saying*, who will come unto me?

5 Behold, I will bring a fear upon you, said the Lord GOD of hosts, from all those that be about you; and you will be driven out every man right forth; and none will gather up him that wanders.

6 And afterward I will bring again the captivity of the children of Ammon, said the LORD.

7 Concerning Edom, thus said the LORD of hosts. *Is* wisdom no more in Teman? Is counsel perished from the prudent? Is their wisdom vanished?

8 Flee you, turn back, dwell deep, O inhabitants of Dedan; for I will bring the calamity of Esau upon him, the time *that* I will visit him.

9 If grape-gatherers come to you, would they not leave *some* gleaning grapes? If thieves by night, they will destroy till they have enough.

10 But I have made Esau bare, I have uncovered his secret places, and he will not be able to hide himself: his seed is spoiled, and his brethren, and his neighbors, and he *is* not.

11 Leave your fatherless children, I will preserve *them* alive; and let your widows trust in me.

12 For thus said the LORD; behold, they whose judgment *was* not to drink of the cup have assuredly drunken; and are you he *that* will altogether go unpunished? You will not go unpunished, but you will surely drink *of it*.

13 For I have sworn by myself, said the LORD, that Bozrah will become a desolation, a reproach, a waste, and a curse; and all the cities thereof will be perpetual wastes.

14 I have heard a rumor from the LORD, and an ambassador is sent unto the heathen, *saying*, Gather you together, and come against her, and rise up to the battle.

15 For, lo, I will make you small among the heathen, *and* despised among men.

16 your terribleness have deceived you, *and* the pride of your heart, O you that dwell in the clefts of the rock, that hold the height of the hill: though you should make your nest as high as the eagle, I will bring you down from thence, said the LORD.

17 Also Edom will be a desolation: everyone that goes by it will be astonished, and will hiss at all the plagues thereof.

18 As in the overthrow of Sodom and Gomorrah and the neighbor *cities* thereof, said the LORD, no man will abide there, neither will a son of man dwell in it.

19 Behold, he will come up like a lion from the swelling of Jordan against the habitation of the strong: but I will suddenly make him run away from her: and who *is* a chosen *man, that* I may appoint over her? For who *is* like me? And who will appoint me the time? And who *is* that shepherd that will stand before me?

20 Therefore hear the counsel of the LORD, that he **has** taken against Edom; and his purposes, that he have purposed against the inhabitants of Teman: Surely the least of the flock will draw them out: surely he will make their habitations desolate with them.

21 The earth is moved at the noise of their fall, at the cry the noise thereof was heard in the Red sea.

22 Behold, he will come up and fly as the eagle, and spread his wings over Bozrah: and at that day will the heart of the mighty men of Edom be as the heart of a woman in her pangs.

23 Concerning Damascus. Hamath is confounded, and Arpad: for they have heard evil tidings: they are fainthearted; *there is* sorrow on the sea; it cannot be quiet.

24 Damascus is waxed feeble, *and* turns herself to flee, and fear have seized on *her*: anguish and sorrows have taken her, as a woman in travail.

25 How is the city of praise not left, the city of my joy!

26 Therefore her young men will fall in her streets, and all the men of war will be cut off in that day, said the LORD of hosts.

---

[1] derision- Hebrew word *sechôq*, meaning *laughter* (in merriment or defiance): scorn, mocked sport. [Strgs#7814]

[2] lit. to *catch* (in a net, trap or pit); *capture* or occupy; also to *choose* (by lot); to *cohere*, caught [Strgs#3920].

27 And I will kindle a fire in the wall of Damascus, and it will consume the palaces of Ben-hadad.

28 Concerning Kedar, and concerning the kingdoms of Hazor, which Nebuchadrezzar king of Babylon will smite, thus said the LORD; Arise ye, go up to Kedar, and spoil the men of the east.

29 Their tents and their flocks will they take away: they will take to themselves their curtains, and all their vessels, and their camels; and they will cry unto them, Fear *is* on every side.

30 Flee, get you far off, dwell deep, O you inhabitants of Hazor, said the LORD; for Nebuchadrezzar king of Babylon have taken counsel against you, and have conceived a purpose against you.

31 Arise, get you up unto the wealthy nation, that dwells without care, said the LORD, which have neither gates or bars, *which* dwell alone.

32 And their camels will be a booty[1], and the multitude of their cattle a spoil: and I will scatter into all winds them *that are* in the utmost corners; and I will bring their calamity from all sides thereof, said the LORD.

33 And Hazor will be a dwelling for dragons, *and* a desolation for ever: there will no man abide there, or *any* son of man dwell in it.

34 The word of the LORD that came to Jeremiah the prophet against Elam in the beginning of the reign of Zedekiah king of Judah, saying,

35 Thus said the LORD of hosts; Behold, I will break the bow of Elam, the chief of their might.

36 And upon Elam will I bring the four winds from the four quarters of heaven, and will scatter them toward all those winds; and there will be no nation where the outcasts of Elam will not come.

37 For I will cause Elam to be dismayed before their enemies, and before them that seek their life: and I will bring evil upon them, *even* my fierce anger, said the LORD; and I will send the sword after them, till I have consumed them:

38 And I will set my throne in Elam, and will destroy from thence the king and the princes, said the LORD.

39 But it will come to pass in the latter days, *that* I will bring again the captivity of Elam, said the LORD.

CHAPTER 50

1 The word that the LORD spoke against Babylon *and* against the land of the Chaldeans by Jeremiah the prophet.

2 Declare you among the nations, and publish, and set up a standard; publish, *and* conceal not: say, Babylon is taken, Bel is confounded, Merodach[2] is broken in pieces; her idols are confounded, her images are broken in pieces.

3 For out of the north there cometh up a nation against her, which will make her land desolate, and none will dwell therein: they will remove, they will depart, both man and beast.

4 In those days, and in that time, said the LORD, the children of Israel will come, they and the children of Judah together, going and weeping: they will go, and seek the LORD their God.

5 They will ask the way to Zion with their faces thitherward, *saying*, Come, and let us join ourselves to the LORD in a perpetual covenant *that* will not be forgotten.

6 My people have been lost sheep: their shepherds have caused them to go astray, they have turned them away *on* the mountains: they have gone from mountain to hill, they have forgotten their resting place.

7 All that found them have devoured them: and their adversaries said, we offend not, because they have sinned against the LORD, the habitation of justice, even the LORD, the hope of their fathers.

8 Remove out of the midst of Babylon, and go forth out of the land of the Chaldeans, and be as the he goats before the flocks.

9 For, lo, I will raise and cause to come up against Babylon an assembly of great nations from the north country: and they will set themselves in array against her; from thence she will be taken: their arrows will *be* as of a mighty expert man; none will return in vain.

10 And Chaldea will be a spoil: all that spoil her will be satisfied, said the LORD.

11 Because you were glad, because you rejoiced, O you destroyers of mine heritage, because you are grown fat as the heifer at grass, and bellow as bulls;

12 Your mother will be sore confounded; she that bare you will be ashamed: behold, the hindermost of the nations will *be* a wilderness, a dry land, and a desert.

13 Because of the wrath of the LORD it will not be inhabited, but it will be wholly desolate: everyone that goes by Babylon will be astonished, and hiss at all her plagues.

14 Put yourselves in array against Babylon round about: all you that bend the bow, shoot at her, spare no arrows: for she have sinned against the LORD.

15 Shout against her round about: she have given her hand: her foundations are fallen, her walls are thrown down: for it *is* the vengeance of the LORD: take vengeance upon her; as she have done, do unto her.

16 Cut off the sower from Babylon, and him that handles the sickle in the time of harvest: for fear of the oppressing sword they will turn everyone to his people, and they will flee everyone to his own land.

17 Israel *is* a scattered sheep; the lions have driven *him* away: first the king of Assyria have devoured him; and last this Nebuchadrezzar king of Babylon have broken his bones.

18 Therefore thus said the LORD of hosts, the God of Israel; Behold, I will punish the king of Babylon and his land, as I have punished the king of Assyria.

19 And I will bring Israel again to his habitation, and he will feed on Carmel and Bashan, and his soul will be satisfied upon mount Ephraim and Gilead.

20 In those days, and in that time, said the LORD, the iniquity of Israel will be sought for, and *there will be* none; and the sins of Judah, and they will not be found: for I will pardon them whom I reserve.

21 Go up against the land of Merathaim, *even* against it, and against the inhabitants of Pekod: waste and utterly destroy after them, said the LORD, and do according to all that I have commanded you.

22 A sound of battle *is* in the land, and of great destruction.

23 How is the hammer of the whole earth cut asunder and broken! how is Babylon become a desolation among the nations!

24 I have laid a snare for you, and you are also taken, O Babylon, and you were not aware: you are found, and also caught, because you have striven against the LORD.

25 The LORD have opened his armory, and have brought forth the weapons of his indignation: for this *is* the work of the Lord GOD of hosts in the land of the Chaldeans.

---

[1] literally- *plunder*: booty, prey, spoil. [Strgs#957]
[2] Merodach – the Babylonian god of war and the patron diety of the city of

Babylon. His name means *your rebellion*.

26 Come against her from the utmost border, open her storehouses: cast her up as heaps, and destroy her utterly: let nothing of her be left.
27 Slay all her bullocks; let them go down to the slaughter: woe unto them! For their day is come, the time of their visitation.
28 The voice of them that flee and escape out of the land of Babylon, to declare in Zion the vengeance of the LORD our God, the vengeance of his temple.
29 Call together the archers against Babylon: all you that bend the bow, camp against it round about; let none thereof escape: recompense her according to her work; according to all that she have done, do unto her: for she have been proud against the LORD, against the Holy One of Israel.
30 Therefore will her young men fall in the streets, and all her men of war will be cut off in that day, said the LORD.
31 Behold, I *am* against you, O *you* most proud, said the Lord GOD of hosts: for your day is come, the time *that* I will visit you.
32 And the most proud will stumble and fall, and none will raise him up: and I will kindle a fire in his cities, and it will devour all round about him.
33 Thus said the LORD of hosts; the children of Israel and the children of Judah *were* oppressed together: and all that took them captives held them fast; they refused to let them go.
34 Their Redeemer *is* strong; the LORD of hosts *is* his name: he will thoroughly plead their cause, that he may give rest to the land, and disquiet the inhabitants of Babylon.
35 A sword *is* upon the Chaldeans, said the LORD, and upon the inhabitants of Babylon, and upon her princes, and upon her wise *men*.
36 A sword *is* upon the liars; and they will dote: a sword *is* upon her mighty men; and they will be dismayed.
37 A sword *is* upon their horses, and upon their chariots, and upon all the mingled people that *are* in the midst of her; and they will become as women: a sword *is* upon her treasures; and they will be robbed.
38 A drought *is* upon her waters; and they will be dried up: for it *is* the land of graven images, and they are mad upon *their* idols.
39 Therefore the wild beasts of the desert with the wild beasts of the islands will dwell *there*, and the owls will dwell therein: and it will be no more inhabited for ever; neither will it be dwelt in from generation to generation.
40 As God overthrew Sodom and Gomorrah and the neighbor *cities* thereof, said the LORD; *so* will no man abide there, neither will any son of man dwell therein.
41 Behold, a people will come from the north, and a great nation, and many kings will be raised up from the coasts of the earth.
42 They will hold the bow and the lance: they *are* cruel, and will not show mercy: their voice will roar like the sea, and they will ride upon horses, *every one* put in array, like a man to the battle, against you, O daughter of Babylon.
43 The king of Babylon have heard the report of them, and his hands waxed feeble: anguish took hold of him, *and* pangs as of a woman in travail.
44 Behold, he will come up like a lion from the swelling of Jordan unto the habitation of the strong: but I will make them suddenly run away from her: and who *is* a chosen *man, that* I may appoint over her? For who *is* like me? And who will appoint me the time? And who *is* that shepherd that will stand before me?
45 Therefore hear you the counsel of the LORD, that he have taken against Babylon; and his purposes, that he have purposed against the land of the Chaldeans: Surely the least of the flock will draw them out: surely he will make *their* habitation desolate with them.
46 At the noise of the taking of Babylon the earth is moved, and the cry is heard among the nations.

CHAPTER 51

1 Thus said the LORD; Behold, I will raise up against Babylon, and against them that dwell in the midst of them that rise up against me, a destroying wind[1];
2 And will send unto Babylon fanners, that will fan her, and will empty her land: for in the day of trouble they will be against her round about.
3 Against *him that* bends let the archer bend his bow, and against *him that* lifts himself up in his brigandine: and spare you not her young men; destroy you utterly all her host.
4 Thus the slain will fall in the land of the Chaldeans and *they that are* thrust through in her streets.
5 For Israel have not *been* forsaken, or Judah of his God, of the LORD of hosts; though their land was filled with sin against the Holy One of Israel.
6 Flee out of the midst of Babylon, and deliver every man his soul: be not cut off in her iniquity; for this *is* the time of the LORD'S vengeance; he will render unto her a recompense.
7 Babylon have *been* a golden cup in the LORD'S hand, that made all the earth drunken: the nations have drunken of her wine; therefore the nations are mad.
8 Babylon is suddenly fallen and destroyed: howl for her; take balm for her pain, if so be she may be healed.
9 We would have healed Babylon, but she is not healed: forsake her, and let us go every one into his own country: for her judgment reaches unto heaven, and is lifted up *even* to the skies.
10 The LORD have brought forth our righteousness: come, and let us declare in Zion the work[2] of the LORD our God.
11 Make bright[3] the arrows; gather the shields[4]: the LORD have raised up the spirit of the kings of the Medes: for his device *is* against Babylon, to destroy it; because it *is* the vengeance of the LORD, the vengeance of his temple.
12 Set up the standard upon the walls of Babylon, make the watch strong, set up the watchmen, prepare the ambushes: for the LORD have both devised[5] and done that which he spoke against the inhabitants of Babylon.
13 O you that dwell upon many waters, abundant in treasures, your end[6] is come, *and* the measure[7] of your covetousness[8].
14 The LORD of hosts have sworn by himself, *saying*, surely I will fill you with men, as with caterpillars; and they will lift up a shout against you.

---

[1] lit. *wind*, resemblance *breath*, a sensible (or even violent) exhalation; figuratively *life, anger, unsubstantiality* [Strgs#7307]. <u>A destroying spirit</u>.
[2] lit. an <u>action</u> (good or bad), *transaction, activity*; by implication a product, property [Strgs#4639].
[3] bright – to *clarify, examine,* <u>piercers</u>, *select* [Strgs#1305].
[4] shield – a *shield* (as controlling protectiong the person) [Strgs#7983]. Derives from a Hebrew root word meaning to *dominate, govern,* implication to *permit* [Strgs#7980].
[5] lit. to plan, consider, imagine, plot think (evil) [Strgs#2 61].
[6] lit. an extremity [Strgs#7093].
[7] lit. a <u>cubit</u>, a *mother, unit* of measure, the *forearm*, door *base* (as a bond of the entrance) [Strgs#520].
[8] covetousness – <u>plunder</u>; by extension *gain* (usually unjust) [Strgs#1215].

Jeremiah

15 He have made the earth by his power, he have established the world by his wisdom, and have stretched out the heaven by his understanding.

16 When he utters *his* voice, *there is* a multitude of waters in the heavens; and he causes the vapors to ascend from the ends of the earth: he makes lightning's with rain, and brings forth the wind out of his treasures.

17 Every man is brutish by *his* knowledge; every founder is confounded by the graven image: for his molten image *is* falsehood, and *there is* no breath in them.

18 They *are* vanity, the work of errors: in the time of their visitation they will perish.

19 The portion of Jacob *is* not like them; for he *is* the former of all things: and *Israel is* the rod of his inheritance: the LORD of hosts *is* his name.

20 you are my battle axe *and* weapons of war: for with you will I break in pieces the nations, and with you will I destroy kingdoms;

21 And with you will I break in pieces the horse and his rider; and with you will I break in pieces the chariot and his rider;

22 With you also will I break in pieces man and woman; and with you will I break in pieces old and young; and with you will I break in pieces the young man and the maid;

23 I will also break in pieces with you the shepherd and his flock; and with you will I break in pieces the husbandman and his yoke of oxen; and with you will I break in pieces captains and rulers.

24 And I will render unto Babylon and to all the inhabitants of Chaldea all their evil that they have done in Zion in your sight, said the LORD.

25 Behold, I *am* against you, O destroying mountain, said the LORD, which destroys all the earth: and I will stretch out mine hand upon you, and roll you down from the rocks, and will make you a burnt mountain.

26 And they will not take of you a stone for a corner, or a stone for foundations; but you will be desolate forever, said the LORD.

27 Set you up a standard in the land, blow the trumpet among the nations, prepare the nations against her, call together against her the kingdoms of Ararat, Minni, and Ashchenaz; appoint a captain against her; cause the horses to come up as the rough caterpillars.

28 Prepare against her the nations with the kings of the Medes, the captains thereof, and all the rulers thereof, and all the land of his dominion.

29 And the land will tremble and sorrow: for every purpose of the LORD will be performed against Babylon, to make the land of Babylon a desolation without an inhabitant.

30 The mighty men of Babylon have forborn to fight, they have remained in *their* holds: their might have failed; they became as women: they have burned her dwelling places; her bars are broken.

31 One post will run to meet another, and one messenger to meet another, to show the king of Babylon that his city is taken at *one* end,

32 And that the passages are stopped, and the reeds they have burned with fire, and the men of war are affrighted.

33 For thus said the LORD of hosts, the God of Israel; the daughter of Babylon *is* like a threshing-floor, *it is* time to thresh her: yet a little while, and the time of her harvest will come.

34 Nebuchadrezzar the king of Babylon have devoured me, he have crushed me, he have made me an empty vessel, he have swallowed me up like a dragon, he have filled his belly with my delicates, he have cast me out.

35 The violence done to me and to my flesh *be* upon Babylon, will the inhabitant of Zion say; and my blood upon the inhabitants of Chaldea, will Jerusalem say.

36 Therefore thus said the LORD; Behold, I will plead your cause, and take vengeance for you; and I will dry up her sea, and make her springs dry.

37 And Babylon will become heaps, a dwelling place for dragons, an astonishment, and an hissing, without an inhabitant.

38 They will roar together like lions: they will yell as lions' whelps.

39 In their heat I will make their feasts, and I will make them drunken, that they may rejoice, and sleep a perpetual sleep, and not wake, said the LORD.

40 I will bring them down like lambs to the slaughter, like rams with he goats.

41 How is Sheshach taken! And how is the praise of the whole earth surprised! How is Babylon become an astonishment among the nations!

42 The sea is come up upon Babylon: she is covered with the multitude of the waves thereof.

43 Her cities are a desolation, a dry land, and a wilderness, a and wherein no man dwells, neither does *any* son of man pass thereby.

44 And I will punish Bel in Babylon, and I will bring forth out of his mouth that which he have swallowed up: and the nations will not flow together any more unto him: yea, the wall of Babylon will fall.

45 My people, go you out of the midst of her, and deliver you every man his soul from the fierce anger of the LORD.

46 And lest your heart faint, and you fear for the rumor that will be heard in the land; a rumor will both come *one* year, and after that in *another* year will *come* a rumor, and violence in the land, ruler against ruler.

47 Therefore, behold, the days come, that I will do judgment upon the graven images of Babylon: and her whole land will be confounded, and all her slain will fall in the midst of her.

48 Then the heaven and the earth, and all that *is* therein, will sing for Babylon: for the spoilers will come unto her from the north, said the LORD.

49 As Babylon have *caused* the slain of Israel to fall, so at Babylon will fall the slain of all the earth.

50 you that have escaped the sword, go away, stand not still: remember the LORD afar off, and let Jerusalem come into your mind.

51 We are confounded, because we have heard reproach: shame have covered our faces: for strangers are come into the sanctuaries of the LORD'S house.

52 Wherefore, behold, the days come, said the LORD, that I will do judgment upon her graven images: and through all her land the wounded will groan.

53 Though Babylon should mount up to heaven, and though she should fortify the height of her strength, *yet* from me will spoilers come unto her, said the LORD.

54 A sound of a cry *cometh* from Babylon, and great destruction from the land of the Chaldeans:

55 Because the LORD have spoiled Babylon, and destroyed out of her the great voice; when her waves do roar like great waters, a noise of their voice is uttered:

56 Because the spoiler is come upon her, *even* upon Babylon, and her mighty men are taken, every one of their bows is broken: for the LORD God of recompenses will surely requite.

57 And I will make drunk her princes, and her wise *men*, her captains, and her rulers, and her mighty men: and they will sleep a perpetual sleep, and not wake, said the King, whose name *is* the LORD of hosts.

58 Thus said the LORD of hosts; the broad walls of Babylon will be utterly broken, and her high gates will be burned with fire; and the people will labor in vain, and the folk in the fire, and they will be weary.

59 The word which Jeremiah the prophet commanded Seraiah the son of Neriah, the son of Maaseiah, when he went with Zedekiah the king of Judah into Babylon in the fourth year of his reign. And *this* Seraiah *was* a quiet prince.

60 So Jeremiah wrote in a book all the evil that should come upon Babylon, *even* all these words that are written against Babylon.

61 And Jeremiah said to Seraiah, when you come to Babylon, and will see, and will read all these words;

62 Then will you say, O LORD, you have spoken against this place, to cut it off, that none will remain in it, neither man or beast, but that it will be desolate forever.

63 And it will be, when you have made an end of reading this book, *that* you will bind a stone to it, and cast it into the midst of Euphrates:

64 And you will say, thus will Babylon sink, and will not rise from the evil that I will bring upon her: and they will be weary. Thus far *are* the words of Jeremiah.

CHAPTER 52

1 Zedekiah *was* one and twenty years old when he began to reign, and he reigned eleven years in Jerusalem. And his mother's name *was* Hamutal the daughter of Jeremiah of Libnah.

2 And he did *that which was* evil in the eyes of the LORD, according to all that Jehoiakim had done.

3 For through the anger of the LORD it came to pass in Jerusalem and Judah, till he had cast them out from his presence, that Zedekiah rebelled against the king of Babylon.

4 And it came to pass in the ninth year of his reign, in the tenth month, in the tenth *day* of the month, *that* Nebuchadrezzar king of Babylon came, he and all his army, against Jerusalem, and pitched against it, and built forts against it round about.

5 So the city was besieged unto the eleventh year of King Zedekiah.

6 And in the fourth month, in the ninth *day* of the month, the famine was sore in the city, so that there was no bread for the people of the land.

7 Then the city was broken up, and all the men of war fled, and went forth out of the city by night by the way of the gate between the two walls, which *was* by the king's garden; (now the Chaldeans *were* by the city round about:) and they went by the way of the plain.

8 But the army of the Chaldeans pursued after the king, and overtook Zedekiah in the plains of Jericho; and all his army was scattered from him.

9 Then they took the king, and carried him up unto the king of Babylon to Riblah in the land of Hamath; where he gave judgment upon him.

10 And the king of Babylon slew the sons of Zedekiah before his eyes: he slew also all the princes of Judah in Riblah.

11 Then he put out the eyes of Zedekiah; and the king of Babylon bound him in chains, and carried him to Babylon, and put him in prison till the day of his death.

---

[1] see Reference Index
[2] lit. *breath*, *life*, *anger*, *unsubstantiality*, a *region* of the sky, *spirit*

12 Now in the fifth month, in the tenth *day* of the month, which *was* the nineteenth year of Nebuchadrezzar king of Babylon, came Nebuzar-adan, captain of the guard, *which* served the king of Babylon, into Jerusalem,

13 And burned the house of the LORD, and the king's house; and all the houses of Jerusalem, and all the houses of the great *men*, burned he with fire:

14 And all the army of the Chaldeans, that *were* with the captain of the guard, brake down all the walls of Jerusalem round about.

15 Then Nebuzar-adan the captain of the guard carried away captive *certain* of the poor of the people, and the residue of the people that remained in the city, and those that fell away, that fell to the king of Babylon, and the rest of the multitude.

16 But Nebuzar-adan the captain of the guard left *certain* of the poor of the land for vinedressers and for husbandmen.

17 Also the pillars of brass that *were* in the house of the LORD, and the bases, and the brasen sea that *was* in the house of the LORD, the Chaldeans brake, and carried all the brass of them to Babylon.

18 The caldrons also, and the shovels, and the snuffers, and the bowls, and the spoons, and all the vessels of brass wherewith they ministered, took they away.

19 And the basons, and the firepans, and the bowls, and the caldrons, and the candlesticks, and the spoons, and the cups; *that* which *was* of gold *in* gold, and *that* which *was* of silver *in* silver, took the captain of the guard away.

20 The two pillars, one sea, and twelve brasen bulls that *were* under the bases, which King Solomon had made in the house of the LORD: the brass of all these vessels was without weight.

21 And *concerning* the pillars, the height of one pillar *was* eighteen cubits; and a fillet of twelve cubits did compass it; and the thickness thereof *was* four fingers: *it was* hollow.

22 And a chapiter[1] of brass *was* upon it; and the height of one chapiter *was* five cubits, with network and pomegranates upon the chapiters round about, all *of* brass. The second pillar also and the pomegranates *were* like unto these.

23 And there were ninety and six pomegranates on a side[2]; *and* all the pomegranates upon the network *were* an hundred round about.

24 And the captain of the guard took Seraiah the chief priest, and Zephaniah the second priest, and the three keepers of the door:

25 He took also out of the city an eunuch, which had the charge of the men of war; and seven men of them that were near the king's person, which were found in the city; and the principal scribe of the host, who mustered the people of the land; and threescore men of the people of the land, that were found in the midst of the city.

26 So Nebuzar-adan the captain of the guard took them, and brought them to the king of Babylon to Riblah.

27 And the king of Babylon smote them, and put them to death in Riblah in the land of Hamath. Thus Judah was carried away captive out of his own land.

28 This *is* the people whom Nebuchadrezzar carried away captive: in the seventh year three thousand Jews and three and twenty:

29 In the eighteenth year of Nebuchadrezzar he carried away captive from Jerusalem eight hundred thirty and two persons:

30 In the three and twentieth year of Nebuchadrezzar Nebuzar-adan the captain of the guard carried away captive of the Jews

---

[Strgs#7307].

seven hundred forty and five persons: all the persons *were* four thousand and six hundred.

31 And it came to pass in the seven and thirtieth year of the captivity of Jehoiachin king of Judah, in the twelfth month, in the five and twentieth *day* of the month, *that* Evil-merodach king of Babylon in the *first* year of his reign lifted up the head of Jehoiachin king of Judah, and brought him forth out of prison,

32 And spoke kindly unto him, and set his throne above the throne of the kings that *were* with him in Babylon,

33 And changed his prison garments: and he did continually eat bread before him all the days of his life.

34 And *for* his diet, there was a continual diet given him of the king of Babylon, [every day a portion][1] until the day of his death, all thedays of his life.

---
[1] lit. the matter of the day in his day.

LAMENTATIONS OF JEREMIAH

CHAPTER 1

1 How doth the city sit solitary, *that was* full of people! *How* is she become as a widow! She *that was* great among the nations, *and* princess among the provinces, *how* is she become tributary!
2 She weeps sore in the night, and her tears *are* on her cheeks: among all her lovers she has none to comfort *her*: all her friends have dealt treacherously with her, they are become her enemies.
3 Judah is gone into captivity because of affliction, and because of great servitude: she dwells among the heathen, she finds no rest: all her persecutors overtook her between the straits.
4 The ways of Zion do mourn, because none come to the solemn feasts: all her gates are desolate: her priests sigh, her virgins are afflicted, and she *is* in bitterness.
5 Her adversaries are the chief, her enemies prosper; for the LORD has afflicted her for the multitude of her transgressions: her children are gone into captivity before the enemy.
6 And from the daughter of Zion all her beauty is departed: her princes are become like harts *that* find no pasture, and they are gone without strength before the pursuer.
7 Jerusalem remembered in the days of her affliction and of her miseries all her pleasant things that she had in the days of old, when her people fell into the hand of the enemy, and none did help her: the adversaries saw her, *and* did mock at her Sabbaths.
8 Jerusalem has grievously sinned; therefore she is removed: all that honored her despise her, because they have seen her nakedness: yes, she sighs, and turns backward.
9 Her filthiness *is* in her skirts; she remembers not her last end; therefore she came down wonderfully: she had no comforter. O LORD, behold my affliction: for the enemy has magnified *himself*.
10 The adversary has spread out his hand upon all her pleasant things: for she has seen *that* the heathen entered into her sanctuary, whom you did command *that* they should not enter into your congregation.
11 All her people sigh, they seek bread; they have given their pleasant things for meat to relieve the soul: see, O LORD, and consider; for I am become vile.
12 *Is it* nothing to you, all you that pass by? Behold, and see if there be any sorrow like unto my sorrow, which is done unto me, wherewith the LORD has afflicted *me* in the day of his fierce anger.
13 From above has he sent fire into my bones, and it prevails against them: he has spread a net for my feet, he has turned me back: he has made me desolate *and* faint all the day.
14 The yoke of my transgressions is bound by his hand: they are wreathed, *and* come up upon my neck: he has made my strength to fall, the Lord has delivered me into *their* hands, *from whom* I am not able to rise up.
15 The Lord has trodden under foot all my mighty *men* in the midst of me: he has called an assembly against me to crush my young men: the Lord has trodden the virgin, the daughter of Judah, *as in* a winepress.
16 For these *things* I weep; mine eye, mine eye runs down with water, because the comforter that should relieve my soul is far from me: my children are desolate, because the enemy prevailed.
17 Zion spreads forth her hands, *and there is* none to comfort her: the LORD has commanded concerning Jacob, *that* his adversaries *should be* round about him: Jerusalem is as a monstrous woman among them.
18 The LORD is righteous; for I have rebelled against his commandment: hear, I pray you, all people, and behold my sorrow: my virgins and my young men are gone into captivity.
19 I called for my lovers, *but* they deceived me: my priests and mine elders gave up the ghost in the city, while they sought their meat to relieve their souls.
20 Behold, O LORD; for I *am* in distress: my bowels are troubled; mine heart is turned within me; for I have grievously rebelled: abroad the sword bereaves, at home *there is* as death.
21 They have heard that I sigh: *there is* none to comfort me: all mine enemies have heard of my trouble; they are glad that you have done *it*: you will bring the day *that* you have called, and they will be like unto me.
22 Let all their wickedness come before you; and do unto them, as you have done unto me for all my transgressions: for my sighs *are* many, and my heart *is* faint.

CHAPTER 2

1 How has the Lord covered the daughter of Zion with a cloud in his anger, *and* cast down from heaven unto the earth the beauty of Israel, and remembered not his footstool in the day of his anger!
2 The Lord has swallowed up all the habitations of Jacob, and has not pitied: he has thrown down in his wrath the strong holds of the daughter of Judah; he has brought *them* down to the ground: he has polluted the kingdom and the princes thereof.
3 He has cut off in *his* fierce anger all the horn of Israel: he has drawn back his right hand from before the enemy, and he burned against Jacob like a flaming fire, *which* devours round about.
4 He has bent his bow like an enemy: he stood with his right hand as an adversary, and slew all *that were* pleasant to the eye in the tabernacle of the daughter of Zion: he poured out his fury like fire.
5 The Lord was as an enemy: he has swallowed up Israel, he has swallowed up all her palaces: he has destroyed his strong holds, and has increased in the daughter of Judah mourning and lamentation.
6 And he has violently taken away his tabernacle, as *if it were of* a garden: he has destroyed his places of the assembly: the LORD has caused the solemn feasts and Sabbaths to be forgotten in Zion, and has despised in the indignation of his anger the king and the priest.
7 The Lord has cast off his altar, he has abhorred his sanctuary, he has given up into the hand of the enemy the walls of her palaces; they have made a noise in the house of the LORD, as in the day of a solemn feast.
8 The LORD has purposed to destroy the wall of the daughter of Zion: he has stretched out a line, he has not withdrawn his hand from destroying: therefore he made the rampart and the wall to lament; they languished together.
9 Her gates are sunk into the ground; he has destroyed and broken her bars: her king and her princes *are* among the Gentiles: the law *is* no *more*; her prophets also find no vision from the LORD.
10 The elders of the daughter of Zion sit upon the ground, *and* keep silence: they have cast up dust upon their heads; they have girded themselves with sackcloth: the virgins of Jerusalem hang down their heads to the ground.
11 Mine eyes do fail with tears, my bowels are troubled, my liver is poured upon the earth, for the destruction of the daughter of my people; because the children and the sucklings swoon in the streets of the city.

12 They say to their mothers, Where *is* corn and wine? When they swooned as the wounded in the streets of the city, when their soul was poured out into their mothers' bosom.
13 What thing will I take to witness for you? What thing will I liken to you, O daughter of Jerusalem? What will I equal to you, that I may comfort you, O virgin daughter of Zion? For your breach *is* great like the sea: who can heal you?
14 Your prophets have seen vain and foolish things for you: and they have not discovered your iniquity, to turn away your captivity; but have seen for you false burdens[1] and causes of banishment[2].
15 All that pass by clap *their* hands at you; they hiss and wag their head at the daughter of Jerusalem, *saying, is* this the city that *men* call The perfection of beauty, The joy of the whole earth?
16 All your enemies have opened their mouth against you: they hiss and gnash the teeth: they say, we have swallowed *her* up: certainly this *is* the day that we looked for; we have found, we have seen *it*.
17 The LORD has done *that* which he had devised; he has fulfilled his word that he had commanded in the days of old: he has thrown down, and has not pitied: and he has caused your enemy to rejoice over you, he has set up the horn of your adversaries.
18 Their heart cried unto the Lord, O wall of the daughter of Zion, let tears run down like a river day and night: give yourself no rest; let not the apple of your eye cease.
19 Arise, cry out in the night: in the beginning of the watches pour out your heart like water before the face of the Lord: lift up your hands toward him for the life of your young children, that faint for hunger in the top of every street.
20 Behold, O LORD, and consider to whom you have done this. Will the women eat their fruit, *and* children of a span long? Will the priest and the prophet be slain in the sanctuary of the Lord?
21 The young and the old lie on the ground in the streets: my virgins and my young men are fallen by the sword; you have slain *them* in the day of your anger; you have killed, *and* not pitied.
22 you have called as in a solemn day my terrors round about, so that in the day of the LORD'S anger none escaped nor remained: those that I have swaddled and brought up has mine enemy consumed.

CHAPTER 3

1 I *am* the man *that* has seen affliction by the rod of his wrath.
2 He has led me, and brought *me into* darkness, but not *into* light.
3 Surely against me is he turned; he turns his hand *against me* all the day.
4 My flesh and my skin has he made old; he has broken my bones.
5 He has built against me, and compassed *me* with gall and travail.
6 He has set me in dark places, as *they that be* dead of old.
7 He has hedged me about, that I cannot get out: he has made my chain heavy.
8 Also when I cry and shout, he shuts out my prayer.
9 He has inclosed my ways with hewn stone, he has made my paths crooked.
10 He *was* unto me *as* a bear lying in wait, *and as* a lion in secret places.
11 He has turned aside my ways, and pulled me in pieces: he has made me desolate.
12 He has bent his bow, and set me as a mark for the arrow.

13 He has caused the arrows of his quiver to enter into my reins.
14 I was a derision to all my people; *and* their song all the day.
15 He has filled me with bitterness, he has made me drunker with wormwood.
16 He has also broken my teeth with gravel stones, he has covered me with ashes.
17 And you have removed my soul far off from peace: I forgot prosperity.
18 And I said, My strength and my hope is perished from the LORD:
19 Remembering mine affliction and my misery, the wormwood and the gall.
20 My soul has *them* still in remembrance, and is humbled in me.
21 This I recall to my mind, therefore have I hope.
22 *It is of* the LORD'S mercies that we are not consumed, because his compassions fail not.
23 *They are* new every morning: great *is* your faithfulness.
24 The LORD *is* my portion, says my soul; therefore will I hope in him.
25 The LORD *is* good unto them that wait for him, to the soul *that* seeks him.
26 *It is* good that *a* man should both hope and quietly wait for the salvation of the LORD.
27 *It is* good for a man that he bear the yoke in his youth.
28 He sits alone and keeps silence, because he has borne *it* upon him.
29 He puts his mouth in the dust; if so be there may be hope.
30 He gives *his* cheek to him that smites him: he is filled full with reproach.
31 For the Lord will not cast off forever:
32 But though he cause grief, yet will he have compassion according to the multitude of his mercies.
33 For he does not afflict willingly nor grieve the children of men.
34 To crush under his feet all the prisoners of the earth,
35 To turn aside the right of a man before the face of the most High,
36 To subvert a man in his cause, the Lord approves not.
37 Who *is* he *that* says, and it comes to pass, *when* the Lord commands *it* not?
38 Out of the mouth of the most High proceeds not evil and good?
39 Wherefore doth a living man complain, a man for the punishment of his sins?
40 Let us search and try our ways, and turn again to the LORD.
41 Let us lift up our heart with *our* hands unto God in the heavens.
42 We have transgressed and have rebelled: you have not pardoned.
43 You have covered with anger, and persecuted us: you have slain, you have not pitied.
44 You have covered yourself with a cloud, that *our* prayer should not pass through.
45 You have made us *as* the offscouring[3] and refuse in the midst of the people.
46 All our enemies have opened their mouths against us.
47 Fear and a snare is come upon us, desolation and destruction.
48 Mine eye runs down with rivers of water for the destruction of the daughter of my people.

---

[1] burdens – to *raise*, *lift*, an *utterance*, *beacon*, *tribute*, a *reproach* [Strgs#4864]. The same word used for sign in **Jer. 6:1** and gifts in **Esther 2:18**.
[2] banishment – is the Hebrew word *maddûach* meaning *seduction*

[Strgs#4065]. Root word *nâdach* meaning to *push off* [Strgs#5080].
[3] offscouring- literally *refuse* (as swept off). [Strgs#5501]

49 Mine eye trickles down, and ceases not, without any intermission,
50 Till the LORD look down, and behold from heaven.
51 Mine eye affects mine heart because of all the daughters of my city.
52 Mine enemies chased me sore, like a bird, without cause.
53 They have cut off my life in the dungeon, and cast a stone upon me.
54 Waters flowed over mine head; *then* I said, I am cut off.
55 I called upon your name, O LORD, out of the low dungeon.
56 You have heard my voice: hide not your ear at my breathing, at my cry.
57 You drew near in the day *that* I called upon you: you said, Fear not.
58 O Lord, you have pleaded the causes of my soul; you have redeemed my life.
59 O LORD, you have seen my wrong: judge you my cause.
60 You have seen all their vengeance *and* all their imaginations against me.
61 You have heard their reproach, O LORD, *and* all their imaginations against me;
62 The lips of those that rose up against me, and their device against me all the day.
63 Behold their sitting down, and their rising up; I *am* their music.
64 Render unto them a recompense, O LORD, according to the work of their hands.
65 Give them sorrow¹ of heart, your curse unto them.
66 Persecute and destroy them in anger from under the heavens of the LORD.

CHAPTER 4

1 How is the gold become dim! *How* is the most fine gold changed! the stones of the sanctuary are poured out in the top of every street.
2 The precious sons of Zion, comparable to fine gold, how are they esteemed as earthen pitchers, the work of the hands of the potter!
3 Even the sea monsters draw out the breast, they give suck to their young ones: the daughter of my people *is become* cruel, like the ostriches in the wilderness.
4 The tongue of the sucking child cleaves to the roof of his mouth for thirst: the young children ask bread, *and* no man breaks *it* unto them.
5 They that did feed delicately are desolate in the streets: they that were brought up in scarlet² embrace dunghills.
6 For the punishment of the iniquity of the daughter of my people is greater than the punishment of the sin of Sodom, that was overthrown as in a moment, and no hands stayed on her.
7 Her Nazarites were purer than snow, they were whiter than milk, they were more ruddy³ in body than rubies, their polishing *was* of sapphire:
8 Their visage is blacker than a coal; they are not known in the streets: their skin cleaves to their bones; it is withered, it is become like a stick.
9 *They that be* slain with the sword are better than *they that be* slain with hunger: for these pine away, stricken through for *want of* the fruits of the field.
10 The hands of the pitiful women have sodden their own children: they were their meat in the destruction of the daughter of my people.
11 The LORD has accomplished his fury; he has poured out his fierce anger, and has kindled a fire in Zion, and it has devoured the foundations thereof.
12 The kings of the earth, and all the inhabitants of the world, would not have believed that the adversary and the enemy should have entered into the gates of Jerusalem.
13 For the sins of her prophets, *and* the iniquities of her priests, that have shed the blood of the just in the midst of her,
14 They have wandered *as* blind *men* in the streets, they have polluted themselves with blood, so that men could not touch their garments.
15 They cried unto them, Depart you; *it is* unclean; depart, depart, touch not: when they fled away and wandered, they said among the heathen, they shall no more sojourn *there*.
16 The anger of the LORD has divided them; he will no more regard them: they respected not the persons of the priests, they favored not the elders.
17 As for us, our eyes as yet failed for our vain help: in our watching we have watched for a nation *that* could not save us.
18 They hunt our steps, that we cannot go in our streets: our end is near, our days are fulfilled; for our end is come.
19 Our persecutors are swifter than the eagles of the heaven: they pursued us upon the mountains, they laid wait for us in the wilderness.
20 The breath of our nostrils, the anointed of the LORD, was taken in their pits, of whom we said, under his shadow we will live among the heathen.
21 Rejoice and be glad, O daughter of Edom, that dwells in the land of Uz; the cup also will pass through unto you: you will be drunken, and will make yourself naked.
22 The punishment of your iniquity is accomplished, O daughter of Zion; he will no more carry you away into captivity: he will visit your iniquity, O daughter of Edom; he will discover your sins.

CHAPTER 5

1 Remember, O LORD, what is come upon us: consider, and behold our reproach.
2 Our inheritance is turned to strangers, our houses to aliens.
3 We are orphans and fatherless, our mothers *are* as widows.
4 We have drunken our water for money; our wood is sold unto us.
5 Our necks *are* under persecution: we labor, *and* have no rest.
6 We have given the hand *to* the Egyptians, *and to* the Assyrians, to be satisfied with bread.
7 Our fathers have sinned, *and are* not; and we have borne their iniquities.
8 Servants have ruled over us: *there is* none that doth deliver *us* out of their hand.
9 We gat⁴ our bread with *the peril of* our lives because of the sword of the wilderness.
10 Our skin was black like an oven because of the terrible famine.
11 They ravished the women in Zion, *and* the maids in the cities of Judah.

---

¹ lit. covering (in a bad sese), blindness or obduracy [Strgs#4044]. Root word mâgan meaning to shield, encompass, to rescue, to hand safely over [Strgs#4042].
² compare **Rev. 17:4**.
³ ruddy– *to show blood* (in the face), that is, *flush* or turn rosy:- be (dyed, made) red. [Strgs#119]
⁴ gat- a primitive root; to *go* or *come* (in a wide variety of applications): - abide, apply, attain, be, befall, + besiege, bring (forth, in, into, to pass), call, carry, certainly, (cause, let, thing for) to come. [Strgs#935]

12 Princes are hanged up by their hand: the faces of elders were not honored.
13 They took the young men to grind, and the children fell under the wood.
14 The elders have ceased from the gate, the young men from their music.
15 The joy of our heart is ceased; our dance is turned into mourning.
16 The crown is fallen *from* our head: woe unto us, that we have sinned!
17 For this our heart is faint; for these *things* our eyes are dim.
18 Because of the mountain of Zion, which is desolate, the foxes walk upon it.
19 Thou, O LORD, remains forever; your throne from generation to generation.
20 Wherefore dost you forget us forever, *and* forsake us so long time?
21 Turn you us unto you, O LORD, and we will be turned; renew our days as of old.
22 But you have utterly rejected us; you are very wroth[1] against us.

---

[1] wroth- to *crack off*, that is, (figuratively) *burst* out in rage: - (be) anger, displease, fret self, (provoke to) wrath (come). [Strgs#7107]

EZEKIEL

CHAPTER 1

1 Now it came to pass in the thirtieth year, in the fourth *month*, in the fifth *day* of the month, as I *was* among the captives by the river of Chebar[1], *that* the heavens were opened, and I saw visions of God.

2 In the fifth *day* of the month, which *was* the fifth year of king Jehoiachin's captivity,

3 [The word of the LORD came expressly unto Ezekiel[2] the priest, the son of Buzi, in the land of the Chaldeans by the river Chebar; and the hand of the LORD was there upon him.][3]

4 And I looked, and, behold, a whirlwind came out of the north, a great cloud[4], and a fire infolding[5] itself, and a brightness *was* about it, and out of the midst thereof as the color of amber, out of the midst of the fire.

5 Also out of the midst thereof *came* the likeness of four living creatures. And this *was* their appearance; they had the likeness of a man.

6 And everyone had four faces, and everyone had four wings.

7 And their feet *were* straight feet; and the sole of their feet *was* like the sole of a calf's foot[6]: and they sparkled like the color of burnished brass.

8 And *they had* the hands of a man under their wings on their four sides; and they four had their faces and their wings.

9 Their wings *were* joined one to another; they turned not when they went[7]; they went everyone straight forward.

10 As for the likeness of their faces, they four had the face of a man, and the face of a lion, on the right side: and they four had the face of an ox on the left side; they four also had the face of an eagle.

11 Thus *were* their faces: and their wings *were* stretched upward; two *wings* of everyone *were* joined one to another, and two covered their bodies.

12 And they went every one straight forward: where the spirit was to go, they went; *and* they turned not when they went.

13 As for the likeness of the living creatures, their appearance *was* like burning coals of fire, *and* like the appearance of lamps: it went up and down among the living creatures; and the fire was bright, and out of the fire went forth lightning.

14 And the living creatures ran and returned as the appearance of a flash of lightning.

15 Now as I beheld the living creatures, behold one wheel upon the earth by the living creatures, with his four faces.

16 The appearance of the wheels and their work *was* like unto the color of a beryl: and they four had one likeness: and their appearance and their work *was* as it were a wheel in the middle of a wheel.

17 When they went, they went upon their four sides: *and* they turned not when they went.

18 As for their rings, they were so high that they were dreadful; and their rings *were* full of eyes round about them four.

19 And when the living creatures went, the wheels went by them: and when the living creatures were lifted up from the earth, the wheels were lifted up.

20 Whithersoever the spirit was to go, they went, there *was* their spirit to go; and the wheels were lifted up over against them: for the spirit of the living creature *was* in the wheels.

21 When those went, *these* went; and when those stood, *these* stood; and when those were lifted up from the earth, the wheels were lifted up over against them: for the spirit of the living creature *was* in the wheels.

22 And the likeness of the firmament upon the heads of the living creature *was* as the color of the terrible crystal, stretched forth over their heads above.

23 And under the firmament *were* their wings straight, the one toward the other: everyone had two, which covered on this side, and every one had two, which covered on that side, their bodies.

24 And when they went, I heard the noise of their wings, like the noise of great waters, as the voice of the Almighty, the voice of speech, as the noise of a host: when they stood, they let down their wings.

25 And there was a voice from the firmament that *was* over their heads, when they stood, *and* had let down their wings.

26 And above the firmament that *was* over their heads *was* the likeness of a throne, as the appearance of a sapphire stone: and upon the likeness of the throne *was* the likeness as the appearance of a man above upon it.

27 And I saw as the color of amber, as the appearance of fire round about within it, from the appearance of his loins even upward, and from the appearance of his loins even downward, I saw as it were the appearance of fire, and it had brightness round about.

28 As the appearance of the bow that is in the cloud in the day of rain, so *was* the appearance of the brightness round about. This *was* the appearance of the likeness of the glory of the LORD. And when I saw *it*, I fell upon my face, and I heard a voice of one that spoke.

CHAPTER 2

1 And he said unto me, Son of man, stand upon your feet, and I will speak unto you.

2 And the spirit entered into me when he spoke unto me, and set me upon my feet, that I heard him that spoke unto me.

3 And he said unto me, Son of man, I send you to the children of Israel, to a rebellious nation that has rebelled against me: they and their fathers have transgressed against me, *even* unto this very day.

4 For *they are* impudent[8] children and stiff-hearted I do send you unto them; and you will say unto them, thus says the Lord GOD.

5 And they, whether they will hear, or whether they will forbear, (for they *are* a rebellious[9] house,) yet will know that there has been a prophet among them.

6 And you, son of man, be not afraid of them, neither be afraid of their words, though briers and thorns *be* with you and you dost dwell among scorpions: be not afraid of their words, or be dismayed[10] at their looks, though they *be* a rebellious house.

---

[1] Chebar- is a river of Mesopotamia. Its name literally means *far off or length*. [Strgs#3529]
[2] Ezekiel- literally means *God strengthens*.
[3] Prophets can be called in Babylon, compare **Rev.18:4**.
[4] compare Hebrews 12:1
[5] infolding- is the Hebrew word *lâqach*, law-kakh'; meaning to *take* (in the widest variety of applications):- accept, bring, buy, carry away, drawn, fetch, get, many, mingle, place, receive, reserve, seize, send for, take away. [Strgs#3947]
[6] compare Lev. 11:1-8
[7] Lit. to walk. [Strgs#3212]
[8] lit. severe, churlish, cruel, grievous, hard, obstinate [Strgs#7186].
[9] rebellious – bitterness or concretely bitter [Strgs#4805].
[10] dismayed – to prostrate, to break down (by violence, confusion and fear [Strgs#2865].

7 And you will speak my words unto them, whether they will hear, or whether they will forbear: for they *are* most rebellious.
8 But you, son of man, hear what I say unto you; Be not you rebellious[1] like that rebellious house: open your mouth, and eat that I give you.
9 And when I looked, behold, an hand *was* sent unto me; and, lo, a roll of a book *was* therein;
10 And he spread it before me; and it *was* written within and without: and *there was* written therein lamentations, and mourning, and woe.

CHAPTER 3

1 Moreover he said unto me, Son of man, eat that you finds; eat this roll, and go speak unto the house of Israel.
2 So I opened my mouth, and he caused me to eat that roll.
3 And he said unto me, Son of man, cause your belly to eat, and fill your bowels with this roll that I give you. Then did I eat *it*; and it was in my mouth as honey for sweetness.
4 And he said unto me, Son of man, go, get you unto the house of Israel, and speak with my words[2] unto them.
5 For you are not sent to a people of a strange speech and of a hard language, *but* to the house of Israel;
6 Not too many people of a strange speech and of a hard language, whose words you canst not understand. Surely, had I sent you to them, they would have hearkened unto you.
7 But the house of Israel will not hearken unto you; for they will not hearken unto me: for all the house of Israel *are* impudent[3] and hardhearted.
8 Behold, I have made your face strong against their faces, and your forehead strong against their foreheads.
9 As an adamant[4] harder than flint have I made your forehead: fear them not, neither be dismayed at their looks, though they *be* a rebellious house.
10 Moreover he said unto me, Son of man, all my words that I will speak unto you receive in your heart, and hear with your ears.
11 And go, get you to them of the captivity, unto the children of your people, and speak unto them, and tell them, Thus says the Lord GOD; whether they will hear, or whether they will forbear.
12 Then the spirit took me up, and I heard behind me a voice of a great rushing, *saying*, Blessed *be* the glory of the LORD from his place.
13 *I heard* also the noise of the wings of the living creatures that touched one another, and the noise of the wheels over against them, and a noise of a great rushing.
14 So the spirit lifted me up, and took me away, and I went in bitterness, in the heat of my spirit; but the hand of the LORD was strong upon me.
15 Then I came to them of the captivity at Tel-abib, that dwelt by the river of Chebar, and I sat where they sat, and remained there astonished among them seven days.
16 And it came to pass at the end of seven days, that the word of the LORD came unto me, saying,
17 Son of man, I have made you a watchman unto the house of Israel: therefore hear the word at my mouth, and give them warning from me.
18 When I say unto the wicked, you will surely die; and you gives him not warning, or speaks to warn the wicked from his wicked way, to save his life; the same wicked *man* will die in his iniquity; but his blood will I require at your hand.
19 Yet if you warn the wicked, and he turn not from his wickedness, or from his wicked way, he will die in his iniquity; but you have delivered your soul.
20 Again, when a righteous *man* does turn from his righteousness, and commit iniquity, and I lay a stumbling block before him, he will die: because you have not given him warning, he will die in his sin, and his righteousness which he has done will not be remembered; but his blood will I require at your hand.
21 Nevertheless if you warn the righteous *man*, that the righteous sin not, and he does not sin, he will surely live, because he is warned; also you have delivered your soul.
22 And the hand of the LORD was there upon me; and he said unto me, Arise, go forth into the plain, and I will there talk with you.
23 Then I arose, and went forth into the plain: and, behold, the glory of the LORD stood there, as the glory which I saw by the river of Chebar: and I fell on my face.
24 Then the spirit entered into me, and set me upon my feet, and spoke with me, and said unto me, Go, shut yourself within your house.
25 But you, O son of man, behold, they will put bands upon you, and will bind you with them, and you will not go out among them:
26 And I will make your tongue cleave to the roof of your mouth, that you will be dumb, and will not be to them a reprover: for they *are* a rebellious[5] house.
27 [But when I speak with you, I will open your mouth, and you will say unto them, Thus says the Lord GOD; He that hears, let him hear; and he that forbears, let him forbear: for they *are* a rebellious house.][6]

CHAPTER 4

1 You also, son of man, take you a tile, and lay it before you, and portray[7] upon it the city, *even* Jerusalem:
2 And lay siege against it, and build a fort against it, and cast a mount against it; set the camp also against it, and set *battering* rams against it round about.
3 Moreover take you unto you an iron pan, and set it *for* a wall of iron between you and the city: and set your face against it, and it will be besieged, and you will lay siege against it. This will *be* a sign to the house of Israel.
4 Lie you also upon your left side, and lay the iniquity of the house of Israel upon it: *according* to the number of the days that you will lie upon it you will bear their iniquity.
5 For I have laid upon you the years of their iniquity, according to the number of the days, three hundred and ninety days: so will you bear the iniquity of the house of Israel.

---

[1] see [Strgs#4805]
[2] compare **Jer. 1:9**
[3] impudent – derives from two Hebrew words the first word being *châzâq* meaning <u>strong</u> (usually in a bad sense, *hard*, *bold*, <u>violent</u>), <u>fortify</u> [Strgs#2389]. The second being *mêtsach*; meaning *to be clear, conspicuous*, the <u>forehead</u> (as open and *prominent*) [Strgs#4696]. Compare **Rev. 13:16**.
[4] lit. <u>priking</u>; pointed, a *thorn*, also (from its keeneness for scratching) a gem, probably the diamond: -brier [Strgs#8068].
[5] lit. bitter [Strgs#4805]
[6] compare **Jer. 1:2-4**
[7] portray- to hack, that is, engrave, by implication to enact (laws being cut in stone or metal tablets in primitive times) or prescribe: -appoint, decree, governor, grave, lawgiver, note, print, set. [Strgs#2710]

Ezekiel

6 And when you have accomplished them, lie again on your right side, and you will bear the iniquity of the house of Judah forty days: I have appointed you [each day for a year.][1]

7 Therefore you will set your face toward the siege of Jerusalem, and your arm will *be* uncovered, and you will prophesy against it.

8 And, behold, I will lay bands upon you, and you will not turn you from one side to another, till you have ended the days of your siege.

9 Take you also unto you wheat, and barley, and beans, and lentiles, and millet, and fitches, and put them in one vessel, and make you bread thereof, *according* to the number of the days that you will lie upon your side, three hundred and ninety days will you eat thereof.

10 And your meat which you will eat will *be* by weight, twenty shekels a day: from time to time will you eat it.

11 You will drink also water by measure, the sixth part of a hin[2]: from time to time will you drink.

12 And you will eat it *as* barley cakes, and you will bake it with dung that cometh out of man, in their sight.

13 And the LORD said, even thus will the children of Israel eat their defiled bread among the Gentiles, where I will drive them.

14 Then said I, Ah Lord GOD! Behold, my soul has not been polluted: for from my youth up even till now have I not eaten of that which dies of itself, or is torn in pieces; neither came there abominable flesh into my mouth.

15 Then he said unto me, Lo, I have given you cow's dung for man's dung, and you will prepare your bread therewith.

16 Moreover he said unto me, Son of man, behold, I will break the staff of bread in Jerusalem: and they will eat bread by weight, and with care; and they will drink water by measure, and with astonishment:

17 That they may want bread and water, and be astonied[3] one with another, and consume away for their iniquity.

CHAPTER 5

1 And you, son of man, take you a sharp knife, take you a barber's razor, and cause *it* to pass upon your head and upon your beard: then take you balances to weigh, and divide the *hair.*

2 You will burn with fire a third part in the midst of the city, when the days of the siege are fulfilled: and you will take a third part, *and* smite about it with a knife: and a third part you will scatter in the wind; and I will draw out a sword after them.

3 You will also take thereof a few in number, and bind them in your skirts.

4 Then take of them again, and cast them into the midst of the fire, and burn them in the fire; *for* thereof will a fire come forth into all the house of Israel.

5 Thus says the Lord GOD; This *is* Jerusalem: I have set it in the midst of the nations and countries *that are* round about her.

6 And she has changed my judgments into wickedness more than the nations, and my statutes more than the countries that *are* round about her: for they have refused my judgments and my statutes, they have not walked in them.

7 Therefore thus says the Lord GOD; Because you multiplied more than the nations that *are* round about you, *and* have not walked in my statutes, neither have kept my judgments, neither have done according to the judgments of the nations that *are* round about you;

8 Therefore thus says the Lord GOD; Behold, I, even I, *am* against you, and will execute judgments in the midst of you in the sight of the nations.

9 And I will do in you that which I have not done, and whereunto I will not do any more the like, because of all your abominations.

10 Therefore the fathers will eat the sons in the midst of you, and the sons will eat their fathers; and I will execute judgments in you, and the whole remnant of you will I scatter into all the winds.

11 Wherefore, *as* I live, says the Lord GOD; Surely, because you have defiled my sanctuary with all your detestable things, and with all your abominations, therefore will I also diminish you; neither will mine eye spare, neither will I have any pity.

12 A third part of you will die with the pestilence, and with famine will they be consumed in the midst of you: and a third part will fall by the sword round about you; and I will scatter a third part into all the winds, and I will draw out a sword after them.

13 Thus will mine anger be accomplished, and I will cause my fury to rest upon them, and I will be comforted: and they will know that I the LORD have spoken *it* in my zeal, when I have accomplished my fury in them.

14 Moreover I will make you waste, and a reproach among the nations that *are* round about you, in the sight of all that pass by.

15 So it will be a reproach and a taunt, an instruction and an astonishment unto the nations that *are* round about you, when I will execute judgments in you in anger and in fury and in furious rebukes. I the LORD have spoken *it.*

16 When I will send upon them the evil arrows of famine, which will be for *their* destruction, *and* which I will send to destroy you: and I will increase the famine upon you, and will break your staff of bread:

17 So will I send upon you famine and evil beasts, and they will bereave you; and pestilence and blood will pass through you; and I will bring the sword upon you. I the LORD have spoken *it.*

CHAPTER 6

1 And the word of the LORD came unto me, saying,

2 Son of man, set your face toward the mountains of Israel, and prophesy against them,

3 And say, you mountains of Israel, hear the word of the Lord GOD; Thus says the Lord GOD to the mountains, and to the hills, to the rivers, and to the valleys; Behold, I, *even* I, will bring a sword upon you, and I will destroy your high places.

4 And your altars will be desolate, and your images will be broken: and I will cast down your slain *men* before your idols.

5 And I will lay the dead carcasses of the children of Israel before their idols; and I will scatter your bones round about your altars.

6 In all your dwelling places the cities will be laid waste, and the high places will be desolate; that your altars may be laid waste and made desolate, and your idols may be broken and cease, and your images may be cut down, and your works may be abolished.

7 And the slain will fall in the midst of you, and you will know that I *am* the LORD.

---

[1] compare Numbers 14:34.
390+40=420,
240 - times,
120 time,
60 half time

[1] Repeated twice: come to pass shortly
[2] see Measurement & Liquid chart
[3] astonied- to stun (or intransitively grow numb), that is, devastate or (figuratively) stupefy (both usually in a passive sense): -make amazed, desolate, be destitute, destroy (self), waste, wonder. Strgs#8074]

8 Yet will I leave a remnant, that you may have *some* that will escape the sword among the nations, when you will be scattered through the countries.

9 And they that escape of you will remember me among the nations where they will be carried captives, because I am broken with their whorish heart, which has departed from me, and with their eyes, which go a whoring after their idols: and they will lothe¹ themselves for the evils which they have committed in all their abominations.

10 And they will know that I *am* the LORD, *and that* I have not said in vain that I would do this evil unto them.

11 Thus says the Lord GOD; Smite with your hand, and stamp with your foot, and say, Alas for all the evil abominations of the house of Israel! for they will fall by the sword, by the famine, and by the pestilence.

12 He that is far off will die of the pestilence; and he that is near will fall by the sword; and he that remains and is besieged will die by the famine: thus will I accomplish my fury upon them.

13 Then will you know that I *am* the LORD, when their slain *men* will be among their idols round about their altars, upon every high hill, in all the tops of the mountains, and under every green tree, and under every thick oak, the place where they did offer sweet savor to all their idols.

14 So will I stretch out my hand upon them, and make the land desolate, yea, more desolate than the wilderness toward Diblath, in all their habitations: and they will know that I *am* the LORD.

CHAPTER 7

1 Moreover the word of the LORD came unto me, saying,

2 Also, you son of man, thus says the Lord GOD unto the land of Israel; An end, the end is come upon the four corners of the land.

3 Now *is* the end *come* upon you, and I will send mine anger upon you, and will judge you according to your ways, and will recompense upon you all your abominations.

4 And mine eye will not spare you, neither will I have pity: but I will recompense your ways upon you, and your abominations will be in the midst of you: and you will know that I *am* the LORD.

5 Thus says the Lord GOD; An evil, an only evil, behold, is come.

6 An end is come, the end is come: it watches² for you; behold, it is come.

7 The morning is come unto you, O you that dwells in the land: the time is come, the day of trouble *is* near, and not the sounding again of the mountains.

8 Now will I shortly pour out my fury upon you, and accomplish mine anger upon you: and I will judge you according to your ways, and will recompense you for all your abominations.

9 And mine eye will not spare, neither will I have pity: I will recompense you according to your ways and your abominations *that* are in the midst of you; and you will know that I *am* the LORD that smites.

10 Behold the day, behold, it is come: the morning is gone forth; the rod has blossomed, pride has budded.

11 Violence is risen up into a rod of wickedness: none of them will *remain*, or of their multitude, or of any of theirs: neither will *there be* wailing for them.

12 The time is come, the day draws near: let not the buyer rejoice, or the seller mourn: for wrath *is* upon all the multitude thereof.

13 For the seller will not return to that which is sold, although they were yet alive: for the vision *is* touching the whole multitude thereof, *which* will not return; neither will any strengthen himself in the iniquity of his life.

14 They have blown the trumpet, even to make all ready; but none goes to the battle: for my wrath *is* upon **the entire** multitude thereof.

15 The sword *is* without, and the pestilence and the famine within: he that *is* in the field will die with the sword; and he that *is* in the city, famine and pestilence will devour him.

16 But they that escape of them will escape, and will be on the mountains like doves of the valleys, all of them mourning, every one for his iniquity.

17 All hands will be feeble, and all knees will be weak *as* water.

18 They will also gird *themselves* with sackcloth, and horror will cover them; and shame will *be* upon all faces, and baldness upon all their heads.

19 They will cast their silver in the streets, and their gold will be removed: their silver and their gold will not be able to deliver them in the day of the wrath of the LORD: they will not satisfy their souls, neither fill their bowels: because it is the stumbling block of their iniquity³.

20 As for the beauty of his ornament, he set it in majesty: but they made the images of their abominations *and* of their detestable things therein: therefore have I set it far from them.

21 And I will give it into the hands of the strangers for a prey, and to the wicked of the earth for a spoil; and they will pollute it.

22 My face will I turn also from them, and they will pollute my secret *place*: for the robbers will enter into it, and defile it.

23 Make a chain: for the land is full of bloody crimes, and the city is full of violence.

24 Wherefore I will bring the worst of the heathen, and they will possess their houses: I will also make the pomp of the strong to cease; and their holy places will be defiled.

25 Destruction cometh; and they will seek peace, and *there will be* none.

26 Mischief will come upon mischief, and rumor will be upon rumor; then will they seek a vision of the prophet; but the law will perish from the priest, and counsel from the ancients.

27 The king will mourn, and the prince will be clothed with desolation, and the hands of the people of the land will be troubled: I will do unto them after their way, and according to their deserts⁴ will I judge them; and they will know that I *am* the LORD.

CHAPTER 8

1 And it came to pass in the sixth year, in the sixth *month*, in the fifth *day* of the month, *as* I sat in mine house, and the elders of Judah sat before me, that the hand of the Lord GOD fell there upon me.

2 Then I beheld, and lo a likeness as the appearance of fire: from the appearance of his loins even downward, fire; and from his loins even upward, as the appearance of brightness, as the color of amber.

3 And he put forth the form of an hand, and took me by a lock of mine head; and the spirit lifted me up between the earth and the heaven, and brought me in the visions of God to Jerusalem, to the

---

¹ lothe- to cut off, be grieved [Strgs#6962]

² watches – the idea of *abruptness* in starting up from sleep, to *awake*, to awaken against you [Strgs#6974].

³ iniquity – *perversity*, (moral) *evil*: fault, mischief, punishment (of iniquity), sin [Strgs#5771]. Money.

⁴ deserts – verdict, *divine law*, sentence, *justice*, right or *privilege* [Strgs#4941].

door of the inner gate that looks toward the north; where *was* the seat of the image of jealousy, which [provokes to jealousy]¹.

4 And, behold, the glory of the God of Israel *was* there, according to the vision that I saw in the plain.

5 Then said he unto me, Son of man, lift up your eyes now the way toward the north. So I lifted up mine eyes the way toward the north, and behold northward at the gate of the altar this image of jealousy in the entry.

6 He said furthermore unto me, Son of man, see you what they do? *Even* the great abominations that the house of Israel commits here, that I should go far off from my sanctuary? But turn you yet again, *and* you will see greater abominations.

7 And he brought me to the door of the court; and when I looked, behold a hole in the wall.

8 Then said he unto me, Son of man, dig now in the wall: and when I had **dug** in the wall, behold a door.

9 And he said unto me, Go in, and behold the wicked abominations that they do here.

10 So I went in and saw; and behold every form of creeping² things, and [abominable beasts]³, and all the idols⁴ of the house of Israel, **portrayed** upon the wall round about.

11 And there stood before them seventy men of the ancients of the house of Israel, and in the midst of them stood Jaazaniah⁵ the son of Shaphan, with every man his censer in his hand; and a thick⁶ cloud of incense went up.

12 Then said he unto me, Son of man, have you seen what the ancients of the house of Israel do in the dark, every man in the chambers of his imagery⁷? For they say, The LORD sees us not; the LORD has forsaken the earth.

13 He said also unto me, Turn you yet again, *and* you will see greater abominations that they do.

14 Then he brought me to the door of the gate of the LORD'S house which *was* toward the north; and, behold, there sat women weeping for Tammuz.

15 Then said he unto me, have you seen *this*, O son of man? Turn you yet again, *and* you will see greater abominations than these.

16 And he brought me into the inner court of the LORD'S house, and, behold, at the door of the temple of the LORD, between the porch and the altar, *were* about five and twenty men, with their backs toward the temple of the LORD, and their faces toward the east; and they worshipped the sun toward the east.

17 Then he said unto me, have you seen *this*, O son of man? Is it a light thing to the house of Judah that they commit the abominations which they commit here? For they have filled the land with violence, and have returned to provoke me to anger: and, lo, they put the branch to their nose.

18 Therefore will I also deal in fury: mine eye will not spare, neither will I have pity: and though they cry in mine ears with a loud voice, *yet* will I not hear them.

CHAPTER 9

1 He cried also in mine ears with a loud voice, saying, Cause them that have charge over the city to draw near, even every man *with* his destroying weapon in his hand.

2 And, behold, six men came from the way of the higher gate, which lies toward the north, and every man a slaughter weapon in his hand; and one man among them *was* clothed with linen, with a writer's inkhorn by his side: and they went in, and stood beside the brasen altar.

3 And the glory of the God of Israel was gone up from the cherub, whereupon he was, to the threshold of the house. And he called to the man clothed with linen, which *had* the writer's inkhorn by his side;

4 And the LORD said unto him, Go through the midst of the city, through the midst of Jerusalem, and set a mark upon the foreheads of the men that sigh and that cry for all the abominations that be done in the midst thereof.

5 And to the others he said in mine hearing, go you after him through the city, and smite: let not your eye spare, neither have you pity:

6 Slay utterly old *and* young, both maids, and little children, and women: but come not near any man upon whom *is* the mark; and begin at my sanctuary. Then they began at the ancient men which *were* before the house.

7 And he said unto them, Defile the house, and fill the courts with the slain: go you forth. And they went forth, and slew in the city.

8 And it came to pass, while they were slaying them, and I was left, that I fell upon my face, and cried, and said, Ah Lord GOD! Will you destroy all the residue of Israel in your pouring out of your fury upon Jerusalem?

9 Then said he unto me, the iniquity of the house of Israel and Judah *is* exceeding great, and the land is full of blood, and the city full of perverseness: for they say, The LORD has forsaken the earth, and the LORD sees not.

10 And as for me also, mine eye will not spare, neither will I have pity, *but* I will recompense their way upon their head.

11 And, behold, the man clothed with linen, which *had* the inkhorn by his side, reported the matter, saying, I have done as you have commanded me.

CHAPTER 10

1 Then I looked, and, behold, in the firmament that *was* above the head of the cherubims there appeared over them as it were a sapphire stone, as the appearance of the likeness of a throne.

2 And he spoke unto the man clothed with linen, and said, Go in between the wheels, *even* under the cherub, and fill your hand with coals of fire from between the cherubims, and scatter *them* over the city. And he went in, in my sight.

3 Now the cherubims stood on the right side of the house, when the man went in; and the cloud filled the inner court.

4 Then the glory of the LORD went up from the cherub, *and stood* over the threshold of the house; and the house was filled with the cloud, and the court was full of the brightness of the LORD'S glory.

5 And the sound of the cherubims' wings was heard *even* to the outer court, as the voice of the Almighty God when he speaks.

6 And it came to pass, *that* when he had commanded the man clothed with linen, saying, Take fire from between the wheels, from between the cherubims; then he went in, and stood beside the wheels.

7 And *one* cherub stretched forth his hand from between the cherubims unto the fire that *was* between the cherubims, and took

---

¹ lit. *erect*, *create*, *sell*, procure, own [Strgs#7069].
² creeping – reptile that glides [Strgs#7431].
³ lit. filthy dumb beast [Strgs#8263+929].
⁴ idols – *log* [Strgs#1544].
⁵ Jaazaniah- Jehovah hears or *heard of Jah.* [Strgs#2970]

⁶ thick – derives from the Hebrew word *'âthâr* meaning *incense* (as increasing to a volume of smoke), worshipper [Strgs#6282]. Compare **Job 33:26**.
⁷ lit. *image*, *figure*, *imagination*, opinion, *conceit* [Strgs#4906]. Compare **Proverbs 18:11**.

thereof, and put *it* into the hands of *him that was* clothed with linen: who took *it*, and went out.

8 And there appeared in the cherubims the form of a man's hand under their wings.

9 And when I looked, behold the four wheels by the cherubims, one wheel by one cherub, and another wheel by another cherub: and the appearance of the wheels *was* as the color of a beryl stone.

10 And *as for* their appearances, they four had one likeness, as if a wheel had been in the midst of a wheel.

11 When they went, they went upon their four sides; they turned not as they went, but to the place where the head looked they followed it; they turned not as they went.

12 And their whole body, and their backs, and their hands, and their wings, and the wheels, *were* full of eyes round about, *even* the wheels that they four had.

13 As for the wheels, it was cried unto them in my hearing, O wheel.

14 And every one had four faces: the first face *was* the face of a cherub, and the second face *was* the face of a man, and the third the face of a lion, and the fourth the face of an eagle.

15 And the cherubims were lifted up. This *is* the living creature that I saw by the river of Chebar.

16 And when the cherubims went, the wheels went by them: and when the cherubims lifted up their wings to mount up from the earth, the same wheels also turned not from beside them.

17 When they stood, *these* stood; and when they were lifted up, *these* lifted up themselves *also*: for the spirit of the living creature *was* in them.

18 Then the glory of the LORD departed from off the threshold of the house, and stood over the cherubims.

19 And the cherubims lifted up their wings, and mounted up from the earth in my sight: when they went out, the wheels also *were* beside them, and *every one* stood at the door of the east gate of the LORD'S house; and the glory of the God of Israel *was* over them above.

20 This *is* the living creature that I saw under the God of Israel by the river of Chebar; and I knew that they *were* the cherubims.

21 Every one had four faces apiece, and every one four wings; and the likeness of the hands of a man *was* under their wings.

22 And the likeness of their faces *was* the same faces which I saw by the river of Chebar, their appearances and themselves: they went every one straight forward.

CHAPTER 11

1 Moreover the spirit lifted me up, and brought me unto the east gate of the LORD'S house, which looks eastward: and behold at the door of the gate five and twenty men; among whom I saw Jaazaniah[1] the son of Azur[2], and Pelatiah[3] the son of Benaiah, princes of the people.

2 Then said he unto me, Son of man, these *are* the men that devise mischief, and give wicked counsel in this city:

3 Which say, *it is* not near; let us build houses: this *city is* the caldron, and we *be* the flesh.

4 Therefore prophesy against them, prophesy, O son of man.

5 And the Spirit of the LORD fell upon me, and said unto me, Speak; Thus says the LORD; Thus have you said, O house of Israel: for I know the things that come into your mind[4], *every* one *of* them.

6 you have multiplied your slain in this city, and you have filled the streets[5] thereof with the slain[6].

7 Therefore thus says the Lord GOD; your slain whom you have laid in the midst of it, they *are* the flesh, and this *city is* the caldron: but I will bring you forth out of the midst of it.

8 you have feared the sword; and I will bring a sword upon you, says the Lord GOD.

9 And I will bring you out of the midst thereof, and deliver you into the hands of strangers, and will execute judgments among you.

10 you will fall by the sword; I will judge you in the border of Israel; and you will know that I *am* the LORD.

11 This *city* will not be your caldron, neither will you be the flesh in the midst thereof; *but* I will judge you in the border of Israel:

12 And you will know that I *am* the LORD: for you have not walked in my statutes, neither executed my judgments, but have done after the manners of the heathen that *are* round about you.

13 And it came to pass, when I prophesied, that Pelatiah the son of Benaiah died. Then fell I down upon my face, and cried with a loud voice, and said, Ah Lord GOD! Will you make a full end of the remnant of Israel?

14 Again the word of the LORD came unto me, saying,

15 Son of man, your brethren, *even* your brethren, the men of your kindred, and all the house of Israel wholly, *are* they unto whom the inhabitants of Jerusalem have said, Get you far from the LORD: unto us is this land given in possession.

16 Therefore say, thus says the Lord GOD; although I have cast them far off among the heathen, and although I have scattered them among the countries, yet will I be to them as a little sanctuary in the countries where they will come.

17 Therefore say, thus says the Lord GOD; I will even gather you from the people, and assemble you out of the countries where you have been scattered, and I will give you the land of Israel.

18 And they will come thither, and they will take away all the detestable things thereof and all the abominations thereof from thence.

19 And I will give them one heart, and I will put a new spirit within you; and I will take the stony heart out of their flesh, and will give them a heart of flesh:

20 That they may walk in my statutes, and keep mine ordinances, and do them: and they will be my people, and I will be their God.

21 But *as for them* whose heart walks after the heart of their detestable things and their abominations, I will recompense their way upon their own heads, says the Lord GOD.

22 Then did the cherubims lift up their wings, and the wheels beside them; and the glory of the God of Israel *was* over them above.

23 And the glory of the LORD went up from the midst of the city, and stood upon the mountain which *is* on the east side of the city.

24 Afterwards the spirit took me up, and brought me in a vision by the Spirit of God into Chaldea, to them of the captivity. So the vision that I had seen went up from me.

25 Then I spoke unto them of the captivity all the things that the LORD had showed me.

---

[1] Jaazaniah – Jah has heard or *heard of Jah* [Strgs#2970].

[2] lit. *helpful*, he that assists [Strgs#5809].

[3] lit. *Jah has delivered* or Jehovah delivers [Strgs#6410].

[4] mind – breath, life, anger, unsubstantiality, spirit [Strgs#7307].

[5] lit. to separate or sever by a wall, outside or outdoor [Strgs#2351].

[6] slain – pierced (especially to death), wounded, polluted, kill, profane, slew [Strgs#2491].

CHAPTER 12

1 The word of the LORD also came unto me, saying,
2 Son of man, you dwell in the midst of a rebellious[1] house, which have eyes to see, and see not; they have ears to hear, and hear not: for they *are* a rebellious[2] house.
3 Therefore, you son of man, prepare you stuff for removing, and remove by day in their sight; and you will remove from your place to another place in their sight: it may be they will consider, though they *be* a rebellious house.
4 Then will you bring forth your stuff by day in their sight, as stuff for removing: and you will go forth at even in their sight, as they that go forth into captivity.
5 Dig you through the wall in their sight, and carry out thereby.
6 In their sight will you bear *it* upon your shoulders, *and* carry *it* forth in the twilight: you will cover your face, that you see not the ground: for I have set you *for* a sign unto the house of Israel.
7 And I did so as I was commanded: I brought forth my stuff by day, as stuff for captivity, and in the even I **dug** through the wall with mine hand; I brought *it* forth in the twilight, *and* I bare *it* upon my shoulder in their sight.
8 And in the morning came the word of the LORD unto me, saying,
9 Son of man, has not the house of Israel, the rebellious house, said unto you, What do you?
10 Say you unto them, Thus says the Lord GOD; This burden *concerns* the prince in Jerusalem, and all the house of Israel that *are* among them.
11 Say, I *am* your sign: like as I have done, so will it be done unto them: they will remove *and* go into captivity.
12 And the prince that *is* among them will bear upon *his* shoulder in the twilight, and will go forth: they will dig through the wall to carry out thereby: he will cover his face, that he see not the ground with *his* eyes.
13 My net also will I spread upon him, and he will be taken in my snare: and I will bring him to Babylon *to* the land of the Chaldeans; yet will he not see it, though he will die there.
14 And I will scatter toward every wind all that *are* about him to help him, and all his bands; and I will draw out the sword after them.
15 And they will know that I *am* the LORD, when I will scatter them among the nations, and disperse them in the countries.
16 But I will leave a few men of them from the sword, from the famine, and from the pestilence; that they may declare all their abominations among the heathen where they come; and they will know that I *am* the LORD.
17 Moreover the word of the LORD came to me, saying,
18 Son of man, eat your bread with quaking, and drink your water with trembling and with carefulness;
19 And say unto the people of the land, thus says the Lord GOD of the inhabitants of Jerusalem, *and* of the land of Israel; they will eat their bread with carefulness, and drink their water with astonishment, that her land may be desolate from all that is therein, because of the violence of all them that dwell therein.
20 And the cities that are inhabited will be laid waste, and the land will be desolate; and you will know that I *am* the LORD.
21 And the word of the LORD came unto me, saying,
22 Son of man, what *is* that proverb *that* you have in the land of Israel, saying, the days are prolonged, and every vision fails?
23 Tell them therefore, Thus says the Lord GOD; I will make this proverb to cease, and they will no more use it as a proverb in Israel; but say unto them, The days are at hand, and the effect of every vision.
24 For there will be no more any vain vision or flattering divination within the house of Israel.
25 For I *am* the LORD: I will speak, and the word that I will speak will come to pass; it will be no more prolonged: for in your days, O rebellious house, will I say the word, and will perform it, says the Lord GOD.
26 Again the word of the LORD came to me, saying,
27 [Son of man, behold, *they of* the house of Israel say, the vision that he sees *is* for many days *to come*, and he prophesies of the times *that are* far off.][3]
28 Therefore say unto them, Thus says the Lord GOD; There will none of my words be prolonged any more, but the word which I have spoken will be done, says the Lord GOD.

CHAPTER 13

1 And the word of the LORD came unto me, saying,
2 Son of man, [prophesy against][4] the prophets of Israel that prophesy, and say you unto them [that prophesy][5] out of their own hearts, Hear you the word of the LORD;
3 Thus says the Lord GOD; Woe unto the foolish prophets, that follow their own spirit, and [have seen nothing][6]
4 O Israel, your prophets are like the foxes in the deserts.
5 You have not gone up into the gaps, neither made up the hedge for the house of Israel to stand in the battle in the day of the LORD.[7]
6 [They have seen vanity[8] and lying divination, saying, The LORD says: and the LORD has not sent them: and they have made others to hope that they would confirm the word.][9]
7 [Have you not seen a vain vision, and have you not spoken a lying divination, whereas you say, The LORD says *it*; albeit I have not spoken?][10]
8 Therefore thus says the Lord GOD; because you have spoken vanity, and seen lies, therefore, behold, I *am* against you, says the Lord GOD.
9 [And mine hand will be upon the prophets that see vanity, and that divine lies: they will not be in the assembly of my people, neither will they be written in the writing of the house of Israel, neither will they enter into the land of Israel; and you will know that I *am* the Lord GOD.][11]
10 Because, even because they have seduced my people, saying, Peace; and *there was* no peace; and one built up a wall, and, lo, others daubed it with untempered[12] *morter*.
11 Say unto them which daub *it* with untempered *morter*, that it will fall: there will be an overflowing shower; and you, O [great hailstones][13], will fall; and a stormy[14] wind will rend *it*.

---

[1] lit. *bitter* [Strgs#2491].
[2] Ibid.
[3] see Jer. 1:12
[4] see Jer. 1:3 & Ez. 13:17
[5] lit. *that are prophets, inspired* man [Strgs#5030]
[6] or *and they have not seen.*
[7] compare **Ps. 106:23**
[8] see Lam. 2:14
[9] contrast to **Jer. 1:2-4, Ez. 4:3, 3:26, Luke 3:2**.
[10] What makes a "Lying Divination" is when prophets say, "God said" and God did not say.
[11] see Lam. 2:14
[12] untempered- to *smear; plaster* (as gummy) or slime; (figuratively) frivolity: -foolish things, unsavory. [Strgs#8602]
[13] lit. *almighty chrystal stones* [Strgs#417&68]
[14] stormy – *hurricane* [Strgs#5591]

12 Lo, when the wall is fallen, will it not be said unto you, Where *is* the daubing wherewith you have daubed *it*?
13 Therefore thus says the Lord GOD; I will even rend *it* with a stormy wind in my fury; and there will be an overflowing shower in mine anger, and great hailstones in *my* fury to consume *it*.
14 [So will I break down the wall that you have daubed with untempered *morter*, and bring it down to the ground, so that the foundation thereof will be discovered, and it will fall, and you will be consumed in the midst thereof: and you will know that I *am* the LORD.]¹
15 Thus will I accomplish my wrath upon the wall, and upon them that have daubed it with untempered *morter*, and will say unto you, The wall *is* no *more*, neither they that daubed it;
16 *To wit*, the prophets of Israel which prophesy concerning Jerusalem, and which see visions of peace for her, and *there is* no peace, says the Lord GOD.
17 Likewise, you son of man, [set your face against the daughters]² of your people, which prophesy out of their own heart; and prophesy you against them,
18 And say, thus says the Lord GOD; Woe to the *women* that sew pillows to all armholes³, and make kerchiefs⁴ upon the head of every stature to hunt souls! Will you hunt⁵ the souls of my people, and will you save the souls alive *that come* unto you?
19 And will you pollute me among my people for handfuls of barley and for pieces of bread, to slay the souls that should not die, and to save the souls alive that should not live, by your lying to my people that hear *your* lies?
20 Wherefore thus says the Lord GOD; Behold, I *am* against your pillows, wherewith you there hunt the souls to make *them* fly, and I will tear them from your arms, and will let the souls go, *even* the souls that you hunt to make *them* fly.
21 Your kerchiefs also will I tear, and deliver my people out of your hand, and they will be no more in your hand to be hunted; and you will know that I *am* the LORD.
22 Because with lies you have made the heart of the righteous sad, whom I have not made sad; and strengthened the hands of the wicked, that he should not return from his wicked way, by promising him life:
23 Therefore you will see no more vanity, or divine divinations: for I will deliver my people out of your hand: and you will know that I *am* the LORD.

CHAPTER 14

1 Then came certain of the elders of Israel unto me, and sat before me.
2 And the word of the LORD came unto me, saying,
3 Son of man, these men have set up their idols in their heart, and put the stumbling block of their iniquity before their face: should I be enquired of at all by them?
4 Therefore speak unto them, and say unto them, Thus says the Lord GOD; Every man of the house of Israel that sets up his idols in his heart, and puts the stumbling block of his iniquity before his face, and cometh to the prophet; I the LORD will answer him that cometh according to the multitude of his idols;
5 That I may take the house of Israel in their own heart, because they are all estranged from me through their idols.
6 Therefore say unto the house of Israel, Thus says the Lord GOD; Repent, and turn *yourselves* from your idols; and turn away your faces from all your abominations.
7 For every one of the house of Israel, or of the stranger that sojourns in Israel, which separates himself from me, and sets up his idols in his heart, and puts the stumbling block of his iniquity before his face, and cometh to a prophet to enquire of him concerning me; I the LORD will answer him by myself:
8 And I will set my face against that man, and will make him a sign and a proverb, and I will cut him off from the midst of my people; and you will know that I *am* the LORD.
9 And if the prophet be deceived when he has spoken a thing, I the LORD have deceived that prophet, and I will stretch out my hand upon him, and will destroy him from the midst of my people Israel.
10 And they will bear the punishment of their iniquity: the punishment of the prophet will be even as the punishment of him that seeks *unto him*;
11 That the house of Israel may go no more astray from me, neither be polluted any more with all their transgressions; but that they may be my people, and I may be their God, says the Lord GOD.
12 The word of the LORD came again to me, saying,
13 Son of man, when the land sins against me by trespassing grievously, then will I stretch out mine hand upon it, and will break the staff of the bread thereof, and will send famine upon it, and will cut off man and beast from it:
14 Though these three men, Noah, Daniel, and Job, were in it, they should deliver *but* their own souls by their righteousness, says the Lord GOD.
15 If I cause [noisome beasts]⁶ to pass through the land, and they spoil it, so that it be desolate, that no man may pass through because of the beasts:
16 *Though* these three men *were* in it, *as* I live, says the Lord GOD, they will deliver neither sons or daughters; they only will be delivered, but the land will be desolate.
17 Or *if* I bring a sword upon that land, and say, Sword, go through the land; so that I cut off man and beast from it:
18 Though these three men *were* in it, *as* I live, says the Lord GOD, they will deliver neither sons or daughters, but they only will be delivered themselves.
19 Or *if* I send a pestilence into that land, and [pour out my fury upon it in blood]⁷, to cut off from it man and beast:
20 Though Noah, Daniel, and Job, *were* in it, *as* I live, says the Lord GOD, they will deliver neither son or daughter; they will *but* deliver their own souls by their righteousness.
21 For thus says the Lord GOD; How much more when I send my four⁸ sore judgments⁹ upon Jerusalem, the sword, and the famine, and the noisome¹⁰ beast, and the pestilence, to cut off from it man and beast?
22 Yet, behold, therein will be left a remnant that will be brought forth, *both* sons and daughters: behold, they will come forth unto you, and [you will see their way]¹¹ and their doings: and you will be

---

¹ No Jesus **2 Tim. 2:19**, God did not seal, these prophets He does not "known" them.
² see Ez. 13:2 & Jer. 1:3.
³ armholes – *uniting*; a joint of the hand (that is, *knuckle*), *partywall* [Strgs#679].
⁴ lit. a *veil* (as *spread* out) [Strgs#4555].
⁵ hunt – to *lie alongside*, to *catch*, to *victual*, sore [Strgs#6679].

⁶ lit. evil beast [Strgs#7451+2416].
⁷ compare Rev. 8:7 & Rev. 16
⁸ see Rev. 6:8
⁹ lit. sentence [Strgs#8201]
¹⁰ noisome – evil [Strgs#7451].
¹¹ see Jer 6:27-30

comforted[1] concerning the evil that I have brought upon Jerusalem, *even* concerning all that I have brought upon it.

23 And they will comfort you, when [you see their ways][2] and their doings: and you will know that I have not done without cause all that I have done in it, says the Lord GOD.

CHAPTER 15

1 And the word of the LORD came unto me, saying,

2 Son of man, what is the vine tree more than any tree, *or than* a branch which is among the trees of the forest?

3 Will wood be taken thereof to do any work? Or will *men* take a pin of it to hang any vessel thereon?

4 Behold, it is cast into the fire for fuel; the fire devours both the ends of it, and the midst of it is burned. Is it meet[3] for *any* work?

5 Behold, when it was whole, it was meet[4] for no work: how much less will it be meet[5] yet for *any* work, when the fire has devoured it, and it is burned?

6 Therefore thus says the Lord GOD; as the vine tree among the trees of the forest, which I have given to the fire for fuel, so will I give the inhabitants of Jerusalem.

7 And I will set my face against them; they will go out from *one* fire, and *another* fire will devour them; and you will know that I *am* the LORD, when I set my face against them.

8 And I will make the land desolate, because they have committed a trespass, says the Lord GOD.

CHAPTER 16

1 Again the word of the LORD came unto me, saying,

2 Son of man, cause Jerusalem to know her abominations,

3 And say, thus says the Lord GOD unto Jerusalem; your birth and your nativity *is* of the land of Canaan; your father *was* an Amorite, and your mother an Hittite.

4 And *as for* your nativity, in the day you were born your navel was not cut, neither were you washed in water to supple you; you were not salted at all, or swaddled at all.

5 None eye pitied you, to do any of these unto you, to have compassion upon you; but you were cast out in the open field, to the loathing of your person, in the day that you were born.

6 And when I passed by you, and saw you polluted in your own blood, I said unto you *when you were* in your blood, Live; yea, I said unto you *when you were* in your blood, Live.

7 I have caused you to multiply as the bud of the field, and you have increased and waxen great, and you are come to excellent ornaments: your breasts are fashioned, and your hair is grown, whereas you were naked and bare.

8 Now when I passed by you, and looked upon you, behold, your time *was* the time of love; and I spread my skirt over you, and covered your nakedness: yea, I swore unto you, and entered into a covenant with you, says the Lord GOD, and you became mine.

9 Then washed I you with water; yea, I thoroughly washed away your blood[6] from you, and I anointed you with oil.

10 I clothed you also with broidered work, and shod you with badgers' skin, and I girded you about with fine linen, and I covered you with silk.

11 I decked you also with ornaments, and I put bracelets upon your hands, and a chain on your neck.

12 And I put a jewel on your forehead, and earrings in your ears, and a beautiful crown upon your head.

13 Thus were you decked with gold and silver; and your raiment *was of* fine linen, and silk, and broidered work; you did eat fine flour, and honey, and oil: and you were exceeding beautiful, and you did prosper into a kingdom.

14 And your renown went forth among the heathen for your beauty: for it *was* perfect through my comeliness, which I had put upon you, says the Lord GOD.

15 But you did trust in your own beauty, and played the harlot because of your renown, and poured out your fornications on every one that passed by; his it was.

16 And of your garments you did take, and deck your high places with divers[7] colors, and played the harlot thereupon: *the like things* will not come, neither will it be *so*.

17 you have also taken your fair jewels of my gold and of my silver, which I had given you, and made to yourself images of men, and did commit whoredom with them,

18 And took your broidered garments, and covered them: and you have set mine oil and mine incense before them.

19 My meat also which I gave you, fine flour, and oil, and honey, *wherewith* I fed you, you have even set it before them for a sweet savor: and *thus* it was, says the Lord GOD.

20 Moreover you have taken your sons and your daughters, whom you have borne unto me, and these have you sacrificed unto them to be devoured. *Is this* of your whoredoms a small matter,

21 That you have slain my children, and delivered them to cause them to pass through *the fire* for them?

22 And in all your abominations and your whoredoms you have not remembered the days of your youth, when you were naked and bare, *and* were polluted in your blood.

23 And it came to pass after all your wickedness, (woe, woe unto you! says the Lord GOD;)

24 *That* you have also built unto you an eminent place, and have made you an high place in every street.

25 You have built your high place at every head of the way, and have made your beauty to be abhorred, and have opened your feet to everyone that passed by, and multiplied your whoredoms.

26 You have also committed fornication with the Egyptians your neighbors, great of flesh; and have increased your whoredoms, to provoke me to anger.

27 Behold, therefore I have stretched out my hand over you, and have diminished your ordinary *food*, and delivered you unto the will of them that hate you, the daughters of the Philistines, which are ashamed of your lewd way.

28 you have played the whore also with the Assyrians, because you were insatiable; yes, you have played the harlot with them, and yet could not be satisfied.

29 you have moreover multiplied your fornication in the land of Canaan unto Chaldea; and yet you were not satisfied herewith.

30 How weak is your heart, says the Lord GOD, seeing you doest all these *things*, the work of an imperious whorish woman;

31 In that you built your eminent place in the head of every way, and make your high place in every street; and have not been as an harlot, in that you scorn hire;

---

[1] When it appears that you do not mourn over the judgement, it is because you know the ways of those who are/were judge.
[2] see note# 6 above
[3] meet- is the Hebrew *ṣālaḥ*, and it is defined as to be powerful, come forcefully; to rush: to prosper, prevail, succeed and avail. [Strgs#6743]
[4] meet- is defined differently than the meet given above. Here it is the Hebrew word *'āśā*, meaning to do, be made, to be done, to caress and sqeeze. [Strgs#6213]
[5] Ibid.
[6] plural *bloods* or drops of blood [Strgs#1818].
[7] literally spotted or patched colors. [Strgs#2921]

32 *But as* a wife that commits adultery, *which* takes strangers instead of her husband!
33 They give gifts to all whores: but you give your gifts to all your lovers, and hires them, that they may come unto you on every side for your whoredom.¹
34 And the contrary is in you from *other* women in your whoredoms, whereas none follows you to commit whoredoms: and in that you give a reward, and no reward is given unto you, therefore you are contrary.
35 Wherefore, O harlot, hear the word of the LORD:
36 Thus says the Lord GOD; because your filthiness was poured out, and your nakedness discovered through your whoredoms with your lovers, and with all the idols of your abominations, and by the blood of your children, which you did give unto them;
37 Behold, therefore I will gather all your lovers, with whom you have taken pleasure, and all *them* that you have loved, with all *them* that you have hated; I will even gather them round about against you, and will discover your nakedness unto them, that they may see all your nakedness.
38 [And I will judge you, as women that break wedlock and shed blood are judged; and I will give you blood in fury and jealousy.]²
39 And I will also give you into their hand, and they will throw down your eminent place, and will break down your high places: they will strip you also of your clothes, and will take your fair jewels, and leave you naked and bare.
40 They will also bring up a company against you, and they will stone you with stones, and thrust you through with their swords.
41 And they will burn your houses with fire, and execute judgments upon you in the sight of many women³: and I will cause you to cease from playing the harlot, and you also will give no hire any more.
42 So will I make my fury toward you to rest, and my jealousy will depart from you, and I will be quiet, and will be no more angry.
43 Because you have not remembered the days of your youth, but have fretted me in all these *things*; behold, therefore I also will recompense your way upon your head, says the Lord GOD: and you will not commit this lewdness above all your abominations.
44 [Behold, every one that uses proverbs will use *this* proverb against you, saying, as *is* the mother, *so is* her daughter.]⁴
45 you are your mother's daughter, that loathes her husband and her children; and you are the sister of your sisters, which loathes their husbands and their children: your mother *was* an Hittite, and your father an Amorite.
46 And your elder sister *is* Samaria, she and her daughters that dwell at your left hand: and your younger sister, that dwells at your right hand, *is* Sodom and her daughters.
47 Yet have you not walked after their ways, or done after their abominations: but, as *if that were* a very little *thing*, you were corrupted more than they in all your ways.
48 *As* I live, says the Lord GOD, Sodom your sister has not done, she or her daughters, as you have done, you and your daughters.
49 [Behold, this was the iniquity of your sister Sodom, pride, fullness of bread, and [abundance of idleness]⁵ was in her and in her daughters, neither did she strengthen the hand of the poor and needy.
50 And they were haughty, and committed abomination before me: therefore I took them away as I saw *good*.
51 Neither has Samaria committed half of your sins; but you have multiplied your abominations more than they, and have justified your sisters in all your abominations which you have done.]⁶
52 you also, which have judged your sisters, bear your own shame for your sins that you have committed more abominable than they: they are more righteous than you: yes, be you confounded also, and bear your shame, in that you have justified your sisters.
53 When I will bring again their captivity, the captivity of Sodom and her daughters, and the captivity of Samaria and her daughters, then *will I bring again* the captivity of your captives in the midst of them:
54 That you may bear your own shame, and may be confounded in all that you have done, in that you are a comfort unto them.
55 When your sisters, Sodom and her daughters, will return to their former estate, and Samaria and her daughters will return to their former estate, then you and your daughters will return to your former estate.
56 For your sister Sodom was not mentioned by your mouth in the day of your pride,
57 Before your wickedness was discovered, as at the time of your reproach of the daughters of Syria, and all *that are* round about her, the daughters of the Philistines, which despise you round about.
58 you have borne your lewdness and your abominations, says the LORD.
59 For thus says the Lord GOD; I will even deal with you as you have done, which have despised the oath in breaking the covenant.
60 Nevertheless I will remember my covenant with you in the days of your youth, and I will establish unto you an everlasting covenant.
61 Then you will remember your ways, and be ashamed, when you will receive your sisters, your elder and your younger: and I will give them unto you for daughters, but not by your covenant.
62 And I will establish my covenant with you; and you will know that I *am* the LORD:
63 That you may remember, and be confounded, and never open your mouth anymore because of your shame, when I am pacified toward you for all that you have done, says the Lord GOD.

CHAPTER 17

1 And the word of the LORD came unto me, saying,
2 Son of man, put forth a riddle, and speak a parable unto the house of Israel;
3 And say, thus says the Lord GOD; A great eagle with great wings, long-winged, full of feathers, which had divers colors, came unto Lebanon, and took the highest branch of the cedar:
4 He cropped off the top of his young twigs, and carried it into a land of traffic; he set it in a city of merchants.
5 He took also of the seed of the land, and planted it in a fruitful field; he placed *it* by great waters, *and* set it *as* a willow tree.
6 And it grew, and became a spreading vine of low stature, whose branches turned toward him, and the roots thereof were under him: so it became a vine, and brought forth branches, and shot forth sprigs.
7 There was also another great eagle with great wings and many feathers: and, behold, this vine did bend her roots toward him, and shot forth her branches toward him, that he might water it by the furrows of her plantation.

---

¹ In **Rev. 18** the Harlot makes the world rich.
² We shed blood when/if we break wedlock from Jesus.
³ compare **Rev. 14:4**
⁴ compare **Rev. 17:5**
⁵ lit. <u>successful repose</u> [Strgs# 7962 + 8252]
⁶ Matthew 10:12-18, 12:32-45; Mark 6:11, 13:9

8 It was planted in a good soil by great waters, that it might bring forth branches, and that it might bear fruit, that it might be a goodly vine.
9 Say you, Thus says the Lord GOD; will it prosper? will he not pull up the roots thereof, and cut off the fruit thereof, that it wither? it will wither in all the leaves of her spring, even without great power or many people to pluck it up by the roots thereof.
10 Yea, behold, *being* planted, will it prosper? Will it not utterly wither, when the east wind touches it? It will wither in the furrows where it grew.
11 Moreover the word of the LORD came unto me, saying,
12 Say now to the rebellious house, Know you not what these *things mean*? Tell *them*, Behold, the king of Babylon is come to Jerusalem, and has taken the king thereof, and the princes thereof, and led them with him to Babylon;
13 And has taken of the king's seed, and made a covenant with him, and has taken an oath of him: he has also taken the mighty of the land:
14 That the kingdom might be base, that it might not lift itself up, *but* that by keeping of his covenant it might stand.
15 But he rebelled against him in sending his ambassadors into Egypt, that they might give him horses and much people. Will he prosper? Will he escape that doeth such *things*? Or will he break the covenant, and be delivered?
16 *As* I live, says the Lord GOD, surely in the place *where* the king *dwells* that made him king, whose oath he despised, and whose covenant he brake, *even* with him in the midst of Babylon he will die.
17 Neither will Pharaoh with *his* mighty army and great company make for him in the war, by casting up mounts, and building forts, to cut off many persons:
18 Seeing he despised the oath by breaking the covenant, when, lo, he had given his hand, and has done all these *things*, he will not escape.
19 Therefore thus says the Lord GOD; *As* I live, surely mine oath that he has despised, and my covenant that he has broken, even it will I recompense upon his own head.
20 And I will spread my net upon him, and he will be taken in my snare, and I will bring him to Babylon, and will plead with him there for his trespass that he has trespassed against me.
21 And all his fugitives with all his bands will fall by the sword, and they that remain will be scattered toward all winds: and you will know that I the LORD have spoken *it*.
22 Thus says the Lord GOD; I will also take of the highest branch of the high cedar, and will set *it*; I will crop off from the top of his young twigs a tender one, and will plant *it* upon an high mountain and eminent:
23 In the mountain of the height of Israel will I plant it: and it will bring forth boughs, and bear fruit, and be a goodly cedar: and under it will dwell all fowl of every wing; in the shadow of the branches thereof will they dwell.
24 And all the trees of the field will know that I the LORD have brought down the high tree, have exalted the low tree, have dried up the green tree, and have made the dry tree to flourish: I the LORD have spoken and have done *it*.

CHAPTER 18

1 The word of the LORD came unto me again, saying,
2 What mean you, that you use this proverb concerning the land of Israel, saying, the fathers have eaten sour grapes, and the children's teeth are set on edge?
3 *As* I live, says the Lord GOD, you will not have *occasion* any more to use this proverb in Israel.
4 Behold, all souls are mine; as the soul of the father, so also the soul of the son is mine: the soul that sins, it will die.
5 But if a man be just, and do that which is lawful and right,
6 *And* has not eaten upon the mountains, neither has lifted up his eyes to the idols of the house of Israel, neither has defiled his neighbor's wife, neither has come near to a menstruous woman,
7 And has not oppressed any, *but* has restored to the debtor his pledge, has spoiled none by violence, has given his bread to the hungry, and has covered the naked with a garment;
8 He *that* has not given forth upon usury, neither has taken any increase, *that* has withdrawn his hand from iniquity, has executed true judgment between man and man,
9 has walked in my statutes, and has kept my judgments, to deal truly; he *is* just, he will surely live, says the Lord GOD.
10 If he beget a son *that is* a robber, a shedder of blood, and *that* doeth the like to *any* one of these *things*,
11 And that doeth not any of those *duties*, but even has eaten upon the mountains, and defiled his neighbor's wife,
12 has oppressed the poor and needy, has spoiled by violence, has not restored the pledge, and has lifted up his eyes to the idols, has committed abomination,
13 Have given forth upon usury, and has taken increase: will he then live? He will not live: he has done all these abominations; he will surely die; his blood will be upon him.
14 Now, lo, *if* he beget a son, that sees all his father's sins which he has done, and considers, and doeth not such like,
15 *That* has not eaten upon the mountains, neither has lifted up his eyes to the idols of the house of Israel, has not defiled his neighbor's wife,
16 Neither has oppressed any, has not **withheld** the pledge, neither has spoiled by violence, *but* has given his bread to the hungry, and has covered the naked with a garment,
17 *That* has taken off his hand from the poor, *that* has not received usury or increase, has executed my judgments, has walked in my statutes; he will not die for the iniquity of his father, he will surely live.
18 *As for* his father, because he cruelly oppressed, spoiled his brother by violence, and did *that* which *is* not good among his people, lo, even he will die in his iniquity.
19 Yet say you, why? Does not the son bear the iniquity of the father? When the son has done that which is lawful and right, *and* has kept all my statutes, and has done them, he will surely live.
20 The soul that sins, it will die. The son will not bear the iniquity of the father, neither will the father bear the iniquity of the son: the righteousness of the righteous will be upon him, and the wickedness of the wicked will be upon him.
21 But if the wicked will turn from all his sins that he has committed, and keep all my statutes, and do that which is lawful and right, he will surely live, he will not die.
22 All his transgressions that he has committed, they will not be mentioned unto him: in his righteousness that he has done he will live.
23 Have I any pleasure at all that the wicked should die? Says the Lord GOD: *and* not that he should return from his ways, and live?
24 But when the righteous turns away from his righteousness, and commits iniquity, *and* does according to all the abominations that the wicked *man* does, will he live? All his righteousness that he

has done will not be mentioned: in his trespass that he has trespassed, and in his sin that he has sinned, in them will he die.
25 Yet you say, the way of the Lord is not equal. Hear now, O house of Israel; is not my way equal? Are not your ways unequal?
26 When a righteous *man* turns away from his righteousness, and commits iniquity, and dies in them; for his iniquity that he has done will he die.
27 Again, when the wicked *man* turns away from his wickedness that he has committed, and doeth that which is lawful and right, he will save his soul alive.
28 Because he considers, and turns away from all his transgressions that he has committed, he will surely live, he will not die.
29 Yet says the house of Israel, The way of the Lord is not equal. O house of Israel, are not my ways equal? Are not your ways unequal?
30 Therefore I will judge you, O house of Israel, every one according to his ways, says the Lord GOD. Repent, and turn *yourselves* from all your transgressions; so iniquity will not be your ruin.
31 Cast away from you all your transgressions, whereby you have transgressed; and make you a new heart and a new spirit: for why will you die, O house of Israel?
32 For I have no pleasure in the death of him that dies, says the Lord GOD: wherefore turn *yourselves*, and live ye.

CHAPTER 19

1 Moreover take you up a lamentation for the princes of Israel,
2 And say, what *is* your mother? A lioness: she lay down among lions, she nourished her whelps among young lions.
3 And she brought up one of her whelps: it became a young lion, and it learned to catch the prey; it devoured men.
4 The nations also heard of him; he was taken in their pit, and they brought him with chains unto the land of Egypt.
5 Now when she saw that she had waited, *and* her hope was lost, then she took another of her whelps, *and* made him a young lion.
6 And he went up and down among the lions, he became a young lion, and learned to catch the prey, *and* devoured men.
7 And he knew their desolate palaces, and he laid waste their cities; and the land was desolate, and the fullness thereof, by the noise of his roaring.
8 Then the nations set against him on every side from the provinces, and spread their net over him: he was taken in their pit.
9 And they put him in ward in chains, and brought him to the king of Babylon: they brought him into holds, that his voice should no more be heard upon the mountains of Israel.
10 your mother *is* like a vine in your blood, planted by the waters: she was fruitful and full of branches by reason of many waters.
11 And she had strong rods for the scepters of them that bare rule, and her stature was exalted among the thick branches, and she appeared in her height with the multitude of her branches.
12 But she was plucked up in fury, she was cast down to the ground, and the east wind dried up her fruit: her strong rods were broken and withered; the fire consumed them.
13 And now she *is* planted in the wilderness, in a dry and thirsty ground.
14 And fire is gone out of a rod of her branches, *which* has devoured her fruit, so that she has no strong rod *to be* a scepter to rule. This *is* a lamentation, and will be for a lamentation.

CHAPTER 20

1 And it came to pass in the seventh year, in the fifth *month*, the tenth *day* of the month, *that* certain of the elders of Israel came to enquire of the LORD, and sat before me.
2 Then came the word of the LORD unto me, saying,
3 Son of man, speak unto the elders of Israel, and say unto them, thus says the Lord GOD; Are you come to enquire of me? As I live, says the Lord GOD, I will not be enquired of by you.
4 will you judge them, son of man, will you judge *them*? Cause them to know the abominations of their fathers:
5 And say unto them, Thus says the Lord GOD; In the day when I chose Israel, and lifted up mine hand unto the seed of the house of Jacob, and made myself known unto them in the land of Egypt, when I lifted up mine hand unto them, saying, I *am* the LORD your God;
6 In the day *that* I lifted up mine hand unto them, to bring them forth of the land of Egypt into a land that I had espied for them, flowing with milk and honey, which *is* the glory of all lands:
7 Then said I unto them, Cast you away every man the abominations of his eyes, and defile not yourselves with the idols of Egypt: I *am* the LORD your God.
8 But they rebelled against me, and would not hearken unto me: they did not every man cast away the abominations of their eyes, neither did they forsake the idols of Egypt: then I said, I will pour out my fury upon them, to accomplish my anger against them in the midst of the land of Egypt.
9 But I wrought for my name's sake, that it should not be polluted before the heathen, among whom they *were*, in whose sight I made myself known unto them, in bringing them forth out of the land of Egypt.
10 Wherefore I caused them to go forth out of the land of Egypt, and brought them into the wilderness.
11 And I gave them my statutes, and showed them my judgments, which *if* a man do, he will even live in them.
12 Moreover also I gave them my Sabbaths, to be a sign between me and them, that they might know that I *am* the LORD that sanctify them.
13 But the house of Israel rebelled against me in the wilderness: they walked not in my statutes, and they despised my judgments, which *if* a man do, he will even live in them; and my Sabbaths they greatly polluted: then I said, I would pour out my fury upon them in the wilderness, to consume them.
14 But I wrought for my name's sake, that it should not be polluted before the heathen, in whose sight I brought them out.
15 Yet also I lifted up my hand unto them in the wilderness, that I would not bring them into the land which I had given *them*, flowing with milk and honey, which *is* the glory of all lands;
16 Because they despised my judgments, and walked not in my statutes, but polluted my Sabbaths: for their heart went after their idols.
17 Nevertheless mine eye spared them from destroying them, neither did I make an end of them in the wilderness.
18 But I said unto their children in the wilderness, walk you not in the statutes of your fathers, neither observe their judgments, or defile yourselves with their idols:
19 I *am* the LORD your God; walk in my statutes, and keep my judgments, and do them;
20 And hallow my Sabbaths; and they will be a sign between me and you, that you may know that I *am* the LORD your God.

21 Notwithstanding the children rebelled against me: they walked not in my statutes, neither kept my judgments to do them, which *if* a man do, he will even live in them; they polluted my Sabbaths: then I said, I would pour out my fury upon them, to accomplish my anger against them in the wilderness.
22 Nevertheless I withdrew mine hand, and wrought for my name's sake, that it should not be polluted in the sight of the heathen, in whose sight I brought them forth.
23 I lifted up mine hand unto them also in the wilderness, that I would scatter them among the heathen, and disperse them through the countries;
24 Because they had not executed my judgments, but had despised my statutes, and had polluted my Sabbaths, and their eyes were after their fathers' idols.
25 Wherefore I gave them also statutes *that were* not good, and judgments whereby they should not live;
26 And I polluted them in their own gifts, in that they caused to pass through *the fire* all that opens the womb, that I might make them desolate, to the end that they might know that I *am* the LORD.
27 Therefore, son of man, speak unto the house of Israel, and say unto them, thus says the Lord GOD; yet in this your fathers have blasphemed me, in that they have committed a trespass against me.
28 *For* when I had brought them into the land, *for* the which I lifted up mine hand to give it to them, then they saw every high hill, and all the thick trees, and they offered there their sacrifices, and there they presented the provocation of their offering: there also they made their sweet savor, and poured out there their drink offerings.
29 Then I said unto them, what *is* the high place whereunto you go? And the name thereof is called Bamah unto this day.
30 Wherefore say unto the house of Israel, Thus says the Lord GOD; Are you polluted after the manner of your fathers? And commit you whoredom after their abominations?
31 For when you offer your gifts, when you make your sons to pass through the fire, you pollute yourselves with all your idols, even unto this day: and will I be enquired of by you, O house of Israel? *As* I live, says the Lord GOD, I will not be enquired of by you.
32 And that which cometh into your mind will not be at all, that you say, we will be as the heathen, as the families of the countries, to serve wood and stone.
33 *As* I live, says the Lord GOD, surely with a mighty hand, and with a stretched out arm, and with fury poured out, will I rule over you:
34 And I will bring you out from the people, and will gather you out of the countries wherein you are scattered, with a mighty hand, and with a stretched out arm, and with fury poured out.
35 And I will bring you into the wilderness of the people, and there will I plead with you face to face.
36 Like as I pleaded with your fathers in the wilderness of the land of Egypt, so will I plead with you, says the Lord GOD.
37 And I will cause you to pass under the rod, and I will bring you into the bond of the covenant:
38 And I will purge out from among you the rebels, and them that transgress against me: I will bring them forth out of the country where they sojourn, and they will not enter into the land of Israel: and you will know that I *am* the LORD.
39 As for you, O house of Israel, thus says the Lord GOD; Go you, serve you every one his idols, and hereafter *also*, if you will not hearken unto me: but pollute you my holy name no more with your gifts, and with your idols.
40 For in mine holy mountain, in the mountain of the height of Israel, says the Lord GOD, there will all the house of Israel, all of them in the land, serve me: there will I accept them, and there will I require your offerings, and the first-fruits of your oblations, with all your holy things.
41 I will accept you with your sweet savor, when I bring you out from the people, and gather you out of the countries wherein you have been scattered; and I will be sanctified in you before the heathen.
42 And you will know that I *am* the LORD, when I will bring you into the land of Israel, into the country *for* the which I lifted up mine hand to give it to your fathers.
43 And there will you remember your ways, and all your doings, wherein you have been defiled; and you will loathes yourselves in your own sight for all your evils that you have committed.
44 And you will know that I *am* the LORD, when I have wrought with you for my name's sake, not according to your wicked ways, or according to your corrupt doings, O you house of Israel, says the Lord GOD.
45 Moreover the word of the LORD came unto me, saying,
46 Son of man, set your face toward the south, and drop your *word* toward the south, and prophesy against the forest of the south field;
47 And say to the forest of the south, Hear the word of the LORD; Thus says the Lord GOD; Behold, I will kindle a fire in you, and it will devour every green tree in you, and every dry tree: the flaming flame will not be quenched, and all faces from the south to the north will be burned therein.
48 And all flesh will see that I the LORD have kindled it: it will not be quenched.
49 Then said I, Ah Lord GOD! They say of me, does he not speak parables?

CHAPTER 21

1 And the word of the LORD came unto me, saying,
2 Son of man, set your face toward Jerusalem, and drop your *word* toward the holy places, and prophesy against the land of Israel,
3 And say to the land of Israel, Thus says the LORD; Behold, I *am* against you, and will draw forth my sword out of his sheath, and will cut off from you the righteous and the wicked.
4 Seeing then that I will cut off from you the righteous and the wicked, therefore will my sword go forth out of his sheath against all flesh from the south to the north:
5 That all flesh may know that I the LORD have drawn forth my sword out of his sheath: it will not return any more.
6 Sigh therefore, you son of man, with the breaking of your loins; and with bitterness sigh before their eyes.
7 And it will be, when they say unto you, wherefore **groan** you? That you will answer, for the tidings; because it comes: and every heart will melt, and all hands will be feeble, and every spirit will faint, and all knees will be weak *as* water: behold, it cometh, and will be brought to pass, says the Lord GOD.
8 Again the word of the LORD came unto me, saying,
9 Son of man, prophesy, and say, thus says the LORD; Say, A sword, a sword is sharpened, and also furbished:

10 It is sharpened to make a sore slaughter; it is furbished that it may glitter: should we then make mirth? It contemns¹ the rod of my son, *as* every tree.
11 And he has given it to be furbished, that it may be handled: this sword is sharpened, and it is furbished, to give it into the hand of the slayer.
12 Cry and howl, son of man: for it will be upon my people, it will *be* upon all the princes of Israel: terrors by reason of the sword will be upon my people: smite therefore upon your thigh.
13 Because *it is* a trial, and what if *the sword* contemn even the rod? it will be no *more*, says the Lord GOD.
14 you therefore, son of man, prophesy, and smite your hands together, and let the sword be doubled the third time, the sword of the slain: it *is* the sword of the great *men that are* slain, which enters into their privy chambers.
15 I have set the point of the sword against all their gates, that *their* heart may faint, and *their* ruins be multiplied: ah! *it is* made bright, *it is* wrapped up for the slaughter.
16 Go you one way or other, *either* on the right hand, *or* on the left, whithersoever your face *is* set.
17 I will also smite mine hands together, and I will cause my fury to rest: I the LORD have said *it*.
18 The word of the LORD came unto me again, saying,
19 Also, you son of man, appoint you two ways, that the sword of the king of Babylon may come: both twain will come forth out of one land: and choose you a place, choose *it* at the head of the way to the city.
20 Appoint a way, that the sword may come to Rabbath² of the Ammonites, and to Judah in Jerusalem the defense³.
21 For the king of Babylon stood at the parting of the way, at the head of the two ways, to use divination: he made *his* arrows bright, he consulted with images, he looked in the liver.
22 At his right hand was the divination for Jerusalem, to appoint captains, to open the mouth in the slaughter, to lift up the voice with shouting, to appoint *battering* rams against the gates, to cast a mount, *and* to build a fort.
23 And it will be unto them as a false divination in their sight, to them that have sworn oaths: but he will call to remembrance the iniquity, that they may be taken.
24 Therefore thus says the Lord GOD; because you have made your iniquity to be remembered, in that your transgressions are discovered, so that in all your doings your sins do appear; because, *I say*, that you are come to remembrance, you will be taken with the hand.
25 And you, profane wicked prince of Israel, whose day is come, when iniquity will *have* an end,
26 Thus says the Lord GOD; Remove the diadem, and take off the crown: this will not *be* the same: exalt *him that is* low, and abase *him that is* high.
27 I will overturn, overturn, overturn, it: and it will be no *more*, until he come whose right it is; and I will give it *him*.
28 And you, son of man, prophesy and say, Thus says the Lord GOD concerning the Ammonites, and concerning their reproach; even say you, The sword, the sword *is* drawn: for the slaughter *it is* furbished, to consume because of the glittering:
29 Whiles they see vanity unto you, whiles they divine a lie unto you, to bring you upon the necks of *them that are* slain, of the wicked, whose day is come, when their iniquity will *have* an end.
30 will I cause *it* to return into his sheath? I will judge you in the place where you were created, in the land of your nativity.
31 And I will pour out mine indignation upon you, I will blow against you in the fire of my wrath, and deliver you into the hand of brutish men, *and* skilful to destroy.
32 you will be for fuel to the fire; your blood will be in the midst of the land; you will be no *more* remembered: for I the LORD have spoken *it*.

CHAPTER 22

1 Moreover the word of the LORD came unto me, saying,
2 Now, you son of man, will you judge, will you judge the bloody city? Yes, you will show her all her abominations.
3 Then say you, thus says the Lord GOD, The city sheds blood in the midst of it, that her time may come, and makes idols against herself to defile herself.
4 you are become guilty in your blood that you have shed; and have defiled yourself in your idols which you have made; and you have caused your days to draw near, and are come *even* unto your years: therefore have I made you a reproach unto the heathen, and a mocking to all countries.
5 *Those that be* near, and *those that be* far from you, will mock you, *which are* infamous *and* much vexed.
6 Behold, the princes of Israel, everyone were in you to their power to shed blood.
7 In you have they set light by father and mother: in the midst of you have they dealt by oppression with the stranger: in you have they vexed the fatherless and the widow.
8 you have despised mine holy things, and have profaned my Sabbaths.
9 In you are men that carry tales to shed blood: and in you they eat upon the mountains: in the midst of you they commit lewdness.
10 In you have they discovered their fathers' nakedness: in you have they humbled her that was set apart for pollution.
11 And one has committed abomination with his neighbor's wife; and another has lewdly defiled his daughter in law; and another in you has humbled his sister, his father's daughter.
12 In you have they taken gifts to shed blood; you have taken usury and increase, and you have greedily gained of your neighbors by extortion, and have forgotten me, says the Lord GOD.
13 Behold, therefore I have smitten mine hand at your dishonest gain which you have made, and at your blood which has been in the midst of you.
14 Can your heart endure, or can your hands be strong, in the days that I will deal with you? I the LORD have spoken *it*, and will do *it*.
15 And I will scatter you among the heathen, and disperse you in the countries, and will consume your filthiness out of you.
16 And you will take your inheritance in yourself in the sight of the heathen, and you will know that I *am* the LORD.
17 And the word of the LORD came unto me, saying,
18 Son of man, the house of Israel is to me become dross: all they *are* brass, and tin, and iron, and lead, in the midst of the furnace; they are *even* the dross of silver.

---

¹ contemns- to *spurn*; also (intransitively) to *disappear*: -abhor, cast away, despise, disdain, vile person, reprobate. [Strgs#3988]
² Rabbath- Hebrew word rabbâh, feminine of great; Rabbah, the name of two places in Palestine, East and West. One being the capital city of the Ammonites located east of the Jordan. [Strgs#7237]
³ defense- to *clip* off; specifically (as denominative from Strgs#1210) to *gather* grapes; also to *be isolated* (that is, *inaccessible* by height or fortification): -cut off, restrain, strong, wall up. [Strgs#1219]

19 Therefore thus says the Lord GOD; because you are all become dross, behold, therefore I will gather you into the midst of Jerusalem.
20 *As* they gather silver, and brass, and iron, and lead, and tin, into the midst of the furnace, to blow the fire upon it, to melt *it*; so will I gather *you* in mine anger and in my fury, and I will leave *you there*, and melt you.
21 Yea, I will gather you, and blow upon you in the fire of my wrath, and you will be melted in the midst thereof.
22 As silver is melted in the midst of the furnace, so will you be melted in the midst thereof; and you will know that I the LORD have poured out my fury upon you.
23 And the word of the LORD came unto me, saying,
24 Son of man, say unto her, you are the land that is not cleansed, or rained upon in the day of indignation.
25 *There is* a conspiracy of her prophets in the midst thereof, like a roaring lion ravening the prey; they have devoured souls; they have taken the treasure and precious things; they have made her many widows in the midst thereof.
26 Her priests have violated my law, and have profaned mine holy things: they have put no difference between the holy and profane, neither have they showed *difference* between the unclean and the clean, and have hid their eyes from my Sabbaths, and I am profaned among them.
27 Her princes in the midst thereof *are* like wolves ravening the prey, to shed blood, *and* to destroy souls, to get dishonest gain.
28 And her prophets have daubed them with untempered *morter*, seeing vanity, and divining lies unto them, saying, thus says the Lord GOD, when the LORD has not spoken.
29 The people of the land have used oppression, and exercised robbery, and have vexed the poor and needy: yea, they have oppressed the stranger wrongfully.
30 And I sought for a man among them, that should make up the hedge, and stand in the gap before me for the land, that I should not destroy it: but I found none.
31 Therefore have I poured out mine indignation upon them; I have consumed them with the fire of my wrath: their own way have I recompensed upon their heads, says the Lord GOD.

CHAPTER 23

1 The word of the LORD came again unto me, saying,
2 Son of man, there were two women, the daughters of one mother:
3 And they committed whoredoms in Egypt; they committed whoredoms in their youth: there were their breasts pressed, and there they bruised the teats of their virginity.
4 And the names of them *were* Aholah[1] the elder, and Aholibah[2] her sister: and they were mine, and they bare sons and daughters. Thus *were* their names; Samaria *is* Aholah, and Jerusalem Aholibah.
5 And Aholah played the harlot when she was mine; and she doted[3] on her lovers, on the Assyrians *her* neighbors,
6 *Which were* clothed with blue, captains and rulers, all of them desirable young men, horsemen riding upon horses.
7 Thus she committed her whoredoms with them, with all them *that were* the chosen men of Assyria, and with all on whom she doted: with all their idols she defiled herself.
8 Neither left she her whoredoms *brought* from Egypt: for in her youth they lay with her, and they bruised the breasts of her virginity, and poured their whoredom upon her.
9 Wherefore I have delivered her into the hand of her lovers, into the hand of the Assyrians, upon whom she doted.
10 These discovered her nakedness: they took her sons and her daughters, and slew her with the sword: and she became famous among women; for they had executed judgment upon her.
11 And when her sister Aholibah saw *this*, she was more corrupt in her inordinate love[4] than she, and in her whoredoms more than her sister in *her* whoredoms.
12 She doted upon the Assyrians *her* neighbors, captains and rulers clothed most gorgeously, horsemen riding upon horses, all of them desirable young men.
13 Then I saw that she was defiled, *that* they *took* both one way,
14 And *that* she increased her whoredoms: for when she saw men portrayed upon the wall, the images of the Chaldeans portrayed with vermilion,
15 Girded with girdles upon their loins, exceeding in dyed attire upon their heads, all of them princes to look to, after the manner of the Babylonians of Chaldea, the land of their nativity:
16 And as soon as she saw them with her eyes, she doted[5] upon them, and sent messengers unto them into Chaldea.
17 And the Babylonians came to her into the bed of love, and they defiled her with their whoredom, and she was polluted with them, and her mind was [alienated from them][6].
18 So she discovered her whoredoms, and discovered her nakedness: then my mind was alienated from her, like as my mind was alienated from her sister.
19 Yet she multiplied her whoredoms, in calling to remembrance the days of her youth, wherein she had played the harlot in the land of Egypt.
20 For she doted upon their paramours, whose flesh *is as* the flesh of asses, and whose issue *is like* the issue of horses.
21 Thus you called to remembrance the mischief[7] of your youth, in bruising your teats[8] by the Egyptians for the paps[9] of your youth.
22 Therefore, O Aholibah, thus says the Lord GOD; Behold, I will raise up your lovers against you, from whom your mind is alienated, and I will bring them against you on every side;
23 The Babylonians, and all the Chaldeans, Pekod, and Shoa, and Koa, *and* all the Assyrians with them: all of them desirable young men, captains and rulers, great lords and renowned, all of them riding upon horses.
24 And they will come against you with chariots, wagons, and wheels, and with an assembly of people, *which* will set against you

---

[1] Aholah- is the Hebrew word *'ohôlâh*, <u>o-hol-aw'</u>; meaning her own tent or *her tent* (that is idolatrous sanctuary). [Strgs#170]
[2] Aholibah- is the Hebrew word *'ohŏlîybâh*, <u>o"-holee-baw'</u>; meaning woman of the tent, the tent is in her or my tent is in her. [Strgs#172]
[3] doted- is the Hebrew word *'âgab*, <u>aw-gab'</u>; meaning to *breathe* after, that is, to love (sensually): -lover. [Strgs#5691]
[4] inordinate love- *love* (abstractly), that is *amorousness*. [Strgs#5691] It comes from the same root word as doted, meaning to *breathe* after (sensually). [Strgs#5689]
[5] doted – <u>breathe</u> after, to <u>love</u> [Strgs#5689]

[6] sexual sins will always cause you to hate the one who defiled you, compare v22
[7] KJV originally used the word lewdness- meaning a *plan*, especially a bad one: -heinous crime, purpose, mischief, thought, wicked (device, mind). [Strgs#2154]
[8] lit. <u>breast</u> [Strgs#1730], its root word means to <u>boil</u>, a *love token, lover, friend* [Strgs#1730].
[9] lit. <u>breast</u> (as in <u>bulging</u>) [Strgs#7699]

buckler and shield and helmet round about: and I will set judgment before them, and they will judge you according to their judgments.

25 And I will set my jealousy against you, and they will deal furiously with you: they will take away your nose and your ears; and your remnant will fall by the sword: they will take your sons and your daughters; and your residue will be devoured by the fire.

26 They will also strip you out of your clothes, and take away your fair jewels.

27 Thus will I make your lewdness to cease from you, and your whoredom *brought* from the land of Egypt: so that you will not lift up your eyes unto them, or remember Egypt any more.

28 For thus says the Lord GOD; Behold, I will deliver you into the hand *of them* whom you hate, into the hand *of them* from whom your mind is alienated:

29 And they will deal with you hatefully, and will take away all your labor, and will leave you naked and bare: and the nakedness of your whoredoms will be discovered, both your lewdness and your whoredoms.

30 I will do these *things* unto you, because you have gone a whoring after the heathen, *and* because you are polluted with their idols.

31 you have walked in the way of your sister; therefore will I give her cup into your hand.

32 Thus says the Lord GOD; you will drink of your sister's cup deep and large: you will be laughed to scorn and had in derision; it contains much.

33 you will be filled with drunkenness and sorrow, with the cup of astonishment and desolation, with the cup of your sister Samaria.

34 you will even drink it and suck *it* out, and you will break the sherds[1] thereof, and pluck off your own breasts: for I have spoken *it*, says the Lord GOD.

35 Therefore thus says the Lord GOD; because you have forgotten me, and cast me behind your back, therefore bear you also your lewdness and your whoredoms.

36 The LORD said moreover unto me; Son of man, will you judge Aholah and Aholibah? Yea, declare unto them their abominations;

37 That they have committed adultery, and blood *is* in their hands, and with their idols have they committed adultery, and have also caused their sons, whom they bare unto me, to pass for them through *the fire*, to devour *them*.

38 Moreover this they have done unto me: they have defiled my sanctuary in the same day, and have profaned my Sabbaths.

39 For when they had slain their children to their idols, then they came the same day into my sanctuary to profane it; and, lo, thus have they done in the midst of mine house.

40 And furthermore, that you have sent for men to come from far, unto whom a messenger *was* sent; and, lo, they came: for whom you did wash yourself, painted your eyes, and decked yourself with ornaments,

41 And sat upon a stately bed, and a table prepared before it, whereupon you have set mine incense and mine oil.

42 And a voice of a multitude being at ease *was* with her: and with the men of the common sort *were* brought Sabeans from the wilderness, which put bracelets upon their hands, and beautiful crowns upon their heads.

43 Then said I unto *her that was* old in adulteries, Will they now commit whoredoms with her, and she *with them*?

Ezekiel

44 Yet they went in unto her, as they go in unto a woman that plays the harlot: so went they in unto Aholah and unto Aholibah, the lewd women.

45 And the righteous men, they will judge them after the manner of adulteresses, and after the manner of women that shed blood; because they *are* adulteresses, and blood *is* in their hands.

46 For thus says the Lord GOD; I will bring up a company upon them, and will give them to be removed and spoiled.

47 And the company will stone them with stones, and dispatch them with their swords; they will slay their sons and their daughters, and burn up their houses with fire.

48 Thus will I cause lewdness to cease out of the land, that all women may be taught not to do after your lewdness.

49 And they will recompense your lewdness upon you, and you will bear the sins of your idols: and you will know that I *am* the Lord GOD.

CHAPTER 24

1 Again in the ninth year, in the tenth month, in the tenth *day* of the month, the word of the LORD came unto me, saying,

2 Son of man, write you the name of the day, *even* of this same day: the king of Babylon set himself against Jerusalem this same day.

3 And utter a parable unto the rebellious house, and say unto them, Thus says the Lord GOD; Set on a pot, set *it* on, and also pour water into it:

4 Gather the pieces thereof into it, *even* every good piece, the thigh, and the shoulder; fill *it* with the choice bones.

5 Take the choice of the flock, and burn also the bones under it, *and* make it boil well, and let them **boil up** the bones of it therein.

6 Wherefore thus says the Lord GOD; Woe to the bloody city, to the pot whose scum *is* therein, and whose scum is not gone out of it! Bring it out piece by piece; let no lot fall upon it.

7 For her blood is in the midst of her; she set it upon the top of a rock; she poured it not upon the ground, to cover it with dust;

8 That it might cause fury to come up to take vengeance; I have set her blood upon the top of a rock, that it should not be covered.

9 Therefore thus says the Lord GOD; Woe to the bloody city! I will even make the pile for fire great.

10 Heap on wood, kindle the fire, consume the flesh, and spice it well, and let the bones be burned.

11 Then set it empty upon the coals thereof, that the brass of it may be hot, and may burn, and *that* the filthiness of it may be molten in it, *that* the scum of it may be consumed.

12 She has wearied *herself* with lies, and her great scum went not forth out of her: her scum will *be* in the fire.

13 In your filthiness *is* lewdness: because I have purged you, and you were not purged, you will not be purged from your filthiness any more, till I have caused my fury to rest upon you.

14 I the LORD have spoken *it*: it will come to pass, and I will do *it*; I will not go back, neither will I spare, neither will I repent; according to your ways, and according to your doings, will they judge you, says the Lord GOD.

15 Also the word of the LORD came unto me, saying,

16 Son of man, behold, I take away from you the desire of your eyes with a stroke: yet neither will you mourn or weep, neither will your tears run down.

---

[1] lit. *a piece of pottery* [Strgs#2789]

17 Forbear to cry, make no mourning for the dead, bind the tire of your head upon you, and put on your shoes upon your feet, and cover not your lips, and eat not the bread of men.

18 So I spoke unto the people in the morning: and at even my wife died; and I did in the morning as I was commanded.

19 And the people said unto me, will you not tell us what these things *are* to us, that you doest *so*?

20 Then I answered them, the word of the LORD came unto me, saying,

21 Speak unto the house of Israel, Thus says the Lord GOD; Behold, I will profane my sanctuary, the excellency of your strength, the desire of your eyes, and that which your soul pities; and your sons and your daughters whom you have left will fall by the sword.

22 And you will do as I have done: you will not cover *your* lips, or eat the bread of men.

23 And your tires will *be* upon your heads, and your shoes upon your feet: you will not mourn or weep; but you will pine away for your iniquities, and mourn one toward another.

24 Thus Ezekiel is unto you a sign: according to all that he has done will you do: and when this comes, you will know that I *am* the Lord GOD.

25 Also, you son of man, will *it* not *be* in the day when I take from them their strength, the joy of their glory, the desire of their eyes, and that whereupon they set their minds, their sons and their daughters,

26 *That* he that escapes in that day will come unto you, to cause you to hear *it* with your ears?

27 In that day will your mouth be opened to him which is escaped, and you will speak, and be no more dumb: and you will be a sign unto them; and they will know that I *am* the LORD.

CHAPTER 25

1 The word of the LORD came again unto me, saying,

2 Son of man, set your face against the Ammonites, and prophesy against them;

3 And say unto the Ammonites, Hear the word of the Lord GOD; Thus says the Lord GOD; Because you said, Aha, against my sanctuary, when it was profaned; and against the land of Israel, when it was desolate; and against the house of Judah, when they went into captivity;

4 Behold, therefore I will deliver you to the men of the east for a possession, and they will set their palaces in you, and make their dwellings in you: they will eat your fruit, and they will drink your milk.

5 And I will make Rabbah a stable for camels, and the Ammonites a couching place for flocks: and you will know that I *am* the LORD.

6 For thus says the Lord GOD; because you have clapped your hands, and stamped with the feet, and rejoiced in heart with all your despite against the land of Israel;

7 Behold, therefore I will stretch out mine hand upon you, and will deliver you for a spoil to the heathen; and I will cut you off from the people, and I will cause you to perish out of the countries: I will destroy you; and you will know that I *am* the LORD.

8 Thus says the Lord GOD; because that Moab and Seir do say, Behold, the house of Judah *is* like unto all the heathen;

9 Therefore, behold, I will open the side of Moab from the cities, from his cities which are on his frontiers, the glory of the country, Beth-jeshimoth, Baal-meon, and Kiriathaim,

10 Unto the men of the east with the Ammonites, and will give them in possession, that the Ammonites may not be remembered among the nations.

11 And I will execute judgments upon Moab; and they will know that I *am* the LORD.

12 Thus says the Lord GOD; because that Edom has dealt against the house of Judah by taking vengeance, and has greatly offended, and revenged himself upon them;

13 Therefore thus says the Lord GOD; I will also stretch out mine hand upon Edom, and will cut off man and beast from it; and I will make it desolate from Teman; and they of Dedan will fall by the sword.

14 And I will lay my vengeance upon Edom by the hand of my people Israel: and they will do in Edom according to mine anger and according to my fury; and they will know my vengeance, says the Lord GOD.

15 Thus says the Lord GOD; because the Philistines have dealt by revenge, and have taken vengeance with a despiteful heart, to destroy *it* for the old hatred;

16 Therefore thus says the Lord GOD; Behold, I will stretch out mine hand upon the Philistines, and I will cut off the Cherethims, and destroy the remnant of the sea coast.

17 And I will execute great vengeance upon them with furious rebukes; and they will know that I *am* the LORD, when I will lay my vengeance upon them.

CHAPTER 26

1 And it came to pass in the eleventh year, in the first *day* of the month, *that* the word of the LORD came unto me, saying,

2 Son of man, because that Tyrus has said against Jerusalem, Aha, she is broken *that was* the gates of the people: she is turned unto me: I will be replenished, *now* she is laid waste:

3 Therefore thus says the Lord GOD; Behold, I *am* against you, O Tyrus, and will cause many nations to come up against you, as the sea causes his waves to come up.

4 And they will destroy the walls of Tyrus, and break down her towers: I will also scrape her dust from her, and make her like the top of a rock.

5 It will be *a place for* the spreading of nets in the midst of the sea: for I have spoken *it*, says the Lord GOD: and it will become a spoil to the nations.

6 And her daughters which *are* in the field will be slain by the sword; and they will know that I *am* the LORD.

7 For thus says the Lord GOD; Behold, I will bring upon Tyrus Nebuchadrezzar king of Babylon, a king of kings, from the north, with horses, and with chariots, and with horsemen, and companies, and much people.

8 He will slay with the sword your daughters in the field: and he will make a fort against you, and cast a mount against you, and lift up the buckler against you.

9 And he will set engines of war against your walls, and with his axes he will break down your towers.

10 By reason of the abundance of his horses their dust will cover you: your walls will shake at the noise of the horsemen, and of the wheels, and of the chariots, when he will enter into your gates, as men enter into a city wherein is made a breach.

11 With the hoofs of his horses will he tread down all your streets: he will slay your people by the sword, and your strong garrisons will go down to the ground.

12 And they will make a spoil of your riches, and make a prey of your merchandise: and they will break down your walls, and

destroy your pleasant houses: and they will lay your stones and your timber and your dust in the midst of the water.
13 And I will cause the noise of your songs to cease; and the sound of your harps will be no more heard.
14 And I will make you like the top of a rock: you will be *a place* to spread nets upon; you will be built no more: for I the LORD have spoken *it*, says the Lord GOD.
15 Thus says the Lord GOD to Tyrus; will not the isles shake at the sound of your fall, when the wounded cry, when the slaughter is made in the midst of you?
16 Then all the princes of the sea will come down from their thrones, and lay away their robes, and put off their broidered garments: they will clothe themselves with trembling; they will sit upon the ground, and will tremble at *every* moment, and be astonished at you.
17 And they will take up a lamentation for you, and say to you, how are you destroyed, *that were* inhabited of seafaring men, the renowned city, which were strong in the sea, she and her inhabitants, which cause their terror *to be* on all that haunt it!
18 Now will the isles tremble in the day of your fall; yea, the isles that *are* in the sea will be troubled at your departure.
19 For thus says the Lord GOD; When I will make you a desolate city, like the cities that are not inhabited; when I will bring up the deep upon you, and great waters will cover you;
20 When I will bring you down with them that descend into the pit, with the people of old time, and will set you in the low parts of the earth, in places desolate of old, with them that go down to the pit, that you be not inhabited; and I will set glory in the land of the living;
21 I will make you a terror, and you will *be* no *more*: though you be sought for, yet will you never be found again, says the Lord GOD.

CHAPTER 27

1 The word of the LORD came again unto me, saying,
2 Now, you son of man, take up a lamentation for Tyrus;
3 And say unto Tyrus, O you that are situate at the entry of the sea, which *are* a merchant of the people for many isles, thus says the Lord GOD; O Tyrus, you have said, I *am* of perfect beauty.
4 your borders *are* in the midst of the seas, your builders have perfected your beauty.
5 They have made all your *ship* boards of fir trees of Senir: they have taken cedars from Lebanon to make masts for you.
6 *Of* the oaks of Bashan have they made your oars; the company of the Ashurites have made your benches *of* ivory, *brought* out of the isles of Chittim.
7 Fine linen with broidered work from Egypt was that which you spreads forth to be your sail; blue and purple from the isles of Elishah was that which covered you.
8 The inhabitants of Zidon and Arvad were your mariners: your wise *men*, O Tyrus, *that* were in you, were your pilots.
9 The ancients of Gebal and the wise *men* thereof were in you your calkers[1]: all the ships of the sea with their mariners were in you to occupy your merchandise.
10 They of Persia and of Lud and of Phut were in your army, your men of war: they hanged the shield and helmet in you; they set forth your comeliness.
11 The men of Arvad with your army *were* upon your walls round about, and the Gammadims were in your towers: they **hung** their shields upon your walls round about; they have made your beauty perfect.

12 Tarshish *was* your merchant by reason of the multitude of all *kind of* riches; with silver, iron, tin, and lead, they traded in your fairs.
13 Javan, Tubal, and Meshech, they *were* your merchants: they traded the persons of men and vessels of brass in your market.
14 They of the house of Togarmah traded in your fairs with horses and horsemen and mules.
15 The men of Dedan *were* your merchants; many isles *were* the merchandise of your hand: they brought you *for* a present horns of ivory and ebony.
16 Syria *was* your merchant by reason of the multitude of the wares of your making: they occupied in your fairs with emeralds, purple, and broidered work, and fine linen, and coral, and agate.
17 Judah, and the land of Israel, they *were* your merchants: they traded in your market wheat of Minnith, and Pannag, and honey, and oil, and balm.
18 Damascus *was* your merchant in the multitude of the wares of your making, for the multitude of all riches; in the wine of Helbon, and white wool.
19 Dan also and Javan going to and fro occupied in your fairs: bright iron, cassia, and calamus, were in your market.
20 Dedan *was* your merchant in precious clothes for chariots
21 Arabia, and all the princes of Kedar, they occupied with you in lambs, and rams, and goats: in these *were they* your merchants.
22 The merchants of Sheba and Raamah, they *were* your merchants: they occupied in your fairs with chief of all spices and with all precious stones, and gold.
23 Haran, and Canneh, and Eden, the merchants of Sheba, Asshur, *and* Chilmad, *were* your merchants.
24 These *were* your merchants in all sorts *of things*, in blue clothes, and broidered work, and in chests of rich apparel, bound with cords, and made of cedar, among your merchandise.
25 The ships of Tarshish did sing of you in your market: and you were replenished, and made very glorious in the midst of the seas.
26 Your rowers have brought you into great waters: the east wind has broken you in the midst of the seas.
27 Your riches, and your fairs, your merchandise, your mariners, and your pilots, your calkers, and the occupiers of your merchandise, and all your men of war, that *are* in you, and in all your company which *is* in the midst of you, will fall into the midst of the seas in the day of your ruin.
28 The suburbs will shake at the sound of the cry of your pilots.
29 And all that handle the oar, the mariners, *and* all the pilots of the sea, will come down from their ships, they will stand upon the land;
30 And will cause their voice to be heard against you, and will cry bitterly, and will cast up dust upon their heads, they will wallow themselves in the ashes:
31 And they will make themselves utterly bald for you, and gird them with sackcloth, and they will weep for you with bitterness of heart *and* bitter wailing.
32 And in their wailing they will take up a lamentation for you and lament over you, *saying*, What *city is* like Tyrus, like the destroyed in the midst of the sea?
33 When your wares went forth out of the seas, you filled many people; you did enrich the kings of the earth with the multitude of your riches and of your merchandise.

---

[1] calkers – a *gap*, *leak* or breach. [Strg#919]

34 In the time *when* you will be broken by the seas in the depths of the waters your merchandise and all your company in the midst of you will fall.
35 All the inhabitants of the isles will be astonished at you, and their kings will be sore afraid, they will be troubled in *their* countenance.
36 The merchants among the people will hiss at you; you will be a terror, and never will *be* any more.

CHAPTER 28

1 The word of the LORD came again unto me, saying,
2 Son of man, say unto the prince of Tyrus, Thus says the Lord GOD; Because your heart *is* lifted up, and you have said, I *am* a God, I sit *in* the seat of God, in the midst of the seas; yet you are a man, and not God, though you set your heart as the heart of God:
3 Behold, you are wiser than Daniel; there is no secret that they can hide from you:
4 With your wisdom and with your understanding you have gotten you riches, and have gotten gold and silver into your treasures:
5 By your great wisdom *and* by your traffic[1] have you increased your riches, and your heart is lifted up because of your riches:
6 Therefore thus says the Lord GOD; because you have set your heart as the heart of God;
7 Behold, therefore I will bring strangers upon you, the terrible of the nations: and they will draw their swords against the beauty of your wisdom, and they will defile your brightness.
8 They will bring you down to the pit, and you will die the deaths of them that are slain in the midst of the seas.
9 will you yet say before him that slays you, I *am* God? But you will *be* a man, and no God, in the hand of him that slays you.
10 [You will die the deaths[2] of the uncircumcised by the hand of strangers: for I have spoken *it*, says the Lord GOD.][3]
11 Moreover the word of the LORD came unto me, saying,
12 Son of man, take up a lamentation upon the king of Tyrus[4], and say unto him, thus says the Lord GOD; you seal up the sum, full of wisdom, and perfect in beauty.
13 You have been in Eden the garden of God; every precious stone *was* your covering, the sardius, topaz, and the diamond, the beryl, the onyx, and the jasper, the sapphire, the emerald, and the carbuncle, and gold: the workmanship of your tambourine and of your pipes was prepared in you in the day that you were created.
14 You are the anointed cherub that covers; and I have set you *so*: you were upon the holy mountain of God; you have walked up and down in the midst of the stones of fire.
15 You were perfect in your ways from the day that you were created, till iniquity was found in you.
16 By the multitude of your merchandise they have filled the midst of you with violence, and you have sinned: therefore I will cast you as profane out of the mountain of God: and I will destroy you, O covering cherub, from the midst of the stones of fire.
17 Your heart was lifted up because of your beauty, you have corrupted your wisdom by reason of your brightness: I will cast you to the ground, I will lay you before kings, that they may behold you.
18 You have defiled your sanctuaries by the multitude of your iniquities, by the iniquity of your traffic; therefore will I bring forth a fire from the midst of you, it will devour you, and I will bring you to ashes upon the earth in the sight of all them that behold you.
19 All they that know you among the people will be astonished at you: you will be a terror, and never will you *be* any more.
20 Again the word of the LORD came unto me, saying,
21 Son of man, set your face against Zidon, and prophesy against it,
22 And say, thus says the Lord GOD; Behold, I *am* against you, O Zidon; and I will be glorified in the midst of you: and they will know that I *am* the LORD, when I will have executed judgments in her, and will be sanctified in her.
23 For I will send into her pestilence, and blood into her streets; and the wounded will be judged in the midst of her by the sword upon her on every side; and they will know that I *am* the LORD.
24 And there will be no more a pricking brier unto the house of Israel, or *any* grieving thorn of all *that are* round about them, that despised them; and they will know that I *am* the Lord GOD.
25 Thus says the Lord GOD; when I will have gathered the house of Israel from the people among whom they are scattered, and will be sanctified in them in the sight of the heathen, then will they dwell in their land that I have given to my servant Jacob.
26 And they will dwell safely therein, and will build houses, and plant vineyards; yea, they will dwell with confidence, when I have executed judgments upon all those that despise them round about them; and they will know that I *am* the LORD their God.

CHAPTER 29

1 In the tenth year, in the tenth *month*, in the twelfth *day* of the month, the word of the LORD came unto me, saying,
2 Son of man, set your face against Pharaoh king of Egypt, and prophesy against him, and against all Egypt:
3 Speak, and say, Thus says the Lord GOD; Behold, I *am* against you, Pharaoh king of Egypt, the great dragon that lies in the midst of his rivers, which has said, My river *is* mine own, and I have made *it* for myself.
4 But I will put hooks in your jaws, and I will cause the fish of your rivers to stick unto your scales, and I will bring you up out of the midst of your rivers, and all the fish of your rivers will stick unto your scales.
5 And I will leave you *thrown* into the wilderness, you and all the fish of your rivers: you will fall upon the open fields you will not be brought together, or gathered: I have given you for meat to the beasts of the field and to the fowls of the heaven.
6 And all the inhabitants of Egypt will know that I *am* the LORD, because they have been a staff of reed to the house of Israel.
7 When they took hold of you by your hand, you did break, and rend all their shoulder: and when they leaned upon you, you **broke**, and made all their loins to be at a stand.
8 Therefore thus says the Lord GOD; Behold, I will bring a sword upon you, and cut off man and beast out of you.
9 And the land of Egypt will be desolate and waste; and they will know that I *am* the LORD: because he has said, The river *is* mine, and I have made *it*.
10 Behold, therefore I *am* against you, and against your rivers, and I will make the land of Egypt utterly waste *and* desolate, from the tower of Syene even unto the border of Ethiopia.
11 No foot of man will pass through it, or foot of beast will pass through it, neither will it be inhabited forty years.

---

[1] traffic- meaning trade (as peddled):- merchandise. [Strgs#7404]. Feminine passive participle of Strgs#7402.
[2] 1st and 2nd death
[3] Note: this prince is already cursed with the second death. Those who say they are 'Gods' are destined for the 2nd death.
[4] Tyrus – *rock, stone, knife, sharp stone* [Strgs#6865 + 6864], compare **Exodus 4:25** (flint), **Ez. 3:9**.

12 And I will make the land of Egypt desolate in the midst of the countries *that are* desolate, and her cities among the cities *that are* laid waste will be desolate forty years: and I will scatter the Egyptians among the nations, and will disperse them through the countries.
13 Yet thus says the Lord GOD; At the end of forty years will I gather the Egyptians from the people where they were scattered:
14 And I will bring again the captivity of Egypt, and will cause them to return *into* the land of Pathros, into the land of their habitation; and they will be there a base kingdom.
15 It will be the basest of the kingdoms; neither will it exalt itself any more above the nations: for I will diminish them, that they will no more rule over the nations.
16 And it will be no more the confidence of the house of Israel, which brings *their* iniquity to remembrance, when they will look after them: but they will know that I *am* the Lord GOD.
17 And it came to pass in the seven and twentieth year, in the first *month*, in the first *day* of the month, the word of the LORD came unto me, saying,
18 Son of man, Nebuchadrezzar king of Babylon[1] caused his army to serve a great service against Tyrus: every head *was* made bald, and every shoulder *was* peeled: yet had he no wages, or his army, for Tyrus, for the service that he had served against it:
19 Therefore thus says the Lord GOD; Behold, I will give the land of Egypt unto Nebuchadrezzar king of Babylon; and he will take her multitude, and take her spoil, and take her prey; and it will be the wages for his army.
20 I have given him the land of Egypt *for* his labor wherewith he served against it, because they wrought for me, says the Lord GOD.
21 In that day will I cause the horn of the house of Israel to bud forth, and I will give you the opening of the mouth in the midst of them; and they will know that I *am* the LORD.

CHAPTER 30

1 The word of the LORD came again unto me, saying,
2 Son of man, prophesy and say, thus says the Lord GOD; Howl you, Woe worth the day!
3 For the day *is* near, even the day of the LORD *is* near, a cloudy day; it will be the time of the heathen.
4 And the sword will come upon Egypt, and great pain will be in Ethiopia, when the slain will fall in Egypt, and they will take away her multitude, and her foundations will be broken down.
5 Ethiopia, and Libya, and Lydia, and all the mingled people, and Chub, and the men of the land that is in league, will fall with them by the sword.
6 Thus says the LORD; they also that uphold Egypt will fall; and the pride of her power will come down: from the tower of Syene will they fall in it by the sword, says the Lord GOD.
7 And they will be desolate in the midst of the countries *that are* desolate, and her cities will be in the midst of the cities *that are* wasted.
8 And they will know that I *am* the LORD, when I have set a fire in Egypt, and *when* all her helpers will be destroyed.
9 In that day will messengers go forth from me in ships to make the careless Ethiopians afraid, and great pain will come upon them, as in the day of Egypt: for, lo, it cometh.
10 Thus says the Lord GOD; I will also make the multitude of Egypt to cease by the hand of Nebuchadrezzar king of Babylon.

11 He and his people with him, the terrible of the nations, will be brought to destroy the land: and they will draw their swords against Egypt, and fill the land with the slain.
12 And I will make the rivers dry, and sell the land into the hand of the wicked: and I will make the land waste, and all that is therein, by the hand of strangers: I the LORD have spoken *it*.
13 Thus says the Lord GOD; I will also destroy the idols, and I will cause *their* images to cease out of Noph; and there will be no more a prince of the land of Egypt: and I will put a fear in the land of Egypt.
14 And I will make Pathros desolate, and will set fire in Zoan, and will execute judgments in No.
15 And I will pour my fury upon Sin, the strength of Egypt; and I will cut off the multitude of No.
16 And I will set fire in Egypt: Sin will have great pain, and No will be rent asunder, and Noph will *have* distresses daily.
17 The young men of Aven and of Pi-beseth will fall by the sword: and these *cities* will go into captivity.
18 At Tehaphnehes also the day will be darkened, when I will break there the yokes of Egypt: and the pomp of her strength will cease in her: as for her, a cloud will cover her, and her daughters will go into captivity.
19 Thus will I execute judgments in Egypt: and they will know that I *am* the LORD.
20 And it came to pass in the eleventh year, in the first *month*, in the seventh *day* of the month, *that* the word of the LORD came unto me, saying,
21 Son of man, I have broken the arm of Pharaoh king of Egypt; and, lo, it will not be bound up to be healed, to put a roller to bind it, to make it strong to hold the sword.
22 Therefore thus says the Lord GOD; Behold, I *am* against Pharaoh king of Egypt, and will break his arms, the strong, and that which was broken; and I will cause the sword to fall out of his hand.
23 And I will scatter the Egyptians among the nations, and will disperse them through the countries.
24 And I will strengthen the arms of the king of Babylon, and put my sword in his hand: but I will break Pharaoh's arms, and he will groan before him with the groanings of a deadly wounded *man*.
25 But I will strengthen the arms of the king of Babylon, and the arms of Pharaoh will fall down; and they will know that I *am* the LORD, when I will put my sword into the hand of the king of Babylon, and he will stretch it out upon the land of Egypt.
26 And I will scatter the Egyptians among the nations, and disperse them among the countries; and they will know that I *am* the LORD.

CHAPTER 31

1 And it came to pass in the eleventh year, in the third *month*, in the first *day* of the month, *that* the word of the LORD came unto me, saying,
2 Son of man, speak unto Pharaoh king of Egypt, and to his multitude; Whom are you like in your greatness?
3 Behold, the Assyrian *was* a cedar in Lebanon with fair branches, and with a shadowing shroud, and of **a** high stature; and his top was among the thick boughs.
4 The waters made him great, the deep set him up on high with her rivers running round about his plants, and sent out her little rivers unto all the trees of the field.

---

[1] see Index

5 Therefore his height was exalted above all the trees of the field, and his boughs were multiplied, and his branches became long because of the multitude of waters, when he shot forth.
6 All the fowls of heaven made their nests in his boughs, and under his branches did all the beasts of the field bring forth their young, and under his shadow dwelt all great nations.
7 Thus was he fair in his greatness, in the length of his branches: for his root was by great waters.
8 The cedars in the garden of God could not hide him: the fir trees were not like his boughs, and the chestnut trees were not like his branches; or any tree in the garden of God was like unto him in his beauty.
9 I have made him fair by the multitude of his branches: so that all the trees of Eden, that *were* in the garden of God, envied him.
10 Therefore thus says the Lord GOD; because you have lifted up yourself in height, and he has shot up his top among the thick boughs, and his heart is lifted up in his height;
11 I have therefore delivered him into the hand of the mighty one of the heathen; he will surely deal with him: I have driven him out for his wickedness.
12 And strangers, the terrible of the nations, have cut him off, and have left him: upon the mountains and in all the valleys his branches are fallen, and his boughs are broken by all the rivers of the land; and all the people of the earth are gone down from his shadow, and have left him.
13 Upon his ruin will all the fowls of the heaven remain, and all the beasts of the field will be upon his branches:
14 To the end that none of all the trees by the waters exalt themselves for their height, neither shoot up their top among the thick boughs, neither their trees stand up in their height, all that drink water: for they are all delivered unto death, to the nether parts of the earth, in the midst of the children of men, with them that go down to the pit.
15 Thus says the Lord GOD; in the day when he went down to the grave I caused a mourning: I covered the deep for him, and I restrained the floods thereof, and the great waters were stayed: and I caused Lebanon to mourn for him, and all the trees of the field fainted for him.
16 I made the nations to shake at the sound of his fall, when I cast him down to hell with them that descend into the pit: and all the trees of Eden, the choice and best of Lebanon, all that drink water, will be comforted in the nether parts of the earth.
17 They also went down into hell with him unto *them that be* slain with the sword; and *they that were* his arm, *that* dwelt under his shadow in the midst of the heathen.
18 To whom are you thus like in glory and in greatness among the trees of Eden? Yet will you be brought down with the trees of Eden unto the nether parts of the earth: you will lie in the midst of the uncircumcised with *them that be* slain by the sword. This *is* Pharaoh and his **entire** multitude, says the Lord GOD.

CHAPTER 32

1 And it came to pass in the twelfth year, in the twelfth month, in the first *day* of the month, *that* the word of the LORD came unto me, saying,
2 Son of man, take up a lamentation for Pharaoh king of Egypt, and say unto him, you are like a young lion of the nations, and you are as a whale in the seas: and you came forth with your rivers, and troubled the waters with your feet, and fouled their rivers.
3 Thus says the Lord GOD; I will therefore spread out my net over you with a company of many people; and they will bring you up in my net.
4 Then will I leave you upon the land, I will cast you forth upon the open field, and will cause all the fowls of the heaven to remain upon you, and I will fill the beasts of the whole earth with you.
5 And I will lay your flesh upon the mountains, and fill the valleys with your height.
6 I will also water with your blood the land wherein you swim, *even* to the mountains; and the rivers will be full of you.
7 And when I will put you out, I will cover the heaven, and make the stars thereof dark; I will cover the sun with a cloud, and the moon will not give her light.
8 All the bright lights of heaven will I make dark over you, and set darkness upon your land, says the Lord GOD.
9 I will also vex the hearts of many people, when I will bring your destruction among the nations, into the countries which you have not known.
10 Yea, I will make many people amazed at you, and their kings will be horribly afraid for you, when I will brandish my sword before them; and they will tremble at *every* moment, every man for his own life, in the day of your fall.
11 For thus says the Lord GOD; the sword of the king of Babylon will come upon you.
12 By the swords of the mighty will I cause your multitude to fall, the terrible of the nations, all of them: and they will spoil the pomp of Egypt, and **the entire** multitude thereof will be destroyed.
13 I will destroy also all the beasts thereof from beside the great waters; neither will the foot of man trouble them anymore, or the hoofs of beasts trouble them.
14 Then will I make their waters deep, and cause their rivers to run like oil, says the Lord GOD.
15 When I will make the land of Egypt desolate, and the country will be destitute of that whereof it was full, when I will smite all them that dwell therein, then will they know that I *am* the LORD.
16 This *is* the lamentation wherewith they will lament her: the daughters of the nations will lament her: they will lament for her, *even* for Egypt, and for all her multitude, says the Lord GOD.
17 It came to pass also in the twelfth year, in the fifteenth *day* of the month, *that* the word of the LORD came unto me, saying,
18 Son of man, wail for the multitude of Egypt, and cast them down, *even* her, and the daughters of the famous nations, unto the nether parts of the earth, with them that go down into the pit.
19 Whom dost you pass in beauty? go down, and be you laid with the uncircumcised.
20 They will fall in the midst of *them that are* slain by the sword: she is delivered to the sword: draw her and all her multitudes.
21 The strong among the mighty will speak to him out of the midst of hell with them that help him: they are gone down, they lie uncircumcised, slain by the sword.
22 Asshur *is* there and all her company: his graves *are* about him: all of them slain, fallen by the sword:
23 Whose graves are set in the sides of the pit, and her company is round about her grave: all of them slain, fallen by the sword, which caused terror in the land of the living.
24 There *is* Elam and all her multitude round about her grave, all of them slain, fallen by the sword, which are gone down uncircumcised into the nether parts of the earth, which caused their terror in the land of the living; yet have they borne their shame with them that go down to the pit.

25 They have set her a bed in the midst of the slain with all her multitude: her graves *are* round about him: all of them uncircumcised, slain by the sword: though their terror was caused in the land of the living, yet have they borne their shame with them that go down to the pit: he is put in the midst of *them that be* slain.
26 There *is* Meshech, Tubal, and all her multitude: her graves *are* round about him: all of them uncircumcised, slain by the sword, though they caused their terror in the land of the living.
27 And they will not lie with the mighty *that are* fallen of the uncircumcised, which are gone down to hell with their weapons of war: and they have laid their swords under their heads, but their iniquities will be upon their bones, though *they were* the terror of the mighty in the land of the living.
28 Yea, you will be broken in the midst of the uncircumcised, and will lie with *them that are* slain with the sword.
29 There *is* Edom, her kings, and all her princes, which with their might are laid by *them that were* slain by the sword: they will lie with the uncircumcised, and with them that go down to the pit.
30 There *be* the princes of the north, all of them, and all the Zidonians, which are gone down with the slain; with their terror they are ashamed of their might; and they lie uncircumcised with *them that be* slain by the sword, and bear their shame with them that go down to the pit.
31 Pharaoh will see them, and will be comforted over all his multitude, *even* Pharaoh and all his army slain by the sword, says the Lord GOD.
32 For I have caused my terror in the land of the living: and he will be laid in the midst of the uncircumcised with *them that are* slain with the sword, *even* Pharaoh and all his multitude, says the Lord GOD.

CHAPTER 33

1 Again the word of the LORD came unto me, saying,
2 Son of man, speak to the children of your people, and say unto them, when I bring the sword upon a land, if the people of the land take a man of their coasts, and set him for their watchman:
3 If when he sees the sword come upon the land, he blow the trumpet, and warn the people;
4 Then whosoever hears the sound of the trumpet, and takes not warning; if the sword come, and take him away, his blood will be upon his own head.
5 He heard the sound of the trumpet, and took not warning; his blood will be upon him. But he that takes warning will deliver his soul.
6 But if the watchman see the sword come, and blow not the trumpet, and the people be not warned; if the sword come, and take *any* person from among them, he is taken away in his iniquity; but his blood will I require at the watchman's hand.
7 So you, O son of man, I have set you a watchman unto the house of Israel; therefore you will hear the word at my mouth, and warn them from me.
8 When I say unto the wicked, O wicked *man*, you will surely die; if you dost not speak to warn the wicked from his way, that wicked *man* will die in his iniquity; but his blood will I require at your hand.
9 Nevertheless, if you warn the wicked of his way to turn from it; if he do not turn from his way, he will die in his iniquity; but you have delivered your soul.

10 Therefore, O you son of man, speak unto the house of Israel; Thus you speak, saying, If our transgressions and our sins *be* upon us, and we pine away in them, how should we then live?
11 Say unto them, *As* I live, says the Lord GOD, I have no pleasure in the death of the wicked; but that the wicked turn from his way and live: turn you, turn you from your evil ways; for why will you die, O house of Israel?
12 [Therefore, you son of man, say unto the children of your people, The righteousness of the righteous will not deliver him in the day of his transgression: as for the wickedness of the wicked, he will not fall thereby in the day that he turn from his wickedness; neither will the righteous be able to live for his *righteousness* in the day that he sins.][1]
13 When I will say to the righteous, *that* he will surely live; if he trust to his own righteousness, and commit iniquity, all his righteousnesses will not be remembered; but for his iniquity that he has committed, he will die for it.
14 Again, when I say unto the wicked, you will surely die; if he turn from his sin, and do that which is lawful and right;
15 *If* the wicked restore the pledge, give again that he had robbed, walk in the statutes of life, without committing iniquity; he will surely live, he will not die.
16 None of his sins that he has committed will be mentioned unto him: he has done that which is lawful and right; he will surely live.
17 Yet the children of your people say, the way of the Lord is not equal: but as for them, their way is not equal.
18 When the righteous turns from his righteousness, and commits iniquity, he will even die thereby.
19 But if the wicked turn from his wickedness, and do that which is lawful and right, he will live thereby.
20 Yet you say, the way of the Lord is not equal. O you house of Israel, I will judge you every one after his ways.
21 And it came to pass in the twelfth year of our captivity, in the tenth *month*, in the fifth *day* of the month, *that* one that had escaped out of Jerusalem came unto me, saying, the city is smitten.
22 Now the hand of the LORD was upon me in the evening, afore he that was escaped came; and had opened my mouth, until he came to me in the morning; and my mouth was opened, and I was no more dumb.
23 Then the word of the LORD came unto me, saying,
24 Son of man, they that inhabit those wastes of the land of Israel speak, saying, Abraham was one, and he inherited the land: but we *are* many; the land is given us for inheritance.
25 Wherefore say unto them, thus says the Lord GOD; you eat with the blood, and lift up your eyes toward your idols[2], and shed blood: and will you possess the land?
26 you stand upon your sword, you work abomination, and you defile everyone his neighbor's wife: and will you possess the land?
27 Say you thus unto them, Thus says the Lord GOD; *As* I live, surely they that *are* in the wastes will fall by the sword, and him that *is* in the open field will I give to the beasts to be devoured, and they that *be* in the forts and in the caves will die of the pestilence.
28 For I will lay the land most desolate, and the pomp of her strength will cease; and the mountains of Israel will be desolate, that none will pass through.
29 Then will they know that I *am* the LORD, when I have laid the land most desolate because of all their abominations which they have committed.

---

[1] All of your righteousness over the years can be lost with one act of sin.

[2] idols – *log* [Strgs#1544]. Note: the root has in it the term for 'dung'.

30 Also, you son of man, the children of your people still are talking against you by the walls and in the doors of the houses, and speak one to another, every one to his brother, saying, Come, I pray you, and hear what is the word that cometh forth from the LORD.

31 And they come unto you as the people cometh, and they sit before you *as* my people, and they hear your words, but they will not do them: for with their mouth they show much love, *but* their heart goes after their covetousness.

32 And, lo, you are unto them as a very lovely song of one that has a pleasant voice, and can play well on an instrument: for they hear your words, but they do them not.

33 And when this cometh to pass, (lo, it will come,) then will they know that a prophet has been among them.

CHAPTER 34

1 And the word of the LORD came unto me, saying,

2 Son of man, prophesy against the shepherds of Israel, prophesy, and say unto them, Thus says the Lord GOD unto the shepherds; Woe *be* to the shepherds of Israel that do feed themselves! should not the shepherds feed the flocks?

3 you eat the fat, and you clothe you with the wool, you kill them that are fed: *but* you feed not the flock.

4 The diseased have you not strengthened, neither have you healed that which was sick, neither have you bound up *that which was* broken, neither have you brought again that which was driven away, neither have you sought that which was lost; but with force and with cruelty have you ruled them.

5 And they were scattered, because *there is* no shepherd: and they became meat to all the beasts of the field, when they were scattered.

6 My sheep wandered through all the mountains, and upon every high hill: yea, my flock was scattered upon all the face of the earth, and none did search or seek *after them*.

7 Therefore, you shepherds, hear the word of the LORD;

8 *As* I live, says the Lord GOD, surely because my flock became a prey, and my flock became meat to every beast of the field, because *there was* no shepherd, neither did my shepherds search for my flock, but the shepherds fed themselves, and fed not my flock;

9 Therefore, O you shepherds, hear the word of the LORD;

10 Thus says the Lord GOD; Behold, I *am* against the shepherds; and I will require my flock at their hand, and cause them to cease from feeding the flock; neither will the shepherds feed themselves anymore; for I will deliver my flock from their mouth, that they may not be meat for them.

11 For thus says the Lord GOD; Behold, I, *even* I, will both search my sheep, and seek them out.

12 As a shepherd seeks out his flock in the day that he is among his sheep *that are* scattered; so will I seek out my sheep, and will deliver them out of all places where they have been scattered in the cloudy and dark day.

13 And I will bring them out from the people, and gather them from the countries, and will bring them to their own land, and feed them upon the mountains of Israel by the rivers, and in all the inhabited places of the country.

14 I will feed them in a good pasture, and upon the high mountains of Israel will their fold be: there will they lie in a good fold, and *in* a fat pasture will they feed upon the mountains of Israel.

15 I will feed my flock, and I will cause them to lie down, says the Lord GOD.

16 I will seek that which was lost, and bring again that which was driven away, and will bind up *that which was* broken, and will strengthen that which was sick: but I will destroy the fat and the strong; I will feed them with judgment.

17 And *as for* you, O my flock, thus says the Lord GOD; Behold, I judge between cattle and cattle, between the rams and the he goats.

18 *Seems it* a small thing unto you to have eaten up the good pasture, but you must tread down with your feet the residue of your pastures? And to have drunk of the deep waters, but you must foul the residue with your feet?

19 And *as for* my flock, they eat that which you have trodden with your feet; and they drink that which you have fouled with your feet.

20 Therefore thus says the Lord GOD unto them; Behold, I, *even* I, will judge between the fat cattle and between the lean cattle.

21 Because you have thrust with side and with shoulder, and pushed all the diseased with your horns, till you have scattered them abroad;

22 Therefore will I save my flock, and they will no more be a prey; and I will judge between cattle and cattle.

23 And I will set up one shepherd over them, and he will feed them, *even* my servant David; he will feed them, and he will be their shepherd.

24 And I the LORD will be their God, and my servant David a prince among them; I the LORD have spoken *it*.

25 And I will make with them a covenant of peace, and will cause the evil beasts to cease out of the land: and they will dwell safely in the wilderness, and sleep in the woods.

26 And I will make them and the places round about my hill a blessing; and I will cause the shower to come down in his season; there will be showers of blessing.

27 And the tree of the field will yield her fruit, and the earth will yield her increase, and they will be safe in their land, and will know that I *am* the LORD, when I have broken the bands of their yoke, and delivered them out of the hand of those that served themselves of them.

28 And they will no more be a prey to the heathen, neither will the beast of the land devour them; but they will dwell safely, and none will make *them* afraid.

29 And I will raise up for them a plant of renown, and they will be no more consumed with hunger in the land, neither bear the shame of the heathen any more.

30 Thus will they know that I the LORD their God *am* with them, and *that* they, *even* the house of Israel, *are* my people, says the Lord GOD.

31 And you my flock, the flock of my pasture, *are* men, *and* I *am* your God, says the Lord GOD.

CHAPTER 35

1 Moreover the word of the LORD came unto me, saying,

2 Son of man, set your face against mount Seir, and prophesy against it,

3 And say unto it, Thus says the Lord GOD; Behold, O mount Seir, I *am* against you, and I will stretch out mine hand against you, and I will make you most desolate.

4 I will lay your cities waste, and you will be desolate, and you will know that I *am* the LORD.

5 Because you have had a perpetual hatred, and have shed *the blood of* the children of Israel by the force of the sword in the time of their calamity, in the time *that their* iniquity *had* an end:

Ezekiel

6 Therefore, *as* I live, says the Lord GOD, I will prepare you unto blood, and blood will pursue you: **although**[1] you have not hated blood, even blood will pursue you.

7 Thus will I make mount Seir most desolate, and cut off from it him that passes out and him that returns.

8 And I will fill his mountains with his slain *men*: in your hills, and in your valleys, and in all your rivers, will they fall that are slain with the sword.

9 I will make you perpetual desolations, and your cities will not return: and you will know that I *am* the LORD.

10 Because you have said, these two nations and these two countries will be mine, and we will possess it; whereas the LORD was there:

11 Therefore, *as* I live, says the Lord GOD, I will even do according to your anger, and according to your envy which you have used out of your hatred against them; and I will make myself known among them, when I have judged you.

12 And you will know that I *am* the LORD, *and that* I have heard all your blasphemies which you have spoken against the mountains of Israel, saying, They are laid desolate, they are given us to consume.

13 Thus with your mouth you have boasted against me, and have multiplied your words against me: I have heard *them*.

14 Thus says the Lord GOD; When the whole earth rejoices, I will make you desolate.

15 As you did rejoice at the inheritance of the house of Israel, because it was desolate, so will I do unto you: you will be desolate, O mount Seir, and all Idumea, *even* all of it: and they will know that I *am* the LORD.

CHAPTER 36

1 Also, you son of man, prophesy unto the mountains of Israel, and say, you mountains of Israel, hear the word of the LORD:

2 Thus says the Lord GOD; Because the enemy has said against you, Aha, even the ancient high places are our's in possession:

3 Therefore prophesy and say, Thus says the Lord GOD; Because they have made *you* desolate, and swallowed you up on every side, that you might be a possession unto the residue of the heathen, and you are taken up in the lips of talkers, and *are* an infamy of the people:

4 Therefore, you mountains of Israel, hear the word of the Lord GOD; Thus says the Lord GOD to the mountains, and to the hills, to the rivers, and to the valleys, to the desolate wastes, and to the cities that are forsaken, which became a prey and derision to the residue of the heathen that *are* round about;

5 Therefore thus says the Lord GOD; Surely in the fire of my jealousy have I spoken against the residue of the heathen, and against all Idumea, which have appointed my land into their possession with the joy of all *their* heart, with despiteful minds, to cast it out for a prey.

6 Prophesy therefore concerning the land of Israel, and say unto the mountains, and to the hills, to the rivers, and to the valleys, Thus says the Lord GOD; Behold, I have spoken in my jealousy and in my fury, because you have borne the shame of the heathen:

7 Therefore thus says the Lord GOD; I have lifted up mine hand, Surely the heathen that *are* about you, they will bear their shame.

8 But you, O mountains of Israel, you will shoot forth your branches, and yield your fruit to my people of Israel; for they are at hand to come.

9 For, behold, I *am* for you, and I will turn unto you, and you will be tilled and sown:

10 And I will multiply men upon you, all the house of Israel, *even* all of it: and the cities will be inhabited, and the wastes will be **built**:

11 And I will multiply upon you man and beast; and they will increase and bring fruit: and I will settle you after your old estates, and will do better *unto you* than at your beginnings: and you will know that I *am* the LORD.

12 Yea, I will cause men to walk upon you, *even* my people Israel; and they will possess you, and you will be their inheritance, and you will no more henceforth bereave them *of men*.

13 Thus says the Lord GOD; Because they say unto you, you *land* devours up men, and have bereaved your nations;

14 Therefore you will devour men no more, neither bereave your nations any more, says the Lord GOD.

15 Neither will I cause *men* to hear in you the shame of the heathen any more, neither will you bear the reproach of the people any more, neither will you cause your nations to fall any more, says the Lord GOD.

16 Moreover the word of the LORD came unto me, saying,

17 Son of man, when the house of Israel dwelt in their own land, they defiled it by their own way and by their doings: their way was before me as the uncleanness of a removed woman.

18 Wherefore I poured my fury upon them for the blood that they had shed upon the land, and for their idols *wherewith* they had polluted it:

19 And I scattered them among the heathen, and they were dispersed through the countries: according to their way and according to their doings I judged them.

20 And when they entered unto the heathen, where they went, they profaned my holy name, when they said to them, These *are* the people of the LORD, and are gone forth out of his land.

21 But I had pity for mine holy name, which the house of Israel had profaned among the heathen, where they went.

22 Therefore say unto the house of Israel, Thus says the Lord GOD; I do not *this* for your sakes, O house of Israel, but for mine holy name's sake, which you have profaned among the heathen, where you went.

23 And I will sanctify my great name, which was profaned among the heathen, which you have profaned in the midst of them; and the heathen will know that I *am* the LORD, says the Lord GOD, when I will be sanctified in you before their eyes.

24 For I will take you from among the heathen, and gather you out of all countries, and will bring you into your own land.

25 Then will I sprinkle clean water upon you, and you will be clean: from all your filthiness, and from all your idols, will I cleanse you.

26 A new heart also will I give you, and a new spirit will I put within you: and I will take away the stony heart out of your flesh, and I will give you an heart of flesh.

27 And I will put my spirit within you, and cause you to walk in my statutes, and you will keep my judgments, and do *them*.

28 And you will dwell in the land that I gave to your fathers; and you will be my people, and I will be your God.

29 I will also save you from all your uncleannesses: and I will call for the corn, and will increase it, and lay no famine upon you.

---

[1] In the original KJV <u>although</u> is translated as sith, a primitive particle; used very widely as demonstrative, interrogative, *whether*, or conditional, *if*,

although. [Strgs#518]

30 And I will multiply the fruit of the tree, and the increase of the field, that you will receive no more reproach of famine among the heathen.
31 Then will you remember your own evil ways, and your doings that *were* not good, and will lothe yourselves in your own sight for your iniquities and for your abominations.
32 Not for your sakes do I *this*, says the Lord GOD, be it known unto you: be ashamed and confounded for your own ways, O house of Israel.
33 Thus says the Lord GOD; In the day that I will have cleansed you from all your iniquities I will also cause *you* to dwell in the cities, and the wastes will be built.
34 And the desolate land will be tilled, whereas it lay desolate in the sight of all that passed by.
35 And they will say, This land that was desolate is become like the garden of Eden; and the waste and desolate and ruined cities *are* become fenced, *and* are inhabited.
36 Then the heathen that are left round about you will know that I the LORD build the ruined *places, and* plant that that was desolate: I the LORD have spoken *it*, and I will do *it*.
37 Thus says the Lord GOD; I will yet *for* this be enquired of by the house of Israel, to do *it* for them; I will increase them with men like a flock.
38 As the holy flock, as the flock of Jerusalem in her solemn feasts; so will the waste cities be filled with flocks of men: and they will know that I *am* the LORD.

CHAPTER 37

1 The hand of the LORD was upon me, and carried me out in the spirit of the LORD, and set me down in the midst of the valley which *was* full of bones,
2 And caused me to pass by them round about: and, behold, *there were* very many in the open valley; and, lo, *they were* very dry.
3 And he said unto me, Son of man, can these bones live? And I answered, O Lord GOD, you know.
4 Again he said unto me, Prophesy upon these bones, and say unto them, O you dry bones, hear the word of the LORD.
5 Thus says the Lord GOD unto these bones; Behold, I will cause breath to enter into you, and you will live:
6 And I will lay sinews upon you, and will bring up flesh upon you, and cover you with skin, and put breath in you, and you will live; and you will know that I *am* the LORD.
7 So I prophesied as I was commanded: and as I prophesied, there was a noise, and behold a shaking, and the bones came together, bone to his bone.
8 And when I beheld, lo, the sinews and the flesh came up upon them, and the skin covered them above: but *there was* no breath in them.
9 Then said he unto me, Prophesy unto the wind, prophesy, son of man, and say to the wind, Thus says the Lord GOD; Come from the four winds, O breath, and breathe upon these slain, that they may live.
10 So I prophesied as he commanded me, and the breath came into them, and they lived, and stood up upon their feet, an exceeding great army.
11 Then he said unto me, Son of man, these bones are the whole house of Israel: behold, they say, Our bones are dried, and our hope is lost: we are cut off for our parts.
12 Therefore prophesy and say unto them, Thus says the Lord GOD; Behold, O my people, I will open your graves, and cause you to come up out of your graves, and bring you into the land of Israel.
13 And you will know that I *am* the LORD, when I have opened your graves, O my people, and brought you up out of your graves,
14 And will put my spirit in you, and you will live, and I will place you in your own land: then will you know that I the LORD have spoken *it*, and performed *it*, says the LORD.
15 The word of the LORD came again unto me, saying,
16 Moreover, you son of man, take you one stick, and write upon it, For Judah, and for the children of Israel his companions: then take another stick, and write upon it, For Joseph, the stick of Ephraim, and *for* all the house of Israel his companions:
17 And join them one to another into one stick; and they will become one in your hand.
18 And when the children of your people will speak unto you, saying, will you not show us what you *meanest* by these?
19 Say unto them, Thus says the Lord GOD; Behold, I will take the stick of Joseph, which *is* in the hand of Ephraim, and the tribes of Israel his fellows, and will put them with him, *even* with the stick of Judah, and make them one stick, and they will be one in mine hand.
20 And the sticks whereon you write will be in your hand before their eyes.
21 And say unto them, Thus says the Lord GOD; Behold, I will take the children of Israel from among the heathen, where they be gone, and will gather them on every side, and bring them into their own land:
22 And I will make them one nation in the land upon the mountains of Israel; and one king will be king to them all: and they will be no more two nations, neither will they be divided into two kingdoms any more at all:
23 Neither will they defile themselves any more with their idols, or with their detestable things, or with any of their transgressions: but I will save them out of all their dwelling places, wherein they have sinned, and will cleanse them: so will they be my people, and I will be their God.
24 And David my servant will *be* king over them; and they all will have one shepherd: they will also walk in my judgments, and observe my statutes, and do them.
25 And they will dwell in the land that I have given unto Jacob my servant, wherein your fathers have dwelt; and they will dwell therein, *even* they, and their children, and their children's children for ever: and my servant David will *be* their prince forever.
26 Moreover I will make a covenant of peace with them; it will be an everlasting covenant with them: and I will place them, and multiply them, and will set my sanctuary in the midst of them for evermore.
27 My tabernacle also will be with them: yea, I will be their God, and they will be my people.
28 And the heathen will know that I the LORD do sanctify Israel, when my sanctuary will be in the midst of them for evermore.

CHAPTER 38

1 And the word of the LORD came unto me, saying,
2 Son of man, set your face against Gog, the land of Magog, the chief prince of Meshech and Tubal, and prophesy against him,
3 And say, Thus says the Lord GOD; Behold, I *am* against you, O Gog, the chief prince of Meshech and Tubal:
4 And I will turn you back, and put hooks into your jaws, and I will bring you forth, and all your army, horses and horsemen, all of

them clothed with all sorts *of armor, even* a great company *with* bucklers and shields, all of them handling swords:

5 Persia, Ethiopia, and Libya with them; all of them with shield and helmet:

6 Gomer, and all his bands; the house of Togarmah of the north quarters, and all his bands: *and* many people with you.

7 Be you prepared, and prepare for yourself, you, and all your company that are assembled unto you, and be you a guard unto them.

8 After many days you will be visited: in the latter years you will come into the land *that is* brought back from the sword, *and is* gathered out of many people, against the mountains of Israel, which have been always waste: but it is brought forth out of the nations, and they will dwell safely all of them.

9 you will ascend and come like a storm, you will be like a cloud to cover the land, you, and all your bands, and many people with you.

10 Thus says the Lord GOD; It will also come to pass, *that* at the same time will things come into your mind, and you will think an evil thought:

11 And you will say, I will go up to the land of unwalled villages; I will go to them that are at rest, that dwell safely, all of them dwelling without walls, and having neither bars or gates,

12 To take a spoil, and to take a prey; to turn your hand upon the desolate places *that are now* inhabited, and upon the people *that are* gathered out of the nations, which have gotten cattle and goods, that dwell in the midst of the land.

13 Sheba, and Dedan, and the merchants of Tarshish, with all the young lions thereof, will say unto you, are you come to take a spoil? Have you gathered your company to take a prey? to carry away silver and gold, to take away cattle and goods, to take a great spoil?

14 Therefore, son of man, prophesy and say unto Gog, Thus says the Lord GOD; in that day when my people of Israel dwells safely, will you not know *it*?

15 And you will come from your place out of the north parts, you, and many people with you, all of them riding upon horses, a great company, and a mighty army:

16 And you will come up against my people of Israel, as a cloud to cover the land; it will be in the latter days, and I will bring you against my land, that the heathen may know me, when I will be sanctified in you, O Gog, before their eyes.

17 Thus says the Lord GOD; are you he of whom I have spoken in old time by my servants the prophets of Israel, which prophesied in those days *many* years that I would bring you against them?

18 And it will come to pass at the same time when Gog will come against the land of Israel, says the Lord GOD, *that* my fury will come up in my face.

19 For in my jealousy *and* in the fire of my wrath have I spoken, Surely in that day there will be a great shaking in the land of Israel;

20 So that the fishes of the sea, and the fowls of the heaven, and the beasts of the field, and all creeping things that creep upon the earth, and all the men that *are* upon the face of the earth, will shake at my presence, and the mountains will be thrown down, and the steep places will fall, and every wall will fall to the ground.

21 And I will call for a sword against him throughout all my mountains, says the Lord GOD: every man's sword will be against his brother.

22 And I will plead against him with pestilence and with blood; and I will rain upon him, and upon his bands, and upon the many people that *are* with him, an overflowing rain, and great hailstones, fire, and brimstone.

23 Thus will I magnify myself, and sanctify myself; and I will be known in the eyes of many nations, and they will know that I *am* the LORD.

CHAPTER 39

1 Therefore, you son of man, prophesy against Gog, and say, Thus says the Lord GOD; Behold, I *am* against you, O Gog, the chief prince of Meshech and Tubal:

2 And I will turn you back, and leave but the sixth part of you, and will cause you to come up from the north parts, and will bring you upon the mountains of Israel:

3 And I will smite your bow out of your left hand, and will cause your arrows to fall out of your right hand.

4 you will fall upon the mountains of Israel, you, and all your bands, and the people that *is* with you: I will give you unto the ravenous birds of every sort, and *to* the beasts of the field to be devoured.

5 you will fall upon the open field: for I have spoken *it*, says the Lord GOD.

6 And I will send a fire on Magog, and among them that dwell carelessly in the isles: and they will know that I *am* the LORD.

7 So will I make my holy name known in the midst of my people Israel; and I will not *let them* pollute my holy name any more: and the heathen will know that I *am* the LORD, the Holy One in Israel.

8 Behold, it is come, and it is done, says the Lord GOD; this *is* the day whereof I have spoken.

9 And they that dwell in the cities of Israel will go forth, and will set on fire and burn the weapons, both the shields and the bucklers, the bows and the arrows, and the hand-staves, and the spears, and they will burn them with fire seven years:

10 So that they will take no wood out of the field, neither cut down *any* out of the forests; for they will burn the weapons with fire: and they will spoil those that spoiled them, and rob those that robbed them, says the Lord GOD.

11 And it will come to pass in that day, *that* I will give unto Gog a place there of graves in Israel, the valley of the passengers on the east of the sea: and it will stop the *noses* of the passengers: and there will they bury Gog and all his multitude: and they will call *it* The valley of Hamon-gog.

12 And seven months will the house of Israel be burying of them, that they may cleanse the land.

13 Yea, all the people of the land will bury *them*; and it will be to them a renown the day that I will be glorified, says the Lord GOD.

14 And they will sever out men of continual employment, passing through the land to bury with the passengers those that remain upon the face of the earth, to cleanse it: after the end of seven months will they search.

15 And the passengers *that* pass through the land, when any sees a man's bone, then will he set up a sign by it, till the buriers have buried it in the valley of Hamon-gog.

16 And also the name of the city will *be* Hamonah. Thus will they cleanse the land.

17 And, you son of man, thus says the Lord GOD; Speak unto every feathered fowl, and to every beast of the field, Assemble yourselves, and come; gather yourselves on every side to my sacrifice that I do sacrifice for you, *even* a great sacrifice upon the mountains of Israel, that you may eat flesh, and drink blood.

18 you will eat the flesh of the mighty, and drink the blood of the princes of the earth, of rams, of lambs, and of goats, of bullocks, all of them fatlings of Bashan.

19 And you will eat fat till you be full, and drink blood till you be drunken, of my sacrifice which I have sacrificed for you.

20 Thus you will be filled at my table with horses and chariots, with mighty men, and with all men of war, says the Lord GOD.

21 And I will set my glory among the heathen, and all the heathen will see my judgment that I have executed, and my hand that I have laid upon them.

22 So the house of Israel will know that I *am* the LORD their God from that day and forward.

23 And the heathen will know that the house of Israel went into captivity for their iniquity: because they trespassed against me, therefore hid I my face from them, and gave them into the hand of their enemies: so fell they all by the sword.

24 According to their uncleanness and according to their transgressions have I done unto them, and hid my face from them.

25 Therefore thus says the Lord GOD; now will I bring again the captivity of Jacob, and have mercy upon the whole house of Israel, and will be jealous for my holy name;

26 After that they have borne their shame, and all their trespasses whereby they have trespassed against me, when they dwelt safely in their land, and none made *them* afraid.

27 When I have brought them again from the people, and gathered them out of their enemies' lands, and am sanctified in them in the sight of many nations;

28 Then will they know that I *am* the LORD their God, which caused them to be led into captivity among the heathen: but I have gathered them unto their own land, and have left none of them anymore there.

29 Neither will I hide my face any more from them: for I have poured out my spirit upon the house of Israel, says the Lord GOD.

CHAPTER 40

1 In the five and twentieth year of our captivity, in the beginning of the year, in the tenth *day* of the month, in the fourteenth year after that the city was smitten, in the selfsame day the hand of the LORD was upon me, and brought me thither.

2 In the visions of God brought he me into the land of Israel, and set me upon a very high mountain, by which *was* as the frame[1] of a city on the south.

3 And he brought me thither, and, behold, *there was* a man, whose appearance *was* like the appearance of brass, with a line[2] of flax in his hand, and a measuring reed; and he stood in the gate.

4 And the man said unto me, Son of man, [behold[3] with your eyes, and hear with your ears[4], and set your heart upon all that I will show you][5]; for to the intent that I might show *them* unto you are you brought **here**: declare all that you see to the house of Israel.[6]

5 [And behold a wall on the outside of the house round about, and in the man's hand a measuring reed of six cubits *long* by the cubit and an hand breadth: so he measured the breadth of the building, one reed; and the height, one reed.][7]

6 Then came he unto the gate which looks toward the east, and went up the stairs[8] thereof, and measured the threshold of the gate, *which was* one reed broad; and the other threshold[9] *of the gate, which was* one reed broad.

7 And *every* [little chamber][10] *was* one reed long, and one reed broad; and between the little chambers *were* five cubits; and the threshold of the gate by the porch of the gate within *was* one reed.

8 He measured also the porch[11] of the gate within, one reed.

9 Then measured he the porch of the gate, eight cubits; and the posts[12] thereof, two cubits; and the porch of the gate *was* inward.

10 And the little chambers of the gate eastward *were* three on this side, and three on that side; they three *were* of one measure: and the posts had one measure on this side and on that side.

11 And he measured the breadth of the entry of the gate, ten cubits; *and* the length of the gate, thirteen cubits.

12 [The space[13] also before the little chambers *was* one cubit *on this side*, and the space *was* one cubit on that side: and the little chambers *were* six cubits on this side, and six cubits on that side.][14]

13 He measured then the gate from the roof of *one* little chamber to the roof of another: the breadth *was* five and twenty cubits, door against door.

14 He made also posts of threescore cubits, even unto the post of the court round about the gate.

15 And from the face of the gate of the entrance unto the face of the porch of the inner gate *were* fifty cubits.

16 And *there were* narrow[15] windows to the little chambers, and to their posts within the gate round about, and likewise to the arches: and windows *were* round about inward: and upon *each* post *were* palm trees.

17 Then brought he me into the outward court, and, lo, *there were* chambers, and a pavement[16] made for the court round about: thirty chambers *were* upon the pavement.

18 And the pavement by the side of the gates over against the length of the gates *was* the lower pavement.

19 Then he measured the breadth from the forefront of the lower gate unto the forefront of the inner court without, an hundred cubits eastward and northward.

20 And the gate of the outward court that looked toward the north, he measured the length thereof, and the breadth thereof.

21 [And the little chambers thereof were three on this side and three on that side; and the posts thereof and the arches thereof were after the measure of the first gate: the length thereof was fifty cubits, and the breadth five and twenty cubits.][17]

---

[1] lit. building [Strgs#4011]

[2] line – *twine* [Strgs#6616], derives from a Hebrew root word meaning to *stuggle* or to *be tortuous* [Strgs#6617].

[3] lit. to see [Strgs#7200].

[4] lit. *broadness* [Strgs#241], to *expand*, to *broaden out the ear*, to *listen* [Strgs#238].

[5] compare Isaiah 6:10

[6] For **Ezekiel 40:4** the Tanakh - The man spoke to me: "Mortal, look closely and listen attentively and note well everything I am going to show you— for you have been brouhht here in order to be shown—and report everything you see to the House of Israel."

[7] height and length of the wall (6 = one reed) = 6x6=36, 36x4=144, compare **Rev. 21:17 & Eze. 43:16**.

[8] stairs – *elevation* (literally a *journey* to a *higher place*, a *thought arising*), *superiority* of station, climactic *progression* [Strgs#4609]. Root means an *elevation*, *acclivity* or *platform*, priority [Strgs#4608].

[9] threshold – *containing*, a *vestibule* (as a limit), a *dish* bowl or bason [Strgs#5592]. Root means to *snatch away*, *termincte*, doorkeeper [Strgs#6505].

[10] comes from the Hebrew root word *tā'âh* meaning to *mark off*, designate [Strgs#8372+8376].

[11] derives from the Hebrew root word *'âlam* meaning to *be tongue tied*, to *tie*, be dumb, put to silence [Strgs#197+481].

[12] lit. *strength*, anything *strong*, a *chief*, a ram [Strgs#352].

[13] space – a *cord* (as *twisted*), a *boundary*, by extension the *territory* inclosed, *limit*, border, *bound* [Strgs#1366].

[14] six cubits = one reed, the same as v7. Six was used here for a reason.

[15] lit. to *close* (the lips or ears), to *contract* [Strgs#331].

[16] lit. a red *hot stone* (for baking), live *coal* [Strgs#7531].

[17] Going under the porch is being filled with the spirit (50) and the reminder of the promised son being born {Issac took 25 years}.

22 And their windows, and their arches, and their palm trees, *were* after the measure of the gate that looks toward the east; and they went up unto it by seven steps; and the arches thereof *were* before them.

23 And the gate of the inner court *was* over against the gate toward the north, and toward the east; and he measured from gate to gate an hundred cubits.

24 After that he brought me toward the south, and behold a gate toward the south: and he measured the posts thereof and the arches thereof according to these measures.

25 And *there were* windows in it and in the arches thereof round about, like those windows: the length *was* fifty cubits, and the breadth five and twenty cubits.

26 And *there were* seven steps to go up to it, and the arches thereof *were* before them: and it had palm trees, one on this side, and another on that side, upon the posts thereof.

27 And *there was* a gate in the inner court toward the south: and he measured from gate to gate toward the south an hundred cubits.

28 And he brought me to the inner court by the south gate: and he measured the south gate according to these measures;

29 And the little chambers thereof, and the posts thereof, and the arches thereof, according to these measures: and *there were* windows in it and in the arches thereof round about: *it was* fifty cubits long, and five and twenty cubits broad.

30 And the arches round about *were* five and twenty cubits long, and five cubits broad.

31 And the arches thereof *were* toward the utter court; and palm trees *were* upon the posts thereof: and the going up to it *had* eight steps.

32 And he brought me into the inner court toward the east: and he measured the gate according to these measures.

33 And the little chambers thereof, and the posts thereof, and the arches thereof, *were* according to these measures: and *there were* windows therein and in the arches thereof round about: *it was* fifty cubits long, and five and twenty cubits broad.

34 And the arches thereof *were* toward the outward court; and palm trees *were* upon the posts thereof, on this side, and on that side: and the going up to it *had* eight steps.

35 And he brought me to the north gate, and measured *it* according to these measures;

36 The little chambers thereof, the posts thereof, and the arches thereof, and the windows to it round about: the length *was* fifty cubits, and the breadth five and twenty cubits.

37 And the posts thereof *were* toward the utter court; and palm trees *were* upon the posts thereof, on this side, and on that side: and the going up to it *had* eight steps.

38 And the chambers and the entries thereof *were* by the posts of the gates, where they washed the burnt offering.

39 And in the porch of the gate *were* two tables on this side, and two tables on that side, to slay thereon the burnt offering and the sin offering and the trespass offering.

40 And at the side without, as one goes up to the entry of the north gate, *were* two tables; and on the other side, which *was* at the porch of the gate, *were* two tables.

41 Four tables *were* on this side, and four tables on that side, by the side of the gate; eight tables, whereupon they slew *their* sacrifices.

42 And the four tables *were* of hewn stone for the burnt offering, of a cubit and an half long, and a cubit and an half broad, and one cubit high: whereupon also they laid the instruments wherewith they slew the burnt offering and the sacrifice.

43 And within *were* hooks, a hand broad, fastened round about: and upon the tables *was* the flesh of the offering.

44 And without the inner gate *were* the chambers of the singers in the inner court, which *was* at the side of the north gate; and their prospect *was* toward the south: one at the side of the east gate having the prospect toward the north.

45 And he said unto me, this chamber, whose prospect *is* toward the south, *is* for the priests, the keepers of the charge of the house.

46 And the chamber whose prospect *is* toward the north *is* for the priests, the keepers of the charge of the altar: these *are* the sons of Zadok[1] among the sons of Levi, which come near to the LORD to minister unto him.

47 So he measured the court, an hundred cubits long, and an hundred cubits broad, foursquare; and the altar *that was* before the house.

48 And he brought me to the porch of the house, and measured *each* post of the porch, five cubits on this side, and five cubits on that side: and the breadth of the gate *was* three cubits on this side, and three cubits on that side.

49 The length of the porch *was* twenty cubits, and the breadth eleven cubits; and *he brought me* by the steps whereby they went up to it: and *there were* pillars by the posts, one on this side, and another on that side.

CHAPTER 41

1 Afterward he brought me to the temple, and measured[2] the posts[3], six cubits broad on the one side, and six cubits broad on the other side, *which was* the breadth of the tabernacle.

2 And the breadth of the door *was* ten cubits; and the sides of the door *were* five cubits on the one side, and five cubits on the other side: and he measured the length thereof, forty cubits: and the breadth, twenty cubits.

3 Then went he inward, and measured the post of the door, two cubits; and the door, six cubits; and the breadth of the door, seven cubits.

4 So he measured the length thereof, twenty cubits; and the breadth, twenty cubits, before the temple: and he said unto me, this *is* the most holy *place*.

5 After he measured the wall of the house, six cubits; and the breadth of *every* side chamber, four cubits, round about the house on every side.

6 And the side chambers *were* three, one over another, and thirty in order; and they entered into the wall which *was* of the house for the side chambers round about, that they might have hold, but they had not hold in the wall of the house.

7 And *there was* an enlarging, and a winding about still upward to the side chambers: for the winding about of the house went still upward round about the house: therefore the breadth of the house *was still* upward, and so increased *from* the lowest *chamber* to the highest by the midst.

---

[1] Zadok – Hebrew word *tsâdôq*, <u>tsaw-doke'</u>; meaning righteous. [Strgs#6659]

[2] measure – to *stretch*, <u>to *measure* (as if by *stretching* a line)</u>, to *be extended*

[Strgs#4058].

[3] lit. *strength* [Strgs#352].

8 I saw also the height of the house round about: the foundations of the side chambers were a full reed of six great cubits.
9 The thickness of the wall, which was for the side chamber without, was five cubits: and that which was left was the place of the side chambers that were within.
10 And between the chambers was the wideness of twenty cubits round about the house on every side.
11 And the doors of the side chambers were toward the place that was left, one door toward the north, and another door toward the south: and the breadth of the place that was left was five cubits round about.
12 Now the building that was before the separate place at the end toward the west was seventy cubits broad; and the wall of the building was five cubits thick round about, and the length thereof ninety cubits.
13 So he measured the house, an hundred cubits long; and the separate place, and the building, with the walls thereof, an hundred cubits long;
14 Also the breadth of the **front** of the house, and of the separate place toward the east, an hundred cubits.
15 And he measured the length of the building over against the separate place which was behind it, and the galleries thereof on the one side and on the other side, an hundred cubits, with the inner temple, and the porches of the court;
16 The door posts, and the narrow windows, and the galleries round about on their three stories, over against the door, cieled[1] with wood round about, and from the ground up to the windows, and the windows were covered;
17 To that above the door, even unto the inner house, and without, and by all the wall round about within and without, by measure.
18 And it was made with cherubims and palm trees, so that a palm tree was between a cherub and a cherub; and every cherub had two faces;
19 So that the face of a man was toward the palm tree on the one side, and the face of a young lion toward the palm tree on the other side: it was made through **the entire** house round about.[2]
20 From the ground unto above the door were cherubims and palm trees made, and on the wall of the temple.
21 The posts of the temple were squared, and the **front** of the sanctuary; the appearance[3] of the one as the appearance of the other.
22 [The altar of wood[4] was three cubits high[5], and the length thereof two cubits; and the corners thereof, and the length thereof, and the walls thereof, were of wood: and he said unto me, This is the table[6] that is before the LORD.][7]
23 And the temple and the sanctuary had two doors.
24 And the doors had two leaves apiece, two turning[8] leaves; two leaves for the one door, and two leaves for the other door.

25 And there were made on them, on the doors of the temple, cherubims and palm trees, like as were made upon the walls; and there were thick planks upon the **front** of the porch without.
26 And there were narrow windows and palm trees on the one side and on the other side, on the sides of the porch, and upon the side chambers of the house, and thick planks.

CHAPTER 42

1 Then he brought me forth into the utter court, the way toward the north: and he brought me into the chamber that was over against the separate place, and which was before the building toward the north.
2 Before the length of an hundred cubits was the north door, and the breadth was fifty cubits.
3 Over against the twenty cubits which were for the inner court, and over against the pavement which was for the utter court, was gallery against gallery in three stories.
4 And before the chambers was a walk of ten cubits breadth inward, a way of one cubit; and their doors toward the north.
5 Now the upper chambers were shorter: for the galleries were higher than these, than the lower, and than the middlemost of the building.
6 For they were in three stories, but had not pillars as the pillars of the courts: therefore the building was straitened more than the lowest and the middlemost from the ground.
7 And the wall that was without over against the chambers, toward the utter court on the forepart of the chambers, the length thereof was fifty cubits.
8 For the length of the chambers that were in the utter court was fifty cubits: and, lo, before the temple were **a** hundred cubits.
9 And from under these chambers was the entry on the east side, as one goes into them from the utter court.
10 The chambers were in the thickness of the wall of the court toward the east, over against the separate place, and over against the building.
11 And the way before them was like the appearance of the chambers which were toward the north, as long as they, and as broad as they: and all their goings out were both according to their fashions[9], and according to their doors.
12 [And according to the doors of the chambers that were toward the south was a door in the head of the way, even the way directly before the wall toward the east, as one enters into them.][10]
13 Then said he unto me, The north chambers and the south chambers, which are before the separate place, they be holy chambers, where the priests that approach unto the LORD will eat the most holy things: there will they lay the most holy things, and the meat offering, and the sin offering, and the trespass offering; for the place is holy.
14 When the priests enter therein, then will they no go out of the holy place into the utter court, but there they will lay their garments

---

[1] ceiled- a board (as chipped thin). [Strgs#7824]. From the same as Strgs#7828, to peel, that is, emaciate; the gull (as thin).
[2] The Septuagint reads, "The face of a man was toward one palm-tree on this side and on that side, and the face of a lion toward another palm-tree on this side and on that side: the house was carved all round." See **Jezekiel XLI:19**
[3] lit. a view, a shape, comeliness, pattern, a vision [Strgs#4758].
[4] lit. a tree (from its firmness) [Strgs#6086]. The cross is the way to see Heaven.
[5] high – elevated (or elated), powerful, arrogant [Strgs#1364].
[6] table – a table (as spread out) [Strgs#7979]. Derives from the root word shâlach meaning to send away [Strgs#7971].

[7] compare **Eze. 44:16**. The Altar of the Cross (Tree): denies self, God powered, offensive, persecution, endurance, no curse, live unto righteousness, we must not come down from the tree by temptation, follows Jesus, daily prayer, bear the tree, not empty prayer with man's wisdom, fasting, hand writing blotted out, unity of body (race), being compelled by others, your title will be seen on the tree, release your mother.
[8] lit. a reversal (i.e open both ways), the backside (of a gem), fold (of a double leaved door), transutation (of a name) [Strgs#4142].
[9] fashion – judicial, verdict [Strgs#4941].
[10] There is a door in the head (mind) of the head (Jesus). He is the head of The Way.

wherein they minister; for they *are* holy; and will put on other garments, and will approach to *those things* which *are* for the people.

15 Now when he had made an end of measuring the inner house, he brought me forth toward the gate whose prospect *is* toward the east, and measured it round about.

16 He measured the east[1] side[2] with the measuring reed, five hundred reeds, with the measuring reed round about.

17 He measured the north[3] side, five hundred reeds, with the measuring reed round about.

18 He measured the south[4] side, five hundred reeds, with the measuring reed.

19 He turned about to the west[5] side, *and* measured five hundred reeds with the measuring reed.

20 [He measured it by the four sides: it had a wall round about, five hundred *reeds* long, and five hundred broad, to make a separation between the sanctuary and the profane place.][6]

CHAPTER 43

1 Afterward he brought me to the gate, *even* the gate that looks toward[7] the east:

2 And, behold, the glory of the God of Israel came from the way[8] of the east: and his voice *was* like a noise of many waters: and the earth shined with his glory.

3 And *it was* according to the appearance of the vision which I saw, *even* according to the vision that I saw when I came to destroy the city: and the visions *were* like the vision that I saw by the river Chebar; and I fell upon my face.

4 And the glory of the LORD came into the house by the way of the gate whose prospect *is* toward the east.

5 So the spirit took me up, and brought me into the inner court; and, behold, the glory of the LORD filled the house.

6 And I heard *him* speaking unto me out of the house; and the man stood by me.

7 And he said unto me, Son of man, the place of my throne, and the place of the soles of my feet, where I will dwell in the midst of the children of Israel for ever, and my holy name, will the house of Israel no more defile, *neither* they, or their kings, by their whoredom, or by the carcasses of their kings in their high places.

8 In their setting of their threshold by my thresholds, and their post by my posts, [and the][9] wall between me and them, they have even defiled my holy name by their abominations that they have committed: wherefore I have consumed them in mine anger.

9 Now let them put away their whoredom, and the carcasses of their kings, far from me, and I will dwell in the midst of them forever.

10 You son of man, show the house to the house of Israel, that they may be ashamed of their iniquities: and let them measure the pattern[10].

11 [And if they be ashamed of all that they have done, show[11] them the form[12] of the house, and the fashion[13] thereof, and the goings out thereof, and the comings in thereof, and all the forms thereof, and all the ordinances[14] thereof, and all the forms thereof, and all the laws thereof: and write *it* in their sight, that they may keep the whole form thereof, and all the ordinances thereof, and do them.][15]

12 [This *is* the law of the house; upon the top of the mountain the whole limit thereof round about will *be* [most holy][16]. Behold, this *is* the law of the house.][17]

13 And these *are* the measures of the altar after the cubits: The cubit *is* a cubit and an [hand breadth][18]; even the bottom[19] will *be* a cubit, and the breadth a cubit, and the border thereof by the edge[20] thereof round about will *be* a span[21]: and this will *be* the higher place of the altar.

14 And from the bottom *upon* the ground *even* to the lower settle[22] will *be* two cubits, and the breadth one cubit; and from the lesser settle *even* to the greater settle will *be* four cubits, and the breadth *one* cubit.

15 So the altar[23] will *be* four cubits; and from the altar and upward will *be* four horns.

16 [And the altar will *be* twelve *cubits* long, twelve broad, square in[24] the four squares[25] thereof.][26]

17 And the settle will *be* fourteen *cubits* long and fourteen broad in the four squares thereof; and the border about it will *be* half a cubit; and the bottom thereof will *be* a cubit about; and his stairs will look toward the east.

18 And he said unto me, Son of man, thus says the Lord GOD; these *are* the ordinances of the altar in the day when they will make it, to offer[27] [burnt offerings][28] thereon, and to sprinkle blood thereon.

19 And you will give to the priests the Levites that be of the seed of Zadok, which approach unto me, to minister unto me, says the Lord GOD, a young[29] bullock for a sin offering.

20 And you will take of the blood thereof, and put *it* on the four horns of it, and on the four corners[30] of the settle, and upon the border round about: thus will you cleanse and purge[31] it.

---

[1] lit. *fore* or front part [Strgs#6921].

[2] lit. *breath*, spirit, *life, anger, unsubstantiality* [Strgs#7307].

[3] lit. hidden [Strgs#6828].

[4] lit. poet, the *south wind* [Strgs#1864], compare **Job 37:17**.

[5] lit. to *roar*, a *sea* (as breaking in *noisy* surf), *river* [Strgs#3220].

[6] 4L=2,000, 500 reeds = 6 cubits (500x6=3,000). 4L= 2,000 reeds= 12,000 cubits.

[7] towards – road (as trodden), a *course* of life or *mode* of action [Strgs#1870].

[8] see note 16.

[9] lit. for a wall

[10] pattern – *admeasurement*, consummation [Strgs#8508].

[11] lit. to know by seeing [Strgs#3045]

[12] form – comes from the Hebrew word *tsûrâh*, is the feminine of *tsûr*, meaning rock, also a form (as if pressed out) [Strgs#6699]. See **Job 28:10**.

[13] fashion – adjustment, structure; by implication *equipage, balance* [Strgs#8498 & 8505].

[14] lit. comes from Hebrew root word meaning enactment by writing, appointment [Strgs#2706].

[15] compare **Matthew 22:37-40**: love God and love neighbor

[16] lit. Holy of Holies

[17] compare **Isaiah 2:2**

[18] hand breadth – to *flatten out* or extend (as a tent, to nurse a child (as *promotive* of *growth*) [Strgs#2946].

[19] lit. bosom, to *inclose* [Strgs#2436].

[20] edge – the idea of *termination*, the *lip* (as a natural boundary), language, a margin [Strgs#8193].

[21] span – is the Hebrew word *zereth* meaning the spread of the fingers [Strgs#2239]. Derives from the Hebrew root word *zârâh* meaning to toss about, to *diffuse*, winnow [Strgs#2219].

[22] lit. surrounding, inclosure, also a *border*, court [Strgs#5835].

[23] Comes from two Hebrew words meaning the mount of God [Strgs#741 & 2025].

[24] in – is the Hebrew word *'el*, the same word used to for God.

[25] lit. *fourth* (part or side) [Strgs#7253].

[26] The alter is 144 cubits, the measure of a man that is sacrificed.

[27] lit. to ascend [Strgs#5927].

[28] burnt offerings – feminine of Strgs#5927. It is defined as a step or collectively stairs, as ascending, holocaust [Strgs#5930].

[29] lit. a son of a Ox [Strgs#1121 & 1241].

[30] corners – angle, pinnacle, chieftain [Strgs#6438].

[31] lit. to cover [Strgs#3722].

21 you will take the bullock also of the sin offering, and he will burn it in the appointed place of the house, without[1] the sanctuary.

22 And on the second day you will offer[2] a kid[3] of the goats[4] without blemish for a sin offering; and they will cleanse the altar, as they did cleanse *it* with the bullock.

23 When you have made an end of cleansing *it*, you will offer a young bullock without blemish, and a ram out of the flock without blemish.

24 And you will offer them before the LORD, and the priests will cast salt upon them, and they will offer them up *for* a burnt offering unto the LORD.

25 Seven days will you prepare every day a goat *for* a sin offering: they will also prepare a young bullock, and a ram out of the flock, without blemish.

26 Seven days will they purge the altar and purify it; and they will consecrate themselves[5].

27 And when these days are expired, it will be, *that* upon the eighth day, and *so* forward, the priests will make your burnt offerings upon the altar, and your peace offerings; and I will accept[6] you, says the Lord GOD.

CHAPTER 44

1 Then he brought me back the way of the gate of the outward sanctuary which looks toward the east; and it *was* shut.

2 Then said the LORD unto me; this gate will be shut, it will not be opened, and no man will enter in by it; because the LORD, the God of Israel, has entered in by it, therefore it will be shut.

3 *It is* for the prince; the prince[7], he will sit in it to eat bread before the LORD; he will enter by the way of the porch of *that* gate, and will go out by the way of the same.

4 Then brought he me the way of the north gate before the house: and I looked, and, behold, the glory of the LORD filled the house of the LORD: and I fell upon my face.

5 And the LORD said unto me, Son of man, mark well, and behold with your eyes, and hear with your ears all that I say unto you concerning all the ordinances of the house of the LORD, and all the laws thereof; and mark well the entering in of the house, with every going forth of the sanctuary.[8]

6 And you will say to the rebellious, *even* to the house of Israel, Thus says the Lord GOD; O you house of Israel, let it suffice you of all your abominations,

7 In that you have brought *into my sanctuary* strangers[9], uncircumcised in heart, and [uncircumcised in flesh][10], to be in my sanctuary, to pollute it, *even* my house, when you offer my bread, the fat and the blood, and they have broken my covenant because of all your abominations.

8 And you have not kept the charge[11] of mine holy things: but you have set keepers of my charge in my sanctuary for yourselves.

9 Thus says the Lord GOD; No stranger, uncircumcised in heart, or uncircumcised in flesh, will enter into my sanctuary, of any stranger that *is* among the children of Israel.[12]

10 And the Levites that are gone away far from me, when Israel went astray, which went astray away from me after their idols[13]; they will even bear their iniquity.

11 Yet they will be ministers in my sanctuary, having charge at the gates of the house, and ministering to the house: they will slay the burnt offering and the sacrifice for the people, and they will stand before them to minister unto them.

12 [Because they ministered unto them before their idols, and [caused the house of Israel to fall into iniquity][14]; therefore have I lifted up mine hand against them, says the Lord GOD, and they will bear their iniquity.][15]

13 And they will not come near unto me, to do the office of a priest unto me, or to come near to any of my holy things, in the most holy *place*: but they will bear their shame, and their abominations which they have committed.

14 But I will make them keepers of the charge of the house, for all the service thereof, and for all that will be done therein.

15 But the priests the Levites, the sons of Zadok[16], that kept the charge of my sanctuary when the children of Israel went astray from me, they will come near to me to minister unto me, [and they will stand before me to offer unto me the fat and the blood][17], says the Lord GOD:

16 They will enter into my sanctuary, and they will come near to my table, to minister unto me, and they will keep my charge.

17 [And it will come to pass, *that* when they enter in at the gates of the inner court, they will be clothed with linen garments; and no wool will come upon them, whiles they minister in the gates of the inner court, and within.][18]

18 They will have linen bonnets upon their heads, and will have linen breeches[19] upon their loins; they will not gird *themselves* with anything that causes sweat.

19 And when they go forth into the utter court, *even* into the utter court to the people, they will put off their garments wherein they ministered, and lay them in the holy chambers, and they will put on other[20] garments; and they will not sanctify the people with their garments.

20 Neither will they shave their heads, or suffer their locks to grow long; they will only poll their heads.

21 Neither will any priest drink wine, when they enter into the inner court.

22 Neither will they take for their wives a widow, or her that is put away: but they will take maidens of the seed of the house of Israel, or a widow that had a priest before.

---

[1] without – to *sever*, separate by a wall, *outside* [Strgs#2351].
[2] offer – is the Hebrew word *kaw-rab'* meaning *to approach* [Strgs#7126].
[3] kid – *shaggy*, a *he goat*, a *faun*, devil, hairy, rough, satyr [Strgs#8163].
[4] lit. a she goat (as strong), goats hair [Strgs#5795].
[5] lit. to fill the hand [Strgs#4390 & 3027].
[6] accept – *to be pleased with* [Strgs#7521].
[7] prince – an *exalted one*, a *king* or *sheik* [Strgs#5387]. Compare the word vapors from **Psalms 135:7** and clouds from **Proverbs 25:14**.
[8] Can not exist the same way one comes in, compare **Ezekiel 46:9**.
[9] strangers – sons of strangers that look strange [Strgs#1121 & 5236].
[10] compare Col. 2:7,13
[11] lit. watch [Strgs#4931].
[12] compare **Acts 5:13**
[13] idols – roll. It is the derivative of a Hebrew root word meaning dung, circumstance, as rolled around, weight, size, great [Strgs#1544 & 1556].
[14] Heb. were for a stumbling block of iniquity unto, see **Eze. 14:3-4**.
[15] God will cause preachers to minister before the people in their shame and they will feel shame but can not quit.
[16] Zadok is allowed to partake of the table of the true cross, compare **Ezekiel 41:22**.
[17] fat = fasting and blood = boldness to enter, compare **Hebrews 10:12**.
[18] wool = sweat, linen = non-sweat. wool = our own righteousness, linen = His righteousness.
[19] breeches – underwear, trousers, in the sense of *hiding*, drawers (from *concealing* the private parts) [Strgs#4370]. Comes from a Hebrew root word meaning *to store away* or lay up in store [Strgs#3647].
[20] lit. to *hinder*, to loiter (that is, *be behind*), procrastinate, be late (slack) [Strgs#312 & 309].

Ezekiel

23 And they will teach my people *the difference* between the holy and profane, and cause them to discern between the unclean and the clean.

24 And in controversy they will stand in judgment; *and* they will judge it according to my judgments: and they will keep my laws and my statutes in all mine assemblies; and they will hallow my Sabbaths.

25 And they will come at no dead person[1] to defile themselves: but for father, or for mother, or for son, or for daughter, for brother, or for sister that has had no husband, they may defile themselves.

26 And after he is cleansed, they will reckon unto him seven days.

27 And in the day that he goes into the sanctuary, unto the inner court, to minister in the sanctuary, he will offer his sin offering, says the Lord GOD.

28 And it will be unto them for an inheritance: I *am* their inheritance: and you will give them no possession in Israel: I *am* their possession.

29 They will eat the meat offering, and the sin offering, and the trespass offering; and every dedicated thing in Israel will be their's.

30 And the first of all the first-fruits of all *things*, and every oblation of all, of every *sort* of your oblations, will be the priest's: you will also give unto the priest the first of your dough, that he may cause the blessing to rest in your house.

31 The priests will not eat of anything that is dead of itself, or torn, whether it be fowl or beast.

CHAPTER 45

1 Moreover, when you will divide by lot the land for inheritance, you will offer an oblation unto the LORD, **a** holy portion of the land: the length will *be* the length of five and twenty thousand *reeds*, and the breadth will *be* ten thousand. This will *be* holy in all the borders thereof round about.

2 Of this there will be for the sanctuary five hundred *in length*, with five hundred *in breadth*, square round about; and fifty cubits round about for the suburbs thereof.

3 And of this measure will you measure the length of five and twenty thousand, and the breadth of ten thousand: and in it will be the sanctuary *and* the most holy *place*.

4 The holy *portion* of the land will be for the priests the ministers of the sanctuary, which will come near to minister unto the LORD: and it will be a place for their houses, and an holy place for the sanctuary.

5 And the five and twenty thousand of length, and the ten thousand of breadth, will also the Levites, the ministers of the house, have for themselves, for a possession for twenty chambers.

6 And you will appoint the possession of the city five thousand broad, and five and twenty thousand long, over against the oblation of the holy *portion*: it will be for the whole house of Israel.

7 And a *portion will be* for the prince on the one side and on the other side of the oblation of the holy *portion*, and of the possession of the city, before the oblation of the holy *portion*, and before the possession of the city, from the west side westward, and from the east side eastward: and the length will *be* over against one of the portions, from the west border unto the east border.

8 In the land will be his possession in Israel: and my princes will no more oppress my people; and *the rest of* the land will they give to the house of Israel according to their tribes.

9 Thus says the Lord GOD; Let it suffice you, O princes of Israel: remove violence and spoil, and execute judgment and justice, take away your exactions from my people, says the Lord GOD.

10 you will have just balances, and a just ephah, and a just bath.

11 The ephah and the bath will be of one measure, that the bath may contain the tenth part of an homer, and the ephah the tenth part of an homer: the measure thereof will be after the homer.

12 And the shekel will *be* twenty gerahs: twenty shekels, five and twenty shekels, fifteen shekels, will be your maneh.

13 This *is* the oblation that you will offer; the sixth part of an ephah of an homer of wheat, and you will give the sixth part of an ephah of an homer of barley:

14 Concerning the ordinance of oil, the bath of oil, you *will offer* the tenth part of a bath out of the cor, *which is* an homer of ten baths; for ten baths *are* an homer:

15 And one lamb out of the flock, out of two hundred, out of the fat pastures of Israel; for a meat offering, and for a burnt offering, and for peace offerings, to make reconciliation for them, says the Lord GOD.

16 All the people of the land will give this oblation for the prince in Israel.

17 And it will be the prince's part *to give* burnt offerings, and meat offerings, and drink offerings, in the feasts, and in the new moons, and in the Sabbaths, in all solemnities of the house of Israel: he will prepare the sin offering, and the meat offering, and the burnt offering, and the peace offerings, to make reconciliation for the house of Israel.

18 Thus says the Lord GOD; In the first *month*, in the first *day* of the month, you will take a young bullock without blemish, and cleanse the sanctuary:

19 [And the priest will take of the blood of the sin offering, and put *it* upon the posts of the house, and upon the four corners of the settle of the altar, and upon the posts of the gate of the inner court.][2]

20 And so you will do the seventh *day* of the month for everyone that **strays**, and for *him that is* simple[3]: so will you reconcile the house.

21 In the first *month*, in the fourteenth day of the month, you will have the Passover, a feast of seven days; unleavened bread will be eaten.

22 And upon that day will the prince prepare for himself and for all the people of the land a bullock *for* a sin offering.

23 And seven days of the feast he will prepare a burnt offering to the LORD, seven bullocks and seven rams without blemish daily the seven days; and a kid of the goats daily *for* a sin offering.

24 And he will prepare a meat offering of an ephah for a bullock, and an ephah for a ram, and an hin of oil for an ephah.

25 In the seventh *month*, in the fifteenth day of the month, will he do the like in the feast of the seven days, according to the sin offering, according to the burnt offering, and according to the meat offering, and according to the oil.

CHAPTER 46

1 Thus says the Lord GOD; The gate of the inner court that looks toward the east will be shut the six working days; but on the Sabbath it will be opened, and in the day of the new moon it will be opened.

---

[1] person – <u>Hebrew word</u> *'âdâm*, meaning a *human being, mankind* [Strgs#120].

[2] Blood is all over the inner place of God, compare **1 Cor. 3:16-17**; **6:16-**

[19].

[3] derives from a Hebrew root word meaning <u>to be open</u> (to everything) [Strgs#6612+6601].

2 And the prince will enter by the way of the porch of *that* gate without, and will stand by the post of the gate, and the priests will prepare his burnt offering and his peace offerings, and he will worship at the threshold of the gate: then he will go forth; but the gate will not be shut until the evening.

3 Likewise the people of the land will worship at the door of this gate before the LORD in the Sabbaths and in the new moons.

4 And the burnt offering that the prince will offer unto the LORD in the Sabbath day will *be* six lambs without blemish, and a ram without blemish.

5 And the meat offering will *be* an ephah for a ram, and the meat offering for the lambs as he will be able to give, and **a** hin of oil to an ephah.

6 And in the day of the new moon *it will be* a young bullock without blemish, and six lambs, and a ram: they will be without blemish.

7 And he will prepare a meat offering, an ephah for a bullock, and an ephah for a ram, and for the lambs according as his hand will attain unto, and **a** hin of oil to an ephah.

8 And when the prince will enter, he will go in by the way of the porch of *that* gate, and he will go forth by the way thereof.

9 [But when the people of the land will come before the LORD in the solemn feasts, he that enters in by the way of the north gate to worship will go out by the way of the south gate; and he that enters by the way of the south gate will go forth by the way of the north gate: he will not return by the way of the gate whereby he came in, but will go forth over against it.]¹

10 And the prince in the midst of them, when they go in, will go in; and when they go forth, will go forth.

11 And in the feasts and in the solemnities the meat offering will be an ephah to a bullock, and an ephah to a ram, and to the lambs as he is able to give, and an hin of oil to an ephah.

12 [Now when the prince will prepare a voluntary burnt offering or peace offerings voluntarily² unto the LORD, *one* will then open him the gate that looks toward the east, and he will prepare his burnt offering and his peace offerings, as he did on the Sabbath day: then he will go forth; and after his going forth *one* will shut the gate.]³

13 you will daily prepare a burnt offering unto the LORD *of* a lamb of the first year without blemish: you will prepare it every morning.

14 And you will prepare a meat offering for it every morning, the sixth part of an ephah, and the third part of an hin of oil, to temper with the fine flour; a meat offering continually by a perpetual ordinance unto the LORD.

15 Thus will they prepare the lamb, and the meat offering, and the oil, every morning *for* a continual burnt offering.

16 Thus says the Lord GOD; if the prince give a gift unto any of his sons, the inheritance thereof will be his sons'; it will *be* their possession by inheritance.

17 But if he give a gift of his inheritance to one of his servants, then it will be his to the year of liberty; after it will return to the prince: but his inheritance will be his sons' for them.

18 Moreover the prince will not take of the people's inheritance by oppression, to thrust them out of their possession; *but* he will give his sons inheritance out of his own possession: that my people be not scattered every man from his possession.

19 After he brought me through the entry, which *was* at the side of the gate, into the holy chambers of the priests, which looked toward the north: and, behold, there *was* a place on the two sides westward.

20 Then said he unto me, This *is* the place where the priests will boil the trespass offering and the sin offering, where they will bake the meat offering; that they bear *them* not out into the utter court, to sanctify the people.

21 Then he brought me forth into the utter court, and caused me to pass by the four corners of the court; and, behold, in every corner of the court *there was* a court.

22 In the four corners of the court *there were* courts joined of forty *cubits* long and thirty broad: these four corners *were* of one measure.

23 And *there was* a row *of building* round about in them, round about them four, and *it was* made with boiling places under the rows round about.

24 Then said he unto me, these *are* the places of them that boil, where the ministers of the house will boil the sacrifice of the people.

CHAPTER 47

1 Afterward he brought me again unto the door of the house; and, behold, waters issued out from under the threshold⁴ of the house eastward: for the forefront of the house *stood toward* the east, and the waters came down from under from the right side of the house, at the south *side* of the altar.

2 Then brought he me out of the way of the gate northward, and led me about the way without unto the utter gate by the way that looks eastward; and, behold, there ran⁵ out waters on the right side⁶.

3 And when the man that had the line in his hand went forth eastward, he measured a thousand cubits, and he brought me through the waters; [the waters *were* to the ankles]⁷.

4 Again he measured a thousand, and brought me through the waters; the waters *were* to the knees. Again he measured a thousand, and brought me through; the waters *were* to the loins.

5 Afterward he measured a thousand; *and it was* a river that I could not pass over: for the waters were risen⁸, waters to swim⁹ in, a river that could not be passed over.

6 And he said unto me, Son of man, have you seen *this*? Then he brought me, and caused me to return to the brink¹⁰ of the river.

7 Now when I had returned, behold, at the bank¹¹ of the river *were* very many trees on the one side and on the other.

8 Then said he unto me, These waters issue out toward the east country, and go down into the desert, and go into the sea: *which being* brought forth into the sea, the waters will be healed.

9 And it will come to pass, *that* everything that lives, which moves, whithersoever the rivers¹² will come, will live: and there will be a very great multitude of fish, because these waters will come thither: for they will be healed; and everything will live where the river cometh.

---

¹ compare Ezekiel 44:5
² voluntarily – spontaneity, abundant gift [Strgs#5071].
³ Voluntary offering will open the shut door for you. It will shut after you go through because it is personal.
⁴ lit. *stretcher* [Strgs#4670]
⁵ a sudden violent outburst.
⁶ lit. *shoulder* [Strgs#3802]
⁷ Translate in Hebrew as '<u>waters of the ankle</u>.'
⁸ risen – *mount up* [Strgs#1342]
⁹ Points to 'He who bring down pride of the fortress,' compare 1 Samuel 25:
¹⁰ brink – *termination*, the *lip* (as a natural boundary), <u>language</u>, a *margin* [Strgs#8193].
¹¹ Ibid.
¹² lit. <u>two rivers</u> [Strgs#5158]. Derives from the Hebrew root word *nâchal*, meaning to *inherit*, to *occupy*, to *bequeath*, *distribute*, *instate* [Strgs#5157].

10 And it will come to pass, *that* the fishers will stand upon it from En-gedi even unto En-eglaim; they will be a *place* to spread forth nets; their fish will be according to their kinds, as the fish of the great sea, exceeding many.
11 But the miry places thereof and the **marshes** thereof will not be healed; they will be given to salt.
12 And by the river upon the bank thereof, on this side and on that side, will grow all trees for meat, whose leaf will not fade, neither will the fruit thereof be consumed: it will bring forth [new fruit][1] according to his months, because their waters they issued out of the sanctuary: and the fruit thereof will be for meat, and the leaf[2] thereof for medicine.
13 Thus says the Lord GOD; this will *be* the border, whereby you will inherit the land according to the twelve tribes of Israel: Joseph will *have two* portions.
14 And you will inherit it, one as well as another: *concerning* the which I lifted up mine hand to give it unto your fathers: and this land will fall unto you for inheritance.
15 And this will *be* the border of the land toward the north side, from the great sea, the way of Hethlon, as men go to Zedad;
16 Hamath, Berothah, Sibraim, which *is* between the border of Damascus and the border of Hamath; Hazar-hatticon, which *is* by the coast of Hauran.
17 And the border from the sea will be Hazar-enan, the border of Damascus, and the north northward, and the border of Hamath. And *this is* the north side.
18 And the east side you will measure from Hauran, and from Damascus, and from Gilead, and from the land of Israel *by* Jordan, from the border unto the east sea. And *this is* the east side.
19 And the south side southward, from Tamar *even* to the waters of strife *in* Kadesh, the river to the great sea. And *this is* the south side southward.
20 The west side also will *be* the great sea from the border, till a man come over against Hamath. This *is* the west side.
21 So will you divide this land unto you according to the tribes of Israel.
22 And it will come to pass, *that* you will divide it by lot for an inheritance unto you, and to the strangers that sojourn among you, which will beget children among you: and they will be unto you as born in the country among the children of Israel; they will have inheritance with you among the tribes of Israel.
23 And it will come to pass, *that* in what tribe the stranger sojourns, there will you give *him* his inheritance, says the Lord GOD.

CHAPTER 48

1 Now these *are* the names of the tribes. From the north end to the coast of the way of Hethlon, as one goes to Hamath, Hazar-enan, the border of Damascus northward, to the coast of Hamath; for these are his sides east *and* west; a *portion for* Dan.
2 And by the border of Dan, from the east side unto the west side, a *portion for* Asher.
3 And by the border of Asher, from the east side even unto the west side, a *portion for* Naphtali.
4 And by the border of Naphtali, from the east side unto the west side, a *portion for* Manasseh.
5 And by the border of Manasseh, from the east side unto the west side, a *portion for* Ephraim.
6 And by the border of Ephraim, from the east side even unto the west side, a *portion for* Reuben.
7 And by the border of Reuben, from the east side unto the west side, a *portion for* Judah.
8 And by the border of Judah, from the east side unto the west side, will be the offering which you will offer of five and twenty thousand *reeds in* breadth, and *in* length as one of the *other* parts, from the east side unto the west side: and the sanctuary will be in the midst of it.
9 The oblation that you will offer unto the LORD will *be* of five and twenty thousand in length, and of ten thousand in breadth.
10 And for them, *even* for the priests, will be *this* holy oblation; toward the north five and twenty thousand *in length*, and toward the west ten thousand in breadth, and toward the east ten thousand in breadth, and toward the south five and twenty thousand in length: and the sanctuary of the LORD will be in the midst thereof.
11 *It will be* for the priests that are sanctified of the sons of Zadok; which have kept my charge, which went not astray when the children of Israel went astray, as the Levites went astray.
12 And *this* oblation of the land that is offered will be unto them a thing most holy by the border of the Levites.
13 And over against the border of the priests the Levites will have five and twenty thousand in length, and ten thousand in breadth: all the length will *be* five and twenty thousand, and the breadth ten thousand.
14 And they will not sell of it, neither exchange, or alienate the firstfruits of the land: for *it is* holy unto the LORD.
15 And the five thousand, that are left in the breadth over against the five and twenty thousand, will be a profane *place* for the city, for dwelling, and for suburbs: and the city will be in the midst thereof.
16 And these will *be* the measures thereof; the north side four thousand and five hundred, and the south side four thousand and five hundred, and on the east side four thousand and five hundred, and the west side four thousand and five hundred.
17 And the suburbs of the city will be toward the north two hundred and fifty, and toward the south two hundred and fifty, and toward the east two hundred and fifty, and toward the west two hundred and fifty.
18 And the residue in length over against the oblation of the holy *portion will be* ten thousand eastward, and ten thousand westward: and it will be over against the oblation of the holy *portion*; and the increase thereof will be for food unto them that serve the city.
19 And they that serve the city will serve it out of all the tribes of Israel.
20 All the oblation will *be* five and twenty thousand by five and twenty thousand: you will offer the holy oblation foursquare, with the possession of the city.
21 And the residue will *be* for the prince, on the one side and on the other of the holy oblation, and of the possession of the city, over against the five and twenty thousand of the oblation toward the east border, and westward over against the five and twenty thousand toward the west border, over against the portions for the prince: and it will be the holy oblation; and the sanctuary of the house will *be* in the midst thereof.
22 Moreover from the possession of the Levites, and from the possession of the city, *being* in the midst *of that* which is the

---

[1] New fruit – *to burst the womb*, bear or *make early fruit* (of woman or tree), to give the *birthright* [Strgs#1069].

[2] leaf – *ascending*, a *leaf* (as *coming up* on a tree) [Strgs#5929].

prince's, between the border of Judah and the border of Benjamin, will be for the prince.

23 As for the rest of the tribes, from the east side unto the west side, Benjamin will *have a portion*.

24 And by the border of Benjamin, from the east side unto the west side, Simeon will *have a portion*.

25 And by the border of Simeon, from the east side unto the west side, Issachar a *portion*.

26 And by the border of Issachar, from the east side unto the west side, Zebulun a *portion*.

27 And by the border of Zebulun, from the east side unto the west side, Gad a *portion*.

28 And by the border of Gad, at the south side southward, the border will be even from Tamar *unto* the waters of strife *in* Kadesh, *and* to the river toward the great sea.

29 This *is* the land which you will divide by lot unto the tribes of Israel for inheritance, and these *are* their portions, says the Lord GOD. **30** And these *are* the [goings out][1] of the city on the north side[2], four thousand and five hundred measures.

31 And the gates of the city will *be* after the names of the tribes of Israel: three gates northward; one gate of Reuben, one gate of Judah, one gate of Levi.

32 And at the east side[3] four[4] thousand and five hundred: and three gates; and one gate of Joseph, one gate of Benjamin, one gate of Dan.

33 And at the south side four thousand and five hundred measures: and three gates; one gate of Simeon, one gate of Issachar, one gate of Zebulun.

34 At the west side four thousand and five hundred, *with* their three gates; one gate of Gad, one gate of Asher, one gate of Naphtali.

35 *It was* round about eighteen thousand *measures*: and the name of the city from *that* day will *be*, The LORD *is* there.

---

[1] going out – (only in plural collective) *exit, boundary, deliverance,* (actively) *source* [Strgs#8444].
[2] side – feminine of *mouth* in a figurative sense, *direction, region, extremity* [Strgs#6285].
[3] Ibid.
[4] lit. to *be four sided* [Strgs#702 & 7251]

DANIEL

CHAPTER 1

1 In the third year of the reign of Jehoiakim king of Judah came Nebuchadnezzar king of Babylon unto Jerusalem, and besieged it.
2 And the Lord gave Jehoiakim king of Judah into his hand, with part of the vessels of the house of God: which he carried into the land of Shinar to the house of his god; and he brought the vessels into the treasure house of his god.
3 And the king spoke unto Ashpenaz[1] the master of his eunuchs, that he should bring certain of the children of Israel, and of the king's seed, and of the princes;
4 Children in whom *was* no blemish, but well favored, and skilful in all wisdom, and cunning in knowledge, and understanding science, and such as *had* ability in them to stand in the king's palace, and whom they might teach the learning and the tongue of the Chaldeans.
5 And the king appointed[2] them a daily provision[3] of the king's meat, and of [the wine which he drank][4]: so nourishing them three years, that at the end thereof they might stand before the king.
6 Now among these were of the children of Judah, Daniel[5], Hananiah[6], Mishael[7], and Azariah[8]:
7 Unto whom the prince of the eunuchs gave[9] names: for he gave unto Daniel *the name* of Belteshazzar[10]; and to Hananiah, of Shadrach[11]; and to Mishael, of Meshach[12]; and to Azariah, of Abed-nego[13].
8 But Daniel purposed[14] in his heart that he would not defile himself with the portion of the king's meat, or with the wine which he drank: therefore he requested of the prince of the eunuchs that he might not defile himself.
9 Now God had brought Daniel into favor and tender love with the prince of the eunuchs.
10 And the prince of the eunuchs said unto Daniel, I fear my lord the king, who has appointed your meat and your drink: for why should he see your faces worse[15] liking than the children which *are* of your sort[16]? Then will you make *me* endanger my head to the king.
11 Then said Daniel to Melzar, whom the prince of the eunuchs had set over Daniel, Hananiah, Mishael, and Azariah,
12 Prove your servants, I beseech you, ten days; and let them give us pulse to eat, and water to drink.
13 Then let our countenances be looked upon before you, and the countenance of the children that eat of the portion of the king's meat: and as you sees, deal with your servants.
14 So he consented to them in this matter, and proved them ten days.
15 And at the end of ten[17] days their countenances appeared fairer and fatter in flesh than all the children which did eat the portion of the king's meat.
16 Thus Melzar took away the portion of their meat, and the wine that they should drink; and gave them pulse.

17 As for these four children, God gave them knowledge and skill in all learning and wisdom: and Daniel had understanding in all visions and dreams.
18 Now at the end of the days that the king had said he should bring them in, then the prince of the eunuchs brought them in before Nebuchadnezzar.
19 And the king communed with them; and among them all was found none like Daniel, Hananiah, Mishael, and Azariah: therefore stood they before the king.
20 And in all matters[18] of wisdom *and* understanding, that the king enquired of them, he found them ten times[19] better than all the magicians *and* astrologers that *were* in all his realm.
21 And Daniel continued *even* unto the first year of king Cyrus.

CHAPTER 2

1 And in the second year of the reign of Nebuchadnezzar Nebuchadnezzar dreamed dreams, wherewith his spirit was troubled, and his sleep brake from him.
2 Then the king commanded to call the magicians, and the astrologers, and the sorcerer's, and the Chaldeans, for to show the king his dreams. So they came and stood before the king.
3 And the king said unto them, I have dreamed a dream, and my spirit was troubled to know the dream.
4 Then spoke the Chaldeans to the king in Syriack, O king, live forever: tell your servants the dream, and we will show the interpretation.
5 The king answered and said to the Chaldeans, The thing is gone from me: if you will not make known unto me the dream, with the interpretation thereof, you will be cut in pieces, and your houses will be made a dunghill.
6 But if you show the dream, and the interpretation thereof, you will receive of me gifts and rewards and great honor: therefore show me the dream, and the interpretation thereof.
7 They answered again and said, Let the king tell his servants the dream, and we will show the interpretation of it.
8 The king answered and said, I know of certainty that you would gain the time, because you see the thing is gone from me.
9 But if you will not make known unto me the dream, *there is but* one decree for you: for you have prepared lying and corrupt words to speak before me, till the time be changed: therefore tell me the dream, and I will know that you can show me the interpretation thereof.
10 The Chaldeans answered before the king, and said, [there is not a man upon the earth that can show the king's matter][20]: therefore *there is* no king, lord, nor ruler, *that* asked such things at any magician, or astrologer, or Chaldean.
11 And *it is* a rare thing that the king requires, and there is none other that can show it before the king, except the gods whose dwelling is not with flesh.
12 For this cause the king was angry and very furious, and commanded to destroy all the wise *men* of Babylon.

---

[1] Ashpenaz- I will make prominent the sprinkled.
[2] appointed – to weigh out [Strgs#4487].
[3] lit. the *matter* of a *spoken thing* [Strgs#1697].
[4] lit. the loine of His drink.
[5] Daniel- God is my Judge or *Judge of God*. [Strgs#1840]
[6] Hananiah- God has favored or *Jah has favored*. [Strgs#2608]
[7] Mishael- who is what God is. [Strgs#4332]
[8] Azariah- Jehovah has helped or *Jah has helped*. [Strgs#5838]
[9] gave – to put, ordain, order, disguise [Strgs#7760]
[10] Belteshazzar- means *lord of the straitened's treasure*. [Strgs#1095]

[11] Shadrach- royal or the great scribe.
[12] Meshach- guest of a king.
[13] Abednego- servant of Nebo. see Index for Nebo.
[14] the same as note 9 above.
[15] worse – sadder, boil, angery; contrast **Rev. 18:3**.
[16] lit. a revolution (of time, an age),a cycle, also *joy* [Strgs#1524].
[17] ten – as an accumulation to the extent of the digits [Strgs#6235].
[18] lit. word by implication a matter of a spoken thing [Strgs#1697].
[19] times – hand.
[20] This statement is not true, compare to **Eph. 4:12**.

13 And the decree went forth that the wise *men* should be slain; and they sought Daniel and his fellows to be slain.
14 Then Daniel answered with counsel and wisdom to Arioch[1] the captain of the king's guard, which was gone forth to slay the wise *men* of Babylon:
15 He answered and said to Arioch the king's captain, Why *is* the decree *so* hasty from the king? Then Arioch made the thing known to Daniel.
16 Then Daniel went in, and desired of the king that he would give him time, and that he would show the king the interpretation.
17 Then Daniel went to his house, and made the thing known to Hananiah, Mishael, and Azariah, his companions:
18 That they would desire mercies of the God of heaven concerning this secret; that Daniel and his fellows should not perish with the rest of the wise *men* of Babylon.
19 [Then was the secret revealed unto Daniel in a night vision. Then Daniel blessed the God of heaven.][2]
20 Daniel answered and said, Blessed be the name of God forever and ever: for wisdom and might are his:
21 And he changes the times and the seasons: he removes kings, and sets up kings: he gives wisdom unto the wise, and knowledge to them that know[3] understanding:
22 He reveals the deep and secret things: he knows what *is* in the darkness, and the light dwells with him.
23 I thank you, and praise you, O you God of my fathers, who have given me wisdom and might, and have made known unto me now what we desired of you: for you have *now* made known unto us the king's matter.
24 Therefore Daniel went in unto Arioch, whom the king had ordained to destroy the wise *men* of Babylon: he went and said thus unto him; Destroy not the wise *men* of Babylon: bring me in before the king, and I will show unto the king the interpretation.
25 Then Arioch brought in Daniel before the king in haste, and said thus unto him, I have found a man of the captives of Judah, that will make known unto the king the interpretation.
26 The king answered and said to Daniel, whose name *was* Belteshazzar, Are you able to make known unto me the dream which I have seen, and the interpretation thereof?
27 Daniel answered in the presence of the king, and said, The secret which the king has demanded cannot the wise *men*, the astrologers, the magicians, the soothsayers, show unto the king;
28 But there is a God in heaven that reveals secrets, and makes known to the king Nebuchadnezzar what will be in the latter days. Your dream, and the visions of your head upon your bed, are these;[4]
29 As for you, O king, your thoughts came *into your mind* upon your bed, what should come to pass hereafter: and he that reveals secrets makes known to you what will come to pass.
30 But as for me, this secret is not revealed to me for *any* wisdom that I have more than any living, but for *their* sakes that will make known the interpretation to the king, and that you might know the thoughts of your heart.

31 You, O king, saw[5], and behold a great image. This great image, whose brightness *was* excellent, stood before you; and the form[6] thereof *was* terrible[7].
32 This image's head *was* of fine gold, his breast and his arms of silver, his belly and his thighs of brass,
33 His legs of iron, his feet part of iron and part of clay.
34 You saw till that a stone was cut out without hands, which smote[8] the image upon his feet *that were* of iron and clay, and **break** them to pieces.
35 Then was the iron, the clay, the brass, the silver, and the gold, broken to pieces together, and became like the chaff of the summer threshing-floors; and the wind carried them away, that no place was found for them: and the stone that smote the image became a great mountain, and filled the whole earth.
36 This *is* the dream; and we will tell the interpretation thereof before the king.
37 You, O king, *are* a king of kings: for the God of heaven has given you a kingdom, power, and strength, and glory.
38 And wheresoever the children of men dwell, the beasts of the field and the fowls of the heaven has he given into your hand, and has made you ruler over them all. You *are* this head of gold.
39 And after you will arise another kingdom inferior to you, and another third kingdom of brass, which will bear rule over all the earth.
40 [And the fourth kingdom will be strong as iron: forasmuch as iron breaks in pieces and subdues all *things*: and as iron that breaks all these, will it break in pieces and bruise.][9]
41 And whereas you saw the feet and toes, part of potters' clay, and part of iron, the kingdom will be divided; but there will be in it of the strength of the iron, forasmuch as you saw the iron mixed with miry clay.
42 And *as* the toes of the feet *were* part of iron, and part of clay, *so* the kingdom will be partly strong, and partly broken.
43 And whereas you saw iron mixed with miry clay, they will mingle themselves with the seed of men: but they will not cleave one to another, even as iron is not mixed with clay.
44 And in the days of these kings will the God of heaven [set up][10] a kingdom, which will never be destroyed: and the kingdom will not be left to other people, *but* it will break in pieces and consume all these kingdoms, and it will stand for ever.
45 Forasmuch as you saw that the stone was cut out of the mountain without hands, and that it brake in pieces the iron, the brass, the clay, the silver, and the gold; the great God has made known to the king what will come to pass hereafter: and the dream *is* certain, and the interpretation thereof sure.
46 Then the king Nebuchadnezzar fell upon his face, and worshipped Daniel, and commanded that they should offer an oblation and sweet odors unto him.
47 The king answered unto Daniel, and said, Of a truth *it is*, that your God *is* a God of gods, and a Lord of kings, and a revealer of secrets, seeing you could reveal this secret.
48 Then the king made Daniel a great man, and gave him many great gifts, and made him ruler over the whole province of Babylon, and chief of the governors over all the wise *men* of Babylon.

---

[1] Arioch- lion like.
[2] The word of the Lord to Daniel established him as a prophet.
[3] lit. to certify, make known, teach. [Strgs#3046]
[4] In **1 Kings 10:3** Solomon 'Told' The Queen of Ethopia all her questions, also compare **John 7:20**.
[5] saw- Hebrew meaning *to exist*; used in a great variety of applications (especially I connection with other words):-be, become, behold, came (to pass), cease, cleave, consider, do , give, judge, labour, mingle (self), seek, take heed, tremble, walk. [Strgs#1934]
[6] lit. to *see*, sight of others [Strgs#7299+7200].
[7] lit. fear, formidable, to crawl, serpent, to creep [Strgs#1763−2119].
[8] smote – to *strike* in pieces, to *arrest*, to *impale*: hand, stay [Stgs#4223].
[9] Legs of iron = victory in war.
[10] setup – appoint, establish, raise up self, rose, stand [Strgs#6966].

49 Then Daniel requested of the king, and he set Shadrach, Meshach, and Abed-nego, over the affairs of the province of Babylon: but Daniel *sat* in the gate of the king.

CHAPTER 3

1 Nebuchadnezzar[1] the king made an image of gold, whose height *was* threescore cubits, *and* the breadth[2] thereof [six cubits][3]: he set it up in the plain of Dura[4], in the province of Babylon.

2 Then Nebuchadnezzar the king sent to gather together the princes, the governors, and the captains, the judges[5], the treasurers, the counselors[6], the sheriffs[7], and all the rulers[8] of the provinces, to come to the dedication[9] of the image which Nebuchadnezzar the king had set up.

3 Then the princes, the governors, and captains, the judges, the treasurers, the counselors, the sheriffs, and all the rulers of the provinces, were gathered together unto the dedication of the image that Nebuchadnezzar the king had set up; and they stood before the image that Nebuchadnezzar had set up.

4 Then an herald[10] cried aloud[11], To you it is commanded, O people, nations[12], and languages,

5 *That* at what time you hear the sound of the **horn**, flute, harp, sackbut, psaltery[13], dulcimer[14], and all kinds[15] of music[16], you fall down and worship the golden image that Nebuchadnezzar the king has set up:

6 And whoso falls not down and worships will the same hour[17] be cast into the midst of a burning fiery furnace.

7 Therefore[18] at that time, when all the people heard the sound of the cornet, flute, harp, sackbut, psaltery, and all kinds of music, all the people, the nations, and the languages, fell down *and* worshipped the golden image that Nebuchadnezzar the king had set up.

8 Wherefore at that time certain Chaldeans[19] came near, and accused[20] the Jews.

9 They spoke and said to the king Nebuchadnezzar, O king, live forever.

10 You, O king, have made a decree, that every man that will hear the sound of the cornet, flute, harp, sackbut, psaltery, and dulcimer, and all kinds of music, will fall down and worship the golden image:

11 And whoso falls not down and worships, *that* he should be cast into the midst of a burning fiery furnace.

12 There are certain Jews whom you have set over the affairs of the province of Babylon, Shadrach, Meshach, and Abed-nego; these men, O king, have not regarded you: they serve[21] not your gods, nor worship the golden image which you have set up.

13 Then Nebuchadnezzar in *his* rage and fury commanded to bring Shadrach, Meshach, and Abed-nego. Then they brought these men before the king.

14 Nebuchadnezzar spoke and said unto them, Is it true[22], O Shadrach, Meshach, and Abed-nego, do not you serve my gods, nor worship the golden image which I have set up?

15 Now if you be ready that at what time you hear the sound of the cornet, flute, harp, sackbut, psaltery, and dulcimer, and all kinds of music, you fall down and worship the image which I have made; *well*: but if you worship not, you will be cast the same hour into the midst of a burning fiery furnace; and who *is* that God that will deliver you out of my hands?

16 Shadrach, Meshach, and Abed-nego, answered and said to the king, O Nebuchadnezzar, we *are* not careful to answer you in this matter.

17 If it be *so*, our God whom we serve is able to deliver us from the burning fiery furnace, and he will deliver *us* out of your hand, O king.

18 But if not, be it known unto you, O king, that we will not serve your gods, nor worship the golden image which you have set up.

19 Then was Nebuchadnezzar full of fury, and the form[23] of his visage[24] was changed against Shadrach, Meshach, and Abed-nego: *therefore* he spoke, and commanded that they should heat the furnace one seven times more than it was wont[25] to be heated.

20 And he commanded the most mighty men that *were* in his army to bind Shadrach, Meshach, and Abed-nego, *and* to cast *them* into the burning fiery furnace.

21 Then these men were bound in their coats, their hosen, and their hats, and their *other* garments, and were cast into the midst of the burning fiery furnace.

22 Therefore because the king's commandment was urgent, and the furnace exceeding hot, the flame of the fire slew those men that took up Shadrach, Meshach, and Abed-nego.

23 And these three men, Shadrach, Meshach, and Abed-nego, fell down bound into the midst of the burning fiery furnace.

24 Then Nebuchadnezzar the king was atoned, and rose up in haste, *and* spoke, and said unto his counselors, Did not we cast three men bound into the midst of the fire? They answered and said unto the king, True, O king.

25 He answered and said, Lo, I see[26] four men loose, walking in the midst of the fire, and [they have no hurt][27]; and the form of the fourth is like the Son of God.

26 Then Nebuchadnezzar came near to the mouth of the burning fiery furnace, *and* spoke, and said, Shadrach, Meshach, and Abed-nego, you servants of the most high God, come forth, and come

---

[1] Nebuchadnezzar – may Nebo protect the crown [Strgs#5020]. Nebo = elevation.

[2] lit. open(ing), *roomy*, to be or make *simple* or (in a sinister way) *delude* [Strgs#6613+6601].

[3] Its 'opening' was/is 'man' (6 cubits), as 6 is the number of man.

[4] Dura – <u>circle</u> or *dwelling* [Strgs#1757].

[5] lit. a *chief*, *diviner* or *astrologer* [Strgs#148].

[6] counselors – <u>one skilled in law</u> [Strgs#1884].

[7] lit. *judicial*, a *lawyer* [Strgs#8614].

[8] lit. *dominations* [Strgs#7984+7983+7980+].

[9] lit. <u>initiations</u>, consecration, <u>to narrow</u>, <u>to discipline</u>, <u>to train up</u> [Strgs#2597+2598+2596].

[10] herald – to *proclaim*, make a proclamation [Strgs#3744+3745]. Lit. <u>Babylon's Preachers</u>.

[11] aloud – an *army*, *strength*, <u>mighty</u> [Strgs#2429].

[12] These are the places were Babylon sits.

[13] or *lyre* [Strgs#6460]

[14] or *bagpipe* (with a double pipe) [Strgs#5481]

[15] kinds – <u>nourished</u> (or <u>fully developed</u>) [Strgs#217+2177].

[16] music – *striking* with the fingers, to *touch* the strings or parts of a musical instrument, <u>lyre</u> [Strgs#2167].

[17] hour - *look*, a *moment*, to *gaze*, to *inspect*, *consider*, *compassionate*, be *nonplussed*, *bewildered*, <u>to gaze for help</u> [Strgs#8159].

[18] therefore – <u>all in front of this</u> [Strgs#6903+1836].

[19] Chaldeans – <u>clod breakers</u> [Strgs#3779].

[20] accused – ate the pieces of [Strgs#7170+399], compare **Dan. 7 7, Rev. 13:2, 2 Tim. 4:17**.

[21] serve – worship, minister, *slice*, *break* open or *pierce*. strike [Strgs#6399+6398].

[22] lit. <u>intentness</u>, a (sinister) *design* [Strgs#6656].

[23] form – an idolatrous *figure*, image [Strgs#6755].

[24] lit. *face* [Strgs#600].

[25] lit. to *gaze* upon, mentally to *dream*, be *usual*, seen on account of dream [Strgs#2370].

[26] Ibid.

[27] lit. they have no hurt or injury in them.

hither. Then Shadrach, Meshach, and Abed-nego, came forth of the midst of the fire.

27 And the princes, governors, and captains, and the king's counselors, being gathered together, saw these men, upon whose bodies the fire had no power[1], nor was a hair of their head singed, neither were their coats changed, nor the smell of fire had passed on them.

28 *Then* Nebuchadnezzar spoke, and said, Blessed *be* the God of Shadrach, Meshach, and Abed-nego, who has sent his angel, and delivered[2] his servants that trusted in him, and have changed the king's word, and yielded their bodies, that they might not serve nor worship any god, except their own God.

29 Therefore I make a decree, That every people, nation, and language, which speak anything amiss against the God of Shadrach, Meshach, and Abed-nego, will be cut in pieces, and their houses will be made a dunghill: because there is no other God that can deliver[3] after this sort.

30 Then the king promoted Shadrach, Meshach, and Abed-nego, in the province of Babylon.

CHAPTER 4

1 Nebuchadnezzar the king, unto all people, nations, and languages, that dwell in all the earth; Peace be multiplied unto you.

2 I thought it good to show the signs and wonders that the high God has wrought toward me.

3 How great *are* his signs! And how mighty *are* his wonders! His kingdom *is* an everlasting kingdom, and his dominion *is* from generation to generation.

4 I Nebuchadnezzar was at rest in mine house, and flourishing in my palace:

5 I saw a dream which made me afraid, and the thoughts upon my bed and the visions of my head troubled me.

6 Therefore made I a decree to bring in all the wise *men* of Babylon before me, that they might make known unto me the interpretation of the dream.

7 Then came in the magicians, the astrologers, the Chaldeans, and the soothsayers: and I told the dream before them; but they did not make known unto me the interpretation thereof.

8 But at the last Daniel came in before me, whose name *was* Belteshazzar, according to the name of my god, and in whom *is* the spirit of the holy gods: and before him I told the dream, *saying*,

9 O Belteshazzar, master of the magicians, because I know that the spirit of the holy gods *is* in you, and no secret troubles you, tell me the visions of my dream that I have seen, and the interpretation thereof.

10 Thus *were* the visions of mine head in my bed; I saw, and behold a tree in the midst of the earth, and the height thereof *was* great.

11 The tree grew, and was strong, and the height thereof reached unto heaven, and the sight thereof to the end of all the earth:

12 The leaves thereof *were* fair, and the fruit thereof much, and in it *was* meat for all: the beasts of the field had shadow under it, and the fowls of the heaven dwelt in the boughs thereof, and all flesh was fed of it.

13 I saw in the visions of my head upon my bed, and, behold, a watcher and an holy one came down from heaven;

14 He cried aloud, and said thus, Hew down the tree, and cut off his branches, shake off his leaves, and scatter his fruit: let the beasts get away from under it, and the fowls from his branches:

15 Nevertheless, leave the stump of his roots in the earth, even with a band of iron and brass, in the tender grass of the field; and let it be wet with the dew of heaven, and *let* his portion *be* with the beasts in the grass of the earth:

16 Let his heart be changed from man's, and let a beast's heart be given unto him; and let seven times pass over him.

17 This matter *is* by the decree of the watchers, and the demand by the word of the holy ones: to the intent that the living may know that the most High rules in the kingdom of men, and gives it to whomsoever he will, and sets up over it the basest of men.

18 This dream I king Nebuchadnezzar have seen. Now you, O Belteshazzar, declare the interpretation thereof, forasmuch as all the wise *men* of my kingdom are not able to make known unto me the interpretation: but you *are* able; for the spirit of the holy gods *is* in you.

19 Then Daniel, whose name *was* Belteshazzar, was atoned for one hour, and his thoughts troubled him. The king spoke, and said, Belteshazzar, let not the dream, or the interpretation thereof, trouble you. Belteshazzar answered and said, My lord, the dream *be* to them that hate you, and the interpretation thereof to your enemies.

20 The tree that you saw, which grew, and was strong, whose height reached unto the heaven, and the sight thereof to all the earth;

21 Whose leaves *were* fair, and the fruit thereof much, and in it *was* meat for all; under which the beasts of the field dwelt, and upon whose branches the fowls of the heaven had their habitation:

22 It *is* you, O king, that are grown and become strong: for your greatness is grown, and reaches unto heaven, and your dominion to the end of the earth.

23 And whereas the king saw a watcher and an holy one coming down from heaven, and saying, Hew the tree down, and destroy it; yet leave the stump of the roots thereof in the earth, even with a band of iron and brass, in the tender grass of the field; and let it be wet with the dew of heaven, and *let* his portion *be* with the beasts of the field, till seven times pass over him;

24 This *is* the interpretation, O king, and this *is* the decree of the most High, which is come upon my lord the king:

25 That they will drive you from men, and your dwelling will be with the beasts of the field, and they will make you to eat grass as oxen, and they will wet you with the dew of heaven, and seven times will pass over you, till you know that the most High rules in the kingdom of men, and gives it to whomsoever he will.

26 And whereas they commanded to leave the stump of the tree roots; your kingdom will be sure unto you, after that you will have known that the heavens do rule.

27 Wherefore, O king, let my counsel be acceptable unto you, and break off your sins by righteousness, and your iniquities by showing mercy to the poor; if it may be a lengthening of your tranquility.

28 All this came upon the king Nebuchadnezzar.

29 At the end of twelve months he walked in the palace of the kingdom of Babylon.

---

[1] power – <u>dominance</u>, ruler, have the mastery [Strgs#7981].
[2] delievered – is the Hebrew word *shezab* meaning to <u>leave</u>, *free* [Strgs#7804].

[3] deliver – is the Hebrew word *netsal* meaning to *extricate*, *to snatch away* [Strgs#5338+5337].

30 The king spoke, and said, Is not this great Babylon, that I have built for the house of the kingdom by the might of my power, and for the honor of my majesty?
31 While the word *was* in the king's mouth, there fell a voice from heaven, *saying*, O king Nebuchadnezzar, to you it is spoken; The kingdom is departed from you.
32 And they will drive you from men, and your dwelling *will be* with the beasts of the field: they will make you to eat grass as oxen, and seven times will pass over you, until you know that the most High rules in the kingdom of men, and gives it to whomsoever he will.
33 The same hour was the thing fulfilled upon Nebuchadnezzar: and he was driven from men, and did eat grass as oxen, and his body was wet with the dew of heaven, till his hairs were grown like eagles' *feathers*, and his nails like birds' *claws*.
34 And at the end of the days I Nebuchadnezzar lifted up mine eyes unto heaven, and mine understanding returned unto me, and I blessed the most High, and I praised and honored him that lives forever, whose dominion *is* an everlasting dominion, and his kingdom *is* from generation to generation:
35 And all the inhabitants of the earth *are* reputed as nothing: and he does according to his will in the army of heaven, and *among* the inhabitants of the earth: and none can stay his hand, or say unto him, **What have you done**?
36 At the same time my reason returned unto me; and for the glory of my kingdom, mine honor and brightness returned unto me; and my counselors and my lords sought unto me; and I was established in my kingdom, and excellent majesty was added unto me.
37 Now I Nebuchadnezzar praise and extol and honor the King of heaven, all whose works *are* truth, and his ways judgment: and those that walk in pride he is able to abase.

CHAPTER 5

1 Belshazzar the king made a great feast to a thousand of his lords, and drank wine before the thousand.
2 Belshazzar, whiles he tasted the wine, commanded to bring the golden and silver vessels which his father Nebuchadnezzar had taken out of the temple which *was* in Jerusalem; that the king, and his princes, his wives, and his concubines, might drink therein.
3 Then they brought the golden vessels that were taken out of the temple of the house of God which *was* at Jerusalem; and the king, and his princes, his wives, and his concubines, drank in them.
4 They drank wine, and praised the gods of gold, and of silver, of brass, of iron, of wood, and of stone.
5 In the same hour came forth fingers of a man's hand, and wrote over against the candlestick upon the plaster of the wall of the king's palace: and the king saw the part of the hand that wrote.
6 Then the king's countenance was changed, and his thoughts troubled him, so that the joints of his loins were loosed, and his knees smote one against another.
7 The king cried aloud to bring in the astrologers, the Chaldeans, and the soothsayers. *And* the king spoke, and said to the wise *men* of Babylon, Whosoever will read this writing, and show me the interpretation thereof, will be clothed with scarlet, and *have* a chain of gold about his neck, and will be the third ruler in the kingdom.
8 Then came in all the king's wise *men*: but they could not read the writing, nor make known to the king the interpretation thereof.
9 Then was king Belshazzar greatly troubled, and his countenance was changed in him, and his lords were atoned.

10 *Now* the queen, by reason of the words of the king and his lords, came into the banquet house: *and* the queen spoke and said, O king, live forever: let not your thoughts trouble you, nor let your countenance be changed:
11 There is a man in your kingdom, in whom *is* the spirit of the holy gods; and in the days of your father light and understanding and wisdom, like the wisdom of the gods, was found in him; whom the king Nebuchadnezzar your father, the king, *I say*, your father, made master of the magicians, astrologers, Chaldeans, *and* soothsayers;
12 Forasmuch as an excellent spirit, and knowledge, and understanding, interpreting of dreams, and showing of hard sentences, and dissolving of doubts, were found in the same Daniel, whom the king named Belteshazzar: now let Daniel be called, and he will show the interpretation.
13 Then was Daniel brought in before the king. *And* the king spoke and said unto Daniel, *Are* you that Daniel, which *are* of the children of the captivity of Judah, whom the king my father brought out of Jewry?
14 I have even heard of you, that the spirit of the gods *is* in you, and *that* light and understanding and excellent wisdom is found in you.
15 And now the wise *men*, the astrologers, have been brought in before me, that they should read this writing, and make known unto me the interpretation thereof: but they could not show the interpretation of the thing:
16 And I have heard of you, that you can make interpretations, and dissolve doubts: now if you canst read the writing, and make known to me the interpretation thereof, you will be clothed with scarlet, and *have* a chain of gold about your neck, and will be the third ruler in the kingdom.
17 Then Daniel answered and said before the king, let your gifts be to yourself, and give your rewards[1] to another; yet I will read the writing unto the king, and make known to him the interpretation.
18 O you king, the most high God gave Nebuchadnezzar your father a kingdom, and majesty, and glory, and honor:
19 And for the majesty that he gave him, all people, nations, and languages, trembled and feared before him: whom he would he slew; and whom he would he kept alive; and whom he would he set up; and whom he would he put down.
20 But when his heart was lifted up, and his mind hardened in pride, he was deposed from his kingly throne, and they took his glory from him:
21 And he was driven from the sons of men; and his heart was made like the beasts, and his dwelling *was* with the wild asses: they fed him with grass like oxen, and his body was wet with the dew of heaven; till he knew that the most high God ruled in the kingdom of men, and *that* he appoints over it whomsoever he will.
22 And you his son, O Belshazzar, have not humbled your heart, though you knew all this;
23 But have lifted up yourself against the Lord of heaven; and they have brought the vessels of his house before you, and you, and your lords, your wives, and your concubines, have drunk wine in them; and you have praised the gods of silver, and gold, of brass, iron, wood, and stone, which see not, nor hear, nor know: and the God in whose hand your breath *is*, and whose *are* all your ways, have you not glorified:
24 Then was the part of the hand sent from him; and this writing was written.

---

[1] reward – a largess [Strgs#5023]

25 And this *is* the writing that was written, MENE, MENE, TEKEL, UPHARSIN.
26 This *is* the interpretation of the thing: MENE; God has numbered your kingdom, and finished it.
27 TEKEL; You are weighed in the balances, and are found wanting.
28 PERES; Your kingdom is divided, and given to the Medes and Persians.
29 Then commanded Belshazzar, and they clothed Daniel with scarlet, and *put* a chain of gold about his neck, and made a proclamation concerning him, that he should be the third ruler in the kingdom.
30 In that night was Belshazzar the king of the Chaldeans slain.
31 And Darius[1] the Median took the kingdom, *being* about threescore and two years old.

CHAPTER 6

1 It pleased Darius to set over the kingdom an hundred and twenty princes, which should be over the whole kingdom;
2 And over these three presidents; of whom Daniel *was* first: that the princes might give accounts unto them, and the king should have no damage.
3 Then this Daniel was preferred above the presidents and princes, because an excellent spirit *was* in him; and the king thought to set him over the whole realm.
4 Then the presidents and princes sought to find occasion against Daniel concerning the kingdom; but they could find none occasion nor fault; forasmuch as he *was* faithful, neither was there any error or fault found in him.
5 Then said these men, We will not find any occasion against this Daniel, except we find *it* against him concerning the law of his God.
6 Then these presidents and princes assembled together to the king, and said thus unto him, King Darius, live forever.
7 All the presidents of the kingdom, the governors, and the princes, the counselors, and the captains, have consulted together to establish a royal statute, and to make a firm decree, that whosoever will ask a petition of any God or man for thirty days, save of you, O king, he will be cast into the den of lions.
8 Now, O king, establish the decree, and sign the writing, that it be not changed, according to the law of the Medes and Persians, which alters not.
9 Wherefore king Darius signed the writing and the decree.
10 Now when Daniel knew that the writing was signed, he went into his house; and his windows being open in his chamber toward Jerusalem, he kneeled upon his knees three times a day, and prayed, and gave thanks before his God, as he did aforetime.
11 Then these men assembled, and found Daniel praying and making supplication before his God.
12 Then they came near, and spoke before the king concerning the king's decree; Have you not signed a decree, that every man that will ask *a petition* of any God or man within thirty days, save of you, O king, will be cast into the den of lions? The king answered and said, the thing *is* true, according to the law of the Medes and Persians, which alters not.
13 Then answered they and said before the king, That Daniel, which *is* of the children of the captivity of Judah, regards not you, O king, nor the decree that you have signed, but makes his petition three times a day.
14 Then the king, when he heard *these* words, was sore displeased with himself, and set *his* heart on Daniel to deliver him: and he labored till the going down of the sun to deliver him.
15 Then these men assembled unto the king, and said unto the king, Know, O king, that the law of the Medes and Persians *is*, That no decree nor statute which the king establishes may be changed.
16 Then the king commanded, and they brought Daniel, and cast *him* into the den of lions. *Now* the king spoke and said unto Daniel, Your God whom you serves continually, he will deliver you.
17 And a stone was brought, and laid upon the mouth of the den; and the king sealed it with his own signet, and with the signet of his lords; that the purpose might not be changed concerning Daniel.
18 Then the king went to his palace, and passed the night fasting: neither were instruments of music brought before him: and his sleep went from him.
19 Then the king arose very early in the morning, and went in haste unto the den of lions.
20 And when he came to the den, he cried with a lamentable voice unto Daniel: *and* the king spoke and said to Daniel, O Daniel, servant of the living God, is your God, whom you serves continually, able to deliver you from the lions?
21 Then said Daniel unto the king, O king, live forever.
22 My God has sent his angel, and has shut the lions' mouths, that they have not hurt me: forasmuch as before him innocence was found in me; and also before you, O king, have I done no hurt.
23 Then was the king exceeding glad for him, and commanded that they should take Daniel up out of the den. So Daniel was taken up out of the den, and no manner of hurt was found upon him, because he believed in his God.
24 And the king commanded, and they brought those men which had accused Daniel, and they cast *them* into the den of lions, them, their children, and their wives; and the lions had the mastery of them, and brake all their bones in pieces or ever they came at the bottom of the den.
25 Then king Darius wrote unto all people, nations, and languages, that dwell in all the earth; Peace[2] be multiplied unto you.
26 I make a decree, That in every dominion of my kingdom men tremble and fear before the God of Daniel: for he *is* the living God, and steadfast forever, and his kingdom *that* which will not be destroyed, and his dominion *will be even* unto the end.
27 He delivers and rescues, and he works signs and wonders in heaven and in earth, who has delivered Daniel from the power of the lions.
28 So this Daniel prospered in the reign of Darius, and in the reign of Cyrus the Persian.

CHAPTER 7

1 In the first year of Belshazzar king of Babylon Daniel had a dream and visions of his head upon his bed: then he wrote the dream, *and* told the sum of the matters.
2 Daniel spoke and said, I saw in my vision by night, and, behold, the four winds of the heaven strove upon the great sea.
3 And four great beasts came up from the sea, diverse one from another.
4 The first *was* like a lion, and had eagle's wings: I beheld till the wings thereof were plucked, and it was lifted up from the earth, and made stand upon the feet as a man, and a man's heart *was* given to it.

---

[1] see Index

[2] peace – is the Hebrew word *shelâm*, meaning *prosperity* [Strgs#8001].

5 And behold another beast, a second, like to a bear, and it **rose** up itself on one side, and *it had* three ribs in the mouth of it between the teeth of it: and they said thus unto it, Arise, devour much flesh.
6 After this I beheld, and lo another, like a leopard, which had upon the back of it four wings of a fowl; the beast had also four heads; and dominion was given to it.
7 After this I saw in the night visions, and behold a fourth beast, dreadful[1] and terrible, and strong exceedingly; and it had great iron teeth: it devoured and brakes in pieces, and stamped the residue with the feet of it: and it *was* diverse from all the beasts that *were* before it; and it had ten horns.
8 I considered the horns, and, behold, there came up among them another little horn, before whom there were three of the first horns plucked up by the roots: and, behold, in this horn *were* eyes like the eyes of man, and a mouth speaking[2] great things.
9 I beheld till the thrones were cast down, and the Ancient of days did sit, whose garment *was* white as snow, and the hair of his head like the pure wool: his throne *was like* the fiery flame, *and* his wheels *as* burning fire.
10 A fiery stream issued and came forth from before him: thousand thousands ministered[3] unto him, and ten thousand times ten thousand stood before him: the judgment was set, and the books were opened.
11 I beheld then because of the voice of the great words which the horn spoke: I beheld *even* till the beast was slain, and his body destroyed, and given to the burning flame.
12 As concerning the rest of the beasts, they had their dominion taken away: yet their lives were prolonged for a season and time.
13 I saw in the night visions, and, behold, *one* like the Son of man came with the clouds of heaven, and came to the Ancient of days, and they brought him near before him.
14 And there was given him dominion, and glory, and a kingdom, that all people, nations, and languages, should serve him: his dominion *is* an everlasting dominion, which will not pass away, and his kingdom *that* which will not be destroyed.
15 I Daniel was grieved in my spirit in the midst of *my* body, and the visions of my head troubled me.
16 I came near unto one of them that stood by, and asked him the truth of all this. So he told me, and made me know the interpretation of the things.
17 These great beasts, which are four, *are* four kings, *which* will arise out of the earth.
18 But the saints of the most High will take the kingdom, and possess the kingdom forever, even forever and ever.
19 Then I would know the truth of the fourth beast, which was diverse from all the others, exceeding dreadful, whose teeth *were of* iron[4], and his nails *of* brass; *which* devoured, brake in pieces, and stamped the residue[5] with his feet;
20 And of the ten horns that *were* in his head, and *of* the other which came up, and before whom three fell[6]; *even of* that horn that had eyes, and a mouth that spoke very great things, whose look[7] *was* more stout[8] than his fellows.
21 I beheld, and the same horn made war with the saints, and prevailed against them;
22 Until the Ancient of days came, and judgment was given to the saints of the most High; and the time came that the saints possessed the kingdom.
23 Thus he said, The fourth beast will be the fourth kingdom upon earth, which will be diverse[9] from all kingdoms, and will devour the whole earth, and will tread it down, and break it in pieces.
24 And the ten horns out of this kingdom *are* ten kings *that* will arise: and another will rise after them; and he will be diverse from the first, and he will subdue three kings.
25 And he will speak *great* words against the most High, and will wear out the saints of the most High, and think to change[10] times and laws: and they will be given into his hand until a time and times and the dividing of time.
26 But the judgment will sit, and they[11] will take away his dominion, to consume and to destroy *it* until[12] the end.
27 And the kingdom and dominion, and the greatness of the kingdom under the whole heaven, will be given to the people of the saints of the most High, whose kingdom *is* an everlasting kingdom, and all dominions will serve and obey him.
28 Hitherto[13] *is* the end of the matter. As for me Daniel, my cogitations much troubled me, and my countenance changed in me: but I kept the matter in my heart.

CHAPTER 8

1 In the third year of the reign of king Belshazzar a vision appeared unto me, *even unto* me Daniel, after that which appeared unto me at the first.
2 And I saw in a vision; and it came to pass, when I saw, that I *was* at Shushan *in* the palace, which *is* in the province of Elam[14]; and I saw in a vision, and I was by the river of Ulai[15].
3 Then I lifted up mine eyes, and saw, and, behold, there stood before the river a ram which had *two* horns: and the *two* horns *were* high; but one *was* higher than the other, and the higher came up last.
4 I saw the ram pushing westward, and northward, and southward; so that no beasts might stand before him, neither *was there any* that could deliver out of his hand; but he did according to his will, and became great.
5 And as I was considering, behold, an he goat came from the west on the face of the whole earth, and touched not the ground: and the goat *had* a [notable horn][16] between his eyes.
6 And he came to the ram that had *two* horns, which I had seen standing before the river, and ran unto him in the fury of his power.
7 And I saw him come close unto the ram, and he was moved with choler against him, and smote the ram, and brake his two horns: and there was no power in the ram to stand before him, but he cast

---

[1] lit. to *slink*, to *fear*, *be formidable*, crawl, serpent, worm [Strgs#1763+2119].
[2] speak – derives from the Hebrew root word *mâlal*, meaning to *speak* (mostly poetical), *utter* [Strgs#4448].
[3] ministered – is the Hebrew word *shemash* the idea of *activity* implied in daylight, to *serve* [Strgs#8120]. Derives from the Hebrew root word *shemesh* meaning to be *brilliant*, the sun, a *ray*, *battlement* [Strgs#8121]. Compare **Matthew 13:43**.
[4] lit. *iron* as cutting, by extension an iron *implement*, axe head [Strgs#6523+1270]. Compare **Rev. 20:4**.
[5] lit. remainder, remnant, rest [Strgs#7606+7605]. Compare **Rev. 12:7**.
[6] Shows how fragile the kingdom will be: iron/way.

[7] lit. vision, a *sight* [Strgs#2376].
[8] stout – great chief, master, domineer [Strgs#7229].
[9] diverse – change, alter, sleep [Strgs#8133]. His diversity is to cdause 'sleep'.
[10] Ibid.
[11] I saw thrones and they that sat....
[12] Strgs#5705
[13] lit. until, like this, is the end of the world [Strgs#5705+3542].
[14] Elam – hidden, distant, eternity, time out of mind [Strgs#5867].
[15] lit. my leaders [Strgs#195]. A river in Persia.
[16] lit. a horn of vision/sight [Strgs#2380+2372].

him down to the ground, and stamped upon him: and there was none that could deliver the ram out of his hand.

8 Therefore the he goat waxed very great: and when he was strong, the great horn was broken; and for it came up four notable ones toward the four winds of heaven.

9 And out of one¹ of them came forth a little² horn, which waxed exceeding great, toward the south, and toward the east, and toward the pleasant *land*.

10 And it waxed great, *even* to the host of heaven; and it cast down *some* of the host and of the stars to the ground, and stamped upon them.

11 Yes, he magnified *himself* even to the prince of the host, and by him the daily *sacrifice* was taken away, and the place of his sanctuary was cast down.

12 And an host was given *him* against the daily *sacrifice* by reason of transgression, and it cast down the truth to the ground; and it practiced, and prospered.

13 Then I heard one saint speaking, and another saint said unto that certain³ *saint* which spoke, How long *will be* the vision concerning the daily *sacrifice*, and the transgression of desolation, to give both the sanctuary and the host to be trodden under foot?

14 And he said unto me, Unto two thousand and three hundred days; then will the sanctuary be cleansed.

15 And it came to pass, when I, *even* I Daniel, had seen the vision, and sought for the meaning, then, behold, there stood before me as the appearance of a man.

16 And I heard a man's voice between *the banks of* Ulai⁴, which called, and said, Gabriel, make this *man* to understand the vision⁵.

17 So he came near where I stood: and when he came, I was afraid, and fell upon my face: but he said unto me, Understand, O son of man: for at the time of the end *will be* the vision.

18 Now as he was speaking with me, I was in a deep sleep on my face toward the ground: but he touched me, and set me upright.

19 And he said, Behold, I will make you know what will be in the last end of the indignation: for at the time appointed the end *will be*.

20 The ram which you saw having *two* horns *are* the kings of Media and Persia.

21 And the [rough goat]⁶ *is* the king of Grecia: and the great horn that *is* between his eyes *is* the first king.

22 Now that being broken, whereas four stood up for it, four kingdoms will stand up out of the nation, but not in his power.

23 And in the latter time of their kingdom, when the transgressors are come to the full, a king of fierce countenance, and understanding dark sentences, will stand up.

24 And his power will be mighty, but not by his own power: and he will destroy wonderfully, and will prosper, and practice, and will destroy the mighty and the holy people.

25 And through his policy also he will cause craft to prosper in his hand; and he will magnify *himself* in his heart, and by peace will destroy many: he will also stand up against the Prince of princes; but he will be broken without hand.

26 And the vision of the evening and the morning which was told *is* true: wherefore shut you up the vision; for it *will be* for many days.

27 And I Daniel fainted, and was sick *certain* days; afterward I rose up, and did the king's business; and I was astonished at the vision, but none understood *it*.

CHAPTER 9

1 In the first year of Darius the son of Ahasuerus⁷, of the seed of the Medes, which was made king over the realm of the Chaldeans;

2 In the first year of his reign I Daniel understood by books the number of the years, whereof the word of the LORD came to Jeremiah the prophet, that he would accomplish seventy years in the desolations of Jerusalem.

3 And I set my face unto the Lord God, to seek by prayer and supplications, with fasting, and sackcloth, and ashes

4 And I prayed unto the LORD my God, and made my confession, and said, O Lord, the great and dreadful God, keeping the covenant and mercy to them that love him, and to them that keep his commandments;

5 We have sinned, and have committed iniquity, and have done wickedly, and have rebelled, even by departing from your precepts and from your judgments:

6 Neither have we hearkened unto your servants the prophets, which spoke in your name to our kings, our princes, and our fathers, and to all the people of the land.

7 O Lord, righteousness *belongs* unto you, but unto us confusion of faces, as at this day; to the men of Judah, and to the inhabitants of Jerusalem, and unto all Israel, *that are* near, and *that are* far off, through all the countries where you have driven them because of their trespass that they have trespassed against you.

8 O Lord, to us *belongs* confusion of face, to our kings, to our princes, and to our fathers, because we have sinned against you.

9 To the Lord our God *belong* mercies and **forgiveness's**, though we have rebelled against him;

10 Neither have we obeyed the voice of the LORD our God, to walk in his laws, which he set before us by his servants the prophets.

11 Yes, all Israel have transgressed your law, even by departing, that they might not obey your voice; therefore the curse is poured upon us, and the oath that *is* written in the Law of Moses the servant of God, because we have sinned against him.

12 And he has confirmed his words, which he spoke against us, and against our judges that judged us, by bringing upon us a great evil: for under the whole heaven has not been done as has been done upon Jerusalem.

13 As *it is* written in the law of Moses, all this evil is come upon us: yet made we not our prayer before the LORD our God, that we might turn from our iniquities, and understand your truth.

14 Therefore has the LORD watched upon the evil, and brought it upon us: for the LORD our God *is* righteous in all his works which he doeth: for we obeyed not his voice.

15 And now, O Lord our God, that have brought your people forth out of the land of Egypt with a mighty hand, and have gotten you renown, as at this day; we have sinned, we have done wickedly.

16 O Lord, according to all your righteousness, I beseech you, let your anger and your fury be turned away from your city Jerusalem, your holy mountain: because for our sins, and for the iniquities of our fathers, Jerusalem and your people *are become* a reproach to all *that are* about us.

---

¹ lit. the *first* [Strgs#259].
² lit. for a short space/time [Strgs#4705].
³ certain – wonderful, secret, a specific *person, distinguish* [Strgs#6422+6423+6395]. Speaks of Jesus.
⁴ Ulai- my leaders (mighties). Of Persian derivation; the *Ulai* (or Eulaeus A), a river of Persia.
⁵ Translate as pattern, a *view, appearance, comeliness* [Strgs#4758]
⁶ compare **Lev. 17:7**
⁷ see Index

17 Now therefore, O our God, hear the prayer of your servant, and his supplications, and cause your face to shine upon your sanctuary that is desolate, for the Lord's sake.
18 O my God, incline your ear, and hear; open your eyes, and behold our desolations, and the city which is called by your name: for we do not present our supplications before you for our **righteousness's**, but for your great mercies.
19 O Lord, hear; O Lord, forgive; O Lord, hearken and do; defer not, for your own sake, O my God: for your city and your people are called by your name.
20 And whiles I *was* speaking, and praying, and confessing my sin and the sin of my people Israel, and presenting my supplication before the LORD my God for the holy mountain of my God;
21 Yes, whiles I *was* speaking in prayer, even the man Gabriel, whom I had seen in the vision at the beginning, [being caused to fly swiftly][1], touched me about the time of the evening oblation.
22 And he informed *me*, and talked with me, and said, O Daniel, I am now come forth to give you skill and understanding.
23 At the beginning of your supplications the commandment came forth, and I am come to show *you*; for you *are* greatly beloved: therefore understand the matter, and consider the vision.
24 Seventy weeks are determined upon your people and upon your holy city, to finish[2] the transgression[3], and to make an end of sins, and to make reconciliation[4] for iniquity, and to bring in everlasting righteousness, and to seal up the vision and prophecy, and to anoint the most Holy.
25 Know therefore and understand, *that* from the going forth of the commandment to restore and to build Jerusalem unto the Messiah the Prince[5] *will be* seven weeks, and threescore and two weeks: the street will be built again, and the wall[6], even in troublous times.
26 And after threescore and two weeks will Messiah be cut off, but not for himself: and the people of the prince that will come will destroy[7] the city and the sanctuary; and the end thereof *will be* with a flood, and unto the end of the war desolations are determined.
27 And he will confirm the covenant with many for one week: and in the midst of the week he will cause the sacrifice and the oblation to cease, and for the overspreading[8] of abominations he will make *it* desolate[9], even until the consummation, and that determined[10] will be poured upon the desolate.

CHAPTER 10

1 In the third year of Cyrus king of Persia a thing was revealed unto Daniel, whose name was called Belteshazzar; and the thing *was* true, but [the time appointed][11] *was* long: and he understood the thing[12], and had understanding of the vision[13].
2 In those days I Daniel was mourning three full weeks.
3 I ate no pleasant bread, neither came flesh nor wine in my mouth, neither did I anoint myself at all, till three whole weeks were fulfilled.
4 And in the four and twentieth day of the first month, as I was by the side of the great river, which *is* Hiddekel[14];
5 Then I lifted up mine eyes, and looked, and behold a certain man clothed in linen, whose loins *were* girded with fine gold[15] of Uphaz[16]:
6 His body also *was* like the beryl, and his face[17] as the appearance of lightning, and his eyes as lamps of fire, and his arms and his feet like in color[18] to polished brass, and the voice of his words like the voice of a multitude.
7 And I Daniel alone saw the vision: for the men that were with me saw not the vision[19]; but a great quaking fell upon them so that they fled to hide themselves.
8 Therefore I was left alone, and saw this great vision, and there remained no strength in me: for my comeliness was turned in me into corruption, and I retained no strength.
9 Yet heard I the voice of his words: and when I heard the voice of his words, then was I in a deep sleep on my face, and my face toward the ground.
10 And, behold, an hand touched me, which set me upon my knees and *upon* the palms of my hands.
11 And he said unto me, O Daniel, a man greatly beloved, understand the words that I speak unto you, and stand upright: for unto you am I now sent. And when he had spoken this word unto me, I stood trembling.
12 Then said he unto me, Fear not, Daniel: for from the first day that you did set your heart to understand, and to [chasten yourself][20] before your God, your words were heard, and I am come for your words.
13 But the prince of the kingdom[21] of Persia [withstood me][22] one and twenty days: but, lo, Michael, one of the chief princes, came to help me; and I remained there with the kings of Persia.
14 Now I am come to make you understand what will befall your people in the latter days: for yet the vision *is* for *many* days.
15 And when he had spoken such words unto me, I set my face toward the ground, and I became dumb[23].
16 And, behold, *one* like the similitude of the sons of men touched my lips: then I opened my mouth, and spoke, and said unto him that stood before me, O my lord, by the vision my sorrows are turned upon me, and I have retained no strength.
17 For how can the servant of this my lord talk with this my lord? For as for me, straightway there remained no strength in me, neither is there breath left in me.

---

[1] lit. *tire, utterly, exhausted* [Strgs#3286+3288].
[2] finish – *restrict, prohibit* [Strgs#3607].
[3] lit. *revolt* (national, moral or religious), rebellion, sin [Strgs#6588]
[4] reconciliation – *to cover*, to *cancel* or *placate* [Strgs#3722].
[5] Prince – a commander, leader [Strgs#5057].
[6] wall – *incised, decision, threshing sledge, determination, eager,* fine gold, pointed things, *threshing instrument* [Strgs#2742]. Compare **Isaiah 28:7, Amos 1:5, Isaiah 41:15, 2 Chron. 7:18, Haggai 2:15, Joel 3:14**.
[7] lit. *decay* [Strgs#7843]
[8] lit. *edge* or *extremity* [Strgs#3671].
[9] Greek translation reads 'and upon the temple shall be an abomination of desolation and upon the wing (extremity) of the abomination one causing desolation.'
[10] determined – to *point sharply*, to *wound*, to be *alert*, to *decide* [Strgs#2782].
[11] lit. *war, hardship, a mass for war, campaign* [Strgs#6635].
[12] lit. *word* [Strgs#1697].
[13] lit. *pattern* [Strgs#4758].
[14] Hiddekel – translate as *rapid* [Strgs#2313]. One of the rivers of Eden which coursed east toward Assyria; better known as the Tigris (the LXX equivalent).
[15] gold – something *carved out, ore*; hence *gold* [Strgs#3800]. Comes from a Hebrew root word meaning to *carve, engrave, inscribe*, *mark* [Strgs#3799].
[16] Uphaz – *desire of fine gold* [Strgs#210].
[17] plural *faces* [Strgs#6440].
[18] lit. *eye* [Strgs#5869]
[19] feminie *vision* or *mirror* [Strgs#4759].
[20] compare **Ps. 35:13**
[21] lit. *rule, dominion* [Strgs#4438].
[22] compare Daniel 10:13
[23] dumb – is the Hebrew word *'ălam* meaning *tongue tied* [Strgs#481]. A sign of understanding is to be tongue tied.

18 Then there came again and touched me *one* like the appearance of a man, and he strengthened me,

19 And said, O man greatly beloved, fear not: peace *be* unto you, be strong, yes, be strong. And when he had spoken unto me, I was strengthened, and said, Let my lord speak; for you have strengthened me.

20 Then said he, Know you wherefore I come unto you? And now will I return to fight with the prince of Persia: and when I am gone forth, lo, the prince of Grecia will come.

21 But I will show you that which is noted in the scripture of truth: and *there is* none that holds with me in these things, but Michael your prince.

CHAPTER 11

1 Also I in the first year of Darius the Mede, *even* I, stood to confirm and to strengthen him.

2 And now will I show you the truth. Behold, there will stand up yet three kings in Persia; and the fourth will be far richer than *they* all: and by his strength through his riches he will stir up all against the realm of Grecia.

3 And a mighty king will stand up, that will rule with great dominion, and do according to his will.

4 And when he will stand up, his kingdom will be broken, and will be divided toward the four winds of heaven; and not to his posterity, nor according to his dominion which he ruled: for his kingdom will be plucked up, even for others beside those.

5 And the king of the south will be strong, and *one* of his princes; and he will be strong above him, and have dominion; his dominion *will be* a great dominion.

6 And in the end of years they will join themselves together; for the king's daughter of the south will come to the king of the north to make an agreement: but she will not retain the power of the arm; neither will he stand, nor his arm: but she will be given up, and they that brought her, and he that begat her, and he that strengthened her in *these* times.

7 But out of a branch of her roots will *one* stand up in his estate, which will come with an army, and will enter into the fortress of the king of the north, and will deal against them, and will prevail:

8 And will also carry captives into Egypt their gods, with their princes, *and* with their precious vessels of silver and of gold; and he will continue *more* years than the king of the north.

9 So the king of the south will come into *his* kingdom, and will return into his own land.

10 But his sons will be stirred up, and will assemble a multitude of great forces: and *one* will certainly come, and overflow, and pass through: then will he return, and be stirred up, *even* to his fortress.

11 And the king of the south will be moved with choler, and will come forth and fight with him, *even* with the king of the north: and he will set forth a great multitude; but the multitude will be given into his hand.

12 *And* when he has taken away the multitude, his heart will be lifted up; and he will cast down *many* ten thousands: but he will not be strengthened *by it*.

13 For the king of the north will return, and will set forth a multitude greater than the former, and will certainly come after certain years with a great army and with much riches.

14 And in those times there will many stand up against the king of the south: also the robbers of your people will exalt themselves to establish the vision; but they will fall.

15 So the king of the north will come, and cast up a mount, and take the most fenced cities: and the arms of the south will not withstand, neither his chosen people, neither *will there be any* strength to withstand.

16 But he that cometh against him will do according to his own will, and none will stand before him: and he will stand in the glorious land, which by his hand will be consumed.

17 He will also set his face to enter with the strength of his whole kingdom, and upright ones with him; thus will he do: and he will give him the daughter of women, corrupting her: but she will not stand *on his side*, neither be for him.

18 After this will he turn his face unto the isles, and will take many: but a prince for his own behalf will cause the reproach offered by him to cease; without his own reproach he will cause *it* to turn upon him.

19 Then he will turn his face toward the fort of his own land: but he will stumble and fall, and not be found.

20 Then will stand up in his estate a raiser of taxes *in* the glory of the kingdom: but within few days he will be destroyed, neither in anger, nor in battle.

21 And in his estate will stand up a vile person, to whom they will not give the honor of the kingdom: but he will come in peaceably, and obtain the kingdom by flatteries.

22 And with the arms of a flood will they be overflown[1] from before him, and will be broken; yes, also the prince of the covenant.

23 And after the league *made* with him he will work deceitfully: for he will come up, and will become strong with a small people.

24 He will enter peaceably even upon the fattest places of the province; and he will do *that* which his fathers have not done, nor his fathers' fathers; he will scatter among them the prey, and spoil, and riches: *yes*, and he will forecast his devices against the strong holds, even for a time.

25 And he will stir up his power and his courage against the king of the south with a great army; and the king of the south will be stirred up to battle with a very great and mighty army; but he will not stand: for they will forecast devices against him.

26 Yes, they that feed of the portion of his meat will destroy him, and his army will overflow: and many will fall down slain

27 And both these kings' hearts *will be* to do mischief, and they will speak lies at one table; but it will not prosper: for yet the end *will be* at the time appointed.

28 Then will he return into his land with great riches; and his heart *will be* against the holy covenant; and he will do *exploits*, and return to his own land.

29 At the time appointed he will return, and come toward the south; but it will not be as the former, or as the latter.

30 For the ships of Chittim will come against him: therefore he will be grieved, and return, and have indignation against the holy covenant: so will he do; he will even return, and have intelligence with them that forsake the holy covenant.

31 And arms[2] will stand on his part, and they will pollute the sanctuary of strength, and will take away the daily *sacrifice*, and they will place[3] the abomination that makes desolate.

---

[1] lit. to gush; by implication to inundate, cleanse; by analogy to gallop, conquer:- frown, (over-) flow (-whelm), rinse, run, rush, (thoroughly) wash (away). [Strgs#7857]

[2] arms – as *stretched* out, *foreleg*, *force* [Strgs#2220]. Derives from a root word meaning to <u>sow a seed</u>, *disseminate*, *plant*, *fructify* [Strgs#2232].

[3] lit. *give* [Strgs#5414]

32 And such as do wickedly against the covenant will he corrupt[1] by flatteries: but the people that do know their God will be strong, and do *exploits*.

33 And they that understand among the people will instruct many: yet they will fall by the sword, and by flame, by captivity, and by spoil, *many* days.

34 Now when they will fall, they will be holpen with a little help: but many will cleave to them with flatteries.

35 And *some* of them of understanding will fall[2], to try them, and to purge[3], and to make *them* white, *even* to the time of the end: because[4] *it is* yet for a time appointed.

36 And the king will do according to his will; and he will exalt himself, and magnify himself above every god, and will speak marvelous things against the God of gods, and will prosper till the indignation be accomplished: for that that is determined will be done.

37 Neither will he regard the God of his fathers, nor the desire of women, nor regard any god: for he will magnify himself above all.

38 But in his estate[5] will he honor the God of forces: and a god whom his fathers knew not will he honor with gold, and silver, and with precious stones, and pleasant things.

39 Thus will he do in the most strong[6] holds with a strange god, whom he will acknowledge *and* increase with glory: and he will cause them to rule over many, and will divide the land for gain.

40 And at the time of the end will the king of the south push at him: and the king of the north will come against him like a whirlwind, with chariots, and with horsemen, and with many ships; and he will enter into the countries, and will overflow and pass over.

41 He will enter also into the glorious land, and many *countries* will be overthrown: but these will escape out of his hand, *even* Edom, and Moab, and the chief of the children of Ammon.

42 He will stretch forth his hand also upon the countries: and the land of Egypt will not escape.

43 But he will have power over the treasures of gold and of silver, and over all the precious things of Egypt: and the Libyans and the Ethiopians *will be* at his steps.

44 But tidings out of the east and out of the north will trouble him: therefore he will go forth with great fury to destroy, and utterly to make away many.

45 And he will plant the tabernacles of his palace between the seas in the glorious holy mountain; yet he will come to his end, and none will help him.

CHAPTER 12

1 And at that time will Michael stand up, the great prince which stands for the children of your people: and there will be a time of trouble, such as never was since there was a nation *even* to that same time: and at that time your people will be delivered, every one that will be found written in the book.

2 And many of them that sleep in the dust of the earth will awake, some to everlasting life, and some to shame *and* everlasting contempt.

3 And they that be wise will shine as the brightness of the firmament; and they that turn many to righteousness as the stars forever and ever.

4 But you, O Daniel, shut up the words, and seal the book, *even* to the time of the end: many will run to and fro, and knowledge will be increased.

5 Then I Daniel looked, and, behold, there stood other two, the one on this side of the bank of the river, and the other on that side of the bank of the river.

6 And *one* said to the man clothed in linen, which *was* upon the waters of the river, How long *will it be to* the end of these wonders?

7 And I heard the man clothed in linen, which *was* upon the waters of the river, when he held up his right hand and his left hand unto heaven, and swore by him that lives forever that *it will be* for a time, times, and an half; and when he will have accomplished to scatter the power of [the holy people][7], all these *things* will be finished.[8]

8 And I heard, but I understood not: then said I, O my Lord, what *will be* the end of these *things*?

9 And he said, Go your way, Daniel: for the words *are* closed up and sealed till the time of the end.

10 Many will be purified, and made white, and tried; but the wicked will do wickedly: and none of the wicked will understand; but the wise will understand.

11 And from the time *that* the daily *sacrifice* will be taken away, and the abomination that makes desolate set up, there will be a thousand two hundred and ninety days.

12 Blessed *is* he that waits, and cometh to the thousand three hundred and five and thirty days.

13 But go you your way till the end *be*: for you will rest, and stand in your lot at the end of the days.

---

[1] lit. case to dissemble.
[2] fall – *totter*, *waver* (through weakness of the legs, especially the ankle) [Strgs#3782]. Compare **Eze. 47:3-4**.
[3] lit. *clarify* [Strgs#1305]
[4] lit. to make *bricks*, to be (or become) *white* [Strgs#3835].
[5] estate – is the Hebrew word *kên* meaning *stand*, pedestal or station [Strgs#3653].
[6] The Septuagint uses the words strong places.
[7] We are the Holy people, compare **1 Peter 1:9**.
[8] All things will be finished when we move as a unit, as one man.

HOSEA

CHAPTER 1

1 The word of the LORD that came unto Hosea[1], the son of Beeri, in the days of Uzziah, Jotham, Ahaz, *and* Hezekiah, kings of Judah, and in the days of Jeroboam the son of Joash, king of Israel.
2 The beginning of the word of the LORD by Hosea. And the LORD said to Hosea, Go, take unto you a wife of whoredoms and children of whoredoms: for the land has committed great whoredom, *departing* from the LORD.
3 So he went and took Gomer[2] the daughter of Diblaim; which conceived, and bare him a son.
4 And the LORD said unto him, Call his name Jezreel[3]; for yet a little *while*, and I will avenge the blood of Jezreel upon the house of Jehu, and will cause to cease the kingdom of the house of Israel.
5 And it will come to pass at that day, that I will break the bow of Israel in the valley of Jezreel.
6 And she conceived again, and bare a daughter. And *God* said unto him, Call her name Lo-ruhamah[4]: for I will no more have mercy upon the house of Israel; but I will utterly take them away.
7 But I will have mercy upon the house of Judah, and will save them by the LORD their God, and will not save them by bow, nor by sword, nor by battle, by horses, nor by horsemen.
8 Now when she had weaned Lo-ruhamah, she conceived, and bare a son.
9 Then said *God*, Call his name Lo-ammi: for you *are* not my people, and I will not be your *God*.
10 Yet the number of the children of Israel will be as the sand of the sea, which cannot be measured nor numbered; and it will come to pass, *that* in the place where it was said unto them, You *are* not my people, *there* it will be said unto them, You *are* the sons of the living God.
11 Then will the children of Judah and the children of Israel be gathered together, and appoint themselves one head, and they will come up out of the land: for great *will be* the day of Jezreel.

CHAPTER 2

1 Say you unto your brethren, Ammi[5]; and to your sisters, Ruhamah[6].
2 Plead with your mother, plead: for she *is* not my wife, neither *am* I her husband: let her therefore put away her whoredoms out of her sight, and her adulteries from between her breasts;
3 Lest I strip her naked, and set her as in the day that she was born, and make her as a wilderness, and set her like a dry land, and slay her with thirst.
4 And I will not have mercy upon her children; for they *be* the children of whoredoms.
5 For their mother has played the harlot: she that conceived them has done shamefully: for she said, I will go after my lovers, that give *me* my bread and my water, my wool and my flax, mine oil and my drink.
6 Therefore, behold, I will hedge up your way with thorns, and make a wall, that she will not find her paths.
7 And she will follow after her lovers, but she will not overtake them; and she will seek them, but will not find *them* then will she say, I will go and return to my first husband; for then *was it* better with me than now.
8 For she did not know that I gave her corn, and wine, and oil, and multiplied her silver and gold, *which* they prepared for Baal.
9 Therefore will I return, and take away my corn in the time thereof, and my wine in the season thereof, and will recover my wool and my flax *given* to cover her nakedness.
10 And now will I discover her lewdness in the sight of her lovers, and none will deliver her out of mine hand.
11 I will also cause all her mirth to cease, her feast days, her new moons, and her Sabbaths, and all her solemn feasts
12 And I will destroy her vines and her fig trees, whereof she has said, These *are* my rewards that my lovers have given me: and I will make them a forest, and the beasts of the field will eat them.
13 And I will visit upon her the days of Baalim, wherein she burned incense to them, and she decked herself with her earrings and her jewels, and she went after her lovers, and forgot me, says the LORD.
14 Therefore, behold, I will allure her, and bring her into the wilderness, and speak comfortably unto her.[7]
15 And I will give her, her vineyards from thence, and the valley of Achor for a door of hope: and she will sing there, as in the days of her youth, and as in the day when she came up out of the land of Egypt.
16 And it will be at that day, said the LORD, *that* you will call me Ishi[8]; and will call me no more Baali[9].
17 For I will take away the names of Baalim out of her mouth, and they will no more be remembered by their name.
18 And in that day will I make a covenant for them with the beasts of the field, and with the fowls of heaven, and *with* the creeping things of the ground: and I will break the bow and the sword and the battle out of the earth, and will make them to lie down safely.
19 And I will betroth you unto me forever; yes, I will betroth you unto me in righteousness, and in judgment, and in loving-kindness, and in mercies.
20 I will even betroth you unto me in faithfulness: and you will know the LORD.
21 And it will come to pass in that day, I will hear, says the LORD, I will hear the heavens, and they will hear the earth;
22 And the earth will hear the corn, and the wine, and the oil; and they will hear Jezreel.
23 And I will sow her unto me in the earth; and I will have mercy upon her that had not obtained mercy; and I will say to *them which were* not my people, You *are* my people; and they will say, You *are* my God.

CHAPTER 3

1 Then said the LORD unto me, Go yet, love a woman beloved of *her* friend, yet an adulteress, according to the love of the LORD

---

[1] Hosea- lit. salvation or *deliverer*. [Strgs#1954]
[2] Gomer- completion [Strgs#1586]
[3] Jezreel- God will sow [Strgs#3157]
[4] Loruhamah- no mercy or not pitied. [Strgs#3819]
[5] Ammi- a *people* (as a congregated *unit*); specifically a *tribe* (as those of Israel); hence (collectively) troops or *attendants*, figuratively a *flock*:-folk, men, nation, people. [Strgs#5971]
[6] Ruhamah- to *fondle*; by implication to love, especially to *compassionate*:- have compassion (on, upon), love, mercy, pity. [Strgs#7355]
[7] compare Rev. 12:14, Lev. 16:8-10 & 16:21-22.
[8] Ishi- is the Hebrew word *îysh* meaning *a man* as an individual or a male person. [Strgs#376]
[9] Baali- is the Hebrew word ba'ălîy, meaning my lord or *my master*. It's a symbolical name of Jehovah. [Strgs#1180]

toward the children of Israel, who look to other gods, and love flagons of wine.

2 So I bought her to me for fifteen *pieces* of silver, and *for* a homer of barley, and an half homer of barley:

3 And I said unto her, You will abide for me many days; you will not play the harlot, and you will not be for *another* man: so *will* I also *be* for you.

4 For the children of Israel will abide many days without a king, and without a prince, and without a sacrifice, and without an image, and without an ephod, and *without* teraphim:

5 Afterward will the children of Israel return, and seek the LORD their God, and David their king; and will fear the LORD and his goodness in the latter days.

CHAPTER 4

1 Hear the word of the LORD, you children of Israel: for the LORD has a controversy with the inhabitants of the land, because *there is* no truth, nor mercy, nor knowledge of God in the land.

2 By swearing, and lying, and killing, and stealing, and committing adultery, they break out, and blood touches blood.

3 Therefore will the land mourn, and every one that dwells therein will languish, with the beasts of the field, and with the fowls of heaven; yes, the fishes of the sea also will be taken away.

4 Yet let no man strive, nor reprove another: for your people *are* as they that strive with the priest.

5 Therefore will you fall in the day, and the prophet also will fall with you in the night, and I will destroy your mother.

6 My people are destroyed for lack of knowledge: because you have rejected knowledge, I will also reject you, that you will be no priest to me: seeing you have forgotten the law of your God, I will also forget your children.

7 As they were increased, so they sinned against me: *therefore* will I change their glory into shame.

8 They eat up the sin of my people, and they set their heart on their iniquity.

9 And there will be, like people, like priest: and I will punish them for their ways, and reward them their doings.

10 For they will eat, and not have enough: they will commit whoredom, and will not increase: because they have left off to take heed to the LORD.

11 Whoredom and wine and new wine take away the heart.

12 My people ask counsel at their stocks, and their staff declares unto them: for the spirit of whoredoms has caused *them* to err, and they have gone a whoring from under their God.

13 They sacrifice upon the tops of the mountains, and burn incense upon the hills, under oaks and poplars and elms, because the shadow thereof *is* good: therefore your daughters will commit whoredom, and your spouses will commit adultery.

14 I will not punish your daughters when they commit whoredom, nor your spouses when they commit adultery: for themselves are separated with whores, and they sacrifice with harlots: therefore the people *that* do not understand will fall.

15 Though you, Israel, play the harlot, *yet* let not Judah offend; and come not you unto Gilgal, neither go you up to Beth-aven, nor swear, The LORD lives.

16 For Israel slides back as a backsliding heifer: now the LORD will feed them as a lamb in a large place.

17 Ephraim *is* joined to idols: let him alone.

18 Their drink is sour: they have committed whoredom continually: her rulers *with* shame do love, Give you.

19 The wind has bound her up in her wings, and they will be ashamed because of their sacrifices.

CHAPTER 5

1 Hear you this, O priests; and hearken, you house of Israel; and give you ear, O house of the king; for judgment *is* toward you, because you have been a snare on Mizpah, and a net spread upon Tabor.

2 And the revolters are profound to make slaughter, though I *have been* a rebuker of them all.

3 I know Ephraim, and Israel is not hid from me: for now, O Ephraim, you commit whoredom, *and* Israel is defiled.

4 They will not frame their doings to turn unto their God: for the spirit of whoredoms *is* in the midst of them, and they have not known the LORD.

5 And the pride of Israel does testify to his face: therefore will Israel and Ephraim fall in their iniquity; Judah also will fall with them.

6 They will go with their flocks and with their herds to seek the LORD; but they will not find *him*; he has withdrawn himself from them.

7 They have dealt treacherously against the LORD: for they have begotten strange children: now will a month devour them with their portions.

8 Blow you the cornet in Gibeah, *and* the trumpet in Ramah: cry aloud *at* Beth-aven, after you, O Benjamin.

9 Ephraim will be desolate in the day of rebuke: among the tribes of Israel have I made known that which will surely be.

10 The princes of Judah were like them that remove the bound: *therefore* I will pour out my wrath upon them like water.

11 Ephraim *is* oppressed *and* broken in judgment, because he willingly walked after the commandment.

12 Therefore *will* I *be* unto Ephraim as a moth, and to the house of Judah as rottenness.

13 When Ephraim saw his sickness, and Judah *saw* his wound, then went Ephraim to the Assyrian, and sent to king Jareb[1]: yet could he not heal you, nor cure you of your wound.

14 For I *will be* unto Ephraim as a lion, and as a young lion to the house of Judah: I, *even* I, will tear and go away; I will take away, and none will rescue *him*.

15 I will go *and* return to my place, till they acknowledge their offence, and seek my face: in their affliction they will seek me early.

CHAPTER 6

1 Come, and let us return unto the LORD: for he has torn, and he will heal us; he has smitten, and he will bind us up.

2 After two days will he revive us: in the third day he will raise us up, and we will live in his sight.

3 Then will we know, *if* we follow on to know the LORD: his going forth is prepared as the morning; and he will come unto us as the rain, as the latter *and* former rain unto the earth.

4 O Ephraim, what will I do unto you? O Judah, what will I do unto you? For your goodness *is* as a morning cloud, and as the early dew it goes away.

5 Therefore have I hewed *them* by the prophets; I have slain them by the words of my mouth: and your judgments *are as* the light *that* goes forth.

---

[1] Jareb- is a symbolical name for Assyria. It comes from two Hebrew words the first being *yârêb* meaning *he will contend* [Strgs#3377]. The second being *rîyb* meaning to *toss*, that is, *grapple*; mostly figuratively to *wrangle* [Strgs#7378]. Putting these words together his name literally means *to contend by grappling*.

6 For I desired mercy, and not sacrifice; and the knowledge of God more than burnt offerings.
7 But they like men[1] have transgressed the covenant: there have they dealt treacherously against me.
8 Gilead *is* a city of them that work iniquity, *and is* polluted with blood.
9 And as troops of robbers wait for a man, *so* the company of priests murder in the way by consent: for they commit lewdness.
10 I have seen an horrible thing in the house of Israel: there *is* the whoredom of Ephraim, Israel is defiled.
11 Also, O Judah, he has set an harvest for you, when I returned the captivity of my people.

CHAPTER 7
1 When I would have healed Israel, then the iniquity of Ephraim was discovered, and the wickedness of Samaria: for they commit falsehood; and the thief comes in, *and* the troop of robbers spoils without.
2 And they consider not in their hearts *that* I remember all their wickedness: now their own doings have beset them about; they are before my face.
3 They make the king glad with their wickedness, and the princes with their lies.
4 They *are* all adulterers, as an oven heated by the baker, *who* ceases from raising after he has kneaded the dough, until it be leavened.
5 In the day of our king the princes have made *him* sick with bottles of wine; he stretched out his hand with scorners.
6 For they have made ready their heart like an oven, whiles they lie in wait: their baker sleeps all the night; in the morning it burns as a flaming fire.
7 They are all hot as an oven, and have devoured their judges; all their kings are fallen: *there is* none among them that calls unto me.
8 Ephraim, he has mixed himself among the people; Ephraim is a cake not turned.
9 Strangers have devoured his strength, and he knows *it* not: yes, gray hairs are here and there upon him, yet he knows not.
10 And the pride of Israel testifies to his face: and they do not return to the LORD their God, nor seek him for all this.
11 Ephraim also is like a silly dove without heart: they call to Egypt, they go to Assyria.
12 When they will go, I will spread my net upon them; I will bring them down as the fowls of the heaven; I will chastise them, as their congregation has heard.
13 Woe unto them! for they have fled from me: destruction unto them! because they have transgressed against me: though I have redeemed them, yet they have spoken lies against me.
14 And they have not cried unto me with their heart, when they howled upon their beds: they assemble themselves for corn and wine, *and* they rebel against me.
15 Though I have bound *and* strengthened their arms, yet do they imagine mischief against me.
16 They return, *but* not to the most High: they are like a deceitful bow: their princes will fall by the sword for the rage of their tongue: this *will be* their derision in the land of Egypt.

CHAPTER 8
1 *Set* the trumpet to your mouth. *He will come* as an eagle against the house of the LORD, because they have transgressed my covenant, and trespassed against my law.
2 Israel will cry unto me, My God, we know you.
3 Israel has cast off *the thing that is* good: the enemy will pursue him.
4 They have set up kings, but not by me: they have made princes, and I knew *it* not: of their silver and their gold have they made them idols, that they may be cut off.
5 Your calf, O Samaria, has cast *you* off; mine anger is kindled against them: how long *will it be* ere they attain to innocency?
6 For from Israel *was* it also: the workman made it; therefore it *is* not God: but the calf of Samaria will be broken in pieces.
7 For they have sown the wind, and they will reap the whirlwind: it has no stalk: the bud will yield no meal: if so be it yield, the strangers will swallow it up.
8 Israel is swallowed up: now will they be among the Gentiles as a vessel wherein *is* no pleasure.
9 For they are gone up to Assyria, a wild ass alone by himself: Ephraim has hired lovers.
10 Yes, though they have hired among the nations, now will I gather them, and they will sorrow a little for the burden of the king of princes.
11 Because Ephraim has made many altars to sin, altars will be unto him to sin.
12 I have written to him the great things of my law, *but* they were counted as a strange thing.
13 They sacrifice flesh *for* the sacrifices of mine offerings, and eat *it; but* the LORD accepts them not; now will he remember their iniquity, and visit their sins: they will return to Egypt.
14 For Israel has forgotten his Maker, and builds temples; and Judah has multiplied fenced cities: but I will send a fire upon his cities, and it will devour the palaces thereof.

CHAPTER 9
1 Rejoice not, O Israel, for joy, as *other* people: for you have gone a whoring from your God, you have loved a reward upon every corn-floor.
2 The floor and the winepress will not feed them, and the new wine will fail in her.
3 They will not dwell in the LORD'S land; but Ephraim will return to Egypt, and they will eat unclean *things* in Assyria.
4 They will not offer wine *offerings* to the LORD, neither will they be pleasing unto him: their sacrifices *will be* unto them as the bread of mourners; all that eat thereof will be polluted: for their bread for their soul will not come into the house of the LORD.
5 What will you do in the solemn day, and in the day of the feast of the LORD?
6 For, lo, they are gone because of destruction: Egypt will gather them up, Memphis will bury them: the pleasant *places* for their silver, nettles will possess them: thorns *will be* in their tabernacles.
7 The days of visitation are come, the days of recompence[2] are come; Israel will know *it*: the prophet *is* a fool, the spiritual man *is* mad, for the multitude of your iniquity, and the great hatred.
8 The watchman of Ephraim *was* with my God: *but* the prophet *is* a snare of a fowler in all his ways, *and* hatred in the house of his God.

---

[1] lit. *adam* or *human being* [Strgs#120]
[2] recompense- a requital, that is, (secure) retribution, (venal) a fee:-reward.

[Strgs#7966]

Hosea

9 They have deeply corrupted *themselves*, as in the days of Gibeah: *therefore* he will remember their iniquity, he will visit their sins.
10 I found Israel like grapes in the wilderness; I saw your fathers as the first-ripe in the fig tree at her first time: *but* they went to Baal-peor, and separated themselves unto *that* shame; and *their* abominations were according as they loved.
11 *As for* Ephraim, their glory will fly away like a bird, from the birth, and from the womb, and from the conception.
12 Though they bring up their children, yet will I bereave them, *that* there will not *be* a man *left*: yes, woe also to them when I depart from them!
13 Ephraim, as I saw Tyrus, *is* planted in a pleasant place: but Ephraim will bring forth his children to the murderer.
14 Give them, O LORD: what will you give? Give them a miscarrying womb and dry breasts.
15 All their wickedness *is* in Gilgal: for there I hated them: for the wickedness of their doings I will drive them out of mine house, I will love them no more: all their princes *are* revolters.
16 Ephraim is smitten, their root is dried up, they will bear no fruit: yes, though they bring forth, yet will I slay *even* the beloved *fruit* of their womb.
17 My God will cast them away, because they did not hearken unto him: and they will be wanderers among the nations.

CHAPTER 10

1 Israel *is* an empty vine, he brings forth fruit unto himself: according to the multitude of his fruit he has increased the altars; according to the goodness of his land they have made goodly images.
2 Their heart is divided; now will they be found faulty: he will break down their altars, he will spoil their images.
3 For now they will say, We have no king, because we feared not the LORD; what then should a king do to us?
4 They have spoken words, swearing falsely in making a covenant: thus judgment springs up as hemlock in the furrows[1] of the field.
5 The inhabitants of Samaria will fear because of the calves of Beth-aven: for the people thereof will mourn over it, and the priests thereof *that* rejoiced on it, for the glory thereof, because it is departed from it.
6 It will be also carried unto Assyria *for* a present to king Jareb: Ephraim will receive shame, and Israel will be ashamed of his own counsel.
7 *As for* Samaria, her king is cut off as the foam upon the water.
8 The high places also of Aven, the sin of Israel, will be destroyed: the thorn and the thistle will come up on their altars; and they will say to the mountains, Cover us; and to the hills, Fall on us.
9 O Israel, you have sinned from the days of Gibeah: there they stood: the battle in Gibeah against the children of iniquity did not overtake them.
10 *It is* in my desire that I should chastise them; and the people will be gathered against them, when they will bind themselves in their two furrows.
11 And Ephraim *is as* an heifer *that is* taught, *and* loves to tread out *the corn*; but I passed over upon her fair neck: I will make Ephraim to ride; Judah will plow, *and* Jacob will break his clods.

12 Sow to yourselves in righteousness, reap in mercy; break up your fallow ground: for *it is* time to seek the LORD, till he come and rain righteousness upon you.
13 You have plowed wickedness[2], you have reaped iniquity[3]; you have eaten the fruit of lies[4]: because you did trust in your way, in the multitude of your mighty men.
14 Therefore will a tumult arise among your people, and all your fortresses will be spoiled, as Shalman spoiled Beth-arbel in the day of battle: the mother was dashed in pieces upon *her* children.
15 So will Beth-el do unto you because of your great wickedness: in a morning will the king of Israel utterly be cut off.

CHAPTER 11

1 When Israel *was* a child, then I loved him, and called my son out of Egypt.
2 *As* they called them, so they went from them: they sacrificed unto Baalim, and burned incense to graven images.
3 I taught Ephraim also to go, taking them by their arms; but they knew not that I healed them.
4 I drew them with cords of a man, with bands of love: and I was to them as they that take off the yoke on their jaws, and I laid meat unto them.
5 He will not return into the land of Egypt, but the Assyrian will be his king, because they refused to return.
6 And the sword will abide on his cities, and will consume his branches, and devour *them*, because of their own counsels.
7 And my people are bent to backsliding from me: though they called them to the most High, none at all would exalt *him*.
8 How will I give you up, Ephraim? *How* will I deliver you, Israel? How will I make you as Admah? *How* will I set you as Zeboim? Mine heart is turned within me, my repentings are kindled together.
9 I will not execute the fierceness of mine anger, I will not return to destroy Ephraim: for I *am* God, and not man; the Holy One in the midst of you: and I will not enter into the city.
10 They will walk after the LORD: he will roar like a lion: when he will roar, then the children will tremble from the west.
11 They will tremble as a bird out of Egypt, and as a dove out of the land of Assyria: and I will place them in their houses, says the LORD.
12 Ephraim compasses me about with lies, and the house of Israel with deceit: but Judah yet rules with God, and is faithful with the saints.

CHAPTER 12

1 Ephraim feeds on wind, and follows after the east wind: he daily increases lies and desolation; and they do make a covenant with the Assyrians, and oil is carried into Egypt.
2 The LORD has also a controversy with Judah, and will punish Jacob according to his ways; according to his doings will he recompense him.
3 He took his brother by the heel in the womb, and by his strength he had power with God:
4 Yes, he had power over the angel, and prevailed: he wept, and made supplication unto him: he found him *in* Beth-el, and there he spoke with us;
5 Even the LORD God of hosts; the LORD *is* his memorial.
6 Therefore turn you to your God: keep mercy and judgment, and wait on your God continually.

---

[1] furrows – to *accumulate*, a <u>bank</u>, ridge or *terrace* [Strgs#8525].
[2] lit. <u>wrong</u> [Strgs#7562].
[3] lit. *evil*, comes from a Hebrew root word meaning *distort* [Strgs#7562+7561]
[4] lies – <u>failure of flesh</u>, emaciation, hypocrisy [Strgs#3585].

7 *He is* a merchant, the balances of deceit *are* in his hand: he loves to oppress.
8 And Ephraim said, Yet I am become rich, I have found me out substance: *in* all my labors they will find none iniquity in me that *were* sin.
9 And I *that am* the LORD your God from the land of Egypt will yet make you to dwell in tabernacles, as in the days of the solemn feast.
10 I have also spoken by the prophets, and I have multiplied visions, and used similitudes, by the ministry of the prophets.
11 *Is there* iniquity *in* Gilead? Surely they are vanity: they sacrifice bullocks in Gilgal; yes, their altars *are* as heaps in the furrows of the fields.
12 And Jacob fled into the country of Syria, and Israel served for a wife, and for a wife he kept *sheep*.
13 And by a prophet the LORD brought Israel out of Egypt, and by a prophet was he preserved.
14 Ephraim provoked *him* to anger most bitterly: therefore will he leave his blood upon him, and his reproach will his Lord return unto him.

CHAPTER 13

1 When Ephraim spoke trembling, he exalted himself in Israel; but when he offended in Baal, he died.
2 And now they sin more and more, and have made them molten images of their silver, *and* idols according to their own understanding, all of it the work of the craftsmen: they say of them, Let the men that sacrifice kiss the calves.
3 Therefore they will be as the morning cloud, and as the early dew that passes away, as the chaff *that* is driven with the whirlwind out of the floor, and as the smoke out of the chimney.
4 Yet I *am* the LORD your God from the land of Egypt, and you will know no god but me: for *there is* no savior beside me.
5 I did know you in the wilderness, in the land of great drought.
6 According to their pasture, so were they filled; they were filled, and their heart was exalted; therefore have they forgotten me.
7 Therefore I will be unto them as a lion: as a leopard by the way will I observe *them*:
8 I will meet them as a bear *that is* bereaved *of her whelps*, and will rend the caul[1] of their heart, and there will I devour them like a lion: the [wild beast][2] will tear them.
9 O Israel, you have destroyed yourself; but in me *is* your help.
10 I will be your king: where *is any other* that may save you in all your cities? And your judges of whom you said, Give me a king and princes?
11 I gave you a king in mine anger, and took *him* away in my wrath.
12 The iniquity of Ephraim *is* bound up; his sin *is* hid.
13 The sorrows of a travailing woman will come upon him: he *is* an unwise son; for he should not stay long in *the place of* the breaking forth of children.
14 I will ransom them from the power of the grave; I will redeem them from death: O death, I will be your plagues; O grave, I will be your destruction: repentance will be hid from mine eyes.
15 Though he be fruitful among *his* brethren, an east wind will come, the wind of the LORD will come up from the wilderness, and his spring will become dry, and his fountain will be dried up: he will spoil the treasure of all pleasant vessels.

16 Samaria will become desolate; for she has rebelled against her God: they will fall by the sword: their infants will be dashed in pieces, and their women with child will be ripped up.

CHAPTER 14

1 O Israel, return unto the LORD your God; for you have fallen by your iniquity.
2 Take with you words, and turn to the LORD: say unto him, Take away all iniquity, and receive *us* graciously: so will we render the calves of our lips.
3 Asshur will not save us; we will not ride upon horses: neither will we say any more to the work of our hands, *You are* our gods: for in you the fatherless finds mercy.
4 I will heal their backsliding, I will love them freely: for mine anger is turned away from him.
5 I will be as the dew unto Israel: he will grow as the lily, and cast forth his roots as Lebanon.
6 His branches will spread, and his beauty will be as the olive tree, and his smell as Lebanon.
7 They that dwell under his shadow will return; they will revive *as* the corn, and grow as the vine: the scent thereof *will be* as the wine of Lebanon.
8 Ephraim *will say*, What have I to do any more with idols? I have heard *him*, and observed him: I *am* like a green fir tree. From me is your fruit found.
9 Who *is* wise, and he will understand these *things*? Prudent, and he will know them? For the ways of the LORD *are* right, and the just will walk in them: but the transgressors will fall therein.

---

[1] caul- *shut up*, that is, the breast (as inclosing the heart); also gold (as generally shut up safely):- gold. [Strgs#5458]

[2] The Beast of the Field

JOEL

CHAPTER 1

1 The word of the LORD that came to Joel[1] the son of Pethuel[2].
2 Hear this, you old men, and give ear, all you inhabitants of the land. Has this been in your days, or even in the days of your fathers?
3 Tell you your children of it, and *let* your children *tell* their children, and their children another generation.
4 That which the palmerworm has left has the locust eaten; and that which the locust has left has the cankerworm eaten; and that which the cankerworm has left has the caterpillar eaten.
5 Awake, you drunkards, and weep; and howl, all you drinkers of wine, because of the new wine; for it is cut off from your mouth.
6 For a nation is come up upon my land, strong, and without number, whose teeth *are* the teeth of a lion, and he has the cheek teeth of a great lion.
7 He has laid my vine waste, and barked my fig tree: he has made it clean bare, and cast *it* away; the branches thereof are made white.
8 Lament like a virgin girded with sackcloth for the husband of her youth.
9 The meat offering and the drink offering is cut off from the house of the LORD; the priests, the LORD'S ministers, mourn.
10 The field is wasted, the land mourns; for the corn is wasted: the new wine is dried up, the oil languishes.
11 Be you ashamed, O you husbandmen; howl, O you vinedressers, for the wheat and for the barley; because the harvest of the field is perished.
12 The vine is dried up, and the fig tree languishes; the pomegranate tree, the palm tree also, and the apple tree, *even* all the trees of the field, are withered: because joy is withered away from the sons of men.
13 Gird yourselves, and lament, you priests: howl, you ministers of the altar: come, lie all night in sackcloth, you ministers of my God: for the meat offering and the drink offering is **withheld** from the house of your God.
14 Sanctify you a fast, call a solemn assembly, gather the elders *and* all the inhabitants of the land *into* the house of the LORD your God, and cry unto the LORD,
15 Alas for the day! For the day of the LORD *is* at hand, and as a destruction from the Almighty will it come.
16 Is not the meat cut off before our eyes, *yea*, joy and gladness from the house of our God?
17 The seed is rotten under their clods, the garners are laid desolate, the barns are broken down; for the corn is withered.
18 How do the beasts groan! The herds of cattle are perplexed, because they have no pasture; yea, the flocks of sheep are made desolate.
19 O LORD, to thee will I cry: for the fire has devoured the pastures of the wilderness, and the flame has burned all the trees of the field.
20 The beasts of the field cry also unto thee: for the rivers of waters are dried up, and the fire has devoured the pastures of the wilderness.

CHAPTER 2

1 Blow you the trumpet in Zion, and sound an alarm in my holy mountain: let all the inhabitants of the land tremble: for the day of the LORD cometh, for *it is* nigh at hand;
2 A day of darkness and of gloominess, a day of clouds and of thick darkness, as the morning spread upon the mountains a great people and a strong; there has not been ever the like, neither will be any more after it, *even* to the years of many generations.
3 A fire devours before them; and behind them a flame burns: the land *is* as the garden of Eden before them, and behind them a desolate wilderness; yea, and nothing will escape them.
4 The appearance of them *is* as the appearance of horses; and as horsemen, so will they run.
5 Like the noise of chariots on the tops of mountains will they leap, like the noise of a flame of fire that devours the stubble, as a strong people set in battle array.
6 Before their face the people will be much pained: all faces will gather blackness.
7 They will run like mighty men; they will climb the wall like men of war; and they will march everyone on his ways, and they will not break their ranks:
8 Neither will one thrust another; they will walk everyone in his path: and *when* they fall upon the sword, they will not be wounded.
9 They will run to and fro in the city; they will run upon the wall, they will climb up upon the houses; they will enter in at the windows like a thief.
10 The earth will quake before them; the heavens will tremble: the sun and the moon will be dark, and the stars will withdraw their shining:
11 And the LORD will utter his voice before his army: for his camp *is* very great: for *he is* strong that executes his word: for the day of the LORD *is* great and very terrible; and who can abide it?
12 Therefore also now, says the LORD, turn you *even* to me with all your heart, and with fasting, and with weeping, and with mourning:
13 And rend your heart, and not your garments, and turn unto the LORD your God: for he *is* gracious and merciful, slow to anger, and of great kindness, and repents him of the evil.
14 Who knows *if* he will return and repent, and leave a blessing behind him; *even* a meat offering and a drink offering unto the LORD your God?
15 Blow the trumpet in Zion, sanctify a fast, call a solemn assembly:
16 Gather the people, sanctify the congregation, assemble the elders, gather the children, and those that suck the breasts: let the bridegroom go forth of his chamber, and the bride out of her closet.
17 Let the priests, the ministers of the LORD, weep between the porch and the altar, and let them say, Spare thy people O LORD, and give not your heritage to reproach, that the heathen should rule over them: wherefore should they say among the people, Where *is* their God?
18 Then will the LORD be jealous for his land, and pity his people.
19 Yea, the LORD will answer and say unto his people, Behold, I will send you corn, and wine, and oil, and you will be satisfied therewith: and I will no more make you a reproach among the heathen:
20 But I will remove far off from you the northern *army*, and will drive him into a land barren and desolate, with his face toward the

---

[1] Joel- Jehovah is God or *Jehovah is his God.* [Strgs#3100]

[2] Pethuel- literally vision or *God or enlarge of God.* [Strgs#6602]

east sea, and his hinder part toward the utmost sea, and his stink will come up, and his ill savor will come up, because he has done great things.

21 Fear not, O land; be glad and rejoice: for the LORD will do great things.

22 Be not afraid, you beasts of the field: for the pastures of the wilderness do spring, for the tree bears her fruit, the fig tree and the vine do yield their strength.

23 Be glad then, you children of Zion, and rejoice in the LORD your God: for he has given you the former rain moderately, and he will cause to come down for you the rain, the former rain, and the latter rain in the first *month*.

24 And the floors will be full of wheat, and the fats will overflow with wine and oil.

25 And I will restore to you the years that the locust has eaten, the cankerworm, and the caterpillar, and the palmerworm, my great army which I sent among you.

26 And you will eat in plenty, and be satisfied, and praise the name of the LORD your God, that has dealt wondrously with you: and my people will never be ashamed.

27 And you will know that I *am* in the midst of Israel, and *that* I *am* the LORD your God, and none else: and my people will never be ashamed.

28 And it will come to pass afterward, *that* I will pour out my spirit upon all flesh; and your sons and your daughters will prophesy, your old men will dream dreams, your young men will see visions:

29 And also upon the servants and upon the handmaids in those days will I pour out my spirit.

30 And I will show wonders in the heavens and in the earth, blood, and fire, and pillars of smoke.

31 The sun will be turned into darkness, and the moon into blood, before the great and the terrible day of the LORD come.

32 And it will come to pass, *that* whosoever will call on the name of the LORD will be delivered: for in mount Zion and in Jerusalem will be deliverance, as the LORD has said, and in the remnant whom the LORD will call.

CHAPTER 3

1 For, behold, in those days, and in that time, when I will bring again the captivity of Judah and Jerusalem,

2 I will also gather all nations, and will bring them down into the valley of Jehoshaphat, and will plead with them there for my people and *for* my heritage Israel, whom they have scattered among the nations, and parted my land.

3 And they have cast lots for my people; and have given a boy for an harlot, and sold a girl for wine, that they might drink.

4 Yes, and what have you to do with me, O Tyre, and Zidon, and all the coasts of Palestine? Will you render me a recompence? And if you recompense me, swiftly *and* speedily will I return your recompence upon your own head;

5 Because you have taken my silver and my gold, and have carried into your temples my goodly pleasant things:

6 The children also of Judah and the children of Jerusalem have you sold unto the Grecians, that you might remove them far from their border.

7 Behold, I will raise them out of the place whither you have sold them, and will return your recompence upon your own head:

8 And I will sell your sons and your daughters into the hand of the children of Judah, and they will sell them to the Sabeans, to a people far off: for the LORD has spoken *it*.

9 Proclaim you this among the Gentiles; Prepare war, wake up the mighty men, let all the men of war draw near; let them come up:

10 Beat your plowshares into swords, and your pruning-hooks into spears: let the weak say, I *am* strong.

11 Assemble yourselves, and come, all you heathen and gather yourselves together round about: thither cause thy mighty ones to come down, O LORD.

12 Let the heathen be wakened, and come up to the valley of Jehoshaphat: for there will I sit to judge all the heathen round about.

13 Put you in the sickle, for the harvest is ripe: come, get you down; for the press is full, the fats overflow; for their wickedness *is* great.

14 Multitudes, multitudes in the valley of decision: for the day of the LORD *is* near in the valley of decision.

15 The sun and the moon will be darkened, and the stars will withdraw their shining.

16 The LORD also will roar out of Zion, and utter his voice from Jerusalem; and the heavens and the earth will shake: but the LORD *will be* the hope of his people, and the strength of the children of Israel.

17 So will you know that I *am* the LORD your God dwelling in Zion, my holy mountain: then will Jerusalem be holy, and there will no strangers pass through her any more.

18 And it will come to pass in that day, *that* the mountains will drop down new wine, and the hills will flow with milk, and all the rivers of Judah will flow with waters, and a fountain will come forth of the house of the LORD, and will water the valley of Shittim

19 Egypt will be a desolation, and Edom will be a desolate wilderness, for the violence *against* the children of Judah, because they have shed innocent blood in their land.

20 But Judah will dwell forever, and Jerusalem from generation to generation.

21 For I will cleanse their blood *that* I have not cleansed: for the LORD dwells in Zion.

AMOS
CHAPTER 1

1 The words of Amos[1], who was among the herdmen of Tekoa, which he saw concerning Israel in the days of Uzziah king of Judah, and in the days of Jeroboam the son of Joash king of Israel, two years before the earthquake.

2 And he said, The LORD will roar from Zion, and utter his voice from Jerusalem; and the habitations of the shepherds will mourn, and the top of Carmel will wither.

3 Thus says the LORD; For three transgressions of Damascus, and for four, I will not turn away *the punishment* thereof; because they have threshed Gilead with threshing instruments of iron:

4 But I will send a fire into the house of Hazael, which will devour the palaces of Ben-hadad.

5 I will break also the bar of Damascus, and cut off the inhabitant from the plain of Aven, and him that holds the scepter from the house of Eden: and the people of Syria will go into captivity unto Kir, says the LORD.

6 Thus says the LORD; For three transgressions of Gaza, and for four, I will not turn away *the punishment* thereof; because they carried away captive the whole captivity, to deliver *them* up to Edom:

7 But I will send a fire on the wall of Gaza, which will devour the palaces thereof:

8 And I will cut off the inhabitant from Ashdod, and him that holds the scepter from Ashkelon, and I will turn mine hand against Ekron[2]: and the remnant of the Philistines will perish, says the Lord GOD.

9 Thus says the LORD; For three transgressions of Tyrus[3], and for four, I will not turn away *the punishment* thereof; because they delivered up the whole captivity to Edom, and remembered not the brotherly covenant:

10 But I will send a fire on the wall of Tyrus, which will devour the palaces thereof.

11 Thus says the LORD; For three transgressions of Edom, and for four, I will not turn away *the punishment* thereof; because he did pursue his brother with the sword, and did cast off all pity, and his anger did tear perpetually, and he kept his wrath for ever:

12 But I will send a fire upon Teman, which will devour the palaces of Bozrah.

13 Thus says the LORD; For three transgressions of the children of Ammon, and for four, I will not turn away *the punishment* thereof; because they have ripped up the women with child of Gilead, that they might enlarge their border:

14 But I will kindle a fire in the wall of Rabbah, and it will devour the palaces thereof, with shouting in the day of battle, with a tempest in the day of the whirlwind:

15 And their king will go into captivity, he and his princes together, says the LORD.

CHAPTER 2

1 Thus says the LORD; For three transgressions of Moab, and for four, I will not turn away *the punishment* thereof; because he burned the bones of the king of Edom into lime:

2 But I will send a fire upon Moab, and it will devour the palaces of Kerioth: and Moab will die with tumult, with shouting, *and* with the sound of the trumpet:

3 And I will cut off the judge from the midst thereof, and will slay all the princes thereof with him, says the LORD.

4 Thus says the LORD; For three transgressions of Judah, and for four, I will not turn away *the punishment* thereof; because they have despised the law of the LORD, and have not kept his commandments, and their lies caused them to err, after the which their fathers have walked:

5 But I will send a fire upon Judah, and it will devour the palaces of Jerusalem.

6 Thus says the LORD; For three transgressions of Israel, and for four, I will not turn away *the punishment* thereof; because they sold the righteous for silver, and the poor for a pair of shoes;

7 That pant after the dust of the earth on the head of the poor, and turn aside the way of the meek: and a man and his father will go in unto the *same* maid, to profane my holy name:

8 And they lay *themselves* down upon clothes laid to pledge by every altar, and they drink the wine of the condemned *in the* house of their god.

9 Yet destroyed I the Amorite before them, whose height *was* like the height of the cedars, and he *was* strong as the oaks; yet I destroyed his fruit from above, and his roots from beneath.

10 Also I brought you up from the land of Egypt, and led you forty years through the wilderness, to possess the land of the Amorite.

11 And I raised up of your sons for prophets, and of your young men for Nazarites. *Is it* not even thus, O you children of Israel? Says the LORD.

12 But you gave the Nazarites wine to drink; and commanded the prophets, saying, Prophesy not.

13 Behold, I am pressed under you, as a cart is pressed *that is* full of sheaves.

14 Therefore the flight will perish from the swift, and the strong will not strengthen his force, neither will the mighty deliver himself:

15 Neither will he stand that handles the bow; and *he that is* swift of foot will not deliver *himself*: neither will he that rides the horse deliver himself.

16 And *he that is* courageous among the mighty will flee away naked in that day, says the LORD.

CHAPTER 3

1 Hear this word that the LORD has spoken against you, O children of Israel, against the whole family which I brought up from the land of Egypt, saying,

2 You only have I known of all the families of the earth: therefore I will punish you for all your iniquities.

3 Can two walk together, except they be agreed?

4 [Will a lion roar in the forest, when he has no prey? Will a young lion cry out of his den, if he have taken nothing?][4]

5 Can a bird fall in a snare upon the earth, where no gin *is* for him? Will *one* take up a snare from the earth, and have taken nothing at all?

6 Will a trumpet be blown in the city, and the people not be afraid? Will there be evil in a city, and the LORD has not done *it*?

7 Surely the Lord GOD will do nothing, but he reveals his secret unto his servants the prophets.

---

[1] Amos- burden or *burdensome*. [Strgs#5986]
[2] Ekron- is the Hebrew word *'eqrôn, ek-rone'*; meaning emigration, torn up by the roots or *eradication*. [Strgs#6138]
[3] see Index
[4] Sometimes there is no roar in worship because we feel that we have to prey or we roar when we feel victory.

8 The lion has roared, who will not fear? The Lord GOD has spoken, who can but prophesy?

9 Publish in the palaces at Ashdod, and in the palaces in the land of Egypt, and say, Assemble yourselves upon the mountains of Samaria, and behold the great tumults in the midst thereof, and the oppressed in the midst thereof.

10 For they know not to do right, says the LORD, who store up violence and robbery in their palaces.

11 Therefore thus says the Lord GOD; An adversary *there will be* even round about the land; and he will bring down your strength from you, and your palaces will be spoiled.

12 Thus says the LORD; As the shepherd takes out of the mouth of the lion two legs, or a piece of an ear; so will the children of Israel be taken out that dwell in Samaria in the corner of a bed, and in Damascus *in* a couch.

13 Hear you, and testify in the house of Jacob, says the Lord GOD, the God of hosts,

14 That in the day that I will visit the transgressions of Israel upon him I will also visit the altars of Beth-el: and the horns of the altar will be cut off, and fall to the ground.

15 And I will smite the winter house with the summer house; and the houses of ivory will perish, and the great houses will have an end, says the LORD.

CHAPTER 4

1 Hear this word, you **heifer** of Bashan, that *are* in the mountain of Samaria, which oppress the poor, which crush the needy, which say to their masters, Bring, and let us drink.

2 The Lord GOD has sworn by his holiness, that, lo, the days will come upon you, that he will take you away with hooks, and your posterity with fishhooks.

3 And you will go out at the breaches, every *cow at that which is* before her; and you will cast *them* into the palace, says the LORD.

4 Come to Beth-el, and transgress; at Gilgal multiply transgression; and bring your sacrifices every morning, *and* your tithes after three years:

5 And offer a sacrifice of thanksgiving with leaven, and proclaim *and* publish the free offerings: for this like you, O you children of Israel, says the Lord GOD.

6 And I also have given you cleanness of teeth in all your cities, and want of bread in all your places: yet have you not returned unto me, says the LORD.

7 And also I have withheld the rain from you, when *there were* yet three months to the harvest: and I caused it to rain upon one city, and caused it not to rain upon another city: one piece was rained upon, and the piece whereupon it rained not withered.

8 So two *or* three cities wandered unto one city, to drink water; but they were not satisfied: yet have you not returned unto me, says the LORD.

9 I have smitten you with blasting and mildew: when your gardens and your vineyards and your fig trees and your olive trees increased, the palmerworm devoured *them*: yet have you not returned unto me, says the LORD.

10 I have sent among you the pestilence after the manner of Egypt: your young men have I slain with the sword, and have taken away your horses; and I have made the stink of your camps to come up unto your nostrils: yet have you not returned unto me, says the LORD.

11 I have overthrown *some* of you, as God overthrew Sodom and Gomorrah, and you were as a firebrand plucked out of the burning: yet have you not returned unto me, says the LORD.

12 Therefore thus will I do unto you, O Israel: *and* because I will do this unto you, prepare to meet your God, O Israel.

13 For, lo, he that forms the mountains, and creates the wind, and declares unto man what *is* his thought, that makes the morning darkness, and treads upon the high places of the earth, The LORD, The God of hosts, *is* his name.

CHAPTER 5

1 Hear you this word which I take up against you, *even* a lamentation, O house of Israel.

2 The virgin of Israel is fallen; she will no more rise: she is forsaken upon her land; *there is* none to raise her up.

3 For thus says the Lord GOD; The city that went out *by* a thousand will leave an hundred, and that which went forth *by* an hundred will leave ten, to the house of Israel.

4 For thus says the LORD unto the house of Israel, Seek you me, and you will live:

5 But seek not Beth-el, or enter into Gilgal, and pass not to Beer-sheba: for Gilgal will surely go into captivity, and Beth-el will come to nought.

6 Seek the LORD, and you will live; lest he break out like fire in the house of Joseph, and devour *it*, and *there be* none to quench *it* in Beth-el.

7 You who turn judgment to wormwood, and leave off righteousness in the earth,

8 *Seek him* that makes the seven stars and Orion, and turns the shadow of death into the morning, and makes the day dark with night: that calls for the waters of the sea, and pours them out upon the face of the earth: The LORD *is* his name:

9 That strengthens the spoiled against the strong, so that the spoiled will come against the fortress.

10 They hate him that rebukes in the gate, and they abhor him that speaks uprightly.

11 Forasmuch therefore as your treading *is* upon the poor, and you take from him burdens of wheat: you have built houses of hewn stone, but you will not dwell in them; you have planted pleasant vineyards, but you will not drink wine of them.

12 For I know your manifold transgressions and your mighty sins: they afflict the just, they take a bribe, and they turn aside the poor in the gate *from their right*.

13 Therefore the prudent will keep silence in that time; for it *is* an evil time.

14 Seek good, and not evil, that you may live: and so the LORD, the God of hosts, will be with you, as you have spoken.

15 Hate the evil, and love the good, and establish judgment in the gate: it may be that the LORD God of hosts will be gracious unto the remnant of Joseph.

16 Therefore the LORD, the God of hosts, the Lord, says thus; Wailing *will be* in all streets; and they will say in all the highways, Alas! alas! and they will call the husbandman to mourning, and such as are skilful of lamentation to wailing.

17 And in all vineyards *will be* wailing: for I will pass through you, says the LORD.

18 Woe unto you that desire the day of the LORD! To what end *is* it for you? The day of the LORD *is* darkness, and not light.

19 As if a man did flee from a lion, and a bear met him; or went into the house, and leaned his hand on the wall, and a serpent bit him.

20 *Will* not the day of the LORD *be* darkness, and not light? Even very dark, and no brightness in it?

21 I hate, I despise your feast days, and I will not smell in your solemn assemblies.
22 Though you offer me burnt offerings and your meat offerings, I will not accept *them*: neither will I regard the peace offerings of your fat beasts.
23 Take you away from me the noise of your songs; for I will not hear the melody of your viols.
24 But let judgment run down as waters, and righteousness as a mighty stream.
25 Have you offered unto me sacrifices and offerings in the wilderness forty years, O house of Israel?
26 But you have borne the tabernacle of your Moloch[1] and Chiun[2] your images, the star of your god, which you made to yourselves.
27 Therefore will I cause you to go into captivity beyond Damascus, says the LORD, whose name *is* The God of hosts.

CHAPTER 6

1 Woe to them *that are* at ease in Zion, and trust in the mountain of Samaria, *which are* named chief of the nations, to whom the house of Israel came!
2 Pass you unto Calneh, and see; and from there go you to Hamath the great: then go down to Gath of the Philistines: *be they* better than these kingdoms? Or their border greater than your border?
3 You that put far away the evil day, and cause the seat of violence to come near;
4 That lie upon beds of ivory, and stretch themselves upon their couches, and eat the lambs out of the flock, and the calves out of the midst of the stall;
5 That chant to the sound of the viol, *and* invent to themselves instruments of music, like David;
6 That drink wine in bowls, and anoint themselves with the chief ointments: but they are not grieved for the affliction[3] of Joseph.
7 Therefore now will they go captive with the first that go captive, and the banquet of them that stretched themselves will be removed.
8 The Lord GOD has sworn by himself, says the LORD the God of hosts, I abhor the excellency of Jacob, and hate his palaces: therefore will I deliver up the city with all that is therein.
9 And it will come to pass, if there remain ten men in one house, that they will die.
10 And a man's uncle will take him up, and he that burns him, to bring out the bones out of the house, and will say unto him that *is* by the sides of the house, *Is there* yet *any* with you? And he will say, No. Then will he say, Hold your tongue: for we may not make mention of the name of the LORD.
11 For, behold, the LORD commands, and he will smite the great house with breaches, and the little house with clefts.
12 Will horses run upon the rock? Will *one* plow *there* with oxen? For you have turned judgment into gall, and the fruit of righteousness into hemlock.
13 You which rejoice in a thing of nought, which say, Have we not taken to us horns by our own strength?

14 But, behold, I will raise up against you a nation, O house of Israel, says the LORD the God of hosts; and they will afflict you from the entering in of Hemath unto the river of the wilderness.

CHAPTER 7

1 Thus has the Lord GOD showed unto me; and, behold, he formed grasshoppers[4] in the beginning of the shooting up of the latter growth; and, lo, *it was* the latter growth after the king's mowings.
2 And it came to pass, *that* when they had made an end of eating the grass of the land, then I said, O Lord GOD, forgive, I beseech you: by whom will Jacob arise? For he *is* small.
3 The LORD repented for this: It will not be, says the LORD.
4 Thus has the Lord GOD showed unto me: and, behold, the Lord GOD called to contend by fire, and it devoured the great deep, and did eat up a part.
5 Then said I, O Lord GOD, cease, I beseech you: by whom will Jacob arise? for he *is* small.
6 The LORD repented for this: This also will not be, says the Lord GOD.
7 Thus he showed me: and, behold, the Lord stood upon a wall *made* by a plumbline[5], with a plumbline in his hand.
8 And the LORD said unto me, Amos, what see thou? And I said, A plumbline. Then said the Lord, Behold, I will set a plumbline in the midst of my people Israel: I will not again pass by them any more:
9 And the high places of Isaac will be desolate, and the sanctuaries of Israel will be laid waste; and I will rise against the house of Jeroboam with the sword.
10 Then Amaziah the priest of Beth-el sent to Jeroboam king of Israel, saying, Amos has conspired against you in the midst of the house of Israel: the land is not able to bear all his words
11 For thus Amos says, Jeroboam will die by the sword, and Israel will surely be led away captive out of their own land.
12 Also Amaziah said unto Amos, O you seer, go, flee you away into the land of Judah, and there eat bread, and prophesy there:
13 But prophesy not again any more at Beth-el: for it *is* the king's chapel, and it *is* the king's court.
14 Then answered Amos, and said to Amaziah, I *was* no prophet, neither *was* I a prophet's son; but I *was* an herdman, and a gatherer of sycomore fruit:
15 And the LORD took me as I followed the flock, and the LORD said unto me, Go, prophesy unto my people Israel.
16 Now therefore hear you the word of the LORD: You said, Prophesy not against Israel, and drop not *your word* against the house of Isaac.
17 Therefore thus says the LORD; Your wife will be an harlot in the city, and your sons and your daughters will fall by the sword, and your land will be divided by line; and you will die in a polluted land: and Israel will surely go into captivity forth of his land.

CHAPTER 8

1 Thus has the Lord GOD showed unto me: and behold a basket of summer fruit.

---

[1] Moloch- the Hebrew word *melek*, meh'-lek; meaning a king: royal [Strgs#4428]. It comes from the Hebrew root word *mâlak*, maw-lak', meaning to reign; inceptively to ascend the throne; causatively to induct into royalty; heance to take counsel: -consult, be (make, set a set up) king, (begin to, make to) reign [Strgs#4427].
[2] Chiun- an image, pillar, properly *a statue*, that is an idol; but used for some heathen deity [Strgs##3594]. Comes from the Hebrew root word *kûn* meaning *to be erect*, hence to set up, in a great variety of applications, whether literal (*establish, fix, prepare, apply*) or figurative (*appoint, render sure, proper* or *prosperous*) [Strgs#3559]
[3] lit. *fracture, ruin*, specifically a *solution* (of a *dream*), breach [Strgs#7667].
[4] lit. locust (from its *grubbing* as a larve) [Strgs#1462]
[5] plumbline- Hebrew *'ănâk*, an-awk'; meaning to *be narrow*; according to most a plumb *line*, and to others a *hook*. [Strgs#594]

2 And he said, Amos, what see thou? And I said, A basket of summer fruit. Then said the LORD unto me, The end is come upon my people of Israel; I will not again pass by them anymore.
3 And the songs of the temple will be howlings in that day, says the Lord GOD: *there will be* many dead bodies in every place; they will cast *them* forth with silence.
4 Hear this, O you that swallow up the needy, even to make the poor of the land to fail,
5 Saying, When will the new moon be gone, that we may sell corn? and the Sabbath, that we may set forth wheat, making the ephah small, and the shekel great, and falsifying the balances by deceit?
6 That we may buy the poor for silver, and the needy for a pair of shoes; *yea*, and sell the refuse of the wheat?
7 The LORD has sworn by the excellency of Jacob, Surely I will never forget any of their works.
8 Will not the land tremble for this, and every one mourn that dwells therein? And it will rise up wholly as a flood; and it will be cast out and drowned, as *by* the flood of Egypt.
9 And it will come to pass in that day, says the Lord GOD, that I will cause the sun to go down at noon, and I will darken the earth in the clear day:
10 And I will turn your feasts into mourning, and all your songs into lamentation; and I will bring up sackcloth upon all loins, and baldness upon every head; and I will make it as the mourning of an only *son*, and the end thereof as a bitter day.
11 Behold, the days come, says the Lord GOD, that I will send a famine in the land, not a famine of bread, or a thirst for water, but of hearing the words of the LORD:
12 And they will wander from sea to sea, and from the north even to the east, they will run to and fro to seek the word of the LORD, and will not find *it*.
13 In that day will the fair virgins and young men faint for thirst.
14 They that swear by the sin of Samaria, and say, Your god, O Dan, lives; and, The manner of Beer-sheba lives; even they will fall, and never rise up again.

CHAPTER 9

1 I saw the Lord standing upon the altar: and he said, Smite the lintel of the door, that the posts may shake: and cut them in the head, all of them; and I will slay the last of them with the sword: he that flees of them will not flee away, and he that escapes of them will not be delivered.
2 Though they dig into hell, there will mine hand take them; though they climb up to heaven, there will I bring them down:
3 And though they hide themselves in the top of Carmel, I will search and take them out thence; and though they be hid from my sight in the bottom of the sea, there will I command the serpent, and he will bite them:
4 And though they go into captivity before their enemies, there will I command the sword, and it will slay them: and I will set mine eyes upon them for evil, and not for good.
5 And the Lord GOD of hosts *is* he that touches the land, and it will melt, and all that dwell therein will mourn: and it will rise up wholly like a flood; and will be drowned, as *by* the flood of Egypt.
6 *It is* he that builds his stories in the heaven, and has founded his troop in the earth; he that calls for the waters of the sea, and pours them out upon the face of the earth: The LORD *is* his name.

7 *Are* you not as children of the Ethiopians unto me, O children of Israel? says the LORD. Have not I brought up Israel out of the land of Egypt? And the Philistines from Caphtor, and the Syrians from Kir?
8 Behold, the eyes of the Lord GOD *are* upon the sinful kingdom, and I will destroy it from off the face of the earth; saving that I will not utterly destroy the house of Jacob, says the LORD.
9 For, lo, I will command, and I will sift the house of Israel among all nations, like as *corn* is sifted in a sieve, yet will not the least grain fall upon the earth.
10 All the sinners of my people will die by the sword, which say, The evil will not overtake or prevent us.
11 In that day will I raise up the tabernacle of David that is fallen, and close up the breaches thereof; and I will raise up his ruins, and I will build it as in the days of old:
12 That they may possess the remnant of Edom, and of all the heathen, which are called by my name, says the LORD that doeth this.
13 Behold, the days come, says the LORD, that the plowman will overtake the reaper[1], and the treader of grapes him that sows seed; and the mountains will drop sweet wine, and all the hills will melt.
14 And I will bring again the captivity of my people of Israel, and they will build the waste cities, and inhabit *them*; and they will plant vineyards, and drink the wine thereof; they will also make gardens, and eat the fruit of them.
15 And I will plant them upon their land, and they will no more be pulled up out of their land which I have given them, says the LORD your God.

---

[1] reaper- *qâtsar*, <u>kaw-tsar'</u>; a primitive root; to *dock off*, that is *curtail* (transitively or intransitively, literally or figuratively); especially to *harvest* (grass or grain): cut down, much discouraged, grieve, harvestman, lothe, mourn, straiten, trouble, vex. [Strgs#7114]

OBADIAH
CHAPTER 1

1 The vision of Obadiah[1]. Thus says the Lord GOD concerning Edom; We have heard a rumor from the LORD, and an ambassador is sent among the heathen, Arise ye, and let us rise up against her in battle.
2 Behold, I have made you small among the heathen: you are greatly despised.
3 The pride of your heart hath deceived you, you that dwell in the clefts of the rock, whose habitation *is* high; that says in his heart, Who will bring me down to the ground?
4 Though you exalt *yourself* as the eagle, and though you set your nest among the stars, there will I bring you down, says the LORD.
5 If thieves came to you, if robbers by night, (how are you cut off!) would they not have stolen till they had enough? If the grape-gatherers came to you, would they not leave *some* grapes?
6 How are *the things* of Esau searched out! *How* are his hidden things sought up!
7 All the men of your confederacy have brought you *even* to the border: the men that were at peace with you have deceived you, *and* prevailed against you; they that eat your bread have laid a wound under you: *there is* none understanding in him.
8 Will I not in that day, says the LORD, even destroy the wise *men* out of Edom, and understanding out of the mount of Esau?
9 And your mighty *men*, O Teman, will be dismayed, to the end that every one of the mount of Esau may be cut off by slaughter.
10 For *your* violence against your brother Jacob shame will cover you, and you will be cut off for ever.
11 In the day that you stood on the other side, in the day that the strangers carried away captive his forces, and foreigners entered into his gates, and cast lots upon Jerusalem, even you *were* as one of them.
12 But you should not have looked on the day of your brother in the day that he became a stranger; neither should you have rejoiced over the children of Judah in the day of their destruction; neither should you have spoken proudly in the day of distress.
13 You should not have entered into the gate of my people in the day of their calamity; yes, you should not have looked on their affliction in the day of their calamity, nor have laid *hands* on their substance in the day of their calamity;
14 Neither should you have stood in the crossway, to cut off those of his that did escape; neither should you have delivered up those of his that did remain in the day of distress.
15 For the day of the LORD *is* near upon all the heathen: as you have done, it will be done unto you: your reward will return upon your own head.
16 For as ye have drunk upon my holy mountain, *so* will all the heathen drink continually, yes, they will drink, and they will swallow down, and they will be as though they had not been.
17 But upon mount Zion will be deliverance, and there will be holiness; and the house of Jacob will possess their possessions.
18 And the house of Jacob will be a fire, and the house of Joseph a flame, and the house of Esau for stubble, and they will kindle in them, and devour them; and there will not be *any* remaining of the house of Esau; for the LORD hath spoken *it*.
19 And *they of* the south will possess the mount of Esau; and *they of* the plain the Philistines: and they will possess the fields of Ephraim, and the fields of Samaria: and Benjamin *will possess* Gilead.
20 And the captivity of this host of the children of Israel *will possess* that of the Canaanites, *even* unto Zarephath[2]; and the captivity of Jerusalem, which *is* in Sepharad[3], will possess the cities of the south.
21 And saviors will come up on mount Zion to judge the mount of Esau; and the kingdom will be the LORD'S.

---

[1] Obadiah- servant of Jehovah or *serving Jah*. [Strgs#5662]
[2] Zarephath- a city on the coast south of Sidon and the residence of Elijah during the last part of the drought; modern 'Sura-fend.' Its name comes from the Hebrew word tsârephath, tsaq-ref-ath' meaning *refinery* or *refinement*. [Strgs#6886]
[3] Sepharad- a place where Israelites were exiled; site unknown. Translate as *separated*. [Strgs#5614]

JONAH
CHAPTER 1

1 Now the word of the LORD came unto Jonah[1] the son of Amittai, saying,
2 Arise, go to Nineveh, that great city, and cry against it; for their wickedness is come up before me.
3 But Jonah rose up to flee unto Tarshish from the presence of the LORD, and went down to Joppa; and he found a ship going to Tarshish: so he paid the fare thereof, and went down into it, to go with them unto Tarshish from the presence of the LORD.[2]
4 But the LORD sent out a great wind into the sea, and there was a mighty tempest in the sea, so that the ship was like to be broken.
5 Then the mariners were afraid, and cried every man unto his god, and cast forth the wares that were in the ship into the sea, to lighten it of them. But Jonah was gone down into the sides of the ship; and he lay, and was fast asleep.
6 So the shipmaster came to him, and said unto him, What **do you mean**, O sleeper? Arise, call upon thy God, if so be that God will think upon us, that we perish not.
7 And they said everyone to his fellow, Come, and let us cast lots, that we may know for whose cause this evil *is* upon us. So they cast lots, and the lot fell upon Jonah.
8 Then said they unto him, Tell us, we pray you, for whose cause this evil *is* upon us; What *is* your occupation? And **where did you come**? What *is* thy country? And of what people *are* you?
9 And he said unto them, I *am* an Hebrew; and I fear the LORD, the God of heaven, which hath made the sea and the dry *land*.
10 Then were the men exceedingly afraid, and said unto him, Why hast you done this? For the men knew that he fled from the presence of the LORD, because he had told them.
11 Then said they unto him, What will we do unto you, that the sea may be calm unto us? for the sea wrought, and was tempestuous.
12 And he said unto them, Take me up, and cast me forth into the sea; so will the sea be calm unto you: for I know that for my sake this great tempest *is* upon you.
13 Nevertheless the men rowed hard to bring *it* to the land; but they could not: for the sea wrought, and was tempestuous[3] against them.
14 Wherefore they cried unto the LORD, and said, We beseech you, O LORD, we beseech you, let us not perish for this man's life, and lay not upon us innocent blood: for you, O LORD, hast done as it pleased you.
15 So they took up Jonah, and cast him forth into the sea: and the sea ceased from her raging.
16 Then the men feared the LORD exceedingly, and offered a sacrifice unto the LORD, and made vows.
17 Now the LORD had prepared a great fish to swallow up Jonah. And Jonah was in the belly of the fish three days and three nights.

CHAPTER 2

1 Then Jonah prayed unto the LORD his God out of the fish's belly,
2 And said, I cried by reason of mine affliction unto the LORD, and he heard me; out of the belly of hell cried I, *and* you heard my voice.
3 For you had cast me into the deep, in the midst of the seas; and the floods compassed me about: all thy billows and thy waves passed over me.
4 Then I said, I am cast out of thy sight; yet I will look again toward thy holy temple.
5 The waters compassed me about, *even* to the soul: the depth closed me round about, the weeds were wrapped about my head.
6 I went down to the bottoms of the mountains; the earth with her bars *was* about me forever: yet have you brought up my life from corruption, O LORD my God.
7 When my soul fainted within me I remembered the LORD: and my prayer came in unto you, into your holy temple.
8 They that observe lying vanities forsake their own mercy.
9 But I will sacrifice unto you with the voice of thanksgiving; I will pay *that* that I have vowed. Salvation *is* of the LORD.
10 And the LORD spoke unto the fish, and it vomited out Jonah upon the dry *land*.[4]

CHAPTER 3

1 And the word of the LORD came unto Jonah the second time, saying,
2 Arise, go unto Nineveh, that great city, and preach unto it the preaching that I bid you.
3 So Jonah arose, and went unto Nineveh, according to the word of the LORD. Now Nineveh was an exceeding great city of three days' journey.
4 And Jonah began to enter into the city a day's journey, and he cried, and said, Yet forty days, and Nineveh will be overthrown.
5 So the people of Nineveh believed God, and proclaimed a fast, and put on sackcloth, from the greatest of them even to the least of them.
6 For word came unto the king of Nineveh, and he arose from his throne, and he laid his robe from him, and covered *him* with sackcloth, and sat in ashes.
7 And he caused *it* to be proclaimed and published through Nineveh by the decree of the king and his nobles, saying, Let neither man or beast, herd or flock, taste any thing: let them not feed, or drink water:
8 But let man and beast be covered with sackcloth, and cry mightily unto God: yes, let them turn everyone from his evil way, and from the violence that *is* in their hands.
9 Who can tell *if* God will turn and repent, and turn away from his fierce anger, that we perish not?
10 And God saw their works, that they turned from their evil way; and God repented of the evil, that he had said that he would do unto them; and he did *it* not.

CHAPTER 4

1 But it displeased Jonah exceedingly, and he was very angry.
2 And he prayed unto the LORD, and said, I pray you, O LORD, *was* not this my saying, when I was yet in my country? Therefore I fled before unto Tarshish[5]: for I knew that you *are* a gracious God, and merciful, slow to anger, and of great kindness, and repent you of the evil.
3 Therefore now, O LORD, take, I beseech you, my life from me; for *it is* better for me to die than to live.
4 Then said the LORD, Doest you well to be angry?

---

[1] Jonah- literally *dove*. [Strgs#3124] see Index.
[2] Jonah paid a fair to go down. He paid a fee to escape the Lord and only ended up going down into a lower place or state.
[3] tempestuous- a primitive root; to *rush* upon; by implication to *toss*: be sore troubled, come out as a whirlwind. [Strgs#5590]
[4] Jonah was released from his hard times once he recognized his place and purpose while still in the whale. God releases us from hard times using His voice after we had cried out to Him and stepping into our purpose.
[5] see Index

5 So Jonah went out of the city, and sat on the east side of the city, and there made him a booth, and sat under it in the shadow, till he might see what would become of the city.

6 And the LORD God prepared a gourd, and made *it* to come up over Jonah, that it might be a shadow over his head, to deliver him from his grief. So Jonah was exceeding glad of the gourd.

7 But God prepared a worm when the morning rose the next day, and it smote the gourd that it withered.

8 And it came to pass, when the sun did arise, that God prepared a vehement east wind; and the sun beat upon the head of Jonah, that he fainted, and wished in himself to die, and said, *It is* better for me to die than to live.

9 And God said to Jonah, Does you well to be angry for the gourd? And he said, I do well to be angry, *even* unto death.

10 Then said the LORD, You hast had pity on the gourd, for the which you hast not labored, neither made it grow; which came up in a night, and perished in a night:

11 And should not I spare Nineveh, that great city, wherein are more than sixscore thousand persons that cannot discern between their right hand and their left hand; and *also* much cattle?[1]

---

[1] **Jonah 4:5-11**- Many believers are more concerned about the plant (lit. that which makes them comfortable) then preach the gospel to people that cannot discern their right hand from their left.

MICAH

CHAPTER 1

1 The word of the LORD that came to Micah[1] the Morasthite in the days of Jotham, Ahaz, *and* Hezekiah, kings of Judah, which he saw concerning Samaria and Jerusalem.
2 Hear, all you people; hearken, O earth, and all that therein is: and let the Lord GOD be witness against you, the Lord from his holy temple.
3 For, behold, the LORD cometh forth out of his place, and will come down, and tread upon the high places of the earth.
4 And the mountains will be molten under him, and the valleys will be cleft, as wax before the fire, *and* as the waters *that are* poured down a steep place.
5 For the transgression of Jacob *is* all this, and for the sins of the house of Israel. What *is* the transgression of Jacob? *is it* not Samaria? And what *are* the high places of Judah? *are they* not Jerusalem?
6 Therefore I will make Samaria as an heap of the field, *and* as plantings of a vineyard: and I will pour down the stones thereof into the valley, and I will discover the foundations thereof.
7 And all the graven images thereof will be beaten to pieces, and all the hires thereof will be burned with the fire, and all the idols thereof will I lay desolate: for she gathered *it* of the hire of an harlot, and they will return to the hire of an harlot.
8 Therefore I will wail and howl, I will go stripped and naked: I will make a wailing like the dragons, and mourning as the owls.
9 For her wound *is* incurable; for it is come unto Judah; he is come unto the gate of my people, *even* to Jerusalem.
10 Declare you *it* not at Gath, weep you not at all: in the house of Aphrah[2] roll yourself in the dust.
11 Pass you away, you inhabitant of Saphir[3], having your shame naked: the inhabitant of Zaanan[4] came not forth in the mourning of Beth-ezel[5]; he will receive of you his standing.
12 For the inhabitant of Maroth[6] waited carefully for good: but evil came down from the LORD unto the gate of Jerusalem.
13 O you inhabitant of Lachish, bind the chariot to the swift beast: she *is* the beginning of the sin to the daughter of Zion: for the transgressions of Israel were found in you.
14 Therefore will you give presents to Moresheth-gath[7]: the houses of Achzib *will be* a lie to the kings of Israel.
15 Yet will I bring an heir unto you, O inhabitant of Mareshah: he will come unto Adullam[8] the glory of Israel.
16 Make you bald, and poll you for your delicate children; enlarge your baldness as the eagle; for they are gone into captivity from you.

CHAPTER 2

1 Woe to them that devise iniquity, and work evil upon their beds! when the morning is light, they practice it, because it is in the power of their hand.
2 And they covet fields, and take *them* by violence; and houses, and take *them* away: so they oppress a man and his house, even a man and his heritage.
3 Therefore thus says the LORD; Behold, against this family do I devise an evil, from which you will not remove your necks; neither will you go haughtily: for this time *is* evil.
4 In that day will *one* take up a parable against you and lament with a doleful lamentation, *and* say, We be utterly spoiled: he has changed the portion of my people: how has he removed *it* from me! Turning away he has divided our fields.
5 Therefore you will have none that will cast a cord by lot in the congregation of the LORD.
6 Prophesy you not, *say they to them that* prophesy: they will not prophesy to them, *that* they will not take shame.
7 O *you that are* named the house of Jacob, is the spirit of the LORD straitened? *Are* these his doings? Do not my words do good to him that walks uprightly?
8 Even of late my people is risen up as an enemy: you pull off the robe with the garment from them that pass by securely as men averse from war.
9 The women of my people have you cast out from their pleasant houses; from their children have you taken away my glory forever.
10 Arise you, and depart; for this *is* not *your* rest: because it is polluted, it will destroy *you*, even with a sore destruction.
11 If a man walking in the spirit and falsehood do lie, *saying*, I will prophesy unto you of wine and of strong drink; he will even be the prophet of this people.
12 I will surely assemble, O Jacob, all of you; I will surely gather the remnant of Israel; I will put them together as the sheep of Bozrah[9], as the flock in the midst of their fold: they will make great noise by reason of *the multitude of* men.
13 The breaker is come up before them: they have broken up, and have passed through the gate, and are gone out by it: and their king will pass before them, and the LORD on the head of them.

CHAPTER 3

1 And I said, Hear, I pray you, O heads of Jacob, and you princes of the house of Israel; *Is it* not for you to know judgment?
2 Who hate the good, and love the evil; who pluck off their skin from off them, and their flesh from off their bones;
3 Who also eat the flesh of my people, and flay their skin from off them; and they break their bones, and chop them in pieces, as for the pot, and as flesh within the caldron.
4 Then will they cry unto the LORD, but he will not hear them: he will even hide his face from them at that time, as they have behaved themselves ill in their doings.
5 Thus says the LORD concerning the prophets that make my people err, that bite with their teeth, and cry, Peace; and he that puts not into their mouths, they even prepare war against him.
6 Therefore night *will be* unto you, that you will not have a vision; and it will be dark unto you, that you will not divine; and the sun will go down over the prophets, and the day will be dark over them.
7 Then will the seers be ashamed, and the diviners confounded: yea, they will all cover their lips; for *there is* no answer of God.

---

[1] Micah- *Mîykâh*, <u>mee-kaw'</u>; *who is like God* [Strgs#4318] an abbreviation of *Mîykâyâh*, <u>me-kaw-yaw'</u>; meaning *who (is) like Jah* [Strgs#4320].
[2] Aphrah- *house to* (i.e. of) *dust.* [Strgs#1036]
[3] Saphir- literally *fair* or *beautiful.* [Strgs#8208]
[4] Zaanan- *sheep pasture.* [Strgs#6630]
[5] Beth-ezel- *house of narrowing* or *house of the side.* [Strgs#1018]
[6] Maroth- literally *bitterness* or *bitter springs*, a place in Palestine. [Strgs#4796]
[7] Moresheth-gath- a place apparently I the neighborhood of Gath and probably the home of the prophet Micah. The name means *possession of Gath.* [Strgs#4182]. Gath meaning *winepress.* [Strgs#1661]
[8] Adullam- a town of the Canaanites allotted to Judah and lying in the lowlands; site of the cave where David hid. The name is defined as *justice of the people.* [Strgs5725]
[9] Bozrah- literally *an enclosure*, that is *sheepfold.* [Strgs#1223]

8 But truly I am full of power by the spirit of the LORD, and of judgment, and of might, to declare unto Jacob his transgression, and to Israel his sin.
9 Hear this, I pray you, you heads of the house of Jacob, and princes of the house of Israel, that abhor judgment, and pervert all equity.
10 They build up Zion with blood, and Jerusalem with iniquity.
11 The heads thereof judge for reward, and the priests thereof teach for hire, and the prophets thereof divine for money: yet will they lean upon the LORD, and say, *Is* not the LORD among us? None evil can come upon us.
12 Therefore will Zion for your sake be plowed *as* a field, and Jerusalem will become heaps, and the mountain of the house as the high places of the forest.

CHAPTER 4
1 But in the last days it will come to pass, *that* the mountain of the house of the LORD will be established in the top of the mountains, and it will be exalted above the hills; and people will flow unto it.
2 And many nations will come, and say, Come, and let us go up to the mountain of the LORD, and to the house of the God of Jacob; and he will teach us of his ways, and we will walk in his paths: for the law will go forth of Zion, and the word of the LORD from Jerusalem.
3 And he will judge among many people, and rebuke strong nations afar off; and they will beat their swords into plowshares, and their spears into pruning hooks: nation will not lift up a sword against nation, neither will they learn war any more.
4 But they will sit every man under his vine and under his fig tree; and none will make *them* afraid: for the mouth of the LORD of hosts has spoken *it*.
5 For all people will walk everyone in the name of his god, and we will walk in the name of the LORD our God forever and ever.
6 In that day, says the LORD, will I assemble her that halts[1], and I will gather her that is driven out, and her that I have afflicted;
7 And I will make her that halted a remnant, and her that was cast far off a strong nation: and the LORD will reign over them in mount Zion from henceforth, even for ever.
8 And you, O tower of the flock, the strong hold of the daughter of Zion, unto you will it come, even the first dominion; the kingdom will come to the daughter of Jerusalem.
9 Now why dost you cry out aloud? *Is there* no king in you? is your counselor perished? For pangs have taken you as a woman in travail.
10 Be in pain, and labor to bring forth, O daughter of Zion, like a woman in travail: for now will you go forth out of the city, and you will dwell in the field, and you will go *even* to Babylon; there will you be delivered; there the LORD will redeem you from the hand of your enemies.
11 Now also many nations are gathered against you, that say, Let her be defiled, and let our eyes look upon Zion.
12 But they know not the thoughts of the LORD, neither understand they his counsel: for he will gather them as the sheaves into the floor.
13 Arise and thresh, O daughter of Zion: for I will make your horn iron, and I will make your hoofs brass: and you will beat in pieces many people: and I will consecrate their gain unto the LORD, and their substance unto the Lord of the whole earth.

CHAPTER 5
1 Now gather yourself in troops, O daughter of troops: he has laid siege against us: they will smite the judge of Israel with a rod upon the cheek.
2 But you, Beth-lehem Ephratah, *though* you be little among the thousands of Judah, *yet* out of you will he come forth unto me *that is* to be ruler in Israel; whose goings forth *have been* from of old, from everlasting.
3 Therefore will he give them up, until the time *that* she which travails has brought forth: then the remnant of his brethren will return unto the children of Israel.
4 And he will stand and feed in the strength of the LORD, in the majesty of the name of the LORD his God; and they will abide: for now will he be great unto the ends of the earth.
5 And this *man* will be the peace, when the Assyrian will come into our land: and when he will tread in our palaces, then will we raise against him seven shepherds, and eight principal men.
6 And they will waste the land of Assyria with the sword, and the land of Nimrod in the entrances thereof: thus will he deliver us from the Assyrian, when he cometh into our land, and when he treads within our borders.
7 [And the remnant of Jacob will be in the midst of many people as a dew from the LORD, as the showers upon the grass, that tarries not for man, or waits for the sons of men.][2]
8 And the remnant of Jacob will be among the Gentiles in the midst of many people as a lion among the beasts of the forest, as a young lion among the flocks of sheep: who, if he go through, both treads down, and tears in pieces, and none can deliver.
9 Your hand will be lifted up upon your adversaries, and all your enemies will be cut off.
10 And it will come to pass in that day, says the LORD, that I will cut off your horses out of the midst of you, and I will destroy your chariots:
11 And I will cut off the cities of your land, and throw down all your strong holds:
12 And I will cut off witchcrafts out of your hand; and you will have no *more* soothsayers:
13 Your graven images also will I cut off, and your standing images out of the midst of you; and you will no more worship the work of your hands.
14 And I will pluck up your groves out of the midst of you: so will I destroy your cities.
15 And I will execute vengeance in anger and fury upon the heathen, such as they have not heard.

CHAPTER 6
1 Hear you now what the LORD says; Arise, contend you before the mountains, and let the hills hear your voice.
2 Hear you, O mountains, the LORD'S controversy, and you strong foundations of the earth: for the LORD has a controversy with his people, and he will plead with Israel.
3 O my people, what have I done unto you? and wherein have I wearied you? Testify against me.
4 For I brought you up out of the land of Egypt, and redeemed you out of the house of servants; and I sent before you Moses, Aaron, and Miriam.
5 O my people, remember now what Balak king of Moab consulted, and what Balaam the son of Beor answered him from Shittim unto Gilgal; that you may know the righteousness of the LORD.

---

[1] halts- to curve, to limp (as it one sided). [Strgs#6760]

[2] compare 1 Peter 1:24, Rev. 8:7 & Is. 51:12

6 Wherewith will I come before the LORD, *and* bow myself before the high God? will I come before him with burnt offerings, with calves of a year old?

7 Will the LORD be pleased with thousands of rams, *or* with ten thousands of rivers of oil? will I give my firstborn *for* my transgression, the fruit of my body *for* the sin of my soul?

8 He has showed you, O man, what *is* good; and what does the LORD require of you, but to do justly, and to love mercy, and to walk humbly with your God?

9 The LORD'S voice cries unto the city, and *the man of* wisdom will see your name: hear you the rod, and who has appointed it.

10 Are there yet the treasures of wickedness in the house of the wicked, and the scant measure *that is* abominable?

11 Will I count *them* pure with the wicked balances, and with the bag of deceitful weights?

12 For the rich men thereof are full of violence, and the inhabitants thereof have spoken lies, and their tongue *is* deceitful in their mouth.

13 Therefore also will I make *you* sick in smiting you, in making *you* desolate because of your sins.

14 You will eat, but not be satisfied; and your casting down *will be* in the midst of you; and you will take hold, but will not deliver; and *that* which you deliver will I give up to the sword.

15 You will sow, but you will not reap; you will tread the olives, but you will not anoint you with oil; and sweet wine, but will not drink wine.

16 For the statutes of Omri[1] are kept, and all the works of the house of Ahab, and you walk in their counsels; that I should make you a desolation, and the inhabitants thereof an hissing: therefore you will bear the reproach of my people.

CHAPTER 7

1 Woe is me! for I am as when they have gathered the summer fruits, as the grape-gleanings of the vintage: *there is* no cluster to eat: my soul desired the first-ripe fruit.

2 The good *man* is perished out of the earth: and *there is* none upright among men: they all lie in wait for blood; they hunt every man his brother with a net.

3 That they may do evil with both hands earnestly, the prince asks, and the judge *asks* for a reward; and the great *man*, he utters his mischievous desire: so they wrap it up.

4 The best of them *is* as a brier: the most upright *is sharper* than a thorn hedge: the day of your watchmen *and* your visitation cometh; now will be their perplexity.

5 Trust you not in a friend, put you not confidence in a guide: keep the doors of your mouth from her that lies in your bosom.

6 For the son dishonors the father, the daughter rises up against her mother, the daughter in law against her mother in law; a man's enemies *are* the men of his own house.

7 Therefore I will look unto the LORD; I will wait for the God of my salvation: my God will hear me.

8 Rejoice not against me, O mine enemy: when I fall, I will arise; when I sit in darkness, the LORD *will be* a light unto me.

9 I will bear the indignation of the LORD, because I have sinned against him, until he plead my cause, and execute judgment for me: he will bring me forth to the light, *and* I will behold his righteousness.

10 Then *she that is* mine enemy will see *it*, and shame will cover her which said unto me, Where is the LORD your God? Mine eyes will behold her: now will she be trodden down as the mire of the streets.

11 *In* the day that your walls are to be built, *in* that day will the decree be far removed.

12 *In* that day *also* he will come even to you from Assyria, and *from* the fortified cities, and from the fortress even to the river, and from sea to sea, and *from* mountain to mountain.

13 Notwithstanding the land will be desolate because of them that dwell therein, for the fruit of their doings.

14 Feed your people with your rod, the flock of your heritage, which dwell solitarily *in* the wood, in the midst of Carmel: let them feed *in* Bashan and Gilead, as in the days of old.

15 According to the days of your coming out of the land of Egypt will I show unto him marvelous *things*.

16 The nations will see and be confounded at all their might: they will lay *their* hand upon *their* mouth, their ears will be deaf.

17 They will lick the dust like a serpent, they will move out of their holes like worms of the earth: they will be afraid of the LORD our God, and will fear because of you.

18 Who *is* a God like unto you, that pardons iniquity, and passes by the transgression of the remnant of his heritage? He retains not his anger forever, because he delights *in* mercy.

19 He will turn again, he will have compassion upon us; he will subdue our iniquities; and you will cast all their sins into the depths of the sea.

20 You will perform the truth to Jacob, *and* the mercy to Abraham, which you have sworn unto our fathers from the days of old.

---

[1] Omri- *heaping* [Strgs#6018]. BDB defines it as *pupil of Jehovah*.

NAHUM
CHAPTER 1

1 The burden of Nineveh. The book of the vision of Nahum[1] the Elkoshite.
2 God *is* jealous, and the LORD revenges; the LORD revenges, and *is* furious; the LORD will take vengeance on his adversaries, and he reserves *wrath* for his enemies.
3 The LORD *is* slow to anger, and great in power, and will not at all acquit *the wicked*: the LORD has his way in the whirlwind and in the storm, and the clouds *are* the dust of his feet.
4 He rebukes the sea, and makes it dry, and dries up all the rivers: Bashan languishes, and Carmel, and the flower of Lebanon languishes.
5 The mountains quake at him, and the hills melt, and the earth is burned at his presence, yea, the world, and all that dwell therein.
6 Who can stand before his indignation? and who can abide in the fierceness of his anger? his fury is poured out like fire, and the rocks are thrown down by him.
7 The LORD *is* good, a strong hold in the day of trouble; and he knows them that trust in him.
8 But with an overrunning flood he will make an utter end of the place thereof, and darkness will pursue his enemies.
9 What do you imagine against the LORD? he will make an utter end: affliction will not rise up the second time.
10 For while *they be* folden together *as* thorns, and while they are drunken *as* drunkards, they will be devoured as stubble fully dry.
11 There is *one* come out of you, that imagines evil against the LORD, a wicked counselor.
12 Thus says the LORD; Though *they be* quiet, and likewise many, yet thus will they be cut down, when he will pass through. Though I have afflicted you, I will afflict you no more.
13 For now will I break his yoke from off you, and will burst your bonds in sunder.
14 And the LORD has given a commandment concerning you, *that* no more of your name be sown: out of the house of your gods will I cut off the graven image and the molten image: I will make your grave; for you are vile.
15 Behold upon the mountains the feet of him that brings good tidings, that publishes peace![2] O Judah, keep your solemn feasts, perform your vows: for the wicked will no more pass through you; he is utterly cut off.

CHAPTER 2

1 He that dashes in pieces is come up before your face: keep the munition[3], watch the way, make *your* loins strong, fortify *your* power mightily.
2 For the LORD has turned away the excellency of Jacob, as the excellency of Israel: for the emptiers[4] have emptied them out, and marred their vine branches.
3 The shield of his mighty men is made red, the valiant men *are* in scarlet: the chariots *will be* with flaming torches in the day of his preparation, and the fir trees will be terribly shaken.
4 The chariots will rage in the streets, they will justle one against another in the broad ways: they will seem like torches, they will run like the lightnings.
5 He will recount his worthies: they will stumble in their walk; they will make haste to the wall thereof, and the defense[5] will be prepared.
6 The gates of the rivers will be opened, and the palace will be dissolved.
7 And Huzzab[6] will be led away captive, she will be brought up, and her maids will lead *her* as with the voice of doves, tambourine upon their breasts.
8 But Nineveh *is* of old like a pool of water: yet they will flee away. Stand, stand, *will they cry*; but none will look back.
9 Take you the spoil of silver, take the spoil of gold: for *there is* none end of the store *and* glory out of all the pleasant furniture.
10 She is empty, and void, and waste: and the heart melts, and the knees smite together, and much pain *is* in all loins, and the faces of them all gather blackness.
11 Where *is* the dwelling of the lions, and the feeding-place of the young lions, where the lion, *even* the old lion, walked, *and* the lion's whelp, and none made *them* afraid?
12 The lion did tear in pieces enough for his whelps, and strangled for his lionesses, and filled his holes with prey, and his dens with ravin[7].
13 Behold, I *am* against you, says the LORD of hosts, and I will burn her chariots in the smoke, and the sword will devour your young lions: and I will cut off your prey from the earth, and the voice of your messengers will no more be heard.

CHAPTER 3

1 Woe to the bloody city! it *is* all full of lies *and* robbery; the prey departs not;
2 The noise of a whip, and the noise of the rattling of the wheels, and of the prancing horses, and of the jumping chariots
3 The horseman lifts up both the bright sword and the glittering spear: and *there is* a multitude of slain, and a great number of carcasses; and *there is* none end of *their* corpses; they stumble upon their corpses:
4 Because of the multitude of the whoredoms of the well-favored harlot, the mistress of witchcrafts, that sells nations through her whoredoms, and families through her witchcrafts.
5 Behold, I *am* against you, says the LORD of hosts, and I will discover your skirts upon your face, and I will show the nations your nakedness, and the kingdoms your shame.
6 And I will cast abominable filth upon you, and make you vile, and will set you as a gazing-stock.
7 And it will come to pass, *that* all they that look upon you will flee from you, and say, Nineveh is laid waste: who will bemoan her? Where will I seek comforters for you?
8 Are you better than populous No, that was situate among the rivers, *that had* the waters round about it, whose rampart *was* the sea, *and* her wall *was* from the sea?
9 Ethiopia and Egypt *were* her strength, and *it was* infinite; Put and Lubim were your helpers.

---

[1] Nahum- means comfort. [Strgs#5151]
[2] compare Romans 10:15
[3] munition- a *hemming* in, that is, (objectively) a *mound* (of siege), or (subjectively) a *rampart* (of protection), (abstractly) *fortification*: -fenced (city) fort, strong hold. [Strgs#4694]
[4] emptiers- Hebrew *bâqaq*, baw-kah'; meaning to *pour out*, that is, to *empty*, figuratively to *depopulate*; by analogy to spread out (as a fruitful vine). [Strgs#1238]
[5] defense- to *entwine* as a screen, by implication to *fence in*, cover over, (figuratively) *protect*. [Strgs#5526]
[6] Huzzab- Hebrew *nâtsab*, naw-tsab'; meaning to *station*, in various applications: appointed, deputy, erect, establish, lay, officer, pillar, rear up, settle, sharpen. [Strgs#5324]
[7] Ravin- Hebrew *terêphâh*, ter-ay-faw'; *prey*, that is flocks devoured by animals: (that which was) torn (of beasts, in pieces). [Strgs#2966]

10 Yet *was* she carried away, she went into captivity: her young children also were dashed in pieces at the top of all the streets: and they cast lots for her honorable men, and all her great men were bound in chains.

11 You also will be drunken: you will be hid, you also will seek strength because of the enemy.

12 All your strong holds *will be like* fig trees with the first-ripe figs: if they be shaken, they will even fall into the mouth of the eater.

13 Behold, your people in the midst of you *are* women: the gates of your land will be set wide open unto your enemies: the fire will devour your bars.

14 Draw you waters for the siege, fortify your strong holds: go into clay, and tread the mortar, make strong the **brickwork**.

15 There will the fire devour you; the sword will cut you off, it will eat you up like the cankerworm: make yourself many as the cankerworm, make yourself many as the locusts.

16 You have multiplied your merchants above the stars of heaven: the cankerworm spoils, and flies away.

17 Your crowned *are* as the locusts, and your captains as the great grasshoppers, which camp in the hedges in the cold day, *but* when the sun arises they flee away, and their place is not known where they *are*.

18 Your shepherds slumber, O king of Assyria: your nobles will dwell *in the dust*: your people is scattered upon the mountains, and no man gathers *them*.

19 *There is* no healing of your bruise; your wound is grievous: all that hear the bruit[1] of you will clap the hands over you: for upon whom has not your wickedness passed continually?

---

[1] bruit- something *heard*, that is, a *sound*, *rumor*, *announcement*; abstractly *audience*: -fame, hear (-ing), loud, report, speech, tidings. [Strgs# 8088]

HABAKKUK

CHAPTER 1

1 The burden which Habakkuk[1] the prophet did see.
2 O LORD, how long will I cry, and you will not hear! *even* cry out unto you *of* violence, and you will not save!
3 Why dost you show me iniquity, and cause *me* to behold grievance? for spoiling and violence *are* before me: and there are *that* raise up strife and contention.
4 Therefore the law is slacked, and judgment does never go forth: for the wicked does compass about the righteous; therefore wrong judgment proceeds.
5 Behold you among the heathen, and regard, and wonder marvelously: for *I* will work a work in your days, *which* you will not believe, though it be told *you*.
6 For, lo, I raise up the Chaldeans, *that* bitter and hasty nation, which will march through the breadth of the land, to possess the dwelling-places *that are* not theirs.
7 They *are* terrible and dreadful: their judgment and their dignity will proceed of themselves.
8 Their horses also are swifter than the leopards, and are more fierce than the evening wolves: and their horsemen will spread themselves, and their horsemen will come from far; they will fly as the eagle *that* haste to eat.
9 They will come all for violence: their faces will sup up *as* the east wind, and they will gather the captivity as the sand.
10 And they will scoff at the kings, and the princes will be a scorn unto them: they will deride every strong hold; for they will heap dust, and take it.
11 Then will *his* mind change, and he will pass over, and offend, *imputing* this his power unto his god.
12 *Are* you not from everlasting, O LORD my God, mine Holy One? we will not die. O LORD, you have ordained them for judgment; and, O mighty God, you have established them for correction.
13 *You are* of purer eyes than to behold evil, and canst not look on iniquity: wherefore looks you upon them that deal treacherously, *and* holds your tongue when the wicked devours *the man that is* more righteous than he?
14 And makes men as the fishes of the sea, as the creeping things, *that have* no ruler over them?
15 They take up all of them with the angle, they catch them in their net, and gather them in their drag: therefore they rejoice and are glad.
16 Therefore they sacrifice unto their net, and burn incense unto their drag; because by them their portion *is* fat, and their meat plenteous.
17 Will they therefore empty their net, and not spare continually to slay the nations?

CHAPTER 2

1 I will stand upon my watch, and set me upon the tower, and will watch to see what he will say unto me, and what I will answer when I am reproved.
2 And the LORD answered me, and said, Write the vision, and make *it* plain upon tables, that he may run that reads it.
3 For the vision *is* yet for an appointed time, but at the end it will speak, and not lie: though it tarry, wait for it; because it will surely come, it will not tarry.

---

[1] Habakkuk- *embrace*. [Strgs#2265]
[2] compare Rev. 16:14-16

4 Behold, his soul *which* is lifted up is not upright in him: but the just will live by his faith.
5 Yea also, because he transgresses by wine, *he is* a proud man, neither keeps at home, who enlarges his desire as hell, and *is* as death, and cannot be satisfied, but gathers unto him all nations, and heaps[2] unto him all people:
6 Will not all these take up a parable against him, and a taunting proverb against him, and say, Woe to him that increases *that which is* not his! how long? and to him that **loads** himself with thick clay!
7 Will they not rise up suddenly that will bite you, and awake that will vex you, and you will be for booties unto them?
8 Because you have spoiled many nations, all the remnant of the people will spoil you; because of men's blood, and *for* the violence of the land, of the city, and of all that dwell therein.
9 Woe to him that covets an evil covetousness to his house, that he may set his nest on high, that he may be delivered from the power of evil!
10 You have consulted shame to your house by cutting off many people, and have sinned *against* your soul.
11 For the stone will cry out of the wall, and the beam out of the timber will answer it.
12 Woe to him that builds a town with blood, and establishes a city by iniquity!
13 Behold, *is it* not of the LORD of hosts that the people will labor in the very fire, and the people will weary themselves for very vanity?
14 For the earth will be filled with the knowledge of the glory of the LORD, as the waters cover the sea.
15 Woe unto him that gives his neighbor drink, that puts your bottle to *him*, and makes *him* drunken also, that you may look on their nakedness!
16 You are filled with shame for glory: drink you also, and let your foreskin be uncovered: the cup of the LORD'S right hand will be turned unto you, and shameful spewing *will be* on your glory.
17 For the violence of Lebanon will cover you, and the spoil of beasts, *which* made them afraid, because of men's blood, and for the violence of the land, of the city, and of all that dwell therein.
18 What profits the graven image that the maker thereof has graven it; the molten image, and a teacher of lies, that the maker of his work trusts therein, to make dumb idols?
19 Woe unto him that says to the wood, Awake; to the dumb stone, Arise, it will teach! Behold, it *is* laid over with gold and silver, and *there is* no breath at all in the midst of it.
20 But the LORD *is* in his holy temple: let all the earth keep silence before him.

CHAPTER 3

1 A prayer of Habakkuk the prophet upon Shigionoth[3].
2 O LORD, I have heard your speech, *and* was afraid: O LORD, revive your work in the midst of the years, in the midst of the years make known; in wrath remember mercy.
3 God came from Teman, and the Holy One from mount Paran. Selah. His glory covered the heavens, and the earth was full of his praise.
4 And *his* brightness was as the light; he had horns coming out of his hand: and there *was* the hiding of his power.
5 Before him went the pestilence, and burning coals went forth at his feet.

---

[3] Shigionoth- literally *aberration*, that is, a dithyramb or rambling poem. [Strgs#7692]

6 He stood, and measured the earth: he beheld, and drove asunder the nations; and the everlasting mountains were scattered, the perpetual hills did bow: his ways *are* everlasting.

7 I saw the tents of Cushan in affliction: *and* the curtains of the land of Midian did tremble.

8 Was the LORD displeased against the rivers? *was* your anger against the rivers? *was* your wrath against the sea, that you did ride upon your horses *and* your chariots of salvation?

9 Your bow was made quite naked, *according* to the oaths of the tribes, *even your* word. Selah. You did cleave the earth with rivers.

10 The mountains saw you, *and* they trembled: the overflowing of the water passed by: the deep uttered his voice, *and* lifted up his hands on high.

11 The sun *and* moon stood still in their habitation: at the light of your arrows they went, *and* at the shining of your glittering spear.

12 You did march through the land in indignation, you did thresh the heathen in anger.

13 [You went forth for the salvation of your people, *even* for salvation with your anointed; you wounded the head out of the house of the wicked, by discovering the foundation unto the neck. Selah.][1]

14 You did strike through with his staves the head of his villages: they came out as a whirlwind to scatter me: their rejoicing *was* as to devour the poor secretly.

15 You did walk through the sea with your horses, *through* the heap of great waters.

16 When I heard, my belly trembled; my lips quivered at the voice: rottenness entered into my bones, and I trembled in myself, that I might rest in the day of trouble: when he comes up unto the people, he will invade them with his troops.

17 Although the fig tree will not blossom, neither *will* fruit *be* in the vines; the labor of the olive will fail, and the fields will yield no meat; the flock will be cut off from the fold, and *there will be* no herd in the stalls:

18 Yet I will rejoice in the LORD, I will joy in the God of my salvation.

19 The LORD God *is* my strength, and he will make my feet like hinds' *feet*, and he will make me to walk upon mine high places. To the chief singer on my stringed instruments.

---

[1] Whenever we 'discover' or 'expose' false foundations. It is like wounding the head of the wicked (beast/satan).

ZEPHANIAH
CHAPTER 1

1 The word of the LORD which came unto Zephaniah[1] the son of Cushi, the son of Gedaliah, the son of Amariah, the son of Hizkiah, in the days of Josiah the son of Amon, king of Judah.
2 I will utterly consume all *things* from off the land, says the LORD.
3 I will consume man and beast; I will consume the fowls of the heaven, and the fishes of the sea, and the stumbling-blocks with the wicked; and I will cut off man from off the land, says the LORD.
4 I will also stretch out mine hand upon Judah, and upon all the inhabitants of Jerusalem; and I will cut off the remnant of Baal from this place, *and* the name of the Chemarims[2] with the priests;
5 And them that worship the host of heaven upon the housetops; and them that worship *and* that swear by the LORD, and that swear by Malcham[3];
6 And them that are turned back from the LORD; and *those* that have not sought the LORD, or enquired for him.
7 Hold your peace at the presence of the Lord GOD: for the day of the LORD *is* at hand: for the LORD has prepared a sacrifice, he has bid his guests.
8 And it will come to pass in the day of the LORD'S sacrifice, that I will punish the princes, and the king's children, and all such as are clothed with strange apparel.
9 In the same day also will I punish all those that leap on the threshold, which fill their masters' houses with violence and deceit.
10 And it will come to pass in that day, says the LORD, *that there will be* the noise of a cry from the fish gate, and an howling from the second, and a great crashing from the hills.
11 Howl, you inhabitants of Maktesh, for all the merchant people are cut down; all they that bear silver are cut off.
12 And it will come to pass at that time, *that* I will search Jerusalem with candles, and punish the men that are settled on their lees: that say in their heart, The LORD will not do good, neither will he do evil.
13 Therefore their goods will become a booty, and their houses a desolation: they will also build houses, but not inhabit *them*; and they will plant vineyards, but not drink the wine thereof.
14 The great day of the LORD *is* near, *it is* near, and haste greatly, *even* the voice of the day of the LORD: the mighty man will cry there bitterly.
15 That day *is* a day of wrath, a day of trouble and distress, a day of wasteness and desolation, a day of darkness and gloominess, a day of clouds and thick darkness,
16 A day of the trumpet and alarm against the fenced cities, and against the high towers.
17 And I will bring distress upon men, that they will walk like blind men, because they have sinned against the LORD: and their blood will be poured out as dust, and their flesh as the dung.
18 Neither their silver or their gold will be able to deliver them in the day of the LORD'S wrath; but the whole land will be devoured by the fire of his jealousy: for he will make even a speedy riddance of all them that dwell in the land.

---

[1] Zephaniah- Jehovah has treasured or *Jah has secreted*. [Strgs#6846]
[2] Chemarims- properly an *ascetic* (as if shrunk with self maceration), that is, an idolatrous priest. [Strgs#3649]
[3] Malcham- Hebrew word *melek*, meh'-lek; meaning *king*. [Strgs#4428]
[4] Ashkelon- a maritime city of the Philistines, southwest of Jerusalem. It means I shall be weighed or *weighing place* (that is, mart). [Strgs#831]
[5] Ashdod- a major Philistine city of the Mediterranean Sea west from Jerusalem, modern Esdud. Its name is defined as powerful or *ravager*.

CHAPTER 2

1 Gather yourselves together, yea, gather together, O nation not desired;
2 Before the decree bring forth, *before* the day pass as the chaff, before the fierce anger of the LORD come upon you, before the day of the LORD'S anger come upon you.
3 Seek you the LORD, all you meek of the earth, which have wrought his judgment; seek righteousness, seek meekness: it may be you will be hid in the day of the LORD'S anger.
4 For Gaza will be forsaken, and Ashkelon[4] a desolation: they will drive out Ashdod[5] at the noon day, and Ekron[6] will be rooted up.
5 Woe unto the inhabitants of the sea coast, the nation of the Cherethites[7]! the word of the LORD *is* against you; O Canaan, the land of the Philistines, I will even destroy you, that there will be no inhabitant.
6 And the sea coast will be dwellings *and* cottages for shepherds, and folds for flocks.
7 And the coast will be for the remnant of the house of Judah; they will feed thereupon: in the houses of Ashkelon will they lie down in the evening: for the LORD their God will visit them, and turn away their captivity.
8 I have heard the reproach of Moab, and the revilings of the children of Ammon, whereby they have reproached my people, and magnified *themselves* against their border.
9 Therefore *as* I live, says the LORD of hosts, the God of Israel, Surely Moab will be as Sodom, and the children of Ammon as Gomorrah, *even* the breeding of nettles, and salt-pits, and a perpetual desolation: the residue of my people will spoil them, and the remnant of my people will possess them.
10 This will they have for their pride, because they have reproached and magnified *themselves* against the people of the LORD of hosts.
11 The LORD *will be* terrible unto them: for he will famish all the gods of the earth; and *men* will worship him, everyone from his place, *even* all the isles of the heathen.
12 You Ethiopians also, you *will be* slain by my sword.
13 And he will stretch out his hand against the north, and destroy Assyria; and will make Nineveh a desolation, *and* dry like a wilderness.
14 And flocks will lie down in the midst of her, all the beasts of the nations: both the cormorant and the bittern will lodge in the upper lintels of it; *their* voice will sing in the windows; desolation *will be* in the thresholds: for he will uncover the cedar work.
15 This *is* the rejoicing city that dwelt carelessly, that said in her heart, I *am*, and *there is* none beside me: how is she become a desolation, a place for beasts to lie down in! Every one that passes by her will hiss, *and* wag his hand.

CHAPTER 3

1 Woe to her that is filthy and polluted, to the oppressing city!
2 She obeyed not the voice; she received not correction; she trusted not in the LORD; she drew not near to her God.

[Strgs#795]
[6] Ekron- the most northerly of the 5 principal cities of the Philistines; located in the lowlands of Judah and later given to Dan. Ekron meaning emigration, torn up by the roots or *eradication*. [Strgs#6138]
[7] Cherethites- a group of foreign mercenary soldiers serving as a bodyguard for king David; also executioners. Either Cretans or proto-Philistines (in general). Their names means *executioner*, or *life guardsman*. [Strgs#3774]

3 Her princes within her *are* roaring lions; her judges *are* evening wolves; they gnaw not the bones till the morrow.

4 Her prophets *are* light *and* treacherous persons: her priests have polluted the sanctuary; they have done violence to the law.

5 The just LORD *is* in the midst thereof; he will not do iniquity: every morning does he bring his judgment to light, he fails not; but the unjust knows no shame.

6 I have cut off the nations: their towers are desolate; I made their streets waste, that none passes by: their cities are destroyed, so that there is no man, that there is none inhabitant.

7 I said, Surely you will fear me, you will receive instruction; so their dwelling should not be cut off, howsoever I punished them: but they rose early, *and* corrupted all their doings.

8 Therefore wait you upon me, says the LORD, until the day that I rise up to the prey: for my determination[1] *is* to gather the nations, that I may assemble the kingdoms, to pour upon them mine indignation, *even* all my fierce anger: for all the earth will be devoured with the fire of my jealousy.

9 For then will I turn to the people a pure language, that they may all call upon the name of the LORD, to serve him with one consent.

10 From beyond the rivers of Ethiopia my suppliants, *even* the daughter of my dispersed, will bring mine offering.

11 In that day will you not be ashamed for all your doings, wherein you have transgressed against me: for then I will take away out of the midst of you them that rejoice in your pride, and you will no more be haughty because of my holy mountain.

12 I will also leave in the midst of you an afflicted and poor people, and they will trust in the name of the LORD.

13 The remnant of Israel will not do iniquity, or speak lies; neither will a deceitful tongue be found in their mouth: for they will feed and lie down, and none will make *them* afraid.

14 Sing, O daughter of Zion; shout, O Israel; be glad and rejoice with all the heart, O daughter of Jerusalem.

15 The LORD has taken away your judgments, he has cast out your enemy: the king of Israel, *even* the LORD, *is* in the midst of you: you will not see evil any more.

16 In that day it will be said to Jerusalem, Fear you not: *and to* Zion, Let not your hands be slack.

17 The LORD your God in the midst of you *is* mighty; he will save, he will rejoice over you with joy; he will rest in his love, he will joy over you with singing.

18 I will gather *them that are* sorrowful for the solemn assembly, *who* are of you, *to whom* the reproach of it *was* a burden.

19 Behold, at that time I will undo all that afflict you: and I will save her that halts, and gather her that was driven out; and I will get them praise and fame in every land where they have been put to shame.

20 At that time will I bring you *again*, even in the time that I gather you: for I will make you a name and a praise among all people of the earth, when I turn back your captivity before your eyes, says the LORD.

---

[1] determination- a verdict, divine law, justice, right, privilege, charge, manner, measure, due order, worthy. [Strgs#4941]

HAGGAI

CHAPTER 1

1 In the second year of Darius the king, in the sixth month, in the first day of the month, came the word of the LORD by Haggai[1] the prophet unto Zerubbabel[2] the son of Shealtiel[3], governor of Judah, and to Joshua the son of Josedech, the high priest, saying,
2 Thus speaks the LORD of hosts, saying, This people say, The time is not come, the time that the LORD'S house should be built.
3 Then came the word of the LORD by Haggai the prophet, saying,
4 *Is it* time for you, O you, to dwell in your cieled[4] houses, and this house *lie* waste?
5 Now therefore thus says the LORD of hosts; Consider your ways.
6 You have sown much, and bring in little; you eat, but you have not enough; you drink, but you are not filled with drink; you clothe you, but there is none warm; and he that earns wages earns wages *to put it* into a bag with holes.
7 Thus says the LORD of hosts; Consider your ways.
8 Go up to the mountain, and bring wood, and build the house; and I will take pleasure in it, and I will be glorified, says the LORD.
9 You looked for much, and, lo, *it came* to little; and when you brought *it* home, I did blow upon it. Why? says the LORD of hosts. Because of mine house that *is* waste, and you run every man unto his own house.
10 Therefore the heaven over you is stayed from dew, and the earth is stayed *from* her fruit.
11 And I called for a drought upon the land, and upon the mountains, and upon the corn, and upon the new wine, and upon the oil, and upon *that* which the ground brings forth, and upon men, and upon cattle, and upon all the labor of the hands.
12 Then Zerubbabel the son of Shealtiel, and Joshua the son of Josedech, the high priest, with all the remnant of the people, obeyed the voice of the LORD their God, and the words of Haggai the prophet, as the LORD their God had sent him, and the people did fear before the LORD.
13 Then spoke Haggai the LORD'S messenger in the LORD'S message unto the people, saying, I *am* with you, says the LORD.
14 And the LORD stirred up the spirit of Zerubbabel the son of Shealtiel, governor of Judah, and the spirit of Joshua the son of Josedech, the high priest, and the spirit of all the remnant of the people; and they came and did work in the house of the LORD of hosts, their God,
15 In the four and twentieth day of the sixth month, in the second year of Darius[5] the king.

CHAPTER 2

1 In the seventh *month*, in the one and twentieth *day* of the month, came the word of the LORD by the prophet Haggai, saying,
2 Speak now to Zerubbabel the son of Shealtiel, governor of Judah, and to Joshua the son of Josedech, the high priest, and to the residue of the people, saying,
3 Who *is* left among you that saw this house in her first glory? and how do you see it now? *is it* not in your eyes in comparison of it as nothing?
4 Yet now be strong, O Zerubbabel, says the LORD; and be strong, O Joshua, son of Josedech, the high priest; and be strong, all you people of the land, says the LORD, and work: for I *am* with you, says the LORD of hosts:
5 *According to* the word that I covenanted with you when you came out of Egypt, so my spirit remains among you: fear you not.
6 For thus says the LORD of hosts; Yet once, it *is* a little while, and I will shake the heavens, and the earth, and the sea, and the dry *land*;
7 And I will shake all nations, and the desire of all nations will come: and I will fill this house with glory, says the LORD of hosts.
8 The silver *is* mine, and the gold *is* mine, says the LORD of hosts.
9 The glory of this latter house will be greater than of the former, says the LORD of hosts: and in this place will I give peace, says the LORD of hosts.
10 In the four and twentieth *day* of the ninth *month*, in the second year of Darius, came the word of the LORD by Haggai the prophet, saying,
11 Thus says the LORD of hosts; Ask now the priests *concerning* the law, saying,
12 If one bear holy flesh in the skirt of his garment, and with his skirt do touch bread, or pottage, or wine, or oil, or any meat, will it be holy? And the priests answered and said, No.
13 Then said Haggai, If *one that is* unclean by a dead body touch any of these, will it be unclean? And the priests answered and said, It will be unclean.
14 Then answered Haggai, and said, So *is* this people, and so *is* this nation before me, says the LORD; and so *is* every work of their hands; and that which they offer there *is* unclean.
15 And now, I pray you, consider from this day and upward, from before a stone was laid upon a stone in the temple of the LORD:
16 Since those *days* were, when *one* came to an heap of twenty *measures*, there were *but* ten: when *one* came to the pressfat[6] for to draw out fifty *vessels* out of the press, there were *but* twenty.
17 I smote you with blasting and with mildew and with hail in all the labors of your hands; yet you *turned* not to me, says the LORD.
18 Consider now from this day and upward, from the four and twentieth day of the ninth *month, even* from the day that the foundation of the LORD'S temple was laid, consider *it*.
19 Is the seed yet in the barn? yea, as yet the vine, and the fig tree, and the pomegranate, and the olive tree, has not brought forth: from this day will I bless *you*.
20 And again the word of the LORD came unto Haggai in the four and twentieth *day* of the month, saying,
21 Speak to Zerubbabel, governor of Judah, saying, I will shake the heavens and the earth;
22 And I will overthrow the throne of kingdoms, and I will destroy the strength of the kingdoms of the heathen; and I will overthrow the chariots, and those that ride in them; and the horses and their riders will come down, everyone by the sword of his brother.
23 In that day, says the LORD of hosts, will I take you, O Zerubbabel, my servant, the son of Shealtiel, says the LORD, and will make you as a signet: for I have chosen you, says the LORD of hosts.

---

[1] Haggai- festive. [Strgs#2292]
[2] Zerubbabel- sown in Babylon or *descended of* (that is, from) *Babylon*. [Strgs#2216]
[3] Shealtiel- *I have asked of God*. [Strgs#7597]
[4] ceiled- *to hide* by covering; specifically *to roof* (passive participle as noun, a roof) or *wainscot*, figuratively to *reserve*: cover, seated. [Strgs#5603]
[5] Darius- see Index
[6] pressfat- Hebrew word yeqeb, yeh'-keb; meaning to excavate; a trough (as dug out); specifically a wine vat (whether the lower one, into which the juice drains; or the upper, in which the grapes are crushed): -fats, presses. [Strgs#3342]

ZECHARIAH

CHAPTER 1

1 In the eighth month, in the second year of Darius, came the word of the LORD unto Zechariah[1], the son of Berechiah[2], the son of Iddo the prophet, saying,
2 The LORD has been sore displeased with your fathers.
3 Therefore say you unto them, Thus says the LORD of hosts; Turn you unto me, says the LORD of hosts, and I will turn unto you, says the LORD of hosts.
4 Be you not as your fathers, unto whom the former prophets have cried, saying, Thus says the LORD of hosts; Turn you now from your evil ways, and *from* your evil doings: but they did not hear, or hearken unto me, says the LORD.
5 Your fathers, where *are* they? and the prophets, do they live for ever?
6 But my words and my statutes, which I commanded my servants the prophets, did they not take hold of your fathers? and they returned and said, Like as the LORD of hosts thought to do unto us, according to our ways, and according to our doings, so has he dealt with us.
7 Upon the four and twentieth day of the eleventh month, which *is* the month Sebat, in the second year of Darius, came the word of the LORD unto Zechariah, the son of Berechiah, the son of Iddo the prophet, saying,
8 I saw by night, and behold a man riding upon a red horse, and he stood among the myrtle trees that *were* in the bottom; and behind him *were there* red horses, speckled, and white.
9 Then said I, O my lord, what *are* these? And the angel that talked with me said unto me, I will show you what these *be*.
10 And the man that stood among the myrtle trees answered and said, These *are they* whom the LORD has sent to walk to and fro through the earth.
11 And they answered the angel of the LORD that stood among the myrtle trees, and said, We have walked to and fro through the earth, and, behold, all the earth sits still, and is at rest.
12 Then the angel of the LORD answered and said, O LORD of hosts, how long will you not have mercy on Jerusalem and on the cities of Judah, against which you have had indignation these threescore and ten years?
13 And the LORD answered the angel that talked with me *with* good words *and* comfortable words.
14 So the angel that communed with me said unto me, Cry thou, saying, Thus says the LORD of hosts; I am jealous for Jerusalem and for Zion with a great jealousy.
15 And I am very sore displeased with the heathen *that are* at ease: for I was but a little displeased, and they helped forward the affliction.
16 Therefore thus says the LORD; I am returned to Jerusalem with mercies: my house will be built in it, says the LORD of hosts, and a line will be stretched forth upon Jerusalem.
17 Cry yet, saying, Thus says the LORD of hosts; My cities through prosperity will yet be spread abroad; and the LORD will yet comfort Zion, and will yet choose Jerusalem.
18 Then lifted I up mine eyes, and saw, and behold four horns.
19 And I said unto the angel that talked with me, What *be* these? And he answered me, These *are* the horns which have scattered Judah, Israel, and Jerusalem.
20 And the LORD showed me four carpenters[3].
21 Then said I, What come these to do? And he spake, saying, These *are* the horns which have scattered Judah, so that no man did lift up his head: but these are come to fray them, to cast out the horns of the Gentiles, which lifted up *their* horn over the land of Judah to scatter it.

CHAPTER 2

1 I lifted up mine eyes again, and looked, and behold a man with a measuring line in his hand.
2 Then said I, **Where are you going**? And he said unto me, To measure Jerusalem, to see what *is* the breadth thereof, and what *is* the length thereof.
3 And, behold, the angel that talked with me went forth, and another angel went out to meet him,
4 And said unto him, Run, speak to this young man, saying, Jerusalem will be inhabited *as* towns without walls for the multitude of men and cattle therein:
5 For I, says the LORD, will be unto her a wall of fire round about, and will be the glory in the midst of her.
6 Ho, ho, *come forth*, and flee from the land of the north, says the LORD: for I have spread you abroad as the four winds of the heaven, says the LORD.
7 Deliver thyself, O Zion, that dwells *with* the daughter of Babylon.
8 For thus says the LORD of hosts; After the glory has he sent me unto the nations which spoiled you: for he that touches you touches the apple of his eye.
9 For, behold, I will shake mine hand upon them, and they will be a spoil to their servants: and you will know that the LORD of hosts has sent me.
10 Sing and rejoice, O daughter of Zion: for, lo, I come, and I will dwell in the midst of you, says the LORD.
11 And many nations will be joined to the LORD in that day, and will be my people: and I will dwell in the midst of you, and you will know that the LORD of hosts has sent me unto you.
12 And the LORD will inherit Judah his portion in the holy land, and will choose Jerusalem again.
13 Be silent, O all flesh, before the LORD: for he is raised up out of his holy habitation.

CHAPTER 3

1 And he showed me Joshua the high priest standing before the angel of the LORD, and Satan standing at his right hand to resist him.
2 And the LORD said unto Satan, The LORD rebuke you, O Satan; even the LORD that has chosen Jerusalem rebuke you: *is* not this a brand[4] plucked out of the fire?
3 Now Joshua was clothed with filthy garments, and stood before the angel.
4 And he answered and spake unto those that stood before him, saying, Take away the filthy garments from him. And unto him he said, Behold, I have caused your iniquity to pass from you, and I will clothe you with change of raiment.

---

[1] Zechariah- *Jehovah remembers* or *Jah has remembered*. [Strgs#2148]
[2] Berechiah- *Jehovah blesses*. [Strgs#1296]
[3] Carpenters- *fabricator* of any material: artificer, craftsman, engraver, maker, mason, skilful smith, workman. [Strgs#2796]
[4] lit. to *rake* together; a *poker* (for *turning* or *gathering* embers) [Strgs#181].

5 And I said, Let them set a fair **turbin** upon his head. So they set a fair **turbin** upon his head, and clothed him with garments. And the angel of the LORD stood by.
6 And the angel of the LORD protested unto Joshua, saying,
7 Thus says the LORD of hosts; If you will walk in my ways, and if you will keep my charge, then you will also judge my house, and will also keep my courts, and I will give you places to walk among these that stand by.
8 Hear now, O Joshua the high priest, you, and your fellows that sit before you: for they *are* men wondered at: for, behold, I will bring forth my servant the BRANCH.
9 For behold the stone that I have laid before Joshua; upon one stone *will be* seven eyes: behold, I will engrave the graving thereof, says the LORD of hosts, and I will remove the iniquity of that land in one day.
10 In that day, says the LORD of hosts, will you call every man his neighbor under the vine and under the fig tree.

CHAPTER 4

1 And the angel that talked with me came again, and waked me, as a man that is wakened out of his sleep,
2 And said unto me, **What do you see**? And I said, I have looked, and behold a candlestick all *of* gold, with [a bowl]¹ upon the top of it, and his seven lamps thereon, and seven pipes to the seven lamps, which *are* upon the top thereof:
3 And two olive trees by it, one upon the right *side* of the bowl², and the other upon the left *side* thereof.
4 So I answered and spake to the angel that talked with me, saying, What *are* these, my lord?
5 Then the angel that talked with me answered and said unto me, Knowest you not what these be? And I said, No, my lord.
6 Then he answered and spake unto me, saying, This *is* the word of the LORD unto Zerubbabel, saying, Not by might, or by power, but by [my spirit]³, says the LORD of hosts.
7 Who *are* you, O great mountain? before Zerubbabel *you will become* a plain: and he will bring forth the headstone *thereof with* shoutings, *crying*, Grace, grace unto it.
8 Moreover the word of the LORD came unto me, saying,
9 The hands of Zerubbabel have laid the foundation of this house; his hands will also finish it; and you will know that the LORD of hosts has sent me unto you.
10 For who has despised the day of small things? for they will rejoice, and will see the plummet⁴ in the hand of Zerubbabel *with* those seven; they *are* the eyes of the LORD, which run to and fro through the whole earth.
11 Then answered I, and said unto him, What *are* these two olive trees upon the right *side* of the candlestick and upon the left *side* thereof?
12 And I answered again, and said unto him, What *be these* two olive branches⁵ which through⁶ the two golden pipes empty the golden *oil* out of themselves?
13 And he answered me and said, **Do you not know what these *are*?** And I said, No, my lord.
14 Then said he, These *are* the two [anointed ones]⁷, that stand by the Lord of the whole earth.

CHAPTER 5

1 Then I turned, and lifted up mine eyes, and looked, and behold a flying roll.
2 And he said unto me, **What do you see**? And I answered, I see a flying roll; the length thereof *is* twenty cubits, and the breadth thereof ten cubits.
3 Then said he unto me, This *is* the curse that goes forth over the face of the whole earth: for every one that steals will be cut off *as* on this side according to it; and every one that swears will be cut off *as* on that side according to it.
4 I will bring it forth, says the LORD of hosts, and it will enter into the house of the thief, and into the house of him that swears falsely by my name: and it will remain in the midst of his house, and will consume it with the timber thereof and the stones thereof.
5 Then the angel that talked with me went forth, and said unto me, Lift up now your eyes, and see what *is* this that goes forth.
6 And I said, What *is* it? And he said, This *is* an ephah⁸ that goes forth. He said moreover, This *is* their resemblance through all the earth.
7 And, behold, there was lifted up a talent of lead: and this *is* a woman that sits in the midst of the ephah.
8 And he said, This *is* wickedness. And he cast it into the midst of the ephah; and he cast the weight of lead upon the mouth thereof.
9 Then lifted I up mine eyes, and looked, and, behold, there came out two women, and the wind *was* in their wings; for they had wings like the wings of a stork: and they lifted up the ephah between the earth and the heaven.
10 Then said I to the angel that talked with me, Whither do these bear the ephah?
11 And he said unto me, To build it an house in the land of Shinar: and it will be established, and set there upon her own base.

CHAPTER 6

1 And I turned, and lifted up mine eyes, and looked, and, behold, there came four chariots out from between two mountains; and the mountains *were* mountains of brass.
2 In the first chariot *were* red horses; and in the second chariot black horses;
3 And in the third chariot white horses; and in the fourth chariot grisled⁹ and bay horses.
4 Then I answered and said unto the angel that talked with me, What *are* these, my lord?
5 And the angel answered and said unto me, These *are* the four spirits of the heavens, which go forth from standing before the Lord of all the earth.
6 The black horses which *are* therein go forth into the north country; and the white go forth after them; and the grisled go forth toward the south country.
7 And the bay went forth, and sought to go that they might walk to and fro through the earth: and he said, Get you hence, walk to and fro through the earth. So they walked to and fro through the earth.
8 Then cried he upon me, and spake unto me, saying, Behold, these that go toward the north country have quieted my spirit in the north country.
9 And the word of the LORD came unto me, saying,

---

¹ lit. her bowl, a *cup* for oil (as *round*) [Strgs#1531].
² lit. a *fountain*, *bowl* or *globe* (as *round*) [Strgs#1543].
³ Symbolic of the golden oil which is the Holy Spirit.
⁴ lit. tin, stone; root word meaning divide or separate [Strgs#68+913].
⁵ branches – a *stream* (as *flowing*), also an *ear* of grain (as *growing* out)

[Strgs#7641].
⁶ lit. by the *hand* [Strgs#3027].
⁷ lit. sons of oil as producing light [Strgs#3323].
⁸ see measurement table
⁹ grisled- *spotted.* [Strgs#1261]

Zachariah

10 Take of *them of* the captivity, *even of* Heldai[1], of Tobijah[2], and of Jedaiah[3], which are come from Babylon, and come you the same day, and go into the house of Josiah the son of Zephaniah;
11 Then take silver and gold, and make crowns, and set *them* upon the head of Joshua the son of Josedech, the high priest;
12 And speak unto him, saying, Thus speaks the LORD of hosts, saying, Behold the man whose name *is* The BRANCH; and he will grow up out of his place, and he will build the temple of the LORD:
13 Even he will build the temple of the LORD; and he will bear the glory, and will sit and rule upon his throne; and he will be a priest upon his throne: and the counsel of peace will be between them both.
14 And the crowns will be to Helem, and to Tobijah, and to Jedaiah, and to Hen the son of Zephaniah, for a memorial in the temple of the LORD.
15 And they *that are* far off will come and build in the temple of the LORD, and you will know that the LORD of hosts has sent me unto you. And *this* will come to pass, if you will diligently obey the voice of the LORD your God.

CHAPTER 7

1 And it came to pass in the fourth year of king Darius, *that* the word of the LORD came unto Zechariah in the fourth *day* of the ninth month, *even* in Chisleu[4];
2 When they had sent unto the house of God Sherezer[5] and Regem-melech[6], and their men, to pray before the LORD,
3 *And* to speak unto the priests which *were* in the house of the LORD of hosts, and to the prophets, saying, Should I weep in the fifth month, separating myself, as I have done these so many years?
4 Then came the word of the LORD of hosts unto me, saying,
5 Speak unto all the people of the land, and to the priests, saying, When you fasted and mourned in the fifth and seventh *month*, even those seventy years, did you at all fast unto me, *even* to me?
6 And when you did eat, and when you did drink, did not you eat *for yourselves*, and drink *for yourselves*?
7 *Should you* not *hear* the words which the LORD has cried by the former prophets, when Jerusalem was inhabited and in prosperity, and the cities thereof round about her, when *men* inhabited the south and the plain?
8 And the word of the LORD came unto Zechariah, saying,
9 Thus speaks the LORD of hosts, saying, Execute true judgment, and show mercy and compassions every man to his brother:
10 And oppress not the widow, or the fatherless, the stranger, or the poor; and let none of you imagine evil against his brother in your heart.
11 But they refused to hearken, and pulled away the shoulder, and stopped their ears, that they should not hear.
12 Yea, they made their hearts *as* an adamant stone, lest they should hear the law, and the words which the LORD of hosts has sent in his spirit by the former prophets: therefore came a great wrath from the LORD of hosts.
13 Therefore it is come to pass, *that* as he cried, and they would not hear; so they cried, and I would not hear, says the LORD of hosts:
14 But I scattered them with a whirlwind among all the nations whom they knew not. Thus the land was desolate after them, that no man passed through or returned: for they laid the pleasant land desolate.

CHAPTER 8

1 Again the word of the LORD of hosts came *to me*, saying,
2 Thus says the LORD of hosts; I was jealous for Zion with great jealousy, and I was jealous for her with great fury.
3 Thus says the LORD; I am returned unto Zion, and will dwell in the midst of Jerusalem: and Jerusalem will be called a city of truth; and the mountain of the LORD of hosts the holy mountain.
4 Thus says the LORD of hosts; There will yet old men and old women dwell in the streets of Jerusalem, and every man with his staff in his hand for very age.
5 And the streets of the city will be full of boys and girls playing in the streets thereof.
6 Thus says the LORD of hosts; If it be marvelous in the eyes of the remnant of this people in these days, should it also be marvelous in mine eyes? says the LORD of hosts.
7 Thus says the LORD of hosts; Behold, I will save my people from the east country, and from the west country;
8 And I will bring them, and they will dwell in the midst of Jerusalem: and they will be my people, and I will be their God, in truth and in righteousness.
9 Thus says the LORD of hosts; Let your hands be strong, you that hear in these days these words by the mouth of the prophets, which *were* in the day *that* the foundation of the house of the LORD of hosts was laid, that the temple might be built.
10 For before these days there was no hire for man, or any hire for beast; neither *was there any* peace to him that went out or came in because of the affliction: for I set all men every one against his neighbor.
11 But now I *will* not *be* unto the residue of this people as in the former days, says the LORD of hosts.
12 For the seed *will be* prosperous; the vine will give her fruit, and the ground will give her increase, and the heavens will give their dew; and I will cause the remnant of this people to possess all these *things*.
13 And it will come to pass, *that* as you were a curse among the heathen, O house of Judah, and house of Israel; so will I save you, and you will be a blessing: fear not, *but* let your hands be strong.
14 For thus says the LORD of hosts; As I thought to punish you, when your fathers provoked me to wrath, says the LORD of hosts, and I repented not:
15 So again have I thought in these days to do well unto Jerusalem and to the house of Judah: fear you not.
16 These *are* the things that you will do; Speak you every man the truth to his neighbor; execute the judgment of truth and peace in your gates:
17 And let none of you imagine evil in your hearts against his neighbor; and love no false oath: for all these *are things* that I hate, says the LORD.
18 And the word of the LORD of hosts came unto me, saying,
19 Thus says the LORD of hosts; The fast of the fourth *month*, and the fast of the fifth, and the fast of the seventh, and the fast of the tenth, will be to the house of Judah joy and gladness, and cheerful feasts; therefore love the truth and peace.

---

[1] Heldai-worldly, *worldliness*. [Strgs#2469]
[2] Tobijah- Jehovah is good or *goodness of Jehovah*. [Strgs#2900]
[3] Jedaiah- Jehovah has known or *Jah has known*. [Strgs#3048]
[4] see Biblical calendar
[5] Sherezer- names means prince of fire. [Strgs#8272]
[6] Regemmelech- *kings heap* [Strgs#7278]. Comes from two Hebrew words the first *Regem* meaning *heap* [Strgs#7276], the second being *melek* meaning *king* or royal [Strgs#4428].

Zachariah

20 Thus says the LORD of hosts; *It will* yet *come to pass*, that there will come people, and the inhabitants of many cities:
21 And the inhabitants of one *city* will go to another, saying, Let us go speedily to pray before the LORD, and to seek the LORD of hosts: I will go also.
22 Yea, many people and strong nations will come to seek the LORD of hosts in Jerusalem, and to pray before the LORD.
23 Thus says the LORD of hosts; In those days *it will come to pass*, that ten men will take hold out of all languages of the nations, even will take hold of the skirt of him that is a Jew, saying, We will go with you: for we have heard *that* God *is* with you.

CHAPTER 9

1 The burden of the word of the LORD in the land of Hadrach, and Damascus *will be* the rest thereof: when the eyes of man, as of all the tribes of Israel, *will be* toward the LORD.
2 And Hamath[1] also will border thereby; Tyrus, and Zidon, though it be very wise.
3 And Tyrus did build herself a strong hold, and heaped up silver as the dust, and fine gold as the mire of the streets.
4 Behold, the Lord will cast her out, and he will smite her power in the sea; and she will be devoured with fire.
5 Ashkelon will see *it*, and fear; Gaza also *will see it*, and be very sorrowful, and Ekron; for her expectation will be ashamed; and the king will perish from Gaza, and Ashkelon will not be inhabited.
6 And a bastard will dwell in Ashdod, and I will cut off the pride of the Philistines.
7 And I will take away his blood out of his mouth, and his abominations from between his teeth: but he that remains, even he, *will be* for our God, and he will be as a governor in Judah, and Ekron as a Jebusite.
8 And I will encamp about mine house because of the army, because of him that passes by, and because of him that returns: and no oppressor will pass through them any more: for now have I seen with mine eyes.
9 Rejoice greatly, O daughter of Zion; shout, O daughter of Jerusalem: behold, your King cometh unto you: he *is* just, and having salvation; lowly, and riding upon an ass, and upon a colt the foal of an ass.
10 And I will cut off the chariot from Ephraim, and the horse from Jerusalem, and the battle bow will be cut off: and he will speak peace unto the heathen: and his dominion *will be* from sea *even* to sea, and from the river *even* to the ends of the earth.
11 As for you also, by the blood of your covenant I have sent forth your prisoners out of the pit wherein *is* no water.
12 Turn you to the strong hold, you prisoners of hope: even today do I declare *that* I will render double unto you;
13 When I have bent Judah for me, filled the bow with Ephraim, and raised up your sons, O Zion, against your sons, O Greece, and made you as the sword of a mighty man.
14 And the LORD will be seen over them, and his arrow will go forth as the lightning: and the Lord GOD will blow the trumpet, and will go with whirlwinds of the south.
15 The LORD of hosts will defend them; and they will devour, and subdue with sling stones; and they will drink, *and* make a noise as through wine; and they will be filled like bowls, *and* as the corners of the altar.
16 And the LORD their God will save them in that day as the flock of his people: for they *will be as* the stones of a crown, lifted up as an ensign upon his land.
17 For how great *is* his goodness, and how great *is* his beauty! corn will make the young men cheerful, and new wine the maids.

CHAPTER 10

1 [Ask you of the LORD rain in the time of the latter rain; *so* the LORD will make bright clouds, and give them showers of rain, to everyone grass in the field.][2]
2 For the idols have spoken vanity, and the diviners have seen a lie, and have told false dreams; they comfort in vain: therefore they went their way as a flock, they were troubled, because *there was* no shepherd.
3 Mine anger was kindled against the shepherds, and I punished the goats: for the LORD of hosts has visited his flock the house of Judah, and has made them as his goodly horse in the battle.
4 Out of him came forth the corner, out of him the nail, out of him the battle bow, out of him every oppressor together.
5 And they will be as mighty *men*, which tread down *their* enemies in the mire of the streets in the battle: and they will fight, because the LORD *is* with them, and the riders on horses will be confounded.
6 And I will strengthen the house of Judah, and I will save the house of Joseph, and I will bring them again to place them; for I have mercy upon them: and they will be as though I had not cast them off: for I *am* the LORD their God, and will hear them.
7 And *they of* Ephraim will be like a mighty *man*, and their heart will rejoice as through wine: yea, their children will see *it* and be glad; their heart will rejoice in the LORD.
8 I will hiss for them, and gather them; for I have redeemed them: and they will increase as they have increased.
9 And I will sow them among the people: and they will remember me in far countries; and they will live with their children, and turn again.
10 I will bring them again also out of the land of Egypt, and gather them out of Assyria; and I will bring them into the land of Gilead and Lebanon; and *place* will not be found for them.
11 And he will pass through the sea with affliction, and will smite the waves in the sea, and all the deeps of the river will dry up: and the pride of Assyria will be brought down, and the scepter of Egypt will depart away.
12 And I will strengthen them in the LORD; and they will walk up and down in his name, says the LORD.

CHAPTER 11

1 Open your doors, O Lebanon, that the fire may devour your cedars.
2 Howl, fir tree; for the cedar is fallen; because the mighty are spoiled: howl, O you oaks of Bashan; for the forest of the vintage is come down.
3 *There is* a voice of the howling of the shepherds; for their glory is spoiled: a voice of the roaring of young lions; for the pride of Jordan is spoiled.
4 Thus says the LORD my God; Feed the flock of the slaughter;
5 Whose possessors slay them, and hold themselves not guilty: and they that sell them say, Blessed *be* the LORD; for I am rich: and their own shepherds pity them not.

---

[1] Hamath- the principle city of upper Syria in the valley of Orontes. Hamath translate as *fortress*. [Strgs#2574]

[2] compare Ps. 28:2, Rev. 8:7 & 9:4.

6 For I will no more pity the inhabitants of the land, says the LORD: but, lo, I will deliver the men every one into his neighbor's hand, and into the hand of his king: and they will smite the land, and out of their hand I will not deliver *them*.
7 And I will feed the flock of slaughter, *even* you, O poor of the flock. And I took unto me two staves; the one I called Beauty, and the other I called Bands; and I fed the flock.
8 Three shepherds also I cut off in one month; and my soul loathed them, and their soul also abhorred me.
9 Then said I, I will not feed you: that that dies, let it die; and that that is to be cut off, let it be cut off; and let the rest eat every one the flesh of another.
10 And I took my staff, *even* Beauty, and cut it asunder, that I might break my covenant which I had made with all the people.
11 And it was broken in that day: and so the poor of the flock that waited upon me knew that it *was* the word of the LORD.
12 And I said unto them, If you think good, give *me* my price; and if not, forbear. So they weighed for my price thirty *pieces* of silver.
13 And the LORD said unto me, Cast it unto the potter: a goodly price that I was **valued** at of them. And I took the thirty *pieces* of silver, and cast them to the potter in the house of the LORD.
14 Then I cut asunder mine other staff, *even* Bands, that I might break the brotherhood between Judah and Israel.
15 And the LORD said unto me, Take unto you yet the instruments of a foolish shepherd.
16 For, lo, I will raise up a shepherd in the land, which will not visit those that be cut off, neither will seek the young one, or heal that that is broken, or feed that that stands still: but he will eat the flesh of the fat, and tear their claws in pieces.
17 Woe to the idol shepherd that leaves the flock! the sword *will be* upon his arm, and upon his right eye: his arm will be clean dried up, and his right eye will be utterly darkened.

CHAPTER 12

1 The burden of the word of the LORD for Israel, says the LORD, which stretches forth the heavens, and **laid** the foundation of the earth, and forms the spirit of man within him.
2 Behold, I will make Jerusalem a cup of trembling unto all the people round about, when they will be in the siege both against Judah *and* against Jerusalem.
3 And in that day will I make Jerusalem a burdensome stone for all people: all that burden themselves with it will be cut in pieces, though all the people of the earth be gathered together against it.
4 In that day, says the LORD, I will smite every horse with astonishment, and his rider with madness: and I will open mine eyes upon the house of Judah, and will smite every horse of the people with blindness.
5 And the governors of Judah will say in their heart, The inhabitants of Jerusalem *will be* my strength in the LORD of hosts their God.
6 In that day will I make the governors of Judah like an hearth of fire among the wood, and like a torch of fire in a sheaf; and they will devour all the people round about, on the right hand and on the left: and Jerusalem will be inhabited again in her own place, *even* in Jerusalem.
7 The LORD also will save the tents of Judah first, that the glory of the house of David and the glory of the inhabitants of Jerusalem do not magnify *themselves* against Judah.
8 In that day will the LORD defend the inhabitants of Jerusalem; and he that is feeble among them at that day will be as David; and the house of David *will be* as God, as the angel of the LORD before them.
9 And it will come to pass in that day, *that* I will seek to destroy all the nations that come against Jerusalem.
10 And I will pour upon the house of David, and upon the inhabitants of Jerusalem, the spirit of grace and of supplications: and they will look upon me whom they have pierced and they will mourn for him, as one mourns for *his* only *son*, and will be in bitterness for him, as one that is in bitterness for *his* firstborn.
11 In that day will there be a great mourning in Jerusalem, as the mourning of Hadadrimmon in the valley of Megiddon
12 And the land will mourn, every family apart; the family of the house of David apart, and their wives apart; the family of the house of Nathan apart, and their wives apart;
13 The family of the house of Levi apart, and their wives apart; the family of Shimei apart, and their wives apart;
14 All the families that remain, every family apart, and their wives apart.

CHAPTER 13

1 In that day there will be a fountain opened to the house of David and to the inhabitants of Jerusalem for sin and for uncleanness.
2 And it will come to pass in that day, says the LORD of hosts, *that* I will cut off the names of the idols out of the land, and they will no more be remembered: and also I will cause the prophets and the unclean spirit to pass out of the land.
3 And it will come to pass, *that* when any will yet prophesy, then his father and his mother that begat him will say unto him, Thou will not live; for you speak lies in the name of the LORD: and his father and his mother that begat him will thrust him through when he prophesies.
4 And it will come to pass in that day, *that* the prophets will be ashamed every one of his vision, when he has prophesied; neither will they wear a rough garment to deceive:
5 But he will say, I *am* no prophet, I *am* an husbandman; for man taught me to keep cattle from my youth.
6 And *one* will say unto him, What *are* these wounds in your hands? Then he will answer, *Those* with which I was wounded *in* the house of my friends.
7 Awake, O sword, against my shepherd, and against the man *that is* my fellow, says the LORD of hosts: smite the shepherd, and the sheep will be scattered: and I will turn mine hand upon the little ones.
8 And it will come to pass, *that* in all the land, says the LORD, two parts therein will be cut off *and* die; but the third will be left therein.
9 And I will bring the third part through the fire, and will refine them as silver is refined, and will try them as gold is tried: they will call on my name, and I will hear them: I will say, It *is* my people: and they will say, The LORD *is* my God.

CHAPTER 14

1 Behold, the day of the LORD cometh, and your spoil will be divided in the midst of you.
2 For I will gather all nations against Jerusalem to battle; and the city will be taken, and the houses rifled, and the women ravished; and half of the city will go forth into captivity, and the residue of the people will not be cut off from the city.
3 Then will the LORD go forth, and fight against those nations, as when he fought in the day of battle.
4 And his feet will stand in that day upon the mount of Olives, which *is* before Jerusalem on the east, and the mount of Olives will cleave in the midst thereof toward the east and toward the west, *and there will be* a very great valley; and half of the mountain will remove toward the north, and half of it toward the south.

5 And you will flee *to* the valley of the mountains; for the valley of the mountains will reach unto Azal[1]: yea, you will flee, like as you fled from before the earthquake in the days of Uzziah king of Judah: and the LORD my God will come, *and* all the saints with you.

6 And it will come to pass in that day, *that* the light will not be clear, *or* dark:

7 But it will be one day which will be known to the LORD, not day, or night: but it will come to pass, *that* at evening time it will be light.

8 And it will be in that day, *that* living waters will go out from Jerusalem; half of them toward the former sea, and half of them toward the hinder sea: in summer and in winter will it be.

9 And the LORD will be king over all the earth: in that day will there be one LORD, and his name one.

10 All the land will be turned as a plain from Geba to Rimmon south of Jerusalem: and it will be lifted up, and inhabited in her place, from Benjamin's gate unto the place of the first gate, unto the corner gate, and *from* the tower of Hananeel unto the king's winepresses. **11** And *men* will dwell in it, and there will be no more utter destruction; but Jerusalem will be safely inhabited.

12 And this will be the plague wherewith the LORD will smite all the people that have fought against Jerusalem; Their flesh will consume away while they stand upon their feet, and their eyes will consume away in their holes, and their tongue will consume away in their mouth.

13 And it will come to pass in that day, *that* a great tumult from the LORD will be among them; and they will lay hold everyone on the hand of his neighbor, and his hand will rise up against the hand of his neighbor.

14 And Judah also will fight at Jerusalem; and the wealth of all the heathen roundabout will be gathered together, gold, and silver, and apparel, in great abundance.

15 And so will be the plague of the horse, of the mule, of the camel, and of the ass, and of all the beasts that will be in these tents, as this plague.

16 And it will come to pass, *that* every one that is left of all the nations which came against Jerusalem will even go up from year to year to worship the King, the LORD of hosts, and to keep the feast of tabernacles.

17 And it will be, *that* whoso will not come up of *all* the families of the earth unto Jerusalem to worship the King, the LORD of hosts, even upon them will be no rain.

18 And if the family of Egypt go not up, and come not, that *have* no *rain*; there will be the plague, wherewith the LORD will smite the heathen that come not up to keep the feast of tabernacles.

19 This will be the punishment of Egypt, and the punishment of all nations that come not up to keep the feast of tabernacles.

20 In that day will there be upon the bells of the horses, HOLINESS UNTO THE LORD; and the pots in the LORD'S house will be like the bowls before the altar.

21 Yea, every pot in Jerusalem and in Judah will be holiness unto the LORD of hosts: and all they that sacrifice will come and take of them, and seethe therein: and in that day there will be no more the Canaanite in the house of the LORD of hosts.

---

[1] Azal- reserved or *noble*. [Strgs#682]

MALACHI

CHAPTER 1

1 The burden of the word of the LORD to Israel by Malachi[1].
2 I have loved you, says the LORD. Yet you say, Wherein have you loved us? *Was* not Esau Jacob's brother? says the LORD: yet I loved Jacob,
3 And I hated Esau, and laid his mountains and his heritage waste for the dragons of the wilderness.
4 Whereas Edom saith, We are impoverished, but we will return and build the desolate places; thus says the LORD of hosts, They will build, but I will throw down; and they will call them, The border of wickedness, and, The people against whom the LORD has indignation forever.
5 And your eyes will see, and you will say, The LORD will be magnified from the border of Israel.
6 A son honors *his* father, and a servant his master: if then I *be* a father, where *is* mine honor? and if I *be* a master, where *is* my fear? says the LORD of hosts unto you, O priests, that despise my name. And you say, Wherein have we despised your name?
7 Ye offer polluted bread upon mine altar; and you say, Wherein have we polluted thee? In that you say, The table of the LORD *is* contemptible.
8 And if you offer the blind for sacrifice, *is it* not evil? and if you offer the lame and sick, *is it* not evil? offer it now unto your governor; will he be pleased with thee, or accept your person? says the LORD of hosts.
9 And now, I pray you, beseech God that he will be gracious unto us: this has been by your means: will he regard your persons? says the LORD of hosts.
10 Who *is there* even among you that would shut the doors for nought? neither do you kindle *fire* on mine altar for nought. I have no pleasure in you, says the LORD of hosts, neither will I accept an offering at your hand.
11 For from the rising of the sun even unto the going down of the same my name *will be* great among the Gentiles; and in every place incense *will be* offered unto my name, and a pure offering: for my name *will be* great among the heathen, says the LORD of hosts.
12 But you have profaned it, in that you say, The table of the LORD *is* polluted; and the fruit thereof, *even* his meat, *is* contemptible.
13 Ye said also, Behold, what a weariness *is it*! and you have snuffed at it, says the LORD of hosts; and you brought *that which was* torn, and the lame, and the sick; thus you brought an offering: should I accept this of your hand? says the LORD.
14 But cursed *be* the deceiver, which has in his flock a male, and vows, and sacrifices unto the Lord a corrupt thing: for I *am* a great King, says the LORD of hosts, and my name *is* dreadful among the heathen.

CHAPTER 2

1 And now, O you priests, this commandment *is* for you.
2 If you will not hear, and if you will not lay *it* to heart, to give glory unto my name, says the LORD of hosts, I will even send a curse upon you, and I will curse your blessings: yea, I have cursed them already, because you do not lay *it* to heart.
3 Behold, I will corrupt your seed, and spread dung[2] upon your faces, *even* the dung of your solemn feasts; and *one* will take you away with it.
4 [And you will know that I have sent this commandment unto you, that my covenant might be with Levi, says the LORD of hosts.
5 My covenant was with him of life and peace; and I gave them to him *for* the fear wherewith he feared me, and was afraid before my name.
6 The law of truth was in his mouth, and iniquity was not found in his lips: he walked with me in peace and equity, and did turn many away from iniquity.][3]
7 For the priest's lips should keep knowledge, and they should seek the law at his mouth: for he *is* the messenger of the LORD of hosts.
8 But you are departed out of the way; you have caused many to stumble at the law; you have corrupted the covenant of Levi, says the LORD of hosts.
9 Therefore have I also made you contemptible and base before all the people, according as you have not kept my ways, but have been partial in the law.
10 Have we not all one father? has not one God created us? why do we deal treacherously every man against his brother, by profaning the covenant of our fathers?
11 Judah has dealt treacherously, and an abomination is committed in Israel and in Jerusalem; for Judah has profaned the holiness of the LORD which he loved, and has married the daughter of a strange god.
12 The LORD will cut off the man that doeth this, the master and the scholar, out of the tabernacles of Jacob, and him that offers an offering unto the LORD of hosts.
13 And this have you done again, covering the altar of the LORD with tears, with weeping, and with crying out, insomuch that he regards not the offering any more, or receives *it* with good will at your hand.
14 Yet you say, Wherefore? Because the LORD has been witness between you and the wife of your youth, against whom you have dealt treacherously: yet *is* she your companion, and the wife of your covenant.
15 And did not he make one? Yet had he the residue of the spirit. And wherefore one? That he might seek a godly seed. Therefore take heed to your spirit, and let none deal treacherously against the wife of his youth.
16 For the LORD, the God of Israel, says that he hates putting away: for *one* covers violence with his garment, says the LORD of hosts: therefore take heed to your spirit, that you deal not treacherously.
17 Ye have wearied the LORD with your words. Yet you say, Wherein have we wearied *him*? When you say, every one that doeth evil *is* good in the sight of the LORD, and he delights in them; or, Where *is* the God of judgment?

CHAPTER 3

1 Behold, I will send my messenger, and he will prepare the way before me: and the Lord, whom you seek, will suddenly come to his temple, even the messenger of the covenant, whom you delight in: behold, he will come, says the LORD of hosts.

---

[1] Malachi- my messenger or *ministrative*. [Strgs#4401]
[2] dung – *excrement* (as *eliminated*) [Strgs#6569]. Derives from a root word meaning to *separate*, to *disperse*, to *wound* [Strgs#6567].
[3] He repented after the encounter with Joseph.

2 But who may abide the day of his coming? and who will stand when he appears? for he *is* like a refiner's fire, and like fullers' **soap**:

3 And he will sit *as* a refiner and purifier of silver: and he will purify the sons of Levi, and purge them as gold and silver, that they may offer unto the LORD an offering in righteousness.

4 Then will the offering of Judah and Jerusalem be pleasant unto the LORD, as in the days of old, and as in former years.

5 And I will come near to you to judgment; and I will be a swift witness against the sorcerers, and against the adulterers, and against false swears, and against those that oppress the hireling in *his* wages, the widow, and the fatherless, and that turn aside the stranger *from his right*, and fear not me, says the LORD of hosts.

6 For I *am* the LORD, I change not; therefore you sons of Jacob are not consumed.

7 Even from the days of your fathers you are gone away from mine ordinances, and have not kept *them*. Return unto me, and I will return unto you, says the LORD of hosts. But you said, Wherein will we return?

8 Will a man rob God? Yet you have robbed me. But you say, Wherein have we robbed thee? In tithes and offerings.

9 Ye *are* cursed with a curse: for you have robbed me, *even* this whole nation.

10 Bring you all the tithes into the storehouse, that there may be meat in mine house, and prove me now herewith, says the LORD of hosts, if I will not open you the windows of heaven, and pour you out a blessing, that *there will* not *be room* enough *to receive it*.

11 And I will rebuke the devourer for your sakes, and he will not destroy the fruits of your ground; neither will your vine cast her fruit before the time in the field, says the LORD of hosts.

12 And all nations will call you blessed: for you will be a delightsome land, says the LORD of hosts.

13 Your words have been stout against me, says the LORD. Yet you say, What have we spoken *so much* against thee?

14 Ye have said, It *is* vain to serve God: and what profit *is it* that we have kept his ordinance, and that we have walked mournfully before the LORD of hosts?

15 And now we call the proud happy; yea, they that work wickedness are set up; yea, *they that* tempt God are even delivered.

16 Then they that feared the LORD spoke often one to another: and the LORD hearkened, and heard *it*, and a book of remembrance was written before him for them that feared the LORD, and that thought upon his name.

17 And they will be mine, says the LORD of hosts, in that day when I make up my jewels; and I will spare them, as a man spares his own son that serves him.

18 Then will you return, and discern between the righteous and the wicked, between him that serves God and him that serves him not.

CHAPTER 4

1 For, behold, the day comes, that will burn as an oven; and all the proud, yea, and all that do wickedly, will be stubble: and the day that comes will burn them up, says the LORD of hosts, that it will leave them neither root or branch.

2 But unto you that fear my name will the Sun of righteousness arise with healing in his wings; and you will go forth, and grow up as calves of the stall.

3 And you will tread down the wicked; for they will be ashes under the soles of your feet in the day that I will do *this*, says the LORD of hosts.

4 Remember you the law of Moses my servant, which I commanded unto him in Horeb for all Israel, *with* the statutes and judgments.

5 Behold, I will send you Elijah the prophet before the coming of the great and dreadful day of the LORD:

6 And he will turn the heart of the fathers to the children, and the heart of the children to their fathers, lest I come and smite the earth with a curse.

THE NEW TESTAMENT
DR. DONALD PEART EXEGESIS

HONOR

It is with great gratitude that I say Jesus Christ, the Son of the living God, is the highest value in my life. I (We) love Him because he loved us first! It is He, the living Christ, who has made me a better person towards Him, towards our fellow humanity and towards all His creation. To Him, be love, wisdom, power, glory, value, riches, strength, praise, fear, reverence, worship, government! It is through Jesus and His Holy Spirit, the Father has demonstrated His great love in which he has loved us, is loving us and shall yet love us to the end. Jesus is Lord; Jesus is King, Jesus is Savior; Jesus is Baptizer! Jesus is Life! Jesus dying for our sins and being resurrected for our salvation is God's Love demonstrated! Jesus, the Lamb of God, is worthy of our worship, worthy of our spirit, soul, and body! Let us glorify God with our spirt, soul and body which are His!

I honor Judy my beautiful wife of 35 years, the wife of my youth, my best friend, an exact prophetess of the Lord Jesus; and our six children (Donald Jr. and his wife Keyanna, Jeshua, Charity, Benjamin, and Jesse) who have experienced the demands of ministry with us; and our grandchildren Skye Marie Peart and Justus John Peart. Honor to my parents Lennox Peart and Millicent Peart who the Lord selected to use as portals to send me into the earth in order for me to complete the will of the Lord Jesus. I also give honor to Harrison Tucker, my father-in-law who exemplified to me that one could work two fulltime jobs while pursuing a college degree. I also value the saints and leaders of Crown of Glory Ministries who have partnered with me through the years to do the will of God, to name a few leaders (in no particular order): George Johnson, Jamal and Trina Dutton, among the first to join our young ministry in 1997; Gaylord and Psalmist Sanora Dutton, Michael and Dian Sumler (who has been with us since 1997), Will and Nichole Brown, Sherone Elden, Tonyette Hall, Anticius and Ja'Nee Bartley, Tia Henry, Donald Jr and Keyanna Peart, Dameon and Tiffany Gibbs, Olen and Kia McCardell, and so on.

I also give honor to the Spirit of Jesus who has been my Teacher and Commander from the beginning. I also honor some men and women of God who have taught me through the years—Dr. Raymond Buie and Ola Buie (exemplary figures with regards to enduring sufferings); Steve and Michelle Daniels (people of wisdom, whose life was the nudge I needed to receive the salvation of Jesus); Dr. Clarice Fluitt (a sweet prophetic psalmist of the Lord and a current apostolic advisor to Judy and me); Dr. Sandra Hayden, who has been an excellent example of worship and love to Judy and me; prophetess Maria Howard (one who flows prophetically in a coat of many beautiful colors); Dr. Turnel Nelson (the mighty preacher of God; whom we (and others) went to see at his home in Trinidad (including seeing his wife) about a month before he went to be with the Lord); Bishop Earl Palmer (a man of planning), Apostle Richard and Prophetess Teresa Scott (full of grace and truth); Apostle Lewis Sanders, Jacksonville, NC, a fruitful man, who provide us a place to stay, at no cost, in a season of intense trials; and Dr. Kelley Varner (my mentor for 13 years who became our apostolic support for about 7 years before he went to be with Christ in 2009). I also make honorable mention of David Dayton of Virginia, a man who demonstrates love, and who, in his home, taught me a principle on release that is still with me to this date; honorable mention to Raj Ramlal, his wife Seeta, Vishnu and Lisa Seepersad of Trinidad, who have become good friends to my wife and me; Dr. Stephen Everett of Florida, a brilliant mind with regards to spiritual understanding; one whom I deem a true "lawyer" or "doctor" ("teacher" of the "law"), according to the Scriptures. I also make honorable mention of Don Nori, a man of God, who have come to demonstrate true love and a broken spirit. Finally, I also honor Dr. Samuel Soleyn of New Mexico, a friend indeed, an attorney by degree, and also an exceptional lawyer of the living God who demonstrates excellent apostolic sagacity.

Sincerely,
Donald Peart

COMMENTS

*John 1:1818 No man has seen God at any time; the **only-born** Son, which is in the bosom of the Father, he has **exegesis-him**.*

Jesus was the first to properly "exegesis" the heavenly Father. Thus, after asking Judith (my wife) to help me with a title for this book, she suggested the idea of including the word "exegesis" in the title for this book. Exegesis by definition mean critical explanation or interpretation of a text, especially of Scriptures. However, "exegesis" is the Greek compound "ek," which means "out-of," that is something having its origin within that something; and "hegeomai," which means, to lead.

Therefore, Jesus was the first to lead us to the Father "out-of" the Scripture. Thus, we are to be careful not to do the opposite of "eisegesis." That is, we are to be careful not to read what we want "into" the Scriptures to make them say what we think it should say, rather than what is being revealed by the Lord "out-of" the Scriptures.

I am reminded of an encounter our Lord Jesus had with a lawyer who had some questions about the Scriptures; and I remember the manner in which Jesus responded to the lawyer. Our Lord's response was very instructive. Jesus enlightened the lawyer (and us) by indicating that the Scriptures are only understood properly based on "how" they are read.

Luke 10:25-26: *25And, **be-perceiving**, a certain lawyer stood up, and tempted him, saying, **Teacher**, what shall I do to inherit **life age**? 26He said **towards him**, what is written in the law? **How are you reading**?*

Thus, for many of the words used in the Scripture I wanted to follow the pattern set by our Lord Jesus who "declared" (exegesis) the Father; by applying the exegesis principle to the **Word of God**. That is, this publication contains **a** "reading-out" of some of the Greek compounds used in the original texts. For example, the Greek word translated "gospel" is the Greek compound "euaggelion" ("eu" (good, well) and "aggello" (to bring a message). Thus, **an** exegesis of this word is **"well-message."** In addition, some words, like one of the Greek words for "healing," ("therapeuo") is transliterated as **"therapy-served;"** because this word expresses being **"served,"** receiving **"therapy," and** a **"servant" ("therapist"),** as used of Moses in Hebrews 3:5.

Also, since I really like the style of the King James translation of the Bible; and the fact that it is classified as "public domain," I have used the King James translation as a base for my **exegesis**. I have used **bold font** for words that I used in translation. I did not change all of the words; and therefore, some words were not enhanced according to this exegesis. In addition, one of the intents with regards to the reading of this publication is to provide some vivid mental pictures while reading. Here is an example.

Mark 1:41: *"And Jesus, **being-gut-compassionate**, out-stretched the hand, and **fastened-to-him**, and says **to-him**, I will; **be-clean!**"*

With that said, another one of the foremost goals of this book is to be as consistent as possible in translation. That is, I pursued translating the same reading for a word throughout the book, with some exceptions. Thus, comparing Scriptures with Scriptures for understanding can be a little easier in light of 1 Corinthians 2:13. Also, if one has this book electronically, he/she can do a search of a particular word to find were its translated similarly; and more than likely, one of those references should also give a contextual definition that should clarify the use of that word in other places. For those with a printed copy, that kind of comparison will have to be done the old fashion way, reading the entire text, and making notes.

This can be exemplified by the Greek word "parakaleo" (to-beside-call) and its associated words. "Parakaleo" is translated in the King James as: "beseech," "call for," "comfort," "desire," "exhort," "entreat," "pray," etcetera. In this exegesis, I have attempted to translate this word as it reads from the Greek compound word, **"beside-call."**

Another example is the Greek word for **authority**. **Authority** (**exousia**) is translated as such (**authority**) throughout this text; thus, a reader can readily compare words and context. It is also worthy to note that some of the sentences may not read well in order to show some of the literal translations (the idea is to provide an exegesis that encourages study and prayer towards our Lord Jesus Christ to ascertain Jesus' wisdom and knowing). The definitions/translations that are used in this exegesis are obviously not the only definitions/translations available.

Finally, I have spent more than 500 hours providing this exegesis; however, please be advised that, as the Lord wills, it is my intent to continue editing and publishing updated editions of this book until I finish the "race" in the "stadiums" the Lord Jesus has determined for me. As you may find some oversight and/or typo within the body of this book, please understand that this exegesis is voluminous and ongoing; and as indicated, it is my determination to provide an updated edition once or twice per year, or as needed. So, if a reader finds any misprint or typo in a particular edition, please pencil in the correct spelling. Please also understand that I wanted to publish the book knowing that there will be other editions, because it is my intent, through the Spirit of Jesus, to help further the spiritual understanding of any who desire to pursue the will of the Father of our Lord Jesus Christ.

May you excel through the Grace of our Lord Jesus Christ; may you accept the Comfort of the Holy Spirit; and may you receive the Love of the Father and His Truth!

Jesus is King! Jesus was born King! The Lord Jesus! Jesus is the Christ, the Son of the living God! Jesus lives in us!

Donald Peart

TABLE OF CONTENTS

THE GOSPEL OF MATTHEW 1
   MATTHEW CHAPTER 1 1
   MATTHEW CHAPTER 2 1
   MATTHEW CHAPTER 3 2
   MATTHEW CHAPTER 4 3
   MATTHEW CHAPTER 5 4
   MATTHEW CHAPTER 6 6
   MATTHEW CHAPTER 7 7
   MATTHEW CHAPTER 8 8
   MATTHEW CHAPTER 9 9
   MATTHEW CHAPTER 10 11
   MATTHEW CHAPTER 11 12
   MATTHEW CHAPTER 12 13
   MATTHEW CHAPTER 13 15
   MATTHEW CHAPTER 14 17
   MATTHEW CHAPTER 15 18
   MATTHEW CHAPTER 16 20
   MATTHEW CHAPTER 17 21
   MATTHEW CHAPTER 18 22
   MATTHEW CHAPTER 19 23
   MATTHEW CHAPTER 20 24
   MATTHEW CHAPTER 21 25
   MATTHEW CHAPTER 22 27
   MATTHEW CHAPTER 23 28
   MATTHEW CHAPTER 24 30
   MATTHEW CHAPTER 25 31
   MATTHEW CHAPTER 26 33
   MATTHEW CHAPTER 27 36
   MATTHEW CHAPTER 28 38
THE GOSPEL OF MARK 40
   MARK CHAPTER 1 40
   MARK CHAPTER 2 41
   MARK CHAPTER 3 42
   MARK CHAPTER 4 43

- MARK CHAPTER 5 45
- MARK CHAPTER 6 46
- MARK CHAPTER 7 48
- MARK CHAPTER 8 50
- MARK CHAPTER 9 51
- MARK CHAPTER 10 53
- MARK CHAPTER 11 55
- MARK CHAPTER 12 56
- MARK CHAPTER 13 58
- MARK CHAPTER 14 59
- MARK CHAPTER 15 62
- MARK CHAPTER 16 63

THE GOSPEL OF LUKE 65
- LUKE CHAPTER 1 65
- LUKE CHAPTER 2 67
- LUKE CHAPTER 3 69
- LUKE CHAPTER 4 70
- LUKE CHAPTER 5 72
- LUKE CHAPTER 6 73
- LUKE CHAPTER 7 75
- LUKE CHAPTER 8 77
- LUKE CHAPTER 9 79
- LUKE CHAPTER 10 82
- LUKE CHAPTER 11 83
- LUKE CHAPTER 12 85
- LUKE CHAPTER 13 88
- LUKE CHAPTER 14 89
- LUKE CHAPTER 15 90
- LUKE CHAPTER 16 91
- LUKE CHAPTER 17 93
- LUKE CHAPTER 18 94
- LUKE CHAPTER 19 95
- LUKE CHAPTER 20 97
- LUKE CHAPTER 21 98
- LUKE CHAPTER 22 100
- LUKE CHAPTER 23 102
- LUKE CHAPTER 24 104

THE GOSPEL OF JOHN ... 107
JOHN CHAPTER 1 ... 107
JOHN CHAPTER 2 ... 108
JOHN CHAPTER 3 ... 109
JOHN CHAPTER 4 ... 110
JOHN CHAPTER 5 ... 112
JOHN CHAPTER 6 ... 114
JOHN CHAPTER 7 ... 116
JOHN CHAPTER 8 ... 117
JOHN CHAPTER 9 ... 119
JOHN CHAPTER 10 ... 121
JOHN CHAPTER 11 ... 122
JOHN CHAPTER 12 ... 124
JOHN CHAPTER 13 ... 125
JOHN CHAPTER 14 ... 127
JOHN CHAPTER 15 ... 128
JOHN CHAPTER 16 ... 129
JOHN CHAPTER 17 ... 130
JOHN CHAPTER 18 ... 131
JOHN CHAPTER 19 ... 132
JOHN CHAPTER 20 ... 134
JOHN CHAPTER 21 ... 135
THE ACTS OF THE APOSTLES ... 137
ACTS CHAPTER 1 ... 137
ACTS CHAPTER 2 ... 138
ACTS CHAPTER 3 ... 139
ACTS CHAPTER 4 ... 140
ACTS CHAPTER 5 ... 142
ACTS CHAPTER 6 ... 144
ACTS CHAPTER 7 ... 144
ACTS CHAPTER 8 ... 147
ACTS CHAPTER 9 ... 148
ACTS CHAPTER 10 ... 150
ACTS CHAPTER 11 ... 152
ACTS CHAPTER 12 ... 153
ACTS CHAPTER 13 ... 154
ACTS CHAPTER 14 ... 156

- ACTS CHAPTER 15 157
- ACTS CHAPTER 16 159
- ACTS CHAPTER 17 161
- ACTS CHAPTER 18 162
- ACTS CHAPTER 19 163
- ACTS CHAPTER 20 165
- ACTS CHAPTER 21 167
- ACTS CHAPTER 22 169
- ACTS CHAPTER 23 170
- ACTS CHAPTER 24 172
- ACTS CHAPTER 25 173
- ACTS CHAPTER 26 174
- ACTS CHAPTER 27 176
- ACTS CHAPTER 28 178
- ROMANS 180
  - ROMANS CHAPTER 1 180
  - ROMANS CHAPTER 2 181
  - ROMANS CHAPTER 3 182
  - ROMANS CHAPTER 4 183
  - ROMANS CHAPTER 5 184
  - ROMANS CHAPTER 6 185
  - ROMANS CHAPTER 7 185
  - ROMANS CHAPTER 8 186
  - ROMANS CHAPTER 9 188
  - ROMANS CHAPTER 10 189
  - ROMANS CHAPTER 11 190
  - ROMANS CHAPTER 12 191
  - ROMANS CHAPTER 13 192
  - ROMANS CHAPTER 14 192
  - ROMANS CHAPTER 15 193
  - ROMANS CHAPTER 16 194
- 1 CORINTHIANS 196
  - 1 CORINTHIANS CHAPTER 1 196
  - 1 CORINTHIANS CHAPTER 2 197
  - 1 CORINTHIANS CHAPTER 3 197
  - 1 CORINTHIANS CHAPTER 4 198
  - 1 CORINTHIANS CHAPTER 5 199

- [1 CORINTHIANS CHAPTER 6](#) 199
- [1 CORINTHIANS CHAPTER 7](#) 200
- [1 CORINTHIANS CHAPTER 8](#) 201
- [1 CORINTHIANS CHAPTER 9](#) 202
- [1 CORINTHIANS CHAPTER 10](#) 203
- [1 CORINTHIANS CHAPTER 11](#) 204
- [1 CORINTHIANS CHAPTER 12](#) 205
- [1 CORINTHIANS CHAPTER 13](#) 206
- [1 CORINTHIANS CHAPTER 14](#) 207
- [1 CORINTHIANS CHAPTER 15](#) 208
- [1 CORINTHIANS CHAPTER 16](#) 210
- [2 CORINTHIANS](#) 212
  - [2 CORINTHIANS CHAPTER 1](#) 212
  - [2 CORINTHIANS CHAPTER 2](#) 212
  - [2 CORINTHIANS CHAPTER 3](#) 213
  - [2 CORINTHIANS CHAPTER 4](#) 214
  - [2 CORINTHIANS CHAPTER 5](#) 214
  - [2 CORINTHIANS CHAPTER 6](#) 215
  - [2 CORINTHIANS CHAPTER 7](#) 216
  - [2 CORINTHIANS CHAPTER 8](#) 217
  - [2 CORINTHIANS CHAPTER 9](#) 217
  - [2 CORINTHIANS CHAPTER 10](#) 218
  - [2 CORINTHIANS CHAPTER 11](#) 219
  - [2 CORINTHIANS CHAPTER 12](#) 220
  - [2 CORINTHIANS CHAPTER 13](#) 221
- [GALATIANS](#) 222
  - [GALATIANS CHAPTER 1](#) 222
  - [GALATIANS CHAPTER 2](#) 222
  - [GALATIANS CHAPTER 3](#) 223
  - [GALATIANS CHAPTER 4](#) 224
  - [GALATIANS CHAPTER 5](#) 225
  - [GALATIANS CHAPTER 6](#) 226
- [EPHESIANS](#) 228
  - [EPHESIANS CHAPTER 1](#) 228
  - [EPHESIANS CHAPTER 2](#) 228
  - [EPHESIANS CHAPTER 3](#) 229
  - [EPHESIANS CHAPTER 4](#) 230

- EPHESIANS CHAPTER 5 231
  - EPHESIANS CHAPTER 6 232
- PHILIPPIANS 234
  - PHILIPPIANS CHAPTER 1 234
  - PHILIPPIANS CHAPTER 2 235
  - PHILIPPIANS CHAPTER 3 236
  - PHILIPPIANS CHAPTER 4 236
- COLOSSIANS 238
  - COLOSSIANS CHAPTER 1 238
  - COLOSSIANS CHAPTER 2 239
  - COLOSSIANS CHAPTER 3 240
  - COLOSSIANS CHAPTER 4 240
- 1 THESSALONIANS 242
  - 1 THESSALONIANS CHAPTER 1 242
  - 1 THESSALONIANS CHAPTER 2 242
  - 1 THESSALONIANS CHAPTER 3 243
  - 1 THESSALONIANS CHAPTER 4 243
  - 1 THESSALONIANS CHAPTER 5 244
- 2 THESSALONIANS 246
  - 2 THESSALONIANS CHAPTER 1 246
  - 2 THESSALONIANS CHAPTER 2 246
  - 2 THESSALONIANS CHAPTER 3 247
- 1 TIMOTHY 248
  - 1 TIMOTHY CHAPTER 1 248
  - 1 TIMOTHY CHAPTER 2 248
  - 1 TIMOTHY CHAPTER 3 249
  - 1 TIMOTHY CHAPTER 4 250
  - 1 TIMOTHY CHAPTER 5 250
  - 1 TIMOTHY CHAPTER 6 251
- 2 TIMOTHY 253
  - 2 TIMOTHY CHAPTER 1 253
  - 2 TIMOTHY CHAPTER 2 253
  - 2 TIMOTHY CHAPTER 3 254
  - 2 TIMOTHY CHAPTER 4 255
- TITUS 257
  - TITUS CHAPTER 1 257
  - TITUS CHAPTER 2 257

- TITUS CHAPTER 3 258
- PHILEMON 259
  - PHILEMON CHAPTER 1 259
- HEBREWS 260
  - HEBREWS CHAPTER 1 260
  - HEBREWS CHAPTER 2 260
  - HEBREWS CHAPTER 3 261
  - HEBREWS CHAPTER 4 262
  - HEBREWS CHAPTER 5 262
  - HEBREWS CHAPTER 6 263
  - HEBREWS CHAPTER 7 264
  - HEBREWS CHAPTER 8 265
  - HEBREWS CHAPTER 9 266
  - HEBREWS CHAPTER 10 267
  - HEBREWS CHAPTER 11 268
  - HEBREWS CHAPTER 12 270
  - HEBREWS CHAPTER 13 271
- JAMES 273
  - JAMES CHAPTER 1 273
  - JAMES CHAPTER 2 273
  - JAMES CHAPTER 3 274
  - JAMES CHAPTER 4 275
  - JAMES CHAPTER 5 276
- 1 PETER 277
  - 1 PETER CHAPTER 1 277
  - 1 PETER CHAPTER 2 278
  - 1 PETER CHAPTER 3 279
  - 1 PETER CHAPTER 4 280
  - 1 PETER CHAPTER 5 280
- 2 PETER 282
  - 2 PETER CHAPTER 1 282
  - 2 PETER CHAPTER 2 282
  - 2 PETER CHAPTER 3 283
- 1 JOHN 285
  - 1 JOHN CHAPTER 1 285
  - 1 JOHN CHAPTER 2 285
  - 1 JOHN CHAPTER 3 286

- 1 JOHN CHAPTER 4 287
- 1 JOHN CHAPTER 5 288
- 2 JOHN 289
  - 2 JOHN CHAPTER 1 289
- 3 JOHN 290
  - 3 JOHN CHAPTER 1 290
- JUDE 291
  - JUDE CHAPTER 1 291
- THE REVELATION OF JESUS CHRIST 293
  - REVELATION OF JESUS CHRIST CHAPTER 1 293
  - REVELATION OF JESUS CHRIST CHAPTER 2 293
  - REVELATION OF JESUS CHRIST CHAPTER 3 295
  - REVELATION OF JESUS CHRIST CHAPTER 4 296
  - REVELATION OF JESUS CHRIST CHAPTER 5 296
  - REVELATION OF JESUS CHRIST CHAPTER 6 297
  - REVELATION OF JESUS CHRIST CHAPTER 7 297
  - REVELATION OF JESUS CHRIST CHAPTER 8 298
  - REVELATION OF JESUS CHRIST CHAPTER 9 299
  - REVELATION OF JESUS CHRIST CHAPTER 10 300
  - REVELATION OF JESUS CHRIST CHAPTER 11 300
  - REVELATION OF JESUS CHRIST CHAPTER 12 301
  - REVELATION OF JESUS CHRIST CHAPTER 13 302
  - REVELATION OF JESUS CHRIST CHAPTER 14 303
  - REVELATION OF JESUS CHRIST CHAPTER 15 304
  - REVELATION OF JESUS CHRIST CHAPTER 16 304
  - REVELATION OF JESUS CHRIST CHAPTER 17 305
  - REVELATION OF JESUS CHRIST CHAPTER 18 306
  - REVELATION OF JESUS CHRIST CHAPTER 19 307
  - REVELATION OF JESUS CHRIST CHAPTER 20 308
  - REVELATION OF JESUS CHRIST CHAPTER 21 309
  - REVELATION OF JESUS CHRIST CHAPTER 22 310
- SYNOPTIC BIO OF DONALD PEART
  - OTHER BOOKS
  - CONTACT INFORMATION

THE GOSPEL OF MATTHEW

MATTHEW CHAPTER 1

1 The **scroll** of the **genesis** of Jesus Christ, the son of David, the son of Abraham.

2 Abraham **birthed** Isaac; and Isaac birthed Jacob; and Jacob **birthed** Judas and his **brothers**;

3 And Judas **birthed** Phares and Zara of Thamar; and Phares **birthed** Esrom; and Esrom **birthed** Aram;

4 And Aram **birthed** Aminadab; and Aminadab **birthed** Naasson; and Naasson birthed Salmon;

5 And Salmon **birthed** Booz of Rachab; and Booz **birthed** Obed of Ruth; and Obed **birthed** Jesse;

6 And Jesse **birthed** David the king; and David the king **birthed** Solomon of her of Urias;

7 And Solomon **birthed** Roboam; and Roboam **birthed** Abia; and Abia birthed Asa;

8 And Asa **birthed** Josaphat; and Josaphat **birthed** Joram; and Joram **birthed** Ozias;

9 And Ozias **birthed** Joatham; and Joatham **birthed** Achaz; and Achaz **birthed** Ezekias;

10 And Ezekias **birthed** Manasses; and Manasses **birthed** Amon; and Amon **birthed** Josias;

11 And Josias **birthed** Jechonias and his **brothers**, **upon the change-house of-**Babylon:

12 And after they were **change-house of-**Babylon, Jechonias **birthed** Salathiel; and Salathiel birthed Zorobabel;

13 And Zorobabel **birthed** Abiud; and Abiud **birthed** Eliakim; and Eliakim **birthed** Azor;

14 And Azor **birthed** Zadok; and Zadok **birthed** Achim; and Achim **birthed** Eliud;

15 And Eliud **birthed** Eleazar; and Eleazar birthed Matthan; and Matthan **birthed** Jacob;

16 And Jacob **birthed** Joseph the husband of Mary, of whom was born Jesus, who is called Christ.

17 So all the generations from Abraham to David, fourteen generations; and from David until the **change-house of-**Babylon, fourteen generations; and from the **change-house of-**Babylon **until the** Christ, fourteen generations.

18 Now the **genesis** of Jesus Christ **thus existed**: when as his mother Mary was **pledged-by souvenir**[1219] to Joseph, before they came together, she was found **in womb-belly holding out-of** the Holy Spirit.

19 Then Joseph her husband, being just, and not willing to make her a **beside-show**,[1220] **planned-counseled to-from-loose her** privately.

20 But while he **in-sacrifice-anger** on these things, **be-perceiving**, the angel of the Lord **shined to-him** in a **trance** saying, Joseph, you son of David, fear not to **beside-take** Mary your wife; **because** that which is conceived in her is **out-of** the Holy Spirit.

21 **Then** she shall **produce Son,** and you shall call his name **Jesus**; **because** he shall save his people from their sins.

22 Now all this **became**, that it might be **filled** which was spoken of the Lord **through** the prophet, saying,

23 **Be-perceiving,** a virgin shall be **holding in womb-belly**, and shall **produce** Son, and they shall call his name Emmanuel, which being **change-translated**, God with us.

24 Then Joseph being-**awaken** from sleep **produced** as the angel of the Lord had **towards-arranged** him, and **beside-take the wife, his.**

25 And knew her not **until** she **produced** her firstborn, **the** Son: and he called his name Jesus.

MATTHEW CHAPTER 2

1 Now when Jesus was born in Bethlehem of Judaea in the days of Herod the king, **be-perceiving**, there **beside-became** wise men from the east **into** Jerusalem,[1221]

2 Saying, where is he that is **produced** King of the Jews? For we have **perceived** his star in the east and are come to worship him.

3 When Herod the king had heard he was **aggravated**, and all Jerusalem with him.

4 And when he had gathered all the **first-rank-priests** and scribes of the people together, he **ascertain-by-inquiry** of them where Christ should be born.

[1219] Lit., to give a reminder
[1220] Or exhibit

[1221] Greek: "Hierosoluma"—priests-peace (hierou-priest, sacred) and salem (peace)

5 Yet, they said **to-him**, in Bethlehem of Judaea: for **in-this-way** it is written **through** the prophet,

6 And you Bethlehem, the land of Juda, are **by-no-means inferior** among the **leaders** of Juda: **because** out of you shall come a **Leader** that shall **Shepherd** my people Israel.

7 Then Herod, when he had **privately-hidden** called the wise men, enquired of them **exactly** what **uninterrupted-time** the star **shined**.

8 And he **dispatched** them into Bethlehem, and said, go and **out-examine**[1222] **exactly** for the young child; and when you have found, **from-message me**, that I may come and worship him also.

9 When they had heard the king, they departed; and, **be-perceiving**, the star, which they saw in the east, **before-lead** them, until it came and stood **upon-above** where the young child was.

10 When they saw the star, they-were-**cheered, great, tremendous**[1223] **cheerfulness**.

11 And when they were come into the house, they **perceived** the child with Mary his mother, and fell, and worshipped him: and when they had opened their **treasures**[1224] they presented **to-him** gifts; gold, and frankincense, and myrrh.

12 And being **apprised**[1225] of God in a **trance** that they should not return to Herod, they **up-spaced** into their own **space another-same** way.

13 And when they were **up-spaced**, **be-perceiving**, the angel of the Lord **shined** to Joseph in a **trance**, saying, arise, and take the child and his mother, and flee into Egypt, and **exist** there until I bring you word: **because** Herod **impending to-**seek the child to **from-ruin**[1226] him.

14 When he arose, he **beside-take** the child and his mother by night, and **up-spaced** into Egypt:

15 And was there until the death of Herod: that it might be **filled** which was spoken **under** the Lord **through** the prophet, saying, out of Egypt have I called **the Son of-me**.

16 Then Herod, when he **perceived** that he was **in-childish-mocked**,[1227] of the wise men, was **sacrifice-angry**, and sent forth, and **up-lift**,[1228] all the boys that were in Bethlehem, and in all the **horizon of-her** from two **years** old and under, **down** the **uninterrupted-**time which he had **exactly beside** the wise men.

17 Then was **filled** that which was spoken by Jeremiah the prophet, saying,

18 In Rama was there a **voice** heard, lamentation, and weeping, and **much** mourning, Rachel weeping her children, and would not be **beside-called**, because they are not.

19 Yet when Herod was **finished**, **behold**, an angel of the Lord **shines** in a dream to Joseph in Egypt,

20 Saying, arise, and **beside-take** the child and his mother, and go into the land of Israel: for they are dead which sought the young child's **soul**.

21 And he arose, and **beside-take** the child and his mother, and came into the land of Israel.

22 But when he heard that Archelaus[1229] did reign in Judaea **instead** of his father Herod, he was afraid to go there: **yet according-to**, being **apprised** of God in a **trance**, he **up-spaced** into the **sections** of Galilee:

23 And he came and **down-house** in a city called Nazareth: that it might be **filled** which was spoken **through** the prophets, He shall be called a Nazarene.

MATTHEW CHAPTER 3

1 In those days came John the Baptist, preaching in the **lonesome** of Judaea,

2 And saying, **be-change-thinking; because** the kingdom of heaven **near-squeezed**.

3 Because, this is he that was spoken of by the prophet **Isaiah**, saying, the **voice** of one crying in the **lonesome**, prepare[1230] you the way of the Lord, **produce** his paths **soon**.[1231]

4 And the same John had his raiment of camel's hair, and a leather **belt** about his loins; and his **food** was locusts and wild honey.

[1222] Or, to test thoroughly by questions
[1223] Neuter plural of "sphodros" (violent, vehement)
[1224] Greek: "thesaurous"—placed into tomorrow
[1225] Greek: "chrematizo," to furnish what is needed, divine response; secular meaning of constituting a business, employ, to bear as a title, to apprise (to give notice, state of affair, inform)
[1226] Greek: "apo" (from) and "alethros" (ruin), to destroy fully

[1227] Greek compound: "empaiktes" (in-sport (mock) as a boy), root means a child as disciplined
[1228] Or lit., assassinate
[1229] Defined as "people-ruling"
[1230] Or, lit., internal preparation
[1231] Or, good-place, level

5 Then **out-passage towards** him Jerusalem, and all Judaea, and all the **about-space of-the** Jordan,

6 And were baptized of him in Jordan, **out-same-saying** their sins.

7 Yet when he saw many of the Pharisees and Sadducees come to his baptism, he said **to** them, **offspring** of vipers, who has **under-show** you to flee from the **swelling-anger impending**?

8 Produce therefore fruits **worthy of-the change-thought.**

9 And **seem** not to say **in** yourselves, we have Abraham to father**; because,** I say **to-you**, that God **is-powerful out-of** these stones to raise up children **to** Abraham.

10 Yet, **already, also,** the axe is laid **to** the root of the trees: therefore, every tree which **is-not producing ideal** fruit is **out-of-cut** and cast into the fire.

11 I indeed baptize you with water into **change-thought;** but he that comes after me is **forceful** than I, whose **sandals** I am not **sufficient**[1232] to bear; he shall baptize you with the Holy Spirit, and fire.

12 Whose **winnowing-fork** in his hand, and he will be thoroughly **cleaning** his floor, and **together-lead** his wheat into the garner; but he will burn up the chaff with **unextinguished** fire.

13 Then comes Jesus from Galilee to Jordan **towards** John, to be baptized of him.

14 But John forbids him, saying, I have need to be baptized of you, and come you **towards** me?

15 And Jesus answering said **to-him, from-let-go**[1233] now: for **in-this-way** it-is **towering** us to **fill** all **righteous-togetherness**. Then he **from-let-go** him.

16 And Jesus, when he was baptized, **up-walked soon** out of the water: and, **be-perceiving,** the heavens had **up-opened to-him,** and he perceived the Spirit of God **down-walking as-if** a dove, and **coming** upon him:

17 And **be-perceiving** a voice from heaven, saying, this is my beloved, **the** Son, in whom I am **good-seem.**

MATTHEW CHAPTER 4

1 Then was Jesus led up of the Spirit into the **lonesome** to be tempted **under** the Devil.

2 And when he had fasted forty days and forty nights, afterward, he was hungry.

3 And when the tempter came **to-him**, he said, if you be Son of**-the** God, **say** that these stones **become** bread.

4 But he answered and said, it is written, man shall not live by bread alone, but by every word that **out-passage through** the mouth of God.

5 Then the Devil **beside-take** him up into the **Holy City**, and **stands** him on a pinnacle of the **priest-place**,

6 And says **to-him**, if you be Son of**-the** God, cast yourself down; **because** it is written, He shall give his angels **command** concerning you: and in hands they shall bear you up, lest you **toward-strike**[1234] your foot against a stone.

7 Jesus **show**[1235] **to-him**, it is written again, you shall not tempt the Lord your God.

8 Again, the Devil **beside-take** him up into an exceeding high mountain, and shows him all the kingdoms of the world, and the glory of them;

9 And says **to-him**, all these things will I give you, **if-on** falling, **you-worship** me.

10 Then says Jesus **to-him, be-under-leading,** Satan; **because** it is written, you shall worship the Lord your God, and **to-him** only **shall-you-be-hired-service.**

11 Then the **Devil** leaves him, and, **be-perceiving,** angels came and **attended to-him.**

12 Now when Jesus had heard that John was **betrayed,**[1236] he **up-spaced** into Galilee;

13 And leaving Nazareth, he came and **down-house into** Capernaum, **beside-sea,** in the **horizon** of Zebulon and Naphtali:

14 That it might be **filled** which was spoken by **Isaiah** the prophet, saying,

15 The land of Zebulon, and the land of Naphtali, the way of the sea, **other-side of-Jordan,** Galilee of the **nations;**

[1232] Lit., to arrive; or, competent as if coming in season, ample in amount, fit in character
[1233] Or lit., release, forgive

[1234] Or, stub, towards-chop
[1235] Greek: "phemi," the root word for fame ("pheme")
[1236] Lit., beside-given

16 The people **who** sat in darkness **perceived Mega Light** and **to-them** which sat in the region and shadow of death light **up-rises.**[1237]

17 From **then** Jesus began to preach, and to say, **change-thought, because** the kingdom of heaven **near-squeeze.**

18 And Jesus, walking by the sea of Galilee, saw two **brothers,** Simon called Peter, and Andrew his brother, casting a net into the sea**; because** they were fishers.

19 And he says **to-them,** follow me, and I will **produce** you fishers of men.

20 And they **shortly** left **the** nets and followed him.

21 And going on from there, he **perceived other-same** two **brothers,** James of Zebedee, and John his brother, in a ship with Zebedee their father, **down-fresh** their nets; and he called them.

22 And they **soon** left the ship and their father and followed him.

23 And Jesus went about all Galilee, teaching in their synagogues, and preaching the **well-message** of the kingdom, and **therapy-served**[1238] all manner of **nausea**[1239] and **every softness**[1240] in the people.

24 And his **hearing** went **into the whole** Syria: and they brought **to-him** all **evil holding** people **to-various nausea** and torments[1241] **together-holding,** and those **demonized,** and those which were **moon-struck,** and **paralytic;**[1242] and he **therapy-served**[1243] them.

25 And there followed him **many** multitudes from Galilee, and Decapolis, and Jerusalem, and Judaea, and **other-side of-Jordan.**

MATTHEW CHAPTER 5

1 And **perceiving** the multitudes, he-**up-walked** into **the** mountain; and when he was **down-seated,** his disciples came **to-him:**

2 And he opened his mouth, and taught them, saying,

3 Happy the poor **to-the** spirit; for theirs is the kingdom of heaven.

4 Happy they that mourn; for they shall be **beside-called.**

5 Happy the **mild**: for they shall inherit the earth.

6 Happy they which hunger and thirst after **righteous-togetherness**; for they shall be filled.

7 Happy the merciful: for **they-shall-obtain-mercy.**

8 Happy the **clean** in **heart**: for they shall see[1244] God.

9 Happy the peacemakers: for they shall be called **sons** of God.

10 Happy they which are **chased on-account-of righteous-togetherness;** for theirs is the kingdom of heaven.

11 Happy are you, when **they-shall-defame**[1245] you, and **chase-you** and shall say **every wicked-hurtful** against you falsely, **on-account-of me.**

12 Be-cheerful, and **jump-for-joy;** for **much** your reward in heaven; for so **they-chased** the prophets which were before you.

13 You are the salt of the earth; but if the salt **becomes-moronic, in what** shall it be salted? **Into nothing is-it-forceful, still;** if not having-being-cast **outside** to be **trampled** under **the** men.

14 You are the light of the world. A city that is **laying** on a **mountain**[1246] **not is-powerful to-be-hidden.**

15 Neither do men light a candle, and put it under a **dry-measure,**[1247] but on a candlestick; and it gives light **to** all that are in the house.

16 Let your light so shine before men, that they may **perceive** your **ideal** works, and glorify your Father which is in **the** heavens.

17 Not you-should-think-by-law that I am come to **down-loosen** the **Law,** or the **Prophets:** I am not come to **down-loosen,** but to **fill.**

18 Amen, because I say **to-you,** until heaven and earth pass, **no not** one **iota** or one **horn** shall pass from the law, until all **becomes.**

19 Whoever therefore shall **loose** one of these least commandments, and shall teach men so, he shall be called the least in the kingdom of heaven; **yet** whoever shall **produce** and teach, the same shall be called **great** in the kingdom of heaven.

[1237] Lit., up-finish
[1238] Or heal, cure, root may be defined as "heat"
[1239] Lit., ship-sickness
[1240] Or., catamite
[1241] Or ordeals
[1242] Or, loosen-beside
[1243] Or, cure, root heat
[1244] Lit., gaze at
[1245] Lit., notorious, name
[1246] Greek: "orous," mountain
[1247] Latin origin, "modios" (English: modius), a certain measure

20 Because, I say **to-you**, that except your **righteous-togetherness** shall exceed the scribes and Pharisees, you shall **not** enter into the kingdom of heaven.

21 You have heard that it was said **to-the originals**, you shall not **murder**; and whoever shall **murder** shall be **liable**[1248] of the **judging**.

22 Yet, I say **to-you**, that whoever is **swelling-anger** with his brother **simulating**[1249] shall be **liable to-the judgement**; and whoever shall say to his brother, **empty,**[1250] shall be in **liable of the Sanhedrin;**[1251] yet, whoever shall say, you are **stupid,**[1252] shall be in **liable into of-the fire Gehenna**.

23 Therefore, if you bring your gift to the **sacrifice-place**, and there remembers that your brother **holds down of**-you;

24 Leave there your gift before the **sacrifice-place**, and **under-lead**; foremost be **through-another-same**[1253] **to-you**r brother, and then come and offer your gift.

25 Well-thought to-your anti-righteous[1254] quickly, whiles you are in the way with him; **lest-when you beside-gives the anti-righteous** to the judge, and the judge **beside-give** you **to-the subservient**[1255] and you be cast into prison.

26 Amen, I say **to-you**, you shall by no means come out there, until you have **given** the **last quadrans**.[1256]

27 You have heard that it was said by them of**-the originals, not you-shall-adultery:**

28 But I say **to-you**, that whoever **looks**[1257] on a woman **towards the on-feel of**-her has already adultery her **in the heart of-him.**

29 And if your right eye **scandalizes**[1258] you, pluck it out, and cast from you; **because** it is **together-carrying** for you that one of your members should **be-from-ruined,**[1259] and not your whole body should be cast into **Gehenna**.

30 And if your right hand **scandalizes** you, cut it off, and cast from you; **because** it is **together-carrying** for you that one of your members should **ruin**, and not your whole body should be cast into **Gehenna**.

31 It has been said, whoever shall **from-loose** his wife, let him give her a **divorce**.[1260]

32 But I say **to-you**, that whoever shall **from-loose** his wife, **beside-exterior of-saying**[1261] **of-prostitution, produces** her to **commit-adultery;** and whoever shall marry her that is **from-loosed commits-adultery.**

33 Again, you have heard that it has been said **of-the originals**, you shall not **swear, yet you-shall-from-give to**-the Lord your oaths.

34 But I say **to-you**, swear not at all; neither **in the** heavens; for it is God's throne:

35 Nor **in** the earth; for it is his footstool; neither by Jerusalem; for it is the **City** of the **great** King.

36 Neither shall you swear **in** your head, because **not you-are-powerful produce** one hair white or black.

37 But let your **saying** be, yes, yes; no, no; **yet** whatever is more than these comes **out**-of **wicked-hurtful.**

38 You have heard that it has been said, an eye **instead of-an-eye,** and a tooth **instead of-a-tooth.**

39 Yet, I say **to-you**, that you **anti-stand** not **wicked-hurtful;** but whoever shall **slap** you on your right cheek, turn **to-him** the other also.

40 And if any man will **judge you**, and **take** your **shirt**, let him have your **garment** also.

41 And whoever shall **courier** you to go a mile,[1262] go with him two.

42 Give **to-him** that asks you, and from him that would borrow of you turn not you away.

43 You have heard that it has been said, you shall love your neighbor, and **detest** your haters.

44 But I say **to-you**, love your **haters**, bless them that **down-pray** you, **produce ideally to-them** that **detest** you, and pray for them which **insult** you, and **chase** you.

[1248] Greek: in-hold, to hold in
[1249] Image, weak (as if simulating others)
[1250] Greek: "raca" a transliteration of a Hebrew word meaning, empty
[1251] Or together (joint) session (sitting)
[1252] Greek: moron
[1253] Or reconcile
[1254] Lit., anti-just, opponent, plaintiff
[1255] Lit., under-oarsman, generally a subordinate
[1256] Latin origin: the fourth (1/4) part of a donkey
[1257] Lit., a voluntary observation
[1258] Or, lit., snared
[1259] Greek: "apo" (from) and "alethros" (ruin), to destroy fully
[1260] Properly: a thing that separates; or lit., to from-stand
[1261] Greek: logos having [onoma (name) and rhema (living voice)]
[1262] Greek: "million" (Latin origin), 1,000 paces

45 That you may be **sons** of your Father which is in heavens: for he makes his sun to rise on the **wicked-hurtful** and on the good and sends rain on the **righteous-ones** and on the **unrighteous-ones**.

46 For if you love them which love you, what reward have you? **Produce** not even the **tax-collector**[1263] the same?

47 And if you **embrace** your **brothers** only, what **produce** you more? Do not even the **tax-collectors in-this-way produce**?

48 Be you therefore **mature**, even as your Father which is in heaven is **mature**.

MATTHEW CHAPTER 6

1 Toward-hold not **to-be-producing** your **pity-mercy** before men, **to-be-a-theatre** of them: otherwise, you have no reward of your Father which is in heavens.

2 Therefore, when you **produce** your **pity-mercy**, do not **trumpet** before you, as the hypocrites **produce** in the synagogues and in the streets, that they may have glory of men. **Amen**, I say **to-you**, they have their reward.

3 But when you **produce pity-mercy**, let not your left hand know what your right hand does:

4 That your **pity-mercy** may be in **the hidden**: and your Father, which **is-looking** in **the hidden**, himself shall **from-give** you **shining**.

5 And when you pray, you shall not be as the hypocrites; for they love to pray standing in the synagogues and **in** the corners of the streets that they may be **shining to-the** men. **Amen**, I say **to-you**, they have their reward.

6 Yet you, when you pray, enter **into your storeroom**, and when you have **locked** your door, pray **to-your** Father which is in **the hidden**; and your Father which **is-looking** in **the hidden** shall **from-giving** you **shining**.

7 Yet when you pray, use not **stutter-sayings**,[1264] as the **nations**; for they **seem** that they shall be heard for their **much-saying**.

8 Not, be-assimilating to-them; for your Father **perceived** what things you have need of, before you ask him.

9 After this manner therefore pray you: Our Father **the-one in the** heavens, **Holy the name of you.**

10 Your kingdom come. Your will **become** in earth, as in heaven.

11 Upon-I-exist,[1265] give us **today** our bread.

12 And **release**[1266] us our debts, as we **release** our debtors.

13 And **not into-carry us** into **probe-testing**, but **rush-rescue** us from **the wicked-hurtful**; for yours is the kingdom, and the power, and the glory, **into the ages**. Amen.

14 For if you **release** men their **beside-falls**, your heavenly Father will also **release** you:

15 But if you **release** not men their **beside-falls**, neither will your Father **release** your **beside-falls**.

16 Moreover when you fast, be not, as the hypocrites, of **bad-temper-gaze**[1267] for they **un-shine**[1268] their faces, that they may **shined to** men **fasting**. **Amen**, I say **to-you**, they have their reward.

17 Yet you, when you fast, anoint your head, and wash your face.

18 That you **shine** not **to** men to fast, but **to-your** Father which is in **the hidden**: and your Father, which **is-looking** in **the hidden**, shall reward you **shining**.

19 Not place-into-tomorrow[1269] for yourselves **treasures** upon earth, where moth and rust **feeding, is-un-shining-it**, and where thieves break through and steal:

20 But **place-into-tomorrow** for yourselves **treasures** in heaven, where neither moth nor rust **feeding, is-un-shining-it**, and where thieves do not **through-burrow**, nor steal:

21 For where your **place-into-tomorrow** is, there will your **heart** be also.

22 The **candle** of the body is the eye; if therefore your eye be **single**;[1270] your whole body shall be light.

[1263] Or, lit., finish-purchase
[1264] Or stammer-saying
[1265] Or, upon-substance, or property
[1266] Lit., to from-let-go, release
[1267] Sullen-face. Sullen-gaze, gloomy-face, gloomy-gaze, sad-face, sad-eye
[1268] Or disguise
[1269] Greek: "thesauros," transliterated as thesaurus, also means a deposit, treasures,
[1270] Haplous, the antonym of "diplous" meaning double

23 But if your eye be **wicked-hurtful**, your whole body shall be darkness. If therefore the light that is in you be darkness, how **much** is that darkness!

24 No-one is-powerful to-two lords to-be-slaving, for either he will hate the one, and love the other; or else he will **anti-hold** to the one, and **down-disposition** the **another-different** you cannot **slave to**-God and mammon.[1271]

25 Through this, I say **to-you, not be-portion-worry** for your **soul,** what you shall eat, or what you shall drink; nor yet for your body, what you shall put on. is not the **soul** more than meat, and the body than **clothing-yourself**?

26 In-look, the **birds** of the **heaven,** for they sow not, neither do they reap, nor gather into barns; yet your heavenly Father feeds them. Are you not **differ**[1272] **more** than they?

27 Which of you by **portion-worrying is-powerful to-** add one cubit **to** his stature?

28 And why **are-you-portion-worrying** for **clothing**? **Down-learn** the lilies of the field, how they grow; they **fatigue** not, neither do they spin.[1273]

29 And yet I say **to-you,** that even Solomon in all his glory was not **clothed** like one of these.

30 Yet, if God so clothe the grass of the field, which today is, and tomorrow is cast into the oven, not much more you, **ones-of-puny-faith**?

31 Therefore **not be-portion-worrying,** saying, what shall we eat? Or what shall we drink? Or what shall we be clothed?

32 (For after all these things do the **nations** seek:) for your heavenly Father knows that you have need of all these things.

33 But seek you **foremost** the kingdom of God, and his **righteous-togetherness**; and all these things shall be added **to-you**.

34 Therefore **not be-portion-worrying** for the tomorrow: **because** tomorrow shall-**portion-worry** for the things of itself. Sufficient **to-the** day the evil **of-her**.

MATTHEW CHAPTER 7

1 Judge not, that you be not judged.

2 Because in which judgment-result[1274] you judge, you shall be judged; and with what measure you **measure,** it shall be measured **to-you** again.

3 And why **are-you-looking** the **shriveled-splinter** that is in your brother's eye, but **not down-mind** the **timber** that is in your own eye?

4 Or how **will** you say **to-you**r brother, let me pull out the **shriveled-splinter** out of your eye; and, **be-perceiving,** a **timber** in your own eye?

5 Hypocrite, first cast out the **timber** out of your own eye; and then shall you see clearly to cast out the **shriveled-splinter** out of your brother's eye.

6 Give not that which is holy **to** the dogs, neither cast you your pearls before swine, lest they trample them under their feet, and **turn** and **break** you.

7 Ask, and it shall be given you; seek, and you shall find; knock, and it shall be opened **to-you:**

8 Because, everyone that asks **takes** and he that seeks finds; and **to-him** that knocks it shall be opened.

9 Or what man is there of you, whom if his son ask bread, will he give him a stone?

10 Or if he asks **for-a**-fish, will he give him a serpent?

11 If you then, being **wicked-hurtful, perceive** how to give good gifts **to-you**r children, how much **rather** shall your Father which is in heaven give good things **to-them** that ask him?

12 Therefore, all things whatever you would that men should **produce to-you, produce** you **also** to them for this is the **Law and the Prophets.**

13 Enter you in at the **narrow**[1275] gate: for **wide-flat** the gate, and **good-spaced** the way, that **from**-leads to **the from-ruin,** and many **are the-ones entering through her**:

14 Because **narrow** the gate, and **tribulation** the way, which leads **to** life, and few there be that find it.

15 Yet, **be-you-towards-holding from the** false prophets, which come **to-you** in sheep's clothing, but inwardly they are **snatching** wolves.

16 You shall know them **from** their fruits. Do men gather grapes of thorns, or figs of **three-cast?**[1276]

[1271] Originally: confidence, wealth personified
[1272] Greek: "diaphero," to through-bear, transliterated as "differ" or "different"
[1273] Spinning yarn for clothing
[1274] Greek: "krima," transliterated as "crime" and also means judgment, verdict
[1275] Narrow with obstacles close by
[1276] Or, thistle, lit., a crow-foot (three pronged obstruction used in war)

17 Even so every good tree **produces** good fruit; but a **rotten** tree **produces wicked-hurtful**[1277] fruit.

18 A good tree **not is-powerful to-produce wicked-hurtful** fruit, neither a **rotten** tree **produces** good fruit.

19 Every tree that **produces** not **ideal** fruit is **chopped-out** and cast into the fire.

20 Therefore by their fruits you shall **upon-know**[1278] them.

21 Not everyone that says **to** me, Lord, Lord, shall enter into the kingdom of heaven; but he that **produces** the will of my Father which is in heavens.

22 Many will say to me in that day, Lord, Lord, have we not prophesied in your name? And in your name have cast out **demons**? And in your name **produce** many **powers**?

23 And then will I **same-say to-them,** I never knew you**, from-space** from me, you that work **the lawlessness**.

24 Therefore, whoever hears these sayings of mine, and **produce** them, I will **assimilate** him **to** a wise man, which **house-built** his house upon a rock:

25 And the rain descended, and the floods came, and the winds blew, and **towards-fell** upon that house; and it fell not: for it was founded upon a rock.

26 And every one that hears these sayings of mine, and **produce** them not, shall be **assimilated** to a **moronic** man, which **house-built** his house upon the sand:

27 And the rain descended, and the floods came, and the winds blew, and **toward-strike**[1279] upon that house; and it fell; and **great** was the fall of it.

28 And **it became**, when Jesus had **together-finished** these sayings, the people were **pounded-out**[1280] upon his **teaching.**

29 For he taught them as having authority, and not as the scribes.

MATTHEW CHAPTER 8

1 When he come down from the mountain **many** multitudes followed him.

2 And, **be-perceiving**, there came a leper and worshipped him, saying, Lord, if you **will**, you-**are-powerful to cleanse me.**

3 And Jesus **out-of-stretch the** hand, and **fastened to-him**, saying, I will; be-clean. And **soon** his leprosy was **cleaned.**

4 And Jesus says **to-him,** see you tell no man; but **under-lead**, show yourself to the priest, and offer the gift that Moses **towards-arrange into** a **witness to-them.**

5 And when Jesus was entered into Capernaum, there came **to-him** a centurion,[1281] **beside-calling** him,

6 And saying, Lord, my **boy** lays at home **paralytic**,[1282] **timidly**[1283] tormented.[1284]

7 And Jesus says **to-him**, I will come and **therapy-served** him.

8 The centurion answered and **showed**[1285] Lord, I am not **sufficient**[1286] that you should come under my roof: but speak the word only, and my **boy** shall be **cured**.

9 Because, I am a man under authority, having soldiers under me: and I say to this, go, and he goes; and to another, come, and he comes; and to my **slave, produce** this, and he **produces.**

10 When Jesus heard, he marveled,[1287] and said **to-them** that followed, **amen**, I say **to-you**, I have not found **the-self**[1288] faith, no, not in Israel.

11 And I say **to-you**, that many shall come from the east and west, and shall **recline**[1289] with Abraham, and Isaac, and Jacob, in the kingdom of heaven.

12 But the **sons** of the kingdom shall be cast out into outer darkness: there shall be weeping and **grating** of teeth.

13 And Jesus said **to** the centurion, **be-you-under-led**; and as you have believed, **let-it-become to-**you. And his **boy** was healed in the **that** hour.

[1277] Greek: "poneros," also means hurtful
[1278] Or exact knowledge
[1279] Or, stub, towards-chop
[1280] Or, out of-pound
[1281] Or, lit., hundred-chief, a hundred-original
[1282] Or beside-loosen
[1283] From the root, to dread
[1284] Or (in) ordeal
[1285] Greek: "phemi," the root word for fame ("pheme")
[1286] Lit., to arrive; or, competent as if coming in season, ample in amount, fit in character
[1287] Lit., look closely at
[1288] Greek: "tosauten," a compound of (tos (the) and autos (self)
[1289] Up-incline

14 And when Jesus was come into Peter's house, he **perceived** his wife's mother **cast**, and **feverish**.[1290]

15 And he **fastened to** her hand, and the fever **released** her: and she arose, and **attended to-them**.

16 When the even was **became**, they brought **to-him** many that were **demonized** and he cast out the spirits **with-word,** and **therapy-served** all that were **evil holders.**

17 That it might be **filled** which was spoken by **Isaiah** the prophet, saying, Himself **took** our **weaknesses**, and bare **nauseas**.[1291]

18 Now when Jesus **perceived many** multitudes **around** him, he gave **order** to **depart into** the other side.

19 And a certain scribe came, and said **to-him**, **Teacher**, I will follow you wherever you go.

20 And Jesus says **to-him**, the foxes have **burrows**, and the birds of the **heaven**, nests; **yet** the Son of man has not where to lay[1292] **the** head.

21 And **another-different** of his disciples said **to-him**, Lord, **permit** me **foremost** to go and bury my father.

22 But Jesus said **to-him**, follow me; and **release** the dead bury their dead.

23 And when he was entered into a ship, his disciples followed him.

24 And, **be-perceiving**, there arose a **great quaking** in the sea, **so** that the ship was covered with the waves: but he was asleep.

25 And his disciples came, and awoke him, saying, Lord, save us, we **from-ruin**.[1293]

26 And he says **to** them, why are you **timid**,[1294] O you of **little-faith**? Then he arose and **rebuke**[1295] the winds and the sea; and there **became** a great calm.[1296]

27 But the men marveled,[1297] saying, what manner of man is this, that even the winds and the sea **under-hear**[1298] him!

28 And when he was come to the other side into the country of the Gergesenes, there met him two **demonized**, coming out of the **remembrance-tomb**, exceeding fierce,[1299] so that no man **forceful to-pass through** that way.

29 And, **be-perceiving**, they cried out, saying, what have we to do with you, Jesus, you Son of God? Are you come **here** to torment[1300] us before the **season**?

30 And there was a good way off from them a herd of many swine feeding.

31 So the **demons asked** him, saying, if you cast us out, **permit** us to go away into the herd of swine.

32 And he said **to** them, **be-under-leading**. And when they were come out, they went into the herd of swine: and, **be-perceiving**, the **entire** herd of swine **violent-impulse** down a **precipice** into the sea, and **from-died** in the waters.

33 And they that kept them fled, and went their ways into the city, and told everything, **of-the demonized**

34 And, **be-perceiving**, the **entire** city came out to **under-anti** Jesus: and when they **perceived** him, they **beside-call** that he would **change-pace**[1301] from the horizon **of-them**.

MATTHEW CHAPTER 9

1 And he **in-stepped** into a ship, and **crossed** over, and came into his own city.

2 And, **be-perceiving**, they brought **to-him** a man **paralytic**,[1302] **laying** on a **cot**;[1303] and Jesus seeing their faith said to the **paralytic**, Son, be **daring**;[1304] your sins **have-been-released**[1305] **of-**you.

3 And, **be-perceiving** certain of the scribes said within themselves, this blasphemes.

4 And Jesus **perceiving** their **in-sacrifice-anger** said, **why that** you **in-sacrifice-anger wicked-hurtfully-hurtful** in your **hearts**?

5 For which is easier, to say, your sins **have-been-released**[1306] you; or to say, arise, and walk?

6 But that you may **perceive** that the Son of man has **authority**[1307] on earth to **release** sins, (then **he says**

[1290] Or to be on fire
[1291] Or ship-sickness
[1292] Or, to slant, to slope, recline
[1293] Greek: "apo" (from) and "alethros" (ruin), to destroy fully
[1294] Timid comes from a root word meaning: to dread
[1295] Tax-upon, charge
[1296] Or smile
[1297] Or, to look at closely
[1298] Or obey
[1299] Or, difficult, ferocious
[1300] Or, to ordeal
[1301] Lit., to change-base
[1302] Or beside-loosen
[1303] Or a recliner
[1304] Or, bold
[1305] Lit., from-let-go
[1306] Or from-let-go
[1307] Authority is a compound word from "ek" (out-of) and "eimi" (-I exist)

to the sick of the **paralytic**,) arise, take up your **cot**, and **be-under-led into your** house.

7 And he arose and departed **into** his house.

8 But when the multitudes **perceived,** they marveled, and glorified God, which had given such **authority to** men.

9 And as Jesus **beside-leading** from there, he **perceived** a man, named Matthew, sitting at the **tax-office** and he says **to-him**, follow me. And he **up-stood** and followed him.

10 And it **became,** as Jesus **reclined** in the house, **be-perceiving**, many **tax-collectors,** and sinners came and **together-reclined to-him** and his disciples.

11 And when the Pharisees **perceived,** they said **to** his disciples, why eat your **Teacher** with **tax-collectors** and sinners?

12 Yet, when Jesus heard, he said to-them, the **ones-holding forcefulness** need not a physician, but they that **evil holders**.

13 Yet, go you and learn **what is: I-am-willing-desire mercy,** and not sacrifice! **Because** I am not come to call the righteous, but sinners **into change-thought**.

14 Then came **to-him** the disciples of John, saying, why do we and the Pharisees fast **much,** but your disciples fast not?

15 And Jesus said **to** them, **not is-powerful** the **sons** of the **bridechamber** mourn, as long as the bridegroom is with them? **Yet,** the days will come, when the bridegroom shall be taken from them, and then shall they fast.

16 No man puts a **patch** of new **rag on** an old garment, for that which is put in to fill it up **lifts** from the garment, and the **split**[1308] is made worse.

17 Neither do men put **new-young** wine into old **leather**: else the **leather-bottles burst** and the wine **spills** out, and the bottles **from-ruin;** but they put **new-young** wine into **new-fresh leather-bottles**, and both are **together-preserved.**

18 While he spoke these things **to**-them, **be-perceiving**, there came a certain **first-rank**,[1309] and worshipped him, saying, my daughter **is-presently** finished; but come and lay your hand upon her, and she shall live.

19 And Jesus arose, and followed him, and his disciples.

20 And, **be-perceiving,** a woman, **having-blood-issue** twelve **years**, came behind, and **fastened to** the hem of his garment:

21 For she said within herself, if I may but **fasten to** his garment, I shall be **safe**.[1310]

22 But Jesus turned, and when he **perceived** her, he said, daughter, **daring,**[1311] your faith has **saved**. And the woman was **safe**[1312] from that hour.

23 And when Jesus came into the **first-rank**, house, and **perceived** the **flutists** and the people making a **disturbance-wail,**

24 He said **to** them, **up-space: because** the **maiden** is not dead, but sleeps. And they **down-laughed him**.

25 But when the people were **out-of cast**, he went in, and **governed her** hand, and the **girl** arose.

26 And the fame hereof went into **that whole** land.

27 And when Jesus **beside-leading there** two blind men followed him, crying, and saying, Son of David, have mercy on us.

28 And when he was come into the house, the blind men came **to-him**: and Jesus says **to-them**, believe you that **I-am-powerful** to **produce** this? They said **to-him**, yes, Lord.

29 Then he **fastened-to** their eyes, saying according **to-your** faith **let-it-become to-**you.

30 And their eyes were opened; and Jesus **in-snorts-with-anger to-them,** saying, see, no-**one let-be-known.**

31 Yet they, when they were departed, **through-fame him** in **that whole** land.

32 As they went out, **be-perceiving,** they brought **to-him** a **man blunted,**[1313] **demonized.**

33 And when the **demon** was cast out, the **blunted**, spoke: and the multitudes marveled, saying, it never **shined in-this-way** in Israel.

34 Yet, the Pharisees said, he casts out **demons** through the **first-rank** of the **demons**

[1308] Lit., schism
[1309] Or, original-rank, beginning-rank
[1310] Or., saved
[1311] Or, courageous
[1312] Or, saved
[1313] Or, deaf-mute, root to chop (choppy), to beat the chest

35 And Jesus went about all the cities and villages, teaching in their synagogues, and preaching the **well-message** of the kingdom, and **therapy-served**[1314] every **nausea** and every **softness**[1315] in the people.

36 But when he **perceived** the multitudes, he **had-gut-compassion about** them, because they **out-of-loosen** and **tossed**, as sheep having no shepherd.

37 Then **he says to** his disciples, the harvest truly plenteous, but the **workers** few;

38 Beg-bind you **then** the Lord of the harvest, that he will send forth **workers** into his harvest.

MATTHEW CHAPTER 10

1 And when he had **towards-called** his twelve disciples, he gave **to-them authority of-**unclean spirits, **as-both to-be-cast-out** them, and to **therapy-served every nausea and every softness**.[1316]

2 Now the names of the twelve apostles are these; **foremost**, Simon, who is called Peter, and Andrew his brother; James, of Zebedee, and John his brother;

3 Philip, and Bartholomew; Thomas, and Matthew the **tax-collector**; James, of Alphaeus, and Lebbaeus, who's **upon-called**[1317] was Thaddaeus;

4 Simon the Canaanite, and Judas Iscariot, who also betrayed[1318] him.

5 These twelve Jesus sent forth, and **beside-message** them, saying, go not into the way of the **nations**, and into city of the Samaritans, **not you-be-entering.**

6 Yet, go rather **towards** the **from-ruin** sheep of the house of Israel.

7 And as you go, preach, saying, the kingdom of heaven is **near-squeeze.**

8 Therapy-served the **weak**, cleanse the lepers, raise the dead, cast out **demons; gratuitously**[1319] you have **gotten, gratuitously** give.

9 Acquire neither gold, nor silver, nor brass in your **belt.**

10 Nor **wallet into** journey, neither two **garments**, neither **sandals**, nor yet **rods, because** the workman is **deserving** of his meat.

11 And into whatever city or town you shall enter, enquire who in it is **deserving**; and there **remain** until **when** you **go-out.**

12 And when you come into a house, **embrace her.**

13 And if the house be **deserving**, let your peace come upon it: **yet** if it be not **deserving**, let your peace return **to-you.**

14 And whoever shall not **welcome** you, nor hear your words, when you depart out of that house or city, shake off the dust of your feet.

15 Amen, I say **to-you**, it shall be more tolerable for the land of Sodom and Gomorrah in the day of **judging**, than for that city.

16 Be-perceiving, I send you forth as sheep in the middle of wolves; be you therefore **disposed** as serpents, and **un-mixed** as doves.

17 Yet, before-hold from men; for they will **betray**[1320] you **into** the **Sanhedrin**, and they will **be whipping** you in their synagogues;

18 And **you-shall-be-led** before **leaders** and kings **on-account-of me**, **into** a **witness to-**them and the **nations.**

19 Yet, when they **betray you, not be-portion-worry** how or what you shall speak; **because** it shall be given you in that hour what you shall speak.

20 Because, it is not you that speak, but the Spirit of your Father which speaks in you.

21 And the brother shall **betray** the brother to death, and the father the child: and the children shall **upon-stand** against parents and cause them to be put to death.

22 And you shall be hated of all **through my name;** but he that **under-remain** to the **finish** shall be saved.[1321]

23 But when they **chase** you in this city, flee you into another; **amen, because** I say **to-you**, you shall not **finish** the cities of Israel, until the Son of man may-be-coming.

24 The disciple is not above **the teacher**, nor the **slave** above his lord.

25 It is **sufficient** for the disciple that he be as his **teacher**, and the **slave** as his lord. If they have called

---

[1314] Or, curing
[1315] Or catamites
[1316] "Malakia," from the root "malakos," soft, catamite
[1317] Or, to entitle, to invoke
[1318] Lit., beside-given
[1319] Or, without a cause
[1320] Lit., beside-given
[1321] Or, safe

the **house-owner** Beelzebub,[1322] how much **rather** them of his household?

26 Fear them not therefore; **because** there is nothing covered, that shall not be revealed; and **hidden,** that shall not be known.

27 What I tell you in darkness, speak you in light: and what you hear in the ear, preach you upon the housetops.

28 And fear not them which kill the body, but **not are-powerful** to kill the soul; **yet** rather, fear him which **is-powerful** to **from-ruin** both soul and body in **Gehenna.**

29 Are not two sparrows sold for a **coin**?[1323] and one **out-of** them shall not fall on the ground without your Father.

30 But the very hairs of your head are all numbered.

31 Fear you not therefore, you are **differing**[1324] than many sparrows.

32 Whoever therefore shall **same-saying in** me before men, **in** him will I confess also before my Father which is in heavens.

33 But whoever shall **contradict** me before men, him will I also **contradict** before my Father which is in heavens.

34 Not do-by-law that I am come to send peace on earth; I came not to send peace, but a sword.

35 For I am come **to-cut into two, a-**man **downing** his father, and the daughter **downing** her mother, and the daughter in law **downing** her mother in law.

36 And a man's **haters the-ones-of-his** household.

37 He that **friends'** father or mother more than me is not **deserving** of me; and he that **friends'** son or daughter **over** me is not **deserving** of me.

38 And he that **takes** not his cross, and follows **behind** me, is not **deserving** of me.

39 He that finds his **soul** shall **from-ruin her**; and he that **from-ruin his soul on-account-of me,** shall find it.

40 He that **welcome** you **welcome** me, and he that **welcome** me **welcome** him that sent me.

41 He that **welcome** a prophet in the name of a prophet shall **take** a prophet's **wages**; and he that **welcome** a **righteous-one into** the name of a **righteous-one** shall **take** a righteous-one's wage.

42 And whoever shall give to drink **to** one of these little ones a cup of **cool,** only in the name of a disciple, **amen** I say **to-you**; he shall **not from-ruin his wage.**

MATTHEW CHAPTER 11

1 And **it became,** when Jesus **finished through-arrange** his twelve disciples, he **changed-step**[1325] **there** to teach and to preach in their cities.

2 Now when John had heard in the prison the works of Christ, he **dispatched** two of his disciples,

3 And said **to-him**, are you he **the-one-coming**, or do we **towards-seem** for **another-different**?

4 Jesus answered and said **to** them, go and **from-message to-**John those things which you do hear and see:

5 The blind receives their sight, and the **limping** walk, the lepers are cleaned, and the **blunted,**[1326] hear, the dead are raised up, and the poor **are-being-evangelized.**

6 And **happy is-he** whoever shall not be **scandal**[1327] in me.

7 And as they departed, Jesus began to say **to** the multitudes concerning John, what went you out into the **lonesome** to see? A reed shaken with the wind?

8 But what went you out **to-be-perceiving**? A man clothed in soft[1328] **garments**? **Be-perceiving,** they that wear **softness** are in kings' houses.

9 But what went you out for **to-be-perceiving**? A prophet? Yes, I say **to-you**, and more than a prophet.

10 For this is, of whom it is written, **be-perceiving,** I send my **angel** before your face, which shall **construct** your way before you.

11 Amen, I say **to-you**, among them that are born of women there has not risen a **larger**[1329] than John the Baptist: **yet** he that is **smaller** in the kingdom of heaven is **larger** than **him.**

[1322] Lord of the flies (another name for Satan)
[1323] Lit., assarius (a roman coin)
[1324] Greek: "diaphero," to through-bear, transliterated as "differ" or "different"
[1325] Or change-base

[1326] Or, deaf-mute, root to chop (choppy), to beat the chest
[1327] Or., lit snared
[1328] Or, catamite garments, effeminate garments
[1329] Larger, especially in age

12 And from the days of John the Baptist until now the kingdom of heaven **is-being-forced**, and **the forceful-ones are-snatching her**.

13 For all the **Prophets and the Law** prophesied until John.

14 And if you will **welcome**, this is **Elijah, impending** to come.

15 He that has ears to hear, hear!

16 But **to what** shall I **assimilate** this generation? It is like **to** children sitting in the markets, and **toward-voicing to** their **kinsman**.

17 And saying, **we-have-flute to-you**, and you have not danced; we have mourned **to-you**, and you have not lamented.[1330]

18 For John came neither eating nor drinking, and they say, he has a **demon**.

19 The Son of man came eating and drinking, and they say, **be-perceiving** a man gluttonous, and a **wine-drinker**, a friend of **tax-collectors** and sinners. But wisdom **was-made-righteous from** her children.

20 Then began him to **defame**[1331] the cities **in which** most of his **powers** were done, because they **not change-thinking**:

21 Woe **to-you**, Chorazin! Woe **to-you**, Bethsaida! For if the **powers**, which **becoming in** you, **became** in Tyre and Sidon, they would have **change-thinking of-old**[1332] in sackcloth and ashes.

22 But I say **to-you**, it shall be more tolerable for Tyre and Sidon at the day of **judging**, than for you.

23 And you, Capernaum, which are **elevated until** heaven, shall be brought down to **Hell**: for if the **powers**, which **is-becoming in** you, had **become** in Sodom, it would have remained until **today.**

24 But I say **to-you**, that it shall be more tolerable for the land of Sodom in the day of **judging**, than for you.

25 In that, the season, Jesus answered and said, I thank you, Father, Lord of heaven and earth, **for** you have hid these things from the wise and **understanding**,[1333] and has revealed them **to infants**

26 Even so, Father; for so it-**became** well-seem in your sight.

27 All things are **beside-given under** me of my Father; and no man **upon-knows**[1334] the Son, **if not** the Father; neither **upon-knows** any man the Father, **if not** the Son, and to whomever the Son **plan-counsels-himself to-reveal.**

28 Come-here towards me, all you that **are-fatigue** and are **loaded**, and I will give you rest.

29 Lift my yoke upon you and learn **from** me; for I am **mild** and **humble** in **heart**; and you shall find rest **to-you**r souls.

30 Because, my yoke **furnish-what-is-needed**,[1335] and my **invoice-load** is light.

MATTHEW CHAPTER 12

1 In that **season** Jesus went on the Sabbath through the **cornfields**; and his disciples were a hungry and began to pluck the **stalk-standing** of corn, and to eat.

2 But when the Pharisees saw, they said **to-him, be-perceiving**, your disciples **produce** that which is not lawful to **produce in** the Sabbath.

3 But he said **to** them, have you not read what David did, when he was hungry, and they that were with him.

4 How he entered into the **House of God,** and did eat the **breads of-the purpose**,[1336] which was not lawful for him to eat, neither for them which were with him, but only for the priests?

5 Or have you not read in the law, how that on the Sabbaths, the priests in the **priest-place** profane[1337] the Sabbath, and are **un-caused-guiltless?**[1338]

6 But I say **to-you**, that in this place is **larger**[1339] than the **priest-place.**

7 But if you had known what **is**, I will have mercy, and not sacrifice, you would not have **down-justice** the **un-caused-guiltless?**

8 For the Son of man is Lord even of the Sabbath.

9 And when he **changed-step** there, he went into their synagogue:

10 And, **be-perceiving**, there was a man who had a withered hand. And they asked him, saying, is it lawful

---

[1330] Or beat the chest in grief
[1331] Lit., notorious, name
[1332] Or long ago
[1333] Or lit., to send-together
[1334] Or, to know exactly

[1335] Or employer
[1336] Lit., before-placed, a placing before or a placing in advance
[1337] Profane by crossing the thresholds
[1338] Or, without a "cause," without-"asking" for something due
[1339] Larger, especially in age

to **therapy-served** on the Sabbaths? That they might accuse[1340] him.

11 And he said **to** them, what man shall there be **out of-you,** that shall have one sheep, and if it falls into a pit on the Sabbaths, will he not **govern** it, and **shall-be-raising-it?**

12 How much then is a man **differing of-s**heep? **So-too,** it is lawful to **produce ideally** on the Sabbaths.

13 Then **he says** to the man, **out-**stretch your hand. And he **out-**stretched; and it was restored **healthy-grow,** like as the **other-same.**

14 Then the Pharisees went out and **got together-plan-counsel to down** him, how they might **from-ruin** him.

15 But when Jesus knew, he **up-space** himself from there; and **many** multitudes followed him, and he **therapy-served** them all;

16 And **rebuke**[1341] them that they should not **produce** him **shine.**

17 That it might be **filled** which was spoken **through** Isaiah[1342] the prophet, saying,

18 Be-perceiving my **boy,** whom I **prefer;** my beloved, in whom my soul is **good-seem**: I will **place** my Spirit upon him, and he shall **from-message judging** to the **nations.**

19 He shall not **quarrel,** nor cry; neither shall any man hear his voice in the streets.

20 A **crushed** reed shall he not break, and **smoldering linen** shall he not **extinguish,** until he **out-of-cast judging to conquest.**

21 And in his name shall the **nations expect.**

22 Then was brought **to-him one-demonized,** blind and **blunted,**[1343] and he **therapy-served**[1344] him, **so-too** that the blind and **blunted,** spoke and saw.

23 And all the people were **ecstasized,**[1345] and said, is not this the son of David?

24 But when the Pharisees heard, they said, this-one does not cast out **demons,** but by Beelzebub the **first-rank,** of the **demons.**

25 And Jesus **perceived** their **in-sacrifice-anger,** and said **to** them, every kingdom divided against itself is brought to desolation; and every city or house divided against itself shall not stand:

26 And if Satan cast out Satan, he is divided against himself; how shall then his kingdom stand?

27 And if I by Beelzebub cast out **demons, through** whom your **sons are-out-casting? Through-this,** they shall be your judges.

28 Yet, if I cast out **demons** by the Spirit of God, then the kingdom of God is **anticipated**[1346] **upon** you.

29 Or else, how **is-powerful any to** enter into **the** house **of-the forceful,** and **through-snatch** his **vessels,** except he **foremost** binds the **forceful?** And then he will **through-snatch** his house.

30 He that is not with me is **downing** me; and he that gathers not with me is-scattering.

31 Through-this, I say to-you, **every** sin and blasphemy shall be **released**[1347] **to-the** men: **yet** the blasphemy **of-**the Spirit shall not be **released to-the** men.

32 And whoever speaks a word **downing** the Son of man, it shall be **released to-him**: but whoever speaks **downing** the Holy Spirit, it shall not be **released to-him,** neither in this **age,** neither in the **impending.**

33 Either **produce** the tree **ideal,** and his fruit **ideal;** or else **produce** the tree **rotten,** and his fruit **rotten; because** the tree is known by fruit.

34 Offspring of vipers, how **are-you-powerful,** to speak good things being **wicked-hurtful?** Because, out of the **surplus**[1348] of the **heart** the mouth speaks.

35 A good man out of the good **placed-into-tomorrow**[1349] of the **heart** brings forth good things: and a **wicked-hurtful** man out of the **wicked-hurtful placed-into-tomorrow** brings forth **wicked-hurtful** things.

36 Yet, I say to-you, that every **non-working** word that men shall speak, they shall give **word about** in the day of **judging.**

[1340] Transliterated as "categorize"
[1341] Tax-upon, charge, upon-value, warn
[1342] Greek for Isaiah
[1343] Or, deaf-mute, root to chop (choppy), to beat the chest
[1344] Or cures
[1345] Greek compound existemi (out-of-stand) from which we take our English ecstasy (overwhelming feelings)
[1346] Or to be beforehand, to precede, to have arrived
[1347] To from-let-go
[1348] Or excess
[1349] Greek: "thesauros," transliterated as thesaurus, also means a deposit, treasure,

37 Because **out-of** your words **you-shall-be righteous** and **out-of** your words you shall be **down-righteous**.

38 Then certain of the scribes and of the Pharisees answered, saying, **Teacher**, we would **perceive** a sign from you.

39 But he answered and said **to** them, a **wicked-hurtful** and adulterous generation seeks after a sign; and there shall no sign be given to it, but the sign of the prophet Jonas.

40 Because, as Jonas was three days and three nights in the whale's belly; so, shall the Son of man be three days and three nights in the **heart** of the earth.

41 The men of Nineveh shall rise in **the judging** with this generation and shall **down-judge** it: because they **change-thinking into** the preaching of Jonas; and, **be-perceiving, more of-**Jonas here.

42 The queen of the south shall rise up in the **judging** with this generation and shall **down-judge** it: for she came from the **extremity** of the earth to hear the wisdom of Solomon; and, **be-perceiving, more of-**Solomon here.

43 When the unclean spirit is **out-coming from** a man, he walks through **un-watered spots,** seeking **up-pause**, and finds none.

44 Then he says, I will return into my house from where I came out; and when he is come, he finds **loitering-leisure,**[1350] swept, and **having-cosmetic.**

45 Then goes he and **is-beside-taking** with himself seven other**-different** spirits more **wicked-hurtful** than himself, and they enter in and **down-house** there: and the last of that man is worse than the **foremost**. Even so shall it be also **to** this **wicked-hurtful** generation.

46 While he yet talked to the people, **be-perceiving, the** mother, and his **brothers** stood without, **seeking** to speak with him.

47 Then one said **to-him, be-perceiving,** your mother, and your **brothers** stand without, **seeking** to speak with you.

48 Yet, he answered and said **to-him** that told him, who is my mother? And who are my **brothers**?

49 And he **out-**stretched his hand toward his disciples, and said, **be-perceiving** my mother and my **brothers!**

50 For whoever shall **produce** the will of my Father which is in **heavens,** he is my brother, and sister, and mother.

MATTHEW CHAPTER 13

1 The same day went Jesus out of the house and sat **beside** the sea.

2 And **many** multitudes were **together-led towards** him, so that he **in-stepped** into a ship, and sat; and the whole multitude stood on the shore.

3 And he spoke many things **to-them** in parables, saying, **be-perceiving,** a Sower went forth to sow;

4 And when he sowed, some fell **beside the way,** and the **birds** came and devoured them up:

5 Some fell upon **rock-like,**[1351] where they had not much earth; and **soon** they **out-of-rise,** because they had no depth of earth;

6 And when the sun **up-rising,** they were scorched; and because they had no root, they withered.

7 And some fell among thorns; and the thorns **up-walked**, and choked them:

8 But other fell into **ideal** ground, and **give** fruit, some a hundred, some sixty, some thirty.

9 Who has ears to hear, hear!

10 And the disciples came, and said **to-him,** why speak you **to-them** in parables?

11 He answered and said **to** them, **for** it is given **to-you** to know the mysteries of the kingdom of heaven, but **to-them** it is not given.

12 For whoever has, **to-him** shall be given, and he shall have more abundance: but whoever has not, from him shall be taken away even that he has.

13 Therefore speak I **to-them** in parables: because they seeing see not; and hearing they hear not, neither do they understand.

14 And **upon** them is **filled** the prophecy of Isaiah, which says, by hearing you shall hear, and shall not understand; and seeing you shall see, and shall not perceive:

15 For this people's **heart** is **thick-fixed**, and ears are **heavy** of hearing, and their eyes they have **down-shut; lest-when** they should **perceive to-the** eyes, and hear **to-the** ears, and should understand **to-the**

[1350] Lit., being schooled, in the sense of not working

[1351] Or stony-perception per the root word given in Strong's dictionary

heart, and should be **reverted**, and I should **cure** them.

16 But **happy** your eyes, for they see: and your ears, for they hear.

17 Amen, because, I say **to-you,** that many prophets and righteous have **on-feel** to **perceive** which you see and have not **perceived**; and to hear which you hear and have not heard.

18 Hear you therefore the parable of the Sower.

19 When anyone hears the word of the kingdom, and understands not, then comes the **wicked-hurtful,** and **snatching** that which was sown in his **heart**. This is he **beside the way being-sown.**

20 Yet, the one on the **rock-like**[1352] **being-sown, this** is he that hears the **Word,** and **soon** with **cheerfulness take** it;

21 Yet, has he no root in himself, but is **toward-season**: **yet,** when tribulation or **chase becomes through** the Word, **soon** he is **scandalized**.[1353]

22 Yet, **the-ones into the thorns being-sown** is he that hears the **Word,** and the **portion-worry** of this **age,** and the **cheating** of riches, choke **the Word,** and he becomes unfruitful.

23 Yet, **the-one on the ideal ground being-sown** is he that hears the **Word,** and understands;[1354] which also **carry-**fruit, and is **producing,** some a hundred, some sixty, some thirty.

24 Another parable **he-beside-place**[1355] to-them, saying, the kingdom of heaven is **assimilated to** a man which sowed **ideal** seed in his field:

25 But while men slept, his **hateful-enemy** came and sowed tares[1356] **up middle of-**the wheat and went his way.

26 But when the **grass** was **sprouted,** and **produced** fruit, then **shined** the tares also.

27 So the **slaves** of the householder came and said **to-him**, Lord, not **ideal** seed you sow in your field? From where **then is-having the** tares?

28 He **showed**[1357] to them, an **enemy-hater, man,** has **produced** this. The **slaves** said **to-him,** will you then that we go and gather them up?

29 But he **showed,** no; lest-**when** you gather up the tares, you root up **simultaneous** the wheat with them.

30 Let both grow together until the harvest: and in the **season** of harvest, I will say to the reapers, gather you together **foremost** the tares, and bind them in bundles to burn them: but gather the wheat into my barn.

31 Another parable **he-beside-placed to-them,** saying, the kingdom of heaven is like to a grain of mustard seed, which a man **takes,** and sowed in his field:

32 Which indeed is the least of all seeds: **yet** when it is grown, it is the **larger** among herbs, and becomes a tree, so that the birds of the **heaven** come and lodge in the branches **of-it.**

33 Another parable spoke he **to** them; the kingdom of heaven is like **to ferment,** which a woman **took,** and hid in three measures of meal, until the whole was **fermented.**

34 All these things spoke Jesus **to** the multitude in parables; and **space-from** a parable spoke he not **to** them:

35 That it might be **filled** which was spoken by the prophet, saying, I will open my mouth in parables; I will **belch** things which have been **hidden** from the **down-casting**[1358] of the world.

36 Then Jesus **released**[1359] the multitude and went into the house: and his disciples came **to-him,** saying, **decipher** to-us the parable of the tares of the field.

37 He answered and said **to** them, He that sows the **ideal** seed is the Son of man;

38 The field is the world; the **ideal** seed are the **sons** of the kingdom; but the tares are the **sons** of the **wicked-hurtful.**

39 The **enemy-hater** that sowed them is the **Devil;** the harvest is the **together-finish of-the age**; and the reapers are the angels.

40 As therefore the tares are gathered and burned in the fire; so, shall it be in the **together-finish of-the age.**

41 The Son of man shall send forth his angels, and they shall gather out of his kingdom all things that

---

[1352] Or stony-perception per the root word given in Strong's dictionary
[1353] Or., lit snared
[1354] Or lit., send-together
[1355] Or deposit
[1356] Or wild rice
[1357] Greek: "phemi," the root word for fame ("pheme")
[1358] Or disruption
[1359] Or to send-from, forgive

scandalizes,[1360] and them which **produce the lawlessness;**

42 And shall cast them into a furnace of fire: there shall be wailing and **grating** of teeth.

43 Then shall the righteous shine forth as the sun in the kingdom of their Father. Who has ears to hear, hear!

44 Again, the kingdom of heavens is like **to treasure**[1361] **hidden** in a field; the which when a man has found, he hides, and **from the cheerfulness of-it,** goes and sells all that he has, and buys[1362] that field.

45 Again, the kingdom of heavens is like **to** a merchant man, seeking **ideal** pearls:

46 Who, when he had found one pearl of **much-valued**, went, and sold all that he had, and bought it.

47 Again, the kingdom of heavens is like **to** a net, which was cast into the sea, and gathered of every **kin.**

48 Which, when it was full, they drew to shore and sat down, and gathered the **ideal** into **pails,** but cast **out** the **rotten.**

49 So shall it be at the **together-finish of-the age;** the angels shall come forth, and **from-defining**[1363] the **wicked-hurtful out-of the middle of-**the **righteous-ones,**

50 And shall cast them into the furnace of fire: there shall be wailing and **grating** of teeth.

51 Jesus says **to** them, have you understood all these things? They say **to-him,** yes, Lord.

52 Then said he **to** them, therefore every scribe **discipled into** the kingdom of heavens is like **to** a man, a householder, who **extracts**[1364] out of his **placed-into-tomorrow new-fresh** and old.

53 And **it became,** when Jesus had finished these parables, he departed there.

54 And when he was come into his own **father-country,** he taught them in their synagogue, **so** that they were **out-of-pounded,** and said, **where** has **this-one** this wisdom, and **the powers**?

55 Is not this the carpenter's son? Is not his mother called Mary? And his **brothers**, James, and Joses, and Simon, and Judas?

56 And his sisters, are they not all with us? Where then has **this-one** all these things?

57 And they were **scandalized**[1365] in him. Yet, Jesus said **to** them, **not** is **a prophet un-valued, if not** in his own **father-country,** and in his own house.

58 And he **produces** not many **powers** there because of their unbelief.

MATTHEW CHAPTER 14

1 At that **season heard** Herod the Tetrarch[1366] **the hearing** of Jesus,

2 And said **to** his **boys,** this is John the Baptist; he is risen from the dead; and therefore, **powers are-in-working** in him.

3 **Because,** Herod had **governed** John, and bound him, and **from-place** in prison **through** Herodias', his brother Philip's wife.

4 For John said **to-him,** it is not lawful for you to have her.

5 And when he would have put him to death, he feared the multitude, because they **held** him as a prophet.

6 But when Herod's birthday was kept, the daughter of Herodias danced **in the middle,** and pleased Herod.

7 **Which-place,** he **same-say** with an oath to give her whatever she would ask.

8 And she, being **before-stepped under** her mother, give me, she-**showed,**[1367] here John Baptist's head in a **plate.**

9 And the king was **distress-saddened:** nevertheless, **through** the oath, and them which **reclined** with him at meat, he **orders** to be given.

10 And he **dispatched,** and beheaded John in the prison.

11 And his head was brought in a **plate** and given to the maiden; and she brought to her mother.

12 And his disciples came, and **lift** the body, and buried it, and went and **from-message** Jesus.

[1360] Or snares
[1361] Greek: "thesauros," transliterated as thesaurus, also means a deposit, treasure,
[1362] Lit., to go to the market, redeem
[1363] From-horizon, from-boundary, separate by boundary
[1364] Or out-casting
[1365] Or, snared
[1366] First-rank-of-fourth-part
[1367] Greek: "phemi," the root word for fame ("pheme")

13 When Jesus heard, he **up-spaced there** by ship into a **lonesome place down privately**; and when the people had heard, they followed him on foot out of the cities.

14 And Jesus went forth, and **perceived many** multitude, and **he-has-gut-compassionate** toward them, and he **therapy-served** their **un-leaving-weakness**.

15 And when it was evening, his disciples came **to-him**, saying, this is a **lonesome** place, and the **hour** is now past; **from-loose** the multitude, that they may go into the villages, and buy[1368] themselves **food**.

16 But Jesus said **to** them, they need not **from-loosed**; you give them to eat.

17 And they say **to-him**, we have here but five loaves, and two fishes.

18 He said, bring them **here** to me.

19 And he **orders** the multitude to sit down on the grass, and **taking** the five loaves, and the two fishes, and looking up **into the** heaven, he blessed, and **broke,** and gave the loaves to disciples, and the disciples to the multitude.

20 And they did all eat and were **fed**: and they **lift** up of the fragments that remained twelve baskets full.

21 And they that had eaten were about five thousand men, **spacing-from** women, and children.

22 And **soon,** Jesus **necessitates** his disciples to **take** into a ship, and to go before him **to** the other side, while he **from-loosed** the multitude.

23 And when he had sent the multitudes away, he-**up-walked** into **the** mountain **according-to privately** pray: and when the evening was come, he was there alone.

24 But the ship was now in the middle of the sea, tossed with waves: for the wind was **contrary**.[1369]

25 And in the fourth watch of the night, Jesus went **to** them, walking on the sea.

26 And when the disciples saw him walking on the sea, they were **agitated**, saying, it is a **phantom**;[1370] and they cried out for fear.

27 But **soon** Jesus spoke **to** them, saying, be **daring**;[1371] it is I; be not afraid.

28 And Peter answered him and said, Lord, if t be you, **order** me come **towards** you on the **waters.**

29 And he said, come. And when Peter was come down out of the ship, he walked on the water, **towards** Jesus.

30 Yet, when **he-is-looking**, the wind **being-forceful**, he was afraid; and beginning to sink, he cried, saying, Lord, save me.

31 And **soon** Jesus **out**-stretched **the** hand, and **upon-take of-him**, and said **to-him, little-faith!** Why into **two-standing**?

32 And when they **in-stepped** into the ship, the wind **tired-cut**.

33 Then they that were in the ship came and worshipped him, saying, **truly you are** Son of-God.

34 And when they were **crossed** over, they came into the land of Gennesaret.

35 And when the men of that place had knowledge of him, they sent out into all that country **about-space** and brought **to-him** all that were **evil holders**.

36 And **asked** him that they might only **fasten to** the hem of his garment: and as many as **fastened** were **through-saved**.

MATTHEW CHAPTER 15

1 Then came to Jesus scribes and Pharisees, which were of Jerusalem, saying,

2 Why do your disciples **beside-step**[1372] the **beside-giving**[1373] of the elders? **Because** they wash not their hands when they eat bread.

3 But he answered and said **to** them, why do you also **beside-step** the commandment of God by your **beside-giving**?

4 For God commanded, saying, **value** your father and mother: and He that **evil-speak** father or mother, let him **finish to**-death.

5 Yet, you say, whoever shall say to father or mother, a gift by whatever you-may-profit **of-me;**

[1368] Lit., to go to the market, redeem
[1369] Greek compound: in-anti, in front of, opposite, antagonistic
[1370] Greek: "phantasma"
[1371] Or, courageous, bold
[1372] Transgress
[1373] Lit., tradition

Matthew

6 And **value** not his father or his mother.[1374] **And you have un-lord** the commandment of God **through** your **beside-giving.**

7 You hypocrites, **ideally** did Isaiah prophesy of you, saying,

8 This people **near-squeeze to-me** with their mouth, and **value** me with lips; but their **heart** is **forward from-holding from** me.

9 But in vain they **revere** me, **teachers,**[1375] teaching commandments of men.

10 And he called the multitude, and said **to-them,** hear, and **synthesize:**[1376]

11 Not that which goes into the mouth **common the** man; but that which **out-passage out-of** the mouth, this **common the** man.

12 Then came his disciples, and said **to-him, have-you-perceived** that the Pharisees were **scandalized,**[1377] after they heard this saying?

13 But he answered and said, every plant, which my heavenly Father has not planted, shall be rooted **out.**

14 Release[1378] them; they be blind **way-**leaders of the blind. And if the blind lead the blind, both shall fall into **deep-hole.**

15 Then answered Peter and said **to-him, decipher** to-us this parable.

16 And Jesus said, are you also **at-this-point not-synthesizing**?

17 No you-thought that whatever enters in at the mouth goes into the belly, and is cast out into the **latrine**?

18 But those things which **out-passage out-of** the mouth come forth from the **heart**; and they **common** the man.

19 For out of the **heart** proceed **wicked-hurtful through-inventory,** murders, adulteries, **prostitutions,** thefts, **false-witness,** blasphemies:

20 These are which **common** a man: but to eat with **un-washed** hands **common** not a man.

21 Then Jesus went **out-of-there,** and **up-spaced** into the **sections** of Tyre and Sidon.

22 And, **be-perceiving,** a woman of Canaan came out of **those horizons,** and cried **to-him,** saying, have mercy on me, Lord, Son of David; my daughter is **evil demonized.**

23 But he answered her not a word. And his disciples came and **asked** him, saying, **form-loose** her; for she cries **behind** us.

24 But he answered and said, I am not sent but **to** the **from-ruin** sheep of the house of Israel.

25 Then came she and worshipped him, saying, Lord, help[1379] me.

26 But he answered and said, it is not **ideal** to take the children's bread, and to cast to **puppies.**

27 And she said, truth, Lord: yet the **puppies** eat of the crumbs which fall from their **lords'** table.

28 Then Jesus answered and said **to** her, O woman, **great** your faith; **let-it-become** to-you even as you will. And her daughter was **cured** from that hour.

29 And Jesus **changed-steps**[1380] from **there and** came **beside** the sea of Galilee; and **up-walked** into **the** mountain, and **down-sat** there.

30 And **many** multitudes came **to-him,** having with them **limping,** blind, **blunted,**[1381] maimed, and many **others-different,** and **tossed** them at Jesus' feet; and he **therapy-served** them.

31 Insomuch that the multitude **marveled,** when they saw the **blunted,** to speak, the maimed **healthy-grow,** the **limping** walk, and the blind see: and they glorified the God of Israel.

32 Then Jesus called his disciples, and said, **I-am-having-gut-compassion** on the multitude, because they **remained** with me now three days, and have nothing to eat: and I will not **from-loose them** fasting, lest they **out-loosed** in the way.

33 And his disciples say **to-him, where** should we have so much bread in the **lonesome,** as to **feed so-many** multitude?

34 And Jesus says **to** them, how many loaves have you? And they said, seven, and a few little fishes.

35 And he **orders** the multitude to **up-fall** on the ground.

[1374] The phrase " and value (honor) not his father and mother" is not found in the Byzantine Texts.
[1375] Didaskontes (nominative case)
[1376] Greek: syniete [sun (together) and hemi (send), to send together facts comprehensively.
[1377] Or, snared
[1378] Or forgive (Greek: from-send)
[1379] To run to a cry for help
[1380] Or change-base
[1381] Or, deaf-mute, root to chop (choppy), to beat the chest

36 And he **takes** the seven loaves and the fishes, and gave thanks, and **broke**, and gave to his disciples, and the disciples to the multitude.

37 And they did all eat and were **fed**; and they **lift** the broken that was left seven baskets full.

38 And they that did eat were four thousand men, **spacing-from** women, and children.

39 And he **from-loosed** the multitude, and **in-stepped into** ship, and came into the **horizon** of Magdala.

MATTHEW CHAPTER 16

1 The Pharisees also with the Sadducees came and tempting desired him that he would show them a sign **out-of the** heaven.

2 He answered and said **to** them, when it is evening, you say, **good-calm**-weather; for the **heaven** is **fire-like**.

3 And in the morning, **storm** today: for the **heavens** is **fire-like** and **gloomy-hate**. Hypocrites, you can **know through-judge** the face of the **heaven**; **yet** the signs of the **seasons not you-are-powerful**?

4 A **wicked-hurtful** and adulterous generation seeks after a sign; and there shall no sign be given **to** it, but the sign of the prophet Jonas. And he left them and departed.

5 And when his disciples were come to the other side, they had forgotten to take bread.

6 Then Jesus said **to** them, **be-seeing** and **towards-hold from** the **ferment** of the Pharisees and of the Sadducees.

7 And they **through-inventoried in** themselves, saying, **that** we **took** no bread.

8 Yet, Jesus **knowing,** he said **to** them, **you-of-little-faith,** why **through-inventory** among yourselves, because **you-took** no bread?

9 Not-yet thought neither remember the five loaves of the five thousand, and how many baskets you-**got**?

10 Neither the seven loaves of the four thousand, and how many baskets you-**took**?

11 How **no thought** that I spoke not **to-you** about bread, that you should **towards-hold from** the **ferment** of the Pharisees and of the Sadducees?

12 Then **synthesized**[1382] they how that he **said** not **towards-hold from** the **ferment** of bread, but of the **teaching** of the Pharisees and of the Sadducees.

13 When Jesus came into the **sections** of Caesarea Philippi, he asked his disciples, saying, whom do men say that the Son of man **is**?

14 And they said, some, John the Baptist some, **Elijah;** and others, **J**eremiah, or one of the prophets.

15 He says **to** them, **yet** who say you that I am?

16 And Simon Peter answered and said, you are the Christ, the Son of the living God.

17 And Jesus answered and said **to-him, ha**ppy are you, Simon Bar-Jona;[1383] for flesh and blood has not revealed **to-you**, but my Father which is in **the** heavens.

18 And I say also **to-you**, that you are Peter, and upon this rock I will **house-build** my Church; and the gates of **Hell** shall not **down-force** it.

19 And I will give to-you the **lockers**[1384] of the kingdom of **the** heavens: and whatever you shall bind on earth shall be bound[1385] in heaven: and whatever you shall loose on earth shall be loosed in **in the** heaven.

20 Then he **through-stalled** his disciples that they should tell no man that he was Jesus the Christ.

21 From **then** Jesus began to show **to** his disciples, how that **it-is-binding** he go **into** Jerusalem, and **emotion** many things of the elders and **first-rank-**priests and scribes, and be killed, and be raised again the third day.

22 Then Peter **toward-took** him, and began to **rebuke**[1386] him, saying, **mercy**[1387] **to-**you, Lord: this shall not be **to-you**.

23 But he turned, and said **to** Peter, **be-under-leading** behind me, Satan; you are a **scandal**[1388] **to** me: for **not you-are-disposed** the things that be of God, but those that be of men.

[1382] Sun (together) and hemi (send), send together mentally
[1383] Of Chaldee origin; lit., son (bar) of dove (Jona); or heir of dove
[1384] Or, keys (as shutting a lock), root: to close
[1385] Bound is perfect tense in the Greek texts
[1386] Tax upon, censure
[1387] Greek: "hileos" associated with "hilasterion," (Mercyseat) an expiatory place, atone, merry-atonement, conciliate, mercy
[1388] Or snare

24 Then said Jesus **to** his disciples, if any will come **behind** me, let him **contradict** himself, and **lifts** his cross, and follow me.

25 Because, whoever will save his **soul** shall **from-ruin** it: and whoever will **from-ruin** his **soul on-account of-me** shall find it.

26 For what is a man profited, if he shall gain the whole world, and **detriment** his own soul? Or what shall a man give in exchange for his soul?

27 Because, impending the Son of man **to-**come in the glory of his Father with his angels; and then he shall **from-give** every man **down the practices** of-him.

28 Amen, I say **to-you,** there be some standing here, which shall not taste of death, until they **perceive** the Son of man coming in his kingdom.

MATTHEW CHAPTER 17

1 And after six days, Jesus **beside-take** Peter, James, and John his brother, and brings them up into a high mountain **privately.**

2 And was **transformed**[1389] before them: and his face did shine as the sun, and his **garments became** white as the light.

3 And, **be-perceiving** there appeared to-them Moses and **Elija**h talking with him.

4 Then answered Peter, and said **to** Jesus, Lord, it is **ideal** for us to be here: if you will, let us **produce** here three tabernacles; one for you, and one for Moses, and one for **Elijah.**

5 While he yet spoke, **be-perceiving,** a bright cloud overshadowed them: and **be-perceiving** a voice out of the cloud, which said, this is my beloved Son, in whom I am **good-seem**; hear you him.

6 And when the disciples heard, they fell on their face, and were **tremendously**[1390] afraid.

7 And Jesus came and **fastened of-them**, and said, arise, and be not afraid.

8 And when they had lifted up their eyes, they **perceived** no man, **if not,** Jesus **Himself**, only.

[1389] Greek: "metamorphoo"
[1390] From "sphodros" (violent, vehement)
[1391] Or tax upon, censure
[1392] Or change-step

9 And as they came down from the mountain, Jesus **commanded** them, saying, tell the vision to no man, until the Son of man be risen again **out-of** the dead.

10 And his disciples asked him, saying, why then say the scribes that **it-is-binding Elijah** come, **foremost**?

11 And Jesus answered and said **to** them, **Elijah** truly **is-coming foremost** and **shall-**restore all things.

12 Yet, I say **to-you**, that **Elijah** is come already, and they knew him not, but have **produce to-him** whatever they **willed**. Likewise, **it-is-impending** also the Son of man **to-emotion** of them.

13 Then the disciples **synthesize** that he spoke **to-them** of John the Baptist.

14 And when they were come to the multitude, there came **to-him** a man, **knee-falling to-him**, and saying,

15 Lord, have mercy on my son: for he is lunatic, and **evil emotion**: for **many** he falls into the fire, and **many** into the water.

16 And I brought him **to-your** disciples, and they **not is-powerful to-therapy-served** him.

17 Then Jesus answered and said, O **un-believing** and perverse generation, how long shall I be with you? How long shall I **tolerate** you? Bring him **here** to me.

18 And Jesus **rebukes**[1391] the **demon**; and he departed out of him: and the child was **therapy-served** from that very hour.

19 Then came the disciples to Jesus **privately**, and said, why **not we-were-powerful to-**cast him out?

20 And Jesus said **to** them, **through** your unbelief: **amen, because,** I say **to-you**, if you have faith as a grain of mustard seed, you shall say **to** this mountain, **change-base**[1392] **within, to-there**; and it shall **change-base**, and nothing shall be **un-powerful to-you**.

21 {**Yet,** this **kind not out-passage if not in to-prayer** and **to-fasting.**}[1393]

22 And while they **up-turned**[1394] in Galilee, Jesus said **to** them, **it-is-impending** the Son of man be betrayed[1395] into the hands of men:

[1393] This verse is not in the oldest Alexandrian texts; see Mark 9:29
[1394] Or, returned
[1395] Lit., beside-given

23 And they shall kill him, and the third day he shall be raised again. And they were **tremendously**[1396] **distress-sadden**.

24 Yet, when they were come to Capernaum, they that **took** tribute[1397] came to Peter, and said, does not your **teacher finish**[1398] the tribute? [1399]

25 He says, yes. And when he was come into the house, Jesus prevented him, saying, what **to-you is-seeming**, Simon? Of whom do the kings of the earth take **finishes**[1400] or **census**?[1401] Of their own **sons**, or of **others-same**?

26 Peter says **to-him, of others-same.** Jesus **showed to-him**, then are the **sons** free.

27 Yet, that not scandalizing[1402] them, go **into** the sea, and cast a hook, and take up the fish that **foremost** comes up; and when you have opened his mouth, you shall find **stander;**[1403] that **take** and give **to-them** for me and you.

MATTHEW CHAPTER 18

1 At the **that hour** came the disciples **to** Jesus, saying, who is the **larger**[1404] in the kingdom of **the** heavens?

2 And Jesus called a child **to-him**, and set him in the **middle** of them,

3 And said, **amen** I say **to-you**, except you be **turn**, and become as children, you shall not enter into the kingdom of **the** heavens.

4 Whoever therefore shall humble himself as this child, the same is **larger** in the kingdom of **the** heavens.

5 And **whoever** shall **welcome** one such child in my name **welcomes** me.

6 But **whoever** shall **scandalize**[1405] one of these little ones which believe in me, it-is-**expedient** for him that a millstone was hanged about his neck, and he were **down-plunge** in **ocean of-**the sea.

7 Woe **to-the** world because of **scandals**![1406] **Because, it-is necessity** that **scandals** come; but woe to that man by whom the **scandal comes**!

8 Yet, if your hand or your foot **scandalize** you, cut them off, and cast from you: it is **ideal** for you to enter into life **limping** or maimed, rather than having two hands or two feet to be cast into **the eternal fire.**

9 And if your eye **scandalizes** you, pluck it out, and cast from you: it is **ideal** for you to enter into life with one eye, rather than having two eyes to be cast into **Gehenna** fire.

10 Be-seeing that you **down-disposition** not one of these little ones; for I say **to-you**, that in heavens their angels do always **be-perceiving** the face of my Father which is in heavens.

11 For the Son of man is come to save that which was **from-ruin**.

12 How **seem you**? If a man has a hundred sheep, and one of them be **seduced**,[1407] does he not leave the ninety and nine, and goes into the mountains, and seek that which is **seduced**?

13 And if so be that he finds it, **amen,** I say **to-you**, he **cheers** more of that, than of the ninety and nine which **not seduced**.

14 Even so it is not the will of your Father which is in heavens, that one of these little ones should **from-ruin**.

15 Moreover if your brother shall **sin into you**, go and **evidence-expose** him between you and him alone: if he shall hear you, you have gained your brother.

16 Yet, if he will not hear you, **beside-take** with you one or two more, that in the mouth of two or three witnesses every **declaration** may be established.

17 And if he shall **mishear** them, tell **to-the** Church: but if he **mishears** the Church, let him be **to-you** as **the nation**[1408] and a **tax-collector**.

18 Amen, I say **to-you**, whatever you shall bind on earth shall be bound in heaven: and whatever you shall loose on earth shall be loosed in heaven.

19 Again I say **to-you**, that if two of you shall agree[1409] on earth **about every practice** that they shall ask, it shall **become** for them of my Father which is in heavens.

20 For where two or three are gathered together in my name, there am I in the **middle** of them.

[1396] Neuter plural of "sphodros" (violent, vehement)
[1397] Two-drachma grasping) coin
[1398] Greek: "telos"
[1399] Lit., two-drachma (grasping) coin
[1400] "Telos" is also used of levy
[1401] Census was associated with tax
[1402] Or snare
[1403] Lit., "stater," a standard of value, or certain coin
[1404] Larger, especially in age
[1405] Or snare
[1406] Snares
[1407] Or roam
[1408] Lit., ethnic
[1409] Greek: symphony

21 Then came Peter **to-him**, and said, Lord, **how-often** shall my brother sin against me, and I **release** him? **Until seven**?

22 Jesus says **to-him**, I say not **to-you**, **until** seven: but, until **seventy-times seven.**

23 Therefore is the kingdom of heaven **assimilated to a man, a king,** who would take **saying** of his **slave**s.

24 And when he had begun to reckon,[1410] one was brought **to-him**, which owed him ten thousand talents.

25 **Yet, not having** to-**pay**,[1411] his lord **orders** him to be sold, and his wife, and children, and all that he had, and payment to be made.

26 The **slave** therefore fell, and worshipped him, saying, Lord, have **long-sacrifice-anger** with me, and I will pay you all.

27 Then the lord of that **slave** was **gut-compassionate,** and **from-**loosed him, and forgave the **loan to-him.**

28 But the same **slave** went out, and found one of his **together-slaves**, which owed him a hundred **denarius**:[1412] and he **governed him**, and **choked**, saying, pay me that you owe.

29 And his **together-slave** fell at his feet, and **beside-call** him, saying, have **long-sacrifice-anger** with me, and I will pay you all.

30 And he **willed** not; but went and cast him into prison, **until** he should pay the **owed**.

31 So when his **together-slaves perceived** what was **becoming**, they were **tremendously**[1413] **distress-sadden,** and came and **through-clearly to-their** lord all that was **becoming**.

32 Then his lord, after that he had called him, said **to-him**, you **wicked-hurtful slave**, I **released** you **of-all the owed** because you **beside-call** me:

33 Not **it-was-binding** you also **to-be-merciful** on your **together-slave**, even as I had **mercy** on you?

34 And his lord was **swelling-anger**, and **beside-give** him to the tormentors, **until** he should **from-give** all that was **owed to-him.**

35 So likewise shall my heavenly Father **produce** also **to-you**, if you from your **hearts release**[1414] not everyone his brother their **beside-fall.**

[1410] Greek: together-lift
[1411] Lit., from-give
[1412] Or, ten she asses (donkeys)

MATTHEW CHAPTER 19

1 And **it became**, when Jesus had finished these sayings, he departed from Galilee, and came into the **horizon** of Judaea **other-side of-the** Jordan;

2 And **many** multitudes followed him; and he **therapy-served** them there.

3 The Pharisees also came **to-him**, **probe-testing** him, and saying **to-him**, is it lawful for a man to put away his wife for every cause?

4 And he answered and said to-them, have you not read, that he which made **from original produced** them male and female,

5 And said, for this cause shall a man leave father and mother, and shall **towards-keeping company** to his wife: and they two shall be **into first** flesh?

6 **So-that,** they are no more two, but **first** flesh. What therefore God has **together-yoke**, let not man **space**.

7 They say **to-him**, why did Moses then command to give a **little-scroll** of-divorce, and **from-loose her**?

8 He says **to** them, Moses because of the **dry-hardness** of your **heart permitted** you **from-loose** your wives: but from the **origin,** it was not so.

9 And I say **to-you,** whoever shall **from-loose** his wife, except for **prostitution**, and shall marry another, **commits-adultery:** and **whoever** marries her, which is **from-loosed commits-adultery.**

10 His disciples say **to-him**, if the **cause** of the man be so with wife, it is not good to marry.

11 But he said **to** them, **not** all **are-spacing** this saying, **but** to whom it is given.

12 For there are some eunuchs, who were so born from mother's womb: and there are some eunuchs, who were made eunuchs of men: and there be eunuchs, which have made themselves eunuchs **through** the kingdom of heavens. He that **is-powerful to-be-spacing,** let him **be-spacing.**

13 Then were there brought **to-him** children, that he should **upon-place** hands **to-**them and pray: **yet** the disciples rebuked them.

[1413] The root for this word carries the idea of violence
[1414] Lit., from-let-go

14 But Jesus said, **release the** children, and **prevent** them not, to come **to** me: for of such is the kingdom of **the** heavens.

15 And he **placed** hands on them and departed **there.**

16 And, **be-perceiving**, one came and said **to-him**, Good **Teacher**, what good thing shall I **produce**, that I may have **eternal** life?

17 And he said **to-him**, why call you me good? None good but one, God: **yet** if **you-are-willing to** enter into life, keep the commandments.

18 He says **to-him**, which? Jesus said, you shall do no murder, **not you-shall-adultery,** you shall not steal, you shall not **false-witness,**

19 **Value** your father and your mother: and you shall love your neighbor as yourself.

20 The young man says **to-him**, all these things have I kept from my youth up: what lack I **still**?

21 Jesus **showed to-him**, if you**-are-willing to**-be **mature**, go, sell that you have, and give to the poor, and you shall have **treasure**[1415] in heaven: and **here,**[1416] follow me.

22 But when the young man heard that saying, he went away **distress-sad**: for he had **many acquisitions**.

23 Then said Jesus **to** his disciples, **amen,** I say **to-you**, that a rich man shall **difficult-eat**[1417] entering into the kingdom of **the** heavens.

24 And again I say **to-you**, it is easier for a camel to go through the eye of a needle, than for a rich man to enter into the kingdom of God.

25 When his disciples heard, they were **tremendously out-of-pounded**, saying, who then **is-powerful to-be-saved**?

26 But Jesus **in-looking**, and said **to** them, with men this is **un-powerful**; **yet,** with God all things are **powerful**.

27 Then answered Peter and said **to-him, be-perceiving**, we have **released** all, and followed you; what shall we have then?

28 Yet, Jesus said **to** them, **amen,** I say **to-you**, that you which have followed me, in the regeneration when the Son of man shall sit in the throne of his glory, you also shall sit upon twelve thrones, **judges-judging,**[1418] the twelve tribes of Israel.

29 And every one that has **release** houses, or **brothers**, or sisters, or father, or mother, or wife, or children, or lands, **on-account of my name**, shall-**be-taking-to-himself** a hundred-**form,**[1419] and shall inherit **eternal** life.

30 But many **foremost** shall be last; and the last **foremost**.

MATTHEW CHAPTER 20

1 For the kingdom of **the** heavens is like to-man, a **house-owner,** which went out in the morning to hire **workers** into his vineyard.

2 And when he had agreed with the **workers** for a **denarius** a day, he sent them into his vineyard.

3 And he went out about the third hour, and **perceived** others standing **un-working** in the marketplace,

4 And said **to** them; go you also into the vineyard, and whatever is **righteous-thing,** I will give you. And they went their way.

5 Again he went out about the sixth and ninth hour and **produce** likewise.

6 And about the eleventh hour he went out, and found others standing **un-working**, and says **to** them, why stand you here all day **un-workers**?

7 They say **to-him, for** no man has hired us. He says **to** them, go you also into the vineyard; and whatever is **righteous-thing, you-shall-take.**

8 So when even was come, the lord of the vineyard says **to** his **manager**, call the **workers**, and **from-give to-them the pay**, beginning from the last to-the **foremost**

9 And when they came about the eleventh hour, they **took** every man a **denarius**.

10 But when the **foremost** came, they **do-by-law** that they should have **taken** more; and they likewise **took** every man a **denarius**.

11 And when they **took, now,** they **grumble** against the **house-owner,**

[1415] Greek: "thesauros," to place into tomorrow, also transliterated as "thesaurus,"
[1416] Imperative "deuro:" hither! Here! To this place!
[1417] Or, fastidious (meticulous about eating); peevish (fretful, worry); difficult-food (eating), impractical
[1418] Greek: "krinontes," present tense, nominative case
[1419] Or lit., hundred-mold (shape, form, fabricate)

12 Saying, these last have **worked first** hour, and you have made them equal **to-us**, which have **lifted** the **weight** and heat of the day.

13 Yet, he answered one of them, and said, **kinsman,** I do you no wrong: did not you **agree**[1420] with me for a **denarius**?

14 Lift up yours and go your way: I will give **to** this last, even as **to-you**.

15 Is it not lawful **to-me** to **produce** what I will with mine? Is your eye **wicked-hurtful** because I am good?

16 So the last shall be **foremost**, and the **foremost** last: **because** many **are** called, but few chosen.

17 And Jesus **up-walking into** Jerusalem he-**beside-took** the twelve disciples **down privately** in the way, and said **to-them,**

18 Be-perceiving, we-**are-up-walking into** Jerusalem; and the Son of man shall be betrayed[1421] to the **first-rank** priests and to the scribes, and they shall **down-judge** him to death,

19 And shall **beside-give** him to the **nations** to **in-childish-mocked,**[1422] and to **whip**, and to crucify; and the third day he shall **up-stand**.

20 Then came **to-him** the mother of Zebedee's **sons** with her sons, worshipping, and **asking** a certain thing of him.

21 And he said **to** her, what will you? She says **to-him, say** that these my two sons may sit, the one **out-of** your right hand, and the other **out-of** the left, in your kingdom.

22 But Jesus answered and said, you **perceive** not what you ask. **Are-you-powerful** to drink of the cup that I am-**impending** to-drink, and to be baptized with the baptism that I am baptized with? They say **to-him, we-are-powerful.**

23 And he says **to** them, you shall drink indeed of my cup, and be baptized with the baptism that I am baptized with: **yet** to sit **out-of** my right hand, and **out-of** my left, is not mine to give, but for whom it is **internally**-prepared of my Father.

24 And when the ten heard, they were **much-grief-ached**[1423] **about** the two **brothers**.

25 Yet, Jesus called them, and said, you know that the **first-ranks,**[1424] of the **nations down-lord** them, and they that are **great, downing-authority** them.

26 Yet, it shall not be so **in** you: but whoever will be **great in** you, let him be your **attendant**.

27 And whoever will be **foremost** among you, let him be your **slave**:

28 Even as the Son of man came not to be **attended** to, but **attend-to,** and to give his **soul a ransom-looser instead of-many**.

29 And as they **out-passage** from Jericho, much multitude followed him.

30 And, **be-perceiving**, two blind men sitting by the way side, when they heard that Jesus passed by, cried out, saying, have mercy on us, O Lord, Son of David.

31 And the multitude **rebuke**[1425] them, **that** they should **be-silent**: but they cried **larger** saying, have mercy on us, Lord, Son of David.

32 And Jesus stood still, and **voiced** them, and said, what will you that I shall **produce to-you**?

33 They say **to-him**, Lord, that our eyes may be opened.

34 So Jesus **had-gut-compassion and fastened to** their eyes: and **soon** their eyes **up-looked**, and they followed him.

MATTHEW CHAPTER 21

1 And when they **near-squeeze to** Jerusalem, and were come to Bethphage,[1426] **towards** the mountain of Olives, then sent Jesus two disciples,

2 Saying **to** them, **be-gone** into the village over against you, and **soon** you shall find a **donkey** tied, and a **colt** with her; loose, and **lead her to**-me.

3 And if any say **anything to**-you, you shall say, the Lord has need of them; and **soon** he will send them.

4 All this was done, that it might be **filled** which was spoken by the prophet, saying,

5 Say-you to-the the daughter of Sion, **be-perceiving**, your King **is-coming** to-you, **mild**, and sitting upon a **donkey**, and a **colt**, the **son of under-yoke**.[1427]

[1420] Greek: symphony
[1421] Lit., beside-given
[1422] Greek compound: "empaiktes" (in-sport (mock) as a boy), root means a child as disciplined
[1423] Or, resentful
[1424] Or, original-rank, beginning-rank
[1425] To tax upon, charge
[1426] House of figs
[1427] Or yoked beast

6 And the disciples went, and **produce** as Jesus **towards-arrange** them,

7 And brought the **donkey**, and the **colt**, and put on them their **garments**, and they seated **on-up of-them**.

8 And a very **most** multitude spread their garments in the way; others cut down branches from the trees and **spread** in the way.

9 And the multitudes that went before, and that followed, cried, saying, Hosanna[1428] to the Son of David: blessed **the-one-coming** in the name of the Lord; Hosanna in the highest.

10 And when he was come into Jerusalem, all the city **quaked**, saying, who is this?

11 And the multitude said, this is Jesus the prophet **from** Nazareth of Galilee.

12 And Jesus went into the **priest-place** of God, and cast out all them **selling** and buying[1429] in the **priest-place**, and **down-turn** the tables of the **coin-dealers**, and the seats of them that sold doves,

13 And said **to-them,** it is written, my house shall be called the house of prayer; but you have **produced** it a **cave** of **plunderers**.[1430]

14 And the blind and the **limping** came **to-him** in the **priest-place**; and he **therapy-served** them.

15 And when the **first-rank-priests** and scribes saw the **marvelous** things that he **produced**, and the children crying in the **priest-place**, and saying, Hosanna to the Son of David; they were **much-grief-ached**.[1431]

16 And said **to-him, are-you-hearing** what these say? And Jesus says **to** them, yes; have you never read, out of the mouth of **babes** and **of-suckling** you have **down-fresh** praise?

17 And he left them and went out of the city into Bethany; and he lodged[1432] there.

18 Now in the morning as he **up-leads** into the city, he hungered.

19 And when he **perceived** a fig tree in the way, he came to it, and found nothing **in her**, but leaves only, and said **to to-her, Not-still out-of you** fruit **may-be-becoming into the age.** And **instantly** the fig tree withered.

20 And when the disciples saw, they marveled, saying, how **instantly** the fig tree withered!

21 Jesus answered and said **to** them, **amen,** I say **to-you,** if you have faith, and **not through-judge**, you shall not only **produce** this to the fig tree, but also if you shall say **to** this mountain, be **lifted,** and be you cast into the sea; **it-shall-be-becoming.**

22 And all things, whatever you shall ask in prayer, believing, you shall **take**.

23 And when he was come into the **priest-place**, the **first-rank-**priests and the elders of the people came **to-him** as he was teaching, and said, **in which** authority **produce** you these things? And who gave you this authority?

24 And Jesus answered and said **to-them,** I also will ask you one thing, which if you tell me, I in likewise will tell you by what authority I **produce** these things.

25 The baptism of John, **which-place** was it, **out-of** heaven, or **out-of** men? And they **through-inventoried beside** themselves, saying, if we shall say, **out-of** heaven; he will say **to-us,** why did you not then believe him?

26 But if we shall say **out-of** men; we fear the people; for all hold John as a prophet.

27 And they answered Jesus, and said, **not we-have-perceived.** And he **showed**[1433] **to** them, neither tell I you **in which** authority I **produce** these things.

28 Yet, what **seem** you? A man had two **children**; and he came to the **foremost**, and said, **child,** go work today in my vineyard.

29 He answered and said, I will not: but afterward he **after-cared** and went.

30 And he came to the second and said likewise. And he answered and said, **I-ego, Lord,** and went not.

31 Which of **the two produced** the will **of-the** father? They say **to-him,** the **foremost**. Jesus says **to** them, **amen,** I say **to-you,** that the **tax-collectors** and the **prostitutes** go into the kingdom of God before you.

32 Because, John came **to-you** in the way of **righteous-togetherness,** and you believed him not: but the **tax-collectors** and the **prostitutes** believed

---

[1428] Save now! or, please save!
[1429] Lit., to go to the market, redeem
[1430] Or robbers
[1431] Resentful
[1432] A yard open to the wind
[1433] Greek: "phemi," the root word for fame ("pheme")

him: and you, when you had **perceived**, not **change-care** afterward, that you might believe him.

33 Hear another parable: there was a certain **house-owner**, which planted a vineyard, and **fenced** it round about, and dug a winepress in it, and **house-built** a tower, and **give** it out to **land-workers**, and **traveled.**

34 And when the **season** of the fruit **near-squeeze,** he sent his **slave**s to the **land-workers**, that they might **take** the fruits of it.

35 And the **land-workers took** his **slave**s, and **skinned**, and killed another, and stoned another.

36 Again, he sent other **slave**s more than the **foremost** and they **produce to-them** likewise.

37 Yet, last of all, he sent **to-them the Son,** saying, they will **regard**[1434] **the Son of-me**.

38 But when the **land-workers** saw the **Son**, they said among themselves, this is the heir; come, let us kill him, and let us **hold-down** his inheritance.

39 And they caught him, and cast out of the vineyard, and **killed.**

40 When the lord therefore of the vineyard comes, what will he **produce to** those **land-workers**?

41 They say **to-him**, he will **from-ruin** those **evil-**men, and will **give** out vineyard **to** other **land-workers**, which shall **give** him the fruits in their seasons.

42 Jesus says **to** them, did you **not-yet** read in the **Scriptures**, the stone which the **house-builders from-seem-test,**[1435] the same is become the head of the corner: this is the Lord's doing, and it is marvelous in our eyes?

43 Through this, I say **to-you**, the kingdom of God shall be **lifted** from you, and given to a nation **producing** the fruits **of-her.**

44 And whoever shall fall on this stone shall be broken; **yet** on **whomever** it shall fall, it will grind him to powder.

45 And when the **first-rank-priests** and Pharisees heard his parables, they **know** that he spoke **about** them.

46 And when they sought to **govern** him, they feared the multitude, because they **held** him **as** a prophet.

[1434] Lit., in-turn (invert),
[1435] Or, rejected

MATTHEW CHAPTER 22

1 And Jesus answered and spoke **to-them** again by parables, and said,

2 The kingdom of heaven **was assimilated to** a certain king, which **produces** a **marriage** for his son,

3 And sent forth his **slave**s to call them that were **called** to the **marriages**: and they **willed not to-come**.

4 Again, he sent forth other **slave**s, saying, tell them which are **called, be-perceiving,** I have prepared my dinner: my oxen and fatlings, **sacrificed,** and all things ready: come**-her into** the **marriages.**

5 But they **not-cared** and went their ways, one to his farm, another to his **merchandising:**

6 And the **remaining-ones governed** his **slave**s, and **insulted**, and **killed**.

7 But when the king heard, **he-was-swelling-angry**: and he **dispatched** his **war-troops**, and **from-ruined** those murderers, and burned up their city.

8 Then **he says** to his **slave**s, the **marriage** is ready, but they which were **called** were not **deserving**.

9 You-be-gone then into the **through-exits** and as many as you shall find, **call into** the **marriage-celebrations.**

10 So those **slave**s went out into the **roads**, and gathered together all as many as they found, both **wicked-hurtful** and good: and the **marriage-celebration** was **filled** with **ones-reclining**[1436]

11 And when the king came in to see the **ones-reclining**, he saw there a man which had not on a **marriage clothe**.[1437]

12 And he says **to-him, kinsman,** how come you here not having a **marriage** garment? And he was **muzzled**.

13 Then said the king to the **attendants**, bind him hand and foot, and **lift him**, and cast into **exterior** darkness; there shall be weeping and **grating** of teeth.

14 For many are called, but few chosen.

15 Then went the Pharisees, and **together-counsel-plan** how they might entangle him in talk.

16 And they sent out **to-him** their disciples with the Herodians, saying, **Teacher,** we **perceived** that you are true, and teach the way of God in truth, neither care

---

[1436] Or lit., up-cline
[1437] Lit., in-down; or, in-sink, in-down-slipping

you for any; **because** you **look** not **into** the **face** of men.

17 Tell us then, what **seems** you? Is it lawful to give **census-tax to** Caesar, or not?

18 But Jesus **knowing** their **wicked-hurtfulness**, and said, why me do-you-**probe-test**, hypocrites?

19 Show me the **census-tax to-do-by-law-money.** And they brought **to-him** a **denarius**.

20 And he says **to** them, who this image and **inscription**?

21 They say **to-him**, Caesar's. Then **he says** to them, **give** then to Caesar the things which are Caesar's; and to God the things that are God's.

22 When they had heard, they marveled, and left him, and went their way.

23 The same day came **to-him** the Saducees, which say that there is no resurrection, and asked him,

24 Saying, **Teacher**, Moses said, if a man dies, having no children, his brother shall marry his wife, and raise up seed **to** his brother.

25 Now there were with us seven **brothers**: and the **foremost**, when he had married a wife, deceased, and having seed left his wife to his brother:

26 Likewise the second also, and the third, **until** the seventh.

27 And last of all the woman died also.

28 Therefore in the resurrection whose wife shall she be of the seven? **Because** they all had her.

29 Jesus answered and said **to** them, you-**are-being-seduced**, not **perceiving** the **Scriptures**, nor the power of God.

30 For in the resurrection they neither marry, nor **beside-marrying**, but are as the angels of God in heaven.

31 Yet, about the resurrection of the dead, have you not read that which was spoken **to-you** by God, saying,

32 I am the God of Abraham, and the God of Isaac, and the God of Jacob? God is not the God of the dead, but of the living.

33 And when the multitude heard, they were **out-of-pounded**[1438] at his **teaching**.

34 But when the Pharisees had heard that he had **muzzled** the Saducees, they were gathered together.

35 Then one of them, a lawyer, asked, **probe-testing** him, and saying,

36 Master, which commandment **great** in the law?

37 Jesus said **to-him**, you shall love the Lord your God with **your whole heart, and with your whole soul, and with your whole deep-thought**.[1439]

38 This is the **foremost** and **great** commandment.

39 And the second is like **to** it, you shall love your neighbor as yourself.

40 On these two commandments hang **whole,** the **Law and the Prophets.**

41 While the Pharisees were gathered together, Jesus asked them,

42 Saying, what **seem** you of Christ? Whose son, is he? They say **to-him**, **of-the** David.

43 He says **to** them, how then does David in **Spirit** call him Lord, saying,

44 The Lord said **to** my Lord, sit you **out-of** my right hand, **until** I make your **enemies-haters** your footstool[1440] of **your feet**?

45 If David then calls him Lord, how is he his son?

46 And no man was-**powerful** to answer him a word, neither **venture** any from that day to-ask-of him anymore.

MATTHEW CHAPTER 23

1 Then spoke Jesus to the multitude, and to his disciples,

2 Saying, the scribes and the Pharisees sit in Moses' seat:

3 All therefore whatever they say you observe, observe, and **produce**; but **produce** not you after their works; **because** they say, and **produce** not.

4 Because they bind heavy **invoiced-load** and **difficult** to be **bear and** lay on men's shoulders; **yet** they will not move them with one of their fingers.

5 Yet all their works they **produce** to be seen of men: they make broad their phylacteries,[1441] and enlarge the **hem** of their garments,

---
[1438] Or, smitten
[1439] Lit., through-mind

[1440] Lit., under-foot
[1441] A guard case for wearing slips of **Scriptures**, the roof means to watch

6 And **friend** the **foremost-recliner** at **expensive-dinners**, and the **foremost**-seats in the synagogues,

7 And **embraced** in the markets, and to be called of men, Rabbi, Rabbi.

8 But you be not called Rabbi: **because** one is your **Teacher**, Christ; and all you are **brothers**.

9 And call no your father upon the earth; **because** one is your Father, which is in **the** heavens.

10 Neither be you called **down-leaders** for one is your **Down-Leader**, Christ.

11 But he that is **larger**[1442] among you shall be your **attendant**.

12 And whoever shall **elevate** himself shall be **humbled**; and he that shall humble himself shall be **elevated**.

13 But woe **to-you**, scribes and Pharisees, hypocrites! For you **lock** the kingdom of heaven **before** men: **because** you neither go in, neither **you release**[1443] them that are entering to go in.

14 Woe to-you, scribes and Pharisees, hypocrites! For you devour widows' houses, and for a **pretense**[1444] make long prayer: therefore, you shall receive the **more-excessive judgment-result**.[1445]

15 Woe **to-you**, scribes and Pharisees, hypocrites! For you **about-lead** sea and land to **produce** one proselyte,[1446] and when he **becomes**, you make him **more-double** the **son** of Gehenna than yourselves.

16 Woe **to-you**, you blind **way-leaders**, which say, **whoever** shall swear by the temple, it is nothing; but whoever shall swear by the gold of the temple, he is **owing**!

17 You **morons** and blind: for which is **larger**,[1447] the gold, or the temple that sanctifies the gold?

18 And, **whoever** shall swear by the **sacrifice-place**, it is nothing; but whoever swears by the gift that is upon it, he **owes it**.

19 Morons and blind: for **which** is **larger**, the gift, or the **sacrifice-place** that **sanctifies** the gift?

20 Whoever therefore shall swear by the **sacrifice-place**, swears by it, and by all things **upon it**.

21 And **whoever** shall swear by the temple, swears by it, and by him that **down-house him**.

22 And he that shall swear by heaven, swears by the throne of God, and by him that **sits upon it**.

23 Woe **to-you**, scribes and Pharisees, hypocrites! for you tithe of **sweet-fragrance**, dill, and cumin,[1448] and have **released** the weightier of the law, **judging**, mercy, and faith: these **it-was-binding to produce**, and not **release those**.

24 You blind **way-leaders**, which strain at a **mosquito**, and swallow a camel.

25 Woe **to-you**, scribes and Pharisees, hypocrites! For you make clean the outside of the cup and of the platter, but within they are full of **snatching** and **un-governed**.

26 You blind Pharisee, cleanse **foremost** that within the cup and platter, that the outside of them may be clean also.

27 Woe **to-you**, scribes and Pharisees, hypocrites For you are like **to whitewashed graves**, which indeed **shines belonging-to-the-hour outwardly**, but are within full of dead bones, and of all uncleanness.

28 Even so, you also outwardly **shine** righteous **to-the** men, but within you are full of hypocrisy and **lawlessness**.

29 Woe **to-you**, scribes and Pharisees, hypocrites! **For** you **house-built** the **graves** of the prophets, and **cosmetic** the **remembrance-tomb** of the **righteous-ones**,

30 And say, if we had been in the days of our fathers, we would not have been **commune** with them in the blood of the prophets.

31 So-that you **are** witnesses **to-yourselves**, that you are the **sons** of them which killed the prophets.

32 Fill you then the measure of your fathers.

33 You serpents, you **offspring** of vipers, how can you escape the **judging** of Gehenna?

34 Through-this be-perceiving, I send **to-you** prophets, and wise men, and scribes: and of them, you shall kill and crucify; and of them shall you **whip** in your synagogues, and **chase** from city to city:

[1442] Larger, especially in age, **great**
[1443] Lit., from-let-go, forgive
[1444] Greek: before-appear, outward show
[1445] Greek: "krima," transliterated as "crime" and also means judgment
[1446] Towards-comer
[1447] Larger, especially in age
[1448] Root: to store or preserve

35 So-that upon you may come all the righteous blood **poured** upon the earth, from the blood of **righteous-one**, Abel, **to** the blood of Zacharias son of Barachias, whom you **murdered** between the temple and the **sacrifice-place**.

36 Amen, I say **to-you**, all these things shall **arrive** on this generation.

37 Jerusalem, Jerusalem, you that kills the prophets, and stone them which are sent **towards** you, how often would I have gathered your children together, even as a hen gathers her chickens under wings, and you would not!

38 Be-perceiving, your house is left **to-you lonesome**.

39 For I say **to-you**, you shall not **perceive** me from **present, until** you shall say, blessed he **coming** in the name of the Lord.

MATTHEW CHAPTER 24

1 And Jesus went out and departed from the **priest-place**:[1449] and his disciples came to show him the **house-buildings** of the **priest-place**.

2 And Jesus said **to** them, see you not all these things? **Amen,** I say **to-you**, there shall not be **released**[1450] here one stone upon another, that shall not be **down-loosed**.

3 And as he sat upon the mountain of Olives, the disciples came **to-him** privately, saying, tell us, when shall these things be? And what the sign of your **presence**, and of the **together-finish of the age**?

4 And Jesus answered and said **to** them, **be-looking** that no man **seduces** you.

5 For many shall come in my name, saying, I am Christ; and shall **seduce** many.

6 Yet you-shall-be-impending to-hear of **battles** and rumors of **battles**: see that you be not **uproar-wailing; because it-is-binding** all **be-becoming**, but the **finish** is not yet.

7 For nation shall rise against nation, and kingdom against kingdom: and there shall be famines, and **plagues**, and **quakes, down spots**.

8 All these the **original** of **pang**.[1451]

9 Then shall they **beside-give** you up to be **troubled** and shall kill you: and you shall be hated of all nations **through my name**.

10 And then shall many be **scandalized**,[1452] and shall betray one another, and shall hate **another-same**.

11 And many **false-prophets** shall rise,[1453] and shall **seduce** many.

12 And **through the lawlessness** shall **increase**, the love of many shall **cool**.

13 But he that shall **under-remain into finish**, the same shall be saved.[1454]

14 And this **well-message** of the kingdom shall be preached in **whole,** the **housed-land, into** a witness **to-all** nations; and then shall the **finish arrive**.

15 When you therefore **perceive** the abomination[1455] of desolation,[1456] spoken of **through** Daniel the prophet, stand in the holy place, (**whoever** reads, let him **have-thought**)

16 Then let them which be in Judaea flee into the mountains:

17 Let him which is on the housetop not come down to **lift** anything out of his house:

18 Neither let him which is in the field return back to take his **garments**.

19 And woe **to-them** that are with child, and **to-them** that give **suckle** in those days!

20 But pray you that your flight be not in the winter,[1457] neither **in** the Sabbath:

21 Because then shall be **great** tribulation, such as **no become** since the **origin**[1458] of the world **until now,** no, **not-yet no may-be-becoming.**

22 And except those days should be shortened, there should no flesh be saved: **yet through** the elect's sake those days shall be shortened.

23 Then if any man shall say **to-you, be-perceiving,** here Christ, or there; believe not.

24 For there shall **rise false-christs, and false-prophets,** and shall **give great signs** and

---

[1449] Or, priest-place, sacred place
[1450] Lit., from-let-go
[1451] Or, pang, sudden pain
[1452] Or, snared
[1453] Third person, plural
[1454] Or, safe
[1455] Stink
[1456] Or, to lay waste, lonesome
[1457] Derived for a word that means to pour, a storm as pouring rain
[1458] Or principality

wonders;[1459] **so too**, if **powerful**, they shall **also seduce** the elect.

25 Be-perceiving, I have **foretold**.

26 Therefore, if they shall say **to-you**, **be-perceiving**, he is in the **lonesome**; go not forth: **be-perceiving**, in the **storerooms**; believe not.

27 Because as the **star-light**[1460] comes out of the east, and shines **until** the west; so, shall-**be** also the **presence** of the Son of man.

28 For wherever the **corpse**[1461] is, there will the eagles be gathered together.

29 Soon after the tribulation of those days shall the sun be darkened, and the moon shall not give her light, and the stars shall fall from heaven, and the powers of the heavens shall be shaken.

30 And then shall **shine** the sign of the Son of man in **the** heaven: and then shall all the tribes of the earth mourn, and they shall see the Son of man coming **upon** the clouds of heaven with power and **much** glory.

31 And he shall send his angels with a **great** voice of a trumpet, and they shall gather together his elect from the four winds, from **extremities** of heaven **until extremities of-them**.

32 Now learn a parable of the fig tree; when his branch is yet tender, and **sprouting** leaves, you know that summer **near-squeeze**:

33 So likewise you, when you shall **perceive** all these things, know that it is **near-squeeze**, at the **doors**.

34 Amen, I say **to-you**, this generation shall not pass, **until** all these things **may-be-becoming**.

35 Heaven and earth shall pass away, **yet** my words shall not pass away.

36 Yet, about that day and hour **no-man has-perceived**, no, not the angels of heaven, but my Father only.

37 Yet, as the days of **Noe**, so **shall-be** also the **presence** of the Son of man.

38 Because, as in the days that were before the flood they were eating and drinking, marrying and **marry-izing**[1462] until the day that Noe entered into the **Ark**.

39 And knew not until the flood came, and **lift** them all away; so, shall-**be** also the **presence** of the Son of man.

40 Then shall two be in the field; the one shall be **being-beside-taken**, and the other **is-being-released**,[1463]

41 Two grinding at the mill; the **first** shall be **being-beside-get**, and the other **being-released.**

42 Awake-watch therefore: for you **perceive** not what hour your Lord **is-coming**.

43 But know this: that if the **house-owner** of the house had **perceived** in what watch the thief would come, he would have **awake-watched**, and would not have **let-be** his house to be **through-burrowed**.

44 Through this, be you also **internally-prepared**: for in such an hour as you **seem** not the Son of man **is-coming**.

45 Who then is a **believing** and wise **slave**, whom his lord has made **down-stands** over his **therapy-served** to give them **food** in due season?

46 Happy that **slave**, whom his lord when he comes shall find so **producing**.

47 Amen, I say **to-you**, that he shall make him **down-stand** over all his goods.

48 Yet, if that evil **slave** shall say in his **heart**, **is-delaying-uninterrupted-time**, my lord **to-be-coming;**

49 And shall begin to **thump the together-slaves**, and to eat and drink with the **being-drunk;**

50 The lord of that **slave** shall **arrive** in a day **which not-ne-is-towards-seeming**, and in an hour that he is not **knowing;**

51 And shall cut him asunder and **place** his **sect on** with the hypocrites: there shall be weeping and **grating** of teeth.

MATTHEW CHAPTER 25

1 Then shall the kingdom of **the heavens** be **assimilated to**-ten virgins, which **took** their lamps, and went forth **into from-meeting**[1464] the bridegroom.

[1459] Greek, "teras" transliterated as "terror;" the archaic definition is "monster" happenings
[1460] Astrape (star-fall), from the root aster (star)
[1461] Greek: "ptoma" (a ruin, a corpse, lifeless body, and alternate of "pipto" to fall)
[1462] Gamizontes is a compound word comprised of gamos (marry)+izein (ize)+ontes (to be), where "ize" means to make or conform to, to act
[1463] Or., from-let-go, forgiven
[1464] Greek: "apantesis," the official welcome of a newly arriving dignitary, by people going out to meet the dignitary and escorting the dignitary back to the origin of the ones who went to meet the dignitary; see also 1 Thessalonians 4:17, Matthew 25:1-6

2 And five of them were **prudently-disposed**,[1465] and five **stupid**.

3 Whoever morons took their lamps, and **took** no oil with them:

4 Yet, the **prudently-disposed took** oil in their vessels with their lamps.

5 While the bridegroom **delayed-uninterrupted-time**, they all **nodded** and slept.

6 Then at-middle of-night a cry **became, be-perceiving**, the bridegroom comes; go you out **into from-meeting** him.

7 Then all those virgins arose, and **cosmetics** their lamps.

8 And the **morons** said **to** the **prudently-disposed,** give us **out-of** your oil; for our lamps **extinguished**.

9 Yet, the **prudently-disposed** answered, saying, **not-ever no** there be not **contentment** for us and you; but go you rather **to-them** that sell, and **buy**[1466] for yourselves.

10 And while they went to buy, the bridegroom came; and they that were ready went in with him to the marriage: and the **door** was **locked**.

11 Afterward also came the **remaining** virgins, saying, Lord, Lord, open to us.

12 But he answered and said, **amen** I say **to-you,** I **perceived** you not.

13 Awake-watch therefore, for you know neither the day nor the hour **in which** the Son of man **is-coming.**

14 For as a man travelling into a far country, called his own **slave**s, and **beside-give to-them** his goods.

15 And **to-one** he gave five talents, **to-one** two, **then** one; **to-everyone down** his **private power**; and **from-people, soon.**

16 Then he that had **took** the five talents went and **worked in them** and **produced other-same** five talents.

17 And likewise **the-one, the** two, he also gained **other-same** two.

18 But he that had **took** one went and **burrowed** in the earth and hid his lord's **silver.**

19 After a **much uninterrupted-time** the lord of those **slave**s comes, and **together-lifts saying** with them.

20 And so he that had **took** five talents came and brought other five talents, saying, Lord, you **gave to-me** five talents: **be-perceiving**, I have gained beside them five talents more.

21 His lord **showed to-him, good,** you **beautiful** and **believing slave**: you have been **believing** over a few things, I will make you **down-stand** many things: enter you into the **cheerfulness** of your **Lord.**

22 He also that **took** two talents came and said, Lord, you **gave to-me** two talents: **be-perceiving** I have gained two other talents beside them.

23 His lord **showed to-him, good,** you **beautiful** and **believing slave**; you have been **believing** over a few things, I will make you **down-stand** many things: enter you into the **cheerfulness** of your **Lord.**

24 Then he which **took** the one talent came and said, Lord, I knew you that you are a hard man, reaping where you have not sown, and gathering where you have not **scattered**:

25 And I was afraid and went and hid your talent in the earth; **be-perceiving you-are-having** yours.

26 His lord answered and said **to-him,** you **wicked-hurtful** and **slow-hesitating slave**, you **perceived** that I reap where I sowed not, and gather where I have not **scattered.**

27 It-was-binding then, you **to-be-throwing** my money to the **bankers,**[1467] and at my coming I should have **provided** mine with **seed-birth-interest.**

28 Lift then, the talent from him, and give to-him which has ten talents.

29 Because, to everyone that has shall be given, and he shall have **excess**: but from him that has not shall be **lifted** even that which he has.

30 And cast you the unprofitable **slave** into **outer** darkness: there shall be weeping and **grating** of teeth.

31 When the Son of man shall come in his glory, and all the holy angels with him, then shall he sit upon the throne of his glory:

32 And before him shall be gathered all nations: and he shall **from-define**[1468] them one from another, as a shepherd **from-defined** sheep from the goats:

33 And he shall **stand** the sheep **out-of** his right hand, but the goats **out-of** the left.

[1465] Or, prudent
[1466] Lit., to go to the market, redeem
[1467] Greek" "trapezites," table, money-broker, banker
[1468] Lit., from-horizon

34 Then shall the King **show to-them out-of** his right hand, **come-here**, you blessed of my Father, inherit the kingdom **internally-prepared** for you from the **down-throw** of the world:

35 For I was a hungry, and you gave me meat: I was thirsty, and you gave me drink: I was a **foreign-lodger**, and you **together-led** me:

36 Naked, and you clothed me: I was sick, and you **bishop**[1469] me: I was in prison, and you came **towards** me.

37 Then shall the righteous answer him, saying, Lord, when **perceived** we you hungering, and **nourished** you? Or thirsty, and gave you drink?

38 When **perceived** we you a **foreign-lodger**, and **together-led** you? Or naked, and clothed you?

39 Or when **perceived** we you **weak**, or in prison, and came **to-you**?

40 And the King shall answer and say **to** them, **amen**, I say **to-you**, inasmuch as you have **produced to-one of** these, the least[1470], **of-my** brothers, **you-have-produce -it to-me.**

41 Then shall he say also **to-them out-of** the left hand, **travel**[1471] from me, **those down-prayed**, into **the eternal** fire, **internally-prepared to-the** Devil and **to-the angels of-him**:

42 For I was hungry, and you gave me no meat: I was thirsty, and you gave me no drink:

43 I was a **foreign-lodger**, and you **together-led** me not: naked, and you clothed me not: **without-strength** and in prison, and you **bishop** me not.

44 Then shall they also answer him, saying, Lord, when saw we you hungry, or athirst, or a **foreign-lodger**, or naked, or **without-strength**, or in prison, and did not **attend to-you**?

45 Then shall he answer them, saying, **amen** I say **to-you**, **as-much-**as you **produce** not to one of the least[1472] of these, you **produce** not to me.

46 And these **from-come**[1473] into **eternal** punishment: but the righteous into **eternal** life.

[1469] Greek compound: upon-peer about, upon-skeptic, upon-scout, upon watch, upon-watch, upon-sentry
[1470] Or, inferior
[1471] Present tense, passive/middle voice
[1472] Or, inferior
[1473] Future tense, middle voice
[1474] Lit., beside-given

MATTHEW CHAPTER 26

1 And **it became**, when Jesus had finished all these sayings, he said to his disciples,

2 You perceived that after two days is the Passover, and the Son of man is betrayed[1474] **into the to-be-crucified**.

3 Then assembled together the **first-rank-priests**, and the scribes, and the elders of the people, to the **yard**[1475] of the **first-rank-priest**, who **is-said** Caiaphas,

4 And consulted that they **govern** Jesus by **trick-bait**,[1476] and kill.

5 But they said, not on the **festival, that no** uproar[1477] **become in** the people.

6 Now when Jesus was in Bethany, in the house of Simon the leper,

7 There came **to-him** a woman having an alabaster[1478] of **heavy-value**, myrrh,[1479] and poured it on his head, as he **reclined**.

8 But when his disciples **perceived**, they had **much-grief-ached**[1480] saying, **into what** this **from-ruin**?

9 Because, this **myrrh was-powerful to-be-**sold for much and given to the poor.

10 Yet Jesus **knowing**, he said **to** them, why **cut-toil** you the woman? **Because** she-**worked an ideal** work **into** me.

11 Because you have the poor always with you; **yet** me you have not always.

12 Because in that she has **thrown** this **myrrh** on my body, she did for my burial.

13 Amen, I say **to-you**, wherever this **well-message** shall be preached in the whole world, shall also this that this woman has **produced**, be told for a memorial of her.

14 Then one of the twelve, called Judas Iscariot, went **to** the **first-rank-priests**,

---

[1475] Yard as open to the wind, the root is the Greek word for "air"
[1476] Greek: dolos
[1477] Or disturbance
[1478] Alabaster is the name of a stone; therefore, a stone vase
[1479] Myrrh is defined as "bitter" tasting
[1480] Or, resentful

15 And said, what will you give me, and I will **betray** him to-you? And they **stand to**-him for thirty pieces of silver.

16 And from **then,** he sought **good-season** to betray him.

17 Now **to-the foremost of-the Unfermented,** the disciples came to Jesus, saying to-him, where will you that we **internally-prepare** for you to eat the **Passover**?

18 And he said, go into the city **towards the so-and-so,** and say **to-him, the teacher** says, **my season is-near-squeezing;** I will **produce** the **Passover** at your house with my disciples.

19 And the disciples **produced** as Jesus had **under-arrange** them; and they **internally-prepared** the **Passover**.

20 Yet, when the evening **became,** he **reclined**[1481] with the twelve.

21 And as they did eat, he said, **amen** I say **to-you,** that one **out-of** you shall betray me.

22 And they were **tremendously distressed-sad,** and began every one of them to say **to-him,** Lord, is it I?

23 Yet, he answered and said, he that **in-baptize**[1482] **with me in the dish, the hand,** the same shall betray me.

24 The Son of man goes as it is written of him: **yet** woe **to** that man by whom the Son of man is betrayed![1483] It had been **ideal** for that man if he had not been born.

25 Then Judas, which betrayed him, answered, and said, **Rabbi,** is it I? He said **to-him,** you have said.

26 And as they were eating, Jesus **taking** bread, and blessed, and **broke,** and gave to the disciples, and said, **take,** eat; this is my body.

27 And he **taking** the cup, and **good-graced,** and gave to them, saying, drink you all of it.

28 For this is my blood of the **New Covenant,** which is **out-poured** for many for the **release**[1484] of sins.

29 But I say **to-you,** I will not drink **presently** of this **offspring** of the vine, until that day when I drink it **new-fresh** with you in my Father's kingdom.

30 And when they **sang-an-hymn,** they went out into the **mountain** of Olives.

31 Then says Jesus **to**-them, all you shall be **scandalized**[1485] in me this night: **because** it is written, I will smite the shepherd, and the sheep of the **sheep-herd** shall be **through-scattered.**

32 But after I am risen again, I will go before you into Galilee.

33 Peter answered and said **to-him,** though all shall be **scandalized in** you, I will never be **scandalized.**

34 Jesus said **to-him, amen** I say **to-you,** that this night, before the **rooster** crow, you shall **contradict** me three.

35 Peter said **to-him, may-be-binding** I should die with you, yet will I not **contradict** you. Likewise, also said all the disciples.

36 Then comes Jesus with them to a **space** called Gethsemane,[1486] and says **to** the disciples, **be-seated,** while I **from-go** and pray.

37 And he **took** with him Peter and the two sons of Zebedee and began to be **distress-sad** and very heavy.

38 Then **he says to**-them, my soul is exceeding **distress-sad,** even **until** death: **remain** here, and **wake-watch** with me.

39 And he went a little further, and fell on his face, and prayed, saying, my Father, if **it-is powerful,** let this cup pass from me; **more,** not as I will, but as you.

40 And he comes **towards** the disciples, and finds them asleep, and says to Peter, **in-this-way not are-you-forceful to-wake** with me **first** hour?

41 Wake-watch and pray, that you enter not into **probe-testing**: the spirit indeed **before-feels,** but the flesh is **without-strength.**

42 He went away **out-of** the **second,** and prayed, saying, my Father, if this cup **not is-powerful to-**pass away from me, except I drink it, your will **become.**

43 And he came and found them asleep again: for their eyes were **weighty**

44 And he **released**[1487] them, and went away again, and prayed **out-of** the **third,** saying the same words.

[1481] Or up-cline
[1482] Lit., in-whelm (to cover wholly with fluid)
[1483] Lit., beside-given
[1484] Lit., from-let-go, forgive

[1485] Or, snared
[1486] Lit., oil-press
[1487] Or, to from-let-go, forgive

45 Then comes he to his disciples, and says **to** them, **remain sleeping,** and **be-resting**: **be-perceiving,** the hour **near-squeeze,** and the Son of man is betrayed[1488] into the hands of sinners.

46 Rise, let us be going: **be-perceiving,** he is **near-squeeze** that does betray me.

47 And while he-**was-speaking, be-perceiving,** Judas, one **of-the** twelve, came, and with him **much** multitude with swords and **trees** from the **first-rank-priests** and elders of the people.

48 Now he that betrayed him gave them a sign, saying, whomever I shall kiss,[1489] **he it-is**; **govern him!**

49 And **soon,** he came to Jesus, and said, **be-cheerful, Rabbi**; and kissed [1490]him.

50 And Jesus said **to-him, kinsman, upon which** are you **present**? Then came they, and laid hands on Jesus, and **governed** him.

51 And, **be-perceiving,** one of them which were with Jesus **out-**stretched **the** hand, and drew his sword,[1491] and struck a **slave** of the **first-rank** priest's, and **off-lift** his ear[1492].

52 Then said Jesus **to-him, away-turn** your sword into his **spot**: for all they that **take** the sword shall **from-ruin in** the sword.

53 Or you-seem that I **not is-powerful** now **to-beside-call** to my Father, and he shall presently **beside-stand** me more than twelve legions of angels?

54 Then how then shall the **Scriptures** be **filled,** that **in-this-way it-is-binding to-become**?

55 In that hour said Jesus to the multitudes, are you come out as **upon** a **robber**[1493] with swords and **trees** to **take** me? I sat daily with you teaching in the **priest-place,** and **not you-governed** me.

56 Yet whole this became, that the **Scriptures** of the prophets might be **filled.** Then all the disciples **released** him and fled.

57 Yet, they that **governed** Jesus **from-led-him** to Caiaphas the **first-rank-**priest, where the scribes and the elders were **together-lead.**

58 Yet, Peter followed him afar off to the **first-rank-**priest's **court-yard,** and went in, and sat with the **subservient-ones**[1494], to-**perceive the finish.**

59 Now the **first-rank-priests,** and elders, and all the **Sanhedrin,** sought **false-witness** against Jesus, to put him to death;

60 But found none: **yes,** though many **false-witnesses** came, found they none. **Yet,** came two **false-witnesses,**

61 And said, this **showed, I-am-powerful** to **down-loose** the temple of God, and to **house-build** it **through** three days.

62 And the **first-rank-priest** arose, and said **to-him,** answer you nothing? What these **are-down-witnessing** you?

63 Yet Jesus **was-silent.** And the **first-rank-priest** answered and said **to-him,** I **out-of-oath** you by the living God, that you tell us whether you be the Christ, the Son of God.

64 Jesus says **to-him,** you have said: **more,** I say **to-you, from present,** you shall see the Son of man sitting **out-of** the right hand of power and coming **on** the clouds **of-the heavens.**

65 Then the **first-rank-priest tear** his **garments,** saying, he **blasphemes**; what further need have we of witnesses? **Be-perceiving,** now you have heard his blasphemy.

66 What **seems to-you**? They answered and said, He is **liable**[1495] of death.

67 Then did they spit **into** his face, and **curtail-with-the-fist** him; **yet** those slapped-him,

68 Saying, prophesy **to-us,** you Christ, who is he that **hit** you?

69 Now Peter sat **outside in the yard**:[1496] and **first girl** came **to-him,** saying, you also **were** with Jesus of Galilee.

70 Yet, he **contradicted** before all, saying, I **perceive** not what you say.

71 And when he was gone out into the **gate, another-same perceived** him, and said **to-them** that were there, **this-one** was also with Jesus of Nazareth.

[1488] Lit., beside-given
[1489] Or, be-friendly
[1490] Down-friend
[1491] Greek: "machariar" sounds like machete
[1492] "Ear" is diminutive in the Greek "little-ear," or an "earlet"
[1493] Root, plunder
[1494] Lit., under-oarsman, generally a subordinate
[1495] Greek: in-hold, to hold in
[1496] A yard as open to the wind, the Greek root is "air"

72 And again he **contradicted** with an oath, I do not **perceive** the man.

73 Yet, after a while came **to-him** they **having-stood**, and said to Peter, **truly** you also are of-them; for your speech **clearly** is **producing you**.

74 Then began he to **down-ban**[1497]. and to swear, I-**perceive** not the man. And **soon** the **roster** voiced.

75 And Peter remembered the **declarations** of Jesus, which said **to-him**, before the **rooster** crow, you shall **from-contradict** me **three**. And he went out and wept[1498] bitterly.[1499]

MATTHEW CHAPTER 27

1 When the morning **becoming, together-planned-counseled, took** all the **first-rank-priests** and elders of the people, **down of-the** Jesus to put him to death:

2 And when they had bound him, they led him away, and **betrayed**[1500] him to Pontius Pilate[1501] the **leader**.

3 Then Judas, which had betrayed him, when he **perceived** that he was **down-judged, after-cared,** and **from-turn** the thirty pieces of silver to the **first-rank-priests** and elders,

4 Saying, I have sinned in that I have betrayed the **innocent**[1502] blood. And they said, what to us? **See you.**

5 And he **flings** the pieces of silver in the temple, and **up-spaced**, and went and **from-choke**-himself.

6 Yet, the **first-rank-priests taking** the silver, and said, it is not lawful for to put them into the **corban**,[1503] because it is the **value** of blood.

7 Yet, they **together-plan-counsel,** and **they-bought**[1504] **out-of** them the potter's field, to bury **foreign-lodgers** in.

8 Through which the field was called, the field of blood, **until** this day.

9 Then was **filled** that which was spoken by **Jeremiah,** the prophet, saying, and they **took** the thirty pieces of silver, the price of him that was valued, whom they of the **sons** of Israel did value;

10 And gave them for the potter's field, as the Lord **under-arranged** me.

11 And Jesus stood before the **leader;** and the **leader** asked him, saying, are you the King of the Jews? And Jesus **showed to-him**, you say.

12 And when he was accused of the **first-rank-priests** and elders, he answered nothing.

13 Then said Pilate **to-him**, hear you not how many things they **down-witness** you?

14 And **not** he answered him **not one declaration;** insomuch that the **leader** marveled, **very**.[1505]

15 Now **according of-festival, it-was-ethics**,[1506] the **leader** to **from-loose to** the people a prisoner, whom they willed.

16 And they had then, **upon-sign, a-prisoner,** called Barabbas.[1507]

17 Then, when they were **gathered-together,** Pilate said **to** them, whom will you that I **from-loose to-you**? Barabbas, or Jesus, which is-**being-said,** Christ?

18 Because, he **perceived** that for **ill-will** they had **betrayed** him.

19 When he was **seated** on the **judgment-step**,[1508] his wife sent **to-him**, saying, you have nothing to do with that **just-man**: for I have **emotion** many things this day in a **trance through** him.

20 But the **first-rank-priests** and elders persuaded the multitude that they should ask Barabbas, and **from-ruin** Jesus.

21 The **leader** answered and said **to** them, **which** of the **two** will you that I **from-loose to-you**? They said, Barabbas.

22 Pilate says **to** them, what shall I **produce** then with Jesus, which **is-being-said,** Christ? All say **to-him**, let him be crucified.

23 And the **leader showed**,[1509] why, what evil has he **produced**? But they cried out the more, saying, let him be crucified.

24 When Pilate **perceived** that he could **gain** nothing, but rather an **uproar**[1510] **is-becoming,** he took water,

---

[1497] Greek: "kataanathematizo," down-anathema (lit., down-up-place)
[1498] Or, sobbed
[1499] Lit., acridity (strong, irritating, unpleasant, pungent (sharp), taste or smell), poison
[1500] Lit., beside-given
[1501] Pilate means: close-presses, firm
[1502] Greek: un-placed (penalty), not-guilty
[1503] Transliterated Hebrew word meaning, something bought near to the altar, to approach
[1504] Lit., to go to the market, redeem
[1505] Or, immensely
[1506] Custom
[1507] Barabbas: Bar (son, heir) and Abba (father)
[1508] Greek: "Bema," a step, foot-breadth, rostrum, tribunal
[1509] Greek: "phemi," the root word for fame ("pheme")
[1510] Or disturbance

and washed **the** hands before the multitude, saying, I am innocent[1511] of the blood of this **just-man:** see you.

25 Then answered all the people, and said, His blood on us, and on our children.

26 Then **from-loosed** he Barabbas **to** them: and when he **whipped** Jesus, he **betrayed-him** to be crucified.

27 Then the soldiers of the **leader beside-getting** Jesus into the **Praetorium,**[1512] and gathered **to-him** the whole **mass-of-men.**[1513]

28 And they stripped him and put on him a scarlet robe.

29 And when they had platted a **victor's-crown** of thorns, they put upon his head, and a **reed** in his right hand: and they **knee-fall** before him, and **in-childish-mocked** him, saying, **be-cheerful,** King of the Jews!

30 And they spit upon him, and **took** the **reed,** and **thumped** him on the head.

31 And after that they had **in-childish-mocked** him, **they-unclothed** the robe from him, and **clothed him** the **garments** of-him, and led him away **to-crucify.**

32 And as they came out, they found a man of Cyrene,[1514] Simon by name: him they **courier-compelled** to **lift** his cross.

33 And when they were come **to** a **spot** called Golgotha, which is to say, a **spot** of a skull,

34 They gave him vinegar to drink **mixed** with gall: and when he had tasted, he **willed not-to-drink.**

35 And they crucified him, and parted his garments, casting **inheritance:** that it might be **filled** which was spoken by the prophet, they parted my garments among them, and upon my vesture did they cast **inheritance.**

36 And sitting down they **guard** him there;

37 And set up over his head his accusation written, this is **Jesus, the King of the Jews.**

38 Then were there two **robbers**[1515] crucified with him, one **out-of** the right hand, and another **out-of** the left.

39 And they that passed by **blasphemed** him, wagging their heads,

40 And saying, you that **down-loose** the temple, and **house-build** in three days, save yourself. If you be the Son of God, **down-step** from the cross.

41 Likewise also the **first-rank-priests in-childish-mocked,** with the scribes and elders, said,

42 He saved others; himself **not he-is-powerful to-save.** If he be the King of Israel, let him now **down-step** from the cross, and we will believe him.

43 He trusted in God; let him **rush-rescue** him now, if he will have him: **because** he said, I am the Son of God.

44 The **robbers**[1516] also, which were crucified with him, **defamed**[1517] him.

45 Now from the sixth hour there was darkness over all the land **until** the ninth hour.

46 And about the ninth hour Jesus cried with a loud voice, saying, Eli, Eli, lama sabachthani? that is to say, My God, my God, why has you forsaken[1518] me?

47 Some of them that stood there, when they heard, said, This voice for Elijah.

48 And **soon** one of them ran, and **taking** a sponge, and filled with vinegar, and put on a **reed,** and gave him to drink.

49 The **remaining-ones** said, **release,** let us **be-perceiving** if Elijah **is-coming** to save him.

50 Jesus, when he had cried again with**-a-sound, released the spirit**.

51 And, **be-perceiving**, the veil of the temple was **split into two** from the top to the bottom; and the earth did quake, and the rocks **split**;

52 And the **remembrance-tomb** were opened; and many bodies of the saints which slept arose,

53 And came out of the **remembrance-tomb** after his resurrection, and went into the **Holy City,** and **emphasize**[1519] **to** many.

54 Yet, the centurion, and they that were with him, **guarding** Jesus, **perceived** the **quaking,** and **the becoming,** they feared **tremendously,** saying, truly this was the Son of God.

[1511] Greek: un-placed, not guilty
[1512] Or governor's courtroom
[1513] Greek: "speira, transliterated "spire" meaning to coil, figuratively a mass of roman military cohort, or a squad of Levitical janitors
[1514] Cyrene is a region of Africa
[1515] Root: to plunder
[1516] Root: to plunder
[1517] Lit., notorious, name
[1518] Or in-down-leave
[1519] Greek: "emphanizo" also transliterated as "emphasize"

55 Yet, many women were there **theatre-spectating** afar off, which followed Jesus from Galilee, **attending to-him.**

56 In whom was Mary Magdalene, and Mary the mother of James and Joses, and the mother of Zebedee's children.

57 When the **evening becoming**, there came a rich man of **Arimathea,** named Joseph, who also himself was Jesus' disciple:

58 He went to Pilate and **requested** the body of Jesus. Then Pilate **ordered** the body to be **from-given.**

59 And when Joseph **took** the body, he wrapped it in a clean linen cloth,

60 And laid it in his own new **remembrance-tomb**, which he had **quarried** out in the rock: and he rolled a **great** stone to the **door** of the **remembrance-tomb** and departed.

61 And there was Mary Magdalene, and the other Mary, sitting over against the **tomb.**

62 Now the **upon-tomorrow**, which followed the **Preparation,** the **first-rank-priests** and Pharisees came together **towards** Pilate,

63 Saying, **Lord,** we remember that **that-one seducer** said, while he was yet alive, after three days I will rise again.

64 Order then that the **tomb** be **secured** until the third day, **not-ever** his disciples come by night, and steal him away, and say **to-the** people, he is risen from the dead: so, the last **seduction** shall be worse than the **foremost.**

65 Pilate **showed to-them,** you have **custody,** go your way, **secure** as you **perceived.**

66 So they went, and **secure**d the **tomb,** sealing the stone, and setting **the custodians**

MATTHEW CHAPTER 28

1 Yet, evening of-Sabbaths, to-the upon-lighting into the first of-Sabbaths, came Mary Magdalene and the other Mary to see the **tomb.**

2 And, **be-perceiving,** there was a **great quake:** for the angel of the Lord descended from heaven and came and rolled back the stone from the door and sat upon it.

3 Yet, his **perception** was like **star-light,**[1520] and his **garment** white as snow:

4 Yet for fear of him the keepers **quaked** and became **as-if** dead.

5 Yet the angel answered and said **to** the women, fear not ye: for I **perceive** that you seek Jesus, which was crucified.

6 He is not here: **because** he is risen, as he said. come, see the **spot** where the Lord **laid.**

7 And go quickly and tell his disciples that he is risen from the dead; and, **be-perceiving,** he goes before you into Galilee; there shall you see him: **be-perceiving,** I have told you.

8 And they departed quickly from the **remembrance-tomb** with fear and **great cheerfulness** and **race** to bring his disciples **from-message.**

9 Yet, as they went to **from-message** his disciples, **be-perceiving,** Jesus met them, saying, **cheer** And they came and **governed** him, the feet, and worshipped him.

10 Then said Jesus **to** them, be not afraid: go **from-message** my **brothers** that they go into Galilee, and there shall they see me.

11 Yet, when they were going, **be-perceiving,** some of the **custodian** came into the city, and **from-message to** the **first-rank-priests** all the **becoming.**[1521]

12 And when they were assembled with the elders, and **together-planned-counsel,** took money sufficient[1522] they gave **to** the soldiers;

13 Saying, say you, His disciples came by night, and stole him while we slept.

14 And if this come to the **leader's** ears, we will persuade him, and **produce** you **un-worry.**

15 So they **took** the money and **produce** as they were taught: and this saying is **through-fame besides** the Jews until this day.

16 Then the eleven disciples went away into Galilee, into a mountain where Jesus had **arranged to-**them.

17 And when they **perceived** him, they worshipped him: **yet** some **two-stand.**

18 And Jesus came and spoke **to** them, saying, all **authority** is given **to-me** in heaven and **on** earth.

[1520] Astrape (star-fall) from the root aster (star)
[1521] Plural
[1522] Lit., to arrive; or, competent as if coming in season, ample in amount, fit in character

19 Go you therefore, and teach all nations, baptizing them **into** the name of the Father, and of the Son, and of the Holy Spirit:

20 Teaching them to **guard** all things whatever I have commanded you: and, **be-perceiving**, I am with you always, **until of-the together-finish of-the ages**. Amen.

THE GOSPEL OF MARK

MARK CHAPTER 1

1 The **original** of the **well-message** of Jesus Christ, the Son of God.

2 As it is written in the prophets, **be-perceiving**, I send my **angel** before your face, which shall **construct** your way before you.

3 The voice of one crying in the **lonesome**, you **internally-prepare** the way of the Lord, **produce** his paths **soon**.

4 John did baptize in the **lonesome** and preach the baptism of **change-thinking** for the **release**[1523] of sins.

5 And there **out-passage towards him** all the land of Judaea, and they of Jerusalem, and were all baptized of him in the river of Jordan, **out-same-saying** their sins.

6 And John was clothed[1524] with camel's hair, and with a **belt** of a skin about his loins; and he did eat locusts and wild honey;

7 And preached, saying, there comes one-**forceful** of-me, after me, the **strap** of whose **sandal** I am not **sufficient**[1525] to **bend** and unloose.

8 I indeed have baptized you **in** water: but he shall baptize you **in** the Holy Spirit.

9 And it **became** in those days that Jesus came from Nazareth of Galilee and was baptized of John **into** Jordan.

10 And **soon** up-**walking from** the water, he-**perceived** the heavens **split**, and the Spirit **as-if** dove **down-walking** upon him:

11 And there came a voice from heaven, you are my beloved Son, in whom I am **good-seem**.

12 And **soon** the Spirit **ejecting** him into the **lonesome**.

13 And he was there in the **lonesome** forty days, **probe-tested under** Satan; and was with the **wild-beasts**; and the angels **attended to-him**.

14 Yet after that John was put in prison, Jesus came into Galilee, **evangelizing** of the kingdom of God,

15 And saying, the **season** is **filled,** and the kingdom of God **has-near-squeezed**: **change-thinking** and believe the **well-message**.

16 Now as he walked **beside** the Sea of Galilee, he-**perceived** Simon, and Andrew his brother casting a net into the sea: **because** they were fishers.

17 And Jesus said **to** them, **here behind** me, and I will **produce** you to become fishers of men.

18 And **soon** they **release** their nets and followed him.

19 And when he had gone **there, a-few,** he-**perceived** James the of Zebedee, and John his brother, who also were in the ship **down-fresh** their nets.

20 And **soon** he called them: and they **released** their father Zebedee in the ship with the **hired** and went **behind** him.

21 And they went into Capernaum; and **soon to-the** Sabbath he entered into the synagogue and taught.

22 And they were **out-of-pounded** at his **teaching**: for he taught them as one that had authority, and not as the scribes.

23 And there was in their synagogue a man **in** an unclean spirit; and he cried out,

24 Saying, **let it be;** what have we to do with you, you Jesus of Nazareth? **Are** you come to **from-loose** us? **I-perceived** you who you are, the **Holy-One** of God.

25 And Jesus **rebuke**[1526] him, saying, **be-muzzled**, and come out of him.

26 And when the unclean spirit had **grasp-spasm** him, and cried with a **great** voice, he came out of him.

27 And they were all **stupefied,**[1527] insomuch that they questioned **towards** themselves, saying, what thing is this? What new **teaching** this? **That according-to** authority he **under-arrange** even the unclean spirits, and they do **under-hear**[1528] him.

28 Yet soon his **hearing** spread **universally into whole about-space of-the** Galilee.

29 And **soon**, when they were come out of the synagogue, they entered into the house of Simon and Andrew, with James and John.

30 Yet, Simon's wife's mother lay sick of a fever, and **soon** they tell him of her.

[1523] Lit., from-let-go
[1524] Lit., in-down; or, in-sink, in-down-slipping
[1525] Lit., to arrive; or, competent as if coming in season, ample in amount, fit in character

[1526] Or, to tax upon
[1527] Stupefy is defined as: un able to think or feel properly
[1528] Or obey

31 And he came and **governed** her by the hand and lifted her up; and **soon** the fever **released** her, and she **attended to-them.**

32 Yet becoming of-evening, when the sun did set, they brought **to-him** all that **evil holders**, and **those demonized**

33 And all the city was gathered together at the **door.**

34 And he **therapy-served** many that were **evil holders to-various nauseas** and cast out many **demons**; and **released** not the **demons** to speak, because they **perceived** him.

35 And in the morning, **in-night, very-much, up-standing**, he went out, and departed into a **lonesome** place, and there prayed.

36 And Simon and they that were with him followed after him.

37 And when they had found him, they said **to-him**, all seek for you.

38 And he said **to** them, let us go into the next towns that I may preach there also: **because into this I-out-came.**

39 And he preached in their synagogues **into whole** Galilee and cast out **demons.**

40 And there came a leper **to-him**, beseeching him, and **knee-falling to-him**, and saying **to-him**, if you will, **you-are-powerful to-**make me clean.

41 And Jesus, **being-gut-compassionate, out-stretched the** hand, and **fastened-to-him**, and says **to-him**, I will; **be-clean!**

42 And as soon as he had spoken, **soon** the leprosy departed from him, and he was cleaned.

43 And he **soon in-snorts-with-anger to-him**, and **soon he-cast-out him**;

44 And says **to-him**, see you say nothing to any man: but go your way, show yourself to the priest, and offer for your cleansing those things which Moses **towards-arrange, into** a **witness to** them.

45 But he went out, and began to publish much, and to-**through-fame** the **saying**, insomuch that Jesus **not-still is-powerful to-enter plainly**[1529] into the city but was **outside** in **lonesome spots**: and they came **toward** him **all-places.**

[1529] Lit, appear
[1530] Exact knowledge

MARK CHAPTER 2

1 And again he entered into Capernaum after days; and it was **heard** that he was **into** the house.

2 And **soon** many were gathered together, **so-that** that there was no **space** to receive, no, not so much as about the **door**: and he **talked** the **Word to** them.

3 And they come **to-him**, bringing one sick of the **paralytic**, which was **lifted under** four.

4 And when they **not is-powerful towards-near-squeeze to-him** for the **multitude, they-un-roof** where he was: and when they had **out-dug**, they **lower** the **mattress on which** the sick of the **paralytic laid.**

5 When Jesus **perceived** their faith, he said **to** the sick of the **paralytic, child** your sins **are-released of-you.**

6 Yet, there were certain of the scribes sitting there, and **through-inventory** in their **hearts,**

7 Why does **this-one in-this-way** speak blasphemies? Who **is-powerful to-release** sins but God only?

8 And **soon** when Jesus **on-knowing**[1530] in his spirit that they so **through-inventoried** within themselves, he said **to** them, why **through-inventoried** you these things in your **hearts**?

9 What is it easier to say to the **paralytic**, your sins **are-released of-you**; or to say, arise, and take up your **mattress**, and walk?

10 But that you may know that the Son of man has **authority** on earth to **release** sins, (he says to the **paralytic,**)

11 I say **to-you**, arise, and take up your **mattress**, and go your way **into your** house.

12 And **soon** he arose, **lift** the bed, and went forth before them all; **so-that** they were all **ecstasized,**[1531] and glorified God, saying, we never **perceived in-this-way.**

13 And he went forth again **beside** the sea; and all the multitude **came towards him**, and he taught them.

14 And as he passed by, he saw Levi **of-the** Alphaeus sitting at the **tax-office** and said **to-him**, follow me. And he **up-stand** and followed him.

15 And it **became**, that, as Jesus **reclined** in his house, many **tax-collectors** and sinners sat also together with

---
[1531] Greek compound existemi (out-of-stand) from which we take our English ecstasy (overwhelming feelings)

Jesus and his disciples: **because** there were many, and they followed him.

16 And when the scribes and Pharisees saw him eat with **tax-collectors** and sinners, they said **to-his** disciples, how is it that he eats and drinks with **tax-collectors** and sinners?

17 When Jesus heard, he says **to-them,** they that are **forceful** have no need of the physician, but they that are **evil holders**: I came not to call the righteous, but sinners to **change-thought**

18 And the disciples of John and of the Pharisees used to fast: and they come and say **to-him**, why do the disciples of John and of the Pharisees fast, but your disciples fast not?

19 And Jesus said **to** them, **is-powerful** the **sons** of the **bride-chamber**, while the bridegroom is with them **to fast**? As long as they have the bridegroom with them, **not they-are-powerful to-fast.**

20 But the days will come, when the bridegroom shall be taken away from them, and then shall they fast in those days.

21 No man also sews a **patch** of **unshrunk** cloth on an old garment: else the **new-fresh patch is-lifting the filling of-the** the old; and the **split**[1532] becomes worse.

22 Yet, no man puts **new-young** wine into old bottles: else the **new-young** wine does **burst** the **leather,** and the wine is spilled, and the bottles will be **from-ruined**: but **new-young** wine is-**cast** into **new-fresh** bottles.

23 And it **became,** that he went through the corn fields on the Sabbath; and his disciples began, to **produce plucking** the **stalk-stand** of corn.

24 And the Pharisees said **to-him, be-perceiving,** why **produce** they on the Sabbath that which is not lawful?

25 And he said **to** them, have you never read what David **produced,** when he had need, and was hungry, he, and they that were with him?

26 How he went into the **House of God** in the days of Abiathar the **first-rank-priest,** and did eat the **breads of-the purpose**[1533] which is not lawful to eat but for the priests, and gave also **to-them** which were with him?

27 And he said **to** them, the Sabbath was made **through** man, and not man **through** the Sabbath:

28 Therefore the Son of man is Lord also of the Sabbath.

MARK CHAPTER 3

1 And he entered again into the synagogue; and there was a man there which had a withered hand.

2 And they watched him, whether he would **therapy-served** him on the Sabbath; that they might accuse him.

3 And he says **to** the man which had the withered hand, **rise into the middle**.

4 And he says **to** them, is it lawful to **good-do** on the Sabbaths, or to **evil-do;** to save life, or to kill? **Yet,** they **were-silent**.

5 And when he **about**-looked on them with **swelling-anger**, being **together-sad** for the hardness of their **hearts**, he says **to-the** man, **out-stretch** your hand. And he **out-stretched**: and his hand was restored **healthy-grown** as the other.

6 And the Pharisees went forth, and **soon together-planned-counsel** with the Herodians **downing** him, how they might **from-ruin**[1534] him.

7 But Jesus **up-space** himself with his disciples to the sea: and **much** multitude from Galilee followed him, and from Judaea,

8 And from Jerusalem, [1535] and from Idumaea,[1536] and **other-side of-the** Jordan; and they **about** Tyre and Sidon, a **many** multitude, when they had heard **how-much** things he **produced,** came **to-him**.

9 And he spoke to his disciples that a small-ship **towards-govern to-him** because of the multitude, lest they should **tribulation**[1537] him.

10 For he had **therapy-served** many; insomuch that they **fell** upon him to **fasten-upon** him, **as-many-as** had **plagues-whipped.**

11 And unclean spirits, when they saw him, **toward-fell to**-him, and cried, saying, you are the Son of God.

12 And he **soon rebukes**[1538] them that they should not **produce** him **shine**.

[1532] Schism
[1533] Lit., before-place, to place before, or to place in advance
[1534] Greek: "apo" (from) and "alethros" (ruin), to destroy fully
[1535] Greek: Priests-peace (hierou-priest, sacred) and salem (peace)
[1536] Greek for Edom
[1537] Root: to crowd, a rut, worn track
[1538] Or tax upon

13 And **he-is-up-walking** into a mountain, and calls whom he **willed**: and they came **to-him**.

14 And he **produced** twelve, that they should be with him, and that he might send them forth to preach,

15 And to have **authority** to **therapy-served nausea**, and to cast out **demons**.

16 And Simon he surnamed Peter;

17 And James the of Zebedee, and John the brother of James; and he named them Boanerges, which is, the sons of thunder:

18 And Andrew, and Philip, and Bartholomew, and Matthew, and Thomas, and James the of Alphaeus, and Thaddaeus, and Simon the Canaanite,

19 And Judas Iscariot, which also betrayed[1539] him: and they went into a house.

20 And the multitude comes together again, **so-that not is-powerful them,** so much as eat bread.

21 And when **the-ones beside of-him**[1540] heard, they went out to **govern** him: **because** they said, **he-was-ecstasized.**[1541]

22 And the scribes which came down from Jerusalem said, **that he-has** Beelzebub, and by the **first-rank**,[1542] of the **demons** casts he out **demons**.

23 And he called them, and said **to-them** in parables, how **is-powerful** Satan cast out Satan?

24 And if a kingdom be divided against itself, that kingdom **not is-powerful to-**stand.

25 And if a house be divided against itself, that house **not is-powerful to-**stand.

26 And if Satan rise up against himself, and be divided, he **not is-powerful to-**stand, but has a **finish**.

27 **Not is-powerful no-one entering** into **the** house **of-the forceful**, and **through-snatch** his **vessels**, except he **foremost** binds the **forceful**; and then he will **through-snatch** his house.

28 Amen I say **to-you**, all sins shall be **released to-the** sons of men, and blasphemies **as-much-as ever** they shall blaspheme:

29 Yet he that shall blaspheme **into** the Holy Spirit has **no release,**[1543] but is **liable**[1544] of **eternal judging:**[1545]

30 That they said, he has an unclean spirit.

31 Then came his **brothers** and his mother, and, standing **outside,** sent **to-him, voicing** him.

32 And the multitude sat about him, and they said **to-him, Be-perceiving**, your mother, and your **brothers, outside, are-seeking you.**

33 And he answered them, saying, who is my mother, or my **brothers**?

34 And he looked round about on them which **sitting** about him, and said, **be-perceiving** my mother and my **brothers!**

35 Because, whoever **produces** the will of God, the same is my brother, and my sister, and mother.

MARK CHAPTER 4

1 And he began again to teach **beside** the sea: and there was gathered **towards him the entire** multitude, so that he entered into a ship, and sat in the sea; and the whole multitude was by the sea on the land.

2 And he taught them many things by parables, and said **to-them** in his **teaching,**

3 Be-you-hearing; **be-perceiving**, there went out a Sower to sow:

4 And it **became**, as he sowed, some fell by the way side, and the **birds** of the **heaven** came and devoured it up.

5 And some fell on **rock-like,**[1546] where it had not much earth; and **soon** it sprang up, because it had no depth of earth;

6 But when the sun was up, it was scorched; and because it had no root, it withered away.

7 And some fell **into the** thorns, and the thorns **up-walked**, and **together-**choked it, and it **gives** no fruit.

8 And other fell on **ideal** ground and did **give** fruit **up-walking** and **grew**; and **carried, one,** thirty, and **one,** sixty, and **one,** a hundred.

9 And he said **to** them, he that has ears to hear, hear!

10 And when he was alone, they that were about him with the twelve asked of him the parable.

[1539] Lit., beside-given
[1540] Genitive case
[1541] Greek compound existemi (out-of-stand) from which we take our English ecstasy (overwhelming feelings)
[1542] Or, original-rank, beginning-rank
[1543] Lit., from-let-go
[1544] Greek: in-hold, to hold in
[1545] Alexandrian Texts read "age sin"
[1546] Or stony-perception per Strong's dictionary

11 And he said to-them, to-you it is given to know the mystery of the kingdom of God: **yet to-them** that are **outside**, all things **are becoming** in parables:

12 That seeing they may see, and not perceive; and hearing they may hear, and not **synthesize**; **not-ever** they should **revert**, and sins should be **released to-them.**

13 And he said **to-them, perceive** you not this parable? And how then will you know all parables?

14 The Sower sows the **Word.**

15 And these are they by the way side, where the **Word** is sown; but when they have heard, Satan comes **soon**, and **lifts** the **Word** that was sown in their **hearts.**

16 And these are they likewise which are sown on **rock-like**;[1547] who, when they have heard the **Word**, **soon take** it with **cheerfulness**;

17 And have no root in themselves, and so **towards-seasons**: afterward, when **tribulation** or **chasing** arises **through the Word**, **soon** they are **scandalized**.[1548]

18 And these are they which are sown among thorns; such as hear the **Word,**

19 And the **portion-worry** of this **age**, and the **cheating** of riches, and the **on-feeling** of other things entering in, choke the **Word**, and it becomes unfruitful.

20 And these are they which are sown on **ideal** ground; such as hear the **Word**, and **beside**-receive, and **carry** fruit, **one**, thirty, **one**, sixty, and **one**, a hundred.

21 And he said **to** them, is a candle brought to be put under a **dry-measure**, or under a **cot**;[1549] and not to be **placed** on a candlestick?

22 For there is nothing **hidden,** which shall not **shine**; neither was anything **from-hidden**, but that it-should-**come into shining.**

23 If any man has ears to hear, hear!

24 And he said **to** them, **be-looking** what you hear: with what measure you **measure**, it shall be measured **to-you**: and **to-you** that hear shall more be **added.**

25 For he that has, **to-him** shall be given: and he that has not, from him shall be **lifted** even that which he has.

26 And he said, so is the kingdom of God, as f a man should cast seed into the ground;

27 And should sleep, and rise night and day, and the seed should **sprout** and **lengthen**, he **perceived** not how.

28 For the earth **fruit-carry automatically**; first the **grass**, then the **stalk-stand,** after that the full corn in the **stalk-stand.**

29 Yet, when the fruit is **beside-gives**, **soon** he puts in the sickle, because the harvest is **beside-stood.**

30 And he said **to-what** shall we **assimilate** the kingdom of God? Or with what **parable** shall we **parable**?

31 As a grain of mustard seed, which, when it is sown **on** the earth, is **smaller** than all the seeds that be in the earth;

32 But when it is sown, **it-is-up-walking**, and becomes **larger**[1550] than all herbs, and **produces great** branches; so that the **birds of-the heaven is-powerful to**-lodge under the **shade** of it.

33 And with many such parables spoke he the **Word to** them, as **they-were-powerful** to hear.

34 But **spacing-from** a parable spoke he not **to-them:** and when they **according-to private**, he expounded[1551] all things to his disciples.

35 And the same day, when the evening **became**, he says **to-them,** let us **through-come** into the **other-side.**

36 And when they had **released**[1552] the multitude, they **beside-get** him even as he was in the ship. And there were also with him other little ships.

37 And **is-becoming** a **great** storm[1553] of wind, and the waves **upon-throw** into the ship, so that it was **already** full.

38 And he was in the **stern** of the ship, asleep on a pillow: and they **woke** him, and say **to-him**, Teacher, **interest** you not that we **from-ruin**?

[1547] Or stony-perception per the root word given in Strong's dictionary
[1548] Snared
[1549] Or (re)cline
[1550] Larger, especially in age
[1551] On-loosed
[1552] Lit., from-let-go
[1553] Lit., whirlwind of-wind

39 And he arose, and **rebuke**[1554] the wind, and said **to** the sea, **be-silent**, be-**muzzled**. And the wind ceased, and there was a **great** calm.[1555]

40 And he said **to** them, why are you so **timid**? How is it that you have no faith?

41 And they feared, **great fear**, and said one to another, **who** is this, that **also** the wind and the sea **under-hear**[1556] him?

MARK CHAPTER 5

1 And they came **into** the other side of the sea, into the country of the Gadarenes.

2 And when he **came out-of** the ship, **soon** there met him out of the **remembrance-tombs** a man with an unclean spirit,

3 Who had **down-house in** the **remembrance-tomb**; and no man **not is-powerful to-**bind him, no, not with chains:

4 Through that he had been often bound with **shackles** and chains, and the chains had been **through-pulled** by him, and the **shackles together-crushed**: neither **was-forceful** any **to-**tame him.

5 And always, night and day, he was in the mountains, and in the **remembrance-tomb**, crying, and cutting himself with stones.

6 But when he saw Jesus afar off, he ran and worshipped him,

7 And cried with a **great** voice, and said, what have I to do with you, Jesus, you Son of the **Highest** God? I **oath** you by God, that you torment me not.

8 For he said **to-him**, come out of the man, you unclean spirit.

9 And he asked him, what is your name? And he answered, saying, my name Legion: for we are many.

10 And he **beside-call** him much that he would not send them away out of the **space**.

11 Now there was there **towards** the mountains a **great** herd of swine feeding.

12 And all the **demons beside-call** him, saying, **dispatched** us into the swine, that we may enter into them.

13 And **soon** Jesus **permitted them**. And the unclean spirits went out and entered into the swine: and the herd **rushed-violently-impulsively** down a **precipice** into the sea, (they were about two thousand) and were choked in the sea.

14 And **those feeding** the swine fled, and **up-message** in the city, and in the country. And they went out to **perceive** what **having-become**

15 And they come to Jesus, and **theatre-spectator** him that was **demonized**, and had the legion, sitting, and clothed, and in **safe-disposition**:[1557] and they were afraid.

16 And they that **perceived, through-lead** them how it **became to-him** that was **demonized**, and **about** the swine.

17 And they began to **beside-call** him to depart out of their **horizon**.

18 And when he was come into the ship, he that had been **demonized beside-called** him that he might be with him.

19 Yet, Jesus **released** him not, but says **to-him**, go home **towards yours**, and **up-message** them **how-much** things the Lord **produced** for you, and has had **mercy** on you.

20 And he departed and began to **preach** in Decapolis **as-much-as the-things** Jesus **produced** for him: and all did marvel.

21 And when Jesus was **crossed** over again by ship **to-the other-side**, much people gathered **to-him**: and he was **beside** the sea.

22 And, **be-perceiving, coming** one of the **first-rank-of-synagogue**, Jairus by name; and when he **perceived** him, he fell **towards** his feet,

23 And **beside-call** him **much**, saying, my little daughter, **at-the-last** is **holding**: come and lay your hands on her, that she may be **saved**; and she shall live.

24 And went with him; and much people followed him, and **together-tribulation**[1558] him.

25 And a certain woman, which had an issue of blood twelve **years**,

---

[1554] Or, to tax-upon
[1555] Or smile
[1556] Or obey

[1557] Or safe-disposition
[1558] Root: to crowd, a rut, worn track

26 And had **emotion** many things of many physicians, and had spent all that she had, and nothing was **gained**, but rather **comes** worse,

27 When she had heard of Jesus, came in the **multitude** behind, and **fastened-to** his garment.

28 Because she said, if I may **fasten-to and-if** his garment, I shall be **saved**.

29 And **soon** the fountain of her blood was dried up; and she **knew** in body that she was **cured** of that **whipping-plague**.

30 And Jesus, **soon** knowing in himself that **power** had gone out of him, **upon-turned** in the **multitude**, and said, who **fastened-to** my **garments**?

31 And his disciples said **to-him**, you see the multitude **together-tribulation** you, and say you, who **fastened-to** me?

32 And he looked round about to **perceive** her that had done this thing.

33 But the woman fearing and trembling, **perceiving** what was **become on** her, came and **fell-towards** him, and told him all the truth.

34 And he said **to** her, daughter, your faith has made you **saved**;[1559] go **into** peace and be **healthy-grown from** your **whipping**-plague.

35 While he yet spoke, there came from the **first-rank-of-synagogue** which said, your daughter is dead: why **flay-strip** you the **Teacher** any further?

36 But Jesus **soon** heard the word that was spoken, he says **to the first-rank-of-synagogue,** be not afraid, only believe.

37 And he **released** no man to follow him, **except,** Peter, and James, and John the brother of James.

38 And he comes **into** the house of the **first-rank**-of-synagogue, and sees the **disturbance**,[1560] and them that wept and **uproar**[1561] much.

39 And when he **entered**, he says **to** them, why make you **disturbance-wail**, and weep? The **girl** is not dead, but sleeps.

40 And they **down-laughed**. But when he had **out-cast all-them**, he **beside-take** the father and the mother of the **girl**, and them that were with him, and enters where the **girl** was **laying**.

41 And he **governed** the **girl** by the hand, and said **to** her, talitha cumi; which is, being interpreted, **little-girl, I-say to-you**, arise.

42 And **soon** the **little-girl** arose and walked; for she was of twelve **years**. And they were **ecstasized**,[1562] with a **great ecstasy**.

43 And he **through-stall** them **soon** that no man should know it; and **said** that something should be given her to eat.

MARK CHAPTER 6

1 And he went out from there and came into his **father-country**; and his disciples follow him.

2 And when the Sabbath was come, he began to teach in the synagogue: and many hearing were **out-of-pounded**,[1563] saying, from where has **this-man** these things? And what wisdom this which is given **to-him**, that even[1564] such **powers** are become through his hands?

3 Is not this the **Technician**, the son of Mary, the brother of James, and Joseph, and of Juda, and Simon? And are not his sisters here with us? And they were **scandalized**[1565] in him.

4 But Jesus said **to** them, a prophet is not **un-valued, except** in his own **father-country,** and among his own **together-kin,** and in his own house.

5 And he **not is-powerful** there to **produce power, except** that he **placed** his hands upon a few **un-leaving-weakness,** and **therapy-served-them**.

6 And he marveled because of their unbelief. And he **around-leading** the villages, **cycle-circling** teaching.

7 And he **toward**-called-**to-him** the twelve, and began to send them two and two; and gave them **authority to-the** unclean spirits;

8 And **beside-message** them that they should **lift** nothing **into** journey,[1566] **except** a rod only; no **wallet**,[1567] no bread, no money in **belt**:

[1559] Or, safe
[1560] Or uproar
[1561] Or disturbance
[1562] Greek compound existemi (out-of-stand) from which we take our English ecstasy (overwhelming feelings)
[1563] Or lit., out-pound
[1564] "Kai" having copulative and cumulative force
[1565] snared
[1566] Or, way, road
[1567] Or bag

9 But **under-bind** sandals; and not **clothing-yourself** [1568] two coats.

10 And he said **to** them, **wherever** you enter into a house, there **remain until** you depart from that place.

11 And whoever shall not **welcome** you, nor hear you, when you **out-passage** there, shake off the dust under your feet **into witness to-them. Amen** I say **to-you**, it shall be more tolerable for Sodom and Gomorrah in the day of **judging,** than for that city.

12 And they went out and preached that men should **change-thought**.

13 And they cast out many **demons** and anointed[1569] with oil many that were **un-leaving-weakness**, and **therapy-served-them**.

14 And king Herod heard; (for his name **became shine**): and he said that John the Baptist was risen **out-of** the dead, and therefore **powers in-work** in him.

15 Others said that it is **Elijah**. And others said that it is a prophet, or as one of the prophets.

16 But when Herod heard, he said, it is John, whom I beheaded: he is risen **out-of** the dead.

17 For Herod himself had sent forth and **governed** John, and bound him in prison for Herodias' sake, his brother Philip's wife: for he had married her.

18 Because John had said **to-Herod**, it is not lawful for you to have your brother's wife.

19 Therefore Herodias had **in-hold**[1570] him, and **willed to** kill him; **and not was-powerful**:

20 Because, Herod feared John, **perceiving** that he was a **righteous** man and a holy, and **together-guard** him; and when he heard him, he did many things, and heard him **sweetly**.

21 And when a **good-season** day **became**, that Herod on his birthdays **produced** an **expensive-dinner** to his **magnates,**[1571] **first-rank-of-thousands,** and **foremost**[1572] of Galilee;

22 And when the daughter of **herself, the** Herodias, came in, and danced, and pleased Herod and them that **together-up-reclined** with him, the king said **to** the **maiden**, ask of me whatever you **will**, and I will give you.

23 And he swore **to** her, whatever you shall ask of me, I will give you, **to** the half of my kingdom.

24 And she went forth, and said **to** her mother, what shall I ask? And she said, the head of John the Baptist.

25 And she came in **soon** with **speed to** the king, and asked, saying, I will that you give me **soon** in a **plate** the head of John the Baptist.

26 And the king was **around-sad; through** his oath, and **the ones-together-up-reclining**, he would not **un-place** her.

27 And **soon** the king sent an executioner, and **under-arrange** his head to be brought: and he went and beheaded him in the prison,

28 And brought his head in a charger and gave it to the **maiden**: and the **maiden** gave it to her mother.

29 And when his disciples heard, they came and **lift** up his **corpse,**[1573] and laid it in a **remembrance-tomb**.

30 And the apostles gathered themselves together **to-**Jesus, and **from-message** him all things, both what they **produced**, and what they had taught.

31 And he said **to** them, come **down privacy** into a **lonesome spot**, and rest a **few** for there were many coming and going, and they had no **good-season** so much as to eat.

32 And they departed into a **lonesome spot** by ship privately.

33 And the people **perceived** them departing, and many knew him, and **on-foot, they-together-ran, from** all **the** cities, and **towards-come** them **to-him**.

34 And Jesus, when he came out, saw much **multitude**, and **had-gut-compassionate** toward them, because they were as sheep not having a shepherd: and he began to teach them many things.

35 And **already of-hour** much **becoming**, his disciples came **towards him**, and said, this is a **lonesome** place, and **already many hour**:

36 Send them away, that they may go into the **field** round, and into the villages, and buy[1574] themselves bread: for they have nothing to eat.

[1568] Lit., in-down; or, in-sink, in-down-slipping
[1569] Or, rubbed
[1570] Or, held-in (against) him
[1571] Or, **great**-ones, or transliterated majesties
[1572] Plural
[1573] Greek: "ptoma" (a ruin, a corpse, lifeless body, and alternate of "pipto" to fall)
[1574] Lit., to go to the market, redeem

37 He answered and said **to** them, give you them to eat. And they say **to-him**, shall we go and buy[1575] two hundred **denarii**[1576] of bread, and give them to eat?

38 He says **to** them, how many loaves have you? Go and **perceive**. And when they knew, they say, five, and two fishes.

39 And he **under-arrange** them to make all **up-recline** by **together-drinking-party** upon the green grass.

40 And they **up-fall** in **leek-rows**, **up** hundred, and **up** fifty.

41 And when he had **taken** the five loaves and the two fishes, he looked up into **the** heaven, and blessed, and **broke** the loaves, and gave to his disciples to **beside-place**[1577] **to-them**; and the two fishes **portioned** he among them all.

42 And they did all eat and were filled.

43 And they **lift** twelve baskets full of the fragments, and **from** the fishes.

44 And they that did eat of the loaves were about five thousand men.

45 And **soon** he **necessitate** his disciples to **take** into the ship, and to go to the other side before **to-**Bethsaida, while he **from-loosed** the people.

46 And when he had **released to-them**, he departed into a mountain to pray.

47 And when evening **becoming**, the ship was in the middle of the sea, and he alone on the land.

48 And he **perceived** them **tormenting** in **the pushing**; for the wind was contrary[1578] to-them: and about the fourth **guard-watch** of the night he comes **towards** them, walking upon the sea, and **willed to-pass** by them.

49 But when they **perceived** him walking upon the sea, they supposed it had been a **phantom**,[1579] and cried out:

50 For they all **perceived** him and were **agitated**. And **soon** he talked with them, and says **to-them**, be-**daring**:[1580] **I am**;[1581] be not afraid.

51 And he **up-walk**ed **towards** them into the ship; and the wind ceased: and they were **excessive** in themselves, **they-ecstasized**, and **marveled**.

52 For they **understood** not **on** the loaves: for their **heart** was hardened.

53 And when they had **crossed** over, they came into the land of Gennesaret, and **towards-anchor**.

54 And when they were come out of the ship, **soon** they knew him,

55 And **around-ran** the whole **about-space** and began to carry about in **mattress** those that were **evil holders**, wherever they heard he was.

56 And wherever he entered, into villages, or cities, or **fields**, they laid the **weak** in the **markets**, and **beside-call** him that they might **fasten-to if-ever** the **hem** of his garment: and as many as **fastened-to-him** were-made-**safe**.[1582]

MARK CHAPTER 7

1 Then **together-lead towards him** the Pharisees, and certain of the scribes, which came from Jerusalem.

2 And when they **perceived** some of his disciples eat bread **with-common**, that is to say, with unwashed, hands, they **blamed**.

3 For the Pharisees, and all the Jews, except **not to-fist** they wash **the hands,** eat not, **governing**[1583] the **beside-giving**[1584] of the elders.

4 And from the market, except they **baptize**, they eat not. And many other things there be, which they have **beside-taken to-be-governed**, the **baptism** of cups, and pots, brass vessels, and of **cot**.[1585]

5 Then the Pharisees and scribes asked him, why walk not your disciples **down** the **beside-giving** of the elders, but eat bread with unwashed hands?

6 He answered and said **to-them, ideally** has **Isaiah** prophesied of you hypocrites, as it is written, this people **value** me with lips, but their **heart is forward from-holding** from me.

7 Yet, in vain do they **revere** me, **teachers, teachings** commandments of men!

[1575] Lit., to go to the market, redeem
[1576] Or ten donkeys
[1577] Or deposit
[1578] Greek compound: in-anti, in front of, opposite, antagonistic
[1579] Greek: phantasma, ghost, spirit, specter
[1580] Or, courageous
[1581] Two Greek words: Ego (I) and eimi (I exists)
[1582] Or, saved, delivered
[1583] Lit., kratountes, nominative; so, it could be translated governors
[1584] Lit., beside-give, transmission, tradition
[1585] Or recliners

8 Because, **releasing** the commandment of God, you **govern to-the beside-giving** of men, the **baptism** of pots and cups: and many other such like things you **produce**.

9 And he said **to** them, **ideally** you **un-place** the commandment of God, that you may **guard** your own **beside-giving**.

10 Because Moses said, **value** your father and your mother; and, whoever **evil-saying-of** father or mother, **to-death they finish**:

11 **Yet,** you say, if a man shall say to his father or mother, corban, which is to say, a gift, by whatever you may be **gained** by me..

12 And you **release** him no more to **produce to-the** father or **to-the** mother;

13 **Un-lording** the Word of God through your **beside-giving,** which you have **beside-given**: and many such like things you **produce**.

14 And when he had **towards-called** all the people, he said **to-them, be-hearing to-me** everyone, and **synthesize**:[1586]

15 There is nothing from **outside** a man entering **into him is-powerful to-common** him: but the things which **out-passage from** him, those are they that **common** the man.

16 If any man has ears to hear, hear!

17 And when he was entered into the house from the people, his disciples asked him **about** the parable.

18 And he says **to** them, are you also **without-synthesizing**? **Not you-thought** that whatever thing from **outside** enters into the man, **not is-powerful to-common** him;

19 **That** it enters not into his **heart**, but into the belly, and **out-passage** into the **latrine, cleansing** all **food**?

20 And he said that which **out-passage** the man, that **commons** the man.

21 For from within, out of the **heart** of men, **out-passage** evil **through-reckoning**, adulteries, **prostitutions**, murders,

22 Thefts, **more-having**,[1587] **wicked-hurtful**ness, **trick-bait, wantonness, wicked-hurtful** eye, blasphemy, **above-appearing, un-disposed**:

23 All these **wicked-hurtful** things **out-passage** within, and **common** the man.

24 And from there he **up-stand** and went into the **change-horizon**[1588] of Tyre and Sidon, and entered into a house, and **he-willed none to-know**: but **not he-is-powerful to-be-hidden.**

25 **Because,** a woman **hearing**, whose young daughter had an unclean spirit, heard of him, and came and **towards**-fell **towards** his feet:

26 The woman was a **Hellenic**,[1589] a Syrophoenician[1590] by **kin**; and she **asked** him that he cast **out** the **demon** out of her daughter.

27 But Jesus said **to** her, **release**[1591] the children **foremost** be filled: for it is not **ideal** to **take** the children's bread, and to cast **to** the **puppies**.

28 And she answered and said **to-him**, Yes, Lord: **and** the **puppies** under the table eat of the children's crumbs.

29 And he said **to** her, **through this** saying **under-lead**; the **demon** is **out-of-gone out-of** your daughter.

30 And when she was come to her house, she found the **demon** gone **out-of,** and her daughter laid upon the **cot**.[1592]

31 And again, departing from the **horizon** of Tyre and Sidon, he came **towards** the sea of Galilee, through the middle of the **horizon** of Decapolis.

32 And they bring **to-him** one that was **blunted**,[1593] **difficult-talking**; and they **beside-call** him to **place** his hand upon him.

33 And he **from-get** him from the multitude, and **cast**[1594] his fingers into his ears, and he spit, and **fastened-to** his tongue;

34 And looking up **into the** heaven, he **groaned**,[1595] and says **to-him**, ephphatha, that is, **be-through-up-opened.**

[1586] Greek: synete (compound of sunieme) to send together into a comprehensive hole
[1587] Or covetousness
[1588] Or change-boundary
[1589] Non-Jew, Greek
[1590] Or Syria-Phoenician (Palm-country)
[1591] Lit., from-let-go
[1592] Or (re)cline
[1593] Or, deaf-mute, root to chop (choppy), to beat the chest
[1594] Or thrust
[1595] Or groan in straits

35 And **soon** his ears **were-through-up-opened**, and the **bands** of his tongue was loosed, and he spoke **straight-erect**.[1596]

36 And he **through-stall** them that they should tell no man: but the more he **through-stalled** them, so much the more-**excessively** they **preached**

37 And were **beyond-excessive out-of-pounded** saying, he **produced** all things **ideal**: he **produces** both the **blunted**, to hear, and the **un-talk** to **talk**.

MARK CHAPTER 8

1 In those days the multitude being **many**, and having nothing to eat, Jesus **towards-called** his disciples, and says **to-them**,

2 **I-am-having-gut-compassion** on the multitude that they have **already toward-remain** with me three days, and have nothing to eat:

3 And if I send them away fasting to their own houses, they will **out-of-loosed** by the way: for **some** of them **arrived** from far.

4 And his disciples answered him, **where is-powerful anyone to-satisfy** these with bread here **on** the **lonesome**?

5 And he asked them, how many loaves have you? And they said, Seven.

6 And he **beside-message** the people to **up-fall** on the ground: and he **took** the seven loaves, and **good-graced**, and **broke,** and gave to his disciples to **beside-place**;[1597] and they did **beside-place to-the** multitude.

7 And they had a few small fishes: and he blessed, and **said, beside-place to-them**.

8 So they did eat and were filled: and they **lift** of the **surplus**[1598] **broken**, seven baskets.

9 And they that had eaten were about four thousand: and he sent them away.

10 And **soon** he entered into a ship with his disciples and came into the **sections** of Dalmanutha.

11 And the Pharisees came forth, and began to question with him, seeking of him a sign from **the** heaven, **probe-testing** him.

12 And he **up-groaned** in his spirit, and says, why does this generation seek after a sign? **Amen,** I say **to-you**, there shall no sign be given **to** this generation.

13 And he **released** them and entering into the ship again departed to the **other-side**.

14 Now **they** forgot to **take** bread, neither had they in the ship with them more than one loaf.

15 And he **through-stalled** them, saying, **be-seeing, be-looking from** the **ferment** of the Pharisees, and the **ferment** of Herod.

16 And they **through-inventory towards one-another**, saying, **that** we have no bread.

17 And when Jesus knew, he says **to** them, why **through-inventory** you, **that** you have no bread? **Not-yet you-thought**, neither **synthesize**? **Is your heart held** hardened?

18 Having eyes, see you not? And having ears, hear you not? And do you not remember?

19 When I **broke** the five loaves among five thousand, how many baskets full of fragments **you-lifted**? They say **to-him**, twelve.

20 And when the seven among four thousand, how many baskets full of fragments **you-lifted**? And they said, seven.

21 And he said **to-them**, how is it that **not-yet you-synthesize**?

22 And he comes to Bethsaida; and they bring a blind man **to-him** and **asked** him to **fasten-to-him**.

23 And he **took** the blind man by the hand and led him out of the town; and when he had spit on his eyes, and **placed** his hands upon him, he asked him if he saw.

24 And he looked up, and said, I see men as trees, walking.

25 After that he **placed the** hands again upon his eyes and made him look up: and he was restored, and **in-looked** every man clearly.

26 And he sent him away to his house, saying, neither go into the town, nor tell any in the town.

27 And Jesus **out-go,** and his disciples, into the towns of Caesarea Philippi: and by the way he asked his disciples, saying **to-them**, whom do men say that I am?

[1596] Greek: "orthos"
[1597] Or deposit
[1598] Or excess

28 And they answered, John the Baptist: but some, **Elijah**; and others, one of the prophets.

29 And he says **to-them, yet** who say you that I am? And Peter answered and says **to-him**, you are the Christ.

30 And he **rebukes**[1599] them that they should tell no man **about** him.

31 And he began to teach them, that **it-is-binding** the Son of man **emotion** many things, and be **from-seem**[1600] of the elders, and the **first-rank-priests**, and scribes, and be killed, and after three days rise again.

32 And he **all-speech**,[1601] that saying, and Peter **towards-get** him, and began to **rebuke** him.

33 But when he had turned about and looked on his disciples, he **rebuked** Peter, saying, **take** you behind me, Satan: for you **disposition** not the things that be of God, but the things that be of men.

34 And when he had **towards-called** the people with his disciples also, he said **to-them, whoever** will come after me, let him **contradict** himself, and **lift** his cross, and follow me.

35 For whoever will save his **soul** shall **from-ruin her**; but whoever shall **from-ruin** his **soul on-account-of me** and the **well-message**, shall save **her**.

36 For what shall it profit a man, if he shall gain the whole world, and **detriment** his own soul?

37 Or what shall a man give in exchange for his soul?

38 Whoever therefore shall be **upon-disfigured** of me and of my words in this adulterous and sinful generation; of him also shall the Son of man be **upon-disfigured**, when he comes in the glory of his Father with the holy angels.

MARK CHAPTER 9

1 And he said **to** them, **amen** I say **to-you**, that there be some of them that stand here, which shall not taste of death, **until** they have **perceived** the kingdom of God come **in** power.

2 And after six days Jesus **took** Peter, and James, and John, and **carry** them up into a high mountain **privately** by themselves: and he was **transformed**[1602] before them.

3 And his **garment** became shining, exceeding white as snow; so, as no fuller[1603] on earth **is-powerful to-**white them.

4 And there **seen to-them Elijah** with Moses: and they were talking with Jesus.

5 And Peter answered and said to Jesus, **Rabbi**, it is **ideal** for us to be here: and let us **produce** three tabernacles; one for you, and one for Moses, and one for **Elijah.**

6 For he **perceived** not what to say; **because** they were sore afraid.

7 And there was a cloud that overshadowed them: and a voice came out of the cloud, saying, this is my beloved Son: hear him.

8 And suddenly, when they had looked round, they **perceived** no man any more, **except** Jesus only with themselves.

9 And as they came down from the mountain, he **through-stalled** them that they should tell no man what things they had **perceived, until** the Son of man were risen **out-of** the dead.

10 And they **governed** that saying with themselves, questioning one with another what the rising **out-of** the dead should mean.

11 And they asked him, saying, why say the scribes that **Elijah, it-is-binding, foremost to-**come?

12 And he answered and told them, **Elijah indeed** comes **foremost**, and restores all things; and how it is written of the Son of man, that he **emotion** many things, and **be-from-nothing.**[1604]

13 But I say **to-you**, that **Elijah** is indeed come, and they **produced to-him** whatever they **will**, as it is written of him.

14 And when he came to disciples, he **perceived much** multitude about them, and the scribes questioning with them.

15 And **soon** all the people, when they **perceived** him, were **out-of-stupefied**,[1605] and running to **embrace** him.

16 And he asked the scribes, what question you with them?

[1599] Or, tax-upon
[1600] Or, rejected
[1601] Free speech
[1602] Greek: "metamorphoo"
[1603] Cloth-dresser
[1604] Make utterly nothing
[1605] Stupefy is defined as: unable to think or feel properly

17 And one **out-**of the multitude answered and said, **Teacher**, I have brought **to-you** my son, which has a dumb spirit;

18 And wherever he **down-take** him, he tears him: and he **froth, a**nd **grate** with his teeth, and **withers**: and I spoke **to-you**r disciples that they should cast him out; and **not they-are-forceful**.

19 He answers him, and says, O **un-believing** generation, how long shall I be with you? How long shall I **tolerate** you? Bring him **towards** me.

20 And they brought him **to-him**: and when he saw him, **soon** the spirit **spasm** him; and he fell on the ground and **rolled frothing**.

21 And he asked his father, **how-much uninterrupted-time** is it since this **became to-him**? And he said, **of-a-child**.

22 And **often** it has cast him into the fire, and into the waters, to **from-ruin** him: but if you **you-are-powerful** do anything, have **gut-compassion** on us, and help[1606] us.

23 Jesus said **to-**him, if **you-are-powerful to-**believe, all things **powerful to-him** that believes.

24 And **soon** the father of the child cried out, and said with tears, Lord, I believe; help **my** unbelief.

25 When Jesus **perceive** that the people came **together-running**, he **rebukes**[1607] the **unclean** spirit, saying **to-him**, you **un-talk** and **blunted**,[1608] spirit, I **upon-arrange** you, come out of him, and enter[1609] no more **into** him.

26 And **screaming**, and **spasm** him **much**, and came out of him: and he was as dead; insomuch that many said, he is dead.

27 But Jesus **governed** him by the hand, and **up-stand** him up; and he arose.

28 And when he was come into the house, his disciples asked him privately, why **not we-are-powerful** cast him out?

29 And he said **to** them, this **kind**[1610] in nothing **is-powerful to-**come-**out**, **if not in** prayer.

30 And they departed there and passed through Galilee; and he would not that any man should know.

31 For he taught his disciples, and said **to-them,** the Son of man is **betrayed**[1611] into the hands of men, and they shall kill him; and after that he is killed, he shall **stand-up** the third day.

32 But **they-did-not-mind** the **declaration** and were afraid to ask him.

33 And he came to Capernaum: and being in the house he asked them, what was it that you **through-inventoried** among yourselves by the way?

34 But they **were-silent**: for by the way they had **through-said**[1612] among themselves, who the **larger.**[1613]

35 And he sat down, and voice the twelve, and says **to-them,** if any man **willing** to be **foremost**, shall be last of all, and **attendant** of all.

36 And he **took** a child, and **stand** him in the middle of them: and when he had **embraced** him, he said **to-them,**

37 Whoever shall **welcome** one of such children in my name, **welcomes** me: and whoever shall **welcome** me, **welcome** not me, but him that sent me.

38 And John answered him, saying, **Teacher**, we saw one casting out **demons** in your name, and he follows not us: and we **prevented** him, because he follows not us.

39 But Jesus said, **prevent** him not: for there is no man who shall **produce power** in my name, which **is-powerful** swiftly **to-speak-evil** of me.

40 For he that is not **downing** us is **for us.**

41 For whoever shall give you a cup of water to drink in my name, because you are **of-**Christ, **amen**, I say **to-you**, he shall not **from-ruin** his **pay**.

42 And whoever shall **scandal**[1614] one of little-ones that believe in me, it is **ideal** for him that a millstone was hanged about his neck, and he were cast into the sea.

43 And if your hand **scandalizes** you, cut it off: it is **ideal** for you to enter into life maimed,[1615] than having two hands to go into **Gehenna** into the fire that never shall be **extinguished**:

[1606] To run to the cry for help
[1607] Or, to tax-upon
[1608] Or, deaf-mute, root to chop (choppy), to beat the chest
[1609] Aorist tense
[1610] Or species

[1611] Lit., beside-given
[1612] Say thoroughly, discuss
[1613] Larger, especially in age
[1614] Snare
[1615] Or rocking

44 Where their worm **finish** not, and the fire is not **extinguished**.

45 And if your foot **scandalizes** you, **amputate it**: it is **ideal** for you to enter **limping** into life, **rather-than** having two feet to be cast into **Gehenna**, into the fire that never shall be **extinguished**:

46 Where their worm **finish** not, and the fire is not **extinguished**.

47 And if your eye **scandalizes** you, pluck it out: it is **ideal** for you to enter into the kingdom of God with one eye, **rather-**than having two eyes to be cast into **Gehenna of-the** fire:

48 Where their worm **finish** not, and the fire is not **extinguished**.

49 For everyone shall be salted with fire, and every sacrifice shall be salted with salt.

50 Salt is-**ideal**: but if the salt becomes **un-salted, in what** will you season[1616] it? Have salt in yourselves and have peace **in one-another.**

MARK CHAPTER 10

1 And he **stood-up** from there and comes into the **horizon** of Judaea by the **other** side of Jordan: and the people resort **towards him** again; and, as he **his-ethics,**[1617] he taught them again.

2 And the Pharisees came **to-him**, and asked him, is it lawful for a man to **from-loose** wife? tempting him.

3 And he answered and said **to** them, what did Moses command you?

4 And they said, Moses **permitted** to write a **little-scroll** of **divorce,** and to **from-loose her.**

5 And Jesus answered and said **to** them, **towards your dry-hardened-heart** he wrote you this **commandment.**

6 But from the **original** of the creation God **produced** them male and female.

7 For this cause shall a man leave his father and mother, and **toward-keep-company towards** his wife;

8 And they two shall be **into first** flesh: so, then they are no more **two,** but **first** flesh.

9 What therefore God has **together-yoked**, let not man put **space**.

10 And in the house his disciples asked him again of the same.

11 And he says **to** them, **whoever** shall **from-loose** his wife, and marry another, commits adultery against her.

12 And if a woman shall **from-loose** her husband, and be married to **another-same,** she commits adultery

13 And they brought children **to-him**, that he should **fasten-to** them: and disciples rebuked those that brought.

14 But when Jesus **perceived**, he was **much-grief-ached**[1618], and said **to** them, **release**[1619] the little children to come **towards** me, and **prevent** them not: for of such is the kingdom of God.

15 Amen I say **to-you, whoever** shall not **welcome** the kingdom of God as a little child, he shall not enter **into her.**

16 And he **embraced them, placed** hands upon them, and blessed them.

17 And when he **out-passage** into the way, there came one running, and **knee-falling to-him**, and asked him, Good **Teacher**, what shall I **produce** that I may inherit **eternal** life?

18 And Jesus said **to-him,** why me **you-say** good? None good but one, God.

19 You-perceived the commandments, **not you-shall-adultery,** do not **murder,** do not steal, do not **be-false-witnessing, from-rob-deprive** not, **value** you father and mother.

20 And he answered and said **to-him, Teacher,** all these have I **watched** from my youth.

21 Then Jesus **in-looking to-him** loved him, and said **to-him,** one thing you **late:**[1620] go your way, sell whatever you have, and give to the poor,[1621] and you shall have **treasure**[1622] in heaven: and come, **lift** the cross, and follow me.

22 And he was sad at that saying and went away **distress-sadden**: for he had **much acquisition**.

[1616] Lit., prepare with stimulating condiments
[1617] Or custom
[1618] Or, resentful
[1619] From-let-go
[1620] Or deficit

[1621] Akin to a word that means to frighten fall) (see Strong's' Concordance #4434)
[1622] Greek: "thesauros," to place into tomorrow, transliterated as "thesaurus,"

23 And Jesus looked round about, and says **to** his disciples, how **difficult-eat**[1623] shall they that have riches enter into the kingdom of God!

24 And the disciples were **stupefied**[1624] at his words. But Jesus answers again, and says **to** them, children, how **difficult-eat** is it for them that **faith-trust** in riches to enter into the kingdom of God!

25 It is easier for a camel to go through the eye of a needle, than for a rich man to enter into the kingdom of God.

26 And they were **out-of-pounded exceedingly**, saying among themselves, who **is-powerful to-be-saved**?

27 And Jesus **in-look** them says, with men, **un-powerful**, but not with God: for with God all things are **powerful**.

28 Then Peter began to say **to-him, be-perceiving**, we have **released** all, and have followed you.

29 And Jesus answered and said, **amen** I say **to-you**, there is no man that has **released**, or **brothers**, or sisters, or father, or mother, or wife, or children, or lands, **on-account-of me**, and the **well-message**.

30 But he shall **take** a **hundred-mold** now in this **season**, houses, and **brothers**, and sisters, and mothers, and children, and lands, with **chases**; and in the **age, the coming, eternal** life.

31 But many **foremost** shall be last; and the last **foremost**.

32 And they were in the way **up-walking into** Jerusalem; and Jesus went before them: and they were **stupefied**; and as they followed, they were afraid. And he **beside-took** again the twelve, and began to tell them what **impending** things **together-walk to-him**,

33 That, **be-perceiving, we-are-up-walking into** Jerusalem; and the Son of man shall be **betrayed**[1625] **to-the first-rank-priests**, and **to-the** scribes; and they shall **down-judge** him to death, and shall **betray** him to the **nations**:

34 And they shall **in-childish-mock**[1626] him, and shall **whip** him, and shall spit upon him, and shall kill him: and the third day he shall **up-stand**.

35 And James and John, the sons of Zebedee, come **to-him**, saying, **Teacher**, we would that you **will produce** for us whatever we shall **request**.

36 And he said **to-them**, what **will** you that I **produce** for you?

37 They said **to-him, give to-us** that we may sit, one **out-of** your right hand, and the other **out-of** your left hand, in your glory.

38 But Jesus said **to** them, you **perceived** not what you ask: **are-you-powerful to-**drink of the cup that I drink of? And be baptized with the baptism that I am baptized with?

39 And they said **to-him, we-are-powerful**. And Jesus said **to-them**, you shall indeed drink of the cup that I drink of; and with the baptism that I am baptized withal shall you be baptized:

40 Yet, to sit **out-of** my right hand and **out-of** my left hand is not mine to give; but for whom it is **internally-prepared**.

41 And when the ten heard, they began to be **much-grief-ached**[1627] with James and John.

42 But Jesus **towards-called** them, and says **to-them**, you **perceived** that they which **seems first-rank of-**the **nations are-down-lord of-them**; and their **great-ones down-authority of-them**.

43 But not so shall it be among you: but whoever will be **great in** you, shall be your **attendant**.

44 And whoever of you will be the **foremost**, shall be **slave** of all.

45 For even the Son of man came not to be **attended**, but **attended-to**, and to give his **soul** a **ransom-loosen instead of-many**.

46 And they came to Jericho: and as he **cut-passage from** Jericho with his disciples and **sufficient**[1628] multitude, blind Bartimaeus,[1629] the son of Timaeus,[1630] sat by the way **towards-begging**.

47 And when he heard that it was Jesus of Nazareth, he began **screaming**, and say, Jesus, you Son of David, have mercy on me.

[1623] Or, fastidious (meticulous about eating); peevish (fretful, worry); difficult-food (eating), impractical
[1624] Stupefy is defined as: un able to think or feel properly
[1625] Lit., beside-given
[1626] Greek compound: "empaiktes" (in-sport (mock) as a boy), root means a child as disciplined
[1627] Or, resentful
[1628] Lit., to arrive; or, competent as if coming in season, ample in amount, fit in character
[1629] Lit., Hebrew: heir (son) of foulness
[1630] Lit., to be foul

48 And many **rebuked** him that he should **be-silent**: but rather, he **screamed** more, Son of David, have mercy on me.

49 And Jesus stood and **said** voice **him.** And they voiced the blind man, saying **to-him,** be **daring,**[1631] rise; he voice**s** you.

50 And he, casting away his garment, **up-stand,** and came **towards** Jesus.

51 And Jesus answered and said **to-him,** what **will** you that I should **produce to-you?** The blind man said **to-him, Rabboni,** that **I-might-be-up-looking.**

52 And Jesus said **to-him,** go your way; your faith has made you **saved.**[1632] And **soon** he**-up-looks,** and followed Jesus in the way.

MARK CHAPTER 11

1 And when they **near-squeeze** to Jerusalem, **to** Bethphage and Bethany, at the **mountain** of Olives, he sends two of his disciples,

2 And says **to** them, go into the village **down-instead**[1633] you: and as soon as you enter into it, you shall find a **colt** tied, **on which no** man sat; loose him, and **lead him.**

3 And if any man says **to-you,** why **are-you-producing** this? Say you that the Lord has need of him; and **soon** he will send him **here.**

4 And they went, and found the **colt** tied by the door **outside on the around-road**; and **they-are-loosing** him.

5 And certain of them that stood there said **to** them, what **are-you- producing,** loosing the **colt?**

6 And they said **to-them** even as Jesus had commanded: and they **released.**

7 And they brought the **colt** to Jesus and cast their garments on him; and he sat upon him.

8 And many spread their garments in the way: and others cut down branches off the trees and **spread-them** in the way.

9 And **the ones-before-leading,** and they that followed, **screaming,** saying, Hosanna;[1634] Blessed he that comes in the name of the Lord:

10 Blessed **the coming** kingdom **in the name of the Lord of-the** father David: Hosanna in the highest.

11 And Jesus entered into Jerusalem, and into the **priest-place**: and when he had looked round about upon all things, and **already evening,** he went out **to** Bethany with the twelve.

12 And the **on-tomorrow,** when they were come from Bethany, he was hungry:

13 And **perceiving** a fig tree afar off having leaves, he came, if **consequently** he might find anything **upon it**: and when he came to it, he found nothing but leaves; for **it-was not** the **season** of figs.

14 And Jesus answered and said **to-it,** no man eat fruit of you hereafter **into the age.** And his disciples heard.

15 And they come to Jerusalem: and Jesus went into the **priest-place,** and began to cast out **those selling and buying**[1635]in the **priest-place,** and overthrew the tables of the **coin-dealers,** and the seats of them that sold doves;

16 And would not **release** that any man should **through-bear**[1636] vessel through the **priest-place.**

17 And he taught, saying **to-them,** is it not written, my house shall be called of all nations the house of prayer? **Yet,** you **produced** it a **cave** of **robbers.**[1637]

18 And the scribes and **first-rank-priests** heard and sought how they might **from-ruin** him: for they feared him, because all the people were **pounded-out**[1638]at his **teaching.**

19 And when **it-became evening,** he **out-passage outside** the city.

20 And in the morning, as they passed by, they **perceived** the fig tree dried up from the roots.

21 And Peter **being-reminded** says **to-him, Rabbi, be-perceiving,** the fig tree which you **down-pray** is withered.

22 And Jesus answering says **to-them, hold** faith **of-God.**

23 Because, amen, I say **to-you,** that whoever shall say **to-the** mountain, be you removed, and be you cast into the sea; and shall not **through-judge** in his **heart**

[1631] Or, courageous
[1632] Or, safe
[1633] Or, facing
[1634] Derived of Hebrew: open-now, safe-now, save-now
[1635] Lit., to go to the market, redeem
[1636] Greek: "diaphero," to through-bear, transliterated as "differ" or "different"
[1637] Root: to plunder
[1638] Or lit., out-of-pound

but shall believe that those things which he says **is-becoming**; he shall have whatever he says.

24 Therefore I say **to-you**, **as-much-as** you **request**, when you pray, believe that **you-are-taking-them**, and **it-shall-be**[1639] **to-you**

25 And when you stand praying, **release,** if you-**are-holding down** any: that your Father also which is in heaven may **release** you, your **beside-falls**.

26 But if you do not **release**[1640] neither will your Father which is in heaven **release** your **beside-falls**.

27 And they come again to Jerusalem: and as he was walking in the **priest-place**, there come **to-him** the **first-rank-priests**, and the scribes, and the elders,

28 And say **to-him**, **in** what authority **you produce** these things? And who gave you this authority to **produce** these things?

29 And Jesus answered and said **to-them,** I will also ask of you one question, and answer me, and I will tell you by what authority I **produce** these things.

30 The baptism of John, was-it **out-of** heaven, or **out-of** men? Answer me.

31 And they **through-inventoried** with themselves, saying, if we shall say, **out-of** heaven; he will say, why then did you not believe him?

32 But if we shall say, **out-of** men; they feared the people: for all **held** John, that he **really-exists** a prophet **he-is**.

33 And they answered and said **to-Jesus,** we cannot **perceive**. And Jesus answering says **to-them,** neither do I tell you by what authority I **produce** these things.

MARK CHAPTER 12

1 And he began to speak **to-them** by parables. A man planted a vineyard, and **fenced,** and **excavated an under-trough,**[1641] and **house-built** a tower, and **give** it out to **land-workers**, and went **from-people**

2 And **near-squeeze the** season he sent to the **land-workers** a **slave**, that he might **take** from the **land-workers** of the fruit of the vineyard.

3 And they **taking him,** and **skinned** him, and **sent-him** empty.

4 And again he sent **towards** them another **slave**; and at him they cast stones, and **they-head**[1642] **him**, and sent **un-valued.**

5 And again he sent another; and him they killed, and many others; **skinning** some, and killing some.

6 Having yet therefore one Son, his beloved, he sent him also last **towards** them, saying, they will **in-turn**[1643] my son.

7 But those **land-workers** said among themselves, this is the heir; come, let us kill him, and the inheritance shall be ours.

8 And they **taking** him, and killed-**him**, and cast-**him** out of the vineyard.

9 What shall therefore the lord of the vineyard **produce**? He will come and **from-ruin** the **land-workers** and will give the vineyard **to** others.

10 And have you not read this scripture; The stone which the **house-builders** rejected[1644] is become **into** the head of the corner:

11 This was the Lord's doing, and it is marvelous in our eyes?

12 And they sought to **govern** him but feared the **multitude**: for they knew that he had spoken the parable **towards** them: and they **released** him and went their way.

13 And they send **towards-him** certain of the Pharisees and of the Herodians, to **hunt-lead** him in words.

14 And when they were come, they say **to-him**, **Teacher,** we **perceived** that you are true, and care for no man: for you **look not into the face** of men, but teach the way of God in truth: is it lawful to give **census-tax** to Caesar, or not?

15 Shall we give, or shall we not give? But he, **perceived** their hypocrisy, said **to-them,** why you **probe-test** me? Bring me a **denarius**, that I may **perceived**.

16 And they brought. And he says **to-them,** whose this image and **inscription**? And they said **to-him**, Caesar's.

[1639] Future tense of "to exist"
[1640] Lit., from-let-go
[1641] Or vat
[1642] Or to sum up
[1643] Or invert with respect
[1644] From-seem

17 And Jesus answering said **to-them, give** to Caesar the things that are Caesar's, and to God the things that are God's. And they marveled at him.

18 Then come **to-him** the Sadducees, which say there is no resurrection; and they asked him, saying,

19 Teacher, Moses wrote **to-us,** if a man's brother dies, and **down-**leave wife, and **release** no children, that his brother should **take** his wife, and **up-stand** seed **to-his** brother.

20 Now there were seven **brothers**: and the **foremost got** a wife and dying **release** no seed.

21 And the second **take** her, and died, neither **release** he any seed: and the third likewise.

22 And the seven had her, and **from-let-go** no seed: last of all the woman died also.

23 In the resurrection therefore, when they shall **up-stand**, whose wife shall she be of them? for the seven had her to wife.

24 And Jesus answering said **to** them, do you not therefore err, because you **perceived** not the **Scriptures**, neither the power of God?

25 For when they shall **up-stand out-of** the dead, they neither marry, nor are given in marriage; but are as the angels which are in **the heavens.**

26 And as touching the dead, that **they-are-being-raised:**[1645] have you not read in the **scroll** of Moses, how in the **thorn-**bush God spoke **to-him,** saying, I[1646] the God of Abraham, and the God of Isaac, and the God of Jacob?

27 He is not the God of the dead, but the God of the living: you therefore **much seduced.**

28 And one of the scribes came, and having heard them **together-seeking,** and perceiving that he had answered them **ideally,** asked him, which is the **foremost** commandment of all?

29 And Jesus answered him, the **foremost** of all the commandments, Hear, Israel; the Lord our God is one Lord:

30 And you shall love the Lord your God with **whole** your **heart,** and with **whole** your soul, and with **whole** your **through-mind,** and you're your **whole force:** this the **foremost** commandment.

31 And the second like, this, you shall love your neighbor as yourself. There is none other commandment **larger**[1647] than these.

32 And the scribe said **to-him, ideal, Teacher,** you have said the truth: for there is one God; and there is none other **more** he:

33 And to love him with the **whole heart,** and with the **whole synthesizing,** and with the **whole** soul, and with the **whole force,** and to love neighbor as himself, is more than all **whole-burnt-offerings** and sacrifices.

34 And when Jesus **perceived** that he answered **mind-holding,** he said **to-him,** you are not far from the kingdom of God. And no man after that **ventured to-**ask him.

35 And Jesus answered and said, while he taught in the **priest-place,** how say the scribes that Christ is the Son of David?

36 For David himself said **in** the Holy Spirit, the Lord said to my Lord, sit you **out-of** my right hand, **until** I make your haters your footstool.

37 David therefore himself **saying** him Lord; and **which-place** is he his son? And the **many multitude** heard him **sweetly.**

38 And he said **to-them** in his **teaching, be-looking** of the scribes, which **willing** to **about-walk** in **robes,** and **embraced** in the marketplaces,

39 And the **foremost-seats** in the synagogues, and the **foremost-reclines in expensive-dinners**:

40 Which **down-eat** widows' houses, and for a **pretense**[1648] make long prayers: these shall **take more-excessive judgment-result.**[1649]

41 And Jesus sat **down-opposite** the **treasury-guard-watch and** beheld how the people cast money into the **placed-into-tomorrow-guard**: and many that were rich cast in much.

42 And there came a certain poor widow, and she threw in two mites,[1650] which make a **farthing.**[1651]

43 And he called **towards,** his disciples, and says **to-them, amen** I say **to-you,** that this poor widow has cast

---

[1645] In the Greek text, this word is present tense and passive voice
[1646] Lit., Ego
[1647] Larger, especially in age
[1648] Greek: before-appear, outward show
[1649] Greek: "krima," transliterated as "crime" and also means judgment
[1650] Greek: "lepton;" a small coin
[1651] Greek: "kodrantes (quadrans), a fourth part of a donkey

more in, than all they which have cast into the **placed-into-tomorrow-guard**:

44 For all did cast in **out-of** their abundance; but she of her **deficit**[1652] did cast in all that she had, all her **livelihood**.

MARK CHAPTER 13

1 And as he **out-passage out-of** the **priest-place**, one of his disciples says **to-him, Teacher, perceive** what stones and what **house-**buildings!

2 And Jesus answering said **to-him, You-are-looking to-these great house-**buildings? There shall not be **released** one stone upon another, that shall not be **down-loosed**.

3 And as he sat upon the **mountain** of Olives **down-opposite** the **priest-place**, Peter, James, John, and Andrew asked him privately,

4 Tell us, when shall these things be? and what the sign when all these things **impending to-be-together-finish**?

5 And Jesus answering them began to say, **be-looking** lest any **seduce** you:

6 For many shall come in my name, saying, I am; and shall **seduce** many.

7 And when you shall hear of **battles** and **rumor-hearings** of **battles**, not **be-you-uproar-wailing**; **because it-is binding to-become**; but the **finish** not yet.

8 For nation shall rise against nation, and kingdom against kingdom: and there shall be **quakes down spots**, and there shall be famines and **agitations**: these the **origin**[1653] of **pang**.[1654]

9 Yet, **be-looking to-you**rselves: for they shall **betray** you up to **Sanhedrin**; and in the synagogues you shall be **skinned**: and you shall be brought before **leaders** and kings for my sake, **into a witness to-**them.

10 And the **well-message it-is-binding, foremost, to-be-preached** among all nations.

11 Yet, when they shall lead, and **betray you, not before-portion-worry** what you shall speak, neither do you **to-be-of-interest**: but whatever shall be given you in that hour, that speak you: **because** it is not you that speak, but the Holy Spirit.

12 Now the brother shall betray the brother **in to** death, and the father the **child**; and children shall **upon-stand on** parents and shall cause them to be put to death.

13 And you shall be **detested** of all **through my name**: but he that shall **under-remain into** the **finish**, the same shall be saved.

14 But when you shall **perceive** the abomination[1655] of desolation,[1656] spoken of by Daniel the prophet, standing where not **it-is-binding**, (let him that reads, **have-thought**,) then let them that be in Judaea flee **into** the mountains:

15 And let him that is on the housetop not go down into the house, neither enter, to **lift** anything out of his house:

16 And let him that is in the field not turn back again for to **lift** his garment.

17 But woe **to-them** that **in belly holding**, and **to-them** that suckle in those days!

18 And pray you that your **fleeing** be not in the winter.[1657]

19 For those days shall be **tribulation**, such as was not from the **original** of the creation which God created **until now**, neither shall **be-becoming.**

20 And except that the Lord had shortened those days, no flesh should be saved:[1658] but **through the elect**, whom he has chosen, he has shortened the days.

21 And then if any man shall say **to-you, be-perceiving**, here is Christ; or, **be-perceiving**, there; believe not:

22 Because, false-christs and false-prophets shall rise, and shall show signs and wonders,[1659] to seduce, if **powerful**, even the elect.

23 But **be-looking, be-perceiving**, I have foretold you all things.

24 But in those days, after **the tribulation**, that the sun shall be darkened, and the moon shall not give her light,

---

[1652] Or want, lateness
[1653] Or principality
[1654] Or, pang, sudden pain
[1655] Or stink
[1656] Or, to lay waste, lonesome
[1657] Or, pouring rain (in winter)
[1658] Or, safe
[1659] Greek word "teras," transliterated "terror," archaic meaning of monster (things)

25 And the stars of heaven shall **out-of-fall,** and the powers that are in **the heavens** shall be shaken.

26 And then shall they see the Son of man coming in the clouds with **much** power and glory.

27 And then shall he send his angels and shall gather together his elect from the four winds, from **extremity of-land until extremity of-heaven.**

28 Now learn a parable of the fig tree; when her branch is yet tender, and **sprout** leaves, you know that summer **near-squeezes**:

29 So you in like manner, when you shall **perceive** these things **becoming,** know that it is **near-squeeze** at the doors.

30 Amen, I say **to-you,** that this generation shall not pass, **until** all these things **become.**

31 Heaven and earth shall pass away: but my words shall not pass away.

32 Yet, about that day and hour **perceive** no man, no, not the angels which are in heaven, neither the Son, **except** the Father.

33 Be-looking, be-sleepless and pray: for you **perceived** not when the **season** is.

34 As a man taking a far journey, who **released** his house, and gave authority to his **slave**s, and to every man his work, and commanded the **door-seer**[1660] to **wake.**

35 Wake you therefore: for you **perceived** not when the **lord** of the house **is-coming,** at evening, or at midnight, or at the **rooster-sounding,** or morning:

36 Not coming suddenly he find you sleeping.

37 And what I say **to-you** I say **to** all, **awake.**

MARK CHAPTER 14

1 After two days was the **Passover,** and of **Unfermented:** and the **first-rank-priests** and the scribes sought how they might **govern** him by **trick-bait** and put to death.

2 But they said, not on the **festival,** lest there be an **uproar**[1661] of the people.

3 And being in Bethany in the house of Simon the leper, as he sat at meat, there came a woman having an alabaster[1662] of **myrrh nard, believe, much-finish;** and she **together-rut**[1663] the **alabaster,** and **down-poured** on his head.

4 And there were some that **much-grief-ached**[1664] within themselves, and said, why was this **from-run** of the **myrrh became**?

5 Because this is-powerful to-be-sold for more than three hundred **denarii,**[1665] and have been given to the poor. And they **in-snorts-with-anger**[1666] against her.

6 And Jesus said, **release** her; why **cut** you her? She **beside-hold worked** an **ideal** work **into** me.

7 Because, you have the poor with you always, and **whenever** you will, **you-are-powerful** to **produce** them good: but me you have not always.

8 What-she-had, she produced: **she-before-takes** to **myrrh** my body **into** the burying.

9 Amen, I say **to-you, wherever** this **well-message** shall be preached **into** the whole world, also that she **produced** shall be spoken of **into** a memorial of her.

10 And Judas Iscariot, one of the twelve, went **to** the **first-rank-priests,** to betray him **to-them.**

11 And when they heard, they were **cheerful,** and promised to give him money. And he sought how, **good-season, betraying** him.

12 And the **foremost Day of Unfermented,** when they killed the **Passover,** his disciples said **to-him,** where **will** you that we go and **internally-prepare** that you may eat the **Passover**?

13 And he sent two of his disciples, and says **to-them,** go you into the city, and there shall meet you a man bearing a pitcher of water: follow him.

14 And wherever he shall go in, say you to the **house-owner** of the house, the **Teacher** says, where is the **guest-chamber,**[1667] where I shall eat the **Passover** with my disciples?

15 And he will show you a **great up-room, spread,** prepared: there make **preparations to-us.**

16 And his disciples **went-out,** and came into the city, and found as he had said **to**-them: and they **internally-prepared** the **Passover.**

17 And in the evening **he-is-coming** with the twelve.

[1660] Or watcher
[1661] Or disturbance
[1662] Alabaster is the name of a stone
[1663] Together-rub, together-path as worn out
[1664] Or, resentful
[1665] Or, ten donkeys, (300 x 10 donkeys)
[1666] Or, in-thundered
[1667] Lit, to down-loose

18 And as they **reclined** and did eat, Jesus said, **amen** I say **to-you**, one **out-**of you which eats with me shall betray me.

19 And they began to be **distress-sad**, and to say **to-him** one by one, **no-any** I? and another, **no-any** I?

20 And he answered and said **to-them**, one **out-of** the twelve, that **in-baptize** with me in the dish.

21 The Son of man indeed goes, as it is written of him: but woe to that man **through** whom the Son of man is betrayed! [1668] **Ideal it-was** for that man if he had never been born.

22 And as they did eat, Jesus **taking** bread, and blessed, and **broke**, and gave to them, and said, **take**, eat: this is my body.

23 And he **taking** the cup, and when he had given thanks,[1669] he gave to them: and they all drank **out-of** it.

24 And he said **to-them**, this is my blood of the New[1670] **Covenant**, which is **outpoured about** many.

25 Amen I say **to-you**, I will drink no more **out-of** the **offspring** of the vine, until that day that I drink it **new-fresh** in the kingdom of God.

26 And when they had sung a hymn, they went out into the **mountain** of Olives.

27 And Jesus says **to** them, all you shall be **scandalized**[1671] because of me this night: for it is written, I will smite[1672] the shepherd, and the sheep shall be scattered.

28 But after that I am risen, I will go before you into Galilee.

29 But Peter **showed to-him**, although all shall be **scandalized, but** not I!

30 And Jesus says **to-him, amen** I say **to-you**, that this day, in this night, before the **rooster** voice twice, you shall **from-contradict** me three.

31 But he spoke the **excessively**, if **it-is-binding to-die** with you, I will not **from-contradict** you. Likewise, also said they all.

32 And they came to a **space** which was named Gethsemane:[1673] and he says to his disciples, sit you here, **until** I shall pray.

33 And he **takes beside** him Peter, James, and John, and began to be **out-of-stupefy**,[1674] and to be **heavy-distressed;**

34 And says **to** them, my soul is **about-sad until** death: **remain** here and **keep-awake**.

35 And he went **before** a little, and fell on the ground, and prayed that, if **it-is powerful**, the hour might pass from him.

36 And he said, Abba,[1675] Father, all things **powerful to-you; beside-carry** this cup from me: **but** not what I will, but what you **will**.

37 And he comes, and finds them sleeping, and says **to-Peter**, Simon, **you-sleep**? **Not you-are-forceful to-wake** one hour?

38 Wake-you and pray, **that not,** you enter into **probe-testing**. The spirit **indeed before-feels**, but the flesh **without-strength**.

39 And again he went away, and prayed, and spoke the same words.

40 And when he returned, he found them asleep again, (for their eyes were heavy,) neither **perceived** they what to answer him.

41 And he comes the **third,** and says **to** them, sleep, and **remain resting**: it is enough,[1676] the hour is come; **be-perceiving**, the Son of man is betrayed[1677] into the hands of sinners.

42 Rise, let us go; **be-perceiving**, he that betrays me **near-squeezed**.[1678]

43 And **soon**, while he yet spoke, **beside-becoming** Judas, one of the twelve, and with him **much** multitude with swords and **trees, beside** the **first-rank-priests** and the scribes and the elders.

44 And he that betrayed him had given them a **together-sign**, saying, **whom-ever** I shall kiss,[1679] **He it-is; govern** him, and lead away safely.[1680]

[1668] Lit., beside-given
[1669] Lit, good-graciousness
[1670] Or, fresh
[1671] Or, snared
[1672] Or to knock
[1673] Oil-press
[1674] Stupefy: unable to think or feel properly
[1675] Abba could be Hebrew words for father ("Ab") and the Hebrew word for come ("ba") compounded—Come-Father, Father
[1676] Lit, from-holding
[1677] Lit., beside-given
[1678] Perfect tense, active voice
[1679] Or, friendly
[1680] Or, without-failing

45 And as soon as he was come, he goes **soon to-him**, and says, **Rabbi, Rabbi**; and kissed[1681] him.

46 And they **upon-take the** hands on him and **governed** him.

47 And one of them that **beside-stood** by drew **the** sword, hit the slave of the **first-rank-priest**, and **released** his **ear**.[1682]

48 And Jesus answered and said **to-them,** are you come out, as against a **robber,**[1683] with swords and **trees** to **take** me?

49 I was daily **towards** you in the **priest-place** teaching, and you **governed** me not: but **that** the **Scriptures be-filled.**

50 And they all **released** him and fled.

51 And there followed him a certain young man, having a linen cloth cast about **upon** naked; and the **youths governed** him:

52 And he **down-leave** the linen and fled from them naked.

53 And they led Jesus **towards** the **first-rank-priest**: and with him were assembled all the **first-rank-priests** and the elders and the scribes.

54 And Peter followed him afar off, **until within into the yard**[1684] of the **first-rank-priest**: and he sat with the **subservient-ones**[1685] and warmed himself **towards** the fire.

55 And the **first-rank-priests** and **whole** the **Sanhedrin** sought for witness against Jesus to put him to death; and found none.

56 For many bare **false-witness** against him, but their **witnesses were not equal.**

57 And there arose certain, and bare **false-witness downing** him, saying,

58 We heard him say, I will **down-loose** this temple that is made with hands, and **through** three days I will **house-build** another made without hands.

59 And **in-this-way,** neither was their witness equal.

60 And the **first-rank-priest** stood up in the middle, and asked Jesus, saying, answer you nothing? What these **down**-witness you?

61 But he-**was-silent** and answered nothing. Again, the **first-rank-priest** asked him, and said **to-him**, are you the Christ, the Son of the Blessed?

62 And Jesus said, I am: and you shall see the Son of man sitting **out-of** the right hand of power and coming **with**[1686] the clouds of-**the** heaven.

63 Then the **first-rank-priest through-break** his clothes, and says, what need we any further witnesses?

64 You have heard the blasphemy. What **shines to-you?** And they all **down-judge** him to be **liable**[1687] of death.

65 And some began to spit on him, and to cover his face, and to **curtail-with-the-fist** him, and to say **to-him**, prophesy: and the **subservient-ones**[1688] did cast **to-slap** him.

66 And as Peter was beneath in the **yard**, there comes **first** of the **girls** of the **first-rank-priest**:

67 And when she **perceived** Peter warming himself, she looked upon him, and said, and you also **were** with Jesus of Nazareth.

68 But he **contradicted**, saying, I **perceived** not neither **acquainted**[1689] what you say. And he went out into the **before-yard**;[1690] and the **rooster** voice.

69 And a maid **perceived** him again and began to say **to-them** that **beside-stood** by this is **out-of** them.

70 And he **contradicted** it again. And a little after, they that **beside-**stood by said again to Peter, **truly** you are of them: **because** you are a Galilean, and your speech **similar**

71 But he began to **ban**[1691] and to swear, I **perceive** not this man of whom you speak.

72 And **out of-second** the **rooster** voice. And Peter **is-reminded** the **declaration** that Jesus said **to-him, that prior** the **rooster** voice twice, you shall **from-contradict** me three. And when he **upon-cast,**[1692] he wept.

[1681] Or down-friend
[1682] Greek: earlet, or earlobe
[1683] One who plunders
[1684] Yard as open to the air or wind
[1685] Lit., under-oarsman, generally a subordinate
[1686] Greek: "meta," after, with
[1687] Greek: in-hold, to hold in
[1688] Lit., under-oarsman, generally a subordinate
[1689] Greek: upon-stand, to put the mind upon, to be acquainted with, comprehend, be present
[1690] Front-yard
[1691] Or anathema
[1692] Reflected

MARK CHAPTER 15

1 And **soon on** the morning the **first-rank-priests producing together-counsel-plan** with the elders and scribes and the whole **Sanhedrin**, and bound Jesus, and **carried-him-away**, and **betrayed**[1693] to Pilate.

2 And Pilate asked him, **are** you the King of the Jews? And he answering said **to-him,** you **have-said.**

3 And the **first-rank-priests** accused him of many things: **yet** he answered nothing.

4 And Pilate asked him again, saying, answer you nothing? **Be-perceiving** how-**much of-you they-are-down-witnessing**

5 **Yet,** Jesus yet answered nothing; so that Pilate marveled.

6 Now at **festivals** he **from-loosed to-them** one prisoner, **whomever** they **requested**.

7 And there was, **said,** Barabbas,[1694] bound with the **together-insurgents,**[1695] who had **produced** murder in the insurrection.

8 And the multitude **up-crying** began **asking, downing he-produced to**-them.

9 But Pilate answered them, saying, you will that I **from-loose to-you** the King of the Jews?

10 For he knew that the **first-rank-priests** had **betrayed** him for **ill-will.**

11 But the **first-rank-priests** moved the people, that he should rather **from-loose** Barabbas **to-them.**

12 And Pilate answered and said again **to-them,** what will you then that I shall **produce, to-whom** you **say** the King of the Jews?

13 And they **screamed** again, crucify him.

14 Then Pilate said **to-them,** why, what evil has he **produced**? And they **screamed** the more exceedingly, crucify him.

15 And Pilate, **plan-counseling suffice**[1696] **produce** the people, **from-loosed** Barabbas **to-them,** and **betrayed**[1697] Jesus, **whipped-him,** to be crucified.

16 And the soldiers led him away into the yard, called Praetorium,[1698] and they **together-call** the whole **mass-of-men.**[1699]

17 And they clothed him with purple, and platted a **victor's-crown** of thorns, and put it about him,

18 And began **to-embrace** him, **cheer,** King of the Jews!

19 And they **thumped** him on the head with a reed, and did spit upon him, and **placing the** knees worshipped him.

20 And when they had **in-childishly-mocked** him, they **unclothed** the purple from him, and **clothed him his private garments,** and led him out to crucify him.

21 And they compel one Simon a Cyrenian, who passed by, coming **from field,** the father of Alexander and Rufus, to bear his cross.

22 And they bring him **to-the** place Golgotha, which is, being interpreted, the place of a skull.

23 And they gave him wine to drink, **having-myrrh:** but he **took-it** not.

24 And when they had crucified him, they parted his garments, casting lots upon them, what every man should **lift.**

25 And it was the third hour, and they crucified him.

26 And the **inscription** of his **cause** was written over, The King of the Jews.

27 And with him they crucify two thieves: the one **out-of** his right hand, and the other **out-of** his left.

28 And the scripture was **filled,** which says, and he was **inventoried** with the **lawless.**

29 And they that passed by **blasphemed** him, wagging their heads, and saying, ah, you that **down-loose** the temple, and **house-build** in three days,

30 Save yourself and come down from the cross.

31 Likewise also the **first-rank-priests in-childish-mocked**[1700] said among themselves with the scribes, he saved others; himself **not he-is-powerful to-**save.

[1693] Lit., beside-given
[1694] Heir (Bar) of father (Abba)
[1695] Lit., together-standing, together-dissension
[1696] Lit., to arrive; or, competent as if coming in season, ample in amount, fit in character
[1697] From-give
[1698] Governor's courtroom
[1699] Greek: "speira, transliterated "spire" meaning to coil, figuratively a mass of roman military cohort, or a squad of Levitical janitors
[1700] Greek compound: "empaiktes" (in-sport (mock) as a boy), root means a child as disciplined

32 Let Christ the King of Israel descend now from the cross, that we may **perceived** and believe. And they that were crucified with him **defamed**[1701] him.

33 And when the sixth hour was come, there **became** darkness over the whole land until the ninth hour.

34 And at the ninth hour Jesus cried with a loud voice, saying, Eloi, Eloi, lama sabachthani? which is, being interpreted, My God, my God, why has you forsaken me?

35 And some of them that **beside**-stood by, when they heard, said, **be-perceiving, he-is-sounding Elijah.**

36 And one ran and filled a sponge full of vinegar, and put on a reed, and gave him to drink, saying, **release**; let us **perceive** whether Elijah will come to **lift** him down.

37 And Jesus **released**[1702] with a **great** voice, and **out-breathe.**

38 And the veil of the temple was **split** in two from the top to the bottom.

39 And when the centurion, which **beside-stood contrary**[1703] **of-him, perceived** that he so **screamed,** and **out-breathed,** he said, truly this man was the Son of God.

40 There were also women looking on afar off: among whom was Mary Magdalene, and Mary the mother of James the less and of Joses, and Salome;

41 (Who also, when he was in Galilee, followed him, and **attended to-him**); and many other women which **together-step to-him into** Jerusalem.

42 And **already** evening **becoming, since** it was the **Preparation, which** is, **before-Sabbath,**

43 Joseph of **Arimathea,** a **well-figured counsellor-planner,** which also **toward-receiving** the kingdom of God, came, and went in **daring to** Pilate, and **asked of-the** body of Jesus.

44 And Pilate marveled if he were already dead: and **toward-calling** the centurion, he asked him **if long-ago he-died.**

45 And when he knew of the centurion, he gave the body to Joseph.

46 And he buying linen, and **lift** him down, and wrapped him in the linen, and laid him in a **remembrance-tomb** which was hewn out of a rock and rolled a stone **to-the** door of the **remembrance-tomb.**

47 And Mary Magdalene and Mary of Joses **theatre-spectated** where he was **placed.**

MARK CHAPTER 16

1 And when the Sabbath **through-becoming,** Mary Magdalene, and Mary, of James, and Salome, bought spices, that they might come and **oil**[1704] him.

2 And very morning the first of the **Sabbaths,** they came **to-the remembrance-tomb** at the rising of the sun.

3 And they said among themselves, who shall roll us away the stone from the door of the **remembrance-tomb**?

4 And when they looked, they **perceived** that the stone was rolled away; **because** it was **tremendously great**

5 And entering into the **remembrance-tomb,** they **perceived** a **youth** sitting **in** the right side, clothed in a long white garment; and they were **out-of-stupefied.**[1705]

6 And he says **to-them,** be not **out-of-stupefied;** you seek Jesus of Nazareth, which was crucified; he is risen; he is not here: **be-perceiving** the **spot** where they **placed** him.

7 But go your way, tell his disciples and Peter that he goes before you into Galilee: there shall you see him, as he said **to-you.**

8 And they went out quickly and fled from the **remembrance-tomb;** for they trembled and were **ecstasized,**[1706] neither said they **to-none nothing, because** they were afraid.

9 Now when was risen early the **foremost** of the **Sabbath,** he **shined foremost** to Mary Magdalene, **from** whom he had **out-of-cast** seven **demons.**

10 She went and **from-message** them that had been with him, as they mourned and wept.

11 And they, when they had heard that he was alive, and had been seen of her, believed not.

12 After that he **shined** in **another-different** form **to** two of them, as they walked, and went into the **field.**

[1701] Lit., notorious, name
[1702] Or forgave
[1703] Greek compound: in-anti, in front of, opposite, antagonistic
[1704] Root: grease, fat
[1705] Unable to think or feel properly
[1706] Overpowering influence (on the mind)

13 And they went and **from-message to** the **remaining-ones**: neither believed they them.

14 Afterward he **shined to** the eleven as they sat at meat and **defamed**[1707] **the unbelief of-them** and **hard-heart**, because they believed not them which had **theatre-spectate** him after he was risen.

15 And he said **to-them, travel** into all the world, and preach the **well-message to-every creation**.

16 He that believes and is baptized shall be saved; but he that believes not shall be **down-judged**.

17 And these signs shall **beside-**follow them that believe; in my name shall they cast out **demons**; they shall speak with **new-fresh** tongues;

18 They shall **lift** serpents; and if they drink any deadly thing, it shall not **hurt-hinder** them; they shall lay hands on the **un-leaving-weakness**, and they **hold ideal-beauty.**

19 So then after the Lord had spoken **to-them**, he **up-taken** into **the** heaven, and sat **out-of** the right hand of God.

20 And they went forth, and preached **universally**, the Lord **together-working** and **stabilizing** the **Word through** signs **on-following.** Amen.

[1707] Lit., notorious, name

THE GOSPEL OF LUKE

LUKE CHAPTER 1

1 **Since-indeed** many have taken in hand to **up-arrange** a **narrative**[1708] of those **practices** which are **fully-burdened** in us,

2 Even as they **beside-give** them **to-us**, which from the **original** becoming **same-seers**, and **subservient-ones**[1709] of the Word.

3 **It-seemed** to me also, having had **exact beside-follow** of all things **from-above**, to write **to-you** in order, **governor** Theophilus,

4 That you may-know the **certainty**[1710] of those things, **which** you have been **catechized**.[1711]

5 **It-became** in the days of Herod, the king of Judaea, a certain priest named Zacharias, **out of-on-day of-**Abia: and his wife of the daughters of Aaron, and her name Elisabeth.

6 And they were both righteous before God, **traveling** in all the commandments and **righteous-deeds** of the Lord blameless.

7 And they had no child, because that Elisabeth was barren, and they both were **before-stepped, in days**.

8 And it **became**, that while he **in the priests-duties** before God in the order **on-day of-him**,

9 According to the **ethics**[1712] of the **priest-duty**, his **lot**[1713] was to burn incense when he went into the temple of the Lord.

10 And the whole multitude of the people were praying **outside** at the **hour** of incense.

11 And there appeared **to-him** an angel of the Lord standing **out-of** the right side of the **sacrifice-place** of incense.

12 And when Zacharias **perceived**, he was **agitated**, and fear fell upon him.

13 But the angel said **toward him**, fear not, Zacharias: **through-that** your **bind-begging** is heard; and your wife Elisabeth shall bear you a son, and you shall call his name John.

14 And you shall have **cheerful** and **jumping**-joy; and many **shall-be-cheerful upon** his **genesis**.

15 For he shall be **great** in the sight of the Lord and shall drink neither wine nor **intoxicant**; and he shall be filled with the Holy Spirit, even from his mother's womb.

16 And many of the **sons** of Israel shall he turn to the Lord their God.

17 And he shall go before him in spirit and power of **Elijah,** to turn the **hearts** of the fathers to the children, and the **un-perusable** to the **disposition** of the **righteous-ones**; **to-internally-prepare** a people **constructed** for the Lord.

18 And Zacharias said **towards** the angel, whereby shall I know this? **Because** I am an old man, and my wife **before-stepped in her days**.

19 And the angel answering said **to-him**, I am Gabriel, that **beside-stand** in the presence of God; and am sent to speak **towards** you, and to **well-message** you these.

20 And, **be-perceiving**, you shall be dumb, and not **is-powerful** to speak, until the day that these things **becomes**, **which not** you believe my words, which shall be **filled into** their season.

21 And the people **toward-seem** for Zacharias, and marveled **in the delaying-uninterrupted-time, him,** in **the** temple.

22 And when he came out, not **he-is-powerful to-**speak **to** them: and they **upon-knew** that he had seen a vision in the temple: for he **through-nodding to** them, and **through-remained blunted**.[1714]

23 And **it became**, that, as soon as the days of his **people-work**[1715] were accomplished, he departed to his own house.

24 And after those days his wife Elisabeth **together-took**,[1716] and **about-hid** herself five months, saying,

25 **In-this-way** has the Lord **produced to-me** in the days **to-which he-upon-perceived,** to **lift** my **defaming**[1717] in men.

26 And in the sixth month the angel Gabriel was sent from God **into** a city of Galilee, named Nazareth,

---

[1708] Or recital; Greek: through-lead
[1709] Lit., under-oarsman, generally a subordinate
[1710] Greek: "a" (negative participle) and "sphallo" (to "fail"), security, certainty
[1711] Greek: "katecho" (down-echo) transliterated as "catechize" (forms of questions and answers used for instructing), reverberate, sound, roar
[1712] Or custom
[1713] Greek: "lagchano" to chance, to determine by lot
[1714] Or, deaf-mute, root, choppy, to beat the chest
[1715] Lit., laos (people)-ergon (work); "liturgy"
[1716] Or, to clasp, to conceive
[1717] Or, notoriety, to name

27 Toward a virgin **given-a-espoused-souvenir** to a man whose name was Joseph, of the house of David; and the virgin's name Mary.

28 And the angel came **towards** her, and said, **cheer you graced**, the Lord with you: blessed are you **in** women.

29 And when she **perceived**, she was **through-agitated** at his saying, and **through-inventoried from-where may-be this enfolding-the arms?**

30 And the angel said **to** her, fear not, Mary: for you have found **grace beside** God.

31 And, **be-perceiving**, you shall **together-take** in your womb, and bring forth a son, and shall call his name **Jesus.**

32 He shall be **great**, and shall be called the Son of the Highest: and the Lord God shall give **to-him** the throne of his father David:

33 And he shall reign over the house of Jacob **into the ages**; and of his kingdom there shall be no **finish**.

34 Then said Mary **to-the** angel, how shall this be, seeing I know not a man?

35 And the angel answered and said **to-her**, The Holy Spirit shall come upon you, and the power of the Highest shall overshadow you: **through-which** also **the Holy** which shall be born **out-**of you shall be called the Son of God.

36 And, **be-perceiving**, your cousin Elisabeth, she has also **together-taken** a son in her old age: and this is the sixth month with her, who was called barren.

37 That not shall-be-un-powerful, beside the God, every Declaration.

38 And Mary said, **be-perceiving** the **slave** of the Lord; **may-it-become to-me** according **to-your** declaration. And the angel departed from her.

39 And Mary arose in those days, and went into the **mountains** with **speed**, into city of Juda;

40 And entered into the house of Zacharias and **enfold-the-arms** Elisabeth.

41 And it **became**, that, when Elisabeth heard the **enfold-the-arms** of Mary, the babe **jumped** in her womb; and Elisabeth was filled **of** the Holy Spirit:

42 And she **up-sound** with a **great** voice, and said, blessed are you **in** women, and blessed the fruit of your womb.

43 And **where** this to me, that the mother of my Lord should come **towards** me?

44 Because, **be-perceiving**, as soon as the voice of your **enfolding-the-arm into my** ears, the babe **jump-for-joy** in my womb.

45 And **happy** she that believed: for there shall be a **maturing** of those things which were told her **beside** the Lord.

46 And Mary said, my soul does magnify the Lord,

47 And my spirit has **jumped-for-joy** in God my Savior.

48 For he has **gazed on** the **humiliation** of his **slave**: because, **be-perceiving**, from **now** all generations shall call me **happy**.

49 For he that is **powerful** has done to me **great** things; and holy his name.

50 And his mercy on them that fear him **into** generation to generation.

51 He **produced government**[1718] with his arm; he has scattered the **above-shining-ones**[1719] in the **through-mind** of their **heart**.

52 He has **down-lift** the **dynasties**[1720] from thrones and **elevate humble-ones**.

53 He has filled the hungry with good things; and the rich he has **out-of-sent** empty.

54 He has **instead-taken**[1721] his **child** Israel, in remembrance of mercy;

55 As he spoke to our fathers, to Abraham, and to his seed **into the age**.

56 And Mary **remain together to-her** about three months and returned **into** her own house.

57 Now Elisabeth **filled the uninterrupted-time of-the to-produce**; and she **birthed** a son.

58 And her neighbors and her **together-kin** heard how the Lord had showed **magnified** mercy upon her; and they **together-cheer to-**her.

59 And it-**became**, that on the eighth day they came to circumcise the child; and they called him Zacharias, after the name of his father.

[1718] Greek: kratos, transliterated as "great" and also means vigor, strength, to use strength, to rule, government, translated as "cracy" in democracy—people(demo)-government (kratos)

[1719] Or, appearing above others
[1720] Or power-ones
[1721] Or, help, support

60 And his mother answered and said, no; but he shall be called John.

61 And they said **to** her, there is none of your **together-kin** that is called by this name.

62 And they **nodded** to his father, how he **will** have him called.

63 And he asked for a writing **tablet,** and wrote, saying, His name is John. And they marveled all.

64 And his mouth was opened **at-the-thing-itself**, and his tongue, and he spoke, and **blessed the** God.

65 And fear **became** on all that **about-housed** them: and all these **declarations** were **through-talked in whole mountains** of Judaea.

66 And all they that heard **placed** in their **hearts**, saying, what **consequently the** child shall be? And the hand of the Lord was with him.

67 And his father Zacharias was filled with the Holy Spirit, and prophesied, saying,

68 Blessed the Lord God of Israel; for he has **bishop**[1722] and **loosed** his people,

69 And has raised up a horn of salvation for us in the house of his **boy** David;

70 As he spoke **through** the mouth of his holy prophets, **from the age,**

71 That we should be saved from our **enemies-haters**, and from the hand of all that **detest** us;

72 To **produce** the mercy to our fathers, and to remember his holy covenant;

73 The oath which he swore to our father Abraham,

74 That he would **give to-us**, we being **rushed-rescue** out of the hand of our **haters**, might **be-hired-service to-**him without fear,

75 In **intrinsic-right** and **righteous-togetherness, before** him, all the days of our life.

76 And you, child, shall be called the prophet of the Highest: for you shall go before the face of the Lord to **internally-prepare** his ways.

77 To give knowledge of salvation **to-his** people by the **releasing** of their sins,

78 Through the **gut-compassion** mercy of our God; **in which** the **East** from **out-of** high has **bishoped** us,

79 Upon-appear to-them that sit in darkness and the shadow of death, to **down-immediate** our feet into the way of peace.

80 And the child grew, and **governs to-spirit,** and was in the **lonesome until** the day of his showing **towards** Israel.

LUKE CHAPTER 2

1 And **it became** in those days, that there went out a **dogma**[1723] from Caesar Augustus, that all the **housed-land** should be taxed.

2 (And this taxing was first made when Cyrenius was **leader** of Syria.)

3 And all went to be taxed, everyone into his own city.

4 And Joseph also **up-walked** from Galilee, out of the city of Nazareth, into Judaea, **to-the** city of David, which is called Bethlehem; (because he was of the house and **fatherhood** of David:)

5 To be taxed with Mary his **to-espoused souvenir,** wife, being **in-swell-with-child.**

6 And so it was, that, while they were there, the days were **filled** that she should be **producing.**

7 And she **produced** her firstborn son, and wrapped him in swaddling clothes, and laid him in a manger; because there was no room for them in the inn.[1724]

8 And there were in the same **space** shepherds **playing-the-flute** in the field, **watching, watch** over their flock by night.

9 And, **be-perceiving**, the angel of the Lord came upon them, and the glory of the Lord shined round about them: and they were **great** afraid.

10 And the angel said **to-them,** fear not: for, **be-perceiving**, I bring you **well-message** of **great cheerfulness**, which shall be to all people.

11 For **to-you** is **produced** this day in the city of David a Savior, which is Christ the Lord.

12 And this a sign **to-you**; you shall find the babe wrapped in swaddling clothes, **laying** in a manger.

13 And suddenly there was with the angel a multitude of the heavenly host praising God, and saying,

---

[1722] Greek compound: upon-peer about, upon-skeptic, upon-scout, upon watch, upon-watch, upon-sentry
[1723] Accepted beliefs, authoritative decrees that are not questioned, from "dokeo," to think, to seem,
[1724] Lit., down-loose

14 Glory to God in the highest, and on earth, peace, well-seem **in** men.

15 And it **became,** as the angels were gone away from them into heaven, the shepherds said one to another, let us now go even **to**-Bethlehem, and **perceive** this thing which **became,** which the Lord has **declared to-us.**

16 And they came with **speed,** and found Mary, and Joseph, and the **baby laying** in a manger.

17 And when they had **perceived,** they made **through-known** the **declaration** which was told them **about** this child.

18 And all they that heard marveled at those things which were told them by the shepherds.

19 But Mary **together-guard** all these things, and **together-cast**[1725] in her **heart.**

20 And the shepherds returned, glorifying, and praising God for all the things that they had heard and **perceived,** as it was told **towards** them.

21 And when eight days were **filled** for the circumcising of the child, his name was called **Jesus,** which was so named of the angel before he was **together-taken** in the womb.

22 And when the days of her **cleansing down** the law of Moses were **filled,** they brought him to Jerusalem,[1726] to **beside-stand** to the Lord;

23 (As it is written in the law of the Lord, every male that opens the womb shall be called holy to the Lord;)

24 And to offer a sacrifice **down** that which is said in the law of the Lord, a pair of turtledoves, or two young pigeons.

25 And, **be-perceiving,** there was a man in Jerusalem, whose name Simeon; and the same man just and **well-taker,**[1727] **toward-receiving** the **beside-call**[1728] of Israel: and the Holy Spirit was upon him.

26 And it was **apprised**[1729] **to-him** by the Holy Spirit, that he should not **perceive** death, before he had **perceived** the Lord's Christ.

27 And he came **in** the Spirit into the **priest-place**: and when the parents brought in the child Jesus, to do for him after the **ethics** of the law,

28 Then **welcomed** he him up in his arms, and blessed God, and said,

29 **Owner,** now **you-from-loose** your **slave** in peace, according **to-your declaration**:

30 For **my** eyes have **perceived** your salvation,

31 Which you have **internally-prepared** before the face of all people;

32 A light **into revelation of-nations**, and the glory of your people Israel.

33 And Joseph and his mother marveled at those things which were spoken **about** him.

34 And Simeon blessed them, and said **to**-Mary his mother, **Be-perceiving,** this-one is-**laid** for the fall and **resurrection**[1730] of many in Israel; and **into** a sign which shall be **disputed**[1731]

35 (Yea, a sword shall pierce through your own soul also,) that the through-**inventory** of many hearts may be revealed.

36 And there was one Anna, a prophetess, the daughter of Phanuel, of the tribe of Asher: she was **before-stepped in many days**, and had lived with a husband seven **years** from her virginity;

37 And she a widow of about **eighty-four years**, which **divorced**[1732] not from the **priest-place,** but **hired-servant to**-fasting and **to-beg-binding** night and day.

38 And she coming in that instant[1733] **instead-same-saying to** the Lord and spoke **about** him to all them that **toward-welcome redemption-loosening** in Jerusalem.

39 And when they had **finished** all things **down** the law of the Lord, they returned into Galilee, to their city Nazareth.

40 And the child grew, and **governed to-spirit,** filled with wisdom: and the grace of God was upon him.

41 Now his parents went to Jerusalem every **year** at the **festival** of the **Passover.**

[1725] Or, combined
[1726] Greek: Priests-peace (hierou-priest, sacred) and salem (peace)
[1727] Eulabes-to take (things) well
[1728] Or consolation
[1729] Greek: "chrematizo," to furnish what is needed, divine response; secular, constituting a business, employ, to bears as a title, to apprise (to give notice, state of affair, inform)
[1730] Or up-standing
[1731] Lit, anti-word, refute, dispute
[1732] Lit., "aphistemi" from-stand, the root word for "apostasies:" feminine of "apostasion" (divorce); a thing that separates.
[1733] On-stand

42 And when he **became** twelve **years** old, they **up-walked into** Jerusalem after the **ethics** of the **festival**.

43 And when **matured** the days, as they returned, the child Jesus **under-remained** in Jerusalem; and Joseph and his mother knew not.

44 But they, **do-by-law** him to have been in the **together-road**,¹⁷³⁴ went a day's journey; and they sought him among **together-kin** and **known**.

45 And when they found him not, they turned back again **into** Jerusalem, seeking him.

46 And it **became**, that after three days they found him in the **priest-place**, sitting in the middle of the **teachers**, both hearing them, and asking them questions.

47 And all that heard him were **ecstasy**¹⁷³⁵ at his **synthesizing** and answers.

48 And when they **perceived** him, they were **out-of-pounded**; and his mother said **to-him**, **child**, why **do-you to-us in-this-way**? **Be-perceiving**, your father and I have sought you **pained**.

49 And he said **to** them, **why** is it that you sought me? **Perceive** you not that **in the things of my Father, it-is-binding to-me to-be**?

50 And they **synthesized**¹⁷³⁶ not the saying which he spoke **to-them**.

51 And he went down with them, and came to Nazareth, and was **subordinate**¹⁷³⁷ **to-them**: but his mother **through-watched** all these **declarations** in her **heart**.

52 And Jesus **progressed**¹⁷³⁸ in wisdom and stature, and **to-grace** with God and man.

LUKE CHAPTER 3

1 Now in the fifteenth **years** of the reign of Tiberius Caesar, Pontius Pilate being **leader** of Judaea, and Herod being tetrarch¹⁷³⁹ of Galilee, and his brother Philip tetrarch of Ituraea and of the **space** of Trachonitis, and Lysanias the tetrarch of Abilene,

2 Annas and Caiaphas being the **first-rank-priests**, the **Word of God** came **to** John the son of Zacharias in the **lonesome**.

3 And he came into all the **space** about Jordan, preaching the baptism of **change-thinking** for the **release**¹⁷⁴⁰ of sins:

4 As it is written in the **scroll** of the words of **Isaiah** the prophet, saying, the voice of one crying in the **lonesome**, **internally-prepare** the way of the Lord, make his paths **soon**.

5 Every valley shall be filled, and every mountain and hill shall be **humbled**; and the **warped-leg into soon**, and the **uneven-rocks** ways **into level**:

6 And all flesh shall see the salvation of God.

7 Then said he to the multitude that **out-passage** to be baptized of him, **offspring** of vipers, who has **under-show** you to flee from the **impending swelling-anger**?

8 **Produce** therefore fruits **deserving** of **change-thought**, and not begin to say within yourselves, we have father Abraham: **because** I say **to-you**, that God **is-powerful out-**of these stones to **wake** children **to-**Abraham.

9 And now also the axe is laid **toward** the root of the trees: every tree therefore **not producing ideal** fruit is **exscind**,¹⁷⁴¹ and cast into the fire.

10 And the **multitude** asked him, saying, what shall we **produce** then?

11 He answers and says **to-them**, he that has two coats, let him **change-give to-him** that has none; and he that has **food**, let him do likewise.

12 Then also came **tax-collectors** to be baptized, and said **to-him**, **teacher**, what shall we do?

13 And he said **to** them, no more than that which is **through-arranged to-**you.

14 And the soldiers likewise **asked** of him, saying, and what shall we do? And he said **to** them, **intimidate**¹⁷⁴² no man, neither be-**fig-informant;**¹⁷⁴³ and be content with your **soldier-rations**.

---

¹⁷³⁴ Greek: "sunodia" (companionship in a journey); "synod" (an assembly of clergy)
¹⁷³⁵ Overwhelming feelings
¹⁷³⁶ Together-send
¹⁷³⁷ Under-arranged
¹⁷³⁸ Before-chop
¹⁷³⁹ Fourth-first-rank
¹⁷⁴⁰ Lit., from-let-go
¹⁷⁴¹ Lit., out-of-cut, to cut out
¹⁷⁴² Lit., through-shake, to shake thoroughly
¹⁷⁴³ Or, a reporter of the law forbidden the exportation of figs, defraud, exact unlawfully, extortion

15 And as the people were **toward-seeming**, and all men **through-inventoried** in their **hearts about** John, whether he was the Christ, or not;

16 John answered, saying **to-all,** I indeed baptize you with water; but one **forceful** than I **comes**, the **straps** of whose **sandals** I am not **sufficient** to unloose: he shall baptize you in the Holy Spirit and fire:

17 Whose **winnowing-fork** in his hand, and he will **thoroughly-cleanse** his floor, and will gather the wheat into his garner; but the chaff he will burn with fire **unextinguished**

18 And many **other-different** things in his **beside-call** he-**good-message to-the** people.

19 But Herod the tetrarch, being **evidence-exposed** by him for Herodias his brother Philip's wife, and for all the **wicked-hurtful-hurts** which Herod had **produced**,

20 Added yet this above all, that he **down-lock** John in **guard-watch**.

21 Now when all the people **became** baptized, **it became**, that Jesus also being baptized, and praying, the heaven was opened,

22 And the Holy Spirit descended **to-bodily perception as-if** a dove upon him, and a voice **becoming out-of** heaven, which said, you are my beloved Son; in you I am **good-seem**.

23 And Jesus himself began to be about thirty **years**, being (as **to-do-by-law**) the son of Joseph, which was of Heli,

24 Which was of Matthat, which was of Levi, which was of Melchi, which was of Janna, which was of Joseph,

25 Which was of Mattathias, which was of Amos, which was of Naum, which was of Esli, which was of Nagge,

26 Which was of Maath, which was of Mattathias, which was of Semei, which was of Joseph, which was of Juda,

27 Which was of Joanna, which was of Rhesa, which was of Zorobabel, which was of Salathiel, which was of Neri,

28 Which was of Melchi, which was of Addi, which was of Cosam, which was of Elmodam, which was of Er,

29 Which was of Jose, which was of Eliezer, which was of Jorim, which was of Matthat, which was of Levi,

30 Which was of Simeon, which was of Juda, which was of Joseph, which was of Jonan, which was of Eliakim,

31 Which was of Melea, which was of Menan, which was of Mattatha, which was the son of Nathan, which was of David,

32 Which was of Jesse, which was of Obed, which was of Booz, which was of Salmon, which was of Naasson,

33 Which was of Aminadab, which was of Aram, which was of Esrom, which was of Phares, which was of Juda,

34 Which was of Jacob, which was of Isaac, which was of Abraham, which was of Thara, which was of Nachor,

35 Which was of Saruch, which was of Ragau, which was of Phalec, which was of Heber, which was of Sala,

36 Which was of Cainan, which was of Arphaxad, which was of Sem, which was of Noe, which was of Lamech,

37 Which was of Mathusala, which was of Enoch, which was of Jared, which was of Maleleel which was of Cainan,

38 Which was of Enos, which was of Seth, which was of Adam, which was of God.

LUKE CHAPTER 4

1 And Jesus being full of the Holy Spirit returned from Jordan, and was led **in** the Spirit into the **lonesome**,

2 Being forty days **probe-tested under** the Devil. And in those days, he did eat nothing: and when they were **together-finished**, afterward **he-hungered**.

3 And the Devil said **to-him**, if you be the Son of God, command this stone that it **become** bread.

4 And Jesus answered him, saying, it is written, that man shall not live by bread alone, but by every **Declaration** of God.

5 And the Devil, taking him up into a high mountain, showed **to-him** all the kingdoms of the **housed-land** in a **stigma**[1744] of **uninterrupted-time**.

6 And the Devil said **to-him,** all this **authority** will I give you, and the glory of them: for that is **betrayed**[1745] **to-me;** and to **whomever,** I will, I give it.

7 If you therefore **will** worship me, all shall be yours.

[1744] Or, mark, to prick, to stick

[1745] Or from-give

8 And Jesus answered and said **to-him**, you **under-lead**[1746] behind me, Satan: **because** it is written, you shall worship the Lord your God, and **to**-him only **shall-you-be-hired-service.**

9 And he led him to Jerusalem, and stand him on a **winglet**[1747] of the **priest-place**, and said **to-him**, if you be the Son of God, cast yourself down from **within**:

10 **Because** it is written, he shall give his angels **command about** you, to **through-watch** you:

11 And in hands they shall **lift you**, **lest** you **toward-strike**[1748] your foot against a stone.

12 And Jesus answering said **to-him**, it is said, you shall not **out-of-probe-test** the Lord your God.

13 And when the Devil had **together-finished** all the **probe-testing**, he **divorces**[1749] from him **until** season.

14 And Jesus returned in the power of the Spirit into Galilee: and there **went-out** a fame of him **down whole** of-the **about-space about him**.

15 And he taught in their synagogues, being glorified **by** all.

16 And he came to Nazareth, where he had been **nurtured**: and, as his **ethics** was, he went into the synagogue on the **Sabbath**, and stood up to read.

17 And there was **given to-him** the **little-scroll** of the prophet **Isaiah**. And when he had opened the **scroll**, he found the **spot** where it was written,

18 The Spirit of the Lord is upon me, because he has anointed me to **evangelize**[1750] **to**-poor; he has sent me to **cure** the **through-crushed** heart, to preach release[1751] to the captives, and recovering of sight to the blind, **release to-them** that are **crushed**,[1752]

19 To preach the **welcomed years** of the Lord.

20 And he closed the **little-scroll**, and he **from-give** to the **subservient**[1753] and sat down. And the eyes of all them that were in the synagogue were **look-stretching to-**him.

21 And he began to say **towards** them, **today** is this Scripture **filled** in your ears.

22 And all witness **to-him** and **marveled upon** the gracious words which **out-passage out-of** his mouth. And they said, is not this Joseph's son?

23 And he said **to-them,** you will surely say **to-me** this **parable**, Physician,[1754] **serve-therapy** yourself: whatever we have heard **becoming** in Capernaum, do also here in your country.

24 And he said, **amen,** I say **to-**you, no prophet is **received** in his **father-country**.

25 Yet I tell you of a truth, many widows were in Israel in the days of **Elijah**, when the heaven was **locked** three **years** and six months, when **great** famine **became** throughout all the land;

26 But **toward** none of them was **Elijah dispatched**, if not, to Sarepta, of Sidon, **to** a woman a widow.

27 And many lepers were in Israel **upon Elisha** the prophet; and none of them was **cleaned**, saving Naaman the Syrian.

28 And all they in the synagogue, when they heard these things, were filled with **sacrifice-anger**,

29 And rose up, and out-**cast him out** of the city, and led him **until** the brow[1755] of the **mountain on which** their city was **house-built**, that they might **down-hang him**.

30 But he passing through the **middle** of them **traveled-beyond**,

31 And came down to Capernaum, a city of Galilee, and taught them **in the Sabbaths**.

32 And they were **out-of-pounded** at his **teaching**: for his word was **in authority**.

33 And in the synagogue, there was a man, who had a spirit of an unclean **demon**, and cried out with a **great** voice,

34 Saying, **let it be**; what have we to do with you Jesus of Nazareth? Are you come to **from-ruin**[1756] us? I **perceive** who you are; the **Holy-One** of God.

35 And Jesus rebuked[1757] him, saying, **be-muzzled**, and come out of him. And when the **demon** had thrown

---

[1746] Lit., one word "hupage," to under-lead, to lead under, go away, etc.
[1747] Or extreme corner
[1748] Or, stub, towards-chop
[1749] Lit., "aphistemi" from-stand, the root word for "apostasies:" feminine of "apostasion" (divorce); a thing that separates.
[1750] Or **well-message**
[1751] Lit., from-let-go
[1752] Or, wrecked, broken
[1753] Lit., under-oarsman, generally a subordinate
[1754] Or, curer, healer
[1755] The eye-"brow," brink of a precipice
[1756] Greek: "apo" (from) and "alethros" (ruin), to destroy fully
[1757] Tax-upon, charge

him in the middle, he came out of him, and **hindering** him not.

36 And they were all **stupefied**, and spoke among themselves, saying, what a word this! For with authority and power he **under-arranges** the unclean spirits, and they come out.

37 And the **echo about** him **out-passage** into every **spot** of the **about-space**.

38 And he **up-stand** out of the synagogue and entered into Simon's house. And Simon's wife's mother was **together-held to-fever, great**; and they **asked** him **about** her.

39 And he stood over her and rebuked the fever; and **it-released** her: and **instantly** she arose and **attended to-them**.

40 Now when the sun was setting, all they that had any **weak** with **various nauseas lead** them **towards him**; and he **upon-placed** his hands on every one of them and **served-therapy** them.

41 And **demons** also came out **from** many, **screaming**, and saying, you are Christ the Son of God. And he rebukes, not **permitting** them to speak for they **perceived** that he was Christ.

42 And when it **became** day, he departed and went into a **lonesome spot**: and the **multitude** sought him, and **until they-came to-him**, and **down-hold**[1758] him, that he should not depart from them.

43 And he said **towards** them, **it-is-binding to-me to-evangelize** the kingdom of God to **other-different** cities also: **that into this** am I sent.

44 And he preached in the synagogues of Galilee.

LUKE CHAPTER 5

1 And **it became**, that, as the **multitude upon-laying to-him** to hear the **Word of God**, he stood by the lake of Gennesaret,

2 And **perceived** two ships standing by the lake: but the fishermen were gone out of them and were **from-plunging the** nets.

3 And he **in-stepped** into one of the ships, which was Simon's, and **asked** him to **upon-up-lead** a **little** from the land. And he sat down and taught the **multitude** out of the ship.

4 Now when he had **paused**, speaking, he said **to** Simon, **upon-up-lead** into the deep, and let down your nets **into catch**.

5 And Simon answering said **to-him, Commander**,[1759] we have **fatigue-cut** all the night, and have **taken** nothing: nevertheless, at your **declaration** I will let down the net.

6 And **producing** this, they **together-locked many** fishes: and their net broke.

7 And they **down-nod to**-partners,[1760] which were in the **other-different** ship, that they should come and **together-take** them. And they came, and filled both the ships, so that they began to sink.

8 When Simon Peter **perceived**, he **towards-fell** at Jesus' knees, saying, depart from me; for I am a sinful man, Lord!

9 For **amazement about-hold him**, and all that were with him, at the **catch** of the fishes which they had **together-taken.**

10 And so also James, and John, the sons of Zebedee, which were **communing** with Simon. And Jesus said **to** Simon, fear not; from **now** you shall catch men.

11 And when they had brought their ships to land, they **released** all, and followed him.

12 And it **became** when he was in **first** city, **be-perceiving** a man full of leprosy: who **perceiving** Jesus fell on his face, and **beg-bind** him, saying, Lord, if you **will**, you-**are-powerful to**-make me clean.

13 And he **out-stretched the** hand, and **fastened to-him**, saying, **I-am-willing: be-clean**. And **soon** the leprosy departed from him.

14 And he **beside-message** him to tell no man: but go, and show yourself to the priest, and offer for your cleansing, **down-as** Moses **towards-arrange, into** a **witness to**-them.

15 But so much the more went there a **saying about** him: and **many** multitudes came together to hear, and to be **served-therapy under** him **from** their **weakness**.

16 And he **under-spacing** himself into the **lonesome** and prayed.

[1758] Or, detained
[1759] Greek: "epistasis," upon-stand," to stand over, to stop, stoppage,
Commander, appointee over, Stopper
[1760] Or, with-holders, sharers

17 And it **became, in first of-the** days, as he was teaching, that there were Pharisees and doctors[1761] sitting by, which were come out of every town of Galilee, and Judaea, and Jerusalem: and the power of the Lord was to **cure** them.

18 And, **be-perceiving**, men brought in a **cot;**[1762] a man which was taken with a **paralytic**: and they sought to bring him in, and to **place** before him.

19 And when they could not find **through which** they might bring him in because of the multitude, they **up-walked** upon the housetop, and let him down through the tiling with **cot** into the **middle** before Jesus.

20 And when he **perceived** their faith, he said **to-him,** man, your sins are **released to-you.**

21 And the scribes and the Pharisees began to **through-inventory,** saying, who is this which speaks blasphemies? Who **is-powerful to-release**[1763] sins, but God alone?

22 But when Jesus **upon-know** their **through-inventory,** he answering said **to** them, what **through-inventory** you in your **hearts**?

23 Whether is **good-cut,** to say, your sins be **released to-**you; or to say, rise and **about-walk**?

24 But that you may **perceive** that the Son of man has **authority** upon earth to **release** sins, (he said **to-the paralytic,**) I say **to-you,** arise, and **lift** your **cot,** and go **into your** house.

25 And **instantly** he rose up before them, and **lift** that **which** he **down-laid on,** and departed to his own house, glorifying God.

26 And they were all **ecstasized,**[1764] and they glorified God, and were filled with fear, saying, we have **perceived paradoxes**[1765] today.

27 And after these things he went forth, and saw a **tax-collector,** named Levi, sitting at the **tax-office**: and he said **to-him,** follow me.

28 And he **down-leave** all, rose up, and followed him.

29 And Levi made him a **great reception** in his house: and there was a **much multitude** of **tax-collectors** and of others that **down-recline** with them.

30 But their scribes and Pharisees **grumbled** against his disciples, saying, why do you eat and drink with **tax-collectors** and sinners?

31 And Jesus answering said **to-them,** they that are **healthy-grown** need not a physician; but they that are **evil holders**.

32 I came not to call the righteous, but sinners to **change-thought.**

33 And they said **towards him,** why do the disciples of John fast often, and make prayers, and likewise of the Pharisees; but yours eat and drink?

34 And he said **to** them, **not you-are-powerful** the **sons** of the **bride-chamber,** while the bridegroom is with them, **to produce fasting,?**

35 But the days will come, when the bridegroom shall be **lifted** from them, and then shall they fast in those days.

36 And he spoke also a parable **to** them; no man puts a piece of **a new-fresh** garment upon an old; if otherwise, then both the **new-fresh** makes a **split,** and the piece that was out of the **new-fresh together-sound**[1766] not with the old.

37 And no man puts new-**young** wine into old bottles; else the **new-young** wine will burst the **leathers,** and be spilled, and the **leathers** shall **from-ruin.**

38 But new wine must be put into **new-young leathers**; and both are preserved.

39 No man also having drunk old **soon wills new-young**: for he says, the old is useful-**employed.**[1767]

LUKE CHAPTER 6

1 And **it became in** the **second-foremost**[1768] Sabbath, that he went through the **sown**; and his disciples plucked the **stalk-stand** of corn, and did eat, rubbing in hands.

2 And certain of the Pharisees said **to**-them, why do you that which is not lawful to do on the Sabbaths?

3 And Jesus answering them said, have you not read so much as this, what David did, when he was hungry, and those-who were with him;

[1761] Lit., Law-teachers
[1762] Or (re)cline
[1763] Lit., from-let-go
[1764] Greek: "ekstasis," transliterated as "ecstasy," out-of-stand, displacement of the mind, strong feelings (good or bad) that absorbs the mind
[1765] Greek: para (beside) and doxa (glory, seeming), transliterated "paradox"
[1766] "Symphony"
[1767] Or furnish what is needed, suitable
[1768] Majority Text. The Alexandrian reads "trough-passing"

4 How he went into the **House of God,** and did take and eat the **breads of-the purpose,**[1769] and gave also **to-them** that were with him; which is not lawful to eat but **only** the priests alone?

5 And he said **to**-them, that the Son of man is Lord also of the Sabbath.

6 And it **became** also on another Sabbath, that he entered into the synagogue and taught: and there was a man whose right hand was withered.

7 And the scribes and Pharisees watched him, whether he would heal in the Sabbath; that they might **accuse** [1770] him.

8 But he **perceived** their **through-inventory** and said to the man which had the withered hand, Rise, and stand in the **middle.** And he arose and stood.

9 Then said Jesus **to**-them, I will ask you one thing; is it lawful on the Sabbath to **good-do**, or to **evil-do**, to save life, or to **from-ruin?**

10 And looking round about upon them all, he said **to**-the man, **out-of-stretch** your hand. And he **produced**: and his hand was restored **healthy-grown** as the **other-same.**

11 And they were filled with **un-mind**;[1771] and **through-talked** one with another what they might do to Jesus.

12 And **it became** in those days, that he went out into a mountain to pray, and **through-night**[1772] in **through-prayer-wish** to God.

13 And when it **became** day, he **towards-sounds** his disciples: and of them he chose twelve, whom also he named apostles;

14 Simon, (whom he also named Peter,) and Andrew his brother, James and John, Philip, and Bartholomew,

15 Matthew and Thomas, James of-the Alphaeus, and Simon called Zealots,

16 And Judas of James, and Judas Iscariot, which also was the traitor.[1773]

17 And he came down with them, and stood in the **spot foot-level**, and the **multitude** of his disciples, and **filled many of-the** people out of all Judaea and Jerusalem, and from the **beside-salted**[1774] of Tyre and Sidon, which came to hear him, and to be **cured** of their **nauseas**;

18 And they that were **multitude-harassed**[1775] from unclean spirits: and they were **served-therapy**.

19 And the whole multitude sought to **fasten to-him**: for there went **power** out of him and **cured** all.

20 And he lifted up his eyes on his disciples, and said, **happy the** poor: for yours is the kingdom of God.

21 Happy the hunger now: for you shall be filled. **happy the** weeping now: for you shall laugh.

22 Happy are you, when men shall hate you, and when they shall **from-define**[1776] you, and shall **defame,**[1777] and cast out your name as **wicked-hurtful**, on-account of-the Son of man.

23 Be-cheerful, in that day, and **joy-jump:** for, be-perceiving, your reward **much** in heaven: for **according-to these** did their fathers **to-the** prophets.

24 But woe **to-you** that are rich! for you have received your **beside-calling**.

25 Woe **to-you** that are full! for you shall hunger. Woe **to-you** that laugh now! for you shall mourn and weep.

26 Woe **to-you,** when all men shall speak **ideal** of you! **According-to these** did their fathers to the **false-prophets.**

27 But I say **to-you** which hear, love your **haters,**[1778] do good **to-them** which **detest**[1779] you,

28 Bless them that **down-curse** you, and **towards-pray-wish** for them which **upon-threat** you.

29 And **to-him** that **thump** you on the cheek **beside-hold** also the **other-same;** and him that **lifts** your cloak **prevent** not **the shirt** also.

30 Give to every man that ask of you; and of him that **lifts** yours ask not again.

31 And as you **will** that men do **to-you**, do you also **to-them** likewise.

32 For if you love them which love you, what thank have **you? Because** sinners also love those that love them.

[1769] Lit., before-place, to place before, or to place in advance
[1770] Lit., categorized
[1771] Or no-mind (irrational behavior)
[1772] Or, to sit up all night
[1773] Lit., before-give
[1774] Or sea-coast
[1775] Or, in-mobbed
[1776] Lit., from-horizon
[1777] Lit., notorious, name
[1778] Passionate dislike
[1779] Intense dislike

33 And if you **good-producing to-them** which **good-producing to-you**, what **grace** have **you**? **Because** sinners also do the same.

34 And if you lend of whom you **expect** to **from-take**, what **grace** have **you**? **Because,** sinners also **lend** to sinners, to **from-take the equal**.

35 But love you your **haters**, and **good-produce**, and lend, **from-expecting** for nothing again; and your **pay** shall be **much**, and you shall be the **sons** of the Highest: for he **furnish-what-is-needed to** the **ungracious** and the **wicked-hurtful**.

36 Become **pity-merciful**, as your Father also **pities-mercifully**.[1780]

37 Judge not, and you shall not be judged: **down-justice** not, and you shall not be **down-justice; from-looses**,[1781] and you shall be **from-loosed**:

38 Give, and it shall be given **to-you**; **ideal** measure, **packed**,[1782] and shaken, and running over, shall men give **into your** bosom. For same measure **to-which** **you-measure** shall be measured **to-you**.

39 And he spoke a parable **to-them, is-powerful** the blind **to-lead** the blind? Shall they not both fall into the ditch?

40 The disciple is not above his **teacher**: but every one that is **down-fresh**[1783] shall be as his **teacher**.

41 And why **be-looking** you the **withered-twig** that is in your brother's eye, but **down-mind** not the **timber** that is in your own eye?

42 Either how **are-you--powerful to-**say **to-your** brother, Brother, let me pull out the **withered-twig** that is in your eye, when you yourself **be-perceiving** not the **timber** that is in your own eye? You hypocrite, cast out first the **timber** out of your own eye, and then shall you see clearly to pull out the **withered-twig** that is in your brother's eye.

43 For an **ideal** tree **produces** not **rotten** fruit; neither does a **rotten** tree **produces ideal** fruit.

44 For every tree is known **out-of** his own fruit. **Because,** of thorns men do not gather figs, nor of a **thorn-bush** gather they grapes.

45 A good man out of the good **placed-into-tomorrow** of his **heart before-carry** that which is good; and an evil man out of the **wicked-hurtful**[1784] **placed-into-tomorrow**[1785] of his **heart before-carry** that which is **wicked-hurtful**: for of the **surplus**[1786] of the **heart** his mouth speaks.

46 And why call you me, Lord, Lord, and **produce** not the things which I say?

47 Whoever comes to me, and hears my sayings, and **produces** them, I will show you to whom he is like:

48 He is like a man which house-built a house, and **dug** deep, and **place** the foundation on a rock: and when the **flood-tide becomes,** the **river towards-tear** that house, and **not is-forceful to-shake** it: for it was founded upon a rock.

49 But he that **hears,** and **produces** not, is like a man that **spacing-from** a foundation **house-**built a house upon the earth; against which the **river towards-tear,** and **soon** it fell; and the **tear** of that house was **great**.

LUKE CHAPTER 7

1 Now when he had **filled** all his **declarations** in the **hearing** of the people, he entered into Capernaum.

2 And a certain centurion's **slave**, who was **in-value to-him**, was **evil holding**, and **impending to-be-finished**.

3 And when he heard of Jesus, he sent **to-him** the elders of the Jews, **asking** him that he would come and **through-save** his slave.

4 And when they came to Jesus, they **beside-called** him **speedily,** saying, that he was **deserving** for whom he should **hold-near** this:

5 For he loves our nation, and he has **house-**built us a synagogue.

6 Then Jesus went with them. And when he was now not far from the house, the centurion **dispatched** friends **to-him,** saying **to-him,** Lord, **flay** not yourself: for I am not **sufficient** that you should enter under my roof:

[1780] the feeling of sorrow and compassion caused by the suffering and misfortunes of other
[1781] Or release
[1782] "Piezo" to pack, to squeeze by hand, to press
[1783] Or, adjusted, mended, framed
[1784] Greek: "poneros," hurtful to others
[1785] Greek: "thesauros," transliterated as thesaurus, also means a deposit, treasure,
[1786] Or excess

Luke

7 **Through-which,** neither myself **deserving** to come **towards** you: but say in a word, and my **boy** shall be **cured**.

8 For I also am a man set under authority, having under me soldiers, and I say **to-one,** go, and he goes; and to another, come, and he **comes**; and to my **slave**, do this, and he does.

9 When Jesus heard these things, he marveled at him, and turned him about, and said **to-the multitude** that followed him, I say **to-you,** I have not found **so-much** faith, no, not in Israel.

10 And they that were **dispatched**, returning to the house, found the **slave healthy-grown** that had been **weak**.

11 And it **became** the day after, that he went into a city called Nain; and many of his disciples went with him, **sufficient and** much **multitude**.

12 Now when he came **near-squeeze** to the gate of the city, **be-perceiving,** there was a dead **out-of-carried,** the **only-born** son of his mother, and she was a widow: and **sufficient multitude** of the city was **together to-her.**

13 And when the Lord **perceived** her, he had **gut-compassion** on her, and said **to** her, **sob**[1787] not.

14 And he came and **fastened to-the** bier: and **the-ones-bearing** stood. And he said, youth, I say **to-you, awake**!

15 And he that was dead sat up and began to speak. And he **gives** him to his mother.

16 And there came a fear on all: and they glorified God, saying, that a **great** prophet is risen up **in** us; and, that God has **bishoped**[1788] his people.

17 And this **saying** went forth **in whole** Judaea about him, and **about** all the **about-space**

18 And the disciples of John **from-message** of-him **about** all these things.

19 And John **toward-calling** two of his disciples **dispatched** to Jesus, saying, **are** you he that should come? Or **toward-seem another-same?**

20 When the men **came to-him,** they said, John Baptist has sent us **to-you,** saying, **are** you he that should come? Or **toward-seem another-same?**

21 And in that same hour he **served-therapy** many of **nauseas** and plagues, and of **wicked-hurtful** spirits; and **to** many blinds he **graced** sight.

22 Then Jesus answering said **to** them, go your way, and **from-message** John what things you have **perceive** and heard; how that the blind see, the **limping** walk, the lepers are **cleaned**, the **blunted**,[1789] hear, the dead are raised, the poor **evangelized**.[1790]

23 And **happy is-he**, whoever shall not be **scandalized**[1791] in me.

24 And when the **angels** of John were departed, he began to speak **to-the** people concerning John, what went you out into the **lonesome** to see? A reed shaken with the wind?

25 But what went you out for to see? A man clothed in **soft** raiment? **Be-perceiving**, they which are **gloriously** appareled, and **living enfeebling**,[1792] **under-original-ones,** are in **the royals**.

26 But what went you out to **perceive**? A prophet? Yea, I say **to-you,** and **more-exceed** than a prophet.

27 This is **about** whom it is written, **Be-perceiving**, I send my **angel** before your face, which shall **be-constructing** your way before you.

28 Because, I say **to-you**, among those that are born of women there is not a **larger**[1793] prophet than John the Baptist: but he that is **smaller** in the kingdom of God is **larger** than he.

29 And all the people that heard, and the **tax-collectors, rendered-righteous** God, being baptized with the baptism of John.

30 But the Pharisees and lawyers rejected the **planned-counsel** of God **un-placed into** themselves, being not baptized **under** him.

31 And the Lord said, **to-whom** then shall **assimilate** the men of this generation? And to what are they **similar**?

32 They are like **to** children sitting in the marketplace, and **toward-sounding one-another,** and saying, we

---

[1787] Or weep
[1788] Greek compound: upon-peer about, upon-skeptic, upon-scout, upon watch, upon-watch, upon-sentry
[1789] Or deaf-mute; root, choppy, to beat the chest
[1790] Or, **well-messaged**
[1791] Or, snared
[1792] From the Greek word "thrupto" to break up or to enfeeble the mind and body by indulgences
[1793] Larger, especially in age

have piped **to-you**, and you have not danced; we have wailed **to-you**, and you have not **sobbed**.

33 For John the Baptist came neither eating bread nor drinking wine; and you say, He has a **demon**.

34 The Son of man is come eating and drinking; and you say, **be-perceiving** a gluttonous man, and a **wine-drinker**,[1794] a friend of **tax-collectors** and sinners!

35 But wisdom is **made-righteous from** all her children.

36 And one of the Pharisees desired him that he would eat with him. And he went into the Pharisee's house and **reclined**.

37 And, **be-perceiving**, a woman in the city, which was a sinner, when she knew that **he-reclined** in the Pharisee's house, brought an alabaster-stone of **myrrh**

38 And stood **beside** his feet, behind, weeping, and began to wash his feet with tears, and did wipe with the hairs of her head, and kissed his feet, and **oil-greased**[1795] with the **myrrh**.

39 Now when the Pharisee which had bidden him **perceived**, he spoke within himself, saying, this man, if he were a prophet, would have known who and **where-from the** woman that **attached** to-him: for she is a sinner.

40 And Jesus answering said **towards him**, Simon, I have somewhat to say **to-you**. And he **showed**, **Teacher**, say on.

41 There was a certain creditor which had two debtors:[1796] the one owed five hundred denarius,[1797] and the other fifty.

42 And when they had nothing to **from-give**, he **graced** them both. tell me therefore, which of them will love him **more**?

43 Simon answered and said, I **under-take** that to whom he **graces more**. And he said **to-him**, you have rightly[1798] judged.

44 And he turned to the woman, and **showed to** Simon, **you-look-at** this woman. I entered **into your** house; you gave me no water for my feet: but she has **moistened** my feet with tears and wiped with the hairs of her head.

45 You gave me no kiss: but this woman since I came in has not **through-leave** to kiss my feet.

46 My head with **olive-oil** you **did not oil**: but this woman has **oiled** my feet with **myrrh**.

47 **This grace,** I say **to-you**, her sins, which are many, are **released**;[1799] for she loved much: but to whom **few** is **released**, loves **few**.

48 And he said **to**-her, your sins are **released**.

49 And the **ones-together-recline** began to say within themselves, who is this that **releases** the sins also?

50 And he said to the woman, your faith has saved[1800] you; go **into** peace.

LUKE CHAPTER 8

1 And **it became down-next**, that he went throughout every city and village, preaching and **evangelizing** the kingdom of God: and the twelve with him,

2 And certain women, which had been **served-therapy from wicked-hurtful** spirits and **weaknesses**, Mary called Magdalene, **from** whom went seven **demons**,

3 And Joanna, the wife of Chuza Herod's **manager**, and Susanna, and many others, which **attended to-him** of their substance.

4 And when much **multitude** were gathered together, and were come **to-him** out of every city, he spoke by a parable:

5 A Sower went out to sow his seed: and as he sowed, some fell by the wayside; and it was **trampled** down, and the **birds of the heaven** devoured it.

6 And **another-different** fell upon a rock; and as soon as it **sprouted**, it withered away, because it **has no** moisture.

7 And **another-different** fell among thorns; and the thorns sprang up with it and choked it.

8 And **another-different** fell on good ground, and **sprouted**, and bear fruit a hundredfold. And when he had said these things, he voiced, he that has ears to hear, hear!

9 And his disciples asked him, saying, what might this parable be?

[1794] Lit.,, a tippler (habitual drinker)
[1795] Fat, or grease
[1796] Lit, use-owing-one
[1797] On denarius is equivalent to ten she asses, or a day's wage
[1798] Greek: "orthos" erect, straight manner
[1799] To from-let-go
[1800] Or, safe

Luke

10 And he said, un**to-you** it is given to know the mysteries of the kingdom of God: but to **remaining** in parables; that seeing they might not see and hearing they might not **synthesize**.[1801]

11 Now the parable is this: The seed is the **Word of God**.

12 Those by the wayside are they that hear; then comes the Devil, and **lifts** the **Word** out of their **hearts**, **that not** they should believe and be saved.

13 They on the rock, which, when they hear, **welcome** the **Word** with **cheer**; and these have no root, which for a **season** believe, and in **season** of **probe-testing divorce**.[1802]

14 And that which fell among thorns are they, which, when they have heard, go forth, and are choked with **portion-worry** and riches and **hedonism** of **livelihood**,[1803] and **carry** not fruit to **maturity**.

15 But that on the **ideal** ground are they, which in an honest and good **heart**, having heard the **Word**, **down-hold**, and **carry** fruit **in under-remaining**.

16 No man, when he has lighted a candle, covers it with a vessel, or puts under a **cot**;[1804] but sets on a candlestick, that they which enter in may see the light.

17 For nothing is **hidden**, that shall not **become shine**; neither **from-hidden**, that shall not be known and come **into shine**.

18 Be-**looking** therefore how you hear: for whoever has, **to-him** shall be given; and whoever has not, from him shall be **lifted** even that which he seems to have.

19 Then came **to-him** the mother and his **brothers**, and **not they-are-powerful to-together-happening to-him** for the **multitude**.

20 And it was **from-message** him which said, your mother and your **brothers** stand **outside**, **willing** to **perceive** you.

21 And he answered and said **toward** them, my mother and my **brothers** are these which hear the **Word of God** and do it.

22 Now **it became in first of the days**, that he went into a ship with his disciples: and he said **to-them**, let us go over **to** the other side of the lake. And they launched.[1805]

23 But as they sailed, he fell asleep: and there came down a storm of wind on the lake; and they were filled and were in **danger**.

24 And they came **to-him**, and awoke him, saying, **Commander, Commander**,[1806] we **from-ruin**.[1807] Then he arose, and rebuked the wind and the **surge** of the water: and they **paused**, and **it-became** calm.[1808]

25 And he said **to** them, where is your faith? And they being afraid **marveled** saying one to another, what manner of man is this! Because he **upon-arrange** even the winds and water, and they **under-hear**[1809] him.

26 And they arrived at the **space** of the Gadarenes, which is **instead-other-side of-the** Galilee.

27 And when he went **out** to land, there met him a certain man out of the city, which had **demons sufficient uninterrupted-time**, and wore no clothes, neither **remained** in house, but in the **remembrance-tomb**.

28 When he **perceived** Jesus, he cried out, and fell down **towards** him, and with a **great** voice said, what have I to do with you, Jesus, you Son of God, **the Highest**? I **beg-bind** you, torment[1810] me not.

29 (**Because** he had **beside-message** the unclean spirit to come out of the man. For **many uninterrupted-times** it had caught him: and he was kept bound with chains and in fetters; and he **broke** the bands and was **pushed under** the demon into the **lonesome**.)

30 And Jesus asked him, saying, what is your name? And he said, Legion: because many **demons** were entered into **him**.

31 And they **beside-called** him that he would not **upon-arrange** them **to-from-go** into the **abyss**.

32 And there was there a herd of **sufficient** swine, feeding, on the mountain: and they **beside-called** him that he would **permit** them to enter into them. And he **permitted** them.

[1801] Greek: together-send
[1802] Lit., "aphistemi" from-stand, the root word for "apostasies:" feminine of "apostasion" (divorce); a thing that separates.
[1803] Or goods
[1804] Or (re)cline
[1805] Lit., up-lead
[1806] Lit., upon-stand, stoppage, appointed over, commander
[1807] Greek: "apo" (from) and "alethros" (ruin), to destroy fully
[1808] Or smile
[1809] Or obey
[1810] Or, torture, ordeal

33 Then went the **demons** out of the man and entered into the swine: and the herd **violent-impulse** down a **precipice** into the lake and were choked.

34 When they that fed **perceived** what was done, they fled, and went and **from-message** in the city and in the **fields**.

35 Then they went out to **perceive** what **became**; and came to Jesus, and found the man, out of whom the **demons** were departed, sitting at the feet of Jesus, clothed, and in **save-disposition**: and they were afraid.

36 They also which **perceived** told them by what means **the demonized** was **saved**.[1811]

37 Then **every fullness** of the **about-space** of the Gadarenes round about **asked** him to depart from them; for they were **together-held** with **great** fear: and he went up into the ship and returned.

38 Now the man out of whom the **demons** were departed **beg-bind** him that he might be with him: but Jesus **from-loosed him**, saying,

39 Return **to-your** own house and show how **much** things God has **produced to-you**. And he went his way and **preached** throughout the whole city how much things Jesus had done **to-him**.

40 And **it became**, that, when Jesus was returned, the **multitude** received him: for they were all **toward-seeming** him.

41 And, **be-perceiving**, there came a man named Jairus, and he was a **first-rank**,[1812] of the synagogue: and he fell down at Jesus' feet, and **beside-called** him that he would come into his house:

42 For he had an **only-born** daughter, about twelve **years** of age, and she lay dying. But as he went the **multitude together-chocked** him.

43 And a woman having a **flux** of blood twelve **years**, which had spent all her **livelihood** upon physicians, neither **forceful** be **served-therapy** of any,

44 Toward-came from-behind and fastened to-the border of his garment: and **instantly** her **flux** of blood **stopped**.[1813]

45 And Jesus said, who **fastened to- me**? When all **contradicted**, Peter and they that were with him said, **Commander**, the multitude **together-hold** you and **from-tribulation**[1814] you, and say you, who **fastened to** me?

46 And Jesus said, somebody has **fastened to-me**: for I **know** that **power** is gone out **from** me.

47 And when the woman **perceived** that she was not **hidden**, she came trembling, and falling down **towards** him, she **from-message to-him** before all the people for what cause she had **fastened to-him**, and how she was **cured instantly**.

48 And he said **to-her**, daughter, be-**daring**:[1815] your faith has **saved you**. Go **into** peace.

49 While he yet spoke, there comes one from the **first-rank-of-**synagogue, saying **to-him**, your daughter is dead; **flay** not the **Teacher**.

50 But when Jesus heard, he answered him, saying, fear not: believe only, and she shall be **saved**.[1816]

51 And when he came into the house, he **released**[1817] no man to go in, **if not** Peter, and James, and John, and the father and the mother of the **girl**.

52 And all wept, and bewailed her: but he said, weep not; she is not dead, but sleeps.

53 And they **down-laughed** him, **perceiving** that she was dead.

54 And he put them all out, and **governed** her by the hand, and **shouted**, saying, **girl**, arise.

55 And her spirit came again, and she **up-stood instantly**: and he **through-arrange** to give her meat.

56 And her parents were **ecstasized**,[1818] but he **beside-message** them that they should tell no man what **having-become**.

LUKE CHAPTER 9

1 Then he called his twelve disciples together, and gave them power and authority over all **demons**, and to **serve-therapy nauseas**.

2 And he sent them to preach the kingdom of God, and to **cure the without-strength**.

[1811] Or, made safe
[1812] Or, original-rank, beginning-rank
[1813] Lit., stood
[1814] To crowd, to wear out
[1815] Or, be-courageous
[1816] Or to be safe
[1817] From-let-go
[1818] Greek compound existemi (out-of-stand) from which we take our English ecstasy (overwhelming feelings)

3 And he said **to-them, lift** nothing for journey, neither **rods**, nor **wallet**, neither bread, neither money; neither have two coats apiece.

4 And whatever house you enter into, there **remain**, and there **depart.**

5 And whoever will not **welcome** you, when you go out of that city, shake off the very dust from your feet for a **witness** against them.

6 And they departed, and went through the towns, preaching the **well-message**, and **serving-therapy universally**.

7 Now Herod the tetrarch heard of all that **becoming** by him: and he was perplexed,[1819] because that it was said of some, that John was risen **out-of** the dead;

8 And of some, that **Elijah** had **shined**; and of others, that one of the **original** prophets was risen again.

9 And Herod said, John have I beheaded: but who is this, of whom I hear such things? And he **sought** to **perceive** him.

10 And the apostles, when they were returned, **through-lead** him all that they had done. And he **took** them and went aside privately into a **lonesome spot** belonging to the city called Bethsaida.

11 And the **multitude**, when they knew, followed him: and he **welcomed** them, and spoke **to-them** of the kingdom of God, and **served-therapy** them that had need of-**cure**.

12 And when the day began to **decline**, then came the twelve, and said **to-him, from-loosed** the multitude away, that they may go into the towns and **field** around, and lodge, and **find provisions**: for we are here in a **lonesome spot**.

13 But he said **to-them,** give you them to eat. And they said, we have no more but five loaves and two fishes; except we should go and buy[1820] **food** for all this people.

14 For they were about five thousand men. And he said to his disciples, **recline them** by fifties in **reclines**.[1821]

15 And they did so and made them all **up-cline**.

16 Then he **took** the five loaves and the two fishes, and looking up **into the** heaven, he blessed them, and broke, and gave to the disciples **to-beside-place**[1822] **to-the** multitude.

17 And they did eat and were all filled: and there was **lifted** of fragments that remained **to-them** twelve baskets.

18 And **it became**, as he was alone praying, his disciples were with him: and he asked them, saying, who say the **multitude** that I am?

19 They answering said, John the Baptist; but some, **Elijah**; and others, that one of the **original** prophets is risen again.

20 He said **to** them, but who say you that I am? Peter answering said, the Christ of God.

21 And he **rebuked** them, and **beside-message** to **tell no-one this.**

22 Saying, **it-is-binding** the Son of man **to-emotion** many things and be **from-seem-test**[1823] of the elders and **first-rank-priests** and scribes, and be slain, and be raised the third day.

23 And he said **toward** all, if any will **to-come** after me, let him **through-contradict** himself, and **lift** his cross daily, and follow me.

24 For whoever will save his **soul** shall **from-ruin**[1824] it: but whoever will **from-ruin** his **soul** for or-account-of me, the same shall save it.

25 For what is a man **profit**, if he gains the whole world, and **detriment**[1825] himself, or be **from-ruin**?

26 For whoever shall be **upon-disfigured** of me and of my words, of him shall the Son of man be **upon-disfigured**, when he shall come in his own glory, and **of-the** Father, and of the holy angels.

27 But I tell you of a truth, there be some standing here, which shall not taste of death, **until** they **perceive** the kingdom of God.

28 And **it became as-if** eight days after these sayings, he **beside-taken** Peter and John and James, and **up-walked** into a mountain to **towards-pray-wish**.

29 And as he **towards-prayed-wished**, the **perception** of his **face** was **another-different**, and his raiment white **out-of-lightning**.

[1819] Lit., through-to have no way out
[1820] Lit., to go to the market, redeem
[1821] Properly: cline
[1822] Or deposit
[1823] Or, rejected, disapprove
[1824] Greek: "apo" (from) and "alethros" (ruin), to destroy fully
[1825] To fine, to injure

30 And, **be-perceiving**, there talked with him two men, which were Moses and **Elijah**:

31 Who appeared in glory and spoke of his **exodus**[1826] which **he-was-impending to-be-filling in** Jerusalem.

32 But Peter and they that were with him were heavy with sleep: and when they were awake, they **perceived** his glory, and the two men that stood with him.

33 And **it became**, as they departed from him, Peter said **to-Jesus, Commander**, it is **ideal** for us to be here: and let us make three tabernacles; one for you, and one for Moses, and one for **Elijah**: not **perceiving** what he said.

34 While he spoke **these-things**, there came a cloud, and overshadowed them: and they feared as they entered into the cloud.

35 And there came a voice out of the cloud, saying, this is my beloved Son: hear him.

36 And when the voice **became**, Jesus was found alone. And they kept **silent**, and **from-message** no man in those days any of those things which they had seen.

37 And **it became**, that on the next day, when they were come down from the **mountain**, much **multitude together-meet** him.

38 And, **be-perceiving**, a man of the **multitude** cried out, saying, **Teacher**, I **beg-bind** you, look upon my son: for he is my **only-born.**

39 And, **be-perceiving,** a spirit **takes** him, and he **suddenly is-screaming;** and it **spasm** him that he foams, and **together-worn**[1827] him **difficultly** departs[1828] from him.

40 And I **beg-bind** your disciples to cast him out; and **not they-are-powerful**.

41 And Jesus answering said, O faithless and perverse generation, how long shall I be with you, and **tolerate** you? Bring your son hither.

42 And as he was yet a coming, the **demon together-spasm,** and **break** him. And Jesus rebuked the unclean spirit, and **cured** the child, and **from-gives** him again to his father.

43 And they were all **out-of-pounded** at the **great-smoothness**[1829] of God. But while they **marveled** everyone at all things which Jesus did, he said **to-his** disciples,

44 Let these sayings sink down **into your** ears: because the Son of man **impending to-be-beside-given** into the hands of men.

45 But **they-did-not-mind** this saying, and it was **beside-covered** from them, that they **sensed** it not: and they feared to ask him of that **declaration**

46 Then there arose a **through-inventory in** them, which of them should be **larger.**[1830]

47 And Jesus, perceiving the **through-inventorying of-their heart, upon-take** a child, and **stood** him by him,

48 And said **to-them**, whoever shall **welcome** this child in my name **welcome** me: and whoever shall **welcome** me **welcome** him that sent me: **because** he that is **smaller** among you all, the same shall be **great**.

49 And John answered and said, **Commander**, we **perceived** one casting out **demons** in your name; and we **prevented** him, because he follows not with us.

50 And Jesus said **to-him, prevent** not: for he that is not **downing** us is for us.

51 And **it became**, when **together-filled the days** that he should be **up-taken**, he **set**[1831] his face to go to Jerusalem,

52 And sent **angels** before his face: and they went, and entered into a village of the Samaritans, to **internally-prepare**[1832] for him.

53 And they did not **welcome** him, because his face was **going into** Jerusalem.

54 And when his disciples James and John **perceived**, they said, Lord, **will** you that we command fire to come down from heaven, and consume[1833] them, even as **Elijah** did?

55 But he turned, and rebuked them, and said, you **perceive** not what manner of spirit you are of.

56 For the Son of man is not come to **from-ruin** men's **souls**, but to save. And they went to **another-different** village.

[1826] Out-way, out-road
[1827] Or together-crush
[1828] Or from-space
[1829] Compound of **great** (great) and leios (smooth)
[1830] Larger, especially in age

[1831] Or Greek sterizo, to set fast, to turn resolutely in a certain direction, to confirm
[1832] Internal preparation
[1833] Up-choose, to use up

57 And **it became**, that, as they went in the way, a certain said **to-him**, Lord, I will follow you wherever you go.

58 And Jesus said **to-him**, foxes have holes, and birds of the heaven nests; but the Son of man has not where to **recline** his head.

59 And he said **to-another-different,** follow me. But he said, Lord, **permit** me **foremost** to go and bury my father.

60 Jesus said **to-him**, **release** the dead to bury their dead: but go you and **through-message** the kingdom of God.

61 And **another-different** also said, Lord, I will follow you; but **permit** me first go **release them**, which are **into** my house.

62 And Jesus said **to-him**, no man, having put his hand to the plough, and looking back, is **soon**[1834] for the kingdom of God.

LUKE CHAPTER 10

1 After these things the Lord **up-show another-different** seventy also and sent them two and two before his face into every city and **spot**, where he himself **impending to-be-coming.**

2 Therefore said he **to-them,** the harvest truly **many**, but the **workers** few: pray you therefore the Lord of the harvest, that he would **out-of-cast**[1835] **workers** into his harvest.

3 Go your ways: **be-perceiving**, I send you forth as lambs **in the middle of-**wolves.

4 Carry neither **pouch** nor **wallet**, nor **sandals**: and **embrace** no man by the way.

5 And into whatever house you enter, **foremost** say, peace to this house.

6 And if the son of peace be there, your peace shall rest upon it: if not, **it-shall-bend**[1836] **upon** you.

7 And in the same house remain, eating and drinking such things as they give: for the **worker** is **deserving** of his **pay**. Go not from house to house.

8 And into whatever city you enter, and they **welcome** you, eat such things as are **beside-place**[1837] **to-you:**

9 And **serve-therapy the without-strength** that are **in her**, and say **to-them,** the kingdom of God is **near-squeeze upon** you.

10 But into whatever city you enter, and they **welcome** you not, go your ways out into the streets of the same, and say,

11 Even the very dust of your city, which **glued**[1838] on us, we do wipe off against you: notwithstanding **be-you-knowing** this, that the kingdom of God is **near-squeezed upon** you.

12 But I say **to-you**, that it shall be more tolerable in that day for Sodom, than for that city.

13 Woe **to-you**, Chorazin! Woe **to-you**, Bethsaida! for if the **powers** had **become** in Tyre and Sidon, which **became** in you, they had **long**-ago **change-thought**, sitting in sackcloth and ashes.

14 But it shall be more tolerable for Tyre and Sidon **in** the **judging**, than for you.

15 And you, Capernaum, which are **elevated** to heaven, shall be thrust down to **Hell.**

16 He that hears you hears me; and he that **un-places**[1839] you **un-places** me; and he that **un-places** me **un-places** him that sent me.

17 And the seventy returned again with **cheerfulness**, saying, Lord, even the **demons** are **subordinate**[1840] **to-us in** your name.

18 And he said **to-them,** I **looked-closely-at**[1841] Satan as **star-light**[1842] **fell**[1843] **out-of** heaven.

19 Be-perceiving, I give **to-you authority** to **trample** on serpents and scorpions,[1844] and over all the power of the **hater**: and nothing shall by any means **unrighteous** you.

20 Notwithstanding in this **cheer** not, that the spirits are **subordinate**[1845] **to-you**; but rather rejoice, because your names are written in **the heavens**

21 In that hour Jesus **much-jumped-for-joy** in spirit, and said, I thank you, Father, Lord of heaven and earth, that you have hid these things from the wise and

---

[1834] Or, good-placed
[1835] Or eject
[1836] Or bow
[1837] Or deposit
[1838] Or, to stick to, to cling, to keep company with
[1839] Or, set aside
[1840] Under-arranged
[1841] Imperfect tense
[1842] Astrapen, from the roots aster (star) and pto (to fall), star-fall
[1843] Aorist tense
[1844] Lit., scatter-penetrate, scatter-venom
[1845] Under-arranged

synthesizing-ones and has revealed them **to children**:[1846] even so, Father; for so it seemed good in your sight.

22 All things are **from-given** to me of my Father: and no man knows who the Son is, but the Father; and who the Father is, but the Son, and to whom the Son will reveal.

23 And he turned **towards** disciples, and said privately, **happy** the eyes which see the things that you see:

24 For I tell you, that many prophets and kings have **willed** to **perceive** those things which you see and have not **perceived**; and to hear those things which you hear and have not heard.

25 And, **be-perceiving**, a certain lawyer stood up, and **probe-tested** him, saying, **Teacher**, what shall I do to inherit **eternal** life?

26 He said **towards him**, what is written in the law? How **are you reading**?

27 And he answering said, you shall love the Lord your God with your **whole** heart, and with your **whole** soul, and **out-of your whole force**, and **out-of your whole through-mind**; and your neighbor as yourself.

28 And he said **to-him**, you have answered right: this **produce**, and you shall live.

29 But he, willing to **righteous** himself, said **towards** Jesus, and who is my neighbor?

30 And Jesus **under-take** said, a certain went down from Jerusalem to Jericho, and fell among thieves, which stripped him of his raiment, and **plague-poundings**[1847] **placing-on-him**, and departed, **released-him, it-happens,**[1848] half-dead.

31 And by **together-chance**[1849] there came down a certain priest that way: and when he **perceived** him, he passed by on the other side.

32 And likewise a Levite, when he was at the place, came and **perceived**, and passed by on the other side.

33 But a certain Samaritan, as he journeyed, came where he was: and when he **perceived** him, **he-had-gut-compassion**,

34 And **went-to-him**, and bound up his **trauma**,[1850] pouring in oil and wine, and set him on his own **domestic-animal**, and brought him to an inn, and **upon-cared** of him.

35 And on the tomorrow when he departed, he **cast-out** two **denarii**,[1851] and gave to the host, and said **to-him**, take care of him; and whatever you spend more, when I come again, I will **from-give** you.

36 Which now of these three, **seem** you, was neighbor **to-him** that fell among the **robbers**?

37 And he said, he that showed **pity-mercy** on him. Then said Jesus **to-him**, go, and **produce** you likewise.

38 Now **it became**, as they went, that he entered into a certain village: and a certain woman named Martha received him into her house.

39 And she had a sister called Mary, which also sat at Jesus' feet, and heard his word.

40 But Martha was **about-spasm-pulled** much **attending**, and came **to-him**, and said, Lord, do you not care that my sister has left me to **attend** alone? **Be-saying to-**her therefore that she helps me.

41 And Jesus answered and said **to-her**, Martha, Martha, you are **portion-worry** and **disturbed** about many things:

42 But one **small** thing is needful: and Mary has chosen that good p**ortion**, which shall not be **lifted** from her.

LUKE CHAPTER 11

1 And **it became**, that, as he was **towards-praying-wishing** in a certain **spot**, when he **paused**, one of his disciples said **towards him**, Lord, teach us to pray, as John also taught his disciples.

2 And he said **to** them, when you **towards-pray-wish**, say, our Father who are in the heavens, **holy** your name. your kingdom come. Your will be-**becoming**, as in heaven, so in earth.

3 The bread of-us, the upon-going, be-giving to-us according-to day.

4 And **release**[1852] us our sins; for we also **release** every one that is indebted to us. And lead us not into **probe-testing**; but **rush-rescue** us from **the wicked-hurtful**.

[1846] Nepiois-child, or non-speaking infants
[1847] Or, strokes, wound, to pound
[1848] Or, hit the mark, chance upon, obtain,
[1849] Sun (together) and kyreo (to happen accidentally); kyreo is from the same root for Lord (kurious)
[1850] Greek: "trauma," to wound
[1851] Two days wage
[1852] Lit., from-let-go

Luke

5 And he said **towards** them, which of you shall have a friend, and shall go **towards him** at midnight, and say **towards him**, Friend, lend me three loaves;

6 For a friend of mine in his journey is come to me, and I have nothing to **beside-place**[1853] **to-**him?

7 And he from within shall answer and say, **weary-cut** me not: the door is now **locked**, and my children are with me in bed; **not I-am-powerful to-**rise and give you.

8 I say **to-you**, though he will not rise and give him, because he is his friend, yet because of his **un-bashfulness** he will rise and give him as many as he needs.

9 And I say **to-you**, ask, and it shall be given you; seek, and you shall find; knock, and it shall be opened **to-you**.

10 For every one that asks **takes**; and he that seeks finds; and **to-him** that knocks it shall be opened.

11 If a son shall ask bread of any of you that is a father, will he give him a stone? Or if a fish, will he for a fish give him a serpent?

12 Or if he shall ask an egg, will he offer him a scorpion?

13 If you then, **under-originating-ones, wicked-hurtful, perceive** how to give good gifts **to-your** children: how much more shall **the** Father **out-of the** heaven give the Holy Spirit **to-them** that ask him?

14 And he was casting out a **demon**, and it was dumb. And **it became** when the **demon** was gone out, the **blunted**,[1854] spoke; and the **multitude marveled**.

15 But some of them said, He casts out **demons** through Beelzebub the **first-rank**,[1855] of the **demons**.

16 And **another-different**,[1856] **probe-testing**, sought of him a sign **out-of** heaven.

17 But he, **perceiving** their **through-mind**, said **to** them, every kingdom divided against itself is brought to desolation; and a house against a house falls.

18 If Satan also be divided against himself, how shall his kingdom stand? Because you say that I cast out **demons in** Beelzebub.

19 And if I **in** Beelzebub cast out **demons**, **in** whom do your sons cast out? Therefore, shall they be your judges.

20 But if I with the finger of God cast out **demons**, no doubt the kingdom of God is **anticipated**[1857] upon you.

21 When a **forceful**, armed, keeps his **yard**, his goods are in peace:

22 But when a **forceful** than he shall come upon him, and **conquer**[1858] him, he **lifts** from him all his **armor on which** he trusted, and **through-gives** his **flays**.

23 He that is not with me is against me: and he that gathered not with me scattering.

24 When the unclean spirit is gone out of a man, he walks through **un-watered spots**, seeking rest; and finding none, he says, I will return **into** my house **where** I came out.

25 And when he **comes**, he finds swept and **having-cosmetic.**

26 Then goes he and **takes** seven other spirits more **wicked-hurtful** than himself; and they enter in, and **down-house** there: and the last of that man is worse than the **foremost**.

27 And **it became**, as he spoke these things, a certain woman of the **multitude** lifted up her voice, and said **to-him**, **happy** the womb that bear you, and the **breasts** which you have suckled.

28 But he said, yes rather, **happy** they that hear the **Word of God**, and **guard** it.

29 And when the **multitude** were gathered thick together, he began to say, this is a **wicked-hurtful** generation: they seek a sign; and there shall no sign be given it, but the sign of Jonas the prophet.

30 For as Jonas was a sign **to** the Ninevites, so shall also the Son of man be to this generation.

31 The queen of the south shall rise up in the **judging** with the men of this generation and condemn them: for she came **out of the extremity** of the earth to hear the wisdom of Solomon; and, **be-perceiving**, more of-Solomon here.

32 The men of **Nineveh** shall rise up in the **judging** with this generation and shall **down-judge** it: for they

---

[1853] Or deposit
[1854] Or, deaf-mute, root to chop (choppy), to beat the chest
[1855] Or, original-rank, beginning-rank
[1856] Plural
[1857] Or to be beforehand, to precede, to have arrived at
[1858] "Nikao," to defeat an enemy

change-thinking at the preaching of Jonas; and, **be-perceiving**, more of-Jonas here.

33 No man, when he has lighted a candle, **places into hiding**, neither under a **dry-measure**, but on a candlestick, that they which come in may see the light.

34 The **candle** of the body is the eye: therefore, when your eye is **single**;[1859] your whole body also is light; **yet, if-ever, it-may-be wicked-hurtful, y**our body also darkness.

35 Spy[1860] therefore that the light which is in you be not darkness.

36 If your whole body therefore full of light, having no **section** dark, the whole shall be light, as when the **star-light**[1861] of a candle does give you light.

37 And as he spoke, a certain Pharisee **asked** him to dine with him: and he went in, and **up-falls.**[1862]

38 And when the Pharisee **perceived,** he marveled that he had not first washed before dinner.

39 And the Lord said **towards him**, now do you Pharisees make clean the outside of the cup and the **plate**; but your **inside** is full of **snatching** and **wicked-hurtfulness.**

40 You **un-disposed**, did not he that made that which is **outside** make that which is within also?

41 But rather give **pity-mercy-togetherness** of such things as you have; and, **be-perceiving**, all things are clean **to-you**.

42 But woe **to-you**, Pharisees! For you tithe **sweet-fragrance** and rue and all manner of herbs and pass over **judging** and the love of God: these **it-was-binding to-produce**, and not to **release**[1863] those.

43 Woe **to-you**, Pharisees! For you love the **foremost-seats** in the synagogues, and **enfolding-the-arms** in the markets.

44 Woe **to-you**, scribes and Pharisees, hypocrites! For you are as graves which appear not, and the men that walk over not **they-have-perceived.**

45 Then answered one of the lawyers, and said **to-him, Teacher**, saying **these-things,** you **insulting** us also.

46 And he said, woe **to-you** also, you lawyers! For you **load** men with **invoice-load difficult-to-lift** and you yourselves **towards-touch** not the **invoice-load** with one of your fingers.

47 Woe **to-you**! For you **house-build** the **remembrance-tomb** of the prophets, and your fathers killed them.

48 Truly you witness that you **together-seem** the **works** of your fathers: for they indeed killed them, and you **house-build** their **remembrance-tomb**.

49 Therefore also said the wisdom of God, I will send them prophets and apostles, and of them they shall **from-kill** and **chase**:

50 That the blood of all the prophets, which was **out-poured** from the **down-casting** of the world, may be **out-searched from** this generation;

51 From the blood of Abel **until** the blood of Zacharias, which **from-ruined** between the **sacrifice-place** and the **house**: **yes,** I say **to-you**, it shall be **out-of-seek from** this generation.

52 Woe **to-you**, lawyers! For you have **lift** the **locker**[1864] of knowledge: you entered not in yourselves, and them that were entering in you **prevented.**

53 And as he said these things **towards** them, the scribes and the Pharisees began to **intimidate,**[1865] **in-hold-him,**[1866] and to **from-mouth him about more**:

54 Lurking[1867] for him and seeking to **beast-hunt** something out of his mouth, that they might accuse him.

LUKE CHAPTER 12

1 In **which**, when there were gathered together an innumerable multitude, insomuch that they **trampling one-another-same**, he began to say **to** his disciples **foremost** of all, **towards-hold** you **from** the **ferment** of the Pharisees, which is hypocrisy.

2 For there is nothing covered, that shall not be revealed; neither **hidden,** that shall not be known.

3 Therefore whatever you have spoken in darkness shall be heard in the light; and that which you have spoken in the ear in closets shall be **preached** upon the housetops.

[1859] Haplous, the antonym of "diplous" meaning double
[1860] Or watch
[1861] Astrape, from the root aster (star) and pto (to fall), star-fall, lightning
[1862] Or, to lean back (up)
[1863] Lit., from-let-go, forgive
[1864] Or key (as if shutting a lock); root: to close
[1865] Or, to timid
[1866] ensnare
[1867] Or, to plot assassination

Luke

4 And I say **to-you** my friends, be not afraid of them that kill the body, and after that have no more that they can do.

5 But I **under-show** you whom you shall fear: fear him, which after he has killed has **authority** to cast into **Gehenna**; yes, I say **to-you**, fear him.

6 Are not five sparrows sold for two farthings, and not one of them is forgotten before God?

7 But even the very hairs of your head are all numbered. Fear not therefore: you are of **differing**[1868] **of-**many sparrows.

8 Also I say **to-you**, whoever shall **same-say**[1869] **in** me before men, him shall the Son of man also **same-say in him** before the angels of God:

9 But he that **contradicts** me before men shall be **contradicted** before the angels of God.

10 And whoever shall speak a word **into** the Son of man, it shall be **released**[1870] **to-him**: but **to-him** that blasphemes **into** the Holy Spirit it shall not be **released.**

11 And when they bring you **upon** the synagogues, and the **first-rank**, and **authorities no portion-worry** how or what thing you shall **answer,**[1871] or what you shall say:

12 For the Holy Spirit shall teach you in the same hour what **it-is-binding** say.

13 And one **out-of** the **multitude** said **to-him**, **Teacher**, speak to my brother, that he divides the inheritance with me.

14 And he said **to-him**, man, who **down-stands** me a **justice** or a divider over you?

15 And he said **towards** them, **be-seeing**, and **watch** of **more-having**:[1872] for a man's life not in the abundance of **his belongings.**

16 And he spoke a parable **to** them, saying, the ground of a certain rich man **good-carries**:

17 And he **through-inventoried** within himself, saying, what shall I do, because I have no room where to **assemble** my fruits?

18 And he said, this will I do: I will pull down my barns, and **house-build great**; and there will I **assemble** all my **generation**[1873] and my goods.

19 And I will say to my soul, soul, you have much goods laid up **into** many **years**; take your ease, eat, drink, **be-good-disposition.**

20 But God said **to-him**, you **un-disposed** this night your soul shall be required **from** you: then whose shall those things be, which you have **internally-prepared**?

21 So he that **places-into-tomorrow**[1874] for himself and is not rich toward God.

22 And he said **to** his disciples, **through this,** I say **towards you, not be-portion-worrying** for your **soul**, what you shall eat; neither for the body, what you shall **clothe.**

23 The **soul** is more **of-the** meat, and the body **of-the** raiment.

24 **Down-mind** the ravens: for they neither sow nor reap; which neither have storehouse nor barn; and God feeds them: how much more are you **different of-**the **birds**?

25 And which of you **portion-worrying is-powerful to-**add to his stature one cubit?

26 If you then be not **is-powerful** to do that thing which is least, why **are-you-portion-worry** for the **remaining**?

27 **Down-mind** the lilies how they grow: they **fatigue** not, they spin[1875] not; and yet I say **to-you**, that Solomon in all his glory was not **clothed** like one of these.

28 If then God so clothe the grass, which is today **being** in the field, and tomorrow is cast into the oven; how much **rather** you, you of little-faith?

29 And seek not you what you shall eat, or what you shall drink, neither be you **a meteor.**[1876]

30 For all these things do the nations of the world seek after: and your Father **perceives** that you have need of these things.

31 But rather seek you the kingdom of God; and all these things shall be added **to-you.**

[1868] Greek: "diaphero," to through-bear, transliterated as "differ" or "different"
[1869] confess
[1870] Lit., from-let-go, forgive
[1871] Greek: "apologeomai" (from-saying) to exculpate (self), to give account, to defend
[1872] Cocetousness
[1873] Majority Texts
[1874] Greek: "thesauros," transliterated as thesaurus, also means a deposit, treasure,
[1875] To spin yarn to make clothing
[1876] Lit., change lift (Greek: "airo")

Luke

32 Fear not, **little-flock;** for it is your Father's well-seem to give you the kingdom.

33 Sell **the belongings** and give **pity-mercy-togetherness;** provide yourselves **pouches not aging, placed-into-tomorrow** in the heavens **un-omitted,** where no thief **near-squeeze,** neither moth corrupts.

34 For where your **placed-into-tomorrow** is, there will your heart be also.

35 Let your loins be **about-belted,** and **candle** burning;

36 And you yourselves like **to** men that **toward-receiving** their lord, when he will **up-loose** from the **marriages;** that when he comes and knocks, they may open **to-him soon.**

37 Happy those **slave**s, whom the lord when he comes shall find watching: **amen** I say **to-you,** that he shall **about-belt** himself, and make them to **recline** to meat, and will **beside-come** and **attend** them.

38 And if he shall come in the second watch, or come in the third watch, and find so, **happy** are those **slave**s.

39 And this **perceive** that if the **house-owner** had known what hour the thief would come, he would have watched, and not have **released** his house to be **through-burrow.**

40 And you then become **internally-prepared:** for the Son of man comes at an hour when you **seem** not.

41 Then Peter said, Lord, speak you this parable **toward us,** or **towards** all?

42 And the Lord said, who then is that **believing** and **disposed**[1877] **house-lawyer,**[1878] whom **the** lord shall **down-stand** over his **serve-therapy,** to give **corn-measure** in season?

43 Happy that **slave,** whom his lord when he comes shall find so doing.

44 Of a truth I say **to-you,** that he will make him **down-stand** over all **his belongings.**

45 Yet, if that **slave** says in his **heart, is-delaying-uninterrupted-time,** my lord **to-be-coming;** and shall begin to beat the **boys** and **girls,** and to eat and drink, and to be drunk;

46 The lord of that **slave shall-arrive** in a day **which not-he-is-toward-seeming** and at an hour **to-which not he-is-knowing,** and will cut him in two, and will **place** him his **section** with the unbelievers.

47 And that **slave,** who knew his lord's will, and not **internally-prepared,** neither did **towards** his will, shall be **skinned** with many.

48 But he that knew not, and did things **deserving** of **plague-poundings,** shall be **skinned** with few. For **to whomever** much is given, of him shall much be required: and to whom men have **beside-placed**[1879] much, of him they will ask the more.

49 I am come to send fire on the earth; and what will I, if it be already kindled?

50 But I have a baptism to be baptized with; and how am I **together-held until** it be **finished**!

51 Seeming-you that I am come to give peace on **earth**? I tell you, no; but rather division:

52 Because from **the now,** there shall be five in one house divided, three against two, and two against three.

53 The father shall be **through-parted upon** the son, and the son **upon** the father; the mother **upon** the daughter, and the daughter **upon** the mother; the mother in law **upon** her daughter in law, and the daughter in law **upon** her mother in law.

54 And he said also to the **multitude,** when you **perceive** a cloud rise out of the west, **soon** you say, there comes a **thunderstorm;** and so, it **becomes.**

55 And when the south wind blow, you say, there will be heat; and **it-is-becoming.**

56 You hypocrites, you can **perceive** the face of the **heaven** and of the earth; but how is it that you do not **seem-test** this **season**?

57 Yes, and why even **from** yourselves judge you not what is **righteous**?

58 When you go with your **plaintiff**[1880] to the **first-rank,**[1881] in the way, give **work**[1882] that you may be **from-change** from him; lest he **drag** you to the judge, and the judge deliver you to the **proctor,** and the **proctor** cast you into prison.

[1877] Or, prudent
[1878] Greek: "oikonomos," the root of "oikonomia" (house-law) transliterated as economy.
[1879] Or deposit
[1880] Lit., anti-just, opponent, instead of justice
[1881] Or, original-rank, beginning-rank
[1882] Occupation

59 I tell you, you shall not depart there, **until** you have **from-give** the very last **stripped**[1883]-**copper**.

LUKE CHAPTER 13

1 There were present at that season some that **from-message** him of the Galileans, whose blood Pilate had **mixed** with their sacrifices.

2 And Jesus answering said **to** them, **seem** you that these Galileans were sinners above all the Galileans, because they **emotion** such things?

3 I tell you, no: but, except you **change-thought**, you shall all likewise **from-ruin**.

4 Or those eighteen, upon whom the tower in Siloam fell, and **killed** them, **seem** you that **theses owe** above all men that **down-house** in Jerusalem?

5 I tell you, no: but, except you **change-thought**, you shall all likewise **from-ruin**.

6 He also spoke this parable; a certain had a fig tree planted in his vineyard; and he came and sought fruit **upon it** and found none.

7 Then said he **to the vine-worker** of his vineyard, **be-perceiving**, these three **years** I come seeking fruit **in** this fig tree, and find none: **you-out-of-chop**; why **is-it-down-working** the ground?

8 And he answering said **to-him**, Lord, **release**[1884] this **year** also, **until** I shall dig about **her**, and **cast manure**:

9 And if **indeed** it **produces** fruit, and if not, **impending** that you-**shall-out-of-chop her**.

10 And he was teaching in one of the synagogues on the Sabbaths.

11 And, **be-perceiving**, there was a woman who had a spirit of **weakness** eighteen **years**, and was **together-bending**, and **not is-powerful to-up-bend into the all-finish**.

12 And when Jesus **perceived** her, he **towards-shout** and said **to-her**, woman, **you-have-been-from-loosed of-the weakness of-you**.

13 And he laid hands on her: and **instantly** she was made **up-erect**, and glorified God.

14 And the **first-rank-of-the-synagogue** answered with **much-grief-ached**,[1885] because that Jesus had healed on the **Sabbath**, and said **to-the** people, there are six days in which **it-is-binding** to work: in them therefore come and be **served-therapy**, and not on the **Sabbath**.

15 The Lord then answered him, and said, you hypocrite, does not each one of you on the Sabbath loose his **bull** or **donkey** from the stall, and lead away to watering?

16 And not **it-is-binding** this woman, being a daughter of Abraham, whom Satan has bound, **be-perceiving**, these eighteen **years**, be loosed from this bond on the **Sabbath**?

17 And when he had said these things, all his **opposing-ones**[1886] were **down-disfigure**d; and all the **multitude cheered** for all the **in-glorious** things that **became** by him.

18 Then said he, unto what is the kingdom of God like? And **to-what** shall I **assimilate** it?

19 It is like a grain of mustard seed, which a man took, and cast into his garden; and it grew, and **became** a **great** tree; and the **birds of the heaven lodged** in the branches of it.

20 And again he said, **to what** shall I **assimilate** the kingdom of God?

21 It is like **ferment**, which a woman **getting** and hid in three measures of meal, **until** the whole was **fermented**.

22 And he went through the cities and villages, teaching, and **travels into** Jerusalem.

23 Then said one **to-him**, Lord, are there few that be saved? And he said **towards** them,

24 Agonize to enter in at the **narrow**[1887] gate:[1888] for many, I say **to-you**, will seek to enter in, and shall not be-**forceful**.

25 When once the **house-owner** is risen up, and has shut to the door, and you begin to stand **outside**, and to knock at the door, saying, Lord, Lord, open **to-us**; and he shall answer and say **to-you**, I **perceive** you not **where** you are:

26 Then shall you begin to say, we have eaten and **drank** in your presence, and you have taught in our streets.

[1883] Scaled copper, very thin copper
[1884] Lit., from-let-go, forgive
[1885] Or, resentful
[1886] Greek: anti-laying outstretched

[1887] Greek: "stenos" narrow from obstacles standing close about, roof: to stand
[1888] Alexandrian Texts: "thura" (door), in lieu of "pule" (gate)

27 But he shall say, I tell you, I **perceive** you not **where you are**; **be-divorced**[1889] from me, all you workers of **unrighteousness**.

28 There shall be weeping and gnashing of teeth, when you shall see Abraham, and Isaac, and Jacob, and all the prophets, in the kingdom of God, and you **cast** out.

29 And they shall **arrive** from the east, and the west, and from the north, and the south, and shall **recline** in the kingdom of God.

30 And, **be-perceiving**, there are **last-ones** who shall be **foremost-ones**, and there are **foremost-ones** which shall be **last-ones**.

31 The same day there came certain of the Pharisees, saying **to-him**, **take** you out, and depart **within**: for Herod **is-willing to-kill y**ou.

32 And he said **to-them**, go you, and tell that fox,[1890] **Be-perceiving**, I cast out **demons**, and I **from-finish** cures today and tomorrow, and the third **I-am-being-matured**.

33 Me, moreover, **it-is-binding to-travel** today, and tomorrow, and the following: for it cannot be that a prophet **be-from-ruin** out of Jerusalem.

34 Jerusalem, Jerusalem, which kills the prophets, and stone them that are sent **to-you**; how often would I have gathered your children together, as a hen does her brood under wings, and you would not!

35 Be-perceiving, your house is **released**[1891] **to-you lonesome**: and **amen** I say **towards** you, you shall not **perceive** me, until **it-arrives** when you shall say, blessed he that **is-coming** in the name of the Lord.

LUKE CHAPTER 14

1 And **it became**, as he went into the house of one of the **first-rank**[1892] Pharisees to eat bread on the **Sabbath**, that they **beside-watched** him.

2 And, **be-perceiving**, there was a certain man before him which had the dropsy.[1893]

3 And Jesus answering spoke **towards** the lawyers and Pharisees, saying, is it lawful to **serve-therapy** on the **Sabbath**?

4 And they held their peace. And he **upon-take-him**, and **cured** him, and **from-loosed-him**;

5 And answered them, saying, which of you shall have a donkey or a **bull shall-be-falling** into a pit, and will not **soon** pull him **up** on the **Sabbath**?

6 And **not-they-are-forceful to-answer** him again **towards** these things.

7 And he put forth a parable to those which were **called**, when he **upon-held** how they chose out the **foremost-recliners**; saying **towards** them,

8 When you are **called** of any **into marriages**, **recline not** in the **foremost-recliner**; lest a more **valuable** man than you be **called** of him;

9 And he that **called** you and him come and say **to-you**, give this man **spot**; and you begin with **disfigurement** to **down-hold** the **last spot**.

10 But when you are **called**, go and **rest into the last spot**; that when he that **called** you **comes**, he may say **to-you**, friend, **toward-step upper**: then shall you have **glory** in the presence of them that **together-recline with-you**.

11 For whoever **elevate** himself shall be **humbled**; and he that humbles himself shall be **elevated**.

12 Then said he also **to-him** that **called** him, when you make a dinner or an **expensive-dinner**,[1894] call not your friends, nor your **brothers**, neither your kinsmen, nor your rich neighbors; lest they also **call** you again, and a **repayment**[1895] **become to-you**.

13 But when you make a **reception**, call the poor, the **crippled**, the **limping**, the blind:

14 And you shall be **happy**; for they cannot **repay** you for you shall be **repaid**[1896] at the resurrection of the **righteous-ones**.

15 And when one of them **together-reclined** with him heard these things, he said **to-him**, **happy-is** he that shall eat bread in the kingdom of God.

16 Then said he **to-him**, a certain man made a **great expensive-dinner**, and **calls** many:

17 And sent his **slave to-the hour of-the expensive-dinner** to say **to-them** that were **called**, come; for all things are now **prepared**.

[1889] Lit., "aphistemi" from-stand, the root word for "apostasies:" feminine of "apostasion" (divorce); a thing that separates.
[1890] "Fox" is feminine in the Greek texts
[1891] Lit., from-let-go
[1892] Or, original-rank, beginning-rank

[1893] Greek: hudropikos (hudor (water) and to look; watery-looking, dropsically
[1894] Supper comes from a root word that means "costly:
[1895] Instead-from-giving
[1896] Greek: instead-from-give

18 And they all **from** one began to **refuse.**[1897] The **foremost** said **to-him**, I have bought a piece of ground, and **I-am-holding necessity to-go** and **perceive** it: I pray you have me excused.

19 And **another-different** said, I have bought five yokes of **bulls**, and I go to **seem-test** them: I pray you have me **refuse.**

20 And **another-different** said, I have married a wife, and therefore **not I-am-powerful to-**come.

21 So that **slave** came, and **from-message** his lord these things. then the **house-owner** being **swelling-angry** said to his **slave**, go out quickly into the streets and lanes of the city, and bring in here the poor, and the **crippled**, and the **limping**, and the blind.

22 And the **slave** said, Lord, **it-became** as you have **upon-arranged**, and yet there is **spot.**

23 And the lord said **towards** the **slave**, go out into the **roads** and hedges, and **necessitate** to come in, that my house may be filled.

24 For I say **to-you**, that none of those men who were **called** shall taste of my **expensive-dinner.**

25 And there went **much** multitudes with him: and he turned, and said **toward** them,

26 If any come to me, and hate not his father, and mother, and wife, and children, and **brothers**, and sisters, **yes**, and his own **soul** also, **not he-is-powerful to-be** my disciple.

27 And whoever **carries not** his cross, and come after me, **not he-is-powerful to-**be my disciple.

28 For which of you, **wills** to **house-build** a tower, **sits** not down **foremost**, and **pebble-vote-count**[1898] the cost, whether he have **toward** the **from-fresh-finish?**

29 Lest, after he has laid the foundation, and is not **forceful** to **out-finish**, all that **be-perceiving** begin to **in-childish-mocked**[1899] him,

30 Saying, this man began to **house-build**, and was not **forceful** to **out-finish.**

31 Or what king, going to make war against **another-different** king, **sits** not down **foremost**, and **counsel-plan** if **he-is powerful in** ten thousand to meet him that comes against him with twenty thousand?

32 Or else, while **him being forward**, he sends an **eldership,**[1900] and **asking towards** peace.

33 So likewise, whoever he be of you that **from-arrange** not all that he **under-first-begin**, **not he-is-powerful to-be** my disciple.

34 Salt good: but if the salt **being-made-stupid,**[1901] in **what** shall it be seasoned?

35 It is neither fit for the land, nor yet for the **manure**, men cast it out. He that has ears to hear, hear!

LUKE CHAPTER 15

1 Then **near-squeezing to-him** all the **tax-collectors** and sinners for to hear him.

2 And the Pharisees and scribes **through-murmured**, saying, this man **towards-welcome** sinners, and eat with them.

3 And he spoke this parable **towards** them saying,

4 What man **out-of** you, having a hundred sheep, if he **from-ruin** one of them, does not leave the ninety and nine in the **lonesome**, and go after that which is **from-ruin**, until he finds it?

5 And when he has found, he **upon-place** on his shoulders, **cheering**.

6 And when he comes home, he calls together friends and neighbors, saying **to-them**, **cheer** with me; for I have found my sheep which was **from-ruined**.

7 I say **to-you**, that likewise **cheer** shall be in heaven over one sinner that **change-thought**, more than over ninety and nine just persons, which need no **change-thought.**

8 Either what woman having ten pieces of silver, if she **from-ruin** one piece, does not light a candle, and sweep the house, and seek **upon-carefully until** she **find-it?**

9 And when she has found, she calls friends and neighbors together, saying, **cheer** with me; for I have found the piece which I had **from-ruin.**

10 Likewise, I say **to-you**, there is **cheerfulness** in the presence of the angels of God over one sinner that **change-thought.**

11 And he said, a certain man had two sons:

[1897] Lit., beside-ask, to beg off, shun, refuse
[1898] Or pebble-count
[1899] Greek compound: "empaiktes" (in-sport (mock) as a boy), root means a child as disciplined
[1900] Or ambassador
[1901] Greek: moron, stupid, dull

12 And the younger of them said to father, father, give me the **section** of goods that **belong to-me**. And he divided **to-them livelihood**.

13 And not many days after the younger son gathered all together, and **traveled** into a far **space**, and there **wasted** his **being**[1902] with **un-saved** living.

14 And when he had spent all, there **became a forceful** famine in that land; and he began to be in want.[1903]

15 And he went and **glued**[1904] himself to a citizen of that **space**; and he **dispatched** him into his fields to feed swine.

16 And he **upon-feeling to-fill** his belly with the **husks-horns** that the swine did eat: and no man gave **to-him**.

17 And when he came **into himself**, he said, how many **wage-earners of** my father have enough bread **in excess**, and I **am-from-ruin** with hunger!

18 I will **up-stand** and go to my father, and will say **to-him**, father, I have sinned against heaven, and before you,

19 And **I-am** no more **deserving** to be called your son: make me as one of your **wage-earners**.

20 And he arose and came to his father. But when he was yet **far from-holding**, his father **perceived** him, and had **gut-compassion,** and ran, and fell on his neck, and kissed him.

21 And the son said **to-him**, father, I have sinned against heaven, and in your sight, and am no more **deserving** to be called your son.

22 But the father said to his **slave**s, bring-out the **foremost** robe, and **clothed**[1905] him; and put a ring on his hand, and **sandals** on **the** feet:

23 And bring **here** the **grain-fed** calf, and **sacrifice**; and let us eat, and be **good-dispositioned**:

24 For this my son was dead, and **up-lives**; he was **from-ruin** and is found. And they began to be **good-disposition**.

25 Now his elder son was in the field: and as he came and **near-squeeze** to the house, he heard **symphony** and dancing.

26 And he called one of the **boys** and **ascertain-by-inquiry** what these things meant.

27 And he said **to-him**, your brother is **arriving**; and your father has **sacrificed** the **grain-fed** calf, because he has **from-get** him **healthy**.

28 And he was **swelling-angry**, and **willed** not **to-enter**: therefore, came his father out, and **beside-called** him.

29 And he answering said **to-the** father, be-**perceiving**, these many **years I-am-slaving to-you**, **not-ever I-beside-came** your commandment: and **not-ever** you gave me a kid, that I might make **good-disposition** with my friends:

30 But as soon as this your son was come, which has devoured your **livelihood** with **prostitutes**, you have **sacrificed** for him the **grain-fed** calf.

31 And he said **to-him**, **child**, you are **always** with me, and all that I have is yours!

32 Yet, it-was-**binding to-be-good-disposition**, and be **cheerful**: **that** your brother was dead, and **up-lives**; and was **from-ruin** and is found.

LUKE CHAPTER 16

1 And he said also **towards** his disciples, there was a certain rich man, who had a **house-lawyer**; and the same was **deviled**[1906] **to-him** that he had **through-scattered** his goods.

2 And he voiced him, and said **to-him**, how is it that I hear this of you? Give a **word** of your **house-law**, because not **you-shall-be** powerful still **to-be a house-lawyer**.

3 Then the **house-lawyer** said within himself, what shall I do? For my lord **lifts** from me the **hose-law**: **to-dig, I-am-not-forceful**; to beg **I-am-being-disfigured**.

4 I **knew** what to do, that, when I am put out of the **house-law**, they may **welcome** me into their houses.

5 So he called every one of his lord's debtors[1907] **to-him**, and said **to-the foremost**, how much owe you **to** my lord?

6 And he said, a hundred measures of oil. And he said **to-him**, **welcome** your bill, and sit down quickly, and write fifty.

[1902] Greek: "ousia," feminine of "on," a present participle of "eimi" (I exist)
[1903] Or, late
[1904] Or, to stick to, to cling, to keep company with
[1905] Lit., in-down; or, in-sink, in-down-slipping
[1906] Greek: "diaballo," the root word for "devil" (diabolos), back-bite, slander
[1907] Or use-owing-ones

7 Then said he to **another-different,** and how much **you owe**? And he said, a hundred measures of wheat. And he said **to-him**, **welcome** your bill, and write **eighty**.

8 And the lord **upon-praised** the **unrighteous house-lawyer**, because he had done **disposed**:[1908] for the **sons** of this world are in their generation **more-disposed** than the **sons** of light.

9 And I say **to-you**, make **to-yourselves** friends of the mammon[1909] of unrighteousness; that, when you **omit**,[1910] they may **welcome** you into **the eternal tabernacles**.

10 He that is **believing** in that which is least is **believing** also in much: and he that is **unrighteous** in the least is **unrighteous** also in much.

11 If therefore you have not been **believing** in the unrighteous mammon, who will **believe to-you** the true?

12 And if you have not been **believing** in that which is **another's-same**, who shall give you that which is your own?

13 No **domestic is-powerful be-slaving to-two** masters: for either he will hate the one and love the **other-different;** or else he will **uphold** to the one, and **down-disposition** the **other-different**. **Not you-are-powerful to-be-slaving to-**God and **to-**mammon.

14 And the Pharisees also, who **under-originals-ones friends-of-silver**, heard all these things: and they**-out-of-nosed**[1911] him.

15 And he said **to-them,** you are they which **righteous-ones,** yourselves, before men; but God knows your **hearts**: for that which is **lofty in** men is abomination[1912] in the sight of God.

16 The **Law and the Prophets** until John: **from then** the kingdom of God is preached, and every man **presses-violently** into it.

17 And it is easier for heaven and earth to pass, than one tittle[1913] of the law to **fall**.

18 Whoever **from-loose** his wife, and marries **another-different, is-committing-adultery:** and whoever marries her that is **from-loosed** from husband **is-committing-adultery**.

19 There was a certain rich man, who was clothed in purple and linen, and **good-disposed, brightly,** every day:

20 And there was a certain **poor** named Lazarus, which was **cast** at his gate, full of sores,

21 And **on-feeling** to be fed with the crumbs which fell from the rich man's table: moreover, the dogs came and licked his sores.

22 And **it became**, that the **poor** died, and was carried by the angels into Abraham's bosom: the rich man also died, and was buried;

23 And in **Hell** he lifts up his eyes, **under-originate-one** in torments, and sees Abraham afar off, and Lazarus in his bosoms.

24 And he voiced and said, father Abraham, have **pity-mercy** on me, and **dispatch** Lazarus, that he may **baptize**[1914] the tip of his finger in water, and cool my tongue; for I am **pained** in this flame.[1915]

25 But Abraham said, **child**, remember that you in your **life from-took** your good things, and likewise Lazarus evil things: but now he is **beside-call**, and you are **pained**.

26 And beside all this, between us and you there is a **great chasm** fixed:[1916] so that they which **willing to-through-step** from **within towards you not is-powerful**; neither they **through-cross towards** us, that from there.

27 Then he said, I **ask** you therefore, father, that you **would-dispatched** him to my father's house:

28 For I have five **brothers**; that he may **through-witnesses to-them, that not** they also come into this **spot** of torment.

29 Abraham says **to-him**, they have Moses and the prophets; let them hear them.

30 And he said, no, father Abraham: but if one went **to-them** from the dead, they will **change-thought**.

31 And he said **to-him**, if they hear not Moses and the prophets, neither will they **believe**, though one rose from the dead.

[1908] Or prudent disposition
[1909] Chaldee for confidence, wealth
[1910] To leave out
[1911] Or, to sneer
[1912] To stink
[1913] Lit., horn-like
[1914] Greek: bapto—to whelm, to cover wholly with fluid
[1915] Greek, "phlox," transliterated as flash, flame, and flux
[1916] Or, stood

LUKE CHAPTER 17

1 Then said he **to** the disciples, it is **un-in-welcome** but that **scandals** will come: but woe through whom they come!

2 **It-is-loose-finish** for him that a **donkey's** mill was hanged about his neck, and **he-is-fling** into the sea, **rather-**than that he should **scandal** one of these little ones.

3 **Towards-hold to-yourselves:** If your brother **sins into** you, rebuke him; and if he **after-mind, release**[1917] him.

4 And if he **sins into** you **seven** in a day, and **seven** in a day turn again **to-you**, saying, I **after-mind**; you shall **release** him.

5 And the apostles said **to-the** Lord, **add to-**our faith!

6 And the Lord said, if you had faith as a grain of mustard seed, you might say **to** this sycamore tree, be **out-of-rooted,** and be planted in the sea; and it **under-heard**[1918] you.

7 But which of you, having a **slave** plowing or **shepherding**, will say **to-him soon**, when he is come from the field, go and **up-fall**?[1919]

8 And will not rather say **to-him, internally-prepare something I-should-be-supping,**[1920] and **belt** yourself, and **attended to-me, until** I have eaten and drank; and afterward, you shall eat and drink?

9 Does he **grace** that **slave** because he did the things that were **through-arranged** him? I **seem** not.

10 So likewise you, when you shall have done all those things which are **through-arranged** you, say, we are **un-used slave**s: we have done that which **we-owed** to do.

11 And **it became**, as he went to Jerusalem, that he passed through the middle of Samaria and Galilee.

12 And as he entered into a certain village, ten men met him that were lepers, who stood afar off:

13 And they lifted up voice**s**, and said, Jesus, **Commander**, have **pity-mercy** on us.

14 And when he **perceived** he said **to-them**, go show yourselves **to-the** priests. And **it became**, that, as they went, they were **cleaned**.

15 And one **out-of** them, when he **perceived** that he was **cured**, turned back, and with a **great** voice glorified God,

16 And fell down on **his-**face at his feet, giving him thanks: and he was a Samaritan.

17 And Jesus answering said, were there not ten **cleaned**? **Yet, where-are** the nine?

18 There are not found that returned to give glory to God, **if not** this **another-same-race.**[1921]

19 And he said **to-him**, arise, go your way: your faith has **saved** you.

20 And when he was **asked** of the Pharisees, when the kingdom of God should come, he answered them and said, the kingdom of God comes not with **beside-carefully-watching**:

21 Neither shall they say, **be-perceiving** here! Or, **be-perceiving** there! For, **be-perceiving**, the kingdom of God is within you.

22 And he said **towards** the disciples, the days will come, when you shall **on-feeling** to **perceive** one of the days of the Son of man, and you shall not see.

23 And they shall say **to-you, be-perceiving** here; or, **be-perceiving** there: go not after, nor **chase**.[1922]

24 For as the **star-light,**[1923] that **is-star-lighting out-of** the under heaven, **is-**shining **into** the under heaven; so, shall also the Son of man be in his day.

25 But **foremost, it-is-binding,** he **emotion** many things, and be **from-seem-test**[1924] **from** this generation.

26 And as **it-became** in the days of **Noah,** so shall it be also in the days of the Son of man.

27 They did eat, they drank, they married, they **out-of-marry-ize**[1925], until the day that **Noah** entered into the **Ark**, and the flood came, and **from-ruin** them all.

28 Likewise also as **it-became** in the days of Lot; they did eat, they drank, they bought,[1926] they sold, they planted, they **house-built;**

[1917] Lit., from-let-go
[1918] Or obey
[1919] Or lean back
[1920] Expensive dinner
[1921] Lit., another (same)-kin
[1922] Or persecute
[1923] Astrape, from the root aster (star)
[1924] Rejected
[1925] Ekgamizontes is a compound word comprised of ek (out-of)+gamos (marry)+izein (ize)+ontes (to be), where "ize" means to make or conform to, to act
[1926] Lit., to go to the market, redeem

29 But the same day that Lot went out of Sodom it rained fire and **God-like-burning**[1927] from heaven, and **from-ruin** all.

30 According-to these shall it be in the day when the Son of man is revealed.

31 In that day, he which shall be upon the housetop, and his **vessels** in the house, let him not come down to **lift it**: and he that is in the field, let him likewise not return **behind**.

32 Remember Lot's wife.

33 Whoever shall seek to **around-make**[1928] his **soul** shall **from-ruin** it; and whoever shall **from-ruin his soul** shall **life-generate** it.

34 I tell you, in that night there shall be two on one **cot**;[1929] the one shall be **being-beside-taken**, and the **other-different** shall be-**released**.[1930]

35 Two shall be grinding together; the one shall be **beside-taken**, and the other **released**.

36 Two shall be in the field; the one shall be **beside-taken**, and the **other-different released**.

37 And they answered and said **to-him**, where Lord? And he said **to** them, **wherever** the body, there will the eagles be gathered together.

LUKE CHAPTER 18

1 And he spoke a parable **to** them, **it-is-binding** that men always to **towards-pray-wish,** and not **out-of-evil**;

2 Saying, there was in a city a judge, which feared not God, neither **in-turn** man:

3 And there was a widow in that city; and she came **to-him**, saying, avenge[1931] me of my **plaintiff.** [1932]

4 And he **willed** not **upon uninterrupted-time**: but afterward he said within himself, though I fear not God, nor **in-turn** man;

5 Yet because this widow **beside-hold** me, I will avenge her, lest by her coming **into finish**, she-**under-gaze,** [1933] **to**-me.

6 And the Lord said, hear what the judge, **the unrighteous,** says.

7 And shall not God **produce avenging** his own elect, which cry day and night **to-him**, though he **long-sacrifice-anger on** them?

8 I tell you that he will **produce avenging** them **swiftly**. Nevertheless, when the Son of man **comes**, shall he find **the** faith on the earth?

9 And he spoke this parable **towards** certain which trusted in themselves that they were righteous, and **out-of-nothing** others:

10 Two men **up-walked** into the **priest-place** to **towards-pray-wish**; the one a Pharisee, and the **other-different** a **tax-collector**.

11 The Pharisee stood and prayed **these-things** with himself, God, I thank you, that I am not as **remaining** men, **snatchers, unrighteous,** adulterers, or even as this **tax-collector**.

12 I fast twice **of the Sabbath**; I give tithes of all that I **acquire**.

13 And the **tax-collector**, standing afar off, **willed** not **to**-lift up so much as eyes **to** heaven, but **beat** upon his **chest**, saying, God be **merry-atoned**[1934] to me a sinner.

14 I tell you; this man went down **into** his house **righteous** than **than-one**: for every one that **elevate** himself shall be **humbled**; and he that humbles himself shall be **elevated**.

15 And they brought **to-him** also infants, that he would **fasten to-them:** but when disciples **perceived**, they rebuked them.

16 But Jesus **towards**-called them, and said, **release**[1935] children to come **towards** me, and **prevent** them not: for of such is the kingdom of God.

17 Amen, I say **to-you**, **whoever** shall not **welcome** the kingdom of God as a child shall **no not** enter **into her**.

18 And a certain **first-rank,**[1936] asked him, saying, Good **Teach**er, what shall I do to inherit **eternal** life?

[1927] Lit., "theion" a place struck by "deity" lightning, God-flashing, God-lightning
[1928] Greek: peri (around) and poieo (make, produce), means to purchase, acquire
[1929] Or (re)cline
[1930] Lit., from-let-go, forgiven
[1931] Or out-of-justice
[1932] Lit., anti-just, opponent, instead of justice
[1933] Or, to hit under the eye
[1934] Greek: "hilaskomai" and means propitious (atonement); atonement-merry; from the same root for "Mercyseat"
[1935] Lit., from-let-go
[1936] Or, original-rank, beginning-rank

19 And Jesus said **to-him**, why call you me good? None good, **if not**, God.

20 You **perceived** the commandments, no adultery, **no murder**, no stealing, **no** false-witnessing, **money-value** your father and your mother.

21 And he said, all these have I **watched** from my youth up.

22 Now when Jesus heard these things, he said **to-him**, yet you lack one thing: sell all that you have, and **give to-the** poor, and you shall have **placed-into-tomorrow**[1937] in heaven: and come, follow me.

23 And when he heard this, he was **about- sorrowful**: for he was very rich.

24 And when Jesus **perceived** that he was **about-sorrowful**, he said, how **difficult-eat**[1938] shall they that have riches enter into the kingdom of God!

25 For it is easier for a camel to go through a needle's eye, than for a rich man to enter into the kingdom of God.

26 And they that heard said, who then **is-powerful to-be-saved**?

27 And he said, the things which are **un-powerful near** men are **powerful near** God.

28 Then Peter said, **be-perceiving**, we have **released**[1939] all, and followed you.

29 And he said **to-them**, amen I say **to-you**, there is no man that has **released**[1940] house, or parents, or **brothers**, or wife, or children, **on-account-of** the kingdom of God,

30 Who shall not **from-take many-fold** more in this **season**, and in the **age** to come, **eternal** life.

31 Then he **beside-take** the twelve, and said **to** them, **be-perceiving**, we **are-up-walking into** Jerusalem, and all things that are written **through** the prophets **to-the** the Son of man shall be **finished**.

32 For he shall be **betrayed**[1941] **to** the **nations**, and shall be **in-childish-mocked**, and **insulted**[1942] and spitted on:

33 And they shall **whip-him** and put him to death: and the third day he shall rise again.

34 And they **synthesized** none of these things: and this **declaration** was **hidden** from them, neither knew they the things which were spoken.

35 And **it became**, that as he **near-squeeze to** Jericho, a certain blind man sat **beside** the way **toward-ask**:

36 And hearing the multitude pass by, he **ascertain-by-inquiry what-this may-be**.

37 And they **from-message to-him**, that Jesus of Nazareth **beside-come**.

38 And he cried, saying, Jesus, you Son of David, have **pity-mercy** on me.

39 And they which went before rebuked him, that **he-should-be-silent**: but he **screamed** more, you Son of David, have **pity-mercy** on me.

40 And Jesus stood, and **order** him to be brought **to-him**: and when he was come near, he asked him,

41 Saying, what **will** you that I shall **produce to-you**? And he said, Lord, that I may **up-look**.

42 And Jesus said **to-him**, **up-look**: your faith has saved you.

43 And **instantly** he **up-look**, and followed him, glorifying God: and all the people, when they **perceived**, gave praise **to** God.

LUKE CHAPTER 19

1 And **having-entered**, he-**through-passed** Jericho.

2 And, **be-perceiving**, a man named Zacchaeus, which was a **first-rank-tax-collectors**, and he was rich.

3 And he sought to **perceive** Jesus who **he-is**; and **not is-powerful from** the multitude, because he was little of stature.

4 And he **before-raced**, and **up-walked on** a sycamore[1943] tree to **perceive** him: **that he-is-impending** to **come-through** that.

5 And when Jesus came to the **spot** he looked up, and **perceived** him, and said **to-him**, Zacchaeus, make haste, and come down; for today **it-is-binding** I **remain** at your house.

[1937] Greek: "thesauros," place into tomorrow, transliterated as "thesaurus"
[1938] Or, fastidious (meticulous about eating); peevish (fretful, worry); difficult-food (eating), impractical
[1939] Release, forgiven
[1940] From-let-go, from-send, forgive
[1941] Beside-give
[1942] Greek: Hubris
[1943] Lit., sykon (fig) and moron (mulberry)

Luke

6 And he **sped**, and came down, and **under-welcome** him **cheerfully**.

7 And when they **perceived**, they all **through grumbled**, saying, that he was gone to be **down-loose**[1944] with a man that is a sinner.

8 And Zacchaeus stood, and said **towards** the Lord; **be-perceiving**, Lord, the half of my **under-original-goods** I give to the poor; and if I **have-fig-informed**[1945] anything from any man, I **from-give quadruple**.

9 And Jesus said **to-him**, today is salvation come to this house, **down-that**, he also is a son of Abraham.

10 For the Son of man is come to seek and to save that which was **from-ruined**.

11 And as they heard these things, he added and spoke a parable, because he was **near-squeeze** to Jerusalem, and because they **seeming** that the kingdom of God **impending instantly to-up-light**.

12 He said therefore, a certain **good-birth** went into a far **space** to **take** for himself a kingdom, and to return.

13 And he called his ten **slave**s, and **gives** them ten pounds, and said **to-them, practice until** I come.

14 Yet, his citizens hated him, and sent an **eldership**[1946] after him, saying, we will not have **this-man** to reign over us.

15 And **it became**, that when he was returned, having **taking** the kingdom, then he **said** these **slave**s to be voiced **to-him**, to whom he had given the **silver**, that he might know **which, which, through-practice**.

16 Then **beside-became** the foremost, saying, Lord, your **weight** has **work-additionally**[1947] ten **weights**.

17 And he said **to-him, good**, you **intrinsic-good slave**: because you have been **believing** in **smallest**, have you authority over ten cities.

18 And the second came, saying, Lord, your **weight** has **produced** five **weights**.

19 And he said likewise **to-him**, be you also **upon-above** five cities.

20 And **another-different** came, saying, Lord, **be-perceiving**, your **weight**, which I have kept laid up in a **sweat-cloth**:

21 For I feared you, because you are an austere[1948] man: you **lift** that you **place not** and reap that you **did** not sow.

22 And he says **to-him**, out of your own mouth will I judge you, you **wicked-hurtful slave**. You **perceived** that I was an austere man, **lifting which I place not**, and reaping that I did not sow:

23 Through why then, gave you not my money into the **table-bank**, that at my coming I might have **practiced it** with **interest-produced**?

24 And he said **to-them** that **beside-stood, lift** from him the **weight**, and give **to-him** that has ten **weights**.

25 (And they said **to-him**, Lord, he has ten **weights**.)

26 For I say **to-you**, that **to everyone** which has shall be given; and from him that has not, even that he has shall be **lifted** from him.

27 Moreover, those **my haters**, which would not that I should reign over them, bring here, and **down-butcher** before me.

28 And when he had spoken **these-things**, he went before, **up-walking into** Jerusalem.

29 And **it became**, when he was **near-squeeze** to Bethphage and Bethany, at the **mountain** called of Olives, he sent two of his disciples,

30 Saying, go you into the village over against; in the which at your entering you shall find a **colt** tied, **on which no man ever sat**: loose him, and bring.

31 And if any man asks you, why are you **loosing**? **In-this-way** you shall say **to-him**: because the Lord has need of him.

32 And they that were sent went their way and found **down-as** he had said **to** them.

33 And as they were **loosing** the **colt**, the **lords of-him** said **to** them, why **loose** you the **colt**?

34 And they said, the Lord has need of him

35 And they brought him to Jesus: and they cast their garments upon the **colt**, and they **mount Jesus upon it**.

36 And as he went, they spread their clothes in the way.

37 And when he was **near-squeeze, already** at the descent of the **mountain** of Olives, the **entire fullness**

[1944] Or a guest
[1945] Or, a reporter of the law forbidden the exportation of figs, defraud, exact unlawfully, extortion
[1946] Or ambassador
[1947] Or towards-work
[1948] "Auster" is transliterated from the Greek "austeros," meaning rough as a gale, harsh, stringent

of the disciples began to **cheer** and praise God with a **great** voice **about** all the **powers** that they had **perceived**;

38 Saying, blessed the King that comes in the name of the Lord: peace in heaven, and glory in the highest.

39 And some of the Pharisees from among the multitude said **towards him**, **Teacher**, rebuke your disciples.

40 And he answered and said **to** them, I tell you that, if these should-**be-silent**, the stones would **scream**.

41 And when he was come near, he **perceived** the city, and wept over it,

42 Saying, if you knew, even you, at least in this your day, the things **toward** your peace! **Yet** now they are **hidden** from your eyes.

43 For the days shall **arrive** upon you, that your **haters** shall cast a trench about you, and **about-circle**, and **together-hold** you on every side,

44 And shall **level you**, and your children within you; and they shall not **release**[1949] in you one stone upon **stone**; because you knew not the **season** of your **bishopric.**[1950]

45 And he went into the **priest-place**, and began to cast out **those-selling in it, and those-buying;**[1951]

46 Saying **to-them**, it is written, my house is the house of prayer: but you have made it a **cave** of **robbers**.

47 And he taught daily in the **priest-place**. But the **first-rank-priests** and the scribes and the **foremost-ones** of the people sought to **from-ruin** him,

48 And could not find what they might do: for all the people were very **out-hung** to hear him.

LUKE CHAPTER 20

1 And **it became, first** of those days, as he taught the people in the **priest-place**, and **evangelized**, the **first-rank-priests** and the scribes **upon-stand** with the elders,

2 And spoke **to-him**, saying, tell us, by what authority do you these things? Or who is he that gave you this authority?

3 And he answered and said **towards** them, I will also ask you one **word;** and answer me:

4 The baptism of John, was it **out-of** heaven, or **out-of** men?

5 And they **together-inventoried towards** themselves, saying, if we shall say, **out-of** heaven; he will say, why not then you believed him?

6 Yet, if we say, **out-of** men; all the people will stone us: for they **believed** that John was a prophet.

7 And they answered that they could not **perceive where**.

8 And Jesus said **to-them**, neither I tell you **in what-kind** authority I do these things.

9 Then began him to speak **towards** the people this parable; a certain man planted a vineyard, and **out-gave** to **land-workers**, and **from-people** for **sufficient uninterrupted**-time.

10 And at the season he sent a **slave** to the **land-workers**, that they should give him of the fruit of the vineyard: but the **land-workers skinned** him and sent away empty.

11 And **he-added, dispatched another-different slave**: and they **skinned** him also, and **un-valued**, and **dispatched** away empty.

12 And **he-added, dispatched** a third: and they **traumatized**[1952] him also, and **out-of-cast.**

13 Then said the lord of the vineyard, what shall I **produce**? I will **dispatch** my beloved son: **maybe** they will **invert** when they **perceive** him.

14 But when the **land-workers perceived** him, they **through-inventoried towards** themselves, saying, this is the heir: come, let us kill him, that the inheritance may **become** ours.

15 So they cast him out of the vineyard and killed. What therefore shall the lord of the vineyard **produce to-them?**

16 He shall come and **from-ruin** these **land-workers** and shall give the vineyard to others. And when they heard, they said, **not may-it-become**.

17 And he **in-looked-at** them, and said, what is this then that is written, the stone which the **house-builders from-seem-test,**[1953] the same is become the head of the corner?

[1949] Lit., from-let-go, forgive
[1950] Greek: "episkope" (upon-peer-about, upon-watch, a sentry, a scout); "episcopate," bishopric, visitation
[1951] Lit., to go to the market, redeem
[1952] Greek: "traumatize" traumatized, to wound
[1953] Rejected

18 Whoever shall fall upon that stone shall be broken; but on **whomever** it shall fall, it will **winnow him**.

19 And the **first-rank-priests** and the scribes the same hour sought to lay hands on him; and they feared the people: for they **knew** that he had spoken this parable **towards** them.

20 And they watched, and sent forth spies,[1954] which should **hypocrite** themselves **just**, that they might **upon-take** of his words, that so they might **betray**[1955] him **to** the **originals** and **to-the** authority **of-the leader**.

21 And they asked him, saying, **Teacher**, we **perceive** that you say and teach **strait-erectly**,[1956] neither **take** you the **face**, but teach the way of God **upon** truth:

22 Is it lawful for us to give **load-tax to** Caesar, or no?

23 But he **down-mind** their **all-working**,[1957] and said **towards** them, why **probe-test** you me?

24 Shew me a **denarius**. Whose image and **inscription** has it? They answered and said, Caesar's.

25 And he said **towards** them, **from-give** therefore **to-Caesar** the things which **of-Caesar**, and **to-**God the things which **of-God**.

26 And **not-they-are-forceful to-upon-take his declarations** before the people: and they marveled at his answer, and **they-were-silenced**.

27 Then came to certain of the Sadducees, which **anti-word**[1958]that there is any resurrection; and they asked him,

28 Saying, **Teacher**, Moses wrote **to-us**, if any man's brother dies, having a wife, and he die without children, that his brother should **take** his wife, and raise up seed **to-his** brother.

29 There were therefore seven **brothers**: and the **foremost take** a wife and died without children.

30 And the second **took** her to wife, and he died childless.

31 And the third **took** her; and in like manner the seven also: and they left no children and died.

32 Subsequently of all, the woman died also.

33 Therefore in the resurrection whose wife of them is she? **Because** seven had her to wife.

34 And Jesus answering said **to-them**, the **sons** of this **age** marry, and are **out-of-**marriage:

35 But **those deserving** to **happen**[1959] that age, and the resurrection **out-of** the dead, neither marry, nor are **out-of-**marriage:

36 Neither **they-are-powerful to-die** any more: **because** they are **similar-to-angels**; and are the **sons** of God, being the **sons** of the resurrection.

37 Now that the dead are raised, even Moses **disclosed** at the **thorn-bush**, when he calls the Lord the God of Abraham, and the God of Isaac, and the God of Jacob.

38 For he is not a God of the dead, but of the living: **because** all **are-living to-him**.

39 Then certain of the scribes answering said, **Teacher**, you have **ideally** said.

40 And after that they dared not ask him **anything**.

41 And he said **towards** them, how say they that Christ is David's son?

42 And David himself says in the **scroll** of Psalms, the **Lord** said **to** my Lord, **be-sitting out-of** my right hand,

43 Until I make your **enemy-haters** your footstool.

44 David therefore calls him Lord, how is he then his son?

45 Then in the **hearing** of all the people he said **to-his** disciples,

46 towards-hold from the scribes, which desire to walk in robes, and **friend embracing** in the markets, and the **foremost-seats** in the synagogues, and the **foremost-recliner** at **expensive-dinners**;

47 Which devour widows' houses, and for a **pretense**[1960] make **great** prayers: the same shall **take more-excessive judgment-result**.[1961]

LUKE CHAPTER 21

1 And he looked up and **perceived** the rich men casting their gifts into the **treasure-guard**.

[1954] In-down-lay
[1955] Or beside-give
[1956] "Otrhos"
[1957] Craftiness

[1958] Or refute, dispute
[1959] Or, hit the mark, chance upon, obtain,
[1960] To appear before, before-appear
[1961] Greek: "krima," transliterated as "crime" and also means judgment

Luke

2 And he **also perceived** a certain **poor-wage-worker** widow casting in there two **peeled-copper**.[1962]

3 And he said, **truly,** I say **to-you**, that this **poor-crouching** widow has cast in more than they all:

4 For all these have of their **excess** cast **into** the offerings of God: but she of her **deficit**[1963] has cast in all the **livelihood** that she had.

5 And as some spoke of the **priest-place**, how it was **cosmetic** with **ideal** stones and gifts, he said,

6 These things which **you-are-beholding,** the days will come, in the which there shall not **be-released**[1964] one stone upon another, that shall not be **down-loosed**.

7 And they asked him, saying, **Teacher**, but when shall these things be? And what sign when these things **impending to-be-becoming**?

8 And he said, **be-looking** that you be not **seduced**: for many shall come in my name, saying, I am; and the **season near-squeeze**: not go after them.

9 But when you shall hear of wars and **instability**,[1965] be not terrified: **because it-is-binding** these things **foremost become**; but the **finish** not **soon**.

10 Then said he **to-them,** nation shall rise **upon** nation, and kingdom **upon** kingdom:

11 And **great quakes down spots**,[1966] and famines, and pestilences;[1966] and **fearful-things** and **great** signs shall there be from heaven.

12 But before all these, they shall lay their hands on you, and **chase**, **betraying into** the synagogues, and into prisons, **being lead** before kings and **leaders on-account-of my name**.

13 And it shall **from-stepping**[1967] **to-you into witness**.

14 Place therefore in your **hearts**, not to **before-care** what you shall **answer**:

15 For I will give you a mouth and wisdom, which all your **anti-laying-ones**[1968] **not shall-be-powerful** to **anti-say** nor **anti-stand**.

16 And you shall be **betrayed**[1969] both by parents, and **brothers**, and **together-kin**, and friends; and of you shall they cause to be put to death.

17 And you shall be **detested** of all **through my name**.

18 But there shall not a hair of your head **from-ruin**.

19 In your **under-remain acquire** you your souls.

20 And when you shall **perceive** Jerusalem **encircled** with armies,[1970] then know that the desolation **of-her** is **near-squeezed**.

21 Then let them which are in Judaea flee to the mountains; and let them which are in the **middle** of it depart out; and let not them that are in the **spaces** enter into **her**.

22 For these be the days of vengeance, that all things which are written may be **filled**.

23 But woe **to-them** that are with child, and **to-them** that give suckle, in those days! **Because** there shall be **great arm-bending-necessity** in the land and **swelling-anger** upon this people.

24 And they shall fall by the edge of the sword and shall be led away captive into all nations: and Jerusalem shall be **trampled** of the **nations**, until the **seasons** of the **nations** be **filled**.

25 And there shall be signs in the sun, and in the moon, and in the stars; and upon the earth **together-hold**[1971] of nations, with **having-no-way-out**; the sea and the waves[1972] **echoing**;

26 Men **from-breathing**[1973] from fear, and **toward-seeming to-**those things which are coming on the **housed-land**: for the powers **of-the** heaven shall be shaken.

27 And then shall they see the Son of man coming in **to-cloud** with power and **much** glory.

28 And when these things begin **to-be-becoming,** then **up-bend,** and lift your heads; for your **from-loose**[1974] **near-squeeze**

29 And he spoke **to-them** a parable; **be-perceiving** the fig tree, and all the trees;

30 When they **already** shoot forth, you see and know **from yourself** that summer is **already near-squeeze**.

[1962] Lit., "lepton" as flake, a peel, something scaled
[1963] Root: to be later, fall short
[1964] Lit., from-let-go, forgive
[1965] Greek: down-standing, inconstant, unstable
[1966] Greek: "loimos," disease, pest, plague
[1967] Lit., disembark, eventuate
[1968] Greek: anti-laying outstretched
[1969] Lit., beside-given
[1970] Or lit., war-feet
[1971] Or anguish
[1972] Lit., vibrating
[1973] Or, breathing out, from-cooling
[1974] Or redemption

31 So likewise you, when you **perceive** these things **becoming**, know you that the kingdom of God is **near-squeeze**.

32 Amen I say **to-you**, this generation shall not pass away, **until** all **may-be-becoming**.

33 Heaven and earth shall pass away: but my words shall not pass away.

34 Yet towards-hold to-yourselves, lest your **hearts** be **weighty** with **skull-vibration,**[1975] and drunkenness,[1976] and **portion-worry to-livelihood,** and that day come upon you **unapparent**[1977].

35 For as a **trap** shall it **become** on all them **sitting** on the face of **all the** earth.

36 Be-sleepless therefore, and **beg-bind in all season**, that you may be **deserving** to escape all these things that **impending to-become,** and to stand before the Son of man.

37 And in the day, he was teaching in the **priest-place**; and at night he went out, and **yard-lodge**[1978] in the mountains that is called of Olives.

38 And all the people came early **towards** him in the **priest-place**, for to hear him.

LUKE CHAPTER 22

1 Now the **Festival** of **Unfermented near-squeezed**, which is called the Passover.

2 And the **first-rank-priests** and scribes sought how they might **up-lift,**[1979] him; for they feared the people.

3 Then entered Satan into Judas, **upon-called**[1980] Iscariot, being **out-of** the number of the twelve.

4 And he went his way, and **together-talked** with the **first-rank-priests** and **generals**,[1981] how he might betray him **to-them.**

5 And they were **cheerful**, and **together-placed** to give him **silver.**

6 And he promised and sought **good-season** to betray him **to-them** in the absence of the multitude.

7 Then came the **Day of Unfermented**, when **it-is-binding** the **Passover** be **sacrificed.**

8 And he sent Peter and John, saying, go and **internally-prepare** us the **Passover**, that we may eat.

9 And they said **to-him**, where **will** you that we **internally-prepare?**

10 And he said **to** them, **be-perceiving**, where you are entered into the city, there shall a man meet you, bearing a pitcher of water; follow him into the house where he enters in.

11 And you shall say **to** the **house-owner**, the **Teacher** says **to-you**, where is the guest-chamber, where I shall eat the **Passover** with my disciples?

12 And he shall show you a **great up-above-ground spread**: there **internally-prepare.**

13 And they went and found as he had said **to** them: and they **internally-prepared** the **Passover.**

14 And when the hour **became**, he **up-falls,**[1982] and the twelve apostles **together to**-him.

15 And he said **towards** them, with **upon-feeling** I have **upon-feel**[1983] to eat this **Passover** with you before I **emotion**:

16 For I say **to-you**, I will not any more eat **of-it** until it be **filled** in the kingdom of God.

17 And he **welcomed** the cup, and gave thanks, and said, **take** this, and divide among yourselves:

18 For I say **to-you**, I will not drink of the **generation** of the vine, until the kingdom of God shall come.[1984]

19 And he **takes** bread, and gave thanks, and **broke** and gave **to-them,** saying, this is my body which is given for you: this do in remembrance of me.

20 Likewise also the cup after **the expensive-dinner**, saying, this cup, the **New Covenant** in my blood, which is **poured-out** for you.

21 But, **be-perceiving**, the hand of him that betrays me with me **upon** the table.

22 And truly the Son of man goes, as it was **defined**[1985] but woe **to** that man by whom he is betrayed! [1986]

23 And they began to **together-enquire,** which of them **impending to-practice** this thing.

[1975] Greek: "kraipale" ["kranion" (skull) and "pale" (vibrate, wrestle)]
[1976] Or meth
[1977] Un-lighted
[1978] Lit., yard as open to the air or wind
[1979] Or lit., assassinate
[1980] Or, to entitle, to invoke
[1981] Greek: "strategois" transliterated as "strategists," a Greek compound war-leader
[1982] Or lean back
[1983] Or lust
[1984] Aoristic (has come, is coming, and shall be coming)
[1985] Greek:," horizon"
[1986] Lit., beside-given

24 And there was also a **friend-quarrel** among them, which of them **is-seeming to be larger**.[1987]

25 And he said **to-them**, the kings of the **nations' exercise-lordship of-**them; and they that **exercise-authority** upon them are called **good-workers**.

26 You, however, not so: but he that is **larger** among you, let him be as the younger; and he that is **leading**, as he that does **attend**.

27 For **who** is **larger,** he that **reclines**, or he that **attends**? **Not** he that **reclines**? But I am **in middle of-you** as he that **attends**.

28 You are they which have **through-remained** with me in my **probe-testing**.

29 And I **covenant to-you** a kingdom, as my Father has **covenanted to-**me;

30 That you may eat and drink at my table in my kingdom and sit on thrones **judges-judging** the twelve tribes of Israel.

31 And the Lord said, Simon, Simon, **be-perceiving**, Satan has **requested** you, that he may sift **you** as wheat:

32 But I have **beg-bind** for you, that your faith not **be-omitted**:[1988] and when you are **reverted** strengthen your **brothers**.

33 And he said **to-him**, Lord, I am **internally-prepared to-traverse** with you, both into prison, and **into** death.

34 And he said, I tell you, Peter, the **rooster** shall not voice this day, before that you shall **three you-shall-be-contradicting** that you **perceive** me.

35 And he said **to-them,** when I sent you without **pouch,** and **wallet,** and **sandals,** not you lacked anything? And they said, nothing.

36 Then said he **to** them, but now, he that has a **pouch,** let him **lift,** and likewise, **wallet**: and he that has no sword, let him sell his garment, and buy[1989] one.

37 Because, I say **to-you,** that this that is written **it-is-binding to-be-finished** in me, and he was **inventoried** among the **lawless**: **because** the things concerning me have **a finish**.

38 And they said, Lord, **be-perceiving**, here two swords. And he said **to-them,** it is **sufficient**.[1990]

39 And he **out-of-came,** and went, **down to the ethics, into** the mountain of Olives; and his disciples also followed him.

40 Then **having-becoming upon** the **spot,** he said **to-**them, **towards-pray-wish** that you enter not into **probe-testing**.

41 And he was withdrawn from them about a stone's cast, and **placing the** knees, and **towards-prayed-wished,**

42 Saying, Father, if you **plan-counsel**, remove this cup from me: nevertheless, not my will, but your, **be-becoming**.

43 And there appeared an angel **to-him** from heaven, **in-forcing** him.

44 And **becoming** in an agony he prayed **out-stretched,** and his sweat **became** as it were **clots** of blood falling down to the ground.

45 And when he **stood-up** from **towards-prayer-wish,** and **came** to his disciples, he found them sleeping for **sorrow-pain,**

46 And said **to-them,** why sleep **you**? **Stand-up** and pray, **that not** you enter into **probe-testing**.

47 And while he yet spoke, **be-perceiving** a multitude, and **the one-being-said,** Judas, one of the twelve, went before them, and **near-squeeze to-the** Jesus to **friend-kiss** him.

48 But Jesus said **to-him,** Judas, you betray the Son of man with a **friend-kiss**?

49 When they which were about him **perceived** what would follow, they said **to-him,** Lord, shall we **hit in** the sword?

50 And one of them **hit** the **slave** of the **first-rank-priest** and **released** his right ear.

51 And Jesus answered and said, **let-be until of-this**. And he **fastened** his ear and **cured** him.

52 Then Jesus said **towards** the **first-rank-priests,** and **generals**[1991] of the **priest-place** and the elders, which were come **to-him, are** you come out, as **on a-robber,** with swords and **trees**?

53 When I was daily with you in the **priest-place, not you-out-stretched the** hands **on** me: but this is your hour, and the **authority of-the** darkness.

[1987] Larger, especially in age
[1988] Lit., leave-out-of
[1989] Lit., to go to the market, redeem
[1990] Lit., to arrive; or, competent as if coming in season, ample in amount, fit in character
[1991] Greek: "strategois" transliterated as "strategists," war-leader

54 Then they **together-take** him, and led-**him,** and **lead**-him into the **first-rank-priest**'s house. And Peter followed afar off.

55 And when they had kindled a fire in the **middle** of the **yard**,[1992] and were **together-down-seated**, Peter **sat-down** in middle of-them.

56 But a certain **girl perceived** him as he sat by the fire, and **look-stretching to-him,** and said, this man was also **together to-him.**

57 And he **contradicted** him, saying, woman, I **perceive** him not.

58 And after a little while **another-different perceived** him, and **showed,** you are also **out-of** them. And Peter said, man, I am not.

59 And **of-through-standing as-if first** hour after **another-same through-forcefully**, saying, of a truth this also was with him: **because** he is a Galilean.

60 And Peter said, man, I **perceive** not what you say. And **instantly**, while he yet spoke, the **rooster** voices.

61 And the Lord turned, and **in-looked** Peter. And Peter remembered the **Word of the Lord**, how he had said **to-him,** before the **rooster** crow, you shall **from-contradict**[1993] me three.

62 And Peter went out and wept bitterly. [1994]

63 And the men that held Jesus **in-childish-mocked**[1995] him, and **skinning.**

64 And when they had blindfolded him, they **thumped** him on the face, and asked him, saying, prophesy, who is it that **hitting** you?

65 And many **other-different** things blasphemously spoke they **into him.**

66 And **as it-became** day, the elders of the people and the **first-rank-priests** and the scribes came together, and led him into their **Sanhedrin**, saying,

67 If **you are** the Christ, tell us? And he said **to-them,** If I tell you, you will not believe:

68 And if I also ask, you will not answer me, nor **from-loose.**

69 From the now, shall the Son of man **be-sitting out-of** the right hand of the power of God.

70 Then said they all, **are** you then the Son of-**the** God? And he **showed towards** them, you **are-say**ing that I am.

71 And they said, what need we any further witness? **Because** we ourselves have heard of his own mouth.

LUKE CHAPTER 23

1 And the whole **fullness** of them **up-stand** and led him **upon the** Pilate.

2 And they began to accuse him, saying, we found this-**one distorting** the nation, and **preventing** to give **load-taxes** to Caesar, saying that he himself is Christ a King.

3 And Pilate asked him, saying, **are** you the King of the Jews? And he answered him and **showed**, you **are-saying.**

4 Then said Pilate to the **first-rank-priests** and the **multitude**, I find no **cause** in this man.

5 And they were **upon-forceful**, saying, he stirs up the people, teaching throughout all Judea, beginning from Galilee **until here.**

6 When Pilate heard of Galilee, he asked whether the man was a Galilean.

7 And as soon as he knew that he belonged to Herod's **authority**, he sent him to Herod, who himself also was at Jerusalem **in these days**.

8 And when Herod **perceived** Jesus, he was **cheerful**: for he was **willing** to **perceive** him **out-of sufficient, through hearing** many things of him; and he **expected** to have **perceived** some **sign becoming** by him.

9 Then he questioned with him in **sufficient** words; but he answered him nothing.

10 And the **first-rank-priests** and scribes stood and **good-stretched**[1996] accused him.

11 And Herod with his men of war **made-him-nothing**, and **in-childish-mocked**, and arrayed him in a **radiant** robe, and sent him again to Pilate.

12 And the same day Pilate and Herod **became** friends **with one-another because**, before they were **haters towards** themselves.

[1992] Yard as open to the air and/or wind
[1993] Or utterly contradict
[1994] Lit., acridity (strong, irritating, unpleasant, pungent (sharp), taste or smell), poison
[1995] Greek: "empaiktes" (in-sport (mock) as a boy)
[1996] Or well-strung manner

Luke

13 And Pilate, when he had called together the **first-rank-priests** and the **first-rank**,[1997] and the people,

14 Said **towards** them, you have brought this man **to** me, as one that perverts the people: and, **be-perceiving**, I, having **up-judged-him** before you, have found no **cause** in this man **of-which** you accuse him:

15 No, nor yet Herod: for I sent you **to-him**; and, **be-perceiving**, nothing **deserving** of death is **practiced to-him**.

16 I will therefore **boy-train** him, and **from-loose-him**.

17 (Yet of **arm-bending-necessity** he must **from-loose** one **to-them** at the **festival**.)

18 Yet, they **up-cried every-full**, saying, **be-lifting this-one** and **from-loose to-us** Barabbas:

19 (Who for a certain **insurrection**[1998] made in the city, and for murder, was cast into prison.)

20 Pilate therefore, willing to **from-loose** Jesus, again, **towards-sound to-them**.

21 But they **upon-sounded**, saying, **crucify! Crucify him!**

22 And he said **towards** them the **third**, why, what evil has he **produce**d? I have found no cause of death in him: I will therefore **boy-train** him, and **from-loose him**.

23 Yet, they **upon-lay** with **great** voices, **asking** that he might be crucified. And the voices of them and of the **first-rank-priests down-forceful**.

24 And Pilate **upon-judged** that it should **become** as they **asked**.

25 And he **from-loosed to-them** him that for **insurrection** and murder was cast into prison, whom they had **asked**; but he **betrayed** Jesus to their will.

26 And as they **from-lead**, they laid hold upon one Simon, a Cyrenian, coming **from** the **field**, and on him they laid the cross, that he might bear **behind** Jesus.

27 And there followed him **many fullness** of people, and of women, which also wailed[1999] and lamented him.

28 But Jesus turning **to-them** said, daughters of Jerusalem, weep not for me, but weep for yourselves, and for your children.

29 For, **be-perceiving**, the days are coming, in the which they shall say, **happy** the barren, and the wombs that never bare, and the **breast** which never gave **suckle**.

30 Then shall they begin to say to the mountains, fall on us; and to the hills, cover us.

31 For if they do these things in a **wet** tree, what shall **become** in the **dry-withered**?

32 And there were also two **other-different, evil-workers, together to-him to-be-lifted up**.[2000]

33 And when they were come to the place, which is called **Skull**,[2001] there they crucified him, and the **evil-workers**, one **out-of** the right hand, and the other **out-of** the left.

34 Then said Jesus, Father, **release**[2002] them; for they **perceived** not what they **produced**. And they parted his **garments**, and cast **inheritance**

35 And the people stood **looking**. And the **first-rank**, also with them **out-nosed**, saying, he saved others; let him save himself, if he be Christ, the chosen of God.

36 And the soldiers also **in-childish-mocked** him, coming **to-him**, and **towards-carrying to-**him vinegar,

37 And saying, if you be the king of the Jews, save yourself.

38 And an inscription also was written over him **to-letters to-Gentiles**, and **to-Romans**,[2003] and **Hebrews, this is the King of the Jews**.

39 And one of the **evil-workers** which were hanged **blasphemed** him, saying, if you be Christ, save yourself and us.

40 But the **other-different** answering rebuked him, saying, do you not fear God, seeing you are in the same **judgment-result**?

41 And we indeed justly **deserve, because of-which we-practiced, from-taking**: yet this man has **practiced nothing un-placed**.

42 And he said, Jesus, Lord, remember me **whenever** you come **into** your kingdom.

43 And Jesus said **to-him**, **amen** I say **to-you**; today shall you be with me in **the** paradise.

[1997] Or, original-rank, beginning-rank
[1998] Lit., standing
[1999] Lit., to strike oneself, beating the chest
[2000] Or lit., assassinate
[2001] Greek: "kranion" transliterated as "cranium" (skull)
[2002] Lit., from-let-go
[2003] Greek: "rhomaikos" transliterated as "Romaic"

44 And it was about the sixth hour, and there was darkness over all the earth until **of-ninth** hour.

45 And the sun was darkened, and the veil of the temple **is-split** in the middle.

46 And when Jesus cried with a **great** voice, he said, Father, **into your** hands **I-beside-place**[2004] my spirit: and having said this, **he-out-breathed-hard**.

47 Now when the centurion **perceived** what **became**, he glorified God, saying, **really** this was a righteous man.

48 And all the **multitude** that came together **upon this theatre-spectacle, theatre-spectating the-things becoming, thump** their **chest**, and **under-returned**.

49 And all those **knowing him**, and the women that followed him from Galilee, stood afar off, **seeing** these things.

50 And, **be-perceiving**, a man named Joseph, a **planner-counsellor, under-originate**; a good man, and **righteous**:

51 (The same had not **together-placed** to the **plan-counsel** and **practices** of them;) of **Arimathea**, a city of the Jews: who also himself **towards-welcome** for the kingdom of God.

52 This went **to**-Pilate **and asked** the body of Jesus.

53 And he **down-lift-it,** and wrapped it in linen, and laid it in a **remembrance-tomb** that was **rock-quarried**, **where no-man no-yet** laid.

54 And that day was the **Preparation,** and the Sabbath **upon-shined**.

55 And the women also, which came with him from Galilee, followed after, and **looked-closely-at** the **remembrance-tomb**, and how his body was **placed**.

56 And they returned, and prepared spices and **myrrh**; and **quite-kept-seat** the Sabbath **down** the commandment.

LUKE CHAPTER 24

1 Yet, **to-the** first **of-the** Sabbath, **of-dawn-rising of-deep**, they came **upon** the **remembrance-tomb**, **bearing** the spices which they had **internally-prepared**, and certain **together to**-them.

[2004] Or deposit
[2005] Perplexed
[2006] Or, incredible story, nonsense
[2007] Warm spring

2 And they found the stone rolled away from the **remembrance-tomb**.

3 And they entered in and found not the body of the Lord Jesus.

4 And **it became**, as they **have-no-way-out**[2005] about **this, be-perceiving**, two men stood by them in **star-fall-lighting** garments:

5 And as they **becoming** afraid, and **incline their** faces to the earth, they said **towards** them, why seek you the living **with** the dead?

6 He is not here, but is risen: remember how he spoke **to-you** when he was **still** in Galilee,

7 Saying, **that it-is-binding** the Son of man be-**betrayed** into the hands of sinful men, and be crucified, and the third day **up-stand**.

8 And they remembered his **declarations**,

9 And returned from the **remembrance-tomb**, and **from-message** all these things **to-the eleven,** and to all the **remaining-ones.**

10 It was Mary Magdalene, and Joanna, and Mary of James, and **remaining-ones** with them, which told these things **towards** the apostles.

11 And their **declarations shined to-them** as **twaddle,**[2006] and they believed them not.

12 Then **up-stood** Peter and ran **upon** the **remembrance-tomb**; and **down-stooped,** he looked-at the **linen** laid **only**, and departed, marveling in himself at that which **became**.

13 And, **be-perceiving**, two of them went that same day to a village called Emmaus,[2007] which was from Jerusalem **sixty stadiums.**[2008]

14 And they **conversed** of all these things which had **together-walked.**

15 And **it became**, that, while they **conversed**[2009] and **together-seeking,** Jesus himself **near-squeeze,** and **together-went to**-them.

16 But their eyes were **governed** that they should not **upon-know** him.

17 And he said **towards** them, what manner of **sayings** these that **you-bandy,**[2010] as you walk, and are **bad-tempter-gazed**?[2011]

[2008] Greek: "stadion," transliterated as stadiums
[2009] Lit, to be in company with
[2010] "Bandy" is defined as: to pass back and forth from one to another
[2011] Sullen-face.(gaze), gloomy-face (gaze),

18 And the one of them, whose name was Cleopas,[2012] answering said **to-him**, **are** you only a **foreign-stranger** in Jerusalem, and has not known the things which are **become in her** in these days?

19 And he said **to-them,** what things? And they said **to-him, about** Jesus of Nazareth, which was a prophet **powerful** in **work** and word before God and all the people:

20 And how the **first-rank**-priests and our **first-rank**, **betrayed** him to be **crime-judged** to death, and have crucified him.

21 But we **expected** that **he** had been **he** which **impending to-be-loosing**[2013] Israel: and beside all this, today is the third day **leading from which these-things became**.

22 Yes, and certain women also of our company **ecstasized us**,[2014] which were **in the rising**[2015] at the **remembrance-tomb**;

23 And when they found not his body, they came, saying, that they had also seen a vision of angels, which said that he was alive.

24 And certain of them which were with us went to the **remembrance-tomb** and found even so as the women had said: but him they **perceived** not.

25 Then he said **towards** them, O! **un-mind-ones**, and slow of **heart** to believe all that the prophets have spoken:

26 Not it-was-binding, Christ to have **emotion** these things, and to enter into his glory?

27 And beginning **from** Moses and **from** all the prophets, he expounded **to**-them in all the **Scriptures** the things **about**[2016] himself.

28 And they **near-squeeze to** the village, where they went: and he made as though he would have gone further.

29 But they **beside-press**[2017] him, saying, **remain** with us: for it is toward **evening**, and the day is **declined**. And he went in to **remain** with them.

30 And **it became**, as he **reclined** with them, he **took** bread, and blessed, and **broke**, and gave **to-them**.

31 And their eyes were opened, and they **upon-knew** him; and he **became un-apparent** out of their sight.

32 And they said one to another, did not our **heart** burn within us, while he talked with us by the way, and while he opened to us the **Scriptures**?

33 And they **up-stood** the same hour, and returned to Jerusalem, and found the eleven **together-hoarded**, and them that were with them,

34 Saying, the Lord is risen indeed, and has appeared to Simon.

35 And they **exegesis**[2018] what things in the way, and how he was known of them in breaking of bread.

36 Yet, as they spoke **these-things,** Jesus himself stood in the **middle** of them, and says **to-them,** peace **to-you.**

37 But they were **in-fear** and frightened and **seemed** that they had seen a spirit.

38 And he said **to-them,** why are you **agitated**? And why **are through-inventories up-walking** in your **hearts**?

39 Be-perceiving my hands and my feet, that it is I myself: handle me, and **perceive**; for a spirit has not flesh and bones, as you see me have.

40 And when he had spoken **this**, he showed them hands and feet.

41 And while they yet believed not for **cheerfulness,** and **marveled,** he said **to-them,** have you here any meat?

42 And they gave him a **section** of a broiled fish, and of a honeycomb.

43 And he **took**, ate before them.

44 And he said **to-them,** these the words which I spoke **to-you**, while I was yet with you, that **it-is-binding** all things be **filled,** which were written in the law of Moses, and the prophets, and the psalms **about** me.

45 Then opened he their **minds,** that they might **synthesize** the Scriptures,

46 And said **to-them, in-this-way** it is written, and **in-this-way it-was-binding the** Christ to **emotion**, and to **up-stand** from the dead **to-the** third day:

[2012] Or, renowned-father, or renown or called (kleos)-all (pas)
[2013] Or redeem
[2014] Greek compound existemi (out-of-stand); English ecstasy (overwhelming feelings)
[2015] Rising of the sun, from the same root word for mountain
[2016] Greek: "peri"
[2017] To violently press, to force
[2018] Or out-of-lead, to lead out

47 And that **change-thinking** and **release** of sins should be preached in his name among all nations, beginning at Jerusalem.

48 And you are witnesses of these things.

49 And, **be-perceiving**, I send the promise of my Father upon you: but **be-seated** in the city of Jerusalem, until you be **clothed**[2019] with power from on high.

50 And he led them out **until into** Bethany,[2020] and he lifted up his hands, and blessed[2021] them.

51 And **it became**, while he blessed them, he was parted[2022] from them, and carried up into heaven.

52 And they worshipped him, and returned to Jerusalem with **great cheerfulness**:

53 And were **through-all** in the **priest-place**, praising and blessing God.

Amen.

[2019] Lit., in-down; or, in-sink, in-down-slipping
[2020] Date-house
[2021] Greek: "eulogy"—good (eu) and word (logos)
[2022] Lit, through-stood

THE GOSPEL OF JOHN

JOHN CHAPTER 1

1 In the **original** was the Word,[2023] and the Word was **towards** God, and the Word was God.

2 The same was in the **original** with God.

3 All things **became** by him; and **spacing-from** him was not anything **became** that **has-become**.

4 In him was **Life**; and the **Life** was the Light of men.

5 And the **Light** shines in darkness; and the darkness **down-take**[2024] it not.

6 There was a man sent **beside** God, whose name John.

7 The same came **into** a witness, **that he-should-**witness **about** the Light, that all through him **should-**believe.

8 He was not that Light, but **that-he-should-**witness **about** that Light.

9 **It-was** the true Light, which light every man that comes into the world.

10 He was in the world, and the world **became through** him, and the world knew him not.

11 He came **into private-things**, and his **private-ones beside-took** him not.

12 **Yet,** as many as **take** him, **to-them** he gave **authority** to become the **children** of God, **to-them** that believe **into** his name:

13 Which were born, not **out-of** blood, nor **out-of** the will of the flesh, nor **out-of** the will of man, but **out-of** God.

14 And the Word **became** flesh, and **tabernacle in** us, (and we **looked-closely-at** his glory, the glory as of the **only-born** of the Father,) full of grace and truth.

15 John witnessed of him, and **screamed**, saying, this was he of whom I spoke, He that comes after me is **in-front of-me:** for he was **foremost of-me.**

16 And of his **filling** have all we **took**, and grace **instead of-**grace.

17 For the law was given **through** Moses, grace and truth **became through** Jesus Christ.

18 No man has seen God **ever;** the **only-born God,**[2025] which is in the bosom of the Father, he has **exegesis-him.**[2026]

19 And this is the **witness** of John, when the Jews sent priests and Levites from Jerusalem[2027] to ask him, who are you?

20 And he **same-say**, and **contradict** not; but **same-say,** I am not the Christ.

21 And they asked him, what then? **Are** you **Elijah**? And he says, I am not. **Are** you that prophet? And he answered, no.

22 Then said they **to-him,** who are you that we may give an answer **to-them** that **dispatched** us? What say you **about** yourself?

23 He **showed,**[2028] I the voice of one crying in the **lonesome**, make **soon**[2029] the way of the Lord, as said the prophet, **Isaiah**.

24 And they which were sent were **out-of** the Pharisees.

25 And they asked him, and said **to-him,** why then **you-are-baptizing,** if you be not that Christ, nor **Elijah,** neither that prophet?

26 John answered them, saying, I baptize with water: but there **stands** one **middle of-you,** whom you **perceived** not;

27 He it is, who coming after me is **in-front-of** me, whose **sandal straps** I am not **deserving** to loose.

28 These things **became** in Bethabara[2030] **other-side of-the** Jordan, where John was baptizing.

29 The **upon-tomorrow** John **sees** Jesus coming **to-him,** and says, **be-perceiving** the Lamb of God, which **lifts** the sin of the world.

30 This is he of whom I said, after me comes a man which is **in-front-of-me** me: for he was **foremost of-me.**

31 And I **perceived** him not: but that he should **shine** to Israel, therefore am I come baptizing with water.

[2023] Logos defined by Heraclitus as divine plan and purpose that orders, coordinate and regulate the universe. Plato and Aristotle define Logos as a sentence having rhema (living voice) and anoma (name).
[2024] Take eagerly, seize
[2025] Alexandrian Texts reads "God" in lieu of "Son" (Majority Texts)
[2026] Exegesis is transliterated from "exegeomai," to lead out-of, to unfold
[2027] Greek: Priests-peace (hierou-priest, sacred) and salem (peace)
[2028] Greek: "phemi," the root word for fame ("pheme")
[2029] Or, good-placed
[2030] Ferry-house

32 And John **witnesses**, saying, I saw the Spirit descending from heaven like a dove, and it **remains** upon him.

33 And I **perceived** him not: but he that **dispatched** me to baptize with water, **that-one** said **to-me**, upon whom you shall **perceive** the Spirit descending, and remaining on him, **this** is **the-one** which baptizes **in** the Holy Spirit.

34 I-also saw and **witnessed** that this is the Son of God.

35 Again the next day after John stood, and two of his disciples.

36 And **in-looked to-the** Jesus as he walked, he says, **be-perceiving** the Lamb of God!

37 And the two disciples heard him speak, and they followed Jesus.

38 Then Jesus turned, and saw them following, and says **to-them,** what seek **you?** They said **to-him**, Rabbi, (which is to say, being-**translated Teacher**,) where **are-you-remaining?**

39 He says **to-them,** come and **perceive.** They came and **perceived** where he **remains** and **remained** with him that day: for it was about the tenth hour.

40 One of the two which heard John, and followed him, was Andrew, Simon Peter's brother.

41 He first finds his own brother Simon, and says **to-him**, we have found the Messiah, which is, being interpreted, the Christ.

42 And he **led** him to Jesus. And when Jesus **in-looked to-**him, he said, you are Simon the son of Jona:[2031] you shall be called Cephas,[2032] which is by **translation, Peter**.[2033]

43 The **upon-tomorrow** Jesus would go forth into Galilee, and finds Philip,[2034] and says **to-him,** follow me.

44 Now Philip was of Bethsaida, the city of Andrew and Peter.

45 Philip finds Nathanael, and says **to-him**, we have found him, of whom Moses in the law, and the prophets, did write, Jesus of Nazareth, the son of Joseph.

46 And Nathanael said **to-him, is-powerful** any good thing out of Nazareth? Philip says **to-him,** come and **perceive.**

47 Jesus **perceived** Nathanael coming **to-him,** and says of him, **be-perceiving** an Israelite indeed, in whom is no **trick-bait**!

48 Nathanael says **to-him, which-place you-know** me? Jesus answered and said **to-him,** before that Philip called you, when you **were** under the fig tree, I **perceived** you.

49 Nathanael answered and says **to-him,** Rabbi, you are the Son of God; you are the King of Israel.

50 Jesus answered and said **to-him, that** I said **to-you,** I **perceived** you under the fig tree, believe **you?** You shall see **great** things than these.

51 And he says **to-him,** amen, amen, I say **to-you, from present** you shall see heaven open, and the angels of God **up-walking** and **down-walking** upon the Son of man.

JOHN CHAPTER 2

1 And the third day there was a marriage in Cana of Galilee; and the mother of Jesus was there:

2 And both Jesus **and his disciples were called** to the marriage.

3 And when they **deficient of-**wine, the mother of Jesus says **to-him,** they have no wine.

4 Jesus says **to-her, what to-me and to-you women? My** hour is not yet **arrived**.

5 His mother says **to** the **attendants**, whatever he says **to-you, produce**.

6 And there were set there six stone **water-pots,** after the manner of the **cleansing** of the Jews, **spacing** two or three **up measures**.[2035]

7 Jesus says **to-them,** fill the **water-pots** with water. And they filled them up **full**.

8 And he says **to-them,** draw out now, and **carry to-the first-rank-three-recliner**.[2036] And they **carried-it**.

9 When the **first-rank-three-recliner** had tasted the water that was made wine, and **perceived** not **where** it was: (but the **attendant** which drew the water

---

[2031] Dove
[2032] The rock
[2033] A large rock

[2034] Fiend of horses
[2035] Greek: "metretes," transliterated as "meter"
[2036] Or, three-original-recliner, three-arch-recliners

perceived;) the **first-rank-three-recliner voicing** the bridegroom,

10 And says **to-him**, every man at the **foremost** does set forth **ideal** wine; and when men have well drunk, then that which is **inferior**.[2037] You have kept the **ideal** wine until now.

11 This **original** of **signs** did Jesus in Cana of Galilee and **shined** his glory; and his disciples believed on him.

12 After this he went down to Capernaum, he, and his mother, and his **brothers**, and his disciples: and they **remained** there not many days.

13 And the Jews' **Passover** was at hand, and Jesus **up-walk into** Jerusalem,

14 And found in the **priest-place** those that sold **bulls** and sheep and doves, and the **money-changers**[2038] sitting:

15 And when he had made a **whip** of small cords, he drove them all out of the **priest-place**, and the sheep, and the **bulls**; and poured out the **coin-dealers** and overthrew the tables.

16 And said **to-them** that sold doves, take these things **from-within-here**; make not my Father's house a house of merchandise.[2039]

17 And his disciples remembered that it was written, the zeal of your house has eaten me up.

18 Then answered the Jews and said **to-him**, what sign show you **to-us**, seeing that you do these things?

19 Jesus answered and said **to-them,** destroy this temple, and in three days I will raise it up.

20 Then said the Jews, forty and six **years** was this temple in **house-building**, and **will** you rear it up in three days?

21 But he spoke of the temple of his body.

22 When therefore he was risen from the dead, his disciples remembered that he had said this **to-them;** and they believed the Scripture, and the word which Jesus had said.

23 Now when he was in Jerusalem at the **Passover**, in the festival, many believed in his name, when they saw the **signs** which he did.

24 But Jesus did not **entrust** himself **to-them,** because he knew all,

25 And needed not that any should **witness** of man: for he knew what was in man.

JOHN CHAPTER 3

1 There was a man of the Pharisees, named Nicodemus, a **first-rank**,[2040] of the Jews:

2 The same came to Jesus by night, and said **to-him**, Rabbi, we **perceived** that you are a teacher come from God: for no man **is-powerful to-be-producing** these **signs which you-are-producing,** except God be with him.

3 Jesus answered and said **to-him, amen, amen,** I say **to-you**, except a man be born **from-above**, **not he-is-powerful to-perceive** the kingdom of God.

4 Nicodemus says **to-him**, how **is-powerful** a man be born when he is old? **Not he-is-powerful to-**enter the **second** into his mother's womb, and be born?

5 Jesus answered, **amen, amen,** I say **to-you**, except a man be born of water and the Spirit, **not he-is-powerful to-**enter into the kingdom of God.

6 That which is born of the flesh is flesh; and that which is born of the Spirit is spirit.

7 Marvel not that I said **to**-you, **it-is-binding** you **to-be-born from-above.**

8 The **Spirit breathe-hard** where it **wills**, and you **hear** the voice **of-it**, but **not you-perceived where** it **comes**, and where it goes: so is every one that is born of the Spirit.

9 Nicodemus answered and said **to-him**, how **is-powerful these to-become**?

10 Jesus answered and said **to-him, are** you a **teacher** of Israel, and know not these things?

11 Amen, amen, I say **to-you**, we speak that we **perceived**, and **witness** that we have seen; and you **take** not our witness.

12 If I have told you **earthly** things, and you believe not, how shall you believe, if I tell you **upon-heavens-things**?

13 And no man has-**up-walked into** heaven, but he that **down-walked out-of** heaven, the Son of man which is in heaven.

[2037] Greek" "elassoni," smaller in size, age, quantity, dignity, inferior,
[2038] Or, clippers, shearers
[2039] Greek: emporium
[2040] Or, original-rank, beginning-rank

14 And as Moses **elevated** the serpent in the **lonesome**, even so **it-is-binding** the Son of man be **elevated**:

15 That whoever believes in him should not **from-ruin**,[2041] but have **eternal** life.

16 For God so loved the world, that he gave his **only-born** Son, that whoever believes **into him** should not **from-ruin** but have **eternal** life.

17 For God sent not his Son into the world to **judge** the world; but that the world through him might be saved.

18 He that believes on him is not **judged**: but he that believes not is **judged** already, because he has not believed in the name of the **only-born** Son of God.

19 And this is the **judging**, that light is come into the world, and men loved darkness rather than light, because their **works** were **wicked-hurtful**.

20 For every one that **practices foul, detest** the light, neither comes to the light, lest his **works** should be **exposed**.

21 But he that **producing** truth comes to the light, that his **works** may **shine**, that they are **worked** in God.

22 After these things Jesus and his disciples came into the land of Judaea; and there he **tarried**[2042] with them and baptized.

23 And John also was baptizing in Aenon[2043] near to Salim, because there was much water there: and they came and were baptized.

24 For John was not yet cast into prison.

25 Then there arose a question between John's disciples and the Jews about **cleansing**.

26 And they came **towards** John, and said **to-him**, Rabbi, he that was with you beyond Jordan, to whom you **have-witnessed, be-perceiving**, the same baptize, and all come **to-him**.

27 John answered and said, a man **not is-powerful to-get** nothing, except it be given him **out-of the** heaven.

28 You yourselves **are-witnessing**, that I said, I am not the Christ, but that I am sent before him.

29 He that has the bride is the bridegroom: but the friend of the bridegroom, which **stands** and hears him, **to-cheer is-cheering** because of the bridegroom's voice: this my **cheerfulness** therefore is filled.

30 Him, **it-is-binding, to-be-growing**, but me **to-decrease**.

31 He that comes from above is above all: he that is **out-**of the earth is **earthly and** speaks **out-of** the earth; he that comes **out-of** heaven is above all.

32 And what he has seen and heard, that he **witnesses**; and no man **takes** his **witness**.

33 The **one-taking** his **witness** has set to his seal that God is true.

34 For he whom God has sent speaks the **declarations** of God: **because** God gives not the Spirit **out-of** measure.

35 The Father loves the Son and has given all things into his hand.

36 He that believes on the Son has **eternal** life: and he that believes not the Son shall not see life: but the **swelling-anger** of God **remains** on him.

JOHN CHAPTER 4

1 When therefore the Lord knew how the Pharisees had heard that Jesus made and baptized more disciples than John,

2 (Though Jesus himself baptized not, but his disciples,)

3 He left Judaea and departed again into Galilee.

4 Yet, **it-is-binding, for-him to-travel** through Samaria.

5 Then **he-is-coming into** to a city of Samaria, which is called Sychar, near to the **space** that Jacob gave to his son Joseph.

6 Now Jacob's **fountain** was there. Jesus, therefore, being wearied with journey, sat **in-this-way** on the **fountain**: it was about the sixth hour.

7 There comes a woman **out-of** Samaria to draw water: Jesus says **to-her**, give me to drink.

8 (For his disciples were **from-come into** the city to buy **food**.)

9 Then says the woman of Samaria **to-him**, how is it that you, being a Jew, ask drink of me, which am a woman of Samaria? **Because** the Jews have no **together-use** with the Samaritans.

[2041] Greek: "apo" (from) and "alethros" (ruin), to destroy fully
[2042] Greek: through-wear
[2043] Hebrew for spring, fountain, eye

10 Jesus answered and said **to-her,** if you **perceive** the gift of God, and who it is that says **to-you**, give me to drink; you would have asked of him, and he would have given you living water.

11 The woman says **to-him, Lord,** you have nothing to draw with, and the well is deep: from **where** then have you **the** living water?

12 Are you **larger**[2044] than our father Jacob, which gave us the well, and drank **of-it** himself, and his children, and his cattle?

13 Jesus answered and said **to-her, whoever** drinks of this water shall thirst again:

14 But whoever drinks of the water that I shall give him shall **not, no, thirst into the age**; but the water that I shall give him shall be in him a **fountain** of water **jumping** into **eternal** life.

15 The woman says **to-him, Lord,** give me this water, that I thirst not, neither come **here** to draw.

16 Jesus says **to** her, **under-lead,** call your husband, and come **from-within-here.**

17 The woman answered and said, I have no husband. Jesus said **to-her,** you have well said, I have no husband:

18 For you have had five husbands; and he whom you now have is not your husband: in that said you truly.

19 The woman says **to-him, Lord,** I **see** that you are a prophet.

20 Our fathers worshipped in this mountain; and you say, that in Jerusalem is the place where **it-is-binding** to worship.

21 Jesus says **to-her,** woman, believe me, the hour **comes**, when you shall neither in this mountain, nor yet at Jerusalem, worship the Father.

22 You worship **what not you-perceived:** we **perceived** what we worship: for salvation is **out-of** the Jews.

23 But the hour **comes,** and now is, when the true worshippers shall worship the Father in spirit and in truth: for the Father seeks such to worship him.

24 The God is Spirit; and they that worship him, **it-is-binding, to-worship** in spirit and truth.

25 The woman says **to-him,** I **perceived** that Messiah **comes,** which is called Christ: when he is come, he will **message** us all things.

26 Jesus says **to-her,** I[2045] am[2046] the one-speaking to-you.

27 And upon this came his disciples, and marveled that he talked with the woman: yet no man said, what seek you? Or, why **are-you-talking** with her?

28 The woman then left her **water-pot,** and went her way into the city, and says to the men,

29 Come, **perceive** a **Man,** which told me all, **as-much-as,** I did: is not this the Christ?

30 Then they went out of the city and came **towards him**.

31 In the mean while his disciples **asked** him, saying, **Rabbi,** eat.

32 But he said **to-them,** I have **food** to eat that you **perceive** not of.

33 Therefore said the disciples one to another, has any man brought him to eat?

34 Jesus says **to-them,** my **food** is to do the will of him that **dispatched** me, and to finish his work.

35 Say not you, there are yet four months, and comes **the** harvest? **Be-perceiving,** I say **to-you,** lift up your eyes, and look on the **spaces**; for they are white already to harvest.

36 And he that reaps receive wages and gathers fruit **to eternal** life: that both he that sows and he that reaps may **cheer** together.

37 Because, in this the saying true, **other-same** sows, and another-**same** reaps.

38 I sent you to reap **not which you-fatigue-cut, other-same fatigue-cut,** and you are entered into their **cut**.

39 And many of the Samaritans of that city believed on him for the saying of the woman, which **witnessed,** he told me all that **as-much-as** I did.

40 So when the Samaritans **came to-him,** they **asked** him that he would **remain** with them: and he **remains** there two days.

41 And many more believed **through** of his word.

[2044] Larger, especially in age
[2045] Greek: "ego"

[2046] Greek: "I exists"

42 And said **to** the woman, now we believe, not **through** your saying: for we have heard ourselves, and **perceived** that this is indeed the Christ, the Savior of the world.

43 Now after two days he departed there and went into Galilee.

44 For Jesus himself **witnessed**, that a prophet has no **value** in his own country.

45 Then when he was come into Galilee, the Galileans **welcomed** him, having seen all the things that he did at Jerusalem at the **festival**: for they also went **into** the **festival.**

46 So Jesus came again into Cana of Galilee, where he made the water wine. And there was a certain **regal**,[2047] whose son was **weak** at Capernaum.

47 When he heard that Jesus **is-arriving** out of Judaea into Galilee, he went **to-him**, and **asked** him that he would come down, and **cure** his son: for he was **impending to-be-from-dying.**

48 Then said Jesus **to-him**, except you **perceive** signs and wonders, you will not believe.

49 The **regal** says **to-him**, Lord, come down **before** my child die.

50 Jesus says **to-him**, go your way; your son lives. And the man believed the word that Jesus spoke **to-him**, and he went his way.

51 And as he was now going down, his **slave**s met him, and **messaged,** saying, your son lives.

52 Then he **ascertain-by-inquiry** of them the hour when he began to **be-well-dressed**.[2048] And they said **to-him**, yesterday at the seventh hour the fever **released** him.

53 So the father knew that at the same hour, in the which Jesus said **to-him**, your son lives: and himself believed, and his whole house.

54 This again the second **sign** Jesus did, when he was come out of Judaea into Galilee.

JOHN CHAPTER 5

1 After this there was a **festival** of the Jews; and Jesus **up-walked into** Jerusalem.

2 Now there is **in** Jerusalem **upon to-the** sheep, a pool, which is called in the Hebrew tongue Bethesda, having five porches.

3 In these **down-laid much fullness of-the weak**, of blind, **of-limping, of-withered, out-of-welcoming** the **stirring** of the water.

4 For an angel **down-walk down** season into the pool, and **agitated** the water: whoever then **foremost,** after the troubling of the water, stepped in became **healthy-grown** of whatever **nausea** he **down-hold**.

5 And a certain man was there, which **held in weakness** thirty and eight **years**.

6 When Jesus **perceived** him **laying-down**, and knew that he had been **already much uninterrupted-time,** he says **to-him, will** you be made **healthy-grown**?

7 The **weak** man answered him, **Lord**, I have no man, when the water is **agitated**, to put me into the pool: but while I am coming, another-same **down-walk** before me.

8 Jesus says **to-him**, rise, take up your **mattress**, and walk.

9 And **soon**, the man **became healthy-grown**, and **lifts** his **mattress**, and walked: and on the same day was the Sabbath.

10 The Jews therefore said **to-him** that was **served-therapy**, it is the Sabbath: it is not lawful for you to carry your **mattress**.

11 He answered them, he that made me **healthy-grown**, the same said **to-me lift** your **mattress**, and **about-pathing**.

12 Then asked they him, what man is that which said **to-you, lift** your **mattress**, and walk?

13 And he that was **cured perceive** not who it was: for Jesus had **out-of-nod**,[2049] a multitude being in **the spot**.

14 Afterward Jesus finds him in the **priest-place**, and said **to-him, be-perceiving**, you are made **healthy-grown**: sin no more, **that no** worse thing **become to-you**.

15 The man departed, and told the Jews that it was Jesus, **who** had made him **healthy-grow**.

[2047] Basilikos: regal, belonging to the sovereign
[2048] Or, neater

[2049] Or, to slip out

16 And therefore did the Jews **chase** Jesus, and sought to **from-kill** him, because he had done these things on the Sabbath.

17 But Jesus answered them, my Father **works until present**, and I work.

18 Therefore the Jews sought the more to kill him, because he not only had broken the Sabbath, but said also that God was his Father, making himself **equal-similar to-God**.

19 Then answered Jesus and said **to** them, **amen, amen**, I say **to-you**, the Son **not is-powerful to-do anything from** himself, but what he **sees** the Father **producing**: because **as-much-as** he **produces**, these also **produces** the Son likewise.

20 For the Father **friends** the Son and shows him all things that himself **produces**: and he will show him **great** works than these, that you may marvel.

21 For as the Father raises the dead and **is-life-producing**; even so the Son **is-life-producing** whom he **wills**.

22 For the Father is-**judging** no man, but has **giving** all **judging to-the** Son:

23 That all should **value** the Son, even as they **value** the Father. He that **value** not the Son **value** not the Father which has **dispatched** him.

24 Amen, amen, I say **to-you**, he that hears my word, and believes on him that **dispatched** me, has **eternal life**, and shall not come into **judging**; but is **change-base out-of the** death **into the** life.

25 Amen, amen, I say **to-you**, the hour is coming, and now is, when the dead shall hear the voice of the Son of God: and they that hear shall live.

26 For as the Father **holds** life in himself; so, has he given to the Son to **hold** life in himself;

27 And has given him authority to **do judging** also, **that** he is the Son of man.

28 Marvel not at this: for the hour is coming, in the which all that are in the **remembrance-tomb** shall hear his voice,

29 And shall **out-passage**; they that have **produce**[2050] good, **into** the resurrection of life; and they that have **practiced**[2051] foul, **into** the resurrection of **judging**.

30 Not I am-powerful from myself to-produce anything: as I hear, I judge: and my **judging** is **righteous**; because I seek not **my** will, but the will of the Father which has **dispatched** me.

31 If I witness **about** myself, my witness is not true.

32 There is another that witness of me; and I **perceive** that the witness which he witness **about** me is true.

33 You sent **towards** John, and he witness **to-the** truth.

34 But I **take** not **witness** from man: but these things I say that you might be saved.

35 He was a burning and a shining light: and you were willing for **an hour** to **jump-for-joy** in his light.

36 But I have **great** witness than of John: for the works which the Father has given me to **mature**, the same works that I **produce**, bear witness of me, that the Father has sent me.

37 And the Father himself, which has **dispatched** me, has witness of me. you have neither heard his voice, **ever**, nor **stared-at** his **perception**.

38 And you have not his word **remaining** in you: for whom he has sent, him you believe not.

39 Search the **Scriptures**; for in them you think you have **eternal life**: and they are they which **witness** of me.

40 And you will not come **towards** me, that you might have life.

41 I receive not **glory** from men.

42 But I know you, that you have not the love of God in you.

43 I am come in my Father's name, and you **take** me not: if another-**same** shall come in his **private** name, him you will **take**.

44 How **are-powerful** you **to-believe**, which **take glory** one of another, and seek not the **glory** that comes from God only?

45 Do not **seem** that I will accuse you **toward** the Father: there is that accuses you, Moses, **into** whom you **expected**.

46 For had you believed Moses, you would have believed me: for he wrote **about** me.

[2050] Greek: "poiesantes" (to do or to make); nominative case and therefore, personified,

[2051] Greek: "praxantes," nominative case and therefore, personified

47 But if you believe not his writings, how shall you believe my **declarations**?

JOHN CHAPTER 6

1 After these things Jesus went over the sea of Galilee, which is of Tiberias.

2 And **much** multitude followed him, because they saw his **signs** which he **produced upon** them that were **weak**.

3 And Jesus went up into a mountain, and there he sat with his disciples.

4 And the **Passover**, a **festival** of the Jews, **near-squeeze**.

5 When Jesus **looked-closely**, and saw **much multitude** come **to-him**, he says **to** Philip, **where** shall we buy bread, that these may eat?

6 And this he said to **probe-test** him: **because** he himself **perceive** what **he-was-impending to-produce**.

7 Philip answered him, two hundred **denarius**[2052] worth of bread is not sufficient for them, that every one of them may take a little.

8 One of his disciples, Andrew, Simon Peter's brother, says **to-him**,

9 There is a lad here, which has five barley **breads**, and two small fishes: but what are they **into** so many?

10 And Jesus said, make the men **up-fall**.[2053] Now there was much grass in the place. So, the men **up-fell**, in number about five thousand.

11 And Jesus **took** the **breads**; and when he had given thanks, he distributed to the disciples, and the disciples **to-them** that were **up-laying** and likewise of the fishes as much as they **willed**.

12 When they were filled, he said **to** his disciples, gather up the **excess** fragments, that nothing be **from-ruin**.

13 Therefore they gathered together and filled twelve baskets with the fragments of the five barley **bread**, **excess to**-them that had eaten.

14 Then those men, when they **perceived** the **sign** that Jesus did, said, this is of a truth that prophet that should come into the world.

15 When Jesus therefore **perceived** that **they-impending to-come** and **snatch him**, to make him a king, he **up-space** again into a mountain himself alone.

16 And when **evening became**, his disciples went down **to** the sea,

17 And entered into a ship and went over the sea toward Capernaum. And it **already became** dark, and Jesus was not come **toward** them.

18 And the sea **arose-through** a **great** wind that blew.

19 Then **when-they-pushed** about **twenty-five** or thirty **stadiums**,[2054] they see Jesus walking on the sea, and **near-squeeze to** the ship: and they **became** afraid.

20 But he says **to-them**, it is I; be not afraid.

21 Then they willingly **took** him into the ship: and **soon** the ship was at the land where they went.

22 The **upon-tomorrow**, when the people which stood on the other side of the sea **perceived** that there was no other boat there, **except** that one **into which** his disciples were entered, and that Jesus went not with his disciples into the boat, but his disciples were gone away alone.

23 (**Yet** there came other boats from Tiberias **near-squeezing to** the **spot** where they-**ate the** bread, after that the Lord had given thanks:)

24 When the **multitude** therefore **perceive** that Jesus was not there, neither his disciples, they also **stepped-in the** ship, and came to Capernaum, seeking for Jesus.

25 And when they had found him on the other side of the sea, they said **to-him**, Rabbi, when **you became here**?

26 Jesus answered them and said, **amen, amen**, I say **to-you**, you seek me, not because you **perceive** the **signs**, but because you did eat of the **breads**, and were **fed**.

27 Work not for the **feeding** which **from-ruin**, but for that **feeding** which **remains into eternal life**, which the Son of man shall give **to-you**: for him has God the Father sealed.

28 Then said they **towards him**, what shall we **produce**, that **we-may-work** the works of God?

[2052] Or ten donkeys worth
[2053] Or lean back

[2054] Greek: "stadion," transliterated as stadiums, root to stand as fixed

29 Jesus answered and said **to-them,** this is the work of God, that you believe **into him** whom he has sent.

30 They said therefore **to-him,** what sign show you then, that we may **perceive,** and believe you? What do you work?

31 Our fathers did eat manna in the **lonesome**; as it is written, He gave them bread from heaven to eat.

32 Then Jesus said **to** them, **amen, amen,** I say **to-you,** Moses gave you not that bread from heaven; but my Father gives you the true bread from heaven.

33 For the bread of God is he which comes down from heaven and gives life **to** the world.

34 Then said they **towards him,** Lord, **always** give us this bread.

35 And Jesus said **to-them,** I am the bread of life: he that comes to me shall never[2055] hunger; and he that believes **into** me shall never thirst.

36 But I said **to-you,** that you also have seen me, and believe not.

37 All that the Father gives me shall come to me; and him that comes to me I will **no not** cast out.

38 For I came down from heaven, not to **produce my** will, but the will of him that **dispatched** me.

39 And this is the Father's will which has **dispatched** me, that of all which he has given me I should **from-ruin** nothing but should **up-stand it in** the last day.

40 And this is the will of him that **dispatched** me, that everyone which **sees**[2056] the Son, and believes on him, may have **eternal life**: and I will **up-stand him in** the last day.

41 The Jews then **grumbled** at him, because he said, I am the bread which came down **out-of** heaven.

42 And they said, is not this Jesus, the son of Joseph, whose father and mother we **perceive**? How is it then that he says, I came down from heaven?

43 Jesus therefore answered and said **to-them, grumble** not **with one-another**.

44 No man **not is-powerful to-come** to me, except the Father which has **dispatched** me **out-of-induced** him: and I will **up-stand him in** the last day.

45 It is written in the prophets, and they shall be all taught of God. Every man therefore that has heard, and has learned of the Father, comes **towards** me.

46 Not that any man has seen the Father, **if not** he, which is **beside** God, he has seen the Father.

47 Amen, amen, I say **to-you,** he that believes on me has **eternal life**.

48 I am that bread of life.

49 Your fathers did eat manna in the **lonesome** and are dead.

50 This is the bread which comes down **out-of** heaven, that a man may eat **of-it,** and not die.

51 I am the living bread which came down from heaven: if any man eats of this bread, he shall live **into the age**: and the bread that I will give is my flesh, which I will give for the life of the world.

52 The Jews therefore **fought towards one-another,** saying, how **is-powerful** this man **to-**give us flesh to eat?

53 Then Jesus said **to-them, amen, amen,** I say **to-you,** except you eat the flesh of the Son of man, and drink his blood, you have no life in you.

54 Whoever eats my flesh, and drinks my blood, has **eternal life**; and I will **up-stand him to-the** last day.

55 For my flesh **truly** is **feeding,** and my blood **truly** is drink.

56 He that eats my flesh, and drinks my blood, **remains** in me, and I in him.

57 As the living Father has sent me, and I live by the Father: so, he that eats me, even he shall live **through** me.

58 This is that bread which came down from heaven: not as your fathers did eat manna and are dead: he that eats of this bread shall live **into the age**.

59 These things said he in the synagogue, as he taught in Capernaum.

60 Many therefore of his disciples, when they had heard, said, this is a hard-**dry** saying; who **is-powerful to-**hear it?

61 When Jesus **perceives** in himself that his disciples **grumbled** at it, he said **to-them,** does this **scandalize**[2057] you?

[2055] Greek is two words, "not no"
[2056] Lit., to be a spectator
[2057] Or snare

62 **If then** you shall see the Son of man **up-walk** where he was **previously**?

63 **The** Spirit **is the life-producer**; the flesh profits nothing: the **declarations** that I speak **to-you**, are spirit, and are life.

64 But there are some **out-of** you that believe not. For Jesus **perceive** from the **original** who they were that believed not, and who should betray him.

65 And he said, **through this I** said **to-you,** that no man **is-powerful to-come towards** me, except it were given **to-him out-of** my Father.

66 **Out-of this,** many of his disciples went **into the** back, and walked no more with him.

67 Then said Jesus **to-the** twelve, will you also **be-under-led**?

68 Then Simon Peter answered him, Lord, **towards** whom shall we go? You have the **declarations** of **eternal life**.

69 And we believe and **have-known** that you are that Christ, the Son of the living God.

70 Jesus answered them, have not I chosen you twelve, and one of you is a devil?[2058]

71 He spoke of Judas Iscariot of Simon: **because** he was **impending to-betray** him, being one **out-of** the twelve.

JOHN CHAPTER 7

1 After these things Jesus walked in Galilee: for he willed not walk in Judea, because the Jews sought to kill him.

2 Now the Jews' **Festival of Tabernacles** was **near-squeeze**.

3 His **brothers** therefore said **to-him**, depart **from-within-there,** and go into Judaea, that your disciples also may **theatre-spectate** the works that you **producing**

4 For no man does anything in **hiding**, and he himself seeks **to-all-speech**.[2059] If you **produce** these things, **shine** yourself to the world.

5 For **not-yet** did his **brothers** believe in him.

6 Then Jesus said **to-them**, my **season** is not yet come: but your **season** is always **internally-prepared**.

7 The world **not is-powerful to-detest** you; but me it **detests**, because I **witness** of it, that the works **of-it** are **wicked-hurtful**.

8 You, **up-walk into** this **festival**: I **not yet up-walk into** this **festival**; for my **season** is not yet **filled**.

9 When he had said these words **to-them**, he **remained** in Galilee.

10 But when his **brothers** were **up-walked**, then he also **up-walked into** the **festival**, not openly, but as it were in **hiding**.

11 Then the Jews sought him at the **festival**, and said, where is he?

12 And there was much **grumbling** among the **multitude** concerning him: for some said, He is good: others said, **no**; but he **is seducing** the people.

13 However, no man spoke **all-speech**[2060] of him for fear of the Jews.

14 Yet, already, **being-the-middle** of the **festival**, Jesus **up-walked** into the **priest-place**, and taught.

15 And the Jews marveled, saying, how **perceived** this man letters, having never learned?

16 Jesus answered them, and said, my **teaching** is not mine, but his that **dispatched** me.

17 If any man will do his will, he shall know of the **teaching**, whether it be of God, or I speak of myself.

18 He that speaks **from** himself seeks his own glory: but he that seeks his glory that **dispatched** him, the same is true, and no unrighteousness is in him.

19 Did not Moses give you the law, and none of you keeps the law? Why go you about to kill me?

20 The people answered and said, you have a **demon**: who goes about to kill you?

21 Jesus answered and said **to-them**, I have **produced** one work, and you all marvel.

22 Moses therefore gave **to-you** circumcision; (not because it is of Moses, but of the fathers;) and you on the Sabbath circumcise a man.

23 If a man on the Sabbath **take** circumcision, that the law of Moses should not be **loosed**; are you **bile-gall** at me, because I have **produce** a man **whole healthy-grow** on the Sabbath?

[2058] Greek diabolos also means backbiter
[2059] Free speech
[2060] Free speech

24 Judge not **down sight-appearance** but judge righteous **judging**.

25 Then said some of them of Jerusalem, is not this he, whom they seek to kill?

26 But, **be-perceiving,** he speaks **all-out-spoken**, and they say nothing **to-him**. Do the **first-rank**,[2061] know **truly** that this is the very Christ?

27 However, we **perceive** this man **where** he is: but when Christ **comes**, no man knows **where** he is.

28 Then **screamed** Jesus in the **priest-place** as he taught, saying, you both **perceived** me, and you **perceived where** I am: and I am not come **from** myself, but he that **dispatched** me is true, whom you **perceive** not.

29 But I **perceive** him: for I am **beside** him, and he has sent me.

30 Then they sought to **squeeze-capture**[2062] him: but no man laid hands on him, because his hour was not yet come.

31 And many of the **multitude** believed on him, and said, when Christ **comes**, will he **produce** more **signs** than these which **this-one** has **produced**?

32 The Pharisees heard that the **multitude grumbled** such things concerning him; and the Pharisees and the **first-rank-priests** sent **subservient-ones**[2063] to **squeeze-capture** him.

33 Then said Jesus **to-them,** yet a little **uninterrupted-time** am I with you, and I go **to-him** that **dispatched** me.

34 You shall seek me, and shall not find: and where I am, **not you-are-powerful to-come.**

35 Then said the Jews **towards** themselves, **where is-impending** he **to-travel**, that we shall not find him? Will he go **to** the **through-scattered**[2064] **of-**the **Hellenic,** and teach the **Hellenics**?

36 What saying is this that he said, you shall seek me, and shall not find: and where I am, **not you-are-powerful to-come?**

37 Yet, in the last day, **the great of-the festival,** Jesus stood and **screamed**, saying, if any man thirst, let him come **towards** me, and drink.

38 He that believes **into** me, as the Scripture has said, out of his belly shall flow[2065] rivers of living water.

39 (But this spoke he of the Spirit, which they that believe **into him is-impending to-be-taking**: **because** the Holy Spirit was not yet; because that Jesus was not yet glorified.)

40 Many of the people therefore, when they heard this saying, said, of a truth this is the Prophet.

41 Others said, this is the Christ. But some said, shall Christ come out of Galilee?

42 Has not the Scripture said that Christ comes **out-of** the seed of David, and out of the town of Bethlehem, where David was?

43 So there was a **split** among the **multitude through** him.

44 And some of them willed **to-squeeze-capture** him; but no man **upon-cast** hands on him.

45 Then came the **subservient-ones** to the **first-rank-priests** and Pharisees; and they said **to** them, why have you not **led** him?

46 The **subservient-ones** answered, **not-yet a** man spoke like this man.

47 Then answered them the Pharisees, are you also **seduced**?

48 Have any **out-of** the **first-rank**, or of the Pharisees believed **into him**?

49 But this people who knows not the law are **upon-down-curse**.[2066]

50 Nicodemus says **towards** them, (he that came to Jesus by night, being one **out-of** them,)

51 Does our law judge man, before it hears him, and know what he does?

52 They answered and said **to-him, are** you also of Galilee? Search, and **perceive** for out of Galilee arises no prophet.

53 And **each-man** went **into** his own house.

JOHN CHAPTER 8

1 Jesus went **into** the **mountain** of Olives.

[2061] Or, original-rank, beginning-rank
[2062] "Piazo," to squeeze, to seize by hand, to press, to arrest, to capture
[2063] Lit., under-oarsman, generally a subordinate
[2064] Or, diaspora, dispersed
[2065] Or, to gush
[2066] Or, upon-curse, what has to go down

2 And early in the morning he came again into the **priest-place**, and all the people came **to-him**; and he sat down and taught them.

3 And the scribes and Pharisees brought **to-him** a woman **down-taken** in adultery; and when they had set her in the middle,

4 They say **to-him**, **Teacher**, this woman was **down-taken** in adultery, **in-itself-theft**.

5 Now Moses in the law commanded us, that such should be stoned: but what say **you**?

6 This they said, **probe-testing** him, that they might have to accuse him. But Jesus stooped down, and with finger wrote on the ground.

7 So when they **upon-remained** asking him, he **up-bend** himself, and said **to-them**, he that is without sin among you, let him **foremost** cast a stone at her.

8 And again he stooped down and wrote on the ground.

9 And they which heard, being **exposed** by conscience, went out one by one, beginning at the eldest, **until** the last: and Jesus was left alone, and the woman standing in the **middle**.

10 When Jesus had **up-bend** himself, and saw none but the woman, he said **to-**her, woman, where are those your accusers? Has no man **down-judge** you?

11 She said, no man, Lord. And Jesus said **to-**her, neither do I **down-judge** you: go, and sin no more.

12 Then spoke Jesus again **to-them**, saying, I am the light of the world: he that follows me shall not walk in darkness, but shall have the light of life.

13 The Pharisees therefore said **to-him**, you **witness** of yourself; your **witness** is not true.

14 Jesus answered and said **to-them**, though I **witness** of myself, **my witness** is true: for I **perceive from-where** I came, and where I go; but you cannot **perceive from-where** I come, and where I go.

15 You **are-judging** after the flesh; **I-am-judging** no man.

16 And yet if I judge, my **judging** is true: for I am not alone, but I and the Father that **dispatched** me.

17 It is also written in your law, that the **witness** of two men is true.

18 I am one that witness of myself, and the Father that **dispatched** me witness **about** me.

19 Then said they **to-him**, where is your Father? Jesus answered, you neither **perceive** me, nor my Father: if you had **perceived** me, you should have **perceive** my Father also.

20 These words spoke Jesus in the **treasure-house**, as he taught in the **priest-place**: and no man **squeeze-capture** him; for his hour was not yet come.

21 Then said Jesus again **to-them**, I go my way, and you shall seek me, and shall die in your sins: where I go, **not you-are-powerful to**-come.

22 Then said the Jews, will he kill himself? Because he says, where I go, **not you-are-powerful to-come.**

23 And he said **to-them**, you are **out-of the downward**; I am **out-of the upward**: you are of this world; I am not of this world.

24 I said therefore **to-you**, that you shall die in your sins: for if you believe not that I am, you shall die in your sins.

25 Then said they **to-him**, who are **you**? And Jesus says **to-them**, even that I said **to-you** from the **origin**.

26 I have many things to say and to judge of you: but he that **dispatched** me is true; and I speak to the world those things which I have heard of him.

27 They understood not that he spoke **to-them** of the Father.

28 Then said Jesus **to-them**, when you have lifted the Son of man, then shall you know that I am, and I **produce** nothing **from** myself; but as my Father has taught me, I speak these things.

29 And he that **dispatched** me is with me: the Father has not **released** me alone; for I do always those things that please him.

30 As he spoke these words, many believed on him.

31 Then said Jesus **towards** those Jews which believed on him, if you **remain** in my word, are you my disciples **truly**;

32 And you shall know the truth, and the truth **shall-free-you**.

33 They answered him, we be Abraham's seed, and **to-no-one slaved**: how says you, **you-shall-become** free?

34 Jesus answered them, **amen**, **amen**, I say **to-you**, whoever **producing**[2067] the sin is the **slave** of **the** sin.

[2067] Present tense, active voice

35 And the **slave** not is-**remaining** in the house **into the age**: the Son is-**remaining into the age**.

36 If the Son therefore shall make you free, you shall be **really** free.

37 I **perceived** that you are Abraham's seed; but you seek to kill me, because my word has no **space** in you.

38 I speak that which I have seen **beside** my Father: and you do that which you have seen **beside** your father.

39 They answered and said **to-him**, Abraham is our father. Jesus says **to-them**, if you were Abraham's children, you would do the works of Abraham.

40 But now you seek to kill me, a man that has told you the truth, which I have heard of God: this did not Abraham.

41 You do the **works** of your father. Then said they **to-him**, we were not born **out-of prostitution**; we have one Father, God.

42 Jesus said **to-them**, if God were your Father, you would love me: for I **proceeded**[2068] and **arrive from** God; neither came I **from** myself, but he sent me.

43 Why do you not **know** my speech, **that not you-are-powerful to-hear** my word?

44 You are **out-of** father the Devil, and the **upon-feelings** of your father you **are-willing to-be-producing**. He was a **man-faced-slayer**[2069] from the **origin**, and **stood** not in the truth, because there is no truth in him. When he speaks **the falsehood**, he speaks **out-of** his **private**:[2070] for he is a **falsifier**, and the father of it.

45 Yet that I tell the truth, you believe me not.

46 Which of you **exposes** me of sin? And if I say the truth, why do you not believe me?

47 He that is **out-of** God hears God's **declarations**: you therefore hear not **that** you are not **out-of** God.

48 Then answered the Jews, and said **to-him**, say we not **ideally** that you are a Samaritan, and has a **demon**?

49 Jesus answered, I have not a **demon**; but I **value** my Father, and you do **un-value** me.

50 And I seek not **my** glory: there is one that seeks and **judging**.

51 Amen, amen, I say **to-you**, if a man keeps my saying, **death not he-shall-be-seeing into the age**.

52 Then said the Jews **to-him**, now we know that you have a **demon** Abraham is dead, and the prophets; and you say, if a man keep my saying, he shall not taste of death **into the age**.

53 Are you **larger**[2071] than our father Abraham, which is dead? And the prophets are dead: who make you yourself?

54 Jesus answered, if I **glorify** myself, my **glory** is nothing: it is my Father that **glories** me; of whom you say, that he is your God:

55 Yet you have not known him; but I **perceive** him: and if I should say, I **perceive** him not, I shall be a **falsifier** like **to-you**: but I **perceive** him and keep his saying.

56 Your father Abraham rejoiced to **perceive** my day: and he **perceive** and was **cheerful**.

57 Then said the Jews **to-him**, you are not yet fifty **years**, and have you seen Abraham?

58 Jesus said **to-them, amen, amen**, I say **to-you**, before Abraham **to-be-becoming**, I am.

59 Then **the lifted** stones to cast at him: but Jesus hid himself, and went out of the **priest-place**, going through the middle of them, and so passed by.

JOHN CHAPTER 9

1 And passing by, **he-perceive** a man which was blind from birth.

2 And his disciples asked him, saying, **Rabbi**, who did sin, this man, or his parents, that he was born blind?

3 Jesus answered, neither has this man sinned, nor his parents: but that the works of God should **shine** in him.

4 It-is-binding I work the works of him that **dispatched** me, while it is day: the night **comes**, when no man **is-powerful to-**work.

5 As long as I am in the world, I am the light of the world.

6 When he had spoken **these-things**, he spat on the ground, and made clay of the spittle, and he anointed the eyes of the blind man with the clay,

---

[2068] Lit., came-out-of
[2069] Or a human killer
[2070] Or, pertaining to self, conferring with self, private
[2071] Larger, especially in age

7 And said **to-him**, go, wash in the pool of Siloam, (which is by **translation**, Sent.) He went his way therefore, and washed, and came seeing.

8 The neighbors therefore, and they which before had seen him that he was blind, said, is not this he that sat and begged?

9 Some said, this is he: others, he is like him: he said, I am.

10 Therefore said they **to-him**, how were your eyes opened?

11 He answered and said, a man that is called Jesus made clay, and anointed **my** eyes, and said **to** me, go to the pool of Siloam, and wash: and I went and washed, and I-**up-looked**.

12 Then said they **to-him**, where is he? He said, I **perceive** not.

13 They brought to the Pharisees him that **once** was blind.

14 And it was the Sabbath when Jesus made the clay and opened his eyes.

15 Then again, the Pharisees also asked him how he had received his sight. he said **to-them**, He put clay upon **my** eyes, and I washed, and do see.

16 Therefore said some of the Pharisees, this man is not of God, because he keeps not the Sabbath. Others said, how **is-powerful** a man that is a sinner do such **signs**? And there was a **split** among them.

17 They say **to** the blind man again, what say you of him, that he has opened your eyes? He said, he is a prophet.

18 But the Jews did not believe concerning him, that he had been blind, and received his sight, until they called the parents **of-him, the one-up-looking**.

19 And they asked them, saying, is this your son, who you say was born blind? How then does he now see?

20 His parents answered them and said, we **perceive** that this is our son, and that he was born blind:

21 But by what means he now sees, we **perceive** not; or who has opened his eyes, we **perceive** not: he is of-stature ask him: he shall speak for himself.

22 These spoke his parents, because they feared the Jews: for the Jews had agreed already, that if any man did confess that he was Christ, he should be put out of the synagogue.

23 Therefore said his parents, he is of stature; ask him.

24 Then again called they the man that was blind, and said **to-him**, give God the praise: we **perceive** that this man is a sinner.

25 He answered and said, whether he be a sinner, I **perceive** not: one thing I **perceive**, that, **being** blind, now I see.

26 Then said they **to-him** again, what did he **to-you**? How opened he your eyes?

27 He answered them, I have told you already, and you did not hear: why **are-you-willing to-**hear again? Will you also be his disciples?

28 Then they **abuse-spear** him, and said, you are his disciple; but we are Moses' disciples.

29 We **perceive** that God spoke **to** Moses: this, we **perceive** not from **where** he is.

30 The man answered and said **to-them, because in this** is a marvelous thing, that you **perceive** not from **where** he is, and he has opened **my** eyes.

31 Now we **perceive** that God hears not sinners: but if any man be **reverence-God**,[2072] and does his will, him he **hears**.

32 Out-of the age, not it was heard that any man opened the eyes of one that was born blind.

33 If this man were not of God, **not he-could-be-powerful to-do not-one-thing**.

34 They answered and said **to-him**, you **were wholly** born in sins,[2073] and **do** you teach us? And they cast him out.

35 Jesus heard that they had cast him out; and when he had found him, he said **to-him**, do you believe **into** the Son of God?

36 He answered and said, who is he Lord, that I might believe **into him**?

37 And Jesus said **to-him**, you have both seen him, and it is he that talks with you.

38 And he **showed**,[2074] Lord, I believe. And he worshipped him.

[2072] Greek: "theosebes." Nominative case, "God-reverer," God-respecter
[2073] Contrast Jesus' opinion in John 9:1-3
[2074] Greek: "phemi," the root word for fame ("pheme")

39 And Jesus said, **into judgment-result**[2075] I am come into this world, that they which see not might see; and that they which see **may-become** blind.

40 And of the Pharisees which were with him heard these words, and said **to-him,** are we blind also?

41 Jesus said **to-them,** if you were blind, you should have no sin: but now you say, we see; therefore, your sin remains.

JOHN CHAPTER 10

1 Amen, amen, I say **to-you,** he that enters not by the door into the sheepfold, but **up-walking** other-way, **that-one** is a thief and a robber.

2 But he that enters in by the door is the shepherd of the sheep.

3 To him the **door-watcher** opens; and the sheep hear his voice: and he calls his own sheep by name and leads them out.

4 And when he puts forth his own sheep, he goes before them, and the sheep follow him: for they **perceive** his voice.

5 And **other-same** will they not follow but will flee from him: for they **perceive** not the voice of **others.**

6 This parable spoke Jesus **to-them:** but they understood not what things they were which he spoke **to** them.

7 Then said Jesus **to-them** again, **amen, amen,** I say **to-you,** I am the door of the sheep.

8 All that came before me are thieves and robbers: but the sheep did not hear them.

9 I am the door: by me if any man enters, he shall be saved, and shall go in and out, and find pasture.

10 The thief comes not, but for to steal, and to **sacrifice,** and to **from-ruin:** I am come that they might have life, and that they might have **excessively.**

11 I am the **ideal** shepherd: the **ideal** shepherd gives his **soul** for the sheep.

12 But he that is a **wageworker,** and not the shepherd, who's own the sheep are not, **sees** the wolf coming, and leaves the sheep, and flees: and the wolf **snatches** them, and scatters the sheep.

13 The **wageworker** flees, because he is a **wageworker** and **not interested about** the sheep.

14 I am the **ideal** shepherd, and know **mine,** and am known of mine.

15 As the Father knows me, even so know I the Father: and I lay down my **soul** for the sheep.

16 And other-same sheep I have, which are not of this **yard:** them also **it-is-binding** I **lead,** and they shall hear my voice; and there shall be **first-flock,** one shepherd.

17 Through this, my Father love me, **for** I lay down my **soul,** that I might **take** it again.

18 No man **lifts** it from me, but I **place it from** myself. I have **authority** to **place it,** and I have **authority** to **take** it again. This commandment **I-got beside** my Father.

19 There was a **split** therefore again **in** the Jews **through** these sayings.

20 And many of them said, he has a **demon** and is **maniac;**[2076] why hear you him?

21 Others said, these are not the **declarations** of him that has a **demon. Is-powerful** a **demon to-**open the eyes of the blind?

22 And it was at Jerusalem the **Dedication,** and it was winter.

23 And Jesus walked in the **priest-place** in Solomon's porch.

24 Then came the Jews round him, and said **to-him, until when you-are-lifting our soul**? If you be the Christ, tell us **all-speech.**[2077]

25 Jesus answered them, I told you, and you believed not: the works that I **produce** in my Father's name, they witness of me.

26 But you believe not, because you are not of my sheep, as I said **to-you.**

27 My sheep hear my voice, and I know them, and they follow me:

28 And I give **to-them** eternal life; and they shall **not be-from-ruin,**[2078] neither shall any **snatch** them out of my hand.

[2075] Greek: "krima," transliterated as "crime" and also means judgment
[2076] Or, raving mad, divination maniac, divining mad
[2077] Or free speech
[2078] Greek: "apo" (from) and "alethros" (ruin), to destroy fully

29 My Father, which gave **to-me,** is **larger**[2079] than all; and **no-one** is-**powerful** to **be-snatching** out of my Father's hand.

30 I and **the** Father are one.

31 Then the Jews **lifted** stones again to stone him.

32 Jesus answered them, many **ideal** works have I showed you from my Father; for which of those works do you stone me?

33 The Jews answered him, saying, not **about ideal** work we stone you; but for blasphemy; and because that you, being a man, make yourself God.

34 Jesus answered them, is it not written in your law, I said, you are gods?

35 If he called them gods, **towards** whom the **Word of God became**, and **not is-powerful-any**[2080] **to-loose the** Scripture.

36 Say you of him, whom the Father has sanctified, and sent into the world, you blaspheme; because I said, I am the Son of God?

37 If I **produce** not the works of my Father, believe me not.

38 But if I **produce**, though you believe not me, believe the works: that you may know, and believe, that the Father in me, and I in him.

39 Therefore they sought again to **squeeze-capture** him: but he escaped out of their hand,

40 And went away again **other-side of-the** Jordan into the **spot** where John **foremost** baptized; and there he **remained**.

41 And many resorted **to-him,** and said, John did no **sign**: but all things that John spoke of this man were true.

42 And many believed **into him** there.

JOHN CHAPTER 11

1 Now a certain was **weak**, Lazarus, of Bethany, the town of Mary and her sister Martha.

2 (It was Mary who **oiled** the Lord with **myrrh**, and wiped his feet with her hair, whose brother Lazarus was **weak**.)

3 Therefore his sisters sent **to-him,** saying, Lord, **be-perceiving**, he whom you **friend** is sick.

4 When Jesus heard, he said, this **weakness** is not to death, but for the glory of God, that the Son of God might be glorified **through it**.

5 Now Jesus loved Martha, and her sister, and Lazarus.

6 When he had heard therefore that he was **weak**, he **remained** two days still in the same **spot** where he was.

7 Then after that **he says to-the** disciples, let us go into Judaea again.

8 The disciples say **to-him, Rabbi,** the Jews **now** sought to stone you; and again, you **are-going there**?

9 Jesus answered, are there not twelve hours in the day? If any man walks in the day, not he **toward-strike,**[2081] because he **sees** the light of this world.

10 But if a man walks in the night, he **toward-strike,** because there is no light in him.

11 These things said he: and after that he says **to-them,** our friend Lazarus sleeps; but I go, that I may awake him out of sleep.

12 Then said his disciples, Lord, if he sleeps, he shall **be-safe**.[2082]

13 Yet, Jesus spoke of his death: but they **seemed** that he had spoken of **laying** in sleep.

14 Then said Jesus **to-them, all-out-spoken,** Lazarus is dead!

15 And I am glad **through you** that I was not there, **that** you may believe; **but** let us go **to-him.**

16 Then said Thomas, which is called Didymus, **to-his together-disciples,** let us also go, that we may die with him.

17 Then when Jesus came, he found **him held** in the **remembrance-tomb** four days already.

18 Now Bethany was **near-squeezed to** Jerusalem, **from** fifteen **stadiums**.[2083]

19 And many of the Jews came to Martha and Mary, to **beside-closure**[2084] them concerning their brother.

20 Then Martha, as soon as she heard that Jesus was coming, went and met him: but Mary sat in the house.

[2079] Larger, especially in age
[2080] Third person, singular
[2081] Or, stub, towards-chop

[2082] Or, saved
[2083] Greek: "stadion," transliterated as stadiums, root to stand as fixed
[2084] Lit., beside-closure, or beside-myth, beside-fable,

21 Then said Martha **to** Jesus, Lord, if you had been here, my brother had not died.

22 But I **perceive**, that even now, whatever you **will** ask of God, God will give you.

23 Jesus says **to-her,** your brother shall rise again.

24 Martha says **to-him,** I **perceive** that he shall rise again in the resurrection **in** the last day.

25 Jesus said **to-her,** I am the resurrection, and the life: he that believes **into** me, though he were dead, yet shall he live:

26 And whoever lives and believes **into** me shall **no not die into the age.** Believe you this?

27 She says **to-him**, yes, Lord: I believe that you are the Christ, the Son of God, which should come into the world.

28 And when she had so said, she went her way, and called Mary her sister secretly, saying, the **Teacher** is come, and **voices** for you.

29 As soon as she heard, she arose quickly, and came **toward him.**

30 Now not yet Jesus **came** into the town but was in that **spot** where Martha met him.

31 The Jews then which were with her in the house, and **beside-closure** her, when they **perceive** Mary, that she rose up hastily and went out, followed her, saying, she goes **into** the **remembrance-tomb** to weep there.

32 Then when Mary was come where Jesus was, and **perceive** him, she fell down at his feet, saying **to-him**, Lord, if you have been here, my brother had not died.

33 When Jesus therefore **perceives** her weeping, and the Jews also weeping which came with her, he **in-snorts-with-anger**[2085] in the spirit, and was **agitated,**

34 And said, where have you laid him? They said **to-him**, Lord, come and **perceive**.

35 Jesus wept.

36 Then said the Jews, **be-perceiving** how he **friend-of** him!

37 And some of them said, **not is-powerful** this man, who opened the eyes of the blind, have caused that even this man should not have died?

38 Jesus therefore again **in-snorts-with-anger** in himself comes to the **remembrance-tomb**. It was a cave, and a stone laid upon it.

39 Jesus said, **lift** the stone. Martha, the sister of him that was dead, says **to-him**, Lord, he stinks **already: because** he has been **four-days.**

40 Jesus says **to-her,** said I not **to-you,** that if you would believe, you should see the glory of God?

41 Then they **lift** the stone where the dead was laid. And Jesus lifted up **the** eyes, and said, Father, I thank you that you have heard me.

42 And I **perceive** that you **hear** me always: but because of the people which stand by I said that they may believe that you have sent me.

43 And when he had spoken **these-things,** he cried with a **great** voice, Lazarus, **here, outside!**

44 And he that was dead came forth, bound hand and foot with **winding-sheets**:[2086] and his **sight-appearance** was bound about with a **sweat-cloth**. Jesus says **to-them,** loose him, and **release** him **to under-lead.**

45 Then many of the Jews which came to Mary, and had seen the things which Jesus did, believed **into him.**

46 But some of them went their ways to the Pharisees and told them what things Jesus had done.

47 Then gathered the **first-rank-priests** and the Pharisees, a **Sanhedrin**, and said, what do we? **That** this, **the Man, is-producing** many **signs.**

48 If we **release him,** all will believe **into** him: and the Romans shall come and take away both our **spot** and nation.

49 And one **out-of** them, Caiaphas, being the **first-rank-priest** that same **year,** said **to-them,** you **perceive** nothing at all,

50 Not-moreover you-through-inventory that it is **together-bear** for us, that one man should die for the people, and that the whole nation not **from-ruin.**

51 And this spoke he not **from** himself: but being **first-rank-priest** that **year,** he prophesied that **it-was-impending the** Jesus **to-die** for that nation.

[2085] Or in-thunders

[2086] Or swathe

52 And not for that nation only, but that also he should gather together in one the children of God that were **through-scattered**.

53 Then from that day forth **they-together-plan-counsel** to-**from-kill him**.

54 Jesus therefore **about-walked** no more **all-speech**[2087] in the Jews; but went **there, into the space,** near-**squeeze** to the **lonesome**, into a city called Ephraim, and there **tarried**[2088] with his disciples.

55 And the Jews' **Passover** was **near-squeezed**: and many **up-walked** out **of-the space** **into** Jerusalem before the **Passover**, to **clean** themselves.

56 Then sought they for Jesus, and spoke **with one-another-same**, as they stood in the **priest-place**, what think you, that he will not come to the **festival**?

57 Now both the **first-rank-priests** and the Pharisees had given a commandment, that, if any man knew where **he-is**, he should **disclose** that they might **squeeze-capture**[2089] him.

JOHN CHAPTER 12

1 Then Jesus six days before the **Passover** came to Bethany, where Lazarus was which was dead, whom he raised from the dead.

2 There they made him an **expensive-dinner**; and Martha **attended**; but Lazarus was one of them that sat at the table with him.

3 Then **took** Mary a pound of **myrrh** of nard, very costly, and **oiled** the feet of Jesus, and wiped his feet with her hair: and the house was filled **out-of** the odor of the myrrh.

4 Then says one of his disciples, Judas Iscariot, Simon's, **the one-impending to-betray** him,

5 Why was not this **myrrh** sold for three hundred **denarii**, and given to the poor?

6 This he said, not that he cared for the poor; but because he was a thief, and had the **tongue-world**,[2090] and **lift** what was **being-cast.**

7 Then said Jesus, **release** her: **into** the day of my burying has she kept this.

8 For the poor **you always** have with you; but me you have not always.

9 Many people of the Jews therefore knew that he was there: and they came not for Jesus' sake only, but that they might **perceive** Lazarus also, whom he had raised **out-of** the dead.

10 But the **first-rank-priests** consulted that they might put Lazarus also to death;

11 That through him many of the Jews **were-under-led** and believed **into** Jesus.

12 Upon-tomorrow many **multitude** that were come to the **festival**, when they heard that Jesus was coming **into** Jerusalem,

13 Got branches of palm trees, and went forth to meet him, and **screamed**, hosanna: blessed the King of Israel **the one-coming** in the name of the Lord.

14 And Jesus, when he had found a young **donkey**, sat **upon it** as it is written,

15 Fear not, daughter of Sion: **be-perceiving**, your King **comes**, sitting on a **colt of-donkey**.

16 These things **knew** not his disciples, **the foremost**: but when Jesus was glorified, then remembered they that these things were written of him, and they had done these things **to-him**.

17 The **multitude** therefore that was with him when he called Lazarus out of his **remembrance-tomb** and raised him from the dead, **witnessed**.

18 For this cause the **multitude** also met him, for that they heard that he had **produced** this **sign**.

19 The Pharisees therefore said among themselves, **look** you how you **profit** nothing? **Be-perceiving**, the world is gone after him.

20 And there were certain **Hellenic out-of the ones-up-walking** to worship **in** the **festival**:

21 The same came therefore to Philip, which was of Bethsaida of Galilee, and **asked** him, saying, **Lord**, we-**are-willing to-perceive** Jesus.

22 Philip comes and tells Andrew: and again, Andrew and Philip tell Jesus.

23 And Jesus answered them, saying, the hour is come, that the Son of man should be glorified.

24 Amen, amen, I say **to-you**, except a corn of wheat fall into the ground and die, it **remains** alone: but if it dies, it **carries** much fruit.

[2087] Or free speech
[2088] Greek: through-wear
[2089] "Piazo," to squeeze, to seize by hand, to press, to arrest, to capture
[2090] Or language (of the) world

25 He that loves his **soul** shall **from-ruin** it; and he that **detest** his **soul** in this world shall **watch** it **into eternal life.**

26 If any man **attended to-me,** let him follow me; and where I am, there shall also my **attendant** be: if any man **attends to-me,** him will **the** Father **value.**

27 Now is my soul **agitated**; and what shall I say? Father, save me from this hour: but **through this** came I **into** this hour.

28 Father, glorify your name. Then came there a voice from heaven, I have both glorified, and will glorify again.

29 The **multitude** therefore, that stood by and heard, said that it thundered: others said, an angel spoke **to-him.**

30 Jesus answered and said, this voice **became** not because of me, but **through you.**

31 Now is the **judging** of this world: now shall the **first-rank,**[2091] of this world be cast out.

32 And I, if I be **elevated out-of** the earth, **I-shall-out-of-induced** all **towards** myself.

33 This he said, **a-sign to-what** death **he-was-impending to-be-from-dying.**

34 The **multitude** answered him, we have heard out of the law that Christ **remains into the age**: and how say you, **it-is-binding** the Son of man be **elevated**? Who is this Son of man?

35 Then Jesus said **to-them,** yet a little while is the light with you. Walk while you have the light, lest darkness **down-take** you: for he that walks in darkness **perceives** not where he goes.

36 While you have light, believe in the light, that you may be the **sons** of light. These things spoke Jesus, and departed, and did hide himself from them.

37 But though he had **produced** so many **signs** before them, yet they believed not **into him:**

38 That the saying of **Isaiah** the prophet might be filled, which he spoke, Lord, who has believed our **hearing**? And to whom has the arm of the Lord been revealed?

39 Therefore, **not they-were-powerful to-**believe, because that **Isaiah** said again,

40 He has blinded their eyes and hardened their **heart**; that they should not **perceive** with eyes, nor **thought to-the heart**, and be **reverted**, and I should **cure** them.

41 These things said **Isaiah**, when he **perceived** his glory, and spoke **about** him.

42 Nevertheless, also **out-of** the **first-rank,** many believed **into him**; but **through** the Pharisees they did not **same-say, that not** they should be put out of the synagogue:

43 For they loved the **glory** of men more than the **glory** of **the** God.

44 Jesus **screamed** and said, he that believes **into** me, believes not **into** me, but **into him** that **dispatched** me.

45 And he that **sees** me **sees** him that **dispatched** me.

46 I am come a light into the world, that whoever believes **into** me should not **remain** in darkness.

47 And if any man hears my **declarations**, and believe not, I judge him not: for I came not to judge the world, but to save the world.

48 He that **un-place**[2092] me, and **take** not my **declarations**, has one that judging him: the word that I have spoken, the same shall judge him in the last day.

49 For I have not spoken **out-of** myself; but the Father which **dispatched** me, he gave me a commandment, what I should say, and what I should speak.

50 And I **perceive** that his commandment is **eternal life**: whatever I speak therefore, even as the Father said **to-me,** so I speak.

JOHN CHAPTER 13

1 Now before the **Festival** of the **Passover,** when Jesus **perceived** that his hour was come that he should **change-base out-of** this world **towards** the Father, having loved his own which were in the world, he loved them **into finish.**

2 And **an-expensive-dinner becoming,** the Devil having now put into the **heart** of Judas Iscariot, Simon's, to betray him.

3 Jesus **perceiving** that the Father had given all things into his hands, and that he was come from God and **under-lead towards** God;

[2091] Or, original-rank, beginning-rank

[2092] Or, set aside

4 He rose **out of-the expensive-dinner** and laid aside his garments; and **took** a towel, and **through-belted** himself.

5 After that he poured water into a basin, and began to wash the disciples' feet, and to wipe with the towel **to-which** he was **through-belted**.

6 Then **he comes towards** Simon Peter: and Peter says **to-him**, Lord, **do-you-wash** my feet?

7 Jesus answered and said **to-him**, what I **produce** you **perceive** not now; but you shall know **after these-things**.

8 Peter says **to-him**, you shall never wash my feet. Jesus answered him, If I wash you not, you have no **section** with me.

9 Simon Peter says **to-him**, Lord, not my feet only, but also **the** hands and **the** head.

10 Jesus says **to-him**, he that is washed needs not **if not** to wash feet, but is clean **wholly**: and you are clean, but not all.

11 For he **perceived** who should betray him; therefore, said he, you are not all clean.

12 So after he had washed their feet, and **took** his garments, and was **up-fall**[2093] again, he said **to-them**, know you what I have **produced to-you**?

13 You call me **Teacher** and Lord: and you say **ideally**; for I am.

14 If I then, Lord and **Teacher**, have washed your feet; you also **owe** to wash **another-same**'s feet.

15 For I have given you an example, that you should **produce** as I have **produced to-you**.

16 **Amen**, **amen**, I say **to-you**, the **slave** is not **larger**[2094] than his lord; neither is an **apostle larger** than **the-one** that **dispatched him**.

17 If you **perceive** these things, happy are you if you **produce** them.

18 I speak not of you all: I **perceive** whom I have chosen: but that the Scripture may be **filled**, he that eats bread with me has lifted his heel **upon** me.

19 Now I tell you before it **becomes**, that, when it-**becomes** you may believe that I am.

20 **Amen**, **amen**, I say **to-you**, he that **takes** **whomever** I **dispatched takes** me; and he that **takes** me **takes** him that **dispatched** me.

21 When Jesus said **these-things**, he was **agitated to-the** spirit, and **witnessed**, and said, **amen**, **amen**, I say **to-you**, that one of you shall betray me.

22 Then the disciples looked one on another, **having-no-way-out** of whom he spoke.

23 Now there was leaning on Jesus' bosom one of his disciples, whom Jesus loved.

24 Simon Peter therefore **nod to-him**, that he should **ascertain-by-inquiry** who it should be **about** whom he spoke.

25 He then **laying** on Jesus' **chest** says **to-him**, Lord, who is it?

26 Jesus answered, he it is, to whom I shall give a sop, when I have **baptized**.[2095] And when he had **in-baptized** the **morsel**, he gave to Judas Iscariot, of Simon.

27 And after the **morsel**, Satan entered **into him**. Then said Jesus **to-him**, **that-which you-are-producing**, **produce** quickly.

28 Now no man at the **recline**[2096] knew for what intent he spoke this **to-him**.

29 For some **seemed**, because Judas had the **tongue-world**,[2097] that Jesus had said **to-him**, buy[2098] what we have need of **into** the festival; or, that he should give something to the poor.

30 He then having **taken** the **morsel** went **soon** out: and it was night.

31 Therefore, when he was gone out, Jesus said, now is the Son of man glorified, and God is glorified in him.

32 If God be glorified in him, God shall also glorify him in himself, and shall **soon** glorify him.

33 Little children, yet a little I am with you. You shall seek me: and as I said **to** the Jews, **where** I go, **not you-are-powerful to-come**; so now I say **to-you**.

34 A new commandment I give **to-you**, that you love **one-another-same**; as I have loved you, that you also love **one-another-same**.

[2093] Or, leaning back
[2094] Larger, especially in age
[2095] Greek: bapto—to whelm, to cover wholly with fluid
[2096] Greek: up-cline
[2097] Or language (of the) world
[2098] Lit., to go to the market, redeem

35 By this shall all know that you are my disciples if you have love **in one-another-same**.

36 Simon Peter said **to-him**, Lord, where **are-you-going**? Jesus answered him, **where** I go, **not-you-are-powerful to-follow** me now; but you shall follow me afterwards.

37 Peter said **to-him**, Lord, why **not I-am-powerful to-**follow you now? I will **place** my **soul over you**.

38 Jesus answered him, **will** you **place your soul over me**? **Amen**, **amen**, I say **to-you**, the **rooster** shall not crow, **until** you have denied me three.

JOHN CHAPTER 14

1 Let not your **heart** be **agitated**: you believe **into** God, believe also **into** me.

2 In my Father's house are many **remaining-places**: [2099] if not, I would have told you. I **traverse** to **internally-prepare** a **spot** for you.

3 And if I **traverse** and **internally-prepare** a **spot** for you, I will come again, and **beside-take** you **towards** myself; that where I am, you may be also.

4 And where I go you **perceive**, and the way you **perceive**.

5 Thomas says **to-him**, Lord, we **perceive** not where you go; and how **are-we-powerful to-perceive** the way?

6 Jesus says **to-him**, I am the **Way**, the **Truth**, and the **Life**: no man comes **towards** the Father, **if not through** me.

7 If you had known me, you should have known my Father also: and from **present** you know him and have seen him.

8 Philip says **to-him**, Lord, show us the Father, and it **content** us.

9 Jesus says **to-him**, have I been so **much uninterrupted-time** with you, and yet have you not known me, Philip? He that has seen me has seen the Father; and how say you, **show** us the Father?

10 Believe you not that I am in the Father, and the Father in me? The words that I speak **to-you** I speak not of myself: but the Father that **remains** in me, he **produces** the works.

11 Believe me that I in the Father, and the Father in me: or else believe me **through the** works.

12 **Amen**, **amen**, I say **to-you**, he that believes **into** me, the works that I **produce** shall he do also; and **great** than these shall he **produce**; because I **traverse towards** my Father.

13 And whatever you shall ask in my name, that will I **produce**, that the Father may be glorified in the Son.

14 If you shall ask **a-thing** in my name, I will **produce**.

15 If you love me, keep my commandments.

16 And I will pray the Father, and he shall give you **another-same Beside-Caller**, that he may **remain** with you **into the age**;

17 The Spirit of **Truth**; whom the world **not is-powerful to-take**, because it **sees** him not, neither knows him: but you know him; for he **remains** with you and shall be in you.

18 I will not **release** you **orphans**: I will come **to-you**.

19 Yet a little while, and the world **sees** me no more; but you see me: because I live, you shall live also.

20 In that day you shall know that I in my Father, and you in me, and I in you.

21 He that has my commandments, and **guards** them, he it is that loves me: and he that loves me shall be loved of my Father, and I will love him, and will **emphasize**[2100] myself **to-him**.

22 Judas says **to-him**, not Iscariot, Lord, how is it that **you-are-impending to-emphasize** yourself **to-us**, and not **to** the world?

23 Jesus answered and said **to-him**, if a man loves me, he will **guard** my words: and my Father will love him, and we will come **towards** him, and **produce remaining beside** him

24 He that loves me not **guards** not my sayings: and the word which you hear is not mine, but the Father's which **dispatched** me.

25 These things have I spoken **to-you**, **remaining beside** you.

26 But the **Beside-Caller**, the Holy Spirit, whom the Father will **dispatch** in my name, he shall teach you all things, and bring all things **to-your** remembrance, whatever I have said **to-you**.

[2099] Greek: "monai" or "mone;" this inflection is used in two places (John 14:2 and John 14:23); "monai," or any of its inflection also means "to stay"

[2100] Greek: "emphanizo" also transliterated as "emphasize"

27 Peace I **release** with you, my peace I give **to-you**: not as the world gives, give I **to-you**. Let not your **heart** be **agitated**, neither let it be **timid**.[2101]

28 You have heard how I said **to-you, I-am-under-leading,** and **I-am-coming towards** you. If you loved me, **you-were-cheerful,** because I said, I **traverse towards** the Father: for my Father is **larger**[2102] than I.

29 And now I have told you before it **becomes** that, when it **becomes**, you might believe.

30 Not still much, I will not talk much with you: for the **first-rank**,[2103] of this world **comes**, and has **no, not-one-thing**[2104] in me.

31 But that the world may know that I love the Father; and as the Father gave me commandment, even so I **produce**. Arise, let us go **within**.

JOHN CHAPTER 15

1 I am the true vine, and my Father is the **Land-Worker**.

2 Every branch in me that **carries** not fruit **he-is-lifting it**: and **every branch in me carrying** fruit, he **cleanses** it, that it may **carry** more fruit.

3 Already, you are clean through the word which I have spoken **to-you**.

4 Remain in me, and I in you. As the branch **not is-powerful to-carry** fruit of itself, except it **remains** in the vine; no more can you, except you **remain** in me.

5 I am the vine, you the branches: he that **remains** in me, and I in him, the same brings forth much fruit: for **spacing** me you **are-powerful to-do not-one-thing**.

6 If a man **remains** not in me, **he-was-cast outside** as a branch, and is withered; and men gather them, and cast into the fire, and they are burned.

7 If you **remain** in me, and my words **remain** in you, you shall ask what you will, and **it-shall-become to-you**.

8 In this is my Father glorified: that you **carry** much fruit; so, shall you be my disciples.

9 As the Father has loved me, so have I loved you: **remain** you in my love.

10 If you **guard** my commandments, you shall **remain** in my love; even as I have **guarded** my Father's commandments and **remain** in his love.

11 These things have I spoken **to-you**, that my **cheerfulness** might remain in you, and your **cheerfulness** might be full.

12 This is my commandment, that you love **another-same**, as I have loved you.

13 Mega love has no man than this, that a man place his **soul over** his friends.

14 You are my friends, if you **produce** whatever I command you.

15 Not still, I call you not **slave**s; for the **slave perceives** not what his lord does: but I have called you friends; for all things that I have heard of my Father I have made known **to-you**.

16 You have not chosen me, but I have chosen you, and **placed** you, that you should go and **carry** fruit, and your fruit should remain: that whatever you shall ask of the Father in my name, he may give it you.

17 These things I command you, that you love **another-same**.

18 If the world **detests** you, you know that it **detested** me before you.

19 If you were of the world, the world would **friend** his own: but because you are not of the world, but I have chosen you out of the world, therefore the world **detests** you.

20 Remember the word that I said **to-you**, the **slave** is not **larger**[2105] than his lord. If they have **chased** me, they will also **chase** you; if they have **guarded** my saying, they will **guard** yours also.

21 But all these things will they **produce into you through my name**, because they **perceive** not him that **dispatched** me.

22 If I had not come and spoken **to-them,** they had not had sin: but now they have no **pretense**[2106] for their sin.

23 He that **detest** me **detest** my Father also.

24 If I had not **produced** among them the works which none other man **produced**, they had not had sin: but

---

[2101] Or dread
[2102] Larger, especially in age
[2103] Or, original-rank, beginning-rank
[2104] Or: double negative, no, not-one-thing, no, nothing
[2105] Larger, especially in age
[2106] Greek: before-appear, outward show

now have they both seen and **detested** both me and my Father.

25 But that the word might be filled that is written in their law, they **detested** me **gratuitously**.[2107]

26 But when the **Beside-Caller** is come, whom I will **dispatch to-you** from the Father, the Spirit of **Truth**, which **out-passage beside** the Father, he shall **witness** of me:

27 And you also **are-witnesses,** because you have been with me from the **origin**.

JOHN CHAPTER 16

1 These things have I spoken **to-you**, that you should not be **scandalized**.[2108]

2 From- synagogues they-shall-produce you: **yes**, the **hour comes**, that whoever kills you will **seem** that he **towards-bear** God's **hired-service**.

3 And these things will they **produce**, because they have not known the Father, nor me.

4 But these things have I told you, that when the **hour** shall come, you may remember that I told you of them. And these things I said not **to-you** at the **origin**, because I was with you.

5 But **now -under-lead to-him** that **dispatched** me; and none of you ask me, **where are-you going?**

6 But because I have said these things **to-you**, sorrow has filled your **heart**.

7 Nevertheless I tell you the truth; it is **together-bear** for you that **I-from-go**: for if **not-I-from-go**, the **Beside-Caller** will not come **to-you**; but if I **traverse**, I will **dispatch** him **to-you**.

8 And when he is come, he will **expose** the world of sin, and of **righteous-togetherness**, and of **judging**:

9 Of sin, because they believe not **into** me.

10 Of **righteous-togetherness**, because I go **towards** my Father, and you see me no more;

11 Of **judging**, because the **first-rank**,[2109] of this world **has-been-judged**.[2110]

12 I have yet many things to say **to-you**, but **not you-are-powerful to-lift** them now.

13 Yet when he, the Spirit of **Truth**, is come, he will **lead** you into all truth: for he shall not speak of himself; but whatever he shall hear, shall he speak: and he will **up-message to-you** things to come.

14 He shall glorify me: for he shall **take** of mine and shall **up-message to-you**.

15 All things that the Father has are mine: therefore, **I said**: that he shall **take** of mine, and shall **up-message to-you.**

16 A little while, and you shall not see me: and again, a little while, and you shall see me, **that I-under-lead towards** the Father.

17 Then said of his disciples among themselves, what is this that he says **to-us**, a little while, and you shall not see me: and again, a little while, and you shall see me: and, because I go **towards** the Father?

18 They said therefore, what is this that he says, a little while? We cannot **perceive** what he says.

19 Now Jesus knew that they **willed** to ask him, and said **to-them, do-you-enquire** among yourselves of that I said, a little while, and you shall not see me: and again, a little while, and you shall see me?

20 Amen, amen, I say **to-you**, that you shall **weep** and lament, but the world shall **cheer**: and you shall be **distress-saddened**, but your **distress-sadness** shall be turned into **cheer**.

21 A woman when she is in travail has sorrow, because her hour is come: but as soon as she **birthed** the child, she remembers no more the **tribulation**, for **cheer** that a man is born into the world.

22 And you now therefore have sorrow: but I will see you again, and your **heart** shall **cheer**, and your **cheerfulness** no man **lifts** from you.

23 And in that day you shall ask me nothing. **Amen, amen**, I say **to-you**, whatever you shall ask the Father in my name, he will give you.

24 Until now have you asked nothing in my name: ask, and you shall **take** that your **cheer** may be **filled.**

25 These things have I spoken **to-you** in proverbs: but the **hour comes**, when I shall no longer speak **to-you** in proverbs, but I shall **up-message** you **all-speech**[2111] of the Father.

[2107] Or, without a cause
[2108] Or, snared, baited trap stick
[2109] Or, original-rank, beginning-rank
[2110] Greek is perfect tense, passive voice
[2111] Or free speech

26 In that day you shall ask in my name: and I say not **to-you**, that I will pray the Father **about** you:

27 For the Father himself **friend** you, because you have **friend** me, and have believed that I **out-of-came beside of-the** God.

28 I-**out-of-came-out out-of** the Father, and **I-have-come** into the world: again, I **release**[2112] the world, and go **towards** the Father.

29 His disciples said **to-him**, **be-perceiving,** now speak you **all-speech,**[2113] and speak no proverb.

30 Now are we **perceive** that you **perceived** all things and need not that any man should ask you: by this we believe that you **out-of-came** from God.

31 Jesus answered them, do you now believe?

32 **Be-perceiving**, the hour **comes**, **yes**, is now come, that you shall be scattered, every man to his own, and shall **release** me alone: and yet I am not alone, because the Father is with me.

33 These things I have spoken **to-you**, that in me you might have peace. In the world, you shall have tribulation: but be **courageous**; I have **conquered**[2114] the world.

JOHN CHAPTER 17

1 These words spoke Jesus, and lifted up his eyes to heaven, and said, Father, the hour is come; glorify your Son, that your Son also may glorify you:

2 As you have given him **authority** over all flesh, that he should give **eternal life** to as many as you have given him.

3 And this is **the eternal life**, that they might know you, the only true God, and Jesus Christ, whom you have sent.

4 I have glorified you on the earth; I have finished the work which you gave me to do.

5 And now, Father, glorify you me **beside** yourself with the glory which I had with you before the world was.

6 I have **shined** your name **to-the** men who you gave me out of the world: yours they were, and you gave them me; and they have **guarded** your word.

7 Now they have known that all things whatever you have given me are of you.

8 For I have given **to-them** the words which you gave me; and they have **taken and** have known **truly** that I came out from you, and they have believed that you sent me.

9 I pray **about** them: I pray not for the world, but **about** them which you have given me; for they are yours.

10 And all mines are yours, and yours are mine; and I am glorified in them.

11 And now I am no more in the world, but these are in the world, and I come **towards** you. Holy Father **guard** through your name those whom you have given me, that they may be one, as we.

12 While I was with them in the world, I **guarded** them in your name: those that you gave me I have **watched**, and none of them is **from-ruin**, but the son of **from-ruin**; that the Scripture might be filled.

13 And now come I **to-you**; and these things I speak in the world, that they might have my **cheerfulness filled in them.**

14 I have given them your word; and the world has **detested** them, because they are not of the world, even as I am not of the world.

15 I pray that you should not take them out of the world, but that you should **guard** them from the **wicked-hurtful**.

16 They are not **out-of** the world, even as I am not **out-of** the world.

17 Sanctify them through your truth: your **Word is Truth.**

18 As you have sent me into the world, even so have I also sent them into the world.

19 And **over them,** I sanctify myself, that they also might be sanctified through the truth.

20 Neither I pray for these alone, but for them also which shall believe on me through their word.

21 That they all may be one; as you, Father, are in me, and I in you, that they also may be one in us: that the world may believe that you have sent me.

22 And the glory which you gave me I have given them; that they may be one, even as we are one:

[2112] Or, to from-let-go, forgive
[2113] Or free speech
[2114] "Nikao," to defeat an enemy

23 I in them, and you in me, that they may be **matured into** one; and that the world may know that you have sent me, and has loved them, as you have loved me.

24 Father, I will that they also, whom you have given me, be with me where I am; that they may **be-perceiving** my glory, which you have given me: for you loved me before the **down-casting** of the world.

25 Righteous Father! The world has not known you: but I have known you, and these have known that you have sent me.

26 And I have **made-known to-them** your name and will **make-it-known** that the love **which** you have loved me may be in them, and I in them.

JOHN CHAPTER 18

1 When Jesus had spoken these words, he went forth with his disciples over the brook Kidron,[2115] where was a garden, into the which he entered, and his disciples.

2 And Judas also, which betrayed[2116] him, **perceive** the **spot**: for Jesus often **together-lead** there with his disciples.

3 Judas then, having **taken** a **mass-of-men**.[2117] and **subservient-ones**[2118] from the **first-rank-priests** and Pharisees, comes there with lanterns, lamps, and weapons.

4 Jesus therefore, **perceiving** all things that should come upon him, went forth, and said **to-them,** whom **are-you-seeking?**

5 They answered him, Jesus of Nazareth. Jesus says **to-them,** I am. And Judas also, which betrayed him, stood with them.

6 As soon then as he had said **to-them,** I am, they went backward, and fell to the ground.

7 Then asked he them again, whom **are-you-seeking?** And they said, Jesus of Nazareth.

8 Jesus answered, I have told you that I am: if therefore you seek me, **release these to-under-lead.**

9 That the saying might be filled, which he spoke, of them which you gave me have I **from-ruin** none.

10 Then Simon Peter having a sword **out-of-induced her**, and **hit** the **first-rank-priest**'s **slave**, and cut off his right ear. The **slave**'s name was Malchus [2119]

11 Then said Jesus **to** Peter, put up your sword into the sheath: the cup which my Father has given me, shall I not drink it?

12 Then the **mass-of-men**, and the captain and **subservient-ones** of the Jews **together-took** Jesus, and bound him,

13 And led him away to Annas **foremost**; for he was father-in-law to Caiaphas, which was the **first-rank-priest** that **year**.

14 Now Caiaphas was he, which gave **together-plan-counsel** to the Jews, that it was **together-bear** that one man should die **over** the people.

15 And Simon Peter followed Jesus, and another disciple: that disciple was known **to** the **first-rank-priest** and **went-in-together to-the** Jesus into the **yard**[2120] of the **first-rank-priest**.

16 But Peter stood at the door **outside**. Then went out that **other-same** disciple, who was known **to** the **first-rank-priest**, and spoke **to** her that kept the door, and brought in Peter.

17 Then says the **girl** that kept the door **to** Peter, **are** not you also of this man's disciples? He says, I am not.

18 And the **slaves** and **subservient-ones** stood there, who had made **coal-fire**; for it was cold: and they warmed themselves: and Peter stood with them and warmed himself.

19 The **first-rank-priest** then asked Jesus of his disciples, and of his **teaching**.

20 Jesus answered him, I spoke **all-speech**[2121] to the world; I **always** taught in the synagogue, and in the **priest-place**, where the Jews always **together-come**[2122] and in **hiding** have I said nothing.

21 Why ask you me? Ask them which heard me, what I have said **to-them: be-perceiving,** they **perceive** what I said.

22 And when he had spoken **these-things**, one of the **subservient-ones** which **beside-stood slap** Jesus

---

[2115] Hebrew origin, "dusky place"
[2116] Lit., beside-given
[2117] Greek: "speira, transliterated "spire" meaning to coil, figuratively a mass of roman military cohort, or a squad of Levitical janitors
[2118] Lit., under-oarsman, generally a subordinate

[2119] Hebrew origin, "king"
[2120] Yard open to the air and/or wind
[2121] Or free speech
[2122] Or convene

with the palm of his hand, saying, **you-are-answering** the **first-rank-priest** so?

23 Jesus answered him, if I have spoken evil, witness of the evil: but if **ideally**, why **are-you-skinning me**?

24 Now Annas had sent him bound **to** Caiaphas, the **first-rank-priest**.

25 And Simon Peter stood and warmed himself. They said therefore **to-him, are** you not also of his disciples? He **contradicted** and said, I am not.

26 One of the **slaves** of the **first-rank-priest**, being kinsman, whose ear Peter cut off, says, did not I **perceive** you in the garden with him?

27 Peter then **contradicted** again: and **soon** the **rooster** voice.

28 Then led they Jesus from Caiaphas **to** the **Praetorium**: and it was early; and they themselves went not into the **Praetorium**,[2123], lest they should be **stained**; but that they might eat the **Passover**.

29 Pilate then went out **towards** them, and said, what accusation **carry** you against this man?

30 They answered and said **to-him**, if he were not an **evil-worker**, we would not have **betrayed**[2124] him **to-you.**

31 Then said Pilate **to** them, you **take** him, and judge him according **to-you**r law. The Jews therefore said **to-him**, it is not lawful for us to put any man to death:

32 That the saying of Jesus might be filled, which he spoke, **a-sign to-what** death **he-was-impending to-be-dying.**

33 Then Pilate entered into the **Praetorium**[2125] again, and called Jesus, and said **to-him, are** you the King of the Jews?

34 Jesus answered him, say you this thing of yourself, or did others tell you **about** me?

35 Pilate answered, Am I a Jew? **Your** own nation and the **first-rank-priests** have **betrayed** you **to** me: what have you **produced**?

36 Jesus answered, My kingdom is not **out-of** this world: if my kingdom were **out-of** this world, then would my **subservient-ones**[2126] **agonize**,[2127] that I should not be **betrayed** to the Jews: but now is my kingdom not **from-within-here.**

37 Pilate therefore said **to-him, are** you a king then? Jesus answered, you say that I am a king. **Into this** was I born, and **into this** came I into the world, that I should witness **to** the truth. Every one that is **out-of** the truth hears my voice.

38 Pilate says **to-him**, what is truth? And when he had said this, he went out again **towards** the Jews, and says **to-them**, I find in him no **cause**.

39 But you have a **together-ethics**, that I should **from-loose to-you** one at the **Passover**: will you therefore that I **from-loose to-you** the King of the Jews?

40 Then cried they all again, saying, not this man, but Barabbas![2128] Now Barabbas was a robber.

JOHN CHAPTER 19

1 Then Pilate therefore **took** Jesus, and **whipped-him**

2 And the soldiers **braided** a **victor's-crown** of thorns, and put on his head, and they put on him a purple robe,

3 And said, **cheer**, King of the Jews! And they **slapped** him with their hands.

4 Pilate therefore went forth again, and says **to-them, be-perceiving**, I bring him forth **to-you**, that you may know that I find no **cause** in him.

5 Then came Jesus forth, wearing the **victor's-crown** of thorns, and the purple robe. And **he-is-saying** to them, **be-perceiving** the man!

6 When the **first-rank-priests** therefore and **subservient-ones**[2129] **perceived** him, they cried out, saying, crucify, crucify. Pilate says **to**-them, you **take** him, and crucify for I find no **cause** in him.

7 The Jews answered him, we have a law, and by our law he **owes** to die, because he made himself the Son of God.

8 When Pilate therefore heard that saying, he was the more afraid.

9 And went again into the **Praetorium**,[2130] and says **to** Jesus, **from-where** are **you**? But Jesus gave him no answer.

[2123] Or governor's courtroom
[2124] Lit., beside-given
[2125] Or governor's courtroom
[2126] Lit., under-oarsman, generally a subordinate
[2127] Or, struggle, fight, compete for a prize
[2128] Hebrew origin, heir, or son of (a) father
[2129] Lit., under-oarsman, generally a subordinate
[2130] Or governor's courtroom

10 Then says Pilate **to-him**, speak you not **to-me**? **Perceive** you not that I have **authority** to crucify you, and have **authority** to **from-loose** you?

11 Jesus answered, you could have no **authority no-not-one**, except it were given you from above: therefore, he that **betrayed**[2131] me to -you have the **greater** sin.

12 And **out-of this** Pilate sought to **from-loose** him: but the Jews **screamed**, saying, if you **from-loose** this man, you are not Caesar's friend: whoever makes himself a king **anti-word**[2132] Caesar.

13 When Pilate therefore heard that saying, he brought Jesus forth, and sat in the **judgment-step,**[2133] **into** a place that is called the Pavement,[2134] but in the Hebrew, Gabbatha.[2135]

14 And it was the **Preparation** of the **Passover**, and about the sixth hour: and he says **to** the Jews, **be-perceiving** your King!

15 But they cried out, **lift-you, lift-you, crucify-you** him. Pilate says **to-them,** shall I crucify your King? The **first-rank-priests** answered, we have no king **if not** Caesar.

16 Then he **betrayed** him therefore **to-them** to be crucified.

17 And he is bearing his cross **out-of-came** into a **spot** called, of-skull, which is called in the Hebrew Golgotha:[2136]

18 Where they crucified him, and two **others-same** with him, **from-within-here and from-within-here**,[2137] and Jesus in the **middle.**

19 And Pilate wrote a title, and **place** on the cross. And the writing was, **Jesus, the Nazarene, the King of the Jews**.

20 This title then read many of the Jews: for the **spot** where Jesus was crucified **near-squeeze** to the city: and it was written, Hebrew, **Hellenic,**[2138] **Roman**.

21 Then said the **first-rank-priests** of the Jews to Pilate, write not, the King of the Jews; but that he said, I am King of the Jews.

22 Pilate answered, what I have written I have written.

23 Then the soldiers, when they had crucified Jesus, **took** his garments, and made four **sections**, to every soldier a **section**; and also, **the** coat: now the coat was without seam,[2139] woven from the top throughout.

24 They said therefore among themselves, let us not **split** it, but cast **lots**[2140] for it, whose it shall be: that the Scripture might be filled, which says, they parted my raiment among them, and for my **garment** they did cast **inheritance**.[2141] These things therefore the soldiers did.

25 Now there stood by the cross of Jesus his mother, and his mother's sister, Mary the of Cleophas,[2142] and Mary Magdalene.[2143]

26 When Jesus therefore **perceives** his mother, and the disciple **beside-standing**, whom he loved, he says **to** his mother, woman, **be-perceiving** your son!

27 Then **he says** to the disciple, **be-perceiving** your mother! And from that disciple hour that **took** her **into the private**.

28 After this, Jesus **perceiving** that all things were now **finished**, that the Scripture might be **filled,** says, I thirst.

29 Now there was set a vessel full of vinegar: and they filled a sponge with vinegar, and **about-placing** hyssop, and **toward-carry** to his mouth.

30 When Jesus therefore had **taken** the vinegar, he said, it is finished: and he **declined** his head, and **beside-gives** the **spirit**

31 The Jews therefore, because it was the **Preparation,** that the bodies should not remain upon the cross on the Sabbath, (for that Sabbath was a **great** day,) **asked** Pilate that their legs might be broken, and they might be **lifted**.

32 Then came the soldiers, and broke the legs of the **foremost**, and of the **other-same** which was crucified **to-him.**

33 But when they came to Jesus, and **perceive** that he was dead already, they **broke** not his legs:

34 But one of the soldiers with a spear pierced his side, and **soon** came out blood and water.

[2131] Lit., beside-given
[2132] Or refute, dispute
[2133] Greek: "Bema," a step, foot-breadth, tribunal
[2134] Lit;, stone-spread
[2135] "Gabbatha" is Hebrew for back
[2136] Skull
[2137] "Enteuthen" also carries the idea of both sides
[2138] Greek: Hellenistically (Greek language)
[2139] Or, un-sewed, a single piece
[2140] Greek: "lagchano" to chance, to determine by lot
[2141] Greek: "kleros," inheritance, inherit
[2142] Hebrew origin, brother of father
[2143] Tower

35 And he that saw **witnessed**, and his **witness** is true: and he **perceives** that **truth he is saying**, that you might believe.

36 For these things **became**, that the Scripture should be **filled**, **no** bone of him shall be **crushed**.

37 And again **another-different** Scripture says, they shall look on him whom they pierced.[2144]

38 And after this Joseph of Arimathaea, being a disciple of Jesus, but **hidden** for fear of the Jews, **asked** Pilate that he might **lift** the body of Jesus: and Pilate **permitted**. He came therefore and **lift** the body of Jesus.

39 And there also came Nicodemus, which at the **foremost** came to Jesus by night, and brought a mixture of myrrh and aloes, about a hundred pound.[2145]

40 Then **took** they the body of Jesus, and **bound** it in linen with the spices, as the **ethics** of the Jews is to bury.

41 Now in the place where he was crucified there was a garden; and in the garden a new **remembrance-tomb**, **in which not-yet no-one was-placed**.

42 There **they placed** Jesus **through** the Jews' **Preparation**; for the **remembrance-tomb near-squeeze**.

JOHN CHAPTER 20

1 Yet, **to-the first of the Sabbaths,** comes Mary Magdalene early, when it was yet dark, **into** the **remembrance-tomb**, and **sees** the stone **lifted** from the **remembrance-tomb**

2 Then **she-is-running**, and **is-coming toward** Simon Peter, and to the **other-same** disciple, whom Jesus loved, and says **towards** them, they have **lifted** the Lord out of the **remembrance-tomb**, and we **perceive** not where they have laid him.

3 Peter therefore went forth, and that other disciple, and came to the **remembrance-tomb**.

4 So they **ran the two alike**: and the **other-same** disciple did **before-raced** Peter and came **foremost into** the **remembrance-tomb**.

5 And he **beside-bend**, saw the linen **laying**; yet he went not in.

6 Then comes Simon Peter following him, and went into the **remembrance-tomb**, and **sees** the linen clothes **laying**,

7 And the **sweat-cloth**, that was about his head, not **laying** with the linen, but wrapped together in a place **spaced-from**.

8 Then went in also that **other-same** disciple, who came **foremost** to the **remembrance-tomb**, and he **perceive**, and believed.

9 For as yet they **perceive** not the Scripture, that **it-is-binding** he rise again from the dead.

10 Then the disciples went away again **towards** themselves.

11 But Mary stood without at the **remembrance-tomb** weeping: and as she wept, she **beside-bend**, into the **remembrance-tomb,**

12 And **sees** two angels in white sitting, the one at the head, and the other at the feet, where the body of Jesus had laid.

13 And they say **to-her**, woman, **why are-you-weeping?** She says **to-them,** because they have **lifted** my Lord, and I **perceive** not where they have **placed** him.

14 And when she had said **these-things**, she turned herself back, and saw Jesus standing, and **perceive** not that it was Jesus.

15 Jesus says **to-her,** woman, **why are-you-weeping?** Whom seek **you?** She, **seeming him to be the garden-seer,** says **to-him**, Lord, if you have **lift-walk**[2146] him, tell me where you have **placed** him, and I will **lift him.**

16 Jesus says **to-her,** Mary. She turned herself, and says **to-him**, Rabboni; which is to say, **Teacher.**

17 Jesus says **to-her, not fasten to-me**; for I am not yet **up-walked** to my Father: but go **towards** my **brothers**, and say **to**-them, **I-am-up-walking towards** my Father, and your Father; and my God, and your God.

18 Mary Magdalene came and **up-message** the disciples that she had seen the Lord, and he had spoken these things **to-her.**

19 Then the day, that evening, **first of-the Sabbaths**, when the doors were **locked** where the disciples were

---

[2144] Greek ek-(out-of) and "kenteo" (prick), the root for "center" ("kentron")

[2145] A Roman pound (about 12 ounces)

[2146] Greek: "bastazo" to lift, from the Greek root "baino" to pace or to walk

assembled for fear of the Jews, came Jesus, and stood in the **middle**, and says **to-them**, Peace **to-you**.

20 And when he had so said, he showed **to-them** the hands and his side. Then were the disciples **cheerful** when they **perceive** the Lord.

21 Then said Jesus **to-them** again, peace **to-you**: as the Father has sent me, even so **I-am-dispatching** you.

22 And when he had said this, he **breathed-in-them**, and says **to-them, take** the Holy Spirit:

23 Whoever sins you **release**[2147] they are **release to-them**; whosoever you **govern**, they are **have-been-governed**.

24 But Thomas, one of the twelve, called Didymus,[2148] was not with them when Jesus came.

25 The **other-same** disciples therefore said **to-him**, we have seen the Lord. But he said **to-them, if not** I shall **perceive** in his hands the **thump-impression**[2149] of the nails and **thrust**[2150] my finger into the **thump-impression** of the nails, and thrust my hand into his side, I will not believe.

26 And after eight days again his disciples were within, and Thomas with them: came Jesus, the doors being **locked**, and stood in the **middle**, and said, peace **to-you**.

27 Then **he says** to Thomas, **bear** your finger, and **be-perceiving** my hands; and **bear** your hand, and thrust into my side: and **become** not **un-believing**, but believing.

28 And Thomas answered and said **to-him**, My Lord, and my God.

29 Jesus says **to-him**, Thomas, because you have seen me, you have believed: **happy** they that have not **perceived** and have believed.

30 And many other signs truly did Jesus in the presence of his disciples, which are not written in this **little-scroll**:

31 But these are written that you might believe that Jesus is the Christ, the Son of God; and that believing you might have life **in his** name.

JOHN CHAPTER 21

1 After these things Jesus **shined** himself again to the disciples at the sea of Tiberias; **he shined, yet in-this-way:**

2 There were together, Simon Peter, and Thomas called Didymus, and Nathanael **the-one from** Cana in Galilee, and **the-ones** of Zebedee, and two **other-same** of his disciples.

3 Simon Peter says **to-them, I-under-lead to-fishing.** They say **to-him**, we also go with you. They **up-walked** and entered into **the boat soon**; and that night they **squeeze-captured** nothing.

4 But when the morning **already became**, Jesus stood on the shore: but the disciples **perceive** not that it was Jesus.

5 Then Jesus says **to-them,** children, have you any meat? They answered him, no.

6 And he said **to-them**, cast the net on the right **section** of the ship, and you shall find. They cast therefore, and now they were not **forceful** to **out-of-induced**[2151] it for the multitude of fishes.

7 Therefore that disciple whom Jesus loved says **to** Peter, it is the Lord. Now when Simon Peter heard that it was the Lord, he **through-belt outer-garment**, (**because** he was naked,) and cast himself into the sea.

8 And the **other-same** disciples came in a little ship; (for they were not far from land, but as it were two hundred cubits,) dragging the net with fishes.

9 As soon then as they were come to land, they saw a **coal-fire** there, and fish laid **upon it**, and bread.

10 Jesus says **to-them**, bring of the fish which you have now **squeeze-captured.**

11 Simon Peter **up walked**, and **out-of-induced**[2152] the net to land full of **great** fishes, a hundred and fifty and three: and for all there were so many, yet the net was not **split**

12 Jesus says **to-them, come-here early-noon-eat**. And none of the disciples **dared** ask him, who are **you? Having-perceive** that it was the Lord.

13 Jesus then **comes**, and **taking** bread, and gives them, and fish likewise.

[2147] Lit., from-let-go
[2148] Double, twin
[2149] Greek word, transliterated as "type" (a die a struck)
[2150] Lit., cast
[2151] Or drag out of
[2152] Or dragged out of

14 This **already** the **third** that Jesus **shined** himself to his disciples, after that he was risen **out-of** the dead.

15 So when they had **early-noon-eaten**, Jesus says to Simon Peter, Simon, of Jonas, you love me more than these? He says **to-him**, yes, Lord; you **perceive** that I **friend** you. He says **to-him**, feed my lambs.

16 He says **to-him** again, **second,** Simon, of Jonas, you love me? He says **to-him**, yes, Lord; you **perceive** that I **friend** you. He says **to-him**, **shepherd** my sheep.

17 He says **to-him** the **third,** Simon, of Jonas, you **fond of-**me? Peter was **distress-saddened** because he said **to-him** the third time, **friend** you me? And he said **to-him**, Lord, you **perceive** all things; you know that I **friend** you. Jesus says **to-him**, feed my sheep.

18 Amen, amen, I say **to-you**, when you **were** young, you **belted** yourself, and walked where you willed: but when you shall be old, you shall **stretch-out** your hands, and another shall **belt** you, and **shall-be-**carrying where not **you-are-willing**.

19 This spoke he, **a-sign, to-what** death he should glorify God. And when he had spoken this, he says **to-him**, follow me.

20 Then Peter, turning about, **sees** the disciple whom Jesus loved following; which also leaned on his **chest in the expensive-dinner**, and said, Lord, who is he that betrays you?

21 Peter **perceive** him says to Jesus, Lord, **yet what to-this-man**?

22 Jesus says **to-him**, If I will that he **remains until** I come, what **to-you**? You follow me!

23 Then went this saying **into** the **brothers,** that that disciple should not die: yet Jesus said not **to-him**, he shall not die; but, if I will that he **remains until I-am-coming,** what **to-you**?

24 This is the disciple who **witnesses** of these things and wrote these things: and we **perceive** that his **witness** is true.

25 And there are also many **other-same** things which Jesus **produced**, the which, if they should be written **down** one, **I-make-like**[2153] the world itself could not **space** the **little-scrolls** that should be written. Amen.

[2153] Or suppose

THE ACTS OF THE APOSTLES

ACTS CHAPTER 1

1 The **foremost saying** have I made, O Theophilus,[2154] of all that Jesus began both to do and teach,

2 Until the day in which he was **up-taken**, after that he through the Holy Spirit had given commandments **to** the apostles whom he had chosen:

3 To whom also he **beside-stood** himself alive after his **emotion** by many **tokens**, being seen of them forty days, and speaking of the things **about** the kingdom of God:

4 And, being **together-assembled** with **them**, **beside-message** them that they should not **depart** from Jerusalem,[2155] but wait for the promise of the Father, which you have heard of me.

5 For John **indeed** baptized with water; but you shall be baptized **in** the Holy Spirit not **after** many **of-these** days.

6 When they therefore **together-came**, they asked of him, saying, Lord, **will** you at this **uninterrupted-time** restore again the kingdom to Israel?

7 And he said **towards** them, it is not for you to know the **uninterrupted-times** or the seasons, which the Father has **placed** in his own **authority**.

8 But you shall **take** power, after that the Holy Spirit is come upon you: and you shall be witnesses **to-me** both in Jerusalem, and in all Judaea, and in Samaria, and **until the last** of-the earth.

9 And when he had spoken these things, while they **looked**, he was **upon-lifted**; and a cloud **under-take** him out of their sight.

10 And while they **looked-stretched** toward heaven as he **traversed**[2156] **be-perceiving**, two men **beside-stood to**-them in white **garment**.

11 Which also said, you men of Galilee, why stand you **in-looking** into heaven? This same Jesus, which is **up-taken** from you into heaven, shall so come in like **turn** as you have seen him go into heaven.

12 Then returned they **into** Jerusalem from the mountain called Olive, which is from Jerusalem - **Sabbath's holding journey-way**.

13 And when they were come in, they **up-walked** into an upper room, where **down-remain** both Peter, and James, and John, and Andrew, Philip, and Thomas, Bartholomew, and Matthew, James of Alphaeus, and Simon the Zealot, and Judas of James.

14 These all **toward-governed** with **same-feeling** in prayer and **beg-binding**, with the women, and Mary the mother of Jesus, and with his **brothers**.

15 And in those days Peter **up-standing**, in the middle of the disciples, and said, (the **multitude** of-names together were about a hundred and twenty,)

16 Men! Brothers! **It-is-binding** this scripture **to-be-filled**, which the Holy Spirit **before-said through** the mouth of David concerning Judas, which was **way-leader to-them** that **together-take** the Jesus.

17 For he was **down-numbered** with us and was **allotted**[2157] the inheritance of this **attendance**.

18 Now this man **acquired** a **space** with the **pay** of **unrighteousness**; and **prone becoming**, his middle **crack-opened**, and all his **intestine-spleen**[2158] **poured**.

19 And it was known **to**-all the **down-housing** at Jerusalem; **so that** that **space** is called in their **private dialect**, Aceldama, that is to say, the **space** of blood.

20 For it is written in the **scroll** of Psalms, let his **upon-yard** be **lonesome**, and let no man **down-house in her**: and his **bishopric**[2159] let another-**different take**.

21 It-is-binding then of these men which have **together-coming to-us in all uninterrupted-time** that the Lord Jesus **came** and **out-came upon** us,

22 Beginning from the baptism of John **until** that same day that he was **up-taken** from us, one must witness with us of his resurrection.

23 And **they-stood** two, Joseph called Barsabas, who was **upon-called**[2160] Justus, and Matthias.

24 And they prayed, and said, you, Lord, which know the **hearts** of all, show whether of these two you have chosen,

---

[2154] God-friend
[2155] Greek: Priests-peace (hierou-priest, sacred) and salem (peace)
[2156] Traverse carries the idea of going back and forth
[2157] Greek: "lagchano" to chance, to determine by lot
[2158] Also defined as "gut-compassion"
[2159] Greek: "episkope" (upon-peer-about, upon-watch, upon-goal, upon-mark, a sentry, a scout), transliterated as "episcopate," bishopric, the office of a bishop, visitation, to visit, oversee, oversight, upon-skeptic
[2160] Or, to entitle, to invoke

25 That he may **take inheritance** of this **attendance** and apostleship, **out-of** which Judas by **beside-step**, **traveled into** his own **spot**.

26 And they gave forth their **inheritance**; and the **inheritance** fell upon Matthias; and he was **together-down-pebble-vote-counted** with the eleven apostles.

ACTS CHAPTER 2

1 And when the day of Pentecost was **together-filled**, they were all with **same-feeling upon the same**.

2 And suddenly there **became** an **echo** from heaven as a **carried violent breath,** and it filled the **whole** house where they were sitting.

3 And there appeared **to-them through-apportioned** tongues like as of fire, and it sat upon each of them.

4 And they were all filled with the Holy **Spirit**, and began to speak with **another-different** tongues, as the Spirit gave them **from-sound**

5 And there were **down-housing** at Jerusalem Jews, **well-taking** men, out of every nation under heaven.

6 Now when this was **voiced,** the **fullness** came together, and were **together-poured,**[2161] because that every man heard them speak in his own **dialect**.

7 And they were all **ecstasized**, and marveled, saying one to another, **be-perceiving**, are not all these which speak, Galileans?

8 And how hear we every man in our own **dialect**, **in which** we were born?

9 Parthians, and Medes, and Elamites, and the **down-housing** in Mesopotamia, and in Judaea, and Cappadocia, in Pontus, and Asia,

10 Phrygia, and Pamphylia, in Egypt, and in the **sections** of Libya about Cyrene, and **upon-foreigners**[2162] of Rome, Jews and proselytes,

11 Cretes and Arabians, we do hear them speak in our tongues the **great** works of God.

12 And they were all **ecstasy,**[2163] and **have-no-way-out**, saying one to another, what **wills** this?

13 **Others-different** mocking said, these men are full of **sweet-wine**.

14 But Peter, standing up with the eleven, lifted up his voice, and **from-sounded to-them,** you men of Judaea, and all you that **down-house** at Jerusalem, be this known **to-you**, and **hear** to my words:

15 For these are not drunk, as you **under-take,** seeing it is the third hour of the day.

16 But this is that which was spoken by the prophet Joel:

17 And **it-shall-be** in the last days, says God, I will pour out **from** my Spirit upon all flesh: and your sons and your daughters shall prophesy, and your young men shall see visions, and your old men shall dream dreams:

18 And on my **male-slave**s and on my **female-slaves** I will pour out in those days **from** my Spirit; and they shall prophesy:

19 And I will **give** wonders in heaven above, and signs in the earth beneath; blood, and fire, and **mist-breathing** of smoke:

20 The sun shall be turned into darkness, and the moon into blood, before that **great** and **epiphany**[2164] day of the Lord come:

21 And **it-shall-be**, whoever shall **upon-call**[2165] the name of the Lord shall be saved.

22 You men of Israel, hear these words; Jesus of Nazareth, a man **from-showed** God among you by **powers**, wonders, and signs, which God did by him in the middle of you, as you, yourselves, also **perceived**.

23 Him, being delivered by the **defined**[2166] counsel and **before-knowing** of God, you have **taken**, and by **lawless** hands have **towards-fastened** and **up-lifted**:[2167]

24 Whom God has **up-stand**, having loosed the **pang**[2168] of **Death:** because it was not **powerful** that he should be **governed under** it.

25 For David spoke concerning him, I **before-saw** the Lord always before my face, for he is **out-of** my right hand, that I should not be **shaken**:

[2161] Greek compound: sun (together) and cheo (pour), to pour together, to comingle promiscuously, throw into disorder, perplex the mind
[2162] Upon public, to make oneself at home in a foreign country
[2163] Greek compound existemi (out-of-stand) from which we take our English ecstasy (overwhelming feelings)
[2164] Greek: "epiphanes" (conspicuous, notable) is the root word for the Greek word "epiphaneia" (upon-shine) transliterated to our English word "epiphany"
[2165] Or, to entitle, to invoke
[2166] Greek:," horizon"
[2167] Or lit., assassinate
[2168] Or, pang, sudden pain

26 Through this, **was-good-disposed** my **heart** and my tongue **jumped-for-joy**; **yet still,** also my flesh shall rest in **expectation**

27 Because you will not leave my soul in **Hell,** neither **will** you give your **Intrinsic-Right-One** to **perceive** corruption.

28 You have made known to me the ways of life; you shall make me full of **good-disposition** with your **face**.

29 Men, **brothers,** let me **all-speech**[2169] of the patriarch David, that he is both **finished** and buried, and his **remembrance-tomb** is with us **to** this day.

30 Therefore **under-originating** a prophet and **perceiving** that God had sworn with an **oath-fence to-him**, that of the fruit of his loins, **down** the flesh, he would **up-stand** Christ to sit on his throne.

31 He **before-perceiving** spoke **about** the resurrection of Christ, that his soul was not left in **Hell**, neither his flesh did **perceive** corruption.

32 This Jesus has God **up-stand**, whereof we all are witnesses.

33 Therefore being by the right hand of God exalted and having received of the Father the promise of the **Holy Spirit**, he has **out-of-poured** this, which you now see and hear.

34 For David is not **up-walked** into the heavens: but he says himself, the Lord said **to** my Lord, sit, you, out**-of** my right hand,

35 Until I make your **haters** your footstool.

36 Therefore let all the house of Israel know assuredly, that God has made that same Jesus, whom you have crucified, both Lord and Christ.

37 Now when they heard, they were **down-pricked** in their **heart**, and said **to** Peter and to the **remaining** apostles, men **brothers,** what shall we do?

38 Then Peter **showed**[2170] **to** them, **change-thought,** and be baptized every one of you in the name of Jesus Christ for the release[2171] of sins, and you shall receive the gift of the Holy **Spirit**.

39 For the promise is **to-you**, and **to-your** children, and to all that are afar off, as many as the Lord our God shall call.

40 And with many **other-different** words did he **witness** and **beside-called**, saying, save yourselves from this **warped-leg** generation.

41 They that gladly **from-welcome** his word were baptized: and the same day there were added about three thousand souls.

42 And they **towards-governed** in the apostles' **teaching** and **communion**, and in breaking of bread, and in prayers.

43 And fear came upon every soul: and many wonders and signs were done by the apostles.

44 And all that believed were together and had all things common.

45 And sold their **acquisitions** and goods, and parted them to all, as every man had need.

46 Besides, **according-to** day **towards-governing same-feeling** in the **priest-place**, and breaking bread from house to house, did eat their **food with-jumping-joy** and **with-un-stoned** of **heart,**

47 Praising God and having favor with all the people. And the Lord added to the Church daily such as should be saved.

ACTS CHAPTER 3

1 Now Peter and John **up-walked** into the **priest-place** at the hour of prayer, the ninth.

2 And a certain man **limping** from his mother's womb, **under-originated,** was carried, whom they laid daily at the gate of the **priest-place,** which is called Beautiful, to ask **pity-mercy** of them that entered into the **priest-place**;

3 Who **perceived** Peter and John **impending to-go-into** the **priest-place** asked **pity-mercy to take**.

4 And Peter, **look-stretching into him** with John, said, look **into** us.

5 And he gave heed **to-them, towards-seem** to **take** something **beside** them.

6 Then Peter said, silver and gold none **under-originate to-me**; but such as I have, give I you: In the name of Jesus Christ of Nazareth rise up and walk.

[2169] Or free speech
[2170] Greek: "phemi," the root word for fame ("pheme")
[2171] Lit., from-let-go

7 And he **squeeze-captured**[2172] him by the right hand and **raised-him:** and **instantly** his feet and ankle **solidified**.

8 And he, **out-of-leaping**, stood, and walked, and entered with them into the **priest-place**, walking, and leaping, and praising God.

9 And all the people **perceiving** him walking and praising God:

10 And they **perceived** that it was he who sat for **pity-mercy** at the gate Beautiful of the **priest-place**: and they were filled with **stupefaction**[2173] and **ecstasy**[2174] at that which had **together-walked to-him**.

11 And as the **limping** man, which was healed **governed** Peter and John, all the people ran together **to-them** in the porch that is called Solomon's, wondering.

12 And when Peter **perceiving**, he answered **to** the people, you men of Israel, why marvel you at this? Or, why **look-stretching** on us, as though by our own power or **good-reverence** we had made this man to walk?

13 The God of Abraham, and of Isaac, and of Jacob, the God of our fathers, has glorified his **Child**[2175] Jesus; whom you delivered up, and **contradicted** him in the presence of Pilate, when he **judged that-one to-from-loose**.

14 Yet you **contradicted** the **Holy-One** and the **Righteous-One and requested** a murderer to be granted **to-you**.

15 And killed the **Origin-Leader** of life, whom God has raised **out-of** the dead; whereof we are witnesses.

16 And his name through faith in his name has made this man **solid**, whom you see and **perceive: yes**, the faith which is by him has given him this **whole-inheritance**[2176] in the presence of you all.

17 And now, **brothers, I-perceived now** that **downing ignorance** you **practiced**, as also your **first-rank**s[2177].

18 But those things, which God **before-down-messaged** by the mouth of all his prophets, that Christ should **emotion**, he has so **filled**.

19 Change-thought therefore, and be **reverted**, that your sins may be **oiled-out**, when the **seasons** of **up-breathing**[2178] shall come from the presence of the Lord.

20 And he shall send Jesus Christ, which before was preached **to-you**:

21 Whom **it-is-binding** the heaven **in-fact welcomed** until the **uninterrupted-times** of **restoration**[2179] of all things, which God has spoken **through** the mouth of all his holy prophets **from ages.**

22 Because Moses **indeed** said **to** the fathers, a prophet shall the Lord your God **up-stand to-you** of your **brothers**, like **to-me;** him shall you hear in all things whatever he shall say **to-you**.

23 And **it-shall-be**, every soul, which will not hear that prophet, shall be **out-of-ruined out of-the** the people.

24 Yes, and all the prophets from Samuel and those that follow after, as many as have spoken, have likewise **before-messaged** of these days.

25 You are the **sons** of the prophets, and of the covenant which God made with our fathers, saying **towards** Abraham, and in your seed shall all the **fatherhoods** of the earth be blessed.

26 Unto-you foremost God, having **up-stand** his **Child**[2180] Jesus, sent him to bless you, in turning away every one of you from **your wicked-hurtfulness**.

ACTS CHAPTER 4

1 And as they spoke **towards** the people, the priests, and the **general**[2181] of the **priest-place**, and the Sadducees, came upon them,

2 Being **through-pained** that they taught the people, and **down-messaged** through Jesus the resurrection **out-of** the dead.

3 And they **upon-cast** them the hands and **placed-them** in **watching into** the next day: for it was now **evening**.

4 Yet, many of them which heard the **Word** believed; and the number of the men was about five thousand.

[2172] "Piazo," to squeeze, to seize by hand, to press, to arrest, to capture
[2173] Or, dumbfounded
[2174] Greek: "ekstasis," transliterated as "ecstasy," out-of-stand, displacement of the mind, strong feelings (good or bad) that absorbs the mind
[2175] The Greek root for "boy" means: to hit, to strike, to smite
[2176] 1 Thessalonians 5:23, James 1:4
[2177] Or original-rank, beginning-rank
[2178] Or recovery of breath, breathing easily
[2179] Greek definition carries the idea of restoration of health, home, or organization
[2180] The Greek root for "boy" is defined as: to hit
[2181] Greek: "strategois" transliterated as "strategists"

5 And **it became upon tomorrow**, that their **first-ranks**,[2182] and elders, and scribes,

6 And Annas the **first-rank-priest**, and Caiaphas, and John, and Alexander, and as many as were of the **kin** of the **first-rank-priest**, were gathered together at Jerusalem.

7 And when they had set them in the middle, they **ascertain-by-inquiry**, by what power, or by what name, have you done this?

8 Then Peter, filled with the **Holy Spirit**, said **towards** them, you **first-ranks**, of the people, and elders of Israel,

9 If we this day be **up-judged** of the **good-work** to the **without-strength** man, by what means he is **saved**;[2183]

10 Be it known **to-you** all, and to all the people of Israel, that by the name of Jesus Christ of Nazareth, whom you crucified, whom God raised **out-of** the dead, **in-this** this man **beside-stand** here before you **healthy-grown**.

11 This is the stone **that** was **made-out-be-nothing** of you **house-builders**, **is-become** the head of the corner.

12 Neither is there salvation in any other: for there is no **other-different** name, under heaven given **in** men, **in which it-is-binding us to-be-saved**.

13 Now when they saw the **all-speech**[2184] of Peter and John, and **down-took** that they were **un-lettered**[2185] and **private-ones**,[2186] they marveled; and they **upon-know**[2187] of them, that they had been with Jesus.

14 Yet, looking, the man who was **served-therapy** standing with them, **they–had** nothing **to-anti-speak**.[2188]

15 But when they had **ordered** them to go out of the Sanhedrin,[2189] they conferred[2190] **towards one-another**

16 Saying, what shall we **produce** to-**thes**e men? For that indeed a **known sign** has **become** by them **shining to-all** them that **down-house** in Jerusalem; and **not-we-are-powerful to-**deny.

17 But that it spread no further among the people, let us threaten them that they speak **to-no** man in this name.

18 And they called them, and **beside-message** them not to **sound** at all nor teach in the name of Jesus.

19 But Peter and John answered and said **towards** them, **if** it be **righteous** in the sight of God to **hear** you more than God, judge you.

20 Because, not we are-powerful not to-speak the things **that** we have **perceived** and heard.

21 So when they had **towards**-threatened, they **from-loosed them**, finding nothing how they might punish them, because of the people: for all glorified God for that which **became,**

22 For the man was above forty **years** old, on whom **became** this **sign of-the cure.**

23 And being **from-loosed**, they went to their **private-ones**, and **from-message** all that the **first-rank-priests** and elders had said **to** them.

24 And when they heard that, they lifted up their voice to God with **same-feeling**, and said, **Owner**, you are God, which has made heaven, and earth, and the sea, and all that is in them:

25 Who by the mouth of your **child** David has said, why did the **nations snort** and the people **be-of-interest of empty**-things?

26 The kings of the earth **beside-stood,** and the **first-ranks**,[2191] were gathered together against the Lord, and against his Christ.

27 For of a truth against your holy **Child** Jesus, whom you have anointed, both Herod, and Pontius Pilate, with the **nations**, and the people of Israel, were gathered together,

28 For to do whatever your hand and your **plan-counsel before-defined** to **become**.

29 And now, Lord, **upon-perceiving** their threatening: and grant **to-your slave**s, that with all **all-speech**[2192] they may speak your word,

---

[2182] Or, original-rank, beginning-rank
[2183] Or, made-safe
[2184] Or free speech
[2185] Or un-write (could not write), illiterate
[2186] Greek: "idiotes," transliterated as "idiots;" and properly means a private learner as opposed to a public debater, also means who confer with oneself privately; negatively, it also means a person who does not have input from others with regards to learning and/or debates, etc.
[2187] Greek: "epiginosko," upon-knowing (exact-knowing)
[2188] Or, to refute, to deny
[2189] Lit., together-sitting
[2190] Greek: together-cast, to cast together, to combine
[2191] Or, original-rank, beginning-rank
[2192] Or free speech

30 By **out-of-stretching** your hand to **cure**; and that signs and wonders may be done by the name of your holy **Child**[2193] Jesus.

31 And when they had **beg-bind**, the **spot** was shaken where they were assembled together; and they were all filled with the **Holy Spirit**, and they spoke the **Word of God** with **all-speech**.[2194]

32 And the multitude of them that believed were of **first heart** and soul: neither said any **one** of **his goods** was his **private**; but they had all things common.

33 And with **great** power gave the apostles witness of the resurrection of the Lord Jesus: and **great** grace was upon them all.

34 Neither was there any **under-originate-goods in** them **in-binding**: for as many as were **acquirers** of **spaces** or houses sold them, and brought the **value** of the things that were sold,

35 And **placed** at the apostles' feet: and **through-giving** was made **to**-every man **down-as** he had need.

36 And Joses, who by the apostles, was **upon-called**[2195] Barnabas,[2196] (which is, being interpreted, the son of **beside-calling**) a Levite, of the **kin** of Cyprus,

37 **Under-originating-goods to-him,** land, sold and brought the money, and laid at the apostles' feet.

ACTS CHAPTER 5

1 But a certain man named Ananias,[2197] with Sapphira[2198] his wife, sold **acquisition**,

2 And **kept-back-for-themselves**[2199] of the **value**, his wife also **being-conscious,** and brought a certain **section**, and **placed** at the apostles' feet.

3 But Peter said, Ananias, why has Satan filled your **heart** to **falsify** to the **Holy Spirit**, and to **kept-back-for-yourselves from the value** of the **space**?

4 While it remained, was it not yours? And after it was sold, was it not in your **authority it-under-originated**? Why has you placed this **practice** in your **heart**? You have not **falsified to**-men, but **to-God.**

5 And Ananias hearing these words fell, and **out-soul**: and **great** fear came on all of them that heard these things.

6 And the young men **up-stood, together-stall**[2200] and **out-of-carried,** and buried.

7 And it was about three hours **through-stood,** when his wife, not **perceiving** what **became, came-into.**

8 And Peter answered **towards** her, tell me whether you **from-give** the **space** for so much? And she said, yes, for so much.

9 Then Peter said **towards** her, how is it that you have **together-agreed** to **probe-test** the Spirit of the Lord? **Be-perceiving**, the feet of them which have buried your husband at the door and shall **out-of-carry** you.

10 Then she-fell **instantly beside** his feet, and **out-soul** and the young men came in, and found her dead, and **out-of carrying,** buried **towards** her husband.

11 And **great** fear came upon all the Church, and upon as many as heard these things.

12 And **through** the hands of the apostles were many signs and wonders **became in** the people; (and they were all with **same-feeling** in Solomon's porch.

13 Yet of-the remaining-ones no man dared to-be-glued[2201] to-them: but the people magnified them.

14 Yet rather, believers were the more added to the Lord, multitudes both of men and women.)

15 Insomuch that they brought forth the **without-strength** into the streets, and **placed** on **cots**[2202] and **mattresses**, that at the least the shadow of Peter passing by might overshadow some of them.

16 There **together-came** also a **fullness** of the about cities **into** Jerusalem, bringing **without-strength,** and them that were **molested under** unclean spirits: and they were **served-therapy** everyone.

17 Then the **first-rank-priest up-stand**, and all they that were with him, (which is the sect of the Sadducees,) and were filled with **zeal**,

18 And laid their hands on the apostles and **placed** them in the **public** prison.

[2193] Boy as hit, struck, smitten
[2194] Or free speech
[2195] Or, to entitle, to invoke
[2196] Son or Heir of Prophet
[2197] Hebrew origin, Jehovah has favored
[2198] Hebrew origin Sapphire, defined as to score with a mark
[2199] Or, to sequestrate for oneself, to embezzle
[2200] Enwrap
[2201] Or, to stick to, to cling, to keep company with
[2202] Or (re)cline

19 But the angel of the Lord by night opened the prison doors, and brought them forth, and said,

20 Go, stand and speak in the **priest-place** to the people all the **declarations** of this life.

21 And when they heard, they entered into the **priest-place under the dawn** and taught. But the **first-rank-priest** came, and they that were with him, and called the **Sanhedrin** together, and all the **aged-senators** of the children of Israel and sent to the prison to have them brought.

22 But when the **subservient-ones**[2203] came, and found them not in the prison, **they-returned, yet they-from-message**,

23 Saying, the prison **indeed** found we **locked** with all **certainty**,[2204] and the keepers standing **outside** before the doors: but when we had opened, we found no man within.

24 Now when the **first-rank-priest** and the **general** of the **priest-place** and the **first-rank-priests** heard these things, they **through-have-no-way-out** of them **what many-become of-this**.

25 Then came one and **from-message** them, saying, **be-perceiving**, the men whom you put in prison are standing in the **priest-place**, and teaching the people.

26 Then went the **general**[2205] with the **subservient-ones**,[2206] and **led them, not with** violence, for they feared the people, lest they should have been stoned.

27 And when they had brought them, they **stand** before the **Sanhedrin**: and the **first-rank-priest** asked them,

28 Saying, did not we **beside-charge, beside-charged** you that you should not teach in this name? And, **be-perceiving**, you have filled Jerusalem with your **teaching**, and **plan-counseled** to bring this man's blood upon us.

29 Then Peter and the apostles said, **it-is-binding** to **be-believing-first to-**God rather than men.

30 The God of our fathers raised up Jesus, whom you **through-hand** and hanged on a tree.

31 Him has God exalted with his right hand a **First-Rank-Leader** and a Savior, for to give **change-thinking** to Israel, and **release**[2207] of sins.

32 And we are his witnesses of these things; and also, the **Holy Spirit**, whom God has given to-those **believing-first to-him**.

33 When they heard, they were **through-sawed**, and **they-planned-counseled** to **up-lift**[2208] them.

34 Then there **up-stand** one in the **Sanhedrin**, a Pharisee, named Gamaliel, a **Doctor**,[2209] had in **valued** among all the people, and **ordered** to put the apostles forth a **bit**;

35 And said **towards** them, you men of Israel, **towards-hold to-yourselves** what you **are-impending** to **practice upon** these men.

36 For before these days **up-stand** Theudas, boasting himself to be somebody; to whom a number of men, about four hundred, joined themselves: who was **up-lifted**; and all, as many as obeyed him, were **through-loosed**, and **into nothing.**

37 After this man, **up-stand** Judas of Gallee in the days of the **taxing-enrolment,** and **divorced**[2210] people, **sufficient**,[2211] **behind** him: he also **from-ruin**;[2212] and all, as many as obeyed him, were **through-scattered**.

38 And now I say **to-you**, **divorce** from these men, and **release**: for if this **plan-counsel**, or this work be of men, it will **down-loosen.**

39 But if it be of God, **not you-are-powerful to-down-loose** it; lest **also** you be found **God-fighters.**

40 And **to-him** they **were-persuaded**: and when they had **towards-called** the apostles, and **skinning**, they commanded that they should not speak in the name of Jesus, and **from-loosed them.**

41 And they departed from the presence of the **Sanhedrin**, **cheerful** that they were **deserving to-be-unvalued over** his name.

42 And daily in the **priest-place**, and **down** house, they **paused** not to teach and **good-messaging** Jesus Christ.

[2203] Lit., under-oarsman, generally a subordinate
[2204] Greek: "a" (negative particle) and "sphallo" (to "fail"), security, certainty
[2205] Greek: "strategois" transliterated as "strategists"
[2206] Lit., under-oarsman, generally a subordinate
[2207] Lit., from-let-go
[2208] Or lit., assassinate
[2209] Lit., law-teacher, 1 Tim 1:7, Luke 5:17
[2210] Lit., "aphistemi" from-stand, the root word for "apostasies:" feminine of "apostasion" (divorce); a thing that separates.
[2211] Lit., to arrive; or, competent as if coming in season, ample in amount, fit in character
[2212] Greek: "apo" (from) and "alethros" (ruin), to destroy fully

ACTS CHAPTER 6

1 And in those days, when the number of the disciples was multiplied, there arose a murmuring of the **Hellenic towards** the Hebrews, because their widows were **beside-looked**[2213] in the daily **attendance**.

2 Then the twelve called the multitude of the disciples, and said, it is not reason that we should leave the **Word of God** and **attend** tables.

3 Then, **brothers**, you, **bishop,**[2214] **out-of** among you seven men, **witnessed**, full of the Holy Spirit and wisdom, whom we may **down-stand** over this **need**

4 But we will give **towards-govern** to prayer, and **attendance** of the **Word**.

5 And the saying pleased the **entire fullness**: and they chose Stephen, a man full of faith and of the **Holy Spirit**, and Philip, and Prochorus, and Nicanor, and Timon, and Parmenas, and Nicolas a proselyte of Antioch:

6 Whom they set before the apostles: and when they had prayed, they laid hands on them.

7 And the **Word of God grew**; and the number of the disciples multiplied in Jerusalem **tremendously**; and a **many multitudes** of the priests **under-hear**[2215] **to-the** faith.

8 And Stephen, full of faith and power, did **great** wonders and **signs in** the people.

9 Then there **up-stand** certain **out-of** the synagogue, which is called of the Libertines,[2216] and Cyrenians, and Alexandrians, and of them of Cilicia and of Asia, **together-seeking** with Stephen.

10 And they were not able to **anti-stand** the wisdom and the **Spirit** by which he spoke.

11 Then they **under-threw**[2217] men, which said, we have heard him speak blasphemous **declarations into** Moses, and God.

12 And they **together-stirred** the people, and the elders, and the scribes, and came upon, and **together-snatched** him, and brought to the **Sanhedrin**,

13 And set up witnesses, **falsifiers,** which said, this man **paused** not to speak blasphemous **declarations** against this holy **spot**, and the law:

14 For we have heard him say, that this Jesus of Nazareth shall **down-loose** this place and shall change the **ethics** which Moses **beside-give** us.

15 And all that sat in the **Sanhedrin look-stretching into him, perceived** his face as it had been the face of an angel.

ACTS CHAPTER 7

1 Then said the **first-rank-priest**, are these things so?

2 And he **showed,**[2218] men, **brothers**, and fathers, hear; the God of glory appeared **to-our** father Abraham, when he was in Mesopotamia, before he **down-housed** in Charran,

3 And said **to-him, take** you out of your country, and from your **together-kin**, and come into the land which I shall show you.

4 Then came he out of the land of the Chaldeans, and **down-housed** in Charran: and from there, when his father was dead,[2219] he **change-house** him into this land, **into which** you now **down-house**.

5 And he gave him no inheritance in it, no, not a **judgment-step;**[2220] yet he promised that he would give it **to-him** for **occupancy,**[2221] and to his seed after him, when he had no child.

6 And God spoke **in-this-way**, that his seed should **foreign-house**[2222] in a **another-same-place** land; and that they would bring them into **slavery**, and evil four hundred **years**.

7 And the nation to whom they shall be in bondage will I judge, said God: and after that shall they come forth, and **be-hired-service to-**me in this **spot**.

8 And he gave him the covenant of circumcision: and so **birthed** Isaac and circumcised him the eighth day; and Isaac Jacob; and Jacob the twelve patriarchs.

[2213] Or overlook, disregard
[2214] Greek compound: upon-peer about, upon-skeptic, upon-scout, upon watch, upon-watch, upon-sentry
[2215] Or obey
[2216] "Libertines" is transliteration of "Libertinos" (a Roman freedman)
[2217] Greek: under-cast, to throw in stealthily, introduce by collision
[2218] Greek: "phemi," the root word for fame ("pheme")
[2219] Abraham father was spiritually dead when he left his father: Terah (Abraham's father was 70 when he had "Abrham" (Genesis 11:26),

Abraham left Haran (Charran) when he was 75 (Genesis 12:4); 70+75=145; so, Abraham father (Terah) was 145 when Abraham left and Terah lived to be 205 (Genesis 11:32); however Acts 7:4 said that Abraham father was dead when Abraham left, since Tarah was still alive physically, Terah must have been spiritually dead.
[2220] Greek: "Bema," a step, foot-breadth, rostrum, tribunal
[2221] Lit., down-hold
[2222] Greek: Beside-house, having a house beside (near), a by-dweller (alien resident)

9 And the patriarchs, **being-zealous betrayed**[2223] Joseph into Egypt: but God was with him,

10 And **He-out-lifted** him out of all his **tribulation** and gave him **grace** and wisdom in the sight of Pharaoh king of Egypt; and **he-down-stand** him **leader** over Egypt and his **whole** house.

11 Now there came a **famine on whole** the land of Egypt and Chanaan, and **great tribulation**: and our fathers found no sustenance.

12 But when Jacob heard that there was **grain** in Egypt, he sent out our fathers **foremost.**

13 And **in** the second Joseph was **up-known**[2224] to his **brothers**; and Joseph's **kin became shine** to Pharaoh.

14 Then sent Joseph, and called his father Jacob to, and all his **together-kin, seventy-five** souls.

15 So Jacob went down into Egypt, and **finished,** he, and our fathers,

16 And were **translated** into Sychem and laid in the **remembrance-tomb** that Abraham bought for a **value** of money of the sons of Emmor of Sychem.

17 But when the **uninterrupted-time** of the promise **near-squeezed,** which God had sworn to Abraham, the people grew and **increased-filled** in Egypt,

18 Until another-**different** king **up-stand,** which **perceived** not Joseph.

19 The same **down-wisdom** our **kin,** and **evil** our fathers, so that they cast out their young children, **into the not life-generating**[2225]

20 In which **season** Moses was born, and was **Urban**[2226] **to-the-God** and nourished up in his father's house three months:

21 And when he was **out-placed,**[2227] Pharaoh's daughter **up-lift** him, and nourished him **to-herself into** son.

22 And Moses was **boy-trained** in all the wisdom of the Egyptians and was **powerful** in words and in **works.**

23 And when he was full forty **years** old, **it-up-walked upon** his **heart** to **bishop**[2228] his **brothers** the children of Israel.

24 And **perceiving** someone's **unrighteousness**, he defended, and avenged[2229] him that was **down-labor-starving,** and **knocked** the Egyptian:

25 Yet, he **do-by-law** his **brothers** would have **synthesized**[2230] how that God by his hand would **save** them: but they **synthesized** not.

26 And the next day he showed himself **to-them** as they **fought,** and **he-together-pushed them into peace,** saying, **men,** you are **brothers**; why do you **unrighteous one-another?**

27 But he that did his neighbor **un-righteously** thrust him away, saying, who **down-stand** you a **first-rank,**[2231] and a **justice** over us?

28 Will you **up-lift**[2232] me, as you **up-lifted** the Egyptian yesterday?

29 Then fled Moses at this saying and **became foreign-house**[2233] in the land of Madian,[2234] where he **birthed** two sons.

30 And when forty **years** were **filled,** there appeared **to-him** in the **lonesome of-the mountain** Sinai an angel of the Lord in a flame of fire, in a **thorn-bush.**

31 When Moses **perceived,** he **marveled**[2235] at the sight: **yet** as he **toward-come** to **down-mind,** the voice of the Lord came **towards him,**

32 I the God of your fathers, the God of Abraham, and the God of Isaac, and the God of Jacob. Then Moses trembled and **dared** not **to-down-mind.**

33 Then said the Lord **to-him, loose** your **sandals** from your feet: for the **spot** where you stand is holy ground.

34 Perceiving, I have **perceived** the **evil** of my people which is in Egypt, and I have heard their groaning, and am come down to **out-lift** them. And now, come, I will send you into Egypt.

[2223] From-give, to give over to
[2224] Or, to know again
[2225] Or, life-parenting, life-birthing
[2226] Greek: "asteios," nominative, derived from a word for "city" (astu); urbane; implication (handsome); see Hebrews 11:23 where Moses is called a "city child" or an urban child, developed, genteel, polished, comely
[2227] Or, exposed
[2228] Greek compound: upon-peer about, upon-skeptic, upon-scout, upon watch, upon-watch, upon-sentry

[2229] Or out-justice
[2230] Or, send-together [sun-hiemi (the root for synthesize)] to combine information into a comprehensive and logical whole
[2231] Or, original-rank, beginning-rank
[2232] Or lit., assassinate
[2233] Greek: Beside-house, having a house beside (near), a by-dweller (alien resident)
[2234] Hebrew means: contention, quarrel, brawling,
[2235] Or, to look at closely

35 This Moses whom they **contradicted**, saying, who made you a **first-rank**,[2236] and a **justice**? The same did God send a **first-rank**, and a **looser** by the hand of the angel which appeared **to-him** in the **thorn**-bush.

36 He **out-of-led** them, after that he **produced** wonders and signs in the land of Egypt, and in the Red Sea,[2237] and in the **lonesome** forty **years**.

37 This is that Moses, who said **to-the** children of Israel, a prophet shall the Lord your God **up-stand to-you out**-of your **brothers**, like **to-me**; him shall you hear.

38 This is he, **becoming** in the Church in the **lonesome** with the angel which spoke **to-him** in the **mountain Sinai,** and our fathers: who **welcomed** the **living** oracles to give **to-us**:

39 To whom our fathers would not obey, but thrust from them, and in their **hearts** turned back again into Egypt,

40 Saying **to** Aaron, make us gods to go before us: **because** this Moses, which **out-of-led** us of the land of Egypt, we **perceived** not what is become of him.

41 And they made a calf in those days, and **up-lead** sacrifice **to-the** idol, and **they-were-good-disposed** in the works of their own hands.

42 Then God turned, and gave them up **to-be-hired-service to**-the host of heaven; as it is written in the **scroll** of the prophets: house of Israel, have you offered to me **butchery** and sacrifices forty **years** in the **lonesome**?

43 You **up-took** the tabernacle of Moloch, and the star of your god Remphan, **types**[2238] which you made to worship them: and I will **change-house** you **upon-that** Babylon.

44 Our fathers had the tabernacle of witness in the **lonesome**, as he had **through-arranged**, speaking **to** Moses, that he should make it **down** the **type**[2239] that he had seen.

45 Which also our fathers **into-led through-welcoming** with Jesus[2240] into the **occupancy**[2241] of the **nations**, whom God **out-of-thrust** before the face of our fathers, **until** the days of David;

46 Who found **grace** before God and **asked** to find a tabernacle for the God of Jacob.

47 But Solomon **house-built** him n house.

48 But not, the Highest **down-house** in temples made with hands; as says the prophet,

49 Heaven is my throne, and earth my footstool **of the feet**: what house will you **house-built** me? says the Lord: or what is the **spot** of my **down-pause**?

50 Has not my hand made all these things?

51 You **stiff-necked** and uncircumcised **heart** and ears, you do always **anti-fall** the Holy **Spirit**: as your fathers, so you.

52 Which of the prophets have not your fathers **chased**? And they have slain them which **before-down-message** of the coming of the **Righteous-One**; of whom you have been now the betrayers and murderers:

53 Who have **taken** the law by the **under-arrangements** of angels and have not **watched-it**.

54 When they heard these things, they were **through-sawn** to the **heart**, and they **grated the teeth on him**.

55 But he, **under-originating** full of the Holy **Spirit**, **look-stretching** into heaven, and **perceived** the glory of God, and Jesus **having-stood out-of** the right hand of God,

56 And said, **be-perceiving**, I see the heavens opened, and the Son of man **having-stood out-of** the right hand of God.

57 Then they **screamed** with a **great** voice, and **together-held** their ears, and **violently-impulsive** upon him with **same-feeling**,

58 And **out-cast outside** of the city and **stoned-cast-him**: and the witnesses **from-placed** their clothes at a young man's feet, whose name was Saul.

59 And they **stoned-cast** Stephen **upon-calling**,[2242] and saying, Lord Jesus, **welcome** my spirit.

60 Yet, placing the knees, **he-screamed** with a **great** voice, Lord, **stand** not this sin **to-them**. And when he had said this, he slept.

[2236] Or, original-rank, beginning-rank
[2237] Hebrew word for defined as "Red" also means "Termination," hence "Termination Sea"
[2238] Or, a die (as struck), thump-impression
[2239] A die as struck, thump-impression
[2240] Or Joshua
[2241] Or down-hold
[2242] Or, to entitle, to invoke

ACTS CHAPTER 8

1 And Saul was **together-good-seeming to** his **up-lift**.[2243] And **in that day,** there **became** a **great chase on** the Church which was at Jerusalem; and they were all **through-scattered**[2244] throughout the **spaces** of Judaea and Samaria, except the apostles.

2 And **well-takers** men **together-provided-for** Stephen and made **great** lamentation over him.

3 As for Saul, he **soiled-maltreated** the Church, entering into every house, and **hauling both** men and women, **betrayed-them into** prison.

4 Therefore they that were **through-scattered** went everywhere **evangelizing** the **Word.**

5 Then Philip went down **into** the city of Samaria, and preached Christ **to-them.**

6 And the people with **same-feeling towards-hold** to those things which Philip spoke, hearing and seeing the **signs** which he did.

7 For unclean spirits, crying with **great** voice, came out of-many **of-the ones-holding**: and many **paralyzed,** and that were **limping,** were **served-therapy.**

8 And there was **great cheer** in that city.

9 But there was a certain man, **named** Simon, which **before-under-begin** in the same city **used-magic,** and **ecstasized** the **nation** of Samaria, **saying** himself is **someone great:**

10 To whom they all **towards-hold,** from the least to the **great,** saying, this man is the **great** power of God.[2245]

11 And **to-him** they had **towards-hold,** because that of **sufficient**[2246] **uninterrupted-time** he had **ecstasized**[2247] them **to-the magic.**

12 But when they believed Philip **evangelizing** the things concerning the kingdom of God, and the name of Jesus Christ, they were baptized, both men and women.

13 Then Simon himself believed also: and when he was baptized, he **towards-govern to-the** Philip, looking besides the **powers** and signs **becoming, he-is-in-ecstasy.**

14 Now when the apostles which were at Jerusalem heard that Samaria had **welcomed** the **Word of God,** they sent **to-them** Peter and John:

15 Who, when they were come down, prayed **concerning** them, that they might **take** the **Holy Spirit**:

16 (For as yet he was **not upon-fallen of-them: yet** only they were baptized, **under-originated into** the name of the Lord Jesus.)

17 Then **they-upon-placed the** hands on them, and they **took** the Holy **Spirit.**

18 And when Simon saw that through **upon-placing** of the apostles' hands the Holy Spirit was given, he offered them **wealth,**

19 Saying, give me also this **authority**, that on **whomever I place** hands, he may **take** the Holy **Spirit.**

20 But Peter said **towards him,** your money **from-ruin** with you, because you have **do-by-law** that the gift of God may be **acquired** with money.

21 You have neither part nor **inheritance** in this **to-saying**: for your **heart** is not **soon**[2248] in the sight of God.

22 Change-thought therefore **from** this your evil, and **beg-bind** God, if perhaps the **upon-mind** of your **heart** may be **released**[2249] **to-you.**

23 Because **I-am-staring-at** you being in the gall[2250] of bitterness,[2251] and the **together-bond** of **unrighteousness.**

24 Then answered Simon, and said, **beg-bind** you to the Lord **over** me, that none of these things which you have spoken come upon me.

25 And they, when they had **through-witnessed** and preached the **Word of the Lord,** returned to Jerusalem, and **evangelized** in many villages of the Samaritans.

[2243] Or lit., assassination
[2244] Or, diaspora, dispersed
[2245] Or, this-man is the power of-the God, the **great**
[2246] Lit., to arrive; or, competent as if coming in season, ample in amount, fit in character
[2247] Greek compound existemi (out-of-stand) from which we take our English ecstasy (overwhelming feelings (good or bad that absorbs the mind)
[2248] Or, straight, good-path, level
[2249] Lit., from-let-go
[2250] Or bile
[2251] Lit., acridity (strong, irritating, unpleasant, pungent (sharp), taste or smell), poison

26 And the angel of the Lord spoke **to** Philip, saying, **up-stand**, and go **down midday on** the way that goes down from Jerusalem **to** Gaza, which is **lonesome**

27 And he **up-stand** and went: and, **be-perceiving**, a man of Ethiopia, a eunuch, **a dynasty**[2252] **of-**Candace queen of the Ethiopians, who had the charge of all her **treasure**, and had come to Jerusalem for to worship,

28 Was returning and sitting in his chariot read **Isaiah** the prophet.

29 Then the Spirit said **to** Philip, **towards-come**, and **glue**[2253] yourself to this chariot.

30 And Philip **towards-running**, and heard him read the prophet **Isaiah**, and said, **know** what you read?

31 And he said, how **am-I-powerful**, except some man should **road-lead** me? And he **beside-called** Philip that he would **up-walk** and **down-**sit with him.

32 The **about-hold** of the Scripture which he read was this, He was led as a sheep to the **butchery**; and like a lamb **un-sounding** before his **shearer**, so opened he not his mouth:

33 In his humiliation his **judging** was **lifted**: and who shall **through-lead** his generation? For his life is **lifted** from the earth.

34 And the eunuch answered Philip, and said, I **beg-bind** you, of whom speaks the prophet this? **About** himself, or of some **other-different** man?

35 Then Philip opened his mouth, and began at the same Scripture, and **evangelized to-him** Jesus.

36 And as they went on **the** way, they came **to** a certain water: and the eunuch **showed**,[2254] see, water; what does **prevent** me to be baptized?

37 And Philip said, if you believe **out-of** whole **of-your heart**, you may. And he answered and said, **I-am-believing** that Jesus Christ is the Son of God.

38 And he **ordered** the chariot to stand: and they went down both into the water, both Philip and the eunuch; and he baptized him.

39 And when they **up-walked** out of the water, the Spirit of the Lord **snatches** Philip, that the eunuch **perceived** him no more: and he went on his way **cheerful**

40 But Philip was found at Azotus: and passing through he **evangelized** in all the cities, **until** he came to Caesarea.

ACTS CHAPTER 9

1 And Saul, yet **in-breathing** threats and **murder** against the disciples of the Lord, went **to** the **first-rank-priest**,

2 And desired of him letters to Damascus to the synagogues, that if he found any of this way, whether they were men or women, he might **lead** them bound **to** Jerusalem.

3 And as he journeyed, he **became near-squeeze** Damascus: and suddenly there **about-star-fall-light** him a light from heaven:

4 And he fell to the earth, and heard a voice saying **to-him**, Saul, Saul, why **are-you-chasing** me?

5 And he said, who are you, Lord? And the Lord said, I am Jesus whom you **chase**: hard for you to kick against the **piercers.**[2255]

6 And he trembling and **stupefied**[2256] said, Lord, what **will** you have me to **produce**? And the Lord **to-him**, **up-stand**, and go into the city, and it shall be told you what **is-binding** you **to-produce.**

7 And the men which journeyed with him stood speechless,[2257] hearing a voice, but seeing no man.

8 And Saul arose from the earth; and when his eyes were opened, he saw no man: but they led him by the hand and brought into Damascus.

9 And he was three days without sight, and neither did eat nor drink.

10 And there was a certain disciple at Damascus, named Ananias;[2258] and **to-him** said the Lord in a vision, Ananias. And he said, **be-perceiving**, I[2259] Lord.

11 And the Lord **toward him**, **up-stand**, and go into the street, which is called **Immediate**,[2260] and enquire in the house of Judas **to-name** Saul, of Tarsus: for, **be-perceiving**, he prays,

---

[2252] Or power-one
[2253] Or, to stick to, to cling, to keep company with
[2254] Greek: "phemi," the root word for fame ("pheme")
[2255] Greek: "kentron," transliterated as "center;" piercer, point, prick, sting
[2256] Stupefy is defined as: un able to think or feel properly
[2257] Greek: in-nod, communicate by gesture
[2258] Jehovah has favored
[2259] Lit., "Ego"
[2260] Greek: "euthus," well-placed, level straight

12 And **he-perceived** in a vision a man named Ananias coming in, and **placing** hand on him, that he might **up-look**.

13 Then Ananias answered, Lord, I have heard by many of this man, how much evil he has done **to-your saints** at Jerusalem:

14 And here he has authority from the **first-rank-priests** to bind all that **upon-call**[2261] your name.

15 But the Lord said **to-him, you-be-going** for he is a chosen vessel **to-me,** to bear my name before the **nations**, and kings, and the children of Israel:

16 For I will show **to-him** how **much** things **is-binding** him **to-emotion** over my name.

17 And Ananias went and entered into the house; and **placing** his hands on him said, brother Saul, the Lord Jesus, the **gazed-one to-you** in the way as you came, has sent me, that you-**should-up-look**, and be filled with the **Holy Spirit**.

18 And **soon** there fell from his eyes as it had been scales: and he-**up-looked instantly**, and **up-stand**, and was baptized.

19 And when he had **taken food**, he **became in-strengthened**. Then was Saul certain days with the disciples which were at Damascus.

20 And **soon** he preached Christ in the synagogues, that he is the Son of God.

21 But all that heard were **ecstasized**,[2262] and said, is not this he that **sack-ravaged** them which **upon-call**[2263] this name in Jerusalem, and came here **into this**, that he might **lead** them bound **to the first-rank-priests**?

22 Yet, Saul **was-more in-powered**, and **together-poured**,[2264] the Jews which **down-housed** at Damascus, **together-embark**[2265] that this is very Christ.

23 And after that many days were **sufficient**,[2266] the Jews **together-planned-counsel** to **up-lift**[2267] him:

24 But their **beside-watch** was known of Saul. And they watched the gates day and night to **up-lift** him.

25 Then the disciples **taking** him by night and let down by the wall in a basket.

26 And when Saul was come to Jerusalem, he-**tried** to **glue**[2268] himself to the disciples: but they were all afraid of him and believed not that he was a disciple.

27 But Barnabas **upon-took** him, and **lead** to the apostles, and **through-lead to-them** how he had **perceived** the Lord in the way, and that he had spoken **to-him**, and how he had preached **all-speech** at Damascus in the name of Jesus.

28 And he was with them **into-traversing** and **out-of-traversing** at Jerusalem.

29 And he **all-out-spoke** in the name of the Lord Jesus and disputed against the **Hellenic**: but they went about to **up-lift** him.

30 When the **brothers** knew, they brought him down to Caesarea, and sent him forth to Tarsus.

31 Then had the Churches rest throughout all Judaea, Galilee, and Samaria and were **house-built**; and walking in the fear of the Lord, and in the **beside-call** of the **Holy Spirit**, were multiplied.

32 And **it became**, as Peter passed throughout all, he came down also to the saints which **down-house** at Lydda.

33 And there he found a certain man named Aeneas, which **down-laid on** his **mattress** eight **years**, and was sick of the **paralytic**.

34 And Peter said **to-him**, Aeneas, Jesus Christ makes you whole: **up-stand**, and make your bed. And he **up-stand** soon.

35 And all that **down-housed** at Lydda and Saron **perceived** him and turned to the Lord.

36 Now there was at Joppa a certain disciple named Tabitha, which by interpretation is called Dorcas: this woman was full of good works and **pity-mercy** which she did.

37 And **it became** in those days, that she was sick, and died: whom when they had washed, they **placed-her** in an upper chamber.

[2261] Or, to entitle, to invoke
[2262] Greek compound existemi (out-of-stand) from which we take our English ecstasy (overwhelming feelings)
[2263] Or, to entitle, to invoke
[2264] Greek compound: sun (together) and cheo (pour), to pour together, to comingle promiscuously, throw into disorder, perplex the mind
[2265] Greek: sun (together) and bibazo (to force), drive-together, unite, together-board a ship
[2266] Lit., to arrive; or, competent as if coming in season, ample in amount, fit in character
[2267] Or lit., assassinate
[2268] Or, to stick to, to cling, to keep company with

38 Yet, Lydda was **near-squeeze** to Joppa, and the disciples had heard that Peter was there, they sent **to-him** two men, **beside-called** that he would not **hesitate** to come to them.

39 Then Peter **up-stand** and went with them. When he was come, they **up-led** him into the upper chamber: and all the widows **beside-stood** by him weeping and showing the coats and garments which Dorcas[2269] made, while she was with them.

40 But Peter **out-cats-them** all **outside** and **placed the knees, a**nd prayed; and turning to the body said, Tabitha,[2270] **be-up-standing**! And she opened her eyes: and when she **perceived** Peter, she sat up.

41 And he gave her hand, and **up-stand her**, and when he had called the saints and widows, **beside-stands** her alive.

42 And it was known throughout all Joppa;[2271] and many believed in the Lord.

43 And **it became**, that he tarried **sufficient**[2272] days in Joppa with one Simon a tanner.

ACTS CHAPTER 10

1 There was a certain man in Caesarea called Cornelius, a centurion of the **mass-of-men**.[2273] called the Italian

2 Good-reverence, and one that feared God with all his house, which gave much **pity-mercy** to the people, and prayed to God **through-all**.

3 He **perceived** in a vision **shining** about the ninth hour of the day an angel of God coming in **towards** him, and saying **to-him**, Cornelius.

4 And when he **look-stretching to-him**, he was **in-fear**, and said, what is it, Lord? And he said **to-him**, your prayers, and your **pity-mercy up-walked into** a memorial[2274] before God.

5 And now **dispatched** men to Joppa, and call for Simon, **who is-upon-called**[2275] Peter:

6 He **foreign-lodged** with one Simon a tanner, whose house is by the **seaside**: he shall tell you what **is-binding** you to do.

7 And when the angel which spoke **to** Cornelius was departed, he voiced two of his **domestics**, and a **good-reverence** soldier of them that **towards-govern to-him**.

8 And when he had **exegesis**[2276] all things **to them**, he sent them to Joppa.

9 On the **tomorrow**, as they went on their **road-travel**, and **near-squeeze to** the city, Peter **up-walked** upon the housetop to pray about the sixth hour:

10 And he became very hungry, and **willed** have eaten: but while they made ready, he fell into **ecstasy**,[2277]

11 And saw heaven opened, and a certain vessel descending **to-him**, as it had been a **great** sheet knit at the four **originals**, and let down to the earth;

12 In which under-originate all manner of **four-footed** of the earth, and **wild-beasts,** and **reptiles**, and **birds** of-the **heaven**.

13 And there came a voice **to-him**, **up-stand**, Peter; **sacrifice**, and eat.

14 But Peter said, not so, Lord; for I have never eaten anything that is common or unclean.

15 And the voice spoke **towards him** again the second, what God has **cleaned**, call not you common.

16 This was done **thrice**: and the vessel was **up-gotten** again into heaven.

17 Now while Peter **through-have-no-way-out** in himself what this vision which he had **perceived may-be**, **be-perceiving**, the men who were sent from Cornelius had **through-ask** for Simon's house, and stood before the gate,

18 And called, and **ascertain-by-inquiry** whether Simon, **the upon-called**[2278] Peter, were **foreign-lodged** there.

19 While Peter **in-sacrifice-anger** on the vision, the Spirit said **to-him**, **be-perceiving**, three men seek you.

20 But, **up-stand** and **take** you down, and go with them, **through-judge** nothing: for I have sent them

---

[2269] Gazelle
[2270] Also means Gazelle
[2271] Beautiful
[2272] Lit., to arrive; or, competent as if coming in season, ample in amount, fit in character
[2273] Greek: "speira, transliterated "spire" meaning to coil, figuratively a mass of roman military cohort, or a squad of Levitical janitors

[2274] Or reminder
[2275] Or, to entitle, to invoke
[2276] Exegesis is transliterated from "exegeomai," to lead-out-of, to unfold
[2277] Greek: "ekstasis," transliterated as "ecstasy," out-of-stand, displacement of the mind, strong feelings (good or bad) that absorbs the mind
[2278] Or, to entitle, to invoke

21 Then Peter went down to the men which were sent **to-him** from Cornelius; and said, **be-perceiving**, I am he whom you seek: what the cause which **you-are-beside-being**?

22 And they said, Cornelius the centurion, a **righteous** man, and one that fear God, and **being-witnesses besides under** the **whole** nation of the Jews, was **apprised**[2279] from God by a holy angel to **change-dispatch** you into his house, and to hear **declarations** of you.

23 Then he called them in, and **foreign-lodged**. And **upon-tomorrow** Peter went away with them, and certain **brothers** from Joppa accompanied him.

24 And the **tomorrow** after they entered into Caesarea. And Cornelius **toward-seeming** them and had **together-called** his **together-kin** and **constrained** friends.

25 And as Peter was coming in, Cornelius **together-meet** him, and fell down **upon** his feet, and worshipped.

26 But Peter **raised him**, saying, stand up; I myself also am a man.

27 And as he **with-talked**[2280] him, he went in, and found many that were come together.

28 And he **showed**[2281] **to-them**, you **acquainted**[2282] how that it is an **un-placed** thing for a man that is a Jew to **keep-company**[2283] or come **towards other-tribe**; but God has showed me that I should not call any man common or unclean.

29 Therefore, I came **without-instead-saying**, as soon as I was sent for, I **ascertain-by-inquiry** therefore for what **saying** you have sent for me?

30 And Cornelius **showed,**[2284] four days ago I was fasting until this hour; and at the ninth hour I prayed in my house, and, **be-perceiving**, a man stood before me in **lamp**[2285] clothing,

31 And **showed,** Cornelius, your prayer is heard, and your **pity-mercy** are in remembrance in the sight of God.

32 Dispatched therefore **into** Joppa, and call **here** Simon, who **upon-called**[2286] Peter; he is **foreign-lodged** in the house of Simon a tanner by the seaside: who, when he **beside-becoming**, shall speak **to-you**.

33 Out-of-auto, therefore I **dispatched to-you**; and you **have ideally produced** that you are come. Now therefore are we all here present before God, to hear all things that are **toward-arrange to-you under the** God.

34 Then Peter opened **the** mouth, and said, of a truth I **down-take** that God is no **respecter-of-persons:**[2287]

35 But in every nation he that fear him, and **works righteous-togetherness**, is **received to-him.**

36 The **Word** which **he**-sent **to** the **sons** of Israel, preaching peace **through** Jesus Christ: (he is Lord of all:)

37 You **have-perceived,** which was **declared** throughout all Judaea, and began from Galilee, after the baptism which John preached;

38 How God anointed Jesus of Nazareth with the Holy Spirit and with power: who **through-came good-worker,**[2288] and **curing** all that were **down-dynasty**[2289] of the Devil; for God was with him.

39 And we are witnesses of all things which he did both in the land of the Jews, and in Jerusalem; whom they **up-lifted**[2290] and hanged on a **tree**:

40 Him God raised up the third day, and **gives in-shine to-become**;

41 Not to all the people, but **to-witnesses beforehand-stretch under the** God, to us, who did eat and drink with him after he **up-stand out-of** the dead.

42 And he **beside-message** us to preach **to-the** people, and to **through-witness** that it is he which was **defined**[2291] of God the Judge of **living** and dead.

43 To him give all the prophets witness, that through his name whoever believes in him shall **take release**[2292] of sins.

[2279] Greek: "chrematizo," to furnish what is needed, divine response; secular meaning of constituting a business, employ, to bears as a title, to apprise (to give notice, state of affair, inform)
[2280] Greek compound: sun (together) and homileo (same)
[2281] Greek: "phemi," the root word for fame ("pheme")
[2282] Greek: upon-stand, to put the mind upon, to be acquainted with, comprehend, be present
[2283] "Kollao" is from the Greek root is "kola"" transliterated as "glue," to stick to, to cling, to keep company with, to be joined
[2284] Greek: "phemi," the root word for fame ("pheme")
[2285] Or, radiant
[2286] Or, to entitle, to invoke
[2287] Greek compound: towards-get (receive)-face
[2288] Or to be philanthropic
[2289] Or down-power-one
[2290] Or lit., assassinate
[2291] Greek:" horizon"
[2292] Lit., from-let-go

44 While Peter yet spoke these **declarations**, the Holy Spirit fell on all **those hearing** the **Word**.

45 And they of the circumcision which believed were **ecstasized**,[2293] as many as came with Peter, because that on the **nations** also was **out-of-poured** the gift of the Holy **Spirit**.

46 For they heard them speak with tongues and magnify God. Then answered Peter,

47 Is-powerful any man **to-prevent** water, that these should not be baptized, which have received the Holy Spirit as well as we?

48 And he **towards-arrange** them to be baptized in the name of the Lord. Then prayed they him to **upon-remain** certain days.

ACTS CHAPTER 11

1 And the apostles and **brothers** that were in Judaea heard that the **nations** had also **welcomed** the **Word of God**.

2 And when Peter **up-walked into** Jerusalem, they that were of the circumcision **through-judged towards** him,

3 Saying, you went in **towards** men uncircumcised, and **ate** with them.

4 But Peter rehearsed from the beginning, and expounded by **down-order to-them**, saying,

5 I was in the city of Joppa praying: and in **ecstasy**[2294] I **perceived** a vision, a certain vessel descended, as it had been a **great** sheet, let down from heaven by four **originals**; and it came even to me:

6 Upon the which when I had **look-stretching**, I **down-minded**, and **perceived four-footed** of the earth, and **wild-beasts**, and **reptiles**, and **birds of-the heaven**.

7 And I heard a voice saying **to me**, **up-stand**, Peter; **sacrifice** and eat.

8 But I said, not so, Lord: for nothing common or unclean has **ever** entered into my mouth.

9 But the voice answered me again from heaven, what God has **cleaned**, call not you common.

10 And this was done **thrice**: and all were drawn up again into heaven.

11 And, **be-perceiving**, **out-of-auto** there were three men already come **upon** the house where I was, sent from Caesarea **towards** me.

12 And the Spirit **told** me go with them, nothing **through-judging**. Yet, these six **brothers** accompanied me, and we entered into the man's house:

13 And he **from-message to-us** how he had **perceived** an angel in his house, which stood and said **to-him**, send men to Joppa, and call for Simon, the **upon-called**[2295] Peter;

14 Who shall tell you **declarations**, whereby you and all your house shall be saved.

15 And as I began to speak, the Holy Spirit **upon-fell** upon them, as on us at the **origin**.

16 Then I remembered the **declaration** of the Lord, how that he said, John indeed baptized with water; but you shall be baptized **in** the Holy **Spirit**.

17 If then as God gave them the **equal** gift as **to-us**, who believed on the Lord Jesus Christ; **who** was I, that **I–was powerful to-prevent** God?

18 When they heard these things, they **kept-their-seat**, and glorified God, saying, then **God has** also to the **nations** granted **change-thinking to** life.

19 How they which were **through-scattered**[2296] upon the **tribulation** that **became on** Stephen travelled as far as Phenice, and Cyprus, and Antioch, preaching the **Word** to none but **to-Jews** only.

20 And some of them were men of Cyprus and Cyrene, which, when they were come to Antioch, spoke **towards** the **Hellenic, evangelizing** the Lord Jesus.

21 And the hand of the Lord was with them: and **many** number believed and turned **upon** the Lord.

22 Then **hearing** of these things came **to** the ears of the Church which was in Jerusalem: and they **out-of-sent** Barnabas, that he should go as far as Antioch.

23 Who, when he came, and had **perceived** the grace of God, was glad, and **beside-called** them all, that with **purpose**[2297] of heart **to-be-toward-remain** in **to-the** Lord.

[2293] Greek compound existemi (out-of-stand) from which we take our English ecstasy (overwhelming feelings)
[2294] Greek: "ekstasis," transliterated as "ecstasy," out-of-stand, displacement of the mind, strong feelings (good or bad) that absorbs the mind
[2295] Or, to entitle, to invoke
[2296] Or, diaspora, dispersed
[2297] Lit., before-place, to place before, or to place in advance

24 For he was a good man, and full of the Holy Spirit and of faith: and **sufficient**[2298] crowd were added **to** the Lord.

25 Then departed Barnabas to Tarsus, for to seek Saul:

26 And when he had found him, **he-led** him **to** Antioch. And **it became**, that a whole **year** they assembled themselves with the Church and taught **sufficient multitude** And the disciples were **apprised**[2299] **both**[2300] Christians **foremost** in Antioch.

27 And in these days came prophets from Jerusalem **into** Antioch.

28 And there **up-stand** one of them named Agabus,[2301] and **signed through** the Spirit that **great famine is-impending upon whole** the **housed-land**: which **became** in the days of Claudius Caesar.

29 Then the disciples, every man **down-as** his **good-travel, defined**[2302] to **dispatched attendance to** the **brothers** which **down-housed** in Judaea:

30 Which also they **produced** and sent it **towards** the elders **through** the hands of Barnabas and Saul.

ACTS CHAPTER 12

1 Now about that **season** Herod the king stretched forth hands to **evil** certain **from** the Church.

2 And he **up-lifted**[2303] James the brother of John with the sword.

3 And because he **perceived** it pleased the Jews, he **added** to **take** Peter also. (Then were the days **of Unfermented**.)

4 And when he **squeezed-captured**[2304] him, he **place-him** in prison, and **beside-give-him** to four quaternions of soldiers to keep him; planned-**counseled** after **Passover** to bring him forth to the people.

5 Peter **indeed then** was kept in prison: but prayer **became out-stretch** of the Church **towards** God for him.

6 And when Herod **impending to-before-lead** him, the same night Peter was sleeping between two soldiers, bound with two chains: and the keepers before the door kept the prison.

7 And, **be-perceiving**, the angel of the Lord **upon-stood,** and a light shined in the prison: and he **knocked** Peter on the side, and raised him up, saying, **up-stand** quickly. And his chains **out-of-fell out-of the** hands.

8 And the angel said **to-him, about-belt** yourself, and **under-bind** on your sandals. And so, he did. And he says **to-him, about-cast** your garment about you, and follow me.

9 And he went out and followed him; and **perceived** not that it was true **what became through** the angel; **yet seemed** he saw a vision.

10 When they were past the **foremost** and the second **prison,** they came **upon** the iron gate that leads **into** the city; which opened **to-them automatically**:[2305] and they went out and passed on through **first** street; and **soon** the angel **divorce**[2306] from him.

11 And when Peter **became into himself,** he said, now I **perceived, truly**, that the Lord has **out-of-sent** his angel and has **out-lifted** me **out-of** the hand of Herod, and all the **toward-seem** of the people of the Jews.

12 And **being-conscious**, he came to the house of Mary the mother of John, **upon-called**[2307] Mark; where **sufficient** were gathered together praying.

13 And as Peter knocked at the door of the gate, a **girl** came to **under-hear**[2308] named Rhoda.

14 And when she **upon-knew** Peter's voice, she opened not the gate for **cheerfulness**, but ran in, and told how Peter stood before the gate.

15 And they said **towards** her, you are **maniac**.[2309] But she **through-forcefully** that it was even so. Then said they, it is his angel.

16 But Peter continued knocking: and when they had opened, and **perceived** him, they were **ecstasized**.[2310]

[2298] Lit., to arrive; or, competent as if coming in season, ample in amount, fit in character
[2299] Greek: "chrematizo," to furnish what is needed, divine response; secular meaning of constituting a business, employ, to bears as a title, to apprise (to give notice, state of affair, inform)
[2300] That is, they were apprised as "both" disciples and Christians at the Church of Antioch
[2301] Locust
[2302] Greek:" horizon"
[2303] Or lit., assassinate
[2304] "Piazo," to squeeze, to seize by hand, to press, to arrest, to capture
[2305] Greek: "automatos," transliterated as automatic
[2306] Lit., "aphistemi" from-stand, the root word for "apostasies:" feminine of "apostasion" (divorce); a thing that separates.
[2307] Or, to entitle, to invoke
[2308] Or obey
[2309] Or, raving mad, divination maniac, divining mad
[2310] Greek existemi (out-of-stand) from which we take our English ecstasy (overwhelming feelings)

17 But he, **gesturing to-them** with the hand **to-be-silent**, **through-lead to-them** how the Lord had brought him out of the prison. And he said, go **from-message** these things **to** James, and to the **brothers**. And he departed and went into another-**different spot**.

18 Yet as it **became** day, there was no **few agitation in** the soldiers, what was become of Peter.

19 And when Herod had sought for him, and found him not, he **up-judged** the guards, **orders them-to-be-from-lead**.[2311] **And he down-came into** Caesarea, and **tarried**.[2312]

20 And Herod was **feeling-fighting** with them of Tyre and Sidon: but they came with **same-feeling to-him**, and, having **persuaded** Blastus[2313] **who upon of-the** the **regal's**,[2314] **bed-room**[2315] desired peace; because their country was nourished by the king's.

21 And upon a set day Herod, **clothed**[2316] in **regal** robe, sat upon his **judgment-step**,[2317] and **public-market-speech towards** them.

22 And the **public upon-voiced**, **of-god** the voice and not of a man.

23 And **instantly** the angel of the Lord smote him, because he gave not God the glory: and **he-became** eaten of worms, and **out-soul**.

24 But the **Word of God** grew and multiplied.

25 And Barnabas[2318] and Saul returned **out-of** Jerusalem, when they had **filled the attendance**, and **together-beside-took** John, **being-upon-called**[2319] Mark.

ACTS CHAPTER 13

1 Now there were in the Church that was at Antioch certain prophets and teachers; as Barnabas, and Simeon that was called Niger,[2320] and Lucius of Cyrene,[2321] and Manaen, **together-nursed** with Herod the tetrarch, and Saul.

2 Yet, of-them, people-worked[2322] to-the Lord, and fasted, the Holy Spirit said, from-defined[2323] to-me Barnabas and Saul into the work which I have towards-called them.

3 And when they had fasted and prayed, and **placed** hands on them, they **from-loosed-them**

4 So they **indeed**, being-**out-dispatched under** the Holy **Spirit**, departed **to** Seleucia; and from there they sailed to Cyprus.

5 And when they were at Salamis, they **down-messaged** the **Word of God** in the synagogues of the Jews: and they had also John, **subservient-one**.[2324]

6 And when they had gone through the isle **to** Paphos, they found a certain **magi**, a **false-prophet**, a Jew, whose name Bar-Jesus:[2325]

7 Which was with the deputy[2326] of the country, Sergius Paulus, a **synthesizing**[2327] man; who called for Barnabas and Saul and **seek** to hear the **Word of God**.

8 But Elymas the **magi** (for so is his name by **translation**) **anti-stood** them, seeking to **distort**[2328] the deputy from the faith.

9 Then Saul, (who also Paul,) filled with the **Holy Spirit**, **look-stretching into him**,

10 And said, O full of all **trick-bait** and all **easy-going-work**,[2329] you son of the Devil, you hater of all **righteous-togetherness**, **will** you not **pause** to **distort** the **soon** ways of the Lord?

11 And now, **be-perceiving**, the hand of the Lord upon you, and you shall be blind, not seeing the sun **until** season. And **instantly** there fell on him **dimness-of-sight** and a darkness; and he went about seeking some to lead him by the hand.

12 Then the deputy, when he **perceived** what **became**, believed, being astonished[2330] **upon** the **teaching** of the Lord.

[2311] Or, put to death
[2312] Greek: through-wear
[2313] A sprout, to germinate, to yield fruit
[2314] Basilikos: regal, belonging to the sovereign
[2315] Greek: "koiton," a bedroom, from "koites" transliterated as "coitus," also means bed, the place of semen, physical union of male and female genitals
[2316] Lit., in-down; or, in-sink, in-down-slipping
[2317] Greek: "Bema," a step, foot-breadth, rostrum, tribunal
[2318] Lit., son or heir of a prophet
[2319] Or, to entitle, to invoke
[2320] Or, black, a Black man (Simon (hearing)) among the prophets and teachers who was involve in the dispatching of Saul through the Holy Spirit
[2321] A region of Africa where Lucius (illuminative) was from who was also among the prophets and teachers who was involve in the dispatching of Saul through the Holy Spirit
[2322] Lit., laos (people)-ergon (work)
[2323] Lit., from-horizon
[2324] Lit., under-oarsman, generally a subordinate
[2325] Son or heir of Jesus
[2326] Lit., instead-under, instead of the highest officer, Roman proconsul
[2327] From the root compound suniemi-together-send
[2328] Or, through-turn, pervert
[2329] Or reckless-work
[2330] Lit., out-pound

13 Now when Paul and his company loosed from Paphos, they came to Perga²³³¹ in Pamphylia: and John **from-space** them returned **into** Jerusalem.

14 But when they departed from Perga, they came to Antioch in Pisidia, and went into the synagogue on the **Sabbath**, and **they-**sat.

15 And after the reading of the **Law and the Prophets** the **first-rank-of-synagogue** sent **wards** them, saying, you men, **brothers**, if you have any word of **beside-calling towards** the people, **be-saying.**

16 Then Paul **up-stand**, and **gesture** with hand said, men of Israel, and you that fear God, **hear**!

17 The God of this people of Israel chose our fathers and **elevated** the people when they as **foreign-stranger** in the land of Egypt, and with a high arm brought he them out of it.

18 And about the **uninterrupted-**time of forty **years** **he-behavior-bear them** in the **lonesome**.

19 And when he **down-lifted** seven nations in the land of Chanaan, he **down-inheritance-gave to-them** their land.

20 And after that he gave judges about the space of four hundred and fifty **years**, until Samuel the prophet.

21 And afterward they desired a king: and God gave **to-them** Saul the son of Cis,²³³² a man of the tribe of Benjamin, by the space of forty **years**.

22 And when he had **translated**²³³³ him, he raised up **to-them** David to be their king; to whom also he gave **witness**, and said, I have found David the of Jesse, a man **downing my heart**, which **shall-be-doing** all my will.

23 Of this man's seed has God **down** promise raised **to-**Israel a Savior, Jesus:

24 When John had **before-preached** his **entrance**,²³³⁴ the baptism of **change-thinking** to all the people of Israel.

25 And as John filled his **race**, he said, whom **under-mind**²³³⁵ you that I am? **Not, I Am**. But, **be-perceiving**, there **comes** one after me, whose **sandal of-the feet** I am not **deserving** to loose.

26 Men, **brothers**, children of the **kin** of Abraham, and whoever among you fears God, **to-you** is the word of this salvation sent.

27 For they that **down-house** at Jerusalem, and their **first-ranks**,²³³⁶ because they **ignoring him and** the voices of the prophets which are read every **Sabbath**, they have filled **judging-him**.

28 And though they found no cause of death, yet **they-asked** Pilate that he should be **up-lifted**²³³⁷

29 And when they had **finished** all that was written of him, they **down-lifted** from the tree, and **placed-him** in a **remembrance-tomb**

30 But God raised him **out-of** the dead:

31 And he was seen many days of them which came up with him from Galilee to Jerusalem, who are his witnesses **towards** the people.

32 And we **well-message**, how that the promise which **becoming towards** the fathers,

33 God has **out-filled** the same **to-us** their children, in that he has **up-stand** Jesus; as it is also written in the second Psalm, you are my Son, **today** I have **birthed** you.

34 Yet that he **up-stand him** from the dead, **not impending to-be-returning into** corruption, he said, I will give you the **intrinsic-rights** of David, the **believing**.

35 Through-which, he says also in another-**different**, you shall not **give** your **Intrinsic-Right-One** to **perceive** corruption.

36 Because indeed, David, after he **subserved**²³³⁸ his **private** generation by the will of God, fell on sleep, and was **added towards** his fathers, and **perceived** corruption:

37 But he, whom God raised again, **perceived** no corruption.

38 Be it known **to-you** therefore, men, **brothers**, that through this man is **down-messaged to-you** the **release**²³³⁹ of sins:

39 And **from** him all that believe are **righteous** from all things, from which **not you-are-powerful to-be-righteous** by the law of Moses.

---

²³³¹ Tower, fortified
²³³² Greek for Hebrew "Kish"
²³³³ To change-stand, to after-stand
²³³⁴ Greek: into-road
²³³⁵ Or, suspicious
²³³⁶ Or, original-rank, beginning-rank
²³³⁷ Or lit., assassinate
²³³⁸ Lit., under-oarsman, generally a subordinate
²³³⁹ To from-let-go

40 Be-looking therefore, lest that come upon you, which is spoken in the prophets.

41 Be-perceiving, you **down-disposition-ones**, and **marvel**, and **un-shined-ones**: for I work a work in your days, a work which you shall in no **not** believe, though a man **out-through-lead** it **to-you**.

42 And when the Jews were gone out of the synagogue, the **nations beside-called** that these **declarations** might be **spoken to-them** the next Sabbath.

43 Now when the congregation was **loosed**, many of the Jews and **reverencing** proselytes followed Paul and Barnabas: who, speaking to them, persuaded them to **remain** in the grace of God.

44 And the **coming Sabbath** came almost the **entire** city together to hear the **Word of God**.

45 But when the Jews **perceived** the multitudes, they were filled with **zeal**, and **disputed**[2340] those things which were spoken by Paul, **anti-saying**, and blaspheming.

46 Then Paul and Barnabas **all-out-spoken**, and said, it was **constraining** that the **Word of God** should **foremost** have been spoken **to-you**: but seeing you **pushed** it from you, and judge yourselves **undeserving** of eternal life, **be-perceiving**, we turn **into** the **nations**.

47 For so has the Lord commanded us, I have set you to be a light of the **nations**, that you should be **into** salvation until the **last** of the earth.

48 And when the **nations** heard this, they were **cheerful**, and glorified the **Word of the Lord**: and as many as were **arranged into eternal life** believed.

49 And the **Word of the Lord differed**[2341] throughout **whole of-the space**.

50 But the Jews **beside-spur**[2342] the **reverencing** and **well-schemed** women, and the **foremost**-men of the city, and raised **chase upon** Paul and Barnabas, and **out-of-cats** them out of their **horizon**.

51 But they shook off the dust of their feet against them and came **into** Iconium.

52 And the disciples were filled with **cheerfulness**, and of-Holy Spirit.

ACTS CHAPTER 14

1 And **it became** in Iconium **down the same, entered they** into the synagogue of the Jews, and so spoke, that **much fullness** both of the Jews and also of the **Hellenic** believed.

2 But the **un-persuadable** Jews **upon-stirred** the **nations** and made their **souls** evil **downing of**-the **brothers**.

3 **Sufficient**[2343] **uninterrupted-time indeed** then **they-tarried**[2344] **all-speech** in the Lord, which gave **witness to** the **Word** of his grace, and granted signs and wonders **to-become through** their hands.

4 But the **fullness** of the city was **split**: and some **together to-the** the Jews, and some **together to-the** the apostles.

5 And when there was a **rush-impulse** made both of the **nations**, and also of the Jews with their **first-ranks**,[2345] to **insult** and to **stone-cast** them,

6 They **being-conscious** fled **to** Lystra and Derbe, cities of Lycaonia, and **the-about-space**.

7 And there they **well-messaged**.

8 And there sat a certain man at Lystra, **un-powerful** in his feet, being a **limper out-of** his mother's womb **under-originating**, who never had **about-walked**:

9 The same heard Paul speak: who **look-stretching and perceiving** him that he had faith to be **saved**

10 Said with a **great** voice, **up-stand** upright on your feet. And he leaped and **about-walked**.

11 And when the **multitude perceived** what Paul had done, they lifted up their voices, saying in the speech of Lycaonia, the gods are come down **towards** us in the **assimilating to-humans**.

12 And they called Barnabas, **Zeus**;[2346] and Paul, **Hermes**,[2347] because he was the **leading** speaker.

13 Then the priest of **Zeus**, which was before their city, brought **bulls** and garlands[2348] **to** the gates, and **he-willed** sacrifice with the **multitude**.

[2340] Lit, anti-word, refute, dispute
[2341] Greek: "diaphero," to through-bear, transliterated as "differ" or "different"
[2342] Or to urge along, to stimulate to hostility
[2343] Lit., to arrive; or, competent as if coming in season, ample in amount, fit in character

[2344] Greek: through-wear, through-rub
[2345] Or, original-rank, beginning-rank
[2346] Greek: "Dis" through
[2347] Translator, interpreter
[2348] Or, wreath, twine, crown

14 When the apostles, Barnabas, and Paul, heard, they **through-tear** their **garments**, and **into-leap into the multitude, screaming,**

15 And saying, **lord**s, why **produce** you these things? We also are men of like-**emotions** with you, and **well-message to-you** that you should turn from these **empty-things**[2349] upon the living God, which made heaven, and earth, and the sea, and all things that are **in them**:

16 Who in **beside-gone-by generations let-be** all nations to **traverse** in their ways.

17 Nevertheless, he left not himself **un-witnessed,** in **good-working,** gave us rain from heaven, and **fruit-carrying** seasons, filling our **hearts** with food and **good-disposition**.

18 And with these sayings **with-difficulty down-rested** they the **multitude, that they not sacrifice to-them.**

19 And there came there Jews from Antioch and Iconium, who persuaded the **multitude**, and, having stoned Paul, **dragged** out of the city, **to-do-by-law** he **died.**

20 Yet, as the disciples **circled** him, he **up-stand,**[2350] and came into the city: and the **upon-tomorrow** he departed with Barnabas to Derbe.

21 And when they **evangelized** to that city, and had taught **sufficiently,**[2351] they returned again **into** Lystra, and Iconium, and Antioch,

22 Confirming[2352] the souls of the disciples, **beside-called** them to **remain** in the faith, and that **it-is-binding** we through much tribulation **into-enter** into the kingdom of God.

23 And when they had **hand-stretch**[2353] them elders in every Church, and had prayed with fasting, they-**beside-placed**[2354] them to the Lord, on whom they believed.

24 And after they had passed throughout Pisidia, they came to Pamphylia.[2355]

25 And when they **spoke** the **Word** in Perga, they went down into Attalia:

26 And there sailed to Antioch, from **where** they had been **beside-given** to the grace of God for the work which they **filled**.

27 And when they **beside-come**, and had gathered the Church together, they **up-message** all that God had **produced** with them, and how he had opened the door of faith **to-the nations**.

28 And there they **tarried**[2356] **not a-few** with the disciples.

ACTS CHAPTER 15

1 And certain men which came down from Judaea taught the **brothers**, except you be circumcised after the **ethics** of Moses, **not you-are-powerful to-be-saved.**

2 When therefore Paul and Barnabas had no **few insurrection**[2357] and **together-seeking** with them, they **under-arranged** that Paul and Barnabas, and certain other of them, should **up-walk into** Jerusalem **to** the apostles and elders about this **seeking**.

3 And being **before-dispatch under** the Church, they passed through Phenice and Samaria, **out-of-through-lead** the conversion of the **nations**: and they caused **great cheerfulness** to all the **brothers**.

4 And when they were come to Jerusalem, they were received of the Church, and the apostles and elders, and they **up-messaged** all things that God had done with them.

5 But there **out-of-up-stand** certain of the sect of the Pharisees which believed, saying, that **it-is-binding** to circumcise them, and to **beside-charge** to **watch** the law of Moses.

6 And the apostles and elders came together for to **perceive about** this **saying**.

7 And when there had been much **together-seeking**, Peter **up-standing**, and said **towards** them, men, **brothers**, you **are-acquainted**[2358] how that a good while ago God made choice among us, that the **nations** by my mouth should hear the word of the **well-message** and believe.

[2349] Or, empty through the idea of unsuccessful search
[2350] "Anastas" also translated "rise again" ("ana"-up/again and "histemi" to stand)
[2351] Lit., to arrive; or, competent as if coming in season, ample in amount, fit in character
[2352] Lit., upon-stand, set fast, to support further, reestablish, or literally to turn resolutely in a certain direction
[2353] Or select
[2354] Or deposit
[2355] All-tribal, every-tribal
[2356] Greek: through-wear
[2357] Lit., standings
[2358] Greek: upon-stand, to put the mind upon, to be acquainted with, comprehend, be present

8 And God, **the heart-knower, witnessed,** giving them the **Holy Spirit, down-as to-us;**

9 And put no **through-judging**[2359] between us and them, **cleansing** their **hearts** by faith.

10 Now therefore why **probe-test** you God, to put a yoke upon the neck of the disciples, which neither our fathers nor we were **forceful** to bear?

11 But we believe that through the grace of the Lord Jesus Christ we shall be saved, even as they.

12 Then all the **fullness silent,** and gave audience to Barnabas and Paul, **exegesis**[2360] what miracles and wonders God had **produced in** the **nations through** them.

13 And after they **were silent,** James answered, saying, men **brothers,** hear me:

14 Simeon has **exegesis** how God at the first **bishoped**[2361] the **nations,** to take out of them a people **upon** his name.

15 And to this **together-sound**[2362] the words of the prophets as it is written,

16 After this I will return,[2363] and will **house-build** again the tabernacle of David, which **fell**;[2364] and I will **house-build** again the **down-dug of-her,** and I will **up-erecting her**:

17 That the **down-remaining** of men might seek after the Lord, and all the **nations,** upon whom my name is **upon-called,**[2365] says the Lord, **the one-producing** all these things.

18 Known **to** God are all his works from **ages.**

19 Through this **I-am-judging,** that we not **near-in-crowd** them, which from among the **nations** are **upon-turned**[2366] **upon** the God:

20 But that we write **to-them,** that they abstain from **soil** of-the idols, and **of-the prostitution,** and things **of-the** strangled, and **of-the** blood.

21 For Moses **out-of original generations** has in every city them that preach him, being read in the synagogues every **Sabbath.**

22 Then **it-seemed to-the** apostles and elders, with the whole Church, to **dispatch** chosen men **out-of them** to Antioch with Paul and Barnabas; Judas **being-upon-called** Barsabas,[2367] and Silas, **leading** men in the **brothers**:

23 And they wrote by them after this manner; the apostles and elders and **the brothers, cheerfulness to** the **brothers** which are of the **nations** in Antioch, Syria, and Cilicia:

24 Since-now, we have heard, that certain which went out from us have **agitated** you with words, subverting[2368] your souls, saying, be circumcised, and keep the law: to whom, **not we-through-stalled**:[2369]

25 It seemed good **to-us, becoming** with **same-feeling,** to **dispatched** chosen men **towards** you with our beloved Barnabas and Paul,

26 Men that have **beside-given** their **souls over** the name of our Lord Jesus Christ.

27 We have sent therefore Judas and Silas, who shall also **from-message** the same things.

28 For it seemed good to the **Holy Spirit,** and to us, to lay upon you no **more weight** than these necessary things:

29 That you **from-hold idol-sacrifices,** and from blood, and from things strangled, and from **prostitution**: **out-of** which if you keep yourselves, **good you-will-be-practicing. Be-strengthened**

30 So when they were **from-loosed,** they came to Antioch: and when they had gathered the **fullness** together, they **upon-give** the epistle:

31 When they had read, they **were-cheerful** for the **beside-calling.**

32 And Judas and Silas, being prophets also themselves, **beside-called** the **brothers** with many words, and confirmed.[2370]

33 And after they **produced uninterrupted-time,** they were **from-loosed**[2371] in peace from the **brothers towards** the apostles.

34 Yet, it **seemed to-the** Silas to **remain** there

[2359] Or discriminate, difference
[2360] Exegesis is transliterated from "exegeomai," to lead out-of, to unfold
[2361] Greek compound: upon-peer about, upon-skeptic, upon-scout, upon watch, upon-watch, upon-sentry
[2362] Or English: symphony
[2363] Or overturn
[2364] Fell is perfect tense feminine (see masculine use in Revelation 9:1)
[2365] Or, to entitle, to invoke
[2366] Revert
[2367] Son or heir of pleasing, or son or heir of interpretation
[2368] To pack up, baggage, to upset, to dismantle
[2369] assigned
[2370] Lit., upon-stand, set fast, to support further, reestablish, or literally to turn resolutely in a certain direction
[2371] Passive voice (the brothers held them until the brothers were finished with prophets)

35 Paul also and Barnabas **tarried**[2372] in Antioch, teaching and **evangelizing** the **Word of the Lord**, with many **others-different** also.

36 And some days after Paul said **to** Barnabas, let us go again and **bishop**[2373] our **brothers** in every city where we have preached the **Word of the Lord**, how they **are-holding**.

37 And Barnabas **planned-counseled-himself** to **together-take** them John, **the-one called** Mark.

38 Yet, Paul, **not he-deserving** to-be-**together-beside-take to-them**, who **divorcing**[2374] from them from Pamphylia,[2375] and **not together-come to**-them **into** the work.

39 And **became beside-acid**[2376] between them, that they **spaced** one from the other: and so, Barnabas **beside-take** Mark, and sailed **into** Cyprus;

40 And Paul **upon-chose** Silas, and departed, **being-beside-given** by the **brothers to** the grace of God.

41 And he went through Syria and Cilicia, confirming[2377] the Churches.

ACTS CHAPTER 16

1 Then he **down-meet**[2378] **into** Derbe and Lystra: and, **be-perceiving**, a certain disciple was there, named **Timothy**, the son of a certain woman, which was a Jewess, and believed; but his father a **Hellenic**:

2 Which was **witnessed under** the **brothers** that were at Lystra and Iconium.

3 Him **willed** Paul to **out-of-come** with him; and **took** and circumcised him **through** the Jews which were in those **spots**: for they **perceived** all that his father was a **Hellenic, under-originated**.

4 And as they went through the cities, they **beside-give** them the **dogmas**[2379] **to-watch**, that were **judged-decided under** the apostles and elders which were at Jerusalem.

5 And so were the Churches **solidified** in the faith and **exceed** in number daily.

6 Now when they had gone throughout Phrygia and the **space** of Galatia, and were **prevented** of the Holy Spirit to preach the **Word** in Asia,

7 After they **came** to Mysia, they **probe-tested** to **traverse** into Bithynia: **and not let-be them the Spirit of Jesus**.

8 And they **beside-passed** Mysia **down-walked** to Troas.

9 And a vision appeared to Paul **through** the night; there stood a man of Macedonia, and **beside-called** him, saying, come over into Macedonia, and help[2380] us.

10 And after he had **perceived** the vision, **soon** we **sought** to go into Macedonia, **together-embark**[2381] that the Lord had called us **to-good-message to-them**.

11 Therefore, **up-leading** from Troas, **we-immediately-ran** to Samothracia, and the next **into** Neapolis;[2382]

12 And from there to Philippi,[2383] which is the **foremost** city of that part of Macedonia, a colony: and we were in that city **tarried**[2384] certain days.

13 And on the Sabbath, we went out of the city by a river side, where prayer **to-do-by-law**; and we sat down and spoke **to-the** women who **together-coming**.

14 And a certain woman named Lydia, a seller of purple, of the city of Thyatira, which **reverenced** God, heard: whose **heart** the Lord **up-opened**, that she **toward-hold to-the** things which were spoken of Paul.

15 And when she was baptized, and her household, she **beside-called**, saying, if you have judged me to be **believing** to the Lord, come into my house, and **remain**. And she **beside-forced** us.

[2372] Greek: through-wear
[2373] Greek compound: upon-peer about, upon-skeptic, upon-scout, upon watch, upon-watch, upon-sentry
[2374] Lit., "aphistemi" from-stand, the root word for "apostasies:" feminine of "apostasion" (divorce); a thing that separates.
[2375] Every-tribal, all-tribal, all tribes
[2376] Greek: "paproxumos," (beside or near-"acid," keen, sharp) transliterated as "paroxysm" dispute, a fit, provoke, sharp contention, sharp outburst
[2377] Lit., upon-stand, set fast, to support further, reestablish, or literally to turn resolutely in a certain direction
[2378] Greek: "katantao," down-opposite, down-instead, down-anti
[2379] Accepted beliefs, authoritative proclamations, decrees, etcetera that is not questioned or doubted, from "dokeo," to think, to seem,
[2380] Run to an urgent distress cry
[2381] Greek: sun (together) and bibazo (to force), drive-together, unite, infer, together-board a ship
[2382] Newtown
[2383] Friend of horses
[2384] Greek: through-wear

16 And **it became**, as we went to prayer, a certain **girl holding**[2385] a spirit of **python**[2386] **from-met** us, which brought her **lords** much **work**[2387] by **divination-maniac**:[2388]

17 The same **down-followed** Paul and us, and **screamed**, saying, these men are the **slaves** of the **Highest** God, which **down-message to-us** the way of salvation.

18 And this did she many days. But Paul, being **through-toil**,[2389] turned and said to the spirit, I command you in the name of Jesus Christ to come out **from** her. And he came out the same hour.

19 And when her **lords perceived** that the **expectation** of their **work**[2390] was gone, they **upon-take** Paul and Silas, and **dragged-them** into the marketplace **upon** the **first-rank**s.[2391]

20 And brought them to the **generals**,[2392] saying, these men, **under-originating,** Jews, **out-of-agitate** our city,

21 And **down-message ethics**, which are not lawful for us to **beside-welcome** neither **to-produce,** being Romans.

22 And the multitude rose up together against them: and the **generals about-break** their clothes and commanded **to-be-rod-beaten.**

23 And when they had **upon-placed plague-poundings to-them,** they cast into prison, **beside-message** the jailor to keep them **securely**:[2393]

24 Who, having **taken** such a **beside-message**, threw them into the inner prison, and made their feet **secured**[2394] **into** the **tree**.

25 And at midnight Paul and Silas prayed and **hymned to** God: **yet** the prisoners heard them.

26 And suddenly there **became** a **great quake,** so that the foundations of the prison were shaken: and **instantly** all the doors were opened, and everyone's bands were **up-send.**[2395]

27 And the keeper of the prison **became out-of-**sleep, and **perceiving** the prison doors open, he drew out his sword, and **he-was-impending to-up-lift**[2396] himself, **to-do-by-law** that the prisoners **out-fled.**

28 But Paul voiced with a **great** voice, saying, not **practice to-yourself evil**: for we are all **within**

29 Then he **asked** for a light, and **into-leap**, and **became** trembling, and **towards-fell to-the** Paul and Silas,

30 And **before-leading** them out, and **showed lords,** what **is-binding** me **to-produce** that **I-may-be-saved**?

31 And they said, believe on the Lord Jesus Christ, and you shall be saved, and your house.

32 And they spoke **to-him** the **Word of the Lord**, and to all that were in his house.

33 And he **beside-take in that** hour of the night and washed **the plague-poundings**; and was baptized, he and all his, **instantly**.

34 And when he had **up-led** them into his house, **he-beside-placed**[2397] **a-table,** and **jumped-for-joy**, believing in God with all his house.

35 And when it **became** day, the **generals** sent the **rod-holders**, saying, **from-loose** those men.

36 And the keeper of the prison **from-messaged** this saying to Paul, the **generals** have sent to **from-loose** you: now therefore depart and go in peace.

37 But Paul **showed towards** them, they have **skinned** us openly **un-down-judged, under-originating** Romans, and have cast into prison; and now they **throw** us out **secretly**? **No! Because,** let them come themselves and **out-lead.**

38 And the **rod-holders up-messaged** these **declarations to** the **generals:** and they feared when they heard that they were Romans.

39 And they came and **beside-called** them, and **out-of-lead**, and **asked-them** to depart out of the city.

40 And they went out of the prison and entered into **the** Lydia: and when they had **perceived** the **brothers**, they **beside-called** them, and departed.

[2385] Or, having
[2386] Or lit., "Ascertainer," from the Greek root, "puth" or "puthanomai," to ascertain-by-inquiry
[2387] Occupation
[2388] Or, diviner, madness, to long for, craving, to rave as a maniac, raving madness
[2389] Greek compound dia (through) and "ponos" (toil); per Strong's the root for "ponos" ("penes") carries the idea of experiencing straitened circumstances in private
[2390] Occupation
[2391] Or, original-rank, beginning-rank
[2392] Greek: "strategois" transliterated as "strategists"
[2393] Lit., un-fail
[2394] Lit., to un-fail
[2395] Or to slacken
[2396] Or lit., assassinate
[2397] Or deposit

ACTS CHAPTER 17

1 Now when they had passed through Amphipolis[2398] and Apollonia,[2399] they came to Thessalonica, where was a synagogue of the Jews:

2 Yet, Paul, **down ethics**, **into-go towards** them, and three **Sabbaths through-said**[2400] with them out of the **Scriptures**,

3 Opening and **beside-placing**,[2401] that **it-was-binding the** Christ **to-emotion**, and **up-stand out-of** the dead; and that this Jesus, whom I **down-messaged to-you**, is **the** Christ.

4 And some of them believed, and **towards-inherited** with Paul and Silas; and of the **reverencing Hellenic** a **much fullness**, and of the **foremost** women, not a few.

5 But the Jews which believed not, **being-zealous**, **towards-take-themselves** certain **wicked-hurtful men** of the **market-place**, and **multitude-producing**, set all the city on a **disturbance-wail**, and **upon-stand** the house of Jason,[2402] and sought to bring them out to the **public.**

6 And when they found them not, they **dragged** Jason and certain **brothers to** the **city-first-ranks distress-crying**, these the **habitable-world**[2403] **have-up-stood**[2404] they are **also present here-within**;

7 Whom Jason has **under-welcomed**: and these all **from-anti** to the **dogmas**[2405] of Caesar **are-practicing another-different, saying** Jesus is **King!**

8 And they **agitated** the **multitude** and the **city-first-ranks**, when they heard these things.

9 And when they had **taken sufficient**[2406] beside Jason, and of the **remaining**, they **from-loosed them**.

10 And the **brothers soon out-of-dispatched** Paul and Silas **through** night **into** Berea: who **beside-becoming** there went into the synagogue of the Jews.

11 These were more **good-birthed** than those in Thessalonica, **who welcomed** the **Word** with all **before-feeling** and **up-judged** the **Scriptures** daily, whether those things **may-be-holding**.

12 Therefore many **out-of** them believed; also, of-the **Hellenic women, the well-schemed**, and of men, not a few.

13 Yet, when the Jews of Thessalonica had **knowing** that the **Word of God** was **down-messaged** of Paul at Berea, they came there also, and **shook** the **multitude**.

14 And then **soon** the **brothers** sent away Paul to go as it were to the sea: but Silas and **Timothy remained** there.

15 And they that **down-standing**[2407] Paul **lead** him to Athens: and **taking** a commandment **towards** Silas and **Timothy** to come **towards** him **quickly**, they departed.

16 Now while Paul **out-of-welcome** for them in Athens, his spirit was **beside-acid**[2408] in him, when he saw the city **down-idolatry**.[2409]

17 Therefore he **through-said**[2410] in the synagogue with the Jews, and with the **reverencing-ones**, and in the market daily **towards** them that **beside-happened**.[2411]

18 Then certain philosophers of the Epicureans,[2412] and of the Stoics, **together-cast to-him**. And some said, what will this **seed-collector**[2413] say? **Yet**, he seems to be a **down-messenger** of **foreign-lodgers' demons**: because he **well-message to-them** Jesus, and the resurrection.

19 And they **take** him, and brought him **to** Areopagus,[2414] saying, **we-are-powerful to-**know what this **new-fresh teaching**, you **are-s**peaking?

20 For you bring certain **foreign-lodge-things** to our ears: we **will to-know** therefore what these things mean.

[2398] Surrounded-city
[2399] Destroyer, from-ruining-one
[2400] Say thoroughly, discuss
[2401] Or deposit
[2402] Or, Healer, curing-one
[2403] Or housed-land
[2404] Or insurrection, to drive out of one's home
[2405] Accepted beliefs, authoritative proclamations, decrees, etcetera that is not questioned or doubted, from "dokeo," to think, to seem,
[2406] Lit., to arrive; or, competent as if coming in season, ample in amount, fit in character
[2407] Or conduct, escort
[2408] Or beside-keen
[2409] Or intense idolatry
[2410] Say thoroughly, discuss
[2411] Or beside-obtain, beside-to hit the target, beside-happenings, beside-chance upon
[2412] Upon-girl-helper
[2413] Or seed picker ("spermologos"—seed (sperm) and lego (so select, to lay forth)
[2414] Compound of "ares" (god of war) and pagos (fixed a tent); pagos was also a hill or rock

21 (For all the Athenians[2415] and **upon-foreigners**[2416] **foreign-lodgers,** which were there, spent their **good-season**[2417] in nothing **another-different,** but either to tell, or to hear some **new-fresh** thing.)

22 Then Paul stood in the middle of **Areopagus,** and **showed,**[2418] you men of Athens, **I-am-looking** that in all things you are **dreading-demonism**[2419]

23 Because through-passing, and beheld your **reverences,** I found a **sacrifice-place** with this inscription, **to-ignorant god.** Whom, **then,** you **are-ignorant good-reverence, this-one I down-message to-you.**

24 God that made the world and all things **in him,** seeing that he is Lord of heaven and earth, **down-house** not in temples made with hands.

25 Neither is **served-therapy** with men's hands, as though he needed anything, seeing he gives to all life, and breath, and all things;

26 And has made of one blood all nations of men to **down-house** on all the face of the earth, and has **defined**[2420] the **seasons before-arranged,** and the **defined-place** of their **down-house.**

27 That they should seek the Lord, **at-least** they **may-rub** him, and find him, though he **under-originating** not far from every one of us:

28 For in him we live, and move,[2421] and have our being; as certain also of your own **poets-producers** have said, for we are also his **kin-race.**

29 Then, we-**under-originating** the **kin-race** of God, we owe not **to-do-by-law** that the Godhead is like **to-gold,** or **to-silver,** or **to-stone, to-engraved-character**[2422] by **tech**[2423] and man's **in-sacrifice-anger.**

30 The indeed uninterrupted-times of this **ignorance,**[2424] God **over-perceived;**[2425] but now, **he-is-beside-message** all men **universally** to **change-thought**:

31 Because he **stands** a day, in the which **he-is-impending to-be-judging** the **housed-land** in **righteous-togetherness in to-Man** whom he has **defined;**[2426] he has **beside-hold faith to-all,** in that he has **up-stand** him **out-of** the dead.

32 And when they heard of the resurrection of the dead, some **throw-out-the-lip**:[2427] and others said, we will hear you again **about** this.

33 So Paul departed **out-of middle of-them.**

34 Yet, certain men **glued**[2428] **to-him,** and believed: among **whom** Dionysius[2429] the Areopagite, and a woman named Damaris,[2430] and **others-different** with them.

ACTS CHAPTER 18

1 After these things Paul **spaced out-of** Athens and came to Corinth.

2 And found a certain Jew named Aquila,[2431] **kin of-Pontus,**[2432] **before-slain**[2433] came from Italy, with his wife Priscilla;[2434] (because that Claudius had **through-arranged** all Jews to **space from** Rome:) and **toward-came to-them.**

3 And because he was of the **like-tech,** he remained with them, and **worked:** for by their **tech,** they were tentmakers.

4 And he **through-said**[2435] in the synagogue every Sabbath and persuaded the Jews and the **Hellenics.**

5 And when Silas and **Timothy** were come from Macedonia, Paul was **together-held to-the Spirit,** and **through-witnesses** to the Jews, Jesus Christ

6 And when they **anti-arranged-**themselves, and blasphemed, he **out-of-shook the garment,** and said

---

[2415] Derived from "athenai" the goddess of wisdom
[2416] Upon public, to make oneself at home in a foreign country
[2417] Or opportune season
[2418] Greek: "phemi," the root word for fame ("pheme")
[2419] Or timid of demons, dreading-demons, fearful of demons, therefore superstition
[2420] Greek:" horizon"
[2421] Or stir
[2422] Greek, "charagma," to carve, to scratch, to etch, sculpture; to engrave or write; akin to "charackter" (character);" "charagma" is used of a serpent's bite by Sophocles; "charagma" also means expressed image character, an engraving.
[2423] Greek: "techne" (trade, craft); from tekton (carpenter, craftsman), these are the root words for "tech," technician, technical, etc.
[2424] Lit., ignoring, ignorance, un-minding
[2425] Or, to overlook
[2426] Greek:" horizon"
[2427] Or jeer at, mock
[2428] Or, to stick to, to cling, to keep company with
[2429] Reveler
[2430] Tame, gentle
[2431] Eagle
[2432] Sea, marine
[2433] Lit., before (recently) and "aphazoa' (butcher), also meaning "recently"
[2434] Latin meaning Ancient
[2435] Say thoroughly, discuss

towards them, your blood upon your own heads, I clean: from **the now** I will **traverse into** the **nations**.

7 And he **change-step there,** and entered into a certain house, named Justus, that **reverenced** God, whose house **together-border** to the synagogue.

8 And Crispus, the **first-rank-of-synagogue**, believed on the Lord with all his house; and many of the Corinthians hearing believed, and were baptized.

9 Then **the Lord spoke** to Paul in the night by a vision, be not afraid, but speak, and **not be silent:**

10 For I am with you, and no man shall **upon-place to-you to-evil**: for I have much people in this city.

11 And he-**is-seated** a **year** and six months, teaching the **Word of God in** them.

12 And when Gallio was the deputy of Achaia, the Jews **down-stood-him** with-**same-feeling to-the** Paul, and led him to the **judgment-step**,[2436]

13 Saying, this **up-persuade** men to **reverence** God **beside** the law.

14 Yet, Paul **is-impending to-be-up-opening the** mouth, Gallio said **towards** the Jews, if it were of **unrighteousness** or **wicked-hurtful easy-going-work**,[2437] O Jews, **down saying I-tolerate**[2438] with you:

15 But if it be a **seeking about** words and names, and your law, look you; for not **I-am-plan-counseling to-be** judge of such.

16 And he **from-drives** them from the **judgment-step**.[2439]

17 Then all the **Hellenic upon-take** Sosthenes, the **first-rank-of-synagogue**, and **thumped-him** before the **judgment-step**. And Gallio **not interesting of-those-things**.

18 And Paul **toward-remain** yet a **sufficient**[2440] days and then **from-arranged** the **brothers**, and sailed there into Syria, and with him Priscilla and Aquila; having **sheared-head** in Cenchrea: **because** he had a **prayer**.

19 And he **meet-against**[2441] to Ephesus and left them there: but he himself entered into the synagogue, and **through-said**[2442] with the Jews.

20 When they **asked-him** to **remain more** with them, not he-**upon-nodded**;

21 But **from-arranged to-them**, saying, **is-binding me entirely coming to-do the festival into** Jerusalem: but I will **up-bend towards** you if God wills. And he **up-lead** from Ephesus.

22 And when he **down-come into** Caesarea, and **up-walked,** and **embraced** the Church, he **down-walked** to Antioch.

23 And after he **produced uninterrupted-time,** he departed, and **through-come** the **space** of Galatia and Phrygia in order, strengthening all the disciples.

24 And a certain Jew named Apollos, **to-the kin**, Alexandria, an **eloquent**[2443] man, **powerful** in the **Scriptures**, **meet-against**[2444] **into** Ephesus.

25 This man was **catechized** in the way of the Lord; and being **zealous to-the** spirit, he spoke and taught **exactly**[2445] the things **about** the Lord, **being-acquainted**[2446] only the baptism of John.

26 And he began to **all-speech** in the synagogue: whom when Aquila and Priscilla had heard, they-**toward-took** him, and expounded[2447] **to-him** the way of God **more-exactly**.[2448]

27 And when he **plan-counseled-himself to-through-come** into Achaia, the **brothers** wrote, **before-turning** the disciples to **from-welcome** him: who, when he **beside-became, together-cast** them much which had believed through **the** grace:

28 Because, **to-the** Jews he-**well-stretched, through-down-exposed**, publicly, **upon**-showing **through** the Scriptures that Jesus is **the** Christ.

ACTS CHAPTER 19

1 And **it became**, that, while Apollos was at Corinth, Paul having passed through the upper **sections** came **into** Ephesus: and finding certain disciples,

---

[2436] Greek: "Bema," a step, foot-breadth, rostrum, tribunal
[2437] Lit., easy (reckless)-work
[2438] Greek: up-hold, to hold oneself up against
[2439] Greek: "Bema," a step, foot-breadth, rostrum, tribunal
[2440] Lit., to arrive; or, competent as if coming in season, ample in amount, fit in character
[2441] Greek: "katantao," down-opposite, down-instead, down-anti
[2442] Say thoroughly, discuss
[2443] Or, an orator, fluent, scholarly
[2444] Greek: "katantao," down-opposite, down-instead, down-anti
[2445] akribos
[2446] Greek: upon-stand, to put the mind upon, to be acquainted with, comprehend, be present
[2447] Out-of-place, place-out
[2448] Greek: "akribesteron" (more-exact) a superlative of "akribos (exact)"

2 He said **towards** them, have you **taken** the Holy Spirit since you believed? And they said **toward him**, we have not so much as heard whether there be any **Holy Spirit**.

3 And he said, **into** what then were you baptized? And they said, **into** John's baptism.

4 Then said Paul, John **indeed** baptized with the baptism of **change-thought**, saying **to-the** people, that they should believe **into** him which should come after him, that is, **into** Christ Jesus.

5 When they heard, they were baptized **into** the name of the Lord Jesus.

6 And when Paul had **placed** hands upon them, the Holy Spirit came **upon** them; and they spoke **both**[2449] with-tongues and prophesied.

7 And all the men were about twelve.

8 And he went into the synagogue, and **all-speech upon** three months, **through-saying**[2450] and persuading the things **about** the kingdom of God.

9 But when **some** were hardened, and believed not, but **evil-saying the Way** before the **fullness**, he **divorced**[2451] from them, and **from-defined**[2452] the disciples, **through-saying**[2453] **down day** in the school of one Tyrannus.[2454]

10 And this **became upon** two **years**; so that all they which **down-house** in Asia heard the **Word of the Lord** Jesus, both Jews and **Hellenics**.

11 Powers, beside the happenings[2455] God did through the hands of Paul.

12 So that from his **skin** were brought **upon** the sick handkerchiefs or aprons, and **from-change** the **nauseas from them, the both,** spirits, **the wicked-hurtful, traveled-out from** them.

13 Then certain of the **wandering**[2456] Jews, **out-of-oath**[2457] **upon-hand** to **name upon** them the name of the Lord Jesus which **holding wicked-hurtful** spirits, saying, we **oath** you **by-the** Jesus whom Paul preaches.

14 And they were seven sons of Sceva, a Jew, **first-rank-**priest, which **produced this**.

15 And the **wicked-hurtful** spirit answered and said, Jesus **I-am-knowing,** and Paul **I-am-acquainted;**[2458] but who are **you**?

16 And the man in whom the **wicked-hurtful** spirit was leaped on them, and **down-lord** them, and **force down** them, so that they fled out of that house naked and **traumatized**.[2459]

17 And this was known to all the Jews and **Hellenics** also **down-housing** at Ephesus; and fear fell on them all, and the name of the Lord Jesus was magnified.

18 And many that believed came, and **out-of-same-say**, and **up-message** their **practices**.

19 Sufficient[2460] of them also which **practicing meddlesome-magic**[2461] **together-carry** their **scrolls** and burned them before all: and they **together-pebble-vote-count** the **value** of them and found fifty thousand of silver.

20 So **down government**[2462] grew the **Word of God** and **was-forceful**.

21 After these things were **filled**, Paul **placed** in the **Spirit,** when he had passed through Macedonia and Achaia, to **traverse into** Jerusalem, saying, after I have been there, **is-binding me** also **to-perceive** Rome.

22 So he sent into Macedonia two of them that **attended to-him, Timothy,** and Erastus; but he himself stayed in Asia for **uninterrupted-time**.

23 And the same **season** there **became agitation, not few,** about that **Way**.

24 For a certain named Demetrius, a silversmith, who made silver shrines for **Artemis, near-hold work**[2463] **to** the **technicians,** not **few**;

[2449] Greek "te" which means and both, which implies some spoke in tongues and some prophesied (compare Acts 19:12 and also see 1 Corinthians 12:30 in the Greek—"not all speak with tongues," therefore some prophesied after being filled with the Holy Spirit)
[2450] Say thoroughly, discuss
[2451] Lit., "aphistemi" from-stand, the root word for "apostasies:" feminine of "apostasion" (divorce); a thing that separates.
[2452] Lit., from-horizon
[2453] Say thoroughly, discuss
[2454] Lordship, lord, controller, supreme authority
[2455] Or, hit the mark, chance upon, obtain,
[2456] Greek: about-coming-going
[2457] Greek: "exorkistes" (exorcist), literally, out-of-oath
[2458] Greek: upon-stand, to put the mind upon, to be acquainted with, comprehend, be present
[2459] Greek: "traumatize" traumatized, to wound
[2460] Lit., to arrive; or, competent as if coming in season, ample in amount, fit in character
[2461] Greek: "periergos," all-working, busy body, meddlesome, magic, superstitious practices
[2462] Greek: kratos, transliterated as "great" and also means vigor, strength, to use strength, to rule, government, translated as "cracy" in democracy—people(demo)-government (kratos), or public-government
[2463] Occupation

25 Whom he **hoarded-together, of like workers**, and said, **men**, you **acquainted**[2464] that **out-of** this **work**[2465] we have our wealth.[2466]

26 Moreover you see and hear, that not alone at Ephesus, but almost throughout all Asia, this Paul has persuaded and turned away **sufficient**[2467] **multitude**, saying that they be no gods, which are-**becoming through** hands:

27 So that not only this our **section** is in danger **into from-evidence-exposure**; but also, that the **priest-place** of the **great** goddess **Artemis impending to-be-inventoried nothing**, and her magnificence should be **down-lifted**, whom all Asia and the **housed-land** worshipped.

28 And when they heard, they were full of **sacrifice-anger**, and **screamed**, saying, **great Artemis**[2468] of the Ephesians.

29 And the whole city was filled with **together-poured**:[2469] and having caught Gaius and Aristarchus, men of Macedonia, Paul's **together-out-public**,[2470] they **violent-impulse-rushed** with **same-feeling** into the theatre.

30 And when Paul would have entered **into** the **public**, **not let-be** him the disciples.

31 And certain of the Asia-**first-rank**, which were his friends, **dispatched toward him**, **beside-called** that he would not **give** himself into the theatre.

32 Some therefore **screamed** one thing, and some another: for the **church** was **together-poured**,[2471] and the **more-ones**[2472] **perceived** not what **on-account-of** they were come together.

33 And they **together-embark** Alexander out of the multitude, the Jews **toward-cast him**. And Alexander **down-sway**[2473] with the hand and **willed to-answer**[2474] to the **public**.

34 But when they knew that he was a Jew all with one voice about the space of two hours **screamed**, **great Artemis**[2475] of the Ephesians.

35 Yet, when the **scribe** had **down-stalled** the **multitude**, he **showing**,[2476] men of Ephesus, what man is there that knows not how that the city of the Ephesians is a **temple-sweeper** of the **great** goddess **Artemis**, and of the which **Zeus-fallen**?

36 Seeing then that these things cannot be spoken against, **binding it-is** you to **under-originating down-stalled**,[2477] and to **practice** nothing **forward-falling**.[2478]

37 For you have brought **here** these men, which are neither **priest-place-robbers**, nor yet blasphemers of your goddess.

38 If indeed then, Demetrius, and the **technician** which are with him, have a **word towards** any man, the **market-place** is open, and there are deputies: let them **in-call**[2479] another-same.

39 But if you **ask** anything about **other-different-things**, it shall be **upon-loosed** in a **lawful**[2480] church.

40 For we are in danger to be **in-called** for this day's **insurrection**[2481] there **under-originate** no cause which we-shall-be-powerful **to-from-give saying** of this **together-turn**.[2482]

41 And when these **sayings**, he **from-loosed** the **church**.

ACTS CHAPTER 20

1 And after the uproar[2483] **paused**, Paul called **to-him** the disciples, and **embraced**, and departed **to-travel** into Macedonia.

2 And when he had **through-coming to-those sections**, and **beside-called them to many sayings**, he came into **the Hellenic**,

---

[2464] Greek: upon-stand, to put the mind upon, to be acquainted with, comprehend, be present
[2465] Occupation
[2466] Lit., well-go
[2467] Lit., to arrive; or, competent as if coming in season, ample in amount, fit in character
[2468] Greek: Artemis, the name of a Grecian goddess borrowed by the Asiatics
[2469] Or commixture
[2470] Fellow-traveler
[2471] Greek compound: sun (together) and cheo (pour), to pour together, to comingle promiscuously, throw into disorder, perplex the mind
[2472] Or majority
[2473] Gesture
[2474] Greek: "apologeomai" (from-saying) to exculpate (self), to give account, to defend
[2475] Greek: Artemis, the name of a Grecian goddess borrowed by the Asiatics
[2476] Greek: "phemi," the root word for fame ("pheme")
[2477] Or quell, put down
[2478] Heady, rashly, etc.
[2479] To bring criminal charges, indict
[2480] Or lit., in-law
[2481] Lit., standings
[2482] Or together-twist, riot
[2483] Or disturbance

3 And **producing** three months; and when the Jews **upon-plane-counseled** for him, as he was-**impending** to sail into Syria, **it-became his opinion** to return through Macedonia.

4 Then together-followed him into Asia Sopater of Berea; and of the Thessalonians, Aristarchus and Secundus; and Gaius of Derbe, and **Timothy**; and of Asia, Tychicus and Trophimus.

5 These, going before, **remained-for** us at Troas.

6 And we **out-of-sailed** from Philippi after the days of **Unfermented** and came **to-them** to Troas in five days, where we **tarried**[2484] seven days.

7 Yet, in the first of the Sabbaths, when the disciples came together to break bread, Paul **through-said**[2485] **to-them, impending** to depart on the **tomorrow**; and **beside-stretch** his **saying** until midnight.

8 And there were **sufficient**[2486] lamps in the upper chamber, where they were gathered together.

9 Then was-sitting in a window a certain young man named Eutychus,[2487] being **down-bear** into a deep sleep: and as Paul was **much through-saying**,[2488] he-**being-down-bear from the** sleep, fell from the **third-roof,** and was **lifted** dead.

10 And Paul went down, and **upon-fell** him, and **embraced** said, **disturbance-wail** not yourselves; for his **soul** is in him.

11 When he therefore **up-walked**, and had broken bread, and eaten, and talked **sufficiently**[2489] even **until radiance**,[2490] so he departed.

12 And **they-lead** the young man alive and were not **measurable beside-called.**

13 And we **before-came into the** ship, and sailed **upon** Assos, there **impending to-up-take** Paul: for so had he **through-arranged, impending** himself **to-travel-by-foot.**

14 And when **he-together-cast**[2491] **to-us** at Assos, we **up-took him**, and came to Mitylene.

15 And we sailed **there and arrived**[2492] over against Chios; and the **another-different**, we **beside-cats** into Samos, and **remained** at Trogyllium; and **holding**, we came to Miletus.

16 For Paul had **judged** to sail by Ephesus, because he would not **uninterrupted-time-wear-rut-path** in Asia: for **he-was-speeding,** if it were **powerful** for him to-become **into** Jerusalem the day of Pentecost.

17 And from Miletus he **dispatched** to Ephesus and called the elders of the Church.

18 And when **they-beside-became towards** him, he said **to-them,** you **are-acquainted,**[2493] from the first day that I came into Asia, **how** I have been with you all **uninterrupted-time,**

19 Slaving **to-**the Lord with all **humility-disposition** and with many tears, and **probe-testing,** which **together-walked to-me in** the **upon-plan-counsel**[2494] of the Jews:

20 How I **under-stalled** nothing that **bear-together,** but have **up-message to-**you, and have taught you publicly, and **down** houses,

21 Through-witnessing both to the Jews, and also to the **Hellenics, to-change-mind into the** God, and faith **into the** Lord **of-us,** Jesus Christ.

22 And now, **be-perceiving,** I **travel** bound **to-the** Spirit **into** Jerusalem, not **perceiving** the things that shall **together-meet** me there:

23 Except that the Holy Spirit witness in every city, saying that bonds and **tribulations are-remaining for-me.**

24 But no **word produce** my **soul valuable to** myself, so that I might **mature** my **race** with **cheerfulness,** and the **attendance,** which I have **taken beside** the Lord Jesus, to **through-witness** the **well-message** of the grace of God.

25 And now, **be-perceiving, I-perceived** that you all, among whom I have **traveled** preaching the kingdom of God, shall see my face no more.

26 Through-which I-am-witnessing to-you this day, that I **clean** from the blood of all.

27 For I have not **under-stalled** to **up-message to-you** all the **plan-counsel** of God.

[2484] Greek: through-wear
[2485] Say thoroughly, discuss
[2486] Lit., to arrive; or, competent as if coming in season, ample in amount, fit in character
[2487] Good-happen
[2488] Say thoroughly, discuss
[2489] Lit., to arrive; or, competent as if coming in season, ample in amount, fit in character
[2490] Lit., a ray of light, to dawn
[2491] Or, combined, converse, consult
[2492] Or, meet-against
[2493] Greek: upon-stand, to put the mind upon, to be acquainted with, comprehend, be present
[2494] Or plots

28 **Towards-hold** therefore **to-yourselves,** and to all the **little-flock, in** the which the Holy Spirit has made you **bishops**[2495] to **shepherd** the Church of God, which he has **around-make**[2496] through his own blood.

29 For I **perceived** this, that after my **from-arrive**[2497] shall **weighty** wolves enter **into you,** not sparing[2498] the **little-flock.**

30 Also of yourselves shall men **up-stand,** speaking **through-turned**[2499] things, to **from-draw**[2500] disciples **behind** them.

31 Therefore **be-awake,** and remember, that three **years** I **paused** not to **thought-place each** one night and day with tears.

32 And now, **brothers, I-am-beside-placing**[2501] you to God, and to the **Word** of his grace, which is-**powerful** to **house-build** you, and to give you an inheritance **in** all them which are sanctified.

33 I have **upon-feel** no man's silver, or gold, or **garment.**

34 Yet, you yourselves know, that these hands have **subserved**[2502] **to** my **needs,**[2503] and **to-them** that were with me.

35 I have **under-**showed you all things, how that so **fatiguing** you **it-is-binding to-instead-take**[2504] the weak, and to remember the words of the Lord Jesus, how he said, it is **happy** to give **rather** than to **be-taking.**

36 And when he had spoken **these things,** he **placed the** knees, and prayed with them all.

37 Yet they-became sufficient[2505] **weepers** and fell on Paul's neck, and kissed him,

38 Being-pained most of all for the words which he spoke, that **impending** they see his face no more. And they **before-dispatch** him **into** the ship.

ACTS CHAPTER 21

1 And **it became,** that after we were **up-led** from them, and had **from-draw,** we came with **soon-race into** Coos, and the following in**to** Rhodes, and from there **into** Patara:

2 And finding a ship **ferrying**[2506] into Phenicia, we **upon-step,** and **were-up-lead.**

3 Now when we had **up-lighten** Cyprus **and leaving** it on the left, and sailed into Syria, and landed at Tyre: for there, the ship was to **unload** her **load.**

4 And finding disciples, we **remained** there seven days: who said to Paul through the Spirit, that he should not **up-walk into** Jerusalem.

5 And when we had **out-of-fresh** those days, we departed and **traveled and they-before-dispatched**, with wives and children, **until outside** of the city: and we **placed the knees upon** the **beach** and prayed.

6 And when **we-embraced one-another-same,** we **upon-step into the** ship; and they returned **into their privacy.**

7 And when we had **through-effect** from Tyre, we came to Ptolemais, and **embraced** the **brothers,** and **remained** with them one day.

8 Yet, the **upon-tomorrow** we that were **about** Paul's departed and came **into** Caesarea: and we entered into the house of Philip the evangelist,[2507] which was of the seven; and **remained** with him.

9 And the same man had four daughters, virgins, **prophetesses.**[2508]

10 And as we **remained** many days, there came down from Judaea a certain prophet, named Agabus.[2509]

11 And when he was come **toward us,** he **lifts** Paul's **belt,** and bound his own hands and feet, and said, **the-yet** says the **Holy Spirit,** so shall the Jews at Jerusalem bind the man that owns this **belt** and shall **betray**[2510] into the hands of the **nations.**

[2495] Greek: "episkopos" (upon-peer-about, upon watch, upon-goal, upon-mark), bishop, visitation, to visit, oversee, oversight, upon-skeptic
[2496] Greek: peri (around) and poieo (make, produce), means to purchase, acquire
[2497] Properly" arrival, to go forth
[2498] Or, not treating leniently
[2499] perverse
[2500] Or, from-pulling
[2501] Or deposit
[2502] Lit., under-oarsman, generally a subordinate
[2503] Or employment
[2504] Or help, support
[2505] Lit., to arrive; or, competent as if coming in season, ample in amount, fit in character
[2506] Lit., to through-cross (pierce)
[2507] Or., lit., good-angel
[2508] "Propheteou:" nominative, plural feminine of "prophetes" ("prophet")
[2509] Lit., Locust (Hebrew)
[2510] Beside-give

12 And when we heard these things, both we, and they of that place, **beside-called** him not to **up-walk into** Jerusalem.

13 Then Paul answered, what **are-you-producing** to weep and **together-crush my heart? Because** I am **internally-prepared** not to be bound only, but also to die at Jerusalem **over** the name of the Lord Jesus.

14 And when he would not be persuaded, **we-were-silent,** saying, the will of the Lord **be-becoming**.

15 And after those days we **up-stepped** our **baggage,**[2511] and **up-walked into** Jerusalem.

16 There went with us also of the disciples of Caesarea, and brought with them one Mnason[2512] of Cyprus, an **original** disciple, with whom we should **foreign-lodge.**

17 And when we were **meet-against**[2513] to Jerusalem, the **brothers** welcomed us **with-pleasure**.

18 And the **upon-being**,[2514] Paul went in with us **to** James; and all the elders were **beside-became**.

19 And when he had **exegesis**[2515] **down each** what things God **produced in** the **nations** by his **attendance**.

20 And when they heard, they glorified the Lord, and said **to-him,** you see, brother, how many thousands of Jews there are which believe; and they all **under-originating zealots** of the law:

21 And they are **catechized** of you, that you teach all the Jews which are among the **nations** to **divorce**[2516] Moses, saying not to circumcise **the** children, neither to walk **to-the ethics**.

22 What is it, therefore? **Entirely, it-is-binding** the **fullness** come together: for they will hear that you are come.

23 Produce therefore this that we say **to-you**: we have four men which have a **prayer** on them;

24 Them **beside-take**, and **clean** yourself with them, and **expense** with them, that they may shave heads: and all may know that those things, whereof they were **catechized about** you, are nothing; but you yourself also **element-walk**,[2517] and keep the law.

25 Yet, **about** the **nations** which believe, we have written **judging** that they **guard** themselves from **idol-sacrifice**, and from **the** blood, and from strangled, and from **prostitution**.

26 Then Paul **beside-take** the men, and the next day **cleaning** himself with them entered into the **priest-place**, to **through-message** the **out-of-filling** of the days of **cleaning**, until that an offering should be offered for every one of them.

27 And when the seven days were **impending to-together-finished**, the Jews which were of Asia, when they saw him in the **priest-place**, **together-poured**,[2518] all the **multitude**, and **upon-cast** hands on him,

28 Screaming, men of Israel, **distress-help**: this is the man, that teach all, **universally,** against the people, and the law, and this **spot**: and further brought **Hellenics** also into the **priest-place** and has **common** this holy **spot**.

29 (For they had seen before with him in the city Trophimus,[2519] an Ephesian, whom they **do-by-law** that Paul had brought into the **priest-place**.)

30 And all the city was **stirred**, and the people ran together: and they **upon-take** Paul, and **out-of-induced**[2520] him out of the **priest-place**: and soon **locked** the doors.

31 And as they **seeking** to kill him, **report up-walked to** the **thousand-first-rank** of the **mass-of-men**,[2521] that all Jerusalem was **together-poured**.[2522]

32 Who **out-of-self beside-take** soldiers and centurions and ran down **upon** them: and when they **perceived** the **thousand-first-rank** and the soldiers, they **paused thumping** Paul.

33 Then the **thousand-first-rank near-squeeze,** and **upon-take** him, and **ordered** to be bound with two chains; and **ascertain-by-inquiry** who he was, and what he had done.

[2511] Or from-vessels
[2512] Mnason is defined as "reminded"
[2513] Greek: "katantao," down-opposite, down-instead, down-anti
[2514] Or supervening
[2515] Exegesis is transliterated from "exegeomai," to lead out-of, to unfold
[2516] Lit., "apostasies:" from-stand; feminine of "apostasion" (divorce); a thing that separates. See 2 Thessalonians 2:3 ("falling away")
[2517] Gk.: stoicheo, to march in rank (keep step), from same root for "element"
[2518] Greek compound: sun (together) and cheo (pour), to pour together, to comingle promiscuously, throw into disorder, perplex the mind
[2519] Nutritive, nourishment
[2520] Or dragged out of
[2521] Greek: "speira," transliterated "spire" meaning to coil, figuratively a mass of roman military cohort, or a squad of Levitical janitors
[2522] Greek compound: sun (together) and cheo (pour), to pour together, to comingle promiscuously, throw into disorder, perplex the mind

34 And **other-same** cried one thing, some **another-same,** among the multitude: and when he **not yet is-powerful to-know** the certainty²⁵²³ for the **uproar,**²⁵²⁴ he **ordered** him to be carried into the **barracks.**²⁵²⁵

35 And when he came upon the stairs, **together thrown,** that he was **lifted** of the soldiers for the violence of the **multitude.**

36 For the **fullness** of the people followed after, **screaming, lift** him!

37 Impending Paul to be led into the **barracks,** he said **to-the thousand-first-rank, it-is-lawful** I speak **to-you?** Who said, **the yet, showing you-are-knowing** Hellenics?

38 Are not you that Egyptian, which before these days made an **up-standing,**²⁵²⁶ and led out into the **lonesome** four thousand men that were **dagger-men?**²⁵²⁷

39 But Paul said, I am a man a Jew of Tarsus, in Cilicia, a citizen of no **un-signed** city; and I **beg-bind** you, **permit** me to speak **towards** the people.

40 And when he **permitted** him, Paul stood on the stairs, and **gestured** with the hand **to-the** people. And when there was made a **much** silence, he **toward-sound** in the Hebrew **dialect,** saying,

ACTS CHAPTER 22

1 Men, **brothers,** and fathers, hear you my **apology**²⁵²⁸ now **towards** you.

2 (And when they heard that he spoke in the Hebrew **dialect** to them, they kept the more silence: and he **showed,**

3 I am **indeed** a man a Jew, born in Tarsus, in Cilicia, yet brought up in this city at the feet of Gamaliel, **boy-trained down exactness** of the law of the fathers, and **under-originating zealot of-the** God, **down-as** you all are this day.

4 And I **chased** this, **the** Way, **until** death, binding and **beside-giving** into prisons both men and women.

5 As also the **first-rank-priest** does bear me witness, and all the elders: from whom also I **welcomed** letters **towards** the **brothers,** and went to Damascus, to bring them which were there bound **into** Jerusalem, for to be **value-guarded.**²⁵²⁹

6 And **it became,** that, as I **traveled,** and was come **near-squeeze to** Damascus about noon, suddenly, **out-of** heaven **about-star-fall-light,**²⁵³⁰ **Light, sufficient,**²⁵³¹ about me.

7 And I fell **into** the **bottom,** and heard a voice saying **to-me,** Saul, Saul, why me you **chase**?

8 And I answered, who are you, Lord? And he said **towards** me, I am Jesus the **Nazarene,** whom you **are-chasing.**

9 And they that were with me saw indeed the Light and **became in-fear**; but they heard not the voice of him that spoke to me.

10 And I said, what shall I do, Lord? And the Lord said **towards** me, **up-stand,** and go into Damascus; and there it shall be told you **about** all things which are **arranged** for you to do.

11 And when I could not see for the glory of that light, being led by the hand of them that were with me, I came into Damascus.

12 And one Ananias, a **well-taker** man **down** the law, having a **witness under** all the Jews which **down-housed,**

13 Came **towards** me, and **upon-stood,** and said **towards** me, brother Saul, **up-look.** And the same hour I **up-looked into him**.

14 And he said, the God of our fathers has **before-hand** you, that you should know his will, and **perceive** that **Righteous-One,** and should hear the voice of his mouth.

15 For you shall be his witness **towards** all men of what you have seen and heard.

16 And now why **you-impending? Up-stand,** and be baptized, and wash away your sins, **upon-calling**²⁵³² the name of the Lord.

17 And **it became,** that, when I **under-turned into** Jerusalem, even while I prayed in the **priest-place,** I was in **ecstasy;**²⁵³³

---

²⁵²³ Lit., to be un-failing
²⁵²⁴ Or disturbance
²⁵²⁵ Or camp
²⁵²⁶ Or, to drive out of one's home
²⁵²⁷ Or assassins
²⁵²⁸ Compound of "apo" (from) and logo (word, saying), also means defense
²⁵²⁹ Or lit., to protect one's honor
²⁵³⁰ Or about-lightning
²⁵³¹ Lit., to arrive; or, competent as if coming in season, ample in amount, fit in character
²⁵³² Or, to entitle, to invoke
²⁵³³ Greek: "ekstasis," transliterated as "ecstasy," out-of-stand, displacement of the mind, strong feelings (good or bad) that absorbs the

18 And **perceived** him saying **to-me, speed,** and **take** you quickly out of Jerusalem: for they will not **beside-welcome** your **witness** about me.

19 And I said, Lord, they **acquainted**[2534] that I imprisoned and **skinning** in every synagogue them that believed **upon you:**

20 And when the blood of your **witness** Stephen was **out-poured,** I also was **upon-standing,** and **together-good-seem** to his **up-lift,**[2535] and kept the **garment** of them that **up-lifted** him.

21 And he said **towards** me, depart: for I will **out-of-send** you far **into** the **nations.**

22 And they gave him **hearing until** this word, and **upon-lifted** their voices, and said, **lift** such a from the earth; for it is not **down-reached**[2536] that he should live.

23 And as they **screamed,** and **throw garments,** and **casting** dust into the air,

24 The **thousand-first-rank ordered** him to be brought into the **barracks,**[2537] and **said** that he should be **up-examined**[2538] by **whipping**; that he might know **through which cause** they **upon-sound to-him.**

25 And as they **before-stretched** him with **straps,** Paul said **towards** the centurion that stood by, is it lawful for you to **whip** a man that is a Roman, and **un-down-judged?**

26 When the centurion heard, he went and told the **thousand-first-rank,** saying, **see** what **you–are-impending to-do:** for this man is a Roman.

27 Then the **thousand-first-rank** came, and said **to-him,** tell me, are you a Roman? He **showed,**[2539] yes.

28 And the **thousand-first-rank** answered, with a **much** sum **acquired** I this **citizenship.** And Paul **showed,** but I was born.

29 Then **soon** they **divorce**[2540] from him **the ones-impending to-be-up-examining** him: and the **thousand-first-rank** also was afraid, after he **upon-knew** that he was a Roman, and because he had bound him.

30 Yet, **to-the tomorrow, plan-counseling to-know the** certainty[2541] **why** he was accused **beside** the Jews, he loosed him from **the** bands, and **ordered** the **first-rank-priests** and all their **Sanhedrin** to **come** and brought Paul down and **stand** him **into** them.

ACTS CHAPTER 23

1 And Paul, **look-stretching to-**the Sanhedrin, said, men, **brothers,** I have **citizen to-all** good conscience **to-the** God until this day.

2 And the **first-rank-priest** Ananias commanded them that **beside-stood** him to **thump** him on the mouth.

3 Then said Paul **towards him,** God **impending to-be-thumping** you, you **lime-whitewashed** wall: and you sit to judge me **down** the law, and **ordering** me to be **thumped beside-law?**[2542]

4 And they that **beside-stood** said, you **spear-abuse** God's **first-rank-priest?**

5 Then **showed** Paul, I **perceived** not, **brothers,** that he was the **first-rank-priest:** for it is written, you shall not speak evil of the **first-rank**[2543] of your people.

6 But when Paul **knew** that the one **section** were Sadducees, and the other-**different** Pharisees, he **screamed** in the **Sanhedrin,** men, **brothers,** I am a Pharisee, the son of a Pharisee: **about** he **expectation** and resurrection of the dead I **am-being-judged**

7 And when he had so said, there arose an **insurrection**[2544] between the Pharisees and the Sadducees: and the **fullness** was **split.**

8 Because the Sadducees say that there is no resurrection, neither angel, nor spirit: but the Pharisees **same-say** both.

9 And there **became** a **great scream**: and the scribes **of-the section of-the** Pharisees' **up-stand,** and **through-fight,** saying, we find no evil in this man: but if a spirit or an angel has spoken **to-him,** let us not **be-God-fighters**.

10 Yet becoming of-much insurrection,[2545] the **thousand-first-rank, feared, lest** Paul should **be-**

[2534] Greek: upon-stand, to put the mind upon, to be acquainted with, comprehend, be present
[2535] Or lit., assassination
[2536] Or befitting
[2537] Or camp
[2538] Investigated, interrogated
[2539] Greek: "phemi," the root word for fame ("pheme")
[2540] Lit., "aphistemi" from-stand, the root word for "apostasies:" feminine of "apostasion" (divorce); a thing that separates.
[2541] Un-fail
[2542] Beside-law can be translated as transgressing
[2543] Or, original-rank, beginning-rank
[2544] Lit., standings
[2545] Lit., standings

through-torn under them, ordered the soldiers down-walk, to snatch him out-of middle of-them, and to lead into the barracks.[2546]

11 And the night upon-being, the Lord stood by him, and said, be daring,[2547] Paul: because as you through-witnessed about me in Jerusalem, so it-is-binding you to witness also at Rome.

12 Yet, when it became day, certain of-the Jews doing together-twist, anathematize,[2548] saying that they would neither eat nor drink until they had killed Paul.

13 And they were more than forty which had made this together-swear.

14 And they toward-came to-the first-rank-priests and elders, and said, we have we-anathematize to anathema, that we will taste nothing until we have slain Paul.

15 Now therefore you with the Sanhedrin emphasize[2549] to the thousand-first-rank that he bring him down to-you tomorrow, as though you impending to-through-know something more-exactly about him: and we, before he near-squeeze, are prepared-internally to up-lift[2550] him.

16 And when Paul's sister's son heard of their ambush,[2551] he went and entered into the barracks, and from-message to-the Paul.

17 Then Paul toward-called one of the centurions to-him, and showed,[2552] bring this young man towards the thousand-first-rank: for he has a certain-thing to from-message to-him.

18 So he beside-take him, and brought to the thousand-first-rank, and showed, Paul, the prisoner, called me to-him, and asked me to bring this young man towards you, who has something to say to-you.

19 Then the thousand-first-rank upon-taking him by the hand, and up-spaced privately, and ascertain-by-inquiry, What is that you has to from-message to-me?

20 And he said, the Jews have agreed[2553] to ask you that you would bring down Paul tomorrow into the Sanhedrin, as though they are-impending to-ascertain-by-inquiry something about him more-exactly.

21 Then, not you be-persuaded to-them: for they-lurk-ambush for him, of them more than forty men, which have bound themselves with anathematize, that they will neither eat nor drink until they have up-lift[2554] him: and now are they internally-prepared, towards-welcome a promise from you.

22 So the thousand-first-rank from-loose the young man, and beside-messaged-him, tell no man that you have emphasized[2555] these things toward me.

23 And he called to-him two centurions, saying, internally-prepared two hundred soldiers to go to Caesarea, and horsemen seventy, and spearmen[2556] two hundred, from the third hour of the night;

24 And beside-stand animals,[2557] that they may upon-step[2558] Paul, to-through-save towards Felix, the leader.

25 And he wrote a letter about-holding this type:[2559]

26 Claudius Lysias to-the governing leader, Felix, be-cheerful.

27 This man was together-taken of the Jews and impending to-be-up-lifted[2560] under them: then came I with an army, and out-of-lifted him, having learned that he was a Roman.

28 And when I-planned-counseled to-known the cause through which they in-called him, I down-lead him into their Sanhedrin:

29 Whom I found to be in-called of questions of their law, but to have nothing in-called deserving of death or of bonds.

30 Then it-was-disclosed to-me the Jews impending upon-plan-counseled[2561] into the man, I dispatched out-of-same to-you, and beside-message to his accusers also to say upon you what they towards him. Strength!

[2546] Or camp
[2547] Or, courageous
[2548] A religious ban or excommunication
[2549] Greek: "emphanizo" – "emphasize"
[2550] Or lit., assassinate
[2551] In-sitting (waiting), in-settled
[2552] Greek: "phemi," the root word for the Greek word transliterated as fame ("pheme")
[2553] Or together-placed
[2554] Or lit., assassinate
[2555] Greek: "emphanizo" also transliterated as "emphasize"
[2556] Lit., right-getters, slingers, spearman as if taking the right
[2557] Or, stand-beside the animals
[2558] Or, to mount
[2559] A die as struck, thump-impression
[2560] Or lit., assassinate
[2561] Or, to plot

31 Then the soldiers, **down through-arranged** them, **up-took** Paul, and brought by night to Antipatris.[2562]

32 On the **tomorrow** they **let-be** the horsemen to **from-go** with him, and **under-turned** to the **camp**:

33 Who, when they came to Caesarea, and **up-gave** the epistle to the **leader**, **beside-stood** Paul also before him.

34 And when the **leader** had read, he asked of what province[2563] he was. And when he **ascertain-by-inquiry** that of Cilicia;

35 I will **through-hear** you, **he-showed**,[2564] whenever your accusers also come. And he **ordered** him to be kept in Herod's **Praetorium**.[2565]

ACTS CHAPTER 24

1 And after five days Ananias the **first-rank-priest** descended with the elders, and a certain orator Tertullus, who **emphasize**[2566] **to-the leader downing** Paul.

2 And when he was called, Tertullus began to accuse, saying, seeing that by you we **happenings**[2567] **peace**, and that **down-erect-things**[2568] **becoming to** this nation **through** your **before-mind**,

3 We **from-welcome** always, and **universally**, **governing** Felix, with all thankfulness.

4 Notwithstanding, that **not upon** further **in-cut** you, I **beside-called** you that you would hear us **briefly upon-fairly-resemble.**

5 For we have found this man, pestilent,[2569] and a **stirrer** of insurrection[2570] among all the Jews throughout the **housed-land**, and a **protestor**[2571] of the sect of the Nazarenes:

6 Who also has gone about to profane[2572] the **priest-place**: whom also we **governed** and would have judged **down** our law.

7 But the **thousand-first-rank** Lysias came, and with **much** violence **from-led** out of our hands,

8 **Ordering** his accusers to come **upon** you: of whom yourself, by **up-judging, shall-be-powerful to-know about** all these things, **of-which we-are-accusing** him.

9 And the Jews also **agreed**, **asserting** that these things were so.

10 Then Paul, after that the **leader** had **nodded to-him** to speak, answered, **I-am-acquainted**[2573] that you have been of many **years** a judge **to** this nation, I do the more **good-feeling answering**[2574] **about** myself

11 Because that you **are-powerful to-know**, that there are **more to-me** twelve days since I-**up-walked in** Jerusalem to worship.

12 And **they neither found me in the priest-place through-saying**[2575] with any man, neither **upon-together-standing, making of-multitude**, neither in the synagogues, nor in the city:

13 Neither **they-are-powerful to-beside-stand** the things **about which** they now accuse me.

14 But this I **same-saying to-you,** that after the **Way** which they call heresy, so **I-am-hired-service to-the** God of my fathers, believing all things which are written in the law and in the prophets:

15 And have **expectation into the** God, which they themselves also **towards-receive**, that **is-impending** a resurrection of the dead, both of the **righteous** and **unrighteous**.

16 And **in this** do I exercise myself, to have **through-all** a conscience **un-toward-strike** toward God, and men.

17 Now after many **years I-beside-became** to bring **pity-mercy** to my nation, and offerings.

18 **In which** certain Jews from Asia found me **clean in** the **priest-place**, neither with multitude, nor with **uproar.**[2576]

19 Who **it-was-binding upon you to-be-present,** and **accusing,** if they had **anything towards** me.

[2562] Anti-father
[2563] Lit., "eparch" (Greek compound—upon-first-rank); governor of a district, Roman praefecture
[2564] Greek: "phemi," the root word for the Greek word transliterated as fame ("pheme")
[2565] Or governor's courtroom
[2566] Greek: "emphanizo"— "emphasize"
[2567] Or, hit the mark, chance upon, obtain,
[2568] Or reforms
[2569] Greek: "loimos," a plague, disease, a pest
[2570] Lit., standings
[2571] Protestor is transliterated from the Greek word "protostates" (before-stand)
[2572] The roof for this word is "threshold"
[2573] Greek: upon-stand, to put the mind upon, to be acquainted with, comprehend, be present
[2574] Greek: "apologeomai" (from-saying) to exculpate (self), to give account, to defend
[2575] Say thoroughly, discuss
[2576] Or disturbance

20 Or else let these **same-say,** if they have found any **unrighteousness** in me, while I stood before the **Sanhedrin,**

21 Except it be **about** this **first** voice, that I **screamed** standing among them, **about** the resurrection of the dead **I-am-being-judged** by you **today.**

22 And when Felix heard these things, having **more-exact perception of-the-things about the Way,** he said, when Lysias the **thousand-first-rank** shall come down, I will **through-know the-things down** you.

23 And he **through-arranged** a centurion to keep Paul, and **relax,**[2577] and that he should **prevent** none of his **private to-be-subservient**[2578] or **towards-come to-him.**

24 And after certain days, when Felix **beside-became** with his wife Drusilla, which was a Jewess, he sent for Paul, and heard him **about** the faith in Christ.

25 Yet he **is-through-saying**[2579] of **righteous-togetherness, in-governance,** and **judgment-result**[2580] **impending,** Felix trembled, and answered, for now, **travel;** when I have a season, **I-shall-change-call**[2581] you.

26 He **expected** also that money should have been given him of Paul, that he might loose him: **through-which** he **changed-dispatched** for him often, and **same-company** with him.

27 Yet, two **years being-filled,** Porcius Festus[2582] **took successor,**[2583] the Felix: and Felix, willing to **down-place** the Jews a **grace,** left Paul bound.

ACTS CHAPTER 25

1 Now when Festus was come into the province,[2584] after three days he **up-walked** from Caesarea to Jerusalem.

2 Yet, **emphasize**[2585] **to-him** the **first-rank-priest** and the **foremost-ones** of the Jews **downing of-the** Paul, and **beside-called** him,

3 And **asked** favor **down** him, that he would **change-dispatch** him **into** Jerusalem, **doing ambush,**[2586] in the way to **up-lift**[2587] him.

4 But Festus answered that Paul should be **guarded** at Caesarea, and that he himself **impending out-passaging, swiftly.**

5 The-ones powerful in you, he-is-showing,[2588] together-down-step-me[2589] and let-them-be-accusing this man, if there be anything un-placed[2590] in him.

6 And when he had **through-rut-path**[2591] in them more than ten days, he **down-stepped to** Caesarea; and **upon-tomorrow** sitting on the **judgment-step,**[2592] commanded Paul to be brought.

7 And when he **beside-became,** the Jews which came down from Jerusalem stood about, and **bear** many and **weighty causes downing** Paul, which they could not **from-show.**[2593]

8 While he **answered**[2594] **of-himself, that** neither **into** the law of the Jews, neither **into** the **priest-place,** nor yet **into** Caesar, anything I-**sinned.**

9 But Festus, willing to **down-place grace to**-the Jews, answered Paul, and said, **will** you **up-walk into** Jerusalem, and there be judged of these things before me?

10 Then said Paul, I stand at Caesar's **judgment-step,**[2595] where **me it-is-binding to-be-judged:** to the Jews **nothing I-am-unrighteous,** as you **more-ideally upon-know.**

11 Because, if **I-am-unrighteous,** or have practiced anything **deserving** of death, I refuse[2596] not to die: but if there be none of these things **of-which** these accuse

---

[2577] Greek: up-send, up-let, ease, to let up, relax
[2578] Lit., under-oarsman, generally a subordinate
[2579] Say thoroughly, discuss
[2580] Greek: "krima," transliterated as "crime" and also means judgment
[2581] Or, to call elsewhere
[2582] Defined as festival
[2583] Greek: Get through-receive (get succession)
[2584] Lit., "eparch" (Greek compound—upon-first-rank); governor of a district, Roman praefecture
[2585] Greek: "emphanizo" also transliterated as "emphasize"
[2586] In-sitting (waiting), in-settled
[2587] Or lit., assassinate

[2588] Greek: "phemi," the root word for the Greek word transliterated as fame ("pheme")
[2589] Or, to go down with
[2590] Or to be out of place
[2591] Greek: through-wear
[2592] Greek: "Bema," a step, foot-breadth, rostrum, tribunal
[2593] O, demonstrate
[2594] Greek: "apologeomai" (from-saying) to exculpate (self), to give account, to defend
[2595] Greek: "Bema," a step, foot-breadth, rostrum, tribunal
[2596] Lit., beside-ask, to beg off, shun, refuse

me, **no-one is-powerful to-grace**[2597] me **to-them.** I **upon-called**[2598] Caesar.

12 Then Festus, when he had **together-talked** with the **together-plan-council,** answered, have you **upon-called**[2599] Caesar? **On** Caesar shall **you-travel.**

13 And after certain days king Agrippa and Bernice **meet-against**[2600] **into** Caesarea **to-embrace, the** Festus.

14 And when **they-tarried**[2601] there many days, Festus **up-placed** Paul's **down to** the king, saying, there is a certain man **down-left** in bonds by Felix:

15 About whom, when I was at Jerusalem, the **first-rank-priests** and the elders of the Jews **emphasized**[2602] **asking down-justice downing** him.

16 To whom I answered; it is not the **ethics** of the Romans to **grace** any man **into from-ruin,** before that he which is accused have the accusers face to face, and have **spot** to answer for himself **about** the **in-calling taken about** him.

17 Therefore, when they **together-came in-place, not placing** delay[2603] **to-the next,** I sat on the **judgment-step,**[2604] and **ordered** the man to be brought.

18 About whom when the accusers stood up, they **upon-bear no cause** of such things as I **under-minded:**

19 But had certain questions **towards** him of their **private dreading-demon,**[2605] and **about certain** Jesus, **who died,** whom Paul **asserts** to be alive.

20 And because I **have-no-way-out about these** questions, I **said if he-be-plan-counseled to-travel into** Jerusalem, and there be judged **about** these.

21 But when Paul had **upon-called**[2606] **to-be-guarded to** the **through-knowing of-the Venerable,**[2607] I **ordered** him to be kept **until** I might **dispatch** him to Caesar.

22 Then Agrippa **showed**[2608] **towards** Festus, I would also hear the man myself. Tomorrow, **he-showed,** you shall hear **of-him.**

23 Then, on the tomorrow, when Agrippa was come, and Bernice, with **much fantasy,**[2609] and was entered into the **hearing-place,** with the **thousand-first-ranks,** and **prominent**[2610] men of the city, at Festus' order Paul was brought.

24 And Festus **showed,** King Agrippa, and all men which are here present with us, you **theatre-spectator** this man, about whom all the **fullness** of the Jews have **in-happenings**[2611] with me, both at Jerusalem, and here, **distress-crying** that not **it-is-binding,** him, **to-be-living not-still.**

25 But when I **down-taken nothing** that he had **practiced deserving** of death, and that he himself has **upon-called**[2612] the **Venerable,**[2613] I have **judged** to **dispatch** him.

26 About whom I have **nothing certain**[2614] to write to-my lord. **Through-which** I have brought him **upon** you, and especially **upon** you, king Agrippa, that, after **up-judging,** I might have **something** to write.

27 For it seems to me **un-logical** to **dispatch** a prisoner, and not **to-sign** the **causes downing** him.

ACTS CHAPTER 26

1 Then Agrippa **showed towards** Paul, you are permitted to speak for yourself. Then Paul **out-of-stretched** the hand, and **answered**[2615] for himself:

2 I **lead** myself happy, king Agrippa, because **I-am-impending to-answer** for myself this day before you **about** all the things **of-which** I am **in-called** of the Jews:

3 Especially, **having-perceived** you to be a **knowing-one** in all **ethics** and questions which are among the Jews: **through-which I-am-beg-binding of-you long-sacrifice-anger** to hear me.

[2597] See Acts 25:9, Paul must have perceived Festus intention
[2598] Or, to entitle, to invoke
[2599] Or, to entitle, to invoke
[2600] Greek: "katantao," down-opposite, down-instead, down-anti
[2601] Greek: through-wear
[2602] Greek: "emphanizo" also transliterated as "emphasize"
[2603] Greek: up-cast, putting off
[2604] Greek: "Bema," a step, foot-breadth, rostrum, tribunal
[2605] Or, timid-of-demons, superstitions
[2606] Or, to entitle, to invoke
[2607] The Greek in all manuscripts reads: "Venerable," in this verse; and is understood to be Caesar Augustus
[2608] Greek: "phemi," the root word for the Greek word transliterated as fame ("pheme")
[2609] Greek: "phantasia," transliterated as fantasy, vain-show, vain-light, vain-appearance
[2610] Greek: out-stand, to stand out, prominence
[2611] Or in-obtain. in-to hit the target, in-chance upon
[2612] Or, to entitle, to invoke
[2613] The Greek in all manuscripts reads: "Venerable," in this verse; and is understood to be Caesar Augustus
[2614] Greek: "asphales," transliterated as "un-failing,"
[2615] Greek: "apologeomai" (from-saying)

Acts

4 My **livelihood out-of** my youth, which was **from the original in** my nation **in** Jerusalem, **acquainted**[2616] all the Jews;

5 Which **before-knew** me **from-above**,[2617] if **they-willing to-be-witnessing**, that **down** the **most-exact** sect of our religion[2618] I lived a Pharisee.

6 And now I stand and am judged for the **expectation** of the promise **becoming** of God **into** our fathers:

7 Into which our twelve tribes, **out-stretched a-hired-servant**, day, and night, **expect** to **meet-against**[2619]. For which **expectation**, king Agrippa, I am **in-called** of the Jews.

8 Why should it be **unbelieving beside** you, **if** God **is-raising** the dead?

9 I **indeed seem to-myself**, that **it-is-binding to-practice** many things contrary[2620] **towards** the name of Jesus of Nazareth.

10 Which thing I also did in Jerusalem: and many of the saints did I **down-lock** in prison, **taking** authority from the **first-rank-priests**; and when they were **up-lifted**,[2621] besides, I gave my **pebble-vote-count**.

11 And I **value-guarded**[2622] them **many** in every synagogue and **necessitated** to blaspheme; and being **excessively in-maniac**[2623] against them, I **chased** even **into outside** cities.

12 In which, also traveled **into** Damascus with authority and **permission** from the **first-rank-priests**,

13 At midday, king, I **perceived** in the way a light **from-heaven**, **over** the brightness of the sun, shining round about me and them which **traveled** with me.

14 Yet, all of-us **down-falling** to the earth, I heard a voice speaking **towards** me, and saying in the Hebrew **dialect**, Saul, Saul, why **are-you chasing** me? Hard for you to kick **towards** the **piercers**.[2624]

15 And I said, who are you, Lord? And he said, I am Jesus whom you **are-chasing**.

16 But **up-stand** and **be-standing** upon your feet: for I **was-seen to-you into** this **before-handed**,[2625] to make you a **subservient**[2626] and a witness both of these things which you have **perceived**, and of those things in the which I will **view to**-you.

17 Out-lifting you **out-of** the people, and **of**-the **nations**, **to** whom now **I-am-sending** you,

18 To open their eyes, **the upon-turning** from darkness **into** light, and the **authority** of Satan **upon the** God, that they may **take release**[2627] of sins, and inheritance among them which are sanctified by faith that is **into** me.

19 Which, king Agrippa, I was not **un-pursuable to-the** heavenly vision:

20 But **I-from-messaged foremost to-them** of Damascus, and at Jerusalem, and throughout all the **space** of Judaea, and to the **nations**, that they should **change-thinking** and **upon-turn** to God and **practice** works **deserving** for **change-thinking**.

21 On-account of-these, the Jews **together-took** me in the **priest-place**, **they-probe-tested**[2628] to **through-handle**.[2629]

22 Having therefore **happening**[2630] **upon-girl-assistant beside** the God, I continue **until** this day, witnessing both to small and **great**, saying **nothing outside** than those which the prophets and Moses did say **impending to-be-becoming**:

23 That Christ should **emotion**, that he should be the **foremost out-of** resurrection **of-dead**, **impending to-down-message** light **to-the** people, and to the **nations**.

24 Yet, he-**answering**[2631] these-things, Festus **showed**[2632] with a **great** voice, Paul, you are **around-turn**;[2633] much learning does make you **maniac**.[2634]

25 But he **showed**, I am not **maniac** Governor Festus; but of truth and **safe-disposition** declarations **I-from-sounded**.

[2616] Greek: "isemi," to know, acquainted with, perceive
[2617] Or, on the top, upward, up-place
[2618] Ceremonial observances
[2619] Greek: "katantao," down-opposite, down-instead,
[2620] Greek compound: in-anti, in front of, opposite, antagonistic
[2621] Or lit., assassinate
[2622] Or lit., to protect one's honor
[2623] Or in-raving mad, in-divination madness
[2624] Greek: "kentron," transliterated as "center;" piercer, point, prick, sting
[2625] Or, pre-handled, to handle for oneself in advance
[2626] Lit., under-oarsman, generally a subordinate
[2627] Lit., from-let-go
[2628] Or, attempted
[2629] Or, to violently lay hands on, to kill
[2630] Or, hit the mark, chance upon, obtain,
[2631] Greek: "apologeomai" (from-saying) to exculpate (self), to give account, to defend
[2632] Greek: "phemi," the root word for fame ("pheme")
[2633] Or, crazed, deranged
[2634] Or, raving mad, divination maniac, divining mad

26 For the king **is-acquainted**[2635] about these things, before whom also I speak **all-out-spoken**: for I am persuaded that none of these things are hidden from him, **because this-thing** was not **practiced** in a corner.

27 King Agrippa, believe you the prophets? I **perceived** that **you–are-believing.**

28 Then Agrippa **showed towards** Paul, **in few you-are-persuading** me to **become** Christian.[2636]

29 And Paul said, I **pray** to God, that not only you, but also all that hear me this day, were both **in few**, and **in much** such as I am, **beside-exterior** these bonds.

30 And when he had spoken **these-things**, the king **up-stand**, and the **leader**, and Bernice,[2637] and they that sat with them:

31 And when they were **up-spaced**, they talked **toward one-another**, saying, this man **practices** nothing **deserving** of death or of bonds.

32 Then **showed** Agrippa **to** Festus, this man **may-be-powerful to-from-loosed**, if he had not **upon-called**[2638] Caesar.

ACTS CHAPTER 27

1 And when it was **judged** that we should sail into Italy, they **beside-gave** Paul and certain other-**different** prisoners **to** , a centurion named Julius of **Venerated**[2639] **mass-of-men**.[2640]

2 And entering into a ship of Adramyttium, we launched, **impending to-sail down** the coasts of Asia; Aristarchus,[2641] a Macedonian of Thessalonica, being with us.

3 And the **beside another-different** we **down-led into** Sidon. And Julius **apprised**[2642] Paul, and **permitted him** to **travel towards** his friends, of-**on-care to-be-happening**.[2643].

4 And when we **up-led** from there, we sailed under Cyprus, because the winds were contrary.[2644]

5 And when we had sailed over the **deep-sea** of Cilicia and Pamphylia, we came to Myra, of Lycia.

6 And there the centurion found a ship of Alexandria sailing into Italy; and he **in-mount** us **into it**.

7 And when we had sailed slowly, **sufficient**[2645] days, and **difficultly becoming down** Cnidus, the wind **not towards-letting-be** us, we sailed under Crete, **down** Salmone;

8 And, **difficultly** passing it, came **into** a **spot** which is called the **Ideal Harbors; near-squeeze to-which** the city Lasea.

9 Now when **sufficient uninterrupted-time through-becoming**, and when sailing was now **hazardous**,[2646] because the fast already past, Paul **beside-praise**,

10 And said **to-them, men**, I **see** that **impending** this voyage with **insult** and much damage, not only of the **load** and ship, but also of our **souls.**

11 Nevertheless the centurion believed the **pilot** and the **boat-heir**, more than those things which were spoken **under** Paul.

12 And because the **harbor** was not **un-immediate**[2647] **under-originating towards beside-wintering,** the **majority placed plan-counseled** to **depart** there also, if **somehow**, **they-are-powerful to-meet-against**[2648] **in**to Phenice, to **beside**-winter; a **harbor** of Crete, and **looking** toward the south-west and north-west.

13 And when the south wind blew softly, **seeming** that they had **governed purpose,**[2649] **lifting**, they sailed close by Crete.

14 But not much **after-change**, there **cast down from**-it a **smoky-stormy** wind, being-called Euroclydon.[2650]

15 And when the ship was **together-snatched**, and **not is-powerful** to-**anti-face to-the** wind, we-**upon-give to-be-carried**.

16 And running under a certain island which is called Clauda, we had **difficult force** to **about-govern to-be-becoming of-the skiff**:[2651]

[2635] Greek: upon-stand, to put the mind upon, to be acquainted with, comprehend, be present
[2636] Anointed ("Christ")-related ("ian"), Christ-related
[2637] Bearer of conquest
[2638] Or, to entitle, to invoke
[2639] Caesar Augustus
[2640] Greek: "speira, transliterated "spire" meaning to coil, figuratively a mass of roman military cohort, or a squad of Levitical janitors
[2641] Dinner-first-rank, best-first-rank, best-ruling
[2642] Or, to inform, to tell, to furnish what is needed
[2643] Or, hit the mark, chance upon, obtain,
[2644] Greek compound: in-anti, in front of, opposite, antagonistic
[2645] Lit., to arrive; or, competent as if coming in season, ample in amount, fit in character
[2646] Upon-failing
[2647] Un-well-placed, un-good-placed
[2648] Greek: "katantao," down-opposite, down-instead
[2649] Lit., before-place, to place before, or to place in advance
[2650] Lit., east-wind-surge of the sea, storm from the east
[2651] A flat boat that is dug out

17 Which when they **lifted**, they **apprised**[2652] **helps-cry**, undergirding the ship; and, fearing lest they should fall into the **sand-drag, lowered the** sail, and so were **carried**.

18 And we are **speedily winter-stormed**, the next, they-**produce out-casting**;

19 Down the third, we **fling with-our-own-hands** the **furniture** of the ship.

20 And when neither **upon-appeared** sun nor stars in many days **winter-storming**, and no **few pouring further laid-on-us**, finally all **expectation** that we should be saved was **about-lifted**.

21 Yet, after **under-originating much fasting** Paul stood in the middle of them and said: **O men! It-is-binding to-be-believing-first to-me**, and not have **up-led** from Crete, and to have gained this **insult** and **damage**.

22 And now I **beside-praise** you to be of **good-feeling**: because there shall be no loss of **soul out-of** you, **more-than of-the** ship.

23 For, there **beside-stood** me this night the angel of God, whose I am, and whom **I-am-hired-serving**,

24 Saying, fear not, Paul; you **it-is-binding to-beside-stand to-Caesar**: and, **be-perceiving**, God has **graced to-you** all them that sail with you.

25 Through-which, men, be **good-feeling**: for I-believe God, that it shall **down the turn it-was-said to-me.**

26 Yet, **it-is-binding to-us** to-**upon-fall into** certain island.

27 But when the fourteenth night **became**, as we **differed**[2653] in Adria, about midnight the shipmen **under-mind** that they **toward-lead** to some **space**;

28 And **cast and** found twenty **stretch-arms**: and when they had gone a **short through-standing**, they **cast** again, and found fifteen **stretch-arms**.

29 Then fearing lest we should **out-fall** upon **uneven-rocks spots** they **threw** anchors **out-of** the **stern** and **prayed-wished to-become** day.

30 And as the shipmen were **seeking** to flee **out-of** the ship, when they had **lower** the **skiff**[2654] into the sea, under **pretense**[2655] as though they **intend-to out-stretch** anchors out of the **prow,**[2656]

31 Paul said to the centurion and to the soldiers, except these **remain** in the ship, **not-you-are-powerful to-be-saved.**

32 Then the soldiers cut off the ropes of the **skiff**[2657] and **let** her **to-out-fall**.

33 And while the day was **impending**, Paul **beside-called** all to take **food**, saying, this day is the fourteenth day that you have **before-watched** and **through-finished** fasting, having **toward-taken** nothing.

34 Through-which I-beside-call you to take **food because** this is **toward** your **salvation is-under-originating**: for there shall not a hair fail **out-of** the head of any of you.

35 And when he had spoken **these-things**, he **took** bread, and gave thanks to God in presence of them all: and when he had broken, he began **eating.**

36 Then were they all of **good-feeling**, and they also **towards-take food**.

37 And we were all in the ship **two-hundred seventy-six** souls.

38 And when they had **crammed food**, they **unloaded** the ship, and cast out the wheat into the sea.

39 And when it **became** day, they knew not the land: but they **down-mind** a certain **bosom** with a shore, into the which they **plan-counseled** if **they-may-be-powerful** to **out-of-pushed** the ship.

40 And when they had **about-lifted** the anchors, they **let-it into** the sea, and **up-send** the rudder[2658] **coupling,**[2659] and hoisted up the mainsail to the wind, and **down-hold into the** shore.

41 About-falling into a **spot** where two seas met, they ran the ship aground; and the **prow**[2660] **stuck**, and remained unmovable, but the **stern**[2661] was broken with the violence of the waves.

[2652] Or, to inform, to tell, to furnish what is needed
[2653] Greek: "diaphero," to through-bear, transliterated as "differ" or "different"
[2654] A flat boat dug out
[2655] Greek: before-appear, outward show
[2656] The forward part of the ship
[2657] Lifeboat
[2658] Greek: "pedal," a helm
[2659] Yoke, the beam of the balance
[2660] The forward part of the ship
[2661] The hinder part of the ship

42 And the soldiers' **plan-counsel became** to kill the prisoners, lest any of them should swim out, and escape.

43 But the centurion, **plane-counseled-himself** to **through-save** Paul, **prevented** them **of-the plan-counsel**; and **orders** that they **being-powerful to-**swim should **from-fling foremost**, and **out-go upon the** land:

44 And the **remaining**, some on **planks**, and some from the ship. And so, **it became**, that they escaped all **through-safe** to land.

ACTS CHAPTER 28

1 And when they were **through-saved**, then they **upon-knew** that the island was called Melita.

2 And the barbarous people **hold-near** us **not the happening**[2662] **philanthropy to-us**: **because** they kindled a fire, and **toward-take all of-us, through the** present rain, and **through** the cold.

3 And when Paul had **together-turned** a **fullness** of sticks, and **placed-on** the fire, there came a viper out of the heat, and **down-fastened** his hand.

4 And when the barbarians **perceived** the **wild-beast hanging out-of** his hand, they said **towards one-another, all,** this man is a murderer, whom, though he **being-through-saved out-of** the sea, yet **justice not let-be to-be-living.**

5 And he shook off the **wild-beast** into the fire, and **emotion** no **evil**.

6 Yet, they **toward-seem** him impending **to-be-on-fire or** fall down dead suddenly: **yet** after they had **toward-seem on much**, and saw **nothing un-placed becoming into him**, they **change-casting**, and said that he was a god.

7 In the same **spot under-originate spaces** of the **foremost-man** of the island, whose name was Publius;[2663] who received us, and **foreign-lodged** us three days **friendly-disposition**.

8 And **it became**, that the father of Publius **together-hold down-laid to-fevers** and **to-dysentery**:[2664]

toward whom Paul entered, and **toward-prayed-wished**, **placed** his hands on him, and **cured** him.

9 So when this **became**, others also in the island, which had **weakness**, **toward-came**, and were **served-therapy**:

10 Who also **valued** us with many **values**; and when we **up-led**, they **upon-placed towards the need**.[2665]

11 And after three months we **up-led** in a ship of Alexandria, which had wintered in the **island,** whose **beside-sign** was **Zeus-girl**.[2666]

12 And landing at Syracuse, we **upon-remained** three days.

13 And from there we **wandered**,[2667] and **meet-against**[2668] **into** Rhegium: and after **first** day the south wind **upon-became**, and we came the next day **into** Puteoli:[2669]

14 Where we found **brothers** and were **beside-called** to **upon-remain** with them seven days: and so, we went **into** Rome.

15 And from there, when the **brothers** heard of us, they **out-of-came** to **from-meet**[2670] us until Appii forum,[2671] and the three taverns: whom when Paul **perceived**, he thanked God, and **took daring**.[2672]

16 And when we came **into** Rome, the centurion **beside-gives** the prisoners to the **soldier-first-rank**: but Paul was **permitted** to **remain** by himself with a soldier that **watched** him.

17 And **it became**, that after three days Paul called the **foremost** of the Jews together: and when they were come together, he said **towards** them, men, **brothers**, though I have **produced** nothing contrary[2673] **to-the** people, or **ethics** of our fathers, yet was I **beside-given** prisoner **out-of** Jerusalem into the hands of the Romans.

18 Who, when they had **up-judged** me, **plan-counseled to-from-loose**, because there was no cause of death **under-originated** in me.

[2662] Or, hit the mark, chance upon, obtain,
[2663] Lit., Popular
[2664] Dysentery, Greek compound "dusenteria," meaning "hard-inside" (hard-bowels)
[2665] Or employment
[2666] Greek compound "dioscuri": zeus (dzyyooce) and korasion (a girl)
[2667] About going
[2668] Greek: "katantao," down-opposite

[2669] Little wells (mineral springs)
[2670] Greek: "apantesis," the official welcome of a newly arriving dignitary, by people going out to meet the dignitary and escorting the dignitary back to the origin of the ones who went to meet the dignitary; see also 1 Thessalonians 4:17, Matthew 25:1-6
[2671] Or, marketplace, a station on the Appian road
[2672] Or, courageous
[2673] Greek compound: in-anti, antagonistic

19 Yet, of-anti-words of-the Jews I-was-necessitated to-**upon-call**[2674] Caesar; not that I had **anything** to accuse my nation.

20 Through this cause **then**, I have **beside-called** you, to **perceive**, and **toward-speak** with because that for the **expectation** of Israel I am **about-laid** with this chain.

21 And they said **to-him**, we neither **welcomed** letters out of Judaea concerning you, neither any of the **brothers** that came **from-messaged** or spoke any **wicked-hurtful** of you.

22 But we **deserve** to hear of you what **is-your-disposition**: for as concerning this sect, we know that **universally** it is **disputed.**

23 And when they had **arranged** him a day, **arrived** many **towards** him into lodging; to whom he **out-placed**[2675] and **through-witness** the kingdom of God, persuading them **about** Jesus, both **from** the law of Moses, and the prophets, from morning **until evening**.

24 And some believed the things which were spoken, and some believed not.

25 And when they agreed not **toward one-another**, they departed, after that Paul had spoken one **declaration**, **ideally** spoke the Holy Spirit **through Isaiah** the prophet **toward** our fathers,

26 Saying, **travel toward** this people, and say, hearing you shall hear, and shall not **synthesize**; and seeing you shall see, and not perceive:

27 For the **heart** of this people is **thick**, and their ears are **heavy** of hearing, and their eyes have they **down-shut**;[2676] lest they should **perceive** with eyes, and hear with ears, and understand with **heart**, and should be **reverted**, and I should **cure** them.

28 Be it known therefore **to-you**, that the salvation of God is sent **to-the nations**, and they will hear it.

29 And when he had said these words, the Jews departed, and had **much together-seeking in** themselves.

30 And Paul **remained** two whole **years** in his own **rented-building**, and **from-received** all that came in **toward him**,

31 Preaching the kingdom of **the** God, and teaching those things which **about** the Lord Jesus Christ, with **every all-speech** no man **hindering** him.

[2674] Or, to entitle, to invoke
[2675] Or, exposed

[2676] Or down-mystery

ROMANS

ROMANS CHAPTER 1

1 Paul, a **slave** of Jesus Christ, called an apostle, **from-defined**[2677] into the **well-message** of God,

2 (Which he had **before-promised through** his prophets in the holy **Scriptures**,)

3 **About** his Son Jesus Christ our Lord, which **became** of the seed of David **down** flesh;

4 And **defined** the Son of God **in** power, **down** Spirit of holiness, by the resurrection **out-of** the dead:

5 By whom we **have-taken** grace and apostleship, for **under-hearing** to the faith **in** all **the** nations, **over** his name:

6 **In** whom are you also called of Jesus Christ:

7 To all that be in Rome, beloved of God, called saints: grace **to-you** and peace from God our Father, and the Lord Jesus Christ.

8 **Foremost**, I thank my God through Jesus Christ for you all, that your faith is **down-message in** the whole world.

9 For God is my witness, whom **I-am-hired-serving in** my spirit in the **well-message** of his Son, that **not-through-leave** I make **reminder** of you always in my **toward-prayers-wishes**.

10 **Always on my toward-prayers-wishes**, if **somehow, already**, I might have a **good-road** by the will of God to come **toward** you.

11 For I **upon-yearn** to **perceive** you, that I may **impart to-you** some spiritual **grace, into to-be-established;**[2678]

12 That is, that I may be **together-beside-call** with you **in one-another-same** faith both of you and me.

13 Yet, I will not have you **ignorant brothers, how much** I **purpose**[2679] to come **to-you**, (but was **prevented here**,) that I might have some fruit **in** you also, even as among other **nations**.

14 I **owe** both to the **Hellenics**, and to the Barbarians; both to the wise, and to the **un-mind**.

15 So, as much as in me is, I **before-feel** to **well-message to-you** that are **in** Rome also.

16 For I am not **upon-disfigured** of the **well-message** of Christ: for it is the power of God **to** salvation to everyone that believes; to the Jew **foremost**, and also to the **Hellenics**.

17 For **in it** the **righteous-togetherness** of God **is-revealed out-of** faith **into** faith: as it is written, the **righteous** shall live **out-of** faith.

18 For the **swelling-anger** of God is revealed from heaven against all **un-good-reverence** and unrighteousness of men, who **down-hold** the truth in unrighteousness.

19 **Through-that the** known of God is **shined** in them, **because** God has **shined to** them.

20 For the invisible things of him from the creation of the world are **down-seen**, being-**thought to-the poems-products,**[2680] his **everlasting** power and **Divinity**; so that they are **without-apologies.**[2681]

21 Because that, when they knew God, they glorified not as God, neither were thankful; but became vain in their **through-inventorying**, and their **rot-synthesizing heart** was darkened.

22 **Asserting** themselves to be wise, they became **dull**,[2682]

23 And changed the glory of the incorruptible God into an image made like to corruptible man, and to birds, and four-footed, and **reptiles**.

24 **Through-which** God also gave them up to uncleanness through the **on-feeling** of-the **hearts**, to **un-value** their bodies **in** themselves:

25 Who changed the truth of God **into the falsehood and** revered and **hired-served to-the creation beside** the Creator, who is blessed **into the ages**. Amen.

26 For this cause, God gave them up **to un-value emotions: because** even their **female** did **after-change-another-same** the **physical** use into that which is **beside growth**:

27 And likewise also the **males**, **release**[2683] the **physical** use of the **female**, **out-of**-burned in their

---

[2677] Lit., from-horizon
[2678] Greek: "sterizo," set fast, stand
[2679] Lit., before-place, to place before, or to place in advance
[2680] Greek: "Poiema," transliterated as "poem;" and also means to make, to produce, to achieve, manufactured
[2681] Lit., "anapologetos," without-from-inventory, without-answers, without defense, "unapologetic"
[2682] Greek: morons
[2683] Or forgive (i.e., justifying the act by self-imposed release)

stretching into **one-another-same**; male in male **down-working** that which is **disfigured-togetherness**,[2684] and **from-taking** in themselves **the instead-pay**[2685] of their **seduction** which **was-binding**.

28 And even as they did not **seem-test to-hold** God in knowledge, God gave them over to a **not-seem-approved**[2686] mind, to do those things which are not **down-arrive**.

29 Being filled with all unrighteousness, **prostitution**, **wicked-hurtfulness, more-having**, evil; full of **ill-will**, murder, **quarrel**,[2687] **trick-bait**, **evil-ethics**; whisperers,[2688]

30 Down-talkers, God-haters, insulters, **above-shiners**,[2689] braggarts, **upon-finders** of evil, **un-perusable** to parents,

31 un-synthesizing, not-together-placed, without-**cherishing, un-spent**,[2690] unmerciful:

32 Who knowing the **righteous-act** of-**the** God, that they which **practice** such things are **deserving** of death, not only do the same, but also **together-good-seem to-**them **practicing**.

ROMANS CHAPTER 2

1 Therefore, you are **without-apologies**, O man, **each who** judges: for **in which** you judge **another-different**, you **down-judging** yourself; for you that judge **practice** the same things.

2 Yet, **we perceive** that the **judgment-result** of God is **down** truth against them **practicing** such things.

3 And you **inventory** this, O man, that judge them which **practices** such things, and do the same, that you shall escape the **judgment-result** of God?

4 Or, **down-disposition** you the riches of his **usefulness** and **tolerance**[2691] and **long-sacrifice-anger; ignoring** that the **usefulness**[2692] of God leads you to **change-thought**?

5 But after your hardness and **un-change-mind heart placed-into-tomorrow to-yourself** swelling-anger in the day of **swelling-anger** and revelation of the **righteous-judgment of-the** God;

6 Who will **from-give** to every man **down** his **works**:

7 To them who by **under-remaining** in **good work**, seek for glory, **value**, and **incorruption**, **eternal life**.

8 But **to-them** that are **out-of stimulations-self-interest**,[2693] and **un-persuaded to-**the truth, **yet persuaded to-the** unrighteousness, **sacrifice-anger**, and **swelling-anger**.

9 Tribulation and **narrow-space**, upon every soul of man that **down-work the** evil, of the Jew **foremost**, and also of the **Hellenics.**

10 But glory, **value**, and peace, to every man that **works** good to the Jew **foremost**, and also to the **Hellenic**:

11 For there is no respect of persons[2694] **beside** God.

12 For as many as have sinned **lawlessly** shall also **be-from-ruin**[2695] lawlessly: and as many as have sinned in the law shall be judged **through** the law;

13 (For not the **hearers** of the law righteous **beside** God, but the **poets-producers** of the law shall be **righteous**.

14 For when the **nations**, which have not the law, do by **growth** the things **of-the** the law, these, having not the law, are a law **to** themselves:

15 Which show the work of the law written in their **hearts**, their conscience also **together-**witness, and **logics**[2696] the mean while accusing or else **apologizing**[2697] **one-another-same**;)

16 In the day when God shall judge the **hidden-things** of men **through** Jesus Christ **down** my **well-message**.

17 Be-perceiving, you are **upon-named** a Jew, and rest in the law, and make your boast of God,

18 And know **the** will and **seem-test** the things that **differ**[2698] being **catechized** out of the law.

19 And are **convinced** that yourself are a **way-leader** of the blind, a light of them which are in darkness,

---

[2684] Compound of ("aschemon" (disfigured) and "sun" (together)) only in Romans 1:27 and Revelation 16:15
[2685] Or anti-pay
[2686] Rejected, reprobate
[2687] Or, electioneering, quarrel, debates
[2688] Or, secret whisperer, akin to falsehood
[2689] Or, appearing above others
[2690] Or un-libation ("aspondos"—un-spent)
[2691] Lit., to hold oneself up against, self-restraint
[2692] Or, to furnish what is needed or used, employed
[2693] Or electioneering, rivalry
[2694] Or acceptor of face, partiality
[2695] Greek: "apo" (from) and "alethros" (ruin), to destroy fully
[2696] Or, to inventory
[2697] Greek: "apologeomai" (from-saying) to exculpate (self), to give account, to defend
[2698] Greek: "diaphero," to through-bear, transliterated as "differ" or "different"

20 A **boy-trainer** of the **undisposed**, a teacher of **infants**, which has the form of **knowing** and of the truth in the law.

21 You therefore which teach **another-different**, teach you not yourself? You that preach a man should not steal, **do** you steal?

22 You that say a man should not **be-committing-adultery, you-are-committing-adultery!** You that **abominating**[2699] idols, **you-are-priest-place-robbing!**[2700]

23 You that make your boast of the law, through **beside-stepping** the law **you-are-un-valuing** God?

24 For the name of God is blasphemed **in** the **nations** through you, as it is written.

25 Because circumcision **indeed** profit, if you keep the law: but if you **beside-step of-law,** your circumcision **has-become** uncircumcision.

26 Therefore if the uncircumcision keeps the **righteous-deeds** of the law, shall not his uncircumcision be **inventoried** for circumcision?

27 And shall not uncircumcision which is **of-growth**, if it **finishes** the law, judge you, who **through** the letter and circumcision **beside-step** the law?

28 Because he is not a Jew, which is **the outward-shine,** neither circumcision, which is **outward-shine** in flesh:

29 But he is a Jew, **in the hidden**; and circumcision of the **heart,** in spirit, not **to-writing**; whose praise not **out-**of men, but **out-**of God.

ROMANS CHAPTER 3

1 What **exceed** then has the Jew? Or what profit of circumcision?

2 Much every way; **foremost,** because that **to-them** were **upon-believed** the oracles of God.

3 For what if some did not believe? Shall their unbelief make the faith of God **down-non-working**?

4 Not may-it-become, yet, let God be true, but every man a **falsifier**; as it is written, that you might be righteous in your sayings, and might **conquer**[2701] when you are judged.

5 But if our unrighteousness **is-together-standing** the **righteous-togetherness** of God, what shall we say? Not God's unrighteous who **upon-carry swelling-anger**? (I speak **down** a man)

6 Not may-it-become: for then, how shall God judge the world?

7 For if the truth of God **exceeds** through my **falsehood into** his glory; why yet am I also judged as a sinner?

8 And not, (as **we-are-blasphemed,** and as some **show**[2702] that we say,) Let us do evil, that good may come? Whose **judgment-result**[2703] is **righteous.**

9 What then? Are we **before-having?**[2704] **Not at-all; because** we have **before-caused** both Jews and **Hellenics** that they are all under sin;

10 As it is written, there is none righteous, no, not one:

11 There is none that understand, there is none that **out-of-**seeks **the** God.

12 They are all **out-cline** of the way, they are together become **unused**; there is none that **produces useful,** no, not one.

13 Their throat is-an open sepulcher; with their tongues they have used **trick-bait**; the poison[2705] of asps under their lips:

14 Whose mouth **is-swell** of **curse-payer** and bitterness:[2706]

15 Their feet **sharp** to **out-pour** blood:

16 Together-crush and **talent-tested**[2707] in their ways:

17 And the way of peace have they not known:

18 There is no fear of God before their eyes.

19 Yet, we **perceive** that **as-much-as** the law says, it says **to-them** who are under the law: that every mouth may be **fenced,** and all the world may become **under-justice**[2708] before God.

20 Therefore by the **works** of the law there shall no flesh be **righteous** in his sight: for by the law the knowledge of sin.

[2699] Root means, to stink
[2700] Or, priest-place-stripping,
[2701] "Nikao," to defeat an enemy
[2702] Greek: "phemi," the root word for fame ("pheme")
[2703] Greek: "krima," "crime" and also means judgment
[2704] Or, privileged

[2705] Or rust
[2706] Lit., acridity (strong, irritating, unpleasant, pungent (sharp), taste or smell), poison
[2707] Talaiporos-Strong's define as weight-tested, balanced-tested; and Thayer defines as bearing-callous, full of callous
[2708] Or, Sentenced, just verdict

21 Yet now, the **righteous-togetherness** of God **spaced-from** the law is **shined,** being witnessed by the **Law and the Prophets;**

22 Even the **righteous-togetherness** of God by faith of Jesus Christ **into** all and upon all them that believe: **because** there is no **through-stall.**[2709]

23 For all have sinned, and come **late** of the glory of God;

24 Being **righteous gift to-the grace of-him** through the **from-loosing**[2710] that is in Christ Jesus:

25 Whom God has **purposed**[2711] a **Merry-Atonement**[2712] through faith in his blood, **into in-show** his **righteous-togetherness** for the **beside-let-go** of sins that are past, through the **tolerance** of God;

26 To **in-show, in the now season,** his **righteous-togetherness**: that he might be **righteous**, and the **making-righteousness the-ones out-of faith** Jesus.

27 Where boasting then? It is **out-of-locked.** By what law? Of works? No, but by the law of faith.

28 Therefore we **inventory** that a man is **righteous** by faith **spaced-from** the **works** of the law.

29 Or, the God of the Jews only? Not also of the **nations**? Yes, of the **nations** also:

30 Since-indeed, one God, which shall **make-righteous** the circumcision **out-of** faith, and uncircumcision through faith.

31 Do we then make void the law through faith? **Not may-it-become.** Yes, we establish the law.

ROMANS CHAPTER 4

1 What shall we say then that Abraham our father, as pertaining to the flesh, has found?

2 For if Abraham were **righteous** by works, he has **boasting,** but not **toward** God.

3 For what says the Scripture? Abraham believed God, and it was **inventoried to-him** for **righteous-togetherness.**

4 Now **to-him** that **works** the **pay** is not **inventoried** of grace but **owed.**

5 But **to-him** that **works** not, but believes on him **makes-righteous** the **irreverent**, his faith is **inventoried** for **righteous-togetherness**.

6 Even as David also **says** the **happiness** of the man, **to-whom** God **inventory righteous-togetherness space-from** works,

7 Happy they whose **lawlessness** are **released,**[2713] and whose sins are covered.

8 Happy the man to whom the Lord will not **inventory** sin.

9 This happiness, then upon the circumcision, or upon the uncircumcision also? **Because,** we say that faith was **inventoried** to Abraham for **righteous-togetherness**.

10 How was it then **inventoried**? When he was in circumcision, or in uncircumcision? Not in circumcision, but in uncircumcision.

11 And he **took** the sign of circumcision, a seal of the **righteous-togetherness** of the faith **in the** uncircumcised: that he might be the father of all them that believe, though they be not circumcised; that **righteous-togetherness** might be **inventoried to-them** also:

12 And the father of circumcision **to-them** who are not of the circumcision only, but who also **element-walk,**[2714] **to-the tracks** of that faith of our father Abraham, **in the** uncircumcised.

13 For the promise, that he should be the heir of the world, not to Abraham, or to his seed, through the law, but through the **righteous-togetherness** of faith.

14 For if they which are of the law heirs, faith is made void, and the promise **emptied.**

15 Because the law **down-works swelling-anger**: for where no law is, no **beside-stepping.**[2715]

16 Therefore **it out-of** faith, that **according-to** grace; **into the to-be stable** the promise to all the seed; not to that only which is of the law, but to that also which is of the faith of Abraham; who is the father of us all,

17 (As it is written, I have **placed** you a father of many nations,) before him whom he believed, God, who **is-**

[2709] Or, distinction, difference
[2710] redemption
[2711] Lit., before-place, to place in advance
[2712] Greek: "hilasterion," an expiatory place, atone, conciliate; translated as the "Mercyseat" in some translation

[2713] Lit., from-let-go
[2714] Gk.: stoicheo, to march in rank (keep step), from same root for "element"
[2715] Or transgression

life-produces to-the dead and calls those things which not **being as existing.**

18 Who **beside expectation,** believed **upon expectation,** that he might become the father of many nations, **down** that which was spoken, so shall your seed be.

19 And being not weak in faith, he **down-mind his body**[2716] **having-died,** about **under-originating** hundred **years** old, **and** the deadness of Sara's womb:

20 He **through-judged** not at the promise of God through unbelief; but was **empowered** in faith, giving glory to God.

21 And **being-fully-burden-wearing** that, what he had promised, **he-is powerful** also to **produce.**

22 And therefore it was **inventoried to-him** for **righteous-togetherness.**

23 Now it was not written, **yet through him only,** that it was **inventoried to-him;**

24 But for us also, to whom **it-is-impending to-be inventoried,** if we believe on him that raised up Jesus our Lord **out-of** the dead;

25 Who was **betrayed**[2717] for our **beside-falls** and was raised again for our justification.

ROMANS CHAPTER 5

1 Therefore being **righteous out-of** faith, we have peace **towards** God through our Lord Jesus Christ:

2 By whom also we have **toward-lead** by faith into this grace **in which** we stand and **boast in expectation** of the glory of God.

3 And not only, but we **boast** in tribulations also: **perceiving** that tribulation **is-down-working under-remaining.**

4 Yet, the **under-remaining, seem-test;** yet the **seem-test, expectation:**

5 Yet, the **expectation** makes not **down-disfigured;** that the love of God is **out-poured** in our **hearts** by the Holy Spirit which is given **to-us.**

6 For when we were yet **without-strength, down season,** Christ died for the **irreverent.**

7 For **difficult** for a righteous man one dies: yet **swiftly** for a good man some would dare to die.

8 But God **together-stand** his love **into** us, in that, while we were yet sinners, Christ died for us.

9 Much more then, being now **righteous** by his blood, we shall be saved from **swelling-anger** through him.

10 For if, when we were **haters,** we were **exchanged**[2718] to God by the death of his Son, much more, being **exchanged** we shall be saved by his life.

11 And not only, but we also **boast** in God through our Lord Jesus Christ, **through** whom we have now **take** the **exchange.**

12 Through this, as-much-as through one man, sin entered into the world, and death **through** sin; and so, death passed **through** all men, for that all have sinned:

13 (For until the law sin was in the world: but sin is not **inventoried** when there is no law.

14 Nevertheless death reigned from Adam **until** Moses, even over them that had not sinned after the similitude of Adam's transgression, who is the **type**[2719] of him **impending.**

15 But not as the **side-fall,** so also is the **grace.** For if through the **side-fall** of one many **died,** much more the grace of God, and the gift **in** grace, by one man, Jesus Christ, has **exceed to** many.

16 And not as **through** one that sinned, the gift: for the **judgment-result**[2720] **out-of** one to **down-judgment,** but the gift **out-of** many **beside-falls into righteous-deed.**

17 For if by one man's **side-fall** death reigned by one; much more they which **take excess** of grace and of the gift of **righteous-togetherness** shall reign in life by one, Jesus Christ.)

18 Therefore, as by the **side-fall** of one upon all men to **down-judging;** even so by the **righteous-deed through** one upon all men **into righteousness** of life.

19 For as by one man's **mishearing**[2721] many were made sinners, so by the **under-hearing of-the One** shall many be made righteous.

20 Moreover, the law entered that the **side-fall was-made-more.** But where sin **was-made-more,** grace did **over-exceed:**

[2716] Genesis 17:17, Genesis 18:11-14
[2717] Or beside -given
[2718] Or change mutually, to down-change,
[2719] A die as struck, thump-impression
[2720] Greek: "krima," "crime" and also means judgment
[2721] Or beside-hearing

21 That as sin has reigned **in the** death, even so, might grace reign through **righteous-togetherness into eternal life through** Jesus Christ our Lord.

ROMANS CHAPTER 6

1 What shall we say then? Shall we **upon-remain** in sin, that grace **should-be-more**?

2 Not may-it-become. How shall we, that are dead to sin, **still live in her**?

3 Or, ignore that so many of us as were baptized into Jesus Christ were baptized into his death?

4 Therefore, we are buried with him **through** baptism into death: that like as Christ was raised **out-of** the dead **through** the glory of the Father, even so we also should walk in **new-freshness of-life**.

5 For if we have been **together-planted** in the likeness of his death, **but also**, we shall be **of-the** resurrection:

6 Knowing this, that our old man is **together-**crucified, that the body of sin might be **down-not-working**, that we should not **still be-slaving to-the** sin.

7 For he that is dead **is-righteous** from **the** sin.

8 Now if we be dead **together to-Christ**, we believe that we shall also **together-live to-him:**

9 Perceiving that Christ being raised **out-of** the dead dies no more; death has no more **lordship of-him.**

10 For in that he died, he died **to-sin** once: but in that he lives, he lives **to-the** God.

11 Likewise you, **inventory** also yourselves to be dead indeed **to-sin**, but alive **to-God** through Jesus Christ our Lord.

12 Let not sin therefore reign in your mortal body, that you should **under-hear**[2722] **to-her** in the **upon-feeling of it.**

13 Neither **beside-stand** you your members instruments of unrighteousness **to-the** sin: but **beside-stand** yourselves **to-God,** as those that are alive from the dead, and your members instruments of **righteous-togetherness to-God.**

14 Because, sin shall not have **lordship** over you: **because** you are not under **law**, but under grace.

15 What then? Shall we sin, **for** we are not under law, but under grace? **Not may-it-become.**

16 Perceive you not, that to whom you **beside-stand** yourselves **slaves** to **under-hear,** his **slaves** you are to whom you **under-hear;** whether of sin **into** death, or of **under-hearing into righteous-togetherness**?

17 But thanks to God, that you were the **slaves** of sin, but you have **under-heard**[2723] **out-of** the **heart** that **type**[2724] of **teaching** which was **beside-given** you.

18 Yet, being-freed from sin, you became the **slaves** of **righteous-togetherness.**

19 I speak **as-a-**man because of the **weakness** of your flesh: for as you have **beside-stand** your members **slaves** to uncleanness and to **lawlessness into the lawlessness**; even so now **beside-stand** your members **slaves** to **righteous-togetherness into** holiness.

20 For when you were the **slaves** of sin, you were free from **righteous-togetherness**.

21 What fruit had you then in those things **on which** you are now **upon-disfigured**? Because the finish **of-those-things,** death.

22 But now **being-free** from sin, and become **slaves** to God, you have your fruit **into** holiness, and the **finish, eternal life.**

23 For the **soldier-ration** of sin, is death, but the **grace** of God, **eternal life,** through Jesus Christ our Lord.

ROMANS CHAPTER 7

1 Or, are-you-ignorant brothers, (for I speak **to-them** that know the law.) how that the law has **lordship** over a man **as-much-as uninterrupted-time**s he lives ?

2 For the woman, **under-man,** is bound by the law to husband so long as he lives; **yet** if the husband **dies**, she is **down-not-work** from the law **of-the** husband.

3 So then if, lives the husband, she **became** to **another-different** man, she shall be **apprised**[2725] an adulteress. but if her husband **dies**, she is free from that law; so that she is no adulteress, though she **became** to **another-different** man.

4 So-too, my **brothers,** you also are become dead to the law by the body of Christ; that **you should-be-**

[2722] Or obey
[2723] Or obey
[2724] Lit., thump-impression, a die as struck, imaged form from striking, transliterated in English as "typing"

[2725] Greek: "chrematizo," to furnish what is needed, divine response; secular meaning of constituting a business, employ, to bears as a title, to apprise (to give notice, state of affair, inform)

becoming to **another-different**, **the-one** who is raised **out-of** the dead, that we should **carry** fruit **to-God**.

5 For when we were in the flesh, the **emotions** of sins, which were by the law, did work in our members to **fruit-carry to-the** death.

6 But now we are **down-not-work** from the law, that being dead **in which** we were **down-held**; that we should serve in **new-freshness** of spirit, and not the oldness of the **writing**.

7 What shall we say then? The law sin? **Not may-it-become**. No, I had not known sin, but **through** the law: **because** I had not **perceived upon-feeling**, except the law had said, you shall not **upon-feel**.

8 Yet, sin, **taking from-violent-impulse-rush** by the commandment, **down-work** in me all **upon-feelings**. For **spacing-from** the law sin **is** dead.

9 For I was alive **spacing-from** the law once: **yet**, when the commandment came, sin **up-lived**, and I died.

10 And the commandment, which **into** life, I found **into** death.

11 For sin, **getting from-violent-impulse-rush through** the commandment, **out-of-seduced** me, and by it **from-kills**.

12 So-that, the law holy, and the commandment holy, and just, and good.

13 Was then that which is good **became** death **to** me? **Not may-it-become**. But sin, that **it-might-shine** sin, **down-working** death in me **through** that which is good; that sin by the commandment might become **over-cast**²⁷²⁶ sinful.

14 For we **perceived** that the law is spiritual: but I am **fleshly, across-traffic-sell** under sin.

15 For that which I **down-work** I **know** not: **because** what **I-am-willing**, that I **practice** not; but what I **detest**, that I **produce**.

16 If then I produce that which I **will** not, I **together-show to** the law that is **ideal**.

17 Now then it is no more I that **down-work** it, but sin that **homing** in me.

18 For I **perceived** that in me (that is, in my flesh,) **is-homing** no good thing: for to will is **beside-laying** with me; yet to **down-work** that which is **ideal** I find not.

19 Because the good that I **will**, I **produce** not: but the evil which I **will** not, that **I-am-practicing**.

20 Now if I **produce** that I **willed** not, it is no more I that **down-work** it, but sin **homing** in me.

21 I find then a law, that, when I **will to-produce ideal**, evil is **beside-laying**.

22 Because I **together-sensual-delight**²⁷²⁷ in the **Law** of God after the **inside** man:

23 But I see **another-different** law in my members, warring against the law of my mind, and bringing me into captivity **to-the** law of sin which is in my members.

24 Weight-calloused²⁷²⁸ man that I am! Who shall **rush-rescue** me **out-of** the body of this death?

25 I thank God through Jesus Christ our Lord. So then **to-thought** I **am-slaving to-law** of God; **yet to-**the flesh **to-law** of sin.

ROMANS CHAPTER 8

1 Consequently, now no **down-judging to-them** which are in Christ Jesus.²⁷²⁹

2 Because, the law of the Spirit **of-the** life in Christ Jesus **frees me** from the law **of-the** sin and **of-the** death.

3 For **un-powerful** the law, in that it was weak through the flesh, **the** God **dispatching** his own Son in the likeness of sinful flesh, and **about** sin, **down-judged** sin in the flesh:

4 That the **righteous-deed** of the law might be filled in us, who **is-walking** not **down** the flesh, but **down** the Spirit.

5 For they **down flesh, being, to-the** things of the flesh **are-disposed**; but they that are **down** the Spirit the things of the Spirit.

6 Because, the disposition of the flesh, death; **yet the disposition of the Spirit,** life, and peace.

7 Because, the disposition of the flesh hates²⁷³⁰ **into** God: **because** it is not **subordinate**²⁷³¹ to the **Law** of God, neither indeed **it-is-powerful**.

---

²⁷²⁶ Or a throw beyond others
²⁷²⁷ Greek compound: sun+hedomai (together-"hedonism")
²⁷²⁸ Talaiporos-Strong's define as weight-tested, balanced-tested; and Thayer defines as bearing-callous, full of callous

²⁷²⁹ Byz and TR texts add "who walk not according to flesh, but according to Spirit"
²⁷³⁰ Or hostile, enemy
²⁷³¹ Under-arranged

8 So then they that are in the flesh **not powerful to-please** God.

9 But you are not in the flesh, but in the Spirit, **if-much** Spirit of God **homes** in you. Now if any man not **is-holding** the Spirit of Christ, he is **not of-him**.

10 And if Christ in you, **in-fact,** the body **is** dead because of sin; but the Spirit life because of **righteous-togetherness**.

11 But if the Spirit of him that raised up Jesus from the dead **is-housing** in you, he that raised **the** Christ from the dead **life-produce to** your **dying** bodies **through** his Spirit **in-housing** in you.

12 Therefore, **brothers**, we **owe** not to the flesh, to live **down** the flesh.

13 For if you live **down** the flesh, **you-are-impending to-die:** but if you through the Spirit do mortify the **practices** of the body, you shall live.

14 Because, as many as are led **to-Spirit** of God, they are the sons of God.

15 Because, you have not **taken** the spirit of **slavery** again to fear; but you have **taken** the Spirit of **son-placing, in which** we **scream,** Abba,[2732] Father.

16 The **same** Spirit **together-witness** with our spirit, that we are the children of God:

17 And if children, then heirs; heirs, **in fact,** of God, and **together-heirs** with Christ; if so be that we **together-emotion,** that we may be also **together-glorified.**

18 For **I-am-inventorying** that the **emotions** of this present **season** not **deserving** with the glory **impending to-be-revealed into** us.

19 For the **from-head-seem** of the creature **from-out-welcome** the revelation of the sons of God.

20 For the **creation** was made **subordinate** to vanity, not willingly, but **through** him who has **subordinated** in **expectation,**

21 Because the **creation** itself also shall be **freed** from the **slavery** of corruption into the **freedom of-the glory** of the children of God.

22 For we **perceived** that the whole creation groans and travails in pain together until now.

23 And not only, but ourselves also, which have the firstfruit of the Spirit, even we ourselves groan within ourselves, waiting for the **son-placing,** the **from-loosing,** of our body.

24 For we are saved by **expectation**: but **expectation** that is seen is not **expectation**: for what a man sees, why does he yet **expect**?

25 But if we **expect** for that we see not, do we **through under-remaining from-welcome.**

26 Likewise, the Spirit also **together-instead-take** our **weaknesses**: for we **perceive** not what we should **towards-pray-wish** for as **is-binding**:[2733] but the Spirit itself makes **over-happening**[2734] for us with groanings which cannot be uttered.

27 And he that searches the **hearts perceives** what the **disposition** of the Spirit, because he makes **in-happenings**[2735] for the saints **down** God.

28 And we know that all things work together for good **to-them** that love God, **to-them** who are the called **down purpose.**[2736]

29 For whom he did foreknow, he also did **before-define** conformed **of-the** image of his Son, that he might be the firstborn among many **brothers**.

30 Moreover whom he did **before-define,** them he also called: and whom he called, them also **he-made-righteous:** and whom **he-made-righteous,** them he also glorified.

31 What shall we then say to these things? If God for us, who against us?

32 He that spared not his own Son, but **from-gave** him for us all, how shall he not with him also freely give us all things?

33 Who shall lay anything to the charge of God's elect? God **making-righteous.**

34 Who he that **down-judges**? Christ that died, yes rather, that is risen again, who is even **in** the right hand of God, who also makes **in-happenings**[2737] **over** us.

35 Who shall **space** us from the love of Christ? Tribulation, or **narrowness**, or **chasing**, or famine, or nakedness, or peril, or sword?

[2732] Abba could be Hebrew words for father ("Ab") and the Hebrew word for come ("ba") compounded—Come-Father, Father
[2733] Or, necessary as binding
[2734] Or over-obtain, over-to hit the target, over-chance upon
[2735] Or in-obtain. in-to hit the target, in-chance upon
[2736] Lit., before-place, to place before, or to place in advance
[2737] Or in-obtain. in-to hit the target, in-chance upon

36 As it is written, **that on-account of-you** we are killed all day long; we are **inventoried** as sheep for the slaughter.

37 But, in all these things we are more than conquerors through him that loved us.

38 For I am persuaded, that neither death, nor life, nor angels, nor **originals,** nor powers, nor things present, nor things **impending,**

39 Nor **high-body** nor depth, nor any other **creation,** shall be **powerful** to **space** us from the love of God, which is in Christ Jesus our Lord.

ROMANS CHAPTER 9

1 I say the truth in Christ, I **falsify** not, my conscience also **together-witnessing** in the Holy **Spirit,**

2 That I have **great** heaviness and **un-through-leave** sorrow in my **heart.**

3 For I could **pray** that myself were **banned** from Christ for my **brothers**, my kinsmen **down** the flesh:

4 Who are Israelites; to whom the **son-placing,** and the glory, and the covenants, and the **legislation,** and the **hired-service,** and the promises.

5 Whose the fathers, and of whom as concerning the flesh, Christ, who is over all, God blessed **into the ages.** Amen.

6 Not as though the **Word of God** has **out-of-fallen. Because these** not all Israel, **the-ones out-of** Israel:

7 Neither, because they are the seed of Abraham, all children: but, in Isaac shall your seed be called.

8 That is, they which are the children of the flesh, these not the children of**-the** God: but the children of the promise are **inventoried into** seed.

9 Because this the word of promise, at this **season** will I come, and Sara shall have a son.

10 Yet not only; but when Rebecca also had conceived[2738] **out-of** one, by our father Isaac;

11 (For being not yet born, neither having done any good or evil, that the **purpose**[2739] of God **down** election **may-be-remaining,** not **out-of** works, but **out-**of him **calling**;)

12 It was said **to-her,** the **larger**[2740] shall **slave to-the inferior**.[2741]

13 As it is written, Jacob have I loved, but Esau have I **detested**.

14 What shall we say then? Unrighteousness with God? **Not may-it-become**.

15 For he says to Moses, I will have mercy on whom I will have mercy, and I will have **pity** on whom I will have **pity**

16 So then, not of him that wills, nor of him that **runs,** but of God **being-merciful.**

17 For the Scripture says **to-the** Pharaoh, even for this same have I raised you up, that I might show my power in you, and that my name might be **through-message in** all the earth.

18 Therefore **he has** mercy on whom he will, and whom he will **he-is-hardening.**

19 You **will** say then **to** me, why does he yet b**l**ame? For who has **anti-stand** his **plan-counsel**?

20 Indeed-beside-sure, O man, who are you that **anti-answer to-the** God? Shall the thing **molded** say **to-him molding,** why have you made me **in-this-way**?

21 Have not the potter **authority** over the clay, of the same **dough** to make one vessel **into value,** and another **to un-value**?

22 Yet, if God, willing to show **the swelling-anger,** and to make his power known, **bear** with much **long-sacrifice-anger** the vessels of **swelling-anger down-fresh** into **from-ruin.**

23 And that he might make known the riches of his glory on the vessels of mercy, which he had **before-prepared-internally into** glory,

24 Even us, whom he has called, not **out-of** the Jews only, but also out-of the **nations**?

25 As he says also in **Hosea,** I will call them my people, which were not my people; and her beloved, which was not loved.

26 And it shall**-be,** in the **spot** where it was said **to** them, you are not my people; there shall they be called the **sons** of the living God.

[2738] Greek: "koites" transliterated as "coitus," also means bed, the place of semen, physical union of male and female genitals
[2739] Lit., before-place, to place before, or to place in advance
[2740] Larger, especially in age, bigger
[2741] "Elassoni," smaller in size, age, quantity, inferior,

27 **Isaiah** also **screamed over** Israel, though the number of the **sons** of Israel be as the sand of the sea, a remnant[2742] shall be saved:

28 For he will **together-finish** the work, and **together-cutting** in **righteous-togetherness**: because a **together-cutting** will the Lord **produce** upon the earth.

29 And as **Isaiah before-said,** except the Lord of **Armies**[2743] had left us a seed, we had been as Sodom, and been **assimilated as** Gomorrah.

30 What shall we say then? That the **nations**, which **chased** not after **righteous-togetherness**, have **down-get righteous-togetherness**, even the **righteous-togetherness** which is **out-of** faith.

31 But Israel, which **chased** after the law of **righteous-togetherness**, has not **anticipated**[2744] to the law of **righteous-togetherness**.

32 Through what? That not **out-of** faith, but as it were **out-of** the works of the law. For they **toward-strike**[2745] **to-the stone of-the toward-strike:**

33 As it is written, **be-perceiving**, I lay in Sion a **toward-strike** stone and rock of **scandal**:[2746] and whoever believes on him shall not be **down-disfigured**.

ROMANS CHAPTER 10

1 Brothers, my heart's well-seem and **beg-binding** to God for Israel is, that they might be saved.

2 For I **witness** that they have a zeal of God, but not **down** knowledge.

3 For they being-**un-thinking** of God's **righteous-togetherness** and going about to establish their own **righteous-togetherness**, have not **subordinated**[2747] themselves **to-the righteous-togetherness** of God.

4 For Christ is the **finish** of the law for **righteous-togetherness** to everyone that believes.

5 For Moses describes the **righteous-togetherness** which is of the law, that the man which does those things shall live by them.

6 But the **righteous-togetherness** which is of faith speaks on this wise, say not in your **heart**, who shall **up-walk** into heaven? (That is, to **down-lead** Christ.)

7 Or, who shall **down-walk** into the **abyss**? (That is, to bring up Christ again from the dead.)

8 But what says it? The **declaration near-squeeze of**-you, in your mouth, and in your heart, that is, the **declaration** of faith, which we preach.

9 That if you shall **same-say** with your mouth the Lord Jesus and shall believe in your heart that God has raised him from the dead, you shall be saved.

10 For with the **heart** man believes **into righteous-togetherness**; and with the mouth **same-saying** is made **into** salvation.

11 For the Scripture says, **whoever** believes on him shall not be **down-disfigured**.

12 For there is no **through-stall**[2748] between the Jew and the **Hellenics**: for the same Lord over all is rich **into** all that **upon-calling**[2749] him.

13 Because, whoever **upon-call** the name of the Lord shall be saved.

14 How then shall they **upon-call into** whom they have not believed? And how shall they believe in him of whom they have not heard? And how shall they hear **spacing-from** a preacher?

15 And how shall they preach, except they be sent? As it is written, how **belonging-to-the-hour** are the feet of them that **evangelize** peace and **evangelize the** good things!

16 But they have not all **under-hear**[2750] the **well-message**? Because Isaiah says, Lord, who has believed our **hearing**?

17 So then faith **out-of** hearing, and hearing **through** the **declaration** of God.

18 But I say, have they not heard? Yes, **indeed**, their **sound** went into all the earth, and their **declarations** to the **extremity of the housed-land.**[2751]

19 But I say, did not Israel know? **Foremost,** Moses says, I will **beside-zealous** by no people, by a nation **not-synthesizing** I will **beside-swelling-anger** you.

20 But **Isaiah** is very bold, and says, I was found of them that sought me not; I was made **in-shine to-them** that asked not after me.

[2742] Down-leave
[2743] Greek: "Saboath," of Hebrew origin, which means "Armies"
[2744] Or to be beforehand, to precede, to have arrived
[2745] Or, stub, towards-chop
[2746] Or snare
[2747] Under-arranged
[2748] Or, distinction, difference
[2749] Or, to entitle, to invoke
[2750] Or obey
[2751] Habitable earth

21 Yet, toward Israel he says, all day long I have **expanded** my hands **to** an **un-persuading** and **a disputing**[2752] people.

ROMANS CHAPTER 11

1 I say then, has God **from-shove** his people? **Not may-it-become.** For I am also an Israelite, of the seed of Abraham, the tribe of Benjamin.

2 God has not **from-shove** his people which he foreknew. **Perceive** you not what the Scripture says of **Elijah**? How he makes **in-happenings**[2753] to God **downing** Israel, saying,

3 Lord, they have killed your prophets, and **dig-down** your **sacrifice-place**s; and I am left alone, and they seek my life.

4 But what says the **apprise**[2754] of God **to-him**? I have **down-leave** to myself seven thousand men, who have not bowed the knee to Baal.

5 Even so then at this present **season** also there is a remnant **down** the election of grace.

6 And if by grace, then no more of works: otherwise, grace is no more grace. But if **out-of** works, then is it no more grace: otherwise, work is no more work.

7 What then? Israel has not **upon-happened** that which he seeks for; but the election has **upon-happened** it, and the rest were **petrified.**

8 (**Down-as** it is written, God has given them the spirit of **through-prick-nudge**, eyes that they should not see, and ears that they should not hear;) **until** this day.

9 And David says, let their table **became** a **trap**, and a **hunt,** and a **scandal,** and a **repayment to** them:

10 Let their eyes be darkened, that they may not see, and bow down their back **through-all**

11 I say then, have they stumbled that they should fall? **Not may-it-become!** But through their **beside-fall** salvation **to-the nations,** for to **beside-zealous them.**

12 Now if the **beside-fall** of them the riches of the world, and the **worsening** of them the riches of the **nations,** how much more their **filling**?

13 For I speak **to-you nations**, inasmuch as I am the apostle of the **nations,** I **glorify my attendance.**

14 If by any means I may **beside-zealous** my flesh and might save **any**[2755] of them.

15 For if the casting away of them the **exchange**[2756] **of-world,** what the **towards-taking**, but life from the dead?

16 For if the firstfruit holy, the **dough** also: and if the root holy, so the branches.

17 And if some of the branches be **broken-out,** and you, being a **field-olive tree**, were grafted **in** them, and with them **together-communion** of the **root** and fatness of the olive tree;

18 Boast not against the branches. But if you boast, you **lift** not the root, but the root you.

19 You **will** say then, the branches were **out-of-broken,** that I might be grafted in.

20 Ideally, because of unbelief they were **out-of-broken, yet** you stand by faith. Be not high-**disposed**, but fear:

21 For if God spared not the **nature-growth** branches, **not you he will spare.**

22 Be-perceiving therefore the **usefulness** and **from-cutting** of God: on them which fell, **from-cutting**; but toward you, **usefulness,** if you **remain** in **usefulness**: otherwise, you also shall be **out-of-cut.**

23 And they also, if they **remain** not still in unbelief, shall be gaffed in: for God is **powerful** to graft them in again.

24 For if you were cut out of the olive tree which is **field** by **nature-growth**, and were grafted **beside growth** into an **ideal-olive tree**: how much more shall these, which **down nature-growth,** be gaffed **to-the** private olive tree?

25 Because, I **will** not **brothers** that you should ignorant **of-the** mystery, lest you should be **disposed beside yourselves**; that **callousness, from section,** became to Israel, until the **filling** of the **nations into-come**.

26 And so all Israel shall be saved: as it is written, there shall **arrive out-of** Sion the Deliverer,[2757] and shall-**from-turn un-good-reverence** from Jacob:

[2752] Lit, anti-word, refute, dispute
[2753] Or in-obtain. in-to hit the target, in-chance upon
[2754] Or, to furnish what is needed, divine response; secular meaning of constituting a business, employ
[2755] Or some
[2756] Or change mutually, to down-change, adjustment, conciliation
[2757] Rush-Rescuer, present/middle/passive

27 For this my covenant **to-them,** when I shall **lift** their sins.

28 As concerning the **well-message**, **haters through you**: but **according-to** the election, beloved **through** the fathers.

29 For the gifts and calling of God **un-regrettable.**[2758]

30 For as you **once were-un-perusable to-the** God, yet now **you-have-mercy** through **they being-un-perusable.**

31 Even so have these also now **un-perusable**, that through your mercy they also **may-have-mercy.**

32 For God has **together-lock** them all in **un-perusable**, that he might have mercy **to** all.

33 O! **Depth** of the riches both of the wisdom and **knowing** of God! How **unsearchable** his **judgment-results,**[2759] and his ways **untraceable!**

34 For who has known the **thought** of the Lord? Or who has **become** his **together-plan-counsellor?**

35 Or who has **before-gives to-him**, and it shall be **repaid**[2760] **to-him** again?

36 For **out-of** him, and through him, and **into him**, **all** things: to whom glory **into the ages**. Amen.

ROMANS CHAPTER 12

1 I **beside-call** you therefore, **brothers, through** the **pity**[2761] of God, that you **beside-stand** your bodies a living sacrifice, holy, acceptable **to**-God, your **logical hired-service.**

2 And be not **together-schemed** to this world: but be you transformed[2762] **to-the up-young-new** of your mind, **into the seem-test by-you** what is the will of God, **the** good, and **well-pleasing,** and **mature**.

3 For I say, through the grace given **to-me**, to **everyone** that is **in** you, not to **be-high-disposed beside which is-binding to-be-disposed**; but **to-be-disposed into save-disposition**, **as** God has **parted** to every man measure of faith.

4 Because as we have many members in one body, and all members have not the same **practice**:

5 So we, many, are one body in Christ, and **down one of-another-same** members.

6 Having then gifts **differing**[2763] **down** the grace that is given to us, whether prophecy, **down** the **up-word** of faith;

7 Or **attendance in the attending**: or he that teach, **in the** teaching.

8 Or he that **beside-call, in beside-calling**: he that gives, **in singleness;**[2764] he that **before-stands** with **speed**; he that shows mercy, in **atonement-merriness.**[2765]

9 Love be **un-hypocritical. From-hate** that which is **wicked-hurtful; glue**[2766] **to-the** good.

10 To-the friendly-brothers into one-another-same with **friend-cherishing;** in **value before-leading**[2767] **one-another-same;**

11 Not **slow** in **speed, zealous to-**spirit; **slaving to-**the Lord.

12 Cheering to-the expectation; under-remain in tribulation; **towards-government to-the towards-prayer-wish.**

13 Communing to the **needs**[2768] of saints; **chase fond-lodging.**[2769]

14 Bless them which **chase** you: bless, and not **down-curse-pray.**

15 Cheer with **ones-cheering**, and weep with them that weep.

16 Into the same **disposition into one-another-same. Dispose** not high things, but **together-lead** to men of **humble disposition**. Be not **disposed beside yourselves.**

17 From-give to no man evil for evil. **Before-mind** things **ideally** in the sight of all men.

18 If **powerful, out-of** you, live peaceably with all men.

19 Beloved, avenge not yourselves, but give **spot to swelling-anger**: for it is written, vengeance[2770] mine; I will repay,[2771] says the Lord.

[2758] Lit., un-changed-care
[2759] Greek: "krima," "crime," judgment
[2760] Greek: instead-from-give
[2761] Greek is plural, and genitive case
[2762] Greek: "metamorphoo"
[2763] Greek: "diaphero," to through-bear, transliterated as "differ" or "different;" excel
[2764] Haplotetes, the antonym of "diplous" meaning double
[2765] Greek: "hilarotes" transliterated as hilarious, and means propitious (atonement); atonement-merry; associated with the "Mercyseat"
[2766] Or stick to, to cling, "keep company" with
[2767] Or prefer, to lead other before yourself
[2768] Or, employment, to furnish what is needed, useful
[2769] Or chase hospitality
[2770] Lit., out-justice
[2771] Greek: instead-from-give

20 Therefore if your **hater** hunger, feed him; if he thirsts, give him drink: for in so **producing,** you shall heap coals of fire on his head.

21 Be not overcome **under** evil but **conquer**[2772] the evil **in the** good.

ROMANS CHAPTER 13

1 Let every soul be **subordinate**[2773] **to** the **superior.**[2774] For there is no **authority if not under** God: the **authority** that be are **arranged under** God.

2 Whoever therefore **anti-arrange to-the authority, anti-stand** the **through-arrangement** of God: and they that **anti-stand** shall **take** to themselves **judgment-result**.

3 For **first-ranks**[2775] are not a **fear** to good works, but to the evil. **Will** you then not be afraid of the **authority**? Do that which is good, and you shall have praise **out-of** the same:

4 For he is the **attendant** of God **to-you into the** good. But if you **produce** that which is evil, be afraid; **because not without-cause he wears** the sword: for he is the **attendant** of God, a revenger to **swelling-anger into him** that **practices** evil.

5 Through-which necessity **to-be-subordinate** not only for **swelling-anger,** but also **through** conscience.

6 Through this, you-are-finishing load-taxes also: **because** they are God's **people-workers,**[2776] **towards-government into the same.**

7 Give therefore to all **the owed: load-taxes** to whom **load-taxes; finish-revenue** to whom **finish-revenue;** fear to whom fear; **value** to whom **value.**

8 Owe no man anything, but to love **one-another-same:** for he that loves **another-different** has **filled** the law.

9 For this, **not you-shall-commit-adultery, not you-shall-murder, not you–shall-steal, not you shall-be-false-witnessing, not you-shall-upon-feeling**; and if any **other-different** commandment, it is **up-head** in this saying, namely, you shall love your neighbor as yourself.

10 Love **works** no ill to his neighbor: therefore, love is the **filling** of the law.

11 And that, **perceiving** the **season,** that **already hour for-us** to awake out of sleep: for now, our salvation **near-squeeze** than when we believed.

12 The night is **forward-chop,**[2777] the day **has-near-squeezed**: let us therefore **from-place** the works of darkness and **be-clothed** the armor of light.

13 Let us walk **good-schemed,** as in the day; not in **laying** and drunkenness, not in **coitus**[2778] and wantonness,[2779] not in **quarrel,**[2780] and **zealousness.**

14 But **be-clothed**[2781] the Lord Jesus Christ, and make not **before-mind** for the flesh, **into the upon-feelings.**

ROMANS CHAPTER 14

1 Him that is weak in the faith **toward-take,** not **into through-judging of through-inventory**.

2 For one believes that he may eat all things: another, who is weak, eats **vegetables**.

3 The one eating, not make-out-to-be-nothing[2782] **him that eats not, the one not eating, but the not Judge the one eating: for God has towards-taken him**.

4 Who are you that judges **another's-same domestic**? To his own **lord** he **stands** or falls. Yes, he shall **stand because** God is **powerful** to make him stand.

5 Who indeed judges a day beside a day? Who yet is-judging every day? Each be-fully-burdened-wear in his **private** mind.

6 He that **disposed** the day, **disposes to** the Lord; and he that **disposes** not the day, to the Lord he **disposes not**. He that eats, eats to the Lord, for he gives God thanks; and he that eats not, to the Lord he eats not, and gives God thanks.

7 For none of us lives **to-himself,** and no man dies **to-himself.**

8 For whether we live, we live **to-**the Lord; and whether we die, we die **to-**the Lord: whether we live therefore, or die, we are the Lord's.

[2772] "Nikao," to defeat an enemy
[2773] Under-arranged
[2774] Lit., huper (above) and echo (to hold)
[2775] Or, original-rank, beginning-rank
[2776] Lit., laos (people)-ergon (work); "liturgist"
[2777] Or, cutting towards, progress

[2778] Greek: "koites" transliterated as "coitus," also means bed, the place of semen,
[2779] Or no control
[2780] Or, electioneering, quarrel, debates
[2781] Lit., in-down; or, in-sink, in-down-slipping
[2782] Or despise

9 Because **into this,** Christ both died, and **up-stand,** and **up-lived,** that he might be Lord both of the dead and living.

10 But why **are** you judging your brother? Or why **are you making-out-to-be-nothing your** brother? **Because** we shall all **beside-stand to-**the **judgment-step**[2783] of Christ.

11 It-is-written, because I live, says the Lord, every knee shall bow to me, and every tongue shall **same-say** to God.

12 So then **each** of us shall give **saying** of himself to God.

13 Let us not therefore judge **one-another-same** anymore: but judge this rather, that no man put a **toward-strike** or **scandal to-the** brother's way.

14 I **perceive,** and am persuaded by the Lord Jesus, that nothing **common** of itself: but **to-him** that **inventory** anything to be **common, to-him common.**

15 But if your brother be **distressed-sad** with your **food, not-still** down love **your-are-walking. From-ruin**[2784] not him with your **food,** for whom Christ died.

16 Then, not let-be-blasphemed your good.

17 For the kingdom of God is not **feeding** and **drinking;** but **righteous-togetherness,** and peace, and **cheerfulness** in the Holy **Spirit.**

18 For he that in these slaves **to-the** Christ **well-pleasing** to God and **seem-approved** of men.

19 Let us therefore chase the things **of-the** peace, and things **of house-building another-same.**

20 For **food down-loose** not the work of God. All things indeed **clean;** but evil for that man who eats with **toward-strike.**[2785]

21 Ideal neither to eat **meat,** nor to drink wine, nor whereby your brother **toward-strike,** or is **scandalized,**[2786] or is made weak.

22 You that have faith? Have **to-yourself** before God. Happy he that **judge** not himself in that thing which he **seem-test.**[2787]

23 And he that **through-judge** is **down-judged** if he eat, because not **out-**of faith: yet everything which not **out-of** faith is sin.

[2783] Greek: "Bema," a step, foot-breadth, rostrum, tribunal
[2784] Greek: "apo" (from) and "alethros" (ruin), to destroy fully
[2785] Or, stub, towards-chop
[2786] Or, snared

ROMANS CHAPTER 15

1 We then that are **powerful owes** to bear the **weakness** of the **un-powerful,** and not to please ourselves.

2 Let every one of us please neighbor **into** good **towards house-building.**

3 For even Christ pleased not himself; but as it is written, the **defaming**[2788] of them that **defamed** you fell **upon** me.

4 For whatever things were **before-written** were written for our **teaching,** that we through **under-remaining** and **beside-calling** of the **Scriptures** might have **expectation.**

5 Now the God of **under-remaining,** and **beside-calling** grant you **the same disposition, in one-another-same down** Christ Jesus:

6 That you may with **same-feeling,** one mouth glorify God, even the Father of our Lord Jesus Christ.

7 Through-which towards-take one-another-same, as Christ also **towards-take** us to the glory of God.

8 Now I say that Jesus Christ was an **attendant** of the circumcision for the truth of God, to **stabilize** the promises **to-the** fathers:

9 And that the **nations** might glorify God for mercy; as it is written, **through this,** I will **out-of-same-saying to-you in** the **nations,** and **psalm**[2789] **to-your** name.

10 And again he says, **be-good-disposed** you **nations,** with his people.

11 And again, praise the Lord, all **nations;** and **upon-praise** him, all **the** people.

12 And again, **Isaiah** says, there shall be a root of Jesse, and he that shall **up-stand** to **be-First-Rank** over the **nations;** in him shall the **nations expect.**

13 Now the God of **expectation.** fill you with all **cheerfulness** and peace in believing, that you may **exceed** in **expectation.,** through the power of the **Holy Spirit.**

14 And I myself also am persuaded of you, my **brothers,** that you also are full of **good-togetherness,**

[2787] Approve with good opinion
[2788] Lit., notorious, name
[2789] To sing with stringed instruments

filled with all **knowing**, **powerful** also to **mind-place**[2790] **one-another-same**.

15 Nevertheless, **brothers**, I have written the more **daring to-you** from **section**, as **up-reminding you**, because of the grace that is given to me **under** God,

16 Into my being, a **people-worker**,[2791] of Jesus Christ to the **nations**, **priest-working** the **well-message** of God, that the offering[2792] up of the **nations** might be **well-towards-welcomed**, being sanctified by the **Holy Spirit**.

17 I have therefore whereof I may **boast** through Jesus Christ in those things **towards** God.

18 For I will not dare to speak of any of those things which Christ has not **down-worked** by me, to make the **nations under-hear**, by word and **work**,

19 In power of-signs and **of-wonders**, in **power** of the Spirit of God; so that from Jerusalem,[2793] and round about **until** Illyricum, I have **filled** the **well-message** of Christ.

20 Yet, **in-this-way**, **being-friend-of-value** to **well-message**, not where Christ was named, **that not** I should **house-build upon another's-same foundation**:

21 But as it is written, to whom he was not **up-message about**, they shall see: and they that have not heard shall understand.

22 For which cause also I have been much **cut-into**[2794] from coming **towards** you.

23 But now having no more **spot** in these **slopes** and having a **upon-yearn** these many **years** to come **towards** you.

24 Whenever I take my **travel** into Spain, I will come **to-you**: for I **expect** to see you in my **through-travel**, and to be **before-dispatch under** you, if **foremost** I be filled **from section of you**.

25 But now **I-travel into** Jerusalem to **attend to-the** saints.

26 For it has **well-seem** them of Macedonia and Achaia to make a certain **communion** for the poor saints which are **in** Jerusalem.

27 It has well-seem them; and **they owe them**; because if the **nations** have been made **commun on** of their **spiritual, they-owe** also to **people-work**,[2795] **to-them** in **flesh-things**.

28 When therefore I have **upon-finish** this, and have sealed **to-them** this fruit, I will come **through** you into Spain.

29 And I **perceive** that, when I come **toward** you, I shall come in the **filling** of the blessing of the **well-message** of Christ.

30 Now I **beside-call** you, **brothers, that through** the Lord Jesus Christ and for the love of the Spirit, that you **together-agonize to-me** in **the towards-prayers-wish** to God **over** me;

31 That I may be **rush-rescued** from them that **un-pursuable** in Judaea; and that my **attendance** which for Jerusalem may be **good-towards-welcome** of the saints;

32 That I may come **to-you in cheerfulness** by the will of God and **together-pause**[2796] **to-you**.

33 Now the God of peace with you all. Amen.

ROMANS CHAPTER 16

1 I **together-stand to-you** Phebe our sister, which is an **attendant** of the Church which is at Cenchrea:

2 That you **toward-welcome** her in the Lord, as **deserving of-the** saints, and that you **beside-stand** her in whatever **practices** she has need of you: for she has been a **patroness**[2797] of many, and of myself also.

3 Embrace Priscilla and Aquila my **together-workers** in Christ Jesus:

4 Who have **over** my **soul under-place** their own necks: **to** whom not only I give thanks, but also all the Churches of the **nations**.

5 Likewise he Church that is in their house. **Embrace** my beloved Epaenetus,[2798] who is the firstfruit of Achaia **to-Christ**.

6 Embrace Mary, who much **fatigue into** us.

[2790] Noutheteo-mind-placing, to warn, to admonish
[2791] Lit., laos (people)-ergon (work); "liturgist"
[2792] Greek: towards-carry
[2793] Hierou-priest, sacred) and salem (peace)
[2794] Lit., in-cut, impede, delayed
[2795] Lit., laos (people)-ergon (work); "liturgy"
[2796] Or, refreshed
[2797] Greek: "prostatis," patroness, (before-stand)
[2798] Lit., On-praise, upon-praise

7 Embrace Andronicus[2799] and Junia,[2800] my kinsmen, and my fellow-prisoners, who are **upon-sign in** the apostles, who also **became** in Christ before me.

8 Embrace Amplias[2801] my beloved in the Lord.

9 Embrace, Urbane, our **together-worker** in Christ, and Stachys[2802] my beloved.

10 Embrace Apelles, **seem-approved** in Christ. **Embrace** them which are **out-**of Aristobulus.'[2803]

11 Embrace Herodion my kinsman. **Embrace** them that be of the of Narcissus, which are in the Lord.

12 Embrace Tryphenaand Tryphosa, who **fatigued** in the Lord. **Embrace** the beloved Persis, which **fatigued** much in the Lord.

13 Embrace Rufus chosen in the Lord, and his mother and mine.

14 Embrace Asyncritus, Phlegon, Hermas, Patrobas, Hermes, and the **brothers** which are with them.

15 Embrace Philologus, and Julia, Nereus, and his sister, and Olympas, and all the saints which are with them.

16 Embrace one-another-same with a holy **friend-kiss.** The Churches of Christ **embrace,** you.

17 Now I **beside-call** you, **brothers, spy**[2804] them which cause **two-stands** and **scandals beside** to the **teaching** which you have learned; and **out-of-cline from** them.

18 For they that are such **slave** not **to-our** Lord Jesus Christ, but their own belly; and **through useful-saying** and **blessings out-of-cheat** the **hearts** of the **not-evil.**[2805]

19 For your **under-hearing** is **from-sufficient into** all. I am **cheerful** therefore **over you:** but yet I would have you wise **to-be into** that which is good, and **un-mixed yet into** evil.

20 Yet, the God of peace shall **together-crush** Satan under your feet shortly. The grace of our Lord Jesus Christ with you. Amen.

21 Timothy my **together-worker,** and Lucius,[2806] and Jason, and Sosipater, my kinsmen, **embrace,** you.

22 I Tertius, who wrote epistle, **embrace** you in the Lord.

23 Gaius my **foreign-lodger,** and of the whole Church, **embrace** you. Erastus the **house-lawyer** of the city, you **embrace,** and Quartus,[2807] **the** brother.

24 The grace of our Lord Jesus Christ with you all. Amen.

25 Now **to-him** that is **of-power** to **strengthen** you **down** my **well-message,** and the preaching of Jesus Christ, **down** the revelation of the mystery, which was **silenced**[2808] **to-uninterrupted-times, to-eternal,**

26 But now **shines, both through** the **prophetic Scriptures, down** the **upon-arrangement** of the **eternal** God, made known **into** all nations **into** the **under-hearing** of faith:

27 To God, only wise, glory through Jesus Christ **into the ages** Amen.

[2799] Man-conqueror
[2800] Or "Junias," feminine noun
[2801] Enlarge
[2802] Grain stalk, corn stalk
[2803] Lit., Best-counsel, dinner-counsel
[2804] Take aim, note, mark, watch, skeptic
[2805] Or innocent
[2806] Illuminative
[2807] Fourth
[2808] Or, hushed

1 CORINTHIANS

1 CORINTHIANS CHAPTER 1

1 Paul, called apostle of Jesus Christ through the will of God, and Sosthenes[2809] **the** brother,

2 Unto the Church of God, which is at Corinth, **to-them** that are sanctified in Christ Jesus, called saints, with all that in every place **upon-calling**[2810] the name of Jesus Christ our Lord, both theirs and ours:

3 Grace **to-you**, and peace, from God our Father, and the Lord Jesus Christ.

4 I thank my God always on your behalf, for the grace of God which is given you by Jesus Christ;

5 That in everything you are enriched by him, in all **saying**, and all **knowing**;

6 Even as the **witness** of Christ was for **stabilized** in you:

7 So that you not **be-late** in **grace**; from-out-welcoming the **revelation** of our Lord Jesus Christ:

8 Who shall also **stabilize** you **to** the **finish**, **un-called-in**[2811] in the day of our Lord Jesus Christ.

9 God is **believing**, by whom you were called **to** the **communion** of his Son Jesus Christ our Lord.

10 Now I **beside-call** you, **brothers**, by the name of our Lord Jesus Christ, that you all speak the same thing, and there be no **splits in** you; but you be **down-fresh** in the same **thought** and in the same **opinion**.

11 For it has been declared **to-me** of you, my **brothers**, by them of Chloe,[2812] that there are **quarrel**,[2813] among you.

12 Now this I say, that every one of you says, I am of Paul; and I of Apollos; and I of Cephas; and I of Christ.

13 is Christ **parted**? Was Paul crucified for you? Or were you baptized in the name of Paul?

14 I thank God that I baptized none of you, but Crispus[2814] and Gaius;

15 Lest any should say that I had baptized **into my** name.

16 And I also baptized the household of Stephanas:[2815] besides, I know not whether I baptized any other.

17 For Christ sent me not to baptize, but to preach the **well-message**: not with wisdom of words, lest the cross of Christ should be **empty**.

18 For the preaching of the cross is **to-them** that **from-ruin**[2816] **moronic**; but **to-us** which are saved it is the power of God.

19 For it is written, I will **from-ruin** the wisdom of the wise, and will bring to nothing the understanding of the **one-who-understands**

20 Where the wise? Where is the scribe? Where the **together-seekers**[2817] of this world? Has not God made **moronic** the wisdom of this world?

21 For after that in the wisdom of God the world by wisdom knew not God, it pleased God by the **moronic** of preaching to save them that believe.

22 For the Jews **ask** a sign, and the Greeks seek wisdom:

23 But we preach Christ, crucified; **to-the** Jews a **scandal**,[2818] and **to** the **Hellenics moronic**.

24 But **to-them** which are called, both Jews and **Hellenics**, Christ the power of God, and the wisdom of God.

25 Because the **moronic** of God is wiser than men; and **without-strength** of God is **forceful** than men.

26 For you see your calling, **brothers**, how that not many wise men **down** the flesh, not many **powerful**, not many **well-birthed**:[2819]

27 But God has chosen the **moronic** things of the world to **down-disfigure** the wise; and God has chosen the **without-strength** things of the world to **down-disfigure** the things which are **forceful**;

28 And **things without-kin** of the world, and things which are **made-nobody**, has God chosen, and things which **not exists**, to **down-un-work** things that **exist**:

29 That no flesh should **boast** in his presence.

30 Yet **out-of** him are you in Christ Jesus, who of God **was-became to-us** wisdom, and **righteous-**

[2809] Safe-strength, saves-strength
[2810] Or, to entitle, to invoke
[2811] Or un-accused
[2812] Defined as "green"
[2813] Or, electioneering, quarrel, debates
[2814] Transliterated as "crisp"

[2815] Crowned
[2816] Greek: "apo" (from) and "alethros" (ruin), to destroy fully
[2817] Or, disputers, investigate jointly
[2818] Or snare
[2819] Or nobles

togetherness, and sanctification, and **from-loosing**:[2820]

31 That, **down-as** it is written, he that **boast**, let him **boast** in the Lord.

1 CORINTHIANS CHAPTER 2

1 And I, **brothers**, when I came **to-you**, came not with **superiority** of speech or of wisdom, **down-messaging to-you** the **witness** of God.

2 For I **judged** not to **perceive** anything among you, **if not** Jesus Christ, and him crucified.

3 And I was with you in weakness, and in fear, and in much trembling.

4 And my speech and my preaching not with **faith** words of man's wisdom, but in **from-show**[2821] of the Spirit and of power:

5 That your faith should not stand in the wisdom of men, but in the power of God.

6 **Yet,** we speak wisdom among them that are **mature**: yet not the wisdom of this **age**, nor of the **first-ranks** of this **age**, that **being-down-un-worked**:

7 But we speak the wisdom of God in a mystery, the hidden, which God **before-defined before** the **ages to** our glory:

8 Which none of the **first-ranks** of this **age** knew: for had they known, they would not have crucified the Lord of glory.

9 But as it is written, eye has not **perceived**, nor ear heard, neither have **up-walked** into the **hearts** of man, the things which God has **internally-prepared** for them that love him.

10 But God has revealed **to-us** by his Spirit: for the Spirit searches all things, yes, the deep things of God.

11 For what man **perceives** the things of a man, **if not** the spirit of man which is in him? Even so the things of God **perceive** no man, but the Spirit of God.

12 Now we have **taken**, not the spirit of the world, but the spirit which is **out-of** God; that we might **perceive** the things that are **graced** to us of God.

13 Which things also we speak, not in the words which man's wisdom teaches, but which the Holy Spirit teaches: **together-judging spiritual to-spiritual.**

14 But the **soulish** man **welcomes** not the things of the Spirit of God: for they are **moronic to-him**: **not he-is-powerful to-know,** because they are spiritually **up-judged**.

15 **Yet, the** spiritual **up-judges** all things, yet he himself is **up-judged** of no man.

16 **Because,** who has known the **thought** of the Lord, that he **shall- together-embark**[2822] him? **Yet,** we have the **thought** of Christ.

1 CORINTHIANS CHAPTER 3

1 And I, **brothers, not powerful to-**speak **to-you** as to spiritual, but as **to** fleshly, as **to non-speaking-infants** in Christ.

2 I have fed you with milk, and not with **food**: for **not-yet** you were **powerful**, neither yet now are you **powerful**.

3 **Because,** you are yet **fleshly: because the-where in** you zealousness, and **quarrel,**[2823] and **two-stands,** are you not **fleshly**, and walk as men?

4 For while one says, I am of Paul; and **another-different**, I of Apollos; are you not **fleshly**?

5 Who then is Paul, and who Apollos, but **attendants** by whom you believed, even as the Lord gave to every man?

6 I have planted, Apollos watered; but God gave the **growth**.

7 So then neither is he that plants anything, neither he that waters; but God that gives the **up-growth**.

8 Now he that plants and he that waters are one. and every man shall receive his **private pay down** his **private cut-labor.**

9 For we are **together-workers** with God: you are God's **land-work**, you God's **house-building**.

10 According to the grace of God, which is given **to** me, as a **first-rank-technician,**[2824] I have **placed** the foundation, and another **house-builds upon it**. But, let every man **look** how he **house-**builds thereupon.

[2820] Or redemption
[2821] Or to show off, demonstration
[2822] Greek: sun (together) and bibazo (to force), drive-together, unite, infer, together-board a ship
[2823] Or, electioneering, quarrel, debates
[2824] Greek is "architekton," transliterated as "architect"

11 For **other-same** foundation **not-one is-powerful to-place beside the-one** laid,[2825] which is Jesus Christ.

12 Yet, if any **house-build** upon this foundation gold, silver, **valuable** stones, **trees**,[2826] hay, stubble;

13 Every man's work shall-**become shine**: for the day shall **make-it-clear**, because it shall be revealed by fire; and the fire shall **seem-test** every man's work of **who-which-sort** it is.

14 If any man's work **remains** which he has **house-build** thereupon, he shall **take pay**.

15 If any man's work shall be burned, he shall be-**injured**: but he, himself, shall be saved; yet so as **through** fire.

16 Perceive you not that you are the temple of God, and the Spirit of God **homing** in you?

17 If any man **corrupts**[2827] the temple of God, him shall God **corrupt**; for the temple of God is holy, which you are.

18 Let no man **out-of-cheat** himself. If any man among you seems to be wise in this **age**, let him become a **moron**, that he may **become** wise.

19 For the wisdom of this world is **moronic** with God. For it is written, He **clutches** the wise in their own **all-working**.[2828]

20 And again, the Lord knows the **inventory** of the wise, that they are **empty**.[2829]

21 Therefore let no man **boast** in men. For all things are yours;

22 Whether Paul, or Apollos, or Cephas, or the world, or life, or death, or things present, or things **impending**, all are yours;

23 And you are Christ's; and Christ God's

1 CORINTHIANS CHAPTER 4

1 Let a man so **inventory** of us, as of the **subservients**[2830] of Christ, and **house-lawyers** of the mysteries of God.

2 Moreover, it is **sought** in **house-lawyers**, that a man be found **believing**.

3 But, with me, it is a very small thing that I should be **up-judged** of you, or of man's **day**: yes, I **up-judge** not **myself.**

4 Because, not I-am-conscious to-myself; but I am not, **in this, made-righteous**: but he that **up-judges** me is the Lord.

5 Therefore judge nothing before **season**, until the Lord come, who both will bring to light the hidden things of darkness and will make **shine** the **plan-counsels** of the **hearts**: and then shall every man have **upon-praise** of God.

6 And these things, **brothers**, I have in a **changed-scheme** to myself and Apollos **through you**; that you might learn in us not to **be-disposed** above that which is written, that no **one over one being-inflated, downing of-another-different.**

7 For who makes you to **through-judge**? And what have you that you **did not take**? Now if you **did take**, why do you boast, as if you have not **taken-it**?

8 Now you **already** full, now you are rich, you have reigned **spacing-from** us: and **owe besides you-reign,** that we also might **together-reign.**

9 For **I-am-seeming** that God has **from-show**[2831] us the apostles last, as **upon-death**: for we become a **theater to** the world, and to angels, and to men.

10 We **morons through** Christ, but you **disposed** in Christ; we **without-strength**, but you **forceful**; you **valued**, but we **un-valued**.

11 Until this present hour we both hunger, and thirst, and are naked, and are **curtail-with-fist**, and **we-are-non-stationary**.

12 And **fatigue-cut**, working with our own hands: being **spear-abuser**, we bless; being **chased**, we **tolerate**[2832] it:

13 Being **blasphemed** we **beside-call**: we are made as the **about-cleanse** of the world, the **scum**[2833] of all things **until** this day.

14 I write not these things to **invert** you, but as my beloved **children** I **mind-place**.

[2825] Greek: to lay in a passive horizontal position
[2826] The oldest Greek texts (Alexandrian texts) for 1 Corinthians 3:12 reads: "valuable trees;" in lieu of "valuable stones"
[2827] Or, to pine, to waste, to rot
[2828] Craftiness
[2829] Or, empty through unsuccessful search
[2830] Lit., under-oarsman, generally a subordinate
[2831] Or exhibit
[2832] Or, to hold oneself up against
[2833] About-rub

15 For though you have ten thousand **boy-leaders** in Christ, yet not many fathers: for in Christ Jesus, I have **birthed** you through the **well-message**.

16 Then, **I-am-beside-calling** you, be you **imitators** of me.

17 For this cause have I **dispatched to-you Timothy**, who is my beloved **child**, and **believing** in the Lord, who shall **remind you** of my ways which be in Christ, as I teach **universally** in every Church.

18 Now some are **inflated**, as though I would not come **towards** you.

19 But I will come **towards you** shortly, if the Lord will, and will know, not the speech of them which are **inflated**, but the power.

20 For the kingdom of God is not in word, but in power.

21 What will **you?** Shall I come **towards** you with a rod, or in love, and the spirit of **mildness**?

1 CORINTHIANS CHAPTER 5

1 It is **heard in you prostitution** and **the-this prostitution** as is not so much as named **in** the **nations**, that one should have his father's wife.

2 And you are **inflated**, and have not rather mourned, that he that has **practiced** this **work** might be **out-lifted out-of middle of-**you.

3 Because, indeed, as absent **to-body**, but present **to-spirit**, have judged already, as though I were present, **the-one** that has so **down-worked**.

4 In the name of our Lord Jesus Christ, when you are gathered together, and my spirit, **together to-the** the power of our Lord Jesus Christ,

5 To **beside-give** such **to-Satan** for the **whole-ruin** of the flesh, that the spirit may be saved in the day of the Lord Jesus.

6 Your **boasting** not good. **Perceive** you not that a little **ferment, ferments** the whole **dough**?

7 Purge out therefore the old **ferment**, that you may be a new-**young dough**, as you are **unfermented**. For even Christ our **Passover** is sacrificed for us:

8 Therefore, let us **keep-the-festival**, not **in** old **ferment**, neither with the **ferment** of evil and **wicked-hurtfulness**; but in **unfermented** of **sun-judged** and truth.

9 I wrote **to-you** in an epistle not to **together-mix** with **paramours**:

10 Yet not altogether with the **paramours** of this world, or with the **more-havers**, or **snatchers**, or with idolaters; for then **you-are-owing to**-go-out of the world.

11 But now I have written **to-you** not to **together-mix**, if any man that is called a brother be a **paramour,** or **more-haver**, or an idolater, or a **spear-abuser**, or a drunkard, or a **snatcher**; with such a one no not to eat.

12 For what have I to do to judge them also that are **outside**? Do not you judge them that are within?

13 But them that are **outside**, God judges. Therefore, **out-of-lift out-of** yourselves that **wicked-hurtful** person.

1 CORINTHIANS CHAPTER 6

1 Dare any of you, having a **practice towards another-different**, **to-be-judged upon** the **unrighteous** and not **upon** the saints?

2 Do you not **perceive** that the saints shall judge the world? And if the world shall be judged by you, are you **un-deserving** to **criterion-judge**[2834] the **least**?

3 Perceive you not that we shall judge angels? How much more things that pertain **to-livelihood**?

4 If then you have **criterion-judgment to-livelihood**, **seat t**hem to judge who are **out-of-nothing** in the Church?

5 I speak **to-your invert**. is it so, that there is not a wise man among you? No, not one that shall be **powerful** to **through-judge** between his **brothers**?

6 But brother **is-judged** with brother, and that **upon** the unbelievers.

7 Now therefore there is utterly a **worsening** among you, because you **crime-judge**[2835] with **yourselves**. Why do you not rather take wrong? Why do you not rather be **from-deprived?**

8 But, you **are-unrighteous,** and **from-deprived** and **these-things to brothers**.

9 Perceive you not that the unrighteous shall not inherit the kingdom of God? Be not **seduced**; neither

---

[2834] Or, to have a tribunal, have a rule of judging

[2835] Greek: "krima," transliterated as "crime" and also means judgment

paramours, nor idolaters, nor adulterers, nor **effeminate,**[2836] nor **male-coitus**[2837]

10 Nor thieves, nor **more-havers**, nor drunkards, nor **spear-abusers**, nor **snatchers**, shall inherit the kingdom of God.

11 And such were some of you: but you are washed, but you are sanctified, but you are **righteous** in the name of the Lord Jesus, and by the Spirit of our God.

12 All things are lawful **to-me,** but all things are not **together-bearing:** all things are lawful for me, but not I[2838] **will-be-authorized** under any.

13 Foods for the belly, and the belly for **foods**: yet God shall **down-work** both it and them. Now the body not **to-the prostitution**, but **to-the** Lord; and the Lord **to-the** body.

14 And God has both raised up the Lord and will also raise up us **through** his own power.

15 Perceive you not that your bodies are the members of Christ? Shall I then **lift** the members of Christ, and make them members of a **prostitute**? **Not may-it-become**.

16 What? **Perceive** you not that he which is **glued**[2839] to a **prostitute** is one body? For two, **shows** he, shall be **first** flesh.

17 But he that is **glued to** the Lord is one spirit.

18 Flee **prostitution**. Every sin that a man does is **outside** the body; **yet** he that **paramour** sins **into** his own body.

19 What? **Perceive** you not that your body is the temple of the Holy Spirit in you, which you have of God, and you are not your own?

20 For you are bought[2840] with **value**: Therefore, glorify God in your body, and in your spirit, which are God's.

1 CORINTHIANS CHAPTER 7

1 Yet, about the things **which** you wrote **to-me: ideal** for a man not to **fasten-to** a woman.

2 Yet, through the prostitutions, let every man have **of-himself** wife, and let every woman have her **private** husband.

3 Let the husband **from-give to** the wife **the owing, well-thought**: and likewise, also the wife **to-the** husband.

4 The wife has not **authority** of her **private** body, but the husband: and likewise, also the husband has not **authority** of his **private** body, but the wife.

5 Not **from-deprive one-another-same, if not** with **together-voice**[2841] toward season, that you may **school to-the fast** and **to-the** prayer; and come together again, that Satan not **probe-test** you for your **un-governed**.

6 Yet, I speak this by **together-knowing**[2842] not of **upon-arrange**.

7 Because, I will that all men were even as I myself. But every man has his **private grace** of God, one after this manner, and another after that.

8 I say therefore to the unmarried and widows, it is **ideal** for them if they **remain** even as I.

9 Yet, if they not **are-in-governing**, let them marry: **because** it is **better-government**[2843] to marry than to burn.

10 Yet, to-the married I **beside-message**, not I, but the Lord, let not the wife **space** from husband:[2844]

11 Yet, if she **space**, let her remain unmarried, or be **exchanged**[2845] to husband: and the husband **not release a** wife.

12 Yet, to the rest speak I, not the Lord: If any brother has a wife that believes not, and she be **together-well-seem** to **home** with him, **not release her**.

13 And the woman which has a husband that believes not, and if he be **together-well-seem** to **home** with her, **not release** him.

14 For the unbelieving husband is sanctified by the wife, and the unbelieving wife is sanctified by the husband: else were your children unclean; but now are they holy.

[2836] Or catamite
[2837] Greek: "arsenokoites" transliterated as "male-coitus;" "coitus also means bed, the place of semen, physical union of genitals
[2838] Lit., "ego"-self-confident, self-image, self-importance, self-esteem
[2839] Or, to stick to, to cling, to keep company with
[2840] Lit., to go to the market, redeem
[2841] Or symphony

[2842] Or with-knowledge
[2843] Greek: "kreisson," neuter of "kreitton," a comparative derivative of "kratos;" translated as "cracy" in democracy—people (demo)-government ('cracy' (kratos))
[2844] Compare 1 Corinthians 11:11
[2845] Or change mutually, to down-change, adjustment, conciliation

15 Yet, if the unbelieving **space**, let him **space**. A brother or a sister is not **enslaved** in such: **yet,** God has called us to peace.

16 For **how perceive** you, wife, whether you shall save your husband? Or how **perceive** you, man, whether you shall save your wife?

17 But as God has **sectioned to-each**, as the Lord has called everyone, so let him walk. And so, I **through-arrange** in all Churches.

18 Is any man called being circumcised? Let him not become **un-upon-pulled**. is any called in uncircumcision? Let him not be circumcised.

19 The circumcision is nothing, and the uncircumcision is nothing, but the **watching** of the commandments of God.

20 Let every man **remain** in the same calling **to-which** he was called.

21 Are you called a **slave**? Care not for it: but if you **are-powerful to-become** free, **use-it**[2846] rather.

22 For he that is called in the Lord, a **slave**, is the Lord's freeman: likewise, also he that is called, free, is Christ's **slave**.

23 You are bought[2847] **of-value**; **not become slaves** of men.

24 Brothers, **each, in which** he is called, **in this remain beside** God.

25 Now concerning virgins I have no **upon-arrange** of the Lord: yet I give my **opinion**, as one that has mercy of the Lord to be **believing**.

26 I **do-by-law** therefore that this is **ideal to-be-under-originating through** the present **necessity,** that **ideal** for a man so **to exist.**

27 Are you bound **to-wife**? Seek not to be loosed. **Are** you loosed from a wife? Seek not a wife.

28 Yet also, if you marry, you has not sinned; and if a virgin marry, she has not sinned. Nevertheless, such shall have trouble in the flesh: but I spare you.

29 Yet, this I **show, brothers**, the **season together-stall**: it remains, that both they that have wives be as though they had none;

30 And they that weep, as though they wept not; and they that **cheerful**, as though they not **cheerful**; and they that buy,[2848] as though not **down-holding**;

31 And they that use[2849] this world, as not **down-use**: for the **scheme** of this world passes away.

32 Yet, I will have you without **portion-worry**. He that is unmarried cares for the things that belong to the Lord, how he may please the Lord:

33 But he that is married cares for the things that are of the world, how he may please **to-the** wife.

34 Has-been-apportion-parted, a wife and a virgin. The unmarried woman cares for the things of the Lord, that she may be holy both in body and in spirit: but she that is married cares for the things of the world, how she may please **to-the** husband.

35 And this I speak for your own **bearing-together**; not that I may cast a **noose** upon you, but for that which is **well-schemed**, and that you may **well-towards-sit** upon the Lord **not-dragged-around**.

36 Yet, if any man **do-by-law** that he behaves himself **un-schemed upon** his virgin, if she **beyond-acme**, and **is-owing to-be-becoming**, let him do what he will, he sins not: **let-them -marry**.

37 Nevertheless he that **stands settled-seated** in his **heart**, having no **necessity**, but has **authority about** his **private** will, and has so **judged** in his **heart** that he will **guard** his virgin, **produces ideally**.

38 So then he that **out-marries produces ideally**; but he that **not out-marries better-governing is-producing**.

39 The wife is bound **upon** the law **as-much uninterrupted-time as** her husband lives; but f her husband **sleeps**, she is **free** to be married to whom she will; only in the Lord.

40 But she is happier if she so **remains,** after my **opinion**: and **I-am-seeming** also that I have the Spirit of God.

1 CORINTHIANS CHAPTER 8

1 Now **concerning** things offered **to**-idols, we **perceive** that we all have **knowing. Knowing inflates**, but love **house-build**.

[2846] Or, to inform, to tell, to furnish what is needed, to use, to employ, apprise
[2847] Lit., to go to the market, redeem
[2848] Lit., to go to the market, redeem
[2849] Or, to inform, to tell, to furnish what is needed, to use, to employ, apprise

2 And if any man **seems** that he **perceives** anything, he knows nothing yet as **it-is-binding** to know.

3 But if any man love God, the same is known of him.

4 **About then,** the **feeding** of **idol-sacrifices**, we **perceive** that an idol nothing in the world, and that none **other-different** God but one.

5 For though there be that are **said** gods, whether in heaven or in earth, (as there be gods many, and lords many,)

6 But to us one God, the Father, **out-**of whom all things, and we **into him**; and one Lord Jesus Christ, **through** whom all things, and we **through** him.

7 **But,** not in every man that **knowing:** for some with conscience of the idol **until present** eat as **idol-sacrifices**; and their conscience being **without-strength** is **stained**.

8 But **food beside-stand** us not to God: for neither, if we eat, are we **excelling**; neither, if we eat not, are we **late**.

9 Yet, **be-looking not** this **authority** of yours become a **toward-strike**[2850] **to-them** that are **without-strength**.

10 For if **anyone perceive** you which has **knowing recline** at meat in the **idol-shrine**, shall not the conscience of him which is weak **house-build** to eat those things which are **idol-sacrifices**;

11 And through your **knowing,** shall the weak brother **from-ruin** for whom Christ died?

12 But when you sin **into** the **brothers**, and **thump** their weak conscience, you sin **into** Christ.

13 **Through-which,** if **feeding scandalizes**[2851] my brother, I will eat no **food** while the world stands, lest I **scandalize** my brother.

1 CORINTHIANS CHAPTER 9

1 Am I not an apostle? Am I not free? Have I not seen Jesus Christ, our Lord? Are not you my work in the Lord?

2 If I be not an apostle **to-others-same, but surely,** I am **to-you:** for the seal of my apostleship are you in the Lord.

3 **My apology**[2852] **to-them** that **up-judging** me is this,

4 Have we not **authority** to eat and to drink?

5 Have we not **authority** to lead about a sister, a wife, as well as other apostles, and the **brothers** of the Lord, and Cephas?

6 Or I only and Barnabas, have we not **authority not** to **work**?

7 Who goes a warring any at his own **soldier-rations**? Who plants a vineyard, and eats not of the fruit **of-him**? Or who **shepherds** a flock, and eats not of the milk of the flock?

8 Say I these things as a man? Or says not the law the same also?

9 For it is written in the law of Moses, you shall not muzzle the mouth of the **bull** that **threshes**. Does God care for **bulls**?

10 Or, **he says** altogether **through-us**? **Through-us**, is written **that on expectation is-owing** he that plow, **to-be-plowing**; and that he that threshes in **expectation** should be **partner**[2853] of his **expectation**.

11 If we have sown **to-you spiritual-things**, a **great** thing if we shall reap your **fleshly-thing**s?

12 If others be **partner** of **the authority** over you, not we rather? Nevertheless, we have not used[2854] this **authority**; but **roof** all things, lest we should **cut-into** the **well-message** of Christ.

13 Do you not **perceive** that they which **works out of-the priest-place-things**[2855] live of the **priest-place**? And they which **toward-sit** at the **sacrifice-place are-together-sharing** with the **sacrifice-place**?

14 Even so has the Lord **through-arranged** that they which **down-message** the **well-message** should live of the **well-message**.

15 But I have used[2856] none of these things: neither have I written these things, that it should be so **become in to-me:** for **ideal** for me to die, than any man should make my **boasting empty**.

16 For though I **evangelize**, I have nothing to **boast** of: **because necessity** is laid upon me; **yes,** woe is to me, if I **evangelize not!**

[2850] Or, stub, towards-chop
[2851] Or snare
[2852] Compound of "apo" (from) and logo (word, saying), also means defense
[2853] Or, with-holder, change-holder, after-holder, sharer
[2854] Or, to inform, to tell, to furnish what is needed, to use, to employ
[2855] Or sacred things
[2856] Or, to inform, to tell, to furnish what is needed, to use, to employ

17 For if I **practice** this thing **voluntarily**, I have **payment**: but if **un-voluntarily**, a **house-law is-trusted-to-me**.²⁸⁵⁷

18 What is my **pay** then? That, when I preach the **well-message**, I may make the **well-message** of Christ without charge, that I abuse²⁸⁵⁸ not my **authority** in the **well-message**.

19 For **being** free from all, yet have I made myself **slave** to all, that I might gain the more.

20 And **to-the** Jews, I became as a Jew that I might gain the Jews; **to-them** that are under law, as under law, that I might gain them that are under law;

21 To them that are **lawless**, as **lawless**, (being not **lawless to-God**, but **in-law**²⁸⁵⁹ to Christ,) that I might gain them that are **lawless**.

22 To the **without-strength** became I as **without-strength**, that I might gain the **without-strength**: **I-have-became** all things to all, that I might by all save some.

23 And this I **produce through** the **well-message**, that **together-communion I-be-become of-it**.

24 Perceive you not that they which **are-running** in a **stadium**,²⁸⁶⁰ indeed, all **are-running**, but one **takes** the prize? So **be-running**, that you may **take**.

25 And every man that **agonize** is **in-governed** in all things. Now they **indeed** to **take** a corruptible²⁸⁶¹ **victor's-crown**; but we an incorruptible.

26 I therefore **so** run, not as **unclear**; **so**, I **fist-box**, not as one that **skins** the air:

27 But **I-under-gaze**²⁸⁶² the body of-me, and **slave-leading**: **not-somehow**, when I have preached **to-others-same**, I myself should be a **not-seem-approved**.

1 CORINTHIANS CHAPTER 10

1 Moreover, **brothers**, I **will** not that you should **not-mind**, how that all our fathers were under the cloud, and all passed through the sea;

2 And were all baptized **into** Moses in the cloud and in the sea;

3 And did all eat the same spiritual **food**;

4 And did all drink the same spiritual drink: for they drank of that spiritual Rock that followed them: and that Rock was Christ.

5 But with many of them God was not **well-seem**: for they were **down-spread** in the **lonesome**.

6 Now these things were our **types**, **into the to-be**, we should not **upon-feelings** after evil things, as they also **on-feel**.

7 Neither be you idolaters, as some of them; as it is written, the people **is-seated** to eat and drink, and **up-stand** to play.

8 Neither let us **prostitutes**, as some of them **prostituted**, and fell in **first** day three and twenty thousand.

9 Neither let us tempt Christ, as some of them also tempted, and were **from-ruined** of serpents.

10 Neither **grumble** you, as some of them also **grumble**, and were **from-ruin** of the **whole-ruin-one**.²⁸⁶³

11 Now all these things **together-stepped to-them** for **types**: and they are written for our **mind-placing**, upon whom the **finishes** of the **ages** are **meet-against**.²⁸⁶⁴

12 So-too, let him that **seems** he **stands look** lest he fall.

13 There has no **probe-testing has-taken** you but such as is to man:²⁸⁶⁵ **yet, believing, the** God, who not **shall-let-be** you be **probe-tested** above **which** you are **powerful**; but will with the **probe-testing** also make a way to escape,²⁸⁶⁶ that you may be **powerful** to **carry**.

14 Through-which, my beloved, flee from idolatry.

15 I speak as to **disposed-ones**; judge you what I **show**.

16 The cup of blessing which we bless, is it not the communion of the blood of Christ? The bread which we break, is it not the communion of the body of Christ?

17 For we many are one bread, one body: for we are all **partner**²⁸⁶⁷ **out-of the** one bread.

---

²⁸⁵⁷ Or, I-have-been-believed
²⁸⁵⁸ Greek: down-use, to overuse, misuse
²⁸⁵⁹ Or, illegally
²⁸⁶⁰ Greek: "stadion," transliterated as stadiums, root to stand as fixed
²⁸⁶¹ Or, to pine, to waste, to rot
²⁸⁶² Or, to hit under the eye

²⁸⁶³ Or destroyer
²⁸⁶⁴ Greek: "katantao," down-opposite, down-instead, down-anti
²⁸⁶⁵ Or "Trial not has-gotten you, if not human ...."
²⁸⁶⁶ Or, exit, out-of-walk, step-out
²⁸⁶⁷ Or, with-holder, change-holder, after-holder, sharer

18 **Be-perceiving,** Israel **down** the flesh: are not they which eat of the sacrifices **communion** of the **sacrifice-place**?

19 What **I-show** then? That the idol is anything, or that which is offered in sacrifice to idols is anything?

20 But **that which** the **nations** sacrifice, they sacrifice to **demons**, and not to God: and I would not that you should have **communion** with **demons**.

21 Not you-are-powerful to-drink the cup of the Lord, and the cup of **demons**: **Not you-are-powerful to-be partners** of the Lord's table, and of the table of **demons**.

22 Do we **beside-zealous the Lord**? Are we **forceful** than he?

23 All things are lawful for me, but all things are not **together-bear**: all things are lawful for me, but all things **house-build** not.

24 Let no man seek his own, but every man **another's-different.**

25 Whatever is sold in the **butchery**, eat, **not up-judging through** conscience:

26 For the earth is the Lord's, and the **filling of-her.**

27 If any of them that believe not **call** you, and you **are-willing** to **travel**; whatever is **beside-place**[2868] **to-you**, eat, **not up-judging through** conscience.

28 Yet, if any man says **to-you**, this is **idol-sacrifice**, eat not **through him** that **disclosed** it, and through conscience: for the earth the Lord's, and the **filling of-it**:

29 Conscience, I say, not your own, but of the **other-different**: **because** why is my **freedom** judged of **another-same** conscience?

30 For if I by grace be a **partner**, why am I **blasphemed** for that for which I give thanks?

31 Whether therefore you eat, or drink, or whatever you do, do all to the glory of God.

32 Give **no-strike**, neither to the Jews, nor to the **Hellenics**, nor to the Church of God:

33 Even as I please **to-all in all-things**, not seeking **of-myself**, but **the together-bearing of-the** many, that they may be saved.

[2868] Or deposit
[2869] Lit., beside-give, transmission, tradition
[2870] Greek: "kata," meaning down

1 CORINTHIANS CHAPTER 11

1 Be you **imitators** of me, even as I also of Christ.

2 Now I praise you, **brothers**, that you remember me in all things, and **down-hold** the **beside-given**[2869] **down-as I-also beside-given to-you**.

3 Yet, **I-am-willing** have you **perceive**, that the head of every man is Christ; and the head of the woman the man; **yet** the head of Christ **the** God.

4 Every man praying or prophesying, having head **down**,[2870] **down-disfigure** his head.

5 But every woman that prays or prophesies **to-un-down-covered her** head, **down-disfigure** her head: for that is even all one as if she were **razor-shaven**.

6 For if the woman not **is-being-down-covered**, let her also be **shear**ed: but if it be **disfigured** for a woman to be **sheared** or **razor-shaven**, let her be **down-covered**.

7 For a man indeed **owes** not to **down-covered** head, **yet** he is the image and glory of God: **yet** the woman **under-originating** the glory of the man.

8 Because, the man is not **out-of** the woman; but the woman **out-of** the man.

9 Neither was the man created **through** the woman, but the woman **through** the man.

10 Through this is-owing the woman to have **authority over the** head **through** the angels.

11 Nevertheless neither is the man **spaced** the woman, neither the woman **spaced**[2871] the man, in the Lord.

12 Because, as the woman **out-of** the man, even so the man also **through** the woman; but all things **out-of** God.

13 Judge in yourselves: is it **towering-up** that a woman prays **to-the** God **un-down-covered**?

14 Does not even nature itself teach you, that, if a man has **long-hair**,[2872] it is an **un-value to-him**?

15 But if a woman has **long-hair,** it is a glory to her: for long-hair is given her **instead** a **clothing.**

16 But if any man seems to be **friend-quarrel**, we have no such **together-ethics**, neither the Churches of God.

[2871] Compare 1 Corinthians 7:10-11
[2872] Greek: "koma" (long hair that needs combing)

17 Now in this that I **beside-message,** I praise not that you come together, not for the **better-government,**[2873] but for the worse.

18 For **foremost** of all, when you come together in the Church, I hear that **under-originating splits in** you; and **I-am-believing** some section of it.

19 Because **it-is-binding** also **splits in** you, that they which are **seem-approved** may **become shine in** you.

20 When you come together **then upon the same**, not **it-is** to eat the Lord's **expensive-dinner**?

21 For in eating **each before-takes** his **private expensive-dinner**: and one is hungry, and another is drunk.

22 What? Have you not houses to eat and to drink in? Or **down-dispose** you the Church of God, and **down-disfigure** them that have not? What shall I say **to-you**? Shall I praise you in this? I praise not.

23 For I have **beside-take** of the Lord that which also I **beside-give to-you**, that the Lord Jesus the night in which he was betrayed[2874] **took** bread:

24 And when he had given thanks, he broke, and said, take, eat: this is my body, which is broken **over** you: this **produce** in remembrance of me.

25 After the same manner also the cup, when he had supped, saying, this cup is the **New Covenant** in my blood: this **produce**, as **many** as you drink, in remembrance of me.

26 For as often as you eat this bread, and drink this cup, you **are-down-messaging** the Lord's death **until which when** he come.

27 So-too, whoever shall eat this bread and drink cup of the Lord, **un-deservingly**, shall be **liable**[2875] of the body and blood of the Lord.

28 But let a man **seem-test** himself, and so let him eat **out-of the** bread and drink **out-of the** cup.

29 For he that eats and drinks **un-deservingly**, eats and drinks **judgment-result**[2876] **to-himself,** not **through-judging** the Lord's body.

30 Through this, many **without-strength** and **un-leaving-weakness** among you, and sleep, **sufficiently.**

31 For if we **through-judge** ourselves, we should not be judged.

32 But when we are judged, we are **boy-trained** of the Lord, that we should not be **down-judged** with the world.

33 So-too, my **brothers,** when you come together to eat, **out-of-welcome one-another-same.**

34 And if any man hunger, let him eat at home; that you come not together **to judgment-result**. And the rest will I **under-arrange** when I come.

1 CORINTHIANS CHAPTER 12

1 Now concerning **spiritual, brothers,** I would not have you **ignorant.**

2 You **perceive** that you were **nations, led towards** these **voiceless** idols, even as you were **from-led**.

3 Through-which, I give you **knowing,** that no man speaking by the Spirit of God calls Jesus **banned**[2877] and no man **is-powerful to**-say Lord Jesus, if not in **the Holy Spirit.**

4 Now there are **apportions** of **grace, yet** the same Spirit.

5 And there are **apportions** of **attendances, and** the same Lord.

6 And there are **apportions** of **in-working, yet** it is the same God which **in-works** all in all.

7 Yet, the **shining** of the Spirit is given to **each towards together-bear.**

8 Because to **whom** is given by the Spirit the word of wisdom; to **another-same** the word of knowledge **down** the same Spirit;

9 Yet, to **another-different,** faith, **in** the same Spirit; to **another-same** the **grace** of **cures in** the same Spirit;

10 Yet, to **another-same,** the **in-working** of **powers**; to **another-same** prophecy; to **another-same through-judging** of spirits; to **another-different, kin** of tongues; to **another-same** the interpretation[2878] of tongues:

11 Yet, all these **works** that one and the same Spirit, **distributing to-own to-each down-as it-is-planned-counseled.**

[2873] Greek: "kreitton," a comparative derivative of "kratos;" translated as "cracy" in democracy—people (demo)-government ('cracy' (kratos)), or public-government
[2874] Lit., beside-given
[2875] Greek: in-hold, to hold in
[2876] Greek: "krima," transliterated as "crime" and also means judgment
[2877] Greek: anathema, banned, excommunicate
[2878] Or translation

12 For as the body is one, and has many members, and all the members of that one body, being many, are one body: so also, **the** Christ.

13 For by one Spirit are we all baptized into one body, whether Jews or **Hellenics**, whether **slave** or free; and have been all made to drink into one Spirit.

14 For the body is not one member, but many.

15 If the foot shall say **that** I am **not** the hand, I am not **out-of** the body; is it therefore not **out-of** the body?

16 And if the ear shall say **that** I am **not** the eye, I am not **out-of** the body; is it therefore not **out-of** the body?

17 If the whole body an eye, where the hearing? If the whole hearing, where the smelling?

18 Yet, now has God **placed** the members **each** of them in the body, **according-as he-wills**.

19 And if they were all one member, where the body?

20 Yet, now many members, yet one body.

21 Yet, the eye **not is-powerful to-**say **to** the hand, I have no need of you: nor again the head to the feet, I have no need of you.

22 But, much more those members of the body, which seem to be **without-strength, under-originating**, are **necessary**:

23 And those of the body, which we **seem** to be **unvalued**, upon these we **about-place excess value**; and our **disfigured, excess well-together-scheme**.[2879]

24 For our **good-schemed** have no need: but God has **together-mingled** the body, having given **excessive value to-the-deficient**:

25 That there should be no **split** in the body; but the members should have the same **portion-worry over one-another-same**.

26 And whether one member **emotion**, all the members **emotion** with it; or one member be **glorified**, all the members **together-cheer the member**.

27 Now you are the body of Christ, and members **out of-section**.

28 And God has **placed** some in the Church, **foremost** apostles, second prophets, third teachers, **upon-there powers**, then **grace** of **cures, instead-takers,**[2880] **steerage**,[2881] **kin** of-tongues.

29 Not all apostles! Not all prophets! Not all teachers! Not all powers!

30 Not all are-having the grace of cures! Not all speak to-tongues! Not all interpret!

31 Yet, be-zealous for the better-government[2882] grace: and still, I show to-you a beyond-throw way.

1 CORINTHIANS CHAPTER 13

1 Though I speak with the tongues of men and of angels, and have not love, I am become **echoing** brass, or a tinkling cymbal.

2 And though I have prophecy, and **perceive** all mysteries, and all **knowing**; and though I have all faith, so that I could remove mountains, and have not love, I am nothing.

3 And though I bestow all my goods to feed, and though I give my body to be burned, and have not love, it profits me nothing.

4 Love is- **long-sacrifice-anger, is-being-useful**; love **is not -zealous**; love **boast** not itself, is not **inflated**,

5 Is not **being-indecent**, seeks not her own, is not **beside-sharp, inventory** no evil;

6 Grace-cheer not in **unrighteousness**, but **together-grace-cheers** in the truth;

7 Roof all things, believes all things, **expects** all things, **under-remain** all things.

8 Love never **falls**: but whether prophecies, they shall **down-non-work**; whether tongues, they shall **pause**; whether **knowing**, it shall **down-non-work**.

9 For we know in **section**, and we prophesy in **section**.

10 But when that which is **mature** is come, then that which is in **section shall-be-down-non-work**.

11 When I was an **infant**, I spoke as an **infant, I-was-disposed** as **an infant, I inventoried** as an **infant**: but when I became a man, I **down-non-work** infant things.

[2879] Or decorum
[2880] Supports, relief, to take a hold of in turn
[2881] Or pilotage

[2882] Greek: "kreitton," a comparative derivative of "kratos," translated as "cracy" in democracy—people (demo)-government ('cracy' (kratos)), or public-government

12 For now we see through a **mirror**, **in enigma**;[2883] but then face to face: now I know **out-of section**; but then shall I know even as also I am known.

13 And now **remains** faith, **expectation**, love, these three; but the **larger**[2884] of these **the** love.

1 CORINTHIANS CHAPTER 14

1 Chase the love, and **zealous for-the spiritual**, but rather that you may prophesy.

2 Because, he that speaks in a tongue speaks not **to-**men, but **to-the** God: for no man is-**hearing yet**, to-spirit he speaks mysteries.

3 Yet, he that prophesy speaks **to** men **house-building**, and **beside-calling**, and **beside-closure**.

4 He that speaks in a tongue **house-builds** himself; but he that prophesies **house-builds** the Church.

5 I **will** that you all spoke with tongues, **yet** rather that you prophesied: for **larger** he that prophesies than he that speaks with tongues, except he interprets, that the Church may receive **house-building**.

6 Yet, now, **brothers**, if I come **to-you** speaking with tongues, what shall I **gain** you, except I shall speak **to-you** either in revelation, or **in knowing**, or in prophesying, or **in teaching**?

7 And even things, **soulless**, giving voice, whether pipe or harp, except they give a **through-stall**[2885] in the **sound**, how shall it be known what is piped or harped?

8 For if the trumpet gives an **unclear** voice, who shall **prepare** himself to the battle?

9 So likewise you, except you utter **through** the tongue words **good-signed**, how shall it be known what is spoken? **Because** you shall speak into the air.

10 There are, **may-be-happening**,[2886] so many **kin** of voices in the world, and none of them **un-voice**.

11 Therefore, if I **perceive** not the **power** of the voice, I shall be **to-him** that speaks a barbarian, and he that speaks a barbarian **in** me.

12 Even so you, **since** as you are **zealots** of **spirits**, seek that you may excel **towards** the **house-building** of the Church.

13 Through-which let him that speaks in a tongue pray that he may interpret.

14 For if I pray in a tongue, my spirit prays, but my **thought** is unfruitful.

15 What is it then? I will pray **to-the** spirit and I will pray with the **thought** also: I will sing **to-the** spirit, and I will sing with the **thought** also.

16 Else when you shall bless **to-the** spirit, how shall he that **up-fills** the **spot** of the **private-ones**[2887] say amen at your giving of thanks, seeing he **perceived** not what you say?

17 For you **indeed** gives thanks **ideally**, but **the other-different** is not **house-built**.

18 I thank my God; I speak with tongues more than you all:

19 Yet in the Church I had rather speak five words **through** my **mind**, that I might **catechize** others also, than ten thousand words in a tongue.

20 Brothers, **not become** children in **disposition**: **but to-the evil, be-infants**, but in **disposition become mature**.

21 In the law it is written, **in other-different-tongues** and **other-different** lips will I speak **to-this** people; and yet for all that will they not hear me, says the Lord.

22 So-too, tongues are **into** a sign, not **to-them** that believe, but **to-them** that believe not: but prophesying not for them that believe not, but for them which believe.

23 If therefore the whole Church be come together **upon the same**, and all speak with tongues, and there come in **private-ones**, or unbelievers, will they not say that you are **maniac**?[2888]

24 But if all prophesy, and there come in one that believes not, or **private-ones**, he is **evidence-exposed** of all, he is not **up-judged under** all:

25 And **these**, the **hidden-things** of his **heart**, **becomes shine**; and so, falling on face he will worship God, and **from-message** that God is in you of a truth.

26 How is it then, **brothers**; when you come together, every one of you have a psalm, has a **teaching**, has a tongue, has a revelation, has an interpretation? Let all things **become towards house-building**.

[2883] Or obscure sayings
[2884] Larger, especially in age
[2885] Or, distinction, difference
[2886] Or, hit the mark, chance upon, obtain,
[2887] Greek: "idiotes," transliterated as "idiots"
[2888] Or, raving mad, divination maniac, divining mad, mad by divination

27 If any man speaks in a tongue, by two, or at the most three, and by **section**;²⁸⁸⁹ and let one interpret.

28 Yet, if there be no interpreter, **let-him-be-silent** in the Church; and let him speak **to-him**self, and to God.

29 Let the prophets speak two or three and let the **others-same through-**judge.

30 If **may-be-be-revealed** to **another-same** that **sits** by, let the **foremost be-silent**.

31 Because, **you-are-powerful down** one, **all to-**prophesy, that all may learn, and all may be **beside-called**.

32 And the spirits of the prophets are **subordinate**²⁸⁹⁰ to the prophets.

33 For God is not of **instability**,²⁸⁹¹ but of peace, as in all Churches of the saints.

34 Let your **wives be-silent** in the Churches: **because** it is not permitted **to-them** to speak;²⁸⁹² but **to-be-subordinate,**²⁸⁹³ as also says the law.

35 And if they will learn anything, let them ask their **private** husbands at home: for it is a **disfigurement** for **wives** to speak²⁸⁹⁴ in the Church.

36 Or, **out-of-came** the **Word of God** from you? Or, **meet-against**²⁸⁹⁵ **into you** only?

37 If any man **seems** to be a prophet, or spiritual,²⁸⁹⁶ let him acknowledge that the things that I write **to-you** are the commandments of the Lord.

38 But if any man **ignorant**, let him be **ignorant**.

39 So-too, **brothers**, **zealous** to prophesy, and **prevent** not to speak with tongues.

40 Let all things **become good-schemed** and **according-to-arrangement**.

1 CORINTHIANS CHAPTER 15

1 Moreover, **brothers**, I **make-known to-you** the **well-message** which I preached **to-you**, which also you have **beside-got**, and **in which** you stand.

2 By which also you are saved, if you **down-hold** what I preached **to-you**, unless you have believed in **without-cause**.

3 For I **beside-give to-you foremost** of all that which I also **beside-take**, how that Christ died for our sins **down** the **Scriptures**;

4 And that he was buried, and that he rose again the third day **down** the **Scriptures**:

5 And that he was seen of Cephas, then of the twelve:

6 After that, he was seen of above five hundred **brothers** at once; of whom the **majority** remains **to** this present, but some sleep.

7 After that, he was seen of James; then of all the apostles.

8 Yet, last of all, **as to-the miscarriage**, he was seen of me also

9 For I am the least of the apostles, that am not **sufficient**²⁸⁹⁷ to be called an apostle, because I **chased** the Church of God.

10 But by the grace of God I am what I am: and his grace which upon me was not **empty**; but I **fatigued excessively** than they all: yet not I, but the grace of God which was with me.

11 Therefore whether I or they, so we preach, and so you believed.

12 Now if Christ be preached that he rose from the dead, how say some **in** you that there is no resurrection of the dead?

13 But if there be no resurrection of the dead, then is Christ not risen:

14 And if Christ be not risen, then our preaching **empty**, and your faith also **empty**.

15 Yes, and we are found **false-witnesses** of God; because we have **witnessed** of God that he raised up Christ: whom he raised not up, if so be that the dead rise not.

16 For if the dead rise not, then is not Christ raised:

17 And if Christ be not raised, your faith **empty**;²⁸⁹⁸ you are yet in your sins.

18 Then they also which are asleep in Christ are **from-ruined**.²⁸⁹⁹

---

²⁸⁸⁹ Or, part, division, share
²⁸⁹⁰ Under-arranged
²⁸⁹¹ Greek: down-standing, inconstant, unstable, confusion
²⁸⁹² An extended or random harangue
²⁸⁹³ Under-arranged
²⁸⁹⁴ An extended or random harangue

²⁸⁹⁵ Greek: "katantao," down-opposite, down-instead, down-ant
²⁸⁹⁶ Greek: "pneumatikos," pneumatics (spiritual people)
²⁸⁹⁷ Lit., to arrive; or, competent as if coming in season, ample in amount, fit in character
²⁸⁹⁸ Or, empty through the idea of unsuccessful search
²⁸⁹⁹ Greek: "apo" (from) and "alethros" (ruin), to destroy fully

19 If in this life only we have **expectation** in Christ, we are of all men **more-pitiful**.

20 But now is Christ risen **out-of** the dead, become the firstfruit of them that slept.

21 Because, since **through** man **the** death, **through** man also the resurrection of the dead.

22 Because as in Adam all die, even so in Christ all **life-produced**.

23 But every man in his own **arrangement: firstfruit Christ;**[2900] afterward they that are Christ's **in** his **presence**.

24 Then the **finish**, when he shall have **beside-give** the kingdom to God, even the Father; when he shall have **down-work** all **originals** and all authority and power.

25 Because, it-is-binding him **to-be-reigning until** he has **placed** all the **haters** under his feet.

26 Last hater **is-being-down-worked, the** death.

27 Because, all he-subordinated under his feet. But when he says all things are **subordinated, it-is-clear** that he is **outside**, which did **subordinate to-him, all.**

28 And when all things shall **be-subordinated**[2901] **to-him**, then shall the Son also himself be **subordinated to-him** that **subordinating to-him**, that God may be all in all.

29 Else what shall they do which are baptized for the dead, if **whole** dead rise not at all? why are they then baptized for the dead?

30 And why stand we in jeopardy every hour?

31 I protest by your **boasting** which I have in Christ Jesus our Lord, I die daily.

32 If **down** men **I-have-fought-with-beasts** at Ephesus, what **gain to-me**, if the dead rise not? Let us eat and drink; for tomorrow we die.

33 Be not **seduced**: evil **ethics** corrupt[2902] good **companionship**.[2903]

34 Out-sober, to **righteous-togetherness**, and sin not; for some have **un-knowing** of God: I speak **to-your inverting.**

35 But some will say, how are the dead raised up? And with what body do they come?

36 You **un-disposed**, that which you sow **life-produces not**, except it die:

37 And that which you sow, you sow not that body that shall be, but **naked** grain, it may **happen**[2904] of wheat, or of some **remaining-ones**

38 Yet, God gives it a body as **he-wills**, and to every seed his **private**[2905] body.

39 All flesh not the same flesh: but one flesh of men, **another-same** flesh of **domestic-animals, another-same** of fishes, another of birds.

40 Also **upon-heavens** bodies, and bodies **upon-earth**: but the glory of the **upon-heavens another-different**, and the of the **upon-earth another-different**.

41 Another-same glory of the sun, and **another-same** glory of the moon, and **another-same** glory of the stars: for star differs[2906] from star in glory.

42 So also the resurrection of the dead. It is sown in corruption; it is raised in incorruption:

43 It is sown in **un-value**; it is raised in glory: it is sown in weakness; it is raised in power:

44 It is sown a **soulish** body; it is raised a spiritual body. There is a **soulish** body, and there is a spiritual body.

45 And so it is written, the **foremost** man Adam **became** a living soul; the last Adam **into life-producing** spirit.

46 But, not **foremost** which is spiritual, but **the soulish**; and afterward **the** spiritual.

47 The **foremost** man of the earth, **soil**: the second man, the Lord **out-of** heaven.

48 As the **soil**, such they also that are **soil-ones**: and as the **upon-heaven**, such they also that are **upon-heavens**.

49 And as **we-wear** the image of the **soil**, we shall also **wear** the image of the **upon-**heaven.

[2900] This is the convention of all the Greek texts in this verse "firstfruit Christ," <u>in lieu</u> of "Christ, the first fruit."
[2901] Under-arranged
[2902] Or, to pine, to waste, to rot
[2903] Or same-crowd
[2904] Or, hit the mark, chance upon, obtain,
[2905] Or own
[2906] Greek: "diaphero," to through-bear, transliterated as 'differ' or "different"

50 Now this I **show, brothers,** that flesh and blood **not are-powerful to-**inherit the kingdom of God; neither corruption inherit incorruption.

51 Be-perceiving, I show you a mystery; we shall not all sleep, but we shall all be changed,

52 In **atom,**²⁹⁰⁷ in the **fling-jerk** of an eye, **in** the last trumpet: for **he-shall-be-trumpeting,** and the dead shall be raised incorruptible, and we shall be changed.

53 For **it-is-binding** this corruptible **to-be-clothed**²⁹⁰⁸ **incorruptible,** and this mortal **to-be-clothed immortal.**

54 So when this corruptible shall-**be-clothed incorruptible,** and this mortal **shall-be-clothed immortal,** then shall **become** the saying that is written, death is swallowed in**to conquest.**

55 Death, where your **piercer?**²⁹⁰⁹ **Hell,** where your **conquest?**

56 The **piercer** of death **the** sin; and the **power of-the** sin the law.

57 But thanks to God, which gives us the **conquest** through our Lord Jesus Christ.

58 Therefore, my beloved **brothers,** be you **settled-seated, un-change-action** always **excelling** in the work of the Lord, **having-perceive** that your **toil-cut** is not **empty** in the Lord.

1 CORINTHIANS CHAPTER 16

1 Now concerning the **contribution**²⁹¹⁰ for the saints, as I have given **through-arrangements** to the Churches of Galatia, even so do you.

2 Upon the first **of-Sabbaths,** let every one of you **place into-tomorrow,** as has **good-road**²⁹¹¹ him, that there be no **contribution** when I come.

3 And when I come, **whomever** you shall **seem-test through** letters, them will I **dispatch** to bring your **grace to** Jerusalem.

4 And if it be **deserving** that I **travel** also, they shall **travel** with me.

5 Now I will come **to-you,** when I shall pass through Macedonia: for I do pass through Macedonia.

6 And **happening**²⁹¹² that I will **remain, yes,** and winter with you, that you may **before-dispatch me** wherever I go.

7 For **not** I-am-willing **now in the beside-way to-be perceiving** you; but I **expect** to **remain some uninterrupted-time** with you if the Lord permit.

8 But I will **remain** at Ephesus until Pentecost.

9 For a **great** door and **in-working** is opened **to** me, and many **opposing-ones.**²⁹¹³

10 Now if **Timothy** come, see that he may be with you without fear: for he **works** the work of the Lord, as I also.

11 Let no man therefore **down-nothing him yet before-dispatch him** in peace, that he may come **towards** me: for **I-am-out-welcoming** him with the **brothers.**

12 Yet, concerning the brother Apollos, I **much beside-called** him to come **to-you** with the **brothers:** but his will was not at all to come **now;** but he will come when he shall have **well-season.**

13 Watch you, stand in the faith, **be-men,** be **governmental!**

14 Let all your things **become** with love.

15 I **beside-call** you, **brothers,** (you **perceive** the house of Stephanas, that it is the firstfruit of Achaia, and they have **arranged** themselves to the **attendant** of the saints,)

16 That you **subordinate**²⁹¹⁴ yourselves **to-such,** and to everyone that **together-work,** and **fatigue.**

17 I am glad of the **presence** of Stephanas and Fortunatus and Achaicus: for that which was lacking on your part they have **up-filled.**

18 For they have refreshed²⁹¹⁵ my spirit and yours: therefore **be-knowing such-as-these.**

19 The Churches of Asia **embrace-you.** Aquila and Priscilla **embrace-you** much in the Lord, **together to-the** Church that is in their house.

20 All the **brothers embrace-you. embrace one another-same** with a holy **friend-kiss.**

21 The **embrace** of Paul with **my** hand.

---

²⁹⁰⁷ Greek: "atomos," "atom," uncut, instant
²⁹⁰⁸ Lit., in-down; or, in-sink, in-down-slipping
²⁹⁰⁹ Greek: "kentron," "center;" piercer, prick, sting
²⁹¹⁰ "Logia," collecting in the commercial sense
²⁹¹¹ To succeed in business affairs, to succeed in reaching
²⁹¹² Or, hit the mark, chance upon, obtain,
²⁹¹³ Greek: anti-laying outstretched
²⁹¹⁴ Under-arranged
²⁹¹⁵ Up-pause

22 If any man **friend** not the Lord Jesus Christ, let him be anathema[2916] Maranatha.[2917]

23 The grace of our Lord Jesus Christ with you.

24 My love with all **of-you** in Christ Jesus. Amen.

[2916] banned

[2917] Chaldean origin, meaning, the Lord has come

2 CORINTHIANS

2 CORINTHIANS CHAPTER 1

1 Paul, an apostle of Jesus Christ **through** the will of God, and Timothy **the** brother, **to** the Church of God, which is at Corinth, with all the saints which are in all Achaia:

2 Grace **to-you** and peace from God our Father, and the Lord Jesus Christ.

3 Blessed **the** God, even the Father of our Lord Jesus Christ, the Father of mercies, and the God of all **beside-call**;

4 Who **beside-call** us in all our tribulation, that we may be **powerful** to **beside-call** them which are in any trouble, **through** the **beside-call which** we ourselves are **beside-called** of God.

5 For as the **emotions** of Christ abound in us, so our **beside-call** also **exceed** by Christ.

6 And whether we be **troubled**, for your **beside-call** and salvation, which is **in-working** in the **under-remaining** of the same **emotions** which we also **emotion**: or whether we be **beside-called**, for your **beside-call** and salvation.

7 And our **expectation** of you **is-stable**, **perceiving**, that as you are **communion** of the **emotions**, so also of the **beside-calling**.

8 For we would not, **brothers**, have you **ignorant over the** trouble which came to us in Asia, that we were pressed **beyond-throw**, above **power**, insomuch that we **out-of-having-no-way-out**, even of life:

9 But we had the **from-crime**[2918] of death in ourselves, that we should not trust in ourselves, but in God which raise the dead:

10 Who **rush-rescued** us **out-of such** death and does **rush-rescue**: in whom we trust that he will yet **rush-rescue**.

11 You also **together-under-working** by **beg-binding** for us, that for the **grace** upon us by the means of many persons thanks may be given by many on our behalf.

12 For our **boasting** is this, the **witness** of our conscience, that in **singleness**;[2919] and **sun-judged of-God**, not with fleshly wisdom, but by the grace of God, we have had our **behavior** in the world, and **exceedingly to-you**-ward.

13 For we write none other things **to-you**, than what you read or acknowledge; and I **expect** you shall acknowledge even to the **finish**.

14 As also you have acknowledged us **from section**, that we are your **boasting**, even as you also ours in the day of the Lord Jesus.

15 And in this **trust**, **I-planned-counseled** to come **towards** you, **foremost**, that you might have a second **grace**;

16 And to pass **through** you into Macedonia, and to come again out of Macedonia **towards** you, and of you to be **before-dispatched into the** Judaea.

17 When I therefore was **plan-counseling-myself these-things**, did I use[2920] lightness? Or the things that **I-planned-counsel, do-I-plan-counsel down** the flesh, that **beside** me there should be yes, yes, and **the no, no**?

18 But **believing** God, our word toward you **became** not yes and **no**.

19 For the Son of God, Jesus Christ, who was preached among you **through** us, **through** me and Silvanus and **Timothy**, **became** not yes and **no**, but in him was yes.

20 For all the promises of God in him, **yes**, and in him Amen, **towards** the glory of God **through** us.

21 Now he which **stabilizes** us with you in Christ, and has anointed us, God.

22 Who has also sealed us and given the **pledge** of the Spirit in our **hearts** .

23 Moreover I **upon-calling**[2921] God for a **witness** upon my soul, that to spare you I came not as yet **into** Corinth.

24 Not for that we have **lordship** over your faith but are **together-workers** of your **cheerfulness**: for by faith, you stand.

2 CORINTHIANS CHAPTER 2

1 But I **judged** this with myself that I would not come again **to-you** in **distress-sadness**.

[2918] Greek: apokrima, originally, sentence from-crime, the result of a judicial judgment
[2919] Haplotetes, the antonym of "diplous" meaning double
[2920] Or, to inform, to tell, to furnish what is needed, to use, to employ
[2921] Or, to entitle, to invoke

2 For if I make you **distress-sad**, who is he then that makes me **good-disposition**, but the same which is made **distress-sad** by me?

3 And I wrote this same **to-you**, lest, when I came, I should have **distress-sadness** from them of whom **it-is-binding to-be-cheerful**; having confidence **upon** you all, that my **cheerfulness** is all of you.

4 For out of much **tribulation** and **together-hold**[2922] of **heart** I wrote **to-you** with many tears; not that you should be **distress-sad**, but that you might know the love which I have **excessively into you**.

5 But if any have-**distressed-sadden**, he has not **distress-sadden** me, but in **section**: that I may not **upon-heavy** you all.

6 Sufficient[2923] to such a man this **rebuke under the many**.

7 So that contrariwise you rather to **release**,[2924] and **beside-call**, lest perhaps such a one should be swallowed **to-the excessive distress-sadness**.

8 Through-which, I **beside-call** you that you would **lordship-ratify** love **into him**.

9 Into this I write that I might know the **seem-test** of you, whether you be obedient in all things.

10 To whom you **grace** anything, I **grace** also: for if I **graced** anything, to whom I **graced**, **through you in the face** of Christ;

11 Lest **the** Satan should **take more-holding**[2925] of us: **because not we ignorant**[2926] his **thoughts**.

12 Yet, when I came to Troas to Christ's **well-message**, and a door was opened **to-me in** the Lord,

13 I had no **up-send** in my spirit, because I found not Titus my brother: but **from-arranging to-**them, I **out-of-came** into Macedonia.

14 Now thanks **to** God, which always cause us to triumph in Christ, and makes **shine** the **odor** of his **knowing** by us in every **spot**.

15 For we are **to-**God a **well-odor** of Christ, in them that are saved, and in them that **from-ruin**:[2927]

16 To the one, the **odor out-of** death **into** death; and to the other the **odor out-of** life **into** life. And who **sufficient**[2928] for these things?

17 For we are not as many, which **retail**[2929] the **Word of God**: but as of **sun-judged**, but as **out-of** God, in the sight of God speak we in Christ.

2 CORINTHIANS CHAPTER 3

1 Do we begin again to **together-stand** ourselves? Or need we, as some, epistles of **together-standing towards** you, or of **together-standing** from you?

2 You are our epistle written in our **hearts**, known, and read of all men:

3 Shined to be the epistle of Christ **attended** by us, written not with ink, but with the Spirit of the living God, not in tables of stone, but in fleshy tables of the **heart**.

4 And such trust have we through Christ **towards** God:

5 Not that we are **sufficient**[2930] of ourselves to **inventory** anything as of ourselves; but our **sufficiency**[2931] **of-the** God;

6 Who also has made us able **attendants** of the **New Covenant**; not of the letter, but of the **Spirit**: for the letter kills, but the **Spirit is-life-producing**.

7 But if the **attendance** of death, written engraved in stones, was **in glory**, so that the **sons** of Israel **not being-powerful to-look-stretch into** the face of Moses **through** the glory of his **face**; which was to be **down-un-worked**:

8 How shall not the **attendance** of the **Spirit shall**-be **in glory**?

9 For if the **attendance** of **down-judging** glory, much more does the **attendance** of **righteous-togetherness** exceed in glory.

10 For even that which was made glorious had no glory in this **section**, by reason of the glory that **beyond-throw**.

11 For if that which is **down-un-worked** glorious, much more that which remains, **in glory**.

[2922] Or anguish
[2923] Lit., to arrive; or, competent as if coming in season, ample in amount, fit in character
[2924] Lit., from-let-go
[2925] Or covet, overreach
[2926] Or lit., not-know, ignore
[2927] Greek: "apo" (from) and "alethros" (ruin), to destroy fully
[2928] Lit., to arrive; or, competent as if coming in season, ample in amount, fit in character
[2929] Huckster (a person who employs showy method to effect sale, win votes, retailer of small articles, sell illegally
[2930] Lit., to arrive; or, competent as if coming in season, ample in amount, fit in character
[2931] Lit., to arrive; or, competent as if coming in season, ample in amount, fit in character

12 Seeing then that we have such **expectation**, we use²⁹³² much **all-out-spoken**:

13 And not as Moses, **placing** a veil over his face, that the **sons** of Israel could not **look-stretch into** to the **finish** of that which is-**being-down-un-worked**

14 But their **thoughts** were blinded: for until this day, the same veil in the reading of the **Old Covenant**; remaining not unveiled which is **down-un-worked** in Christ.

15 But even **until** this day, when Moses is read, the veil is upon their **heart.**

16 Nevertheless when it shall turn to the Lord, the vail shall be **about-lifting**.

17 Now the Lord is **the** Spirit: and where the Spirit of the Lord, there **freedom.**

18 But we all, with **unveiled** face **down-mirroring** the glory of the Lord, are **transformed**²⁹³³ into the same image from glory **into** glory, as **from** the Spirit of the Lord.

2 CORINTHIANS CHAPTER 4

1 Therefore seeing we have this **attendance** as we have mercy, **not we-are-out-of-evil**;²⁹³⁴

2 But have **from-say**²⁹³⁵ the hidden things of **disfigurement**, not walking in **all-working**,²⁹³⁶ nor handling the **Word of God trick-bating**; but by manifestation of the truth **together-standing** ourselves to every man's conscience in the sight of God.

3 But if our **well-message is hidden**, it is **hidden to-them** that are **being-from-ruined**:²⁹³⁷

4 In whom the god of this **age** has blinded the **thoughts** of them which believe not, lest the light **of-the well-message of-the glory of-the** Christ, who is the image of God.

5 For we preach not ourselves, but Christ Jesus the Lord; and ourselves your **slave**s for Jesus' sake.

6 For God, who **upon-arranged** the light to shine out of darkness, has shined in our **hearts, towards** the light of the **knowing** of the glory of God in the face of Jesus Christ.

7 But we have this **placed-into-tomorrow**²⁹³⁸ in **ostraca**²⁹³⁹ vessels, that the **beyond-throw** of the power may be of God, and not of us.

8 Troubled on every side, yet not **narrow-room**²⁹⁴⁰ **have-no-way-out**, but not **out-of-having-no-way-out**.

9 Chased, but not **in-down-left**; cast down, but not **from-ruin**;

10 Always bearing about in the body the dying of the Lord Jesus, that the life also of Jesus might **shine** in our body.

11 For we which live are always **beside-given to** death **through** Jesus, that the life also of Jesus might **shine** in our **dying** flesh.

12 So then death **in-works** in us, but life in you.

13 We having the same spirit of faith, **down** it is written, I believed, and therefore have I spoken; we also believe, and therefore speak;

14 Perceiving that he which raised up the Lord Jesus shall raise up us also by Jesus and shall **beside-stand** with you.

15 For all things **through-you**, that the **more** grace might through the thanksgiving of many **exceed into** the glory of God.

16 For which cause we **not out-of-evil**; but though our outward man **corrupts**, yet the inward is **up-fresh** day by day.

17 For our light **tribulation**, which is but for a moment, **down-working down** us **beyond-throw into beyond-throw eternal** weight of glory.

18 While we **spy**²⁹⁴¹ not at the things which are seen, but at the things which are not seen: for the things which are seen **are-toward-season,** but the things which are not seen, **eternal.**

2 CORINTHIANS CHAPTER 5

1 For we **perceive** that if our **on-land** house of **of-the** tabernacle were **down-loosed**, we have a **house-building** of God, a house not made with hands, **eternal,** in the heavens.

---

²⁹³² Or, to inform, to tell, to furnish what is needed, to use, to employ
²⁹³³ Greek: "metamorphoo"
²⁹³⁴ Intrinsic bad
²⁹³⁵ Renounce, to say off for oneself
²⁹³⁶ Craftiness
²⁹³⁷ Greek: "apo" (from) and "alethros" (ruin), to destroy fully

²⁹³⁸ Greek: "thesauros," transliterated as thesaurus, also means a deposit, treasure,
²⁹³⁹ Greek: ostrakinos, transliterated "ostraca"-potsherd used as a writing surface, also the derivative of "oyster"
²⁹⁴⁰ Or, hemmed in
²⁹⁴¹ Or, skeptic, mark, scope

2 For in this we groan,²⁹⁴² **upon-yearn** to be clothed upon with our **house-location**²⁹⁴³ which is **out-of** heaven:

3 If so be that being clothed²⁹⁴⁴ we shall not be found naked.

4 For we that are in tabernacle do groan, being **weighty**: not for that **we-are-willing to-be-unclothed,** but clothed upon, that **dying** might be swallowed up of life.

5 Now he that has **down-work** us for the selfsame thing, God, who also has given **to-us** the **pledge** of the Spirit.

6 Therefore always **daring, perceiving** that, while we are **in-public** in the body, we are **out-of-public** from the Lord:

7 (For we walk by faith, not by **perception**:)

8 We are **daring,** and **well-seem** rather to be **out-of-public out-of** the body, and to be **in-public towards** the Lord.

9 Through-which, we friend-of-value that, whether **in-public** or **out-of-public**, we may be **well-pleasing to**-him.

10 Because is-binding all us to-shine before the **judgment-step**²⁹⁴⁵ of Christ; that everyone may-**be-provided** the things **through the** body, **towards which it-practices**, whether good or **evil.**

11 Perceiving therefore the **fear** of the Lord, we persuade men; but we **shined to** God; and I trust also **shined** in your consciences.

12 For we **together-stand** not ourselves again **to-you** but give you **from-urge** to **boast** on our behalf, that you may have **towards** them which **boast** in **face**, and not in **heart.**

13 Because, whether we be **ecstasized,**²⁹⁴⁶ to God: or whether we be **safe-disposition, to-you.**

14 For the love of Christ **together-holds**²⁹⁴⁷ us; because we **in-this-way** judge, that if one died for all, then were all dead:

15 And he died for all, that they which live should not **still** live **to-themselves,** but **to-him** which died for them, and rose.

16 So-too, from now, perceive we no man after the flesh: **yes**, though we have known Christ after the flesh, yet now, **not-still we-are-knowing.**

17 Therefore if any man in Christ, a new-**young creation**: **original** things are passed away; **be-perceiving,** all things **has-became** new.

18 And all things of God, who has **exchanged**²⁹⁴⁸ us **to-him**self by Jesus Christ and has given to us the **attendance** of **exchange.**

19 How that, that God was in Christ, **exchanging** the world **to-himself,** not **inventorying** their **beside-falls to** them; and has **placed to-us** the word of **exchange.**

20 Now then we are **elders** for Christ, as though God did **beside-call** by us: we pray in Christ's stead, be you **exchange** to God.

21 For he has made him sin for us, who knew no sin; that we might **become** the **righteous-togetherness** of God in him.

2 CORINTHIANS CHAPTER 6

1 We then, **together-workers, beside-call** also that you **welcome** not the grace of God **into empty.**

2 (For he says, I have heard you in a **season welcomed**, and in the day of salvation have I **distress-cry-helped** you: **be-perceiving,** now the **season of well-towards-welcome; be-perceiving,** now, the day of salvation.)

3 Giving no **toward-strike** in anything, that the **attendance** be not blamed:

4 But in all **together-standing** ourselves as the **attendants** of God, in much **under-remaining,** in **tribulations,** in **necessities,** in **cramp-spaces,**

5 In **plague-poundings,** in imprisonments, in **instability,**²⁹⁴⁹ in **cut-labors,** in **sleeplessness,** in fasting.

6 By **cleanness, in knowing, in long-sacrifice-anger, in usefulness, in** the Holy Spirit, **in** love **un-hypocritical.**

7 In the **Word of Truth, in** the power of God, **through** the armor of **righteous-togetherness** on the right hand and on the left,

---

²⁹⁴² In straights, narrow
²⁹⁴³ Oikeo (house) and terion (a location where something happens)
²⁹⁴⁴ Lit., in-down; or, in-sink, in-down-slipping
²⁹⁴⁵ Greek: "Bema," a step, foot-breadth, rostrum, tribunal
²⁹⁴⁶ Greek compound existemi (out-of-stand) from which we derive our English ecstasy (overwhelming feelings)
²⁹⁴⁷ Or, to compress
²⁹⁴⁸ Or change mutually, to down-change, adjustment, conciliation
²⁹⁴⁹ Greek: down-standing, inconstant, unstable, confusion

8 Through-glory and un-value, through difficult-fame and well-fame: as seducers, and true;

9 As un-minded-ones,²⁹⁵⁰ and being-known; as dying, and, be-perceiving, we live; as boy-trained, and not killed;

10 As distressed-sad, yet cheerful-ones; as poor, yet making many rich; as having nothing, and down-hold all things.

11 You Corinthians, our mouth is open to-you, our heart is broad.²⁹⁵¹

12 You are not narrow-space in us, but you are narrow-space in your own gut-compassions.

13 Now for an instead-pay in the same, (I speak as to-children,) be you also broaden.

14 Be you not different-yoked with unbelievers: for what partnership has righteous-togetherness with lawlessness? And what communion has light towards darkness?

15 And what symphony²⁹⁵² has Christ with Belial?²⁹⁵³ Or what part has he that believes with an unbeliever?

16 And what together-down-place²⁹⁵⁴ has the temple of God with idols? For you are the temple of the living God; as God has said, I will in-house in them, and in-walk; and I will be their God, and they shall be my people.

17 Through which, come out of-middle of-them, and be you from-defined,²⁹⁵⁵ says the Lord, and not fasten-to the unclean; and I will into-welcome you,

18 And will be a Father into you, and you shall be into my sons and daughters, says the Lord All-Governor.²⁹⁵⁶

2 CORINTHIANS CHAPTER 7

1 Having therefore these promises, beloved, let us cleanse ourselves from all stain of the flesh and spirit, maturing holiness in the fear of God.

2 Space us; we have unrighteous no man, we have corrupted²⁹⁵⁷ no man, we have more-hold²⁹⁵⁸ no man.

3 I speak not to down-judge: for I have said before that you are in our hearts into together-die and to-be-together-living.

4 Much my all-speech toward you, much my boasting of you: I am filled with beside-call, I am over-exceeding cheerful on all our tribulation.

5 For, when we were come into Macedonia, our flesh had no up-sending,²⁹⁵⁹ but we were troubled in all; outside fighting, inside, fears.

6 Nevertheless God, that beside-call those that are cast down, beside-calls us in the presence of Titus;

7 And not by his presence only, but in the beside-calling to which he beside-called upon you, when he up-message us your upon-yearning, your moaning, your zeal toward me; so that I cheered the rather

8 For though I made you distress-sad with a letter, I do not change-care,²⁹⁶⁰ though also I-after-care for I perceive that the same epistle towards you has made you distress-sad.

9 Now I cheer, not that you were made distress-sad, but that you distress-sad into change-thought: for you were made distress-sad down God, that in nothing you-are-detriment out-of us.

10 For down God, you sadden into change-thinking to salvation not to be change-cared, of: but the distress-sadness of the world down-works death.

11 For be-perceiving this selfsame thing, that you distress-sad according-to God how-much speed it in-worked to-you, but apology²⁹⁶¹ of yourselves, but, much-grief, but fear, but upon-yearning, but zeal, but vengeance! In all, you have together-stood yourselves to be clean in this practice.

12 Consequently, though I wrote to-you, not on-account-of the unrighteous-one,²⁹⁶² nor on-account-of the injured-one, account-of the speed over you may-shine in the sight of God.

13 Therefore we were beside-called in your beside-calling: yet, and more-excessive we cheered for the

---

²⁹⁵⁰ Or unknown
²⁹⁵¹ Or, spread out, flat
²⁹⁵² Or together-voice
²⁹⁵³ Hebrew origin: failure to ascend, worthless, without profit, **wicked-hurtfulness**
²⁹⁵⁴ Or agreement, deposit
²⁹⁵⁵ Lit., from-horizon
²⁹⁵⁶ Greek compound "Pankrator," pan (all, entire, every) and krator from kratos (government, rule, strong), all-governing, etc.; think of democracy, demo (people)-kratos (government, rule, etc.). "kratos" is also transliterated as "great."
²⁹⁵⁷ Or, to pine, to waste, to rot
²⁹⁵⁸ Or covet, overreach, more-have
²⁹⁵⁹ Or ease, to let up
²⁹⁶⁰ Or regret, or after care
²⁹⁶¹ "Apo" (from) and logo (word, saying), defense
²⁹⁶² Lit., un-justly, injuring

cheerfulness of Titus, because his spirit was **up-paused**[2963] by you all.

14 For if I have boasted anything **to-him** of you, I am not **down-disfigured**; but as we spoke all things **to-you** in truth, even so our boasting, which before Titus, **became** truth.

15 And his **gut-compassion** is **more-exceeding into you**, while he remembers the **under-hearing** of you all, how with fear and trembling you **welcomed** him.

16 **I–am-cheerful** therefore that I have **courage** in you in all.

2 CORINTHIANS CHAPTER 8

1 Moreover, **brothers**, **we-make-known to-you** the grace of God **given in** the Churches of Macedonia.

2 How that in a **much seem-test of tribulations** of their **exceeding cheerfulness** and their deep poverty **exceeded into** the riches of their **singleness**.[2964]

3 **That down** power, I **witnessed**, and beyond power, **self-choice**.

4 Praying us with much **beside-call** that we would **welcome** the **grace**, and the **communion** of the **attending** to the saints.

5 And, not as we **expected**, but **foremost** gave **themselves** to the Lord, and **to-us through** the will of God.

6 Insomuch that we **beside-call** Titus, that as he **before-in-original**, so he would also finish **into you** the same grace also.

7 Therefore, as you **exceed** in every-thing, faith, and **word**, and **knowing**, and all **speed, and in the out-of you in us love,** that you **exceed in** this grace also.

8 I speak not by **upon-arrangement**, but **through the speed** of **others-different**, and to **seem-test** the **legitimate-birth** of your love.

9 For you know the grace of our Lord Jesus Christ, that, though he was rich, yet **through you** he became poor, that you through his poverty might be rich.

10 And **in this**, I give **opinion**: for this is **together-bear** for you, **who not only to-produce**, but also **to-be-willing before-in-original, from last-year.**

11 Now therefore **finish** the **producing**; that as a **before-feeling** to will, so a **upon-finish** also out of that which you have.

12 For if the **before-feeling is-before-laid, down-as** a man has, **well-towards-welcome**, not **down-as** that he has not.

13 For not that **other-same be-up-sending**,[2965] and you **troubled**.

14 But **out-of** equality, now at this **season** your **surplus**[2966] for their **deficit**, that their **surplus** also may be for your **deficit**: that there may be equality:

15 As it is written, he that much, **nothing more**; and he that had **few,** not **inferior**.

16 But thanks to God, which **gives** the same **speed over you in** the **heart** of Titus.

17 For indeed he **welcomed** the **beside-call**; yet **under-originating** more-**speedy**, of his **self-choice** he went **to-you**.

18 And **we-together-dispatched** the brother, whose praise in the **well-message through** all the Churches;

19 And not only, but who was also **hand-stretched** of the Churches **together-out-of-public**[2967] **of-us** with this grace, which is **attended under** us **toward** the glory of the same Lord, and your **before-feeling**:

20 **Stall** this, that no man should blame us in this **stout-plumpness** which is **attended under** us:

21 **Before-thinking idealness**, not only in the sight of the Lord, but also in the sight of men.

22 And **we-together-dispatched to-them** the brother, whom we have **much, much, seem-tested speedy to-be, yet** now much **speedy**, upon **much trust into you**.

23 Whether of Titus, my **communion-one** and **together-workers** concerning you: or our **brothers, the apostles** of the Churches, the glory of Christ.

24 Then, **in-show** you to them, and before the Churches, the **in-show** of your love, and of our boasting **over you**.

2 CORINTHIANS CHAPTER 9

1 Because indeed, concerning the **attending** to the saints, it is **excessive** for me to write **to-you**:

[2963] Or, refreshed
[2964] Haplotetes, the antonym of "diplous" meaning double
[2965] Or, ease, to let up
[2966] Or excess
[2967] Or-fellow traveler

2 For I **perceive** the **before-feeling of-you,** for which I boast of you **to-them** of Macedonia, that Achaia was **beside-vessel** a **years** ago; and your zeal has **stimulated**[2968] very many.

3 Yet have I **dispatched** the **brothers**, lest our boasting of you should be **empty** in this **section**; that, as I said, you may be **prepared-internally**:

4 Lest-**somehow** if they of Macedonia come with me, and find you **un-beside-vessel**, we (that we say not, you) should be **down-disfigured** in this same **substructure**[2969] of-boasting.

5 Therefore I **lead** it **constraining** to **beside-call** the **brothers**, that they would go before **to-you**, and **before-down-fresh** your **blessing**, whereof you had **before-down-message**, that the same might be **internally prepared**, as a **blessing**, and not as **more-having**.[2970]

6 But this, he which sows sparingly shall reap also sparingly; and he which sows **blessing** shall reap also **blessing**.

7 Every man **down-as** he **before-lifted** in his **heart**, not **distress-sadly**, or of **necessity**: for God loves a **merry-atonement**[2971] giver.

8 And God is **powerful** to make all grace **exceed into you**; that you, always having all **self-sufficiency** in all, may **exceed into** every good work:

9 (As it is written, He has **scattered**; he has given to the **starving**: his **righteous-togetherness** remains **into the age**.

10 Now he that **supplies** seed to the **Sower** both **supplies** bread for **feeding**, and multiply your seed sown, and **grows** the **generations**[2972] of your **righteous-togetherness**;)

11 Being enriched in everything **into** all **singleness**,[2973] which **down-work** through us thanksgiving to God.

12 For the **attendance** of this **people-work**[2974] not only **toward-filling** the **deficit** of the saints, but **exceeds** also **through** many thanksgivings **to-the** God;

13 Through the **seem-test** of this **attending** they glorify God for your **same-saying subordination into** the **well-message** of Christ, and for **singleness of-the communion into** them, and **into** all;

14 And by their **beg-binding over** you, which **upon-yearn for** you **through** the **beyond-throw** grace of God **upon** you.

15 Thanks **to** God **upon** his **indescribable** gift.

2 CORINTHIANS CHAPTER 10

1 Now I Paul myself **beside-call** you by the **mildness** and **upon-resemble**[2975] of Christ, who in presence, **indeed**, humble **in** you, but being absent am **courageous into you**:

2 Yet, I **beg-bind** that I may not be **daring** when I am present with that **trust**, **to-which** I **inventory** to be **daring** against some, which **inventory** us as if we walked **down** the flesh.

3 For though we walk in the flesh, we do not war **down** the flesh:

4 (For the weapons of our war not **fleshy**, but **powerful towards** God to the **down-lifting** of **fortifications**;)

5 Down-lifting inventories, and every **high-body**[2976] that **upon-lift** itself against the **knowing** of God, and **captivating** every **thought into** the **under-hearing** of Christ;

6 And in **internal-preparation having** to revenge all **mishearing**,[2977] when your **under-hearing** is filled.

7 Do you look on things **down face**? If any man trust **to-himself** that he is Christ's, let him of himself **inventory** this again, that, as he Christ's, even so we Christ's.

8 For though I should boast somewhat **excessively** of our authority, which the Lord has given us for **house-building**, and not for your **down-lifting**, not I-shall-be-**disfigured**:

9 That I may not seem as if I would **out-of-fear** you **through** letters.

[2968] To stimulate to anger
[2969] Greek: "hupostasis," under-stand," substrate, substance (real existence)
[2970] Covetousness, greed
[2971] Greek: "hilaros" associated with hilarious, and means propitious, atonement-merry; associated with the Greek word for "Mercyseat" (Merry-Atonement).
[2972] Or, offspring's, products
[2973] Haplotetes, the antonym of "diplous" meaning double
[2974] Lit., laos (people)-ergon (work); "liturgy"
[2975] Or reasonable, fairness through identifying with (resembling)
[2976] Greek compound "hupsoma," huper (over, elevated) and soma (body)
[2977] Or beside-hearing

10 For letters, **they-show**[2978], weighty and **forceful**; but bodily presence **without-strength**, and speech **out-of-nothing**.

11 Let such a one **inventory** this, that, such as we are in word **through** letters when we are absent, such also in **work** we are present.

12 For we **venture** not **to-in-judge**, or **together-judging** ourselves with some that **together-stand** themselves: but they **measure** themselves **in** themselves, and **together-judging** themselves **to-**themselves, **not synthesizing**.[2979]

13 But we will not boast of things **un-measured**, but **down** the measure of the **standard**[2980] which God has **sectioned**[2981] to us, a measure to **upon-arrive until** you.

14 Because not as not we-upon-arrive into you, we-beyond-out-stretched ourselves, because we are over-out-stretching[2982] ourselves **until** you also, in the **well-message** of Christ:

15 Not boasting of things **un-measured**, of **another-same cut-toils**; but having **expectation**, when your faith is **grown**, that we shall be **magnified**[2983] by you **down** our **standard surplus**,

16 To preach the **well-message** in the **over-there of-you**, not **internally-preparing into the** boasting in another-**same standard**.

17 Yet, he that **boast**, let him **boast** in the Lord.

18 For not he that **together-stand** himself is **seem-approved**, but whom the Lord **together-stands**.

2 CORINTHIANS CHAPTER 11

1 Would to God you could **tolerate** me a little in **the un-disposition**: and indeed, **tolerate** with me.

2 For I am **zealous** over you with **God's zealousness**: because I have **jointed** you to one husband, a chaste virgin, to **beside-stand to-the** Christ.

3 But I fear, lest by any means, as the serpent **out-of-cheat** Eve through his **all-working**,[2984] so your **thoughts** should be corrupted[2985] from the **singleness**[2986] that is in Christ.

4 For if he that **comes** preaches **another-same** Jesus, whom we have not preached, or you **welcome another-different** spirit, which you have not **taken**, or **another-different well-message**, which you have not **welcome**, you might **ideally tolerate**.

5 For I **inventory** I was not **deficient of-the** apostles over much.

6 But though **private-one**,[2987] in saying, yet not in **knowing**; but we have, **in all, shined in** you **into all-things**.

7 Have I **sinned** in **humbling** myself that you might be **elevated**, because I have **well-messaged to-you** the **well-message** of God **gratuitously**?[2988]

8 I robbed other Churches, **getting solider-ration**, to do you **attendance**.

9 And when I was present with you, and **lacked**, I was **down-numbed** to no man: for that which was lacking to me the **brothers** which came from Macedonia **towards-up-fill**: and in all I have **guard** myself **weightless to-you**, and **I-shall-be-guarded**.

10 As the truth of Christ is in me, no man shall **fence** me of this boasting in the regions of Achaia.

11 Why? Because I love you not? God **perceives**.

12 But what **I-produce, also I-produce,** that I may **out-of-cut from-urge** them which **will's to from-urge**; that **in which** they **boast**, they may be found **down-as also** we.

13 Because the-such false-apostles, **trick-bait** workers, **changed-scheming** themselves into the apostles of Christ.

14 And no marvel; for Satan himself is **changed-schemed** into an angel of light.

15 Therefore no **great-thing** if his **attendants** also **changed-scheme** as the **attendants** of **righteous-togetherness**; whose **finish** shall be **down** their works.

16 I say again, let no man think me **un-disposed**; if otherwise, yet as **un-disposed welcome** me, that I may boast myself a little.

[2978] Greek: "phemi," the root word for fame ("pheme")
[2979] Combining into a comprehensive logical whole related to understanding
[2980] Greek: "kanon" (straight reed); transliterated as "canon," a standard of measure
[2981] Or portioned
[2982] Or to be beforehand, to precede, to have arrived
[2983] Or, **great**
[2984] Craftiness
[2985] Or, to pine, to waste, to rot
[2986] Haplotetes, the antonym of "diplous" meaning double
[2987] Greek: "idiotes," transliterated as "idiots"
[2988] Or, without a cause

17 That which I speak, I speak not **down** the Lord, but as it were **un-disposed**, in this **substructure**[2989] of boasting.

18 Seeing that many **boast** after the flesh, I will **boast** also.

19 For you **tolerate the un-disposed sweetly**, seeing you are **disposed.**

20 For you **tolerate**, if a man **down-slave you**, if a man **down-eat**, if a man **takes**, if a man **up-lift** himself, if a man **skin** you **into** the face.

21 I speak as concerning **un-value**, as though we had been weak. **Yet, in which** any is **daring**, (I speak **un-disposed**,) I am **daring** also.

22 Are they Hebrews? **I-also**. Are they Israelites? **I-also**. Are they the seed of Abraham? **I-also**.

23 Are they **attendants** of Christ? (I speak as a **beside-disposed**) I **exceed**; in **to-labor-cut beyond-throw**, in **to-plague-poundings, above-throw, in to-prisons more-exceeding**, in deaths, **much**.

24 Of the Jews, **five, I-take** forty, **beside first.**

25 Three **I-was-beaten-with-rods,** once was I stoned, **three** shipwreck, a night and a day **I have-produced** in the deep;

26 Journeys, **many**, perils of waters, perils of robbers, perils by **kin**, perils by the **nations**, perils in the city, perils in the **lonesome**, perils in the sea, perils **in false-brothers;**

27 In **labor-cuts** and **difficult-toil**, in **sleeplessness, many**, in hunger and thirst, in fast **many**, in cold and nakedness.

28 Beside-exterior those things that are **space-from**, that which **comes** upon me **down day**, the **portion-worry** of all the Churches.

29 Who is weak, and I am not weak? Who is **scandalized**, and I burn not?

30 If **it-is-binding to-boast**, I will **boast** of the things which concern **my weakness.**

31 The God and Father of our Lord Jesus Christ, which is blessed **into the ages, perceive** that not **I-am-falsifying.**

32 In Damascus, the **Ethnarch**[2990] under Aretas the king **before-stared** the city of Damascenes, **willing to squeeze-capture**[2991] me:

33 And through a window in a basket **I-was-lowered** by the wall, and **out-of-fled** his hands.

2 CORINTHIANS CHAPTER 12

1 It is not **together-bearing** for me to **boast**. I will come **into** visions and revelations of the Lord.

2 I-perceived a man in Christ **before** fourteen **years** ago, (whether in the body, I cannot **perceive**; or whether out of the body, I cannot **perceive**: God **perceives**;) such a one **snatched until** third heaven.

3 And **I-perceived** such a man, (whether in the body, or out of the body, I cannot **perceive**: God **perceives**;)

4 How that he was **snatched** into paradise, and heard **un-expressed declarations**, which it is not lawful for a man to **talk**.

5 Over such an one will I **boast**: yet of myself I will not **boast**, but in **my weaknesses**

6 For though **I-am-willing** to **boast**, I shall not be **un-disposed**; for I will say the truth: but **I-spare**, lest any man should **inventory** of me above that which he **sees** me, or he **hears out-of** me.

7 And **that not I-may-be-lifted beyond-throw** through the **beyond-throw** of the revelations, there was given to me a thorn in the flesh, the **angel**,[2992] **of-Satan** to **fist-chastise**[2993] me, **that not I-be-over-lifted.**

8 Over, this thing I **beside-call** the Lord **three**, that it might **divorce**[2994] from me.

9 And he said **to-me**, my grace is **sufficient** for you: for my **power** is **matured** in weakness. **Sweetly**, therefore will I rather **boast** in my **weaknesses**, that the power of Christ may **upon-tent** me.

10 Therefore I take **well-seem** in **weakness**, in **insults**, in **necessities**, in **chases**, in **cramp-spaces over** Christ: for when I am weak, then **I-am powerful.**

11 I am become **un-disposed** in **boasting**; you have **necessitated** me: for I ought to have been **together-stood** of you: for in nothing am I **behind-late to-those** apostles **over much**, though I be nothing.

[2989] Greek: "hupostasis," under-stand," substrate
[2990] Or, Ethnic-first-rank, ethnic-principality, ethnic-original, ethnic-first, ethnic-chief
[2991] "Piazo," to squeeze, to seize by hand, to press, to arrest, to capture
[2992] Nominative
[2993] Greek: "kolaphizo" from the root for "kalazo" (curtail), to curtail by chastisement
[2994] Lit., "aphistemi" from-stand, the root word for "apostasies:" feminine of "apostasion" (divorce); a thing that separates.

12 Indeed, the signs of an apostle were **down-worked in** you in all **under-remaining, in** to-**signs,** and to-**wonders,** and to-**powers.**

13 Because, what is-there which you-were-inferior to **remaining** Churches, except that I myself was not **down-numb to-you**? **Be-gracious to-me to-this unrighteousness.**

14 Be-perceiving, the **third** I am **internally-prepared** to come **to-you**; and I will not be **down-numb to-you**: for I seek not yours, but you: for the children **owes** not **place-into-tomorrow** for the parents, but the parents for the children.

15 And I will very **sweetly** spend and be spent for you; though the **more-excessively** I love you, the less I be loved.

16 But be it so, I did not **down-weight** you: nevertheless, **under-originating all-working,** I caught you with **trick-bait.**

17 Did I **more-have**[2995] of you by any of them whom I sent **to-you?**

18 I **beside-call** Titus, and **together-dispatched** the brother. Did Titus **more-have** of you? Walked we not in the **selfsame Spirit?** Not in the same **footprints?**

19 Again, **you-are-seeming** that we **answer**[2996] **to-you?** We speak before God in Christ: but all things, beloved, for your **house-building.**

20 For I fear, lest, when I come, I shall not find you such as I **will,** and I shall be found **to-you** such as not **you-are-willing:** lest quarrel,[2997] **zeal, sacrifice-angers, stimulations,**[2998] **down-talk,** whisperings, **inflations, instability.**[2999]

21 Not when I come again, my God will humble me **in** you, and I shall **grieve** many which have **before-sinned** and have not **change-thinking** of the uncleanness, prostitution, and **wantonness** which **they-practiced.**

2 CORINTHIANS CHAPTER 13

1 This the third I am coming **to-you**. In the mouth of two or three witnesses shall every **declaration** be **stand.**

2 I-before-speak, and **I-am-systematically-predicting,**[3000] as if I were present, the second; and being absent now I write **to-them** which **have-before-sinned,** and to all **remaining,** that, if I come again, I will not spare:

3 Since you seek a **seem-test** of Christ speaking in me, **who toward** is not weak, but is **powerful** in you.

4 For though he was crucified through weakness, yet he lives **out-of** the power of God. For we also are weak in him, but we shall live **together to-him** by the power of God **into you**.

5 Probe-test yourselves, whether you **are** in the faith; **seem-test** yourselves. Know you not yourselves, how that Jesus Christ is in you, except you be **un-seem-test?**[3001]

6 But I **expect** that you shall know that we are not **not-seem-tested.**[3002]

7 Now I pray **towards** God that you **produce** no evil; not that we should **shine seem-tested,** but that you should **produce** that which is **ideal,** though we be as **not-seem-tested.**

8 Because, not we-are-powerful anything **down** the truth, but **over** the truth.

9 For we are **cheerful,** when we are weak, and you are **powerful**: and this also we **pray,** your **down-freshness.**

10 Therefore I write these things being absent, lest being present I should use, **from-single-cut, down** the power which the Lord has given me **into house-building,** and not **into down-lifting.**

11 Finally, **brothers, cheer!** Be **down-fresh,** be **beside-called,** be **the same disposition,** live in peace; and the God of love and peace shall be with you.

12 Embrace one-another-same with a holy **friend-kiss.**

13 All the saints **embrace,** you.

14 The grace of the Lord Jesus Christ, and the love of God, and the communion of the **Holy Spirit,** with you all. Amen!

[2995] Or covet, overreach, greedy
[2996] Greek: "apologeomai" (from-saying) to exculpate (self), to give account, to defend
[2997] Or, electioneering, quarrel, debates
[2998] Or to arouse curiosity (intrigue)
[2999] Down-standing, inconstant, unstable, confusion
[3000] Before-(systematically) speak
[3001] Rejected, reprobate
[3002] Rejected, reprobate

GALATIANS

GALATIANS CHAPTER 1

1 Paul, an apostle, (not **from** men, neither **through** man, but **through** Jesus Christ, and God the Father, who raised him **out-of** the dead.)

2 And all the **brothers** which are with me, **to-the** Churches of Galatia:

3 Grace **to-you** and peace from God the Father, and our Lord Jesus Christ,

4 Who gave himself for our sins, that he might **out-of-lift** us from this present **wicked-hurtful age down** the will of God and our Father:

5 To whom glory **into the ages of the ages**. Amen.

6 I marvel that you are so soon **translated** from him that called you **in** the grace of Christ **into another-different well-message**:

7 Which is not **another-same**; but there be some that **agitate** you and would pervert the **well-message** of Christ.

8 But though we, or an angel from heaven, preach any other **well-message to-you beside** which we have **well-messaged to-you**, let him be **banned**.[3003]

9 As we said before, so say I now again, if any preach any other **well-message to-you** than that you have **beside-taken**, let him be **banned**.

10 Presently, because of men **I-believe**, or **the** God? Or do I seek to please men? **Because**, if I yet pleased men, I should not be the **slave** of Christ.

11 Yet **I-make-known to-you**, brothers, that the **well-message** which was **evangelized under** me is not **down** man.

12 **Because**, I neither **beside-took** it **beside** man, neither was I taught, but by the revelation of Jesus Christ.

13 **Because**, you have heard of my **behavior once** in the **Judaism**, how that **beyond-throw**, I **chased** the Church of God, and **ravaged her**.

14 And profited in the **Judaism** above many my **co-primes** in my **kin**, excessive **zealot**, **under-originating**, of the **beside-giving**[3004] of my fathers

15 But when it pleased God, who **from-defined**[3005] me from my mother's womb, and called **through** his grace,

16 To reveal his Son in me, that I might **well-message** him among the **nations**; **soon** I **added**[3006] not with flesh and blood:

17 Neither went I up **into** Jerusalem[3007] **to-them** which were apostles before me; but I went into Arabia and returned again **into** Damascus.

18 **Thereupon,** after three years I went up to Jerusalem to **history**[3008] Peter and **remained toward** him **ten-five** days.

19 But **another-different** of the apostles **I-perceived** none, **if not,** James the Lord's brother.

20 Now the things which I write **to-you, be-perceiving**, before God, I **falsify** not.

21 **Thereupon,** I came into the regions of Syria and Cilicia;

22 And was **not-minded to-**face **to-Churches** of Judaea, which were in Christ:

23 Yet, they had heard only, that he which **chased** us **once** now **well-message** the faith which he **once ravaged**.

24 And they glorified God in me.

GALATIANS CHAPTER 2

1 **Thereupon, ten-four years** after I **up-walked** again **into** Jerusalem[3009] with Barnabas, and **together-beside-taking,** Titus.

2 Yet, I-**up-walk** by revelation, and **up-placed to-them** that **well-message** which I preach **in** the **nations,** but privately **to-them** which were of **seem-tested** lest by any means **I-am-racing**, or **I-ran, into empty**.

3 **Also** neither Titus, who was with me, being a **Hellenic**, was **necessitated** to be circumcised:

4 And that because of **false-brothers beside-into-lead**[3010] who **beside-into-came, down-scope**[3011] out

---
[3003] Or anathema
[3004] Lit., beside-give, transmission, tradition
[3005] Or. From-horizon
[3006] Greek: towards-up-place, to lay up additionally
[3007] Greek: Priests-peace (hierou-priest, sacred) and salem (peace)

[3008] Greek: "historeo"—from a derivative "eido" (to perceive) and "rheo" (to flow as water; i.e., rhetoric)
[3009] Greek: Priests-peace (hierou-priest, sacred) and Salem (peace)
[3010] Or, smuggled in
[3011] Or spy

our **freedom** which we have in Christ Jesus, that they might **enslave us**.

5 To whom, not, **towards hour we-imaged**³⁰¹² to-the **under-arranging**; that the truth of the **well-message should-be-through-remaining towards** you.

6 But of these who seemed to be somewhat, (whatever they were, it makes no **difference**³⁰¹³ to me: God accepts no man's person:) for they who seemed, **added**³⁰¹⁴ nothing to me:

7 But contrariwise, when they **perceived** that the **well-message** of the Uncircumcision was committed **to-me**, **down-as** of the Circumcision **to** Peter;

8 (For he that **in-worked** in Peter to the apostleship of the Circumcision, the same was **in-worked** in me **into the nations**.)

9 And when James, Cephas, and John, who seemed to be pillars,³⁰¹⁵ **knowing** the grace that was given **to-me**, they gave to me and Barnabas the right hands of **communion**; that we **into** the **nations**, and they **into** the Circumcision.

10 Only that we should remember the poor; the same which I also was **speedy** to **produce**.

11 **Yet** when Peter was come to Antioch, I **anti-stand** him to the face, because he was to be **down-know**.

12 **Because** before **some** came from James, he did eat with the **nations**: but when they were come, he **under-stall** and **from-defined**³⁰¹⁶ himself, fearing them which were **out-of** the circumcision.

13 And the other Jews **together-hypocrite to-him**; insomuch that Barnabas also was **together-led-from** with their **hypocrisy**.

14 **Yet** when **I-perceived** that **not they-straight-footed toward** the truth of the **well-message**, I said to Peter before all, if you, being a Jew, **under-originating, as-the-nations are-living,** and not as do the Jews, why **are-you-necessitating** the nations to **Judaize?**³⁰¹⁷

15 We Jews by nature, and not sinners of the nations,

16 **Having-perceived** that a man is not **righteous** by the works of the law, but by the faith of Jesus Christ, even we have believed **into** Jesus Christ, that we might be **righteous out-of** the faith of Christ, and not by the works of the law: for **out-of** the works of the law shall no flesh be **righteous**.

17 But if, while we seek to be **righteous in** Christ, we ourselves also are found sinners, is therefore Christ the **attendant** of sin? **Not may-it-become**.

18 For if I **house-build** again the things which I **down-loosed**, I make myself a **beside-stepper**.

19 For I through the law am dead to the law, that **I-should-be-living** to God.

20 I am **together-crucified** Christ, **yet I-live**; yet not I, but Christ lives in me: and the life which I now live in the flesh I live by the faith **to-the of-the** Son **of-the** God, who loved me, and gave himself **over** me.

21 I do not **un-place** the grace of God; **because** if **righteous-togetherness** by the law, then Christ **died gratuitously**.³⁰¹⁸

GALATIANS CHAPTER 3

1 O **un-mind** Galatians, who has **malign**³⁰¹⁹ you, that you should not **be-persuaded of-the** truth, **down** eyes Jesus Christ has been **before-written**, crucified **in** you?

2 This only would I learn of you, **take** you the Spirit **out-of** the works of the law, or **out-of** the hearing of faith?

3 Are you so **un-minded**? Having **in-original to-**Spirit, are you now **upon-finish to-the** flesh?

4 Have you **emotion** so many things **without-basis**? If yet **without-cause**.

5 He therefore that **supplies to-you** the Spirit, and **in-work powers**³⁰²⁰ in you, **out-of** works of the law, or **out of** the hearing of faith?

6 Even as Abraham believed God, and it was **inventoried to-him** for **righteous-togetherness**.

7 Know you therefore that they which are **out-of** faith, **these** are the **sons** of Abraham.

8 And the Scripture, **before-perceiving** that God would **make-righteous** the **nations out-of** faith, **before-good-message to-Abraham**, "in you shall all nations be blessed."

---

³⁰¹² Or, imaged, yield, to be weak to resemble, I am like (Strong's #1502, #1503, #1504)
³⁰¹³ Greek: "diaphero," to through-bear, transliterated as "differ" or "different"
³⁰¹⁴ Greek: towards-up-place, to lay up additionally,
³⁰¹⁵ Lit., styles
³⁰¹⁶ Lit., from-horizon
³⁰¹⁷ Or, become a Judean
³⁰¹⁸ Or, without a cause
³⁰¹⁹ Speak about someone in a spiteful critical manner
³⁰²⁰ Or miracles

9 So then they which be **out-of** faith are blessed with **believing** Abraham.

10 For as many as are **out-of** the works of the law are under the **down-prayer; because** it is written, **down-prayed** every one that **remains** not in all things which are written in the **little-scroll** of the law to do them.

11 Yet that no man is **righteous** by the law in the sight of God, **is-clear,** for, the **righteous** shall live **out-of** faith.

12 And the law is not **out-of** faith: but the man that does them shall live in them.

13 Christ has **out-of-market** us from the **down-prayer** of the law, being made a curse for us: for it is written, **down-prayed** everyone that hangs on a tree:

14 That the blessing of Abraham might come on the **nations** through Jesus Christ; that we might receive the promise of the Spirit through faith.

15 Brothers, I speak **down** men; **like-as** man's **lordship-ratify a covenant**, no man **in-un-placing**, or **upon-through-arranging.** [3021]

16 Now to Abraham and his seed were the promises **spoken**. He says not, and to seeds, as of many; but as of one, and **to-your** seed, which is Christ.

17 Yet this I say, the covenant, that was **before-lordship-ratified under the** God in Christ, the law, which was four hundred and thirty **years** after, cannot **un-lordship-ratify,** [3022] that it should make the promise **into the down-un-work.**

18 For if the inheritance is **out-of** the law, no more **out-of** promise; **yet** God **graced** to Abraham by promise.

19 Why then the law? It was **added** [3023] because of **beside-stepping**, until the seed should come to whom the promise was made; **through-arranged through** angels in the hand of a mediator.

20 Now a mediator is not of one, but God is one.

21 Therefor, the law down the promises of God? **Not may-it-become! Because,** if **was-given** law **the being-powerful to-life-produce, really, righteous-togetherness** should have been **out-of** the law.

22 Yet the Scripture has **together-locked** all under sin, that the promise **out-of** faith of Jesus Christ might be given **to-them** that believe.

23 Yet before faith came, we were **before-stared-at** under the law, **together-locked** into the faith **impending to-be-revealed.**

24 So-too, the law was our **boy-leader** into Christ, that **we-might-be-made-righteous out-of** faith.

25 Yet after that faith is come, we are **not-still** under a **boy-leader**.

26 For you are all the **sons** of God **through the** faith in Christ Jesus.

27 Because as many of you as have been baptized into Christ have **clothe-yourself** [3024] Christ.

28 There is neither Jew nor **Hellenics**, there is neither **slave** nor free, there is neither male nor female, **because** you are all one in Christ Jesus.

29 And if you **of-Christ,** then are you Abraham's seed, and heirs according-to the promise.

GALATIANS CHAPTER 4

1 Now I say, the heir, **as-much-as uninterrupted-time,** he is an **infant**, differs [3025] nothing from a **slave**, though he be lord of all.

2 But is under **managers** [3026] and **house-lawyers** until the **purpose** [3027] of the father.

3 Even so we, when we were **infants**, were in **slavery** under the **elements** [3028] of the world:

4 But when the **filling** of the **uninterrupted-time came,** God **out-of-sent** his Son, **birthed** of a woman, **birthed** under the law,

5 To **out-of-market-place** [3029] them that were under the law, that we might **take** the **son-placing**.

6 That now you are sons, God has **out-of-sent** the Spirit of his Son into **your hearts, screaming,** [3030] Abba, [3031] Father.

7 So-too, you are no more a **slave,** but son, and if son, then an heir of God through Christ.

[3021] Supplement
[3022] Or invalidate
[3023] Or, to place additionally
[3024] Lit., in-down; or, in-sink, in-down-slipping, in-slip
[3025] Greek: "diaphero," to through-bear, transliterated as "differ" or "different"
[3026] Lit., upon-turn
[3027] Lit., before-place, to place before, or to place in advance

[3028] Or, any first thing, something orderly in arrangement (Gal 4 3, 4:9; Col 2:8, 20; Heb 5:12; 2 Peter 3:10, 12; compare Acts 21:24, Rom 4:12, Gal 5:25, Gal 6:16, Phil 3:16)
[3029] Compare "towards-market" in Hebrews 5:10
[3030] Greek "krazon," transliterated as crazy
[3031] Abba could be Hebrew words for father ("Ab") and the Hebrew word for come ("ba") compounded—Come-Father, Father

8 Also then, when you **perceived** not God, **you-were-slaved to-them** which by nature are no gods.

9 Yet now, after that you have known God, or rather are known **under** God, how **upon-turn**[3032] you again to the **without-strength** and **poor elements**[3033] **to-which** you **will** again to be in **slavery**?

10 You **beside-watch**[3034] days, and months, and **seasons**, and **years**.

11 I am afraid of you, lest I have **fatigue-cut, into you, without-cause**.

12 Brothers, I **beg-bind** you, **be as I; and-I as you**; you have not **unrighteous** me.

13 You **perceived** how through **weakness** of the flesh I **well-message** you **before**.

14 And my **probe-testing** which was in my flesh you **not out-of-nothing**,[3035] **not-yet spit-out**; but **welcomed** me as an angel of God, as Christ Jesus.

15 Where then the **happiness of-you**? Because, **I-am-witnessing of-you**, that, if **powerful**, you would have **out-dug** your own eyes, and have given them to me.

16 Am I therefore become your **hate, being-true to-you**?

17 They-are-being **zealous over-you**, not **ideally**; also, they-are-willing **out-lock** you, **that you-may-be-zealous over-them**.

18 Yet, **ideal to-be-zealous** always in **to-ideal**, and not only when I am present **towards** you.

19 My children, of whom I travail in birth again until Christ be formed in you.

20 I **willed** to be present **towards** you now, and to **change** my voice; that **I-have-no-way-out in** you.

21 Tell me, you that **willing** to be under the law, do you not hear the law?

22 For it is written, that Abraham had two sons, the one by a **girl**, the **one out-of** a freewoman.

23 Also he of the **girl** was born **down** the flesh; but he of the freewoman **through** the promise.

24 Which things are an allegory: **because** these are the two covenants; the one from the **mountain** Sinai, **which born into slavery,** which is Agar.

25 For this Agar is **mountain** Sinai in Arabia, and **together-element**[3036] to Jerusalem[3037] which now is and is **slaving** with her children.

26 But Jerusalem[3038] which is above is free, which is the mother of us all.

27 Because it is written, **be-good-dispositioned,** you **sterile** that **brings-forth, burst-forth** and **distress-call**, you that travail not; **that** the **lonesome** has many more children than she which has a husband.

28 Now we, **brothers**, as Isaac was, are the children of promise.

29 But as then he that was born after the flesh **chased** him **down** the Spirit, even so now.

30 Also what says the Scripture? Cast out the **girl** and her son, **because** the son of the **girl** shall not be heir with the son of the freewoman.

31 So then, **brothers**, we are not children of the **girl**, but of the **freewoman**.

GALATIANS CHAPTER 5

1 Stand therefore **to-the-freedom** Christ **has-freed us** and be not **yoked** again **of-slavery**.

2 Be-perceiving, I Paul say **to-you,** that if you be circumcised, Christ shall profit you nothing.

3 Yet, **I-am-witnessing** again to every man that is circumcised, that he is a debtor to do the whole law.

4 Christ is **down-un-worked from** you, whoever of you are **righteous in** the law; you are **out-of-fall** from grace.

5 Because we **to-Spirit** wait for the **expectation** of **righteous-togetherness out-of** faith.

6 Because, in Jesus Christ, neither circumcision **forces** anything, nor uncircumcision; but faith which **in-work through** love.

7 You did **run ideally**; who did **cut-into**[3039] you that you should not **be-persuaded to-the** truth?

[3032] Or revert
[3033] Or, any first thing, something orderly in arrangement (Gal 4:3, 4:9; Col 2:8, 20; Heb 5:12; 2 Peter 3:10, 12; compare Acts 21:24, Rom 4:12, Gal 5:25, Gal 6:16, Phil 3:16)
[3034] Or inspect, comparer Mark 3:2
[3035] Or scorn
[3036] Or together-in line
[3037] "Hierosoluma"—priests-peace (hierou-priest, sacred) and salem (peace)
[3038] Jerusalem in the Old Testament is plural (dual) —Est. 2:6, 2 Chron. 25:1, etc.
[3039] Lit., in-cut, impede, delayed

8 This persuasion not of him that **is-calling** you.

9 A little **ferment, ferment** the whole **dough**.

10 I have confidence in you **in** the Lord, that you will not be **else disposed**; **yet** he that **agitate** you shall bear his **judgment-result**,³⁰⁴⁰ whosoever **he-may-be**.

11 And I, **brothers**, if I yet preach circumcision, why **am-I-being chased**? Then is the **scandal**³⁰⁴¹ of the cross **is-down-un-work**.

12 Also, owing they-shall-from-cut³⁰⁴² themselves which **up-stand**³⁰⁴³ you.

13 Because, **brothers**, you have been called **upon freedom**; only not **freedom into from-start** to the flesh, but **through** love **be-slaving to-one-another-same.**

14 Because all the law is **filled** in one **saying**, in this; you shall love your neighbor as yourself.

15 Yet, if you bite and **eat another-same, be-you-looking** that you be not consumed one of another.

16 I say then, walk **to-Spirit,** and you shall not **finish** the **upon-feelings** of the flesh.

17 For the flesh **in-on-feeling down** the Spirit, and the Spirit **down** the flesh: and these are **opposing-ones**³⁰⁴⁴ the one to the other; so that you cannot do the things that you **will**.

18 Yet if you be led **to-Spirit,** you are not under the law.

19 Yet the works of the flesh are **shining,** which are adultery, **prostitution,** uncleanness, **wantonness.**³⁰⁴⁵

20 Idolatry, **drugging**³⁰⁴⁶ hatred, **quarrel,**³⁰⁴⁷ **zealousness, sacrifice-anger, stimulations,**³⁰⁴⁸ **two-stands, sect-preference.**

21 Ill-will, murders, drunkenness,³⁰⁴⁹ **laying-outstretch,**³⁰⁵⁰ and such like; **I-am-systematically-predicting,**³⁰⁵¹ **down-as I-before-said**, that they which **practice** such things shall not inherit the kingdom of God.

22 Yet, the fruit of the Spirit is love, **cheerfulness,** peace, **long-sacrifice-anger, usefulness, good-togetherness,** faith,

23 Mildness, **in-governed**: against such there is no law.

24 And they that are **of-Christ** have crucified the flesh **together to**-the emotions and **upon-feelings**

25 If we live **to-Spirit,** let us also **element-walk,**³⁰⁵² to-Spirit.

26 Let us not become vain-glorifying, **before-calling-to-oneself,**³⁰⁵³ ill-will to-one-another.

GALATIANS CHAPTER 6

1 Brothers, if a man be **before-taken** in a **side-fall,** you which are spiritual, **down-fresh** such a one in spirit of **mildness; spy** yourself, **not** you also be **probe-tested**.

2 Lift you **one-another's-same weight,** and so **up-fill** the law of **the** Christ.

3 For if a man **seems** to be something, when he is nothing, he **disposition-misleading**³⁰⁵⁴ himself.

4 But let every man **seem-test** his own work, and then shall he have **boast** in himself alone, and not in **another-different**.

5 For every man shall **lift** his own **invoice-load**

6 Let him that is **catechize** the **Word** communicate **to-the one-catechizing** in all good things.

7 Be not **seduced**; God is not **snouted**: for whatever a man sows, that shall he also reap.

8 For he that sow **into** his flesh shall of the flesh reap corruption; but he that sow **into** the Spirit shall of the Spirit reap **eternal life**.

9 And let us not **be-out-of-evil** in **ideal** doing; **because** in **private** season we shall reap if we **out-of-loose** not.

10 As we have therefore **season,** let us **work** good **towards** all, especially **towards** them who are of the household of faith.

---

³⁰⁴⁰ Greek: "krima" transliterated as crime and also means judgment
³⁰⁴¹ Or, snare, bent trap-stick
³⁰⁴² Or amputate
³⁰⁴³ Or properly: to drive out of home, to disturb
³⁰⁴⁴ Greek: anti-laying outstretched
³⁰⁴⁵ Or, unlimited sexual relationships, no control
³⁰⁴⁶ Or pharmacy
³⁰⁴⁷ Or, electioneering, quarrel, debates
³⁰⁴⁸ Or to arouse curiosity (intrigue)
³⁰⁴⁹ Greek: meth
³⁰⁵⁰ Or, letting loose
³⁰⁵¹ Before-(systematically) speak
³⁰⁵² Gk.: stoicheo, to march in rank (keep step), from same root for "element"
³⁰⁵³ Or, challenging
³⁰⁵⁴ Or, mind-misleading, mind-cheater, disposition-cheater

11 **Be-perceiving how-full-grown**[3055] a letter I have written **to-you** with **my** hand.

12 As many as **will to-good-face** in the flesh, they **necessitate** you to be circumcised; **that not they-may-be-chased** for the cross of Christ.

13 For neither they themselves who are circumcised **watch** the law; but **will you to-be-circumcised,** that they may **boast** in your flesh.

14 Yet, **not may-it-become** that I should **boast,** if not in the cross of our Lord Jesus Christ, **through** whom the world is crucified **to-me, and-I**[3056] **to-the** world.

15 Because in Christ Jesus neither circumcision, anything, **is-forceful,** nor uncircumcision, but a new **creation.**

16 And as many as **element-walk,**[3057] **to-this rod-standard**, peace on them, and mercy, and on the Israel of **the-**God.

17 Of-the remaining, let no man **cut** me: for I **near-hold** in my body the **stigma**[3058] of the Lord Jesus.

18 Brothers, the grace of our Lord Jesus Christ with your spirit. Amen.

[3055] Or, how much (as indefinite), dignity, adult
[3056] "Kago" a Greek compound kia (and) and ego (self-esteem, self-confident, self-importance, etc.)
[3057] Greek "stoicheo" -to march in rank (keep step), from same root for "element"
[3058] Greek "stigma" - to mark or puncture for recognition of ownership, to scar, to brand, the Greek letter representing "6" (relating to "man")

EPHESIANS

EPHESIANS CHAPTER 1

1 Paul, an apostle of Jesus Christ by the will of God, to the saints which are at Ephesus, and to the **believing** in Christ Jesus:

2 Grace **to-you**, and peace, from God our Father, and the Lord Jesus Christ.

3 Blessed[3059] the God and Father of our Lord Jesus Christ, who has blessed us with all spiritual blessings in **the** heavenly in Christ:

4 **Down-as** he has chosen us in him before the **down-casting** of the world, that we should be holy and without blame **down-before** him in love:

5 Having **before-defined**[3060] us **into son-placed through** Jesus Christ **into himself, down** the **well-seem** of his will,

6 **Into** the praise of the glory of his grace, **in which** he has **graced** us in the Beloved.

7 In whom we have **from-loosed** through his blood, the **release**[3061] of **beside-falls, down** the riches of his grace.

8 **Which** he has abounded **into** us in all wisdom and **prudent-disposition**.

9 Having made known **to-us** the mystery of his will, **down well-seem** which he has **preplaced** in himself:

10 That in the **house-law** of the fullness of **seasons** he **up-head** all things in Christ, both which are in heaven, and which are on earth; in him:

11 In whom also **we-have-an-inheritance, before-defined, down** the **preplacement**[3062] of him who **in-works** all things **down** the **plan-counsel** of his will:

12 **Into we-exist**, us, **into** the praise of his glory, **before-expected** in Christ.

13 In whom you also, after that you heard the **Word** of **Truth**, the **well-message** of your salvation: in whom also **having-believed,** you were sealed with that Holy Spirit of promise,

14 Who is the **down-payment** of our inheritance **into** the **from-loose** of the **around-make**[3063] **into** the praise of his glory.

15 **Through this,** I also, after I heard of your faith in the Lord Jesus, and love **into** all the saints,

16 **Paused** not to give thanks for you, making **remembrance** of you in my prayers.

17 That the God of our Lord Jesus Christ, the Father of glory, may give **to-you** the spirit of wisdom and revelation in the knowledge of him:

18 The eyes of your **heart** being enlightened that you may **perceive** what the **expectation** of his calling and what the riches of the glory of his inheritance in the saints;

19 And what the **beyond-throw great** of his power **into us** who believe, **down** the **energy** of-the **government**[3064] of-the force of-him,

20 Which he **in-worked** in Christ, when he raised him from the dead, and **seated-him in** his right hand in the **heavens.**

21 **Up-above** all original, and **authority,** and **power,** and **lord,** and every name that is named, not only in this **age,** but also in **the-one impending**:

22 And has **subordinate**[3065] all under his feet, and gave him, the head, over all to the Church,

23 Which is his body, the **filling** of him **filling** all in all.

EPHESIANS CHAPTER 2

1 And you who were dead in **beside-falls** and sins;

2 **In which when** you **about-walked down** the **age** of this world, **down** the **first-rank**[3066] of the **authority** of the air, the spirit that now **in-works** in the sons of-**un-persuadable**:

3 Among whom also we all had our **behavior**, once, in the **on-feeling** of our flesh, **producing** the **will** of the flesh and of the **deep-thoughts**; and were by nature the children of **swelling-anger**, even as **the remaining-ones**.

4 But God, who is rich in mercy, for his **much** love **with which** he loved us,

---

[3059] Greek: "eulogetos" (good-speaking, well-speaking, good-word, well-word)
[3060] Or. Before-horizon, pre-defined, predestined
[3061] Lit., from-let-go
[3062] Or before-place, to place before, or to place in advance, purpose
[3063] Greek: peri (around) and poieo (make, produce), means to purchase, acquire
[3064] Greek: kratos, transliterated as "great" and also means vigor, strength, to use strength, to rule, government, translated as "cracy" in democracy—people(demo)-government (kratos), or public-government
[3065] Under-arranged
[3066] Or, original-rank, beginning-rank

5 Even when we were dead in **beside-falls**, has **together-life-produced** us with Christ (by grace you are saved).

6 And has **together-raised-us** and **together-seated-us** in **the** heavens in Christ Jesus:

7 That in the ages to come he might show the **beyond-throw** riches of his grace in **his-usefulness** toward us through Christ Jesus.

8 **Because,** by grace you are saved through faith and that not **out-of** yourselves, the gift of God:

9 Not **out-of** works, lest any man should boast.

10 For we are his **poem-products,**³⁰⁶⁷ created in Christ Jesus **into** good works, which God has **before-internally-prepared** that we should **together-walk** in them.

11 Therefore remember, that you **formerly nations** in the flesh, **ones-being-said**, Uncircumcision, by that which is called the Circumcision in the flesh **hand-made**.

12 That at that **season** you were **spaced-from** Christ, being **from-another-same** of-the **citizenship** of Israel, and **foreign-lodger** from the covenants of promise, having no **expectation**, and **atheist** in the world.

13 **Yet** now in Christ Jesus you who sometimes were far off **became near-squeezed in** the blood of Christ.

14 For he is our peace, who has **made** both one, and has **loosed** the **middle-wall** of **fence**.

15 Having **down-un-worked** in his flesh the **hate**, the law of commandments, in **dogmas,**³⁰⁶⁸ for to **create** in himself of **two into** one **new-fresh** man, making peace.

16 And that he might **from-down-change** both **to** God in one body by the cross, having slain the **hate in it**.

17 And came and **well-messaged** peace **to-you** which were afar off, and **to-them near-squeezed**.

18 For through him we both have **towards-lead in** one Spirit **towards** the Father.

19 Now therefore you are no more **foreign-lodger** and **foreign-household**³⁰⁶⁹ but **together-citizens** with the saints, and of the household of God.

20 And **being-house-built** upon the foundation of the apostles and prophets, Jesus Christ himself being the **extreme-corner**

21 In whom all the **house-building together-joint-laid** together grows into a holy temple in the Lord:

22 In whom you also are **together-house-built into a down-house-location**³⁰⁷⁰ **of-the** God **in** the Spirit.

EPHESIANS CHAPTER 3

1 **On this grace,** I Paul, the prisoner of Jesus Christ **over** you **the nations**,

2 If you have heard of the **house-law** of the grace of God which is given **to-me into you**.

3 How that by revelation he made known **to-me** the mystery; (as I wrote afore in few words,

4 Whereby, when you read, **you-are-powerful to-thought** my **synthesis**³⁰⁷¹ in the mystery of Christ)

5 Which in **another-different generations** was not made known **to-the** sons of men, as it is now revealed **to** his holy apostles and prophets **in** the Spirit;

6 That the **nations** should be **together-heirs,** and **together-bodies,** and **together-partners**³⁰⁷² of his promise in Christ **through** the **well-message**:

7 **Of which** I **became** an **attendant, down** the gift of the grace of God given **to-me down** the **energy** of his power.

8 **To-me,** who the least of all saints, is this grace given, that I should **well-message** among the **nations** the **untraceable** riches of Christ;

9 And to **enlighten** what the **communion** of the mystery, which from **the ages** has been hid in God, who created all things **through** Jesus Christ:

10 **That now, to-the originals** and **authorities,** in heavens, **may-be-known through** the Church the **various** wisdom of God,

11 **Down preplaced**³⁰⁷³ **of-the ages** which he **made** in Christ Jesus our Lord:

---

³⁰⁶⁷ Greek: "Poiema," transliterated as "poem;" and also means to make, to do, to produce, to achieve
³⁰⁶⁸ Greek: Accepted beliefs, authoritative proclamations, decrees, etcetera that is not questioned or doubted, from "dokeo," to think, to seem,
³⁰⁶⁹ Greek: Beside-house, having a house beside (near), a by-dweller (alien resident)

³⁰⁷⁰ Greek: kate (down), oikeo (house) and terion (a location where something happens)— see also Rev. 18:2
³⁰⁷¹ Combining into a comprehensive and logical whole [Greek compound "sun" (together) and "hiemi" (to put, to send)]
³⁰⁷² Or together-with-holders, together-sharers
³⁰⁷³ Or before-place, to place before, or to place in advance, purposed

12 In whom we have **all-speech**[3074] and **toward-lead** with **trust** by the faith of him.

13 Through which I desire that you not **out-of-bad** in my tribulations for you, which is your glory.

14 Of-this grace I bow my knees **towards** the Father of our Lord Jesus Christ,

15 Of whom **every fatherhood** in heavens and earth **is-being-named**.

16 That he would grant you, **down** the riches of his glory, **to-power, be-governed through** his Spirit into the **inside** man.

17 That Christ may **down-house** in your **hearts through** faith; that you, being rooted and **founded** in love,

18 That **you-should-be-forceful to-down-take** with all saints what is the **width**,[3075] and length, and depth,[3076] and **elevation**.

19 Besides, to know the love of Christ, which **is-a-beyond-throw of-the** knowing, that **you-may-be-filled** with all the **filling of-the** God.

20 Now **to-him** that is **powerful, over** all, **producing exceeding** that we ask or **thought, down** the power that **in-works** in us,

21 To-him, glory in the Church by Christ Jesus **into all the generations of-the age of-the ages**. Amen.

EPHESIANS CHAPTER 4

1 I therefore, the prisoner of the Lord, **beside-call** you that you walk **deserving** of the **calling** of-which you are called,

2 With all **humble-disposition** and **mildness**, with **long-sacrifice-anger**, tolerating **one-another-same** in love.

3 Speeding, to **guard** the **oneness** of the Spirit in the **together-bond** of peace.

4 One body, and one Spirit, even as you are called in one **expectation** of your calling.

5 One Lord, **first** faith, one baptism,

6 One God and Father of all, who **upon** all, and through all, and in you all.

7 Yet to each one of us **was-given** grace **down** the measure of the gift **of-the** Christ.

8 Through-which he says when he **up-walked into elevation, he-captures captivity,** and gave gifts to-the men.

9 (Now that he **up-walked**, what is it but that he also **down-walked, before-most,** into the lower **sections** of the earth?

10 He that **down-walked** is the same also that **up-walked over-up** all heavens, that he may fill all things.)

11 And **He** gave **in-fact**,[3077] the apostles, **yet the** prophets; **yet-the** evangelist,[3078] **yet the shepherds** and teachers;

12 Towards the **down-fresh** of the saints, for the work of the ministry, for the **house-building** of the body of Christ:

13 Until we all **down-against into** the **oneness** of the faith, and of the knowledge of the Son of God, **into** a **mature** man, **into** the measure **of**-stature[3079] **of-the filling of-the** Christ:

14 That **no-not-still** we-may-be **infants**, being-surged, carried about with every wind of **teaching**, by the **cube-gambling** of men, **all-working**,[3080] **towards the change-road**[3081] **of-the seducing.**

15 Yet being-true-ones, in love, may grow **into him** in all things, **who** is the head, **the** Christ:

16 Out of-whom the **entire** body **together-joint-laid** and **together-embark**[3082] **through every joint of-the supply,**[3083] **down** the energy in the measure **of-one each section, growth** of the body **into the house-building** of itself in love.

17 This I say therefore, and **witness** in the Lord, that you **no-not-still about-walk down** as also the **nations** walk, in the vanity of their mind,

18 Having the **deep-thoughts**[3084] darkened, **from-another-same, of-the** the life **of-the** God through the **ignoring** that is in them, **through** the **callous-petrifying** of their **heart:**

[3074] Or free speech
[3075] Lit., platos ("flat," "plot")
[3076] Lit., bathos ("bath"); root to walk, base
[3077] Or, indeed
[3078] Or., lit., good-angel
[3079] Or, state or time of greatest strength, best quality, mature age
[3080] Craftiness
[3081] Greek: "method"
[3082] Greek: sun (together) and bibazo (to force), drive-together, unite, infer, together-board a ship
[3083] Or upon-choir-leader
[3084] Through-mind

19 Who **being-from-pain**[3085] have given themselves over **to unrestrained-sensual-brutality,** into **work**[3086] of-every uncleanness in more-having.

20 Yet, you have not so learned **the** Christ;

21 If so be that you have heard him, and have been taught **in** him, as the truth is in Jesus:

22 That you **from-place down** the former **behavior** the old man, which is corrupt[3087] **down** the **cheating upon-feelings** ;

23 And be **up-new-young** in the spirit of your **thought**.

24 And that you **clothe-yourself**[3088] the **new-fresh** man, **down** God is created in **righteous-togetherness** and **intrinsic-right of-the truth**.

25 Through-which, from-place falsehood, speak every man truth with his neighbor: for we are members **of-another-same**.

26 You-are-swelling-angry, and sin not: let not the sun **upon-sink** upon your **beside-swelling-anger:**

27 Neither give **spot** to the **Devil**.

28 Let him that **is-stealing** steal no more: but rather let him **fatigue-cut**, working with hands the good, that he may have to **change-give to-him** that needs.[3089]

29 Let no **rotten saying out-passage** your mouth, but that which is good **toward house-building**, that it may give grace **to the hearers**.

30 And not **distress-sadden** the Holy Spirit of God, whereby you are sealed into the day **of-from-loosing**.

31 Let all bitterness,[3090] and **sacrifice-anger,** and **swelling-anger**, and **loud-cries**, and **blasphemy**, be **lifted** from you, with all **evil**.

32 Yet, into one-another-same, **furnish-what-is-needed**,[3091] **gut-compassions, grace to-yourselves**, even as God **in Christ** has **graced** you.

EPHESIANS CHAPTER 5

1 Be-becoming, then, **imitators** of God, as **beloved** children.

2 And **about-walk** in love, as Christ also loved us and has given himself for us an offering and a sacrifice to God **into** an **odor of-good-odor**.

3 Yet, prostitution, and all uncleanness, or **more-having**, let it not be once named **in** you, as **towering-up** saints.

4 Neither **disfigurement**, nor **stupid-saying,** nor **witticism,** which are not **proper**[3092] but rather giving of thanks.

5 For this you know that no **paramour**, no unclean person, nor **more-have** man, who is an idolater, has any inheritance in the kingdom of Christ and of God.

6 Let no man **cheat** you with **empty** sayings: for because of these things comes the **swelling-anger** of God upon the children of **un-persuadable-ness**.

7 Be not you therefore **together-partners**[3093] **of-them**.

8 Because you were **once** darkness, but now light in the Lord; walk as children of light:

9 (For the fruit **of-the Spirit**[3094] is in all **good-togetherness** and **righteous-togetherness** and truth.)

10 Seem-testing what is **well-pleasing to** the Lord.

11 And have no **together-communion** with the unfruitful works of darkness, but rather **evidence-expose**.

12 For it is **disfigured** even to speak of those things, which are done of them in secret.

13 But all things that are **evidence-exposed is-made-to-shine under** the light: **because** whatever **makes-shine** is light.

14 Through this, he says, awake you that sleep, and arise from the dead, and Christ shall give you light.

15 See then that you walk **exactly**, not as **unwise**, but as wise,

16 Out-of-market-buy the **season**, because the days are **wicked-hurtful**.

17 Through this, not become **imprudent-disposition**, but **synthesize** what the will of the Lord.

[3085] Or past feelings
[3086] Occupation
[3087] Or, to pine, to waste, to rot
[3088] Lit., in-down; or, in-sink, in-down-slipping
[3089] Lit., employment
[3090] Lit., acridity (strong, irritating, unpleasant, pungent (sharp), taste or smell), poison
[3091] Lit. employ
[3092] Upon-arrive
[3093] Or together-with-holders, together-sharers
[3094] Alexandrian Texts reads "Light" in lieu of "Spirit"

18 And be not drunk with wine, **in which** is **un-save** but **be-filled in** the Spirit;

19 Speaking **to-yourselves** in psalms and hymns and spiritual songs, singing and making melody in your **heart** to the Lord;

20 Giving thanks always **over** all things **to** God and the Father in the name of our Lord Jesus Christ;

21 Subordinating[3095] yourselves **to-one-another-same** in the fear of God.

22 Wives, **subordinate** yourselves **to-your** private husbands, as **to-the** Lord.

23 That the husband is the head of the wife, even as Christ is the head of the Church: and he is the savior of the body.

24 Also, as the Church is **subordinate to** Christ, so the wives to their **private** husbands in everything.

25 Husbands, love your wives, even as Christ also loved the Church, and **beside-gave** himself **over her;**

26 That he might sanctify and clean **her** with the washing of water **in declaration,**

27 That he might **beside-stand her to-himself in-glory the** Church, not having **stain**, or wrinkle, or any such thing; but that it should be holy and without blemish.

28 So **owe** men to love their wives as their own bodies. He that loves his wife loves himself.

29 Because no man yet hated his own flesh; but **out-of-nourishes** and cherishes[3096] **her**, even as the Lord the Church:

30 For we are members of his body, **out-of** his flesh, and **out-of** his bones.

31 This instead, a man shall leave his father and mother, and shall be joined[3097] **towards** his wife, and they two shall be **into first** flesh.

32 This is a **great** mystery: **but I-am-speaking into** Christ and the Church.

33 More also, let every one of you **down** so love his wife even as himself; and the wife that she **fear the** husband.

[3095] Under-arranged
[3096] Or brood over; therefore, affectionate
[3097] Or. Keep company with
[3098] Or obey
[3099] Or obey

EPHESIANS CHAPTER 6

1 Children, **under-hear**[3098] your parents in the Lord; for this is **righteous**.

2 Value your father and mother; (which is the **foremost** commandment with promise.)

3 That it may be **good** with you, and **you-exists long-uninterrupted-time** on the earth.

4 And, you fathers, not **beside-swelling-anger** your children but bring them up in the **out-of-nourishment** and **thought-placing** of the Lord.

5 Slaves, **under-hear**[3099] **to-them** that are **lords down** the flesh, with fear and trembling, in **singleness**[3100] **of-your heart**, as **to** Christ;

6 Not with **eye-slavery**, as men-pleasers; but as the **slave**s of Christ, doing the will of God from the **heart.**

7 With **well-mind, slaving**, as to the Lord, and not to men:

8 Having-perceived that whatever good thing any man does, the same shall he receive of the Lord, whether **slave** or free.

9 And, you **lords, produce** the same things **towards** them, **desists threats; perceiving** that your **Lord** also is in heaven; neither is there respect of persons with him.

10 Finally, my **brothers, be-empowered** in the Lord, and in the **government**[3101] of his **force**.

11 Clothe-yourself the **every-armor** of God that you may be **powerful** to stand against the **methods**[3102] of the **Devil**.

12 For we **wrestle-vibrate** not **towards** flesh and blood, but **towards originals, towards authorities, towards world-governments of the darkness, towards** spiritual **of-the wicked-hurtfulness in the heavens**.

13 Through this, take the **every-armor of-the** God that you may be **powerful** to **anti-stand** in the **wicked-hurtful** day, and having **down-worked** all, stand.

14 Stand therefore, having your loins girded about with truth, and **clothe-yourself** the breastplate of **righteous-togetherness**.

[3100] Haplotetes, the antonym of "diplous" meaning double
[3101] Greek: kratos, to rule, translated as "cracy" in democracy—people (demo)-government (kratos),
[3102] Lit., change-road

15 And your feet **sandaled** with the **internal-preparation** of the **well-message** of peace.

16 Above all, **up-take** the **door-shield** of faith, **in which** you shall be **powerful** to **extinguish** all the fiery **missiles** of the **wicked-hurtful**.

17 And **welcome** the helmet[3103] of salvation, and the **Sword** of the Spirit, which is the **Declaration** of God:

18 Towards-praying-wishing always **through** all **towards-prayer-wish** and **beg-binding** in the Spirit, and **this, no-sleep**[3104] **into the self** with all **towards-government** and **beg-binding** for all saints.

19 And for me, that **sayings**[3105] may be given **to**-me, that I may open my mouth **to-all-speech**[3106] to make known the mystery of the **well-message**,

20 For which I am an **elder** in **chains** that **in it** I may **all-out-spoken**, as **it-is-binding** to speak.

21 But that you also may **perceive down me**, how **I-am-practicing.** Tychicus, a beloved brother and **believing attendant** in the Lord, shall make known **to-you** all things:

22 Whom I have **dispatched towards** you **into the same**, that **you-my-perceive about us**, and **he-may-beside-call** your **hearts** .

23 Peace to the **brothers**, and love with faith, from God the Father and the Lord Jesus Christ.

24 Grace with all them that love our Lord Jesus Christ in **incorruptly**. Amen

---

[3103] Lit., about-head, all-around-the-head
[3104] Or watching
[3105] Or words
[3106] Or free speech

PHILIPPIANS

PHILIPPIANS CHAPTER 1

1 Paul and **Timothy**, the **slaves** of Jesus Christ, to all the saints in Christ Jesus which are at Philippi, **together, bishops**[3107] and **attendant**.

2 Grace **to-you**, and peace, from God our Father, and the Lord Jesus Christ.

3 I thank my God upon every remembrance of you,

4 Always, in every **beg-binding** of mine **over** all **of-you, producing beg-binding** with **cheerfulness**,

5 For your **communion** in the **well-message** from the **foremost** day until now;

6 Being confident of this very thing that he which has **in-begun** a good work in you **shall-be-upon-finishing** until the day of Jesus Christ:

7 Even as it is **righteous** for me **to-be-disposed over** all **of-you**, because I have you in my **heart**; inasmuch as both in my bonds, and in the **apology**[3108] and **sure-walk** of the **well-message**, you all are **together-communion** of my grace.

8 For God is my **witness**, how **I-upon-yearn** after you all in the **spleen**[3109] of Jesus Christ.

9 And this I pray, that your love may abound yet more and more in knowledge and all **sensing**;

10 That you may **seem-test** things that **differ**;[3110] that you may be **sun-judged** and **un-toward-strike** into the day of Christ;

11 Being filled with the fruits of **righteous-togetherness**, which are **through** Jesus Christ, **into** the glory and praise of God.

12 But **I-am-plan-counseling-myself** you should **know, brothers**, that the things **down into** the **toward-chopping**[3111] of the **well-message**;

13 So that my bonds in Christ **shine** in all the **Praetorium**,[3112] and in all **the remaining-ones**

14 And many of the **brothers** in the Lord, confident **to** my bonds, are much more **bold-venture** to speak the **Word** without fear.

15 Some indeed preach Christ even of **ill-will** and **quarrel**,[3113] and some also of **good-seem**:

16 The one preaches Christ **out-of stimulations**,[3114] not **cleanly, supposing-** to add **tribulation** to my bonds:

17 But the other of love, **perceiving** that I am set for the **apology**[3115] of the **well-message**.

18 What then? **More, to-every turn**, whether in **pretense**,[3116] or in truth, Christ is preached; and I this **I-am-cheerful, yes**, and **will-be-cheerful**.

19 For **I-perceived** that this shall **from-step** to my salvation through your **beg-binding**, and the supply of the Spirit of Jesus Christ,

20 **Down** my **from-head-seem** and **expectation**, that in nothing **I-shall-be-disfigured**, but with all **all-speech**,[3117] as always, now also Christ shall be great in my body, whether **through** life, or **through** death

21 For to me to live Christ, and to die gain.

22 But if I live in the flesh, this the fruit of my **work**: yet what I shall **prefer, I know** not.

23 For **I-am-together-held out-of the** two, having an **on-feeling** to **up-loose**, and to be with Christ; which is **much** better:

24 Nevertheless to **remain** in the flesh **up-bending-arm**[3118] **through** you.

25 And having this confidence, **I-perceived** that **I-shall-remain** and **shall-be-together-remaining to-all** you, **into** the **toward-cut** and **cheerfulness of-the** faith;

26 That your **boasting** may be more abundant in Jesus Christ **through** me by my **presence toward** you again.

27 Only let your **citizenship** be **deserving of-the well-message** of Christ: that whether I come and **perceive** you, or else be absent, I may hear **about you**, that you stand in one spirit, **first soul, together-contending** for the faith of the **well-message**;

[3107] Greek: "episkopos" (upon-peer-about, upon watch, upon-goal, upon-mark), bishop, visitation, to visit, oversee, oversight, upon-skeptic
[3108] Compound of "apo" (from) and logo (word, saying), also means defense
[3109] Or gut
[3110] Greek: "diaphero," to through-bear, transliterated as "differ" or "different"
[3111] Or, progress, advancement, profit
[3112] Or governor's courtroom
[3113] Or, electioneering, quarrel, debates
[3114] Or to arouse curiosity (intrigue)
[3115] Compound of "apo" (from) and logo (word, saying), also means defense
[3116] Greek: before-appear, outward show
[3117] Or free speech
[3118] Or necessary, constraining

28 And in nothing **frighten** by your **opposing-ones**[3119]: which is **to-them** an **in-showing** of-**from-ruin**, but **to-you** of salvation, and that **from** God.

29 For **to-you** it is **graced over** Christ, not only to believe **into him**, but also to **emotion over him.**

30 Having the same **agony** which you **perceived** in me, and now hear in me.

PHILIPPIANS CHAPTER 2

1 If **then** any **beside-call** in Christ, if any **beside-closure** of love, if any **communion** of the Spirit, if any **gut-compassions** and **pity**,

2 Fulfill you my **cheer**, that you be **same disposition**, having the same love, **together-soul**, of one **disposition**.

3 Nothing **down stimulations**,[3120] or vainglory; but in **humble-disposition** let each **lead one-another-same superior**[3121] **to-themselves.**

4 Spy not every man on his own things, but every man also on the things of **another-different**.

5 Let this **disposition** be in you, which was also in Christ Jesus:

6 Who, **under-originating** in the form of God, **lead-himself** not robbery to be equal **to-**God:

7 But **emptied himself**, and **taking in** the form of a **slave**, and **becoming** in the **likeness** of men:

8 And being found in **scheme** as a man, he humbled himself, and became obedient **until** death, even the death of the cross.

9 Through-which God also has **above-elevated**, him, and given him a name which is above every name:

10 That at the name of Jesus every knee should bow, **upon-heavens**, and **upon-earth**, and **down-ground**;[3122]

11 And every tongue should **out-of-same-say** that Lord Jesus Christ **into** the glory of God the Father.

12 So-too, my beloved, as you have always **under-heard**,[3123] not as in my presence only, but now much more in my absence, **down-work** your own salvation with fear and trembling.

13 For it is God which **in-work** you both to will and to **work over the well-seem.**

14 Do all things **spaced-from grumbling** and **through-inventory**:

15 That you may be **un-blamed** and **unmixed**, the **children** of God, **un-flawed**, in the **middle** of a crooked and **warped-leg** generation, **in** whom you shine as lights in the world;

16 Holding the **Word of Life**; that I may **boast** in the day of Christ, that I have not **raced into empty**, neither **fatigue-cut into empty.**

17 Yea, and if I be **spent** upon the sacrifice and **people-work**[3124] of your faith, **I-am-cheerful**, and **I-am-together-cheerful** with you all.

18 And into the same you are **cheerful** and **be-together-cheerful** with me.

19 But **I expect** in the Lord Jesus to **dispatch Timothy briefly to-you**, that I also may be of **well-soul**, when I know **about you.**

20 Because I have no man **equal-soul**, who **genuine-birth portion-worry the-things about you.**

21 For all seek **the-things of-themselves**, not the things which are Jesus Christ's.

22 But you know the **seem-test** of him, that, as a **child** with the father, he has **slaved together-with** me in the **well-message**.

23 Him therefore I **expected** to **dispatch** presently, so, soon as I shall **perceived** how it will go **about** me.

24 But **I-have-confidence** in the Lord that I also myself shall come **briefly**

25 Yet I **lead** it **up-bend-arm**[3125] to **dispatch to-you** Epaphroditus, **the** brother, and **together-worker**, and **together-warrior**, but your **apostle**, and he that **people-worked**,[3126] of my **employment**.

26 For he **upon-yearn** you all, and was **to-be-in-distress**, because that you had heard that he had been sick.

27 For indeed he was sick **beside-near to-death**: but God had mercy on him; and not on him only, but on me also, lest I should **hold** sorrow upon sorrow.

[3119] Greek: anti-laying outstretched
[3120] Or to arouse curiosity (intrigue)
[3121] Lit., to hold oneself above (huper (above) and echo (to hold)
[3122] Greek compound-kata(down) and chthon (ground), subterranean
[3123] Or obey
[3124] Lit., laos (people)-ergon (work); "liturgy"
[3125] Constraining, necessary
[3126] Lit., laos (people)-ergon (work); "liturgist"

28 I **dispatch** him therefore **speedily**, that, when you see him again, **you-may-be-cheerful**, and that I may be **un-sorrowful**.

29 Towards-welcome him therefore in the Lord with all **cheerfulness**; and hold such in **value**.

30 That through the work of Christ he was **until** death he-near-squeezed, **besides-plan-counseling**[3127] **to-the soul**, that **he-may-up-fill** your **deficit of-the people-work**[3128] toward me.

PHILIPPIANS CHAPTER 3

1 To the remaining, my **brothers**, **be-cheerful** in the Lord; to write the same things **to-you**, to me indeed not **slow-hesitation**, but for you **certainty**.[3129]

2 Beware of dogs, beware of evil workers, beware of the **down-cutters**.

3 For we are the circumcision, **hired-servants to-**God **to-**spirit, and **boasting** in Christ Jesus, and have no confidence in the flesh.

4 Though I might also have **trust** in the flesh. If any other man **seems** that he might trust in the flesh, I more.

5 Circumcised the eighth day of the **kin** of Israel, the tribe of Benjamin, a Hebrew **out-of** the Hebrews; **down** the law, a Pharisee;

6 Concerning **zealousness**, **chasing** the Church; touching the **righteous-togetherness** which is in the law, **un-blamable**.

7 But **which-things** were gain to me, those, **I-lead loss** for Christ.

8 Yes **indeed-surely**, and **I-lead** all things loss for the **superiority**[3130] of the knowledge of Christ Jesus my Lord: **through** whom I have **detriment** all things, and do **lead** them **refuse**, that I may **gain** Christ.

9 And be found in him, not having **my righteous-togetherness**, which is of the law, but that which is through the faith of Christ, the **righteous-togetherness** which is **out-of** God **upon the** faith:

10 That I may know him, and the power of his resurrection, and the **communion** of his **emotions**, being made **together-conformed to-his** death;

11 If by any means I might **meet-against**[3131] **into** the resurrection **out-of** the dead.

12 Not as though I had already **took**, either were already **matured**: but I **chase** if that I may **down-take** that for which also I am **down-taken** of Christ Jesus.

13 Brothers, I **inventory** not myself to have **down-taken**: but one thing, forgetting those things which are behind, and **upon-out-stretching to-the-things** which are **in-front**,

14 Down the scoped-end-mark, I-chase the prize of-the above calling of God in Christ Jesus.

15 Let us therefore, as many as be mature be **this** disposed: and if in anything you be **another-different disposition**, God shall reveal even this **to-you**.

16 Nevertheless, whereto we have **anticipated**,[3132] the same rod-standard, **element-walk**,[3133] the same **disposition**

17 Brothers, be **together-imitators** of me, and **spy** them which walk so as you have us for a **type**.

18 (For many walk, of whom I have told you often, and now tell you even weeping, the **haters** of the cross of Christ:

19 Whose end **from-ruin**, whose God **the** belly,[3134] and glory in their **disfigurement**, **these earthly disposed**)

20 For our **citizenship** in heavens, **under-originating**: from where also we **from-out-of-welcome** the Savior, the Lord Jesus Christ:

21 Who shall **change-scheme** our **humiliating** body, that it may be **together-formed** like **to** his glorious body, **down** the **energy** whereby he is **powerful** even to **subordinate**[3135] all things **to-himself**.

PHILIPPIANS CHAPTER 4

1 Therefore, my **brothers** beloved and **upon-yearn**, my **cheerfulness** and **victor's-crown**, so **stand** in the Lord, beloved.

2 I **beside-call** Euodias, and beseech Syntyche, that they be of the **self-same disposition** in the Lord.

3 And I **ask** you also, **legitimately-birth**, **together-yoke**, **together-take** those women which **together-**

[3127] To consult amiss
[3128] Lit., laos (people)-ergon (work); "liturgy"
[3129] Greek: "asphales," transliterated as "un-failing,"
[3130] Lit., to hold oneself above (huper (above) and echo (to hold)
[3131] Greek: "katantao," down-opposite, down-instead, down-anti

[3132] Or to be beforehand, to precede, to have arrived
[3133] Gk.: stoicheo, to march in rank (keep step), from same root for "element"
[3134] Or womb
[3135] Under-arranged

compete with me in the **well-message**, with Clement also, and **remaining-ones of-my together-worker**, whose names in the **Scroll of Life**.

4 **Be-cheering** in the Lord always: again, I say, **be-cheering**

5 Let your **upon-yielding**³¹³⁶ be known to all men. The Lord **near-squeezes**.

6 Not **be-portion-worrying**; but in everything by **towards-prayer-wish** and **beg-binding** with thanksgiving let your requests be made known **towards** God.

7 And the peace of God, which **superior-to**³¹³⁷ every thought, shall **watch** your **hearts** and minds through Christ Jesus.

8 Finally, **brothers**, whatever things are true, whatever things **reverencing**, whatever things **righteous**, whatever things **clean**, whatever things **towards-friendly**, whatever things **good-fame**; if any **excellent-quality**,³¹³⁸ and if any **on-praise, inventory** these things.

9 Those things, which you have both learned, and received, and heard, and seen in me, **practice**: and the God of peace shall be with you.

10 But **I-was-cheered** in the Lord **great**, that now once your **disposition over** me has **blossomed**; **upon which you-were-disposed**, however, **you had-no-season**.

11 Not that I speak **down-as** want: for I have learned, in **which I am**, to be **self-sufficient**.

12 **I-have-perceived** both how to **be-humbled**, **I-have-perceived** how to abound: everywhere and in all things **mystery-initiated** both to be full and to be hungry, both to abound and to-**be-wanting**

13 **All-things I-have-force in the Christ empowering me.**

14 Notwithstanding **ideally you-produced**, **together-communicated** my **tribulation**.

15 Now you Philippians **perceived** also, that in the **original** of the **well-message**, when I departed from Macedonia, no Church communicated with me **into word of-giving and of-receiving**, but you only.

16 For even in Thessalonica you **dispatched** once and **twice into** my **employment**.

17 Not because **I-seek** a gift: but I **seek** fruit that may abound **into your saying**.

18 But I have all, and abound: I am full, having **welcomed** of Epaphroditus the things **beside** you, an odor of a **good-odor**, a sacrifice acceptable, **well-pleasing** to God.

19 But my God shall **fill** all your **employment down** his riches in glory by Christ Jesus.

20 Now **to-God** and our Father glory **into the ages of-the ages**. Amen.

21 **Embrace** every saint in Christ Jesus; the **brothers** which are with me **embrace** you.

22 All the saints **embrace** you, **especially** they that are of Caesar's household.

23 The grace of our Lord Jesus Christ with you all. Amen.

---

³¹³⁶ Or upon-simulate, to be weak to, yield (Strong's #1909 + #1502, #1503, #1504)

³¹³⁷ Lit., to hold oneself above [huper (above) and echo (to hold)]

³¹³⁸ Or excellent character, manly excellence, property of a thing

COLOSSIANS

COLOSSIANS CHAPTER 1

1 Paul, an apostle of Jesus Christ **through** the will of God, and **Timothy** our brother,

2 To the saints and **believing brothers** in Christ which are at Colosse: Grace be **to-you**, and peace, from God our Father and the Lord Jesus Christ.

3 We give thanks to God and the Father of our Lord Jesus Christ, praying always **about** you,

4 Since we heard of your faith in Christ Jesus, and of the love which you have **into** all the saints,

5 For the **expectation** which is **from-placed** for you in **the** heavens, whereof you heard before in the **Word of the Truth** of the **well-message**;

6 Which is come **into you**, as it is in all the world; and **fruit-bearing**, as it does also in you, since the day you heard of it, and knew the grace of **the** God in truth:

7 As you also learned of Epaphras our **beloved together-slave**, who is for you a **believing attendant** of Christ;

8 Who also declared **to-us** your love in Spirit.

9 **Through this** we also, since the day we heard it, do not **paused** to pray for you, and to **request** that you might be filled with the knowledge **of-the** will **of-him**, in all wisdom and **synthesizing**[3139] **spiritual**.

10 That you might walk **deserving** of the Lord **to** all pleasing, **fruit-carrying** in every good work, and **growing** in the knowledge **of-the** God;

11 **Empowered** with all **power**, **down** his glorious **government**,[3140] **to** all **under-remaining** and **long-sacrifice-anger** with **cheerfulness**;

12 Giving thanks **to** the Father, which has made us **arrived into the portion** of the inheritance of the saints in light:

13 Who has **rush-rescued** us from the **authority** of darkness, and has translated us into the kingdom **of-the** Son **of-his love**:

14 In whom we have **from-loose** through his blood, even the **release**[3141] of sins:

15 Who is the image of the invisible God, the firstborn of every **creation**!

16 **That in** him were all things created, that are in **the** heavens, and that are **upon** earth, visible and invisible, whether they be thrones, or **lords**, or **originals**, or **authority**: all things were created **through** him, and **into him**:

17 And he is before all things; and **in** him all things **together-stand**.

18 And he is the **Head** of the **Body,** the Church; who is the **Original**, the **Firstborn out-of** the dead; that in all things he might have the preeminence.

19 For it **well-seem** the Father that in him should all **filling down-house**;

20 And, having made peace through the blood of his cross, **through** him to **from-down-change**[3142] all things **to-himself**; by him, I say, whether they be things in earth, or things in **the** heavens.

21 And you, that were sometimes **from-another-same** and **haters** in your **deep-thoughts** by wicked-**hurtful** works, yet now has he **from-down-changed**

22 In the body of his flesh through death, to **beside-stand** you holy, unblemished, and **un-called-in**[3143] in his sight:

23 If you **upon-remain** in the faith **founded** and **settled-seated** and be **not change-moved** away from the hope of the **well-message**, which you have heard, and which was preached **in** every **creation** which is under **the** heaven; whereof I Paul am made an **attendant.**

24 Who now **cheerful** in my **emotions** for you, and fill up that which is **deficient** of the **tribulations** of Christ in my flesh for his **Body's** sake, which is the Church:

25 Whereof I am made an **attendant**, **down** the **house-law** of God, which is given to me for you, to **fill** the Word of God;

26 Even the mystery which has been hid from **the** ages and from the generations, but now is **shining** to his saints:

27 To whom God **wills to-make-known** what is the riches of the glory of this mystery among the **nations**, which is Christ in you, the **expectation** of glory:

[3139] Combining into a comprehensive and logical whole
[3140] Greek: kratos, transliterated as "great" and also means vigor, strength, to use strength, to rule, government, translated as "cracy" in democracy—people(demo)-government (kratos), or public-government
[3141] Lit., from-let-go
[3142] Or exchange
[3143] Or un-accused

28 Whom we **down-message thought-placing** every man, and teaching every man in all wisdom; that we may **beside-stand** every man **mature** in Christ Jesus:

29 Into which I-am-fatigue-cut, agonizing down his energy, in-working in me powerfully.

COLOSSIANS CHAPTER 2

1 For I **will** that you **perceive stature** [3144] **agony** I have for you, and for them at Laodicea, and for as many as have not seen my face in the flesh.

2 That their **hearts** might be **beside-call, being-together-embark** [3145] in love, and **into** all riches of the **full-burden-wearing** of **synthesizing, into** the knowledge of the mystery **of-the** God, **and Father**, and **of-the** Christ;

3 In whom are **hidden** all the **treasures** [3146] of wisdom and **knowing.**

4 And this I say, lest any man should **beside-inventory** you with **faith-words.**

5 For though I be absent in the flesh, yet am I with you **to-the** spirit, **cheerful** and **looking of-**your order, and the **stability** of your faith in Christ.

6 As you have therefore **beside-taken** Christ Jesus the Lord, so **about-walk** in him:

7 Rooted and **upon-house-built** in him, and **secure-based** in the faith, as you have been taught, abounding **in him** with thanksgiving.

8 Look, let no man **strip-lead** you through philosophy and **empty cheating, down** the **beside-giving** [3147] of men, after the **elements** [3148] of the world, and not **down** Christ.

9 For in him **down-house** all the **filling** of the **Deity,** bodily.

10 And you are in him **having-being-filled**, who is the head of all **originals** and **authority.**

11 In whom also you are circumcised with the circumcision made without hands, in **the from-unclothing of-the** body of the sins of the flesh, **in** the circumcision of Christ:

12 Buried with him in baptism, **in which you-were-together-raised** through the faith of the **energy** of God, who has raised him **out-of** the dead.

13 And you, being dead in your sins and the uncircumcision of your flesh, has he **together-life-produced**, having **graced** all your **beside-falls.**

14 Out-of-oiled the **downing us** handwriting **of-the dogmas** [3149] that was **under-in-opposite** [3150] **to-us,** and **lifted** it out of the **middle, towards-nailing** it to his cross.

15 And having **from-unclothe originals and authorities**; he made a show of them **to-all-speech,** [3151] triumphing [3152] over them in it.

16 Let no man therefore judge you in **feeding**, or in drink, or in **section** of a **festivals**, or of the **young-month**, or of Sabbath.

17 Which are a shadow of things **impending**; **yet** the **Body** is **of-the** Christ.

18 Let no man **down-arbitrate** you in **will-humility** and **religion** of angels, **in-stepping** into those things which he has not seen, **without-cause, being-inflated** under the thought **of-his flesh,**

19 And not **governing** the Head, **out-of whom** all the **Body through joints** and **together-bonds** having **supply**, and **together-embark,** [3153] **grows** with the **growth of-the** God.

20 If then, you are dead with Christ from the **elements** [3154] of the world, why, as though living in the world, **are-you-being-seem-dogmatized.** [3155]

21 (**Fasten** not; taste not; handle not;

22 Which all are **into corruption from the using**) after the commandments and **teachings** of men?

23 Which things have indeed a **word** of wisdom in **will-religion**, and humility, and **not-sparing** of the body;

[3144] Or, one of the same age, as big as, full age
[3145] Greek: sun (together) and bibazo (to force), drive-together, unite, infer, together-board a ship
[3146] Greek: thesaurus (place-into-tomorrow), treasures
[3147] Lit., beside-give, transmission, tradition
[3148] Or, any first thing, something orderly in arrangement (Gal 4:3, 4:9; Col 2:8, 20; Heb 5:12; 2 Peter 3:10, 12; compare Acts 21:24, Rom 4:12, Gal 5:25, Gal 6:16, Phil 3:16)
[3149] Accepted beliefs, authoritative proclamations, decrees, etcetera that is not questioned or doubted, from "dokeo," to think, to seem,

[3150] Contrary, opposed, against
[3151] Or free speech
[3152] I.e., to parade captives and spoils of war, publicly
[3153] Greek: sun (together) and bibazo (to force), drive-together, unite, infer, together-board a ship
[3154] Or, any first thing, something orderly in arrangement (Gal 4:3, 4:9; Col 2:8, 20; Heb. 5:12; 2 Peter 3:10, 12; compare Acts 21:24, Rom 4:12, Gal 5:25, Gal 6:16, Phil 3:16)
[3155] Accepted beliefs, authoritative proclamations, decrees, etcetera that is not questioned or doubted, from "dokeo," to think, to seem,

not in any **value towards full-remaining**[3156] of the flesh.

COLOSSIANS CHAPTER 3

1 If you then **were-together-risen to-the** Christ, seek those things which are above, where Christ sits **in** the right hand of God.

2 Set your **disposition** on things above, not on things on the earth.

3 For you **from-died**, and your life is **hidden together to-the** Christ in God.

4 When Christ, who is our life, shall **shine**, then shall you also **shine together to-him** in glory.

5 Deaden therefore your members which are upon the earth; **prostitution**, uncleanness, **emotions**, evil **upon-feelings**, and **more-having**, which is idolatry.

6 Through-which the **swelling-anger** of God **is-coming** on the **sons of-the un-persuadable**

7 In **whom** you also **about-walk, then,** when you lived in them.

8 But now you also **from-place** all these; **swelling-anger, sacrifice-anger, evil,** blasphemy, **disfigured-words** out of your mouth.

9 Falsify not **into one-another-same,** seeing that you have **unclothed** the old man with his **practices**.

10 And have **clothed-yourself,** the new-man, which is **new-fresh into** knowledge **down** the image of him that created him:

11 Where there is neither **Hellenic** nor Jew, circumcision nor un-circumcision, Barbarian, Scythian, **slave** nor free: but Christ is all, and in all.

12 Clothe-yourself therefore, as the elect of God, holy and beloved, **gut-compassions** of **pity, usefulness, humble-disposition,** gentleness, **long-sacrifice-anger.**

13 Forbearing **one-another-same,** and **gracing selfsame-ones,** if any man has a **blame towards** any: even as Christ **graced** you, so also you.

14 And **upon** all these things put on love, which is the **together-bond** of **maturity**.

15 And let the peace of God **arbitrate** in your **hearts, into** which also you are called in one **Body:** and be you thankful.

16 Let the Word of Christ **in-house** you richly, in all wisdom; teaching and **thought-placing yourselves to-psalms and to-hymns and to-spiritual** songs, singing **in** grace in your **hearts** to the Lord.

17 And whatever you **produce** in word or **work,** all in the name of the Lord Jesus, giving thanks to God and the Father **through** him.

18 Wives, **subordinate**[3157] yourselves **to-your private** husbands, as it is **proper**[3158] in the Lord.

19 Husbands, love your wives, and be not bitter[3159] **towards** them.

20 Children, **under-hear**[3160] your parents in all things: for this is **well-pleasing to-the** the Lord.

21 Fathers, not **stimulate**[3161] your children that not **they-become-un-feeling.**[3162]

22 Slaves **under-hear,** in all things, your **lords down** the flesh; not with **eye-slavery,** as **men-pleasers;** but in **singleness**[3163] **of-heart,** fearing God:

23 And whatever you **produce, out-of soul** work, as to the Lord, and not **to-men;**

24 Having-perceived that **from** the Lord you shall **from-take** the reward of the inheritance: **because to-the Lord Christ you-are-slaving.**

25 But the unrighteousness **shall-be-provided** that **unrighteousness** and there is no respect of persons.

COLOSSIANS CHAPTER 4

1 Lords, give **to-your slaves** that which is **righteous** and equal; knowing that you also have a **Lord** in heaven.

2 Towards-govern in prayer and **stay-awake** in the same with thanksgiving.

3 Simultaneously praying also for us, that God would open **to-us** a door of **saying,** to speak the mystery of Christ, for which I am also in bonds:

4 That I may make it **shine,** as **is-binding** to speak.

[3156] Greek: plesmone—pletho (fill) and mene (remain)
[3157] Under-arranged
[3158] Upon-arrive
[3159] Lit., acridity (strong, irritating, unpleasant, pungent (sharp), taste or smell), poison
[3160] Or obey
[3161] To stimulate to anger
[3162] Or without passion
[3163] Haplotetes, the antonym of "diplous" meaning double

Colossians

5 **About-walk** in wisdom toward them that are **outside**, **out-of-market-buy**[3164] the **season**.

6 Let your **saying** be always with grace, seasoned with salt, that you may **perceive** how **it-is-binding** to answer every man.

7 All **the-things down me,** Tychicus **make-known to-you,** who is a beloved brother, and a **believing attendant** and **together-slave** in the Lord:

8 Whom I have **dispatched towards** you for the **same-thing,** that he might know **the-things about you,** and **beside-call** your **hearts.**

9 Together, with-Onesimus,[3165] a **believing** and beloved brother, who is **out-of** you. They shall make known **to-you** all things here.

10 Aristarchus[3166] my **together-captive embrace** you, and Marcus, **a kin** to Barnabas, (**about** whom you **welcomed** commandments: if he come **to-you,** receive him).

11 And Jesus, which is called Justus, who are of the circumcision. These only are my **together-workers into** the kingdom of God, which have been a **paragoric**[3167] **to-me.**

12 Epaphras, who is one of you, a **slave** of Christ, **embrace** you, always **agonizing over** you in **towards-prayers-wishes** that you may stand **mature** and **filled** in all the will of God.

13 For **I-am-witnessing to-him** that he has **much zeal** for you, and them that are in Laodicea, and them in Hierapolis.

14 Luke, the beloved physician, and Demas, **embrace** you.

15 Embrace the **brothers** which are in Laodicea, and Nymphas, and the Church which is in his house.

16 And when this epistle is read **beside** you, **produce** that it be read also in the Church of the Laodiceans; and that you read the epistle **out-of** Laodicea.

17 And say to Archippus, **look** to the ministry which you have **beside-taken** in the Lord, that you **fill** it.

18 The **embrace to-the** hand of me Paul. Remember my bonds. Grace be with you.

Amen.

[3164] Out-buying, out-going-to-market, redeem, rescue
[3165] Profitable
[3166] Male-rule (first in rank or power), best-rule

[3167] "Paregoria," transliterated as "paregoric" soothing medication; but literally means beside-market place, or beside the place of assembly

1 THESSALONIANS

1 THES. CHAPTER 1

1 Paul, and Silvanus, and **Timothy, to-the** Church of the Thessalonians in God the Father, and the Lord Jesus Christ; grace **to-you,** and peace, from God our Father, and the Lord Jesus Christ.

2 We give thanks to God always for you all, **remembering** you in our prayers.

3 Remembering **not-through-leaving** your work of faith, and labor of love, and **under-remaining** of **expectation** in our Lord Jesus Christ, in the sight of God and our Father.

4 **Having-perceived,** brothers' beloved, your election of God.

5 For our **well-message** came not **into you** in word only, but also in power, and in the **Holy Spirit,** and in much **full-burden-wearing** as **you-perceived** what manner of men we were **in** you **through-you.**

6 And you became **imitators** of us, and of the Lord, having **welcomed** the **Word** in much **tribulation,** with **cheerfulness** of the **Holy Spirit.**

7 So that you were examples to all that believe in Macedonia and Achaia.

8 For from you **out-of-echo** the **Word of the Lord,** not only in Macedonia and Achaia, but also in every **spot** your faith **towards God** is **out-come**; so that we need not to speak anything.

9 For they **from-message** of us what manner of **into-way** we had **towards** you, and how you **reverted** to **the** God from idols **to-be-slaving to-God,** the living and true.

10 And to **up-remaining** for his Son **out-of** heaven, whom he raised from the dead, Jesus, which **rush-rescue** us from the **swelling-anger, the coming.**

1 THES. CHAPTER 2

1 For yourselves, **brothers, perceived** our **into-way towards** you that it was not **empty:**

2 But even after that we had **before-emotion,** and **insulted,** as **you-perceived,** at Philippi, we were **all-speech** in our God to speak **to-you** the **well-message** of God with much **agony.**

3 For our **beside-call** not **of-seduction,** nor of uncleanness, nor in **trick-bait.**

4 But as we were **seem-tested** of God to be put in trust with the **well-message,** even so we speak; not as **agreeable to-men,** but God, which **seem-test** our **hearts** .

5 For neither **once** we used flattering words, as **you-perceived,** nor a **pretense**[3168] of **more-having,** God witness.

6 Nor of men sought, we **glory,** neither of you, nor of others-**same, being-powerful in weight to-be,** as the apostles of Christ.

7 But, we were **gentle-speech in** you, even as a nurse **warm-brood** her children:

8 **In-this-way, yearning of-you,** we **well-seemed** to have **given to-you,** not the **well-message** of God only, but also our own souls, because you were **beloved to-us.**

9 For you remember, **brothers,** our **cut-fatigue** and **toil-difficulty; working** night and day, because we would not be **upon-heavy towards** any of you, we preached **into you** the **well-message** of God.

10 You witnesses, and God, how **intrinsically-right** and **justly** and **un-blamable we-became to-you** that believe:

11 As **you-perceived** how we **call-near** and **beside-closure each** of you, as a father his children,

12 **And into the witnessing** you would walk **deserving** of God, who hath called you **into** his kingdom and **glory.**

13 **Through this** also thank we God **not-through-leaving,** because, when you **beside-took** the **Word of God** which you heard of us, you **welcomed** not the word of men, but as it is in truth, the **Word of God,** which **in-work** also in you that believe.

14 For you, **brothers,** became **imitators** of the Churches of God which in Judaea are in Christ Jesus: for you also have **emotion** like things of your own countrymen, even as they of the Jews.

15 Who both killed the Lord Jesus, and their own prophets, and have **out-of-chased** us; and they please not God, and are contrary[3169] to all men:

[3168] Or before-show, outward showing

[3169] Greek compound: in-anti, antagonistic

16 **Preventing** us to speak to the **nations** that they might be saved, to fill up their sins always: for the **swelling-anger** is **anticipated** upon them **into finish**.

17 But we, **brothers**, **being-orphaned** from you for **season of-hour** in presence, not in **heart**, **speed** the **more-exceedingly** to **perceive** your face with **much on-feeling**.

18 Through-which we would have come **towards you**, even I Paul, once and again; but Satan **cut-into** us.

19 For what our **expectation**, or **cheerfulness**, or **victor's-crown** of **boasting**? Not even you **before** our Lord Jesus Christ **in** his **presence**?

20 For you are our glory and **cheerfulness**.

1 THES. CHAPTER 3

1 Through-which when we could **no-further roof-over**, **we-good-seem** to be left at Athens alone.

2 And **dispatched** Timothy, our brother, and **attendant** of God, and our **together-worker** in the **well-message** of Christ, to establish you, and to **beside-call** you **over** your faith:

3 That no man should **be-swayed** by these **tribulations**; for yourselves **perceived** that **into this** we **lay**.

4 Because, when we were with you, **we-before-speak**[3170] **to-you** that **we-are-impending to-be-troubled**; even as **it-became**, and **you-perceived**.

5 Through this, when I could no longer **roof-over**, I **dispatched** to know your faith, lest by some means the **Tempter**[3171] have tempted you, and our **toil-cut** be into **empty**.

6 But now when Timothy came from you **to-us** and brought us **well-message** of your faith and love, and that you have good remembrance of us always, **upon-yearning to-perceive** us, as we also you.

7 Therefore, **brothers**, we were **called-near** over you in all our **tribulation** and **necessity** by your faith:

8 For now we live, if you **stand** in the Lord.

9 For what thanks **are-we-powerful to-repay to-the** God **about** you, for all the **cheerfulness which** we **cheer through you** before our God?

[3170] systematically predict
[3171] Prober, tester, probe-testing

10 Night and day **beg-binding out-excessive into the perceiving of-your** face, and **down-equip** that which is **deficit** in your faith.

11 Now God himself and our Father, and our Lord Jesus Christ, **down-straighten** our way **to-you**.

12 And the Lord make you to increase and abound in love **into one-another-same**, and **into** all, even as we **into you**:

13 Into the **establishment of-your hearts un-blamable** in holiness before God, even our Father, **in** the **presence** of our Lord Jesus Christ with all his saints.

1 THES. CHAPTER 4

1 The remaining then **brothers** we **request** you, and **call-near** by the Lord Jesus, that as you have **beside-taken beside** us how **it-is binding** you to **about-walk** and **to-be-agreeable to-God**, that rather **you-may-be exceeding**.

2 For **you-perceived** what **beside-message** we gave you by the Lord Jesus.

3 For this is the will of God, your sanctification that you should abstain from **prostitution**.

4 That every one of you should **perceive** how to **acquire** his vessel in sanctification and **value**.

5 Not in the **emotions of-on-feeling**, even as the **nations** which **perceived** not God:

6 That **not over-stepping** and **more-have**[3172] in **to-the practice** his brother; **through-that** the Lord the avenger of all such, as we also have **before-said to-you** and **through-witnesses**.

7 For God has not called us **into** uncleanness, but **in** holiness.

8 He therefore that **un-placing**, **un-placing** not man, but God, who hath also given **into** us his Holy Spirit.

9 But as touching **brotherly-friendship** you need not that I write **to-you**; for you, yourselves, are **God-taught into** loving **one-another-same**.

10 And **because** you **produce this into** all the **brothers** which are in all Macedonia; **yet** we **call-near** you, **brothers**, that you **rather to-be-exceeding**.

[3172] Or covet, overreach

1 Thessalonians

11 And that you **friend-value** to be **quiet-seated**, and **practice** your own, and to work with your own hands, as we **beside-message** you;

12 That you may walk **well-formed** toward them that are **outside**, and **no-one need you-may-be-having**.

13 But I would not have you **ignorant brothers**, concerning them which are asleep, that you **distress-sadden** not, even as **the remaining** which have no **expectation**.

14 For if we believe that Jesus died and rose again, even so them also which sleep in Jesus will God **lead together to-him**.

15 For this we say **to-you** in the **Word of the Lord**, that we **the living and about-remaining into** the **presence** of the Lord shall not **anticipate** them which are asleep.

16 For the Lord, himself, shall descend from heaven **in shout-order, in** voice of **an** archangel, and **in trumpet** of God; and the dead in Christ shall rise **before-most**.

17 Then, we **the living and about-remaining shall-be-snatched simultaneously together to-them** in clouds, **into meeting**[3173] the Lord **into** air;[3174] and so shall we **always together to-**Lord.

18 So-too beside-call another-same in these words.

1 THES. CHAPTER 5

1 But of the **uninterrupted-times** and the **set-seasons, brothers**, you have no **use** that I write **to-you**.

2 For yourselves **have-perceived exactly** that the day of the Lord, so, **it-is-coming** as a thief in the night.

3 For when they shall say, peace and **certainty**,[3175] then **un-apparent whole-ruin** comes upon them, as **pang**[3176] upon a woman with child; and **not they-out-of-fleeing**.

4 But you, **brothers**, are not in darkness, that that day should **down-take** you as a thief.

5 You are all the **sons** of light, and the **sons** of the day; we are not of the night, nor of darkness.

6 Consequently then let us not sleep, as **the remaining**; but let us watch and be **sober**.

7 For they that sleep, sleep in the night; and they that be drunk are drunk in the night.

8 But let us, who are of the day, be sober, **clothe-yourself** breastplate of faith and love, and for a helmet,[3177] the **expectation** of salvation.

9 For God hath not **placed** us to **swelling-anger**, but to **around-make**[3178] **of-salvation through** our Lord Jesus Christ.

10 Who died for us, that, whether we wake or sleep, we should live **simultaneous with to-him**.

11 Through-which, beside-call one-another-same, and **house-build** one the one, **down-as you-are-producing**.

12 And we **request** you, **brothers**, to **perceive** them which **fatigue-cut in** you, and **stand-before** you in the Lord, and **thought-placing** you.

13 And to **lead** them **over out-of-excessive** in love **through** the work. **Be-at-peace in** yourselves.

14 Now **we-beside-call** you, **brothers, thought-place** them that are **unarranged, beside-closure the little-soul**,[3179] support the **without-strength**, be **long-sacrifice-anger** toward all.

15 See that none **from-give** evil **opposite** evil **to-any**; but **always chase** that which is good, **also into one-another**, and **into** all.

16 Be-cheerful always.

17 Pray **without-through-leaving**.

18 In everything give thanks: for this is the will of God in Christ Jesus **into you**.

19 The Spirit not **be-you-extinguishing**.

20 Not **make-out-to be-nothing** prophesying.

21 Test-seem all things; **down-hold** that which is **ideal**.

22 Hold-from all **perception** of **wicked-hurtful**.

23 Yet the God himself **of-the** peace sanctify you **whole-finish**; and your **whole-inheritance**[3180] the-

---

[3173] Greek: "apantesis," the official welcome of a newly **arriving** dignitary, by people going out to meet the dignitary and escorting the dignitary back to the origin of the ones who went to meet the dignitary; see also Acts 28:14-16, Matthew 25:1-6

[3174] Greek root for this word means to breathe

[3175] Greek: "a" (negative participle) and "sphallo" (to "fail"), security, certainty

[3176] Or, pang, sudden pain

[3177] Lit., About-head

[3178] Greek: peri (around) and poieo (make, produce), means to purchase acquire

[3179] Or diminutive-soul (underdeveloped soul)

[3180] Acts 3:16, James 1:4

spirit and **the-soul** and **the-body** be **guarded** blameless **in** the **presence** of our Lord Jesus Christ.

24 Believing he that calls you, who also **shall-be-doing.**

25 Brothers, pray **about** us.

26 Embrace all the brothers with a holy **friend-kiss.**

27 I **oath** you by the Lord that this epistle be read **to** all the holy brothers.

28 The grace of our Lord Jesus Christ with you. Amen!

2 THESSALONIANS

2 THES. CHAPTER 1

1 Paul, and Silvanus, and Timothy, **to-the** Church of the Thessalonians in God our Father, and the Lord Jesus Christ.

2 Grace **to-you**, and peace, from God our Father and the Lord Jesus Christ.

3 We **owe** to thank God always **about** you, **brothers**, as it is **deserving**; because that your faith **over-growing**, and the **love** of every one of you all **into one-another-same** abounds.

4 So that we ourselves **boast** in you in the Churches of God for your **under-remaining** and faith in all your **chasings** and tribulations that you **hold-up**.

5 **In-show** of the righteous **judging** of God **into the down-deserving**, you, of the kingdom of God, for which you also **are-emotional**.

6 **If-even** righteousness beside God to repay[3181] tribulation **to-them** that trouble you;

7 And **to-you** who are troubled **up-send** with us, **in the revelation of-the** Lord Jesus from heaven with his angels **of-power**.

8 In fire **of-blaze** giving vengeance[3182] on them that **perceived** not God, and that **under-hearing**[3183] not the **well-message** of our Lord Jesus Christ:

9 **Who-any** righteously **shall-pay-the-price** with eternal **whole-ruin** from the **face** of the Lord, and from the glory of his **force**!

10 When he shall come **to-be-glorified** in his saints, and to be **marveled** in all them that believe (because our **witness** among you was believed) in that day.

11 **Into which** also we pray always for you, that our God would **deem-you-deserving of-the** calling, and **fill** all the **well-seem of-good-togetherness**, and the work of faith **in** power:

12 That the name of our Lord Jesus Christ may be glorified in you, and you in him, **down** the grace of our God and the Lord Jesus Christ.

2 THES. CHAPTER 2

1 Yet we **request** you, brothers, by the **presence** of our Lord Jesus Christ, and our **upon-assembling** on him.

2 That you be not soon shaken **from the thought**, or be **uproar-wailing**, neither **through** spirit, nor **through** word, nor **through** letter as from us, as that the day **of the Lord has-in-stood**.

3 Let no man **out-cheat** you by any **turn, that** except there come **the divorce**[3184] **foremost**, and that man of **lawlessness**[3185] be revealed, the son of **from-ruin**;

4 **The opposing-one**[3186] and **over-lifts** himself **upon** all that is called God, or that is **reverenced**; so that he as God **seated into** the temple of God, **showing-off** himself that he is God.

5 Remember you not, that, when I was yet **towards** you, **I–said to-you these-things**?

6 And now you **perceived** what **down-holds**[3187] **into the being-revealed in to**-his **season**.

7 **Because**, the mystery **of-the lawlessness** already **is-in-working** only **the one-down-holding**, until **out of-middle it-became**.

8 And then shall that **lawless** be revealed, whom the Lord shall consume **to-the** Spirit of his mouth and shall **down-not-working to**-the epiphany[3188] of his **presence**.

9 Whose presence is according-to the energy of-the Satan in all to-power and to-signs and to wonders of-falsehood,

10 And **in** all **cheating** of **unrighteousness** in them that **from-ruin**;[3189] instead **of-which the love of the truth**, they welcomed **not** that they might be saved

11 And **through this**, God **shall-dispatch**[3190] **to-them energy of-seduction, into the belief to-the falsehood**.

12 That they all **may-be-judged** who believed not the truth, but **well-seeming in the unrighteousness**.

13 But we **owe to-be-thanking** always to God **about** you, brothers, beloved of the Lord, because God

---

[3181] Greek: instead-from-give
[3182] Lit., out-or-righteousness
[3183] Or obey
[3184] Lit., "apostasies:" from-stand; feminine of "apostasion" (divorce); a thing that separates.
[3185] Alexandrian Text: man of lawlessness
[3186] Greek: anti-laying outstretched

[3187] Or occupancy (occupy) Strong's #2722 and #2697 (a derivative of #2722)
[3188] "Epiphany" is a transliteration of the Greek compound "epiphaneia" (upon-shine)
[3189] Greek: "apo" (from) and "alethros" (ruin), to destroy fully
[3190] Greek: "pempo," emphasizing the point of departure

preferred you from the **original into** salvation through sanctification of the Spirit and belief of the truth.

14 Into which he called you by our **well-message**, to the **around-make**[3191] of the **glory** of our Lord Jesus Christ.

15 Consequently, brothers, stand, and **be-governing** the **beside-giving**[3192] which you have been taught, whether **through** word, or **through** our epistle.

16 Now our Lord Jesus Christ himself, and God, even our Father, the **one-loving** us, and has given **eternal beside-call,** and good **expectation in** grace,

17 Beside-call your **hearts,** and **stand** you in every good word and work.

2 THES. CHAPTER 3

1 The remaining, brothers, pray for us, that the **Word of the Lord may-be-running**, and be **glorified**, even as **towards** you:

2 And that we may be **rush-rescued** from **unplaced** and **wicked-hurtful** men; **Because not** all **of- the** faith.

3 But the Lord is **believing**, who shall **stand** you, and **guard** from **the wicked-hurtful**.

4 Yet we-believing in the Lord **upon** you that you both **produce** and **will-produce** the things which we **beside-message to-you**.

5 And the Lord **down-straighten** your **hearts** into the love of God, and **into the under-remaining** for Christ.

6 Now we **beside-message** you, brothers, in the name of our Lord Jesus Christ that you **stall** yourselves from every brother that walks **un-arranged**, and not after the **beside-giving** which he received **beside** us.

7 For yourselves **perceived** how **it-is-binding to-imitate** us; for not **we-un-arranged in** you.

8 Neither did we eat any man's bread **gratuitously**; but **cut-fatigue** with **work** and **toil-difficulty** night and day, that we might not be **heavy towards** any of you:

9 Not because we **hold** no **authority**, but to make ourselves a **type into you** to **imitate** us.

10 For even when we were **towards** you, this we **beside-message** you, that if any would not work, neither should he eat.

11 For we hear that there are some which walk among you **un-arranged**, working not at all, but are **meddlesome-magicians**.[3193]

12 Now them that are such we **beside-message** and **beside-call through** our Lord Jesus Christ, that with **quiet-seated** they work, and eat their own bread.

13 But you, brothers, be not **out-of-bads** in **ideal-producing**.

14 And if any man **under-hear**[3194] not our word **through** this epistle, **sign-mark** that man, and **not together-up-mix** with him, that he may **in-vert**.

15 Yet not as a **hater be-leading** but **thought-place** as a brother.

16 Now the Lord **of-the** peace, himself, give you peace **through all, in all spots**. The Lord with all **of-you**.

17 The **embrace** of Paul with **my** hand, which is the **sign** in every epistle: so, I write.

18 The grace of our Lord Jesus Christ with you all. **Amen!**

[3191] Greek: peri (around) and poieo (make, produce), means to purchase, acquire
[3192] Lit., beside-give, transmission, tradition
[3193] Greek: "periergos," all-working, busy body, meddlesome, magic, superstitious practices
[3194] Or obey

1 TIMOTHY

1 TIMOTHY CHAPTER 1

1 Paul, an apostle of Jesus Christ **down** the **decree**[3195] of God our Savior, and Lord Jesus Christ, which is our **expectation**.

2 **To-Timothy, legitimately-birth child** in the faith: Grace, mercy, and peace, from God our Father and Jesus Christ our Lord.

3 As I **beside-called** you **toward-remain** still at Ephesus, when I went into Macedonia, that you **beside-message** some that they **not different-teach**,

4 Neither **holding** to **myths**[3196] and **un-passed-through** genealogies, which minister questions, rather than **God's house-law**[3197] which is in faith.

5 Now the **finish** of the **beside-message** is **love** out of a **clean heart,** and of a good conscience, and of faith **un-hypocritical**.

6 From which some having **deviated** have **revert to vain-saying.**

7 **Willer** to be **law-teachers**;[3198] **not thoughtful** what they say, nor **about which** they **through-established**.

8 **Yet** we know that the law is **ideal**, if **any use**[3199] it lawfully.

9 **Having-perceived** this, that the law is not **placed** for a righteous man, but for the lawless and **insubordinate**, for the **irreverent** and for sinners, for **not-right (intrinsically)** and profane, for **father-threshers** and **mother-thresher**, for **man-faced-slayer**,

10 For **paramour**, for **male-coitus**[3200] for **enslavers,**[3201] for **falsifiers**, for **oaths** and if there be any **another-different** that is **opposing**[3202] to **healthy-growth teaching**;

11 According to the glorious **well-message** of the **happy** God, which **I was-believed**.

12 And I **have grace to-the-one,** Christ Jesus our Lord, who has **empowered** me, for that he **believed me,** putting me into the **service.**

13 Who was before a blasphemer, and a **chaser,** and **hubristic**;[3203] but **I-obtained-mercy,** because I did it **ignorantly,** in unbelief.

14 And the grace of our Lord was **over-more** with faith and love which is in Christ Jesus.

15 This is a **believing** saying, and **deserving** of all acceptations, that Christ Jesus came into the world to save sinners; of whom I am **foremost**.

16 Yet through this, **I-obtained-mercy,** that in me foremost Jesus Christ might show forth all **long-sacrifice-anger,** for an **under-type of-the ones-impending to-believe upon** him **into eternal life.**

17 Yet to-the the King **of-the ages, incorruptible,** invisible, the only wise God, be **value** and glory **into the ages of the ages**. Amen.

18 This **beside-message I-am-beside-placing**[3204] **to-you,** child, Timothy, **down** the prophecies which **before-lead** you, that you **in** them may-war **the ideal** warfare;

19 Holding faith, and a good conscience, which some having **from-shoved** concerning faith have made shipwreck:

20 Of whom is Hymenaeus and Alexander; whom I have **beside-given to-the** Satan that they may be **boy-trained** not to blaspheme.

1 TIMOTHY CHAPTER 2

1 I **beside-call** therefore, that, **foremost** of all, **beg-binding** prayers, **in-happenings**,[3205] and giving of thanks, be made **over** all men.

2 For kings, and for all that are in **superiority**; that we may lead a **tranquil-lonesome** and **quite-seated livelihood** in all **good-reverence** and **serious-reverence.**

3 For this is **ideal** and **from-welcome** in the sight of God our Savior;

4 Who will have all men to be saved, and to come **into** the knowledge of the truth.

5 For there is one God, and one mediator **of-God** and men, the man Christ Jesus.

[3195] Lit., upon-arrangement
[3196] False mysteries (hence attempting to teach mysteries as do the true apostles and prophets)
[3197] All of the oldest text reads "house-law;" the more recent copy of a text used to translate the King James reads: "God's house-building"
[3198] Or, properly, doctors
[3199] Or, to inform, to tell, to furnish what is needed, to use, to employ
[3200] Greek: "arsenokoites" transliterated as "male-coitus;" "coitus also means bed, the place of semen, physical union of male and female genitals
[3201] Lit., "man-foot," to enslave by bringing man to his feet, to kidnap
[3202] Greek: anti-laying outstretched
[3203] Insulter
[3204] Or deposit
[3205] Or in-obtain. in-to hit the target, in-chance upon

6 Who gave himself an **instead-loose** for all, to be witnessed **to-own to-seasons**.

7 Into which I am **placed** a preacher, and an apostle, (I speak the truth in Christ, and **falsify** not), a teacher of the **nations** in faith and **truth**.

8 I-plan-counseled-myself therefore that men pray **in** every **spot**, lifting up **intrinsically-right** hands, **spaced-from swelling-anger** and **through-inventory**.

9 In like manner also, that women, in **apparel,**[3206] **cosmetics** themselves **with-change un-perceiving** and a **safe-disposition**, not **cosmetics in braids**, or gold, or pearls, or **much-finished clothing.**

10 But (which **towers up** women **promising God-reverence**) **through** good works.

11 Let the woman learn in **silence-seated** with all **subordination**.

12 But I **permit**[3207] not a woman[3208] to teach, nor **self-authoritative**[3209] **of-the** man,[3210] but to be in **silence-seated**.

13 For Adam was **foremost** formed, then Eve.

14 And Adam was not **cheated**, but the woman being **cheated** was in **beside-stepping**.

15 Notwithstanding, she shall be saved through **childbirth**, if they **remain** in faith and **love** and holiness with **safe-disposition**.

1 TIMOTHY CHAPTER 3

1 This is a **believing** saying, if a man **grasping-crave bishopric,**[3211] **he-is-upon-feeling of-ideal** work.

2 A **bishop,**[3212] **it-is-binding** then, **to-be-un-arrested**, the husband of **first** wife, sober, **safe-disposition, cosmetic, friendly-lodger, didactic.**[3213]

3 Not **beside-wine**, no **smiter**, no **disfigured-gain**; but **upon-yield,**[3214] not a **fighter, not-friendly-to-silver.**

4 One that **before-stand** well his own house, having his children in **subordination** with all **serious-reverence**.

5 (For if a man know not how to **before-stand** his own house, how shall he **be-upon-interest** of the Church of God?)

6 Not a novice, **not-enveloping-in-smoke**, that not he fall into the **judgment-result**[3215] of the Devil.

7 Moreover **it-is-binding**, he has **an ideal witness** of them which are **outside**; that not he fall into **defame** and the **fixed-trap** of the Devil.

8 Likewise must the **attendants** be **serious-reverent**, not **two-saying**, not given to much wine, **not holding disfigured-gain**.

9 Holding the mystery of the faith in a **clean** conscience.

10 And let these also **foremost** be **seem-tested**; then let them **attended** being found **un-called-in.**[3216]

11 Even so must their wives be **serious-reverent**, not **devils**, sober, **believing** in all things.

12 Let the **attendants** be the husbands of **first** wife, **before-standing** their children and their own houses **ideally**.

13 Because, ideally, they that **are-through-attendants around-make**[3217] to themselves a good **stair-step**, and **much all-speech**[3218] in the faith which is in Christ Jesus.

14 These things write I **to-you**, **expecting** to come **to-you** swiftly

15 But if **I-am-slow**, that you **may-perceive** how **it-is-binding** to behave yourself in the **House of God**, which is the Church of the living God, the pillar and **support-seat** of the truth.

16 And **same-saying great** is the mystery of **good-reverence**: Who[3219] **shined** in the flesh, **righteous** in

---

[3206] Greek: "katastole," root, to put down, to quell, to quite, to appease
[3207] Or transfer
[3208] Or wife
[3209] The Greek word authenteo originally meant "one who commits suicide"—(auto—"self," and theno—suicide (to kill with one own hands); the meaning evolved to mean "a self-worker," or a "acting on one's own." We now take our English word "authentic" (self-authoritative) from this Greek word.
[3210] Or husband
[3211] Greek: "episkope" (upon-peer-about, upon-watch, upon-goal, upon-mark, a sentry, a scout), transliterated as "episcopate," bishopric, the office of a bishop, visitation, to visit, oversee, oversight, upon-skeptic
[3212] Greek: "episkopos" (upon-peer-about, upon watch, upon-goal, upon-mark), bishop, visitation, to visit, oversee, oversight, upon-skeptic
[3213] Or apt to teach
[3214] Or, upon-image, to be weak to simulate (Strong's #1909 + #1502, #1503, #1504)
[3215] Greek: "krima," transliterated as "crime" and also means judgment
[3216] Or un-accused
[3217] Greek: peri (around) and poieo (make, produce), means to purchase, acquire
[3218] Or free speech
[3219] Alexandrian Texts reads "Who" in lieu of "God," see 1 John 1:18 for comparison between the texts

the Spirit, seen of angels, preached **in to-nations**, **upon-believed** in the world, **up-taken** into glory.

1 TIMOTHY CHAPTER 4

1 Now the Spirit speaks **explicitly** that in the **under seasons** shall **divorce**[3220] some **of-the** faith, **towards-holding-ones to-seducing** spirits, and **to-teachings of demons**;

2 In hypocrisy of false-saying; having **burn-branded** their **private** conscience.

3 **Preventing marrying,** to abstain from **foods**, which God has created to be **taken** with thanksgiving of them which believe and know the truth.

4 For every creature of God is **ideal**, and nothing to be refused, if it be received with thanksgiving:

5 For it is sanctified by the **Word of God** and **in-happenings**.[3221]

6 These things **place-under** the brothers; you shall be an **ideal attendant** of Jesus Christ, **in-fed** in the words of faith and of **ideal teaching, which you have followed.**

7 But refuse[3222] profane and **old-wives-view** and **be-naked-exercising** yourself rather **to good-reverence**.

8 Because, bodily **naked-exercise** profits **towards few-things; yet, good-reverence** is profitable **towards** all things, having promise of the life that now is, and **the impending.**

9 This is a **believing** saying and **deserving** of all **from-welcome.**

10 For **into this,** we both **cut-fatigue** and **defamed**,[3223] because we **expect** in the living God, who is the Savior of all men, especially of those that believe.

11 These things **beside-message** and teach.

12 Let no man despise your youth; but become a **type of-the** believers, in word, in **behavior** in love, in spirit, in faith, in **cleanness.**

13 Until I come, **towards-hold** to reading, to **beside-calling**, to **teaching**.

14 Neglect not the **grace** that is in you, which was given you by prophecy, with the laying on of the hands of the **eldership**.

15 **Be-of-interest upon these things; that your progress may shine to all.**

16 Hold **to-yourself**, and **to-the teaching; upon-remain to-them:** for in **producing** this you shall both save yourself, and them that hear you.

1 TIMOTHY CHAPTER 5

1 **An elder, not upon-pound,** but **beside-call** him as a father; and the younger men as **brothers;**

2 The **presbytesses**[3224] as mothers; the younger as sisters, with all **cleanness**.

3 **Value** widows that are widows indeed.

4 But if any widow has children or **descendants**,[3225] let them learn foremost to show **good-reverence** at home, and to **repay** their **before-parents**:[3226] for that is **ideal** and acceptable **in-view of-the** God.

5 Now she that is a widow indeed, and **alone-remain**, **expect on the** God, and **towards-remaining** in **bird-begging** and prayers night and day.

6 But she, **being-voluptuous, has-died living**.

7 And these things give **beside-message** that they may be **un-arrested**.

8 But if any not **before-thoughtful** for his own, and especially for those of his own house, he has **contradicted** the faith, and is worse than an **un-believer**.

9 Let not a widow be **down-lay forth**[3227] **inferior**[3228] **sixty** years old, having been the wife of one man,

10 **Ideal witness** for **ideal** works; if she **nourished-children,** if she has **welcomed-strangers,** if she has washed the saints' feet, if she have **upon-satisfy** the **troubled**, if she have followed every good work.

11 But the younger widows refuse:[3229] for whenever they **down-luxurious**[3230] **to-the** Christ, they will marry;

12 Holding **judgment-result,**[3231] because they have **un-placed** their **foremost** faith.

[3220] Lit., "aphistemi" from-stand, the root word for "apostasies:" feminine of "apostasion" (divorce); a thing that separates.
[3221] Or in-obtain. in-to hit the target, in-chance upon, intersession
[3222] Lit., beside-ask, to beg off, shun, refuse
[3223] Lit., notorious, name
[3224] Greek: "presbuteras," the feminine of presbytery (elder)
[3225] Out-parents
[3226] Or, grandparents, "progenitors"
[3227] Or enroll
[3228] Greek "elassoni," smaller in size, age, quantity, dignity, inferior,
[3229] Lit., beside-ask, to beg off, shun, refuse
[3230] Or down-straining (based on probably root)
[3231] Greek, "krima," transliterated as "crime;" but also means judgment for crime

13 **At-the-same** they learn to be idle, wandering[3232] from house to house; and not only idle, but **gossiper** also and **meddlesome-magicians**,[3233] speaking things **not binding**.

14 I-plan-counsel-myself therefore that the younger women marry, bear children, **be-home-owning**, give **no-violent impulse-stare** to the **opposing-ones**[3234] of-**spear-abusing grace**.

15 For some are already **reverted behind** Satan.

16 If any man or woman that believes have widows, let them relieve them, and let not the Church be **weighed-down**; that it may relieve them that are **really** widows.

17 The elders that **before-stand ideally** be counted **deserving** of double **value**, especially they who **fatigue-cut** in the **Word** and **teaching**.

18 For the Scripture says, you shall not muzzle the **bull** that threshes out the corn. And the **worker deserves** his **wages**.

19 Downing an elder, an accusation,[3235] not **beside-welcome**, but **upon** two or three witnesses.

20 Yet, those sinning-ones **evidence-expose** before all that **the remaining** also **may-hold** fear.

21 I-through-witness you **in-view** God, and the Lord Jesus Christ, and the elect angels, that you **watch** these things **spaced-from prejudice**,[3236] producing nothing by **bias**.[3237]

22 Lay hands **swiftly** on no man, neither **communion** of other men's sins: **guard** yourself **clean**.

23 Drink no longer water, but use[3238] little wine, **through** your stomach's and your often **weakness**.

24 Some men's sins are **before-evident**, going before to **judging**; and some men they follow after.

25 Likewise also the **ideal** works of some are **before-evident**; and they that are otherwise **not powerful to-be hidden**.

[3232] About going
[3233] Greek: "periergos," all-working, busy body, meddlesome, magic, superstitious practices
[3234] Greek: anti-laying outstretched
[3235] Transliterated as "categorizing"
[3236] Greek: prokrimatos (before-judge)
[3237] Lit., toward-slope, leaning towards, incline
[3238] Or, to inform, to tell, to furnish what is needed, to use, to employ

1 TIMOTHY CHAPTER 6

1 Let as many **slaves** as are under the yoke count their own **owners deserving** of all **value**, that the name of God and his **teaching** be not blasphemed.

2 And they that have believing **owners**, let them not **down-disposition-them**, because they are **brothers**; but rather **be-slaving-them**, because they are **believing** and beloved, **instead-take**[3239] of the **good-work**. These things teach and **beside-call**.

3 If any man **another-different-teaching**, and **approach** not to **healthy-grow** words, even the words of our Lord Jesus Christ, and to the **teaching** which is **down good-reverence**;

4 He-is-**envelope-in-smoke**, not-being-acquainted,[3240] but **being-nauseated** about questions and **fighting-words**, out-of which becomes ill-will, quarrel,[3241] blaspheming, wicked-hurtful under-thoughts,[3242]

5 Beside-through-rut of men of corrupt **thoughts**, and **deprived** of the truth, **do-by-law** that gain is **good-reverence**: from such **divorce**[3243] yourself.

6 Yet, good-reverence with **self-sufficiency** is great gain.

7 Because, we brought nothing into this world, and it is certain **not we-are-powerful to-out-carry a-thing**.

8 And having **nourishment** and **shelter** let us **to-these be-content**.

9 Yet they that **plan-counsel-themselves to-be-rich** fall into **probe-testing** and a **trap-fix**, and into many **upon-feelings un-thoughtful** and **hindering**, which **sink-down**[3244] men in **whole-ruin** and **from-ruin**.

10 For the **friend-of-silver** is the root of all evil: which while some **grasping-crave**, they **were-seduced** from the faith, and **through-pierced** themselves through with many sorrows.

11 O! **Yet** you, man of God, flee these things; and **chase righteous-togetherness**, **good-reverence**, faith, love, **under-remaining**, **gentleness**.

[3239] Or, help, support
[3240] Greek: upon-stand, to put the mind upon, to be acquainted with, comprehend, be present
[3241] Or, electioneering, quarrel, debates
[3242] Or suspicions
[3243] Lit., "aphistemi" from-stand, the root word for "apostasies:" feminine of "apostasion" (divorce); a thing that separates.
[3244] Or submerge

12 **Agonize** the **ideal agony** of faith, lay hold on **eternal life, into which** you are also called, and has **same-say** a good **same-say** before many witnesses.

13 I–am-beside-messaging you, in-view of-the God, **the One life-producing** all things, and before Christ Jesus, who before Pontius Pilate witnessed a good **same-saying**.

14 That you **guard** this commandment without **stain, un-arrested**, until the **epiphany**[3245] of our Lord Jesus Christ:

15 Whom in his **own seasons,** he shall show, who is the **happy** and only **Dynasty,**[3246] the King of **kings,** and Lord **of-the ones-being-lords.**

16 Who only has immortality, **homing** in the light which no man can approach **to**; whom no man has **perceived,** nor **is-powerful** to **perceive**: to whom be **value** and **government,**[3247] eternal. Amen.

17 Beside-message them that are rich in **now age,** that they be not **high-dispositioned,** nor **expect** in uncertain riches, but in the living God, who **near-holds to-us** richly all things to enjoy;

18 Be-good-worker, rich in **ideal** works, **good-givers, communicative;**

19 Placing-into-tomorrow for themselves an **ideal** foundation **into the impending,** that **they-upon-take the eternal life.**

20 O! Timothy, **watch** that which is **deposited to-you,** avoiding profane and **vain-voices,** and **anti-placings** of **false-name knowing.**

21 Which some **upon-messaging** have **deviated about** the faith. Grace be with you.

Amen.

[3245] "Epiphany" is a transliteration of the Greek compound "epiphaneia" (upon-shine)
[3246] Or Power-One
[3247] Greek: kratos, transliterated as "great" and also means vigor, strength, to use strength, to rule, government, translated as "cracy" in democracy— people(demo)-government (kratos), or public-government

2 TIMOTHY

2 TIMOTHY CHAPTER 1

1 Paul, an apostle of Jesus Christ **through** the will of God, **down** the promise of life which is in Christ Jesus,

2 To Timothy, my beloved **child**: Grace, mercy, and peace, from God the Father and Christ Jesus our Lord.

3 **I-have-graciousness to-the** God, **to-whom I-am-hired-serving** from my forefathers with **clean** conscience, that without **lacking**, I have remembrance of you in my **beg-bindings** night and day.

4 **Upon-longing** to **perceive** you, **remembering** your tears, that I may be filled with **cheerfulness**.

5 When I **remember** the **un-hypocritical** faith that is in you, which **in-home foremost** in your grandmother Lois, and your mother Eunice; and I am persuaded that in you also.

6 **Through** which cause, **I-am-reminding you** that you **up-live-firing**[3248] the **grace** of God, which is in you **through** the **upon-placing** of my hands.

7 **Because,** God has not given us the spirit of **timidity** but of power, and of love, and of a **safe-disposition**.[3249]

8 Be not therefore **upon-disfigured** of the **witness** of our Lord, nor of me his prisoner: but **you-together-evilly-emotion** of the **well-message down** the power of God;

9 Who has saved us, and called us with a holy calling, not **down** our works, but **down** his own **purpose**[3250] and grace, which was given us in Christ Jesus before **uninterrupted-times eternal**.

10 But is now made-**to-shine** by the **epiphany**[3251] of our Savior Jesus Christ, who has **down-idle** death, and has brought life and **incorruptibility** to light through the **well-message**:

11 Into which I am **placed** a preacher, and an apostle, and a teacher of the **nations**.

12 **Through** which cause I also **emotion** these things; nevertheless, I am not **upon-disfigured**: for I know whom I have believed and am persuaded that he is **powerful** to **watch** that which I have **deposited** into that day.

13 Hold fast the **under-type** of **healthy-grow** words, which you have heard of me, in faith and love which is in Christ Jesus.

14 That **ideal** thing which was **down-deposited to-you watch** by the Holy Spirit which **homes** in us.

15 This you **perceived** that all they which are in Asia be turned away from me; of whom are Phygellus and Hermogenes.

16 The Lord give mercy **to-the** house of Onesiphorus;[3252] for **much he up-cools** me and was not **upon-disfigured** of my chain:

17 But, when he was in Rome, he sought me out **speedily**, and found me.

18 The Lord **give to-him** that he may find mercy of the Lord in that day: and in many things he **attended-to** at Ephesus, you know better.

2 TIMOTHY CHAPTER 2

1 **You then,** my **child, be-empowered** in the grace that is in Christ Jesus.

2 And the things that you have heard **beside** me **through** many witnesses, you **beside-place**[3253] the same to **believing** men, who shall be **sufficient**[3254] to teach **another-different** also.

3 You then **evilly-emotion**, as an **ideal** soldier of Jesus Christ.

4 No man that wars **entwine** himself with the **practices**[3255] of this **livelihood**; that the **soldier should-be-pleasing**.

5 And if a man also **competes**, yet is he not **victory-crowned**, except he **competes** lawfully.

6 The **land-toiler it-is-binding foremost to-be-change-taking** of-the fruits.

7 **Be-thoughtful the-things I-am-saying;** and the Lord give you **synthesizing** in all things.

8 Remember that Jesus Christ of the seed of David was raised **out-of** the dead **down** my **well-message**:

[3248] Lit., up-living-one-fire
[3249] Or safe-disposition
[3250] Lit., before-place, or to place in advance
[3251] "Epiphany" (upon-shine)
[3252] Profit-carrying

[3253] Or deposit
[3254] Lit., to arrive; or, competent as if coming in season, ample in amount, fit in character
[3255] Greek: "pragmateria," transaction, negotiation, business

9 In-which I-emotion, as an **evil-worker**, until **chains-bound**; but the **Word of God** is not **chain-bound**.

10 Through-this I-under-remain all things through the elect that they may also happen[3256] of-the salvation which is in Christ Jesus with **eternal** glory.

11 It is a **believing** saying: for if we **died** with him, we shall also live with him:

12 If we **under-remain**, we shall **together-reign**: if we **contradict**[3257] him, he also will **contradict** us.

13 If we believe not, yet he **remains believing**: he **not he-is-powerful to-deny**[3258] himself.

14 These **be-under-reminding, through-witnessing in-view** of-the Lord that they **not word-fight** to no **use**, but to the **catastrophe** of the **hearers**.

15 Speed yourself seem-approved beside-standing to-the God, a **worker not-upon-disfigured, straight-cutting** the **Word of Truth**.

16 But profane and **vain-voices about-stand**[3259] for they will **drive-forward to** more **un-good-reverence**.

17 And their word **as-gangrene law**[3260] **shall-be-holding** of whom is Hymenaeus and Philetus;

18 Who concerning the truth have **deviated**, saying that the resurrection is past already; and **overturn** the faith of some.

19 Nevertheless the foundation of God stands **solid**, having this seal, the Lord knows them that are his. And, let everyone that names the name of Christ **divorce**[3261] **unrighteousness**.

20 But in a **great** house there are not only vessels of gold and of silver, but also of wood and of **earthenware**; and some **into value**, and some to **un-value**.

21 If any then **clean** himself from these, he shall be a vessel **to value,** sanctified, and **good-useful** for the **owner's** use, and prepared **into** every good work.

22 Flee also youthful **upon-feelings** : but chase **righteous-togetherness**, faith, love, peace, with them that **upon-call**[3262] the Lord out of a **clean heart**.

23 But **morons** and **un-boy-trained questionings**[3263] **refuse,**[3264] **having-perceived** that they **birth fights**.

24 And the **slave** of the Lord **it-is-binding** not to **fight**; but be gentle **towards** all men, **didactic,**[3265] patient,

25 In **mildness, boy-training** those **that-anti-through-place-themselves;**[3266] if God will give them **change-thought** to the acknowledging of the truth.

26 And that they **be-up-sober** out of the **trap** of the Devil, who are **live-caught under** him **into** his will.

2 TIMOTHY CHAPTER 3

1 This know also, that in the last days **difficult seasons** shall **in-stand**.

2 For men shall be **friend-of-selves,**[3267] **friend-of-silver, braggart,**[3268] **over-shiners,**[3269] **blasphemers, unpersuadable** to parents, un-graceful, **un-intrinsic-right,**

3 **Un-affectionate, un-spent,**[3270] **devils, un-governed**[3271] **fierce,**[3272] **un-friend-of-good,**

4 Traitors, **rash,**[3273] **smoldering,**[3274] **friends-of-hedonism** rather than **friends-God**;

5 Having a form of **good-reverence** but **contradict** the power **of-her**: from such **from-turn**.

6 **Out of these** are they which **in-slip** into houses, and **capture little-women pileup** with sins, led away with **various upon-feelings** ,

7 Ever learning, and **not-yet powerful** to come to the knowledge of the truth.

8 Now as Jannes and Jambres **anti-stand** Moses, so do these also **anti-stand** the truth: men of **down-corrupt thoughts, not-seem-approved about** the faith.

[3256] Or, hit the mark, chance upon, obtain,
[3257] Or deny
[3258] Or contradicts
[3259] Middle voice in the Greek and means to avoid, to shun, stand all about
[3260] Greek: "Nomen," feminine of nomos (law)
[3261] Lit., "aphistemi" from-stand, the root word for "apostasies:" feminine of "apostasion" (divorce); a thing that separates.
[3262] Or, to entitle, to invoke
[3263] Seekers, searchers, meaningless seeking, speculations
[3264] Lit., beside-ask, to beg off, shun, refuse
[3265] Instructive
[3266] Or anti-covenant-themselves
[3267] Selfish
[3268] Ostentatious: vulgar display to attract or impress
[3269] Or, appearing above others
[3270] Greek: "spendo" to pour out a libation
[3271] Or uncontrollable
[3272] Or, un-mild (not-pleasant to the senses), savage
[3273] Greek: before-falling
[3274] Or envelope in smoke

9 But they shall proceed no further: for their **unthoughtfulness** shall be **out-of-clear to-all,** as theirs also was.

10 But you **have-beside-followed** my **teaching, the leading, purpose,**[3275] the faith, **long-sacrifice-anger,** love, **under-remaining,**

11 Chasings, emotions, which **became to-me in** Antioch, **in** Iconium, **in** Lystra; what **chasings** I **under-carry**: but out of them all the Lord **rush-rescued** me.

12 Yes, and all that will live **good-reverent** in Christ Jesus **shall-be-chased.**

13 But **wicked-hurtful** men and **wailing-wizards** shall **progress** worse and worse, **seducing,** and **being-seduced.**

14 But **you remain** in the things which you have learned and have been **persuaded** of, **perceiving** of whom you have learned them;

15 And that from an **infant**[3276] you have **perceived** the **priestly Scriptures,** which are **powerful** to make you wise **into** salvation through faith which is in Christ Jesus.

16 All Scripture is **God-breathed,** and is profitable for **teaching,** for **evidence-exposing,** for **upon-up-straighten,** for **training** in **righteous-togetherness:**

17 That the man of God may be **fresh, out-of-freshness towards** all good works.

2 TIMOTHY CHAPTER 4

1 I **am-through-witnessing in-view of-the** God, and the Lord Jesus Christ, who **impending to-be-judging** the **living** and the dead **down** his **epiphany**[3277] and his **kingdom;**

2 Preach the **Word; be-upon-standing good-season, un-season; evidence-expose,** rebuke, **beside-call in** all **long-sacrifice-anger** and **teaching.**

3 For the **season** will come when they will not **hold-up healthy-grow teaching**; but **down** their own **upon-feelings** shall they **pileup** to themselves teachers, having **tickled**[3278] the hearing;

4 And the truth they shall **from-turn the hearing** and shall be turned **to myths.**[3279]

5 But **you be-sober!** In all **evilly-emotion,** produce the work of an evangelist,[3280] **fully-burden-wear** your ministry.

6 For I am now ready to be **spent**, and the **season** of my **up-loose** is **upon-stand**

7 I have **agonized** an ideal **agony,** I have finished my **race,** I have **guarded** the faith:

8 Remaining, there is **reserved** for me a **victor's-crown** of **righteous-togetherness,** which the Lord, the righteous judge, shall give **to-me in** that day: and not to me only, but **to-all** them also that **loved** his **epiphany.**

9 Be-speedy to come **swiftly towards** me:

10 For Demas has forsaken me, having loved this **now age,** and is **traveled into** Thessalonica; Crescens to Galatia, Titus **into** Dalmatia.

11 Only Luke is with me. Take Mark and **lead** him with you: for he is **good-useful** to me for the **attendance.**

12 And Tychicus have I sent to Ephesus.

13 The **cloak** that I left at Troas with Carpus, when you come, bring with you, and the **little-scroll,** but especially the **membrane.**

14 Alexander the coppersmith **in-show** me much evil; the Lord reward him **down** his works:

15 Of whom be you **watch** also; for he has **very-much anti-stand** our words.

16 In the foremost apology[3281] no man **together-beside-became,** but all men forsook me: I pray God that it may not be **inventoried to-them.**

17 Yet the Lord **beside-stood to-me and empowered** me; that **through** me the preaching **might-be-fully-burdened-worn,** and that all the **nations** might hear: and I was **rush-rescued** out of the mouth of the lion.

18 And the Lord shall **rush-rescue** me from every **wicked-hurtful** work and will **save** me **into** his heavenly kingdom: to whom be glory **into the ages of-the ages.** Amen.

19 Embrace Prisca and Aquila, and the household of Onesiphorus.

20 Erastus **remained** at Corinth; but Trophimus have I left at Miletum sick.

[3275] Lit., before-place, or to place in advance
[3276] "Brephos," an infant or properly an unborn baby
[3277] "Epiphany" (upon-shine)
[3278] Or, scratched
[3279] False mysteries
[3280] Or., lit., good-angel
[3281] Also means defense

21 **Be-speedy** to come before winter. Eubulus **embrace** you, and Pudens, and Linus, and Claudia, and all the **brothers**.

22 The Lord Jesus Christ be with your spirit. Grace be with you. Amen.

TITUS

TITUS CHAPTER 1

1 Paul, a **slave** of God, and an apostle of Jesus Christ, **down** the faith of God's elect, and the knowledge of the truth which is after **good-reverence**;

2 Upon expectation of **eternal life**, which promised **the un-falsifying** God, before **uninterrupted-times eternal**.

3 But has in **seasons shined** his Word through preaching, which **I believed down** the **decree** of God our Savior;

4 To Titus, **legitimate-birth child down** the common faith: grace, mercy, peace, from God the Father and the Lord Jesus Christ our Savior.

5 For this cause left I you in Crete, that you should **up-straighten** the things that are **lacking**, and **place-down** elders in every city, as I **under-arranged to-you**.

6 If any be **un-called-in**,[3282] the husband of **first** wife, having **believing** children not accused of **un-saved** or **un-arranged-under**.

7 For a **bishop**[3283] **it-is-binding to-be-un-called-in**,[3284] as the **house-lawyer** of God; not **self-hedonist**, not **swelling-anger**, not **staying-near-wine**, no **smiter**, not given to **disfigured-gain**.

8 But a **friendly-lodger**, a **friend-of-good**, **safe-disposition**, **righteous**, **intrinsically-right**, **in-hold**.[3285]

9 **Opposite-hold** the **believing** Word as he has been taught, that **he-may-be powerful in the healthy-grow teaching** both to **beside-call** and to **evidence-expose** the **disputers**.[3286]

10 For there are many **un-under-arranged** and **vain-talkers** and **disposition-misleader**,[3287] especially they of the circumcision:

11 Who **it-is-binding to-be-gagged**,[3288] who **overturn** whole houses, teaching things which **not is-binding**, **of-shame** gain **through-grace**.

12 One **out-of** themselves, a prophet of their own, said, the Cretians **ever falsifiers**, evil **wild-beasts, idle womb**.[3289]

13 This witness is true. **Through-which cause evidence-expose** them **from-single-cut**, that they may **heathy-grow** in the faith;

14 Not **holders** to Jewish **myths**, and commandments of men, that turn from the truth.

15 **To** the **clean** all things **clean**: but **to-them** that are **contaminated** and unbelieving nothing **clean**; but even their **thought** and conscience is **contaminated**.

16 They **same-say** that they **perceived** God; but in works they **contradict**, being **stink**, and **unpersuadable**, and **towards** every good work **not-seem-approved**.[3290]

TITUS CHAPTER 2

1 But you speak the things which **towers up healthy-grow teaching**.

2 That the **elders** be sober, **serious-reverence**, **safe-disposition**, **healthy-growing to-faith, to-love, to-under-remaining**.

3 The **presbytesses**[3291] likewise, that in **demeanor** as **priests-towering-up**,[3292] not **devils**, not **been-enslaved** to much wine, **ideal-teachers**.

4 That **they-safe-disposition** the young women, to **friend** their husbands, to **friend** their children,

5 **Safely-disposed**, **holy**, **home-seers**, good, **subordinate**[3293] to their **private** husbands, that the **Word of God** be not blasphemed.

6 Young men likewise **beside-call** to be **safe-disposition**.

7 **About** all things, **beside-hold** yourself a **type** of **ideal** works; in **the teaching** show **incorruptibleness, serious-reverence**.

[3282] Or un-accused
[3283] Greek: "episkopos" (upon-peer-about, upon watch, upon-goal, upon-mark), bishop, visitation, to visit, oversee, oversight, upon-skeptic
[3284] Or un-accused
[3285] Or self-control
[3286] Lit, anti-word, refute, dispute
[3287] Or, disposition-cheater, mind-misleader
[3288] Lit., upon-mouth
[3289] Or lit., non-working pregnancy
[3290] Or rejected, reprobate
[3291] Transliterated from the Greek: presbutidas ("senioresses"-noun, feminine, plural of "presbutes" (elder, senior, old man))
[3292] Or priest-fitting
[3293] Under-arranged

8 **Healthy-grown** speech **not-down-know**; that he that is contrary³²⁹⁴ **may-be-in-turned**, having no **foul** thing to say of you.

9 Slaves be **subordinate to** their **private owners**, to please well in all; not **disputing**.³²⁹⁵

10 Not **kept-back-for-themselves**,³²⁹⁶ but showing all good **faith**; that they may **cosmetic** the **teaching** of God our Savior in all things.

11 For the grace of God, **the** salvation, **upon-shined** to all men.

12 Boy-training us that **contradicting un-good-reverence** and worldly³²⁹⁷ **upon-feelings**, we should live **safely-disposed**, righteously, and **good-reverence**, in this present **age**.

13 Toward-welcome the happy expectation, and the glorious **epiphany**³²⁹⁸ of the **great** God and our Savior Jesus Christ.

14 Who gave himself for us, that he might **loose** us from all **lawlessness** and **cleaning to-himself** a people **about-exists**,³²⁹⁹ zealots of **ideal** works.

15 These things speak, and **beside-call**, and expose with **every upon-arrange**. Let no man **about-dispose**, you.

TITUS CHAPTER 3

1 Under-remind them to be **subordinate**³³⁰⁰ to **originals** and **authorities, to-believe-first**, to be **internally-prepared** to every good work,

2 Blaspheme no-one, be **non-fighters, upon-yield**,³³⁰¹ showing all **mildness towards** all men.

3 For we ourselves also were sometimes **un-thoughtful, unpersuadable, seduced, slaving to-various upon-feelings** and **to-hedonism, through-leading** in **evil** and envy, hateful, **detesting one-another-same**.

4 But however, the **usefulness** and **philanthropist** of God our Savior **upon-appeared**.

5 Not **out-of** works of **righteous-togetherness** which we have **produced**, but **down** his mercy he saved us, by the **bath** of **rebirth**, and **up-young-new** of the Holy Spirit;

6 Which he **poured upon** us **richly** through Jesus Christ our Savior;

7 That **righteous-ones, to-that** grace, we should be made heirs **down** the **expectation** of **eternal life**.

8 Faithful the saying, and **about** these things **I-plan-counseled-myself** that you **through-confirm**, that they which have believed in God **be-disposed** to **before-stand ideal** works. These things are ideal and profitable **to-the** men.

9 But avoid **moronic** questions, and genealogies, and **quarrel**,³³⁰² and **fighting** about the law; for they are unprofitable and **empty**.³³⁰³

10 A man that is a heretic after the first and second **thought-placing, refuse**.³³⁰⁴

11 Having-perceived that he that is such is **perverted**, and sins, **self-down-judged**.

12 When I shall **dispatch** Artemas **towards you**, or Tychicus, **speedily** come **towards** me **into** Nicopolis: for I have **judged** to winter there.

13 Zenas, the lawyer, and Apollos **speedily before-dispatch** that nothing be **lacking** to-them.

14 And let ours' also learn to **before-stand ideal** works for **constraining** uses, that they be not unfruitful.

15 All that are with me, **embrace**, you. **Embrace** them that **friend** us in the faith. Grace with you all. Amen.

---

³²⁹⁴ Greek compound: in-anti, in front of, opposite, antagonistic
³²⁹⁵ Lit, anti-word, refute, dispute
³²⁹⁶ Or, to sequestrate for oneself, to embezzle
³²⁹⁷ Kosmikos: pertaining to a ordered system, as opposed to a particular part, systemic (set of things working together)
³²⁹⁸ "Epiphany" is a transliteration of the Greek compound "epiphaneia" (upon-shine)
³²⁹⁹ A compound of Greek word made up of "peri" (about) and "eimi" (I exists); therefore, being beyond usual, special
³³⁰⁰ Under-arranged
³³⁰¹ Or. Upon-image, to be weak to, yield (Strong's #1909 + #1502, #1503, #1504)
³³⁰² Or, electioneering, quarrel, debates
³³⁰³ Or, empty through the idea of unsuccessful search
³³⁰⁴ Lit., beside-ask, to beg off, shun, refuse

PHILEMON

PHILEMON CHAPTER 1

1 Paul, a prisoner of Jesus Christ, and Timothy **the** brother, **to-Philemon** our dearly beloved, and **together-worker**.

2 And **to-the** beloved Apphia, and Archippus our **together-soldier**, and to the Church in your house:

3 Grace **to-you**, and peace, from God our Father and the Lord Jesus Christ.

4 I thank my God, **producing reminder** of you always **upon** my prayers,

5 Hearing of your love and faith, which **you-have** towards the Lord Jesus, and **into** all saints.

6 That the **communion** of your faith may become **in-working** by the **knowledge** of every good thing which is in you in Christ Jesus.

7 For we have **cheerfulness** and **beside-call** in your love, because the **gut-compassions** of the saints are **up-paused through** you, brother.

8 **Through-which**, though I might be much **all-speech**[3305] in Christ to **upon-arrange**[3306] you that which is **proper**,[3307]

9 **Through love**, I rather **beside-call**[3308] you, being such a one as Paul the **elder**, and now also a prisoner of Jesus Christ.

10 **I-beside-call about** my son Onesimus, whom I have **birthed** in my bonds:

11 Who sometimes was **useless to-you**, but now **good-use to-you** and to me:

12 Whom I have **up-dispatched**[3309] **to-you**; therefore, receive him, that is, **my gut-compassions**

13 Whom **I-plan-counseled** towards myself to **down-hold**, that **beyond-you**, that **over you**, he might have **attended to-me** in the **bond-chains** of the **well-message**:

14 But **spaced-from** your **opinion I-will to-produce** nothing; that your **good** should not as **down** of **necessity**, but **down voluntary**.

15 For **shortly**, **through this**, **he-departed** for an **hour**, that you should receive him **eternally**.

16 Not now as a **slave**, but above a **slave**, a brother, beloved, especially to me, but how much more **to-you**, both in the flesh, and in the Lord?

17 If you **hold** me therefore **communion**,[3310] receive him as myself.

18 If he has **unrighteous** you, or owes you, put that on my **upon-word**.

19 I Paul have written with **my** hand, I will **pay-the-price**: albeit I do not say **to-you** how you **towards-owe** to me even yourself.

20 Yes, brother, let me have **gratified-advantage** of you in the Lord: **up-rest** my **gut-compassions** in the Lord.

21 Having **persuasion** in your **under-hearing**, I wrote **to-you**, **having-perceived** that **you-shall-do** over which **I-am-saying**.

22 But **simultaneously internally-prepare** me also a lodging: for **I-am-expecting** that through your prayers I shall be **graced to-you**.

23 **Embrace, you.** Epaphras, my **together-prisoner** in Christ Jesus.

24 Marcus, Aristarchus, Demas, Lucas, my **together-worker**.

25 The grace of our Lord Jesus Christ with your spirit. Amen.

[3305] Or free speech
[3306] Or decree
[3307] Upon-arrive
[3308] Or call near
[3309] Or send back, send again
[3310] Or partner

HEBREWS

HEBREWS CHAPTER 1

1 God, who at **much-turn** and in **much-portion** spoke **of-old** to the fathers **in** the prophets,

2 **On the last of these** days spoke **to-us in** Son,[3311] whom **he-places** heir of-all, **through** whom also he made the **ages.**

3 Who being the **from-ray-of-light**[3312] of his glory, and the **character-engraver**[3313] **of-the substructure**[3314] **of-Him, carrying** all things, **then, to-the declaration** of his power, when he had **through** himself purged our sins, sat down **in** the right hand of the **Great-togetherness**[3315] on high.

4 Becoming so-much better-government[3316] than the angels, as he has by inheritance a **differing**[3317] name **beside them.**

5 Because **to-which** of the angels said he **at-any-time**, you are my Son, this day have I[3318] **birthed** you? And again, I will be **into him** a Father, and he shall be **into** me Son?

6 And again, when he **into-leads** the **firstborn** into the **housed-land**, he says, and let all the angels of God worship him.

7 And **towards** the angels he says, who **produces** his angels spirits, and his **people-workers**,[3319] flame of fire.

8 Yet, **toward** the Son, he says, your throne, **the** God, is **into the age of the ages**, a **rod** of **soon**[3320] is the **rod** of your kingdom.

9 **You-loved righteous-togetherness**, and hated **lawlessness, through-this**, God, even your God, has anointed you with the **olive-oil of jumping-joy beside** your **partners.**[3321]

10 And, you, Lord, in the **original** has **founded** the earth; and the heavens are the works of your hands.

11 They **shall-be-from-ruined**;[3322] but you **through-remain**; and they all **shall-be-old** as a garment.

12 And as a **covering** shall you fold them, and they shall be changed; **yet** you are the same, and your years **not shall-be-omitted**.

13 Yet **towards** which of the angels said he **at-any-time**, sit **out-of** my right hand, until I **place** your **haters** footstool **of-the feet of-you**?

14 Are they not all **people-worker**[3323] spirits, sent into **attendant**[3324] **through** them who **are-impending to-be-heirs** of salvation?

HEBREWS CHAPTER 2

1 **Through this, it-is-binding** to **more towards-hold** to the things which we have heard, **not-ever** we should let them **beside-flow.**[3325]

2 **Because,** if the word spoken by angels was **stable**, and every **beside-step** and **mishearing**[3326] took **righteous wage-give.**[3327]

3 How shall we **out-of-flee**, if we neglect so **prime-same** salvation, which **originally taken**, spoken **through** the Lord, and was **stabilized into** us **under** them that heard him.

4 God also **together-witnessing**, both with **to-signs** and **to-wonders**, and with **various powers**, and **distributions** of the **Holy Spirit**, **down** his own will.

5 Because, not **to-**angels has **he-subordinate**[3328] the **housed-land impending, about** which we **are-speaking.**

6 Yet, someone, somewhere **witnesses,** saying, what is man, that **you-are-being-reminded** of him? Or the son of man, that you **bishop**[3329] him?

[3311] Compare corporate son in Galatians 4:7
[3312] Or from-dawn
[3313] Exact representation, pressed image, originally a tool used for engraving, hence a stamp or impress used on a coin or seal
[3314] Greek: "hupostasis," under-stand," substrate, substance (a real being), substantial quality, nature
[3315] Greek compound: **great** (big) and sun (together); Big-togetherness, great-togetherness
[3316] Greek: "kreitton," a comparative derivative of "kratos;" ("cracy") in democracy—people (demo) and government ('cracy') (kratos)),
[3317] Greek: "diaphero," to through-bear, transliterated as "differ" or "different"
[3318] Ego-self-esteem, self-importance,
[3319] Laos (people)-ergon (work); lit., "liturgic"
[3320] Greek "eu" (good) "tithemi" (place); lit., straight, soon, level
[3321] Greek: meta (change or with)-echo (to hold or to have); "with-holders," sharers
[3322] Greek: "apo" (from) and "alethros" (ruin), to destroy fully
[3323] Lit., laos (people)-ergon (work); "liturgist"
[3324] Or through-run on errands, deacons
[3325] Or flow or run like water, run by, flow by
[3326] Or beside-hearing
[3327] Or reward
[3328] Under-arranged
[3329] Greek compound: upon-peer about, upon-skeptic

7 You-**inferior** him **briefly beside some** angels; you **victory-crowned** him with glory and **value**, and **down-stand** him over the works of your hands:

8 You subordinated all under his feet. **Because** in **the subordinated all to-him, nothing, he-releases**[3330] **un-subordinate to-him. Yet** now we see not yet all **subordinate to-him.**

9 Yet briefly, beside some angels, we see Jesus **inferior, through** the **emotions of-the** death, **victory-crowned** with glory and **value**; that he by the grace of God should taste death **over** every man.

10 For it-**towers-up to-him, through** whom **the all-things,** and **through** whom **the all-things,** many sons **into** glory, **leading** the **Original-Leader** of their salvation **mature** through **emotions**.

11 For both he that sanctifies, and they who are sanctified are all **out-of** one; **through** which cause he is not **upon-disfigured** to call them **brothers,**

12 Saying, I will **from-message** your name to my **brothers,**[3331] in the **middle** of the Church will I **hymn to-you.**

13 And again, I will put my trust in him. And again, **be-perceiving,** I and the children which God has given me.

14 Since then as the children are **communion** of flesh and blood, he also himself **beside-near partner**[3332] of the same; that through **the-death he-should-be-down-working** him that **held** the **government of-the** death, that is, the **Devil.**

15 And **from-change** them who through fear of death were, all their **living, liable**[3333] to **slavery.**

16 Because not binding, the nature of angels to **he-upon-take;** but **he-upon-take of-the** seed of Abraham.

17 Which-place, in all things **he-owed to-the brothers to-be-assimilated,** that he **become** a merciful and **believing First-Rank-Priest** in things **towards** the God, **to-be-merry-atoning**[3334] for the sins of the people.

18 Because in that he **emotion** being **probe-tested,** he is **powerful** to **help**[3335] **to-them** that are **probe-tested.**

HEBREWS CHAPTER 3

1 Which-place, holy **brothers, partners**[3336] of the heavenly calling, **down-thought** the Apostle and **First-Rank-Priest** of our **same-saying,** Christ Jesus;

2 Who was **believing to-him** that **produced** him, as also Moses was **believing** in all his house.

3 For this man was **deserving** of more glory than Moses, inasmuch as he who has **constructed**[3337] the house has more **value** than the house.

4 For every house is **constructed** by some man; but he that **construct** all things is God.

5 And Moses **indeed** was **believing** in **whole of-his** house, as a **therapist,** for a **witness** of those things **which-shall-be** spoken.

6 But Christ as Son over his own house; whose house are we if we **down-hold** the **all-speech**[3338] and the **boasting** of the **expectation stable until finish.**

7 Through-which (as the **Holy Spirit** says, today if you will hear his voice,

8 Harden not your **hearts,** as in the **beside-bitterness,** in the day of **probe-testing** in the **lonesome:**

9 When your fathers **probe-tested** me, **seem-test** me, and saw my works forty **years.**

10 Through-which I was grieved with that generation, and said, they always **are-seduced** in their **heart; yet** they have not known my ways.

11 So I swore in my **swelling-anger** if **they-shall**-enter into my **down-pause.**)

12 Be-looking, brothers, lest there be in any of you a **wicked-hurtful heart** of unbelief, in **divorcing**[3339] from the living God.

13 But **beside-call yourselves** daily, **until which,** it is called today; **that none** be hardened **out-of to-cheating of-the** sin.

[3330] Or forgive, from-let go
[3331] Lit., "brother of the same womb" (and so through the entire New Testament)
[3332] Greek: meta (with, or change)-echo (hold, to have)
[3333] Or, to in-hold, or hold in
[3334] Greek: "hilaskomai" and means propitious (atonement); atonement-merry; from the same root for "Mercyseat"
[3335] Lit., to run to the cry (help)
[3336] Or, with-holders, sharers
[3337] Greek: down-vessel, to prepare thoroughly
[3338] Or free speech
[3339] Lit., "aphistemi" from-stand, the root for "apostasies;" feminine of "apostasion" (divorce)

14 For **we-become partners**[3340] of Christ if we **down-hold** the **original** of-the **substructure**[3341] **stable until-finish.**

15 In the being-said, today if you will hear his voice, harden not your **hearts**, as in the **beside-bitterness.**

16 Because some, when they had heard, did **beside-bitter, but** not all that came out of Egypt **through** Moses.

17 Yet to-whom was he **towards-irked** forty **years**? Was it not with them that had sinned, whose carcasses fell in the **lonesome**?

18 Yet to whom swore he that they should not enter into his **down-pause**, but **to-them** that **were-un-persuadable**?

19 So **we-are-looking** that **not they-powerful to-**enter **through** unbelief.

HEBREWS CHAPTER 4

1 Let us therefore fear, lest a promise **down-remaining** of entering into his **down-pause**, any of you should seem **to-be-late.**

2 Because we-are evangelized, as well as them; but the **Word of-the hearing** did not profit them, not being **together-mingle** with faith in them that heard it.

3 For we which have believed do enter into **down-pause**, as he said, as I have sworn in my **swelling-anger** if they shall enter into my rest: although the works **became** from the **down-casting** of the world.

4 For he spoke **somewhere about** the seventh day, **in-this-way**, and God did rest in the seventh day from all his works.

5 And in this, again, if they shall enter into my **down-pause.**

6 Since, then it-from-remain that some enter **into it**, and they to whom it was **formerly evangelized** entered not in **through being-un-persuadable.**

7 Again, he **defines**[3342] a certain day, saying in David, today, after **so-much** time; as it is said, today if you will hear his voice, harden not your **hearts** .

8 For if Jesus[3343] had given them **down-pause**, then would he not, **another-same**, have spoken of **after-change**[3344] day.

9 Consequently, is-from-remaining a **Sabbath** to the people of God.

10 For he that is entered into his **down-pause**, he also has **down-paused** from his own works, as God did from his.

11 Be-speedy, then, to enter into that **down-pause**, that not in the **selfsame under-show of-the should-fall of-un-persuadable.**

12 Because, the **Word of God** is **living,** and **in-working,** and **cut above every two-mouth** sword, **through-arriving**[3345] **until parting** of soul and spirit **joining both also** marrow and is **decisive-judge**[3346] of the **in-thought** and **in-sacrifice-anger** of the **heart.**

13 Neither is there any **creation** that is **un-shined** in his sight; **yet** all things are naked and opened[3347] to-the eyes of him **towards** whom **to-us the** Word.

14 Seeing then that we have a **Great First-Rank-Priest**, that is **through-come** the heavens, Jesus the Son **of-the** God, **we-govern** our **same-saying.**

15 Because, we have not a **First-Rank-Priest** which **not powerful to-be together-emotion**[3348] with the **together-emotions**[3349] of our **weakness; yet** was in all points **probe-tested** like as we are yet **spaced-from** sin.

16 Let us therefore **towards-come to-all-speech**[3350] to the **Throne of Grace,** that we may **take** mercy, and find grace to help[3351] into **good-season.**

HEBREWS CHAPTER 5

1 Because every **original** priest taken from among men is **down-standing** for men in things **towards** God, that he may offer both gifts and sacrifices **over** sins:

2 Being-powerful to-measure-emotions to-the ignorant, and on them that are **seduced**; for that he himself also is **around-laid** with **weakness.**

3 And **through this** he **owes**, as **about** the people, so also **about** himself, to offer for sins.

[3340] Or, with-holders, sharers
[3341] Greek: "hupostasis," under-stand," substrate
[3342] Greek: horizon, to mark out a bound, to specify, to define
[3343] Or Joshua
[3344] Greek: "meta"
[3345] Or penetrating

[3346] Greek: "kritikos," transliterated critical; decisive, discerner, judge
[3347] To seize or expose the throat or neck
[3348] Greek: sun (together) and pathos (emotion); transliterated, "sympathy"
[3349] Lit., sympathy
[3350] Or free speech
[3351] Lit., to run to a cry for help

4 And no man **is-taking** this **value to-himself,** but he that is called **under** God, as was Aaron.

5 So also, Christ glorified not himself to be made **First-Rank-Priest**; but he that said **to-him,** you are my Son, today have I **birthed** you.

6 As he says also in **another-different**, you are a **Priest, into the age, down** the order of Melchizedek.

7 Who in the days of his flesh, when he had offered up **beg-bindings** and **olive-branch-supplications** with **forceful screaming** and tears **towards** him that was **powerful** to save him **out-of** death and was heard in that he **well-take**.³³⁵²

8 Though he were Son yet learned he **under-hearing from** the things which he **emotion.**

9 And **being-matured,** he became the **causer** of **eternal** salvation **to** all them that **under-hear**³³⁵³ him;

10 **Towards-market-place**³³⁵⁴ **under** God a **First-Rank-Priest, down** the order of Melchizedek.

11 **About**³³⁵⁵ whom we have many things to say, and **difficult-translated**, seeing you are **lazy** of hearing.

12 **Because** when **through** the **uninterrupted**-time you **owe** to be teachers, you **hold need** that one teach you again **what-is** the **elements**³³⁵⁶ **of-the original of-the** oracles of God; and are become such as have need of milk, and not of **stiff food.**

13 For every one that **partner**³³⁵⁷ **of-milk** is **un-probe-tested** in the Word of **righteous-togetherness**: for he is **an infant.**

14 But **stiff food to-them** that are **mature**, even those who **through habit**³³⁵⁸ have their senses **naked-exercised** to **through-judge** both **ideal** and evil.

HEBREWS CHAPTER 6

1 **Through-which** leaving the **original** of the **Word** of Christ, **let-us-be-carried upon the Mature-One**; not **down-casting** again the foundation of **change-thought**³³⁵⁹ from dead works, and of faith **upon** God,

2 Of the **teaching** of baptisms, **both** of laying on of hands, and of resurrection **both** of the dead, and of **eternal judgment-result.**³³⁶⁰

3 And this will we do, if God permit.³³⁶¹

4 **Because un-powerful** for those who were once enlightened, and have tasted **both** of the heavenly gift, and were made **partners**³³⁶² of the **Holy Spirit**,

5 And have tasted the **ideal Declaration** of God, and the powers of the **age impending**,

6 If they shall **beside-fall**, to **up-fresh** them again **into change-thought**; **the-ones-up-crucifying to-themselves** the Son of God, and **beside-exhibit-him.**³³⁶³

7 For the earth which drinks in the rain that come often upon it, and brings forth herbs **well-placed** for them **through** whom it is **land-worked, change-taking** blessing from God:

8 **Yet** that which bears thorns and **three-cast**³³⁶⁴ is **not-seem-approved** and is **near-squeeze to down-curse**; whose **finish** is **into** burn.

9 **Yet**, beloved, we are persuaded **better-government** things of you, and **holds of-salvation**, though we speak **in-this-way.**

10 **Because** God is not unrighteous to forget your work and **cut** of love, which you have showed toward his name, in that you have **attended to-the** saints, and **are-attendants.**

11 And we **upon-feel** that every one of you do show the same **speed towards the full-burden-wearing of-the expectation until** the **finish.**

12 That you be not **lazy**, but **imitators** of them who through faith and **long-sacrifice-anger** inherit the promises.

13 **Because** when God made promise to Abraham, because he could swear by no greater, he swore **down himself,**

14 Saying, **truly,** blessing I will bless you, and multiplying I will multiply you.

---

³³⁵² Or, to take it well (Greek compound: "eu" (good) and lambano (to get, or to take))
³³⁵³ Or obey
³³⁵⁴ Or towards-speaking to an assembly; also compare "out-of-market-place" in Galatians 4:5
³³⁵⁵ Greek: "peri"—all about, all around
³³⁵⁶ Or, any first thing, something orderly in arrangement (Gal 4:3, 4:9; Col 2:8, 20; Heb 5:12; 2 Peter 3:10, 12; compare Acts 21:24, Rom 4:12, Gal 5:25, Gal 6:16, Phil 3:16)
³³⁵⁷ Or, with-holder, change-holder, after-holder
³³⁵⁸ Root: to hold
³³⁵⁹ Or after-mind
³³⁶⁰ Greek: "krima," "crime" and also means judgment
³³⁶¹ Or transfer
³³⁶² Or, with-holders, sharers
³³⁶³ Or beside-specimen-him
³³⁶⁴ Or, a crow-foot (three pronged obstruction used in war), thistles

15 And so, after he had **long-sacrifice-anger,** he **upon-happened of-the** promise.

16 Because men **indeed** swear by the **great,** and an oath for **stabilization** is **to-them** an **extremity** of all **anti-word**.

17 In which God, **counseling-himself more-abundantly** to show **to-the** heirs of promise the immutability of his counsel, **mediated** it by an oath:

18 That by two immutable **practices**, in which **un-powerful**[3365] for God to **falsify,** we might have a forceful **beside-calling,** who have fled **to-government of-the before-laid expectation**:

19 Which we have as an anchor of the soul, both **certainty**[3366] and **stable,** and which enters into **that interior of-the** veil.

20 Where the **before-racer over** us entered, even Jesus, **became** a **First-Rank-Priest into the age down** the order of Melchizedek.

HEBREWS CHAPTER 7

1 For this Melchizedek, king of Salem, priest of the **Highest** God, who **together-met** Abraham returning from the **cutting** of the kings and blessed him.

2 To whom also Abraham **tenth from all** parts; **foremost** being by **translation** King of **righteous-togetherness,** and also King of Salem,[3367] which is, King of peace.

3 Un-fathered, un-mothered, un-genealogy, having neither **original** of days, nor **finish** of life; **yet from-similar to-the** Son of God; **remains** a priest **into the through-carry**.

4 Looking how-**full-grown**[3368] this man was, to-whom even the patriarch Abraham **gives** tenth **out-of** the **extreme-piles**.

5 And **indeed** they that are **out-of** the sons of Levi, **the priesthood taking,** have a commandment **to-from-tenth** of the people **down** the law, that is, of their **brothers,** though they come out of the loins of Abraham:

6 Yet, he whose **genealogy** is not **out of-**them **has-tenth the** Abraham and blessed him that had the promises.

7 Yet, spacing-from all **anti-word,** the **inferior**[3369] is blessed **under** the **better-government**.

8 And here men that die **takes** tithes; **yet** there he of whom it is witnessed that he lives.

9 And as I may so say, Levi also, who **takes** tithes, **has-tenth through** Abraham.

10 Because, he was yet in the loins of his father, when Melchizedek **together-meet** him.

11 If indeed maturing were **through** the Levitical **priest-togetherness, (because upon** it the people **were-legislated**[3370]) what further need was there that **another-different** priest should rise after the order of Melchizedek, and not be **said down** the order of Aaron?

12 Because, the **priest-togetherness** being **translated,** there **is-becoming** of **necessity,** a **translation** also of the law.

13 Because, he of whom these things are spoken of **another-different** tribe **partnered,**[3371] **from whom** no man **towards-hold** at the **sacrifice-place**.

14 Because, it-is-before-clear that our Lord **up-finish** out of Juda; **into** which tribe Moses spoke nothing **about** priesthood.

15 And **it-is** still **more-abundantly** if **down the resemblance** of Melchizedek there arises **another-different** priest,

16 Who is **become** not after the law of a **fleshly** commandment, but after the power of an **un-down-loosed** life.

17 Because he-is-witnessing, you are a priest **into the age down** the order of Melchizedek.

18 Because there is **indeed** an **un-placing**[3372] of the commandment **before-leading** for the **without-strength** and **un-profitableness of-her**.

19 For the law made nothing **mature,** but the **upon-into-leading** of a **better-government expectation** did; **through** the which we draw **near-squeeze to-the** God.

20 And inasmuch as not **space-from** an oath he **became** priest:

[3365] Impossible, unable
[3366] Greek: "asphales," transliterated as "un-failing,"
[3367] Salem was the original name for Jerusalem
[3368] Or, how much (as indefinite), dignity, adult

[3369] Greek" "elassoni," smaller in size, age, quantity, dignity, inferior,
[3370] Or, law-placed
[3371] Or, with-holder, change-holder, after-holder, sharer
[3372] Or cancel

21 (**Yet** with the oath **through** him that said **towards** him, the Lord swore and will not **regret**,[3373] you are **Priest into the age down** the order of Melchizedek:)

22 Down so much, Jesus **became of-better-government covenant in-limb.**[3374]

23 And they **indeed became** many priests, because they were **prevented** to **beside-remain through** death.

24 Yet, this man, because he **remains into the age**, has an **un-beside-step**[3375] **priest-togetherness**.

25 Which-place he is **powerful** also to save them **into** the **every-finish** that come **to** God **through** him, **always living in-happenings**[3376] **over** them.

26 Because such a **First-Rank-Priest towers-up to-us**, who is **intrinsically-right, not-evil, not-contaminated, space from** sinners, and **became elevated of-the** heavens.

27 Who not is-holding down daily, necessity, as those **first-rank-priest**s, to offer up sacrifice, **foremost over** his own sins, and then **of-those of-the** people's; for this he did once, when he **offered-up** himself.

28 Because, the law **down-stand** men **original-priests** which have **weakness**; but the **Word** of the oath, which was **after** the law, Son, **into the age, matured**.

HEBREWS CHAPTER 8

1 Now of the things which we have spoken this is the **Head:** We have such a **First-Rank-Priest**, who is set in the right hand of the throne of the **Great-togetherness**[3377] in the heavens;

2 People-worker[3378] of the **holies**, and of the true tabernacle, which the Lord **peg-fixed,** and not man.

3 For every **original-priest into the** offer **both** gifts and sacrifices **is-down-placed; which-place** it is of **constraint** that this man have **something** also to offer.

4 Because, if he were on earth, he should not be a priest, **exists the** priests that offer gifts **down** the law.

5 Who **to-under-show**[3379] and **to-shadow are-hired-service of-the heavens,** as Moses was **apprised**[3380] of God when **impending** to **upon-finish** the tabernacle: for, **be-seeing, he says,** that you make[3381] all things **down** the **type**[3382] showed[3383] **to-you** in the mount.

6 Yet, now has he **happen**[3384] a **different**[3385] **of-the people-work**,[3386] by how much also he is the Mediator of a **better-government** covenant, which was **legislated**[3387] upon **better-government** promises.

7 For if that **foremost** had been **un-blamable**, then should no **spot** have been sought for the second.

8 Because blaming to-them, he says, **be-perceiving**, the days come, says the Lord, when I will **together-finish** a New Covenant[3388] with the house of Israel and with the house of Judah:

9 Not **down** the covenant that I **produced** with their fathers in the day when I **upon-take** them by the hand to lead them out of the land of Egypt; because they **in-remain** not in my covenant, and I **un-cared of-them**, says the Lord.

10 That this is the covenant that **I-shall-be-covenanting** with the house of Israel after those days, says the Lord; I will **give** my laws into their **deep-thoughts**, and write them in their **hearts**; and I will be **into** them a God, and they shall be **into** me a people:

11 And they shall not teach every man his neighbor, and every man his brother, saying, know the Lord; **that** all shall **perceive** me, from the **micro** to the **great**.

12 For **I-shall-be merry-atonement**[3389] to their **unrighteousness**, and their sins and their **lawlessness** not **I-will**-remember **still**.

13 In that he says, a **New Covenant,** he has made the **foremost, antique,** and **senile-aged, near-squeeze disappeared**.

[3373] Or, lit., change-care
[3374] Or, pledge, as if articulated by a member
[3375] Or, non-transgressed
[3376] Or in-obtain. in-to hit the target, in-chance upon
[3377] Greek compound: **great** (big) and sun (together); Big-togetherness, great-togetherness
[3378] Lit., laos (people)-ergon (work); "liturgist"
[3379] Copy, example
[3380] Greek: "chrematizo," to furnish what is needed, divine response; secular: constituting a business, to give notice, state of affair, inform
[3381] Or do
[3382] Greek: "tupos" transliterated as "type," a die (as struck)
[3383] Greek: "phemi," the root word for fame ("pheme")
[3384] Or, hit the mark, chance upon, obtain,
[3385] Greek: "diaphero," to through-bear, "differ" or "different"
[3386] Lit., laos (people)-ergon (work); "liturgy"
[3387] Or, law-placed
[3388] Or, lit., through-place
[3389] Greek: "hileos" associated with "hilasterion," (Mercyseat) an expiatory place, atone, conciliate

HEBREWS CHAPTER 9

1 Then **indeed** the **foremost** had also **righteous-deeds of-hired-service**, and a worldly[3390] **holy-place**.

2 For there was a tabernacle **constructed**; the **foremost, in which** was the candlestick, and the table, and the **pre-placement**[3391] **of-the breads**; which is called the **holy-place**.

3 And after the second veil, the tabernacle which is called the **Holy of-Holies**

4 Which had the golden censer, and the **Ark** of the Covenant overlaid **every-which** with gold, **in which** was the golden pot[3392] that had manna, and Aaron's rod that **sprouted**, and the **plates**[3393] of the covenant.

5 And **up-over** it, the cherubs of glory shadowing the **Merry-Atonement**, of which we cannot now speak **down section.**

6 Yet, when **these-things** were **in-this-way constructed**, the priests went always into the **foremost** tabernacle, **upon-finishing** the **hired-service** of God.

7 Yet, into the second went the **first-rank-priest** alone once, **yearly**, not **spaced-from** blood, which he offered for himself, and for the **ignorance** of the people:

8 This, the **Holy Spirit making-clear** that the way into the **holies not-yet shined** while the **foremost** tabernacle was standing:[3394]

9 Which was a **parable into the season** then present, **down** which were offered both gifts and sacrifices, that **not is-powerful** to-**mature** him that did the **hired-service, down** the conscience.

10 Only in **foods** and drinks, and **different**[3395] **baptisms,** and **righteous-deeds of-flesh**, upon-laid them until the **season** of reformation[3396].

11 Yet, Christ being come an **Original-Priest** of good things **impending**, by a **great** and **mature** tabernacle, not made with hands, that is to say, not of this **creation.**

12 Neither **through** the blood of goats and calves, **yet, through** his own blood he entered once into the **holies**, having **found eternal loosing.**

13 Because, if the blood of bulls and of goats, and the ashes of a heifer sprinkling the **common**, sanctifies **towards the cleaning** of the flesh:

14 How much more shall the blood of Christ, who through the **eternal** Spirit offered himself **un-blamed to-the** God, **clean** your conscience from dead works **to-be-hired-service to-the** living God?

15 And **through this,** he is the Mediator of the **New Covenant,** that by means of death, **into from-loosing** of the **beside-steps** that were under the **foremost covenant**, they which are called might **take the** promise **of-the eternal** inheritance.

16 For where a **covenant** is, there must also of **necessity** be the death of the **one-being-covenanted**.

17 For a **covenant** is **stable** after men are dead; otherwise, it is of no **force** at all while the **one-being-covenanted** lives.

18 Which-place neither the **foremost covenant** was **in-fresh-new**[3397] **spaced-from** blood.

19 Because when Moses had spoken every **in-finish**[3398] to all the people **down** the law, he **took** the blood of calves and of goats, with water, and scarlet wool, and hyssop, and sprinkled both the **little-scroll** and all the people.

20 Saying, this is the blood of the **covenant** which God has **in-finished towards** you.

21 And yet, he sprinkled with blood both the tabernacle, and all the vessels of the **of-the people-work.**[3399]

22 And almost all things **are-being-cleaned in** blood **down** the law; and **spaced-from blood-out-pouring, not is-becoming release.**[3400]

23 It was therefore **necessity** that the **under-show** of things in the heavens should be **cleaned** with these; **yet** the heavenly things themselves with **better-government** sacrifices **beside** these.

24 Because, Christ is not entered into the **holies** made with hands, which are the **antitype** of the true; but into

---

[3390] Kosmikos: pertaining to a ordered system, as opposed to a particular part, systemic (set of things working together)
[3391] Lit., before-place, or to place in advance, purposed
[3392] Greek: "stamnos," compare English "stamina."
[3393] Greek: "plax," English, "plate"
[3394] The Greek word for "standing" ("stasis") is also translated as insurrection in the New Testament.
[3395] Greek: "diaphero," to through-bear, transliterated as "differ" or "different"
[3396] Lit., through-erecting, to straighten thoroughly
[3397] Dedicated, inaugurated
[3398] Or, in-limit, commandment
[3399] Lit., laos (people)-ergon (work); "liturgy"
[3400] To from-let-go

heaven itself, now to **emphasize**[3401] in the **face** of God **over** us:

25 Nor yet that he should offer himself **often**, as the **original-priest** enters into the **holies according-to years in** blood of **another's**.

26 For then **it-is-binding** he often **to-emotion from** the **down-casting** of the world; **yet** now once, **upon together-finish** of the **ages,** has he **shined** to **un-place**[3402] sin **through** the sacrifice of himself.

27 And as it is **from-laid**[3403] **to** men once to die, **yet,** after this the **judgment.**

28 So Christ was, once, offered **into the up-carrying** of many sins; and **to-them from-out-of-welcome** him, **shall-he-be-viewed out-of** second, **spaced-from** sin, **into** salvation.

HEBREWS CHAPTER 10

1 For the law having a shadow of good things **impending,** and not the selfsame image of the **practices,** never **is-powerful** with those sacrifices which they offered **down yearly, through-carry to-**make the **towards-comers mature.**

2 Thereupon, would they not have **paused** to be offered? **Through the not-any should-still have conscience of sins,** the **hired-servants,** once **cleaned.**

3 But in those, is an **up-reminding** of sins **down yearly.**

4 Because un-powerful the blood of bulls and of goats **to-be-from-lifting** sins.

5 Through-which, when he **comes** into the world, he says, sacrifice and offering **not you-willed,** but a body you have **down-fresh**[3404] **to-**me:

6 In **whole-burnt-offerings** and sacrifices for sin, **not you-good-seem.**

7 Then said I, **be-perceiving, I-am-arriving** (in the volume of the **little-scroll** it is written of me,) to do your will, God.

8 Above when he said, sacrifice and offering and **whole-burnt-offerings** and **about** sin, you-**willed** not,

neither had **good-seem**, which are offered **down** the law.

9 Then said he, **be-perceiving, I-am-arriving** to **produce** your will, God. He **up-lift**[3405] the **foremost,** that he may **stand** the second.

10 In which will, we **have-been-sanctified** through the offering of the body of Jesus Christ **upon-once.**

11 And every priest **stands** daily, **people-working,**[3406] and offering oftentimes the same sacrifices, which never **is-powerful to-about-lift**[3407] sins:

12 But this man, after he had offered **first** sacrifice **over** sins, **into the through-carry, seated in** the right hand of God.

13 The remaining-ones out-of-welcoming until his **haters be-placed a-footstool of-his feet.**

14 Because **to-first** offering, he has **matured into the through-carry** them that are sanctified.

15 Yet, the Holy Spirit also is a witness **to-us, after: because** he **before-said,**

16 This is the covenant that I will **covenant towards** them after those days, says the Lord, **giving** my laws **upon** their **hearts**, and **upon** their **deep-thoughts**[3408] will I write them;

17 And their sins and **lawlessness I will not** remember, **still.**

18 Now where **release**[3409] of these is, there is no more offering **about** sin.

19 Having therefore, **brothers, all-speech** to enter into the holiest by the blood of Jesus,

20 By a **freshly-slain**[3410] and living way, which he has **dedicated** for us, through the veil, that is to say, his flesh;

21 And having a **Priest, Mega,** over the **House of God;**

22 Let us draw near with a true **heart** in **full-burden** of faith, having our **hearts** sprinkled from **consciousness of-wicked-hurtful**, and our bodies washed with **clean** water.

[3401] Greek: "emphanizo," "emphasize"
[3402] Or cancel
[3403] Or, reserved
[3404] Or down-equip, adjust, repair, frame
[3405] A violent taking away; lit., assassination
[3406] Lit., laos (people)-ergon (work); i.e., "liturgy"
[3407] To remove all around
[3408] Lit., through-mind
[3409] To from-let-go
[3410] Greek: towards-slain, recently slain, freshly-slain

23 Let us **down-hold** the **same-saying** of our **expectation** without wavering; (for he is **believing** that promised;)

24 And let us **down-thought**[3411] **another-same** into **sharpen-beside of-love** and **of-good** works:

25 Not **in-down-leaving** the **together-assembling of-themselves,** as the **ethics** of some; but **beside-calling**: and so much more, as you see the day **near-squeezing.**

26 Because, if we sin **voluntarily** after that we have **taken** the knowledge of the truth, there remains no more sacrifice **about** sins,

27 But a certain fearful **out-of-welcoming** of **judging** and fiery **zealousness, impending to-devour** the **under-contrary.**[3412]

28 He that **un-placed** Moses' law died **spaced-from** mercy under two or three witnesses:

29 Of how much **seem-you worse,** shall he be-**deserving worth-guardian,**[3413] who has **trample-down** the Son of God, and has **lead** the blood of the **Covenant, in which** he was sanctified, **common,** and has **insulted** the Spirit of **Grace?**

30 For we **perceive** him that has said, vengeance belongs **to-me, I**[3414] will **repay,**[3415] says the Lord. And again, the Lord shall judge his people.

31 It is a fearful thing to fall into the hands of the living God.

32 But call to remembrance the former days, in which, after you were illuminated, you **under-remain many struggles**[3416] of **emotions**;

33 This indeed, while you were made a **theater** both by **defamation** and **tribulations**; and while you became **communion** of them that were **overturned.**

34 Because you had **sympathy**[3417] of me in my bonds, and **towards-welcome** joyfully the **snatching** of your **belonging,** knowing in yourselves that you have in heaven a **better-government** and a **remaining belonging.**

35 Cast not away therefore your **all-out-spoken,** which has **great wages-from-give.**

36 Because, you have need of **under-remain,** that, after you have **produced** the will of God, you might **be-provided** the promise.

37 For yet a little while, and he that **is-coming** will **arrive** and **not shall-be-delayed-uninterrupted-time.**

38 Now the **righteous** shall live **out-of** faith: but if any man **under-stall,** my soul shall have no **well-seem** in him.

39 But we are not of them who **under-stall to from-ruin**; but of them that believe to the **around-make**[3418] of the soul.

HEBREWS CHAPTER 11

1 Yet faith is the **substructure**[3419] of things **expected,** the **exposing** of **practices** not seen.

2 Because in this, the elders **witnessed.**

3 To-faith we-mind that the **ages** were **down-fresh with-Declaration**[3420] of God, so that things which are seen were not **become out-of** things which do **shine.**

4 To-faith Abel offered **to-God** more sacrifice than Cain, by which he witnessed that he was righteous, God **witnessing** of his gifts: and **through** it, he being dead yet speaks.

5 To-faith Enoch was translated that he should not see death; and was not found, because God had translated him: for before his translation he had this **witness,** that he pleased God.

6 But **spaced-from** faith **un-powerful** to please him: for he that **comes** to God **it-is-binding to-**believe that he is, and that he **is-becoming a Rewarder**[3421] of them that **out-of-seeking** him.

7 To-faith Noah, being **apprised**[3422] of God of things not seen as yet, **well-take-it, constructed** an Ark to the saving of his house; by the which he **down-judge** the world, and became heir of the **righteous-togetherness** which is **down** faith.

[3411] To think from up to down to a conclusion
[3412] Or, under-in-anti, under-opposite
[3413] Worth-assigned guardian that punishes
[3414] Ego-self-esteem, self-importance
[3415] Greek: instead-from-give
[3416] Or, athletics, contend, strive, compete
[3417] Or together-emotion
[3418] Greek: peri (around) and poieo (make, produce), means to purchase, acquire
[3419] Greek: "hupostasis," under-stand," substrate
[3420] Dative case: to-Declaration or with-Declaration
[3421] Greek compound: pay-from-giver
[3422] Greek: "chrematizo," to furnish what is needed, divine response (oracle); secular meaning of constituting a business, employ, to bears as a title, to apprise (to give notice, state of affair, inform)

8 To-faith Abraham, when he was called to go out into a place which he **is-impending to-take** for an inheritance, **under-heard**;³⁴²³ and he went out, not **acquainted**³⁴²⁴ where he went.

9 To-faith he **foreign-stranger** in the land of promise, as in a **another's-same**, **down-housing**³⁴²⁵ in tabernacles with Isaac and Jacob, the heirs with him of the same promise:

10 Because, **he-out-welcome** a city which has foundations, whose **Technician** and **Public-Worker** is God.

11 To-faith also Sara herself **took** strength to **down-cast** seed and **took** a child when she was **beside season of-prime**,³⁴²⁶ because she **leads** him **believing** who had promised.

12 Through which were-birthed, from one, and him, as dead, so many as the stars of the **heaven** in **fullness**, and **as-if** the sand which is by the shore **of-the** sea **un-numbered**.

13 These all died in faith, not having **taken** the promises, but having **perceived** them afar off, and were persuaded of them, and **embrace** them, and **same-say** that they were **foreign-lodgers** and **foreign-sojourner**³⁴²⁷ upon the earth.

14 For they that say such things **emphasize**³⁴²⁸ that they seek a **father-country**.

15 And **indeed**, if they **remembered** from **where** they came out, they might have had **season** to have **up-bend**.

16 But now they **stretch-for** a **better-government**, that is, a heavenly: **through-which** God is not **upon-disfigured** to be **upon-called**³⁴²⁹ their God: for he has **internally-prepared** for them a city.

17 To-faith Abraham, when he was **probe-tested**, offered up Isaac: and he that had **up-welcomed** the promises offered up his **only-born**,

18 Of whom it was said, that in Isaac shall your seed be called:

19 Inventorying that **the** God was **powerful to awake, also out-of** the dead; from **where** also he **provided-for** him in a **parable**.

20 To-faith Isaac blessed Jacob and Esau **about** things **impending**.

21 To-faith Jacob, when he was a dying, blessed both the sons of Joseph; and worshipped, leaning upon the top of his **rod**.

22 To-faith Joseph, when he **finished**, **reminded about** the exodus³⁴³⁰ of the **sons** of Israel; and gave commandment **about**³⁴³¹ his bones.

23 To-faith Moses, when he was born, was **hidden** three months of his parents, because they saw he was an **urban**³⁴³² child; and they were not afraid of the king's **through-arrangement**.

24 To-faith Moses, when he **became great**, **contradicts** to be called the son of Pharaoh's daughter;

25 Preferring, rather, **to-be-together-evil-hold** with the people of God, than **having from-enjoyment**³⁴³³ **of-sin toward-**season.

26 Leading the **defamation of-the** Christ **great** riches, than the **placed-into-tomorrow** in Egypt: **because** he **from-looked** into the **pay-from-giving**

27 To-faith he forsook Egypt, not fearing the **sacrifice-anger** of the king: for he **governed**, as seeing him who is invisible.

28 To-faith he **does**³⁴³⁴ the **Passover**, and the sprinkling of blood, **that not the destroyer**³⁴³⁵ **of-the** firstborns should **finger-handle** them.

29 To-faith they **through-step** the Red sea as **through** dry land: which **probe-testing took** the Egyptians drowned.

30 To-faith the walls of Jericho fell, after they were **encircled upon** seven days.

31 To-faith the **prostitute** Rahab not **together-ruined** with **those unpersuaded**, when she **welcomed** the spies with peace.

---

³⁴²³ Or obey
³⁴²⁴ Greek: upon-stand, to put the mind upon, to be acquainted with, comprehend, be present
³⁴²⁵ Or, permanently dwelling
³⁴²⁶ Or, stature, age, as big as, how much
³⁴²⁷ Lit., beside-upon-public, to reside in a foreign country
³⁴²⁸ Greek: "emphanizo" also transliterated as "emphasize"
³⁴²⁹ Or, to entitle, to invoke

³⁴³⁰ Lit., out-road
³⁴³¹ Lit., peri
³⁴³² Greek: "asteios" (urban or city), developed genteel, polished, comely; Acts 7:20
³⁴³³ Lit., "apo" (from) and "lauo" (enjoy), full enjoyment
³⁴³⁴ Or, to make
³⁴³⁵ Or whole-ruining-one

32 And what shall I more say? **Because time is-upon-lacking** me to **through-lead** about of-Gideon, and **of-Barak**, and **of-Samson**, and **of-Jephthae**; of-David also, and Samuel, and **of-the** prophets:

33 Who through faith **down-agonize**[3436] kingdoms, worked **righteous-togetherness, upon-happened** promises, **fenced** the mouths of lions,

34 Extinguished the power of fire, escaped the edge of the sword, out of weakness were made **powerful**, became forceful in battle, **declined**[3437] the **battle-array**[3438] of **foreign-strangers**.

35 Women **took** their dead raised to life again: and **others-same** were **stretched-beaten**,[3439] not **towards-welcoming from-loosing**; that they **may-happen**[3440] **of-better-government** resurrection:

36 And **others-different took** trial **of-in-childish-mockery**[3441] and **whipping, yet still**, of **chains-bound** and imprisonment:

37 They were stoned, they were sawn, were **probe-tested**, were **murdered in** the sword: they **about-going** in **sheep-skins** and **goat skins**; being **late-last, troubled, evil-holdings**;

38 (Of whom the world was not **deserving**:) they wandered in **lonesome**, and in mountains, and in **caves** and **holes** of the earth.

39 And these all, **being-witnessed** through **the** faith, not **provided** the promise:

40 God **before-looked** some **better-government** for us, that they **spaced-from** us should not be **matured**.

HEBREWS CHAPTER 12

1 Indeed-because-then we are also **laid-about** with **so-much** cloud of witnesses, let us **from-place** every **bending-mass**, and **the popular**[3442] sin, and through **under-remaining be-running** the **agony**[3443] that is **laid**-before us,

2 Looking **to** Jesus the **Origin-Leade**r and **Mature-one** of our faith, who for the **cheerfulness** that was **before-laid** him **under-remained** the cross, **down-dispositioned** the **disfigurement**, and **sat-down** in the right hand of the throne of God.

3 Because, up-inventory him that **under-remain** such **anti-word** of sinners against himself, **that not** you be **toil**-weary and **out-of-loosed** in your **souls**.

4 You have not yet **instead-down-stand until** blood, **agonizing towards** sin.

5 And you have forgotten the **beside-calling** which **through-saying**[3444] **to-you** as **to-sons**, my son, not **little-care**[3445] the **boy-training** of the Lord, nor **out-of-loosed** when you are **evidence-exposed** of him:

6 For whom the Lord loves he **boy-trains** and **whips** every son whom he **beside-welcomes**.

7 If you **under-remain boy-training**, God **towards-carry** you as sons, **because** what son is he whom the father **boy-trains** not?

8 But if you be **spaced-from boy-training**, whereof all are **partners**,[3446] then are you bastards,[3447] and not sons.

9 Furthermore we have had fathers of our flesh which **boy-trains** us, and we gave them **invert**: shall we not much rather be **subordinate**[3448] **to** the Father of spirits, and live?

10 For they **indeed** for a few days **boy-train** us **down** their **seeming**; but he for **bearing-together**, that we might be **change-take** of his holiness.

11 Now, no **boy-training** for the present seems to be **cheerful**, but **distress-sadness**: nevertheless, **later** it **gives** the peaceable fruit of **righteous-togetherness to-them** which are **naked-exercised through her**.

12 Through-which up-erect the hands which hang down, and the **paralyzed** knees.

13 And **produce erect** paths for your feet, lest that which is **limping be-out-of-turned**, but let it rather be **cured**.

14 Chase peace with all men, and holiness, **of-which spaced-from** no man shall see the Lord:

[3436] Or down-struggle
[3437] Or route
[3438] Or, camp, barracks, battle-array
[3439] The Greek word "tumpanizo" (tympanum) carries the idea of beating a drum
[3440] Or, hit the mark, chance upon, obtain,
[3441] Greek compound: "empaiktes" (in-sport (mock) as a boy), root means a child as disciplined

[3442] Gk.: good (well)-about-standing, well-admired, much admired, skillfully surrounding (retard running)
[3443] Or a place of assemble as if led, from the root "ago," to lead
[3444] Say thoroughly, discuss
[3445] Lit., to have "little" regard
[3446] Lit., with-holders, with-have, sharers
[3447] Or spurious, illegitimate sons
[3448] Under-arranged

15 Being-bishops,[3449] not any man being-late-ones from the grace of God; not any root of bitterness,[3450] sprouting, in-mob[3451] you, and through this, many be stained.

16 Lest there be any paramour, or profane person, as Esau, who for first feeding, from-give[3452] his birthright.

17 For you are-aware how that afterward, when he would have inherited the blessing, he was from-seem:[3453] for he found no spot of change-thought, though he out-of-seek it with tears.

18 For you are not towards-come to the mountain being-rub-touched, and having-burned with fire, nor to gloom-cloud, and darkness, and sacrifice-storm,[3454]

19 And the echo of a trumpet, and the voice of declarations; which voice, they that heard refused that the word should not be added to-them:

20 (For they could not bear that which was through-stalling, and if so much as a wild-beast finger-handle the mountain, it shall be stoned, or down-shoot with a dart,

21 And so terrible was the phantom-appearing, that Moses said, I-am out-of-fear and in-tremors)

22 But you are toward-come to-mountain Sion, and to-city of the living God, the upon-heaven Jerusalem,[3455] and to an innumerable company of angels,

23 To the all-market-assembly[3456] and Church of the firstborns, which are written in heaven, and to God the Judge of all, and to the spirits of righteous-ones made-mature,

24 And to Jesus, the Mediator of the New Covenant, and to the blood of sprinkling, that speaks better-government than that of Abel.

25 See that you refuse not him that speaks. For if they escaped not who refuse him that apprised on earth, much more shall not we escape, if we turn away from him that speaks from heaven:

26 Whose voice then shook the earth; but now he has promised, saying, yet once more I quake not the earth only, but also heaven.

27 And this word, yet once more, make-it-plain the translating of those things that are shaken, as of things that are made, that those things which cannot be shaken may remain.

28 Through-which a kingdom which cannot be shaken we beside-took, let us have grace, through which we-are-hired-service, good-pleasing to-the God, with timidity-dread and well-taking:

29 For our God is a consuming fire.

HEBREWS CHAPTER 13

1 Let friendly-brother remain.

2 Be not forgetful to friendly-loge: for thereby some have foreign-lodged angels unawares.

3 Remember them that are in chains-bonds, as chain-bound with them; and them which evil-holding, as being yourselves also in the body.

4 Marriage is valuable in all, and the bed[3457] un-stained: but paramours and adulterers God will judge.

5 Let your behavior without-friend-of-money; and be content with such things as you have: for he has said, I will never up-send you, nor out-of-down-leave you.

6 So that we may boldly say, the Lord is my helper, and I will not fear what man shall do to me.

7 Remember them which lead you, who have spoken to-you the Word of God: whose faith imitate, up-theatre-spectate the exit of their behavior.

8 Jesus Christ the same yesterday, and today, and into the ages.

9 Be not carried about with various and foreign-lodger teachings. For it is a good thing that the heart be stabilized with grace; not with foods, which have not profited the ones-about-walking.[3458]

10 We have a sacrifice-place, whereof they have no authority to eat, the-ones hired-servants to-the tabernacle.

[3449] "Episkopeo" (upon-peer-about, upon-skeptic
[3450] Lit., acridity, pungent (sharp), taste or smell)
[3451] Or crowd
[3452] Or, to give away
[3453] Rejected, reprobate
[3454] Or, heat-storm, smoke-storm, anger-storm
[3455] "Hierosoluma"—priests-peace (hierou-priest, sacred) and salem (peace)
[3456] Or mass meeting
[3457] Greek: "koites" transliterated as "coitus," also means bed, the place of semen, physical union of male and female genitals
[3458] Or about-treading (a path)

11 For the bodies of those **living-ones**, whose blood is brought into the **Holies** by the **first-rank-priest** for sin, are burned **outside** the **camp**.

12 Through-which Jesus also, that he might sanctify the people with his own blood, **emotion outside** the gate.

13 Let us go forth therefore **to-him outside** the **camp**, bearing his **defamation**.

14 For here have we no **remaining** city, but we **are-upon-seeking the one-impending**.

15 Through him therefore let us offer the sacrifice of praise to God **through-all**, that is, the fruit of our lips **same-saying** his name.

16 But to **good-producing** and to communion forget not: for with such sacrifices God is **well-pleased**.

17 Be-persuaded to-them that **lead** you, and **under-yield**[3459] yourselves: for they **sleepless over** your souls, as they that must give **Word**, that they may **produce** it with **cheer**, and not with **groans**:[3460] **Because** that is **un-loosed-finish** for you.

18 Pray for us: for we trust we have an **ideal** conscience, in all things willing to **behave ideally**.

19 But **I-beside-call** you the rather to **produce** this, that I may be restored **to-you** the sooner.

20 Now the God of peace, that **up-leads out-of** the dead our Lord Jesus, that **Mega Shepherd** of the sheep, through the blood of the **Eternal Covenant,**

21 Make you **down-fresh** in every good work to **produce** his will, **producing** in you that which is **well-pleasing** in his sight, through Jesus Christ; to whom be glory **into the ages of the ages**. Amen.

22 And I **beside-call** you, **brothers**, **tolerate** the word of **beside-calling**: for I have written a letter **to-you** in **short** words.

23 Know you that our brother Timothy is **from-loosed**; with whom, if he comes shortly, I will see you.

24 Embrace all them that **stand-before** you, and all the saints. They **from** Italy **embrace** you.

25 Grace be with you all. Amen.

[3459] Or under-simulate, under-weak to

[3460] Or, straits, narrowness, obstacles

JAMES

JAMES CHAPTER 1

1 James, a **slave** of God and of the Lord Jesus Christ, to the twelve tribes **the through-scattered,**[3461] **cheer.**

2 My **brothers, lead** it all **cheerfulness** when you **about-fall** into **various probes-testing.**

3 Knowing, that the **seem-testing** of your faith **down-work under-remaining.**

4 But let **under-remaining** have **mature** work, that you may be **mature** and **whole-inherit,**[3462] **lacking** nothing.

5 If any of you lack wisdom, let him ask of God, that gives to all **single**[3463] and **defame** not; and it shall be given him.

6 But let him ask in faith, **not through-judging.** For he that **through-judges simulates**[3464] a **surge** of the sea, **by-the-wind** and tossed.

7 For let not that man **make-like** he shall **take** anything of the Lord.

8 A **double-soul** man unstable in all his ways.

9 Let the **humble** brother **boast** in that he is **elevated.**

10 But the rich, in **the humiliation of-him**, because as the flower of the grass he shall pass away.

11 For the sun is soon risen with a burning heat, but it withers the grass, and the flower **of-him out-of-falls,** and the grace of the **good-tower-up** of it **from-ruin;** so also, shall the rich man fades in his **travels.**

12 **Happy** the man that **under-remain probe-testing;** for when he is **seem-approved** he shall **take** the **victor's-crown** of life, which the Lord has promised **to-them** that love him.

13 Let no man say when he is **probe-tested,** I am **probe-rested** of God: for God cannot be **probe-tested** with evil, neither **probe-test** he any man:

14 But every man is **probe-tested,** when he is **out-of-induced** of his own **upon-feelings,** and **trick-bait.**

15 Then when **upon-feelings** has **together-take,** it **produces** sin: and sin, when it is finished, **from-pregnant** death.

16 **Not be-seduced,** my beloved **brothers.**

17 Every good gift and every **mature** gift is from above, and comes down from the Father of lights, with whom is no **mutation,** neither **reverting from-shade.**

18 **By-plan-counsel, he-from-pregnant** us with the **Word of Truth,** that we should be **some**[3465] **first-fruit** of his creatures.

19 **So-too,** my beloved **brothers,** let every man be swift to hear, slow to speak, slow to **swelling-anger.**

20 For the **swelling-anger** of man **down-work** not the **righteous-togetherness** of God.

21 **Through-which from-place** all **dirtiness** and **surplus** of evil, and **welcome** with **mildness** the **implanted** Word, which is **powerful** to save your souls.

22 But be you **poets-producers** of the **Word,** and not **hearers** only, **beside-inventorying** yourselves.

23 For if any be a **hearer** of the **Word,** and not a **poet,** he **simulates to-a-man down-thinking** his **genesis**[3466] face in a **mirror.**

24 Because he **down-minds** himself, and goes his way, and **soon** forgets what-**kind** of man he was.

25 But **whoever peer** into the **mature Law of-the Freedom,** and **beside-remain,** he being not a forgetful **hearer,** but a **poets-producers** of the work, this man shall be **happy** in his **producing.**

26 If any man among you seems to be religious, and bridles not his tongue, but **cheat** his own **heart;** this man's religion **is-empty.**[3467]

27 **Clean** religion and **un-soiled** before God and the Father is this, to **bishop**[3468] the **orphans:** and widows in their **tribulation,** to keep himself **un-stained** from the world.

JAMES CHAPTER 2

1 My **brothers,** have not the faith of our Lord Jesus Christ, of glory, with respect of persons.

[3461] Or, diaspora, dispersed
[3462] Acts 3:16; 1 Thessalonians 5:23
[3463] Haplotetes, the antonym of "diplous" meaning double
[3464] Or, imaged, weak to, yield (Strong's #1502, #1503, #1504)
[3465] Greek: "tina," and inflection of "tis," meaning "some" or any person or object
[3466] Or generation
[3467] Or, empty through unsuccessful search
[3468] Greek: upon-peer about, upon-skeptic,

2 For if there come **to-your synagogue** a man with a gold ring, in **radiant clothing**, and there come in also a poor man in **dirty clothing**.

3 And you **upon-gazed** him that wear the **radiant** clothing, and say **to-him**, sit you here **ideally**; and say to the poor, you stand there, or sit here under my footstool.

4 Are you not then **through-judging**³⁴⁶⁹ in yourselves, and are become judges of **wicked-hurtful through-inventory**?

5 **Hear**, my beloved **brothers**, has not God chosen the poor of this world rich in faith, and heirs of the kingdom which he has promised **to-them** that love him?

6 But you have **un-value** the poor. Do not rich men **down-dynasty** you, and **out-of-induced**³⁴⁷⁰ you **into criteria**?

7 Do not they blaspheme that **ideal** name **upon-called**³⁴⁷¹ **over you**?

8 If you **finish** the **Regal**³⁴⁷² **Law down** the Scripture, you shall love your neighbor as yourself, you do **ideally**.

9 But if you have respect to persons, you commit sin, and are **evidence-exposed** of the **Law** as **beside-steppers**.

10 For whoever shall **guard** the whole **Law**, and yet **trip** in one, he is **liable** of-all.

11 For he that said, do not **adultery**, said also, do not **murder**. Now if **you-adultery** not, yet if you **murder**, you are become a **beside-stepper** of the **Law**.

12 So speak you, and so **produce**, as they **impending to-be-judged** by the Law **of-Freedom**.

13 For he shall have **judging without-mercy**, that has showed no mercy; and mercy **down-boast of-judging**.

14 What **the** profit, my **brothers**, though a man say he has faith, and have not works? **Is-powerful the** faith **to-save** him?

15 If a brother or sister be naked, **under-originating**, and **lacking** daily food,

16 And one of you say **to-them**, depart in peace, be you warmed and **fodder**; **not** you give them not those things which are **necessary** to the body; what does profit?

17 Even so faith, if it has not works, is dead, **down herself**.

18 **Else** a man may say, you have faith, and I have works; show me your faith **spaced-from** ³⁴⁷³ your works, and I will show you my faith **out-of** my works.

19 You believe that there is one God; you do **ideally**. The **demons** also believe, and **bristle**.

20 But will you know, O **empty** man, that faith **spaced-from** works is dead?

21 Was not Abraham our father **made-righteous** by works, when he had offered Isaac his son upon the **sacrifice-place**?

22 See you how faith **together-word** with his works and **out-of the** works was **the** faith made **mature**?

23 And the Scripture was **filled** which says, Abraham believed **the** God, and it was **inventoried to-him** for **righteous-togetherness**; and he was called the Friend of God.

24 You see then how that **out-of** works a man **is-being-righteous,** and not **out-of** faith only.

25 **But also like-as,** was not Rahab, the **prostitute, made-righteous out-of** works, when she had **welcomed** the **angels**, and had sent out **another-different** way?

26 For as the body **apart-from** the spirit is dead; **in-this-way also,** faith **spaced-from** works is dead.

JAMES CHAPTER 3

1 My **brothers, become** not many **teachers, having-perceived** that we shall receive the **larger judgment-result.**³⁴⁷⁴

2 For in **much-things** we **trip** all. If any man **trips** not in word, **this-one mature** man, **powerful** also to bridle the whole body.

3 **Be-perceiving**, we put **bridles** in the horses' mouths **toward persuading them to-us**; and we **change-lead** their whole body.

4 **Be-perceiving** also the ships, **such-as-this, being-pushed** of **dry** winds, yet are they **change-lead** under

---

³⁴⁶⁹ Or discriminate
³⁴⁷⁰ Or drag out of
³⁴⁷¹ Or, to entitle, to invoke
³⁴⁷² Basilikos: regal, belonging to the sovereign
³⁴⁷³ Or., lit., room,
³⁴⁷⁴ Greek: krima, transliterated crime

a-small rudder,³⁴⁷⁵ wherever the **straighten rush-impulse.**

5 Even so, the tongue is a **micron** member, and **great-boaster.** Be-perceiving, a puny³⁴⁷⁶ fire **up-fasten-to a-statured forest!**

6 And the tongue **is-fire,** a world of **unrighteousness;** so is the tongue among our members, that it **stains** the whole body, and **blazing** the **wheel** of **genesis**; and **being-blazed** under the Gehenna.

7 For every **nature** of **wild**-beasts, and of birds, and of **reptiles,** and **of-things-in-salt,** is tamed, and has been tamed **to the nature** of mankind:

8 But the tongue **no-one is-powerful of-man to-**tame; an **un-down-hold** evil, full of **rust, death-carrying.**

9 In her bless we God, even the Father; and **in-her down-curse** we men, which are made after the similitude of God.

10 Out of the same mouth **is-out-coming** blessing and **down-cursing.** My **brothers,** these things **need** not **to-be-coming.**

11 Does a fountain send forth at the same place sweet and bitter?³⁴⁷⁷

12 Not is-powerful the fig tree, my **brothers,** bear olives? Or a **grape**-vine, figs? So, no fountain **produce** both salt water and fresh.

13 Who wise man and **adept**³⁴⁷⁸ among you? Let him show out of **ideal behavior** his works with **mildness**³⁴⁷⁹ of wisdom.

14 But if you have bitter **zealousness** and **stimulations,**³⁴⁸⁰ in your **hearts, down-boast** not, and **falsify** not **downing** the truth.

15 This wisdom descends not from above, but earthly, **soulish, demonical.**

16 For where **zealousness** and **stimulations,** there **instability,**³⁴⁸¹ and every **foul practice.**

17 But the wisdom that is from above is **foremost clean,** then peaceable, **upon-yield,**³⁴⁸² **good-persuasion,** full **of-mercy,** and good fruits, **un-through-judging,** and **un-hypocritical.**

18 And the fruit of **righteous-togetherness** is sown in peace of them that **producing** peace.

JAMES CHAPTER 4

1 Which-place polemic-battles and fighting **in** you? **Not within out-of** the **hedonism** of-you that war in your members?

2 You-on-feel and have not: you **murder,** and **zealous** to have, and **not powerful to-be-on-happening**: you fight and **polemic**-battle, yet you have not, because you ask not.

3 You ask, and **take** not, because you ask **evilly,** that you may **spend** upon your **hedonism.**

4 You adulterers and adulteresses, not you **heave-perceived** that the friendship of the world is **hate of-the God**? Whoever therefore **plan-counsel to-be** a friend of the world is the **hater** of God.

5 Do you **seem** that the Scripture says in vain, the Spirit that **down-house** in us **upon-yearn** towards **envy**?³⁴⁸³

6 But he gives **great** grace. **Through-which** he says, the God **against**-arrange the **over-shining-ones,**³⁴⁸⁴ but gives grace **to-humble-ones.**

7 Subordinate³⁴⁸⁵ yourselves **then** to God. **Anti-stand** the Devil, and he will flee from you.

8 Squeeze-near to God, and he will **squeeze-near to-you. Cleanse-your** hands, you sinners; and **make-clean-your hearts double-soul.**

9 Talent-test,³⁴⁸⁶ and **mourn-emotion,** and **sob**: let your laughter be turned to **mourning-emotions,** and **cheerfulness** to **down-shine**

10 Humble yourselves in the sight of the Lord, and he shall **elevate you.**

11 Not down-talk another-same, brothers. He that **down-talks of-brother,** and **judges** his brother, **down-talk** of the law, and judges the law: but if you judge the law, **you-are** not a **poets-producers** of the law, but a judge.

---

³⁴⁷⁵ Greek: pedalion transliterated as "pedal," a helm
³⁴⁷⁶ Or few
³⁴⁷⁷ Lit., irritating, unpleasant taste or smell, poison
³⁴⁷⁸ Lit., upon-place, as in to place the mind upon
³⁴⁷⁹ That which is pleasant to the senses
³⁴⁸⁰ Or to arouse curiosity (intrigue)
³⁴⁸¹ Greek: down-standing, unstable, confusion

³⁴⁸² Or upon-weak to, upon-yield
³⁴⁸³ Or, ill-will
³⁴⁸⁴ Or, appearing above others
³⁴⁸⁵ Under-arranged
³⁴⁸⁶ Talaiporos-Strong's define as weight-tested, balanced-tested; and Thayer defines as bearing-callous, full of callous

12 There is one **Legislator**, who is **powerful** to save and to **from-ruin**: who are you that judges **the another-different**?

13 **Be-leading** now, you that say, today or tomorrow we will go into such a city, and **produce** there **a year**, and **we-shall-be-merchandise**, and **shall-be-gaining**.

14 Who not **are-acquainted-with**[3487] **the-things of-the** tomorrow. For what your life? It is even a **mist that shines** for a **few, yet thereupon, it-un-shines**.

15 Instead, say you, if the Lord will, we shall live, and **produce** this, or that.

16 But now you **boast** in your **bragging**; all such boasting is **wicked-hurtful**.

17 Therefore **to-him having-perceived** to do **ideally**, and **produce** not, **to-him** it is sin.

JAMES CHAPTER 5

1 Be-leading now, you rich men, weep, and howl for your **talent-test**[3488] that shall **upon-come**.

2 Your riches are **putrefied**,[3489] and your garments are **moth-eaten**.

3 Your gold and silver are **down-rusted**; and the rust of them shall be a witness against you and shall eat your flesh as it were fire. You have **placed-into-tomorrow**[3490] in last days.

4 Be-perceiving, the **wages** of the **workers** who have **collected** your fields, **the-ones having-been-deprived, is-screaming**; and the **call-for-aid** of them which have reaped are entered into the ears of the Lord of **Armies**.

5 You-effeminate on the earth, and **you-voluptuous**; you have nourished your **hearts**, as in a day of **butchery**.

6 You have **down-righted, you-murdered** the **righteous**; he does not **against-arrange** you.

7 Be-long-sacrifice-anger, therefore, **brothers, until of-the presence** of the Lord. **Be-perceiving**, the **land-worker** waits for the **valuable** fruit of the earth, and has **long-sacrifice-anger** for it, until he **takes** the early and latter.

8 Be-long-sacrifice-anger; **establish** your **hearts**; for the **presence** of the Lord **near-squeezes**.

9 Groan not **brothers downing another-same**, lest you be **down-judged**: **be-perceiving**, the **Judge** stands before the doors.

10 Take, my **brothers**, the prophets, who have spoken in the name of the Lord, for an **under-show** of **evilly-emotion**, and of **long-sacrifice-anger**.

11 Be-perceiving, we count them happy which **under-remain**. You have heard of the **under-remaining** of Job and have seen the **finish** of the Lord; that the Lord is very **much-gut-compassions**, and **pity-merciful**.[3491]

12 But before all things, my **brothers**, swear not, neither by heaven, neither by the earth, neither by any other oath: but let your yes be yes; and no, no; lest you fall **under judging**.

13 Is any among you **evilly-emotion**? Let him pray. Is any **good-feeling**? Let him **play-music**.

14 Is any **weak** among you? Let him call for the elders of the Church; and let them pray over him, **oiling** him **with-olive-oil** in the name of the Lord:

15 And the prayer of faith shall save the **toil-tired**, and the Lord shall **awaken** him; and if he has **produced** sins, **it-will-release** him.

16 Out-of-same-saying[3492] the **beside-fall to-one-another-same**, and pray **for one-another-same, that you-may-be-cured**. The **in-working** prayer of a righteous man **forces** much.

17 Elijah was a man subject to **like-emotions** as we are, and **with-prayer he-prayed** that it might not rain: and it rained not on the earth by the space of three **years** and six months.

18 And he prayed again, and the heaven gave rain, and the earth **germinated** her fruit.

19 Brothers, if any of you **being-seduced** from the truth, and one **revert** him;

20 Be-knowing, that **the-one-reverting** a sinner **out-of seduction of-way of-him**, , shall save a soul **out-of** death, and shall **cover filling** of sins.

[3487] Greek: upon-stand, to put the mind upon
[3488] Talaiporos-Strong's define as weight-tested, balanced-tested; and Thayer defines as bearing-callous, full of callous
[3489] Or, rotted
[3490] "Thesauros," transliterated as thesaurus, treasure,
[3491] Pity: a feeling of sorrow and compassion caused by sufferings and misfortune
[3492] Confess

but **beside-gave** himself **to-him** that judges righteously.

24 Who his own self **up-carry** our sins in his body on the tree that we, **from-birth**³⁵¹³ **to-the** sins, should live **to-righteous-togetherness**: by whose **moles**³⁵¹⁴ you were **cured**.

25 For you were as sheep **seduced**; but are now **reverted upon** the Shepherd and **Bishop**³⁵¹⁵ of your souls.

1 PETER CHAPTER 3

1 Likewise, you wives, be **subordinate**³⁵¹⁶ **to-your private** husbands; that, if any **are-un-persuadable to-the Word**, they also may without the Word be **gained** by the **behavior** of the wives.

2 While they **upon-inspect** your **clean behavior in** fear.

3 Of-whom not let-it-be the outside of braiding of hair, and about-placing of gold, or putting-on of **world garments**.

4 But let it be the hidden man³⁵¹⁷ of the **heart,** in that which is not corruptible, even a **mild**³⁵¹⁸ and quiet³⁵¹⁹ spirit, which is in the sight of **the God extremely-expensive.**³⁵²⁰

5 Because, **in-this-way both-somewhere,** the holy women also, who **expected upon the** God, **cosmetic**³⁵²¹ themselves, being **subordinate to** their **private** husbands:

6 As Sara **under-heard** Abraham, calling him lord: whose **children** you are, **good-producing**, and are not afraid with any **alarm**.

7 Likewise, you husbands, **together-home** with them **down knowing**, giving **value to** the **feminine-wife,** as **to** the weaker vessel, and as being **together-heirs** of the grace of life; that your prayers be not **out-chopped**.

8 Yet the finish, be you all of **same-disposition, sympathetic**³⁵²² **friend-brothers, good-gut-compassions,** be **friendly-disposition**:

9 Not **giving** evil for evil, or **spear-abuse** for **spear-abuse**: but contrariwise **well-speaking**; **having-perceived** that **into this** you are called, that you should inherit blessing.³⁵²³

10 For he that will love life, and **perceive** good days, let him **pause** his tongue from evil, and his lips that they speak no **trick-bait**:

11 Let him **out-cline from** evil, and do good; let him seek peace, and **chase** it.

12 For the eyes of the Lord are over the righteous, and his ears are open **into** their **beg-binding**: but the face of the Lord is **upon** them that **produce** evil.

13 And who is he that will **evil** you, if you be **imitators** of that which is good?

14 But **also,** if you **emotion through righteous-togetherness**, happy are you: and be not afraid of their **fear,** neither be **agitated**;

15 But sanctify the Lord God in your **hearts**: and be **internally-prepared** always to give an **apology**³⁵²⁴ to every man that asks you a **word** of the **expectation** that is in you with **mildness** and fear:

16 Having a good conscience; that, **in which they-down-talk** you, as of **evil-producers**, they may be **down-disfigured** that **insult** your good **behavior** in Christ.

17 For it is **better-government,**³⁵²⁵ if the will of God be so, that you **emotion** for **good-producing,** than for **evil-producing**.

18 For Christ also has once suffered **about** sins, the **Righteous-One** for the **unrighteous-ones,** that he might **lead** us **to-the** God, **being-put-to-death to-flesh,** but **life-producer to-the** Spirit:

19 In which also he **traveled**³⁵²⁶ and preached **to-the** spirits in prison.

20 To-un-persuadable-ones, somewhere-both when the **long-sacrifice-anger** of God **from-welcome** in the days of Noah, while the **Ark** was **being-**

---

³⁵¹³ Greek compound from apo (from) and ginomai (birth, to become)
³⁵¹⁴ From Greek, molops (transliterated as mole-face or welt-face); and also means a "black eye," welt, or to soften (moisten) by beating or work
³⁵¹⁵ Greek: "episkopos" (upon-peer-about, upon watch, upon-goal, upon-mark), bishop, visitation, to visit, oversee, oversight, upon-skeptic
³⁵¹⁶ Under-arranged
³⁵¹⁷ Greek: "anthropos"—man-faced
³⁵¹⁸ That which is pleasant to the sense
³⁵¹⁹ Quietness by keeping one's seat
³⁵²⁰ Lit. much-finish
³⁵²¹ Greek: kosmeo, to put in proper order
³⁵²² Together-emotion
³⁵²³ Greek: "eulogetos" (good-speaking, well-speaking, good-word, well-word)
³⁵²⁴ Compound of "apo" (from) and logo (word, saying), also means defense
³⁵²⁵ Greek: "kreitton," a comparative derivative of "kratos;" translated as "cracy" in democracy—people (demo)-government ('cracy') (kratos))
³⁵²⁶ Or, traversed

constructing, **in which** few, that is, eight souls were saved **through** water.

21 Antitype **to-which** baptism does also now save us (not the **from-placing** of the **dirt** of the flesh, but the **inquiry** of a good conscience **into** God,) **through** the resurrection of Jesus Christ:

22 Who is **traveled** into heaven and is **in** the right hand of **the** God; angels and authorities and powers **subordinate to-him**.

1 PETER CHAPTER 4

1 Then, as Christ has **emotion** for us in the flesh, arm yourselves likewise with the same **in-thought**: for he that has **emotion** in the flesh has **paused** from sin;

2 Into the not-still to-men to-upon-feelings, but to-will of-God to remaining uninterrupted-time in flesh, livelihood

3 For **sufficient** the **beside-came uninterrupted-time** of our **livelihood**, the **plan-counsel** of the **nations** to have **down-work** traveled in **unrestrained-sensual-brutality upon-feelings** , wine-bubbles, laying-outstretched, drinking-bouts, and un-placed idolatries:

4 In which they-foreign-lodging you, not **of-together-racing into** the same **effusion** of **un-save**, blaspheming.

5 Who shall give word **to-him** that is **internally-prepared** to judge the **living** and the dead.

6 For **into this** was **evangelized** them that are dead, that **they-being-judged**[3527] **down** men **to-flesh** but live **down** God **to**-spirit.

7 But the **finish** of all things is **near-squeezing**; **be-saved-disposition**, and **sober into the prayers**.

8 And above all things have **out-stretched love** among yourselves: for **love** shall cover the multitude of sins.

9 Friendly-lodgers into one-another-same without **grumbling**.

10 As every man has **taken grace**, even so **attend** the same **into yourself**, as **ideal house-lawyers** of the **various grace** of God.

11 If any man speaks, as the oracles of God; if any man **attend**, let him do it as of the **force** which God **supplies**: that **the** God in all things may be glorified through Jesus Christ, to whom be **glory** and **government into the ages of the ages**. Amen.

12 Beloved, **not foreign-lodging to-the ignition**[3528] in you which **became probe-testing to-you**, as though **of-foreign-lodger together-walking with-you**:

13 But **be-cheerful**, inasmuch as you are **communion to-the** Christ's **emotions**; that, when his glory shall be revealed, you may be **cheerful jumping-for-joy**.

14 If you be **defamed**[3529] for the name of Christ, happy are you that the glory and **of-the** God Spirit **up-pause** you: **down indeed them**, he is **blasphemed**, but **down** yours he is glorified.

15 But let none of you **emotion** as a murderer, or as a thief, or as an **evil-producer**, or as **another-same-bishop**.

16 Yet, if any man **emotions** as a Christian, let him not be **disfigured**; but let him glorify **the** God **in this section**.

17 For the **season** is come that **judgment-result**[3530] must begin **from the House of God**: and if it **foremost** begin **from** us, what shall the **finish** be of-the **un-persuadable-ones to-the well-message** of-the God?

18 And if the righteous **difficultly is-being-saved**, where shall the **un-reverent** and the sinner **shine**?

19 So-that also, let them that **emotion down** the will of God **beside-place**[3531] their souls **to-him** in **good-producing**, as **to believing** Creator.

1 PETER CHAPTER 5

1 The elders which are among you I **beside-call**, who am also an elder, and a witness of the **emotions** of Christ, and also a partaker of the glory **impending to-be-revealed**:

2 Shepherd the **little-flock of-the** God, which is in you, **being-bishops**,[3532] not by **compulsion**, but **voluntarily**; not **disfigured-gain**, but **before-feeling**.

3 Neither as being **down-lords** over God's **inheritance**, but being **types** to the **little-flock**

4 And when the **Chief-Shepherd** shall **shine**, **you-shall-be provided** an **unfading victor's-crown** of glory.

[3527] Aorist, passive, third person
[3528] Firing, igniting
[3529] Lit., notorious, name
[3530] Greek: "krima," transliterated as "crime" and also means judgment
[3531] Or deposit
[3532] Greek: "episkopeo" (upon-peer-about, upon-watch, upon-goal, upon-mark, a sentry, a scout), visitation, to visit, oversee, oversight, upon-skeptic (see Hebrews 12:15 for the same word)

5 Likewise, you younger, **subordinate**[3533] yourselves to the elder. Yes, all of you be **subordinate to-one-another-same and** be humility-disposed in-girded: for God **against-arrange** the **above-shining-ones**,[3534] and gives grace to the humble.

6 Humble yourselves, therefore, under the **government** hand **of-the** God, that he may **elevate** you in **season**:

7 Casting all your **portion-worry** upon him; for he **is-interested about** you.

8 Be sober, be **awake**; because your **ant-righteous**,[3535] the Devil, as a roaring lion, walks about, seeking whom he may **swallow**:

9 Whom **anti-stand stiff**[3536] in the faith, **having-perceived** that the same **emotions** are **upon-finish** in your **brothers** that are in the world.

10 But the God of all grace, who has called us **into his eternal** glory, **in** Christ Jesus, after that you have **emotion a few, down-mend** you, **establish**, strengthen, **foundation-you.**

11 To him be glory and **government**[3537] **into the ages of the ages**. Amen.

12 Through Silvanus, a **believing** brother **to-you**, as **I-am inventorying**, I have written **a-few, beside-calling**, and **upon-witnessing** that this is the true grace of **the** God **into which you-have-stood.**

13 Embrace you, **she in** Babylon, **together-elected** and Marcus my son.

14 Embrace one-another-same with a **friendly-kiss** of **love**. Peace be with you all that are in Christ Jesus. Amen.

[3533] Under-arranged
[3534] Or, appearing above others
[3535] Lit., anti-just, opponent, instead of justice
[3536] Greek: steros (like steroids)
[3537] Greek: kratos vigor, strength, to use strength, to rule, government, translated as "cracy" in democracy—people(demo)-government (kratos)

2 PETER

2 PETER CHAPTER 1

1 Simon Peter, a **slave,** and an apostle of Jesus Christ, **to-them** that have **allotted**[3538] **equal-value** faith with us through the **righteous-togetherness** of-the God and our Savior Jesus Christ:

2 Grace and peace be multiplied **to-you in** knowledge **of-the** God, and of Jesus our Lord,

3 As his divine power has given **to-us** all things that **towards** life and **good-reverence,** through the knowledge of him that has called us **to-with-own** glory and **excellent-quality.**

4 Through which are given **to-us great** and **valuable** promises: that **through** these **you-may-become communing-ones** of the divine nature, having **from-fleeing** the corruption that is in the world through **on-feeling.**

5 And beside this, **beside-carry-inward** all **speed, supply to-you**r faith **excellent-quality**; and to **excellent-quality knowing.**

6 And to **knowing in-governing**;[3539] and to **in-governing under-remain**; and to **under-remain good-reverence.**

7 And to **good-reverence friendly-brothers**; and to **friendly-brothers love.**

8 Because, if these things **to-you under-originating,** and **more,** they make neither **idle** nor unfruitful in the knowledge of our Lord Jesus Christ.

9 Because he-whom is **not beside-present** these things is blind, and **closed-eyes,** and has forgotten that he was purged from his old sins.

10 Through-which the rather, **brothers, be-speedy** to make your calling and election **stable**: for if you do these things, you shall **no not trip**.

11 For so an entrance shall be **supplied to-you** richly into the **eternal** kingdom of our Lord and Savior Jesus Christ.

12 Through-which I will not be negligent to put you always in remembrance of these things, though you **perceived,** and be established in the present truth.

13 Yet, **righteous I-am-leading,** as long as I am in this tabernacle, **to-wake** you in remembrance.

14 Perceiving that **swiftly** I must put off my tabernacle, even as our Lord Jesus Christ has **made-clear to-me**.

15 Moreover **I-shall-be-speedy** that you may be able after my **exodus**[3540] to have these things always in remembrance.

16 For we have not followed cunningly devised **myths,** when we made known **to-you** the power and **presence** of our Lord Jesus Christ but were **on-viewers** of **that great.**[3541]

17 For he received from God the Father **value** and glory, when there came such a voice **to-him** from the **great-tower** glory, this is my beloved Son, into whom I am well **good-seem**.

18 And this voice which came **out-of** heaven we heard, when we were with him in the holy **mountain.**

19 We have also a more-**stable** word of prophecy; **to-which you are-**producing ideally that you **holding-ones,** as **to** a **lamp** that shines in a **dirty** place, until the day **through-shine,** and the **light-bringer** arise in your **hearts:**

20 Knowing this **foremost** that **every** prophecy of the Scripture **not is-becoming of-private upon-loosing.**[3542]

21 For the prophecy came not **at-any-place** by the will of man: but holy men of God spoke **being-carried** by the **Holy Spirit.**

2 PETER CHAPTER 2

1 And yet became false-prophets also **in** the people, even as there shall be **false-teachers in** you, who **beside-into-lead** in heresies[3543] **from-ruin,** even **contradicting** the **Owner** that bought them, and bring upon themselves swift **from-ruin.**

2 And many shall follow their **from-ruin** ways; **through** whom the **Way of Truth shall-be-blasphemed.**

3 And through **more-having** shall they with **molded**[3544] words make merchandise of you: whose **judgment-result**[3545] **not out-of-old is-non-working,** and their **from-ruin nods** not.

[3538] Greek: "lagchano" to chance, to determine by lot
[3539] Or self-control
[3540] Out-way
[3541] Greek: **great**leiotos
[3542] Greek: "epilusis," upon-loose, "explanation"
[3543] Personal choice, specific opinion
[3544] Greek is transliterated as "plastic."
[3545] Greek: "krima," transliterated as "crime" and also means judgment

4 For if God spared not the angels that sinned, but cast down to **Tartarus**, **beside-gave** into chains of **gloom**, to be **kept into judging**.

5 And spared not the **original** world, but **watched** Noah the eighth, a preacher of **righteous-togetherness**, bringing in the flood upon the world of the **un-reverent**;

6 And turning the cities of Sodom and Gomorrah into ashes **down-judged** with **a catastrophe, an-under-show to** those **impending having-placed un-reverencing**.

7 And **rush-rescue righteous** Lot, **down-pain** with the **unrestrained-sensual-brutality** behavior of the **un-placed**:

8 (For that righteous **in-down-housing in** them, in seeing and hearing, **tortured** righteous soul day **out-of** day with **lawless works**;)

9 The Lord **perceives** how to **rush-rescue** the **–good-reverencing-one** out of **probe-testing**, and **guarding** the **unrighteous-ones, being-punished**,[3546] **into** the day of **judging**:

10 But **very-much** them that walk **behind** the flesh in the **upon-feelings** of **contamination**, and **down-disposing lords. Daring, self-hedonism** they are not afraid to **blaspheme glories**.

11 **The-where** angels, which are greater in power and **force**, bring not **blasphemy judging** against them before the Lord.

12 But these, as natural **illogical living-ones, birthed for capture** and **corruption, blaspheme** the things that **they-are-ignorant-of**; and shall **be corrupted** in their own corruption.

13 And **shall-be-provided** the **wage** of **unrighteousness**, they that **lead hedonism** to **enfeeble**,[3547] in the day. **Stain** and blame, **in-enfeebling**, with their own **cheating together-good-having** with you.

14 Having eyes full of **adulteress**, and that **cannot-down-pause** from sin; **bait-tricking unfixed** souls: a **heart** they have **naked-exercised** with **more-having**; **down-cursed** children:

15 Which have **down-leave** the **well-placed**[3548] **Way**, and are **seduced**, following the way of Balaam[3549] of Bosor, who loved the **wage** of **unrighteousness**.

16 But was **evidence-exposed** for his **beside-law**;[3550] the dumb **donkey sounded** with man's voice **prevented** the **beside-disposition**[3551] of the prophet.

17 These are **fountains** without water, clouds **being-pushed** with a **whirlwind**; to whom the **gloom** of **the** darkness is reserved **into an-age**.

18 For when they **sound over-bulk**ed vanity, they **trick-bait** through the **upon-feelings** of the flesh, **to-unrestrained-sensual-brutality**, those that were **really** escaped from them who **behaved** in **seduction**.

19 While they promise them **freedom**, they themselves are the **slaves under-originating of-the** corruption: for of whom a man is **made-inferior**, of the same **has-been-slaved**.

20 For if after they have **fled** the **contamination** of the world **in** the knowledge of the Lord and Savior Jesus Christ, they are again **entwined**, and **made-inferior**, the latter end is worse with them than the beginning.

21 For it had been **better-government**[3552] for them not to have known the way of **the righteous-togetherness**, than, after they have known, to turn **out-of** the holy commandment **given to-them**.

22 But it is **together-walked to-them to-the** true **parable**, the dog turned to his **private** vomit; and the sow that was washed to her wallowing in the **mud**.

2 PETER CHAPTER 3

1 This second epistle, beloved, already **I-am-writing to-you**; in which **I-trough-wake** your **sun-judged deep-thoughts** by way of remembrance:

2 That you may **remember** the words which were spoken before by the holy prophets, and of the commandment of us the apostles of the Lord and Savior:

3 Knowing this **foremost**, that there shall come in the last days, **in-childish-mockers**,[3553] **traveling down** their **private upon-feelings**,

---

[3546] Middle voice, present tense
[3547] From the Greek word "thrupto" to break up or to enfeeble the mind and body by indulgences
[3548] Or **soon**
[3549] "Way of Balaam"-Num. 22:32 w/Num 22:22-32
[3550] Or outlawry

[3551] Or lit., insanity, mis-thinking
[3552] Greek: "kreitton," a comparative derivative of "kratos;" translated as "cracy" in democracy—people (demo)-government ('cracy' (kratos))
[3553] Greek compound: "empaiktes" (in-sport (mock) as a boy), root means a child as disciplined

4 And saying, where is the promise of his **presence**? For since the fathers fell asleep, all things **through-remaining** from the **original** of the creation.

5 For this they willingly **hide**, that **to-the Word of-the** God the heavens were **out-of-old,** and the earth **out-of** water and **through** water **together-stood**:

6 Through which the world that then was, being **down-surge** with water, **from-ruin**:[3554]

7 But the heavens and the earth, which are now, by the same **Word** are kept in store, reserved **to** fire **into** the day of **judging** and **from-ruin** of **irreverent** men.

8 But, beloved, be not **hidden** of this one thing, that **first**[3555] day with the Lord as a thousand **years**, and a thousand **years** as **first** day.

9 The Lord is not **slow** concerning his promise, as some men count **slowness**; but is **long-sacrifice-anger** to **into you** not willing that any should **from-ruin**, but that all should come to **changed-thought**.

10 But the day of the Lord **shall-arrive** as a thief in the night; in which the heavens shall pass away with a **booming-whirl**, and the **elements**[3556] **loosed** with fervent heat, the earth also and the works that are **in her** shall be **down-burned**.

11 Of-these like-this all shall be **loosed, from-where it-is-binding to-be-under-originating** you in holy **behavior** and **well-reverence**,

12 Toward-seeming and **speeding** the **presence** of the day **of-the** God, **through which** the heavens being on fire shall be **loosed**, and the **elements** shall melt with fervent heat?

13 Nevertheless we, **down** his promise, **towards-seeming new-fresh** heavens and a **new-fresh** earth, **in which down-homing righteous-togetherness**.

14 Through-which, beloved, seeing that you **toward-seem** such things, **be-speed**y that you may be found of him in peace, **un-stained**, and blameless.

15 And **of-the long-sacrifice-anger** of our Lord salvation; even as our beloved brother Paul also **down** the wisdom given **to-him** has written **to-you.**

16 As also in all epistles, speaking in them **about** these things; in which are some things **difficult-to-thought**, which they that are **un-discipled** and **unfixed** twist, as also the other **Scriptures**, **to** their own **from-ruin**.

17 You **then**, beloved, **before-knowing**, **watch that not** you also, **being-lead-off-together** with the **seduction** of the **unplaced**, **out-of-fall** your **private stability**.

18 But grow in grace, and knowledge of our Lord and Savior Jesus Christ. To him **the** glory both now and **into** day **of-age**. Amen.

[3554] Greek: "apo" (from) and "alethros" (ruin), to destroy fully
[3555] Or lit., "first" (Greek: mia) in both places in this verse
[3556] Or, any first thing, something orderly in arrangement (Gal 4:3, 4:9; Col 2:8, 20; Heb 5:12; 2 Peter 3:10, 12; compare Acts 21:24, Rom 4:12, Gal 5:25, Gal 6:16, Phil 3:16)

1 JOHN

1 JOHN CHAPTER 1

1 That which was from the **origin**, which we have heard, which we have seen with our eyes, which we have **gazed**, and our hands have handled, **about** the Word of life;

2 (For the life **shined**, and we have seen it, and bear witness, and show **to-you** that **eternal life**, which was with the Father, and **shined to-us**).

3 That which we have seen and heard we **from-message to-you**, that you also may have **communion** with us: and truly our **communion** is with the Father, and with his Son Jesus Christ.

4 And these things we write **to-you**, that your **cheerfulness** may be full.

5 This then is the message which we have heard of him, and **up-message to-you**, that **the** God is light, and in him is no darkness at all.

6 If we say that we have **communion** with him, and walk in darkness, we **falsify**, and do not the truth:

7 But if we walk in the light, as he is in the light, we have **communion** with **one-another-same**, and the blood of Jesus Christ his Son cleans us from **every** sin.

8 If we say that we have no sin, we **seduce** ourselves, and the truth is not in us.

9 If we **same-say** our sins, he is **believing** and **righteous** to **release**[3557] us our sins, and to cleans us from all unrighteousness.

10 If we say that we have not sinned, **we-produce** him a **falsifier**, and his **Word** is not in us.

1 JOHN CHAPTER 2

1 My **children**, these things I write **to-you**, that you sin not. And if any man sin, we have a **Beside-Caller** with the Father, Jesus Christ the **Righteous-One**:

2 And he is the **Merry-Atoner**[3558] for our sins: and not for ours only, but also for the sins of the whole world.

3 And **in this** we know that we know him if we keep his commandments.

4 He that says, I know him, and keeps not his commandments, is a **falsifier**, and the truth is not in him.

5 But **whoever** keeps his **Word**, in him **truly** is the love **of-the** God **matured**: **in this** know we that we are in him.

6 He that **says he remains** in him **owes down-as** that-one about-walked, he this-way about-walk.

7 **Brothers**, I write no **new-fresh** commandment **to-you**, but an old commandment which you had from the **origin**. The old commandment is the word which you have heard from the **origin**

8 Again, a **new-fresh** commandment I write **to-you**, which thing is true in him and in you: because the darkness is past, and the true light **already** shines.

9 He that **he says** is in the light, and **detest**-hates his brother, is in darkness even until now.

10 He that loves his brother abides in the light, and there is no **scandal**[3559] in him.

11 But he that **detest-hates** his brother is in darkness, and walks in darkness, and knows not where he goes, because that darkness has blinded his eyes.

12 I write **to-you**, **children**, because your sins are **release**[3560] you **through his name**.

13 I write **to-you**, fathers, because you have known him that is from the **origin**. I write **to-you**, **young**, because you have **conquered**[3561] the **wicked-hurtful**. I write **to-you**, **children**, because you have known the Father.

14 I have written **to-you**, fathers, because you have known him that is from the **origin**. I have written **to-you**, young men, because you are strong, and the **Word of God remains** in you, and you have **conquered** the **wicked-hurtful**.

15 Love not the world, neither the things that are in the world. If any man loves the world, the love of the Father is not in him.

16 For all that is in the world, the **upon-feelings** of the flesh, and the **upon-feelings** of the eyes, and the **bragging** of **livelihood**, is not **out-of** the Father, but is **out-of** the world.

[3557] Lit., from-let-go
[3558] Greek: "hilasmos" associated with "hilasterion," an expiatory place, atoning-one, conciliate; can translated as the "Mercyseat."
[3559] Or, lit., a bent trap stick, snare
[3560] Lit., from-let-go
[3561] "Nikao," to defeat an enemy

17 And the world passes away, and the **upon-feelings of-him**: but he that **produces** the will of God **remains into the age**.

18 Children, it is the last **hour**: and as you have heard that antichrist shall come, even now are there many antichrists; whereby we know that it is the last **hour**.

19 They **out-of-came out-of** us, but they were not **out of-**us; for if they had been **out-of** us, they would no doubt have **remained** with us: but they **out-of-came**, that they **shine** that they were not all **out-of us**.

20 But you have an **anointing** from the Holy One, and **you-have-perceived** all things.

21 Not I-have-written to-you because you **perceived** not the truth, but because you **perceived** it, and that **every falsehood** is **not out-of** the truth.

22 Who is a **falsifier,** but he that **contradicts** that Jesus is the Christ? He is antichrist that **contradicts** the Father and the Son.

23 Whoever **contradicts** the Son, the same has not the Father: **the one-same-saying** the Son has the Father also.

24 Let that therefore **remain** in you, which you have heard from the **origin**. If that which you have heard from the **origin** shall remain in you, you also shall **remain** in the Son, and in the Father.

25 And this is the promise that he has promised us, **the eternal life.**

26 These-things I-have-written to-you about them that seduce you.

27 But the anointing which you have **taken from** him **remains** in you, and you need not that any man **teaches** you: but as the **self-same** anointing teaches you **about** all things, and is truth, and is not **falsehood**, and **down-as** it has taught you, you shall **remain** in him.

28 And now, children, **remain** in him; that, when he shall **shine,** we may have **all-speech,**³⁵⁶² and not be **disfigured** before him **in his presence.**

29 If you know that he is righteous, you know that every one that does **righteous-togetherness** is born of him.

1 JOHN CHAPTER 3

1 Be-perceiving, what manner of love the Father has **given** upon us, that we should be called the **children** of God: therefore, the world knows us not, because it knew him not.

2 Beloved now are we the **children** of God, and not yet **shine** what we shall be: but **we-perceived** that, when he shall **shine**, we shall be like him; for we shall see him as he is.

3 And every man that has this **expectation** in him **cleanse** himself, even as he is **clean**.

4 Whoever producing the-her sin **also is- producing lawlessness**: for **the-her** sin is the **lawlessness**.

5 And **you-perceived** that he **shined to-lift** our sins; and in him is no sin.

6 Whoever remains in him sins not: whoever sins have not seen him, neither known him.

7 Children, let no man **seduce** you: he that **produces righteous-togetherness** is righteous, even as he is righteous.

8 The-one producing sin is **out-of** the Devil, for the Devil sins from the **origin**. **Into this** the Son of God **shined**, that **he-should-be-loosing** the works of the Devil.

9 Whoever is born **out-of the** God **not is-producing** sin; for his seed remains in him: and he **not is-powerful to-be-sinning,** because he is born **out-of the** God.

10 In this the children of God **shines**, and the children of the **Devil**: whoever **produces** not **righteous-togetherness** is not **out-of the** God, neither he that loves not his brother.

11 For this is the message that you heard from the **origin**, that we should love **one-another-same**.

12 Not as Cain, who was **out-of the wicked-hurtful** and **butchered** his brother. And **why butchered** he him? Because his own works were **wicked-hurtful** and his brother's righteous.

13 Marvel not, my **brothers**, if the world **detest-hate** you.

14 We know that we have passed **out-of** death **into the** life, because we love the **brothers**. He that loves not his brother **is-remaining** in death.

15 Whoever **detest-hate** his brother is a **man-faced-slayer**: and you know that no **man-face-slayer** has **eternal life remaining** in him.

---

³⁵⁶² Free speech

16 **In this we-know** the love, because he laid down his **soul over** us: and we **owe** to lay down our **souls over** the **brothers**.

17 But **whoever** has this world's **livelihood**, and see his brother have **employment-need,** and **locks** his **gut-compassions** from him, how **remains** the love of God in him?

18 My children, let us not love in word, neither in tongue; but **with-work** and **with-truth**.

19 And **in this** we know that we are **out-of** the truth and **shall-persuade** our **hearts** before him.

20 For if our **heart down-know** us, God is **larger**[3563] than our **heart,** and knows **all**.

21 Beloved, if our **heart down-knows** us not, then have we **all-speech** toward God.

22 And whatever we ask, we **take from** him, because we keep his commandments, and do those things that are **agreeable** in his sight.

23 And this is his commandment: that we should believe **to-the** name of his Son Jesus Christ, and love **one-another-same,** as he gave us commandment.

24 And he that keeps his commandments **remains** in him, and he in him. And **in this** we know that he **remains** in us, **out-of** the Spirit which he has given us.

1 JOHN CHAPTER 4

1 Beloved, believe not every spirit, but **seem-test**[3564] the spirits whether they are **out-of the** God: because many false prophets are gone out into the world.

2 In this know you the Spirit of God: every spirit that **same-saying** that Jesus Christ is come in the flesh is **out-of the** God:

3 And every spirit that **not same-saying** that Jesus Christ **came** in the flesh is not **out-of the** God: and this is **of-the** antichrist, **which** you have heard that **it-is-coming**; and **now** is already in the world.

4 You are **out-of the** God **children** and have **conquered**[3565] them: because **larger**[3566] is he that is in you, than he that is in the world.

5 They are **out-of** the world: therefore, **they speak out-of** the world, and the world hears them.

6 We are **out-of the** God: he that knows **the** God hears us; he that is not **out-of the** God hears not us. **Out-of this we-know** the Spirit of Truth, and the spirit **of-the seducer**.

7 Beloved, let us love one another: for love is **out-of the** God; and every one that loves is born **out-of the** God, and knows **the** God.

8 He that loves not **knew** not **the** God; for **the** God is love.

9 In this **shined** the love **of-the** God **in** us, because that **the** God sent his **only-born** Son into the world, that we might live through him.

10 In this is **the** love, not that we loved **the** God, but that he loved us, and sent his Son to be the **Merry-Atoner**[3567] for our sins.

11 Beloved, if **the** God so loved us, we **owe** also to love **one-another-same.**

12 No man has **gazed** God at any time. If we love one another, **the** God **remains** in us, and his love is **matured** in us.

13 In this we know that we **remain** in him, and he in us, because he has given us **out-of** his Spirit.

14 And we have seen and do **witness** that the Father sent the Son to be the Savior of the world.

15 Whoever shall **same-say** that Jesus is the Son of God, **the** God **remains** in him, and he in **the** God.

16 And we have known and believed the love that **the** God has **in** us. **The** God is love; and he that **remains** in **the** love **remains** in **the** God, and **the** God in him.

17 In this is love **matured with us**, that we may have **all-speech** in the **day of judging:** because as he is, so are we in this world.

18 There is no fear in **the** love; but **the mature** love casts out fear: because fear has torment. He that fear is not made **mature** in **the** love.

19 We love him, because he first loved us.

20 If a man say, I love **the** God, and **detest-hates** his brother, he is a **falsifier**: for he that loves not his brother whom he has seen, how **is-he-powerful to-love** God whom he has not seen?

[3563] Larger, especially in age
[3564] Test comes from a root word that means "to seem." Seem means the impression of being, that which appears to the observation of your understanding

[3565] "Nikao," to defeat an enemy
[3566] Larger, especially in age
[3567] Greek: "hilasmos" associated with "hilasterion," an expiatory place, atone, conciliate; can translated as the "Mercyseat."

21 And this commandment have we from him, that he who loves **the** God love his brother also.

1 JOHN CHAPTER 5

1 **Whoever** believes that Jesus is the Christ is born **out-of** God: and every one that loves him that **births** loves him also that is **birthed out-of** him.

2 By this we know that we love the children of God, when we love God, and **guard** his commandments.

3 For this is the love of God, that we keep his commandments: and his commandments are not **heavy**.

4 For **everything** born **out-of** God **conquers**[3568] the world: and this is the **conquest** that **conquers** the world, **the** faith **of-us**.

5 Who is he that **conquers** the world, but he that believes that Jesus is the Son of God?

6 This is he that came **through** water and blood, even Jesus Christ; not **in the** water only, but **in the** water and **the** blood. And it is the Spirit that witness because the Spirit is **the Truth.**

7 For there are three that **witnesses**.[3569]

8 The Spirit, and the water, and the blood: and these three **into the** one **exists**.

9 If we **take** the witness of men, the witness of-**the** God is **larger**:[3570] for this is the witness of-**the** God which he has **witnessed** of his Son.

10 He that believes **into** the Son **of-the** God has the witness in himself: he that believes not **the** God has made him a **falsifier**; because he believes not the **witness** that **the** God gave of his Son.

11 And this is the **witness** that **the** God has given to us **eternal life**, and this life is in his Son.

12 He that has the Son has **the** life; and he that has not the Son of God has not **the** life.

13 These things have I written **to-you** that believe **into** the name of the Son of God; that **you-may-perceive** that you have **eternal life**, and that you may believe **into** the name of the Son of God.

14 And this is the **all-speech** that we have in him, that, if we ask anything **down** his will, he hears us:

15 And if we-**perceived** that he hears us, whatever we ask, we-**perceive** that we have the **request** that we **ask** of him.

16 If any man sees his brother sin a sin which is not **towards** death, he shall ask, and he shall give him life for them that sin not **towards** death. There is a sin **towards** death: I do not say that he shall pray for **that**.

17 All unrighteousness is sin: and there is a sin not **towards** death.

18 **We-perceived** that everyone birthed **out-of the** God sins not; but he that is **born out-of the** God keeps himself, and that **wicked-hurtful not is-attaching of-him**.

19 And we-**perceived** that we are **out-of the** God, and the whole world **lays**[3571] in **the wicked-hurtful**.

20 And we-**perceived** that the Son of God is **arriving**, and has given us **deep-thought**,[3572] that we may know him that is true, and we are in him that is true, even in his Son Jesus Christ. This is the true God, and **the eternal life**.

21 **Children,** keep yourselves from idols. Amen.

[3568] "Nikao," to defeat an enemy
[3569] KJV add in heaven, the Father, the Word, and the Holy Spirit: and these three are one;" the oldest manuscripts excluded
[3570] Larger, especially in age
[3571] Greek: to lay outstretched in a horizontal passive position
[3572] Lit., through-mind

2 JOHN

2 JOHN CHAPTER 1

1 The elder **to** the elect **Lady**[3573] and her children, whom I love in the truth; and not I only, but also all they that have known the truth;

2 Through the truth which **remains** in us and shall be with us **into the age**.

3 Grace be with you, mercy, peace, **beside** God the Father, and **beside** the Lord Jesus Christ, the Son of the Father, in truth and love.

4 I-grace-cheered much that I found **out-of** your children walking in truth, as we have **taken** a commandment from the Father.

5 And now I **interrogate** you, **Lady**,[3574] not as though I wrote a **new-fresh** commandment to-you, but that which we had from the **origin**, that we love **one-another-same**.

6 And this is love that we **about-walk down** his commandments. This is the commandment, that, as you have heard from the **origin**, you should **about-walk** in it.

7 For many **seducers** are entered into the world, who confess not that Jesus Christ is **coming** in flesh. This is **the seducer** and **the** antichrist.

8 Look **to-yourselves**, that we **not from-ruin**[3575] those things which we have **worked**, but that we **from-take** a full reward.

9 Whoever **beside-steps**, and **remains** not in the **teaching** of Christ, has not God. He that **remains** in the **teaching** of Christ, he has both the Father and the Son.

10 If there come any **to-you**, and bring not this **teaching**, receive him not into house, neither bid him **grace-cheer:**

11 For he that **says to-him grace-cheer'** is **communion to-the works of-him, the wicked-hurtful**.

12 Having many things to write **to-you**, I would not with paper and ink: but I trust to come **to-you**, and speak **mouth** to **mouth**, that our **cheerfulness** may be full.

13 The children of your elect sister **embrace** you. Amen.

[3573] Greek "kuria" feminine of "kurios"-Lord, and "Lady" represents the corporate "Lady," the Church John writes to. There is also a "sister" corporate Church (see verse 13).

[3574] Greek "kuria" feminine of "kurios"-Lord
[3575] Greek: "apo" (from) and "alethros" (ruin), to destroy fully

3 JOHN

3 JOHN CHAPTER 1

1 The elder **to-the** beloved Gaius, whom I love in the truth.

2 Beloved, I **pray about** all things that you may prosper[3576] and be **healthy-growing, down-as** your soul prospers.

3 For I **cheered much**, when the **brothers** came and **witnessed** of the truth that is in you, even as you walk in the truth.

4 I have no **great cheerfulness of-these** than to hear that my children walk in truth.

5 Beloved, **believing, you-are-producing** whatever you **worked into** the **brothers**, and to **foreign-lodgers**;

6 Who **witnessed** of your love before the Church: whom if you **before-dispatch deserving of-the God**, you shall **produce ideally**:

7 Because that **over His name**, they went forth, taking nothing of the **nations**.

8 We therefore **owe to-from-take** such, that **together-workers we-may-be-becoming** to the truth.

9 I wrote **to-the** Church: but Diotrephes, who **friends-to-be-foremost of-them**, not **upon-welcome** us.

10 Through this, if I come, I will remember his **works** which he **produces, bubble-babbling** us with **wicked-hurtful** words: and not content **upon these**, neither he himself **upon-welcome** the **brothers**, and **prevents the-ones plan-counseling**, and **out-of-casts** them **out-of** the Church.

11 Beloved, **not imitate** that which is evil, but that which is good. **The good-producing** is **out-of** God: but **the evil-producing** has not seen God.

12 Demetrius **has-being-witnesses** of all, and of the truth itself: **Yet we also are-witnessing**; and you **perceive** that our **witness** is true.

13 I had many things to write, but I will not **through** ink and **reed**[3577] write **to-you**:

14 But I **expect** I shall **soon perceive** you, and we shall speak **mouth towards mouth**. Peace **to-you**. Our friends **embrace** you. **Embrace** the friends **down** name.

[3576] Lit., good-road, to help on the road

[3577] Or pen

JUDE

JUDE CHAPTER 1

1 Jude, the **slave** of Jesus Christ, and brother of James, **to-them** that are sanctified by God the Father, and **watched-guarded** in Jesus Christ, called.

2 Mercy **to-you**, and peace, and love, be multiplied.

3 Beloved, when I gave all **speed** to write **to-you** of the common salvation, it was **necessity** for me to write **to-you**, and **beside-call** that you should **into-struggle** for the faith which was once delivered **to-the** saints.

4 For there are certain men **beside-into-sink**,[3578] who were **before-written into** this **judgment-result**[3579], **irreverent** men, **translating** the grace of our God into **unrestrained-sensual-brutality**, and **contradicting** the only **Owner**, God, and our Lord Jesus Christ.

5 I will therefore put you in remembrance, though you **have-perceived** this, how that the Lord, having saved the people out of the land of Egypt, **the second, from-ruined**[3580] them that believed not.

6 And the angels which **watch-guarded** not their **origin**, but left their **private house-location**[3581] he has **watch-guarded** in everlasting[3582] chains under **gloom-cloud** to the **judging** of the **great** day.

7 Even as Sodom and Gomorrah, and the cities about them in like **turn, out-of-prostitutes,** and **from-going behind another-different** flesh, are **before-laid an example of eternal fire, the vengeance, under-holding.**

8 Likewise also these dreamers **contaminate** the flesh, **un-placing lords,** and **blaspheme glories**.

9 Yet Michael the archangel, when **through-judged** with the **Devil** he **through-said**[3583] about the body of Moses, **dare** not **judging to-bring-on** him **blasphemy**, but said, the Lord rebuke you.

10 But these **blaspheme** those things which they **perceived** not; but what they **are-acquainted**[3584] **physically**, as **illogical living-ones**, in **these** things they corrupt[3585] themselves.

11 Woe **to-them**! For they have **traveled** in the way of Cain, and **out-of-poured to-the** error of Balaam[3586] for reward, and **from-ruined**[3587] in the **anti-word** of **Korah.**

12 These are **reefs-ledge** in your **loves,** when they **festival** with you, **shepherding** themselves without fear; clouds without water, carried about of winds; trees **wane-late-hour,** without fruit, twice dead, plucked up by the roots.

13 Raging waves of the sea, foaming out their own **disfigurement; planet** stars, to whom is reserved the **gloom-cloud** of darkness **into the age.**

14 And Enoch also, the seventh from Adam, prophesied of these, saying, **be-perceiving**, the Lord comes **in** ten thousand of his saints.

15 To-do judging, downing of-all, and to **evidence-expose** all that are **irreverent about** them, of all their **irreverent works of-which they-are-irreverent**, and of all their **hard-dry**,[3588] which **irreverent** sinners have **talk-down of-him**.

16 These are **grumblers, blaming-fate,** walking after their own **upon-feelings,** and their mouth speaks **over-bulging-things, marveling faces of-useful-gain, through-favor.**[3589]

17 But, beloved, remember the **declarations** which were **before-spoken** of the apostles of our Lord Jesus Christ.

18 How that they told you there should be **in-childish-mockers**,[3590] in the last **uninterrupted-time,** who should walk after their own **irreverent upon-feelings**.

19 These **are the-ones** who **from-define**[3591] themselves, **soulish, not holding** the Spirit.

20 But you, beloved, **house-build** yourselves **to-the holiest** faith **of-you**, praying in the **Holy Spirit.**

[3578] Or slip in
[3579] Greek: "krima," transliterated as "crime" and also means judgment
[3580] Greek: "apo" (from) and "alethros" (ruin), to destroy fully
[3581] Oikeo (house) and terion (a location where something happens)—2 Cor. 5:2
[3582] Or lit., un-seen, un-perceived
[3583] Say thoroughly, discuss
[3584] Greek: upon-stand, to put the mind upon, to be acquainted with, comprehend, be present
[3585] Or, to pine, to waste, to rot
[3586] "Error of Balaam"-Numbers 22:20-21
[3587] Greek: "apo" (from) and "alethros" (ruin), to destroy fully
[3588] Or, fierce-hard, dry-tough, harsh, severe
[3589] Or ... to faces of useful-gain, favor; or ... [having] faces [in] grace, [because] of useful-gain
[3590] Greek compound: "empaiktes" (in-sport (mock) as a boy), root means a child as disciplined
[3591] Lit., from-through-define, from-through-horizon, from-through-boundary, to separate by boundary

21 **Watch-guard** yourselves in the love of God, **towards-welcome** the **pity-mercy** of our Lord Jesus Christ **into eternal life**.

22 And **some, indeed,** have compassion, making a difference:

23 **Yet some,** save with fear, **snatching-them out-of** the fire; **detest-hating down** the garment **stained from** the flesh.

24 Now **to-him** that is **powerful** to **watch** you from **tripping**, and to present faultless before the presence of his glory with **jumping-joy**.

25 To the only wise God our Savior, glory, and **great-togetherness**,[3592] **government**[3593] and **authority,** both now and **into all the ages**. Amen.

[3592] Greek compound: **great** (big) and sun (together); Big-togetherness, great-togetherness

[3593]

THE REVELATION OF JESUS CHRIST

REVELATION CHAPTER 1

1 Revelation of Jesus Christ, which God gave **to-him**, to show to his **slaves'** things which **it-is-binding to-swiftly become**; and he sent and signified through his angel to his **slave** John.

2 Who **witnessed** of the **Word of God**, and of the **witness** of Jesus Christ, and of all things that he saw.

3 **Happy** is he that **again-knows,** and they that hear the words of this prophecy, and **guard** those things which are written **in her**; because the **season near-squeezes.**

4 John to the seven Churches which are in Asia; grace **to-you**, and peace, from him **Who is, and Who was, and Who is-coming**; and from the seven **Spirits** which are before his throne;

5 And from Jesus Christ, the **Believing Witness,** the **Firstborn** of the dead, and the **First-rank**[3594] of the kings of the earth. To him **who loves** us, and washed us from our sins in his own blood,

6 And has made us **a kingdom** and priests to God and his Father; **to-him** glory and **government**[3595] **into the ages of the ages**. Amen.

7 **Be-perceiving**, he **is-coming** with clouds; and every eye shall see him, and they which pierced him; and all **tribes** of the earth shall **grieve-struck** because of him. Even so, amen!

8 I am Alpha and Omega,[3596] says the Lord **God**, who is, and who was, and who **is-coming**, the **All-Governor.**[3597]

9 I John, who also am your brother, and **together-partner** in tribulation, and in the kingdom and **under-remaining** of Jesus Christ, was in the island that is called Patmos, for the **Word of God**, and for the **witness** of Jesus Christ.

10 **I-became in** the Spirit **in** the Lord's Day, and heard behind me a **great** voice, as of a trumpet.

11 Saying, I am Alpha and Omega, the First and the Last; and, what you see, write in a **little-scroll**, and **dispatch** to the seven Churches; to Ephesus, and to Smyrna, and to Pergamos, and to Thyatira, and to Sardis, and to Philadelphia, and to Laodicea.

12 And I turned to see the voice that spoke with me. And being turned, I saw seven golden candlesticks.

13 And in the **middle** of the seven candlesticks **like to-Son** of man, clothed[3598] with a garment down to the foot, and **girded** about the **breast** with a golden **pocket-belt.**

14 His head and hairs white like wool, as white as snow; and his eyes as a flame of fire.

15 And his feet like to **copper-frankincense**, as if they burned in a furnace, and his voice as the voice of many waters.

16 And he had in his right hand seven stars; and **out-of** his mouth **out-passage** a sharp **two-mouth** sword; and his **face** as the sun **shining** in his **power.**

17 And when **I-perceived** him, I fell at his feet as dead. And he laid his right hand upon me, saying to me, fear not; I am the First and the Last.

18 **And the Living-One**, and was dead; and, **be-perceiving**, I am alive **into the ages of the ages**, amen; and have the keys[3599] of **Hell** and of **Death.**

19 Write the things which **you-perceived**, and the things which are, and the things **impending becoming after these.**

20 The mystery of the seven stars which you saw in my right hand, and the seven golden candlesticks. The seven stars are the angels of the seven Churches; and the seven candlesticks which you saw are the seven Churches.

REVELATION CHAPTER 2

1 To the angel of the Church of Ephesus[3600] write; these things say he that **governs** the seven stars in his right hand, who walks in the **middle** of the seven golden candlesticks.

2 **I-perceived** your **works**, and your **cutting-fatigue**, and your **under-remaining**, and how **not you-are-**

[3594] Or, original-rank, beginning-rank
[3595] Greek: kratos, transliterated as "great" and also means vigor, strength, to use strength, to rule, government, translated as "cracy" in democracy—people(demo)-government (kratos)
[3596] The King James add "beginning (origin) and the end (finish)"
[3597] Greek: "Pankrator," pan (all) and krator from kratos (government, rule, strong), kratos is transliterated as "cracy," in democracy (people-government, people-rule)
[3598] Lit., in-down; or, in-sink, in-down-slipping
[3599] Lit., lockers
[3600] Ephesus (Upon-within—(epi (upon) + eso (inside))

powerful **to-bear** them which are **evil**; and you have **probe-tested** them which **say** they are apostles, and are not, and have found them **falsifiers.**

3 And has **lifted,** and has **under-remained,** and through my name has **cut-fatigued,** and has not **wearied.**

4 Nevertheless I have **down** you, because you have left your first love.

5 Remember therefore from **which-place** you are fallen, and **change-thought**, and do the first works; or else I will come **to-you swiftly,** and will remove your candlestick out of his place, except you **change-thought.**

6 But this you have, that you **detest-hate** the works of the Nicolaitans,³⁶⁰¹ which I also **detest-hate.**

7 He that has an ear, hear what the Spirit says to the Churches! **To-the one-conquering**³⁶⁰² will I give to eat of the tree of life, which is in the **middle** of the paradise of God.

8 And to the angel of the Church in Smyrna³⁶⁰³ write; these things say the First and the Last, which was dead, and is alive.

9 I know your **works,** and tribulation, and **beggary,** (but you are rich); and the blasphemy of them which say they are Jews, and are not, but the synagogue of Satan.

10 Fear none of those things which **you-are-impending to-emotion; be-perceiving,** the Devil shall cast **out-of** you into prison, that you may be **probe-tested**; and you shall have tribulation ten days; be you **believing** to death, and I will give you a **victor's-crown** of life.

11 He that has an ear, hear what the Spirit says to the Churches! **The one-conquering** shall not be **unrighteous**³⁶⁰⁴ **out-**of the **Second Death.**

12 And to the angel of the Church in Pergamos³⁶⁰⁵ write these things say he which has the sharp sword with two-edges.

13 I know your works, and where you **down-house,** where Satan's **throne** and **you-are-governing** my name, and have not denied my faith, even in those days **in which** Antipas³⁶⁰⁶ my **believing** witness, who was slain among you, where Satan **down-house.**

14 But I have a few things **down** you, because you have the **ones-governing** the **teaching** of Balaam,³⁶⁰⁷ who taught Balak to cast **scandals**³⁶⁰⁸ before the **sons** of Israel, **eating idol-sacrifices**, and **prostitution.**

15 So have you also the **ones-governing** the **teaching** of the Nicolaitans,³⁶⁰⁹ which thing I **detest-hate.**

16 Change-thought; or else **I-am-coming to-you swiftly** and will fight against them with the sword of my mouth.

17 He that has an ear, hear what the Spirit says to the Churches! **To-the one-conquering**³⁶¹⁰ will I give to eat of the hidden manna, and will give him a white **pebble-vote**, and in the **pebble-vote** a **new-fresh** name written, which no man knows except he who **takes**.

18 And to the angel of the Church in Thyatira³⁶¹¹ write; these things say the Son of God, who has his eyes like to a flame of fire, and his feet like **copper-incense.**

19 I know your **works**, and love, and **attendance**, and faith, and your **under-remaining**, and your **works**; and the last more than the first.

20 Notwithstanding I **have down you, that** you **are-letting-be wife**³⁶¹² **Jezebel,** which calls herself a prophetess, **and** teach and **seduce** my **slave**s to **prostitution** and to eat **idol-sacrifices.**

21 And I gave her uninterrupted-time to change-thought; and not willing to change-thought of her prostitution.

22 Be-perceiving, I will cast her into a **cot**;³⁶¹³ and **them-adultery** with her into **great** tribulation, except they **change-thought out-of** their **works.**

23 And I will kill her children with death; and all the Churches shall know that I am he who searches the **kidneys** and **hearts;** and I will give to every one of you **down to-your works.**

24 But **to-you** I say, and to the rest in Thyatira, as many as have not this **teaching**, and which have not known

---

³⁶⁰¹ Conquering-laity, conquering-people
³⁶⁰² "Nikao," to defeat an enemy
³⁶⁰³ Smyrna—myrrh
³⁶⁰⁴ Or, injured
³⁶⁰⁵ Pergamos—much-marriage (per (much) gamos (marriage), a city in Turkey
³⁶⁰⁶ Greek compound: "anti" (against) and "pas" (all); meaning anti-all, anti-everything
³⁶⁰⁷ "Teaching of Balaam"—Num. 31:16 w/Num. 25
³⁶⁰⁸ Snares, trap stick, trap trigger
³⁶⁰⁹ Conquering-laity, conquering-people
³⁶¹⁰ "Nikao," to defeat an enemy
³⁶¹¹ Thyatira—meaning unknown, maybe "daughter," a city in Turkey
³⁶¹² Some texts reads "your wife"
³⁶¹³ Or (re)cline

the depths of Satan, as they speak; I will **cast** upon you no **other-same weight**.

25 But that which you have, **govern** until I **arrive**.

26 And **the one-conquering**, and keeps my **works** to the **finish**, **to-him** will I give **authority** over the nations.

27 And he shall **shepherd** them **in to-rod** of iron; as the vessels, **the pottery together-crushed**; even as I-**have-taken beside** my Father.

28 And I will give him the morning star.

29 He that has an ear, hear what the Spirit says to the Churches.

REVELATION CHAPTER 3

1 And to the angel of the Church in Sardis[3614] write these things **he says** that has the seven Spirits of God, and the seven stars; I know your **works**, that you have a name that you live and are dead.

2 Be watchful, and **stand-fast the-things** which remain, that are **impending** to die; for I have not found your **works filled** before **my** God.

3 Remember therefore how you have **taken** and heard, and **guard**, and **change-thought**. If therefore you shall not watch, I **shall-arrive** on you as a thief, and you shall not know what hour I will **arrive** upon you.

4 **Nevertheless** you have a few names in Sardis which have not **soiled** their garments; and they shall **about-walk** with me in white; for they are **deserving**.

5 **The one-conquering**,[3615] the same shall be clothed in white **garment**; and I will not **out-of-oil** his name **out-of** the Scroll of Life, but I will **same-say** his name before my Father, and before his angels.

6 He that has an ear, hear what the Spirit says to the Churches!

7 And to the angel of the Church in Philadelphia[3616] write these things **he says** that is Holy, he that is **True**, he that has the **locker** of David, **he that opens, and none locks, and locking none open.**

8 I **perceived** your **works**; **be-perceiving**, I have set before you an open door, and **no-one is-powerful to-lock** it; for you have a little strength, and have **guarded** my **Word**, and has not **contradicted** my name.

9 **Be-perceiving**, I will make them of the synagogue of Satan, which say they are Jews, and are not, but **are-falsifying**; **be-perceiving**, I will make them **arrive** and worship before your feet, and to know that I have loved you.

10 Because you have **guarded** the **Word** of my **under-remaining**, I also will **guard** you **out-of** the hour of **probe-testing**, which **impending to-be-coming** upon whole the **housed-land**[3617] to **probe-test** them that **down-house** upon the earth.

11 **Be-perceiving**, I come **swiftly**; **govern what** you have, that no man takes your **victor's-crown**.

12 **The one-conquering** will I make a pillar[3618] in the temple of my God, and he shall go no more out; and I will write upon him the name of my God, and the name of the city of my God, **new-fresh** Jerusalem,[3619] which **is-descending** out of heaven from my God; and my **new-fresh** name.

13 He that has an ear, hear what the Spirit says to the Churches!

14 And to the angel of the Church of the Laodiceans[3620] write; these things say the Amen, the **Believing** and **True Witness**, the **Origin** of the creation of God.

15 I know your works, that you are neither cold nor hot; **you-owe** to be cold or hot.

16 So then because you are warm and neither cold nor hot, **I-am-impending to-vomit** you out of my mouth.

17 Because you say, I am rich, and increased with goods, and have need of nothing; and **perceive** not that you are **talent-tested**,[3621] and **pity-mercy**, and **beggar**, and blind, and naked.

18 **I-plan-counsel** you to buy of me gold **fired** in the fire, that you may be rich; and white **garment**, that you may be clothed, and the **disfigure** of your nakedness not **shine**; and **in-anoint** eyes with **plaster**, that you may see.

19 As many as I love, I **evidence-expose** and **boy-train**; be zealous therefore, and **change-thought**.

20 **Be-perceiving**, I stand at the door, and knock; if any man hears my voice, and opens the door, I will come **into him**, and will **dine** with him, and he with me.

[3614] Sardis—blood red, flesh
[3615] "Nikao," to defeat an enemy
[3616] Philadelphia—fond-of-brothers (brothers of the same womb)
[3617] Plural in the Greek texts
[3618] Greek: "style"
[3619] "Hierosoluma"—priests-peace (hierou-priest, sacred) and salem (peace)
[3620] Laodiceans—people-of-justice, people-of-vengeance, people-of-right
[3621] Talaiporos-Strong's define as weight-tested, balanced-tested; and Thayer defines as bearing-callous, full of callous

21 The **one-conquering**[3622] will I grant to sit with me in my throne, even as I also **conquered**, and **down-seated** with my Father in his throne!

22 He that has an ear, hear what the Spirit says to the Churches!

REVELATION CHAPTER 4

1 After this I **perceived**, and, **be-perceiving**, a door opened in heaven; and the first voice which I heard as it were of a trumpet talking with me; which said, **up-walk here,** and I will show you things which **it-is-binding to-become after these**.

2 And **soon** I was in **to-Spirit** and **perceived** a throne was **laid** in heaven, and **him-sitting** on the throne.

3 And he that **is-sitting** was to look upon like jasper and a sardine stone; and a rainbow round about the throne, like **seeing** an emerald.

4 And round about the throne twenty-four **thrones;** and upon the **thrones I-perceived twenty-four** elders sitting, clothed in white garment; and they had on their heads **victor's-crowns** of gold.

5 And out of the throne **is-out-of-passaging star-fall-lights**[3623] and thunders and voices; and seven **Lamps** of fire burning before the thrones which are the seven Spirits of God.

6 And before the throne a sea of glass like **ice-frost** and in the middle of the throne, and round about the throne, four **living-things** full of eyes before and behind.

7 And the first **living-thing** like a lion, and the second **living-thing** like a calf, and the third **living-thing** had a face as a man, and the fourth **living-thing** like a flying eagle.

8 And the four **living-things** one down one **of-them**, had **up wings, six, encircled;** and full of eyes within; and they **up-pause** not day and night, saying, **holy, holy, holy**[3624] **Lord God All-Governor,** [3625] Who was, and Who is, and **Who** is **coming.**

9 And **whenever** those **living-things** give glory and **value** and thanks **to-the one-sitting** on the throne, **to-the one-**living **into the ages of the ages.**

10 The **twenty-four** elders **sitting** on the throne fall down before him, and worship him that lives **into the ages of the ages**, and cast their **victor's-crowns** before the throne, saying:

11 You are **deserving, our Lord and God**, to receive glory, value, and power; for you have created all things, and **through** your **will** they **existed** and were created.

REVELATION CHAPTER 5

1 And I saw in the **right** of **him-sitting** on the throne a **little-scroll** written inside and on the back, sealed with seven seals.

2 And I saw a **forceful** angel proclaiming with a **great** voice, who is **deserving** to open the **little-scroll**, and to loose the seals **of-it**?

3 And no man in heaven, or in earth, neither under the earth, was **powerful** to open the **little-scroll**, neither to look **at-same.**

4 And I wept much, because no man was found **deserving** to open and to read the **little-scroll**, neither to look **at-same.**

5 And one of the elders says to me, weep not, **be-perceiving,** the Lion of the tribe of Judah, the Root of David, has **conquered**[3626] to open the **little-scroll**, and the seven seals **of-it**.

6 And **I-perceived, and be-perceiving,** in the middle of the throne and of the four **living-things**, and in the middle of the elders, stood a Lamb as **having-been-slain**, having seven horns and seven eyes, which are the seven Spirits of God sent forth into all the earth.

7 And he came and **took** the **little-scroll out-of** the right of him **sitting** upon the throne.

8 And when he had taken the **little-scroll**, the four **living-things** and **twenty-four** elders fell down before the Lamb, having every one of them harps, and golden **bowls** full of **incense**, which are the prayers of saints.

9 And they **are-singing** a **new-fresh** song, saying, you are **deserving** to take the **little-scroll**, and to open the seals **of-it**; for you were slain, and have **bought**[3627] us **to-the** God **in** your blood **out-of** every **tribe**, and tongue, and people, and nation;

[3622] "Nikao," to defeat an enemy
[3623] Astrape, from the root aster (star) and pto (fall)
[3624] Byzantine Texts repeats this nine times in lieu of three times
[3625] Greek: "Pankrator," pan (all) and krator from kratos (government, rule, strong), kratos is transliterated as "cracy," in democracy (people-government, people-rule)
[3626] "Nikao," to defeat an enemy
[3627] Lit., to go to the market, redeem

10 And have made **them** to our God **a kingdom**[3628] and priests; and **they** shall reign on the earth.

11 And I beheld, and I heard the voice of many angels round about the throne and the **living-things** and the elders; and the number of them was ten thousands, times ten thousands, and thousands of thousands;

12 Saying with a loud voice, **deserving** is the Lamb that was slain to **take** power, and riches, and wisdom, and strength, and **value**, and glory, and blessing.

13 And every creature which is in heaven, and on the earth, and under the earth, and such as are in the sea, and all that are in them, I heard saying, blessing, and **value**, and glory, and **government**, [3629] **to-him** that sits upon the throne, and to the Lamb **into the ages of the ages**. Amen.

14 And the four **living-things** said, amen. And the elders fell down and worshipped.[3630]

REVELATION CHAPTER 6

1 And I saw when the Lamb opened **first out-of** the **seven** seals, and I heard, as it were the noise of thunder, one of the four **living-things** saying, come and **look**.

2 And **I-perceived**, and **be-perceiving,** a white horse and he sitting on him had a bow; and a **victor's-crown** was given **to-him**; and he went forth conquering, and to conquer.

3 And when he had opened the second seal, I heard the second **living-thing** say, come.

4 And there went out **another-same horse fire-like** and **it-was-given to-him-sitting** on him to take peace from the earth, and that they should kill **one-another-same**; and there was given **to-him** a **great** sword.

5 And when he had opened the third seal, I heard the third **living-thing** say, come and **look**. And **I-perceived**, and **be-perceiving,** a black horse; and **he-sitting** on him had a **yoke** in his hand.

6 And I heard a voice in the middle of the four **living-thing** say, a measure of wheat for a **denarius**, and three measures of barley for a **denarius**; and the oil and the wine not **you-should-hurt**.

7 And when he had opened the fourth seal, I heard the voice of the fourth **living-thing** say, come and **look**.

8 And **I-perceived**, and **be-perceiving,** a **greenish** horse; and his name that **sitting** on him was Death, and Hell followed with him. And **authority** was given **to-them** over the fourth part of the earth, to kill **in** sword, and **in** hunger, and **in** death, and **under** the **wild-beasts** of the earth.

9 And when he had opened the fifth seal, **I-perceived** under the **sacrifice-place** the souls of them that were slain **through** the **Word of God**, and **through** the **witness** which they held.

10 And they **screamed** with a **great** voice, saying, how long, **the Owner**, **Holy** and **True,** do you not judge and avenge our blood on them that **down-house** on the **earth**?

11 And white robes were given to every one of them; and it was said to them, that they should **pause** yet for a **micro uninterrupted-time**, until their fellow **slaves** also and their **brothers impending to-be-killed,** as they, should be **filled.**

12 And **I-perceived** when he had opened the sixth seal, and **be-perceiving,** there was a **great quake**; and the sun became black as sackcloth of hair, and the moon became as blood.

13 And the stars of heaven fell to the earth, even as a fig tree cast her **unripe** figs, when she is **quaked** of a **great** wind.

14 And the heaven departed as a **little-scroll** when it is **coiled**; and every mountain and island were moved **out-of** their places.

15 And the kings of the earth, and the **great great-men**, and the **rich-men**, and the **chief-of thousands**, and the **powerful**, and every **slave**, and every **free-man**, hid themselves in the dens and in the rocks of the mountains.

16 And said to the mountains and rocks, fall on us, and hide us from the face of **him-sitting** on the throne, and from the **swelling-anger** of the Lamb.

17 For the **great** day of his **swelling-anger** is come; and who shall be **powerful** to stand?

REVELATION CHAPTER 7

1 And after these things **I-perceived** four angels standing on the four corners of the earth, **governing**

[3628] Or kings
[3629] Greek: kratos; vigor, strength, to use strength, to rule, government, translated as "cracy" in democracy—people(demo)-government (kratos)

[3630] The M texts and the Alexandrian texts exclude "living-one into the ages of the ages"

the four winds of the earth, that the wind should not blow on the earth, nor on the sea, nor on any tree.

2 And I saw **another-same** angel **up-walking** from **up-finished sun**, having the seal of the living God; and he **screamed** with a **great** voice to the four angels, to whom it was given to **unrighteous**³⁶³¹ the earth and the sea,

3 Saying, **unrighteous** not the earth, neither the sea, nor the trees, until we have sealed the **slaves** of our God in their foreheads.³⁶³²

4 And I heard the number of them which were sealed; a hundred forty-four thousand sealed **out-of** all the tribes of the **sons** of Israel.

5 Out-of the tribe of Judah sealed twelve thousand. **Out-of** the tribe of Reuben sealed twelve thousand. **Out-of** the tribe of Gad sealed twelve thousand.

6 Out-of the tribe of Asher sealed twelve thousand. **Out-of** the tribe of Naphtali sealed twelve thousand. **Out-of** the tribe of Manasseh sealed twelve thousand.

7 Out-of the tribe of Simeon sealed twelve thousand. **Out-of** the tribe of Levi sealed twelve thousand. **Out-of** the tribe of Issachar sealed twelve thousand.

8 Out-of the tribe of Zebulon sealed twelve thousand. **Out-of** the tribe of Joseph sealed twelve thousand. **Out-of** the tribe of Benjamin sealed twelve thousand.

9 After this **I-perceived**, and, **be-perceiving** a **much** multitude, which no man **is-powerful to-**number, of all nations, and **tribes**, and people, and tongues, stood before the throne, and before the Lamb, clothed with white robes, and palms in their hands;

10 And **screamed** with a **great** voice, saying, salvation to our God which sits upon the throne, and to the Lamb.

11 And all the angels stood round about the throne, and the elders and the four **living-things**, and fell before the throne on their faces, and worshipped God,

12 Saying, amen! **The** blessing, and **the** glory, and **the** wisdom, and **the** thanksgiving, and **the** value, and **the** power, and **the forcefulness** to our God **into the ages of ages,** amen!

13 And one of the elders answered, saying to me, what are these which are arrayed in white robes, and where came they?

14 And I said **to-him, my Lord,** you **perceived.** And he said to me, these are they which **are-coming** out of the **great** tribulation, and have washed their robes, and made them white in the blood of the Lamb.

15 Therefore are they before the throne of God, and **hired-service to-him,** day and night, in his temple; and he **that-is-sitting** on the throne shall **tabernacle over** them.

16 They shall hunger no more, neither thirst anymore; neither shall the sun **fall** on them, nor any heat.

17 For the Lamb, **the up middle** of the throne, shall **shepherd** them, and shall lead them **upon living fountains of waters;** and God shall **out-of-oil** all tears from their eyes.

REVELATION CHAPTER 8

1 And when he had opened the seventh seal, there was **hush** in heaven **as** half an hour.

2 And I saw the seven angels which stood before God; and **to-them** were given seven trumpets.

3 And another angel came and stood at the **sacrifice-place**, having **golden frankincense**; and there was given **to-him** much incense, that he should **give to-the** prayers of all saints upon the golden **sacrifice-place** which was before the throne.

4 And the **smoke** of the incense **to-the** the prayers of the saints, **up-walked** before God **out-of** the angel's hand.

5 And the angel **took** the **frankincense** and filled it with fire of the **sacrifice-place** and cast into the earth; and there **became** voices, and thunders, and **star-fall-lights,**³⁶³³ and a **quake**.

6 And the seven angels who had the seven trumpets **internally-prepared** themselves to **trumpet**.

7 The first angel **trumpeted**, and there followed hail and fire **mixed in** blood, and they were cast upon the earth; **a third of the earth was down-burned,** and the third of trees was **down-burned**, and all green grass was **down-burned**.

8 And the second angel **trumpeted**, and as it were a **great** mountain burning with fire was cast into the sea; and the third of the sea became blood.

---

³⁶³¹ Or, injured
³⁶³² Greek: "mataops," to change (meta)-eyes (ops), to change-face (ops), after-face, after-eyes, beyond-face, beyond-eyes
³⁶³³ Astrape, from the root aster (star) and pto (to fall)

9 And the third part of the creatures which were in the sea, **having soul,** died and the third of the ships were **through-rotted.**

10 And the third angel **trumpeted,** and there fell a **great** star from heaven, burning as it were a lamp, and it fell upon the third of the rivers, and upon the fountains of waters.

11 And the name of the star is called **Absinth**;[3634] and the third of the waters became **absinth;** and many men died **out-of** the waters, because they were made **bitter.** [3635]

12 And the fourth angel **trumpeted,** and the third of the sun was **pounded,** and the third of the moon, and the third of the stars; **that** the third of them was **obscured,** and the day **shine**[3636] not for a third of it, and the night **like-as.**

13 And **I-perceived,** and heard an **eagle** flying **in** the **mid-heaven,** saying with a loud voice, woe, woe, woe, to the **ones-down-housing upon** the earth **out-of** the **remaining** voices of the trumpet of the three angels, **impending to-be-trumpeting**!

REVELATION CHAPTER 9

1 And the fifth angel **trumpeted,** and **I-perceived** a star **out-of** heaven fell[3637] **into** the earth; and **to-him** was given[3638] the **locker** of the **well of-the abyss.**

2 And he opened[3639] the **well of-the abyss**; and **up-walked** smoke out of the pit, as the smoke of a **great** furnace; and the sun and the air were **obscured out-of** the smoke of the **well.**

3 And there came out of the smoke locusts upon the earth; and **to-them** was given **authority,** as the scorpions[3640] of the earth have **authority**.

4 And it was commanded them that they should not **unrighteous**[3641] the grass of the earth, neither any green thing, neither any tree; but only those men which have not the seal of God on their foreheads.[3642]

5 And **to-them** it was given that they should not kill them, but that they should be tormented five months; and their torment as the torment of a scorpion, when he strikes a man.

6 And in those days shall men seek death and shall not find it; and shall-**be-upon-feeling** to die, and death shall flee from them.

7 And the shapes of the locusts like to horses **internally-prepared** to battle; and on their heads as it were **victor's-crown** like gold, and their faces as the faces of men.

8 And they had hair as the hair of women, and their teeth were as of lions.

9 And they had **chest,** as it were **chest** of iron; and the voice of their wings as the voice of chariots of many horses **running into** battle.

10 And they had tails like to scorpions, and there were stings[3643] in their tails; and their **authority to-unrighteous**[3644] men five months.

11 And they had a king over them, the angel of the **abys**s, whose name **to-him Hebrew,** Abaddon, but in the **Hellenic** has a name, Apollyon.

12 One woe is past; **be-perceiving, are-come** two woes more **after these.**

13 And the sixth angel **trumpeted,** and I heard a voice from the four horns of the golden **sacrifice-place** which is before God,

14 Saying to the sixth angel which had the trumpet, loose[3645] the four angels which are bound in the **great** river Euphrates.[3646]

15 And the four angels were loosed, which were **internally-prepared into** an hour, and a day, and a month and a **years, that from-kill** the third of men.

16 And the number of the army of the horsemen **ten-thousands of-ten-thousands,**[3647] and I heard the number of them.

17 And **in-this-way I-perceived** the horses in the vision, and **them-sitting** on them, having **chest** of fire, and of **hyacinth,** and **God-fire-similarity**[3648] and the heads of the horses as the heads of lions; and **out-of**

[3634] Defined as: un-drinkable
[3635] Lit., acridity (strong, irritating, unpleasant, pungent (sharp), taste or smell), poison
[3636] Or lighten
[3637] Fell is perfect tense masculine (see feminine use in Acts 15:16)
[3638] Aorist tense, a past event with ongoing repetition
[3639] Aorist tense
[3640] Skorpios: from "skorpizo" (scatter, dissipate) and "ios" (rust, venom, poison)
[3641] Or, injured
[3642] Greek: "mataops," to change (meta)-eyes (ops), to change-face (ops), after-face, after-eyes, beyond-face, beyond-eyes
[3643] Greek: "kentron," transliterated as "center;" piercer, point, prick, sting
[3644] Or, injured
[3645] Loose also means to reduce to the constituent (component, ingredient, element) particles (minute portions) (Strong's #3089 w/#4486)
[3646] Hebrew definition means: to break forth, to gush
[3647] 100,000,000; King James read: 200,000,000
[3648] Lit., "theiodes" from "theion," a place struck by "deity" lightning and "eidos," a view, a form

their mouths **out-of-passage** fire and smoke and **God-fire**.

18 By these three was the third of men killed, **out-of** the fire, and the smoke, and the **God-fire**[3649] which **out-passage out-of** their mouths.

19 For **the authority of the horses** in their mouth, and in their tails; for their tails like to serpents, and had heads, and with them they do hurt.

20 And the rest of the men which were not killed by these **plague-poundings**, not **they-changed-thought** of the **works** of their hands, that they should not worship **demons**, and idols of gold, and silver, and brass, and stone, and of wood; which neither **powerful to-look**, nor hear, nor walk.

21 Neither **they-change-thought out-of** their murders, nor **out-of** their **drug-potions**, nor **out-of** their **prostitution**, nor **out-of** their thefts.

REVELATION CHAPTER 10

1 And **I-perceived** another **forcible** angel come down from heaven, clothed with a cloud; and a rainbow upon his head, and his face as the sun, and his feet as pillars of fire.

2 And he had in his hand a **little-scroll** open; and he set his right foot upon the sea and left on the earth.

3 And **screamed** with a **great** voice, as a lion roars; and when he had **screamed**, seven thunders uttered their voices.

4 And when the seven thunders had **spoken** their voices, **I-was-impending** to write; and I heard a voice from heaven saying to me, seal up those things which the seven thunders **spoke**, and write them not.

5 And the angel which I saw stand upon the sea and upon the earth lifted up his **right** hand to heaven.

6 And swore by him that lives **into the ages of-the ages**, who created heaven, and the things **in it**, and the earth, and the things that are **in her**, and the sea, and the things which are **in her**, that there should be **uninterrupted-time**[3650] no longer.

7 But in the days of the voice of the seventh angel, **whenever he-is-impending to-be-trumpeting**, the mystery of God **was-finished**,[3651] as he has **evangelized** to his **slaves** the prophets.

8 And the voice which I heard from heaven spoke to me again, and said, go take the **little-scroll** which is open in the hand of the angel which stands upon the sea and upon the earth.

9 And I went to the angel, and said **to-him**, give me the **little-scroll**. And he said to me, take and eat it up; and it shall make your belly bitter,[3652] but it shall be in your mouth sweet as honey.

10 And **I-took** the **little-scroll** out of the angel's hand and ate it; and it was in my mouth sweet as honey; and as soon as I had eaten it, my belly was bitter.

11 And **they**[3653] said **to-me**, you, **it-is-binding to-**prophesy again **upon** many peoples, and nations, and tongues, and kings.

REVELATION CHAPTER 11

1 And there was given me a reed likened to a rod saying, rise and measure the temple of God, and the **sacrifice-place**, and **them-worshiping in-him**.

2 But the court which is **outside** the temple **out-of-cast outside and** measure **her** not; for it is given to the **nations**; and the Holy City **they-shall-trample** foot forty-two months.

3 And I will **give** to my two witnesses, and **they shall prophesy** a thousand two hundred **sixty** days, clothed in sackcloth.

4 These are the two olive trees, and the two candlesticks standing before the **Lord** of the earth.

5 And if any man will **unrighteous**[3654] them, **fire out-of-passage out-of their mouth and** devours their **enemy-haters**; and if any man will **unrighteous**[3655] them, **it-is-binding he** in this manner be killed.

6 These have **authority** to **lock** heaven that it rains not in the days of their prophecy; and have **authority upon** waters to turn them to blood, and to smite the earth with **every plague-pounding, as-many-times if they-should-will**.

7 And when they shall have finished **the witness**, the **wild**-beast, **the one-up-walking out-of the abyss**,

---

[3649] Lit., "theion" a place struck by "deity" lightning, God-flashing, God-lightning
[3650] "Chronos," uninterrupted time, study Galatians 4
[3651] Aorist tense (past action, with no limit on time or repetition)
[3652] Lit., acridity (strong, irritating, unpleasant, pungent (sharp), taste or smell), poison
[3653] All manuscript reads "they" (plural)
[3654] Or, injured
[3655] Or injure

shall **do battle with** them, and shall **conquer** them, and kill them.

8 And their **corpse**[3656] in the street of the **great** city, which spiritually is called Sodom and Egypt, **wherever**[3657] also **their** Lord was crucified.

9 And they of the people and **tribes**, tongues, and nations see their **corpse** three days and a half and shall not **release**[3658] their **corpse** to be put in **remembrance-tomb**.

10 And they that **down-house** upon the earth shall **cheer** over them, and **shall-be-well-disposed**, and shall **dispatch** gifts to **one-another-same**; because these two prophets tormented[3659] them that dwelt on the earth.

11 And after three days and a half the Spirit of **Life out-of** God entered into them, and they stood upon their feet; and **great** fear fell upon them which saw them.

12 And they heard a **great** voice from heaven saying to them, **up-walk here**. And they **up-walked** to heaven in a cloud; and their **enemy-haters theatre-spectate** them.

13 And **in that hour** was there a **great quake**, and the tenth of the city fell and in the **quake** were **killed names of-men** seven thousand; and the remnant **became in-fear** and gave glory to the God of heaven.

14 The second woe is past; **be-perceiving** the third woe **is-coming shortly**.

15 And the seventh angel **trumpeted**; and there **became great** voices in heaven, saying, the **kingdom** of this world **became of-our** Lord, and of his Christ; and he shall reign **into the ages of ages**.

16 And the twenty-four elders, **the-ones sitting** before God on their **thrones**, fell upon their faces, and worshipped God.

17 Saying, we give you thanks, Lord God **All-Governor, Who is, and Who was;**[3660] because you have taken **to-you** your **great** power and have reigned.

18 And the nations were **swelling-angry**, and your **swelling-anger** is come, and the season of the dead, **being-**judged,[3661] and that you should give reward to-your **slave**s the prophets, and to the saints, and them that fear your name, small and **great**; and should **through-rot** them which **through-rotting** the earth.

19 And the temple of God was opened in heaven, and there was seen in his temple the **Ark of-the Covenant of the Lord**; and there were **star-fall-lights,**[3662] and voices, and thunders, and a **quake,** and **great** hail.

REVELATION CHAPTER 12

1 And there appeared a **great** wonder in heaven; a woman clothed with the sun and the moon under her feet and upon her head a **victor's-crown** of twelve stars.

2 And she **in belly holding, screamed,** travailing, and **tormented**[3663] **to-produce**.

3 And there appeared another wonder in heaven; and **be-perceiving** a **great fiery-red** dragon, having seven heads[3664] and ten horns, and seven **royal-crowns** upon his heads.

4 And his tail **dragged** the third of the stars of heaven and did cast them to the earth; and the dragon stood before the woman **who-impending to-produce, to-eat-down** her child **whenever she-produced.**

5 And she **produced a son, a male, who is-impending to-shepherd** all nations **in to-rod** of iron; and her child **is-snatched towards** God, and his throne.

6 And the woman fled into the **lonesome**, where she has a **spot internally-prepared from** God that **they-should-nourish** her there a thousand two hundred sixty days.

7 And there **became a-battle** in heaven; Michael and his angels **battled** against the dragon; and the dragon **battled** and his angels.

8 And **not they-are-forceful**; neither was **a spot** found **for him** anymore in heaven.

9 And the **great** dragon was cast out, that **original** serpent, called the Devil, and Satan, **the-one seducing** the **whole housed-land**; he was cast out into the earth, and his angels were cast out with him.

[3656] Greek: "ptoma" (a ruin, a corpse, lifeless body, and alternate of "pipto" to fall)
[3657] Gk.: hopou—whichever (spot), whatever, wherever
[3658] Greek: from-let go, to forgive
[3659] Lit., to test validity of metal
[3660] None of the oldest texts (Byzantine or Alexandrian) add "and who is coming"
[3661] Aorist, passive
[3662] Astrape: star-fall, from the root aster (star) and pto (to fall)
[3663] Lit., to test or examine for validity
[3664] Corporate Satan possible 7 heads: principalities, authorities, powers, thrones, lords, world-governments of darkness, spiritual hurtful-ones (Ephesians 1:21, Colossians 1:16, Ephesians 6:12)

10 And I heard a **great** voice saying in heaven, now is come salvation, and **power,** and the kingdom of our God, and the **authority** of his Christ; for the accuser of our **brothers** is cast down, which accused³⁶⁶⁵ them before our God day and night.

11 And they **conquered**³⁶⁶⁶ him **through** the blood of the Lamb and **through** the word of their **witness**; and they loved not their **souls until** death.

12 Through this, be-well-disposed you heavens, and you that **tabernacle** in them. Woe to the **ones-down-housing** the earth and of the sea! For the Devil is come down **towards** you, having **great sacrifice-anger**, because he **perceives** that he has but a **few**³⁶⁶⁷ **season**.

13 And when the dragon saw that he was cast to the earth, he **chased** the woman, **any-who produced the male.**

14 And to the woman were given two wings of a **great** eagle that **she-may-fly** into the **lonesome**, into her **spot**, where she is nourished for a **season**, and **seasons**, and half a **season** from the face of the serpent.

15 And the serpent cast out of his mouth water as a flood after the woman, that he might cause her to be **river-burdened**.

16 And the earth **ran-to the-distress-cry of-the** woman, and the earth opened her mouth, and swallowed up the flood which the dragon cast out of his mouth.

17 And the dragon was **swelling-angry** with the woman and went to **do battle** with the **remaining-ones** of her seed, which **guard** the commandments of God, and have the **witness** of Jesus. **And he**³⁶⁶⁸ **stood upon the sand of the sea.**

REVELATION CHAPTER 13

1 And **I-perceived** a **wild-beast up-walking out-of** the sea, **having ten horns and seven heads**, and upon his horns ten **royal-crowns,** and upon his heads the **names** of blasphemy.

2 And the **wild-beast** which I saw was like a leopard, and his feet **like** a bear, and his mouth **like** the mouth of a lion; and the dragon gave him his power, and his **throne**, and **great** authority.

3 And **I-perceived first** of his heads as it were **butchered** to death; and his **plague-pounding of-the death** was **therapeutic**; and **marveled** the **whole earth behind** the **wild-beast.**

4 And they worshipped the dragon which gave **authority** to the **wild-beast;** and they worshipped the **wild-beast,** saying, who like to the **wild-beast**? Who is **powerful** to **battle** with him?

5 And there was given **to-him** a mouth speaking **great** things and blasphemies; and **authority** was given **to-him** to **make-war** forty-two months.

6 And he opened his mouth in blasphemy **towards** God, to blaspheme his name, and his tabernacle, **them that tabernacle in heaven.**

7 And it was given **to-him** to **do battle**³⁶⁶⁹ with the saints, and to **conquer**³⁶⁷⁰ them; and **authority** was given him over all **tribe**, **and people,** and tongues, and nations.

8 And all that **down-house** upon the earth shall worship him, whose names are not written in the **Scroll** of Life of the Lamb slain from the foundation of the world.

9 If any man has an ear, hear!

10 If anyone into captivity, into captivity he under-leads; **if anyone in sword is-killing it-is-binding himself in sword be-killed.** Here is the **under-remaining** and the faith of the saints.

11 And **I-perceived another-same wild-beast up-walking out-of** the earth; and he had two horns like a lamb, and he spoke as a dragon.

12 And **he-is-producing** all the **authority** of the **foremost wild-beast** before him, and **he-is-producing** the earth and them which **down-house in her** to worship the **before-most wild-beast** whose **plague-pounding of-death** was **therapeutic.**

13 And **he-is-producing great signs**, so that fire **he-is-producing down-coming** from heaven **into** the earth in the **face** of men.

---

³⁶⁶⁵ "Katagoros," transliterated as "category"
³⁶⁶⁶ "Nikao," to defeat an enemy
³⁶⁶⁷ Or, puny
³⁶⁶⁸ The Alexandrian Text reads "he" as in the dragon stood upon the sand …." The Byzantine texts read: "I" in lieu of "he"
³⁶⁶⁹ Greek: "polemos,: transliterated as "polemic," also means strong and critical attack by speech or writing
³⁶⁷⁰ "Nikao," to defeat an enemy

14 And **seducing those**[3671] **down-housing** on the earth by those **signs** which **he-was-given** to **produce** in the **face** of the **wild-beast**; saying **to-them** that **down-house** on the earth, that they should **produce** an image **to-the wild-beast**, which had the **plague-pounding of-the** sword and did live.

15 And **he was-given to-give spirit** to the image of the **wild-beast** that the image of the **wild-beast** should both speak and **produce that** as many as would not worship the image of the **wild-beast** should be killed.

16 And **he-is-producing** all, both small and **great**, rich, and poor, free and bond, to **give to-them**[3672] an **engraved-character**[3673] upon their **right**, or **upon** their foreheads.[3674]

17 And that no man **may-be-powerful to-buy**[3675] or sell, **if not the-one having** the **engraved-character**, the name of the **wild-beast**, or the number of his name.

18 Here is wisdom. Let him that has **thought, pebble-vote-count**[3676] the number of the **wild-beast**; **number because man's it-is**; and his number **six hundred sixty six**[3677]

REVELATION CHAPTER 14

1 And **I-perceived** and **be-perceiving, the** Lamb stood on the mountain Zion, and with him a hundred **forty-four** thousand, having **his name**[3678] and his Father's name written on their foreheads.

2 And I heard a voice from heaven, as the voice of many waters, and as the voice of a **great** thunder; and I heard the voice of harpers harping with their harps.

3 And **they-are-singing as** a **new-fresh** song before the throne, and before the four **living-things**, and the elders; and **no-one is-powerful to-disciple** that song **if-not** the hundred forty-four thousand, which were **bought**[3679] from the earth.

4 These are they which were not **soiled** with women; for they are virgins. These are they which follow the Lamb wherever he goes. These were **bought**[3680] from **the** men, the first-fruit to God and to the Lamb.

5 And in their mouth was found no **falsehood**; for they are without fault.

6 And I saw another angel **flying** in the **mid-heaven**, having the **eternal well-message** to **evangelize** them that **down-house** on the earth, and to every nation, and **tribe**, and tongue, and people,

7 Saying with a **great** voice, fear God, and give glory **to-him**; for the hour of his **judging** is come; and worship him that **produced** heaven, and earth, and the sea, and the fountains of waters.

8 And there followed **another-same** angel, saying, **Babylon, the great,** is **fallen; she has** made all nations drink of the wine of the **sacrifice-anger** of her **prostitution**.

9 And the third angel followed them, saying with a **great** voice, if any man worships the **wild-beast** and his image, and **take an engraved-character**[3681] upon his forehead,[3682] or **upon** his hand.

10 The same shall drink of the wine of the **sacrifice-anger** of God, which is **blended, un-governed,**[3683] into the cup of his **swelling-anger**, and he shall be tormented with fire and **God-fire**[3684] in the presence of the holy angels, and in the presence of the Lamb.

11 And the smoke of their torment **up-walks into the ages of ages**; and they have no **up-pause** day or night, **the-ones worshipping** the **wild-beast** and his image, and whoever **takes** the **engraved-character** of his name.

12 Here is the **under-remaining** of the saints **keeping** the commandments of God, and the faith of Jesus.

13 And I heard a voice from heaven saying to me, write, **happy**[3685] the dead who die in the Lord from now; yes, says the Spirit that they may **up-pause** from their **weariness**; and their **works** do follow them.

[3671] Majority Texts reads "my-own-people" in lieu of "the-ones;"
[3672] Or to-themselves (reflexive pronoun)
[3673] Greek, "charagma," to carve, to scratch, to etch, sculpture; to engrave or write; akin to "charackter (character);" "charagma" is used of a serpent's bite by Sophocles; "charagma" also means expressed image (or pressed image), character, an engraving, exact image.
[3674] Greek: "mataops," to change (meta)-eyes (ops), to change-face (ops), after-face, after-eyes, beyond-face, beyond-eyes
[3675] Lit., to go to the market, redeem
[3676] Or pebble-count
[3677] Greek Orthodox Texts: (χξς)—chi (χ)-xi (ξ)-stigma (ς); 600-60-6. Alexandrian Texts: six hundred sixty six
[3678] "His name" is in all the oldest texts
[3679] Lit., to go to the market, redeem
[3680] Lit., to go to the market, redeem
[3681] Greek, "charagma," to carve, to scratch, to etch, sculpture; to engrave or write; akin to "charackter (character);" "charagma" is used of a serpent's bite by Sophocles; "charagma" also means expressed image character, an engraving.
[3682] Greek: "mataops," to change (meta)-eyes (ops), to change-face (ops), after-face, after-eyes, beyond-face, beyond-eyes
[3683] Or, un-held
[3684] Lit., "theion" a place struck by "deity" lightning, God-flashing, God-lightning
[3685] The dead in the Lord has happy emotions

14 And **I-perceived**, and **be-perceiving,** a white cloud, and upon the cloud **sitting-one** like **to-Son** of man, having on his head a golden **victor's-crown,** and in his hand a **keen gathering-hook**.

15 And **another-same** angel came out of the temple, **screaming** with a **great** voice **to-him sitting** on the cloud, **dispatch** your **gathering-hook,** and reap; for the **hour** is come to reap; for the harvest of the earth is **withered**.

16 And he **sitting upon** the cloud **threw** his **gathering-hook upon** the earth; and the earth was reaped.

17 And **another-same** angel came **out-of** the temple, which is in heaven, he also having a **keen gathering-hook**.

18 And **another-same** angel **out-of-came out-of** the **sacrifice-place,** which had **authority** over fire; and cried with a loud cry **to-him** that had the **keen gathering-hook,** saying, **dispatch** your **keen gathering-hook,** and gather the clusters of the vine of the earth; for her grapes are **pointed-ripe.**

19 And the angel **threw** in his **gathering-hook** into the earth, and gathered the vine of the earth, and cast into the **great** winepress of the **sacrifice-anger** of God.

20 And the winepress was **trampled outside** the city, and blood came out of the winepress, **until** the horses' bridles, **from** a thousand six hundred **stadiums.**[3686]

REVELATION CHAPTER 15

1 And **I-perceived** another sign in heaven, **great** and marvelous, seven angels having the seven last **plague-poundings;** for in them is filled up the **sacrifice-anger** of God.

2 And I saw as it were a sea of glass **mixed** with fire; and them that **conquered**[3687] **out-of** the **wild**-beast, and **out-of** his image[3688] **and out-of** the number of his name, stand **upon** the sea of glass, having the harps of God.

3 And they sing the song of Moses the **slave** of God, and the song of the Lamb, saying, **great** and marvelous your works, Lord God **All-Governor**; just and true your ways, you King of **nations.**

4 Who shall not fear you, Lord, and glorify your name? For **only-you Right-One**[3689]: for all nations shall **arrive** and worship before you; for your **righteous-deeds are-made-to-shine.**

5 And after that **I-perceived,** and, **be-perceiving,** the temple of the tabernacle of the **witness** in heaven was opened.

6 And the seven angels came out of the temple, having the seven plagues, clothed[3690] in **clean** and white linen, and having their **chest belted** with golden **pocket-belt.**

7 And one of the four **living-things** gave to the seven angels, seven golden **bowls swelling** of the **sacrifice-anger** of God, who lives **into the ages of ages.**

8 And the temple was **swelled** with smoke **out-of** the glory of God, and **out-of** his power; and no man was **powerful** to enter into the temple, until the seven **plague-poundings** of the seven angels were **finished**.

REVELATION CHAPTER 16

1 And I heard a **great** voice out of the temple saying to the seven angels, go your ways, and pour out the **seven bowls** of the **sacrifice-anger** of God **into** the earth.

2 And the first went and poured out his **bowl upon** the earth; and **became bad** and **hurtful ulcers into** the men which had the **engraved-character**[3691] of the **wild-beast** and them which worshipped his image.

3 And the second angel poured out his **bowl into** the sea; and it became as the blood of a **dead-one** and every living soul died in the sea.

4 And the third angel poured out his **bowl** upon the rivers and fountains of waters; and they became blood.

5 And I heard the angel of the waters say, you are righteous, **Who is,** and **Who was,** and **the Right-One,** [3692] because you have judged **these-things.**

[3686] Greek: "stadion," transliterated as stadiums, root to stand as fixed
[3687] "Nikao," to defeat an enemy
[3688] The King James add "mark" after "image; however, "mark" is not found in the Byzantine Texts (Majority Texts); neither is it found in the Alexandrian Texts; Both Byzantine and the Alexandrian texts are considered the older text. The King James is from recent copies from the older texts.
[3689] Intrinsically right
[3690] Lit., in-down; or, in-sink, in-down-slipping
[3691] Greek, "charagma," to carve, to scratch, to etch, sculpture; to engrave or write; akin to "charackter" (character);" "charagma" is used of a serpent's bite by Sophocles; "charagma" also means expressed image character, an engraving.
[3692] Alexandrian and Majority Texts

6 For they have **out-of-poured** the blood of saints and prophets, and you have given them blood to drink; for they are **deserving**.

7 And I heard the sacrifice-place say, even so, Lord God, **All-Governor**, true and righteous your **judging**.

8 And the fourth angel poured out his **bowl** upon the sun; and **it-was-given to-him** to scorch men with fire.

9 And men were scorched with **great** heat, and blasphemed the name of God, which has **authority** over these **plague-poundings**; and not **they-change-though** to give him glory.

10 And the fifth angel poured out his **bowl** upon the **throne** of the **wild-beast;** and his kingdom was full of darkness; and they **chewed** their tongues for pain.

11 And blasphemed the God of heaven, because of their pains[3693] and their **ulcers**, and not **they-changed-thought out-of** their **works.**

12 And the sixth angel poured out his **bowl** upon the **great** river Euphrates; and the water **of-him** was dried up, that the way of the kings **from** the **up-finished sun** might be **internally-prepared.**

13 And **I-perceived** three unclean spirits like frogs **out-of** the mouth of the dragon, and **out-of** the mouth of the **wild-**beast, and **out-of** the mouth of the false prophet.

14 For they are the spirits of **demons producing signs, out-of-passaging upon** the kings of the whole **housed-land,**[3694] to gather them to the battle of **that day, the great,** of God **the All-Governor.**[3695]

15 Be-perceiving, I-am-coming as a thief. **Happy** he that watch, and **guard** his garments, lest he walk naked, and they **look-at** his **disfigured-togetherness.**[3696]

16 And he gathered them together into a **spot** called in the Hebrew tongue **Armageddon.**

17 And the seventh angel poured out his **bowl** into the air; and there came a **great** voice out of the temple of heaven, from the throne, saying, **it-has-become.**

18 And there were voices, and thunders, and **star-fall-lights;**[3697] and there was a **great quake,** such as was not since men were upon the earth, a **quake such-as-this**, so **great**.

19 And the **great** city was divided into three **sections**, and the cities of the nations' fell; and **great** Babylon came in remembrance before God, to give to her the cup of the wine of the **sacrifice-anger of-his swelling-anger**.

20 And every island fled away, and the mountains were not found.

21 And there fell upon men a **great** hail **out-of** heaven, **talent-weight;**[3698] and men blasphemed God because of the **plague-poundings** of the hail; for the plague **of-her** was **great, vehemently-violent**.

REVELATION CHAPTER 17

1 And there came one of the seven angels which had the seven **bowls,** and talked with me, saying to me, come **here;** I will show **to-you** the **judgment-result**[3699] of the **great prostitute** that sits upon many waters.

2 With whom the kings of the earth have **prostituted**, and the **ones-down-housing** the earth have been made drunk with the wine of her **prostitution**.

3 So he carried me away **in Spirit** into the **lonesome**; and **I-perceived** a woman **sitting** upon a scarlet colored **wild-beast, swelling** of-names **of-blasphemy**, having seven heads and ten horns.

4 And the woman was arrayed in purple and scarlet color, and **gilded** with gold and **valuable** stones and pearls, having a golden cup in her hand full of **stink** and **un-cleansed** of her **prostitution of the earth.**

5 And upon her forehead[3700] a name written, **mystery Babylon, the great, the mother of prostitutes and stinks** of the earth.

6 And **I-perceived** the woman drunk with the blood of the saints, and with the blood of the **witness** of Jesus; and when **I-perceived** her, I **marveled** with **great marvel**.

7 And the angel said to me, why did you marvel? I will tell you the mystery of the woman, and of the **wild-beast** that carries her, which has the seven heads and ten horns.

[3693] "Ponos," from a root "peno," toil for daily substance, starving,
[3694] Alexandrian and Majority Texts
[3695] Greek: "Pankrator," pan (all) and krator from kratos ("cratic," "cracy" government, rule, strong),
[3696] This is a compound word ("aschemon" (disfigured) and "sun" (together)) only used in Romans 1:27 and Revelation 16:15

[3697] Astrape, from the root aster (star) and pto (to fall)
[3698] The root for "talent-like" means a balance as supporting weight, a "talent" as a sum of money
[3699] Greek: "krima," transliterated as "crime" and also means judgment
[3700] Greek: "mataops," to change (meta)-eyes (ops), to change-face (ops), after-face, after-eyes, beyond-face, beyond-eyes

8 The **wild**-beast that you saw was and is not; and **is-impending up-walking out-of** the **abyss** and **are-under-leading** into **from-ruin**; and they that **down-house** on the earth shall **marvel**, whose names were not written in the **Little-Scroll** of Life from the foundation of the world, **the ones-looking-at** the **wild-beast** that was, and is not, **and-yet is.**

9 And here the **thought** which has wisdom. The seven heads are seven mountains, **upon** which the woman **is-sitting**.

10 And **they-are** seven kings; five are fallen, and one is, the other is not yet come; and **whenever** he comes, **it-is-binding** he remain **few**.[3701]

11 And the **wild-beast** that was, and is not, even he is the eighth, and is **out-of** the seven, and **is-under-leading** into **from-ruin**.

12 And the ten horns which **you-perceived** are ten kings, **who** have **taken** no kingdom as yet; but **are-taking authority** as kings **first** hour with the **wild-beast.**

13 These **are-having first opinion** and **are-through-giving** their **authority** and **power** to the **wild-beast.**

14 These shall make war with the Lamb, and the Lamb shall **conquer**[3702] them; for he is Lord of lords, and King of kings; and they that are with him called, and chosen, and **believing**.

15 And he says to me, the waters which **you-perceived**, where the **prostitute is-sitting**, are peoples, and multitudes, and nations, and tongues.

16 And the ten horns which you saw **and** the **wild-beast**; these shall **detest-hate** the **prostitute**, and shall make her desolate and naked, and shall eat her flesh, and burn her with fire.

17 **Because**, God **give into** their **hearts** to **produce the opinion of him**, and to **produce first opinion**, and **to-give** their kingdom **to-the wild-beast**, until the words of-the God **shall-be-finished**.[3703]

18 And the woman which **you-perceived** is **the city, the great**, having **a kingdom** over the kings of the earth.

REVELATION CHAPTER 18

1 And after these things I saw **another-same** angel come down from heaven, having **great authority**; and the earth was **illuminated out-of** his glory.

2 And he **screamed** with a **great** voice, saying, Babylon the **great** is fallen, is fallen, and is become the **down-house-location**[3704] of demons, and the **prison** of every unclean spirit, and a **prison** of every unclean and hateful **bird**.

3 For all nations have drunk of the wine of the **sacrifice-anger** of her **prostitution,** and the kings of the earth have **prostituted** with her, and the merchants of the earth are waxed rich through the **power** of her **straining**.

4 And I heard another voice from heaven, saying, come **out-of** her, my people, that you be not **together-communion** of her sins, and that you **take** not of her **plague-poundings**.

5 For her sins have **glued**[3705] to heaven, and God has remembered her **unrighteousness**.

6 Reward her even as she rewarded, and double to her double **down** her works. In the cup which she has filled fill to her double.

7 How much she has glorified herself, and lived **straining**, so much torment and sorrow give her; for she says in her **heart**, I sit a queen, and am no widow, and shall see no sorrow.

8 Therefore shall her **plague-poundings arrive** in **first** day, death, and mourning, and famine; and she shall be burned with fire; for **forcible** the Lord God who **has judged** her.

9 And the kings of the earth, **prostitute with her** and lived **straining** with her, shall bewail her, and lament for her, when they shall see the smoke of her burning.

10 Standing afar off for the fear of her torment, saying, **woe, woe,** that **great** city Babylon, that **forcible** city! For in **first** hour is your **judging** come.

11 And the merchants of the earth shall weep and mourn over her; for no man buys their merchandise **no-longer.**

12 The merchandise of gold, and silver, and **valuable** stones, and of pearls, and linen, and purple, and silk,

---

[3701] Or, puny
[3702] "Nikao," to defeat an enemy
[3703] Aorist tense

[3704] Greek: kate (down), oikeo (house) and terion (a location where something happens)— see also Eph. 2:22
[3705] Or, to stick to, to cling, to keep company with

and scarlet, and all **thyine**[3706] **tree**, and all manner vessels **of-elephant**, and all manner vessels of most **valuable trees**, and of brass, and iron, and marble,

13 And cinnamon, and **incense**, and **myrrh**, and frankincense, and wine, and oil, and flour, and wheat, and **acquisitions**,[3707] and sheep, and horses, and chariots, and **bodies**, and souls of men.

14 And the fruits that your soul **upon-feel** are departed from you and all things which were **fat** and **radiant** are departed from you, and you shall **not-still** find them.

15 The merchants of these things, which were made rich by her, shall stand afar off for the fear of her torment, **sobbing** and wailing,

16 And saying, **woe, woe,** that **great** city, that was clothed in linen, and purple, and scarlet, and **gilded** with gold, and **valuable** stones, and pearls!

17 For in **first** hour **so-much** riches are come to nothing. And every **navigator**, and all **those upon spot sailing**, and sailors, and as many as **worked** by sea, stood afar off,

18 And **screamed** when they saw the smoke of her burning, saying, what like to this **great** city!

19 And they cast dust on their heads, and **screamed**, weeping, and wailing, saying, **woe, woe,** that **great** city, **in which** were made rich all that had ships in the sea **out-of** her **expensiveness**! For in **first** hour is she made **lonesome**![3708]

20 Rejoice over her, the heaven, **and the saints, and the** apostles and **the** prophets; for God has **judged your judgment-result**[3709] **out-of** her.

21 And a **forcible** angel **lifts** a stone like a **great** millstone, and cast into the sea, saying, **in-this-way**, with violence shall that **great** city Babylon be thrown down, and shall **not-still** be found.

22 And the voice of harpers, and musicians, and of pipers, and trumpeters, shall be heard no more at all in you; and no **technician**, of whatever **tech**, shall be found any more in you; and the voice of a millstone shall be heard no more at all in you.

23 And the light of a candle shall shine no more at all in you; and the voice of the bridegroom and of the bride shall be heard no more at all in you; for your merchants were the **great** men of the earth; for by your **drugs** were all nations **seduced**.

24 And in her was found the blood of prophets, and of saints, and of all that were slain upon the earth.

REVELATION CHAPTER 19

1 And after these things I heard **something like** a **great** voice of much people in heaven, saying, alleluia; salvation, and glory, and **value**, and power, to the Lord our God.

2 For true and righteous his **judging**; for he has judged the **great prostitute,** which did **corrupt**[3710] the earth **in** her **prostitution**, and has avenged the blood of his **slaves** at her hand.

3 And again they said, alleluia; and her smoke **is-up-walking into the ages of ages.**

4 And the twenty-four elders and the four **living-things** fell down and worshipped God that **is-sitting** on the throne, saying, amen; alleluia.

5 And a voice came out of the throne, saying, praise our God, all you his **slaves**, and you that fear him, both **micro** and **great**.

6 And I heard as it were the voice of a **much** multitude, and as the voice of **much water** and as the voice of **forcible** thunders, saying, alleluia, for the Lord God **All-Governor**[3711] reigns.

7 Let us be glad and rejoice and give **glory to-him**; for the marriage of the Lamb **came**[3712] and his wife has made herself **internally-prepared**.

8 And to her was granted that she should be **clothed** in linen, clean and **radiant**; for the linen is the **righteous-deeds** of saints.

9 And he says to me, write: **happy the-ones** which are called **into expensive-dinner of-the** marriage of the Lamb. And he says to me, these are the true sayings of God.

10 And I fell at his feet to worship him. And he said to me, **you-see** not, I am your **together-slave**, and of your **brothers** that have the **witness** of Jesus, worship God; for the **witness** of Jesus is the spirit of prophecy.

[3706] Greek: "thuinos," transliterated as "thyine;" root (thuo): to rush, breathe hard, blow, smoke, sacrifice
[3707] Or domestic animals
[3708] Or, devastated
[3709] Greek: "krima," transliterated as "crime" and also means judgment
[3710] Or, to pine, to waste, to rot
[3711] Greek: "Pankrator," pan (all) and krator from kratos (government, rule, strong), kratos is transliterated as "cracy," in democracy (people-government, people-rule)
[3712] Aorist tense

11 And **I-perceived** heaven opened, and **be-perceiving**, a white horse; and **the-one sitting** upon him called **Believing** and True, and in **righteous-togetherness** he does judge and war.

12 His eyes as a flame of fire, and on his head many **royal-crowns**, **having names**³⁷¹³ written and a name written, that no man knew, **if not him**.

13 And he **was-clothed** with **garment baptized**³⁷¹⁴ in blood; and his name is called the **Word of God**.

14 And the armies in heaven followed him upon white horses, clothed³⁷¹⁵ in **clean white linen**.

15 And **out-of** his mouth **out-of-passage** a sharp sword, that **in her** he should **hit** the nations; and he shall **shepherd** them **in to-rod** of iron; and he **is-trampling**³⁷¹⁶ the winepress of the **sacrifice-anger and swelling-anger** of-the **All-Governor, the** God.

16 And he has on **garment** and on his thigh a name written, King of kings, and Lord of lords.

17 And I saw **one** angel standing in the sun; and he **screamed** with a **great** voice, saying to all the **birds** that fly in **mid-heaven**, come, and gather yourselves together to the **great expensive-dinner of the God**.

18 That you may eat the flesh of kings, and the flesh of captains, and the flesh of **forcible** men, and the flesh of horses, and of them that sit on them, and the flesh of all, free and slaves, both small and **great**.

19 And I saw the **wild-beast,** and the kings of the earth, and their armies, gathered together to **produce battle with** him that sat on the horse, and **with** his army.

20 And the **wild-beas**t was **squeeze-captured**,³⁷¹⁷ and with him the false prophet that **produced** signs before him, with which he **seduced** them that **took** the **engraved-character**³⁷¹⁸ of the **wild-beast,** and them that worshipped his image. These both were cast alive into a lake of fire burning with **God-fire.**³⁷¹⁹

21 And the **remaining-ones** were slain with the sword which **out-of-passage out-of** his mouth of him **sitting** upon the horse; and all the **birds** were filled with their flesh.

REVELATION CHAPTER 20

1 And **I-perceived** an angel come down from heaven, having the **locker** of the bottomless pit and a **great** chain in his hand.

2 And he **governed** the dragon, that **original** serpent, which is the Devil, and Satan, and bound him a thousand **years**.

3 And cast him into the **abyss**, and **locked him**, and **seal up-above** him, that he should not still **seduce** the nations, **until** the thousand **years finished**; and after these **it-is-binding** he **be-loosed** a **small time**.

4 And I saw thrones, and they **seated** upon them, and **judgment-result**³⁷²⁰ was given to them; and the souls of them that were beheaded³⁷²¹ through the witness of Jesus, and through the **Word of God**, and **any-who** had not worshipped the **wild-beast,** neither his image, neither had **taken the engraved-character**³⁷²² on their foreheads,³⁷²³ or **upon** their hands; and **they-lived** and **they-kings** with Christ **the** thousand **years**.

5 But the rest of the dead **up-lived** not until the thousand **years** were finished. This is the **foremost** resurrection.

6 Happy and holy he that has **section** in the **foremost** resurrection; on such the **Second Death** has no **authority**, but they shall be priests of God and of Christ and **shall-be-kings** with him a thousand **years**.

7 And when the thousand **years** are **finished**, Satan shall be loosed out of his prison.

8 And shall go out to **seduce** the nations which are in the four **corners** of the earth, **the** Gog, and **the** Magog, **to-together-lead** them **into** battle: the number of whom as the sand of the sea.

9 And they **up-walked** on the **width**³⁷²⁴ of the earth, and **circle** the **camp** of the saints, and the beloved

---

³⁷¹³ Per Majority Texts
³⁷¹⁴ Greek: bapto—to whelm, to cover wholly with fluid
³⁷¹⁵ Lit., in-down; or, in-sink, in-down-slipping
³⁷¹⁶ Present tense
³⁷¹⁷ "Piazo," to squeeze, to seize by hand, to press, to arrest, to capture
³⁷¹⁸ Greek, "charagma," to carve, to scratch, to etch, sculpture; to engrave or write; akin to "charackter" (character);" "charagma" is used of a serpent's bite by Sophocles; "charagma" also means expressed image character, an engraving.
³⁷¹⁹ Lit., "theion" a place struck by "deity" lightning, God-flashing, God-lightning

³⁷²⁰ Greek: "krima," transliterated as "crime," also means judgment; the suffix "ma" means the result of judgment
³⁷²¹ Or, axed, to ax off the head
³⁷²² Greek, "charagma," to carve, to scratch, to etch, sculpture; to engrave or write; akin to "charackter" (character);" "charagma" is used of a serpent's bite by Sophocles; "charagma" also means expressed image character, an engraving.
³⁷²³ Greek: "mataops," to change (meta)-eyes (ops), to change-face (ops), after-face, after-eyes, beyond-face, beyond-eyes
³⁷²⁴ Greek: "platos" from "platus," "flat," "plot,"

City; and fire came down from God out of heaven, and **down-eat** them.

10 And the Devil that **seduced** them was cast into the lake of fire and **God-fire,** where **also** the **wild-beast** and the false prophet and shall be tormented day and night **into the ages of the ages.**

11 And **I-perceived** a **great** white throne, and him that sat on it, from whose face the earth and the heaven fled away; and there was found no place for them.

12 And **I-perceived** the dead, small and **great,** stand before **the throne**; and the **little-scrolls** were opened; and **another-same Little-Scroll** was opened, which is of Life; and the dead were judged out of those things which were written in the **little-scrolls, down** their **works.**

13 And the sea gave up the dead which were in **her**; and **Death** and **Hell gave** up the dead which were in them; and they were judged **each down** their **works.**

14 And **Death** and **Hell** were cast into the lake of fire. This is the **Second Death, the lake of fire.**

15 And **if-any** was not found written in the **Scroll** of Life was cast into the lake of fire.

REVELATION CHAPTER 21

1 And **I-perceived** a **new-fresh** heaven and a **new-fresh** earth; for the **former** heaven and the **former** earth were passed away; and there was no more sea.

2 And **I perceived** the **Holy City, Holy**[3725] **Jerusalem,**[3726] coming down from God out of heaven, **internally-prepared** as a bride **cosmetic** for her husband.

3 And I heard a **great** voice out of heaven saying, **be-perceiving,** the tabernacle of God with men, and he will **tabernacle** with them, and they shall be his people, and God himself shall be with them, their God.

4 And God shall **out-of-oil** all tears from their eyes; and there shall be no more death, neither sorrow, nor crying, neither shall there be any more pain; for the **before-most** things are **from-gone.**

5 And **the-one sitting** on the throne said, **be-perceiving,** I **produce** all things **new-fresh.** And he said to me, write; for these words are true and **believing.**

6 And he said to me, **it-has-become.** I am Alpha and Omega, the **Origin,** and the **Finish.** I will give **to-him** that is athirst of the fountain of the water of life **gratuitously.**[3727]

7 The one-conquering,[3728] **I shall give him these things**; and I will be his God, and **he shall be to me, Son.**

8 But the **timid,** and unbelieving, and the **stink,** and murderers, and **paramours,** and **druggists,** and **image-servants,** and all **falsifiers,** shall have their **section** in the lake which burns with fire and **God-fire**[3729] which is the **Second Death.**

9 And there came one of the seven angels which had the seven **bowls** full of the seven last **plague-poundings,** and talked with me, saying, come **here,** I will show you **the woman, the Lamb's Bride.**

10 And he carried me away in the **Spirit** to a **great** and high mountain, and showed me the **City, the great,**[3730] **the Holy Jerusalem,** descending **out-of** the heaven from **the God.**

11 Having the glory of God; and her light like to a stone **valuable,** even like a jasper stone, **crystallized.**[3731]

12 And had a wall, **great** and high, **having** twelve gates, and at the gates twelve angels, and names written **upon it**, which are of the twelve tribes of the **sons** of Israel.

13 On the east three gates; on the north three gates; on the south three gates; and on the west three gates.

14 And the wall of the city had twelve foundations, and in them the **twelve** names of the twelve apostles of the Lamb.

15 And he that talked with me had a golden reed to measure the city, and the gates **of-her**, and the wall **of-her.**

16 And the city lays **four-cornered,** and the length is as much as the breadth; and he measured the city **to-the** reed, **upon stadiums,**[3732] twelve thousand. The length, the breadth, and the height **of-her** are **equal.**

[3725] Holy Jerusalem in all the oldest Greek texts (Byzantine or Majority Texts, Alexandrian Texts)
[3726] "Hierosoluma"—priests-peace (hierou-priest, sacred) and salem (peace)
[3727] Or, without a cause
[3728] "Nikao," to defeat an enemy
[3729] Lit., "theion" God-flashing, God-lightning
[3730] Byzantine texts
[3731] Or, frost, frozen, ice, rock-crystal
[3732] Greek: "stadion," stadiums, to stand as fixed, 600 Greek feet, 1/8th of a Roman mile, 404.5 Cubits

17 And he measured the wall **of-her**, a hundred **forty-four** cubits, the measure of a man, that is, of the angel.

18 And the **in-building** of the wall of it was jasper; and the city clean gold, like to **clean** glass.

19 And the foundations of the wall of the city **cosmetic** with all **valuable** stones. The first foundation jasper;[3733] the second, **blue-stone**;[3734] the third, **copper-like**; the fourth, a **green-stone**;[3735]

20 The fifth, **red-vein**;[3736] the sixth, **red**;[3737] the seventh, **gold-stone**; the eighth, beryl;[3738] the ninth, a topaz;[3739] the tenth, a **gold-leek**; the eleventh, a **hyacinth**; the twelfth, an **un-drunk**.[3740]

21 And the twelve gates twelve pearls; **up each one of-the** gate was **out-of** one pearl; and the **plat** of the city was **clean** gold, **as** transparent glass.

22 And **I-perceived** no temple **in her**; for the Lord God All-Governor and the Lamb is the temple **of-her**.

23 And the city had no need of the sun, neither of the moon, to shine; for the **very** glory of God did lighten it, and the Lamb the **Lamp of-her**.

24 And the nations shall walk in the light **of-her**; and the kings of the earth do bring their glory and **value of the nations to Him.**

25 And the gates of it shall not be **locked** at all by day; for there shall be no night there.

26 And they shall bring the glory and **value** of the nations into **her that they may enter in**.

27 And there shall in no **not** enter into it anything that **common**, or **one-making stink, or falsehood**; but they which are written in the Lamb's **Little-scroll** of Life.

REVELATION CHAPTER 22

1 And he showed me a river of water of life, **shining** as crystal, **out-of-passage out-of** the throne of God and of the Lamb.

2 In the middle of the street of it, **within and within**[3741] of the river, the tree of life, **producing** twelve fruits, **from-giving** her fruit **one each** month; and the leaves of the tree for the **therapy-serving** of the nations.

3 And there shall be no more **down-up-placed**; but the throne of God and of the Lamb shall be in **her**; and his **slaves shall-be-hired-serving to-him**.

4 And they shall see his face, and his name in their foreheads.

5 And there shall be no night there; and they need no candle, neither light of the sun; for the Lord God gives them light; and **they-shall-be kings into the ages of ages**.

6 And he said to me, these sayings **believing** and true; and the Lord God of the **spirits**[3742] of prophets sent his angel to show to his **slaves** the things which **it-is-binding** shortly **to-become.**

7 Be-perceiving, I-am-coming swiftly happy he that **guards** the sayings of the prophecy of this **little-scroll**

8 And I John the one-who-hearing and the one-looking-at these things. And when I heard and saw, I fell down to worship before the feet of the angel which showed me these things.

9 Then **he says** to me, **see not**; I am your **together-slave**, and of your **brothers**, the prophets, and of them which **guard** the sayings of this **little-scroll**; worship God.

10 And he says to me, seal not the sayings of the prophecy of this **little-scroll**; for the **season near-squeezes**.

11 He that is **unrighteous**, let him be **unrighteous** still; and he which is **soiled**, let him be **soiled** still; and he that **produces righteous**, let him be **produce righteous** still; and he that is holy, let him be holy still.

12 And, **be-perceiving, I-am-coming swiftly**; and my reward with me, to give every man **as his works** shall be.

13 I am the First and the Last, the Origin and the Finish.

14 Happy those washing their robes that they may have **authority** to the tree of life and may enter in through the gates into the city.

[3733] Per Revelation 21:11, jasper is frost-like, ice-like
[3734] Sapphire
[3735] Greek: "smaragdos" (emerald)
[3736] "Sardonyx:" "sard" (red, or blood red) and "onyx" (vein); or red-fingernail, or red-claw
[3737] Greek: sardius, red, blood red
[3738] The ancient Greeks designated beryl for any green stone
[3739] Topaz means "to seek (Ethiopian origin)"
[3740] Amethyst (un-drunk)
[3741] Whenever "enteuthen" is used twice, joined with "and;" it carries the idea of "both sides"
[3742] The oldest texts (Majority and Alexandrian)

15 Outside **are-dogs**, and **druggists**, and **paramour**, and murderers, and **image-servants**, and whoever **friends** and makes **falsehood**.

16 I Jesus have **dispatched** my angel to **witness to-you** these things in the Churches. I am the root and the **kin** of David, the **Bright and Morning Star**.

17 And the Spirit and the **Bride** say, **come**. And let him that hears say, come. And let him that is **thirsty** come. And whoever will, let him take the water of life **gratuitously**.[3743]

18 For I **witness** to every man that hears the words of the prophecy of this **little-scroll,** if any man shall add to these things, God shall add **to-him** the **plague-poundings** that are written in this **little-scroll**.

19 And if any man shall take away from the words of the **little-scroll** of this prophecy, **may God take away** his **section** out of the **Tree of Life,** and out of the **Holy City**, and the things which are written in this book.

20 He **witnessing** these things say, **yes, I-am-coming swiftly**. Amen. **Yes, be-you-coming,** Lord Jesus.

21 The grace of our Lord Jesus Christ with all **the saints**. Amen.

[3743] Or, without a cause

SYNOPTIC BIO OF DONALD PEART

Donald Peart is married to Judith Peart. They are the parents of Donald Jr and his wife Keyanna; Jeshua, Charity, Benjamin, and Jesse. Donald and Judith have been serving the Lord Jesus and declaring the well-message of Jesus since 1986. Over the years, the Lord Jesus has worked various manifestations of signs, wonders, and miracles through them.

The vision the Lord has impressed upon them is summed up in Ephesians 4:11-16. They have founded and currently shepherd Crown of Glory Ministries, in which Jesus is Lord. The ministry is located in Randallstown, Maryland.

Through the Grace of the Lord Jesus, Donald and Judith Peart have published over 35 books; and they have distributed their books in at least 29 States in the USA and several nations; to include, but not limited to, Greenland, Tanzania, Uganda, Trinidad, Jamaica, Philippines, India, Peru, Bahamas, United Kingdom, Germany, Netherlands, Italy, Mexico, Canada, South Africa, Ghana, Nigeria, Kenya, Australia, China, France, Sierra Leon, Pakistan, and Brazil.

Donald and Judith also travel as a team to refresh and build up Jesus' Church, and to also aid in structuring competent prophetic administrators for the work of Jesus' towards His goal. Donald Peart has also advised and developed "five-fold" ministries since 1990. In addition to ministering in various States in America, he and his wife has traveled abroad to Japan, Korea, Puerto Rico, Bahamas, Trinidad and Tobago, and Jamaica, West Indies, the country of his birth.

Judith earned a Bachelor of Science degree in Early Childhood Education. Donald graduated from Baltimore Polytechnic High School, in Baltimore Maryland. He also earned an Associate of Arts degree in Pre-Engineering, a Bachelor of Science degree in Civil Engineering, a Master of Divinity, a Master of Science in Construction Management, and a Doctorate in Theology.

OTHER BOOKS

- Poiema, by Judith Peart
- Wisdom from Above, by Judith Peart
- Procreation, Understanding Sex, and Identity, by Judith Peart
- 100 Nevers, by Judith Peart
- The Shattered and the Healing by Judith Peart
- The Lamb, by Donald Peart
- Jesus' Resurrection, Our Inheritance, by Donald Peart.
- Sexuality, By Donald Peart
- Forgiven 490 Times, by Donald Peart w/Judith Peart!
- The Days of the Seventh Angel, By Donald Peart
- The Torah (The Principle) of Giving, by Donald Peart
- The Time Came, by Donald Peart
- The Last Hour, the First Hour, the Forty-Second Generation, by Donald Peart
- Vision Real, by Donald Peart
- The False Prophet, Alias, Another Beast V1, by Donald Peart
- "The Beast," by Donald Peart
- Son of Man Prophesy Against the false prophet, by Donald Peart
- The Dragon's Tail, Prophets who Teaches Lies, by Donald Peart
- The Work of Lawlessness Revealed, by Donald Peart
- When the Lord Made the Tempter, by Donald Peart
- Examining Doctrine, Volume 1, by Donald Peart
- Exousia, Your God Given Authority, by Donald Peart
- The Numbers of God, by Donald Peart
- The Completions of the Ages ... by Donald Peart
- The Revelation of Jesus Christ, by Donald Peart
- Jude—Translation and Commentary, by Donald Peart
- Obtaining the Better Resurrection, by Donald Peart
- Manifestations from Our Lord Jesus ...by Donald and Judith Peart
- The New Testament, Dr. Donald Peart Exegesis
- Dr. Donald Peart New Testament Exegesis II (without footnotes)
- The Tree of Life, By Dr. Donald Peart
- The Spirit and Power of John, the Baptist by Dr. Donald Peart
- The Shattered and the Healing by Judith Peart
- Is She Married to a Husband? by Donald Peart
- The Ugliest Man God Made by Donald Peart
- Does Answering the Call of God Impact Your Children? by Donald Peart
- Victory Out of the Beast-the Harvest of the Earth by Donald Peart
- Melchizedek by Donald Peart
- Butter and Honey, Understanding How to Choose the Good and Refuse Evil by Donald Peart
- Wholly Maturing, Wholly Inheriting, Spirit, Soul, and Body, by Donald Peart
- Angels and the Supernatural by Donald Peart
- Ezekiel-the House-the City-the Land (Interpreting the Patterns) by Donald Peart
- The Prophetic Patterns of the Two Witnesses, by Donald Peart
- Born a Second Time (Spirit with the Spirit), by Donald Peart
- The Sweet Incense of Prayer by Donald Peart

- Her Seed vs his Seed (Outlined Notes by Donald Peart)
- Melchizedek Order, the Matured Priesthood (Outlined Notes by Donald Peart)
- The Next One Thousand Years-Before-During-After by Donald Peart

CONTACT INFORMATION

Crown of Glory Ministries
P.O. Box 1041 Randallstown, MD 21133
donaldpeart7@gmail.com